CHIRAANE CHIYAYAYA

찌라아너 찌야야야

NEW TESTAMENT

치뗌보 신약 성경 / Chitembo New Testament

발행 / Publisher
도서출판 동연 / Dongyeonpress

번역 / Translation
치뗌보 성경번역 위원회 / Chitembo Bible Translation Committee

사업 총괄 / Project Director
최관신 선교사 (작은손 선교회) / Koanshin Choi, Missionary of HfL

치뗌보 문자 변환 / Chitembo Script Conversion
김찬호 안수집사 (노량진장로교회) / Chanho Kim, Deacon of Noryangjin Presbyterian Church

표기 체계 연구 / Chitembo Jeongeum Writing System Research
연구 책임자 / Chief Researcher
소강춘 교수 (전주대학교 / 전 국립국어원장) / Prof. Kangchoon Soh (Jeonju University / Former President, National Institute of Korean Language)

연구원 / Researchers
김주원 교수 (서울대학교) / Prof. Juwon Kim (Seoul National University)
고동호 교수 (전북대학교) / Prof. Dongho Ko (Jeonbuk National University National University)
박한상 교수 (홍익대학교) / Prof. Hansang Park (Hongik University)

연구 보조원 / Research Assistants
심재홍 (서울대학교) / Jaehong Shim (Seoul National University)
최정혜 (전북대학교) / Jeonghye Choi (Jeonbuk National University)

치뗌보어 번역 / Translation (BMCC)
현지 책임자 / Local Coordinator
Prof. Ahadi Bilungulira Aristote

현지 번역 / Field Translators
Heritier Byakumbwa Crispin
David Balumisa Israel
Munguiko Biteri Luc
Kitumani Mukara Georges
Kuhombire Mastora Sylvain
Katondo Kapalata David
Sandra Kataulwa Merose
Imani Kamuteire Rene

감수 / Review
Ps. Balumisa Mirimba

후원 / Sponsors
샌프란시스코 금문장로교회 (조은석 목사) / Golden Gate Presbyterian Church, San Francisco (Rev. Eunseok Cho)
서울 노량진장로교회 (여충호 목사) / Noryangjin Presbyterian Church, Seoul, Korea (Rev. Chungho Yeo)
군산 성광교회 (차상영 목사) / Sungkwang Presbyterian Church, Gunsan, Korea (Rev. Sangyoung Cha)
원암문화재단 (이기남 이사장) / Wonam Cultural Foundation, Jeonju, Korea (President Kinam Lee)
작은손 선교회 (고재찬 장로) / Hands For The Littles, Korea (Elder Jaechan Ko)
부름독서회 (4대) / Bureum Reading Club, Korea (4th Cohort)
예수간호대학교 (27회 동문) / Jesus University, Jeonju, Korea (Class of 27th)

CHIRAANE CHIYAYAYA

찌라아너 찌야야야

New Testament

HfL
Hands for the Littles   동연

Bya bilyemo | 뱌 비려모 | INDEX

Matayo

마다요

Matthew

**MWASI MUBUYABUYA WA Yesu Kirisito
N'NGOKWA YAANJIKWA NA MATAYO**

꽈시 무부야부야 와 여수 기리시도
누오과 야아꺼과 나 마다요

Matayo Chikono 1	마다요 찌고노 1	Matthew Chapter 1[NIV]

Elubuto Iwa Kirisito ashokaamo	*어루빕명 꽈 기리시도 아쏘가아모*	*The Genealogy of Jesus*

1. yesu kirisito e lubuto lw'ashokaamo lululuno, yeine abaa womwa lubuto lwa mwami daudi. daudi nai abaa womwa lubuto lwa aburahamu

1. 여수 기리시도 어 루부도 꽈쏘가아모 루루루노, 여이너 아바아 오마 루부도 꽈 마미 다우디. 다우디 나이 아바아 오마 루부도 꽈 아부라하무

1. A record of the genealogy of Jesus Christ the son of David, the son of Abraham:

2. Aburahamu abuta Isaka. Na Isaka era kubuta yakobo, na Yakobo era kubuta Yuda na banyakabo

2. 아부라하무 아부다 이사가. 나 이사가 어라 구부다 야고보, 나 야고보 어라 구부다 유다 나 바냐가보

2. Abraham was the father of Isaac, Isaac the father of Jacob, Jacob the father of Judah and his brothers,

3. na yuda era kubuta peresi na sera kutamari. na peresi era kubuta hesironi. na hesironi era kubuta aramu.

3. 나 유다 어라 구부다 퍼러시 나 서라 구다마리. 나 퍼러시 어라 구부다 허시로니. 나 허시로니 어라 구부다 아라무.

3. Judah the father of Perez and Zerah, whose mother was Tamar, Perez the father of Hezron, Hezron the father of Ram,

4. na aramu era kubuta aminadabu. na aminadabu era kubuta nasoni. na nasoni era kubuta salumoni.

4. 나 아라무 어라 구부다 아미나다부. 나 아미나다부 어라 구부다 나소니. 나 나소니 어라 구부다 사루모니.

4. Ram the father of Amminadab, Amminadab the father of Nahshon, Nahshon the father of Salmon,

5. na salumoni era kubuta bowasi ku rahabu. na bowasi era kubuta obedi ku ruta. na obeti era kubuta yese.

5. 나 사루모니 어라 구부다 보와시 구 라하부. 나 보와시 어라 구부다 오버디 구 루다. 나 오버디 어라 구부다 여서.

5. Salmon the father of Boaz, whose mother was Rahab, Boaz the father of Obed, whose mother was Ruth, Obed the father of Jesse,

6. na yese era kubuta mwami Daudi. na Daudi era kubuta solomono kumukasi muuma

6. 나 여서 어라 구부다 마미 다우디. 나 다우디 어라 구부다 소로모노 구무가시

6. and Jesse the father of King David. David was the father of Solomon, whose

olawabaamuka ulyi

무우마 오파와바아무가 우뤠

mother had been Uriah's wife,

7. na solomono era kubuta rehobowamu. na rehobowamu era kubuta asa.

7. 나 소로모노 어라 구부다 러호보와무. 나 러호보와무 어라 구부다 아사.

7. Solomon the father of Rehoboam, Rehoboam the father of Abijah, Abijah the father of Asa,

8. na asa era kubuta yosafati. na yosafati era kubuta yoramu. na yoramu era kubuta usiya

8. 나 아사 어라 구부다 요사파디. 나 요사파디 어라 구부다 요라무. 나 요라무 어라 구부다 우시야

8. Asa the father of Jehoshaphat, Jehoshaphat the father of Jehoram, Jehoram the father of Uzziah,

9. na usiya era kubuta yotamu. Na yotamu era kubuta ahasi. na aasi era kubuta esekiya.

9. 나 우시야 어라 구부다 요다무. 나 요다무 어라 구부다 아하시. 나 아아시 어라 구부다 어서기야.

9. Uzziah the father of Jotham, Jotham the father of Ahaz, Ahaz the father of Hezekiah,

10. na esekiya era kubuta manasi. na manasi era kubuta amoni. na amoni era kubuta yosiya

10. 나 어서기야 어라 구부다 마나시. 나 마나시 어라 구부다 아모니. 나 아모니 어라 구부다 요시야

10. Hezekiah the father of Manasseh, Manasseh the father of Amon, Amon the father of Josiah,

11. na yosiya era kubuta yekoniaya na banyakabo mango e baisiraeli basimbibwaa mwa bita, na kw'ekibwa mwa chio chebabiloni.

11. 나 요시야 어라 구부다 여고니아야 나 바냐가보 마꼬어 바이시라어삐 바시삐봐와 봐 비다, 나 궈기봐 봐 찌오 쩌바비로니.

11. and Josiah the father of Jeconiah and his brothers at the time of the exile to Babylon.

12. na mango babaa bera bekibwaayi yekoniya, era kubuta salatiyeri. na salatiyeri era kubuta sorobabeli.

12. 나 마꼬 바바아 버라 버기봐아에 여고니야, 어라 구부다 사퐈디여리. 나 사퐈디여리 어라 구부다 소로바버삐.

12. After the exile to Babylon: Jeconiah was the father of Shealtiel, Shealtiel the father of Zerubbabel,

13. na sorobabeli era kubuta abihuti. na abihuti era kubuta eliyakimu. na eliyakimu era kubuta asori

13. 나 소로바버삐 어라 구부다 아비후디. 나 아비후디 어라 구부다 어삐야기무. 나 어삐야기무 어라 구부다 아소리

13. Zerubbabel the father of Abiud, Abiud the father of Eliakim, Eliakim the father of Azor,

14. na asori era kubuta satoke. na satoke era kubuta akimu. na akimu era kubuta elihuti.

15. na elihuti era kubuta eliyaseri. na eliyaseri era kubuta matani. na matani era kubuta yakobo.

16. na yakobo era kubuta yosefu.oyo yesefu iwabaa eba wa mariya. na mariya iwabutaa Yesu ola werikirwe mbu ikirisito.

17. Rero, kutengera ku aburahamu kuikiraku mwami Daudi, kwabaa nyibuto ekumi nene. Na kutengera ku Daudi kuikira mango ebaisiraeli bekibwaa e babiloni, kwabaa sinji nyibuto ekumi nene. Na kutengera kwa kwekibwa bekibwaa ebabiloni, kuikira kwa kubutwa kwa Kirisito, kwahubaa kuba sinji nyibuto ekumi nene

E kubutwa kwa Yesu Kirisito

18. E kubutwa kwa Yesu Kirisito, bacha kukwabaa: mariya inyina abaa ahambalyirwa na yosefu. na mango yosefu abaaatasa kumuisa, mariya era kulorekanako kwa ete bukure. Obu bukure e kaabo kurengera ebuashi

14. 나 아소리 어라 구부다 사도거. 나 사도거 어라 구부다 아기무. 나 아기무 어라 구부다 어삐후디.

15. 나 어삐후디 어라 구부다 어삐야서리. 나 어삐야서리 어라 구부다 마다니. 나 마다니 어라 구부다 야고보.

16. 나 야고보 어라 구부다 요서푸.오요 여서푸 이와바아 어바 와 마리야. 나 마리야 이와부다아 여수 오라 워리기뤄 뿌 이기리시도.

17. 러로, 구더뻐라 구 아부라하무 구이기라구 마미 다우디, 과바아 네부도 어구미 너너. 나 구더뻐라 구 다우디 구이기라 마꼬 어바이시라어삐 버기봐아 어 바비뽀니, 과바아 시찌 네부도 어구미 너너. 나 구더뻐라 과 궈기봐 버기봐아 어바비뽀니, 구이기라 과 구부돠 과 기리시도, 과후바아 구바 시찌 네부도 어구미 너너

어 구부돠 과 여수 기리시도

18. 어 구부돠 과 여수 기리시도, 바짜 구과바아: 마리야 이네나 아바아 아하빠레롸 나 요서푸. 나 마꼬 요서푸 아바아아다사 구무이사, 마리야 어라 구뽀러가나고 과 어더 부구러. 오부 부구러 어 가아보 구러뻐라 어부아씨 붜무찌마

14. Azor the father of Zadok, Zadok the father of Akim, Akim the father of Eliud,

15. Eliud the father of Eleazar, Eleazar the father of Matthan, Matthan the father of Jacob,

16. and Jacob the father of Joseph, the husband of Mary, of whom was born Jesus, who is called Christ.

17. Thus there were fourteen generations in all from Abraham to David, fourteen from David to the exile to Babylon, and fourteen from the exile to the Christ.

The Birth of Jesus Christ

18. This is how the birth of Jesus Christ came about: His mother Mary was pledged to be married to Joseph, but before they came together, she was found to be with child through the Holy Spirit.

bwemuchima mubuya-buya

19. yosefu iwabaa wamuhambalyira abaa mundju mubuya era muhondo sa Ongo, na atasimaa mbu echise mariya honyi. bushi noku, erakuhonda amureke kwa bubisho-bisho.

20. abere yosefu anachilyi aanyisa kwei myasi, malaika muuma wa enawechwu era kumupamukira mwa biroto. era kumubura mbu yosefu mwenyi Daudi utobaa kuisa mariya bushi e bukure bw'ete abwekire kurengera ebuashi bwemuchima mubuya-buya.

21. angabuta mwana wa busana. Oyu mwana ungamwelyika mbu I Yesu bushi iukanunula ebandju bai mwa bibi byabo.

22. ebi byoshi byabaa bacha, chasiya echinwa chiberere cha enawetu abaa atechire mira kurengera emurebi wai mbu

23. mumvaa emunyere ola utafuraa kumenya mulume angeka bukere. na mwobu bukure, angabuta mwana wa busana noyo mwana

---

무부야-부야

19. 요서푸 이와바아 와무하빠꼐라 아바아 무뚜 무부야 어라 무호또 사 오꼬, 나 아다시마아 뿌 어찌서 마리야 호네. 부씨 노구, 어라구교호따 아무러거 과 부비쏘-비쏘.

20. 아버러 요서푸 아나찌꼐 아아네사 꿔이 먀시, 마꽈이가 무우마 와 어나워쭈 어라 구무파무기라 먀 비로도. 어라 구무부라 뿌 요서푸 뭐네 다우디 우도바아 구이사 마리야 부씨 어 부구러 뭐더 아뭐기러 구러꺼라 어부아씨 뭐무찌마 무부야-부야.

21. 아까부다 먀나 와 부사나. 오유 먀나 우까뭐꼐가 뿌 이 여수 부씨 이우가누누꽈 어바뚜 바이 먀 비비 뱌보.

22. 어비 뵤씨 뱌바아 바짜, 짜시야 어찌나 찌버러러 짜 어나워두 아바아 아더찌러 미라 구러꺼라 어무러비 와이 뿌

23. 무빠아 어무녀러 오꽈 우다푸라아 구머냐 무루머 아꺼가 부거러. 나 몸부 부구러, 아까부다 먀나 와 부사나 노요 먀나 바까뭐리가

---

19. Because Joseph her husband was a righteous man and did not want to expose her to public disgrace, he had in mind to divorce her quietly.

20. But after he had considered this, an angel of the Lord appeared to him in a dream and said, "Joseph son of David, do not be afraid to take Mary home as your wife, because what is conceived in her is from the Holy Spirit.

21. She will give birth to a son, and you are to give him the name Jesus, because he will save his people from their sins."

22. All this took place to fulfill what the Lord had said through the prophet:

23. "The virgin will be with child and will give birth to a son, and they will call him Immanuel"--which means, "God with us."

bangamwerika esina lya emanuweri. Emanuwelyi, kukuteta mbu: ongo aliuma netu.

어시나 퍄 어마누워리.
어마누워뤠, 구구더다 뿌: 오꼬 아쀠우마 너두.

24. abere yosefu asuka, era kunaira ngokwa malaika wa enawetu anamuburaa, era kunaisa mukai.

24. 아버러 요서푸 아수가, 어라 구나이라 꼬과 마퐈이가 와 어나워두 아나무부라아, 어라 구나이사 무가이.

24. When Joseph woke up, he did what the angel of the Lord had commanded him and took Mary home as his wife.

25. si ataonjiraa nai kuikira mango mariya abutaa oyu mwana webusana. Noyu mwana, yesefu era kunamwerika esina lya Yesu.

25. 시 아다오찌라아 나이 구이기라 마꼬 마리야 아부다아 오유 뫄나 워부사나. 노유 뫄나, 여서푸 어라 구나뭐리가 어시나 퍄 여수.

25. But he had no union with her until she gave birth to a son. And he gave him the name Jesus.

Matayo Chikono 2
E bandju b'e bwenge baika kw'emba Yesu

마다요 찌고노 2
어 바뚜 버 붸머 바이가 궈빠 여수

Matthew Chapter 2[NIV]

1. Yesu abuchwaa mwa musi mueke w'e betelehemu, mwachio che yudeya. Mwesi suku, mwami herode iwabaa w'emire. Era nyuma sekubuchwa kwa yesu, mwa musi we yerusalemu mwera kuulukira bandju bebwenge ba babaa batengerakwa lunda esuba lyende lyaulukira.

1. 여수 아부쫘아 뫄 무시 무어거 워 버더쩌허무, 뫄찌오 쩌 유더야. 뭐시 수구, 뫄미 허로더 이와바아 워미러. 어라 뉴마 서구부쫘 과 여수, 뫄 무시 워 여루사쩌무 뭐라 구우루기라 바뚜 버붸머 바 바바아 바더꺼라과 루따 어수바 쪄떠 퍄우루기라.

1. After Jesus was born in Bethlehem in Judea, during the time of King Herod, Magi from the east came to Jerusalem

2. Abu bandju bera kubusa mbu. kulyi mwana ola wabuchirwe mbu iungaba mwami webayuda, rero ngai ualyi? bushi chwalolaa kwa ngununu yai yapamukira era

2. 아부 바뚜 버라 구부사 뿌. 구뤠 마나 오퐈 와부찌뤄 뿌 이우빠바 마미 워바유다, 러로 빠이 우아뤠? 부씨 쫘뢰퐈아 과 꾸누누 야이 야파무기라 어라 수바 쪄떠 퍄우루기라,

2. and asked, "Where is the one who has been born king of the Jews? We saw his star in the east and have come to worship him."

suba lyende lyaulukira, bacha 바짜 쫘이기러 구뭐빠.
chwaikire kumwemba.

3. Mwami herode mwa
kunomva bacha,ebwenge
bwera kumusungulyira
alauma na besha yerusalemu
boshi.

3. 뫄미 허로더 뫄 구노빠
바짜,어붜어 붜라
구무수우쮀라 아쫘우마 나
버싸 여루사쪄무 보씨.

3. When King Herod heard
this he was disturbed, and
all Jerusalem with him.

4. Bushi noku, era kwamaala
ebakulu-kulu bebakuhanyi
nebakangilyisi be mwaso,
boshi. era kubabusa mbu:
ewashe Kirisito ngai uabaa
emire abuchirwe?

4. 부씨 노구, 어라 과마아쫘
어바구루-구루 버바구하니
너바가쮀리쎼시 버 뫄소, 보씨.
어라 구바부사 뿌: 어와써
기리시도 쐐이 우아바아
어미러 아부찌뤄?

4. When he had called
together all the people's
chief priests and teachers
of the law, he asked them
where the Christ was to be
born.

5. Nabo mbu: mwa musi
webetelehemu, mwa chio
cheyudeya. bushi ei myasi
iemurebi abaa aanjikire mira
mbu:

5. 나보 뿌: 뫄 무시
워버더쩌허무, 뫄 찌오
쩌유더야. 부씨 어이 먀시
이어무러비 아바아 아아씨기러
미라 뿌:

5. "In Bethlehem in Judea,"
they replied, "for this is
what the prophet has
written:

6. Nao betelehemu mwa chio
che yudeya, woyo, ata
umueke mwa musi Yoshi ye
yudeya, bushi uungatengera
mwemwami. noyu mwami
iukemangira e bandju banyi
be isiraeli.

6. 나오 버더쩌허무 뫄 찌오
쩌 유더야, 오요, 아다
우무어거 뫄 무시 요씨 여
유더야, 부씨 우우쐐더쩌라
뭐뫄미. 노유 뫄미
이우거마쐐라 어 바쭈 바니 버
이시라어쮜.

6. " 'But you, Bethlehem,
in the land of Judah, are
by no means least among
the rulers of Judah; for out
of you will come a ruler
who will be the shepherd
of my people Israel.'"

7. Herode kukwera kwamaala
abu bandju bebwenge
kwabubosho-boshi, chasiya
bamubure mangochi balolaa
kweingununu.

7. 허로더 구꿔라 과마아쫘
아부 바쭈 버붜어 과부보쏘-
보씨, 짜시야 바무부러 마꼬찌
바론쫘아 꿔이우꾸누누.

7. Then Herod called the
Magi secretly and found
out from them the exact
time the star had
appeared.

8. Chasinda, era kubachwuma
ebetelehemu na ababura
mbu: muyaa kubusilyisa
kubuya emyasi era luulu soyu
mwana. Na mango mungaba

8. 짜시따, 어라 구바쭈마
어버더쩌허무 나 아바부라 뿌:
무야아 구부시쩨사 구부야
어먀시 어라 루우루 소유
뫄나. 나 마꼬 무쐐바

8. He sent them to
Bethlehem and said, "Go
and make a careful search
for the child. As soon as
you find him, report to

mwamulolyireko,
mwananyibura chasiya nanyi
nyiye kumwemba.

9. Abu bandju bebwenge,
mango babaa bera bomvaa
emyasi ya mwami, bera
kuchiuma. Era ngununu
balolaako era esuba lyende
lyaulumikira, yabaa yenjire
yabahondorera. Yesu
kwimanga ala mwana abaa
ali.

10. Ei ngununu, mango
bahubaa kuilolaako, bera
kumowa busese.

11. Mw'olu, bera kwengilyira
mwa nyumba, bera kulola
kwa mwana alyi alauma na
nyina mariya. bera kukoma e
mafi bwemere. chasinda, bera
kuboola ehao sabo, bera
kuchwula emwana enyembo,
e horo, nekasuku, nemarashi.

12. Chasinda, Ongo era
kubabura mwa biroto
mbubatachihubaa era mwa
herode. Mwa kufuluka era
mwabo, bera kwera barenga
muinji njira.

13. Abu bandju bebwenge,
mango babaa bera
bachiumaa, malaika
w'enawechwu era kuikira
yosefu mwa biroto. Era

마무로쿼레러고, 뫄나네부라
짜시야 나네 네여 구뭐빠.

9. 아부 바뉴 버붜어, 마꼬
바바아 버라 보빠아 어먀시 야
뫄미, 버라 구찌우마. 어라
꾸누누 바로쫘아고 어라
어수바 켜떠 쨔우루미기라,
야바아 여찌러 야바호또러라.
여수 귀마뼈 아쫘 뫄나 아바아
아찌.

10. 어이 꾸누누, 마꼬
바후바아 구이로쫘아고, 버라
구모와 부서서.

11. 모루, 버라 궈삐레라 뫄
뉴빠, 버라 구로쫘 과 뫄나
아레 아쫘우마 나 네나
마리야. 버라 구고마 어 마삐
붜머러. 짜시따, 버라 구보오쫘
어하오 사보, 버라 구쭈쫘
어뫄나 어녀뽀, 어 호로,
너가수구, 너마라씨.

12. 짜시따, 오꼬 어라
구바부라 뫄 비로도
뿌바다찌후바아 어라 뫄
허로더. 뫄 구푸루가 어라
뫄보, 버라 궈라 바러뼈
무이찌 찌라.

13. 아부 바뉴 버붜어, 마꼬
바바아 버라 바찌우마아,
마쫘이가 워나워쭈 어라
구이기라 요서푸 뫄 비로도.
어라 구무부라 뿌: 요서푸

me, so that I too may go
and worship him."

9. After they had heard
the king, they went on
their way, and the star
they had seen in the east
went ahead of them until
it stopped over the place
where the child was.

10. When they saw the
star, they were overjoyed.

11. On coming to the
house, they saw the child
with his mother Mary, and
they bowed down and
worshiped him. Then they
opened their treasures and
presented him with gifts of
gold and of incense and of
myrrh.

12. And having been
warned in a dream not to
go back to Herod, they
returned to their country
by another route.

13. When they had gone,
an angel of the Lord
appeared to Joseph in a
dream. "Get up," he said,
"take the child and his

kumubura mbu: yosefu bachwukaa utole emwana na nyina, muhaire e misiri. mwikalaayi, kuikira emango nyingahuba kubabura mbu mufulukaa, bushi herode angaika kuhonda emwana, chasiya amwite.

14. Bushi noku, yosefu era kubachwuka mwobu buchwufu, era kutola emwana na nyina, era kunahaira nabo e misiri.

15. Era kw'ikalayi kuikira mango herodeti afaa. mwolu mwechinwa cheraa chaberera cha enawetu abaa atechire mira kurengera emerebi mbu: namaalaa emwana wanyi afuluke kutenga emisiri.

E bana bebusana b'echiwa e betelehemu

16. Mango herode alolaa kw'abu bandju bebwenge bamwengeere, era kusinana busese. Era kuchwuma ebandju mwa musi webetelehemu nomwa ndambi sao soshi, baye kw'ita ebana boshi kutengera kwa chwubonjo-bonjo kuikira kw'aba bete myaka ebilyi. Ekuishirira wei myaka ebilyi, kwatenganaa nemyesi era ebandju bebwenge

바쪽가아 우도뿨 어마나 나 네나, 무하이러 어 미시리. 뮈가꽈아에, 구이기라 어마꼬 네꽈후바 구바부라 뿌 무푸루가아, 부씨 허로더 아꽈이가 구호따 어마나, 짜시야 아뮈더.

14. 부씨 노구, 요서푸 어라 구바쭈가 모부 부쭈푸, 어라 구도꽈 어마나 나 네나, 어라 구나하이라 나보 어 미시리.

15. 어라 귀가꽈에 구이기라 마꼬 허로더디 아파아. 모루 뭐찌놔 쩌라아 짜버러라 짜 어나워두 아바아 아더찌러 미라 구러꺼라 어머러비 뿌: 나마아꽈아 어마나 와네 아푸루거 구더꽈 어미시리.

어 바나 버부사나 버찌와 어 버더꿔행뮬

16. 마꼬 허로더 아룬꽈아 과부 바뉴 버붜꺼 바뮈꺼어러, 어라 구시나나 부서서. 어라 구쭈마 어바뉴 꽈 무시 워버더꿔허무 노꽈 따뻬 사오 소씨, 바여 귀다 어바나 보씨 구더꺼라 과 쭈보꼬-보꼬 구이기라 과바 버더 먀가 어비뻬. 어구이씨리라 워이 먀가 어비뻬, 과더꽈나아 너며시 어라 어바뉴 버붜꺼 바무부다아.

mother and escape to Egypt. Stay there until I tell you, for Herod is going to search for the child to kill him."

14. So he got up, took the child and his mother during the night and left for Egypt,

15. where he stayed until the death of Herod. And so was fulfilled what the Lord had said through the prophet: "Out of Egypt I called my son."

16. When Herod realized that he had been outwitted by the Magi, he was furious, and he gave orders to kill all the boys in Bethlehem and its vicinity who were two years old and under, in accordance with the time he had learned from the Magi.

bamubutaa.

17. Rero, echinwa chera kwelyi chaberera cha chatechwaa na murebi yeremiya mbu:

18. Malyira manene, mwomvikere mwa musi w'e rama. Raeli alyilyira ebana bai busese, atanahonda kusiranyisibwa, bushi abu bana batachilyio.

17. 러로, 어찌놔 쩌라 궈레 짜버러라 짜 짜더좌아 나 무러비 여러미야 뿌:

18. 마쩨라 마너너, 몸삐거러 뫄 무시 워 라마. 라어쩨 아쩨쩨라 어바나 바이 부서서, 아다나호따 구시라네시봐, 부씨 아부 바나 바다찌쩨오.

17. Then what was said through the prophet Jeremiah was fulfilled:

18. "A voice is heard in Ramah, weeping and great mourning, Rachel weeping for her children and refusing to be comforted, because they are no more."

Yosefu atenga nemwana e misiri

요서푸 아더따 너꽈나 어 미시리

19. Mango herode abaa era afaa, ei misiri kanji malaika w'enawechwu era kuikira yosefu mwa biroto.

20. Era kumubura mbu: bachwukaa utole e mwana na nyina, ufuluke mwa chio cheisiraeli, bushi ba babaa bahonda kw'ita oyo mwana bafire mira.

21. Yosefu era kunabachwuka, era kutola emwana na nyina, na bafuluka mwa chio che isiraeli.

22. Si mango yosefu omvaa kwa arikelao iwerire wema eyuteya mwetwe lyeshe heroti, era kwobaa kuyayi. Era nyuma sekuburwa mwa biroto, era kwere aya mwa

19. 마꼬 허로더 아바아 어라 아파아, 어이 미시리 가찌 마쫘이가 워나워쭈 어라 구이기라 요서푸 뫄 비로도.

20. 어라 구무부라 뿌: 바쭈가아 우도뤄 어 뫄나 나 네나, 우푸루거 뫄 찌오 쩌이시라어쩨, 부씨 바 바바아 바호따 귀다 오요 뫄나 바피러 미라.

21. 요서푸 어라 구나바쭈가, 어라 구도꽈 어뫄나 나 네나, 나 바푸루가 뫄 찌오 쩌 이시라어쩨.

22. 시 마꼬 요서푸 오빠아 과 아리거꽈오 이워리러 워마 어유더야 뮈뛰 쪄써 허로디, 어라 곤바아 구야에. 어라 뉴마 서구부롸 뫄 비로도, 어라 궈러 아야 뫄 찌오 쩌

19. After Herod died, an angel of the Lord appeared in a dream to Joseph in Egypt

20. and said, "Get up, take the child and his mother and go to the land of Israel, for those who were trying to take the child's life are dead."

21. So he got up, took the child and his mother and went to the land of Israel.

22. But when he heard that Archelaus was reigning in Judea in place of his father Herod, he was afraid to go there. Having been warned in a dream,

chio ch'e kalilaya.

23. Aikireyi, era kuya kubera mwa musi we nasareti. Mwolo, mw'e chinwa chaberereaa, cha chatechwaa kurengera ebarebi mbu: akende elyikibwa mbu mwesha nasareti.

가ᄈ|롸야.

23. 아이기러에, 어라 구야 구버라 뫄 무시 워 나사러디. 몰론, 뭐 찌놔 짜버러라아, 짜 짜더쫘아 구러ᄰ라 어바러비 뿌: 아거ᄄ 어ᄙ기봐 뿌 뭐싸 나사러디.

he withdrew to the district of Galilee,

23. and he went and lived in a town called Nazareth. So was fulfilled what was said through the prophets: "He will be called a Nazarene."

Matayo Chikono 3
E myasi era yowana mubatisayi endee akangilyisa e bandju

1. Mw'esi suku, yowana mubatisayi aulukiraa mwa buyeye, bwe yudeya ahubanganyisa e bandju mbu:

2. Mubindjukaa mutenge mwa bibi byenyu bushi e bwami b'okwa nguba bulyi ofu.

3. Oyu yohana inoyu imurebi isaya ahambalaako mbu: e mundju ola ulyi mwa buyeye enjire ateta na murenge munene mbu: mukunganyisaa enawechwu e njira: mulambaatanyaa ala angarenga.

4. Yowana, e njimba sai sabaaa sikunganyisibwe mu boya bwa nyama nguma mbu ingamiya, kanji end'achimina

마다요 찌고노 3
*어 먀시 어라 요와나
무바디사에 어ᄄ앤 아가ᄈ|ᄙᄈ
어 바뚜*

1. 뭐시 수구, 요와나 무바디사에 아우루기라아 뫄 부여여, 붜 유더야 아후바ᄈ네사 어 바뚜 뿌:

2. 무비뚜가아 무더ᄰ 뫄 비비 벼뉴 부씨 어 봐미 보과 우바 부ᄙ 오푸.

3. 오유 요하나 이노유 이무러비 이사야 아하빠롸아고 뿌: 어 무뚜 오롸 우ᄙ 뫄 부여여 어ᄈ러 아더다 나 무러ᄰ 무너너 뿌: 무구ᄈ네사아아 어나워쭈 어 ᄈ라: 무롸빠아다냐아 아롸 아ᄈ러ᄰ.

4. 요와나, 어 ᄈ빠 사이 사바아 시구ᄈ네시붜 무 보야 봐 냐마 우마 뿌 이ᄈ미야, 가ᄈ 어ᄄ찌미나 무가바 와

Matthew Chapter 3[NIV]

1. In those days John the Baptist came, preaching in the Desert of Judea

2. and saying, "Repent, for the kingdom of heaven is near."

3. This is he who was spoken of through the prophet Isaiah: "A voice of one calling in the desert, 'Prepare the way for the Lord, make straight paths for him.' "

4. John's clothes were made of camel's hair, and he had a leather belt around his waist. His food

mukaba wa luu mwa mbiji. Ebilyo byae byabaa e miuku n'e buki.

5. E bandju bendee bamuikiranga kutengera e yerusalemu, nomwa chio choshi che yudeya, nokwa nyinda soshi selwishi lw'e yorodani.

6. Abu bandju babaa benjire bachiaya changanama kwa bibi byabo.yowana nai, era kunde ababatisa mwolu lwishi.

7. Si mango yowana alolaa kwa bafarisayo nebasandukayo benjire bamuikiranga banene, chasiya ababatise, era kunde ababura mbu: mwabo mulyi nga buko bwa njoka; rero, nde iwabalosise e njira yekufufumuka e buchinjibusi bwa Ongo bwa bw'eshire?

8. Bushi n'oku, mundaa mwalosa kurengera emyanya yenyu kwa mwabindjukire kutenga mwa bibi byenyu,

9. Kanji mutendaa mwachitonga mbu: chwubano, aburahamu ihokulu wechwu, rero, nababura kwa Ongo angaala kukulyira aburahamu e bana na mwamano makoi!

루우 꽈 삐지. 어비룐 뱌어 뱌바아 어 미우구 너 부기.

5. 어 바쭈 버떠어 바무이기라꺄 구더꺼라 어 여루사쩌무, 노꽈 찌오 쪼씨 쩌 유더야, 노과 네따 소씨 서뤼씨 뤄 요로다니.

6. 아부 바쭈 바바아 버찌러 바찌아야 짜꺄나마 과 비비 뱌보.요와나 나이, 어라 구떠 아바바디사 몰루 뤼씨.

7. 시 마꼬 요와나 아롤콰아 과 바파리사요 너바사뚜가요 버찌러 바무이기라꺄 바너너, 짜시야 아바바디서, 어라 구떠 아바부라 뿌: 뫄보 무뤠 꺄 부고 봐 쪼가; 러로, 떠 이와바롼시서 어 찌라 여구푸푸무가 어 부찌찌부시 봐 오꼬 봐 뷔씨러?

8. 부씨 노구, 무따아 뫄롼사 구러꺼라 어먀냐 여뉴 과 뫄비뿌기러 구더꺄 꽈 비비 벼뉴,

9. 가찌 무더따아 뫄찌도꺄 뿌: 쭈바노, 아부라하무 이호구루 워쭈, 러로, 나바부라 과 오꼬 아꺄아콰 구구쩨라 아부라하무 어 바나 나 뫄마노 마고이!

was locusts and wild honey.

5. People went out to him from Jerusalem and all Judea and the whole region of the Jordan.

6. Confessing their sins, they were baptized by him in the Jordan River.

7. But when he saw many of the Pharisees and Sadducees coming to where he was baptizing, he said to them: "You brood of vipers! Who warned you to flee from the coming wrath?

8. Produce fruit in keeping with repentance.

9. And do not think you can say to yourselves, 'We have Abraham as our father.' I tell you that out of these stones God can raise up children for Abraham.

10. Ekakuma kabikirwe mira kwa kukondera emichi kwanabisina; rero chira muchi woshi ola uteka bifuma bibuya, angakonjibwa, na kuumwa mwa mulyiro.

11. Nyono nenjire nababatisa mwa meshi, kwa kulosa kwa mwabindjukire kutenga mwa bibi byenyu. Si era nyuma sanyi, kuchilyi kungaika unji mundju ola unyirenzise ebuashi. Oyu mundju, chiro ndete kwa nyilyi kwa kungachwuma namukongola ebirato. yeke ungababatisa kwa muchima mubuya-buya,nokwa mulyiro.

12. Rero, era ete elwelyi mwamino sai,kwa kwelula ebichi mwa bulo.obu bulo,angalundabo mwa ngulyi yai. Si ebichi byeke, angaumaabi mwa mulyiro. Oyu mulyiro, atakasime chiro na hicha.

E kubatisibwa kwa Yesu

13. Mwaamu mango, Yesu era kutenga mwa chio chekalilaya. Era kuikira yowana kwa lwishi lweyorotani chasiya amubatise.

14. Si yowana era kuereka kunana mbu: chacha

10. 어가구마 가비기뤄 미라 과 구고떠라 어미찌 과나비시나; 러로 찌라 무찌 오씨 오라 우더가 비푸마 비부야, 아까고찌봐, 나 구우봐 봐 무뤠로.

11. 뇨노 너찌러 나바바디사 봐 머씨, 과 구로사 과 봐비뿌기러 구더봐 봐 비비 벼뉴. 시 어라 뉴마 사네, 구찌뤠 구까이가 우찌 무뚜 오롸 우네러씨서 어부아씨. 오유 무뚜, 찌로 떠더 과 네뤠 과 구까쭈마 나무고꼬롸 어비라도. 여거 우까바바디사 과 무찌마 무부야-부야,노과 무뤠로.

12. 러로, 어라 어더 어뤄뤠 봐미노 사이,과 궈루롸 어비찌 봐 부로.오부 부로,아까루따보 봐 우뤠 야이. 시 어비찌 벼거, 아까우마아비 봐 무뤠로. 오유 무뤠로, 아다가시머 찌로 나 히짜.

어 구바디시봐 과 여수

13. 봐아무 마꼬, 여수 어라 구더까 봐 찌오 쩌가뤼라야. 어라 구이기라 요와나 과 뤼씨 뤄요로다니 짜시야 아무바디서.

14. 시 요와나 어라 구어러가 구나나 뿌: 짜짜 어와뤠야, 시

10. The ax is already at the root of the trees, and every tree that does not produce good fruit will be cut down and thrown into the fire.

11. "I baptize you with water for repentance. But after me will come one who is more powerful than I, whose sandals I am not fit to carry. He will baptize you with the Holy Spirit and with fire.

12. His winnowing fork is in his hand, and he will clear his threshing floor, gathering his wheat into the barn and burning up the chaff with unquenchable fire."

13. Then Jesus came from Galilee to the Jordan to be baptized by John.

14. But John tried to deter him, saying, "I need to be

ewalyiya, si nyono nyi nyemire kubatisibwa nao, rero, kute kuuwelyire wanyi ikira?

뇨노 네 녀미러 구바디시봐 나오, 러로, 구더 구우워쪠러 와네 이기라?

baptized by you, and do you come to me?"

15. Yesu nai mbu: rekaa bibe bacha tanga, bushi bichwemire chwuire byoshi bya bichwungenene era muhonda sa Ongo. Yowana era kwire emerera.

15. 여수 나이 뿌: 러가아 비버 바짜 다따, 부씨 비쭤미러 쭈이러 뵤씨 뱌 비쭈어너너 어라 무호따 사 오꼬. 요와나 어라 귀러 어머러라.

15. Jesus replied, "Let it be so now; it is proper for us to do this to fulfill all righteousness." Then John consented.

16. Mango Yesu abaa era abatisibwaa, era kutenga mwameshi.unao-unao, e nguba kuna kubookala. Era kulola kwa muchima wa Ongo andaala nga chiruka, na chamuumbilyirako.

16. 마꼬 여수 아바아 어라 아바디시봐아, 어라 구더까 꽈머씨.우나오-우나오, 어 꾸바 구나 구보오가꽈. 어라 구로꽈 과 무찌마 와 오꼬 아따아꽈 따 찌루가, 나 짜무우삐쩨라고.

16. As soon as Jesus was baptized, he went up out of the water. At that moment heaven was opened, and he saw the Spirit of God descending like a dove and lighting on him.

17. Kanji kwa nguba kwera kutengera murenge ola wabaa wateta mbu: onola, imuala wanyi musiirwa, uchwula unyisimise.

17. 가찌 과 꾸바 궈라 구더따라 무러따 오꽈 와바아 와더다 뿌: 오노꽈, 이무아꽈 와네 무시이롸, 우쭈꽈 우네시미서.

17. And a voice from heaven said, "This is my Son, whom I love; with him I am well pleased."

Matayo Chikono 4
Yesu aerekibwa n'e musimu

마다요 찌고노 4
여수 아어러기봐 너 무시무

Matthew Chapter 4[NIV]

1. Era nyuma sebi, emuchima mubuya-buya era kweka Yesu mwa buyeye, chasiya wamusimu amuereke.

1. 어라 뉴마 서비, 어무찌마 무부야-부야 어라 궈가 여수 꽈 부여여, 짜시야 와무시무 아무어러거.

1. Then Jesus was led by the Spirit into the desert to be tempted by the devil.

2. Yesu era kumala suku mane, ebuchwufu n'e mushi, busira kulya. chasinda, e businya bwera kumusimba.

2. 여수 어라 구마꽈 수구 마너, 어부쭈푸 너 무씨, 부시라 구꺄. 짜시따, 어 부시냐 붜라 구무시빠.

2. After fasting forty days and forty nights, he was hungry.

3. Mwolu, wamusimu era kuika kumuereka. Era kumubura mbu: akaba unalyi muala wa Ongo, buraa mano makoi mahumbe mikati.

3. 몰루, 와무시무 어라 구이가 구무어러가. 어라 구무부라 뿌: 아가바 우나례 무아롸 와 오꼬, 부라아 마노 마고이 마후뻐 미가디.

3. The tempter came to him and said, "If you are the Son of God, tell these stones to become bread."

4. Yesu era kumwakula mbu: si byanjikirwe mwa maanjiko mabuya-buya mbu: bya mundju alya, byeine ata bingachwuma aba muuma-uma. si ende aba muuma-uma mwa kukulyikira chira chinwa cha chatenga mwa bunu bwa Ongo.

4. 여수 어라 구꽈구롸 뿌: 시 뱌찌기뤄 뫄 마아찌고 마부야-부야 뿌: 뱌 무뚜 아럈, 벼이너 아다 비꺄쭈마 아바 무우마-우마. 시 어떠 아바 무우마-우마 뫄 구구례기라 찌라 찌놔 짜 짜더뼈 뫄 부누 봐 오꼬.

4. Jesus answered, "It is written: 'Man does not live on bread alone, but on every word that comes from the mouth of God.'"

5. Chasinda, wamusimu era kweka Yesu mwa musi mubuya-buya we yerusalemu. Era kumwemanza kwa ngangamo se luhulwa Ongo, na amubura mbu:

5. 짜시따, 와무시무 어라 궈가 여수 뫄 무시 무부야-부야 워 여루사뿌무. 어라 구뭐마싸 꽈 뼈꺄모 서 루후꽈 오꼬, 나 아무부라 뿌:

5. Then the devil took him to the holy city and had him stand on the highest point of the temple.

6. Akaba unalyi mwana wa ongo, uchiumaa alashi, bushi byanjikirwe mbu: Ongo angabura e bamalaika bai bakwangilyire, ekuulu kwao kungesha kuchihuta kwekoi.

6. 아가바 우나례 뫄나 와 오꼬, 우찌우마아 아롸씨, 부씨 뱌찌기뤄 뿌: 오꼬 아꺄부라 어 바마롸이가 바이 바과삐례러, 어구우릍 과오 구뼈싸 구찌후다 궈고이.

6. "If you are the Son of God," he said, "throw yourself down. For it is written: " 'He will command his angels concerning you, and they will lift you up in their hands, so that you will not strike your foot against a stone.'"

7. Yesu nai mbu: si byanjikirwe kanji mbu: utendaa waereka enawenyu Ongo.

7. 여수 나이 뿌: 시 뱌찌기뤄 가찌 뿌: 우더따아 와어러가 어나워뉴 오꼬.

7. Jesus answered him, "It is also written: 'Do not put the Lord your God to the test.'"

8. Wamusimu, era

8. 와무시무, 어라 구뭐루시사

8. Again, the devil took

kumwerusisa ku butala-tala bwa ndJulungu nguma irerere. Era kumulosa e mami moshi mebutala, nebuare bwamo.

9. Era kumubura mbu: akaba ungafukama era muhondo sanyi wanyera, ebi byoshi useneko, nyingakweresabi.

10. Yesu nai mbu: eu musimu tengaa mwameho manyi. Bushi byanjikirwe mbu: undaa wera enawenyu Ongo, na kunde wamukorera yeine oshao.

11. Chasinjire, wamusimu era kwire amureka. Ebamalaika bera kuika kumuasa.

Yesu atangilyisa emulyiomo wai ekalilaya

12. Mango Yesu omvaa emwasi kwa yowana bamuumire mwa buroko, era kutenga aola, na aya ekalilaya.

13. Era kutenga enasareti, aya kwekala mwa musi wekaperinaumu. Oyu musi, achwula kwa musike senyanja y'e kalilaya, kwa lunda lw'e chio cha sabuloni n'e cha nafutali.

14. Byabaa bacha chasiya chachinwa chiberebere, cha chabaa chatechirwe mira

---

구 부다꾜-다꽈 봐 뚜루루우 꾸마 이러러러. 어라 구무로사 어 마미 모씨 머부다꽈, 너부아러 봐모.

9. 어라 구무부라 뿌: 아가바 우꽈푸가마 어라 무호또 사니 와녀라, 어비 뵤씨 우서너고, 네꽈궈러사비.

10. 여수 나이 뿌: 어우 무시무 더꽈아 먀머호 마니. 부씨 뱌찌기뤄 뿌: 우따아 워라 어나워뉴 오꼬, 나 구떠 와무고러라 여이너 오싸오.

11. 짜시찌러, 와무시무 어라 귀러 아무러가. 어바마꽈이가 버라 구이가 구무아사.

여수 아다꾀꿰뻡 어무꿰엡명 와이 어가꿰꽈앳

12. 마꼬 여수 오꽈아 어꽈시 과 요와나 바무우미러 꽈 부로고, 어라 구더꽈 아오꽈, 나 아야 어가꿰꽈야.

13. 어라 구더꽈 어나사러디, 아야 궈가꽈 먀 무시 워가퍼리나우무. 오유 무시, 아쭈꽈 과 무시거 서냐짜 여 가꿰꽈야, 과 루따 뤄 찌오 짜 사부로니 너 짜 나푸다꿰.

14. 뱌바아 바짜 짜시야 짜찌놔 찌버러버러, 짜 짜바아 짜더찌뤄 미라 구러꺼라

---

him to a very high mountain and showed him all the kingdoms of the world and their splendor.

9. "All this I will give you," he said, "if you will bow down and worship me."

10. Jesus said to him, "Away from me, Satan! For it is written: 'Worship the Lord your God, and serve him only.'"

11. Then the devil left him, and angels came and attended him.

12. When Jesus heard that John had been put in prison, he returned to Galilee.

13. Leaving Nazareth, he went and lived in Capernaum, which was by the lake in the area of Zebulun and Naphtali--

14. to fulfill what was said through the prophet Isaiah:

kurengera murebi isaya mbu: 무러비 이사야 뿌:

15. Echio cha sabuloni, n'e cha nafutali, kukulyikira enjira yerekere kwa nyanja, kwa lunda lw'e lwishi lw'e yorotani, mwa chio chekalilaya. Eyera, yiebandju besinji mbaa bachwula.

15. 어찌오 짜 사부로니, 너 짜 나푸다찌, 구구쩨기라 어찌라 여러거러 과 냐짜, 과 루따 뤄 뤼씨 뤄 요로다니, 마 찌오 쩌가찌롸야. 어여라, 에어바쭈 버시찌 빠아 바쭈롸.

15. "Land of Zebulun and land of Naphtali, the way to the sea, along the Jordan, Galilee of the Gentiles--

16. Ebandju ba babaa balyi mwa musimya, balolyire ku bulangare bunene. Ba babaa balyi mwa chio chemusimya munene w'e lufu nabo, baikilyirwe n'e bulangare.

16. 어바쭈 바 바바아 바쩨 마 무시먀, 바로쩨러 구 부롸따러 부너너. 바 바바아 바쩨 마 찌오 쩌무시먀 무너너 워 루푸 나보, 바이기쩨뤄 너 부롸따러.

16. the people living in darkness have seen a great light; on those living in the land of the shadow of death a light has dawned."

17. Kutengera amu mango, Yesu era kutangilyisa kunde ahubanganyisa e bandju mbu: murekaa e bibi byenyu, bushi e bwami bokwa nguba bwera bulyi ofu.

17. 구더꺼라 아무 마꼬, 여수 어라 구다찌쩨사 구꺼 아후바꺼네사 어 바쭈 뿌: 무러가아 어 비비 벼뉴, 부씨 어 봐미 보과 꾸바 뭐라 부쩨 오푸.

17. From that time on Jesus began to preach, "Repent, for the kingdom of heaven is near."

Yesu alondola e banafunzi babere-bere

여수 아로또롸 어 바나푸씨 바버러-버러

18. Lusuku luuma mango Yesu abaa arenga kwa musike s'e nyanja yekalilaya, era kulola ku bafubi babilyi ba bula buuma: simoni ola bendee belyika mbu ipetero na andereya. Abu babilyi, babaa bena echwusira mwa nyanja.

18. 루수구 루우마 마꼬 여수 아바아 아러따 과 무시거 서 냐짜 여가찌롸야, 어라 구로롸 구 바푸비 바비쩨 바 부롸 부우마: 시모니 오롸 버떠어 버쩨가 뿌 이퍼더로 나 아떠러야. 아부 바비쩨, 바바아 버나 어쭈시라 마 냐짜.

18. As Jesus was walking beside the Sea of Galilee, he saw two brothers, Simon called Peter and his brother Andrew. They were casting a net into the lake, for they were fishermen.

19. Yesu era kubabura mbu: munyikulyikiraa, nyingabaira kuba bafubi ba bandju.

19. 여수 어라 구바부라 뿌: 무네구쩨기라아, 네따바이라 구바 바푸비 바 바쭈.

19. "Come, follow me," Jesus said, "and I will make you fishers of men."

20. Unao-unao, bera kureka

20. 우나오-우나오, 버라

20. At once they left their

echwusira chwabo, na bamukulyikira.

21. Mango Yesu abaa era achifundaa era muhondo hicha, era kulola ku banji bafubi babilyi ba bula buuma: yakobo na yowana. Abu babilyi, babaa balyi mwa bwato aalauma n'eshe wabo sebedayo. Bakunganya echwusira chwabo. Nabo, Yesu era kubamaala.

22. Unao-uno, bera kureka obu bwato, banareka n'eshe wabo, na bakukulyikira yesu.

Yesu akangilyisa e bandju alamya n'e balwala

23. Yesu abaa enjire asungula mwa chio choshi ch'e kalilaya. Mwechi chio, era kunde engilyira mwa mashenge m'e bayuda. Mwesi nyuhu, era kunde ahubanganyisa e bandju e mwasi mubuya-buya w'e bwami bokwa nguba. Era kunde alamya n'e bandju ba babaa bete chira bulwala neba babaa baremere.

24. Engulu yai, yera kuhandabana busese mwa chio choshi che suriya. Bushi noku, e bandju bera kunde bamureteranga e balwala

구러가 어쭈시라 좌보, 나 바무구레기라.

21. 마꼬 여수 아바아 어라 아찌푸따아 어라 무호또 히짜, 어라 구르롸 구 바찌 바푸비 바비레 바 부라 부우마: 야고보 나 요와나. 아부 바비레, 바바아 바레 뫄 바도 아아롸우마 너써 와보 서버다요. 바구꺄냐 어쭈시라 좌보. 나보, 여수 어라 구바마아롸.

22. 우나오-우노, 버라 구러가 오부 봐도, 바나러가 너써 와보, 나 바구구레기라 여수.

여수 아가삐레뻽 어 바쭈 아롸맹 너 바콰롸

23. 여수 아바아 어찌러 아수우롸 뫄 찌오 쪼씨 쩌 가뤼롸야. 뭐찌 찌오, 어라 구떠 어삐레라 뫄 마써어 머 바유다. 뭐시 뉴후, 어라 구떠 아후바까네사 어 바쭈 어 뫄시 무부야-부야 워 봐미 보과 꾸바. 어라 구떠 아롸먀 너 바쭈 바 바바아 버더 찌라 부콰롸 너바 바바아 바러머러.

24. 어우루 야이, 여라 구하따바나 부서서 뫄 찌오 쪼씨 쩌 수리야. 부씨 노구, 어 바쭈 버라 구떠 바무러더러롸 어 바롸롸 보씨 바 바바아

nets and followed him.

21. Going on from there, he saw two other brothers, James son of Zebedee and his brother John. They were in a boat with their father Zebedee, preparing their nets. Jesus called them,

22. and immediately they left the boat and their father and followed him.

23. Jesus went throughout Galilee, teaching in their synagogues, preaching the good news of the kingdom, and healing every disease and sickness among the people.

24. News about him spread all over Syria, and people brought to him all who were ill with various diseases, those suffering

boshi ba babaa balyibukire
na chira bulwala, n'e bihwasi,
n'e luungu, na ba babaa
baremere. Abu boshi, Yesu
era kunde anabalamya.

25. Echera chera kuchwuma
bandju banene busese kunde
bamukulyikira. Abu bandju,
babaa batengera mwa chio
chekalilaya, neche tekapoli,
nomwa musi we yerusalemu,
nomwa chio che yudeya.
Nokwa mushilyilya welwishi
lwe yorodani.

Matayo Chikono 5
*Yesu akangilyisa e bandju
kwa ndjulungu*

1. Mango Yesu alolaa kwa
luamba lw'e bandju, era
kwerukira kwa ndjulungu.
Abere era ekalaa, e banafunzi
bai bera kuchifunda ofu nai.

2. Era kutangilyisa
abakangilyisa mbu:

3. Bahanyirwe ba beshi kwa
balyi bakene bemuchima,
bushi ebwami bokwa nguba
bulyi bwabo.

4. Bahanyirwe ba balyi mwa
malyira, bushi Ongo
angabasesa emuchima.

5. Bahanyirwe ba bachwula
barembu, bushi bangeresibwa

바레부기러 나 찌라 부롸롸,
너 비화시, 너 루우우, 나 바
바바아 바러머러. 아부 보씨,
여수 어라 구떠 아나바롸먀.

25. 어쩌라 쩌라 구쭈마 바뉴
바너너 부서서 구떠
바무구쩨기라. 아부 바뉴,
바바아 바더뻐라 먀 찌오
쩌가뤼롸야, 너쩌 더가포뢰,
노와 무시 워 여루사뻐무,
노와 찌오 쩌 유더야. 노과
무씨뤠랴 워뤼씨 뤄 요로다니.

마다요 찌고노 5
*여수 아가뼤뤠뼵 어 바뉴 과
뉴뤄우*

1. 마오 여수 아뢰롸아 과
루아빠 뤄 바뉴, 어라
궈루기라 과 뉴뤄우. 아버러
어라 어가롸아, 어 바나푸씨
바이 버라 구찌푸따 오푸
나이.

2. 어라 구다뼤뤠사
아바가뼤뤠사 뿌:

3. 바하니뤄 바 버씨 과 바뤠
바거너 버무찌마, 부씨 어봐미
보과 우바 부뤠 봐보.

4. 바하니뤄 바 바뤠 먀
마뤠라, 부씨 오꼬 아까바서사
어무찌마.

5. 바하니뤄 바 바쭈롸 바러뿌,
부씨 바뻐러시봐 어찌오 구바

---

severe pain, the demon-
possessed, those having
seizures, and the
paralyzed, and he healed
them.

25. Large crowds from
Galilee, the Decapolis,
Jerusalem, Judea and the
region across the Jordan
followed him.

Matthew Chapter 5[NIV]

1. Now when he saw the
crowds, he went up on a
mountainside and sat
down. His disciples came
to him,

2. and he began to teach
them saying:

3. "Blessed are the poor in
spirit, for theirs is the
kingdom of heaven.

4. Blessed are those who
mourn, for they will be
comforted.

5. Blessed are the meek,
for they will inherit the

echio kuba mwandju.

6. Bahanyirwe ba bachwusa ebusinya nechami chekuira bya bichwungenene era muhondo sa Ongo, bushi Ongo angabeucha.

7. Bahanyirwe ba bende bafira ebanji ebonjo, bushi nabo Ongo angabafira bonjo.

8. Bahanyirwe ba bachwusa emuchima ola ukomisibwe, bushi bakalola ku Ongo.

9. Bahanyirwe ba bende bareta eboolo, bushi bangelyikibwa bana ba Ongo.

10. Bahanyirwe ba balyibusibwa bushi bende baira bya bichwungenene era muhondo sa Ongo, bushi ebwami bokwa nguba bulyi bwabo.

11. Muahanyirwe emango e bandju bende ba bakamba na kubalyibusa na kubasinga chira mwasi mubi bushi nanyi.

12. Mundaa mwamowa na kuchiterera busese, bushi Ongo ababikilyire lwembo lunene kwa nguba. Kunoku kubanalyibusaa e barebi ba babahondoreraa.

E munyu n'e bulangare bw'e butala

13. Mwabo mulyi nga munyu

뫄뚜.

6. 바하니뤄 바 바쭈사 어부시냐 너짜미 쩌구이라 뱌 비쭈어너너 어라 무호또 사 오꼬, 부씨 오꼬 아빠버우짜.

7. 바하니뤄 바 버떠 바피라 어바찌 어보쪼, 부씨 나보 오꼬 아빠바피라 보쪼.

8. 바하니뤄 바 바쭈사 어무찌마 오롸 우고미시붜, 부씨 바가로롸 구 오꼬.

9. 바하니뤄 바 버떠 바러다 어보오롣, 부씨 바껴레기봐 바나 바 오꼬.

10. 바하니뤄 바 바레부시봐 부씨 버떠 바이라 뱌 비쭈어너너 어라 무호또 사 오꼬, 부씨 어봐미 보과 꾸바 부뼤 봐보.

11. 무아하니뤄 어마꼬 어 바뚜 버떠 바 바가빠 나 구바뼤부사 나 구바시꺄 찌라 뫄시 무비 부씨 나니.

12. 무따아 뫄모와 나 구찌더러라 부서서, 부씨 오꼬 아바비기꼐러 뤄뽀 루너너 과 꾸바. 구노구 구바나레부사아 어 바러비 바 바바호또러라아.

어 무뉴 너 부롸뺘란 붜 부다롸

13. 뫄보 무뼤 꺄 무뉴

---

earth.

6. Blessed are those who hunger and thirst for righteousness, for they will be filled.

7. Blessed are the merciful, for they will be shown mercy.

8. Blessed are the pure in heart, for they will see God.

9. Blessed are the peacemakers, for they will be called sons of God.

10. Blessed are those who are persecuted because of righteousness, for theirs is the kingdom of heaven.

11. "Blessed are you when people insult you, persecute you and falsely say all kinds of evil against you because of me.

12. Rejoice and be glad, because great is your reward in heaven, for in the same way they persecuted the prophets who were before you.

13. "You are the salt of the

webutala. Rero akaba emunyu angaesa ebuloke bwai, chi bangabikamo kanji ahube kuloka? Oyu munyu, atachete mufa usibya si anera wa kusheshibwa era butala, chasinda anakandangwa n'e bandju.

14. Mwabo mulyi bulangare bwebutala. E musi ola uimbirwe kwa ndjulungu, atangachibisha.

15. Kanji kutalyi mundju ola ungakoresa etara chasinda analyifunyikira echitonga. Si ende abikalyi kwa kakondo cha siya lyilomekere ebandju boshi ba balyi mwa nyumba.

16. Kuno ku kwebulangare bwenyu bwemire kunde bwalomekera ebandju, chasiya bende balola kwa myanya yenyu ibuya, nabo bende batonga eho wenyu ola ulyi kwa nguba.

Yesu akangilyisa era lulu s'e mwaso wa musa

17. Mutendaa mwaanyasi mbu naikire kuhandjula emwaso wa musa, nesi emyasi era yatechwaa nebarebi. Ndaikire bushi nyibihandjule, si naikire chasiya ebi byoshi bibirere.

18. Kubinali, nababura kwa

워부다롸. 러로 아가바 어무뉴 아빠어사 어부로거 봐이, 찌 바빠비가모 가찌 아후버 구론가? 오유 무뉴, 아다쩌더 무파 우시뱌 시 아너라 와 구써씨봐 어라 부다롸, 짜시따 아나가따꽈 너 바뉴.

14. 롸보 무레 부롸빠러 붜부다롸. 어 무시 오롸 우이삐뤄 과 뚜루우, 아다빠찌비싸.

15. 가찌 구다레 무뿌 오롸 우빠고러사 어다라 짜시따 아나레푸네기라 어찌도꽈. 시 어떠 아비가레 과 가고또 짜 시야 레로머거러 어바뉴 보씨 바 바레 롸 뉴빠.

16. 구노 구 궈부롸빠러 붜뉴 붜미러 구떠 봐로머거라 어바뉴, 짜시야 버떠 바로롸 과 먀냐 여뉴 이부야, 나보 버떠 바도꽈 어호 워뉴 오롸 우레 과 우바.

여수 아가삐레뻽 어라 룰루 서 롸소 와 무사

17. 무더따아 롸아냐시 뿌 나이기러 구하뉴롸 어롸소 와 무사, 너시 어먀시 어라 야더꽈아 너바러비. 따이기러 부씨 니비하뉴뤄, 시 나이기러 짜시야 어비 뵤씨 비비러러.

18. 구비나삐, 나바부라 과

---

earth. But if the salt loses its saltiness, how can it be made salty again? It is no longer good for anything, except to be thrown out and trampled by men.

14. "You are the light of the world. A city on a hill cannot be hidden.

15. Neither do people light a lamp and put it under a bowl. Instead they put it on its stand, and it gives light to everyone in the house.

16. In the same way, let your light shine before men, that they may see your good deeds and praise your Father in heaven.

17. "Do not think that I have come to abolish the Law or the Prophets; I have not come to abolish them but to fulfill them.

18. I tell you the truth,

buendera enguba nebutala bikaba bichirio, kutali chiro na ka erufu kauna nesi chitamukiro chiuma che mwaso cha chikakuibwa, kuikira byoshi biberere.

19. Bushi noku mwoyu mwaso, chira mundju woshi ola ungakena emuomba ola usenekeko nga mueke kurenza ilyikabo, chasinda anakangilyisa e banji mbu nabo baukenaa oyu mundju iukaba mueke mwa bwami bokwa nguba. Si ola ukachwundao na kuukangilyisa banji nabo bendaa bauchwunda, oyola iukaba mukulu-kulu mwa bwami bokwa nguba.

20. Rero nababura kwa akaba mutenjire mwaira bya bichwungenene era muhondo sa Ongo kurenza ebafarisayo nebakangilyisi bemwaso, mutakengilyire chiro na hicha mwa bwami bokwa nguba.

Yesu akangilyisa era luulu s'e kusinana

21. Mwomvaa kwa bahokulu benyu baburwaa mbu: utendaa weta. Bushi e mundju ola wechire

부어떠라 어우바 너부다롸 비가바 비찌리오, 구다뙤 찌로 나 가 어루푸 가우나 너시 찌다무기로 찌우마 쩌 롸소 짜 찌가구이봐, 구이기라 뵤씨 비버러러.

19. 부씨 노구 모유 롸소, 찌라 무뚜 옷씨 오롸 우까거나 어무오빠 오롸 우서너거고 롸 무어거 구러싸 이레가보, 짜시따 아나가띠레사 어 바찌 뿌 나보 바우거나아 오유 무뚜 이우가바 무어거 롸 봐미 보과 우바. 시 오롸 우가쭈따오 나 구우가띠레사 바찌 나보 버따아 바우쭈따, 오요롸 이우가바 무구루-구루 롸 봐미 보과 우바.

20. 러로 나바부라 과 아가바 무더찌러 롸이라 뱌 비쭈어너너 어라 무호또 사 오꼬 구러싸 어바파리사요 너바가띠레시 버롸소, 무다거띠레러 찌로 나 히짜 롸 봐미 보과 우바.

여수 아가띠레뻽 어라 루윰루 서 구시나나

21. 모빠아 과 바호구루 버뉴 바부롸아 뿌: 우더따아 워다. 부씨 어 무뚜 오롸 워찌러 무레가보, 어미러

until heaven and earth disappear, not the smallest letter, not the least stroke of a pen, will by any means disappear from the Law until everything is accomplished.

19. Anyone who breaks one of the least of these commandments and teaches others to do the same will be called least in the kingdom of heaven, but whoever practices and teaches these commands will be called great in the kingdom of heaven.

20. For I tell you that unless your righteousness surpasses that of the Pharisees and the teachers of the law, you will certainly not enter the kingdom of heaven.

21. "You have heard that it was said to the people long ago, 'Do not murder, and anyone who murders

mulyikabo, emire kuchinjibusibwa.

22. Si nyono nababura kwa akaba emundju angasinanyira munyakabo, oyu mundju emire kuchinjibusibwa. Kanji ola ungakamba munyakabo mbu: ulyi mbuta nai emire kuchinjibusibwa mwa karubanda kechwu. Nola wabura munyakabo mbu; ulyi musire, oyola nai emire uumwa mwa mulyiro wesuku nemango.

23. Rero akaba ungaba waya kuchwula Onga kwa kahaha kemichwulo, na wakengera kwa munyakenyu akwete kumwasi murebe,

24. Urekaa tanga ei michwulo yao era muhondo s'e kahaha, wanaya kwomvikana nai. Chasinda, wanere wabaha kwana ei michwulo yao.

25. Kanji akaba mundju murebe angaba akusitakire, womvikanaa nai fuba mango muchilyi mwa njira yekuya era muhondo sebaishi bemanja. Bitabere bacha, oyu mundju angakwana era mwebaishi bemanja, nabo banakubika mwamino sabasula, chasinda nabo anakuuma mwa buroko.

구찌찌부시봐.

22. 시 뇨노 나바부라 과 아가바 어무뚜 아빠시나니네라 무냐가보, 오유 무뚜 어미러 구찌찌부시봐. 가찌 오꽈 우빠가빠 무냐가보 뿌: 우레 뿌다 나이 어미러 구찌찌부시봐 꽈 가루바따 거쭉. 노라 와부라 무냐가보 뿌; 우레 무시러, 오요꽈 나이 어미러 우우꽈 꽈 무레로 워수구 너마꼬.

23. 러로 아가바 우빠바 와야 구쭈꽈 오빠 과 가하하 거미쭉로, 나 와거꺼라 과 무냐거뉴 아궈더 구꽈시 무러버,

24. 우러가아 다빠 어이 미쭉로 야오 어라 무호또 서 가하하, 와나야 곰삐가나 나이. 짜시따, 와너러 와바하 과나 어이 미쭉로 야오.

25. 가찌 아가바 무뚜 무러버 아빠바 아구시다기러, 옴삐가나아 나이 푸바 마꼬 무찌레 꽈 띠라 여구야 어라 무호또 서바이씨 버마짜. 비다버러 바짜, 오유 무뚜 아빠과나 어라 뭐바이씨 버마짜, 나보 바나구비가 꽈미노 사바수꽈, 짜시따 나보 아나구우마 꽈 부로고.

will be subject to judgment.'

22. But I tell you that anyone who is angry with his brotherwill be subject to judgment. Again, anyone who says to his brother, 'Raca,' is answerable to the Sanhedrin. But anyone who says, 'You fool!' will be in danger of the fire of hell.

23. "Therefore, if you are offering your gift at the altar and there remember that your brother has something against you,

24. leave your gift there in front of the altar. First go and be reconciled to your brother; then come and offer your gift.

25. "Settle matters quickly with your adversary who is taking you to court. Do it while you are still with him on the way, or he may hand you over to the judge, and the judge may hand you over to the officer, and you may be thrown into prison.

26. Kubinalyi, nababura kwa utangatenga mwobu buroko akaba utasa kuonga e mwinda woshi.

Yesu akangirisa era lulu sekubanda ekiri

27. Mwomvaa kwa byatechwaa mbu: utendaa wabanda ekilyi.

28. Si nyono nababura kwa akaba emulume angachwumbikisa emukasi kwa kuchifisai, elyi abanjire ekilyi noyu mukasi mwa muchima wai. Elyiho lyao lyemalyo akaba lyingachwuma.

29. E lyiho yao ly'e malyo lyika kuilyira Kubi wana lyi kula, bushi Chitera chao chuuma chingaera e mubilyi woshi akuya mwa mulyiro.

30. Na kuboko kwao kw'e malyo kuka Kuilyira kubi, ukuishaa ne ku kuuma bure, chasiya chitera chwuma chikwera Kasi utaya mwa mulyiro n'e mubilyi wao. woshi.

31. Kanji batechire kwa, mundju akareka mukasi waye, ana mulangikira e malyikanuko

---

26. 구비나레, 나바부라 과 우다꺼더꺼 모부 부로고 아가바 우다사 구오꺼 어 뮈따 옷씨.

여수 아가꺼릇뻽 어라 루루 서구바따 어기리

27. 모빠아 과 뱌더쫘아 뿌: 우더따아 와바따 어기레.

28. 시 뇨노 나바부라 과 아가바 어무루머 아꺼쭈삐기사 어무가시 과 구찌피사이, 어레 아바찌러 어기레 노유 무가시 뫄 무찌마 와이. 어레호 랴오 려마뢷 아가바 레꺼쭈마.

29. 어 레호 야오 뤼어 마뢷 레가 구이레라 구비 와나 레 구롸, 부씨 찌더라 짜오 쭈우마 찌꺼어라 어 무비레 옷씨 아구야 뫄 무레로.

30. 나 구보고 과오 궈 마뢷 구가 구이레라 구비, 우구이싸아 너 구 구우마 부러, 짜시야 찌더라 쭈마 찌궈라 가시 우다야 뫄 무레로 너 무비레 와오. 옷씨.

31. 가찌 바더찌러 과, 무뿌 아가러가 무가시 와여, 아나 무롸꺼기라 어 마레가누고

---

26. I tell you the truth, you will not get out until you have paid the last penny.

27. "You have heard that it was said, 'Do not commit adultery.'

28. But I tell you that anyone who looks at a woman lustfully has already committed adultery with her in his heart.

29. If your right eye causes you to sin, gouge it out and throw it away. It is better for you to lose one part of your body than for your whole body to be thrown into hell.

30. And if your right hand causes you to sin, cut it off and throw it away. It is better for you to lose one part of your body than for your whole body to go into hell.

31. "It has been said, 'Anyone who divorces his wife must give her a certificate of divorce.'

32. Selyi nyono nababura, chira ola warekire mukasi waye itabere kumyasi ya kumusimba naungi mulume (e kilyi) amuilyire muckilyikilyi nola unga muhwera oyo mukasi warekibwa naye analyi mukilyikilyi.

33. Kanji mwomvire kwa bandju ba miramira ba baburaa, utenda wa chikulyinja e bisha, kweine uilyira nyamusinda bya wateta.

34. Kweine nyono nababulyire kwa mutachikulyinza kandju, chira ingaba Kwa nguba bushi e nguba chi chifumbi che bwami bwa Ongo.

35. Kalyi kwa chino, kuva bushi khwenda bikira e maulu mae, kasi kwa Jerusalemu Kwa bushi imusi we bwami bukulu.

36. Ka utachikulyinza etchwe Lyao bushi utangaa kwira lufilyi Iwao luuma Kuba emvi kalyi kuba Eyerafulu.

37. Kwa bushi e myasi yenyu iban kanangana kwa kanangana kutalyi kutalyi elyi kutanalyi bushi bya bitalyi bacha elyi byatengera era mwe musimu.

38. Kanji mwomvire khwa

---

32. 서레 뇨노 나바부라, 찌라 오롸 와러기러 무가시 와여 이다버러 구먀시 야 구무시빠 나우삐 무루머 (어 기롈) 아무이뻬러 무시기뼤기뼤 노롸 우꼬 무훠라 오요 무가시 와러기봐 나여 아나뼤 무기뼤기뼤.

33. 가찌 몰뻬러 과 바뚜 바 미라미라 바 바부라아, 우더따 와 찌구뼤짜 어 비싸, 궈이너 우이뼤라 냐무시따 뱌 와더다.

34. 궈이너 뇨노 나바부뼤러 과 무다찌구뼤싸 가뚜, 찌라 이꽈바 과 우바 부씨 어 우바 찌 찌푸뻬 쩌 봐미 봐 오꼬.

35. 가뼤 과 찌노, 구바 부씨 구훠따 비기라 어 마우루 마어, 가시 과 저루사뻐무 과 부씨 이무시 워 봐미 부구루.

36. 가 우다찌구뼤싸 어쭤 럐오 부씨 우다꼬아 귀라 루피뼤 이와오 루우마 구바 어뻬 가뼤 구바 어여라푸루.

37. 과 부씨 어 먀시 여뉴 이바누 가나꽈나 과 가나꽈나 구다뼤 구다뼤 어뼤 구다나뼤 부씨 뱌 비다뼤 바짜 어뼤 뱌더꺼라 어라 뭐 무시무.

38. 가찌 몰뻬러 구화

---

32. But I tell you that anyone who divorces his wife, except for marital unfaithfulness, causes her to become an adulteress, and anyone who marries the divorced woman commits adultery.

33. "Again, you have heard that it was said to the people long ago, 'Do not break your oath, but keep the oaths you have made to the Lord.'

34. But I tell you, Do not swear at all: either by heaven, for it is God's throne;

35. or by the earth, for it is his footstool; or by Jerusalem, for it is the city of the Great King.

36. And do not swear by your head, for you cannot make even one hair white or black.

37. Simply let your 'Yes' be 'Yes,' and your 'No,' 'No'; anything beyond this comes from the evil one.

38. "You have heard that it

batetaa kwa lyiho kwa lyiho na lyino kwa lyino,

39. Kweine nyono naba bulyire kwa mutashiikana ne mundju mubi kweine e mundju ola unga kumaasa kwe tama lye malyo, umualyulyira ne lyindji,

40. Ne mundju ola unga kutonganya ne kunyaa e ropu yao, umuvekera ne kabutura nako.

41. Nola unga kulyibicha chichiro chuuma cha njira wana enda naye e cha kabilyi.

42. Eunga kuema muwaa nola unga chihomba era musao wanesha kumurekera.

43. Kaa mumvire kwa batetaa. Kwa usima e mulungu wao wanaya ne murenda wao.

44. Kiveine nyono nababulyire musimaa ne barenda benyu, mwenda mwemera nabala babalyibusa.

45. Elyi mwabona e Kwamalyibwa bana ba tata wenyu ola ulyi kwa nguba bushi yeke enda koresesa e suba e babi ne babuya, enda tosesa ne neula ba babete e mwaso nabala bateete

바더다아 과 레호 과 레호 나 레노 과 레노,

39. 궈이너 뇨노 나바 부레러 과 무다씨이가나 너 무뚜 무비 궈이너 어 무뚜 오롸 우꽈 구마아사 궈 다마 려 마룐, 우무아려유레라 너 레씨,

40. 너 무뚜 오롸 우꽈 구도꺄냐 너 구냐아 어 로푸 야오, 우무버거라 너 가부두라 나고.

41. 노롸 우꽈 구레비짜 찌찌로 쭈우마 짜 띠라 와나 어따 나여 어 짜 가비레.

42. 어우꽈 구어마 무와아 노롸 우꽈 찌호빠 어라 무사오 와너싸 구무러거라.

43. 가아 무삐러 과 바더다아. 과 우시마 어 무루꾸 와오 와나야 너 무러따 와오.

44. 기버이너 뇨노 나바부레러 무시마아 너 바러따 버뉴, 뭐따 뭐머라 나바꽈 바바레부사.

45. 어레 꽈보나 어 과마레봐 바나 바 다다 워뉴 오롸 우레 과 꾸바 부씨 여거 어따 고러서사 어 수바 어 바비 너 바부야, 어따 도서사 너 너우롸 바 바버더 어 꽈소 나바꽈 바더어더 꽈소.

was said, 'Eye for eye, and tooth for tooth.'

39. But I tell you, Do not resist an evil person. If someone strikes you on the right cheek, turn to him the other also.

40. And if someone wants to sue you and take your tunic, let him have your cloak as well.

41. If someone forces you to go one mile, go with him two miles.

42. Give to the one who asks you, and do not turn away from the one who wants to borrow from you.

43. "You have heard that it was said, 'Love your neighbor and hate your enemy.'

44. But I tell you: Love your enemies and pray for those who persecute you,

45. that you may be sons of your Father in heaven. He causes his sun to rise on the evil and the good, and sends rain on the righteous and the unrighteous.

mwaso.

46. Bushi, mukasima ba babasimire mungabona lyeembo luchiye? bushi ne babusi b'e mbarata nabo bataira bacha?

47. Kanji mukana kesa ba balyi banyakenyu chiye chi mwailyire kurenza e banji? Ne banji bandju babataly bemeresi nabo bataira bacha?

48. Kasi mwabo mubaa Kanangana ngokwa cho wenyu ola ulyi kwa nguba atchwula karangana.

---

46. 부씨, 무가시마 바 바바시미러 무까보나 쪄어뽀 루찌여? 부씨 너 바부시 버 빠라다 나보 바다이라 바짜?

47. 가찌 무가나 거사 바 바레 바냐거뉴 찌여 찌 마이레러 구러싸 어 바찌? 너 바씨 바뚜 바바다뤼 버머러시 나보 바다이라 바짜?

48. 가시 꽈보 무바아 가나까나 쯔과 쪼 워뉴 오롸 우뤠 과 우바 아쭈롸 가라까나.

---

46. If you love those who love you, what reward will you get? Are not even the tax collectors doing that?

47. And if you greet only your brothers, what are you doing more than others? Do not even pagans do that?

48. Be perfect, therefore, as your heavenly Father is perfect.

Matayo Chikono 6

Yesu akangilyisa era luuku s'e kuasa e bakene

1. Mumenyaa, mutenda mwaira e mabuya era muhundo s'e bandju chasiya muchilose era muhondo sabo. Bushi mukaira bacha, kutachilyi lwembo lusibya lwa mungabona era mw'eho wenyu ola ulyi kwa nguba.

2. bushi noku, emango waasa e bakene, utendaa wabanda mwa kaperere ngokwe batebanyi bende baira mwa mashenge mabo nomwa njira, chasiya e bandju bende

---

마다요 찌고노 6

여수 아가끼레쁩 어라 루욥꼴 서 구아사 어 바거너

1. 무머냐아, 무더따 먀이라 어 마부야 어라 무후또 서 바뚜 짜시야 무찌로써 어라 무호또 사보. 부씨 무가이라 바짜, 구다찌뤠 뤄뽀 루시뱌 롸 무까보나 어라 뭐호 워뉴 오롸 우뤠 과 우바.

2. 부씨 노구, 어마쪼 와아사 어 바거너, 우더따아 와바따 롸 가퍼러러 쯔궈 바더바네 버떠 바이라 롸 마써꺼 마보 노롸 띠라, 짜시야 어 바뚜 버떠 바바도까, 구비나뤠,

---

Matthew Chapter 6[NIV]

1. "Be careful not to do your 'acts of righteousness' before men, to be seen by them. If you do, you will have no reward from your Father in heaven.

2. "So when you give to the needy, do not announce it with trumpets, as the hypocrites do in the synagogues and on the streets, to be honored by

babatonga, kubinalyi, nababura kwa beke baboonyire e lwambo mira.

3. si woyo mango waasa e bakene, e mino yao y'e marembe itendaa yamenya cha y'e malyo yaira.

4. Rero amu mubaya undaa wamaira mwa bubisho-bisho n'eho wao i usene mwabubisho-bisho kwebya waira, angakwemba.

Yesu akangilyisa era luulu s'e kuema Ongo

5. mango mwema Ongo, mutendaa mwaba nga batebanyi, bushi beke mwa kuba bema, bachwula basimire kwemanga mwa mashenge mabo, nomwa mahanganyisa m'e njira chasiya balorekaneko n'e bandju. Kubinalyi, nababura kwa babonyire e lwembo lwabo mira.

6. si woyo mango wahonda kwema Ongo wangilyiraa mwa chumba chao, wanachinga e lwisi, wanere wema eho ola utasenekeko. Noyu eho, i usene kwebya waira weine, angakwemba.

7. kanji mango mwema Ongo, mutendaamwateteresa myasi era itete mufa, ngokwa

나바부라 과 버거 바보오네러 어 롸뫈 미라.

3. 시 옷요 마꼬 와아사 어 바거너, 어 미노 야오 여 마러뻐 이더따아 야머냐 짜 여 마룐 야이라.

4. 러로 아무 무바야 우따아 와마이라 뫄 부비쏘-비쏘 너호 와오 이 우서너 뫄부비쏘-비쏘 궈뱌 와이라, 아까궈빠.

여수 아가끼레뻽 어라 룲욬룮 서 구어마 오꼬

5. 마꼬 뭐마 오꼬, 무더따아 뫄바 까 바더바네, 부씨 버거 뫄 구바 버마, 바쭈롸 바시미러 궈마까 뫄 마써꺼 마보, 노뫄 마하까네사 머 찌라 짜시야 바롤러가너고 너 바쭈. 구비나레, 나바부라 과 바보네러 어 뤄뫈 롸보 미라.

6. 시 옷요 마꼬 와호따 궈마 오꼬 와끼레라아 뫄 쭈빠 짜오, 와나찌까 어 뤼시, 와너러 워마 어호 오롸 우다서너거고. 노유 어호, 이 우서너 궈뱌 와이라 워이너, 아까궈빠.

7. 가찌 마꼬 뭐마 오꼬, 무더따아뫄더더러사 먀시 어라 이더더 무파, 꼬과 어 바쭈 바

men. I tell you the truth, they have received their reward in full.

3. But when you give to the needy, do not let your left hand know what your right hand is doing,

4. so that your giving may be in secret. Then your Father, who sees what is done in secret, will reward you.

5. "And when you pray, do not be like the hypocrites, for they love to pray standing in the synagogues and on the street corners to be seen by men. I tell you the truth, they have received their reward in full.

6. But when you pray, go into your room, close the door and pray to your Father, who is unseen. Then your Father, who sees what is done in secret, will reward you.

7. And when you pray, do not keep on babbling like pagans, for they think they

e bandju ba bateshi Ongo bende baira. Bushi beke, bende baanyisambu Ongo angomvabo bushi n'e bwingi bw'e binwa byabo.	바더씨 오끄 버머 바이라. 부씨 버거, 버머 바아니에사뿌 오끄 아끄빠보 부씨 너 뷔끼 뭐 비냐 쨔보.	will be heard because of their many words.
8. Abu bandju, mwabo mutendaa mweyabo, bushi eho wenyuaneshi bya mulaireko inabe mutasa kumwema.	8. 아부 바쭈, 먀보 무더따아 뭐야보, 부씨 어호 워뉴아너씨 뱌 무꽈이러고 이나버 무다사 구뭐마.	8. Do not be like them, for your Father knows what you need before you ask him.
9. Rero, bacha ku mundaa mwema : Ongo tata u ulyi kwa nguba, esina lyao liye ngulu.	9. 러로, 바짜 구 무따아 뭐마 : 오끄 다다 우 우레 과 꾸바, 어시나 랴오 끼여 꾸루.	9. "This, then, is how you should pray: " 'Our Father in heaven, hallowed be your name,
10. e bwami bwao, bubahaa. Ekuhonda kwao, ku kwindaa kwanaba muno butala, ngokwa nguba.	10. 어 봐미 봐오, 부바하아. 어구호따 과오, 구 귀따아 과나바 무노 부다꽈, 끄과 꾸바.	10. your kingdom come, your will be done on earth as it is in heaven.
11. uchwweresaa e bilyo byechwu bya chira lusuku.	11. 우쫘워러사아 어 비료 벼쭈 뱌 찌라 루수구.	11. Give us today our daily bread.
12. undaa wachwubabalyira e bibi byechwu, ngokwa nechwu chwende chwababalyira ba bende bachwukorera e mabi.	12. 우따아 와쭈바바꼐라 어 비비 벼쭈, 끄과 너쭈 쮀머 쫘바바꼐라 바 버머 바쭈고러라 어 마비.	12. Forgive us our debts, as we also have forgiven our debtors.
13. utendaa wareka chwengilyire mwa miereko si undaa wachwutabala ku wamusimu. Bushi woyo, uena e bwami, e buashi, n'e ngulu, e suku n'e mango, bibe bacha.	13. 우더따아 와러가 쮀끼꼐러 뫄 미어러고 시 우따아 와쭈다바꽈 구 와무시무. 부씨 요요, 우어나 어 봐미, 어 부아씨, 너 꾸루, 어 수구 너 마끄, 비버 바짜.	13. And lead us not into temptation, but deliver us from the evil one.'
14. Yesu era ku teta kanji mbu: akaba mungende mwa babalyira e banji e mabi ma	14. 여수 어라 구 더다 가찌 뿌: 아가바 무꺼머 뫄 바바꼐라 어 바찌 어 마비 마	14. For if you forgive men when they sin against you, your heavenly Father will

babakorere, eho wenyu ola ulyi kwa nguba nai angababababalyira.

15. si akaba mutangababalyira e banji, eho wenyu ola ulyi kwa nguba nai atakabababalyire.

Yesu akangilyisa era luulu s'e memo ma mende mairwa busira kulya

16. Mango mulyi mwa memo ma mende mairwa busira kulya, mutendaa mwachilosa nga ba basinanyire ngokwe batebanyi bende baira. Bushi beke, bende ba sinya e buso kwabo, chasiya balose ebandu kwa bali mwa'mu memo. Kubinalyi, nababura kwa babonyire e lwembo lwabo mira.

17. si woyo mango uli mwa'mu memo, undaa wowa era buso, wanasanura ne'mviri sao,

18. e bandju bangesha kumenya kwa kasi ulyi mwamu memo. Si oyu mwasi aneshibwe n'eho wao ola utasenekeko. Noyu eho i usene kwebya waira weine, angakwemba.

Yesu akangilyisa era luulu s'e buare

19. Yesu era kuhuba kuteta

바바고러러, 어호 워뉴 오꽈 우쮀 과 우바 나이 아꿔바바바바쮀라.

15. 시 아가바 무다꿔바바바쮀라 어 바찌, 어호 워뉴 오꽈 우쮀 과 우바 나이 아다가바바바바쮀러.

여수 아가삐쮀뻽 어라 루욥루 서 머모 마 머뻐 마이롸 부시라 구꺄

16. 마꼬 무쮀 뫄 머모 마 머뻐 마이롸 부시라 구꺄, 무더꿔아 뫄찌로사 꿔 바 바시나녜러 꼬궈 바더바네 버뻐 바이라. 부씨 버거, 버뻐 바 시냐 어 부소 과보, 짜시야 바로서 어바뚜 과 바삐 뫄무 머모. 구비나쮀, 나바부라 과 바보녜러 어 뤠또 꽈보 미라.

17. 시 오요 마꼬 우삐 뫄무 머모, 우따아 오와 어라 부소, 와나사누라 너뻬리 사오,

18. 어 바뚜 바꿔싸 구머냐 과 가시 우쮀 뫄무 머모. 시 오유 므와시, 아너씨붜 너호 와오 오꽈 우다서너거고. 노유 어호 이 우서너 궈뱌 와이라 워이너, 아꿔궈빠.

여수 아가삐쮀뻽 어라 루욥루 서 부아러

19. 여수 어라 구후바 구더다

also forgive you.

15. But if you do not forgive men their sins, your Father will not forgive your sins.

16. "When you fast, do not look somber as the hypocrites do, for they disfigure their faces to show men they are fasting. I tell you the truth, they have received their reward in full.

17. But when you fast, put oil on your head and wash your face,

18. so that it will not be obvious to men that you are fasting, but only to your Father, who is unseen; and your Father, who sees what is done in secret, will reward you.

19. "Do not store up for

mbu: mutendaa mwachibikira e buare muno butala, bushi e kaembe n'e luhwarenge byende byakumbyabo. N'e besi bende bachwula e nyumba na beba.

20. si mundaa mwachibikira e buare kwa nguba, bushi okola kweke e kaembe n'e luhwarenge bitangaala kukumbya, n'e besi batangaala kuchwula na kwiba.

21. Bushi ala bikulo byao bilyi w'e muchima wao nao ende anaba.

E meho ku kamore k'e mubilyi

22. Emeho kukamore k'e mubilyi. Akaba e meho mao machilyi machwungenene, e mubilyi wao woshi, anaba mwa bulangare.

23. si akaba e meho mao mauchire, e mubilyi wao woshi anaba mwa musimya. Rero, akaba e bulangare bwa bulyi mwa ndanda Sao bungabindjuka musimya anere aba munene busese.

E kokurera Ongo nesi e bikulo

24. kutalyi mundju ola ungaala kukorera ba enawabo babilyi. Bushi kuika

뿌: 무더따아 꽈찌비기라 어 부아러 무노 부다꽈, 부씨 어 가어뻐 너 루화러러 벼버 뱌구뺘보. 너 버시 버떠 바쭈꽈 어 뉴빠 나 버바.

20. 시 무따아 꽈찌비기라 어 부아러 과 우바, 부씨 오고꽈 귀거 어 가어뻐 너 루화러러 비다아아꽈 구구뺘, 너 버시 바다아아꽈 구쭈꽈 나 귀바.

21. 부씨 아꽈 비구로 뱌오 비레 워 무찌마 와오 나오 어떠 아나바.

어 머호 구 가모러 거 무비레

22. 어머호 구가모러 거 무비레. 아가바 어 머호 마오 마찌레 마쭈뻐너너, 어 무비레 와오 올씨, 아나바 꽈 부꽈아러.

23. 시 아가바 어 머호 마오 마우찌러, 어 무비레 와오 올씨 아나바 꽈 무시먀. 러로, 아가바 어 부꽈아러 봐 부레 꽈 따따 사오 부빠비쭈가 무시먀 아너러 아바 무너너 부서서.

어 고구러라 오꼬 너시 어 비구로

24. 구다레 무뚜 오라 우빠아꽈 구고러라 바 어나와보 바비레. 부씨 구이가

yourselves treasures on earth, where moth and rust destroy, and where thieves break in and steal.

20. But store up for yourselves treasures in heaven, where moth and rust do not destroy, and where thieves do not break in and steal.

21. For where your treasure is, there your heart will be also.

22. "The eye is the lamp of the body. If your eyes are good, your whole body will be full of light.

23. But if your eyes are bad, your whole body will be full of darkness. If then the light within you is darkness, how great is that darkness!

24. "No one can serve two masters. Either he will hate the one and love the

anahombe muuma anasima e unji. Nesi angaba luuma-luuma na muuma na kukena e unji. Mutangaala kukorera Ongo, mukorere n'e bikulo.

Yesu akangilyisa era lulu s'e kuchanya

25. Bushi noku, nababura kwa mutendaa mwachanya bushi n'e kalamo kenyu mwa kuchibusa mbu: chi chwungalya, chichwungamwa, nesi chi chwungembala? Si e kalamo, ku kete mufa kurenza e bilyo, n'e mubilyi, iwete mufa kurenza e njimba.

26. mulolaa kwa milonge! Itainga, itashebula, itachwusa na ngulyi. Sichiro bacha, eho wenyu ola ulyi kwa nguba, ende analyisai. rero mwabo, kasi ata mumwete mufa munene kurenza ei milonge?

27. ewashe! Nde mu mwabo, ola bushi n'e kuchanyakwai angaala kuchibikira lunji lusuku luuma kwa kalamo kai?

28. Chi chachwuma mwachanya bushi n'e njimba? Mulola kwa bwaso bo mw'eshwa bwende bwahowa. Obu bwaso, butakola butanachilanjira na njimba.

29. si chiro bacha, nababura

아나호뻐 무우마 아나시마 어우씨. 너시 아빠바 루우마-루우마 나 무우마 나 구거나 어 우씨. 무다빠아롸 구고러라 오꼬, 무고러러 너 비구롣.

여수 아가삐쩨뻽 어라 룻루 서 구짜냐

25. 부씨 노구, 나바부라 과 무더따아 뫄짜냐 부씨 너 가롸모 거뉴 뫄 구찌부사 뿌: 찌 쭈아럌, 찌쭈까마, 너시 찌 쭈어빠롸? 시 어 가롸모, 구 거더 무파 구러싸 어 비룐, 너 무비레, 이워더 무파 구러싸 어 찌빠.

26. 무롣롸아 과 미롣어뻐! 이다이빠, 이다써부뽜, 이다쭈사 나 우레. 시찌로 바짜, 어호 워뉴 오라 우레 과 우빠, 어떠 아나레사이. 러로 뫄보, 가시 아다 무뭐더 무파 무너너 구러싸 어이 미롣어뻐?

27. 어와써! 떠 무 뫄보, 오롸 부씨 너 구짜냐과이 아빠아롸 구찌비기라 룻씨 룻수구 룻우마 과 가롸모 가이?

28. 찌 짜쭈마 뫄짜냐 부씨 너 찌빠? 무롣롸 과 보소 보 뭐수화 뷔떠 뵤호와. 오부 뵤소, 부다고뽜 부다나찌뽜씨라 나 찌빠.

29. 시 찌로 바짜, 나바부라 과

other, or he will be devoted to the one and despise the other. You cannot serve both God and Money.

25. "Therefore I tell you, do not worry about your life, what you will eat or drink; or about your body, what you will wear. Is not life more important than food, and the body more important than clothes?

26. Look at the birds of the air; they do not sow or reap or store away in barns, and yet your heavenly Father feeds them. Are you not much more valuable than they?

27. Who of you by worrying can add a single hour to his life?

28. "And why do you worry about clothes? See how the lilies of the field grow. They do not labor or spin.

29. Yet I tell you that not

kwa anabe na mwami solomono mwa buare bwai boshi, atembalaaluchimba lwa lungahuhanyisimbwa n'e bukome bwobu bwaso!

30. e bichi byo mw'ehwa byende byalorekanako lwarero na mishangya byanaumwa mwa mulyiro. Si chiro bacha, Ongo ende embasabi njimba sa sikomire. Rero kute atabembase kubuya busese, mubandju b'e bwemeresi bueke?

31. bushi noku, mutendaa mwachanya mbu: chi chwungalya, chi chwungamwa, nesi chi chwungembala!

32. ebi byoshi, e bandju ba bateshi Ongo bu bende bachilyibusa mwa kuhondabi. Eho wenyu ola ulyi kwa nguba aneshi kubuya-buya kwa mubilaireko.

33. mundaa mwahonda tanga e bwami bwa Ongo, na kuhondabya bichwungenene era muhondo sai, nai angaberesa ebi binji byoshi.

34. bushi noku, mutendaa mwachanya bushi nebya bingaba mishangya, bushi ebyera, bingachihonda byeine. Chira lusuku, luneete

아나버 나 먀미 소롣모노 먀 부아러 봐이 보씨, 아더빠랴아루찌빠 똬 루꺄후하네시꽈 너 부고머 보부 봐소!

30. 어 비찌 뵤 뭐화 벼더 뱌로러가나고 똬러로 나 미싸야 뱌나우뫄 먀 무쪠로. 시 찌로 바짜, 오꼬 어더 어빠사비 찌빠 사 시고미러. 러로 구더 아다버빠서 구부야 부서서, 무바뚜 버 뷔머러시 부어거?

31. 부씨 노구, 무더따아 먀짜냐 뿌: 찌 쭈꺄랴, 찌 쭈꺄뫄, 너시 찌 쭈꺄빠랴!

32. 어비 뵤씨, 어 바뚜 바 바더씨 오꼬 부 버더 바찌례부사 먀 구호따비. 어호 워뉴 오라 우쪠 과 꾸바 아너씨 구부야-부야 과 무비꽈이러고.

33. 무따아 먀호따 다꺄 어 봐미 봐 오꼬, 나 구호따뱌 비쭈어너너 어라 무호또 사이, 나이 아꺄버러사 어비 비찌 뵤씨.

34. 부씨 노구, 무더따아 먀짜냐 부씨 너뱌 비꺄바 미싸야, 부씨 어벼라, 비꺄찌호따 벼이너. 찌라 룻수구, 루너어더 어마이

even Solomon in all his splendor was dressed like one of these.

30. If that is how God clothes the grass of the field, which is here today and tomorrow is thrown into the fire, will he not much more clothe you, O you of little faith?

31. So do not worry, saying, 'What shall we eat?' or 'What shall we drink?' or 'What shall we wear?'

32. For the pagans run after all these things, and your heavenly Father knows that you need them.

33. But seek first his kingdom and his righteousness, and all these things will be given to you as well.

34. Therefore do not worry about tomorrow, for tomorrow will worry about itself. Each day has enough trouble of its own.

emai malyibuko.

마레부고.

Matayo Chikono 7
*Yesu akangilyisa era luulu
s'e kuchinjibusa e banji*

1. Mutendaa mwachinjibusa e
banji, Ongo angesha
kubachinjibusa nenyu.
2. bushi kwa mwende
mwachinjibusa e banji, ku
Ongo nai akanabachinjibusa.
Kanji kwa mwende
mwarengera e banji, ku Ongo
nai akanabarengera.
3. Chi chachwuma walola kwa
kaaha k'e muchi ka kalyi
mwalyiho lya mulyikenyu, si
utalolyire kwa muchi ola ulyi
mwa lyao?
4. nesi kute ungabura
mulyikenyu mbu: iraa
nyikukule e kachi ka kalyi
mwa liho lyao, noku mwa
lyao weke muchilyi muchi?
5. E umutebanyi! Ukulaa
tanga e muchi ola ulyi mwa
lyiho lyao, elyi walola kubuya
kwa ungakula e kachi ka kalyi
mwa lyamulyikenyu!

6. mutendaa mweresa e
ngunda e bindju bibuya-buya
singesha kubabindjukira na
sababerenganga. Kanji
mutendaa mwauma engulube

마다요 찌고노 7
*여수 아가삐레뻽 어라 루읍루
서 구찌씨뵙뻽 어 바찌*

1. 무더따아 뫄찌찌부사 어
바찌, 오오 아머싸
구바찌찌부사 너뉴.
2. 부씨 과 뮈머 뫄찌찌부사
어 바찌, 구 오오 나이
아가나바찌찌부사. 가찌 과
뮈머 뫄러머라 어 바찌, 구
오오 나이 아가나바러머라.
3. 찌 짜쭈마 와로라 과
가아하 거 무찌 가 가레
뫄레호 랴 무레거뉴, 시
우다로레러 과 무찌 오라 우레
뫄 랴오?
4. 너시 구더 우까부라
무레거뉴 뿌: 이라아 네구구머
어 가찌 가 가레 뫄 삐호
랴오, 노구 뫄 랴오 워거
무찌레 무찌?
5. 어 우무더바네! 우구꽈아
다까 어 무찌 오라 우레 뫄
레호 랴오, 어레 와로꽈
구부야 과 우까구꽈 어 가찌
가 가레 뫄 랴무레거뉴!

6. 무더따아 뮈러사 어 우까
어 비뿌 비부야-부야 시머싸
구바비뿌기라 나
사바버러까까. 가찌 무더따아
뫄우마 어위뤁버 어 미고푸

Matthew Chapter 7[NIV]
Judging Others

1. "Do not judge, or you
too will be judged.

2. For in the same way
you judge others, you will
be judged, and with the
measure you use, it will be
measured to you.

3. "Why do you look at
the speck of sawdust in
your brother's eye and pay
no attention to the plank
in your own eye?

4. How can you say to
your brother, 'Let me take
the speck out of your eye,'
when all the time there is
a plank in your own eye?
5. You hypocrite, first take
the plank out of your own
eye, and then you will see
clearly to remove the
speck from your brother's
eye.

6. "Do not give dogs what
is sacred; do not throw
your pearls to pigs. If you
do, they may trample
them under their feet, and

e mikofu yenyu y'e chichiro chinene, singesha kulyibatangai.

E kwema n'e kweresibwa

7. Mundaa mwema, elyi mweresibwa. Mundaa mwahonda, elyi mwabona. Mundaa mwakongota, elyi bababoorera e lwisi.

8. bushi chira mundju ola wema iwende weresibwa, nola wahonda iwende wabona, nola wakongota ibende baboorera e lwisi.

9. Nde mu mwabo ola ungeresa e mwana wai ekoi mango amwema e mukati?

10. Nesi amwerese e njoka mango amwema efi?

11. Chiro angaba mbu muchwula bandju babi, si muchwula mwishi kweresa e bana benyu e bindju bya bikomire. Rero eho wenyu ola ulyi kwa nguba, kute angafundjwa kweresa ba bende bamwema e bindju bya bikomire busese?

12. Byoshi bya mwahonda e banji bandju babailyiraa, nenyu bi mundaa mwanabailyiraa, nenyu bi mundaa mwanabairira. Bushi e byera by'e mwaso wa musa n'e bitabo by'e barebi

여뉴 여 찌찌로 찌너너, 시ㅿㅓ싸 구레바다ㅿㅏ이.

어 궈마 너 궈러시봐

7. 무따아 뭐마, 어레 뭐러시봐. 무따아 먀호따, 어레 와보나. 무따아 먀고ㅉ다, 어레 바바보오러라 어 ㄹ위시.

8. 부씨 찌라 무뚜 오롸 워마 이워떠 워러시봐, 노롸 와호따 이워떠 와보나, 노롸 와고ㅉ다 이버떠 바보오러라 어 ㄹ위시.

9. 떠 무 먀보 오롸 우ㅿ어러사 어 먀나 와이 어고이 마ㅉ 아뭐마 어 무가디?

10. 너시 아뭐러서 어 쪼가 마ㅉ 아뭐마 어피?

11. 찌로 아ㅺ아바 뿌 무쭈롸 바뚜 바비, 시 무쭈롸 뮈씨 궈러사 어 바나 버뉴 어 비뚜 뱌 비고미러. 러로 어호 워뉴 오롸 우레 과 ㄴ우바, 구더 아ㅺ아푸좌 궈러사 바 버너 바뭐마 어 비뚜 뱌 비고미러 부서서?

12. 뵤씨 뱌 먀호따 어 바찌 바뚜 바바이ㅃ레라아, 너뉴 비 무따아 먀나바이ㅃ레라아. 너뉴 비 무따아 먀나바이리라. 부씨 어 벼라 벼 먀소 와 무사 너 비다보 벼 바러비 비쭈롸 비더찌러.

then turn and tear you to pieces.

Ask, Seek, Knock

7. "Ask and it will be given to you; seek and you will find; knock and the door will be opened to you.

8. For everyone who asks receives; he who seeks finds; and to him who knocks, the door will be opened.

9. "Which of you, if his son asks for bread, will give him a stone?

10. Or if he asks for a fish, will give him a snake?

11. If you, then, though you are evil, know how to give good gifts to your children, how much more will your Father in heaven give good gifts to those who ask him!

12. So in everything, do to others what you would have them do to you, for this sums up the Law and the Prophets.

bichwula bitechire.

<table>
<tr><td>

E nyisi ebilyi

13. Mundaa mwengilyira mwa lwisi lwa lufundeerere. Bushi e lwisi lwa lwerekere mwa muero luchwula luneneire, n'e njira y'e kuyamo itachwusa byangiko. Nei njira, e bandju ba benjire barengamo, balyi banene.

14. Si e lwisi lwa lwerekere mwa kalamo lweke, luchwula lufundeerere. N'e njira y'e kuyamo ichwusa byangiko. Nei njira, e bandju ba benjire barengamo, balyi baeke.

E barebi b'e bisha

15. Mundaa mwachilanga kwa barebi, b'e bisha. Bushi bende babaikira bachilyire nga mbulyi, si mwa michima yabo balyi nga nyishibwabwa sa sikalyiire busese.

16. abu barebi mungende mwabamesherera kurengera e myanya yabo. Bushi e chwutenge-tenge chwuteka bifuma bya misabibu nesi bya tini.

17. Kubinalyi, chira muchi mubuya, ende eka bifuma bibuya. Na chira muchi mubi, ende eka bifuma bibi.

</td><td>

어 내슙 어비례

13. 무따아 뭐(메)례라 꽈 뤼시 꽈 루푸떠어러러. 부씨 어 뤼시 꽈 뤄러거러 꽈 무어로 루쭈꽈 루너너이러, 너 띠라 여 구야모 이다쭈사 뱌(메)고. 너이 띠라, 어 바쭈 바 버띠러 바러(까)모, 바례 바너너.

14. 시 어 뤼시 꽈 뤄러거러 꽈 가꽈모 뭐거, 루쭈꽈 루푸떠어러러. 너 띠라 여 구야모 이쭈사 뱌(메)고. 너이 띠라, 어 바쭈 바 버띠러 바러(까)모, 바례 바어거.

어 바러비 버 비싸

15. 무따아 꽈찌꽈까 과 바러비, 버 비싸. 부씨 버머 바바이기라 바찌례러 (까) 뿌례, 시 꽈 미찌마 야보 바례 (까) 네씨봐봐 사 시가례이러 부서서.

16. 아부 바러비 무(머)떠 꽈바머써러라 구러(머)라 어 먀냐 야보. 부씨 어 쭈더(머)- 더(머) 쭈더가 비푸마 뱌 미사비부 너시 뱌 디니.

17. 구비나례, 찌라 무찌 무부야, 어떠 어가 비푸마 비부야. 나 찌라 무찌 무비, 어떠 어가 비푸마 비비.

</td><td>

The Narrow and Wide Gates

13. "Enter through the narrow gate. For wide is the gate and broad is the road that leads to destruction, and many enter through it.

14. But small is the gate and narrow the road that leads to life, and only a few find it.

A Tree and Its Fruit

15. "Watch out for false prophets. They come to you in sheep's clothing, but inwardly they are ferocious wolves.

16. By their fruit you will recognize them. Do people pick grapes from thornbushes, or figs from thistles?

17. Likewise every good tree bears good fruit, but a bad tree bears bad fruit.

</td></tr>
</table>

18. Emuchi mubuya atangeka bifuma bibi. N'e muchi mubi, atangeka bifuma bibuya.

19. Chira muchi ola uteka bifuma bibuya, ende akonjibwa na kuumwa mwa mulyiro.

20. Bushi noku, abu barebi b'e bisha, mungende mwabamenyerera kurengera e myanya yabo.

E bandju ba batakengilyire mwa bwami bokwa nguba

21. Ata chira mundju ola wende wanyibura mbu: enawechwu, enawechwu! iukengilyira mwa bwami bokwa nguba, si ola wende waira e kuhonda kwa tata ola ulyi kwa nguba.

22. Mango e lusuku lw'e buchinjibusi lukaika, bandju banene bakanyibura mbu: Enawechwu, enawechwu! Si kw'e sina lyao ku chwendee chwareba, na kw'elyi sina ku chwendee chwambula e bihwasi na kuira bisomerano binene!

23. Chasinda, nyikababura mbu: Mwabo, ndafuraa kubamenya chiro na hicha! Mutengaa mwameho manyi, mu bakosi b'e mabi.

18. 어무찌 무부야 아다꺼가 비푸마 비비. 너 무찌 무비, 아다꺼가 비푸마 비부야.

19. 찌라 무찌 오꽈 우더가 비푸마 비부야, 어떠 아고찌봐 나 구우와 꽈 무레로.

20. 부씨 노구, 아부 바러비 버 비싸, 무꺼떠 꽈바머녀러라 구러꺼라 어 먀냐 야보.

어 바뉴 바 바다거꺼이레랸 꽈 봐미 보과 꾸밍

21. 아다 찌라 무뉴 오꽈 워떠 와네부라 뿌: 어나워쭈, 어나워쭈! 이우거꺼이레라 꽈 봐미 보과 꾸바, 시 오꽈 워떠 와이라 어 구호따 과 다다 오꽈 우레 과 꾸바.

22. 마꼬 어 루수구 뤄 부찌찌부시 루가이가, 바뉴 바너너 바가네부라 뿌: 어나워쭈, 어나워쭈! 시 궈 시나 랴오 구 쭤떠어 쫘러바, 나 궈레 시나 구 쭤떠어 쫘뿌꽈 어 비화시 나 구이라 비소머라노 비너너!

23. 짜시따, 네가바부라 뿌: 꽈보, 따푸라아 구바머냐 찌로 나 히짜! 무더꽈아 꽈머호 마네, 무 바고시 버 마비.

18. A good tree cannot bear bad fruit, and a bad tree cannot bear good fruit.

19. Every tree that does not bear good fruit is cut down and thrown into the fire.

20. Thus, by their fruit you will recognize them.

21. "Not everyone who says to me, 'Lord, Lord,' will enter the kingdom of heaven, but only he who does the will of my Father who is in heaven.

22. Many will say to me on that day, 'Lord, Lord, did we not prophesy in your name, and in your name drive out demons and perform many miracles?'

23. Then I will tell them plainly, 'I never knew you. Away from me, you evildoers!'

E muanyi w'e baimbi babilyi — 어 무아네 워 바이삐 바비페 — *The Wise and Foolish Builders*

24. Rero chira mundju ola womva kwene myasi yanyi na kuichwunda, angahuhanyisibwa na mundju wa bwenge, ola waimbaa e nyumba yai kw'e koi.

24. 러로 찌라 무뚜 오롸 옴바 궈너 먀시 야네 나 구이쭈따, 아까후하네시봐 나 무뚜 와 붜,, 오롸 와이빠아 어 뉴빠 야이 궈 고이.

24. "Therefore everyone who hears these words of mine and puts them into practice is like a wise man who built his house on the rock.

25. Emvula yera kutowa, e nyishi sera kw'ehula, n'e chiusi chikalyiire chera kuchihuta kwei nyumba. Si chiro bacha, itakundjukaa, bushi yabaa isimikire kw'e koi.

25. 어뿌롸 여라 구도와, 어네씨 서라 궈후롸, 너 찌우시 찌가페이러 쩌라 궈이 뉴빠. 시 찌로 바짜, 이다구뚜가아, 부씨 야바아 이시미기러 궈 고이.

25. The rain came down, the streams rose, and the winds blew and beat against that house; yet it did not fall, because it had its foundation on the rock.

26. Si chira mundju ola womvire kwei myasi yanyi, busira kuichwunda, yeke ahuhanyisibwe n'e mbuta, era yaimbaa eyai kwa mishee.

26. 시 찌라 무뚜 오롸 옴삐러 궈이 먀시 야네, 부시라 구이쭈따, 여거 아후하네시붜 너 뿌다, 어라 야이빠아 어야이 과 미써어.

26. But everyone who hears these words of mine and does not put them into practice is like a foolish man who built his house on sand.

27. Emvula yera kutowa, enyishi sera kw'ehula, n'e chiusi chikalyiire chera kuchihuta kui. unao-unao era nyumba, kuna kukundjuka na yahandjukala.

27. 어뿌롸 여라 구도와, 어네씨 서라 궈후롸, 너 찌우시 찌가페이러 쩌라 궈찌후다 구이. 우나오-우나오 어라 뉴빠, 구나 구구뚜가 나 야하뚜가롸.

27. The rain came down, the streams rose, and the winds blew and beat against that house, and it fell with a great crash."

E buashi bwa Yesu
어 부아씨 봐 여수

28. Mango Yesu abaa era amalaa kukangilyisa e bandju ei myasi, bera kusanwa busese.

28. 마꼬 여수 아바아 어라 아마롸아 구가삐페사 어 바뚜 어이 먀시, 버라 구사놔 부서서.

28. When Jesus had finished saying these things, the crowds were amazed at his teaching,

29. basanwaa, bushi yeke atendee abakangilyisa babo

29. 바사놔아, 부씨 여거 아더떠어 아바가삐페사 바보

29. because he taught as one who had authority,

b'e mwaso, si endee abakangilyisa nga mundju ola wete buashi.

버 뫄소, 시 어떠어 아바가삐레사 꽈 무뚜 오꽈 워더 부아씨.

and not as their teachers of the law.

Matayo Chikono 8

마다요 찌고노 8

Matthew Chapter 8[NIV]

Yesu alamya e mubenzi-benzi

여수 아꽈맸 어 무버씨-버씨

The Man With Leprosy

1. Era nyuma sebi, Yesu era kwandaala kwei ndjulungu. Abere era andaalako, bandju banene busese bera kumukulyikira.

1. 어라 뉴마 서비, 여수 어라 과따아꽈 궈이 뚜루꾸. 아버러 어라 아따아꽈고, 바뉴 바너너 부서서 버라 구무구레기라.

1. When he came down from the mountainside, large crowds followed him.

2. Mwolu, mubenzi-benzi muuma era kumuikira. Oyu mubenzi-benzi, era kukoma e mafi era muhondo sa yesu. Era kumubura mbu: Enawechwu! Akaba uhonjire, unganyilamya.

2. 뫄루, 무버씨-버씨 무우마 어라 구무이기라. 오유 무버씨, 어라 구고마 어 마피 어라 무호또 사 여수. 어라 구무부라 뿌: 어나워쭈! 아가바 우호찌러, 우까네꽈먀.

2. A man with leprosy came and knelt before him and said, "Lord, if you are willing, you can make me clean."

3. Yesu era kunanula e kuboko na amuumako. Era kumubura mbu: Nechi! Nahonda ulame! unao-unao, ola mubenzi-benzi kuna kulama.

3. 여수 어라 구나누꽈 어 구보고 나 아무우마고. 어라 구무부라 뿌: 너찌! 나호따 우라머! 우나오-우나오, 오라 무버씨-버씨 구나 구꽈마.

3. Jesus reached out his hand and touched the man. "I am willing," he said. "Be clean!" Immediately he was cured of his leprosy.

4. Chasinda, Yesu era kumuchichika mbu: Umenyaa! Utaereresaa wabura mundju asibya kwei myasi! Si uyaa kuchilosa era mwa kuhanyi, wanaana n'e michwulo kwa kulosa kwa walamire mira, kukulyikana

4. 짜시따, 여수 어라 구무찌찌가 뿌: 우머냐아! 우다어러러사아 와부라 무뚜 아시뱌 궈이 먀시! 시 우야아 구찌로사 어라 뫄 구하네, 와나아나 너 미쭈로 과 구로사 과 와꽈미러 미라, 구구레가나 노과 뫄소 와 무사 아쭈꽈

4. Then Jesus said to him, "See that you don't tell anyone. But go, show yourself to the priest and offer the gift Moses commanded, as a testimony to them."

nokwa mwaso wa musa achwula atechire.

아더찌러.

E bwemeresi bw'e mukulu-kulu w'e basula b'e baroma

어 붜머러시 붜 무구룹-구룹 워 바수퐈 버 바로마

The Faith of Centurion

5. Mango Yesu abaa era engilyira mwa musi w'e kaperinaumu, kwera kuulukira mukulu-kulu muuma w'e basula b'e baroma. Oyu mukulu-kulu, era kuika kwema Yesu mbu amuasaa. Era kumubura mbu:

5. 마꼬 여수 아바아 어라 어삐레라 퐈 무시 워 가퍼리나우무, 궈라 구우룹기라 무구룹-구룹 무우마 워 바수퐈 버 바로마. 오유 무구룹-구룹, 어라 구이가 궈마 여수 뿌 아무아사아. 어라 구무부라 뿌:

5. When Jesus had entered Capernaum, a centurion came to him, asking for help.

6. Enawechwu! Emukosi wanyi aremere, na mw'e chine chihangi, kuonjira kuanaonjire mwa nyumba, bushi alyibuka busese.

6. 어나워쭈! 어무고시 와네 아러머러, 나 뭐 찌너 찌하삐, 구오찌라 구아나오찌러 퐈 뉴빠, 부씨 아레부가 부서서.

6. "Lord," he said, "my servant lies at home paralyzed and in terrible suffering."

7. Yesu era kumwakula mbu: nyingaika kumulamya.

7. 여수 어라 구뫄구퐈 뿌: 네삐이가 구무퐈먀.

7. Jesus said to him, "I will go and heal him."

8. si oyu mukulu-kulu nai mbu: Nanga enawechwu! Ndete kwa nyilyi kwa kungachwuma wengilyira mwa mwanyi. Rero walyiya, woyo unatetaa chinwa chiuma oshao, n'e mukosi wanyi angalama.

8. 시 오유 무구룹-구룹 나이 뿌: 나뺘 어나워쭈! 떠더 과 네레 과 구꺄쭈마 워삐레라 퐈 뫄네. 러로 와레야, 오요 우나더다아 찌놔 찌우마 오싸오, 너 무고시 와네 아꺄라먀.

8. The centurion replied, "Lord, I do not deserve to have you come under my roof. But just say the word, and my servant will be healed.

9. Bushi nanyi, nyilyi era bufulyi sa banji bakulu-kulu. Nyete na basula ba bachwula era bufulyi sanyi. Nende nanabura muuma mbu: Endaa! Nai, unao-unao anaenda. Nanabura n'e unji

9. 부씨 나네, 네레 어라 부푸레 사 바찌 바구룹-구룹. 녀더 나 바수퐈 바 바쭉퐈 어라 부푸레 사네. 너떠 나나부라 무우마 뿌: 어따아! 나이, 우나오-우나오 아나어따. 나나부라 너 우찌 뿌: 바하아!

9. For I myself am a man under authority, with soldiers under me. I tell this one, 'Go,' and he goes; and that one, 'Come,' and he comes. I say to my servant, 'Do

mbu: Bahaa! Nai, unao-unao anabaha. N'e mukosi wanyi nai, kwa nanamubilyire ku ende anaira.

10. Yesu omvire bacha, era kusanwa busese. Era kwire abura e bandju ba babaa bamukulyikire mbu: kubinalyi! Nababura kwa mwa baisiraeli boshi, ndafuraa kulola chiro ne uma kwola wete bwemeresi bungana ng'e bono, muroma!

11. Ndababisha, bandju banene bakatengera mwa bisiki byoshi, kwa kwingilyira mwa bwami bwokwa nguba. Abu bandju, bakalya alauma na aburahamu, na isaka, na yakobo.

12. Si ba bachirembaa mbu bu bakaba besha obu bwami bakaumwa era butala mwa musimya munene. Noyu musimya, bakalyira na kulola kwa kasibu.

13. Chasinda, Yesu era kubura oyu mukulu-kulu mbu: Endaa! Kwa bwemeresi bwao bulyi, kubinganaba. Mwechi chihangi chinechi ola mukosi wai, kuna kulama.

나이, 우나오-우나오 아나바하. 너 무고시 와네 나이, 과 나나무비쩨러 구 어떠 아나이라.

10. 여수 오쎄러 바짜, 어라 구사놔 부서서. 어라 귀러 아부라 어 바뉴 바 바바아 바무구쩨기러 뿌: 구비나쩨! 나바부라 과 봐 바이시라어쩨 보씨, 따푸라아 구쪼롸 찌로 너 우마 굠롸 워더 붜머러시 부싸나 우어 보노, 무로마!

11. 따바비싸, 바뉴 바너너 바가더쩌라 봐 비시기 뵤씨, 과 귀쎄쩨라 봐 봐미 보과 우바. 아부 바뉴, 바가꺄 아꽈우마 나 아부라하무, 나 이사가, 나 야고보.

12. 시 바 바찌러빠아 뿌 부 바가바 버싸 오부 봐미 바가우꽈 어라 부다롸 봐 무시먀 무너너. 노유 무시먀, 바가쩨라 나 구쪼롸 과 가시부.

13. 짜시따, 여수 어라 구부라 오유 무구루루-구루 뿌: 어따아! 과 붜머러시 봐오 부쩨, 구비꺄나바. 뭐찌 찌하쩨 찌너찌 오롸 무고시 와이, 구나 구롸마.

this,' and he does it."

10. When Jesus heard this, he was astonished and said to those following him, "I tell you the truth, I have not found anyone in Israel with such great faith.

11. I say to you that many will come from the east and the west, and will take their places at the feast with Abraham, Isaac and Jacob in the kingdom of heaven.

12. But the subjects of the kingdom will be thrown outside, into the darkness, where there will be weeping and gnashing of teeth."

13. Then Jesus said to the centurion, "Go! It will be done just as you believed it would." And his servant was healed at that very hour.

Yesu alamya balwala banene 여수 **아꽈맸 바꽈꽈 바너너** *Jesus Heals Many*

14. Era nyuma s'ebi, Yesu era 14. 어라 뉴마 서비, 여수 어라 14. When Jesus came into

kwingilyira mwa mwa petero.
Era kubuana nasala wa
petero achilambikire kwa
njingo bushi abaa asimbirwe
n'e hushira.

15. Yesu era kumuuma kwa
mino, unao-unao era hushira
kuna kulama. Oyu mukasi era
kubachwuka na aya
kumutekera e bilyo.

16. Abere lwera luolo-olo,
bera kuretera Yesu bandju
banene. Abu bandju, babaa
basimbirwange na bihwasi.
Ebi bihwasi, Yesu era kunde
aambulabi mwa kunateta
oshao. N'e balwala boshi
nabo, era kunde anabalamya.

17. Byabaa bacha, chasiya
cha chinwa chiberere, cha
murebi Isaya atetaa mbu:
Ekaa e malyibuko mechwu
moshi, era kweka n'e malwala
mechwu.

*Yesu ana eano kwaba
bahonda kumukulyikira*

18. Mango Yesu alolaa
bandju banene bamusungure,
era kubura e banafunzi bai
mbu bahabukiraa kwa unji
mushilyilya w'e nyanja.

19. Mwolu, mukangilyisi
muuma w'e mwaso era
kuchifunda ofu nai. Era

귀끼레라 꽈 꽈 퍼더로. 어라
구부아나 나사꽈 와 퍼더로
아찌꽈삐기러 과 띠꼬 부씨
아바아 아시삐뤄 너 후씨라.

15. 여수 어라 구무우마 과
미노, 우나오-우나오 어라
후씨라 구나 구꽈마. 오유
무가시 어라 구바쭈가 나 아야
구무더거라 어 비뇬.

16. 아버러 뤄라 루오르르-오르르,
버라 구러더라 여수 바쭈
바너너. 아부 바쭈, 바바아
바시삐롸어 나 비화시. 어비
비화시, 여수 어라 구떠
아아뿌꽈비 꽈 구나더다
오싸오. 너 바꽈꽈 보씨 나보,
어라 구떠 아나바꽈먀.

17. 뱌바아 바짜, 짜시야 짜
찌놔 찌버러러, 짜 무러비
이사야 아더다아 뿌: 어가아
어 마레부고 머쭉 모씨, 어라
궈가 너 마꽈꽈 머쭉.

*여수 아나 어아노 과바 바호따
구무구레굿띱*

18. 마꼬 여수 아르꽈아 바쭈
바너너 바무수꾸러, 어라
구부라 어 바나푸씨 바이 뿌
바하부기라아 과 우찌
무씨레꺄 워 냐짜.

19. 모루, 무가끼레시 무우마
워 꽈소 어라 구찌푸따 오푸
나이. 어라 구무부라 뿌:

Peter's house, he saw
Peter's mother-in-law lying
in bed with a fever.

15. He touched her hand
and the fever left her, and
she got up and began to
wait on him.

16. When evening came,
many who were demon-
possessed were brought to
him, and he drove out the
spirits with a word and
healed all the sick.

17. This was to fulfill what
was spoken through the
prophet Isaiah: "He took
up our infirmities and
carried our diseases."

*The Cost of Following
Jesus*

18. When Jesus saw the
crowd around him, he
gave orders to cross to the
other side of the lake.

19. Then a teacher of the
law came to him and said,
"Teacher, I will follow you

kumubura mbu: Mukangilyisi! chira era ungende wanaya, nanyi nyingende nakukulyikira.

20. Yesu era kumwakula mbu: e miterelyi ichwusa nyikunda, n'e milonge ichwusa machwu. Si nyi mwana w'e mundju nyeke, ndachwusa chiro na chisiki cha kuonjiramo!

21. Chasinda, unji mwanafunzi muuma wa Yesu nai era kumubura mbu: enawechwu! unyirekaa tanga nyiye kutaba tata.

22. Yesu era kumwakula mbu: rekaa e bafu bende bataba bafu balyikabo. Si woyo, unyikulyikiraa!

Yesu akalikiira emulaba

23. Era nyuma s'ebi, Yesu era kwerukira mwa bwato, e banafunzi bai bera kuenda nai.

24. Abere baika kwa nyanja, kwera kuulukira mulaba munene. Bushi noku, e meshi mera kutangilyisa machiumanga mwobu bwato. Si mwechi chihangi, Yesu yeke abaa aonjire.

25. Abu banafunzi bai, bera kwire baya kumususa. Bera kumubura mbu: Enawechwu!

무가삐레시! 찌라 어라 우꺼꺼 와나야, 나니 네꺼꺼 나구구뻬기라.

20. 여수 어라 구꽈구꽈 뿌: 어 미더러뻬 이쭈사 네구따, 너 미로꺼 이쭈사 마쭈. 시 니 꽈나 워 무뿌 녀거, 따쭈사 찌로 나 찌시기 짜 구오찌라모!

21. 짜시따, 우찌 꽈나푸씨 무우마 와 여수 나이 어라 구무부라 뿌: 어나워쭉! 우네러가아 다꺼 네여 구다바 다다.

22. 여수 어라 구꽈구꽈 뿌: 러가아 어 바푸 버꺼 바다바 바푸 바뻬가보. 시 오요, 우네구뻬기라아!

여수 아가삐굿윌띱 어무꽈밍

23. 어라 뉴마 서비, 여수 어라 궈루기라 와 바도, 어 바나푸씨 바이 버라 구어따 나이.

24. 아버러 바이가 과 냐짜, 궈라 구우루기라 무꽈바 무너너. 부씨 노구, 어 머씨 머라 구다삐레사 마찌우마꺼 모부 바도. 시 뭐찌 찌하삐, 여수 여거 아바아 아오찌러.

25. 아부 바나푸씨 바이, 버라 궈러 바야 구무수사. 버라 구무부라 뿌: 어나워쭉!

---

wherever you go."

20. Jesus replied, "Foxes have holes and birds of the air have nests, but the Son of Man has no place to lay his head."

21. Another disciple said to him, "Lord, first let me go and bury my father."

22. But Jesus told him, "Follow me, and let the dead bury their own dead."

23. Then he got into the boat and his disciples followed him.

24. Without warning, a furious storm came up on the lake, so that the waves swept over the boat. But Jesus was sleeping.

25. The disciples went and woke him, saying, "Lord, save us! We're going to

chwasika, uchwulamyaa!

좌시가, 우쭈라먀아!

drown!"

26. Nai mbu: era! chi chachwuma mwobaa? kubinalyi, e bwemeresi bwenyu bukeire! era kwire emanga, na akalyiira oyu mulaba n'e meshi mera nyanja, kuna kuorera.

26. 나이 뿌: 어라! 찌 짜쭈마 모바아? 구비나레, 어 뭐머러시 뭐뉴 부거이러! 어라 귀러 어마빠, 나 아가레이라 오유 무빠바 너 머씨 머라 냐짜, 구나 구오러라.

26. He replied, "You of little faith, why are you so afraid?" Then he got up and rebuked the winds and the waves, and it was completely calm.

27. Abu bandju bera kusanwa busese. Bera kutangilyisa bateta mbu: Ewashee! mundju muchiye ono? Ola mulaba n'e nyanja nabi byamuchwunda!

27. 아부 바쭈 버라 구사놔 부서서. 버라 구다삐레사 바더다 뿌: 어와써어! 무뉴 무찌여 오노? 오라 무빠바 너 냐짜 나비 뱌무쭈따!

27. The men were amazed and asked, "What kind of man is this? Even the winds and the waves obey him!"

Yesu alamya bandju babilyi ba babaa basimbirwe n'e bihwasi

여수 아빠맸 바쭈 바비레 바 바바아 바시삐룸 너 비화시

28. Mango Yesu abaa era ahabukaa e nyanja, era kuika mwa chio ch'e baketari. Era kubuana bandju babilyi ba babaa batengera kwa shinda. Abo bandju, babaa basimbirwe na bihwasi. Ebi bihwasi, byera kubaira bakalyi busene. Bushi noku, kwabaa kutachilyi mundju usibya ola wendee waereresa arenga ofu nabo.

28. 마꼬 여수 아바아 어라 아하부가아 어 냐짜, 어라 구이가 마 찌오 쩌 바거다리. 어라 구부아나 바쭈 바비레 바 바바아 바더꺼라 과 씨따. 아보 바쭈, 바바아 바시삐뤄 나 비화시. 어비 비화시, 벼라 구바이라 바가레 부서너. 부씨 노구, 과바아 구다찌레 무뉴 우시뱌 오라 워떠어 아러빠 오푸 나보.

28. When he arrived at the other side in the region of the Gadarenes, two demon-possessed men coming from the tombs met him. They were so violent that no one could pass that way.

29. Abu bandju bera kutangilyisa bachilakangira mbu: Eu mwenyi Ongo! Chi wachwuhondako?

29. 아부 바쭈 버라 구다삐레사 바찌꽈가이라 뿌: 어우 뭐네 오꼬! 찌 와쭈호따고?

29. "What do you want with us, Son of God?" they shouted. "Have you come here to torture us before

waikire kuchwulyibusa era muhondo s'e suku s'e buchinjibusi?

30. Ofu n'echi chisiki, abaa arenga buso bunene bwa ngulube.

31. Ebi bihwasi, byera kwire byema Yesu mbu: akaba wachwambula, uchwuchwumaa mwobu buso bw'e ngulube.

32. Nai mbu: Muyaamo! Ebi bihwasi kuna kubatengako na byachiuma mwesa ngulube. Bwa buso boshi, unao-unao kuna kwandaalyira mwa Nyanja, na sasikiramo.

33. Ebangere b'esi ngulube balolyire bacha, bera kuhaira kwa musi, bera kubalyira e bandju kwa myasi Yoshi era Yesu akorere ba bandju babilyi babaa basimbirwe n'e bihyasi.

34. chasinjire, besha mwa musi boshi, bera kulyibichira era Yesu abaa alyi. Bamulolyireko, bera kumwema busese mbu atengaa mwa chio chabo.

와이기러 구쭈쩨부사 어라 무호또 서 수구 서 부찌찌부시?

30. 오푸 너찌 찌시기, 아바아 아러꽈 부소 부너너 봐 우루버.

31. 어비 비화시, 벼라 귀러 벼마 여수 뿌: 아가바 와쫘뿌롸, 우쭈쭈마아 모부 부소 붜 우루버.

32. 나이 뿌: 무야아모! 어비 비화시 구나 구바더꽈고 나 뱌찌우마 뭐사 우루버. 봐 부소 보씨, 우나오-우나오 구나 과따아쩨라 마 냐쨔, 나 사시기라모.

33. 어바꺼러 버시 우루버 바로쩨러 바짜, 버라 구하이라 과 무시, 버라 구바쩨라 어 바쭈 과 먀시 요씨 어라 여수 아고러러 바 바쭈 바비쩨 바바아 바시삐뤄 너 비햐시.

34. 짜시찌러, 버싸 마 무시 보씨, 버라 구쩨비찌라 어라 여수 아바아 아쩨. 바무로쩨러고, 버라 구뭐마 부서서 뿌 아더꽈아 마 찌오 짜보.

the appointed time?"

30. Some distance from them a large herd of pigs was feeding.

31. The demons begged Jesus, "If you drive us out, send us into the herd of pigs."

32. He said to them, "Go!" So they came out and went into the pigs, and the whole herd rushed down the steep bank into the lake and died in the water.

33. Those tending the pigs ran off, went into the town and reported all this, including what had happened to the demon-possessed men.

34. Then the whole town went out to meet Jesus. And when they saw him, they pleaded with him to leave their region.

Matayo Chikono 9	**마다요 찌고노 9**	**Matthew Chapter 9[NIV]**
Yesu alamya e mundju ola ureemere	*여수 아ᄙᅪ맸 어 무ᅜᅮ 오ᄙᅪ 우러어머러*	
1. Era nyuma s'ebi, Yesu era kwerukira mwa bwato. Abere era ahabukaa e nyanja, era kuhuba mwa musi ola akulyiraamo.	1. 어라 뉴마 서비, 여수 어라 궈루기라 와 봐도. 아버러 어라 아하부가아 어 냐ᅜᅡ, 어라 구후바 와 무시 오ᄙᅪ 아구ᄙᅦ라아모.	1. Jesus stepped into a boat, crossed over and came to his own town.
2. Bandju bauma bera kumuretera mundju ola wabaa uremeere. Oyu mundju, abaa aonjire kwa chipoyo. Mango Yesu alolaa kwa bwemeresi bwabu bandju, era kwire abura ola wabaa uremeere mbu: Emwana wanyi! Usesaa e muchima! Ebibi byao byababalyirwe.	2. 바ᅜᅮ 바우마 버라 구무러더라 무ᅜᅮ 오ᄙᅪ 와바아 우러머어러. 오유 무ᅜᅮ, 아바아 아오ᅜᅵ러 과 찌포요. 마ᅌᅩ 여수 아롤ᄙᅪ아 과 붜머러시 봐부 바ᅜᅮ, 어라 귀러 아부라 오ᄙᅪ 와바아 우러머어러 뿌: 어뫄나 와네! 우서사아 어 무찌마! 어비비 뱌오 뱌바바ᄙᅦ뤄.	2. Some men brought to him a paralytic, lying on a mat. When Jesus saw their faith, he said to the paralytic, "Take heart, son; your sins are forgiven."
3. Mwolu, bauma mwa bakangilyisi b'e mwaso bera kutangilyisa bachitetembya mbu: Ebasa! Ono mundju enjire akamba Ongo!	3. 뫼루, 바우마 와 바가ᅇᅵᄙᅦ시 버 와소 버라 구다ᅇᅵᄙᅦ사 바찌더더뺘 뿌: 어바사! 오노 무ᅜᅮ 어ᅜᅵ러 아가빠 오ᅌᅩ!	3. At this, some of the teachers of the law said to themselves, "This fellow is blaspheming!"
4. Si Yesu bushi abaa amenyire e mianyisa yabo, era kubabusa mbu: Ewashe! Chi chachwuma mwaanyisa bulyio bacha mwa michima yenyu?	4. 시 여수 부씨 아바아 아머녜러 어 미아녜사 야보, 어라 구바부사 뿌: 어와써! 찌 짜쭈마 와아녜사 부ᄙᅧ오 바짜 와 미찌마 여뉴?	4. Knowing their thoughts, Jesus said, "Why do you entertain evil thoughts in your hearts?
5. Rero, munyiburaa! Chiye chi chibofoire kuteta: elyi e kubura e mundju mbu: Ebibi byao byababalyirwe nesi e kumubura mbu: Emangaa	5. 러로, 무녜부라아! 찌여 찌 찌보포이러 구더다: 어ᄙᅦ 어 구부라 어 무ᅜᅮ 뿌: 어비비 뱌오 뱌바바ᄙᅦ뤄 너시 어 구무부라 뿌: 어마ᅌᅡ아	5. Which is easier: to say, 'Your sins are forgiven,' or to say, 'Get up and walk'?

uende?

6. Nahonda mumenyerere kubuya-buya kwanyi mwana w'e mundju nyete e buashi bw'e kubabalyira e bibi by'e bandju muno butala. Chasinda, Yesu era kubura echi chirema mbu: Kuno namurenge! Emangaa, utole n'e chipoyo chao, uchiendere kwa wao.

7. Oyu mundju, era kwimanga na achenderera kwa wai.

8. Mango e bandju balolaa bacha, bera kwobaa busese. Chasinda, bera kutangilyisa batonga Ongo iweresaa e bandju e buashi bwa bulyi ngobu.

Yesu amaala matayo

9. Mango Yesu abaa era atengaa aola, era kubuana mufuchisi muuma wa mbarata mbu i matayo. Oyu matayo, abaa ekese mwa nyumba yai y'e kufuchisisa mw'e mbarata. Yesu era kumubura mbu: Matayo! nyikulyikira! unao-unao, era kwimanga kuna kumukulyikira.

10. Chasinda, Yesu era kuya kulya mwa mwa matayo. Mwei nyumba, mwera

우어떠?

6. 나호따 무머녀러러 구부야-부야 과내 똬나 워 무뚜 녀더어 부아씨 붜 구바바뤠라 어 비비 벼 바뚜 무노 부다짜. 짜시따, 여수 어라 구부라 어찌 찌러마 뿌: 구노 나무러떠! 어마따아, 우도뤄 너 찌포요 짜오, 우쩌떠러 과 와오.

7. 오유 무뚜, 어라 귀마까 나 아쩌떠러라 과 와이.

8. 마꼬 어 바뚜 바로쫘아 바짜, 버라 고바아 부서서. 짜시따, 버라 구다띠뤠사 바도따 오꼬 이워러사아 어 바뚜 어 부아씨 봐 부뤠 꼬부.

여수 아마아쫘 마다요

9. 마꼬 여수 아바아 어라 아더따아 아오쫘, 어라 구부아나 무푸찌시 무우마 와 빠라다 뿌 이 마다요. 오유 마다요, 아바아 어거서 똬 뉴빠 야이 여 구푸찌시사 뭐 빠라다. 여수 어라 구무부라 뿌: 마다요! 니구뤠기라! 우나오-우나오, 어라 귀마까 구나 구무구뤠기라.

10. 짜시따, 여수 어라 구야 구쨔 똬 똬 마다요. 뭐이 뉴빠, 뭐라 궈띠뤠라 바푸찌시

6. But so that you may know that the Son of Man has authority on earth to forgive sins...." Then he said to the paralytic, "Get up, take your mat and go home."

7. And the man got up and went home.

8. When the crowd saw this, they were filled with awe; and they praised God, who had given such authority to men.

9. As Jesus went on from there, he saw a man named Matthew sitting at the tax collector's booth. "Follow me," he told him, and Matthew got up and followed him.

10. While Jesus was having dinner at Matthew's house, many tax collectors and

kwengilyira bafuchisi banene ba mbarata, na banji bakosi ba mabi. Abu boshi bera kulya alauma na Yesu n'e banafunzi bai.

11. Mango e bafarisayo balolaa bacha, bera kubura e banafunzi bai mbu: Chi chachwuma e mukangilyisi wenyu alya alauma n'e banafuchisi b'e mbarata n'e banji bakosi b'e mabi?

12. Yesu omvire bacha, era kubabura mbu: babahaalukire ata bu bende bahonda e muhake, si e balwala bubende bamuhonda!

13. Rero, muyaa kuchikangilyisa tanga kute mano maanjiko mabuya-buya machwula matechire: Nyono, ndahonda mbu munyichwulyiraa michwulo, si nyisimire munde mwafirina e bonjo. Bushi ndaikaa kwamaala ba bachwula bachwunngenene era muhondo sa Ongo, si naikaa bushi n'e bakosi b'e mabi.

Yesu abusibwa bushi n'e memo ma mende mairwa busira kulya

14. Lusuku luuma, e banafunzi ba yowana baikiraa yesu. Bera kumubusa mbu: e

바너너 바 빠라다, 나 바씨 바고시 바 마비. 아부 보씨 버라 구꺄 아꽈우마 나 여수 너 바나푸씨 바이.

11. 마꼬 어 바파리사요 바로꽈아 바짜, 버라 구부라 어 바나푸씨 바이 뿌: 찌 짜쭈마 어 무가께레시 워뉴 아꺄 아꽈우마 너 바나푸찌시 버 빠라다 너 바씨 바고시 버 마비?

12. 여수 오쁘러 바짜, 어라 구바부라 뿌: 바바하아루끼러 아다 부 버너 바호따 어 무하거, 시 어 바꽈꽈 부버너 바무호따!

13. 러로, 무야아 구찌가께레사 다꺄 구더 마노 마아찌고 마부야-부야 마쭈꽈 마더찌러: 뇨노, 따호따 뿌 무네쭈레라아 미쭈로, 시 내시미러 무너 꽈피리나 어 보쪼. 부씨 따이가아 과마아꽈 바 바쭈꽈 바쭈누쩌너너 어라 무호또 사 오꼳, 시 나이가아 부씨 너 바고시 버 마비.

여수 아부시봐 부씨 너 머모 마 머너 마이꽈 부시라 구꺄

14. 루수구 루우마, 어 바나푸씨 바 요와나 바이기라아 여수. 버라

"sinners" came and ate with him and his disciples.

11. When the Pharisees saw this, they asked his disciples, "Why does your teacher eat with tax collectors and 'sinners'?"

12. On hearing this, Jesus said, "It is not the healthy who need a doctor, but the sick.

13. But go and learn what this means: 'I desire mercy, not sacrifice.' For I have not come to call the righteous, but sinners."

14. Then John's disciples came and asked him, "How is it that we and the

walyiya, chwubano n'e bafarisayo, chwende chwaya mwa memo ma mende mairwa busira kulya. Rero chichende chachwuma abanafunzi bao beke bataira bacha?

15. Yesu na imbu: Mango e bandju bende balalyikibwa kwa buya, kute ku bangalosa e businane, noku banachilyi alauma n'e muya mulume? si mwa suku sa seshire, angakulyibwa mwa kachi-kachi kabo. Mwesi suku, mu bangere bende bengilyira mwamu memo.

16. Kutalyi mundju ola ungalanjira e chiraka chiyayaya kwa chiramba. Akaba angaira bacha, echi chiraka chana berenga echi chiramba. Chasinda, e chiramba chana tandjukala.

17. Kanji batabika e divai iyayaya mwa bikunguisa by'e hao s'e nyuu. Bushi akaba bangaira bacha, ei divai mango ingaya, yanaberengasi na yasheshekala. N'esi hao nasi, sanakumba. Si e divai iyayaya, yende yabikikwa mwa hao s'e nyuu siyayaya, ebi bibilyi bilangibwe kubuya!

구무부사 뿌: 어 와쩨야, 쭈바노 너 바파리사요, 쭤떠 좌야 뫄 머모 마 머너 마이롸 부시라 구쨔. 러로 찌쩌떠 짜쭈마 아바나푸씨 바오 버거 바다이라 바짜?

15. 여수 나 이뿌: 마꼬 어 바쭈 버떠 바라쩨기봐 과 부야, 구더 구 바꽈로사 어 부시나너, 노구 바나찌쩨 아꽈우마 너 무야 무루머? 시 뫄 수구 사 서씨러, 아꽈구쩨봐 뫄 가찌-가찌 가보. 뭐시 수구, 무 바꺼러 버떠 버꾀쩨라 뫄무 머모.

16. 구다쩨 무꾸 오꽈 우꽈꽈씨라 어 찌라가 찌야야야 과 찌라빠. 아가바 아꽈이라 바짜, 어찌 찌라가 짜나 버러꽈 어찌 찌라빠. 짜시따, 어 찌라빠 짜나 다꾸가꽈.

17. 가찌 바다비가 어 디바이 이야야야 뫄 비구꾀이사 벼 하오 서 뉴우. 부씨 아가바 바꽈이라 바짜, 어이 디바이 마꼬 이꽈야, 야나버러꽈시 나 야써써가꽈. 너시 하오 나시, 사나구빠. 시 어 디바이 이야야야, 여떠 야비기과 뫄 하오 서 뉴우 시야야야, 어비 비비쩨 비꽈꾀붜 구부야!

Pharisees fast, but your disciples do not fast?"

15. Jesus answered, "How can the guests of the bridegroom mourn while he is with them? The time will come when the bridegroom will be taken from them; then they will fast.

16. "No one sews a patch of unshrunk cloth on an old garment, for the patch will pull away from the garment, making the tear worse.

17. Neither do men pour new wine into old wineskins. If they do, the skins will burst, the wine will run out and the wineskins will be ruined. No, they pour new wine into new wineskins, and both are preserved."

Yesu alamya mukasi omwola na munyere muuma

여수 아빠맲 무가시 오모똬 나 무녀러 무우마

18. Mango Yesu abaa anachilyi ahambala nabu bandju, kwera kuulukira mukulu-kulu muuma wa muyuda. Oyu mukulu-kulu era kufukama era muhondo sa yesu, na amubura mbu: ewalyiya! mwalyi wanyi, era atowaa e muchima. Si chiro bacha, unayaa kumuumako, ahube muuma-uma.

18. 마꼬 여수 아바아 아나찌레 아하빠똬 나부 바쭈, 궈라 구우룹기라 무구룹-구룹 무우마 와 무유다. 오유 무구룹-구룹 어라 구푸가마 어라 무호또 사 여수, 나 아무부라 뿌: 어와레야! 뫄레 와네, 어라 아도와아 어 무찌마. 시 찌로 바짜, 우나야아 구무우마고, 아후버 무우마-우마.

18. While he was saying this, a ruler came and knelt before him and said, "My daughter has just died. But come and put your hand on her, and she will live."

19. Bushi noku Yesu n'e banafunzi bai bera kuchiuma bakulyikira oyu mukulu-kulu.

19. 부씨 노구 여수 너 바나푸씨 바이 버라 구찌우마 바구레기라 오유 무구룹-구룹.

19. Jesus got up and went with him, and so did his disciples.

20. Mwolu, mukasi muuma ola wabaa wamala myaka ekumi n'e bilyi ete bulwala bwa kutengwa na mikira, era kubaha katola nyuma akulyikire yesu. Oyu mikasi, era kuuma kwa musike w'e luchimba lwa yesu,

20. 모룹, 무가시 무우마 오똬 와바아 와마라 먀가 어구미 너 비레 어더 부똬똬 봐 구더똬 나 미기라, 어라 구바하 가도똬 뉴마 아구레기러 여수. 오유 미가시, 어라 구우마 과 무시거 워 루찌빠 똬 여수,

20. Just then a woman who had been subject to bleeding for twelve years came up behind him and touched the edge of his cloak.

21. Bushi abaa achitetembya mbu: akaba nyinganauma kwa luchimba lwai oshao, elyi nalalamire.

21. 부씨 아바아 아찌더더빠 뿌: 아가바 네꺼나우마 과 루찌빠 똬이 오싸오, 어레 나똬똬미러.

21. She said to herself, "If I only touch his cloak, I will be healed."

22. Abere wa mukasi era amuumako, unao-unao Yesu kuna kubindjuka era nyuma. Amulolyireko, era kumubura mbu: Emwalyi wanyi, sesaa e muchima! E bwemeresi bwao

22. 아버러 와 무가시 어라 아무우마고, 우나오-우나오 여수 구나 구비뿌가 어라 뉴마. 아무로레러고, 어라 구무부라 뿌: 어똬레 와네, 서사아 어 무찌마! 어

22. Jesus turned and saw her. "Take heart, daughter," he said, "your faith has healed you." And the woman was healed from that moment.

bwakulamise! unao-unao, oyu mukasi kuna kulama.

23. Chasinda, Yesu era kuika ala mwola mukulu-kulu, era kubuanao luamba lwa bandju balyi mwa rungu-rungu, n'e banji babanda mwa chwuperere bemba e nyimbo s'e malyira.

24. Yesu era kubabura mbu: Mutengaa ano! ono munyere atafire, kuonjira ku aonjire! abu bandju bomvire bacha, bera kumushekera.

25. Abere e bandju bera bakulyibwaa aola, Yesu era kwire engilyira mwa chumba chomwa ndanda. Era kuachilyira oyu munyere kwa mino, unao-unao kuna kubachwuka.

26. Ei myasi, yera kuhandabana mwechi chio choshi.

Yesu alamya bauta habilyi

27. Mango Yesu abaa era atengaa aola, bauta babilyi bera kumukulyikira. Abu bauta, babaa bamulakangira mbu: Emwenyi daudi! uchwufiraa e bonjo!

28. Mango Yesu abaa era engilyiraa mwa nyumba, ba bauta bera kumuikira. Era

---

뭐머러시 봐오 봐구퐈미서! 우나오-우나오, 오유 무가시 구나 구퐈마.

23. 짜시따, 여수 어라 구이가 아퐈 모퐈 무구룹-구루, 어라 구부아나오 루아빠 퐈 바쮸 바레 퐈 루웂-루웂, 너 바찌 바바따 퐈 쮸퍼러러 버빠 어 네뽀 서 마레라.

24. 여수 어라 구바부라 뿌: 무더빠아 아노! 오노 무녀러 아다피러, 구오찌라 구 아오찌러! 아부 바쮸 보뼤러 바짜, 버라 구무써거라.

25. 아버러 어 바쮸 버라 바구레봐아 아오퐈, 여수 어라 귀러 어삐레라 퐈 쮸빠 쪼봐 따따. 어라 구아찌레라 오유 무녀러 과 미노, 우나오-우나오 구나 구바쪼가.

26. 어이 먀시, 여라 구하따바나 뭐찌 찌오 쪼씨.

여수 아퐈맸 바우다 하비레

27. 마끄 여수 아바아 어라 아더빠아 아오퐈, 바우다 바비레 버라 구무구레기라. 아부 바우다, 바바아 바무퐈가삐라 뿌: 어뭐니 다우디! 우쪽피라아 어 보쪼!

28. 마끄 여수 아바아 어라 어삐레라아 퐈 뉴빠, 바 바우다 버라 구무이기라. 어라

---

23. When Jesus entered the ruler's house and saw the flute players and the noisy crowd,

24. he said, "Go away. The girl is not dead but asleep." But they laughed at him.

25. After the crowd had been put outside, he went in and took the girl by the hand, and she got up.

26. News of this spread through all that region.

27. As Jesus went on from there, two blind men followed him, calling out, "Have mercy on us, Son of David!"

28. When he had gone indoors, the blind men came to him, and he

kubabusa mbu: Ewashe! echi mwanyema, munemerere kwa nyigaala kuirachi? nabo mbu: nechi enawechwu! chwemerere.

구바부사 뿌: 어와써! 어찌 뫄녀마, 무너머러러 과 내가아퐈 구이라찌? 나보 뿌: 너찌 어나워쭈! 쮜머러러.

asked them, "Do you believe that I am able to do this?" "Yes, Lord," they replied.

29. Yesu era kubauma kwa meho. Era kubabura mbu: kwa bwemeresi bwenyu bulyi, ku binabaa.

29. 여수 어라 구바우마 과 머호. 어라 구바부라 뿌: 과 뭐머러시 붜뉴 부쮀, 구 비나바아.

29. Then he touched their eyes and said, "According to your faith will it be done to you";

30. Unao-unao e meho mabo kuna kusibukala. Yesu era kuba chichika mbu: Mumenyaa! mutaereresaa mwa bura chiro na mundju asibya kwene myasi!

30. 우나오-우나오 어 머호 마보 구나 구시부가랴. 여수 어라 구바 찌찌가 뿌: 무머냐아! 무다어러러사아 뫄 부라 찌로 나 무뚜 아시뱌 궈너 먀시!

30. and their sight was restored. Jesus warned them sternly, "See that no one knows about this."

31. Si beke, bera ku chiuma baenda babalyikisisa e bandju e myasi ya Yesu mwechi chio choshi.

31. 시 버거, 버라 구 찌우마 바어따 바바쮀기시사 어 바뚜 어 먀시 야 여수 뭐찌 찌오 쪼씨.

31. But they went out and spread the news about him all over that region.

Yesu alamya e musuru

여수 아퐈먲 어 무수루

32. Abere abu bauta babilyi bera bachiumaa, e bandju bera kuretera Yesu mundju muuma ola wabaa usimbirwe na chihwasi, unao-unao Yesu era kwambulachi.

32. 아버러 아부 바우다 바비쮀 버라 바찌우마아, 어 바뚜 버라 구러더라 여수 무뚜 무우마 오퐈 와바아 우시삐뤄 나 찌화시, 우나오-우나오 여수 어라 과뿌퐈찌.

32. While they were going out, a man who was demon-possessed and could not talk was brought to Jesus.

33. Oyu mundju kuna kutangilyisa ateta. E bandju boshi bera kusanwa busese mbu: alibwe! Mw'e chine chio choshi ch'e baisiraeli, mutafuraa kulorekanako mwasi ola ulyi ng'ono chiro na hicha!

33. 오유 무뚜 구나 구다삐쮀사 아더다. 어 바뚜 보씨 버라 구사놔 부서서 뿌: 아뤼붸! 뭐 찌너 찌오 쪼씨 쩌 바이시라어삐, 무다푸라아 구뢴러가나고 먀시 오퐈 우쮀 꾸오노 찌로 나 히짜!

33. And when the demon was driven out, the man who had been mute spoke. The crowd was amazed and said, "Nothing like this has ever been seen in Israel."

34. Si e bafarisayo beke bera kuteta mbu: aaye! si kwa buashi bw'e mukulu-kulu w'e bihwasi ku enjire ambulabi!

E bakosi bachilyi baeke

35. Yesu abaa enjire asungula mwa misi inenene nomwa chwumbara chwoshi, aenda akangilyisa e bandju mwa mashenge m'e bayuda. Mwamu mashenge, abaa enjire abahubanganyisa e mwasi mubuya-buya w'e bwami bokwa nguba. Era kunde alamya na chira malwala mwa kachi-kachi kabo.

36. Mango alolaa kwa luamba lw'e bandju, era kubafira bonjo bushi babaa balyibuka kanji babaa barembire busese. Babaa balyi nga mbulyi sa sitete mungere.

37. Chasinjire, era kubura e banafunzi bai mbu: e myaka yelyire inene, si e bakosi b'e kuishebula bakeire.

38 Bushi noku mwemaa ena e myaka achwume banji bakosi mw'ehwa lyai.

---

34. 시 어 바파리사요 버거 버라 구더다 뿌: 아아여! 시 과 부아씨 붜 무구루-구루 워 비화시 구 어찌러 아뿌꽈비!

어 바고시 바찌레 바어거

35. 여수 아바아 어찌러 아수꾸꽈 뫄 미시 이너너너 노뫄 쭈빠라 쫀씨, 아어따 아가끼레사 어 바뉴 뫄 마써꺼 머 바유다. 뫄무 마써꺼, 아바아 어찌러 아바후바까네사 어 마시 무부야-부야 워 봐미 보과 꾸바. 어라 구떠 아라먀 나 찌라 마꽈꽈 뫄 가찌-가찌 가보.

36. 마꼬 아로꽈아 과 루아빠 뤄 바뉴, 어라 구바피라 보뽀 부씨 바바아 바레부가 가찌 바바아 바러뻬러 부서서. 바바아 바쩨 까 뿌쩨 사 시더더 무꺼러.

37. 짜시찌러, 어라 구부라 어 바나푸씨 바이 뿌: 어 먀가 여쩨러 이너너, 시 어 바고시 버 구이써부꽈 바거이러.

38 부씨 노구 뭐마아 어나 어 먀가 아쭈머 바찌 바고시 뭐화 꽈이.

---

34. But the Pharisees said, "It is by the prince of demons that he drives out demons."

35. Jesus went through all the towns and villages, teaching in their synagogues, preaching the good news of the kingdom and healing every disease and sickness.

36. When he saw the crowds, he had compassion on them, because they were harassed and helpless, like sheep without a shepherd.

37. Then he said to his disciples, "The harvest is plentiful but the workers are few.

38. Ask the Lord of the harvest, therefore, to send out workers into his harvest field."

Matayo Chikono 10

Yesu achwuma e ndjumwa sai ekumi n'ebilyi mwa mulyimo

1. Lukusu luuma Yesu amaalaa e banafunzi bai ekumi na babilyi, era kuberesa e buashi bw'e kwambula e bihwasi, n'e kulamya chira bulwala.

2. Esi ndjumwa ekumi n'ebilyi e masina mabo mu mamamo : e muberebere i simoni ola wasulwaa e sina lya petero, na munyakabobu i andereya, na yakobo mwenyi sebetayo, na munyakabo mbu i yowani,

3. Na filipo, na baritolomayo, na tomasi, na matayo mufuchisi w'e mbarata, na yakobo mwenyi alufayo, na tateo,

4. Na simoni wo mwachikembe ch'e baseloti, na yuda isikariyota, ola warenganya yesu.

5. Esi ndjumwa e kumi n'ebilyi, Yesu era kusichwuma mwa mulyimo. Era kuburasi mbu: mutendaa mwaya era mwe bandju b'e sinji mbaa, kanji mutengilyira mu chiro na musi w'e basamariya.

마다요 찌고노 10

여수 아쭈띱 어 뚜뭏 사이 어구미 너비쩨 와 무레명

1. 루구수 루우마 여수 아마아꽈아 어 바나푸씨 바이 어구미 나 바비쩨, 어라 구버러사 어 부아씨 뭐 과뿌꽈 어 비화시, 너 구꽈먀 찌라 부꽈꽈.

2. 어시 뚜꽈 어구미 너비쩨 어 마시나 마보 무 마마모 : 어 무버러버러 이 시모니 오꽈 와수꽈아 어 시나 꺄 퍼더로, 나 무냐가보부 이 아너러야, 나 야고보 뭐네 서버다요, 나 무냐가보 뿌 이 요와니,

3. 나 피쩨포, 나 바리도로꽈마요, 나 도마시, 나 마다요 무푸찌시 워 빠라다, 나 야고보 뭐네 아루파요, 나 다더오,

4. 나 시모니 오 꽈찌거뻐 쩌 바서쁜디, 나 유다 이시가리요다, 오꽈 와러꺄냐 여수.

5. 어시 뚜꽈 어 구미 너비쩨, 여수 어라 구시쭈마 꽈 무쩨모. 어라 구부라시 뿌: 무더따아 꽈야 어라 뭐 바뚜 버 시찌 빠아, 가찌 무더삐쩨라 무 찌로 나 무시 워 바사마리야.

Matthew Chapter 10[NIV]

1. He called his twelve disciples to him and gave them authority to drive out evil spirits and to heal every disease and sickness.

2. These are the names of the twelve apostles: first, Simon (who is called Peter) and his brother Andrew; James son of Zebedee, and his brother John;

3. Philip and Bartholomew; Thomas and Matthew the tax collector; James son of Alphaeus, and Thaddaeus;

4. Simon the Zealot and Judas Iscariot, who betrayed him.

5. These twelve Jesus sent out with the following instructions: "Do not go among the Gentiles or enter any town of the Samaritans.

6. Si mundaa mwanaya era mw'e baisiraeli oshao, bushi balyi nga mbulyi sa saelyire.

7. Nera mungende mwarenga yoshi, mundaa mwahubanganyisa e bandju mbu: e bwami bokwa nguba bulyi ofu!

8. Mundaa mwalamya e balwala, mwanende mwomola n'e bafu, n'e kulamya e babenzi-benzi, na kunde mwaambula e bihwasi. Rero, bushi mweresibwe kwa buha, nenyu mundaa mwana kwa buha.

9. Mutekaa chiro na luteya lusibya mwa mifuko yenyu.

10. Kanji, mutekaa hao, nesi njimba ebilyi, nesi birato, nesi kachi, bushi kwemire e mukosi kunde eresibwa e lwembo lwai.

11. Mango mungende mwengilyira mwa musi abe munene nesi mueke, mwanahonda e mundju ola ungemerera kubahuukasa. Mwanabera mwa mwai kuikira mango mungatenga mwoyu musi.

12. Mumango mungende mwengilyira mu nyumba irebe, mwanalamusa

6. 시 무따아 먀나야 어라 뭐 바이시라어뤼 오싸오, 부씨 바뤠 따 뿌뤠 사 사어뤠러.

7. 너라 무어너 먀러꽈 요씨, 무따아 먀후바따네사 어 바뚜 뿌: 어 봐미 보과 우바 부뤠 오푸!

8. 무따아 먀꽈먀 어 바꽈꽈, 먀너너 모모꽈 너 바푸, 너 구꽈먀 어 바버씨-버씨, 나 구떠 먀아뿌꽈 어 비화시. 러로, 부씨 뭐러시붜 과 부하, 너뉴 무따아 먀나 과 부하.

9. 무더가아 찌로 나 뤂더야 뤂시뱌 먀 미푸고 여뉴.

10. 가찌, 무더가아 하오, 너시 찌빠 어비뤠, 너시 비라도, 너시 가찌, 부씨 궈미러 어 무고시 구떠 어러시봐 어 뭐뽀 꽈이.

11. 마꼬 무어너 뭐띠뤠라 먀 무시 아버 무너너 너시 무어거, 먀나호따 어 무뚜 오꽈 우어머러라 구바후우가사. 먀나버라 먀 꽈이 구이기라 마꼬 무따더따 모유 무시.

12. 무마꼬 무어너 뭐띠뤠라 무 뉴빠 이러버, 먀나꽈무사 버싸모 뿌:

6. Go rather to the lost sheep of Israel.

7. As you go, preach this message: 'The kingdom of heaven is near.'

8. Heal the sick, raise the dead, cleanse those who have leprosy,drive out demons. Freely you have received, freely give.

9. Do not take along any gold or silver or copper in your belts;

10. take no bag for the journey, or extra tunic, or sandals or a staff; for the worker is worth his keep.

11. "Whatever town or village you enter, search for some worthy person there and stay at his house until you leave.

12. As you enter the home, give it your greeting.

beshamo mbu:

13. mubaa n'e boolo! aka ba besha mwei nyumba babahukasise, mubarekeraa obu boolo. Na akaba bananyire kubahuukasa, mufulukanaa obu boolo bwenyu.

13. 무바아 너 보오롣! 아가 바 버싸 뭐이 뉴빠 바바후가시서, 무바러거라아 오부 보오롣. 나 아가바 바나니러 구바후우가사, 무푸루가나아 오부 보오롣 뷔뉴.

13. If the home is deserving, let your peace rest on it; if it is not, let your peace return to you.

14. Kanji akaba besha munyumba irebe nesi besha musi murebe banganana kubahuukasa na kubomvilyisa mutengaamo. Mwa kutengamo, mwanakunguta e mukungu ola ulyi kwa bihando byenyu.

14. 가찌 아가바 버싸 무뉴빠 이러버 너시 버싸 무시 무러버 바까나나 구바후우가사 나 구보삐레사 무더까아모. 꽈 구더까모, 꽈나구꾸다 어 무구꾸 오꽈 우레 과 비하또 벼뉴.

14. If anyone will not welcome you or listen to your words, shake the dust off your feet when you leave that home or town.

15. Kubinalyi, nababura kwa mango e lusuku lw'e buchinjibusi lukaika, besha oyu musi bakachinjibusibwa busese kurenza besha sodoma n'e koroma.

15. 구비나레, 나뱌부라 과 마끄 어 룰수구 뤄 부찌찌부시 룩가이가, 버싸 오유 무시 바가찌찌부시봐 부서서 구러꽈 버싸 소도마 너 고로마.

15. I tell you the truth, it will be more bearable for Sodom and Gomorrah on the day of judgment than for that town.

E bandju bakalyibusibwa bushi na Yesu

어 바뉴 바가레뵙습뵙 부씨 나 여수

16. Mumenyaa! nabachwumire nga mbulyi mwa kachi-kachi kenyishibwabwa. Bushi noku, mubaa bakalange nga njoko, kanji mwanaba barembu nga biruka.

16. 무머냐아! 나바쪽미러 까뿌레 꽈 가찌-가찌 거네씨봐봐. 부씨 노구, 무바아 바가꺄어 까 쪼고, 가찌 꽈나바 바러뿌 까 비루가.

16. I am sending you out like sheep among wolves. Therefore be as shrewd as snakes and as innocent as doves.

17. Muchilangaa bushi e bandju bangende babeka era muhondo s'e baishi b'e manja, bangende ba

17. 무찌꺄아 부씨 어 바뉴 바꺼떠 바버가 어라 무호또 서 바이씨 버 마쨔, 바꺼떠 바 바후찌사 꽈 쪽찌 꽈 마써어

17. "Be on your guard against men; they will hand you over to the local councils and flog you in

bahuchisa mwa chwuchi mwa mashenge mabo.

마보.

their synagogues.

18. Kanji, bangende babeka era muhondo s'e bakulu-kulu n'e bami bushi nanyi, chasiya mube babei banyi era muhondo sabo, n'era muhondo s'e bandju b'e sinje mbaa.

18. 가찌, 바꺼떠 바버가 어라 무호또 서 바구루-구루 너 바미 부씨 나니, 짜시야 무버 바버이 바네 어라 무호또 사보, 너라 무호또 서 바뚜 버 시뻐 빠아.

18. On my account you will be brought before governors and kings as witnesses to them and to the Gentiles.

19. Si mango bangende babeke era muhondo s'abu bakulu-kulu, mutendaa mwachibusa mbu: chi chwungateta nesi kuute chwungateta. Bushi mw'ebi bihangi, Ongo angaberesa e binwa bya mungateta.

19. 시 마꼬 바꺼떠 바버거 어라 무호또 사부 바구루-구루, 무더따아 마찌부사 뿌: 찌 쪼까더다 너시 구우더 쪼까더다. 부씨 뭐비 비하끼, 오꼬 아까버러사 어 비놔 뱌 무까더다.

19. But when they arrest you, do not worry about what to say or how to say it. At that time you will be given what to say,

20. N'ebi binwa, bitatenge era mwenyu, si e muchima w'eho iungateta mwa ndanda senyu.

20. 너비 비놔, 비다더꺼 어라 뭐뉴, 시 어 무찌마 워호 이우까더다 마 따따 서뉴.

20. for it will not be you speaking, but the Spirit of your Father speaking through you.

21. E mundju angechisa munyakabo. N'eshe w'e mwana angechisa e mwana wai, n'e bana nabo bangabindjukira e basere babo na kubechisa.

21. 어 무뚜 아꺼찌사 무냐가보. 너써 워 모나 아꺼찌사 어 모나 와이, 너 바나 나보 바까비뚜기라 어 바서러 바보 나 구버찌사.

21. "Brother will betray brother to death, and a father his child; children will rebel against their parents and have them put to death.

22. E bandju boshi bangabahomba bushi nanyi. Si ola ungasesa e muchima kuikira kwa businda anganunulyibwa.

22. 어 바뚜 보씨 바까바호빠 부씨 나니. 시 오꽈 우까서사 어 무찌마 구이기라 과 부시따 아까누누뤠봐.

22. All men will hate you because of me, but he who stands firm to the end will be saved.

23. Mango bangende babalyibusa mu musi murebe, mwanahaira mu unji.

23. 마꼬 바꺼떠 바바뤠부사 무 무시 무러버, 모나하이라 무 우찌. 구비나뤠, 나바부라

23. When you are persecuted in one place, flee to another. I tell you

Kubinalyi, nababura kwa
mutamale kusungula mwa
misi yoshi y'e isiraeli era
muhondo nyi mwana w'e
mundju ndasa kufuluka.

24. E mwanafunzi atachwula
arenzise e mukangilyisi wai,
n'e muanda nai, atachwula
arenzise enawabo.

25. Si kukomire e mwanafunzi
ende aba ng'e mukangilyisi
wai. N'e muanda nai
kukomire ende aba nga
enawabo. Akaba ena mwa
nyumba bangamukena na
kumwelyika mbu i belisebuli,
rero si kubanganelyika na
besha mwa mwai e masina
mabi busese bacha.

E kw'obaa e bandju

26. Yesu era kuteta kanji
mbu: abu bandju, mutendaa,
mwobaabo. Bushi kutalyi
kandju kasibya ka kabishirwe
ka katakabihulwe. Kanji
kutalyi na mwasi usibya ola
ubishirwe, ola utakamenyeke.

27. Chira mwasi ola
nababuraa mwa musimya,
mundaa mwabalao
changanama e suba
lyimenze. N'e mwasi ola
mwomvaa mwa byoo, munda
mwabalao na murenge
munene mwimenze

과 무다마러 구수꾸롸 먀 미시
요씨 여 이시라어삐 어라
무호또 네 먀나 워 무뚜 따사
구푸루가.

24. 어 먀나푸씨 아다쭈롸
아러씨서 어 무가삐레씨 와이,
너 무아따 나이, 아다쭈롸
아러씨서 어나와보.

25. 시 구고미러 어 먀나푸씨
어떠 아바 우어 무가삐레씨
와이. 너 무아따 나이
구고미러 어떠 아바 까
어나와보. 아가바 어나 먀
뉴빠 바까무거나 나 구뭐레가
뿌 이 버삐서부삐, 러로 시
구바까너레가 나 버싸 먀 마이
어 마시나 마비 부서서 바짜.

어 고밍씰 어 바뚜

26. 여수 어라 구더다 가찌 뿌:
아부 바뚜, 무더따아, 모바아보.
부씨 구다레 가뚜 가시뱌 가
가비씨뤄 가 가다가비후뤄.
가찌 구다레 나 먀시 우시뱌
오롸 우비씨뤄, 오롸
우다가머녀거.

27. 찌라 먀시 오롸
나바부라아 먀 무시먀, 무따아
먀바롸오 짜까나마 어 수바
레머써. 너 먀시 오롸 모빠아
먀 뵤오, 무따 마바롸오 나
무러꺼 무너너 뮈머써
과까까모 서 뉴빠.

the truth, you will not
finish going through the
cities of Israel before the
Son of Man comes.

24. "A student is not
above his teacher, nor a
servant above his master.

25. It is enough for the
student to be like his
teacher, and the servant
like his master. If the head
of the house has been
called Beelzebub, how
much more the members
of his household!

26. "So do not be afraid of
them. There is nothing
concealed that will not be
disclosed, or hidden that
will not be made known.

27. What I tell you in the
dark, speak in the daylight;
what is whispered in your
ear, proclaim from the
roofs.

kwangangamo s'e nyumba.

28. Mutendaa mwobaa e bandju ba bangeta e mubilyi oshao, si batangaala kuita e muchima. Si mundaa mwobaa Ongo, bushi yeke ete e buashi bw'e kuita e mubilyi n'e muchima mwa mulyiro w'e suku n'e mango.

29. Ewashe, si benjire bausa bitera-mbua bibilyi ku chikoroto chiuma oshao! si chiro bacha, kutalyi chiro na chitera-mbuwa chiuma cha chingatowera alashi busira e kuhonda kw'eho wenyu.

30. Nenyu, Ongo anachwula eshi e muanjo w'e mvilyi senyu soshi.

31. Bushi noku, mutendaa mwobaa, bushi mwabo mu mwete mufa munene kurenza bitera-mbuwa binene.

32. Chira mundju ola wanyemerera era muhondo s'e bandju, nanyi nyikamwemerera era muhondo sa tata olaulyi kwa nguba.

33. Si ola wa nyinana era muhondo s'e bandju, nanyi nyikamunana era muhondo sa tata ola ulyi kwa nguba.

Yesu aretaa e malyikano

---

28. 무더따아 몸바아 어 바뚜 바 바꺼다 어 무비례 오싸오, 시 바다꺼아라 구이다 어 무찌마. 시 무따아 몸바아 오꼬, 부씨 여거 어더 어 부아씨 붜 구이다 어 무비례 너 무찌마 롸 무례로 워 수구 너 마꼬.

29. 어와써, 시 버찌러 바우사 비더라-뿌아 비비례 구 찌고로도 찌우마 오싸오! 시 찌로 바짜, 구다례 찌로 나 찌더라-뿌와 찌우마 짜 찡까도워라 아라씨 부시라 어 구호따 궈호 워뉴.

30. 너뉴, 오꼬 아나쭈라 어씨 어 무아쪼 워 쁘례 서뉴 소씨.

31. 부씨 노구, 무더따아 몸바아, 부씨 롸보 무 뭐더 무파 무너너 구러싸 비더라- 뿌와 비너너.

32. 찌라 무쭈 오라 와녀머러라 어라 무호또 서 바뚜, 나니 네가뭐머러라 어라 무호또 사 다다 오라우례 과 꾸바.

33. 시 오라 와 네나나 어라 무호또 서 바뚜, 나니 네가무나나 어라 무호또 사 다다 오라 우례 과 꾸바.

여수 아러다아 어 마례—녁

---

28. Do not be afraid of those who kill the body but cannot kill the soul. Rather, be afraid of the One who can destroy both soul and body in hell.

29. Are not two sparrows sold for a penny? Yet not one of them will fall to the ground apart from the will of your Father.

30. And even the very hairs of your head are all numbered.

31. So don't be afraid; you are worth more than many sparrows.

32. "Whoever acknowledges me before men, I will also acknowledge him before my Father in heaven.

33. But whoever disowns me before men, I will disown him before my Father in heaven.

34. Yesu era kuendekera ateta mbu: mwaanyisa mbu nabahire kureta boolo kuno butala? nyono ndabahire kureta boolo si malyikano!

35. Bushi nabahire kulyikanya e mundju n'eshe, n'e munyere na nyina, n'e mwasana na nasala.

36. Rero, abarenda b'e mundju, bakanaba besha mwa mwai.

37. Ola uchwula usimire eshe nesi nyina kunyirenza, oyola atangaba mundju wanyi. Nola uchwula usimire muala wai nesi mwalyi kunyirenza, oyola nai atangaba mundju wanyi.

38. Nola utasa kweka e musalaba wai ananyikulyikire, oyola nai atangaba mundju wanyi.

39. Bushi noku, ola wahonda kulamya e kalamo kai angaesako. Si ola ungaesako bushi nanyi, yeke angahuba kukabona.

E lwembo lwa ba bakahuukasa e banafunzi ba Yesu

34. 여수 어라 구어떠거라 아더다 뿌: 마아니사 뿌 나바히러 구러다 보오롣 구노 부다꺄? 뇨노 따바히러 구러다 보오롣 시 마례가노!

35. 부씨 나바히러 구례가냐 어 무뚜 너써, 너 무녀러 나 내나, 너 먀사나 나 나사꺄.

36. 러로, 아바러따 버 무뚜, 바가나바 버싸 먀 먀이.

37. 오꺄 우쭈꺄 우시미러 어써 너시 내나 구네러싸, 오요꺄 아다까바 무뚜 와네. 노꺄 우쭈꺄 우시미러 무아꺄 와이 너시 먀례 구네러싸, 오요꺄 나이 아다까바 무뚜 와네.

38. 노꺄 우다사 궈가 어 무사꺄바 와이 아나네구례기러, 오요꺄 나이 아다까바 무뚜 와네.

39. 부씨 노구, 오꺄 와호따 구꺄먀 어 가꺄모 가이 아까어사고. 시 오꺄 우까어사고 부씨 나네, 여거 아까후바 구가보나.

어 뤄뽀 꽈 바 바가후우가사 어 바나푸씨 바 여수

34. "Do not suppose that I have come to bring peace to the earth. I did not come to bring peace, but a sword.

35. For I have come to turn " 'a man against his father, a daughter against her mother, a daughter-in-law against her mother-in-law -

36. a man's enemies will be the members of his own household.'

37. "Anyone who loves his father or mother more than me is not worthy of me; anyone who loves his son or daughter more than me is not worthy of me;

38. and anyone who does not take his cross and follow me is not worthy of me.

39. Whoever finds his life will lose it, and whoever loses his life for my sake will find it.

40. Ola wabahuukasa, elyi nyi ahuukasise nola wanyihuukasise, elyi ahuukasise ola wanyichwumaa.

41. Ola wahuukasa e murebi bushi alyi murebi, oyola akembibwa nga murebi. Nola wahuukasa e mundju mubuya-buya bushi alyi mubuya-buya, nai akembibwa nga mundju mubuya-buya.

42. Kubinalyi, nababura kwa e mundju ola ukeresa muuma mwa bano batoto ngumbu ya meshi ma maha bushi alyi mwanafunzi wanyi, oyu mundju akabona e lwembo lwai.

Matayo Chikono 11

1. Abere Yesu era amalaa kubura e banafunzi bai ekumi na babilyi ei myasi, era kutenga mw'echi chisiki. Era kuya mwa misi y'e kalilaya aenda akangilyisa n'e kuhubanganyisa e bandju e mwasi mubuya-buya.

2. Mw'esi suku, yowana mubatisayi abaa aminyirwe mwa buroko. Era kumva e ngulu y'e myasi era Kirisito

40. 오꽈 와바후우가사, 어쩨네 아후우가시서 노꽈 와네후우가시서, 어쩨 아후우가시서 오꽈 와네쭈마아.

41. 오꽈 와후우가사 어 무러비 부씨 아쩨 무러비, 오요꽈 아거삐봐 까 무러비. 노꽈 와후우가사 어 무쭈 무부야-부야 부씨 아쩨 무부야-부야, 나이 아거삐봐 까 무쭈 무부야-부야.

42. 구비나쩨, 나바부라 꽈 어 무쭈 오꽈 우거러사 무우마 꽈 바노 바도도 응뿌 야 머씨 마 마하 부씨 아쩨 꽈나푸씨 와네, 오유 무쭈 아가보나 어 뤄뽀 꽈이.

마다요 찌고노 11

1. 아버러 여수 어라 아마꽈아 구부라 어 바나푸씨 바이 어구미 나 바비쩨 어이 먀시, 어라 구더까 뭐찌 찌시기. 어라 구야 꽈 미시 여 가리꽈야 아어따 아가까레사 너 구후바까네사 어 바쭈 어 꽈시 무부야-부야.

2. 뭐시 수구, 요와나 무바디사에 아바아 아미네뤄 꽈 부로고. 어라 구빠 어 우뿌 여 먀시 어라 기리시도 어씨러

40. "He who receives you receives me, and he who receives me receives the one who sent me.

41. Anyone who receives a prophet because he is a prophet will receive a prophet's reward, and anyone who receives a righteous man because he is a righteous man will receive a righteous man's reward.

42. And if anyone gives even a cup of cold water to one of these little ones because he is my disciple, I tell you the truth, he will certainly not lose his reward."

Matthew Chapter 11[NIV]

1. After Jesus had finished instructing his twelve disciples, he went on from there to teach and preach in the towns of Galilee.

2. When John heard in prison what Christ was doing, he sent his disciples

enjire aira. Bushi n'oku, era kuchwuma bauma mwa banafunzi bai,

3. era kubabura mbu: muyaa kubusa Yesu mbu: Elyi unoyu ola wabaa wemire kubaha, nesi tulyinjira unji?

4. Yesu nai mbu: muyaa kubura yowana bya mwomvire n'e kuchilolerako:

5. E bauta balola, n'e birema byaenda, n'e babenzi-benzi balamisibwa, n'e basuru bomva, n'e bafu benjire bomwoka, n'e bakene benjire bahubanganyisibwa e Mwasi mubuya-buya.

6. Aahanyirwe e mundju ola utakaese e bwemeresi bwai ku nyono!

Yesu ateta era lulu sa yowana mubatisayi

7. Mango abu banafunzi ba yowana babaa bera bachiumaa, Yesu era kutangilyisa abura e luamba lw'e bandju bushi n'e myasi ya yowani mbu: Chi mwayaa kutangula mwa buyeye? Elyi lusheke lwa lwabaa lw'ekibaa-ekibwa n'e chiusi? Nanga!

8. Kasi chi mwayaa kutangula? Elyi mundju ola wabaa wembesi e njimba sa sikomire? Nanga! Si ba bende

아이라. 부씨 노구, 어라 구쭈마 바우마 뫄 바나푸씨 바이,

3. 어라 구바부라 뿌: 무야아 구부사 여수 뿌: 어레 우노유 오롸 와바아 워미러 구바하, 너시 두쩨띠라 우찌?

4. 여수 나이 뿌: 무야아 구부라 요와나 뱌 모삐러 너 구찌뢰쩌러라고:

5. 어 바우다 바뢰롸, 너 비러마 뱌어따, 너 바버씨-버씨 바롸미시봐, 너 바수루 보빠, 너 바푸 버띠러 보모가, 너 바거너 버띠러 바후바꺄네시봐 어 뫄시 무부야-부야.

6. 아아하네뤄 어 무뚜 오롸 우다가어서 어 뭬머러시 봐이 구 뇨노!

여수 아더다 어라 룰루 사 요와나 무바디사에

7. 마꼬 아부 바나푸씨 바 요와나 바바아 버라 바찌우마아, 여수 어라 구다삐레사 아부라 어 루아빠 뭬 바뚜 부씨 너 먀시 야 요와니 뿌: 찌 먀야아 구다우롸 뫄 부여여? 어레 루써거 롸 롸바아 뭬기바아-어기봐 너 찌우시? 나꺄!

8. 가시 찌 먀야아 구다우롸? 어레 무뚜 오롸 와바아 워뻐시 어 띠빠 사 시고미러? 나꺄! 시 바 버떠 버빠롸 어 띠빠

3. to ask him, "Are you the one who was to come, or should we expect someone else?"

4. Jesus replied, "Go back and report to John what you hear and see:

5. The blind receive sight, the lame walk, those who have leprosyare cured, the deaf hear, the dead are raised, and the good news is preached to the poor.

6. Blessed is the man who does not fall away on account of me."

7. As John's disciples were leaving, Jesus began to speak to the crowd about John: "What did you go out into the desert to see? A reed swayed by the wind?

8. If not, what did you go out to see? A man dressed in fine clothes? No, those who wear fine clothes are

b'embala e njimba sikomire bachwula mwa nyumba s'e bami!

9. Rero! Chi mwayaa kutangula kasi? Elyi murebi? Nechi! Nababura kwa alyi murebi, si kanji arenzise e murebi.

10. Bushi yowana inoyu I e maanjiko mabuya-buya machwula matechire era lulu sai mbu: nachwumire e ndjumwa yanyi ikuhondorere, chasiya ikukunganyisise e njira

11. kubinalyi, nababura kwa mwa butala boshi mutafura kuba mundju ola urenzise yowana mubatisayi. Si chiro bacha, ola ulyi mueke mwa bwami b'okwa nguba, imukulu-kulu kumurenza.

12. Kutengera e suku sa yowana mubatisayi abaa enjire ahubanganyisa e bandju e chinwa cha Ongo kuikira lwarero, e bandju benjire balwisa e Bwami b'okwa nguba. Obu Bwami, e ndjwalyi si senjire saereka kusimbabo kwa misi.

13. Ei myasi Yoshi yatechwa mwa mwaso ya musa n'e barebi boshi kuikira kwa suku ya yowana.

시고미러 바쭈롸 롸 뉴빠 서 바미!

9. 러로! 찌 롸야아 구다뭐롸 가시? 어레 무러비? 너찌! 나바부라 과 아레 무러비, 시 가찌 아러씨서 어 무러비.

10. 부씨 요와나 이노유 이 어 마아찌고 마부야-부야 마쭈롸 마더찌러 어라 루루 사이 뿌: 나쭈미러 어 뚜롸 야니 이구호또러러, 짜시야 이구구빠네시서 어 찌라

11. 구비나레, 나바부라 과 롸 부다롸 보씨 무다푸라 구바 무뚜 오롸 우러씨서 요와나 무바디사에. 시 찌로 바짜, 오롸 우레 무어거 롸 봐미 보과 뭐바, 이무구루루-구루 구무러싸.

12. 구더뻐라 어 수구 사 요와나 무바디사에 아바아 어찌러 아후바빠네사 어 바뚜 어 찌놔 짜 오꼬 구이기라 롸러로, 어 바뚜 버찌러 바뤼사 어 봐미 보과 뭐바. 오부 봐미, 어 꽈레 시 서찌러 사어러가 구시빠보 과 미시.

13. 어이 먀시 요씨 야더좌 롸 꽈소 야 무사 너 바러비 보씨 구이기라 과 수구 야 요와나.

in kings' palaces.

9. Then what did you go out to see? A prophet? Yes, I tell you, and more than a prophet.

10. This is the one about whom it is written: " 'I will send my messenger ahead of you, who will prepare your way before you.'

11. I tell you the truth: Among those born of women there has not risen anyone greater than John the Baptist; yet he who is least in the kingdom of heaven is greater than he.

12. From the days of John the Baptist until now, the kingdom of heaven has been forcefully advancing, and forceful men lay hold of it.

13. For all the Prophets and the Law prophesied until John.

14. Rero, ei myasi akaba mungemererai, mumenyererraa kwa e murebi Eliya ola batetaa kwa akabaha, I yowana.

14. 러로, 어이 먀시 아가바 무어머러라이, 무머녀러라아과 어 무러비 어쬐야 오롸 바더다아 과 아가바하, 이 요와나.

14. And if you are willing to accept it, he is the Elijah who was to come.

15. Ola wete machi, omvaa!

15. 오롸 워더 마찌, 오빠아!

15. He who has ears, let him hear.

16. Yesu era kuteta kanji mbu: E bandju b'e sine suku, nyingabahuhanya na chiye? Balyi nga banaba bekese mw'e soko babanjirana e chwushembe mbu:

16. 여수 어라 구더다 가찌 뿌: 어 바쭈 버 시너 수구, 네까바후하냐 나 찌여? 바레 까 바나바 버거서 뭐 소고 바바찌라나 어 쭈써뻐 뿌:

16. "To what can I compare this generation? They are like children sitting in the marketplaces and calling out to others:

17. chwabaomberaa e ngoma, si mutasinaa! Kanji chwabembiraa e nyimbo s'e chilyiyo si mutalyiraa!

17. 쫘바오뻐라아 어 꼬마, 시 무다시나아! 가찌 쫘버뻬라아 어 네뽀 서 찌레요 시 무다레라아!

17. " 'We played the flute for you, and you did not dance; we sang a dirge and you did not mourn.'

18. Bushi yowana mango abahaa, abaa atenjire alya atanamwa. E bandju bera kunde bateta mbu asimbirwe na bilwasi.

18. 부씨 요와나 마꼬 아바하아, 아바아 아더찌러 아꺄 아다나똬. 어 바쭈 버라 구더 바더다 뿌 아시뻐뤄 나 비쫘시.

18. For John came neither eating nor drinking, and they say, 'He has a demon.'

19. Nyi mwana w'e Mundju nanyi mango naikaa, nabaa n'enjire nalya n'e kumwa. E bandju bera kunde bateta mbu: mulolaa! Ono mundju I ndarenza kalyo, alyi na mutamisi! Kanji alyi mwira w'e bafuchisi b'e mbarata n'e banji bakosi b'e mabi! Si chiro bacha, e bwenge bwa Ongo bw'enjire bwanalorekanako kurengera e milyimo yai.

19. 네 똬나 워 무쭈 나네 마꼬 나이가아, 나바아 너찌러 나꺄 너 구똬. 어 바쭈 버라 구더 바더다 뿌: 무로쫘아! 오노 무쭈 이 따러싸 가룐, 아레 나 무다미시! 가찌 아레 뮈라 워 바푸찌시 버 빠라다 너 바찌 바고시 버 마비! 시 찌로 바짜, 어 뷔꺼 봐 오꼬 뷔찌러 봐나롣러가나고 구러꺼라 어 미레모 야이.

19. The Son of Man came eating and drinking, and they say, 'Here is a glutton and a drunkard, a friend of tax collectors and "sinners." ' But wisdom is proved right by her actions."

*E misi era yananaa
kwemerera Yesu*

20. Era nyuma s'ebi, Yesu era
kutangilyisa e kalyiira e misi
era airaa mu bisomerano
binene busese, bushi
beshamo batabindjulaa e
myanya yabo ibi. Era kuteta
mbu:

21. buanya ku woyo u musi
w'e korasini! Na buanya ku
woyo u musi w'e betesaida!
Bushi naira bisomerano mwa
ndanda senyu. Ebi
bisomerano, akaba
nyingabiilyire mwa musi w'e
tiro, n'e w'e sitoni, besha
mw'ei misi beke bangembere
mira e mbweka na kwakaba e
lufufu, kwa kulosa kwa
babindjukire kutenga mwa
bibi byabo.

22. Rero nababura kwa e
lusuku lwa Ongo
akachinjibusa e bandju,
mwabo mukachinjibusibwa
busese kurenza besha mwa
musi w'e tiro n'e w'e sitona.

23. Nao umusi w'e
kaperinaumu, elyi waanyisa
mbu ungerusibwa kuikira kwa
nguba? Bitabe bacha!
Kwandaasibwa ku
ungandaasibwa kuikira e
kusimu. Bushi e bisomerano

어 미시 어라 야나나아
궈머러라 여수

20. 어라 뉴마 서비, 여수 어라
구다삐쩨사 어 가쩨이라 어
미시 어라 아이라아 무
비소머라노 비너너 부서서,
부씨 버싸모 바다비쭈롸아 어
먀냐 야보 이비. 어라 구더다
뿌:

21. 부아냐 구 오요 우 무시
워 고라시니! 나 부아냐 구
오요 우 무시 워 버더사이다!
부씨 나이라 비소머라노 똬
따따 서뉴. 어비 비소머라노,
아가바 네삐비이쩨러 똬 무시
워 디로, 너 워 시도니, 버싸
뭐이 미시 버거 바써뻐러 미라
어 뭐가 나 과가바 어 루푸푸,
과 구로사 과 바비쭈기러
구더삐 똬 비비 뱌보.

22. 러로 나바부라 과 어
루수구 롸 오꼬 아가찌찌부사
어 바쭈, 똬보 무가찌찌부시봐
부서서 구러싸 버싸 똬 무시
워 디로 너 워 시도나.

23. 나오 우무시 워
가퍼리나우무, 어레 와아니사
뿌 우꺼루시봐 구이기라 과
꾸바? 비다버 바짜!
과따아시봐 구 우꺼따아시봐
구이기라 어 구시무. 부씨 어
비소머라노 뱌 뱌이쩨봐 어라

20. Then Jesus began to
denounce the cities in
which most of his miracles
had been performed,
because they did not
repent.

21. "Woe to you, Korazin!
Woe to you, Bethsaida! If
the miracles that were
performed in you had
been performed in Tyre
and Sidon, they would
have repented long ago in
sackcloth and ashes.

22. But I tell you, it will be
more bearable for Tyre
and Sidon on the day of
judgment than for you.

23. And you, Capernaum,
will you be lifted up to the
skies? No, you will go
down to the depths. If the
miracles that were
performed in you had
been performed in Sodom,

bya byailyibwa era mwao akaba bingailyibwe mwa musi w'e sodoma, oyu musi angabere anachilyio kuikira Iwarero.

24. Bushi n'oku, nababura kwa e lusuku lwa Ongo akachinjibusa e bandju, woyo ukachinjibusibwa busese kurenza besha sodoma!

먀오 아가바 비까이레붜 먀 무시 워 소도마, 오유 무시 아까버러 아나찌레오 구이기라 꽈러로.

24. 부씨 노구, 나바부라 과 어 루수구 꽈 오꼬 아가찌띠부사 어 바뉴, 오요 우가찌띠부시봐 부서서 구러싸 버싸 소도마!

it would have remained to this day.

24. But I tell you that it will be more bearable for Sodom on the day of judgment than for you."

Yesu atonga Ongo

여수 아도마 오꼬

25. Mw'esi suku, Yesu era kuteta kanji mbu: Ongo tata, woyo u Ena e nguba n'e butala! Nakutonga bushi ene myasi waibishaa e bandju b'e bwenge na ba basomire. Si waibihulyire e bana batoto.

26. Nechi tata! Ebi byoshi binatenganyire ne kuhonda kwao.

27. Tata anyeresise byoshi mira. Kutalyi mundju ola wishi e Mwana kureka tata yeine, nesi kutalyi ola wishi tata kureka e mwana yeine na chira mundju ola oyu mwana ahonda alose Tata.

25. 뭐시 수구, 여수 어라 구더다 가찌 뿌: 오꼬 다다, 오요 우 어나 어 꾸바 너 부다꽈! 나구도마 부씨 어너 먀시 와이비싸아 어 바뉴 버 붜꺼 나 바 바소미러. 시 와이비후레러 어 바나 바도도.

26. 너찌 다다! 어비 뵤씨 비나더마니러 너 구호따 과오.

27. 다다 아녀러시서 뵤씨 미라. 구다레 무뿌 오꽈 위씨 어 먀나 구러가 다다 여이너, 너시 구다레 오꽈 위씨 다다 구러가 어 먀나 여이너 나 찌라 무뿌 오꽈 오유 먀나 아호따 아뤄서 다다.

25. At that time Jesus said, "I praise you, Father, Lord of heaven and earth, because you have hidden these things from the wise and learned, and revealed them to little children.

26. Yes, Father, for this was your good pleasure.

27. "All things have been committed to me by my Father. No one knows the Son except the Father, and no one knows the Father except the Son and those to whom the Son chooses to reveal him.

E kutamukira era mwa Yesu

어 구다무기라 어라 꽈 여수

28. Muboshi mu mwalyibuka n'e misio isito, mubahaa ene mwanyi, nanyi nyigabatamusa.

28. 무보씨 무 꽈레부가 너 미시오 이시도, 무바하아 어너 꽈네, 나네 네가바다무사.

28. "Come to me, all you who are weary and burdened, and I will give you rest.

29. Mundaa mwanyichwunda na kunde mwakulyikira e myasi nenjire nabakangilyisa, bushi nyeke nyichwula murembu, na wamuchima mulomvu. Mukaira bacha, mungamuka.

30. Ekukulyikira e myasi yanyi kutakoochire, n'e musio ola nyingabesa nao atasitoire.

29. 무따아 먀네쭈따 나 구떠 꽈구꼐기라 어 먀시 너찌러 나바가삐꼐사, 부씨 녀거 니쭈라 무러뿌, 나 와무찌마 무로뿌. 무가이라 바짜, 무까무가.

30. 어구구꼐기라 어 먀시 야네 구다고오찌러, 너 무시오 오롸 네까버사 나오 아다시도이러.

29. Take my yoke upon you and learn from me, for I am gentle and humble in heart, and you will find rest for your souls.

30. For my yoke is easy and my burden is light."

Matayo Chikono 12
Yesu I Mukulu-kulu w'e sabato

마다요 찌고노 12
여수 이 무구루-구루 워 사바도

Matthew Chapter 12[NIV]

1. Era nyuma sa suku sieke, lusuku luuma lwa sabato, Yesu n'e banafunzi bai babaa barenga mu mahwa ma bulo. Abu banafunzi babaa bafa businya, echera chera kuchwuma benjire baenda bapolola e bulo, na babulya.

1. 어라 뉴마 사 수구 시어거, 루수구 루우마 롸 사바도, 여수 너 바나푸씨 바이 바바아 바러까 무 마화 마 부로. 아부 바나푸씨 바바아 바파 부시냐, 어쩌라 쩌라 구쭈마 버찌러 바어따 바포로롸 어 부로, 나 바부랴.

1. At that time Jesus went through the grainfields on the Sabbath. His disciples were hungry and began to pick some heads of grain and eat them.

2. e bafarisayo balolyire bacha, bera kubura Yesu mbu: cho! Ulolaa kwebine e banafunzi bao baira, n'oku e Mwaso wechwu atachwula emerere mbu chwundaa chwaira bacha e lusuku lw'e sabato!

2. 어 바파리사요 바로례러 바짜, 버라 구부라 여수 뿌: 쪼! 우로롸아 궈비너 어 바나푸씨 바오 바이라, 노구 어 먀소 워쭈 아다쭈롸 어머러러 뿌 쭈따아 쫘이라 바짜 어 루수구 뤄 사바도!

2. When the Pharisees saw this, they said to him, "Look! Your disciples are doing what is unlawful on the Sabbath."

3. Yesu nai mbu: Ewashe! Mutafuraa kusoma kasi kute ku mwami Daudi airaa mango abaa afa e businya

3. 여수 나이 뿌: 어와써! 무다푸라아 구소마 가시 구더 구 먀미 다우디 아이라아 마꼬 아바아 아파 어 부시냐

3. He answered, "Haven't you read what David did when he and his companions were hungry?

alauma n'e bandju bai?

4. Engilyiraa nabo mwa nyumba ya Ongo. Bera kulya e mikati era bandju babaa bachwulyire Ongo. E mikati ilyi ngei babaa batemererwe kunde balyai, kureka e bakuhanyi beine.

5. Kanji munyiburaa: Mutasa kusoma mwa mwaso wa musa, kwa chira lusuku lwa sabato e bakuhanyi ba bende bakola mwa luhu lwa Ongo benjire besha mwa mwaso ola werekere olu lusuku? Si batenjire baajimbwa kwa bakolyire chibi!

6. Nababura kwa anola alyi mukulu-kulu ola urenzise e luhu lwa Ongo!

7. Mwabo, muteshi ono mwasi kute ku achwula atechire: nyisimire munde mwafirana bonjo, si ndalaire kwa michwulo yenyu. Akaba mungamenyire echera, utangachinjibusise ba batete mabi.

8. bushi nyi mwana w'e Mundju nyi ena e Sabato.
Yesu alamya e mundju e lukusu lw'e sabato

9. Yesu era kutenga mw'echi chisiki, era kuyakwingilyira mwa bushenge bw'e bayuda.

아라우마 너 바쮸 바이?

4. 어삐레라아 나보 뫄 뉴빠 야 오꼬. 버라 구꺄 어 미가디 어라 바쮸 바바아 바쭈레러 오꼬. 어 미가디 이레 쩌이 바바아 바더머러뤄 구떠 바꺄이, 구러가 어 바구하네 버이너.

5. 가찌 무네부라아: 무다사 구소마 뫄 뫄소 와 무사, 과 찌라 루수구 롸 사바도 어 바구하네 바 버떠 바고꽈 뫄 루후 롸 오꼬 버찌러 버싸 뫄 뫄소 오롸 워러거러 오루 루수구? 시 바더찌러 바아지꽈 과 바고레러 찌비!

6. 나바부라 과 아노롸 아레 무구루-구루 오롸 우러씨서 어 루후 롸 오꼬!

7. 뫄보, 무더씨 오노 뫄시 구더 구 아쭈롸 아더찌러: 네시미러 무떠 뫄피라나 보쪼, 시 따롸이러 과 미쭈로 여뉴. 아가바 무까머네러 어쩌라, 우다까찌찌부시서 바 바더더 마비.

8. 부씨 네 뫄나 워 무뚜 네 어나 어 사바도.
여수 아롸맸 어 무뚜 어 루꼴숩 뤄 사바도

9. 여수 어라 구더까 뮈찌 찌시기, 어라 구야귀삐레라 뫄 부써삐 뷔 바유다.

---

4. He entered the house of God, and he and his companions ate the consecrated bread--which was not lawful for them to do, but only for the priests.

5. Or haven't you read in the Law that on the Sabbath the priests in the temple desecrate the day and yet are innocent?

6. I tell you that one greater than the temple is here.

7. If you had known what these words mean, 'I desire mercy, not sacrifice,' you would not have condemned the innocent.

8. For the Son of Man is Lord of the Sabbath."

9. Going on from that place, he went into their synagogue,

10. Mw'obu bushenge, mwabaa mulyi mundju muuma ola wabaa iremere e mino. Mwabaa mulyi na banji bandju ba babaa bahonda kuereka yesu. Mw'olu, bera kumubusa mbu: chwuburaa: e Mwaso wechwu achwemerere mbu chwulamyaa mundju e lusuku lw'e sabato?

11. Yesu nai mbu: akaba muuma mu mwabo e mbulyi yai ingatowera mwa fumbu e lusuku lw'e sabato, atangaikulamo olu lusuku?

12. Rero, si e mundju iwete mufa munene kurenza e mbulyi! Bushi n'oku, e Mwaso achwemerere kwa chwindaa chwaira e mabuya e lusuku lw'e sabato.

13. 'chasinda, Yesu era kubura oyu mundju wabaa uremere mino mbu: Nanulaa e mino yao. Nai mwa kunananulai, unao-unao, yera kulama nayaba nga ilyikabo.

14. Bushi n'oku, e Bafarisayo bera kutenga aola, na baya kuira e lwango lw'e kuita yesu.
E mwanda ola walondolyibwe na Ongo

10. 모부 부써떠, 꽈바아 무레 무뚜 무우마 오꽈 와바아 이러머러 어 미노. 꽈바아 무레 나 바찌 바뚜 바 바바아 바호따 구어러가 여수. 모루, 버라 구무부사 뿌: 쭈부라아: 어 꽈소 워쭈 아쮜머러러 뿌 쭈꽈먀아 무뚜 어 루수구 뭐 사바도?

11. 여수 나이 뿌: 아가바 무우마 무 마보 어 뿌레 야이 이꽈도워라 꽈 푸뿌 어 루수구 뭐 사바도, 아다꽈이구꽈모 오루 루수구?

12. 러로, 시 어 무뚜 이워더 무파 무너너 구러싸 어 뿌레! 부찌 노구, 어 꽈소 아쮜머러러 과 쮜빠아 쫘이라 어 마부야 어 루수구 뭐 사바도.

13. 짜시따, 여수 어라 구부라 오유 무뚜 와바아 우러머러 미노 뿌: 나누꽈아 어 미노 야오. 나이 꽈 구나나누꽈이, 우나오-우나오, 여라 구꽈마 나야바 까 이레가보.

14. 부찌 노구, 어 바파리사요 버라 구더까 아오꽈, 나 바야 구이라 어 꽈오 뭐 구이다 여수.
어 꽈따 오꽈 와룬또레붕 나 오꼬

10. and a man with a shriveled hand was there. Looking for a reason to accuse Jesus, they asked him, "Is it lawful to heal on the Sabbath?"

11. He said to them, "If any of you has a sheep and it falls into a pit on the Sabbath, will you not take hold of it and lift it out?

12. How much more valuable is a man than a sheep! Therefore it is lawful to do good on the Sabbath."

13. Then he said to the man, "Stretch out your hand." So he stretched it out and it was completely restored, just as sound as the other.

14. But the Pharisees went out and plotted how they might kill Jesus.

15. Olo lwango lw'e bafarisayo mango Yesu amenyaalo, era kutenga mw'echi chisiki. Bandju banene bera kumukulyikira. Ba babaa balyi balwala mubo, era kubalamya boshi.

16. si era kubachichika busese mbu batamukanganaa kwa bandju.

17. Ei myasi yabaa bacha, chasiya cha chinwa chibe, cha Ongo atetaa kurengera murebi isaya mbu:

18. mulolaa! Onola imuanda wanyi nachilondorere, imwana wanyi musiirwa, kanji iuchwula unyisimise! Nyingamweresa e Muchima wanyi, angahubanganyisa n'e bandju b'e mbaa soshi e myasi y'e kanangana.

19. atakende aira bwaka na mundju nesi kuira lwayo. Kutalyi ola ukomva e murenge wai mwa nama.

20. Kanji atakafume mwa lusheke lwa luchionyire, nesi atakasimye e kamore ka kahonda kusima. Atakaire ebyera, kuikira e mango e mwasi Yoshi era ichwungenene era muhomdo sa Ongo.

---

15. 오로 롸끄 뤄 바파리사요 마끄 여수 아머냐아룬, 어라 구더따 뭐찌 찌시기. 바뚜 바너너 버라 구무구레기라. 바 바바아 바레 바롸롸 무보, 어라 구바롸먀 보씨.

16. 시 어라 구바찌찌가 부써서 뿌 바다무가따나아 과 바뚜.

17. 어이 먀시 야바아 바짜, 짜시야 짜 찌놔 찌버, 짜 오끄 아더다아 구러꺼라 무러비 이사야 뿌:

18. 무론롸아! 오노롸 이무아따 와네 나찌론또러러, 이뫄나 와네 무시이롸, 가찌 이우쭈롸 우네시미서! 네따뭐러사 어 무찌마 와네, 아까후바따네사 너 바뚜 버 빠아 소씨 어 먀시 여 가나따나.

19. 아다거떠 아이라 봐가 나 무뚜 너시 구이라 롸요. 구다레 오라 우고빠 어 무러꺼 와이 뫄 나마.

20. 가찌 아다가푸머 뫄 루써거 롸 루찌오네러, 너시 아다가시며 어 가모러 가 가호따 구시마. 아다가이러 어벼라, 구이기라 어 마끄 어 뫄시 요씨 어라 이쭈꺼너너 어라 무호무도 사 오끄.

---

15. Aware of this, Jesus withdrew from that place. Many followed him, and he healed all their sick,

16. warning them not to tell who he was.

17. This was to fulfill what was spoken through the prophet Isaiah:

18. "Here is my servant whom I have chosen, the one I love, in whom I delight; I will put my Spirit on him, and he will proclaim justice to the nations.

19. He will not quarrel or cry out; no one will hear his voice in the streets.

20. A bruised reed he will not break, and a smoldering wick he will not snuff out, till he leads justice to victory.

21. N'e sina lyai ly'e bandu boshi bakalangalyira.

E bandju bateta mbu Yesu i belisebuli

22. Chasinda, bera kuretera Yesu mundju muuma ola wabaa usimbirwe n'e bihwasi. Ebi bihwasi, byabaa byamuiilyire muuta kanji musuru. Oyu mundju, Yesu era kululamya kuikira kwa chihangi atangilyisa ateta n'e kulola.

23. Ei myasi, yera kushishasa e bandju boshi. Bera kutangilyisa bateta mbu: Ono mundju anganaba mwenyi Daudi?

24. Si mango e Bafarisayo bomvaa bacha, bera kuteta mbu: Oyu mundju, i mukulu-kulu w'e bihwasi mbu I belisebuli iwenjire wamweresa e buashi bw'e kwambulabi!

25. Si Yesu bushi abaa amenyire mira e mianyisa yabo, era kubarura mbu: akaba bandju ba bwami buuma bangalwa beine kwa beine, elyi obu bwami bwahandjukere. Na akaba bandju ba musi muuma nesi ba ngumo nguma nabo bagalwa beine kwa beine,

21. 너 시나 랴이 려 바뚜 보씨 바가꺄꺄례라.

어 바뚜 바더다 뿌 여수 이 버리섈뷈리

22. 짜시따, 버라 구러더라 여수 무뚜 무우마 오꺄 와바아 우시뻬뤄 너 비화시. 어비 비화시, 뱌바아 뱌무이이례러 무우다 가찌 무수루. 오유 무뚜, 여수 어라 구루꺄먀 구이기라 과 찌하삐 아다뻬례사 아더다 너 구론꺄.

23. 어이 먀시, 여라 구씨싸사 어 바뚜 보씨. 버라 구다뻬례사 바더다 뿌: 오노 무뚜 아까나바 뭐네 다우디?

24. 시 마꼰 어 바파리사요 보빠아 바짜, 버라 구더다 뿌: 오유 무뚜, 이 무구룰-구룰 워 비화시 뿌 이 버리서부리 이워찌러 와뭐러사 어 부아씨 뷔 과뿌꺄비!

25. 시 여수 부씨 아바아 아머네러 미라 어 미아네사 야보, 어라 구바루라 뿌: 아가바 바뚜 바 봐미 부우마 바꺄꽌 버이너 과 버이너, 어레 오부 봐미 봐하뚜거러. 나 아가바 바뚜 바 무시 무우마 너시 바 꾸모 꾸마 나보 바가꽌 버이너 과 버이너, 아부 바뚜 구이가

21. In his name the nations will put their hope."

22. Then they brought him a demon-possessed man who was blind and mute, and Jesus healed him, so that he could both talk and see.

23. All the people were astonished and said, "Could this be the Son of David?"

24. But when the Pharisees heard this, they said, "It is only by Beelzebub, the prince of demons, that this fellow drives out demons."

25. Jesus knew their thoughts and said to them, "Every kingdom divided against itself will be ruined, and every city or household divided against itself will not stand.

abu bandju kuika banahandabane.

26. Na akaba wamusimu nai, angachambula yeine, elyi e bwami bwai nabo bwahandjukere.

27. Mwabo mwenjire mwateta mbu nenjire naambula e bihwasi kwa buashi bwa belisebuli. Rero, e bandju b'omwa chikembe chenyu nabo, kwa buashi bwande ku benjire baambulabi? Abu bandju benyu beine bu bangabalosa kwa mwauwirwe.

28. Si nyonyo nenjire naambula e bihwasi kwa buashi bw'e muchima wa Ongo. Nechi chi chilosise kwa bwami bwa Ongo bwaikire mira mwa kachi-kachi kenyu!

29. kutalyi ola ungaala kwengilyira mwa nyumba y'e mundju ola wete e misi, amunyae n'e bindju byai, akaba atasa kumumina. Si mwa kuba era amuminaa, mu mango angamunvaa e bindju byai byoshi.

30. Ola utalyi kwa lunda lwanyi, elyi alyi murenda wanyi. N'ola utanyiasa kulunda-lunda, elyi kuhandabanya ku

바나하따바너.

26. 나 아가바 와무시무 나이, 아까짜뿌롸 여이너, 어뤠 어 봐미 봐이 나보 봐하누거러.

27. 롸보 뭐찌러 롸더다 뿌 너찌러 나아뿌롸 어 비화시 과 부아씨 봐 버릐서부릐. 러로, 어 바누 보와 찌거뻐 쩌뉴 나보, 과 부아씨 봐너 구 버찌러 바아뿌롸비? 아부 바누 버뉴 버이너 부 바까바로사 과 롸우위뤄.

28. 시 뇨뇨 너찌러 나아뿌롸 어 비화시 과 부아씨 붜 무찌마 와 오꼬. 너찌 찌찌로시서 과 봐미 봐 오꼬 봐이기러 미라 롸 가찌-가찌 거뉴!

29. 구다뤠 오롸 우까아롸 궈끠뤠라 롸 뉴빠 여 무뿌 오롸 워더 어 미시, 아무냐어 너 비뉴 뱌이, 아가바 아다사 구무미나. 시 와 구바 어라 아무미나아, 무 마꼬 아까무빠아 어 비뉴 뱌이 뵤씨.

30. 오롸 우다뤠 과 룬따 롼네. 어뤠 아뤠 무러따 와네. 노롸 우다네아사 구루따-루따, 어뤠 구하따바냐 구 아하따바냐.

26. If Satan drives out Satan, he is divided against himself. How then can his kingdom stand?

27. And if I drive out demons by Beelzebub, by whom do your people drive them out? So then, they will be your judges.

28. But if I drive out demons by the Spirit of God, then the kingdom of God has come upon you.

29. "Or again, how can anyone enter a strong man's house and carry off his possessions unless he first ties up the strong man? Then he can rob his house.

30. "He who is not with me is against me, and he who does not gather with me scatters.

ahandabanya.

31. Bushi n'oku, nababura kwa e bandju bakababalyirwa e bibi byabo byoshi n'e ngambo sabo soshi. Si ola ukakamba e muchima mubuya-buya yeke, atakababalyirwe chiro na hicha.

31. 부씨 노구, 나바부라 과 어 바쭈 바가바바롈롸 어 비비 뱌보 보씨 너 까뽀 사보 소씨. 시 오롸 우가가빠 어 무찌마 무부야-부야 여거, 아다가바바롈뤄 찌로 나 히짜.

31. And so I tell you, every sin and blasphemy will be forgiven men, but the blasphemy against the Spirit will not be forgiven.

32. N'ola ukakamba e Mwana w'e mundju, akababalyirwa. Si ola ukakamba e Muchima mubuya-buya, atakababalyirwe chiro na hicha. Atakababalyirwe mw'e sine suku nesi mwa suku sa s'eshire.

32. 노롸 우가가빠 어 모나 워 무쭈, 아가바바롈롸. 시 오롸 우가가빠 어 무찌마 무부야-부야, 아다가바바롈뤄 찌로 나 히짜. 아다가바바롈뤄 뭐 시너 수구 너시 뫄 수구 사 서씨러.

32. Anyone who speaks a word against the Son of Man will be forgiven, but anyone who speaks against the Holy Spirit will not be forgiven, either in this age or in the age to come.

E muchi n'e bifuma byai

어 무찌 너 비푸마 뱌이

33. akaba e muchi alyi mubuya, ende eka na bifuma bibuya. Na akaba e muchi alyi mubi, ende eka na bifuma bibi. Rero, chira muchi ende amenyeka kurengera e bifuma byai.

33. 아가바 어 무찌 아뤠 무부야, 어떠 어가 나 비푸마 비부야. 나 아가바 어 무찌 아뤠 무비, 어떠 어가 나 비푸마 비비. 러로, 찌라 무찌 어떠 아머녀가 구러뻐라 어 비푸마 뱌이.

33. "Make a tree good and its fruit will be good, or make a tree bad and its fruit will be bad, for a tree is recognized by its fruit.

34. Mwabo mulyi buko bwa njoka! Kute mu bandju babi mungaala kuteta myasi ibuya? Bushi e mundju ende ateta e myasi era yehwire mwa muchima wai!

34. 뫄보 무뤠 부고 봐 쪼가! 구더 무 바쭈 바비 무까아꽈 구더다 먀시 이부야? 부씨 어 무쭈 어떠 아더다 어 먀시 어라 여휘러 뫄 무찌마 와이!

34. You brood of vipers, how can you who are evil say anything good? For out of the overflow of the heart the mouth speaks.

35. E mundju mubuya ende alosa e mabuya ma matenga

35. 어 무쭈 무부야 어떠 아론사 어 마부야 마 마더꽈

35. The good man brings good things out of the

mwa muchima wai mubuya. N'e mundju mubi nai ende alosa e mabi ma matenga mwamuchima wai mubi.

36. Nababura kwa e lusuku lw'e buchinjibusi, e bandju bakatongana bushi na chira mwasi wabuha-buha ola bateta.

37. Bushi chira mundju, e binwa byai bi bikachwuma asingana nesi achinjibusibwa.

E Bafarisayo bema Yesu e chisomerano

38. Era nyuma s'ebi, bafarisayo na bakangilyisi b'e Mwaso bauma, bera kubura Yesu mbu: mukangilyisi! Chw'ahonda uchwulose chisomerano chiuma.

39. Yesu na imbu: e bandju b'e sine suku, balyi babi, kanji batachwunjire Ongo! b'ahonda balole ku chisomerano, si kutalyi chisomerano chisibya cha bangalolako kureka cha murebi yona.

40. Rero, kwa yona amalaa suku ehachwu, e mushi n'e buchwufu alyi mwa bula bw'efi inene, kunoku ku nanyi nyi mwana w'e mundju, nyingamala suku ehachwu, e

와 무찌마 와이 무부야. 너 무뚜 무비 나이 어떠 아르사 어 마비 마 마더빠 마무찌마 와이 무비.

36. 나바부라 과 어 루수구 뤄 부찌찌부시, 어 바뚜 바가도빠나 부씨 나 찌라 와부하-부하 오롸 바더다.

37. 부씨 찌라 무뚜, 어 비놔 뱌이 비 비가쭈마 아시빠나 너시 아찌찌부시봐.

어 바파리사요 버마 여수 어 찌소머라노

38. 어라 뉴마 서비, 바파리사요 나 바가삐레시 버 마소 바우마, 버라 구부라 여수 뿌: 무가삐레시! 좌아호따 우쭈로서 찌소머라노 찌우마.

39. 여수 나 이뿌: 어 바뚜 버 시너 수구, 바레 바비, 가찌 바다쭈찌러 오꼬! 부아호따 바르퓌러 구 찌소머라노, 시 구다레 찌소머라노 찌시뱌 짜 바까르퐈고 구러가 짜 무러비 요나.

40. 러로, 과 요나 아마퐈아 수구 어하쭈, 어 무씨 너 부쭈푸 아레 똬 부퐈 뭐피 이너너, 구노구 구 나니 내 똬나 워 무뚜, 내빠마퐈 수구 어하쭈, 어 무씨 너 부쭈푸

good stored up in him, and the evil man brings evil things out of the evil stored up in him.

36. But I tell you that men will have to give account on the day of judgment for every careless word they have spoken.

37. For by your words you will be acquitted, and by your words you will be condemned."

38. Then some of the Pharisees and teachers of the law said to him, "Teacher, we want to see a miraculous sign from you."

39. He answered, "A wicked and adulterous generation asks for a miraculous sign! But none will be given it except the sign of the prophet Jonah.

40. For as Jonah was three days and three nights in the belly of a huge fish, so the Son of Man will be three days and three nights in the heart of the

mushi n'e buchwufu nyilyi mwa shinda.

네레 봐 씨따.

earth.

41. E lusuku lwa Ongo akachinjibusa e bandju, besha ninawi bakemanga era muhondo s'e bandju b'e sine suku chasiya babachinjibuse, bushi mango yona abahubanganyisaa e chinwa cha Ongo, bera kubindjuka batenga mwa bibi byabo. Rero, mumenyereraa kwa anola alyi ola urenzise yona!

41. 어 루우수구 봐 오꼬 아가찌찌부사 어 바뉴, 버싸 니나위 바거마빠 어라 무호또 서 바뉴 버 시너 수구 짜시야 바바찌찌부서, 부씨 마꼬 요나 아바후바빠네사아 어 찌놔 짜 오꼬, 버라 구비뉴가 바더빠 봐 비비 뱌보. 러로, 무머녀러라아 과 아노봐 아레 오봐 우러씨서 요나!

41. The men of Nineveh will stand up at the judgment with this generation and condemn it; for they repented at the preaching of Jonah, and now one greater than Jonah is here.

42. Mw'esi suku s'e buchinjibusi, mwamikasi w'e chio ch'e seba, nai akemanga era muhondo s'e bandju b'e sine suku chasiya abachinjibuse, bushi atengeraa bure aya kumvilyisa kwa myasi y'e bwenge bwa mwami solomono. Rero, mumenyereraa kwa anola alyi ola urenzise solomono!

42. 뭐시 수구 서 부찌찌부시, 뫄미가시 워 찌오 쩌 서바, 나이 아거마빠 어라 무호또 서 바뉴 버 시너 수구 짜시야 아바찌찌부서, 부씨 아더빠라아 부러 아야 구뻐례사 과 먀시 여 붸뻐 봐 뫄미 소로모노. 러로, 무머녀러라아 과 아노봐 아레 오봐 우러씨서 소로모노!

42. The Queen of the South will rise at the judgment with this generation and condemn it; for she came from the ends of the earth to listen to Solomon's wisdom, and now one greater than Solomon is here.

Yesu akangilyisa era luulu s'e kualuka kw'e bihwasi

여수 아가삐레뻽 어라 루웁루 서 구아루― 궈 비화시

43. Mango e chihwasi chende chatenga kwa mundju, chende chaya kusungula-sungula mwa buyeye chahonda e chisiki ala chingatamukira. Mwa kuinao,

43. 마꼬 어 찌화시 쩌너 짜더빠 과 무뉴, 쩌너 짜야 구수뿌봐-수뿌봐 봐 부여여 짜호따 어 찌시기 아봐 찌빠다무기라. 봐 구이나오,

43. "When an evil spirit comes out of a man, it goes through arid places seeking rest and does not find it.

44. chanachitetembya mbu:

44. 짜나찌더더뺘 뿌:

44. Then it says, 'I will

nyingafuluka mwa nyumba yanyi era natengeraamo, mwa kuikamo, chende chabuana italyi mu mundju, ibisibwe, inakunganyisibwe kubuya.	네까푸루가 와 뉴빠 야네 어라 나더꺼라아모, 와 구이가모, 쩌떠 짜부아나 이다례 무 무뚜, 이비시붜, 이나구까네시붜 구부야.	return to the house I left.' When it arrives, it finds the house unoccupied, swept clean and put in order.
45. Bushi n'oku, echi chihwasi chanere chaya kureta binji bihwasi bilyinda bya bibiire busese kurenzachi. Byoshi byanegilyira mwei nyumba na byachekalyiramo. Oyu mundju anere aba kubi busese kurenza kwa abaa alyi lyebere. E bandju b'e sine suku nabo, ku binganababera bacha, bushi balyi babi busese.	45. 부씨 노구, 어찌 찌화시 짜너러 짜야 구러다 비찌 비화시 비례따 뱌 비비이러 부서서 구러싸찌. 뵤씨 뱌너지례라 뭐이 뉴빠 나 뱌쩌가례라모. 오유 무뚜 아너러 아바 구비 부서서 구러싸 과 아바아 아례 려버러. 어 바뚜 버 시너 수구 나보, 구 비까나바버라 바짜, 부씨 바례 바비 부서서.	45. Then it goes and takes with it seven other spirits more wicked than itself, and they go in and live there. And the final condition of that man is worse than the first. That is how it will be with this wicked generation."

Nde i nyina wa Yesu na bande bu banyakabo	***떠 이 네깁 와 여수 나 바떠 부 바냐가보***	
46. Abere Yesu anachilyi ahambala n'e luamba lw'e bandju, banyakabo na nyina bera kuika. Bera kwimangira era butala, bushi babaa bahonda bahambale nai.	46. 아버러 여수 아나찌례 아하빠롸 너 루아빠 뤄 바뚜, 바냐가보 나 네나 버라 구이가. 버라 귀마끼라 어라 부다롸, 부씨 바바아 바호따 바하빠려 나이.	46. While Jesus was still talking to the crowd, his mother and brothers stood outside, wanting to speak to him.
47. Mw'olu, mundju muuma era kumubura mbu: nyoko na banyakenyu babano balyi era butala, bahonda bahambale nao.	47. 모루, 무뚜 무우마 어라 구무부라 뿌: 뇨고 나 바냐거뉴 바바노 바례 어라 부다롸, 바호따 바하빠려 나오.	47. Someone told him, "Your mother and brothers are standing outside, wanting to speak to you."

48. Yesu na imbu: Nde i malyi? na bande bu banyakechwu?	48. 여수 나 이뿌: 떠 이 마례? 나 바떠 부 바냐거쭈?	48. He replied to him, "Who is my mother, and who are my brothers?"
49. Chasinda, era kwerekesa e mino era banafunzi bai babaa balyi. Era kuteta mbu: mulolaa! banola bu bamalyi kanji bu banyakechwu!	49. 짜시따, 어라 궈러거사 어 미노 어라 바나푸씨 바이 바바아 바례. 어라 구더다 뿌: 무로롸아! 바노롸 부 바마례 가찌 부 바냐거쭈!	49. Pointing to his disciples, he said, "Here are my mother and my brothers.
50. bushi chira mundju ola wende waira e kuhonda kwa tata ola ulyi kwa nguba, oyola imunyakechwu na imwalyi wechwu kanji i malyi.	50. 부씨 찌라 무뉴 오롸 워떠 와이라 어 구호따 과 다다 오롸 우례 과 응구바, 오요롸 이무냐거쭈 나 이뫄례 워쭈 가찌 이 마례.	50. For whoever does the will of my Father in heaven is my brother and sister and mother."
Matayo Chikono 13	**마다요 찌고노 13**	**Matthew Chapter 13[NIV]**
E muanyi w'e muinzi	*어 무아네 워 무이씨*	
1. Mw'olu lusuku, Yesu era kutenga mwa nyumba na aya kwikala kwa musike s'e nyanja, chasiya akangilyise e bandju.	1. 모루 루수구, 여수 어라 구더까 뫄 뉴빠 나 아야 귀가롸 과 무시거 서 냐짜, 짜시야 아가끼레서 어 바뉴.	1. That same day Jesus went out of the house and sat by the lake.
2. Bandju banene busese bera kumusungula. Bushi n'oku, era kwerukira mwa bwato n'e kalamo. Abu bandju nabo, bera kushiba bemenze kwa musike s'e nyanja.	2. 바뉴 바너너 부서서 버라 구무수우롸. 부씨 노구, 어라 궈루기라 뫄 봐도 너 가롸모. 아부 바뉴 나보, 버라 구씨바 버머쩌 과 무시거 서 냐짜.	2. Such large crowds gathered around him that he got into a boat and sat in it, while all the people stood on the shore.
3. Era kubakangilyisa myasi inene mwa mianyi. Era kubabura mbu: kwabaa muinzi muuma ola wayaa kuinga e mbuto mw'ehwa lyai.	3. 어라 구바가끼레사 먀시 이너너 뫄 미아네. 어라 구바부라 뿌: 과바아 무이씨 무우마 오롸 와야아 구이까 어 뿌도 뭐화 랴이.	3. Then he told them many things in parables, saying: "A farmer went out to sow his seed.

4. Abere era ainga ei mbuto, siuma sera kutowera kwa musike s'e njira. E milonge yera kuika na yalyasi.

5. E sinji, sera kutowera mwa makoi ala abaa atalyi lutaka lunene. Esi mbuto, sera kumera fuba bushi e lutaka lwabaa lukeire.

6. Si mango e suba lyakolaa, lyera kwocha ei myaka, na yoma bushi e misi-misi yabaa itasimikire mwa chitaka.

7. E sinji mbuto, sera kutowera mwa myaka era yete mawa. Ei myaka yete mawa mango yakulaa, yera kufundeeresasi.

8. Si e sinji seke, sera kutowera mwa lutaka lwa lukomire, sera kweka e bifuma. Siuma sera kweka eyana, n'e sinji chirachwu, n'e sinji mahachwu.

9. Ola wete machi m'e kumva, omvaa!

Cha chachwumaa Yesu ende ateta mwa mianyi

10. Era nyuma s'ebi, e banafunzi ba Yesu bera kumuikira na bamubusa mbu: e Waliya! chi chenjire chachwuma wateta n'e bandju mwa mianyi?

---

4. 아버러 어라 아이꺄 어이 뿌도, 시우마 서라 구도워라 과 무시거 서 찌라. 어 미르어 여라 구이가 나 야랴시.

5. 어 시찌, 서라 구도워라 롸 마고이 아롸 아바아 아다뤠 루다가 루너너. 어시 뿌도, 서라 구머라 푸바 부씨 어 루다가 롸바아 루거이러.

6. 시 마꼬 어 수바 랴고롸아, 려라 곧짜 어이 먀가, 나 요마 부씨 어 미시-미시 야바아 이다시미기러 롸 찌다가.

7. 어 시찌 뿌도, 서라 구도워라 롸 먀가 어라 여더 마와. 어이 먀가 여더 마와 마꼬 야구롸아, 여라 구푸떠어러사시.

8. 시 어 시찌 서거, 서라 구도워라 롸 루다가 롸 루고미러, 서라 귀가 어 비푸마. 시우마 서라 귀가 어야나, 너 시찌 찌라쭈, 너 시찌 마하쭈.

9. 오롸 워더 마찌 머 구빠, 오빠아!

짜 짜쭈립씹 여수 어떠 아더다 롸 미아네

10. 어라 뉴마 서비, 어 바나푸씨 바 여수 버라 구무이기라 나 바무부사 뿌: 어 와뤼야! 찌 쩌찌러 짜쭈마 와더다 너 바쭈 롸 미아네?

---

4. As he was scattering the seed, some fell along the path, and the birds came and ate it up.

5. Some fell on rocky places, where it did not have much soil. It sprang up quickly, because the soil was shallow.

6. But when the sun came up, the plants were scorched, and they withered because they had no root.

7. Other seed fell among thorns, which grew up and choked the plants.

8. Still other seed fell on good soil, where it produced a crop--a hundred, sixty or thirty times what was sown.

9. He who has ears, let him hear."

10. The disciples came to him and asked, "Why do you speak to the people in parables?"

11. Nai mbu: Mwabo mwabonyire e muisha w'e kumenyerera e myasi ibishirwe yomwa bwami b'okwa nguba. Si e banji beke, batabonaao.

12. Bushi e mundju ola wete kandju, iwende weresibwa e kanji, anere aata binene. Si ola utete kandju yeke, anganyaibwa naka achirembaa kuata.

13. Rero, echera chi chenjire chachwuma nateta nabo mwa mianyi. Bushi abu bandju, chiro angaba mbu benjire bachwumbikisa si batalola, kanji benjire bomvilyisa si batomva, batanamenyerera.

14. Bushi n'oku, e myasi era isaya arebaa yaberere kubo. Bacha ku atetaa : Ekumva, mukende mwomva, si mutakamenyerere chiro na hicha. N'e kuchwumbukisa, mukende mwachwumbikisa, si mutakalole chiro na hicha.

15. Bushi bano bandju bailyire e michima yabo kuba isibu, basibise e machi mabo, chasiya batalolaa, batanomvaa, nesi batanyialukiraa.

11. 나이 뿌: 먀보 먀보니러러 어 무이싸 워 구머녀러라 어 먀시 이비씨뤄 요먀 봐미 보과 우바. 시 어 바찌 버거, 바다보나아오.

12. 부씨 어 무뉴 오롸 워더 가뉴, 이워떠 워러시봐 어 가찌, 아너러 아아다 비너너. 시 오롸 우더더 가뉴 여거, 아까냐이봐 나가 아찌러빠아 구아다.

13. 러로, 어쩌라 찌 쩌찌러 짜쭈마 나더다 나보 먀 미아니. 부씨 아부 바뉴, 찌로 아까바 뿌 버찌러 바쭈뻬기사 시 바다롸라, 가찌 버찌러 보뻬뤠사 시 바도빠, 바다나머녀러라.

14. 부씨 노구, 어 먀시 어라 이사야 아러바아 야버러러 구보. 바짜 구 아더다아 : 어구빠, 무거떠 모빠, 시 무다가머녀러러 찌로 나 히짜. 너 구쭈뿌기사, 무거떠 먀쭈뻬기사, 시 무다가롸뻐 찌로 나 히짜.

15. 부씨 바노 바뉴 바이뤠러 어 미찌마 야보 구바 이시부, 바시비서 어 마찌 마보, 짜시야 바다롸랴아, 바다노빠아, 너시 바다네아루기라아.

11. He replied, "The knowledge of the secrets of the kingdom of heaven has been given to you, but not to them.

12. Whoever has will be given more, and he will have an abundance. Whoever does not have, even what he has will be taken from him.

13. This is why I speak to them in parables: "Though seeing, they do not see; though hearing, they do not hear or understand.

14. In them is fulfilled the prophecy of Isaiah: " 'You will be ever hearing but never understanding; you will be ever seeing but never perceiving.

15. For this people's heart has become calloused; they hardly hear with their ears, and they have closed their eyes. Otherwise they might see with their eyes, hear with their ears,

understand with their hearts and turn, and I would heal them.'

16. Si mwabo, mwaahanyirwe bushi e meho menyu malola n'e machi menyu momva!

16. 시 먀보, 먀아하니뤄 부씨 어 머호 머뉴 마뤄롸 너 마찌 머뉴 모빠!

16. But blessed are your eyes because they see, and your ears because they hear.

17. Kubinalyi, nababura kwa kulyi barebi banene na bandju banene ba babaa bachwula bachwunjire Ongo, bahondaa balole kw'ene myasi museneko, si chiro bakaikolako. Kanji bahondaa bomve kui, si chiro bakayumvako.

17. 구비나뤠, 나바부라 과 구꿰 바러비 바너너 나 바꾸 바너너 바 바바아 바쭈꽈 바쭈찌러 오꼬, 바호따아 바뤈러 궈너 먀시 무서너고, 시 찌로 바가이고꽈고. 가찌 바호따아 보뻐 구이, 시 찌로 바가유빠고.

17. For I tell you the truth, many prophets and righteous men longed to see what you see but did not see it, and to hear what you hear but did not hear it.

Yesu aanulula e muanyi w'e muinzi

여수 아아누뤀꽈 어 무아네 워 무이씨

18. Mwiraa mwomvilyisa kw'oyu muanyi w'e muinzi atechire :

18. 뮈라아 모뻬꿰사 고유 무아네 워 무이씨 아더찌러 :

18. "Listen then to what the parable of the sower means:

19. E mbuto sa satoweraa kwa musike s'e njira, sihuhanyisibwe n'e bandju ba bende bomva e chinwa ch'e bwami bwa Ongo, si batamenyererachi. Chasinda, e Musimu anaika anakulachi mwa michima yabo.

19. 어 뿌도 사 사도워라아 과 무시거 서 찌라, 시후하네시붸 너 바꾸 바 버너 보빠 어 찌놔 쩌 봐미 봐 오꼬, 시 바다머녀러라찌. 짜시따, 어 무시무 아나이가 아나구꽈찌 먀 미찌마 야보.

19. When anyone hears the message about the kingdom and does not understand it, the evil one comes and snatches away what was sown in his heart. This is the seed sown along the path.

20. N'e sinji sa satoweraa mwa makoi, sihuhanyisibwe n'e bandju ba bende bomva e Chimwa cha Ongo, unao-unao bana angilyirachi na

20. 너 시찌 사 사도워라아 먀 마고이, 시후하네시붸 너 바꾸 바 버너 보빠 어 찌먀 짜 오꼬, 우나오-우나오 바나 아삐꿰라찌 나 뤀모오 뤀너너.

20. The one who received the seed that fell on rocky places is the man who hears the word and at once receives it with joy.

86 Matayo / 마다요 / Matthew

lumoo lunene.

21. Si echi chinwa chitasimika mwa michima yabo. Mango bende balola kwa malae, nesi balibuka bushi n'e Chinwa cha Ongo, unao-unao banareka e bwemeresi bwabo.

22. N'e sinji mbuto sa satoweraamwa mawa, sihuhanyisibwe n'e bandju ba bende bomva e Chinwa cha Ongo. Si e mianya yomuno butala, ne kusima kuhumira e buare, byende byafundeeresa echi chinwa mwa michima yabo. Bushi n'oku, chiteka bifuma.

23. N'e sinji sa satoweraa mwa lutaka lwa lukomire seke, sihuhanyisibwe n'e bandju ba bende bomva e Chinwa cha Ongo na kumenyererachi. Chasinda, echi chinwa chaneka e bifuma mwa michima yabo. Bauma, baneka bifuma eyana, n'e banji mahachwu.

E muanyi w'e bichi bibi

24. Yesu era kuisha unji muanyi muuma mbu: e Bwami b'okwa nguba buhuhanyisibwe na mundju muuma ola waingaa mbuto ibuya mw'ehwa lyai.

21. 시 어찌 찌놔 찌다시미가 뫄 미찌마 야보. 마꼬 버너 바로꽈 과 마꽈어, 너시 바뤼부가 부씨 너 찌놔 짜 오꼬, 우나오-우나오 바나러가 어 붜머러시 봐보.

22. 너 시찌 뿌도 사 사도워라아뫄 마와, 시후하네시붜 너 바뚜 바 버너 보빠 어 찌놔 짜 오꼬. 시 어 미아냐 요무노 부다꽈, 너 구시마 구후미라 어 부아러, 벼버 뱌푸떠어러사 어찌 찌놔 뫄 미찌마 야보. 부씨 노구, 찌더가 비푸마.

23. 너 시찌 사 사도워라아 뫄 루다가 꽈 루고미러 서거, 시후하네시붜 너 바뚜 바 버너 보빠 어 찌놔 짜 오꼬 나 구머녀러라찌. 짜시따, 어찌 찌놔 짜너가 어 비푸마 뫄 미찌마 야보. 바우마, 바너가 비푸마 어야나, 너 바찌 마하쭈.

어 무아네 워 비찌 비비

24. 여수 어라 구이싸 우찌 무아네 무우마 뿌: 어 봐미 보과 꼬바 부후하네시붜 나 무뚜 무우마 오꽈 와이까아 뿌도 이부야 뭐화 랴이.

21. But since he has no root, he lasts only a short time. When trouble or persecution comes because of the word, he quickly falls away.

22. The one who received the seed that fell among the thorns is the man who hears the word, but the worries of this life and the deceitfulness of wealth choke it, making it unfruitful.

23. But the one who received the seed that fell on good soil is the man who hears the word and understands it. He produces a crop, yielding a hundred, sixty or thirty times what was sown."

24. Jesus told them another parable: "The kingdom of heaven is like a man who sowed good seed in his field.

25. Si lusuku luuma buchwufu mango e bandju boshi babaa baonjire mira, e murenda wai era kuika kuinga e bischi bibi mwa bulo, chasinda era kuchiendera.	25. 시 ᄙᅮ수구 ᄙᅮ우마 부쭈푸 마ᅌᅩ 어 바ᅜᅮ 보씨 바바아 바오ᅜᅵ러 미라, 어 무러ᄓᅡ 와이 어라 구이가 구이ᅌᅡ 어 비찌 비비 뫄 부ᄙᅩ, 짜시ᄓᅡ 어라 구쩌ᄓᅥ라.	25. But while everyone was sleeping, his enemy came and sowed weeds among the wheat, and went away.
26. abere obu bulo bwamera na kueta, ebi bichi bibi nabi, byera kulorekanako.	26. 아버러 오부 부ᄙᅩ 봐머라 나 구어다, 어비 비찌 비비 나비, 벼라 구ᄙᅩ러가나고.	26. When the wheat sprouted and formed heads, then the weeds also appeared.
27. e bakosi b'en'ehwa, bera kuya kumubusa mbu: e Waliya, si mbuto ibuya ichwaingaa mw'ehwa lyao? Rero, ebi bichi bibi ngai u byatengire?	27. 어 바고시 버너화, 버라 구야 구무부사 뿌: 어 와ᄙᅵ야, 시 뿌도 이부야 이쫘이ᅌᅡ아 뭐화 ᄙᅣ오? 러로, 어비 비찌 비비 ᅌᅡ이 우 뱌더ᅌᅵ러?	27. "The owner's servants came to him and said, 'Sir, didn't you sow good seed in your field? Where then did the weeds come from?'
28. Nai mbu: Murenda iwailyire bacha. Bera kuhuba kumubusa mbu: Elyi wahonda chwuye kubikulyisanga?	28. 나이 뿌: 무러ᄓᅡ 이와이ᄙᅨ러 바짜. 버라 구후바 구무부사 뿌: 어ᄙᅨ 와호ᄓᅡ 쭈여 구비구ᄙᅨ사ᅌᅡ?	28. " 'An enemy did this,' he replied. "The servants asked him, 'Do you want us to go and pull them up?'
29. Nai mbu: Nanga! akaba mungaya kubikulyisa, kulyi mango mungabikulyisanga alauma n'e bulo.	29. 나이 뿌: 나ᅌᅡ! 아가바 무ᅌᅡ야 구비구ᄙᅨ사, 구ᄙᅨ 마ᅌᅩ 무ᅌᅡ비구ᄙᅨ사ᅌᅡ 아ᄙᅡ우마 너 부ᄙᅩ.	29. " 'No,' he answered, 'because while you are pulling the weeds, you may root up the wheat with them.
30. Bushi n'oku, murekaa byoshi bikulyire alauma, kuikira mwa suku s'e kushebula. Mw'esi suku mu nyingabura e bandju b'e kushebula mbu: Mukulyisangaa tanga e bichi, mwanaminabi chwukanda-	30. 부씨 노구, 무러가아 뵤씨 비구ᄙᅨ러 아ᄙᅡ우마, 구이기라 뫄 수구 서 구써부ᄙᅡ. 뭐시 수구 무 네ᅌᅡ부라 어 바ᅜᅮ 버 구써부ᄙᅡ 뿌: 무구ᄙᅨ사ᅌᅡ아 다ᅌᅡ 어 비찌, 뫄나미나비 쭈가ᄓᅡ-쭈가ᄓᅡ 짜시야 비여 꼬찌봐. 짜시ᄓᅡ, 뫄나ᄙᅮᄓᅡ-ᄙᅮᄓᅡ	30. Let both grow together until the harvest. At that time I will tell the harvesters: First collect the weeds and tie them in bundles to be burned; then gather the wheat and bring it into my barn.' "

chwukanda chasiya biye kwochibwa. Chasinda, mwanalunda-lunda e bulo mwanabikabo mwa ngulyi yanyi.

어 부로 먀나비가보 뫄 우쪠야네.

E muanyi w'e kafuma k'e haradani

어 무아네 워 가푸마 거 하라다니

31. Yesu era kubaishira unji muanyi muuma mbu: e Bwami b'okwa nguba buhuhanyisibwe na kafuma kaeke k'e haradani ka mundju muuma atolaa na aya kukainga mw'ehwa lyai.

31. 여수 어라 구바이씨라 우찌 무아네 무우마 뿌: 어 봐미 보과 우바 부후하네시붜 나 가푸마 가어거 거 하라다니 가 무뚜 무우마 아도롸아 나 아야 구가이뫄 뭐화 랴이.

31. He told them another parable: "The kingdom of heaven is like a mustard seed, which a man took and planted in his field.

32. Aku kafuma, ku kachwula kaeke kurenza e chwunji chwoshi. Si mango kende kamera kende kahuba muchi munene kurenza einji myaka yoshi yo mw'ehwa, kuikira e chihangi e milonge yende yaika kuimba e machwu kwa matabi mao.

32. 아구 가푸마, 구 가쭈롸 가어거 구러싸 어 쭈찌 쭈씨. 시 마꼬 거더 가머라 거더 가후바 무찌 무너너 구러싸 어이찌 먀가 요씨 요 뭐화, 구이기라 어 찌하뻬 어 미론워 여더 야이가 구이빠 어 마쭈 과 마다비 마오.

32. Though it is the smallest of all your seeds, yet when it grows, it is the largest of garden plants and becomes a tree, so that the birds of the air come and perch in its branches."

E muanyi w'e chachu

어 무아네 워 짜쭈

33. Kanji Yesu era kuisha unji muanyi muuma mbu: e Bwami b'okwa nguba buhuhwanyisibwe na chachu cha mukasi muuma atola. Echi chachu, era kuhoonganyachi mu biyanga bihachwu binenene bya shano ya bulo, kuikira chera kuimbya ei shano yoshi.

33. 가찌 여수 어라 구이싸 우찌 무아네 무우마 뿌: 어 봐미 보과 우바 부후화네시붜 나 짜쭈 짜 무가시 무우마 아도롸. 어찌 짜쭈, 어라 구호오꺄냐찌 무 비야꺄 비하쭈 비너너너 뱌 싸노 야 부로, 구이기라 쩌라 구이빠 어이 싸노 요씨.

33. He told them still another parable: "The kingdom of heaven is like yeast that a woman took and mixed into a large amount of flour until it worked all through the dough."

34. Ei myasi yoshi Yesu

34. 어이 먀시 요씨 여수

34. Jesus spoke all these

aburaai e luamba lw'e bandju mwa mianyi. Abaa atenjire ababura mwasi usibiya busira kubaishira muanyi.

35. Abaa enjire aira bacha, chasiya e chinwa chiberere, cha chatechwaa n'e murebi mbu: nyingende nateta nabo mwa mianyi, nyingabafulyira n'e myasi era yabaa ibishirwe kutengera e kubumbwa kw'e butala.

Yesu aanulula e muanyi w'e bichi bibi

36. Era nyuma s'ebi, Yesu era kureka e luamba lw'e bandju, na engilyira mwa nyumba. E banafunzi bai bera kuya kumubura mbu: waliya! ola muanyi w'e bichi bibi bya byabaa bilyi mw'ehwa, uchwuanululyiraao.

37. Yesu nai mbu: oyu waingaa e mbuto sibuya, alyi nyono nyi mwana w'e Mundju.

38. N'ehwa, bulyi e butala. N'esi mbuto sibuya, sihuhanyisibwe n'e bandju b'omwa bwami bwa Ongo. N'ebi bichi bibi, bihuhanyisibwe n'e bandju ba wamusimu.

39. N'e murenda ola waikaa kuinga ebi bichi, alyi

아부라아이 어 루아빠 뤄 바뚜 와 미아니. 아바아 아더찌러 아바부라 마시 우시비야 부시라 구바이씨라 무아니.

35. 아바아 어찌러 아이라 바짜, 짜시야 어 찌놔 찌버러러, 짜 짜더좌아 너 무러비 뿌: 네뻐러 나더다 나보 뫄 미아니, 네뻐바부풀레라 너 먀시 어라 야바아 이비씨뤄 구더뻐라 어 구부빠 궈 부다뫄.

여수 아아누루뫄 어 무아니 워 비찌 비비

36. 어라 뉴마 서비, 여수 어라 구러가 어 루아빠 뤄 바뚜, 나 어삐레라 뫄 뉴빠. 어 바나푼씨 바이 버라 구야 구무부라 뿌: 와뤼야! 오롸 무아니 워 비찌 비비 뱌 뱌바아 비뤠 뭐화, 우쭈아누루뤠라아오.

37. 여수 나이 뿌: 오유 와이빠아 어 뿌도 시부야, 아뤠 뇨노 네 뫄나 워 무뚜.

38. 너화, 부뤠 어 부다뫄. 너시 뿌도 시부야, 시후하네시붜 너 바뚜 보뫄 뫄미 봐 오꼬. 너비 비찌 비비, 비후하네시붜 너 바뚜 바 와무시무.

39. 너 무러따 오롸 와이가아 구이빠 어비 비찌, 아뤠

things to the crowd in parables; he did not say anything to them without using a parable.

35. So was fulfilled what was spoken through the prophet: "I will open my mouth in parables, I will utter things hidden since the creation of the world."

36. Then he left the crowd and went into the house. His disciples came to him and said, "Explain to us the parable of the weeds in the field."

37. He answered, "The one who sowed the good seed is the Son of Man.

38. The field is the world, and the good seed stands for the sons of the kingdom. The weeds are the sons of the evil one,

39. and the enemy who sows them is the devil.

wamusimu. N'e kushebula, kuhuhanyisibwe n'e businda bw'e butala. N'e bandju b'e kushebula, bahuhanyisibwe n'e bamalaika.

40. Rero, ng'okwa e bichi bibi byende byakulyisibwa chasiya byochibwe mwa mulyiro, ku bikanaba bacha kwa businda bw'e butala.

41. Bushi nyi Mwana w'e Mundju nyikachwuma e bamalaika banyi mwa bwami bwanyi, baye kulunda-lunda e bandju boshi ba bende bashiilyisa e banji mwa mabi alauma n'e banji boshi ba bende bakola e mabi.

42. chasinda abu bandju babi, e bamalaika bakaumabo mwa marunga m'e mulyiro. Na mw'oyu mulyiro, bakalyira na kulola kwa kasibu.

43. Si e bandju babuya beke, bakaba balangala ng'e suba mwa bwami bw'eshe wabo. Ola wete e machi, omvaa!

E muanyi w'e bindju by'e chichiro chinene

44. e Bwami b'okwa nguba, buhuhanyisibwe na bikulo bya byabaa bibishirwe mw'ehwa. Ebi bikulo, mundju

---

와무시무. 너 구써부롸, 구후하니시붜 너 부시따 붜 부다롸. 너 바쭈 버 구써부롸, 바후하니시붜 너 바마롸이가.

40. 러로, 우오과 어 비찌 비비 벼떠 뱌구례시봐 짜시야 뵤찌붜 마 무롈로, 구 비가나바 바짜 과 부시따 붜 부다롸.

41. 부씨 네 뫄나 워 무뚜 니가쭈마 어 바마롸이가 바니 마 봐미 보네, 뱌여 구루따-루따 어 바쭈 보씨 바 버떠 바씨이롈사 어 바찌 마 마비 아롸우마 너 바찌 보씨 바 버떠 바고롸 어 마비.

42. 짜시따 아부 바쭈 바비, 어 바마롸이가 바가우마보 뫄 마루꺄 머 무롈로. 나 뫄유 무롈로, 바가롈라 나 구로롸 과 가시부.

43. 시 어 바쭈 바부야 버거, 바가바 바롸꺄롸 우어 수바 마 봐미 붜써 와보. 오롸 워더 어 마찌, 오빠아!

어 무아네 워 비뿌 벼 찌찌로 찌너너

44. 어 봐미 보과 우바, 부후하니시붜 나 비구로 뱌 뱌바아 비비씨뤄 뭏화. 어비 비구로, 무뚜 무우마 어라

The harvest is the end of the age, and the harvesters are angels.

40. "As the weeds are pulled up and burned in the fire, so it will be at the end of the age.

41. The Son of Man will send out his angels, and they will weed out of his kingdom everything that causes sin and all who do evil.

42. They will throw them into the fiery furnace, where there will be weeping and gnashing of teeth.

43. Then the righteous will shine like the sun in the kingdom of their Father. He who has ears, let him hear.

44. "The kingdom of heaven is like treasure hidden in a field. When a man found it, he hid it

muuma era kubuulabi, unao-
unao era kuhuba kubishabi.
Oyu mundju, era kumwowa
busese, na aya kuusa e
bindju byai byoshi, chasinda
era kuula elyi ehwa.

45. E bwami b'okwa nguba
buhuhanyisibwe kanji na
muchimbusi muuma ola
wabaa wahonda kuya kuula
makoi ma chichiro chinene.

46. Mango alolaa kukoi
lyiuma lya chichiro chinene,
era kuya kuusa e bindju byai
byoshi na aulalyi.

E muanyi w'e kasira

47. e bwami b'okwa nguba
kanji buhuhanyisibwe na
kasira ka balobi bauma
baumaa mwa nyanja, kera
kusimba chira mulala w'efi.

48. Mango kabaa k'ehwire,
abu balobi bera kukalulyira
kwa musike s'e nyanja.
Chasinda, bera kwekala na
batangilyisa balondola efi.
Bera kubika sa sabaa sikomire
mwa bitonga, nesa sabaa
sibiire, bera kusikabulyira.

49. Rero, kubikanaba bacha
kwa businda bw'e butala. E
bamalaika bakabaha
kulyikanya e bandju babi n'e
babuya.

구부우꽈비, 우나오-우나오
어라 구후바 구비싸비. 오유
무뚜, 어라 구모와 부서서, 나
아야 구우사 어 비뚜 뱌이
뵤씨, 짜시따 어라 구우꽈
어레 어화.

45. 어 봐미 보과 꾸바
부후하네시붸 가찌 나
무찌뿌시 무우마 오라 와바아
와호따 구야 구우꽈 마고이 마
찌찌로 찌너너.

46. 마꼬 아롤롸아 구고이
레우마 랴 찌찌로 찌너너,
어라 구야 구우사 어 비뚜
뱌이 뵤씨 나 아우꽈레.

어 무아네 워 가시라

47. 어 봐미 보과 꾸바 가찌
부후하네시붸 나 가시라 가
바르비 바우마 바우마아 뫄
냐짜, 거라 구시빠 찌라
무꽈꽈 워피.

48. 마꼬 가바아 거휘러, 아부
바르비 버라 구가루레라 과
무시거 서 냐짜. 짜시따, 버라
궈가꽈 나 바다삐레사
바르또꽈 어피. 버라 구비가
사 사바아 시고미러 뫄
비도꾸, 너사 사바아 시비이러,
버라 구시가부레라.

49. 러로, 구비가나바 바짜 과
부시따 붜 부다꽈. 어
바마꽈이가 바가바하 구레가냐
어 바뚜 바비 너 바부야.

again, and then in his joy
went and sold all he had
and bought that field.

45. "Again, the kingdom of
heaven is like a merchant
looking for fine pearls.

46. When he found one of
great value, he went away
and sold everything he
had and bought it.

47. "Once again, the
kingdom of heaven is like
a net that was let down
into the lake and caught
all kinds of fish.

48. When it was full, the
fishermen pulled it up on
the shore. Then they sat
down and collected the
good fish in baskets, but
threw the bad away.

49. This is how it will be at
the end of the age. The
angels will come and
separate the wicked from
the righteous

50. Bakauma e bandju babi mwa marunga m'e mulyiro. Na mw'oyu mulyiro, bakalola kwa kasibu.

E muanyi w'e bindju biyayaya n'e by'okwa mira

51. Yesu era kubusa e banafunzi bai mbu: Ewashe, elyi mwomvire ei myasi yoshi? Nabo mbu: Eee, chwomvire.

52. Chasinda, era kubabura mbu: Rero, chira mukangilyisi w'e mwaso ola ulyi mwanafunzi mwa bwami b'okwa nguba, ahuhanyisibwe n'ena nyumba, ola wende wakula e bindu biyayaya n'e by'okwa mira mwa buare bwai.

Besha Nasareti bakena Yesu

53. Mango Yesu abaa era amalaa kuisha ei mianyi yoshi, era kutenga mw'echi chisiki,

54. era kuya mwa musi ola akulyiraamo. Aikiremo, era kutangilyisa akangilyisa e bandju mwa bushenge bwabo. Abo bandju, bera kusanwa na batangilyisa babusanya mbu: Ono mundju, ngaiu akulyire buno bwenge, n'e bine bisomerano byoshi?

---

50. 바가우마 어 바뚜 바비 똬 마루까 머 무레로. 나 모유 무레로, 바가로콰 과 가시부.

어 무아네 워 비뚜 비야야야 너 뵤콰 미라

51. 여수 어라 구부사 어 바나푸씨 바이 뿌: 어와써, 어레 몸비러 어이 먀시 요씨? 나보 뿌: 어어어, 쫌비러.

52. 짜시따, 어라 구바부라 뿌: 러로, 찌라 무가끼레시 워 똬소 오라 우레 마나푸씨 똬 봐미 보콰 꾸바, 아후하네시붸 너나 뉴빠, 오라 워떠 와구콰 어 비뚜 비야야야 너 뵤콰 미라 똬 부아러 봐이.

버싸 나사러디 바거나 여수

53. 마꼬 여수 아바아 어라 아마콰아 구이싸 어이 미아네 요씨, 어라 구더꺼 뭐찌 찌시기,

54. 어라 구야 똬 무시 오콰 아구레라아모. 아이기러모, 어라 구다끼레사 아가끼레사 어 바뚜 똬 부써꺼 봐보. 아보 바뚜, 버라 구사놔 나 바다끼레사 바부사냐 뿌: 오노 무뚜, 꽈이우 아구레러 부노 붸꺼, 너 비너 비소머라노 뵤씨?

---

50. and throw them into the fiery furnace, where there will be weeping and gnashing of teeth.

51. "Have you understood all these things?" Jesus asked. "Yes," they replied.

52. He said to them, "Therefore every teacher of the law who has been instructed about the kingdom of heaven is like the owner of a house who brings out of his storeroom new treasures as well as old."

53. When Jesus had finished these parables, he moved on from there.

54. Coming to his hometown, he began teaching the people in their synagogue, and they were amazed. "Where did this man get this wisdom and these miraculous powers?" they asked.

55. Onola kasi ata imuala w'ola murenga wende wakunganya e bindju mwa mbao? Na mariya ata i nyina? Na yakobo, na yosufu, na simoni, na yuda, ata bu banyakabo?

55. 오노라 가시 아다 이무아롸 올롸 무러롸 워떠 와구뫄냐 어 비뿌 마 빠오? 나 마리야 아다 이 니나? 나 야고보, 나 요수푸, 나 시모니, 나 유다, 아다 부 바냐가보?

55. "Isn't this the carpenter's son? Isn't his mother's name Mary, and aren't his brothers James, Joseph, Simon and Judas?

56. Na balyiwabo boshi, si chwuchwula alauma nabo kuno! Rero, ene myasi yoshi, ngai u akulyirei?

56. 나 바례와보 보씨, 시 쭈쭈롸 아롸우마 나보 구노! 러로, 어너 먀시 요씨, 뫄이 우 아구레러이?

56. Aren't all his sisters with us? Where then did this man get all these things?"

57. Echera chera kuchwuma batamwemerera. Si Yesu era kubabura mbu: E murebi achwusa echwunda mwa bisiki byoshi, si mwa musi wabo n'omwa ngumo yabo, ende akenyibwa.

57. 어쩌라 쩌라 구쭈마 바다뭐머러라. 시 여수 어라 구바부라 뿌: 어 무러비 아쭈사 어쭈따 마 비시기 뵤씨, 시 마 무시 와보 노롸 꾸모 야보, 어러 아거네봐.

57. And they took offense at him. But Jesus said to them, "Only in his hometown and in his own house is a prophet without honor."

58. Rero, bushi besha nasareti bananaa mbu batangemerera, Yesu nai chiro akaira bisomerano binene eyera.

58. 러로, 부씨 버싸 나사러디 바나나아 뿌 바다머머러라, 여수 나이 찌로 아가이라 비소머라노 비너너 어여라.

58. And he did not do many miracles there because of their lack of faith.

Matayo Chikono 14
Yowana mubatisayi echibwa

마다요 찌고노 14
요와나 무바디사에 어찌봐

Matthew Chapter 14[NIV]

1. Mw'esi suku, herodi iwabaa w'emire mwa chio ch'e kalilaya. Era kumva kwa ngulu ya yesu.

1. 뭐시 수구, 허로디 이와바아 워미러 마 찌오 쩌 가리롸야. 어라 구빠 과 꾸루 야 여수.

1. At that time Herod the tetrarch heard the reports about Jesus,

2. bushi n'oku, era kubura e bashamuka bai mbu: oyola, alyi yowana mubatisayi iwomokire mwa bafu! N'echi chi chichwumire aata e

2. 부씨 노구, 어라 구부라 어 바싸무가 바이 뿌: 오요롸, 아레 요와나 무바디사에 이오모기러 마 바푸! 너찌 찌 찌쭈미러 아아다 어 부아씨 뭐

2. and he said to his attendants, "This is John the Baptist; he has risen from the dead! That is why miraculous powers are at

buashi bw'e kuira ebisomerano.

3. Rero, herodi abaa aminyise yowana. Era kumuuma mwa buroko bushi na herotiya muka firipo. Oyu firipo abaa munyakabo herodi.

4. Yowana abaa enjire abura herodi mbu: Oyu herotiya, e Mwaso wechwu atakwemerere mbu umuhweraa!

5. Bushi n'oku, herodi era kuhonda kwita yowana. Si abaa enjire obaa e bandju, bushi babaa beshi kwa yowana alyi murebi.

6. Mango e lusuku lukulu lw'e kukengera e kubuchwa kwa herodi lwaikaa, mwalyi wa herotiya era kusina era muhondo s'e bandju ba balalyikwaa. Oku kusina kwai, kwera kusimisa herodi busese.

7. Mw'olu, era kumulaanya mwa kulaisa kwa choshi cha angamwema, anganamweresachi.

8. Oyu munyere era nyuma s'e kwema nyina eano, era kwire abura herodi mbu: Unano-unano, unyeresaa echwe lya yowana mubatisayi

구이라 어비소머라노.

3. 러로, 허로디 아바아 아미네서 요와나. 어라 구무우마 뫄 부로고 부씨 나 허로디야 무가 피리포. 오유 피리포 아바아 무냐가보 허로디.

4. 요와나 아바아 어찌러 아부라 허로디 뿌: 오유 허로디야, 어 뫄소 워쭈 아다궈머러러 뿌 우무훠라아!

5. 부씨 노구, 허로디 어라 구호따 귀다 요와나. 시 아바아 어찌러 오바아 어 바뚜, 부씨 바바아 버씨 과 요와나 아레 무러비.

6. 마꼬 어 루수구 루구루 뭐 구거꺼라 어 구부좌 과 허로디 꽈이가아, 뫄레 와 허로디야 어라 구시나 어라 무호또 서 바뚜 바 바꽈레과아. 오구 구시나 과이, 궈라 구시미사 허로디 부서서.

7. 모루, 어라 구무꽈아냐 뫄 구꽈이사 과 쪼씨 짜 아꽈뭐마, 아꽈나뭐러사찌.

8. 오유 무녀러 어라 뉴마 서 궈마 네나 어아노, 어라 귀러 아부라 허로디 뿌: 우나노-우나노, 우녀러사아 어쮀 랴 요와나 무바디사에 과 빠러.

work in him."

3. Now Herod had arrested John and bound him and put him in prison because of Herodias, his brother Philip's wife,

4. for John had been saying to him: "It is not lawful for you to have her."

5. Herod wanted to kill John, but he was afraid of the people, because they considered him a prophet.

6. On Herod's birthday the daughter of Herodias danced for them and pleased Herod so much

7. that he promised with an oath to give her whatever she asked.

8. Prompted by her mother, she said, "Give me here on a platter the head of John the Baptist."

kwa mbare.

9. Echera chera kusibusa mwami. Si bushi n'e kulaisa kwa abaa alaisise mira era muhondo s'abu babalyikwa, era kutete mbu oyu munyere banamweresaa elyi echwe.

9. 어쩌라 쩌라 구시부사 롸미. 시 부씨 너 구롸이사 과 아바아 아롸이시서 미라 어라 무호또 사부 바바뢔과, 어라 구더더 뿌 오유 무녀러 바나뭐러사아 어뢔 어쭤.

9. The king was distressed, but because of his oaths and his dinner guests, he ordered that her request be granted

10. Era kuchwuma mundju muuma mwa buroko mbu aendaa kuisha echwe lya yowana.

10. 어라 구쭘마 무뚜 무우마 롸 부로고 뿌 아어따아 구이싸 어쭤 롸 요와나.

10. and had John beheaded in the prison.

11. Elyi echwe, bera kulyireta kwa mbare na balyeresa ola munyere. Wamunyere nai, era kulyekera nyina.

11. 어뢔 어쭤, 버라 구뢔러다 과 빠러 나 바뤄러사 오롸 무녀러. 와무녀러 나이, 어라 구뤼거라 니나.

11. His head was brought in on a platter and given to the girl, who carried it to her mother.

12. chasinda, e banafunzi ba yowana bera kuika kutola e chirunda chai, na baya kutabachi. Ei myasi, bera kuya kuibalyira yesu.

12. 짜시따, 어 바나푸씨 바 요와나 버라 구이가 구도롸 어 찌루따 짜이, 나 바야 구다바찌. 어이 먀시, 버라 구야 구이바뢔라 여수.

12. John's disciples came and took his body and buried it. Then they went and told Jesus.

Yesu eucha bandju byumbi bitano

여수 어우짜 바뚜 뷰삐 비다노

13. Mango Yesu omvaa kwei myasi, era kutenga aola mwa bwato aya mu chisiki chai yeine. E bandju balolyire bacha, bera kutenganga kwa misi yabo na bamukulyikira n'e maulu.

13. 마꼬 여수 오빠아 궈이 먀시, 어라 구더따 아오롸 롸 봐도 아야 무 찌시기 짜이 여이너. 어 바뚜 바롤뢔러 바짜, 버라 구더따까 과 미시 야보 나 바무구뢔기라 너 마우루.

13. When Jesus heard what had happened, he withdrew by boat privately to a solitary place. Hearing of this, the crowds followed him on foot from the towns.

14. Abere atenga mwa bwato, era kubuana bandju banene, era kubafira bonjo. Ba babaa

14. 아버러 아더따 롸 봐도, 어라 구부아나 바뚜 바너너, 어라 구바피라 보쪼. 바

14. When Jesus landed and saw a large crowd, he had compassion on them

balyi balwala mwa kachi-kachi kabo, era kubalamya.

15. Mango lwabaa lwera luolo-olo, e banafunzi bai bera kuya kumubura mbu: Enawechwu! Mwa buyeye muno chwulyi, kanji n'e buchwufu bwelyire. bushi n'oku, urekaa bano bandju baye kwa misi, baule e bilyo.

16. Yesu nai mbu: Abu bandju, batemire kuenda. Mubeine mubawaa e bilyo.

17. Nabo mbu: ewaliya! Anola chwunete mikati etano n'efi ebilyi ashao!

18. Yesu era kubabura mbu: munyireteraabi.

19. Chasinda, era kubura e bandju mbu bafumbamiraa kwa bichi. Era kutola era mikati etano n'e s'efi ebilyi, era kuchwumbikisa kwa nguba, na atonga Ongo. Era kubiishanga, na kubyeresa abu banafunzi bai. Nabo, bera kubiabiranga e bandju.

20. Abu bandju boshi, bera kulya na kuneuta. Mango e banafunzi balunda-lundaa bya byashibaa, byera kwihusa bitonga ekumi na bibilyi.

바바아 바레 바똬꽈 뫄 가찌-가찌 가보, 어라 구바꽈먀.

15. 마꼬 똴바바아 뤄라 루오오론-오론, 어 바나푸씨 바이 버라 구야 구무부라 뿌: 어나워쭈! 뫄 부여여 무노 쭈레, 가찌 너 부쭈푸 붸레러. 부씨 노구, 우러가아 바노 바뉴 바여 과 미시, 바우뭐 어 비료.

16. 여수 나이 뿌: 아부 바뉴, 바더미러 구어따. 무버이너 무바와아 어 비료.

17. 나보 뿌: 어와뤼야! 아노꽈 쭈너더 미가디 어다노 너피 어비례 아싸오!

18. 여수 어라 구바부라 뿌: 무니러더라아비.

19. 짜시따, 어라 구부라 어 바뉴 뿌 바푸빠미라아 과 비찌. 어라 구도꽈 어라 미가디 어다노 너 서피 어비례, 어라 구쭈삐기사 과 꾸바, 나 아도꽈 오꼬. 어라 구비이싸꽈, 나 구벼러사 아부 바나푸씨 바이. 나보, 버라 구비아비라꽈 어 바뉴.

20. 아부 바뉴 보씨, 버라 구꺅 나 구너우다. 마꼬 어 바나푸씨 바루따-루따아 뱌 뱌씨바아, 벼라 귀후사 비도꽈 어구미 나 비비례.

and healed their sick.

15. As evening approached, the disciples came to him and said, "This is a remote place, and it's already getting late. Send the crowds away, so they can go to the villages and buy themselves some food."

16. Jesus replied, "They do not need to go away. You give them something to eat."

17. "We have here only five loaves of bread and two fish," they answered.

18. "Bring them here to me," he said.

19. And he directed the people to sit down on the grass. Taking the five loaves and the two fish and looking up to heaven, he gave thanks and broke the loaves. Then he gave them to the disciples, and the disciples gave them to the people.

20. They all ate and were satisfied, and the disciples picked up twelve basketfuls of broken pieces that were left over.

21. Mwa bandju ba balyaa ebi bilyo, mwabaa mulyi balume bangaika ku byumbi bitano, busira kuanja e bakasi n'e bana.

Yesu alambaira kwa Nyanja

22. Era nyuma s'ebi, Yesu era kubura e banafunzi bai mbu berukiraa mwa bwato, bamuhondorere kwa mushilyiyla w'e nyanja. Nai era kushiba alauma n'e luamba lw'e bandju.

23. Abere era alaabo, era kwerukira yeine kwa ndjulungu aya kwema Ongo. E buchwufu bwera kwera anachilyi yeine kwei ndjulungu.

24. Mw'echi chihangi, e bwato bwabaa bwaika burerere kusibu n'e mushilyiyla. E chiusi chabaa chatengerera muhondo sabo. Bushi n'oku, e mulaba era kutangilyisa aurutanganya obu bwato.

25. Abere lumbulyi-mbulyi, Yesu era kuika ala banafunzi babaa balyi, aenda alaambaira kwa Nyanja.

26. E banafunzi mango balolaa kwa alambaira kwa Nyanja, bera kuchwungwa. Berakuchilakangira busese

21. 마 바뚜 바 바꺄아 어비 비뢴, 마바아 무뤠 바루머 바까이가 구 뷰뻬 비다노, 부시라 구아짜 어 바가시 너 바나.

여수 아롸빠일띰 과 냐짜

22. 어라 뉴마 서비, 여수 어라 구부라 어 바나푸씨 바이 뿌 버루기라아 마 봐도, 바무호또러러 과 무씨뤠꺄 워 냐짜. 나이 어라 구씨바 아롸우마 너 루아빠 뤄 바뚜.

23. 아버러 어라 아롸아보, 어라 궈루기라 여이너 과 뚜루우 아야 궈마 오꼬. 어 부쭈푸 붜라 궈라 아나찌뤠 여이너 궈이 뚜루우.

24. 뭐찌 찌하삐, 어 봐도 봐바아 봐이가 부러러러 구시부 너 무씨뤠꺄. 어 찌우시 짜바아 짜더꺼러라 무호또 사보. 부씨 노구, 어 무쫘바 어라 구다삐뤠사 아우루다까냐 오부 봐도.

25. 아버러 루뿌뤠-뿌뤠, 여수 어라 구이가 아롸 바나푸씨 바바아 바뤠, 아어따 아롸아빠이라 과 냐짜.

26. 어 바나푸씨 마꼬 바뢰쫘아 과 아롸빠이라 과 냐짜, 버라 구쭈꽈. 버라구찌쫘가삐라 부서서 뿌:

21. The number of those who ate was about five thousand men, besides women and children.

22. Immediately Jesus made the disciples get into the boat and go on ahead of him to the other side, while he dismissed the crowd.

23. After he had dismissed them, he went up on a mountainside by himself to pray. When evening came, he was there alone,

24. but the boat was already a considerable distance from land, buffeted by the waves because the wind was against it.

25. During the fourth watch of the night Jesus went out to them, walking on the lake.

26. When the disciples saw him walking on the lake, they were terrified. "It's a ghost," they said, and

mbu: Musimu yolaee!

27. Unao-unao, Yesu era kubabura mbu: Musesaa e muchimaa! Nyono onola! Mutobaa.

28. Petero era kumwakula mbu: Enawechwu! Akaba analyi woyo, unyiburaa nyibahe au ulyi nalambaira kwa meshi.

29. Nai mbu: Bahaa! Petero kuna kutenga mwa bwato aya ala Yesu abaa alyi aenda alambaira kwa meshi.

30. Si mango alolaa kwa chiusi chakalyiire, era kw'obaa, na atangilyisa asika. Era kuchilakangira mbu: Enawechwu! Unyitabalaa!

31. Unao-unao Yesu era kunanula e mino na amutola. Era kumubura mbu: Echera! Chi cheraa chachwuma wahungwa-hungwa? Unalyi mundju wa bwemeresi bueke!

32. Mango Yesu na petero babaa bera bahubaa kwerukira mwa bwato, echi chusi chera kuorera.

33. Bushi n'oku, e banafunzi ba babaa balyi mw'obu bwato bera kufukama era muhondo sa Yesu na bateta mbu: Kubinalyi! Unalyi mwana wa Ongo!

무시무 요롸어어!

27. 우나오-우나오, 여수 어라 구바부라 뿌: 무서사아 어 무찌마아! 뇨노 오노롸! 무도바아.

28. 퍼더로 어라 구꽈구롸 뿌: 어나워쭈! 아가바 아나례 오요, 우네부라아 네바허 아우 우뤠 나롸빠이라 과 머씨.

29. 나이 뿌: 바하아! 퍼더로 구나 구더따 롸 봐도 아야 아롸 여수 아바아 아례 아어따 아롸빠이라 과 머씨.

30. 시 마꼬 아륻롸아 과 찌우시 짜가례이러, 어라 고바야, 나 아다삐례사 아시가. 어라 구찌롸가삐라 뿌: 어나워쭈! 우네다바롸아!

31. 우나오-우나오 여수 어라 구나누롸 어 미노 나 아무도롸. 어라 구무부라 뿌: 어쩌라! 찌 쩌라아 짜쭈마 와후꽈-후꽈? 우나례 무뿌 와 붜머러시 부어거!

32. 마꼬 여수 나 퍼더로 바바아 버라 바후바아 궈루기라 롸 봐도, 어찌 쭈시 쩌라 구오러라.

33. 부씨 노구, 어 바나푸씨 바 바바아 바례 모부 봐도 버라 구푸가마 어라 무호또 사 여수 나 바더다 뿌: 구비나례! 우나례 롸나 와 오꼬!

cried out in fear.

27. But Jesus immediately said to them: "Take courage! It is I. Don't be afraid."

28. "Lord, if it's you," Peter replied, "tell me to come to you on the water."

29. "Come," he said. Then Peter got down out of the boat, walked on the water and came toward Jesus.

30. But when he saw the wind, he was afraid and, beginning to sink, cried out, "Lord, save me!"

31. Immediately Jesus reached out his hand and caught him. "You of little faith," he said, "why did you doubt?"

32. And when they climbed into the boat, the wind died down.

33. Then those who were in the boat worshiped him, saying, "Truly you are the Son of God."

Yesu alamya e balwala   여수 아퐈맺 어 바퐈퐈

34. Abere Yesu n'e banafunzi bai bera bahabukaa ei Nyanja, bera kuika mwa chio ch'e kenesareti.	34. 아버러 여수 너 바나푸씨 바이 버라 바하부가아 어이 냐짜, 버라 구이가 와 찌오 쩌 거너사러디.	34. When they had crossed over, they landed at Gennesaret.
35. Besha mw'echi chio mango bamenyereraa yesu, bera kuchwuma e mwasi mw'ebi bitambi byoshi. Bushi n'oku, bera kumuretengeranga e balwala boshi.	35. 버싸 뭐찌 찌오 마꼬 바머녀러라아 여수, 버라 구쭈마 어 퐈시 뭐비 비다삐 뵤씨. 부씨 노구, 버라 구무러더어라까 어 바퐈퐈 뵤씨.	35. And when the men of that place recognized Jesus, they sent word to all the surrounding country. People brought all their sick to him
36. Bera kumwema mbu emereraa chiro e balwala bende banauma kwa musike w'e luchimba lwai. Boshi ba baumaako, bera kunalama.	36. 버라 구뭐마 뿌 어머러라아 찌로 어 바퐈퐈 버떠 바나우마 과 무시거 워 루찌빠 롸이. 뵤씨 바 바우마아고, 버라 구나퐈마.	36. and begged him to let the sick just touch the edge of his cloak, and all who touched him were healed.

Matayo Chikono 15   **마다요 찌고노 15**   **Matthew Chapter 15[NIV]**

E myanya era bahokulu b'e Bayuda bendee bakangilyisa   어 먀냐 어라 바호구루 버 바유다 버떠앤 바가끼레삡

1. Era nyuma s'ebi, e bafarisayo n'e bakangilyisi b'e mwaso bera kuikira Yesu batengera mwa musi w'e Yerusalemu. Bera kumubusa mbu:	1. 어라 뉴마 서비, 어 바파리사요 너 바가끼레시 버 퐈소 버라 구이기라 여수 바더어라 와 무시 워 여루사퍼무. 버라 구무부사 뿌:	1. Then some Pharisees and teachers of the law came to Jesus from Jerusalem and asked,
2. chi chenjire chachwuma e banafunzi bao batachwunda e myanya era bahokulu bechwu bachwurekeraa? Bushi beke batenjire bowa kwa mino era muhondo s'e kulya kukulyikana nei myanya!	2. 찌 쩌찌러 짜쭈마 어 바나푸씨 바오 바다쭈따 어 먀냐 어라 바호구루 버쭈 바쭈러거라아? 부씨 버거 바더찌러 보와 과 미노 어라 무호또 서 구퍄 구구레가나 너이 먀냐!	2. "Why do your disciples break the tradition of the elders? They don't wash their hands before they eat!"

3. Yesu era kubakula mbu: Nenyu, chi chenjire chachwuma mwaisha mwa muombi wa Ongo, bushi n'e kukulyikira n'e myanya yenyu?

4. Si mwishi kwa Ongo atetaa mbu: Undaa wachwunda eho na nyoko. kanji era kuteta mbu: Ola ukakamba eshe nesi nyina, emire kwichibwa.

5. Si mwabo, mwenjire mwateta mbu e mundju anganabura eshe nesi nyina mbu: Bya nyingakweresise kwa kukuasa, nabichwulyire Ongo mira.

6. Mwa kuira bacha, mu mwenjire mwateta mbu e mundju atendaa achwunda eshe. Na ku mwenjire mwakena e chinwa cha Ongo bacha bushi n'e kukulyikira e myanya yenyu!

7. emu batebanyi! Isaya atetaa kanangana, mango arebaa era lulu senyu mbu:

8. bano bandju, kwa bieta ku bende banyichwunda. Si e michima yabo ichwula bure nanyi!

9. bushi e kwera kwa bende banyera, kunalyi kwa buha! N'e myanya era bende bakangilyisa, inalyi myasi

---

3. 여수 어라 구바구롸 뿌: 너뉴, 찌 쩌찌러 짜쪼마 롸이싸 롸 무오삐 와 오꼬, 부씨 너 구구례기라 너 먀냐 여뉴?

4. 시 뮈씨 과 오꼬 아더다아 뿌: 우따아 와쪼따 어호 나 뇨고. 가찌 어라 구더다 뿌: 오롸 우가가빠 어써 너시 니나, 어미러 귀찌봐.

5. 시 롸보, 뭐찌러 롸더다 뿌 어 무뿌 아꺄나부라 어써 너시 니나 뿌: 뱌 네꺄궈러시서 과 구구아사, 나비쪼레러 오꼬 미라.

6. 롸 구이라 바짜, 무 뭐찌러 롸더다 뿌 어 무뿌 아더다아 아쪼따 어써. 나 구 뭐찌러 롸거나 어 찌놔 짜 오꼬 바짜 부씨 너 구구레기라 어 먀냐 여뉴!

7. 어무 바더바네! 이사야 아더다아 가나꺄나, 마꼬 아러바아 어라 룰루 서뉴 뿌:

8. 바노 바쭈, 과 비어다 구 버떠 바네쪼따. 시 어 미찌마 야보 이쪼롸 부러 나네!

9. 부씨 어 궈라 과 버떠 바녀라, 구나레 과 부하! 너 먀냐 어라 버떠 바가꼐레사, 이나레 먀시 어라야이롸아 너

---

3. Jesus replied, "And why do you break the command of God for the sake of your tradition?

4. For God said, 'Honor your father and mother' and 'Anyone who curses his father or mother must be put to death.'

5. But you say that if a man says to his father or mother, 'Whatever help you might otherwise have received from me is a gift devoted to God,'

6. he is not to 'honor his father' with it. Thus you nullify the word of God for the sake of your tradition.

7. You hypocrites! Isaiah was right when he prophesied about you:

8. " 'These people honor me with their lips, but their hearts are far from me.

9. They worship me in vain; their teachings are but rules taught by men.'"

erayairwaa n'e bandju. 바뚜.

Bya byende byabika e singa mwa mundju

바 벼너 뱌비가 어 시마 뫄 무뚜

10. Chasinda, Yesu era kwamaala e luamba lw'e bandju. Era kubabura mbu: Mumvilyisaa kubuya chasiya mumenyererebine nahonda kubabura.

10. 짜시따, 여수 어라 과마아롸 어 루아빠 뤄 바뚜. 어라 구바부라 뿌: 무쀠쥐쎄사아 구부야 짜시야 무머녀러러비너 나호따 구바부라.

10. Jesus called the crowd to him and said, "Listen and understand.

11. Bya byende byaya mwa bunu bwe mundju, ata bi byende byamubiba mw'e singa. Si bya byende byatengamo.

11. 뱌 벼너 뱌야 뫄 부누 붸 무뚜, 아다 비 벼너 뱌무비바 뭐 시마. 시 뱌 벼너 뱌더마모.

11. What goes into a man's mouth does not make him 'unclean,' but what comes out of his mouth, that is what makes him 'unclean.' "

12. E banafunzi bai kukwera kumubura mbu: e Waliya, uteshi kwa ei myasi yao yasubisire e bafarisayo?

12. 어 바나푸씨 바이 구궈라 구무부라 뿌: 어 와뤼야, 우더씨 과 어이 먀시 야오 야수비시러 어 바파리사요?

12. Then the disciples came to him and asked, "Do you know that the Pharisees were offended when they heard this?"

13. Yesu nai mbu: Chira mbuto Yoshi akaba itaingwaa na tata ola ulyi kwa nguba, ichilyi ingachungulyibwa.

13. 여수 나이 뿌: 찌라 뿌도 요씨 아가바 이다이꽈아 나 다다 오롸 우뤠 과 꾸바, 이찌뤠 이꺄쭈꾸뤠봐.

13. He replied, "Every plant that my heavenly Father has not planted will be pulled up by the roots.

14. Bushi n'oku abu bafarisayo, mutendaa mwabalaako, bushi balyi bemangisi bauta ba batandaisa banji bauta! Rero, akaba e muuta angatandaisa muuta mulyikabo, boshi kwa banalyi babilyi bangatowera mwafumbi!

14. 부씨 노구 아부 바파리사요, 무더따아 뫄바롸아고, 부씨 바뤠 버마쀠시 바우다 바 바다따이사 바찌 바우다! 러로, 아가바 어 무우다 아꺄다따이사 무우다 무뤠가보, 보씨 과 바나뤠 바비뤠 바마도워라 뫄푸쀠!

14. Leave them; they are blind guides. If a blind man leads a blind man, both will fall into a pit."

15. Petero era kwire amubura

15. 퍼더로 어라 귀러

15. Peter said, "Explain the

mbu: e Waliya, ola muanyi, uchwuanululyiraao.

16. Yesu nai mbu: Nenyu mutanasa kuata e bwenge bw'e kumenyerera?

17. Si mutaabukire kwa byoshi bya byende byengilyira mwa bunu bw'e mundju, byende byandalyira mwa bula, chasinda byanatengamo mwa kuya era chala.

18. Si e binwa bya byende byatenga mwa bunu, mwa muchima mu byende byatengera. N'ebi bi byende byabika e mundju mw'e singa,

19. Bushi mwa muchima mu mwende mwatengera e mianyisa ibi, n'e buichi, n'e buhungu, n'e bwisi, n'e kwekerana e bisha, n'e kwamaana e banji bulio.

20. Ebi byoshi, bi byende byabika e mundju mw'e singa. Si e kulya busira kwowa kwa mino, kutangamubika mw'e singa.

E bwemeresi bw'e mukananakasi

21. Yesu era kutenga mw'echi chisiki aya mwa chio ch'e tiro n'e ch'e sitona.

22. Aikireyi, Mukananakasi

아무부라 뿌: 어 와삐야, 오롸 무아네, 우쭈아누루룰레라아오.

16. 여수 나이 뿌: 너뉴 무다나사 구아다 어 붸어 붜 구머녀려라?

17. 시 무다아부기러 과 뵤씨 뱌 벼너 벼삐쩨라 롸 부누 붜 무뚜, 벼너 뱌따쩨라 롸 부롸, 짜시따 뱌나더쌰모 롸 구야 어라 짜롸.

18. 시 어 비놔 뱌 벼너 뱌더쌰 롸 부누, 롸 무찌마 무 벼너 뱌더쌰라. 너비 비 벼너 뱌비가 어 무뚜 뭐 시쌰,

19. 부씨 롸 무찌마 무 뭐너 롸더쌰라 어 미아네사 이비, 너 부이찌, 너 부후우, 너 뷔시, 너 궈거라나 어 비싸, 너 과마아나 어 바찌 부릐오.

20. 어비 뵤씨, 비 벼너 뱌비가 어 무뚜 뭐 시쌰. 시 어 구롸 부시라 고와 과 미노, 구다쌰무비가 뭐 시쌰.

어 붸머러시 붜 무가나나가시

21. 여수 어라 구더쌰 뭐찌 찌시기 아야 롸 찌오 쩌 디로 너 쩌 시도나.

22. 아이기러에, 무가나나가시

parable to us."

16. "Are you still so dull?" Jesus asked them.

17. "Don't you see that whatever enters the mouth goes into the stomach and then out of the body?

18. But the things that come out of the mouth come from the heart, and these make a man 'unclean.'

19. For out of the heart come evil thoughts, murder, adultery, sexual immorality, theft, false testimony, slander.

20. These are what make a man 'unclean'; but eating with unwashed hands does not make him 'unclean.' "

21. Leaving that place, Jesus withdrew to the region of Tyre and Sidon.

22. A Canaanite woman

muuma w'eyi, era kumuikira aenda achilakangira mbu: enawechwu, mwenyi Daudi, unyifiraa bonjo! Mwalyi wanyi, e bihwasi byamulyibusa busese!

23. Si yesu, chiro akamwakula kandju, e banafunzi bai bera kuchifunda ofu nai, na bamubura mbu: ono mukasi achwuira ku lwayo lunene. Umuburaa achwukule kw'e mufubya tulo!

24. Era kwakula mbu: Nachwumwaa kwa lubaa lw'e baisiraeli oshao, bushi n'e kulola kwa baelyire nga mbulyi.

25. Si wamukasi, era kuika kukoma e mafi era muhondo sa yesu. Era kumwema n'e bonjo mbu: Enawechwu, unyiasaa!

26. Nai mbu: Bitemire kutola e bilyo by'e bana, na kubiuma e ngunda.

27. Oyu mukasi nai mbu: nechi enawechwu! Kubinalyi bacha. Si engunda nasi, sende sanalya e bukombo-kombo bwa bwatowanga kwa mesa m'enawabo.

28. Yesu era kumwakula mbu: ewu mukasi, e bwemeresi

무우마 워에, 어라 구무이기라 아어따 아찌꽈가끠라 뿌: 어나워쭈, 뭐네 다우디, 우네피라아 보쪼! 마꿰 와네, 어 비화시 뱌무꿰부사 부서서!

23. 시 여수, 찌로 아가뫄구꽈 가뉴, 어 바나푸씨 바이 버라 구찌푸따 오푸 나이, 나 바무부라 뿌: 오노 무가시 아쭈이라 구 꽈요 루너너. 우무부라아 아쭈구뭐 궈 무푸뱌 두로!

24. 어라 과구꽈 뿌: 나쭈뫄아 과 루바아 뤄 바이시라어끠 오싸오, 부씨 너 구로꽈 과 바어꿰러 꽈 뿌꿰.

25. 시 와무가시, 어라 구이가 구고마 어 마피 어라 무호또 사 여수. 어라 구뭐마 너 보쪼 뿌: 어나워쭈, 우네아사아!

26. 나이 뿌: 비더미러 구도꽈 어 비뾰 벼 바나, 나 구비우마 어 꾸따.

27. 오유 무가시 나이 뿌: 너찌 어나워쭈! 구비나꿰 바짜. 시 어꾸따 나시, 서떠 사나꺄 어 부고뾰-고뾰 봐 봐도와꽈 과 머사 머나와보.

28. 여수 어라 구뫄구꽈 뿌: 어웉 무가시, 어 붜머러시

from that vicinity came to him, crying out, "Lord, Son of David, have mercy on me! My daughter is suffering terribly from demon-possession."

23. Jesus did not answer a word. So his disciples came to him and urged him, "Send her away, for she keeps crying out after us."

24. He answered, "I was sent only to the lost sheep of Israel."

25. The woman came and knelt before him. "Lord, help me!" she said.

26. He replied, "It is not right to take the children's bread and toss it to their dogs."

27. "Yes, Lord," she said, "but even the dogs eat the crumbs that fall from their masters' table."

28. Then Jesus answered, "Woman, you have great

bwao butanga amaanyibwa!
Bushi n'oku, kwa wahonda,
ku biree byanaba. Mw'echi
chihangi chinechi, mwalyi
w'ola mukasiera kulama.

봐오 부다까 아마아네봐! 부씨
노구, 과 와호따, 구 비러어
뱌나바. 뭐찌 찌하께 찌너찌,
마쪠 올꽈 무가시어라 구꽈마.

faith! Your request is
granted." And her
daughter was healed from
that very hour.

Yesu alamya balwala banene
여수 아꽈맸 바꽈꽈 바너너

29. era nyuma s'ebi, Yesu era
kuya kurenga kwa musike s'e
nyanja y'e kalilaya. Era
kwerukira kwa ndjulungu, na
ekalako.

29. 어라 뉴마 서비, 여수 어라
구야 구러까 과 무시거 서
냐짜 여 가꾀꽈야. 어라
궈루기라 과 쭈룩우, 나
어가꽈고.

29. Jesus left there and
went along the Sea of
Galilee. Then he went up
on a mountainside and sat
down.

30. Bikembe binene bya
bandju byera kumuikira. Bera
kumuretera birema, na
nyaata, na basuru, na banji
balwala banene. abu boshi,
bera kubabika era muhondo
sa yesu, nai era kubalamya.

30. 비거뻐 비너너 뱌 바쭈
뱌라 구무이기라. 버라
구무러더라 비러마, 나 냐아다,
나 바수루, 나 바찌 바꽈꽈
바너너. 아부 보씨, 버라
구바비가 어라 무호또 사
여수, 나이 어라 구바꽈먀.

30. Great crowds came to
him, bringing the lame,
the blind, the crippled, the
mute and many others,
and laid them at his feet;
and he healed them.

31. E bandju, bera kusanwa
busese mwa kulola kwa
basuru bateta, n'e birema
alauma n'e nyaata saenda
sishimire, n'e bauta balola,
bera kunde batonga Ongo
w'e Baisiraeli.

31. 어 바쭈, 버라 구사놔
부서서 뫄 구룬꽈 과 바수루
바더다, 너 비러마 아꽈우마
너 냐아다 사어따 시씨미러,
너 바우다 바룬꽈, 버라 구떠
바도까 오꼬 워 바이시라어삐.

31. The people were
amazed when they saw
the mute speaking, the
crippled made well, the
lame walking and the
blind seeing. And they
praised the God of Israel.

Yesu eucha bandju byumbi bine
여수 어우짜 바쭈 뷰뻬 비너

32. Yesu era kwamaala e
banafunzi bai, era kubabura
mbu: Bano bandju boshi,
nabafilyire bonjo, bushi suku
ehachwu sine chwamala
alauma nabo, batete na kalyo
kasibya. Rero, ndahonda

32. 여수 어라 과마아꽈 어
바나푸씨 바이, 어라 구바부라
뿌: 바노 바쭈 보씨,
나바피쩨러 보쪼, 부씨 수구
어하쭈 시너 쫘마꽈 아꽈우마
나보, 바더더 나 가뀬 가시뱌.
러로, 따호따 구바꽈아

32. Jesus called his
disciples to him and said,
"I have compassion for
these people; they have
already been with me
three days and have
nothing to eat. I do not

kubalaa batanalyire bangesha kurengukalyira mwa njira n'e businya.

33. E banafunzi bai bera kumubusa mbu: e Waliya, si buyeye buno chwulyimo! Ngai uchwungakula e bilyo bya bingeucha bano bandju bangana bacha?

34. Yesu era kubabusa mbu: mwete mikati enga? Nabo mbu: chwete mikati elyinda, n'efi sieke-eke, si sikeire.

35. Abu bandju boshi, Yesu era kubabura mbu bafumbamiraa alashi,

36. era kutola era mikati, n'e s'efi. Abere era atongaa Ongo, era kubiishanga, era kubyeresa abu banafunzi bai, nabo bera kubiabiranga e bandju.

37. E bandju boshi bera kulya na kwiuta. Mango e banafunzi balundaa-lundaa bya byashibaa, byera kwihusa bitonga bilyinda.

38. Ba balyaa ebi bilyo, babaa balyi balume byumbi bine, busira kuaja e bakasi n'e bana.

39. Chasinjire, Yesu era kulaa abu bandju. Era kwerukira

바다나쪠러 바떠싸 구러우가쪠라 뫄 찌라 너 부시냐.

33. 어 바나푸씨 바이 버라 구무부사 뿌: 어 와쪠야, 시 부여여 부노 쭈례모! 따이 우쭈따구롸 어 비료 뱌 비떠우짜 바노 바뉴 바따나 바짜?

34. 여수 어라 구바부사 뿌: 뭐더 미가디 어꽈? 나보 뿌: 쮜더 미가디 어례따, 너피 시어거-어거, 시 시거이러.

35. 아부 바뉴 보씨, 여수 어라 구바부라 뿌 바푸빠미라아 아꽈씨,

36. 어라 구도롸 어라 미가디, 너 서피. 아부러 어라 아도꽈아 오꼬, 어라 구비이싸따, 어라 구벼러사 아부 바나푸씨 바이, 나보 버라 구비아비라따 어 바뉴.

37. 어 바뉴 보씨 버라 구랴 나 귀우다. 마꼬 어 바나푸씨 바루따아-루따아 뱌 뱌씨바아, 벼라 귀후사 비도따 비례따.

38. 바 바랴아 어비 비료, 바바아 바례 바루머 뷰뻬 비너, 부시라 구아자 어 바가시 너 바나.

39. 짜시찌러, 여수 어라 구롸아 아부 바뉴. 어라

want to send them away hungry, or they may collapse on the way."

33. His disciples answered, "Where could we get enough bread in this remote place to feed such a crowd?"

34. "How many loaves do you have?" Jesus asked. "Seven," they replied, "and a few small fish."

35. He told the crowd to sit down on the ground.

36. Then he took the seven loaves and the fish, and when he had given thanks, he broke them and gave them to the disciples, and they in turn to the people.

37. They all ate and were satisfied. Afterward the disciples picked up seven basketfuls of broken pieces that were left over.

38. The number of those who ate was four thousand, besides women and children.

39. After Jesus had sent the crowd away, he got

mwa bwato aya mwa bimbi
by'e Makatani.

귀루기라 뫄 봐도 아야 뫄
비뻬 벼 마가다니.

into the boat and went to
the vicinity of Magadan.

Matayo Chikono 16

1. lusuku luuma e Bafarisayo
n'e Basandukayo baikiraa
yesu, Babaa bahonda
bamuereke ; Bera kumwema
mbu aba?lyiraa chisomerano
chiuma cha chalosa
kanangana kwa e buashi
bwai butengire kwa nguba.
2. Yesu era kubakula mbu: E
bihangi by'e luolo-olo,
mwende mwateta mbu mwa
chanya mulyi bwange,
mishangya bungacha kubuya.
3. N'e bihangi by'e
mishangya-shangya, mwende
mwateta mbu: Enguba
y'enyire, lwarero e mvula
ingatowa Mango mwende
mwachwumbikisa kwa nguba,
mwende mwa menyerera e
bihangi bya bingaba. Rero
bine bihangi mulyimo, kute
mutangabimenyerera?
4. E bandju b'e sine suku
balyi babi, kanji
batachwunjire Ongo! Benjire
bema e chisomerano, si cha
bangalosibwa chinalyi cha
cha murebi Yona oshao
Chasinda, Yesu era kubareka
na achendera.

마다요 찌고노 16

1. 루수구 루우마 어
바파리사요 너 바사뚜가요
바이기라아 여수, 바바아
바호따 바무어러거 ; 버라
구뭐마 뿌 아바?쩨라아
찌소머라노 찌우마 짜 짜로사
가나꾸나 과 어 부아씨 봐이
부더띠러 과 우바.
2. 여수 어라 구바구꽈 뿌: 어
비하띠 벼 루우로르-오르, 뭐머
마더다 뿌 뫄 짜냐 무쩨 봐어,
미싸꺅 부꾸짜 구부야.
3. 너 비하띠 벼 미싸꺅-싸꺅,
뭐머 마더다 뿌: 어우바
여니러, 꽈러로 어 뿌꽈
이꾸도와 마꼬 뭐머
뫄쭈뻬기사 과 우바, 뭐머 뫄
머녀러라 어 비하띠 뱌
비꾸바. 러로 비너 비하띠
무쩨모, 구더
무다꾸비머녀러라?

Matthew Chapter 16[NIV]

1. The Pharisees and
Sadducees came to Jesus
and tested him by asking
him to show them a sign
from heaven.
2. He replied, "When
evening comes, you say, 'It
will be fair weather, for the
sky is red,'
3. and in the morning,
'Today it will be stormy, for
the sky is red and
overcast.' You know how
to interpret the
appearance of the sky, but
you cannot interpret the
signs of the times.
4. A wicked and adulterous
generation looks for a
miraculous sign, but none
will be given it except the
sign of Jonah." Jesus then
left them and went away.

4. 어 바뚜 버 시너 수구 바쩨
바비, 가찌 바다쭈띠러 오꼬!
버띠러 버마 어 찌소머라노,
시 짜 바꾸로시봐 찌나쩨 짜
짜 무러비 요나 오싸오
짜시따, 여수 어라 구바러가
나 아쩌떠라.

E chachu ch'e Bafarisayo n'e 어 짜쭈 쩌 바파리사요 너
Basandukayo 바사누—위

5. Mango e banafunzi ba Yesu babaa bera bahabukaa e nyanja, babaa bebilyire kueka e mikati.

5. 마꼬 어 바나푸씨 바 여수 바바아 버라 바하부가아 어 냐짜, 바바아 버비쩨러 구어가 어 미가디.

5. When they went across the lake, the disciples forgot to take bread.

6. Yesu era kubabura mbu: Mundaa mwachilanga kwa chachu ch'e Bafarisayo n'e ch'e Basadukayo

6. 여수 어라 구바부라 뿌: 무따아 뫄찌롸ㅁㅏ 과 짜쭈 쩌 바파리사요 너 쩌 바사두가요

6. "Be careful," Jesus said to them. "Be on your guard against the yeast of the Pharisees and Sadducees."

7. Abu banafunzi, bera kutangilyisa baburana mbu: atechire bacha, bushi chwutarechire e mikati

7. 아부 바나푸씨, 버라 구다ㅁㅣ쩨사 바부라나 뿌: 아더찌러 바짜, 부씨 쭈다러찌러 어 미가디

7. They discussed this among themselves and said, "It is because we didn't bring any bread."

8. Ebi babaa baburana bacha, Yesu era kubimenyerera. Bushi n'oku, era kubabura mbu: munalyi bandju ba bwemesi bueke! Chi chachwuma mwachitetembya mbu mutete mikati?

8. 어비 바바아 바부라나 바짜, 여수 어라 구비머녀러라. 부씨 노구, 어라 구바부라 뿌: 무나쩨 바뉴 바 붜머시 부어거! 찌 짜쭈마 뫄찌더더ㅃㅏ 뿌 무더더 미가디?

8. Aware of their discussion, Jesus asked, "You of little faith, why are you talking among yourselves about having no bread?

9. Mutanasa kumenyerera? mutachikengere ba bandju byumbi bitano kwa beutaa era mikati etano, na bitonga binga bimwalunda-lundaa bya byeshibaa?

9. 무다나사 구머녀러라? 무다찌거ㅁㅓ러 바 바뉴 뷰ㅁㅔ 비다노 과 버우다아 어라 미가디 어다노, 나 비도ㅁㅏ 비ㅁㅏ 비뫄루따-루따아 뱌 뼈씨바아?

9. Do you still not understand? Don't you remember the five loaves for the five thousand, and how many basketfuls you gathered?

10. Nesi mutachikengere ba banji bandju byumbi bine nabo, kwa beutaa era mikati elyinda, na bitonga binga bi mwalunda-lundaa bya byeshibaa?

10. 너시 무다찌거ㅁㅓ러 바 바찌 바뉴 뷰ㅁㅔ 비너 나보, 과 버우다아 어라 미가디 어쩨따, 나 비도ㅁㅏ 비ㅁㅏ 비 뫄루따-루따아 뱌 뼈씨바아?

10. Or the seven loaves for the four thousand, and how many basketfuls you gathered?

11. Rero, chi chachwuma mwaanyisa mbu bya nateta byerekere e mikati? Nababura kwa mundaa mwachilanga ne chachu ch'e bafarisayo n'e basandukayo

12. E banafunzi bera kwire bamenyerera kwa kasi Yesu abaa atateta era luulu s'e kuchilanga era luulu s'e chachu, si abaa ababura kwa bendaa bachilanga ne myasi y'e bafarisayo n'e basandukayo.

Petero ateta kwa Yesu I Mwana wa Ongo

13. Era nyuma s'ebi, Yesu era kuya mwa bimbi byekaisariya Firipi; era kubusa e banafunzi bai mbu: Ewashe, e bandju benjire bateta mbu nyi Mwana w'e Mwundju, nyi nde?

14. Nabo mbu: Bauma benjire bateta mbu u Yowana Mubatisayi, n'e banji mbu Eliya, n'e banji mbu u Yeremiya, nesi mbu ulyimuuma mwa banji barebi bokwa mira.

15. Yesu kukwera kubabusa mbu: Nenyu mwenjire mwateta mbu nyilyi nde?

11. 러로, 찌 짜쭈마 뫄아니네사 뿌 뱌 나더다 벼러거러 어 미가디? 나바부라 과 무따아 마찌롸꺄 너 짜쭈 쩌 바파리사요 너 바사뚜가요

12. 어 바나푸씨 버라 귀러 바머녀러라 과 가시 여수 아바아 아다더다 어라 루우루 서 구찌롸꺄 어라 루우루 서 짜쭈, 시 아바아 아바부라 과 버따아 바찌롸꺄 너 먀시 여 바파리사요 너 바사뚜가요.

퍼더로 아더다 과 여수 이 뫄나 와 오꾜

13. 어라 뉴마 서비, 여수 어라 구야 뫄 비삐 벼가이사리야 피리피; 어라 구부사 어 바나푸씨 바이 뿌: 어와써, 어 바뚜 버찌러 바더다 뿌 네 뫄나 워 무뚜, 네 떠?

14. 나보 뿌: 바우마 버찌러 바더다 뿌 우 요와나 무바디사에, 너 바찌 뿌 어뤼야, 너 바찌 뿌 우 여러미야, 너시 뿌 우레무우마 뫄 바찌 바러비 보과 미라.

15. 여수 구궈라 구바부사 뿌: 너뉴 뭐찌러 뫄더다 뿌 네레 떠?

11. How is it you don't understand that I was not talking to you about bread? But be on your guard against the yeast of the Pharisees and Sadducees."

12. Then they understood that he was not telling them to guard against the yeast used in bread, but against the teaching of the Pharisees and Sadducees.

13. When Jesus came to the region of Caesarea Philippi, he asked his disciples, "Who do people say the Son of Man is?"

14. They replied, "Some say John the Baptist; others say Elijah; and still others, Jeremiah or one of the prophets."

15. "But what about you?" he asked. "Who do you say I am?"

16. Simoni petero era kumwakula mbu: Woyo, u Kirisito! Mwana wa Ongo w'e kalamo.

17. Yesu era kumubura mbu: Simoni mwenyi Yona, waahanyirwe. Bushi oyu mwasi kutalyi mundju ola wakulosiseo, si Tata ola ulyi kwa nguba.

18. Nanyi nera nakubura kwa woyo u Petero, kukuteta mbu e koi. Na kwelyine koi, ku nyingaimba e luhu lwanyi. N'olu luhu, e buashi bw'e kusimu butakaluime chiro na hicha.

19. Kanji nyingakweresa e funguro s'e Bwami b'okwa nguba. Byoshi bya ukende wanana muno butala Ongo nai akende anabinana. Na byoshi bya ukende wemerera, muno butala, Ongo nai akende anabyemerera.

20. Chasinda, Yesu era kubura e banafunzi bai mbu bataburaa mundju usibya kwai Kirisito.

Yesu ateta era luulu s'e kufa n'e kwomoka kwai

21. Kutengera mwamu mango, Yesu era kutangilyisa abura e banafunzi bai busira kubabisha, kwa bimwemire

16. 시모니 퍼더로 어라 구꾸구꽈 뿌: 우요, 우 기리시도! 뫄나 와 오꼬 워 가꽈모.

17. 여수 어라 구무부라 뿌: 시모니 뭐네 요나, 와아하니뤄. 부씨 오유 뫄시 구다레 무뚜 오라 와구로시서오, 시 다다 오라 우레 과 우바.

18. 나네 너라 나구부라 과 우요 우 퍼더로, 구구더다 뿌 어 고이. 나 궈레너 고이, 구 네아이빠 어 루후 똬네. 노루 루후, 어 부아씨 뷔 구시무 부다가루이머 찌로 나 히짜.

19. 가찌 네아궈러사 어 푸우로 서 봐미 보과 우바. 뵤씨 뱌 우거떠 와나나 무노 부다꽈 오꼬 나이 아거떠 아나비나나. 나 뵤씨 뱌 우거떠 워머러라, 무노 부다꽈, 오꼬 나이 아거떠 아나뷔머러라.

20. 짜시따, 여수 어라 구부라 어 바나푸씨 바이 뿌 바다부라아 무뚜 우시뱌 과이 기리시도.

여수 아더다 어라 뿌윱뿌 서 구꽈 너 교명— 과이

21. 구더떠라 뫄무 마꼬, 여수 어라 구다삐쎄사 아부라 어 바나푸씨 바이 부시라 구바비쌰, 과 비뭐미러 아여

16. Simon Peter answered, "You are the Christ, the Son of the living God."

17. Jesus replied, "Blessed are you, Simon son of Jonah, for this was not revealed to you by man, but by my Father in heaven.

18. And I tell you that you are Peter, and on this rock I will build my church, and the gates of Hades will not overcome it.

19. I will give you the keys of the kingdom of heaven; whatever you bind on earth will be bound in heaven, and whatever you loose on earth will be loosed in heaven."

20. Then he warned his disciples not to tell anyone that he was the Christ.

21. From that time on Jesus began to explain to his disciples that he must go to Jerusalem and suffer

aye e Yerusalemu. N'eyi, e bashamuka b'e Bayuda, n'e bakulukulu b'e bakuhanyi, n'e bakangilyisi b'e Mwaso bangamulyibusa busese. Chasinda, angechibwa, n'okwa lusuku lwa kahachwu angomoka.

22. petero kukwera kumweka ala musike, na atangilyisa amubura na bute bunene mbu: Enawechwu! Ongo akuimiraa e byera, bitakuikiraa chiro na hicha!

23. Si Yesu kuna kubindjuka, na amubura mbu: Eu Musimu! Tengaa mwa meho manyi! Kunyiteya ku wanyiteya, bushi e mianyisa yao itatenga era mwa Ongo, si inalyi ya mundju.

24. Yesu kukwera kubura e banafunzi bai mbu: Akaba e mundju ahonda kunyikulyikira, arekaa kunde aanyisa era luulu sai yeine, emire kweka e musalaba wai, anyikulyikire.

25. Bushi, e mundju ola wahonda kulamya e kalamo kai, angakaesa. Si ola ungana e kalamo kai bushi nanyi, yeke angahuba kukabona.

26. Mutoloke muchiye ola mundju angabona mwa kuata

어 여루사꿔무. 너에, 어 바싸무가 버 바유다, 너 바구루구루 버 바구하니, 너 바가꿰레시 버 꽈소 바까무레부사 부서서. 짜시따, 아꺼찌봐, 노과 루수구 꽈 가하쭈 아꼬모가.

22. 퍼더로 구꿔라 구뭐가 아꽈 무시거, 나 아다꿰레사 아무부라 나 부더 부너너 뿌: 어나워쭈! 오꼬 아구이미라아 어 벼라, 비다구이기라아 찌로 나 히짜!

23. 시 여수 구나 구비뿌가, 나 아무부라 뿌: 어우 무시무! 더꽈아 꽈 머호 마네! 구네더야 구 와네더야, 부씨 어 미아네사 야오 이다더꽈 어라 꽈 오꼬, 시 이나꿰 야 무뿌.

24. 여수 구꿔라 구부라 어 바나푸씨 바이 뿌: 아가바 어 무뿌 아호따 구네구꿰기라, 아러가아 구떠 아아네사 어라 루우루 사이 여이너, 어미러 꿔가 어 무사꽈바 와이, 아네구꿰기러.

25. 부씨, 어 무뿌 오꽈 와호따 구꽈먀 어 가라모 가이, 아꽈가어사. 시 오꽈 우꽈나 어 가꽈모 가이 부씨 나네, 여거 아꽈후바 구가보나.

26. 무도루거 무찌여 오꽈 무뿌 아꽈보나 꽈 구아다 어

many things at the hands of the elders, chief priests and teachers of the law, and that he must be killed and on the third day be raised to life.

22. Peter took him aside and began to rebuke him. "Never, Lord!" he said. "This shall never happen to you!"

23. Jesus turned and said to Peter, "Get behind me, Satan! You are a stumbling block to me; you do not have in mind the things of God, but the things of men."

24. Then Jesus said to his disciples, "If anyone would come after me, he must deny himself and take up his cross and follow me.

25. For whoever wants to save his life will lose it, but whoever loses his life for me will find it.

26. What good will it be for a man if he gains the

e bindju byoshi by'omwa butala, aesise n'e kalamo kai? Na chiye chi e mundju angahuba kwana kwa kununula e kalamo kai?

27. Natechire bacha, bushi nyi Mwana w'e Mundju nyikabaha mwa bulangare bwa Tata alauma n'e bamalaika bai. Kanji nyikemba chira mundju kukulyikana n'e mikorere yai.

28. Kubinalyi, nababura kwa mwa bano bandju balyi analo, mulyi bauma ba batakafe batasa kulola kwa nyi Mwana w'e Mundju naika nga Mwami.

Matayo Chikono 17
Yesu abindjulwa e huhe

1. Mango kwabaa kwarenga suku ndachwu, Yesu era kutola Petero, na Yakobo na Yowana, munyakabo Yakobo. Era kwerukira nabo ku ndjulungu nguma irerere, bera kuberako beine.

2. Abere bera balyi kwei ndjulungu, Yesu era kubindjulwa e huhe mwa meho mabo. E buso bwai, bwera kulangala ng'e suba. N'e njimba sai nasi, sera kwengengenya busese nga

---

비쭈 뵤씨 뵤뫄 부다꽈, 아어시서 너 가꽈모 가이? 나찌여 찌 어 무뚜 아꺄후바 과나 과 구누누꽈 어 가꽈모 가이?

27. 나더찌러 바짜, 부씨 네 뫄나 워 무뚜 네가바하 뫄 부꽈꺄러 봐 다다 아꽈우마 너 바마꽈이가 바이. 가찌 네거빠 찌라 무뚜 구구레가나 너 미고러러 야이.

28. 구비나레, 나바부라 과 뫄 바노 바뚜 바레 아나로, 무레 바우마 바 바다가퍼 바다사 구꾜꽈 과 네 뫄나 워 무뚜 나이가 꺄 뫄미.

마다요 찌고노 17
여수 아비뚜꽈 어 후허

1. 마꼬 과바아 과러꺄 수구 따쭉, 여수 어라 구도꽈 퍼더로, 나 야고보 나 요와나, 무냐가보 야고보. 어라 꿔루기라 나보 구 뚜루우 우마 이러러러, 버라 구버라고 버이너.

2. 아버러 버라 바레 꿔이 뚜루우, 여수 어라 구비뚜꽈 어 후허 뫄 머호 마보. 어 부소 봐이, 붜라 구꽈꺄라 우어 수바. 너 띠빠 사이 나시, 서라 꿔꺼머냐 부서서 꺄 부꽈꺄러.

---

whole world, yet forfeits his soul? Or what can a man give in exchange for his soul?

27. For the Son of Man is going to come in his Father's glory with his angels, and then he will reward each person according to what he has done.

28. I tell you the truth, some who are standing here will not taste death before they see the Son of Man coming in his kingdom."

Matthew Chapter 17[NIV]

1. After six days Jesus took with him Peter, James and John the brother of James, and led them up a high mountain by themselves.

2. There he was transfigured before them. His face shone like the sun, and his clothes became as white as the light.

bulangare.

3. Unao-unao, e banafunzi bera kulola ku musa na Eliya bahambala na Yesu.

3. 우나오-우나오, 어 바나푸씨 버라 구로라 구 무사 나 어뤼야 바하빠라 나 여수.

3. Just then there appeared before them Moses and Elijah, talking with Jesus.

4. Bushi n'oku, Petero era kwire abura Yesu mbu: Enawechwu! kukomire chwubere anola. Kanji akaba uhonjire, nyingaimbireo bitala bihachwu : Chiuma chao, n'e chinji cha Musa, n'e chinji cha Eliya

4. 부씨 노구, 퍼더로 어라 귀러 아부라 여수 뿌: 어나워쭈! 구고미러 쭈버러 아노꽈. 가찌 아가바 우호찌러, 니빠이삐러오 비다꽈 비하쭈 : 찌우마 짜오, 너 찌찌 짜 무사, 너 찌찌 짜 어뤼야

4. Peter said to Jesus, "Lord, it is good for us to be here. If you wish, I will put up three shelters--one for you, one for Moses and one for Elijah."

5. Mango Petero abaa anachilyi ateta, unao-unao kwera kuulukira lumbumbu lwalangala, kuna kubasungula. Mw'olu lumbumbu, mwera kuulukira murenge muuma ola wabaa wateta mbu: Onola iMwana wanyi musiirwa, iuchwula unyisimise. Mundaa mwamumvilyisa!

5. 마꼬 퍼더로 아바아 아나찌레 아더다, 우나오-우나오 귀라 구우루기라 루뿌뿌 콰꽈빠꽈, 구나 구바수꽈꽈. 몰루 루뿌뿌, 뭐라 구우루기라 무러꺼 무우마 오꽈 와바아 와더다 뿌: 오노꽈 이뫄나 와니 무시이롸, 이우쭈꽈 우니시미서. 무따아 마무뻬례사!

5. While he was still speaking, a bright cloud enveloped them, and a voice from the cloud said, "This is my Son, whom I love; with him I am well pleased. Listen to him!"

6. Abu banafunzi mango bomvaa bacha, bera kwobaa busese, kuna kukumbaala kafulyi-bwembe.

6. 아부 바나푸씨 마꼬 보빠아 바짜, 버라 곱바아 부서서, 구나 구구빠아꽈 가푸레-붸뻐.

6. When the disciples heard this, they fell facedown to the ground, terrified.

7. Si Yesu era kuchifunda ofu nabo, era kubaumako na ababura mbu: Mutobaa, mwimangaa!

7. 시 여수 어라 구찌푸따 오푸 나보, 어라 구바우마고 나 아바부라 뿌: 무도바아, 뮈마까아!

7. But Jesus came and touched them. "Get up," he said. "Don't be afraid."

8. Abere bemusa e meho, chiro bakachilola ku unji mundju, kureka Yesu yeine

8. 아버러 버무사 어 머호, 찌로 바가찌로꽈 구 우찌 무뚜, 구러가 여수 여이너

8. When they looked up, they saw no one except Jesus.

oshao.

오싸오.

9. Mango Yesu n'e banafunzi bai babaa bera baandaala kwei ndjulungu, era kubachichika mbu: Ebi mwera kulolako, mutaburaabi mundju usibya kuikira mango nyi Mwana w'e Mundju nyingaba nomwokire mira.

9. 마꼬 여수 너 바나푸씨 바이 바바아 버라 바아따아꽈 궈이 뚜루꾸, 어라 구바찌찌가 뿌: 어비 뭐라 구롤롸고, 무다부라아비 무뚜 우시뱌 구이기라 마꼬 내 뫄나 워 무뚜 네까바 노모기러 미라.

9. As they were coming down the mountain, Jesus instructed them, "Don't tell anyone what you have seen, until the Son of Man has been raised from the dead."

10. Chasinda, e bafunzi ba Yesu bera kumubusa mbu: WAlyiya! Chi chenjire chachwuma e bakangilyisi b'e Mwaso bateta mbu byemire Eliya abahe tanga?

10. 짜시따, 어 바푸씨 바 여수 버라 구무부사 뿌: 와레야! 찌 쩌찌러 짜쭈마 어 바가끼레시 버 뫄소 바더다 뿌 벼미러 어릐야 아바허 다까?

10. The disciples asked him, "Why then do the teachers of the law say that Elijah must come first?"

11. Yesu era kubakula mbu: kubinalyi, byemire Eliya abahe tanga, akungaye e myasi yoshi.

11. 여수 어라 구바구꽈 뿌: 구비나레, 벼미러 어릐야 아바허 다까, 아구까여 어 먀시 요씨.

11. Jesus replied, "To be sure, Elijah comes and will restore all things.

12. Si rero nababura kwa Eliya aikire mira, si e bandju batamumenyereraa. Bera kumuilyira ng'okwa babaa banahonjire. Anabe nanyi nyi Mwana w'e Mundju, ku banganyilyibusa bacha.

12. 시 러로 나바부라 과 어릐야 아이기러 미라, 시 어 바뚜 바다무머녀러라아. 버라 구무이레라 꽃오과 바바아 바나호찌러. 아나버 나내 내 뫄나 워 무뚜, 구 바까나내레부사 바짜.

12. But I tell you, Elijah has already come, and they did not recognize him, but have done to him everything they wished. In the same way the Son of Man is going to suffer at their hands."

13. unao-unao, abu banafunzi bai bera kwire bamenyerera kwa kasi Yesu, mwa kubahambalyira era luulu sa Eliya, abaa ateta era luulu sa Yowana Mubastisayia.

13. 우나오-우나오, 아부 바나푸씨 바이 버라 귀러 바머녀러라 과 가시 여수, 뫄 구바하빠레라 어라 루우루 사 어릐야, 아바아 아더다 어라 루우루 사 요와나 무바시사에아.

13. Then the disciples understood that he was talking to them about John the Baptist.

Yesu ambula e chihwasi ch'e luungu kwa mwana

여수 아뿌퐈 어 찌화시 쩌 룿윾 과 똬나

14. Yesu n'e banafunzi bai bera kunaendekera n'e luendo na baika ala luamba lw'e bandju lwabaa lulyi. Mundju muuma era kuchifunda ofu na Yesu, era kufukama era muhondo sai.

14. 여수 너 바나푸씨 바이 버라 구나어떠거라 너 룾어또 나 바이가 아퐈 룾아빠 뭐 바뚜 퐈바아 룿레. 무뚜 무우마 어라 구찌푸따 오푸 나 여수, 어라 구푸가마 어라 무호또 사이.

14. When they came to the crowd, a man approached Jesus and knelt before him.

15. Era kumubura mbu: Enawechwu, ufiraa e mwana wanyi bonjo bushi achwusa bulwala bwa luungu. Obu bulwala, bwamulosise kwa kasibu. Enjire akumbaalyiranga mwa mulyiro, n'omwa meshi.

15. 어라 구무부라 뿌: 어나워쭈, 우피라아 어 똬나 와네 보쪼 부씨 아쭈사 부퐈퐈 봐 룿우쿠. 오부 부퐈퐈, 봐무뢰씨서 과 가시부. 어찌러 아구빠아줴라㈜ 똬 무풰로, 노똬 머씨.

15. "Lord, have mercy on my son," he said. "He has seizures and is suffering greatly. He often falls into the fire or into the water.

16. Namureteraa e banafunzi bao mbu bamulamye, si pyo!

16. 나무러더라아 어 바나푸씨 바오 뿌 바무퐈며, 시 표!

16. I brought him to your disciples, but they could not heal him."

17. Yesu era kubaakula mbu: Aaye! mu bandju b'e sine suku mulyi babi, kanji mutete na bwemeresi busibya! nyikaendekera kuba nenyu, na kunde nomvilyisa e myasi yenyu kuikira mango chi? Nyireteraa oyu mwana anola!

17. 여수 어라 구바아구퐈 뿌: 아아여! 무 바뚜 버 시너 수구 무풰 바비, 가찌 무더더 나 뭐머러시 부시뱌! 네가어떠거라 구바 너뉴, 나 구떠 노뻬풰사 어 먀시 여뉴 구이기라 마꼬 찌? 네러더라아 오유 똬나 아노퐈!

17. "O unbelieving and perverse generation," Jesus replied, "how long shall I stay with you? How long shall I put up with you? Bring the boy here to me."

18. Yesu era kukalyiira e chihwasi cha chabaa chilyi kw'oyu mwana, na chamutengako. Unao-unao kuna kulama.

18. 여수 어라 구가줴이라 어 찌화시 짜 짜바아 찌풰 고유 똬나, 나 짜무더㈜고. 우나오-우나오 구나 구퐈마.

18. Jesus rebuked the demon, and it came out of the boy, and he was healed from that moment.

19. Chasinda, e banafunzi ba Yesu bera kuchifunda ala

19. 짜시따, 어 바나푸씨 바 여수 버라 구찌푸따 아퐈

19. Then the disciples came to Jesus in private

abaa alyi yeine, na bamubusa mbu: e Waliya! Cha chihwasi, chi chachwumaa chwubeke chwafundjwa kwambulachi?

20. Nai mbu: Bushi e bwemeresi bwenyu bulyi bueke. Kubinalyi nababura kwa chiro angaba mbu e bwemeresi bwenyu bungaba bueke nga hya kafuma hieke busese, munganabura ene ndjulungu mbu: Tengaa anola, uye kuchikoma wala, nai inganayao. Kutanganachiba kandju kasibya ka katangaalyikana era mulyi.

21. Si e chihwasi cha chilyi ng'echi, chabaa chitangambulwa busira memo ma mende mairwa busira kulya

Yesu ateta kanji era luulu s'e kufa n'e kwomoka kwai

22. Lusuku luuma, mango e banafunzi babaa babuananyire e Kalilaya, Yesu era kubabura mbu: Nyi Mwana w'e Mundju nyinganyibwa mwa mino s'e bandju.

23. N'abu bandju, banganyiita, si e lusuku lwa kahachwu nyingomwoka, e banafunzi bai bomvire bacha,

아바아 아쪠 여이너, 나 바무부사 뿌: 어 와쬐야! 짜 찌화시, 찌 짜쭐마아 쭈버거 좌푸쫘 과뿌꽈찌?

20. 나이 뿌: 부씨 어 붜머러시 붜뉴 부쪠 부어거. 구비나쪠 나바부라 과 찌로 아까바 뿌 어 붜머러시 붜뉴 부까바 부어거 까 햐 가푸마 히어거 부서서, 무까나부라 어너 뚜루꾸 뿌: 더까아 아노쫘, 우여 구찌고마 와쫘, 나이 이까나야오. 구다까나찌바 가뚜 가시뱌 가 가다까아쪠가나 어라 무쪠.

21. 시 어 찌화시 짜 찌쪠 꾸어찌, 짜바아 찌다까뿌꽈 부시라 머모 마 머떠 마이롸 부시라 구꺄

여수 아더다 가찌 어라 루울루 서 구파 너 꾜명— 과이

22. 루수구 루우마, 마꼬 어 바나푸씨 바바아 바부아나니러 어 가쬐꺄야, 여수 어라 구바부라 뿌: 니 마나 워 무뚜 니까니봐 마 미노 서 바뚜.

23. 나부 바뚜, 바까네이다, 시 어 루수구 꽈 가하쭈 니꼬모가, 어 바나푸씨 바이 보쀄러 바짜, 버라 구뇨꽈

and asked, "Why couldn't we drive it out?"

20. He replied, "Because you have so little faith. I tell you the truth, if you have faith as small as a mustard seed, you can say to this mountain, 'Move from here to there' and it will move. Nothing will be impossible for you."

21 None

22. When they came together in Galilee, he said to them, "The Son of Man is going to be betrayed into the hands of men.

23. They will kill him, and on the third day he will be raised to life." And the disciples were filled with

bera kunyongwa busese. 부서서. grief.

Yesu na petero bafuta e mbarata y'e Luhu lwa Ongo

여수 나 퍼더로 바푸다 어 빠띱닛 여 루훌 롸 오꼬

24. Chasinda, Yesu n'e banafunzi bai bera kuya mwa musi w'e Kaperinaumu. Baikiremo, e bafuchisi b'e mbarata y'e luhu lwa Ongo, bera kuikira petero, na bamubusa mbu: Ewashe, elyi e mukangilyisi wenyu nai, ende afuta e mbarata y'e luhu lwa Ongo?

24. 짜시따, 여수 너 바나푸씨 바이 버라 구야 롸 무시 워 가퍼리나우무. 바이기러모, 어 바푸찌시 버 빠라다 여 루후 롸 오꼬, 버라 구이기라 퍼더로, 나 바무부사 뿌: 어와써, 어레 어 무가끼레시 워뉴 나이, 어떠 아푸다 어 빠라다 여 루후 롸 오꼬?

24. After Jesus and his disciples arrived in Capernaum, the collectors of the two-drachma tax came to Peter and asked, "Doesn't your teacher pay the temple tax?"

25. Petero na imbu: Eee! Ende afutai Petero mwa kunengilyira mwa nyumba, abere atanasa kuteta chiro na mwasi, Yesu era kumubusa mbu: Ewashe Simoni, kute usene? E bami bobuno butala mango bende bafuchisa e mbarata, elyi bende bafuchisa e bana b'e chio, nesi e baenyi?

25. 퍼더로 나 이뿌: 어어어! 어떠 아푸다이 퍼더로 롸 구너끼레라 롸 뉴빠, 아버러 아다나사 구더다 찌로 나 롸시, 여수 어라 구무부사 뿌: 어와써 시모니, 구더 우서너? 어 바미 보부노 부다롸 마꼬 버떠 바푸찌사 어 빠라다, 어레 버떠 바푸찌사 어 바나 버 찌오, 너시 어 바어니?

25. "Yes, he does," he replied. When Peter came into the house, Jesus was the first to speak. "What do you think, Simon?" he asked. "From whom do the kings of the earth collect duty and taxes--from their own sons or from others?"

26. Petero na imbu: bende bafuchisa e baenyi oshao Yesu kukwera kumubura mbu e bana b'e chio bata bandju ba kunde bafuta mbarata.

26. 퍼더로 나 이뿌: 버떠 바푸찌사 어 바어니 오싸오 여수 구궈라 구무부라 뿌 어 바나 버 찌오 바다 바뚜 바 구떠 바푸다 빠라다.

26. "From others," Peter answered. "Then the sons are exempt," Jesus said to him.

27. Si chiro bacha, chwutahonda kusibusa bano bandju. Bushi n'oku, uyaa kwa nyanja, wanaumaa e ndobi mwa meshi. N'efi era

27. 시 찌로 바짜, 쭈다호따 구시부사 바노 바뚜. 부씨 노구, 우야아 과 냐짜, 와나우마아 어 또비 롸 머씨. 너피 어라 우까나다끼라

27. "But so that we may not offend them, go to the lake and throw out your line. Take the first fish you catch; open its mouth and

unganatangira kusimba, uiboolaa e bunu, ungalolamo ku chikoroto cha buteya. Echi chikoroto, uberesaachi kwa kufuta e mbarata yanyi n'e yao.

구시빠, 우이보오롸아 어 부누, 우ᄽᅡ로롸모 구 찌고로도 짜 부더야. 어찌 찌고로도, 우버러사아찌 과 구푸다 어 빠라다 야네 너 야오.

you will find a four-drachma coin. Take it and give it to them for my tax and yours."

Matayo Chikono 18
E mukulu-kulu mwa Bwami b'okwa nguba

마다요 찌고노 18
어 무구루-구루 와 봐미 보과 우밍

Matthew Chapter 18[NIV]

1. Mw'echi chihangi, e banafunzi ba Yesu bera kumuikira mbu: e Walyiya! nde i mukulu-kulu ku balyikabo mwa bwami b'okwa nguba?

1. 뭐찌 찌하이, 어 바나푸씨 바 여수 버라 구무이기라 뿌: 어 와례야! 떠 이 무구루-구루 구 바례가보 와 봐미 보과 우바?

1. At that time the disciples came to Jesus and asked, "Who is the greatest in the kingdom of heaven?"

2. Yesu era kwamala mwana mutoto muuma, era kumubika mwa kachi-kachi kabo.

2. 여수 어라 과마롸 뫄나 무도도 무우마, 어라 구무비가 와 가찌-가찌 가보.

2. He called a little child and had him stand among them.

3. Era kuteta mbu kubinalyi, nababura kwa akaba mutangabindjula e myanya yenyu mube nga bana batoto, mutakengilyire chiro na hicha mwa Bwami b'okwa nguba.

3. 어라 구더다 뿌 구비나례, 나바부라 과 아가바 무다ᄽᅡ비누롸 어 먀냐 여뉴 무버 ᄽᅡ 바나 바도도, 무다거ᄭᅵ례러 찌로 나 히짜 와 봐미 보과 우바.

3. And he said: "I tell you the truth, unless you change and become like little children, you will never enter the kingdom of heaven.

4. Rero, chira mundju ola ulyi murembu ng'ono mwana mutoto, iukaba mukulu-kulu mwa Bwami b'okwa nguba.

4. 러로, 찌라 무뚜 오라 우레 무러뿌 우오노 뫄나 무도도, 이우가바 무구루-구루 와 봐미 보과 우바.

4. Therefore, whoever humbles himself like this child is the greatest in the kingdom of heaven.

5. N'ola wahuukasa e mwana ola ulyi ng'ono kw'e sina lyanyi, elyi nyono nyi ahuukasise.

5. 노롸 와후우가사 어 뫄나 오라 우레 우오노 궈 시나 롸네, 어레 뇨노 네 아후우가시서.

5. "And whoever welcomes a little child like this in my name welcomes me.

E kuchilanga kwa mabi

어 구찌롸까 과 마비

6. Mwa bano bana batoto banyemerere, akaba mundju murebe angachwuma muuma mubo aya mwa bibi, kungabere kukulu kw'oyu mundju aminyirwe lusho lunene mw'e osi, aumwe mwa nyanja.

6. 뫄 바노 바나 바도도 바녀머러러, 아가바 무뉴 무러버 아까쭈마 무우마 무보 아야 뫄 비비, 구까버러 구구루 꼬유 무뉴 아미녜뤄 루쏘 루너너 뭐 오시, 아우뭐 뫄 냐쨔.

6. But if anyone causes one of these little ones who believe in me to sin, it would be better for him to have a large millstone hung around his neck and to be drowned in the depths of the sea.

7. Buanya kwa butala, bushi n'e myasi yehwiremo y'e kushiilyisa e bandju mwa mabi! Ei myasi itanganaina, si buanya kwa mundju ola yatengerako!

7. 부아냐 과 부다롸, 부씨 너 먀시 여휘러모 여 구씨이례사 어 바뉴 뫄 마비! 어이 먀시 이다까나이나, 시 부아냐 과 무뉴 오롸 야더꺼라고!

7. "Woe to the world because of the things that cause people to sin! Such things must come, but woe to the man through whom they come!

8. Akaba e kuboko kwao nesi e kuulu kwao, bingachwuma waira mabi, ubiishaa wanabiuma bure nao! Bushi kukomire wengilyire mwa kalamo k'e kunalyi wete kuboko kuuma nesi kuulu kuuma, wakuata maboko mabilyi nesi maulu mabilyi, chasinda uumwe, mwa mulyiro w'e suku n'e mango.

8. 아가바 어 구보고 과오 너시 어 구우루 과오, 비까쭈마 와이라 마비, 우비이싸아 와나비우마 부러 나오! 부씨 구고미러 워끼례러 뫄 가롸모 거 구나례 워더 구보고 구우마 너시 구우루 구우마, 와구아다 마보고 마비례 너시 마우루 마비례, 짜시따 우우뭐, 뫄 무례로 워 수구 너 마꼬.

8. If your hand or your foot causes you to sin, cut it off and throw it away. It is better for you to enter life maimed or crippled than to have two hands or two feet and be thrown into eternal fire.

9. Na akaba elyiho lyao nalyi lyingachwuma waira mabi, omwolaalyi, wanalyiuma bure nao! Bushi kukomire wengilyire mwa kalama k'e kunalyi wete lyiho lyiuma, wakuata meho mabilyi chasinda uumwe mwa mulyiro w'e suku n'e mango.

9. 나 아가바 어례호 랴오 나례 례까쭈마 와이라 마비, 오모롸아례, 와나례우마 부러 나오! 부씨 구고미러 워끼례러 뫄 가롸마 거 구나례 워더 례호 례우마, 와구아다 머호 마비례 짜시따 우우뭐 뫄 무례로 워 수구 너 마꼬.

9. And if your eye causes you to sin, gouge it out and throw it away. It is better for you to enter life with one eye than to have two eyes and be thrown into the fire of hell.

E muanyi w'e mbulyi era yaeraa

10. Mumenyaa, mungesha kunde mwakena muuma mwa bano bana batoto, bushi nababura kw'e bamalaika babo, e suku soshi bachwula balyi era muhondo sa Tata ola ulyi kwa nguba.

11. Mumenyaa kwa nyi Mwana w'e Mundju naikaa muno butala, chasiya nyinunule ba babaa baelyire.

12. Kute musene? Akaba mundju murebe angaba ete mbulyi sai eyana, na mw'esi mbulyi, nguma yanaera. Elyi atangareka tanga esi sinji chenda na mwenda kwa ndjulungu, aye kuhonda ei nguma yaelyire?

13. Kubinalyi, nababura kwa akaba angabonai, angamowerai busese kurenza sa sinji chenda na mwenda sa sitaeraa.

14. Kunoko-kunoko, ku Eho mwenyu nai ola ulyi kwa nguba atahonda mbu chiro na muuma mwa bano bana batato aeraa.

Eano bushi n'ola wakukorere e mabi

15. Akaba munyakwenyu

어 무아네 워 뿌쩨 어라 야어라아

10. 무머냐아, 무써싸 구더 마거나 무우마 롸 바노 바나 바도도, 부씨 나바부라 궈 바마좌이가 바보, 어 수구 소씨 바쭈롸 바레 어라 무호또 사 다다 오라 우쩨 과 우바.

11. 무머냐아 과 네 뫄나 워 무뚜 나이가아 무노 부다롸, 짜시야 네누누쩌 바 바바아 바어쩨러.

12. 구더 무서너? 아가바 무뚜 무러버 아싸바 어더 뿌쩨 사이 어야나, 나 뭐시 뿌쩨, 우마 야나어라. 어쩨 아다롸러가 다싸 어시 시찌 쩌따 나 뭐따 과 뚜루우, 아여 구호따 어이 우마 야어쩨러?

13. 구비나쩨, 나바부라 과 아가바 아싸보나이, 아싸모워라이 부서서 구러싸 사 시찌 쩌따 나 뭐따 사 시다어라아.

14. 구노고-구노고, 구 어호 뭐뉴 나이 오라 우쩨 과 우바 아다호따 뿌 찌로 나 무우마 롸 바노 바나 바다도 아어라아.

어아노 부씨 노롸 와구고러러 어 마비

15. 아가바 무냐궈뉴

---

10. "See that you do not look down on one of these little ones. For I tell you that their angels in heaven always see the face of my Father in heaven.

11 None

12. "What do you think? If a man owns a hundred sheep, and one of them wanders away, will he not leave the ninety-nine on the hills and go to look for the one that wandered off?

13. And if he finds it, I tell you the truth, he is happier about that one sheep than about the ninety-nine that did not wander off.

14. In the same way your Father in heaven is not willing that any of these little ones should be lost.

15. "If your brother sins

angakukorera mabi, umuenderaa weine chasiya umulose e mabi mai mango mulyi mu babilyi oshao. Akakumvira, mwanahuba kuba mwa buuma.

16. Si akaba anganana kukumva, utolaa unji mundju muuma nesi babilyi, wanaenda nabo chasiya chira chinwa chimenyeke kanangana kwa bubei bwa bandju babilyi nesi bahachwu.

17. Abu bandju nabo, akaba anganana kubomba, ufulyiraa e bemeresi kw'oyu mwasi. Na akaba atangomvira e bemeresi nabo, mwanere mwamutola nga mundju ola uteshi Ongo, kanji nga mufichisi wa mbarata.

18. Kubinalyi, nababura kwa byoshi bya mukende mwemeresanyako muno butala, bikende byemererwa n'okwa nguba. Na byoshi bya mukende mwanana muno butala, bikende byananyibwa n'okwa nguba.

19. Kubinalyi, nababura kanji kwa muno butala, akaba bandju babilyi mwa kachi-kachi kenyu bangemeresanya kwa kwema chindju chirebe,

아까구고러라 마비, 우무어떠라아 워이너 짜시야 우무른서 어 마비 마이 마꼬 무뤠 무 바비뤠 오싸오. 아가구뻬라, 먀나후바 구바 먀 부우마.

16. 시 아가바 아까나나 구구빠, 우도쫘아 우찌 무뚜 무우마 너시 바비뤠, 와나어따 나보 짜시야 찌라 찌뇨 찌머녀거 가나꺄나 과 부버이 봐 바쭈 바비뤠 너시 바하쭉.

17. 아부 바쭈 나보, 아가바 아까나나 구보빠, 우푸뤠라아 어 버머러시 굥유 먀시. 나 아가바 아다꼬뻬라 어 버머러시 나보, 먀너러 먀무도쫘 까 무뚜 오쫘 우더씨 오꼬, 가찌 까 무피찌시 와 빠라다.

18. 구비나뤠, 나바부라 과 뵤씨 뱌 무거떠 뭐머러사냐고 무노 부다쫘, 비거떠 벼머러롸 노과 꾸바. 나 뵤씨 뱌 무거떠 먀나나 무노 부다쫘, 비거떠 뱌나니봐 노과 꾸바.

19. 구비나뤠, 나바부라 가찌 과 무노 부다쫘, 아가바 바쭈 바비뤠 봐 가찌-가찌 거뉴 바꺼머러사냐 과 궈마 찌뚜 찌러버, 다다 오쫘 우뤠 과

against you, go and show him his fault, just between the two of you. If he listens to you, you have won your brother over.

16. But if he will not listen, take one or two others along, so that 'every matter may be established by the testimony of two or three witnesses.'

17. If he refuses to listen to them, tell it to the church; and if he refuses to listen even to the church, treat him as you would a pagan or a tax collector.

18. "I tell you the truth, whatever you bind on earth will bebound in heaven, and whatever you loose on earth will be loosed in heaven.

19. "Again, I tell you that if two of you on earth agree about anything you ask for, it will be done for you by my Father in heaven.

tata ola ulyi kwa nguba, anganaberesachi.

우바, 아빠나버러사찌.

20. Bushi ala bandju babilyi nesi bahachwu babuananyire kw'e sina lyanyi, elyi nanyi nyilyi mwa kachi-kachi kabo.

20. 부씨 아라 바쭈 바비례 너시 바하쭈 바부아나네러 궈 시나 랸니, 어레 나니 네례 마 가찌-가찌 가보.

20. For where two or three come together in my name, there am I with them."

E muanyi w'e mukosi ola wananaa kubabalyira mulyikabo

어 무아네 워 무고시 오롸 와나나아 구바바례딥 무뤠—볃

21. Era nyuma s'ebi, petero era kuchifunda ofu na Yesu, era kumubusa mbu: Enawechwu, akaba munyakechwu enjire anyikorera mabi, kanga ku binyemire kumubabalyira? Elyi kuikira ku kalyinda?

21. 어라 뉴마 서비, 퍼더로 어라 구찌푸따 오푸 나 여수, 어라 구무부사 뿌: 어나워쭈, 아가바 무냐거쭈 어찌러 아네고러라 마비, 가빠 구 비녀미러 구무바바뤠라? 어뤠 구이기라 구 가뤠따?

21. Then Peter came to Jesus and asked, "Lord, how many times shall I forgive my brother when he sins against me? Up to seven times?"

22. Yesu nai mbu: Nanga! Ndakubire mbu umubabalyiraa kalyinda oshao, si kalyinda kalyi malyinda.

22. 여수 나이 뿌: 나빠! 따구비러 뿌 우무바바뤠라아 가뤠따 오싸오, 시 가뤠따 가뤠 마뤠따.

22. Jesus answered, "I tell you, not seven times, but seventy-seven times.

23. Bushi n'oku, e bwami b'okwa nguba buhuhanyisibwe na mwami muuma ola wabaa wahonda amenye e muanjo w'e minda yai era bakosi bai babaa bemire kumufua.

23. 부씨 노구, 어 봐미 보과 우바 부후하네시붜 나 뫄미 무우마 오라 와바아 와호하 아머녀 어 무아쪼 워 미따 야이 어라 바고시 바이 바바아 버미러 구무푸아.

23. "Therefore, the kingdom of heaven is like a king who wanted to settle accounts with his servants.

24. Mwa kutangilyisa oyu mulyimo, bera kumuretera mukosi muuma ola wabaa ulyi mu mwinda wai munene wa biuma ekumi bya talanda.

24. 뫄 구다삐례사 오유 무뤠모, 버라 구무러더라 무고시 무우마 오롸 와바아 우뤠 무 뮈따 와이 무너너 와 비우마 어구미 뱌 다롸따.

24. As he began the settlement, a man who owed him ten thousand talents was brought to him.

25. Rero, oyu mukosi bushi

25. 러로, 오유 무고시 부씨

25. Since he was not able

abaa atangaala kufuwa oyu mwinda, enawabo era kwire ateta mbu wamukosi ausibwaa nga kaungu, na Mukai, n'e bana bai alauma n'e bindju byai byoshi, chasiya amufuwe e mwinda wai.

26. Oyu mukosi era kuifukama era muhondo s'enawabo, na kumwema mbu: Walyiya, unyilyinjira! Nyingakufuwa e mwinda wao woshi.

27. Enawabo era kumufira bonjo, era kumubabalyira kw'oyu mwinda, chasinda era kumureka aende.

28. Abere wamukosi era aulukaa, era kubuanana na mukosi mulyikabo ola wabaa ulyi mu mwinda wai mueke wa bikoroto eyana. Unao-unao, kuna kumusimbira ala mate na amubura mbu: Nyifuwaa e mwinda wanyi fuba!

29. Oyu mukosi mulyikabo, era kufukama era muhondo sai, na kumwema mbu: walyiya, unyibabalyiraa! Nyingakufuwa e mwinda wao.

아바아 아다까아롸 구푸와 오유 뮈따, 어나와보 어라 귀러 아더다 뿌 와무고시 아우시봐아 까 가우꾸, 나 무가이, 너 바나 바이 아롸우마 너 비뉴 뱌이 뵤씨, 짜시야 아무푸워 어 뮈따 와이.

26. 오유 무고시 어라 구이푸가마 어라 무호또 서나와보, 나 구뭐마 뿌: 와레야, 우네쎄씨라! 니까구푸와 어 뮈따 와오 오씨.

27. 어나와보 어라 구무피라 보쪼, 어라 구무바바례라 교유 뮈따, 짜시따 어라 구무러가 아어떠.

28. 아버러 와무고시 어라 아우루가아, 어라 구부아나나 나 무고시 무뤠가보 오롸 와바아 우뤠 무 뮈따 와이 무어거 와 비고로도 어야나. 우나오-우나오, 구나 구무시뻬라 아롸 마더 나 아무부라 뿌: 네푸와아 어 뮈따 와네 푸바!

29. 오유 무고시 무뤠가보, 어라 구푸가마 어라 무호또 사이, 나 구뭐마 뿌: 와레야, 우네바바례라아! 네까구푸와 어 뮈따 와오.

to pay, the master ordered that he and his wife and his children and all that he had be sold to repay the debt.

26. "The servant fell on his knees before him. 'Be patient with me,' he begged, 'and I will pay back everything.'

27. The servant's master took pity on him, canceled the debt and let him go.

28. "But when that servant went out, he found one of his fellow servants who owed him a hundred denarii. He grabbed him and began to choke him. 'Pay back what you owe me!' he demanded.

29. "His fellow servant fell to his knees and begged him, 'Be patient with me, and I will pay you back.'

30. Si era kunana, na aya kumuuma mwa buroko aberemo kuikira e mango angamufuwa e mwinda wai.

30. 시 어라 구나나, 나 아야 구무우마 와 부로고 아버러모 구이기라 어 마꼬 아빠무푸와 어 뮈따 와이.

30. "But he refused. Instead, he went off and had the man thrown into prison until he could pay the debt.

31. Bakosi balyikabo balolyire bacha, bera kuyongwa busese. Bera kuya kubura enawabo kwei myasi Yoshi.

31. 바고시 바레가보 바로레러 바짜, 버라 구요꽈 부서서. 버라 구야 구부라 어나와보 귀이 먀시 요씨.

31. When the other servants saw what had happened, they were greatly distressed and went and told their master everything that had happened.

32. Enawabo kukwera kuchwumisa ola mukosi, era kumubura mbu: Woyo ulyi mukosi mubi! Nyono nakubabalyiraa e mwinda wao woshi, bushi wanyemaa e bonjo!

32. 어나와보 구궈라 구쭈미사 오꽈 무고시, 어라 구무부라 뿌: 오요 우레 무고시 무비! 뇨노 나구바바레라아 어 뮈따 와오 올씨, 부씨 와녀마아 어 보쪼!

32. "Then the master called the servant in. 'You wicked servant,' he said, 'I canceled all that debt of yours because you begged me to.

33. Rero nao, chi cheraa chachwuma utababalyira mulyikenyu ng'okwa nanyi nakubabalyiraa?

33. 러로 나오, 찌 쩌라아 짜쭈마 우다바바레라 무레거뉴 꾸오과 나네 나구바바레라아?

33. Shouldn't you have had mercy on your fellow servant just as I had on you?'

34. Oyu enawabo era kufa bute bunene. Era kwire ateta mbu bamuuma mwa buroko bamulose kwa kasibu, kuikira mango angafua oyu mwinda wai woshi.

34. 오유 어나와보 어라 구파 부더 부너너. 어라 귀러 아더다 뿌 바무우마 와 부로고 바무로써 과 가시부, 구이기라 마꼬 아빠푸아 오유 뮈따 와이 올씨.

34. In anger his master turned him over to the jailers to be tortured, until he should pay back all he owed.

35. Chasinjire, Yesu era kuteta mbu: Nenyu, ku Tata ola ulyi kwa nguba akanabaira bacha, akaba chira muuma mu mwabo atakende ababalyira

35. 짜시찌러, 여수 어라 구더다 뿌: 너뉴, 구 다다 오꽈 우레 과 꾸바 아가나바이라 바짜, 아가바 찌라 무우마 무 먀보 아다거꺼 아바바레라

35. "This is how my heavenly Father will treat each of you unless you forgive your brother from your heart."

munyakabo kwa muchima wai woshi.

Matayo Chikono 19

1. Mango Yesu abaa era amalaa kuteta ei myasi, era kutenga e kalilaya. Era kuya mwa chio ch'e yuteya kwa unji mushilyilya w'e lwishi lw'e yorodani.

2. Bandju banene busese bera kumukulyikira, na ba babaa balyi balwala, era kubalamya.

3. Bafarisayo bauma bera kumuikira chasiya bamuereke. Bera kumubusa mbu: Ewashe, elyi e mwaso wechwu achwula emerere mbu e mundju anganaulusa mukai bushi na chira mwasi?

4. Yesu nai mbu: mutafura kusoma kute kw'e maanjiko machwula matechire mbu: kutengera mira Ongo abumbaa e mulume n'e mukasi.

5. Chasinda, era kuteta mbu: Echera chi chende chachwuma e mulume areka eshe na nyina, anaimba e bwai buhosi buna mukai. Abu babilyi, banere baba mundju muuma,

마다요 찌고노 19

1. 마꼬 여수 아바아 어라 아마롸아 구더다 어이 먀시, 어라 구더꽈 어 가삐롸야. 어라 구야 먀 찌오 쩌 유더야 과 우찌 무씨레랴 워 뤼씨 뤄 요로다니.

2. 바쭈 바너너 부서서 버라 구무구레기라, 나 바 바바아 바레 바롸롸, 어라 구바롸먀.

3. 바파리사요 바우마 버라 구무이기라 짜시야 바무어러거. 버라 구무부사 뿌: 어와써, 어레 어 먀소 워쭈 아쭈롸 어머러러 뿌 어 무쭈 아꽈나우룩사 무가이 부씨 나 찌라 먀시?

4. 여수 나이 뿌: 무다푸라 구소마 구더 궈 마아찌고 마쭈롸 마더찌러 뿌: 구더꺼라 미라 오꼬 아부빠아 어 무루머 너 무가시.

5. 짜시따, 어라 구더다 뿌: 어쩌라 찌 쩌더 짜쭈마 어 무루머 아러가 어써 나 니나, 아나이빠 어 봐이 부호시 부나 무가이. 아부 바비레, 바너러 바바 무쭈 무우마,

Matthew Chapter 19[NIV]

1. When Jesus had finished saying these things, he left Galilee and went into the region of Judea to the other side of the Jordan.

2. Large crowds followed him, and he healed them there.

3. Some Pharisees came to him to test him. They asked, "Is it lawful for a man to divorce his wife for any and every reason?"

4. "Haven't you read," he replied, "that at the beginning the Creator 'made them male and female,'

5. and said, 'For this reason a man will leave his father and mother and be united to his wife, and the two will become one flesh'?

6. Rero, batachibe babilyi, si banere baba mundju muuma. Bushi n'oku, bya Ongo abikaa alauma, kutabaa chiro na mundju ola ukabilyikanya.

7. Kanji abu bafarisayo, bera kumubusa mbu: Chi cheraa chachwuma musa ateta mbu e mulume endaa eresa mukai e maruba m'e kulyikana e mango ahonda kumuulusa?

8. Yesu nai mbu: Musa abemereraa mbu mundaa mwarekana na bakasi benyu, bushi n'e machi menyu masibu. Si kutengera mira, bitabaa bacha.

9. Rero nyono nababura kwa akaba e mundju angarekana na mukai busira kumusimba mu lusingi, chasinda anahwera unji, onyu mundju, amenyaa kwa abanjire ekilyi.

10. E banafunzi ba Yesu kukwera kumubura mbu: Ewaliya, akaba e lusingi lweine lu lungachwuma e mulume arekana na mukai, kasi e kuhwera kutete mufa usibya!

11. Yesu na imbu: oyu mwasi ata e bandju boshi bu bangaaala kwemererao, si ba Ongo aneresise e misi oshao.

---

6. 러로, 바다찌버 바비례, 시 바너러 바바 무뚜 무우마. 부씨 노구, 뱌 오꼬 아비가아 아꽈우마, 구다바아 찌로 나 무뚜 오꽈 우가비례가냐.

7. 가찌 아부 바파리사요, 버라 구무부사 뿌: 찌 쩌라아 짜쭉마 무사 아더다 뿌 어 무루머 어따아 어러사 무가이 어 마루바 머 구례가나 어 마꼬 아호따 구무우루사?

8. 여수 나이 뿌: 무사 아버머러라아 뿌 무따아 꽈러가나 나 바가시 버뉴, 부씨 너 마찌 머뉴 마시부. 시 구더꺼라 미라, 비다바아 바짜.

9. 러로 뇨노 나바부라 과 아가바 어 무뚜 아꽈러가나 나 무가이 부시라 구무시빠 무 루시꺼, 짜시따 아나훠라 우씨, 오뉴 무뚜, 아머냐아 과 아바찌러 어기례.

10. 어 바나푸씨 바 여수 구궈라 구무부라 뿌: 어와퀴야, 아가바 어 루시꺼 뤄이너 루 루꽈쭉마 어 무루머 아러가나 나 무가이, 가시 어 구훠라 구더더 무파 우시뱌!

11. 여수 나 이뿌: 오유 먀시 아다 어 바뚜 보씨 부 바꽈아아꽈 궈머러라오, 시 바 오꼬 아너러시서 어 미시 오싸오.

---

6. So they are no longer two, but one. Therefore what God has joined together, let man not separate."

7. "Why then," they asked, "did Moses command that a man give his wife a certificate of divorce and send her away?"

8. Jesus replied, "Moses permitted you to divorce your wives because your hearts were hard. But it was not this way from the beginning.

9. I tell you that anyone who divorces his wife, except for marital unfaithfulness, and marries another woman commits adultery."

10. The disciples said to him, "If this is the situation between a husband and wife, it is better not to marry."

11. Jesus replied, "Not everyone can accept this word, but only those to whom it has been given.

12. Bushi n'oku, bandju bauma katangaala kuhwera bushi babuchwaa balyi ngone. E banji batahwera bushi e bandju babailyire ngone. Kulyi na banji ba bachinjire kuhwera bushi n'e kukorera e bwami b'okwa nguba. Rero, ola ungaala kwemerera oyu mwasi, emereraao.

12. 부씨 노구, 바뀨 바우마 가다ㄲ아아롸 구훠라 부씨 바부쫘아 바뤠 잉너. 어 바띠 바다훠라 부씨 어 바뀨 바바이뤠러 잉너. 구뤠 나 바띠 바 바찌띠러 구훠라 부씨 너 구고러라 어 봐미 보과 ㅇ우바. 러로, 오롸 우ㄲ아아롸 궈머러라 오유 뫄시, 어머러라아오.

12. For some are eunuchs because they were born that way; others were made that way by men; and others have renounced marriagebecause of the kingdom of heaven. The one who can accept this should accept it."

Yesu aahanyira e bana batoto

여수 아아하네띱 어 바나 바도도

13. Chasinda, bandju bauma bera kuretera Yesu e bana batoto chasiya ababike kw'e mino mwa kubemera. Si e banafunzi bai, bera kukalyiira abu bandju.

13. 짜시따, 바뀨 바우마 버라 구러더라 여수 어 바나 바도도 짜시야 아바비거 궈 미노 뫄 구버머라. 시 어 바나푸띠 바이, 버라 구가뤠이라 아부 바뀨.

13. Then little children were brought to Jesus for him to place his hands on them and pray for them. But the disciples rebuked those who brought them.

14. Yesu kukwera kubura abu banafunzi bai mbu: Murekaa e bana batoto babahe era nyilyi, mutendaa mwabangika, bushi e bandju ba balyi nga bano bana batoto, bu besha e bwami b'okwa nguba.

14. 여수 구궈라 구부라 아부 바나푸띠 바이 뿌: 무러가아 어 바나 바도도 바바허 어라 네뤠, 무더따아 뫄바ㄲ이가, 부씨 어 바뀨 바 바뤠 ㄲ아 바노 바나 바도도, 부 버싸 어 봐미 보과 ㅇ우바.

14. Jesus said, "Let the little children come to me, and do not hinder them, for the kingdom of heaven belongs to such as these."

15. Yesu era kuahanyira abu bana mwa kubabika kw'e mino. Chasinjire, era kutenga mw'echi chisiki.

15. 여수 어라 구아하네라 아부 바나 뫄 구바비가 궈 미노. 짜시찌러, 어라 구더ㄲ아 뭐찌 찌시기.

15. When he had placed his hands on them, he went on from there.

Yesu ateta era luulu s'e buare n'e bwami bwa Ongo

여수 아더다 어라 루읍루 서 부아러 너 봐미 봐 오ㅇ오

16. Era nyuma s'ebi, mutabana muuma era kuikira

16. 어라 뉴마 서비, 무다바나 무우마 어라 구이기라 여수,

16. Now a man came up to Jesus and asked,

yesu, era kumubusa mbu: Mukangilyisi, mabuya machiye mu nyemire kuira, chasiya nyibone e kalamo k'e suku n'e mango?

17. Yesu nai mbu: Chi chachwuma wanyibusa era luulu s'e mabuya? Si kunalyi muuma oshao iuchwula mubuya! Rero, akaba wahonda kwingilyira mwa kalamo k'e kunalyi, undaa wachwunda e miomba ya Ongo.

18. Oyu mutabana era kumubusa mbu: Mwaso muchiye kasi? Yesu na imbu: utendaa weta, utendaa waira lusingi utendaa weba, utendaa wafula bisha,

19. Undaa wachwunda eho na nyoko, na kusima e banji ng'okwa uchwula uchisimire weine.

20. Wamutabana na imbu: Ei miomba yoshi, n'elyisa nende naichwunda. Chiye cha nyemire kuhuba kuira?

21. Yesu nai mbu: akaba wahonda kuba mundju ola ulumilyire, uyaa kuusa e bindju byao byoshi, n'e buteya bwa bingafa, wanaabirabo e bakene. Ukaira bacha, ungaba elyi

---

어라 구무부사 뿌: 무가ᄲᅦ시, 마부야 마찌여 무 녀미러 구이라, 짜시야 네보너 어 가꽈모 거 수구 너 마ᄋᆞ?

17. 여수 나이 뿌: 찌 짜쭘마 와네부사 어라 루우루루 서 마부야? 시 구나쩨 무우마 오싸오 이우쭈라 무부야! 러로, 아가바 와호따 귀ᄲᅦ쩨라 마 가꽈모 거 구나쩨, 우따아 와쭈따 어 미오빠 야 오ᄋᆞ.

18. 오유 무다바나 어라 구무부사 뿌: 뫄소 무찌여 가시? 여수 나 이뿌: 우더따아 워다, 우더따아 와이라 루시ᄲᅵ 우더따아 워바, 우더따아 와푸꽈 비싸,

19. 우따아 와쭈따 어호 나 뇨고, 나 구시마 어 바찌 ᄆᆞ오과 우쭈꽈 우찌시미러 워이너.

20. 와무다바나 나 이뿌: 어이 미오빠 요씨, 너쩨사 너떠 나이쭈따. 찌여 짜 녀미러 구후바 구이라?

21. 여수 나이 뿌: 아가바 와호따 구바 무뚜 오꽈 우루미쩨러, 우야아 구우사 어 비뿌 뱌오 뵤씨, 너 부더야 봐 비까파, 와나아비라보 어 바거너. 우가이라 바짜, 우까바 어쩨 와비기리뤄 어 뫄뚜 과

"Teacher, what good thing must I do to get eternal life?"

17. "Why do you ask me about what is good?" Jesus replied. "There is only One who is good. If you want to enter life, obey the commandments."

18. "Which ones?" the man inquired. Jesus replied, " 'Do not murder, do not commit adultery, do not steal, do not give false testimony,

19. honor your father and mother,' and 'love your neighbor as yourself.'"

20. "All these I have kept," the young man said. "What do I still lack?"

21. Jesus answered, "If you want to be perfect, go, sell your possessions and give to the poor, and you will have treasure in heaven. Then come, follow me."

wabikirirwe e mwandju kwa nguba. Chasinda, wanere wabaha kunyikulyikira.

ᄋ구바. 짜시따, 와너러 와바하 구네구ᄙᅦ기라.

22. Ola mutabana omvire bacha, era kuchiendera na businane bunene bushi abaa ete bikulo binene busese.

22. 오ᄙᅡ 무다바나 오삐러 바짜, 어라 구쩌떠라 나 부시나너 부너너 부씨 아바아 어더 비구ᄙᅩ 비너너 부서서.

22. When the young man heard this, he went away sad, because he had great wealth.

23. Yesu era kwire abura e banafunzi bai mbu: Kubinalyi, nababura kwa kukoochire busese kwa muare kwingilyira mwa bwami b'okwa nguba!

23. 여수 어라 귀러 아부라 어 바나푸ᄡᅵ 바이 ᄜᅮ: 구비나ᄙᅦ, 나바부라 과 구고오찌러 부서서 과 무아러 귀ᅌ이ᄙᅦ라 뫄 봐미 보과 ᄋ구바!

23. Then Jesus said to his disciples, "I tell you the truth, it is hard for a rich man to enter the kingdom of heaven.

24. Kanji nababura kwa kusibuire e ngamiya kurenga mwa chichwure ch'e singe, si kanji kusibuire busese kwa muare kwingilyira mwa bwami bwa Ongo!

24. 가ᄡᅵ 나바부라 과 구시부이러 어 ᅌ아미야 구러ᅌ아 뫄 찌쭈러 쩌 시ᅌ어, 시 가ᄡᅵ 구시부이러 부서서 과 무아러 귀ᅌ이ᄙᅦ라 뫄 봐미 봐 오ᄋ고!

24. Again I tell you, it is easier for a camel to go through the eye of a needle than for a rich man to enter the kingdom of God."

25. E banafunzi bomvire bacha, bera kusanwa busese. Bera kutangilyisa bateta mbu: Ewashe! Rero mundju muchiye ola unganunulyibwa?

25. 어 바나푸ᄡᅵ 보삐러 바짜, 버라 구사놔 부서서. 버라 구다ᅌ이ᄙᅦ사 바더다 ᄜᅮ: 어와써! 러로 무ᄂ주 무찌여 오ᄙᅡ 우ᅌ아누누ᄙᅦ봐?

25. When the disciples heard this, they were greatly astonished and asked, "Who then can be saved?"

26. Yesu era kubachwumbukisa na ababura mbu: oyu mwasi atangaalyikana kwa bandju, si era mwa Ongo, byoshi byende byaalyikana.

26. 여수 어라 구바쭈ᄜᅮ기사 나 아바부라 ᄜᅮ: 오유 뫄시 아다ᅌ아아ᄙᅦ가나 과 바ᄂ주, 시 어라 뫄 오ᄋ고, 뵤씨 벼ᄕᅥ 뱌아ᄙᅦ가나.

26. Jesus looked at them and said, "With man this is impossible, but with God all things are possible."

27. Petero kukwera kumubusa mbu: Enawechwu, ulolaa! chwubano chwarekire byoshi chwakukulyikira. Rero, chiye chi chwukabona?

27. 퍼더로 구궈라 구무부사 ᄜᅮ: 어나워쭈, 우ᄙᅩᄙᅡ아! 쭈바노 쫘러기러 뵤씨 쫘구구ᄙᅦ기라. 러로, 찌여 찌 쭈가보나?

27. Peter answered him, "We have left everything to follow you! What then will there be for us?"

28. Yesu era kubakula mbu: kubinalyi, mwa butala buyayaya nyi mwana w'e mundju nyikekala kwa ndebe yanyi y'e bulangare. N'enyu kwa munalyi ekumi na babilyi, mu mwanyikulyikiraa mukekala kwa bifumbi ekumi na bibilyi by'e bwami, kwa kuchinjibusa embaa ekumi n'ebilyi s'e baisiraeli.

29. Na chira mundju ola warekire e nyumba yai, nesi banyakabo, nesi balyiwabo, nesi eshe, nesi nyina, nesi e bana bai, nesi ehwa lyai bushi nanyi, akabona lwembo lunene ku kalyi eyana kw'ebya arekire. Chasinda, akabona n'e kalamo k'e suku n'e mango.

30. Bushi n'oku, banene mwaba balyi babere-bere lwarero, bakaba basinda-sinda. Na banene mwaba balyi basinda-sinda lwarero, bakaba babere-bere.

28. 여수 어라 구바구롸 뿌: 구비나레, 롸 부다롸 부야야야 네 뫄나 워 무뚜 네거가롸 과 떠버 야니 여 부롸따러. 너뉴 과 무나레 어구미 나 바비레, 무 뫄네구레기라아 무거가롸 과 비푸삐 어구미 나 비비레 벼 봐미, 과 구찌찌부사 어빠아 어구미 너비레 서 바이시라어뤼.

29. 나 찌라 무뚜 오롸 와러기러 어 뉴빠 야이, 너시 바냐가보, 너시 바레와보, 너시 어써, 너시 내나, 너시 어 바나 바이, 너시 어화 롸이 부씨 나네, 아가보나 뤄뫃 루너너 구 가레 어야나 궈뱌 아러기러. 짜시따, 아가보나 너 가롸모 거 수구 너 마꼬.

30. 부씨 노구, 바너너 뫄바 바레 바버러-버러 롸러로, 바가바 바시따-시따. 나 바너너 뫄바 바레 바시따-시따 롸러로, 바가바 바버러-버러.

28. Jesus said to them, "I tell you the truth, at the renewal of all things, when the Son of Man sits on his glorious throne, you who have followed me will also sit on twelve thrones, judging the twelve tribes of Israel.

29. And everyone who has left houses or brothers or sisters or father or mother or children or fields for my sake will receive a hundred times as much and will inherit eternal life.

30. But many who are first will be last, and many who are last will be first.

Matayo Chikono 20
E muanyi w'e bakosi b'o mw'ehwa ly'e misabibu
1. E bwami b'okwa nguba buhuhanyisibwe n'ono

마다요 찌고노 20
어 무아네 워 바고시 보 뭐화 려 미사비부
1. 어 봐미 보과 응바 부후하네시붜 노노 무아네 :

Matthew Chapter 20[NIV]

1. "For the kingdom of heaven is like a landowner

muanyi : kwabaa mundju muuma ola wabaa wete ehwa lya misabibu. Oyu mundju, era kuchiuma lumbulyi-mbulyi aya kuhonda bandju ba kukola mw'elyi ehwa lyai.

2. Era kulaana nabo kwa angende emba chira mundju chikoroto chiuma cha buteya bwa dinari ku lusuku luuma. Chasinda era kubachwuma mw'ehwa lyai.

3. Abere mwa saa ehachwu s'e mishangya-shangya, era kuhuba kuchiuma. Era kulola ku banji bandju balyi mwa nama busira mulyimo asibya.

4. Era kubabura mbu: Nenyu muyaa kukola mw'ehwa lyanyi ly'e misabibu, nyingabemba ng'okwa binemire.

5. Chasinda, bera kuchiuma. Abere e suba limenzi, kanji era kuchiuma na achwuma banji bandju mw'ehwa lyai. Mango sabaa sera saa mwenda samushi era kunahuba kuira bacha.

6. Abere mwa saa ekumi na nguma s'e luolo-olo, kanji era kuchiuma, era kulola ku banji bandju balyi mwa nama. Era kubabusa mbu: Ewashe! chi chichwumire mwamala

과바아 무뚜 무우마 오라 와바아 워더 어화 랴 미사비부. 오유 무뚜, 어라 구찌우마 루뿌레-뿌레 아야 구호따 바뚜 바 구고롸 뭐레 어화 랴이.

2. 어라 구롸아나 나보 과 아뻐더 어빠 찌라 무뚜 찌고로도 찌우마 짜 부더야 봐 디나리 구 루수구 루우마. 짜시따 어라 구바쭈마 뭐화 랴이.

3. 아버러 롸 사아 어하쭈 서 미싸꺄-싸꺄, 어라 구후바 구찌우마. 어라 구롣롸 구 바찌 바뚜 바레 롸 나마 부시라 무레모 아시뱌.

4. 어라 구바부라 뿌: 너뉴 무야아 구고롸 뭐화 랴네 려 미사비부, 네꺄버빠 꾸오과 비너미러.

5. 짜시따, 버라 구찌우마. 아버러 어 수바 리머씨, 가찌 어라 구찌우마 나 아쭈마 바찌 바뚜 뭐화 랴이. 마꼬 사바아 서라 사아 뭐따 사무씨 어라 구나후바 구이라 바짜.

6. 아버러 롸 사아 어구미 나 꾸마 서 루오롣-오르, 가찌 어라 구찌우마, 어라 구롣롸 구 바찌 바뚜 바레 롸 나마. 어라 구바부사 뿌: 어와써! 찌 찌쭈미러 롸마롸 어무러어러러

who went out early in the morning to hire men to work in his vineyard.

2. He agreed to pay them a denarius for the day and sent them into his vineyard.

3. "About the third hour he went out and saw others standing in the marketplace doing nothing.

4. He told them, 'You also go and work in my vineyard, and I will pay you whatever is right.'

5. So they went. "He went out again about the sixth hour and the ninth hour and did the same thing.

6. About the eleventh hour he went out and found still others standing around. He asked them, 'Why have you been standing here all day long

emureerere woshi anola busira mulyimo usibya?

7. Nabo mbu: Bushi kutalyi mundju ola wachweresise mulyimo. Nai mbu: Nenyu, muyaa kukola mw'ehwa lyanyi.

8. Abere lwera luolo-olo, oyu en'ehwa era kubura e mwemangisi w'e mulyimo wai mbu: wamaala e bakosi, waneresa chira mundju elwai lwembo. N'omwa kubemba, utangilyiraa kwa basinda-sinda, wanasinjira kwa babere-bere.

9. Ba bakosi ba bengilyiraa mwa mulyimo mwa saa ekumi na nguma s'e luolo-olo, bera kuika. chira muuma era kubona chikoroto chiuma cha buteya.

10. Ba babatangilyisaa e mulyimo e mishangya-shangya nabo, bera kuika. bera kuchichinga mbu beke bangeresibwa mwango munene. si Nabo, chira mundju era kunabona chikoroto chiuma cha buteya oshao.

11. Abere bera babonaa olu lwembo, bera kuata buyongwa bunene bushi na en'ehwa mwa kuteta mbu:

오씨 아노꽈 부시라 무뤠모 우시뱌?

7. 나보 뿌: 부씨 구다뤠 무뚜 오꽈 와쮀러시서 무뤠모. 나이 뿌: 너뉴, 무야아 구고꽈 뭐화 랴니.

8. 아버러 뤄라 루오뢴-오뢴, 오유 어너화 어라 구부라 어 뭐마삐시 워 무뤠모 와이 뿌: 와마아꽈 어 바고시, 와너러사 찌라 무뚜 어꽈이 뤄뽀. 노롸 구버빠, 우다삐레라아 과 바시따-시따, 와나시찌라 과 바버러-버러.

9. 바 바고시 바 버삐레라아 롸 무뤠모 롸 사아 어구미 나 응마 서 루오뢴-오뢴, 버라 구이가. 찌라 무우마 어라 구보나 찌고로도 찌우마 짜 부더야.

10. 바 바바다삐뤠사아 어 무뤠모 어 미싸꺄-싸꺄 나보, 버라 구이가. 버라 구찌찌꽈 뿌 버거 바뤄러시봐 롸꼬 무너너. 시 나보, 찌라 무뚜 어라 구나보나 찌고로도 찌우마 짜 부더야 오싸오.

11. 아버러 버라 바보나아 오루 뤄뽀, 버라 구아다 부요꽈 부너너 부씨 나 어너화 롸 구더다 뿌:

---

doing nothing?'

7. " 'Because no one has hired us,' they answered. "He said to them, 'You also go and work in my vineyard.'

8. "When evening came, the owner of the vineyard said to his foreman, 'Call the workers and pay them their wages, beginning with the last ones hired and going on to the first.'

9. "The workers who were hired about the eleventh hour came and each received a denarius.

10. So when those came who were hired first, they expected to receive more. But each one of them also received a denarius.

11. When they received it, they began to grumble against the landowner.

12. Era! Bano bakosi wera wanasindaa kubika mwa mulyimo, si saa nguma ibanakolyire oshao! Rero, kute ungabemba kuuma nechwu, n'oku chwatamire chwakola e murerere woshi kw'e suba lyikalyiire bacha?

13. Si en'ehwa era kuakula muuma mubo mbu: E mwira wanyi, ndakukangire! Si chwalaana kwa ungakorera chikoroto chiuma cha buteya!

14. Rero, tolaa e lwembo lwao, unaende! Byanyisimisaa nyeine kweresa e mukosi ola wasinda kuika e lwembo lwa lunalyi ng'e lwao.

15. Weke waanyisise mbu ndete e buashi bw'e kukoresa e bikulo byanyi ng'okwa nyinahonjire? Nesi, wafire mufula bushi nyilyi mundju mubuya?

16. Yesu era kuteta kanji mbu: Kubinalyi, ba balyi basinda-sinda bakaba babere-bere. Na ba balyi babere-bere, bakaba basinda-sinda.

Yesu ateta e bwakahachwu era lulu s'e kufa n'e kwomoka kwai

12. 어라! 바노 바고시 워라 와나시따아 구비가 먀 무레모, 시 사아 꾸마 이바나고레러 오싸오! 러로, 구더 우까버빠 구우마 너쭈, 노구 쫘다미러 쫘고라 어 무러러러 오씨 궈 수바 레가레이러 바짜?

13. 시 어너화 어라 구아구꽈 무우마 무보 뿌: 어 뮈라 와니, 따구가끼러! 시 쫘라아나 과 우까고러라 찌고로도 찌우마 짜 부더야!

14. 러로, 도라아 어 뤄뽀 쫘오, 우나어떠! 뱌네시미사아 녀이너 궈러사 어 무고시 오롸 와시따 구이가 어 뤄뽀 쫘 루나레 꾸어 쫘오.

15. 워거 와아네시서 뿌 떠더 어 부아씨 붜 구고러사 어 비구롣 뱌네 꾸오과 네나호찌러? 너시, 와피러 무푸롸 부씨 네레 무뉴 무부야?

16. 여수 어라 구더다 가찌 뿌: 구비나레, 바 바레 바시따-시따 바가바 바버러-버러. 나 바 바레 바버러-버러, 바가바 바시따-시따.

여수 아더다 어 봐가하쭈 어라 루루 서 구파 너 굠명— 과이

12. 'These men who were hired last worked only one hour,' they said, 'and you have made them equal to us who have borne the burden of the work and the heat of the day.'

13. "But he answered one of them, 'Friend, I am not being unfair to you. Didn't you agree to work for a denarius?

14. Take your pay and go. I want to give the man who was hired last the same as I gave you.

15. Don't I have the right to do what I want with my own money? Or are you envious because I am generous?'

16. "So the last will be first, and the first will be last."

17. Lusuku luuma, Yesu abaa alyi mwa njira y'e kwerukira mwa musi w'e yeresulamu. Era kutola e banafunzi bai ekumi na babilyi na abeka ala musike. Era kubabura mbu:

18. Mumenyaa! chwabo bano chwahonda kwerukira mwa musi w'e yerusalemu. Mw'oyu musi, nyi mwana w'e mundju nyinganyibwa mwa uino s'e bakulu-kulu b'e bakuhanyi, n'e bakangilyisi b'e mwaso. Abu bandju, banganyichinjibusa chasiya nyichibwe.

19. Kanji banganyana mwa mino s'e bandju ba bateshi Ongo, nabo banganyishekera na kunyipunda busese mwa chwuchi. Chasinda, banganyimanyika kwa musalaba. Si e lusuku lwa kahachwu, nyingomwoka.

Muka sebetayo emera e baala e bukulu-kulu

20. Era nyuma s'ebi, muka Sebetayo alauma na baala baikiraa Yesu. Wamukasi era kukoma e mafi era muhondo sa Yesu amwema mwasi muuma.

21. Yesu era kumubusa mbu: Mango ungaba mwa bwami

17. 루수구 루우마, 여수 아바아 아례 똬 찌라 여 궈루기라 똬 무시 워 여러수롸무. 어라 구도롸 어 바나푸씨 바이 어구미 나 바비레 나 아버가 아롸 무시거. 어라 구바부라 뿌:

18. 무머냐아! 좌보 바노 좌호따 궈루기라 똬 무시 워 여루사러무. 모유 무시, 니 뫄나 워 무뚜 네빠네봐 똬 우이노 서 바구루루-구루 버 바구하네, 너 바가삐레시 버 똬소. 아부 바뚜, 바빠네찌찌부사 짜시야 네찌붜.

19. 가찌 바빠냐나 똬 미노 서 바뚜 바 바더씨 오꼬, 나보 바빠네써거라 나 구네푸따 부서서 똬 쭈찌. 짜시따, 바빠네마네가 꽈 무사롸바. 시 어 루수구 롸 가하쭈, 네꼬모가.

무가 서버다요 어머라 어 바아롸 어 부구루루-구루

20. 어라 뉴마 서비, 무가 서버다요 아롸우마 나 바아롸 바이기라아 여수. 와무가시 어라 구고마 어 마피 어라 무호또 사 여수 아뭐마 똬시 무우마.

21. 여수 어라 구무부사 뿌: 마꼬 우빠바 똬 봐미 봐오,

17. Now as Jesus was going up to Jerusalem, he took the twelve disciples aside and said to them,

18. "We are going up to Jerusalem, and the Son of Man will be betrayed to the chief priests and the teachers of the law. They will condemn him to death

19. and will turn him over to the Gentiles to be mocked and flogged and crucified. On the third day he will be raised to life!"

20. Then the mother of Zebedee's sons came to Jesus with her sons and, kneeling down, asked a favor of him.

21. "What is it you want?" he asked. She said, "Grant

bwao, wemereraa kwa bano
baala banyi babilyi, bu
bangekala ofu nau. Muuma
kwa lunda lw'e malyo, n'e
unji kwa lw'e marembe.
22. Yesu nai mbu: Ebi
mwenjire mwanyema,
mutabishi. Mungaala kumwa
e ngumbu y'e malyibuko era
nyingamwa? Nabo mbu:
Nechi, chwungaala.
23. Yesu era kubabura mbu:
Kubinalyi, ei ngumbu
munganamwai! Si, e kuikasa
e bandju kwa lunda lwanyi
lw'e malyo, nesi lw'e
marembe, bitanyerekere. Ba
bakekala mw'ebi bisiki, tata
yeine abakunganyisisebi mira.
24. Mango abu banji
banafunzi ekumi bomvaa
bacha, bera kuyongwa
busese bushi n'abu bana
babilyi ba Sebetayo.
25. Bushi n'oku, Yesu kukwera
kwamaala e banafunzi boshi
alauma, na ababura mbu:
Mwishi kwa mwa bandju b'e
sinji mbaa, e balyi bende
babalyibusa.
26. Si bitendaa byaba bacha
mwa kachi-kachi kenyu.
Mumenyaa kwa ola wahonda
kuba mukulu-kulu mu

워머러라아 과 바노 바아꽈
바네 바비쩨, 부 바꺼가꽈
오푸 나우. 무우마 과 룬따 뤄
마룐, 너 우찌 과 뤄 마러뼈.
22. 여수 나이 뿌: 어비 뭐찌러
먀녀마, 무다비씨. 무꺼아꽈
구꽈 어 웅뿌 여 마쩨부고
어라 니꺼먀? 나보 뿌: 너찌,
쭈꺼아꽈.
23. 여수 어라 구바부라 뿌:
구비나쩨, 어이 웅뿌
무꺼나마이! 시, 어 구이가사
어 바쭈 과 룬따 꽌네 뤄
마룐, 너시 뤄 마러뼈,
비다녀러거러. 바 바거가꽈
뭐비 비시기, 다다 여이너
아바구꺼네시서비 미라.
24. 마꼬 아부 바찌 바나푸씨
어구미 보빠아 바짜, 버라
구요꽈 부서서 부씨 나부 바나
바비쩨 바 서버다요.
25. 부씨 노구, 여수 구궈라
과마아꽈 어 바나푸씨 보씨
아꽈우마, 나 아바부라 뿌:
뮈씨 과 먀 바쭈 버 시찌
빠아, 어 바쩨 버너
바바쩨부사.
26. 시 비더따아 뱌바 바짜 먀
가찌-가찌 거뉴. 무머냐아 과
오꽈 와호따 구바 무구룹-구룹
무 뫄보, 어미러 구바 무아따

that one of these two sons
of mine may sit at your
right and the other at your
left in your kingdom."
22. "You don't know what
you are asking," Jesus said
to them. "Can you drink
the cup I am going to
drink?" "We can," they
answered.
23. Jesus said to them,
"You will indeed drink
from my cup, but to sit at
my right or left is not for
me to grant. These places
belong to those for whom
they have been prepared
by my Father."
24. When the ten heard
about this, they were
indignant with the two
brothers.
25. Jesus called them
together and said, "You
know that the rulers of the
Gentiles lord it over them,
and their high officials
exercise authority over
them.
26. Not so with you.
Instead, whoever wants to
become great among you
must be your servant,

mwabo, emire kuba muanda wenyu.

27. Kanji ola wahonda kuba mubere-bere mu mwabo, kwemire ende abakorera.	27. 가찌 오롸 와호따 구바 무버러-버러 무 뫄보, 줘미러 어떠 아바고러라.	27. and whoever wants to be first must be your slave--
28. Bushi nyi mwana w'e mundju ndabahaa chasiya bende banyikorera, si nabahaa kwa kunde nakorera e banji na kwana e kalamo kanyi, chasiya nyinunule bandju banene.	28. 부씨 네 뫄나 워 무뚜 따바하아 짜시야 버떠 바네고러라, 시 나바하아 과 구떠 나고러라 어 바찌 나 과나 어 가꽈모 가네, 짜시야 네누누뤄 바뚜 바너너.	28. just as the Son of Man did not come to be served, but to serve, and to give his life as a ransom for many."

Yesu alamya bauta babilyi   *여수 아꽈맺 바우다 바비례*

29. Abere Yesu n'e banafunzi bai bera batenga mwa musi w'e yeriko, bandju banene busese bera kumukulyikira.	29. 아버러 여수 너 바나푸씨 바이 버라 바더따 뫄 무시 워 여리고, 바뚜 바너너 부서서 버라 구무구쩨기라.	29. As Jesus and his disciples were leaving Jericho, a large crowd followed him.
30. Kwa musike s'e njira, kwabaa kwekese bauta babilyi. Abu bauta, mango bomvaa kwa Yesu iwarenga, bera kuchilakangira mbu: Enawechwu, mwenyi daudi! Uchwufiraa bonjo!	30. 과 무시거 서 띠라, 과바아 줘거서 바우다 바비례. 아부 바우다, 마꼬 보빠아 과 여수 이와러따, 버라 구찌꽈가꺼라 뿌: 어나워쭈, 뭐네 다우디! 우쭈피라아 보쪼!	30. Two blind men were sitting by the roadside, and when they heard that Jesus was going by, they shouted, "Lord, Son of David, have mercy on us!"
31. Mango e bandju bomvaa bacha, bera kubakalyiira mbu basiraa. Si abu bauta, bera kunaendekera balakanga mbu: Enawechwu, mwenyi Daudi! Uchwufiraa bonjo!	31. 마꼬 어 바뚜 보빠아 바짜, 버라 구바가께이라 뿌 바시라아. 시 아부 바우다, 버라 구나어떠거라 바꽈가꼬 뿌: 어나워쭈, 뭐네 다우디! 우쭈피라아 보쪼!	31. The crowd rebuked them and told them to be quiet, but they shouted all the louder, "Lord, Son of David, have mercy on us!"
32. Yesu era kwire emanga na amaalabo. Era kubabusa mbu: Ewashe! Chi mwahonda nyibailyire?	32. 여수 어라 귀러 어마따 나 아마아꽈보. 어라 구바부사 뿌: 어와써! 찌 뫄호따 네바이께러?	32. Jesus stopped and called them. "What do you want me to do for you?" he asked.

33. Nabo mbu: Enawechwu, chwahonda e meho mechwu masibukale.

34. Yesu era kubafira bonjo, era kubauma kwa meho, unao-unao e meho mabo kuna kusibukala. Chasinjire, nabo bera kumukulyikira.

33. 나보 뿌: 어나워쭈, 좌호따어 머호 머쭈 마시부가뻐.

34. 여수 어라 구바피라 보쪼, 어라 구바우마 과 머호, 우나오-우나오 어 머호 마보 구나 구시부가뻐. 짜시찌러, 나보 버라 구무구레기라.

33. "Lord," they answered, "we want our sight."

34. Jesus had compassion on them and touched their eyes. Immediately they received their sight and followed him.

Matayo Chikono 21
Yesu engilyira mwa musi w'e yerusalemu

1. Mango Yesu n'e banafunzi bai babaa bera balyi ofu n'e musi w'e Yerusalemu, bera kuika mwa w'e Betefake, ofu n'e ndjulungu y'e Miseituni. Yesu era kuchwuma banafunzi babilyi,

2. era kubabura mbu: Muyaa mwa musi ulyi era muhondo senyu. Mango mungaikamo, unao-unao mugabuana ndokomu nguma n'e chana chai biminyilyirwe alauma. Esi ndokomu, muboolasi, chasinda mwananyireterasi.

3. Na kukaba mundju ola ungababusa mwasi era lulu sesi ndokomu, mwanamwakula mbu enawechwu ete bweera bwasi. Unao-unao, oyu mumdju angabareka muende nasi.

마다요 찌고노 21
여수 어삐레띱 롸 무시 워 여루사뻐물

1. 마꼬 여수 너 바나푸씨 바이 바바아 버라 바께 오푸 너 무시 워 여루사뻐무, 버라 구이가 롸 워 버더파게, 오푸 너 뚜루우우 여 미서이두니. 여수 어라 구쭈마 바나푸씨 바비께,

2. 어라 구바부라 뿌: 무야아 롸 무시 우께 어라 무호또 서뉴. 마꼬 무빠이가모, 우나오-우나오 무가부아나 또고무 우마 너 짜나 짜이 비미네께뤄 아롸우마. 어시 또고무, 무보오롸시, 짜시따 롸나네러더라시.

3. 나 구가바 무뚜 오롸 우빠바부사 롸시 어라 루루 서시 또고무, 롸나롸구롸 뿌 어나워쭈 어더 붜어라 봐시. 우나오-우나오, 오유 무무주 아빠바러가 무어떠 나시.

Matthew Chapter 21[NIV]

1. As they approached Jerusalem and came to Bethphage on the Mount of Olives, Jesus sent two disciples,

2. saying to them, "Go to the village ahead of you, and at once you will find a donkey tied there, with her colt by her. Untie them and bring them to me.

3. If anyone says anything to you, tell him that the Lord needs them, and he will send them right away."

4. Ebyera byabaa bacha, chasiya cha chinwa chiberere cha enawechwu atetaa kurengera emurebi mbu:

4. 어벼라 뱌바아 바짜, 짜시야4. 짜 찌놔 찌버러러 짜 어나워쭈 아더다아 구러써라 어무러비 뿌:

4. This took place to fulfill what was spoken through the prophet:

5. Muburaa besha mwa musi w'e Sayunu mbu: Mulolaa, e mwami wenyu abahire ene mwenyu. Alyi mulomvu, kanji ekese kwa ndokomu. Nei ndokomu, chichilyi chana.

5. 무부라아 버싸 뫄 무시 워 사유누 뿌: 무로똬아, 어 뫄미 워뉴 아바히러 어너 뭐뉴. 아쩨 무로뿌, 가찌 어거서 과 또고무. 너이 또고무, 찌찌쩨 짜나.

5. "Say to the Daughter of Zion, 'See, your king comes to you, gentle and riding on a donkey, on a colt, the foal of a donkey.'"

6. Abu banafunzi bai babilyi, bera kuchiuma na baira ngokwa Yesu anababuraa.

6. 아부 바나푸씨 바이 바비쩨, 버라 구찌우마 나 바이라 꼬과 여수 아나바부라아.

6. The disciples went and did as Jesus had instructed them.

7. Bera kunareta ei ndokomu alauma n'e chana chai. Bera kuhashika kw'e makochi mabo, chasinda Yesu era kwire ekala kui.

7. 버라 구나러다 어이 또고무 아퐈우마 너 짜나 짜이. 버라 구하씨가 궈 마고찌 마보, 짜시따 여수 어라 귀러 어가퐈 구이.

7. They brought the donkey and the colt, placed their cloaks on them, and Jesus sat on them.

8. Bandju banene busese bera kuhashikanga e njimba sabo mwa njira, n'e banji bera kuishanga e mangarara bera kumahashikanga mwa njira.

8. 바쭈 바너너 부서서 버라 구하씨가꺄 어 찌빠 사보 뫄 찌라, 너 바찌 버라 구이싸꺄 어 마꺄라라 버라 구마하씨가꺄 뫄 찌라.

8. A very large crowd spread their cloaks on the road, while others cut branches from the trees and spread them on the road.

9. E bandju ba babaa bahondorere Yesu n'e banji ba babaa bamukulyikire, berakutangilyisa bateta na murenge munene mbu: "Hosana, Mwenyi Daudi! Ongo aahanyiraa ono weshire kw'e sina lyai! Ongo atongwe kwa nguba!

9. 어 바쭈 바 바바아 바호또러러 여수 너 바찌 바 바바아 바무구쩨기러, 버라구다쁴쩨사 바더다 나 무러쩌 무너너 뿌: "호사나, 뭐네 다우디! 오꼬 아아하네라아 오노 워씨러 궈 시나 퍄이! 오꼬 아도워 과 우바!

9. The crowds that went ahead of him and those that followed shouted, "Hosanna to the Son of David!" "Blessed is he who comes in the name of the Lord!" "Hosanna in the highest!"

10. Mango Yesu abaa era engilyiraa mwa musi w'e yerusalemu, oyu musi woshi era kuba mu lwayo lunene. E bandju bera kutangilyisa babusanya mbu: Ewashe! inde ono?

11. Eluamba lw'e bandju ba babaa balyi na Yesu bera kuakula mbu: Onola, I Yesu, murebi womwa musi w'e Nasareti, mwa chio ch'e Kalilaya.

Yesu akolokanya e bachimbusi mwa luhu lwa Ongo

12. Chasinda, Yesu era kuigira mwa chibuwa ch'e luhu lwa Ongo. Aikiremo, era kubuana e bandju ba babaa bausa, n'e banji baula. Abu boshi, era kubakolokanya. Ba babaa bainganyanga e buteya, era kubindjulanga e mesa mabo, era kubindjulanga n'e bifumbi by'e bandju ba babaa bausa e biruka.

13. Chasinda, era kubabura mbu: e Maanjiko Mabuya-buya matechire mbu: E nyumba yanyi ikende yelyikibwa mbu nyumba ya memo. Si mwabo, mwaihubise nyumba ya bihumisi!

10. 마꼬 여수 아바아 어라 어삐레라아 뫄 무시 워 여루사뻐무, 오유 무시 올씨 어라 구바 무 쫘요 루너너. 어 바뉴 버라 구다삐레사 바부사냐 뿌: 어와써! 이떠 오노?

11. 어루아빠 뤄 바뉴 바 바바아 바레 나 여수 버라 구아구롸 뿌: 오노라, 이 여수, 무러비 오뫄 무시 워 나사러디, 뫄 찌오 쩌 가삐롸야.

여수 아고쪼—냇 어 바찌뿌습 뫄 루훌 롸 오꼬

12. 짜시따, 여수 어라 구이지라 뫄 찌부와 쩌 루후 롸 오꼬. 아이기러모, 어라 구부아나 어 바뉴 바 바바아 바우사, 너 바찌 바우롸. 아부 보씨, 어라 구바고쪼가냐. 바 바바아 바이아냐꺄 어 부더야, 어라 구비뿌롸꺄 어 머사 마보, 어라 구비뿌롸꺄 너 비푸쎄 벼 바뉴 바 바바아 바우사 어 비루가.

13. 짜시따, 어라 구바부라 뿌: 어 마아찌고 마부야-부야 마더찌러 뿌: 어 뉴빠 야니 이거떠 여레기봐 뿌 뉴빠 야 머모. 시 뫄보, 마이후비서 뉴빠 야 비후미시!

10. When Jesus entered Jerusalem, the whole city was stirred and asked, "Who is this?"

11. The crowds answered, "This is Jesus, the prophet from Nazareth in Galilee."

12. Jesus entered the temple area and drove out all who were buying and selling there. He overturned the tables of the money changers and the benches of those selling doves.

13. "It is written," he said to them, " 'My house will be called a house of prayer,' but you are making it a 'den of robbers.'"

14. Mwa chibuwa ch'olu luhu, bauta bauma na bireme, bera kuikira yesu. Nai, era kubalamya.

15. Si e bakulu-kulu b'e bakuhanyi, n'e bakangilyisi b'e mwaso mango balolaa bacha, bera kuaya busese mwa kulola kwa bisomerano bya Yesu airaa, nomwa kumva kwa bana bateta na nurenge munene mwa luhu lwa Ongo mbu: Hosana Mwenyi Daudi!

16. Bushi n'oku, bera kubusa Yesu mbu: Ewashe, ei myasi e bana bateta utayumvire? Yesu nai mbu: Nechi! Nyinomvire! Mubeke mutafura kusoma kwa maanjiko Mabuya-buya machwula matechire mbu: Kurengera ebunu bw'e bana batoto, N'e bw'e chwubonjo-bonjo, Ku wende wahubanganyisa e bandju engulu yao.

17. Chasinda, Yesu era kureka abu bandju, era kuya kuchionjilyira mwa musi w'e Betaniya.

Yesu atakira e muchi w'e tini

18. Abere mwei mishangya-shangya, mango Yesu abaa era ahuba e yerusalemu, era

14. 먀 찌부와 쪼루 루후, 바우다 바우마 나 비러머, 버라 구이기라 여수. 나이, 어라 구바쨔먀.

15. 시 어 바구루-구루 버 바구하네, 너 바가삐쎼시 버 뫄소 마꼬 바르롸아 바짜, 버라 구아야 부서서 먀 구른쫘 과 비소머라노 뱌 여수 아이라아, 노뫄 구빠 과 바나 바더다 나 누러ㅁ 무너너 먀 루후 쫘 오꼬 뿌: 호사나 뭐네 다우디!

16. 부씨 노구, 버라 구부사 여수 뿌: 어와써, 어이 먀시 어 바나 바더다 우다유삐러? 여수 나이 뿌: 너찌! 니노삐러! 무버거 무다푸라 구소마 과 마아찌고 마부야-부야 마쭈롸 마더찌러 뿌: 구러ㅁ라 어부누 뭐 바나 바도도, 너 뭐 쭈보쪼-보쪼, 구 워떠 와후바꺄니사 어 바쭈 어꾸루 야오.

17. 짜시따, 여수 어라 구러가 아부 바쭈, 어라 구야 구찌오찌쎼라 먀 무시 워 버다니야.

여수 아다기라 어 무찌 워 디니

18. 아버러 뭐이 미싸꺄-싸꺄, 마꼬 여수 아바아 어라 아후바 어 여루사러무, 어라 구파

14. The blind and the lame came to him at the temple, and he healed them.

15. But when the chief priests and the teachers of the law saw the wonderful things he did and the children shouting in the temple area, "Hosanna to the Son of David," they were indignant.

16. "Do you hear what these children are saying?" they asked him. "Yes," replied Jesus, "have you never read, " 'From the lips of children and infants you have ordained praise'?"

17. And he left them and went out of the city to Bethany, where he spent the night.

18. Early in the morning, as he was on his way back to the city, he was hungry.

kufa businya.

19. Era kulola ku muchi muuma wa tini kwa musike s'e njira, era kuchifunda ofu nao. Si chiro akabuana ku chifuma chisibya, si e bihoho byeine oshao. Bushi n'oku, era atakira oyu muchi mbu: Bushi si utanachekaa chifuma chisibya! Unao-unao, ola muchi kuna kooma.

20. mango e banafunzi ba Yesu balola kw'ebi, bera kusanwa busese. Bera kumubusa mbu: Ewashe! Kute ku ono muchi w'e tini era anaikaa oma bacha?

21. Yesu nai mbu: kubinalyi! Nababura kwa akaba mutangahungwa-hungwa mwa bwemeresi bwenyu, nenyu munganaala kuira ngokuno nera kukorera Ono muchi. Anabe ne n'e ndjulungu, munganaburai mbu iyaa kuchikoma mwa Nyanja, binganabako.

22. kanji akaba mungaata e bwemeresi, choshi cha mungema Ongo, anganaberesachi.

E bandju babusa Yesu era lulu s'e buashi bwai

23. Era nyuma s'ebi, Yesu era kuhuba kwegilyira mwa luhu

부시냐.

19. 어라 구로롸 구 무찌 무우마 와 디니 과 무시거 서 띠라, 어라 구찌푸따 오푸 나오. 시 찌로 아가부아나 구 찌푸마 찌시뱌, 시 어 비호호 벼이너 오싸오. 부씨 노구, 어라 아다기라 오유 무찌 뿌: 부씨 시 우다나쩌가아 찌푸마 찌시뱌! 우나오-우나오, 오롸 무찌 구나 고오마.

20. 마꼬 어 바나푸씨 바 여수 바로롸 궈비, 버라 구사놔 부서서. 버라 구무부사 뿌: 어와써! 구더 구 오노 무찌 워 디니 어라 아나이가아 오마 바짜?

21. 여수 나이 뿌: 구비나레! 나바부라 과 아가바 무다빠후꽈-후꽈 마 붜머러시 붜뉴, 너뉴 무빠나아롸 구이라 꼬구노 너라 구고러라 오노 무찌. 아나버 너 너 뚜루우, 무빠나부라이 뿌 이야아 구찌고마 마 냐자, 비빠나바고.

22. 가찌 아가바 무빠아다 어 붜머러시, 쪼씨 짜 무꺼마 오꼬, 아빠나버러사찌.

어 바뚜 바부사 여수 어라 루뚜 서 부아씨 봐이

23. 어라 뉴마 서비, 여수 어라 구후바 궈지례라 마 루후 꽈

---

19. Seeing a fig tree by the road, he went up to it but found nothing on it except leaves. Then he said to it, "May you never bear fruit again!" Immediately the tree withered.

20. When the disciples saw this, they were amazed. "How did the fig tree wither so quickly?" they asked.

21. Jesus replied, "I tell you the truth, if you have faith and do not doubt, not only can you do what was done to the fig tree, but also you can say to this mountain, 'Go, throw yourself into the sea,' and it will be done.

22. If you believe, you will receive whatever you ask for in prayer."

23. Jesus entered the temple courts, and, while

Iwa Ongo na akangilyisa e bandju. E bakulu-kulu b'e bakuhanyi, n'e bashamuka b'e bayuda bera kumuikira n'e kumubusa mbu: Ewashe, bine wenjire waira, wabiira ku misi ichiye? Na nde iwakuwerei?

24. Yesu na imbu: Nanyi nababusa chinwa chiuma, nenyu mukanyakula, nyigabambura ku buashi buchiye ku neinjire naira ene myasi.

25. Ebuashi bwa yowana endee abatisa mw'e bandju, ngai yi bwatengeraa? Munyiburaa, akaba era mwa Ongo nesi kwa bandju! Bera kuya nama. Bera kuburana mbu: chwukamwakula mbu bwatengaa kwa nguba, angachwubusa mbu: Rero, chi cheraa chachwuma mutamwemerera?

26. Na chwukamwakula mbu kwa bandju, chwobaa bano bandju bachilunjire anola. Bushi boshi babaa baneshi kanangana kwa yowana anabaa murebi.

27. Bushi n'oku, bera kumwakula mbu: chwuteshi! Yesunai mbu: Nanyi, ndabarure ku buashi buchiye

오꼬 나 아가삐쪠사 어 바뚜. 어 바구루-구루 버 바구하네, 너 바싸무가 버 바유다 버라 구무이기라 너 구무부사 뿌: 어와써, 비너 워찌러 와이라, 와비이라 구 미시 이찌여? 나 떠 이와구워러이?

24. 여수 나 이뿌: 나네 나바부사 찌놔 찌우마, 너뉴 무가냐구롸, 네가바뿌라 구 부아씨 부찌여 구 너이찌러 나이라 어너 먀시.

25. 어부아씨 봐 요와나 어떠어 아바디사 뭐 바뚜, 까이 에 봐더꺼러아아? 무네부라아, 아가바 어라 뫄 오꼬 너시 과 바뚜! 버라 구야 나마. 버라 구부라나 뿌: 쭈가뫄구롸 뿌 봐더꺼아아 과 꾸바, 아꺼쭈부사 뿌: 러로, 찌 쩌라아 쨔쭈마 무다뭐머러라?

26. 나 쭈가뫄구롸 뿌 과 바뚜, 쭈바아 바노 바뚜 바찌룬찌러 아노롸. 부씨 보씨 바바아 바너씨 가나꺼나 과 요와나 아나바아 무러비.

27. 부씨 노구, 버라 구뫄구롸 뿌: 쭈더씨! 여수나이 뿌: 나네, 따바루러 구 부아씨 부찌여 너찌러 나이라 어너 먀시.

he was teaching, the chief priests and the elders of the people came to him. "By what authority are you doing these things?" they asked. "And who gave you this authority?"

24. Jesus replied, "I will also ask you one question. If you answer me, I will tell you by what authority I am doing these things.

25. John's baptism--where did it come from? Was it from heaven, or from men?" They discussed it among themselves and said, "If we say, 'From heaven,' he will ask, 'Then why didn't you believe him?'

26. But if we say, 'From men'--we are afraid of the people, for they all hold that John was a prophet."

27. So they answered Jesus, "We don't know." Then he said, "Neither will I tell you by what authority

ku nenjire naira ene myasi.

Muanyi w'e bana babilyi　무아네 워 바나 바비례

28. Yesu era kuhuba kuteta mbu: kute musene kw'ono mwasi? Kwabaa mulume muuma ola wabaa wete bana bai babilyi. Oyu mulume, era kubura e fula yai mbu: E mwana wanyi, lwarero uyaa kureerera wakola mw'ehwa lyechwu ly'e misabibu.

28. 여수 어라 구후바 구더다 뿌: 구더 무서너 고노 먀시? 과바아 무루머 무우마 오롸 와바아 워더 바나 바이 바비례. 오유 무루머, 어라 구부라 어 푸롸 야이 뿌: 어 므나 와네, 롸러로 우야아 구러어러라 와고롸 뭐화 려쭈 려 미사비부.

28. "What do you think? There was a man who had two sons. He went to the first and said, 'Son, go and work today in the vineyard.'

29. Nai mbu: Ndachiikireyi! Si era nyuma, era kuhubya e muchima, na aya kukola.

29. 나이 뿌: 따찌이기러에! 시 어라 뉴마, 어라 구후뱌 어 무찌마, 나 아야 구고롸.

29. " 'I will not,' he answered, but later he changed his mind and went.

30. Chasinda, wamulume era kubura e mutoto ng'okwa anaburaa e fula. Oyu mutoto, era kwakula mbu: Nechi tata, nayayi! Si chiro akayayi.

30. 짜시따, 와무루머 어라 구부라 어 무도도 꾸오과 아나부라아 어 푸롸. 오유 무도도, 어라 과구롸 뿌: 너찌 다다, 나야에! 시 찌로 아가야에.

30. "Then the father went to the other son and said the same thing. He answered, 'I will, sir,' but he did not go.

31. Rero! Mwa bano bana babilyi, nde iwairaa ng'okwa eshe abaa ahonda? Nabo mbu: E fula. Bushi n'oku, Yesu era kuteta mbu: Kubinalyi, nababura kwa e bafuchisi b'e mbarata n'e bihungukasi bu bangaba babere-bere kwingilyira mwa bwami bwa Ongo era muhondo senyu.

31. 러로! 과 바노 바나 바비례, 떠 이와이라아 꾸오과 어써 아바아 아호따? 나보 뿌: 어 푸롸. 부씨 노구, 여수 어라 구더다 뿌: 구비나례, 나바부라 과 어 바푸찌시 버 빠라다 너 비후우가시 부 바꺄바 바버러- 버러 귀삐례라 과 봐미 봐 오꼬 어라 무호또 서뉴.

31. "Which of the two did what his father wanted?" "The first," they answered. Jesus said to them, "I tell you the truth, the tax collectors and the prostitutes are entering the kingdom of God ahead of you.

32. Bushi yowana mango abaikiraa chasiya abalose bya bichwungenene era muhondo sa Ongo,

32. 부씨 요와나 마꼬 아바이기라아 짜시야 아바로써 뱌 비쭈어너너 어라 무호또 사 오꼬, 무다뭐머러라아. 시 어

32. For John came to you to show you the way of righteousness, and you did not believe him, but the

I am doing these things.

mutamwemereraa. Si e bafuchisi b'e mbarata n'e bihungukasi, beke bamwemereraa. Chiro angabambu nyu, kanji mutanamwemereraa."

E mwanyi w'e bainzi babi

33. Yesu era kuteta mbu: Mumvilyisaa kw'ono unji muanyi: kwabaa mulume muuma ola waingaa ehwa lyai lya misabibu. Ely'ehwa, era kulyisungusa e lusito, era kuchima n'ala bagende bakanjira e chwufuma chw'e misabibu. Era kuimbira n'e balanzi bai chitala cha chitowamire busese. Chasinda, era kulyibwesa bainzi bauma, na abalama.

Chikaya cha kukanjira mw'e misabibu

34. Abere e suku s'e kushebula saika, era kuchwuma e bakosi bai era abu bainzi balyi, chasiya bamwerese ewai mwango kwa myaka.

35. Si abu bainzi bera kusimba abu bakosi bai. Muuma, bera kumupunda busese, n'e unji bera kumuita, n'e wakahachwu bera kumuita mwa kumuumanga e makoi.

바푸찌시 버 빠라다 너 비후꾸가시, 버거 바뭐머러라아. 찌로 아빠바뿌 뉴, 가찌 무다나뭐머러라아."

어 꽈네 워 바이씨 바비

33. 여수 어라 구더다 뿌: 무뻐레사아 고노 우찌 무아네: 과바아 무루머 무우마 오롸 와이빠아 어화 랴이 랴 미사비부. 어려화, 어라 구레수꾸사 어 루시도, 어라 구찌마 나롸 바거떠 바가씨라 어 쭈푸마 쭤 미사비부. 어라 구이뻬라 너 바롼씨 바이 찌다롸 짜 찌도와미러 부서서. 짜시따, 어라 구레붜사 바이씨 바우마, 나 아바롸마.

찌가야 짜 구가씨띱 뭐 미사비부

34. 아버러 어 수구 서 구써부롸 사이가, 어라 구쭈마 어 바고시 바이 어라 아부 바이씨 바레, 짜시야 바뭐러서 어와이 먀꼬 과 먀가.

35. 시 아부 바이씨 버라 구시빠 아부 바고시 바이. 무우마, 버라 구무푼따 부서서, 너 우찌 버라 구무이다, 너 와가하쭈 버라 구무이다 먀 구무우마빠 어 마고이.

tax collectors and the prostitutes did. And even after you saw this, you did not repent and believe him.

33. "Listen to another parable: There was a landowner who planted a vineyard. He put a wall around it, dug a winepress in it and built a watchtower. Then he rented the vineyard to some farmers and went away on a journey.

34. When the harvest time approached, he sent his servants to the tenants to collect his fruit.

35. "The tenants seized his servants; they beat one, killed another, and stoned a third.

36. Era nyuma s'ebi, en'ehwa era kuhuba kuchwuma banji bakosi banene kurenza ba babere. Si nabo, abu bainzi bera kubakorera cha banakoreraa ba babere-bere.

37. Chasinjire, era kwire abachwumira muala wai, mwa kuanyisa mbu: Ono muala wanyi, yeke bagamuchwunda.

38. Si ba bainzi balolyire kw'oyu muala, bera kuteta mbu: Onola, iukalya e mwandju w'eshe. Muira chwumwite, chasiya chwuchishibanyireo.

39. Bushi n'oku, bera kumusimba, na bamukululyira kwa musike s'ehwa, chasinda bera kumwita.

40. Yesu kukwera kubusa mbu: Rero, oyu en'ehwa mango akafuluka, kute ku akaira abu bainzi?

41. Nabo mbu: Abu bandju babi, aketabo busira kubafira bonjo. Nely'ehwa lyai, anere abwesalyi banji bainzi ba bakende bamweresa ewai mwango kwa myaka mwa kushebula.

42. Chasinda, Yesu era kubabusa mbu: Mutafuraa kusoma kwa maanjiko mabuya-buya machwula

36. 어라 뉴마 서비, 어너화 어라 구후바 구쭈마 바찌 바고시 바너너 구러싸 바 바버러. 시 나보, 아부 바이씨 버라 구바고러라 짜 바나고러라아 바 바버러-버러.

37. 짜시찌러, 어라 귀러 아바쭈미라 무아꽈 와이, 꽈 구아네사 뿌: 오노 무아꽈 와네, 여거 바가무쭈따.

38. 시 바 바이씨 바로레러 고유 무아꽈, 버라 구더다 뿌: 오노꽈, 이우가꺄 어 꽈뚜 워써. 무이라 쭈뮈더, 짜시야 쭈찌씨바네러오.

39. 부씨 노구, 버라 구무시빠, 나 바무구루레라 과 무시거 서화, 짜시따 버라 구뮈다.

40. 여수 구궈라 구부사 뿌: 러로, 오유 어너화 마꼬 아가푸루가, 구더 구 아가이라 아부 바이씨?

41. 나보 뿌: 아부 바쭈 바비, 아거다보 부시라 구바피라 보쏘. 너껴화 꺄이, 아너러 아붜사레 바찌 바이씨 바 바거러 바뭐러사 어와이 마꼬 과 먀가 꽈 구써부꽈.

42. 짜시따, 여수 어라 구바부사 뿌: 무다푸라아 구소마 과 마아찌고 마부야- 부야 마쭈꽈 마더찌러? 어고이

36. Then he sent other servants to them, more than the first time, and the tenants treated them the same way.

37. Last of all, he sent his son to them. 'They will respect my son,' he said.

38. "But when the tenants saw the son, they said to each other, 'This is the heir. Come, let's kill him and take his inheritance.'

39. So they took him and threw him out of the vineyard and killed him.

40. "Therefore, when the owner of the vineyard comes, what will he do to those tenants?"

41. "He will bring those wretches to a wretched end," they replied, "and he will rent the vineyard to other tenants, who will give him his share of the crop at harvest time."

42. Jesus said to them, "Have you never read in the Scriptures: " 'The stone the builders rejected has

matechire? Ekoi lya baimbi balangulaa, lilyahubire ekoi linene ly'e musingi. Enawechwu iwanairaa bacha. N'echi chilyi chisomerano chinene ku chwubano.

43. Bushi n'oku, nababura kwa mwabo Ongo angabanyaa e bwami bwai, anere eresabo banji bandju ba bagende baira e kuhonda kwai.

44. Nelyi koi, ola ukatowera kulyi, akafunyikira. N'ola likatowera, likamufungolanga.

45. Mango e bakulu-kulu b'e bakuhanyi, n'e Bafarisayo bomvaa kwei mianyi ya yesu, bera kwire bamenyerera kwa abaa ateta era lulu saabo.

46. Bushi n'oku, bera kuhonda njira yakumusimba, sibera kwobaa e bandju, bushi abu bandju babaa batolyire Yesu nga murebi.

Matayo Chikono 22
E muanyi w'e lyinye ly'e buya

1. Yesu era kunaendekera ateta nabu bandju mwa mianyi. Era kubabura mbu:
2. e Bwami b'okwa nguba

퍄 바이뻬 바꺄우꽈아, 뤼퍄후비러 어고이 뤼너너 뼈 무시삐. 어나워쭈 이와나이라아 바짜. 너찌 찌뤠 찌소머라노 찌너너 구 쭈바노.

43. 부씨 노구, 나바부라 과 꺄보 오꼬 아까바냐아 어 봐이, 아너러 어러사보 바찌 바뚜 바 바거떠 바이라 어 구호따 과이.

44. 너뤠 고이, 오퐈 우가도워라 구뤠, 아가푸네기라. 노퐈 뤼가도워라, 뤼가무푸꼬꽈까.

45. 마꼬 어 바구루-구루 버 바구하네, 너 바파리사요 보빠아 궈이 미아네 야 여수, 버라 귀러 바머녀러라 과 아바아 아더다 어라 루루 사아보.

46. 부씨 노구, 버라 구호따 찌라 야구무시빠, 시버라 곧바아 어 바뚜, 부씨 아부 바뚜 바바아 바도뤠러 여수 까 무러비.

마다요 찌고노 22
어 무아네 워 뤠녯 뼈 부야

1. 여수 어라 구나어떠거라 아더다 나부 바뚜 꽈 미아네. 어라 구바부라 뿌:
2. 어 봐미 보과 꾸바

become the capstone; the Lord has done this, and it is marvelous in our eyes'?

43. "Therefore I tell you that the kingdom of God will be taken away from you and given to a people who will produce its fruit.

44. He who falls on this stone will be broken to pieces, but he on whom it falls will be crushed."

45. When the chief priests and the Pharisees heard Jesus' parables, they knew he was talking about them.

46. They looked for a way to arrest him, but they were afraid of the crowd because the people held that he was a prophet.

Matthew Chapter 22[NIV]

1. Jesus spoke to them again in parables, saying:
2. "The kingdom of heaven

buhuhanyisibwe na mwami muuma ola wakuganyisaa muala wai e lyinye ly'e buya.

3. Oyu mwami, era kuchwuma e banda bai mbu bayaa kwamaala e bandju ba abaa alalyikire kwa buya. Si abu bandju, chiro bakachiikira.

4. Chasinda, era kuchwuma baɲji baanda. Era kubabura mbu: Muyaa kubura e bandju ba nalalyikaa kwa buya mbu: Muyaa kubura e bandju ba nalalyikaa kwa buya mbu: natenjire e ngaafu sanyi mira, na sinji nyama sa sinunyire. Rero mubahaa kwa buya, bushi e bindju byoshi byakunganyisibwe mira!

5. Si abu balalyikwaa, chiro bakalaa kw'ebi. Bera kuchiiranga mwa byabo : muuma era kuya mw'ehwa lyai, n'e unji mwa buchimbusi,

6. N'e banji bera kutola abu baanda, bera kubapunda busese, chasinda bera kubeta.

7 Oyu mwami, era kufa bute bunene. Era kwire achwuma e basula bai mbu bayaa kusikya abu bechi na kwocha e musi wabo.

8. Era nyuma s'ebi, era

부후하네시붜 나 뫄미 무우마 오꽈 와구가네사아 무아꽈 와이 어 레녀 려 부야.

3. 오유 뫄미, 어라 구쭈마 어 바따 바이 뿌 바야아 과마아꽈 어 바뉴 바 아바아 아꽈레기러 과 부야. 시 아부 바뉴, 찌로 바가찌이기라.

4. 짜시따, 어라 구쭈마 바찌 바아따. 어라 구바부라 뿌: 무야아 구부라 어 바뉴 바 나꽈레가아 과 부야 뿌: 무야아 구부라 어 바뉴 바 나꽈레가아 과 부야 뿌: 나더찌러 어 ꬰ아푸 사니 미라, 나 시찌 냐마 사 시누네러. 러로 무바하아 과 부야, 부씨 어 비뉴 뵤씨 뱌구ꬰ네시붜 미라!

5. 시 아부 바꽈레과아, 찌로 바가꽈아 궈비. 버라 구찌이라ꬰ 뫄 뱌보 : 무우마 어라 구야 뭐화 랴이, 너 우찌 뫄 부찌뿌시,

6. 너 바찌 버라 구도꽈 아부 바아따, 버라 구바푸따 부서서, 짜시따 버라 구버다.

7 오유 뫄미, 어라 구파 부더 부너너. 어라 귀러 아쭈마 어 바수꽈 바이 뿌 바야아 구시갸 아부 버찌 나 곷짜 어 무시 와보.

8. 어라 뉴마 서비, 어라

---

is like a king who prepared a wedding banquet for his son.

3. He sent his servants to those who had been invited to the banquet to tell them to come, but they refused to come.

4. "Then he sent some more servants and said, 'Tell those who have been invited that I have prepared my dinner: My oxen and fattened cattle have been butchered, and everything is ready. Come to the wedding banquet.'

5. "But they paid no attention and went off-- one to his field, another to his business.

6. The rest seized his servants, mistreated them and killed them.

7. The king was enraged. He sent his army and destroyed those murderers and burned their city.

8. "Then he said to his

kubura e baanda bai mbu: Ebilyo by'e buya byaire mira, si e bandju ba nalalyikaa atabubalairwaabi.

9. Bushi n'oku, mwiree mwaya mwa myengere, e bandju boshi ba munganabuana, mubaburaa babahe kwa buya.

10. Abu baanda bera kunaya mwa mwengere, bera kubuanyanya e bandju boshi ba babuanaa, e babi n'e babuya. Enyumba y'e kulyira mw'e lyinye yera kwehula mw'e baenyi.

11. Oyu mwami, mango engilyiraa mwei nyumba chasiya alole kwa baenyi, era kulola ku mundju muuma ola wabaa utembesi enjimba s'e buya.

12. Era kumubusa mbu: E mwira wanyi, kute wengilyira muno utembese n'e njimba s'e buya? Oyu mundju, chiro akamwakula kandju.

13. Bushi n'oku, mwami era kubura e baanda bai mbu: Ono mundju, mumuminaa e mabiko n'e maulu, chasinda mwanamuuma era butala mwa musimya! Na mwoyu musimya, mu angalyilyira na kulola kwa kasibu.

구부라 어 바아따 바이 뿌: 어비료 벼 부야 뱌이러 미라, 시 어 바쭈 바 나롸레가아 아다부바뽜이로아비.

9. 부씨 노구, 뮈러어 뫄야 뫄 며꺼러, 어 바쭈 보씨 바 무꺼나부아나, 무바부라아 바바허 과 부야.

10. 아부 바아따 버라 구나야 뫄 뭐꺼러, 버라 구부아냐냐 어 바쭈 보씨 바 바부아나아, 어 바비 너 바부야. 어뉴빠 여 구레라 뭐 레녀 여라 궈후꽈 뭐 바어네.

11. 오유 뫄미, 마꼬 어끼레라아 뭐이 뉴빠 짜시야 아로꺼 과 바어네, 어라 구로꽈 구 무쭈 무우마 오꽈 와바아 우더뼈시 어끼빠 서 부야.

12. 어라 구무부사 뿌: 어 뮈라 와네, 구더 워끼레라 무노 우더뼈서 너 띠빠 서 부야? 오유 무쭈, 찌로 아가뫄구꽈 가꾸.

13. 부씨 노구, 뫄미 어라 구부라 어 바아따 바이 뿌: 오노 무쭈, 무무미나아 어 마비고 너 마우루, 짜시따 뫄나무우마 어라 부다꽈 뫄 무시먀! 나 모유 무시먀, 무 아까레레라 나 구로꽈 과 가시부.

servants, 'The wedding banquet is ready, but those I invited did not deserve to come.

9. Go to the street corners and invite to the banquet anyone you find.'

10. So the servants went out into the streets and gathered all the people they could find, both good and bad, and the wedding hall was filled with guests.

11. "But when the king came in to see the guests, he noticed a man there who was not wearing wedding clothes.

12. 'Friend,' he asked, 'how did you get in here without wedding clothes?' The man was speechless.

13. "Then the king told the attendants, 'Tie him hand and foot, and throw him outside, into the darkness, where there will be weeping and gnashing of teeth.'

14. Chasinjire, Yesu era kuteta mbu: E bandju ba balalyikirwe balyi banene, siba balondolyibwe, balyi baeke.

E kufuta e mbarata ya mwami kaisario

15. era nyuma s'ebi, e bafarisayo bera kuya kuira lwango lwa kuteya Yesu mwasi kurengera e binwa byai.

16. Bera kumuchwumira banafunzi babo bauma alauma na banji bandju bomwa chikembe cha herodi. Bera kuika kubusa Yesu mbu: Mukangilyisi, chwishi kwa wende wateta myasi ya kanagana, kanji wende wakangilyisa e bandju e myasi ya Ongo era bemire kunde bakulyikira kwa binemire. Kanji utobaa na mundju asibya, utanobalyisibwa na bukulu-kulu bwa mundju.

17. Rero, uchwubiraa kute usene kw'ono mwasi: E mwaso wechwu achwula emerere nesi atemerere kunde chwafuta e mbarata era mwa mwami kaisario?

18. Si Yesu bushi abaa amenyerere emyanyisa yabo

---

14. 짜시찌러, 여수 어라 구더다 뿌: 어 바뚜 바 바꽈레기뤄 바례 바너너, 시바 바론또레붜, 바례 바어거.

어 구푸다 어 빠띱닛 야 똬미 가이사리오

15. 어라 뉴마 서비, 어 바파리사요 버라 구야 구이라 꽈오 꽈 구더야 여수 마시 구러뻐라 어 비놔 뱌이.

16. 버라 구무쭈미라 바나푸씨 바보 바우마 아꽈우마 나 바찌 바뚜 보봐 찌거뻐 짜 허로디. 버라 구이가 구부사 여수 뿌: 무가예레시, 쮜씨 과 워떠 와더다 먀시 야 가나가나, 가찌 워떠 와가예레사 어 바뚜 어 먀시 야 오꼬 어라 버미러 구떠 바구레기라 과 비너미러. 가찌 우도바아 나 무뚜 아시뱌, 우다노바레시봐 나 부구루-구루 봐 무뚜.

17. 러로, 우쭈비라아 구더 우서너 굔노 먀시: 어 먀소 워쭈 아쭈꽈 어머러러 너시 아더머러러 구떠 꽈푸다 어 빠라다 어라 봐 똬미 가이사리오?

18. 시 여수 부씨 아바아 아머녀러러 어먀네사 야보

---

14. "For many are invited, but few are chosen."

15. Then the Pharisees went out and laid plans to trap him in his words.

16. They sent their disciples to him along with the Herodians. "Teacher," they said, "we know you are a man of integrity and that you teach the way of God in accordance with the truth. You aren't swayed by men, because you pay no attention to who they are

17. Tell us then, what is your opinion? Is it right to pay taxes to Caesar or not?"

18. But Jesus, knowing their evil intent, said, "You

ibi, era kubaakula mbu: Emu batebanyi, chi chachwuma mwanyiteya bacha?

19. Munyilosaa e buteya bwa mwende mwana kwa kufuta e mbarata. Bera kumuretera chikoroto chiuma cha buteya.

20. Yesu era kubabusa mbu: Ewashe! Chine chihuhanyi, n'e lyine sina bilyi bya nde? Nabo mbu:

21. Bilyi bya mwami kaisari. Yesu era kwire ababura mbu: Rero, mundaa mweresa kaisari bya bilyi byai, mwaneresa na Ongo bya bilyi byai.

22. Abu bandju bomvire bacha, bera kusanwa busese. Bera kumureka na bachiendera.

E basadukayo babusa Yesu era lulu s'e kwomoka

23. Mw'olu lusuku lunolu, Basadukayo bauma nabo bera kuikira Yesu. Abu basadukayo bu bende bateta mbu e bafu batakomwoke. Bera kumubusa mbu:

24. Mukangilyisi, Musa atetaa mbu: Akaba e mundju angafa busira kureka mwana asibya, kwemire mulumuna wai engire e muhumba-kasi weshibire, chasiya abuchire

이비, 어라 구바아구롸 뿌: 어무 바더바네, 찌 짜쭈마 뫄네더야 바짜?

19. 무네롸사아 어 부더야 봐 뭐떠 뫄나 과 구푸다 어 빠라다. 버라 구무러더라 찌고로도 찌우마 짜 부더야.

20. 여수 어라 구바부사 뿌: 어와써! 찌너 찌후하네, 너 레너 시나 비레 뱌 떠? 나보 뿌:

21. 비레 뱌 뫄미 가이사리. 여수 어라 귀러 아바부라 뿌: 러로, 무따아 뭐러사 가이사리 뱌 비레 뱌이, 뫄너러사 나 오꼬 뱌 비레 뱌이.

22. 아부 바뚜 보삐러 바짜, 버라 구사놔 부서서. 버라 구무러가 나 바쩌떠라.

어 바사두가요 바부사 여수 어라 루루 서 교명—

23. 모루 루수구 루노루, 바사두가요 바우마 나보 버라 구이기라 여수. 아부 바사두가요 부 버떠 바더다 뿌 어 바푸 바다고모거. 버라 구무부사 뿌:

24. 무가삐레시, 무사 아더다아 뿌: 아가바 어 무뚜 아까파 부시라 구러가 뫄나 아시뱌, 궈미러 무루무나 와이 어삐러 어 무후빠-가시 워씨비러, 짜시야 아부찌러 무구루 와이

hypocrites, why are you trying to trap me?

19. Show me the coin used for paying the tax." They brought him a denarius,

20. and he asked them, "Whose portrait is this? And whose inscription?"

21. "Caesar's," they replied. Then he said to them, "Give to Caesar what is Caesar's, and to God what is God's."

22. When they heard this, they were amazed. So they left him and went away.

23. That same day the Sadducees, who say there is no resurrection, came to him with a question.

24. "Teacher," they said, "Moses told us that if a man dies without having children, his brother must marry the widow and have children for him.

mukulu wai e bana

어 바나

25. Rero, mwa kachi-kachi kechwu, mwabaa batabana balyinda ba bula buuma. Efula yera kuhwera mukasi, era kufa busira kubuta mwana. Mulumuna wai era kwengira oyu muhumba-kasi.

25. 러로, 뫄 가찌-가찌 거쭈, 뫄바아 바다바나 바레따 바 부꽈 부우마. 어푸꽈 여라 구훠라 무가시, 어라 구파 부시라 구부다 뫄나. 무루무나 와이 어라 궈끼라 오유 무후빠-가시.

25. Now there were seven brothers among us. The first one married and died, and since he had no children, he left his wife to his brother.

26. Oyu mulumuna nai, kunoku ku byanabaa. Byera kunaba bacha, nokwa wa kahachwu kuikira kwa wa kalyinda.

26. 오유 무루무나 나이, 구노구 구 뱌나바아. 벼라 구나바 바짜, 노과 와 가하쭈 구이기라 과 와 가레따.

26. The same thing happened to the second and third brother, right on down to the seventh.

27. Era nyuma s'e kufa kwabu batabana boshi, ola muhumba-kasi nai, era kufa.

27. 어라 뉴마 서 구파 과부 바다바나 보씨, 오꽈 무후빠-가시 나이, 어라 구파.

27. Finally, the woman died.

28 Rero, e lusuku lwa bafu bakwomoka, oyu mukasi akere aba wande? Bushi abu batabana balyinda boshi, banamuhweraa!

28 러로, 어 루수구 롸 바푸 바고모가, 오유 무가시 아거러 아바 와떠? 부씨 아부 바다바나 바레따 보씨, 바나무훠라아!

28. Now then, at the resurrection, whose wife will she be of the seven, since all of them were married to her?"

29. Yesu era kubakula mbu: Mwauwirwe busese, bushi n'e kutamenya e Maanjiko Mabuya-buya, nesi e buashi bwa Ongo.

29. 여수 어라 구바구꽈 뿌: 뫄우위뤄 부서서, 부씨 너 구다머냐 어 마아찌고 마부야- 부야, 너시 어 부아씨 봐 오꼬.

29. Jesus replied, "You are in error because you do not know the Scriptures or the power of God.

30. Bushi mango e bafu bakomwoka, e balume n'e bakasi batakachihwerane, si bakaba nga bamalaika bokwa nguba!

30. 부씨 마꼬 어 바푸 바고모가, 어 바루머 너 바가시 바다가찌훠라너, 시 바가바 빠 바마롸이가 보과 꾸바!

30. At the resurrection people will neither marry nor be given in marriage; they will be like the angels in heaven.

31. Kanji bushi n'e myasi y'e kwomoka kw'e bafu, mutafura kusoma ene myasi Ongo ababuraa mbu:

31. 가찌 부씨 너 먀시 여 고모가 궈 바푸, 무다푸라 구소마 어너 먀시 오꼬 아바부라아 뿌:

31. But about the resurrection of the dead-- have you not read what God said to you,

32. Nyono nyi Ongo wa iburahamu, na wa isaka, na wa yakobo. Yesu era kuhuba kuteta mbu: Ongo atachwula Ongo w'e bafu, si achwula Ongo w'e bandju basene!

33. Eluamba lw'e bandju lomvire bacha, lwera kusanwa busese bushi n'e myasi era Yesu abaa akangilyisa.

E muomba munene kurenza ilyikabo

34. e bafarisayo mango bomvaa kwa Yesu aimire abu basadukayo, bera kubuanana.

35. Mukangilyisi muuma w'e mwaso mwa kachi-kachi kabo, era kuereka Yesu mbu:

36. Mukangilyisi, mwa Mwaso woshi, muomba muchiye imunene kurenza ilyikabo?

37. Yesu nai mbu: Usimaa Enawenyu Ongo mwa muchima wao woshi, n'omwa mianyisa yao Yoshi, n'omwa bwenge bwao boshi.

38. Oyu muomba imunene busese kanji imubere-bere.

39. N'e muomba wakabilyi nao analyi ngoyu mubere-bere na bacha ku achwula atechire: Usimaa mulyikenyu ng'okwa uchwula uchisimire.

40. Ene miomba ebilyi, iminyire e myasi Yoshi era

---

32. 뇨노 네 오꼬 와 이부라하무, 나 와 이사가, 나 와 야고보. 여수 어라 구후바 구더다 뿌: 오꼬 아다쭈롸 오꼬 워 바푸, 시 아쭈롸 오꼬 워 바뉴 바서너!

33. 어루아빠 뤄 바뉴 로삐러 바짜, 뤄라 구사놔 부서서 부씨 너 먀시 어라 여수 아바아 아가삐레사.

어 무오빠 무너너 구러싸 이쩨—별

34. 어 바파리사요 마꼬 보빠아 과 여수 아이미러 아부 바사두가요, 버라 구부아나나.

35. 무가삐레시 무우마 워 뫄소 뫄 가찌-가찌 가보, 어라 구어러가 여수 뿌:

36. 무가삐레시, 뫄 뫄소 올씨, 무오빠 무찌여 이무너너 구러싸 이쩨가보?

37. 여수 나이 뿌: 우시마아 어나워뉴 오꼬 뫄 무찌마 와오 올씨, 노뫄 미아네사 야오 요씨, 노뫄 붜어 봐오 보씨.

38. 오유 무오빠 이무너너 부서서 가찌 이무버러-버러.

39. 너 무오빠 와가비쩨 나오 아나쩨 꼬유 무버러-버러 나 바짜 구 아쭈롸 아더찌러: 우시마아 무쩨거뉴 꾸오과 우쭈롸 우찌시미러.

40. 어너 미오빠 어비쩨, 이미네러 어 먀시 요씨 어라

---

32. 'I am the God of Abraham, the God of Isaac, and the God of Jacob'? He is not the God of the dead but of the living."

33. When the crowds heard this, they were astonished at his teaching.

34. Hearing that Jesus had silenced the Sadducees, the Pharisees got together.

35. One of them, an expert in the law, tested him with this question:

36. "Teacher, which is the greatest commandment in the Law?"

37. Jesus replied: " 'Love the Lord your God with all your heart and with all your soul and with all your mind.'

38. This is the first and greatest commandment.

39. And the second is like it: 'Love your neighbor as yourself.'

40. All the Law and the Prophets hang on these

ichwula yanjikirwe mwa mwaso wa musa n'omwa bitabo by'e barebi.

Kirisito alyi mwenyi nde?

41. Mango abu bafarisayo babaa banachilyi babuananyire, Yesu era kubabusa mbu:

42. Ewashe! Kute mwanyisa era lulu sa Kirisito? Oyu Kirisito, alyi mwenyi nde? Nabo mbu: Alyi mwenyi mwami Daudi.

43. Yesu kukwera kubabusa kanji mbu: Rero, kute ku Daudi era atetambu Kirisito alyi Enawabo, n'oku oyu Daudi abaa akoresibwa n'e Muchima Mubuya-buya? Bacha kwatetaa:

44. Enawechwu Ongo aburaa enawechwu mbu: Wikalaa kwa lunda lwanyi lw'e malyo, Kuikira nyibike e barenda bao Kuba chisimachiro chao.

45. Akaba Daudi ende Elyika Kirisito mbu: Enawechwu, rero kute kw'oyu Kirisito angaba muala wai?

46. Mango Yesu abaa era amalaa kuteta ei myasi, kutabaa mundju asibya ola walaa kumwakula chiro na mwasi. Nakutengera mw'esi suku, kutabaa mundju asibya

이쭈롸 야찌기뤄 마 마소 와 무사 노와 비다보 벼 바러비.

기리시도 아레 뭐네 떠?

41. 마꼬 아부 바파리사요 바바아 바나찌레 바부아나니레, 여수 어라 구바부사 뿌:

42. 어와써! 구더 먀네사 어라 루루 사 기리시도? 오유 기리시도, 아레 뭐네 떠? 나보 뿌: 아레 뭐네 먀미 다우디.

43. 여수 구궈라 구바부사 가찌 뿌: 러로, 구더 구 다우디 어라 아더다뿌 기리시도 아레 어나와보, 노구 오유 다우디 아바아 아고러시봐 너 무찌마 무부야-부야? 바짜 과더다아:

44. 어나워쭈 오꼬 아부라아 어나워쭈 뿌: 위가롸아 과 루따 롸네 뤄 마료, 구이기라 네비거 어 바러따 바오 구바 찌시마찌로 짜오.

45. 아가바 다우디 어떠 어레가 기리시도 뿌: 어나워쭉, 러로 구더 궈유 기리시도 아까바 무아롸 와이?

46. 마꼬 여수 아바아 어라 아마롸아 구더다 어이 먀시, 구다바아 무뚜 아시뱌 오롸 와롸아 구꽈구롸 찌로 나 먀시. 나구더뻐라 뭐시 수구, 구다바아 무뚜 아시뱌 오롸

two commandments."

41. While the Pharisees were gathered together, Jesus asked them,

42. "What do you think about the Christ? Whose son is he?" "The son of David," they replied.

43. He said to them, "How is it then that David, speaking by the Spirit, calls him 'Lord'? For he says,

44. " 'The Lord said to my Lord: "Sit at my right hand until I put your enemies under your feet." '

45. If then David calls him 'Lord,' how can he be his son?"

46. No one could say a word in reply, and from that day on no one dared to ask him any more questions.

ola waereresaa kanji
kumubusa mwasi.

와어러러사아 가찌 구무부사
꽈시.

Matayo Chikono 23

Yesu akangilyisa era lulu s'e bubi bw'e Bafarisayo n'e bakangilyisi b'e Mwaso

1. Era nyuma s'ebi, Yesu era kubura e luamba lw'e bandju n'e banafunzi bai mbu:

2. E bakangilyisi b'e Mwaso n'e bafarisayo, beresibwe e mulyimo w'e kunde bakangilyisa e bandju e Mwaso wa musa.

3. Bushi n'oku, mwemire kunde mwachwundabo na kuira e myasi Yoshi era bagende bababura Si chiro bacha, mutendaa mwakulyikira e myanya yabo, bushi bya bende bateta ata bi bende baira.

4. Bende bakanyira e banji e misio era isitoire na kubesai kwa bichwuo, si beine batanaereresa babikako e mutoke wabo.

5. Bya bende baira byoshi, bende babiira chasiya balorekaneko era muhondo s'e bandju. Beke, bende baneneya echwusanduku

마다요 찌고노 23

여수 아가삐레뻽 어라 루루 서 부비 뷔 바파리사요 너 바가삐레습 버 꽈소

1. 어라 뉴마 서비, 여수 어라 구부라 어 루아빠 뤄 바쭈 너 바나푸씨 바이 뿌:

2. 어 바가삐레시 버 꽈소 너 바파리사요, 버러시뷔 어 무레모 워 구너 바가삐레사 어 바쭈 어 꽈소 와 무사.

3. 부씨 노구, 뭐미러 구너 꽈쭈따보 나 구이라 어 먀시 요씨 어라 바거너 바바부라 시 찌로 바짜, 무더따아 꽈구레기라 어 먀냐 야보, 부씨 뱌 버너 바더다 아다 비 버떠 바이라.

4. 버떠 바가네라 어 바찌 어 미시오 어라 이시도이러 나 구버사이 과 비쭈오, 시 버이너 바다나어러러사 바비가고 어 무도거 와보.

5. 뱌 버떠 바이라 뵤씨, 버떠 바비이라 짜시야 바로러가너고 어라 무호또 서 바쭈. 버거, 버떠 바너너야 어쭈사뚜구 짠 버떠 버빠꽈 어라 마꽈㘽 너시

Matthew Chapter 23[NIV]

1. Then Jesus said to the crowds and to his disciples:

2. "The teachers of the law and the Pharisees sit in Moses' seat.

3. So you must obey them and do everything they tell you. But do not do what they do, for they do not practice what they preach.

4. They tie up heavy loads and put them on men's shoulders, but they themselves are not willing to lift a finger to move them.

5. "Everything they do is done for men to see: They make their phylacteries wide and the tassels on their garments long;

chwa bende bembala era malanga nesi kwa maboko. Kanji e maropo ma bende bembala machwusa mirera irerere kwa kulosa kwa beke bachwula bachwunjire e Mwaso wa Ongo.

6. Mwa bisiki by'e lyinye, bachwula basimire kwikala kwa bifumbi by'e chwunda. N'omwa mashenge mabo, bachwula basimire kwikala kwa bifumbi by'era muhondo.

7. Kanji bachwula basimire e bandju bende ba bakesa n'e chwunda mwa bisiki by'e nyibuanano na kunde babelyika mbu: Mukangilyisi!

8. Si mwabo, mutendaa mwemerera babelyika mbu: Mukangilyisi!. bushi muboshi munalyi bauma,na mukangilyisi muuma oshao imunete.

9. kanji muno butala, mutendaa mwelyika mundju murebe mbu: tata bushi munete Eho wenyu muuma oshao ola uchwula kwa nguba.

10. Mutendaa mwemerera babelyika mbu: Mukulu-kulu!, bushi munete mukulu-kulu muuma oshao ikirisito.

11. Rero, ola ulyi mukulu-kulu

과 마보고. 가찌 어 마로포 마 버떠 버빠꽈 마쭈사 미러라 이러러러 과 구롣사 과 버거 바쭈꽈 바쭈찌러 어 뫄소 와 오으.

6. 뫄 비시기 벼 레녀, 바쭈꽈 바시미러 귀가꽈 과 비푸뻬 벼 쭈따. 노뫄 마써써 마보, 바쭈꽈 바시미러 귀가꽈 과 비푸뻬 벼라 무호또.

7. 가찌 바쭈꽈 바시미러 어 바뉴 버떠 바 바거사 너 쭈따 뫄 비시기 벼 내부아나노 나 구떠 바버레가 뿌: 무가ᄱᅵ레시!

8. 시 뫄보, 무더따아 뭐머러라 바버레가 뿌: 무가ᄱᅵ레시!. 부씨 무보씨 무나레 바우마,나 무가ᄱᅵ레시 무우마 오싸오 이무너더.

9. 가찌 무노 부다라, 무더따아 뭐레가 무뚜 무러버 뿌: 다다 부씨 무너더 어호 워뉴 무우마 오싸오 오라 우쭈꽈 과 위바.

10. 무더따아 뭐머러라 바버레가 뿌: 무구루-구루!, 부씨 무너더 무구루-구루 무우마 오싸오 이기리시도.

11. 러로, 오꽈 우레 무구루-

6. they love the place of honor at banquets and the most important seats in the synagogues;

7. they love to be greeted in the marketplaces and to have men call them 'Rabbi.'

8. "But you are not to be called 'Rabbi,' for you have only one Master and you are all brothers.

9. And do not call anyone on earth 'father,' for you have one Father, and he is in heaven.

10. Nor are you to be called 'teacher,' for you have one Teacher, the Christ.

11. The greatest among

mwa kachi-kachi kenyu emire kuba muanda wenyu.

구루 마 가찌-가찌 거뉴 어미러 구바 무아따 워뉴.

you will be your servant.

12. E mundju woshi ola wacherusa, angandaasibwa. ola wachandaasa yeke, angerusibwa.

12. 어 무뚜 오씨 오롸 si와쩌루사, 아빠따아시봐. 시 오롸 와짜따아사 여거, 아꺼루시봐.

12. For whoever exalts himself will be humbled, and whoever humbles himself will be exalted.

Yesu atakira e Bafarisayo n'e Bakangilyisi b'e Mwaso

여수 아다기라 어 바파리사요 너 바가삐례습 버 마소

13. Mulyi baanya mu bakangilyisi b'e Mwaso nenyu mu Bafarisayo. Mulyi batebanyi! Bushi mwenjire mwaminyira e bandju e njira y'e kwengilyira mwa Bwami b'okwa nguba, n'oku mubeine mutengiliyiramo. Na mango e bandju benjire bahonda kwengilyira mwobu Bwami, mwabo mwenjire mwabangika

13. 무례 바아냐 무 바가삐례시 버 마소 너뉴 무 바파리사요. 무례 바더바네! 부씨 뭐띠러 마미니라 어 바뚜 어 띠라 여 궈삐례라 마 봐미 보꽈 꾸바, 노구 무버이너 무더삐례라모. 나 마꼬 어 바뚜 버띠러 바호따 궈삐례라 모부 봐미, 마보 뭐띠러 뭐바삐가

13. "Woe to you, teachers of the law and Pharisees, you hypocrites! You shut the kingdom of heaven in men's faces. You yourselves do not enter, nor will you let those enter who are trying to.

14. Mulyi baanya mu bakangilyisi b'e Mwaso nenyu mu Bafarisayo! Mulyi batebanyi! Mwenjire mwanyaa e bikulo by'e bahumbakasi, si era nyuma mwanaya kuira memo marerere, chasiya mulorekaneko era muhondo s'e bandju. Bushi n'oku, Ongo akabachinjibusa busese kurenza e banji bandju boshi.

14. 무례 바아냐 무 바가삐례시 버 마소 너뉴 무 바파리사요! 무례 바더바네! 뭐띠러 마냐아 어 비구로 벼 바후빠가시, 시 어라 뉴마 마나야 구이라 머모 마러러러, 짜시야 무뢰러가너고 어라 무호또 서 바뚜. 부씨 노구, 오꼬 아가바찌띠부사 부서서 구러싸 어 바찌 바뚜 보씨.

14 None

15. Mulyi baanya mu bakangilyisi b'e Mwaso nenyu mu Bafarisayo! Mulyi

15. 무례 바아냐 무 바가삐례시 버 마소 너뉴 무 바파리사요! 무례 바더바네!

15. "Woe to you, teachers of the law and Pharisees, you hypocrites! You travel

batebanyi! Mwenjire mwasungula e butala boshi mwahabuka n'e nyanja, Chasiya mubindjule mundju muuma kuba womwa chikembe chenyu. Oyu mundju mwa kuba mwamubonyire, mwanamuhubya mundju ola wemire kuchinjibusibwa era kusimu kabilyi kubarenza.

16. Mulyi banya mu bakulu-kulu bauta! Mwende mwateta mbu: Akaba e mundju angalaisa kw'e sina ly'e luhu lwa Ongo, elyi kutalyi mwasi usibya. Si akaba angalaisa kw'e sina ly'e horo era ilyi mwolu luhu, oyu mundju emire kuira kukulyikana n'okwa alaisaa.

17. Mwabo mulyi mbuta kanji mulyi bauta! Rero, chi chirenzise chilyikabo, elyi e horo era ilyi kwa luhu lwa Ongo, nesi olu luhu lweine? Si olu luhu lu luchwumire e horo yaba ibuya-buya!

18. Kanji mwenjire mwateta mbu: Akaba e mundju angalaisa kw'e sina ly'e kahaha k'e michwulo, elyi atailyire mwasi usibya. Si akaba angalaisa kw'e sina ly'e michwulo era ilyi kwako

---

뭐찌러 뫄수우꽈 어 부다꽈 보씨 뫄하부가 너 냐짜, 짜시야 무비뉴꺼 무뿌 무우마 구바 올와 찌거뻐 쩌뉴. 오유 무뿌 와 구바 뫄무보네러, 뫄나무후뱌 무뿌 오롸 워미러 구찌찌부시봐 어라 구시무 가비쪠 구바러싸.

16. 무쪠 바냐 무 바구루-구루 바우다! 뭐떠 뫄더다 뿌: 아가바 어 무뿌 아까퐈이사 궈 시나 쪄 루후 꽈 오꼬, 어레 구다쪠 뫄시 우시뱌. 시 아가바 아까퐈이사 궈 시나 쪄 호로 어라 이쪠 몰루 루후, 오유 무뿌 어미러 구이라 구구쪠가나 노과 아퐈이사아.

17. 뫄보 무쪠 뿌다 가찌 무쪠 바우다! 러로, 찌 찌러씨서 찌쪠가보, 어레 어 호로 어라 이쪠 과 루후 꽈 오꼬, 너시 오루 루후 뭐이너? 시 오루 루후 루 루쭈미러 어 호로 야바 이부야-부야!

18. 가찌 뭐찌러 뫄더다 뿌: 아가바 어 무뿌 아까퐈이사 궈 시나 쪄 가하하 거 미쭈로, 어레 아다이쪠러 뫄시 우시뱌. 시 아가바 아까퐈이사 궈 시나 쪄 미쭈로 어라 이쪠 과고 가하하, 어미러 구이라

---

over land and sea to win a single convert, and when he becomes one, you make him twice as much a son of hell as you are.

16. "Woe to you, blind guides! You say, 'If anyone swears by the temple, it means nothing; but if anyone swears by the gold of the temple, he is bound by his oath.'

17. You blind fools! Which is greater: the gold, or the temple that makes the gold sacred?

18. You also say, 'If anyone swears by the altar, it means nothing; but if anyone swears by the gift on it, he is bound by his oath.'

kahaha, emire kuira kukulyikana nokwa alaisaa.

구구레가나 노과 아롸이사아.

19. Emu bauta! Chi chirenzise chilyikabo? Elyi e michwulo nesi e kahaha k'e michwulo ku kende kachwuma ei michwulo yaba ibuya-buya!

19. 어무 바우다! 찌 찌러씨서 찌레가보? 어레 어 미쭈로 너시 어 가하하 거 미쭈로 구 거떠 가쭈마 어이 미쭈로 야바 이부야-부야!

19. You blind men! Which is greater: the gift, or the altar that makes the gift sacred?

20. Bushi n'oku, mango e mundju ende alaisa kw'e sina ly'e kahaha k'e michwulo, elyi alaisire n'okwa byoshi bya bilyiko.

20. 부씨 노구, 마꼬 어 무뚜 어떠 아롸이사 궈 시나 려 가하하 거 미쭈로, 어레 아롸이시러 노과 뵤씨 뱌 비레고.

20. Therefore, he who swears by the altar swears by it and by everything on it.

21. N'ola walaisa kw'e sina ly'e luhu, elyi alaisise kw'e sina ly'olu luhu n'okwa e sina lya Ongo lya lyichwula lyolu luhu.

21. 노롸 와롸이사 궈 시나 려 루후, 어레 아롸이시서 궈 시나 뤼오루 루후 노과 어 시나 랴 오꼬 랴 레쭈롸 료루 루후.

21. And he who swears by the temple swears by it and by the one who dwells in it.

22. N'ola walaisa kw'e sina ly'e nguba, elyi alaisise n'okwa e sina ly'e ndebe ya Ongo, n'okwa lya Ongo iwekeseko.

22. 노롸 와롸이사 궈 시나 려 꾸바, 어레 아롸이시서 노과 어 시나 려 떠버 야 오꼬, 노과 랴 오꼬 이워거서고.

22. And he who swears by heaven swears by God's throne and by the one who sits on it.

23. Mulyi baanya mu bakangilyisi b'e Mwaso nenyu mu bafarisayo! Mulyi batebayi! Mwende mwachwula Ongo e chiuma ch'e kumi ch'e bichi bya byende byachwuma e bilyo byaloka. Si mwenjire mwareka e myasi era yete mufa mwa mwaso, ngokuno: E kuira bya bichwungenene era muhondo sa Ongo, n'e kufirana e bonjo, n'e

23. 무레 바아냐 무 바가삐레시 버 므소 너뉴 무 바파리사요! 무레 바더바이! 뭐떠 마쭈롸 오꼬 어 찌우마 찌 구미 찌 비찌 뱌 벼떠 뱌쭈마 어 비뵤 뱌로가. 시 뭐삐러 마러가 어 먀시 어라 여더 무파 뫄 므소, 꼬구노: 어 구이라 뱌 비쭈머너너 어라 무호또 사 오꼬, 너 구피라나 어 보꼬, 너 구쭈따 오꼬. 어벼라, 비 뫄바아 뭐미러 구떠 뫄이라아 부시라 구러가

23. "Woe to you, teachers of the law and Pharisees, you hypocrites! You give a tenth of your spices--mint, dill and cummin. But you have neglected the more important matters of the law--justice, mercy and faithfulness. You should have practiced the latter

kuchwunda Ongo. Ebyera, bi
mwabaa mwemire kunde
mwairaa busira kureka ebi
binji.

24. Emu bakulu-kulu bauta!
Mwende mwahongola e susi
mwa meshi, si mwenjire
mwamira e ngamiya!

25. Mulyi baanya mu
bakangilyisi b'e Mwaso nenyu
mu Bafarisayo. Mulyi
batebanyi! Mwende
mwalonga e ngumbu n'e
mbare kwa muongo, si mwa
ndanda mwende mwaba
mwehwire e bindju bya
mwabonaa mwa bwisi
n'omwa buhuma-huma.

26. Eu Muuta w'e Mufarisayo!
Ulongaa tanga mwa ndanda
s'e ngumbu, mwa bacha e
muongo wai nao
anganakoma.

27. Mulyi baanya mu
bakangilyisi b'e Mwaso nenyu
mu bafarisayo. Mulyi
batembanyi! Muhuhanyisibwe
n'e shinda sa basingwire n'e
pemba. Esi shinda, sende
salorekanako kwa muongo
nga sikomire, kasi mwa
ndanda makinya ma bafu
mumehwiremo na binji
bindju bya bibolyire.

28. Nenyu, kumunalyi bacha.

어비 비찌.

24. 어무 바구루-구루 바우다!
뭐떠 뫄호꼬꽈 어 수시 뫄
머씨, 시 뭐찌러 뫄미라 어
까미야!

25. 무레 바아냐 무
바가삐레시 버 뫄소 너뉴 무
바파리사요. 무레 바더바네!
뭐떠 뫄로꽈 어 우뿌 너 빠러
과 무오꼬, 시 뫄 따따 뭐떠
뫄바 뭐휘러 어 비뉴 뱌
뫄보나아 뫄 뷔시 노뫄
부후마-후마.

26. 어우 무우다 워
무파리사요! 우로꽈아 다까 뫄
따따 서 우뿌, 뫄 바짜 어
무오꼬 와이 나오 아꽈나고뫄.

27. 무레 바아냐 무
바가삐레시 버 뫄소 너뉴 무
바파리사요. 무레 바더빠네!
무후하네시붸 너 씨따 사
바시뀌러 너 퍼빠. 어시 씨따,
서떠 사로러가나고 과 무오꼬
꽈 시고미러, 가시 뫄 따따
마기냐 마 바푸 무머휘러모 나
비찌 비뉴 뱌 비보레러.

28. 너뉴, 구무나레 바짜. 뫄

24. You blind guides! You
strain out a gnat but
swallow a camel.

25. "Woe to you, teachers
of the law and Pharisees,
you hypocrites! You clean
the outside of the cup and
dish, but inside they are
full of greed and self-
indulgence.

26. Blind Pharisee! First
clean the inside of the cup
and dish, and then the
outside also will be clean.

27. "Woe to you, teachers
of the law and Pharisees,
you hypocrites! You are
like whitewashed tombs,
which look beautiful on
the outside but on the
inside are full of dead
men's bones and
everything unclean.

28. In the same way, on

Mwa meho m'e bandju, muchwula musenekeko nga ba bachwungenene era muhondo sa Ongo. Si mwa ndanda senyu, muchwula mwehwire butebanyi na chira bubi.

머호 머 바쭈, 무쭈라 무서너거고 까 바 바쭈꺼너너 어라 무호또 사 오ᄋ. 시 마 따따 서뉴, 무쭈라 뭐휘러 부더바네 나 찌라 부비.

the outside you appear to people as righteous but on the inside you are full of hypocrisy and wickedness.

29. Mulyi baanya, mu bakangilyisi b'e Mwaso nenyu mu Bafarisayo! Mulyi batebanyi! Mwende mwaimbira e shinda s'e barebi, n'e kubika e bulyimbi kwa shinda s'e banji bandju babuya.

29. 무레 바아냐, 무 바가끼레시 버 마소 너뉴 무 바파리사요! 무레 바더바네! 뭐떠 마이삐라 어 씨따 서 바러비, 너 구비가 어 부레삐 과 씨따 서 바찌 바쭈 바부야.

29. "Woe to you, teachers of the law and Pharisees, you hypocrites! You build tombs for the prophets and decorate the graves of the righteous.

30. kanji mwenjire mwateta mbu: Akaba chwungabere mwa suku sa bahokulu bechwu, chwutangemeresanyise nabo mwa lwango lw'e kushesha e mikira y'e barebi.

30. 가찌 뭐찌러 마더다 뿌: 아가바 쭈까버러 마 수구 사 바호구루 버쭈, 쭈다꺼머러사니서 나보 마 꽈ᄋ 뭐 구써싸 어 미기라 여 바러비.

30. And you say, 'If we had lived in the days of our forefathers, we would not have taken part with them in shedding the blood of the prophets.'

31. Mwa kuteta bacha, mwalosise mubeine kwa kasi munalyi bana b'e bandju ba beeta e barebi.

31. 마 구더다 바짜, 마로시서 무버이너 과 가시 무나레 바나 버 바쭈 바 버어다 어 바러비.

31. So you testify against yourselves that you are the descendants of those who murdered the prophets.

32. Rero, muendekeraa kuira e mulyimo ola bahokulu benyu batangilyisa!

32. 러로, 무어떠거라아 구이라 어 무레모 오라 바호구루 버뉴 바다꾸레사!

32. Fill up, then, the measure of the sin of your forefathers!

33. Mwabo, mulyi buko bwa njoka! Kute mukafufumuka e buchinjibusi bw'era kusimu?

33. 마보, 무레 부고 봐 쪼가! 구더 무가푸푸무가 어 부찌찌부시 뭐라 구시무?

33. "You snakes! You brood of vipers! How will you escape being condemned to hell?

34. Bushi n'oku,

34. 부씨 노구, 네까바쭈미라

34. Therefore I am sending

nyingabachwumira barebi na banji bandju ba bete e bwenge, na bakangilyisi. Bauma mubo mungabeta, n'e banji munga banyika kwa misalaba, n'e banji mungabapunda n'e chwuchi mwa mashenge menyu na kubaiya mu chira musi.

35. Mumenyereraa kwa e mikira y'e bandju babuya-buya boshi ba bechibwaa muno butala busira chibi chisibya, ikaba kw'echwe ly'enyu. Oku kwichibwa, kwatangilyiraa ku Abeli, iwabaa uchwungenene era muhondo sa Ongo, kuikira ku sakariya mwenyi barakiya imwechiraa mwa luhu lwa Ongo, ala kachi-kachi k'e Chisiki chibuya-buya n'e kahaha k'e michwulo.

36. kubinalyi, nababura kw'e bandju b'e sine suku bu bangabusibwa kw'ebi bisibu byoshi.

Yesu alyilyira besha yerusalemu

37. Alyibwe besha yerusalemu! Mwabo mwende mweta e barebi, na mango Ongo ende abachwumira e bandju, mwende mwabeta mwa kubaumanga e makoi.

바러비 나 바찌 바뚜 바 버더어 뭐어, 나 바가삐레시. 바우마 무보 무까버다, 너 바찌 무까 바네가 과 미사꽈바, 너 바찌 무까바푸따 너 쭈찌 꽈 마써어 머뉴 나 구바이야 무 찌라 무시.

35. 무머녀러라아 과 어미기라 여 바뚜 바부야-부야 보씨 바 버찌봐아 무노 부다꽈 부시라 찌비 찌시뱌, 이가바 궈줘 려뉴. 오구 귀찌봐, 과다삐레라아 구 아버삐, 이와바아 우쭈어너너 어라 무호또 사 오꼬, 구이기라 구 사가리야 뭐니 바라기야 이무찌라아 꽈 루후 꽈 오꼬, 아꽈 가찌-가찌 거 찌시기 찌부야-부야 너 가하하 거 미쭈론.

36. 구비나레, 나바부라 궈 바뚜 버 시너 수구 부 바까부시봐 궈비 비시부 뵤씨.

여수 아레레띱 버싸 여루사퍼물

37. 아레붜 버싸 여루사퍼무! 꽈보 뭐머 뭐다 어 바러비, 나 마꼬 오꼬 어너 아바쭈미라 어 바뚜, 뭐머 꽈버다 꽈 구바우마까 어 마고이. 삐소 시너너, 나바아 너찌러 나호따

you prophets and wise men and teachers. Some of them you will kill and crucify; others you will flog in your synagogues and pursue from town to town.

35. And so upon you will come all the righteous blood that has been shed on earth, from the blood of righteous Abel to the blood of Zechariah son of Berekiah, whom you murdered between the temple and the altar.

36. I tell you the truth, all this will come upon this generation.

37. "O Jerusalem, Jerusalem, you who kill the prophets and stone those sent to you, how often I have longed to gather your children together, as

Mbiso sinene, nabaa nenjire nahonda nyibakomberere ng'okwa e ngoko yende yakomberera e chwunyau chwai mwa bibaba, si mwabo chiro mukemerera!

네바고뻐러러 우오과 어 꼬고 여떠 야고뻐러라 어 쭈냐우 쫘이 마 비바바, 시 뫄보 찌로 무거머러라!

a hen gathers her chicks under her wings, but you were not willing.

38. Mumenyereraa kubuya kw'e nyumba yenyu ingeshiba muhaka.

38. 무머녀러라아 구부야 궈 뉴빠 여뉴 이꺼씨바 무하가.

38. Look, your house is left to you desolate.

39. Nababura kwa kutengera lwarero, mutachinyiloleko kuikira e mango mungateta mbu: Aahane ono weshire kw'e sina lya Enawechwu!

39. 나바부라 과 구더꺼라 롸러로, 무다찌니로꺼고 구이기라 어 마꼬 무꺼더다 뿌: 아아하너 오노 워씨러 궈 시나 랴 어나워쭈!

39. For I tell you, you will not see me again until you say, 'Blessed is he who comes in the name of the Lord.'"

M   Mambo Chikono 24
E luhu lwa Ongo lungahandjulyibwa

마다요 찌고노 24
어 루훌 롸 오꼬 루꺼핍뉴쩨봡

Matthew Chapter 24[NIV]

1. Mango Yesu abaa atenga mwa luhu lwa Ongo, e banafunzi bai bera kumuikira chasiya bamulose olu luhu kwa luimbirwe.

1. 마꼬 여수 아바아 아더꺼 뫄 루후 롸 오꼬, 어 바나푸씨 바이 버라 구무이기라 짜시야 바무로서 오루 루후 과 루이삐뤄.

1. Jesus left the temple and was walking away when his disciples came up to him to call his attention to its buildings.

2. si Yesu era kubaakula mbu: Kubinalyi, nababura kw'ebi byoshi museneko anola, kutalyi chiro n'e koi lya lyikashiba era lulu sa lyilyikabo. Byoshi bingahandjulibwa!

2. 시 여수 어라 구바아구롸 뿌: 구비나례, 나바부라 궈비 뵤씨 무서너고 아노롸, 구다례 찌로 너 고이 랴 례가씨바 어라 루루 사 례레가보. 뵤씨 비꺼하뉴찌봐!

2. "Do you see all these things?" he asked. "I tell you the truth, not one stone here will be left on another; every one will be thrown down."

Bya bikaba mwa suku lw'e businda

뱌 비가바 뫄 수구 뤄 부시따

3. Mango Yesu abaa ekese kwa ndjulungu y'e Miseituni,

3. 마꼬 여수 아바아 어거서 과 뉴루웅우 여 미서이두니, 어

3. As Jesus was sitting on the Mount of Olives, the

e banafunzi bai bera
kumuikira ala abaa alyi yeine.
Bera kumubusa mbu:
Enawechwu, uchwuburaa
mangochi ei myasi ikaba, na
chi chikachwulosa by'e kuika
kwao, n'e by'e businda bw'e
butala!

4. Yesu nai mbu: Mumenyaa!
Kutabaa mundju usibya ola
ukabengeera,

5. bushi bandju banene
bakabaha mw'e sina lyanyi.
Abu bandju, bakende
bachitonga mbu: Nyono nyi
Kirisito! bakengeera na
bandju banene.

6. Mw'esi suku, mukomva e
bandju bateteresa era lulu s'e
bita mwa bisiki byoshi. Si
mutobaa bushi ebi byoshi
kwemire biike. Si ebyera,
bikababitatechire mbu e
businda bw'e butala bwaikire.

7. Chio chiuma chikaya
kutabalyira e chinji. Na
bwami buuma bukaya
kutabalyira e bunji. Bio
binene bikaika mu bulyio, n'e
musisi akende arenga mubi.

8. Ei myasi Yoshi, ikanaba nga
ndagilyiso yamukero.

9. E bandju bakabahomba
bushi nanyi. Bakende
babaana chasiya

바나푸씨 바이 버라
구무이기라 아라 아바아 아레
여이너. 버라 구무부사 뿌:
어나워쭈, 우쭈부라아 마꼬찌
어이 먀시 이가바, 나 찌
찌가쭈로사 벼 구이가 과오,
너 벼 부시따 붜 부다롸!

4. 여수 나이 뿌: 무머냐아!
구다바아 무뚜 우시뱌 오롸
우가버어어라,

5. 부씨 바쭈 바너너 바가바하
붜 시나 럐네. 아부 바쭈,
바거떠 바찌도롸 뿌: 뇨노 네
기리시도! 바거뻐어라 나 바쭈
바너너.

6. 뭐시 수구, 무고빠 어 바쭈
바더더러사 어라 룰루 서 비다
롸 비시기 뵤씨. 시 무도바아
부씨 어비 뵤씨 궈미러
비이거. 시 어벼라,
비가바비다더찌러 뿌 어
부시따 붜 부다롸 봐이기러.

7. 찌오 찌우마 찌가야
구다바뻬라 어 찌찌. 나 봐미
부우마 부가야 구다바뻬라 어
부찌. 비오 비너너 비가이가
무 부뻬오, 너 무시시 아거떠
아러롸 무비.

8. 어이 먀시 요씨, 이가나바
롸 따지뻬소 야무거로.

9. 어 바쭈 바가바호빠 부씨
나니. 바거떠 바바아나 짜시야
무뻬부시붜 부서서 무너찌붜.

disciples came to him
privately. "Tell us," they
said, "when will this
happen, and what will be
the sign of your coming
and of the end of the
age?"

4. Jesus answered: "Watch
out that no one deceives
you.

5. For many will come in
my name, claiming, 'I am
the Christ,' and will
deceive many.

6. You will hear of wars
and rumors of wars, but
see to it that you are not
alarmed. Such things must
happen, but the end is still
to come.

7. Nation will rise against
nation, and kingdom
against kingdom. There
will be famines and
earthquakes in various
places.

8. All these are the
beginning of birth pains.

9. "Then you will be
handed over to be
persecuted and put to

mulyibusibwe busese munechibwe.

10. mw'esi suku, bandju banene bakareka e bwemeresi bwabo. E bandju beine kwa beine, bakende barenganyana na kuhombana.

11. Barebi banene ba bisha bakaulukira. Abu barebi bakengeera bandju banene.

12. kanji bushi n'e mabi kuendekera maluwa busese, enzii ya bandju banene ikandaalyira.

13. Si ola uasesa e muchima kuikira kwa businda, akanunulyibwa.

14. Rero, ono Mwasi mubuya-buya w'e Bwami b'okwa nguba, akahubanganyisibwa mwa butala boshi, bube bubei kwa bandju b'e mbaa soshi. Chasinda, e businda bwanere bwaika.

E malyibuko masibu

15. Mw'esi suku, mukalola kw'ola bende belyika mbu Mubalasimwa kuhandjula alyi mwa chisiki chibuya-buya. Oyu murenda, imurebi Danyeli abaa atechireko mira. Ola wasoma ene myasi,

10. 뭐시 수구, 바쭈 바너너 바가러가 어 뭐머러시 봐보. 어 바쭈 버이너 과 버이너, 바거러 바러까냐나 나 구호빠나.

11. 바러비 바너너 바 비싸 바가우루기라. 아부 바러비 바거꺼어라 바쭈 바너너.

12. 가찌 부씨 너 마비 구어떠거라 마루와 부서서, 어씨이 야 바쭈 바너너 이가따아레라.

13. 시 오라 우아서사 어 무찌마 구이기라 과 부시따, 아가누누레봐.

14. 러로, 오노 마시 무부야-부야 워 봐미 보과 꾸바, 아가후바까네시봐 뫄 부다롸 보씨, 부버 부버이 과 바쭈 버 빠아 소씨. 짜시따, 어 부시따 봐너러 봐이가.

어 마레뷔겔 마시부

15. 뭐시 수구, 무가로롸 곤롸 버떠 버레가 뿌 무바롸시뫄 구하꾸롸 아레 뫄 찌시기 찌부야-부야. 오유 무러따, 이무러비 다녀픠 아바아 아더찌러고 미라. 오롸 와소마 어너 먀시, 아머녀러라아

death, and you will be hated by all nations because of me.

10. At that time many will turn away from the faith and will betray and hate each other,

11. and many false prophets will appear and deceive many people.

12. Because of the increase of wickedness, the love of most will grow cold,

13. but he who stands firm to the end will be saved.

14. And this gospel of the kingdom will be preached in the whole world as a testimony to all nations, and then the end will come.

15. "So when you see standing in the holy place 'the abomination that causes desolation,' spoken of through the prophet Daniel--let the reader understand--

amenyereraa kwanitechire.　과니더찌러.

16. Rero, e bandju ba bakaba balyi e yudeya, bahairaa mwa miruko.　16. 러로, 어 바뚜 바 바가바 바레 어 유더야, 바하이라아 똬 미루고.　16. then let those who are in Judea flee to the mountains.

17. Elyi e mundju akaba alyi kwa ngangamo s'e nyumba atachandaalyiraa mwa ndanda kutola kandju kasibya.　17. 어레 어 무뚜 아가바 아레 과 까까모 서 뉴빠 아다짜따아아레라아 똬 따따 구도똬 가뚜 가시뱌.　17. Let no one on the roof of his house go down to take anything out of the house.

18. N'elyi akaba alyi mw'ehwa, atachifulukaa kwa musi mbu aya kutola e luchimba lwai　18. 너레 아가바 아레 뭐화, 아다찌푸루가아 과 무시 뿌 아야 구도똬 어 루찌빠 똬이　18. Let no one in the field go back to get his cloak.

19. Mw'esi suku, bukaba buanya kwa bakasi ba bakaba bete makure naba bakaba boonza!　19. 뭐시 수구, 부가바 부아냐 과 바가시 바 바가바 버더 마구러 나바 바가바 보오싸!　19. How dreadful it will be in those days for pregnant women and nursing mothers!

20. Mwemaa Ongo, oku kuhaa kwenyu kutabaa mwa suku s'e mvula nesi lusuku lwa sabato.　20. 뭐마아 오꼬, 오구 구하아 궈뉴 구다바아 똬 수구 서 뿌똬 너시 루수구 똬 사바도.　20. Pray that your flight will not take place in winter or on the Sabbath.

21. Bushi esi suku sikaba sa malyibuko manene busese ma matafuraa kuba kutengera e kubumbwa kw'e butala kuikira lwarero. Kanji e malyibuko ma malyi ng'ama matakachibe.　21. 부씨 어시 수구 시가바 사 마레부고 마너너 부서서 마 마다푸라아 구바 구더꺼라 어 구부똬 궈 부다똬 구이기라 똬러로. 가찌 어 마레부고 마 마레 우아마 마다가찌버.　21. For then there will be great distress, unequaled from the beginning of the world until now--and never to be equaled again.

22. Esi suku, akaba Ongo atangasiilyire sieke, kutalyi chiro na mundju asibya ola unganunulyibwe. Si asiilyire sieke, bushi n'e bandju bai ba achilondorere.　22. 어시 수구, 아가바 오꼬 아다까시이레러 시어거, 구다레 찌로 나 무뚜 아시뱌 오똬 우까누누레붜. 시 아시이레러 시어거, 부씨 너 바뚜 바이 바 아찌롣또러러.　22. If those days had not been cut short, no one would survive, but for the sake of the elect those days will be shortened.

23. Mw'esi suku, akaba mundju murebe angababura mbu: Mulolaa! Kirisito yono ulyi wano! nesi mbu: Yola ulyi wala! oyu mundju, mutamwemereraa,

24. bushi kukaulukira bandju ba bakende bafula bisha mbu bu bera Kirisito alauma na barebi ba bisha. Abu boshi, bakende baira bisomerane binene, chasiya akaba bingaalyikana bengeere e bandju ba Ongo alondore.

25. Mumenyaa! Nababilyire ei myasi Yoshi era muhondo iike.

26. Bushi n'oku, akaba e mundju angababura mbu: Mulolaa! Rero Kirisito yola ulyi mwa buyeye! , mutayaayi. Nesi akababura mbu: yono uchibishire mwa chumba! , mutamwemereraa.

27. Bushi e kubaha kwanyi nyi mwana w'e Mundju, kukabaa ng'okwa kalyimya-lyimya kende kalomeka mwa chanya choshi.

28. Chira chisiki cha chilyi mu chirunda, ch'enzu sende saya kuchilundamo.

Ekubaha kw'e Mwana w'e Mundju

29. Era nyuma s'e malyibuko

---

23. 뭐시 수구, 아가바 무뚜 무러버 아빠바부라 뿌: 무롣롸아! 기리시도 요노 우레 와노! 너시 뿌: 요롸 우레 와롸! 오유 무뚜, 무다뭐머러라아,

24. 부씨 구가우루기라 바뚜 바 바거떠 바푸롸 비싸 뿌 부 버라 기리시도 아롸우마 나 바러비 바 비싸. 아부 보씨, 바거떠 바이라 비소머라너 비너너, 짜시야 아가바 비빠아레가나 버뻐어러 어 바뚜 바 오꼬 아롣또러.

25. 무머냐아! 나바비롖러 어이 먀시 요씨 어라 무호또 이이거.

26. 부씨 노구, 아가바 어 무뚜 아빠바부라 뿌: 무롣롸아! 러로 기리시도 요롸 우레 롸 부여여! , 무다야아에. 너시 아가바부라 뿌: 요노 우찌비씨러 롸 쭈빠! , 무다뭐머러라아.

27. 부씨 어 구바하 과네 네 롸나 워 무뚜, 구가바아 응오과 가롖먀-료먀 거떠 가롣머가 롸 짜냐 쪼씨.

28. 찌라 찌시기 짜 찌레 무 찌루따, 쩌부 서떠 사야 구찌룬따모.

어구바하 궈 롸나 워 무뚜

29. 어라 뉴마 서 마롖부고

---

23. At that time if anyone says to you, 'Look, here is the Christ!' or, 'There he is!' do not believe it.

24. For false Christs and false prophets will appear and perform great signs and miracles to deceive even the elect--if that were possible.

25. See, I have told you ahead of time.

26. "So if anyone tells you, 'There he is, out in the desert,' do not go out; or, 'Here he is, in the inner rooms,' do not believe it.

27. For as lightning that comes from the east is visible even in the west, so will be the coming of the Son of Man.

28. Wherever there is a carcass, there the vultures will gather.

29. "Immediately after the

m'esi suku, E suba lyikahuba musimya, N'e mwesi atakachikole, E ngununu nasi sikatowanga kwa nguba. Na byoshi bya byete e bushi kwa nguba, bikalyingitana.

30. Chasinda, e kalorero k'e kubaha kwanyi nyi Mwana w'e Mundju, kakalorenako kwa nguba. N'e bandju b'e mbaa soshi s'omwa butala, bakaba mwa malyira. Bakalola kwa nyi Mwana w'e Mundju natenga kwa nguba nyilyi mwa lumbumbu n'e buashi na bulangare bunene.

31. E kaperere kanene kakabanjibwamo. Chasinda, nyikachwuma e bamalaika banyi baye kwa nyinda soshi s'e butala, kubuanyanya e bandju banyi ba nalondolaa.

E muanyi w'e muchi w'e tini

32. Muchikangilyisaa kurengera e munyi w'e muchi w'e tini. Oyu muchi, mango e matabi mao mende matanganyika n'e bichi bya byatabaana, mwende mwateta mbu e chianyiro chibuya chilyi ofu.

33. Rero, mango mukalola kw'ei myasi Yoshi,

머시 수구, 어 수바 레가후바 무시먀, 너 뭐시 아다가찌고러 어 우누누 나시 시가도와꺄 나 뵤씨 뱌 벼더 어 부씨 과 우바, 비가례이다나.

30. 짜시따, 어 가로러로 거 구바하 과네 니 뫄나 워 무뚜 가가로러나고 과 우바. 너 바쭈 버 빠아 소씨 소뫄 부다꺄, 바가바 뫄 마례라. 바가로꺄 과 니 뫄나 워 무뚜 나더꺄 과 우바 네례 뫄 루뿌뿌 너 부아씨 나 부꺄어러 부너너.

31. 어 가퍼러러 가너너 가가바찌봐모. 짜시따, 네가쭈마 어 바마꺄이가 바니 바여 과 네따 소씨 서 부다꺄, 구부아냐냐 어 바쭈 바니 바 나로또꺄아.

어 무아니 워 무찌 워 디니

32. 무찌가이례사아 구러꺄라 어 무네 워 무찌 워 디니. 오유 무찌, 마꼬 어 마다비 마오 머떠 마다꺄네가 너 비찌 뱌 뱌다바아나, 뭐떠 뫄더다 뿌 어 찌아네로 찌부야 찌례 오푸.

33. 러로, 마꼬 무가로꺄 궈이 먀시 요씨, 뫄나머녀러라 과

distress of those days " 'the sun will be darkened, and the moon will not give its light; the stars will fall from the sky, and the heavenly bodies will be shaken.'

30. "At that time the sign of the Son of Man will appear in the sky, and all the nations of the earth will mourn. They will see the Son of Man coming on the clouds of the sky, with power and great glory.

31. And he will send his angels with a loud trumpet call, and they will gather his elect from the four winds, from one end of the heavens to the other.

32. "Now learn this lesson from the fig tree: As soon as its twigs get tender and its leaves come out, you know that summer is near.

33. Even so, when you see all these things, you know

mwanamenyerera kwa nyi mwana w'e Mundju, n'era nyilyi kwa chiso.

34. Kubinalyi, nababura kw'e bandju b'e sine suku batafe boshi era muhondo ei myasi Yoshi itasa kuba.

35. E nguba n'e butala bikarenga, si e binwa byanyi byeke bitakarenge chiro na hicha.

Ongo yeine iuneshi e lusuku lw'e businda

36. Si kutalyi mundju usibya ola wishi olu lusuku nesi echihangi chei myasi ikaba. Anabe n'e bamalaika b'okwa nguba, nanyi nyi Mwana w'e Mundju chwutaneshi, si tata yeine iuneshi.

37. kwa byabaa mwa suku sa Nowa, kubikanaba kanji kwa lusuku lw'e kuika kwanyi nyi Mwana w'e Mundju.

38. Bushi era muhondo s'e suku s'e mwihuso, e bandju babaa benjire balya n'e kumwa, babaa benjire bahwera n'e kuhwelyibwa, kuikira e lusuku lwa Nowa engilyiraa mwa bwato.

39. Abu bandju, batamenyaa cha chingaba kuikira mango oyu mwihuso aikaa kubasikya

네 먄나 워 무뚜, 너라 네쩨 과 찌소.

34. 구비나쪠, 나바부라 궈 바뚜 버 시너 수구 바다퍼 보씨 어라 무호또 어이 먀시 요씨 이다사 구바.

35. 어 꾸바 너 부다꽈 비가러꺄, 시 어 비놔 뱌네 벼거 비다가러뻐 찌로 나 히짜.

오꼬 여이너 이우너씨 어 룹숩꼴 뤄 부시따

36. 시 구다쩨 무뚜 우시뱌 오꽈 위씨 오루 루수구 너시 어찌하삐 쩌이 먀시 이가바. 아나버 너 바마꽈이가 보과 꾸바, 나네 네 먄나 워 무뚜 쭈다너씨, 시 다다 여이너 이우너씨.

37. 과 뱌바아 꽈 수구 사 노와, 구비가나바 가찌 과 루수구 뤄 구이가 과네 네 먄나 워 무뚜.

38. 부씨 어라 무호또 서 수구 서 뮈후소, 어 바뚜 바바아 버찌러 바꺄 너 구꽈, 바바아 버찌러 바눠라 너 구눠쩨봐, 구이기라 어 룹수구 꽈 노와 어삐쩨라아 꽈 봐도.

39. 아부 바뚜, 바다머냐아 짜 찌꽈바 구이기라 마꼬 오유 뮈후소 아이가아 구바시꺄

that it is near, right at the door.

34. I tell you the truth, this generation will certainly not pass away until all these things have happened.

35. Heaven and earth will pass away, but my words will never pass away.

36. "No one knows about that day or hour, not even the angels in heaven, nor the Son, but only the Father.

37. As it was in the days of Noah, so it will be at the coming of the Son of Man.

38. For in the days before the flood, people were eating and drinking, marrying and giving in marriage, up to the day Noah entered the ark;

39. and they knew nothing about what would happen until the flood came and

boshi. kubikanahuba kuba bacha mango nyi Mwana w'e Mundju nyikafuluka.

보씨. 구비가나후바 구바 바짜 마꼬 네 모나 워 무뚜 네가푸루가.

took them all away. That is how it will be at the coming of the Son of Man.

40. Mw'amu mango, bandju babilyi bakaba balyi mw'ehwa, muuma akekibwa, n'e unji akarekibwa.

40. 뫄무 마꼬, 바뚜 바비례 바가바 바례 뭐화, 무우마 아거기봐, 너 우찌 아가러기봐.

40. Two men will be in the field; one will be taken and the other left.

41. bakasi babilyi bakaba bashera ku lusho luuma, muuma akekibwa n'e unji akarekibwa.

41. 바가시 바비례 바가바 바써라 구 루쏘 루우마, 무우마 아거기봐 너 우찌 아가러기봐.

41. Two women will be grinding with a hand mill; one will be taken and the other left.

42. Bushi n'oku, muchilangaa, bushi muteshi e lusuku lwa Enawenyu akafuluka.

42. 부씨 노구, 무찌롸아, 부씨 무더씨 어 루수구 롸 어나워뉴 아가푸루가.

42. "Therefore keep watch, because you do not know on what day your Lord will come.

43. Mumvilyisaa ene myasi kubuya: Ena e nyumba akaba angamenyire bihangi bichiye buchwufu by'e mwisi angaika kuiba, atangaonjire chasiya alange e nyumba yai bangesha kuichwula.

43. 무삐례사아 어너 먀시 구부야: 어나 어 뉴빠 아가바 아꺼머네러 비하끼 비찌여 부쭈푸 벼 뮈시 아꺼이가 구이바, 아다꺼오찌러 짜시야 아라꺼 어 뉴빠 야이 바꺼싸 구이쭈롸.

43. But understand this: If the owner of the house had known at what time of night the thief was coming, he would have kept watch and would not have let his house be broken into.

44. Nenyu mundaa mwekalaa mwachikunganyise, bushi nyi Mwana w'e Mundju nyikabaha mwa chihangi cha muteshi.

44. 너뉴 무따아 뭐가롸아 짜찌구꺼네서, 부씨 네 모나 워 무뚜 네가바하 뫄 찌하꺼 짜 무더씨.

44. So you also must be ready, because the Son of Man will come at an hour when you do not expect him.

E mukosi ola ungachinyiirwa n'ola utangachinyiirwa

어 무고시 오라 우꺼쭘네일롭 노롸 우다꺼쭘네일롭

45. Nde imukosi mwenge ola enawabo achinyiire, ola angaira kuba mwimangisi wa balyikabo, chasiya ende

45. 떠 이무고시 뭐어 오롸 어나와보 아찌네이러, 오롸 아꺼이라 구바 뮈마꺼시 와 바례가보, 짜시야 어떠

45. "Who then is the faithful and wise servant, whom the master has put in charge of the servants

eresabo e bilyo kwa bihangi bikomire?

46. Oyu mukosi, aahanyirwe akaba enawabo angafuluka mwa lubalamo, anamubuana anachilyi akola oyu mulyimo.

47. Kubinalyi, nababura kw'oyu enawabo angamuira kuba mwimangisi w'e bikulo byai byoshi.

48. Si akaba oyu mukosi angaba mubi, na kuchitetera mbu:

49. Chasinda, anere atangilyisa kunde apunda bakosi balyikabo, na kunde alya n'e kumwa n'e batamisi.

50. Rero, enawabo akafuluka e lusuku n'e chihangi cha ateshi.

51. Bushi n'oku, enawabo akamupunda busese na kumuchinjibusa ng'okwa bendebachinjibusa e batebanyi. Chasinda, akamuuma mwa chisiki cha akalyilyiramo na kulola kwa kasibu.

어러사보 어 비룐 과 비하삐 비고미러?

46. 오유 무고시, 아아하니뤄 아가바 어나와보 아까푸루가 뫄 루바쫘모, 아나무부아나 아나찌레 아고롸 오유 무레모.

47. 구비나레, 나바부라 굮유 어나와보 아까무이라 구바 뮈마삐시 워 비구로 뱌이 뵤씨.

48. 시 아가바 오유 무고시 아까바 무비, 나 구찌더더라 뿌:

49. 짜시따, 아너러 아다삐레사 구떠 아푸따 바고시 바레가보, 나 구떠 아쨔 너 구뫄 너 바다미시.

50. 러로, 어나와보 아가푸루가 어 루수구 너 찌하삐 짜 아더씨.

51. 부씨 노구, 어나와보 아가무푸따 부서서 나 구무찌띠부사 우오과 버떠바찌띠부사 어 바더바네. 짜시따, 아가무우마 뫄 찌시기 짜 아가레레라모 나 구롼롸 과 가시부.

in his household to give them their food at the proper time?

46. It will be good for that servant whose master finds him doing so when he returns.

47. I tell you the truth, he will put him in charge of all his possessions.

48. But suppose that servant is wicked and says to himself, 'My master is staying away a long time,'

49. and he then begins to beat his fellow servants and to eat and drink with drunkards.

50. The master of that servant will come on a day when he does not expect him and at an hour he is not aware of.

51. He will cut him to pieces and assign him a place with the hypocrites, where there will be weeping and gnashing of teeth.

Matayo Chikono 25
E muanyi w'e banyere e

마다요 찌고노 25
어 무아내 워 바녀러 어 구미

Matthew Chapter 25[NIV]

kumi

1. Rero, e Bwami b'okwa nguba bungahuhanyisibwa na mwanyi wa banyere ekumi. Abu banyere batolaa e matara mabo baya kulyinjira muya mulume.

2. Batano mubo sabaa mbuta, n'e banji batano babaa bete bwenge.

3. Esi mbuta, sera kutola e matara mabo busira kw'eka e bitorolyi by'e kubikamo.

4. Si ba babaa bete bwenge beke, bera kutola e matara mabo, na kw'eka e bitorolyi.

5. Oyu muya mulume mushi n'e kwelyisa, ba banyere ekumi boshi bera kusindaana na baonjira.

6. Abere kachi-kachi ka buchwufu, e murenge era kumvikana mbu: Muya mulume eshire! Muyaa kumuhuukasa!

7. Unao-unao, ba banyere boshi bera kusuka, na batangilyisa bakunganya e marata mabo.

8. Sa mbuta, sera kubura ba babaa bete bwenge mbu: muchwuerese kwa bitorolyi byenyu, bushi e matara mechwu mahonda kusima.

---

1. 러로, 어 봐미 보과 우바 후까후하네시봐 나 마네 와 바녀러 어구미. 아부 바녀러 바도꽈아 어 마다라 마보 바야 구레찌라 무야 무루머.

2. 바다노 무보 사바아 뿌다, 너 바찌 바다노 바바아 버더 붸꺼.

3. 어시 뿌다, 서라 구도꽈 어 마다라 마보 부시라 궈가 어 비도로레 벼 구비가모.

4. 시 바 바바아 버더 붸꺼 버거, 버라 구도꽈 어 마다라 마보, 나 궈가 어 비도로레.

5. 오유 무야 무루머 무씨 너 궈레사, 바 바녀러 어구미 보씨 버라 구시따아나 나 바오찌라.

6. 아버러 가찌-가찌 가 부쭈푸, 어 무러꺼 어라 구뻬가나 뿌: 무야 무루머 어씨러! 무야아 구무후우가사!

7. 우나오-우나오, 바 바녀러 보씨 버라 구수가, 나 바다끼레사 바구까냐 어 마라다 마보.

8. 사 뿌다, 서라 구부라 바 바바아 버더 붸꺼 뿌: 무쭈어러서 과 비도로레 벼뉴, 부씨 어 마다라 머쭈 마호따 구시마.

---

1. "At that time the kingdom of heaven will be like ten virgins who took their lamps and went out to meet the bridegroom.

2. Five of them were foolish and five were wise.

3. The foolish ones took their lamps but did not take any oil with them.

4. The wise, however, took oil in jars along with their lamps.

5. The bridegroom was a long time in coming, and they all became drowsy and fell asleep.

6. "At midnight the cry rang out: 'Here's the bridegroom! Come out to meet him!'

7. "Then all the virgins woke up and trimmed their lamps.

8. The foolish ones said to the wise, 'Give us some of your oil; our lamps are going out.'

9. si nabo mbu: Nanga! Bine bitorilyi chwete, bitangachwulumira chwuboshi. Muyaa era mw'e bachimbusi, muchiulyire e byenyu.

10. Abere sa mbuta sinachilyi saya kuula e bitorolyi, ola muya mulume kuna kuika. Ba banyere batano ba babaa bachikunganyise mira, bera kwengilyira mwa linye ly'e buya alauma nai. Chasinda, e lwisi lwera kuchingibwa.

11. Era nyuma s'ebi, sa mbuta nasi sera kuika. Sera kutangilyisa salakanga mbu: Enawechwu! Enawechwu! Uchwuchungulyiraa!

12. Si muya mulume era kubaakula mbu: Nababura kanangana kwa ndabeshi!

13. Chasinjire, Yesu era kuhuba kuteta mbu: Rero, muchilanga-langa, bushi muteshi e lusuku nesi e chihangi nyikafuluka.

E muanyi w'e bakosi bahachwu

14. e bwami b'okwa nguba, chwungabuhuhanya na mwanyi wa mundju muuma ola wabaa wahonda kubalama. Oyu mundju, era kwamaala e bakosi bai na

9. 시 나보 뿌: 나까! 비너 비도리례 쭤더, 비다까쭈루미라 쭈보씨. 무야아 어라 뭐 바찌뿌시, 무찌우례러 어 벼뉴.

10. 아버러 사 뿌다 시나찌례 사야 구우꽈 어 비도로례, 오꽈 무야 무루머 구나 구이가. 바 바녀러 바다노 바 바바아 바찌구까네서 미라, 버라 궈끼례라 꽈 끼녀 껴 부야 아꽈우마 나이. 짜시따, 어 뤼시 뤄라 구찌끼봐.

11. 어라 뉴마 서비, 사 뿌다 나시 서라 구이가. 서라 구다끼례사 사꽈가까 뿌: 어나워쭈! 어나워쭈! 우쭈쭈우례라아!

12. 시 무야 무루머 어라 구바아구꽈 뿌: 나바부라 가나까나 과 따버씨!

13. 짜시찌러, 여수 어라 구후바 구더다 뿌: 러로, 무찌꽈까-꽈까, 부씨 무더씨 어 루수구 너시 어 찌하끼 네가푸루가.

어 무아네 워 바고시 바하쭈

14. 어 봐미 보과 으바, 쭈까부후하냐 나 뫄네 와 무뚜 무우마 오꽈 와바아 와호따 구바꽈마. 오유 무뚜, 어라 과마아꽈 어 바고시 바이 나 아바러거라 어 비구로 뱌이 뿌

9. " 'No,' they replied, 'there may not be enough for both us and you. Instead, go to those who sell oil and buy some for yourselves.'

10. "But while they were on their way to buy the oil, the bridegroom arrived. The virgins who were ready went in with him to the wedding banquet. And the door was shut.

11. "Later the others also came. 'Sir! Sir!' they said. 'Open the door for us!'

12. "But he replied, 'I tell you the truth, I don't know you.'

13. "Therefore keep watch, because you do not know the day or the hour.

14. "Again, it will be like a man going on a journey, who called his servants and entrusted his property to them.

abarekera e bikulo byai mbu ba bikoresaa.

바 비고러사아.

15. Era kweresa mukosi muuma talanda etano n'e unji ebilyi, n'e unji, talanda nguma. Oyu mundju, airaa bacha kukulyikana n'e misi ya chira mukosi. Chasinda, era kubalama.

15. 어라 궈러사 무고시 무우마 다꽈따 어다노 너 우찌 어비례, 너 우찌, 다꽈따 꾸마. 오유 무뚜, 아이라아 바짜 구구례가나 너 미시 야 찌라 무고시. 짜시따, 어라 구바꽈마.

15. To one he gave five talents of money, to another two talents, and to another one talent, each according to his ability. Then he went on his journey.

16. Unao-unao, e mukosi ola weresibwaa talanda etano, era kuya kuchimbula musi. Era kuinguka sinji etano.

16. 우나오-우나오, 어 무고시 오꽈 워러시봐아 다꽈따 어다노, 어라 구야 구찌뿌꽈 무시. 어라 구이우가 시찌 어다노.

16. The man who had received the five talents went at once and put his money to work and gained five more.

17. Ola weresibwaa talanda ebilyi, nai era kuya kuchimbula musi. Era kuinguka sinji ebilyi.

17. 오꽈 워러시봐아 다꽈따 어비례, 나이 어라 구야 구찌뿌꽈 무시. 어라 구이우가 시찌 어비례.

17. So also, the one with the two talents gained two more.

18. Si ola weresibwaa talanda nguma, yeke era kuya kuchima fumbi, na abishamo era talanda y'enawabo.

18. 시 오꽈 워러시봐아 다꽈따 우마, 여거 어라 구야 구찌마 푸삐, 나 아비싸모 어라 다꽈따 여나와보.

18. But the man who had received the one talent went off, dug a hole in the ground and hid his master's money.

19. Abere kwarenga suku sinene, oyu enawabo era kufuluka. Era kwamaala e bakosi bai bamubire kute bakoresaa e bikulo byai.

19. 아버러 과러꽈 수구 시너너, 오유 어나와보 어라 구푸루가. 어라 과마아꽈 어 바고시 바이 바무비러 구더 바고러사아 어 비구로 뱌이.

19. "After a long time the master of those servants returned and settled accounts with them.

20. Emukosi ola weresibwa talanda etano era kureta muinguke wa sinji etano. Era kuteta mbu: Ewalyiya, wanyirekeraa talanda etano, rero ulolaa, sinji etano sine

20. 어무고시 오꽈 워러시봐 다꽈따 어다노 어라 구러다 무이우거 와 시찌 어다노. 어라 구더다 뿌: 어와례야, 와니러거라아 다꽈따 어다노, 러로 우로꽈아, 시찌 어다노

20. The man who had received the five talents brought the other five. 'Master,' he said, 'you entrusted me with five talents. See, I have gained

naungukire.

21. Enawabo nai mbu: Nechi! Ulyi mukosi mubuya, kanji utanalyi mukongobanya! Wailyire kubuya! Rero bushi utabaa mukongobanya kwa bikulo bieke, nyingere nakuiramwimangisi wa bikulo binene. Bushi n'oku, wiraa wabaha, umowe alauma nanyi!

22. Ola weresibwaa talanda ebilyi, nai era kuika. Era kuteta mbu: e Walyiya! Wanyirekeraa talanda ebilyi, rero ulolaa sinji ebilyi sine naingukire.

23. Enawabo nai mbu: Nechi! Ulyi mukosi mubuya, kanji utanalyi mukongobanya! Wailyire kubuya! Rero bushi utabaa mukongobanya kwa bikulo bieke, nyingere nakuira mwimangisi wa bikulo binene. Bushi n'oku, wireewabaha, umowe alauma nanyi!

24. Chasinjire, ola weresibwaa talanda nguma, nai era kuika. Era kuteta mbu: e walyiya, nyishi kwa uchwula mulume musibu, woyo ulyi nga mundju ola wende washebula bya ataingaa, na kulunda-lunda bya atahandabanyaa.

시너 나우꾸기러.

21. 어나와보 나이 뿌: 너찌! 우레 무고시 무부야, 가찌 우다나레 무고꼬바냐! 와이레러 구부야! 러로 부씨 우다바아 무고꼬바냐 과 비구로 비어거, 네꺼러 나구이라뮈마삐시 와 비구로 비너너. 부씨 노구, 위라아 와바하, 우모워 아꽈우마 나니!

22. 오꽈 워러시봐아 다꽈따 어비레, 나이 어라 구이가. 어라 구더다 뿌: 어 와레야! 와네러거라아 다꽈따 어비레, 러로 우르꽈아 시찌 어비레 시너 나이꾸기러.

23. 어나와보 나이 뿌: 너찌! 우레 무고시 무부야, 가찌 우다나레 무고꼬바냐! 와이레러 구부야! 러로 부씨 우다바아 무고꼬바냐 과 비구로 비어거, 네꺼러 나구이라 뮈마삐시 와 비구로 비너너. 부씨 노구, 위러어와바하, 우모워 아꽈우마 나니!

24. 짜시찌러, 오꽈 워러시봐아 다꽈따 꾸마, 나이 어라 구이가. 어라 구더다 뿌: 어 와레야, 네씨 과 우쭈꽈 무루머 무시부, 오요 우레 꽈 무뚜 오꽈 워떠 와써부꽈 뱌 아다이꽈아, 나 구루따-루따 뱌 아다하따바냐아.

five more.'

21. "His master replied, 'Well done, good and faithful servant! You have been faithful with a few things; I will put you in charge of many things. Come and share your master's happiness!'

22. "The man with the two talents also came. 'Master,' he said, 'you entrusted me with two talents; see, I have gained two more.'

23. "His master replied, 'Well done, good and faithful servant! You have been faithful with a few things; I will put you in charge of many things. Come and share your master's happiness!'

24. "Then the man who had received the one talent came. 'Master,' he said, 'I knew that you are a hard man, harvesting where you have not sown and gathering where you have not scattered seed.

25. Bushi n'oku, nera kwobaa, na naya kubisha e talanda yao mwa chitaka. Rero, era talanda yao iyene.

26. Enawabo nai mbu: ulyi mukosi mubi, kanji unalyi ndambaara! Ewashe, wabaa wishi kwa nende nashebula bya ndaingaa, n'okwa nende nalunda-lunda bya ndahandabanyaa!

27. Chi cheraa chachwuma utanyibikira e bikulo byanyi mwa nyumba era bende balangira mw'e buteya, chasiya mango nyingafuluka, nyibitoreremo alauma n'e muunguke wabi?

28. Chasinda era kuteta mbu: Mumunyaaa ei talanda, mwaneresai ono wete talanda ekumi.

29. Bushi ola wete iwende waneresibwa, anere aba mwa muako. Si ola utete kandju, akanyaibwa n'eka achirembaa kuata.

30. Kanji, oyu mukosi utete mufa usibya, mumuuma era butala mwa musimya. Na mwoyu musimya, e bandju bakalyira na kulola kwa kasibu.

25. 부씨 노구, 너라 곱바아, 나 나야 구비싸 어 다롸따 야오 뫄 찌다가. 러로, 어라 다롸따 야오 이여너.

26. 어나와보 나이 뿌: 우레 무고시 무비, 가찌 우나레 따빠아라라! 어와써, 와바아 위씨 과 너더 나써부롸 뱌 따이꺄아, 노과 너더 나루따-루따 뱌 따하따바냐아!

27. 찌 쩌라아 짜쭈마 우다네비기라 어 비구롣 뱌네 뫄 뉴빠 어라 버더 바롸끼라 뭐 부더야, 짜시야 마꼬 네꺄푸룩가, 네비도러러모 아롸우마 너 무우욱거 와비?

28. 짜시따 어라 구더다 뿌: 무무냐아아 어이 다롸따, 먀너러사이 오노 워더 다롸따 어구미.

29. 부씨 오롸 워더 이워떠 와너러시봐, 아너러 아바 뫄 무아고. 시 오롸 우더더 가뚜, 아가냐이봐 너가 아찌러빠아 구아다.

30. 가찌, 오유 무고시 우더더 무파 우시뱌, 무무우마 어라 부다롸 뫄 무시먀. 나 모유 무시먀, 어 바뚜 바가레라 나 구롣롸 과 가시부.

25. So I was afraid and went out and hid your talent in the ground. See, here is what belongs to you.'

26. "His master replied, 'You wicked, lazy servant! So you knew that I harvest where I have not sown and gather where I have not scattered seed?

27. Well then, you should have put my money on deposit with the bankers, so that when I returned I would have received it back with interest.

28. " 'Take the talent from him and give it to the one who has the ten talents.

29. For everyone who has will be given more, and he will have an abundance. Whoever does not have, even what he has will be taken from him.

30. And throw that worthless servant outside, into the darkness, where there will be weeping and gnashing of teeth.'

E buchinjibusi bw'e bandju 어 부찌씨븝슙 붜 바쭈

31. Mango nyi mwana w'e Mundju nyikabaha mwa bulangare bwanyi alauma n'e bamalaika boshi, nyikekala kwa ndebe yanyi y'e bwami.

31. 마꼬 네 뫄나 워 무뚜 네가바하 뫄 부퐈따러 봐니 아퐈우마 너 바마퐈이가 보씨, 네거가퐈 과 떠버 야니 여 봐미.

31. "When the Son of Man comes in his glory, and all the angels with him, he will sit on his throne in heavenly glory.

32. E bandju boshi bakabuanana era muhondo sanyi, nanyi nyikalyikanyabo mu bikembe bibilyi ng'okwa e mungere ende alyikanya e mbulyi n'e mbene.

32. 어 바쭈 보씨 바가부아나나 어라 무호또 사니, 나니 네가레가냐보 무 비거뻐 비비쀄 으오과 어 무뻐러 어뻐 아쀄가냐 어 뿌쀄 너 뻐너.

32. All the nations will be gathered before him, and he will separate the people one from another as a shepherd separates the sheep from the goats.

33. Nyikabika e mbulyi kwa lunda lwanyi lw'e malyo, n'e mbene kwa lw'e marembe.

33. 네가비가 어 뿌쀄 과 루따 퐈니 뤄 마푠, 너 뻐너 과 뤄 마러뻐.

33. He will put the sheep on his right and the goats on his left.

34. Chasinda, nyikabura ba bakaba balyi kwa lunda lwanyi lw'e malyo mbu: Mubahaa, mu mwaahanyirwe na tata, mwengilyire mwa bwami bwa abakunganyisaa kuntengera e kububwa kw'e butala.

34. 짜시따, 네가부라 바 바가바 바쀄 과 루따 퐈니 뤄 마푠 뿌: 무바하아, 무 뫄아하니뤄 나 다다, 뭐삐쀄러 뫄 봐미 봐 아바구퐈니사아 구누더뻐라 어 구부봐 궈 부다퐈.

34. "Then the King will say to those on his right, 'Come, you who are blessed by my Father; take your inheritance, the kingdom prepared for you since the creation of the world.

35. Bushi mango nabaa nafa e businya, mwera kunyeresa e bilyo, na mango nabaa nafa e chami, mwera kunyeresa eby'e kumwa, na mango nabaa nyilyi muenyi, mwera kunyihuukasa.

35. 부씨 마꼬 나바아 나파 어 부시냐, 뭐라 구녀러사 어 비푠, 나 마꼬 나바아 나파 어 짜미, 뭐라 구녀러사 어뻐 구뫄, 나 마꼬 나바아 네쀄 무어니, 뭐라 구네후우가사.

35. For I was hungry and you gave me something to eat, I was thirsty and you gave me something to drink, I was a stranger and you invited me in,

36. Kanji mango nabaa nainyire e luchimba, mwera kunyeresalo, na mango nabaa nyilyi mulwala, mwera kunyiasa, na mango nabaa

36. 가찌 마꼬 나바아 나이니러 어 루찌빠, 뭐라 구녀러사뢰, 나 마꼬 나바아 네쀄 무퐈퐈, 뭐라 구네아사, 나 마꼬 나바아 네쀄 뫄

36. I needed clothes and you clothed me, I was sick and you looked after me, I was in prison and you came to visit me.'

nyilyi mwa buroko, mwerakuya kunyitangula.

37. Chasinda abu babaa bachwunjire Ongo bakanyakula mbu: enawechwu! Mangochi chwakulolaako wafa businya chwera kukweresa e bilyo, nesi mangochi wabaa wafa chami, chwera kukweresa eby'e kumwa?

38. Na mangochi wabaa ulyi muenyi, chwera kukuhuukasa? Nesi mangochi wainaa e luchuimba, chwera kukweresalo?

39. Na mangochi chwakulolaako walaka, nesi ulyi mwa buroko, chwera kuya kukutangula?

40. Oyu mwami akabakura mbu: Kubinalyi, nababura kwa ebi byoshi, mango mwendee mwabikoreraa ola ulyi mueke mwa bano bunyakechwu, mumenyereraa kwa nyi mwendee mwakorerabi.

41. Chasinda, abu bakaba balyi kwa lunda lwanyi lw'e mwarembe, beke nyikababura mbu: Mutengaa mwa meho manyi, mu Ongo atakire! Muya mwa mulyiro ola utakasime e suku n'e mango.

부로고, 뭐라구야 구네다꽈라.

37. 짜시따 아부 바바아 바쭈찌러 오오 바가냐구꽈 뿌: 어나워쭈! 마오찌 좌구론꽈아고 와파 부시냐 쭤라 구궈러사 어 비료, 너시 마오찌 와바아 와파 짜미, 쭤라 구궈러사 어벼 구꽈?

38. 나 마오찌 와바아 우레 무애네, 쭤라 구구후우가사? 너시 마오찌 와이나아 어 루쭈이빠, 쭤라 구궈러사론?

39. 나 마오찌 좌구론꽈아고 와꽈가, 너시 우레 꽈 부로고, 쭤라 구야 구구다꽈라?

40. 오유 꽈미 아가바구라 뿌: 구비나레, 나바부라 과 어비 뵤씨, 마오 뭐떠어 꽈비고러라아 오꽈 우레 무어거 꽈 바노 부냐거쭈, 무머녀러라아 과 네 뭐떠어 꽈고러라비.

41. 짜시따, 아부 바가바 바레 과 루따 꽈네 뭐 꽈러뻐, 버거 네가바부라 뿌: 무더까아 꽈 머호 마네, 무 오오 아다기러! 무야 꽈 무레로 오꽈 우다가시머 어 수구 너 마오. 오유 무레로, 아구까네시붜

37. "Then the righteous will answer him, 'Lord, when did we see you hungry and feed you, or thirsty and give you something to drink?

38. When did we see you a stranger and invite you in, or needing clothes and clothe you?

39. When did we see you sick or in prison and go to visit you?'

40. "The King will reply, 'I tell you the truth, whatever you did for one of the least of these brothers of mine, you did for me.'

41. "Then he will say to those on his left, 'Depart from me, you who are cursed, into the eternal fire prepared for the devil and his angels.

Oyu mulyiro, akunganyisibwe mira bushi na Wamusimu n'e bamalaika bai!

42. Bushi mango nabaa nafa e businya, chiro mukanyeresa e bilyo. Na mango nabaa nafa chami, chiro mukanyeresa eby'e kumwa,

43. na mango nabaa nyilyi muenyi, chiro mukanyihuukasa, na mango nainaa e luchimba, chiro mukanyeresalo. Kanji mango nabaa nyilyi mulwala, na mango nabaa nyilyi mwa buroko, chiro mukaya kunyitangula.

44. Nabo bakamubusa mbu: Enawechwu! Mangochi chwakulolaako wafa businya, nesi wafa chami, nesi ulyi muenyi, nesi wainyire e luchimba, nesi ulyi mulwala, nesi ulyi mwa buroko, chiro chwukaika kukuasa?

45. Nanyi nyikaabakula mbu: kubinalyi, nababura kw'ebi byoshi, mango mutendee mwabikorera ola ulyi mueke mwa bano banyakwechwu, mumenyeraa kwa ata nyi mwendee mwabiilyira.

미라 부씨 나 와무시무 너 바마롸이가 바이!

42. 부씨 마꼬 나바아 나파 어 부시냐, 찌로 무가녀러사 어 비료. 나 마꼬 나바아 나파 짜미, 찌로 무가녀러사 어벼 구롸,

43. 나 마꼬 나바아 네쀄 무어니, 찌로 무가네후우가사, 나 마꼬 나이나아 어 루찌빠, 찌로 무가녀러사로. 가찌 마꼬 나바아 네쀄 무롸롸, 나 마꼬 나바아 네쀄 롸 부로고, 찌로 무가야 구네다우롸.

44. 나보 바가무부사 뿌: 어나워쭈! 마꼬찌 좌구로롸아고 와파 부시냐, 너시 와파 짜미, 너시 우레 무어니, 너시 와이네러 어 루찌빠, 너시 우레 무롸롸, 너시 우레 롸 부로고, 찌로 쭈가이가 구구아사?

45. 나네 네가아바구롸 뿌: 구비나쀄, 나바부라 궈비 뵤씨 마꼬 무더떠어 롸비고러라 오롸 우레 무어거 롸 바노 바냐궈쭈, 무머녀라아 과 아다 네 뭐떠어 롸비이쀄라.

42. For I was hungry and you gave me nothing to eat, I was thirsty and you gave me nothing to drink,

43. I was a stranger and you did not invite me in, I needed clothes and you did not clothe me, I was sick and in prison and you did not look after me.'

44. "They also will answer, 'Lord, when did we see you hungry or thirsty or a stranger or needing clothes or sick or in prison, and did not help you?'

45. "He will reply, 'I tell you the truth, whatever you did not do for one of the least of these, you did not do for me.'

46. Chasinda, abu bandju bakaya mwa buchinjibusi bw'e suku n'e mango. Si ba bachwunjire Ongo beke, bakaya mwa kalamo k'e suku n'e mango.

46. 짜시따, 아부 바쭈 바가야 봐 부찌찌부시 붜 수구 너 마꼬. 시 바 바쭈찌러 오꼬 버거, 바가야 봐 가꺄모 거 수구 너 마꼬.

46. "Then they will go away to eternal punishment, but the righteous to eternal life."

Matayo Chikono 26
E lwango lw'e kusimba Yesu

마다요 찌고노 26
어 꽈꼬 뤄 구시빠 여수

Matthew Chapter 26[NIV]

1. Mango Yesu abaa era amalaa kuteta ei myasi Yoshi, era kubura ebanafunzi bai mbu:

1. 마꼬 여수 아바아 어라 아마꺄아 구더다 어이 먀시 요씨, 어라 구부라 어바나푸씨 바이 뿌:

1. When Jesus had finished saying all these things, he said to his disciples,

2. Si mwishi kwa era nyuma sa suku ebilyi, e lusuku lukulu lw'e pasaka lungaika. Mumenyereraa kwa nyi mwana w'e Mundju nyingaanyibwa chasiya nyimanyikibwe kwa musalaba.

2. 시 뮈씨 과 어라 뉴마 사 수구 어비례, 어 루수구 루구루 뤄 파사가 루꽈이가. 무머녀러라아 과 네 마나 워 무뚜 네꽈아네봐 짜시야 네마네기붜 과 무사꽈바.

2. "As you know, the Passover is two days away--and the Son of Man will be handed over to be crucified."

3. E bakulu-kulu b'e bakuhanyi, n'e bashamuka b'e bayuda, bera kubuanana mwa mw'e mukulu-kulu w'e bakuhanyi mbu I kayafa.

3. 어 바구루-구루 버 바구하네, 너 바싸무가 버 바유다, 버라 구부아나나 봐 뭐 무구루-구루 워 바구하네 뿌 이 가야파.

3. Then the chief priests and the elders of the people assembled in the palace of the high priest, whose name was Caiaphas,

4. Mw'olu lubuanana mu bera kuya lwango lwa kusimba Yesu kwa bubisho-bisho, chasiya bamwite.

4. 몰루 루부아나나 무 버라 구야 꽈꼬 꽈 구시빠 여수 과 부비쏘-비쏘, 짜시야 바뮈더.

4. and they plotted to arrest Jesus in some sly way and kill him.

5. Si bera kuteta mbu: Tutamusimbaa e lusuku lukulu lw'e pasaka, kungesha kuba lwayo lunene mwa

5. 시 버라 구더다 뿌: 두다무시빠아 어 루수구 루구루 뤄 파사가, 구꺼싸 구바 꽈요 루너너 봐 바뚜.

5. "But not during the Feast," they said, "or there may be a riot among the people."

bandju.

Mukasi muuma akaba Yesu e marashi

6. Abere Yesu alyi mwa musi w'e betaniya, era kwengira mwa mwa mulume muuma mbu I simoni. Oyu simoni abaa mubenzi-benzi.

7. Mango babaa bera balya, mukasi muuma era kufunda ofu na yesu. Oyu mukasi, abaa ete mulangi wa marashi ma chichiro chinene busese. Era kumakaba Yesu kw'echwe.

8. E banafunzi bai balolyire bacha, bera kuhongwa busese, na batangilyisa bachitetembya mbu: Ebase! Chi chachwumire ono mukasi aesa mano marashi basha?

9. Si mabaa mangausibwe ku chichiro chinene n'e buteya bwa mangafire, bungaasise e bakene!

10. Obu buyongwa, Yesu era kubumenyerera. Bushi n'oku, era kubabusa mbu: chi chachwuma mwalyibusa ono mukasi bacha? si mabuya mano anyikorere!

11. e bakene bakanaba nenyu e suku soshi, si nyono

무가시 무우마 아가바 여수 어 마라씨

6. 아버러 여수 아쩨 먀 무시 워 버다니야, 어라 궈에라 먀 먀 무루머 무우마 뿌 이 시모니. 오유 시모니 아바아 무버씨-버씨.

7. 마꼬 바바아 버라 바랴, 무가시 무우마 어라 구푸따 오푸 나 여수. 오유 무가시, 아바아 어더 무퐈에 와 마라씨 마 찌찌로 찌너너 부서서. 어라 구마가바 여수 궈쮀.

8. 어 바나푸씨 바이 바롤쩨러 바짜, 버라 구호꽈 부서서, 나 바다에쩨사 바찌더더빠 뿌: 어바서! 찌 짜쭐미러 오노 무가시 아어사 마노 마라씨 바싸?

9. 시 마바아 마꽈우시붜 구 찌찌로 찌너너 너 부더야 봐 마꽈피러, 부꽈아시서 어 바거너!

10. 오부 부요꽈, 여수 어라 구부머녀러러. 부씨 노구, 어라 구바부사 뿌: 찌 짜쭐마 꽈쩨부사 오노 무가시 바짜? 시 마부야 마노 아네고러러!

11. 어 바거너 바가나바 너뉴 어 수구 소씨, 시 뇨노 따가버

6. While Jesus was in Bethany in the home of a man known as Simon the Leper,

7. a woman came to him with an alabaster jar of very expensive perfume, which she poured on his head as he was reclining at the table.

8. When the disciples saw this, they were indignant. "Why this waste?" they asked.

9. "This perfume could have been sold at a high price and the money given to the poor."

10. Aware of this, Jesus said to them, "Why are you bothering this woman? She has done a beautiful thing to me.

11. The poor you will always have with you, but

ndakabe nenyu e suku soshi.

12. Ono mukasi anyakabire mano marashi, bushi n'e kukunganya e kutabwa kwanyi.

13. kubinalyi, nababura kwa mwa butala boshi, mu chira chisiki cha bakende bahubanganya mw'e mwasi mubuya-buya, bakende bahambala era luulu s'e mwasi ono mukasi ailyire. Bushi n'oku, ono mukasi akende akengerwa.

Yuda ahonda kurenganya Yesu

14. Mw'esi suku, muuma mwa banafunzi ekumi na babilyi ba Yesu mbu i yuda isikariota, era kuya era mw'e bakulu-kulu b'e bakuhanyi.

15. Era kubabusa mbu: Chi munganyeresa, akaba nyingabawa Yesu? Bera kumweresa bikorota mahachwu bya buteya.

16. kutengera amu mango, yuda era kutangilyisa ahonda kute angabawa Yesu.

Yesu alya e pasaka alauma n'e banafunzi bai

17. Mango e lusuku lubere lw'e suku sikulu s'e mikati era

너뉴 어 수구 소씨.

12. 오노 무가시 아냐가비러 마노 마라씨, 부씨 너 구구빠냐 어 구다봐 과니.

13. 구비나뤠, 나바부라 과 똬 부다뽜 보씨, 무 찌라 찌시기 짜 바거머 바후바빠냐 뭐 똬시 무부야-부야, 바거머 바하빠뫄 어라 룽우뤃 서 똬시 오노 무가시 아이쪠러. 부씨 노구, 오노 무가시 아거머 아거뭐랴.

유다 아호빠 구러빠냇 여수

14. 뭐시 수구, 무우마 똬 바나푸씨 어구미 나 바비뤠 바 여수 뿌 이 유다 이시가리오다, 어라 구야 어라 뭐 바구룽-구룽 버 바구하니.

15. 어라 구바부사 뿌: 찌 무빠녀러사, 아가바 네빠바와 여수? 버라 구뭐러사 비고로댜 마하쭉 뱌 부더야.

16. 구더뺘라 아무 마쯧, 유다 어라 구다삐쪠사 아호빠 구더 아빠바와 여수.

여수 아뺘 어 파사가 아뺘웁립 너 바나푸씨 바이

17. 마쯧 어 룽수구 루버러 뭐 수구 시구룽 서 미가디 어라

---

you will not always have me.

12. When she poured this perfume on my body, she did it to prepare me for burial.

13. I tell you the truth, wherever this gospel is preached throughout the world, what she has done will also be told, in memory of her."

14. Then one of the Twelve--the one called Judas Iscariot--went to the chief priests

15. and asked, "What are you willing to give me if I hand him over to you?" So they counted out for him thirty silver coins.

16. From then on Judas watched for an opportunity to hand him over.

17. On the first day of the Feast of Unleavened

italyi mu chachu lwaikaa, e banafunzi ba Yesu bera kumuikira na bamubusa mbu: Enawechwu, ngai u wahonda chwuye ku kukunganyisisa e bilyo by'e pasaka?

18. Nai mbu: Muyaa mwa musi, ala mwa mundju murebe. Oyu mundju, mungamubura mbu: e Mukangilyisi wechwu atechire mbu e bihangi bya abaa alanga bilyi ofu. Rero, angalyira e bilyo by'e pasaka mwa mwao alauma n'e banafunzi bai.

19. Abu banafunzi bera kunaira ng'okwa Yesu anababuraa, bera kukuganya e bilyo by'e pasaka.

20. Mango lwabaa lwera luolo-olo, Yesu era kuikala alya e bilyo alauma n'e banafunzi bai ekumi na babilyi.

21. Abere bera balya, era kubabura mbu: kubinalyi, nababura kwa muuma mu mwabo anganyirenganya.

22. Oyu mwasi, era kusibusa e banafunzi busese. Bushi n'oku, chira muuma era kutangilyisa amubusa mbu: Enawechwu! Elyi nyono!

23. Yesu nai mbu: Ola

이다뤠 무 짜쭈 롸이가아, 어 바나푸씨 바 여수 버라 구무이기라 나 바무부사 뿌: 어나워쭈, 롸이 우 와호따 쭈여 구 구구꺄네시사 어 비료 벼 파사가?

18. 나이 뿌: 무야아 롸 무시, 아롸 롸 무뚜 무러버. 오유 무뚜, 무꺄무부라 뿌: 어 무가삐뤠시 워쭈 아더찌러 뿌 어 비하삐 뱌 아바아 아롸아 비뤠 오푸. 러로, 아꺄뤠라 어 비료 벼 파사가 롸 롸오 아롸우마 너 바나푸씨 바이.

19. 아부 바나푸씨 버라 구나이라 꾸오과 여수 아나바부라아, 버라 구구가냐 어 비료 벼 파사가.

20. 마오 롸바아 뤄라 루오로-오로, 여수 어라 구이가롸 아꺄 어 비료 아롸우마 너 바나푸씨 바이 어구미 나 바비뤠.

21. 아버러 버라 바꺄, 어라 구바부라 뿌: 구비나뤠, 나바부라 과 무우마 무 롸보 아꺄내러꺄냐.

22. 오유 롸시, 어라 구시부사 어 바나푸씨 부서서. 부씨 노구, 찌라 무우마 어라 구다삐뤠사 아무부사 뿌: 어나워쭈! 어뤠 뇨노!

23. 여수 나이 뿌: 오롸

Bread, the disciples came to Jesus and asked, "Where do you want us to make preparations for you to eat the Passover?"

18. He replied, "Go into the city to a certain man and tell him, 'The Teacher says: My appointed time is near. I am going to celebrate the Passover with my disciples at your house.' "

19. So the disciples did as Jesus had directed them and prepared the Passover.

20. When evening came, Jesus was reclining at the table with the Twelve.

21. And while they were eating, he said, "I tell you the truth, one of you will betray me."

22. They were very sad and began to say to him one after the other, "Surely not I, Lord?"

23. Jesus replied, "The one

watobesa alauma nanyi, iunganyirenganya.

24. Nyi Mwana w'e mundju nyingafa, kukulyikana n'okwa byanjikirwe era luulu sanyi. Si buanyi kwa mundju ola unganyirenganya! oyu mundju, kungakomire atangabuchirwe!

25. Yuda iwamurenganyaa, nai era kubusa mbu: Mukangilyisi! Elyi nyono? Yesu na imbu: weine watechire!

26. Mango babaa banachilyi balya, Yesu era kutola e mukati era kuteta mbu akoko era mwa Ongo. Era kuishanga muo, era kweresao e banafunzi bai. Chasinda, era kubabura mbu: Mutolaa ono mukati mulyeo, bushi alyi e mubilyi wanyi.

27. Era nyuma s'ebi, era kutola e ngumbu, era kuteta mbu akoko era mwa Ongo. Era kuberesai na ababura mbu: Mumwaa muboshi,

28. bushi enere ilyi e mikira yanyi, ya kulosa e chilaano cha Ongo airaa n'e lubaa lwai. Ei mikira, ingasheshekala kwa kununula bandju banene, chasiya bababalyirwe e bibi

와도버사 아꽈우마 나니, 이우ㅁ나네러ㅁ냐.

24. 네 뫄나 워 무뚜 네ㅳ파, 구구뤠가나 노과 뱌찌기뤄 어라 루우루 사니. 시 부아네 과 무뚜 오롸 우ㅁ나네러ㅳ냐! 오유 무뚜, 구ㅁ고미러 아다ㅃ부찌뤄!

25. 유다 이와무러ㅁ냐아, 나이 어라 구부사 뿌: 무가ㅁ례시! 어레 뇨노? 여수 나 이뿌: 워이너 와더찌러!

26. 마ㅇ 바바아 바나찌레 바랴, 여수 어라 구도롸 어 무가디 어라 구더다 뿌 아고고 어라 뫄 오ㅇ. 어라 구이싸ㅁ 무오, 어라 궈러사오 어 바나푸씨 바이. 짜시따, 어라 구바부라 뿌: 무도롸아 오노 무가디 무뤼오, 부씨 아레 어 무비레 와니.

27. 어라 뉴마 서비, 어라 구도롸 어 ㅇ뿌, 어라 구더다 뿌 아고고 어라 뫄 오ㅇ. 어라 구버러사이 나 아바부라 뿌: 무뫄아 무보씨,

28. 부씨 어너러 이레 어 미기라 야니, 야 구로사 어 찌롸아노 짜 오ㅇ 아이라아 너 루바아 롸이. 어이 미기라, 이ㅁ써써가롸 과 구누누롸 바뚜 바너너, 짜시야

who has dipped his hand into the bowl with me will betray me.

24. The Son of Man will go just as it is written about him. But woe to that man who betrays the Son of Man! It would be better for him if he had not been born."

25. Then Judas, the one who would betray him, said, "Surely not I, Rabbi?" Jesus answered, "Yes, it is you."

26. While they were eating, Jesus took bread, gave thanks and broke it, and gave it to his disciples, saying, "Take and eat; this is my body."

27. Then he took the cup, gave thanks and offered it to them, saying, "Drink from it, all of you.

28. This is my blood of the covenant, which is poured out for many for the forgiveness of sins.

byabo.

바바바쩨뤄 어 비비 뱌보.

29. Nababura kwa kutengera lwarero ndakachimwe tifai, kuikira e lusuku lwa chwukamwa e tifai iyayaya mwa bwami bwa tata.

29. 나바부라 과 구더떠라 꽈러로 따가찌뭐 디파이, 구이기라 어 루수구 꽈 쭈가뫄 어 디파이 이야야야 뫄 봐미 봐 다다.

29. I tell you, I will not drink of this fruit of the vine from now on until that day when I drink it anew with you in my Father's kingdom."

30. Abere bera bemba, bera kuya kwa ndjulungu y'e Miseituni.

30. 아버러 버라 버빠, 버라 구야 과 뚜루우우 여 미서이두니.

30. When they had sung a hymn, they went out to the Mount of Olives.

Yesu ateta kwa petero angamunana

여수 아더다 과 퍼더로 아빠뮬낌낍

31. Chasinda, Yesu era kubura e banafunzi bai mbu: Mwobuno buchwufu, muboshi munganyirekerera. Bushi byanjikirwe mbu: Nyingeta e mungere w'e mbulyi. N'e buso bw'esi mbulyi, bungahandabana.

31. 짜시따, 여수 어라 구부라 어 바나푸씨 바이 뿌: 모부노 부쭈푸, 무보씨 무빠너러거러라. 부씨 뱌찌기뤄 뿌: 네떠다 어 무떠러 워 뿌뤠. 너 부소 붜시 뿌뤠, 부빠하따바나.

31. Then Jesus told them, "This very night you will all fall away on account of me, for it is written: " 'I will strike the shepherd, and the sheep of the flock will be scattered.'

32. Si chiro bacha, mango nyigomwoka, nyingabahonderera e kalilaya.

32. 시 찌로 바짜, 마꼬 네고모가, 네빠바호떠러라 어 가리꽈야.

32. But after I have risen, I will go ahead of you into Galilee."

33. Petero era kumubura mbu: Chiro angaba mbu e banji boshi bangakureka, nyono ndakureke chiro na hicha!

33. 퍼더로 어라 구무부라 뿌: 찌로 아빠바 뿌 어 바찌 보씨 바빠구러가, 뇨노 따구러거 찌로 나 히짜!

33. Peter replied, "Even if all fall away on account of you, I never will."

34. Yesu na imbu: kubinalyi, nakubura kwa mwobuno buchwufu, era muhondo s'e luasi kubika, ungaba wachaakana nyono kahachwu.

34. 여수 나 이뿌: 구비나뤠, 나구부라 과 모부노 부쭈푸, 어라 무호또 서 루아시 구비가, 우빠바 와짜아가나 뇨노 가하쭈.

34. "I tell you the truth," Jesus answered, "this very night, before the rooster crows, you will disown me three times."

35. Petero na imbu: akaba binyemire kufira alauma nao, nemerere. Si e kukunana ku ndangakunana chiro na hicha! E banji banafunzi boshi nabo, bera kunateta bacha.

Yesu ema Ongo e ketesemane

36. Era nyuma s'ebi, Yesu n'e banafunzi bai bera kuya mu chisiki chiuma cha chelyikirwe mbu ketesemane. Baikiremo, Yesu era kubabura mbu: Mwikalaa tanga anola, kuno naya kwema Ongo.

37. Yesu era kuenda na petero na baala ba sebetayo babilyi. Era kuata businane n'e bwenge bwera kumusungulyira.

38. Bushi n'oku, era kubabura mbu: Buno businane bwahonda kunyita. Rero, muberaa anola, mutaonjiraa.

39. Chasinda, era kuchifunda era muhondo hicha, era kufukama, e buso bwai bwera kuikira kwanachitaka. Era kutangilyisa ema Ongo mbu: Tata! akaba bingaalyikana, ene ngumbu ya mano malyibuko, unyiimiraai! Si chiro bacha, bitabaa ng'okwa

35. 퍼더로 나 이뿌: 아가바 비녀미러 구피라 아쫘우마 나오, 너머러러. 시 어 구구나나 구 따빠구나나 찌로 나 히짜! 어 바찌 바나푸씨 보씨 나보, 버라 구나더다 바짜.

여수 어마 오꼬 어 거더서마너

36. 어라 뉴마 서비, 여수 너 바나푸씨 바이 버라 구야 무 찌시기 찌우마 짜 쩌쩨기뤄 뿌 거더서마너. 바이기러모, 여수 어라 구바부라 뿌: 뮈가쫘아 다빠 아노쫘, 구노 나야 궈마 오꼬.

37. 여수 어라 구어따 나 퍼더로 나 바아쫘 바 서버다요 바비쩨. 어라 구아다 부시나너 너 붜어 붜라 구무수꾸쩨라.

38. 부씨 노구, 어라 구바부라 뿌: 부노 부시나너 봐호따 구네다. 러로, 무버라아 아노쫘, 무다오찌라아.

39. 쌰시따, 어라 구찌푸따 어라 무호또 히짜, 어라 구푸가마, 어 부소 바이 붜라 구이기라 과나찌다가. 어라 구다삐쩨사 어마 오꼬 뿌: 다다! 아가바 비빠아쩨가나, 어너 꾸뿌 야 마노 마쩨부고, 우네이미라아이! 시 찌로 바짜, 비다바아 꾸오과 나호따, 시

35. But Peter declared, "Even if I have to die with you, I will never disown you." And all the other disciples said the same.

36. Then Jesus went with his disciples to a place called Gethsemane, and he said to them, "Sit here while I go over there and pray."

37. He took Peter and the two sons of Zebedee along with him, and he began to be sorrowful and troubled.

38. Then he said to them, "My soul is overwhelmed with sorrow to the point of death. Stay here and keep watch with me."

39. Going a little farther, he fell with his face to the ground and prayed, "My Father, if it is possible, may this cup be taken from me. Yet not as I will, but as you will."

nahonda, si e kuhonda kwao
ku kunabaa.

40. Yesu era kuhuba ala
arekaa e banfunzi bai, era
kubabuana baonjire. Era
kubura petero mbu: Ewashe,
kute mwanafunjirwe kuima e
chwulo chiro na saa nguma?

41. Rero, mutachionjira
mweme Ongo, mungesha
kwengilyiraa mwa miereko,
bushi e muchima asimikire, si
e mubilyi ainyire e misi.

42. Yesu era kubareka kanji,
era kuya kwema Ongo e
bwakabilyi mbu: E Tata akaba
ene ngumbu y'e malyibuko
itanganyirengera busira
kumwai, rero e kuhonda
kwao ku kunabaa!

43. Abere era ahubaa ala
banafunzi bai babaa balyi, era
kubabuana kanji baonjire,
bushi echwulo chwabaa
chwulyi chwunene mwa
meho mabo.

44. Bushi n'oku, era kuhuba
kubareka na aya kwema
Ongo e bwakahachwu. Era
kunahubilyira amu memo.

45. Chasinda, era kuhuba ala
e banafunzi bai babaa balyi,
era kubabura mbu: Ewashe,
munachilyi muonjire

어 구호따 과오 구 구나바아.

40. 여수 어라 구후바 아롸
아러가아 어 바누푸씨 바이,
어라 구바부아나 바오찌러.
어라 구부라 퍼더로 뿌:
어와써, 구더 뫄나푸씨뤄
구이마 어 쭈륻 찌로 나 사아
으마?

41. 러로, 무다찌오씨라 뭐머
오꼬, 무뻐싸 궈끼뤠라아 뫄
미어러고, 부씨 어 무찌마
아시미기러, 시 어 무비뤠
아이니러 어 미시.

42. 여수 어라 구바러가 가찌,
어라 구야 궈마 오꼬 어
봐가비뤠 뿌: 어 다다 아가바
어너 으뿌 여 마뤠부고
이다빠네러뻐라 부시라
구롸이, 러로 어 구호따 과오
구 구나바아!

43. 아버러 어라 아후바아
아롸 바나푸씨 바이 바바아
바뤠, 어라 구바부아나 가찌
바오찌러, 부씨 어쭈륻 좌바아
쭈뤠 쭈너너 뫄 머호 마보.

44. 부씨 노구, 어라 구후바
구바러가 나 아야 궈마 오꼬
어 봐가하쭈. 어라
구나후비뤠라 아무 머모.

45. 짜시따, 어라 구후바 아롸
어 바나푸씨 바이 바바아
바뤠, 어라 구바부라 뿌:
어와써, 무나찌뤠 무오찌러

---

40. Then he returned to
his disciples and found
them sleeping. "Could you
men not keep watch with
me for one hour?" he
asked Peter.

41. "Watch and pray so
that you will not fall into
temptation. The spirit is
willing, but the body is
weak."

42. He went away a
second time and prayed,
"My Father, if it is not
possible for this cup to be
taken away unless I drink
it, may your will be done."

43. When he came back,
he again found them
sleeping, because their
eyes were heavy.

44. So he left them and
went away once more and
prayed the third time,
saying the same thing.

45. Then he returned to
the disciples and said to
them, "Are you still
sleeping and resting?

mwatamuka? Rero, mulolaa! e bihangi byaikire mira! Nyi Mwana w'e Mundju nyiganyibwa mwa mino s'e mabi.

46. Mubachwuka chwuende! Ola unganyana, yono wera ulyi ofu!

Yesu asimbwa

47. Abere Yesu anachilyi ateta, yuda, muuma mwa banafunzi bai ekumi na babilyi era kuika. Oyu yuda, abaa alyi na bandju banene ba babaa bete e mwombo n'e bakulu-kulu b'e bakuhanyi, n'e bashamuka b'e bayuda.

48. yuda, iwayaa kwana Yesu, abaa abalosise mira echimenyeso cha angakoresa. Echi chi menyeso kwabaa kuteta mbu: Ola nyingobera elyi iyoyu, mwanamusimba!

49. Unao-unao, yuda era kuchifunda ofu na Yesu. Era kumubura mbu: Mukangilyisi, nakulamusise! Chasinda era kumuobera.

50. Si Yesu era kumubura mbu: E mwira wanyi! Cha chakurechire, uiraachi. Ba bandju kuna kusimba yesu.

마다무가? 러로, 무뢰롸아! 어 비하삐 뱌이기러 미라! 네 롸나 워 무뚜 네가네봐 롸 미노 서 마비.

46. 무바쭈가 쭈어떠! 오롸 우빠나냐, 요노 워라 우레 오푸!

여수 아시빠

47. 아버러 여수 아나찌레 아더다, 유다, 무우마 롸 바나푸씨 바이 어구미 나 바비레 어라 구이가. 오유 유다, 아바아 아레 나 바뚜 바너너 바 바바아 버더 어 모뾰 너 바구루-구루 버 바구하네, 너 바싸무가 버 바유다.

48. 유다, 이와야아 과나 여수, 아바아 아바뢰시서 미라 어찌머녀소 짜 아빠고러사. 어찌 찌 머녀소 과바아 구더다 뿌: 오롸 네꼬버라 어레 이요유, 모나무시빠!

49. 우나오-우나오, 유다 어라 구찌푸따 오푸 나 여수. 어라 구무부라 뿌: 무가삐레시, 나구롸무시서! 짜시따 어라 구무오버라.

50. 시 여수 어라 구무부라 뿌: 어 뭐라 와네! 짜 짜구러찌러, 우이라아찌. 바 바뚜 구나 구시빠 여수.

Look, the hour is near, and the Son of Man is betrayed into the hands of sinners.

46. Rise, let us go! Here comes my betrayer!"

47. While he was still speaking, Judas, one of the Twelve, arrived. With him was a large crowd armed with swords and clubs, sent from the chief priests and the elders of the people.

48. Now the betrayer had arranged a signal with them: "The one I kiss is the man; arrest him."

49. Going at once to Jesus, Judas said, "Greetings, Rabbi!" and kissed him.

50. Jesus replied, "Friend, do what you came for." Then the men stepped forward, seized Jesus and arrested him.

51. Mw'olu, mundju muuma mwa ba babaa balyi na yesu, era kuhohola e bombo bwai, kuna kubuhuta e kaungu k'e mukulu-kulu w'e bakuhanyi, na amuisha e kuchi.

52. si Yesu era kumubura mbu: Fulusaa e bombo bwao mwa lupota. Bushi chira mundju ola wende walwa n'e bombo, nai mwa bombo mu akanechibwa!

53. Mwabo muteshi kwa nyingema tata mbu anyiasaa, na unano-unano ananyichwumire bamalaika banene kubikembe ekumi na bibilyi?

54. Si akaba anganyichwumirabo, rero kute kw'e maanjiko mabuya-buya mangaberera? Amu Maanjiko, machwula matechire mbu ene myasi yoshi, byemire inabe bacha!

55. Chasinda, Yesu era kubusa abu bandju mbu: chi chachwumire mwanyibahira n'e mwombo n'e ngonyi, nga bandju ba baya kusimba chihumisi? Si chira lusuku nabaa nenjire nareerera mwa luhu lwa Ongo nakagilyisa e bandju, si chiro mukanyisimba.

51. 몰루, 무뚜 무우마 롸 바바아 바레 나 여수, 어라 구호호롸 어 보뽀 봐이, 구나 구부후다 어 가우우 거 무구루-구루 워 바구하네, 나 아무이싸 어 구찌.

52. 시 여수 어라 구무부라 뿌: 푸루사아 어 보뽀 봐오 롸 루뽀다. 부씨 찌라 무뚜 오롸 워떠 와롸 너 보뽀, 나이 롸 보뽀 무 아가너찌봐!

53. 롸보 무더씨 과 네어마 다다 뿌 아네아사아, 나 우나노-우나노 아나네쭈미러 바마롸이가 바너너 구비거뻐 어구미 나 비비레?

54. 시 아가바 아아네쭈미라보, 러로 구더 궈 마아찌고 마부야-부야 마아버러라? 아무 마아찌고, 마쭈롸 마더찌러 뿌 어너 먀시 요씨, 벼미러 이나버 바쨔!

55. 쨔시따, 여수 어라 구부사 아부 바뚜 뿌: 찌 쨔쭈미러 롸네바히라 너 모뽀 너 오네, 아 바뚜 바 바야 구시빠 찌후미시? 시 찌라 루수구 나바아 너찌러 나러어러라 롸 루후 롸 오꼬 나가지레사 어 바뚜, 시 찌로 무가네시빠.

51. With that, one of Jesus' companions reached for his sword, drew it out and struck the servant of the high priest, cutting off his ear.

52. "Put your sword back in its place," Jesus said to him, "for all who draw the sword will die by the sword.

53. Do you think I cannot call on my Father, and he will at once put at my disposal more than twelve legions of angels?

54. But how then would the Scriptures be fulfilled that say it must happen in this way?"

55. At that time Jesus said to the crowd, "Am I leading a rebellion, that you have come out with swords and clubs to capture me? Every day I sat in the temple courts teaching, and you did not arrest me.

56. Bine byoshi byabere, chasiya e myasi yoshi iberere era barebi batetaa mwa maanjiko mabuya-buya. Chasinda, e banfunzi bai boshi bera kumureka na bachihaira.

Yesu atongana era muhondo s'e karubanda k'e bayuda

57. Abu bandju, mango babaa bera basimbaa yesu, bera kumweka era mw'e mukulu-kulu w'e bakuhanyi mbu i kayafa. Ebakangilyisi b'e Mwaso, n'e bashamuka b'e bayuda babaa babuanayireyi.

58. Si petero era kukulyikira Yesu katola nyuma. Nai era kwengira mwa chikalyi ch'e mukulu-kulu w'e bakuhanyi. Era kwekala mwa chibuwa alauma n'e balanzi, chasiya alole era e myasi ya Yesu ingasinjira.

59. Abu bakulu-kulu b'e bakuhanyi, n'e bashamuka boshi b'e karubanda k'e bayuda, bera kuhonda myasi ya bisha era bangemangirako chasiya bete Yesu.

---

56. 비너 보씨 뱌버러, 짜시야 어 먀시 요씨 이버러러 어라 바러비 바더다아 뫄 마아찌고 마부야-부야. 짜시따, 어 바누푸씨 바이 보씨 버라 구무러가 나 바찌하이라.

여수 아도빠낍 어라 무호쏘 서 가루바따 거 바유다

57. 아부 바뚜, 마꼬 바바아 버라 바시빠아 여수, 버라 구뭐가 어라 뭐 무구루-구루 워 바구하니 뿌 이 가야파. 어바가삐레시 버 뫄소, 너 바싸무가 버 바유다 바바아 바부아나에러에.

58. 시 퍼더로 어라 구구레기라 여수 가도꽈 뉴마. 나이 어라 궈삐라 뫄 찌가레 쩌 무구루-구루 워 바구하니. 어라 궈가꽈 뫄 찌부와 아라우마 너 바꽈씨, 짜시야 아뤄뻐 어라 어 먀시 야 여수 이빠시찌라.

59. 아부 바구루-구루 버 바구하니, 너 바싸무가 보씨 버 가루바따 거 바유다, 버라 구호따 먀시 야 비싸 어라 바뻐마삐라고 짜시야 버더 여수.

---

56. But this has all taken place that the writings of the prophets might be fulfilled." Then all the disciples deserted him and fled.

57. Those who had arrested Jesus took him to Caiaphas, the high priest, where the teachers of the law and the elders had assembled.

58. But Peter followed him at a distance, right up to the courtyard of the high priest. He entered and sat down with the guards to see the outcome.

59. The chief priests and the whole Sanhedrin were looking for false evidence against Jesus so that they could put him to death.

60. Bandju banene bera kuika kumusinga myasi, si chiro bacha, bera kunaina cha bangemangirako chasiya bamwite. Chasinjire, bandju babilyi bera kuika.

61. na bateta mbu: Ono mundju atetaa mbu angahandjula e luhu lwa Ongo na kuhuba kuluimba ku suku ehachwu.

62. Emukulu-kulu w'e bakuhanyi kukwera kwimanga na abusa Yesu mbu: Ewashe, utakure chiro na mwasi usibya kw'ebi byoshi bano bandju bakusitakireko?

63. Si Yesu chiro akamwakula kandju. Oyu mukulu-kulu w'e bakuhanyi, era kuhuba kumubura mbu: Nakwema kw'e sina lya Ongo w'e kalamo, uchwulaisisaa akaba woyo u Kirisito, mwenyi Ongo.

64. Yesu era kumwakula mbu: Weine watechire mira! Rero, nababura muboshi kwa kutengera lwarero, mungalola kwa nyi mwana w'e Mundju nyekese kwa lunda lw'e malyo ma Ongo w'e buashi. Kanji mungalola kwa nabaha natenga kwa nguba mwa lumbumbu.

60. 바쭈 바너너 버라 구이가 구무시꿔 먀시, 시 찌로 바쨔, 버라 구나이나 쨔 바꺼마꿰라고 쨔시야 바뮈더. 쨔시찌러, 바쭈 바비레 버라 구이가.

61. 나 바더다 뿌: 오노 무쭈 아더다아 뿌 아꽈하누꽈 어 루후 롸 오꼬 나 구후바 구루이빠 구 수구 어하쭈.

62. 어무구루루-구루 워 바구하네 구궈라 귀마꽈 나 아부사 여수 뿌: 어와써, 우다구러 찌로 나 뫄시 우시뱌 궈비 뵤씨 바노 바쭈 바구시다기러고?

63. 시 여수 찌로 아가뫄구꽈 가뚜. 오유 무구루루-구루 워 바구하네, 어라 구후바 구무부라 뿌: 나궈마 궈 시나 랴 오꼬 워 가롸모, 우쭈롸이시사아 아가바 오요 우 기리시도, 뭐네 오꼬.

64. 여수 어라 구꽈구꽈 뿌: 워이너 와더찌러 미라! 러로, 나바부라 무보씨 과 구더꺼라 롸러로, 무꽈르꽈 과 네 뫄나 워 무쭈 녀거서 과 루따 뤄 마뤄 마 오꼬 워 부아씨. 가찌 무꽈르꽈 과 나바하 나더꽈 과 꼬바 뫄 루뿌뿌.

60. But they did not find any, though many false witnesses came forward. Finally two came forward

61. and declared, "This fellow said, 'I am able to destroy the temple of God and rebuild it in three days.' "

62. Then the high priest stood up and said to Jesus, "Are you not going to answer? What is this testimony that these men are bringing against you?"

63. But Jesus remained silent. The high priest said to him, "I charge you under oath by the living God: Tell us if you are the Christ, the Son of God."

64. "Yes, it is as you say," Jesus replied. "But I say to all of you: In the future you will see the Son of Man sitting at the right hand of the Mighty One and coming on the clouds of heaven."

65. Oyu mukulu-kulu w'e bakuhanyi omvire bacha, kuna kuchiberengangira kw'e njimba. Era kuteta mbu: Ono mundju akambire Ongo! Bunji bubeyi buchiye bwa chwuchilyi chwahonda? Si mwera kuchumvira mubeine kwa akamba Ongo!

66. Rero kute musene? Nabo mbu: Emire kwichibwa!

67. Mw'olu, bauma bera kutangilyisa bamuchirangako era buso, na kumuhutanga e bifundo. N'e banji bera kumumaasanga,

68. na kumubura mbu: Era Kirisito, rebaa nde iwakuhuchire!

Petero anana Yesu

69. Mw'echi chihangi, petero abaa ekese mwa chibuwa. Muandakasi muuma era kuchifunda ofu nai. Era kumubura mbu: Nao, wabaa ulyi alauma na Yesu, mwesha kalilaya.

70. Si petero era kunana era muhondo s'e bandju boshi ba babaa balyiaola, era kuteta mbu: Ebi wahonda kuteta, ndabishi!

71. Era nyuma s'ebi, petero era kutenga aola, era kuya

65. 오유 무구룩-구룩 워 바구하네 오삐러 바짜, 구나 구찌버러와끼라 궈 띠빠. 어라 구더다 뿌: 오노 무뚜 아가삐러 오끄! 부찌 부부에 부찌여 봐 쭈찌레 좌호따? 시 뭐라 구쭈삐라 무버이너 과 아가빠 오끄!

66. 러로 구더 무서너? 나보 뿌: 어미러 귀찌봐!

67. 모룩, 바우마 버라 구다끼레사 바무찌라끄고 어라 부소, 나 구무후다까 어 비푸또. 너 바찌 버라 구무마아사까,

68. 나 구무부라 뿌: 어라 기리시도, 러바아 떠 이와구후찌러!

퍼더로 아나나 여수

69. 뭐찌 찌하끼, 퍼더로 아바아 어거서 봐 찌부와. 무아까가시 무우마 어라 구찌푸따 오푸 나이. 어라 구무부라 뿌: 나오, 와바아 우레 아뫄우마 나 여수, 뭐싸 가삐뫄야.

70. 시 퍼더로 어라 구나나 어라 무호또 서 바뚜 보씨 바 바바아 바레아오뫄, 어라 구더다 뿌: 어비 와호따 구더다, 따비씨!

71. 어라 뉴마 서비, 퍼더로 어라 구더까 아오뫄, 어라

65. Then the high priest tore his clothes and said, "He has spoken blasphemy! Why do we need any more witnesses? Look, now you have heard the blasphemy.

66. What do you think?" "He is worthy of death," they answered.

67. Then they spit in his face and struck him with their fists. Others slapped him

68. and said, "Prophesy to us, Christ. Who hit you?"

69. Now Peter was sitting out in the courtyard, and a servant girl came to him. "You also were with Jesus of Galilee," she said.

70. But he denied it before them all. "I don't know what you're talking about," he said.

71. Then he went out to the gateway, where

kwa chiso ch'e chikalyi. Unji muandakasi muuma nai, era kumulolako, era kubura e bandju ba babaa balyi aola mbu: Ono mundju abaa alyi alauma na Yesu w'e nasareti.

72. Si petero era kuhuba kunana mbu: nalaisise kwa ndeshi oyu mundju!

73. Era nyuma hicha, abu bandju ba babaa bemenze aola, bera kuchifunda ofu na petero, na bamubura mbu: kanangana unalyi muuma wabo, bushi e mitetere yao inachilosise!

74. Chasinjire, petero era kutangilyisa ateta mbu: Akaba nafula bisha, nyife shabyo! nalaisise kw'oyu mundju ndamwishi! unao-unao, aluasi kuna kubika.

75. petero era kwire akengera e myasi Yesu amuburaa mbu: era muhondo e luasi lubike, ungaba wanyinana kahachwu. bushi n'oku, era kuuluka era butala, na atangilyisa alyira na businane bunene.

구야 과 찌소 쩌 찌가레. 우씨 무아따가시 무우마 나이, 어라 구무로꽈고, 어라 구부라 어 바뚜 바 바바아 바레 아오꽈 뿌: 오노 무뚜 아바아 아레 아꽈우마 나 여수 워 나사러디.

72. 시 퍼더로 어라 구후바 구나나 뿌: 나꽈이시서 과 떠씨 오유 무뚜!

73. 어라 뉴마 히짜, 아부 바뚜 바 바바아 버머써 아오꽈, 버라 구찌푸따 오푸 나 퍼더로, 나 바무부라 뿌: 가나꽈나 우나레 무우마 와보, 부씨 어 미더더러 야오 이나찌로시서!

74. 짜시찌러, 퍼더로 어라 구다삐레사 아더다 뿌: 아가바 나푸꽈 비싸, 니퍼 싸뵤! 나꽈이시서 교유 무뚜 따뮈씨! 우나오-우나오, 아루아시 구나 구비가.

75. 퍼더로 어라 귀러 아거꺼라 어 먀시 여수 아무부라아 뿌: 어라 무호또 어 루아시 루비거, 우빠바 와니나나 가하쫗. 부씨 노구, 어라 구우루가 어라 부다꽈, 나 아다삐레사 아레라 나 부시나너 부너너.

---

another girl saw him and said to the people there, "This fellow was with Jesus of Nazareth."

72. He denied it again, with an oath: "I don't know the man!"

73. After a little while, those standing there went up to Peter and said, "Surely you are one of them, for your accent gives you away."

74. Then he began to call down curses on himself and he swore to them, "I don't know the man!" Immediately a rooster crowed.

75. Then Peter remembered the word Jesus had spoken: "Before the rooster crows, you will disown me three times." And he went outside and wept bitterly.

Matayo Chikono 27
Yesu ekibwa era muhondo sa pilato

마다요 찌고노 27
여수 어기봐 어라 무호또 사 피꽈명

Matthew Chapter 27[NIV]

---

1. Abere lumbulyi-mbulyi, abakulu-kulu boshi b'e bakuhanyi alauma n'e bashamuka b'e bayuda, bera kuisha elwango lw'e kwita yesu.

2. Bushi n'oku, bera kumumina na baya kumwana mwa mino se mukulu-kulu w'e muroma mbu i pilato.

Yuda achinyiya

3. Mango yuda iwarenganya yesu, alolaa kwa Yesu achinjibusibwe, era kuchiaya. Mw'olu, era kutola bya bikoroto mahachwu by'e buteya, era kubyalulyira e bakulu-kulu b'e bakuhanyi n'e bashamuka b'e bayuda.

4. Era kubabura mbu: nakolyire mabi mwa kwana e mundju ola utailyire chibi chisibya. Nabo mbu: e byera bitachichwerekere, byanera byao ebi!

5. Yuda era kukabula bya bikoroto mwa luhu lwa Ongo. Chasinda, era kuya kuchinyiya.

6. E bakulukulu b'e bakuhanyi bera kutola-tola ebi bikoroto. Bera kuteta mbu: kukulyikana n'e mwaso wechwu, buno buteya kutemire mbu: chwubikaabo mwa sanduku

1. 아버러 루뿌쪠-뿌쪠, 아바구루-구루 보씨 버 바구하네 아쫘우마 너 바싸무가 버 바유다, 버라 구이싸 어롸오 뤄 귀다 여수.

2. 부씨 노구, 버라 구무미나 나 바야 구꽈나 와 미노 서 무구루-구루 워 무로마 뿌 이 피롸도.

유다 아찌네옛

3. 마오 유다 이와러꺄냐 여수, 아르롸아 과 여수 아찌찌부시붜, 어라 구찌아야. 모루, 어라 구도롸 뱌 비고로도 마하쭈 벼 부더야, 어라 구뱌루쪠라 어 바구루-구루 버 바구하네 너 바싸무가 버 바유다.

4. 어라 구바부라 뿌: 나고쪠러 마비 와 과나 어 무뚜 오롸 우다이쪠러 찌비 찌시뱌. 나보 뿌: 어 벼라 비다찌쭤러거러, 뱌너라 뱌오 어비!

5. 유다 어라 구가부롸 뱌 비고로도 와 루후 롸 오오. 짜시따, 어라 구야 구찌네야.

6. 어 바구루루구루 버 바구하네 버라 구도롸-도롸 어비 비고로도. 버라 구더다 뿌: 구구쪠가나 너 와소 워쭈, 부노 부더야 구더미러 뿌: 쭈비가아보 와 사누구 여 루후

1. Early in the morning, all the chief priests and the elders of the people came to the decision to put Jesus to death.

2. They bound him, led him away and handed him over to Pilate, the governor.

3. When Judas, who had betrayed him, saw that Jesus was condemned, he was seized with remorse and returned the thirty silver coins to the chief priests and the elders.

4. "I have sinned," he said, "for I have betrayed innocent blood." "What is that to us?" they replied. "That's your responsibility."

5. So Judas threw the money into the temple and left. Then he went away and hanged himself.

6. The chief priests picked up the coins and said, "It is against the law to put this into the treasury, since it is blood money."

y'e luhu lwa Ongo, bushi bulyi buteya bwa bwasheshire mikira.

7. Bushi n'oku, bera kuisha lwango lwa kukoresa obu buteya mwa kuula ehwa lya murenga muuma, chasiya bende batabamo e baenyi.

8. Echera chi chichwumire ely'ehwa lyelyikibwa kuikira lwarero mbu ehwa lya mikira.

9. Mw'olu, e myasi yera kuberera era murebi yeremia ateta mbu: batolaa bikoroto mahachwu bya buteya kukulyikana n'e chichiro cha baisiraeli balinganyaa n'echwe lyai.

10. Bera kuula ehwa lya murenga muuma ng'okwa enawechwu ananyiburaa.

Pilato achinjibusa Yesu

11. Abere pilato era atonganya yesu, era kumubusa mbu: ewashe, woyo u mwami w'e bayuda? Yesu na imbu weine watechire mira!

12. Chasinda abu bakulu-kulu b'e bakuhanyi n'e bashamuka b'e bayuda, bera kutangilyisa basindaira Yesu e myasi busese. Si chiro akabakula kandju.

롸 오꼬, 부씨 부례 부더야 봐 봐써씨러 미기라.

7. 부씨 노구, 버라 구이싸 롸오 롸 구고러사 오부 부더야 마 구우롸 어화 롸 무러마 무우마, 짜시야 버너 바다바모 어 바어니.

8. 어쩌라 찌 찌쭈미러 어쪄화 려례기봐 구이기라 롸러로 뿌 어화 롸 미기라.

9. 모루, 어 먀시 여라 구버러라 어라 무러비 여러미아 아더다 뿌: 바도롸아 비고로도 마하쭈 뱌 부더야 구구례가나 너 찌찌로 짜 바이시라어릐 바쮜마냐아 너쭤 롸이.

10. 버라 구우롸 어화 롸 무러마 무우마 우오과 어나워쭈 아나네부라아.

피롸명 아찌찌쀀뻽 여수

11. 아버러 피롸도 어라 아도마냐 여수, 어라 구무부사 뿌: 어와써, 오요 우 롸미 워 바유다? 여수 나 이뿌 워이너 와더찌러 미라!

12. 짜시따 아부 바구루루-구루 버 바구하니 너 바싸무가 버 바유다, 버라 구다쮜례사 바시따이라 여수 어 먀시 부서서. 시 찌로 아가바구롸 가뚜.

---

7. So they decided to use the money to buy the potter's field as a burial place for foreigners.

8. That is why it has been called the Field of Blood to this day.

9. Then what was spoken by Jeremiah the prophet was fulfilled: "They took the thirty silver coins, the price set on him by the people of Israel,

10. and they used them to buy the potter's field, as the Lord commanded me."

11. Meanwhile Jesus stood before the governor, and the governor asked him, "Are you the king of the Jews?" "Yes, it is as you say," Jesus replied.

12. When he was accused by the chief priests and the elders, he gave no answer.

13. Bushi n'oku, pilato era kuhuba kumubusa mbu: Ewashe, ei myasi yoshi benjire bakusitakako, utayumvire?

14. Si mw'ebi byoshi, Yesu ataakula chiro na chinwa chisibya. Echera chera kuchwuma, oyu mukulu-kulu asanwa busese.

15. Chira lusuku lw'e pasaka, e mukulu-kulu w'e chio abaa achwusa mwanya wa kuboorera e bandju mundju muuma wa buroko ola basimire.

16. Mwesi siku, mundju muuma mbu ibaraba, abaa aminyirwe. Oyu baraba, abaa aire ngulu busese bushi n'e mabi mai.

17. Abere e bandju bera bachilundaa alauma, pilato era kubabusa mbu: nde i mwahonda nyibaboorere? baraba nesi Yesu ola bende belyika mbu Kirisito?

18. Abusaa bacha, bushi abaa eshi kwa bamureteraa Yesu bushi n'e mufula.

19. Abere pilato anachilyi ekese kwa ndebe yai y'e kuishira kw'e manja, mukai era kumuchwumira e mwasi mbu: utachibikaa mwa myasi

13. 부씨 노구, 피롸도 어라 구후바 구무부사 뿌: 어와써, 어이 먀시 요씨 버찌러 바구시다가고, 우다유삐러?

14. 시 뭐비 뵤씨, 여수 아다아구롸 찌로 나 찌놔 찌시뱌. 어쩌라 쩌라 구쭈마, 오유 무구루-구루 아사놔 부서서.

15. 찌라 루수구 뤄 파사가, 어 무구루-구루 워 찌오 아바아 아쭈사 마냐 와 구보오러라 어 바쭈 무뚜 무우마 와 부로고 오롸 바시미러.

16. 뭐시 시구, 무뚜 무우마 뿌 이바라바, 아바아 아미니뤄. 오유 바라바, 아바아 아이러 우루 부서서 부씨 너 마비 마이.

17. 아버러 어 바쭈 버라 바찌룬따아 아롸우마, 피롸도 어라 구바부사 뿌: 떠 이 롸호따 네바보오러러? 바라바 너시 여수 오롸 버떠 버롁가 뿌 기리시도?

18. 아부사아 바쨔, 부씨 아바아 어씨 과 바무러더라아 여수 부씨 너 무푸라.

19. 아버러 피롸도 아나찌롁 어거서 과 떠버 야이 여 구이씨라 궈 마쨔, 무가이 어라 구무쭈미라 어 마시 뿌: 우다찌비가아 마 먀시 위오유

13. Then Pilate asked him, "Don't you hear the testimony they are bringing against you?"

14. But Jesus made no reply, not even to a single charge--to the great amazement of the governor.

15. Now it was the governor's custom at the Feast to release a prisoner chosen by the crowd.

16. At that time they had a notorious prisoner, called Barabbas.

17. So when the crowd had gathered, Pilate asked them, "Which one do you want me to release to you: Barabbas, or Jesus who is called Christ?"

18. For he knew it was out of envy that they had handed Jesus over to him.

19. While Pilate was sitting on the judge's seat, his wife sent him this message: "Don't have anything to do with that

y'oyu mundju ola utete chibi chisibya! bushi muno buchwufu, nalotaa biroto era luulu sai, byera kunyilyibusa busese!

20. si abu bakulu-kulu b'e bakuhanyi, n'e bashamuka b'e bayuda, bera kushilyisa e bandju mbu bemaa baraba aboolwe, na Yesu echibwe.

21. Pilato era kuhuba kubabusa mbu: Mwa bano bandju babilyi, nde i mwahonda nyibaboorere? nabo mbu: Baraba.

22. Era kubabusa kanji mbu: Rero, kute mwahonda nyiiraa ono Yesu ola bende belyika mbu Kirisito? boshi bera kwakula mbu: Amanyikibwaa kwa musalaba.

23. Pilato era kuhuba kubabusa mbu: Mabi machiye kasi mu ailyire? si bera kuendekera balakanga busese mbu: Amanyikibwaa kwa musalaba!

24. Mango pilato alolaa kwa kutachilyi cha angachihuba kuira, n'e kulola kwa lwayo lwabaa lwaendekera lwa luwa mwa bandju, era kwire atola e meshi, era kowa kwa mino era muhondo s'abu bandju boshi. Era kuteta mbu:

무뚜 오콰 우더더 찌비 찌시뱌! 부씨 무노 부쭈푸, 나루다아 비로도 어라 루우루 사이, 벼라 구네레부사 부서서!

20. 시 아부 바구루-구루 버 바구하네, 너 바싸무가 버 바유다, 벼라 구씨레사 어 바뚜 뿌 버마아 바라바 아보오뤄, 나 여수 어찌붸.

21. 피콰도 어라 구후바 구바부사 뿌: 콰 바노 바뚜 바비레, 더 이 마호따 네바보오러러? 나보 뿌: 바라바.

22. 어라 구바부사 가찌 뿌: 러로, 구더 마호따 네이라아 오노 여수 오콰 버더 버레가 뿌 기리시도? 보씨 벼라 과구콰 뿌: 아마네기봐아 과 무사콰바.

23. 피콰도 어라 구후바 구바부사 뿌: 마비 마찌여 가시 무 아이레러? 시 벼라 구어떠거라 바콰가까 부서서 뿌: 아마네기봐아 과 무사콰바!

24. 마꼬 피콰도 아로콰아 과 구다찌레 짜 아까찌후바 구이라, 너 구로콰 과 콰요 콰바아 콰어떠거라 콰 루와 바뚜, 어라 귀러 아도콰 어 머씨, 어라 고와 과 미노 어라 무호또 사부 바뚜 보씨. 어라 구더다 뿌: 어미기라 위오노

innocent man, for I have suffered a great deal today in a dream because of him."

20. But the chief priests and the elders persuaded the crowd to ask for Barabbas and to have Jesus executed.

21. "Which of the two do you want me to release to you?" asked the governor. "Barabbas," they answered.

22. "What shall I do, then, with Jesus who is called Christ?" Pilate asked. They all answered, "Crucify him!"

23. "Why? What crime has he committed?" asked Pilate. But they shouted all the louder, "Crucify him!"

24. When Pilate saw that he was getting nowhere, but that instead an uproar was starting, he took water and washed his hands in front of the crowd. "I am innocent of this man's blood," he said.

Emikira y'ono mundju itabaa kw'echwe lyanyi, si ibaa kw'echwe lyenyu!	무뚜 이다바아 궈쭤 꺄네, 시 이바아 궈쭤 뗘뉴!	"It is your responsibility!"

25. E bandju boshi bera kwakula mbu: Nechi! e mikira yai ibaa kw'echwe lyechwu, n'okwa ly'e bana bechwu!

25. 어 바뚜 보씨 버라 과구꽈 뿌: 너찌! 어 미기라 야이 이바아 궈쭤 뗘쭈, 노과 뗘 바나 버쭈!

25. All the people answered, "Let his blood be on us and on our children!"

26. Pilato kukwera kubaboorera baraba, era kuteta mbu bapundaa Yesu mwa chwuchi. Chasinda, era kuberesai baye kumumanyika kwa musalaba.

26. 피꽈도 구궈라 구바보오러라 바라바, 어라 구더다 뿌 바푸따아 여수 쭈찌. 짜시따, 어라 구버러사이 바여 구무마네가 과 무사꽈바.

26. Then he released Barabbas to them. But he had Jesus flogged, and handed him over to be crucified.

E basula bashekera Yesu
어 바수꽈 바써거라 여수

27. Era nyuma s'ebi, e basula b'e mukulu-kulu pilato, bera kweka Yesu mwa chikalyi chabo. Echikembe choshi ch'e basula, chera kumusungula.

27. 어라 뉴마 서비, 어 바수꽈 버 무구룩-구룩 피꽈도, 버라 궈가 여수 꽈 찌가레 짜보. 어찌거뻐 쪼씨 쩌 바수꽈, 쩌라 구무수우꽈.

27. Then the governor's soldiers took Jesus into the Praetorium and gathered the whole company of soldiers around him.

28. abu basula, bera kumukongola e njimba sai, na bamwembasa e ropo lya mwola.

28. 아부 바수꽈, 버라 구무고꼬꽈 어 띠빠 사이, 나 바뭐빠사 어 로포 꺄 모꽈.

28. They stripped him and put a scarlet robe on him,

29. Bera kuluka e nzita mwa matabi ma mete mawa, na bamwembasai kw'echwe. Bera kumubika n'e chikoma mwa mino y'e malyo. Chasinda, bera kunde bakoma e mafi era muhondo sai mwa kumushekera mbu: chwakulamusise mwami w'e bayuda!

29. 버라 구룩가 어 씨다 꽈 마다비 마 머더 마와, 나 바뭐빠사이 궈쭤. 버라 구무비가 너 찌고마 꽈 미노 여 마료. 짜시따, 버라 구떠 바고마 어 마피 어라 무호또 사이 꽈 구무써거라 뿌: 쭈구꽈무시서 꽈미 워 바유다!

29. and then twisted together a crown of thorns and set it on his head. They put a staff in his right hand and knelt in front of him and mocked him. "Hail, king of the Jews!" they said.

30. bera kumuchirangako,

30. 버라 구무찌라꽈고, 짜시따

30. They spit on him, and

chasinda bera kutola cha chikoma na batangilyisa bamuhutangachi kw'echwe.

버라 구도ᄙᅡ 짜 찌고마 나 바다ᅇᅵᄙᅦ사 바무후다ᅇᅡ찌 궈쭤.

took the staff and struck him on the head again and again.

31. Mango babaa bera bamalaa kumushekera, bera kumukongola ly'e ropo, na bahuba kumwembasa e njimba sai. Chasinda, bera kuchiuma baya kumumanyika kwa musalaba.

31. 마ᅌᅩ 바바아 버라 바마ᄙᅡ아 구무써거라, 버라 구무고ᅌᅩᄙᅡ ᄙᅧ 로포, 나 바후바 구뭬빠사 어 ᄡᅵ빠 사이. 짜시따, 버라 구찌우마 바야 구무마네가 과 무사ᄙᅡ바.

31. After they had mocked him, they took off the robe and put his own clothes on him. Then they led him away to crucify him.

Yesu amanyikibwa kwa musalaba

여수 아마네긋봅 과 무사ᄙᅡ밍

32. Abere abu basula bera batenga mwa musi, bera kubuanana na mundju muuma w'omwa musi w'e kurene mbu I simoni. Oyu simoni, bera kumwesa e musalaba wa yesu.

3.2 아버러 아부 바수ᄙᅡ 버라 바더ᅇᅡ 뫄 무시, 버라 구부아나나 나 무ᅜᅮ 무우마 오뫄 무시 워 구러너 뿌 이 시모니. 오유 시모니, 버라 구뭬사 어 무사ᄙᅡ바 와 여수.

32. As they were going out, they met a man from Cyrene, named Simon, and they forced him to carry the cross.

33. Chasinda, bera kuika kwa kachwulungu ka bende belyika mbu kolokota kukuteta mbu kachwulungu k'e kangasi.

33. 짜시따, 버라 구이가 과 가쭐루웅 가 버떠 버ᄙᅦ가 뿌 고로고다 구구더다 뿌 가쭐루웅 거 가ᅇᅡ시.

33. They came to a place called Golgotha (which means The Place of the Skull).

34. Bera kweresa Yesu tifai era ihoonganyisibwe na mafu ma malula busese. Si mango atomaa kumo, era kuinana.

34. 버라 궈러사 여수 디파이 어라 이호오ᅇᅡ네시붸 나 마푸 마 마루ᄙᅡ 부서서. 시 마ᅌᅩ 아도마아 구모, 어라 구이나나.

34. There they offered Jesus wine to drink, mixed with gall; but after tasting it, he refused to drink it.

35. Abere abu basula bera bamumanyikaa kwa musalaba, bera kuabana e njimba sai mwa kwesherasi e choore.

35. 아버러 아부 바수ᄙᅡ 버라 바무마네가아 과 무사ᄙᅡ바, 버라 구아바나 어 ᄡᅵ빠 사이 뫄 궈써라시 어 쪼오러.

35. When they had crucified him, they divided up his clothes by casting lots.

36. Chasinda, bera kwekala aola, balanga yesu.

36. 짜시따, 버라 궈가ᄙᅡ 아오ᄙᅡ, 바ᄙᅡᅇᅡ 여수.

36. And sitting down, they kept watch over him there.

37. N'era lulu s'echwe Iyai, bera kubika kw'e chihaki cha babaa banjikire kw'e myasi era bamusitakire. Ei myasi yabaa itechire mbu: onola I yesu, mwami w'e bayuda.

37. 너라 루루 서쭤 쨔이, 버라 구비가 궈 찌하기 짜 바바아 바찌기러 궈 먀시 어라 바무시다기러. 어이 먀시 야바아 이더찌러 뿌: 오노롸 이 여수, 롸미 워 바유다.

37. Above his head they placed the written charge against him: THIS IS JESUS, THE KING OF THE JEWS.

38. Bihumusi bibilyi nabi byabaa byamanyikibwe kwa misalaba ala musike sa yesu. Muuma kwa lunda lw'e malyo, n'e unji kwa lw'e marembe.

38. 비후무시 비비례 나비 뱌바아 뱌마네기붸 과 미사롸바 아롸 무시거 사 여수. 무우마 과 루따 뤄 마룐, 너 우찌 과 뤄 마러뻐.

38. Two robbers were crucified with him, one on his right and one on his left.

39. E bandju ba babaa barenga aola, bera kunde bamukamba-kamba, na kusinya e machwe mabo,

39. 어 바뉴 바 바바아 바러꺄 아오롸, 버라 구떠 바무가빠-가빠, 나 구시냐 어 마쭤 마보,

39. Those who passed by hurled insults at him, shaking their heads

40. Na kumubura mbu: era, si woyo uwabaa wahonda kuhandjula e luhu lwa Ongo, na ku suku ehachwu, uhube kuimbalo! Rero, akaba unalyi mwana wa Ongo, weine uchilamyaa, uchandaase kw'oyu musalaba!

40. 나 구무부라 뿌: 어라, 시 오요 우와바아 와호따 구하뉴롸 어 루후 롸 오꼬, 나 구 수구 어하쭈, 우후버 구이빠룐! 러로, 아가바 우나례 롸나 와 오꼬, 워이너 우찌롸먀아, 우짜따아서 굥유 무사롸바!

40. and saying, "You who are going to destroy the temple and build it in three days, save yourself! Come down from the cross, if you are the Son of God!"

41. Mw'olu, e bakulu-kulu b'e bakuhanyi, n'e bakangalyisi b'e mwaso, alauma n'e bashamuka b'e bayuda, nabo bera kunamushekera mbu:

41. 모루, 어 바구루-구루 버 바구하네, 너 바가꺄례시 버 롸소, 아롸우마 너 바싸무가 버 바유다, 나보 버라 구나무써거라 뿌:

41. In the same way the chief priests, the teachers of the law and the elders mocked him.

42. Abaa enjire alamya e banji, si yeine afunjirwe kuchilamya! Si I mwami w'e baisiraeli! Rero, achandasaa kw'oyu musalaba, nechwu chwumwemerere!

42. 아바아 어찌러 아롸먀 어 바찌, 시 여이너 아푸찌뤄 구찌롸먀! 시 이 롸미 워 바이시라어례! 러로, 아짜따사아 굥유 무사롸바, 너쭉 쭉뭐머러러!

42. "He saved others," they said, "but he can't save himself! He's the King of Israel! Let him come down now from the cross, and we will believe in him.

43. Abaa alangalyire Ongo kanji abaa enjire ateta mbu alyi mwana wai. Rero, akaba oyu Ongo achwula amusimire, amununulaa lwarero!

44. Ebihumusi bya byamanyikibwaa ala musike sa Yesu , nabi byabaa byanamushekera.

E kufa kwa Yesu

45. Era nyuma s'ebi, e musimya era kuhukira e chio choshi kutengera kachi-kachi ka mushi kuikira mwa saa mwenda.

46. Abere e saa mwenda sahonda kuika, Yesu era kulakanga na murenge munene mbu: Eloi! Eloi! Lama sabakitani! Kukuteta mbu: Ongo tata! Ongo tata! Chi chachwumire wanyirekerera?

47. Bandju bauma mw'eba babaa balyi aola, bomvire bacha, bera kuteta mbu: Amaala Eliya.

48. Unao-unao, muuma mubo era kulyibita aya kureta chiraka na alobekachi mwa ngala y'e tifaia. Echi chiraka, era kuminyirachi kwa lusheke, na erusisachi Yesu chasiya amwe.

---

43. 아바아 아쨔ᄲ쩨러 오ᄭ 가찌 아바아 어찌러 아더다 뿌 아쩨 뫄나 와이. 러로, 아가바 오유 오ᄭ 아쭈ᄲ 아무시미러, 아무누누롸아 ᄘᅪ러로!

44. 어비후무시 뱌 뱌마네기봐아 아쫘 무시거 사 여수 , 나비 뱌바아 뱌나무써거라.

어 구파 과 여수

45. 어라 뉴마 서비, 어 무시먀 어라 구후기라 어 찌오 쪼씨 구더ᄧ라 가찌-가찌 가 무씨 구이기라 뫄 사아 뭐따.

46. 아버러 어 사아 뭐따 사호따 구이가, 여수 어라 구쫘가ᄲ 나 무러ᄧ 무너너 뿌: 어로이! 어로이! 라마 사바기다니! 구구더다 뿌: 오ᄭ 다다! 오ᄭ 다다! 찌 짜쪼미러 와네러거러라?

47. 바쭈 바우마 뭐바 바바아 바쩨 아오ᄧ, 보뻬러 바짜, 버라 구더다 뿌: 아마아쫘 어리야.

48. 우나오-우나오, 무우마 무보 어라 구레비다 아야 구러다 찌라가 나 아로버가찌 뫄 ᄲᅡᄧ 여 디파이아. 어찌 찌라가, 어라 구미네라찌 과 루써거, 나 어루시사찌 여수 짜시야 아뭐.

---

43. He trusts in God. Let God rescue him now if he wants him, for he said, 'I am the Son of God.' "

44. In the same way the robbers who were crucified with him also heaped insults on him.

45. From the sixth hour until the ninth hour darkness came over all the land.

46. About the ninth hour Jesus cried out in a loud voice, "Eloi, Eloi, lama sabachthani?"--which means, "My God, my God, why have you forsaken me?"

47. When some of those standing there heard this, they said, "He's calling Elijah."

48. Immediately one of them ran and got a sponge. He filled it with wine vinegar, put it on a stick, and offered it to Jesus to drink.

49. Si e banji bera kuteta mbu: Murekaa chwulole akaba Eliya angaika kumununula!

50. Yesu era kuhuba kulakanga na murenge munene. Chasinjire era kutowa e muchima.

51. Unao-unao, e ngwaya era yabaa ya yahumba mwa luhu lwa Ongo yera kubereka mu byande bibilyi, kutengera mwa chanya kuikira alashi. Echio chera kulyingitana busese, e bilyimbi byera kuberekanga,

52. N'e shinda nasi, sera kubookalanga. Na bemeresi banene ba babaa bafire mira, bera kwomoka.

53. Batenganga mwa chinda. Era nyuma s'e kwomoka kwa yesu, abu bandju bera kwengilyira mwa musi mubuya-buya w'e yerusalemu, bandju banene bera kubalolako.

54. E mukulu-kulu w'e basula alauma n'e basula bai ba babaa balanga yesu, mango balolaa kwa musisi arenga mwa chio, na kw'ebi binji byoshi bya byabere, bera kwobaa busese. Bera kutangilyisa bateta mbu:

49. 시 어 바찌 버라 구더다 뿌: 무러가아 쭈로쩌 아가바 어찌야 아까이가 구무누누롸!

50. 여수 어라 구후바 구롸가까 나 무러쩌 무너너. 짜시찌러 어라 구도와 어 무찌마.

51. 우나오-우나오, 어 꽈야 어라 야바아 야 야후빠 마 루후 롸 오꼬 여라 구버러가 무 뱌너 비비쩨, 구더쩌라 롸 짜냐 구이기라 아롸씨. 어찌오 쩌라 구쩨미다나 부서서, 어 비쩨뻬 벼라 구버러가까,

52. 너 씨따 나시, 서라 구보오가롸까. 나 버머러시 바너너 바 바바아 바피러 미라, 버라 곰오가.

53. 바더까까 마 찌따. 어라 뉴마 서 곰오가 과 여수, 아부 바쭈 버라 궈미쩨라 롸 무시 무부야-부야 워 여루사쩌무, 바쭈 바너너 버라 구바롣롸고.

54. 어 무구루-구루 워 바수롸, 아롸우마 너 바수롸 바이 바 바바아 바롸까 여수, 마오 바롣롸아 과 무시시 아러까 롸 찌오, 나 궈비 비찌 뵤씨 뱌 뱌버러, 버라 곰바아 부서서. 버라 구다미쩨사 바더다 뿌: 구비나쩨, 오노 무뿌 아바아

49. The rest said, "Now leave him alone. Let's see if Elijah comes to save him."

50. And when Jesus had cried out again in a loud voice, he gave up his spirit.

51. At that moment the curtain of the temple was torn in two from top to bottom. The earth shook and the rocks split.

52. The tombs broke open and the bodies of many holy people who had died were raised to life.

53. They came out of the tombs, and after Jesus' resurrection they went into the holy city and appeared to many people.

54. When the centurion and those with him who were guarding Jesus saw the earthquake and all that had happened, they were terrified, and exclaimed, "Surely he was the Son of God!"

kubinalyi, ono mundju abaa analyi mwana wa Ongo!

아나레 모나 와 오꼬!

55. Aola abaa alyi bakasi banene balyi bure hicha, bachwumbikisa. Abu bakasi, bu babaa bakulyikire Yesu kutengera e kalilaya, kanji bu bendee bamukunganyisa e bilyo.

55. 아오롸 아바아 아레 바가시 바너너 바레 부러 히짜, 바쭈뻬기사. 아부 바가시, 부 바바아 바구레기러 여수 구더^꺼라 어 가^리랴야, 가찌 부 버^뻐어 바무구^까네사 어 비료.

55. Many women were there, watching from a distance. They had followed Jesus from Galilee to care for his needs.

56. Mwa kachi-kachi kabo, mwabaa mulyi mariya w'e makatala, na mariya nyina wa yakobo kanji I nyina wa yosefu, na nyina wa benyi sebetayo.

56. 뫄 가찌-가찌 가보, 뫄바아 무레 마리야 워 마가다롸, 나 마리야 니나 와 야고보 가찌 이 니나 와 요서푸, 나 니나 와 버네 서버다요.

56. Among them were Mary Magdalene, Mary the mother of James and Joses, and the mother of Zebedee's sons.

Yesu atabwa

여수 아다봐

57. Mango lwabaa lwera luolo-olo, kwera kuika mulume muuma wa muare w'omwa musi w'e Arimateya mbu I yosefu. Oyu yosefu nai, abaa achwula mwanafunzi wa yesu.

57. 마꼬 롸바아 뤄라 루오로-오로, 궈라 구이가 무루머 무우마 와 무아러 옴롸 무시 워 아리마더야 뿌 이 요서푸. 오유 요서푸 나이, 아쭈롸 뫄나푸씨 와 여수.

57. As evening approached, there came a rich man from Arimathea, named Joseph, who had himself become a disciple of Jesus.

58. Era kuya era mwa Pilato chasiya amweme e chirunda cha yesu. Chasinda, Pilato era kunateta mbu bamweresaachi.

58. 어라 구야 어라 뫄 피롸도 짜시야 아뭐머 어 찌루따 짜 여수. 짜시따, 피롸도 어라 구나더다 뿌 바뭐러사아찌.

58. Going to Pilate, he asked for Jesus' body, and Pilate ordered that it be given to him.

59. Yosefu era kutola echi chirunda, na abunga-bungilyicha mu ngwaya iyayaya.

59. 요서푸 어라 구도롸 어찌 찌루따, 나 아부^까-부^삐레짜 무^꽈야 이야야야.

59. Joseph took the body, wrapped it in a clean linen cloth,

60. Era kutabachi mwa shinda yai iyayaya. Ei shinda, abaa achichimilyirei mwa chilyimbi.

60. 어라 구다바찌 뫄 씨따 야이 이야야야. 어이 씨따, 아바아 아찌찌미레러이 뫄

60. and placed it in his own new tomb that he had cut out of the rock.

Era kukululyira e koi linene kwa chiso chai, chasinda era ku chiendera.

61. Mw'ebi bihangi, Mariya w'e Makatala, n'ola unji Mariya, babaa bekese aola, bachwumbikisa kwa shinda.

E basula balanga e shinda

62. Olu lusuku lu lwabaa lw'e kuchikunganya kwa lusuku lw'e sabato lwera kurenga. Abere mwei mishangya, e bakulu-kulu b'e bakuhanyi n'e bafarisayo bera kubuanana ala mwa Pilato.

63. Bera kumubura mbu: Ewalyiya! chwakengere kwa ka kakalange kw'ola mulume, mango kabaa kachilyi mw'e muka katetaa mbu: Era nyuma s'e kufa kwanyi, nyingomwoka e lusuku lwa kahachwu.

64. Bushi n'oku, uburaa e basula kwa balanga e shinda kuikira kw'olu lusuku lwa kahachwu. Bushi bitabere bacha e banafunzi bai bangaya kwiba e chirunda chai, chasinda banaya kwengeera e bandju mbu omwokire mwa bafu. Obu bwengeere bu bungere bwaba bubi busese kurenza bwa bubere.

찌례삐. 어라 구구루루레라 어고이 리너너 과 찌소 짜이, 짜시따 어라 구 쩌러라.

61. 뭐비 비하끼, 마리야 워 마가다콰, 노콰 우씨 마리야, 바바아 버거서 아오콰, 바쭈삐기사 과 씨따.

어 바수콰 바콰까 어 씨따

62. 오루 루수구 루 콰바아 뤄 구찌구까냐 과 루수구 뤄 사바도 뤄라 구러까. 아버러 뭐이 미싸꺄, 어 바구루-구루 버 바구하니 너 바파리사요 버라 구부아나나 아콰 뫄 피콰도.

63. 버라 구무부라 뿌: 어와례야! 쫘거꺼러 과 가 가가콰꺼 곤콰 무루머, 마꼬 가바아 가찌레 뭐 무가 가더다아 뿌: 어라 뉴마 서 구파 과니, 네꼬모가 어 루수구 콰 가하쭈.

64. 부씨 노구, 우부라아 어 바수콰 과 바콰까 어 씨따 구이기라 곤루 루수구 콰 가하쭈. 부씨 비다버러 바짜 어 바나푸씨 바이 바꽈야 귀바 어 찌루따 짜이, 짜시따 바나야 귀꺼어라 어 바쭈 뿌 오모기러 뫄 바푸. 오부 뭐꺼어러 부 부꺼러 뫄바 부비 부서서 구러싸 뫄 부버러.

He rolled a big stone in front of the entrance to the tomb and went away.

61. Mary Magdalene and the other Mary were sitting there opposite the tomb.

62. The next day, the one after Preparation Day, the chief priests and the Pharisees went to Pilate.

63. "Sir," they said, "we remember that while he was still alive that deceiver said, 'After three days I will rise again.'

64. So give the order for the tomb to be made secure until the third day. Otherwise, his disciples may come and steal the body and tell the people that he has been raised from the dead. This last deception will be worse than the first."

65. Pilato era kubakula mbu: Si mwete basula! Mwekaabo kwa shinda, baye kulangai ng'okwa munasimire.

66. Chasinjire, bera kuchiuma baya kwa shinda. Bera kuhuta e kashe kw'e koi lya lyabaa lihukire ei shinda, na bareka kw'e balanzi.

65. 피파도 어라 구바구꽈 뿌: 시 뭐더 바수꽈! 뭐가아보 과 씨따, 바여 구꽈빠이 꾸오과 무나시미러.

66. 짜시찌러, 버라 구찌우마 바야 과 씨따. 버라 구후다 어 가써 궈 고이 꺄 꺄바아 찌후기러 어이 씨따, 나 바러가 궈 바꽈씨.

65. "Take a guard," Pilate answered. "Go, make the tomb as secure as you know how."

66. So they went and made the tomb secure by putting a seal on the stone and posting the guard.

Matayo Chikono 28
E kwomoka kwa Yesu

마다요 찌고노 28
어 굠명— 과 여수

Matthew Chapter 28[NIV]

1. E lusuku lw'e sabato, lwera kurenga. Abere mwei mishangya lumbulyi-mbulyi lwa lweinga, Mariya w'e makatala alauma n'ola unji Mariya, bera kuya kutangula e shinda.

1. 어 루수구 뭐 사바도, 뭐라 구러꽈. 아버러 뭐이 미싸야 루뿌레-뿌레 꽈 뭐이꽈, 마리야 워 마가다꽈 아꽈우마 노꽈 우씨 마리야, 버라 구야 구다꾸꽈 어 씨따.

1. After the Sabbath, at dawn on the first day of the week, Mary Magdalene and the other Mary went to look at the tomb.

2. Unao-unao, mwa chio mwera kurenga musisi munene. Mw'olu, malaika muuma wa enawechwu era kwandaala atenga kwa nguba, era kuchifunda ofu n'e hinda. Era kufumira ly'e koi era musike, na e kala kulyi.

2. 우나오-우나오, 꽈 찌오 뭐라 구러꽈 무시시 무너너. 몰루, 마꽈이가 무우마 와 어나워쭈 어라 과따아꽈 아더꽈과 꾸바, 어라 구찌푸따 오푸 너 히따. 어라 구푸미라 려 고이 어라 무시거, 나 어 가라 구레.

2. There was a violent earthquake, for an angel of the Lord came down from heaven and, going to the tomb, rolled back the stone and sat on it.

3. Oyu malaika abaa alangala busese nga kalyimya-limya, n'e njimba sai, sabaa salangala pe-pe-pe.

3. 오유 마꽈이가 아바아 아꽈꽈꽈 부서서 꽈 가레먀-리먀, 너 찌먀 사이, 사바아 사꽈꽈꽈 퍼-퍼-퍼.

3. His appearance was like lightning, and his clothes were white as snow.

4. Ba balanzi balolyire bacha, bera kwobabaa busese, na atangilyisa bakukumana

4. 바 바꽈씨 바로레러 바짜, 버라 굡바바아 부서서, 나 아다꾀레사 바구구마나

4. The guards were so afraid of him that they shook and became like

kuikira e bihangi baba nga bafu.

구이기라 어 비하삐 바바 까 바푸.

dead men.

5. Oyu malaika era kubura abu bakasi mbu: Mutobaa, bushi nyishi kwa mwabahire kuhonda yesu, ola bamanyikaa kwa musalaba.

5. 오유 마롸이가 어라 구부라 아부 바가시 뿌: 무도바아, 부씨 내씨 과 꽈바히러 구호따 여수, 오롸 바마네가아 과 무사롸바.

5. The angel said to the women, "Do not be afraid, for I know that you are looking for Jesus, who was crucified.

6. Atachilyi anola! Omwokire kukulyikana n'okwa abaa atechire mira. Mubahaa muchilorere ala babaa bamuonjisise.

6. 아다찌례 아노롸! 오모기러 구구페가나 노과 아바아 아더찌러 미라. 무바하아 무찌롣러러 아롸 바바아 바무오찌시서.

6. He is not here; he has risen, just as he said. Come and see the place where he lay.

7. Rero mwiree mwaenda fuba kubura e banafunzi bai mbu omwokire, abahondorere mira e kalilaya. Eyera, yi bangamulorerako. Ebyera binabaa nahonda nyibabure!

7. 러로 뮈러어 꽈어따 푸바 구부라 어 바나푸씨 바이 뿌 오모기러, 아바호또러러 미라 어 가삐롸야. 어여라, 에 바까무롣러라고. 어벼라 비나바아 나호따 네바부러!

7. Then go quickly and tell his disciples: 'He has risen from the dead and is going ahead of you into Galilee. There you will see him.' Now I have told you."

8. Mw'echi chihangi chinechi, abu bakasi bera kutenga kwa shinda bafa buba, si babaa bamowa busese. Bera kulyibita baya kufulyira e banafunzi ba Yesu kw'oyu mwasi.

8. 뭐찌 찌하삐 찌너찌, 아부 바가시 버라 구더까 과 씨따 바파 부바, 시 바바아 바모와 부서서. 버라 구레비다 바야 구푸페라 어 바나푸씨 바 여수 교유 꽈시.

8. So the women hurried away from the tomb, afraid yet filled with joy, and ran to tell his disciples.

9. unao-unao, Yesu era kubapamukirako na abalamusa mbu: bwachere! Nabo bera kuchifunda ofu nai, bera kumuata kwa bihando mwa kumwera.

9. 우나오-우나오, 여수 어라 구바파무기라고 나 아바롸무사 뿌: 봐쩌러! 나보 버라 구찌푸따 오푸 나이, 버라 구무아다 과 비하또 꽈 구뭐라.

9. Suddenly Jesus met them. "Greetings," he said. They came to him, clasped his feet and worshiped him.

10. Chasinda, Yesu era kubabura mbu: Mutobaa! Muyaa kubura banyakechwu

10. 짜시따, 여수 어라 구바부라 뿌: 무도바아! 무야아 구부라 바냐거쭈 과

10. Then Jesus said to them, "Do not be afraid. Go and tell my brothers to

kwa banyibuanaa e kalilaya. Eyera yi banganyilorerako.

E balanzi bafula e mwasi w'e bisha

11. Abere abu banachilyi mwa njira, basula bauma mwa ba babaa balanga e shinda bera kuya mwa musi. Bera kubalyikisisa e bakulu-kulu b'e bakuhanyi e myasi Yoshi era yabere.

12. Bushi n'oku, abu bakulu-kulu bera kubuanana alauma n'e bashamuka b'e bayuda na baya lwango. Bera kweresa abu basula buteya bunene,

13. Na kubabura mbu: Mwabo, mungateta mbu: E banafunzi bai baikaa kumwiba mwa buchwufu mango chwabaa chwaonjire.

14. E mukulu-kulu Pilato nai akomva kw'ono mwasi, chwubeine chwungamubandako. Bikaba bacha, oyu mwasi atachibaretere bwaka.

15. Babasula bera kunatola obu buteya. Bera kunaira ng'okwa banaburwaa. Oyu mwasi, era kunahandabana mwa bayuda kuikira lwarero.

Yesu achwuma e banafunzi

바네부아나아 어 가찌뢔야. 어여라 에 바까네뤄러라고.

어 바좌씨 바푸좌 어 뫄시 워 비싸

11. 아버러 아부 바나찌례 뫄 띠라, 바수좌 바우마 뫄 바 바바아 바좌까 어 씨따 버라 구야 뫄 무시. 버라 구바례기시사 어 바구루-구루 버 바구하네 어 먀시 요씨 어라 야버러.

12. 부씨 노구, 아부 바구루-구루 버라 구부아나나 아좌우마 너 바싸무가 버 바우다 나 바야 쫜오. 버라 궈러사 아부 바수좌 부더야 부너너,

13. 나 구바부라 뿌: 뫄보, 무까더다 뿌: 어 바나푸씨 바이 바이가아 구뮈바 뫄 부쭈푸 마꼬 쫘바아 쫘오찌러.

14. 어 무구루-구루 피좌도 나이 아고빠 곰노 뫄시, 쭈버이너 쭈까무바따고. 비가바 바쨔, 오유 뫄시 아다찌바러더러 봐가.

15. 바바수좌 버라 구나도좌 오부 부더야. 버라 구나이라 꾸오과 바나부뢔아. 오유 뫄시, 어라 구나하따바나 뫄 바우다 구이기라 쫜러로.

여수 아쭈립 어 바나푸씨 바이

go to Galilee; there they will see me."

11. While the women were on their way, some of the guards went into the city and reported to the chief priests everything that had happened.

12. When the chief priests had met with the elders and devised a plan, they gave the soldiers a large sum of money,

13. telling them, "You are to say, 'His disciples came during the night and stole him away while we were asleep.'

14. If this report gets to the governor, we will satisfy him and keep you out of trouble."

15. So the soldiers took the money and did as they were instructed. And this story has been widely circulated among the Jews to this very day.

bai mwa mulyimo　　　**와 무레명**

16. Era nyuma s'ebi, e banafunzi ekumi na muuma ba yesu, bera kuya e kalilaya. Bera kwirukira kwa ndjulungu era Yesu abaa abalosise mira.

16. 어라 뉴마 서비, 어 바나푸씨 어구미 나 무우마 바 여수, 버라 구야 어 가삐꽈야. 버라 귀루기라 과 쭈루우 어라 여수 아바아 아바론시서 미라.

16. Then the eleven disciples went to Galilee, to the mountain where Jesus had told them to go.

17. Mango bamulolaako, bera kufukama era muhondo sai. Si bauma mubo, chiro bakaika bemerera.

17. 마꼬 바무론꽈아고, 버라 구푸가마 어라 무호또 사이. 시 바우마 무보, 찌로 바가이가 버머러라.

17. When they saw him, they worshiped him; but some doubted.

18. Chasinjire, Yesu era kuchifunda ofu nabo, era kubabura mbu: Neresibwe e buashi boshi kwa nguba n'okwa butala.

18. 짜시찌러, 여수 어라 구찌푸따 오푸 나보, 어라 구바부라 뿌: 너러시붜 어 부아씨 보씨 과 우바 노과 부다꽈.

18. Then Jesus came to them and said, "All authority in heaven and on earth has been given to me.

19. Bushi n'oku, muenderaa e bandju b'e mbaa soshi, chasiya babe banafunzi banyi. Mundaa mwabatisabo kw'e sina lya tata, n'e ly'e mwana, n'e ly'e muchima mubuya-buya.

19. 부씨 노구, 무어떠라아 어 바뚜 버 빠아 소씨, 짜시야 바버 바나푸씨 바네. 무따아 뫄바디사보 궈 시나 꺄 다다, 너 려 모나, 너 려 무찌마 무부야-부야.

19. Therefore go and make disciples of all nations, baptizing them in the name of the Father and of the Son and of the Holy Spirit,

20. Mundaa mwakangilyisabo kunde baira e myasi Yoshi era nababuraa. Kanji mumenyereraa kwa nyikanaendekera kuba alauma nenyu kuikira kwa businda bw'e butala.

20. 무따아 꽈가삐레사보 구떠 바이라 어 먀시 요씨 어라 나바부라아. 가찌 무머녀러라아 과 네가나어떠거라 구바 아꽈우마 너뉴 구이기라 과 부시따 붜 부다꽈.

20. and teaching them to obey everything I have commanded you. And surely I am with you always, to the very end of the age."

Mariko

마리고

Mark

**MWASI MUBUYABUYA WA YESU KIRISITO
N'NGOKWA AANJIKWA NA MARIKO**

와시 무부야부야 와 여수 기리시도
우오과 아아쩌과 나 마리고

Mariko Chikono1

Yowana mubatisayi
akunganyisisa Yesu e njira

1. Anola w'e Mwasi Mubuya-buya wa Yesu kirisito, Mwenyi Ongo atangilyire.
2. Ng'okwa bichwula byajikirwe mwa chitabo cha murebi isaya mbu: Nyono nyi Ongo, nyingachwuma e ndjumwa yanyi ikuhondorere, Chasiya ikukunganyisise e njira.
3. Mundju muuma alyi mwa buyeye e njire ateta na murenge munene mbu: Mukunganyisisaa enawechwu enjira! Mulambaatanyaa ala angarenga!
4. Rero, yowana mubatisayi era kuulukira mwa buyeye bw'e yuteda. Abaa enjire ahubanganyisa e bandju mbu babindjukaa batenge mwa bibi byabo, babatisibwe, na Ongo angababalyirabo.
5. Besha mwa chio ch'e yudeya na besha mwa musi w'e yerusalemu boshi bera kunde baikiranga yowana. Abu bandju, babaa benjire bachiaya changanama kwa

마리고 찌고노1

요와나 무바디사에
아구꾸네시시사 여수 어 찌라

1. 아노롸 워 마시 무부야-부야 와 여수 기리시도, 뭐네 오꼬 아다삐레러.
2. 꼬과 비쭈롸 뱌지기뤄 마 찌다보 짜 무러비 이사야 뿌: 뇨노 네 오꼬, 네꺄쭈마 어 뚜뫄 야네 이구호또러러, 짜시야 이구구꾸네시서 어 찌라.
3. 무뚜 무우마 아뤠 마 부여여 어 찌러 아더다 나 무러꺼 무너너 뿌: 무구꾸네시시사아 어나워쭈 어찌라! 무롸빠아다냐아 아롸 아꺄러꺄!
4. 러로, 요와나 무바디사에 어라 구우루기라 마 부여여 붜유더다. 아바아 어찌러 아후바꺄네사 어 바뚜 뿌 바비뚜가아 바더꺼 마 비비 뱌보, 바바디시붜, 나 오꼬 아꺄바바뤠라보.
5. 버싸 마 찌오 쩌 유더야 나 버싸 마 무시 워 여루사꺼무 보씨 버라 구꺼 바이기라꺄 요와나. 아부 바뚜, 바바아 버찌러 바찌아야 짜꺄나마 과 비비 뱌보, 나이 어라 구꺼

Mark Chapter 1[NIV]

1. The beginning of the gospel about Jesus Christ, the Son of God.
2. It is written in Isaiah the prophet: "I will send my messenger ahead of you, who will prepare your way"--

3. "a voice of one calling in the desert, 'Prepare the way for the Lord, make straight paths for him.' "

4. And so John came, baptizing in the desert region and preaching a baptism of repentance for the forgiveness of sins.

5. The whole Judean countryside and all the people of Jerusalem went out to him. Confessing their sins, they were baptized by him in the Jordan River.

bibi byabo, nai era kunde abatisabo mwa lwishi lw'e yorodani.

6. Yowana endee embala njimba sa silanjirwe mwa boya bwa nyama nguma mbu i ngamiya. Kanji endee embala na mukaba wa luu mwa binji. N'e bilyo byai, byabaa e miuku n'e buki.

7. Abaa enjire ahubanganyisa e bandju mbu: Ola ubahire era nyuma sanyi, anyirenzise e buashi, chiro ndete kwa nyilyi kwa kungachwuma nenamilyira era muhondo sai, chasiya nyiboole e milyisi y'e birato byai.

8. Nyono nenjire nababatisa mwa meshi. Si yeke angende ababatisa kwa muchima mubuya-buya.

E kubatisibwa kwa Yesu n'e kurekibwa kwai

9. Mw'esi suku, Yesu era kutenga e Nasareti, mwa chio ch'e kalilaya, yowana era kumubatisa mwa lwishi lw'e yorodani.

10. Abere Yesu era atenga mwa meshi, unao-unao era kulola kwa nguba yabookala, n'e muchima mubuya-buya era kumwandaalyira nga chiruka.

아바디사보 뫄 뤼씨 뤄 요로다니.

6. 요와나 어떠어 어빠롸 띠빠사 시롼씨뤄 뫄 보야 봐 냐마 우마 뿌 이 빠미야. 가찌 어떠어 어빠롸 나 무가바 와 루우 뫄 비찌. 너 비료 뱌이, 뱌바아 어 미우구 너 부기.

7. 아바아 어찌러 아후바빠네사 어 바뚜 뿌: 오롸 우바히러 어라 뉴마 사니, 아네러씨서 어 부아씨, 찌로 떠더 과 네뤠 과 구꾸쭈마 너나미뤠라 어라 무호또 사이, 짜시야 네보오뤄 어 미뤠시 여 비라도 뱌이.

8. 뇨노 너찌러 나바바디사 뫄 머씨. 시 여거 아꺼떠 아바바디사 과 무찌마 무부야-부야.

어 구바디시봐 과 여수 너 구러기봐 과이

9. 뭐시 수구, 여수 어라 구더빠 어 나사러디, 뫄 찌오 쩌 가뤼롸야, 요와나 어라 구무바디사 뫄 뤼씨 뤄 요로다니.

10. 아버러 여수 어라 아더빠 뫄 머씨, 우나오-우나오 어라 구롤롸 과 우바 야보오가롸, 너 무찌마 무부야-부야 어라 구뫄따아뤠라 빠 찌루가.

---

6. John wore clothing made of camel's hair, with a leather belt around his waist, and he ate locusts and wild honey.

7. And this was his message: "After me will come one more powerful than I, the thongs of whose sandals I am not worthy to stoop down and untie.

8. I baptize you with water, but he will baptize you with the Holy Spirit."

9. At that time Jesus came from Nazareth in Galilee and was baptized by John in the Jordan.

10. As Jesus was coming up out of the water, he saw heaven being torn open and the Spirit descending on him like a dove.

11. Mwei nguba mwera kumvikana murenge muuma ola wabaa wateta mbu: Woyo, u muala wanyi musiirwa, u uchwula unyisimise!

12. unao-unao, e muchima mubuya-buya era kweka Yesu mwa buyeye.

13. Mw'obu buyeye, era kumalamo suku mane aerekibwa na Wamusimu. Era kuberamo alauma n'e nyama s'omwerungu, chasinda e bamalaika bera kuika kumuasa.

Yesu amaala e banafunzi babere-bere

14. Era nyuma sa yowana kuumwaa mwa buroko, Yesu era kuya e kaliliya. Abaa enjire ahubanganyisa e bandju e mwasi mubuya-buya wa Ongo.

15. Era kunde ababura mbu: E bihangi byaikire mira, n'e bwami bwa Ongo bulyi ofu! bushi n'oku, muchiayaa kwa bibi byenyu, mwemerere e mwasi mubuya-buya mwa michima yenyu!

16. Mango Yesu abaa arenga kwa musike s'e nyanja ye'kalilaya, era ku balobi babilyi, simoni na munyakabo mbu i andereya. Babaa bena e

11. 뭐이 꿔바 뭐라 구뻬가나 무러꺼 무우마 오롸 와바아 와더다 뿌: 오요, 우 무아롸 와니 무시이라, 우 우쭈롸 우네시미서!

12. 우나오-우나오, 어 무찌마 무부야-부야 어라 궈가 여수 롸 부여여.

13. 묘부 부여여, 어라 구마롸모 수구 마너, 아어러기봐 나 와무시무. 어라 구버라모 아롸우마 너 냐마 소뭐루위, 짜시따 어 바마롸이가 버라 구이가 구무아사.

여수 아마아롸 어 바나푸씨 바버러-버러

14. 어라 뉴마 사 요와나 구우뫄아 롸 부로고, 여수 어라 구야 어 가삐릐야. 아바아 어찌러 아후반뺘네사 어 바뚜 어 롸시 무부야-부야 와 오꼬.

15. 어라 구너 아바부라 뿌: 어 비하삐 뱌이기러 미라, 너 뫄미 봐 오꼬 부쩨 오푸! 부씨 노구, 무찌아야아 과 비비 벼뉴, 뭐머러러 어 롸시 무부야-부야 롸 미찌마 여뉴!

16. 마꼬 여수 아바아 아러꽈 과 무시거 서 냐뱌 여가삐롸야, 어라 구 바로비 바비쪠, 시모니 나 무냐가보 뿌 이 아너러야. 바바아 버나

11. And a voice came from heaven: "You are my Son, whom I love; with you I am well pleased."

12. At once the Spirit sent him out into the desert,

13. and he was in the desert forty days, being tempted by Satan. He was with the wild animals, and angels attended him.

14. After John was put in prison, Jesus went into Galilee, proclaiming the good news of God.

15. "The time has come," he said. "The kingdom of God is near. Repent and believe the good news!"

16. As Jesus walked beside the Sea of Galilee, he saw Simon and his brother Andrew casting a net into the lake, for they were

kasira mwa nyanja.	어 가시라 와 냐따.	fishermen.
17. Yesu era kubabura mbu: munyikulyikiraa, nyingabaira kuba balobi ba bandju.	17. 여수 어라 구바부라 뿌: 무네구레기라아, 네까바이라 구바 바로비 바 바뉴.	17. "Come, follow me," Jesus said, "and I will make you fishers of men."
18. Unao-unao, bera kureka twa chwusira chwabo na bamukulyikira.	18. 우나오-우나오, 버라 구러가 돠 쭈시라 쫘보 나 바무구레기라.	18. At once they left their nets and followed him.
19. Abere Yesu era achifundaa era muhondo hicha, era kulola ku yakobo na munyakabo mbu i yawana, benyi sebetayo. Abu babilyi, babaa balyi mwa bwato bakuganya echwusira kwabo.	19. 아버러 여수 어라 아찌푸따아 어라 무호또 히짜, 어라 구로롸 구 야고보 나 무냐가보 뿌 이 야와나, 버녜 서버다요. 아부 바비례, 바바아 바례 와 봐도 바구가냐 어쭈시라 과보.	19. When he had gone a little farther, he saw James son of Zebedee and his brother John in a boat, preparing their nets.
20. Unao-unao, Yesu era kubamaala. Bera kureka eshe wabo se betayo mw'obu bwato alauma n'e bakosi bai, na bakukulyikira Yesu.	20. 우나오-우나오, 여수 어라 구바마아롸. 버라 구러가 어써 와보 서 버다요 뫄부 봐도 아롸우마 너 바고시 바이, 나 바구구레기라 여수.	20. Without delay he called them, and they left their father Zebedee in the boat with the hired men and followed him.
Yesu ambula e bihwasi kwa mundju	***여수 아뿌롸 어 비화시 과 무뉴***	
21. Era nyuma s'ebi, Yesu n'e banafunzi bai bera kuya mwa musi w'e kaperinaumu. Mango elusuku lwe'sabato lwaikaa, Yesu era kwengilyira mwa bushenge bw'e Bayuta na atangilyisa akangilyisa e bandju.	21. 어라 뉴마 서비, 여수 너 바나푸씨 바이 버라 구야 와 무시 워 가퍼리나우무. 마오 어루수구 뤄사바도 롸이가아, 여수 어라 궝이레라 와 부써어 붜 바유다 나 아다이레사 아가이레사 어 바뉴.	21. They went to Capernaum, and when the Sabbath came, Jesus went into the synagogue and began to teach.
22. Ei myasi yai, yera kushishasa busese e bandju ba babaa bamomvilyisa, bushi yeke atendee abakangilyisi ng'e bakangilyisi babo b'e mwaso, si edee abakangilyisa	22. 어이 먀시 야이, 여라 구씨싸사 부서서 어 바뉴 바 바바아 바모삐레사, 부씨 여거 아더떠어 아바가이레시 어 바가이레시 바보 버 와소, 시 어더어 아바가이레사 아 무뉴	22. The people were amazed at his teaching, because he taught them as one who had authority, not as the teachers of the law.

nga mundju ola wete buashi.

오롸 워더 부아씨.

23. mw'obu bushenge, mwabaa mulyi mundju muuma ola wabaa usimbirwe n'e bihwasi. Unao-unao, oyu mundju era kuuma emurenge mbu:

23. 몹부 부써어, 먀바아 무레 무뚜 무우마 오롸 와바아 우시삐뤄 너 비화시. 우나오-우나오, 오유 무뚜 어라 구우마 어무러어 뿌:

23. Just then a man in their synagogue who was possessed by an evil spirit cried out,

24. Eu Yesu w'e nasareti, chi wachwuhondako? Elyi wabahire kuchwusikya? nyikuishi kubuya! woyo u mubuya-buya ola Ongo achwumire!

24. 어우 여수 워 나사러디, 찌 와쭈호따고? 어레 와바히러 구쭈시갸? 니구이씨 구부야! 오요 우 무부야-부야 오롸 오꼬 아쭈미러!

24. "What do you want with us, Jesus of Nazareth? Have you come to destroy us? I know who you are--the Holy One of God!"

25. Yesu era kukalyiira echi chihwasi busese mbu: Siraa, unatenge kw'ono mundju!

25. 여수 어라 구가례이라 어찌 찌화시 부서서 뿌: 시라아, 우나더어 교노 무뚜!

25. "Be quiet!" said Jesus sternly. "Come out of him!"

26. cha chihwasi, kuna kukukumanya ola mundju busese na chamutengako chaenda chalakanga na murenge munene. anaambulabi, nabi byanamuchwunda!

26. 짜 찌화시, 구나 구구구마냐 오롸 무뚜 부서서 나 짜무더따고 짜어아따 짜롸가꺄 나 무러어 무너너. 아나아뿌롸비, 나비 뱌나무쭈따!

26. The evil spirit shook the man violently and came out of him with a shriek.

27. E bandju boshi kuna kutungwa na batangilyisa babusanya mbu: Ewashe, bi byera bichiye bine? kubinalyi, ene myasi iyayaya Yesu enjire akangirisa e bandju, yete buashi! Anabe n'e bihwasi enjire

27. 어 바뚜 보씨 구나 구두꽈 나 바다찌레사 바부사냐 뿌: 어와써, 비 벼라 비찌여 비너? 구비나레, 어너 먀시 이야야야 여수 어찌러 아가끼리사 어 바뚜, 여더 부아씨! 아나버 너 비화시 어찌러

27. The people were all so amazed that they asked each other, "What is this? A new teaching--and with authority! He even gives orders to evil spirits and they obey him."

28. Bushi n'oku, engulu ya Yesu, yera kwire yahandabana mwa chio choshi ch'e kalilaya.

28. 부씨 노구, 어우루 야 여수, 여라 귀러 야하따바나 꽈 찌오 쪼씨 쩌 가리라야.

28. News about him spread quickly over the whole region of Galilee.

Yesu alamya balwala banene	***여수 아콰마 바뽜콰 바너너***	
29. Era nyuma s'ebi, Yesu era kutenga mw'obu bushenge alyi na yakobo na yowana. Bera kuingilyira mwa nyumba ya simoni na andereya.	29. 어라 뉴마 서비, 여수 어라 구더까 모부 부써어 아레 나 야고보 나 요와나. 버라 구이끼레라 뫄 뉴빠 야 시모니 나 아떠러야.	29. As soon as they left the synagogue, they went with James and John to the home of Simon and Andrew.
30. Yesu aikiremo, bera kumubura mbu nasala wa simoni alyi kwa njingo, bushi e hushira yabaa yamusimbire.	30. 여수 아이기러모, 버라 구무부라 뿌 나사콰 와 시모니 아레 과 찌오, 부씨 어 후씨라 야바아 야무시삐러.	30. Simon's mother-in-law was in bed with a fever, and they told Jesus about her.
31. Yesu kukwera kuchifunda ofu nai, era kumusimbira kwa mino na amwemanza. Unao-unao, era kushira kuna kulama. Wamukasi, era kutangilyisa abatekera e bilyo.	31. 여수 구궈라 구찌푸따 오푸 나이, 어라 구무시삐라 과 미노 나 아뭐마싸. 우나오-우나오, 어라 구씨라 구나 구콰마. 와무가시, 어라 구다끼레사 아바더거라 어 비료.	31. So he went to her, took her hand and helped her up. The fever left her and she began to wait on them.
32. abere lwera loolo-olo, e suba lyachirowire mira, e bandju bera kureteranga Yesu e balwala boshi, na ba babaa basimbirwe n'e bihwasi.	32. 아버러 뤄라 로오로-오로, 어 수바 콰찌로위러 미라, 어 바쭈 버라 구러더라까 여수 어 바뽜콰 보씨, 나 바 바바아 바시삐뤄 너 비화시.	32. That evening after sunset the people brought to Jesus all the sick and demon-possessed.
33. Besha mw'oyu musi boshi, bera kuya kuchilunda kwa chiso chei nyumba.	33. 버싸 모유 무시 보씨, 버라 구야 구찌루따 과 찌소 쩌이 뉴빠.	33. The whole town gathered at the door,
34. Yesu era kulamya bandju banene ba babaa bete chira bulwala. Era kwambula na bihwasi binene, kanji chiro akemerera mbu bindaa byateta bushi byabaa bichwula bimwishi.	34. 여수 어라 구콰마 바쭈 바너너 바 바바아 버더 찌라 부뽜콰. 어라 과뿌콰 나 비화시 비너너, 가찌 찌로 아거머러라 뿌 비따아 뱌더다 부씨 뱌바아 비쭈콰 비뮈씨.	34. and Jesus healed many who had various diseases. He also drove out many demons, but he would not let the demons speak because they knew who he was.
Yesu akangilyisa e bandju e kalilaya	***여수 아가끼레사 어 바쭈 어 가리콰야***	
35. Abere mwei mishangya	35. 아버러 뭐이 미싸꺄	35. Very early in the

lumbulyi-mbulyi, Yesu era kusuka. Era kutenga mwa nyumba na aya kwema Ongo mu chisiki chai yeine.

36. Chasinda, simoni na balyikabo bera kuya kumuhonda.

37. bamulolyireko, bera kumubura mbu: ewalyia! e bandju boshi bakuhonda!

38. Si na imbu: chwuyaa mwa inji misi era ilyi ofu, chasiya nyihubanganyise beshayi e Chinwa cha Ongo, bushi echera chi chachwumaa nabaha.

39. Bushi n'oku, Yesu era kwire aya kusungula mw'echi chio choshi ch'e kalilaya, era kunde akangilyisa e bandju mwa mashenge m'e Bayuda na kunde aambula e bihwasi.

Yesu alamya e mubenzi-benzi

40. Lusuku luuma, mubenzi-benzi muuma aikiraa Yesu. Oyu mubenzi-benzi, era kukoma e mafi era muhondo sa Yesu na amwema mbu: Akaba uhonjire, unganyilamya!

41. Yesu era kumufira bonjo. Era kunanula e mino, era

루뿌쩨-뿌쩨, 여수 어라 구수가. 어라 구더빠 뫄 뉴빠 나 아야 궈마 오꼬 무 찌시기 짜이 여이너.

36. 짜시따, 시모니 나 바쩨가보 버라 구야 구무호따.

37. 바무론쩨러고, 버라 구무부라 뿌: 어와쩨아! 어 바쭈 보씨 바구호따!

38. 시 나 이뿌: 쭈야아 뫄 이씨 미시 어라 이쩨 오푸, 짜시야 네후바빠네서 버싸에 어 찌놔 짜 오꼬, 부씨 어쩌라 찌 짜쭉마아 나바하.

39. 부씨 노구, 여수 어라 귀러 아야 구수우롸 뭐찌 찌오 쪼씨 쩌 가쀠롸야, 어라 구더 아가삐쩨사 어 바쭈 뫄 마써뻐 머 바유다 나 구더 아아뿌롸 어 비화시.

여수 아롸먀 어 무버씨-버씨

40. 루수구 루우마, 무버씨-버씨 무우마 아이기라아 여수. 오유 무버씨-버씨, 어라 구고마 어 마피 어라 무호또 사 여수 나 아뭐마 뿌: 아가바 우호찌러, 우빠네쩨먀!

41. 여수 어라 구무피라 보쪼. 어라 구나누롸 어 미노, 어라

morning, while it was still dark, Jesus got up, left the house and went off to a solitary place, where he prayed.

36. Simon and his companions went to look for him,

37. and when they found him, they exclaimed: "Everyone is looking for you!"

38. Jesus replied, "Let us go somewhere else--to the nearby villages--so I can preach there also. That is why I have come."

39. So he traveled throughout Galilee, preaching in their synagogues and driving out demons.

40. A man with leprosy came to him and begged him on his knees, "If you are willing, you can make me clean."

41. Filled with compassion, Jesus reached out his hand

kumuumako na amubura mbu: Nahonda ulame!

42. Unao-unao bya bibenzi, kuna kulama.

43. Yesu era kumubura mbu aendaa. Era kumuchichika mbu:

44. utaburaa mundju asibya kw'ene myasi! si uyaa kuchilosa era mwa kuhanyi. Chasinda, wanana e michwulo y'e kulosa kwa walamire mira, ng'okwa e mwaso wa musa achwula atechire.

45. Si oyu mundju mango abaa era achiumaa, era kutangilyisa abalyikisa ei myasi mwa bisiki byoshi. Bushi n'oku, Yesu atachialaa kwengilyira changanama mu musi murebe. Era kunde abera bure n'e bandju mu chisiki chai yeine. Si chiro bacha, e bandju bera kunde banamuikiranga batengera mwa bisiki byoshi.

구무우마고 나 아무부라 뿌: 나호따 우쫘머!

42. 우나오-우나오 뱌 비버씨, 구나 구쫘마.

43. 여수 어라 구무부라 뿌 아아따아. 어라 구무찌찌가 뿌:

44. 우다부라아 무뚜 아시뱌 궈너 먀시! 시 우야아 구찌로사 어라 뫄 구하네. 쫘시따, 와나나 어 미쭈론 여 구론사 꽈 와쫘미러 미라, 꼬과 어 뫄소 와 무사 아쭈쫘 아더찌러.

45. 시 오유 무뚜 마꼬 아바아 어라 아찌우마아, 어라 구다삐레사 아바페기사 어이 먀시 뫄 비시기 뵤씨. 부씨 노구, 여수 아다찌아쫘아 궈삐레라 쫘까나마 무 무시 무러버. 어라 구떠 아버라 부러 너 바뚜 무 찌시기 쫘이 여이너. 시 찌로 바짜, 어 바뚜 버라 구떠 바나무이기라꽈 바더뼈라 뫄 비시기 뵤씨.

and touched the man. "I am willing," he said. "Be clean!"

42. Immediately the leprosy left him and he was cured.

43. Jesus sent him away at once with a strong warning:

44. "See that you don't tell this to anyone. But go, show yourself to the priest and offer the sacrifices that Moses commanded for your cleansing, as a testimony to them."

45. Instead he went out and began to talk freely, spreading the news. As a result, Jesus could no longer enter a town openly but stayed outside in lonely places. Yet the people still came to him from everywhere.

Mariko Chikono 2
Yesu alamya e mundju ola ureemere

1. Era nyuma sa suku burebe, Yesu era kuika kanji mwa musi w'e kaperinaumu. Mango e bandju bomvaa mbu alyi mwa

마리고 찌고노 2
여수 아쫘먀 어 무뚜 오쫘 우러어머러

1. 어라 뉴마 사 수구 부러버, 여수 어라 구이가 가찌 뫄 무시 워 가퍼리나우무. 마꼬 어 바뚜 보빠아 뿌 아레 뫄

Mark Chapter 2[NIV]

1. A few days later, when Jesus again entered Capernaum, the people heard that he had come

nyumba,	뉴빠,	home.
2. banene mubo bera kuya kuchilundamo, kuikira e chihangi ala angekala unji mundju kwa chiso, nao era kunaina. Abu boshi, Yesu abaa abakangilyisa e chinwa cha Ongo.	2. 바너너 무보 버라 구야 구찌ᄙᅮᄠᅡ모, 구이기라 어 찌하ᅇᅵ 아ᄙᅪ 아ᅇᅥ가ᄙᅪ 우ᄣᅵ 무ᅜᅮ 과 찌소, 나오 어라 구나이나. 아부 보씨, 여수 아바아 아바가ᅇᅵᄙᅦ사 어 찌놔 짜 오ᅌᅩ.	2. So many gathered that there was no room left, not even outside the door, and he preached the word to them.
3. Mw'olu, bandju bane bera kureteera Yesu mundju muuma ola wabaa ureemere.	3. 뫄ᄙᅮ, 바ᅜᅮ 바너 버라 구러더어라 여수 무ᅜᅮ 무우마 오ᄙᅪ 와바아 우러어머러.	3. Some men came, bringing to him a paralytic, carried by four of them.
4. Si bushi n'e bwingi bw'e bandju, chiro bakaala kumuisa era muhondo sa Yesu. Bushi n'oku, bera kwire bachwula kwa butala-tala bw'e nyumba, kwa lyima ala yesu abaa analyi. Na mw'echi chichwure mu barenzesaa e chipoyo ch'oyu mundju abaa alyiko.	4. 시 부씨 너 뷔ᅇᅵ 붜 바ᅜᅮ, 찌로 바가아ᄙᅪ 구무이사 어라 무호ᄠᅩ 사 여수. 부씨 노구, 버라 귀러 바쭈ᄙᅪ 과 부다ᄙᅪ-다ᄙᅪ 붜 뉴빠, 과 ᄙᅦ마 아ᄙᅪ 여수 아바아 아나ᄙᅦ. 나 뭐찌 찌쭈러 무 바러ᄴᅥ사아 어 찌포요 쪼유 무ᅜᅮ 아바아 아ᄙᅦ고.	4. Since they could not get him to Jesus because of the crowd, they made an opening in the roof above Jesus and, after digging through it, lowered the mat the paralyzed man was lying on.
5. Mango Yesu alolaa kwa bwemeresi bwabu bandju, era kwire abura ola wabaa ureemere mbu: E mwana wanyi! E bibi byao byababalyirwe.	5. 마ᅌᅩ 여수 아로ᄙᅪ아 과 붜머러시 봐부 바ᅜᅮ, 어라 귀러 아부라 오ᄙᅪ 와바아 우러어머러 뿌: 어 뫄나 와니! 어 비비 뱌오 뱌바바ᄙᅦ뤄.	5. When Jesus saw their faith, he said to the paralytic, "Son, your sins are forgiven."
6. Mwei nyumba mwabaa mulyi bakangilyisi bauma b'e mwaso. Bera kutangilyisa bachibusa mwa michima yabo mbu:	6. 뭐이 뉴빠 뫄바아 무ᄙᅦ 바가ᅇᅵᄙᅦ시 바우마 버 뫄소. 버라 구다ᅇᅵᄙᅦ사 바찌부사 뫄 미찌마 야보 뿌:	6. Now some teachers of the law were sitting there, thinking to themselves,
7. Ono mundju, si kukamba ku akambire Ongo! Bushi kutalyi ola ungaala kubabalyira e bibi, kureka Ongo yeine!	7. 오노 무ᅜᅮ, 시 구가빠 구 아가뻬러 오ᅌᅩ! 부씨 구다ᄙᅦ 오ᄙᅪ 우ᅇᅡ아ᄙᅪ 구바바ᄙᅦ라 어 비비, 구러가 오ᅌᅩ 여이너!	7. "Why does this fellow talk like that? He's blaspheming! Who can forgive sins but God

alone?"

8. Rero, ebi babaa bachibusa mwa michima yabo, unao-unao Yesu kuna kubimenyerera. Bushi n'oku, era kwire ababusa mbu: Ewashe! chi chachwuma mwachibusa bacha mwa michima yenyu?

9. Munyiburaa! chiye chi chibofoire kuteta mw'ene myasi ebilyi: elyi e kubura ono mundju mbu e bibi byai byababalyibwe, nesi e kumubura mbu emangaa atole e chipoyo chai anaende!

10. Rero, nahonda mumenye kwa nyonyo nyi mwana w'e Mundju nyete e buashi bw'e kubabalyira e bibi muno butala. Yesu kukwera kubura ola wabaa ureemere mbu:

11. nyinatechire, woyo w'emangaa, utole n'e chipoyo chao, unafuluke n'okwa wao!

12. Unao-unao, ola Mundju kuna kw'emanga, kuna kutola e chipoyo chai, na aya era butala mwanameho mabo. Boshi bera kusanwa busese. Chasinda, bera kutangilyisa batonga Ongo mbu: chwutafuraa kulola ku bilyi

8. 러로, 어비 바바아 바찌부사 마 미찌마 야보, 우나오-우나오 여수 구나 구비머녀러라. 부씨 노구, 어라 귀러 아바부사 뿌: 어와써! 찌 짜쭈마 먀찌부사 바짜 마 미찌마 여뉴?

9. 무네부라아! 찌여 찌 찌보포이러 구더다 뭐너 먀시 어비레: 어레 어 구부라 오노 무뚜 뿌 어 비비 뱌이 뱌바바레붜, 너시 어 구무부라 뿌 어마뺘아 아도뤄 어 찌포요 짜이 아나어떠!

10. 러로, 나호따 무머녀 과 뇨뇨 네 먀나 워 무뚜 녀더 어 부아씨 붜 구바바레라 어 비비 무노 부다롸. 여수 구궈라 구부라 오롸 와바아 우러어머러 뿌:

11. 네나더찌러, 오요 워마뺘아, 우도뤄 너 찌포요 짜오, 우나푸뤃거 노과 와오!

12. 우나오-우나오, 오롸 무뚜 구나 궈마뺘, 구나 구도롸 어 찌포요 짜이, 나 아야 어라 부다롸 먀나머호 마보. 보씨 버라 구사놔 부서서. 짜시따, 버라 구다삐레사 바도뺘 오꼬 뿌: 쭈다푸라아 구로롸 구 비레 바짜 찌로 너 우마!

8. Immediately Jesus knew in his spirit that this was what they were thinking in their hearts, and he said to them, "Why are you thinking these things?

9. Which is easier: to say to the paralytic, 'Your sins are forgiven,' or to say, 'Get up, take your mat and walk'?

10. But that you may know that the Son of Man has authority on earth to forgive sins . . . ." He said to the paralytic,

11. "I tell you, get up, take your mat and go home."

12. He got up, took his mat and walked out in full view of them all. This amazed everyone and they praised God, saying, "We have never seen anything like this!"

bacha chiro n'e uma!

Yesu abura lawi amukukulyikiraa

여수 아부라 롸위
아무구구꼐기라아

13. Era nyuma s'ebi, Yesu era kuya kanji kwa musike s'e nyanja y'e kalilaya. E luamba loshi lw'e bandju lwera kumuikira, na atangilyisa abakangilyisa.

13. 어라 뉴마 서비, 여수 어라 구야 가찌 과 무시거 서 냐짜 여 가쯰롸야. 어 루아빠 로씨 뤄 바뚜 뤄라 구무이기라, 나 아다삐레사 아바가삐레사.

13. Once again Jesus went out beside the lake. A large crowd came to him, and he began to teach them.

14. Mango abaa alyi mwa luendo, era kulola ku mundju muuma mbu i lawi, mwenyi alufayo. Oyu lawi abaa ekese mwa chisiki cha bendee bafuchisa mw'e mbarata. Yesu era kumubura mbu: Unyikulyikiraa! Lawi kuna kubachwuka na amukulyikira.

14. 마꼬 아바아 아레 롸 루어또, 어라 구로롸 구 무뚜 무우마 뿌 이 롸위, 뭐니 아루파요. 오유 롸위 아바아 어거서 롸 찌시기 짜 버뻐어 바푸찌사 뭐 빠라다. 여수 어라 구무부라 뿌: 우니구꼐기라아! 롸위 구나 구바쭈가 나 아무구꼐기라.

14. As he walked along, he saw Levi son of Alphaeus sitting at the tax collector's booth. "Follow me," Jesus told him, and Levi got up and followed him.

15. chasinda, Yesu era kuya kulya kwa bilyo mwa mwa lawi. Na mw'ei nyumba, mwabaa mulyi na bafuchisi banene ba mbarata na banji bandju ba babaa bachwusa ngulu ibi. Abu boshi, babaa balya alauma na Yesu n'e banafunzi bai, bushi banene mwaba balyi ngabo, bu bendee bamukulyikira.

15. 짜시따, 여수 어라 구야 구롸 과 비료 롸 롸 롸위. 나 뭐이 뉴빠, 마바아 무레 나 바푸찌시 바너너 바 빠라다 나 바찌 바뚜 바 바바아 바쭈사 우루 이비. 아부 보씨, 바바아 바롸 아롸우마 나 여수 너 바나푸씨 바이, 부씨 바너너 롸바 바레 빠보, 부 버뻐어 바무구꼐기라.

15. While Jesus was having dinner at Levi's house, many tax collectors and "sinners" were eating with him and his disciples, for there were many who followed him.

16. Mango e bakangilyisi b'e Mwaso b'omva chikembe ch'e bafarisayo balolaa kwa yesu alya n'e bafuchisi b'e mbarata n'e banji bandju ba babaa bachwusa ngulu ibi, bera

16. 마꼬 어 바가삐레시 버 롸소 보빠 찌거뻐 쩌 바파리사요 바로롸아 과 여수 아롸 너 바푸찌시 버 빠라다 너 바찌 바뚜 바 바바아 바쭈사 우루 이비, 버라 귀러

16. When the teachers of the law who were Pharisees saw him eating with the "sinners" and tax collectors, they asked his disciples: "Why does he eat with tax

kwire babusa e banafunzi bai mbu: Era! Chi chingagchwuma e mukangilyisi wenyu alya n'e bafuchisi b'e mbarata n'e banji bandju ba bachwusa ngulu ibi?

17. Yesu omvire bacha, era kwire ababura mbu: Ba bahaalukire batahonda muhake, si e balwala! Rero, nanyi ndabahire kwamaala ba bachwngenene era muhondo sa Ongo, si e bandju b'e mabi!

E meno ma mende mairwa busira kulya

18. Lusuku luuma, e banafunzi ba yowana mubatisayi n'e bafarisayo, babaa balyi mwa memo ma mende mairwa busira kulya bandju bauma bera kuikira yesu, na bamubusa mbu: chichichwuma e banafunzi ba yowana n'e bafarisayo baya mwa memo ma mende mairwa busira kulya, si ebao beke pyo!

19. Yesu nai mbu: Mwaanyisa mbu e bandju ba balalyikirwe kwa buya bangachima e bilyo mango muya mulume achilyi alauma nabo? Nanga! Mango muya mulume achilyi alauma nabo, batangaala kuchima e bilyo.

20. Si oyu muya mulume,

바부사 어 바나푸씨 바이 뿌: 어라! 찌 찌까쭈마 어 무가끼례시 워뉴 아랴 너 바푸찌시 버 빠라다 너 바찌 바뉴 바 바쭈사 응룰 이비?

17. 여수 오삐러 바짜, 어라 귀러 아바부라 뿌: 바 바하아루기러 바다호따 무하거, 시 어 바롸롸! 러로, 나네 따바히러 과마아롸 바 바쫘어너너 어라 무호또 사 오끄, 시 어 바뉴 버 마비!

어 머노 마 먼더 마이롸 부시라 구퍄

18. 루수구 루우마, 어 바나푸씨 바 요와나 무바디사에 너 바파리사요, 바바아 바례 뫄 머모 마 먼더 마이롸 부시라 구퍄 바뉴 바우마 버라 구이기라 여수, 나 바무부사 뿌: 찌찌쭈마 어 바나푸씨 바 요와나 너 바파리사요 바야 뫄 머모 마 먼더 마이롸 부시라 구퍄, 시 어바오 버거 표!

19. 여수 나이 뿌: 뫄아네사 뿌 어 바뉴 바 바롸례기뤄 과 부야 바까찌마 어 비룐 마꼬 무야 무루머 아찌례 아롸우마 나보? 나까! 마꼬 무야 무루머 아찌례 아롸우마 나보, 바다까아롸 구찌마 어 비룐.

20. 시 오유 무야 무루머,

---

collectors and 'sinners'?"

17. On hearing this, Jesus said to them, "It is not the healthy who need a doctor, but the sick. I have not come to call the righteous, but sinners."

18. Now John's disciples and the Pharisees were fasting. Some people came and asked Jesus, "How is it that John's disciples and the disciples of the Pharisees are fasting, but yours are not?"

19. Jesus answered, "How can the guests of the bridegroom fast while he is with them? They cannot, so long as they have him with them.

20. But the time will come

kukaba lusuku lwa akakulyibwa mwa kachi-kachi kabo. Rero mw'olu lusuku, mu bakaya mwa memo ma mende mairwa busira kulya.

21. Kutalyi ola ungalanjira echiraka chiyayaya kwa chiramba. Akaba angaira bacha, echi chiraka chiyayaya chanere chaberenga ala chalanjilyirwe kwa chiramba. Aola, echi chiramba chanere chanatandukala.

22. kanji kutalyi ola ungabika e chibabe ch'e tifai mwa bikunguisa by'e hao s'e nyuu. Bushinakaba bangaira bacha, echi chibabe kuika chinaberenge esi hao. Mw'olu, esi hao n'echi chibabe byoshi byanakumba. Si e chibabe, mwa hao s'e nyuu sa sichilyi siyayaya mu bende babikachi!

Yesu i Mukulu-kulu w'e sabato

23. Lusuku luuma lwa sabato, Yesu n'e banafunzi bai babaa barenga mu mahwa ma bulo. E banafunzi beke, bera kutangilyisa baenda bapolola kw'obu bulo.

24. e bafarisayo balolyire bacha, bera kumubura mbu: Ulolaa! chi chingachwuma e

구가바 루수구 롸 아가구레봐 롸 가찌-가찌 가보. 레로 모롵 루수구, 무 바가야 롸 머모 마 머머 마이롸 부시라 구롂.

21. 구다레 오라 우빠롸찌라 어찌라가 찌야야야 과 찌라빠. 아가바 아빠이라 바짜, 어찌 찌라가 찌야야야 짜너러 짜버러빠 아롸 짜롸찌레뤄 과 찌라빠. 아오롸, 어찌 찌라빠 짜너러 짜나다뚜가롸.

22. 가찌 구다레 오롸 우빠비가 어 찌바버 쩌 디파이 롸 비구우이사 벼 하오 서 뉴우. 부씨나가바 바빠이라 바짜, 어찌 찌바버 구이가 찌나버러빠 어시 하오. 몰루, 어시 하오 너찌 찌바버 뵤씨 뱌나구빠. 시 어 찌바버, 롸 하오 서 뉴우 사 시찌레 시야야야 무 버너 바비가찌!

여수 이 무구룰-구룰 워 사바도

23. 루수구 루우마 롸 사바도, 여수 너 바나푸찌 바이 바바아 바러빠 무 마화 마 부롢. 어 바나푸찌 버거, 버라 구다삐레사 바어빠 바포롤롸 교부 부롢.

24. 어 바파리사요 바롤레러 바짜, 버라 구무부라 뿌: 우롤롸아! 찌 찌빠쭈마 어

when the bridegroom will be taken from them, and on that day they will fast.

21. "No one sews a patch of unshrunk cloth on an old garment. If he does, the new piece will pull away from the old, making the tear worse.

22. And no one pours new wine into old wineskins. If he does, the wine will burst the skins, and both the wine and the wineskins will be ruined. No, he pours new wine into new wineskins."

23. One Sabbath Jesus was going through the grainfields, and as his disciples walked along, they began to pick some heads of grain.

24. The Pharisees said to him, "Look, why are they doing what is unlawful on

banafunzi bao baira bya mwaso wechwu achwula ananyise kuira e lusuku lw'e sabato?

25. Yesu nai mbu: mutafura kusoma chiro na hicha kwa mwami Daudi airaa mango abaa ahonda abone e bilyo, bushi n'e businya bwa abaa afa alauma n'e bandju bai?

26. Engilyiraa mwa nyumba ya Ongo! Era kutola e mikati era bandju babaa bachwulyire Ongo. Era kulya, chasinda era kweresa banyawai kui, n'oku ei mikati e bakuhanyi ba Ongo beine bu babaa bemire kunde balyai. airaa e byera mango Abitari abaamukulu-kulu w'e bakuhanyi.

27. Yesu era kuhuba kubabura mbu: E lusuku lw'e sabato lwairaa bushi n'e bandju. Si e bandju batairwaa bushi nalo.

28. Echera chi chichwumire mwemire kumenyerera kwa e lusuku lw'e sabato nalo, nyono nyi mwana w'e mundju, nyi enalo.

Mariko Chikono 3
Yesu alamya e mundju alusuku lw'e sabato

바나푸씨 바오 바이라 뱌 먀소 워쭈 아쭈롸 아나니써 구이라 어 루수구 뤄 사바도?

25. 여수 나이 뿌: 무다푸라 구소마 찌로 나 히짜 과 먀미 다우디 아이라아 마꼬 아바아 아호따 아보너 어 비료, 부씨 너 부시냐 봐 아바아 아롸우마 너 바뚜 바이?

26. 어삐례라아 먀 뉴빠 야 오꼬! 어라 구도롸 어 미가디 어라 바뚜 바바아 바쭈례러 오꼬. 어라 구롸, 짜시따 어라 궈러사 바냐와이 구이, 노구 어이 미가디 어 바구하니 바 오꼬 버이너 부 바바아 버미러 구떠 바롸이. 아이라아 어 벼라 마꼬 아비다리 아바아무구루루-구루 워 바구하니.

27. 여수 어라 구후바 구바부라 뿌: 어 루수구 뤄 사바도 롸이라아 부씨 너 바뚜. 시 어 바뚜 바다이롸아 부씨 나로.

28. 어쩌라 찌 찌쭈미러 뭐미러 구머녀러라 과 어 루수구 뤄 사바도 나로, 뇨노 네 뫄나 워 무뚜, 네 어나로.

마리고 찌고노 3
여수 아롸먀 어 무뚜 아루수구 뤄 사바도

---

the Sabbath?"

25. He answered, "Have you never read what David did when he and his companions were hungry and in need?

26. In the days of Abiathar the high priest, he entered the house of God and ate the consecrated bread, which is lawful only for priests to eat. And he also gave some to his companions."

27. Then he said to them, "The Sabbath was made for man, not man for the Sabbath.

28. So the Son of Man is Lord even of the Sabbath."

Mark Chapter 3[NIV]

1. Era nyuma s'ebi, Yesu era kwengilyira kanji mwa bushenge bw'e bayuda. Mw'obu bushenge, mwabaa mulyi mundju muuma ola wabaa ureemere e mino.

2. E bandju ba babaa balyimo, bera kusindera Yesu balole akaba angamulamya e lusuku lw'e sabato, babone cha bangemangirako bamusitake.

3. Yesu era kubura oyu mundju wabaa ureemere e mino mbu: Emangaa muno kachi-kachi k'e bandju.

4. Chasinda, Yesu era kubusa abu bandju mbu: Chiye chi e Mwaso wechwu achwula emerere mbu chwundaa chwaira e lusuku lw'e sabato? kuira e mabuya nesi e mabi? kulamya e mundju nesi kumwita? Abu bandju, bera kuchisilyira.

5. Yesu era kubasindera na bute bunene. Abaa asibukire busese bushi babaa benjire baira e michima yabo kuba isibu. Era kwire abura oyu mundju mbu: Nanulaa e mino yao. Era kunanulai, era mino kuna kulama.

6. Unao-unao, e bafarisayo

1. 어라 뉴마 서비, 여수 어라 궈삐레라 가찌 롸 부써어 붜 바유다. 모부 부써어, 롸바아 무레 무뚜 무우마 오롸 와바아 우러어머러 어 미노.

2. 어 바쭈 바 바바아 바레모, 버라 구시떠라 여수 바로러 아가바 아빠무롸먀 어 루수구 뤄 사바도, 바보너 짜 바뻐마삐라고 바무시다거.

3. 여수 어라 구부라 오유 무뚜 와바아 우러어머러 어 미노 뿌: 어마빠아 무노 가찌-가찌 거 바쭈.

4. 짜시따, 여수 어라 구부사 아부 바쭈 뿌: 찌여 찌 어 롸소 워쭈 아쭈롸 어머러러 뿌 쭈따아 쫘이라 어 루수구 뤄 사바도? 구이라 어 마부야 너시 어 마비? 구롸먀 어 무뚜 너시 구뮈다? 아부 바쭈, 버라 구찌시레라.

5. 여수 어라 구바시떠라 나 부더 부너너. 아바아 아시부기러 부서서 부씨 바바아 버찌러 바이라 어 미찌마 야보 구바 이시부. 어라 귀러 아부라 오유 무뚜 뿌: 나누롸아 어 미노 야오. 어라 구나누롸이, 어라 미노 구나 구롸마.

6. 우나오-우나오, 어

1. Another time he went into the synagogue, and a man with a shriveled hand was there.

2. Some of them were looking for a reason to accuse Jesus, so they watched him closely to see if he would heal him on the Sabbath.

3. Jesus said to the man with the shriveled hand, "Stand up in front of everyone."

4. Then Jesus asked them, "Which is lawful on the Sabbath: to do good or to do evil, to save life or to kill?" But they remained silent.

5. He looked around at them in anger and, deeply distressed at their stubborn hearts, said to the man, "Stretch out your hand." He stretched it out, and his hand was completely restored.

6. Then the Pharisees went

kuna kutenga mw'obu bushenge, na baya kubuanana n'e bandju b'omwa chikembe cha herodi, baire e lwango lw'e kuita Yesu.

바파리사요 구나 구더께 모부 부써어, 나 바야 구부아나나 너 바꾸 보뫄 찌거뻐 짜 허로디, 바이러 어 롸오 뤄 구이다 여수.

out and began to plot with the Herodians how they might kill Jesus.

Bandju banene baikiranga Yesu

바꾸 바너너 바이기라까 여수

7. Yesu nai alauma n'e banafunzi bai bera kutenga aola na baya kwa musike s'e nyanja y'e kalilaya. Bandju banene bera kumukulyikira. Abu bandju babaa batengera mwa chio ch'e kalilaya, n'e ch'e yudeya,

7. 여수 나이 아롸우마 너 바나푸씨 바이 버라 구더까 아오롸 나 바야 과 무시거 서 냐짜 여 가리롸야. 바꾸 바너너 버라 구무구례기라. 아부 바꾸 바바아 바더꺼라 뫄 찌오 쩌 가리롸야, 너 쩌 유더야,

7. Jesus withdrew with his disciples to the lake, and a large crowd from Galilee followed.

8. n'omwa musi w'e yerusalemu, n'omwa chio ch'e itumeya, n'omwa bio by'okwa nyinda s'e lwishi lw'e yorodani, n'omwa bimbi by'e musi w'e tiro n'e w'e sitona. Baikirangaa Yesu bacha, bushi babaa b'omvire mira e ngulu y'e myasi Yoshi era abaa enjire aira.

8. 노뫄 무시 워 여루사러무, 노뫄 찌오 쩌 이두머야, 노뫄 비오 뷔오과 녜따 서 뤼씨 뤄 요로다니, 노뫄 비삐 벼 무시 워 디로 너 워 시도나. 바이기라까아 여수 바짜, 부씨 바바아 보삐러 미라 어 응루 여 먀시 요씨 어라 아바아 어찌러 아이라.

8. When they heard all he was doing, many people came to him from Judea, Jerusalem, Idumea, and the regions across the Jordan and around Tyre and Sidon.

9. Yesu kukwera kubura e banfunzi bai mbu bekalaa bamukunganyisise bwato bueke, olu luamba lw'e bandju lungesha kumufundeeresa.

9. 여수 구궈라 구부라 어 바누푸씨 바이 뿌 버가롸아 바무구까녜시서 봐도 부어거, 오루 루아빠 뤄 바꾸 루꺼싸 구무푸떠어러사.

9. Because of the crowd he told his disciples to have a small boat ready for him, to keep the people from crowding him.

10. Atetaa bacha bushi abaa enjire alamya bandju banene. Rero, abalwala boshi bera kunde bafumirana chasiya baike ala alyi bamuumeko.

10. 아더다아 바짜 부씨 아바아 어찌러 아롸먀 바꾸 바너너. 러로, 아바롸롸 보씨 버라 구떠 바푸미라나 짜시야 바이거 아롸 아례 바무우머고.

10. For he had healed many, so that those with diseases were pushing forward to touch him.

11. Ba babaa basimbirwe n'e bihwasi nabo, mango bendee bamulolako, bera kunde bafukama era muhondo sai, n'e kunde balakanga mbu: woyo u Mwana wa Ongo!

12. si Yesu era kunde akalyiira ebi bihwasi busese kwa bitamukanganaa kwa bandju.

Yesu alondola e ndjumwa ekumi n'ebilyi

13. Chasinda, Yesu era kwerukira kwa ndjulungu. Era kwamaala bandju ba yeine abaa ahonjire. Abu bandju, bera kunaya ala abaa alyi.

14. Baikireo, era kulondola ekumi na babilyi mubo, era kubelyika mbu ndjumwa. Airaa bacha, chasiya babe nai, na kunde abachwuma kuya kuhubanganyisa e bandju e Mwasi Mubuya-buya.

15. Era kuberesa n'e buashi bw'e kunde bambula e bihwasi.

16. E masina m'esi ndjumwa ekumi n'ebilyi mu mamano: Simoni ola Yesu asulaa esina lya petero,

17. na yakobo, na yowana. Abu babilyi, babaa benyi sebetayo kanji bu yesu asulaa

---

11. 바 바바아 바시삐뤄 너 비화시 나보, 마오 버떠어 바무뢰라고, 버라 구떠 바푸가마 어라 무호또 사이, 너 구떠 바꽈가까 뿌: 오요 우 뫄나 와 오꼬!

12. 시 여수 어라 구떠 아가뻬이라 어비 비화시 부서서 과 비다무가까나아 과 바뚜.

여수 아또또꽈 어 뿌뫄 어구미 너비쪠

13. 짜시따, 여수 어라 궈루기라 과 뚜루우. 어라 과마아꽈 바뚜 바 여이너 아바아 아호찌러. 아부 바뚜, 버라 구나야 아꽈 아바아 아쪠.

14. 바이기러오, 어라 구뢰또꽈 어구미 나 바비쪠 무보, 어라 구버쪠가 뿌 뚜뫄. 아이라아 바짜, 짜시야 바버 나이, 나 구떠 아바쭈마 구야 구후바까니네사 어 바뚜 어 뫄시 무부야-부야.

15. 어라 구버러사 너 부아씨 뭐 구떠 바뿌꽈 어 비화시.

16. 어 마시나 머시 뚜뫄 어구미 너비쪠 무 마마노: 시모니 오꽈 여수 아수꽈아 어시나 꺄 퍼더로,

17. 나 야고보, 나 요와나. 아부 바비쪠, 바바아 버니 서버다요 가찌 부 여수

---

11. Whenever the evil spirits saw him, they fell down before him and cried out, "You are the Son of God."

12. But he gave them strict orders not to tell who he was.

13. Jesus went up on a mountainside and called to him those he wanted, and they came to him.

14. He appointed twelve-- designating them apostles- -that they might be with him and that he might send them out to preach

15. and to have authority to drive out demons.

16. These are the twelve he appointed: Simon (to whom he gave the name Peter,

17. James son of Zebedee and his brother John (to them he gave the name

esina lya bowanereke kukuteta mbu: Bana ba bete misi nga murasano.

아수퐈아 어시나 퍄 보와너러거 구구더다 뿌: 바나 바 버더 미시 꽈 무라사노.

Boanerges, which means Sons of Thunder

18. Era kulondola na andereya na filipo, na balitolomayo, na matayo, na tomasi, na yakobo mwenyi alufayo, na tateo, na simoni w'omwa chikembe ch'e baseloti,

18. 어라 구론또롸 나 아떠러야, 나 피뤼포, 나 바뤼도로꽈마요, 나 마다요, 나 도마시, 나 야고보 뭐네 아루파요, 나 다더오, 나 시모니 요꽈 찌거뻐 쩌 바서로디,

18. Andrew, Philip, Bartholomew, Matthew, Thomas, James son of Alphaeus, Thaddaeus, Simon the Zealot

19. na yuda isikariyota, ola warenganyaa Yesu.

19. 나 유다 이시가리요다, 오롸 와러꽈냐아 여수.

19. and Judas Iscariot, who betrayed him.

Banyakambo Yesu baya kumutola

바냐가뽀 여수 바야 구무도롸

20. Era nyuma s'ebi, Yesu era kuhuba mwa nyumba. Luamba lwa bandju banene bera kuhuba kubuananamo kuikira echihangi Yesu n'e banafunzi bai bera kwa bangalya.

20. 어라 뉴마 서비, 여수 어라 구후바 꽈 뉴빠. 루아빠 롸 바쭈 바너너 버라 구후바 구부아나나모 구이기라 어찌하꾀 여수 너 바나푸씨 바이 버라 과 바까퍄.

20. Then Jesus entered a house, and again a crowd gathered, so that he and his disciples were not even able to eat.

21. Mango banyakabo yesu bomvaa kwei myasi, bera kuteta mbu: Aaye! E bwenge bwamukongobanyire! Bushi n'oku, bera kwire baya kumutola.

21. 마꼬 바냐가보 여수 보빠아 궈이 먀시, 버라 구더다 뿌: 아아여! 어 붜꺼 봐무고꼬바니러! 부씨 노구, 버라 궈러 바야 구무도롸.

21. When his family heard about this, they went to take charge of him, for they said, "He is out of his mind."

E bakangilyisi b'e Mwaso belyika Yesu mbu i belisebuli

어 바가꾀레시 버 꽈소 버뻬가 여수 뿌 이 버뤼서부뤼

22. E bakangilyisi b'e mwaso ba batengeraa e yerusalemu, babaa benjire babura e bandju mbu Yesu asimbirwe na belisebuli kanji mbu oyu belisebuli, iuchwula mukulu-kulu w'e bihwasi, na kwa

22. 어 바가꾀레시 버 꽈소 바 바더꺼라아 어 여루사뻐무, 바바아 버찌러 바부라 어 바쭈 뿌 여수 아시뻬뤄 나 버뤼서부뤼 가찌 뿌 오유 버뤼서부뤼, 이우쭈롸 무구루-구루 워 비화시, 나 과 부아씨

22. And the teachers of the law who came down from Jerusalem said, "He is possessed by Beelzebub! By the prince of demons he is driving out demons."

buashi bwai ku Yesu enjire ambulabi.

23. Abu bakangilyisi b'e Mwaso, Yesu era kwire amaalabo, era kubabura mwa mianyi mbu: kute wamusimu angachambula yeine?

24. Akaba bandju ba bwami buuma bangachibaanya, elyi obu bwami bwa handjukere.

25. na akaba bandju ba ngumo nguma nabo, bangabangana beine kwa beine, ei ngumo kuika nai inahandjukale.

26. Rero wamusimu nai, akaba angachambula yeine, n'e bwami bwai akaba bungalyikana, nai atangachiata misi. Chasinda, obu bwami bwai nabo elyi bwahandjukere.

27. kutalyi ola ungaala kwengilyira mwa nyumba y'e mundju ola wete misi amunyae ne bindju byai akaba atasa kumusalyinga. Si mwa kuba era amusalyingaa, mu mango era angamunyaa e bindju byai byoshi.

28. kubinalyi, nababura kwa e bandju bangababalyirwa e bibi byabo byoshi n'e ngambo sabo soshi sa bende bakamba Ongo.

봐이 구 여수 어찌러 아뿌롸비.

23. 아부 바가찌레시 버 뫄소, 여수 어라 귀러 아마아롸보, 어라 구바부라 뫄 미아네 뿌: 구더 와무시무 아까짜뿌롸 여이너?

24. 아가바 바뉴 바 봐미 부우마 바까찌바아냐, 어레 오부 봐미 봐 하뉴거러.

25. 나 아가바 바뉴 바 꾸모 꾸마 나보, 바까바까나 버이너 과 버이너, 어이 꾸모 구이가 나이 이나하뉴가러.

26. 러로 와무시무 나이, 아가바 아까짜뿌롸 여이너, 너 봐미 봐이 아가바 부까레가나, 나이 아다까찌아다 미시. 짜시따, 오부 봐미 봐이 나보 어레 봐하뉴거러.

27. 구다레 오라 우까아롸 귀찌레라 뫄 뉴빠 여 무뉴 오롸 워더 미시 아무냐어 너 비뉴 뱌이 아가바 아다사 구무사레까. 시 뫄 구바 어라 아무사레까아, 무 마꼬 어라 아까무냐아 어 비뉴 뱌이 보씨.

28. 구비나레, 나바부라 과 어 바뉴 바까바바레롸 어 비비 뱌보 보씨 너 까뫃 사보 소씨 사 버더 바가빠 오꼬.

23. So Jesus called them and spoke to them in parables: "How can Satan drive out Satan?

24. If a kingdom is divided against itself, that kingdom cannot stand.

25. If a house is divided against itself, that house cannot stand.

26. And if Satan opposes himself and is divided, he cannot stand; his end has come.

27. In fact, no one can enter a strong man's house and carry off his possessions unless he first ties up the strong man. Then he can rob his house.

28. I tell you the truth, all the sins and blasphemies of men will be forgiven them.

29. Si ola ukaereresa akamba e Muchima mubuya-buya, oyola yeke atakababalyirwe chiro na hicha, bushi ebi bibi byai bikanaendekera kubao e suku n'e mango.

30. Yesu ababuraa bacha, bushi batetaa mbu: Ahwabirwe.

Bande bu banyakabo Yesu

31. Chasinda, balumuna ba Yesu alauma na nyina bera kuika, na bemanga era butala. Abere banachilyi bemenze, bera kumuchwuma kw'e mundju mbu abahaa.

32. Mwei nyumba mwabaa mulyi bandju banene ba babaa basungwire Yesu. Bera kumubura mbu: Umvaa! Nyoko na balumuna bao balyi era butala bakuhonda.

33. Yesu nai: Nde i malyi? Na bande bu balumuna banyi?

34. Chasinda, era kusungusa e meho mw'aba babaa bamusungwire. Era kuteta mbu: Banola bu bamalyi kanji bu na balumuna banyi.

35. Bushi chira ola wende waira e kuhonda kwa Ongo, i munyakechwu, kanji i mwalyi wechwu, kanji ina malyi.

29. 시 오라 우가어러러사 아가빠 어 무찌마 무부야-부야, 오요똬 여거 아다가바바뤠뤄 찌로 나 히짜, 부씨 어비 비비 뱌이 비가나어떠거라 구바오 어 수구 너 마꼬.

30. 여수 아바부라아 바짜, 부씨 바더다아 뿌: 아화비뤄.

바떠 부 바냐가보 여수

31. 짜시따, 바루무나 바 여수 아똬우마 나 네나 버라 구이가, 나 버마까 어라 부다똬. 아버러 바나찌뤠 버머써, 버라 구무쭈마 궈 무뚜 뿌 아바하아.

32. 뭐이 뉴빠 마바아 무뤠 바뚜 바너너 바 바바아 바수뀌러 여수. 버라 구무부라 뿌: 우빠아! 뇨고 나 바루무나 바오 바뤠 어라 부다똬 바구호따.

33. 여수 나이: 떠 이 마뤠? 나 바떠 부 바루무나 바네?

34. 짜시따, 어라 구수꾸사 어 머호 뫄바 바바아 바무수뀌러. 어라 구더다 뿌: 바노똬 부 바마뤠 가찌 부 나 바루무나 바네.

35. 부씨 찌라 오라 워떠 와이라 어 구호따 과 오꼬, 이 무냐거쭈, 가찌 이 뫄뤠 워쭉, 가찌 이나 마뤠.

29. But whoever blasphemes against the Holy Spirit will never be forgiven; he is guilty of an eternal sin."

30. He said this because they were saying, "He has an evil spirit."

31. Then Jesus' mother and brothers arrived. Standing outside, they sent someone in to call him.

32. A crowd was sitting around him, and they told him, "Your mother and brothers are outside looking for you."

33. "Who are my mother and my brothers?" he asked.

34. Then he looked at those seated in a circle around him and said, "Here are my mother and my brothers!

35. Whoever does God's will is my brother and sister and mother."

Mariko Chikono 4

E muanyi w'e muinzi

1. Yesu era kuya kanji kwa musike s'e nyanja y'e kalilaya na antagiliyisa e bandju. Bandju banene bera kumusungula. Bushi n'oku, era kwerukira mwa bwato bwa bwabaa bwemenzi kwa nyanja na ekalamo. N'e bandju bera kushiba kwa musike.

2. yesu era kubakangilyisa myasi inene mwa mianyi. Mw'ei mianyi, era kubabura mbu:

3. mumvilyisaa! kwabaa muinzi muuma ola wayaakuhuiraa e mbuto mw'ehwa lyai.

4. Abere era ahuirasi, siuma sera kutowangiranga kwa musike s'e njira. E milonge yera kuika na yachilyirasi.

5. E sinji sera kutowera mwa chwukoi-koi, ala abaa atalyi lutaka lunene. Sera kumera fuba bushi e lutaka lwabaa lukeire.

6. Si mango e suba lyakolaa, lyera kocha ei myaka na yoma, bushi emisi-misi yai yabaa itasiumikire mwa chitaka.

7. E sinji sera kutowera mwa mihulyi-hulyi. Ei mihulyi-hulyi, mango yameraa yera kuitasi,

---

마리고 찌고노 4

어 무아니 워 무이씨

1. 여수 어라 구야 가찌 과 무시거 서 냐짜 여 가끠롸야 나 아누다지꼐사 어 바뚜. 바뚜 바너너 버라 구무수꾸롸. 부씨 노구, 어라 궈루기라 롸 봐도 봐 봐바아 붜머씨 과 냐짜 나 어가꽈모. 너 바뚜 버라 구씨바 과 무시거.

2. 여수 어라 구바가끠꼐사 먀시 이너너 롸 미아네. 뭐이 미아네, 어라 구바부라 뿌:

3. 무삐꼐사아! 과바아 무이씨 무우마 오롸 와야아구후이라아 어 뿌도 뭐화 랴이.

4. 아버러 어라 아후이라시, 시우마 서라 구도와끠라꽈 과 무시거 서 끠라. 어 미뢰어 여라 구이가 나 야찌꼐라시.

5. 어 시찌 서라 구도워라 롸 쭈고이-고이, 아꽈 아바아 아다꼐 루다가 루너너. 서라 구머라 푸바 부씨 어 루다가 꽈바아 루거이러.

6. 시 마꼬 어 수바 랴고롸아, 려라 고짜 어이 먀가 나 요먀, 부씨 어미시-미시 야이 야바아 이다시우미기러 롸 찌다가.

7. 어 시찌 서라 구도워라 롸 미후꼐-후꼐. 어이 미후꼐-후꼐, 마꼬 야머라아 여라

Mark Chapter 4[NIV]

1. Again Jesus began to teach by the lake. The crowd that gathered around him was so large that he got into a boat and sat in it out on the lake, while all the people were along the shore at the water's edge.

2. He taught them many things by parables, and in his teaching said:

3. "Listen! A farmer went out to sow his seed.

4. As he was scattering the seed, some fell along the path, and the birds came and ate it up.

5. Some fell on rocky places, where it did not have much soil. It sprang up quickly, because the soil was shallow.

6. But when the sun came up, the plants were scorched, and they withered because they had no root.

7. Other seed fell among thorns, which grew up and choked the plants, so that

---

chiro sikacheka bifuma.

찌로 시가쩌가 비푸마.

they did not bear grain.

8. E sinji sera kutowera mwa lutaka lwa lwete e buinu. Esera seke, sera kumera. Mango sakulaa, siuma musi sera kweka bifuma mahachwu-mahachwu, n'e sinji chirachwu-chirachwu, n'e sinji eyana-eyana.

8. 어 시찌 서라 구도워라 롸 루다가 롸 뤄더 어 부이누. 어서라 서거, 서라 구머라. 마꼬 사구꽈아, 시우마 무시 서라 꿔가 비푸마 마하쭈-마하쭈, 너 시찌 찌라쭈-찌라쭈, 너 시찌 어야나-어야나.

8. Still other seed fell on good soil. It came up, grew and produced a crop, multiplying thirty, sixty, or even a hundred times."

9. Chasinda, Yesu kukwera kuteta mbu: Rero, ola wete machi m'e kumva, omvaa!

9. 짜시따, 여수 구꿔라 구더다 뿌: 러로, 오꽈 워더 마찌 머 구빠, 오빠아!

9. Then Jesus said, "He who has ears to hear, let him hear."

Cha chachwumaaa Yesu ende ateta mwa mianyi

짜 짜쭈마아아 여수 어떠 아더다 롸 미아니

10. Mango Yesu abaa era alyi yeine, e ndjumwa sai ekumi n'e bilyi alauma n'e banji bandju ba babaa banusungwire, bera kumubusa mbu: e Waliya! Ei mianyi wera kuteta, uchwuanululyiraai.

10. 마꼬 여수 아바아 어라 아떼 여이너, 어 뚜롸 사이 어구미 너 비떼 아꽈우마 너 바찌 바뚜 바 바바아 바누수뀌러, 버라 구무부사 뿌: 어 와뤼야! 어이 미아니 워라 구더다, 우쭈아누루뤠라아이.

10. When he was alone, the Twelve and the others around him asked him about the parables.

11. Yesu na imbu: Mwabo, mwalosibwe mira e myasi era ibishirwe mwa bwami bwa Ongo. Si e banji ba batachwula mwa chikembe chenyu beke, mwa mianyi mu n'enjire nabahambalyira

11. 여수 나 이뿌: 롸보, 롸로시붸 미라 어 먀시 어라 이비씨뤠 롸 봐미 봐 오꼬. 시 어 바찌 바 바다쭈롸 롸 찌거뻐 쩌뉴 버거, 롸 미아니 무 너찌러 나바하빠뤠라

11. He told them, "The secret of the kingdom of God has been given to you. But to those on the outside everything is said in parables

12. chasiya bende bachwumbikisa si batalolaa, Kanji bende bomva, si batamenyereraa, Bushi akaba bangenjiree balola banamenyerere,

12. 짜시야 버떠 바쭈삐기사 시 바다로롸아, 가찌 버떠 보빠, 시 바다머녀러라아, 부씨 아가바 바뤄찌러러어 바로롸 바나머녀러러, 바까아루기뤠러 오꼬, 나이 아까바바뤠러보.

12. so that, " 'they may be ever seeing but never perceiving, and ever hearing but never understanding; otherwise they might turn and be

Bangaalukilyire Ongo, Nai angababalyirebo.

forgiven!'"

Yesu aanulula e muanyi w'e muinzi

여수 아아누루파 어 무아니 워 무이씨

13. Chasinda, Yesu era kubura e bandju mbu: Akaba mutomvire oyu muanyi, rero kute mungomva einji Yoshi?

13. 짜시따, 여수 어라 구부라 어 바쭈 뿌: 아가바 무도뻬러 오유 무아니, 러로 구더 무꼬빠 어이찌 요씨?

13. Then Jesus said to them, "Don't you understand this parable? How then will you understand any parable?

14. E mbuto sa muinzi aingaa, chilyi e Chinwa cha Ongo.

14. 어 뿌도 사 무이씨 아이까아, 찌레 어 찌놔 짜 오꼬.

14. The farmer sows the word.

15. E mbuto sa satoweraa kwa musike s'e njira, sihuhanyisibwe n'e bandju ba bende bomva e chinwa cha Ongo. Unao-unao, wamusimu Anaika kukulachi mwa michima yabo.

15. 어 뿌도 사 사도워라아 과 무시거 서 찌라, 시후하네시붜 너 바쭈 바 버떠 보빠 어 찌놔 짜 오꼬. 우나오-우나오, 와무시무 아나이가 구구롸찌 뫄 미찌마 야보.

15. Some people are like seed along the path, where the word is sown. As soon as they hear it, Satan comes and takes away the word that was sown in them.

16. N'esa satoweraa mwa chwukoi-koi, si sihuhanyisibwe n'e bandju ba bende b'omva e chinwa cha Ongo, n'e kwangilyirachi na lumoo.

16. 너사 사도워라아 뫄 쭈꼬이-고이, 시 시후하네시붜 너 바쭈 바 버떠 보빠 어 찌놔 짜 오꼬, 너 과이레라찌 나 루모오.

16. Others, like seed sown on rocky places, hear the word and at once receive it with joy.

17. si chitasimika mwa michima yabo, bushi mango bende balola kwa malae nesi kwa malyibuko bushi nachi, unao-unao banareka e bwemeresi bwabo. Aola, bahuhanyisibwe n'e mbuto sa misi-misi yasi itasimikaa mwa chitaka.

17. 시 찌다시미가 뫄 미찌마 야보, 부씨 마꼬 버떠 바로롸 과 마롸어 너시 과 마레부고 부씨 나찌, 우나오-우나오 바나러가 어 붜머러시 봐보. 아오롸, 바후하네시붜 너 뿌도 사 미시-미시 야시 이다시미가아 뫄 찌다가.

17. But since they have no root, they last only a short time. When trouble or persecution comes because of the word, they quickly fall away.

18. N'esa satoweraa mwa mihoi-hoi, sihuhanisibwe n'e

18. 너사 사도워라아 뫄 미호이-호이, 시후하니시붜 너

18. Still others, like seed sown among thorns, hear

bandju ba bende bomva e
Chinwa cha Ongo,

19. Si e mianya yomuno
butala, n'e kusima e buare, na
inji myasi y'e buhuma-huma,
byende byafunderesa echi
chinwa mwa michima yabo.
Bushi n'oku, chiteka bifuma.

20. N'esa satoweraa mwa
lutaka lwa lwete buinu, seke
sihuhanyisibwe n'e bandju ba
bende bomva e chinwa cha
Ongo n'e kwemererachi, na
kunalyinda beka e bifumu.
Bauma baneka bifuma
mahachwu-mahachwu, n'e
banji chirachwu-chirachwu, n'e
banji eyana-eyana.

E muanyi w'e tara

21. kanji Yesu era kubabura
mbu: Ewashe! E mundju
angareta e tara kanji
alyifunyikire e chitonga nesi
abikelyi mwa buhanjingo?
Nanga! Kwa kakondo ku ende
abikalyi.

22. Kunoku ku byoshi bya
bibishirwe bikabihulwa
changanama. Na chira mwasi
woshi ola ubishirwe, nao
akamenyeka changanama.

23. Rero, ola wete e machi me
kumva, omvaa!

24. Yesu era kuhuba kubabura
mbu: Ei myasi momvire,

바쭈 바 버더 보빠 어 찌냐 짜
오꼬,

19. 시 어 미아냐 요무노
부다쫘, 너 구시마 어 부아러,
나 이찌 먀시 여 부후마-후마,
벼떠 뱌푸떠러사 어찌 찌냐 뫄
미찌마 야보. 부씨 노구,
찌더가 비푸마.

20. 너사 사도워라아 뫄
루다가 뢔 뤄떠 부이누, 서거
시후하녜시붸 너 바쭈 바 버떠
보빠 어 찌냐 짜 오꼬 너
궈머러라찌, 나 구나레따 버가
어 비푸무. 바우마 바너가
비푸마 마하쭈-마하쭈, 너
바찌 찌라쭈-찌라쭈, 너 바찌
어야나-어야나.

어 무아니 워 다라

21. 가찌 여수 어라 구바부라
뿌: 어와써! 어 무뚜 아꺄러다
어 다라 가찌 아레푸네기러
찌도꽈 너시 아비거레 뫄
부하찌꼬? 나꽈! 과 가고또 구
어떠 아비가레.

22. 구노구 구 뵤씨 뱌
비비씨뤄 비가비후꽈
짜꽈나마. 나 찌라 뫄시 온씨
오꽈 우비씨뤄, 나오
아가머녀가 짜꽈나마.

23. 러로, 오꽈 워더 어 마찌
머 구빠, 오빠아!

24. 여수 어라 구후바
구바부라 뿌: 어이 먀시

the word;

19. but the worries of this
life, the deceitfulness of
wealth and the desires for
other things come in and
choke the word, making it
unfruitful.

20. Others, like seed sown
on good soil, hear the
word, accept it, and
produce a crop--thirty, sixty
or even a hundred times
what was sown."

21. He said to them, "Do
you bring in a lamp to put
it under a bowl or a bed?
Instead, don't you put it on
its stand?

22. For whatever is hidden
is meant to be disclosed,
and whatever is concealed
is meant to be brought out
into the open.

23. If anyone has ears to
hear, let him hear."

24. "Consider carefully what
you hear," he continued.

muimenyererea kubuya-buya! 모삐러, 무이머녀러라아
Bushi bya mwende mwailyira e구부야-부야! 부씨 뱌 뭐더
banji, bi Ongo nai 마이쩨라 어 바지, 비 오꼬
akanabailyira. kanji yeke 나이 아가나바이쩨라. 가찌
akanarengeresa. 여거 아가나러ᄊ러러사.

25. Bushi ola wete kandju, 25. 부씨 오라 워더 가꾸,
iwende waneresibwa e kanji, si이워떠 와너러시봐 어 가찌,
ola utete kandju yeke, 시 오롸 우더더 가꾸 여거,
akanyaibwa n'eka achirembaa 아가냐이봐 너가 아찌러빠아
kuata. 구아다.

E muanyi w'e mbuto sa **어 무아내 워 뿌도 사**
sachimererea **사찌머러라아**

26. Yesu era kuteta kanji mbu: 26. 여수 어라 구더다 가찌 뿌:
e Bwami bwa Ongo, 어 봐미 봐 오꼬,
chwungabuhuhanya na 쭝까부후하냐 나 무아내 와
muanyi wa mundju muuma 무뿌 무우마 오라 와이ᄭ아 어
ola waingaa e mbuto 뿌도 뭐화 랴이.
mw'ehwa lyai.

27. Ei mbuto yera kumera 27. 어이 뿌도 여라 구머라
yanalyinda yakula e mushi n'e 야나쩨따 야구롸 어 무씨 너
buchwufu, mango abaa enjire 부쭈푸, 마꼬 아바아 어찌러
aba asene nesi aonjire. Chiro 아바 아서너 너시 아오찌러.
akamenyerera kute ku ei 찌로 아가머녀러라 구더 구
mbuto yameraa. 어이 뿌도 야머라아.

28. Mumenyererea kw'e lutaka28. 무머녀러라아 궈 루다가
lweine, lu lwende lwamesa e 뤄이너, 루 뤄떠 롸머사 어
myaka: yende yeka e bihoho 먀가: 여떠 여가 어 비호호
tanga, yaneka e milyimba 다ᄄ, 야너가 어 미쩨빠
chasinda e chwufuma mwa 짜시따 어 쭈푸마 뫄 마쩨빠.
malyimba.

29. Na mango ochwu 29. 나 마꼬 오쭈 쭈푸마 쮜떠
chwufuma chwende chwaba 쫘바 쮜쩨러, 무 마꼬 어 무뿌
chwelyire, mu mango e 어떠 아써부롸쪼, 부씨 어
mundju ende ashebulachwo, 수구 서 구써부롸 사이기러.
bushi e suku s'e kushebula

"With the measure you use, it will be measured to you-- and even more.

25. Whoever has will be given more; whoever does not have, even what he has will be taken from him."

26. He also said, "This is what the kingdom of God is like. A man scatters seed on the ground.

27. Night and day, whether he sleeps or gets up, the seed sprouts and grows, though he does not know how.

28. All by itself the soil produces grain--first the stalk, then the head, then the full kernel in the head.

29. As soon as the grain is ripe, he puts the sickle to it, because the harvest has come."

saikire.

E muanyi w'e kafuma k'e aradani

어 무아니 워 가푸마 거 아라다니

30. Yesu era kuendekera ateta mbu: e Bwami bwa Ongo, chwungabuhuhanya na chiye? Nesi chwungabuhambalako mu muanyi muchiye?

30. 여수 어라 구어떠거라 아더다 뿌: 어 봐미 봐 오꼬, 쭈빠부후하냐 나 찌여? 너시 쭈빠부하빠롸고 무 무아니 무찌여?

30. Again he said, "What shall we say the kingdom of God is like, or what parable shall we use to describe it?

31. Obu bwami, buchwula buhuhanyisibwe n'e kafuma k'e aradani. Aku kafuma, ku kachwula kaeke busese kurenza e chwunji chwufuma chwoshi chwa chwende chwaingwa muno butala.

31. 오부 봐미, 부쭈롸 부후하네시붜 너 가푸마 거 아라다니. 아구 가푸마, 구 가쭈롸 가어거 부서서 구러싸 어 쭈찌 쭈푸마 쪼씨 좌 쮀떠 좌이롸 무노 부다롸.

31. It is like a mustard seed, which is the smallest seed you plant in the ground.

32. Si mango kende kaba kaingirwe mira, kanamera, kanere katabaana kurenza einji myaka Yoshi yomw'ehwa. Chasinda, kanaata matabi manenene, kuikira kwa chihangi e milonge inganaimba e machwu mabo kwamu matabi.

32. 시 마꼬 거떠 가바 가이삐뤄 미라, 가나머라, 가너러 가다바아나 구러싸 어이찌 먀가 요씨 요뭐화. 짜시따, 가나아다 마다비 마너너너, 구이기라 과 찌하삐 어 미뢰떠 이빠나이빠 어 마쭈 마보 과무 마다비.

32. Yet when planted, it grows and becomes the largest of all garden plants, with such big branches that the birds of the air can perch in its shade."

33. Yesu abaa enjire akangilyisa e bandju mu inji mianyi inene era ilyi ngei, kukulyikana n'okwa babaa bangaala kumva.

33. 여수 아바아 어찌러 아가삐레사 어 바뉴 무 이찌 미아니 이너너 어라 이뤠 떠이, 구구뤠가나 노과 바바아 바삐아롸라 구빠.

33. With many similar parables Jesus spoke the word to them, as much as they could understand.

34. Kutalyi chinwa chisibya cha ababuraa busira kutetachi mwa muanyi. Si mango endee aba alyi yeine alauma n'e banafunzi bai, mu mango endee abaanululyira e myasi

34. 구다뤠 찌놔 찌시뱌 짜 아바부라아 부시라 구더다찌 롸 무아니. 시 마꼬 어떠어 아바 아뤠 여이너 아롸우마 너 바나푼씨 바이, 무 마꼬 어떠어 아바아누룩뤠라 어

34. He did not say anything to them without using a parable. But when he was alone with his own disciples, he explained everything.

Yoshi.

먀시 요씨.

Yesu abanda kwa mulaba

여수 아바따 과 무콰바

35. Mw'olu lusuku lunolu, abere lwera luolo-olo, Yesu era kubura e banfunzi bai mbu: chwuhabukiraa kwa unji mushilyilya w'e nyanja.
36. E banafunzi bera kureka e luamba lw'e bandju, bera kw'engilyira mwa bwato bwa Yesu abaa alyimo, na bachiuma. Bera kuenzikanya na manji mato.
37. Kwei nyanja, kwera kuulukira chiusi chisibu. Bwa bwato, e mulaba kuna kutangilyisa aurutanganyabo, kuikira e chihangi e meshi mabaa mahonda kw'ehulamo.
38. Mw'echi chihangi Yesu yeke abaa aonjire kwa lunda lw'era nyuma s'e bwato, asheyamire. E banafunzi bai bera kumususa na kumubura mbu: Mukangilyisi! Elyi utasene kwa kusika ku chwasikira muno?
39. Yesu era kusuka, era kukalyiira echi chiusi na kubura e nyanja mbu: Oreraa, unasire! Unao-unao, ola mulaba kuna kuorera. N'e nyanja na yaba pi!
40. Chasinda, Yesu era kubusa

35. 모루 루수구 루노루, 아버러 뤄라 루오로-오르, 여수 어라 구부라 어 바누푸씨 바이 뿌: 쭈하부기라아 과 우씨 무씨례퍄 워 냐짜.
36. 어 바나푸씨 버라 구러가 어 루아빠 뤄 바뉴, 버라 궈쯰례라 콰 바도 바 여수 아바아 아레모, 나 바찌우마. 버라 구어씨가냐 나 마찌마도.
37. 궈이 냐짜, 궈라 구우루기라 찌우시 찌시부. 봐 봐도, 어 무콰바 구나 구다쯰례사 아우루다꺄냐보, 구이기라 어 찌하쯰 어 머씨 마바아 마호따 궈후콰모.
38. 뭐찌 찌하쯰 여수 여거 아바아 아오찌러 과 루따 뤄라 뉴마 서 봐도, 아써야미러. 어 바나푸씨 바이 버라 구무수사 나 구무부라 뿌: 무가쯰례시! 어쩨 우다서너 과 구시가 구 쫘시기라 무노?
39. 여수 어라 구수가, 어라 구가쩨이라 어찌 찌우시 나 구부라 어 냐짜 뿌: 오러라아, 우나시러! 우나오-우나오, 오콰 무콰바 구나 구오러라. 너 냐짜 나 야바 피!
40. 짜시따, 여수 어라 구부사

35. That day when evening came, he said to his disciples, "Let us go over to the other side."
36. Leaving the crowd behind, they took him along, just as he was, in the boat. There were also other boats with him.
37. A furious squall came up, and the waves broke over the boat, so that it was nearly swamped.
38. Jesus was in the stern, sleeping on a cushion. The disciples woke him and said to him, "Teacher, don't you care if we drown?"
39. He got up, rebuked the wind and said to the waves, "Quiet! Be still!" Then the wind died down and it was completely calm.
40. He said to his disciples,

e banafunzi bai mbu: chi chachwumaa mwobaa bacha? Mutanafuraa kuata bwemeresi?

어 바나푸씨 바이 뿌: 찌 짜쭈마아 모바아 바짜? 무다나푸라아 구아다 뭐머러시?

"Why are you so afraid? Do you still have no faith?"

41. Abu banafunzi bera kobaa busese. Bushi n'oku, bera kutangilyisa babusanya mbu: Ewashe! iwera mundju muchiye ono, ola e mulaba n'e nyanja nabi byamuchwunda!

41. 아부 바나푸씨 버라 고바아 부서서. 부씨 노구, 버라 구다삐레사 바부사냐 뿌: 어와써! 이워라 무뚜 무찌여 오노, 오똬 어 무똬바 너 냐짜 나비 뱌무쭈따!

41. They were terrified and asked each other, "Who is this? Even the wind and the waves obey him!"

Mariko Chikono 5
Yesu ambula e bihwasi kwa mundju

마리고 찌고노 5
여수 아뿌똬 어 비화시 꽈 무뚜

Mark Chapter 5[NIV]

1. Mango Yesu n'e banafunzi bai babaa bera bahabukaa e nyanja, bera kuika mwa chio ch'e bakerasi.

1. 마꼬 여수 너 바나푸씨 바이 바바아 버라 바하부가아 어 냐짜, 버라 구이가 먀 찌오 쩌 바거라시.

1. They went across the lake to the region of the Gerasenes.

2. Abere Yesu era atenga mwa bwato, unao-unao mundju muuma ola wabaa usimbirwe n'e bihwasi, kuna kupamukira era muhondo sai atengera kwa shinda.

2. 아버러 여수 어라 아더뽜 먀 봐도, 우나오-우나오 무뚜 무우마 오똬 와바아 우시삐뤄 너 비화시, 구나 구파무기라 어라 무호또 사이 아더뚸라 꽈 씨따.

2. When Jesus got out of the boat, a man with an evil spirit came from the tombs to meet him.

3. Oyu mundju, kw'esi shinda ku abaa era anachwula. Kanji kutabaa chiro na mundju usibya ola wabaa ungachiala chiro kumusalyinga n'e mareure.

3. 오유 무뚜, 궈시 씨따 구 아바아 어라 아나쭈라. 가찌 구다바아 찌로 나 무뚜 우시뱌 오똬 와바아 우까찌아똬 찌로 구무사뤠뺘 너 마러우러.

3. This man lived in the tombs, and no one could bind him any more, not even with a chain.

4. Bushi chira mango e bandju bendee bamuminyira e byuma mwa maulu, n'e mareure mwamino, ebi byoshi era

4. 부씨 찌라 마꼬 어 바뚜 버떠어 바무미네라 어 뷰마 먀 마우루, 너 마러우러 먀미노, 어비 뵤씨 어라 구떠

4. For he had often been chained hand and foot, but he tore the chains apart and broke the irons on his

kunde anabikonolanga.
Kutabaa chiro na mundju
usibya ola wabaa w'ete misi
y'e kuchimuala.

5. Oyu mundju, kusungula ku
endee anasungula-sungula e
mushi n'e butufu kw'esi shinda
n'omwa miruko. Kanji endee
achilakangira n'e
kuchikomanga n'e makoi.

6. Abere alola ku Yesu
mamererere, era
kumulyibichira na akoma e
mafi era muhondo sai.

7. Era kulakanga busese mbu:
Eu Yesu mwenyi Ongo ola
uchwula kwa nguba, chi
wanyihondako? Nakwema
kw'esina lya Ongo,
utanyilyibusaa!

8. Atetaa bacha bushi Yesu
abaa enjire amukalyiira mbu:
Eu chihwasi, tengaa kw'ono
mundju!

9. Chasinda, Yesu era
kumubusa mbu: Esina lyao,
unde? Nai mbu: Esina lyanyi
nyi chwulyi bengi, bushi
chwuchwula banene.

10. Oyu mundju, era
kunaendekera ema Yesu
busese mbu ataambulyiraa ebi
bihwasi mu chinji chio.

11. Mw'echi chisiki ofu n'e
ndjulungu, mwabaa mwalyira

아나비고노롸啊. 구다바아
찌로 나 무뚜 우시뱌 오롸
와바아 워더 미시 여
구찌무아啊.

5. 오유 무뚜, 구수워롸 구
어떠어 아나수워롸-수워롸 어
무씨 너 부두푸 궈시 씨따
노롸 미루고. 가찌 어떠어
아찌롸가삐라 너 구찌고마啊
너 마고이.

6. 아버러 아뢰롸 구 여수
마머러러러, 어라
구무뤠비찌라 나 아고마 어
마피 어라 무호또 사이.

7. 어라 구롸가啊 부서서 뿌:
어우 여수 뭐네 오꼬 오롸
우쭈롸 과 우바, 찌
와네호따고? 나궈마 궈시나 롸
오꼬, 우다네뤠부사아!

8. 아더다아 바짜 부씨 여수
아바아 어찌러 아무가뤠이라
뿌: 어우 찌화시, 더啊아 교노
무뚜!

9. 짜시따, 여수 어라 구무부사
뿌: 어시나 롸오, 우떠? 나이
뿌: 어시나 롸네 니 쭈뤠 버삐,
부씨 쭈쭈롸 바너너.

10. 오유 무뚜, 어라
구나어떠거라 어마 여수
부서서 뿌 아다아뿌뤠라아
어비 비화시 무 찌찌 찌오.

11. 뭐찌 찌시기 오푸 너
뚜루우, 마바아 마뤠라 부소

feet. No one was strong
enough to subdue him.

5. Night and day among
the tombs and in the hills
he would cry out and cut
himself with stones.

6. When he saw Jesus from
a distance, he ran and fell
on his knees in front of
him.

7. He shouted at the top of
his voice, "What do you
want with me, Jesus, Son of
the Most High God? Swear
to God that you won't
torture me!"

8. For Jesus had said to
him, "Come out of this
man, you evil spirit!"

9. Then Jesus asked him,
"What is your name?" "My
name is Legion," he replied,
"for we are many."

10. And he begged Jesus
again and again not to
send them out of the area.

11. A large herd of pigs
was feeding on the nearby

buso bunene bwa ngulube.

부너너 봐 우루버.

hillside.

12. Ebi bihwasi, byera kwema Yesu mbu: Mw'esi ngulube mu uchwemereraa chwengilyire.

12. 어비 비화시, 벼라 궈마 여수 뿌: 뭐시 우루버 무 우쭤머러라아 쭤[의]레러.

12. The demons begged Jesus, "Send us among the pigs; allow us to go into them."

13. Yesu era kwemerera. Bya bihwasi kukwera kutenga kw'ola mundju na byaya kwengilyira mw'esa ngulube. Obu buso boshi bwasi, kuna kwandaala na sachirowanga mwa Nyanja na sasikiramo. Esi ngulube sabaa singaika ku byumbi bibilyi.

13. 여수 어라 궈머러라. 뱌 비화시 구궈라 구더[꺄] 교꽈 무뚜 나 뱌야 궈[의]레라 뭐사 우루버. 오부 부소 보씨 봐시, 구나 과따아꽈 나 사찌로와[꺄] 꽈 냐짜 나 사시기라모. 어시 우루버 사바아 시[꺄]이가 구 뷰[삐] 비비레.

13. He gave them permission, and the evil spirits came out and went into the pigs. The herd, about two thousand in number, rushed down the steep bank into the lake and were drowned.

14. Chasinda, e bangere b'esi ngulube bera kulyibichira mwa musi n'omwa chwumbara, baya kufulyira e bandju kwa myasi era yabere. E bandju bera kunaika baya kuchilorera kw'ebya byabere.

14. 짜시따, 어 바[어]러 버시 우루버 버라 구레비찌라 꽈 무시 노뫄 쭘빠라, 뱌야 구푸레라 어 바뚜 과 먀시 어라 야버러. 어 바뚜 버라 구나이가 뱌야 구찌[론]러라 궈뱌 뱌버러.

14. Those tending the pigs ran off and reported this in the town and countryside, and the people went out to see what had happened.

15. Abere baika ala Yesu abaa alyi, bera kulola kw'ola mundju wabaa usimbirwe n'e bihwasi ekese, era alyi muuma-uma, era embese n'e njimba. Bushi n'oku, bera kw'obaa.

15. 아버러 바이가 아꽈 여수 아바아 아레, 버라 구로꽈 교꽈 무뚜 와바아 우시[삐]뤄 너 비화시 어거서, 어라 아레 무우마-우마, 어라 어버서 너 찌[빠]. 부씨 노구, 버라 교바아.

15. When they came to Jesus, they saw the man who had been possessed by the legion of demons, sitting there, dressed and in his right mind; and they were afraid.

16. Ba bachiloreraa kwa myasi Yoshi era yaikiraa oyu mundju n'era yaikiraa esi ngulube, bera kubalyira ba basindaa kuika kwei myasi.

16. 바 바찌[론]러라아 과 먀시 요씨 어라 야이기라아 오유 무뚜 너라 야이기라아 어시 우루버, 버라 구바[례]라 바 바시따아 구이가 궈이 먀시.

16. Those who had seen it told the people what had happened to the demon-possessed man--and told about the pigs as well.

17. Bushi n'oku, bera

17. 부씨 노구, 버라

17. Then the people began

kutangilyisa bema Yesu busese mbu atengaa mwa chio chabo.

구다삐레사 버마 여수 부서서 뿌 아더빠아 마 찌오 짜보.

to plead with Jesus to leave their region.

18. Abere Yesu era erukira mwa bwato, oyu mundju wabaa usimbirwe n'e bihwasi era kumwema mbu baendaa alauma nai.

18. 아버러 여수 어라 어루기라 마 봐도, 오유 무뚜 와바아 우시삐뤄 너 비화시 어라 구뭐마 뿌 바어따아 아꽈우마 나이.

18. As Jesus was getting into the boat, the man who had been demon-possessed begged to go with him.

19. Yesu chiro akemerera. Si era kumubura mbu: Uhubaa kwa wao, uye kubura banyakwenyu e myasi Yoshi era enawenyu akukorere, n'okwa akufilyire bonjo.

19. 여수 찌로 아거머러라. 시 어라 구무부라 뿌: 으후바아 과 와오, 우여 구부라 바냐궈뉴 어 먀시 요씨 어라 어나워뉴 아구고러러, 노과 아구피쩨러 보쪼.

19. Jesus did not let him, but said, "Go home to your family and tell them how much the Lord has done for you, and how he has had mercy on you."

20. Chasinjire, Oyu mundju era kwire achiuma, na atangilyisa abalyira e bandju b'omwa chio ch'e tekapoli, e myasi Yoshi era Yesu amukoreraa. E bandju boshi ba bomvaa kwei myasi, bera kusawa busese.

20. 짜시찌러, 오유 무뚜 어라 귀러 아찌우마, 나 아다삐레사 아바쩨라 어 바뚜 보먀 찌오 쩌 더가포리, 어 먀시 요씨 어라 여수 아무고러라아. 어 바뚜 보씨 바 보빠아 궈이 먀시, 버라 구사와 부서서.

20. So the man went away and began to tell in the Decapolishow much Jesus had done for him. And all the people were amazed.

Yesu alamya mukasi muuma omwola na mwalyi wa yairo

여수 아꽈먀 무가시 무우마 오모꽈 나 꽈쩨 와 야이로

21. Era nyuma s'ebi, Yesu era kuhabukira kwa unji mushilyilya we nyanja mwa bwato. Abere era alyi kwa musike sei Nyanja, bandju banene bera kumusungula.

21. 어라 뉴마 서비, 여수 어라 구하부기라 과 우씨 무씨쩨랴 워 냐짜 마 봐도. 아버러 어라 아쩨 과 무시거 서이 냐짜, 바뚜 바너너 버라 구무수꿔롸.

21. When Jesus had again crossed over by boat to the other side of the lake, a large crowd gathered around him while he was by the lake.

22. Mw'olu, mukulu-kulu muuma w'omwa bushenge bw'e bayuda mbu I yairo, era kuika aola. Oyu yairo, mango alolaa ku Yesu, era kukoma e mafi era muhondo sai.

22. 모루, 무구루-구루 무우마 요먀 부써뻐 붸 바유다 뿌 이 야이로, 어라 구이가 아오롸. 오유 야이로, 마꼬 아로꽈아 구 여수, 어라 구고마 어 마피 어라 무호또 사이.

22. Then one of the synagogue rulers, named Jairus, came there. Seeing Jesus, he fell at his feet

23. Era kumwema busese mbu: Mwalyi wanyi mutoto ahonda kutowa e muchima. Rero, nakwema ubahe umubike kw'e mino alame, ahube kuba muuma-uma.

24. Bushi n'oku, Yesu era kuenda nai. Lwa luamba lw'e bandju lwera kukulyikira Yesu baenda bamufundeeresa.

25. Mw'abu bandju namo, mwabaa mulyi mukasi muuma ola wabaa wamala myaka ekumi n'ebilyi ete bulwala bwa kutengwa n'e mikira.

26. Oyu mukasi abaa alyibukire busese bushi n'e kuhakilyirwa na bahake banene. Era kunalyinda aesa e bikulo byai byoshi si chiro atalamaa. Obu bulwala bwai, kuendekera ku bwanaendekeraa bwamusera.

27. Rero, mango omvaa kwa ngulu ya Yesu, era kwire engilyira mwa luamba lw'e bandju alyi era nyuma sai. Chasinda, era kuuma kwa luchimba lwa Yesu,

28. bushi abaa enjire aenda ateta mbu: Akaba nyinganauma chiro kwa luchimba lwai, elyi nanalamire!

29. Unao-unao, kuna kumva kwa e bulwala bwai

---

23. 어라 구뭐마 부서서 뿌: 뫄레 와네 무도도 아호따 구도와 어 무찌마. 러로, 나귀마 우바허 우무비거 귀 미노 아롸마, 아후버 구바 무우마-우마.

24. 부씨 노구, 여수 어라 구어따 나이. 롸 루아빠 뤄 바뚜 뤄라 구구레기라 여수 바어따 바무푸너어러사.

25. 뫄부 바뚜 나모, 뫄바아 무레 무가시 무우마 오롸 와바아 와마롸 먀가 어구미 너비레 어더 부퐈롸 봐 구더와 너 미기라.

26. 오유 무가시 아바아 아레부기러 부서서 부씨 너 구하기뤠롸 나 바하거 바너너. 어라 구나뤠따 아어사 어 비구로 뱌이 보씨 시 찌로 아다롸마아. 오부 부퐈롸 봐이, 구어떠거라 구 봐나어거라아 봐무서라.

27. 러로, 마꼬 오빠아 과 꾸루 야 여수, 어라 귀러 어삐뤠라 뫄 루아빠 뤄 바뚜 아뤠 어라 뉴마 사이. 짜시따, 어라 구우마 과 루찌빠 롸 여수,

28. 부씨 아바아 어찌러 아어따 아더다 뿌: 아가바 네까나우마 찌로 과 루찌빠 롸이, 어레 나나롸미러!

29. 우나오-우나오, 구나 구빠 과 어 부퐈롸 봐이 봐롸미러.

---

23. and pleaded earnestly with him, "My little daughter is dying. Please come and put your hands on her so that she will be healed and live."

24. So Jesus went with him. A large crowd followed and pressed around him.

25. And a woman was there who had been subject to bleeding for twelve years.

26. She had suffered a great deal under the care of many doctors and had spent all she had, yet instead of getting better she grew worse.

27. When she heard about Jesus, she came up behind him in the crowd and touched his cloak,

28. because she thought, "If I just touch his clothes, I will be healed."

29. Immediately her bleeding stopped and she

bwalamire.

felt in her body that she was freed from her suffering.

30. Yesu nai uano-unao, era kumenya kwa kulyi misi era yamutengiremo. Bushi n'oku, era kubindjuka era nyuma mwa luamba, na abusa mbu: Nde iwaumire kwa luchimba lwanyi?

30. 여수 나이 우아노-우나오, 어라 구머냐 과 구레 미시 어라 야무더삐러모. 부씨 노구, 어라 구비쭈가 어라 뉴마 와 루아빠, 나 아부사 뿌: 떠 이와우미러 과 루찌빠 똬니?

30. At once Jesus realized that power had gone out from him. He turned around in the crowd and asked, "Who touched my clothes?"

31. E banafunzi bai nabo mbu: e Walyiya, si weine usene kwa bandju akufundeeresise! Rero, kute kanji wera ungachwubusa mbu nde iwakuumireko?

31. 어 바나푸씨 바이 나보 뿌: 어 와레야, 시 워이너 우서너 과 바쭈 아구푸떠어러시서! 러로, 구더 가찌 워라 우똬쭉부사 뿌 떠 이와구우미러고?

31. "You see the people crowding against you," his disciples answered, "and yet you can ask, 'Who touched me?' "

32. Si Yesu era kusungusa e meho mwa bandju ba babaa bamusungwire, chasiya alole nde iwailyire bacha.

32. 시 여수 어라 구수꾸사 어 머호 와 바쭈 바 바바아 바무수쮜러, 짜시야 아로퍼 떠 이와이레러 바짜.

32. But Jesus kept looking around to see who had done it.

33. Ola mukasi era kw'obaa, na atangilyisa akukumana bushi abaa amenyire mira byoshi bya byamuikirire. Bushi n'oku, era kuya kuchihunda mwa maulu ma Yesu na amubura e myasi yai Yoshi kanagana.

33. 오똬 무가시 어라 교바아, 나 아다삐레사 아구구마나 부씨 아바아 아머니러 미라 뵤씨 뱌 뱌무이기리러. 부씨 노구, 어라 구야 구찌후따 와 마우루 마 여수 나 아무부라 어 먀시 야이 요씨 가나가나.

33. Then the woman, knowing what had happened to her, came and fell at his feet and, trembling with fear, told him the whole truth.

34. Yesu kukwera kumubura mbu: Mwalyi wanyi, e bwemeresi bwao bwakulamise! Uchienderaa n'e boolo. Obu bulwala bwao, bwalamire!

34. 여수 구궈라 구무부라 뿌: 똬레 와니, 어 붜머러시 봐오 봐구똬라미서! 우쩌떠라아 너 보오론. 오부 부똬라 봐오, 봐똬미러!

34. He said to her, "Daughter, your faith has healed you. Go in peace and be freed from your suffering."

35. Abere Yesu anachilyi ateta,

35. 아버러 여수 아나찌레

35. While Jesus was still

kwera kuika ndjumwa sa sabaa satengera ala mwa yairo. Esi ndjumwa, sera kubura yairo mbu: Aaye walyiya! Mwalyi wao era atowaa e muchima. Utachitamyaa e mukagilyisi!

36. Si Yesu chiro akalaa kw'ebi. Era kubura yairo mbu: Utobaa, e bwemeresi bu unaataa!

37. Yesu atemereraa mbu kubaa ola waenda nai kureka petero, na yakobo, na yowana munyakabo yakobo.

38. Baikire ala mwa yairo, Yesu era kubuanao lwayo lunene, bushi e bandju babaa balyira n'e kuchilakangira busese.

39. Era kw'engilyira mwa nyumba na abura e bandju mbu: chi chachwuma mwaira e lwayo n'e kulyira bacha? Ono mwana atafire, si kuonjire ku kaonjire!

40. Abu bandju, bera kutangilyisa bamushekera. si Yesu era kubaulusa boshi era butala. Era kushiba n'e banafunzi bai bahachwu, n'e basere b'oyu munyere. Era kwengira mwa chumba cha chirunda ch'e mwana chabaa chilyi.

아더다, 궈라 구이가 뚜와 사 사바아 사더꺼라 아꽈 뫄 야이로. 어시 뚜꽈, 서라 구부라 야이로 뿌: 아아여 와레야! 마레 와오 어라 아도와아 어 무찌마. 우다찌다먀아 어 무가지꼐시!

36. 시 여수 찌로 아가롸아 궈비. 어라 구부라 야이로 뿌: 우도바아, 어 붜머러시 부 우나아다아!

37. 여수 아더머러라아 뿌 구바아 오롸 와어따 나이 구러가 퍼더로, 나 야고보, 나 요와나 무냐가보 야고보.

38. 바이기러 아꽈 뫄 야이로, 여수 어라 구부아나오 꽈요 루너너, 부씨 어 바뚜 바바아 바레라 너 구찌롸가꺼라 부서서.

39. 어라 궈꺼레라 뫄 뉴빠 나 아부라 어 바뚜 뿌: 찌 짜쭈마 뫄이라 어 꽈요 너 구레라 바짜? 오노 뫄나 아다피러, 시 구오찌러 구 가오찌러!

40. 아부 바뚜, 버라 구다꺼레사 바무써거라. 시 여수 어라 구바우루사 보씨 어라 부다롸. 어라 구씨바 너 바나푸씨 바이 바하쭈, 너 바서러 보유 무녀러. 어라 궈꺼라 뫄 쭈빠 짜 찌루따 쩌 뫄나 짜바아 찌꼐.

speaking, some men came from the house of Jairus, the synagogue ruler. "Your daughter is dead," they said. "Why bother the teacher any more?"

36. Ignoring what they said, Jesus told the synagogue ruler, "Don't be afraid; just believe."

37. He did not let anyone follow him except Peter, James and John the brother of James.

38. When they came to the home of the synagogue ruler, Jesus saw a commotion, with people crying and wailing loudly.

39. He went in and said to them, "Why all this commotion and wailing? The child is not dead but asleep."

40. But they laughed at him. After he put them all out, he took the child's father and mother and the disciples who were with him, and went in where the child was.

41. Era kumusimbira kwa mino na amubura mbu: Talita kumu! kukuteta mbu: Eu munyere, nyinatechire mbu usukaa!

42. Unao-unao, ola munyere kuna kubachwuka na atangilyisa achendera. Abaa ete miaka ekumi n'ebilyi. Ba bandju balolyire bacha, bera kusanwa busese.

43. Si Yesu era kubachichika busese kwa batabalyira mundju usibya kwei myasi. Chasinda, era kuteta mbu beresaa oyu mwana kwa bilyo.

Mariko Chikono 6
Besha mwa musi wabo Yesu bamukena

1. Yesu n'e banafunzi bai bera kutenga mw'echi chisiki, na baya mwa musi wai w'e kabuchwa.

2. Mango e lusuku lw'e sabato lwaikaa, era kutangilyisa akangilyisa e bandju mwa bushenge bw'e bayuda. Mango e bandju babaa bamumvilyisa, banene mubo bera kusanwa busese. Bera kutangilyisa babusanya mbu: Ono mundju, ngai uakulyire ene myasi Yoshi? N'obuno bwenge nde iwamweresisebo?

41. 어라 구무시삐라 과 미노 나 아무부라 뿌: 다리다 구무! 구구더다 뿌: 어우 무녀러, 네나더찌러 뿌 우수가아!

42. 우나오-우나오, 오롸 무녀러 구나 구바쭈가 나 아다삐레사 아쩌너라. 아바아 어더 미아가 어구미 너비레. 바 바뚜 바로레러 바짜, 버라 구사놔 부서서.

43. 시 여수 어라 구바찌찌가 부서서 과 바다바레라 무뚜 우시뱌 궈이 먀시. 짜시따, 어라 구더다 뿌 버러사아 오유 뫄나 과 비료.

마리고 찌고노 6
버싸 롸 무시 와보 여수 바무거나

1. 여수 너 바나푸씨 바이 버라 구더따 뮈찌 찌시기, 나 바야 롸 무시 와이 워 가부좌.

2. 마오 어 루수구 뤄 사바도 롸이가아, 어라 구다삐레사 아가삐레사 어 바뚜 롸 부써뻐 뷔 바유다. 마오 어 바뚜 바바아 바무뻬레사, 바너너 무보 버라 구사놔 부서서. 버라 구다삐레사 바부사냐 뿌: 오노 무뚜, 삐이 우아구레러 어너 먀시 요씨? 노부노 뷔뻐 떠 이와뭐러시서보? 너 비너 비소머라노 어찌러 아이라,

41. He took her by the hand and said to her, "Talitha koum!" (which means, "Little girl, I say to you, get up!").

42. Immediately the girl stood up and walked around (she was twelve years old). At this they were completely astonished.

43. He gave strict orders not to let anyone know about this, and told them to give her something to eat.

Mark Chapter 6[NIV]

1. Jesus left there and went to his hometown, accompanied by his disciples.

2. When the Sabbath came, he began to teach in the synagogue, and many who heard him were amazed. "Where did this man get these things?" they asked. "What's this wisdom that has been given him, that he even does miracles!

N'e bine bisomerano enjire aira, ngai uakulyire e buashi bw'e kuirabi?

3. Si ola murenga w'e kukola embao onola! Si Mariya i nyina! Na yakobo, na yose, na yuda, na simon bu balumuna! Na balyiwabo, si ku chwunachwulanabo kuno! Echera chera kuchwuma batamwemerera.

4. Yesu kukwera kubabura mbu: Emurebi ataina echwunda mwa bisiki byoshi, si mwa musi wabo, na mu banyakabo, n'omwa mwai mu ataneresibwalyi.

5. Yesu chiro akaira chisomerano chisibya mw'oyu musi, si balwala baeke bu analamyaa mwa kubabika kw'e mino.

6. Era kusanwa busese, bushi abu bandju bananaa mbu batangemerera. Era nyuma s'ebi, Yesu era kunde asungula kwa misi aenda akangilyisa e bandju.

Yesu achwuma e ndjumwa sai ekumi n'e bilyi

7. Era kwamaala e ndjumwa sai ekumi n'ebilyi, era kubachwuma babilyi-babilyi na aberesa e buashi bw'e kwambula e bihwasi.

따이 우아구꿰러러 어 부아씨 뭐 구이라비?

3. 시 오꽈 무러까 워 구고꽈 어빠오 오노꽈! 시 마리야 이 내나! 나 야고보, 나 요서, 나 유다, 나 시모누 부 바룰무나! 나 바꿰와보, 시 구 쭈나쭈꽈나보 구노! 어쩌라 쩌라 구쭈마 바다뭐머러라.

4. 여수 구궈라 구바부라 뭉: 어무러비 아다이나 어쭈따 마 비시기 뵤씨, 시 마 무시 와보, 나 무 바냐가보, 노마 마이 무 아다너러시봐꿰.

5. 여수 찌로 아가이라 찌소머라노 찌시뱌 모유 무시, 시 바꽈꽈 바어거 부 아나꽈먀아 마 구바비가 궈 미노.

6. 어라 구사놔 부서서, 부씨 아부 바쭈 바나나아 뭉 바다꺼머러라. 어라 뉴마 서비, 여수 어라 구떠 아수우꽈 과 미시 아어따 아가꿰러사 어 바쭈.

여수 아쭈마 어 뚜꽈 사이 어구미 너 비꿰

7. 어라 과마아꽈 어 뚜꽈 사이 어구미 너비꿰, 어라 구바쭈마 바비꿰-바비꿰 나 아버러사 어 부아씨 뭐 과뿡꽈 어 비화시.

---

3. Isn't this the carpenter? Isn't this Mary's son and the brother of James, Joseph, Judas and Simon? Aren't his sisters here with us?" And they took offense at him.

4. Jesus said to them, "Only in his hometown, among his relatives and in his own house is a prophet without honor."

5. He could not do any miracles there, except lay his hands on a few sick people and heal them.

6. And he was amazed at their lack of faith. Then Jesus went around teaching from village to village.

7. Calling the Twelve to him, he sent them out two by two and gave them authority over evil spirits.

8. Era kubachichika mbu: Mwa lubalamo lwenyu, mutekaa chiro na kandju kasibya, nga mbamba, nesi hao, nesi luteya mwa mifuko yenyu, nesi lunji luchimba lwa kuinganya.

8. 어라 구바찌찌가 뿌: 마루바라모 뭐뉴, 무더가아 찌로 나 가뚜 가시뱌, 까 빠빠, 너시 하오, 너시 루더야 마 미푸고 여뉴, 너시 루찌 루찌빠 롸 구이까냐.

8. These were his instructions: "Take nothing for the journey except a staff--no bread, no bag, no money in your belts.

9. Si ekachi k'e kuenderako keine oshao ku munekaa, mwanembala ne birato.

9. 시 어가찌 거 구어떠라고 거이너 오싸오 구 무너가아, 롸너빠롸 너 비라도.

9. Wear sandals but not an extra tunic.

10. Yesu era kuhuba kubabura mbu: Na mango bangende babahuukasa mu nyumba irebe, muberaamo, kuikira e mango mungatenga mw'oyu musi.

10. 여수 어라 구후바 구바부라 뿌: 나 마꼬 바떠더 바바후우가사 무 뉴빠 이러버, 무버라아모, 구이기라 어 마꼬 무까더따 모유 무시.

10. Whenever you enter a house, stay there until you leave that town.

11. Kanji akaba besha musi murebe banganana kubahuukasa nesi kubomvilyisa, mutengaamo. Si mwa kutengamo, mukungutaa e mukungu ola ulyi kwa bihando byenyu. Obola bungaba bubei kw'abu bandju.

11. 가찌 아가바 버싸 무시 무러버 바까나나 구바후우가사 너시 구보삐레사, 무더따아모. 시 롸 구더따모, 무구우다아 어 무구우 오롸 우례 과 비하또 벼뉴. 오보롸 부까바 부버이 과부 바뚜.

11. And if any place will not welcome you or listen to you, shake the dust off your feet when you leave, as a testimony against them."

12. Esi ndjumwa sera kwire sachiuma saenda sahubanganyisa e bandju mbu babindjukaa batenge mwa bibi byabo.

12. 어시 뚜롸 서라 귀러 사찌우마 사어따 사후바까네사 어 바뚜 뿌 바비뚜가아 바더떠 롸 비비 뱌보.

12. They went out and preached that people should repent.

13. Bera kunde baambula na bihwasi binene, na kulamya balwala banene mwa kubakaba e mafuta.

13. 버라 구떠 바아뿌롸 나 비화시 비너너, 나 구롸먀 바롸롸 바너너 마 구바가바 어 마푸다.

13. They drove out many demons and anointed many sick people with oil and healed them.

Herodi echisa yowana mubatisayi

허로디 어찌사 요와나 무바디사에

14. Mw'esi suku, engulu ya Yesu yera kumvikana busese mwa bandju boshi, kuikira kwa chihangi mwami herodi nai era kunomva kui. Bandju bauma bera kunde bateta mbu: yowana mubatisayi iwomokire. Neshi, chi chichwumire aata e buashi bw'e kuira e bisomerano.

15. Si e banji beke, bera kunde bateta mbu: Oyola i Eliya. N'e banji mbu: Oyola alyi murebi kuuma n'e barebi b'okwa mira.

16. herodi nai mango omvaa kwei myasi, era kuteta mbu: Oyola alyi yowana mubatisayi ola natetaa mbu baishaa echwe, iwomokire!

17. Herodi atetaa bacha, bushi yeine iwabaa wabwilyire e bandju mira mbu basimbaa yowana bamumine n'e mareure, bamuume n'omwa buroko. Airaa ebyera, bushi abaa atolyire herotiya muka firipo na amuhwera. N'oku oyu firipo abaa munyakabo herodi.

18. yowana era kwire ende abura herodi mbu: e Mwaso wechwu atemerere mbu utolaa muka munyakenyu!

19. Bushi n'oku, herotiya era

---

14. 뭐시 수구, 어우루 야 여수 여라 구뻬가나 부서서 뫄 바뚜 뽀씨, 구이기라 과 찌하삐 먀미 허로디 나이 어라 구노빠 구이. 바뚜 바우마 버라 구너 바더다 뿌: 요와나 무바디사에 이오모기러. 너씨, 찌 찌쭈미러 아아다 어 부아씨 붜 구이라 어 비소머라노.

15. 시 어 바찌 버거, 버라 구너 바더다 뿌: 오요롸 이 어뤼야. 너 바찌 뿌: 오요롸 아레 무러비 구우마 너 바러비 보과 미라.

16. 허로디 나이 마꼬 오빠아 귀이 먀시, 어라 구더다 뿌: 오요롸 아레 요와나 무바디사에 오롸 나더다아 뿌 바이싸아 어쭤, 이오모기러!

17. 허로디 아더다아 바짜, 부씨 여이너 이와바아 와뷔레러 어 바뚜 미라 뿌 바시빠아 요와나 바무미너 너 마러우러, 바무우머 노봐 부로고. 아이라아 어벼라, 부씨 아바아 아도레러 허로디야 무가 피리포 나 아무훠라. 노구 오유 피리포 아바아 무냐가보 허로디.

18. 요와나 어라 귀러 어더 아부라 허로디 뿌: 어 뫄소 워쭈 아더머러러 뿌 우도롸아 무가 무냐거뉴!

19. 부씨 노구, 허로디야 어라

---

14. King Herod heard about this, for Jesus' name had become well known. Some were saying, "John the Baptist has been raised from the dead, and that is why miraculous powers are at work in him."

15. Others said, "He is Elijah." And still others claimed, "He is a prophet, like one of the prophets of long ago."

16. But when Herod heard this, he said, "John, the man I beheaded, has been raised from the dead!"

17. For Herod himself had given orders to have John arrested, and he had him bound and put in prison. He did this because of Herodias, his brother Philip's wife, whom he had married.

18. For John had been saying to Herod, "It is not lawful for you to have your brother's wife."

19. So Herodias nursed a

kubikira yowana mungo munene. Era kuhonda amwichise, si chiro akaala, 20. bushi herodi abaa enjire obaa yowana. Kanji abaa eshi kwa alyi mundju olaa uchwungenene era muhondo sa Ongo, kanji alyi mubuya-buya. Bushi n'oku, era kunde amulanga. Kanji abaa achwula asimire kunde omvilyisa e myasi ya yowana, chiro angaba mbu yendee yamusungulyisa e bwenge.

21. Lusuku luuma, herotiya era kubona enjira y'e kwita yowana. Olu lusuku, lwabaa lusuku lukulu lw'e kukengera e kubuchwa kwa herodi. Bushi n'oku, herodi era kuira lyinye na alalyika e bashamuka alauma n'e bakulu-kulu b'e basula, na banji bakulu-kulu b'e chio ch'e kalilaya.

22. Abere bera banalyi mw'elyi lyinye, mwalyi wa herotiya era kwengilyira mwa chai na atangilyisa asina. Oku kusina kwai, kwera kusimisa mwami herodi n'e bandju ba abaa alalyikire bushi n'oku, era kwire abura oyu munyere mbu: Choshi cha unasimire chi unanyemaa, nyinganakweresachi.

구비기라 요와나 무꼬 무너너. 어라 구호따 아뮈쩌서, 시 쩌로 아가아꽈,
20. 부씨 허로디 아바아 어찌러 오바아 요와나. 가찌 아바아 어씨 과 아레 무뚜 오꽈라 우쭝꺼너너 어라 무호또 사 오꼬, 가찌 아레 무부야-부야. 부씨 노구, 어라 구떠 아무꽈따. 가찌 아바아 아쭈꽈 아시미러 구떠 오쀄레사 어 먀시 야 요와나, 쩌로 아까바 뿌 여떠어 야무수꿀레사 어 붸꺼.

21. 루수구 루우마, 허로디야 어라 구보나 어찌라 여 귀다 요와나. 오루 루수구, 꽈바아 루수구 루구루 뤄 구거꺼라 어 구부좌 과 허로디. 부씨 노구, 허로디 어라 구이라 레녀 나 아꽈레가 어 바싸무가 아꽈우마 너 바구루-구루 버 바수꽈, 나 바찌 바구루-구루 버 찌오 쩌 가꿰꽈야.

22. 아버러 버라 바나레 뭐레 레녀, 꽈레 와 허로디야 어라 궈꿰레라 꽈 짜이 나 아다삐레사 아시나. 오구 구시나 과이, 궈라 구시미사 꽈미 허로디 너 바뚜 바 아바아 아꽈레기러 부씨 노구, 어라 궈러 아부라 오유 무녀러 뿌: 쪼씨 짜 우나시미러 찌 우나녀마아, 네까나궈러사찌.

grudge against John and wanted to kill him. But she was not able to,
20. because Herod feared John and protected him, knowing him to be a righteous and holy man. When Herod heard John, he was greatly puzzled; yet he liked to listen to him.

21. Finally the opportune time came. On his birthday Herod gave a banquet for his high officials and military commanders and the leading men of Galilee.

22. When the daughter of Herodias came in and danced, she pleased Herod and his dinner guests. The king said to the girl, "Ask me for anything you want, and I'll give it to you."

23. Kanji era kulaisa mbu: choshi cha ungananyema nyingakweresachi, anabe chimbi ch'e bwami bwanyi.

24. Oyu munyere, kuna kuchiuma aya kwema nyina eano mbu: E mama! Chi nyemaa? Nyina na imbu: Echwe lya yowana mubatisayi lyiunemaa.

25. Unao-unao, wamunyere kuna kuhuba malyibita era mwa mwami. Era kumubura mbu: Unao-unao nahonda unyerese echwe lya yowana mubatisayi kwa mbare.

26. mwami omvire bacha, era kusibuka busese. Si bushi n'e kulaisa kwa abaa alaisise mira era muhondo s'e bandju ba abaa alalyikire, era kuina kute angachinana oyu mwasi.

27. Unao-unao, era kuchwuma musula wai muuma mbu ayaa kumuterera echwe lya yowana mubatisayi. Oyu musula, kuna kuchiuma aya mwa buroko, era kuisha echwe lya yowana.

28. Chasinda, era kuretalyi kwa mbare, na angirisalyi ola munyere. Nai era kulyeresa nyina.

29. Mango e banafunzi ba

---

23. 가찌 어라 구롸이사 뿌: 쪼씨 짜 우꽈나녀마 네꿔러러사찌, 아나버 찌삐 쩌 봐미 봐네.

24. 오유 무녀러, 구나 구찌우마 아야 궈마 네나 어아노 뿌: 어 마마! 찌 녀마아? 네나 나 이뿌: 어쭤 럐 요와나 무바디사에 레우너마아.

25. 우나오-우나오, 와무녀러 구나 구후바 마뻬비다 어라 마미. 어라 구무부라 뿌: 우나오-우나오 나호따 우녀러서 어쭤 럐 요와나 무바디사에 과 빠러.

26. 마미 오뻬러 바짜, 어라 구시부가 부서서. 시 부씨 너 구롸이사 과 아바아 아롸이시서 미라 어라 무호또 서 바뚜 바 아바아 아롸뻬기러, 어라 구이나 구더 아꽈찌나나 오유 마시.

27. 우나오-우나오, 어라 구쭈마 무수롸 와이 무우마 뿌 아야아 구무더러라 어쭤 럐 요와나 무바디사에. 오유 무수롸, 구나 구찌우마 아야 마 부로고, 어라 구이싸 어쭤 럐 요와나.

28. 짜시따, 어라 구러다뻬 과 빠러, 나 아꿰리사뻬 오롸 무녀러. 나이 어라 구뗘러사 네나.

29. 마꼬 어 바나푸씨 바

---

23. And he promised her with an oath, "Whatever you ask I will give you, up to half my kingdom."

24. She went out and said to her mother, "What shall I ask for?" "The head of John the Baptist," she answered.

25. At once the girl hurried in to the king with the request: "I want you to give me right now the head of John the Baptist on a platter."

26. The king was greatly distressed, but because of his oaths and his dinner guests, he did not want to refuse her.

27. So he immediately sent an executioner with orders to bring John's head. The man went, beheaded John in the prison,

28. and brought back his head on a platter. He presented it to the girl, and she gave it to her mother.

29. On hearing of this,

yowana bomvaa kw'oyu uta na mwasi, bera kuika kutola e chirunda chai na baya kutabachi.

Yesu eucha bandju byumbi bitano

30. Mango e ndjumwa sa Yesu safulukiraa era abaa alyi, sera kutangilyisa samubalyikisisa e myasi yoshi era sairaa, na byoshi bya sakangilyisa e bandju.

31. Bandju banene bamuikirangaa n'e banji bafulukanga, kuikira e chihangi Yesu n'e ndjumwa sai bainaa n'e chihangi ch'e kulya. Bushi n'oku, Yesu era kwire abura e ndjumwa sa imbu: Muiraa chwuye mu chechwu chisiki chwubeine, mutamuke hicha.

32. Bera kwire bengilyira mwa bwato na baya mu chabo chisiki beine.

33. Si bandju banene bera kulola kwa baende, na bamenyerera era baire. Bera kutenganga mwa misi yoshi, na balyibichirangayi mwa maulu. Abu bandju bera kuba babere-bere kuikayi era muhondo Yesu n'e ndjumwa sai baike.

34. Mango Yesu abaa era

요와나 보빠아 교유 우다 나 마시, 버라 구이가 구도똬 어 찌루따 짜이 나 바야 구다바찌.

여수 어우짜 바뿌 뷰삐 비다노

30. 마꼬 어 뿌롸 사 여수 사푸루기라아 어라 아바아 아레, 서라 구다삐레사 사무바레기시사 어 먀시 요씨 어라 사이라아, 나 뵤씨 뱌 사가삐레사 어 바뿌.

31. 바뿌 바너너 바무이기라빠아 너 바찌 바푸루가빠, 구이기라 어 찌하삐 여수 너 뿌롸 사이 바이나아 너 찌하삐 쩌 구랴. 부씨 노구, 여수 어라 귀러 아부라 어 뿌롸 사 이뿌: 무이라아 쭈여 무 쩌쭈 찌시기 쭈버이너, 무다무거 히짜.

32. 버라 귀러 버삐레라 롸 롸도 나 바야 무 짜보 찌시기 버이너.

33. 시 바뿌 바너너 버라 구론똬 과 바어너, 나 바머녀러라 어라 바이러. 버라 구더빠빠 롸 미시 요씨, 나 바레비찌라빠에 롸 마우룹. 아부 바뿌 버라 구바 바버러-버러 구이가에 어라 무호또 여수 너 뿌롸 사이 바이거.

34. 마꼬 여수 아바아 어라

John's disciples came and took his body and laid it in a tomb.

30. The apostles gathered around Jesus and reported to him all they had done and taught.

31. Then, because so many people were coming and going that they did not even have a chance to eat, he said to them, "Come with me by yourselves to a quiet place and get some rest."

32. So they went away by themselves in a boat to a solitary place.

33. But many who saw them leaving recognized them and ran on foot from all the towns and got there ahead of them.

34. When Jesus landed and

atenga mwa bwato, era kulola kw'olu luamba lw'e bandju. Era kubafira bonjo bushi babaa balyi nga mbulyi sa sainyire mungere. Era kutangilyisa abakangilyisa myasi inene.

35. Abere lwera luolo-olo, e banafunzi bai bera kuya kumubura mbu: Enawechwu, mwa buyeye muno chwulyi, kanji n'e buchwufu bwelyire.

36. Rero, ungarekire bano bandju baye mwa mahwa n'okwa misi era ilyi ofu, baule bya bangalya.

37. Yesu na imbu: mubeine muberesaa e bilyo! Nabo mbu: si e bilyo bya bingeucha bano bandju boshi bingafa bikoroto maana mabilyi ma buteya. Rero, wahonda chwutole buteya bungana bucha, chwuye kubaulyira e bilyo?

38. Yesu era kubabusa mbu: Mikati enga i muete? Muyaa kuhona tanga. Abere bera bahonaa, bera kumwakula mbu: Mikati etano, n'efi ebilyi bi chwunete oshao.

39. Yesu era kukwera kubabura mbu bekasa e

아더까 꽈 봐도, 어라 구로라 교루 루아빠 뭐 바뇨. 어라 구바피라 보뇨 부씨 바바아 바레 까 뿌레 사 사이니레러 무어러. 어라 구다삐레사 아바가삐레사 먀시 이너너.

35. 아버러 뭐라 루오로-오로, 어 바나푸씨 바이 버라 구야 구무부라 뿌: 어나워쭈, 꽈 부여여 무노 쪼레, 가찌 너 부쭈푸 붜레러.

36. 러로, 우까러기러 바노 바뇨 바여 꽈 마화 노과 미시 어라 이레 오푸, 바우퍼 뱌 바까퍄.

37. 여수 나 이뿌: 무버이너 무버러사아 어 비료! 나보 뿌: 시 어 비료 뱌 비꺼우짜 바노 바뇨 보씨 비까파 비고로도 마아나 마비레 마 부더야. 러로, 와호따 쪼도러 부더야 부까나 부짜, 쪼여 구바우레라 어 비료?

38. 여수 어라 구바부사 뿌: 미가디 어까 이 무어더? 무야아 구호나 다까. 아버러 버라 바호나아, 버라 구꽈구롸 뿌: 미가디 어다노, 너피 어비레 비 쪼너더 오싸오.

39. 여수 어라 구궈라 구바부라 뿌 버가사 어 바뚜

saw a large crowd, he had compassion on them, because they were like sheep without a shepherd. So he began teaching them many things.

35. By this time it was late in the day, so his disciples came to him. "This is a remote place," they said, "and it's already very late.

36. Send the people away so they can go to the surrounding countryside and villages and buy themselves something to eat."

37. But he answered, "You give them something to eat." They said to him, "That would take eight months of a man's wages! Are we to go and spend that much on bread and give it to them to eat?"

38. "How many loaves do you have?" he asked. "Go and see." When they found out, they said, "Five--and two fish."

39. Then Jesus directed them to have all the people

Mariko	마리고	Mark
bandju boshi bikembe-bikembe kwa bichi.	보씨 비거뻐-비거뻐 과 비찌.	sit down in groups on the green grass.
40. Abu bandju bera kwekalanga bikembe-bikembe by'eyana-eyana, na bya matano-matano.	40. 아부 바쭈 버라 궈가쫘쩌 비거뻐-비거뻐: 벼야나-어야나, 나 뱌 마다노-마다노.	40. So they sat down in groups of hundreds and fifties.
41. chasinda, era mikati etano n'e s'efi ebilyi, Yesu era kubitola. Era kuchwumbikisa kwa nguba, na atonga Ongo. Era kuishanga mwa mikati n'e kuyeresa e banafunzi bai baabirangei e bandju boshi. Efi nasi, era kusiabiranga abu bandju boshi.	41. 쨔시따, 어라 미가디 어다노 너 서피 어비례, 여수 어라 구비도쫘. 어라 구쭈뻬기사 과 꾸바, 나 아도쩌 오꼬. 어라 구이싸쩌 쫘 미가디 너 구여러사 어 바나푸씨 바이 바아비라쩌이 어 바쭈 보씨. 어피 나시, 어라 구시아비라쩌 아부 바쭈 보씨.	41. Taking the five loaves and the two fish and looking up to heaven, he gave thanks and broke the loaves. Then he gave them to his disciples to set before the people. He also divided the two fish among them all.
42. E bandju boshi bera kulya na beuta.	42. 어 바쭈 보씨 버라 구쨩 나 버우다.	42. They all ate and were satisfied,
43. Mango e banafunzi batola-tolaa e bimbi-imbi by'e mikati n'e by'efi bya byashibaa, byoshi byera kwihusa bitonga ekumi na bibilyi.	43. 마꼬 어 바나푸씨 바도쫘-도쫘아 어 비뻬-이뻬 벼 미가디 너 벼피 뱌 뱌씨바아, 보씨 벼라 귀후사 비도쩌 어구미 나 비비례.	43. and the disciples picked up twelve basketfuls of broken pieces of bread and fish.
44. N'e balume ba balyaa ebi bilyo, babaa balyi byumbi bitano.	44. 너 바루머 바 바쨔아 어비 비료, 바바아 바례 뷰뻬 비다노.	44. The number of the men who had eaten was five thousand.
Yesu alambaira kwa nyanja	**여수 아쫘빠이라 과 냐쨔**	
45. Era nyuma s'ebi, Yesu era kubura e banfunzi bai mbu berukiraa mwa bwato, bamuhondorere kwa unji mushilyilya w'e nyanja, kwa lunda lw'e musi w'e betesaida. Nai era kushiba alaa olu luamba lw'e bandju.	45. 어라 뉴마 서비, 여수 어라 구부라 어 바누푸씨 바이 뿌 버루기라아 뫄 봐도, 바무호또러러 과 우찌 무씨쩨쨔 워 냐쨔, 과 루따 뭐 무시 워 버더사이다. 나이 어라 구씨바 아쫘아 오루 루아빠 뭐 바쭈.	45. Immediately Jesus made his disciples get into the boat and go on ahead of him to Bethsaida, while he dismissed the crowd.
46. Mango abaa era alaaabo,	46. 마꼬 아바아 어라	46. After leaving them, he

era kwerukira kwa ndjulungu, aya kwema Ongo.

47. Abere lwera luumbilyiro, bwa bwato bw'e banafunzi bwabaa bwera bulyi mwa kachi-kachi k'e nyanja, si Yesu yeke abaa achilyi kwa musike s'e nyanja yeine.

48. Era kulola kwa banafunzi bai balyibuka n'e kuruwa e bwato, bushi e chiusi chabaa chabaangika. Na mango bwabaa bwahonda kucha, Yesu era kuika ala babaa balyi aenda alambaira kwa nyanja. Era kuhonda kubahabuka.

49. Mango e banafunzi bai bamulolaako alambaira kwa nyanja, bera kuchichinga mbu alyi musimu. Unao-unao, bera kutangilyisa bachilakangira busese,

50. Bushi mango bamulolaako boshi, e buba bwera kubasimba busese. Si unao-unao, Yesu era kubabura mbu: Musesaa e muchima! nyono onola! mutobaa!

51. Chasinda, era kwerukira mw'obu bwato, cha chiusi kuna kuumba. E banafinzi bera kusanwa busese,

52. Bushi cha chisomerano ch'e mikati nachi, batamenyereraa kute ku

아꽈아아보, 어라 궈루기라 과 뉴루우, 아야 궈마 오온.

47. 아버러 뤄라 루우쁴레로, 봐 봐도 붜 바나푸씨 봐바아 붜라 부뤠 뫄 가찌-가찌 거 냐짜, 시 여수 여거 아바아 아찌뤠 과 무시거 서 냐짜 여이너.

48. 어라 구롣꽈 과 바나푸씨 바이 바뤠부가 너 구루와 어 봐도, 부씨 어 찌우시 짜바아 짜바아삐가. 나 마온 봐바아 봐호따 구꽈, 여수 어라 구이가 아꽈 바바아 바뤠 아어따 아꽈빠이라 과 냐짜. 어라 구호따 구바하부가.

49. 마온 어 바나푸씨 바이 바무롣꽈아고 아꽈빠이라 과 냐짜, 버라 구찌찌삐아 뿌 아뤠 무시무. 우나오-우나오, 버라 구다삐뤠사 바찌꽈가삐라 부서서,

50. 부씨 마온 바무롣꽈아고 보씨, 어 부바 붜라 구바시빠 부서서. 시 우나오-우나오, 여수 어라 구바부라 뿌: 무서사아 어 무찌마! 뇨노 오노꽈! 무도바아!

51. 짜시따, 어라 궈루기라 모부 봐도, 짜 찌우시 구나 구우빠. 어 바나피씨 버라 구사놔 부서서,

52. 부씨 짜 찌소머라노 쩌 미가디 나찌, 바다머녀러라아 구더 구 짜바아 찌더찌러.

went up on a mountainside to pray.

47. When evening came, the boat was in the middle of the lake, and he was alone on land.

48. He saw the disciples straining at the oars, because the wind was against them. About the fourth watch of the night he went out to them, walking on the lake. He was about to pass by them,

49. but when they saw him walking on the lake, they thought he was a ghost. They cried out,

50. because they all saw him and were terrified. Immediately he spoke to them and said, "Take courage! It is I. Don't be afraid."

51. Then he climbed into the boat with them, and the wind died down. They were completely amazed,

52. for they had not understood about the loaves; their hearts were

chabaa chitechire. Byabaa bacha, bushi e michima yabo yabaa ilyi isibu.

냐바아 바짜, 부씨 어 미찌마 야보 야바아 이레 이시부.

hardened.

Yesu alamya e balwala mwa chio ch'e kenasareti

여수 아라먀 어 바롸롸 롸 찌오 쩌 거나사러디

53. Mango Yesu n'e banafunzi bai babaa bera bahabukaa e nyanja, bera kuika mwa chio ch'e kenasareti. Bera kuminyira e bwato bwabo kwa musike s'e nynja.

53. 마꼬 여수 너 바나푸씨 바이 바바아 버라 바하부가아 어 냐짜, 버라 구이가 롸 찌오 쩌 거나사러디. 버라 구미네라 어 봐도 봐보 과 무시거 서 네짜.

53. When they had crossed over, they landed at Gennesaret and anchored there.

54. Abere bera batengaamo, unao-unao e bandju bera kumenyerera Yesu.

54. 아버러 버라 바더롸아모, 우나오-우나오 어 바뚜 버라 구머녀러라 여수.

54. As soon as they got out of the boat, people recognized Jesus.

55. Bushi n'oku, bera kulyibichiranga mw'echi chio chosi, chasiya bamureterange e balwala kwa bipoyo mu chira chisiki cha bendee bomva mbu alyimo.

55. 부씨 노구, 버라 구레비찌라롸 뭐찌 찌오 쪼시, 짜시야 바무러더라뼈 어 바롸롸 과 비포요 무 찌라 찌시기 짜 버떠어 보빠 뿌 아레모.

55. They ran throughout that whole region and carried the sick on mats to wherever they heard he was.

56. Na chira chisiki cha Yesu endee arengamo, abe mwa misi inenene nesi kwa misi yeeke-eke, nesi mwa chwumbara, e bandju bera kunde babikanga e balwala babo mwa nama, chasiya abalamye. Abu balwala, nabo bera kunde bamwema mbu abemereraa baume chiro kwa musike w'e luchimba lwai oshao. Na boshi ba bendee baluumako, bera kunde banalama

56. 나 찌라 찌시기 짜 여수 어떠어 아러롸모, 아버 롸 미시 이너너너 너시 과 미시 여어거-어거, 너시 롸 쭈빠라, 어 바뚜 버라 구떠 바비가꺄 어 바롸롸 바보 롸 나마, 짜시야 아바롸며. 아부 바롸롸, 나보 버라 구떠 바뭐마 뿌 아버머러라아 바우머 찌로 과 무시거 워 루찌빠 롸이 오싸오. 나 보씨 바 버떠어 바루우마고, 버라 구떠 바나롸마.

56. And wherever he went-- into villages, towns or countryside--they placed the sick in the marketplaces. They begged him to let them touch even the edge of his cloak, and all who touched him were healed.

Mariko Chikono 7

Yesu ateta era luulu s'e myanya y'e kabuchwa

1. E Bafarisayo na bakangilyisi bauma b'e Mwaso batengeraa e Yerusalemu na bachilunda era muhondo sa Yesu.

2. Bera kulola kwa bauma mwa banafunzi bai balya n'e mino sa silyi kw'e singa, kukuteta mbu batowaa kwa mino kukulyikana n'e myanya y'e tini lyabo.

3. Batetaa bacha, bushi e Bafarisayo n'e banji bayuda boshi bachwula bachwunjire e myanya ya bahokulu babo. Ei myanya, itachwula yemerere mbu e mundju endaa alya busira kwowa kwa mino ng'okwa byemire.

4. kanji, mango bende baba batenga mw'e soko, batangalya busira kuchikomya tanga. Bende bakulyikira na inji myanya inene, ngakuno e kulonga e ngumbu, n'e mareya, n'e nyungu sa sikunganyisibwe mwa milyinga.

5. bushi n'oku, abu bafarisayo n'e bakangilyisi b'e Mwaso, bera kubusa Yesu mbu: Chi chichwumire e banafunzi bao

마리고 찌고노 7

여수 아더다 어라 루우루 서 먀냐 여 가부좌

1. 어 바파리사요 나 바가끠레시 바우마 버 마소 바더꺼라아 어 여루사꺼무 나 바찌루따 어라 무호또 사 여수.

2. 버라 구로좌 과 바우마 좌 바나푸씨 바이 바쨔 너 미노 사 시레 궈 시까, 구구더다 뿌 바도와아 과 미노 구구레가나 너 먀냐 여 디니 쨔보.

3. 바더다아 바짜, 부씨 어 바파리사요 너 바찌 바우다 보씨 바쭈좌 바쭈끠러 어 먀냐 야 바호구루 바보. 어이 먀냐, 이다쭈좌 여머러러 뿌 어 무뚜 어따아 아쨔 부시라 고와 과 미노 꼬과 벼미러.

4. 가찌, 마꼬 버꺼 바바 바더꺼 뭐 소고, 바다꺼쨔 부시라 구찌고먀 다까. 버꺼 바구레기라 나 이끼 먀냐 이너너, 꺼구노 어 구로꺼 어 꿔뿌, 너 마러야, 너 뉴꿔 사 시구꺼네시붜 좌 미레까.

5. 부씨 노구, 아부 바파리사요 너 바가끠레시 버 마소, 버라 구부사 여수 뿌: 찌 찌쭈미러 어 바나푸씨 바오 버거

Mark Chapter 7[NIV]

1. The Pharisees and some of the teachers of the law who had come from Jerusalem gathered around Jesus and

2. saw some of his disciples eating food with hands that were "unclean," that is, unwashed.

3. (The Pharisees and all the Jews do not eat unless they give their hands a ceremonial washing, holding to the tradition of the elders.

4. When they come from the marketplace they do not eat unless they wash. And they observe many other traditions, such as the washing of cups, pitchers and kettles.)

5. So the Pharisees and teachers of the law asked Jesus, "Why don't your disciples live according to

beke batachwunda e myanya ya bahokulu bechwu? Bushi benjire balya n'e mino sa silyi kw'e singa!

6. Yesu na imbu: Emu batebanyi! Isaya arebaa kanangana era luulu senyu mango aanjikaa mbu: Bano bandju, kwa bieta ku bende bananyichwunda. Si e michima yabo ichwula bure nanyi!

7. Bushi e kunyera kwabo, kunachwula kwa buha! N'e miomba era bende bakangilyisa, bandju bu banaiiraa.

8. Yesu era kunaendekera ababura mbu: Mwabo, mwende mwareka e miomba ya Ongo, bushi n'e kukulyikira e myanya era yairwaa n'e bandju.

9. kanji era kubabura mbu: Kubinalyi, mutemanga kureka e mionba ya Ongo, bushi n'ekukulyikira e myanya yenyu.

10. Si muchwula mwishi kwa musa atetaa mbu: Undaa wachwunda eho na nyoko. kanji era kuteta mbu: Ola wakambire eshe nesi nyina, emire kwichibwa.

11. Si mwabo, mwende

바다쭈따 어 먀냐 야 바호구루 버쭈? 부씨 버찌러 바뺘 너 미노 사 시레 궈 시까!

6. 여수 나 이뿌: 어무 바더바네! 이사야 아러바아 가나까나 어라 루우루루 서뉴 마꼬 아아찌가아 뿌: 바노 바쭈, 과 비어다 구 버너 바나네쭈따. 시 어 미찌마 야보 이쭈롸 부러 나네!

7. 부씨 어 구녀라 과보, 구나쭈롸 과 부하! 너 미오빠 어라 버너 바가끼레사, 바쭈 부 바나이이라아.

8. 여수 어라 구나어떠거라 아바부라 뿌: 뫄보, 뭐러 뭐러가 어 미오빠 야 오꼬, 부씨 너 구구레기라 어 먀냐 어라 야이롸아 너 바쭈.

9. 가찌 어라 구바부라 뿌: 구비나레, 무더마꺄 구러가 어 미오빠 야 오꼬, 부씨 너구구레기라 어 먀냐 여뉴.

10. 시 무쭈롸 뮈씨 과 무사 아더다아 뿌: 우따아 와쭈따 어호 나 뇨고. 가찌 어라 구더다 뿌: 오롸 와가삐러 어써 너시 네나, 어미러 귀찌봐.

11. 시 뫄보, 뭐더 뫄더다 과

the tradition of the elders instead of eating their food with 'unclean' hands?"

6. He replied, "Isaiah was right when he prophesied about you hypocrites; as it is written: " 'These people honor me with their lips, but their hearts are far from me.

7. They worship me in vain; their teachings are but rules taught by men.'

8. You have let go of the commands of God and are holding on to the traditions of men."

9. And he said to them: "You have a fine way of setting aside the commands of God in order to observe your own traditions!

10. For Moses said, 'Honor your father and your mother,' and, 'Anyone who curses his father or mother must be put to death.'

11. But you say that if a

mwateta kwa e mundju anganabura eshe nesi nyina mbu: Bya nyingakuasise nabi byabere koribani, kukuteta mbu byachwulyirwe Ongo mira.

12. Rero mwa kuira bacha, mu mwende mwanga e mundju mbu ataasaa eshe nesi nyina.

13. Ei myanya bahokulu benyu babarekeraa mango mwenjire mwakangilyisanyai, yanachwuma mutalaa kwa chinwa cha Ongo. Kanji mwenjire mwaira na inji myasi inene era ilyi ngei!

Bya byende byaira e mundju kuba mubi

14. Era nyuma s'ebi, Yesu era kuhuba kwamaala e luamba lw'e bandju, era kubabura mbu: Muboshi munyumvilyisaa kubuya, mumerere n'e bine nahonda kubabura:

15. Bya byende byengilyira mwa mundju, ata bi byende byamubika mw'e singa. Si bya byende byamutengamo.

16. Ola wete machi m'e kumva, omvaa!

17. chasinda, Yesu era kureka olu luamba lw'e bandju. Abere era engilyiraa mwa nyumba, e

어 무뚜 아빠나부라 어써 너시 네나 뿌: 뱌 네까구아시서 나비 뱌버러 고리바니, 구구더다 뿌 뱌쭈레뤄 오꼬 미라.

12. 러로 뫄 구이라 바쨔, 무 뭐떠 뫄빠 어 무뚜 뿌 아다아사아 어써 너시 네나.

13. 어이 먀냐 바호구루 버뉴 바바러거라아 마꼬 뭐찌러 뫄가삐레사냐이, 야나쭈마 무다꽈아 꽈 찌놔 쨔 오꼬. 가찌 뭐찌러 뫄이라 나 이찌 먀시 이너너 어라 이레 빠이!

뱌 벼떠 뱌이라 어 무뚜 구바 무비

14. 어라 뉴마 서비, 여수 어라 구후바 과마아꽈 어 루아빠 뤄 바뚜, 어라 구바부라 뿌: 무보씨 무뉴삐레사아 구부야, 무머러러 너 비너 나호따 구바부라:

15. 뱌 벼떠 벼삐레라 뫄 무뚜, 아다 비 벼떠 뱌무비가 뭐 시빠. 시 뱌 벼떠 뱌무더빠모.

16. 오꽈 워더 마찌 머 구빠, 오빠아!

17. 쨔시따, 여수 어라 구러가 오루 루아빠 뤄 바뚜. 아버러 어라 어삐레라아 뫄 뉴빠, 어

man says to his father or mother: 'Whatever help you might otherwise have received from me is Corban' (that is, a gift devoted to God),

12. then you no longer let him do anything for his father or mother.

13. Thus you nullify the word of God by your tradition that you have handed down. And you do many things like that."

14. Again Jesus called the crowd to him and said, "Listen to me, everyone, and understand this.

15. Nothing outside a man can make him 'unclean' by going into him. Rather, it is what comes out of a man that makes him 'unclean.' "

16. None

17. After he had left the crowd and entered the house, his disciples asked

banafunzi bai bera kumubusa mbu kute ku oyu muanyi atechire.	바나푸ᅜᅵ 바이 버라 구무부사 ᄜᅮ 구더 구 오유 무아녜 아더찌러.	him about this parable.
18. Nai mbu: nenyu mutanafuraa kubookala e bwenge? Si mutabukire kwa byoshi bya byende byengilyira mwa mundju ata bi bingachwuma aba mubi!	18. 나이 ᄜᅮ: 너뉴 무다나푸라아 구보오가ᄙᅪ 어 붸ᅇᅥ? 시 무다부기러 과 뵤씨 뱌 벼ᄕᅥ 벼ᅇᅵᄙᅨ라 뫄 무ᅜᅮ 아다 비 비ᅇᅡ쭈마 아바 무비!	18. "Are you so dull?" he asked. "Don't you see that nothing that enters a man from the outside can make him 'unclean'?
19. Bushi ebyera bitengilyira mwa muchima wai, si mwa bula mu byende byaya, chasinda byanatengamo mwa kuya era chala. Mwa kuteta bacha, Yesu abaa alosa kwa e bilyo byoshi binganalyibwa	19. 부씨 어벼라 비더ᅇᅵᄙᅨ라 뫄 무찌마 와이, 시 뫄 부ᄙᅡ 무 벼ᄕᅥ 뱌야, 짜시ᄕᅡ 뱌나더ᅇᅡ모 뫄 구야 어라 짜ᄙᅡ. 뫄 구더다 바짜, 여수 아바아 아ᄙᅩ사 과 어 비ᄙᅭ 뵤씨 비ᅇᅡ나ᄙᅨ봐	19. For it doesn't go into his heart but into his stomach, and then out of his body." (In saying this, Jesus declared all foods "clean.")
20. Yesu era kuhuba kuteta mbu: Bya byende byaira e mundju kuba mubi, bilyi bya byende byatenga mwa muchima wai.	20. 여수 어라 구후바 구더다 ᄜᅮ: 뱌 벼ᄕᅥ 뱌이라 어 무ᅜᅮ 구바 무비, 비ᄙᅨ 뱌 벼ᄕᅥ 뱌더ᅇᅡ 뫄 무찌마 와이.	20. He went on: "What comes out of a man is what makes him 'unclean.'
21. Bushi mwa muchima w'e mundju mu mwende mwatengera e mianyisa ibi era yende yachwuma e mundju aya mwa buhungu, n'omwa bwisi, n'omwa bwichi,	21. 부씨 뫄 무찌마 워 무ᅜᅮ 무 뭐ᄕᅥ 뫄더ᅇᅥ라 어 미아녜사 이비 어라 여ᄕᅥ 야쭈마 어 무ᅜᅮ 아야 뫄 부후ᅇᅮ, 노뫄 뷔시, 노뫄 뷔찌,	21. For from within, out of men's hearts, come evil thoughts, sexual immorality, theft, murder, adultery,
22. n'omwa lusingi, n'omwa buhuma-huma, n'e mungo, n'omwa butebanyi, n'e kuata myanya ibi, n'e mufula, n'e ngambo, n'e rume, n'e buuta.	22. 노뫄 루시ᅇᅵ, 노뫄 부후마-후마, 너 무ᅇᅩ, 노뫄 부더바녜, 너 구아다 먀냐 이비, 너 무푸ᄙᅡ, 너 ᅇᅡᄜᅩ, 너 루머, 너 부우다.	22. greed, malice, deceit, lewdness, envy, slander, arrogance and folly.
23. Amu mabi moshi, mwa muchima w'e mundju mu mende manatenga, kanji mu	23. 아무 마비 모씨, 뫄 무찌마 워 무ᅜᅮ 무 머ᄕᅥ 마나더ᅇᅡ, 가ᅜᅵ 무 머ᄕᅥ 마나무이라 구바	23. All these evils come from inside and make a man 'unclean.' "

mende manamuira kuba mubi. 무비.

E bwemeresi bw'e Musuriyakasi

어 뭐머러시 뭐 무수리야가시

24. Era nyuma s'ebi, Yesu era kutenga aola, na aya mwa bimbi by'e musi w'e Tiro. Era kwengilyira mu nyumba nguma, si atasimaa mbu e bandju bamenyaa kwa alyimo. Si chiro bacha, oku kuchibisha kwai kutaalyikanaa.

24. 어라 뉴마 서비, 여수 어라 구더꽈 아오롸, 나 아야 롸 비뻬 벼 무시 워 디로. 어라 궈삐레라 무 뉴빠 으마, 시 아다시마아 뿌 어 바쭈 바머냐아 과 아레모. 시 찌로 바짜, 오구 구찌비싸 과이 구다아레가나아.

24. Jesus left that place and went to the vicinity of Tyre. He entered a house and did not want anyone to know it; yet he could not keep his presence secret.

25. Mw'olu, mukasi muuma era kumva e ngulu ya Yesu. Oyu mukasi, mwalyi wai abaa asimbirwe nue bihwasi. Unao-unao, era kwire aya kuchihunda mwa maulu ma Yesu.

25. 몰루, 무가시 무우마 어라 구빠 어 으루 야 여수. 오유 무가시, 퐈레 와이 아바아 아시뻬뤄 누어 비화시. 우나오-우나오, 어라 귀러 아야 구찌후따 롸 마우뤀 마 여수.

25. In fact, as soon as she heard about him, a woman whose little daughter was possessed by an evil spirit came and fell at his feet.

26. Oyu mukasi abaa Mukilyikikasi, mwesha mwa musi wue Foinikiya, mwa chio ch'e suriya. Era kwema Yesu mbu amwambulyira e chihwasi cha chabaa chilyi ku mwalyi wai.

26. 오유 무가시 아바아 무기레기가시, 뭐싸 롸 무시 우어 포이니기야, 롸 찌오 쩌 수리야. 어라 궈마 여수 뿌 아뫄뿌레라 어 찌화시 짜 짜바아 찌레 구 뫄레 와이.

26. The woman was a Greek, born in Syrian Phoenicia. She begged Jesus to drive the demon out of her daughter.

27. Si Yesu era kumwakula mbu: Urekaa ebana beute tanga! Bushi kutakomire kutola ebilyo by'e bana na kubiuma e ngunda.

27. 시 여수 어라 구뫄구롸 뿌: 우러가아 어바나 버우더 다꽈! 부씨 구다고미러 구도롸 어비뿐 벼 바나 나 구비우마 어 으따.

27. "First let the children eat all they want," he told her, "for it is not right to take the children's bread and toss it to their dogs."

28. Wamukasi na imbu: Enawechwu! kubinalyi bacha. Si anabe n'e ngunda nasi, sende sanalya e bukombo-kombo bwa bana bende

28. 와무가시 나 이뿌: 어나워쭈! 구비나레 바짜. 시 아나버 너 으따 나시, 서떠 사나퍄 어 부고뽀-고뽀 롸 바나 버떠 바도사꽈 과 머사.

28. "Yes, Lord," she replied, "but even the dogs under the table eat the children's crumbs."

batosanga kwa mesa.

29. Yesu kukwera kumubura mbu: Bushi wakuira bacha, ufulukaa kwa wao. Echi chihwasi chatengire ku mwalyi wao mira.

30. Mango oyu mukasi aikaa kwa wai, era kubuana mwalyi wai achilambikire kwa njingo, n'echa chihwasi chamutengireko mira.

Yesu alamya e musuru

31. Era nyuma s'ebi, Yesu era kutenga mw'ebi bimbi by'e musi w'e tiro. Era kurenga mwa musi w'e sitona na erengera kwa lunda lw'e nyanja y'e kalilaya, mwa chio ch'e tekapoli.

32. Bera kumuretera mundju muuma ola wabaa ufire e machi kanji abaa mutefu-tefu. Bera kwema Yesu mbu amubikaa kw'e mino.

33. Yesu era kwire amukula mwa luamba lw'e bandju, na kuchifunda nai bure hicha. Chasinda, era kumubika e mitoke mwa machi, era kuchira-chira kwa mino na amuuma kwa lulyimi.

34. Era kuchwumbikisa kwa nguba, na abura oyu mundju na murenge munene mbu:

29. 여수 구궈라 구무부라 뿌: 부씨 와구이라 바짜, 우푸루가아 과 와오. 어찌 찌화시 짜더삐러 구 롸쎄 와오 미라.

30. 마ᄋ 오유 무가시 아이가아 과 와이, 어라 구부아나 롸쎄 와이 아찌롸삐기러 과 찌ᄋ, 너짜 찌화시 짜무더삐러고 미라.

여수 아롸먀 어 무수루

31. 어라 뉴마 서비, 여수 어라 구더ᄊ 뭐비 비삐 벼 무시 워 디로. 어라 구러ᄊ 롸 무시 워 시도나 나 어러ᄊ라 과 룬따 뭐 냐짜 여 가쎄롸야, 롸 찌ᄋ 쩌 더가포리.

32. 버라 구무러더라 무뚜 무우마 오롸 와바아 우피러 어 마찌 가니 아바아 무더푸-더푸. 버라 궈마 여수 뿌 아무비가아 궈 미노.

33. 여수 어라 귀러 아무구롸 롸 루아빠 뭐 바쭈, 나 구찌푼따 나이 부러 히짜. 짜시따, 어라 구무비가 어 미도거 롸 마찌, 어라 구찌라-찌라 과 미노 나 아무우마 과 루쎄미.

34. 어라 구쭈삐기사 과 ᄋ바, 나 아부라 오유 무뚜 나 무러ᄊ 무너너 뿌: 어파다!

29. Then he told her, "For such a reply, you may go; the demon has left your daughter."

30. She went home and found her child lying on the bed, and the demon gone.

31. Then Jesus left the vicinity of Tyre and went through Sidon, down to the Sea of Galilee and into the region of the Decapolis.

32. There some people brought to him a man who was deaf and could hardly talk, and they begged him to place his hand on the man.

33. After he took him aside, away from the crowd, Jesus put his fingers into the man's ears. Then he spit and touched the man's tongue.

34. He looked up to heaven and with a deep sigh said to him, "Ephphatha!" (which

Efata! (kukuteta mbu: Sibukalaa!)

35. Unao-unao, e machi mw'ola mundju kuna kusibukala. N'e lulyimi lwai nalo, kuna kubookala, na atangilyisa ateta kubuya.

36. Yesu era kuchichika e bandju kwa bataburaa mundju usibya kw'oyu mwasi. Si echera chitachwumaa bataendekera bahandabanyao mwa bandju.

37. E bandju bera kusanwa busese. Bera kunde bateta mbu: Byoshi bya Yesu enjire airaa, binakomire ngachi! Anabe n'aba bafire e machi, enjire achwuma bomva. N'e basuru, enjire achwuma bateta!

Mariko Chikono 8
Yesu eucha bandju byumbi bine

1. Mw'esi suku, bandju banene busese bera ku buanana kanji. Mango babaa batachete kalyo, Yesu era kwamaala e banafunzi bai na aburabo mbu:

2. Bano bandju boshi, nabafilyire bonjo, bushi suku ehachwu sine bamala alauma nanyi, batachete na kalyo

---

(구구더다 뿌: 시부가롸아!)

35. 우나오-우나오, 어 마찌 몰롸 무뿌 구나 구시부가롸. 너 루쩨미 롸이 나로, 구나 구보오가롸, 나 아다삐쩨사 아더다 구부야.

36. 여수 어라 구찌찌가 어 바뚜 과 바다부라아 무뿌 우시뱌 교유 마시. 시 어쩌라 찌다쭈마아 바다어떠거라 바하따바냐오 똬 바뚜.

37. 어 바뚜 버라 구사놔 부서서. 버라 구떠 바더다 뿌: 뵤씨 뱌 여수 어찌러 아이라아, 비나고미러 똬찌! 아나버 나바 바피러 어 마찌, 어찌러 아쭈마 보빠. 너 바수루, 어찌러 아쭈마 바더다!

마리고 찌고노 8
여수 어우짜 바뚜 뷰삐 비너

1. 뭐시 수구, 바뚜 바너너 부서서 버라 구 부아나나 가찌. 마꼬 바바아 바다쩌더 가룐, 여수 어라 과마아롸 어 바나푸씨 바이 나 아부라보 뿌:

2. 바노 바뚜 보씨, 나바피쩨러 보쪼, 부씨 수구 어하쭈 시너 바마롸 아롸우마 나니, 바다쩌더 나 가룐 가시뱌.

---

means, "Be opened!").

35. At this, the man's ears were opened, his tongue was loosened and he began to speak plainly.

36. Jesus commanded them not to tell anyone. But the more he did so, the more they kept talking about it.

37. People were overwhelmed with amazement. "He has done everything well," they said. "He even makes the deaf hear and the mute speak."

Mark Chapter 8[NIV]

1. During those days another large crowd gathered. Since they had nothing to eat, Jesus called his disciples to him and said,

2. "I have compassion for these people; they have already been with me three days and have nothing to

kasibya.

3. Rero, ndangalaabo batanalyire bangesha kurengukalyiranga mwa njira n'e businya, bushi bauma mubo batengerengaa burerere.

4. E banafunzi bai bera kumwakula mbu: Enawechwu! Si mwa buyeye muno chwulyi! Rero, ngai uchwungakula e bilyo bya bingeucha bano bandju boshi?

5. Yesu era kubabusa mbu: Mikati enga i mwete? nabo mbu: Elyinda.

6. Yesu era kubura e bandju mbu bekalaa alashi. Era kutola ei mikate elyinda. Na atonga Ongo. Chasinda, era kuishanga mui na eresai e banafunzi bai baabirei abu bandju. E banafunzi nabo, bera kunayabira e bandju boshi.

7. Babaa bete n'efi sieke, kanji sieke-eke. Yesu era kutonga Ongo kanji bushi nasi, na abura e banfunzi bai mbu nasi basibanyaa.

8. Abu bandju boshi bera kulya na beuta. Chasinda, e banafunzi bera kutola-tola e bimbi-imbi bya byashibaa, byera kwehusa bitonga

3. 러로, 따까라아보 바다나쩨러 바어싸 구러우가쩨라까 먀 띠라 너 부시냐, 부씨 바우마 무보 바더어러까아 부러러러.

4. 어 바나푸씨 바이 버라 구꽈구꽈 뿌: 어나워쭈! 시 먀 부여여 무노 쭈레! 러로, 까이 우쭈까구꽈 어 비뾷 뱌 비어우짜 바노 바꾸 보씨?

5. 여수 어라 구바부사 뿌: 미가디 어까 이 뭐더? 나보 뿌: 어레따.

6. 여수 어라 구부라 어 바꾸 뿌 버가꽈아 아꽈씨. 어라 구도꽈 어이 미가더 어레따. 나 아도꽈 오꼬. 짜시따, 어라 구이싸까 무이 나 어러사이 어 바나푸씨 바이 바아비러이 아부 바꾸. 어 바나푸씨 나보, 버라 구나야비라 어 바꾸 보씨.

7. 바바아 버더 너피 시어거, 가찌 시어거-어거. 여수 어라 구도꽈 오꼬 가찌 부씨 나시, 나 아부라 어 바누푸씨 바이 뿌 나시 바시바냐아.

8. 아부 바꾸 보씨 버라 구꺄 나 버우다. 짜시따, 어 바나푸씨 버라 구도꽈-도꽈 어 비뻬-이뻬 뱌 뱌씨바아, 벼라 궈후사 비도꽈 비레따.

eat.

3. If I send them home hungry, they will collapse on the way, because some of them have come a long distance."

4. His disciples answered, "But where in this remote place can anyone get enough bread to feed them?"

5. "How many loaves do you have?" Jesus asked. "Seven," they replied.

6. He told the crowd to sit down on the ground. When he had taken the seven loaves and given thanks, he broke them and gave them to his disciples to set before the people, and they did so.

7. They had a few small fish as well; he gave thanks for them also and told the disciples to distribute them.

8. The people ate and were satisfied. Afterward the disciples picked up seven basketfuls of broken pieces that were left over.

bilyinda.

9. E bandju ba balyaa ebi bilyo, babaa bangaika ku byumbi bine. Chasinda, Yesu era kubalaa.

10. Unao-unao era kwerukira mwa bwato, alauma n'e banafunzi bai. Bera kuya mwa chio ch'e talimanuta.

E bafarisayo bema Yesu e chisomerano

11. Era nyuma s'ebi, e bafarisayo bera kuikira Yesu na batangilyisa bamuenza e bwaka. Bera kumuiereka mwa kumwema mbu abailyira chisomerano chiuma, cha chilosise kanangana kwa e buashi bwai bunatengire kwa nguba.

12. Yesu era kutookala busese, na ateta mbu: chi chingachwuma e bandju b'e sine suku bahonda kulola ku chisomerano? kubinalyi, nababura kwa kutalyi chisomerano chisibya chabangalosibwa!

13. chasinda, era kureka abu bandju, era kuhuba kw'erukira mwa bwato na ahabuka e nyanja.

9. 어 바뚜 바 바랴아 어비 비료, 바바아 방까이가 구 뷰뻬 비너. 짜시따, 여수 어라 구바랴아.

10. 우나오-우나오 어라 궈루기라 먀 봐도, 아꽈우마 너 바나푸씨 바이. 버라 구야 먀 찌오 쩌 다뤼마누다.

어 바파리사요 버마 여수 어 찌소머라노

11. 어라 뉴마 서비, 어 바파리사요 버라 구이기라 여수 나 바다삐께사 바무어싸 어 봐가. 버라 구무이어러가 먀 구뭐마 뿌 아바이께라 찌소머라노 찌우마, 짜 찌론시서 가나싸나 과 어 부아씨 봐이 부나더삐러 과 꾸바.

12. 여수 어라 구도오가꽈 부서서, 나 아더다 뿌: 찌 찌꺄쭈마 어 바뚜 버 시너 수구 바호따 구룬꽈 구 찌소머라노? 구비나께, 나바부라 과 구다께 찌소머라노 찌시뱌 짜바싸룬시봐!

13. 짜시따, 어라 구러가 아부 바뚜, 어라 구후바 궈루기라 먀 봐도 나 아하부가 어 냐짜.

9. About four thousand men were present. And having sent them away,

10. he got into the boat with his disciples and went to the region of Dalmanutha.

11. The Pharisees came and began to question Jesus. To test him, they asked him for a sign from heaven.

12. He sighed deeply and said, "Why does this generation ask for a miraculous sign? I tell you the truth, no sign will be given to it."

13. Then he left them, got back into the boat and crossed to the other side.

E chachu ch'e Bafarisayo n'e 어 짜쭈 쩌 바파리사요 너 짜

cha herodi **허로디**

14. E banafunzi ba Yesu babaa b'ebiliyire kweka e mikati, si muuma pwere ibabaa banete mwa bwato.

14. 어 바나푸씨 바 여수 바바아 버비례러 궈가 어 미가디, 시 무우마 풔러 이바바아 바너더 와 봐도.

14. The disciples had forgotten to bring bread, except for one loaf they had with them in the boat.

15. Yesu era kubabura mbu: Mundaa mwachilanga kwa chachu ch'e Bafarisayo n'e cha herodi.

15. 여수 어라 구바부라 뿌: 무따아 뫄찌롸빠 과 짜쭈 쩌 바파리사요 너 짜 허로디.

15. "Be careful," Jesus warned them. "Watch out for the yeast of the Pharisees and that of Herod."

16. Abu banafunzi bera kutangilyisa baburana mbu: Atechire bacha bushi chwutete e mikati.

16. 아부 바나푸씨 버라 구다삐례사 바부라나 뿌: 아더찌러 바짜 부씨 쭈더더 어 미가디.

16. They discussed this with one another and said, "It is because we have no bread."

17. Ebi babaa baburana bacha, Yesu era kubimenyerera. Bushi n'oku, era kubabura mbu: chi chachwuma mwaburana mbu mutete mikati? Mutanasa kumva? Nesi mutanasa kumenyereraa? E michima yenyu inachilyi isibu?

17. 어비 바바아 바부라나 바짜, 여수 어라 구비머녀러라. 부씨 노구, 어라 구바부라 뿌: 찌 짜쭈마 뫄부라나 뿌 무더더 미가디? 무다나사 구빠? 너시 무다나사 구머녀러라아? 어 미찌마 여뉴 이나찌례 이시부?

17. Aware of their discussion, Jesus asked them: "Why are you talking about having no bread? Do you still not see or understand? Are your hearts hardened?

18. Mwete meho, mutanalola? Mwete n'e machi, mutanomva? Mutachikengere

18. 뭐더 머호, 무다나르빠? 뭐더 너 마찌, 무다노빠? 무다찌거어러

18. Do you have eyes but fail to see, and ears but fail to hear? And don't you remember?

19. Kwa mango naishangangaa era mikati etano, era yeuchaa ba bandju byumbi bitano? Rero, mango mwatola-tola ebimbi-imbi bya byashibaa, mwehusaa bitonga binga? Nabo mbu: Ekumi na bibilyi.

19. 과 마꼬 나이싸빠빠아 어라 미가디 어다노, 어라 여우짜아 바 바뚜 뷰삐 비다노? 러로, 마꼬 뫄도롸-도롸 어비삐-이삐 뱌 뱌씨바아, 뭐후사아 비도빠 비빠? 나보 뿌: 어구미 나 비비례.

19. When I broke the five loaves for the five thousand, how many basketfuls of pieces did you pick up?" "Twelve," they replied.

20. Era kuhuba kubabusa mbu: 20. 어라 구후바 구바부사 뿌: 20. "And when I broke the

kanji era mikati elyinda nai, si yeuchaa bandju byumbi bine! Na mango mwatola-tolaa ebimbi-imbi bya byashibaa, mw'ehusaa bitonga binga? Nabo mbu: Bilyinda.

21. Yesu kukwera kubabusa mbu: Mutanasa kumva?

Yesu alamya e muuta mwa musi w'e betesaita

22. Era nyuma s'ebi, Yesu n'e banfunzi bai bera kuika mwa musi w'e betesaita. E bandju bera kumuretera muuta muuma, na bamwema busese mbu amuumaako.

23. Yesu era kusimbira oyu muuta kwa mino, na amukula mwa musi. Era kumuchira-chira mwa meho na amubika kw'e mino. Chasinda, era kumubusa mbu: Kulyi kandu ka useneko?

24. Nai mwa kwemusa e meho, era kuteta mbu: Nyisene kwa bandju, balyi nga michi si baenda.

25. Yesu kanji era kumuuma kwa meho. Rero mera kulama, na atangilyisa alola kwa bindju byoshi kubuya-buya.

26. Chasinda, Yesu era kumubura mbu: Wera

가씨 어라 미가디 어레따 나이, 시 여우짜아 바뚜 뷰삐 비너! 나 마꼬 꽈도롸-도롸아 어비삐-아삐 뱌 뱌씨바아, 뭐후사아 비도꺄 비꺄? 나보 뿌: 비레따.

21. 여수 구궈라 구바부사 뿌: 무다나사 구꺄?

여수 아꽈먀 어 무우다 꽈 무시 워 버더사이다

22. 어라 뉴마 서비, 여수 너 바누푸씨 바이 버라 구이가 꽈 무시 워 버더사이다. 어 바뚜 버라 구무러더라 무우다 무우마, 나 바뭐마 부서서 뿌 아무우마아고.

23. 여수 어라 구시뻬라 오유 무우다 꽈 미노, 나 아무구꽈 꽈 무시. 어라 구무찌라-찌라 꽈 머호 나 아무비가 궈 미노. 짜시따, 어라 구무부사 뿌: 구레 가뚜 가 우서너고?

24. 나이 꽈 궈무사 어 머호, 어라 구더다 뿌: 네서너 과 바뚜, 바레 꺄 미찌 시 바어따.

25. 여수 가씨 어라 구무우마 과 머호. 러로 머라 구꽈마, 나 아다삐레사 아롸 과 비뚜 뵤씨 구부야-부야.

26. 짜시따, 여수 어라 구무부라 뿌: 워라 우꺄푸루가

---

seven loaves for the four thousand, how many basketfuls of pieces did you pick up?" They answered, "Seven."

21. He said to them, "Do you still not understand?"

22. They came to Bethsaida, and some people brought a blind man and begged Jesus to touch him.

23. He took the blind man by the hand and led him outside the village. When he had spit on the man's eyes and put his hands on him, Jesus asked, "Do you see anything?"

24. He looked up and said, "I see people; they look like trees walking around."

25. Once more Jesus put his hands on the man's eyes. Then his eyes were opened, his sight was restored, and he saw everything clearly.

26. Jesus sent him home, saying, "Don't go into the

ungafuluka kwa wao, si utachihubaa mwa musi.

과 와오, 시 우다찌후바아 마 무시.

village."

Petero ateta mbu Yesu I kirisito

퍼더로 아더다 뿌 여수 이 기리시도

27. Era nyuma s'ebi, Yesu era kutenga mw'echi chisiki alauma n'e banafunzi bai. Era kuya mwa misi era ichwula ofu n'e musi w'e kaisariya firipi. Abere banachilyi mwa luendo, Yesu era kubabusa mbu: Ewashe! E bandju benjire bateta mbu nyi nde kasi?

27. 어라 뉴마 서비, 여수 어라 구더빠 뭐찌 찌시기 아라우마 너 바나푸씨 바이. 어라 구야 마 미시 어라 이쭈라 오푸 너 무시 워 가이사리야 피리피. 아버러 바나찌레 마 루어또, 여수 어라 구바부사 뿌: 어와써! 어 바뉴 버찌러 바더다 뿌 네 떠 가시?

27. Jesus and his disciples went on to the villages around Caesarea Philippi. On the way he asked them, "Who do people say I am?"

28. Nabo mbu: Bauma benjire bateta mbu u Yowana Mubatisayi n'e banji mbu u Eliya, n'e banji mbu ulyi muuma mwa barebi.

28. 나보 뿌: 바우마 버찌러 바더다 뿌 우 요와나 무바디사에 너 바찌 뿌 우 어찌야, 너 바찌 뿌 우레 무우마 마 바러비.

28. They replied, "Some say John the Baptist; others say Elijah; and still others, one of the prophets."

29. Yesu era kuhuba kubabusa mbu: rero, nenyu mwenjire mwateta mbu nyi nde? Petero era kumwakula mbu: Woyo u kirisito!

29. 여수 어라 구후바 구바부사 뿌: 러로, 너뉴 뭐찌러 마더다 뿌 네 떠? 퍼더로 어라 구마구꽈 뿌: 오요 우 기리시도!

29. "But what about you?" he asked. "Who do you say I am?" Peter answered, "You are the Christ."

30. Yesu era kubachichika mbu bataerereresaa bafulyira chiro na mundju asibya kw'ei myasi.

30. 여수 어라 구바찌찌가 뿌 바다어러러사아 바푸레라 찌로 나 무뚜 아시뱌 궈이 먀시.

30. Jesus warned them not to tell anyone about him.

Yesu ateta era lulu s'e kufa n'e kwomoka kwai

여수 아더다 어라 뤃루 서 구파 너 고모가 과이

31. Chasinda, Yesu era kutangilyisa akangilyisa e banafunzi bai mbu: Nyi Mwana w'e mundju, byemire nyilyibusibwe mu njira sinene. E bashamuka b'e bayuda, n'e bakulu-kulu b'e bakuhanyi

31. 짜시따, 여수 어라 구다삐레사 아가삐레사 어 바나푸씨 바이 뿌: 네 마나 워 무뚜, 벼미러 네레부시붜 무 찌라 시너너. 어 바싸무가 버 바유다, 너 바구루-구루 버 바구하니 아짜우마 너

31. He then began to teach them that the Son of Man must suffer many things and be rejected by the elders, chief priests and teachers of the law, and that he must be killed and

alauma n'e bakangilyisi b'e Mwaso baganyinana. Chasinda nyingechibwa, si kwa lusuku lwa kahachwu nyingwomoka.

32. Ei myasi, Yesu aburaai e banafunzi bai changanama. Bushi n'oku, Petero era kumweka ala musike na atangilyisa amubandako mbu atatetaa bacha!

33. Si Yesu kuna kubindjuka na asindera e banafunzi bai. Era kukalyiira petero mbu: Eu Musimu! Tenga mwa meho manyi, bushi ei mianyisa yao, ata era mwa Ongo yi yatenga, si inalyi ya bandju!

34. chasinda, Yesu era kwamala lwa luamba lw'e bandju alauma n'e banafunzi bai, era kubabura mbu: Ola wahonda kunyikulyikira, arekaa kunde aanyisa era lulu sai yeine, eke n'e musalaba wai, ananyikulyikire.

35. Bushi ola wahonda kulamya e kalamo kai, akakaesa. N'ola ukaesako bushi nanyi, na bushi n'e Mwasi mubuya-buya, yeke akahuba kukabona.

36. Ola waesise e kalamo kai, rero mutoloke muchiye angachibona chiro angaata e bindju byoshi by'omwa

바가삐레시 버 먀소 바가니나나. 짜시따 네삐찌봐, 시 과 루수구 똬 가하쭈 네뭐오모가.

32. 어이 먀시, 여수 아부라아이 어 바나푸씨 바이 짜삐나마. 부씨 노구, 퍼더로 어라 구뭐가 아똬 무시거 나 아다삐레사 아무바따고 뿌 아다더다아 바짜!

33. 시 여수 구나 구비뚜가 나 아시떠라 어 바나푸씨 바이. 어라 구가레이라 퍼더로 뿌: 어우 무시무! 더따 똬 머호 마네, 부씨 어이 미아네사 야오, 아다 어라 똬 오꼬 에 야더따, 시 이나레 야 바뚜!

34. 짜시따, 여수 어라 과마똬 똬 루아빠 뭐 바뚜 아똬우마 너 바나푸씨 바이, 어라 구바부라 뿌: 오라 와호따 구네구레기라, 아러가아 구떠 아아네사 어라 루루 사이 여이너, 어거 너 무사똬바 와이, 아나네구레기러.

35. 부씨 오라 와호따 구똬먀 어 가똬모 가이, 아가가어사. 노똬 우가어사고 부씨 나네, 나 부씨 너 먀시 무부야-부야, 여거 아가후바 구가보나.

36. 오라 와어시서 어 가똬모 가이, 러로 무도뢰거 무찌여 아까찌보나 찌로 아까아다 어 비뚜 뵤씨 뷔오똬 부다똬?

after three days rise again.

32. He spoke plainly about this, and Peter took him aside and began to rebuke him.

33. But when Jesus turned and looked at his disciples, he rebuked Peter. "Get behind me, Satan!" he said. "You do not have in mind the things of God, but the things of men."

34. Then he called the crowd to him along with his disciples and said: "If anyone would come after me, he must deny himself and take up his cross and follow me.

35. For whoever wants to save his life will lose it, but whoever loses his life for me and for the gospel will save it.

36. What good is it for a man to gain the whole world, yet forfeit his soul?

butala?

37. N'omwa kuhonda kununula aku kalamo kai, chiye chi angana?

38. Mumenyereraa kwa bandju ba lwarero batachwusa bwemeresi kanji batalaire ku Ongo. Bushi n'oku, akaba e mundju anganyifira honyi, afirasi n'e myasi yanyi era muhondo sabo, nanyi nyi Mwana w'e Mundju nyikamufirasi mango nyikabaha alauma n'e bamalaika banyi babuya-buya mwa bulangare bwa tata.

37. 노와 구호따 구누누롸 아구 가롸모 가이, 찌여 찌 아빠나?

38. 무머녀러라아 과 바뚜 바 롸러로 바다쭈사 뷔머러시 가찌 바다롸이러 구 오꼬. 부씨 노구, 아가바 어 무뚜 아빠네피라 호네, 아피라시 너 먀시 야네 어라 무호또 사보, 나네 내 뫄나 워 무뚜 네가무피라시 마꼬 네가바하 아롸우마 너 바마롸이가 바네 바부야-부야 뫄 부롸빠러 봐 다다.

37. Or what can a man give in exchange for his soul?

38. If anyone is ashamed of me and my words in this adulterous and sinful generation, the Son of Man will be ashamed of him when he comes in his Father's glory with the holy angels."

Mariko Chikono 9

1. Kanji Yesu era kubura abu bandju mbu: Kubinalyi, nababura kwa mwa bano bandju balyi anola, bauma mubo batakafe batasa kulola kwa bwami bwa Ongo bwaika n'e buashi.

Yesu abindjulwa e huhe

2. Era nyuma sa suku ndachwu, Yesu era kutola petero, na yakobo, na yowana. Era kwerukira nabo ku ndjulungu nguma irerere, bera kuberako beine. Abere bera balyiko, Yesu era kubindjulwa e huhe mwa na meho mabo.

마리고 찌고노 9

1. 가찌 여수 어라 구부라 아부 바뚜 뿌: 구비나쩨, 나바부라 과 뫄 바노 바뚜 바쩨 아노롸, 바우마 무보 바다가퍼 바다사 구론롸 과 뫄미 봐 오꼬 봐이가 너 부아씨.

여수 아비뿌롸 어 후허

2. 어라 뉴마 사 수구 따쭉, 여수 어라 구도롸 퍼더로, 나 야고보, 나 요와나. 어라 궈루기라 나보 구 뚜룩우 꾸마 이러러러, 버라 구버라고 버이너. 아버러 버라 바쩨고, 여수 어라 구비뿌롸 어 후허 뫄 나 머호 마보.

Mark Chapter 9[NIV]

1. And he said to them, "I tell you the truth, some who are standing here will not taste death before they see the kingdom of God come with power."

2. After six days Jesus took Peter, James and John with him and led them up a high mountain, where they were all alone. There he was transfigured before them.

3. Enjimba sai sera kulangala na kwengengenya busese. N'ola ungaala kulangasa enjimba bacha muno butala chiro atanalyi.

4. Unao-unao, abu banafunzi kuna kulola ku musa na eliya bahambala na Yesu.

5. Petero na balyikabo bera kuina cha bangateta bushi n'ekuchwungwa busese. Petero era kwire abura Yesu mbu:

6. Mukangilyisi, kungakomire chwubere anola, chwuimbeo bitala bihachwu: chiuma chingaba chao, n'e chinji chanaba cha musa, n'e chinji chigaba cha eliya.

7. chasinda, kwera kuulukira lumbumbu kuna kubahukira. Mulo, mwera kuulukira murenge ola wabaa wateta mbu: Onola I mwana wanyi musiirwa. Mundaa mwamomvilyisa!

8. Abu banafunzi bera kuuma e meho yeyi n'eyi, si chiro bakachilola ku unji mundju alauma nabo, kureka Yesu yeine.

9. Abere bera bandaala kwei ndjulungu, Yesu era

---

3. 어찌빠 사이 서라 구롸꽈롸 나 궈꺼꺼냐 부서서. 노롸 우꽈아롸 구롸꽈사 어찌빠 바짜 무노 부다롸 찌로 아다나꿰.

4. 우나오-우나오, 아부 바나푸씨 구나 구론롸 구 무사 나 어릐야 바하빠롸 나 여수.

5. 퍼더로 나 바꿰가보 버라 구이나 짜 바꽈더다 부씨 너구쭝꽈 부서서. 퍼더로 어라 귀러 아부라 여수 뿌:

6. 무가찌꿰시, 구꽈고미러 쭈버러 아노롸, 쭈이뻐오 비다롸 비하쭈: 찌우마 찌꽈바 짜오, 너 찌찌 짜나바 짜 무사, 너 찌찌 찌가바 짜 어릐야.

7. 짜시따, 궈라 구우루기라 루뿌뿌 구나 구바후기라. 무롣, 뭐라 구우루기라 무러꺼 오롸 와바아 와더다 뿌: 오노롸 이 마나 와네 무시이롸. 무따아 먀모삐꿰사!

8. 아부 바나푸씨 버라 구우마 어 머호 여에 너에, 시 찌로 바가찌론롸 구 우씨 무뚜 아롸우마 나보, 구러가 여수 여이너.

9. 아버러 버라 바따아롸 궈이 누루우, 여수 어라 구바찌찌가

---

3. His clothes became dazzling white, whiter than anyone in the world could bleach them.

4. And there appeared before them Elijah and Moses, who were talking with Jesus.

5. Peter said to Jesus, "Rabbi, it is good for us to be here. Let us put up three shelters--one for you, one for Moses and one for Elijah."

6. (He did not know what to say, they were so frightened.)

7. Then a cloud appeared and enveloped them, and a voice came from the cloud: "This is my Son, whom I love. Listen to him!"

8. Suddenly, when they looked around, they no longer saw anyone with them except Jesus.

9. As they were coming down the mountain, Jesus

kubachichika mbu: Ebi mwera kulolako, mutaburaabi chiro na mundju usibya kuikira mango nyi Mwana w'e Mundju nyingaba n'omwokire.

10. Rero oyu mwasi, abu banafunzi bera kunasilyira kuo. Si bera kutangilyisa babusanya mbu: Oku kw'omwoka, kukwera kuteta kute?

E banafunzi babusa Yesu era lulu s'e kubaha kwa eliya

11. Era nyuma s'ebi, e banafunzi ba Yesu bera kumubusa mbu: ewalyiya, chi chenjire chachwuma e bakangilyisi b'e Mwaso bateta mbu byemire eliya abahe tanga?

12. Yesu nai mbu: kubinalyi, byemire eliya abahe tanga, ekale akunganyise e myasi Yoshi. Rero, chi chichwumire e Maanjiko mabuya-buya mateta mbu e mwana w'e mundju emire alyibusibwe busese na kukenyibwa?

13. Nababura kwa eliya aikire mira, si e bandju bamukoreraa byoshi bya babaa banahonjire kukulyikana n'okwa Maanjiko mabuya-buya machwula matechire era lulu sai.

Yesu ambula e chihwasi kwa

뿌: 어비 뭐라 구로짜고, 무다부라아비 찌로 나 무뚜 우시뱌 구이기라 마꼬 네 뫄나 워 무뚜 네빠바 노모기러.

10. 러로 오유 뫄시, 아부 바나푸씨 버라 구나시레라 구오. 시 버라 구다삐레사 바부사냐 뿌: 오구 꾜모가, 구궈라 구더다 구더?

어 바나푸씨 바부사 여수 어라 룰루 서 구바하 과 어리야

11. 어라 뉴마 서비, 어 바나푸씨 바 여수 버라 구무부사 뿌: 어와레야, 찌 쩌찌러 짜쭈마 어 바가삐레시 버 뫄소 바더다 뿌 벼미러 어리야 아바허 다빠?

12. 여수 나이 뿌: 구비나레, 벼미러 어리야 아바허 다빠, 어가뻐 아구빠니서 어 먀시 요씨. 러로, 찌 찌쭈미러 어 마아찌고 마부야-부야 마더다 뿌 어 뫄나 워 무뚜 어미러 아레부시붜 부서서 나 구거네봐?

13. 나바부라 과 어리야 아이기러 미라, 시 어 바뚜 바무고러라아 뵤씨 뱌 바바아 바나호찌러 구구뻬가나 노과 마아찌고 마부야-부야 마쭈라 마더찌러 어라 룰루 사이.

여수 아뿌꽈 어 찌화시 과

gave them orders not to tell anyone what they had seen until the Son of Man had risen from the dead.

10. They kept the matter to themselves, discussing what "rising from the dead" meant.

11. And they asked him, "Why do the teachers of the law say that Elijah must come first?"

12. Jesus replied, "To be sure, Elijah does come first, and restores all things. Why then is it written that the Son of Man must suffer much and be rejected?

13. But I tell you, Elijah has come, and they have done to him everything they wished, just as it is written about him."

mwana	*뫄나*	
14. Mango Yesu n'abu banafunzi bahachwu, baikaa ala banji banafunzi babaa balyi, bera kulola ku bandju banene babasungwire, bushi babaa baenda e bwaka n'e bakangilyisi b'e mwaso.	14. 마오 여수 나부 바나푸씨 바하쭈, 바이가아 아롸 바찌 바나푸씨 바바아 바례, 버라 구로롸 구 바뉴 바너너 바바수위러, 부씨 바바아 바어따 어 봐가 너 바가이례시 버 뫄소.	14. When they came to the other disciples, they saw a large crowd around them and the teachers of the law arguing with them.
15. Abu bandju boshi, mango balolaa ku Yesu, bera kusanwa busese. Unao-unao, bera kulyibita baye kumuhuukasa.	15. 아부 바뉴 보씨, 마오 바로롸아 구 여수, 버라 구사놔 부서서. 우나오-우나오, 버라 구례비다 바여 구무후우가사.	15. As soon as all the people saw Jesus, they were overwhelmed with wonder and ran to greet him.
16. Yesu era kubusa e banafunzi bai mbu: Bwaka buchiye bu mwaenda na bano bandju?	16. 여수 어라 구부사 어 바나푸씨 바이 뿌: 봐가 부찌여 부 뫄어따 나 바노 바뉴?	16. "What are you arguing with them about?" he asked.
17. Si mundju muuma mwa luamba era kumwakula mbu: Mukangilyisi, nakuretere e mwana wanyi, bushi asimbirwe na chihwasi. N'echi chihwasi, chamuhubise musuru.	17. 시 무뉴 무우마 뫄 루아빠 어라 구뫄구롸 뿌: 무가이례시, 나구러더러 어 뫄나 와네, 부씨 아시삐뤄 나 찌화시. 너찌 찌화시, 짜무후비서 무수루.	17. A man in the crowd answered, "Teacher, I brought you my son, who is possessed by a spirit that has robbed him of speech.
18. Na mu chira chisiki cha chamusimbilyiremo, chende chamuhundanga kwa chitaka, n'e fula lyanamuchwumba kwa bunu. Chasinda, anatangilyisa akuutanga e meno, na anyanyaala. Nera kubura e banafunzi bao mbu bambulaachi, si pyo!	18. 나 무 찌라 찌시기 짜 짜무시삐례러모, 쩌떠 짜무후따아 과 찌다가, 너 푸롸 랴나무쭈빠 과 부누. 짜시따, 아나다이례사 아구우다아 어 머노, 나 아냐냐아롸. 너라 구부라 어 바나푸씨 바오 뿌 바뿌롸아찌, 시 표!	18. Whenever it seizes him, it throws him to the ground. He foams at the mouth, gnashes his teeth and becomes rigid. I asked your disciples to drive out the spirit, but they could not."
19. Yesu era kuteta mbu: Aaye! Mu bandju b'e sine	19. 여수 어라 구더다 뿌: 아아여! 무 바뉴 버 시너 수구,	19. "O unbelieving generation," Jesus replied,

suku, mutete bwemeresi! nyikaenderera kuba nenyu na kunde nomva e myasi yenyu kuikira mangochi? Nyireteraa oyu mwana anola!

20. Bera kunamureterai. cha chihwasi, mwa kunanola kuYesu, kuna kukukumanya ola mwana busese, kuna kumuhunda kwa chitaka, era kupuka-pukira alashi n'e fula lyamuchwumba kwa bunu.

21. Yesu kukwera kubusa eshe mbu: Ono mwana ende aba bacha kutengera mangochi? nai mbu: Kutengera elyana etoto lyai.

22. Chira mango, chende chamuumanga mwa mulyiro, n'omwa meshi, chasiya chimwite. Rero, uchwufiraa bonjo utuase, akaba ungaala!

23. Yesu na imbu: Chi chachwumire wateta mbu akaba nyingaala? Umenyereraa kwa byoshi byende byanaalyikana kw'ola wete bwemeresi!

24. Unao-unao, eshe w'e mwana kuna kuiteta na murenge munene mbu: Nemerere! Si unyiasaa e bwemeresi bwanyi buendekere kuba bunene.

무더더 뭐머러시! 네가어떠러라 구바 너뉴 나 구떠 노빠 어 먀시 여뉴 구이기라 마꼬찌? 네러더라아 오유 뫄나 아노롸!

20. 버라 구나무러더라이. 짜 찌화시, 뫄 구나노롸 구여수, 구나 구구구마냐 오롸 뫄나 부서서, 구나 구무후따 과 찌다가, 어라 구푸가-푸기라 아롸씨 너 푸롸 랴무쭈빠 과 부누.

21. 여수 구궈라 구부사 어써 뿌: 오노 뫄나 어너 아바 바짜 구더꺼라 마꼬찌? 나이 뿌: 구더꺼라 어랴나 어도도 랴이.

22. 찌라 마꼬, 쩌너 짜무우마꺼 뫄 무레로, 노뫄 머씨, 짜시야 찌뮈더. 러로, 우쭈피라아 보쪼 우두아서, 아가바 우꺼아롸!

23. 여수 나 이뿌: 찌 짜쭈미러 와더다 뿌 아가바 네꺼아롸? 우머녀러라아 과 뵤씨 벼너 뱌나아꼐가나 꾜롸 워더 뭐머러시!

24. 우나오-우나오, 어써 워 뫄나 구나 구이더다 나 무러꺼 무너너 뿌: 너머러러! 시 우니아사아 어 뭐머러시 봐니 부어떠거러 구바 부너너.

"how long shall I stay with you? How long shall I put up with you? Bring the boy to me."

20. So they brought him. When the spirit saw Jesus, it immediately threw the boy into a convulsion. He fell to the ground and rolled around, foaming at the mouth.

21. Jesus asked the boy's father, "How long has he been like this?" "From childhood," he answered.

22. "It has often thrown him into fire or water to kill him. But if you can do anything, take pity on us and help us."

23. " 'If you can'?" said Jesus. "Everything is possible for him who believes."

24. Immediately the boy's father exclaimed, "I do believe; help me overcome my unbelief!"

25. Mango Yesu alolaa kwa bandju baendekera bachilunda aola, era kukalyiira cha chihwasi mbu: Eu chihwasi, u wahubise ono mwana musuru n'e kumusiba e machi, natechire mbu umutengaako! Kanji siutanachimuhubiilyiraa!

25. 마꼬 여수 아로롸아 과 바쭈 바어떠거라 바찌루따 아오롸, 어라 구가례이라 짜 찌화시 뿌: 어우 찌화시, 우 와후비서 오노 뫄나 무수루 너 구무시바 어 마찌, 나더찌러 뿌 우무더까아고! 가찌 시우다나찌무후비이례라아!

25. When Jesus saw that a crowd was running to the scene, he rebuked the evil spirit. "You deaf and mute spirit," he said, "I command you, come out of him and never enter him again."

26. Echi chihwasi, kuna kulakanga na murenge munene, na chakukukumanya ola mwana busese. Chasinda, chera kumutengako. Wamwana era kwire aba ng'ola wafire. Bushi n'oku, bandju banene bera kutangilyisa bateta mbu: Aaye, afire mira.

26. 어찌 찌화시, 구나 구롸가까 나 무러머 무너너, 나 짜구구구마냐 오롸 뫄나 부서서. 짜시따, 쩌라 구무더까고. 와뫄나 어라 귀러 아바 꼬롸 와피러. 부씨 노구, 바쭈 바너너 버라 구다끼례사 바더다 뿌: 아아여, 아피러 미라.

26. The spirit shrieked, convulsed him violently and came out. The boy looked so much like a corpse that many said, "He's dead."

27. Si Yesu era kumusimbira kwa mino amwemuse, na abachwuka.

27. 시 여수 어라 구무시삐라 과 미노 아뭐무서, 나 아바쭈가.

27. But Jesus took him by the hand and lifted him to his feet, and he stood up.

28. Era nyuma s'ebi, mango Yesu abaa era engilyiraa mwa nyumba, alyi yeine n'e banafunzi bai, bera kumubusa mbu: ewalyiya! Echi chihwasi, chi chachwumaa chwubeke chwafundjwa kwambulachi?

28. 어라 뉴마 서비, 마꼬 여수 아바아 어라 어끼례라아 뫄 뉴빠, 아례 여이너 너 바나푸씨 바이, 버라 구무부사 뿌: 어와례야! 어찌 찌화시, 찌 짜쭈마아 쭈버거 쫘푸쫘 과뿌롸찌?

28. After Jesus had gone indoors, his disciples asked him privately, "Why couldn't we drive it out?"

29. Nai mbu: Echihwasi cha chilyi ng'echi, chende chanaambulwa kurengera ememo oshao.

29. 나이 뿌: 어찌화시 짜 찌례 꺼찌, 쩌너 짜나아뿌롸 구러꺼라 어머모 오싸오.

29. He replied, "This kind can come out only by prayer."

Yesu ateta kanji era lulu s'e kufa n'e kwomoka kwai

여수 아더다 가찌 어라 루루 서 구파 너 고모가 과이

30. Yesu n'e banafunzi bai

30. 여수 너 바나푸씨 바이

30. They left that place and

bera kutenga aola, bera kurega mwa chio ch'e kalilaya. Si atahondaa e bandju bamenye ala alyi, 31. bushi abaa akangilyisa e banafunzi bai. Era kubabura mbu: nyimwana w'e Mundju nyinganyibwa mwa mino s'e bandju. N'abu bandju bu banganyita. Si kwa lusuku lwa kahachwu nying'omoka.

32. Si ei myasi, e banfunzi bai chiro bakamenyerera kute yabaa itechire, bera kufa buba bwa kumubusa mwasi.

E mukulu-kulu mwa b'okwa nguba

33. Yesu n'e banafunzi bai bera kuika mwa musi w'e kaperinaumu. Abere bera balyi mwa nyumba, era kubabusa mbu: Mango mwabaa mulyi mwa njira, chi mwabaa mwaenzanya kw'e bwaka?

34. Bera kusira, bushi mango babaa balyi mwa njira, babaa baenzanya e bwaka mbu nde I mukulu-kulu wa balyikabo.

35. Yesu era kwire ekala, na amaala e ndjumwa sai ekumi n'ebilyi na aburasi mbu: Akaba e mundju angahonda kuba mubere-bere, emire achiire kuba musinda-sinda wa

버라 구더빠 아오롸, 버라 구러가 롸 찌오 쩌 가뤼롸야. 시 아다호빠아 어 바뚜 바머녀 아롸 아레,

31. 부씨 아바아 아가끼레사 어 바나푸씨 바이. 어라 구바부라 뿌: 네똬나 워 무뚜 네아니봐 롸 미노 서 바뚜. 나부 바뚜 부 바빠니다. 시 꽈 루수구 롸 가하쭈 네꼬모가.

32. 시 어이 먀시, 어 바누푸씨 바이 찌로 바가머녀러라 구더 야바아 이더찌러, 버라 구파 부바 롸 구무부사 마시.

어 무구뿌-구뿌 롸 보과 우바 응구바

33. 여수 너 바나푸씨 바이 버라 구이가 롸 무시 워 가퍼리나우무. 아버러 버라 바레 롸 뉴빠, 어라 구바부사 뿌: 마꼬 롸바아 무레 롸 씨라, 찌 롸바아 롸어싸냐 꿔 봐가?

34. 버라 구시라, 부씨 마꼬 바바아 바레 롸 씨라, 바바아 바어싸냐 어 봐가 뿌 떠 이 무구뿌-구뿌 롸 바레가보.

35. 여수 어라 귀러 어가롸, 나 아마아롸 어 뚜롸 사이 어구미 너비레 나 아부라시 뿌: 아가바 어 무뚜 아까호따 구바 무버러-버러, 어미러 아찌이러 구바 무시따-시따 와 바레가보

passed through Galilee. Jesus did not want anyone to know where they were, 31. because he was teaching his disciples. He said to them, "The Son of Man is going to be betrayed into the hands of men. They will kill him, and after three days he will rise."

32. But they did not understand what he meant and were afraid to ask him about it.

33. They came to Capernaum. When he was in the house, he asked them, "What were you arguing about on the road?"

34. But they kept quiet because on the way they had argued about who was the greatest.

35. Sitting down, Jesus called the Twelve and said, "If anyone wants to be first, he must be the very last, and the servant of all."

balyikabo boshi, abe na muanda wabo.

보씨, 아버 나 무아따 와보.

36. Chasinda, era kutola mwana mutoto muuma, era kumwemanza mwa kachi-kachi kabo na amuobera. Era kubabura mbu:

36. 짜시따, 어라 구도롸 뫄나 무도도 무우마, 어라 구뭐마싸 롸 가찌-가찌 가보 나 아무오버라. 어라 구바부라 뿌:

36. He took a little child and had him stand among them. Taking him in his arms, he said to them,

37. E mundju ola ungahuukasa e mwana mutoto ola ulyi ng'ono kw'e sina lyanyi, elyi nyi ahuukasise. N'ola wanyihuukasise, ata nyeine nyi ahuukasise, si ahuukasise n'ola wanyichwumaa.

37. 어 무뚜 오롸 우꾸후우가사 어 뫄나 무도도 오롸 우레 끄노 궈 시나 롸네, 어레 니 아후우가시서. 노롸 와네후우가시서, 아다 녀이너 니 아후우가시서, 시 아후우가시서 노롸 와네쭈마아.

37. "Whoever welcomes one of these little children in my name welcomes me; and whoever welcomes me does not welcome me but the one who sent me."

Ola uta murenda wechwu elyi alyi mwira wechwu

오롸 우다 무러따 워쭈 어레 아뻬 뮈라 워쭈

38. Yowana era kubura Yesu mbu: Mukangilyisi, chwalolaa ku mundju muuma enjire aambula e bihwasi kw'e sina lyao. Si chwabaa chwenjire chwamwanga, bushi atachwula w'omwa chikembe chechwu.

38. 요와나 어라 구부라 여수 뿌: 무가찌레시, 쫘로롸아 구 무뚜 무우마 어찌러 아아뿌롸 어 비화시 궈 시나 롸오. 시 쫘바아 쮜찌러 쫘뫄따, 부씨 아다쭈롸 요뫄 찌거뻬 쩌쭈.

38. "Teacher," said John, "we saw a man driving out demons in your name and we told him to stop, because he was not one of us."

39. Yesu na imbu: Si mutachimwangaa, bushi ola ungaira echisomerano kw'e sina lyanyi, atangachiteta bulyio era luulu sanyi.

39. 여수 나 이뿌: 시 무다찌뫄꾸아아, 부씨 오롸 우꾸아이라 어찌소머라노 궈 시나 롸네, 아다꾸아찌더다 부레오 어라 루우루 사네.

39. "Do not stop him," Jesus said. "No one who does a miracle in my name can in the next moment say anything bad about me,

40. Bushi ola uta murenda wechwu, elyi alyi kwa lunda lwechwu.

40. 부씨 오롸 우다 무러따 워쭈, 어레 아뻬 과 루따 뤄쭈.

40. for whoever is not against us is for us.

41. kubinalyi, nababura kwa ola ukaberesa ngumbu ya meshi bushi mulyibandju ba

41. 구비나레, 나바부라 과 오롸 우가버러사 꾸뿌 야 머씨 부씨 무레바뿌 바 기리시도,

41. I tell you the truth, anyone who gives you a cup of water in my name

kirisito, oyola atakaine e lwembo lwai chiro hicha.

E kuchalanga kwa mabi

42. Mwa bano bana batoto banyemerere, e mundju ola ungachwuma muuma mubo engilyira mwa bibi, kungabere kukulu kw'oyu mundju aminyirwe lusho lunene mw'e osi, aumwe mwa nyanja.

43. Rero, e mino yao akaba ingachwuma waira mabi, uishaai. bushi kungakubera kukulu wengilyire mwa chisiki ch'e kalamo wete mino nguma, wakuata mino ebilyi, chasinda uumwe era kusimu mwa mulyiro ola utasima.

44. Eyi kusimu, ichwula mifunyu era itafa, ichwula na mulyiro ola utasima.

45. N'e kuulu kwao, akaba kungachwuma waira mabi, uishaako. Bushi kungakubera kukulu wengilyire mwa chisiki ch'e kalamo wete kuulu kuuma, wakuata maulu mabilyi, chasinda uumwe era kusimu.

46. Eyi kusimu, ichwula mifunyu era itafa, ichwula na mulyiro ola utasima.

47. N'e lyiho lyao nalyi, akaba lyingachwuma wengira mwa

오요롸 아다가이너 어 뤄뽀 롸이 찌로 히짜.

어 구짜롸아 과 마비

42. 롸 바노 바나 바도도 바녀머러러, 어 무뚜 오롸 우까쭈마 무우마 무보 어끼레라 롸 비비, 구까버러 구구루 교유 무뚜 아미니뤄 루쏘 루너너 뭐 오시, 아우뭐 롸 냐짜.

43. 러로, 어 미노 야오 아가바 이까쭈마 와이라 마비, 우이싸아이. 부씨 구까구버라 구구루 워끼레러 롸 찌시기 쩌 가롸모 워더 미노 으마, 와구아다 미노 어비레, 짜시따 우우뭐 어라 구시무 롸 무레로 오롸 우다시마.

44. 어에 구시무, 이쭈롸 미푸뉴 어라 이다파, 이쭈롸 나 무레로 오롸 우다시마.

45. 너 구우루 과오, 아가바 구까쭈마 와이라 마비, 우이싸아고. 부씨 구까구버라 구구루 워끼레러 롸 찌시기 쩌 가롸모 워더 구우루 구우마, 와구아다 마우루 마비레, 짜시따 우우뭐 어라 구시무.

46. 어에 구시무, 이쭈롸 미푸뉴 어라 이다파, 이쭈롸 나 무레로 오롸 우다시마.

47. 너 레호 롸오 나레, 아가바 레까쭈마 워끼라 롸 비비,

because you belong to Christ will certainly not lose his reward.

42. "And if anyone causes one of these little ones who believe in me to sin, it would be better for him to be thrown into the sea with a large millstone tied around his neck.

43. If your hand causes you to sin, cut it off. It is better for you to enter life maimed than with two hands to go into hell, where the fire never goes out.

44. None

45. And if your foot causes you to sin, cut it off. It is better for you to enter life crippled than to have two feet and be thrown into hell.

46. None

47. And if your eye causes you to sin, pluck it out. It is

bibi, womwolaalyi. Bushi kungakubera kukulu wengilyire mwa chisiki ch'e kalamo wete lyiho lyiuma, wakuata meho mabilyi, chasinda uumwe era kusimu.

48. Eyi kusimu, ichwula mifunyu era itafa, ichwula na mulyiro ola utasima.

49. Rero, chira mundju akakomisibwa mwa kurenzibwa mwa mulyiro, ng'okwa e michwulo nai yende yakomisibwa mwa kulunga mw'e munyu.

50. E munyu, kachwula kandju kabuya. Si akaba angaesa e buloke bwai, kutachilyi cha bangabikamo chasiya ahube kuloka. Rero nenyu mubaa nga munyu ola uchete buloke, kanji mubaa n'e boolo mwa kachi-kachi kenyu.

오모롸아레. 부씨 구꺄구버라 구구루 워삐레러 롸 찌시기 쩌 가롸모 워더 레호 레우마, 와구아다 머호 마비레, 짜시따 우우뭐 어라 구시무.

48. 어에 구시무, 이쭈롸 미퓨뉴 어라 이다파, 이쭈롸 나 무레로 오롸 우다시마.

49. 러로, 찌라 무뚜 아가고미시봐 롸 구러시봐 롸 무레로, 꼬과 어 미쭈로 나이 여뉴 야고미시봐 롸 구루꺄 뭐 무뉴.

50. 어 무뉴, 가쭈롸 가뚜 가부야. 시 아가바 아꺄어사 어 부로거 봐이, 구다찌레 짜 바꺄비가모 짜시야 아후버 구로가. 러로 너뉴 무바아 꺄 무뉴 오롸 우쩌더 부로거, 가찌 무바아 너 보오로 롸 가찌-가찌 거뉴.

---

better for you to enter the kingdom of God with one eye than to have two eyes and be thrown into hell,

48. where " 'their worm does not die, and the fire is not quenched.'

49. Everyone will be salted with fire.

50. "Salt is good, but if it loses its saltiness, how can you make it salty again? Have salt in yourselves, and be at peace with each other."

Mariko Chikono 10
Yesu akangilyisa era luulu s'e kulyikanuka mwa buhosi

1. Yesu era kutenga mw'echi chisiki, era kuya mwa chio ch'e yudeya, kwa unji mushilyilya w'e lwishi lw'e yorodani. Aikireyi, kanji bandju banene bera kubuanana ala abaa alyi. Era kutangilyisa abakangilyisa kanji ng'okwa abaa achwula

---

마리고 찌고노 10
여수 아가삐레사 어라 루우루 서 구레가누가 롸 부호시

1. 여수 어라 구더꺄 뭐찌 찌시기, 어라 구야 롸 찌오 쩌 유더야, 과 우찌 무씨레롸 워 뤼씨 뤄 요로다니. 아이기러에, 가찌 바뚜 바너너 버라 구부아나나 아롸 아바아 아레. 어라 구다삐레사 아바가삐레사 가찌 꼬과 아바아 아쭈롸

Mark Chapter 10[NIV]

1. Jesus then left that place and went into the region of Judea and across the Jordan. Again crowds of people came to him, and as was his custom, he taught them.

akomere.

2. Bafarisayo bauma bera kumuikira chasiya bamuereke. Bera kumubusa mbu: Ewashe! e Mwaso wechwu achwula emerere mbu e mulume aulusaa mukai?

3. Yesu na imbu: Muomba muchiye i Musa abarekeraa?

4. Nabo mbu: Musa eresaa e mulume eloso lw'e kunaanjikira mukai e maruba m'e kulyikana nai, chasinda anamuulusa.

5. Yesu era kubabura mbu: E michima yenyu isibu iyachwumaa Musa abaanjikira oyu muomba.

6. Si mwa ndangilyiso mango Ongo abumbaa byoshi, abumbaa e mulume n'e mukasi.

7. Echera chi chikachwuma e mulume areka eshe na nyina, anaimba e bwai buhosi buna mukai.

8. Abu babilyi banere bahuba mundju muuma. Atola, batachilyi babilyi si bera balyi mundju muuma.

9. Bushi n'oku, bya Ongo abikire alauma, kutabaa chiro na mundju usibya ola ukabilyikanya.

아고머러.

2. 바파리사요 바우마 버라 구무이기라 짜시야 바무어러거. 버라 구무부사 뿌: 에와써! 어 마소 워쭈 아쭈롸 어머러러 뿌 어 무루머 아우루사아 무가이?

3. 여수 나 이뿌: 무오빠 무찌여 이 무사 아바러거라아?

4. 나보 뿌: 무사 어러사아 어 무루머 어로소 뤄 구나아찌기라 무가이 어 마루바 머 구레가나 나이, 짜시따 아나무우루사.

5. 여수 어라 구바부라 뿌: 어 미찌마 여뉴 이시부 이야쭈마아 무사 아바아찌기라 오유 무오빠.

6. 시 마 따삐레소 마오 오오 아부빠아 뵤씨, 아부빠아 어 무루머 너 무가시.

7. 어쩌라 찌 찌가쭈마 어 무루머 아러가 어써 나 니나, 아나이빠 어 봐이 부호시 부나 무가이.

8. 아부 바비레 바너러 바후바 무뚜 무우마. 아도롸, 바다찌레 바비레 시 버라 바레 무뚜 무우마.

9. 부씨 노구, 뱌 오오 아비기러 아롸우마, 구다바아 찌로 나 무뚜 우시뱌 오롸 우가비레가냐.

---

2. Some Pharisees came and tested him by asking, "Is it lawful for a man to divorce his wife?"

3. "What did Moses command you?" he replied.

4. They said, "Moses permitted a man to write a certificate of divorce and send her away."

5. "It was because your hearts were hard that Moses wrote you this law," Jesus replied.

6. "But at the beginning of creation God 'made them male and female.'

7. 'For this reason a man will leave his father and mother and be united to his wife,

8. and the two will become one flesh.' So they are no longer two, but one.

9. Therefore what God has joined together, let man not separate."

10. Mango Yesu n'e banafunzi bai babaa bera bengilyiraa mwa nyumba, nabo bera kumubusa kanji era lulu s'oyu mwasi.

11. Era kubaakula mbu: Akaba e mulume angaulusa Mukai, chasinda anahwera unji, amenyaa kwa abanjire ekilyi.

12. N'e mukasi nai, akaba angachikula mwa mwai, chasinda anahwelyibwa na unji mulume, nai anamenyaa kwa abanjire ekilyi.

Yesu aahanyira e bana batoto

13. Lusuku luuma, bandju bauma bareteraa Yesu bana batoto, ababike kw'e mino. Si e banafunzi bai, bera kukalyiira abu bandju.

14. mango Yesu alolaa bacha, era kuaya busese. Era kwire abura e banfunzi bai mbu: Murekaa e bana batoto babahe ene nyilyi! Mutabangaa, bushi e bandju ba balyi ng'abo, bu besha e Bwami bwa Ongo.

15. Kubinalyi, nababura kwa akaba e mundju atangamerera e myasi y'e bwami bwa Ongo nga mwana mutoto, atakengilyiremo chiro na

10. 마꼬 여수 너 바나푸씨 바이 바바아 버라 버삐쩨라아 와 뉴빠, 나보 버라 구무부사 가찌 어라 루루 소유 먀시.

11. 어라 구바아구꽈 뿌: 아가바 어 무루머 아까우루사 무가이, 짜시따 아나훠라 우씨, 아머냐아 과 아바찌러 어기쩨.

12. 너 무가시 나이, 아가바 아까찌구꽈 마 먀이, 짜시따 아나훠쩨봐 나 우씨 무루머, 나이 아나머냐아 과 아바찌러 어기쩨.

여수 아아하니라 어 바나 바도도

13. 루수구 루우마, 바뚜 바우마 바러더라아 여수 바나 바도도, 아바비거 궈 미노. 시 어 바나푸씨 바이, 버라 구가쩨이라 아부 바뚜.

14. 마꼬 여수 아로콰아 바짜, 어라 구아야 부서서. 어라 귀러 아부라 어 바누푸씨 바이 뿌: 무러가아 어 바나 바도도 바바허 어너 네쩨! 무다바까아, 부씨 어 바뚜 바 바쩨 우아보, 부 버싸 어 봐미 봐 오꼬.

15. 구비나쩨, 나바부라 과 아가바 어 무뚜 아다까머러라 어 먀시 여 봐미 봐 오꼬 까 마나 무도도, 아다거끼쩨러모 찌로 나 히짜.

10. When they were in the house again, the disciples asked Jesus about this.

11. He answered, "Anyone who divorces his wife and marries another woman commits adultery against her.

12. And if she divorces her husband and marries another man, she commits adultery."

13. People were bringing little children to Jesus to have him touch them, but the disciples rebuked them.

14. When Jesus saw this, he was indignant. He said to them, "Let the little children come to me, and do not hinder them, for the kingdom of God belongs to such as these.

15. I tell you the truth, anyone who will not receive the kingdom of God like a little child will never enter it."

hicha.

16. chasinda era kuobera abu bana, era kubabika kw'e mino na abaahanyira.

16. 짜시따 어라 구오버라 아부 바나, 어라 구바비가 궈 미노 나 아바아하녜라.

16. And he took the children in his arms, put his hands on them and blessed them.

E muare ema Yesu eano

어 무아러 어마 여수 어아노

17. Mango Yesu abaa era achiuma, mundju muuma era kumuikira aenda alyibita. Era kukoma e mafi era muhondo sai, era kumubusa mbu: Mukangilyisi mubuya! Chi n'emire kuira chasiya nyibone e kalamo k'e suku n'e mango?

17. 마꼬 여수 아바아 어라 아찌우마, 무쭈 무우마 어라 구무이기라 아어따 아례비다. 어라 구고마 어 마피 어라 무호또 사이, 어라 구무부사 뿌: 무가찌레시 무부야! 찌 너미러 구이라 짜시야 네보너 어 가롸모 거 수구 너 마꼬?

17. As Jesus started on his way, a man ran up to him and fell on his knees before him. "Good teacher," he asked, "what must I do to inherit eternal life?"

18. Yesu na mbu: Chi chachwuma wanyelyika mbu mubuya? Si kutalyi mundju mubuya kureka Ongo yeine oshao!

18. 여수 나 뿌: 찌 짜쭈마 와녀례가 뿌 무부야? 시 구다례 무쭈 무부야 구러가 오꼬 여이너 오싸오!

18. "Why do you call me good?" Jesus answered. "No one is good--except God alone.

19. Si wishi kwa miomba ichwula itechire mbu: Utendaa weta, utendaa wabanda ekilyi, utendaa weba. Utendaa wekerana bisha, utendaa watebana, undaa wachwunda eho na nyoko.

19. 시 위씨 과 미오빠 이쭈롸 이더찌러 뿌: 우더따아 워다, 우더따아 와바따 어기례, 우더따아 워바. 우더따아 워거라나 비싸, 우더따아 와더바나, 우따아 와쭈따 어호 나 뇨고.

19. You know the commandments: 'Do not murder, do not commit adultery, do not steal, do not give false testimony, do not defraud, honor your father and mother.'"

20. Oyu mundju, era kumwakula mbu: Mukangilyisi! Kutengera elyana etoto lyanyi, ei miomba Yoshi, n'elyisa nende naikulyikira.

20. 오유 무쭈, 어라 구뫄구롸 뿌: 무가찌레시! 구더꺼라 어랴나 어도도 롸네, 어이 미오빠 요씨, 너례사 너떠 나이구례기라.

20. "Teacher," he declared, "all these I have kept since I was a boy."

21. Yesu era kumusindera na meho ma nzii, era kumubura mbu: Uchilyi uinyire mwasi muuma oshao. Uyaa kuusa e

21. 여수 어라 구무시떠라 나 머호 마 씨이, 어라 구무부라 뿌: 우찌례 우이네러 뫄시 무우마 오싸오. 우야아 구우사

21. Jesus looked at him and loved him. "One thing you lack," he said. "Go, sell everything you have and

bindju byao byoshi. N'e buteya bwa bingafa, wanaabira'bo ebakene. Ukaira bacha, ungaba eri wabikiriwe mwandu kwa nguba. Chasinda, wanere wabaha kunyikulyikira.

22. Oyu mundju mango omvaa bacha, e buso bwai kuna kwina, era kuchiendera asibukire busese, bushi abaa ete bikulo binene.

23. Yesu era kuchwumbikisa e banafunzi bai ba babaa bamusungure. Era kubabura mbu: E muare, e kwingilyira kwai mwa bwami bwa Ongo kukoochire busese!

24. E banfunzi bomvire bacha, bera kusanwa busese. Si Yesu era kuhuba kubabura mbu: E bana banyi, e kwengilyira mwa bwami bwa Ongo, kukoochire busese!

25. Kusibuire e ngamiya kurenga mwa chichwure ch'e singe, si kanji kusibuire busese kwa muare kwingilyira mwa bwami bwa Ongo!

26. E banafunzi kanji bomvire bacha, bera kunaendekera basanwa busese, na batangilyisa babusanya mbu: Ewashe! Rero, nde kasi iukere wanunulyibwa?

어 비쭈 뱌오 뵤씨. 너 부더야 봐 비까파, 와나아비라보 어바거너. 우가이라 바짜, 우까바 어리 와비기리워 마뚜 과 꾸바. 짜시따, 와너러 와바하 구니구레기라.

22. 오유 무뚜 마꼬 오빠아 바짜, 어 부소 봐이 구나 귀나, 어라 구쩌떠라 아시부기러 부서서, 부씨 아바아 어더 비구로 비너너.

23. 여수 어라 구쭈삐기사 어 바나푸씨 바이 바 바바아 바무수꾸러. 어라 구바부라 뿌: 어 무아러, 어 귀끼레라 과이 먀 봐미 봐 오꼬 구고오찌러 부서서!

24. 어 바누푸씨 보삐러 바짜, 버라 구사놔 부서서. 시 여수 어라 구후바 구바부라 뿌: 어 바나 바네, 어 귀끼레라 먀 봐미 봐 오꼬, 구고오찌러 부서서!

25. 구시부이러 어 까미야 구러까 먀 찌쭈러 쩌 시어, 시 가찌 구시부이러 부서서 과 무아러 귀끼레라 먀 봐미 봐 오꼬!

26. 어 바나푸씨 가찌 보삐러 바짜, 버라 구나어떠거라 바사놔 부서서, 나 바다끼레사 바부사냐 뿌: 어와써! 러로, 떠 가시 이우거러 와누누레봐?

give to the poor, and you will have treasure in heaven. Then come, follow me."

22. At this the man's face fell. He went away sad, because he had great wealth.

23. Jesus looked around and said to his disciples, "How hard it is for the rich to enter the kingdom of God!"

24. The disciples were amazed at his words. But Jesus said again, "Children, how hard it is to enter the kingdom of God!

25. It is easier for a camel to go through the eye of a needle than for a rich man to enter the kingdom of God."

26. The disciples were even more amazed, and said to each other, "Who then can be saved?"

27. Yesu era kubachwumbikisa na ababura mbu: kwa bandju, ebyera bitangaalyikana, si ku Ongo bitalyi bacha. Buchi era mwai yeke, byoshi byende byanaalyikana.

28. Petero kukwera kumubura mbu: e Walyiya, ulolaa! chwubano chwarekire byoshi chasiya chwukukulyikire.

29. Yesu nai mbu: kubinalyi, nababura kwa akaba e mundJu angareka e nyumba yai, nesi banyakabo, nesi balYiwabo, nesi nyina, nesi eshe, nesi e bana bai nesi e mahwa mai bushi nanyi na bushi n'e Mwasi mubuya-buya,

30. Oyola, mango anachilyi muno butala, angabona lwembo lunene ku kalyi eyana. Angabona: e nyumba, na banyakabo, na balyiwabo, na banyina, n'e bana, n'e mahwa. Si chiro bacha, angalola n'okwa malyibuko. N'omwa suku sa sikaika, mu akere abona e kalamo k'e suku n'e mango.

31. Bandju banene ba balyi babere-bere lwarero, bakaba basinda-sinda. Na ba balyi basinda-sinda, bakaba babere-bere.

27. 여수 어라 구바쭈삐기사 나 아바부라 뿌: 과 바쭈, 어벼라 비다까아레가나, 시 구 오꼬 비다레 바짜. 부찌 어라 똬이 여거, 뵤씨 벼떠 뱌나아레가나.

28. 퍼더로 구궈라 구무부라 뿌: 어 와레야, 우로롸아! 쭈바노 쫘러기러 뵤씨 짜시야 쭈구구레기러.

29. 여수 나이 뿌: 구비나레, 나바부라 과 아가바 어 무뚜 아까러가 어 뉴빠 야이, 너시 바냐가보, 너시 바레와보, 너시 네나, 너시 어써, 너시 어 바나 바이 너시 어 마화 마이 부씨 나네 나 부씨 너 똬시 무부야-부야,

30. 오요롸, 마꼬 아나찌레 무노 부다롸, 아까보나 뤔뽀 루너너 구 가레 어야나. 아까보나: 어 뉴빠, 나 바냐가보, 나 바레와보, 나 바네나, 너 바나, 너 마화. 시 찌로 바짜, 아까로롸 노과 마레부고. 노와 수구 사 시가이가, 무 아거러 아보나 어 가롸모 거 수구 너 마꼬.

31. 바쭈 바너너 바 바레 바버러-버러 똬러로, 바가바 바시따-시따. 나 바 바레 바시따-시따, 바가바 바버러-버러.

27. Jesus looked at them and said, "With man this is impossible, but not with God; all things are possible with God."

28. Peter said to him, "We have left everything to follow you!"

29. "I tell you the truth," Jesus replied, "no one who has left home or brothers or sisters or mother or father or children or fields for me and the gospel

30. will fail to receive a hundred times as much in this present age (homes, brothers, sisters, mothers, children and fields--and with them, persecutions) and in the age to come, eternal life.

31. But many who are first will be last, and the last first."

Yesu ateta e bwakahachwu era lulu s'e kufa n'e komoka kwai

여수 아더다 어 봐가하쭈 어라 루루 서 구파 너 고모가 과이

32. Mango yesu n'e banafunzi bai babaa balyi mwa njira b'erukira e Yerusalemu, Yesu abaa abahondorere. Abu banafunzi babaa bachaanya, n'e banji bandju ba babaa balyi nabo, babaa bafa buba. Yesu era kuhuba kutola endjumwa sai ekumi n'ebilyi, era kutangilyisa aburasi e myasi era ingamuikira.

32. 마꼬 여수 너 바나푼씨 바이 바바아 바레 뫄 찌라 버루기라 어 여루사쩌무, 여수 아바아 아바호또러러. 아부 바나푼씨 바바아 바짜아냐, 너 바찌 바뚜 바 바바아 바레 나보, 바바아 바파 부바. 여수 어라 구후바 구도롸 어뚜뫄 사이 어구미 너비례, 어라 구다삐례사 아부라시 어 먀시 어라 이따무이기라.

32. They were on their way up to Jerusalem, with Jesus leading the way, and the disciples were astonished, while those who followed were afraid. Again he took the Twelve aside and told them what was going to happen to him.

33. Era kubabura mbu: Mulolaa, chwubano bano chwera chwerukira mwa musi w'e Yerusalemu. Na mw'oyu musi, mu nyono nyi Mwana w'e Mundju nyingaanyibwa mwa mino s'e bakulu-kulu b'e bakuhanyi, n'e bakangilyisi b'e mwaso. Banganyichijibusa chasiyanyichibwe. Chasinda, banganyana mwa mino s'e bandju ba bateshi Ongo.

33. 어라 구바부라 뿌: 무롤롸아, 쭈바노 바노 쭤라 쭤루기라 뫄 무시 워 여루사쩌무. 나 모유 무시, 무 뇨노 네 뫄나 워 무뚜 네따아네봐 뫄 미노 서 바구루-구루 버 바구하네, 너 바가삐례시 버 뫄소. 바따네찌지부사 짜시야네찌붸. 짜시따, 바따냐나 뫄 미노 서 바뚜 바 바더씨 오꼬.

33. "We are going up to Jerusalem," he said, "and the Son of Man will be betrayed to the chief priests and teachers of the law. They will condemn him to death and will hand him over to the Gentiles,

34. Abola, banganyishekera na kunyichirako, banganyihuta echwuchi, chasinda banganyita. Si kwa lusuku lwa kahachwu, nyingomwoka.

34. 아보롸, 바따네써거라 나 구네찌라고, 바따네후다 어쭈찌, 짜시따 바따네다. 시 과 루수구 롸 가하쭈, 네꼬모가.

34. who will mock him and spit on him, flog him and kill him. Three days later he will rise."

Benyi sebetayo bachihondera e bukulu-kulu

버네 서버다요 바찌호떠라 어 부구루-구루

35. Era nyuma s'ebi, baala ba sebetayo, yakobo na yowana

35. 어라 뉴마 서비, 바아롸 바 서버다요, 야고보 나 요와나

35. Then James and John, the sons of Zebedee, came

bera kuikira Yesu na bamubura mbu: Mukangilyisi, chwete mwasi muuma ola chwakwema uchwuilyire.

36. Yesu era kubabusa mbu: Chi mwahonda nyibailyire?

37. nabo mbu: Cha chwahonda chi ch'e chine: mango ungaba mw'echwunda lyao, wemereraa chwikale alauma nao muuma kwa lunda lw'e malyo, n'e unji kwa lw'e marembe.

38. Yesu nai mbu: Era! Bya mwema, mutabishi! Elyi mungaala kumwa e ngubu y'e malyibuko era nyigamwa? Na mango nyingabatisibwa mwa malyibuko, nenyu mungaala kubatisibwa mumo?

39. Nabo mbu: Nechi, chwungaala. Yesu kukwera kubabura mbu: kubinalyi, e ngumbu y'e malyibuko era nyingamwa, nenyu munganamwa kui. Na mango nyingabatisibwa mwa malyibuko, nenyu munganabatisibwa mumo.

40. Si e kwikasa e bandju kwa lunda lwanyi lw'e malyo nesi lw'e marembe, bitanyerekere. Ebi bisiki, Ongo yeine iwabikunganyisise e bandju ba alondore mira.

버라 구이기라 여수 나 바무부라 뿌: 무가끼레시, 쮀더 마시 무우마 오라 쫘궈마 우쭈이레러.

36. 여수 어라 구바부사 뿌: 찌 먀호따 네바이레러?

37. 나보 뿌: 짜 좌호따 찌 쩌 찌너: 마꼬 우까바 뭐쭈따 랴오, 워머러라아 쮀가러 아꽈우마 나오 무우마 과 루따 뤄 마뙨, 너 우찌 과 뤄 마러뻐.

38. 여수 나이 뿌: 어라! 뱌 뭐마, 무다비씨! 어레 무까아꽈 구와 어 우부 여 마레부고 어라 네가마? 나 마꼬 네까바디시봐 먀 마레부고, 너뉴 무까아꽈 구바디시봐 무모?

39. 나보 뿌: 너찌, 쭈까아꽈. 여수 구궈라 구바부라 뿌: 구비나레, 어 우뿌 여 마레부고 어라 네까먀, 너뉴 무까나봐 구이. 나 마꼬 네까바디시봐 먀 마레부고, 너뉴 무까나바디시봐 무모.

40. 시 어 귀가사 어 바뚜 과 루따 꽈네 뤄 마뙨 너시 뤄 마러뻐, 비다녀러거러. 어비 비시기, 오꼬 여이너 이와비구까네시서 어 바뚜 바 아롣또러 미라.

to him. "Teacher," they said, "we want you to do for us whatever we ask."

36. "What do you want me to do for you?" he asked.

37. They replied, "Let one of us sit at your right and the other at your left in your glory."

38. "You don't know what you are asking," Jesus said. "Can you drink the cup I drink or be baptized with the baptism I am baptized with?"

39. "We can," they answered. Jesus said to them, "You will drink the cup I drink and be baptized with the baptism I am baptized with,

40. but to sit at my right or left is not for me to grant. These places belong to those for whom they have been prepared."

41. Sa sinji ndjumwa ekumi mango somvaa bacha, sera kuaya yakobo na yowana.

42. Bushi n'oku, Yesu kukwera kwamaala boshi na ababura mbu: Si mwishi kwa mwa bandju ba bateshi Ongo, e bami babo bende babaenza mwa bine. N'e bakulu-kulu babo, bende babalyibusa.

43. Si mwabo, bitaendaa byaba bacha mwa kachi-kachi kenyu. Bushi olawahonda kuba mukulu-kulu mu mwabo, emire abe muanda wenyu.
44. N'ola wahonda kuba mubere-bere mu mwabo, emire abe kaungu ka boshi.
45. Bushi nyi Mwana w'e Mundju nanyi ndabahaa mbu bendaa banyikorera. Si nabahaa nyinde nakorerana na kwana e kalamo kanyi, nyinunule bandju banene

Yesu alamya baritolomayo
46. Chasinda, Yesu n'e banafunzi bai bera kuika mwa musi w'e Yeriko. Mango babaa bera batengamo, bandju banene busese bera kubakulyikira. Kwa musike s'e njira, kwabaa kwekese muuta muuma ola wabaa wenjire

41. 사 시찌 뿌똬 어구미 마꼬 소빠아 바짜, 서라 구아야 야고보 나 요와나.

42. 부씨 노구, 여수 구궈라 과마아똬 보씨 나 아바부라 뿌: 시 뮈씨 과 똬 바쭈 바 바더씨 오꼬, 어 바미 바보 버떠 바바어싸 똬 비너. 너 바구루-구루 바보, 버떠 바바쩨부사.

43. 시 똬보, 비다어따아 뱌바 바짜 똬 가찌-가찌 거뉴. 부씨 오똬와호따 구바 무구루-구루 무 똬보, 어미러 아버 무아따 워뉴.
44. 노똬 와호따 구바 무버러- 버러 무 똬보, 어미러 아버 가우꾸 가 보씨.
45. 부씨 네 똬나 워 무쭈 나니 따바하아 뿌 버따아 바네고러라. 시 나바하아 네떠 나고러라나 나 과나 어 가똬모 가니, 네누누쩌 바쭈 바너너

여수 아똬먀 바리도똔마요
46. 짜시따, 여수 너 바나푼씨 바이 버라 구이가 똬 무시 워 여리고. 마꼬 바바아 버라 바더따모, 바쭈 바너너 부서서 버라 구바구쩨기라. 과 무시거 서 찌라, 과바아 궈거서 무우다 무우마 오똬 와바아 워찌러 워머러사 어 부더야.

41. When the ten heard about this, they became indignant with James and John.

42. Jesus called them together and said, "You know that those who are regarded as rulers of the Gentiles lord it over them, and their high officials exercise authority over them.

43. Not so with you. Instead, whoever wants to become great among you must be your servant,

44. and whoever wants to be first must be slave of all.

45. For even the Son of Man did not come to be served, but to serve, and to give his life as a ransom for many."

46. Then they came to Jericho. As Jesus and his disciples, together with a large crowd, were leaving the city, a blind man, Bartimaeus (that is, the Son of Timaeus), was sitting by the roadside begging.

wemeresa e buteya.
Oyumuuta iwabaa
baritolomayo, mwenyi timayo.

47. Mango omvaa kwa Yesu w'e Nasareti iwarenga, era kutangilyisa alakanga na murenge munene mbu: e Walyiya! Yesu mwenyi Daudi, unyifiraa bonjo!

48. Bandju banene bera kumukalyiiranga mbu asiraa. Si era kunaendekera alakanga na murenge munene mbu: e Walyiya! Mwenyi Daudi, unyifiraa bonjo!

49. Yesu era kwimanga, na ateta mbu: Mumwamaalaa. Bera kunamwamaala na bamubura mbu: Sesaa e muchima wimange! Akwamaere.

50. Ola muuta, kuna kuuma e kochi lyai era musike, kuna kubanzukala na aya ala Yesu abaa alyi.

51. Yesu era kumubusa mbu: Chi wahonda nyikuilyire? Nai mbu: Mukangilyisi, nahonda nyihube kulola.

52. Yesu kukwera kumubura mbu: Uendaa, e bwemeresi bwao bwakulamise. Unao-unao kuna kuhuba kulola, na atangilyisa akulyikira Yesu.

오유무우다 이와바아
바리도ᄙ마요, 뭐네 디마요.

47. 마ᄭ 오빠아 과 여수 워 나사러디 이와러ᄭ, 어라 구다ᄞ례사 아ᄽ가ᄭ 나 무러ᄙ 무너너 뿌: 어 와ᄙ야! 여수 뭐네 다우디, 우네피라아 보ᅑ!

48. 바ᄍ 바너너 버라 구무가ᄙ이라ᄭ 뿌 아시라아. 시 어라 구나어ᄠ거라 아ᄽ가ᄭ 나 무러ᄙ 무너너 뿌: 어 와ᄙ야! 뭐네 다우디, 우네피라아 보ᅑ!

49. 여수 어라 귀마ᄭ, 나 아더다 뿌: 무뫄마아ᄽ아. 버라 구나뫄마아ᄽ 나 바무부라 뿌: 서사아 어 무찌마 위마ᄠ! 아과마어러.

50. 오ᄽ 무우다, 구나 구우마 어 고찌 ᄽ이 어라 무시거, 구나 구바누가ᄽ 나 아야 아ᄽ 여수 아바아 아ᄙ.

51. 여수 어라 구무부사 뿌: 찌 와호ᄯ 네구이례러? 나이 뿌: 무가ᄞ례시, 나호ᄯ 네후버 구ᄛᄽ.

52. 여수 구궈라 구무부라 뿌: 우어ᄯ아아, 어 붜머러시 봐오 봐구ᄽ미서. 우나오-우나오 구나 구후바 구ᄛᄽ, 나 아다ᄞ례사 아구ᄙ기라 여수.

47. When he heard that it was Jesus of Nazareth, he began to shout, "Jesus, Son of David, have mercy on me!"

48. Many rebuked him and told him to be quiet, but he shouted all the more, "Son of David, have mercy on me!"

49. Jesus stopped and said, "Call him." So they called to the blind man, "Cheer up! On your feet! He's calling you."

50. Throwing his cloak aside, he jumped to his feet and came to Jesus.

51. "What do you want me to do for you?" Jesus asked him. The blind man said, "Rabbi, I want to see."

52. "Go," said Jesus, "your faith has healed you." Immediately he received his sight and followed Jesus along the road.

Mark Chapter 11[NIV]

Yesu engiliyira mwa musi w'e Yerusalemu　여수 어삐쩨라 롸 무시 워 여루사펴무

1. Mango Yesu n'e banafunzi bai babaa bahonda kuika mwa musi w'e Yerusalemu, bera kuika mwa bimbi by'e musi w'e betefake n'e w'e betaniya, ofu n'e ndjulungu y'e Miseituni. Yesu era kuchwuma banafunzi bai babilyi.

1. 마꼬 여수 너 바나푸씨 바이 바바아 바호따 구이가 롸 무시 워 여루사쩌무, 버라 구이가 롸 비삐 벼 무시 워 버더파거 너 워 버다니야, 오푸 너 뚜루우 여 미서이두니. 여수 어라 구쭈마 바나푸씨 바이 바비쩨.

1. As they approached Jerusalem and came to Bethphage and Bethany at the Mount of Olives, Jesus sent two of his disciples,

2. Era kubabura mbu: Muyaa mwa musi yola ulyi era muhondo senyu. Mango mungaikamo, mungabuana chana cha ndokomu chiminyirwe, chitafuraa kwerukibwako na mundju. Rero, muboolaachi mwananyireterachi.

2. 어라 구바부라 뿌: 무야아 롸 무시 요롸 우쩨 어라 무호또 서뉴. 마꼬 무빠이가모, 무빠부아나 짜나 짜 또고무 찌미네뤄, 찌다푸라아 궈루기바고 나 무뚜. 러로, 무보오롸아찌 롸나네러더라찌.

2. saying to them, "Go to the village ahead of you, and just as you enter it, you will find a colt tied there, which no one has ever ridden. Untie it and bring it here.

3. Na kukaba mundju ola ungababusa mbu: chi chachwuma mwaira bacha?, mumwakulaa mbu: Enawechwu ete bwera bwachi, si atemange kufulusachi.

3. 나 구가바 무뚜 오롸 우빠바부사 뿌: 찌 짜쭈마 롸이라 바짜?, 무롸구롸아 뿌: 어나워쭈 어더 붜라 봐찌, 시 아더마뼈 구푸루사찌.

3. If anyone asks you, 'Why are you doing this?' tell him, 'The Lord needs it and will send it back here shortly.' "

4. Abu banafunzi bera kunachiuma, bera kunabuana cha chana ch'e ndokomu chiminyirirwe ku chiso cha nyumba nguma, kwa musike s'e njira. Abere bera banaboolachi,

4. 아부 바나푸씨 버라 구나찌우마, 버라 구나부아나 짜 짜나 쩌 또고무 찌미네리뤄 구 찌소 짜 뉴빠 우마, 과 무시거 서 찌라. 아버러 버라 바나보오롸찌,

4. They went and found a colt outside in the street, tied at a doorway. As they untied it,

5. bandju bauma mwa babaa

5. 바뚜 바우마 롸 바바아

5. some people standing

balyi aola, bera kubabusa mbu: Era! Chi mwaboorera echi chana ch'e ndokomu?

6. nabo bera kubaakula ng'okwa Yesu anababuraa. Abu bandju bera kubareka baende.

7. Abere bera bareteraa Yesu echi chana ch'e ndokomu, bera kuhashika kw'e njimba sabo, chasinda Yesu era kw'ekala kuchi.

8. Bandju banene bera kuhashikanga e njimba sabo mwa njira, n'e banji bera kuya kuishanga e matabi m'e michi mwa mahwa na batangilyisa bama hashikanga mwa njira kwa kumuhuukasa n'echwunda.

9. E bandju ba babaa bahondorere Yesu na ba babaa bamukulyikire, babaa baenda bateta na murenge munene mbu: Hosana! Ono wabahire kw'e sina lya enawechwu, aahanyirwa!

10. N'e bwami bwa hokulu wechwu Daudi bwa bweshire nabo, buahanyirwa. Ongo atongwe kwa nguba!

11. Mango Yesu abaa era aikaa mwa musi w'e yerusalemu, era kwengilyira mwa chibuwa ch'e luhu lwa

바례 아오롸, 버라 구바부사 뿌: 어라! 찌 먀보오러라 어찌 짜나 쩌 또고무?

6. 나보 버라 구바아구롸 꼬과 여수 아나바부라아. 아부 바뚜 버라 구바러가 바어떠.

7. 아버러 버라 바러더라아 여수 어찌 짜나 쩌 또고무, 버라 구하씨가 궈 띠빠 사보, 짜시따 여수 어라 궈가롸 구찌.

8. 바뚜 바너너 버라 구하씨가꽈 어 띠빠 사보 먀 띠라, 너 바찌 버라 구야 구이싸꽈 어 마다비 머 미찌 먀 마화 나 바다삐레사 바마 하씨가꽈 먀 띠라 과 구무후우가사 너쭈따.

9. 어 바뚜 바 바바아 바호또러러 여수 나 바 바바아 바무구레기러, 바바아 바어따 바더다 나 무러꺼 무너너 뿌: 호사나! 오노 와바히러 궈 시나 롸 어나워쭈, 아아하네롸!

10. 너 봐미 봐 호구루 워쭈 다우디 봐 뷔씨러 나보, 부아하네롸. 오꼬 아도줘 과 우봐!

11. 마꼬 여수 아바아 어라 아이가아 먀 무시 워 여루사롸무, 어라 궈삐레라 먀 찌부와 쩌 루후 꽈 오꼬. 어라

there asked, "What are you doing, untying that colt?"

6. They answered as Jesus had told them to, and the people let them go.

7. When they brought the colt to Jesus and threw their cloaks over it, he sat on it.

8. Many people spread their cloaks on the road, while others spread branches they had cut in the fields.

9. Those who went ahead and those who followed shouted, "Hosanna!" "Blessed is he who comes in the name of the Lord!"

10. "Blessed is the coming kingdom of our father David!" "Hosanna in the highest!"

11. Jesus entered Jerusalem and went to the temple. He looked around at everything, but since it was

Ongo. Era kusonga byoshi bya byabaa bilyimo. Bushi lwabaa lwera luolo-olo, era kwire aya mwa musi w'e betaniya alauma n'e ndjumwa sai ekumi n'ebilyi.

Yesu atakira e muchi w'e tini

12. Abere mwei mishangya, mango babaa bera batenga e Betaniya, Yesu era kufa businya.

13. Era kulola ku muchi muuma wa tini kwa marerere. Oyu muchi abaa ete bihoho binene. Era kwire aya kuhona elyi angabona ku bifuma. Si mango aikaa ofu nao, chiro akabuana ku kandju kasibya, si ebi bihoho byeine oshao, bushi sitabaa suku s'e muchi w'e tini kweka bifuma.

14. Bushi n'oku ola muchi, Yesu era kutakirao mbu: Kutengera lwarero, si kutachibaa chiro na mundju usibya ola akalya kwa bifuma byao! Ei myasi, e banafunzi bai bera kunomva kui.

Yesu akolokanya e bachimbusi mwa luhu lwa Ongo

15. Era nyuma s'ebi, Yesu n'e banafunzi bai bera kuika mwa

구소咖 뵤씨 뱌 뱌바아 비례모. 부씨 꽈바아 뭐라 루오로-오로, 어라 귀러 아야 꽈 무시 워 버다니야 아꽈우마 너 뚜꽈 사이 어구미 너비쩨.

여수 아다기라 어 무찌 워 디니

12. 아버러 뭐이 미싸咖야, 마꼬 바바아 버라 바더咖 어 버다니야, 여수 어라 구파 부시냐.

13. 어라 구로꽈 구 무찌 무우마 와 디니 과 마러러러. 오유 무찌 아바아 어더 비호호 비너너. 어라 귀러 아야 구호나 어레 아까보나 구 비푸마. 시 마꼬 아이가아 오푸 나오, 찌로 아가부아나 구 가뚜 가시뱌, 시 어비 비호호 뼈이너 오싸오, 부씨 시다바아 수구 서 무찌 워 디니 꿔가 비푸마.

14. 부씨 노구 오꽈 무찌, 여수 어라 구다기라오 뿌: 구더咖라 꽈러로, 시 구다찌바아 찌로 나 무뚜 우시뱌 오꽈 아가꺄 과 비푸마 뱌오! 어이 먀시, 어 바나푸씨 바이 버라 구노빠 구이.

여수 아고똔가냐 어 바찌뿌시 꽈 루후 꽈 오꼬

15. 어라 뉴마 서비, 여수 너 바나푸씨 바이 버라 구이가 꽈

---

already late, he went out to Bethany with the Twelve.

12. The next day as they were leaving Bethany, Jesus was hungry.

13. Seeing in the distance a fig tree in leaf, he went to find out if it had any fruit. When he reached it, he found nothing but leaves, because it was not the season for figs.

14. Then he said to the tree, "May no one ever eat fruit from you again." And his disciples heard him say it.

15. On reaching Jerusalem, Jesus entered the temple

musi w'e Yerusalemu. Era kwengilyira mwa chibuwa ch'e luhu lwa Ongo, na atangilyisa akolokanya ba babaa bausa e bindju na ba babaa babiula. Era kubindjulanga e mesa ma ba babaa bainganyanga e buteya, n'e bifumbi byaba babaa bausa e biruka.

16. Mw'echi chibuwa ch'e luhu lwa Ongo, Yesu chiro akanachemerera mbu kubaa mundju ola wahuba kurenganamo kandju.

17. Chasinda, era kutangilyisa abakangilyisa mbu: e Maanjiko Mabuya-buya bacha ku machwula matechire: E nyumba yanyi, ikende yelyikibwa nyumba ya memo kwa bandju b'e mbaa soshi. Si mwabo, mwelyire mwaihubya ku ba chisiki cha bihumisi!

18. E bakulu-kulu b'e bakuhanyi, n'e bakangilyisi b'e Mwaso, bomvire kwei myasi, bera kutangilyisa bahonda kute bangeta Yesu. Si bera kumwobaa, bushi e bandju boshi bendee basanwa busese n'ebyedee akangilyisa.

19. Abere lwera luolo-olo, Yesu n'e banafunzi bai bera kutenga mw'oyu musi.

Yesu akangilyisa era luula s'e

무시 워 여루사퍼무. 어라 귀ㅁ례라 뫄 찌부와 쩌 루후 롸 오끄, 나 아다ㅁ례사 아고ㄹ가냐 바 바바아 바우사 어 비뉴 나 바 바바아 바비우롸. 어라 구비뉴쫘ㅁ 어 머사 마 바 바바아 바이ㅁ냐ㅁ 어 부더야, 너 비푸쀄 뱌바 바바아 바우사 어 비루가.

16. 뭐찌 찌부와 쩌 루후 롸 오끄, 여수 찌로 아가나쩌머러라 뿌 구바아 무뉴 오롸 와후바 구러ㅁ나모 가뉴.

17. 짜시따, 어라 구다ㅁ례사 아바가ㅁ례사 뿌: 어 마아찌고 마부야-부야 바짜 구 마쭈롸 마더찌러: 어 뉴빠 야니, 이거러 여레기롸 뉴빠 야 머모 과 바뉴 버 빠아 소씨. 시 뫄보, 뭐레러 뫄이후뱌 구 바 찌시기 짜 비후미시!

18. 어 바구루-구루 버 바구하네, 너 바가ㅁ례시 버 뫄소, 보쀄러 귀이 먀시, 버라 구다ㅁ례사 바호따 구더 바ㅁ다 여수. 시 버라 구모바아, 부씨 어 바뉴 보씨 버ㅁ어 바사뇨 부서서 너벼더어 아가ㅁ례사.

19. 아버러 뤄라 루오로ㄹ-오ㄹ르, 여수 너 바나푸씨 바이 버라 구더ㅁ 모유 무시.

여수 아가ㅁ례사 어라 뤄우롸

area and began driving out those who were buying and selling there. He overturned the tables of the money changers and the benches of those selling doves,

16. and would not allow anyone to carry merchandise through the temple courts.

17. And as he taught them, he said, "Is it not written: " 'My house will be called a house of prayer for all nations'? But you have made it 'a den of robbers.'"

18. The chief priests and the teachers of the law heard this and began looking for a way to kill him, for they feared him, because the whole crowd was amazed at his teaching.

19. When evening came, they went out of the city.

kwema Ongo n'e bwemeresi 서 궈마 오꼬 너 뭐머러시

20. Abere mwei mishangya-shangya, mango Yesu n'e banafunzi bai babaa barenga, bera kulola kw'ola muchi w'e tini omire mira kuikira kwanamisi-misi.

20. 아버러 뭐이 미싸야-싸야, 마꼬 여수 너 바나푸씨 바이 바바아 바러따, 버라 구로꽈 교꽈 무찌 워 디니 오미러 미라 구이기라 과나미시-미시.

20. In the morning, as they went along, they saw the fig tree withered from the roots.

21. Petero kukwera kukengera kwa Yesu atakiraa oyu muchi. Era kumubura mbu: Mukangilyisi! Ulolaa, ola muchi w'e tini watakiraa omire!

21. 퍼더로 구궈라 구거어라 과 여수 아다기라아 오유 무찌. 어라 구무부라 뿌: 무가삐레시! 우로꽈아, 오꽈 무찌 워 디니 와다기라아 오미러!

21. Peter remembered and said to Jesus, "Rabbi, look! The fig tree you cursed has withered!"

22. Yesu era kwire abura e banfunzi bai mbu: Mwemereraa Ongo.

22. 여수 어라 귀러 아부라 어 바누푸씨 바이 뿌: 뭐머러라아 오꼬.

22. "Have faith in God," Jesus answered.

23. Kubinalyi, nababura kwa e mundju angabura ene ndjulungu mbu: Tengaa anola uchiume mwa Nyanja. Akaba angateta ei myasi busira kuhungwa-hungwa mwa muchima, si ete bwemeresi kw'ebi atechire binganaba, kuika binabe.

23. 구비나레, 나바부라 과 어 무뚜 아따부라 어너 뚜루우 뿌: 더따아 아노꽈 우찌우머 꽈 냐짜. 아가바 아까더다 어이 먀시 부시라 구후꽈-후꽈 꽈 무찌마, 시 어더 뭐머러시 궈비 아더찌러 비따나바, 구이가 비나버.

23. "I tell you the truth, if anyone says to this mountain, 'Go, throw yourself into the sea,' and does not doubt in his heart but believes that what he says will happen, it will be done for him.

24. Bushi n'oku, nababura kwa chira kandju ka mwema Ongo, mundaa mwaata e bwemeresi kwa mwabonyireko mira. Aola, mwanere mweresibwako.

24. 부씨 노구, 나바부라 과 찌라 가뉴 가 뭐마 오꼬, 무따아 마와다 어 뭐머러시 꽈보네러고 미라. 아오꽈, 마너러 뭐러시바고.

24. Therefore I tell you, whatever you ask for in prayer, believe that you have received it, and it will be yours.

25. Na mango mungende mwema Ongo, mwete na mwasi na mundju murebe, mumubabalyiraa tanga. Aola, eho wenyu ola uchwula kwa

25. 나 마꼬 무꺼떠 뭐마 오꼬, 뭐더 나 먀시 나 무뚜 무러버, 무무바바레라아 다따. 아오꽈, 어호 워뉴 오꽈 우쭈꽈 과 꾸바, 나이 아너러 아바바레라

25. And when you stand praying, if you hold anything against anyone, forgive him, so that your Father in heaven may

nguba, nai anere ababalyira e
mabi menyu.

어 마비 머뉴.

forgive you your sins."

26. Si akaba mutangende mwabababalyira e banji, nenyu eho ola uchwula kwa nguba atakababalyire e mabi menyu.
E bandju babusa Yesu era lulu s'e buashi bwai

26. 시 아가바 무다꺼러 마바바바레라 어 바찌, 너뉴 어호 오롸 우쭈롸 과 우바 아다가바바레러 어 마비 머뉴.
어 바뚜 바부사 여수 어라 뚜루 서 부아씨 봐이

26. None

27. Yesu n'e banafunzi bai bera kuhuba kuya mwa musi w'e yerusalemu. Abere era asungula mwa chibuawa ch'e luhu lwa Ongo, e bakulu-kulu b'e bakuhanyi, n'e bakangilyisi b'e Mwaso, alauma n'e bashamuka b'e Bayuda bera kumuikira.

27. 여수 너 바나푸씨 바이 버라 구후바 구야 마 무시 워 여루사퍼무. 아버러 어라 아수우롸 마 찌부아와 쩌 루후 롸 오꼬, 어 바구루-구루 버 바구하니, 너 바가삐레씨 버 롸소, 아롸우마 너 바싸무가 버 바유다 버라 구무이기라.

27. They arrived again in Jerusalem, and while Jesus was walking in the temple courts, the chief priests, the teachers of the law and the elders came to him.

28. Bera kumubusa mbu: Ewashe, bine wenjire waira, wabiira ku loso luchiye? Na nde iwakuwerelo?

28. 버라 구무부사 뿌: 어와쎄, 비너 워찌러 와이라, 와비이라 구 로소 루찌여? 나 떠 이와구워러로?

28. "By what authority are you doing these things?" they asked. "And who gave you authority to do this?"

29. Yesu nai mbu: Nanyi nababusa mwasi muuma. Na mukanyakula kuo, nanyi nyingababura ku loso luchiye ku nenjire naira ene myasi.

29. 여수 나이 뿌: 나니 나바부사 마시 무우마. 나 무가냐구롸 구오, 나니 네꺼바부라 구 로소 루찌여 구 너찌러 나이라 어너 먀시.

29. Jesus replied, "I will ask you one question. Answer me, and I will tell you by what authority I am doing these things.

30. E loso lwa yowana endee abatisa mw'e bandju nalo, ngai u lwatengeraa? Era mwa Ongo nesi kwa bandju? Munyakulaa!

30. 어 로소 롸 요와나 어떠어 아바디사 뭐 바뚜 나로, 꽈이 우 롸더꺼라아? 어라 마 오꼬 너시 과 바뚜? 무냐구롸아!

30. John's baptism--was it from heaven, or from men? Tell me!"

31. Abu bakulu-kulu bera kuya nama. Bera kutangilyisa baburana mbu:

31. 아부 바구루-구루 버라 구야 나마. 버라 구다삐레사 바부라나 뿌: 쭈가뫄구롸 뿌

31. They discussed it among themselves and said, "If we say, 'From

chwukamwakula mbu era mwa Ongo yilwatengeraa, nai angachwubusa mbu: Chi cheraa chachwuma chwutamwerera?

32. Na chwukamwakula mbu kwa bandju ku lwatengeraa... Bateta bacha, bushi babaa bobaa e bandju, bushi boshi babaa batolyire yowana nga murebi wa kanangana.

33. Bushi n'oku, bera kwire baakula Yesu mbu: chwuteshi. Nai era kwire ababura mbu: Nanyi, ndababure ku loso luchiye ku nenjire naira ene myasi.

Mariko Chikono 12
E muanyi w'e bainzi babi

1. Era nyuma s'ebi, Yesu era kutangilyisa ahambalyira e bandju mwa mianyi. Era kuteta mbu: kwabaa mulume muuma ola waingaa ehwa lyai lya misabibu. Elyi ehwa, era kulyisungusa e lusito, era kuchima n'e fumbi era bagende bakanjira mw'e chwufuma chw'e misabibu. Era kuimbira n'e balanzi belye ehwa, chitala cha chitowamire. Chasinda, era kulyibwesa bainzi bauma, na abalama.

어라 뫄 오꼬 에꽈더꺼라라아, 나이 아까쭈부사 뿌: 찌 쩌라아 짜쭈마 쭈다뭐러라?

32. 나 쭈가뫄구꽈 뿌 과 바꾸 구 꽈더꺼라라아... 바더다 바짜, 부씨 바바아 보바아 어 바꾸, 부씨 보씨 바바아 바도꿰러 요와나 꽈 무러비 와 가나까나.

33. 부씨 노구, 버라 귀러 바아구꽈 여수 뿌: 쭈더씨. 나이 어라 귀러 아바부라 뿌: 나니, 따바부러 구 로소 루찌여 구 너찌러 나이라 어너 먀시.

마리고 찌고노 12
어 무아니 워 바이씨 바비

1. 어라 뉴마 서비, 여수 어라 구다끼꿰사 아하빠꿰라 어 바꾸 뫄 미아네. 어라 구더다 뿌: 과바아 무루머 무우마 오라 와이까아 어화 랴이 꺄 미사비부. 어레 어화, 어라 구꿰수꾸사 어 루시도, 어라 구찌마 너 푸삐 어라 바거꺼 바가찌라 뭐 쭈푸마 쭤 미사비부. 어라 구이삐라 너 바꽈씨 버쪄 어화, 찌다꽈 짜 찌도와미러. 짜시따, 어라 구꿰붜사 바이씨 바우마, 나 아바꽈마.

---

heaven,' he will ask, 'Then why didn't you believe him?'

32. But if we say, 'From men'...." (They feared the people, for everyone held that John really was a prophet.)

33. So they answered Jesus, "We don't know." Jesus said, "Neither will I tell you by what authority I am doing these things."

Mark Chapter 12[NIV]

1. He then began to speak to them in parables: "A man planted a vineyard. He put a wall around it, dug a pit for the winepress and built a watchtower. Then he rented the vineyard to some farmers and went away on a journey.

2. abere e suku s'e kushebula saika, era kuchwuma mukosi wai muuma era abu bainzi balyi, bamwerese ewai mwango kwa myaka.	2. 아버러 어 수구 서 구써부콰 사이가, 어라 구쭈마 무고시 와이 무우마 어라 아부 바이씨 바레, 바뭐러서 어와이 마꼬 과 먀가.	2. At harvest time he sent a servant to the tenants to collect from them some of the fruit of the vineyard.
3. Si oyu mukosi, abu bainzi bera kumusimba, bera kumupunda, na bamufulusa mino buha.	3. 시 오유 무고시, 아부 바이씨 버라 구무시빠, 버라 구무푸따, 나 바무푸루사 미노 부하.	3. But they seized him, beat him and sent him away empty-handed.
4. Oyu en'ehwa, era kuhuba kubachwumira unji mukosi. Oyola nai bera kumusimba, bera kumuhuchiranga kw'echwe na kumukena.	4. 오유 어너화, 어라 구후바 구바쭈미라 우찌 무고시. 오요콰 나이 버라 구무시빠, 버라 구무후찌라마 궈쭤 나 구무거나.	4. Then he sent another servant to them; they struck this man on the head and treated him shamefully.
5. Chasinda, en'ehwa era kuchwuma unji mukosi. Oyola yeke bera kumwita. Era kunaendekera abachwumira banjibakosi banene. bauma mubo, abu bainzi bera kubapunda, n'e banji bera kubeta.	5. 짜시따, 어너화 어라 구쭈마 우찌 무고시. 오요콰 여거 버라 구뮈다. 어라 구나어떠거라 아바쭈미라 바찌바고시 바너너. 바우마 무보, 아부 바이씨 버라 구바푸따, 너 바찌 버라 구버다.	5. He sent still another, and that one they killed. He sent many others; some of them they beat, others they killed.
6. Ena ehwa era kunashiba na muala wai musiirwa oshao. Era kwire abachwumira oyu muala wai mwa kuteta mbu: Nyishi kwa ono muala wanyi yeke, bangamuchwunda.	6. 어나 어화 어라 구나씨바 나 무아콰 와이 무시이롸 오싸오. 어라 귀러 아바쭈미라 오유 무아콰 와이 콰 구더다 뿌: 네씨 과 오노 무아콰 와니 여거, 바꽈무쭌따.	6. "He had one left to send, a son, whom he loved. He sent him last of all, saying, 'They will respect my son.'
7. Si abu bainzi, bamulolyireko, bera kutangilyisa baburana mbu: Onola I ukalya e mwandju w'eshe. Muiraa chwumwite, chasiya chwuchishibanyireo!	7. 시 아부 바이씨, 바무로례러고, 버라 구다삐레사 바부라나 뿌: 오노콰 이 우가캬 어 콰뮤 워써. 무이라아 쭈뮈더, 짜시야 쭈찌씨바네러오!	7. "But the tenants said to one another, 'This is the heir. Come, let's kill him, and the inheritance will be ours.'

8. Bushi n'oku, bera kusimba oyu muala na bamwita. Chasinda, bera kuuma e chirunda chai kwa musike s'ehwa.

9. Yesu kukwera kubusa abu bandju mbu: Rero oyu en'ehwa, kute akaira abu bainzi? Akaika kuitabo, chasinda aneresalyi banji bainzi.

10. Kanji era kubabura mbu: Mutafuraa kusoma kwa maanjiko mabuya-buya machwula matechire mbu: Ekoi lya baimbi balangulaa, Lyilyahubire koi lyinene ly'e kuimbirako.

11. Enawechwu iwanairaa bacha. N'echi, chilyi chisomerano ku chwubano.

12. Abu bakulu-kulu mango bamenyereraa kwa Yesu aishire oyu muanyi bushi nabo, bera kuhonda enjira y'e kumusimba. Si bushi babaa bobaa e luamba lw'e bandju, bera kumureka na bachiendera.

E kufuta e mbarata ya mwami kaisari

13. Era nyuma s'ebi, abu bakulu-kulu bera kuchwumira Yesu bafarisayo bauma na banji bandju b'omwa

---

8. 부씨 노구, 버라 구시빠 오유 무아꽈 나 바뮈다. 짜시따, 버라 구우마 어 찌루따 짜이 과 무시거 서화.

9. 여수 구궈라 구부사 아부 바뉴 뿌: 러로 오유 어너화, 구더 아가이라 아부 바이씨? 아가이가 구이다보, 짜시따 아너러사쩨 바찌 바이씨.

10. 가찌 어라 구바부라 뿌: 무다푸라아 구소마 과 마아찌고 마부야-부야 마쭈꽈 마더찌러 뿌: 어고이 랴 바이삐 바꽈우꽈아, 레랴후비러 고이 레너너 뤼어 구이삐라고.

11. 어나워쭈 이와나이라아 바짜. 너찌, 찌레 찌소머라노 구 쭈바노.

12. 아부 바구루-구루 마꼬 바머녀러라아 과 여수 아이씨러 오유 무아네 부씨 나보, 버라 구호따 어찌라 여 구무시빠. 시 부씨 바바아 보바아 어 루아빠 뤄 바뉴, 버라 구무러가 나 바쩌떠라.

어 구푸다 어 빠라다 야 꽈미 가이사리

13. 어라 뉴마 서비, 아부 바구루-구루 버라 구쭈미라 여수 바파리사요 바우마 나 바찌 바뉴 보꽈 찌거뻐 짜

---

8. So they took him and killed him, and threw him out of the vineyard.

9. "What then will the owner of the vineyard do? He will come and kill those tenants and give the vineyard to others.

10. Haven't you read this scripture: " 'The stone the builders rejected has become the capstone;

11. the Lord has done this, and it is marvelous in our eyes'?"

12. Then they looked for a way to arrest him because they knew he had spoken the parable against them. But they were afraid of the crowd; so they left him and went away.

13. Later they sent some of the Pharisees and Herodians to Jesus to catch him in his words.

chikembe cha herodi, chasiya bamuteya mwasi, bamusimbire kwa chinwa cha angateta.

14. Abu bandju, bera kuika kubusa Yesu mbu: Mukangilyisi, chwishi kwa wende wateta myasi ya kanangana, kanji wende wakangilyisa e bandju e myasi ya Ongo era bemire kunde bakulyikira kwa binemire. Kanji utobaa na mundju usibya, bushi utalaa ku bukulu-kulu bwa mundju. Rero, uchwuburaa kute usene kw'ono mwasi: E mwaso wechwu achwula emerere nesi atemerere kunde chwafuta e mbarata era mwa mwami kaisari? Esi mbarata, chwemire kunde chwafutasi nesi nanga?

15. Si Yesu bushi abaa eshi kwa abu bandju bachwula batebanyi, era kubabura mbu: Chi chachwuma mwanyiteya e myasi bacha? munyireteraa chikorota chiuma cha buteya bwa dinari, nyilole kuchi.

16. Bera kumuretera chiuma. Era kubabusa mbu: Chine chihuhanyi n'e lyine sina bilyi kw'e chine chikoroto, bilyi byande? Nabo mbu: Bilyi bya mwami kaisari.

17. Yesu kukwera kubabura

허로디, 짜시야 바무더야 먀시, 바무시삐러 과 찌놔 짜 아까더다.

14. 아부 바뉴, 버라 구이가 구부사 여수 뿌: 무가삐레시, 쮜씨 과 워떠 와더다 먀시 야 가나까나, 가찌 워떠 와가삐레사 어 바뉴 어 먀시 야 오꼬 어라 버미러 구떠 바구레기라 과 비너미러. 가찌 우도바아 나 무뉴 우시뱌, 부씨 우다똬아 구 부구루-구루 봐 무뉴. 러로, 우쭈부라아 구더 우서너 교노 먀시: 어 먀소 워쭈 아쭐라 어머러러 너시 아더머러러 구떠 좌푸다 어 빠라다 어라 먀 먀미 가이사리? 어시 빠라다, 쮀미러 구떠 좌푸다시 너시 나까?

15. 시 여수 부씨 아바아 어씨 과 아부 바뉴 바쭐롸 바더바네, 어라 구바부라 뿌: 찌 짜쭐마 먀네더야 어 먀시 바짜? 무네러더라아 찌고로다 찌우마 짜 부더야 봐 디나리, 네로뻐 구찌.

16. 버라 구무러더라 찌우마. 어라 구바부사 뿌: 찌너 찌후하네 너 레너 시나 비레 궈 찌너 찌고로도, 비레 뱌뻐? 나보 뿌: 비레 뱌 먀미 가이사리.

17. 여수 구궈라 구바부라 뿌:

14. They came to him and said, "Teacher, we know you are a man of integrity. You aren't swayed by men, because you pay no attention to who they are; but you teach the way of God in accordance with the truth. Is it right to pay taxes to Caesar or not?

15. Should we pay or shouldn't we?" But Jesus knew their hypocrisy. "Why are you trying to trap me?" he asked. "Bring me a denarius and let me look at it."

16. They brought the coin, and he asked them, "Whose portrait is this? And whose inscription?" "Caesar's," they replied.

17. Then Jesus said to

mbu: Rero, mundaa mweresa kaisari bya bilyi byai, mwaneresa na Ongo bya bilyi byai. Oyu mwakure wa Yesu, era kubashishasa busese.

E bandju babusa era luulu s'e kwomoka

18. Era nyuma s'ebi, basadukayo bauma bera kuikira Yesu. Abu basadukayo, bu bende bateta mbu e bafu batakomwoke. Bera kumubusa mbu:

19. Mukangilyisi, musa atetaa mwa Mwaso wechwu mbu akaba e mundju angafa busira kubuta mwana usibya na mukai, byemire mulumuna wai engire e muhumba-kasi weshibire, chasiya abuchire mukulu wai e bana.

20. Rero, kwabaa batabana balyinda ba bula buuma. Efula yera kuhwera mukasi. Ei fula, yera kufa busira kubuta mwana usibya.

21. Mulumuna ola wabaa umuhubako, era kwengira oyu muhumba-kasi. Nai era kufa busira kumubutako. Byera kunaba bacha kwa wa kahachwu,

22. Na ku boshi kwa babaa banalyi balyinda. Abu balume balyinda boshi kwa banatolaa

러로, 무따아 뭐러사 가이사리 뱌 비쩨 뱌이, 뫄너러사 나 오꼬 뱌 비쩨 뱌이. 오유 뫄구러 와 여수, 어라 구바씨싸사 부서서.

어 바뉴 바부사 어라 루우루 서 고모가

18. 어라 뉴마 서비, 바사두가요 바우마 버라 구이기라 여수. 아부 바사두가요, 부 버떠 바더다 뿌 어 바푸 바다고모거. 버라 구무부사 뿌:

19. 무가찌레시, 무사 아더다아 뫄 마소 워쭈 뿌 아가바 어 무뉴 아꾸파 부시라 구부다 뫄나 우시뱌 나 무가이, 벼미러 무루무나 와이 어찌러 어 무후빠-가시 워씨비러, 짜시야 아부찌러 무구루 와이 어 바나.

20. 러로, 과바아 바다바나 바쩨따 바 부좌 부우마. 어푸좌 여라 구훠라 무가시. 어이 푸좌, 여라 구파 부시라 구부다 뫄나 우시뱌.

21. 무루무나 오좌 와바아 우무후바고, 어라 궈찌라 오유 무후빠-가시. 나이 어라 구파 부시라 구무부다고. 벼라 구나바 바짜 과 와 가하쭉,

22. 나 구 보씨 과 바바아 바나레 바쩨따. 아부 바루머 바쩨따 보씨 과 바나도좌아

them, "Give to Caesar what is Caesar's and to God what is God's." And they were amazed at him.

18. Then the Sadducees, who say there is no resurrection, came to him with a question.

19. "Teacher," they said, "Moses wrote for us that if a man's brother dies and leaves a wife but no children, the man must marry the widow and have children for his brother.

20. Now there were seven brothers. The first one married and died without leaving any children.

21. The second one married the widow, but he also died, leaving no child. It was the same with the third.

22. In fact, none of the seven left any children. Last of all, the woman died too.

oyu mukasi, kutabaa chiro na muuma ola wamubutaaku mwana usibya. Chasinjire, ola mukasi nai, era kufa.

23. Rero, e lusuku e bafu bakwomoka, oyu mukasi akere aba wande? Bushi abu balume balyinda boshi, banamuhweraa.

24. Yesu na imbu: Mwauwirwe busese, bushi muteshi e myasi era y'anjikirwe mwa maanjiko mabuya-buya, kanji muteshi n'e buashi bwa Ongo.

25. Bushi mango e bafu bakomwoka, bakaba nga bamalaika b'okwa nguba. Batakachihwere nesi kuhwelyibwa.

26. Kanji, bushi n'e myasi yerekere e kwomoka kw'e bafu, mutafura kusoma mwa Mwaso wa musa, e mwasi era itechire era luulu s'e haka lya lyabaa lyakorera? Ongo aburaa Musa mbu: Nyono nyi Ongo wa abrahamu, na wa isaka, na wa yakobo.

27. Yesu era kunaendekera ateta mbu: Ongo atachwula Ongo wa bafu, si achwula Ongo w'e bandju ba basene! Rero, mwabo mwauwirwe busese!

오유 무가시, 구다바아 찌로 나 무우마 오롸 와무부다아구 마나 우시뱌. 짜시찌러, 오롸 무가시 나이, 어라 구파.

23. 러로, 어 루수구 어 바푸 바곰모가, 오유 무가시 아거러 아바 와떠? 부씨 아부 바루머 바레따 보씨, 바나무훠라아.

24. 여수 나 이뿌: 똬우위뤄 부서서, 부씨 무더씨 어 먀시 어라 야찌기뤄 똬 마아찌고 마부야-부야, 가찌 무더씨 너 부아씨 봐 오꼬.

25. 부씨 마꼬 어 바푸 바고모가, 바가바 까 바마롸이가 보과 읏바. 바다가찌훠러 너시 구훠레봐.

26. 가찌, 부씨 너 먀시 여러거러 어 꼬모가 궈 바푸, 무다푸라 구소마 똬 똬소 와 무사, 어 똬시 어라 이더찌러 어라 루우룰 서 하가 랴 랴바아 랴고러라? 오꼬 아부라아 무사 뿌: 뇨노 내 오꼬 와 아부라하무, 나 와 이사가, 나 와 야고보.

27. 여수 어라 구나어떠거라 아더다 뿌: 오꼬 아다쭐라 오꼬 와 바푸, 시 아쭐롸 오꼬 워 바뚜 바 바서너! 러로, 똬보 똬우위뤄 부서서!

23. At the resurrection whose wife will she be, since the seven were married to her?"

24. Jesus replied, "Are you not in error because you do not know the Scriptures or the power of God?

25. When the dead rise, they will neither marry nor be given in marriage; they will be like the angels in heaven.

26. Now about the dead rising--have you not read in the book of Moses, in the account of the bush, how God said to him, 'I am the God of Abraham, the God of Isaac, and the God of Jacob'?

27. He is not the God of the dead, but of the living. You are badly mistaken!"

E muomba munene kureza ilyikabo

어 무오빠 무너너 구러자 이레가보

28. Mukangilyisi muuma w'e Mwaso, abaa omvire kwa Yesu aenda e bwaka, n'okwa aakula kubuya abu basadukayo. Bushi n'oku, era kuchifunda ofu nai, na amubusa mbu: e Walyiya! Mwa miombi yoshi, muomba muchiye I uchwula urenzise einji yoshi?

28. 무가삐레시 무우마 워 뫄소, 아바아 오삐러 과 여수 아어따 어 봐가, 노과 아아구꽈 구부야 아부 바사두가요. 부씨 노구, 어라 구찌푸따 오푸 나이, 나 아무부사 뿌: 어 와레야! 뫄 미오삐 요씨, 무오빠 무찌여 이 우쭈꽈 우러씨서 어이찌 요씨?

28. One of the teachers of the law came and heard them debating. Noticing that Jesus had given them a good answer, he asked him, "Of all the commandments, which is the most important?"

29. Yesu na imbu: E muomba mubere-bere I yono: Mubenyi isiraeli mumvaa! Enawechwu Ongo, yeine ina Enawechwu.

29. 여수 나 이뿌: 어 무오빠 무버러-버러 이 요노: 무버네 이시라어리 무빠아! 어나워쭈 오꼬, 여이너 이나 어나워쭈.

29. "The most important one," answered Jesus, "is this: 'Hear, O Israel, the Lord our God, the Lord is one.

30. Oyu Enawenyu Ongo, undaa wamusima mwa muchima wao woshi, n'omwa mianyisa yao yoshi, n'omwa bwenge bwao boshi, n'okwa misi yao yoshi.

30. 오유 어나워뉴 오꼬, 우따아 와무시마 뫄 무찌마 와오 온씨, 노뫄 미아니사 야오 요씨, 노뫄 붸어 봐오 보씨, 노과 미시 야오 요씨.

30. Love the Lord your God with all your heart and with all your soul and with all your mind and with all your strength.'

31. N'e muomba wakabilyi, I yono: Undaa wasima na mulyikenyu ng'okwa achwula uchisimire weine. Ei miomba ebilyi, kutalyi inji era irenzisei.

31. 너 무오빠 와가비레, 이 요노: 우따아 와시마 나 무레거뉴 꼬과 아쭈꽈 우찌시미러 워이너. 어이 미오빠 어비레, 구다레 이찌 어라 이러씨서이.

31. The second is this: 'Love your neighbor as yourself.' There is no commandment greater than these."

32. Oyu mukangilyisi w'e Mwaso, era kwire abura Yesu mbu: N'echi, mukangilyisi watechire kubuya kwa kulyi Ongo muuma oshao, kutachilyi na unji.

32. 오유 무가삐레시 워 뫄소, 어라 귀러 아부라 여수 뿌: 너찌, 무가삐레시 와더찌러 구부야 과 구레 오꼬 무우마 오싸오, 구다찌레 나 우찌.

32. "Well said, teacher," the man replied. "You are right in saying that God is one and there is no other but him.

33. Kubinalyi, e mundju emire kunde asima Ongo mwa muchima wai woshi, n'omwa bwenge bwai boshi, n'okwa misi yai yoshi. Kanji emire kunde asima mulyikabo ng'okwa achwula achisimire yeine. Ekuira bacha ku kukulu kwa kwana e michwulo era isiresibwe, nesi einji michwulo yoshi.

34. Mango Yesu alolaa kwa oyu mukangilyisi akwire na bwenge, era kwire amubura mbu: Woyo utalyi bure n'e Bwami bwa Ongo. Era nyuma s'ebi, chiro kukachiba mundju usibya ola waereresaa ahuba kubusa Yesu mwasi.

Kirisito I Enawabo Daudi

35. Mango Yesu abaa akangilyisa e bandju mwa chibuwa ch'e luhu lwa Ongo, era kubabusa mbu: Che ch'enjire chachwuma e bakangilyisi b'e Mwaso bateta mbu kirisito alyi Mwenyi mwami Daudi?

36. Si Daudi yeine bushi abaa akoresibwa n'e Muchima mubuya-buya, atetaa mbu: Enawechwu Ongo aburaa enawechwu mbu: Wikalaa kwa lunda lwanyi lw'e malyo, kuikira nyibike e barenda bao

---

33. 구비나례, 어 무뚜 어미러 구떠 아시마 오꼬 롸 무찌마 와이 옻씨, 노롸 붜뻐 바이 보씨, 노과 미시 야이 요씨. 가찌 어미러 구떠 아시마 무레가보 꼬과 아쭈롸 아찌시미러 여이너. 어구이라 바짜 구 구구루 과 과나 어 미쭈론 어라 이시러시붸, 너시 어이찌 미쭈론 요씨.

34. 마꼬 여수 아로롸아 과 오유 무가삐례시 아귀러 나 붜뻐, 어라 귀러 아무부라 뿌: 오요 우다례 부러 너 봐미 봐 오꼬. 어라 뉴마 서비, 찌로 구가찌바 무뚜 우시뱌 오롸 와어러러사아 아후바 구부사 여수 마시.

기리시도 이 어나와보 다우디

35. 마꼬 여수 아바아 아가삐례사 어 바뚜 롸 찌부와 쩌 루후 롸 오꼬, 어라 구바부사 뿌: 쩌 쩌찌러 짜쭈마 어 바가삐례시 버 롸소 바더다 뿌 기리시도 아례 뭐니 롸미 다우디?

36. 시 다우디 여이너 부씨 아바아 아고러시봐 너 무찌마 무부야-부야, 아더다아 뿌: 어나워쭈 오꼬 아부라아 어나워쭈 뿌: 위가롸아 과 루따 롸네 뤄 마론, 구이기라 네비거 어 바러따 바오 구바

---

33. To love him with all your heart, with all your understanding and with all your strength, and to love your neighbor as yourself is more important than all burnt offerings and sacrifices."

34. When Jesus saw that he had answered wisely, he said to him, "You are not far from the kingdom of God." And from then on no one dared ask him any more questions.

35. While Jesus was teaching in the temple courts, he asked, "How is it that the teachers of the law say that the Christ is the son of David?

36. David himself, speaking by the Holy Spirit, declared: " 'The Lord said to my Lord: "Sit at my right hand until I put your enemies under your feet." '

kuba chisimachiro chao.

37. Daudi yeine atetaa mbu kirisito alyi enawabo. Rero, kute kw'oyu kirisito angahuba kuba mwana wai? Bandju banene busese babaa b'enjire bomvilyisa e mwasi ya Yesu na lumoo lunene.

Yesu akangilyisa era luulu s'e bubi bw'e bakangilyisi b'e mwaso

38. Mango abaa enjire abakangilyisa, era kunde ababura mbu: Mundaa mwachilanga kwa bakangilyisi b'e Mwaso, bushi bachwula basimire kutamba bembese maropo marerere, kanji bachwula basime kunde bakesibwa n'e chwunda mwa bisiki by'e nyibuanano.

39. Kanji mwa mashenge mabo, bachwula basimire kwikala mwa bifumbi by'era muhondo. N'omwa bisiki by'e lyinye, bachwula basimire kwikala kwa bifumbi by'e chwunda.

40. Bende banyaa e bikulo by'e bahumbakasi, na kunde baira memo marerere chasiya balorekaneko era muhondo s'e bandju. Bushi n'oku, Ongo akabachinjibusa busese!

찌시마찌로 짜오.

37. 다우디 여이너 아더다아 뿌 기리시도 아례 어나와보. 러로, 구더 교유 기리시도 아까후바 구바 뫄나 와이? 바쭈 바너너 부서서 바바아 버찌러 보메레사 어 뫄시 야 여수 나 루모오 루너너.

여수 아가끼레사 어라 루우루 서 부비 붜 바가끼레시 버 뫄소

38. 마오 아바아 어찌러 아바가끼레사, 어라 구떠 아바부라 뿌: 무따아 뫄찌라까 과 바가끼레시 버 뫄소, 부씨 바쭈라 바시미러 구다빠 버뻐서 마로포 마러러러, 가찌 바쭈라 바시머 구떠 바거시봐 너 쭈따 뫄 비시기 벼 네부아나노.

39. 가찌 뫄 마셔꺼 마보, 바쭈라 바시미러 귀가라 뫄 비푸삐 벼라 무호또. 노뫄 비시기 벼 레녀, 바쭈라 바시미러 귀가라 과 비푸삐 벼 쭈따.

40. 버떠 바냐아 어 비구로 벼 바후빠가시, 나 구떠 바이라 머모 마러러러 짜시야 바로러가너고 어라 무호또 서 바쭈. 부씨 노구, 오오 아가바찌찌부사 부서서!

37. David himself calls him 'Lord.' How then can he be his son?" The large crowd listened to him with delight.

38. As he taught, Jesus said, "Watch out for the teachers of the law. They like to walk around in flowing robes and be greeted in the marketplaces,

39. and have the most important seats in the synagogues and the places of honor at banquets.

40. They devour widows' houses and for a show make lengthy prayers. Such men will be punished most severely."

E michwulo y'e muhumba-kasi	***어 미쭈로 여 무후빠-가시***	
41. Chasinda, Yesu era kwekala alangusa kwa sanduku era bende bachwulyira mw'e michwulo. Era kulola kwa bandju benjire babika e buteya mwei sanduku. Baare banene bera kubikamu buteya bunene.	41. 짜시따, 여수 어라 궤가라 아라우사 과 사뚜구 어라 버떠 바쭈레라 뭐 미쭈로. 어라 구로롸 과 바쭈 버찌러 바비가 어 부더야 뭐이 사뚜구. 바아러 바너너 버라 구비가무 부더야 부너너.	41. Jesus sat down opposite the place where the offerings were put and watched the crowd putting their money into the temple treasury. Many rich people threw in large amounts.
42. Muhumba-kasi muuma wa mukene nai era kuika. Oyu muhumba-kasi nai, era kubika bikoroto bibilyi bya buteya mwei sanduku. Ebi bikoroto, byabaa bikunganyisibwe mwa milyinga, kanji byabaa byete mufa mueke busese.	42. 무후빠-가시 무우마 와 무거너 나이 어라 구이가. 오유 무후빠-가시 나이, 어라 구비가 비고로도 비비레 뱌 부더야 뭐이 사뚜구. 어비 비고로도, 뱌바아 비구까네시붜 뫄 미레아, 가찌 뱌바아 벼더 무파 무어거 부서서.	42. But a poor widow came and put in two very small copper coins,worth only a fraction of a penny.
43. Yesu kukwera kwamaala e banafunzi bai, era kubabura mbu: Kubinalyi, nababura kwa Ono muhumbakasi w'e mukene iwachwulyire Ongo binene kurenza e banji bandju boshi.	43. 여수 구궈라 과마아롸 어 바나푸찌 바이, 어라 구바부라 쁘: 구비나레, 나바부라 과 오노 무후빠가시 워 무거너 이와쭈레러 오꼬 비너너 구러싸 어 바찌 바쭈 보씨.	43. Calling his disciples to him, Jesus said, "I tell you the truth, this poor widow has put more into the treasury than all the others.
44. Bushi ebanji boshi bachwulaa Ongo e mwango ola watalaa kwa bikulo byabo. Si ono muhumba-kasi mwa bukene bwai yeke, achwulyire Ongo byoshi bya bingamuasise kulama.	44. 부씨 어바찌 보씨 바쭈롸아 오꼬 어 뫄꼬 오롸 와다롸아 과 비구로 뱌보. 시 오노 무후빠-가시 뫄 부거너 봐이 여거, 아쭈레러 오꼬 뵤씨 뱌 비까무아시서 구롸마.	44. They all gave out of their wealth; but she, out of her poverty, put in everything--all she had to live on."

Mariko Chikono 13

Yesu ateta kwa e luhu lwa Ongo lungahandjulyibwa

1. Mango Yesu abaa era atenga mwa chibuya ch'e luhu lwa Ongo, mwanafunzi wai muuma era kumubura mbu: Mukangilyisi, ulolaa kw'ene nyumba ingana! ulolaa n'okwa makoi ma maiimbire!

2. Yesu na imbu: Usene kwei nyumba yoshi? Rero, kutashibe koi era luulu sa lyilyikabo, byoshi bingahandjulyibwa!

Bya bikaika mwa suku s'e businda

3. Mango Yesu abaa ekese kwa ndjulungu y'e Miseituni, kwa lunda lw'era luhu lwa Ongo lulyi, petero, na yakobo, na yowana, na andereya, bera kumuikira ala abaa alyi yeine. Bera kumubusa mbu:

4. Enawechwu! Uchwubura, mangochi ei myasi ikaba, na kalorero kachiye, kukakachwulosa kwa ebi byoshi byahonda kuba.

5. Yesu era kutangilyisa ababura mbu: Mumenyaa! kutabaa mundju usibya ola ukabengeera!

6. Bushi bandju banene

마리고 찌고노 13

여수 아더다 과 어 루후 똬 오꼬 루빠하뚜쀀똬

1. 마꼬 여수 아바아 어라 아더빠 똬 찌부야 쩌 루후 똬 오꼬, 모나푸씨 와이 무우마 어라 구무부라 뿌: 무가삐쀀시, 우뢰똬아 궈너 뉴빠 이빠나! 우뢰똬아 노과 마고이 마 마이이쀀러!

2. 여수 나 이뿌: 우서너 궈이 뉴빠 요씨? 러로, 구다씨버 고이 어라 루우루 사 레레가보, 뵤씨 비빠하뚜쀀똬!

뱌 비가이가 똬 수구 서 부시따

3. 마꼬 여수 아바아 어거서 과 뚜루우 여 미서이두니, 과 루따 뭐라 루후 똬 오꼬 루레, 퍼더로, 나 야고보, 나 요와나, 나 아떠러야, 버라 구무이기라 아롸 아바아 아뤠 여이너. 버라 구무부사 뿌:

4. 어나워쭈! 우쭈부라, 마꼬찌 어이 먀시 이가바, 나 가뢰러로 가찌여, 구가가쭈뢰사 과 어비 뵤씨 뱌호따 구바.

5. 여수 어라 구다삐쀀사 아바부라 뿌: 무머냐아! 구다바아 무뚜 우시뱌 오롸 우가버어어라!

6. 부씨 바뚜 바너너 바가바하

Mark Chapter 13[NIV]

1. As he was leaving the temple, one of his disciples said to him, "Look, Teacher! What massive stones! What magnificent buildings!"

2. "Do you see all these great buildings?" replied Jesus. "Not one stone here will be left on another; every one will be thrown down."

3. As Jesus was sitting on the Mount of Olives opposite the temple, Peter, James, John and Andrew asked him privately,

4. "Tell us, when will these things happen? And what will be the sign that they are all about to be fulfilled?"

5. Jesus said to them: "Watch out that no one deceives you.

6. Many will come in my

bakabaha mw'e sina lyanyi. Abu bandju, bakende bachitonga mbu: Nyono nyi kirisito! Bakengeera bandju banene.

7. Mw'esi suku, mukomva e bandju bateteresa era lulu s'e bita mwa bisiki byoshi, si mutobaa bushi ebi byoshi kwemire biike. Si ebyera, bikaba bitatechire mbu e businda bw'e butala bwaikire.

8. Chio chiuma chikaya kutabalyira e chinji. Na bwami buuma bukaya kutabalyira e bunji. Mubisiki binene, mukarenga misisi, mukaika na bulyio. Ebi byoshi, bikanaba nga ndagilyiso y'e mukero.

9. Si mwabo, muchilangaa bushi mungende mwekibwa era muhondo s'e baishi b'e manja babachinjibuse. Bangende babapunjira mwa mashenge, na kunde mwekibwa era muhondo s'e bakulu-kulu b'e chio, n'era muhondo s'e bami bushi nanyi. Bushi n'oku, mungaba babei banyi era muhondo sabo.

10. Bushi byemire e Mwasi mubuya-buya ahubanganyisibwe tanga kwa bandju b'e mbaa soshi.

뭐 시나 쨔네. 아부 바뉴, 바거뻐 바찌도빠 뿌: 뇨노 니 기리시도! 바거뻐어라 바뉴 바너너.

7. 뭐시 수구, 무고빠 어 바뉴 바더더러사 어라 룰루 서 비다 뫄 비시기 뵤씨, 시 무도바아 부씨 어비 뵤씨 궈미러 비이거. 시 어벼라, 비가바 비다더찌러 뿌 어 부시따 붜 부다꽈 봐이기러.

8. 찌오 찌우마 찌가야 구다바꼐라 어 찌찌. 나 봐미 부우마 부가야 구다바꼐라 어 부찌. 무비시기 비너너, 무가러빠 미시시, 무가이가 나 부꼐오. 어비 뵤씨, 비가나바 빠 따지꼐소 여 무거로.

9. 시 먀보, 무찌꽈빠아 부씨 무뻐너 뭐기봐 어라 무호또 서 바이씨 버 먀쨔 바바찌찌부서. 바뻐너 바바푸찌라 뫄 마써뻐, 나 구너 뭐기봐 어라 무호또 서 바구루-구루 버 찌오, 너라 무호또 서 바미 부씨 나니. 부씨 노구, 무꽈바 바버이 바네 어라 무호또 사보.

10. 부씨 벼미러 어 먀시 무부야-부야 아후바꽈네시붜 다빠 과 바뉴 버 빠아 소씨.

name, claiming, 'I am he,' and will deceive many.

7. When you hear of wars and rumors of wars, do not be alarmed. Such things must happen, but the end is still to come.

8. Nation will rise against nation, and kingdom against kingdom. There will be earthquakes in various places, and famines. These are the beginning of birth pains.

9. "You must be on your guard. You will be handed over to the local councils and flogged in the synagogues. On account of me you will stand before governors and kings as witnesses to them.

10. And the gospel must first be preached to all nations.

11. Na mango bangende babasimba chasiya babeke era muhondo s'e baishi b'e manja, mutendaa mwachibusa mbu chi mungateta. Si e binwa bya mungeresibwa mw'echi chihangi bi munatetaa. N'ebi binwa, bitatenge mwa ndanda senyu, si e Muchima mubuya-buya iungaberesabi.

12. E mundju akechisa munyakabo. N'eshe w'e mwana akechisa e mwana wai. N'e bana nabo, bakahuba ngabo s'e basere babo, na kubechisa.

13. E bandju boshi, bakabahomba bushi nanyi. Si ola ukasesa e muchima kuikira kwa businda, akanunulyibwa.

E malyibuko masibu

14. Yesu era kuendekera ateta mbu: Mw'esi suku mukalola kw'ola bende belyika mbu Mubalasi w'e kuhandjula emenze mwa chisiki cha abaa atemire kubamo. Ola wasoma ene myasi, amenyereraa kwa itechire. Rero, ba kakaba balyi e yudeya, bahairaa mwa miruko.

15. N'ola ukaba ulyi kwa butala-tala bw'e nyumba yai, atachandaalaa mbu aya kutola kandju mwa nyumba.

11. 나 마꼬 바뻐떠 바바시빠 짜시야 바버거 어라 무호또 서 바이씨 버 마짜, 무더따아 꽈찌부사 뿌 찌 무까더다. 시 어 비뇨 뱌 무뻐러시봐 뭐찌 찌하삐 비 무나더다아. 너비 비뇨, 비다더뻐 뫄 따따 서뉴, 시 어 무찌마 무부야-부야 이우까버러사비.

12. 어 무뚜 아거찌사 무냐가보. 너써 워 뫄나 아거찌사 어 뫄나 와이. 너 바나 나보, 바가후바 까보 서 바서러 바보, 나 구버찌사.

13. 어 바뚜 보씨, 바가바호빠 부씨 나니. 시 오꽈 우가서사 어 무찌마 구이기라 과 부시따, 아가누누쪠봐.

어 마쪠부고 마시부

14. 여수 어라 구어떠거라 아더다 뿌: 뭐시 수구 무가로꽈 교꽈 버떠 버쪠가 뿌 무바꽈시 워 구하쭈꽈 어머써 뫄 찌시기 짜 아바아 아더미러 구바모. 오꽈 와소마 어너 먀시, 아머녀러라아 과 이더찌러. 러로, 바 바가바 바쪠 어 유더야, 바하이라아 뫄 미루고.

15. 노꽈 우가바 우쪠 과 부다꽈-다꽈 붜 뉴빠 야이, 아다짜따아꽈라아 뿌 아야 구도꽈 가뚜 뫄 뉴빠.

11. Whenever you are arrested and brought to trial, do not worry beforehand about what to say. Just say whatever is given you at the time, for it is not you speaking, but the Holy Spirit.

12. "Brother will betray brother to death, and a father his child. Children will rebel against their parents and have them put to death.

13. All men will hate you because of me, but he who stands firm to the end will be saved.

14. "When you see 'the abomination that causes desolation'standing where it does not belong--let the reader understand--then let those who are in Judea flee to the mountains.

15. Let no one on the roof of his house go down or enter the house to take anything out.

16. N'ola ukaba ulyi mw'ehwa, nai atachifulukaa kwa wai mbu aya kutola e kochi lyai.

17. Mw'esi suku, bukaba buanya kwa bakasi ba bakaba bete e makure na ba bakaba bonza!

18. Ebi byoshi, mundaa mwema Ongo chasiya bitabaa mwa suku s'e mbeo.

19. Bushi esi suku, sikaba sa malyibuko manene busese ma matafuraa kuba, kutengera mango Ongo abumbaa e butala kuikira lwarero. Kutakachibe na manji malyibuko ma malyi ngamo.

20. Rero esi suku, akaba enawechwu atangailyiresi kuba sieke, kutangabere chiro na mundju usibya ola unganunulyibwe. Si asiilyire sieke bushi n'e bandju bai ba achilondorere.

21. Rero mw'esi suku, akaba mundju murebe angababura mbu: Mulolaa! Kirisito yono ulyi wano! nesi mbu: Mulolaa! Yola ulyi wala! mutamwemereraa.

22. Bushi kukaulukira bandju ba bakende bafula bisha mbu bubera Kirisito, kwanaulukira na barebi ba bisha. Abu boshi, bakende baira bisomerano,

16. 노퐈 우가바 우쮀 뭐화, 나이 아다찌푸루가아 과 와이 뿌 아야 구도롸 어 고찌 퍄이.

17. 뭐시 수구, 부가바 부아냐 과 바가시 바 바가바 버더 어 마구러 나 바 바가바 보쌰!

18. 어비 뵤씨, 무따아 뭐마 오꼬 짜시야 비다바아 뫄 수구 서 뻐오.

19. 부씨 어시 수구, 시가바 사 마쮀부고 마너너 부서서 마 마다푸라아 구바, 구더꺼라 마꼬 오꼬 아부빠아 어 부다퐈 구이기라 퐈러로. 구다가찌버 나 마찌 마쮀부고 마 마쮀 까모.

20. 러로 어시 수구, 아가바 어나워쭈 아다꺄이쮀러시 구바 시어거, 구다꺄버러 찌로 나 무뚜 우시뱌 오퐈 우꺄누누쮀붜. 시 아시이쮀러 시어거 부씨 너 바뚜 바이 바 아찌론또러러.

21. 러로 뭐시 수구, 아가바 무뚜 무러버 아꺄바부라 뿌: 무론퐈아! 기리시도 요노 우쮀 와노! 너시 뿌: 무론퐈아! 요퐈 우쮀 와퐈! 무다뭐머러라아.

22. 부씨 구가우루기라 바뚜 바 바거떠 바푸퐈 비싸 뿌 부버라 기리시도, 과나우루기라 나 바러비 바 비싸. 아부 뵤씨, 바거떠

16. Let no one in the field go back to get his cloak.

17. How dreadful it will be in those days for pregnant women and nursing mothers!

18. Pray that this will not take place in winter,

19. because those will be days of distress unequaled from the beginning, when God created the world, until now--and never to be equaled again.

20. If the Lord had not cut short those days, no one would survive. But for the sake of the elect, whom he has chosen, he has shortened them.

21. At that time if anyone says to you, 'Look, here is the Christ!' or, 'Look, there he is!' do not believe it.

22. For false Christs and false prophets will appear and perform signs and miracles to deceive the elect--if that were possible.

chasiya akaba bingaalyikana bengeere n'e bandju ba Ongo alondore. 바이라 비소머라노, 짜시야 아가바 비까아쩨가나 버어어러 너 바뉴 바 오꼬 아르또러.

23. Si mwabo, mumenyaa bushi nababilyire ei myasi Yoshi mira! 23. 시 뫄보, 무머냐아 부씨 나바비쩨러 어이 먀시 요씨 미라! 23. So be on your guard; I have told you everything ahead of time.

E kubaha kw'e Mwana w'e mundju
어 구바하 귀 뫄나 워 무뿌

24. Yesu era kuteta kanji mbu: Mw'esi suku, era nyuma s'amu malyibuko, Esuba, lyikahuba musimya. N'e mwesi, atakachikole. 24. 여수 어라 구더다 가찌 뿌: 뭐시 수구, 어라 뉴마 사무 마쩨부고, 어수바, 쩨가후바 무시먀. 너 뭐시, 아다가찌고꺼. 24. "But in those days, following that distress, " 'the sun will be darkened, and the moon will not give its light;

25. E ngununu nasi, sikatowanga kwa nguba. Na byoshi bya byete e buashi kwa nguba, bikalyingitana. 25. 어 웅누누 나시, 시가도와까 과 웅바. 나 뵤씨 벼더 어 부아씨 과 웅바, 비가쩨끼다나. 25. the stars will fall from the sky, and the heavenly bodies will be shaken.'

26. Chasinda mw'esi suku, e bandju bakalola kwa by'e mwana w'e Mundju, n'eshire mwa lumbumbu, nyete na buashi bunene na bulangare. 26. 짜시따 뭐시 수구, 어 바뉴 바가로꽈 과 벼 뫄나 워 무뿌, 너씨러 뫄 루뿌뿌, 녀더 나 부아씨 부너너 나 부라까러. 26. "At that time men will see the Son of Man coming in clouds with great power and glory.

27. Nyikachwuma e bamalaika banyi bahandabane mwa butala boshi, n'okwa nguba Yoshi chasiya babuanyanye e bandju boshi ba nalondoere. 27. 네가쭈마 어 바마꽈이가 바네 바하따바너 뫄 부다꽈 보씨, 노과 웅바 요씨 짜시야 바부아냐녀 어 바뉴 보씨 바 나로또어러. 27. And he will send his angels and gather his elect from the four winds, from the ends of the earth to the ends of the heavens.

E muanyi w'e muchi w'e tini
어 무아니 워 무찌 워 디니

28. Muchikangilyisaa kurengera e muanyi w'e muchi w'e tini: oyu muchi, mango e matabi mao mende matanganyika n'e bichi byao byatabaana, mwende mwamenyerera kwa kasi e 28. 무찌가끼쩨사아 구러꺼라 어 무아네 워 무찌 워 디니: 오유 무찌, 마꼬 어 마다비 마오 머더 마다까네가 너 비찌 뱌오 뱌다바아나, 뭐더 뫄머녀러라 과 가시 어 찌아네로 찌부야 찌쩨 오푸. 28. "Now learn this lesson from the fig tree: As soon as its twigs get tender and its leaves come out, you know that summer is near.

chianyiro chibuya chilyi ofu.

29. kunoku, mango mukalola kw'ei myasi Yoshi, mwanamenyerera kwa nyi mwana w'e Mundju nera nyilyi ofu busese.

30. Kubinalyi, nababura kw'e bandju b'e sine suku batafe boshi era muhondo ei myasi Yoshi itasa kuba.

31. E nguba n'e butala bikarenga, si e myasi yanyi yeke, itakarenge chiro na hicha.

Ongo yeine iuneshi e lusuku lw'e businda

32. Kutalyi mundju usibya ola wishi olu lusuku nesi e chihangi cha ei myasi ikaba. Anabe n'e bamalaika b'okwa nguba, nanyi nyi Mwana w'e mundju, kutalyi ola wishi, si tata yeine iuneshi.

33. Mumenyaa! Muchilangaa bushi muteshi mangochi ei myasi ikaba.

34. Ebyera bikaba nga muanyi wa mundju muuma ola wabaa wabalama. Oyu mundju, era kurekera e baanda bai e nyumba, chasiya bemangirei. Era kweresa chira mukosi ewai mulyimo. Chasinda, era kubura e mulanzi w'e lwisi mbu achilanga-langaa.

29. 구노구, 마꼬 무가로꽈 궈이 먀시 요씨, 뫄나머녀러라 과 네 뫄나 워 무뚜 너라 네쩨 오푸 부서서.

30. 구비나쩨, 나바부라 궈 바뚜 버 시너 수구 바다퍼 보씨 어라 무호또 어이 먀시 요씨 이다사 구바.

31. 어 꾸바 너 부다꽈 비가러꽈, 시 어 먀시 야네 여거, 이다가러꺼 찌로 나 히짜.

오꼬 여이너 이우너씨 어 루수구 뤄 부시따

32. 구비꿰 무뚜 우시뱌 오라 위씨 오루 루수구 너시 어 찌하ꙓ 짜 어이 먀시 이가바. 아나버 너 바마꽈이가 보과 꾸바, 나네 네 뫄나 워 무뚜, 구다쩨 오라 위씨, 시 다다 여이너 이우너씨.

33. 무머냐아! 무찌꽈아아 부씨 무더씨 마꼬찌 어이 먀시 이가바.

34. 어벼라 비가바 꽈 무아네 와 무뚜 무우마 오라 와바아 와바꽈마. 오유 무뚜, 어라 구러거라 어 바아따 바이 어 뉴빠, 짜시야 버마ꙓ러이. 어라 궈러사 찌라 무고시 어와이 무쩨모. 짜시따, 어라 구부라 어 무꽈씨 워 뤼시 뿌 아찌꽈마-꽈ꙓ아.

29. Even so, when you see these things happening, you know that it is near, right at the door.

30. I tell you the truth, this generation will certainly not pass away until all these things have happened.

31. Heaven and earth will pass away, but my words will never pass away.

32. "No one knows about that day or hour, not even the angels in heaven, nor the Son, but only the Father.

33. Be on guard! Be alert! You do not know when that time will come.

34. It's like a man going away: He leaves his house and puts his servants in charge, each with his assigned task, and tells the one at the door to keep watch.

35. Rero nenyu muchilanga-langaa! Bushi muteshi e bihangi bya ena e nyumba akafuluka. Kulyi mango angaika luolo-olo, nesi kachi-kachi ka buchwufu, nesi mango e nyaasi sende sabika, nesi mishangya-shangya.

36. Bushi n'oku, muchilanga-langaa angesha kubapamukirako chimbate, anababuana mwaonjire.

37. Ei myasi nababwilyire, naitechire bushi n'e bandju boshi: Muchilanga-langaa!

Mariko Chikono 14
E lwango lw'e kwita Yesu

1. kwabaa kweshiba suku ebilyi, e lusuku lukulu lw'e pasaka, n'e lw'e mikati era italyi mu chachu siike. E bakulu-kulu b'e bakuhanyi alauma n'e bakangilyisi b'e mwaso, bera kuhonda kute bangasimba Yesu kwa bubisho-bisho, chasiya bamwite.

2. Si babaa bateta mbu: chwutamusimbaa e lusuku lukulu, kungesha kuba lwayo lunene mwa bandju.

Mukasi muuma akaba Yesu e marashi

3. Mango Yesu abaa era alyi

---

35. 러로 너뉴 무찌롸아-롸아아! 부씨 무더씨 어 비하께 뱌 어나 어 뉴빠 아가푸루가. 구레 마꼬 아와이가 루오로로-오로, 너시 가찌-가찌 가 부쭈푸, 너시 마꼬 어 냐아시 서떠 사비가, 너시 미싸꺄-싸꺄.

36. 부씨 노구, 무찌롸아-롸아아 아꺼싸 구바파무기라고 찌빠더, 아나바부아나 뫄오찌러.

37. 어이 먀시 나바뷔레러, 나이더찌러 부씨 너 바쭈 보씨: 무찌롸아-롸아아!

마리고 찌고노 14
어 롸꼬 뤄 귀다 여수

1. 과바아 궈씨바 수구 어비레, 어 루수구 루구루 뤄 파사가, 너 뤄 미가디 어라 이다레 무 짜쭈 시이거. 어 바구루루-구루 버 바구하네 아롸우마 너 바가께레시 버 뫄소, 버라 구호따 구더 바까시빠 여수 과 부비쏘-비쏘, 짜시야 바뮈더.

2. 시 바바아 바더다 뿌: 쭈다무시빠아 어 루수구 루구루, 구꺼싸 구바 롸요 루너너 뫄 바쭈.

무가시 무우마 아가바 여수 어 마라씨

3. 마꼬 여수 아바아 어라

---

35. "Therefore keep watch because you do not know when the owner of the house will come back-- whether in the evening, or at midnight, or when the rooster crows, or at dawn.

36. If he comes suddenly, do not let him find you sleeping.

37. What I say to you, I say to everyone: 'Watch!' "

Mark Chapter 14[NIV]

1. Now the Passover and the Feast of Unleavened Bread were only two days away, and the chief priests and the teachers of the law were looking for some sly way to arrest Jesus and kill him.

2. "But not during the Feast," they said, "or the people may riot."

3. While he was in Bethany,

mwa musi w'e betaniya, era kwengiliyira mwa mwa mulume muuma mbu I simoni. Oyu simoni, abaa mubenzi-benzi. Abere Yesu era alya, kwera kuulukira mukasi muuma ete mulangi ola wabaa ukunganyisibwe mukoi lya lyikomire. Mw'oyu mulangi, mwabaa mulyi marashi ma chichiro chinene. Amu marashi, mabaa makunganyisibwe mwa bwaso bw'e muchi w'e narito, kanji mabaa matahoonganyisibwe. Chasinda, ola mukasi kuna kufuna echwe ly'ola mulangi, na atangilyisa aakaba Yesu e marashi kw'echwe.

4. Bandju bauma mwa ba babaa balyi aola, bera kuaya busese. Bera kutangilyisa babusanya mbu: Chi chachwumire bakumbya mano marashi bacha?

5. Si mangafire dinari maana mahachwu, chasinda, banasiabira e bakene! Bushi n'oku, bera kukalyiira oyu mukasi busese.

6. Si Yesu era kubabusa mbu: Chi chachwuma mwalyibusa ono mukasi bacha? Muchimurekeraa, bushi mabuya mano anyikorere.

아레 똬 무시 워 버다니야, 어라 궈삐레라 똬 똬 무루머 무우마 뿌 이 시모니. 오유 시모니, 아바아 무버씨-버씨. 아버러 여수 어라 아럈, 궈라 구우루기라 무가시 무우마 어더 무똬삐 오라 와바아 우구싸네시붜 무고이 럈 레고미러. 뫄유 무똬삐, 똬바아 무레 마라씨 마 찌찌로 찌너너. 아무 마라씨, 마바아 마구싸네시붜 똬 봐소 붜 무찌 워 나리도, 가씨 마바아 마다호오싸네시붜. 짜시따, 오라 무가시 구나 구푸나 어줴 뛰오똬 무똬삐, 나 아다삐레사 아아가바 여수 어 마라씨 궈줘.

4. 바뚜 바우마 똬 바 바바아 바레 아오똬, 버라 구아야 부서서. 버라 구다삐레사 바부사냐 뿌: 찌 짜쭈미러 바구꺄 마노 마라씨 바짜?

5. 시 마싸피러 디나리 마아나 마하쭈, 짜시따, 바나시아비라 어 바거너! 부씨 노구, 버라 구가레이라 오유 무가시 부서서.

6. 시 여수 어라 구바부사 뿌: 찌 짜쭈마 똬레부사 오노 무가시 바짜? 무찌무러거라아, 부씨 마부야 마노 아네고러러.

---

reclining at the table in the home of a man known as Simon the Leper, a woman came with an alabaster jar of very expensive perfume, made of pure nard. She broke the jar and poured the perfume on his head.

4. Some of those present were saying indignantly to one another, "Why this waste of perfume?

5. It could have been sold for more than a year's wages and the money given to the poor." And they rebuked her harshly.

6. "Leave her alone," said Jesus. "Why are you bothering her? She has done a beautiful thing to me.

7. E bakene, bakanaendekera kuba mwa kachi-kachi kenyu e suku soshi. Kanji munganabaasa e bihangi byoshi bya muhonjire. Si nyono, ndakabe nenyu e suku soshi.

7. 어 바거너, 바가나어떠거라 e구바 똬 가찌-가찌 거뉴 어 수구 소씨. 가찌 무꽈나바아사 어 비하삐 뵤씨 뱌 무호찌러. 시 뇨노, 따가버 너뉴 어 수구 소씨.

7. The poor you will always have with you, and you can help them any time you want. But you will not always have me.

8. Rero, ono mukasi ailyire ng'okwa abaa anganaala, bushi aakabire e marashi kwa mubilyi wanyi tanga kwa kukunganya e kutabwa kwanyi.

8. 러로, 오노 무가시 아이레러 꼬과 아바아 아꽈나아똬, 부씨 아아가비러 어 마라씨 과 무비레 와니 다따 과 구구꽈냐 어 구다봐 과니.

8. She did what she could. She poured perfume on my body beforehand to prepare for my burial.

9. Kubinalyi, nababura kwa mwa butala boshi, mu chira chisiki cha bakende bahubanganya mw'e Mwasi mubuya-buya, bakende bahambala era luulu s'e mwasi ola ono mukasi ailyire. Bushi n'oku, e bandju batakamwebilyire.

9. 구비나뗴, 나바부라 과 똬 부다똬 보씨, 무 찌라 찌시기 짜 바거떠 바후바꽈냐 뭐 마시 무부야-부야, 바거떠 바하빠똬 어라 루우루 서 마시 오똬 오노 무가시 아이뗴러. 부씨 노구, 어 바쭈 바다가뭐비뗴러.

9. I tell you the truth, wherever the gospel is preached throughout the world, what she has done will also be told, in memory of her."

Yuda isikariota ahonda kute angarenganya Yesu

유다 이시가리오다 아호따 구더 아꽈러꽈냐 여수

10. Era nyuma s'ebi, yuda isikariota, muuma mwa ndjumwa ekumi n'ebilyi sa Yesu, era kuya era mw'e bakulu-kulu b'e bakuhanyi aberese Yesu.

10. 어라 뉴마 서비, 유다 이시가리오다, 무우마 똬 쭈꽈 어구미 너비뗴 사 여수, 어라 구야 어라 뭐 바구루-구루 버 바구하니 아버러서 여수.

10. Then Judas Iscariot, one of the Twelve, went to the chief priests to betray Jesus to them.

11. Abu bakulu-kulu b'e bakuhanyi bomvire bacha, bera kumowa busese. Bera kumulaanya mbu bangamweresa buteya. Yuta

11. 아부 바구루-구루 버 바구하니 보뻐러 바짜, 버라 구모와 부서서. 버라 구무똬아냐 뿌 바빠뭐러사 부더야. 유다 어라 귀러

11. They were delighted to hear this and promised to give him money. So he watched for an opportunity to hand him over.

era kwire atangilyisa ahonda e bihangi bikomire bya angaberesamu Yesu.

Yesu alya e pasaka alauma n'e banafunzi bai

12. E lusuku lubere-bere lw'e suku sikulu s'e mikati era italyi mu chachu lwera kuika. Olu lusuku, lu bendee batenda mw'e mbulyi s'e kulya kwa pasaka. E banafunzi ba Yesu bera kumubusa mbu: Enawechwu, ngaiu wahonda chwuye kukukunganyisa e bilyo by'e pasaka?

13. Yesu kukwera kuchwuma banafunzi bai babilyi, era kubabura mbu: Muyaa mwa musi, mungabuana mulume muuma ola wete ereya lya meshi. Oyu mulume, mumukulyikiraa.

14. N'e nyumba era angengilyiramo, muburaa enai mbu: e Mukangilyisi abusise mbu ngaiu e chumba chai chilyi cha angalyira mw'e lyinye ly'e pasaka alauma n'e banafunzi bai?

15. Oyu ena nyumba angabalosa chumba chiuma chinene ch'okwa ngangamo. Mw'echi chumba, mungabuana e bindju byoshi byakunganyisibwe mira. Rero

아다삐뗴사 아호따 어 비하삐 비고미러 뱌 아빠버러사무 여수.

여수 아랴 어 파사가 아꽈우마 너 바나푸씨 바이

12. 어 루수구 루버러-버러 뤄 수구 시구루 서 미가디 어라 이다뗴 무 짜쭈 뤄라 구이가. 오루 루수구, 루 버너어 바더따 뭐 뿌뤠 서 구랴 과 파사가. 어 바나푸씨 바 여수 버라 구무부사 뿌: 어나워쭈, 따이우 와호따 쭈여 구구구따네사 어 비료 벼 파사가?

13. 여수 구궈라 구쭈마 바나푸씨 바이 바비뤠, 어라 구바부라 뿌: 무야아 뫄 무시, 무따부아나 무루머 무우마 오꽈 워더 어러야 랴 머씨. 오유 무루머, 무무구뤠기라아.

14. 너 뉴빠 어라 아떠삐뗴라모, 무부라아 어나이 뿌: 어 무가삐뤠시 아부시서 뿌 따이우 어 쭈빠 짜이 찌뤠 짜 아따뤠라 뭐 레녀 뤼어 파사가 아꽈우마 너 바나푸씨 바이?

15. 오유 어나 뉴빠 아따바로사 쭈빠 찌우마 찌너너 쪼과 따까모. 뭐찌 쭈빠, 무따부아나 어 비부 보씨 뱌구따네시붜 미라. 러로 뭐이 뉴빠 무 무따쭈구따네사

12. On the first day of the Feast of Unleavened Bread, when it was customary to sacrifice the Passover lamb, Jesus' disciples asked him, "Where do you want us to go and make preparations for you to eat the Passover?"

13. So he sent two of his disciples, telling them, "Go into the city, and a man carrying a jar of water will meet you. Follow him.

14. Say to the owner of the house he enters, 'The Teacher asks: Where is my guest room, where I may eat the Passover with my disciples?'

15. He will show you a large upper room, furnished and ready. Make preparations for us there."

mwei nyumba mu mungachwukunganyisa e bilyo by'e pasaka.

어 비뢰 벼 파사가.

16. Abu banafunzi babilyi bera kunachiuma baya mwa musi bera kunabuana e bindju byoshi byakunganyisibwe mira ng'okwa Yesu anababuraa. Bera kutangilyisa bateka e bilyo by'e pasaka.

16. 아부 바나푸씨 바비례 버라 구나찌우마 바야 뫄 무시 버라 구나부아나 어 비뚜 뵤씨 뱌구꽈네시붜 미라 은과 여수 아나바부라아. 버라 구다삐례사 바더가 어 비뢰 벼 파사가.

16. The disciples left, went into the city and found things just as Jesus had told them. So they prepared the Passover.

17. Mango lwabaa lwera luolo-olo, Yesu era kuika alauma n'e ndjumwa sai ekumi n'ebilyi.

17. 마꼬 롸바아 뤄라 루오로-오로, 여수 어라 구이가 아롸우마 너 뚜뫄 사이 어구미 너비례.

17. When evening came, Jesus arrived with the Twelve.

18. Abere bera balya, Yesu era kubabura mbu: Kubinalyi, nababura kwa muuma mu mwabo ola nalya nai anganyirenganya.

18. 아버러 버라 바뺘, 여수 어라 구바부라 뿌: 구비나례, 나바부라 과 무우마 무 뫄보 오롸 나뺘 나이 아까네러까냐.

18. While they were reclining at the table eating, he said, "I tell you the truth, one of you will betray me--one who is eating with me."

19. E banfunzi bomvire bacha, bera kusibuka busese, na batangilyisa bamubusa muuma-muuma: Elyi nyono?

19. 어 바누푸씨 보삐러 바짜, 버라 구시부가 부서서, 나 바다삐례사 바무부사 무우마-무우마: 어레 뇨노?

19. They were saddened, and one by one they said to him, "Surely not I?"

20. Yesu nai mbu: Analyi muuma mwa kachi-kachi kenyu kwa munalyi ekumi na babilyi, ola watobesa mu mbare nguma nanyi.

20. 여수 나이 뿌: 아나례 무우마 뫄 가찌-가찌 거뉴 과 무나례 어구미 나 바비례, 오롸 와도버사 무 빠러 우마 나니.

20. "It is one of the Twelve," he replied, "one who dips bread into the bowl with me.

21. Nyi Mwana w'e Mundju nyingechibwa, kukulyikana n'okwa Maanjiko Mabuya-buya machwula matechire era lulu sanyi. Si buanya kwa mundju ola unganyirenganya.

21. 네 뫄나 워 무뚜 네어찌봐, 구구레가나 노과 마아찌고 마부야-부야 마쭈롸 마더찌러 어라 루루 사니. 시 부아냐 과 무뚜 오롸 우까네러까냐. 오유 무뚜, 구까고미러

21. The Son of Man will go just as it is written about him. But woe to that man who betrays the Son of Man! It would be better for him if he had not been

Oyu mundju, kungakomire atangabuchirwe!

아다따부찌뤄!

born."

22. Abere bera balya, Yesu era kutola e mukati na ateta mbu akoko era mwa Ongo. Era kuishanga muo, na eresao e banfunzi bai. Era kuteta mbu: Mutolaa, onola I mubilyi wanyi.

22. 아버러 버라 바퍄, 여수 어라 구도롸 어 무가디 나 아더다 뿌 아고고 어라 뫄 오꼬. 어라 구이싸꽈 무오, 나 어러사오 어 바누푸씨 바이. 어라 구더다 뿌: 무도롸아, 오노롸 이 무비레 와니.

22. While they were eating, Jesus took bread, gave thanks and broke it, and gave it to his disciples, saying, "Take it; this is my body."

23. Chasinda, era kutola n'e ngumbu, era kutonga Ongo, na aberesai. boshi bera kumwa kui.

23. 짜시따, 어라 구도롸 너 우뿌, 어라 구도꽈 오꼬, 나 아버러사이. 보씨 버라 구꽈 구이.

23. Then he took the cup, gave thanks and offered it to them, and they all drank from it.

24. Yesu era kubabura mbu: Enera I mikira yanyi, mikira y'e chilaano era ingasheshekala bushi na bandju banene.

24. 여수 어라 구바부라 뿌: 어너라 이 미기라 야니, 미기라 여 찌롸아노 어라 이까써써가롸 부씨 나 바뚜 바너너.

24. "This is my blood of the covenant, which is poured out for many," he said to them.

25. kubinalyi, nababura kwa ndakachimwe tifai, kuikira e lusuku lwa nyikamwai buyayaya mwa bwami bwa Ongo.

25. 구비나레, 나바부라 과 따가찌뭐 디파이, 구이기라 어 루수구 롸 네가마이 부야야야 뫄 봐미 봐 오꼬.

25. "I tell you the truth, I will not drink again of the fruit of the vine until that day when I drink it anew in the kingdom of God."

26. Abere bera bamalaa kwimba e nyimbo s'e kutonga Ongo, bera kwerukira kwa ndjulungu y'e Miseituni.

26. 아버러 버라 바마롸아 귀빠 어 네뽀 서 구도꽈 오꼬, 버라 궈루기라 과 뚜루우 여 미서이두니.

26. When they had sung a hymn, they went out to the Mount of Olives.

Yesu ateta kwa petero angachakanai

여수 아더다 과 퍼더로 아까짜가나이

27. Chasinda, Yesu era kwire abura e banfunzi bai mbu: Muboshi munganyirekerera, bushi byanjikirwe mbu: Nyingeta e mungere, n'e mbulyi singahandabana.

27. 짜시따, 여수 어라 귀러 아부라 어 바누푸씨 바이 뿌: 무보씨 무꽈네러거러라, 부씨 뱌찌기뤄 뿌: 네꺼다 어 무꺼러, 너 뿌레 시까하따바나.

27. "You will all fall away," Jesus told them, "for it is written: " 'I will strike the shepherd, and the sheep will be scattered.'

28. Si chiro bacha, mango nyingomwoka, nyingahondorera e kalilaya.

29. Petero era kumubura mbu: Walyiya! Chiro angaba mbu e banji boshi bangakurekerera, si nyono ndakurekerere chiro na hicha!

30. Yesu nai mbu: Kubinalyi, nakubura kwa mwobuno buchwufu, era muhondo s'e luasi kubika kabilyi, ungaba wachakana nyono kahachwu.

31. Si petero era kunaendekera ateta mwa kulaisa mbu: Akaba binyemire kufira alauma nao, nanemerere. Si e kunana ku ndangakunana chiro na hicha! N'e banji boshi nabo, bera kunateta bacha.

Yesu ema Ongo e ketesemame

32. Era nyuma s'ebi, Yesu n'e banafunzi bai bera kuika mu chisiki chiuma cha chelyikirwe mbu ketesemani. Era kubabura mbu: Mwikalaa anola tanga, nyiye kwema Ongo.

33. Era kuenda na petero, na yakobo, na yowana. Era kutangilyisa aata businane na kulyibuka busese mwa muchima.

---

28. 시 찌로 바짜, 마꼬 네꼬몰가, 네까호또러라 어 가삐랴야.

29. 퍼더로 어라 구무부라 뿌: 와례야! 찌로 아까바 뿌 어 바찌 보씨 바까구러거러라, 시 뇨노 따구러거러러 찌로 나 히짜!

30. 여수 나이 뿌: 구비나례, 나구부라 과 모부노 부쭈푸, 어라 무호또 서 루아시 구비가 가비례, 우까바 와짜가나 뇨노 가하쭈.

31. 시 퍼더로 어라 구나어떠거라 아더다 뫄 구꽈이사 뿌: 아가바 비녀미러 구피라 아꽈우마 나오, 나너머러러. 시 어 구나나 구 따까구나나 찌로 나 히짜! 너 바찌 보씨 나보, 버라 구나더다 바짜.

여수 어마 오꼬 어 거더서마머

32. 어라 뉴마 서비, 여수 너 바나푸씨 바이 버라 구이가 무 찌시기 찌우마 짜 쩌례기뤄 뿌 거더서마니. 어라 구바부라 뿌: 뮈가꽈아 아노꽈 다까, 네여 궈마 오꼬.

33. 어라 구어따 나 퍼더로, 나 야고보, 나 요와나. 어라 구다삐례사 아아다 부시나너 나 구례부가 부서서 뫄 무찌마.

---

28. But after I have risen, I will go ahead of you into Galilee."

29. Peter declared, "Even if all fall away, I will not."

30. "I tell you the truth," Jesus answered, "today-- yes, tonight--before the rooster crows twice you yourself will disown me three times."

31. But Peter insisted emphatically, "Even if I have to die with you, I will never disown you." And all the others said the same.

32. They went to a place called Gethsemane, and Jesus said to his disciples, "Sit here while I pray."

33. He took Peter, James and John along with him, and he began to be deeply distressed and troubled.

34. Era kubabura mbu: Buno businane bwahonda kunyita. Rero, muberaa anola, mutaonjire.

35. chasinda, era kuchifunda era muhondo hicha, na achihunda kwa chitaka. Era kutangilyisa ema Ongo mbu akaba bingalyikana, ebi bihangi by'e malyibuko, bitamuikiraa.

36. Era kuteta mbu: Aba, tata, era mwao byoshi byende byaalyikana. Ei ngumbu y'e malyibuko, unyiimiraai. Si chiro bacha, e kuhonda kwao ku kunabaa, si ata e kuhonda kwanyi.

37. Chasinda, Yesu era kuhuba ala banfunzi bai babaa balyi, era kubuana baonjire. Era kwire abura petero mbu: Era simoni! Waonjire? Wanafafunjirwe kuima e chwulo chiro na saa nguma?

38. Rero mutachionjiraa, mweme Ongo, mungesha kwengilyira mwa miereko. Bushi e muchima asimikire, si e mubilyi ainyire misi!

39. Yesu era kubareka kanji, era kuya kwema Ongo mwa kuhubilyira ei myasi.

---

34. 어라 구바부라 뿌: 부노 부시나너 봐호따 구네다. 러로, 무버라아 아노롸, 무다오찌러.

35. 짜시따, 어라 구찌푸따 어라 무호또 히짜, 나 아찌후따 과 찌다가. 어라 구다삐레사 어마 오꼬 뿌 아가바 비까레가나, 어비 비하삐 벼 마레부고, 비다무이기라아.

36. 어라 구더다 뿌: 아바, 다다, 어라 뫄오 뵤씨 벼너 뱌아레가나. 어이 으뿌 여 마레부고, 우네이미라아이. 시 찌로 바짜, 어 구호따 과오 구 구나바아, 시 아다 어 구호따 과니.

37. 짜시따, 여수 어라 구후바 아롸 바누푸씨 바이 바바아 바레, 어라 구부아나 바오찌러. 어라 귀러 아부라 퍼더로 뿌: 어라 시모니! 와오찌러? 와나푸찌뤄 구이마 어 쭈롤 찌로 나 사아 으마?

38. 러로 무다찌오찌라아, 뭐머 오꼬, 무뻐싸 궈삐레라 뫄 미어러고. 부씨 어 무찌마 아시미기러, 시 어 무비레 아이네러 미시!

39. 여수 어라 구바러가 가찌, 어라 구야 궈마 오꼬 뫄 구후비레라 어이 먀시.

---

34. "My soul is overwhelmed with sorrow to the point of death," he said to them. "Stay here and keep watch."

35. Going a little farther, he fell to the ground and prayed that if possible the hour might pass from him.

36. "Abba, Father," he said, "everything is possible for you. Take this cup from me. Yet not what I will, but what you will."

37. Then he returned to his disciples and found them sleeping. "Simon," he said to Peter, "are you asleep? Could you not keep watch for one hour?

38. Watch and pray so that you will not fall into temptation. The spirit is willing, but the body is weak."

39. Once more he went away and prayed the same thing.

40. Abere ahuba kanji ala banafunzi bai babaa balyi, era kubabuana kanji baonjire, bushi e meho mabo mabaa masitoire bushi n'e chwulo. Bera kwire baina cha bangamwakula.

41. Mango Yesu ahubaa kufuluka e bwakahachwu ala e banafunzi babaa balyi, era kubabura mbu: Ewashe, munachilyi muonjire mwatamuka? Oshao! Rero e bihangi byaikire. Nyi Mwana w'e Mundju banyanyire mira mwa mino s'e bandju b'e mabi.

42. Mubachwukaa chwuendee! Mulolaa ola wanyana, yono wera ulyi ofu!

Yesu asimbwa

43. Abere Yesu anachilyi ateta, unao-unao, yuda muuma mwa ndjumwa ekumi n'ebilyi sa Yesu, kuna kupamukira. Abaa alyi na bandju banene ba babaa bete e mombo n'e chwuchi mwa mino. Abu bandju, babaa bachwumirwe n'e bakulu-kulu b'e bakuhanyi, n'e bakangilyisi b'e mwaso, n'e bashamuka b'e bayuda.

44. Yuda abaa abalosise mira kute angarenganya Yesu. Era kubabura mbu: Ola

40. 아버러 아후바 가찌 아꽈 바나푸씨 바이 바바아 바레, 어라 구바부아나 가찌 바오찌러, 부씨 어 머호 마보 마바아 마시도이러 부씨 너 쭈론. 버라 귀러 바이나 짜 바꽈구꽈.

41. 마꼬 여수 아후바아 구푸루가 어 봐가하쭈 아라 어 바나푸씨 바바아 바레, 어라 구바부라 뿌: 어와써, 무나찌레 무오찌러 봐다무가? 오싸오! 러로 어 비하삐 뱌이기러. 니 마나 워 무뚜 바냐니러 미라 봐 미노 서 바뚜 버 마비.

42. 무바쭈가아 쭈어떠어! 무론꽈라 오꽈 와냐나, 요노 워라 우레 오푸!

여수 아시꽈

43. 아버러 여수 아나찌레 아더다, 우나오-우나오, 유다 무우마 봐 뚜와 어구미 너비레 사 여수, 구나 구파무기라. 아바아 아레 나 바뚜 바너너 바 바바아 버더 어 모뽀 너 쭈찌 봐 미노. 아부 바뚜, 바바아 바쭈미뤄 너 바구루- 구루 버 바구하니, 너 바가삐레시 버 마소, 너 바싸무가 버 바유다.

44. 유다 아바아 아바론시서 미라 구더 아꽈러꽈냐 여수. 어라 구바부라 뿌: 오꽈

40. When he came back, he again found them sleeping, because their eyes were heavy. They did not know what to say to him.

41. Returning the third time, he said to them, "Are you still sleeping and resting? Enough! The hour has come. Look, the Son of Man is betrayed into the hands of sinners.

42. Rise! Let us go! Here comes my betrayer!"

43. Just as he was speaking, Judas, one of the Twelve, appeared. With him was a crowd armed with swords and clubs, sent from the chief priests, the teachers of the law, and the elders.

44. Now the betrayer had arranged a signal with them: "The one I kiss is the

nyingaombera, elyi I yoyu. Mumusimbaa, mumweke mumulangire kubuya.

45. Mango yuda aikaa ala Yesu abaa alyi, unao-unao kuna kuchifunda ofu nai na amubura mbu: Mukangilyisi! Chasinda, era kumuobera.

46. Abu bandju, kuna kusimba Yesu na bamumina.

47. Si muuma mwaba babaa balyi aola, kuna kuhohola e bombo bwai, kuna kuisha e kuchi ly'e kaungu k'e mukulu-kulu w'e bakuhanyi.

48. Yesu kukwera kubabusa mbu: Chi chachwumire mwaika kunyisimba mwete e mombo n'e chwuchi nga bandju babaya kusimba chihumisi?

49. Chira lusuku, nabaa nenjire naba alauma nenyu mwa luhu lwa Ongo nabakangilyisa, si chiro mukanyisimba. Si ene myasi yabere, chasiya bya bichwula byanjikirwe mwa maanjiko Mabuya-buya biberere.

50. Unao-unao, e banafunzi bai boshi kuna kumureka na bachihaira.

네까오뻐라, 어레 이 요유. 무무시빠아, 무뭐거 무무롸끼러 구부야.

45. 마꼬 유다 아이가아 아롸 여수 아바아 아레, 우나오-우나오 구나 구찌푸따 오푸 나이 나 아무부라 뿌: 무가끼레시! 짜시따, 어라 구무오버라.

46. 아부 바뉴, 구나 구시빠 여수 나 바무미나.

47. 시 무우마 뫄바 바바아 바레 아오롸, 구나 구호호롸 어 보뽀 봐이, 구나 구이싸 어 구찌 뤼어 가우꾸 거 무구루-구루 워 바구하니.

48. 여수 구궈라. 구바부사 뿌: 찌 짜쭈미러 뫄이가 구네시빠 뭐더 어 모뽀 너 쭈찌 까 바뉴 바바야 구시빠 찌후미시?

49. 찌라 루수구, 나바아 나바 아롸우마 너뉴 뫄 루후 오꼬 나바가끼레사, 시 찌로 무가네시빠. 시 어너 먀시 야버러, 짜시야 뱌 비쭈롸 뱌찌기뤄 뫄 마아찌고 마부야-부야 비버러러.

50. 우나오-우나오, 어 바나푸씨 바이 보씨 구나 구무러가 나 바찌하이라.

man; arrest him and lead him away under guard."

45. Going at once to Jesus, Judas said, "Rabbi!" and kissed him.

46. The men seized Jesus and arrested him.

47. Then one of those standing near drew his sword and struck the servant of the high priest, cutting off his ear.

48. "Am I leading a rebellion," said Jesus, "that you have come out with swords and clubs to capture me?

49. Every day I was with you, teaching in the temple courts, and you did not arrest me. But the Scriptures must be fulfilled."

50. Then everyone deserted him and fled.

51. Mutabana muuma abaa aenda akulyikire Yesu, achihukire ka ngwaya. Oyu mutabana, ba bandju bera kuereka kumusimba,

52. Si era kuhunukala kuna kubarekera ka k'e ngwaya, kuna kuchiuma aenda ahaa butambara.

Yesu atongana era muhondo s'e karubanda k'e bayuda

53. Abu bandju, bera kweka Yesu ala mw'e mukulu-kulu w'e bakuhanyi. Aola, uebakulu-kulu b'e bakuhanyi boshi, n'e bashamuka b'e Bayuda alauma n'e bakangilyisi b'e Mwaso babaa babuananyire.

54. Petero abaa aenda akulyikira Yesu marerere, kuikira era kunengirira mwa chibuwa ch'e nyumba y'e mukulu-kulu w'e bakuhanyi. Era kwekala alauma n'e balanzi, akalukala kwa mulyiro.

55. Abu bakulu-kulu b'e bakuhanyi alauma n'e banji bakulu-kulu boshi b'omwa karubanda k'e bayuda, babaa bahonda e chinwa cha bangemangirako chasiya b'echise Yesu. Si bera kuinachi.

56. Bandju banene bera kunde bamusinga myasi ya bisha, si

51. 무다바나 무우마 아바아 아어따 아구쀄기러 여수, 아찌후기러 가 꽈야. 오유 무다바나, 바 바뉴 버라 구어러가 구무시빠,

52. 시 어라 구후누가파 구나 구바러거라 가 거 꽈야, 구나 구찌우마 아어따 아하아 부다빠라.

여수 아도따나 어라 무호또 서 가루바따 거 바우다

53. 아부 바뉴, 버라 궈가 여수 아꽈 뭐 무구루-구루 워 바구하네. 아오꽈, 우어바구루-구루 버 바구하네 보씨, 너 바싸무가 버 바우다 아꽈우마 너 바가찌쀄시 버 마소 바바아 바부아나네러.

54. 퍼더로 아바아 아어따 아구쀄기라 여수 마러러러, 구이기라 어라 구너찌리라 꽈 찌부와 쩌 뉴빠 여 무구루-구루 워 바구하네. 어라 궈가꽈 아꽈우마 너 바꽈씨, 아가루가꽈 과 무쀄로.

55. 아부 바구루-구루 버 바구하네 아꽈우마 너 바찌 바구루-구루 보씨 보꽈 가루바따 거 바우다, 바바아 바호따 어 찌놔 짜 바꺼마찌라고 짜시야 버찌서 여수. 시 버라 구이나찌.

56. 바뉴 바너너 버라 구꺼 바무시빠 먀시 야 비싸, 시

51. A young man, wearing nothing but a linen garment, was following Jesus. When they seized him,

52. he fled naked, leaving his garment behind.

53. They took Jesus to the high priest, and all the chief priests, elders and teachers of the law came together.

54. Peter followed him at a distance, right into the courtyard of the high priest. There he sat with the guards and warmed himself at the fire.

55. The chief priests and the whole Sanhedrin were looking for evidence against Jesus so that they could put him to death, but they did not find any.

56. Many testified falsely against him, but their

ei myasi yabo babaa batenjire baiteta kuuma.

57. Chasinjire, bauma mubo bera kwimanga, na batangilyisa bamusindaira myasi ya bisha mbu:

58. Ono mundju, chwachumviraa chwubeine kwa ateta mbu: Luno luhu lwa Ongo, lwaibwaa n'e bandju. Nyono, nyingahandjulalo n'era nyuma sa suku ehachwu, nanaimba e lunji lwa lungaba lutaimbirwe n'e bandju.

59. Si chiro bacha, ei myasi yabo babaa batenjire baiteta kuuma.

60. E mukulu-kulu w'e bakuhanyi kukwera kubachwuka mwa kachikachi k'e bandju na abusa Yesu mbu: Ei myasi yoshi bano bandju bakusitakilyire, utanakure chiro na kandju kasi bya kui?

61. Si Yesu era kuchisilyira, chiro akamwakula kandju. Oyu mukulu-kulu era kuhuba kumubusa mbu: Elyi woyo u kirisito, mwana wa Ongo ola chwende chwaahanyisa?

62. Yesu na imbu: Eee i nyono! Mungalola kwa nyi Mwana w'e Mundju nyekese kwa lunda lw'e malyo ma Ongo w'e

어이 먀시 야보 바바아 바더띠러 바이더다 구우마.

57. 짜시띠러, 바우마 무보 버라 귀마까, 나 바다끼레사 바무시따아이라 먀시 야 비싸 뿌:

58. 오노 무뚜, 좌쭈삐라아 쭈버이너 과 아더다 뿌: 루노 루후 롸 오꼬, 롸이봐아 너 바뚜. 뇨노, 네까하뚜롸르 너라 뉴마 사 수구 어하쭈, 나나이빠 어 루찌 롸 루까바 루다이삐뤄 너 바뚜.

59. 시 찌로 바짜, 어이 먀시 야보 바바아 바더띠러 바이더다 구우마.

60. 어 무구루-구루 워 바구하네 구귀라 구바쭈가 롸 가찌가찌 거 바뚜 나 아부사 여수 뿌: 어이 먀시 요씨 바노 바뚜 바구시다기레러, 우다나구러 찌로 나 가뚜 가시 바 구이?

61. 시 여수 어라 구찌시레라, 찌로 아가마구롸 가뚜. 오유 무구루-구루 어라 구후바 구무부사 뿌: 어레 오요 우 기리시도, 뫄나 와 오꼬 오롸 쭤떠 좌아하네사?

62. 여수 나 이뿌: 어어어 이 뇨노! 무까로롸 과 네 뫄나 워 무뚜 녀거서 과 루따 뤄 마롣 마 오꼬 워 부아씨. 가찌

statements did not agree.

57. Then some stood up and gave this false testimony against him:

58. "We heard him say, 'I will destroy this man-made temple and in three days will build another, not made by man.' "

59. Yet even then their testimony did not agree.

60. Then the high priest stood up before them and asked Jesus, "Are you not going to answer? What is this testimony that these men are bringing against you?"

61. But Jesus remained silent and gave no answer. Again the high priest asked him, "Are you the Christ, the Son of the Blessed One?"

62. "I am," said Jesus. "And you will see the Son of Man sitting at the right hand of the Mighty One

buashi. Kanji mungalola kwa natenga kwa nguba mwa lumbumbu.

무까롸 과 나더아 과 우바 롸 루뿌뿌.

and coming on the clouds of heaven."

63. Si mango oyu mukulu-kulu w'e bakuhanyi omvaa bacha, kuna kuchiberengangira kw'e njimba. Era kuteta mbu: Rero, bubei buchiye bwa chwuchilyi chwahonda bushi n'onu mundju?

63. 시 마꼬 오유 무구루-구루 워 바구하니 오빠아 바짜, 구나 구찌버러아라 궈 띠빠. 어라 구더다 뿌: 러로, 부찌여 봐 쭈찌레 좌호따 부씨 노누 무뚜?

63. The high priest tore his clothes. "Why do we need any more witnesses?" he asked.

64. Si mubeine mwachwumvilyire mira kwa akamba Ongo. Kute musene? E bandju boshi, bera kuteta mbu emire kwichibwa.

64. 시 무버이너 뫄쭈삐레러 미라 과 아가빠 오꼬. 구더 무서너? 어 바뚜 보씨, 버라 구더다 뿌 어미러 귀찌봐.

64. "You have heard the blasphemy. What do you think?" They all condemned him as worthy of death.

65. Bauma mw'abu bandju, bera kutangilyisa bachira ku Yesu. Bera kumuhukira e buso, chasinda bera kumumaasanga na kumubura mbu: Rero, rebaa nde iwakumaasise! E basula nabo, bera kumutola na batangilyisa bamumaasanga.

65. 바우마 뫄부 바뚜, 버라 구다레사 바찌라 구 여수. 버라 구무후기라 어 부소, 짜시따 버라 구무마아사꽈 나 구무부라 뿌: 러로, 러바아 떠 이와구마아시서! 어 바수꽈 나보, 버라 구무도꽈 나 바다레사 바무마아사꽈.

65. Then some began to spit at him; they blindfolded him, struck him with their fists, and said, "Prophesy!" And the guards took him and beat him.

Petero anana Yesu

퍼더로 아나나 여수

66. Mango petero abaa anachilyi era masina mwa chibuwa ch'e chikalyi, muandakasi muuma w'e mukulu-kulu w'e bakuhanyi era kuika ala abaa alyi.

66. 마꼬 퍼더로 아바아 아나찌레 어라 마시나 뫄 찌부와 쩌 찌가레, 무우마 워 무구루-구루 워 바구하니 어라 구이가 아꽈 아바아 아레.

66. While Peter was below in the courtyard, one of the servant girls of the high priest came by.

67. Era kulola ku petero akalukala kwa mulyiro. Oyu muandakasi, era kumuchwumbikisa na

67. 어라 구롸 구 퍼더로 아가루가꽈 과 무레로. 오유 무아따가시, 어라 구무쭈삐기사 나 아무부라 뿌:

67. When she saw Peter warming himself, she looked closely at him. "You also were with that

amubura mbu: Nao wabaa ulyi alauma na Yesu, mwesha Nasareti.

나오 와바아 우레 아롸우마 여수, 뭐싸 나사러디.

Nazarene, Jesus," she said.

68. Si petero era kunana, na ateta mbu: Ei myasi wahonda kuteta ndaishi, kanji ndanaimenyerere. Chasinda, petero era kuuluka na aya kwa chiso ch'e chikalyi. Unao-unao, eluasi kuna kubika.

68. 시 퍼더로 어라 구나나, 나 아더다 뿌: 어이 먀시 와호따 구더다 따이씨, 가찌 따나이머녀러러. 짜시따, 퍼더로 어라 구우루가 나 아야 과 찌소 쩌 찌가레. 우나오-우나오, 어루아시 구나 구비가.

68. But he denied it. "I don't know or understand what you're talking about," he said, and went out into the entryway.

69. Oyu muandakasi mango alolaa kanji kwa petero emenze kw'echi chiso, era kubura e bandju babaa balyi aola mbu: Ono mundju, alyi muuma mubo!

69. 오유 무아따가시 마꼬 아루롸아 가찌 과 퍼더로 어머써 궈찌 찌소, 어라 구부라 어 바뚜 바바아 바레 아오롸 뿌: 오노 무뚜, 아레 무우마 무보!

69. When the servant girl saw him there, she said again to those standing around, "This fellow is one of them."

70. Si petero kanji era kunana. Era nyuma hicha, abu bandju nabo bera kubura petero mbu: kubinalyi, unalyi muuma mubo bushi nao ulyi mwesha kalilaya!

70. 시 퍼더로 가찌 어라 구나나. 어라 뉴마 히짜, 아부 바뚜 나보 버라 구부라 퍼더로 뿌: 구비나레, 우나레 무우마 무보 부씨 나오 우레 뭐싸 가리롸야!

70. Again he denied it. After a little while, those standing near said to Peter, "Surely you are one of them, for you are a Galilean."

71. Bushi n'oku, Petero era kutangilyisa achakana na kulaisa busese mbu: Ono mundju mwenjire mwamaana, nalaisise kwa ndamwishi. Rero, akaba nafula bisha, nyife shambyo!

71. 부씨 노구, 퍼더로 어라 구다삐레사 아짜가나 나 구롸이사 부서서 뿌: 오노 무뚜 뭐찌러 마마아나, 나롸이시서 과 따뮈씨. 러로, 아가바 나푸롸 비싸, 네퍼 샴뵤!

71. He began to call down curses on himself, and he swore to them, "I don't know this man you're talking about."

72. Unao-unao, e luasi kuna kubika e bwakabilyi. Petero kukwera kukengera era myasi Yesu amuburaa mbu: Era muhondo s'e luasi kubika kabilyi, ungaba wanyinana

72. 우나오-우나오, 어 루아시 구나 구비가 어 봐가비레. 퍼더로 구궈라 구거꺼라 어라 먀시 여수 아무부라아 뿌: 어라 무호또 서 루아시 구비가 가비레, 우까바 와네나나

72. Immediately the rooster crowed the second time. Then Peter remembered the word Jesus had spoken to him: "Before the rooster crows twice you will disown

kahachwu. Petero kuna
kutangilyisa alyira.

가하쭉. 퍼더로 구나
구다ᄈ레사 아례라.

me three times." And he
broke down and wept.

Mariko Chikono 15
*Yesu atongana era muhondo
sa pilato*

1. Abere mwei mishagya
lumbulyi-mbulyi, e bakulu-
kulu b'e bakuhanyi, n'e
bakangilyisi b'e mwaso,
alauma n'e bashamuka b'e
bayuda, kukuteta mbu e
karubanda koshi k'e bayuda
kera kubuanana, baishe e
lwango. Mw'olu, bera
kusalyinga Yesu, na baya
kumwana era mw'e mukulu-
kulu w'e muroma mbu I pilato

2. Pilato era kubusa Yesu mbu:
Elyi woyo u mwami w'e
bayuda? Yesu na imbu: Weine
watechire mira!

3. E bakulu-kulu b'e bakuhanyi
bera kutangilyisa basitaka
yesu ku myasi inene.

4. Bushi n'oku, Pilato era
kumubusa kanji mbu: Ene
myasi yoshi benjire
bakusitakako, utana akure
chiro na kandju kasibya?

5. Si Yesu chiro akamwakula
kandju. Pilato era kwire

마리고 찌고노 15
*여수 아도ᄞ나 어라 무호또 사
피꽈도*

1. 아버러 뭐이 미싸갸
루뿌레-뿌레, 어 바구루-구루
버 바구하네, 너 바가ᄈ레시
버 마소, 아꽈우마 너
바싸무가 버 바유다, 구구더다
뿌 어 가루바따 고씨 거
바유다 거라 구부아나나,
바이써 어 꽈오. 몰루, 버라
구사레ᄞ 여수, 나 바야
구꽈나 어라 뭐 무구루-구루
워 무로마 뿌 이 피꽈도

2. 피꽈도 어라 구부사 여수
뿌: 어레 오요 우 꽈미 워
바유다? 여수 나 이뿌: 워이너
와더찌러 미라!

3. 어 바구루-구루 버
바구하네 버라 구다ᄈ레사
바시다가 여수 구 먀시
이너너.

4. 부씨 노구, 피꽈도 어라
구무부사 가찌 뿌: 어너 먀시
요씨 버찌러 바구시다가고,
우다나 아구러 찌로 나 가뿌
가시뱌?

5. 시 여수 찌로 아가마구꽈
가뿌. 피꽈도 어라 귀러

Mark Chapter 15[NIV]

1. Very early in the
morning, the chief priests,
with the elders, the
teachers of the law and the
whole Sanhedrin, reached a
decision. They bound Jesus,
led him away and handed
him over to Pilate.

2. "Are you the king of the
Jews?" asked Pilate. "Yes, it
is as you say," Jesus replied.

3. The chief priests accused
him of many things.

4. So again Pilate asked
him, "Aren't you going to
answer? See how many
things they are accusing
you of."

5. But Jesus still made no
reply, and Pilate was

asanwa busese.

Pilato ateta mbu yesu echibwaa

6. Chira lusuku lukulu lwa pasaka, pilato abaa achwusa mwanya wa kunde aboorera e bandju mundju muuma wa buroko ola bamwemire.

7. Rero mwa buroko, mwabaa mulyi mundju muuma mbu I baraba. Oyu baraba, abaa aminyilyirwe alauma na banji bechi, bushi na lubanja lwa kwita bandju mwa lwayo lwa lwabaa mwa musi.

8. E luamba lw'e bandju lwera kwerukira ala mwa pilato. Bera kutangilyisa bamwema mbu abailyiraa kanji ng'okwa ende anabailyira.

9. Pilato era kubabusa mbu: Mwahonda nyibaboorere e mwami w'e bayuda?

10. Ateta bacha, bushi abaa amenyire kwa abu bakulu-kulu b'e bakuhanyi bamureteraa Yesu bushi n'e mufula.

11. Si abu bakulu-kulu b'e bakuhanyi bera kushiilyisa olu luamba lw'e bandju mbu ababooreraa baraba.

12. Pilato era kuhuba kubusa e luamba lw'e bandju mbu: Rero, kute mwahonda nyiire ono mundju mwenjire

아사놔 부서서.

피꽈도 아더다 뿌 여수 어찌봐아

6. 찌라 루수구 루구루루 꽈 파사가, 피꽈도 아바아 아쭈사 뫄냐 와 구떠 아보오러라 어 바뚜 무뚜 무우마 와 부로고 오꽈 바뭐미러.

7. 러로 꽈 부로고, 뫄바아 무쩨 무뚜 무우마 뿌 이 바라바. 오유 바라바, 아바아 아미네레뤄 아꽈우마 나 바찌 버찌, 부씨 나 루바짜 꽈 귀다 바뚜 뫄 꽈요 꽈 꽈바아 뫄 무시.

8. 어 루아빠 뤄 바뚜 뤄라 귀루기라 아꽈 뫄 피꽈도. 버라 구다삐레사 바뭐마 뿌 아바이쩨라아 가찌 꼬과 어떠 아나바이쩨라.

9. 피꽈도 어라 구바부사 뿌: 뫄호따 네바보오러러 어 뫄미 워 바유다?

10. 아더다 바짜, 부씨 아바아 아머네러 과 아부 바구루-구루 버 바구하네 바무러더라아 여수 부씨 너 무푸꽈.

11. 시 아부 바구루-구루 버 바구하네 버라 구씨이쩨사 오루 루아빠 뤄 바뚜 뿌 아바보오러라아 바라바.

12. 피꽈도 어라 구후바 구부사 어 루아빠 뤄 바뚜 뿌: 러로, 구더 뫄호따 네이러 오노 무뚜 뭐찌러 뭐쩨가 뿌

amazed.

6. Now it was the custom at the Feast to release a prisoner whom the people requested.

7. A man called Barabbas was in prison with the insurrectionists who had committed murder in the uprising.

8. The crowd came up and asked Pilate to do for them what he usually did.

9. "Do you want me to release to you the king of the Jews?" asked Pilate,

10. knowing it was out of envy that the chief priests had handed Jesus over to him.

11. But the chief priests stirred up the crowd to have Pilate release Barabbas instead.

12. "What shall I do, then, with the one you call the king of the Jews?" Pilate asked them.

mwelyika mbu I mwami w'e Bayuda?	이 와미 워 바유다?	
13. Bera kwakula na murenge munene mbu: Umumanyikaa kwa musalaba!	13. 버라 과구롸 나 무러어 무너너 뿌: 우무마네가아 과 무사롸바!	13. "Crucify him!" they shouted.
14. Pilato era kuhuba kubabusa mbu: Chibi chichiye chi ailyire? Si bera kunaendekera balakanga busese mbu: Umumanyikaa kwa musalaba!	14. 피롸도 어라 구후바 구바부사 뿌: 찌비 찌찌여 찌 아이례러? 시 버라 구나어떠거라 바롸가까 부서서 뿌: 우무마네가아 과 무사롸바!	14. "Why? What crime has he committed?" asked Pilate. But they shouted all the louder, "Crucify him!"
15. Chasinda, pilato bushi abaa ahonda kusimisa e bandju, era kubaboorera baraba. Era kuhuchisa Yesu echwuchi, chasinda era kumwana bamumanyike kwa musalaba.	15. 짜시따, 피롸도 부씨 아바아 아호따 구시미사 어 반쭈, 어라 구바보오러라 바라바. 어라 구후찌사 여수 어쭈찌, 짜시따 어라 구와나 바무마네거 과 무사롸바.	15. Wanting to satisfy the crowd, Pilate released Barabbas to them. He had Jesus flogged, and handed him over to be crucified.
E basula bashekera Yesu	***어 바수롸 바셔거라 여수***	
16. Era nyuma s'ebi, e basula bera kweka Yesu mwa chikalyi ch'e mukulu-kulu w'e chio. Bera kwamaala e chikembe chabo choshi.	16. 어라 뉴마 서비, 어 바수롸 버라 궈가 여수 와 찌가례 쩌 무구루-구루 워 찌오. 버라 과마아롸 어 찌거뻐 짜보 쪼씨.	16. The soldiers led Jesus away into the palace (that is, the Praetorium) and called together the whole company of soldiers.
17. Bera kwembasa Yesu eropo lya mwola, bera kuluka n'e nzita mwa matabi ma mabaa mete mawa na bamwembasai kw'echwe.	17. 버라 궈빠사 여수 어로포 롸 모롸, 버라 구루가 너 씨다 와 마다비 마 마바아 머더 마와 나 바워빠사이 궈쭤.	17. They put a purple robe on him, then twisted together a crown of thorns and set it on him.
18. Bera kutangilyisa bamukesa mbu: chwakulamusise mwami w'e Bayuda!	18. 버라 구다이레사 바무거사 뿌: 쫘구롸무시서 와미 워 바유다!	18. And they began to call out to him, "Hail, king of the Jews!"
19. Bera kumuhutanga elusheke kw'echwe, na	19. 버라 구무후다아 어루써거 궈쭤, 나 바무찌라고. 짜시따,	19. Again and again they struck him on the head

bamuchirako. Chasinda, bera kukoma e mafi na bafukama era muhondo sai, bamushekera.

20. Abere bera bamalaa kumushekera, bera kumukongola ly'e ropo na bahuba kumwebasa e njimba sai. Chasinda, bera kumweka era butala baya kumumanyika kwa musalaba.

Yesu amanyikibwa kwa musalaba

21. Mango babaa bera balyi mwa njira, bera kubuana mundju muuma mbu I simoni, abaa atenga era mahwa. Oyu simoni, abaa mwesha mwa musi w'e kurene, kanji iwabaa eshe wa alesanduro na rufu. E basula bera kumwesa e musalaba wa Yesu kwa misi.

22. Abu basula, bera kweka Yesu mwa chisiki cha bende belyika mbu kolokota kukuteta mbu: Chisiki ch'e kangasi.

23. Bera kumweresa difai era yabaa ihoonganyisibwe mw'e mane-mane, si era kuinana.

24. Chasinda, bera kumumanyika kwa musalaba. E njimba sai, bera kusiabana mwa kushieshera e choore bamenye lwa chira muuma

---

버라 구고마 어 마피 나 바푸가마 어라 무호또 사이, 바무써거라.

20. 아버러 버라 바마콰아 구무써거라, 버라 구무고꼬콰 뤼어 로포 나 바후바 구뭐바사 어 띠빠 사이. 짜시따, 버라 구뭐가 어라 부다콰 바야 구무마네가 과 무사콰바.

여수 아마네기봐 과 무사콰바

21. 마꼬 바바아 버라 바레 콰 띠라, 버라 구부아나 무뚜 무우마 뿌 이 시모니, 아바아 아더빠 어라 마화. 오유 시모니, 아바아 뭐싸 콰 무시 워 구러너, 가찌 이와바아 어써 와 아꿔사뚜로 나 루푸. 어 바수콰 버라 구뭐사 어 무사콰바 와 여수 과 미시.

22. 아부 바수콰, 버라 궈가 여수 콰 찌시기 짜 버너 버레가 뿌 고꼬고다 구구더다 뿌: 찌시기 쩌 가까시.

23. 버라 구뭐러사 디파이 어라 야바아 이호오까네시붜 뭐 마너-마너, 시 어라 구이나나.

24. 짜시따, 버라 구무마네가 과 무사콰바. 어 띠빠 사이, 버라 구시아바나 콰 구씨어써라 어 쪼오러 바머녀 콰 찌라 무우마 무보 아꿔가.

---

with a staff and spit on him. Falling on their knees, they paid homage to him.

20. And when they had mocked him, they took off the purple robe and put his own clothes on him. Then they led him out to crucify him.

21. A certain man from Cyrene, Simon, the father of Alexander and Rufus, was passing by on his way in from the country, and they forced him to carry the cross.

22. They brought Jesus to the place called Golgotha (which means The Place of the Skull).

23. Then they offered him wine mixed with myrrh, but he did not take it.

24. And they crucified him. Dividing up his clothes, they cast lots to see what each would get.

mubo angeka.

25. Mango bamanyikaa Yesu kwa musalaba, sabaa sera saa ehachwu sa mishangya-shangya.

26. Bera kwanjika n'okwa chihaki e myasi era yabaa yalosa cha chachwumire bachinjibusa Yesu. Ei myasi yabaa itechire mbu: e Mwami w'e bayuda.

27. Abu basula, bamanyikaa na bihumusi bibilyi kwa misalaba ala musike sa Yesu. Muuma kwa lunda lwai lw'e malyo n'e unji kwa lw'e marembe.

28. Mw'olu, e myasi era Maanjiko Mabuya-buya machwula matechire, yera kuberera. Ei myasi bacha kuichwula itechire: Bamubikaa mwa muanjo w'e bandju b'e mabi.

29. E bandju ba babaa benjire barenga aola, bera kunde bamukamba na kasinya e machwe mabo. Bera kunde bamu bura mbu: Era? Si uwabaa wenjire wateta mbu ungahandjula e luhu lwa Ongo, na ku suku ehachwu ungahuba kuimba e lunji!

30. Rero, uchinunulaa weine, uchandaase kw'oyu musalaba!

25. 마꼬 바마네가아 여수 과 무사꽈바, 사바아 서라 사아 어하쭉 사 미싸꺄-싸꺄.

26. 버라 과찌가 노과 찌하기 어 먀시 어라 야바아 야로사 짜 짜쭉미러 바찌찌부사 여수. 어이 먀시 야바아 이더찌러 뿌: 어 먀미 워 바유다.

27. 아부 바수꽈, 바마네가아 나 비후무시 비비꼐 과 미사꽈바 아꽈 무시거 사 여수. 무우마 과 루따 꽈이 뭐 마뤈 너 우찌 과 뭐 마러뻐.

28. 몰루, 어 먀시 어라 마아찌고 마부야-부야 마쭈꽈 마더찌러, 여라 구버러라. 어이 먀시 바짜 구이쭈꽈 이더찌러: 바무비가아 먀 무아쪼 워 바뚜 버 마비.

29. 어 바뚜 바 바바아 버찌러 바러꽈 아오꽈, 버라 구떠 바무가빠 나 가시냐 어 마꿔 마보. 버라 구떠 바무 부라 뿌 어라? 시 우와바아 워찌러 와더다 뿌 우꽈하뚜꽈 어 루후 꽈 오쪼, 나 구 수구 어하쭉 우꽈후바 구이빠 어 루찌!

30. 러로, 우찌누누꽈아 워이너, 우짜따아서 교유

25. It was the third hour when they crucified him.

26. The written notice of the charge against him read: THE KING OF THE JEWS.

27. They crucified two robbers with him, one on his right and one on his left.

28. None

29. Those who passed by hurled insults at him, shaking their heads and saying, "So! You who are going to destroy the temple and build it in three days,

30. come down from the cross and save yourself!"

무사꽈바!

31. E bakulu-kulu b'e bakuhanyi, n'e bakangilyisi b'e Mwaso, nabo babaa bashekera Yesu. Bera kutangilyisa baburana mbu: Cho! Abaa enjire anunula e banji, si yeine afunjirwe kuchinunula!

32. Rero akaba I kirisito, mwami w'e Baisiraeli, achandaasaa kw'oyu musalaba nechwu chwuchilorere, chwumwemerere. Ebi bihumusi, bya byamanyikibwa ala musike sa Yesu, nabi byabaa byamukamba.

E kufa kwa Yesu

33. Mango kabaa kera kachi-kachi ka mushi, e musimya era kuhukira e chio choshi kuikira saa mwenda.

34. Abere mwei saa mwenda, Yesu era kuchilakangira na murenge munene mbu: Eloi, Eloi. Lama sabatani. Ku kuteta mbu: Ongo tata, Ongo tata, chi chachwumire wanyirekerera?

35. Bandju bauma mw'aba babaa balyi aola, bomvire bacha, bera kuteta mbu: Munvaa bechwu! Amaala Eliya.

31. 어 바구루-구루 버 바구하니, 너 바가삐레시 버 꽈소, 나보 바바아 바써거라 여수. 버라 구다삐꿰사 바부라나 뿌: 쪼! 아바아 어찌러 아누누꽈 어 바찌, 시 여이너 아푸찌뤄 구찌누누꽈!

32. 러로 아가바 이 기리시도, 꽈미 워 바이시라어릐, 아짜따아사아 교유 무사꽈바 너쭈 쭈찌롤러러, 쭈뭐머러러. 어비 비후무시, 뱌 뱌마네기봐 아꽈 무시거 사 여수, 나비 뱌바아 뱌무가빠.

어 구파 과 여수

33. 마오 가바아 거라 가찌-가찌 가 무씨, 어 무시먀 어라 구후기라 어 찌오 쪼씨 구이기라 사아 뭐따.

34. 아버러 뭐이 사아 뭐따, 여수 어라 구찌꽈가기라 나 무러어 무너너 뿌: 어로이, 어로이. 꽈마 사바다니. 구 구더다 뿌: 오오 다다, 오오 다다, 찌 짜쭈미러 와네러거러라?

35. 바쭈 바우마 꽈바 바바아 바레 아오꽈, 보삐러 바짜, 버라 구더다 뿌: 무빠아 버쭈! 아마아꽈 어릐야.

31. In the same way the chief priests and the teachers of the law mocked him among themselves. "He saved others," they said, "but he can't save himself!

32. Let this Christ, this King of Israel, come down now from the cross, that we may see and believe." Those crucified with him also heaped insults on him.

33. At the sixth hour darkness came over the whole land until the ninth hour.

34. And at the ninth hour Jesus cried out in a loud voice, "Eloi, Eloi, lama sabachthani?"--which means, "My God, my God, why have you forsaken me?"

35. When some of those standing near heard this, they said, "Listen, he's calling Elijah."

36. Muuma mubo, era kulyibita aya kulobeka e chiraka mwa ngala y'e difai, era kuminyirachi kwa lusheke. Chasinda, era kwerusisa chi Yesu amwe. Era kuteta mbu: Murekaa chwulole akaba Eliya angaika kumwandaasa kwa musalaba.

37. Si Yesu era kuhuba kulakanga na murenge munene, chasinda era kutowa e muchima.

38. Mw'olu, e gwaya era yabaa yahumba mwa luhu lwa Ongo, unao-unao kuna kubereka mu bimbi bibilyi, kutengera era lulu kuikira era masina.

39. Aola abaa alyi mukulu-kulu muuma wa basula b'e baroma, emenze era muhondo sa Yesu. Oyu mukulu-kulu, mango alolaa kwa Yesu atowa e muchima, era kuire ateta mbu: Kubinalyi, ono mundu anabaa mwana wa Ongo!

40. Bakasi bauma nabo, babaa bemenze marerere, bachwumbikisa. Mw'abu bakasi, mwabaa mulyi Mariya w'e makatala, na Salome, na mariya nyina wa yakobo na yose.

36. 무우마 무보, 어라 구레비다 아야 구로버가 어찌라가 과 빠꽈 여 디파이, 어라 구미네라찌 과 루써거. 짜시따, 어라 귀루시사 찌 여수 아뭐. 어라 구더다 뿌: 무러가아 쭈론러 아가바 어리야 아까이가 구꽈따아사 과 무사꽈바.

37. 시 여수 어라 구후바 구꽈가까 나 무러꺼 무너너, 짜시따 어라 구도와 어 무찌마.

38. 모루, 어 과야 어라 야바아 야후빠 과 루후 꽈 오꼬, 우나오-우나오 구나 구버러가 무 비뻬 비비레, 구더꺼라 어라 루루 구이기라 어라 마시나.

39. 아오꽈 아바아 아레 무구루-구루 무우마 와 바수꽈 버 바로마, 어머써 어라 무호또 사 여수. 오유 무구루-구루, 마꼬 아론꽈아 과 여수 아도와 어 무찌마, 어라 구이러 아더다 뿌: 구비나레, 오노 무뚜 아나바아 뫄나 와 오꼬!

40. 바가시 바우마 나보, 바바아 버머써 마러러러, 바쭈뻬기사. 꽈부 바가시, 꽈바아 무레 마리야 워 마가다꽈, 나 사론머, 나 마리야 네나 와 야고보 나 요서.

36. One man ran, filled a sponge with wine vinegar, put it on a stick, and offered it to Jesus to drink. "Now leave him alone. Let's see if Elijah comes to take him down," he said.

37. With a loud cry, Jesus breathed his last.

38. The curtain of the temple was torn in two from top to bottom.

39. And when the centurion, who stood there in front of Jesus, heard his cry and saw how he died, he said, "Surely this man was the Son of God!"

40. Some women were watching from a distance. Among them were Mary Magdalene, Mary the mother of James the younger and of Joses, and Salome.

41. Abu bakasi, bu babaa benjire bakulyikira Yesu na kunde bamukunganyisa e bilyo mango abaa alyi e kalilaya. Kanji kwabaa kulyi na banji bakasi banene, ba berukiraa nai eYerusalemu.

41. 아부 바가시, 부 바바아 버찌러 바구꼐기라 여수 나 구떠 바무구꽈네사 어 비료 마꼬 아바아 아례 어 가삐라야. 가찌 과바아 구꼐 나 바찌 바가시 바너너, 바 버루기라아 나이 어여루사쩌무.

41. In Galilee these women had followed him and cared for his needs. Many other women who had come up with him to Jerusalem were also there.

Yesu atabwa

여수 아다봐

42. Mango lwabaa lwera luolo-olo, kwera kuulukira mulume muuma mbu I Yosefu, mwesha mwa musi w'e Arimateya. Oyu yosefu, abaa achwusa echwunda mwa karubanda k'e bayuta. Kanji endee alangalyira ekuika kw'e bwami bwa Ongo.

42. 마꼬 똬바아 뭐라 루오로- 오로, 궈라 구우루기라 무루머 무우마 뿌 이 요서푸, 뭐싸 뫄 무시 워 아리마더야. 오유 요서푸, 아바아 아쭈사 어쭈따 뫄 가루바따 거 바유다. 가찌 어떠어 아똬꺄쪠라 어구이가 궈 봐미 봐 오꼬.

42. It was Preparation Day (that is, the day before the Sabbath). So as evening approached,

43. Rero bushi olu lusuku lu lwabaa lw'e kuchikunganya kwa lusuku lw'e sabato, Yosefu era kusesa e muchima na aya era mwa pilato, amweme e chirunda cha Yesu.

43. 러로 부씨 오루 루수구 루 똬바아 뭐 구찌구꽈냐 과 루수구 뭐 사바도, 요서푸 어라 구서사 어 무찌마 나 아야 어라 뫄 피똬도, 아뭐머 어 찌루따 짜 여수.

43. Joseph of Arimathea, a prominent member of the Council, who was himself waiting for the kingdom of God, went boldly to Pilate and asked for Jesus' body.

44. Pilato era kusanwa busese mwa kumva mbu Yesu afire mira. Bushi n'oku, era ku chwumisa ola mukulu-kulu w'e basula, amubuse akaba kwarenga bihangi binene Yesu afire.

44. 피똬도 어라 구사놔 부서서 뫄 구빠 뿌 여수 아피러 미라. 부씨 노구, 어라 구 쭈미사 오라 무구루-구루 워 바수똬, 아무부서 아가바 과러꺄 비하끼 비너너 여수 아피러.

44. Pilate was surprised to hear that he was already dead. Summoning the centurion, he asked him if Jesus had already died.

45. Oyu mukulu-kulu w'e basula era kumubura kwa Yesu afire mira. Pilato era kwire emerera mbu yosefu anatolaa

45. 오유 무구루-구루 워 바수똬 어라 구무부라 과 여수 아피러 미라. 피똬도 어라 귀러 어머러라 뿌 요서푸

45. When he learned from the centurion that it was so, he gave the body to Joseph.

echi chirunda.

아나도꽈아 어찌 찌루따.

46. Yosefu era kuya kuula e ngwaya, era kwandaasa e chirunda cha Yesu kwa musalaba, na abunga-bungira chi mwei ngwaya. Era kutaba chi mwa chinjifwa cha chabaa chichimirwe mw'ekoi. Chasinda, kwa chiso chinjifwa, era kukunungulyira kw'ekoi.

46. 요서푸 어라 구야 구우꽈 어 꽈야, 어라 과따아사 어 찌루따 짜 여수 과 무사꽈바, 나 아부꽈-부꾀라 찌 뭐이 꽈야. 어라 구다바 찌 마 찌찌꽈 짜 짜바아 찌찌미뤄 뭐고이. 짜시따, 과 찌소 찌찌꽈, 어라 구구누우꿔레라 궈고이.

46. So Joseph bought some linen cloth, took down the body, wrapped it in the linen, and placed it in a tomb cut out of rock. Then he rolled a stone against the entrance of the tomb.

47. Mariya w'e Makatala, na mariya nyina wa yose, babaa bachwumbikisa e chisiki cha Yesu atabwaamo.

47. 마리야 워 마가다꽈, 나 마리야 네나 와 요서, 바바아 바쭈삐기사 어 찌시기 짜 여수 아다바아모.

47. Mary Magdalene and Mary the mother of Joses saw where he was laid.

Mariko Chikono 16
E kwomoka kwa Yesu

마리고 찌고노 16
어 고모가 과 여수

Mark Chapter 16[NIV]

1. Mango e lusuku lw'e sabato lwabaa lwera lwarengaa, mariya w'e Makalata, na Salome, na mariya nyina wa yakobo, bera kuula marashi, baye kumakaba e chirunda cha Yesu.

1. 마오 어 루수구 뤄 사바도 꽈바아 뤄라 꽈러꽈아, 마리야 워 마가꽈다, 나 사로머, 나 마리야 네나 와 야고보, 버라 구우꽈 마라씨, 바여 구마가바 어 찌루따 짜 여수.

1. When the Sabbath was over, Mary Magdalene, Mary the mother of James, and Salome bought spices so that they might go to anoint Jesus' body.

2. Abere lweinga lumbulyi-mbulyi, e suba lyichilyi lyauluka, abu bakasi bera kulamukira kwa shinda.

2. 아버러 뤄이꽈 루뿌꿰레-뿌꿰어 수바 꿰찌꿰 꺅우루가, 아부 바가시 버라 구꽈무기라 과 씨따.

2. Very early on the first day of the week, just after sunrise, they were on their way to the tomb

3. Babaa baenda babusanya mbu: Ly'ekoi lya lyilyi kwa chiso ch'e shinda, nde iungachwukunungulyiralyi?

3. 바바아 바어따 바부사냐 뿌: 뤼어고이 꺅 꿰꿰 과 찌소 쩌 씨따, 터 이우꽈쭈구누우꿰라꿰?

3. and they asked each other, "Who will roll the stone away from the entrance of the tomb?"

4. Batetaa bacha, bushi elyi koi lyabaa lyinene busese. Si abere bemuse e meho, kuna kulola kwa lyasiikirwe mira.

5. Abu bakasi mango bengiraa mwa shinda, bera kubuanamo mutabana muuma ekese kwa lunda lw'e malyo, embese eropo lyalangala Pe-Pe-Pe! Bamulolyireko, kuna kuchihalyima.

6. Oyu mutabana, era kubabura mbu: Mutobaa! Nyishi kwa mwahonda Yesu w'e Nasareti ola bamanyikaa kwa musalaba. Atachilyi anola, awomokire mira. Muchiloreraa mu beine ala babaa bamubikire.

7. Rero muyaa kubura petero n'e banji banafunzi mbu abahondorere e kalilaya. Eyera, yi mungamulorerako, kukulyikana n'okwa anababuraa.

8. Unao-unao, ba bakasi kuna kutenga kwa shinda malyibita. Babaa bakukumana na kusanywa busese. Rero bushi n'e kufa buba bunene, chiro bakabura mundju mwasi usibya.

Yesu apamukira ku Mariya w'e Makata

---

4. 바더다아 바짜, 부씨 어레고이 랴바아 레너너 부서서. 시 아버러 버무서 어 머호, 구나 구로꽈 과 랴시이기뤄미라.

5. 아부 바가시 마꼬 버삐라아 마 씨따, 버라 구부아나모 무다바나 무우마 어거서 과 루따 뤄 마뾰, 어뻐서 어로포 랴꽈까꽈 퍼-퍼-퍼! 바무로레러고, 구나 구찌하레마.

6. 오유 무다바나, 어라 구바부라 뿌: 무도바아! 네씨 과 마호따 여수 워 나사러디 오꽈 바마네가아 과 무사꽈바. 아다찌레 아노꽈, 아오모기러미라. 무찌로러라아 무 버이너 아꽈 바바아 바무비기러.

7. 러로 무야아 구부라 퍼더로 너 바찌 바나푸씨 뿌 아바호또러러 어 가삐꽈야. 어여라, 에 무까무로러라고, 구구레가나 노과 아나바부라아.

8. 우나오-우나오, 바 바가시 구나 구더까 과 씨따 마레비다. 바바아 바구구마나 나 구사네와 부서서. 러로 부씨 너 구파 부바 부너너, 찌로 바가부라 무뚜 와시 우시뱌.

여수 아파무기라 구 마리야 워 마가다

---

4. But when they looked up, they saw that the stone, which was very large, had been rolled away.

5. As they entered the tomb, they saw a young man dressed in a white robe sitting on the right side, and they were alarmed.

6. "Don't be alarmed," he said. "You are looking for Jesus the Nazarene, who was crucified. He has risen! He is not here. See the place where they laid him.

7. But go, tell his disciples and Peter, 'He is going ahead of you into Galilee. There you will see him, just as he told you.' "

8. Trembling and bewildered, the women went out and fled from the tomb. They said nothing to anyone, because they were afraid.

9. Abere lweinga lumbulyi-mbulyi, Yesu era omwokaa, era kupamukira tanga ku mariya w'e Makatala ola ambulaa ku bihwasi bilyinda.

10. Oyu Mariya, era kuya kubalyira e banfunzi ba Yesu kw'oyu mwasi. Abu banafunzi, babaa banachilyi balyilyira Yesu na businane bunene.

11. Na mango bomvaa kwa mariya ababura mbu Yesu alyi muuma-uma, anamulolyireko, chiro bakamwemerera.

Yesu apamukira ku banafunzi bai babilyi

12. Era nyuma s'ebi, banafunzi babilyi ba Yesu babaa baya mwa kambara. Yesu era kupamukirako mu lyinji ehuhe.

13. Bera kufuluka baya kubakulyira balyikabo kw'oyu mwasi. Si nabo chirobakabemerera.

Yesu apamukira kwa djumwa sai ekumi na nguma

14. Chasinda, Yesu era kupamukira e ndjumwa sai ekumi na nguma mango babaa balya. Era kubakalyiira busese bushi n'e kutaata e bwemeresi, kanji bushi n'e kuira e michima yabo kuba

9. 아버러 뤄이빠 루뿌쩨-뿌쩨, 여수 어라 오모가아, 어라 구파무기라 다빠 구 마리야 워 마가다뫄 오뫄 아뿌롸아 구 비화시 비쩨따.

10. 오유 마리야, 어라 구야 구바쩨라 어 바누푸씨 바 여수 교유 뫄시. 아부 바나푸씨, 바바아 바나찌쩨 바쩨쩨라 여수 나 부시나너 부너너.

11. 나 마꼬 보빠아 과 마리야 아바부라 뿌 여수 아쩨 무우마-우마, 아나무로쩨러고, 찌로 바가뭐머러라.

여수 아파무기라 구 바나푸씨 바이 바비쩨

12. 어라 뉴마 서비, 바나푸씨 바비쩨 바 여수 바바아 바야 뫄 가빠라. 여수 어라 구파무기라고 무 쩨찌 어후허.

13. 버라 구푸루가 바야 구바구쩨라 바쩨가보 교유 뫄시. 시 나보 찌로바가버머러라.

여수 아파무기라 과 주뫄 사이 어구미 나 우마

14. 짜시따, 여수 어라 구파무기라 어 뚜뫄 사이 어구미 나 우마 마꼬 바바아 바퍅. 어라 구바가쩨이라 부서서 부씨 너 구다아다 어 뭐머러시, 가찌 부씨 너 구이라 어 미찌마 야보 구바

9. When Jesus rose early on the first day of the week, he appeared first to Mary Magdalene, out of whom he had driven seven demons.

10. She went and told those who had been with him and who were mourning and weeping.

11. When they heard that Jesus was alive and that she had seen him, they did not believe it.

12. Afterward Jesus appeared in a different form to two of them while they were walking in the country.

13. These returned and reported it to the rest; but they did not believe them either.

14. Later Jesus appeared to the Eleven as they were eating; he rebuked them for their lack of faith and their stubborn refusal to believe those who had seen him after he had risen.

isibu. Abakalyiira bacha, bushi batemereraa e myasi yaba bamulolaako era nyuma s'e kwomoka kwai.

15. Chasinjire, Yesu era kwire ababura mbu: Muyaa mwa butala boshi, muhubanganyise e bandju boshi e Mwasi Mubuya-buya.

16. Chira mundju ola ungemerera na kubatisibwa anganunulyibwa. Si ola utemerere, yeke angachinjibusibwa.

17. Na ba bangemerera, bagende baira bine bisomerano: bangende baambula e bihwasi kw'e sina lyanyi na kunde bateta mu manji mateta.

18. Kanji akaba bangasimba e njoka, nesi bamwa cha chingeta e mundju, batafe kandju. Bagende balamya n'e balwala mwa kubabika kw'e mino.

Yesu erusibwa kwa nguba

19. Mango enawechwu Yesu abaa era amalaa kubura e banfunzi bai ei myasi, era kwerusibwa kwa nguba. Era kuya kwikala kwa lunda lw'e malyo ma Ongo.

20. E banafunzi, bera kuya

이시부. 아바가꼐이라 바짜, 부씨 바더머러라아 어 먀시 야바 바무로롸아고 어라 뉴마서 고모가 과이.

15. 짜시띠러, 여수 어라 귀러 아바부라 뿌: 무야아 뫄 부다라 보씨, 무후바까네서 어 바뚜 보씨 어 먀시 무부야-부야.

16. 찌라 무뚜 오롸 우꺼머러라 나 구바디시봐 아꺼누누꼐봐. 시 오롸 우더머러러, 여거 아꺼찌띠부시봐.

17. 나 바 바꺼머러라, 바거머 바이라 비너 비소머라노: 바꺼머 바아뿌롸 어 비화시 귀 시나 럇네 나 구머 바더다 무 마찌 마더다.

18. 가찌 아가바 바꺼시빠 어 쪼가, 너시 바뫄 짜 찌머다 어 무뚜, 바다퍼 가뚜. 바거머 바롸먀 너 바꽈라 뫄 구바비가 귀 미노.

여수 어루시봐 과 우바

19. 마꼬 어나워쭈 여수 아바아 어라 아마꽈아 구부라 어 바누푸씨 바이 어이 먀시, 어라 귀루시봐 과 우바. 어라 구야 귀가롸 과 루따 뤄 마료 마 오꼬.

20. 어 바나푸씨, 버라 구야

15. He said to them, "Go into all the world and preach the good news to all creation.

16. Whoever believes and is baptized will be saved, but whoever does not believe will be condemned.

17. And these signs will accompany those who believe: In my name they will drive out demons; they will speak in new tongues;

18. they will pick up snakes with their hands; and when they drink deadly poison, it will not hurt them at all; they will place their hands on sick people, and they will get well."

19. After the Lord Jesus had spoken to them, he was taken up into heaven and he sat at the right hand of God.

20. Then the disciples went

kuhubanganya e Mwasi Mubuya-buya mwa bisiki byoshi. Enawechwu i Yesu era kunde akola alauma nabo na kuberesa e buashi bw'e kunde baira e bisomerano, kwa kulosa kwa e mwasi era benjire bahubanganyisa e bandju inalyi ya kanangana.

구후바까냐 어 먀시 무부야-부야 먀 비시기 뵤씨. 어나워쭈 이 여수 어라 구떠 아고꽈 아꽈우마 나보 나 구버러사 어 부아씨 붜 구떠 바이라 어 비소머라노, 과 구룬사 과 어 먀시 어라 버띠러 바후바까네사 어 바뚜 이나쩨 야 가나까나.

out and preached everywhere, and the Lord worked with them and confirmed his word by the signs that accompanied it.

Luka

루가

Luke

**MWASI MUBUYABUYA N'NGOKWA
AKOROTOLA LUKA**

마시 무부야부야 우오과
아고로도쫘 루가

Luka Chikono 1

1. Kwabushi bandju banene babikire e maboko mabo kukunganya e myasi y'e bya byailyibwaa muno chio chechwu,

2. n'ngokwa bachwureteraa e babeyi n'e bakosi kutengera kwa ndangilyiso soyo mwasi,

3. Nalolaa kanangana kwabushi nakulyikiraa e myasi y'e tenene ya byoshi kutengera kwa ndangilyiso kukukorotera walyia Teofile,

4. w'ekale wamenyerere e kanangana k'e myasi era w'elyisibwaa.

Sakaria n' Elizabeti

5. Mango Heroti abaa emire mwa chio ch'e Bayuda, kwabaa mulume muuma mbu I Sakariya. Abaa muuma mwa Bayuda ba bendaa bekera Ongo e michwulo, w'omwa chikembe cha kuhanyi mukulu-kulu Abiya. Mukai Elizabeti,

루가 찌고노 1

1. 과부씨 바꾸 바너너 바비기러어 마보고 마보 구구꺄냐 어 먀시 여 뱌 뱌이레봐아 무노 찌오 쩌쭈,

2. 우꼬과 바쭈러더라아 어 바버에 너 바고시 구더뻐라 과 따삐레소 소요 먀시,

3. 나롸라아 가나꺄나 과부씨 나구뻬기라아 어 먀시 여 더너너 야 뵤씨 구더뻐라 과 따삐레소 구구고로더라 와뻬아 더오피뻐,

4. 워가뻐 와머녀러러 어 가나꺄나 거 먀시 어라 워뻬시봐아.

사가리아 우 어삐잉박듯

5. 마꼬 허로디 아바아 어미러 롸 찌오 쩌 바우다, 과바아 무루머 무우마 뿌 이 사가리야. 아바아 무우마 뫄 바유다 바 버따아 버거라 오꼬 어 미쭈롼, 요먀 찌거뻐 쨔 구하네 무구루-구루 아비야. 무가이 어삐자버디, 아바아 요먀 루후

Luke Chapter 1[NIV]

1. Many have undertaken to draw up an account of the things that have been fulfilled among us,

2. just as they were handed down to us by those who from the first were eyewitnesses and servants of the word.

3. Therefore, since I myself have carefully investigated everything from the beginning, it seemed good also to me to write an orderly account for you, most excellent Theophilus,

4. so that you may know the certainty of the things you have been taught.

5. In the time of Herod king of Judea there was a priest named Zechariah, who belonged to the priestly division of Abijah; his wife Elizabeth was also a descendant of Aaron.

abaa w'omwa luhu lwa Aroni, I wabaa kuhanyi wa Ongo mubere-bere w'e bana b'e Isiraeli.

6. Sakariya n'Elisabeti babaa babuya era muhondo sa Ongo n'e kunemerera e myaso yai yoshi mwa kalamo kabu. Kanji Ongo yeine anachiloreraa kwa mikorere yabu.

7. Si bainaa e buta, bushi Elizabeti abaa ngumba. Kanji e myaka bombi babaa bera bete yabaa itangachichwuma babuta.

8. Mango e lusuku lw'e chikembe cha Sakariya kwa kuchwulyira Ongo mwa Luhu lwa ikaa, era kulondolwa na balyikabu.

9. Bushi n'oku, olu lusuku I wabaa ulyi mwa Luhu lwa Ongo* akalanga e marashi ma maukira Ongo.

10. Echi chihangi Sakariya abaa alyi mwa mulyimo mw'olu Luhu, e bandju boshi b'eshibaa era butala b'ema Ongo.

11. Abere Sakariya era analyi mwa mulyimo, unao-unao e ndonyi ya Ongo kuna kumupamukira ku. Era kwimanga kwa lunda lw'e

---

꽈 아로니, 이 와바아 구하네 와 오꼬 무버러-버러 워 바나 버 이시라어삐.

6. 사가리야 너삐사버디 바바아 바부야 어라 무호또 사 오꼬 너 구너머러라 어 먀소 야이 요씨 먀 가랴모 가부. 가찌 오꼬 여이너 아나찌뢰러라아 과 미고러러 야부.

7. 시 바이나아 어 부다, 부씨 어삐자버디 아바아 꾸빠. 가찌 어 먀가 보뻬 바바아 버라 버더 야바아 이다꽈찌쭈마 바부다.

8. 마꼬 어 루수구 뤄 찌거뻐 짜 사가리야 과 구쭈쩨라 오꼬 먀 루후 꽈 이가아, 어라 구로또꽈 나 바레가부.

9. 부씨 노구, 오루 루수구 이 와바아 우레 먀 루후 꽈 오꼬* 아가꽈까 어 마라씨 마 마우기라 오꼬.

10. 어찌 찌하삐 사가리야 아바아 아레 먀 무레모 모루 루후, 어 바뚜 보씨 버씨바아 어라 부다꽈 버마 오꼬.

11. 아버러 사가리야 어라 아나레 먀 무레모, 우나오-우나오 어 또네 야 오꼬 구나 구무파무기라 구. 어라 귀마까 과 루따 뤄 마룬 머 가하하 가

---

6. Both of them were upright in the sight of God, observing all the Lord's commandments and regulations blamelessly.

7. But they had no children, because Elizabeth was barren; and they were both well along in years.

8. Once when Zechariah's division was on duty and he was serving as priest before God,

9. he was chosen by lot, according to the custom of the priesthood, to go into the temple of the Lord and burn incense.

10. And when the time for the burning of incense came, all the assembled worshipers were praying outside.

11. Then an angel of the Lord appeared to him, standing at the right side of the altar of incense.

malyo m'e kahaha ka bende
b'ochera kw'e marashi ma
maukira Ongo.

12. Sakariya amuhunjire kw'e
meho, kuna kuchihalima. Era
kusimbibwa na buba bunene.

13. S'e ndonyi ya Ongo y'era
kumubura: "Sakariya, utobaaa!
malyira mau m'e kuina e buta
mawere, bushi Ongo
am'omvire. Mukasi wau
Elizabeti angakubuchira mwana
wa busana, n'nau ugamwilyika e
sina mbu I Yowana.

14. Ekubuchibwa kw'oyu
mwana kukakusimisa busese, na
bandju banene bakaata lumoo
lunene bushi nai.

15. Kanji akaba mundju usitoire
era muhondo sa Ongo. Atakabe
mundju wa kumwa kapinda,
nesi manji mafu ma
makoochire. Akaata e Muchima
Mubuya-buya kutengera e
kubuchwa kwai.

16. Kanji akaalusa banene mu
benyi Isiraeli mwa maboko ma
Ongo I Enawabu.

17. Akabaha nga ndjumwa ya
Ongo, kanji aka koresibwa na
muchima ukomire kuuma na
murebi Eliya. Akachwuma e
basere basimana n'e bana babu,
n'e kuhubya babuya ba

버떠 보쩌라 궈 마라씨 마
마우기라 오꼬.

12. 사가리야 아무후찌러 궈
머호, 구나 구찌하리마. 어라
구시뻬봐 나 부바 부너너.

13. 서 또네 야 오꼬 여라
E구무부라: "사가리야,
우도바아아! 어 마례라 마우 머
구이나 어 부다 마워러, 부씨
오꼬 아모뼤러. 무가시 와우
어쀠자버디 아빠구부찌라 모나
와 부사나, 우나우 우가뮈례가
어 시나 뿌 이 요와나.

14. 어구부찌봐 교유 모나
구가구시미사 부서서, 나 바뚜
바너너 바가아다 루모오 루너너
부씨 나이.

15. 가찌 아가바 무뚜
우시도이러 어라 무호또 사
오꼬. 아다가버 무뚜 와 구봐
가피따, 너시 마찌 마푸 마
마고오찌러. 아가아다 어 무찌마
무부야-부야 구더뚜라 어
구부좌 과이.

16. 가찌 아가아루사 바너너 무
버네 이시라어쀠 뫄 마보고 마
오꼬 이 어나와부.

17. 아가바하 빠 뚜뫄 야 오꼬,
가찌 아가 고러시봐 나 무찌마
우고미러 구우마 나 무러비
어쀠야. 아가쭈마 어 바서러
바시마나 너 바나 바부, 너
구후뱌 바부야 바 바찌찌러 어

12. When Zechariah saw
him, he was startled and
was gripped with fear.

13. But the angel said to
him: "Do not be afraid,
Zechariah; your prayer
has been heard. Your
wife Elizabeth will bear
you a son, and you are
to give him the name
John.

14. He will be a joy and
delight to you, and
many will rejoice
because of his birth,

15. for he will be great
in the sight of the Lord.
He is never to take wine
or other fermented
drink, and he will be
filled with the Holy Spirit
even from birth.

16. Many of the people
of Israel will he bring
back to the Lord their
God.

17. And he will go on
before the Lord, in the
spirit and power of
Elijah, to turn the hearts
of the fathers to their
children and the

bachinjire e myasi ya Ongo.Bushi n'oku, akachwuma e bandju bachikunganya mwa kulyinjira Enawechwu

18. Si Sakariya ea kubura malaika: "Chi chinganyilosa kw'echi watechire chilyi cha kanangana? Ulolaa kwa nyono nera mungumwa na mukasi wanyi era muekulu.

19. Unao-unao, e ndonyi ya Ongo y'era kumwakula: "Ilyi uteshi kwa nyono nyi ndonyi Gabuliere, nyi nyichwula mukosi w'omwa Bwami bwa Ongo? Yeine I wanyichwumire mbu nyikufuliraa n'e kukuisa kw'ono mwasi mubuya.

20. Nyisene kwa utahondaa kwemerera ene myasi nera kukubura n'noku itakekale itanabaa. Echera chi chingachwuma wahuba kachwuma kuikira mango oyu mwana akabutwa.

21. Mw'ebi bihangi byoshi, e bandju ba babaa bema era butala n'e kulinjira Sakariya basanwaa busese, bushi erisaa mwa Luhu lwa Ongo.

22. Abere Sakariya era auluka mwa Luhu lwa Ongo, chiro

먀시 야 오꼬.부씨 노구, 아가쭈마 어 바쭈 바찌구까냐 먀 구레찌라 어나워쭈

18. 시 사가리야 어아 구부라 마롸이가: "찌 찌까네로사 궈찌 와더찌러 찌레 짜 가나까나? 우르롸아 과 뇨노 너라 무우롸 나 무가시 와네 어라 무어구루.

19. 우나오-우나오, 어 또네 야 오꼬 여라 구롸구롸: "이레 우더씨 과 뇨노 네 또네 가부리어러, 네 네쭈롸 무고시 요롸 봐미 봐 오꼬? 여이너 이 와네쭈미러 뿌 네구푸리라아 너 구구이사 교노 먀시 무부야.

20. 네서너 과 우다호따아 궈머러라 어너 먀시 너라 구구부라 우노구 이다거가뻐 이다나바아. 어쩌라 찌 찌까쭈마 와후바 가쭈마 구이기라 마꼬 오유 롸나 아가부돠.

21. 뭐비 비하끼 뵤씨, 어 바쭈 바 바바아 버마 어라 부다롸 너 구뀌찌라 사가리야 바사놔아 부서서, 부씨 어리사아 롸 루후 롸 오꼬.

22. 아버러 사가리야 어라 아우루가 롸 루후 롸 오꼬, 찌로

---

disobedient to the wisdom of the righteous--to make ready a people prepared for the Lord."

18. Zechariah asked the angel, "How can I be sure of this? I am an old man and my wife is well along in years."

19. The angel answered, "I am Gabriel. I stand in the presence of God, and I have been sent to speak to you and to tell you this good news.

20. And now you will be silent and not able to speak until the day this happens, because you did not believe my words, which will come true at their proper time."

21. Meanwhile, the people were waiting for Zechariah and wondering why he stayed so long in the temple.

22. When he came out, he could not speak to

akachiala kubabura kandju, bushi abaa era alyi kachwuma. Kanji abaa era anabahambalyisa mwa mino. E bandju boshi bera kumenyerera kwa achimananyire na Ongo.

23. Mango e bihangi bya Sakariya by'e kukola mwa Luhu lwa Ongo byabaa byawere, era kuhuba kwa wai.

24. Era nyuma sa suku sitaanjirwe, Elisabeti era kuba mukure. Era kuira myesi etano busira kuuluka. Mw'esi siku, era kunde anateta mmbu:

25. "Enawechwu Ongo atongwe, bushi anyikulire e honyi s'e buumba era muhondo s'e bandju.

아가찌아꽈 구바부라 가뚜, 부씨 아바아 어라 아뢰 가쭈마. 가찌 아바아 어라 아나바하빠뤠사 뫄 미노. 어 바뚜 보씨 버라 구머녀러라 과 아찌마나니러 나 오꼬.

23. 마꼬 어 비하삐 뱌 사가리야 뱌 구고꽈 뫄 루후 꽈 오꼬 뱌바아 뱌워러, 어라 구후바 과 와이.

24. 어라 뉴마 사 수구 시다아찌뤄, 어삐사버디 어라 구바 무구러. 어라 구이라 며시 에다노 부시라 구우루가. 뭐시 시구, 어라 구떠 아나더다 무뿌:

25. "어나워쭈 오꼬 아도꿔, 부씨 아네구뤼러 어 호네 서 부우빠 어라 무호또 서 바뚜.

them. They realized he had seen a vision in the temple, for he kept making signs to them but remained unable to speak.

23. When his time of service was completed, he returned home.

24. After this his wife Elizabeth became pregnant and for five months remained in seclusion.

25. "The Lord has done this for me," she said. "In these days he has shown his favor and taken away my disgrace among the people."

Eburebi bw'ekubutwa kwa Yesu

어부러비 붜구부돠 과 여수

26. Abere e bukure bwa Elisabeti bwaika mwa myesi ndachwu, Ongo era kuchwuma e ndonyi Gabuliere kuhambala na munyere muuma mbu I Mariya, w'mwa musi w'eNasareti, mwa chio ch'eKalilaya.

27. Oyu munyere abaa ahambalyirwa na mutabana muuma mbu I Yosefu, w'omwa chirongo cha Daudi.

26. 아버러 어 부구러 봐 어삐사버디 봐이가 뫄 며시 따쭈, 오꼬 어라 구쭈마 어 또네 가부뤼어러 구하빠꽈 나 무녀러 무우마 뿌 이 마리야, 우뫄 무시 워나사러디, 뫄 찌오 쩌가삐롸야.

27. 오유 무녀러 아바아 아하빠뤠라 나 무다바나 무우마 뿌 이 요서푸, 요뫄 찌로꼬 짜 다우디.

26. In the sixth month, God sent the angel Gabriel to Nazareth, a town in Galilee,

27. to a virgin pledged to be married to a man named Joseph, a descendant of David.

Endonyi y'olukira ku Maria

28. Abere gabuliere aika ala Mariya abaa ekesi, era kumubura: "Bolo Mariya, Enawetu Ongo akweresise muisha munene, kanji alyi alauma nau.

29. Mango Mariya omvaa bacha, e muchima era kumuya bure. Era kutangilyisa achibusa, chi chingachwuma e ndonyi amulamusa bacha.

30. gabuliere alolyire bacha, era kubura Mariya: Utobaaa Mariya, natechire kanji: Ongo akweresise muisha munene.

31. N'noyu muisha I yono: Kutarenge kanga utabere mukure. Chasinda, ungabuta mwana wa busana n'e kumwirika esina mbu I Yesu.

32. Akaba mukulu-kulu munene n'e kwirikwa Mwenyi Ongo utula kwa nguba. Kanji Enawechwu Ongo yeine akamweresa e bwami bwa hokulu wai Daudi,

33. Akema e siku n'e mango mwa lubaa lwa Isiraeli. Kanji e Bwimi bwai butakawe.

34. Abere Kabuliere era amalaa kuteta, Mariya era Kumubusa:

어또네 요룮굿띱 구 마리아

28. 아버러 가부퓌어러 아이가 아롸 마리야 아바아 어거시, 어라 구무부라: "보뢴 마리야, 어나워두 오꼬 아궈러시서 무이싸 무너너, 가찌 아뤠 아롸우마 나우.

29. 마꼬 마리야 오빠아 바짜, 어 무찌마 어라 구무야 부러. 어라 구다삐레사 아찌부사, 찌 찌빠쭈마 어 또니 아무롸무사 바짜.

30. 가부퓌어러 아뢴레러 바짜, 어라 구부라 마리야: 우도바아아 마리야, 나더찌러 가찌: 오꼬 아궈러시서 무이싸 무너너.

31. 우노유 무이싸 이 요노: 구다러뼈 가빠 우다버러 무구러. 짜시따, 우빠부다 뫄나 와 부사나 너 구뮈리가 어시나 뿌 이 여수.

32. 아가바 무구룪-구룮 무너너 너 귀리과 뭐네 오꼬 우두롸 과 꾸바. 가찌 어나워쭈 오꼬 여이너 아가뭐러사 어 봐미 봐 호구룮 와이 다우디,

33. 아거마 어 시구 너 마꼬 뫄 룪바아 롸 이시라어뤼. 가찌 어 뷔미 봐이 부다가워.

34. 아버러 가부퓌어러 어라 아마롸아 구더다, 마리야 어라

The virgin's name was Mary.

28. The angel went to her and said, "Greetings, you who are highly favored! The Lord is with you."

29. Mary was greatly troubled at his words and wondered what kind of greeting this might be.

30. But the angel said to her, "Do not be afraid, Mary, you have found favor with God.

31. You will be with child and give birth to a son, and you are to give him the name Jesus.

32. He will be great and will be called the Son of the Most High. The Lord God will give him the throne of his father David,

33. and he will reign over the house of Jacob forever; his kingdom will never end."

34. "How will this be," Mary asked the angel,

Kute nyono nyingaba mukure ndeshi na chiro na mulume?

35. Kabuliere nai era kumwakula: Muchima Mubuya-buya angakwandaalira, kanji e buashi bwa Ongo bungaba alauma nau n'e kukulang. Echera chi chingatuma ola ungabutwa akaba Mubuya-buya, kanji erikwa Mwana wa Ongo.

36. Si weine wishi kwa munyakenytu Elisabeti, ete bukure bwa myesi ndatu, chiro angaba mbu era muekulu kanji atula ngumba.

37. Umenyererаа kwa kutalyi cha chitangaalikana na Ongo."

38. Mango Mariya abaa era omvaa ebi byoshi, era kwakula Kabuliere: "Nyono nyiri muanda - kasi wa Ongo, ndangaisha mwa cha atechire, binabaa ng'okwa watechire. "hasinjire, bera kulikanuka.

Mariya atabira Elisabeti

39. Mw'esi siku, Mariya atachibandaa kana ataambirire kwa misi y'omwa miruko y'e Yuteya.

40. Aikire yi, era kuya mwa nyumba ya Sakariya n'e kukesa Elisabeti.

구무부사: 구더 뇨노 네까바 무구러 떠씨 나 찌로 나 무루머?

35. 가부피어러 나이 어라 구꽈구꽈: 무찌마 무부야-부야 아까과따아뀌라, 가찌 어 부아씨 봐 오꼬 부까바 아꽈우마 나우 너 구구꽈우. 어쩌라 찌 찌까두마 오꽈 우까부돠 아가바 무부야-부야, 가찌 어리과 꽈나 와 오꼬.

36. 시 워이너 위씨 과 무냐거네두 어뤼사버디, 어더 부구러 봐 며시 따두, 찌로 아까바 뿌 어라 무어구루 가찌 아두꽈 우빠.

37. 우머녀러라아 과 구다뤠 짜 찌다까아뀌가나 나 오꼬."

38. 마꼬 마리야 아바아 어라 오빠아 어비 뵤시, 어라 과구꽈 가부피어러: "뇨노 네리 무아따 - 가시 와 오꼬, 따까이싸 꽈 짜 아더찌러, 비나바아 꼬과 와더찌러. "하시찌러, 버라 구뀌가누가.

마리야 아다비라 어뤼뻽박듯

39. 뭐시 시구, 마리야 아다찌바빠아 가나 아다아뻬리러 과 미시 요꽈 미루고 여 유더야.

40. 아이기러 에, 어라 구야 꽈 뉴빠 야 사가리야 너 구거사 어뤼사버디.

"since I am a virgin?"

35. The angel answered, "The Holy Spirit will come upon you, and the power of the Most High will overshadow you. So the holy one to be born will be called the Son of God.

36. Even Elizabeth your relative is going to have a child in her old age, and she who was said to be barren is in her sixth month.

37. For nothing is impossible with God."

38. "I am the Lord's servant," Mary answered. "May it be to me as you have said." Then the angel left her.

39. At that time Mary got ready and hurried to a town in the hill country of Judea,

40. where she entered Zechariah's home and greeted Elizabeth.

41. Abere Elisabeti na Mariya bera bakesanya, emwana ola wabaa uli mwa bula bwa Elisabeti era kuchihaanya busese. Unao-unao, e Muchima Mubuya-buya era kumwandalyira.

42. Mw'echi chihangi, Elizabeti era kuteta na murenge munene: Ongo akuahanyire kurenza e bakasi boshi, kanji e ngahanyi sai singanaba kwa mwana ola ungabuchwa!

43. Nyilyi nde nyono w'e kukesibwa nau u nyina w'Enawechwu!

44. Utasene? Mango chwera kulamusanya, e mwana ola ulyi mwa bula bwanyi era kuchihaanya busese n'e kumoa.

45. Bolo era mwau, bushi wemereraa kw'e bya waburwaa kutenga era mwa Ongo binganaba kanangana."

Elwimbo lwa Mariya

46. Mariya era kuteta: "Nyono natongire Ongo mwa muchima wanyi woshi, I Enawetu kwa bubuya bwai,

47. kanji namoire mwa muchima wayi, bushi Ongo I Mulamya wanyi.

48. Yeine I wahondaa

---

41. 아버러 어뤼사버디 나 마리야 버라 바거사냐, 어마나 오롸 와바아 우뤼 먀 부롸 봐 어뤼사버디 어라 구찌하아냐 부서서. 우나오-우나오, 어 무찌마 무부야-부야 어라 구먀따쩨라.

42. 뭐찌 찌하삐, 어뤼자버디 어라 구더다 나 무러뻐 무너너: 오꼬 아구아하네러 구러싸 어 바가시 보씨, 가찌 어 빠하네 사이 시빠나바 과 먀나 오롸 우빠부쫘!

43. 네쩨 떠 뇨노 워 구거시봐 나우 우 네나 워나워쭈!

44. 우다서너? 마꼬 쮀라 구롸무사냐, 어 먀나 오롸 우레 먀 부롸 봐네 어라 구찌하아냐 부서서 너 구모아.

45. 보로 어라 먀우, 부씨 워머러라아 궈 뱌 와부롸아 구더빠 어라 먀 오꼬 비빠나바 가나빠나."

어뤼뽀 롸 마리야

46. 마리야 어라 구더다: "뇨노 나도삐러 오꼬 먀 무찌마 와네 오씨, 이 어나워두 과 부부야 봐이,

47. 가찌 나모이러 먀 무찌마 와에, 부씨 오꼬 이 무롸먀 와네.

48. 여이너 이 와호따아

---

41. When Elizabeth heard Mary's greeting, the baby leaped in her womb, and Elizabeth was filled with the Holy Spirit.

42. In a loud voice she exclaimed: "Blessed are you among women, and blessed is the child you will bear!

43. But why am I so favored, that the mother of my Lord should come to me?

44. As soon as the sound of your greeting reached my ears, the baby in my womb leaped for joy.

45. Blessed is she who has believed that what the Lord has said to her will be accomplished!"

46. And Mary said: "My soul glorifies the Lord

47. and my spirit rejoices in God my Savior,

48. for he has been

kunyiahanyira mango alolaa kwa burembu bwanyi nyi muanda - kasi wai. Kutengera lwarero, namenyire kw'ebandu boshi, e mukulu n'e mutoto, bakanyibura mbu nyete emuisha,

49. bushi Ongo, I Muala byoshi, anyikorere binene. Esina lyai lyinaldyi lyibuya -buya.

50. Ebihangi byoshi akanaba w'e kuahanyira boshi ba bamutunjire.

51. Akolire mirimo isitoire mwa misi y'emaboko mai, ahandabanyaa ebandu b'echirume-rume,

52. I wende wakula ba balya ebwami, kanji I wende wemikaebarebu.

53. Eresaa ba babaa bafire n'ebusinya bilyo binene, si afulusaa ebaare busira kandu;

54. Abahaa kuasa ebandju bai b'e lubaa lw'e Isiraeli, atanarekaa n'e bonjo bwai.

55. Echera kanangana chi analaanyaa bahokulu betu, kutengera ku Aburahamu

구네아하네라 마오 아로콰아 과 부러뿌 봐네 네 무아따 - 가시 와이. 구더떠라 콰러로, 나머네러 귀바뚜 보씨, 어 무구룹 너 무도도, 바가네부라 뿌 녀더 어무이싸,

49. 부씨 오오, 이 무아꽈 뵤씨, 아네고러러 비너너. 어시나 꺄이 레나룹두에 레부야 -부야.

50. 어비하삐 뵤씨 아가나바 워 구아하네라 보씨 바 바무두찌러.

51. 아고꾀러 미리모 이시도이러 꽈 미시 여마보고 마이, 아하따바냐아 어바뚜 버찌루머-루머,

52. 이 워떠 와구꽈 바 바퍄 어봐미, 가찌 이 워떠 워미가어바러부.

53. 어러사아 바 바바아 바피러 너부시냐 비뾰 비너너, 시 아푸루사아 어바아러 부시라 가뚜;

54. 아바하아 구아사 어바뚜 바이 버 루바아 뤄 이시라어쾨, 아다나러가아 너 보쪼 봐이.

55. 어쩌라 가나꽈나 찌 아나꽈아냐아 바호구룹 버두, 구더떠라 구 아부라하무

mindful of the humble state of his servant. From now on all generations will call me blessed,

49. for the Mighty One has done great things for me-- holy is his name.

50. His mercy extends to those who fear him, from generation to generation.

51. He has performed mighty deeds with his arm; he has scattered those who are proud in their inmost thoughts.

52. He has brought down rulers from their thrones but has lifted up the humble.

53. He has filled the hungry with good things but has sent the rich away empty.

54. He has helped his servant Israel, remembering to be merciful

55. to Abraham and his descendants forever, even as he said to our

kuikira ku bahukulisa bai boshi esuku n'emango.

56. Mariya amalaa myesi e hachwu era mwa Elisabeti.Chasinjire, era kuhuba era mwabu.

E kubuchwa kwa Yowana

57. Ebihangi by'ekubuta kwa Elisabeti byera kuika. Era kubut mwana wa busana.

58. Mango ebalungu bai na banyakabu bomvaa kwa Ongo amuahanyire kwa kumweresa ebutu, bamoaa busese al'auma nai.

59. Abere emwana aira suku munane abuchirwe, berakuya kumurenza mwa muya w'e kumonya e bana b'ebusana mwa Isiraeli. Kanji bahondaa kumwirika esina ly'eshe Sakariya.

60. Si nyina atahondaa erikwe eri sina. Era kubabura: "Esina ly'e mwana I Yowana."

61. Nabu bera kumwakula: "Si mwa chirongo chenyu mutatula mundju w'elyikirwe elyi sina!

62. Chasinjire, bera kubusa eshe nai mwa mino ng'okwa bendaa banahambala nai; Bra kumubusa: E sina lichie uhonjire kwilyika e mwana wachwuly

---

구이기라 구 바후구삐사 바이 보씨 어수구 너마꼬.

56. 마리야 아마꽈아 며시 어 하쭈 어라 꽈 어삐사버디.짜시찌러, 어라 구후바 어라 꽈부.

어 구부꽈 과 요와나

57. 어비하삐 벼구부다 과 어삐사버디 벼라 구이가. 어라 구부 꽈나 와 부사나.

58. 마꼬 어바루꾸 바이 나 바냐가부 보빠아 과 오꼬 아무아하너러 과 구뭐러사 어부두, 바모아아 부서서 아꽈우마 나이.

59. 아버러 어꽈나 아이라 수구 무나너 아부찌뤄, 버라구야 구무러싸 꽈 무야 워 구모냐 어 바나 버부사나 꽈 이시라어삐. 가찌 바호따아 구뮈리가 어시나 뤼어써 사가리야.

60. 시 니나 아다호따아 어리궈 어리 시나. 어라 구바부라: "어시나 뤼어 꽈나 이 요와나."

61. 나부 버라 구꽈구꽈: "시 꽈 찌로꼬 쩌뉴 무다두꽈 무뚜 워레기뤄 어레 시나!

62. 짜시찌러, 버라 구부사 어써 나이 꽈 미노 꼬과 버따아 바나하빠꽈 나이; 부라 구무부사: 어 시나 삐쩌 우호찌러 귀레가 어 꽈나

---

fathers."

56. Mary stayed with Elizabeth for about three months and then returned home.

57. When it was time for Elizabeth to have her baby, she gave birth to a son.

58. Her neighbors and relatives heard that the Lord had shown her great mercy, and they shared her joy.

59. On the eighth day they came to circumcise the child, and they were going to name him after his father Zechariah,

60. but his mother spoke up and said, "No! He is to be called John."

61. They said to her, "There is no one among your relatives who has that name."

62. Then they made signs to his father, to find out what he would like to name the child.

63. Sakariya era kubema hya chimbi hya chihaki anjike kw'esina ly'emwana. Era kwanjika mmbu: "E sina ly'e mwana I Yowayi. "Abere boshi balola bacha, bera kusanwa busese.

64. Unao-unao, e bunu bwa Sakariya bwera kubookala, kuna kutangirisa ateta n'e kutonga Ongo busese.

65. Bushi n'oku, e balungu bai boshi bobaaa busese. Kanji oyu mwasi era kumvikana mwa bandju boshi b'e chio ch'e Yudedea.

66. Boshi ba bomvaa kw'oyu mwasi basanwaa, bera kutetera mwa michima: "Ono mwana wabuchirwe ikaba ndwalyi! "Ku binalyi, bushi mwa kalamo ka Yowana, Ongo anabaa alauma nai.

Sakariya atonga Ongo

67. Sakariya, eshe w'e mwana, era kwandaalirwa n'e Muchima Mubuya-buya, kuna kutangiris ahambala nga murebi mmbu:

68. "Enawetu atongwe, I Ongo w'elsiraeli, bushi aasise e bandju bai n'e kubanunula mwa bucha.

63. 사가리야 어라 구버마 햐 찌뻬 햐 찌하기 아찌거 궈시나 뤼어모나라. 어라 과찌가 무뿌: "어 시나 뤼어 모나 이 요와에. "아버러 보씨 바뢰롸 바짜, 버라 구사놔 부서서.

64. 우나오-우나오, 어 부누 봐 사가리야 뷔라 구보오가롸, 구나 구다삐리사 아더다 너 구도까 오꼬 부서서.

65. 부씨 노구, 어 바루꾸 바이 보씨 보바아아 부서서. 가찌 오유 롸시 어라 구뻬가나 롸 바쭈 보씨 버 찌오 쩌 유더더아.

66. 보씨 바 보빠아 교유 롸시 바사놔아, 버라 구더더라 롸 미찌마: "오노 롸나 와부찌뤄 이가바 똬례! "구 비나례, 부씨 롸 가롸모 가 요와나, 오꼬 아나바아 아롸우마 나이.

사가리야 아도까 오꼬

67. 사가리야, 어써 워 롸나, 어라 과따아퓌롸 너 무찌마 무부야-부야, 구나 구다삐리수 아하빠롸 까 무러비 무뿌:

68. "어나워두 아도꿔, 이 오꼬 워이시라어퓌, 부씨 아아시서 어 바쭈 바이 너 구바누누롸 롸 부짜.

63. He asked for a writing tablet, and to everyone's astonishment he wrote, "His name is John."

64. Immediately his mouth was opened and his tongue was loosed, and he began to speak, praising God.

65. The neighbors were all filled with awe, and throughout the hill country of Judea people were talking about all these things.

66. Everyone who heard this wondered about it, asking, "What then is this child going to be?" For the Lord's hand was with him.

67. His father Zechariah was filled with the Holy Spirit and prophesied:

68. "Praise be to the Lord, the God of Israel, because he has come and has redeemed his

people.

69. Kwa kulosa chi, achwuchwumilyire e Mulamya ola wete e buashi mwa luhu lwa Daudi I wabaa muanda wai.

70. Ebye byoshi, e barebi ba Ongo bana bihambalaa ku kutengera mira.

71. Achwuchwumilyire ola ukachwununula kutenga mwa maboko m'e ngabo sechwu n'e barenda bechwu.

72. Alosaa e bonjo bwai ku bahokulu bechwu, kanji atebilyiraa e bilaano byai bibuya-buya.

73. Ku binalyi, Ongo alaisaa mwa meho ma hokulu wechwu Aburahamu,

74. mbu akachwukula mwa bucha bw'e ngabo sechwu,

Chwumutonga busira buba.

75. Kanji ahondaa chwube babuya-buya era muhondo sai n'e kumukorera ng'okwa anahonjire mwa kalamo kechwu koshi.

76. N'nau mwana wanyi, ukaba murebi wa Ongo, bushi woyu u ukaulukira era muhondo sa enawechwu n'e kukunganya e njira yai.

69. 과 구로사 찌, 아쭈쭈미례러 어 무롸먀 오롸 워더 어 부아씨 롸 루후 롸 다우디 이 와바아 무아따 와이.

70. 어벼 뵤씨, 어 바러비 바 오꼬 바나 비하빠롸나 구 구더러라 미라.

71. 아쭈쭈미례러 오롸 우가쭈누누롸 구더롸 롸 마보고 머 빠보 서쭈 너 바러따 버쭉.

72. 아로사아 어 보쪼 봐이 구 바호구루 버쭉, 가찌 아더비례라아 어 비롸아노 뱌이 비부야-부야.

73. 구 비나례, 오꼬 아롸이사아 롸 머호 마 호구루 워쭉 아부라하무,

74. 뿌 아가쭈구롸 롸 부짜 붜 빠보 서쭉,

쭈물명롸 부시라 부바.

75. 가찌 아호따아 쭈버 바부야-부야 어라 무호또 사이 너 구무고러라 꼬과 아나호찌러 롸 가롸모 거쭉 고씨.

76. 우나우 뫄나 와네, 우가바 무러비 와 오꼬, 부씨 오유 우 우가우루기라 어라 무호또 사 어나워쭉 너 구구빠냐 어 찌라 야이.

69. He has raised up a horn of salvation for us in the house of his servant David

70. (as he said through his holy prophets of long ago),

71. salvation from our enemies and from the hand of all who hate us--

72. to show mercy to our fathers and to remember his holy covenant,

73. the oath he swore to our father Abraham:

74. to rescue us from the hand of our enemies, and to enable us to serve him without fear

75. in holiness and righteousness before him all our days.

76. And you, my child, will be called a prophet of the Most High; for you will go on before the Lord to prepare the

77. Woyu u ukakanga e lubaa lwai kwa eshire kubanunula mwa kubabalyira e bibi byabu.

78. Enawechwu Ongo achwusa muchima wa chamba chinene. Bushi n'oku, angachwuchwumira kutengera kwa nguba ola uhuhire ng'e suba lya kahalalo;

79. kwa kulomekera ba bachilyi mwa musimya n'na ba bobaa e lufu, ilyi chwuboshi chwabona e bununusi kutenga era mw'e Mulamya."

80. Yowana era kwihuka, n'e muchima wai era kunasera. Atabaa ofu na bandju kuikira e lusuku achilosaa era muhondo s'e bana b'e Isiraeli.

Luka Chikono 2
kubuchwa kwa Yesu

1. Mango Kaisari Okisito abaa mwami mukulu-kulu mwa bio byoshi by'e Baroma babaa bemire mu, era kuteta mbu e masina m'ebandju boshi mw'ebi bio, manjikwaa.

2. E kwanjika e masina kubere-bere kulyi ng'oku, kwairwaa mango Korineli abaa emire mwa chio ch'e Suriya.

---

77. 오유 우 우가가까 어 루바아 똬이 과 어씨러 구바누누똬 뫄 구바바레라 어 비비 뱌부.

78. 어나워쭈 오꼬 아쭈사 무찌마 와 짜빠 찌너너. 부씨 노구, 아까쭈쭘미라 구더꺼라 과 꾸바 오라 우후히러 꺼 수바 랴 가하꺄로;

79. 과 구로머거라 바 바찌레 뫄 무시먀 우나 바 보바아 어 루푸, 이레 쭈보씨 쫘보나 어 부누누시 구더꺼 어라 뭐 무꺄먀."

80. 요와나 어라 귀후가, 너 무찌마 와이 어라 구나서라. 아다바아 오푸 나 바뉴 구이기라 어 루수구 아찌로사아 어라 무호또 서 바나 버 이시라어리.

루가 찌고노 2
구부쫘 과 여수

1. 마꼬 가이사리 오기시도 아바아 뫄미 무구루-구루 뫄 비오 뵤씨 벼 바로마 바바아 버미러 무, 어라 구더다 뿌 어 마시나 머바뉴 보씨 뭐비 비오, 마찌과아.

2. 어 과찌가 어 마시나 구버러-버러 구레 꼬구, 과이롸아 마꼬 고리너리 아바아 어미러 뫄 찌오 쩌 수리야.

---

way for him,

77. to give his people the knowledge of salvation through the forgiveness of their sins,

78. because of the tender mercy of our God, by which the rising sun will come to us from heaven

79. to shine on those living in darkness and in the shadow of death, to guide our feet into the path of peace."

80. And the child grew and became strong in spirit; and he lived in the desert until he appeared publicly to Israel.

Luke Chapter 2[NIV]

1. In those days Caesar Augustus issued a decree that a census should be taken of the entire Roman world.

2. (This was the first census that took place while Quirinius was governor of Syria.)

3. Bushi n'oku, e bandju boshi bera kuenda kuchanjikisa, chira mundju mwa musi wai w'e kabuchwa.

4. Yosefu nai era kutengera e Galilaya mwa musi w'e Nasareti, era kwirukira e Yuteya mwa musi ola Daudi abuchirwaa mu wirikirwe Betelehemu, bushi abaa w'omwa luhu lwa Daudi.

5. Mwa kuya kuchanjikisa, aendaa na Mariya, I munyere abaa ahambalyira, nai ilyi alyi karembe-rembe.

6. Abere baika e Betelehemu, e bukure bwa Mariya abaa ete bwera kutangirisa bwaluma.

7. Era kubuta e lubere lwai, mwana wa busana, era kumubika mwa Chasinjire, era kumuonjisa mwa mbare sa bifuana byende byalyira mu, bushi bainaa ala bangaonjira mwa nyumba y'e baenyi. biresi.

E ndonyi ya hambala n'e bangere be mbulyi

8. Mw'echi chio ch'e Yudeya, e bangere babaa bakeresa e bifuana byabu e butufu boshi, ofu n'e musi w'e Betelehemu.

9. Unao-unao, e ndonyi ya

---

3. 부씨 노구, 어 바뚜 보씨 버라 구어따 구짜씨기사, 찌라 무뚜 먀 무시 와이 워 가부쫘.

4. 요서푸 나이 어라 구더꺼라 어 가쀄꽈야 먀 무시 워 나사러디, 어라 귀루기라 어 유더야 먀 무시 오꽈 다우디 아부찌꽈아 무 위리기뤄 버더꺼허무, 부씨 아바아 요먀 루후 꽈 다우디.

5. 먀 구야 구짜씨기사, 아어따아 나 마리야, 이 무녀러 아바아 아하빠꿰라, 나이 이레 아꿰 가러뻐-러뻐.

6. 아버러 바이가 어 버더꺼허무, 어 부구러 봐 마리야 아바아 어더 붸라 구다삐리사 봐루마.

7. 어라 구부다 어 루버러 꽈이, 먀나 와 부사나, 어라 구무비가 먀 짜시삐러, 어라 구무오씨사 먀 빠러 사 비푸아나 벼뻐 뱌꿰라 무, 부씨 바이나아 아꽈 바꽈오씨라 먀 뉴빠 여 바이네. 비러시.

어 또네 야 하빠꽈 너 바뻐럔 버 뿌꿰

8. 뭐찌 찌오 쩌 유더야, 어 바뻐러 바바아 바거러사 어 비푸아나 뱌부 어 부두푸 보씨, 오푸 너 무시 워 버더꺼허무.

9. 우나오-우나오, 어 또네 야

---

3. And everyone went to his own town to register.

4. So Joseph also went up from the town of Nazareth in Galilee to Judea, to Bethlehem the town of David, because he belonged to the house and line of David.

5. He went there to register with Mary, who was pledged to be married to him and was expecting a child.

6. While they were there, the time came for the baby to be born,

7. and she gave birth to her firstborn, a son. She wrapped him in cloths and placed him in a manger, because there was no room for them in the inn.

8. And there were shepherds living out in the fields nearby, keeping watch over their flocks at night.

9. An angel of the Lord

Ongo y'era kubapamukira ku, n'e bulangare bwa Ongo bwera kubamorekera. Balolyire bacha, bera kufa buba bunene;

10. Si e ndonyi ya Ongo y'era kubabura: "Mutobaaa, bushi nyibeere mwasi mubuya ola ukasimisa busese ebana b'elsiraeli boshi.

11. Mw'obuno butufu, e Mulamya wenyu abuchirwe mwa musi wa Tauti, n'esina lyai I Mununusi* Enawenyu, ola wachwumwaa na Ongo.

12. Cha chingabalosa Okwa I yoyu, chi chichine: Mungabuana e mwana alyi mwa biresi kanji aonjisibwe mwa mbare sa bifuana byende byalyira mu."

13. Unao-unao, e bangere bera kulola kw'ola malaika alyi na banji e ndonyi sa Ongo sinene kutenga kwa nguba ba babaa batonga Ongo, n'e kuteta:

14. "Ongo atongwe kwa nguba, n'na ba bemererwe nai mwa butala boshi babonaa e bolo"

15. Abere e ndonyi n'e bangere balyikanuka, e ndonyi s'era kuhuba kwa nguba, n'e bangere bera kutangilyisa bahambala: "chwiraa chwaya e Betelehemu tuchilorere kanangana cha chabere, ch'enawechwu Ongo

오꼬 여라 구바파무기라 구, 너 부롸아러 봐 오꼬 뭐라 구바모러거라. 바론레러 바짜, 버라 구파 부바 부너너;

10. 시 어 또네 야 오꼬 여라 구바부라: "무도바아아, 부씨 네버어러 마시 무부야 오라 우가시미사 부서서 어바나 버이시라어뤼 보씨.

11. 모부노 부두푸, 어 무롸먀 워뉴 아부찌뤄 봐 무시 와 다우디, 너시나 랴이 이 무누누시* 어나뮤, 오롸 와쭈마아 나 오꼬.

12. 짜 찌아바르사 오과 이 요유, 찌 찌찌너: 무아부아나 어 마나 아레 봐 비러시 가찌 아오찌시붜 봐 빠러 사 비푸아나 벼너 뱌레라 무."

13. 우나오-우나오, 어 바어러 버라 구론롸 교롸 마롸이가 아레 나 바찌 어 또네 사 오꼬 시너너 구더아 과 꾸바 바 바바아 바도아 오꼬, 너 구더다:

14. "오꼬 아도꿔 과 꾸바, 우나 바 버머러뤄 나이 뫄 부다롸 보씨 바보나아 어 보론"

15. 아버러 어 또네 너 바어러 바레가누가, 어 또네 서라 구후바 과 꾸바, 너 바어러 버라 구다이레사 바하빠롸: "쮀라아 좌야 어 버더러후무 두찌론러러 가나아나 짜 짜버러, 쩌나워쭈 오꼬 어라 구쭈마 어 또네 사이

appeared to them, and the glory of the Lord shone around them, and they were terrified.

10. But the angel said to them, "Do not be afraid. I bring you good news of great joy that will be for all the people.

11. Today in the town of David a Savior has been born to you; he is Christ the Lord.

12. This will be a sign to you: You will find a baby wrapped in cloths and lying in a manger."

13. Suddenly a great company of the heavenly host appeared with the angel, praising God and saying,

14. "Glory to God in the highest, and on earth peace to men on whom his favor rests."

15. When the angels had left them and gone into heaven, the shepherds said to one another, "Let's go to Bethlehem and see this thing that has happened, which the

era kuchwuma e ndonyi sai mbu bachwuburaa."

16. Unao-unao, bera kunalyibichira yi, bera kuhonda, bera kunalyinda babuana Mariya na Yosefu, kanji bera kulola kwa mwana aonjire mwa mbare sa bifuana byende byalyira mu.

17. Mango e bangere bamulolaa ku, bera kuenda kubalyira e bandju boshi kwa myasi era e ndonyi ya Ongo abahambalyiraa ku kwa kubuchwa kw'oyu mwana.

18. Boshi ba bomvaa kwa myasi era yafulwaa n'e bangere, basanwaa busese.

19. Mariya yeke abaa aneshi ei myasi yoshi, si ailangaa kwa muchima.

20. Chasinjire, e bangere bera kuhuba Mwa mulyimo wabu, baenda batonga Ongo n'e kumuahanyisa kw'ebya e ndonyi sa Ongo sababuraa kanji banabilola ku.

Yesu elyikwa e sina
21. Abere Yesu aira suku munane abuchirwe, Mariya na Yosefu bera kumweka mwa muya w'e kumonya e bana b'e

뿌 바쭈부라아."

16. 우나오-우나오, 버라 구나쪠비찌라 에, 버라 구호따, 버라 구나쪠따 바부아나 마리야 나 요서푸, 가찌 버라 구롤롸 과나 아오씨러 뫄 빠러 사 비푸아나 벼떠 뱌쪠라 무.

17. 마꼬 어 바꺼러 바무롤롸아 구, 버라 구어따 구바쪠라 어 바쭈 보씨 과 먀시 어라 어 또니 야 오꼬 아바하빠쪠라아 구 과 구부쫘 교유 뫄나.

18. 보씨 바 보빠아 과 먀시 어라 야푸꽈아 너 바꺼러, 바사놔아 부서서.

19. 마리야 여거 아바아 아너씨 어이 먀시 요씨, 시 아이롸꽈아 과 무찌마.

20. 짜시찌러, 어 바꺼러 버라 구후바 뫄 무쪠모 와부, 바어따 바도꺄 오꼬 너 구무아하네사 궈뱌 어 또니 사 오꼬 사바부라아 가찌 바나비롤롸 구.

여수 어쪠굣 어 시나
21. 아버러 여수 아이라 수구 무나너 아부찌뤄, 마리야 나 요서푸 버라 구뭐가 뫄 무야 워 구모냐 어 바나 버 부사나 뫄

Lord has told us about."

16. So they hurried off and found Mary and Joseph, and the baby, who was lying in the manger.

17. When they had seen him, they spread the word concerning what had been told them about this child,

18. and all who heard it were amazed at what the shepherds said to them.

19. But Mary treasured up all these things and pondered them in her heart.

20. The shepherds returned, glorifying and praising God for all the things they had heard and seen, which were just as they had been told.

21. On the eighth day, when it was time to circumcise him, he was named Jesus, the name

busana mwa Isiraeli. Bera kumwilyika e sina Iya Yesu, ng'okwa e ndonyi ya Ongo yanaburaa Mariya era muhondo s'ekuba mukure.

Kw'emerwa kwa Yesu na Simeoni

22. Yosefu na Mariya bayaa kuchikomya mwa Luhu lwa Ongo kukulyikana n'e Mwaso wa Ongo ola Bayuda beresibwaa na Musa. Bera kweka e mwana e Yerusalemu eresibwe Ongo.

23. Bamwekaa yi, bushi mwa Mwaso wa Ongo byabaa byanjikirwe mbu chira lubere lwa musana lukaba mwango wa Ongo.

24. Kanji banaa e michwulo kukulyikana n'okwa Mwaso wa Ongo abaa atechire: chwurenge chwubilyi, nesi byana bibilyi bya biruka.

25. Mwa musi w'e Yerusalemu mwabaa muchwula mutambo muuma mbu I Simeonyi. Oyu Simeonyi abaa achwula mundju w'e kunalyi era muhondo sa Ongo 'e kumuchwunda. Alyinjiraa e kubuchwa kw'ola ukanunula e lubaa lw'e Isiraeli,

26. N'e Muchima Mubuya-buya

이시라어삐. 버라 구뮈쩨가 어 시나 쨔 여수, 끄과 어 또네 야 오끄 야나부라아 마리야 어라 무호또 서구바 무구러.

귀머롸 과 여수 나 시머오니

22. 요서푸 나 마리야 바야아 구찌고먀 롸 루후 롸 오끄 구구쩨가나 너 롸소 와 오끄 오롸 바유다 버러시봐아 나 무사. 버라 귀가 어 먀나 어 여루사쩌무 어러시붜 오끄.

23. 바뭐가아 에, 부씨 롸 롸소 와 오끄 뱌바아 뱌찌기뤄 뿌 찌라 루버러 롸 무사나 루가바 롸끄 와 오끄.

24. 가찌 바나아 어 미쭈론 구구쩨가나 노과 롸소 와 오끄 아바아 아더찌러: 쭈러뻐 쭈비쩨, 너시 뱌나 비비쩨 뱌 비루가.

25. 롸 무시 워 여루사쩌무 롸바아 무쭈롸 무다뽀 무우마 뿌 이 시머오네. 오유 시머오네 아바아 아쭈롸 무뚜 워 구나쩨 어라 무호또 사 오끄 어 구무쭈따. 아쩨찌라아 어 구부좌 교롸 우가누누롸 어 루바아 뤄 이시라어삐,

26. 너 무찌마 무부야-부야

the angel had given him before he had been conceived.

22. When the time of their purification according to the Law of Moses had been completed, Joseph and Mary took him to Jerusalem to present him to the Lord

23. (as it is written in the Law of the Lord, "Every firstborn male is to be consecrated to the Lord"),

24. and to offer a sacrifice in keeping with what is said in the Law of the Lord: "a pair of doves or two young pigeons."

25. Now there was a man in Jerusalem called Simeon, who was righteous and devout. He was waiting for the consolation of Israel, and the Holy Spirit was upon him.

26. It had been revealed

abaa achwula alauma nai. Kanji abaa amubilyire mbu atakafe busira kulola kwa Mununusi ola ukachwumwa n'Enawechwu.

27. Kw'olu lusuku, e Muchima Mubuya-buya wa Ongo era kweka Simeoni mwa Luhu lwa Ongo. Mango e basere ba Yesu bamwekaa mu baire kwa Mwaso achwula atechire,

28. Oyu Simeoni era kwangilyira e mwana, era kutangilyisa atonga Ongo, n'e kuteta:

29. "Mw'echine chihangi Enawechwu, wera unganyireka nyi muanda wau nyichifire mwa bolo kukulyikana n'e mwasi wau ola wabaa wanyibwilyire.

30. Enawechwu, nachilorere nyeine kwa mwana ola wachwumire kununula e bandju.

31. Weine u wamulondere abe Mununusi era muhondo s'e bandju boshi.

32. Oyu Mununusi I ukaba bulangare bwa bukachwuma wamenyeka mwa ba baachwula Bayuda, kanji bu bukareta e chwunda kwa bandju bau, benyi Isiraeli."

33. Ebasere ba Yesu basanwaa

아바아 아쭈롸 아롸우마 나이. 가찌 아바아 아무비쩨러 뿌 아다가퍼 부시라 구롣롸 과 무누누시 오롸 우가쭈롸 너나워쭉.

27. 교루 루수구, 어 무찌마 무부야-부야 와 오꼬 어라 궈가 시머오니 롸 루후 롸 오꼬. 마꼬 어 바서러 바 여수 바뭐가아 무 바이러 과 먀소 아쭈롸 아더찌러,

28. 오유 시머오니 어라 과ㄲ레라 어 먀나, 어라 구다ㄲ레사 아도롸 오꼬, 너 구더다:

29. "뭐찌너 찌하ㄲ 어나워쭉, 워라 우ㄲ나네러가 네 무아따 와우 네찌피러 먀 보로 구구ㄲ레가나 너 먀시 와우 오롸 와바아 와니뷔쩨러.

30. 어나워쭉, 나찌로러러 녀이너 과 먀나 오롸 와쭉미러 구누누롸 어 바뉴.

31. 워이너 우 와무롣너러 아버 무누누시 어라 무호또 서 바뉴 보씨.

32. 오유 무누누시 이 우가바 부롸ㄲ러라 봐 부가쭈마 와머녀가 먀 바 바아쭈롸 바유다, 가찌 부 부가러다 어 쭈따 과 바뉴 바우, 버네 이시라어릐."

33. 어바서러 바 여수 바사놔아

---

to him by the Holy Spirit that he would not die before he had seen the Lord's Christ.

27. Moved by the Spirit, he went into the temple courts. When the parents brought in the child Jesus to do for him what the custom of the Law required,

28. Simeon took him in his arms and praised God, saying:

29. "Sovereign Lord, as you have promised, you now dismiss your servant in peace.

30. For my eyes have seen your salvation,

31. which you have prepared in the sight of all people,

32. a light for revelation to the Gentiles and for glory to your people Israel."

33. The child's father and

bushi n'e myasi Simeoni atetaa era lulu sa Yesu.

34. Simeoni era kubaahanyira, era kubura Mariya, nyina w'e mwana: "Ulolaa! Oo musana akachwuma banene mwa lubaa lw'e Isiraeli bakumbaala, kanji akemusa banene mubu. Akalosa e bandju e kuhonda kwa Ongo si bakamuhomba.

35. Kuika mianyisa ya banene era yabishibwaa imenyeke. N'nau ukalyibuka ng'ola washingirwe e fumo mwa muchima."

36. Mw'echi chihangi, muekulu wa mukasi mbu I Ana, era kuchifunda ala Mariya na Yosefu babaa balyi. Abaa murebi wa Ongo, mwalyi wa Fanuwere w'omwa chirongo cha Asheri. Abere amala myaka elyinda ahwelyirwe, era kufirwa n'e mulume.

37. Abaa muhumba-kasi kuikira myaka lunane n'ene. Atarekaa kukorera Ongo mwa Luhu Iwai. Abaa achwula mu e mushi n'e buchwufu ema Ongo n'e kureka e kulya.

38. Mango alolaa ku Yesu, era kutangirisa atongwa Ongo, kanji era kuanyikisisa e bandju

부씨 너 먀시 시머오니 아더다아 어라 루루 사 여수.

34. 시머오니 어라 구바아하네라, 어라 구부라 마리야, 네나 워 뫄나: "우로좌아! 오오 무사나 아가쭈마 바너너 뫄 루바아 뤄 이시라어뤠 바구빠아좌, 가찌 아거무사 바너너 무부. 아가로사 어 바뚜 어 구호따 과 오끄 시 바가무호빠.

35. 구이가 미아녜사 야 바너너 어라 야비씨봐아 이머녀거. 우나우 우가뤠부가 끄좌 와씨삐뤄 어 푸모 뫄 무찌마."

36. 뭐찌 찌하삐, 무어구루 와 무가시 뿌 이 아나, 어라 구찌푼따 아좌 마리야 나 요서푸 바바아 바뤠. 아바아 무러비 와 오끄, 뫄뤠 와 파누워러 요뫄 찌로끄 짜 아쎄리. 아버러 아마좌 먀가 어뤠따 아훠뤠뤄, 어라 구피라 너 무루머.

37. 아바아 무후빠-가시 구이기라 먀가 루나너 너너. 아다러가아 구고러라 오끄 뫄 루후 꽈이. 아바아 아쭈좌 무 어 무씨 너 부쭈푸 어마 오끄 너 구러가 어 구랴.

38. 마끄 아로좌아 구 여수, 어라 구다삐리사 아도꽈 오끄, 가찌 어라 구아네기시사 어

mother marveled at what was said about him.

34. Then Simeon blessed them and said to Mary, his mother: "This child is destined to cause the falling and rising of many in Israel, and to be a sign that will be spoken against,

35. so that the thoughts of many hearts will be revealed. And a sword will pierce your own soul too."

36. There was also a prophetess, Anna, the daughter of Phanuel, of the tribe of Asher. She was very old; she had lived with her husband seven years after her marriage,

37. and then was a widow until she was eighty-four. She never left the temple but worshiped night and day, fasting and praying.

38. Coming up to them at that very moment, she gave thanks to God

e myasi ya Yesu, ba babaa balinjira ola ukanunula e bana b'e Isiraeli mwa bucha bwabu.

39. Mango e basere ba Yesu bamalaa e mulyimo baenderaa, kukulyikana n'e Mwaso wa Ongo, bera kuuluka mwa musi wabu w'e Nasareti, mwa chio ch'e Kalilaya.

40. Yesu era kunaendekerana ehuka n'e kukula. Abaa ete bwenge bunene, kanji Ongo anamuahanyiraa.

E mwana Yesu ebilyirwa mwa luhu lwa Ongo

41. Chira mwaka, Mariya na Yosefu bendaa baya e Yerusalemu kwa lusuku lukulu lwilyikirwe Pasaka.
42. Abere Yesu era ete myaka ekumi n'ebilyi, abu basere bai bera kuya nai e Yerusalemu ng'okwa bendaa banaira kw'olu lusuku lukulu.
43. Mango e suku s'e Pasaka sabaa sawere, e basere ba Yesu bera kufuluka. Si yeke era kushiba e Yerusalemu batanamenyire.

44. Bera kumala mureerere wa mutenga baenda batanamulola

바꾸 어 먀시 야 여수, 바 바바아 바쀠씨라 오꽈 우가누누꽈 어 바나 버 이시라어쀠 먀 부짜 봐부.

39. 마꼬 어 바서러 바 여수 바마꽈아 어 무쀄모 바어떠라아, 구구쀄가나 너 먀소 와 오꼬, 버라 구우루가 먀 무시 와부 워 나사러디, 먀 찌오 쩌 가쀠꽈야.

40. 여수 어라 구나어떠거라나 어후가 너 구구꽈. 아바아 어더 붜어 부너너, 가찌 오꼬 아나무아하니러아.

어 꽈나 여수 어비쀄롭 먀 루훌 꽈 오꼬

41. 찌라 꽈가, 마리야 나 요서푸 버따아 바야 어 여루사쩌무 과 루수구 루구루 뤼쀄기뤄 파사가.
42. 아버러 여수 어라 어더 먀가 어구미 너비쀄, 아부 바서러 바이 버라 구야 나이 어 여루사쩌무 꼬과 버따아 바나이라 교루 루수구 루구루.
43. 마꼬 어 수구 서 파사가 사바아 사워러, 어 바서러 바 여수 버라 구푸루가. 시 여거 어라 구씨바 어 여루사쩌무 바다나머니러.

44. 버라 구마꽈 무러어러러 와 무더따 바어따 바다나무론꽈 구,

and spoke about the child to all who were looking forward to the redemption of Jerusalem.

39. When Joseph and Mary had done everything required by the Law of the Lord, they returned to Galilee to their own town of Nazareth.

40. And the child grew and became strong; he was filled with wisdom, and the grace of God was upon him.

41. Every year his parents went to Jerusalem for the Feast of the Passover.
42. When he was twelve years old, they went up to the Feast, according to the custom.
43. After the Feast was over, while his parents were returning home, the boy Jesus stayed behind in Jerusalem, but they were unaware of it.

44. Thinking he was in their company, they

ku, bushi bamenyaa mbu analyi mwa luamba lw'e bandju ba babaa balyi nabu. Baalolyire kwa atalyi nabu, kuna kutangilyisa bamuhondera mu banyakabu na bera babu.

45. Si chiro bakamulola ku. Bushi n'oku, bera kuhuba e Yerusalemu kumuhondera yi.

46. Abere bamala kahachwu bamuhonda, bera kumubuana mwa Luhu lwa Ongo. Abaa ekesi alauma n'e bakangilyisi b'e Mwaso abomvilyisa. Kanji abaa ababusa ku inji myasi.

47. Boshi ba bomvaa bya ateta bera kusanwa bushi n'e bwenge bwai n'na kwa endaa aba akula.

48. Mango e basere bai bamulolaa ku, bera kusanwa busese. Nyina era kumubusa: "E mwana wanyi, chi chachwumire wachwuira bacha? Si chwuna eho, chwabaa chwera chwachianya busese mwa kukuhonda!"

49. Yesu era kubaakula: "Chi chinachwuma mwanyihonda bacha? Kasi mutamenyaa kwa kunyemire nyibe mwa bya bya Tata?

50. Si bya abaa abura e basere bai, batabimenyereraa.

부씨 바머냐아 뿌 아나레 똬 루아빠 뤄 바누 바 바바아 바레 나부. 바아로레러 과 아다레 나부, 구나 구다삐레사 바무호떠라 무 바냐가부 나 버라 바부.

45. 시 찌로 바가무로롸 구. 부씨 노구, 버라 구후바 어 여루사뿌무 구무호떠라 에.

46. 아버러 바마롸 가하쭈 바무호따, 버라 구무부아나 똬 루후 롸 오꼬. 아바아 어거시 아롸우마 너 바가삐레시 버 뫄소 아보삐레사. 가찌 아바아 아바부사 구 이찌 먀시.

47. 보씨 바 보빠아 뱌 아더다 버라 구사뇨 부씨 너 뭐떠 봐이 우나 과 어따아 아바 아구롸.

48. 마꼬 어 바서러 바이 바무로롸아 구, 버라 구사뇨 부서서. 네나 어라 구무부사: "어 뫄나 와니, 찌 짜쭈미러 와쭈이라 바짜? 시 쭈나 어호, 쫘바아 쭤라 쫘찌아냐 부서서 똬 구구호따!"

49. 여수 어라 구바아구롸: "찌 찌나쭈마 뫄네호따 바짜? 가시 무다머냐아 과 구녀미러 네버 똬 뱌 뱌 다다?

50. 시 뱌 아바아 아부라 어 바서러 바이, 바다비머녀러라아.

traveled on for a day. Then they began looking for him among their relatives and friends.

45. When they did not find him, they went back to Jerusalem to look for him.

46. After three days they found him in the temple courts, sitting among the teachers, listening to them and asking them questions.

47. Everyone who heard him was amazed at his understanding and his answers.

48. When his parents saw him, they were astonished. His mother said to him, "Son, why have you treated us like this? Your father and I have been anxiously searching for you."

49. "Why were you searching for me?" he asked. "Didn't you know I had to be in my Father's house?"

50. But they did not understand what he was

saying to them.

51. era kuandola alauma nabo kuya e nazareti era kukula n'e kubachwunda. N'nei myasi yoshi, nyina endaa anailanga mwa muchima wai.

52. Yesu nai, era kuendekera ehuka n'e kuata e bwenge. Kanji era kunde anasimisa Ongo alauma n'e bandju.

51. 어라 구아또롸 아롸우마 나보 구야 어 나자러디 어라 구구롸 너 구바쭈따. 우너이 먀시 요씨, 니나 어따아 아나이롸까 먀 무찌마 와이.

52. 여수 나이, 어라 구어떠거라 어후가 너 구아다 어 뷔꺼. 가찌 어라 구떠 아나시미사 오꼬 아롸우마 너 바뚜.

51. Then he went down to Nazareth with them and was obedient to them. But his mother treasured all these things in her heart.

52. And Jesus grew in wisdom and stature, and in favor with God and men.

Luka Chikono 3
E ndangilyiso y'e milyimo ya yowana mubatisai

1. Mango Tiberiyo Kaisari, mwami mukulu -- kulu w'e Baroma, abaa ema myaka ekumi n'etano mwa bio byoshi bya byabaa bilyi mwa bucha bw'e Baroma, babano bu babaa bemire mwa bio bya Bayuda babaa bachwula mu: Ponso Pilato abaa mutambo mwa chio ch'e Yudeya, na Heroti mwa chio ch'e Galilaya. Mukulu wai Firipo nai, abaa mutambo mwa chio ch'e Itureya n'ech'e Tarakoniti. Na Lisanyiyasi I wabaa mutambo mwa chio ch'e Abilenyi.

루가 찌고노 3
어 따뗴쎈 여 미뗴명 야 요와나 무바디사이

1. 마꼬 디버리요 가이사리, 먀미 무구루 -- 구루 워 바로마, 아바아 어마 먀가 어구미 너다노 먀 비오 뵤씨 뱌 뱌바아 비뗴 먀 부짜 뷔 바로마, 바바노 부 바바아 버미러 먀 비오 뱌 바유다 바바아 바쭈롸 무: 포누소 피롸도 아바아 무다뾪 먀 찌오 쩌 유더야, 나 허로디 먀 찌오 쩌 가뢰롸야. 무구루 와이 피리포 나이, 아바아 무다뾪 먀 찌오 쩌 이두러야 너쩌 다라고니디. 나 뢰사네야시 이 와바아 무다뾪 먀 찌오 쩌 아비뻐니.

Luke Chapter 3[NIV]

1. In the fifteenth year of the reign of Tiberius Caesar--when Pontius Pilate was governor of Judea, Herod tetrarch of Galilee, his brother Philip tetrarch of Iturea and Traconitis, and Lysanias tetrarch of Abilene--

2. Mw'esi siku, Hana na Kayafa bu babaa bakulu-kulu b'ebakuhanyi ba Ongo.* Mw'amu mango mu Yowanyi nai, muala wa Sakariya, omvaa emurenge wa Ongo mwa buyeye.

2. 뭐시 시구, 하나 나 가야파 부 바바아 바구루-구루 버바구하니 바 오꼬.* 뭐무 마꼬무 요와니 나이, 무아빠 와 사가리야, 오빠아 어무러뻐 와 오꼬 와 부여여.

2. during the high priesthood of Annas and Caiaphas, the word of God came to John son of Zechariah in the desert.

3. Bushi n'oku, Yowanyi era kutangilyisa arenza e mwamu mwa chio choshi ch'e muchisi w'e Yorotanyi, era kunde ateta: "Murekaa e bibi byenyu, kanji muiraa nyibabatise. Mukaira bacha, Ongo angabibabalyira."

3. 부씨 노구, 요와네 어라 구다삐례사 아러싸 어 뭐무 와 찌오 쪼씨 쩌 무찌시 워 요로다니, 어라 구떠 아더다: "무러가아 어 비비 벼뉴, 가찌 무이라아 네바바디서. 무가이라 바짜, 오꼬 아꽈비바바뼤라."

3. He went into all the country around the Jordan, preaching a baptism of repentance for the forgiveness of sins.

4. Emyasi ya Yowanyi yanalosaa kwa I murebi Isaya abaa emaana mango anjikaa mmbu: "Mumvaa e mundju ola wabarangira mwa buyeye, atechire mmbu: "Mubaa nga njira ikomire, kanji ilambaatanyisibwe era Enawetu angarenga mu.

4. 어먀시 야 요와네 야나로사아 과 이 무러비 이사야 아바아 어마아나 마꼬 아찌가아 무뿌: "무빠아 어 무뚜 오롸 와바라삐라 와 부여여, 아더찌러 무뿌: "무바아 꽈 찌라 이고미러, 가찌 이롸빠아다네시붜 어라 어나워두 아꽈러롸 무.

4. As is written in the book of the words of Isaiah the prophet: "A voice of one calling in the desert, 'Prepare the way for the Lord, make straight paths for him.

5. Chira mubanda, Ongo akawihusa. Kanji,chira ndjulungu na chira kachwulungu, akabihubya malambo. Enjira sichionyire sikaonyolwa, n'na sa silyi mw'e chwukubo sikatendera.

5. 찌라 무바따, 오꼬 아가위후사. 가찌,찌라 뚜루꾸 나 찌라 가쫄루꾸, 아가비후뱌 마롸몐. 어찌라 시찌오네러 시가오뇨롸, 우나 사 시뼤 뭐 쭈구보 시가더뻐라.

5. Every valley shall be filled in, every mountain and hill made low. The crooked roads shall become straight, the rough ways smooth.

6. N'e bandju boshi bakamenyerera kwa Ongo ahonda e kubakula mwa bibi byenyu!

6. 너 바뚜 보씨 바가머녀러라 과 오꼬 아호따 어 구바구롸 와 비비 벼뉴!

6. And all mankind will see God's salvation.' "

7. Bikembe binene bya bandju

7. 비거뻐 비너너 뱌 바뚜

7. John said to the

byendaa byaikira Yowana mbu ababatisaa. Si nai era kunde abura ba babaa batabindjure e myanya yabu kanangana mmbu: "Mwabu mulyi kuuma n'e njoka! Nde I wabatebire mbu mukafuma Ongo mwa buchinjibusi bwai bwa bweshire?

8. Akaba mwahonda kubatisibwa, mubindulaa emyanya yenyu. Mwendaa mwaira emabuya kwa kulosa kwa mwarekire elwenyu. Kanji, mutendaa mwachitonga mmbu: "Ongo atakatutonganye bushi tuli benyi Aburahamu. "dababisha, mano makoi musene ku, Ongo angamahubya bana ba Aburahamu.

9. Mwabu mulyi ng'e michi na Ongo alyi ng'e mukonji. Ekakuma ka katenga kwa luchaso u kera kali kwa kukondera emichi al'auma n'emiuna yai. Chira muchi woshi ola utete bifuma bikomire, oyu mukonji angauishanga n'e kuuma u kwa mulyiro."

10. Bandju bauma mwa luamba bera kunde bamubusa: "Kute chwiraa chwaira kwa kulosa kwa chwabindjure e myanya yechwu?"

벼따아 뱌이기라 요와나 뿌 아바바디사아. 시 나이 어라 구떠 아부라 바 바바아 바다비뿌러 어 먀냐 야부 가나꺄나 무뿌: "뫄부 무레 구우마 너 쪼가! 떠 이 와바더비러 뿌 무가푸마 오꼬 뫄 부찌찌부시 봐이 봐 뿨씨러?

8. 아가바 뫄호따 구바디시봐, 무비뚜꽈아 어먀냐 여뉴. 뭐따아 뫄이라 어마부야 과 구로사 과 뫄러기러 어뤠뉴. 가찌, 무더따아 뫄찌도따 무뿌: "오꼬 아다가두도따녀 부씨 두뤼 버니 아부라하무. "다바비싸, 마노 마고이 무서너 구, 오꼬 아꺄마후뱌 바나 바 아부라하무.

9. 뫄부 무레 꺼 미찌 나 오꼬 아레 꺼 무고찌. 어가구마 가 가더따 과 루짜소 우 거라 가뤼 과 구고떠라 어미찌 아꽈우마 너미우나 야이. 찌라 무찌 오씨 오꽈 우더더 비푸마 비고미러, 오유 무고찌 아꽈우이싸꺄 너 구우마 우 과 무레로."

10. 바뉴 바우마 뫄 루아빠 버라 구더 바무부사: "구더 쮜라아 쫘이라 과 구로사 과 쫘비뿌러 어 먀냐 여쭈?"

crowds coming out to be baptized by him, "You brood of vipers! Who warned you to flee from the coming wrath?

8. Produce fruit in keeping with repentance. And do not begin to say to yourselves, 'We have Abraham as our father.' For I tell you that out of these stones God can raise up children for Abraham.

9. The axe is already at the root of the trees, and every tree that does not produce good fruit will be cut down and thrown into the fire."

10. "What should we do then?" the crowd asked.

11. Nai era kuba akula: "Ola wete njimba ebilyi, atebilyiraa kweresa mulyikabu luuma akaba atangalubona; n'nola wete e bilyo eresaa ola wainyire cha alya."

12. Bafuchisi bauma b'embarata nabu bera kuikira Yowana mbu ababatisaa. Bera kumubusa: "Walyiya, n'nechwu, chi chwuiraa kwa kulosa kwa chwabindjure e myanya yechwu?"

13. Yowana era kuba akula: "Mutendaa mwaholosa e mundju bikulo binene kurenza bya Reta emire."

14. Chasinjire, basula bauma nabu bera kumubusa: "N'nechwu kasi, chi chwuiraa?" Yowana era kuba akula: "Mutendaa mwanyaa e mundju hya hilyi hyai, kanji mutendaa mwasinga e mundju cha atairaa. Kanji mwendaa mwamoera e lwembo lwenyu."

15. E bandju boshi ba babahaa kubachisibwa, babaa bachibusa mwa michima mbu ilyi atangaba Yowana I Mununusi waikire.

16. Bushi n'oku, Yowana era kubabura boshi: "Nyono nababatisa n'e meshi, si ola

---

11. 나이 어라 구바 아구롸: "오롸 워더 띠빠 어비롔, 아더비롔라아 궈러사 무뢔가부 루우마 아가바 아다까루보나; 우노롸 워더 어 비뾰 어러사아 오롸 와이네러 짜 아롺."

12. 바푸찌시 바우마 버빠라다 나부 버라 구이기라 요와나 뿌 아바바디사아. 버라 구무부사: "와롔야, 우너쭈, 찌 쭈이라아 과 구로사 과 좌비뿌러 어 먄냐 여쭈?"

13. 요와나 어라 구바 아구롸: "무더따아 먀호뢴사 어 무뚜 비구롼 비너너 구러싸 뱌 러다 어미러."

14. 짜시띠러, 바수롸 바우마 나부 버라 구무부사: "우너쭈 가시, 찌 쭈이라아?" 요와나 어라 구바 아구롸: "무더따아 먀냐아 어 무뚜 햐 히롔 하이, 가찌 무더따아 먀시까 어 무뚜 짜 아다이라아. 가찌 뭐따아 먀모어라 어 뤄뽀 뤄뉴."

15. 어 바뚜 보씨 바 바바하아 구바찌시봐, 바바아 바찌부사 마 미찌마 뿌 이롔 아다까바 요와나 이 무누누시 와이기러.

16. 부씨 노구, 요와나 어라 구바부라 보씨: "뇨노 나바바디사 너 머씨, 시 오롸

---

11. John answered, "The man with two tunics should share with him who has none, and the one who has food should do the same."

12. Tax collectors also came to be baptized. "Teacher," they asked, "what should we do?"

13. "Don't collect any more than you are required to," he told them.

14. Then some soldiers asked him, "And what should we do?" He replied, "Don't extort money and don't accuse people falsely--be content with your pay."

15. The people were waiting expectantly and were all wondering in their hearts if John might possibly be the Christ.

16. John answered them all, "I baptize you with water. But one more

---

wabahire I wete e buashi kunyirenza. Chiro nyono ndanalyi mwa ba bangaba baanda bai.Yeke akabati e bandju n'e mulyiro w'e Muchima Mubuya - buya.

17. Kanji era anete e lwelyi kwa kwelula e mupunge. Era nyuma s'e kwelula u, akaubika mwa ngulyi, si akakabula e bichi mwa mulyiro ola utakasime."

18. Mango Yowana abaa ahubanganyisa e bandju e Mwasi Mubuya-buya, atebilyiraa n'e kubawa manji maano manene.

19. Ebyera bitachwumaa mwami Heroti ataira mabi manene n'e kuikira arendesa Herotiya, muka munyakabu. Bushi n'oku, Yowana era kumukemera.

20. Echinji chibi cha Heroti airaa chirengerese, chabaa cha ch'e kuminyisa Yowana.

E kubatisibwa kwa Yesu

21. Abere Yowana amala kubatisa boshi ba babindjulaa e myanya yabu, era kubatisa na Yesu. Mango Yesu abaa era abatisibwaa, era kwema Ongo. Unao-unao, n'e nguba kuna kulangala.

와바히러 이 워더 어 부아씨 구네러싸. 찌로 뇨노 따나레 롸 바 바까바 바아따 바이.여거 아가바디 어 바뚜 너 무레로 워 무찌마 무부야 - 부야.

17. 가찌 어라 아너더 어 뤄레 과 궈루롸 어 무푸꺼. 어라 뉴마 서 궈루롸 우, 아가우비가 롸 꾸레, 시 아가가부롸 어 비찌 무레로 오롸 우다가시머."

18. 마꼬 요와나 아바아 아후바까네사 어 바뚜 어 롸시 무부야-부야, 아더비레라아 너 구바와 마찌 마아노 마너너.

19. 어벼라 비다쭈마아 뫄미 허로디 아다이라 마비 마너너 너 구이기라 아러꺼사 허로디야, 무가 무냐가부. 부씨 노구, 요와나 어라 구무거머라.

20. 어찌씨 찌비 짜 허로디 아이라아 찌러꺼러서, 짜바아 짜 쩌 구미네사 요와나.

어 구바디시봐 과 여수

21. 아버러 요와나 아마롸 구바디사 보씨 바 바비누롸아 어 먀냐 야부, 어라 구바디사 나 여수. 마꼬 여수 아바아 어라 아바디시봐아, 어라 궈마 오꼬. 우나오-우나오, 너 꾸바 구나 구롸까롸.

powerful than I will come, the thongs of whose sandals I am not worthy to untie. He will baptize you with the Holy Spirit and with fire.

17. His winnowing fork is in his hand to clear his threshing floor and to gather the wheat into his barn, but he will burn up the chaff with unquenchable fire."

18. And with many other words John exhorted the people and preached the good news to them.

19. But when John rebuked Herod the tetrarch because of Herodias, his brother's wife, and all the other evil things he had done,

20. Herod added this to them all: He locked John up in prison.

21. When all the people were being baptized, Jesus was baptized too. And as he was praying, heaven was opened

22. N'e Muchima Mubuya-buya amuumbilyira ku nga mulonge. E murenge era kutenga kwa nguba n'e kumvika mmbu: "Woyu, u Muala wanyi nyinachwusa, kanji u nyisima busese.

E chirongo cha Yesu

23. Yesu atangilyisaa e mulyimo wai mango abaa era ete byanda mahatu. E bandju bendaa baanyisa mbu achwula muala wa Yosefu. Na Yosefu abaa muala wa Heli,
24. na Heli abaa muala wa Matati, na Matati abaa muala wa Lawi, na Lawi abaa muala wa Melki, na Melki abaa muala wa Yana, na Yana abaa muala wa Yosefu,
25. na Yosefu abaa muala wa Matatia,na Matatia abaa muala wa Amosi,na Amosi abaa muala wa Nahumu,na Nahumu abaa muala wa Esli,na Esli abaa muala wa Nega,
26. na Nega abaa muala wa Mati, na Mati abaa muala wa Matatia, na Matatia abaa muala wa Simei, na Simei abaa muala wa Yosefu,na Yosefu abaa muala wa Yuda,
27. na Yuda abaa muala a Yohana, na Yohana abaa muala

---

22. 너 무찌마 무부야-부야 아무우뻬례라 구 까 무르꺼. 어 무러꺼 어라 구더까 과 꾸바 너 구뻬가 무뿌: "오유, 우 무아꽈 와니 니나쭈사, 가찌 우 네시마 부서서.

어 찌로끄 짜 여수

23. 여수 아다끼례사아 어 무레모 와이 마끄 아바아 어라 어더 뱌따 마하두. 어 바뉴 버따아 바아네사 뿌 아쭈꽈 무아꽈 와 요서푸. 나 요서푸 아바아 무아꽈 와 허뤼,
24. 나 허뤼 아바아 무아꽈 와 마다디, 나 마다디 아바아 무아꽈 와 꽈위, 나 꽈위 아바아 무아꽈 와 머뤄기, 나 머뤄기 아바아 무아꽈 와 야나, 나 야나 아바아 무아꽈 와 요서푸,
25. 나 요서푸 아바아 무아꽈 와 마다디아,나 마다디아 아바아 무아꽈 와 아모시,나 아모시 아바아 무아꽈 와 나후무,나 나후무 아바아 무아꽈 와 어수뤼,나 어수뤼 아바아 무아꽈 와 너가,
26. 나 너가 아바아 무아꽈 와 마디, 나 마디 아바아 무아꽈 와 마다디아, 나 마다디아 아바아 무아꽈 와 시머이, 나 시머이 아바아 무아꽈 와 요서푸,나 요서푸 아바아 무아꽈 와 유다,
27. 나 유다 아바아 무아꽈 아 요하나, 나 요하나 아바아

---

22. and the Holy Spirit descended on him in bodily form like a dove. And a voice came from heaven: "You are my Son, whom I love; with you I am well pleased."

23. Now Jesus himself was about thirty years old when he began his ministry. He was the son, so it was thought, of Joseph, the son of Heli,
24. the son of Matthat, the son of Levi, the son of Melki, the son of Jannai, the son of Joseph,
25. the son of Mattathias, the son of Amos, the son of Nahum, the son of Esli, the son of Naggai,
26. the son of Maath, the son of Mattathias, the son of Semein, the son of Josech, the son of Joda,
27. the son of Joanan, the son of Rhesa, the

---

wa Kesa, na Kesa abaa muala wa Serubali, na Serubali abaa muala a Salichiere, na Salichiere abaa muala wa Ati,

28. na Ati abaa muala wa Kosamu, na Kosamu abaa muala wa Elimatamu, na Elimatamu abaa muala wa Eri

29. na Eri abaa muala wa Yose, na Yose abaa muala wa Eliyeseri, na Eliyeseri abaa muala wa Yoremu, na Yoremu abaa muala wa Matati, na Matati abaa muala wa Lawi,

30. na Lawi abaa muala wa Simeonyi, na Simeonyi abaa muala wa Yuta, na Yuta abaa muala wa Yosefu, na Yosefu abaa muala wa Yonanu, na onanu abaa muala wa Eliyakimu,

31. na Eliyakimu abaa mula wa Meleya, na Meleya abaa muala a Menana, na Menana abaa muala wa Matata, na Matata abaa mula wa Natanyi, na Natanyi abaa muala wa Daudi,

32. na Daudi abaa muala wa Yese, na Yese abaa muala wa Obeti, na Obeti abaa muala wa Nasonyi,

무아쫘 와 거사, 나 거사 아바아 무아쫘 와 서루바쮜, 나 서루바쮜 아바아 무아쫘 아 사쮜쩌러, 나 사쮜쩌러 아바아 무아쫘 와 아디,

28. 나 아디 아바아 무아쫘 와 고사무, 나 고사무 아바아 무아쫘 와 어쮜마다무, 나 어쮜마다무 아바아 무아쫘 와 어리

29. 나 어리 아바아 무아쫘 와 요서, 나 요서 아바아 무아쫘 와 어쮜여서리, 나 어쮜여서리 아바아 무아쫘 와 요러무, 나 요러무 아바아 무아쫘 와 마다디, 나 마다디 아바아 무아쫘 와 쫘위,

30. 나 쫘위 아바아 무아쫘 와 시머오네, 나 시머오네 아바아 무아쫘 와 유다, 나 유다 아바아 무아쫘 와 요서푸, 나 요서푸 아바아 무아쫘 와 요나누, 나 오나누 아바아 무아쫘 와 어쮜야기무,

31. 나 어쮜야기무 아바아 무쫘 와 머러야, 나 머러야 아바아 무아쫘 아 머나나, 나 머나나 아바아 무아쫘 와 마다다, 나 마다다 아바아 무쫘 와 나다네, 나 나다네 아바아 무아쫘 와 다우디,

32. 나 다우디 아바아 무아쫘 와 여서, 나 여서 아바아 무아쫘 와 오버디, 나 오버디 아바아 무아쫘 와 나소네,

son of Zerubbabel, the son of Shealtiel, the son of Neri,

28. the son of Melki, the son of Addi, the son of Cosam, the son of Elmadam, the son of Er,

29. the son of Joshua, the son of Eliezer, the son of Jorim, the son of Matthat, the son of Levi,

30. the son of Simeon, the son of Judah, the son of Joseph, the son of Jonam, the son of Eliakim,

31. the son of Melea, the son of Menna, the son of Mattatha, the son of Nathan, the son of David,

32. the son of Jesse, the son of Obed, the son of Boaz, the son of Salmon, the son of Nahshon,

33. na Nasonyi abaa muala wa Aminatabu, na Aminatabu, na Aminatabu abaa muala wa Aramu, na Aramu abaa muala wa Esironyi, na Esironyi abaa muala waPerisi, na Perisi abaa muala wa Yuta,

34. na Yuta abaa muala wa Yakobo, na Yakobo abaa uala wa Isaka, an Isaka abaa muala wa Aburahamu, na Aburahamu abaa muala wa Tera, na Tera abaa muala wa Naori,

35. na Naori abaa muala wa Seruku, na Seruku abaa muala wa Rewu, na Rewu abaa muala wa Peleki, na Peleki abaa muala wa Eberi, na Ebri abaa muala wa Sela,

36. na sela abaa muala wa Kainana, na Kainama abaa muala wa Arufaksadi,na Arufaksadi abaa muala wa Semu, na Semu abaa muala wa Nowa, na Nowa abaa muala wa Lameki,

37. na Lameki abaa muala wa Metusaeli,na Metusaeli abaa muala wa Enoka,na Enoka abaa muala wa Yareti,na Yareti abaa muala wa Mahaleli, na Mahaleli abaa muala wa Kainana,

33. 나 나소네 아바아 무아롸 와 아미나다부, 나 아미나다부, 나 아미나다부 아바아 무아롸 와 아라무, 나 아라무 아바아 무아롸 와 어시로네, 나 어시로네 아바아 무아롸 와퍼리시, 나 퍼리시 아바아 무아롸 와 유다,

34. 나 유다 아바아 무아롸 와 야고보, 나 야고보 아바아 우아롸 와 이사가, 아누 이사가 아바아 무아롸 와 아부라하무, 나 아부라하무 아바아 무아롸 와 더라, 나 더라 아바아 무아롸 와 나오리,

35. 나 나오리 아바아 무아롸 와 서루구, 나 서루구 아바아 무아롸 와 러웅, 나 러웅 아바아 무아롸 와 퍼러기, 나 퍼러기 아바아 무아롸 와 어버리, 나 어부리 아바아 무아롸 와 서롸,

36. 나 서롸 아바아 무아롸 와 가이나나, 나 가이나마 아바아 무아롸 와 아루파구사디,나 아루파구사디 아바아 무아롸 와 서무, 나 서무 아바아 무아롸 와 노와, 나 노와 아바아 무아롸 와 롸머기,

37. 나 롸머기 아바아 무아롸 와 머두사어릐,나 머두사어릐 아바아 무아롸 와 어노가,나 어노가 아바아 무아롸 와 야러디,나 야러디 아바아 무아롸 와 마하퍼릐, 나 마하퍼릐 아바아 무아롸 와 가이나나,

33. the son of Amminadab, the son of Ram, the son of Hezron, the son of Perez, the son of Judah,

34. the son of Jacob, the son of Isaac, the son of Abraham, the son of Terah, the son of Nahor,

35. the son of Serug, the son of Reu, the son of Peleg, the son of Eber, the son of Shelah,

36. the son of Cainan, the son of Arphaxad, the son of Shem, the son of Noah, the son of Lamech,

37. the son of Methuselah, the son of Enoch, the son of Jared, the son of Mahalalel, the son of Kenan,

38. NA Kainama abaaa muala wa Enosi, na Enosi abaa muala wa Seti, na Seti abaa muala wa Adamu, na Adamu abaa muala wa Ongo.

38. 나 가이나마 아바아아 무아똬 와 어노시, 나 어노시 아바아 무아똬 와 서디, 나 서디 아바아 무아똬 와 아다무, 나 아다무 아바아 무아똬 와 오꼬.

38. the son of Enosh, the son of Seth, the son of Adam, the son of God.

Luka Chikono 4
E musimu ereka Yesu

루가 찌고노 4
어 무시무 어러가 여수

Luke Chapter 4[NIV]

1. Mango Yesu abaa era atengaa era abatisibwaa, mwa Iwishi Iw'e Yorotanyi, e Muchima Mubuya-buya ola abaa era anete, era kumweka mwa buyeye.

1. 마꼬 여수 아바아 어라 아더까아 어라 아바디시봐아, 롸 뤼씨 뤄 요로다니, 어 무찌마 무부야-부야 오똬 아바아 어라 아너더, 어라 구뭐가 롸 부여여.

1. Jesus, full of the Holy Spirit, returned from the Jordan and was led by the Spirit in the desert,

2. Amalaa mu suku mane busira kulya, kanji Shetanyi era kumuereka.

2. 아마똬아 무 수구 마너 부시라 구꺄, 가찌 써다네 어라 구무어러가.

2. where for forty days he was tempted by the devil. He ate nothing during those days, and at the end of them he was hungry.

3. Abere ebusinya bwanamualire, Shetanyi era kumubura: "Akaba woyu uneshi kwa uli Mwenyi Ongo, buraa line ekoi mbu likuhubiraa biryo;

3. 아버러 어부시냐 봐나무아뤼러, 써다네 어라 구무부라: "아가바 옹유 우너씨 과 우뤼 뭐네 오꼬, 부라아 뤼너 어고이 뿌 뤼구후비라아 비료;

3. The devil said to him, "If you are the Son of God, tell this stone to become bread."

4. 'Yesu era kumwakula: "eChinwa cha Ongo chitula chitechire mbu ekalamo k'emundu katangaboneka mwa biryo byeine.

4. 여수 어라 구롸구꺄: "어찌놔 짜 오꼬 찌두똬 찌더찌러 뿌 어가똬모 거무뚜 가다까보너가 롸 비료 벼이너.

4. Jesus answered, "It is written: 'Man does not live on bread alone.'"

5. Kanji Shetnyi era kumweka ala ammanukire, kuna kumulosa ebio byoshi by'omwa butala,

5. 가찌 써두네 어라 구뭐가 아똬 아무마누기러, 구나 구무로사 어비오 뵤씨 뷔오롸

5. The devil led him up to a high place and showed him in an

부다꽈,

instant all the kingdoms of the world.

6. Era kumubura: "Nyingakuwa e buashi bw'e kwemangira ebi byoshi usene ku, n'e chwunda lyabi. Umenyererereraa kwa neresibwe bi, kanji nyinganabyeresa ola nyinasimire.

6. 어라 구무부라: "네꽈구와 어부아씨 붜 궈마꞉라 어비 뵤씨 우서너 구, 너 쭈따 랴비. 우머녀러러라아 과 너러시붜 비, 가띠 네꽈나벼러사 오꽈 네나시미러.

6. And he said to him, "I will give you all their authority and splendor, for it has been given to me, and I can give it to anyone I want to.

7. Akaba unganyichwunda, nyingakweresa e bwami n'e bikulo byoshi by'ebi bio."

7. 아가바 우꽈네쭈따, 네꽈궈러사 어 봐미 너 비구로 뵤씨 벼비 비오."

7. So if you worship me, it will all be yours."

8. Yesu nai era kumwakula: "e Chinwa cha Ongo chichwula chitechire mbu uchwundaa Ongo I Enawenyu, kanji unamutongaa yeine.

8. 여수 나이 어라 구꽈구라: "어 찌놔 짜 오꼬 찌쭈꽈 찌더찌러 뿌 우쭈따아 오꼬 이 어나워뉴, 가띠 우나무도꽈아 여이너.

8. Jesus answered, "It is written: 'Worship the Lord your God and serve him only.'"

9. Chasinjire, Shetanyi era kweka Yesu mwa musi w'e Yerusalemu. Era kumwirusa kwa ngangamo s'e Luhu lwa Ongo n'e kuhuba kumubura: "Akaba woyu uneshi kwa uli Mwenyi Ongo, uchikabulaa era eshi,

9. 짜시찌러, 써다네 어라 궈가 여수 뫄 무시 워 여루사꺼무. 어라 구뮈루사 과 꽈꽈모 서 룻후 꽈 오꼬 너 구후바 구무부라: "아가바 오유 우너씨 과 우뤼 뭐네 오꼬, 우찌가부라아 어라 어씨,

9. The devil led him to Jerusalem and had him stand on the highest point of the temple. "If you are the Son of God," he said, "throw yourself down from here.

10. Bushi eChinwa cha Ongo chitula chitechire mmbu: "Ongo akabura ebamalaika bai mbu bakutabalaa.

10. 부씨 어찌놔 짜 오꼬 찌두꽈 찌더찌러 무뿍: "오꼬 아가부라 어바마꽈이가 바이 뿍 바구다바꽈아.

10. For it is written: " 'He will command his angels concerning you to guard you carefully;

11. Kanji chinatula chitechire mmbu: Bakakwangirira mwa maboko mabu unesha kutoera kw'ekoi n'ekufunyika ekuulu.

11. 가띠 찌나두꽈 찌더찌러 무뿍: 바가과꞉리라 뫄 마보고 마부 우너싸 구도어라 궈고이 너구푸네가 어구우룻.

11. they will lift you up in their hands, so that you will not strike your foot against a stone.'"

12. Si Yesu era kumwakula: "e Chinwa cha Ongo chichwula chitechire mmbu: "Utanaereresa

12. 시 여수 어라 구꽈구라: "어 찌놔 짜 오꼬 찌쭈꽈 찌더찌러 무뿍: "우다나어러러사 와어러가

12. Jesus answered, "It says: 'Do not put the Lord your God to the

waereka Enawenyu Ongo.	어나워뉴 오옹.	test.'"
13. Abere Shetanyi amala kuereka Yesu ekwai kwoshi busira kumuala era kumureka tanga.	13. 아버러 써다네 아마ᄙᅡ 구어러가 여수 어과이 곷씨 부시라 구무아ᄙᅡ 어라 구무러가 다ᅇᅡ.	13. When the devil had finished all this tempting, he left him until an opportune time.
14. Yesu era kuhuba mwa chio ch'e Galilaya. Kanji ebuashi bw'e Muchima Mubuya-buya bwabaa bunalyi alauma nai mwa mulyimo wai. Engulu yai yera kunamala echi chio choshi.	14. 여수 어라 구후바 뫄 찌오 쩌 가ᄙᅵᄙᅡ야. 가ᄭᅵ 어부아씨 붜 무찌마 무부야-부야 봐바아 부나ᄙᅦ 아ᄙᅡ우마 나이 뫄 무ᄙᅦ모 와이. 어우루 야이 여라 구나마ᄙᅡ 어찌 찌오 쪼씨.	14. Jesus returned to Galilee in the power of the Spirit, and news about him spread through the whole countryside.
15. Mango endaa akangilyisa e Chinwa cha Ongo mwa bihaala by'e Bayuda, e bandju boshi bendaa bamuwa e ngulu.	15. 마옹 어따아 아가ᅇᅵᄙᅦ사 어 찌놔 짜 오옹 뫄 비하아ᄙᅡ 벼 바유다, 어 바쭈 보씨 버따아 바무와 어 우루.	15. He taught in their synagogues, and everyone praised him.
Yesu mwa nazareti	*여수 뫄 나자러디*	
16. Yesu era kuya mwa musi w'e Nasareti era akulyiraa. Era kwingira mwa chihaala ch'e Bayuta e lusuku lw'e Sabato* ng'okwa endaa anaira. Aikire mu, bera kumubura mbu emangaa abasomere e Chinwa cha Ongo.	16. 여수 어라 구야 뫄 무시 워 나사러디 어라 아구ᄙᅦ라아. 어라 귀ᅇᅵ라 뫄 찌하아ᄙᅡ 쩌 바유다 어 루수구 뤄 사바도* 옹과 어따아 아나이라. 아이기러 무, 버라 구무부라 뿌 어마ᅇᅡ아 아바소머러 어 찌놔 짜 오옹.	16. He went to Nazareth, where he had been brought up, and on the Sabbath day he went into the synagogue, as was his custom. And he stood up to read.
17. Unao-unao, bera kumweresa e chibungo ch'e Chitabo cha murebi Isaya anjikaa. Abee bungula chi, kuna kuikira ala banjikire mmbu:	17. 우나오-우나오, 버라 구뭐러사 어 찌부옹 쩌 찌다보 짜 무러비 이사야 아ᄭᅵ가아. 아버어 부우ᄙᅡ 찌, 구나 구이기라 아ᄙᅡ 바ᄭᅵ기러 무뿌:	17. The scroll of the prophet Isaiah was handed to him. Unrolling it, he found the place where it is written:
18. "eMuchima Mubuya-buya wa Ongo ali al'auma nanyi. Bushi n'oku, anyilondwere mbu nyihubanganyisaa e bakene e	18. "어무찌마 무부야-부야 와 오옹 아ᄙᅵ 아ᄙᅡ우마 나니. 부씨 노구, 아네론뚜워러 뿌 네후바ᅇᅡ네사아 어 바거너 어	18. "The Spirit of the Lord is on me, because he has anointed me to preach good news to the

Mwasi Mubuya-buya. Anyichwumire mbu nyiburaa e bandju b'e mulyisi kwa bakaboolwa, e bauta kwa bakalola, n'na ba balyi mwa bucha kwa bakanunulyibwa.

19. Kanji anyichwumire mbu nyihambalyiraa e bandju kw'e suku s'e chamba cha Ongo kwa bandju saikire.

20. Abere Yesu era amalaa kusoma, era kubunga e chibungo ch'e Chitabo. Era kuchialulyira e mulanzi w'e chihaala, era kwikala bushi. Chasinjire, e bandju boshi bera kumuchwumbikisa.

21. Yesu era kutangilyiisa ababura: "Kutengera lwarero, echi Chinwa cha Ongo cha nera kubasomera, chaikire ku Mwabu kanangana."

22. Boshi bera kuwa Yesu engulu n'ekusanwa kwa binwa bikomire bya byendaa byatenga mwa bunu bwai. Bera kutangirisa bateta mmbu: "Si mwenyi Yosefu ono wateta bine binwa bikomie bacha!"

23. Bushi n'oku, Yesu era kubabura: "Nyineshi kwa munganyitea mw'ono muso: E muhake, chihakilyiraa weine!;"Twomvire kwa bisomerano byoshi bya wairaa

마시 무부야-부야. 아네쭈미러 뿌 네부라아 어 바쭈 버 무레시 과 바가보오롸, 어 바우다 과 바가르롸, 우나 바 바레 마 부짜 과 바가누누레봐.

19. 가찌 아네쭈미러 뿌 네하빠레라아 어 바쭈 귀 수구 서 짜빠 짜 오꼬 과 바쭈 사이기러.

20. 아버러 여수 어라 아마롸아 구소마, 어라 구부롸 어 찌부꼬 쩌 찌다보. 어라 구찌아루루레라 어 무롸씨 워 찌하아롸, 어라 귀가롸 부씨. 짜시찌러, 어 바쭈 보씨 버라 구무쭈뻬기사.

21. 여수 어라 구다뻬이사 아바부라: "구더뻐라 롸러로, 어찌 찌놔 짜 오꼬 짜 너라 구바소머라, 짜이기러 구 마부 가나뽜나."

22. 보씨 버라 구와 여수 어꾸루 너구사놔 과 비놔 비고미러 뱌 벼뽜아 뱌더뾰 마 부누 봐이. 버라 구다뻬리사 바더다 무뿟: "시 뭐네 요서푸 오노 와더다 비너 비놔 비고미어 바짜!"

23. 부씨 노구, 여수 어라 구바부라: "네너씨 과 무뾰네더아 모노 무소: 어 무하거, 찌하기뻬라아 워이너!;"돔뻬러 과 비소머라노 보씨 뱌 와이라아 어

poor. He has sent me to proclaim freedom for the prisoners and recovery of sight for the blind, to release the oppressed,

19. to proclaim the year of the Lord's favor."

20. Then he rolled up the scroll, gave it back to the attendant and sat down. The eyes of everyone in the synagogue were fastened on him,

21. and he began by saying to them, "Today this scripture is fulfilled in your hearing."

22. All spoke well of him and were amazed at the gracious words that came from his lips. "Isn't this Joseph's son?" they asked.

23. Jesus said to them, "Surely you will quote this proverb to me: 'Physician, heal yourself! Do here in your hometown what we have

e Kaperinaumu, rero ubiiraa n'omuno musi wenyu."

24. Era kunaendekerana ababura: "Nateta kanangana kwa kutali murebi ola bende bomva mwa musi ola akuliraa mu.

25. Kanji nababwirire, ku binali, mukengeraa kwa mwa suku sa murebi Eliya, mwa chio ch'e Isiraeli mwabaa bahumba -kasi banene. Mw'esi suku, kwabaaa businya bunene bushi n'echanda cha chakolaa myaka ehachwu na chimbi busira kureka chisiki.

26. Si Ongo ataumaa Eliya kuasa chiro na muuma mubu kureka ola wabaaa uchwula mwa musi w'e Serepata, mwa chio ch'e Sitona, burerere n'e isiraeli.

27. Kanji munamenyereraa kwa mwa chio ch'e Isiraeli mwanabaa babenzi-benzi banene mwa suku sa murebi Elisha nai. Si chiro na muuma ola walamisibwaa nai kureka Namani w'omwa chio ch'e burerere, e Suriya."

28. Mango boshi ba babaa bali mwa chihaala bombaa kw'ebi binwa, e bute bwera kubasimba busese.

29. Chasinjire, bera kwimuka

가퍼리나우무, 러로 우비이라아 노무노 무시 워뉴."

24. 어라 구나어떠거라나 아바부라: "나더다 가나까나 과 구다삐 무러비 오라 버너 보빠 꽈 무시 오라 아구삐라아 무.

25. 가찌 나바뷔리러, 구 비나삐, 무거꺼라아 과 꽈 수구 사 무러비 어삐야, 꽈 찌오 쩌 루시라어삐 꽈바바아 바후빠 - 가시 바너너. 뭐시 수구, 과바아아 부시냐 부너너 부씨 너짜따 짜 짜고라아 먀가 어하쭈 나 찌삐 부시라 구러가 찌시기.

26. 시 오꼬 아다우마아 어삐야 구아사 찌로 나 무우마 무부 구러가 오라 와바아아 우쭈꽈 꽈 무시 워 서러파다, 꽈 찌오 쩌 시도나, 부러러러 너 이시라어삐.

27. 가찌 무나머녀러라아 과 꽈 찌오 쩌 이시라어삐 꽈나바아 바버씨-버씨 바너너 꽈 수구 사 무러비 어삐싸 나이. 시 찌로 나 무우마 오라 와꽈미시봐아 나이 구러가 나마니 요꽈 찌오 쩌 부러러러, 어 수리야."

28. 마꼬 보씨 바 바바아 바삐 꽈 찌하아꽈 보빠아 궈비 비놔, 어 부더 뷔라 구바시빠 부서서.

29. 짜시찌러, 버라 귀무가 보씨

heard that you did in Capernaum.' "

24. "I tell you the truth," he continued, "no prophet is accepted in his hometown.

25. I assure you that there were many widows in Israel in Elijah's time, when the sky was shut for three and a half years and there was a severe famine throughout the land.

26. Yet Elijah was not sent to any of them, but to a widow in Zarephath in the region of Sidon.

27. And there were many in Israel with leprosy in the time of Elisha the prophet, yet not one of them was cleansed--only Naaman the Syrian."

28. All the people in the synagogue were furious when they heard this.

29. They got up, drove

boshi n'e kumusimba. Bera kutangilyisa bamukululyira era nyuma s'e lusito lw'e musi n'e kumwe ka kwa ngangamo s'e kachwulungu abaa aimbirwe ku. Babaa bahonda bamufumi mwa kabanda.

30. Si Yesu era kurenga mwa kachi-kachi kabu, busira kumuuma ku, kuna kuchiendera.

Yesu akula e bihwasi bibi

31. Bushi n'oku, Yesu era kwandalyira mwa musi w'e Kaperinaumu, mwa chio ch'e Galilaya. Era kukangirisa e bandju e Chinwa cha Ongo mwa chihaala ch'e Bayuda chira lusuku lwa Sabato.

32. E bandju bera kusanwa busese mango bomvaa kwa enjire ahubanganyisa bu e Chinwa cha Ongo n'e buashi.

33. Mw'echi chihaala ch'e Bayuda mwabaa mulyi mundju muuma ola wete e bihwasi. Chihwasi chiuma chera kutangilyisa chalakanga:

34. "Hah! Chiye chi woyu Yesu u mwesha Nasareti wachwuhonda ku? Kuchwukolokanya ku wabahilyire? Nyineshi kwa woyu unalyi Mubuya-buya ola watenga era wa Ongo!"

너 구무시빠. 버라 구다삐례사 바무구루쩨라 어라 뉴마 서 루시도 뤄 무시 너 구뭐 가 과 까까모 서 가쭈루우 아바아 아이삐뤄 구. 바바아 바호따 바무푸미 롸 가바따.

30. 시 여수 어라 구러꽈 롸 가찌-가찌 가부, 부시라 구무우마 구, 구나 구쩌떠라.

여수 아구꽈 어 비화시 비비

31. 부씨 노구, 여수 어라 과따쩨라 롸 무시 워 가퍼리나우무, 롸 찌오 쩌 가삐꽈야. 어라 구가끼리사 어 바뉴 어 찌놔 짜 오꼬 롸 찌하아꽈 쩌 바유다 찌라 루수구 롸 사바도.

32. 어 바뉴 버라 구사놔 부서서 마꼬 보빠아 과 어찌러 아후바바네사 부 어 찌놔 짜 오꼬 너 부아씨.

33. 뭐찌 찌하아꽈 쩌 바유다 롸바아 무쩨 무뿌 무우마 오꽈 워더 어 비화시. 찌화시 찌우마 쩌라 구다삐쩨라 짜라가까:

34. "하! 찌여 찌 오유 여수 우 뭐싸 나사러디 와쭈호따 구? 구쭈고로가냐 구 와바히쩨러? 네너씨 과 오유 우나레 무부야-부야 오꽈 와더까 어라 와 오꼬!"

him out of the town, and took him to the brow of the hill on which the town was built, in order to throw him down the cliff.

30. But he walked right through the crowd and went on his way.

31. Then he went down to Capernaum, a town in Galilee, and on the Sabbath began to teach the people.

32. They were amazed at his teaching, because his message had authority.

33. In the synagogue there was a man possessed by a demon, an evilspirit. He cried out at the top of his voice,

34. "Ha! What do you want with us, Jesus of Nazareth? Have you come to destroy us? I know who you are--the Holy One of God!"

35. Unao-unao, Yesu era kukalyiira chi mmbu: "Siraa unatenge kw'oyu mundju!"Mw'echi chihangi, echi chihwasi chera kuhunda ola mundju kwa chitaka mwa meho m'e bandju boshi. Cherakumutenga ku busira kumubabasa.

36. E bandJu boshi bera kusanwa busese n'e kutangiLYisa babusanya: "Kute angaata e buashi bw'e kwambula e bihwAsi mwa kunateta mmbu: "Siraa, unatenge kw'oyu mundJu,"na byatenga?"

37. Bushi n'oku, Yesu era kunaya ngulu mwa chio choshi ch'e Kaperinaumu.

Yesu alamya nasala wa simoni

38. Yesu era kutenga mwa chihaala ch'e BayuDa n'e kuya mwa nyumba ya Simonyi. Aikire mu, era kubuana nasala wa Simoni akukumana 'ekayao. Besha mu, bera kwema Yesu ebonjo mbu amulamyaa.

39. Yesu era kuchifunda era ulwala abaa ali, era kuteta n'e murenge w'e bukalyi mbu e kayao katengaa mwa mulwala. Unao-unao, era kunalama. Abere era alamaa, era kutangilyisa abahondera ebiryo.

---

35. 우나오-우나오, 여수 어라 구가레이라 찌 무뿌: "시라아 우나더꺼 교유 무뚜!"뭐찌 찌하꾀, 어찌 찌화시 쩌라 구후따 오롸 무뚜 과 찌다가 롸 머호 머 바뉴 보씨. 쩌라구무더꺼 구 부시라 구무바바사.

36. 어 바뉴 보씨 버라 구사놔 부서서 너 구다꾀레사 바부사냐: "구더 아꺼아다 어 부아씨 붜 과뭏롸 어 비화시 롸 구나더다 무뚜: "시라아, 우나더꺼 교유 무뚜,"나 뱌더꺼?"

37. 부씨 노구, 여수 어라 구나냐 우루 롸 찌오 쪼씨 쩌 가퍼리나우무.

여수 아롸뫳 나사롸 와 시모니

38. 여수 어라 구더꺼 롸 찌하아롸 쩌 바유다 너 구야 롸 뉴빠 야 시모네. 아이기러 무, 어라 구부아나 나사롸 와 시모니 아구구마나 어가야오. 버싸 무, 버라 궈마 여수 어보쪼 뿌 아무롸먀아.

39. 여수 어라 구찌푸따 어라 우롸롸 아바아 아리, 어라 구더다 너 무러꺼 워 부가레 뿌 어 가야오 가더꺼아 롸 무롸롸. 우나오-우나오, 어라 구나라마. 아버러 어라 아롸마아, 어라 구다꾀레사 아바호더라 어비료.

---

35. "Be quiet!" Jesus said sternly. "Come out of him!" Then the demon threw the man down before them all and came out without injuring him.

36. All the people were amazed and said to each other, "What is this teaching? With authority and power he gives orders to evil spirits and they come out!"

37. And the news about him spread throughout the surrounding area.

38. Jesus left the synagogue and went to the home of Simon. Now Simon's mother-in-law was suffering from a high fever, and they asked Jesus to help her.

39. So he bent over her and rebuked the fever, and it left her. She got up at once and began to wait on them.

40. Mango lwabaa lwera luoloolo, chira mundju areteraa Yesu ewai mulwala, kanji chira mulwala abaa alumwa kwai. Yesu era kubemera n'e kubika emino kw'etwe lya chira mulwala. Boshi bera kunalama.

41. Kwabaa na banji bandu banene ba bihwasi byatengaa ku byaenda byalakanga mmbu: "woyu utula Mwenyi Ongo. "yatetaa bacha, bushi byabaa bineshi kwa abaa ali mununusi.* Si Yesu endaa abikaliira, kanji atendaa abyemerera bitete bacha.

42. Abere yera mishangya - shangya, Yesu era kutenga mwa musi w'eKaperinaumu n'ekuya bure 'ebandu; Bushi n'oku, bandu banene bera kutangirisa bamuhonda. Mango bamuchimanaa, chiro bakahonda achibatenge ku.

43. Si Yesu era kubabura: "Ndangekala ndahubanganyise eMwasi Mubuya-buya w'eBwimi bwa Ongo mwa inji misi, bushi echera chi chatumaa Ongo anyituma"

44. Yesu endaa anaendekerana ahubanganya eMwasi Mubuya-buya wa Ongo mwa bihaala* by'eBayuta.

40. 마꼬 롸바아 뤄라 루오로오로, 찌라 무뚜 아러더라아 여수 어와이 무롸롸, 가찌 찌라 무롸롸 아바아 아루뫄 과이. 여수 어라 구버머라 너 구비가 어미노 궈뚸 롸 찌라 무롸롸. 보씨 버라 구나롸마.

41. 과바아 나 바찌 바두 바너너 바 비화시 뱌더꽈아 구 뱌어따 뱌퐈가꺄 무뿌: "오유 우두롸 뭐네 오꼬. "야더다아 바짜, 부씨 뱌바아 비너씨 과 아바아 아뤼 무누누시.* 시 여수 어따아 아비가뀌이라, 가찌 아더따아 아벼머러라 비더더 바짜.

42. 아버러 여라 미싸꺄 - 싸꺄, 여수 어라 구더꺄 뫄 무시 워가퍼리나우무 너구야 부러 어바뚜; 부씨 노구, 바뚜 바너너 버라 구다삐리사 바무호따. 마꼬 바무찌마나아, 찌로 바가호따 아찌바더꺼 구.

43. 시 여수 어라 구바부라: "따꺼가퐈 따후바꺄네서 어뫄시 무부야-부야 워뷔미 봐 오꼬 뫄 이찌 미시, 부씨 어쩌라 찌 짜두마아 오꼬 아니두마"

44. 여수 어따아 아나어떠거라나 아후바꺄냐 어뫄시 무부야-부야 와 오꼬 뫄 비하아퐈* 벼바우다.

40. When the sun was setting, the people brought to Jesus all who had various kinds of sickness, and laying his hands on each one, he healed them.

41. Moreover, demons came out of many people, shouting, "You are the Son of God!" But he rebuked them and would not allow them to speak, because they knew he was the Christ.

42. At daybreak Jesus went out to a solitary place. The people were looking for him and when they came to where he was, they tried to keep him from leaving them.

43. But he said, "I must preach the good news of the kingdom of God to the other towns also, because that is why I was sent."

44. And he kept on preaching in the synagogues of Judea.

Luka Chikono 5

Kufuba efi sinene

1. Lusuku luuma, Yesu abaa emenzi kwa musike s'enyanja y'e jenerazeti. Bandju banene bera kumusungula n'ekumufundeeresa. Ba baa bahonda bomvilyise kw'ahubanganya e Chinwa cha Ongo.

2. Mw'echi chihangi, Yesu era kulangusa ku mato mabilyi ma bafubi era musike s''enyanja. Besha mu babaa batengire mumu, bera balonga etusira twabu;

3. Yesu era kwirukira mu bwato buuma, bushi n'ebwingi bw'ebandu. Bwabaa bwa Simonyi Petero. Era kubura ena bu mbu abukulaa kwa mukono abufunde mwa nyanja. Yesu era kwikala mw'obu bwato n'ekutangirisa ahubanganyisa ebandu eChinwa cha Ongo.

4. Abere Yesu era amalaa kuhubnganya eChinwa cha Ongo, era kubura Simonyi: "Fundaa ebwato ala esibe liri, kanji woyu na balikenyu mukabulaa etusira twenyu mwa meshi mufube."

루가 찌고노 5

구푸바 어피 시너너

1. 루수구 루우마, 여수 아바아 어머씨 과 무시거 서냐짜 여 저너라저디. 바쭈 바너너 버라 구무수꾸롸 너구무푸떠어러사. 바 바아 바호따 보뻬레서 과후바아냐 어 찌놔 짜 오꼬.

2. 뭐찌 찌하삐, 여수 어라 구롸꾸사 구 마도 마비레 마 바푸비 어라 무시거 수어냐짜. 버싸 무 바바아 바더삐러 무무, 버라 바로야 어두시라 돠부;

3. 여수 어라 귀루기라 무 봐도 부우마, 부씨 너뷔삐 뭐바뚜. 봐바아 봐 시모네 퍼더로. 어라 구부라 어나 부 뿌 아부구꽈아 과 무고노 아부푸떠 뫄 냐짜. 여수 어라 귀가롸 모부 봐도 너구다삐리사 아후바야네사 어바뚜 어찌놔 짜 오꼬.

4. 아버러 여수 어라 아마롸야 구후부야냐 어찌놔 짜 오꼬, 어라 구부라 시모네: "뿌따아 어바도 아롸 어시버 뤼리, 가찌 오유 나 바뤼거뉴 무가부롸아 어두시라 뚸뉴 뫄 머씨 무푸버."

Luke Chapter 5[NIV]

1. One day as Jesus was standing by the Lake of Gennesaret,with the people crowding around him and listening to the word of God,

2. he saw at the water's edge two boats, left there by the fishermen, who were washing their nets.

3. He got into one of the boats, the one belonging to Simon, and asked him to put out a little from shore. Then he sat down and taught the people from the boat.

4. When he had finished speaking, he said to Simon, "Put out into deep water, and let down the nets for a catch."

5. Simonyi era kumwakula: "Emanzi Enawetu! Bubuno bwnacha twafuba busira n'ekwita elimboolo! Si bushi woyu u watechire ku, nyinganahubya etusira mwa meshi."

6. Abere Simonyi na balikabu bera bakabulaa etusia twabu mwa meshi, bera kwita efi sinene. Bushi n'ebwingi bwasi, etusira twabaa twera twahonda kubereka.

7. Buhi n'oku, bera kwemaala balikabu ba babaa bali mwa bunji bwato mbu babahaa babaase. Emato mabu mombi mera kwihula efi. Mera kunde mabura manenama bushi n'ebusito bwasi.

8. Mango Simonyi alolaa kwa bwingi bw'efi, na akoma emafi era muhondo sa Yesu. Era kuteta: "Enawetu, Nyono nyiri mukosi wa mabi. Bushi n'oku, ndangemanga of unau."

9. Atetaa bacha, bushi asimbwaa na buba bunene al'auma na balikabu boshi mango balolaa kwa bwingi bw'efi.

10. Baala Sebetayo nabu, Yakobo na Yowanyi bu babaa bali mwa bunji bwato, bera kusimbwa na buba bunene

---

5. 시모네 어라 구꽈구꽈:
"어마씨 어나워두! 부부노 부우나짜 돠푸바 부시라 너귀다 어뤠뽀오롿! 시 부씨 오유 우 와더찌러 구, 네꺄나후뱌 어두시라 돠 머씨."

6. 아버러 시모네 나 바뤼가부 버라 바가부롸아 어두시아 돠부 돠 머씨, 버라 귀다 어피 시너너. 부씨 너뷔삐 봐시, 어두시라 돠바아 뚸라 돠호따 구버러가.

7. 부히 노구, 버라 궈마아꽈 바뤼가부 바 바바아 바뤼 돠 부찌 봐도 뿌 바바하아 바바아서. 어마도 마부 모삐 머라 귀후꽈 어피. 머라 구떠 마부라 마너나마 부씨 너부시도 봐시.

8. 마꼬 시모네 아로롸아 과 뷔삐 뷔피, 나 아고마 어마피 어라 무호또 사 여수. 어라 구더다: "어나워두, 뇨노 네리 무고시 와 마비. 부씨 노구, 따꺼마꺄 오푸 우나우."

9. 아더다아 바짜, 부씨 아시꽈아 나 부바 부너너 아꽈우마 나 바뤼가부 보씨 마꼬 바로롸아 과 뷔삐 뷔피.

10. 바아꽈 서버다요 나부, 야고보 나 요와네 부 바바아 바뤼 돠 부찌 봐도, 버라 구시꽈 나 부바 부너너 구우마 나

---

5. Simon answered, "Master, we've worked hard all night and haven't caught anything. But because you say so, I will let down the nets."

6. When they had done so, they caught such a large number of fish that their nets began to break.

7. So they signaled their partners in the other boat to come and help them, and they came and filled both boats so full that they began to sink.

8. When Simon Peter saw this, he fell at Jesus' knees and said, "Go away from me, Lord; I am a sinful man!"

9. For he and all his companions were astonished at the catch of fish they had taken,

10. and so were James and John, the sons of Zebedee, Simon's partners. Then Jesus said

kuuma na balikabu. Si Yesu era kubura Simonyi: "Utobaaa, bushi kutengera lwarero, utakachifube efi si bandu bu ukere wende wahonda."

11. Unao-unao, bera kuya kuminyira emato mabu kwa mukono w'enyanja. Bera kureka bya babaa banet byoshi n'ekukulikira Yesu.

Yesu alamya e mubenzi-benzi

12. Lusuku luuma, Yesu abaa alyi mu musi muuma w'e Galilaya. Abere era alyi mu, mundju muuma wafire n'e bibenzi era kubaha. Mango Mulwala alolaa ku Yesu, era kukoma e mafi era muhondo sai n'e kumwema e bonjo mmbu: "Enawechwu, akaba ungahonda kunyilamya, nyinganalama."

13. Yesu era kumubika kw'e mino, era kuteta: "Nemerere, ulamaa; Unao-unao bya bibenzi na byalama byoshi.

14. Chasinjire, Yesu era kumubura: Utabalyiraa mundju mwasi mwa njia, si uyaa tanga kuchilosa era mwa kuhanyi wa Ongo akulole ku. Kanji uendaa kweresa Ongo emitulo ng'okwa Musa anjikaa, iri e bandju boshi

바뀌가부. 시 여수 어라 구부라 시모네: "우도바아아, 부씨 구더뗘라 똬러로, 우다가찌푸버 어피 시 바뚜 부 우거러 워떠 와호따."

11. 우나오-우나오, 버라 구야 구미네라 어마도 마부 과 무고노 워냐짜. 버라 구러가 뱌 바바아 바너두 뵤씨 너구구뤼기라 여수.

여수 아꽈맨 어 무버씨-버씨

12. 루수구 루우마, 여수 아바아 아뗴 무 무시 무우마 워 가삐뢔랴. 아버러 어라 아뗴 무, 무뚜 무우마 와피러 너 비버씨 어라 구바하. 마꼬 무똴꽈 아뢴꽈아 구 여수, 어라 구고마 어 마피 어라 무호또 사이 너 구뭐마 어 보쪼 무뿌: "어나워쭈, 아가바 우꽈호따 구네꽈먀, 네꽈나꽈마."

13. 여수 어라 구무비가 궈 미노, 어라 구더다: "너머러러, 우꽈마아; 우나오-우나오 뱌 비버씨 나 뱌꽈마 뵤씨.

14. 짜시찌러, 여수 어라 구무부라: 우다바뼤라아 무뚜 꽈시 똬 씨아, 시 우야아 다꽈 구찌론사 어라 똬 구하네 와 오꼬 아구뢴뻐 구. 가찌 우어따아 궈러사 오꼬 어미두뢴 꼬과 무사 아찌가아, 이리 어

to Simon, "Don't be afraid; from now on you will catch men."

11. So they pulled their boats up on shore, left everything and followed him.

12. While Jesus was in one of the towns, a man came along who was covered with leprosy. When he saw Jesus, he fell with his face to the ground and begged him, "Lord, if you are willing, you can make me clean."

13. Jesus reached out his hand and touched the man. "I am willing," he said. "Be clean!" And immediately the leprosy left him.

14. Then Jesus ordered him, "Don't tell anyone, but go, show yourself to the priest and offer the sacrifices that Moses commanded for your cleansing, as a testimony

bamenyerera kwa walamire"

바쑤 보씨 바머녀러라 과
와쫘미러"

to them."

15. Echea chitatumaa Yesu ataya ngulu chira lusuku. Kanji bandu banene bendaa bamushemba, bushi babaa bahonda bome kwa Chinwa cha Ongo n'ekulamisibwa nai.

15. 어쩌아 찌다두마아 여수 아다야 우루 찌라 루수구. 가찌 바쑤 바너너 버따아 바무써빠, 부씨 바바아 바호따 보머 과 찌놔 짜 오꼬 너구콰미시봐 나이.

15. Yet the news about him spread all the more, so that crowds of people came to hear him and to be healed of their sicknesses.

16. Chiro angaba mbu endaa akola bacha, abaa anakomere kuya era itali ofu na bandu kwemera yi Ongo.

16. 찌로 아까바 뿌 어따아 아고콰 바짜, 아바아 아나고머러 구야 어라 이다뤼 오푸 나 바쑤 귀머라 에 오꼬.

16. But Jesus often withdrew to lonely places and prayed.

Yesu alamya e mundju utambukere e bitera

여수 아쫘맫 어 무뿌 우다뿌걔랸 어 비더라

17. Lusuku luuma, Yesu abaa ahubanganyisa e bandju e chinwa cha Ongo mwa nyumba. Bafarisayo bauma na bakangirisi ba Mwaso bauma b'e chio choshi ch'e Galilaya, n'eYuteya, 'eYerusalemu nabu babaa bekesi bamumvirisa. Ongo era kumweresa ebuashi bw'ekulamya ebalwala.

17. 루수구 루우마, 여수 아바아 아후바까니사 어 바쑤 어 찌놔 짜 오꼬 콰 뉴빠. 바파리사요 바우마 나 바가끼리시 바 뫄소 바우마 버 찌오 쪼씨 쩌 가뤼콰야, 너유더야, 어여루사쩌무 나부 바바아 버거시 바무쀼리사. 오꼬 어라 구뭐러사 어부아씨 뷔구콰먀 어바쫘콰.

17. One day as he was teaching, Pharisees and teachers of the law, who had come from every village of Galilee and from Judea and Jerusalem, were sitting there. And the power of the Lord was present for him to heal the sick.

18. Bandju bauma bera kuika bete chirema kwa chipoyo; Bahondaa bamwingirise mwa nyuma Yesu amulole ku.

18. 바쑤 바우마 버라 구이가 버더 찌러마 과 찌포요; 바호따아 바뮈끼리서 뫄 뉴마 여수 아무로뤄 구.

18. Some men came carrying a paralytic on a mat and tried to take him into the house to lay him before Jesus.

19. Si bainaa ala banamurenzesa bushi n'ekuluwa kw'e bandju. Bushi n'oku, bera kumwirukana kwa ngangamo s'e nyumba. Bera kuhanda kwa matebura, na bamurenzesa mwa chiture. Bera kumwandaasisa n'e chipoyo chai mwa kachi-kachi k'e bandju ala Yesu abaa alyi.

20. Abere Yesu alola kwa bwemeresi bwabu kui, era kubura oyu mulwala: "Ebibi byau byababalirwe mwira wanyi."

21. Ebakangirisi b'e Mwaso n'eBafarisayo ba babaa bali mwa nyumba bera kutangirisa bachitetembya: "Ono mundu al inde i wateta bya bitangaretwa? Kulyi mundju ola ungababalire ebii kureka Ongo yeine?"

22. Mango Yesu amenyereraa e mianyisa yabu, era kubabura: "Nyono ndasene cha chingatuma mwaanyisa bacha mwa michima yenyu.

23. Munyiburaa chiye chi chitangaalikana mw'e bine binwa bibiri: Ekubura emulwala mbu e bibi byai byababalyirwe,nesi e kumubura mbu emukaa aende.

19. 시 바이나아 아롸 바나무러써사 부씨 너구루와 귀 바뚜. 부씨 노구, 버라 구뮈루가나 과 까아모 서 뉴빠. 버라 구하따 과 마더부라, 나 바무러써사 뫄 찌두러. 버라 구뫄따아시사 너 찌포요 짜이 뫄 가찌-가찌 거 바뚜 아롸 여수 아바아 아레.

20. 아버러 여수 아로롸 과 붜머러시 봐부 구이, 어라 구부라 오유 무롸롸: "어비비 뱌우 뱌바바뤼뤠 뮈라 와네."

21. 어바가삐리시 버 뫄소 너바파리사요 바 바바아 바뤼 뫄 뉴빠 버라 구다삐리사 바찌더더뺘: "오노 무뚜 아루 이떠 이 와더다 뱌 비다삐러돠? 구레 무뚜 오롸 우까바바뤼러 어비이 구러가 오꼬 여이너?"

22. 마꼬 여수 아머녀러라아 어 미아네사 야부, 어라 구바부라: "뇨노 따서너 짜 찌까두마 뫄아네사 바짜 뫄 미찌마 여뉴.

23. 무네부라아 찌여 찌 찌다까아삐기가나 뭐 비너 비뇨 비비리: 어구부라 어무롸롸 뿌 어 비비 뱌이 뱌바바레뤠,너시 어 구무부라 뿌 어무가아 아어떠.

19. When they could not find a way to do this because of the crowd, they went up on the roof and lowered him on his mat through the tiles into the middle of the crowd, right in front of Jesus.

20. When Jesus saw their faith, he said, "Friend, your sins are forgiven."

21. The Pharisees and the teachers of the law began thinking to themselves, "Who is this fellow who speaks blasphemy? Who can forgive sins but God alone?"

22. Jesus knew what they were thinking and asked, "Why are you thinking these things in your hearts?

23. Which is easier: to say, 'Your sins are forgiven,' or to say, 'Get up and walk'?

24. Bushi n'oku, nahonda nyibalose kw'ebuashi bwanyi nyi Mwana w'e Mundju butalyi kwa kulamya kweine muno butala, si n'ekubabalira ebibi. "hasinjire, Yesu era kubura cha chirema: "Nyi atechire, batulaa e chipoyo chau ufuluke kwa wau."

25. Unao-unao, era Kwimuka banasene, era kubatula echipoyo chai cha abaa alakira ku. Era kuhuba kwa wai aenda atonga Ongo.

26. Boshi ba babaa bali mw'ei nyumba, bera kusanwa busese n'e kutona Ongo. Bushi n'e buba bunene, bera kutangirisa bateta: "Bya chwalolyire ku lwarero bitangaanyikisibwa.

Yesu alondola Matayo

27. Chasinjire, Yesu era kutenga mwa musi. Aikire mwa njira, era kubuana mufuchisi wa mbarata muuma mbu i Matayo. Abaa ali mwa mulimo wai w'ekufuchisa embarata. Yesu era kumubura: "Unyemisaa."

28. Unao-unao,Matayo era kwimuka n'e kureka e mulyimo wai, kuna kuhuba mwanda wa Yesu.

29. Chasinjire, Matayo era kutekera Yesu bilyo binene kwa kulosa e lumoo lwai. Kanji era

---

24. 부씨 노구, 나호따 네바로서 뀌부아씨 봐네 네 마나 워 무뚜 부다쩨 과 구꽈먀 뀌이너 무노 부다라, 시 너구바바삐라 어비비. "하시찌러, 여수 어라 구부라 짜 찌러마: "네 아더찌러, 바두꽈라 어 찌포요 짜우 우푸루거 과 와우."

25. 우나오-우나오, 어라 귀무가 바나서너, 어라 구바두꽈 어찌포요 짜이 짜 아바아 아꽈기라 구. 어라 구후바 과 와이 아어따 아도따 오꼬.

26. 보씨 바 바바아 바삐 뮈이 뉴빠, 버라 구사놔 부서서 너 구도나 오꼬. 부씨 너 부바 부너너, 버라 구다삐리사 바더다: "뱌 좌로쩨러 구 꽈러로 비다따아네기시봐.

여수 아로또꽈 마다요

27. 짜시찌러, 여수 어라 구더따 꽈 무시. 아이기러 꽈 찌라, 어라 구부아나 무푸찌시 와 빠라다 무우마 뿌 이 마다요. 아바아 아삐 꽈 무삐모 와이 워구푸찌사 어빠라다. 여수 어라 구무부라: "우녀미사아."

28. 우나오-우나오,마다요 어라 귀무가 너 구러가 어 무쩨모 와이, 구나 구후바 꽈따 와 여수.

29. 짜시찌러, 마다요 어라 구더거라 여수 비뢰 비너너 과 구로사 어 루모오 꽈이. 가찌

---

24. But that you may know that the Son of Man has authority on earth to forgive sins...." He said to the paralyzed man, "I tell you, get up, take your mat and go home."

25. Immediately he stood up in front of them, took what he had been lying on and went home praising God.

26. Everyone was amazed and gave praise to God. They were filled with awe and said, "We have seen remarkable things today."

27. After this, Jesus went out and saw a tax collector by the name of Levi sitting at his tax booth. "Follow me," Jesus said to him,

28. and Levi got up, left everything and followed him.

29. Then Levi held a great banquet for Jesus at his house, and a large

Kunalalika bafuchisi banene ba mbarata al'auma na banji bandu.

30. Mango Bafarisayo bauma na bakangirisi ba Mwaso auma balolaa bacha, bera kutangilyisa bachitetembya n'e kubura abanafunzi ba Yesu: "Chi chingatuma mwalya n'e kumwa al'auma n'e bandju babi ng'e bafuchisi b'e mbarata?"

31. Si Yesu era kubakula: "Ba bahaalukire baahonda muhake, si e balwala bu bende bamuhonda.

32. Ndabahire kuhonda e bandju ba bera bali babuya, si nabahire kuhonda ba bachiri babi, bareke ebibi bnaalukire Ongo."

33. Kanji eBafarisayo bera kubura Yesu: "Ebanafunzi ba Yowana kuuma na ba betu bende bema chira mango. Kanji kuli mango bende banareka ekulya esuku bema. Si ba bau beke bende balya n'e kumwa mw'e suku sa silyi ng'esi. Chi chingatuma baira bacha?"

34. Yesu era kubakula: "Ndeshi kute mungateta mbu ba balalikwaa kwa buya batalyaa n'oku emuya mulume achiri al'auma nabu.

어라 구나롸뀌가 바푸찌시 바너너 바 빠라다 아롸우마 나 바찌 바뚜.

30. 마꼬 바파리사요 바우마 나 바가삐리시 바 뫄소 아우마 바룐롸아 바짜, 버라 구다삐레사 바찌더더빠 너 구부라 아바나푸씨 바 여수: "찌 찌마두마 뫄랴 너 구뫄 아롸우마 너 바뚜 바비 삐 바푸찌시 버 빠라다?"

31. 시 여수 어라 구바구롸: "바 바하아루뀌러 바아호따 무하거, 시 어 바롸롸 부 버너 바무호따.

32. 따바히러 구호따 어 바뚜 바 버라 바뀌 바부야, 시 나바히러 구호따 바 바찌리 바비, 바러거 어비비 부나아루뀌러 오꼬."

33. 가찌 어바파리사요 버라 구부라 여수: "어바나푸씨 바 요와나 구우마 나 바 버두 버머 바마 찌라 마꼬. 가찌 구뀌 마꼬 버머 바나러가 어구롸 어수구 버마. 시 바 바우 버거 버머 바롸 너 구뫄 뭐 수구 사 시뤠 삐시. 찌 찌마두마 바이라 바짜?"

34. 여수 어라 구바구롸: "떠씨 구더 무마더다 뿌 바 바롸뀌과아 과 부야 바다롸아 노구 어무야 무루머 아찌리 아롸우마 나부.

crowd of tax collectors and others were eating with them.

30. But the Pharisees and the teachers of the law who belonged to their sect complained to his disciples, "Why do you eat and drink with tax collectors and 'sinners'?"

31. Jesus answered them, "It is not the healthy who need a doctor, but the sick.

32. I have not come to call the righteous, but sinners to repentance."

33. They said to him, "John's disciples often fast and pray, and so do the disciples of the Pharisees, but yours go on eating and drinking."

34. Jesus answered, "Can you make the guests of the bridegroom fast while he is with them?

35. Si kukaba sinji suku oyu muya mulume akekibwa. Mw'esi suku, bakareka ekulya, bushi n'ekumulirira."

36. Yesu era kubaishira ono muso: "Kutalyi mundju ola unakula e murera kwas luchimba lwai luyayaya n'ekuulanjira kwa chiramba. Ola ungaira bacha, angaba aberengire eluchimba lwi luyayaya, kanji emurera watenga kulu atangahuhana n'echi chiramba."

37. Kanji Yesu era kunaisha ono unji uso: "Kutali mundu ola ungabika emafu mai m'e chibabe mwa chikunguisa ch'ehao y'eluu pera bende babika mw'emafu.

38. Ola ungaira bacha, angatuma e chibabe chaberenga ei hao yai n'emafu mwa hao iyayaya.

39. Mulyi kuuma n'ola ungaba wamwere kwa muyo ola utangachisima e chibabe. Bacha k'ola wamwere kwa muyo ende ateta: "Mafumano".

---

35. 시 구가바 시찌 수구 오유 무야 무루머 아거기봐. 뭐시 수구, 바가러가 어구꺄, 부씨 너구무찌리라."

36. 여수 어라 구바이씨라 오노 무소: "구다뤠 무뚜 오롸 우나구롸 어 무러라 과수 루찌빠 롸이 루야야야 너구우롸씨라 과 찌라빠. 오라 우꺄이라 바짜, 아꺄바 아버러끼러 어루찌빠 뤼 루야야야, 가찌 어무러라 와더꺄 구루 아다꺄후하나 너찌 찌라빠."

37. 가찌 여수 어라 구나이싸 오노 우찌 우소: "구다뤼 무뚜 오롸 우꺄비가 어마푸 마이 머 찌바버 뫄 찌구뀌이사 쩌하오 여루우 퍼라 버뻐 바비가 뭐마푸.

38. 오롸 우꺄이라 바짜, 아꺄두마 어 찌바버 짜버러꺄 어이 하오 야이 너마푸 뫄 하오 이야야야.

39. 무뤠 구우마 노롸 우꺄바 와뭐러 과 무요 오롸 우다꺄찌시마 어 찌바버. 바짜 고롸 와뭐러 과 무요 어떠 아더다: "마푸마노".

---

35. But the time will come when the bridegroom will be taken from them; in those days they will fast."

36. He told them this parable: "No one tears a patch from a new garment and sews it on an old one. If he does, he will have torn the new garment, and the patch from the new will not match the old.

37. And no one pours new wine into old wineskins. If he does, the new wine will burst the skins, the wine will run out and the wineskins will be ruined.

38. No, new wine must be poured into new wineskins.

39. And no one after drinking old wine wants the new, for he says, 'The old is better.' "

Luka Chikono 6
Yesu y'enaesabato

룩가 찌고노 6
여수 여나어사바도

Luke Chapter 6[NIV]

1. Lusuku luuma lwa Sabato, Yesu n'ebanafunzi bai babaa barenga mwa mahwa m'emupunge ola werire. Mwa kurenga, ebanafunzi bai bera kutangirisas baupolola. Bera kuusinganya mwa mino, bera kuukuuta.

2. Aola, Bafarisayo* bauma bera kubusa mbu: "Chi chachwuma Mwaira bacha? Si eMwaso* wetu atula ananyise ekukola elusuku lw'eSabato!

3. Yesu era kubakula: "Kasi mutafuraa kusoa bya Tuti airaa al'auma na ba babaa bamwerekesise mango babaa bafire n'ebusinya?

4. Si ayaa mwa Nyumba ya Ongo, era kutola emikati batuliraa Ongo. Era kuilya yoshi al'auma na ba babaa bamwereketise, chiro angaba mbu eMwaso wetu atula ananyise chira mundu kulya ebi biyo kureka ebakuhanyi ba Ongo beine!

5. Kanji Yesu akubabua: "Nyono nyi Mwana w'eMundu nyi nyete ebuashi kwa Sabato.* "

Mundju utambukere e kuboko

6. Lunji lusuku luuma lwa Sabato,* Yesu ayaa mu chihaala chiuma ch'eBayuta. Era kutangirisa akangirisa ebandu.

1. 루수구 루우마 롸 사바도, 여수 너바나푸씨 바이 바바아 바러롸 롸 마화 머무푸어 오롸 워리러. 롸 구러롸, 어바나푸씨 바이 버라 구다삐리사수 바우포롣롸. 버라 구우시삐냐 롸 미노, 버라 구우구우다.

2. 아오롸, 바파리사요* 바우마 버라 구부사 뿌: "찌 짜쭈마 롸이라 바짜? 시 어롸소* 워두 아두롸 아나내서 어구고롸 어루수구 뤄사바도!

3. 여수 어라 구바구롸: "가시 무다푸라아 구소아 뱌 두디 아이라아 아롸우마 나 바 바바아 바뭐러거시서 마꼬 바바아 바피러 너부시냐?

4. 시 아야아 롸 뉴빠 야 오꼬, 어라 구도롸 어미가디 바두삐리라아 오꼬. 어라 구이꺄 요씨 아롸우마 나 바 바바아 바뭐러거디서, 찌로 아까바 뿌 어롸소 워두 아두롸 아나내서 찌라 무뚜 구꺄 어비 비요 구러가 어바구하네 바 오꼬 버이너!

5. 가찌 여수 아구바부아: "뇨노 네 마나 워무뚜 네 녀더 어부아씨 과 사바도.* "

무뚜 우다뿌개랸 어 구보고

6. 룩찌 루수구 루우마 롸 사바도,* 여수 아야아 무 찌하아롸 찌우마 쩌바유다. 어라 구다삐리사 아가삐리사 어바뚜.

1. One Sabbath Jesus was going through the grainfields, and his disciples began to pick some heads of grain, rub them in their hands and eat the kernels.

2. Some of the Pharisees asked, "Why are you doing what is unlawful on the Sabbath?"

3. Jesus answered them, "Have you never read what David did when he and his companions were hungry?

4. He entered the house of God, and taking the consecrated bread, he ate what is lawful only for priests to eat. And he also gave some to his companions."

5. Then Jesus said to them, "The Son of Man is Lord of the Sabbath."

6. On another Sabbath he went into the synagogue and was teaching, and a man was

Omola, mwabaa muli mundu muuma uremere emino y'emalyo.

7. Bakangisi bauma b'eMwaso na Bafarisayo * bauma bera kumutmbikisa balole iri angalamya oyu mundu elusuku lw'eSabato, bushi babaa bahonda babone emyasi bangamutonganya ku.

8. Si ebi babaa baanyisa, Yesu abimenyereraa. Echera cherakutuma abura oyu wabaa uremere emino mmbu: "Emukaa wimange mwa kachi-kachi k'eandu. "ra kunemanga mwa kachi-kachi kabu;

9. Yesu era kubusa ebandu boshi: "eMwaso* wetu atula emerere ekuira emabuya elusuku lw'eSabato nesi ekuira mu emabi? Kanji atula emerere ekulamya emundu nesi ekumwita?"

10. Era kubasonga boshi, era kubura cha chirema: "Nanulaa ekuboko kwau. "ai mango ananulaa ku, emino yai yera kunalama.

11. Chasinjire, ebakangirisi b'eMwaso n'eBafarisayo bera kusinana busese. Bera kutangirisa babusanya mbu kute ku bangamuteranya.

오모롸, 롸바아 무뤼 무뚜 무우마 우러머러 어미노 여마료.

7. 바가삐시 바우마 버롸소 나 바파리사요 * 바우마 버라 구무두뻬기사 바롣뻐 이리 아까롸먀 오유 무뚜 어루수구 뭐사바도, 부씨 바바아 바호따 바보너 어먀시 바까무도뺘냐 구.

8. 시 어비 바바아 바아니네사, 여수 아비머녀러라아. 어쩌라 쩌라구두마 아부라 오유 와바아 우러머러 어미노 무뿌: "어무가아 위마뻐 롸 가찌-가찌 거아뚜. "라 구너마빠 롸 가찌-가찌 가부;

9. 여수 어라 구부사 어바뚜 보씨: "어롸소* 워두 아두롸 어머러러 어구이라 어마부야 어루수구 뭐사바도 너시 어구이라 무 어마비? 가찌 아두롸 어머러러 어구롸먀 어무뚜 너시 어구뮈다?"

10. 어라 구바소뺘 보씨, 어라 구부라 짜 찌러마: "나누롸아 어구보고 과우. "아이 마꼬 아나누롸아 구, 어미노 야이 여라 구나롸마.

11. 짜시찌러, 어바가삐리시 버롸소 너바파리사요 버라 구시나나 부서서. 버라 구다삐리사 바부사냐 뿌 구더 구 바빠무더라냐.

there whose right hand was shriveled.

7. The Pharisees and the teachers of the law were looking for a reason to accuse Jesus, so they watched him closely to see if he would heal on the Sabbath.

8. But Jesus knew what they were thinking and said to the man with the shriveled hand, "Get up and stand in front of everyone." So he got up and stood there.

9. Then Jesus said to them, "I ask you, which is lawful on the Sabbath: to do good or to do evil, to save life or to destroy it?"

10. He looked around at them all, and then said to the man, "Stretch out your hand." He did so, and his hand was completely restored.

11. But they were furious and began to discuss with one another what they might do to Jesus.

Yesu alondola e Baanda	*여수 아롤또롸 어 바아따*	
12. Mw'esi suku, Yesu n'ebanafunzi* bai bera kwirukira kwa katulungu. Ebutufu bwera kumuchera ku ema Ongo.	12. 뭐시 수구, 여수 너바나푸씨* 바이 버라 귀루기라 과 가두룰우. 어부두푸 붜라 구무쩌라 구 어마 오옹.	12. One of those days Jesus went out to a mountainside to pray, and spent the night praying to God.
13. Abere yera mishangya - shangya, Yesu era kwemaala eanafunzi bai, era kulondola ekumi na babiri mubu. Era kuberika"ndumwa.* "	13. 아버러 여라 미싸ᅇᅣ - 싸ᅇᅣ, 여수 어라 궈마아롸 어아나푸씨 바이, 어라 구롤또롸 어구미 나 바비리 무부. 어라 구버리가"뚜뫄.* "	13. When morning came, he called his disciples to him and chose twelve of them, whom he also designated apostles:
14. N'emasina mabu mu mamano: Simonyi, ola Yesu asulaa esina lya Petero, na ulumuna wai Andereya, na Yakobo, na Yowanyi, na Firipo na Baritolomayo,	14. 너마시나 마부 무 마마노: 시모네, 오롸 여수 아수롸아 어시나 랴 퍼더로, 나 우루무나 와이 아떠러야, 나 야고보, 나 요와네, 나 피리포 나 바리도롤마요,	14. Simon (whom he named Peter), his brother Andrew, James, John, Philip, Bartholomew,
15. na Matayo, na Tomasi, na Yakobo mwenyi Alufayo, na Simonyi i wabaa wahonda echio chabu chitenge mwa bucha bw'e Baroma.	15. 나 마다요, 나 도마시, 나 야고보 뭐네 아루파요, 나 시모네 이 와바아 와호따 어찌오 짜부 찌더ᅇᅥ 뫄 부짜 붜 바로마.	15. Matthew, Thomas, James son of Alphaeus, Simon who was called the Zealot,
16. Na Yuta mwenyi Yakobo, na Yuta Isikariyota i waalukiraa Yesu ngabo.	16. 나 유다 뭐네 야고보, 나 유다 이시가리요다 이 와아루기라아 여수 ᅇᅡ보.	16. Judas son of James, and Judas Iscariot, who became a traitor.
17. Mango Yesu abaa era alondolaa endumwa* ekumi n'ebiri, era kwendaalira kwa kalambo ali al'auama nasi. Aola nau, abuanaa u chikembe cha banafunzi bai na banji bandu banene busese ba batengeraa mwa chio choshi ch'eYuteya. N'eanji batengeraa mwa musi w'e Tiro n'ew'eSitona, i misi	17. 마옹 여수 아바아 어라 아롤또롸아 어뚜뫄* 어구미 너비리, 어라 궈따아리라 과 가롸뽀 아리 아롸우아마 나시. 아오롸 나우, 아부아나아 우 찌거뻐 짜 바나푸씨 바이 나 바찌 바뚜 바너너 부서서 바 바더ᅇᅥ라아 뫄 찌오 쪼씨 쩌유더야. 너아찌 바더ᅇᅥ라아 뫄 무시 워 디로 너워시도나, 이	17. He went down with them and stood on a level place. A large crowd of his disciples was there and a great number of people from all over Judea, from Jerusalem, and from the coast of Tyre and Sidon,

y'era musike s'enyanja; n'ebanj batengeraa eYerussalemu.

미시 여라 무시거 서냐짜; 너바뚜 바더뻐라아 어여루싸뻐무.

---

18. Abu boshi babahaa bomvirisise Yesu, banalamisibwe emalwala mabu. Ba babaa balibukire 'ebihwasi, nabu bera kunalamisibwa.

19. Abu boshi bendaa bahonda bamuume ku, bushi buashi bunene bwendaa bwamutenga mu, n'noku ku kwendaa kwabalamya boshi.

18. 아부 보씨 바바하아 보뻬리시서 여수, 바나똬미시붜 어마똬똬 마부. 바 바바아 바뀌부기러 어비화시, 나부 버라 구나똬미시봐.

19. 아부 보씨 버따아 바호따 바무우머 구, 부씨 부아씨 부너너 붜따아 봐무더꺄 무, 우노구 구 궈따아 과바똬먀 보씨.

18. who had come to hear him and to be healed of their diseases. Those troubled by evil spirits were cured,

19. and the people all tried to touch him, because power was coming from him and healing them all.

E bandju baahanyirwe n'e bete e bwanya

어 바뚜 바아하네뤔 너 버더 어 봐냐

20. Yesu era kusonga ebanafunzi bai, era kutangirisa ababura: "Mwaahanyirwe mu mutete kwa muli, bushi muli besha mwa Bwami bwa Ongo.

20. 여수 어라 구소꺄 어바나푸씨 바이, 어라 구다뻬리사 아바부라: "뫄아하네뤔 무 무더더 과 무뤼, 부씨 무뤼 버싸 똬 봐미 봐 오꼰.

20. Looking at his disciples, he said: "Blessed are you who are poor, for yours is the kingdom of God.

21. Mwaahanyirwe mu mwafa ebusinya lwarero, bushi mukachiuta. Mwaahanyirwe mu mwalakanga, bushi mukachisheka.

21. 뫄아하네뤔 무 똬파 어부시냐 똬러로, 부씨 무가찌우다. 뫄아하네뤔 무 똬똬가꺄, 부씨 무가찌써가.

21. Blessed are you who hunger now, for you will be satisfied. Blessed are you who weep now, for you will laugh.

22. Mwaahanyirwe mango e bandju bababikire kw'eburenda, banabatakire, banabanane,

22. 뫄아하네뤔 마꼬 어 바뚜 바바비기러 궈부러따, 바나바다기러, 바나바나너,

22. Blessed are you when men hate you, when they exclude you

banaberike bandu babi mbu bushi muli banyi nyi Mwana w'eMundu.

23. Kw'olu lusuku, muchitereraa, bushi mubikirirwe lwembo lunene kwa nguba. Munakengeraa kwa ku n'oku ku bahokulu babu bendaa balibusa ebarebi.

24. Si mu baare, muli banya, bushi mwabonyie elwenyu lumoo mira.

25. N'nenyu mu muchiuchie lwarero muli banya, bushi mukachifa businya. N'nenyu mu mwasheka lwarero muli banya, bushi mukachirira 'ekuchilakagira.

26. Muli banya mango ebandu boshi bangabatonga, bushi ku n'oku ku bahokulu babu bendaa banatona ebarebi b'ebisha.

Kulosa e masimane

27. Si Mwabu mu munyumvirisise, chichine chi nababura: Ba bali ngao senyu, mwendaa mwbasima. N'na ba batula babahombire, mwendaa mwabalosa emabuya.

28. Ba bende babatakira, mwendaa mwema Ongo abaahanyire. N'na ba bende

바나버리거 바뚜 바비 뿌 부씨 무뀌 바니 네 뫄나 워무뚜.

23. 교뤄 뤄수구, 무찌더러라아, 부씨 무비기리뤄 뤔뽀 뤄너너 과 꾸바. 무나거꺼라아 과 구 노구 구 바호구뤄 바부 버따아 바뀌부사 어바러비.

24. 시 무 바아러, 무뀌 바냐, 부씨 뫄보니어 어뤄뉴 뤄모오 미라.

25. 우너뉴 무 무찌우쩌 꽈러로 무뀌 바냐, 부씨 무가찌파 부시냐. 우너뉴 무 뫄쎄가 꽈러로 무뀌 바냐, 부씨 무가찌리라 어구찌꽈가지라.

26. 무뀌 바냐 마꼬 어바뚜 보씨 바따바도꽈, 부씨 구 노구 구 바호구뤄 바부 버따아 바나도나 어바러비 버비싸.

구뤼뽀 어 마시마너

27. 시 뫄부 무 무뉴뻐리시서, 찌찌너 찌 나바부라: 바 바뀌 꽈오 서뉴, 뭐따아 무우바시마. 우나 바 바두꽈 바바호뻐러, 뭐따아 뫄바뢰사 어마부야.

28. 바 버떠 바바다기라, 뭐따아 뭐마 오꼬 아바아하니러. 우나 바 버떠 아바뀌부사, 뭐따아

and insult you and reject your name as evil, because of the Son of Man.

23. "Rejoice in that day and leap for joy, because great is your reward in heaven. For that is how their fathers treated the prophets.

24. "But woe to you who are rich, for you have already received your comfort.

25. Woe to you who are well fed now, for you will go hungry. Woe to you who laugh now, for you will mourn and weep.

26. Woe to you when all men speak well of you, for that is how their fathers treated the false prophets.

27. "But I tell you who hear me: Love your enemies, do good to those who hate you,

28. bless those who curse you, pray for those who mistreat you.

abalibusa, mwendaa mwabemera era mwa Ongo.	뫄버머라 어라 뫄 오ᅌ고.	
29. Mango emundu angakumaasisa kw'etama ly'emalyo, umuteaa n'ely'marembe. Na mango emundu angkwema ekandu utamwemaa ku, nesi mango emundu angachitorera ka kali kau, utachimwemaa ku.	29. 마ᅌ고 어무뚜 아ᅇ까구마아시사 궈다마 뤼어마료, 우무더아아 너뤼마러뻐. 나 마ᅌ고 어무뚜 아꾸궈마 어가뚜 우다뭐마아 구, 너시 마ᅌ고 어무뚜 아ᅇ까찌도러라 가 가리 가우, 우다찌뭐마아 구.	29. If someone strikes you on one cheek, turn to him the other also. If someone takes your cloak, do not stop him from taking your tunic.
30. Umua chira ola wakuemire, nola wahonda kukuyyaa uta honda akualylyire	30. 우무아 찌라 오라 와구어미러, 노라 와호따 구구위야아 우다 호따 아구아뤼레러	30. Give to everyone who asks you, and if anyone takes what belongs to you, do not demand it back.
31. N'na kwa mungahonda ebandu ba bairire ku mwendaa mwanabairira nabu.	31. 우나 과 무ᅇ까호따 어바뚜 바 바이리러 구 뭐따아 뫄나바이리라 나부.	31. Do to others as you would have them do to you.
32. Akaba munganairira emabuya ba bende banabairira mu, nzimwa ichie mungabona? Si ebakosi b'emabi nabu ku bende banairirana bacha!	32. 아가바 무ᅇ까나이리라 어마부야 바 버떠 바나바이리라 무, 찌뫄 이쪄 무ᅇ까보나? 시 어바고시 버마비 나부 구 버떠 바나이리라나 바짜!	32. "If you love those who love you, what credit is that to you? Even 'sinners' love those who love them.
33. Nenyui muka bailyira kubusya ba baira e mabuya elyi bu buya buchiye mwalosise; Bushi, ne bakosi be mabi nabo bende banasima ba babasimire.	33. 너뉴이 무가 바이레라 구부샤 바 바이라 어 마부야 어레 부 부야 부찌여 뫄로시서; 부씨, 너 바고시 버 마비 나보 버떠 바나시마 바 바바시미러.	33. And if you do good to those who are good to you, what credit is that to you? Even 'sinners' do that.
34. Mango munganenjika ba munalangalire kwa bu bangababafua, nzimwa ichie mungabona? Si ebakosi b'emabi nabu bende benjika ba banganababafua!	34. 마ᅌ고 무ᅇ까너찌가 바 무나라ᅇ까리러 과 부 바ᅇ까바푸아, 찌뫄 이쪄 무ᅇ까보나? 시 어바고시 버마비 나부 버떠 버찌가 바 바ᅇ까나바푸아!	34. And if you lend to those from whom you expect repayment, what credit is that to you? Even 'sinners' lend to 'sinners,' expecting to be

repaid in full.

35. Si Mwabu mwendaa mwasima ba bali ngabo senyu; mwendaa mwakola emabuya. Kanji mwendaa mwenjika chira mundu busira kulangalira mbu bangabafua; bushi mubikirirwe lwembo lunene, mukanaba bana ba Ongo, bushi i utula Nyangola - mabuya kwa ba batateta akoko n'na kwa bakosi b'emabi.

36. Mwendaa mwanaata ebonjo kwa bandu ng'okwa Eho w'okwa nguba abuchwusa.

37. Mutendaa mwalyana e lubanja ilyi nenyu mutachilyibwa e lwenyu. Mutendaa mwachinjibusa e banji ilyi nenyu mutachichinjibusibwa. Si mwendaa mwachinjibusa ebanji iri nenyu mutachichinjibusibwa. Si mwendaa mwababalyirana ilyi nenyu mwaba bakubabalirwa.

38. Mwendaa mwana ilyi nenyu Ongo ende aberesa. N'na cha mungeresibwa chingasindairwa n'e kwihusa e hao senyu kwa na meno. Kwa mwarengera e banji ku Ongo akanabarengera." Yesu aishira e

35. 시 뫄부 뭐따아 뫄시마 바 바뀌 까보 서뉴; 뭐따아 뫄고롸 어마부야. 가찌 뭐따아 뭐찌가 찌라 무뚜 부시라 구롸마뤼라 뿌 바까바푸아; 부씨 무비기리뤄 뤄뽀 루너너, 무가나바 바나 바 오꼬, 부씨 이 우두롸 냐꼬롸 - 마부야 과 바 바다더다 아고고 누나 과 바고시 버마비.

36. 뭐따아 뫄나아다 어보쪼 과 바뚜 꼬과 어호 요과 꾸바 아부쭈사.

37. 무더따아 뫄럐나 어 루바쌰 이뻬 너뉴 무다찌뼤봐 어 뤄뉴. 무더따아 뫄찌찌부사 어 바찌 이뻬 너뉴 무다찌찌찌부시봐. 시 뭐따아 뫄찌찌부사 어바찌 이리 너뉴 무다찌찌찌부시봐. 시 뭐따아 뫄바바뼤라나 이뻬 너뉴 뫄바 바구바바뤼롸.

38. 뭐따아 뫄나 이뻬 너뉴 오꼬 어떠 아버러사. 우나 짜 무뻐러시봐 찌까시따이롸 너 귀후사 어 하오 서뉴 과 나 머노. 과 뫄러뻐라 어 바찌 구 오꼬 아가나바러뻐라." 여수 아이씨라 어 바뚜 어미아네

35. But love your enemies, do good to them, and lend to them without expecting to get anything back. Then your reward will be great, and you will be sons of the Most High, because he is kind to the ungrateful and wicked.

36. Be merciful, just as your Father is merciful.

37. "Do not judge, and you will not be judged. Do not condemn, and you will not be condemned. Forgive, and you will be forgiven.

38. Give, and it will be given to you. A good measure, pressed down, shaken together and running over, will be poured into your lap. For with the measure you

bandju emianyi

39. Kanji Yesu era kubaishira, ono muanyi: "Si mutabukire kwa muuta atatandaisa muuta mulyikabu, kuika bombi banatoere mwa fumbi!

40. Kutali mwanafunzi* ola ngarenza emukangirisi wai. Si emwanafunzi ola wamalire kukangirisibwa kubuya-buya i wera ungaba ng'emukangirisi wai.

41. Chi chingatuma wanalola kwa kaha k'emuchi ka kali mwa liho lya mulikenyu, si utasene kwa muchi uli mwa lyau liho?

42. Na kute ungabura mulikenyu mmbu: "Emunyaketu, rekaa nyikukule ekaha ka kakuli mwa liho, na weine utasene kwa muchi mwa lyau! Eu hakubisha mabi, tangiraa kukula emuchi ola uli mwa lyau liho, chasinda wera ngakula ekaha ka kali mwaliho lya mulikeyu." Emunduende amenyekera kwa mikorere yai

43. Kanji Yesu era kuteta: "Kutali muchi mubuya ola ungaata bifuma bibi, kutali na muchi

39. 가찌 여수 어라 구바이씨라, 오노 무아니: "시 무다부기러 과 무우다 아다다따이사 무우다 무레가부, 구이가 보쎄 바나도어러 똬 푸쎄!

40. 구다찌 똬나푸씨* 오똬 따러싸 어무가찌리시 와이. 시 어똬나푸씨 오똬 와마찌러 구가쎄리시봐 구부야-부야 이 워라 우따바 엉어무가쎄리시 와이.

41. 찌 찌따두마 와나로똬 과 가하 거무찌 가 가찌 똬 찌호 쨔 무찌거뉴, 시 우다서너 과 무찌 우찌 똬 쨔우 찌호?

42. 나 구더 우따부라 무찌거뉴 무뿌: "어무냐거두, 러가아 내구구뻐 어가하 가 가구찌 똬 찌호, 나 워이너 우다서너 과 무찌 똬 쨔우! 어우 하구비싸 마비, 다쎄라아 구구똬 어무찌 오똬 우찌 똬 쨔우 찌호, 짜시따 워라 까구똬 어가하 가 가찌 똬찌호 쨔 무찌거유." 어무뚜어떠 아머녀거라 과 미고러러 야이

43. 가찌 여수 어라 구더다: "구다찌 무찌 무부야 오똬 우따아다 비푸마 비비, 구다찌

use, it will be measured to you."

39. He also told them this parable: "Can a blind man lead a blind man? Will they not both fall into a pit?

40. A student is not above his teacher, but everyone who is fully trained will be like his teacher.

41. "Why do you look at the speck of sawdust in your brother's eye and pay no attention to the plank in your own eye?

42. How can you say to your brother, 'Brother, let me take the speck out of your eye,' when you yourself fail to see the plank in your own eye? You hypocrite, first take the plank out of your eye, and then you will see clearly to remove the speck from your brother's eye.

43. "No good tree bears bad fruit, nor does a bad tree bear good fruit.

mubi ola ungaata bifuma bibuya.

나 무찌 무비 오꽈 우까아다 비푸마 비부야.

44. Chira muchiende amenyekera kwa bifuma byau. Bataokola byambamba kwa katenge-tenge. Batanauka ngobya kwa chishembeere.

44. 찌라 무쩌머 아머녀거라 과 비푸마 뱌우. 바다오고꽈 뱌빠빠 과 가더머-더머. 바다나우가 꼬뱌 과 찌써뻐어러.

44. Each tree is recognized by its own fruit. People do not pick figs from thornbushes, or grapes from briers.

45. Ku n'oku ku n'oku, emundu mubuya maiende alosa emabuya ma matenga mwa muchima wai. N'e mundju mubi, e mabi ma mende matenga mwa bubi bwehwire mwamuchima wai. Ebunu bwa chira mundju bwende bwateta bya byehwire mwa muchima wai. "

45. 구 노구 구 노구, 어무뚜 무부야 마이어머 아로사 어마부야 마 마더꽈 마 무찌마 와이. 너 무뚜 무비, 어 마비 마 머머 마더꽈 마 부비 붜휘러 뫄무찌마 와이. 어부누 봐 찌라 무뚜 붜떠 봐더다 뱌 벼휘러 뫄 무찌마 와이. "

45. The good man brings good things out of the good stored up in his heart, and the evil man brings evil things out of the evil stored up in his heart. For out of the overflow of his heart his mouth speaks.

E nyumba kwa lutandalyi

어 뉴빠 과 루닛따례

46. Yesu era kunaendekerana ateta: "Chi chichwuma mwende mwanyibura: "Enawetu, enawetu, mutanaira n'na bya nende nababura?

46. 여수 어라 구나어떠거라나 아더다: "찌 찌쭈마 뭐떠 뫄네부라: "어나워두, 어나워두, 무다나이라 우나 뱌 너떠 나바부라?

46. "Why do you call me, 'Lord, Lord,' and do not do what I say?

47. Chira mundu ola wende waya era nyiri ananyumve, aire n'na bya nateta, nabalosa kwa alyi.

47. 찌라 무뚜 오꽈 워떠 와야 어라 내리 아나뉴뻐, 아이러 우나 뱌 나더다, 나바로사 과 아례.

47. I will show you what he is like who comes to me and hears my words and puts them into practice.

48. Ali ng'e mundju ola watangilyisaa achima echibanja busese, chasinda era kulunda kw'e makoi ma aimbiraa kw'ei nyumba, si chiro ikahaala bushi

48. 아삐 떠 무뚜 오꽈 와다삐례사아 아찌마 어찌바싸 부서서, 짜시따 어라 구루따 궈 마고이 마 아이삐라아 궈이 뉴빠, 시 찌로 이가하아꽈 부씨

48. He is like a man building a house, who dug down deep and laid the foundation on rock. When a flood came, the

yabaa iserire.

야바아 이서리러.

torrent struck that house but could not shake it, because it was well built.

49. Si chira mundu ola ungachiremba mbu ende omva e binwa byanyi atanabichwunda, alyi ng'e mundju ola waimbaa e nyumba yai kwa chitaka buha-buha busira kuibika kwa makoi. Abere e mwihuso achihuta kui, yera kunakundjuka unao-unao, yera kunahandjukala yoshi.

49. 시 찌라 무뚜 오롸 우까찌러빠 뿌 어너 오빠 어 비놔 뱌네 아다나비쭌따, 아뤠 꺼 무뚜 오롸 와이빠아 어 뉴빠 야이 과 찌다가 부하-부하 부시라 구이비가 과 마고이. 아버러 어 뮈후소 아찌후다 구이, 여라 구나구뚜가 우나오-우나오, 여라 구나하뚜가꽈 요씨.

49. But the one who hears my words and does not put them into practice is like a man who built a house on the ground without a foundation. The moment the torrent struck that house, it collapsed and its destruction was complete."

Luka Chikono 7
Yesu alamya e mucha w'emukulu-kuku w'e basula
1. Abere Yesu era amalaa kukangirisa e bandju bya abaa abakangirisa byoshi, era kuya mwa musi w'eKaperinaumu.

루가 찌고노 7
여수 아꽈맸 어 무짜 워무구루-구구 워 바수꽈
1. 아버러 여수 어라 아마꽈아 구가끼리사 어 바뚜 뱌 아바아 아바가끼리사 뵤씨, 어라 구야 꽈 무시 워가퍼리나우무.

Luke Chapter 7[NIV]
1. When Jesus had finished saying all this in the hearing of the people, he entered Capernaum.

2. Mw'iyu musi mwabaa muli mukulu-kulu muuma w'ebasula b'eBaroma. Oyu mukulu-kulu abaa ete muanda wai ola abaa asimire busese. N'noyu muanda abaa alinga kufa n'ebulwala.

2. 뮈유 무시 뫄바아 무끼 무구루-구루 무우마 워바수꽈 버바로마. 오유 무구루-구루 아바아 어더 무아따 와이 오롸 아바아 아시미러 부서서. 우노유 무아따 아바아 아끼까 구파 너부롸꽈.

2. There a centurion's servant, whom his master valued highly, was sick and about to die.

3. Mango oyu mukulu-kulu omvaa mbu Yesu ali eKaperinaumu, era kumutumira bashamuka bauma b'eBayuta.

3. 마꼬 오유 무구루-구루 오빠아 뿌 여수 아끼 어가퍼리나우무, 어라 구무두미라 바싸무가 바우마

3. The centurion heard of Jesus and sent some elders of the Jews to him, asking him to come

버바유다.

and heal his servant.

4. Mango abu bashamuka baikaa ala Yesu ali, bera kumwema ebonjo abahe kulamya yu muanda. Bera kumubura: "Kukomire ulamye emuanda w'oyu mutambo.

4. 마꼬 아부 바싸무가 바이가아 아꽈 여수 아삐, 버라 구뭐마 어보쪼 아바허 구꽈먀 유 무아따. 버라 구무부라: "구고미러 우꽈며 어무아따 요유 무다뜨.

4. When they came to Jesus, they pleaded earnestly with him, "This man deserves to have you do this,

5. Achwula achwusimire, kanji i wachwuimbiraa e chihaala ch'omuno musi wechwu."

5. 아쭈라 아쭈시미러, 가찌 이 와쭈이삐라아 어 찌하아꽈 쪼무노 무시 워쭈."

5. because he loves our nation and has built our synagogue."

6. Abere Yesu omwa bacha, era kuenda nabu. Babere bera bali ofu n''enyumba y'oyu mukulu-kulu, nai era kutuma bera bai mbu bamubwiriraa Yesu mmbu: "Enawetu, emukulu-kulu atutumire mbu utachitamyaa mbu waya mwa mwai, bushi ata mundu ola woyu ungengirira mwa m

6. 아버러 여수 오먀 바짜, 어라 구어따 나부. 바버러 버라 바삐 오푸 우어뉴빠 요유 무구루-구루, 나이 어라 구두마 버라 바이 뿌 바무뷔리라아 여수 무뿌: "어나워두, 어무구루-구루 아두두미러 뿌 우다찌다먀아 뿌 와야 롸 마이, 부씨 아다 무뚜 오꽈 오유 우꺼끼리라 롸 무

6. So Jesus went with them. He was not far from the house when the centurion sent friends to say to him: "Lord, don't trouble yourself, for I do not deserve to have you come under my roof.

7. Echera chi chanatumaa yeine ataika ene uli. Si woyu unatetaa chinwa chiuma n'emuanda wai angalama.

7. 어쩌라 찌 짜나두마아 여이너 아다이가 어너 우삐. 시 오유 우나더다아 찌놔 찌우마 너무아따 와이 아까꽈마.

7. That is why I did not even consider myself worthy to come to you. But say the word, and my servant will be healed.

8. Kanji atechire mbu atula era bufuli s'ebuashi bwa banji bandu. Si nai atula emangirire basula. Akabura muuma bu aendaa,ende anaenda. Kanji akabura eunji mbu abahaa,ende anabaha. Akabura emuanda wai mbu airaa ekandu, kuika anakaire."

8. 가찌 아더찌러 뿌 아두꽈 어라 부푸삐 서부아씨 봐 바찌 바뚜. 시 나이 아두꽈 어마끼리러 바수꽈. 아가부라 무우마 부 아어따아,어너 아나어따. 가찌 아가부라 어우찌 뿌 아바하아,어너 아나바하. 아가부라 어무아따 와이 뿌 아이라아 어가뚜, 구이가

8. For I myself am a man under authority, with soldiers under me. I tell this one, 'Go,' and he goes; and that one, 'Come,' and he comes. I say to my servant, 'Do this,' and he does it."

9. Yesu omvira bacha, era kusanwa n'emitetere y'oyu mukulu-kulu w'ebasula. Era kusong echikembe ch'ebandu ba babaa bamwiisise, era kubabura: "Ndafuraa kulola ku mundu wete ebwemeresi ku Nyono buli ng'obuno mwa lubaa lw'eBayuta b'omwa chio ch'elsiraeli."

10. Abere ba batumwaa bera bafuluka kwa musi, bera kuburwa mbu ola muanda alamire, anahaalukire.

Yesu omola e mwana w'emuhumba - kasi

11. Mw'ei mishangya, Yesu n'ebanafunzi ai na luamba lunene lwa bandu, bayaa mu musi muuma mbu i Nainyi.

12. Abere aika kwa chiso ch'elusito lw'emusi, kwera kubaha chikembe cha bandu. Babaa bete chirunda cha mutabana mwa sanduku. Abaa chuha, na nyina abaa muhumba-kasi. Bandu banene b'emusi babaa bali nai.

13. Yesu amulolire ku, era kumufira bonjo bunene. Erar kumubura: "Utaliraa!"

아나가이러."

9. 여수 오삐라 바짜, 어라 구사놔 너미더더러 요유 무구룹-구룹 워바수꽈. 어라 구소웃 어찌거뻐 쩌바뚜 바 바바아 바뮈이시서, 어라 구바부라: "따푸라아 구롤롸 구 무뚜 워더 어붸머러시 구 뇨노 부뙤 오부노 꽈 루바아 뤄바유다 보꽈 찌오 쩌이시라어뙤."

10. 아버러 바 바두뫄아 버라 바푸루가 과 무시, 버라 구부롸 뿌 오롸 무아따 아롸미러, 아나하아룹기러.

여수 오모꽈 어 꽈나 워무후빠 - 가시

11. 뭐이 미싸꺄, 여수 너바나푸씨 아이 나 루아빠 루너너 꽈 바뚜, 바야아 무 무시 무우마 뿌 이 나이네.

12. 아버러 아이가 과 찌소 쩌룹시도 뤄무시, 궈라 구바하 찌거뻐 짜 바뚜. 바바아 버더 찌루따 짜 무다바나 꽈 사뚜구. 아바아 쭈하, 나 니나 아바아 무후빠-가시. 바뚜 바너너 버무시 바바아 바뙤 나이.

13. 여수 아무롤뙤러 구, 어라 구무피라 보쪼 부너너. 어라루 구무부라: "우다뙤라아!"

---

9. When Jesus heard this, he was amazed at him, and turning to the crowd following him, he said, "I tell you, I have not found such great faith even in Israel."

10. Then the men who had been sent returned to the house and found the servant well.

11. Soon afterward, Jesus went to a town called Nain, and his disciples and a large crowd went along with him.

12. As he approached the town gate, a dead person was being carried out--the only son of his mother, and she was a widow. And a large crowd from the town was with her.

13. When the Lord saw her, his heart went out to her and he said, "Don't cry."

14. Yesu era kuchifunda era sanduku yabaa iri, era kuiuma ku. Ba baaa baee bea kwemanga.; Yesu era kuteta: "Eu mutabana, sukaa!"

15. Unao-unao, ola wabaa ufir era kunasisimuka na ekala bushi. Era kutangirisa ahambala. Yesu era kumualulira nyina.

16. Mango ebandu boshi balolaa bacha, bera kubaa, babaa batonga Ongo n'ekuteta: "Murebi sutoire i waikire mwa kachi-kachi ketu. Kanji Ongo aikire kununula ebandu bai!"

17. Echi Yesu airaa chera kumenyeka mwa chio choshi ch'eYuteya n'ebinji bio bya al'auma nachi.

Kubusa kw'e ngulyikisa sa Yowana

18. Ebanafunzi ba Yowanyi nabu bera kumubalia kw'oyu mwasi. Yowanyi era kubarangira babiri mubu.

19. Era kubatuma era Yesu abaa ali mbu bamubusaa akaba i Mununusi* ola watetwaa mbu akaba wabahire, nesi akaba balinjiraa unji.

---

14. 여수 어라 구찌푸따 어라 사뚜구 야바아 이리, 어라 구이우마 구. 바 바아아 바어어 꿔마따.; 여수 어라 구더다: "어우 무다바나, 수가아!"

15. 우나오-우나오, 오라 와바아 우피루 어라 구나시시무가 나 어가꽈 부씨. 어라 구다삐리사 아하빠롸. 여수 어라 구무아루삐리라 니나.

16. 마오 어바뚜 보씨 바로롸아 바짜, 버라 구바아, 바바아 바도꽈 오오 너구더다: "무러비 수도이러 이 와이기러 먀 가찌-가찌 거두. 가찌 오오 아이기러 구누누꽈 어바뚜 바이!"

17. 어찌 여수 아이라아 쩌라 구머녀가 먀 찌오 쪼씨 쩌유더야 너비찌 비오 뱌 아꽈우마 나찌.

구부사 궈 우레굿삡 사 요와나

18. 어바나푸씨 바 요와네 나부 버라 구무바삐아 교유 먀시. 요와네 어라 구바라삐라 바비리 무부.

19. 어라 구바두마 어라 여수 아바아 아삐 뿌 바무부사아 아가바 이 무누누시* 오롸 와더돠아 뿌 아가바 와바히러, 너시 아가바 바삐찌라아 우찌.

---

14. Then he went up and touched the coffin, and those carrying it stood still. He said, "Young man, I say to you, get up!"

15. The dead man sat up and began to talk, and Jesus gave him back to his mother.

16. They were all filled with awe and praised God. "A great prophet has appeared among us," they said. "God has come to help his people."

17. This news about Jesus spread throughout Judea and the surrounding country.

18. John's disciples told him about all these things. Calling two of them,

19. he sent them to the Lord to ask, "Are you the one who was to come, or should we expect someone else?"

20. Abere baika ala Yesu abaa ali, bera kumubura mbu: "Yowanyi Mubatisasyi atutumire ene uli mbu utuburaa akaba woyu u Mununusi* ola watetwaa mbu ukabaha u wabahire, nesi akaba tulinjiraa unji."

21. Mw'echi chihangi, Yesu era kulamya bandu banene ba babaa bete chira bulwala, n'ebanji ebihwasi. Era kweresa bauta banene emuisha w'ekulola.

22. Chasinjire, era kwakula e baanda ba Yowana: "Muyaa kuanyikisisa Yowanyi bya mwalolyire ku n'ebya momvire. Ebauta bera balola, n'e birema byera byaenda, n'ebabenzi-benzi balamire, n'ebanyabitu bera bomva, n'ebafu bomokire, n'na ba batete kwa bali benjir bahubanganyisibwa eMwasi Mubuya-buya.

23. Aahanyirwe ola utakaese ebwemeresi bwai ku Nyono!"

24. Abere abu banafunzi ba Yowanyi bera bafulukaa, Yesu era kutangirisa abura eluamba lw'ebandu kwa myasi ya Yowanyi: "Mango mwayaa mwa buyeye, chi mwaenderaa kusonga? Kasi atabaa mundu

20. 아버러 바이가 아롸 여수 아바아 아쮜, 버라 구무부라 뿌: "요와네 무바디사수에 아두두미러 어너 우뤼 뿌 우두부라아 아가바 오유 우 무누누시* 오롸 와더돠아 뿌 우가바하 우 와바히러, 너시 아가바 두쮜찌라아 우찌."

21. 뭐찌 찌하삐, 여수 어라 구롸먀 바뚜 바너너 바 바바아 버더 찌라 부콲롸, 너바찌 어비화시. 어라 궈러사 바우다 바너너 어무이싸 워구르롸.

22. 짜시찌러, 어라 과구롸 어 바아따 바 요와나: "무야아 구아네기시사 요와네 뱌 마로레러 구 너뱌 모메러. 어바우다 버라 바로롸, 너 비러마 벼라 뱌어따, 너바버씨-버씨 바롸미러, 너바냐비두 버라 보빠, 너바푸 보모기러, 우나 바 바더더 과 바뤼 버찌루 바후바꺄네시봐 어롸시 무부야-부야.

23. 아아하네뤄 오롸 우다가어서 어붜머러시 봐이 구 뇨노!"

24. 아버러 아부 바나푸씨 바 요와네 버라 바푸루가아, 여수 어라 구다삐리사 아부라 어루아빠 뤄바뚜 과 먀시 야 요와니: "마꼬 먀야아 먀 찌 먀어떠라아 구소꽈? 가시 아다바아 무뚜 오롸 우뤼 꺄

20. When the men came to Jesus, they said, "John the Baptist sent us to you to ask, 'Are you the one who was to come, or should we expect someone else?' "

21. At that very time Jesus cured many who had diseases, sicknesses and evil spirits, and gave sight to many who were blind.

22. So he replied to the messengers, "Go back and report to John what you have seen and heard: The blind receive sight, the lame walk, those who have leprosy are cured, the deaf hear, the dead are raised, and the good news is preached to the poor.

23. Blessed is the man who does not fall away on account of me."

24. After John's messengers left, Jesus began to speak to the crowd about John: "What did you go out into the desert to see? A reed swayed by the

ola uli nga chioka cha chende chasinyira ebuha n'embusi i mwabuana mu?

25. Kanji nababusa:Chi mwayaa kulola ku? Kasi abaa mundu wete njimba sa sisitoire i mwalolaa ku? Si mutabukire kwa ba bende bembala enjimba sa sisitoire n'ekuba mwa muako, wa nyumba s'baare mu batula!

26. Na chi mwaendaa kulola ku kasi? Abaa murebi? Ku binali, abaa murebi Kanji abaa arenzise na murebi.

27. Oyola i wahambalwaa ku mwa Manjiko ma Ongo mmbu: "Umenyaa kwa nakutuirire emuanda wanyi era muhondo sau, i ungakukunganyisa enjira."

28. Yesu era kunaendekerana ateta: Nababura kwa mwa bandu boshi, kutali ola urenzise Yowanyi,si ola ungaba uli mueke mwa Bwami bwa Ongo, amurenzise.

29. Ebandu boshi ba babatisibwaa na Yowanyi al'auma n'ebafuchisi b'embarata ba bomvaa ba ateta, bera kuenyerera kwa Ongo anali mubuya.

찌오가 짜 쩌떠 짜시니라 어부하 너뿌시 이 먀부아나 무?

25. 가찌 나바부사:찌 먀야아 구로똬 구? 가시 아바아 무뚜 워더 띠빠 사 시시도이러 이 먀로똬아 구? 시 무다부기러 과 바 버떠 버빠똬 어찌빠 사 시시도이러 너구바 먀 무아고, 와 뉴빠 수바아러 무 바두똬!

26. 나 찌 먀어따아 구로똬 구 가시? 아바아 무러비? 구 비나삐, 아바아 무러비 가찌 아바아 아러씨서 나 무러비.

27. 오요똬 이 와하빠똬아 구 먀 마찌고 마 오꼬 무뿌: "우머냐아 과 나구두이리러 어무아따 와니 어라 무호또 사우, 이 우까구구까네사 어찌라."

28. 여수 어라 구나어떠거라나 아더다: 나바부라 과 먀 바뚜 보씨, 구다삐 오똬 우러씨서 요와네,시 오똬 우까바 우삐 무어거 먀 바미 바 오꼬, 아무러씨서.

29. 어바뚜 보씨 바 바바디시봐아 나 요와네 아똬우마 너바푸찌시 버빠라다 바 보빠아 바 아더다, 버라 구어녀러라 과 오꼬 아나삐 무부야.

wind?

25. If not, what did you go out to see? A man dressed in fine clothes? No, those who wear expensive clothes and indulge in luxury are in palaces.

26. But what did you go out to see? A prophet? Yes, I tell you, and more than a prophet.

27. This is the one about whom it is written: " 'I will send my messenger ahead of you, who will prepare your way before you.'

28. I tell you, among those born of women there is no one greater than John; yet the one who is least in the kingdom of God is greater than he."

29. (All the people, even the tax collectors, when they heard Jesus' words, acknowledged that God's way was right, because they had been baptized by John.

30. Si e Bafarisayo * al'auma n'ebakangirisi b'eMwaso* beke bananaa ekuhonda kwa Ongo. Bushi n'oku, bera kuchinanyira mbu batangabatisibwa na Yowanyi.

31. Yesu era kunaendekerana ateta: Nde i nyingalingamanya n'ebandu ba lwarero, na bande bu bahuhire?

32. Bahuhire nga bana ba bali mwa nama, ba babanjirana etushembe mbu bauma baomberaa balikabu engoma, si batasinaa, kanji mbu babaa bemba enyimbo s'emalira, si bataliraa.

33. Mango Yowanyi Mubatisayi abahaa, atendaa alya biryo bitungenene na mafu maire, mwera kunde mwateta mmbu: Ete bihwasi.

34. Mango Nyono nyi mwana w'eMundu naikire, nenjire nalya nanamwa. Si mwera mwenjire mwatera mbu Nyono nyi ndarenza kalyo, nyi mutamisi, nyi mwira w'e bafuchisi b'e mbarata, n'e banji ba hakuira mabi.

35. Si ekuhonda kwa Ongo kwende kwanamenyeka kwakuli kubuya n'na ba amwemerere."

Mukasi w'e byaa

30. 시 어 바파리사요 * 아꽈우마 너바가끼리시 버뫄소* 버거 바나나아 어구호따 과 오끄. 부씨 노구, 버라 구찌나네라 뿌 바다까바디시봐 나 요와네.

31. 여수 어라 구나어떠거라나 아더따다: 떠 이 네까끼까마냐 너바뚜 바 꽈러로, 나 바더 부 바후히러?

32. 바후히러 까 바나 바 바끼 뫄 나마, 바 바바찌라나 어두쎠뻐 뿌 바우마 바오뻐라아 바끼가부 어끄마, 시 바다시나아, 가찌 뿌 바바아 버빠 어네뽀 서마끼라, 시 바다끼라아.

33. 마끄 요와네 무바디사에 아바하아, 아더따아 아꺄 비료 비두꺼너너 나 마푸 마이러, 뭐라 구떠 뫄더다 무뿌: 어더 비화시.

34. 마끄 뇨노 네 뫄나 워무뚜 나이기러, 너찌러 나꺄 나나뫄. 시 뭐라 뭐찌러 뫄더라 뿌 뇨노 네 따러꽈 가류, 네 무다미시, 네 뭐라 워 바푸찌시 버 빠라다, 너 바찌 바 하구이라 마비.

35. 시 어구호따 과 오끄 궈떠 과나머녀가 과구끼 구부야 우나 바 아뭐머러러."

무가시 워 뱌아

30. But the Pharisees and experts in the law rejected God's purpose for themselves, because they had not been baptized by John.)

31. "To what, then, can I compare the people of this generation? What are they like?

32. They are like children sitting in the marketplace and calling out to each other: " 'We played the flute for you, and you did not dance; we sang a dirge, and you did not cry.'

33. For John the Baptist came neither eating bread nor drinking wine, and you say, 'He has a demon.'

34. The Son of Man came eating and drinking, and you say, 'Here is a glutton and a drunkard, a friend of tax collectors and "sinners." '

35. But wisdom is proved right by all her children."

36. Mufarisayo muuma mbu i Simonyi, w'omwa musi w'eNainyi emaalaa Yesu mbu abahaa alye kwa biryo mwa mwai. Abere Yesu aika mu, era kutangirisa alya nai.

37. Mw'oyu musi, mwabaa mutula nyumba y'oyu Mufarisayo, chera kuika mu chete mulangi wa marashi.

38. Chera kwikala al'auma n'eihando bya Yesu chalirira u. Emihonya y'emalira machi yera kubilobya. Chera kutangiririsa chahangula i mwa mviri sachi. Chera kufukama, chera kunalinda chaobera ebihando bya Yesu. Chasinjire, chera kubiakaba emarashi

39. Ola Mufarisayo wemaalaa Yesu mwa mwai alolire bacha, era kutangilyisa achitetembya mwa muchima wai: "Akaba ono mundju abaa alyi murebi angamenyerere akaba ono mukasi wamuumire ku ali mundu muchie. "yu Mufarisayo yeke abaa eshi kwa oyu mukasi abaa atula mukosi wa mabi.

40. Yesu alolire bacha, era mukubura: "Simonyi, nyete

36. 무파리사요 무우마 뿌 이 시모네, 요뫄 무시 워나이네 어마아쫘아 여수 뿌 아바하아 아쳐 과 비료 뫄 마이. 아버러 여수 아이가 무, 어라 구다삐리사 아쨔 나이.

37. 모유 무시, 뫄바아 무두쫘 뉴빠 요유 무파리사요, 쩌라 구이가 무 쩌더 무쫘삐 와 마라씨.

38. 쩌라 귀가쫘 아쫘우마 너이하또 뱌 여수 짜쳐리리라 우. 어미호냐 여마쳐리라 마찌 여라 구비롣뱌. 쩌라 구다삐리리사 짜하우쫘 이 뫄 삐리 사찌. 쩌라 구푸가마, 쩌라 구나쳐따 짜오버라 어비하또 뱌 여수. 짜시찌러, 쩌라 구비아가바 어마라씨

39. 오롸 무파리사요 워마아쫘아 여수 뫄 마이 아롣쪠러 바짜, 어라 구다삐레사 아찌더더빠 뫄 무찌마 와이: "아가바 오노 무뚜 아바아 아쪠 무러비 아꺄머녀려러 아가바 오노 무가시 와무우미러 구 아쪠 무뚜 무쩌. "유 무파리사요 여거 아바아 어씨 과 오유 무가시 아바아 아두쫘 무고시 와 마비.

40. 여수 아롣쪠러 바짜, 어라 무구부라: "시모네, 녀더 뫄시

36. Now one of the Pharisees invited Jesus to have dinner with him, so he went to the Pharisee's house and reclined at the table.

37. When a woman who had lived a sinful life in that town learned that Jesus was eating at the Pharisee's house, she brought an alabaster jar of perfume,

38. and as she stood behind him at his feet weeping, she began to wet his feet with her tears. Then she wiped them with her hair, kissed them and poured perfume on them.

39. When the Pharisee who had invited him saw this, he said to himself, "If this man were a prophet, he would know who is touching him and what kind of woman she is--that she is a sinner."

40. Jesus answered him, "Simon, I have

mwasi ola nakubura. "ai era kumwakula: "Hambalaa Mukangirisi."

41. Yesu era kumuishira ono muanyi: "Kwabaa balume babiri ba bachinjikaa bikulo"bya mutambo muuma. Ola mubere-bere abaa angaalwire maana matano, si eunji angaalwire matano.

42. Babere bainyire kwa bangafua en'ebikulo, era kubabalira bombi. Mw'abu bombi, nde i wabaa ungasimire en'ebikulo busese?

43. Simoni era kwakula: "Naanyisise kw'ola ababaliraa wahombwaa binene mw'abu bombi. "esu era kumubura: "Watechire kwa binganaba."

44. Yesu era kusonga ola mukasi n'ekubura Simonyi: "Nengiriraa muno mwa utanaambaa chiro n'ekamata k'emeshi k'ekurenza kwa bihando, si ono mukasi usene ku, yeke anyosise ebihando mwa mihonya yai, kanji era kubihangula mwa mviri sai.

45. Utanyihuukasaa mango aikaa, si yeke kutengera ala naikiraa muno, kuobera ku

오롸 나구부라. "아이 어라 구뫄구꽈: "하빠롸아 무가삐리시."

41. 여수 어라 구무이씨라 오노 무아네: "과바아 바루머 바비리 바 바찌끼가아 비구롣"뱌 무다뽀 무우마. 오롸 무버러-버러 아바아 아빠아뤼러 마아나 마다노, 시 어우씨 아빠아뤼러 마다노.

42. 바버러 바이니러 과 바빠푸아 어너비구롣, 어라 구바바삐라 보삐. 먀부 보삐, 떠 이 와바아 우빠시미러 어너비구롣 부서서?

43. 시모니 어라 과구꽈: "나아네시서 교꽈 아바바삐리아아 와호빠아 비너너 먀부 보삐. "어수 어라 구무부라: "와더찌러 과 비빠나바."

44. 여수 어라 구소빠 오롸 무가시 너구부라 시모네: "너삐리라아 무노 먀 우다나아빠아 찌로 너가마다 거머씨 거구러싸 과 비하또, 시 오노 무가시 우서너 구, 여거 아뇨시서 어비하또 먀 미호냐 야이, 가찌 어라 구비하우꽈 먀 삐리 사이.

45. 우다네후우가사아 마꼬 아이가아, 시 여거 구더뼈라 아꽈 나이기라아 무노, 구오버라

something to tell you."
"Tell me, teacher," he said.

41. "Two men owed money to a certain moneylender. One owed him five hundred denarii, and the other fifty.

42. Neither of them had the money to pay him back, so he canceled the debts of both. Now which of them will love him more?"

43. Simon replied, "I suppose the one who had the bigger debt canceled." "You have judged correctly," Jesus said.

44. Then he turned toward the woman and said to Simon, "Do you see this woman? I came into your house. You did not give me any water for my feet, but she wet my feet with her tears and wiped them with her hair.

45. You did not give me a kiss, but this woman, from the time I entered,

achiri anaobera ebihando byanyi.

46. Utanyakabaa chiro n'ekamata k'emafuta mm'etwe, si yeke marashi mu anyakire kwa bihando."

47. Bushi n'oku, umvaa kwa nakubura: Chiro angabambu ebibi by'ono mukasi byabaa binene, byoshi byababalirwe, bushi n'ekunyisima busese mwa kunyitunda kwai."

48. Chasinjire Yesu era kubura oyu mukasi: "Ebibi byau byababalirwe."

49. Ba babaa bali nai kwa mesa bera kutangirisa nabu bachibusa: "I wera nde ono nai, ola ungababalira ebibi?"

50. Kanji era kubura ola mukasi: "Ebwemeresi bwau bwakulamise, uendaa n'ebolo."

구 아찌리 아나오버라 어비하또 뱌네.

46. 우다냐가바아 찌로 너가마다 거마푸다 무머뭐, 시 여거 마라씨 무 아냐기러 과 비하또."

47. 부씨 노구, 우빠아 과 나구부라: 찌로 아까바뿌 어비비 뷔오노 무가시 뱌바아 비너너, 뵤씨 뱌바바리뤄, 부씨 너구네시마 부서서 뫄 구네두따 과이."

48. 짜시찌러 여수 어라 구부라 오유 무가시: "어비비 뱌우 뱌바바뤼뤄."

49. 바 바바아 바뤼 나이 과 머사 버라 구다삐리사 나부 바찌부사: "이 워라 떠 오노 나이, 오라 우까바바뤼라 어비비?"

50. 가찌 어라 구부라 오꽈 무가시: "어붜머러시 봐우 봐구꽈미서, 우어따아 너보뢴."

has not stopped kissing my feet.

46. You did not put oil on my head, but she has poured perfume on my feet.

47. Therefore, I tell you, her many sins have been forgiven--for she loved much. But he who has been forgiven little loves little."

48. Then Jesus said to her, "Your sins are forgiven."

49. The other guests began to say among themselves, "Who is this who even forgives sins?"

50. Jesus said to the woman, "Your faith has saved you; go in peace."

Luka Chikono 8
Mwanyi w'e muinzi w'e mbuto

1. Mw'esi suku, Yesu ayaa mwa misi n'okwa misi Endaa ahuhanganyisa ebandu eMwasi Mubuya-buya ola utechire era

뿌가 찌고노 8
꽈내 워 무이씨 워 뿌명

1. 뭐시 수구, 여수 아야아 꽈 미시 노과 미시 어따아 아후하꽈네사 어바뚜 어꽈시 무부야-부야 오꽈 우더찌러

Luke Chapter 8[NIV]

1. After this, Jesus traveled about from one town and village to another, proclaiming the

luulu s'eVwami bwa Ongo. Abaa ali al'auma n'endumwa* sai ekumi n'ebiri.

2. Kanji abaa ali na bakasi bauma ba ambulaa kw'ebibwasi, n'ebanji ba alamyaa emalwala. Bauma mubu, babaa: Mariya, i wasulwaa esina lya Mandarina, ola waambulwaa kw'ebihwasi birinda,

3. Na Shanyi, ola eba wai Chusa i wabaa wimangirire emirimo mwa Nyumba ya Heroti, na Susana, na banji bakasi banene. Abu boshi bu bendaa batabala Yesu n'ndumwa sai mwa bikulo byabo

4. Ebandju bendaa batengera mu chira musi, bera kuchilunda al'auma na Yesu. Mango eluamba lw'ebandu lwabaa lwera lwaneneyaa, Yesu era kubaishira ono muanyi:

5. "Muinzi muuma ayaa kuhuira mbuto yai. Abere era ahuiraembuto, njimi siuma sera kutoera mwa njira, ebihando by'ebandu byera kusisinoola. Chasinjire, e milonge yera kusilya.

6. sinji njimi sera kutoera kwa makoi. Abere sera sameraa,

어라 루우루 서봐미 봐 오꼬. 아바아 아뤼 아라우마 너뚜똬* 사이 어구미 너비리.

2. 가찌 아바아 아뤼 나 바가시 바우마 바 아뿌라아 궈비봐시, 너바찌 바 아롸먀아 어마똬롸. 바우마 무부, 바바아: 마리야, 이 와수롸아 어시나 랴 마따리나, 오롸 와아뿌똬아 궈비화시 비리따,

3. 나 싸네, 오롸 어바 와이 쭈사 이 와바아 위마끼리러 어미리모 봐 뉴빠 야 허로디, 나 수사나, 나 바찌 바가시 바너너. 아부 보씨 부 버따아 바다바롸 여수 우뚜똬 사이 봐 비구론 뱌보

4. 어바뉴 버따아 바더꺼라 무 찌라 무시, 버라 구찌루따 아라우마 나 여수. 마꼬 어루아빠 뤄바뉴 똬바아 뤄라 똬너너야아, 여수 어라 구바이씨라 오노 무아네:

5. "무이씨 무우마 아야아 구후이라 뿌도 야이. 아버러 어라 아후이라어뿌도, 찌미 시우마 서라 구도어라 봐 찌라, 어비하또 벼바뉴 벼라 구시시노오라. 짜시찌러, 어 미로꺼 여라 구시랴.

6. 시찌 찌미 서라 구도어라 과 마고이. 아버러 서라 사머라아,

good news of the kingdom of God. The Twelve were with him,

2. and also some women who had been cured of evil spirits and diseases: Mary (called Magdalene) from whom seven demons had come out;

3. Joanna the wife of Cuza, the manager of Herod's household; Susanna; and many others. These women were helping to support them out of their own means.

4. While a large crowd was gathering and people were coming to Jesus from town after town, he told this parable:

5. "A farmer went out to sow his seed. As he was scattering the seed, some fell along the path; it was trampled on, and the birds of the air ate it up.

6. Some fell on rock, and when it came up, the

sera kema bushi sainaa e meshi mwa chitaka.

7. Esinji sera kutoera mwa mihulyi-hulyi. Mwa kumerera al'auma n'ei mihulyi-hulyi, sera kusika.

8. Esinji njimi sera kutoera mwa butaka bukomire. Abere sakula, sera kweka eana lya njimi. "ango Yesu abaa era atetaa bacha, era kubachichika: "Ola wete matwi m'e komva, omvaa!"

9. E baanda bai bera kunde bamubusa mbu chiye ci abaaa ateta mw'oyu muanyi.

10. Yesu era kubakula: "Mwabu mu mweresibwe emuishas w'ekumenya bya by'omwa Bwami bwa Ongo, si ebanji bemire kubiburwa mwa Mianyi iri"Ba bende bachiremba mbu bete meho batalolaa, n'na ba bende bachiremba mbu bete matwi batomvaa"

11. Kanji Yesu era kubura ebanafunzi bai: "Mweraa momva kw'ono muanyi atechire. Embuto i ihuhanisibwe n'eChinwa cha Ongo.

12. Enjira ihuhanisibwe ng'ebandu bauma ba bomvaa kw'echi chinwa. Chasinjire,

서라 거마 부씨 사이나아 어머씨 롸 찌다가.

7. 어시찌 서라 구도어라 롸 미후레-후레. 롸 구머러라 아롸우마 너이 미후레-후레, 서라 구시가.

8. 어시찌 찌미 서라 구도어라 롸 부다가 부고미러. 아버러 사구롸, 서라 궈가 어아나 랴 찌미. "아꼬 여수 아바아 어라 아더다아 바짜, 어라 구바찌찌가: "오롸 워더 마뒤 머 고빠, 오빠아!"

9. 어 바아따 바이 버라 구떠 바무부사 뿌 찌여 씨 아바아아 아더다 모유 무아네.

10. 여수 어라 구바구롸: "롸부 무 뭐러시붜 어무이싸수 워구머냐 뱌 뷔오롸 봐미 봐 오꼬, 시 어바찌 버미러 구비부롸 롸 미아네 이리"바 버떠 바찌러빠 뿌 버더 머호 바다로롸아, 우나 바 버떠 바찌러빠 뿌 버더 마뒤 바도빠아"

11. 가지 여수 어라 구부라 어바나푸씨 바이: "뭐라아 모빠 교노 무아네 아더찌러. 어뿌도 이 이후하니시붜 너찌뇨 짜 오꼬.

12. 어찌라 이후하니시붜 꺼바뚜 바우마 바 보빠아 궈찌 찌뇨. 짜시찌러, 써다네 어라

plants withered because they had no moisture.

7. Other seed fell among thorns, which grew up with it and choked the plants.

8. Still other seed fell on good soil. It came up and yielded a crop, a hundred times more than was sown." When he said this, he called out, "He who has ears to hear, let him hear."

9. His disciples asked him what this parable meant.

10. He said, "The knowledge of the secrets of the kingdom of God has been given to you, but to others I speak in parables, so that, " 'though seeing, they may not see; though hearing, they may not understand.'

11. "This is the meaning of the parable: The seed is the word of God.

12. Those along the path are the ones who hear, and then the devil

Shetanyi era kubakula chi kwa muchima bangesha kwemerera chi banunulibwe.

구바구롸 찌 과 무찌마 바어싸 궈머러라 찌 바누누뤼붸.

comes and takes away the word from their hearts, so that they may not believe and be saved.

13. Ba bahuhanyisibwe n'enjimi sa satoeraa ala mako mali bu bende bomvirisa eChinwa cha Ongo n'ekwemerera chi n'elumoo. Si chitasera mwa michima yabu. Abola bu bende bareka ekimisa eChinwa cha Ongo, bushi n'ebwemeresi bwabu bueke mango emuereko ende abaikira.

13. 바 바후하니시붸 너찌미 사 사도어라아 아롸 마고 마뤼 부 버떠 보뻬리사 어찌놔 쨔 오꼬 너궈머러라 찌 너루모오. 시 찌다서라 롸 미찌마 야부. 아보롸 부 버떠 바러가 어기미사 어찌놔 쨔 오꼬, 부씨 너붸머러시 봐부 부어거 마꼬 어무어러고 어더 아바이기라.

13. Those on the rock are the ones who receive the word with joy when they hear it, but they have no root. They believe for a while, but in the time of testing they fall away.

14. Enjimi sa satoeraa mwa mihuliehuli sihuhanyisibwe na ba bende bomva eChinwa cha Ongo. Si bende baina kwa bangakula mwa bwemeresi, bushi n'emalibuko m'ebutala, nesi ebuare n'emuako mwa kalamo kabu.

14. 어찌미 사 사도어라아 롸 미후뤼어후뤼 시후하네시붸 나 바 버떠 보빠 어찌놔 쨔 오꼬. 시 버떠 바이나 과 바꺄구롸 롸 붸머러시, 부씨 너마뤼부고 머부다롸, 너시 어부아러 너무아고 롸 갸꺄모 가부.

14. The seed that fell among thorns stands for those who hear, but as they go on their way they are choked by life's worries, riches and pleasures, and they do not mature.

15. Enjimi sa satoeraa mwa butaka bukomire, sihuhanyisibwe n'ebandu ba bende bomva eChinwa cha Ongo n'e kubika chi kubuya-buya mwa michima yabu. Abola bu bende bakula mwa bwemeresi bwabu kanangana."

15. 어찌미 사 사도어라아 롸 부다가 부고미러, 시후하네시붸 너바뚜 바 버떠 보빠 어찌놔 쨔 오꼬 너 구비가 찌 구부야-부야 롸 미찌마 야부. 아보롸 부 버떠 바구롸 롸 붸머러시 봐부 가나냐나."

15. But the seed on good soil stands for those with a noble and good heart, who hear the word, retain it, and by persevering produce a crop.

16. Kanji Yesu era kuteta: "Kutalyi mundju ola ungakoresa etara kanji alibike mw'erea nesi mwa buhanjingo. Si kutula

16. 가찌 여수 어라 구더다: "구다뤠 무뚜 오롸 우꺄고러사 어다라 가찌 아뤼비거 뭐러아 너시 롸 부하찌오. 시 구두롸

16. "No one lights a lamp and hides it in a jar or puts it under a bed. Instead, he puts it on a

kwemire alihumbye kwa nguliro iri ba bengirira mwa nyuma balole kwa bulanare.

귀미러 아삐후뼈 과 우삐로 이리 바 버삐리라 먀 뉴마 바로뤄 과 부롸나러.

stand, so that those who come in can see the light.

17. Kutali kandu ka kabishirwe ka katakabihulwe. Kanji kutali kandu ka bubisho-bisho ka katakamenyeke kanangana.

17. 구다삐 가뚜 가 가비씨뤄 가 가다가비후뤄. 가씨 구다삐 가뚜 가 부비쏘-비쏘 가 가다가머녀거 가나싸나.

17. For there is nothing hidden that will not be disclosed, and nothing concealed that will not be known or brought out into the open.

18. Bushi n'oku, mumenyereraa kubuya-buya mwenjire mwomva, bushi ola ukaba womvire mira era luulu s'eBwami bwa Ongo, Ongo akamweresa binene. Si ola utakahond komva n'ekuchikangirisa, akanyaibwa n'na hya akaba achirembire komva."

18. 부씨 노구, 무머녀러라아 구부야-부야 뭐찌러 뭄빠, 부씨 오라 우가바 옴삐러 미라 어라 루우루 서봐미 봐 오오, 오오 아가뭐러사 비너너. 시 오라 우다가호뚜 곰빠 너구찌가삐리리사, 아가냐이봐 우나 햐 아가바 아찌러뻬러 곰빠."

18. Therefore consider carefully how you listen. Whoever has will be given more; whoever does not have, even what he thinks he has will be taken from him."

Nyina na banyakabo Yesu

내낍 나 바냐가보 여수

19. Lusuku luuma, balumuna ba Yesu na nyina bayaa era ali, Chiro bakaikirira ofu nai, bushi n'ekuluwa kw'ebandu.

19. 루수구 루우마, 바루무나 바 여수 나 니나 바야아 어라 아삐, 찌로 바가이기리라 오푸 나이, 부씨 너구루와 궈바뚜.

19. Now Jesus' mother and brothers came to see him, but they were not able to get near him because of the crowd.

20. Ebandju bera kumubura: "Nyoko na banyakenyu bali era butala, bahonda bakulole ku."

20. 어바뚜 버라 구무부라: "뇨고 나 바냐거뉴 바삐 어라 부다라, 바호따 바구로뤄 구."

20. Someone told him, "Your mother and brothers are standing outside, wanting to see you."

21. Yesu era kwakula: "Mali na banyakeru bali ba bende bomva eChinwa cha Ongo n'ekuira kwa chitechire."

21. 여수 어라 과구라: "마삐 나 바냐거루 바삐 바 버뻐 봄빠 어찌냐 짜 오오 너구이라 과 찌더찌러."

21. He replied, "My mother and brothers are those who hear God's word and put it into

practice."

Yesu abanda kwa nyanja

22. Lusuku luuma, Yesu erukiraa mwa bwato al'auma n'e baanda sai. Era kusibura: "Tuhabukiraa kwa unji mukono w'e nyanja. "era kunaenda.

23. Abere bera baruwa e bwato, Yesu era kuonjira. Unao-unao, emulaba erakuchihuta kwa nyanja. Emeshi mera kuya mwa bwato, bera kuba mu bisibu. Babaa balinga kufa.

24. Bera kuya kususa Yesu na bamubura: "Mukangirisi, Mukangirisi, tafa! Nai era kutalimuka na akalyiira e chusi al'auma n'e mulaba. Nabi byera kuwa, n'e nyanja kuna kuorera.

25. Chasinjire, Yesu era kubusa e ndjumwa sai: "Ngae u e bwemeresi bwenyu bulyi?" Si bera kufa buba, kanji bera kussanwa busese. Bera kutangilyisa babusanya. "nde ono mundju I waikira abura e mbusi n'e mulaba e Chinwa binamumve?"

Emundju w'e bihwasi bibi

여수 아바따 과 냐짜

22. 룻수구 루우마, 여수 어루기라아 똬 봐도 아짜우마 너 바아따 사이. 어라 구시부라: "두하부기라아 과 우찌 무고노 워 냐짜. "어라 구나어따.

23. 아버러 버라 바루와 어 봐도, 여수 어라 구오찌라. 우나오-우나오, 어무짜바 어라구찌후다 과 냐짜. 어머씨 머라 구야 똬 봐도, 버라 구바 무 비시부. 바바아 바뤼빠 구파.

24. 버라 구야 구수사 여수 나 바무부라: "무가삐리시, 무가삐리시, 다파! 나이 어라 구다뤼무가 나 아짜레이라 어 쭈시 아짜우마 너 무짜바. 나비 벼라 구와, 너 냐짜 구나 구오러라.

25. 짜시찌러, 여수 어라 구부사 어 뚜봐 사이: "빠어 우 어 붜머러시 붜뉴 부뤠?" 시 버라 구파 부바, 가찌 버라 구싸냐 부서서. 버라 구다삐레사 바부사냐. "떠 오노 무뚜 이 와이기라 아부라 어 뿌시 너 무짜바 어 찌냐 비나무뼈?"

어무뚜 워 비화시 비비

---

22. One day Jesus said to his disciples, "Let's go over to the other side of the lake." So they got into a boat and set out.

23. As they sailed, he fell asleep. A squall came down on the lake, so that the boat was being swamped, and they were in great danger.

24. The disciples went and woke him, saying, "Master, Master, we're going to drown!" He got up and rebuked the wind and the raging waters; the storm subsided, and all was calm.

25. "Where is your faith?" he asked his disciples. In fear and amazement they asked one another, "Who is this? He commands even the winds and the water, and they obey him."

26. Era nyuma s'ebi, Yesu n'e ndjumwa sai bera kuhabukira mwa chio ch'e Bakerasi, mashirirya n'e chio ch'e Galilaya.

27. Abere batenga mwa bwato, bera kubuanana na mulume ola wabaaa usimbirwe n'e bihwasi. Oyu mulume abaa w'omwa musi w'e Kerasi. Abaa atachionjira na mu nyumba si kwa shinda. Kanji abaa atachimbala na luchimba.

28. Alolyire ku Yesu era kuira e miwarenge, era kukumbaala mwa maulu maye ne kuteta kwa murenge munene, chinete nao Yesu, mwala wa Ongo alyi era luulu? na kuemere utangilyibusaa.

29. Echihwasi cha chabaa chimuli ku, chendaa chashiba chamunyianga. Mwa kumulanga, endaa aminwa mwa bureure n'ebyuma, si endaa abikonolanga. Kanji echi chihwasi chendaa chamweka era itula bandu. Yesu amulolire ku, era kubura chi: "Tengaa kw'oyu mundu uye bure!

30. Yesu era kumubusa: "Esina lyau unde?" Nai era kwakula: "Nyono, nyi"chwulyi bengi.

26. 어라 뉴마 서비, 여수 너 뚜똬 사이 버라 구하부기라 똬 찌오 쩌 바거라시, 마씨리랴 너 찌오 쩌 가쀠뢔야.

27. 아버러 바더똬 똬 봐도, 버라 구부아나나 나 무루머 오똬 와바아아 우시삐뤄 너 비화시. 오유 무루머 아바아 요똬 무시 워 거라시. 아바아 아다찌오씨라 나 무 뉴빠 시 과 씨따. 가찌 아바아 아다찌빠뢔 나 루찌빠.

28. 아뢰레러 구 여수 어라 구이라 어 미와러뗘, 어라 구구빠아뢔 똬 마우루 마여 너 구더다 과 무러뗘 무너너, 찌너더 나오 여수, 뫌똬 와 오꼬 아레 어라 루우루? 나 구어머러 우다삐레부사아.

29. 어찌화시 짜 짜바아 찌무쀠 구, 쩌따아 짜씨바 짜무네아뽜. 똬 구무뢔뽜, 어따아 아미뇨 똬 아비고노뢔뽜. 가찌 어찌 찌화시 쩌따아 짜뭐가 어라 이두뢔 바뚜. 여수 아무뢰쀠러 구, 어라 구부라 찌: "더똬아 교유 무뚜 우여 부러!

30. 여수 어라 구무부사: "어시나 뢔우 우떠?" 나이 어라 과구뢔: "뇨노, 네"쭈레 버쀠. "더다아

26. They sailed to the region of the Gerasenes, which is across the lake from Galilee.

27. When Jesus stepped ashore, he was met by a demon-possessed man from the town. For a long time this man had not worn clothes or lived in a house, but had lived in the tombs.

28. When he saw Jesus, he cried out and fell at his feet, shouting at the top of his voice, "What do you want with me, Jesus, Son of the Most High God? I beg you, don't torture me!"

29. For Jesus had commanded the evil spirit to come out of the man. Many times it had seized him, and though he was chained hand and foot and kept under guard, he had broken his chains and had been driven by the demon into solitary places.

30. Jesus asked him, "What is your name?" "Legion," he replied,

"tetaa bacha bushi abaa asimbirwe na bihwasi binene.

31. Byendaa byema Yesu mbu atabyambulaa mbu era kusimu vi biyaa.

32. Aola abaa ali buso bunene bwa ngulube, bwabulirwa kwa katulungu. Ebi bihwasi byera kwema Yesu ebonjo abyemerere biye mw'esi ngulube. Nai era kubyemerera.

33. Ebihwasi byera kutenga kw'oyu mundju na byaya mw'esi ngulube. Ebuso bwasi boshi bwera kwendaalira malibita era nyanja ilyi, kuna kutoera mui. Sera kunasika soshi.

34. Ebangere basi balolire bache, bera kuhaira mwa musi n'omwa mahwa kubura ebandu kw'oyu mwasi.

35. Ebandu bera kunaenda kulola kw'ebya byabaa. Bera kuika ala Yesu abaa alyi, bera kubuana ola bihwasi byatengaa ku ekesi bushi mwa maulu ma Yesu. Kanji abaa embesi enjimba era analyi muuma - uma. Bera kubaa.

바짜 부씨 아바아 아시삐뤄 나 비화시 비너너.

31. 벼따아 벼마 여수 뿌 아다뱌뿌콰아 뿌 어라 구시무 비 비야아.

32. 아오콰 아바아 아뤼 부소 부너너 봐 응구루버, 봐부뤼라 과 가두루우. 어비 비화시 벼라 궈마 여수 어보쪼 아벼머러러 비여 뭐시 응구루버. 나이 어라 구벼머러라.

33. 어비화시 벼라 구더봐 교유 무뚜 나 뱌야 뭐시 응구루버. 어부소 봐시 보씨 뭐라 궈따아뤼라 마뤼비다 어라 냐짜 이레, 구나 구도어라 무이. 서라 구나시가 소씨.

34. 어바뭐러 바시 바론뤼러 바쩌, 버라 구하이라 봐 무시 노봐 마화 구부라 어바뚜 교유 봐시.

35. 어바뚜 버라 구나어따 구론콰 궈뱌 뱌바아. 버라 구이가 아콰 여수 아바아 아레, 버라 구부아나 오콰 비화시 뱌더봐아 구 어거시 부씨 봐 마우루 마 여수. 가찌 아바아 어삐시 어찌빠 어라 아나레 무우마 - 우마. 버라 구바아.

because many demons had gone into him.

31. And they begged him repeatedly not to order them to go into the Abyss.

32. A large herd of pigs was feeding there on the hillside. The demons begged Jesus to let them go into them, and he gave them permission.

33. When the demons came out of the man, they went into the pigs, and the herd rushed down the steep bank into the lake and was drowned.

34. When those tending the pigs saw what had happened, they ran off and reported this in the town and countryside,

35. and the people went out to see what had happened. When they came to Jesus, they found the man from whom the demons had gone out, sitting at Jesus' feet, dressed and in his right mind; and they were afraid.

36. Ba bachiloreraa kwa bihwasi byambulwa kw'oyu mundju, bera kuanyikisa ba batengaa kwa musi.

37. Besha e chio ch'e Kerasi boshi bera kubura Yesu mbu abatengeraa mwa chio chabu, bushi bobaaa busese. Kanji Yesu n'endumwa* sai bera kwirukira mwa bwato bahube era batengeraa.

38. Ola ebihwasi byatengaa ku yeke, abaa ema Yesu mbu aendaa nai. Si Yesu era kumualusa n'ekumubura mmbu:

39. "Hubaa kwa wau, uende kuanyikisa byoshi bya Ongo akuiririre. "ai era kunaya mwa musi woshi aenda aanyikisisa ebandu byoshi bya Yesu amuiriraa.

Mwalyi wa Yairo

40. Mwa kufuluka kwa Yesu e Galilaya, ahuukasibwaa na bandu banene, bushi boshi babaa bamulinjira.

41. Unao-unao, mukulu-kulu muuma w'echihaala ch'eBayuta* mbu i Yairo, era kuika n'ekukoma emafi era muhondo s'ebihando bya Yesu. Abaa amwema ebonjo mbu engiriraa mwa mwai,

36. 바 바찌ᄅ러라아 과 비화시 뱌뿌봐 교유 무뚜, 버라 구아네기시사 바 바더빠아 과 무시.

37. 버싸 어 찌오 쩌 거라시 보씨 버라 구부라 여수 뿌 아바더뻐라아 봐 찌오 짜부, 부씨 보바아아 부서서. 가찌 여수 너뿌봐* 사이 버라 귀루기라 봐 봐도 바후버 어라 바더뻐라아.

38. 오롸 어비화시 뱌더빠아 구 여거, 아바아 어마 여수 뿌 아어따아 나이. 시 여수 어라 구무아ᄅ루사 너구무부라 무뿌:

39. "후바아 과 와우, 우어버 구아네기사 뵤씨 뱌 오꼬 아구이리리러. "아이 어라 구나야 봐 무시 옴씨 아어따 아아네기시사 어바뚜 뵤씨 뱌 여수 아무이리라아.

꽈뻬 와 야이로

40. 봐 구푸ᄅ루가 과 여수 어 가삐꽈야, 아후우가시봐아 나 바뚜 바너너, 부씨 보씨 바바아 바무ᄅ리찌라.

41. 우나오-우나오, 무구룩-구룩 무우마 워찌하아꽈 쩌바유다* 뿌 이 야이로, 어라 구이가 너구고마 어마피 어라 무호또 서비하또 뱌 여수. 아바아 아뮤마 어보쪼 뿌 어삐리라아 봐 꽈이,

36. Those who had seen it told the people how the demon-possessed man had been cured.

37. Then all the people of the region of the Gerasenes asked Jesus to leave them, because they were overcome with fear. So he got into the boat and left.

38. The man from whom the demons had gone out begged to go with him, but Jesus sent him away, saying,

39. "Return home and tell how much God has done for you." So the man went away and told all over town how much Jesus had done for him.

40. Now when Jesus returned, a crowd welcomed him, for they were all expecting him.

41. Then a man named Jairus, a ruler of the synagogue, came and fell at Jesus' feet, pleading with him to come to his house

42. bushi mwali wai abaa ali mareka-reka. Abaa mwana wa chuha, wa ofu myaka ekumi n'ebiri. Mango Yesu abaa era aya era mwa Yairo, ebandu babaa baenda bamufundeeresa.

43. Mw'echi chihangi, mukasi muuma era kuulukira era nyumba sa Yesu. Oyu mukasi abaa aira myaka ekumi n'ebiri atenga emikira. Abaa amalire ebikulo byai byoshi kwa bahake, si batamulamyaa.

44. Aikire ala Yesu abaa ali, era kuuma kwa musike w'e luchimba lwa Yesu. Unao-unao emikira yai chiro ikachitoanga.

45. Yesu nai era kubusa: "Nde i wanyiumire ku?" Abere ebandu boshi bera bachakanaa. Petero ku kwera kumubura: "Mukangirisi! Ebandu ba bakusungwire bu bakufundeeresise."

46. Kanji Yesu era kuteta: "Kuli mundu ola wanyiumire ku, bushi ebuashi bwanyi bwandaalire."

47. Oyu mukasi alolire kwa Yesu amumenyerere, era kuya era abaa ali akukumana n'ebuba. Era kukoma e mafi era muhondo sai. Era kuuanyikisisa mwa kachi-kachi k'ebandu

---

42. 부씨 뫄뤼 와이 아바아 아뤼 마러가-러가. 아바아 뫄나 와 쭈하, 와 오푸 먀가 어구미 너비리. 마꼬 여수 아바아 어라 아야 어라 뫄 야이로, 어바뚜 바바아 바어따 바무푸떠어러사.

43. 뭐찌 찌하삐, 무가시 무우마 어라 구우루끼라 어라 뉴빠 사 여수. 오유 무가시 아바아 아이라 먀가 어구미 너비리 아더빠 어미기라. 아바아 아마뤼러 어비구로 뱌이 뵤씨 과 바하거, 시 바다무뢔먀아.

44. 아이기러 아롸 여수 아바아 아뤼, 어라 구우마 과 무시거 워 루찌빠 롸 여수. 우나오-우나오 어미기라 야이 찌로 이가찌도아롸.

45. 여수 나이 어라 구부사: "떠 이 와네우미러 구?" 아버러 어바뚜 뵤씨 버라 바짜가나아. 퍼더로 구 궈라 구무부라: "무가끼리시! 어바뚜 바 바구수윅러 부 바구푸떠어러시서."

46. 가찌 여수 어라 구더다: "구뤼 무뚜 오롸 와네우미러 구, 부씨 어부아씨 봐니 봐따아뤼러."

47. 오유 무가시 아롣뤼러 과 여수 아무머녀러러, 어라 구야 어라 아바아 아뤼 아구구마나 너부봐. 어라 구고마 어 마피 어라 무호또 사이. 어라 구우아네기시사 뫄 가찌-가찌

---

42. because his only daughter, a girl of about twelve, was dying. As Jesus was on his way, the crowds almost crushed him.

43. And a woman was there who had been subject to bleeding for twelve years, but no one could heal her.

44. She came up behind him and touched the edge of his cloak, and immediately her bleeding stopped.

45. "Who touched me?" Jesus asked. When they all denied it, Peter said, "Master, the people are crowding and pressing against you."

46. But Jesus said, "Someone touched me; I know that power has gone out from me."

47. Then the woman, seeing that she could not go unnoticed, came trembling and fell at his feet. In the presence of all the people, she told

boshi cha chatumaa amuuma ku na kute ku alamaa unao-unao.

48. Yesu era kumubura: "Mama, e bwemeresi bwau bwakulamise, uendaa n'e boolo."

49. Mango Yesu abaa anachiri ateta, emundu era kutenga era mwa Yairo amwetere emwasi mmbu: "Enawechwu, cha chikumi chau chera chatoaa emuchima, utachitamyaa e Mukangirisi mbu abahaa."

50. Yesu omvire bacha, era kubura Yairo: "Utobaaa, angalamisibwa akaba wete e bwemeresi."

51. Yesu aikir kwa wa yairo, chiro akemerera kwingirira mwa nyumba na unji mundu, kureka Petero, na Yowanyi, na Yakobo, n'ebasere b'emwana.

52. Boshi b babuanyibwaa mwa nyumba, babaa balira n'ekuchinyianga, bushi n'e lufu lw'oyu munyere. Si Yesu era kubabura: "Murekaa ekulira, ono munyre atafire, si aonjire!".

53. Bomvire bacha, bera kusanwa nai, bushi beke babaa

거바뚜 보씨 짜 짜두마아 아무우마 구 나 구더 구 아꽈마아 우나오-우나오.

48. 여수 어라 구무부라: "마마, 어 붜머러시 봐우 봐구꽈미서, 우어따아 너 보오론."

49. 마오 여수 아바아 아나찌리 아더다, 어무뚜 어라 구더꽈 어라 꽈 야이로 아뭐더러 어꽈시 무뿌: "어나워쭈, 짜 찌구미 짜우 쩌라 짜도아아 어무찌마, 우다찌다먀아 어 무가끼리시 뿌 아바하아."

50. 여수 오삐러 바짜, 어라 구부라 야이로: "우도바아아, 아까꽈미시봐 아가바 워더 어 붜머러시."

51. 여수 아이기루 과 와 야이로, 찌로 아거머러라 귀끼리라 꽈 뉴빠 나 우찌 무뚜, 구러가 퍼더로, 나 요와네, 나 야고보, 너바서러 버마나.

52. 보씨 부 바부아니붜아 꽈 뉴빠, 바바아 바뤼라 너구찌네아꽈, 부씨 너 루푸 루요유 무녀러. 시 여수 어라 구바부라: "무러가아 어구꿔라, 오노 무녜러 아다피러, 시 아오찌러!".

53. 보삐러 바짜, 버라 구사놔 나이, 부씨 버거 바바아 바너씨

why she had touched him and how she had been instantly healed.

48. Then he said to her, "Daughter, your faith has healed you. Go in peace."

49. While Jesus was still speaking, someone came from the house of Jairus, the synagogue ruler. "Your daughter is dead," he said. "Don't bother the teacher any more."

50. Hearing this, Jesus said to Jairus, "Don't be afraid; just believe, and she will be healed."

51. When he arrived at the house of Jairus, he did not let anyone go in with him except Peter, John and James, and the child's father and mother.

52. Meanwhile, all the people were wailing and mourning for her. "Stop wailing," Jesus said. "She is not dead but asleep."

53. They laughed at him, knowing that she was

baneshi kw'oyu munyere afire.

54. Yesu nai era kwimusa emino y'oyu munyere, era kuuma e murenge: "Emwa, sukaa!"

55. Unao-unao, emuchima wai kuna kusisimuka, era kunemuka. Yesu era kubura e bandju mbu bamuwaa e bilyo.

56. Ebasere b'oyu munyere bera kussanwa busese. Yesu era kubanga mbu batabura mundju bya byarengire.

교유 무녀러 아피러.

54. 여수 나이 어라 귀무사 어미노 요유 무녀러, 어라 구우마 어 무러꺼: "어뫄, 수가아!"

55. 우나오-우나오, 어무찌마 와이 구나 구시시무가, 어라 구너무가. 여수 어라 구부라 어 바뚜 뿌 바무와아 어 비료.

56. 어바서러 보유 무녀러 버라 구쌰놔 부서서. 여수 어라 구바꽈 뿌 바다부라 무뚜 뱌 뱌러삐러.

dead.

54. But he took her by the hand and said, "My child, get up!"

55. Her spirit returned, and at once she stood up. Then Jesus told them to give her something to eat.

56. Her parents were astonished, but he ordered them not to tell anyone what had happened.

Luka Chikono 9

1. Lusuku luuma, Yesu emaalaa e baanda baye e kumi n'e bilyi. Era kuseresa emisi n'ebuashi bw'e kwambula e bihwasi n'e kulamya e balwala;

2. Era kusituma kuhubanganyisa ebandu e Mwasi Mubuya-buya w'e Bwami bwa Ongo n'e kulamya e balwala.

3. Era muhondo s'e kuenda, Yesu era kusibura: "Mwa lubalamo lwenyu, mutekaa kachi, nesi chimbesa. Mutekaa bilyo, nesi butea; Kutalyi wimbalaa na njimba ebilyi.

4. Kanji mango e mundju

루가 찌고노 9

1. 루수구 루우마, 여수 어마아롸아 어 바아따 바여 어 구미 너 비례. 어라 구서러사 어미시 너부아씨 붜 과뿌롸 어 비화시 너 구롸먀 어 바꽈롸;

2. 어라 구시두마 구후바꽈네사 어바뚜 어 뫄시 무부야-부야 워 봐미 봐 오꼬 너 구롸먀 어 바꽈롸.

3. 어라 무호또 서 구어따, 여수 어라 구시부라: "뫄 루바롸모 뤄뉴, 무더가아 가찌, 너시 찌뻐사. 무더가아 비료, 너시 부더아; 구다레 위빠롸아 나 띠빠 어비례.

4. 가찌 마꼬 어 무뚜 어머러러

Luke Chapter 9[NIV]

1. When Jesus had called the Twelve together, he gave them power and authority to drive out all demons and to cure diseases,

2. and he sent them out to preach the kingdom of God and to heal the sick.

3. He told them: "Take nothing for the journey-- no staff, no bag, no bread, no money, no extra tunic.

4. Whatever house you

emerere mbu muberaa mwa mwai, munaberaa mu kuikira e lusuku lw'e kuya mwa unji musi.

5. Si e bandju bakanana mbu mutaberaa kwa musi wabu, mwanatenga ku. Si mwa kutenga ku, mwanabakunguchira e mukungu w'e bihando, ku kubalosa kwa Ongo akabachinjibua bushi n'ebubi bwabu."

6. Abere endumwa* sera somvaa bacha, sera kuchiuma n'e kuya ku chira musi saenda sahubanganyisa e bandju e Mwasi Mubuya-buya wa Ongo n'e kulamya e balwala.

7. Si Herodi nai i wabaa mutambo w'e Galilaya, mango omvaa kw'ebye byoshi Yesu n'e ndjumwa sai benjire baira, e muchima era kumuya bure, bushi bandju bauma bendaa bateta mbu Yowana i womokire.

8. N'e banji bendaa bateta mbu murebi Eliya alorekanyire ku kanji. N'e banji nabu mbu muuma mwa barebi ba mira - mira i womokire.

9. Si Heroti era kuchibusa: "Kutasa kurengasuku naishire echwe lya Yowana kanangana, I wera nde ono mundju utatenga

뿌 무버라아 뫄 뫄이, 무나버라아 무 구이기라 어 루수구 뤄 구야 뫄 우찌 무시.

5. 시 어 바뉴 바가나나 뿌 무다버라아 과 무시 와부, 뫄나더빠 구. 시 뫄 구더빠 구, 뫄나바구우찌라 어 무구우 워 비하또, 구 구바로사 과 오꼬 아가바찌찌부아 부씨 너부비 뫄부."

6. 아버러 어뚜뫄* 서라 소빠아 바짜, 서라 구찌우마 너 구야 구찌라 무시 사어따 사후바빠네사 어 바뉴 어 뫄시 무부야-부야 와 오꼬 너 구롸먀 어 바빠롸.

7. 시 허로디 나이 이 와바아 무다뗘 워 가뤼롸야, 마꼬 오빠아 궈벼 뵤씨 여수 너 뚜뫄 사이 버찌러 바이라, 어 무찌마 어라 구무야 부러, 부씨 바뉴 바우마 버따아 바더다 뿌 요와나 이 오모기러.

8. 너 바찌 버따아 바더다 뿌 무러비 어뤼야 아로러가네러 구 가찌. 너 바찌 나부 뿌 무우마 뫄 바러비 바 미라 - 미라 이 오모기러.

9. 시 허로디 어라 구찌부사: "구다사 구러빠수구 나이씨러 어쮜 롸 요와나 가나빠나, 이 워라 떠 오노 무뚜 우다더빠 뫄

enter, stay there until you leave that town.

5. If people do not welcome you, shake the dust off your feet when you leave their town, as a testimony against them."

6. So they set out and went from village to village, preaching the gospel and healing people everywhere.

7. Now Herod the tetrarch heard about all that was going on. And he was perplexed, because some were saying that John had been raised from the dead,

8. others that Elijah had appeared, and still others that one of the prophets of long ago had come back to life.

9. But Herod said, "I beheaded John. Who, then, is this I hear such things about?" And he

mwa bunu bw'e bandju?" Bushi n'oku, Herodi era kuhonda alole ku Yesu.

부누 뭐 바뚜?" 부씨 노구, 허로디 어라 구호따 아르러 구 여수.

tried to see him.

Yesu alyisa byumbi bitanu bya bandju

여수 아레뻽 뷰삐 비다누 뱌 바뚜

10. Mango e baanda ba Yesu safulukaa era sachwumwaa, sera kutangirisa samuanyikisa emulimo sakolire. Yesu omvire bacha, era satumwaa, sera kutangirisa samuanyikisa e mulyimo sakolyire. Yesu omvire bacha, era kusibura mbu sirekaa e luamba simwimise mwa musi welyikirwe Betesaida.

10. 마꼬 어 바아따 바 여수 사푸루가아 어라 사쭈뫄아, 서라 구다삐리사 사무아네기사 어무삐모 사고삐러. 여수 오삐러 바짜, 어라 사두뫄아, 서라 구다삐리사 사무아네기사 어 무뻬모 사고뼤러. 여수 오삐러 바짜, 어라 구시부라 뿌 시러가아 어 루아빠 시뮈미서 뫄 무시 워뼤기뭐 버더사이다.

10. When the apostles returned, they reported to Jesus what they had done. Then he took them with him and they withdrew by themselves to a town called Bethsaida,

11. Mango e bikembe by'e bandju byomvaa kwa Yesu n'e ndjumwa sai yi baire eyi, bera kumwimisa. Abere bera babuana Yesu, era kubamoera n'e kutangilyisa abahubanganyisa era luulu s'e Bwimi bwa Ongo. Era kulamya ba babaa balyi balwala mubu.

11. 마꼬 어 비거뻐 뱌 바뚜 뵤빠아 과 여수 너 뚜뫄 사이 에 바이러 어에, 버라 구뮈미사. 아버러 버라 바부아나 여수, 어라 구바모어라 너 구다삐뼤사 아바후바삐네사 어라 루우루 서 뷔미 봐 오꼬. 어라 구롸먀 바 바바아 바뼤 바뫄쫘 무부.

11. but the crowds learned about it and followed him. He welcomed them and spoke to them about the kingdom of God, and healed those who needed healing.

12. Abere esuba lyera lyasoka, endumwa sa Yesu sera kumuikira n'ekumubura: "Ano chwulyi alyi are n'e misi; Bushi n'oku, kungakomire ubure e bandju bahube kwa musi n'omwa mahwa mabu, bahonde ala bangaonjira n'na bya bangalya.

12. 아버러 어수바 뼈라 꺄소가, 어뚜뫄 사 여수 서라 구무이기라 너구무부라: "아노 쭈레 아뼤 아러 너 미시; 부씨 노구, 구꼬고미러 우부러 어 바뚜 바후버 과 무시 노뫄 마화 마부, 바호떠 아롸 바꼬오삐라 우나 뱌 바꼬꺄.

12. Late in the afternoon the Twelve came to him and said, "Send the crowd away so they can go to the surrounding villages and countryside and find food and lodging, because we are in a remote place here."

13. Yesu nai era kubabura: "Mubeine mubahonderaa bya

13. 여수 나이 어라 구바부라: "무버이너 무바호떠라아 뱌

13. He replied, "You give them something to eat."

balya. Nabu bera kumwakula: "Kutalyi kalyo ka chwete anaola kureka ene mikati etano n'esine efi ebilyi. Ngaba uchwuburaa chwuye kuula e bilyo bya bano bandju boshi bangeuta.	바랴. 나부 버라 구뫄구라: "구다례 가료 가 쮜더 아나오라 구러가 어너 미가디 어다노 너시너 어피 어비례. 까바 우쭈부라아 쭈여 구우라 어 비료 뱌 바노 바쭈 보씨 바꺼우다.	They answered, "We have only five loaves of bread and two fish--unless we go and buy food for all this crowd."
14. Aola, abaa alyi "Mwikasaa e bandju bikembe bya matano-matano."	14. 아오라, 아바아 아례 "뮈가사아 어 바쭈 비거뻬 뱌 마다노-마다노."	14. (About five thousand men were there.) But he said to his disciples, "Have them sit down in groups of about fifty each."
15. Ebanafunzi bera kumomva kwa Yesu ababuraa n'e kwikasa e bandju.	15. 어바나푸찌 버라 구모빠 과 여수 아바부라아 너 귀가사 어 바쭈.	15. The disciples did so, and everybody sat down.
16. Chasinjire, Yesu era kutola era mikati etano n'na s'efi ebilyi n'e kuchwumbikisa kwa nguba n'e kutangilyisa atonga Ongo. Era kubiishanga n'e kubyeresa e baanda bai babiabire e bandju.	16. 짜시찌러, 여수 어라 구도라 어라 미가디 어다노 우나 서피 어비례 너 구쭈삐기사 과 우바 너 구다끼례사 아도까 오끄. 어라 구비이싸까 너 구벼러사 어 바아따 바이 바비아비러 어 바쭈.	16. Taking the five loaves and the two fish and looking up to heaven, he gave thanks and broke them. Then he gave them to the disciples to set before the people.
17. Chira mundju era kuneuta. E baanda bera kwihusa bitonga ekumi na bibilyi by'e bilyo bya bandju bafundwaa.	17. 찌라 무쭈 어라 구너우다. 어 바아따 버라 귀후사 비도까 어구미 나 비비례 벼 비료 뱌 바쭈 바푸놔아.	17. They all ate and were satisfied, and the disciples picked up twelve basketfuls of broken pieces that were left over.
Yesu I kristo	*여수 이 기리시도*	
18. Lusuku luuma, Yesu abaa ema Ongo, n'e baanda bai babaa balyi ala musike. Abere Yesu amala kwema, e baanda bera kuchifunda ala abaa alyi.	18. 루수구 루우마, 여수 아바아 어마 오끄, 너 바아따 바이 바바아 바례 아라 무시거. 아버러 여수 아마라 궈마, 어 바아따 버라 구찌푸따 아라	18. Once when Jesus was praying in private and his disciples were with him, he asked them, "Who do the crowds say

Nai era kubabusa: "E bandju benjire bateta mbu Nyono nyinde,"

19. Bera kumwakula: "Bauma benjire bateta mbu u Yowana Mubatisayi, n'e banji mbu u Eliya, n'e banji nabu mbu ulyi muuma mwa barebi ba mira-mira ola womokire."

20. Yesu omvire bacha, era kubabusa: "N'nenyu kasi, mwenjire mwateta mbu nyilyi nde?" Petero era kumwakula: "Ulyi Mununusi* ola watengaa era mwa Ongo.

21. Yesu era kubabura mbu bataereeresaa Babura mundju kwa I Mununusi ola watengire era mwa Ongo.

22. Kanji era kuteta: "Kwemire Nyono nyi Mwana w'e Mundju nyiribusibwe kusibu n'ekulairwa n'ebashamuka, n'ebakulu-kulu b'ebakuhanyi ba Ongo* n'ebakangirisi b'eMwaso.* Kanji nyikechibwa, na ku suku ehatu nyikomola."

23. Chasinjire, era kubabura boshi: "Akaba emundu ahonda anyikulikire, arekaa kuira ekuhonda kwai emerere n'e kweka e musalaba w'e malibuko mai bushi nanyi chira lusuku, ananyikulikire.

아바아 아레. 나이 어라 구바부사: "어 바뚜 버찌러 바더다 뿌 뇨노 네떠,"

19. 버라 구꽈구꽈: "바우마 버찌러 바더다 뿌 우 요와나 무바디사에, 너 바찌 뿌 우 어릐야, 너 바찌 나부 뿌 우레 무우마 뫄 바러비 바 미라-미라 오꽈 오모기러."

20. 여수 오뻬러 바짜, 어라 구바부사: "우너뉴 가시, 뭐찌러 뫄더다 뿌 네레 떠?" 퍼더로 어라 구꽈구꽈: "우레 무누누시* 오꽈 와더꽈아 어라 뫄 오꼬.

21. 여수 어라 구바부라 뿌 바다어러러사아 바부라 무뚜 과 이 무누누시 오꽈 와더삐러 어라 뫄 오꼬.

22. 가찌 어라 구더다: "궈미러 뇨노 네 뫄나 워 무뚜 네리부시붸 구시부 너구꽈이롸 너바싸무가, 너바구루-구루 버바구하네 바 오꼬* 너바가꿰리시 버뫄소.* 가찌 네거찌봐, 나 구 수구 어하두 네고모꽈."

23. 짜시찌러, 어라 구바부라 보씨: "아가바 어무뚜 아호꽈 아네구꿰기러, 아러가아 구이라 어구호따 과이 어머러러 너 궈가 어 무사꽈바 워 마삐부고 마이 부씨 나네 찌라 루수구, 아나네구꿰기러.

I am?"

19. They replied, "Some say John the Baptist; others say Elijah; and still others, that one of the prophets of long ago has come back to life."

20. "But what about you?" he asked. "Who do you say I am?" Peter answered, "The Christ of God."

21. Jesus strictly warned them not to tell this to anyone.

22. And he said, "The Son of Man must suffer many things and be rejected by the elders, chief priests and teachers of the law, and he must be killed and on the third day be raised to life."

23. Then he said to them all: "If anyone would come after me, he must deny himself and take up his cross daily and follow me.

24. Mumenyereraa kw'emundu ola wanana e kunyikulikira bushi n'ekuhondakulamya ekalamo kai, atakabone ekalamo k'e suku n'e mango. Si ola ukakaesa bushi nanyi, akabona ka k'e suku n'e mango.

25. Kanji akaba mundju angabona ebibuya byoshi by'e butala si abe aesise ekalamo kai, mutoloke muchie angotola?

26. Mumenyereraa kw'emundu ola ukanyifira ehonyi, kanji asifire n'ebinwa byanyi, n'nanyi nyi Mwana w'eMundu nyikamufira si mango nyikabaha mw'etunda lyanyi, lina lya Tata. Kanji lyina echwunda ly'e ndonyi sa Ongo babuiya-buya.

27. Kanji nababura kanangana: Bauma mu Mwabu mulyi ano batakafe batasa kulola kwa Bwami bwa Ongo.

Yesu abilwa e malanga

28. Abere kwarenga einga Yesu ahambere bacha, era kubura Petero, na Yowanyi na Yakobo mbu berukiraa nai kwa ndjulungu kwema Ongo.

29. Mango abaa era ema Ongo, e malanga mai mera kuhuba

---

24. 무머녀러라아 궈무뚜 오콰 와나나 어 구네구뀌기라 부씨 너구호따구콰먀 어가콰모 가이, 아다가보너 어가콰모 거 수구 너 마꼬. 시 오콰 우가가어사 부씨 나니, 아가보나 가 거 수구 너 마꼬.

25. 가찌 아가바 무뚜 아꽈보나 어비부야 뵤씨 벼 부다콰 시 아버 아어시서 어가콰모 가이, 무도로꺼 무쩌 아꼬도콰?

26. 무머녀러라아 궈무뚜 오콰 우가네피라 어호네, 가찌 아시피러 너비봐 뱌네, 우나네 네 마나 워무뚜 네가무피라 시 마꼬 네가바하 뭐두따 콰네, 뤼나 콰 다따. 가찌 레나 어쭈따 뤼어 또네 사 오꼬 바부이야- 부야.

27. 가찌 나바부라 가나꽈나: 바우마 무 꽈부 무쩨 아노 바다가퍼 바다사 구로콰 과 봐미 봐 오꼬.

여수 아비콰 어 마콰까

28. 아버러 과러꽈 어이꽈 여수 아하뻐러 바짜, 어라 구부라 퍼더로, 나 요와네 나 야고보 뿌 버루기라아 나이 과 뚜루우 궈마 오꼬.

29. 마꼬 아바아 어라 어마 오꼬, 어 마콰꽈 마이 머라

---

24. For whoever wants to save his life will lose it, but whoever loses his life for me will save it.

25. What good is it for a man to gain the whole world, and yet lose or forfeit his very self?

26. If anyone is ashamed of me and my words, the Son of Man will be ashamed of him when he comes in his glory and in the glory of the Father and of the holy angels.

27. I tell you the truth, some who are standing here will not taste death before they see the kingdom of God."

28. About eight days after Jesus said this, he took Peter, John and James with him and went up onto a mountain to pray.

29. As he was praying, the appearance of his

kunji-kunji, n'e njimba sai sera kulangala busese.

30. Unao-unao, kwera kupamukira balume babilyi ba babaa bahambala nai mw'obu bulangare. Muuma abaa alyi Musa n'e unji alyi Eliya.

31. Abu balume ba bapamukiraa mw'obu bulangare bwa Ongo, babaa bahambala na Yesu era luulu s'e bisibu n'e lufu lwa lungamuikira e Yerusalemu yi angamalyira e mulyimo wai.

32. Mw'echi chihangi, Petero na balyikabu babaa bashushukire kwa chwulo. Abere bera basisimuka, berakulola ku Yesu n'abu balume babilyi basungwirwe n'e bulangare bwa Ongo.

33. Abere abu balume babilyi bera bachiumaa, Petero era kubura Yesu: "Walyiya, kukomire chwuere anola. Chwungaimba bitala bihachwu: chiuma chingaba chau, n'e chinji chingaba cha Musa, n'e chinji chingaba cha Eliya."

34. Abere Petero anachiri ahambala bacha, elumbumbu lwera kubaha n'ekubahukira

구후바 구찌-구찌, 너 띠빠 사이 서라 구꽈빠꽈 부서서.

30. 우나오-우나오, 꿔라 구파무기라 바루머 바비쩨 바 바바아 바하빠꽈 나이 모부 부꽈라러. 무우마 아바아 아쩨 무사 너 우찌 아쩨 어뤼야.

31. 아부 바루머 바 바파무기라아 모부 부꽈라러 봐 오꼬, 바바아 바하빠꽈 나 여수 어라 루우루 서 비시부 너 루푸 꽈 루꽈무이기라 어 여루사꺼무 에 아까마쩨라 어 무쩨모 와이.

32. 뭐찌 찌하삐, 퍼더로 나 바쩨가부 바바아 바수쑤기러 과 쭈로. 아버러 버라 바시시무가, 버라구뢰꽈 구 여수 나부 바루머 바비쩨 바수뉘뤄 너 부꽈라러 봐 오꼬.

33. 아버러 아부 바루머 바비쩨 버라 바찌우마아, 퍼더로 어라 구부라 여수: "와쩨야, 구고미러 쭈어러 아노꽈. 쭈꽈이빠 비다꽈 비하쭈: 찌우마 찌꽈바 짜우, 너 찌찌 찌꽈바 짜 무사, 너 찌찌 찌꽈바 짜 어뤼야."

34. 아버러 퍼더로 아나찌리 아하빠꽈 바짜, 어루뿌뿌 뤄라 구바하 너구바후기라 보씨. 어

face changed, and his clothes became as bright as a flash of lightning.

30. Two men, Moses and Elijah,

31. appeared in glorious splendor, talking with Jesus. They spoke about his departure, which he was about to bring to fulfillment at Jerusalem.

32. Peter and his companions were very sleepy, but when they became fully awake, they saw his glory and the two men standing with him.

33. As the men were leaving Jesus, Peter said to him, "Master, it is good for us to be here. Let us put up three shelters--one for you, one for Moses and one for Elijah." (He did not know what he was saying.)

34. While he was speaking, a cloud appeared and enveloped

boshi. E ndjumwa sera kubaa mango ssalolaa kwa lumbumbu lwabahukira.

35. E murenge wa Ongo era kumvika mw'olu lumbumbu mmbu: "Onola i Muala wanyi ola natumire kuba Mununusi* wenyu. Mwendaa mwomva bya atela."

36. Abere oyu murenge era omvikanaa, endumwa* sera kulola kwa Yesu yeine i washibire aola. Sera kunasira busira kuhambalira mundu kw'ebi ssalolaa ku kuika mango Yesu abaa atachiri nasi muno butala.

E mwana w'e bihwasi bibi

37. Mw'ei mishangya, Yesu n'esi ndjumwa sai ehachwu bera kutenga kwa ndjulungu. Luamba lunene lw'e bandju lwabahaa kumulinjira.

38. Mw'olu luamba, mulume muuma era kwemaala: "Mukangirisi, nakwemire ebonjo. Unyiloreraa ku muala wanyi w'echuha.

39. Ulolaa, echihwasi chenjire chamusimba n'ekumulakangya, kanji chanamurenula, n'efula lyamutumba kwa bunu. Chenjire chamutenga ku iri champunjire - punjire emubiri.

뚜뫄 서라 구바아 마꼬 싸쁘롸아 과 루뿌뿌 롹바후기라.

35. 어 무러꺼 와 오꼬 어라 구뻬가 모루 루뿌뿌 무뿌: "오노롸 이 무아롸 와네 오롸 나두미러 구바 무누누시* 워뉴. 뭐따아 모빠 뱌 아더롸."

36. 아버러 오유 무러꺼 어라 오뻬가나아, 어뚜뫄* 서라 구쁘롸 과 여수 여이너 이 와씨비러 아오롸. 서라 구나시라 부시라 구하빠뤠라 무뚜 궈비 싸쁘롸아 구 구이가 마꼬 여수 아바아 아다찌리 나시 무노 부다롸.

어 뫄나 워 비화시 비비

37. 뭐이 미싸뺘, 여수 너시 뚜뫄 사이 어하쭈 버라 구더뺘 과 뚜루우. 루아빠 루너너 뤄 바뚜 롹바하아 구무뤠찌라.

38. 모루 루아빠, 무루머 무우마 어라 궈마아롸: "무가뼈리시, 나궈미러 어보쪼. 우네쁘러라아 구 무아롸 와네 워쭈하.

39. 우쁘롸아, 어찌화시 쩌찌러 짜무시빠 너구무롸가뺘, 가찌 짜나무러누롸, 너푸롸 랴무두빠 과 부누. 쩌찌러 짜무더뺘 구 이리 짜무푸찌러 - 푸찌러 어무비리.

---

them, and they were afraid as they entered the cloud.

35. A voice came from the cloud, saying, "This is my Son, whom I have chosen; listen to him."

36. When the voice had spoken, they found that Jesus was alone. The disciples kept this to themselves, and told no one at that time what they had seen.

37. The next day, when they came down from the mountain, a large crowd met him.

38. A man in the crowd called out, "Teacher, I beg you to look at my son, for he is my only child.

39. A spirit seizes him and he suddenly screams; it throws him into convulsions so that he foams at the mouth. It scarcely ever leaves him and is destroying

him.

40. Naburaa ebanafunzi bau mbu bambulaa echi chihwasi, si bafundwaa."

40. 나부라아 어바나푸씨 바우 뿌 바뿌롸아 어찌 찌화시, 시 바푸봐아."

40. I begged your disciples to drive it out, but they could not."

41. Yesu omvire bacha, era kubanda endulu: "Mwabu mu bandu b'esine suku muta bemeresi, kanji muli babi. Ndachete suku sinene nenyu, kanji ndangachiendekerna nomva ebyenyu ku suku sinene. "ra kubura eshe w'emwana: "Nyireteraa emwana wau anola."

41. 여수 오삐러 바짜, 어라 구바따 어뚜루: "뫄부 무 바뚜 버시너 수구 무다 버머러시, 가찌 무뤼 바비. 따쩌더 수구 시너너 너뉴, 가찌 따싸쩌너거루나 노빠 어벼뉴 구수구 시너너. "라 구부라 어써 워뫄나: "니러더라아 어뫄나 와우 아노롸."

41. "O unbelieving and perverse generation," Jesus replied, "how long shall I stay with you and put up with you? Bring your son here."

42. Abere emwana abaha, echihwasi chera kumusimba n'ekumuhunda kwa chitaka, kuna kumurenguka n'ekutangirisa chamukukumanya. Si Yesu era kukalira chi n'ekwambula chi. Era kulamya ola mwana n'ekumweresa eshe.

42. 아버러 어뫄나 아바하, 어찌화시 쩌라 구무시빠 너구무후따 과 찌다가, 구나 구무러우가 너구다삐리사 짜무구구마냐. 시 여수 어라 구가쀠라 찌 너과뿌롸 찌. 어라 구롸먀 오롸 뫄나 너구뭐러사 어써.

42. Even while the boy was coming, the demon threw him to the ground in a convulsion. But Jesus rebuked the evil spirit, healed the boy and gave him back to his father.

43. E bandju boshi basanwaa n'ebuashi bunene bwa Ongo bwa balolaa kwa Mango chira mundu abaa asanwa n'na bya Yesu endaa akola, Yesu nai era kubura ebbanafunzi bai:

43. 어 바뚜 보씨 바사놔아 너부아씨 부너너 봐 오꼬 봐 바르롸아 과 마꼬 찌라 무뚜 아바아 아사놔 우나 뱌 여수 어따아 아고롸, 여수 나이 어라 구부라 어부바나푸씨 바이:

43. And they were all amazed at the greatness of God. While everyone was marveling at all that Jesus did, he said to his disciples,

44. "Muteyaa ematwi mumve kwa binwa nababura mwa kano kabangi: Nyono nyi Mwana w'eMundu nyinganyibwamwa maboko m'ebalume."

44. "무더야아 어마뒤 무뻐 과 비놔 나바부라 뫄 가노 가바삐: 뇨노 니 뫄나 워무뚜 네싸네봐뫄 마보고 머바루머."

44. "Listen carefully to what I am about to tell you: The Son of Man is going to be betrayed into the hands of men."

45. Si batomvaa ebi binwa bya

45. 시 바도빠아 어비 비놔 뱌

45. But they did not

abaa ababura n'ekumenyerera kwa bitechire, bushi Ongo ababishaa ekubimenyerera. Bera kufa n'ebuba bw'ekubusa Yesu kubi.

N'nde I mukulu-kulu?

46. Endjumwa* sa Yesu satangirisaa bwaka bwa kubusanya mbu nde I mukulu-kulu musi.

47. Si Yesu abaa amenyerere emianyis ayasi mira. Era kutola emwanamutoto n'ekumubika al'auma nai.

48. Era kusibura: "Ola ungangirira ono mwana bushi n'esina lyanyi iiri anyangirire. N'nola unganyangirira, iri ola wanyitumire I angirire. Mwiraa mwamenyerera kw'ola ungachihubya mueke mu muboshi I mukulu-kulu."

49. Yowana ku kwera kuteta: "Enawechwu, chwalolaa ku mundu muuma ola wabaa wenjire aambula e bihwasi mw'esina lyau, si twabaa twenjire twamwanga, bushi atakulyikana nechwu."

50. Yesu era kumubura: "Lunji lusuku mutachimwangaa, bushi ola uta murenda wenyu ilyi alyi

아바아 아바부라 너구머녀러라 과 비더찌러, 부씨 오꼬 아바비싸아 어구비머녀러라. 버라 구파 너부바 붜구부사 여수 구비.

우뻐 이 무구루루-구루루?

46. 어뚜뫄* 사 여수 사다삐리사아 봐가 봐 구부사냐 뿌 뻐 이 무구루루-구루루 무시.

47. 시 여수 아바아 아머녀러러 어미아네수 아야시 미라. 어라 구도뢔 어뫄나무도도 너구무비가 아뢔우마 나이.

48. 어라 구시부라: "오뢔 우꺼리라 오노 뫄나 부씨 너시나 뢔네 이이리 아냐꺼리러러 우노뢔 우꺼냐꺼리라, 이리 오뢔 와내두미러 이 아꺼리러. 뮈라아 뫄머녀러라 교뢔 우꺼찌후뱌 무어거 무 무보씨 이 무구루루-구루루."

49. 요와나 구 궈라 구더다: "어나워쭈, 좌뢰롸아 구 무뚜 무우마 오뢔 와바아 워찌러 아아뿌뢔 어 비화시 뭐시나 뢔우, 시 돠바아 뛰찌러 돠뫄뢔, 부씨 아다구레가나 너쭈."

50. 여수 어라 구무부라: "루찌 루수구 무다찌뫄까아, 부씨 오뢔 우다 무러따 워뉴 이레 아레

understand what this meant. It was hidden from them, so that they did not grasp it, and they were afraid to ask him about it.

46. An argument started among the disciples as to which of them would be the greatest.

47. Jesus, knowing their thoughts, took a little child and had him stand beside him.

48. Then he said to them, "Whoever welcomes this little child in my name welcomes me; and whoever welcomes me welcomes the one who sent me. For he who is least among you all--he is the greatest."

49. "Master," said John, "we saw a man driving out demons in your name and we tried to stop him, because he is not one of us."

50. "Do not stop him," Jesus said, "for whoever is not against you is for

w"okwa lunda lw'e Basamariya bauma banana kwemerera Yesu.

51. Esuku sa Yesu s'e kwekibwa kwa nguba sabaa saikire. Bushi n'oku, era kulola kwa binamwemire erukire eYerusalemu.

52. Era kutuma endumwa* simuhondorere, simukunganyise ala angaikira. Abere sera siri mwa njira, sera kwingirira mu musi muuma w'eBasamariya;*

53. Si besha kw'oyu musi bera kusibura: "Tutahonda Yesu kw'ono musi, bushi eYerusalemu yi a"

54. Endumwa sai, Yakobo na Yowanyi, somvire bacha, sera kuteta: "Enawetu, uhonjire tutete bu emuliro atengaa kwa nguba abasikye?"

55. E muchima Waye era bindjuka unao era kuemuka . Era kuteta kwa bamua e bilyo.

56. E basere baye bera kusomerwa busese, kweine era kubabura kwa bataburaa mundju cha chabaa.

E kukulyikira Yesu

57. Abere Yesu n'e baanda bai bera balyi mwa njira, mundju muuma era kumubura: "Nyikende nakwemisa era ukende wanarenga yoshi."

우오과 루따 뤄 바사마리야 바우마 바나나 궈머러라 여수.

51. 어수구 사 여수 서 궈기봐 과 꾸바 사바아 사이기러. 부씨 노구, 어라 구뢰퐈 과 비나뭐미러 어루기러 어여루사퍼무.

52. 어라 구두마 어뚜꽈* 시무호또러러, 시무구꽈네서 아퐈 아까이기라. 아버러 서라 시리 꽈 띠라, 서라 귀끼리라 무 무시 무우마 워바사마리야;*

53. 시 버싸 교유 무시 버라 구시부라: "두다호따 여수 교노 무시, 부씨 어여루사퍼무 에 아"

54. 어뚜꽈 사이, 야고보 나 요와네, 소삐러 바쨔, 서라 구더다: "어나워두, 우호띠러 두더더 부 어무뢰로 아더꽈아 과 꾸바 아바시겨?"

55. 어 무찌마 와여 어라 비뿌가 우나오 어라 구어무가 . 어라 구더다 과 바무아 어 비료.

56. 어 바서러 바여 버라 구소머롸 부서서, 궈이너 어라 구바부라 과 바다부라아 무뚜 쨔 쨔바아.

어 구구쀄굿띱 여수

57. 아버러 여수 너 바아따 바이 버라 바뤠 꽈 띠라, 무뚜 무우마 어라 구무부라: "네거머 나궈미사 어라 우거머 와나러꽈 요씨."

---

you."

51. As the time approached for him to be taken up to heaven, Jesus resolutely set out for Jerusalem.

52. And he sent messengers on ahead, who went into a Samaritan village to get things ready for him;

53. but the people there did not welcome him, because he was heading for Jerusalem.

54. When the disciples James and John saw this, they asked, "Lord, do you want us to call fire down from heaven to destroy them?"

55. But Jesus turned and rebuked them,

56. and they went to another village.

57. As they were walking along the road, a man said to him, "I will follow you wherever you go."

58. Yesu omvire bacha, era kumubura: "Emiterelyi itusa ala yende yabunda, n'emilonge yanaata ematu; si Nyono nyi Mwana w'e Mundju nyeke ndachwusa ala nyingaonjira."

59. Kanji era kubura unji mundju muuma: "Unyemisaa." "yu mundu era kuteta: "Waliya, unyirekaa tanga nyiende kutaba tata."

60. Yesu era kumwakula: "rekaa ebafu beine batabe ebafu babu, si woyu uendaa kufulira eandu eyasi y'eBwami bwa Ongo."

61. Unji mundu muuma era kubura Yesu: "Enawetu, nyikende nakwemisa, si unyirekaa tanga nyiende kulaa engumu yanyi."

62. Yesu era kumubura: "E mundju ola ungaba watangilyise e kuchika atangachiba wa kulola era nyuma. Ola waira bacha, atangaba wa kukorera e Bwami bwa Ongo."

58. 여수 오삐러 바짜, 어라 구무부라: "어미더러레 이두사 아라 여떠 야부따, 너미쁘어 야나아다 어마두; 시 뇨노 네 모나 워 무뚜 녀거 따쭈사 아라 네까오씨라."

59. 가찌 어라 구부라 우찌 무뚜 무우마: "우녀미사아." "유 무뚜 어라 구더다: "와쀠야, 우네러가아 다까 니어어 구다바 다다."

60. 여수 어라 구뫄구뫄: "러가아 어바푸 버이너 바다버 어바푸 바부, 시 오유 우어따아 구푸쀠라 어아뚜 어야시 여봐미 봐 오꼬."

61. 우찌 무뚜 무우마 어라 구부라 여수: "어나워두, 네거떠 나꿔미사, 시 우네러가아 다까 니어떠 구꽈아 어꾸무 야네."

62. 여수 어라 구무부라: "어 무뚜 오롸 우까바 와다삐레써 어 구찌가 아다까찌바 와 구롸 어라 뉴마. 오롸 와이라 바짜, 아다까바 와 구고러라 어 봐미 봐 오꼬."

58. Jesus replied, "Foxes have holes and birds of the air have nests, but the Son of Man has no place to lay his head."

59. He said to another man, "Follow me." But the man replied, "Lord, first let me go and bury my father."

60. Jesus said to him, "Let the dead bury their own dead, but you go and proclaim the kingdom of God."

61. Still another said, "I will follow you, Lord; but first let me go back and say good-by to my family."

62. Jesus replied, "No one who puts his hand to the plow and looks back is fit for service in the kingdom of God."

Luka Chikono 10
Yesu achwuma bandju malyinda

1. Era nyuma s'ebi, Enawetu era

룩가 찌고노 10
여수 아쭈립 바뚜 마뻬따

1. 어라 뉴마 서비, 어나워두

Luke Chapter 10[NIV]

1. After this the Lord

kulondola banji banafunzi malinda na babiri. Era kubatuababiri-babiri bamuhondorere mu chira musi ola lyeine abaa ahonda aye mu.

어라 구쯔또롸 바찌 바나푸씨 마뤼따 나 바비리. 어라 구바두아바비리-바비리 바무호또러러 무 찌라 무시 오꽈 려이너 아바아 아호따 아여 무.

appointed seventy-two others and sent them two by two ahead of him to every town and place where he was about to go.

2. Era muhondo s'ekubatuma, bacha ku abaa enjire ababura: "Emyaka era yerire iri inene, si ebakosi b'ekuishebula bu bakeire. Bushi n'oku, mwemaa en'emyaka atume banji bakosi mw'ehwa lyai bishebule.

2. 어라 무호또 서구바두마, 바짜 구 아바아 어찌러 아바부라: "어먀가 어라 여리러 이리 이너너, 시 어바고시 버구이써부꽈 부 바거이러. 부씨 노구, 뭐마아 어너먀가 아두머 바찌 바고시 뭐화 랴이 비써부뤄.

2. He told them, "The harvest is plentiful, but the workers are few. Ask the Lord of the harvest, therefore, to send out workers into his harvest field.

3. Muchiumaa: Si Mumenyereraa kwa nabatuma mwa bandu na byana bya mbuli mwa kachi-kachi k'ebishibwabwa.

3. 무찌우마아: 시 무머녀러라아 꽈 나바두마 뫄 바뉴 나 뱌나 뱌 뿌뤼 뫄 가찌-가찌 거비씨뫄뫄.

3. Go! I am sending you out like lambs among wolves.

4. Mutekaa lutea, nesi mbweka. Ebirato mwimbesi bi munekaa, mutakesaa undu bihangi binene mwa njira.

4. 무더가아 루더아, 너시 뭦가. 어비라도 뮈뻐시 비 무너가아, 무다거사아 우뿌 비하띠 비너너 뫄 찌라.

4. Do not take a purse or bag or sandals; and do not greet anyone on the road.

5. Mango mungengirira mu nyumba irebe, mukesaa besha mui n'ebolo.

5. 마꼬 무꺼끼리라 무 뉴빠 이러버, 무거사아 버싸 무이 너보로.

5. "When you enter a house, first say, 'Peace to this house.'

6. Akaba mw'ei nyumba mungaba mundju ola wahonda ebolo, ebolo bwa Ongo bwa mwahonda ekwana, oyola I unabubona. Bitali bacha ebolo bwenyu bwanabaalukira.

6. 아가바 뭐이 뉴빠 무꽈바 무뿌 오꽈 와호따 어보로, 어보로 봐 오꼬 봐 마호따 어과나, 오요롸 이 우나부보나. 비다뤼 바짜 어보로 뭐뉴 뫄나바아루기라.

6. If a man of peace is there, your peace will rest on him; if not, it will return to you.

7. Muberaa mw'ei nyumba, munalye n'ekumwa bya besha mui bangaberesa, bushi

7. 무버라아 뭐이 뉴빠, 무나뤄 너구꽈 뱌 버싸 무이 바꽈버러사, 부씨 벼미러

7. Stay in that house, eating and drinking whatever they give you,

byemire emukosi abone elwembo lwai. Mutatengaa mu nyumba mbu mwaya mu inji.

8. N'akaba mungangirirwa kubuya mu chira musi mungengirira mu, mulyaa bya bangaberesa mu,

9. mulamye ebalwala bamu, munababure: 'e Bwimi bwa Ono bwaikire ofu nenyu"

10. Batabangirire kubuya mu chira musi mungengirira mu, muyaa mwa nama munatete mmbu:

11. Chwabakunguchilyire e mukungu w'e musi wenyu ola wayaa kwa bihando byetu, ku kubalosa kwa Ongo akabachinjibusa bushi n'ebubi bwenyu. Si chichine chi mumenyerera: eBwimi bwa Ongo bwabaikirire mira.

12. Nababura: Elusuku lw'e buchinjibusi bwa Ongo, besha e musi w'e Sotomo bakatonanyisibwa kueke kurenza besha oyu musi."

13. "Kanji Mumenyereraa kwa besha mwa musi w'eKorasinyi n'ew'e Betesaita ali banya, bushi ebisomerano bya byairirwe mwa kachi-kachi kabu bingairirwe mwa musi w'eTiro

어무고시 아보너 어뤄쁘 롸이. 무다더빠아 무 뉴빠 뿌 롸야 무 이찌.

8. 나가바 무빠삐리롸 구부야 무 찌라 무시 무뻐삐리라 무, 무롸아 뱌 바빠버러사 무,

9. 무롸며 어바뽜라 바무, 무나바부러: 어 뷔미 봐 오노 봐이기러 오푸 너뉴"

10. 바다바삐리러 구부야 무 찌라 무시 무뻐삐리라 무, 무야아 롸 나마 무나더더 무뿌:

11. 쫘바구꾸찌레러 어 무구꾸 워 무시 워뉴 오롸 와야아 과 비하또 벼두, 구 구바로사 과 오꼬 아가바찌찌부사 부씨 너부비 붜뉴. 시 찌찌너 찌 무머녀러라: 어뷔미 봐 오꼬 봐바이기리러 미라.

12. 나바부라: 어루수구 뤄 부찌찌부시 봐 오꼬, 버싸 어 무시 워 소도모 바가도나네시봐 구어거 구러싸 버싸 오유 무시."

13. "가찌 무머녀러라아 과 버싸 롸 무시 워고라시네 너워 버더사이다 아뢰 바냐, 부씨 어비소머라노 뱌 뱌이리뤄 롸 가찌-가찌 가부 비빠이리뤄 롸 무시 워디로 너워 시도나, 버싸

for the worker deserves his wages. Do not move around from house to house.

8. "When you enter a town and are welcomed, eat what is set before you.

9. Heal the sick who are there and tell them, 'The kingdom of God is near you.'

10. But when you enter a town and are not welcomed, go into its streets and say,

11. 'Even the dust of your town that sticks to our feet we wipe off against you. Yet be sure of this: The kingdom of God is near.'

12. I tell you, it will be more bearable on that day for Sodom than for that town.

13. "Woe to you, Korazin! Woe to you, Bethsaida! For if the miracles that were performed in you had been performed in Tyre

n'ew'e Sitona, besha mui bangembere ebikunyia n'e kwikala mwa lufufu, kwa kulossa kwa bahonda kubindjula emyanya yabu.

무이 바꺼뻐러 어비구네아 너 귀가꺄 뫄 루푸푸, 과 구로싸 과 바호따 구비뚜꺄 어먀냐 야부.

and Sidon, they would have repented long ago, sitting in sackcloth and ashes.

14. Bushi n'oku, besha e misi y'eTiro n'e Sitona, bakachinjibusibwa kueke kurenza besha Korasinyi na besha Betesaita, bushi beke balolaa kwa naira e bisomerano, si batabindulaa emyanya yabu.

14. 부씨 노구, 버싸 어 미시 여디로 너 시도나, 바가찌찌부시봐 구어거 구러싸 버씨 고라시네 나 버싸 버더사이다, 부씨 버거 바로꽈아 과 나이라 어 비소머라노, 시 바다비뚜꽈아 어먀냐 야부.

14. But it will be more bearable for Tyre and Sidon at the judgment than for you.

15. Na besha mwa musi w'eKaperinaumu, baanyisa mbu bakeresibwa ebuashi bw'ekuika kwa nguba bushi nanabaa al'auma nabu? Chitangaalikana, kuika banalinde baika era bafu ba bateshi Ongo bende baya kulibukira!"

15. 나 버싸 뫄 무시 워가퍼리나우무, 바아네사 뿌 바거러시봐 어부아씨 붜구이가 과 꾸바 부씨 나나바아 아꽈우마 나부? 찌다꽈아찌가나, 구이가 바나찌러 바이가 어라 바푸 바 바더씨 오꼬 버떠 바야 구찌부기라!"

15. And you, Capernaum, will you be lifted up to the skies? No, you will go down to the depths.

16. Kanji Yesu era kubura ebanafunzi bai: "Ola waBomvire ilyi nyi omvire, si ola waabananyire ilyi nyi ananyire, n'nola wanyinanyire ilyi ola wanyichwumaa I ananyire. "ra nyuma s'ebi, bera kuchiuma.

16. 가찌 여수 어라 구부라 어바나푸씨 바이: "오꽈 와보뻐러 이레 니 오뻐러, 시 오꽈 와아바나네러 이레 니 아나네러, 우노꽈 와네나네러 이레 오꽈 와네쭈마아 이 아나네러. "라 뉴마 서비, 버라 구찌우마.

16. "He who listens to you listens to me; he who rejects you rejects me; but he who rejects me rejects him who sent me."

Kufuluka kw'e bandju malyinda

구푸루— 귀 바꾸 마레따

17. Abere ba banafunzi malinda na babiri bamala emulimo, bera kufuluka na lumoo lunene. Bera kutea: "Enawechwu, mano

17. 아버러 바 바나푸씨 마찌따 나 바비리 바마라 어무찌모, 버라 구푸루가 나 루모오 루너너. 버라 구더아: "어나워쭈, 마노

17. The seventy-two returned with joy and said, "Lord, even the demons submit to us in

twabaa twenjire twambula ebihwasi mw'esina lyau, byabaa byenjire byanemerera bya chwabibura."

18. Bushi n'oku, Yesu era kubabura: "Ku binalyi, n'nanyi nabaa nyisene kw Shetanyi atoa kwa nguba ng'okwa chikengu chende chatoa kwa nguba.

19. Muenyereraa, naberesise e buashi bw'e kusinool e misi y'oyu muenda. Mw'obu buashi mu mungende mwalibata enjoka n'engutu. Kutachiri n'echa chingabababasa.

20. Si chiro e bihwasi bingemerera bya mwabibura, echera cheine chitatumaa mwamoa, si mumoaa bushi emasina menyu manjikirw era mwa Ongo.

21. Mw'echi chihangi, eMuchima Mubuya-buya era kweresa Yesu lumoo lunene. Yesu era kuangirisa ema Ongo: "eTata, Enawechwu, woyu u En'enguba n'ebutala; nakutongire mwa kulola kwa binwa bya wabishaa ba bachwula benge, wabikangire ba batula balonjirwe. Ku binalyi Tata, weine u waondaa kwa ku bibaa bacha!"

22. Era nyuma s'ekwema, era kubura ebandu: "Tata ameresise

마노 돠바아 뛰찌러 돠뿌롸 어비화시 뭐시나 쨔우, 뱌바아 벼찌러 뱌너머러라 뱌 쫘비부라."

18. 부씨 노구, 여수 어라 구바부라: "구 비나뤠, 우나네 나바아 니셔너 구 써다네 아도아 과 꾸바 꼬과 찌거우 쩌러 짜도아 과 꾸바.

19. 무어녀러라아, 나버러시서 어 부아씨 뷔 구시노오루 어 미시 요유 무어따. 모부 부아씨 무 무꺼러 뫄쀠바다 어쪼가 너꾸두. 구다찌리 너짜 찌꺄바바바사.

20. 시 찌로 어 비화시 비꺼머러라 뱌 뫄비부라, 어쩌라 쩌이너 찌다두마아 뫄모아, 시 무모아아 부씨 어마시나 머뉴 마찌기루 어라 뫄 오꼬.

21. 뭐찌 찌하삐, 어무찌마 무부야-부야 어라 궈러사 여수 루모오 루너너. 여수 어라 구아삐리사 어마 오꼬: "어다다, 어나워쭈, 오유 우 어너꾸바 너부다롸; 나구도삐러 뫄 구뢴롸 과 비놔 뱌 와비싸아 바 바쭈롸 버꺼, 와비가삐러 바 바두롸 바롿찌뤄. 구 비나뤠 다다, 워이너 우 와오따아 과 구 비바아 바짜!"

22. 어라 뉴마 서궈마, 어라 구부라 어바뚜: "다다

your name."

18. He replied, "I saw Satan fall like lightning from heaven.

19. I have given you authority to trample on snakes and scorpions and to overcome all the power of the enemy; nothing will harm you.

20. However, do not rejoice that the spirits submit to you, but rejoice that your names are written in heaven."

21. At that time Jesus, full of joy through the Holy Spirit, said, "I praise you, Father, Lord of heaven and earth, because you have hidden these things from the wise and learned, and revealed them to little children. Yes, Father, for this was your good pleasure.

22. "All things have been committed to me by my

byoshi. Kutali munu ola uchwula unyishi kureka Tata eine. Kanji kutalyi ola uchwula wishi Tata kureka Nyono nyeine, n'na ba nyeine nyisimire bamumenye."

23. Chasinjire, Yesu era kwerekera era anafunzi ai babaa bali. Era kubabura beine: "Emeho ma masene kuuma n'okwa musene bahondaa balole kw'ebya musen ku, si batabilolaa ku. Kanji bahondaa bomve kw'ebya mwenjie mwomva ku, si batabyumvaa ku."

24. Buishi naba bulyire kwa barebi banene na bami banga hondjire balole kwabya mwalolako mwaabu kweine batalolyire, ne kuumva bya mwomvireko mwabo sibata biomvireko.

E muanyi bushi n'e Musamariya mubuya

25. Mukangilyisi muuma w'e Mwasiemukaa n'e kutea Yesu e chinwa. Era kumubusa: "Walyiya, chiye chi nyingaira nyibone e kalamo k'esuku n'e mango?"

26. Yesu era kumwakula: "Kute kw'e Mwaso* wetu atula anjikirwe? Na kute ku wende

---

아머러시서 뵤씨. 구다뤼 무누 오롸 우쭈롸 우니씨 구러가 다다 어이너. 가찌 구다뤠 오롸 우쭈롸 위씨 다다 구러가 노노 녀이너, 우나 바 녀이너 네시미러 바무머녀."

23. 짜시찌러, 여수 어라 궈러거라 어라 아나푸씨 아이 바바아 바뤼. 어라 구바부라 버이너: "어머호 마 마서너 구우마 노과 무서너 바호따아 바롸뤄 궈뱌 무서누 구, 시 바다비롸라아 구. 가찌 바호따아 보뻐 궈뱌 뭐찌어 모빠 구, 시 바다뷰빠아 구."

24. 부이씨 나바 부뤠러 과 바러비 바너너 나 바미 바까 호찌러 바롸뤄 과뱌 뫄롸뽜고 뫄아부 궈이너 바다롸뤠러, 너 구우빠 뱌 모뻬러고 뫄보 시바다 비오뻬러고.

어 무아네 부씨 너 무사마리야 무부야

25. 무가띠뤠시 무우마 워 뫄시어무가아 너 구더아 여수 어 찌놔. 어라 구무부사: "와뤠야, 찌여 찌 네까이라 네보너 어 가뽜모 거수구 너 마꼬?"

26. 여수 어라 구뫄구롸: "구더 궈 뫄소* 워두 아두롸 아찌기뤄? 나 구더 구 워떠

Father. No one knows who the Son is except the Father, and no one knows who the Father is except the Son and those to whom the Son chooses to reveal him."

23. Then he turned to his disciples and said privately, "Blessed are the eyes that see what you see.

24. For I tell you that many prophets and kings wanted to see what you see but did not see it, and to hear what you hear but did not hear it."

25. On one occasion an expert in the law stood up to test Jesus. "Teacher," he asked, "what must I do to inherit eternal life?"

26. "What is written in the Law?" he replied. "How do you read it?"

womva u mwa kuusoma?"

올빠 우 마 구우소마?"

27. Oyu mukangirisi w'eMwaso* era kumwakula: "Atul atechire mmbu: Usimaa Enawenyu I Ongo n'emuchima wau woshi, n'emisi yau yoshi, n'emianyisa yau yoshi, n'e bwenge bwa boshi.b Kanji simaa mulikenyu ng'okwa weine utula uchisiire."

27. 오유 무가끼리시 워마소* 어라 구마구롸: "아두루 아더찌러 무뿌: 우시마아 어나워뉴 이 오꼬 너무찌마 와우 오씨, 너미시 야우 요씨, 너미아네사 야우 요씨, 너 붸뻐 봐 보씨.부 가찌 시마아 무뤼거뉴 꼬과 워이너 우두롸 우찌시이러."

27. He answered: " 'Love the Lord your God with all your heart and with all your soul and with all your strength and with all your mind'; and, 'Love your neighbor as yourself.'"

28. Chasinjire, Yesu era kuteta: "Wakwire kubuya, ebi wera kutea bi wendaa waira ubone ekalamo."

28. 짜시찌러, 여수 어라 구더다: "와귀러 구부야, 어비 워라 구더아 비 워따아 와이라 우보너 어가롸모."

28. "You have answered correctly," Jesus replied. "Do this and you will live."

29. Oyu mukangirisi w'e Mwaso abaa ahonda ach?rese emwaso, kanji era kubusa Yeu: "Nande I wera mulyikechwu?"

29. 오유 무가끼리시 워 마소 아바아 아호따 아찌?러서 어마소, 가찌 어라 구부사 여우: "나떠 이 워라 무뤠거쭈?"

29. But he wanted to justify himself, so he asked Jesus, "And who is my neighbor?"

30. Yesu era kuhuba kumubura mwa muanyi: "Munu muuma abaa atenga eYerusalemu endaalira eYriko. Era kupapamukira ku bihumusi. Byera kumunyaa byoshi bya abaa ee n'ekumupunda. Byera kuchiendera byamurekire mareka-reka.

30. 여수 어라 구후바 구무부라 마 무아네: "무누 무우마 아바아 아더빠 어여루사뻐무 어따아뤼라 어위리고. 어라 구파파무기라 구 비후무시. 벼라 구무냐아 뵤씨 뱌 아바아 어어 너구무푸따. 벼라 구쩌떠라 뱌무러기러 마러가-러가.

30. In reply Jesus said: "A man was going down from Jerusalem to Jericho, when he fell into the hands of robbers. They stripped him of his clothes, beat him and went away, leaving him half dead.

31. Kuhanyi wa Ongo muuma abaa abandaala mwel njira. Amuhunjire kw'emeho, era kwambuka busira kumuasa.

31. 구하네 와 오꼬 무우마 아바아 아바따아롸 뭬이 찌라. 아무후찌러 귀머호, 어라 과뿌가 부시라 구무아사.

31. A priest happened to be going down the same road, and when he saw the man, he passed by on the other side.

32. Mulawai c muuma nai era kuika aola. ALolire kw'oyu

32. 무롸와이 시 무우마 나이 어라 구이가 아오롸. 아로뤼러

32. So too, a Levite, when he came to the

mundu, nai era kwambuka.

교유 무뚜, 나이 어라 과뿌가.

place and saw him, passed by on the other side.

33. Si Musamariya muuma ola wabaa uli wa lubalamo, era kuika ala oyu mundu abaa ali. Amulolire ku, era kumufira bonjo bunene.

33. 시 무사마리야 무우마 오롸 와바아 우뤼 와 루바롸모, 어라 구이가 아롸 오유 무뚜 아바아 아뤼. 아무롣뤼러 구, 어라 구무피라 보쪼 부너너.

33. But a Samaritan, as he traveled, came where the man was; and when he saw him, he took pity on him.

34. Era kuchifunda ofu nai, era kuufuka elutuku n'emafua kwa biulu n'ekubimina. Era kumubika kwa ndokomo yai, era kumweka mwa nyumba y'ebaenyi alangibwe mu.

34. 어라 구찌푸따 오푸 나이, 어라 구우푸가 어루두구 너마푸아 과 비우루 너구비미나. 어라 구무비가 과 또고모 야이, 어라 구뭐가 뫄 뉴빠 여바어니 아롸삐붜 무.

34. He went to him and bandaged his wounds, pouring on oil and wine. Then he put the man on his own donkey, took him to an inn and took care of him.

35. Abee mw'ei mishangya, era kukula butea bwa bungakorerwa mibisi ebiri, era kuburekera en'enyumba y'ebaenyi n'ekumubura: 'Ulangaa ono mundu kubuya. N'ebunji butea bwa ungamuesa ku, nyi nyingakualulira bu mango nyingafuluka!"

35. 아버어 뭐이 미쌰야, 어라 구구롸 부더아 봐 부빠고러롸 미비시 어비리, 어라 구부러거라 어너뉴빠 여바어니 너구무부라: 우롸뫄아 오노 무뚜 구부야. 너부찌 부더아 봐 우빠무어사 구, 네 네빠구아루뤼라 부 마꼬 네빠푸루가!"

35. The next day he took out two silver coins and gave them to the innkeeper. 'Look after him,' he said, 'and when I return, I will reimburse you for any extra expense you may have.'

36. Yesu ku kwera kubusa oyu mukangirisi w'eMwaso:* "Ku woyu, mweabu bahatu nde I usene ku nga I wabaa mulikabu w'oyu wapundwaa n'ebihumusi?"

36. 여수 구 귀라 구부사 오유 무가삐리시 워뫄소:* "구 오유, 뭐아부 바하두 떠 이 우서너 구 빠 이 와바아 무뤼가부 요유 와푸똬아 너비후무시?"

36. "Which of these three do you think was a neighbor to the man who fell into the hands of robbers?"

37. Oyu mukangirisi w'eMwaso era kumwakula: "Ola wamufiraa ebonjo. "esu era kumubura: "Uendaa, n'nau ku wendaa waira bacha.

37. 오유 무가삐리시 워뫄소 어라 구뫄구롸: "오롸 와무피라아 어보쪼. "어수 어라 구무부라: "우어따아, 우나우 구 워따아 와이라 바짜.

37. The expert in the law replied, "The one who had mercy on him." Jesus told him, "Go and do likewise."

38. Mango Yesu n'ebanafnzi bai babaa banachiri mwa luendo lw'ekwirukira eYerusalemu, bera kuya ku musi muuma. Mukasi muuma mbu I Marata era kumuhuukasa mwa mwai.

38. 마오 여수 너바나푸씨 바이 바바아 바나찌리 마 루어또 뤄귀루기라 어여루사쩌무, 버라 구야 구 무시 무우마. 무가시 무우마 뿌 이 마라다 어라 구무후우가사 마 마이.

38. As Jesus and his disciples were on their way, he came to a village where a woman named Martha opened her home to him.

39. N'noyo mukasi abaa ete mulumuna wai mbu I Mariya. Oyola abaa ekesi ala musike s'ebihando bya Yesu. Abaa omwirisa bya Yesu abaa ateta.

39. 우노요 무가시 아바아 어더 무루무나 와이 뿌 이 마리야. 오요롸 아바아 어거시 아롸 무시거 서비하또 뱌 여수. 아바아 오뮈리사 뱌 여수 아바아 아더다.

39. She had a sister called Mary, who sat at the Lord's feet listening to what he said.

40. Si Marata yeke abaa aluirirwe n'emulimon w'ekuteka ebiryo, era kuika ala Yesu abaa ali, era kumubura: "Kungakomie umenyerere kwa mulumuna wanyi anyirekere emulimo w'kuteka nyene. Umuburaa abahe kunyiasa."

40. 시 마라다 여거 아바아 아루이리뤄 너무쮜모누 워구더가 어비료, 어라 구이가 아롸 여수 아바아 아쮜, 어라 구무부라: "구꽈고미어 우머녀러러 과 무루무나 와네 아네러거러 어무쮜모 우구더가 녀너. 우무부라아 아바허 구네아사."

40. But Martha was distracted by all the preparations that had to be made. She came to him and asked, "Lord, don't you care that my sister has left me to do the work by myself? Tell her to help me!"

41. Yesu era kumwakula: "Marata, Marata, woyu wachiribusa ku bindu binene.

41. 여수 어라 구꽈구롸: "마라다, 마라다, 오유 와찌리부사 구 비뚜 비너너.

41. "Martha, Martha," the Lord answered, "you are worried and upset about many things,

42. Chindju chiuma chi chilyi ch'emutoloke chi chichine: Mariya yeke alondwere cha chikomire busese, n'nechi chi atakanyaibwe.

42. 찌뚜 찌우마 찌 찌뤠 쩌무도로꺼 찌 찌찌너: 마리야 여거 아루뚜워러 짜 찌고미러 부서서, 우너찌 찌 아다가냐이붜.

42. but only one thing is needed. Mary has chosen what is better, and it will not be taken away from her."

Yesu akanga e baanda baye kuema Ongo

1. Lusuku luuma, Yesu abaa emera mu chisiki chiuma. Abere era amalaa, mwanafunzi* wai muuma era kumubura: "Enawetu, utukagirisaa ekwema Ongo, ng'okwa Yowanyi nai akangirisaa ebanafunzi bai."

2. Yesu era kubabura: "Mango mwema, bacha ku mwenda mwateta: Tata, esina lyau linamenyekaa n'ebandu boshi kwa litula libuya-buya!* eBwimi bwau buikaa!

3. Wendaa watweresa ebiryo byetu bya chira lusuku.

4. Wendaa watubabalira ebibi byetu, ng'okwa n'netu twende twababalira chira mundu ola watuiririre emabi. Utaturekereraa twaimwa na chira muereko."

5. Kanji era kubabura: "Mu Mwabu, nde ola mwalungu wai angaendera kachi-kachi ka butufu anamubure: E munyaketu, unyihombaa mikati ehatu,

6. bushi naikirirwe na mwira wanyi ola wanyitambirire, si nainyire 'ekalyo ka nyingamweresa.

여수 아가까 어 바아따 바여 구어마 오꼬

1. 루수구 루우마, 여수 아바아 어머라 무 찌시기 찌우마. 아버러 어라 아마롸아, 마나푸씨* 와이 무우마 어라 구무부라: "어나워두, 우두가지리사아 어궈마 오꼬, 꼬과 요와네 나이 아가끼리사아 어바나푸씨 바이."

2. 여수 어라 구바부라: "마꼬 뭐마, 바짜 구 뭐따 마더다: 다다, 어시나 랴우 뢰나머녀가아 너바뚜 보씨 과 뢰두롸 뢰부야-부야!* 어뷔미 봐우 부이가아!

3. 워따아 와뚸러사 어비료 벼두 뱌 찌라 루수구.

4. 워따아 와두바바뢰라 어비비 벼두, 꼬과 우너두 뛰떠 롸바바뢰라 찌라 무뚜 오롸 와두이리리러 어마비. 우다두러거러라아 돠이뫄 나 찌라 무어러고."

5. 가찌 어라 구바부라: "무 뫄부, 떠 오롸 마루꾸 와이 아까어떠라 가찌-가찌 가 부두푸 아나무부러: 어 무냐거두, 우네호빠아 미가디 어하두,

6. 부씨 나이기리뤄 나 뭐라 와네 오롸 와네다삐리러, 시 나이네러 어가룐 가 네까뭐러사.

---

1. One day Jesus was praying in a certain place. When he finished, one of his disciples said to him, "Lord, teach us to pray, just as John taught his disciples."

2. He said to them, "When you pray, say: " 'Father, hallowed be your name, your kingdom come.

3. Give us each day our daily bread.

4. Forgive us our sins, for we also forgive everyone who sins against us. And lead us not into temptation.' "

5. Then he said to them, "Suppose one of you has a friend, and he goes to him at midnight and says, 'Friend, lend me three loaves of bread,

6. because a friend of mine on a journey has come to me, and I have nothing to set before him.'

7. Akaba ola uli mwa nymba angamwakula mmbu: Unyirekaa kw'elwayo mano mango, nachingire mira. Kanji Nyono n'ebana banyi twaonjire mira. Ndangachiala kwimuka mbu nyikweresaa i."

8. Yesu era kunaendekerana ateta: "Ndababisha, chiro mbu atangemuka amwrese i bushi ali mwalungu wai, angemuka anamuwe byoshi bya ahonda bushi n'ekuchanda kwai.

9. Chichine chi nababura: Mwendaa mwema Ongo bya mwahonda, iriende abawa bi. Mwendaa mwahonda bya muinyire, na Ongo anabaasa kubibona. Mwendaa mwemaala kwa Iwisi, iri Ongoende anabaasa kubibona.Mwendaa mwemaala kwa Iwisi, iri Ongoende abachungulira.

10. Ku binali, ola wemire i wende weresibwa, n'nola wahonda i wende wabona, n'nola wemaala kwa Iwisi i wende wanachungulirwa.

11. Mu Mwabu, nde mulume ola muala wai angema efi amuwe emongi areke ekumuwa efi?

12. Nesi ola muala wai angema

7. 아가바 오라 우릐 먀 네빠 아아먀구꽈 무뿌: 우녜러가아 궈꽈요 마노 마꼬, 나찌에러 미라. 가찌 뇨노 너바나 바녜 돠오찌러 미라. 따아찌아꽈 귀무가 뿌 네궈러사아 이."

8. 여수 어라 구나어떠거라나 아더다: "따바비싸, 찌로 뿌 아다어무가 아무우러서 이 부씨 아릐 먀루우 와이, 아어무가 아나무워 뵤씨 뱌 아호따 부씨 너구짜따 과이.

9. 찌찌너 찌 나바부라: 뭐따아 뭐마 오꼬 뱌 먀호따, 이리어머 아바와 비. 뭐따아 먀호따 뱌 무이녜러, 나 오꼬 아나바아사 구비보나. 뭐따아 뭐마아꽈 과 이위시, 이리 오꼬어머 아나바아사 구비보나.뭐따아 뭐마아꽈 과 뤼시, 이리 오꼬어머 아바쭈우릐라.

10. 구 비나릐, 오라 워미러 이 워떠 워러시봐, 우노꽈 와호따 이 워떠 와보나, 우노꽈 워마아꽈 과 뤼시 이 워떠 와나쭈우릐롸.

11. 무 먀부, 떠 무루머 오라 무아꽈 와이 아어마 어피 아무워 어모에 아러거 어구무와 어피?

12. 너시 오라 무아꽈 와이

7. "Then the one inside answers, 'Don't bother me. The door is already locked, and my children are with me in bed. I can't get up and give you anything.'

8. I tell you, though he will not get up and give him the bread because he is his friend, yet because of the man's boldness he will get up and give him as much as he needs.

9. "So I say to you: Ask and it will be given to you; seek and you will find; knock and the door will be opened to you.

10. For everyone who asks receives; he who seeks finds; and to him who knocks, the door will be opened.

11. "Which of you fathers, if your son asks for a fish, will give him a snake instead?

12. Or if he asks for an

ei amuwe engutu?

13. Akaba wabu mu mutula babi mungamenyerera ekweresa ebana benyu bya bilomire, chi chingatuma Tata ola utula kwa nguba alaira kwana eMuchima Mubuya-buya kwa ba bamwema u!"

E bandju b'elyika yesu mbu musimu

14. Lusuku luuma, Yesu abaa ambula echihwasi ku mundu muuma era muhondo s'eluamba l'ebandu cha chamuhubyaa katuma. Abere echi chihwasi chatenga, ka katuma kera kutagiisa kateta. Abu bandu bera kusanwa busese.

15. Bauma mubu bera kutangirisa bateta era luulu sa Yesu: "Belisebuli i mukulu-kulu w'ebihwasi i wamweresise ebuashi bw'ekwambula ebihwasi."

16. N'ebanji babaa bamutea, bera kumwema mbu aabairiraa chisomerao chiuma ch'ekulosa kwa atumwaa na Ongo.

17. Si bushi Yesu abaa ammenyerere emianyisa yabu, era kubabura: "Chira bwami bwa bungachibaanya bweine,

---

아뼈마 어이 아무워 어우두?

13. 아가바 와부 무 무두롸 바비 무뻐머녀러라 어궈러사 어바나 버뉴 뱌 비롸미러, 찌 찌뻐두마 다다 오롸 우두롸 과 우바 아롸이라 과나 어무찌마 무부야-부야 과 바 바뭐마 우!"

어 바쭈 버뼤— 여수 뿌 무시무

14. 루수구 루우마, 여수 아바아 아뿌롸 어찌화시 구 무뚜 무우마 어라 무호또 서루아빠 루어바뚜 짜 짜무후뱌아 가두마. 아버러 어찌 찌화시 짜더빠, 가 가두마 거라 구다지이사 가더다. 아부 바뚜 버라 구사놔 부서서.

15. 바우마 무부 버라 구다뼤리사 바더다 어라 루우루 사 여수: "버뼤서부뤼 이 무구루-구루 워비화시 이 와뭐러시서 어부아씨 뭐과뿌롸 어비화시."

16. 너바찌 바바아 바무더아, 버라 구뭐마 뿌 아아바이리라아 찌소머라오 찌우마 쩌구롣사 과 아두마아 나 오꽁.

17. 시 부씨 여수 아바아 아무머녀러러 어미아니에사 야부, 어라 구바부라: "찌라 봐미 봐 부빠찌바아냐 뭐이너, 구이가

---

egg, will give him a scorpion?

13. If you then, though you are evil, know how to give good gifts to your children, how much more will your Father in heaven give the Holy Spirit to those who ask him!"

14. Jesus was driving out a demon that was mute. When the demon left, the man who had been mute spoke, and the crowd was amazed.

15. But some of them said, "By Beelzebub, the prince of demons, he is driving out demons."

16. Others tested him by asking for a sign from heaven.

17. Jesus knew their thoughts and said to them: "Any kingdom divided against itself will

---

kuika bunahandukale. Akaba n'ebandu ba ngumu nguma bangabangana beine kwa beine, ei ngumu nai kuika inahandukale.

18. Akaba ebambali ba Shetanyi nabu bangalwa beine kwa beine, kute ebwami bwai bungachemanga? Natechire ebi bushi mwatechire mbu Belisebuli i wanyeresise ebuashi bw'ekwambula ebihwasi.

19. Akaba mungatetamb Nyono nambula ebihwasi mwa buashi bwa Belisebuli, benyi wenyu nabu bende bambula bi mwa buashi bwande? Bushi n'oku, beine bu bakabatonganya kw'ei mitetere yenyu.

20. Si Nyono, mwa buashi bwa Ongo mu nenjire nambula ebihwasi. Echera chi chilosise kw'eBwimi bwa Ongo bwabaikirire.

21. Mango emunyake ola wete efumo n'embenzi angalanga enyumba yai, ebikulo byai bingalangwa kubuya.

22. Si akaba unji munyake kumurenza angaika, angamuima amunyae n'ebya abaa alangalire mwa kulwa, aabe na byoshi bya amunyaaa.

부나하뚜가뻐. 아가바 너바뚜 바꾸무 꾸마 바꽈바꽈나 버이너 과 버이너, 어이 꾸무 나이 구이가 이나하뚜가뻐.

18. 아가바 어바빠뤼 바 써다니 나부 바꽈롸 버이너 과 버이너, 구더 어봐미 봐이 부꽈쩌마까? 나더찌러 어비 부씨 뫄더찌러 뿌 버뤼서부뤼 이 와녀러시서 어부아씨 붜과뿌롸 어비화시.

19. 아가바 무꽈더다뻐 뇨노 나뿌롸 어비화시 뫄 부아씨 봐 버뤼서부뤼, 버네 워뉴 나부 버떠 바뿌롸 비 뫄 부아씨 봐떠? 부씨 노구, 버이너 부 바가바도꽈냐 귀이 미더더러 여뉴.

20. 시 뇨노, 뫄 부아씨 봐 오꼬 무 너찌러 나뿌롸 어비화시. 어쩌라 찌 찌롣시서 귀뷔미 봐 오꼬 봐바이기리러.

21. 마꼬 어무냐거 오롸 워더 어푸모 너뻐씨 아꽈롸꽈 어뉴빠 야이, 어비구롣 뱌이 비꽈롸꽈 구부야.

22. 시 아가바 우찌 무냐거 구무러롸 아꽈이가, 아꽈무이마 아무냐어 너뱌 아바아 아롸꽈뤼러 뫄 구꽈, 아아버 나 뵤씨 뱌 아무냐아아.

be ruined, and a house divided against itself will fall.

18. If Satan is divided against himself, how can his kingdom stand? I say this because you claim that I drive out demons by Beelzebub.

19. Now if I drive out demons by Beelzebub, by whom do your followers drive them out? So then, they will be your judges.

20. But if I drive out demons by the finger of God, then the kingdom of God has come to you.

21. "When a strong man, fully armed, guards his own house, his possessions are safe.

22. But when someone stronger attacks and overpowers him, he takes away the armor in which the man trusted and divides up the spoils.

23. Ola utatula nanyi ali ngabo yanyi, n'nola utanyiasa kulunda ali muhandabanyi".

23. 오라 우다두롸 나네 아뤼 빠보 야네, 우노롸 우다네아사 구루따 아뤼 무하따바네".

23. "He who is not with me is against me, and he who does not gather with me, scatters.

24. Kanji Yesu era kunaendekerana ateta: "Mango echihwasi chende chatenga kwa mundu, chende charenga-renga era itatula bandu, chahonda ala chingatamukira. Chitabonyire yi, chanera chateta mmbu: "Nyingaaluka nyihube mwa mundu wanyi ola natengeraa mu.

24. 가찌 여수 어라 구나어떠거라나 아더다: "마꼬 어찌화시 쩌떠 짜더따 과 무뚜, 쩌떠 짜러따-러따 어라 이다두롸 바뚜, 짜호따 아롸 찌따다무기라. 찌다보네러 에, 짜너라 짜더다 무뿌: "네따아루가 네후버 롸 무뚜 와네 오롸 나더떠라아 무.

24. "When an evil spirit comes out of a man, it goes through arid places seeking rest and does not find it. Then it says, 'I will return to the house I left.'

25. Mwa kufulula, chanabuana ekalamo k'oyu mundu kakunganyisibwe.

25. 롸 구푸루롸, 짜나부아나 어가롸모 고유 무뚜 가구따네시붜.

25. When it arrives, it finds the house swept clean and put in order.

26. Bushi n'oku, chanera chalunga binji bihwasi birinda bya bibiire kurenza chi; mwakuba byera byengiriraa byoshi, byanabera mu. Ekalamo k'oyu mundu kanera kabia kurenza ka kabere-bere."

26. 부씨 노구, 짜너라 짜루따 비찌 비화시 비리따 뱌 비비이러 구러싸 찌; 롸구바 뼈라 뼈끼리라아 뵤씨, 뱌나버라 무. 어가롸모 고유 무뚜 가너라 가비아 구러싸 가 가버러-버러."

26. Then it goes and takes seven other spirits more wicked than itself, and they go in and live there. And the final condition of that man is worse than the first."

27. Abere Yesu era amalaa kuteta ebi byoshi, mukasi muuma mwa luamba era kuuma emurenge, era kubura Yesu: "Emukasi ola wakubutaa n'ekukonza aahanyirwe."

27. 아버러 여수 어라 아마롸아 구더다 어비 뵤씨, 무가시 무우마 롸 루아빠 어라 구우마 어무러떠, 어라 구부라 여수: "어무가시 오롸 와구부다아 너구고싸 아아하네뤄."

27. As Jesus was saying these things, a woman in the crowd called out, "Blessed is the mother who gave you birth and nursed you."

28. Yesu era kumwakula: "Ku binali, si ba bende bomvirisa echinwa cha Ongo n'ekuira kwa chihonjire bu baahanyirwe kanangana. "

28. 여수 어라 구꽈구롸: "구 비나뤼, 시 바 버더 보뻬리사 어찌놔 짜 오꼬 너구이라 과 찌호찌러 부 바아하네뤄 가나꽈나. "

28. He replied, "Blessed rather are those who hear the word of God and obey it."

Yesu abura e bandju bushi n'e chisomerane cha Yona

29. Mango e bandju babaa bera bachilunda ofu na Yesu, era kutangirisa ateta: "Mwabu mu bandju ba lwarero muli bandju babi: Mwenjire mwahonda echisomerano, si ndakabairire chi, kureka ekalorero ka murebi Yonakeine.

30. Kwa binwa bya Yona byanabaa kalorero ku besha Nyinawi, kw'ebinwa byanyi nyi Mwana w'e Mundju nabi bikanaba kalorero ku Mwabu mu bandu ba lwarero.

31. Si mwishi mwami Solomono nai! Lusuku luuma, emwami-kasi wemaa mwa chio ch'eSaba atengeraa ita ofu mwa butala kumvirisa ebinwa by'ebwenge bwai bunene. Oyu mwami-kasi akomokera kuuma nenyu mu bandju ba lwarero e lusuku lw'e buchinjibusi. Oyola i ukabatonganya, bushi ola mwomvire kwa byai anola i usitoire kurenza Solomono, n'nenyu mutenjire mwahonda kubyemerera.

32. Mango elusuku lw'ebuchinjibusi lukaika, besha Nyinawi nabu bakomokera kuuma nenyu mu bandu ba lwarero. Abola bu

여수 아부라 어 바뚜 부씨 너 찌소머라너 짜 요나

29. 마꼬 어 바뚜 바바아 버라 바찌룬따 오푸 나 여수, 어라 구다삐리사 아더다: "뫄부 무 바뚜 바 롸러로 무뤼 바뚜 바비: 뭬찌러 뫄혼따 어찌소머라노, 시 따가바이리러 찌, 구러가 어가뢰러로 가 무러비 요나거이너.

30. 과 비놔 뱌 요나 뱌나바아 가뢰러로 구 버싸 네나위, 궈비놔 뱌니 네 뫄나 워 무뚜 나비 비가나바 가뢰러로 구 뫄부 무 바뚜 바 롸러로.

31. 시 뮈씨 뫄미 소뢰모노 나이! 루수구 루우마, 어뫄미-가시 워마아 뫄 찌오 쩌사바 아더뼈라아 이다 오푸 뫄 부다롸 구뼈리사 어비놔 벼붸뻐 뫄이 부너너. 오유 뫄미-가시 아고모거라 구우마 너뉴 무 바뚜 바 롸러로 어 루수구 뤄 부찌찌부시. 오요롸 이 우가바도꺄냐, 부씨 오롸 모뼤러 과 뱌이 아노롸 이 우시도이러 구러싸 소뢰모노, 누너뉴 무더찌러 뫄호따 구벼머러라.

32. 마꼬 어루수구 뤄부찌찌부시 루가이가, 버싸 네나위 나부 바고모거라 구우마 너뉴 무 바뚜 바 롸러로. 아보롸 부 바가바도나냐 부씨 버거

29. As the crowds increased, Jesus said, "This is a wicked generation. It asks for a miraculous sign, but none will be given it except the sign of Jonah.

30. For as Jonah was a sign to the Ninevites, so also will the Son of Man be to this generation.

31. The Queen of the South will rise at the judgment with the men of this generation and condemn them; for she came from the ends of the earth to listen to Solomon's wisdom, and now one greater than Solomon is here.

32. The men of Nineveh will stand up at the judgment with this generation and condemn it; for they

bakabatonanya bushi beke bachiayaa kwa bibi byabu mango Yona abahubanganyisaa. N'noku bya mwahubanganyisibwa anola bi bisitoire kurenza bya bya Yona, n'neny mu mwanana ekubyemerera.

33. Yesu era kunaendekarana ateta: "Kutali mundu ola ungakoresa etara kanji alibishe, nesi alifunyikire n'echitonga, si lyende lyabikwa ala amanukire iri ebandu ba bengirira mwa nyumba balole kwa bulangare.

34. Eliho lyau li lichwula ng'etara ly'e mubilyi wau. Mango elibo lyau lingaba lihaalukire, ungalola kubuya. N'nau wera ungaba mwa bulanare.SI akaba eliho lya lingabia,utangalola kubuya. Alola, wera ungaba mwa musimya.

35. Umenyereraa kubuya buya akaba ebulangare bwa wachitongera butali musimya.

36. Akaba wabonyire e bulangare busira chiro n'e y'e kasimya, ekalamo kau koshi kangamoreka kw'etaralyende lyakumorekera."

바찌아야아 과 비비 뱌부 마꼬 요나 아바후바까네사아. 우노구 뱌 마후바까네시봐 아노롸 비 비시도이러 구러싸 뱌 뱌 요나, 누너네 무 뫄나나 어구벼머러라.

33. 여수 어라 구나어떠가라나 아더다: "구다찌 무뚜 오롸 우까고러사 어다라 가찌 아찌비써, 너시 아찌푸네기러 너찌도꺄, 시 쪄떠 쨔비과 아롸 아마누기러 이리 어바뚜 바 버찌리라 뫄 뉴빠 바로뤄 과 부롸꺄러.

34. 어찌호 쨔우 찌 찌쭈롸 꺼다라 뤼어 무비레 와우. 마꼬 어찌보 쨔우 찌까바 찌하아루기러, 우까로롸 구부야. 우나우 워라 우까바 뫄 부롸나러.시 아가바 어찌호 쨔 찌까비아,우다까로롸 구부야. 아로롸, 워라 우까바 뫄 무시먀.

35. 우머녀러라아 구부야 부야 아가바 어부롸꺄러 봐 와찌도꺼라 부다찌 무시먀.

36. 아가바 와보네러 어 부롸꺄러 부시라 찌로 너 여 가시먀, 어가꺄모 가우 고씨 가까모러가 궈다라쪄너 쨔구모러거라."

repented at the preaching of Jonah, and now one greater than Jonah is here.

33. "No one lights a lamp and puts it in a place where it will be hidden, or under a bowl. Instead he puts it on its stand, so that those who come in may see the light.

34. Your eye is the lamp of your body. When your eyes are good, your whole body also is full of light. But when they are bad, your body also is full of darkness.

35. See to it, then, that the light within you is not darkness.

36. Therefore, if your whole body is full of light, and no part of it dark, it will be completely lighted, as when the light of a lamp shines on you."

Buanya bw'e bafarisayo

37. Abere Yesu era amalaa kuhambala, Mufarisayo muuma era kumubura mbu abahaa kulya mwa mwai. Yesu aikire mu, era kwikala ofu n'ebilyo.

38. Oyu Mufarisayo alolire kwa Yesu alya atoire n'e mino kukulikana n'emyanya y'e Bafarisayo, era kusanwa.

39. Yesu era kumubura: "Ulolaa kwa mutula Mwabu mu Baarisayo,* mwende mwalangasa emuongo w'engumbu n'emuongo w'embare busira kulonga endanda, n'noku mwa michima yenyu mutula mwehwire ebukumbatanya n'ebukali.

40. Mabu mutula mbuta! Muteshi kw'ola wabumbaa emuongo i wabumbaa n'endanda?

41. Mwendaa mwawa ebakene kw'ebya mwete mw'esi ngumbu n'nesi mbare, n'nechi chi chingauma ebyenyu byoshi byakoma eamuhondo sa Ongo.

42. Si mulyi banya, mu Bafarisayo, bushi mwende mwana echiuma ch'e kumi ch'ehoo n'esheya, nesi cha chisi nyanyi, n'noku mwende mwanana ekuira emabuya, kanji

부아냐 붜 바파리사요

37. 아버러 여수 어라 아마롸아 구하빠롸, 무파리사요 무우마 어라 구무부라 뿌 아바하아 구꺄 뫄 마이. 여수 아이기러 무, 어라 귀가롸 오푸 너비료.

38. 오유 무파리사요 아롤뤼러 과 여수 아꺄 아도이러 너 미노 구구뤼가나 너먀냐 여 바파리사요, 어라 구사놔.

39. 여수 어라 구무부라: "우론롸아 과 무두라 뫄부 무 바아리사요,* 뭐떠 뫄롸까사 어무오꼬 워뿌뿌 너무오꼬 워빠러 부시라 구론꺄 어따따, 우노구 뫄 미찌마 여뉴 무두롸 뭐휘러 어부구빠다냐 너부가뤼.

40. 마부 무두롸 뿌다! 무더씨 교롸 와부빠아 어무오꼬 이 와부빠아 너따따?

41. 뭐따아 뫄와 어바거너 귀뱌 뭐더 뭐시 우뿌 우너시 빠러, 우너찌 찌 찌까우마 어벼뉴 뵤씨 뱌고마 어아무호또 사 오꼬.

42. 시 무레 바냐, 무 바파리사요, 부씨 뭐더 뫄나 어찌우마 쩌 구미 쩌호오 너써야, 너시 짜 찌시 냐네, 우노구 뭐더 뫄나나 어구이라 어마부야, 가찌 무다두사

37. When Jesus had finished speaking, a Pharisee invited him to eat with him; so he went in and reclined at the table.

38. But the Pharisee, noticing that Jesus did not first wash before the meal, was surprised.

39. Then the Lord said to him, "Now then, you Pharisees clean the outside of the cup and dish, but inside you are full of greed and wickedness.

40. You foolish people! Did not the one who made the outside make the inside also?

41. But give what is inside the dish to the poor, and everything will be clean for you.

42. "Woe to you Pharisees, because you give God a tenth of your mint, rue and all other kinds of garden herbs, but you neglect justice

mutatusa n'emasimano nga ma ma Ongo. Ekwana echiuma ch'e kumi kutabiire, si kukomire mwende mwaira emabuya n'ekuata emasimano nga ma ma Ongo.

너마시마노 꽈 마 마 오꼬. 어과나 어찌우마 쩌 구미 구다비이러, 시 구고미러 뭐떠 꽈이라 어마부야 너구아다 어마시마노 꽈 마 마 오꼬.

and the love of God. You should have practiced the latter without leaving the former undone.

43. Muli banya, mu Bafarisayo,* bushi musiira kwikala kwa bifumbi by'era muhondo mwa bihaala,* kanji musiira ekukesibwa ala bandu batula baluire.

43. 무삐 바냐, 무 바파리사요,* 부씨 무시이라 귀가꽈 과 비푸뻬 벼라 무호또 꽈 비하아꽈,* 가찌 무시이라 어구거시봐 아꽈 바뚜 바두꽈 바루이러.

43. "Woe to you Pharisees, because you love the most important seats in the synagogues and greetings in the marketplaces.

44. Muli banya, bushi mutula kuuma 'eshinda sa sitaseneke ku, n'ebandu bende balibatanga si batanammenyire ebubi buli musi."

44. 무삐 바냐, 부씨 무두꽈 구우마 어씨따 사 시다서너거 구, 너바뚜 버너 바삐바다꽈 시 바다나무머네러 어부비 부삐 무시."

44. "Woe to you, because you are like unmarked graves, which men walk over without knowing it."

Buanya bw'e bandju be miaso 부아냐 붸 바뚜 버 미아소

45. Muuma mwa bakangirisi b'eMwaso* era kumwakula: "E Waliya, mwa kuteta kuli ng'oku, n'netu watukambire."

45. 무우마 꽈 바가기리시 버꽈소* 어라 구꽈구꽈: "어 와삐야, 꽈 구더다 구삐 꼬구, 우너두 와두가뻬러."

45. One of the experts in the law answered him, "Teacher, when you say these things, you insult us also."

46. Yesu era kumubura: "N'nenyu muli banya, mu bakangirisi b'eMwaso,* bushi mwende mwesa ebandu emisio era isitoire, si mubeine mutanaba nga mwaereresa mwaira ku mutoke wenyu muuma mubaase.

46. 여수 어라 구무부라: "우너뉴 무삐 바냐, 무 바가삐리시 버꽈소,* 부씨 뭐떠 뭐사 어바뚜 어미시오 어라 이시도이러, 시 무버이너 무다나바 꽈 꽈어러러사 꽈이라 구 무도거 워뉴 무우마 무바아서.

46. Jesus replied, "And you experts in the law, woe to you, because you load people down with burdens they can hardly carry, and you yourselves will not lift one finger to help them.

47. Muli banya, bushi mwende mwaimbira eshinda s'ebarebi na beho bu betaa bu.

47. 무삐 바냐, 부씨 뭐떠 꽈이뻬라 어씨따 서바러비 나 버호 부 버다아 부.

47. "Woe to you, because you build tombs for the prophets, and it was your forefathers

who killed them.

48. Ku kutea mbu n'nenyu muneshi bya beho bairaa kanji unabyemerere, bushi beke bu betaa ebarebi, n'nenyu mu mwenjire mwaimbira eshinda sabu.

49. Bushi n'oku, Ongo mwa bwenge bwai atetaa: Nyikabatumira e barebi n'e baanda, si bakea bauma mubu, bakalibussa n'ebanji.

50. Echera chi chikatuma mu bandju ba lwarero mwachinjibusibwa, bushi n'ekwita ebarebi kutengera ekubumbwa kw'ebutala.

51. Kutengera kwa mikira ya Abeli kuikira kw'era ya Sakariyad i wanafiraa mwa chibua ch'eLuhu lwa Ongo.* Ku binali, ndababisha, emikira yabu bandu boshi ikaba kw'etwe lyenyu mu bandu ba lwarero.

52. Muli banya, mu bakangirisi b'eMwaso,* bushi mwaminyirire ebanji bandu enjira era ingatuma bamenyerera Ongo kanangana. Mwabu mutahonda kuya mw'ei njira, kanji mwende

48. 구 구더아 뿌 우너뉴 무너씨 뱌 버호 바이라아 가찌 우나벼머러러, 부씨 버거 부 버다아 어바러비, 우너뉴 무 뭐찌러 뫄이삐라 어씨따 사부.

49. 부씨 노구, 오꼬 뫄 붜머 봐이 아더다아: 네가바두미라 어 바러비 너 바아따, 시 바거아 바우마 무부, 바가삐부싸 너바찌.

50. 어쩌라 찌 찌가두마 무 바쭈 바 꽈러로 뫄찌찌부시봐, 부씨 너귀다 어바러비 구더꺼라 어구부꽈 궈부다꽈.

51. 구더꺼라 과 미기라 야 아버리 구이기라 궈라 야 사가리야두 이 와나피라아 뫄 찌부아 쩌루후 꽈 오꼬.* 구 비나찌, 따바비싸, 어미기라 야부 바뚜 보씨 이가바 궈뛰 려뉴 무 바뚜 바 꽈러로.

52. 무삐 바냐, 무 바가끼리시 버뫄소,* 부씨 뫄미네리러 어바찌 바뚜 어찌라 어라 이까두마 바머녀러라 오꼬 가나꽈나. 뫄부 무다호따 구야 뭐이 찌라, 가찌 뭐떠 뫄따 바

48. So you testify that you approve of what your forefathers did; they killed the prophets, and you build their tombs.

49. Because of this, God in his wisdom said, 'I will send them prophets and apostles, some of whom they will kill and others they will persecute.'

50. Therefore this generation will be held responsible for the blood of all the prophets that has been shed since the beginning of the world,

51. from the blood of Abel to the blood of Zechariah, who was killed between the altar and the sanctuary. Yes, I tell you, this generation will be held responsible for it all.

52. "Woe to you experts in the law, because you have taken away the key to knowledge. You yourselves have not entered, and you have

mwanga ba bahonda baye mui."

바호따 바여 무이."

hindered those who were entering."

53. Chasinjire, Yesu era kuuluka mw'ei nyumba. Kutengera olu lusuku, ebakangirisi b'eMwaso n'eBafarisayo* bera kutangirisa bamukunza busese n'ekuhonda bamukule mu inji myasi inene.

53. 짜시찌러, 여수 어라 구우루가 뭐이 뉴빠. 구더꺼라 오루 루수구, 어바가끼리시 버꽈소 너바파리사요* 버라 구다끼리사 바무구싸 부서서 너구호따 바무구꺼 무 이찌 먀시 이너너.

53. When Jesus left there, the Pharisees and the teachers of the law began to oppose him fiercely and to besiege him with questions,

54. Babaa bamutea bomve chinwa chibi cha chingatenga mwa bunu.

54. 바바아 바무더아 보뻐 찌놔 찌비 짜 찌까더아 먀 부누.

54. waiting to catch him in something he might say.

Luka Chikono 12
Yesu anga e bandju e butebanyi

1. Mw'echi chihangi, bandju banene busese babaa achilunjire aola. Bera kutangirisa bafundeeresanya bushi n'e bwingi bwabu. Era kubura e baanda bai tanga: "Mutendaa mwachibika mwa myasi y'e butebanyi bw'e kubisha - bisha bw'eBafarisayo.*

루가 찌고노 12
여수 아빠 어 바뉴 어 부더바니

1. 뭐찌 찌하끼, 바뉴 바너너 부서서 바바아 아찌루찌러 아오꽈. 버라 구다끼리사 바푸떠어러사냐 부씨 너 뷔끼 봐부. 어라 구부라 어 바아따 바이 다따: "무더따아 꽈찌비가 꽈 먀시 여 부더바니 뷔 구비싸 - 비싸 뷔바파리사요.*

Luke Chapter 12[NIV]

1. Meanwhile, when a crowd of many thousands had gathered, so that they were trampling on one another, Jesus began to speak first to his disciples, saying: "Be on your guard against the yeast of the Pharisees, which is hypocrisy.

2. Kutali cha chibishirwe cha chitakabihukale. Kanji kutali cha bubisho-bisho cha chitakamenyeke.

2. 구다끼 짜 찌비씨뤄 짜 찌다가비후가꺼. 가찌 구다끼 짜 부비쏘-비쏘 짜 찌다가머녀거.

2. There is nothing concealed that will not be disclosed, or hidden that will not be made

3. Bushi n'oku, choshi cha mukaba mwaahambalaa mwa musimya, chikumvibwa changanama. N'na cha mwatetaa mwa byooo mwa chumba, chikatetwa mu chira chisiki.

4. Yesu era kunaendekerana ateta: "Nababura mu muli bea banyi: Mutendaa mwobaa bala bangeta emubilyi n'nera nyuma s'echi btangachiala kuira chinji. 5. Nahonda e kubalosa nde i mwendaa mwobaa: Mwendaa mwobaa Ongo i unganyaa e kalamo k'e mundju kanji i wete e buashi bw'ekuuma emundu mwa muliro w'esuku n'e mango. Kanji nababwirire, oyola i mwendaa mwobaa.

6. Si mwishi kwa bitera - mbua bitano, butea bubiri bu byende byanaulwa! Si chiro na chiuma cha chende chebilyirwa mubi era muhondo sa Ongo.

7. Mutachanyaa, bushi murenzise bitera-mbua binene era muhondo sa Ongo.Kanji Mumenyereraa kwa n'e bwingi w'e mviri senyu soshi sa kw'echwe, Ongo atula abwishi."

3. 부씨 노구, 쪼씨 짜 무가바 뫄아하빠롸아 뫄 무시먀, 찌구삐봐 짜꺼나마. 우나 짜 뫄더다아 뫄 뵤오오 뫄 쭈빠, 찌가더돠 무 찌라 찌시기.

4. 여수 어라 구나어떠거라나 아더다: "나바부라 무 무뤼 버아 바네: 무더따아 모봐아 바라 바꺼다 어무비뤠 우너라 뉴마 서찌 부다꺼찌아뢰 구이라 찌씨. 5. 나호따 어 구바로사 떠 이 뭐따아 모봐아: 뭐따아 모봐아 오꼬 이 우꺼냐아 어 가뢰모 거 무쭈 가찌 이 워더 어 부아씨 뷔구우마 어무뚜 뫄 무뤼로 워수구 너 마꼬. 가찌 나바뷔리러, 오요롸 이 뭐따아 모봐아.

6. 시 뮈씨 과 비더라 - 뿌아 비다노, 부더아 부비리 부 벼너 뱌나우롸! 시 찌로 나 찌우마 짜 쩌떠 쩌비뤠롸 무비 어라 무호또 사 오꼬.

7. 무다쨔냐아, 부씨 무러씨서 비더라-뿌아 비너너 어라 무호또 사 오꼬.가찌 무머녀러라아 과 너 뷔삐 워 삐리 서뉴 소씨 사 궈줘, 오꼬 아두롸 아뷔씨."

3. What you have said in the dark will be heard in the daylight, and what you have whispered in the ear in the inner rooms will be proclaimed from the roofs.

4. "I tell you, my friends, do not be afraid of those who kill the body and after that can do no more. 5. But I will show you whom you should fear: Fear him who, after the killing of the body, has power to throw you into hell. Yes, I tell you, fear him.

6. Are not five sparrows sold for two pennies? Yet not one of them is forgotten by God.

7. Indeed, the very hairs of your head are all numbered. Don't be afraid; you are worth more than many sparrows.

8. Kanji Yesu era kubabura: "Chira mundju ola unganyemerera era muhondo s'ebandu Nyono nyi Mwana w'eMundu, n'nanyi nyikamwemerera era muhondo s'e bamalaika ba Ongo.

9. Ola unganyinana era muhondo s'ebandu, akananyibwa nanyi era muhondo s'e ndonyi sa Ongo.

10. Na chira mundju ola ukateta chinwa chibi ku Nyono nyi Mwana w'e Mundju, akababalyirwa. Si ola ukakena eMuchima Mubuya-buya, atakababalirwe.

11. Mango banbabeka mwa bihaala* mutongane, nesi era muhondo s'ebasusu, nesi era m uhondo s'ebakulu-kulu, mutababalaa mbu kuteku mungatongana, nesi chi mungateta.

12. Mutachitamyaa, bushi eMuchima Mubuya-buya angabakanga chi mungateamw'ebi bihangi."

E muanyi bushi n'e muare w'e mbuta

13. Mundu muuma mwa luamba era kubura Yesu: "E Waliya, unyibwiriraa munyaketu mbu tuabaa emwandu ola tata

8. 가찌 여수 어라 구바부라: "찌라 무뚜 오롸 우꺼녀머러라 어라 무호또 서바뚜 뇨노 네 꽈나 워무뚜, 우나네 네가뭐머러라 어라 무호또 서 바마라이가 바 오꼬.

9. 오라 우꺼네나나 어라 무호또 서바뚜, 아가나네봐 나네 어라 무호또 서 또네 사 오꼬.

10. 나 찌라 무뚜 오롸 우가더다 찌놔 찌비 구 뇨노 네 꽈나 워 무뚜, 아가바바롊롸. 시 오롸 우가거나 어무찌마 무부야-부야, 아다가바바찓뤄.

11. 마꼬 바빠버가 뫄 비하아꽈* 무도꺼너, 너시 어라 무호또 서바수수, 너시 어라 무 우호또 서바구룹-구룹, 무다바바롸아 뿌 구더구 무꺼도꺼나, 너시 찌 무꺼더다.

12. 무다찌다먀아, 부씨 어무찌마 무부야-부야 아꺼바가꺼 찌 무꺼더아뭐비 비하꼐."

어 무아네 부씨 너 무아러 워 뿌닛

13. 무뚜 무우마 뫄 루아빠 어라 구부라 여수: "어 와찌야, 우네뷔리라아 무냐거두 뿌 두아바아 어꽈뚜 오롸 다다

8. "I tell you, whoever acknowledges me before men, the Son of Man will also acknowledge him before the angels of God.

9. But he who disowns me before men will be disowned before the angels of God.

10. And everyone who speaks a word against the Son of Man will be forgiven, but anyone who blasphemes against the Holy Spirit will not be forgiven.

11. "When you are brought before synagogues, rulers and authorities, do not worry about how you will defend yourselves or what you will say,

12. for the Holy Spirit will teach you at that time what you should say."

13. Someone in the crowd said to him, "Teacher, tell my brother to divide the inheritance

aturekeraa."

14. Yesu era kumwakula: "E washi! Nde i wanyiiraa muishi wa manja w'ekubaabira ebyenyu?"

15. Era kubabura boshi: "MUmenyaa, munachilange kwa kusima ebuare, bushi ekalamo k'emundu katatengera mwa bwingi bw'ebikulo byai chiro angaba muare."

16. Chasinjire, Yesu era kubaishira ono muanyi: "Kwabaa muare muuma ola mmahwa mai mesaa myaka inene.

17. Era kutangirisa aanyisa n'ekuchibusa: "Kute nyingaira kuno ndachete ala nyingabika emyaka yanyi?

18. Era kuteta mmbu: Bacha ku nyingaira: Nyingangula enguli sanyi n'ekwinga sa sinenene, na mw'esi mu nyingere nabika emupunge n'einji myaka yanyi.

19. Chasind, nyingerre nachibura: Nyono, nera nete bikulo binen bya bikamala myaka inene, nyingere natamuka, nyilye, nyimwe, nyinalaukale!

아두러거라아."

14. 여수 어라 구꽈구꽈: "어 와씨! 떠 이 와네이라아 무이씨 와 마짜 워구바아비라 어벼뉴?"

15. 어라 구바부라 보씨: "무머냐아, 무나찌꽈어 과 구시마 어부아러, 부씨 어가꽈모 거무뚜 가다더어라 뫄 뷔이 뷔비구로 뱌이 찌로 아꽈바 무아러."

16. 짜시찌러, 여수 어라 구바이씨라 오노 무아니: "과바아 무아러 무우마 오꽈 무마화 마이 머사아 먀가 이너너.

17. 어라 구다삐리사 아아네사 너구찌부사: "구더 네아이라 구노 따쩌더 아꽈 네꽈비가 어먀가 야네?

18. 어라 구더다 무뿌: 바짜 구 네꽈이라: 네꽈우꽈 어우뤼 사네 너귀꽈 사 시너너너, 나 뭐시 무 네어러 나비가 어무푸어 너이찌 먀가 야네.

19. 짜시뚜, 네어루러 나찌부라: 뇨노, 너라 너더 비구로 비너 뱌 비가마꽈 먀가 이너너, 네어러 나다무가, 네뗘, 네뭐, 네나꽈우가꺼!

with me."

14. Jesus replied, "Man, who appointed me a judge or an arbiter between you?"

15. Then he said to them, "Watch out! Be on your guard against all kinds of greed; a man's life does not consist in the abundance of his possessions."

16. And he told them this parable: "The ground of a certain rich man produced a good crop.

17. He thought to himself, 'What shall I do? I have no place to store my crops.'

18. "Then he said, 'This is what I'll do. I will tear down my barns and build bigger ones, and there I will store all my grain and my goods.

19. And I'll say to myself, "You have plenty of good things laid up for many years. Take life easy; eat, drink and be merry." '

20. Si Ongo era kumubura: Uli mbuta woyu, uteshi kwa kalamo kau kakwemibwamw'obuno butufu? Ebi wakolaa byoshi bikere byaba byande?

21. Ebyera bi byende byaikira ola wende wahonda kuchiira muare n'ebuare bwai bu buteshibwe mwa meho ma Ongo."

Chemire kulangalyira Ongo

22. Yesu era kubura ebanafunzi bai: "Echera chi chatuma nahonda ekubabura mbu mutendaa mwachanya mwa kalamo kenyu mbu chi mungalya, nesi chi mungembala.

23. Mumenyereraa kw'e kalamo katula Karenzise ebiryo, n'emubiri achwula arenzise enjimba.

24. Mulolaa kwa bikoma bitula: bikona bitula: Btainga, bitanashebula, bitatusa ala bingabika kalyo, si Ongoende alisa bi. Mwabu mutula murenzise ei milonge!

25. Nande mu Mwabu, mwa kuchanya kwai, ola ungaata ebuashi bw'e kubika e koro

20. 시 오꼬 어라 구무부라: 우뾔 뿌다 오유, 우더씨 과 가꽈모 가우 가귀미봐모부노 부두푸? 어비 와고롸아 뵤씨 비거러 뱌바 뱌떠?

21. 어벼라 비 벼떠 뱌이기라 오꽈 워떠 와호따 구찌이라 무아러 너부아러 봐이 부 부더씨붜 뫄 머호 마 오꼬."

쩌미러 구꽈꽈뤠띱 오꼬

22. 여수 어라 구부라 어바나푸씨 바이: "어쩌라 찌 짜두마 나호따 어구바부라 뿌 무더따아 뫄짜냐 뫄 가꽈모 거뉴 뿌 찌 무꽈꺄, 너시 찌 무꺼빠라.

23. 무머녀러라아 궈 가꽈모 가두꽈 가러씨서 어비료, 너무비리 아쭈꽈 아러씨서 어찌빠.

24. 무뢰롸아 과 비고마 비두꽈: 비고나 비두꽈: 부다이꽈, 비다나써부꽈, 비다두사 아꽈 비꽈비가 가룐, 시 오꼬어떠 아쬐사 비. 뫄부 무두꽈 무러씨서 어이 미뢰꺼!

25. 나떠 무 뫄부, 뫄 구짜냐 과이, 오꽈 우꽈아다 어부아씨 붜 구비가 어 고로 쬐우마 과

20. "But God said to him, 'You fool! This very night your life will be demanded from you. Then who will get what you have prepared for yourself?'

21. "This is how it will be with anyone who stores up things for himself but is not rich toward God."

22. Then Jesus said to his disciples: "Therefore I tell you, do not worry about your life, what you will eat; or about your body, what you will wear.

23. Life is more than food, and the body more than clothes.

24. Consider the ravens: They do not sow or reap, they have no storeroom or barn; yet God feeds them. And how much more valuable you are than birds!

25. Who of you by worrying can add a single hour to his life?

liuma kwa kalamo kai? 가라모 가이?

26. Akaba mutangaaata ebuashi bw'e kuira lyiuma kwa kalamo kai? Akaba mutangaata e buashi bw'ekuira n'ehy'ekandu hieke, chi chingatuma mwachanya kwa binji?

26. 아가바 무다빠아아다 어부아씨 붜 구이라 레우마 과 가라모 가이? 아가바 무다빠아다 어 부아씨 붜구이라 너혀가뿌 히어거, 찌 찌빠두마 뫄짜냐 과 비찌?

26. Since you cannot do this very little thing, why do you worry about the rest?

27. Mulolaa kwa bwaso nabu butula: Butakola, butachiirira na njimba; si nababura kwa Solomono atembalaa luchimba lukomire nga chiro na lwaso luuma, chiro angaba mbu aataa etunda.

27. 무로롸아 과 봐소 나부 부두롸: 부다고롸, 부다찌이리라 나 찌빠; 시 나바부라 과 소로모노 아더빠롸아 루찌빠 루고미러 빠 찌로 나 롸소 루우마, 찌로 아빠바 뿌 아아다아 어두따.

27. "Consider how the lilies grow. They do not labor or spin. Yet I tell you, not even Solomon in all his splendor was dressed like one of these.

28. N'akaba Ongo angembasa ebichi by'omwa musitu bya bingaba u lwarero na mishangya biumwe mwa mulir, kute atangabembasa eba hakuina bulangalire?

28. 나가바 오꼬 아꺼빠사 어비찌 뷔오뫄 무시두 뱌 비빠바 우 롸러로 나 미싸꺄 비우뭐 뫄 무릐루, 구더 아다빠버빠사 어바 하구이나 부롸빠릐러?

28. If that is how God clothes the grass of the field, which is here today, and tomorrow is thrown into the fire, how much more will he clothe you, O you of little faith!

29. N'nenyu mutendaa mwekala mwachanya mwa kuhonda cha mungalya n'necha mungamwa.

29. 우너뉴 무더따아 뭐가롸 뫄짜냐 뫄 구호따 짜 무빠랴 우너짜 무빠뫄.

29. And do not set your heart on what you will eat or drink; do not worry about it.

30. Ba batatula beshi Ongo mw'obuno butala bu bende bahonda bacha, si Mwabu mubeke, Eho achwula eshi kwa mutusa bwera bw'ebi.

30. 바 바다두롸 버씨 오꼬 모부노 부다롸 부 버더 바호따 바짜, 시 뫄부 무버거, 어호 아쭈롸 어씨 과 무두사 붜라 뷔비.

30. For the pagan world runs after all such things, and your Father knows that you need them.

31. Mwendaa mwahonda tanga eBwami bwai, chasinda mungende mweresibwa ebi binji."

31. 뭐따아 뫄호따 다빠 어봐미 봐이, 짜시따 무꺼더 뭐러시봐 어비 비찌."

31. But seek his kingdom, and these things will be given to you as well.

32. "Mutobaaa mu muli luamba lueke, bushi Eho asimaa e kuberesa e buare bw'omwa Bwami bwai.

33. Muusaa bya mwete, muase 'ebakene. Ehao sa sitakakunguwe si mwendaa mwachiirira, kanji kwa nguba kui mwendaa mwachibikira ebikulo bya bitakawe. Okola kweke kutangaika mwisi, n'ekaembe katangaesha bi.

34. Mumenyereraa kw'ala bikulo bya mundu biri w'emuchima waiende anaba."

Kufuka kwa Yesu
35. "Mwa kulinjira cha chingabaikira, emikoba y'e njimba senyu s'e mulimo indaa yekala iminyirwe, n'etumore twenyu twendaa twekala twakorera.

36. Kanji mwendaa mwaba nga baanda ba balinjira enawabu ola watenga kwa buya, bushi mango angaika anabarangire kwa lwisi, unao-unao banamuchungulira.

37. Baahanyirwe e baanda b'enawabu angaika bachiri balanga. Ku binali, nababwirire kwa akembala enjimba

---

32. "무도바아아 무 무뤼 루아빠 루어거, 부씨 어호 아시마아 어 구버러사 어 부아러 부요마 봐미 봐이.

33. 무우사아 뱌 뭐더, 무아서 어바거너. 어하오 사 시다가구꾸워 시 뭐따아 꽈찌이리라, 가찌 과 꾸바 구이 뭐따아 꽈찌비기라 어비구뢰 뱌 비다가워. 오고꽈 궈거 구다빠이가 뮈시, 너가어뻐 가다빠어싸 비.

34. 무머녀러라아 과꽈 비구뢰 뱌 무뚜 비리 워무찌마 와이어떠 아나바."

구푸가 과 여수
35. "뫄 구뤼찌라 짜 찌빠바이기라, 어미고바 여 찌빠 서뉴 서 무뤼모 이따아 여가꽈 이미내뤄, 너두모러 뛰뉴 뛰따아 뛰가꽈 돠고러라.

36. 가찌 뭐따아 뫄바 빠 바아따 바 바뤼찌라 어나와부 오꽈 와더빠 과 부야, 부씨 마꾸 아빠이가 아나바라삐러 과 뤼시, 우나오-우나오 바나무쭈꾸뤼라.

37. 바아하니뤄 어 바아따 버나와부 아빠이가 바찌리 바꽈빠. 구 비나뤼, 나바뷔리러 과 아거빠꽈 어찌빠 서무뤼모

---

32. "Do not be afraid, little flock, for your Father has been pleased to give you the kingdom.

33. Sell your possessions and give to the poor. Provide purses for yourselves that will not wear out, a treasure in heaven that will not be exhausted, where no thief comes near and no moth destroys.

34. For where your treasure is, there your heart will be also.

35. "Be dressed ready for service and keep your lamps burning,

36. like men waiting for their master to return from a wedding banquet, so that when he comes and knocks they can immediately open the door for him.

37. It will be good for those servants whose master finds them watching when he

s'emulimo abawe ebiryo.

아바워 어비료.

comes. I tell you the truth, he will dress himself to serve, will have them recline at the table and will come and wait on them.

38. Baahanyirwe ebaanda b'enawabu angaika kachi-kachi ka butufu, nesi bwalinga kucha banachiri balanga."

38. 바아하네뤄 어바아따 버나와부 아까이가 가찌-가찌 가 부두푸, 너시 봐리까 구짜 바나찌리 바라까."

38. It will be good for those servants whose master finds them ready, even if he comes in the second or third watch of the night.

39. "Si mUmenyaa kw'akaba en'enyumba angamenyire e chihangi cha mwisi angaika, atangarekire enyumba yai ipomolwe n'e besi.

39. "시 무머냐아 과가바 어너뉴빠 아까머네러 어 찌하이 짜 뮈시 아까이가, 아다까러기러 어뉴빠 야이 이포모뤄 너 버시.

39. But understand this: If the owner of the house had known at what hour the thief was coming, he would not have let his house be broken into.

40. N'nenyu mwendaa mwachilanga, bushi mwa chihangi cha mukaba muteshi mu Nyono nyi Mwana w'e Mundju nyikabaha."

40. 우너뉴 뭐따아 뫄찌라까, 부씨 뫄 찌하이 짜 무가바 무더씨 무 뇨노 네 뫄나 워 무뚜 네가바하."

40. You also must be ready, because the Son of Man will come at an hour when you do not expect him."

41. Petero ku kwera kubusa Yesu: "Enawechwu, oyu muanyi wera kuisha, tubano tu anerekere nesi erekere ebandu boshi?"

41. 퍼더로 구 궈라 구부사 여수: "어나워쭈, 오유 무아네 워라 구이싸, 두바노 두 아너러거러 너시 어러거러 어바뚜 보씨?"

41. Peter asked, "Lord, are you telling this parable to us, or to everyone?"

42. Na Yesu era kumwakula: "Nde muanda ungaba ulangalirwe n'enawabu ola Wabalamire, aate n'ebwenge, ola ungaina kutaba mukulu-kulu wa balikabu abawe

42. 나 여수 어라 구뫄구라: "떠 무아따 우까바 우라까리뤄 너나와부 오라 와바라미러, 아아더 너붸어, 오라 우까이나 구다바 무구루-구루 와 바리가부 아바워 너비료 어

42. The Lord answered, "Who then is the faithful and wise manager, whom the master puts in charge of his servants to give them their food

n'ebiryo e chihangi asimire?

찌하삐 아시미러?

allowance at the proper time?

43. Aahanyirwe oyu muanda, bushi enawabu mwa kubalamuka akamubuana achiri akola bacha.

43. 아아하니뤄 오유 무아따, 부씨 어나와부 똬 구바쫘무가 아가무부아나 아찌리 아고똬 바짜.

43. It will be good for that servant whom the master finds doing so when he returns.

44. Ku binali, nababura kw'enawabu akamuira mukulu-ku w'ekwemangira ebikulo bya byoshi.

44. 구 비나삐, 나바부라 꿔나와부 아가무이라 무구루루-구 워꿔마삐라 어비구로 뱌 뵤씨.

44. I tell you the truth, he will put him in charge of all his possessions.

45. Si akaba oyu muanda angatangirisa ateta mwa muchima wai mmbu: 'Enawetu erisise mwa angatangirisa atela mwa muchima wai mmbu: 'Enawetu erisise mwa lubalamo, ateshi n'ebya naira,' n'ekutangirisa apunda ebanji baanda, ebalume n'ebakasi, n'ekutangirisa alya n'ekumwa n'e kutamira

45. 시 아가바 오유 무아따 아빠다삐리사 아더다 똬 무찌마 와이 무뿌: 어나워두 똬 아빠다삐리사 아더똬 똬 무찌마 와이 무뿌: 어나워두 어리시서 똬 루바쫘모, 아더씨 너뱌 나이라, 너구다삐리사 아푸따 어바찌 바아따, 어바루머 너바가시, 너구다삐리사 아꺄 너구똬 너 구다미라

45. But suppose the servant says to himself, 'My master is taking a long time in coming,' and he then begins to beat the menservants and maidservants and to eat and drink and get drunk.

46. enawabu akafuluka elusuku lwa atamulanga n'echihangi cha ateshi. Akamulosa kwa kasibu, kanji akamuanja nga muuma mwa ba batangalangalirwa.

46. 어나와부 아가푸루가 어루수구 똬 아다무쫘빠 너찌하삐 짜 아더씨. 아가무로사 과 가시부, 가찌 아가무아짜 똬 무우마 똬 바 바다빠쫘빠찌롸.

46. The master of that servant will come on a day when he does not expect him and at an hour he is not aware of. He will cut him to pieces and assign him a place with the unbelievers.

47. Emuanda ungaba wishi e kuhonda kw'e nawabu, atachikunganyise, nesi atairire ku, akahutwa tuchi tunene."

47. 어무아따 우빠바 위씨 어 구호따 꿔 나와부, 아다찌구빠니세, 너시 아다이리러 구, 아가후똬 두찌 두너너."

47. "That servant who knows his master's will and does not get ready or does not do what his master wants will be beaten with many blows.

48. "i ola ungaba uteshi ekuhonda kw'enawabu, akaira bya bingatuma ahutwa, akahutwa kueke. Ola weresiwaa binene, akemibwa na binene. N'nola wabikisibwaa binene, akabusibwa binene busese."

E kanangana kenda kareta e malyikanuko

49. Kanji Yesu era kubura ebanafunzi bai: "Nabahire kuuma emuliro w'ebuchinjibusi bw'ebandu mwa butala, kanji nyingasimire era aangirisa akorera.

50. Kuli bubatiso bwa malibuko bwa binyemire nyibone bushi n'obu buchinjibusi, kanji nyisiterwe kuika mango bukanyiikira.

51. Mwishi mbu bolo bu nabahire kwana mwa butala? Naanga, nababura kwa malikano mu narechire.

52. Kutengera lwarero, mu nyumba nguma mukaba malikano ma bandu batano, bahatu lunda na babiri lunda bushi nanyi.

48. "이 오꽈 우빠바 우더씨 어구호따 궈나와부, 아가이라 뱌 비빠두마 아후돠, 아가후돠 구어거. 오꽈 워러시와아 비너너, 아거미봐 나 비너너. 우노꽈 와비기시봐아 비너너, 아가부시봐 비너너 부서서."

어 가나빠낍 거따 가러다 어 마레—높겔

49. 가끼 여수 어라 구부라 어바나푸씨 바이: "나바히러 구우마 어무뢰로 워부찌띠부시 봐바뚜 마 부다꽈, 가끼 네빠시미러 어라 아아삐리사 아고러라.

50. 구뢰 부바디소 봐 마뢰부고 봐 비녀미러 네보너 부씨 노부 부찌띠부시, 가끼 네시더뤄 구이가 마꾜 부가네이기라.

51. 뮈씨 뿌 보로 부 나바히러 과나 마 부다꽈? 나아빠, 나바부라 과 마뢰가노 무 나러찌러.

52. 구더어라 꽈러로, 무 뉴빠 우마 무가바 마뢰가노 마 바뚜 바다노, 바하두 룬따 나 바비리 룬따 부씨 나니.

48. But the one who does not know and does things deserving punishment will be beaten with few blows. From everyone who has been given much, much will be demanded; and from the one who has been entrusted with much, much more will be asked.

49. "I have come to bring fire on the earth, and how I wish it were already kindled!

50. But I have a baptism to undergo, and how distressed I am until it is completed!

51. Do you think I came to bring peace on earth? No, I tell you, but division.

52. From now on there will be five in one family divided against each other, three against two and two against three.

53. Emulume n'emuala batakomvane, emukasi n'emwali batakomvane, emukasi n'emwasana.

53. 어무루머 너무아롸 바다고뻐너, 어무가시 너뫄뀌 바다고뻐너, 어무가시 너뫄사나.

53. They will be divided, father against son and son against father, mother against daughter and daughter against mother, mother-in-law against daughter-in-law and daughter-in-law against mother-in-law."

54. Kanji Yesu abaa enjire abura eluamba lw'ebandu: "Mango mwende mwalola elumbumbu lwatenga era esuba lyende lyasokera muno chio chetu, unao-unao mwende mwateta mmbu: 'Emvula yesire.' Kanangana, yende yanatoa.

54. 가찌 여수 아바아 어찌러 아부라 어루아빠 뤄ㅣ바뚜: "마오 뮈떠 마롤롸 어루뿌뿌 롸더꽈 어라 어수바 펴러 꺄소거라 무노 찌오 쩌두, 우나오-우나오 뮈떠 마더다 무뿌: 어뿌롸 여시러. 가나꺄나, 여떠 야나도아.

54. He said to the crowd: "When you see a cloud rising in the west, immediately you say, 'It's going to rain,' and it does.

55. Mutula bateebanyi! Mutula mwishi ebianyiro by'echitaka n'enguba, si kute mutangamenyerera kuana chine chianyiro muli mu?"

5.5 무두롸 바더어바니! 무두롸 뮈씨 어비아니로 벼찌다가 너꾸바, 시 구더 무다꺄머녀러라 구아나 찌너 찌아니로 무뀌 무?"

55. And when the south wind blows, you say, 'It's going to be hot,' and it is.

56. Emu batebanyi, mumenyire e huhe lye chiuo ne nguba kute kubilyi kasi mwende mwaba muteshi kwa bilyi?

56. 어무 바더바니, 무머니러 어 후허 려 찌우오 너 꾸바 구더 구비례 가시 뮈떠 뫄바 무더씨 과 비례?

56. Hypocrites! You know how to interpret the appearance of the earth and the sky. How is it that you don't know how to interpret this present time?

57. "Chi chingatuma nenyu mubeine mutamenyerera ekuira cha chiri chibuya?

57. "찌 찌꺄두마 너뉴 무버이너 무다머녀러라 어구이라 쨔 찌리 찌부야?

57. "Why don't you judge for yourselves what is right?

58. Mango ungaba waya kutongana n'emurenda watu era mw'emukulu-kulu, uira emisi yau umalane nai mwa njira angesha kukuisa era muhondo s'emususu, n'emususu akwane era mw'emusula, n'emusula akuume mwa mulisi.

59. Nakubura: Utangatenga mu kuika mango ukanaba wanyire elutea lusinda - sinda.

Luka Chikono 13

1. Mw'echi chihangi, bandu bauma baikiraa Yesu. Bera kumuanyikisisa kwa PIlato echisaa Bakalilaya bauma mwa Luhu lwa Ongo.

2. Yesu era kubabussa: "Mwaanyisise bu abu Bakalilaya bu babaa bakosi b'emabi kurenza ebanji Bakalilya bushi bu babonaa elufu luli ng'olu?

3. Naanga. Nababura, ku muboshi mukanafa bacha akaba utarekire ebii byenyu n'ekualukira Ongo;

---

58. 마꼬 우빠바 와야 구도빠나 너무러따 와두 어라 뭐무구루-구루, 우이라 어미시 야우 우마빠너 나이 봐 띠라 아뻐싸 구구이사 어라 무호또 서무수수, 너무수수 아과너 어라 뭐무수롸, 너무수롸 아구우머 봐 무뤼시.

59. 나구부라: 우다빠더빠 무 구이가 마꼬 우가나바 와네러 어루더아 루시따 - 시따.

루가 찌고노 13

1. 뭐찌 찌하삐, 바뚜 바우마 바이기라아 여수. 버라 구무아네기시사 과 피꽈도 어찌사아 바가삐꽈야 바우마 봐 루후 롸 오꼬.

2. 여수 어라 구바부싸: "봐아네시서 부 아부 바가삐꽈야 부 바바아 바고시 버마비 구러싸 어바찌 바가삐꽈 부씨 부 바보나아 어루푸 루뤼 꼬루?

3. 나아빠. 나바부라, 구 무보씨 무가나파 바짜 아가바 우다러기러 어비이 벼뉴 너구아루기라 오꼬;

---

58. As you are going with your adversary to the magistrate, try hard to be reconciled to him on the way, or he may drag you off to the judge, and the judge turn you over to the officer, and the officer throw you into prison.

59. I tell you, you will not get out until you have paid the last penny."

Luke Chapter 13[NIV]

1. Now there were some present at that time who told Jesus about the Galileans whose blood Pilate had mixed with their sacrifices.

2. Jesus answered, "Do you think that these Galileans were worse sinners than all the other Galileans because they suffered this way?

3. I tell you, no! But unless you repent, you too will all perish.

4. 'Kanji mukengeraa ba banji bandu ekumi na munane ba bafaa mwa musi w'eSilowamu mango elusito lwabasuukiraa. Mwaayisise mbu abola bu babaa bakosi b'emabi kurenza besha Yerusalemu boshi?

5. Naanga. Nababura, n'nenu muboshi ku mukanafa kwa bafaa akaba mutangareka ebii byenyu n'ekualukira Ongo."

E muanyi w'e muchi mbusira bifuma

6. Yesu era kuisha ono unji muanyi: "Mundu muuma aataa muchi wai wa bifuma ola wabaa uingirwe mw'ehwa lyai. Lusuku luuma, era kuya kuhondera kw'efima, si atabonaa ku chiro na kandu.

7. Bushi n'oku, era kubura emundu wai w'emulimo: 'Ulolaa, myaka ehatu ene nende naika kuhondera ebifuma kw'ono muchi, si ndabona ku kandu.

8. Ishaa u! Chi chingatuma atamisa ebutaka buha? Nai era kumwakula: 'Waliya, uhuba kureka u ono mwaka, nyingaendekerana nashekerera u.

4. 가찌 무거꺼라아 바 바찌 바뚜 어구미 나 무나너 바 바파아 뫄 무시 워시뢰와무 마꼬 어루시도 롸바수우기라아. 뫄아에시서 뿌 아보롸 부 바바아 바고시 버마비 구러싸 버싸 여루사꺼무 보씨?

5. 나아빠. 나바부라, 우너누 무보씨 구 무가나파 과 바파아 아가바 무다빠러가 어비이 벼뉴 너구아루기라 오꼬."

어 무아네 워 무찌 뿌습띱 비푸마

6. 여수 어라 구이싸 오노 우찌 무아네: "무뚜 무우마 아아다아 무찌 와이 와 비푸마 오롸 와바아 우이삐뤄 뭐화 랴이. 루수구 루우마, 어라 구야 구호떠라 궈피마, 시 아다보나아 구 찌로 나 가뚜.

7. 부씨 노구, 어라 구부라 어무뚜 와이 워무삐모: 우뢰롸아, 먀가 어하두 어너 너떠 나이가 구호떠라 어비푸마 교노 무찌, 시 따보나 구 가뚜.

8. 이싸아 우! 찌 찌빠두마 아다미사 어부다가 부하? 나이 어라 구무구롸: 와삐야, 우후바아 구러가 우 오노 뫄가, 네빠어떠거라나 나써거러라 우.

4. Or those eighteen who died when the tower in Siloam fell on them--do you think they were more guilty than all the others living in Jerusalem?

5. I tell you, no! But unless you repent, you too will all perish."

6. Then he told this parable: "A man had a fig tree, planted in his vineyard, and he went to look for fruit on it, but did not find any.

7. So he said to the man who took care of the vineyard, 'For three years now I've been coming to look for fruit on this fig tree and haven't found any. Cut it down! Why should it use up the soil?'

8. " 'Sir,' the man replied, 'leave it alone for one more year, and I'll dig around it and fertilize it.

9. Kuli mango anganana bifuma mwa suku sa seshire, na atanyire bifuma, wanaisha u."

Yesu alamya e mukasi uchionyire e moongo e lw'e sabato

10. Lusuku luuma lwa Sabato,* Yesu abaa akangirisa mu chihaala chiuma ch'eBayuta.*

11. Omola, mwabaa muli mukasi muuma ola chihwasi charemasaa ku myaka ekumi na munane. Abaa era anachionyire, abaa atanganachiala kwinamuka chiro na hicha.

12. Yesu amulolire ku, era kumwamaaha, abahe.

13. Era kumubika kw'emino, nai kuna kwinamuka. Era kumubura: "Mama, walamisibwe e burema bwau. "nao-unao, era kutangilyisa atonga Ongo.

14. Si emukulu-kulu w'e chihaala* era kusibuka, bushi Yesu alamyaa emundu elusuku lw'eSabato.* Era kutangirisa abura ba babaa bali mu: "Suku ndatu si situla s'ekukolibwa mu. Mw'esi mu mwendaa mwaika kulamisibwa, si ata elusuku lw'eSabato."

---

9. 구삐 마꼬 아빠나나 비푸마 뫄 수구 사 서씨러, 나 아다니러 비푸마, 와나이싸 우."

여수 아라맸 어 무가시 우찌오녜랸 어 모오꼬 어 뭐 사바도

10. 루수구 루우마 롸 사바도,* 여수 아바아 아가삐리사 무 찌하아롸 찌우마 쩌바유다.*

11. 오모롸, 뫄바아 무삐 무가시 무우마 오롸 찌화시 짜러마사아 구 먀가 어구미 나 무나너. 아바아 어라 아나찌오네러, 아바아 아다빠나찌아롸 귀나무가 찌로 나 히짜.

12. 여수 아무롣삐러 구, 어라 구뫄마아하, 아바허.

13. 어라 구무비가 궈미노, 나이 구나 귀나무가. 어라 구무부라: 마마, 와롸미시붜 어 부러마 봐우. "나오-우나오, 어라 구다삐례사 아도와 오꼬.

14. 시 어무구룪-구룪 워 찌하아롸* 어라 구시부가, 부씨 여수 아롸먀아 어무뚜 어룪수구 뭐사바도.* 어라 구다삐리사 아부라 바 바바아 바삐 무: "수구 따두 시 시두롸 서구고삐봐 무. 뭐시 무 뭐따아 마이가 구롸미시봐, 시 아다 어룪수구 뭐사바도."

---

9. If it bears fruit next year, fine! If not, then cut it down.' "

10. On a Sabbath Jesus was teaching in one of the synagogues,

11. and a woman was there who had been crippled by a spirit for eighteen years. She was bent over and could not straighten up at all.

12. When Jesus saw her, he called her forward and said to her, "Woman, you are set free from your infirmity."

13. Then he put his hands on her, and immediately she straightened up and praised God.

14. Indignant because Jesus had healed on the Sabbath, the synagogue ruler said to the people, "There are six days for work. So come and be healed on those days, not on the Sabbath."

15. Yesu era kumwakula: "Mutula batebanyi, nde mu Mwabu ola utangakeresa engaafu yai nesi alise endokomo yai anaimwese elusuku lw'eSabato?

16. Ono mukasi ali w'omwa luhu lwa Aburahamu, na i Shetanyi aminaa ku myaka ekumi na munane. Si elusuku lw'eSabato lu abaa emire kuboolwa mw'amu malibujo!'"

17. abere era atetaa echi, ebarenda bai boshi bera kufa honyi. Si ebanji bandu boshi beke baoeraa ebisomerano byoshi bya byairwaa nai.

Yesu ahuhanya e Bwami bwa Ongo

18. Yesu era kuteta: "Kute kw'e Bwami bwa Ongo butula buhuhire? Na chiye chi nyingalingamanya nabu?
19. Butula buhuhire nga kafuma kaeke ka mundu ahuiraa mw'ehwa lyai. Abere kakula, kera kuhuba muchi, n'emilongge yera kunaimba ematu mabu kwa ndabi sau."

15. 여수 어라 구꽈구꽈: "무두꽈 바더바네, 떠 무 꽈부 오꽈 우다까거러사 어까아푸 야이 너시 아쮜서 어또고모 야이 아나이뭐서 어루수구 뭐사바도?

16. 오노 무가시 아쮜 요꽈 루후 꽈 아부라하무, 나 이 써다네 아미나아 구 먀가 어구미 나 무나너. 시 어루수구 뭐사바도 루 아바아 어미러 구보오꽈 꽈무 마쮜부조!"

17. 아버러 어라 아더다아 어찌, 어바러따 바이 보씨 버라 구파 호네. 시 어바찌 바뚜 보씨 버거 바오어라아 어비소머라노 뵤씨 뱌 뱌이뢰아 나이.

여수 아후하냐 어 봐미 봐 오꼬

18. 여수 어라 구더다: "구더 궈 봐미 봐 오꼬 부두꽈 부후히러? 나 찌여 찌 네까쮜까마냐 나부?
19. 부두꽈 부후히러 까 가푸마 가어거 가 무뚜 아후이라아 뭐화 랴이. 아버러 가구꽈, 거라 구후바 무찌, 너미론우거 여라 구나이빠 어마두 마부 과 따비 사우."

15. The Lord answered him, "You hypocrites! Doesn't each of you on the Sabbath untie his ox or donkey from the stall and lead it out to give it water?

16. Then should not this woman, a daughter of Abraham, whom Satan has kept bound for eighteen long years, be set free on the Sabbath day from what bound her?"

17. When he said this, all his opponents were humiliated, but the people were delighted with all the wonderful things he was doing.

18. Then Jesus asked, "What is the kingdom of God like? What shall I compare it to?

19. It is like a mustard seed, which a man took and planted in his garden. It grew and became a tree, and the birds of the air perched in its branches."

20. Kanji era kubusa: "Chiye chi nyingalingamanya n'eBwami bwo Ongo?

21. Butula nga bufumu bwa bwende bwaimbya eshano y'emikati, bwa mukasi angahoonganya na bitonga bihatu by'eshano y'emikati bunaiimbye yoshi."

E lwisi lw'eke lw'e Bwami bwa Ongo

22. Mango Yesu abaa anachiri aendekerana n'eluendo kw'ekwirukira eYerusalemu, endaa arenga mwa misi n'okwa misi akangirisa ebandu.

23. Mundu muuma era kumubusa: "Enawetu, baeke beine bu bakananunulibwa?" Yesu era kumwakula:

24. 'Muiraa emisi mwingirire mwa Bwami bwa Ongo chiro enjira y'ekuya mubu mwingirire mwa Bwami bwa Ongo chiro enjira y'e kuya mubu ingakeya-keya, bushi nababura kwa banene bakahonda ekwingirira mubu, si batakaale.

25. Kukaika chihangi cha en'enyumba akaba achingire elwisi n'nenyu mukaba mwimenzi era butala. Chasinda, mukatangirisa mwemaala kwa lwisi n'ekutela: 'Waliya, achingire elwisi n'nenyu

20. 가찌 어라 구부사: "찌여 찌 네까찌까마냐 너봐미 보 오꼬?

21. 부두롸 까 부푸무 봐 붸머 봐이뺘 어싸노 여미가디, 봐 무가시 아까호오까냐 나 비도까 비하두 벼싸노 여미가디 부나이이뼈 요씨."

어 뤼습 뤼개 뤄 봐미 봐 오꼬

22. 마꼬 여수 아바아 아나찌리 아어떠거라나 너뤄어또 궈귀루기라 어여루사뼈무, 어따아 아러까 봐 미시 노과 미시 아가찌리사 어바뚜.

23. 무뚜 무우마 어라 구무부사: "어나워두, 바어거 버이너 부 바가나누누찌봐?" 여수 어라 구뫄구롸:

24. 무이라아 어미시 뮈찌리러 봐 봐미 봐 오꼬 찌로 어찌라 여구야 무부 뮈찌리러 봐 봐미 봐 오꼬 찌로 어찌라 여 구야 무부 이까거야-거야, 부씨 나바부라 과 바너너 바가호따 어귀찌리라 무부, 시 바다가아뼈.

25. 구가이가 찌하찌 짜 어너뉴뺘 아가바 아찌찌러 어뤼시 은너뉴 무가바 뮈머씨 어라 부다롸. 짜시따, 무가다뼈리사 뭐마아롸 과 뤼시 너구더롸: 와뢰야, 아찌찌러 어뤼시 은너뉴 무가바 뮈머씨

20. Again he asked, "What shall I compare the kingdom of God to?

21. It is like yeast that a woman took and mixed into a large amount of flour until it worked all through the dough."

22. Then Jesus went through the towns and villages, teaching as he made his way to Jerusalem.

23. Someone asked him, "Lord, are only a few people going to be saved?" He said to them,

24. "Make every effort to enter through the narrow door, because many, I tell you, will try to enter and will not be able to.

25. Once the owner of the house gets up and closes the door, you will stand outside knocking and pleading, 'Sir, open the door for us.' "But he will answer, 'I don't know

mukaba mwimenzi era butala. Chasinda, mukatangirisa mwemaala kwa lwisi n'ekuteta: 'Waliya, utuchunguliraa!' Mwa kubakula akateta: Ndeshi muli besha ngae.'

26. N'nenyu mukatangirisa mwateta: 'Era! Si twalyaa n'ekumwa al'auma nau, kanji wendda wakangirisisa mwa nama s'emisi yetu!'

27. Nai mwa kubakula akateta: 'Munyitengeraa aola, bushi ndeshi muli besha ngae, mu baosi b'emabi."

28. Kanji Yesu era kuteta: "Si mukalangusa ku Aburahamu yeke, na Isaka, na Yakobo, n'ebarebi boshi mwa Bwami bwa Ongo. Si mwabu mutakengirire mu. Bushi n'oku, mukalira n'ekukuutanga emeno.

29. Ebandu bakatengera era suba lyende lyaulukira, n'nera lyende lyasokera, n'nera luulu s'echio, n'nera masina sachi. Abola beke bu bakalya mwa Bwami bwa Ongo.

30. Mmenyereraa kwa kuli babere-bere ba bakahuba basinda - sinda, kwanaba na basindad-sinda ba bakahuba babere-bere."

어라 부다꽈. 짜시따, 무가다삐리사 뭐마아꽈 과 뛰시 너구더다: '와꾀야, 우두쭈꾸꾀리라아!' 꽈 구바구꽈 아가더다: 떠씨 무꾀 버싸 까어.

26. 우너뉴 무가다삐리사 꽈더다: 어라! 시 돠랴아 너구꽈 아꽈우마 나우, 가찌 워뚜다 와가삐리시사 꽈 나마 서미시 여두!

27. 나이 꽈 구바구꽈 아가더다: 무네더꺼라아 아오꽈, 부씨 떠씨 무꾀 버싸 까어, 무 바오시 버마비."

28. 가찌 여수 어라 구더다: "시 무가꽈꾸사 구 아부라하무 여거, 나 이사가, 나 야고보, 너바러비 보씨 꽈 봐미 봐 오꼬. 시 꽈부 무다거삐리러 무. 부씨 노구, 무가꾀라 너구구우다까 어머노.

29. 어바뚜 바가더꺼라 어라 수바 려너 꺄우루끼라, 우너라 려너 꺄소거라, 우너라 루우루 서찌오, 우너라 마시나 사찌. 아보꽈 버거 부 바가꺄 꽈 봐미 봐 오꼬.

30. 무머녀러라아 과 구꾀 바버러-버러 바 바가후바 바시따 - 시따, 과나바 나 바시따두-시따 바 바가후바 바버러-버러."

you or where you come from.'

26. "Then you will say, 'We ate and drank with you, and you taught in our streets.'

27. "But he will reply, 'I don't know you or where you come from. Away from me, all you evildoers!'

28. "There will be weeping there, and gnashing of teeth, when you see Abraham, Isaac and Jacob and all the prophets in the kingdom of God, but you yourselves thrown out.

29. People will come from east and west and north and south, and will take their places at the feast in the kingdom of God.

30. Indeed there are those who are last who will be first, and first who will be last."

Yesu alyira bushi Yerusalemu   여수 아레띱 부씨 여루사뿌물

31. Mw'echi chihangi, Bafarisayo* bauma bera kuchifunda ofu na Yesu. Bera kumubura: "Utengaa anolal uchiendere, bushi Heroti ahonda akwete."

31. 뭐찌 찌하삐, 바파리사요* 바우마 버라 구찌푸따 오푸 나 여수. 버라 구무부라: "우더따아 아노롸루 우쩌떠러, 부씨 허로디 아호따 아궈더."

31. At that time some Pharisees came to Jesus and said to him, "Leave this place and go somewhere else. Herod wants to kill you."

32. Nai era kubabura: "Muendaa kunyibwirira oyu mutereri mbu lwarero na mishangya nyingembula ebihwasi nyilamye n'ebalwala, n'elusuku lwa kahutu nyingaba namalire bya nahonda nyiire.

32. 나이 어라 구바부라: "무어따아 구네뷔리라 오유 무더러리 뿌 롸러로 나 미싸땨 네떠뿌롸 어비화시 네롸며 너바롸롸, 너루수구 롸 가후두 네따바 나마찌러 뱌 나호따 네이러.

32. He replied, "Go tell that fox, 'I will drive out demons and heal people today and tomorrow, and on the third day I will reach my goal.'

33. Binyemire lwarero, na mishangya, na lishisho nyibe mwa luendo, bushi chitangaalikana emurebi uli nga Nyono kufira mu unji musi kureka e Yeussalemu."

33. 비녀미러 롸러로, 나 미싸땨, 나 찌씨쏘 네버 롸 루어또, 부씨 찌다따아뤼가나 어무러비 우뤼 따 뇨노 구피라 무 우찌 무시 구러가 어 여우싸뿌무."

33. In any case, I must keep going today and tomorrow and the next day--for surely no prophet can die outside Jerusalem!

34. Mango Yesu abaa alinga kuika mwa musi w'eYerusaleu, era kuteta: "E mu besha Yerusalemu! Mwabu mu mwende mwahuta ebarebi emakoi ba mwende mwatumirwa chasia mubete! Kanga ku nende nahonda kubakomberera ng'okwa ngoko yende yakomberera ebana bai, si mutahonda!

34. 마꼬 여수 아바아 아뤼따 구이가 롸 무시 워여루사뿌우, 어라 구더다: "어 무 버싸 여루사뿌우! 롸부 무 뭐떠 롸후다 어바러비 어마고이 바 뭐떠 롸두미롸 짜시아 무버더! 가따 구 너떠 나호따 구바고뻐러라 오과 오고 여떠 야고뻐러라 어바나 바이, 시 무다호따!

34. "O Jerusalem, Jerusalem, you who kill the prophets and stone those sent to you, how often I have longed to gather your children together, as a hen gathers her chicks under her wings, but you were not willing!

35. Mulolaa, Ongo abarekerere al'auma n'emusi wenyu. Ndababisha, mutakachinyilole ku chiro na hicha, kuikira mango mukaba mwera mwateta mmbu: 'Aahanyirwe ola wabahire mw'esina ly'Enawechwu.

35. 무르꽈아, 오꼬 아바러거러러 아꽈우마 너무시 워뉴. 따바비싸, 무다가찌네로꺼 구 찌로 나 히짜, 구이기라 마꼬 무가바 뭐라 마더다 무뿌: '아아하니뤄 오꽈 와바히러 뭐시나 뤼어나워쭉.

35. Look, your house is left to you desolate. I tell you, you will not see me again until you say, 'Blessed is he who comes in the name of the Lord.'"

Luka Chikono 14
E mundju wa lumwa mwa bula

루가 찌고노 14
어 무뿌 와 룸뫄 뫄 부꽈

Luke Chapter 14[NIV]

1. Lusuku luuma lwa Sabato, Yesu ayaa kulya mwa nyumba ya mukulu-kulu muuma w'eBafarisayo.* Omola mwabaa muli na banji Bafarisayo n'ebakangirisi b'eMwaso* ba babaa bamuloeresa.

1. 루수구 루우마 꽈 사바도, 여수 아야아 구꺄 뫄 뉴빠 야 무구루-구루 무우마 워바파리사요.* 오모꽈 뫄바아 무뤼 나 바찌 바파리사요 너바가끼리시 버뫄소* 바 바바아 바무로어러사.

1. One Sabbath, when Jesus went to eat in the house of a prominent Pharisee, he was being carefully watched.

2. Kanji mwabaa muli mulume muumba era muhondo sa Yesu ola wabaa uimbire emubiri woshi.

2. 가찌 뫄바아 무뤼 무루머 무우빠 어라 무호또 사 여수 오꽈 와바아 우이삐러 어무비리 오씨.

2. There in front of him was a man suffering from dropsy.

3. Yesu era kubusa ebakangirisi b'eMwaso n'eBafarisayo: "eMwaso wa Musa tula emererre ekulamya elusuku lw'eSabato* nsi naana?"

3. 여수 어라 구부사 어바가끼리시 버뫄소 너바파리사요: "어뫄소 와 무사 두꽈 어머러루러 어구꽈먀 어루수구 뤄사바도* 씨 나아나?"

3. Jesus asked the Pharisees and experts in the law, "Is it lawful to heal on the Sabbath or not?"

4. Chiro bakamwakula. Yesu era kuuma kw'oyu mulwala, kunakumulamya. Era kumubura mbu aendaa.

4. 찌로 바가뫄구꽈. 여수 어라 구우마 교유 무꽈꽈, 구나구무꽈먀. 어라 구무부라 뿌 아어따아.

4. But they remained silent. So taking hold of the man, he healed him and sent him away.

5. Kanji Yesu era kubabusa: "Nde mu Mwabu ola muala wai, nesi engaafu yai ingaba yatoere mwa chitomu aine kulibichira kuikula mu chiro lungaba lusuku lwa Sabato?"

6. Kanji chiro bakaala kumwakula kw'echi.

E bisiki byera muhondo

7. Mango Yesu alolaa kwa ba balalikwaa benjire bachihoa eifumbi by'era muhondo, era kubabura ene myasi:

8. 'Mango mundu murebe angaba akulalikire kwa buya, utendaa wachihoa echifumbi ch'era muhondo, kuta kuika unji mundu ola utnjirwe ku woyu ola walalikwaa.

9. Ungachichingira ola wabalalikaa era akubura: 'Sheeraa oyu mundu.' Aola, wera ungasinda kwa chifumbi ch'era nyuma n'e honyi.

10. Si mango ungaba walalikirwe, uchihoaa echifumbi ch'era nyuma. Aola u ola wakulalikaa angakubwirira: 'E mwira wanyi, chifundaa ene muhondo.' Echera chingatuma ba walya nabu boshi bakweresa etunda.

---

5. 가찌 여수 어라 구바부사: "떠 무 뫄부 오롸 무아롸 와이, 너시 어꽈아푸 야이 이꽈바 야도어러 뫄 찌도무 아이너 구뤼비찌라 구이구롸 무 찌로 루꽈바 루수구 롸 사바도?"

6. 가찌 찌로 바가아롸 구뫄구롸 궈찌.

어 비시기 벼라 무호또

7. 마꼬 여수 아롣롸아 과 바 바롸뤼과아 버찌러 바찌호아 어이푸삐 벼라 무호또, 어라 구바부라 어너 먀시:

8. 마꼬 무뚜 무러버 아꽈바 아구롸뤼기러 과 부야, 우더따아 와찌호아 어찌푸삐 쩌라 무호또, 구다 구이가 우찌 무뚜 오롸 우두찌뤄 구 오유 오롸 와롸뤼과아.

9. 우꽈찌찌삐라 오롸 와바롸뤼가아 어라 아구부라: 써어라아 오유 무뚜. 아오롸, 워라 우꽈시따 과 찌푸삐 쩌라 뉴마 너 호네.

10. 시 마꼬 우꽈바 와롸뤼기뤄, 우찌호아아 어찌푸삐 쩌라 뉴마. 아오롸 우 오롸 와구롸뤼가아 아꽈구뷔리라: 어 뮈라 와네, 찌푸따아 어너 무호또. 어쩌라 찌꽈두마 바 와퍄 나부 보씨 바궈러사 어두따.

---

5. Then he asked them, "If one of you has a son or an ox that falls into a well on the Sabbath day, will you not immediately pull him out?"

6. And they had nothing to say.

7. When he noticed how the guests picked the places of honor at the table, he told them this parable:

8. "When someone invites you to a wedding feast, do not take the place of honor, for a person more distinguished than you may have been invited.

9. If so, the host who invited both of you will come and say to you, 'Give this man your seat.' Then, humiliated, you will have to take the least important place.

10. But when you are invited, take the lowest place, so that when your host comes, he will say to you, 'Friend, move up to a better place.' Then you will be honored in the presence of all your

11. Umenyereraa kw'ola wende wacherusa akakenyibwa, n'nola wende wachirembya, akatunjibwa."

12. Yesu era kubura n'ola wamulalikaa: "Mango ungaba watekire biryo,utendaa walalika ba banali basere bau, nesi ba banali baare mwa balung bau, bushi wishi kwa abola b bangakulalika banakualulire cha waberesaa.

13. Akaba ungaba watekire biryo, ulalikaa e bakene, n'e bakonyi, n'e birema, n'e bauta.

14. Ukaira bacha, ukaahanyirwa na Ongo, bushi abola beke batangabona cha bangakualulira. N'nau Ongo akakualulira mango ba bairaa emabuya bakomoka."

Lyinye lyinene

15. Muuma mwa ba babaa balyaomvire bacha, era kuteta: "Aahanyirwe ola ukalya biryo mwa Bwami bwa Ongo!"

16. Yesu era kumwakula mw'ono muanyi: "Mundu muuma atekaa biryo binene,

---

11. 우머녀러라아 교롸 워머 와쩌루사 아가거네봐, 우노롸 워머 와찌러뺘, 아가두띠봐."

12. 여수 어라 구부라 노롸 와무롸뤼가아: "마꼬 우까바 와더기러 비료,우더따아 와롸뤼가 바 바나뤼 바서러 바우, 너시 바 바나뤼 바아러 콰 바루우 바우, 부씨 위씨 과 아보롸 부 바까구롸뤼가 바나구아루뤼러 짜 와버러사아.

13. 아가바 우까바 와더기러 비료, 우롸뤼가아 어 바거너, 너 바고네, 너 비러마, 너 바우다.

14. 우가이라 바짜, 우가아하네롸 나 오꼬, 부씨 아보롸 버거 바다까보나 짜 바까구아루뤼라. 우나우 오꼬 아가구아루뤼라 마꼬 바 바이라아 어마부야 바고모가."

뗴넷 뗴날날

15. 무우마 퐈 바 바바아 바럇오쁴러 바짜, 어라 구더다: "아아하네뤄 오롸 우가꺄 비료 퐈 봐미 봐 오꼬!"

16. 여수 어라 구뫄구롸 모노 무아니: "무뚜 무우마 아더가아 비료 비너너, 어라 구롸뤼가 나

---

fellow guests.

11. For everyone who exalts himself will be humbled, and he who humbles himself will be exalted."

12. Then Jesus said to his host, "When you give a luncheon or dinner, do not invite your friends, your brothers or relatives, or your rich neighbors; if you do, they may invite you back and so you will be repaid.

13. But when you give a banquet, invite the poor, the crippled, the lame, the blind,

14. and you will be blessed. Although they cannot repay you, you will be repaid at the resurrection of the righteous."

15. When one of those at the table with him heard this, he said to Jesus, "Blessed is the man who will eat at the feast in the kingdom of God."

16. Jesus replied: "A certain man was preparing a great

era kulalika na bandju banene. 바쭈 바너너.

17. Mango ebiryo byabaa byera byayaa, era kutuma emuanda wai mbu aendaa kumubwirira ba babaa balalikirwe bacha: 'Mwiraa mwabaha, bushi ebiryo byaire.'

18. Si chira muuma mubu era kuchilairra ekuika. Bera kuchiremba balosa bya byatumaa bataika: la mubere - bere era kumubura: 'Naulire ehwa, binyemire nyiye kulitangula. Nakwemire unyibabalire.'

19. N'eunji era kutata: 'Naulire mbanzi ekumi s'ekunyichikira, near naya kuhona akaba singakola. Nakwemire unyibabalire.'

20. N'eunji era kuteta: 'Nyichiri mwa buya. Bushi n'oku, ndangaala kubaba.'

21. Oyu muanda mwa kufuluka, era kuanyikisisa enawabu ebi byoshi. Bushi n'oku, ebute bwera kusimba oyu en'enyumba. Era kubura emuanda wai: 'Endaa fuba mwamusi woshi ubinge ebakene, n'ebakonyi, n'ebirema, n'ebauta.'

17. 마꼬 어비료 뱌바아 벼라 뱌야아, 어라 구두마 어무아따 와이 뿌 아어따아 구무뷔리라 바 바바아 바쫘뤼기뤄 바짜: 뮈라아 뫄바하, 부씨 어비료 뱌이러.

18. 시 찌라 무우마 무부 어라 구찌쫘이라 어구이가. 버라 구찌러빠 바로사 뱌 뱌두마아 바다이가: 롸 무버러 - 버러 어라 구무부라: 나우쀠러 어화, 비녀미러 내여 구쀠다우쫘. 나꿔미러 우네바바쀠러.

19. 너우씨 어라 구다다: 나우쀠러 빠씨 어구미 서구네찌기라, 너라 나야 구호나 아가바 시꼬쫘. 나꿔미러 우네바바쀠러.

20. 너우씨 어라 구더다: 네찌리 뫄 부야. 부씨 노구, 따꼬아쫘 구바바.

21. 오유 무아따 뫄 구푸루가, 어라 구아네기시사 어나와부 어비 뵤씨. 부씨 노구, 어부더 뭐라 구시빠 오유 어너뉴빠. 어라 구부라 어무아따 와이: 어따아 푸바 뫄무시 오씨 우비꼬 어바거너, 너바고네, 너비러마, 너바우다.

17. At the time of the banquet he sent his servant to tell those who had been invited, 'Come, for everything is now ready.'

18. "But they all alike began to make excuses. The first said, 'I have just bought a field, and I must go and see it. Please excuse me.'

19. "Another said, 'I have just bought five yoke of oxen, and I'm on my way to try them out. Please excuse me.'

20. "Still another said, 'I just got married, so I can't come.'

21. "The servant came back and reported this to his master. Then the owner of the house became angry and ordered his servant, 'Go out quickly into the streets and alleys of the town and bring in the poor, the crippled, the blind and the lame.'

22. Abere kwarenga chihangi, oyu muanda era kuteta: 'Waliya,kwa wabaa wahonda kwairirwe, si ebandu batanasa kwihula mwa nyumba.'

23. Chasinjire, en'enyumba era kubura oyu muanda: 'Endaa ur?nge mu chira njira n'na mwa mahwa unanjirire ebandu babahe enyumba yanyi ihule.

24. Ndababisha, chiro na muuma mwa ba balalikwaa ola ukalya kwa biryo byanyi natekaa."

E kukulyikira Yesu kuta kubofu

25. Yesu abaa akulikirwe na bandu banene angahonda kunyikulikira,

26. anyisimaa kurenza eshe na nyina, na mukai, n'ebana bai, na banyakabu, na baliwabu. Kanji anyisimaa kurenza ekalamo kai yeine. Atairire bacha, atangaba mwanafunzi* wanyi.

27. Ola utangemerera kweka emusalaba w'emalibuko mai bushi nanyi ananyimise, atangaba mwanafunzi* wanyi.

28. Kute k'ola wahonda kuimba nyumba inene mu Mwabu angaira? Mumenyereraa kwa angekala tanga, ahole e bikulo

---

22. 아버러 과러까 찌하삐, 오유 무아따 어라 구더다: 와쯰야,과 와바아 와호따 과이리뤄, 시 어바뚜 바다나사 귀후꽈 뫄 뉴빠.

23. 짜시찌러, 어너뉴빠 어라 구부라 오유 무아따: 어따아 우루?꺼 무 찌라 띠라 우나 뫄 마화 우나찌리러 어바뚜 바바허 어뉴빠 야네 이후뿨.

24. 따바비싸, 찌로 나 무우마 뫄 바 바롸쯰과아 오라 우가꺄 과 비료 뱌네 나더가아."

어 구구쩨굿띱 여수 구다 구보푸

25. 여수 아바아 아구쯰기뤄 나 바뚜 바너너 아까호따 구네구쮜기라,

26. 아네시마아 구러싸 어써 나 네나, 나 무가이, 너바나 바이, 나 바냐가부, 나 바쯰와부. 가찌 아네시마아 구러싸 어가꽈모 가이 여이너. 아다이리러 바짜, 아다까바 뫄나푸씨* 와네.

27. 오롸 우다꺼머러라 궈가 어무사꽈바 워마쯰부고 마이 부씨 나네 아나네미서, 아다까바 뫄나푸씨* 와네.

28. 구더 고꽈 와호따 구이빠 뉴빠 이너너 무 뫄부 아까이라? 무머녀러라아 과 아꺼가꽈 다꽈, 아호뿨 어

---

22. " 'Sir,' the servant said, 'what you ordered has been done, but there is still room.'

23. "Then the master told his servant, 'Go out to the roads and country lanes and make them come in, so that my house will be full.

24. I tell you, not one of those men who were invited will get a taste of my banquet.' "

25. Large crowds were traveling with Jesus, and turning to them he said:

26. "If anyone comes to me and does not hate his father and mother, his wife and children, his brothers and sisters--yes, even his own life--he cannot be my disciple.

27. And anyone who does not carry his cross and follow me cannot be my disciple.

28. "Suppose one of you wants to build a tower. Will he not first sit down and estimate the cost to

bya bingawera kui, analole akaba angabibona kuikira ihule.	비구로 뱌 비와워라 구이, 아나로러 아가바 아가비보나 구이기라 이후러.	see if he has enough money to complete it?
29. Bacha ku bangateta: 'Kute ono mundu atangirisaa kuimba enyumba ataale n'e kwihusa i!'	29. 바짜 구 바가더다: 구더 오노 무뚜 아다기리사아 구이빠 어뉴빠 아다아러 너 귀후사 이!	29. For if he lays the foundation and is not able to finish it, everyone who sees it will ridicule him,
30. Nekuteta, ono mundju atonderaa aimba eteete na misi ya kumala.	30. 너구더다, 오노 무쭈 아도떠라아 아이빠 어더어더 나 미시 야 구마라.	30. saying, 'This fellow began to build and was not able to finish.'
		31. "Or suppose a king is about to go to war against another king. Will he not first sit down and consider whether he is able with ten thousand men to oppose the one coming against him with twenty thousand? 32. If he is not able, he will send a delegation while the other is still a long way off and will ask for terms of peace.
33. Ku binalyi, kutalyi mundju mu Mwabu ola ungaba mwanafunzi wanyi akaba nai atangabeka tanga ekalamo kai mwa maboko manyi."	33. 구 비나레, 구다레 무쭈 무 와부 오라 우가바 와나푸씨 와네 아가바 나이 아다가버가 다가 어가라모 가이 와 마보고 마니."	33. In the same way, any of you who does not give up everything he has cannot be my disciple.
34. Kanji Yesu era kubura abu bandju: "Mumenyereraa kw'emunyu atula akomire. Si akaba emunyu w'ene mwetu	34. 가지 여수 어라 구부라 아부 바쭈: "무머녀러라아 귀무뉴 아두라 아고미러. 시 아가바 어무뉴 워너 뭐두	34. "Salt is good, but if it loses its saltiness, how can it be made salty again?

angaesa ebuloke, chi chingalokya u kanji?

35. Era angakabulwa kwa chafu, bushi atangachiata mufa kwa butaka n'na kwa myaka ya mw'ehwa. Ola wete ematwi m'ekomva, omvaa bya nateta.

아까어사 어부롣거, 찌 찌까롣갸 우 가찌?

35. 어라 아까가부롸 과 짜푸, 부씨 아다까찌아다 무파 과 부다가 우나 과 먀가 야 뭐화. 오롸 워더 어마뒤 머고빠, 오빠아 뱌 나더다.

35. It is fit neither for the soil nor for the manure pile; it is thrown out. "He who has ears to hear, let him hear."

Luka Chikono 15
E mbulyi ya yaeraa

1. Lusuku luuma, ebafuchisi b'e mbarata na banji bandu babi babaa benjire bachifunda ofu ne Yesu bamumvirise.

2. Mango eBafarisayo* n'ebakangirisi b'eMwaso* bendaa balola bacha, bera kunde batangirisa bachitetembya mmbu: "Onolaende ahuukasa ebandu babi n'ekunalya nabu!"

3. Bushi n'oku, Yesu era kubabusa mw'ono muso:

4. "Nde muuma mu Mwabu ola ungaba walanga mbuli eana, akaesa nguma musi aine kutareka cha chenda na mwenda mwa lusito, aende kuhonda era kutareka cha chenda na mwenda mwa lusito, aende kuhonda era yaerire kwa bituo aenda amoa.

5. Chasinda kumulolako enda amubika kwa bitchwuwe byaye

루가 찌고노 15
어 뿌쩨 야 야어라아

1. 루수구 루우마, 어바푸찌시 버 빠라다 나 바찌 바뚜 바비 바바아 버찌러 바찌푸따 오푸 너 여수 바무뻬리서.

2. 마꼬 어바파리사요* 너바가끼리시 버먀소* 버따아 바롣롸 바짜, 버라 구너 바다끼리사 바찌더더빠 무뿌: "오노롸어너 아후우가사 어바뚜 바비 너구나랴 나부!"

3. 부씨 노구, 여수 어라 구바부사 모노 무소:

4. "떠 무우마 무 먀부 오롸 우까바 와롸까 뿌찌 어아나, 아가어사 꾸마 무시 아이너 구다러가 짜 쩌따 나 뭐따 먀 루시도, 아어너 구호따 어라 구다러가 짜 쩌따 나 뭐따 먀 루시도, 아어너 구호따 어라 야어리러 과 비두오 아어따 아모아.

5. 짜시따 구무롣롸고 어따 아무비가 과 비쭈워 뱌여 너

Luke Chapter 15[NIV]

1. Now the tax collectors and "sinners" were all gathering around to hear him.

2. But the Pharisees and the teachers of the law muttered, "This man welcomes sinners and eats with them."

3. Then Jesus told them this parable:

4. "Suppose one of you has a hundred sheep and loses one of them. Does he not leave the ninety-nine in the open country and go after the lost sheep until he finds it?

5. And when he finds it, he joyfully puts it on his

ne lumoo.

루모오.

shoulders

6. and goes home. Then he calls his friends and neighbors together and says, 'Rejoice with me; I have found my lost sheep.'

7. Yesu ku kwera kubabura: "Kw'e lumoo lungaba kwa nguba bacha mango mundu mubi muuma angareka eii byai n'ekualukira Ongo, kurenza bandu babuya chenda na mwenda ba batangachiata bwera bwa kualukira Ongo."

7. 여수 구 궈라 구바부라: "궈 루모오 루까바 과 꾸바 바짜 마꼬 무뚜 무비 무우마 아까러가 어이이 뱌이 너구아루기라 오꼬, 구러싸 바뚜 바부야 쩌따 나 뭐따 바 바다까찌아다 붜라 봐 구아루기라 오꼬."

7. I tell you that in the same way there will be more rejoicing in heaven over one sinner who repents than over ninety-nine righteous persons who do not need to repent.

E bikulo bya byaeraa

어 비구로 뱌 뱌어라아

8. Kanji Yesu era kubabusa: "Nde mukasi ungaba wete butea bwai ekumi akaesa luuma mubu lwa lungakorerwa mubisi wa mutenga aine kutakoresa ekaore n'ekubisa enyumba aluhonde kubuya-buya kuikira mango angalutola?

8. 가찌 여수 어라 구바부사: "떠 무가시 우까바 워더 부더아 봐이 어구미 아가어사 루우마 무부 꽈 루까고러롸 무비시 와 무더까 아이너 구다고러사 어가오러 너구비사 어뉴빠 아루호떠 구부야-부야 구이기라 마꼬 아까루도롸?

8. "Or suppose a woman has ten silver coins and loses one. Does she not light a lamp, sweep the house and search carefully until she finds it?

9. Mango angaba alutolire, kuika anemaale bera bai, n'ebalung bai, n'ekubabura: 'Mumoaa al'auma nanyi, bushi natolire elutea lwa lwanyieraa.'"

9. 마꼬 아까바 아루도쬐러, 구이가 아너마아꿔 버라 바이, 너바루우 바이, 너구바부라: 무모아아 아꽈우마 나니, 부씨 나도쬐러 어루더아 꽈 꽈네어라아."

9. And when she finds it, she calls her friends and neighbors together and says, 'Rejoice with me; I have found my lost coin.'

10. Yesu ku kwera kubabura: "Ku e bamalaika ba Ongo bangaata e lumoo bacha mango mundu mubi muuma angareka ebii byai n'ekualukira

10. 여수 구 궈라 구바부라: "구 어 바마꽈이가 바 오꼬 바까아다 어 루모오 바짜 마꼬 무뚜 무비 무우마 아까러가 어비이 뱌이 너구아루기라

10. In the same way, I tell you, there is rejoicing in the presence of the angels of God over one sinner who repents."

Ongo."

E mwana ola waeraa

11. Yesu era kuishira eBafarisayo* n'ebakangirisi b'eMwaso* ono muanyi: "Kwabaa mulume muuma ola wabaa wete baala bai babiri.

12. lusuku luuma, ola mutoto mubu era kubura eshe: 'tata? nahonda unyerese ewanyi mwandu mwa bikulo byau kuno uchilyi u. eshe era kwemerera kuabira abu baala bai babiri ebikulo bya abaa ete.

13. Era nyuma sa suku sieke, ola mutoto era kuusa e wai mwango, na aya mu chio cha burerere. Aikire yi, era kumalira ebikulo byai mwa myasi y'ebuha-buha.

14. Abere atanachete kandju, echio cha abaa ali mu chera kuya mw'ebulio. Bushi n'oku, era kutangirisa aina hya angalya.

15. Era kuendera mutambo muuma wa mw'echi chio amweme emulimo. Nai era kumutuma mwa mahwa mai mbu aendaa kumulangira engulube.

16. Endaa ahonda chiro alye

어 꽈나 오꽈 와어라아

11. 여수 어라 구이씨라 어바파리사요* 너바가끼리시 버꽈소* 오노 무아니: "과바아 무루머 무우마 오꽈 와바아 워더 바아꽈 바이 바비리.

12. 루수구 루꾸마, 오꽈 무도도 무부 어라 구부라 어써: 다다? 나호따 우녀러서 어와니 꽈뚜 꽈 비구롣 뱌우 구노 우찌롄 우. 어써 어라 궈머러라 구아비라 아부 바아꽈 바이 바비리 어비구롣 뱌 아바아 어더.

13. 어라 뉴마 사 수구 시어거, 오꽈 무도도 어라 구우사 어 와이 꽈꼬, 나 아야 무 찌오 짜 부러러러. 아이기러 에, 어라 구마꼐라 어비구롣 뱌이 꽈 먀시 여부하-부하.

14. 아버러 아다나쩌더 간쮸, 어찌오 짜 아바아 아뀌 무 쩌라 구야 뭐부뀌오. 부씨 노구, 어라 구다꼐리사 아이나 햐 아꺄꽈.

15. 어라 구어떠라 무다뽀 무우마 와 뭐찌 찌오 아뭐머 어무뀌모. 나이 어라 구무두마 꽈 마화 마이 뿌 아어따아 구무꽈꼐라 어꾸루버.

16. 어따아 아호따 찌로 아뼈

11. Jesus continued: "There was a man who had two sons.

12. The younger one said to his father, 'Father, give me my share of the estate.' So he divided his property between them.

13. "Not long after that, the younger son got together all he had, set off for a distant country and there squandered his wealth in wild living.

14. After he had spent everything, there was a severe famine in that whole country, and he began to be in need.

15. So he went and hired himself out to a citizen of that country, who sent him to his fields to feed pigs.

16. He longed to fill his

kwa bihuu bya ngulube sendaa salya, si kutali ola wamuwaa bi.

과 비후우 뱌 우ㄹ루버 서따아 사꺄, 시 구다삐 오롸 와무와아 비.

stomach with the pods that the pigs were eating, but no one gave him anything.

17. Era kutangirisa achibusa: 'Ebakosi ba tata bataonjira batalire, chi chingatuma Nyono naorera ene n'ebusinya?

17. 어라 구다삐리사 아찌부사: 어바고시 바 다다 바다오찌라 바다삐리러, 찌 찌까두마 뇨노 나오러라 어너 너부시냐?

17. "When he came to his senses, he said, 'How many of my father's hired men have food to spare, and here I am starving to death!

18. Nyingahuba era musi. Bacha ku nyingabura tata: Tata, nairire mabi era muhondo sa Ongo n'nera muhondo sau.

18. 네까후바 어라 무시. 바짜 구 네까부라 다다: 다다, 나이리러 마비 어라 무호또 사 오꼬 우너라 무호또 사우.

18. I will set out and go back to my father and say to him: Father, I have sinned against heaven and against you.

19. Ndangachilorekana ku nga mwana wau; wiraa wanyitola nga muuma mwa bakosi bau!'"

19. 따까찌로러가나 구 까 마나 와우; 위라아 와네도롸 까 무우마 뫄 바고시 바우!"

19. I am no longer worthy to be called your son; make me like one of your hired men.'

20. Oyu mutabana kuna kuhuba era musi: "Abere achiri burerere mwa chifuna, eshe era kumumenyerera, era kumufira bonjo bunene, era kumulibichira, kuna kumuumbikira na lumoo lunene.

20. 오유 무다바나 구나 구후바 어라 무시: "아버러 아찌리 부러러러 뫄 찌푸나, 어써 어라 구무머녀러라, 어라 구무피라 보꼬 부너너, 어라 구무삐비찌라, 구나 구무우삐기라 나 루모오 루너너.

20. So he got up and went to his father. "But while he was still a long way off, his father saw him and was filled with compassion for him; he ran to his son, threw his arms around him and kissed him.

21. Si oyu muala era kumubura: 'Tata, nairire mabi era m uhondo ssa Ongo n'era muhondo sau. Ndangachilorekana ku nga mwana wau.'

21. 시 오유 무아롸 어라 구무부라: 다다, 나이리러 마비 어라 무 우호또 싸 오꼬 너라 무호또 사우. 따까찌로러가나 구 까 뫄나 와우.

21. "The son said to him, 'Father, I have sinned against heaven and against you. I am no longer worthy to be called your son.'

22. Si eshe era kubura ebaanda

22. 시 어써 어라 구부라

22. "But the father said to

bai: 'Muretaa eluchimba lukomire kusibu fuba,munamwimbase lu. Mumwimbasaa n'echianga kwa mutoke, mumwimbase n'ebirato.

23. Muretaa n'echana ch'engaafu cha chinunyire, munatende chi, tulye tunamoe.

24. Mumenyereraa kw'ono muala wanyi anyiberaa ng'ola wafire, kasi u achiri. Abaa aerire, si abonekire.' Chasinjire, bera kutangirisa balya n'ekumoa.

25. "Ala wai w'efula abaa achiri era mahwa. Abere era afuluka achiri mwa chifuna ch'emusi, era komva engoma n'enyimbo sahumbire.

26. Era kwemaala muanda muumda muuma amubuse chiye chi chabere kwa musi.

27. Nai era kumubura: 'Mulumuna watu aikire, n'eho echire echana ch'e ngaafu cha chinunyire, bushi muala wai aikire achiri anahaalukire.'

28. Ebute bwera kumusimba, atahonda n'ekwingirira mwa nyumba. Eshe era kuulka n'ekutangirisas amukoberesas.

29. Nai era kubura eshe: 'Ulolaa

어바아따 바이: 무러다아 어루찌빠 루고미러 구시부 푸바,무나뮈빠서 루. 무뮈빠사아 과 무도거, 무뮈빠서 너비라도.

23. 무러다아 너짜나 쩌빠아푸 짜 찌누네러, 무나더뜨 찌, 두쪄 두나모어.

24. 무머녀러라아 교노 무아따 와네 아네버라아 꼬쫘 와피러, 가시 우 아찌리. 아바아 아어리러, 시 아보너기러. 짜시찌러, 버라 구다삐리사 바쨔 너구모아.

25. "아쫘 와이 워푸쫘 아바아 아찌리 어라 마화. 아버러 어라 아푸루가 아찌리 뫄 찌푸나 쩌무시, 어라 고빠 어꼬마 너네뽀 사후삐러.

26. 어라 궈마아쫘 무아따 무우무다 무우마 아무부서 찌여 찌 짜버러 과 무시.

27. 나이 어라 구무부라: 무루무나 와두 아이기러, 너호 어찌러 어짜나 쩌 빠아푸 짜 찌누네러, 부씨 무아쫘 와이 아이기러 아찌리 아나하아루기러.

28. 어부더 붜라 구무시빠, 아다호따 너귀삐리라 뫄 뉴빠. 어써 어라 구우루가 너구다삐리사수 아무고버러사수.

29. 나이 어라 구부라 어써:

---

his servants, 'Quick! Bring the best robe and put it on him. Put a ring on his finger and sandals on his feet.

23. Bring the fattened calf and kill it. Let's have a feast and celebrate.

24. For this son of mine was dead and is alive again; he was lost and is found.' So they began to celebrate.

25. "Meanwhile, the older son was in the field. When he came near the house, he heard music and dancing.

26. So he called one of the servants and asked him what was going on.

27. 'Your brother has come,' he replied, 'and your father has killed the fattened calf because he has him back safe and sound.'

28. "The older brother became angry and refused to go in. So his father went out and pleaded with him.

29. But he answered his

kwa m yaka ingana wanyikoresa. Kanji ndafuraa kuisha mu chinwa cha watechire, si utafuraa kumba nemwana w'embenembu nanyi nyimoaa al'auma nab era banyi.

30. Si kuno muala wau, ola wamalire ebikulo byau kwa bakasi aikire, wamw?chirire echana ch'engaafu cha chinunyire!'

31. Eshe era kumwakula: 'Emanzi mwana wanyi! Tu nau tu tutula esuku soshi, n'ebyanyi byoshi bitula byau.
32 Kwabaa kun?mire elumoo lube, bushi mulumuna wau abaa ng'ola wafire, kasi u achiri Kanji abaa aerire, si abonekire.'"

Lula Chikono 16
1. Yesu aishira ebanafunzi bai ono unji muanyi: "Kwabaa mulanzi muuma. Oyu mulanzi abaa emangirire bikulo bya muare muuma. Oyu muare era kuburw mbu oyu wabaa wemangirire ebikulo byai abikoresise kubi.
2. En'ebikulo era kumwemaala,

우르롸아 과 무 야가 이꺄나 와네고러사. 가찌 따푸라아 구이싸 무 찌냐 짜 와더찌러, 시 우다푸라아 구빠 너뫄나 워뻐너뿌 나네 네모아아 아롸우마 나부 어라 바네.

30. 시 구노 무아롸 와우, 오롸 와마쀠러 어비구롣 뱌우 과 바가시 아이기러, 와무우?찌리러 어쨔나 쩌꺄아푸 짜 찌누네러!

31. 어써 어라 구뫄구롸: 어마씨 뫄나 와네! 두 나우 두 두두롸 어수구 소씨, 너뱌네 뵤씨 비두롸 뱌우.
32 과바아 구누?미러 어루무오오 루버, 부씨 무루무나 와우 아바아 꾀롸 와피러, 가시 우 아찌리. 가찌 아바아 아어리러, 시 아보너기러."

룩가 찌고노 16
1. 여수 아이씨라 어바나푸씨 바이 오노 우찌 무아네: "과바아 무롸씨 무우마. 오유 무롸씨 아바아 어마삐리러 비구롣 뱌 무아러 무우마. 오유 무아러 어라 구부루 뿌 오유 와바아 워마삐리러 어비구롣 뱌이 아비고러시서 구비.
2. 어너비구롣 어라

---

father, 'Look! All these years I've been slaving for you and never disobeyed your orders. Yet you never gave me even a young goat so I could celebrate with my friends.

30. But when this son of yours who has squandered your property with prostitutes comes home, you kill the fattened calf for him!'

31. " 'My son,' the father said, 'you are always with me, and everything I have is yours.

32. But we had to celebrate and be glad, because this brother of yours was dead and is alive again; he was lost and is found.'"

Luke Chapter 16[NIV]
1. Jesus told his disciples: "There was a rich man whose manager was accused of wasting his possessions.

2. So he called him in

era kumubura: 'Wishi kwa nenjire nomva emyasi ibi yoshi era wenjire waira? Umenyereraa kwa kutengera lwarero, utakachilange e bikulo byanyi. Bushi n'oku, unyilosaa kute ku wakoresise bya nakweresaa.'

3. Oyu mulanziomvire bacha, era kutangirisa achibussa: 'Kute nyingere naira kuno en'ebikulo ananyire mbu ndachemangiraa ebikulo byai? Ekuinga, ndangaala ku; n'ekwemeresa naku,kunganyita honyi.

4. Namenyire kwa nyingere naira, iri ebandu bende banyihuukasa mwa manyumba mabu mango nyingabanakolokanyisibwe mwa manyumba mabu mango nyingaba nakolokanyisibwe mwa mulimo.'

5. Bushi n'oku, era kwemaala muuma-muuma mwa ba babaa bete emwinda w'enawabu. Era kubusa ola mubere-bere: 'Unyiburaa mwinda wa manga w'enawetu i uli mu.'

6. Nai era kwakula: 'Nyiri mu mwinda wa mirengof eana ya mafuta.' Oyu mulanzi era kumubura: 'Utolaa ekaratasi wikale, 'e kwanjika mbu uli mu mwinda wa mirengo Matano.'

구뭐마아롸, 어라 구무부라: 위씨 과 너찌러 노빠 어먀시 이비 요씨 어라 워찌러 와이라? 우머녀러라아 과 구더꺼라 꽈러로, 우다가찌꽈꺼 어 비구롣 뱌네. 부씨 노구, 우네롣사아 구더 구 와고러시서 뱌 나궈러사아.

3. 오유 무퐈씨오뻬러 바짜, 어라 구다삐리사 아찌부싸: 구더 네꺼러 나이라 구노 어너비구롣 아나네러 뿌 따쩌마삐라아 어비구롣 뱌이? 어구이꺄, 따꺼아아롸 구; 너궈머러사 나구,구꺼네다 호네.-

4. 나메네러 과 네꺼러 나이라, 이리 어바뚜 버떠 바네후우가사 롸 마뉴빠 마부 마꼬 네꺼바나고롣가네시붜 롸 마뉴빠 마부 마꼬 네꺼바 나고롣가네시붜 롸 무뢰모.

5. 부씨 노구, 어라 궈마아롸 무우마-무우마 롸 바 바바아 버더 어뮈따 워나와부. 어라 구부사 오롸 무버러-버러: 우네부라아 뮈따 와 마꺼 워나워두 이 우뢰 무.

6. 나이 어라 과구꽈: 네리 무 뮈따 와 미러꼬푸 어아나 야 마푸다. 오유 무퐈씨 어라 구무부라: 우도퐈아 어가라다시 위가뤄, 어 과씨가 뿌 우뢰 무 뮈따 와 미러꼬 마다노.

and asked him, 'What is this I hear about you? Give an account of your management, because you cannot be manager any longer.'

3. "The manager said to himself, 'What shall I do now? My master is taking away my job. I'm not strong enough to dig, and I'm ashamed to beg-

4. I know what I'll do so that, when I lose my job here, people will welcome me into their houses.'

5. "So he called in each one of his master's debtors. He asked the first, 'How much do you owe my master?'

6. " 'Eight hundred gallons of olive oil,' he replied. "The manager told him, 'Take your bill, sit down quickly, and make it four hundred.'

7. Kanji era kubusa eunji: 'N'nau uli mu mwinda wa manga?' Era kumwakula: Nyiri mu mwinda wa mbweka eana sa shano ya marondo.' Oyu mulanzi era kumubura: Utolaa ekaratasi n'ekwanjika mbu uli mu mwinda wa mbweka lunane.

8. Ena e bikulo ombire bya oyu mulanzi mubi enjire aira era kumutonga bushi n'ebukalange bwai bw'e kumenyerera cha chingamuikira. Mulolaa kw'e bandju b'obuno butala bende bamenyerera bya bingabaikira muno butala, si ba batula bachirembire mbu bali bandu b'ebulangare bwa Ongo beke, batamenyerera bya biri era muhondo.

9. Yesu era kunaendekerana ateta: "N'nanyi nababura: Mango mungaba mwete ebikulo by'omuno butala, mwendaa mwakoma ebwira na chira mundu mubi, mubone e bwira era mwa Ongo, mango bikaba bitachibetere mulimo.

10. N'emundu ola walanga kubi bya byete mutoloke mueke, anganalanga kubi bya byete mutoloke munene.

7. 가찌 어라 구부사 어우찌: 우나우 우뾔 무 뮈따 와 마빠? 어라 구꽈구롸: 네리 무 뮈따 와 뾔가 어아나 사 싸노 야 마로또. 오유 무퐈씨 어라 구무부롸: 우도퐈아 어가라다시 너과찌가 뿌 우뾔 무 뮈따 와 뾔가 루나너.

8. 어나 어 비구롤 오뼤러 뱌 오유 무퐈씨 무비 어찌러 아이라 어라 구무도빠 부씨 너부가퐈꺼 봐이 붜 구머녀러라 짜 찌빠무이기라. 무롣퐈아 궈 바뚜 보부노 부다퐈 버떠 바머녀러라 뱌 비빠바이기라 무노 부다퐈, 시 바 바두퐈 바찌러뻬러 뿌 바뾔 바뚜 버부퐈빠러 봐 오꼬 버거, 바다머녀러라 뱌 비리 어라 무호또.

9. 여수 어라 구나어떠거라나 아더다: "우나니 나바부라: 마꼬 무빠바 뭐더 어비구롤 뷔오무노 부다퐈, 뭐따아 꽈고마 어뷔라 나 찌라 무뚜 무비, 무보너 어 뷔라 어라 꽈 오꼬, 마꼬 비가바 비다찌버더러 무뾔모.

10. 너무뚜 오퐈 와퐈빠 구비 뱌 벼더 무도롣거 무어거, 아빠나퐈빠 구비 뱌 벼더 무도롣거 무너너.

7. "Then he asked the second, 'And how much do you owe?' " 'A thousand bushels of wheat,' he replied. "He told him, 'Take your bill and make it eight hundred.'

8. "The master commended the dishonest manager because he had acted shrewdly. For the people of this world are more shrewd in dealing with their own kind than are the people of the light.

9. I tell you, use worldly wealth to gain friends for yourselves, so that when it is gone, you will be welcomed into eternal dwellings.

10. "Whoever can be trusted with very little can also be trusted with much, and whoever is dishonest with very little will also be dishonest with much.

11. Akaba mutanaba babuya mwa kulanga ebikulo by'omuno butal, Ongo nai atanganaberesa ebulanzi bw'e buare b'okwa nguba.

12. N'akaba mutangalanga bya by'e unji, nde i wera ungachiberesa bya mwabikirirwe kwa nguba?

13. Kutali kaungu ka kangakorera benawabu babiri, bushi akaba kangasima muuma mubu kanamutunde, kangaba kohombire oyu unji n'ekumukena. Mutangakorera Ongo kanji mukorere n'ebikulo."

Yesu era kuakula e Bafarisayo

14. E Bafarisayo,* babaa bombirisa ebi byoshi Yesu abaa ateta. Babaa bera bamushekera, bushi bu batula basimire ebikulo.

15. Na Yesu era kubabura: "Mwabu mwende mwachilosa era muhondo s'e bandju kwa mubeine u munatula babuya, si Ongo atula eshi bya mwaanyisa. Mumenyereraa kwa ata chira mundu ola ebandu beresa etunda i wende wasimisa Ongo.

16. Ebyanda by'e Mwaso wa

---

11. 아가바 무다나바 바부야 꽈구꽈싸 어비구롣 뷔오무노 부다루, 오꼬 나이 아다꽈나버러사 어부꽈씨 뭐 부아러 보과 우바.

12. 나가바 무다꽈꽈꽈 뱌 벼 우찌, 떠 이 워라 우꽈찌버러사 뱌 꽈비기리뤄 과 우바?

13. 구다뛰 가우꾸 가 가꽈고러라 버나와부 바비리, 부씨 아가바 가꽈씨마 무우마 무부 가나무두떠, 가꽈바 고호뻬러 오유 우찌 너구무거라. 무다꽈고러라 오꼬 가찌 무고러러 너비구롣."

여수 어라 구아구꽈 어 바파리사요

14. 어 바파리사요,* 바바아 보뻬리사 어비 뵤씨 여수 아바아 아더다. 바바아 버라 바무써거라, 부씨 부 바두꽈 바시미러 어비구롣.

15. 나 여수 어라 구바부라: "꽈부 뭐떠 꽈찌롣사 어라 무호또 서 바뚜 과 무버이너 우 무나두꽈 바부야, 시 오꼬 아두꽈 어씨 뱌 꽈아니사. 무머녀러라아 과 아다 찌라 무뚜 오꽈 어바뚜 버러사 어두따 이 워떠 와시미사 오꼬.

16. 어뱌따 벼 꽈소 와

---

11. So if you have not been trustworthy in handling worldly wealth, who will trust you with true riches?

12. And if you have not been trustworthy with someone else's property, who will give you property of your own?

13. "No servant can serve two masters. Either he will hate the one and love the other, or he will be devoted to the one and despise the other. You cannot serve both God and Money."

14. The Pharisees, who loved money, heard all this and were sneering at Jesus.

15. He said to them, "You are the ones who justify yourselves in the eyes of men, but God knows your hearts. What is highly valued among men is detestable in God's sight.

16. "The Law and the

Musa n'e by'e barebi byasinjiraa ku Yowanyi Mubatisayi. Kutengera ku Yowanyi, eMwasi Mubuya-buya ola utechire era luulu s'eBwimi bwa Ongo, kuhubanganyisibwa ku nahubanganyisibwa. Bushi n'oku, bandu banene bende banahonda bengirire mubu.

17. Mumenyereraa kw'enguba n'echitaka bikerenga, si e Mwaso wa Ongo atakftenge ku chiro n'ekambesha.

18. Na mwasi muuma mw'oyu Mwaso i yono: Chira mulume ola ungaulusa mukai n'e kuhwera unji mukasi, ilyi abanjire ekilyi. N'e mulume ola ungahwera emukasi ola waulusibwe n'eba wai iri nai anabanjire e kilyi."

Emuare buna Lusaro

19. Kanji Yesu era kuisha ono unji muanyi: "Kwabaa muare muuma. Oyu muare endaaambala njimba sa sisitoire, kanji sa salangala busese. Abaa atula mwa muako, kanji abaa atlya biryo bya buha-buha.

20. Kwa chiso ch'enyumba y'oyu muare, kwarekibwaa mukene muuma mbu i Lasaro. Abaa ete biulu binene.

벼 바러비 뱌시띠라아 구 요와네 무바디사에. 구더ᄄ라 구 요와네, 어뫄시 무부야-부야 오ᄈ라 우더찌러 어라 루우루 서뷔미 봐 오읃, 구후바ᄊ네시봐 구 나후바ᄊ네시봐. 부씨 노구, 바뚜 바너너 버더 바나호ᄄ라 버띠리러 무부.

17. 무머녀러라아 귀욷바 너찌다가 비거러따, 시 어 뫄소 와 오읃 아다구푸더떠 구 찌로 너가ᄈ러싸.

18. 나 뫄시 무우마 모유 뫄소 이 요노: 찌라 무루머 오라 우따우루사 무가이 너 구훠라 우찌 무가시, 이ᄈ레 아바찌러 어기ᄈ레. 너 무루머 오라 우따훠라 어무가시 오ᄈ라 와우루시붜 너바 와이 이리 나이 아나바찌러 어 기ᄈ레."

어무아러 부나 루ᄈᄈ렌

19. 가찌 여수 어라 구이싸 오노 우찌 무아네: "과바아 무아러 무우마. 오유 무아러 어ᄄ라아아빠ᄈ라 찌빠 사 시시도이러, 가찌 사 사빠따ᄈ라 부서서. 아바아 아두ᄈ라 뫄 무아고, 가찌 아바아 아두ᄈ려 비료 뱌 부하-부하.

20. 과 찌소 쩌뉴빠 요유 무아러, 과러기봐아 무거너 무우마 뿌 이 빠사로. 아바아 어더 비우루 비너너.

Prophets were proclaimed until John. Since that time, the good news of the kingdom of God is being preached, and everyone is forcing his way into it.

17. It is easier for heaven and earth to disappear than for the least stroke of a pen to drop out of the Law.

18. "Anyone who divorces his wife and marries another woman commits adultery, and the man who marries a divorced woman commits adultery.

19. "There was a rich man who was dressed in purple and fine linen and lived in luxury every day.

20. At his gate was laid a beggar named Lazarus, covered with sores

21. Endaa ahonda alye ebukombo-kombo bw'ebiryo bwa bwendaa bwatoa kwa mesa m'oyu muare. Si kanji engunda se ndaa sabaha kumulamba-lamba ebiulu.

21. 어따아 아호따 아ᄙᅧ 어부고뽀-고뽀 뤄비료 봐 뤄따아 봐도아 과 머사 모유 무아러. 시 가찌 어우따 서 따아 사바하 구무ᄙᅡ빠-ᄙᅡ빠 어비우ᄙᅮ.

21. and longing to eat what fell from the rich man's table. Even the dogs came and licked his sores.

22. Abere elusuku lw'ekufa kwa Lasaro lwaika, era kut?bwa. Emuchima wai era kwekibwa n'ebamalaika ha Ongo kwa nguba ekae mwa lutungu lwa Aburahamu. Wamuare nai era kufa, na bamutaba.

22. 아버러 어ᄙᅮ수구 ᄙᅯ구파 과 ᄙᅡ사로 ᄙᅪ이가, 어라 구두?봐. 어무찌마 와이 어라 궈기봐 너바마ᄙᅡ이가 하 옹고 과 ᆼ구바 어가어 뫄 ᄙᅮ둥구 ᄙᅪ 아부라하무. 와무아러 나이 어라 구파, 나 바무다바.

22. "The time came when the beggar died and the angels carried him to Abraham's side. The rich man also died and was buried.

23. Abere era anali era anali era bafu ba bateshi Ongo bende bya, kanji era analibuka busese, era kwimusa emeho. Era kulangusa ku Aburahamu ali burerere, na Lasaro ali mwa lutungu lwai.

23. 아버러 어라 아나ᄙᅵ 어라 아나ᄙᅵ 어라 바푸 바 바더씨 옹고 버떠 뱌, 가찌 어라 아나ᄙᅵ부가 부서서, 어라 귀무사 어머호. 어라 구ᄙᅡᆼ구사 구 아부라하무 아ᄙᅵ 부러러러, 나 ᄙᅡ사로 아ᄙᅵ 뫄 ᄙᅮ둥구 ᄙᅪ이.

23. In hell, where he was in torment, he looked up and saw Abraham far away, with Lazarus by his side.

24. Era kuuma emurenge: E tata Aburahamu, unyifiraa ebonjo. bushi kufa ku nera nafa n'emuliro. Unyibwiriraa Lasaro abike emutoke wai mwa meshi, chiro anyiretere mumata muuma wamu, manyibike ehy'emwaha kwa lulimi.'

24. 어라 구우마 어무렁거: 어 다다 아부라하무, 우녜피라아 어본조. 부씨 구파 구 너라 나파 너무ᄙᅵ로. 우녜뷔리라아 ᄙᅡ사로 아비거 어무도거 와이 뫄 머씨, 찌로 아녜러더러 무마다 무우마 와무, 마녜비거 어혀뫄하 과 ᄙᅮᄙᅵ미.

24. So he called to him, 'Father Abraham, have pity on me and send Lazarus to dip the tip of his finger in water and cool my tongue, because I am in agony in this fire.'

25. Aburahamu nai era kumwakula: E mwana wanyi! Utachikengere kwa wabonaa bindu binene bibuya mwa kalamo kau na Lasaro i wabaa walola kwa Ongo? Lwarero nai

25. 아부라하무 나이 어라 구뫄구ᄙᅡ: 어 뫄나 와녜! 우다찌겅거러 과 와보나아 빈두 비너너 비부야 뫄 가ᄙᅡ모 가우 나 ᄙᅡ사로 이 와바아 와로ᄙᅡ 과 옹고? ᄙᅪ러로 나이

25. "But Abraham replied, 'Son, remember that in your lifetime you received your good things, while Lazarus received bad things, but now he is

era atamukira anola, si nau u wera walibuka.

26. Kanji Umenyaa kwa ala kachi-kachi kenyu netu abikirwe mubanda munene ola utangatuma ba bahonda ekutenga ene tuli baye eyi muli, nesi ba bahonda ekutenga eyi muli bahabukire ene tuli.

27. Kanji wamuare era kuteta: E tata, mwa ngumu yetu muchiri balumuna banyi batano. Nakwemire, uhimhaa wnyit umirire Lasaro era bali,

28. anyikengese bu bangaira kwa nendaa naira bata kuikira nabu mw'echine chisiki cha mano malibuko nyiri mu.

29. Kanji Aburaharnu era kumwakula: Abu banyakenyu batusa eMwaso' wa Musa n'emanjiko m'ebarebi kwa kubakengesa. bendaa baira kwa matula matechire.

30. Nai era kubura Aburahamu: Naanga tula Aburahamu, abola batomva. Nyishi kwa akaba muuma mwa ba bafire i ungabaendera, banganabindula emyanya yabu.

31. Chasinjire, Aburahimu era kumubura: Akaba

어라 아다무기라 아노꽈, 시 나우 우 워라 와쀠부가.

26. 가찌 우머냐아 과 아꽈 가찌-가찌 거뉴 너두 아비기뤄 무바따 무너너 오꽈 우다꺼두마 바 바호따 어구더꺼 어너 두쀠 바여 어에 무쀠, 너시 바 바호따 어구더꺼 어에 무쀠 바하부기러 어너 두쀠.

27. 가찌 와무아러 어라 구더다: 어 다다, 꽈 꾸무 여두 무찌리 바루무나 바니 바다노. 나궈미러, 우히무하아 우니두 우미리러 꽈사로 어라 바쀠,

28. 아니거꺼서 부 바까이라 과 너따아 나이라 바다 구이기라 나부 뭐찌너 찌시기 짜 마노 마쀠부고 내리 무.

29. 가찌 아부라하루누 어라 구꽈구꽈: 아부 바냐거뉴 바두사 어꽈소 와 무사 너마찌고 머바러비 과 구바거꺼사. 버따아 바이라 과 마두꽈 마더찌러.

30. 나이 어라 구부라 아부라하무: 나아까 두꽈 아부라하무, 아보꽈 바도빠. 내씨 과 아가바 무우마 꽈 바 바피러 이 우까바어떠라, 바까나비뿌꽈 어먀냐 야부.

31. 짜시찌러, 아부라히무 어라 구무부라: 아가바 바다꺼머러라

comforted here and you are in agony.

26. And besides all this, between us and you a great chasm has been fixed, so that those who want to go from here to you cannot, nor can anyone cross over from there to us.'

27. "He answered, 'Then I beg you, father, send Lazarus to my father's house,

28. for I have five brothers. Let him warn them, so that they will not also come to this place of torment.'

29. "Abraham replied, 'They have Moses and the Prophets; let them listen to them.'

30. " 'No, father Abraham,' he said, 'but if someone from the dead goes to them, they will repent.'

31. "He said to him, 'If they do not listen to

batangemerera kwa Mwaso wa Musa n'emanjiko m'ebarebi bitula byemire, batanganasiya bemerera n'e myasi yafulwa n'ola w'omokire.

Luka Chikono 17
Yesu akangilyisa

1. Yesu era kubura ehanafunzi bai: "Chitangaalikana emuereko w'ekubika emundu mwa bibi ekale atamuikirire. Si Mumenyereraa kwa bungaba bwanya kw'ola ungareterana oyu muereko!

2. Kungaba kukulu kw'oyu mundu aminyirwe ekoi ly'elusho mw'eosi akabulwe n'omwa nyanja, wa kubika chiro muuma mwa bano bana mwa bwemeresi mwa bibi.

3. Bushi n'oku, chira muuma mu Mwabu achilanga-langaa! Si akaba munyakenyu angakuirira emabi, umulesaa kwa airire kubi, n'akaba angachiaya, umibabaliraa.

4. Kanji akaba angakuirira emabi kalinda kwa lusuku luuma, kanji anaike kukwema ebubabalire kalinda, unamubabaliraa."

5. Era nyuma s'ebi, endumwa sa Yesu sera kumubura: "Utuasaa

루가 찌고노 17
여수 아가삐뻬뻽

1. 여수 아라 구부라 어하나푸씨 바이: "찌다아아삐가나 어무어러고 워구비가 어무뚜 와 비비 어가뻐 아다무이기리러. 시 무머녀러라아 과 부빠바 봐냐 교꽈 우빠러더라나 오유 무어러고!

2. 구빠바 구구루 교유 무뚜 아미네뤄 어고이 뤼어루쏘 뭐오시 아가부뤄 노와 냐쌰, 와 구비가 찌로 무우마 와 바노 바나 와 붸머러시 와 비비.

3. 부씨 노구, 찌라 무우마 무 뫄부 아찌꽈빠-꽈아아! 시 아가바 무냐거뉴 아꽈구이리라 어마비, 우무뻐사아 과 아이리러 구비, 나가바 아빠찌아야, 우미바바삐리아.

4. 가찌 아가바 아꽈구이리라 어마비 가삐따 과 루수구 루우마, 가찌 아나이거 구궈마 어부바바삐러 가삐따, 우나무바바삐리아."

5. 어라 뉴마 서비, 어뚜와 사 여수 서라 구무부라:

Luke Chapter 17[NIV]

1. Jesus said to his disciples: "Things that cause people to sin are bound to come, but woe to that person through whom they come.

2. It would be better for him to be thrown into the sea with a millstone tied around his neck than for him to cause one of these little ones to sin.

3. So watch yourselves. "If your brother sins, rebuke him, and if he repents, forgive him.

4. If he sins against you seven times in a day, and seven times comes back to you and says, 'I repent,' forgive him."

5. The apostles said to the Lord, "Increase our

Moses and the Prophets, they will not be convinced even if someone rises from the dead.' "

tuate bwemeresi bunene ku Ongo."

6. Nai era kubabura: "Akaba mungaachire ebwemeresi chiro bungana nga hya kafuma hya hingakula, hinahube muchi munene, mungenjire Mwabura n'emuchi mbu achishingulaa mwa chitaka aye kuchikoma mwa nyanja amere mu, anganabemerere.

7. Yesu era kubusa ebanafunzi bai: "Akaba muuma mu Mwabu angaba ete muanda wai ola wMuluka luoloolo era mahwa, nesi afuluka kukeresa ebifuana, chingaalikana amibure mbu ajkiraa kulya? Naanga!

8. Chichine chi angamubura: Utekaa bya nyingalya, chasinda ungembala kubuya, unyibikire ebiryo kwa mbare, n'ebinji byoshi bya nyingalya kuikira mango nyingamala kulya. Era businda, n'nau ungere walya.

9. Mwishi mbu angawa oyu muanda wai enzimwa kwa bushi airaa kwa anamubiiraa? Naanga!

10. N'nenyu, mango mungaba mwairire ekandu ka Ongo angababura mbu muiraa, hacha ku mwendaa mwateta: Tubano tunali baanda oshi au Bya

---

"우두아사아 두아더 뭐머러시 부너너 구 오끄."

6. 나이 어라 구바부라: "아가바 무까아찌러 어뭐머러시 찌로 부아나 까 햐 가푸마 햐 히까구롸, 히나후버 무찌 무너너, 무꺼찌러 뫄부라 너무찌 뿌 아찌씨꾸롸아 뫄 찌다가 아여 구찌고마 뫄 냐쨔 아머러 무, 아까나버머러러.

7. 여수 어라 구부사 어바나푸씨 바이: "아가바 무우마 무 뫄부 아까바 어더 무아따 와이 오롸 우무루가 루오로오로 어라 마햐, 너시 아푸루가 구거러사 어비푸아나, 찌까아뤼가나 아미부러 뿌 아j기라아 구꺄? 나아까!

8. 찌찌너 찌 아까무부라: 우더가아 뱌 네까꺄, 짜시따 우꺼빠롸 구부야, 우네비기러 어비료 과 빠러, 너비찌 뵤씨 뱌 네까꺄 구이기라 마끄 네까마롸 구꺄. 어라 부시따, 우나우 우꺼러 와꺄.

9. 뮈씨 뿌 아까와 오유 무아따 와이 어씨뫄 과 부씨 아이라아 과 아나무비이라아? 나아까!

10. 우너뉴, 마끄 무까바 뫄이리러 어가뉴 가 오끄 아까바부라 뿌 무이라아, 하쨔 구 뭐따아 마더다: 두바노 두나뤼 바아따 오씨 아우 뱌

---

faith!"

6. He replied, "If you have faith as small as a mustard seed, you can say to this mulberry tree, 'Be uprooted and planted in the sea,' and it will obey you.

7. "Suppose one of you had a servant plowing or looking after the sheep. Would he say to the servant when he comes in from the field, 'Come along now and sit down to eat'?

8. Would he not rather say, 'Prepare my supper, get yourself ready and wait on me while I eat and drink; after that you may eat and drink'?

9. Would he thank the servant because he did what he was told to do?

10. So you also, when you have done everything you were told to do, should say, 'We are unworthy servants; we

tunganaala kuira bi twairire."

두까나아꽈 구이라 비 돠이리러."

have only done our duty.' "

Babenzi-benzi ekumi

바버씨-버씨 어구미

11. Mango Yesu abaa anachiri mwa luendo lw'ekwirukira eYerusalemu, era kurengera mwa. lubibi lw'echio ch'eSamariya n'ech'eKalilaya.

11. 마꼬 여수 아바아 아나찌리 꽈 루어또 뤄귀루기라 어여루사뤄무, 어라 구러꺼라 꽈. 뤼비비 뤄찌오 쩌사마리야 너쩌가꾀꽈야.

11. Now on his way to Jerusalem, Jesus traveled along the border between Samaria and Galilee.

12. Abere era ah ofu na musi muuma, era kubi.ianana na babenzi-benzi ekumi. Bera kwemanga marerere nai,

12. 아버러 어라 아후 오푸 나 무시 무우마, 어라 구비.이아나나 나 바버씨-버씨 어구미. 버라 꿔마꺄 마러러러 나이,

12. As he was going into a village, ten men who had leprosymet him. They stood at a distance

13. kuna kutangirisa balakanga inmbu: "Enawetu Yesu, utufiraa ebonjo!"

13. 구나 구다꾀리사 바꽈가꺄 이누뿌: "어나워두 여수, 우두피라아 어본쪼!"

13. and called out in a loud voice, "Jesus, Master, have pity on us!"

14. Yesu abalorie ku, era kubabura: "Muendaa, muchilose mubeine era bakuhanyi ba Ongo* bali, balole akaba mwalamire. "bere bera banali mwa luendo baya yi, bera kunalma.

14. 여수 아바뢰리어 구, 어라 구바부라: "무어따아, 무찌뢴써 무버이너 어라 바구하네 바 오끄* 바꾀, 바뢰꿔 아가바 꽈꽈미러. "버러 버라 바나꾀 꽈 루어또 바야 에, 버라 구나뤂마.

14. When he saw them, he said, "Go, show yourselves to the priests." And as they went, they were cleansed.

15. Muuma mubu yeke alolire kwa alamire, era kuhuba era Yesu abaa ahaenda tonga Ongo na murenge munene.

15. 무우마 무부 여거 아뢴꾀러 과 아꽈미러, 어라 구후바 어라 여수 아바아 아하어따 도꺄 오끄 나 무러꺼 무너너.

15. One of them, when he saw he was healed, came back, praising God in a loud voice.

16. Kwa kulosa Yesu elumoo iwai, era kukoma emafi era muhondo sai Era kutangirisa muwa engulu. Oyu mundu atbaa Muyuta, si ibaa Musamariya.

16. 과 구뢰사 여수 어뤂모오 이와이, 어라 구고마 어마피 어라 무호또 사이 어라 구다꾀리사 무와 어꿔뤂. 오유 무뚜 아두바아 무유다, 시 이바아 무사마리야.

16. He threw himself at Jesus' feet and thanked him--and he was a Samaritan.

17. Yesu nai ku kwera kubura ba bhaa bali aola: "Si babenzi-

17. 여수 나이 구 꿔라 구부라 바 부하아 바꾀 아오꽈: "시

17. Jesus asked, "Were not all ten cleansed?

benzi ekumi bu nalamyaa! Kute ku hi banji mwenda batachibahire!

18. Kutanabonekire chiro na muuma mubu ola waalukire era nyuma atonge Ongo ng'okwa ono uti Muyuta airire?"

19. Chasinjire, Yesu era kumubura: "Imangaa uende n'ebolo, bushi ebwemeresi bwau ku Nyono bwakununwire."

Ekufulaka kwa Yesu

20. e Bafarisayo* babusaa Yesu: Mongochi Ongo akabaha kwema mwa butala?" Yesu era kubakula"e Bwami bwa Ongo butachwula mbu kuika e bandju banalolaa n'e meho kwa bwa ikire.

21. Mumenyereraa kw'e Bwimi bwa Ongo bwera buli kwa bandu boshi. Bushi n'oku, e bandju batakatete mmbu: Anola u e Bwimi bwai, bulyi nesi Wala u eBwimi bwai buli!".

22. Kanji Yesu era kubura ebanafunzi bai: "kukaba suku sa mukahonda ekunyilola ku chiro lusuku luuma nyi Mwana w'eMundu, si mutakafure kunyilola ku.

23. Ebandu bakababura: Mulolaa, wala u e Mwana w'e Mundju alyi, Mutanaereresa

---

바버씨-버씨 어구미 부 나꺄먀아! 구더 구 히 바찌 뭐따 바다찌바히러!

18. 구다나보너기러 찌로 나 무우마 무부 오꽈 와아루기러 어라 뉴마 아도꺼 오꼬 꼬과 오노 우디 무유다 아이리러?"

19. 짜시찌러, 여수 어라 구무부라: "이마까아 우어꺼 너보로, 부씨 어붜머러시 봐우 구 뇨노 봐구누니위러."

어구푸꽈— 과 여수

20. 어 바파리사요* 바부사아 여수: 모꼬찌 오꼬 아가바하 꿔마 봐 부다꽈?" 여수 어라 구바구꽈"어 봐미 봐 오꼬 부다쭈라 뿌 구이가 어 바뚜 바나로꽈아 너 머호 과 봐 이기러.

21. 무머녀러라아 꿔 뷔미 봐 오꼬 뭐라 부꿰 과 바뚜 보씨. 부씨 노구, 어 바뚜 바다가더더 무뿌: 아노꽈 우 어 뷔미 봐이, 부레 너시 와꽈 우 어뷔미 봐이 부꿰!".

22. 가찌 여수 어라 구부라 어바나푸씨 바이: "구가바 수구 사 무가호따 어구네론꽈 구 찌로 루수구 루우마 네 먀나 워무뚜, 시 무다가푸러 구네론꽈 구.

2.3 어바뚜 바가바부라: 무론꽈아, 와꽈 우 어 먀나 워 무뚜 아레, 무다나어러러사 뿌

Where are the other nine?

18. Was no one found to return and give praise to God except this foreigner?"

19. Then he said to him, "Rise and go; your faith has made you well."

20. Once, having been asked by the Pharisees when the kingdom of God would come, Jesus replied, "The kingdom of God does not come with your careful observation,

21. nor will people say, 'Here it is,' or 'There it is,' because the kingdom of God is within you."

22. Then he said to his disciples, "The time is coming when you will long to see one of the days of the Son of Man, but you will not see it.

23. Men will tell you, 'There he is!' or 'Here he is!' Do not go running off

mbu mwaya u, neci mbu Mwalbichira u.	뫄야 우, 너씨 뿌 뫄루비찌라 우.	after them.
24. Mumenyereraa kwa mango Nyono nyi Mwana w'e Mundju nyikafuluka, nyikalorekana ku ng'okwa chikengu chende chetenga kwa nguba n'ekulangasa e butala boshi.	24. 무머녀러라아 과 마ᅌᅩ 뇨노 네 뫄나 워 무뚜 네가푸루가, 네가로러가나 구 ᅌᅩ과 찌거ᅌᅮ 쩌떠 쩌더ᅌᅡ 과 ᅌᅮ바 너구ᄙᅡᅌᅡ사 어 부다ᄙᅡ 보씨.	24. For the Son of Man in his day will be like the lightning, which flashes and lights up the sky from one end to the other.
25. Si kunyemire nyiribuke busese tanga, nyinalairwe nenyu mu bandu ba Lwarero.	25. 시 구녀미러 네리부거 부서서 다ᅌᅡ, 네나ᄙᅡ이뤄 너뉴 무 바뚜 바 롸러로.	25. But first he must suffer many things and be rejected by this generation.
26. Kwa bandu banabaa mwa suku sa Nowa, mtihondo s'emeshi kwihula mwa butala boshi, ku bikanaba mamgo Nyono nyi Mwana w'eMundu nyikafuluka.	26. 과 바뚜 바나바아 뫄 수구 사 노와, 무디호또 서머씨 귀후ᄙᅡ 뫄 부다ᄙᅡ 보씨, 구 비가나바 마무고 뇨노 네 뫄나 워무뚜 네가푸루가.	26. "Just as it was in the days of Noah, so also will it be in the days of the Son of Man.
27. Mw'esi suku sa Nowa ebandu bendaa balya banamwa, bendaa bahwera banahwerwa, kuikira elusuku Nowa engiriraa mwa bwato hwui bunene. Chasinda, emvula inene yera kutoa. Enyishi soshi sera kwiliuia n'ekumira endulungu soshi. Ebandu boshi bera kunasika. kureka engumu ya Nowa yeine.	27. 뭐시 수구 사 노와 어바뚜 버따아 바ᄙᅣ 바나뫄, 버따아 바훠라 바나훠롸, 구이기라 어루수구 노와 어ᅌᅵ리라아 뫄 봐도 후우이 부너너. 짜시따, 어뿌ᄙᅡ 이너너 여라 구도아. 어네씨 소씨 서라 귀ᄙᅵ우이아 너구미라 어뚜루ᅌᅮ 소씨. 어바뚜 보씨 버라 구나시가. 구러가 어ᅌᅮ무 야 노와 여이너.	27. People were eating, drinking, marrying and being given in marriage up to the day Noah entered the ark. Then the flood came and destroyed them all.
28. Kanji ku byanabaa bacha inwa suku sa Loti: Ebandu bendaa blya b?namwa, bendaa baula banausa, bendaa bainga banaimba.	28. 가ᄶᅵ 구 뱌나바아 바짜 이놔 수구 사 로디: 어바뚜 버따아 부ᄙᅣ 부?나뫄, 버따아 바우ᄙᅡ 바나우사, 버따아 바이ᅌᅡ 바나이빠.	28. "It was the same in the days of Lot. People were eating and drinking, buying and selling, planting and building.
29. Amu mango, Ongo era	29. 아무 마ᅌᅩ, 오ᅌᅩ 어라	29. But the day Lot left

kutosa emuliro uli nga mvula ya lutwa elusuku engumo ya Loti yabaa yera yatengaa awa musi w'eSotomo. Oyu muliro era kusikya ebandu boshi b'oyu musi.

구도사 어무삐로 우삐 롸 뿌롸 야 루돠 어루수구 어뜨모 야 롼디 야바아 여라 야더롸아 아와 무시 워소도모. 오유 무삐로 어라 구시갸 어바뚜 보씨 보유 무시.

Sodom, fire and sulfur rained down from heaven and destroyed them all.

30. Bushi n'emuako uli ng'oyu, ebandu bakaba batachikunganyise elusuku Nyono nyi Mwana w'eMundu nyikafuluka.

30. 부씨 너무아고 우삐 꼬유, 어바뚜 바가바 바다찌구뫄네서 어루수구 뇨노 네 뫄나 워무뚜 네가푸루가.

30. "It will be just like this on the day the Son of Man is revealed.

31. "Mukengeraa kwa muka Loti afaa bushi n'ekulola era nyumba. Olu lusuku, ola Ukaba utalyi mwa nyumba yai arekire n'e bikayi byaimui, atakachibone bihangi bya Kuhuba mui mbu abitole.

31. "무거뭐라아 과 무가 롣디 아파아 부씨 너구뢴롸 어라 뉴빠. 오루 루수구, 오롸 우가바 우다레 뫄 뉴빠 야이 아러기러 너 비가에 뱌이무이, 아다가찌보너 비하뗘 뱌 구후바 무이 뿌 아비도뤄.

31. On that day no one who is on the roof of his house, with his goods inside, should go down to get them. Likewise, no one in the field should go back for anything.

32. N'nola ukaba waire era mahwa, atakachiale kufuluka *Kwa musi, si yi akere anarengera eyi ahaa.*

32. 우노롸 우가바 와이러 어라 마화, 아다가찌아뤄 구푸루가 *과 무시, 시 에 아거러 아나러뫄띱 어에 아하아.*

32. Remember Lot's wife!

33. Ola ukahonda kulanga E kalamo kai k'omuno butala n'ekulaira kunyikulikira, atakabone ekalamo k'esuku n'amango. Si oa kakases bushi nayi, akabona ka k'e suku n'a mango.

33. 오롸 우가호따 구라뫄 어 가롸모 가이 고무노 부다롸 너구롸이라 구네구뤼기라, 아다가보너 어가롸모 거수구 나마꼬. 시 오아 가가서수 부씨 나에, 아가보나 가 거 수구 나 마꼬.

33. Whoever tries to keep his life will lose it, and whoever loses his life will preserve it.

34. Chichine chi muenyereraa: Olu lusuku, bandju babiri bakaba baonje ku njingo Nguma batufu; nyikeka muuma mwa lmoo lwani, nyiareka na mua achinjbusibwe.

34. 찌찌너 찌 무어녀러라아: 오루 루수구, 바뚜 바비리 바가바 바오쩌 구 찌꼬 뭉마 바두푸; 네거가 무우마 롸 루모오 롸니, 네아러가 나 무아 아찌뚜부시붜.

34. I tell you, on that night two people will be in one bed; one will be taken and the other left.

35. Bakasi babiri bakaba bashira al'auma; nyikeka muuma mwa lumoo lwanyi, Nyikareka na muuma achinjibusibwe.

36. Balume babiri bakaba bakola mw'ehwa; nyikeka muuma mwa lumoo lwanyi, nyikareka na muuma achinjibusibwe".

37. Ebanafunzi bomvire bacha, bera kubusa Yesu: "Enawechwu,ngaeu ukaikira?" Nai era kubakula mwa muso: "Ala echirunda chikaba chiri, w'e bikona bikanehula."

35. 바가시 바비리 바가바 바씨라 아롸우마; 네거가 무우마 뫄 루모오 똬네, 네가러가 나 무우마 아찌띠부시붜.

36. 바루머 바비리 바가바 바고롸 뭐화; 네거가 무우마 뫄 루모오 똬네, 네가러가 나 무우마 아찌띠부시붜".

37. 어바나푸씨 보삐러 바짜, 버라 구부사 여수: "어나워쭈,까어우 우가이기라?" 나이 어라 구바구롸 뫄 무소: "아롸 어찌루따 찌가바 찌리, 워 비고나 비가너후롸."

35. Two women will be grinding grain together; one will be taken and the other left."

36 None

37. "Where, Lord?" they asked. He replied, "Where there is a dead body, there the vultures will gather."

Luka Chikono 18
Emurusu n'emuhumba-kasi

1. Kanji Yesu aishiraa ebanafunzi bai ono unji muanyi. Abaa wa kubalosa kwa bendaa bema Ongo busira kutama.

2. Era kutangirisa ahambala: "Kwabaa muishi wa manja mu musi muuma. Abaa atatunda Ongo, kanji abaa atanaanja na unji mundu.

3. Kanji mw'oyu musi mwabaa mutula muhumba-kasi muuma ola wendaa washiba waikira oyu muishi w'emanja n'e kumubura "Unyiishiraa kubuya elubanja

루가 찌고노 18
어무루수 너무후빠-가시

1. 가찌 여수 아이씨라아 어바나푸씨 바이 오노 우찌 무아네. 아바아 와 구바로사 과 버따아 버마 오꼬 부시라 구다마.

2. 어라 구다끼리사 아하빠롸: "과바아 무이씨 와 마짜 무 무시 무우마. 아바아 아다두따 오꼬, 가찌 아바아 아다나아짜 나 우찌 무뚜.

3. 가찌 모유 무시 뫄바아 무두롸 무후빠-가시 무우마 오롸 워따아 와씨바 와이기라 오유 무이씨 워마짜 너 구무부라: "우네이씨라아

Luke Chapter 18[NIV]

1. Then Jesus told his disciples a parable to show them that they should always pray and not give up.

2. He said: "In a certain town there was a judge who neither feared God nor cared about men.

3. And there was a widow in that town who kept coming to him with the plea, 'Grant me justice against my adversary.'

nyitusa n'emurenda wanyi", 구부야 어루바짜 네두사
너무러따 와네",

4. Si suku sita sieke sanarengaa analaire kumuishira lu. Chasinjire, oyu muishi w'e manja era kuanyisa mwa muchima wai mmbu: "Nyishi kwa Nyono ndatunda Ongo, kanji ndaanja na unji mundu.

4. 시 수구 시다 시어거 사나러꽈아 아나빠이러 구무이씨라 루. 짜시찌러, 오유 무이씨 워 마짜 어라 구아네사 꽈 무찌마 와이 무뿌: "네씨 과 뇨노 따두따 오꼬, 가찌 따아짜 나 우찌 무뚜.

4. "For some time he refused. But finally he said to himself, 'Even though I don't fear God or care about men,

5. Si oku ono muhumba-kasai anyibikire kwa shoko, nyingamuishira elubanja lwai kubuya, bushi ndairire bacha, atakanyikule kw'ekaaso."

5. 시 오구 오노 무후빠-가사이 아네비기러 과 쏘고, 네까무이씨라 어루바짜 꽈이 구부야, 부씨 따이리러 바짜, 아다가네구뻐 궈가아소."

5. yet because this widow keeps bothering me, I will see that she gets justice, so that she won't eventually wear me out with her coming!' "

6. Kanji Yesu era kuteta: "Mwomvire e mitetere y'e muishi w'e manja mubi?

6. 가찌 여수 어라 구더다: "모뻐러 어 미더더러 여 무이씨 워 마짜 무비?

6. And the Lord said, "Listen to what the unjust judge says.

7. Mulolaa kw'oyu muishi w'emanja mubi aishiraa oyu muhumba-kasi elubanja lwai kubuya! chi chingatuma Ongo nai atabaishira elubanja kubuya kuuma n'ebanji ba alondolaa, bu bende bamwema emushi n'ebutufu, kanji atusa n'emuchima kubu?

7. 무로꽈아 교유 무이씨 워마짜 무비 아이씨라아 오유 무후빠-가시 어루바짜 꽈이 구부야! 찌 찌빠두마 오꼬 나이 아다바이씨라 어루바짜 구부야 구우마 너바찌 바 아로또꽈아, 부 버떠 바뭐마 어무씨 너부두푸, 가찌 아두사 너무찌마 구부?

7. And will not God bring about justice for his chosen ones, who cry out to him day and night? Will he keep putting them off?

8. Nyono nababura kwa akabaishira elubanja kubuya fuba-fuba. Si nyono nyi Mwana w'e Mundju ndeshi akaba nyikabiiana chiro mwemeresi ola ukilhnda waika kwa businda o mango nyikafuluka!".

8. 뇨노 나바부라 과 아가바이씨라 어루바짜 구부야 푸바-푸바. 시 뇨노 네 뫄나 워 무뚜 떠씨 아가바 네가비이아나 찌로 뭐머러시 오랴 우기루후따 와이가 과 부시따 오 마꼬 네가푸루가!".

8. I tell you, he will see that they get justice, and quickly. However, when the Son of Man comes, will he find faith on the earth?"

Mufasiriyo n'e mufuchisi w'e mbarata

9. Kanji Yesu era kuisha ono unji muanyi kwa ba bendaa kabena ebanji bandju n'ekuchitonga kwa beine bu bende banaira kwa Mwaso wa Musa atula emire.

10. Era kuteta: "Balume babiri bayaa kwemera Ongo mwa Luhu lwai. Muuma mubu abaa Mufarisayo,* n'e unjiabaa mufuchisi wa mbarata.

11. Baikire mwa Luhu lwa Ongo,* bacha kw'e Mufarisayo atangirisaa achitonga mwa kwema anemenzi: Ongo, natechire mbu akoko era ulyi, bushi Nyono ndatula mubi kuuma n'e banji bandju. Beke hatula besi, kanji barenzi, kanji babanzi b'ekiri. Kanji ndatula kuuma n'ono mufuchisi w'embarata mubi ola uli muno.

12. N'ende nareka suku e bilyi ndalya nw'einga mango nema; nende nana echiuma ch'ekurni cha byoshi bya nende nabona.

13. Si emufuchisi w'embarata yeke, emangiraa marerere n'ebanji. Chiro atanahendaa atumbikise n'omwa chanya. Kwa kulosa ekuchiaya kwai, era kubika emino sai kwa chifuba n'ekuteta mmbu: Ongo,

무파시리요 너 무푸찌시 워 빠띱닛

9. 가찌 여수 어라 구이싸 오노 우찌 무아네 과 바 버빠아 가버나 어바찌 바뚜 너구찌도꽈 과 버이너 부 버너 바나이라 과 꽈소 와 무사 아두꽈 어미러.

10. 어라 구더다: "바루머 바비리 바야아 궈머라 오꼬 꽈 루후 똬이. 무우마 무부 아바아 무파리사요,* 너 우찌아바아 무푸찌시 와 빠라다.

11. 바이기러 꽈 루후 똬 오꼬,* 바짜 궈 무파리사요 아다삐리사아 아찌도꽈 꽈 궈마 아너머씨: 오꼬, 나더찌러 뿌 아고고 어라 우뤠, 부씨 뇨노 따두꽈 무비 구우마 너 바찌 바뚜. 버거 하두꽈 버시, 가찌 바러씨, 가찌 바바씨 버기리. 가찌 따두꽈 구우마 노노 무푸찌시 워빠라다 무비 오꽈 우뤼 무노.

12. 너떠 나러가 수구 어 비뤠 따뺘 누워이꽈 마꼬 너마; 너떠 나나 어찌우마 쩌구루니 짜 뵤씨 뱌 너떠 나보나.

13. 시 어무푸찌시 워빠라다 여거, 어마삐라아 마러러러 너바찌. 찌로 아다나허따아 아두뻬기서 노꽈 짜냐. 과 구로사 어구찌아야 과이, 어라 구비가 어미노 사이 과 찌푸바 너구더다 무뿌: 오꼬,

9. To some who were confident of their own righteousness and looked down on everybody else, Jesus told this parable:

10. "Two men went up to the temple to pray, one a Pharisee and the other a tax collector.

11. The Pharisee stood up and prayed about himself: 'God, I thank you that I am not like other men--robbers, evildoers, adulterers--or even like this tax collector.

12. I fast twice a week and give a tenth of all I get.'

13. "But the tax collector stood at a distance. He would not even look up to heaven, but beat his breast and said, 'God, have mercy on me, a sinner.'

unyifiraa ebonjo, bushi nyitula mukosi wa bibi.

우네피라아 어보쪼, 부씨 내두꽈 무고시 와 비비.

14. Yesu ku kwera kuteta: "Ndababisha, oyu mufuchisi w'embarata afulukaa kwa wai ababalirwe na Ongo. Si e Mufarisayo yeke atababalirwaa, bushi ola wende wacherusa yeine akendaasibwa. Si ola wende wachirembya akerusibwa."

14. 여수 구 궈라 구더다: "따바비싸, 오유 무푸찌시 웨빠라다 아푸루가아 과 와이 아바바뤼뤄 나 오꼬. 시 어 무파리사요 여거 아다바바뤼로아, 부씨 오꽈 워떠 와쩌루사 여이너 아거따아시봐. 시 오꽈 워떠 와찌러빠 아거루시봐."

14. "I tell you that this man, rather than the other, went home justified before God. For everyone who exalts himself will be humbled, and he who humbles himself will be exalted."

Yesu aahanyira e bana batoto

여수 아아하네삐 어 바나 바도도

15. Kanji ebandu bareterangaa Yesu ebana batoto mbu abaumaa ku abaahanyire. Ebanafunzi bai balolire bacha, bera kunde babakaliiranga.

15. 가찌 어바뚜 바러더라꽈아 여수 어바나 바도도 뿌 아바우마아 구 아바아하네러. 어바나푼씨 바이 바롤뤼러 바짜, 버라 구떠 바바가뤼이라꽈.

15. People were also bringing babies to Jesus to have him touch them. When the disciples saw this, they rebuked them.

16. Si Yesu era kubarangira abu bana n'ekubura ebanafunzi bai: "Murekaa ebana batoto babahe ene nyiri, mutabengaa, bushi eBwami bwa Ongo bunatula kwa ba bali ng'abu.

16. 시 여수 어라 구바라삐라 아부 바나 너구부라 어바나푼씨 바이: "무러가아 어바나 바도도 바바허 어너 니리, 무다벵까아, 부씨 어봐미 봐 오꼬 부나두꽈 과 바 바삐 꾸아부.

16. But Jesus called the children to him and said, "Let the little children come to me, and do not hinder them, for the kingdom of God belongs to such as these.

17. Ku binali, mu nabura: Ola uikatunde Ongo ng'okwa mwana mutoto,ende atunda ebasere bai atikaike mwa Bwami bwai chiro na hicha."

17. 구 비나뤼, 무 나부라: 오꽈 우이가두떠 오꼬 꼬과 모나 무도도,어떠 아두따 어바서러 바이 아디가이거 꽈 봐미 봐이 찌로 나 히짜."

17. I tell you the truth, anyone who will not receive the kingdom of God like a little child will never enter it."

Yesu n'eMundju we bikulo binene

여수 너무뚜 워 비구롯 비너너

18. Kwabaa muare muuma, kanji mukulu-kulu w'echihaala

18. 과바아 무아러 무우마, 가찌 무구룰-구루 워찌하아꽈

18. A certain ruler asked him, "Good teacher, what

ch'eBayuta. Lusuku luuma, era kubura Yesu: "Mukangirisi, nyishi kwa woyu utula mundu mubuya, wiraa wanyibura: Chi nyingaira nyibone ekalamo k'esuku n'e mango?"

19. Yesu era kumwakula: "Si wishi kwa kutati.ila mubuya kureka Ongo yeine! Chi chera chingatiima wnyfrika mubuya?

20. Kanji u wabusa mbu chi uiraa, si utula wishi eMwaso* wa Ongo: Utendaa wabanda ekiri, utabaa mwichi wa bandu, utendaa weba, utendaa wsinga emundu cha atafraa. Wendaa wtunda eho na nyoko."

21. Oyu mundu era kwekula: "Ebi byoshi nende nanabijra kutengera elyana etoto Iyanyi."

22. Yesu omvire bacha, era kumubura: "Kwakushibira kuira chinji chindu chiuma: Uhubaa kwa wau, wanausa byoshi bya wete, uabire ebakene ebutea bingafa. Ukalra bacha, ungabona bikulo binene kwa nguba. Chasinda, unyikulikiraa iibe mwanafunzi wanyi"

23. Si mango oyu mukulu-kulu omvaa mbu ailsaa ebyai byoshi atiula na muare, era kusinana busese.

쩌바유다. 루수구 루우마, 어라 구부라 여수: "무가끼리시, 네씨 과 오유 우두롸 무뚜 무부야, 위라아 와네부라: 찌 네까이라 네보너 어가롸모 거수구 너 마꼬?"

19. 여수 어라 구롸구롸: "시 위씨 과 구다디.이롸 무부야 구러가 오꼬 여이너! 찌 쩌라 찌까디이마 우네푸리가 무부야?

20. 가찌 우 와부사 뿌 찌 우이라아, 시 우두롸 위씨 어롸소* 와 오꼬: 우더따아 와바따 어기리, 우다바아 뮈찌 와 바뚜, 우더따아 워바, 우더따아 우시까 어무뚜 짜 아다푸라아. 워따아 우두따 어호 나 뇨고."

21. 오유 무뚜 어라 궈구롸: "어비 뵤씨 너떠 나나비jra 구더꺼라 어롸나 어도도 랴네."

22. 여수 오삐러 바짜, 어라 구무부라: "과구씨비라 구이라 찌찌 찌뚜 찌우마: 우후바아 과 와우, 와나우사 뵤씨 뱌 워더, 우아비러 어바거너 어부더아 비까파. 우가루라 바짜, 우까보나 비구로 비너너 과 꾸바. 짜시따, 우네구뀌기라아 이이버 마나푸씨 와네"

23. 시 마꼬 오유 무구루-구루 오빠아 뿌 아이루사아 어뱌이 뵤씨 아디우롸 나 무아러, 어라 구시나나 부서서.

---

must I do to inherit eternal life?"

19. "Why do you call me good?" Jesus answered. "No one is good--except God alone.

20. You know the commandments: 'Do not commit adultery, do not murder, do not steal, do not give false testimony, honor your father and mother.'"

21. "All these I have kept since I was a boy," he said.

22. When Jesus heard this, he said to him, "You still lack one thing. Sell everything you have and give to the poor, and you will have treasure in heaven. Then come, follow me."

23. When he heard this, he became very sad, because he was a man of great wealth.

---

24. Yesu alolire kw'oyu mutambo asinanyire busese, era kuteta: "Kutkabe kubofu kwa baare kwingirira mwa Bwami bwa Ongo!

25. Ekuulukana kw'engaafu mwa chiture ch'esinge ku kubofu kwa muare kwingirira mwa Bwanii bwa Ongo."

26. Ba bomvaa kwa Yesu teta bacha, bera kwire bebusa: Nande i ukere wengirira mw'obu Bwami bwa Ongo?

27. Yesu era kubakula: "Cha chitangaalikana n'ebandu era mwa Ongo yeke, chingaalikana."

28. Petero naiomvire bacha, era kuteta: "Ulolaa kwa tubano twarekire bya twataa byoshi bushi n'ekukukulikira."

29. Yesu ku kwera'ubura ebanafunzi bai: "Ku binali, nebabura kwa kutali ola ungahondosa e Bwami bwa Ongo kurenza enyumba yai, nesi mukai, nesi banyakabu, nesi ebasere bai, nesi ebana bai,

30. aine kutabona binene kw'ebi muno butala, abone n'ekalamo k'esuku n'emango mwa suku seshire."

Emiasi y'e kufa kwa Yesu

24. 여수 아로찌러 교유 무다뽀 아시나니러 부서서, 어라 구더다: "구두가버 구보푸 과 바아러 귀띠리라 뫄 봐미 봐 오꼬!

25. 어구우루가나 궈꺼아푸 뫄 찌두러 쩌시뻐 구 구보푸 과 무아러 귀띠리라 뫄 봐니이 봐 오꼬."

26. 바 보빠아 과 여수 더다 바짜, 버라 귀러 버부사: 나너 이 우거러 워띠리라 모부 봐미 봐 오꼬?

27. 여수 어라 구바구꽈: "짜 찌다꺼아찌가나 너바뚜 어라 뫄 오꼬 여거, 찌꺼아찌가나."

28. 퍼더로 나이오뻐러 바짜, 어라 구더다: "우로꽈아 과 두바노 돠러기러 뱌 돠다아 뵤씨 부씨 너구구구찌기라."

29. 여수 구 궈라우부라 어바나푸씨 바이: "구 비나찌, 너바부라 과 구다찌 오꽈 우꺼아호또사 어 봐미 봐 오꼬 구러싸 어뉴빠 야이, 너시 무가이, 너시 바냐가부, 너시 어바서러 바이, 너시 어바나 바이,

30. 아이너 구다보나 비너너 궈비 무노 부다꽈, 아보너 너가꽈모 거수구 너마꼬 뫄 수구 서씨러."

어미아시 여 구파 과 여수

24. Jesus looked at him and said, "How hard it is for the rich to enter the kingdom of God!

25. Indeed, it is easier for a camel to go through the eye of a needle than for a rich man to enter the kingdom of God."

26. Those who heard this asked, "Who then can be saved?"

27. Jesus replied, "What is impossible with men is possible with God."

28. Peter said to him, "We have left all we had to follow you!"

29. "I tell you the truth," Jesus said to them, "no one who has left home or wife or brothers or parents or children for the sake of the kingdom of God

30. will fail to receive many times as much in this age and, in the age to come, eternal life."

31. Era nyuma s'ebi, Yesu era kubura endumwa* sai: "Mumenyereraa, eYerusalemu ene tweia twerukira. Byoshi bya byanjikwaa n'ebarebi era luulu sanyi nyi.Mwana w'eMundu, eyera yi byernire bibe.

32. Ku kuteta rnbu eBayuta bangnyibika mwa maboko m'ebandu ha bataniia Bayuta. Aboa bu bangnyishekera, bananyikambe, bananyichire ku.

33. Mango bangaba banyihuyaise, banganyita. Si ku suku ehatu, nyingemolwa."

34. Si endumwasitomvaa chiro na hicha mw'ebi binwa Yesu abaa eteta. Kanji sitiienyereraa kute kw'ei niyasi yabaa itechire. Chiro sitanamenyereraa era luulu sa myasi ichie Yesu abaa ahambala ku.

Emunta we yeriko

35. Chasinda, Yesu era kunaendekerana n'e luendo iwai lw'e kwilukira e yerusalemu. Abere era ah ofu n'emusi w'e Yeriko, muuta muuma nai abaa ekesi kwa musike snpra emeresa.

36. Abere oyu muutaomva kwa lusindo lw'ebandu ba babaa bali na Yesu, era kubusa bu

---

31. 어라 뉴마 서비, 여수 어라 구부라 어뚜뫄* 사이: "무머녀러라아, 어여루사뻐무 어너 뛰이아 뛰루기라. 뵤씨 뱌 뱌찌과아 너바러비 어라 룬우룬 사네 네.뫄나 워무뚜, 어여라 에 벼루니러 비버.

32. 구 구더다 루뿌 어바유다 바읶네비가 뫄 마보고 머바뚜 하 바다니이아 바유다. 아보아 부 바읶네써거라, 바나네가뻐, 바나네찌러 구.

33. 마꼬 바꺄바 바네후야이서, 바꺄니다. 시 구 수구 어하두, 네뻐모꽈."

34. 시 어뚜뫄시도빠아 찌로 나 히짜 뭐비 비놔 여수 아바아 어더다. 가찌 시디이어녀러라아 구더 궈이 니야시 야바아 이더찌러. 찌로 시다나머녀러라아 어라 룬우룬 사 먀시 이쩌 여수 아바아 아하빠롸 구.

어무누다 워 여리고

35. 짜시따, 여수 어라 구나어더거라나 너 룬어또 이와이 뭐 귀룬기라 어 여루사뻐무. 아버러 어라 아후 오푸 너무시 워 여리고, 무우다 무우마 나이 아바아 어거시 과 무시거 수누p라 어머러사.

36. 아버러 오유 무우다오빠 과 룬시또 뭐바뚜 바 바바아 바뛰 나 여수, 어라 구부사 부 뿌 찌

---

31. Jesus took the Twelve aside and told them, "We are going up to Jerusalem, and everything that is written by the prophets about the Son of Man will be fulfilled.

32. He will be handed over to the Gentiles. They will mock him, insult him, spit on him, flog him and kill him.

33. On the third day he will rise again."

34. The disciples did not understand any of this. Its meaning was hidden from them, and they did not know what he was talking about.

35. As Jesus approached Jericho, a blind man was sitting by the roadside begging.

36. When he heard the crowd going by, he asked what was happening.

mbu chi chabere.

짜버러.

37. Bera kt.nnubur inhu Yesu mwesha Nasareti i werenga.

37. 버라 구두.누누부루 이누후 여수 뭐싸 나사러디 이 워러까.

37. They told him, "Jesus of Nazareth is passing by."

38. omvire bacha, ku kwera kutitna emurenge: "Yesu, mwenyi Tauti, unyifiraa ebonjo!

38. 오뻬러 바짜, 구 궈라 구디두나 어무러꺼: "여수, 뭐네 다우디, 우네피라아 어보쪼!

38. He called out, "Jesus, Son of David, have mercy on me!"

39. Ba babaa hahondorere eluamba lw'ebandu babaa bamukaliira mbu asiraa. Si kanji naendekeranaa auma emurenge kusimbu: "E Mwenyi Tauti, unyifiraa ebonjo."

39. 바 바바아 하호또러러 어루아빠 뤄바뚜 바바아 바무가꿰이라 뿌 아시라아. 시 가찌 나어떠거라나아 아우마 어무러꺼 구시뿌: "어 뭐네 다우디, 우네피라아 어보쪼."

39. Those who led the way rebuked him and told him to be quiet, but he shouted all the more, "Son of David, have mercy on me!"

40. Yesu era kwemanga. Era kuteta mbu banittal i. Ahere aika ofu na Yesu, Yesu era kumubusa:

40. 여수 어라 궈마까. 어라 구더다 뿌 바니따루 이. 아허러 아이가 오푸 나 여수, 여수 어라 구무부사:

40. Jesus stopped and ordered the man to be brought to him. When he came near, Jesus asked him,

41. "Chi wanona nyikuirire?" Oyu muuta era kumw? kula: Enawechwu, nahonda nyilole kanji buyayaya.

41. "찌 와노나 네구이리러?" 오유 무우다 어라 구무우? 구꽈: 어나워쭈, 나호따 네로러 가찌 부야야야.

41. "What do you want me to do for you?" "Lord, I want to see," he replied.

42. Yesu ku kwera kumubura: "Ebwemweresi! Hubaa kulola hwakuniinwire! Hubaa kulola buyayaya.

42. 여수 구 궈라 구무부라: "어붜뭐러시! 후바아 구로꽈 화구니이니위러! 후바아 구로꽈 부야야야.

42. Jesus said to him, "Receive your sight; your faith has healed you."

43. Unao-unao, era kunalola buyayaya. Era kwirnisa Yesu aenda atonga Ongo Mano ebandu boshi balalaa kw'ebya hyabere, nabu bera kutonga Ongo.

43. 우나오-우나오, 어라 구나로꽈 부야야야. 어라 귀루니사 여수 아어빠 아도까 오꼬 마노 어바뚜 보씨 바꽈꽈아 궈뱌 햐버러, 나부 버라 구도까 오꼬.

43. Immediately he received his sight and followed Jesus, praising God. When all the people saw it, they also praised God.

Luka Chikono 19
Yesu buna zakayo

1. Yesu abaa era ahabuka emusi w'eYeriko.

2. Mw'oyu musi mwobaa mutala mulume muuna.mbu i Sakayo. Abaa mukulu-kulu. w'e bafuchisi b'embarata Kanji baa muare.

3. Abere Yesu era arenga, Sakayo nai era kuhonda amumenye. Si abaa atangaala kumulola ku bushi n'eluamba lw'ebandu, kanji bushiabaa atula mufu-mufu.

4 .Alolire bacha, ku kwera kulibichira era muhondo muchi abaa ali u Yesu angarenga.

5. Mango Yesu aikaa ala Sakayoabaa ali kwa muchi, era kutumbikisa mwa chanya n'ekumubura: "Sakayo, wendaalaa fuba, bushi binyemire nyibe mwau lwarero."

6. Sakayo era kunandala kwa muchi fuba-fuba, era kwngirira Yesu mwa mwai n'elumoo.

7. Ba babaa bali bali aole balolire bacha, bera kutangirisa bachitetembya: "Mwa mw'e mukosi w'e bibi mu Yesu aire kuonjira!"

루가 찌고노 19
여수 부나 자가요

1. 여수 아바아 어라 아하부가 어무시 워여리고.

2. 모유 무시 모바아 무다꽈 무루머 무우나.뿌 이 사가요. 아바아 무구루-구루. 워 바푸찌시 버빠라다 가찌 바아 무아러.

3. 아버러 여수 어라 아러꽈, 사가요 나이 어라 구호따 아무머녀. 시 아바아 아다꽈아꽈 구무롣꽈 구 부씨 너루아빠 뤄바뚜, 가찌 부씨아바아 아두꽈 무푸-무푸.

4. 아롣리러 바짜, 구 궈라 구끄비찌라 어라 무호또 무찌 아바아 아뤼 우 여수 아꽈러꽈.

5. 마꼬 여수 아이가아 아꽈 사가요아바아 아뤼 과 무찌, 어라 구두삐기사 뫄 짜냐 너구무부라: "사가요, 워따아꽈라아 푸바, 부씨 비녀미러 니버 뫄우 꽈러로."

6. 사가요 어라 구나따꽈 과 무찌 푸바-푸바, 어라 구끼리라 여수 뫄 마이 너루모오.

7. 바 바바아 바뤼 바뤼 아오뻐 바롣끄러 바짜, 버라 구다끼리사 바찌더더꽉: "뫄 뭐 무고시 워 비비 무 여수 아이러 구오끼라!"

Luke Chapter 19[NIV]

1. Jesus entered Jericho and was passing through.

2. A man was there by the name of Zacchaeus; he was a chief tax collector and was wealthy.

3. He wanted to see who Jesus was, but being a short man he could not, because of the crowd.

4. So he ran ahead and climbed a sycamore-fig tree to see him, since Jesus was coming that way.

5. When Jesus reached the spot, he looked up and said to him, "Zacchaeus, come down immediately. I must stay at your house today."

6. So he came down at once and welcomed him gladly.

7. All the people saw this and began to mutter, "He has gone to be the guest of a 'sinner.' "

8. Abere bera bali mwa nyiirnba, Sakayo era kwemanga era muhondo sa Yesu kuna kuteta: "omvaa, Enawetu: Ola nanyaa kai, nyingya kumuiulira ku kane. Kanji nyinganaya kuabira ebakene chimbi kwa bikulo byanyi."

9. Yesu ku kwera kubura ba babaa bali aola: "Lwarero, ebunuriusi bwaikirire ene ngumu y'ono mundu, bushi nai anete ebwemeresi ng'obwa bw'eho wenyu Aburahamu.
10. Mumenyereraa kubuya-buya kwa Nyono nyi Mwana w'eMundu nbahire kuhonda ola waerire nyimununule."

E muanyi wa muare muuma n'e bambalyi

11. Mango Yesu abaa alinga kwingirira mwa musi w'eYerusalemu, ebandu babaa bamumvirisa. Kanji abu bandu babaa bera bnyisa mbu eBwimi bwa Ongo butachimange kuika. Bushi n'oku, Yesu era kubaishira ono muanyi:
12. "Kwabaa mulusi muuma ola wabaa whonda kubalamira mu chio cha burerere emikirwe mu, siabaa angahuba kufuluka kwema mwa chio chai.

---

8. 아버러 버라 바삐 뫄 네이루빠, 사가요 어라 귀마뽜 어라 무호또 사 여수 구나 구더다: "오빠아, 어나워두: 오롸 나냐아 가이, 네먀 구무이우삐라 구 가너. 가찌 네뽜나야 구아비라 어바거너 찌삐 과 비구롣 뱌니."

9. 여수 구 궈라 구부라 바 바바아 바삐 아오롸: "롸러로, 어부누리우시 봐이기리러 어너 뿌무 요노 무뚜, 부씨 나이 아너더 어뭐머러시 끄봐 뷔호 워뉴 아부라하무.
10. 무머녀러라아 구부야-부야 과 뇨노 네 뫄나 워무뚜 빠히러 구호따 오롸 와어리러 네무누누뤄."

어 무아네 와 무아러 무우마 너 바빠뤠

11. 마꼬 여수 아바아 아뤼뽜 귀삐리라 뫄 무시 워여루사뭐무, 어바누 바바아 바무뻬리사. 가찌 아부 바뚜 바바아 버라 부네사 뿌 어뷔미 봐 오꼬 부다찌마뭐 구이가. 부씨 노구, 여수 어라 구바이씨라 오노 무아네:
12. "과바아 무룻시 무우마 오롸 와바아 우호따 구바롸미라 무 찌오 짜 부러러러 어미기뤄 무, 시아바아 아뽜후바 구푸룻가 궈마 뫄 찌오 짜이.

---

8. But Zacchaeus stood up and said to the Lord, "Look, Lord! Here and now I give half of my possessions to the poor, and if I have cheated anybody out of anything, I will pay back four times the amount."

9. Jesus said to him, "Today salvation has come to this house, because this man, too, is a son of Abraham.
10. For the Son of Man came to seek and to save what was lost."

11. While they were listening to this, he went on to tell them a parable, because he was near Jerusalem and the people thought that the kingdom of God was going to appear at once.
12. He said: "A man of noble birth went to a distant country to have himself appointed king and then to return.

13. Era muhondo s'ekuenda, era kubarangira ekumi mwa baanda bai. Era kweresa boshi chikanda cha butea, era kubura mbu: "Munyichimbuliraa kuikira mango nyikfuluka". Era kuhima.

14. Si oyu mulusiabaa atasimirwe n'ehandu b'omwa chio thai. Bushi n'oku, hera kumutumira endumwa* mwa chio cha abaa: emikirwa mu rnbu batahenda be mwarni wabu."

15. "Era kuneresibwa obu bwami chiro angaba mbu bamulairaa. Abere afuluka, era kwamaala ba baanda ekumi, bushi abaa ahonda amenyerere emutoloke ola wabonekire mwa buchimbusi kwa bairaa.

16. Ola mubere-bere emkuiba n'ekuteta: "Enawetu, elutea lwa wambaa lwabuchire sinji ekumi"

17. Mwami era kumubura: "Wakolire! uli muanda mubuya. Ungere wemangira misi ekumi inenene, bushi wakolaa kubuya mwa hy'ekandu hieke"

18. Ola wakabiri nai era kuika n'ekuteta: "Enawetu lwa lutea lwau lwabuchire sinji etano".

13. 어라 무호또 서구어따, 어라 구바라삐라 어구미 똬 바아따 바이. 어라 궈러사 보씨 찌가따 짜 부더아, 어라 구부라 뿌: "무네찌뿌삐라아 구이기라 마ᆢ오 네구푸루가". 어라 구히마.

14. 시 오유 무루시아바아 아다시미뤄 너하뚜 보와 찌오 따이. 부씨 노구, 허라 구무두미라 어뚜똬* 똬 찌오 짜 아바아: 어미기롸 무 루뿌 바다허따 버 롸루니 와부."

15. "어라 구너러시봐 오부 봐미 찌로 아까바 뿌 바무똬이라아. 아버러 아푸루가, 어라 과마아롸 바 바아따 어구미, 부씨 아바아 아호따 아머녀러러 어무도롣거 오롸 와보너기러 똬 부찌뿌시 과 바이라아.

16. 오롸 무버러-버러 어무구이바 너구더다: "어나워두, 어루더아 똬 와빠아 똬부찌러 시찌 어구미"

17. 똬미 어라 구무부라: "와고삐러! 우삐 무아따 무부야. 우꺼러 워마삐라 미시 어구미 이너너너, 부씨 와고롸아 구부야 똬 혀가뚜 히어거"

18. 오롸 와가비리 나이 어라 구이가 너구더다: "어나워두 똬 루더아 똬우 똬부찌러 시찌 어다노".

13. So he called ten of his servants and gave them ten minas.'Put this money to work,' he said, 'until I come back.'

14. "But his subjects hated him and sent a delegation after him to say, 'We don't want this man to be our king.'

15. "He was made king, however, and returned home. Then he sent for the servants to whom he had given the money, in order to find out what they had gained with it.

16. "The first one came and said, 'Sir, your mina has earned ten more.'

17. " 'Well done, my good servant!' his master replied. 'Because you have been trustworthy in a very small matter, take charge of ten cities.'

18. "The second came and said, 'Sir, your mina has earned five more.'

19. Mwami era kubura oyu unji nai: "N'nau ungere wemangira misi etano inenene.

20. Eunji nai era kuika n'ekuteta: Enawetu, nakuretere lwa lutea lwau, nabishaa lu burerere mwa kamba.

21. Nabaa nakubaa busese, bushi utula mulume musibu. wende wachitorera ka utakoreraa, kanji wende washebula bya utaingaa.

22. Mwami era kumubura: Woyu uli muanda mubi. Bushi n'oku, nyingakuchinjibusa kukulikana n'ei mitetere yau y'e bisha. Akaba wabaa wishi kwa Nyono' nyitula mulume musibu nende n?chitorera, kanji nende n?shebula bya ndaingaa;

23. chi chachwumaa utalumba weresise e bachimbusi olu lwanyi? Nyishi kwa mwa kufuluka banganyilulire lu al'auma n'emutoloke.'

24. Chasinjire, oyu mwami era kubura ba babaa bali aola: Mumunyaa olu lutea mulwerese ola wete butea ekumi.

25. Nabu bera kumubura:

---

19. 마미 어라 구부라 오유 우찌 나이: "우나우 우꺼러 워마삐라 미시 어다노 이너너너.

20. 어우찌 나이 어라 구이가 너구더다: 어나워두, 나구러더러 꽈 루더아 꽈우, 나비싸아 루 부러러러 꽈 가빠.

21. 나바아 나구바아 부서서, 부씨 우두꽈 무루머 무시부. 워꺼 와찌도러라 가 우다고러라아, 가찌 워꺼 와써부꽈 뱌 우다이꺼아.

22. 마미 어라 구무부라: 오유 우뤼 무아따 무비. 부씨 노구, 네꺼구찌찌부사 구구뤼가나 너이 미더더러 야우 여 비싸. 아가바 와바아 위씨 과 뇨노 네두꽈 무루머 무시부, 너꺼 누?찌도러라, 가찌 너꺼 누?써부꽈 뱌 따이꺼아;

23. 찌 짜쭈마아 우다루빠 워러시서 어 바찌뿌시 오루 꽈네? 네씨 과 와 구푸루가 바꺼네루뤼러 루 아꽈우마 너무도롱거.

24. 짜시찌러, 오유 마미 어라 구부라 바 바바아 바뤼 아오꽈: 무무냐아 오루 루더아 무꿔러서 오꽈 워더 부더아 어구미.

25. 나부 버라 구무부라:

---

19. "His master answered, 'You take charge of five cities.'

20. "Then another servant came and said, 'Sir, here is your mina; I have kept it laid away in a piece of cloth.

21. I was afraid of you, because you are a hard man. You take out what you did not put in and reap what you did not sow.'

22. "His master replied, 'I will judge you by your own words, you wicked servant! You knew, did you, that I am a hard man, taking out what I did not put in, and reaping what I did not sow?

23. Why then didn't you put my money on deposit, so that when I came back, I could have collected it with interest?'

24. "Then he said to those standing by, 'Take his mina away from him and give it to the one who has ten minas.'

25. " 'Sir,' they said, 'he

Enawetu, si oyola abonyire butea ekumi mira!

26. Oyu mwami ku kwera kuteta: Mumvaa kwa nbabura: ola ukakoresa n'ebwenge keresibwaa, akeresibwa na binji. Si ola utakakorese n'ebwenge keresibwaa; akanyaibwa ku.

27. Kanji oyu mwami era kuteta: Ebarenda banyi, ba batahondaa nyibe mwami wabu, muberetaa anola munabakerere mwa meho manyi."

Yesu aye ika eYerusalemu

28. Mango Yesu abaa era amalaa kuisha oyu muanyi, era kunaendekerana n'eluendo lwai lw'ekwirukira eYerusalemu. Abaa ahondorere eluamba lw'ebandu.

29. Abere aika ofu n'emusi w'eBetefake n'ew'eBetanyiya, mwa ndambi s'ekatulungu k'emichi y'eMiseitunyi,* era kutuma banafunzi babiri mmbu:

30. "Muyaa kwa musi uli era muhondo setu. Mango mungaika ku, mungabuana ndokomu ilyi kwa lukoba, kanji itafuraa kwikalwa ku na mundu. Mungaboola i n'e kureta i.

31. N'akaba kungaba ola ungababusa mbu chi chatuma mwaboola i, bacha ku

어나워두, 시 오요롸 아보니러 부더아 어구미 미라!

26. 오유 꽈미 구 궈라 구더다: 무빠아 과 빠부라: 오롸 우가고러사 너붜꿔 거러시봐아, 아거러시봐 나 비찌. 시 오롸 우다가고러서 너붜꿔 거러시봐아; 아가냐이봐 구.

27. 가찌 오유 꽈미 어라 구더다: 어바러따 바니, 바 바다호따아 니버 꽈미 와부, 무버러다아 아노롸 무나바거러러 꽈 머호 마니."

여수 아여 이가 어여루사뻐물

28. 마꼬 여수 아바아 어라 아마롸아 구이싸 오유 무아네, 어라 구나어떠거라나 너루어또 롸이 뤄귀루기라 어여루사뻐무. 아바아 아호또러러 어루아빠 뤄바뚜.

29. 아버러 아이가 오푸 너무시 워버더파거 너워버다니에야, 꽈 따삐 서가두룩우 거미찌 여미서이두네,* 어라 구두마 바나푸씨 바비리 무뿌:

30. "무야아 과 무시 우뢰 어라 무호또 서두. 마꼬 무꽈이가 구, 무꽈부아나 또고무 이뤠 과 룩고바, 가찌 이다푸라아 귀가꽈 구 나 무뚜. 무꽈보오롸 이 너 구러다 이.

31. 나가바 구꽈바 오롸 우꽈바부사 뿌 찌 짜두마 꽈보오롸 이, 바짜 구

already has ten!'

26. "He replied, 'I tell you that to everyone who has, more will be given, but as for the one who has nothing, even what he has will be taken away.

27. But those enemies of mine who did not want me to be king over them--bring them here and kill them in front of me."

28. After Jesus had said this, he went on ahead, going up to Jerusalem.

29. As he approached Bethphage and Bethany at the hill called the Mount of Olives, he sent two of his disciples, saying to them,

30. "Go to the village ahead of you, and as you enter it, you will find a colt tied there, which no one has ever ridden. Untie it and bring it here.

31. If anyone asks you, 'Why are you untying it?' tell him, 'The Lord needs

mungemwakula: Enawetu ete bwera bwai."

무꺼뫄구꽈: 어나워두 어더 뭐라 봐이."

it.' "

32. Ebanafunzi ba batumwaa bera kunaenda. Bya baburwaa na Yesu bi banalolaa ku.

32. 어바나푸씨 바 바두뫄아 버라 구나엔따. 뱌 바부롸아 나 여수 비 바나롼라아 구.

32. Those who were sent ahead went and found it just as he had told them.

33. Mango babaa bera baboola era ndokomu, besha i bera kubusa mbu: "Chi chatuma mwaboola ei ndokomu?"

33. 마꼬 바바아 버라 바보오롸 어라 또고무, 버싸 이 버라 구부사 뿌: "찌 짜두마 뫄보오롸 어이 또고무?"

33. As they were untying the colt, its owners asked them, "Why are you untying the colt?"

34. Ebanafunzi bera kubakula: "Enawetu ete bwera bwai."

34. 어바나푸씨 버라 구바구롸: "어나워두 어더 뭐라 봐이."

34. They replied, "The Lord needs it."

35. Chasinjire, bera kuretera i Yesu. Bera kubika emakochi mabu kui, na bakambachisa ku Yesu.

35. 짜시찌러, 버라 구러더라 이 여수. 버라 구비가 어마고찌 마부 구이, 나 바가빠찌사 구 여수.

35. They brought it to Jesus, threw their cloaks on the colt and put Jesus on it.

36. Mango Yesu abaa era anali mwa luendo, ebandu nabu babaa benjire bamuhashikira emakochi mabu mwa njira kwa kumweresa etunda.

36. 마꼬 여수 아바아 어라 아나뤼 뫄 룬어또, 어바뚜 나부 바바아 버찌러 바무하씨기라 어마고찌 마부 뫄 찌라 과 구뭐러사 어두따.

36. As he went along, people spread their cloaks on the road.

37. Abere Yesu era ahonda kuminuka ekatulungu k'emichi y'e Miseitunyi, ebanafunzi boshi babaa baenda bamoa busese. Babaa batonga Ongo na murenge munene, bushi ebisomerano byoshi bya balolaa ku byabaa bilosise ebuashi bwai.

37. 아버러 여수 어라 아호따 구미누가 어가두룽우 거미찌 여 미서이두네, 어바나푸씨 보씨 바바아 바어따 바모아 부서서. 바바아 바도따 오꼬 나 무러꺼 무너너, 부씨 어비소머라노 뵤씨 뱌 바롼롸아 구 뱌바아 비롼시서 어부아씨 봐이.

37. When he came near the place where the road goes down the Mount of Olives, the whole crowd of disciples began joyfully to praise God in loud voices for all the miracles they had seen:

38. Bacha ku babaa baenda bateta: "E mwami wabahire aahanyirwe mw'esina ly'Enawetu Ongo. Ebolo bubaa ala kachi-kachi ka Ongo n'e bandju, na Ongo atengwe!"

38. 바짜 구 바바아 바어따 바더다: "어 뫄미 와바히러 아아하네뤄 뭐시나 뤼어나워두 오꼬. 어보롼 부바아 아꽈 가찌-가찌 가 오꼬 너 바뚜, 나 오꼬 아더워!"

38. "Blessed is the king who comes in the name of the Lord!" "Peace in heaven and glory in the highest!"

39. Bafarisayo* bauma, ba babaa bali mwa luamba lw'ebandu, bera kubura Yesu: "Mukangirisi, kaliiraa ebanafunzi bau bareke ekuteta bacha."

40. Nai era kubakula: Momvaa kwa nababura: Akaba abola batanganyitonga, emakoi mu manganyitonga anola!'

41. Yesu era kuika ofu n'emusi w'eYerusalemu. Abere ahunda emeho kuu, era kuulirira.

42. Era kutangirisa ateta: Akaba nenyu mu besha Yerusalemu mungamenyerere kuikira Iwarero cha chingabanunwire, Ongo angabawere chi! Si ababishire chi. Emeho menyu matangafura kulola kuchi, bushi mwenyilaire.

43. Mumenyereraa kw'esuku sikabaikira sa barenda benyu bakabasungula, banabasikye al'auma n'ebana benyu. Bakabasungula, banabatanganyire n'okwa nyinda soshi.

44. Bakahanda emusi wenyu banabasikye al'auma n'ebana benyu. Batakereke ekoi ku linji mwa musi, bushi mutamenyereraa ebihangi

39. 바파리사요* 바우마, 바 바바아 바뤼 뫄 루아빠 이워바뚜, 버라 구부라 여수: "무가삐리시, 가뤼이라아 어바나푸씨 바우 바러거 어구더다 바짜."

40. 나이 어라 구바구롸: 모빠아 과 나바부라: 아가바 아보롸 바다빠네도쫘, 어마고이 무 마빠네도쫘 아노롸!

41. 여수 어라 구이가 오푸 너무시 워여루사퍼무. 아버러 아후따 어머호 구우, 어라 구우뤼리라.

42. 어라 구다삐리사 아더다: 아가바 너뉴 무 버싸 여루사퍼무 무빠머녀러러 구이기라 쫜러로 쨔 찌빠바누니위러, 오꾀 아빠바워러 찌! 시 아바비씨러 찌. 어머호 머뉴 마다빠푸라 구뢴롸 구찌, 부씨 뭐네롸이러.

43. 무머녀러라아 궈수구 시가바이기라 사 바러따 버뉴 바가바수꾸롸, 바나바시겨 아롸우마 너바나 버뉴. 바가바수꾸롸, 바나바다빠네러 노과 네따 소씨.

44. 바가하따 어무시 워뉴 바나바시겨 아롸우마 너바나 버뉴. 바다거러거 어고이 구 쮀찌 뫄 무시, 부씨 무다머녀러라아 어비하삐 오꾀

39. Some of the Pharisees in the crowd said to Jesus, "Teacher, rebuke your disciples!"

40. "I tell you," he replied, "if they keep quiet, the stones will cry out."

41. As he approached Jerusalem and saw the city, he wept over it

42. and said, "If you, even you, had only known on this day what would bring you peace--but now it is hidden from your eyes.

43. The days will come upon you when your enemies will build an embankment against you and encircle you and hem you in on every side.

44. They will dash you to the ground, you and the children within your walls. They will not leave one stone on another,

Ongo abahire. kubanunula."

아바히러. 구바누누롸."

Yesu akomya e Luhu lwa Ongo

여수 아고먀 어 루흘 롸 오끄

45. Mango Yesu abaa era alyi mwa musi w'eYerusalemu, era kwingirira mwa chibua ch'eLuhu lwa Ongo.* Aikire mu, era kuikira akolokanya ebachimbusi mulu, bushi babaa bachimbulira mulu kubi.

45. 마끄 여수 아바아 어라 아뤠 롸 무시 워여루사뤄무, 어라 귀끼리라 롸 찌부아 쩌루후 롸 오끄.* 아이기러 무, 어라 구이기라 아고롼냐 어바찌뿌시 무루, 부씨 바바아 바찌뿌뤼라 무룩 구비.

45. Then he entered the temple area and began driving out those who were selling.

46. Era kubabura: "Bacha ku eChinwa cha Ongo chitula chitechire: Enyumba yanyi itula nyumba ya kwemera mu Ongo. Si Mwabu mwaihubise nga chisiki cha bihumusi byende byabuananyira mu.,"

46. 어라 구바부롸: "바짜 구 어찌놔 짜 오끄 찌두롸 찌더찌러: 어뉴빠 야네 이두롸 뉴빠 야 궈머라 무 오끄. 시 롸부 롸이후비서 까 찌시기 짜 비후무시 벼떠 뱌부아나니라 무.,"

46. "It is written," he said to them, " 'My house will be a house of prayer'; but you have made it 'a den of robbers.'"

47. Chira lusuku, Yesu abaa enjire akangirisa mwa Luhu lwa Ongo.* Ebakulu-kulu b'e bakuhanyi ba Ongo, n'e bakangilyisi b'eMwaso, * al'auma n'ebashamuka, babaa benjire bahonda bamwichise.

47. 찌라 루수구, 여수 아바아 어찌러 아가끼리사 롸 루후 롸 오끄.* 어바구룩-구룩 버 바구하네 바 오끄, 너 바가끼뤠시 버뫄소, * 아롸우마 너바싸무가, 바바아 버찌러 바호따 바뮈찌서.

47. Every day he was teaching at the temple. But the chief priests, the teachers of the law and the leaders among the people were trying to kill him.

48. Si batabonaa kwa bangamuika ku, bushi e bandju boshi babaa benjire bamusungula bamuteire e machi.

48. 시 바다보나아 과 바꺄무이가 구, 부씨 어 바뚜 보씨 바바아 버찌러 바무수웃롸 바무더이러 어 마찌.

48. Yet they could not find any way to do it, because all the people hung on his words.

Luka Chikono 20
E buaka bushi n'e buashi bwa Yesu

루가 찌고노 20
어 부아가 부씨 너 부아씨 봐 여수

Luke Chapter 20[NIV]

1. Lusuku luuma, Yesu abaa akangilyisa ebandu mwa chibua ch'e luhu lwa Ongo n'e kubabahubanganyisa e mwasi Mubuya-buya wa Ongo. E bakulu-kulu b'ebakuhanyi ba Ongo n'e bakangilyisi b'e Mwaso, al'auma n'e bashamuka b'e Bayuda bera. Kupamukira.

2. Bera kumubusa: "Uchwuburaa, kwa loso lwande ku wenjire waira bacha, nesi nde i wakweresise e buashi bz'ekuira ebi."

3. Yesu era kubakula: "N'nanyi nahonda kubabusa mwasi muuma, munyakulaa:

4. Ebushi bw'ebubatiso bwa Yowanyi bwatengeraa era mwa Ongo, nesi kwa bandju?"

5. Bomvire bacha, bera kutangilyisa bakusanya n'e kuteta: "chwukateta mbu Ongo i wamweresaa bu, nai angatabusa mbu chi cheraa chachwuma chwutamwemerera.

6. Kanji chwukateta mbu e dandju bu bamweresa bu, e luamba loshi lulyi ano lungachwita n'e makoi, bushi luchwula lwishi kwa Yowana era buashi bwa Yowana a baa anachwula murebi."

7. Chasinjire, bera kumwakula: "chwuteshi era buashi bwa

---

1. 루수구 루우마, 여수 아바아 아가ㅁ떼레사 어바뚜 뫄 찌부아 쩌 루후 롸 오ㅇㅇ 너 구바바후바ㅆ나네사 어 뫄시 무부야-부야 와 오ㅇㅇ. 어 바구루-구루 버바구하네 바 오ㅇㅇ 너 바가ㅁ떼레시 버 뫄소, 아롸우마 너 바싸무가 버 바유다 버라. 구파무기라.

2. 버라 구무부사: "우쭈부라아, 과 로소 롸너 구 워찌러 와이라 바짜, 너시 떠 이 와궈러시서 어 부아씨 부저구이라 어비."

3. 여수 어라 구바구꽈: "우나네 나호따 구바부사 뫄시 무우마, 무냐구꽈아:

4. 어부씨 붜부바디소 봐 요와네 봐더ㅁ라아 어라 뫄 오ㅇㅇ, 너시 과 바뚜?"

5. 보ㅁ러러 바짜, 버라 구다ㅁ레사 바구사냐 너 구더다: "쭈가더다 뿌 오ㅇㅇ 이 와뭐러사아 부, 나이 아ㅁ다부사 뿌 찌 쩌라아 짜쭈마 쭈다뭐머러라.

6. 가찌 쭈가더다 뿌 어 다뚜 부 바뭐러사 부, 어 루아빠 로씨 루레 아노 루아쮜다 너 마고이, 부씨 루쭈꽈 뤼씨 과 요와나 어라 부아씨 봐 요와나 아 바아 아나쭈꽈 무러비."

7. 짜시찌러, 버라 구뫄구꽈: "쭈더씨 어라 부아씨 봐 요뫄나

---

1. One day as he was teaching the people in the temple courts and preaching the gospel, the chief priests and the teachers of the law, together with the elders, came up to him.

2. "Tell us by what authority you are doing these things," they said. "Who gave you this authority?"

3. He replied, "I will also ask you a question. Tell me,

4. John's baptism--was it from heaven, or from men?"

5. They discussed it among themselves and said, "If we say, 'From heaven,' he will ask, 'Why didn't you believe him?'

6. But if we say, 'From men,' all the people will stone us, because they are persuaded that John was a prophet."

7. So they answered, "We don't know where it was

Yomwana bwatengeraa."

봐더ᄢ라아."

from."

8. Yesu nai ku kwera kubura mbu: "N'nanyi ndagababura kwa buashi bwande ku nenjire naira bacha."

8. 여수 나이 구 궈라 구부라 뿌: "우나니 따가바부라 과 부아씨 봐더 구 너찌러 나이라 바짜."

8. Jesus said, "Neither will I tell you by what authority I am doing these things."

E bainzi babi

어 바이씨 바비

9. Yesu era kutangilyisa aishira e bandju ono unji muanyi: "Kwabaa mulume muuma ola waingaa ehwa iyai lya misabibu. Era kulirekera ebalanzi n'e kubabura mbu bakende bamwerasa kwa bifuma bifuma mwa kushebula. Chasinjire, era kubalamira mu chio cha burere ku sukusinene.

9. 여수 어라 구다ᄳ례사 아이씨라 어 바쭈 오노 우씨 무아네: "과바아 무루머 무우마 오롸 와이ᄭ아 어화 이야이 ᄙ 미사비부. 어라 구ᄙ러거라 어바ᄍ씨 너 구바부라 뿌 바거러 바뭐라사 과 비푸마 비푸마 뫄 구써부롸. 짜시찌러, 어라 구바ᄍ미라 무 찌오 짜 부러러 구 수구시너너.

9. He went on to tell the people this parable: "A man planted a vineyard, rented it to some farmers and went away for a long time.

10. Abere esuku s'ekushebula aika, en'ehwa era kutumira abu balanwi emuanda wai bawerese ewai mwango w'ebifuma. Ebalanzi bamulolire ku, bera kumupunda n'ekumukolokanya busira kufulukana kandu.

10. 아버러 어수구 서구써부롸 아이가, 어너화 어라 구두미라 아부 바ᄍ니위 어무아따 와이 바워러서 어와이 뫄ᄭ 워비푸마. 어바ᄍ씨 바무ᄙ러 구, 버라 구무푸따 너구무고ᄅ가냐 부시라 구푸ᄙ루가나 가뚜.

10. At harvest time he sent a servant to the tenants so they would give him some of the fruit of the vineyard. But the tenants beat him and sent him away empty-handed.

11. En'ehwa alolire bacha, era kutuma unji muanda, nai bera kunamupunda, bera kumukamba-kamba n'ekumufulusa emuanda wa kahatu. Bamulolire ku nai, bera kumubabasa n'e kuuma era musike s'ehwa.

11. 어너화 아ᄅᄙ러 바짜, 어라 구두마 우찌 무아따, 나이 버라 구나무푸따, 버라 구무가빠-가빠 너구무푸루사 어무아따 와 가하두. 바무ᄙ러 구 나이, 버라 구무바바사 너 구우마 어라 무시거 서화.

11. He sent another servant, but that one also they beat and treated shamefully and sent away empty-handed.

12. He sent still a third, and they wounded him

and threw him out.

13. En'ehwa ku kwera kuchibusa: kute nyinatusa, kanji ola nyisima busese, ngaba i bangatunda.

13. 어너화 구 궈라 구찌부사: 구더 네나두사, 가찌 오롸 네시마 부서서, 빠바 이 바빠두따.

13. "Then the owner of the vineyard said, 'What shall I do? I will send my son, whom I love; perhaps they will respect him.'

14. Abere ebalanzi bahunda oyu muala wai kw'emeho, bera kuya iwango n'ekuteta: "Onola i ena ono mwandju. Akaba tungamwita, tungachihokorera u."

14. 아버러 어바롸씨 바후따 오유 무아롸 와이 궈머호, 버라 구야 이와꼬 너구더다: "오노롸 이 어나 오노 먀쭈. 아가바 두빠뮈다, 두빠찌호고러라 우."

14. "But when the tenants saw him, they talked the matter over. 'This is the heir,' they said. 'Let's kill him, and the inheritance will be ours.'

15. Bushi n'oku, bera kumweka kwa musike s'ehwa kuna kumwita. "esu era kubusa e bandju: "Munyiburaa, kute ena eri ehwa era angira abu balanwi?

15. 부씨 노구, 버라 구뭐가 과 무시거 서화 구나 구뮈다. "어수 어라 구부사 어 바쭈: "무네부라아, 구더 어나 어리 어화 어라 아삐라 아부 바롸니위?

15. So they threw him out of the vineyard and killed him. "What then will the owner of the vineyard do to them?

16. Akabaha n'ekubasikya, kanji akeresa banji bandu e bulanzi bw'elyi ehwa lyai. "a babaa balyi aola bomvire bacha, bera kuteta: "Kutemire bya bilyi bacha biike."

16. 아가바하 너구바시갸, 가찌 아거러사 바찌 바뚜 어 부롸씨 뷔레 어화 랴이. "아 바바아 바레 아오롸 보삐러 바짜, 버라 구더다: "구더미러 뱌 비레 바짜 비이거."

16. He will come and kill those tenants and give the vineyard to others." When the people heard this, they said, "May this never be!"

17. Si Yesu era kubatumbira ku n'e kuteta "Kute chine Chinwa cha Ongo chihonjire ekuteta: Ekoi iya baimbi bakabulaa era musike iyahibire iy'ekuimbira, n'nola likatoera, likamufungola kw'eri ekoi akafunyikanga, n'nola likatoera, likamufungola."

17. 시 여수 어라 구바두삐라 구 너 구더다 "구더 찌너 찌놔 짜 오꼬 찌호삐러 어구더다: 어고이 이야 바이삐 바가부롸아 어라 무시거 이야히비러 이여구이삐라, 우노롸 삐가도어라, 삐가무푸꼬롸 궈리 어고이 아가푸네가빠, 우노롸 삐가도어라, 삐가무푸꼬롸."

17. Jesus looked directly at them and asked, "Then what is the meaning of that which is written: " 'The stone the builders rejected has become the capstone'?

18. Chira mundju ola watoera kwelyine koi, anga funyika-funyika, hola lyinga toweraka lyinga mu sina sina.

19. Bushi n'oku, ebakangirisi b'emwaso, al'auma n'ebakulu-kulu b'e bakuhanyi ba Ongo, bamenyereraa kwa aishire oyu muanyi bushi nabu. Bera kuhonda bamusimbe unao-unao, si bera kubaa ebandu.

Kufuta e mbarata era mwa Kaisari?

20. Abu bakangirisi b'eMwaso al'auma n'ebakulu-kulu b'ebakuhanyi ba Ongo banaedekeraa baloreresa Yesu bamuhonde kw'emyasi. Babaa bahonda bamwane era mw'emukulu-kulu w'eMuroma ola wabaa wemire mwa chio ch'eBayuita. Bera kumutuma kwebandu mwa bubisho-bisho ba babaa bachirembire mbu bu bu batula babuya, bomvirise bya angende ateta bamusimbire kubi.

21. Abu balume bera kumubura: "Mukangirisi, twishi kwa kwa binali ku wende wanakangirisa ebandu enjira ya Ongo kwa binali.

18. 찌라 무뉴 오라 와도어라 궈레너 고이, 아까 푸네가-푸네가, 호꽈 레까 도워라가 레까 무 시나 시나.

19. 부씨 노구, 어바가끼리시 버뫄소, 아꽈루마 너바구룹-구룹 버 바구하네 바 오꼬, 바머녀러라아 과 아이씨러 오유 무아네 부씨 나부. 버라 구호따 바무시뻐 우나오-우나오, 시 버라 구바아 어바뚜.

구푸다 어 빠띱닛 어라 꽈 가이사리?

20. 아부 바가끼리시 버뫄소 아꽈루마 너바구룹-구룹 버바구하네 바 오꼬 바나어더거라아 바뢰러러사 여수 바무호너 궈먀시. 바바아 바호따 바뫄너 어라 뭐무구룹-구룹 워무로마 오라 와바아 워미러 꽈 찌오 쩌바유이다. 버라 구무두마 궈바뚜 꽈 부비쏘-비쏘 바 바바아 바찌러뻐러 뿌 부 부 바두꽈 바부야, 보뻐리서 뱌 아꺼너 아더다 바무시뻐러 구비.

21. 아부 바루머 버라 구무부라: "무가끼리시, 뒤씨 과 과 비나삐 구 워떠 와나가끼리사 어바뚜 어찌라 야 오꼬 과 비나삐.

18. Everyone who falls on that stone will be broken to pieces, but he on whom it falls will be crushed."

19. The teachers of the law and the chief priests looked for a way to arrest him immediately, because they knew he had spoken this parable against them. But they were afraid of the people.

20. Keeping a close watch on him, they sent spies, who pretended to be honest. They hoped to catch Jesus in something he said so that they might hand him over to the power and authority of the governor.

21. So the spies questioned him: "Teacher, we know that you speak and teach what is right, and that you do not show partiality but teach

the way of God in accordance with the truth.

22. Wiraa watubura: eMwaso wetu atula emerere tufute embarata era mwa kaisari, nesi naanga?

23. Yesu era kumenyerera kwa kumutea ku babaa bamutea. Bushi n'oku, era kubabura:

24. "Munyilosaa echichere ch'elutea. Chihuhanyi chande, nesi esina iyande bi biri ku?" Bera kumwakula: "echihuhani cha kaisari n'esina iyai bi bibiri ku."

25. Nai ku kwera kubabura: "bushi n'oku, mwendaa mweresa kaisari bya biri byai, na ongo, mwenende mwamweresa bya biri byai."

26. chiro bakatola Yesu ku mwasi era muhondo s'ebandu ba babaa bali aola. Bera kunaina cha bangateta bushi n'ekusanwa n'ebya a bakulaa.

Yesu ahambala kw'akomoka

27. Era nyuma s'ebi, bauma mwa basandukayo [bu bende bateta kwakomoka kutatula], babu bera kuchifunda ala Yesu abaa ali kwa kumutea emwasi. Bera kumubasa:

22. 위라아 와두부라: 어꽈소 워두 아두꽈 어머러러 두푸더 어빠라다 어라 꽈 가이사리, 너시 나아까?

23. 여수 어라 구머녀려라 과 구무더아 구 바바아 바무더아. 부씨 노구, 어라 구바부라:

24. "무네로사아 어찌쩌러 쩌루더아. 찌후하니 짜떠, 너시 어시나 이야떠 비 비리 구?" 버라 구꽈구꽈: "어찌후하니 짜 가이사리 너시나 이야이 비 비비리 구."

25. 나이 구 꿔라 구바부라: "부씨 노구, 뭐따아 뭐러사 가이사리 뱌 비리 뱌이, 나 오꼬, 뭐너떠 꽈뭐러사 뱌 비리 뱌이."

26. 찌로 바가도꽈 여수 구 꽈시 어라 무호또 서바누 바 바바아 바삐 아오꽈. 버라 구나이나 짜 바까더다 부씨 너구사놔 너뱌 아 바구꽈아.

여수 아하빠꽈 과고모가

27. 어라 뉴마 서비, 바우마 꽈 바사누가요 [부 버너 바더다 과고모가 구다두꽈], 바부 버라 구찌푼따 아꽈 여수 아바아 아삐 과 구무더아 어꽈시. 버라 구무바사:

22. Is it right for us to pay taxes to Caesar or not?"

23. He saw through their duplicity and said to them,

24. "Show me a denarius. Whose portrait and inscription are on it?"

25. "Caesar's," they replied. He said to them, "Then give to Caesar what is Caesar's, and to God what is God's."

26. They were unable to trap him in what he had said there in public. And astonished by his answer, they became silent.

27. Some of the Sadducees, who say there is no resurrection, came to Jesus with a question.

28. "Mukangirisi, musa atwanjikiraa mbu akaba munyakabu mundu angafa busira kubuta, mundu angola emuhumba-kasi ola arekaa, anamubute kw'ebana, emubuto wa munyakabu angaera."

29. kanji bera kumubura: "kwabaa batabana balinda ba bula buuma. Efula yera kuhwera, yera kufa busira kubuta.

30. ewakabiri, nai era kwingira oyu muhumba-kasi, se era kufa busira kubuta nai.

31. chasinda, ewakahatu. Boshi kwa banabaa balinda, bera kunafa busira kubuta mwana kw'oyu mukasi.

32. chasinjire, ola muhumba-kasi nai era kufa.

33. wiraa watubura: oyu mukasi akere abawande mwa 'abu batabana balinda mango ebandu bakomoka! Twakubusise bacha, bushi ahwerwaa na chira muuma mubu!"

34. Yesu era kubaakula: "Ebandu b'omuno butala bende bahwera, n'ebanji bahweribwa,

28. "무가끼리시, 무사 아돠찌기라아 뿌 아가바 무냐가부 무뚜 아까파 부시라 구부다, 무뚜 아끄롸 어무후빠-가시 오롸 아러가아, 아나무부더 궈바나, 어무부도 와 무냐가부 아까어라."

29. 가찌 버라 구무부라: "과바아 바다바나 바뀌따 바 부롸 부우마. 어푸롸 여라 구훠라, 여라 구파 부시라 구부다.

30. 어와가비리, 나이 어라 귀끼라 오유 무후빠-가시, 서 어라 구파 부시라 구부다 나이.

31. 짜시따, 어와가하두. 보씨 과 바나바아 바뀌따, 버라 구나파 부시라 구부다 모나 교유 무가시.

32. 짜시찌러, 오롸 무후빠-가시 나이 어라 구파.

33. 위라아 와두부라: 오유 무가시 아거러 아바와뭐 롸 아부 바다바나 바뀌따 마끄 어바뚜 바고모가! 돠구부시서 바짜, 부씨 아훠롸아 나 찌라 무우마 무부!"

34. 여수 어라 구바아구롸: "어바뚜 보무노 부다롸 버더 바훠라, 너바씨 바훠리봐,

28. "Teacher," they said, "Moses wrote for us that if a man's brother dies and leaves a wife but no children, the man must marry the widow and have children for his brother.

29. Now there were seven brothers. The first one married a woman and died childless.

30. The second

31. and then the third married her, and in the same way the seven died, leaving no children.

32. Finally, the woman died too.

33. Now then, at the resurrection whose wife will she be, since the seven were married to her?"

34. Jesus replied, "The people of this age marry and are given in marriage.

35. si mwa komoka, ba bolorekanyire ku na ongo kwa bu baka mwa butala butala bwabahire, batakahwere ne si kuhweribwa.

36. bushi n'oku, batakachiife. Bakere baba kuuma n'ebamalaika. Kanji bu bali bana ba ongo ba akaka amwere.

37. Musa nai etetaa kanangana kwa bafu bakomoka ala anjikaa kwa ongo ahambalaa nai kutengera mw'ehaka iya iyakoreraa. Anjikirwe kwa enawetu ongo acherikaa mbu i congo wa aburahamu, na isaka, na yakobo.

38. chi chitumire ongo atula ongo wa ba basese, si atatula wa ba befire. Kanji mwa meho ma ongo, aburahamu, na isaka, na yakobo, na boshi ba bakomoka, bali u!

39. abere e bandju bomwa Yesu akwire eBasandukayo, bakangirisi bauma b'emwaso bera kuteta: "Mukangirisi, watechire kwa binali."

40. Bushi n'oku, batamubusa ku unjimwasi wa kumutea.

35. 시 뫄 고모가, 바 보로러가네러 구 나 오꼬 과 부 바가 뫄 부다롸 부다롸 봐바히러, 바다가훠러 너 시 구훠리봐.

36. 부씨 노구, 바다가찌이퍼. 바거러 바바 구우마 너바마롸이가. 가찌 부 바뤼 바나 바 오꼬 바 아가가 아뭐러.

37. 무사 나이 어더다아 가나꽈나 과 바푸 바고모가 아롸 아찌가아 과 오꼬 아하빠롸아 나이 구더뻐라 뭐하가 이야 이야고러라아. 아찌기뤄 과 어나워두 오꼬 아쩌리가아 뿌 이 고꼬 와 아부라하무, 나 이사가, 나 야고보.

38. 찌 찌두미러 오꼬 아두롸 오꼬 와 바 바서서, 시 아다두롸 와 바 버피러. 가찌 뫄 머호 마 오꼬, 아부라하무, 나 이사가, 나 야고보, 나 보씨 바 바고모가, 바뤼 우!

39. 아버러 어 바쭈 보뫄 여수 아귀러 어바사뚜가요, 바가뀌리시 바우마 버뫄소 버라 구더다: "무가뀌리시, 와더찌러 과 비나뤼."

40. 부씨 노구, 바다무부사 구 우찌뫄시 와 구무더아.

35. But those who are considered worthy of taking part in that age and in the resurrection from the dead will neither marry nor be given in marriage,

36. and they can no longer die; for they are like the angels. They are God's children, since they are children of the resurrection.

37. But in the account of the bush, even Moses showed that the dead rise, for he calls the Lord 'the God of Abraham, and the God of Isaac, and the God of Jacob.'

38. He is not the God of the dead, but of the living, for to him all are alive."

39. Some of the teachers of the law responded, "Well said, teacher!"

40. And no one dared to ask him any more

E buuma bwa Yesu buna Daudi

41. kanji Yesu era kubusa ba beteta mbu eMununusi ali mwenyi tauti?

42. Si mwishi kwa tauti yeine anjikaa mwa chitabo ch'eNyimbo mmbu: chi chingatuma mbu eMunusi ali mweyi Tauti? Yeine anjikaa chitabo ch'eNyimbo mmbu: "Enawetu ongo aburaa Enawetu: wikalaa kwa malyo manyi,

43. n'nanyi nyibe naima ebarenda bau kanji nyibabike mwa bihando byau."

44. Akaba tauti amuburaa mbu ali enawabu, kute kanji angaba mwenyi Tauti oshi au?"

45. Cha sinjire, era kubura ebanafunzi bai n'ebandu boshi banomvire:

46. "Mutendaa mwabu kuuma n'ebakangirisi b'eMwaso, bu batula basiire e kwembala enjimba sisitoire. Kanji bu batula basiiren'ekukesibwa mwa kachi-k'ebandu. Kanji bu batula basiire ekwimbala enjimba sisitoire. Kanji bu batula basiire n'e kukesibwa mwa kachi-kachi

---

어 부우마 봐 여수 부나 다우디

41. 가찌 여수 어라 구부사 바 버더다 뿌 어무누누시 아뤼 뭐네 다우디?

42. 시 뮈씨 과 다우디 여이너 아찌가아 봐 찌다보 쩌네뽀 무뿌: 찌 찌빠두마 뿌 어무누시 아뤼 뭐에 다우디? 여이너 아찌가아 찌다보 쩌네뽀 무뿌: "어나워두 오꼬 아부라아 어나워두: 위가꽈라 과 마룐 마네,

43. 우나네 네버 나이마 어바러따 바우 가찌 네바비거 봐 비하또 뱌우."

44. 아가바 다우디 아무부라아 뿌 아뤼 어나와부, 구더 가찌 아빠바 뭐네 다우디 오씨 아우?"

45. 짜 시찌러, 어라 구부라 어바나푸씨 바이 너바뚜 보씨 바노뻬러:

46. "무더따아 뫄부 구우마 너바가삐리시 버뫄소, 부 바두꽈 바시이러 어 궈빠꽈 어찌빠 시시도이러. 가찌 부 바두꽈 바시이러너구거시봐 봐 가찌-거바뚜. 가찌 부 바두꽈 바시이러 어귀빠꽈 어찌빠 시시도이러. 가찌 부 바두꽈 바시이러 너 구거시봐 봐 가찌-

---

41. Then Jesus said to them, "How is it that they say the Christis the Son of David?

42. David himself declares in the Book of Psalms: "'The Lord said to my Lord: "Sit at my right hand

43. until I make your enemies a footstool for your feet." '

44. David calls him 'Lord.' How then can he be his son?"

45. While all the people were listening, Jesus said to his disciples,

46. "Beware of the teachers of the law. They like to walk around in flowing robes and love to be greeted in the marketplaces and have the most important seats in the synagogues and -the places of honor at

k'ebandu. K'e bandju.

47. Kanji bu batula basire n'e kwikala mwa bisiki by'era muhondo mwa bihaala, n'kuchihoa ebifumbi birerere balose kwa bu banatula bandju babuya, n'noku bu bamamire bya by'e bahumba-kasi. Abola bu bak?chinjibusibwa kurenza e banji."

가찌 거바뚜. 거 바뚜.

47. 가찌 부 바두롸 바시러 너 귀가롸 롸 비시기 벼라 무호또 롸 비하아롸, 누구찌호아 어비푸뻬 비러러러 바로서 과 부 바나두롸 바뚜 바부야, 누노구 부 바마미러 뱌 벼 바후빠-가시. 아보롸 부 바구?찌찌부시봐 구러싸 어 바찌."

banquets.

47. They devour widows' houses and for a show make lengthy prayers. Such men will be punished most severely."

Luka Chikono 21
E michwulo y'e muhumbakasi

1. Abere Yesu achiri mwa chibua ch'eluhu lwa ongo, era kutumbikisa kwa bare benjire babika emitulo yabu mwa ngulubwa y'emitulo.

2. Era kulola na ku mukene muuma wa Muhumba-kasi, atosema twa bichere tubiri mw'ei ngulubwa y'e michwulo.

3. Yesu alolire bacha, era kubura ba babaa bali aola: "nababura kanangana: ono mukene w'emuhuma-kasi anyire mitulo inene kurenza emitulo y'ebanji boshi.

4. natechire bacha, bushi e banji boshi banyire e michwulo y'e butea bwa bwatalaa kwa bakoresaa. Si ono Muhumba-kasi yeke anyire loshi iwa abaa anete."

루가 찌고노 21
어 미쭈롣 여 무후빠—습

1. 아버러 여수 아찌리 롸 찌부아 쩌루후 롸 오꼬, 어라 구두뻬기사 과 바러 버찌러 바비가 어미두롣 야부 롸 응우룹봐 여미두롣.

2. 어라 구롣롸 나 구 무거너 무우마 와 무후빠-가시, 아도서마 돠 비쩌러 두비리 뭐이 응우룹봐 여 미쭈롣.

3. 여수 아롣찌러 바짜, 어라 구부라 바 바바아 바뤼 아오롸: "나바부라 가나까나: 오노 무거너 워무후마-가시 아니러 미두롣 이너너 구러싸 어미두롣 여바찌 보씨.

4. 나더찌러 바짜, 부씨 어 바찌 보씨 바니러 어 미쭈롣 여 부더아 봐 봐다롸아 과 바고러사아. 시 오노 무후빠-가시 여거 아니러 롣씨 이와 아바아 아너더."

Luke Chapter 21[NIV]

1. As he looked up, Jesus saw the rich putting their gifts into the temple treasury.

2. He also saw a poor widow put in two very small copper coins.

3. "I tell you the truth," he said, "this poor widow has put in more than all the others.

4. All these people gave their gifts out of their wealth; but she out of her poverty put in all she had to live on."

Kureba bushi n'e kuhandjukala kw'e luhu lwa ongo e yerusalemu

구러바 부씨 너 구하뉴—롸 궈 루홀 롸 오끄 어 여루사풔물

5. Banafunzi bauma babaa bahambala mbu e Luhu iwa ongo Iwaimbirwe kubuya n'emakoi makomire. Kanji mbu iwatonyire n'emitulo bende beresa ongo.Yesu omvire bacha, ku kwera kuteta:

5. 바나푸씨 바우마 바바아 바하빠롸 뿌 어 루후 이와 오끄 이와이삐뤄 구부야 너마고이 마고미러. 가찌 뿌 이와도네러 너미두롣 버떠 버러사 오끄.여수 오뻬러 바짜, 구 궈라 구더다:

5. Some of his disciples were remarking about how the temple was adorned with beautiful stones and with gifts dedicated to God. But Jesus said,

6. "kw'ei nyumba mwatumbikisa tacha, kutak ekale ekoi chiro na liuma busira kuhanjibwa n'ebandu mwa suku sikabaha.

6. "궈이 뉴빠 뫄두삐기사 다짜, 구다구 어가뤄 어고이 찌로 나 찌우마 부시라 구하찌봐 너바뚜 뫄 수구 시가바하.

6. "As for what you see here, the time will come when not one stone will be left on another; every one of them will be thrown down."

7. mango ebanafunzi ba Yesu bomvya bacha,bera kumubusa: "mukangirisi,mangochi ebi by'ekuhanda eluhu lwa ongo bikaba,na chiye chi chikalosa kwa byeshire?

7. 마끄 어바나푸씨 바 여수 보뺘 바짜,버라 구무부사: "무가뀌리시,마끄찌 어비 벼구하따 어루후 롸 오끄 비가바,나 찌여 찌 찌가롣사 과 벼씨러?

7. "Teacher," they asked, "when will these things happen? And what will be the sign that they are about to take place?"

8. Yesu era kubakula: "mumenyaa mungatebwa. Bandju banene bakabaha mw'e sina iyanyi. bakatangisira bateta mbu bu bera banunusi,n'ebihangi byabu byaikire. Si mutanaereresa mwabakulikira.

8. 여수 어라 구바구롸: "무머냐아 무꺼더봐. 바뚜 바너너 바가바하 뭐 시나 이야네. 바가다뀌시라 바더다 뿌 부 버라 바누누시,너비하뀌 뱌부 뱌이기러. 시 무다나어러러사 뫄바구뀌기라.

8. He replied: "Watch out that you are not deceived. For many will come in my name, claiming, 'I am he,' and, 'The time is near.' Do not follow them.

9. mango mukomva ebandubateta-tete era luulu s'endambala mwa bio al'aumu n'elwayo mza kachi-kachi k'ebandu,mutobaa. Kwemire

9. 마끄 무고빠 어바부바더다- 더더 어라 루우루 서따빠롸 뫄 비오 아라우무 너롸요 무자 가찌-가찌 거바뚜,무도바아. 궈미러 어벼라 비이거 다따,시

9. When you hear of wars and revolutions, do not be frightened. These things must happen first, but the end will not

ebyera biike tanga,si butakafire kuba businga bw'e butala."

부다가피러 구바 부시ﾞﾞﾞ 뭐 부다ﾞﾞ."

come right away."

10. chichine chi mumenyereraa: ebirongo kwa birongo,n'echio kwa chio bikalwa.

10. 찌찌너 찌 무머녀러라아: 어비로꼬 과 비로꼬,너찌오 과 찌오 비가ﾞﾞ.

10. Then he said to them: "Nation will rise against nation, and kingdom against kingdom.

11. mu bisiki binene,ebandu bakalibula kusibu bushi n'emisisi isibu-isibu y'echitaka,n'ebulio, na malwalwa ma ma kaufira. N'nokwa nguba bukatenga binene kubaisa,al'auma n'ebishishalo.

11. 무 비시기 비너너,어바뚜 바가ﾞﾞ부ﾞﾞ 구시부 부씨 너미시시 이시부-이시부 여찌다가,너부ﾞﾞ오, 나 마ﾞﾞ라ﾞﾞ 마 마 가우피라. 우노과 ﾞﾞ바 부가더ﾞﾞ 비너너 구바이사,아ﾞﾞ라우마 너비씨ﾞﾞﾞﾞ.

11. There will be great earthquakes, famines and pestilences in various places, and fearful events and great signs from heaven.

12. "si era muhondo ebi byoshi bibe, e bandju babamine, ne kubalibusa. Bakabana mwa bihaala mutongane, ne kubakabula mwa mulisi. Kanji bakabana mutongananyisibwe era muhondo s'e bakulu-kulu be binji bio bushi nanyi.

12. "시 어라 무호또 어비 뵤씨 비버, 어 바ﾞﾞ 바바미너, 너 구바ﾞﾞ부사. 바가바나 ﾞﾞ 비하아ﾞﾞ 무도ﾞﾞ너, 너 구바가부ﾞﾞ ﾞﾞ 무ﾞﾞ시. 가찌 바가바나 무도ﾞﾞ나네시붜 어라 무호또 서 바구루ﾞ-구루ﾞ 버 비ﾞﾞ 비오 부씨 나네.

12. "But before all this, they will lay hands on you and persecute you. They will deliver you to synagogues and prisons, and you will be brought before kings and governors, and all on account of my name.

13. mumenyereraa kw'ebasere benyu nabu, nesi banyakenyu, nesi ebalungu benyu,

13. 무머녀러라아 궈바서러 버뉴 나부, 너시 바냐거뉴, 어바루ﾞﾞ 버뉴,

13. This will result in your being witnesses to them.

14. nesi bera benyu, bakanabana era muhondo s'ebakulu-kulu. na bauma mumwabu bakechibwa bihangi by'e kuanyikisisa ebandu byoshi bya mwllolaa ku era lulu sanyi.

14. 너시 버라 버뉴, 바가나바나 어라 무호또 서바구루ﾞ-구루ﾞ. 나 바우마 무ﾞﾞ부 바거찌봐 비하ﾞﾞ 벼 구아네기시사 어바뚜 뵤씨 뱌 무우루ﾞﾞ로ﾞﾞ라아 구 어라 루ﾞﾞ루ﾞﾞ 사네.

14. But make up your mind not to worry beforehand how you will defend yourselves.

15. bushi n'oku, mutendaa mwachanya mbu chiye chi mungateta mwa kutongana,

15. 부씨 노구, 무더ﾞﾞ아 ﾞﾞ짜냐 ﾞﾞ 찌여 찌 무ﾞﾞ더다 ﾞﾞ 구도ﾞﾞ나,

15. For I will give you words and wisdom that none of your adversaries

		will be able to resist or contradict.
16. bushi nyeine nyi nyikabaasa kubona cha mukateta. nyikabawa n'ebwenge bwa bukatuma mwabona cha mungabura e barenda benyu,	16. 부씨 녀이너 네 네가바아사 구보나 짜 무가더다. 네가바와 너붸어 봐 부가두마 뫄보나 짜 무까부라 어 바러따 버뉴,	16. You will be betrayed even by parents, brothers, relatives and friends, and they will put some of you to death.
17. baine na cha bangateta, nesi cha bangabaenza ku mwaka.	17. 바이너 나 짜 바까더다, 너시 짜 바까바어싸 구･뫄가.	17. All men will hate you because of me.
18. si kutakachibe chiro na lufiri luuma kw'echwe lyenyu lwa mukaba mwaesie.	18. 시 구다가찌버 찌로 나 루피리 루우마 궈쮜 려뉴 롸 무가바 뫄어시어.	18. But not a hair of your head will perish.
19. musimikaa, bushi mukaira bacha mukabona ekalamo k'esuku n'e suku.	19. 무시미가아, 부씨 무가이라 바짜 무가보나 어가롸모 거수구 너 수구.	19. By standing firm you will gain life.
20. kanji Yesu era kuteta: mango mukalola kwa,musi w'e yerusalem era asungulwa n'e ngabo,mwanamenyera kw'ebihangi by'ekuhanjibwa kwau biri ofu.	20. 가찌 여수 어라 구더다: 마오 무가로롸 과,무시 워 여루사러무 어라 아수우롸 너 아보,뫄나머녀라 궈비하이 벼구하지봐 과우 비리 오푸.	20. "When you see Jerusalem being surrounded by armies, you will know that its desolation is near.
21. bishi n'oku,ba bakaba bali muu batengaa muu, n'na ba bakaba bali mwa tumbara,batachifulukiraa muu. ku kuteta mbu mbesha mwa tumbara, batachifulukiraa muu.ku kuteta mbu besha mwa chio ch'ebayuta boshi bahairaa kwa ndjulungu.	21. 비씨 노구,바 바가바 바리 무우 바더까아 무우, 우나 바 바가바 바리 뫄 두빠라,바다찌푸루기라아 무우. 구 구더다 뿌 뻐싸 뫄 두빠라, 바다찌푸루기라아 무우.구 구더다 뿌 버싸 뫄 찌오 쩌바유다 보씨 바하이라아 과 누루우.	21. Then let those who are in Judea flee to the mountains, let those in the city get out, and let those in the country not enter the city.
22. Mumenyereraa kw'esi suku sikaba suku sa buchinjibusi bwa ongo kwa bayuta,kukulikana n'okwa chinwa cha ongo chitula	22. 무머녀러라아 궈시 수구 시가바 수구 사 부찌지부시 봐 오오 과 바유다,구구리가나 노과 찌놔 짜 오오 찌두롸	22. For this is the time of punishment in fulfillment of all that has been written.

chitechire.

23. esi suku sikaba suku sa malibuko manene. Ebakasi ba bakaba bali basito, n'na ba bakaba bete etubonjo-bonjo bakalibuka kusibu. besha mwa chio bakaba mu malibuko manene, bushi ebuchinjibusi bwa ongo bukaba bunene kubu.

24. kanji ba batatula bayuta bu bakasikya bauma mubu n'emombo, beke n'ebanji kuminyirwa mu binji bio. abola bu bakakumbya emusi w'eyerusalem busese, kuikira mango nabu ebihangi bya ongo abawaa bikawa

25. Yesu era kunaendekerana ateta: era muhondo s'ekufuluka kwanyi, kukaba bishishalo mw'esuba, n'omwa ngununu. Kanji enyanja ikafwanga. ebyera bi bikalosa ebandu boshi kwa kwabahire bya kubaisa.

26. ebandu b'omwa butala boshi bakere baina kwa baira, bushi ongo akaba atenganyishe esuba n'e mwesi, n'engununu.bushi n'oku,bandu bauma bakachichinjibalira bushi n'ebuba mango bakaba bamenyerere bya byera byabanga mwa butala boshi.

27. Era nyuma s'ebi,ebandu

찌더찌러.

23. 어시 수구 시가바 수구 사 마뤼부고 마너너. 어바가시 바 바가바 바뤼 바시도, 우나 바 바가바 버더 어두보쪼-보쪼 바가뤼부가 구시부. 버싸 롸 찌오 바가바 무 마뤼부고 마너너, 부씨 어부찌찌부시 롸 오꼬 부가바 부너너 구부.

24. 가찌 바 바다두롸 바유다 부 바가시꺄 바우마 무부 너모뽀, 버거 너바찌 구미네롸 무 비찌 비오. 아보롸 부 바가구뺘 어무시 워여루사꺼무 부서서, 구이기라 마꼬 나부 어비하삐 뱌 오꼬 아바와아 비가와

25. 여수 어라 구나어떠거라나 아더다: 어라 무호또 서구푸뿌가 과내, 구가바 비씨싸로 뭐수바, 노롸 우누누. 가찌 어냐짜 이가퐈빠. 어벼라 비 비가로사 어바뚜 보씨 과 과바히러 뱌 구바이사.

26. 어바뚜 보롸 부다롸 보씨 바거러 바이나 과 바이라, 부씨 오꼬 아가바 아더빠네써 어수바 너 뭐시, 너우누누.부씨 노구,바뚜 바우마 바가찌찌찌바뤼라 부씨 너부바 마꼬 바가바 바머녀러러 뱌 벼라 뱌바빠 롸 부다롸 보씨.

27. 어라 뉴마 서비,어바뚜

---

23. How dreadful it will be in those days for pregnant women and nursing mothers! There will be great distress in the land and wrath against this people.

24. They will fall by the sword and will be taken as prisoners to all the nations. Jerusalem will be trampled on by the Gentiles until the times of the Gentiles are fulfilled.

25. "There will be signs in the sun, moon and stars. On the earth, nations will be in anguish and perplexity at the roaring and tossing of the sea.

26. Men will faint from terror, apprehensive of what is coming on the world, for the heavenly bodies will be shaken.

27. At that time they will

---

bakalola kwa nyono nyi mwana w'emundu nabanire mwa lumbumbu n'ebuashi, al'auma n'etunda.

28. mango ebi bishishalo bikaba byera byalorekana ku, musesaa emichima muate n'emunyiiro, bushi ebununusi bwenyu bukaba buli ofu.

29. Era nyuma s'ebi,Yesu era kubura ebandu mw'ono muso: "Mwendaa mwalola kwa muchi ola utula werikirwe mbu mutinyi atula, nesi mwanalola kwa inji michi yoshi itula.

30. mango yende yaba yahokosise ene mwetu, mwende,mwanamenyerera kwa mibi kwa ongo buli ofu.

31. E nguba ne butala bikarenga selyi e myasi yanyi itakarenga.

32. nababura kanangana kwa bauma mu mwabu mu bandu ba iwarero batakafe batalolaa kw'amu malibuko.

33. Enguba n'ebutala bikarenga, si e binwa byanyi bitakarenge chiro na hicha."

34. Yesu era kubura ebanafunzi bai: "muchilangaa,emianyisa yenyu itabaa mwa

바가뢔롸 과 뇨노 네 뫄나 워무뚜 나바니러 와 루뿌뿌 너부아씨, 아롸우마 너두따.

28. 마꼬 어비 비씨싸로 비가바 벼라 뱌롤러가나 구, 무서사아 어미찌마 무아더 너무네이로, 부씨 어부누누시 붸뉴 부가바 부뤼 오푸.

29. 어라 뉴마 서비,여수 어라 구부라 어바뚜 뫄노 무소: "뭐따아 뫄롤롸 과 무찌 오롸 우두롸 워리기뤄 뿌 무디네 아두롸, 너시 뫄나롸롸 과 이찌 미찌 요씨 이두롸.

30. 마꼬 여떠 야바 야호고시서 어너 뭐두, 뭐떠,뫄나머녀러라 과 미비 과 오꼬 부뤼 오푸.

31. 어 우바 너 부다롸 비가러따 서뤠 어 먀시 야네 이다가러따.

32. 나바부라 가나따나 과 바우마 무 뫄부 무 바뚜 바 이와러로 바다가퍼 바다롨롸아 과무 마뤼부고.

33. 어우바 너부다롸 비가러따, 시 어 비놔 뱌네 비다가러떠 찌로 나 히짜."

34. 여수 어라 구부라 어바나푸씨 바이: "무찌롸따아아,어미아네사 여뉴

see the Son of Man coming in a cloud with power and great glory.

28. When these things begin to take place, stand up and lift up your heads, because your redemption is drawing near."

29. He told them this parable: "Look at the fig tree and all the trees.

30. When they sprout leaves, you can see for yourselves and know that summer is near.

31. Even so, when you see these things happening, you know that the kingdom of God is near.

32. "I tell you the truth, this generation will certainly not pass away until all these things have happened.

33. Heaven and earth will pass away, but my words will never pass away.

34. "Be careful, or your hearts will be weighed down with dissipation,

kumwa,n'ekutamira. kanji mutalaa kwa kuonda ekalamo k'umuno butala oshi au,elusuku iw'ebuchinjibushi luta kuika mutanachikunganyise.

35. olu lusuku, ebandu boshi mwa butala bakasimbwa ng'okwa kasira kende kafuba efi mwa lwishi.

36. muboolaa emeho, n'ekunde mwema mwema ongo iri mwaata emisi y'e kuima. Musesaa n'emichima mw'ebi byoshi bya bikaika, mwimange n'omwa meho manyi nyi mwa na w'emundu busira honyi."

37. mw'esi suku, Yesu endaa akangilyisa e bandju mwa chibua ch'e luhuu iw'e yerusalemu emushi. Si e buchwufu,endaa aya kuonjira kwa kachwulungu kerikirwe mbu miseituni.

38. na chira lumbuli-mbuli, ebandu boshi ba bendaa bamumvirisa,bendaa bahuba kubaha muchi baya kumumvirisa.

이다바아 꽈 구꽈,너구다미라. 가찌 무다꽈아 과 구오따 어가꽈모 구우무노 부다꽈 오씨 아우,어루수구 이워부찌찌부씨 루다 구이가 무다나찌구까니서.

35. 오루 루수구, 어바뚜 보씨 꽈 부다꽈 바가시까 오과 가시라 거꺼 가푸바 어피 꽈 뤼씨.

36. 무보오꽈아 어머호, 너구꺼 뭐마 뭐마 오꼬 이리 꽈아다 어미시 여 구이마. 무서사아 너미찌마 뭐비 뵤씨 뱌 비가이가, 뮈마꺼 노꽈 머호 마네 네 꽈 나 워무뚜 부시라 호네."

37. 뭐시 수구, 여수 어따아 아가찌레사 어 바뚜 꽈 찌부아 쩌 루후우 이워 여루사꺼무 어무씨. 시 어 부쭈푸,어따아 아야 구오찌라 과 가쭈루우 거리기뤄 뿌 미서이두니.

38. 나 찌라 루뿌찌-뿌찌, 어바뚜 보씨 바 버따아 바무뻬리사,버따아 바후바 구바하 무찌 바야 구무뻬리사.

drunkenness and the anxieties of life, and that day will close on you unexpectedly like a trap.

35. For it will come upon all those who live on the face of the whole earth.

36. Be always on the watch, and pray that you may be able to escape all that is about to happen, and that you may be able to stand before the Son of Man."

37. Each day Jesus was teaching at the temple, and each evening he went out to spend the night on the hill called the Mount of Olives,

38. and all the people came early in the morning to hear him at the temple.

Luka Chikono 22
Yuda a chirana Yesu
1. Elusuku lukulu lw'e mikati itali mu bufumu byekuimbya,

루가 찌고노 22
유다 아 찌라나 여수
1. 어루수구 루구루 뤄 미가디 이다뤼 무 부푸무 벼구이빠,

Luke Chapter 22[NIV]
1. Now the Feast of Unleavened Bread, called

iwa iwerikiwe pasaka iwabaa luli ofu.

2. E bakulu-kulu b'ebakuhanyi ba ongo, al'auma n'e bakakangirisi b'emwaso, berakuhonda kute bangetisa Yesu mwa bubisho-bisho, bushi babaa bobaa e bandju.

3. mw'echi chihangi, shetanyi ku kwera kuya mwa muchima wa yuta, i werikwaa mbu i isikariota. Oyu yuta abaa muuma mwa nduma ekumi n'ebiri sa Yesu.

4. Era kuya kuhambala n'ebakulu-kulu b'ebakuhanyi ba ongo, al'auma n'ebalanzi b'eluhu lwa ongo. Ayaa kuhambala nabu kute ku angabaisaku Yesu.

5. Bera kusima, bera kunaana nai kwa bangamweresa ebutea bushi n'oyu mulimo.

6. yuta era kwemerera. Era kunatangirisa ahonda echihangi cha angarenganya mu Yesu era bali busira ebanji bandu kumenya.

7. E lusuku lukulu iw'epasaka iwera kuika. Olu lusuku,kwabaa kwemire bakere ebyana by'embuli by'epasaka

8. Yesu era kutuma petero na yowanyi, era kubabura:

이와 이워리기워 파사가 이와바아 루삐 오푸.

2. 어 바구루-구루 버바구하네 바 오꼬, 아라우마 너 바가까리시 버뫄소, 버라구호따 구더 바뼈디사 여수 똬 부비쏘-비쏘, 부씨 바바아 보바아 어 바뚜.

3. 뭐찌 찌하삐, 써다네 구 궈라 구야 똬 무찌마 와 유다, 이 워리과아 뿌 이 이시가리오다. 오유 유다 아바아 무우마 똬 뚜마 어구미 너비리 사 여수.

4. 어라 구야 구하빠롸 너바구루-구루 버바구하네 바 오꼬, 아라우마 너바꽈씨 버루후 꽈 오꼬. 아야아 구하빠롸 나부 구더 구 아꺄바이사구 여수.

5. 버라 구시마, 버라 구나아나 나이 과 바꺄뭐러사 어부더아 부씨 노유 무삐모.

6. 유다 어라 궈머러라. 어라 구나다뼈리사 아호따 어찌하삐 쨔 아꺄러꺄냐 무 여수 어라 바삐 부시라 어바찌 바뚜 구머냐.

7. 어 루수구 루꾸루 이워파사가 이워라 구이가. 오루 루수구,과바아 궈미러 바거러 어뱌나 벼뿌삐 벼파사가

8. 여수 어라 구두마 퍼더로 나 요와네, 어라 구바부라: "뭐따아

the Passover, was approaching,

2. and the chief priests and the teachers of the law were looking for some way to get rid of Jesus, for they were afraid of the people.

3. Then Satan entered Judas, called Iscariot, one of the Twelve.

4. And Judas went to the chief priests and the officers of the temple guard and discussed with them how he might betray Jesus.

5. They were delighted and agreed to give him money.

6. He consented, and watched for an opportunity to hand Jesus over to them when no crowd was present.

7. Then came the day of Unleavened Bread on which the Passover lamb had to be sacrificed.

8. Jesus sent Peter and John, saying, "Go and

"mwendaa mututekere ebiryo bya tungalya kwa pasaka."

9. bera kumubusa: "ngae u onjire tubitekere?"

10. era kubakula: mango mungaba mwera mwengirira mwa musi w'eyerusalemu,mungabuana,na mulume ola wete erea lya meshi. Mumukulirikaamwa nyumba era angengirira mu.

11. mwa kuika mui,mungabura ena mu mbu nyono namwemire abalose ala chumba chiri cha nyono n'ebanafunzi banyi tungalira mw'ebiryoby'epasaka.

12. Anga balosa kur businda bunene byera ndonga se nyumba itoamire cha chikunganyisibwe mira mu kunganyisa omola.

13. Bera kuenda bera kuna bwaana kwanababuraa, bera ku kunyisisa mwe Pasaka.

14. mango by'epasaka byaikaa,Yesu n'endumwa sai bera kwikala kwa mesa.

15. era kababura: "nabaa nyete mbuha inene y'ekula ene pasaka al'auma nenyu era muhondo s'emalibuko manyi

---

무두더거러 어비료 뱌 두꺄꺄 과 파사가."

9. 버라 구무부사: "꺄어 우 오찌러 두비더거러?"

10. 어라 구바구꺄: 마꼬 무꺄바 뭐라 뭐꺼리리라 과 무시 워여루사꺼무,무꺄부아나,나 무루머 오라 워더 어러아 꺄 머씨. 무무구끼리가아와 뉴빠 어라 아꺼끼리라 무.

11. 꽈 구이가 무이,무꺄부라 어나 무 뿌 뇨노 나뭐미러 아바뢰서 아꽈 쭈빠 찌리 짜 뇨노 너바나푸씨 바니 두꺄끼라 뭐비료벼파사가.

12. 아꺄 바뢰사 구루 부시꽈 부너너 벼라 또꺄 서 뉴빠 이도아미러 짜 찌구꺄네시붜 미라 무 구꺄네사 오모꽈.

13. 버라 구어꽈 버라 구나 봐아나 과나바부라아, 버라 구 구네시사 뭐 파사가.

14. 마꼬 벼파사가 뱌이가아,여수 너뚜꽈 사이 버라 귀가꽈 과 머사.

15. 어라 가바부라: "나바아 녀더 뿌하 이너너 여구꽈 어너 파사가 아꽈우마 너뉴 어라 무호또 서마끼부고 마니

---

make preparations for us to eat the Passover."

9. "Where do you want us to prepare for it?" they asked.

10. He replied, "As you enter the city, a man carrying a jar of water will meet you. Follow him to the house that he enters,

11. and say to the owner of the house, 'The Teacher asks: Where is the guest room, where I may eat the Passover with my disciples?'

12. He will show you a large upper room, all furnished. Make preparations there."

13. They left and found things just as Jesus had told them. So they prepared the Passover.

14. When the hour came, Jesus and his apostles reclined at the table.

15. And he said to them, "I have eagerly desired to eat this Passover with you before I suffer.

16. si cha babura kanangana chiri chichine: ndakachirye inji pasaka kuikira mango ongo akanunula e bandju bai mango akema kanangana mwa butala boshi.

17. abere atola engumbu, era kutonga ongo era kubabura: "mwangiriraa ene ngumbu y'e hande y'e bifuma by'e misabibu muihangire muboshi.

18. kanji echinji cha nababura kanangananga chiri chichine: ndakachimwe ku inji hande iri ng'ei kutengera chine chihangi, kuikira mango ebwimi bwa ongo bukaika."

19. kanji era kutola emukati, era kutonga ongo, era kuishanga u n'e kukaabira u, era kubabura: "onola ali mubiri wanyi wanyirwe bushi nenyu: ku mwendaa mwaira bachi iri mwindemwanyikengera.

20. abere bera bamalaa kulya ebi biryo by'epasaka, kanji era kutola inji ngumbu n'e kubabura: "ene ngumbu chili chilaamo chiyayaya cha ongo n'ebandu kwa mikira yani era ingashescekala bushinenyu.

21. mumenyereraa kwola Unganyirenganya ali ola twalira nai al'auma.

16. 시 짜 바부라 가나까나 찌리 찌찌너: 따가찌루여 이찌 파사가 구이기라 마꼬 오꼬 아가누누꽈 어 바뚜 바이 마꼬 아거마 가나까나 꽈 부다꽈 보씨.

17. 아버러 아도꽈 어우뿌, 어라 구도꽈 오꼬 어라 구바부라: "마끼리라아 어너 꾸뿌 여 하떠 여 비푸마 벼 미사비부 무이하끼러 무보씨.

18. 가찌 어찌찌 짜 나바부라 가나까나까 찌리 찌찌너: 따가찌뭐 구 이찌 하떠 이리 꺼이 구더꺼라 찌너 찌하끼, 구이기라 마꼬 어뷔미 봐 오꼬 부가이가."

19. 가찌 어라 구도꽈 어무가디, 어라 구도꽈 오꼬, 어라 구이싸까 우 너 구가아비라 우, 어라 구바부라: "오노꽈 아뤼 무비리 와네 와네뤄 부씨 너뉴: 구 뭐따아 마이라 바찌 이리 뭐떠마네거러라.

20. 아버러 버라 바마꽈아 구꺄 구도꽈 이찌 꾸뿌 너 구바부라: "어너 꾸뿌 찌뤼 찌꽈아모 찌야야야 짜 오꼬 너바뚜 과 미기라 야니 어라 이까써수시어가꽈 부씨너뉴.

21. 무머녀러라아 곤꽈 우까네러까냐 아뤼 오꽈 돠뤼라 나이 아라우마.

16. For I tell you, I will not eat it again until it finds fulfillment in the kingdom of God."

17. After taking the cup, he gave thanks and said, "Take this and divide it among you.

18. For I tell you I will not drink again of the fruit of the vine until the kingdom of God comes."

19. And he took bread, gave thanks and broke it, and gave it to them, saying, "This is my body given for you; do this in remembrance of me."

20. In the same way, after the supper he took the cup, saying, "This cup is the new covenant in my blood, which is poured out for you.

21. But the hand of him who is going to betray me is with mine on the

table.

22. Nyono nyi Mwana w'eMungu, nyiri mu kuchiendera kukulikana n'ekubonda kwa Ongo. Si bwanya kwa mundu ola wanyirenganyise."

22. 뇨노 네 뫄나 워무우, 네리 무 구쩌뻐라 구구뤼가나 너구보따 과 오앳. 시 봐냐 과 무뚜 오라 와니러따니서."

22. The Son of Man will go as it has been decreed, but woe to that man who betrays him."

23. Endumwa sai somvire becha, sera kubunya mbu nde musi ola ungaira oyu mwasi.

23. 어뚜뫄 사이 소뻬러 버짜, 서라 구부냐 뿌 떠 무시 오뫄 우뫄이라 오유 뫄시.

23. They began to question among themselves which of them it might be who would do this.

24. Chasinda, kwera kuba bwaka kachi-kacha k'endumwa sa Yesu. Bwabaa bwa kumenyerera nde I useneke ku nga I ungaba mukulu-kulu usi.

24. 짜시따, 궈라 구바 봐가 가찌-가짜 거뚜뫄 사 여수. 봐바아 봐 구머녀러라 떠 이 우서너거 구 뫄 이 우뫄바 무구룹-구룹 우시.

24. Also a dispute arose among them as to which of them was considered to be greatest.

25. Yesu alolire bacha, era kusibura: "Ebami bomuno butala, kwa bandu ku bende balira ebwami. Kanji abu bami, b'omuno butala, kwa bandu ku bende balira ebwami. Kanji abu bami, bende bahonda berikwe mbu bu, ba nyangola mabuka."

25. 여수 아로뤼러 바짜, 어라 구시부라: "어바미 보무노 부다뫄, 과 바뚜 구 버떠 바뤼라 어봐미. 가찌 아부 바미, 보무노 부다뫄, 과 바뚜 구 버떠 바뤼라 어봐미. 가찌 아부 바미, 버떠 바호따 버리궈 뿌 부, 바 냐앗뫄 마부가."

25. Jesus said to them, "The kings of the Gentiles lord it over them; and those who exercise authority over them call themselves Benefactors.

26. Si bitali bacha ku mwabu. Chira mundu ola ungaba mukulu-kulu mu mwabu, alorekanaa ku nga I mueke. N'nola wemangirire ebanji, achiiraa muanda wabu.

26. 시 비다뤼 바짜 구 뫄부. 찌라 무뚜 오라 우뫄바 무구룹-구룹 무 뫄부, 아로러가나아 구 뫄 이 무어거. 누노뫄 워마뼈리러 어바찌, 아찌이라아 무아따 와부.

26. But you are not to be like that. Instead, the greatest among you should be like the youngest, and the one who rules like the one who serves.

27. Munyiburaa, nde I mukulu-kulu wa mulikabu mwa bano bandu babiri: Ola walya I mukulu-kulu! Rero, mumenyereraa kwa nyeke nachiirire nga muanda mwa kachi-kachi kenyu.

27. 무네부라아, 떠 이 무구ᄙᅮ-구ᄙᅮ 와 무ᄙᅵ가부 뫄 바노 바뚜 바비리: 오ᄙᅡ 와ᄙᅣ 이 무구ᄙᅮ-구ᄙᅮ! 러로, 무머녀러라아 과 녀거 나찌이리러 ᅁᅡ 무아따 뫄 가찌-가찌 거뉴.

27. For who is greater, the one who is at the table or the one who serves? Is it not the one who is at the table? But I am among you as one who serves.

28. Si nyishi kwa mwabu mu mwekere al'auma nanyi esuku soshi mwa malibuko manyi.

28. 시 네씨 과 뫄부 무 뭐거러 아ᄙᅡ우마 나네 어수구 소씨 뫄 마ᄙᅵ부고 마네.

28. You are those who have stood by me in my trials.

29. Bushi n'oku, n'nanyi nyikaberesa ebuashi bw'ekwima kwa bandu boshi, ng'okwa Tata amberesaa bu.

29. 부씨 노구, 우나네 네가버러사 어부아씨 붜귀마 과 바뚜 보씨, ᅁᅩ과 다다 아뻐러사아 부.

29. And I confer on you a kingdom, just as my Father conferred one on me,

30. Mukende mwalira kwa bifumbi by'eBwami, wmine kwa birongo ekumi na bibiri by'e bana b'e Isiraeli."

30. 무거떠 뫄ᄙᅵ라 과 비푸뻬 벼봐미, 우미너 과 비로ᅁᅩ 어구미 나 비비리 벼 바나 버 이시라어ᄙᅵ."

30. so that you may eat and drink at my table in my kingdom and sit on thrones, judging the twelve tribes of Israel.

31. Yesu era kubura Simonyi Petero: "Simonyi, Simonyi, ulolaa kwa Shetanyi aire kwema Ongo eloso iz'ekubelula nga mupunge chasia abareke.

31. 여수 어라 구부라 시모네 퍼더로: "시모네, 시모네, 우ᄙᅩᄙᅡ아 과 써다네 아이러 궈마 오ᅁᅩ 어ᄙᅩ소 이저구버ᄙᅮᄙᅡ ᅁᅡ 무푸ᅁᅥ 짜시아 아바러거.

31. "Simon, Simon, Satan has asked to sift you as wheat.

32. Si nyono nakwemeraa era mwa Ongo ebwemersi bwau bungesha kuwa. N'nau, mango ungaba waalukire era nyiri, usesaa banyakenyu mwa bwemeresi".

32. 시 뇨노 나궈머라아 어라 뫄 오ᅁᅩ 어붜머시 봐우 부ᅁᅥ싸 구와. 우나우, 마ᅁᅩ 우ᅁᅡ바 와아ᄙᅮ기러 어라 네리, 우서사아 바냐거뉴 뫄 붜머러시".

32. But I have prayed for you, Simon, that your faith may not fail. And when you have turned back, strengthen your brothers."

33. Petero era kubura Yesu: "Enawechwu, nemerere kuya mwa mulyisi a l'auma nau, nesi kufira al'auma nau."

33. 퍼더로 어라 구부라 여수: "어나워쭈, 너머러러 구야 뫄 무ᄙᅨ시 아 ᄙᅡ우마 나우, 너시 구피라 아ᄙᅡ우마 나우."

33. But he replied, "Lord, I am ready to go with you to prison and to death."

34. Yesu era kumubura: "Nakubura Petero, ku kwarero eluasi lutabike utachiakana kahatu mbu utanyishi."

35. kanji Yesu era kubusa endumwa * sai: "mango nabatumaa busira hao,nesi birato, kuli cha,mwainaa? Bera kumwakula mbu naanga.

36. Yesu ku kwera kubabura: ene myasi yanjikwaa mwa chitabo cha ongo yemire imenyekana ku nyono.bacha ku ichwula itechire: aanjirwaa a l'auma n'ebandu ba batakulikira mwaso.

37. si kwa businda,kuika ene myasi inyierekereibe.rero,kutengera iwarero,ola utusa hao, nesi mbweka, aitolaa. n'ola utatusa bombo, ausaa ekochi lyai abuule.

38. endumwa sera kumbura: enawetu,anola ali,mombo mabiri. nai era kubabura: Murekaa bacha

Gestemani

39. Yesu era kuukula mwa babaa balira n'ekwirukira kwa katulungu k'emiseitunyi ng'okwa endaa anaira.endumwa sai sera kumulikira ku.

34. 여수 어라 구무부라: "나구부라 퍼더로, 구 과러로 어루아시 루다비거 우다찌아가나 가하두 뿌 우다네씨."

35. 가찌 여수 어라 구부사 어뚜똬 * 사이: "마꼬 나바두마아 부시라 하오,너시 비라도, 구쀠 짜,마이나아? 버라 구똬구똬 뿌 나아똬.

36. 여수 구 궈라 구바부라: 어너 먀시 야찌과아 똬 찌다보 짜 오꼬 여미러 이머녀가나 구 뇨노.바짜 구 이쭈똬 이더찌러: 아나찌롸아 아 롸우마 너바뚜 바 바다구쀠기라 뫄소.

37. 시 과 부시따,구이가 어너 먀시 이네어러거러이버.러로,구더쩌라 이와러로,오랴 우두사 하오, 너시 뭐가, 아이도롸아. 노랴 우다두사 보뽀, 아우사아 어고찌 롸이 아부우뤄.

38. 어뚜똬 서라 구뿌라: 어나워두,아노똬 아쀠,모뽀 마비리. 나이 어라 구바부라: 무러가아 바짜

거수더마니

39. 여수 어라 구우구똬 똬 바바아 바쀠라 너귀루기라 과 가두루꾸 거미서이두네 꼬과 어따아 아나이라.어뚜똬 사이 서라 구무쀠기라 구.

34. Jesus answered, "I tell you, Peter, before the rooster crows today, you will deny three times that you know me."

35. Then Jesus asked them, "When I sent you without purse, bag or sandals, did you lack anything?" "Nothing," they answered.

36. He said to them, "But now if you have a purse, take it, and also a bag; and if you don't have a sword, sell your cloak and buy one.

37. It is written: 'And he was numbered with the transgressors'; and I tell you that this must be fulfilled in me. Yes, what is written about me is reaching its fulfillment."

38. The disciples said, "See, Lord, here are two swords." "That is enough," he replied.

39. Jesus went out as usual to the Mount of Olives, and his disciples followed him.

40. abere aika ku,era kubura endumwa sai: mwemaa ongo mungesha kuya mwa muereko.

41. era kuchifunda bure hicha nabu,areya ng'ala mundu angauma ekoi mwa kuboko abaa ema ongo akomire n'emafi.

42. era kutangiri ateta: tata,ukahonda utwalaa bure nanyi emalibuko makoochire ma manganyiikira ekohonda kwau ku kubaa, si ekwanyi kutabaa.

43. unao-unao,emalaika era kumuikira atenga kwa nguba,era kumweresa emisi.

44. chasinda,Yesu era kunaendekerena ema ongo busese na chifufu chinene echuka chai chera kuba nga mikira,chabaa chatoangira kwa chitaka.

45. mango Yesu abaa era amalaa kwema ongo, era kuya ala ndumwa sai sabaa siri.era kusibuana saonjire n'ebusinane.

46. etra kasibusa: chi chatumire mwaonjira? Musukaa mweme ongo mungesha kuya mwa muereko.

Yuda arenganya Yesu

---

40. 아버러 아이가 구,어라 구부라 어두꽈 사이: 뭐마아 오꼬 무꺼싸 구야 뫄 무어러고.

41. 어라 구찌푸따 부러 히짜 나부,아러야 우가꽈 무뚜 아까우마 어고이 뫄 구보고 아바아 어마 오꼬 아고미러 너마피.

42. 어라 구다띠리 아더다: 다다,우가호따 우돠똬아 부러 나니 어마띠부고 마고오찌러 마 마까네이기라 어고호따 과우 구 구바아, 시 어과네 구다바아.

43. 우나오-우나오,어마똬이가 어라 구무이기라 아더꽈 과 꾸바,어라 구뭐러사 어미시.

44. 짜시따,여수 어라 구나어떠거러나 어마 오꼬 부서서 나 찌푸푸 찌너너 어쭈가 짜이 쩌라 구바 까 미기라,짜바아 짜도아띠라 과 찌다가.

45. 마꼬 여수 아바아 어라 아마똬아 궈마 오꼬, 어라 구야 아꽈 뚜뫄 사이 사바아 시리.어라 구시부아나 사오찌러 너부시나너.

46. 어두라 가시부사: 찌 짜두미러 뫄오찌라? 무수가아 뭐머 오꼬 무꺼싸 구야 뫄 무어러고.

유다 아러까넷 여수

---

40. On reaching the place, he said to them, "Pray that you will not fall into temptation."

41. He withdrew about a stone's throw beyond them, knelt down and prayed,

42. "Father, if you are willing, take this cup from me; yet not my will, but yours be done."

43. An angel from heaven appeared to him and strengthened him.

44. And being in anguish, he prayed more earnestly, and his sweat was like drops of blood falling to the ground.

45. When he rose from prayer and went back to the disciples, he found them asleep, exhausted from sorrow.

46. "Why are you sleeping?" he asked them. "Get up and pray so that you will not fall into temptation."

47. mango Yesu abaa anachiri ateta, luamba lunene lwa balume lwera kuulukira. yuta, i muuma mwa ndumwa sai ekumi n'ebiri abaa abohonderere. era kuchifunda ofu Yesu amuebere.

48. Yesu ku kwera kumbura: "yuda, mwa kuobera mu wera wanyama nyi mwana w'emundu?"

49. endumwa sa Yesu salolire kwa bya byeshire bisibuire sera kuteta: "enawetu, kwemire tukomange bu"

50. muuma mubu kuna kuisha ekuta kw'emalyo kw'emuanda w'emukulu-kulu munene w'e bakuhanyi ba ongo.

51. Yesu era kubabura: "murekeraa aola. "ra kuuma k'okwa kutu, na kwalama.

52. chasinjire,Yesu era kubura abakulu - kulu b'e bakuhanyi ba ongo, n'ebakulu -kulu b'ebalanzi b'eluhu lwa ongo, n'e bashamuka, babahaa kumusimba mmbu: "chi chatumire mwanyibahira n'emombo al'auma n'e manjinga nga nyitula chitula chihumusi?

53. chira lusuku,nendaa

47. 마꼬 여수 아바아 아나찌리 아더다, 루아빠 루너너 롸 바루머 뤄라 구우루기라. 유다, 이 무우마 뫄 뚜뫄 사이 어구미 너비리 아바아 아보호떠러러. 어라 구찌푸따 오푸 여수 아무어버러.

48. 여수 구 궈라 구뿌라: "유다, 뫄 구오버라 무 워라 와냐마 네 뫄나 워무뿌?"

49. 어뚜뫄 사 여수 사롣뤼러 과 뱌 벼쎄러 비시부이러 서라 구더다: "어나워두, 궈미러 두고마떠 부"

50. 무우마 무부 구나 구이싸 어구다 궈마뢷 궈무아빠 워무구루-구루 무너너 워 바구하네 바 오꼬.

51. 여수 어라 구바부라: "무러거라아 아오롸. "라 구우마 고과 구두, 나 과롸마.

52. 짜시찌러,여수 어라 구부라 아바구루 - 구루 버 바구하네 바 오꼬, 너바구루 -구루 버바롸씨 버루후 롸 오꼬, 너 바싸무가, 바바하아 구무시빠 무뿌: "찌 짜두미러 뫄네바히라 너모뽀 아롸우마 너 마찌꼬 뫄 네두롸 찌두롸 찌후무시?

53. 찌라 루수구,너따아

47. While he was still speaking a crowd came up, and the man who was called Judas, one of the Twelve, was leading them. He approached Jesus to kiss him,

48. but Jesus asked him, "Judas, are you betraying the Son of Man with a kiss?"

49. When Jesus' followers saw what was going to happen, they said, "Lord, should we strike with our swords?"

50. And one of them struck the servant of the high priest, cutting off his right ear.

51. But Jesus answered, "No more of this!" And he touched the man's ear and healed him.

52. Then Jesus said to the chief priests, the officers of the temple guard, and the elders, who had come for him, "Am I leading a rebellion, that you have come with swords and clubs?

53. Every day I was with

nareerera nenyu mwa luhu lwa ongo si mutanyiumaa ku. si chinera chiri chihangi chenyu al'auma na shetanyi,cha ongo abawere mw'ebuashi bw'e buashi bw'ekunyisimba."

54. mango babaa bera basimbaa Yesu, bera kumweka mwa nyumba y'emukulu-kulu munene w'ebakuhanyi ba ongo. Na petero abaa abakulikire katola -nyuma, marerere.

Petero achakana Yesu

55. bandju bauma babaa bauhire emulire mwa kachi-kachi k'echibua ch'emukulu-kulu w'ebakuhanyi ba ongo. babaa bekesi basungwire u. petero nai era kwikala al'auma nabu.

56. muanda -kasi muuma era kulola ku petero ekesi mwa changasi ch'emuliro. era kumutumbikisa, kuna kubura e bandju: onola nai abaa atula na Yesu

57. si petero era kuchakana n'ekuteta: ndeshi oyu mundju mama.

58. era nyuma hicha, unji mundu ola wabaa uli aola, era kumulola ku, kuna kutangirisa ateta: n'nau unali muuma mwa banafunzi ba Yesu si petero era kwakula oyu muuma nabu

나러어러라 너뉴 똬 루후 똬 오꼬 시 무다네우마아 구. 시 찌너라 찌리 찌하삐 쩌뉴 아꽈우마 나 써다네,짜 오꼬 아바워러 뭐부아씨 뭐 부아씨 뭐구네시빠."

54. 마꼬 바바아 버라 바시빠아 여수, 버라 구뭐가 똬 뉴빠 여무구루루-구루 무너너 워바구하네 바 오꼬. 나 퍼더로 아바아 아바구삐기러 가도똬 - 뉴마, 마러러로.

퍼더로 아짜가나 여수

55. 바뚜 바우마 바바아 바우히러 어무삐러러 똬 가찌-가찌 거찌부아 쩌무구루루-구루 워바구하네 바 오꼬. 바바아 버거시 바수뀌러 우. 퍼더로 나이 어라 귀가꽈 아꽈우마 나부.

56. 무아따 -가시 무우마 어라 구로꽈 구 퍼더로 어거시 똬 짜빠시 쩌무삐로. 어라 구무두삐기사, 구나 구부라 어 바뚜: 오노꽈 나이 아바아 아두꽈 나 여수

57. 시 퍼더로 어라 구짜가나 너구더다: 떠씨 오유 무뚜 마마.

58. 어라 뉴마 히짜, 우씨 무뚜 오꽈 와바아 우삐 아오꽈, 어라 구무로꽈 구, 구나 구다삐리사 아더다: 우나우 우나삐 무우마 똬 바나푸씨 바 여수 시 퍼더로 어라 과구꽈 오유

you in the temple courts, and you did not lay a hand on me. But this is your hour--when darkness reigns."

54. Then seizing him, they led him away and took him into the house of the high priest. Peter followed at a distance.

55. But when they had kindled a fire in the middle of the courtyard and had sat down together, Peter sat down with them.

56. A servant girl saw him seated there in the firelight. She looked closely at him and said, "This man was with him."

57. But he denied it. "Woman, I don't know him," he said.

58. A little later someone else saw him and said, "You also are one of them." "Man, I am not!" Peter replied.

무우마 나부

59. abere kwarenga nga saa nguma,unji mulume ere kusera ku petero n'ekuteta: bita bisha, oku ono mulume ali mwesha kalilaya, nai abaa anatula na Yesu.

60. chasinjire, petero era kumwakula n'ekuteta: eu mulume, ndeshi cha wateta. unao, abere atanasa kumala kuteta, eluasi kuna kubika.

61. Yesu era kualula eosi lyai atumbikise petero.petero amuhunjire kw'emeho era kukengera echinwa cha Yesu amuburaa mbu e luasi lutabike atachakana kahatu mbu atamwishi.

62. petero era kutenga mwa chibua nera kutangirisha alira na businane bunene mwa muchima

Malyibuko ma Yesu

63. e balanzi ba babaa balanga Yesu bera kunde bamushekera n'e kumupunda.

64. abere bamumina emeho mwa murembe, bera kunde bamubusa: eburebi bwau bukukangaa nde I wakupunjire!

65. babaa benjire bateta na inji

---

59. 아버러 과러까 까 사아 꾸마,우찌 무루머 어러 구서라 구 퍼더로 너구더다: 비다 비싸, 오구 오노 무루머 아찌 뭐싸 가찌라야, 나이 아바아 아나두꽈 나 여수.

60. 짜시찌러, 퍼더로 어라 구꽈구꽈 너구더다: 어우 무루머, 떠씨 짜 와더다. 우나오, 아버러 아다나사 구마꽈 구더다, 어루아시 구나 구비가.

61. 여수 어라 구아루꽈 어오시 꽈이 아두삐기서 퍼더로.퍼더로 아무후찌러 귀머호 어라 구거꺼라 어찌놔 짜 여수 아무부라아 뿌 어 루아시 루다비거 아다짜가나 가하두 뿌 아다뮈씨.

62. 퍼더로 어라 구더까 꽈 찌부아 너라 구다삐리싸 아찌라 나 부시나너 부너너 꽈 무찌마

마쀔븸곌 마 여수

63. 어 바꽈씨 바 바바아 바랑가 여수 버라 구더 바무써거라 너 구무푸따.

64. 아버러 바무미나 어머호 꽈 무러삐, 버라 구더 바무부사: 어부러비 봐우 부구가까아 너 이 와구푸찌러!

65. 바바아 버찌러 바더다 나

---

59. About an hour later another asserted, "Certainly this fellow was with him, for he is a Galilean."

60. Peter replied, "Man, I don't know what you're talking about!" Just as he was speaking, the rooster crowed.

61. The Lord turned and looked straight at Peter. Then Peter remembered the word the Lord had spoken to him: "Before the rooster crows today, you will disown me three times."

62. And he went outside and wept bitterly.

63. The men who were guarding Jesus began mocking and beating him.

64. They blindfolded him and demanded, "Prophesy! Who hit you?"

65. And they said many

myasi inene ya kumushekera.

Yesu atongana

66. abere mw'ei mishangya-shangya, ebashamuka b'ebayuta, n'e bakuhanyi ba ongo, al'auma n'ebangirisi b'eMwaso,* bera kubuanana. Yesu era kurechibwa mw'olu lubunano lwabu.

67. Bera kutangirisa bamusa: "utuburaa iri woyu una Mununusi.* "Nai era kubakula: "chiro nyingababura kwa nyi Mununusi* mutangemerera.

68. Kanji chiro nyingababusa cha chatuma mutemerera, mutanganyakula.

69. si Mumenyereraa kwa era nyuma sa bihangi bieke, nyono nyi Mwana w'eMundu, emalyo ma ongo chi chingaba chisiki chanyi"

70. Boshi ku kwera kumubusa: "mwabu mu mwatechire ku."

71. chasinjire, bera kuteta: "Nde kanji i tungachibusa kwa myasi y'ono mundju? si tubeine twachumvirire kwa achitetera!"

이찌 먀시 이너너 야 구무써거라.

여수 아도먀낍

66. 아버러 뭐이 미싸먀-싸먀, 어바싸무가 버바유다, 너 바구하네 바 오꼬, 아쫘우마 너바삐리시 버뫄소,* 버라 구부아나나. 여수 어라 구러찌봐 몰루 루부나노 롸부.

67. 버라 구다삐리사 바무사: "우두부라아 이리 오유 우나 무누누시.* "나이 어라 구바구롸: "찌로 네꽈바바부라 과 네 무누누시* 무다꺼머러라.

68. 가찌 찌로 네꽈바부사 짜 짜두마 무더머러라, 무다꺄냐구롸.

69. 시 무머녀러라아 과 어라 뉴마 사 비하삐 비어거, 뇨노 네 모나 워무뚜, 어마룐 마 오꼬 찌 찌꽈바 찌시기 짜내"

70. 보씨 구 궈라 구무부사: "뫄부 무 뫄더찌러 구."

71. 짜시찌러, 버라 구더다: "떠 가찌 이 두꽈찌부사 과 먀시 요노 무뚜? 시 두버이너 돠쭈삐리러 과 아찌더러라!"

other insulting things to him.

66. At daybreak the council of the elders of the people, both the chief priests and teachers of the law, met together, and Jesus was led before them.

67. "If you are the Christ," they said, "tell us." Jesus answered, "If I tell you, you will not believe me,

68. and if I asked you, you would not answer.

69. But from now on, the Son of Man will be seated at the right hand of the mighty God."

70. They all asked, "Are you then the Son of God?" He replied, "You are right in saying I am."

71. Then they said, "Why do we need any more testimony? We have heard it from his own lips."

Luka Chikono 23	루가 찌고노 23	Luke Chapter 23[NIV]
Era muhondo sa pilato buna erode	*어라 무호또 사 피롸뎡 부나 어로더*	
1. E luamba loshi iw'e bashamuka b'e Bayuta n'ebakuhanyi ba ongo al'auma n'ebakangirisi	1. 어 루아빠 로씨 이워 바싸무가 버 바유다 너바구하네 바 오끙 아롸우마 너바가ᅇ이리시	1. Then the whole assembly rose and led him off to Pilate.
2. b'e Mwaso* lwera kutangirisa bamwekera e bisha n'e kuteta: "Twabuanaa ono mundju enjire ana e bandju betu kubi. Enjire ange bu mbu batendaa bafuta embarata sa mwami kiasari. Kanji enjire achitonga mbu i Mununusi* Kanji mbu imwami w'elsiraeli. "	2. 버 뫄소* 이워라 구다ᅇ이리사 바뭐거라 어 비싸 너 구더다: "돠부아나아 오노 무뉴 어ㅆ지러 아나 어 바뉴 버두 구비. 어ㅆ지러 아ᅇ어 부 뿌 바더따아 바푸다 어빠라다 사 뫄미 기아사리. 가ㅆ지 어ㅆ지러 아찌도ᅇ아 뿌 이 무누누시* 가ㅆ지 뿌 이뫄미 우'어루시라어뢰. "	2. And they began to accuse him, saying, "We have found this man subverting our nation. He opposes payment of taxes to Caesar and claims to be Christ, a king."
3. pilato nai ku kwera kubusa Yesu: "woyu u watechire ku."	3. 피롸도 나이 구 궈라 구부사 여수: "오유 우 와더찌러 구."	3. So Pilate asked Jesus, "Are you the king of the Jews?" "Yes, it is as you say," Jesus replied.
4. pilato oivirebacha, era kubura e bakulu - kulu b'ebakuhanyi ba ongo al'aume n'eluamba loshi: "Nalolire kwa kutali chinwa cha chingatuma ono mundu achinjisibusibwa"	4. 피롸도 오이비러바짜, 어라 구부라 어 바구루 - 구루 버바구하네 바 오끙 아롸우머 너루아빠 로씨: "나로뢰러 과 구다뢰 찌놔 짜 찌ᅇ아두마 오노 무뚜 아찌ㅆ시부시봐"	4. Then Pilate announced to the chief priests and the crowd, "I find no basis for a charge against this man."
5. si bera kunachanda n'ekuteta: "Ekukangiri kw'ono mundju kwenjire kwakaramya e bandju mwa chio choshi ch'yuteta. ekalilaya yi atangirisisaa, yono waluisa n'omuno Yelusalemu."	5. 시 버라 구나짜따 너구더다: "어구가ᅇ이리 교노 무뉴 궈ㅆ지러 과가라먀 어 바뉴 뫄 찌오 쪼씨 찌유더다. 어가뢰롸야 에 아다ᅇ이리시사아, 요노 와루이사 노무노 여루사러무."	5. But they insisted, "He stirs up the people all over Judeaby his teaching. He started in Galilee and has come all the way here."
6. Mango Pilato omvaa bya bandu babaa bateta, era	6. 마끙 피롸도 오빠아 뱌 바뚜 바바아 바더다, 어라 구바부사	6. On hearing this, Pilate asked if the man was a

kubabusa iri Yesu atula mwesha kalilaya

이리 여수 아두꽈 뭐싸 가꾀꽈야

Galilean.

7. Abare amenyerera kwa Yesu atula w'omwa chio cha Heroti, eKalilaya era kumutuma era mwa Heroti bushi nai mwaku kabiri abaa ali mwa musi w'eYerusalemu.

7. 아바러 아머녀러라 과 여수 아두꽈 요먀 찌오 짜 허로디, 어가꾀꽈야 어라 구무두마 어라 먀 허로디 부씨 나이 먀구 가비리 아바아 아꾀 먀 무시 워여루사꿔무.

7. When he learned that Jesus was under Herod's jurisdiction, he sent him to Herod, who was also in Jerusalem at that time.

8. Mango mwami Heroti alolaa ku Yesu, era kumoa busese bushi a baa omvire kwa ngulu yai. Kanji kutengera suku sinene endaa a honda amulole ku. A baa alinjirire kulola ku chisomerano cha chairwa nai.

8. 마꼬 먀미 허로디 아론꽈아 구 여수, 어라 구모아 부서서 부씨 아 바아 오삐러 과 꾸루 야이. 가찌 구더꺼라 수구 시너너 어따아아 아 호따 아무론꺼러 구. 아 바아 아꾀찌리러 구론꽈 구 찌소머라노 짜 짜이롸 나이.

8. When Herod saw Jesus, he was greatly pleased, because for a long time he had been wanting to see him. From what he had heard about him, he hoped to see him perform some miracle.

9. era kubusa Yesu myasi inene si Yesu atamwakulaa.

9. 어라 구부사 여수 먀시 이너너, 시 여수 아다먀구꽈아.

9. He plied him with many questions, but Jesus gave him no answer.

10. Ebakulu-kulu b'ebakuhanyi ba ongo, al'auma n'ebakangirisi b'emwaso, babaa bali ala Heroti abaa abaa abusisa Yesu, Abola bu babaa basindaira Yesu emyasi busesu.

10. 어바구루-구루 버바구하네 바 오꼬, 아꽈우마 너바가꾀리시 버먀소, 바바아 바꾀 아꽈 허로디 아바아 아바아 아부시사 여수, 아보꽈 부 바바아 바시따이라 여수 어먀시 부서수.

10. The chief priests and the teachers of the law were standing there, vehemently accusing him.

11. chasinda, Heroti a l'auma n'ebasula bai bera kushekera Yesu n'ekumuhunda enguwo. Era kubura abu basula mbu bembasaa Yesu eluchimba lwalangala. Era kubabura mbu bamuhubyaa era mwa pilato.

11. 짜시따, 허로디 아 꽈우마 너바수꽈 바이 버라 구써거라 여수 너구무후따 어우오. 어라 구부라 아부 바수꽈 뿌 버빠사아 여수 어루찌빠 꽈꽈까라. 어라 구바부라 뿌 바무후뱌아 어라 먀 피꽈도.

11. Then Herod and his soldiers ridiculed and mocked him. Dressing him in an elegant robe, they sent him back to Pilate.

12. olu lusuku, Heroti na Pilato bera kuhuba bera, n'noku babaa batomvana.

12. 오루 루수구, 허로디 나 피꽈도 버라 구후바 버라, 우노구 바바아 바도빠나.

12. That day Herod and Pilate became friends-- before this they had been enemies.

Yesu era muhondo sa pilato bwakabiyi

여수 어라 무호또 사 피꽈명 봐가비에

13. Mango Yesu aisibwaa era mwa pilato, era kubuanyanya ebakulu-kulu b'ebakuhanyi ba Ongo, alauma n'ebanji bakulu - kulu, n'ebanji bandu.

13. 마꼬 여수 아이시봐아 어라 마 피꽈도, 어라 구부아냐냐 어바구루-구루 버바구하니 바 오꼬, 아꽈우마 너바찌 바구루 - 구루, 너바찌 바두.

13. Pilate called together the chief priests, the rulers and the people,

14. Era kubabura: "Mwanyiretere ono mundu mbu I wenjire wana ebandu kubi. Bushi n'oku, dera kumubusa era muhondo senyu, si ndalolire ku chinwa chibi kui kw'ebi byoshi mwatechire era lulu sai.

14. 어라 구바부라: "콰네러더러 오노 무뚜 뿌 이 워찌러 와나 어바뚜 구비. 부씨 노구, 더라 구무부사 어라 무호또 서뉴, 시 따로찌러 구 찌놔 찌비 구이 꿔비 뵤씨 마더찌러 어라 루루 사이.

14. and said to them, "You brought me this man as one who was inciting the people to rebellion. I have examined him in your presence and have found no basis for your charges against him.

15. mulolaa kwa Heroti nai atutumire I bushi atamulolire ku bubi. N'nanyi nyisene kwa kutali chibi cha airier cha chingatuma echibwa.

15. 무로꽈아 과 허로디 나이 아두두미러 이 부씨 아다무로찌러 구 부비. 우나네 내서너 과 구다찌 찌비 짜 아이리어루 짜 찌까두마 어찌봐.

15. Neither has Herod, for he sent him back to us; as you can see, he has done nothing to deserve death.

16. Bushi n'oku, mango nyigaba na muhuchisise etchi,nyiamubooresa achiendere."

16. 부씨 노구, 마꼬 네가바 나 무후찌시서 어찌,네아무보오러사 아쩌러러."

16. Therefore, I will punish him and then release him."

17. chira lusuku lukulu lwa iwa pasak,* Pilata ebooresa mundu muuma wa mulisi kwa kusimisa eBayuta.

17. 찌라 루수구 루구루 꽈 이와 파사구,* 피꽈다 어보오러사 무뚜 무우마 와 무찌시 과 구시미사 어바유다.

17. None

18. si boshi bera kuuma

18. 시 보씨 버라 구우마

18. With one voice they

emirenge n'ekuteta: "witaa Yesu utuboorere Baraba!"

19. Oyu baraba a kabulwaa mwa mulisi busi bushi lusuku luumaabaa ali mwa ba babikaa ebandu mw'ematwi masibu, kanji bushi etaa mundu.

20. Kanji Pilato era kunaendekerana ababura kwa Yesu atete chibi, si ahonda amuboorese.

21. si boshi bera kunde banauma emirenge n'ekuteta: "umumanyikaa kwa musalaba! umumanyikaa kwa musalaba!"

22. kanji Pilato era kubabusa ebwa kahatu: "Mabi machie ono mundu airire? Nono ndalolire ku chnwa kw'ono mundu cha chigatuma echibwa. Mango nyingaba namuhuchisise atuchi, nyingemubooresa achiendere."

23. si boshi bera kunde baunde emirenge busese n'ekunde bema Pilato mbu mbu amumanyikaa kwa musalaba. Era kwe merera kuisha elubanja kwa bandju banamwemaa.

24. Pilato era kumu chingibusa elyi e kuhonda kwabo kubaa.

25. Era kubaboorera baraba bema, n'noku i wakabulwaa

어미러뻐 너구더다: "위다아 여수, 우두보오러러 바라바!"

19. 오유 바라바 아 가부똬아 똬 무삐시 부시 부씨 루수구 루우마아바아 아삐 똬 바 바비가아 어바뚜 뭐마뒤 마시부, 가찌 부씨 어다아 무뚜.

20. 가찌 피똬도 어라 구나어뻐거라나 아바부라 과 여수 아더더 찌비, 시 아호따 아무보오러서.

21. 시 보씨 버라 구떠 바나우마 어미러뻐 너구더다: "우무마네가아 과 무사똬바! 우무마네가아 과 무사똬바!"

22. 가찌 피똬도 어라 구바부사 어봐 가하두: "마비 마쩌 오노 무뚜 아이리러? 노노 따로삐러 구 찌놔 교노 무뚜 짜 찌가두마 어찌봐. 마오 네까바 나무후찌시서 아두찌, 네뻐무보오러러사 아쩌떠러."

23. 시 보씨 버라 구떠 바우떠 어미러뻐 부서서 너구떠 버마 피똬도 뿌 뿌 아무마네가아 과 무사똬바. 어라 궈 머러라 구이싸 어루바짜 과 바뚜 바나뭐마아.

24. 피똬도 어라 구무 찌삐부사 어레 어 구호따 과보 구바아.

25. 어라 구바보오러라 바라바 버마, 우노구 이 와가부똬아

---

cried out, "Away with this man! Release Barabbas to us!"

19. (Barabbas had been thrown into prison for an insurrection in the city, and for murder.)

20. Wanting to release Jesus, Pilate appealed to them again.

21. But they kept shouting, "Crucify him! Crucify him!"

22. For the third time he spoke to them: "Why? What crime has this man committed? I have found in him no grounds for the death penalty. Therefore I will have him punished and then release him."

23. But with loud shouts they insistently demanded that he be crucified, and their shouts prevailed.

24. So Pilate decided to grant their demand.

25. He released the man who had been thrown

mw'ematwi masiby, kanji i wetaa. Si era kubawa Yesu yeke bamuire kwa baa nanahonda.

뭐마뒤 마시뷔, 가찌 이 워다아. 시 어라 구바와 여수 여거 바무이러 과 바아 나나호따.

into prison for insurrection and murder, the one they asked for, and surrendered Jesus to their will.

Yesu kwa chimanyi

여수 과 찌마네

26. Mango ebasula babaa bera bekaa Yesu ete n'emusalaba, bera kubuanana na mundu muuma w'omwa musi w'kurene mbu i simonyi. Abaa etenga mwa kambara. Bera kumusimba, bera kumwesa emusalaba ola Yesu abaa ete. Bera kumubura mbu amu lulikiraa.

26. 마꼬 어바수똬 바바아 버라 버가아 여수 어더 너무사똬바, 버라 구부아나나 나 무뚜 무우마 요똬 무시 우구러너 뿌 이 시모네. 아바아 어더까 똬 가빠라. 버라 구무시빠, 버라 구뭐사 어무사똬바 오똬 여수 아바아 어더. 버라 구무부라 뿌 아무 루뛰기라아.

26. As they led him away, they seized Simon from Cyrene, who was on his way in from the country, and put the cross on him and made him carry it behind Jesus.

27. Bandju banene, al'auma n'ebakasi, babaa bakulikire Yesu. Abu bakasi babaa bamulira n'e kuchinyianga.

27. 바뚜 바너너, 아똬우마 너바가시, 바바아 바구뛰기러 여수. 아부 바가시 바바아 바무뛰라 너 구찌네아까.

27. A large number of people followed him, including women who mourned and wailed for him.

28. Yesu era kubasonga n'ekubabura: "Emu bamama b'eyerusalemu, mutaliraa bushi n'emalibuko manyi meine, si n'nenyu muchiririraa, mulirire n'ebana benyu.

28. 여수 어라 구바소까 너구바부라: "어무 바마마 버여루사꺼무, 무다뛰리라아 부씨 너마뛰부고 마니 머이너, 시 우너뉴 무찌리리라아, 무뛰리러 너바나 버뉴.

28. Jesus turned and said to them, "Daughters of Jerusalem, do not weep for me; weep for yourselves and for your children.

29. Mumenyereraa kwa mwa suku sibahire, bacha ku ebandu bakateta: "Engumba saahanyirwe, n'na ba batafuraa kubuta, n'na batafuraa kuonza"

29. 무머녀러라아 과 똬 수구 시바히러, 바짜 구 어바뚜 바가더다: "어우빠 사아하네뤄, 우나 바 바다푸라아 구부다, 우나 바다푸라아 구오싸"

29. For the time will come when you will say, 'Blessed are the barren women, the wombs that never bore and the breasts that never nursed!'

30. kanji bakangirisa bema

30. 가찌 바가끼리사 버마

30. Then " 'they will say

endulungu ebonjo mmbu: "Mutufumbiraa!"

31. Yesu era kunaendekerana a babura: "Akaba banganyiira bacha nyi nyitulanga muchi mubishi-bishi, kute bingaba akaba mu muli nga michi yomire mu lwaikirire?"

32. Bihumusi bibiri na byekibwaa a l'auma na Yesu.

33. Ebandu boshi bera luika kwa katulungu kerikirwe mbu kaangasi Okola ku bamanyiiraa Yesu kwa musalaba a l'auma n'ebi bihumusi bibiri, chiuma kwa musalaba a l'auma 'ebi bihumusi bibiri, chiuma kwa maiyo mai, n'echinji, kwa marembe.

34. chasinda, Yesu era kutangirisa eteta: "E tata, ubababaliraa, bushi bateshi bya baira!"Ebasula baabaa enjimba sai mwa kusikubira echiore.

35. Aolaabaa emenzi bandu ba babaa batumbikisa byoshi bya byarenga. Ebakulu - kulu b'e bayuda nabu babaa bamushekera n'ekuteta: "Endaa alamya ebanji; nai achilamyaa yeine tulole, akaba ina

어뚜루우 어보쪼 무뿌: "무두푸삐라아!"

31. 여수 어라 구나어떠거라나 아 바부라: "아가바 바빠네이라 바짜 니 네두똬까 무찌 무비씨-비씨, 구더 비빠바 아가바 무 무삐 까 미찌 요미러 무 이와이기리러?"

32. 비후무시 비비리 나 벼기봐아 아 똬우마 나 여수.

33. 어바뚜 보씨 버라 루이가 과 가두루우 거리기뤄 뿌 가아까시 오고똬 구 바마네라아 여수 과 무사똬바 아 똬우마 너비 비후무시 비비리, 찌우마 과 무사똬바 아 똬우마 어비 비후무시 비비리, 찌우마 과 마이요 마이, 너찌찌, 과 마러뻐.

34. 짜시따, 여수 어라 구다삐리사 어더다: "어 다다, 우바바바삐라아, 부씨 바더씨 뱌 바이라!"어바수똬 바아바아 어찌빠 사이 똬 구시구비라 어찌오러.

35. 아오똬아바아 어머씨 바뚜 바 바바아 바두삐기사 보씨 뱌 뱌러똬. 어바구루 - 구루 버 바유다 나부 바바아 바무써거라 너구더다: "어따아 아똬먀 어바씨; 나이 아찌똬먀아 여이너 두르뤄,

to the mountains, "Fall on us!" and to the hills, "Cover us!" '

31. For if men do these things when the tree is green, what will happen when it is dry?"

32. Two other men, both criminals, were also led out with him to be executed.

33. When they came to the place called the Skull, there they crucified him, along with the criminals-- one on his right, the other on his left.

34. Jesus said, "Father, forgive them, for they do not know what they are doing." And they divided up his clothes by casting lots.

35. The people stood watching, and the rulers even sneered at him. They said, "He saved others; let him save himself if he is the Christ of God, the Chosen One."

Mununusi* ola walondolwa na ongo!" 아가바 이나 무누누시* 오롸 와로또롸 나 오꼬!"

36. kanji ebasula bera kuhonda kumweresa. Ehanda era ikaliire y'ebifuma by'emisabibu n'ekumubura:

36. 가찌 어바수롸 버라 구호따 구뭐러사. 어하따 어라 이가쀠이러 여비푸마 벼미사비부 너구무부라:

36. The soldiers also came up and mocked him. They offered him wine vinegar

37. "Akaba woyu una mwami w'elubaa lw'ebayuta, uchilamyaa weine tutole"

37. "아가바 오유 우나 롸미 워루바아 이워바유다, 우찌롸먀아 워이너 두도러"

37. and said, "If you are the king of the Jews, save yourself."

38. babaa banjikire kwa chihaki, ala luulu s'echwe iyai mmbu: "onola i mwami w'elubaa iw'Ebayuta."

38. 바바아 바찌기러 과 찌하기, 아롸 루우루루 서쮀 이야이 무뿌: "오노롸 이 롸미 워루바아 이워바유다."

38. There was a written notice above him, which read: THIS IS THE KING OF THE JEWS.

Emwisi kwa chimanyi aalukira Yesu. 어뮈시 과 찌마네 아아루꿋띱 여수.

39. Muuma mwa bihumusi bya byabaa bimanyikirwe kwa misalaba a l'auma na Yesu, era kukamba Yesu n'ekuteta: "si nambu woyu u. Utula Mununusi! Chi chingatuma utachilamya weine, n'netu utulamye?

39. 무우마 와 비후무시 뱌 뱌바아 비마네기뤄 과 미사롸바 아 롸우마 나 여수, 어라 구가빠 여수 너구더다: "시 나뿌 오유 우. 우두롸 무누누시! 찌 찌빠두마 우다찌롸먀 워이너, 우너두 우두롸며?

39. One of the criminals who hung there hurled insults at him: "Aren't you the Christ? Save yourself and us!"

40. Si mukabu yeke era kumukaliira busese n'ekuteta: "Woyu utanachubaa Ongo chiro angaba mbu emalibuko mai n'emetu muna mauma lwarero?

40. 시 무가부 여거 어라 구무가쀠이라 부서서 너구더다: "오유 우다나쭈바아 오꼬 찌로 아빠바 뿌 어마쀠부고 마이 너머두 무나 마우마 이와러로?

40. But the other criminal rebuked him. "Don't you fear God," he said, "since you are under the same sentence?

41. Tubano tunganachinjibusibwe al'auma netu atairaa na chiro na mwasi mubi."

41. 두바노 두빠나찌찌부시뷔 아롸우마 너두 아다이라아 나 찌로 나 롸시 무비."

41. We are punished justly, for we are getting what our deeds deserve. But this man has done nothing wrong."

42. Chasinjire, era nai era kumwakula "Nyono utanyibiriraa

42. 짜시찌러, 어라 나이 어라 구꽈구롸 "뇨노 우다네비리라아

42. Then he said, "Jesus, remember me when you

mwa Bwimi bwau."

43. Chasinjire, era kubura Yesu "Nyono utanyibiraa mwa kamangana: Lwarero ungaba al'auma nanyi mwa chisiki ch'e lumoo!"

Yesu era kushika e muchima

44. Abere yalinga kuba saa ndutu, e suba Iyera kusima.

45. Emusimya era kuba mwa chio choshi kuikira saa mwenda. Unao-unao, engwaya inene era yabaa yahumba mwa Luhu iwa Ongo, yera kubereka byande bibiri.

46. Chasinjire, Yesu era kuchilakangira busese n'ekuteta: "Tata, nabikire emuchina wanyi mwa maboko mau. "bere amala kuteta bacha, kuna kutoa emuchima."

47. Mango emukulu-kulu w'ebasula alolaa kw'ebwa byabare, era kutangirisa atonga Ongo n'ekuteta: "Ona mundu abaa kulola kwa beta Yesu, kanji banalola

48. Ebanji bandu boshi Yesu beke, kanji banalola kw'ebya byarengaa byoshi, bera kufulukanga na businane bunene.

와 뷔미 봐우."

43. 짜시띠러, 어라 구부라 여수 "뇨노 우다니비라아 마 가마꺄나: 똫러로 우꺄바 아똫우마 나니 마 찌시기 쩌 루모오!"

여수 어라 구씨가 어 무찌마

44. 아버러 야삐꺄 구바 사아 뚜두, 어 수바 이여라 구시마.

45. 어무시먀 어라 구바 먀 찌오 쪼씨 구이기라 사아 우나오-우나오, 어꺄야 이너너 어라 야바아 야후빠 먀 루후 이와 오꾟, 여라 구버러가 뱌떠 비비리.

46. 짜시띠러, 여수 어라 구찌똫가삐라 부서서 너구더다: "다다, 나비기러 어무찌나 와네 먀 마보고 마우. "버러 아마똫 구더다 바짜, 구나 구도아 어무찌마."

47. 마꾟 어무구루-구루 워바수똫 아똟똫아 궈봐 뱌바러, 어라 구다띠리사 아도꺄 오꾟 너구더다: "오나 무뚜 아바아 구롣똫 과 버다 여수, 가찌 바나롣똫

48. 어바찌 바뚜 보씨 여수 버거, 가찌 바나롣똫 궈뱌 뱌러꺄아 뵤씨, 버라 구푸루루가꺄 나 부시나너 부너너.

come into your kingdom."

43. Jesus answered him, "I tell you the truth, today you will be with me in paradise."

44. It was now about the sixth hour, and darkness came over the whole land until the ninth hour,

45. for the sun stopped shining. And the curtain of the temple was torn in two.

46. Jesus called out with a loud voice, "Father, into your hands I commit my spirit." When he had said this, he breathed his last.

47. The centurion, seeing what had happened, praised God and said, "Surely this was a righteous man."

48. When all the people who had gathered to witness this sight saw what took place, they beat their breasts and

went away.

49. Si ba babaa beshi Yesu beke, al'auma n'ebakisi ba batengeraa nai ekalilaya, babaa bemenzi marerere, batumbikisa bya byarenga kuikira kwa businda.

49. 시 바 바바아 버씨 여수 버거, 아쩌우마 너바기시 바 바더써라아 나이 어가쯰쫘야, 바바아 버머씨 마러러러, 바두쎼기사 뱌 뱌러쌰 구이기라 과 부시따.

49. But all those who knew him, including the women who had followed him from Galilee, stood at a distance, watching these things.

Yesu atabwa

여수 아다봐

50. Era nyuma s'ebi, kwera kupamukira mulume muuma mbu i Yosefu.

50. 어라 뉴마 서비, 궈라 구파무기라 무루머 무우마 뿌이 요서푸.

50. Now there was a man named Joseph, a member of the Council, a good and upright man,

51. Abaa mwesha mwa musi w'e Bayuda b'e Arimatayi. Kanji abaa atunjire e Mwaso wa Musa. Kutengera suku sinene, abaa alinjira eBwimi bwa Ongo buike. Abaa atula muuma w'omwa lubuanano iw'ebashamuka, si yeke atabaa mu lwango luuma n'eBayuta mwa lufu lwa Yesu.

51. 아바아 뭐싸 뫄 무시 워 바유다 버 아리마다에. 가씨 아바아 아두찌러 어 뫄소 와 무사. 구더써라 수구 시너너, 아바아 아쯰찌라 어뷔미 봐 오꼬 부이거. 아바아 아두쫘 무우마 요뫄 루부아나노 이워바싸무가, 시 여거 아다바아 무 쫜꼬 루우마 너바유다 뫄 루푸 쫜 여수.

51. who had not consented to their decision and action. He came from the Judean town of Arimathea and he was waiting for the kingdom of God.

52. Era kunaya kukula chi kwa musalaba. Abere era kulaa chi al'auma na ba bamuasaa, bera kubika chi mwa chirimbi. Kanji chaba chitafuraa kutabibwa mu mundu.

52. 어라 구나야 구구쫘 찌 과 무사쫘바. 아버러 어라 구쫘아 찌 아쫘우마 나 바 바무아사아, 버라 구비가 찌 뫄 찌리쎼. 가씨 쨔바 찌다푸라아 구다비봐 무 무뚜.

52. Going to Pilate, he asked for Jesus' body.

53. Then he took it down, wrapped it in linen cloth and placed it in a tomb cut in the rock, one in which no one had yet been laid.

54. Yesu atabibwaa lusuku lwa katano, n'esabato yabaa yera iri ofu.

54. 여수 아다비봐아 루수구 꽈 가다노, 너사바도 야바아 여라 이리 오푸.

54. It was Preparation Day, and the Sabbath was about to begin.

55. Ba bakasi b'ekalilaya, bera kwerekesa Yosefu kutaba Yesu. Bera kutumbikisa echinjifwa n'ekulola kwa chirunda cha Yesu chabikwa mu.

55. 바 바가시 버가삐꽈야, 버라 궈러거사 요서푸 구다바 여수. 버라 구두삐기사 어찌씨꽈 너구뢷라 과 찌루따 짜 여수 짜비과 무.

55. The women who had come with Jesus from Galilee followed Joseph and saw the tomb and how his body was laid in it.

56. Chasinjire, bera kufuluka kwa musi baye kukunganya ebichi bya byauuka al'aum n'e marashi m'e kulanga emubiri wa Yesu angesha kubola. Si bera kutamuka elusuku iw'e Sabato kukulikana n'okwa Mwaso wabu abaa atula atechire.

56. 짜시찌러, 버라 구푸루가 과 무시 바여 구구꺄냐 어비찌 뱌 뱌우우가 아뢰우무 너 마라씨 머 구꽈꺄 어무비리 와 여수 아꺼싸 구보꽈. 시 버라 구다무가 어루수구 이워 사바도 구구쬐가나 노과 꽈소 와부 아바아 아두꽈 아더찌러.

56. Then they went home and prepared spices and perfumes. But they rested on the Sabbath in obedience to the commandment.

Luka Chikono 24
K'omoka kwa Yesu

루가 찌고노 24
고모가 과 여수

Luke Chapter 24[NIV]

1. Abere lware lw'einga lumbuli-mbuli, ba bakasi bera kulamukira kwa chinjifwa. Kanji babaa bete ma marashi babaa bakunganyise

1. 아버러 꽈러 뤄이마 뤂쀠-뿌쀠, 바 바가시 버라 구꽈무기라 과 찌씨꽈. 가찌 바바아 버더 마 마라씨 바바아 바구꺄네서

1. On the first day of the week, very early in the morning, the women took the spices they had prepared and went to the tomb.

2. Baikire ku, bera kubauana ekoi lya lyende lyafunyikira echiso ch'echinjifwa lyakunungwirwe.

2. 바이기러 구, 버라 구바우아나 어고이 꺄 쪄러 꺄푸네기라 어찌소 쩌찌씨꽈 꺄구누쮜뤄.

2. They found the stone rolled away from the tomb,

3. Mango bangilyiraa Muchi, bera kubuana e chirunda cha Yesu chitachiri mu.

3. 마꼬 바삐레라아 무찌, 버라 구부아나 어 찌루따 짜 여수 찌다찌리 무.

3. but when they entered, they did not find the body of the Lord Jesus.

4. Abere baanyisa, bainyire ku bangaira, unao-unao bamalaika babiri bera kubapamukira ku. Babaa b?mbesi njimba salangala busese.

5. Ba bakasi babahunjire kw'emeho, bera kusimbibwa na buba buba bunene. Bera kukoma n'emeho mwa chitaka. Abu bamalaika bera kubabura: "chi al'auma nenyu ekalilaya.

0

7. si mwishi kwa ababuraa mbu kwemire imwana we mundju anyibwe mwa maboko m'e bandju babi, Anamanyikibwe kwa musalaba, n'elusuku lwa kahatu omoke!"

8. Bushi n'oku, abu bakasi bera kukengera ei myasi ya Yesu.

9. Abere bera betengaa kwa chinji bandu byoshi bya balolaa ku.

10. Ebakasi ba bafuliraa endumwa* kw'oyu mwasi bu babaa babano: Mariya makatala, na shanyi, na mariya

---

4. 아버러 바아네사, 바이네러 구 바꺄이라, 우나오-우나오 바마꺄이가 바비리 버라 구바파무기라 구. 바바아 부?뻐시 띠빠 사꺄꺄꺄 부서서.

5. 바 바가시 바바후찌러 궈머호, 버라 구시뻬봐 나 부바 부바 부너너. 버라 구고마 너머호 와 찌다가. 아부 바마꺄이가 버라 구바부라: "찌 아꺄우마 너뉴 어가꾀꺄야.

0

7. 시 뮈씨 과 아바부라아 뿌 궈미러 이뫄나 워 무뚜 아네붜 와 마보고 머 바뚜 바비, 아나마네기붜 과 무사꺄바, 너꾸수구 꺄 가하두 오모거!"

8. 부씨 노구, 아부 바가시 버라 구거꺼라 어이 먀시 야 여수.

9. 아버러 버라 버더꺄아 과 찌찌 바뚜 뵤씨 뱌 바로꺄아 구.

10. 어바가시 바 바푸꾀라아 어누뫄* 교유 뫄시 부 바바아 바바노: 마리야 마가다꺄, 나 싸네, 나 마리야 네나 와

---

4. While they were wondering about this, suddenly two men in clothes that gleamed like lightning stood beside them.

5. In their fright the women bowed down with their faces to the ground, but the men said to them, "Why do you look for the living among the dead?

6. He is not here; he has risen! Remember how he told you, while he was still with you in Galilee:

7. 'The Son of Man must be delivered into the hands of sinful men, be crucified and on the third day be raised again.' "

8. Then they remembered his words.

9. When they came back from the tomb, they told all these things to the Eleven and to all the others.

10. It was Mary Magdalene, Joanna, Mary the mother of James, and the others with them who

nyina wa yakobo, na banji bakasi.	야고보, 나 바찌 바가시.	told this to the apostles.
11. Si emyasi y'abu bakasi yaberaa e ndjumwa nga biroto.chiro batanemereraa kwa ingaba ya kanangana.	11. 시 어먀시 야부 바가시 야버라아 어 뀻뫄 까 비로도.찌로 바다너머러라아 과 이까바 야 가나까나.	11. But they did not believe the women, because their words seemed to them like nonsense.
12. Petero yeke, era kulola kwa mikunjo babungiraa kwa chirunda cha Yesu oshi au. Era kuhuba kwa wai asanyirwe bungiraa kwa chirunda cha Yesu oshi au. Era kuhuba kwa wai asanyirwe busese n'e bya byabaa.	12. 퍼더로 여거, 어라 구로롸 과 미구뇨 바부찌라아 과 찌루따 짜 여수 오씨 아우. 어라 구후바 과 와이 아사니뤄 부찌라아 과 찌루따 짜 여수 오씨 아우. 어라 구후바 과 와이 아사네뤄 부서서 너 뱌 뱌바아.	12. Peter, however, got up and ran to the tomb. Bending over, he saw the strips of linen lying by themselves, and he went away, wondering to himself what had happened.
Era kuulukira kubaanda babilyi b'e emaus	***어라 구우루긋띱 구바아따 바비쀄 버 어마우수***	
13. kw'olu lusuku lw'einga, babiri mwa banafunzi ba Yesu babaa bendaalira ku musi muuma mbu I Emau. Oyu musiabaa ali ku bilometere ekumi na chiuma n'eyerusalemu.	13. 교루 루수구 뤄이까, 바비리 뫄 바나푸씨 바 여수 바바아 버따아뢰라 구 무시 무우마 뿌 이 어마우. 오유 무시아바아 아뢰 구 비로머더러 어구미 나 찌우마 너여루사뤄무.	13. Now that same day two of them were going to a village called Emmaus, about seven miles from Jerusalem.
14. Babaa baenda bahambala era lulu s'e myasi y'e lufu lwa Yesu.	14. 바바아 바어따 바하빠롸 어라 루루 서 먀시 여 루푸 롸 여수.	14. They were talking with each other about everything that had happened.
15. Abere bera banali mw'oyu muhambare, Yesu yeine era kuulukira n'ekutangirisa aezikanya nabu.	15. 아버러 버라 바나뢰 뫄유 무하빠러, 여수 여이너 어라 구우루기라 너구다찌리사 아어지가냐 나부.	15. As they talked and discussed these things with each other, Jesus himself came up and walked along with them;
16. si batamumenyerera, bushi ongo abasibyaa emeho	16. 시 바다무머녀러라, 부씨 오오 아바시뱌아 어머호	16. but they were kept from recognizing him.

bangesha kumumenyerera. 바어싸 구무머녀러라.

17. Yesu era kubabusa: "Myasi ichie mwaenda mwahambala ku?" Bera kwimanga batanahaalukire.

17. 여수 어라 구바부사: "먀시 이쩌 먀어따 먀하빠롸 구?" 버라 귀마빠 바다나하아루기러.

17. He asked them, "What are you discussing together as you walk along?" They stood still, their faces downcast.

18. Muuma mw'abu banafunzi mbu I cheleopa, era kumwakula: "Umundju wabaa ulyi mwa yerusalemu kute weke u utanamenyire bya byarengire mu mwa kano kabiri?

18. 무우마 먀부 바나푸씨 뿌 이 쩌러오파, 어라 구뫄구롸: "우무뉴 와바아 우레 먀 여루사러무 구더 워거 우 우다나머네러 뱌 뱌러삐러 무 뫄 가노 가비리?

18. One of them, named Cleopas, asked him, "Are you only a visitor to Jerusalem and do not know the things that have happened there in these days?"

19. na Yesu era kubabusa: ' myasi ichie yarengire mu kasi?" Bera kumwakula: iri myasi era yerekere Yesu mwesha nasareti. Abana atula murebi, kanjiabaa ete ebuashi mw'ebya endaa aira, n'na bya endaa ateta era muhondo sa Ongo n'era muhondo s'e bandju boshi.

19. 나 여수 어라 구바부사: 먀시 이쩌 야러삐러 무 가시?" 버라 구뫄구롸: 이리 먀시 어라 여러거러 여수 뭐싸 나사러디. 아바나 아두롸 무러비, 가찌아바아 어더 어부아씨 뭐뱌 어따아 아이라, 우나 뱌 어따아 아더다 어라 무호또 사 오꼬 너라 무호또 서 바뉴 보씨.

19. "What things?" he asked. "About Jesus of Nazareth," they replied. "He was a prophet, powerful in word and deed before God and all the people.

20. Ebakulu - kulu b'ebakuhayika ba Ongo a l'auma n'e banji bakulu- kulu betu bamwanaa era mw'e baromabaisha e lwango mbu afaa chasinda abu baroma bera kumumanyika kwa musalaba

20. 어바구룰 - 구룰 버바구하에가 바 오꼬 아 롸우마 너 바찌 바구룰- 구룰 버두 바뫄나아 어라 뭐 바로마바이싸 어 롹오 뿌 아파아 짜시따 아부 바로마 버라 구무마네가 과 무사롸바

20. The chief priests and our rulers handed him over to be sentenced to death, and they crucified him;

21. Tubano twabaa tulangalire kwa I okanunula ebana b'eisraeli mwa busha bw'eberenda babu na iwarero lu lusuku iwa kahatu kutengera

21. 두바노 돠바아 두롸빠리러 과 이 오가누누롸 어바나 버이수라어피 먀 부싸 뭐버러따 바부 나 이와러로 룩 룩수구 이와 가하두 구더빠러

21. but we had hoped that he was the one who was going to redeem Israel. And what is more, it is the third day since all

ei myasi yarengere

22. kanji kuli bakasi bauma b'o,mwa luamba iwetu iw'ebanafunzi ba balamukiraa era chinjifwa nabu ba batunyisi n'emyasi babafulukana yi

23. Bushi mbu bamalaika babapamukiraa ku, bera kubabura mbu Yesu ali muuma uma

24. Banafunzi bauma mu tubano nabu banayaa era chinjifwa bera kulola ng'okwa abu bakasi banatetaa, nabu batanamulolaa ku"

25. Yesu ku kwera kubura abu banafunzi: "kute Mwabu mutomva! Nyesene ng'emichima yenyu itahondaa kwemera emyasi batetaa era muhondo.

26. Muteshi kwabaa kwemire eMununusi* alibuke era muhondo s'ekuya mw'etunda iyai?"

27. chasinjire, Yesu era kubaanyikisisa bya byatetwaa era lulu sai mwa manjiko ma ongo. Era kutangirira kwa bitabo bya Musa, kuikira n'okwa bitabo byoshi by'e barebi.

28. Abere bera bali ofu n'oyu musi abu banafunzi babiri babaa b?ya ku, Yesu yeke era

---

어이 먀시 야러꺼러

22. 가찌 구뀌 바가시 바우마 보,먀 루아빠 이워두 이워바나푸씨 바 바꽈무기라아 어라 찌찌퐈 나부 바 바두네시 너먀시 바바푸루가나 에

23. 부씨 뿌 바마퐈이가 바바파무기라아 구, 버라 구바부라 뿌 여수 아뀌 무우마 우마

24. 바나푸씨 바우마 무 두바노 나부 바나야아 어라 찌찌퐈 버라 구뢰콰 꼬과 아부 바가시 바나더다아, 나부 바다나무뢰콰아 구"

25. 여수 구 궈라 구부라 아부 바나푸씨: "구더 먀부 무도빠! 녀서너 꺼미찌마 여뉴 이다호따아 궈머라 어먀시 바더다아 어라 무호또.

26. 무더씨 과바아 궈미러 어무누누시* 아뀌부거 어라 무호또 서구야 뭐두따 이야이?"

27. 짜시찌러, 여수 어라 구바아네기시사 뱌 뱌더돠아 어라 루루 사이 먀 마찌고 마 오꼬. 어라 구다띠리라 과 비다보 뱌 무사, 구이기라 노과 비다보 뵤씨 벼 바러비.

28. 아버러 버라 바뀌 오푸 노유 무시 아부 바나푸씨 바비리 바바아 부?야 구, 여수

---

this took place.

22. In addition, some of our women amazed us. They went to the tomb early this morning

23. but didn't find his body. They came and told us that they had seen a vision of angels, who said he was alive.

24. Then some of our companions went to the tomb and found it just as the women had said, but him they did not see."

25. He said to them, "How foolish you are, and how slow of heart to believe all that the prophets have spoken!

26. Did not the Christ have to suffer these things and then enter his glory?"

27. And beginning with Moses and all the Prophets, he explained to them what was said in all the Scriptures concerning himself.

28. As they approached the village to which they were going, Jesus acted

kulorekana ku ng'ola wabaa uchiri waya are.	여거 어라 구로러가나 구 오ᄭᅩᄙᅪ 와바아 우찌리 와야 아러.	as if he were going farther.
29. si abu banafunzi batahondaa abareke. Bera kumubura: "ushibaa al'auma netu bushi ebutufu bwahonda kwira. "mvire bacha, era kwingirira mwa nyumba era babaa b?ya mu, era kwikala a l'auma nabu.	29. 시 아부 바나푸ᄡᅵ 바다호따아 아바러거. 버라 구무부라: "우씨바아 아ᄙᅪ우마 너두 부씨 어부두푸 봐호따 귀라. "삐러 바짜, 어라 귀ᅇᅵ리라 뫄 뉴빠 어라 바바아 부?야 무, 어라 귀가ᄙᅪ 아 ᄙᅪ우마 나부.	29. But they urged him strongly, "Stay with us, for it is nearly evening; the day is almost over." So he went in to stay with them.
30. Mangoabaa era ali kwa mesa nabu, era kutola emukati, era kutonga ongo, era ukishanga u n'ekubaabira u.	30. 마ᄭᅩ아바아 어라 아ᄙᅴ 과 머사 나부, 어라 구도ᄙᅪ 어무가디, 어라 구도ᅇᅡ 오ᄭᅩ, 어라 우기싸ᅇᅡ 우 너구바아비라 우.	30. When he was at the table with them, he took bread, gave thanks, broke it and began to give it to them.
31. unao-unao, emeho mabu kuna kubookala, na bamenyerera kwa kasi Yesu I uli nabu. Si mwe'echi chihangi, atachilorekanaa ku nabu.	31. 우나오-우나오, 어머호 마부 구나 구보오가ᄙᅪ, 나 바머녀러라 과 가시 여수 이 우ᄙᅵ 나부. 시 뭐어찌 찌하ᅇᅵ, 아다찌로러가나아 구 나부.	31. Then their eyes were opened and they recognized him, and he disappeared from their sight.
32. Abu babiri bera kutangirisa baburana: "ku binali, Yesu I twalolire ku! Utera kulola kwa chira muuma mu tubabire?ata lumoo lunene mwa muchima mango era kuba?tuhambalira mwa njira kw'ebya byatetwa bushi nai mwa manjiko ma ongo?"	32. 아부 바비리 버라 구다ᅇᅵ리사 바부라나: "구 비나ᄙᅵ, 여수 이 돠로ᄙᅵ러 구! 우더라 구로ᄙᅪ 과 찌라 무우마 무 두바비러?아다 루모오 루너너 뫄 무찌마 마ᄭᅩ 어라 구바?두하빠ᄙᅵ라 뫄 ᄡᅵ라 궈뱌 뱌더돠 부씨 나이 뫄 마ᄡᅵ고 마 오ᄭᅩ?"	32. They asked each other, "Were not our hearts burning within us while he talked with us on the road and opened the Scriptures to us?"
33. Mw'echi chihangi. Abu banafunzi babiri bera kwimuka ala babaa balira n'ekuhuba eyerusalemu. Baikire yi,bera kuchimana endumwa* ekumi na nguma mwa lubuanano a	33. 뭐찌 찌하ᅇᅵ. 아부 바나푸ᄡᅵ 바비리 버라 귀무가 아ᄙᅪ 바바아 바ᄙᅵ라 너구후바 어여루사ᄙᅥ무. 바이기러 예,버라 구찌마나 어뚜롸* 어구미 나 ᅌᅮ마 뫄 루부아나노 아 ᄙᅪ우마	33. They got up and returned at once to Jerusalem. There they found the Eleven and those with them, assembled together

l'auma na banji banafunzi.

34. Bera kubura abu banafunzi babiLlyi: "

35. Abu banafunzi babiLYi nabu bera kuanyikisisa bya balolaa ku mwa njira y'eEmau, na kute bamenyerera Yesu mabgo abaabiraa emukati.

Yesu olukira kwa baanda

36. Abere abu banafunzi babiri banachiri baanyikisa, Yesu kuna kupamukira mwaa kachi-kachi kabu boshi n'ekubakesa mmbu: "Bolo!"

37. Balolire bacha, bera kusimbibwa na buba bunene, bushi b?chichingaa mbu musimu I balolire ku.

38. si Yesu era kubabusa: "chichatuma mwasimbibwa n'ebuba, na chi chatuma mwachikebwa mwa michima yenyu mwa kunyilola ku?

39. Musongaa kwa nzuu mwa biaha byanyi n'na kwa bihando byanyi, mwanyimenyerera, bushi emusimu atatusa munyofu na makinya ng'okwa munyisene ku.

40. Mango abaa abura bu bacha, era kubalosa ebiaha n'bihando n'ebihando byai.

나 바찌 바나푸씨.

34. 버라 구부라 아부 바나푸씨 바비루쩨: "

35. 아부 바나푸씨 바비레 나부 버라 구아네기시사 뱌 바로롸아 구 마 찌라 여어마우, 나 구더 바머녀러라 여수 마부고 아바아비라아 어무가디.

여수 오룩굿띱 과 바아따

36. 아버러 아부 바나푸씨 바비리 바나찌리 바아네기사, 여수 구나 구파무기라 마아 가찌-가찌 가부 보씨 너구바거사 무뿌: "보로!"

37. 바로찌러 바짜, 버라 구시삐봐 나 부바 부너너, 부씨 부?찌찌까아 뿌 무시무 이 바로찌러 구.

38. 시 여수 어라 구바부사: "찌짜두마 먀시삐봐 너부바, 나 찌 짜두마 먀찌거봐 마 미찌마 여뉴 마 구네론퐈 구?

39. 무소까아 과 누우 먀 비아하 뱌네 우나 과 비하또 뱌네, 먀네머녀러라, 부씨 어무시무 아다두사 무뇨푸 나 마기냐 꼬과 무네서너 구.

40. 마꼬 아바아 아부라 부 바짜, 어라 구바론사 어비아하 우비하또 너비하또 뱌이.

---

34. and saying, "It is true! The Lord has risen and has appeared to Simon."

35. Then the two told what had happened on the way, and how Jesus was recognized by them when he broke the bread.

36. While they were still talking about this, Jesus himself stood among them and said to them, "Peace be with you."

37. They were startled and frightened, thinking they saw a ghost.

38. He said to them, "Why are you troubled, and why do doubts rise in your minds?

39. Look at my hands and my feet. It is I myself! Touch me and see; a ghost does not have flesh and bones, as you see I have."

40. When he had said this, he showed them his hands and feet.

41. Batachilaa kw'ebya Yesu abaa abura bu bachi n'elumoo al'auma N'ekusanwa. Yesu ku kwera kubusa bu iri bangabona biryo.

42. Nabu bera kumwanfirisa chimbi ch'efi yochirwe.

43. Era kwangirira I n'e kulya I banasene.

44. Era kubabura: "mukengeraaebinwa byanyi bya nendaa nababura era muhondo s'e kufa kwanyi mmbu: kwemire bike kanangana byoshi byanjikwaa era lulu sanyi mwa mwaso* wa Musa, n'omwa wanjiko m'ebarebi, n'omwa chitabo ch'enyimbo."

45. chasinda, Yesu era kubaboola ebukengere bw'ekumekumenyerera bya byanjikwaa mw'echi chitabo cha ongo: kwemire eMununusi*

46. Alibuke, anafe, na ku suku ehatu, omoke.

47. n'na mw'e sina iyai mu ilyi ongo ababalira. N'eyerusalemu yi bakatangirira.

41. 바다찌롸아 궈뱌 여수 아바아 아부라 부 바찌 너루모오 아롸우마 너구사놔. 여수 구 궈라 구부사 부 이리 바꺄보나 비료.

42. 나부 버라 구뫄삐리사 찌삐 쩌피 요찌뤄.

43. 어라 과삐리라 이 너 구꺄 이 바나서너.

44. 어라 구바부라: "무거꺼라아어비놔 뱌네 뱌 너따아 나바부라 어라 무호또 서 구파 과네 무뿌: 궈미러 비거 가나꺄나 뵤씨 뱌찌과아 어라 루루 사네 뫄 뫄소* 와 무사, 노뫄 와찌고 머바러비, 노뫄 찌다보 쩌네뽀."

45. 짜시따, 여수 어라 구바보오롸 어부거꺼러 붜구머구머녀러라 뱌 뱌찌과아 뭐찌 찌다보 짜 오꼬: 궈미러 어무누누시*

46. 아쀠부거, 아나퍼, 나 구 수구 어하두, 오모거.

47. 우나 뭐 시나 이야이 무 이쀀 오꼬 아바바바쀠라. 너여루사뻐무 에 바가다삐리라.

41. And while they still did not believe it because of joy and amazement, he asked them, "Do you have anything here to eat?"

42. They gave him a piece of broiled fish,

43. and he took it and ate it in their presence.

44. He said to them, "This is what I told you while I was still with you: Everything must be fulfilled that is written about me in the Law of Moses, the Prophets and the Psalms."

45. Then he opened their minds so they could understand the Scriptures.

46. He told them, "This is what is written: The Christ will suffer and rise from the dead on the third day,

47. and repentance and forgiveness of sins will be preached in his name to all nations, beginning at Jerusalem.

48. si mubeine mwachilorere kw'ebya byarengire era lulu sanyi! Kwemire mubianyikisise abu bandju boshi.

49. nyeine nyikabatumira eMuchima Mubuya-buya ola tata abalaayaa. Si mwikalaa muno musi w'eyerusalemu kukira mango ebuashi bw'oyu muchima wa ongo bukabandaailire"

Yesu aya kwa Nguba

50. Chasinjire, Yesu era kutenga n'ebabafunzi bai eyerusalemu, era kubeka ofu n'e musi w'e Betanyiya. Baikire yi, era kwemusa emaboko mwa chanya, era kubaahayira.

51. Mangoabaa anachiri abaahanyira, era kurekana nabu, chasinda era kwekibwa kwekibwa kwa Nguba.

52. Abere nabu bera ba bamukomeraa emafi n'e kumuchwunda, bera kufuluka eyerusalemu na lumoo lunene.

53. Bera kunde banabuanana batonga ongo mwa luhu iwai.

48. 시 무버이너 꽈찌로러러 궈뱌 뱌러삐러 어라 루루 사니! 궈미러 무비아네기시서 아부 바쭈 보씨.

49. 녀이너 네가바두미라 어무찌마 무부야-부야 오꽈 다다 아바꽈아야아. 시 뮈가꽈아 무노 무시 워여루사꿔무 구기라 마꼬 어부아씨 부요유 무찌마 와 오꼬 부가바따아이삐러"

여수 아야 과 꿍밍

50. 짜시띠러, 여수 어라 구더빠 너바바푸씨 바이 어여루사꿔무, 어라 구버가 오푸 너 무시 워 버다니야. 바이기러 에, 어라 궈무사 어마보고 꽈 짜냐, 어라 구바아하에라.

51. 마꼬아바아 아나찌리 아바아하니라, 어라 구러가나 나부, 짜시따 어라 궈기봐 궈기봐 과 꿍바.

52. 아버러 나부 버라 바 바무고머라아 어마피 너 구무쭈따, 버라 구푸루가 어여루사꿔무 나 루모오 루너너.

53. 버라 구떠 바나부아나나 바도빠 오꼬 꽈 루후 이와이.

48. You are witnesses of these things.

49. I am going to send you what my Father has promised; but stay in the city until you have been clothed with power from on high."

50. When he had led them out to the vicinity of Bethany, he lifted up his hands and blessed them.

51. While he was blessing them, he left them and was taken up into heaven.

52. Then they worshiped him and returned to Jerusalem with great joy.

53. And they stayed continually at the temple, praising God.

Yoana

요아나

John

E MWASI MUBUYA-BUYA WA YESU KIRISITO
N'NGOKWA AANJIKWA NA YOWANA

어 꽈시 무부야-부야 와 여수 기리시도
우오과 아아찌과 나 요와나

Yoana Chikono 1

1. Mwa ndangilyiso, era muhondo s'e kubumba chira kandju, wachinwa abaa era anachwulao. Kanji mw'esi suku, wachinwa abaa alyi alauma na Ongo, kanji iwanabaa Ongo kanangana.

2. Kutengera esi suku soshi, buna Ongo bu babaa banachwula.

3. Ongo abumbaa e bindju byoshi, kurengera wachinwa. Rero, kutalyi chiro na kandju kasibya ka kabumbwaa busirai.

4. Mw'oyu wachimwa, mu mwabaa muchwula e kalamo. N'aku kalamo, bu bwabaa bulangare kwa bandju.

5. Obu bulangare, bwendee bwalomeka mwa musimya. N'e musimya chiro akaala kusimyabo.

6. Rero, Ongo achwumaa mundju muuma mbu I Yowana.

7. Oyu Yowana, abahaa kuhambala kwa bya achiloreraako era luulu s'obu bulangare, chasiya mwa kumurengera ko, e bandju boshi bemerere mwa michima yabo.

요아나 찌고노 1

1. 마 따삐레소, 어라 무호또 서 구부빠 찌라 가꾸, 와찌놔 아바아 어라 아나쭈롸오. 가찌 뭐시 수구, 와찌놔 아바아 아뤠 아롸우마 나 오꼬, 가찌 이와나바아 오꼬 가나까나.

2. 구더뻐라 어시 수구 소씨, 부나 오꼬 부 바바아 바나쭈롸.

3. 오꼬 아부빠아 어 비쭈 보씨, 구러뻐라 와찌놔. 러로, 구다뤠 찌로 나 가꾸 가시뱌 가 가부꽈아 부시라이.

4. 모유 와찌똬, 무 뫄바아 무쭈롸 어 가롸모. 나구 가롸모, 부 봐바아 부롸꺼러 과 바꾸.

5. 오부 부롸꺼러, 뭐뻐어 봐로머가 뫄 무시먀. 너 무시먀 찌로 아가아롸 구시먀보.

6. 러로, 오꼬 아쭈마아 무누 무우마 뿌 이 요와나.

7. 오유 요와나, 아바하아 구하빠롸 과 뱌 아찌로러라아고 어라 루우루 소부 부롸꺼러, 짜시야 뫄 구무러꺼라 고, 어 바꾸 보씨 버머러러 뫄 미찌마 야보.

John Chapter 1[NIV]

1. In the beginning was the Word, and the Word was with God, and the Word was God.

2. He was with God in the beginning.

3. Through him all things were made; without him nothing was made that has been made.

4. In him was life, and that life was the light of men.

5. The light shines in the darkness, but the darkness has not understood it.

6. There came a man who was sent from God; his name was John.

7. He came as a witness to testify concerning that light, so that through him all men might believe.

8. Yowana, ata iwabaa obu bulangare, si abahaa kuteta e myasi era achiloreraako era luulu s'obu bulangare.

9. Wachinwa iwabaa bulangare bw'e kanangana. Obu bulangare bwaikire mwa butala na bu bwende bwalomekera e bandju boshi.

10. Si mango abaa era alyi muno butala, beshamo chiro bakamumenyerera, n'oku iwabumbaabo.

11. Aikaa n'omwa lubaa lwabo, si banyakabo nabo chiro bakanamuhuukasa.

12. Si boshi ba bamuhuukasaa na kumwemerera mwa michima yabo beke abaresise e buashi bw'e kuba bana ba Ongo.

13. N'oku kuba bana ba Ongo, kutalyi ng'okwa e bandju bende babuchwa, nesi kuhondjwa kwa mubilyi, nesi kuhonda kwa mundju murebe, si Ongo yeine iwabailyire kuba bana bai.

14. Wachinwa ahubire mundju. Era kuba n'omwa kachi-kachi kechwu, ete na bonjo bunene na myasi ya kanangana. chwera kunalola n'okwa bulangare bwai bwa abaa

8. 요와나, 아다 이와바아 오부 부라까러, 시 아바하아 구더다 어 먀시 어라 아찌로러라아고 어라 루우루 소부 부라까러.

9. 와찌냐 이와바아 부라까러 뭐 가나까나. 오부 부라까러 봐이기러 뫄 부다꽈 나 부 뭐떠 봐로머거라 어 바뚜 보씨.

10. 시 마꼬 아바아 어라 아꼐 무노 부다꽈, 버싸모 찌로 바가무머녀러라, 노구 이와부빠아보.

11. 아이가아 노뫄 루바아 꽈보, 시 바냐가보 나보 찌로 바가나무후우가사.

12. 시 보씨 바 바무후우가사아 나 구뭐머러라 뫄 미찌마 야보 버거 아바러시서 어 부아씨 뭐 구바 바나 바 오꼬.

13. 노구 구바 바나 바 오꼬, 구다꼐 꼬과 어 바뚜 버거 바부좌, 너시 구호꽈 과 무비꼐, 너시 구호따 과 무뚜 무러버, 시 오꼬 여이너 이와바이꼐러 구바 바나 바이.

14. 와찌냐 아후비러 무뚜. 어라 구바 노뫄 가찌-가찌 거쭈, 어더 나 보쪼 부너너 나 먀시 야 가나까나. 쭤라 구나로꽈 노과 부라까러 봐이 봐 아바아 아쭈사. 오부

8. He himself was not the light; he came only as a witness to the light.

9. The true light that gives light to every man was coming into the world.

10. He was in the world, and though the world was made through him, the world did not recognize him.

11. He came to that which was his own, but his own did not receive him.

12. Yet to all who received him, to those who believed in his name, he gave the right to become children of God--

13. children born not of natural descent, nor of human decision or a husband's will, but born of God.

14. The Word became flesh and made his dwelling among us. We have seen his glory, the glory of the One and Only, who came from the Father, full of grace and

achwusa. Obu bulangare, Ongo tata yeine iweresaabo e mwana wai w'e chihwa.

15. Yowana ahambalaa kwa bya yeine achiloreraako era luulu s'oyu mwana wa Ongo. Atetaa na murenge munene mbu: Ono mundju inatetaa era luulu sa imbu: angabaha era nyuma sanyi, si anyirenzise bushi mango nabaa ndasa kubuchibwa, yeke abaa anachwulao.

16. Achwusa na bonjo bunene ngachi. Rero bushi n'obu bonjo, chwuboshi chwabonyire ewechwu mwango wa ngahanyi sinene busese.

17. Ongo achweresaa e mwaso kurengera musa. Si e bonjo n'e myasi y'e kanangana byeke, abiretaa kurengera Yesu kirisito.

18. Kutalyi ola ufuraa kulola ku Ongo chiro na hicha. Si oyu mwana wai w'e chihwa anachwula Ongo, ola achwula alauma na Ongo tata. Kanji yeine iwanachwulosisei.

Yowana mubatisayi ana e bubeyi

19. Lusuku luuma, e bakulu-kulu b'e bayuda b'e yerusalemu bachwumaa e

부꽈꺄러, 오꼬 다다 여이너 이워러사아보 어 꽈나 와이 워 찌화.

15. 요와나 아하빠꺄아 과 뱌 여이너 아찌롸러라아고 어라 루우루 소유 꽈나 와 오꼬. 아더다아 나 무러뻐 무너너 뿌: 오노 무뿌 이나더다아 어라 루우루 사 이뿌: 아빠바하 어라 뉴마 사니, 시 아네러씨서 부씨 마꼬 나바아 따사 구부찌봐, 여거 아바아 아나쭈꽈오.

16. 아쭈사 나 보쪼 부너너 꽈찌. 러로 부씨 노부 보쪼, 쭈보씨 쫘보니러 어워쭈 꽈꼬 와 꽈하네 시너너 부서서.

17. 오꼬 아쭤러사아 어 꽈소 구러뻐라 무사. 시 어 보쪼 너 먀시 여 가나꽈나 벼거, 아비러다아 구러뻐라 여수 기리시도.

18. 구다레 오꽈 우푸라아 구롸 구 오꼬 찌로 나 히짜. 시 오유 꽈나 와이 워 찌화 아나쭈꽈 오꼬, 오꽈 아쭈꽈 아꽈우마 나 오꼬 다다. 가찌 여이너 이와나쭈롸시서이.

요와나 무바디사에 아나 어 부버에

19. 루수구 루우마, 어 바구루-구루 버 바유다 버 여루사뻐무 바쭈마아 어

truth.

15. John testifies concerning him. He cries out, saying, "This was he of whom I said, 'He who comes after me has surpassed me because he was before me.' "

16. From the fullness of his grace we have all received one blessing after another.

17. For the law was given through Moses; grace and truth came through Jesus Christ.

18. No one has ever seen God, but God the One and Only, who is at the Father's side, has made him known.

19. Now this was John's testimony when the Jews of Jerusalem sent priests and

bakuhanyi, n'e balawi era mwa Yowana, bamubuse mbu inde. Era kuhambala e myasi era abaa eshi.

바구하네, 너 바롸위 어라 뫄 요와나, 바무부서 뿌 이떠. 어라 구하빠롸 어 먀시 어라 아바아 어씨.

Levites to ask him who he was.

20. Era kubaakula changanama busira kubabisha mbu: Nyono, ata nyi kirisito.

20. 어라 구바아구롸 짜꺄나마 부시라 구바비싸 뿌: 뇨노, 아다 네 기리시도.

20. He did not fail to confess, but confessed freely, "I am not the Christ."

21. Nabo bera kwire bamubusa mbu: Rero, u wera nde? Elyi u eliya? Nai mbu: Nanga, ata nyi Eliya. Bera kumubusa kanji mbu: Elyi ulyi murebi wa Ongo? Nai mbu: Nanga!

21. 나보 버라 귀러 바무부사 뿌: 러로, 우 워라 떠? 어레 우 어릐야? 나이 뿌: 나꺄, 아다 네 어릐야. 버라 구무부사 가찌 뿌: 어레 우레 무러비 와 오꼬? 나이 뿌: 나꺄!

21. They asked him, "Then who are you? Are you Elijah?" He said, "I am not." "Are you the Prophet?" He answered, "No."

22. Chasinjire, bera kwire bamubusa mbu: Ewashe! Woyo, uwera mundju muchiye kasi? Uchwuburaa chi watechire era lulu sao weine, chwumenye cha chwungabura ba bachwuchwumaa.

22. 짜시찌러, 버라 귀러 바무부사 뿌: 어와써! 요요, 우워라 무뿌 무찌여 가시? 우쭈부라아 찌 와더찌러 어라 루루 사오 워이너, 쭈꺄녀 짜 바쭈쭈마아.

22. Finally they said, "Who are you? Give us an answer to take back to those who sent us. What do you say about yourself?"

23. Yowani era kwire abakula ng'okwa murebi isaya itetaa mbu: Nyono, nyilyi mundju ola wabarangira mwa buyeye mbu: Mukunganyisisaa enawechwu enjira kubuya-buya.

23. 요와니 어라 귀러 아바구롸 꼬과 무러비 이사야 이더다아 뿌: 뇨노, 네레 무뿌 오롸 와바라끼라 뫄 부여여 뿌: 무구꺄네시사아 어나워쭈 어찌라 구부야-부야.

23. John replied in the words of Isaiah the prophet, "I am the voice of one calling in the desert, 'Make straight the way for the Lord.' "

24. Bauma mwa ba batumwaa era mwa yowana, babaa bafarisayo.

24. 바우마 뫄 바 바두뫄아 어라 뫄 요와나, 바바아 바파리사요.

24. Now some Pharisees who had been sent

25. Abu bafarisayo, bera kumubusa mbu: Akaba ata u kirisito, nesi ata u Eliya, uta na murebi, rero chi chera chenjire

25. 아부 바파리사요, 버라 구무부사 뿌: 아가바 아다 우 기리시도, 너시 아다 우 어릐야, 우다 나 무러비, 러로

25. questioned him, "Why then do you baptize if you are not the Christ, nor Elijah, nor the Prophet?"

chachwuma wabatisa e bandju?

26. Nai mbu: Nyono, nenjire nabatisa e bandju mwa meshi. Si mwa kachi-kachi kenyu mulyi mundju muuma ola muteshi.

27. Oyu mundju, angabaha era nyuma sanyi. Si ndete kwa nyilyi kwa kungachwuma naboola e milyisi y'e birato byai.

28. Ei myasi Yoshi yabaa ala Yowana endee abatisisa e bandju, mwa musi w'e betaniya, kwa lunji lunda lw'e lwishi lw'e yorotani.

Yowana ana e bubei era lulu sa Yesu

29. Abere mwei mishangya, Yowana era kulola ku Yesu abaha ofu nai. Era kubura e bandju mbu: Onola i mwana w'e mbulyi wa Ongo, ola wende wakula e bibi by'e bandju b'omwa butala!

30. Mango nababuraa mbu mundju muuma angabaha era nyuma sanyi, onola i nabaa namaana. Kanji natetaa mbu Anyirenzise, bushi mango nabaa ndasa kubuchwa, yeke abaa anachwulao.

31. Anabe nanyi nabaa ndanamwishi. Si naikire

찌 쩌라 쩌찌러 짜쭈마 와바디사 어 바뉴?

26. 나이 뿌: 뇨노, 너찌러ᅦ 나바디사 어 바뉴 먀 머씨. 시 먀 가찌-가찌 거뉴 무쀀 무뿨 무우마 오롸 무더씨.

27. 오유 무뉴, 아까바하 어라 뉴마 사네. 시 떠더 과 네레 과 구까쭈마 나보오롸 어 미쀀시 여 비라도 뱌어ᅦ.

28. 어이 먀시 요씨 야바아 아롸 요와나 어떠어 아바디시사 어 바뉴, 먀 무시 워 버다니야, 과 루찌 루따 뤄 뤼씨 뤄 요로다니.

요와나 아나 어 부버이 어라 뤂뤂 사 여수

29. 아버러 뭐이 미싸꺄, 요와나 어라 구로롸 구 여수 아바하 오푸 나이. 어라 구부라 어 바뉴 뿌: 오노롸 이 먀나 워 뿌쀀 와 오오, 오라 워떠 와구롸 어 비비 벼 바뉴 보와 부다롸!

30. 마오 나바부라아 뿌 무뿨 무우마 아까바하 어라 뉴마 사네, 오노롸 이 나바아 나마아나. 가찌 나더다아 뿌 아네러씨서, 부씨 마오 나바아 따사 구부좌, 여거 아바아 아나쭈롸오.

31. 아나버 나네 나바아 따나뮈씨. 시 나이기러

---

26. "I baptize with water," John replied, "but among you stands one you do not know.

27. He is the one who comes after me, the thongs of whose sandals I am not worthy to untie."

28. This all happened at Bethany on the other side of the Jordan, where John was baptizing.

29. The next day John saw Jesus coming toward him and said, "Look, the Lamb of God, who takes away the sin of the world!

30. This is the one I meant when I said, 'A man who comes after me has surpassed me because he was before me.'

31. I myself did not know him, but the reason I came

kubatisa e bandju mwa meshi, chasiya nyimukangane kwa lubaa lw'e baisiraeli.

32. Yowana era kuteta kanji era luulu sa yesu mbu: Nalolaa kwa muchima mubuya-buya andaala nga chiruka atenga kwa nguba, na amuumbilyirako.

33. Nyono nabaa ndanga mumenyire. Si ola wanyichwumaa mbu nyindaa na batisa e bandju mwa meshi, iwanyiburaa mbu ola nyingalola e muchima mubuya-buya andaalyira na amuumbilyirako, oyola i ukende wabatisa e bandju kwa njira y'e muchima mubuya-buya.

34. Rero ei myasi yoshi, nyeine nanachilorere kui. Kubinalyi nababura kwa ono mundju ina mwana wa Ongo kanangana.

E banafunzi babere-bere ba yesu

35. Mwei mishangya, yowana abaa anachilyi mw'echi chisiki na banafunzi bai babilyi.

36. Mango alolaa kwa Yesu arenga, era kuteta mbu: Mulolaa! Onola i mwana w'e mbulyi wa Ongo.

37. Ba banafunzi babilyi

구바디사 어 바뚜 꽈 머씨, 짜시야 네무가까너 과 루바아 뭐 바이시라어리.

32. 요와나 어라 구더다 가찌 어라 루우루 사 여수 뿌: 나로라아 과 무찌마 무부야-부야 아따아꽈 꽈 찌루가 아더꽈 과 꾸바, 나 아무우삐레라고.

33. 뇨노 나바아 따꽈 무머네러. 시 오꽈 와네쭈마아 뿌 네따아 나 바디사 어 바뚜 꽈 머씨, 이와네부라아 뿌 오꽈 네꽈로꽈 어 무찌마 무부야-부야 아따아레라 나 아무우삐레라고, 오요꽈 이 우거러 와바디사 어 바뚜 과 찌라 여 무찌마 무부야-부야.

34. 러로 어이 먀시 요씨, 녀이너 나나찌로러러 구이. 구비나레 나바부라 과 오노 무뚜 이나 뫄나 와 오꼬 가나꽈나.

어 바나푸씨 바버러-버러 바 여수

35. 뭐이 미싸꺄, 요와나 아바아 아나찌레 뭐찌 찌시기 나 바나푸씨 바이 바비레.

36. 마꼬 아로꽈아 과 여수 아러꽈, 어라 구더다 뿌: 무로꽈라! 오노꽈 이 뫄나 워 뿌레 와 오꼬.

37. 바 바나푸씨 바비레

baptizing with water was that he might be revealed to Israel."

32. Then John gave this testimony: "I saw the Spirit come down from heaven as a dove and remain on him.

33. I would not have known him, except that the one who sent me to baptize with water told me, 'The man on whom you see the Spirit come down and remain is he who will baptize with the Holy Spirit.'

34. I have seen and I testify that this is the Son of God."

35. The next day John was there again with two of his disciples.

36. When he saw Jesus passing by, he said, "Look, the Lamb of God!"

37. When the two disciples

bomvire bacha, kuna kukulyikira Yesu.

38. Yesu mwa kubindjuka, era kulola kwa bamukulyikira. Era kubabusa mbu: Chi mwahonda? Nabo mbu: Rabi, ngai yi uchwula? (Rabi kukuteta mbu mukangilyisi.)

39. Nai mbu: Mubahaa, mulole ala nyichwula. Kwa banalyi babilyi, bera kuchiuma baya kulola ala yesu abaa achwula. Olu lusuku loshi, bera kubera alauma nai. Kanji ebi bihangi byabaa byera bya saa ng'ekumi sa luolo-olo.

40. Abu babilyi ba bomvaa kwei myasi ya yowana, bu bakulyikira Yesu. Muuma mubo iwabaa Andereya, munyakabo Simoni Petero.

41. Andereya kuna kuya kufulyira tanga oyu munyakabo kw'oyu mwasi. Amulolyireko, era kumubura mbu: Era! chwalolyire ku masiya! (Masiya kukuteta mbu kirisito).

42. Chasinda, era kweka simoni era mwa Yesu. Yesu era kumuchwumbikisa, na amubura mbu: Woyo u simoni mwenyi Yowana. Rero kutengera lwarero bakere

---

보삐러 바짜, 구나 구구쩨기라 여수.

38. 여수 먀 구비뿌가, 어라 구쁘롸 과 바무구쩨기라. 어라 구바부사 뿌: 찌 먀호따? 나보 뿌: 라비, 아이 에 우쭈롸? (라비 구구더따 뿌 무가삐쩨시.)

39. 나이 뿌: 무바하아, 무르러 아롸 네쭈롸. 과 바나쩨 바비쩨, 버라 구찌우마 바야 구르롸 아롸 여수 아바아 아쭈롸. 오루 루수구 로씨, 버라 구버라 아롸우마 나이. 가찌 어비 비하삐 뱌바아 벼라 뱌 사아 어구미 사 루오로로-오로로.

40. 아부 바비쩨 바 보빠아 궈이 먀시 야 요와나, 부 바구쩨기라 여수. 무우마 무보 이와바아 아너러야, 무냐가보 시모니 퍼더로.

41. 아너러야 구나 구야 구쁘쩨라 따아 오유 무냐가보 교유 먀시. 아무르쩨러고, 어라 구무부라 뿌: 어라! 좌로쩨러 구 마시야! (마시야 구구더따 뿌 기리시도).

42. 짜시따, 어라 궈가 시모니 어라 먀 여수. 여수 어라 구무쭈삐기사, 나 아무부라 뿌: 오요 우 시모니 뭐네 요와나. 러로 구더러라 롸러로 바거러 버떠 바궈쩨가

---

heard him say this, they followed Jesus.

38. Turning around, Jesus saw them following and asked, "What do you want?" They said, "Rabbi" (which means Teacher), "where are you staying?"

39. "Come," he replied, "and you will see." So they went and saw where he was staying, and spent that day with him. It was about the tenth hour.

40. Andrew, Simon Peter's brother, was one of the two who heard what John had said and who had followed Jesus.

41. The first thing Andrew did was to find his brother Simon and tell him, "We have found the Messiah" (that is, the Christ).

42. And he brought him to Jesus. Jesus looked at him and said, "You are Simon son of John. You will be called Cephas" (which, when translated, is Peter).

bende bakwelyika mbu u kefa.
(Kefa mwa manji mateta
kukuteta mbu Petero).

뿌 우 거파. (거파 와 마찌
마더다 구구더다 뿌 퍼더로).

*Yesu amaala Filipo na
Natanaeli mwa mulyimo*

여수 아마아빠 피삐펠 나
나다나어삐 와 무레명

43. Abere mwei mishangya,
Yesu era kulola kwa kukomire
aye e kalilaya. Era kubuana
Filipo, na amubura mbu:
unyikulyikiraa!

43. 아버러 뭐이 미싸야, 여수
어라 구로빠 과 구고미러
아여 어 가삐빠야. 어라
구부아나 피삐포, 나
아무부라 뿌: 우네구레기라아!

43. The next day Jesus
decided to leave for Galilee.
Finding Philip, he said to
him, "Follow me."

44. Oyu Filipo, abaa mwesha
mwa musi w'e betesaita.
Mw'oyu musi, mu Andereya,
na Petero nabo babaa
bachwula.

44. 오유 피삐포, 아바아 뭐싸
와 무시 워 버더사이다. 모유
무시, 무 아떠러야, 나 퍼더로
나보 바바아 바쭈빠.

44. Philip, like Andrew and
Peter, was from the town of
Bethsaida.

45. Chasinda, Filipo era
kubuana Natanaeli. Era
kumubura mbu: chwalolyire
kwa mundju ola bitabo by'e
mwaso wa musa n'e by'e
barebi bichwula byanjikire era
lulu sai. N'oyu mundju i Yesu,
mwenyi Yosefu, mwesha mwa
musi w'e nasareti.

45. 짜시따, 피삐포 어라
구부아나 나다나어삐. 어라
구무부라 뿌: 쫘로레러 과
무뿌 오빠 비다보 벼 뫄소 와
무사 너 벼 바러비 비쭈빠
뱌찌기러 어라 루루 사이.
노유 무뿌 이 여수, 뭐네
요서푸, 뭐싸 와 무시 워
나사러디.

45. Philip found Nathanael
and told him, "We have
found the one Moses wrote
about in the Law, and about
whom the prophets also
wrote--Jesus of Nazareth,
the son of Joseph."

46. Natanaeli omvire bacha,
kukwera kubusa Filipo mbu:
Ewashe! Enasareti nayi
inganatenga kandju kabuya?
Filipo nai mbu: Woyo, kubaha
ku unabaha uchilorere!

46. 나다나어삐 오뻬러 바짜,
구궈라 구부사 피삐포 뿌:
어와써! 어나사러디 나에
이빠나더빠 가뚜 가부야?
피삐포 나이 뿌: 오요, 구바하
구 우나바하 우찌로러러!

46. "Nazareth! Can anything
good come from there?"
Nathanael asked. "Come and
see," said Philip.

47. Mango Yesu alolaa kwa
Natanaeli abaha era alyi, era
kuteta era lulu sai mbu:
Mulolaa! Ono mundju analyi
muisiraeli tenene, n'omwa

47. 마꼬 여수 아로빠아 과
나다나어삐 아바하 어라
아레, 어라 구더다 어라 루루
사이 뿌: 무로빠아! 오노 무뿌
아나뻬 무이시라어삐 더너너,

47. When Jesus saw
Nathanael approaching, he
said of him, "Here is a true
Israelite, in whom there is
nothing false."

muchima wai mutalyi chiro na butebanyi busibya!

48. Natanaeli, era kubusa Yesu mbu: kute ku unyishi kasi? Yesu nai mbu: Mango Filipo abaa atasa kukwamaala, nabaa nakulolyireko mira mango wabaa wekesi mwa chisina ch'e muchi w'e tini.

49. Natanaeli era kwire amubura mbu: mukangilyisi, woyo unalyi mwana wa Ongo! Kanji woyo u mwami w'e baisiraeli!

50. Yesu kukwera kumubusa mbu: Nyono e kukubura kwa nabaa nakulolyireko mira mango wabaa wekese mwa chasina ch'e muchi w'e tini, ku kwachwumire wemerera mwa muchima wao? Rero, uchilyi ungalola ku inji myasi inene era irenzise eyera!

51. Chasinjire, Yesu era kuteta kanji mbu: Kubinalyi! Nababura kwa kuika munalole kwa nguba yabookala. Kanji mungalola n'okwa bamalaika ba Ongo benjire batenga kwa nguba banyaandalyira nyi mwana w'e mundju, chasinda banahuba kw'erukirako.

노뫄 무찌마 와이 무다레 찌로 나 부더바네 부시뱌!

48. 나다나어뤼, 어라 구부사 여수 뿌: 구더 구 우네씨 가시? 여수 나이 뿌: 마꼬 삐뤼포 아바아 아다사 구과마아뽜, 나바아 나구룐롌러고 미라 마꼬 와바아 워거시 뫄 찌시나 쩌 무찌 워 디니.

49. 나다나어뤼 어라 귀러 아무부라 뿌: 무가삐롌시, 오요 우나뢰 뫄나 와 오꼬! 가찌 오요 우 뫄미 워 바이시라어뤼!

50. 여수 구궈라 구무부사 뿌: 뇨노 어 구구부라 과 나바아 나구룐롌러고 미라 마꼬 와바아 워거서 뫄 짜시나 쩌 무찌 워 디니, 구 과쭈미러 워머러라 뫄 무찌마 와오? 러로, 우찌뢰 우뽜룐뽜 구 이찌 먀시 이너너 어라 이러씨서 어여라!

51. 짜시띠러, 여수 어라 구더다 가찌 뿌: 구비나뢰! 나바부라 과 구이가 무나룐뿌 과 우바 야보오가뽜. 가찌 무뽜룐뽜 노과 바마뽜이가 바 오꼬 버찌러 바더뽜 과 우바 바냐아따롌라 네 뫄나 워 무뚜, 짜시따 바나후바 궈루기라고.

48. "How do you know me?" Nathanael asked. Jesus answered, "I saw you while you were still under the fig tree before Philip called you."

49. Then Nathanael declared, "Rabbi, you are the Son of God; you are the King of Israel."

50. Jesus said, "You believe because I told you I saw you under the fig tree. You shall see greater things than that."

51. He then added, "I tell you the truth, you shall see heaven open, and the angels of God ascending and descending on the Son of Man."

Yoana Chikono 2

1. Abere kwarenga suku ebilyi kwera kuba buya mwa musi w'e kana, mwa chio ch'e kalilaya. Nyina wa Yesu, abaa alyi eyera,

2. Yesu n'e banafunzi bai nabo, babaa balalyikirwe kw'obu buya.

3. Abere e difai yera yawaa, nyina wa Yesu era kwire amubura mbu: Batachete inji difai!

4. Yesu omvire bacha, era kumwakula mbu: E mama, oyu mwasi atanyerekere. Si e bihangi byanyi bitasa kuika!

5. Unao-unao, nyina wa Yesu era kubura e bakosi b'e buya ba babaa batanza e difai mbu: Choshi cha angababura, chi munairaa!

6. Aola, abaa alyi mareya ndachwu manenene, ma mabaa makunganyisibwe mwa makoi. Rero e mareya ma malyi ng'ama mw'e bayuda bendee babika mw'e meshi m'e kuchikomya era muhondo sa Ongo. Na mu chira e reya mwabaa mungaya milangi eyana ya meshi.

7. Yesu era kubura abu bakosi mbu: mano mareya moshi, mwehusaa mw'e meshi. Bera

요아나 찌고노 2

1. 아버러 과러까 수구 어비레, 궈라 구바 부야 똬 무시 워 가나, 똬 찌오 쩌 가리라야. 네나 와 여수, 아바아 아레 어여라,

2. 여수 너 바나푸씨 바이 나보, 바바아 바롸레기뤄 교부 부야.

3. 아버러 어 디파이 여라 야와아, 네나 와 여수 어라 궈러 아무부라 뿌: 바다쩌더 이찌 디파이!

4. 여수 오뻬러 바짜, 어라 구똬구롸 뿌: 어 마마, 오유 롸시 아다녀러거러. 시 어 비하끼 뱌네 비다사 구이가!

5. 우나오-우나오, 네나 와 여수 어라 구부라 어 바고시 버 부야 바 바바아 바다싸 어 디파이 뿌: 쪼씨 짜 아까바부라, 찌 무나이라아!

6. 아오롸, 아바아 아레 마러야 따쭈 마너너너, 마 마바아 마구까네시붜 똬 마고이. 러로 어 마러야 마 마레 우아마 뭐 바유다 버떠어 바비가 뭐 머씨 머 구찌고먀 어라 무호또 사 오꼬. 나 무 찌라 어 러야 똬바아 무까야 미롸끼 어야나 야 머씨.

7. 여수 어라 구부라 아부 바고시 뿌: 마노 마러야 모씨, 뭐후사아 뭐 머씨. 버라

John Chapter 2[NIV]

1. On the third day a wedding took place at Cana in Galilee. Jesus' mother was there,

2. and Jesus and his disciples had also been invited to the wedding.

3. When the wine was gone, Jesus' mother said to him, "They have no more wine."

4. "Dear woman, why do you involve me?" Jesus replied, "My time has not yet come."

5. His mother said to the servants, "Do whatever he tells you."

6. Nearby stood six stone water jars, the kind used by the Jews for ceremonial washing, each holding from twenty to thirty gallons.

7. Jesus said to the servants, "Fill the jars with water"; so they filled them to the brim.

kunehusa mw'e meshi kuikira
kwana meno.

구너후사 뭐 머씨 구이기라
과나 머노.

8. Chasinda, Yesu era kwire
ababura mbu: Mwiree
mwafoma kw'amu meshi,
mwekeremo ola w'emangilyire
e buya. Bera kunamwekeramo.

8. 짜시따, 여수 어라 귀러
아바부라 뿌: 뮈러어 뫄포마
과무 머씨, 뭐거러모 오롸
워마삐께러 어 부야. 버라
구나뭐거라모.

8. Then he told them, "Now
draw some out and take it
to the master of the
banquet." They did so,

9. Abere era atomaa kumo,
era kuchichinga mabindjukire
difai mira, si chiro akamenya
era matengeraa. E bakosi ba
bafomaa kw'amu meshi, beine
bu babaa baneshi era
matengeraa. Oyu wabaa
w'emangilyire e buya, unao-
unao kuna kuchwumisa muya
mulume.

9. 아버러 어라 아도마아
구모, 어라 구찌찌꺄
마비뿌기러 디파이 미라, 시
찌로 아가머냐 어라
마더꺼라아. 어 바고시 바
바포마아 과무 머씨, 버이너
부 바바아 바너씨 어라
마더꺼라아. 오유 와바아
워마삐께러 어 부야, 우나오-
우나오 구나 구쭈미사 무야
무루머.

9. and the master of the
banquet tasted the water
that had been turned into
wine. He did not realize
where it had come from,
though the servants who
had drawn the water knew.
Then he called the
bridegroom aside

10. Era kumubura mbu: Era! Si
wishi kwa e bandju boshi, e
difai era ilokire i bende
batanzisa tanga ba
balalyikwaa. Na mango abu
balalyikwaa bende baba
bamwere busese, banere
batanza e mvenya. Si weke,
unachilyi ulangire e difai era
ilokire kuikira mano mango!

10. 어라 구무부라 뿌: 어라!
시 위씨 과 어 바쭈 보씨, 어
디파이 어라 이롸기러 이
버꺼 바다씨사 다꺄 바
바꽈레과아. 나 마꼬 아부
바꽈레과아 버꺼 바바 바뭐러
부서서, 바너러 바다싸 어
뻐냐. 시 워거, 우나찌께
우꽈삐러 어 디파이 어라
이롸기러 구이기라 마노
마꼬!

10. and said, "Everyone
brings out the choice wine
first and then the cheaper
wine after the guests have
had too much to drink; but
you have saved the best till
now."

11. Ei myasi Yesu airaa e kana,
mwa chio ch'e kalilaya, chi
chabaa chisomerano chai
chibere-bere. Mw'olu, era
kulosa e bwashi bwai. Bushi
n'oku, e banafunzi bai bera

11. 어이 먀시 여수 아이라아
어 가나, 뫄 찌오 쩌
가삐꽈야, 찌 짜바아
찌소머라노 짜이 찌버러-버러.
몰루, 어라 구롸사 어 봐씨
봐이. 부씨 노구, 어 바나푸씨

11. This, the first of his
miraculous signs, Jesus
performed in Cana of
Galilee. He thus revealed his
glory, and his disciples put
their faith in him.

kumwemerera mwa michima yabo.

12. Era nyuma s'ebi, Yesu era kwandaalyira mwa musi w'e kaperinaumu alyi na nyina, na banyakabo, alauma n'e banafunzi bai. Bera kuberayi suku sieke.

Yesu akolokanya abachimbusi mwa chibuwa ch'e luhu lwa Ongo

13. E lusuku lukulu lw'e pasaka y'e bayuda, mango lwabaa lwahonda kuika, Yesu era kw'erukira e yerusalemu.

14. Aikire mwa chibuwa ch'e luhu lwa Ongo, era kubuana bandju bauma bausisamo e ngaafu, n'e mbulyi, n'e biruka. N'e banji babaa bekese bainganyanga e buteya kwa mesa.

15. Yesu kukwera kutola-tola e milyisi, na aunga mw'e lukoba. Ba bandju boshi, alauma n'e ngaafu sabo, n'e mbulyi sabo, kuna kutangilyisa akolokanyabo mw'echi chibuwa ch'e luhu lwa Ongo. Chasinda, ba babaa bainganyanga e buteya nabo, era kusheshanga obu buteya bwabo na kubindjulanga e mesa ma babaa

---

바이 버라 구뭐머러라 뫄 미찌마 야보.

12. 어라 뉴마 서비, 여수 어라 과따아롐라 뫄 무시 워 가퍼리나우무 아롐 나 니나, 나 바냐가보, 아좌우마 너 바나푸씨 바이. 버라 구버라에 수구 시어거.

여수 아고론―냇 아바찌뿌습 뫄 찌부와 쩌 룿훌 똬 오꼬

13. 어 룿수구 룿구룿 뤂 파사가 여 바유다, 마꼬 똬바아 똬호따 구이가, 여수 어라 궈루기라 어 여루사쩌무.

14. 아이기러 뫄 찌부와 쩌 룿후 똬 오꼬, 어라 구부아나 바뉴 바우마 바우시사모 어 까아푸, 너 뿌롐, 너 비루가. 너 바찌 바바아 버거서 바이까냐까 어 부더야 과 머사.

15. 여수 구궈라 구도똬-도똬 어 미롐시, 나 아우까 뮈 룿고바. 바 바뉴 보씨, 아좌우마 너 까아푸 사보, 너 뿌롐 사보, 구나 구다삐롐사 아고론가냐보 뭐찌 찌부와 쩌 룿후 똬 오꼬. 짜시따, 바 바바아 바이까냐까 어 부더야 나보, 어라 구써싸까 오부 부더야 뫄보 나 구비뉴좌까 어 머사 마 바바아 바부이까네시사고.

---

12. After this he went down to Capernaum with his mother and brothers and his disciples. There they stayed for a few days.

13. When it was almost time for the Jewish Passover, Jesus went up to Jerusalem.

14. In the temple courts he found men selling cattle, sheep and doves, and others sitting at tables exchanging money.

15. So he made a whip out of cords, and drove all from the temple area, both sheep and cattle; he scattered the coins of the money changers and overturned their tables.

babuinganyisisako.

16. Ba babaa bausa e biruka nabo, era kubabura mbu: Mukulaa bine byoshi anola! si mutanachiereresaa mwahubya e nyumba ya tata kuba e soko!

16. 바 바바아 바우사 어 비루가 나보, 어라 구바부라 뿌: 무구롸아 비너 뵤씨 아노롸! 시 무다나쪄러러사아 뫄후뱌 어 뉴빠 야 다다 구바 어 소고!

16. To those who sold doves he said, "Get these out of here! How dare you turn my Father's house into a market!"

17. Mw'olu, e banafunzi bai bera kukengera e myasi era ichwula y'anjikirwe mwa maanjiko mabuya-buya mbu: Ongo tata! e nzii era nyichwusa kwa nyumba yao, ikanyimala.

17. 모루, 어 바나푸씨 바이 버라 구거ㄲ러라 어 먀시 어라 이쭈롸 야ㅉ기뤄 뫄 마아찌고 마부야-부야 뿌: 오꼬 다다! 어 씨이 어라 네쭈사 과 뉴빠 야오, 이가네마롸.

17. His disciples remembered that it is written: "Zeal for your house will consume me."

18. E bayuda bera kwire babusa Yesu mbu: Bine wera kuira, chisomerano chichiye cha ungaira cha chingachwulosa kanangana kwa wete e loso lw'e kubiira?

18. 어 바유다 버라 귀러 바부사 여수 뿌: 비너 워라 구이라, 찌소머라노 찌찌여 짜 우ㅇ가이라 짜 찌ㅇ가쭈로사 가나ㅇ가나 과 워더 어 로소 뤄 구비이라?

18. Then the Jews demanded of him, "What miraculous sign can you show us to prove your authority to do all this?"

19. Yesu na imbu: Luno luhu lwa Ongo, muhandjulaalo, na mu suku ehachwu mungalola kwa nahuba kuimbalo.

19. 여수 나 이뿌: 루노 루후 롸 오꼬, 무하ㄴ쭈롸아로, 나 무 수구 어하쭈 무ㅇ가로롸 과 나후바 구이빠로.

19. Jesus answered them, "Destroy this temple, and I will raise it again in three days."

20. Nabo mbu: Si luno luhu lwa Ongo, ku myaka mane na ndachwu ku lwehulyiraa! Rero, weke mbu ungahuba kuimbalo ku suku ehachwu oshao?

20. 나보 뿌: 시 루노 루후 롸 오꼬, 구 먀가 마너 나 따쭈 구 뤄후례라아! 러로, 워거 뿌 우ㅇ가후바 구이빠로 구 수구 어하쭈 오싸오?

20. The Jews replied, "It has taken forty-six years to build this temple, and you are going to raise it in three days?"

21. Si eluhu lwa Yesu abaa amaana, abaa ateta era luulu s'e mubilyi wai.

21. 시 어루후 롸 여수 아바아 아마아나, 아바아 아더다 어라 루우루 서 무비례 와이.

21. But the temple he had spoken of was his body.

22. Na mango Yesu abaa era omwoka abu banafunzi bera kwire bakengera kwa atetaa era luulu s'oyu mwasi. Bushi n'oku, bera kw'emerera e maanjiko mabuya-buya mwa michima yabo, n'e myasi era Yesu atetaa.

Yesu achwula eshi byoshi bya bilyi mwa muchima w'e mundju

23. Mango yesu abaa alyi e yerusalemu mwa suku sikulu se pasaka, era kunde aira bisomerano binene. Mwa kulola kw'e bisomerano, bandju banene busese bera kumwemerera mwa michima yabo.

24. Si chiro bacha, Yesu atendee abalangalyira bushi abaa achwula abeshi boshi kubuya-buya.

25. Kanji abaa atahonda mbu bamufulyiraa mwasi era lulu sa mundju murebe, bushi byoshi bya bilyi mwa michima y'e bandju abaa anabishi.

22. 나 마꼬 여수 아바아 어라 오모가 아부 바나푸씨 버라 귀러 바거어라 과 아더다아 어라 루우루 소유 먀시. 부씨 노구, 버라 귀머러라 어 마아찌고 마부야-부야 먀 미찌마 야보, 너 먀시 어라 여수 아더다아.

여수 아쭈라 어씨 뵤씨 뱌 비뻬 뫄 무찌마 워 무뚜

23. 마꼬 여수 아바아 아뻬 어 여루사뤄무 뫄 수구 시구루 서 파사가, 어라 구떠 아이라 비소머라노 비너너. 뫄 구뢷꽈 귀 비소머라노, 바뚜 바너너 부서서 버라 구뭐머러라 뫄 미찌마 야보.

24. 시 찌로 바짜, 여수 아더떠어 아바롸꽈뻬라 부씨 아바아 아쭈꽈 아버씨 뵤씨 구부야-부야.

25. 가찌 아바아 아다호따 뿌 바무푸뤠라아 먀시 어라 루루 사 무뚜 무러버, 부씨 뵤씨 뱌 비뻬 뫄 미찌마 여 바뚜 아바아 아나비씨.

22. After he was raised from the dead, his disciples recalled what he had said. Then they believed the Scripture and the words that Jesus had spoken.

23. Now while he was in Jerusalem at the Passover Feast, many people saw the miraculous signs he was doing and believed in his name.

24. But Jesus would not entrust himself to them, for he knew all men.

25. He did not need man's testimony about man, for he knew what was in a man.

Yoana Chikono 3
Yesu ahambala na Nikotemu

1. Kwabaa mulume muuma mbu I Nikotemu. Oyu Nikotemu, abaa muuma mwa

요아나 찌고노 3
여수 아하빠랴 나 니고더무

1. 과바아 무루머 무우마 뿌 이 니고더무. 오유 니고더무, 아바아 무우마 뫄 바싸무가

John Chapter 3[NIV]

1. Now there was a man of the Pharisees named Nicodemus, a member of

bashamuka b'e bayuda, kanji abaa achwula w'omwa chikembe ch'e bafarisayo.

2. Lusuku luuma buchwufu, Nikotemu era kuikira Yesu. Era kumubura mbu: Mukangilyisi, chwishi kwa Ongo akuchwumire kwa kunde wakangilyisa e bandju. Bushi bino bisemerano wenjire waira, kutalyi ola ungaala kubira akaba Ongo atalyi alauma nai.

3. Yesu era kumubura mbu: Kubinalyi, chechine chi nakubura: akaba e mundju atabuchirwe e bwakabilyi, atangengilyira chiro na hicha mwa bwami bwa Ongo.

4. Nikotemu kukwera ku mubusa mbu: Ewashe! E mundju ola wera mungumwa, kute ku angabuchibwa kanji? Achilyi angahuba mwa bula bwa nyina, abuchibwe kanji?

5. Yesu nai mbu: Kubinalyi, nakubura kw'e mundju atangengilyira mwa bwami bwa Ongo, akaba atasa kubuchibwa kurengera e meshi na kurengera e muchima mubuya-buya.

6. Bya by'e mubilyi, kwa njira y'e mubilyi ku byende byanabuchwa. N'e by'e

버 바유다, 가찌 아바아 아쭈콰 오콰 찌거뻐 쩌 바파리사요.

2. 루수구 루우마 부쭈푸, 니고더무 어라 구이기라 여수. 어라 구무부라 뿌: 무가삐레시, 쮜씨 과 오꼬 아구쭈미러 과 구떠 와가삐레사 어 바쭈. 부씨 비노 비서머라노 워찌러 와이라, 구다레 오콰 우까아콰 구비라 아가바 오꼬 아다레 아콰우마 나이.

3. 여수 어라 구무부라 뿌: 구비나레, 쩌찌너 찌 나구부라: 아가바 어 무뚜 아다부찌뤄 어 봐가비레, 아다떠삐레라 찌로 나 히짜 콰 봐미 봐 오꼬.

4. 니고더무 구궈라 구 무부사 뿌: 어와써! 어 무뚜 오콰 워라 무우콰, 구더 구 아까부찌봐 가찌? 아찌레 아까후바 콰 부콰 봐 니나, 아부찌붜 가찌?

5. 여수 나이 뿌: 구비나레, 나구부라 궈 무뚜 아다떠삐레라 콰 봐미 봐 오꼬, 아가바 아다사 구부찌봐 구러떠라 어 머씨 나 구러떠라 어 무찌마 무부야-부야.

6. 뱌 벼 무비레, 과 찌라 여 무비레 구 벼떠 뱌나부좌. 너 벼 무찌마 무부야-부야 나비, spirit.

the Jewish ruling council.

2. He came to Jesus at night and said, "Rabbi, we know you are a teacher who has come from God. For no one could perform the miraculous signs you are doing if God were not with him."

3. In reply Jesus declared, "I tell you the truth, no one can see the kingdom of God unless he is born again."

4. "How can a man be born when he is old?" Nicodemus asked. "Surely he cannot enter a second time into his mother's womb to be born!"

5. Jesus answered, "I tell you the truth, no one can enter the kingdom of God unless he is born of water and the Spirit.

6. Flesh gives birth to flesh, but the Spirit gives birth to spirit.

muchima mubuya-buya nabi, kwa njira y'e muchima mubuya-buya ku byende byanabuchwa.

7. E kukubura kwa mwemire mubuchibwe e bwakabilyi kutachwumaa wasanwa.

8. E chiusi, era chisimire yi chende cha naya. Na chiro unomva kwa charenga, utangamenya era chatengera nesi era Chaya. Rero, kubinachwula bacha ku chira mundju ola ubuchirwe kwa njira y'e muchima mubuya-buya.

9. Nikotemu era kumubusa kanji mbu: Ei, myasi kute ku ingaalyikana?

10. Yesu na imbu: Era Nikotemu! Rero ei myasi, kute ku utaishi?

11. Kubinalyi, nakubura kwa e myasi era chwenjire chwateta, chwuishi kubuya-buya. Kanji e myasi era chwenjire chw'anyira e bubei, inalyi era chwachiloreraako. Si chiro bacha obu bubei, mwabo mutenjire mwabwemerera.

12. Mango nenjire nabahambalyira era luulu s'e myasi yo muno butala, mutenjire mwanyemerera. Rero mango

---

과 띠라 여 무찌마 무부야-부야 구 벼떠 뱌나부좌.

7. 어 구구부라 과 뭐미러 무부찌붜 어 봐가비레 구다쭈마아 와사놔.

8. 어 찌우시, 어라 찌시미러 에 쩌떠 짜 나야. 나 찌로 우노빠 과 짜러까, 우다까머냐 어라 짜더꺼라 너시 어라 짜야. 러로, 구비나쭈좌 바짜 구 찌라 무뚜 오라 우부찌뤄 과 띠라 여 무찌마 무부야-부야.

9. 니고더무 어라 구무부사 가찌 뿌: 어이, 먀시 구더 구 이까아레가나?

10. 여수 나 이뿌: 어라 니고더무! 러로 어이 먀시, 구더 구 우다이씨?

11. 구비나레, 나구부라 과 어 먀시 어라 쭤찌러 좌더다, 쭈이씨 구부야-부야. 가찌 어 먀시 어라 쭤찌러 좌네라 어 부버이, 이나레 어라 좌찌로러라아고. 시 찌로 바짜 오부 부버이, 먀보 무더찌러 먀붜머러라.

12. 마꼬 너찌러 나바하빠레라 어라 루우루 서 먀시 요 무노 부다좌, 무더찌러 먀녀머러라. 러로 마꼬 니까바하빠레라 어라

---

7. You should not be surprised at my saying, 'You must be born again.'

8. The wind blows wherever it pleases. You hear its sound, but you cannot tell where it comes from or where it is going. So it is with everyone born of the Spirit."

9. "How can this be?" Nicodemus asked.

10. "You are Israel's teacher," said Jesus, "and do you not understand these things?

11. I tell you the truth, we speak of what we know, and we testify to what we have seen, but still you people do not accept our testimony.

12. I have spoken to you of earthly things and you do not believe; how then will you believe if I speak of heavenly things?

nyingabahambalyira era luulu s'e myasi y'okwa nguba, kute mungemererai?

루우루 서 먀시 요과 꾸바, 구더 무꺼머러라이?

13. Kutalyi mundju ola ufuraa kwerukira kwa nguba, kunyireka nyi mwana w'e mundju, nyi n'andaalaa kutengako.

13. 구다례 무뚜 오롸 우푸라아 궈루기라 과 꾸바, 구네러가 네 먀나 워 무뚜, 네 나따아롸아 구더꺼고.

13. No one has ever gone into heaven except the one who came from heaven--the Son of Man.

14. Rero, ng'okwa Musa erusaa e njoka kwa muchi era yabaa ikunganyisibwe mwa mulyinga mwa buyeye, kunoku ku nyi mwana w'e mundju nanyi nyemire nyerusibwe.

14. 러로, 으과 무사 어루사아 어 쪼가 과 무찌 어라 야바아 이구꺼네시뷔 먀 무레꺼 먀 부여여, 구노구 구 네 먀나 워 무뚜 나네 녀미러 녀루시뷔.

14. Just as Moses lifted up the snake in the desert, so the Son of Man must be lifted up,

15. Chasiya chira mundju woshi ola unganyemerera mwa muchima wai, abone e kalamo k'e suku n'e mango.

15. 짜시야 찌라 무뚜 오씨 오롸 우꺼녀머러라 먀 무찌마 와이, 아보너 어 가롸모 거 수구 너 마꼬.

15. that everyone who believes in him may have eternal life.

16. Ongo, bushi asimaa e butala busese, ku kwachwuma achwumaa e mwana wai w'e chihwa, chasiya chira mundju woshi ola wamwemerere ataeraa, si abone e kalamo k'e siku n'e mango.

16. 오꼬, 부씨 아시마아 어 부다롸 부서서, 구 과쭈마 아쭈마아 어 먀나 와이 워 찌화, 짜시야 찌라 무뚜 오씨 오롸 와뭐머러러 아다어라아, 시 아보너 어 가롸모 거 시구 너 마꼬.

16. "For God so loved the world that he gave his one and only Son, that whoever believes in him shall not perish but have eternal life.

17. Bushi Ongo atatchwuma e mwaala mwa butala bushi achinyibuse e butala chasiya e butala bu nunulyibwe kumurengera.

17. 부씨 오꼬 아다쭈마 어 먀아롸 먀 부다롸 부씨 아찌네부서 어 부다롸 짜시야 어 부다롸 부 누누레뷔 구무러꺼라.

17. For God did not send his Son into the world to condemn the world, but to save the world through him.

18. Chira mundju woshi ola unganyemerera nyi mwana wa Ongo, atakachinjibusibwe. Si ola utanyememerere, yeke

18. 찌라 무뚜 오씨 오롸 우꺼녀머러라 네 먀나 와 오꼬, 아다가찌띠부시뷔. 시 오롸 우다녀머머러러, 여거

18. Whoever believes in him is not condemned, but whoever does not believe stands condemned already

achinjibusibwe mira, bushi atanyemerere nyi mwana w'e chihwa wa Ongo.

19. Rero, cha chikachwuma e bandju bachinjibusibwa chi chechine: e bulangare bwaikire mira mwa butala, si e bandju batasimaabo. Si bushi n'e mabi ma bende bakola, bera kuchisimira e musimya.

20. Chira mundju woshi ola wende wakola e mabi, atachwula asimire e bulangare. Kanji atomva chiro kuchifunda era obu bulangare bulyi, bushi e mabi mai mangesha kulorekanako changanama.

21. Si ola wende waira bya bichwungenene era muhondo sa Ongo, yeke ende aya era obu bulangare bulyi, chasiya e bandju boshi balole kwa ebi enjire aira bitenganyire n'e kuhonda kwa Ongo.

Yowana mubatisayi ateta era luulu sa Yesu

22. Era nyuma s'ebi, Yesu era kuya mwa chio ch'e yudeya alauma n'e banafunzi bai. Bera kuberayi, Yesu era kunde abatisisayi e bandju.

23. Mwesi suku sinesi, Yowana nai abaa enjire abatisa e

아찌찌부시뷔 미라, 부씨 아다녀머러러 네 뫄나 워 찌화 와 오꼬.

19. 러로, 짜 찌가쭈마 어 바뚜 바찌찌부시봐 찌 쩌찌너: 어 부롸꺼러 봐이기러 미라 뫄 부다롸, 시 어 바뚜 바다시마아보. 시 부씨 너 마비 마 버너 바고롸, 버라 구찌시미라 어 무시먀.

20. 찌라 무뚜 올씨 오롸 워떠 와고롸 어 마비, 아다쭈롸 아시미러 어 부롸꺼러. 가찌 아도빠 찌로 구찌푸따 어라 오부 부롸꺼러 부레, 부씨 어 마비 마이 마꺼싸 구로러가나고 짜꺼나마.

21. 시 오롸 워떠 와이라 뱌 비쭈어너너 어라 무호또 사 오꼬, 여거 어떠 아야 어라 오부 부롸꺼러 부레, 짜시야 어 바뚜 보씨 바로꺼러 과 어비 어찌러 아이라 비더꺼네러 너 구호따 과 오꼬.

요와나 무바디사에 아더다 어라 룹윱루 사 여수

22. 어라 뉴마 서비, 여수 어라 구야 뫄 찌오 쩌 유더야 아꽈우마 너 바나푸씨 바이. 버라 구버라에, 여수 어라 구떠 아바디시사에 어 바뚜.

23. 뭐시 수구 시너시, 요와나 나이 아바아 어찌러 아바디사

---

because he has not believed in the name of God's one and only Son.

19. This is the verdict: Light has come into the world, but men loved darkness instead of light because their deeds were evil.

20. Everyone who does evil hates the light, and will not come into the light for fear that his deeds will be exposed.

21. But whoever lives by the truth comes into the light, so that it may be seen plainly that what he has done has been done through God."

22. After this, Jesus and his disciples went out into the Judean countryside, where he spent some time with them, and baptized.

23. Now John also was baptizing at Aenon near

bandju mwa musi w'e ainoni, ofu n'e musi w'e salimu, bushi eyera yeke yi yabaa ilyi meshi manene. E bandju babaa benjire bamuikiranga, nai era kunde ababatisa.

24. Mwesi suku, Yowana abaa atasa kuumwa mwa buroko
25. Lusuku luuma, banafunzi bauma ba Yowana bayaa bwaka na muyuda muuma, era luulu s'e mwiya w'e kuchikomya.
26. Bushi n'oku, bera kwire baikira Yowana na bamubura mbu: Mukangilyisi, ungachikengera ola mundju wabaa ulyi alauma nao kwa mushilyilya w'e lwishi lw'e yorotani, ola watetaa era luulu sai? ulolaa! yola nai wera wenjire wabatisa e bandju. Rero, e bandju boshi kumuikiranga ku bera benjire banamuikiranga!
27. Yowana na imbu: Kutalyi kandju kamundju angabona, akaba ata Ongo iwamweresisiko.
28. Si mu beine mwomvaa kwa natetaa mbu ata nyi kirisito, si Ongo anyichwumaa nyimuhondorere.
29. Muya mulume i uchwula

어 바뚜 뫄 무시 워 아이노니, 오푸 너 무시 워 사뤼무, 부씨 어여라 여거 에 야바아 이뤠 머씨 마너너. 어 바뚜 바바아 버찌러 바무이기라꺄, 나이 어라 구떠 아바바디사.

24. 뭐시 수구, 요와나 아바아 아다사 구우뫄 뫄 부로고
25. 루수구 루우마, 바나푸씨 바우마 바 요와나 바야아 봐가 나 무유다 무우마, 어라 루우루 서 뮈야 워 구찌고먀.
26. 부씨 노구, 버라 귀러 바이기라 요와나 나 바무부라 뿌: 무가삐뤠시, 우꺄찌거뻐라 오꽈 무뚜 와바아 우뤠 아롸우마 나오 과 무씨뤠꺄 워 뤼씨 뤄 요로다니, 오꽈 와더다아 어라 루우루 사이? 우로롸아! 요롸 나이 워라 워찌러 와바디사 어 바뚜. 러로, 어 바뚜 보씨 구무이기라꺄 구 버라 버찌러 바나무이기라꺄!
27. 요와나 나 이뿌: 구다뤠 가뚜 가무뚜 아꺄보나, 아가바 아다 오꼬 이와뭐러시서고.
28. 시 무 버이너 뫃빠아 과 나더다아 뿌 아다 니 기리시도, 시 오꼬 아네쭈마아 네무호또러러.
29. 무야 무루머 이 우쭈꽈

Salim, because there was plenty of water, and people were constantly coming to be baptized.

24. (This was before John was put in prison.)
25. An argument developed between some of John's disciples and a certain Jew over the matter of ceremonial washing.
26. They came to John and said to him, "Rabbi, that man who was with you on the other side of the Jordan--the one you testified about--well, he is baptizing, and everyone is going to him."
27. To this John replied, "A man can receive only what is given him from heaven.
28. You yourselves can testify that I said, 'I am not the Christ but am sent ahead of him.'
29. The bride belongs to the

ena e muya mukasi. Si mwira w'e muya mulume ende aba emenze ofu nai amuteire e machi, na mango ende omva wa muya mulume, ende amowa busese, rero nanyi namoire, n'olu lumoo lwanyi lwelyire lwanaberera.

30. Oyu mundju mwera kuteta era luulu sai, byemire aendekere eruka busese, nanyi inyiendekere nandaalyira busese.

Ola watengaa kwa nguba i uchwula era luulu sa byoshi

31. Yowana era kunaendekera ateta mbu: Ola wabahire kutenga kwa nguba, i unachwula era luulu sa byoshi. Si e mundju w'omwa butala, anachwula w'omwa butala. N'e myasi era ende ateta nai, inachwula y'omwa butala. Si ola watengaa kwa nguba yeke, i unachwula era luulu sa byoshi.

32. N'e myasi era achiloreraako na kuchwumvirako, yenjire anateta. Si chiro bacha ei myasi yai, kutalyi ola wenjire wemererai.

33. chira mundju ola wemerere ei myasi yai, kukuteta mbu nai emerere

어나 어 무야 무가시. 시 뮈라 워 무야 무루머 어머 아바 어머써 오푸 나이 아무더이러 어 마찌, 나 마꼬 어머 오빠 와 무야 무루머, 어머 아모와 부서서, 러로 나니 나모이러, 노루 루모오 꽈네 뤄뤠러 꽈나버러라.

30. 오유 무뚜 뭐라 구더다 어라 루우루 사이, 벼미러 아어머거러 어루가 부서서, 나네 이니어머거러 나따아뤠라 부서서.

오꽈 와더따씹 과 우밍 이 우쭈꽈 어라 루읍루 사 뵤씨

31. 요와나 어라 구나어머거러 아더다 뿌: 오꽈 와바히러 구더따 과 우바, 이 우나쭈꽈 어라 루우루 사 뵤씨. 시 어 무뚜 옴와 부다꽈, 아나쭈꽈 옴꽈 부다꽈. 너 먀시 어라 어머 아더다 나이, 이나쭈꽈 요꽈 부다꽈. 시 오꽈 와더따아 과 우바 여거, 이 우나쭈꽈 어라 루우루 사 뵤씨.

32. 너 먀시 어라 아찌뢰러라아고 나 구쭈뻬라고, 여씨러 아나더다. 시 찌로 바짜 어이 먀시 야이, 구다뤠 오꽈 워찌러 워머러라이.

33. 찌라 무뚜 오꽈 워머러러 어이 먀시 야이, 구구더다 뿌 나이 어머러러 과 오꼬

bridegroom. The friend who attends the bridegroom waits and listens for him, and is full of joy when he hears the bridegroom's voice. That joy is mine, and it is now complete.

30. He must become greater; I must become less.

31. "The one who comes from above is above all; the one who is from the earth belongs to the earth, and speaks as one from the earth. The one who comes from heaven is above all.

32. He testifies to what he has seen and heard, but no one accepts his testimony.

33. The man who has accepted it has certified that God is truthful.

kwa Ongo anachwula wa kanangana.

34. Ola wachwumirwe na Ongo, kuika ende ateta e myasi ya Ongo, bushi Ongo lwende wamweresa e muchima mubuya-buya busira kumu horera.

35. Ongo tata achwula asimire e mwana wai ngachi, rero amweresise e bindju byoshi.

36. N'oyu mwana wai, chira mundju ola wamwemerere mwa muchima wai kuika anabone e kalamo k'e suku n'e mango. Si ola utamwemerere, yeke atakaboneko, n'e businane bwa Ongo bukanaendekera kuba kw'echwe lyai.

아나쭈콰 와 가나까나.

34. 오라 와쭈미뤄 나 오꼬, 구이가 어떠 아더다 어 먀시야 오꼬, 부씨 오꼬 뤄떠 와뭐러사 어 무찌마 무부야-부야 부시라 구무 호러라.

35. 오꼬 다다 아쭈콰 아시미러 어 마나 와이 까찌, 러로 아뭐러시서 어 비뉴 뵤씨.

36. 노유 마나 와이, 찌라 무뿌 오라 와뭐머러러 마 무찌마 와이 구이가 아나보너 어 가꽈모 거 수구 너 마꼬. 시 오라 우다뭐머러러, 여거 아다가보너고, 너 부시나너 봐 오꼬 부가나어떠거라 구바 귀꿔 랴이.

---

34. For the one whom God has sent speaks the words of God, for God gives the Spirit without limit.

35. The Father loves the Son and has placed everything in his hands.

36. Whoever believes in the Son has eternal life, but whoever rejects the Son will not see life, for God's wrath remains on him."

Yoana Chikono 4
Yesu ahambala n'e musamariya-kasi

1. Mw'esi suku, e bafarisayo bera kumva e mwasi kwa Yesu yeke enjire abona banafunzi banene kurenza Yowana, enjire anabatisabo.

2. Si chirobacha, Yesu yeine aba atenjire abatisa abu bandju, si e banafunzi bai bu babaa benjire babatisabo.

요아나 찌고노 4
여수 아하빠꽈 너 무사마리야-가시

1. 뭐시 수구, 어 바파리사요 버라 구빠 어 먀시 과 여수 여거 어찌러 아보나 바나푸씨 바너너 구러싸 요와나, 어찌러 아나바디사보.

2. 시 찌로바짜, 여수 여이너 아바 아더찌러 아바디사 아부 바뉴, 시 어 바나푸씨 바이 부 바바아 버찌러

John Chapter 4[NIV]

1. The Pharisees heard that Jesus was gaining and baptizing more disciples than John,

2. although in fact it was not Jesus who baptized, but his disciples.

바바디사보.

3. Mango Yesu omvaa kw'oyu mwasi, era kwire atenga e yudeya, na ahuba kanji e kalilaya.

4. Mwa kuyayi, byera kumwema arengere tanga mwa chio ch'e samariya.

5. Chasinda era kuika ku kamusi kauma kw'omwa chio ch'e samariya, ka bende b'elyika mbu sikari. Aku k'e musi, kachwula ofu n'ehwa lya Yakobo eresaa muala wai Yosefu.

6. Mw'echi chisiki, Yakobo achimaa mu chitomu. Yesu aikire kw'echi chitomu era kwi kala kwa musike sachi bushi abaa atamire busese. Kanji sabaa sahonda kuba saa ndachwu sa mushi.

7. Mw'echi chihangi, e banafunzi bai babaa bera bayaa mwa musi kuuula e bilyo.

8. Kw'echi chitomu, kwera kuika musamariya-kasi muuma aya kufoma. Yesu amulolireko, era kumubura mbu: unyeresaa kwa meshi nyimwe.

9. Oyu mukasi nai mbu: Ewashe! Woyo u muyuda,

3. 마꾜 여수 오빠아 교유 꽈시, 어라 귀러 아더꽈 어 유더먀, 나 아후바 가찌 어 가삐랴먀.

4. 꽈 구야에, 벼라 구뭐마 아러꺼러 다꽈 꽈 찌오 쩌 사마리야.

5. 짜시따 어라 구이가 구 가무시 가우마 교꽈 찌오 쩌 사마리야, 가 버떠 버뻬가 뿌 시가리. 아구 거 무시, 가쭈꽈 오푸 너화 꺄 야고보 어러사아 무아꽈 와이 요서푸.

6. 뭐찌 찌시기, 야고보 아찌마아 무 찌도무. 여수 아이기러 궈찌 찌도무 어라 귀 가꽈 과 무시거 사찌 부씨 아바아 아다미러 부서서. 가찌 사바아 사호따 구바 사아 따쭈 사 무씨.

7. 뭐찌 찌하삐, 어 바나푸씨 바이 바바아 버라 바야아 꽈 무시 구우우꽈 어 비꾜.

8. 궈찌 찌도무, 궈라 구이가 무사마리야-가시 무우마 아야 구포마. 여수 아무로삐러고, 어라 구무부라 뿌: 우녀러사아 과 머씨 니뭐.

9. 오유 무가시 나이 뿌: 어와써! 오요 우 무유다, 나네

3. When the Lord learned of this, he left Judea and went back once more to Galilee.

4. Now he had to go through Samaria.

5. So he came to a town in Samaria called Sychar, near the plot of ground Jacob had given to his son Joseph.

6. Jacob's well was there, and Jesus, tired as he was from the journey, sat down by the well. It was about the sixth hour.

7. When a Samaritan woman came to draw water, Jesus said to her, "Will you give me a drink?"

8. (His disciples had gone into the town to buy food.)

9. The Samaritan woman said to him, "You are a Jew

nanyi nyi musamariya-kasi, kute unganayema meshi m'e kumwa? Atetaa bacha, bushi e bayuda babaa batalyira alauma n'e basamariya.

10. Yesu nai mbu: Akaba ungamenyire e lwembo lwa Ongo ende ana, kanji akaba ungamenyire ola wakwema e meshi, u ungamwemiremo, nai angakweresise e meshi ma mende mareta e kalamo.

11. Ola mukasi nai mbu: Ewaliya si utete chikai cha kufomamo, na mw'echine chitomu e meshi malyi era mubi busese! Rero, amu meshi ma mende mareta e kalamo, ngai yi ungere wamakula?

12. Chine chitomu, hokulu wechwu Yakobo iwachweresaachi. Kanji yeine alauma n'e bana bai, n'e bifuana byai bamwaa kwa meshi machi. Rero, woyo waanyisa mbu uwera urenzise Yakobo?

13. Yesu nai mbu: Chira mundju woshi ola wende wamwa kwa mano meshi, achilyi akafa chami.

14. Si ola wamwere kwa meshi ma nyingamweresa, yeke atakachife chami chiro na hicha. Bushi amu meshi,

---

내 무사마리야-가시, 구더 우까나녀마 머씨 머 구꽈? 아더다아 바짜, 부씨 어 바유다 바바아 바다쩨라 아꽈우마 너 바사마리야.

10. 여수 나이 뿌: 아가바 우까머네러 어 뤄뽀 롸 오꼬 어떠 아나, 가찌 아가바 우까머네러 오롸 와궈마 어 머씨, 우 우까뭐미러모, 나이 아까궈러시서 어 머씨 마 머떠 마러다 어 가꽈모.

11. 오롸 무가시 나이 뿌: 어와쮀야 시 우더더 찌가이 짜 구포마모, 나 뭐찌너 찌도무 어 머씨 마레 어라 무비 부서서! 러로, 아무 머씨 마 머떠 마러다 어 가꽈모, 까이 에 우꺼러 와마구꽈?

12. 찌너 찌도무, 호구루 워쭈 야고보 이와쭤러사아찌. 가찌 여이너 아롸우마 너 바나 바이, 너 비푸아나 뱌이 바뫄아 과 머씨 마찌. 러로, 오요 와아네사 뿌 우워라 우러씨서 야고보?

13. 여수 나이 뿌: 찌라 무뚜 옴씨 오롸 워떠 와뫄 과 마노 머씨, 아찌레 아가파 짜미.

14. 시 오롸 와뭐러 과 머씨 마 네까뭐러사, 여거 아다가찌퍼 짜미 찌로 나 히짜. 부씨 아무 머씨, 마까바

---

and I am a Samaritan woman. How can you ask me for a drink?" (For Jews do not associate with Samaritans.)

10. Jesus answered her, "If you knew the gift of God and who it is that asks you for a drink, you would have asked him and he would have given you living water."

11. "Sir," the woman said, "you have nothing to draw with and the well is deep. Where can you get this living water?

12. Are you greater than our father Jacob, who gave us the well and drank from it himself, as did also his sons and his flocks and herds?"

13. Jesus answered, "Everyone who drinks this water will be thirsty again,

14. but whoever drinks the water I give him will never thirst. Indeed, the water I give him will become in him

---

mangaba nga shokororo mwa ndanda sai, na mu mangamweresa e kalamo k'e suku n'e mango.

꽈 쏘고로로 꽈 따따 사이, 나 무 마꽈뭐러사 어 가꽈모 거 수구 너 마꼬.

a spring of water welling up to eternal life."

15. Oyu mukasi, era kubura Yesu mbu: Ewalyiya! Unyeresaa kw'amu meshi, chasiya sindachifaa chami. Aola, ndakachiike kw'e chine chitomu kufoma e meshi kanji.

15. 오유 무가시, 어라 구부라 여수 뿌: 어와례야! 우녀러사아 과무 머씨, 짜시야 시따찌파아 짜미. 아오꽈, 따가찌이거 궈 찌너 찌도무 구포마 어 머씨 가찌.

15. The woman said to him, "Sir, give me this water so that I won't get thirsty and have to keep coming here to draw water."

16. Yesu kukwera kumubura mbu: Uyaa kwamala e bao ubahe nai anola.

16. 여수 구궈라 구무부라 뿌: 우야아 과마꽈 어 바오 우바허 나이 아노꽈.

16. He told her, "Go, call your husband and come back."

17. Ola mukasi mbu: si ndachwusa mulume! Yesu era kumubura mbu: E kuteta kwa utachwusa mulume waakure kubuya,

17. 오꽈 무가시 뿌: 시 따쭈사 무루머! 여수 어라 구무부라 뿌: 어 구더다 과 우다쭈사 무루머 와아구러 구부야,

17. "I have no husband," she replied. Jesus said to her, "You are right when you say you have no husband.

18. bushi waba na balume batano, n'oyu ulyi nai lwarero chiro ata n'eba wao. Rero ebi watechire, binalyi bya kanangana.

18. 부씨 와바 나 바루머 바다노, 노유 우례 나이 꽈러로 찌로 아다 너바 와오. 러로 어비 와더찌러, 비나례 뱌 가나꽈나.

18. The fact is, you have had five husbands, and the man you now have is not your husband. What you have just said is quite true."

19. Chasinda oyu mukasi era kwire abura Yesu mbu: e walyiya nalolyire mira kwa unalyi murebi.

19. 짜시따 오유 무가시 어라 궈러 아부라 여수 뿌: 어 와례야 나꼬례러 미라 과 우나례 무러비.

19. "Sir," the woman said, "I can see that you are a prophet.

20. Bahokulu bechwu babaa benjire berera Ongo kw'ene ndjulungu. Si mu bayuda mubeke, mwende mwateta mbu kwemire kunde chwaya kwerera Ongo e yerusalemu.

20. 바호구루 버쭈 바바아 버찌러 버러라 오꼬 궈너 뚜루꾸. 시 무 바유다 무버거, 뭐너 뫄더다 뿌 궈미러 구너 쫘야 궈러라 오꼬 어 여루사꿔무.

20. Our fathers worshiped on this mountain, but you Jews claim that the place where we must worship is in Jerusalem."

21. Yesu nai mbu: E mama! Ene myasi nakubura

21. 여수 나이 뿌: 어 마마! 어너 먀시 나구부라

21. Jesus declared, "Believe me, woman, a time is

iwemereeraa: mwa suku s'eshire, abe kw'ene ndjulungu nesi e yerusalemu, ata yi mukende mwerera tata.

22. Mu basamariya mwende mwera bya muteshi. Si chwu bayuda, chwubeke chwende chwera bya chwishi, bushi e bununusi ku chwubano ku bufula bushokire.

23. Si e suku s'eshire saikire na mira, ba bende bera tata kanangana, bangende bamwera kwa njira y'e muchima mubuya-buya n'omwa myasi y'e kanangana. Mwabacha, ba balyi ng'abo bu tata ahonda.

24. Rero, oku Ongo achwula muchima mubuya-buya, byemire n'e bandju ba bende bamwera, bamwere kurengera e muchima mubuya-buya, n'omwa myasi y'e kanangana.

25. Oyu mukasi, era kubura Yesu mbu: Nyono nyishi kwa masiya, ola bende berika mbu kirisito, achilyi akabaha. Na mango akaika, mu mango akachwubura ei myasi Yoshi.

26. Yesu nai mbu: Rero oyu waamana i nyono nyi nahambala nao!

Basamariya banene bemerera Yesu

이워머러라야: 먀 수구 서씨러, 아버 궈너 쭈루우 너시 어 여루사꺼무, 아다 에 무거러 뭐러라 다다.

22. 무 바사마리야 뭐떠 뭐라 뱌 무더씨. 시 쭈 바유다, 쭈버거 쮜떠 쮜라 뱌 쮜씨, 부씨 어 부누누시 구 쭈바노 구 부푸롸 부쏘기러.

23. 시 어 수구 서씨러 사이기러 나 미라, 바 버너 버라 다다 가나와나, 바꺼러 바뭐라 과 씨라 여 무찌마 무부야-부야 노롸 먀시 여 가나와나. 뫄바쨔, 바 바레 우아보 부 다다 아호따.

24. 러로, 오구 오꼬 아쭈롸 무찌마 무부야-부야, 벼미러 너 바쭈 바 버떠 바뭐라, 바뭐러 구러꺼라 어 무찌마 무부야-부야, 노롸 먀시 여 가나와나.

25. 오유 무가시, 어라 구부라 여수 뿌: 뇨노 내씨 과 마시야, 오롸 버너 버리가 뿌 기리시도, 아찌레 아가바하. 나 마꼬 아가이가, 무 마꼬 아가쭈부라 어이 먀시 요씨.

26. 여수 나이 뿌: 러로 오유 와아마나 이 뇨노 네 나하빠롸 나오!

바사마리야 바너너 버머러라 여수

coming when you will worship the Father neither on this mountain nor in Jerusalem.

22. You Samaritans worship what you do not know; we worship what we do know, for salvation is from the Jews.

23. Yet a time is coming and has now come when the true worshipers will worship the Father in spirit and truth, for they are the kind of worshipers the Father seeks.

24. God is spirit, and his worshipers must worship in spirit and in truth."

25. The woman said, "I know that Messiah" (called Christ) "is coming. When he comes, he will explain everything to us."

26. Then Jesus declared, "I who speak to you am he."

27. Mw'echi chihangi, ba banafunzi ba Yesu bera kufuluka era bayaa mwa musi. Bamubuanyire ahambala n'oyu mukasi, bera kusamwa busese. Si kutabaa chiro na muuma mubo, ola waereresa amubusa mbu chiye chi ahonda, nesi chi chachwuma ahambala n'oyu mukasi.

28. Unao-unao, ola mukasi kuna kureka ereya lyai aola, na afuluka mwa musi. Era kuya kubura e bandju mbu:

29. Ebechwu! mubahaa mulole kw'ola wanyibilyire byoshi bya nairaa. Ono mundju, atanganaba i kirisito?

30. Bushi n'oku, abu bandju bera kutenganga mwa musi na baya era Yesu abaa alyi.

31. Mw'echi chihangi, e banafunzi ba Yesu bera kumwema busese mbu: Nyete e bilyo by'e kulya, si mwabo mutabiishi!

32. Era kubabura, nyono nyeete e bilyo bya mutangamenya mwabo.

33. Bomvire bacha, bera kutangilyisa babusanya mbu: Ewashe! Elyi kulyi mundju ola wamureterere e bilyo mira?

27. 뭐찌 찌하에, 바 바나푸씨 바 여수 버라 구푸루가 어라 바야아 뫄 무시. 바무부아네러 아하빠롸 노유 무가시, 버라 구사뫄 부서서. 시 구다바아 찌로 나 무우마 무보, 오롸 와어러러사 아무부사 뿌 찌여 찌 아호따, 너시 찌 짜쭈마 아하빠롸 노유 무가시.

28. 우나오-우나오, 오롸 무가시 구나 구러가 어러야 랴이 아오롸, 나 아푸루가 뫄 무시. 어라 구야 구부라 어 바뉴 뿌:

29. 어버쭈! 무바하아 무로러 교롸 와네비레러 뵤씨 뱌 나이라아. 오노 무뿌, 아다에나바 이 기리시도?

30. 부씨 노구, 아부 바뉴 버라 구더에꺄 뫄 무시 나 바야 어라 여수 아바아 아레.

31. 뭐찌 찌하에, 어 바나푸씨 바 여수 버라 구뭐마 부서서 뿌: 녀더 어 비료 뼈 구롸, 시 뫄보 무다비이씨!

32. 어라 구바부라, 뇨노 녀어더 어 비료 뱌 무다에머냐 뫄보.

33. 보뻬러 바짜, 버라 구다에레사 바부사냐 뿌: 어와써! 어레 구레 무뿌 오롸 와무러더러러 어 비료 미라?

27. Just then his disciples returned and were surprised to find him talking with a woman. But no one asked, "What do you want?" or "Why are you talking with her?"

28. Then, leaving her water jar, the woman went back to the town and said to the people,

29. "Come, see a man who told me everything I ever did. Could this be the Christ?"

30. They came out of the town and made their way toward him.

31. Meanwhile his disciples urged him, "Rabbi, eat something."

32. But he said to them, "I have food to eat that you know nothing about."

33. Then his disciples said to each other, "Could someone have brought him food?"

34. Yesu era kubabura mbu: E bilyo byanyi, kulyi kuira e kuhonda kw'ola wanyichwumaa na kumalyilyisa e mulyimo ola anyeresaa.

35. Si mu mwende mwateta mbu: Myesi ene oshao y'e myaka yende yanaira mwa chitaka na chwaishebula. Si nyono, chechine chi nababura musungusaa e meho mw'ehwa! E myaka yelyire mira, kushebulai ku kwanashiba.

36. Ola washebula, abonyire e lwembo lwai. Kanji kulunda ku enjire analunda-lunda e bandju nga myaka babone e kalamo k'e suku n'e mango. Rero aola, e muinzi n'ola washebula bana moera alauma.

37. Kubinalyi kwa bende bateta mbu: Muuma ende ainga, n'e unji anashebula.

38. Rero nenyu, nabachwumaa kuya kushebula e myaka era mutakoreraa. Ei myaka, banji bandju bu bashikirai e ndjubano, si mwabo mu mwera mwalya e mutoloke w'e tamo lyabo.

39. Mw'oyu musi w'e sikari, e myasi era oyu mukasi atetaa yera kuchwuma basamariya

34. 여수 어라 구바부라 뿌: 어 비료 뱌네, 구레 구이라 어 구호따 교卦 와네쭈아아 나 구마례례사 어 무례모 오卦 아녀러사아.

35. 시 무 뭐떠 卦더다 뿌: 며시 어너 오싸오 여 먀가 여떠 야나이라 卦 찌다가 나 좌이써부라. 시 뇨노, 쩌찌너 찌 나바부라: 무수우사아 어 머호 뭐화! 어 먀가 여례러 미라, 구써부라이 구 과나씨바.

36. 오卦 와써부卦, 아보네러 어 뭐뽀 卦이. 가찌 구루따 구 어찌러 아나루따-루따 어 바쭈 까 먀가 바보너 어 가卦모 거 수구 너 마꼬. 러로 아오卦, 어 무이씨 노卦 와써부卦 바나 모어라 아卦우마.

37. 구비나례 과 버너 바더다 뿌: 무우마 어너 아이까, 너 우찌 아나써부라.

38. 러로 너뉴, 나바쭈마아 구야 구써부라 어 먀가 어라 무다고러라아. 어이 먀가, 바찌 바쭈 부 바씨기라이 어 쭈바노, 시 뫄보 무 뭐라 卦卦 어 무도로거 워 다모 랴보.

39. 모유 무시 워 시가리, 어 먀시 어라 오유 무가시 아더다아 여라 구쭈마

34. "My food," said Jesus, "is to do the will of him who sent me and to finish his work.

35. Do you not say, 'Four months more and then the harvest'? I tell you, open your eyes and look at the fields! They are ripe for harvest.

36. Even now the reaper draws his wages, even now he harvests the crop for eternal life, so that the sower and the reaper may be glad together.

37. Thus the saying 'One sows and another reaps' is true.

38. I sent you to reap what you have not worked for. Others have done the hard work, and you have reaped the benefits of their labor."

39. Many of the Samaritans from that town believed in him because of the woman's

banene bemerera Yesu mwa michima yabo. Bushi ababuraa mbu: Ono mundju anyibilyire mira byoshi bya nairaa.

40. Mango abu basamariya babaa bera baikaa ala Yesu abaa alyi, bera kumwema busese mbu aberaa alauma nabo. Era kwire amala suku ebilyi eyera.

41. Rero bushi n'e myasi era Yesu yeine abaa ateta, banji bandju banene nabo, bera kumwemerera mwa michima yabo ;

42. Bera kubura oyu mukasi mbu: Ata e myasi wachwuburaa yeine oshao iyachwumire chwamwemerera. Si chwamwemerere bushi chwachwumvilyire chwubeine e myasi yai. Kanji chwuneshi kanangana kw'ono mundju, ina mununusi w'e butala.

Yesu alamya mwana wa mukungu muuma

43. Mango Yesu abaa era amalaa esi suku ebilyi, era kutenga mw'oyu musi na aya e kalilaya.

44. Byabaa bacha, bushi yeine abaa atechire mira kw'e murebi ateresibwa e chwunda mwa chio chabo.

바사마리야 바너너 버머러라 여수 꽈 미찌마 야보. 부씨 아바부라아 뿌: 오노 무뚜 아니비쀄러 미라 뵤씨 뱌 나이라아.

40. 마꼬 아부 바사마리야 바바아 버라 바이가아 아꽈 여수 아바아 아쀄, 버라 구뭐마 부서서 뿌 아버라아 아꽈우마 나보. 어라 귀러 아마꽈 수구 어비쀄 어여라.

41. 러로 부씨 너 먀시 어라 여수 여이너 아바아 아더다, 바찌 바뚜 바너너 나보, 버라 구뭐머러라 꽈 미찌마 야보 ;

42. 버라 구부라 오유 무가시 뿌: 아다 어 먀시 와쭈부라아 여이너 오싸오 이야쭈미러 꽈뭐머러라. 시 꽈뭐머러러 부씨 꽈쭈쀄레러 쭈버이너 어 먀시 야이. 가찌 쭈너씨 가나꽈나 교노 무뚜, 이나 무누누시 워 부다꽈.

여수 아꽈맺 꽈나 와 무구우 무우마

43. 마꼬 여수 아바아 어라 아마꽈아 어시 수구 어비쀄, 어라 구더꽈 모유 무시 나 아야 어 가쀄꽈야.

44. 뱌바아 바짜, 부씨 여이너 아바아 아더찌러 미라 궈 무러비 아더러시봐 어 쭈따 꽈 찌오 짜보.

testimony, "He told me everything I ever did."

40. So when the Samaritans came to him, they urged him to stay with them, and he stayed two days.

41. And because of his words many more became believers.

42. They said to the woman, "We no longer believe just because of what you said; now we have heard for ourselves, and we know that this man really is the Savior of the world."

43. After the two days he left for Galilee.

44. (Now Jesus himself had pointed out that a prophet has no honor in his own country.)

45. Mango Yesu aikaa e kalilaya, beshayi bera kumuhuukasa kubuya. Bushi nabo mango bayaa e yerusalamu kwa lusuku lukulu lw'e pasaka, bachiloreraa kwa myasi yoshi era airaayi.

46. Chasinda, Yesu era kuhuba kanji mwa musi w'e kana, mwa chio ch'e kalilaya. Mw'oyu musi, mu abindjulaa e meshi kuba difai. Omola, mwabaa muchwula mukungu muuma wa mwami. Oyu mukungu, muala wai abaa alakira mwa musi w'e kapernaumu.

47. Oyu mukungu, mango omvaa kwa Yesu aikire e kalilaya mira, atengera e yudeya era kuya era abaa alyi. Era kumwema busese mbu andalyiraa e kaperinaumu, aye kulamya muala wai, bushi abaa ahonda kutowa e muchima.

48. Yesu kukwera kumubura mbu: Mwabo mutemerera, mutasa kulola ku bisomerano!

49. Oyu mukungu na imbu: Enawechwu! wandalyiraa ala mwanyi, kuno e mwana wanyi atasa kutowa e muchima.

50. Yesu na imbu: Fulukaa kwa

45. 마꼬 여수 아이가아 어 가삐꽈야, 버싸에 버라 구무후우가사 구부야. 부씨 나보 마꼬 바야아 어 여루사롸무 과 루수구 루구루 뭐 파사가, 바찌뽀러라아 과 먀시 요씨 어라 아이라아에.

46. 짜시따, 여수 어라 구후바 가찌 뫄 무시 워 가나, 뫄 찌오 쩌 가삘롸야. 뫄유 무시, 무 아비뉴롸아 어 머씨 구바 디파이. 오모롸, 뫄바아 무쭈롸 무구우 무우마 와 뫄미. 오유 무구우, 무아롸 와이 아바아 아롸기라 뫄 무시 워 가퍼루나우무.

47. 오유 무구우, 마꼬 오빠아 과 여수 아이기러 어 가삘꽈야 미라, 아더꺼라 어 유더야 어라 구야 어라 아바아 아례. 어라 구뭐마 부서서 뿌 아따례라아 어 가퍼리나우무, 아여 구롸먀 무아롸 와이, 부씨 아바아 아호따 구도와 어 무찌마.

48. 여수 구궈라 구무부라 뿌: 뫄보 무더머러라, 무다사 구룐롸 구 비소머라노!

49. 오유 무구우 나 이뿌: 어나워쭈! 와따례라아 아롸 마네, 구노 어 뫄나 와네 아다사 구도와 어 무찌마.

50. 여수 나 이뿌: 푸루가아

45. When he arrived in Galilee, the Galileans welcomed him. They had seen all that he had done in Jerusalem at the Passover Feast, for they also had been there.

46. Once more he visited Cana in Galilee, where he had turned the water into wine. And there was a certain royal official whose son lay sick at Capernaum.

47. When this man heard that Jesus had arrived in Galilee from Judea, he went to him and begged him to come and heal his son, who was close to death.

48. "Unless you people see miraculous signs and wonders," Jesus told him, "you will never believe."

49. The royal official said, "Sir, come down before my child dies."

50. Jesus replied, "You may

wao, e mwana wao alamire mira. Oyu mukungu, era kwemerera e myasi era Yesu amuburaa chasinda era kuchiuma.

51. Abere anachilyi mwa njira andalyira kwa wai, e bakosi bai bera kubaha kumulyinjira na bamubura mbu: Walyiya! e mwana alamire mira!

52. Era kubabusa mbu: Era! e mwana alamaa mu bihangi bichiye? Nabo mbu: Alamaa e hushira mw'eolo, mwa saa elyinda s'e mushi.

53. Unao-unao, eshe w'oyu mwana era kukengera kwa mw'echi chihangi mu Yesu anamuburaa mbu e mwana wai alamire. Bushi n'oku, yeine alauma na besha mwa mwai boshi, bera kwemerera Yesu mwa michima yabo.

54. Echera chi chabaa chisomerano cha kabilyi cha Yesu airaa e kalilaya mango abaa era atengaa e yudeya.

과 와오, 어 먀나 와오 아꽈미러 미라. 오유 무구꾸, 어라 궈머러라 어 먀시 어라 여수 아무부라아 짜시따 어라 구찌우마.

51. 아버러 아나찌레 먀 띠라 아따레라 과 와이, 어 바고시 바이 버라 구바하 구무페띠라 나 바무부라 뿌: 와레야! 어 먀나 아꽈미러 미라!

52. 어라 구바부사 뿌: 어라! 어 먀나 아꽈마아 무 비하삐 비찌여? 나보 뿌: 아꽈마아 어 후씨라 뭐오로, 먀 사아 어레따 서 무씨.

53. 우나오-우나오, 어써 오유 먀나 어라 구거에라 과 뭐찌 찌하삐 무 여수 아나무부라아 뿌 어 먀나 와이 아꽈미러. 부찌 노구, 여이너 아꽈우먀 나 버싸 먀 먀이 보씨, 버라 궈머러라 여수 먀 미찌마 야보.

54. 어쩌라 찌 짜바아 찌소머라노 짜 가비레 짜 여수 아이라아 어 가꾀꽈야 마오 아바아 어라 아더꽈아 어 유더야.

---

go. Your son will live." The man took Jesus at his word and departed.

51. While he was still on the way, his servants met him with the news that his boy was living.

52. When he inquired as to the time when his son got better, they said to him, "The fever left him yesterday at the seventh hour."

53. Then the father realized that this was the exact time at which Jesus had said to him, "Your son will live." So he and all his household believed.

54. This was the second miraculous sign that Jesus performed, having come from Judea to Galilee.

Yoana Chikono 5
Yesu alamya e chirema kwa chitomu ch'e Betesaida

요아나 찌고노 5
여수 아꽈됐 어 찌러마 과 찌도무 쩌 버더사이다

John Chapter 5[NIV]

1. Era nyuma s'ebi, Yesu era kwerukira mwa musi w'e yerusalemu, aye kwa lusuku lukulu lw'e bayuda.

2. Mw'oyu musi, mwabaa muchwula chitomu chiuma cha bendee b'elyika mwa chieburaniya mbu: Betesaida, Echi chitomu, chichwula ofu n'e chiso cha chelyikirwe mbu: Chiso cha mbulyi kanji echi chitomu, chichwula chisungurwe na bisusu bitano.

3. Mw'ebi bisusu, mwabaa mulyi balwala banene bachilambikirange kwa mikeka. Mubo, mwaba mulyi bauta, na ba baremere e nungo. Abu balwala, bendee balyinjira e meshi m'e chitomu malyingitanyisibwe,

4. Bushi malaika muuma wa Ongo abaa enjire andaalyira mumo chira chihangi na alyingitanyamo. Mwa kuba era amalyingitanyaa, e mulwala ola wendee watangira kwandaalyiramo, iwendee wanalama e malwala mai moshi.

5. Kw'echi chitomu, kwabaa kulyi mundju muuma ola wabaa wamala myaka mahachwu na munane alyibuka n'e bulwala.

1. 어라 뉴마 서비, 여수 어라 궈루기라 마 무시 워 여루사뤄무, 아여 과 루수구 루구루 뤄 바유다.

2. 모유 무시, 마바아 무쭈롸 찌도무 찌우마 짜 버너어 버레가 마 쩌부라니야 뿌: 버더사이다, 어찌 찌도무, 찌쭈롸 오푸 너 찌소 짜 쩌레기뤄 뿌: 찌소 짜 뿌레 가찌 어찌 찌도무, 찌쭈롸 찌수우뤄 나 비수수 비다노.

3. 뭐비 비수수, 마바아 무레 바롸롸 바너너 바찌롸삐기라뭐 과 미거가. 무보, 마바 무레 바우다, 나 바 바러머러 어 누꼬. 아부 바롸롸, 버너어 바레찌라 어 머씨 머 찌도무 마레삐다네시붸,

4. 부씨 마롸이가 무우마 와 오꼬 아바아 어찌러 아따아레라 무모 찌라 찌하끼 나 아레삐다냐모. 콰 구바 어라 아마레삐다냐아, 어 무롸롸 오롸 워너어 와다끼라 과따아레라모, 이워너어 와나롸마 어 마롸롸 마이 모씨.

5. 궈찌 찌도무, 과바아 구레 무쭈 무우마 오롸 와바아 와마롸 먀가 마하쭈 나 무나너 아레부가 너 부롸롸.

1. Some time later, Jesus went up to Jerusalem for a feast of the Jews.

2. Now there is in Jerusalem near the Sheep Gate a pool, which in Aramaic is called Bethesda and which is surrounded by five covered colonnades.

3. Here a great number of disabled people used to lie--the blind, the lame, the paralyzed.

4. None

5. One who was there had been an invalid for thirty-eight years.

6. Mango Yesu amulolaako alyi kwa mukeka, era kumenyerera kwa amala suku sinene alyibuka n'obu bulwala. Bushi n'oku, era kumubusa mbu: Ewashe! Wahonda ulame?

7. Nai mbu: e walyiya! Mango e meshi m'e chitomu mende malyingitanyisibwa nyeke nende naina e mundju ola unganyandaasisa mumo. Na mango nende naereka kwandalyiramo, unao-unao unji mundju ananyitangira.

8. Yesu kukwera kumubura mbu: Bachwukaa utole e mukeka wao unaende.

9. Unao-unao, ola mulwala kuna kulama, kuna kutola e mukeka wai, na atangilyisa aenda. Rero e lusuku ebyera byabaa, lwabaa lusuku lwa sabato.

10. Bushi n'oku, e bayuda bera kubura oyu mundju walamisibwaa mbu: Era! Si lwarero lulyi lusuku lwa sabato, n'e mwaso wechwu atemerere mbu wekaa oyu mukeka wao!

11. Nai mbu: ola wanyilamyaa iwanyiburaa mbu nyitolaa e mukeka wanyi nyinaende.

6. 마꼬 여수 아무로꽈아고 아레 과 무거가, 어라 구머녀러라 과 아마꽈 수구 시너너 아레부가 노부 부꽈꽈. 부씨 노구, 어라 구무부사 뿌: 어와써! 와호따 우꽈머?

7. 나이 뿌: 어 와레야! 마꼬 어 머씨 머 찌도무 머떠 마레[삐]다네시봐 녀거 너떠 나이나 어 무뚜 오라 우까냐따아시사 무모. 나 마꼬 너떠 나어러가 과따레라모, 우나오-우나오 우씨 무뚜 아나니[삐]라.

8. 여수 구궈라 구무부라 뿌: 바쭈가아 우도뤄 어 무거가 와오 우나어떠.

9. 우나오-우나오, 오라 무꽈꽈 구나 구꽈마, 구나 구도꽈 어 무거가 와이, 나 아다[삐]레사 아어따. 러로 어 루수구 어뼈라 뱌바아, 꽈바아 루수구 꽈 사바도.

10. 부씨 노구, 어 바우다 버라 구부라 오유 무뚜 와꽈미시봐아 뿌: 어라! 시 꽈러로 루레 루수구 꽈 사바도, 너 마소 워쭈 아더머러러 뿌 워가아 오유 무거가 와오!

11. 나이 뿌: 오라 와네꽈먀아 이와네부라아 뿌 니도꽈아 어 무거가 와네 니나어떠.

6. When Jesus saw him lying there and learned that he had been in this condition for a long time, he asked him, "Do you want to get well?"

7. "Sir," the invalid replied, "I have no one to help me into the pool when the water is stirred. While I am trying to get in, someone else goes down ahead of me."

8. Then Jesus said to him, "Get up! Pick up your mat and walk."

9. At once the man was cured; he picked up his mat and walked. The day on which this took place was a Sabbath,

10. and so the Jews said to the man who had been healed, "It is the Sabbath; the law forbids you to carry your mat."

11. But he replied, "The man who made me well said to me, 'Pick up your mat and walk.' "

12. Chasinda abu bayuda bera kuhuba kumubusa mbu: Ola wakuburaa mbu utolaa e mukeka wao, unaende i nde?

13. Si oyu mundju, atamenyaa nde iwamulamise, bushi Yesu abaa era aereraa mwa luamba lw'e bandju ba babaa balyi aola.

14. Era nyuma s'ebi, Yesu era kubuana ola mundju mwa luhu lwa Ongo. Era kumubura mbu: E mwira wanyi! Si usene kwa walamire! Rero, si utachiereresaa waira mabi, ungesha kulola ku malyio ma marenzise ma wabaa wete.

15. Oyu mundju, era kutenga aola na aya kubura ba bayuda mbu Yesu iwamulamyaa.

16. Rero bushi Yesu airaa ei myasi e lusuku lw'e sabato, e bayuda bera kutangilyisa bamulyibusa.

17. Si Yesu era kubabura mbu: Tata kukola ku anachilyi akola kuikira lwarero. Rero, nanyi kukola ku nanakola.

18. Bushi n'oku, abu bayuda bera kuhonda enjira soshi s'e kwita Yesu. Byabaa bacha, ata bushi n'e kutachwunda e lusuku lw'e sabato oshao, si

---

12. 짜시따 아부 바유다 버라 구후바 구무부사 뿌: 오꽈 와구부라아 뿌 우도꽈라 어 무거가 와오, 우나애떠 이 떠?

13. 시 오유 무뚜, 아다머냐아 떠 이와무꽈미서, 부씨 여수 아바아 어라 아어러라아 꽈 루아빠 뤄 바뉴 바 바바아 바꿰 아오꽈.

14. 어라 뉴마 서비, 여수 어라 구부아나 오꽈 무뚜 꽈 루후 꽈 오꼬. 어라 구무부라 뿌: 어 뮈라 와니! 시 우서너 과 와꽈미러! 러로, 시 우다쩌러러사아 와이라 마비, 우꺼싸 구로꽈 구 마꿰오 마 마러씨서 마 와바아 워더.

15. 오유 무뚜, 어라 구더꽈 아오꽈 나 아야 구부라 바 바유다 뿌 여수 이와무꽈먀아.

16. 러로 부씨 여수 아이라아 어이 먀시 어 루수구 뤄 사바도, 어 바유다 버라 구다꿰레사 바무꿰부사.

17. 시 여수 어라 구바부라 뿌: 다다 구고꽈 구 아나찌레 아고꽈 구이기라 꽈러로. 러로, 나니 구고꽈 구 나나고꽈.

18. 부씨 노구, 아부 바유다 버라 구호따 어찌라 소씨 서 귀다 여수. 뱌바아 바짜, 아다 부씨 너 구다쭈따 어 루수구 뤄 사바도 오싸오, 시 부씨

---

12. So they asked him, "Who is this fellow who told you to pick it up and walk?"

13. The man who was healed had no idea who it was, for Jesus had slipped away into the crowd that was there.

14. Later Jesus found him at the temple and said to him, "See, you are well again. Stop sinning or something worse may happen to you."

15. The man went away and told the Jews that it was Jesus who had made him well.

16. So, because Jesus was doing these things on the Sabbath, the Jews persecuted him.

17. Jesus said to them, "My Father is always at his work to this very day, and I, too, am working."

18. For this reason the Jews tried all the harder to kill him; not only was he breaking the Sabbath, but he was even calling God his

bushi kanji endee achilyingamanya na Ongo mwa kunde achitonga mbu Ongo achwula eshe.

가찌 어떠어 아찌쩨까마냐
오꼬 마 구떠 아찌도꽈 뿌
오꼬 아쭈꽈 어써.

own Father, making himself equal with God.

E buashi bw'e mwana wa Ongo

어 부아씨 붜 뫄나 와 오꼬

19. Chasinda Yesu era kuhuba kubusa abu bayuda mbu: Kubinalyi nababura kwa nyono nyi mwana wa Ongo, kutalyi kandju kasibya ka nyingaala kuira kwa kuhonda kwanyi nyeine. Si bya nyisene kwa tata aira, bi nanyi nenjire nanaira. Bushi choshi cha tata ende aira, chi nanyi nyi mwana wai nenjire nanaira.

19. 짜시따 여수 어라 구후바 구부사 아부 바유다 뿌: 구비나쪠 나바부라 과 뇨노 네 뫄나 와 오꼬, 구다쪠 가꾸 가시뱌 가 네까아꽈 구이라 과 구호따 과네 녀이너. 시 뱌 네서너 과 다다 아이라, 비 나네 너찌러 나나이라. 부씨 쪼씨 짜 다다 어떠 아이라, 찌 나네 네 뫄나 와이 너찌러 나나이라.

19. Jesus gave them this answer: "I tell you the truth, the Son can do nothing by himself; he can do only what he sees his Father doing, because whatever the Father does the Son also does.

20. Oku tata achwula anyisimire nyi mwana wai, ende anyilosa byoshi by'ende aira. Kanji achilyi akanyilosa na myasi inene kurenza ene museneko, kuikira kwa chihangi mukasanwa busese.

20. 오구 다다 아쭈꽈 아네시미러 네 뫄나 와이, 어떠 아네로사 뵤씨 벼떠 아이라. 가찌 아찌쩨 아가네로사 나 먀시 이너너 구러꽈 어너 무서너고, 구이기라 과 찌하께 무가사놔 부서서.

20. For the Father loves the Son and shows him all he does. Yes, to your amazement he will show him even greater things than these.

21. Rero ng'okwa tata ende omwola e bafu, na bahuba kuba bauma-uma, kunoku ku nyi mwana wai nanyi, nyingeresa e kalamo ba nyisimire kweresako.

21. 러로 오꽈 다다 어떠 오모꽈 어 바푸, 나 바후바 구바 바우마-우마, 구노구 구 네 뫄나 와이 나네, 네떠러사 어 가꽈모 바 네시미러 궈러사고.

21. For just as the Father raises the dead and gives them life, even so the Son gives life to whom he is pleased to give it.

22. Kanji kutalyi chiro na mundju usibya ola Tata achinjibusise si e buashi boshi bw'e kuchinjibusa e bandju, nyono nyi mwana wai nyi eresisebo mira.

22. 가찌 구다쩨 찌로 나 무뚜 우시뱌 오라 다다 아찌찌부시서 시 어 부아씨 보씨 뭐 구찌찌부사 어 바뚜, 뇨노 네 마나 와이 네 어러시서보 미라.

22. Moreover, the Father judges no one, but has entrusted all judgment to the Son,

23. Chasiya e bandju boshi bende banyichwunda ng'okwa bachwula banamuchwunjire. Bushi n'oku, ola utanyichwunjire nyi mwana, elyi atachwunjire na tata bushi iwanyichwumaa.

23. 짜시야 어 바뚜 보씨 버떠 바네쭈따 꼬과 바쭈롸 바나무쭈씨러. 부씨 노구, 오롸 우다네쭈씨러 네 마나, 어쎄 아다쭈씨러 나 다다 부씨 이와네쭈마아.

23. that all may honor the Son just as they honor the Father. He who does not honor the Son does not honor the Father, who sent him.

24. Kubinalyi, nababura kwa ola ungomva e myasi yanyi, na kwemerera ola wanyichwuma, oyola iukabona e kalamo k'e suku n'e mango. Kanji yeke atakachichinjibusibwe, si afufumukire e lufu na abona e kalamo.

24. 구비나쎄, 나바부라 과 오롸 우꼬빠 어 먀시 야네, 나 줘머러라 오롸 와네쭈마, 오요롸 이우가보나 어 가롸모 거 수구 너 마꼬. 가찌 여거 아다가찌찌찌부시붜, 시 아푸푸무기러 어 루푸 나 아보나 어 가롸모.

24. "I tell you the truth, whoever hears my word and believes him who sent me has eternal life and will not be condemned; he has crossed over from death to life.

25. Kanji kubinalyi, na babura kwa e lusuku lungaika, lwaikire na mira, lwa bafu bangomva e murenge wanyi nyi mwana wa Ongo. Na ba bangomvao bangabona e kalamo.

25. 가찌 구비나쎄, 나 바부라 과 어 루수구 룽아이가, 롸이기러 나 미라, 롸 바푸 바꼬빠 어 무러쩌 와네 네 마나 와 오꼬. 나 바 바꼬빠오 바꺼보나 어 가롸모.

25. I tell you the truth, a time is coming and has now come when the dead will hear the voice of the Son of God and those who hear will live.

26. Bushi ng'okwa tata achwusa e buashi bw'e kwana aku kalamo, kunoku ku nanyi anyeresise nyi mwana wai e buashi bw'e kwanako.

26. 부씨 꼬과 다다 아쭈사 어 부아씨 뭐 과나 어 가롸모, 구노구 구 나네 아녀러시서 네 마나 와이 어 부아씨 뭐 과나고.

26. For as the Father has life in himself, so he has granted the Son to have life in himself.

27. Kanji e buashi bw'e kuchinjibusa e bandju, nyono nyi mwana wai nyi eresisebo, bushi nyi mwana w'e mundju.

28. Mutasanwaa bushi n'ene myasi, bushi e bihangi bingaika bya bandju boshi ba balyi mwa shinda, bangaomva kwa murenge wanyi,

29. Na bomwoka ba bendee baira e mabuya mubo bangabona e kalamo. Si ba bendee baira e mabi beke, kuchinjibusibwa ku bakachinjibusiwa.

E bandju bateta era luulu s'e buashi bwa Yesu

30. Nyono kutalyi cha nyingaira kwa kuhonda kwanyi nyeine, n'e kuchinjibusa e bandju nako, nende nanairako ng'okwa tata anyibilyire. Bushi n'oku, obu buchinjibusi bwanyi bunachwula bwa kanangana, bushi ndaira e kuhonda kwanyi, si nende naira e kuhonda kw'ola wanyichwumaa.

31. Rero akaba nyingenjire na teta era luulu sanyi nyeine ei myasi nenjire nateta itangenjire yanaba ya kanangana.

27. 가찌 어 부아씨 뷔 구찌띠부사 어 바뚜, 뇨노 내 마나 와이 네 어러시서보, 부씨 네 마나 워 무뚜.

28. 무다사놔아 부씨 너너 먀시, 부씨 어 비하끼 비까이가 뱌 바뚜 보씨 바 바레 먀 씨따, 바까오빠 과 무러꺼 와네,

29. 나 보모가 바 버떠어 바이라 어 마부야 무보 바까보나 어 가꺄모. 시 바 버떠어 바이라 어 마비 버거, 구찌띠부시봐 구 바가찌띠부시와.

어 바뚜 바더다 어라 뤂읍룪 서 부아씨 봐 여수

30. 뇨노 구다레 짜 네까이라 과 구호따 과네 녀이너, 너 구찌띠부사 어 바뚜 나고, 너떠 나나이라고 꼬과 다다 아네비레러. 부씨 노구, 오부 부찌띠부시 봐네 부나쭈꽈 봐 가나까나, 부씨 따이라 어 구호따 과네, 시 너떠 나이라 어 구호따 곱꽈 와네쭈마아.

31. 러로 아가바 네꺼찌러 나 더다 어라 뤂우룪 사네 녀이너 어이 먀시 너찌러 나더다 이다꺼찌러 야나바 야 가나까나.

27. And he has given him authority to judge because he is the Son of Man.

28. "Do not be amazed at this, for a time is coming when all who are in their graves will hear his voice

29. and come out--those who have done good will rise to live, and those who have done evil will rise to be condemned.

30. By myself I can do nothing; I judge only as I hear, and my judgment is just, for I seek not to please myself but him who sent me.

31. "If I testify about myself, my testimony is not valid.

32. Si kulyi unji ola wenjire wateta e myasi era eshi era luulu sanyi, bushi nyineshi kwei myasi inalyi ya kanangana.

33. Anabe mango mwachwumaa e bandju era mwa Yowana e myasi era atetaa era luulu sanyi yanabaa ya kanangana.

34. Kuta kuteta mbu nyilaire ku mundju ola wateta era luulu sanyi si nenjire nababura ene myasi chasiya mununulyibwe.

35. Yowana abaa alyi nga tara lya lyakorera chasiya lyilomekere e bandju. N'obu bulangare bwai, mwabo mwera kunamoerabo kubihangi bieke oshao.

36. Si chiro bacha, nyete inji myasi era yenjire yateta era luulu sanyi. Nei myasi irenzise era Yowana atetaa. Bushi tata anyibikire mwa mulyimo mira chasiya nyimalyilyiseo. N'ebya nenjire naira bi byenjire byalosa kanangana kwa iwananyichwumaa.

37. Rero oku tata iwanyichwumaa, nai enjire anateta era luulu sanyi kanangana. Si e murenge wai

---

32. 시 구뤠 우찌 오롸 워찌러 와더다 어 먀시 어라 어찌 어라 루우루 사니, 부찌 네너찌 궈이 먀시 이나뤠 야 가나꺄나.

33. 아나버 마꼬 뫄쭈마아 어 바쭈 어라 뫄 요와나 어 먀시 어라 아더다아 어라 루우루 사니 야나바아 야 가나꺄나.

34. 구다 구더다 뿌 네롸이러 구 무뿌 오롸 와더다 어라 루우루 사니 시 너찌러 나바부라 어너 먀시 짜시야 무누누뤠뷔.

35. 요와나 아바아 아뤠 꺄 다라 랴 랴고러라 짜시야 뤠로머거러 어 바쭈. 노부 부퐈꺄러 봐이, 뫄보 뭐라 구나모어라보 구비하꺼 비어거 오싸오.

36. 시 찌로 바짜, 녀더 이찌 먀시 어라 여찌러 야더다 어라 루우루 사니. 너이 먀시 이러찌서 어라 요와나 아더다아. 부찌 다다 아네비기러 뫄 무뤠모 미라 짜시야 네마뤠뤠서오. 너뱌 너찌러 나이라 비 벼찌러 뱌로사 가나꺄나 과 이와나네쭈마아.

37. 러로 오구 다다 이와네쭈마아, 나이 어찌러 아나더다 어라 루우루 사니 가나꺄나. 시 어 무러꺼 와이

---

32. There is another who testifies in my favor, and I know that his testimony about me is valid.

33. "You have sent to John and he has testified to the truth.

34. Not that I accept human testimony; but I mention it that you may be saved.

35. John was a lamp that burned and gave light, and you chose for a time to enjoy his light.

36. "I have testimony weightier than that of John. For the very work that the Father has given me to finish, and which I am doing, testifies that the Father has sent me.

37. And the Father who sent me has himself testified concerning me. You have never heard his voice nor

---

imutafuraa kumvako chiro n'euma. Kanji mutafuraa kulola kwa achwula ahuhire.

이무다푸라아 구빠고 찌로 너우마. 가찌 무다푸라아 구른롸 과 아쭈롸 아후히러.

seen his form,

38. N'e chinwa chai, chitenjire chasimika mwa michima yenyu, bushi mutenjire mwanyemerera mwa michima yenyu nyi achwumaa.

38. 너 찌놔 짜이, 찌더띠러 짜시미가 롸 미찌마 여뉴, 부씨 무더띠러 뫄녀머러라 롸 미찌마 여뉴 니 아쭈마아.

38. nor does his word dwell in you, for you do not believe the one he sent.

39. Muchwusa bashiru ngachi mwa kunde mwachikangilyisa e maanjiko Mabuya-buya, bushi mwende mwaanyisa mbu mw'ebi mu mungabonera e kalamo k'e suku n'e mango. Rero mumenyereraa kwa amu maanjiko mabuuya-buya, mu menjire mateta era luulu sanyi!

39. 무쭈사 바씨루 께찌 롸 구떠 뫄찌가께레사 어 마아찌고 마부야-부야, 부씨 뭐떠 뫄아네사 뿌 뭐비 무 무꺄보너라 어 가롸모 거 수구 너 마꼬. 러로 무머녀러러라아 과 아무 마아찌고 마부우야-부야, 무 머띠러 마더다 어라 루우루 사니!

39. You diligently study the Scriptures because you think that by them you possess eternal life. These are the Scriptures that testify about me,

40. Si chiro bacha, mutenjire mwahonda kubaha era nyilyi, mubone e kalamo.

40. 시 찌로 바짜, 무더띠러 뫄혼따 구바하 어라 니레, 무보너 어 가롸모.

40. yet you refuse to come to me to have life.

41. Nyono ndahonda mbu e bandju bendaa banyitonga.

41. 뇨노 따호따 뿌 어 바쭈 버따아 바네도꺄.

41. "I do not accept praise from men,

42. Si mwabo nyichwula nyibeshi kubuya! kanji nyishi kwa mutachwula musimire Ongo.

42. 시 뫄보 네쭈라 네버씨 구부야! 가찌 네씨 과 무다쭈롸 무시미러 오꼬.

42. but I know you. I know that you do not have the love of God in your hearts.

43. Nyono nabahire kw'e sina lya tata, si mwabo mutahonda kunyihuukasa. Si akaba unji mundju iwabahire kw'e sina lyai yeine, yeke kuika munamuhukase.

43. 뇨노 나바히러 궈 시나 랴 다다, 시 뫄보 무다호따 구네후우가사. 시 아가바 우찌 무뿌 이와바히러 궈 시나 랴이 여이너, 여거 구이가 무나무후가서.

43. I have come in my Father's name, and you do not accept me; but if someone else comes in his own name, you will accept him.

44. Mwabo muchwula musimire kunde mweresanya e chwunda, si mutahonda kubona e chwunda lya lyatenga era mwa Ongo yeine. Rero, kute mungaala kwemerera mwa muchima yenyu?

45. Mutachichingaa mbu nyi nyingabasitaka era mwa tata. Ola ungabasitaka alyi musa, bushi imuchwula mulangalyire.

46. Akaba muchwula mwemerere musa, nanyi munganyemerere bushi e myasi era aanjika ichwula itechire era luulu sanyi.

47. Si akaba mutenjire mwemerera bya Musa aanjika, rero kute mungemerera e myasi era nenjire nateta?

---

44. 먀보 무쭈롸 무시미러 e구떠 뭐러사냐 어 쭈따, 시 무다호따 구보나 어 쭈따 롸 롸더따 어라 먀 오꼬 여이너. 러로, 구더 무까아롸 궈머러라 먀 무찌마 여뉴?

45. 무다찌찌까아 뿌 니 네까바시다가 어라 먀 다다. 오롸 우까바시다가 아레 무사, 부씨 이무쭈롸 무롸까레러.

46. 아가바 무쭈롸 뭐머러러 무사, 나니 무까나녀머러러 부씨 어 먀시 어라 아아찌가 이쭈롸 이더찌러 어라 루우루 사니.

47. 시 아가바 무더찌러 뭐머러라 뱌 무사 아아찌가, 러로 구더 무꺼머러라 어 먀시 어라 너찌러 나더다?

---

44. How can you believe if you accept praise from one another, yet make no effort to obtain the praise that comes from the only God?

45. "But do not think I will accuse you before the Father. Your accuser is Moses, on whom your hopes are set.

46. If you believed Moses, you would believe me, for he wrote about me.

47. But since you do not believe what he wrote, how are you going to believe what I say?"

Yoana Chikono 6

Yesu alyisa bandju byumbi bitano

1. Era nyuma s'ebi, Yesu era kutenga aola na ahabuka e nyanja y'e kalilaya. (Ei nyanja, ibende belyika kanji mbu nyanja y'e tiberiya)

요아나 찌고노 6

여수 아쩨뻽 바뉴 뷰뻬 비다노

1. 어라 뉴마 서비, 여수 어라 구더꺼 아오롸 나 아하부가 어 냐쨔 여 가꺼롸야. (어이 냐쨔, 이버떠 버쩨가 가찌 뿌 냐쨔 여 디버리야)

John Chapter 6[NIV]

1. Some time after this, Jesus crossed to the far shore of the Sea of Galilee (that is, the Sea of Tiberias),

2. Bandju banene bera kumukulyikira, bushi beine bendee bachilorera kwa bisomerano by'endee aira mwa kulamya e balwala.	2. 바쭈 바너너 버라 구무구레기라, 부씨 버이너 버떠어 바찌로러라 과 비소머라노 벼떠어 아이라 뫄 구라먀 어 바롸라.	2. and a great crowd of people followed him because they saw the miraculous signs he had performed on the sick.
3. Yesu era kwerukira kwa ndjulungu na ekelako alauma n'e banafunzi bai.	3. 여수 어라 궈루기라 과 쭈루우 나 어거라고 아라우마 너 바나푸씨 바이.	3. Then Jesus went up on a mountainside and sat down with his disciples.
4. N'e lusuku lukulu lw'e pasaka y'e bayuda lwabaa lulyi ofu.	4. 너 루수구 루구루 뤄 파사가 여 바유다 롸바아 루레 오푸.	4. The Jewish Passover Feast was near.
5. Mango Yesu emusaa e meho, era kulola ba bandju bamukulyikire banene, bushi n'oku, era kubusa Filipo mbu: Era Filipo ngai uchwungaulyira e mikati era bano bandju boshi bangalya?	5. 마오 여수 어무사아 어 머호, 어라 구로라 바 바쭈 바무구레기러 바너너, 부씨 노구, 어라 구부사 피리포 뿌: 어라 피리포 ㅇ가이 우쭈ㅇ가우레라 어 미가디 어라 바노 바쭈 보씨 바ㅇ가랴?	5. When Jesus looked up and saw a great crowd coming toward him, he said to Philip, "Where shall we buy bread for these people to eat?"
6. Abusaa bacha, bushi abaa ahonda omve kute Filipo angaakula. Si yeine abaa amenyire mira changaira.	6. 아부사아 바짜, 부씨 아바아 아호따 오뻐 구더 피리포 아ㅇ가아구라. 시 여이너 아바아 아머네러 미라 짜ㅇ가이라.	6. He asked this only to test him, for he already had in mind what he was going to do.
7. Filipo na imbu: Ewalyiya! chiro chwungaula mikati ya maana mabilyi ma dinari. Itangalumilyira bano bandju boshi, kuikira kwa chihangi chira muuma mubo abone chiro n'e kambesha.	7. 피리포 나 이뿌: 어와레야! 찌로 쭈ㅇ가우라 미가디 야 마아나 마비레 마 디나리. 이다ㅇ가루미레라 바노 바쭈 보씨, 구이기라 과 찌하ㅇ기 찌라 무우마 무보 아보너 찌로 너 가뻐싸.	7. Philip answered him, "Eight months' wages would not buy enough bread for each one to have a bite!"
8. Unji mwanafunzi muuma wa Yesu, mbu i Andereya munyakabo Simoni Petero, nai era kuteta mbu:	8. 우찌 뫄나푸씨 무우마 와 여수, 뿌 이 아떠러야 무냐가보 시모니 퍼더로, 나이 어라 구더다 뿌:	8. Another of his disciples, Andrew, Simon Peter's brother, spoke up,

9. Anola alyi musana muuma ola wete mikati etano oshao, era ikunganyisibwe mwa shayiri. Eti n'efi ebilyi oshao. Rero bano bandju bangana bacha, bi bilyo bingabalumilyirebi?

10. Yesu na imbu: Muburaa e bandju boshi bekale alashi. E bandju boshi bera kunekala, bushi aola abaa alyi bichi binene mw'abu bandju, e balume beine oshao, babaa bangaika ku byumbi bitano.

11. Chasinda Yesu era kwire atola era mikati etano, era kutonga Ongo na ayabiranga abu bandju. S'efi nasi era kubaabirangasi, kukulyikana n'okwa chira muuma abaa anahonda.

12. Abere abu bandju boshi bera beutaa, Yesu kukwera kubura e banafunzi bai mbu balunda-lundaa e bilyo byoshi bya byeshibire, bingesha kufa buha.

13. Chasinda bera kutangilyisa balunda-lunda bya byashibaa kwera mikate etano era yabaa ikunganyisibwe mwa shayiri, byera kw'ehusa bitonga ekumi na babilyi.

9. 아노롸 아레 무사나 무우마 오롸 워더 미가디 어다노 오싸오, 어라 이구까네시붜 뫄 싸에리. 어디 너피 어비레 오싸오. 러로 바노 바쭈 바까나 바짜, 비 비료 비까바루미레러비?

10. 여수 나 이뿌: 무부라아 어 바쭈 보씨 버가꿔 아롸씨. 어 바쭈 보씨 버라 구너가롸, 부씨 아오롸 아바아 아레 비찌 비너너 뫄부 바쭈, 어 바루머 베이너 오싸오, 바바아 바까이가 구 뷰뻬 비다노.

11. 짜시따 여수 어라 귀러 아도롸 어라 미가디 어다노, 어라 구도까 오꼬 나 아야비라까 아부 바쭈. 서피 나시 어라 구바아비라까시, 구구레가나 노과 찌라 무우마 아바아 아나호따.

12. 아버러 아부 바쭈 보씨 버라 버우다아, 여수 구궈라 구부라 어 바나푸씨 바이 뿌 바루따-루따아 어 비료 뵤씨 뱌 벼씨비러, 비꺼싸 구파 부하.

13. 짜시따 버라 구다끠레사 바루따-루따 뱌 뱌씨바아 궈라 미가더 어다노 어라 야바아 이구까네시붜 뫄 싸에리, 벼라 궈후사 비도까 어구미 나 바비레.

9. "Here is a boy with five small barley loaves and two small fish, but how far will they go among so many?"

10. Jesus said, "Have the people sit down." There was plenty of grass in that place, and the men sat down, about five thousand of them.

11. Jesus then took the loaves, gave thanks, and distributed to those who were seated as much as they wanted. He did the same with the fish.

12. When they had all had enough to eat, he said to his disciples, "Gather the pieces that are left over. Let nothing be wasted."

13. So they gathered them and filled twelve baskets with the pieces of the five barley loaves left over by those who had eaten.

14. Abu bandju, mango balolaa kw'echi chisomerano Yesu airaa, bera kutangilyisa bateta mbu: Kubinalyi ono mundju analyi ola murebi bendee bateta kwa akabaha muno butala!

15. Unao-unao, Yesu era kumenyerera kwa bahonda kumwemika kwa misi abe mwami wabo.bushi n'oku, era kwire atenga aola na aya kanji kwa ndjulungu yeine.

Yesu alambaira kwa nyanja

16. Abere lwera luolo-olo, e banafunzi ba Yesu bera kwandaalyira kanji kwa nyanja.

17. Bera kwerukira mwa bwato, na batangilyisa bahabuka e nyanja, baye mwa musi w'e kaperinaumu. Yesu abaa atasa kubabuana, n'oku e buchwufu bwabaa bw'elyire mira.

18. Rero, kwa meshi kwera kuchihuta kausi kasibu, e mulaba era kwire aba kwa nyanja.

19. Abere e banafunzi bera bahabuka bilometere bingaika kubitano nesi ndachwu, bera kulola ku Yesu era alyi ofu n'e bwato, aenda alambaira kwa nyanja. Bushi n'oku, bera kw'obaa.

---

14. 아부 바쭈, 마꼬 바로쫘아 궈찌 찌소머라노 여수 아이라아, 버라 구다삐레사 바더다 뭊: 구비나레 오노 무뿌 아나레 오똬 무러비 버떠어 바더다 과 아가바하 무노 부다똬!

15. 우나오-우나오, 여수 어라 구머녀러라 과 바호따 구뭐미가 과 미시 아버 뫄미 와보.부씨 노구, 어라 궈러 아더꽈 아오똬 나 아야 가찌 과 쭈루우 여이너.

여수 아똬빠윌띱 과 냐짜

16. 아버러 뤄라 루오로로-오르, 어 바나푸씨 바 여수 버라 과따아뤠라 가찌 과 냐짜.

17. 버라 궈루기라 뫄 봐도, 나 바다삐레사 바하부가 어 냐짜, 바여 뫄 무시 워 가퍼리나우무. 여수 아바아 아다사 구바부아나, 노구 어 부쭈푸 봐바아 붜뤠러 미라.

18. 러로, 과 머씨 궈라 구찌후다 가우시 가시부, 어 무똬바 어라 궈러 아바 과 냐짜.

19. 아버러 어 바나푸씨 버라 바하부가 비로머더러 비꽈이가 구비다노 너시 따쭉, 버라 구로똬 구 여수 어라 아레 오푸 너 봐도, 아어따 아똬빠이라 과 냐짜. 부씨 노구, 버라 교바아.

---

14. After the people saw the miraculous sign that Jesus did, they began to say, "Surely this is the Prophet who is to come into the world."

15. Jesus, knowing that they intended to come and make him king by force, withdrew again to a mountain by himself.

16. When evening came, his disciples went down to the lake,

17. where they got into a boat and set off across the lake for Capernaum. By now it was dark, and Jesus had not yet joined them.

18. A strong wind was blowing and the waters grew rough.

19. When they had rowed three or three and a half miles, they saw Jesus approaching the boat, walking on the water; and they were terrified.

20. Si Yesu era kubabura mbu: Nyono ono, mutobaaa!

21. Bera kuhonda bamweke mwa bwato. Si unao-unao obu bwato bwabaa bwaikire mira kwa musike s'e nyanja, ala babaa baya.

E bandju bahonda Yesu

22. Abere mwei mishangya, e bandju ba bashibaa kwa unji mushilyilya w'e nyanja, bera kukengera kwa kasi bwato buuma oshao bu bwabaa bunalyi aola. Kanji bera kumenya kwa Yesu aterukiraa mwa bwato alauma n'e banafunzi bai, si beine bu banachiumaa.

23. Mw'olu, kwera kuulukira manji mato ma mabaa matengera mwa musi w'e tiberiya. Amu mato, mera kuika ofu n'ala abu bandju balyiraa era mikati mango enawechwu abaa era atongaa Ongo bushi nai.

24. Abu bandju balolyire kwa Yesu n'e banafunzi bai batachilyi aola, bera kwire berukiranga mw'amu mato baye kumuhondera e kaperenaumu.

Yesu I mukati ola wende wana e kalamo

---

20. 시 여수 어라 구바부라 뿌: 뇨노 오노, 무도바아아!

21. 버라 구호따 바뭐거 먀 봐도. 시 우나오-우나오 오부 봐도 봐바아 봐이기러 미라 과 무시거 서 냐짜, 아퐈 바바아 바야.

어 바뚜 바호따 여수

22. 아버러 뭐이 미싸뺘, 어 바뚜 바 바씨바아 과 우찌 무씨례럐 워 냐짜, 버라 구거뻐라 과 가시 봐도 부우마 오싸오 부 봐바아 부나례 아오퐈. 가찌 버라 구머냐 과 여수 아더루기라아 먀 봐도 아퐈우마 너 바나푸씨 바이, 시 버이너 부 바나찌우마아.

23. 몰루, 귀라 구우루기라 마찌 마도 마 마바아 마더뻐라 먀 무시 워 디버리야. 아무 마도, 머라 구이가 오푸 나퐈 아부 바뚜 바례라아 어라 미가디 마꼬 어나워쭈 아바아 어라 아도퐈아 오꼬 부씨 나이.

24. 아부 바뚜 바로례러 과 여수 너 바나푸씨 바이 바다찌례 아오퐈, 버라 귀러 버루기라꽈 먀무 마도 바여 구무호뻐라 어 가퍼러나우무.

여수 이 무가디 오퐈 워뻐 와나 어 가퐈명

---

20. But he said to them, "It is I; don't be afraid."

21. Then they were willing to take him into the boat, and immediately the boat reached the shore where they were heading.

22. The next day the crowd that had stayed on the opposite shore of the lake realized that only one boat had been there, and that Jesus had not entered it with his disciples, but that they had gone away alone.

23. Then some boats from Tiberias landed near the place where the people had eaten the bread after the Lord had given thanks.

24. Once the crowd realized that neither Jesus nor his disciples were there, they got into the boats and went to Capernaum in search of Jesus.

25. Mango abu bandju babuanaa Yesu kwa mushilyilya w'e nyanja bera kumubusa mbu: Mukangilyisi! Mangochi waikaa enera?

26. Nai mbu: Kubinalyi, nababura kwa mutanyihonda bushi mwa lolaa kwa bisomerano bya naira. Si nyishi kwa e mikati era mwalyaa na mweuta iyachwuma mwanyihonda bacha!

27. Rero, mutendaa mwachikorera e bilyo bya byende byaamba si mundaa mwakorera e bilyo bya byende byelyisa, kanji binabaretere e kalamo k'e suku n'e mango. E byera byeke bi bilyo nyi mwana w'e mundju nyingaberesa. Bushi nyi mwana w'e mundju, Ongo tata anyibikire kw'e kalorero mira k'e kulosa kwa achwula anyilangalyire.

28. Chasinda, bera kubusa Yesu mbu: Rero chi chwuiraa, chwukole e milyimo era Ongo achwula asimire?

29. Nai mbu: E mulyimo ola Ongo ahonda I yono: Munyemereraa mwa michima yenyu nyono nyi yeine achwumaa.

25. 마꼬 아부 바뉴 바부아나아 여수 과 무씨뤠랴 워 냐짜 베라 구무부사 뿌: 무가꼐쀄시! 마꼬찌 와이가아 어너라?

26. 나이 뿌: 구비나뤠, 나바부라 과 무다네호따 부씨 와 뤄롸아 과 비소머라노 뱌 나이라. 시 네씨 과 어 미가디 어라 뫄랴아 나 뭐우다 이야쭈마 먀네호따 바짜!

27. 러로, 무더따아 뫄찌고러라 어 비뤞 뱌 벼뻐 뱌아빠 시 무따아 먀고러라어 비뤞 뱌 벼뻐 벼뤠사, 가찌 비나바러더러 어 가꽈모 거 수구 너 마꼬. 어 벼라 벼거 비 비뤞 네 마나 워 무뿌 네꽈버러사. 부씨 네 먀나 워 무뿌, 오꼬 다다 아네비기러 궈 가뤄러로 미라 거 구뤈사 과 아쭈꽈 아네꽈꽈뤠러.

28. 짜시따, 버라 구부사 여수 뿌: 러로 찌 쭈이라아, 쭈고뤄 어 미뤠모 어라 오꼬 아쭈꽈 아시미러?

29. 나이 뿌: 어 무뤠모 오라 오꼬 아호따 이 요노: 무녀머러라아 뫄 미찌마 여뉴 뇨노 네 여이너 아쭈마아.

25. When they found him on the other side of the lake, they asked him, "Rabbi, when did you get here?"

26. Jesus answered, "I tell you the truth, you are looking for me, not because you saw miraculous signs but because you ate the loaves and had your fill.

27. Do not work for food that spoils, but for food that endures to eternal life, which the Son of Man will give you. On him God the Father has placed his seal of approval."

28. Then they asked him, "What must we do to do the works God requires?"

29. Jesus answered, "The work of God is this: to believe in the one he has sent."

30. Bera kuhuba kumubusa mbu: Chisomerano chichiye ungaira nechwu mwa kulola kuchi chwukwemerere? Rero, mwasi muchiye I ungaira?

31. Bahokulu bechwu beke, mana mu bendee balya mwa buyeye, kukulyikana ng'okwa maanjiko mabuya-buya machwula matechire mbu: Abaa enjire aberesa e mukati ola watenga kwa nguba, chasiya bende balyao.

32. Yesu nai mbu: Kubinalyi, nababura kwa oyu mukati wendee watenga kwa nguba, ata musa iwendee waberesao. si e mukati w'e kunalyi ola watenga kwa nguba, tata iwenjire waberesao.

33. Bushi oyu mukati Ongo ende eresa e bandju analyi nyono nyinatengire kwa nguba, chasiya nyiretere e bandju b'omwa butala e kalamo.

34. Bushi n'oku, bera kwire bamubura mbu: E walyiya! Oyu mukati, utangende wachweresao e suku soshi!

35. Yesu kukwera kubabura mbu: Nyono nyi mukati w'e kalamo. Akaba e mundju angabaha ene nyilyi ananyemerere mwa muchima

---

30. 버라 구후바 구무부사 뿌: 찌소머라노 찌찌여 우빠이라 너쭈 뫄 구룰롸 구찌 쭈궈머러러? 러로, 마시 무찌여 이 우빠이라?

31. 바호구루 버쭈 버거, 마나 무 버떠어 바럐 뫄 부여여, 구구레가나 꼬과 마아찌고 마부야-부야 마쭐롸 마더찌러 뿌: 아바아 어찌러 아버러사 어 무가디 오롸 와더빠 과 꾸바, 짜시야 버떠 바럐오.

32. 여수 나이 뿌: 구비나레, 나바부라 과 오유 무가디 워떠어 와더빠 과 꾸바, 아다 무사 이워떠어 와버러사오. 시 어 무가디 워 구나레 오롸 와더빠 과 꾸바, 다다 이워찌러 와버러사오.

33. 부씨 오유 무가디 오꼬 어떠 어러사 어 바쭈 아나레 뇨노 니나더삐러 과 꾸바, 짜시야 니러더러 어 바쭈 보뫄 부다롸 어 가롸모.

34. 부씨 노구, 버라 귀러 바무부라 뿌: 어 와레야! 오유 무가디, 우다뻐러 와쭤러사오 어 수구 소씨!

35. 여수 구궈라 구바부라 뿌: 뇨노 니 무가디 워 가롸모. 아가바 어 무쭈 아빠바하 어너 니레 아나녀머러러 뫄 무찌마 와이, 오요롸

---

30. So they asked him, "What miraculous sign then will you give that we may see it and believe you? What will you do?

31. Our forefathers ate the manna in the desert; as it is written: 'He gave them bread from heaven to eat.'"

32. Jesus said to them, "I tell you the truth, it is not Moses who has given you the bread from heaven, but it is my Father who gives you the true bread from heaven.

33. For the bread of God is he who comes down from heaven and gives life to the world."

34. "Sir," they said, "from now on give us this bread."

35. Then Jesus declared, "I am the bread of life. He who comes to me will never go hungry, and he who believes in me will never be thirsty.

wai, oyola atakachife businya, nesi chami chiro na hicha.

아다가찌퍼 부시냐, 너시 짜미 찌로 나 히짜.

36. Si ng'okwa nanababuraa: Chiro angaba mwanyilolyireko mira, si mutanyemerere mwa michima yenyu.

36. 시 꼬과 나나바부라아: 찌로 아빠바 뫄네뜨레러고 미라, 시 무다녀머러러 봐 미찌마 여뉴.

36. But as I told you, you have seen me and still you do not believe.

37. Si chiro bacha e bandju boshi ba tata anyeresise, kuika bakanabaha era nyilyi. Nabo, ndakabaume era butala chiro na hicha.

37. 시 찌로 바짜 어 바뚜 보씨 바 다다 아녀러시서, 구이가 바가나바하 어라 네레. 나보, 따가바우머 어라 부다롸 찌로 나 히짜.

37. All that the Father gives me will come to me, and whoever comes to me I will never drive away.

38. Bushi cha chachwumaa natenga kwa nguba, kutabaa kuira e kuhonda kwanyi nyeine, Si ekuhonda kw'ola wanyichwumaa.

38. 부씨 짜 짜쭈마아 나더빠 과 꾸바, 구다바아 구이라 어 구호따 과네 녀이너, 시 어구호따 교롸 와네쭈마아.

38. For I have come down from heaven not to do my will but to do the will of him who sent me.

39. N'e kuhonda kw'oyu wanyichwumaa, kulyi kuteta mbu ndaesaa chiro na muuma mw'aba anyeresise, si nyibomwole kwa lusuku lw'e businda.

39. 너 구호따 교유 와네쭈마아, 구레 구더다 뿌 따어사아 찌로 나 무우마 뫄바 아녀러시서, 시 네보모뤄 과 루수구 뤄 부시따.

39. And this is the will of him who sent me, that I shall lose none of all that he has given me, but raise them up at the last day.

40. Kubinalyi tata ahonjire mbu chira mundju woshi ola unganyilolako nyi mwana wai n'e kunyimerera mwa muchima wai, abonaa e kalamo k'e suku n'e mango. Na kwa lusuku lw'e businda, nyikamwomola.

40. 구비나레 다다 아호찌러 뿌 찌라 무뚜 오씨 오롸 우빠네뜨롸고 네 뫄나 와이 너 구네머러라 봐 무찌마 와이, 아보나아 어 가롸모 거 수구 너 마꼬. 나 과 루수구 뤄 부시따, 네가모모롸.

40. For my Father's will is that everyone who looks to the Son and believes in him shall have eternal life, and I will raise him up at the last day."

41. Rero bushi Yesu abaa enjire ateta mbu I mukati watengaa kwa nguba, e

41. 러로 부씨 여수 아바아 어찌러 아더다 뿌 이 무가디 와더빠아 과 꾸바, 어 바유다

41. At this the Jews began to grumble about him because he said, "I am the

bayuda bera kutangilyisa kunde bamusibukira.

42. Bera kwire bende bateta mbu: Ewashe! ono mundju kasi Ata I Yesu, mwenyi Yosefu? si eshe na nyina chwubeshi! Rero kute era enjire achitonga mbu kwa nguba ku atengaa?

43. Yesu era kubabura mbu: Murekaa kunde mwasibukirana mwa kachi-kachi kenyu!

44. Kutalyi ola ungabaha ene nyilyi, akaba tata ola wanyichwumaa atasa kumureta. N'ola ungabaha ene nyilyi, nyikamwomola kwa lusuku lw'e businda.

45. Bushi bichwula byanjikirwe mwa bitabo by'e barebi mbu: E bandju boshi, Ongo yeine I ukabakangilyisa. Rero, chira mundju woshi ola wende womvilyisa e myasi ya tata, na kuichwunda, oyola iwende wabaha ene nyilyi.

46. Ndatechire mbu kulyi mundju ola ufuraa kulola ku tata, kunyireka nyi natengaa era achwula. Nyono nyeine oshao nyi nera nyinamulolyireko.

47. Kubinalyi, nababura kwa

버라 구다ᄁ레사 구떠 바무시부기라.

42. 버라 귀러 버머 바더다 뿌: 어와써! 오노 무뚜 가시 아다 이 여수, 뭐내 요서푸? 시 어써 나 니나 쭈버씨! 러로 구더 어라 어찌러 아찌도까 뿌 과 우바 구 아더까아?

43. 여수 어라 구바부라 뿌: 무러가아 구떠 뫄시부기라나 뫄 가찌-가찌 거뉴!

44. 구다레 오라 우까바하 어너 내레, 아가바 다다 오꽈 와내쭈마아 아다사 구무러다. 노꽈 우까바하 어너 내레, 네가모모꽈 과 루수구 뭐 부시따.

45. 부씨 비쭈꽈 뱌찌기뤄 뫄 비다보 벼 바러비 뿌: 어 바뚜 보씨, 오꼬 여이너 이 우가바가끼레사. 러로, 찌라 무뚜 올씨 오꽈 워떠 올뻬레사 어 먀시 야 다다, 나 구이쭈따, 오요꽈 이워떠 와바하 어너 내레.

46. 따더찌러 뿌 구레 무뚜 오꽈 우푸라아 구로꽈 구 다다, 구네러가 네 나더까아 어라 아쭈꽈. 뇨노 녀이너 오싸오 네 너라 니나무로ᄙᅦ러고.

47. 구비나레, 나바부라 과

---

bread that came down from heaven."

42. They said, "Is this not Jesus, the son of Joseph, whose father and mother we know? How can he now say, 'I came down from heaven'?"

43. "Stop grumbling among yourselves," Jesus answered.

44. "No one can come to me unless the Father who sent me draws him, and I will raise him up at the last day.

45. It is written in the Prophets: 'They will all be taught by God.' Everyone who listens to the Father and learns from him comes to me.

46. No one has seen the Father except the one who is from God; only he has seen the Father.

47. I tell you the truth, he

ola wanyemerere mwa muchima wai, kuika anabone e kalamo k'e suku n'e mango.

48. Nyono nyi mukati w'e kalamo.

49. Abu bahokulu benyu chiro angaba mbu bendee balya e mana mwa buyeye, kufa ku bendee banafanga.

50. Si oyu mukati watengaa kwa nguba weke akaba e mundju angalyao, atakafe chiro na hicha.

51. Rero oyu mukati w'e kalamo ola watengaa kwa nguba, alyi nyono akaba e mundju angalyao, angaata e kalamo k'e suku n'e mango. Kanji oyu mukati nyingeresa e bandju, alyi e mubilyi wanyi. N'oyu mubilyi, nyinganao chasiya e bandju bomwa butala babone e kalamo.

52. Bushi n'oku, abu bayuda kuna kutangilyisa baenzanya e bwaka busese. Bera kuteta mbu: ono mundju, kute angachweresa e mubilyi wai mbu ichwiraa chwalya?

53. Yesu kukwera kubabura mbu: kubinalyi, nababura kwa akaba mutangalya e mubilyi wanyi nyi mwana w'e mundju, na kumwa e mikira yanyi, mutangabona e kalamo k'e

오라 와녀머러러 먀 무찌마 와이, 구이가 아나보너 어 가라모 거 수구 너 마꼬.

48. 뇨노 네 무가디 워 가라모.

49. 아부 바호구루 버뉴 찌로 아꾜바 뿌 버떠어 바랴 어 마나 먀 부여여, 구파 구 버떠어 바나파꺄.

50. 시 오유 무가디 와더꺄아 과 꾸바 워거 아가바 어 무뚜 아꾜챠오, 아다가퍼 찌로 나 히짜.

51. 러로 오유 무가디 워 가라모 오라 와더꺄아 과 꾸바, 아례 뇨노 아가바 어 무뚜 아꾜챠오, 아꾜아다 어 가라모 거 수구 너 마꼬. 가찌 오유 무가디 네어러사 어 바뚜, 아례 어 무비례 와네. 노유 무비례, 네꺄나오 짜시야 어 바뚜 보먀 부다랴 바보너 어 가라모.

52. 부씨 노구, 아부 바유다 구나 구다꾀례사 바어싸냐 어 봐가 부서서. 버라 구더다 뿌: 오노 무뚜, 구더 아꾜쮜러사 어 무비례 와이 뿌 이쮜라아 쫘쨔?

53. 여수 구궈라 구바부라 뿌: 구비나례, 나바부라 과 아가바 무다꺄챠 어 무비례 와네 네 먀나 워 무뚜, 나 구콰 어 미기라 야네, 무다꺄보나 어 가라모 거

who believes has everlasting life.

48. I am the bread of life.

49. Your forefathers ate the manna in the desert, yet they died.

50. But here is the bread that comes down from heaven, which a man may eat and not die.

51. I am the living bread that came down from heaven. If anyone eats of this bread, he will live forever. This bread is my flesh, which I will give for the life of the world."

52. Then the Jews began to argue sharply among themselves, "How can this man give us his flesh to eat?"

53. Jesus said to them, "I tell you the truth, unless you eat the flesh of the Son of Man and drink his blood, you have no life in you.

suku n'e mango.

수구 너 마꼬.

54. Ola walya e mubilyi wanyi, na kumwa e mikira yanyi, oyola yeke iwete aku kalamo. N'oyu, inyikwomola kwa lusuku lw'e businda.

54. 오꽈 와꺄 어 무비레 와네, 나 구꽈 어 미기라 야네, 오요꽈 여거 이워더 아구 가라모. 노유, 이네굧모꽈 과 루수구 뤄부시따.

54. Whoever eats my flesh and drinks my blood has eternal life, and I will raise him up at the last day.

55. Bushi e mubilyi wanyi, binalyi bilyo bya kanangana, n'e mikira yanyi nai, binalyi bya kumwa bya kanangana.

55. 부씨 어 무비레 와네, 비나레 비룐 뱌 가나꽈나, 너 미기라 야네 나이, 비나레 뱌 구꽈 뱌 가나꽈나.

55. For my flesh is real food and my blood is real drink.

56. Bushi n'oku, ola ungalya kwa mubilyi wanyi, na kumwa kwa mikira yanyi, oyola I ungaba mwa buuma nanyi, nanyi nanaba mwa buuma nai.

56. 부씨 노구, 오꽈 우까꺄 과 무비레 와네, 나 구꽈 과 미기라 야네, 오요꽈 이 우까바 뫄 부우마 나네, 나네 나나바 뫄 부우마 나이.

56. Whoever eats my flesh and drinks my blood remains in me, and I in him.

57. Tata iwanyichwuma achwula muuma-uma, nanyi nyilyi muuma-uma kwa buashi bwai. Rero kunoku ku ola walya kwa mubilyi wanyi nai, anganaba muuma-uma kwa buashi bwanyi.

57. 다다 이와네쭈마 아쭈꽈 무우마-우마, 나네 네레 무우마-우마 과 부아씨 봐이. 러로 구노구 구 오꽈 와꺄 과 무비레 와네 나이, 아까나바 무우마-우마 과 부아씨 봐네.

57. Just as the living Father sent me and I live because of the Father, so the one who feeds on me will live because of me.

58. Nyono nyi mukati watengaa kwa nguba. N'oyu mukati weke, atalyi ng'ola baahokulu benyu bendee balya mwa buyeye, n'e kunde bafanga. Si ono mukati, ola ungalyao, yeke angabona e kalamo k'e suku n'e mango.

58. 뇨노 네 무가디 와더꽈아 과 우바. 노유 무가디 워거, 아다레 꼬꽈 바아호구루 버뉴 버떠어 바꺄 뫄 부여여, 너 구떠 바파꽈. 시 오노 무가디, 오꽈 우까꺄오, 여거 아까보나 어 가꽈모 거 수구 너 마꼬.

58. This is the bread that came down from heaven. Your forefathers ate manna and died, but he who feeds on this bread will live forever."

59. Ei myasi yoshi, Yesu atetaai mango abaa akangilyisa e bandju mwa bushenge bw'e bayuda, mwa musi w'e kaperinaumu.

Banene mwa banafunzi ba Yesu bamureka

60. Mango e banafunzi ba Yesu nabo bomvaa kwei myasi banene mubo bera kutangilyisa bateta mbu: Aaye! ene myasi ikoochire busese! kutalyi ola ungaala kwemererai.

61. Unao-unao, Yesu era kumenyerera kwa abu banafunzi bai benjire basibuka bushi n'ebi. Bushi n'oku, era kwire ababusa mbu: Ene myasi, yabalumire kwa muchima?

62. Rero kute ku bingaba mango mungalola kwa nyi mwana w'e mundju nerukira kanji era nabaa nyichwula?

63. Mumenyereraa kw'e mundju yeine atangachialyira kandju. Si e muchima mubuya-buya iwende wana e kalamo. Ei myasi nababilyire, ilyi y'e muchima mubuya-buya, kanji iyende yana e kalamo.

---

59. 어이 먀시 요씨, 여수 아더다아이 마꼬 아바아 아가삐레사 어 바뚜 뫄 부써어 붜 바유다, 뫄 무시 워 가퍼리나우무.

바너너 뫄 바나푸씨 바 여수 바무러가

60. 마꼬 어 바나푸씨 바 여수 나보 보빠아 귀이 먀시 바너너 무보 버라 구다삐레사 바더다 뿌: 아아여! 어너 먀시 이고오찌러 부서서! 구다레 오롸 우꽈아롸 궈머러라이.

61. 우나오-우나오, 여수 어라 구머녀러라 과 아부 바나푸씨 바이 버찌러 바시부가 부씨 너비. 부씨 노구, 어라 아바부사 뿌: 어너 먀시, 야바루미러 과 무찌마?

62. 러로 구더 구 비꽈바 마꼬 무꽈로롸 과 네 뫄나 워 무뚜 너루기라 가찌 어라 나바아 네쭈롸?

63. 무머녀러라아 귀 무뚜 여이너 아다꽈찌아레라 가뚜. 시 어 무찌마 무부야-부야 이워떠 와나 어 가퍄모. 어이 먀시 나바비레러, 이레 여 무찌마 무부야-부야, 가찌 이여떠 야나 어 가퍄모.

---

59. He said this while teaching in the synagogue in Capernaum.

60. On hearing it, many of his disciples said, "This is a hard teaching. Who can accept it?"

61. Aware that his disciples were grumbling about this, Jesus said to them, "Does this offend you?

62. What if you see the Son of Man ascend to where he was before!

63. The Spirit gives life; the flesh counts for nothing. The words I have spoken to you are spirit and they are life.

64. Si chiro bacha, bauma mu mwabo batanasa kunyemerera mwa michima yabo. Yesu atetaa bacha bushi abaa aneshi kutengera mira ba babaa batasa kumwemerera. Kanji abaa aneshi, ola ukamurenganya.

65. Yesu era kuhuba kuteta mbu: Echera chi chachwumaa nababura kwa kutalyi ola ungabaha ene nyilyi, akaba ata tata iwamweresise obu buashi.

66. Rero, kutengera amu mango, banene mwa banafunzi bai bera kumureka na bachienderanga. Chiro bakende banachimukulyikira.

67. Bushi n'oku, Yesu era kwire abusa e ndjumwa sai ekumi n'ebilyi mbu: Ewashe! nenyu mwa kunyireka mu munalyi?

68. Simoni Petero era kumwakula mbu: Enawechwu, era mwande yi chwungachiya kanji? si woyo, u wete e myasi era yende yana e kalamo k'e suku n'e mango!

69. chwubeine chwemerere mira, kanji chwuneshi kanangana kwa woyo una mubuya-buya, ola Ongo achwumire.

64. 시 찌로 바짜, 바우마 무 먀보 바다나사 구녀머러라 먀 미찌마 야보. 여수 아더다아 바짜 부씨 아바아 아너씨 구더꺼라 미라 바 바바아 바다사 구뭐머러라. 가찌 아바아 아너씨, 오롸 우가무러꺼냐.

65. 여수 어라 구후바 구더다 뿌: 어쩌라 찌 짜쭈마아 나바부라 과 구다뤠 오롸 우꺄바하 어너 네뤠, 아가바 아다 다다 이와뭐러시서 오부 부아씨.

66. 러로, 구더꺼라 아무 마꼬, 바너너 먀 바나푸씨 바이 버라 구무러가 나 바쩌꺼라꺄. 찌로 바거꺼 바나찌무구뤠기라.

67. 부씨 노구, 여수 어라 귀러 아부사 어 뚜꽈 사이 어구미 너비뤠 뿌: 어와써! 너뉴 먀 구녀러가 무 무나뤠?

68. 시모니 퍼더로 어라 구꽈구꽈 뿌: 어나워쭈, 어라 먀너 에 쭈꺄찌야 가찌? 시 요요, 우 워더 어 먀시 어라 여꺼 야나 어 가꽈모 거 수구 너 마꼬!

69. 쭈버이너 쮜머러러 미라, 가찌 쭈너씨 가나꺄나 과 오요 우나 무부야-부야, 오롸 오꼬 아쭈미러.

64. Yet there are some of you who do not believe." For Jesus had known from the beginning which of them did not believe and who would betray him.

65. He went on to say, "This is why I told you that no one can come to me unless the Father has enabled him."

66. From this time many of his disciples turned back and no longer followed him.

67. "You do not want to leave too, do you?" Jesus asked the Twelve.

68. Simon Peter answered him, "Lord, to whom shall we go? You have the words of eternal life.

69. We believe and know that you are the Holy One of God."

70. Yesu na imbu: Ewashe! si nyono nyeine nyinabalondolaa kwa munalyi ekumi na babilyi! si chiro bacha, muuma mu mwabo alyi musimu!

71. Yesu atetaa bacha bushi na Yuda, mwenyi Simoni isikariyota. Oyu Yuda, chiro angaba mbu abaa muuma mwa ndjumwa ekumi n'ebilyi sa Yesu, si iwabaa unganamurenganya.

70. 여수 나 이뿌: 어와써! 시 뇨노 녀이너 네나바뢰또롸아 과 무나쩨 어구미 나 바비쩨! 시 찌로 바짜, 무우마 무 먀보 아쩨 무시무!

71. 여수 아더다아 바짜 부씨 나 유다, 뭐네 시모니 이시가리요다. 오유 유다, 찌로 아까바 뿌 아바아 무우마 먀 뚜먀 어구미 너비쩨 사 여수, 시 이와바아 우까나무러까냐.

70. Then Jesus replied, "Have I not chosen you, the Twelve? Yet one of you is a devil!"

71. (He meant Judas, the son of Simon Iscariot, who, though one of the Twelve, was later to betray him.)

Yoana Chikono 7
Banyakabo Yesu nabo batamwemerera

1. Era nyuma s'ebi, Yesu era kuya kusungula mwa chio ch'e kalilaya. Atahondaa kurenga mwa ch'e yudeya, bushi e bakulu-kulu b'e bayuda beyi, babaa bahonda e njira y'e kumwita.

2. Mango e lusuku lukulu lw'e bayuda lwa lwelyikirwe mbu lusuku lukulu lw'e bitala lwabaa lulyi ofu kuika,

3. Banyakabo Yesu bera kumubura mbu: Utengaa anola, uye e yudeya e banafunzi bao, nabo bachilorere kwa bisomerano bya wenjire waira.

요아나 찌고노 7
바냐가보 여수 나보 바다뭐머러라

1. 어라 뉴마 서비, 여수 어라 구야 구수꾸롸 먀 찌오 쩌 가삐롸야. 아다호따아 구러까 먀 쩌 유더야, 부씨 어 바구루루-구루루 버 바유다 버에, 바바아 바호따 어 찌라 여 구뮈다.

2. 마꼬 어 루수구 루구루루 뤄 바유다 롸 뤄뤠기뤄 뿌 루수구 루구루루 뤄 비다롸 롸바아 루쩨 오푸 구이가,

3. 바냐가보 여수 버라 구무부라 뿌: 우더까아 아노롸, 우여 어 유더야 어 바나푸씨 바오, 나보 바찌뢰러러 과 비소머라노 뱌 워찌러 와이라.

John Chapter 7[NIV]

1. After this, Jesus went around in Galilee, purposely staying away from Judea because the Jews there were waiting to take his life.

2. But when the Jewish Feast of Tabernacles was near,

3. Jesus' brothers said to him, "You ought to leave here and go to Judea, so that your disciples may see the miracles you do.

4. Bushi ola wahonda amenyeke mwa bandju, bitemire ende aira e mulyimo wai mwa bubisho-bisho. Rero nao, oku wenjire wakola e milyimo era ilyi ngei, uyaa kuchilosa changanama era muhondo s'e bandju boshi.

5. Abu banyakabo batetaa bacha, bushi nabo babaa batachwula bamwemerere mwa michima yabo.

6. Bushi n'oku, Yesu era kubabura mbu: E bihangi byoshi binachwula bikomire!

7. Mwabo, e bandju b'omwa butala batangabahomba. Si nyeke banyihombire mira, bushi n'enjire nabatabula kwa myanya yabo ilyi ibi.

8. Bushi n'oku, mwabo muyaa kwa lusuku lukulu, si nyono ndafura kuyako. Bushi e bihangi bya bikomire ku nyono, bitasa kuika.

9. Mango Yesu abaa era amalaa kuteta ei myasi, era kuchishibira e kalilaya.

Yesu aya kwa lusuku lukulu lw'e bitala

10. Mango banyakabo babaa bera bachiumaa baya kwa lusuku lukulu, nai era kuyayi.

---

4. 부씨 오빠 와호따 아머녀거 봐 바뉴, 비더미러 어떠 아이라 어 무레모 와이 봐 부비쏘-비쏘. 러로 나오, 오구 워찌러 와고꽈 어 미레모 어라 이레 어이, 우야아 구찌로사 짜아나마 어라 무호또 서 바뉴 보씨.

5. 아부 바냐가보 바더다아 바짜, 부씨 나보 바바아 바다쭈꽈 바뭐머러러 봐 미찌마 야보.

6. 부씨 노구, 여수 어라 구바부라 뿌: 어 비하께 뵤씨 비나쭈꽈 비고미러!

7. 꽈보, 어 바뉴 보꽈 부다꽈 바다까바호빠. 시 녀거 바네호뻬러 미라, 부씨 너찌러 나바다부꽈 과 먀냐 야보 이레 이비.

8. 부씨 노구, 꽈보 무야아 과 루수구 루구루, 시 뇨노 따푸라 구야고. 부씨 어 비하께 뱌 비고미러 구 뇨노, 비다사 구이가.

9. 마꼬 여수 아바아 어라 아마꽈아 구더다 어이 먀시, 어라 구찌씨비라 어 가삐꽈야.

여수 아야 과 루슙꼴 루꼴루 뤼 비다꽈

10. 마꼬 바냐가보 바바아 버라 바찌우마아 바야 과 루수구 루구루, 나이 어라

---

4. No one who wants to become a public figure acts in secret. Since you are doing these things, show yourself to the world."

5. For even his own brothers did not believe in him.

6. Therefore Jesus told them, "The right time for me has not yet come; for you any time is right.

7. The world cannot hate you, but it hates me because I testify that what it does is evil.

8. You go to the Feast. I am not yet going up to this Feast, because for me the right time has not yet come."

9. Having said this, he stayed in Galilee.

10. However, after his brothers had left for the Feast, he went also, not

Si ayaayi kwa bubisho-bisho busira kuchilosa changanama kwa bandju.

11. Mw'olu lusuku lukulu, e bayuda babaa basungula-sungula bamuhonda. Bera kunde babusilyisa mbu: Ola mulume, ngai u alyi?

12. E bandju ba babaa behwire aola, babaa baenzanya e bwaka mwa byooo era luulu sa Yesu. Bauma babaa benjire bateta mbu: Achwula mundju mubuya. Si e banji beke mbu: Bisha byenyu! si enjire engeera e bandju!

13. Si mwa kuteta era luulu sai, kutabaa chiro na mundju ola waereresaa ateta changanama, bushi babaa bobaa e bakulu-kulu b'e bayuda.

14. Mango e bandju babaa bera balyi mwa kachi-kachi k'esi suku sikulu, Yesu era kuya mwa luhu lwa Ongo, na atangilyisa akangilyisabo.

15. Abu bakulu-kulu b'e bayuda, mwa kunomva kwa akangilyisa, bera kusanwa busese. Bera kutangilyisa bateta mbu: Ewashe! ene myasi yoshi, kute ono mundju amenyaai, n'oku atarengire ku

구야에. 시 아야아에 과 부비쏘-비쏘 부시라 구찌로사 짜𝅭나마 과 바뚜.

11. 몰루 루수구 루구루, 어 바유다 바바아 바수꾸롸-수꾸롸 바무호따. 버라 구떠 바부시례사 뿌: 오롸 무루머, 𝅭아이 우 아례?

12. 어 바뚜 바 바바아 버휘러 아오롸, 바바아 바어싸냐 어 봐가 먀 뵤오오 어라 루우루루 사 여수. 바우마 바바아 버지러 바더다 뿌: 아쭈롸 무뚜 무부야. 시 어 바찌 버거 뿌: 비싸 벼뉴! 시 어찌러 어뻐어라 어 바뚜!

13. 시 먀 구더다 어라 루우루루 사이, 구다바아 찌로 나 무뚜 오롸 와어러러사아 아더다 짜𝅭나마, 부씨 바바아 보바아 어 바구루-구루 버 바유다.

14. 마꼬 어 바뚜 바바아 버라 바례 먀 가찌-가찌 거시 수구 시구루, 여수 어라 먀 루후 롸 오꼬, 나 아다𝅭례사 아가𝅭례사보.

15. 아부 바구루-구루 버 바유다, 먀 구노뺘 과 아가𝅭례사, 버라 구사놔 부서서. 버라 구다𝅭례사 바더다 뿌: 어와써! 어너 먀시 요씨, 구더 오노 무뚜 아머냐아이, 노구 아다러𝅭러

publicly, but in secret.

11. Now at the Feast the Jews were watching for him and asking, "Where is that man?"

12. Among the crowds there was widespread whispering about him. Some said, "He is a good man." Others replied, "No, he deceives the people."

13. But no one would say anything publicly about him for fear of the Jews.

14. Not until halfway through the Feast did Jesus go up to the temple courts and begin to teach.

15. The Jews were amazed and asked, "How did this man get such learning without having studied?"

masomo?

16. Yesu era kubaakula mbu: Ene myasi nenjire nabakangilyisa, itatengire era mwanyi, si itengire era mw'ola wanyichwumaa.

17. N'ola ungahonda kumenyerera akaba ei myasi nenjire nakangilyisa itengire era mwa Ongo, nesi ilyi ya kuchitonga kwanyi, byemire abe ola usimire kuira e kuhonda kwa Ongo.

18. Ola wateta era luulu sai yeine, ende aba achihondera e chwunda lyai yeine. Si ola wahonda e chwunda ly'ola wamuchwumaa, oyola yeke iwende wateta e myasi y'e kanangana. Kanji mwa ndanda sai mutachwula butebanyi busibya.

19. Si Musa aberesaa e mwaso! si chiro bacha, kutalyi chiro na muuma mu mwabo ola wende wachwundao. Rero, chi chera chachwuma mwahonda kunyita?

20. Olu luamba lw'e bandju lwera kumwakula mbu: wahwabirwe! nde iwahonda kukwita?

21. Yesu na imbu: chisomerano chiuma chi nanairaa oshao, chera

구 마소모?

16. 여수 어라 구바아구꽈 뿌: 어너 먀시 너찌러 나바가끼레사, 이다더끼러 어라 마네, 시 이더끼러 어라 몰꽈 와네쭈마아.

17. 노꽈 우까호따 구머녀러라 아가바 어이 먀시 너찌러 나가끼레사 이더끼러 어라 마 오꼬, 너시 이레 야 구찌도까 과네, 벼미러 아버 오꽈 우시미러 구이라 어 구호따 과 오꼬.

18. 오꽈 와더다 어라 루우루 사이 여이너, 어머 아바 아찌호떠라 어 쭈따 꺄이 여이너. 시 오꽈 와호따 어 쭈따 뤼오꽈 와무쭈마아, 오요꽈 여거 이워머 와더다 어 먀시 여 가나까나. 가찌 마 따따 사이 무다쭈꽈 부더바네 부시뱌.

19. 시 무사 아버러사아 어 마소! 시 찌로 바짜, 구다레 찌로 나 무우마 무 마보 오꽈 워머 와쭈따오. 러로, 찌 쩌라 짜쭈마 마호따 구네다?

20. 오루 루아빠 뤄 바누 뤄라 구마구꽈 뿌: 와화비뤄! 떠 이와호따 구귀다?

21. 여수 나 이뿌: 찌소머라노 찌우마 찌 나나이라아 오싸오, 쩌라 구쭈마 무보씨

16. Jesus answered, "My teaching is not my own. It comes from him who sent me.

17. If anyone chooses to do God's will, he will find out whether my teaching comes from God or whether I speak on my own.

18. He who speaks on his own does so to gain honor for himself, but he who works for the honor of the one who sent him is a man of truth; there is nothing false about him.

19. Has not Moses given you the law? Yet not one of you keeps the law. Why are you trying to kill me?"

20. "You are demon-possessed," the crowd answered. "Who is trying to kill you?"

21. Jesus said to them, "I did one miracle, and you are all astonished.

kuchwuma muboshi mwasanwa.

22. Si oku Musa abarekeraa e muomba w'e kunde mwamonya e bana benyu b'e busana, mwabo mwera mwenjire mwanamonyabo n'e lusuku lw'e sabato. (si kanangana, oyu muomba atatengaa era mwa Musa, si era mwa bahokulu benyu)

23. Rero, akaba mungamonya e mwana e lusuku lw'e sabato, chasiya muchwunde oyu muomba wa Musa, chi chera chachwuma mwanyisibukira bushi nalamyaa e mundju e lusuku lw'e sabato?

24. bushi n'oku, murekaa kunde mwachinjibusa e banji mwa kunabalolako oshao, si mund

E bandju bachibusa akaba Yesu ina kirisito

25. Chasinda bandju bauma b'omwa musi w'e yerusalemu, bera kutangilyisa babusanya mbu: Ewashe! ono mundju kasi ata ibahonda kwita?

26. Rero, kute kw'enjire ateta changanama nabo batanamubusa chiro na mwasi usibya? Abunya e bakulu-kulu bechwu bamenyire kanangana kwa ina kirisito!

뫄사놔.

22. 시 오구 무사 아바러거라아 어 무오빠 워 구떠 뫄모냐 어 바나 버뉴 버부사나, 뫄보 뭐라 뭐찌러 뫄나모냐보 너 루수구 뤄 사바도. (시 가나까나, 오유 무오빠 아다더까아 어라 뫄 무사, 시 어라 뫄 바호구루 버뉴)

23 러로, 아가바 무까모냐 어 뫄나 어 루수구 뤄 사바도, 짜시야 무쭌떠 오유 무오빠 와 무사, 찌 쩌라 짜쭈마 뫄네시부기라 부씨 나롸먀아 어 무쭈 어 루수구 뤄 사바도?

24. 부씨 노구, 무러가아 구떠 뫄찌찌부사 어 바찌 뫄 구나바롤롸고 오싸오, 시 무뚜

어 바쭈 바찌부사 아가바 여수 이나 기리시도

25. 짜시따 바쭈 바우마 보뫄 무시 워 여루사뤄무, 버라 구다이례사 바부사냐 뿌: 어와쎄! 오노 무쭈 가시 아다 이바호따 귀다?

26. 러로, 구더 궈찌러 아더다 짜까나마 나보 바다나무부사 찌로 나 뫄시 우시뱌? 아부냐 어 바구루-구루 버쭈 바머네러 가나까나 과 이나 기리시도!

22. Yet, because Moses gave you circumcision (though actually it did not come from Moses, but from the patriarchs), you circumcise a child on the Sabbath.

23. Now if a child can be circumcised on the Sabbath so that the law of Moses may not be broken, why are you angry with me for healing the whole man on the Sabbath?

24. Stop judging by mere appearances, and make a right judgment."

25. At that point some of the people of Jerusalem began to ask, "Isn't this the man they are trying to kill?

26. Here he is, speaking publicly, and they are not saying a word to him. Have the authorities really concluded that he is the Christ?

27. Ono mundju chwishi era atengera. Si mango kirisito yeke akabaha, kutalyi ola ukamenya era akaba atengera.

27. 오노 무뉴 쮜씨 어라 아더꺼라. 시 마꼬 기리시도 여거 아가바하, 구다례 오랴 우가머냐 어라 아가바 아더꺼라.

27. But we know where this man is from; when the Christ comes, no one will know where he is from."

28. Mango Yesu abaa anachilyi akangilyisa e bandju mwa chibuwa ch'e luhu lwa Ongo, era kuteta na murenge munene mbu: Mwabo, mwenjire mwateta mbu munyishi, mwishi n'era natenga! Ndabahire kwa buashi bwanyi nyeine, si ola wanyichwumaa achwula wa kanangana. Rero, mwabo mutamwishi.

28. 마꼬 여수 아바아 아나찌례 아가끼례사 어 바뉴 뫄 찌부와 쪄 루후 롸 오꼬, 어라 구더다 나 무러꺼 무너너 뿌: 뫄보, 뭐찌러 뫄더다 뿌 무네씨, 뮈씨 너라 나더까! 따바히러 과 부아씨 봐네 녀이너, 시 오랴 와네쭈마아 아쭈랴 와 가나까나. 러로, 뫄보 무다뮈씨.

28. Then Jesus, still teaching in the temple courts, cried out, "Yes, you know me, and you know where I am from. I am not here on my own, but he who sent me is true. You do not know him,

29. Si nyono nyeke, nyimwishi kubuya bushi era mwai yi natengaa, kanji iwananyichwumaa.

29. 시 뇨노 녀거, 네뮈씨 구부야 부씨 어라 뫄이 에 나더까아, 가찌 이와나네쭈마아.

29. but I know him because I am from him and he sent me."

30. Ebi Yesu atetaa, byera kuchwuma bauma mw'abu bandju bahonde kumusimba si kutalyi ola wamubikaa kw'e mino, bushi e chihangi chai chabaa chitasa kuika.

30. 어비 여수 아더다아, 벼라 구쭈마 바우마 뫄부 바뉴 바호떠 구무시빠 시 구다례 오랴 와무비가아 궈 미노, 부씨 어 찌하끼 짜이 짜바아 찌다사 구이가.

30. At this they tried to seize him, but no one laid a hand on him, because his time had not yet come.

31. Si mw'olu luamba lunolu, bandju banene, beke bera kumwemerera mwa michima yabo. Bera kutangilyisa bateta mbu: Mango kirisito akaika mwishi akende aira bisomerano binene kurenza bya ono mundju enjire aira?

31. 시 모루 루아빠 루노루, 바뉴 바너너, 버거 버라 구뭐머러라 뫄 미찌마 야보. 버라 구다끼례사 바더다 뿌: 마꼬 기리시도 아가이가 뮈씨 아거떠 아이라 비소머라노 비너너 구러싸 뱌 오노 무뉴 어찌러 아이라?

31. Still, many in the crowd put their faith in him. They said, "When the Christ comes, will he do more miraculous signs than this man?"

E mukulu-kulu w'e bayuda
achwuma e balanzi baye
kusimba Yesu

어 무구루-구루 워 바유다
아쭈립 어 바롸씨 바여
구시빠 여수

32. E myasi era bandju babaa bateteresanga mwa byooo era luulu sa Yesu, e bafarisayo nabo bera kumva kui. Bushi n'oku, abu bafarisayo alauma n'e bakulu-kulu b'e bakuhanyi bera kwire achwuma e balanzi baye kumusimba.

32. 어 먀시 어라 바뉴 바바아 바더더러사까 뫄 뵤오오 어라 루우루 사 여수, 어 바파리사요 나보 버라 구빠 구이. 부씨 노구, 아부 바파리사요 아롸우마 너 바구루-구루 버 바구하네 버라 귀러 아쭈마 어 바롸씨 바여 구무시빠.

32. The Pharisees heard the crowd whispering such things about him. Then the chief priests and the Pharisees sent temple guards to arrest him.

33. Yesu era kuteta mbu: nyichilyi alauma nenyu ku suku sieke oshao, chasinda nyingafuluka era mw'ola wanyichwumaa.

33. 여수 어라 구더다 뿌: 네찌레 아롸우마 너뉴 구 수구 시어거 오싸오, 짜시따 네까푸루가 어라 몰롸 와네쭈마아.

33. Jesus said, "I am with you for only a short time, and then I go to the one who sent me.

34. Rero mwabo munganyihonda si mutachinyiloleko. Bushi ala nyingaba nyilyi, mutangaaala kuikao.

34. 러로 뫄보 무까네호따 시 무다찌네롤러고. 부씨 아롸 네까바 네레, 무다까아아롸 구이가오.

34. You will look for me, but you will not find me; and where I am, you cannot come."

35. E bakulu-kulu b'e bayuda bomvire bacha, bera kutangilyisa babusanya mbu: Ewashe! ono mundju ngai u angaya kuikira chwutangachimulolako? Elyi angaya era mwa banyakechwu bayuda ba bahandabanyire mwa bakiriki, chasiya akangilyiise abu bakariki nabo?

35. 어 바구루-구루 버 바유다 보삐러 바짜, 버라 구다삐레사 바부사냐 뿌: 어와써! 오노 무뿌 까이 우 아까야 구이기라 쭈다까찌무롤롸고? 어레 아까야 어라 뫄 바냐거쭈 바유다 바 바하따바네러 뫄 바기리기, 짜시야 아가삐레서 아부 바가리기 나보?

35. The Jews said to one another, "Where does this man intend to go that we cannot find him? Will he go where our people live scattered among the Greeks, and teach the Greeks?

36. Kanji mango enjire ateta mbu chwubano chwungamuhonda, si

36. 가찌 마꼬 어끼러 아더다 뿌 쭈바노 쭈까무호따, 시 쭈다찌무롤러고, 부씨

36. What did he mean when he said, 'You will look for me, but you will not find

chwutachimuloleko, bushi
chwutangaala kuika ala
angaba alyi, kukwera kuteta
kuto ku?

*E meshi ma mende maana e
kalamo*

37. E lusuku lusinda lw'esi
suku sikulu, lwera kuika. Olu
lusuku, lu lwabaa lusuku
lunene ku silyikabo. Mw'olu
Yesu era kubachwuka na
atangilyisa ateta na murenge
munene mbu: Akaba kulyi
mundju ola wafa chami,
abahaa ene nyilyi, amwe.

38. Ola unganyemerera mwa
muchima wai, e shokororo s'e
meshi ma mende maana e
kalamo singende sashoka
mwa muchima wai, ng'okwa
maanjiko mabuya-buya
machwula matechire.

39. Ei myasi Yesu abaa ateta,
yabaa era luulu s'e muchima
mubuya-buya, ola ba
bangamwemerera bangabona.
Rero, oku Ongo abaa atasa
kwerusa Yesu mw'e chwunda
lyai, chi chachwumaa abaa
atasa kuchwuma e muchima
mubuya-buya.

*E bandju nabo
baberekanamo bushi na Yesu*

40. Bauma mw'abu bandju,
mango bomvaa kwei myasi,

쭈다꺄아롸 구이가 아롸
아꺄바 아레, 구궈라 구더다
구도 구?

*어 머씨 마 머떠 마아나 어
가롸명*

37. 어 루수구 루시따 뤄시
수구 시구루, 뤄라 구이가.
오루 루수구, 루 롸바아
루수구 루너너 구 시레가보.
모루 여수 어라 구바쭈가 나
아다띠레사 아더다 나 무러꺼
무너너 뿌: 아가바 구레 무뚜
오롸 와파 짜미, 아바하아
어너 니레, 아뭐.

38. 오롸 우꺄녀머러라 롸
무찌마 와이, 어 쏘고로로 서
머씨 마 머떠 마아나 어
가롸모 시꺼떠 사쏘가 롸
무찌마 와이, 끄과 마아찌고
마부야-부야 마쭈롸 마더찌러.

39. 어이 먀시 여수 아바아
아더다, 야바아 어라 루우루
서 무찌마 무부야-부야, 오롸
바 바꺄뭐머러라 바꺄보나.
러로, 오구 오끄 아바아
아다사 궈루사 여수 뭐 쭈따
랴이, 찌 짜쭈마아 아바아
아다사 구쭈마 어 무찌마
무부야-부야.

*어 바뚜 나보 바버러가나모
부씨 나 여수*

40. 바우마 뫄부 바뚜, 마끄
보빠아 궈이 먀시, 버라

me,' and 'Where I am, you
cannot come'?"

37. On the last and greatest
day of the Feast, Jesus stood
and said in a loud voice, "If
anyone is thirsty, let him
come to me and drink.

38. Whoever believes in me,
as the Scripture has said,
streams of living water will
flow from within him."

39. By this he meant the
Spirit, whom those who
believed in him were later to
receive. Up to that time the
Spirit had not been given,
since Jesus had not yet been
glorified.

40. On hearing his words,
some of the people said,

bera kutangilyisa bateta mbu: Kubinalyi ono mundju I murebi chwende chwalyinjira!

41. E banji nabo mbu: Ono mundju I kirisito! Si e banji, beke bera kuteta mbu: Ewashe! E kalilaya nayi inganatenga kirisito?

42. Si e maanjiko mabuya-buya machwula matechire mbu kirisito mwa lubuto lwa mwami Daudi mu akashoka! N'omwa musi w'e betelehemu mu akabuchirwa, na mu Daudi abaa anachwula!

43. Bushi n'oku ba bandju kuna kuberekanamo bushi na Yesu!

44. Bauma mubo, babaa bera bahonda bamumine, si kutaba chiro na mundju usibya ola wamubikaa kw'e mino.

E bakulu-kulu b'e bayuda nabo banana kw'emerera Yesu

45. Chasinda, ba balanzi bera kufuluka era mwa ba bakulu-kulu b'e bakuhanyi na ba farisayo. Bera kubusa abu balanzi mbu: chi chachwumire mutareta Yesu?

46. Nabo mbu: Aaye chwutafuraa kulola kw'ola wateta ng'oyu mulume!

47. Abu bafarisayo bera kwire

구다삐레사 바다다 뿌: 구비나레 오노 무뚜 이 무러비 쭤떠 쫘레찌라!

41. 어 바찌 나보 뿌: 오노 무뚜 이 기리시도! 시 어 바찌, 버거 버라 구더다 뿌: 어와써! 어 가삐쫘야 나에 이빠나더빠 기리시도?

42. 시 어 마아찌고 마부야-부야 마쭈쫘 마더찌러 뿌 기리시도 뫄 루부도 롸 뫄미 다우디 무 아가쏘가! 노뫄 무시 워 버더쩌허무 무 아가부찌롸, 나 무 다우디 아바아 아나쭈쫘!

43. 부씨 노구 바 바뚜 구나 구버러가나모 부씨 나 여수!

44. 바우마 무보, 바바아 버라 바호따 바무미너, 시 구다바 찌로 나 무뚜 우시뱌 오쫘 와무비가아 궈 미노.

어 바구루-구루 버 바유다 나보 바나나 궈머러라 여수

45. 쨔시따, 바 바쫘씨 버라 구푸루가 어라 뫄 바 바구루-구루 버 바구하네 나 바 파리사요. 버라 구부사 아부 바쫘씨 뿌: 찌 쨔쭈미러 무다러다 여수?

46. 나보 뿌: 아아여 쭈다푸라아 구롣롸 교롸 와더다 꼬유 무룹머!

47. 아부 바파리사요 버라

"Surely this man is the Prophet."

41. Others said, "He is the Christ." Still others asked, "How can the Christ come from Galilee?

42. Does not the Scripture say that the Christ will come from David's family and from Bethlehem, the town where David lived?"

43. Thus the people were divided because of Jesus.

44. Some wanted to seize him, but no one laid a hand on him.

45. Finally the temple guards went back to the chief priests and Pharisees, who asked them, "Why didn't you bring him in?"

46. "No one ever spoke the way this man does," the guards declared.

47. "You mean he has

bababusa mbu: Era! Nenyu, anabengeere?

귀러 바바부사 뿌: 어라! 너뉴, 아나버어어러?

deceived you also?" the Pharisees retorted.

48. Kutalyi chiro na mukulu-kulu muuma, nesi mufarisayo muuma, ola mwomvaa mbu nai amwemerere?

48. 구다레 찌로 나 무구루-구루 무우마, 너시 무파리사요 무우마, 오롸 모빠아 뿌 나이 아뭐머러러?

48. "Has any of the rulers or of the Pharisees believed in him?

49. Aaye! Bano bandju balyi anola, beke batachwula beshi kute e mwaso wa Musa achwula atechire. Bakomirwe shambyo!

49. 아아여! 바노 바뉴 바레 아노롸, 버거 바다쭈롸 버씨 구더 어 뫄소 와 무사 아쭈롸 아더찌러. 바고미뤄 쌰뾰!

49. No! But this mob that knows nothing of the law--there is a curse on them."

50. Nikotemu, ola mulume waikiraaYesu nai abaa alyi mwabu bafarisayo. Era kubusa balyikabo mbu.

50. 니고더무, 오롸 무루머 와이기라아여수 나이 아바아 아레 뫄부 바파리사요. 어라 구부사 바레가보 뿌.

50. Nicodemus, who had gone to Jesus earlier and who was one of their own number, asked,

51. Ewashe! E mwaso wechwu achwula emerere mbu chwundaa chwachinjibusa e mundju chwutasa na kumumvilyisa, chwumenye cha ailyire?

51. 어와써! 어 뫄소 워쭈 아쭈롸 어머러러 뿌 쭈따아 쫘찌지부사 어 무뉴 쭈다사 나 구무삐레사, 쭈머녀 짜 아이레러?

51. "Does our law condemn anyone without first hearing him to find out what he is doing?"

52. Nabo mbu: nao achwula mwesha kalilaya? Uyaa kusoma e maanjiko mabuya-buya tanga chasinda ungalola kwa e kalilaya itafuraa kutenga murebi!

52. 나보 뿌: 나오 아쭈롸 뭐싸 가리라야? 우야아 구소마 어 마아찌고 마부야-부야 다까 짜시따 우까로롸 과 어 가리라야 이다푸라아 구더까 무러비!

52. They replied, "Are you from Galilee, too? Look into it, and you will find that a prophet does not come out of Galilee."

53. Chasinjire, chira mundju era kufuluka kwa wai.

53. 짜시찌러, 찌라 무뉴 어라 구푸루가 과 와이.

53. Then each went to his own home.

Yoana Chikono 8

Yesu ababalyira e chihungukasi

요아나 찌고노 8

여수 아바바레띱 어 찌후우—습

John Chapter 8[NIV]

1. Era nyuma s'ebi, Yesu era kuya kwa ndjulungu y'e

1. 어라 뉴마 서비, 여수 어라 구야 과 뉴루우 여

1. But Jesus went to the Mount of Olives.

miseituni.	미서이두니.	
2. Abere mwei mishangya lumbulyi-mbulyi, era kuya kanji mwa luhu lwa Ongo. E bandju boshi ba babaa balyi aola, mango babaa bera bachifundaa ofu nai, era kwekala na atangilyisa abakangilyisa.	2. 아버러 뭐이 미싸쨔 루뿌뤠-뿌뤠, 어라 구야 가찌 뫄 루후 롸 오꼬. 어 바뉴 보씨 바 바바아 바뤠 아오롸, 마꼬 바바아 버라 바찌푸따아 오푸 나이, 어라 궈가롸 나 아다찌뤠사 아바가찌뤠사.	2. At dawn he appeared again in the temple courts, where all the people gathered around him, and he sat down to teach them.
3. Mw'olu, e bakangilyisi b'e mwaso, n'e bafarisayo bera kureta mukasi muuma ola wasimbwaa mwa lusingi bera kumwemanza era muhondo s'e bandju boshi	3. 모루, 어 바가찌뤠시 버 뫄소, 너 바파리사요 버라 구러다 무가시 무우마 오롸 와시뽜아 뫄 루시찌 버라 구뭐마싸 어라 무호또 서 바뉴 보씨	3. The teachers of the law and the Pharisees brought in a woman caught in adultery. They made her stand before the group
4. Na ababura Yesu mbu: Mukangilyisi! Ono mukasi asimbirwe mwa lusingi.	4. 나 아바부라 여수 뿌: 무가찌뤠시! 오노 무가시 아시삐뤄 뫄 루시찌.	4. and said to Jesus, "Teacher, this woman was caught in the act of adultery.
5. Mwa mwaso wechwu, Musa achwuburaa mbu e bakasi ba balyi ng'abano, chwundaa chwetabo mwa kubahutanga e makoi. Rero nao, kute ku watechire?	5. 뫄 뫄소 워쭈, 무사 아쭈부라아 뿌 어 바가시 바 바뤠 우아바노, 쭌따아 쮜다보 뫄 구바후다까 어 마고이. 러로 나오, 구더 구 와더찌러?	5. In the Law Moses commanded us to stone such women. Now what do you say?"
6. Baburaa Yesu bacha, bushi babaa bahonda bamuteye mwa si babone e chinwa cha bangemangirako mwa kumusitaka. Si Yesu era kwinamilyira, na atangilyisa aanjika n'e mutoke kwa chitaka.	6. 바부라아 여수 바짜, 부씨 바바아 바호따 바무더여 뫄 시 바보너 어 찌놔 짜 바꺼마찌라고 뫄 구무시다가. 시 여수 어라 귀나미뤠라, 나 아다찌뤠사 아아찌가 너 무도거 과 찌다가.	6. They were using this question as a trap, in order to have a basis for accusing him. But Jesus bent down and started to write on the ground with his finger.
7. Na mango baendekeraa bamubusa, era kwenamuka na ababura mbu: Ola utafuraa	7. 나 마꼬 바어떠거라아 바무부사, 어라 궈나무가 나 아바부라 뿌: 오롸	7. When they kept on questioning him, he straightened up and said to

kuira bibi mu mwabo, I ubaa mubere kuhuta ono mukasi ekoi.

8. Kanji era kwinamilyira na aendekera aanjika kwa chitaka.

9. Abu bandju bomvire bacha, berakutenga aola muuma-muuma, kutengera kwa bangumwa tanga kuikira kwa banji bandju. Ola mukasi yeine oshao iwanashibaa aola, emenze era muhondo sa Yesu.

10. Yesu kanji era kwenamuka, na amubusa mbu: E mama! Abu bera kukusitaka, ngai u balyi? Kutalyi chiro na muuma mubo ola wakuchinjibusise?

11. Nai mbu: nanga enawechwu! Kutalyi! Yesu kukwera kumubura mbu: Anabe nanyi, ndakuchinjibusa. Rero, wera ungaenda, si kutengera lwarero, si utachiira bibi kanji.

Yesu iwarechire e bulangare mwa butala

12. Yesu era kubura e bandu kanji mbu: Nyono nyi bulangare bw'e butala. Ola unganyikulyikira, angabona e bulangare bwa bwende bwareta e kalamo. Mwa bacha, atakachiende mwa

우다푸라아 구이라 비비 무 뫄보, 이 우바아 무버러 구후다 오노 무가시 어고이.

8. 가찌 어라 귀나미쪠라 나 아어떠거라 아안찌가 과 찌다가.

9. 아부 바뉴 보쎄러 바짜, 버라구더꽈 아오꽈 무우마-무우마, 구더꺼라 과 바꾸꽈 다꽈 구이기라 과 바찌 바뉴. 오꽈 무가시 여이너 오싸오 이와나씨바아 아오꽈, 어머써 어라 무호또 사 여수.

10. 여수 가찌 어라 궈나무가, 나 아무부사 뿌: 어 마마! 아부 버라 구구시다가, 까이 우 바레? 구다례 찌로 나 무우마 무보 오꽈 와구찌찌이라 비비 와구찌찌부시서?

11. 나이 뿌: 나꽈 어나워쭈! 구다례! 여수 구궈라 구무부라 뿌: 아나버 나녜, 따구찌찌부사. 러로, 워라 우꽈어따, 시 구더꺼라 꽈러로, 시 우다찌이라 비비 가찌.

여수 이와러찌러 어 부꽈꽈랸 꽈 부다꽈

12. 여수 어라 구부라 어 바뉴 가찌 뿌: 뇨노 네 부꽈꺼러 붜 부다꽈. 오꽈 우꽈네구레기라, 아꽈보나 어 부꽈꺼러 봐 붜떠 버러다 어 가꽈모. 꽈 바짜, 아다가쩌떠 꽈 무시먀 찌로 나 히짜.

them, "If any one of you is without sin, let him be the first to throw a stone at her."

8. Again he stooped down and wrote on the ground.

9. At this, those who heard began to go away one at a time, the older ones first, until only Jesus was left, with the woman still standing there.

10. Jesus straightened up and asked her, "Woman, where are they? Has no one condemned you?"

11. "No one, sir," she said. "Then neither do I condemn you," Jesus declared. "Go now and leave your life of sin."

12. When Jesus spoke again to the people, he said, "I am the light of the world. Whoever follows me will never walk in darkness, but will have the light of life."

musimya chiro na hicha.

13. Bushi n'oku, e bafarisayo bera kumubusa mbu: Era! kute weine uwenjire wateta era luulu sao? Rero, ebi wenjire wateta bitalyi bya kanangana.

14. Yesu na imbu: Chiro angaba mbu nenjire na teta era lulu sanyi nyeine, ebi nenjire nateta binalyi bya kanangana, bushi nyishi era natengaa, n'era naya muteshiyi.

15. Mwabo mwende mwachinjibusa e banji kukulyikana n'e mianyisa y'e bandju. Si nyono ndenjire nachinjibusa mundju usibya.

16. Si akaba nyingenjire nachinjibusa e bandju, nyeke nyingenjire nachinjibusabo mwa myasi y'e kanangana, bushi ata nyeine nyi nyichwula, si chwuchwula alauma na tata ola wanyichwumaa.

17. Anabe n'omwa mwaso wenyu, si bichwula byanjikirwe mbu akaba bandju babilyi bangateta era luulu sa mwasi murebe ola beine bachiloreraako, oyola i uchwula w'e kanangana!

13. 부씨 노구, 어 바파리사요 버라 구무부사 뿌: 어라! 구더 워이너 우워찌러 와더다 어라 루루우루 사오? 러로, 어비 워찌러 와더다 비다쪠 뱌 가나까나.

14. 여수 나 이뿌: 찌로 아까바 뿌 너찌러 나 더다 어라 루루루 사네 녀이너, 어비 너찌러 나더다 비나쪠 뱌 가나까나, 부씨 네씨 어라 나더까아, 너라 나야 무더씨에.

15. 뫄보 뭐떠 뫄찌찌부사 어 바찌 구구레가나 너 미아네사 여 바쭈. 시 뇨노 떠찌러 나찌찌부사 무뿌 우시뱌.

16. 시 아가바 네꺼찌러 나찌찌부사 어 바쭈, 녀거 네꺼찌러 나찌찌부사보 뫄 먀시 여 가나까나, 부씨 아다 녀이너 네 네쭈꽈, 시 쭈쭈꽈 아꽈우마 나 다다 오꽈 와네쭈마아.

17. 아나버 노뫄 뫄소 워뉴, 시 비쭈꽈 뱌찌기뤄 뿌 아가바 바쭈 바비쪠 바까더다 어라 루우루 사 뫄시 무러버 오꽈 버이너 바찌로러라아고, 오요꽈 이 우쭈꽈 워 가나까나!

13. The Pharisees challenged him, "Here you are, appearing as your own witness; your testimony is not valid."

14. Jesus answered, "Even if I testify on my own behalf, my testimony is valid, for I know where I came from and where I am going. But you have no idea where I come from or where I am going.

15. You judge by human standards; I pass judgment on no one.

16. But if I do judge, my decisions are right, because I am not alone. I stand with the Father, who sent me.

17. In your own Law it is written that the testimony of two men is valid.

18. Bushi n'oku nyono nenjire na teta era luulu sanyi nyeine na tata ola wanyichwumaa, nai enjire anateta era luulu sanyi.

19. Bera kwire bamubusa mbu: Oyu eho, ngai unai achwula? na imbu: Mwabo, mutanyishi tata nai mutanamwishi! bushi akaba munganyimenyire, nai munganamumenyire.

20. Ei myasi yoshi, Yesu atetaaai, mango abaa akangilyisa e bandju mwa chibua ch'e luhu lwa Ongo, ofu n'e sanduku y'e kuchwulyira mw'e michwulo. Si kutalyi chiro na mundju usibya ola wamusimbaa, bushi e chihanga chai chabaa chitasa kuika.

21. Yesu era kubura abu bandju kanji mbu: nyono kuchiendera ku nyilyimo. Na chiro angaba mbu munganyihonda, kufa ku munganashiba mwafira mwa bibi byenyu! Rero eyi nyingaya, mutangaala kuikayi.

22. Bushi n'oku, e bakulu-kulu b'e bayuda bera kwire babusanya mbu: Ono mundju atechire mbu chwutangaala kuika era angaya, elyi

18. 부씨 노구 뇨노 너찌러 나 더다 어라 루우루루 사니 뇨이네어너 나 다다 오롸 와네쭈마아, 나이 어찌러 아나더다 어라 루우루루 사니.

19. 버라 귀러 바무부사 뿌: 오유 어호, 와이 우나이 아쭈롸? 나 이뿌: 마보, 무다네씨 다다 나이 무다나뮈너! 부씨 아가바 무까네머네러, 나이 무까나무머네러.

20. 어이 먀시 요씨, 여수 아더다아아이, 마꼬 아바아 아가삐레사 어 바쭈 마 찌부아 쩌 루후 롸 오꼬, 오푸 너 사뚜구 여 구쭈레라 뮈 미쭈롣. 시 구다레 찌로 나 무뚜 우시뱌 오롸 와무시빠아, 부씨 어 찌하꺄 짜이 짜바아 찌다사 구이가.

21. 여수 어라 구부라 아부 바쭈 가찌 뿌: 뇨노 구쩌떠라 구 네레모. 나 찌로 아까바 뿌 무까네호따, 구파 구 무까나씨바 마피라 마 비비 벼뉴! 러로 어에 네까야, 무다꺄아롸 구이가에.

22. 부씨 노구, 어 바구루-구루 버 바유다 버라 귀러 바부사냐 뿌: 오노 무뚜 아더찌러 뿌 쭈다꺄아롸 구이가 어라 아꺄야, 어레

18. I am one who testifies for myself; my other witness is the Father, who sent me."

19. Then they asked him, "Where is your father?" "You do not know me or my Father," Jesus replied. "If you knew me, you would know my Father also."

20. He spoke these words while teaching in the temple area near the place where the offerings were put. Yet no one seized him, because his time had not yet come.

21. Once more Jesus said to them, "I am going away, and you will look for me, and you will die in your sin. Where I go, you cannot come."

22. This made the Jews ask, "Will he kill himself? Is that why he says, 'Where I go, you cannot come'?"

kuchikonola ku angaya
kuchikonola?

구찌고노롸 구 아까야
구찌고노롸?

23. Yesu na imbu: Mwabo munalyi bo muno butala, si nyono, ndachiberere w'omuno butala, si nyichiberere w'okwa nguba.

23. 여수 나 이뿌: 롸보 무나레 보 무노 부다롸, 시 뇨노, 따찌버러러 오무노 부다롸, 시 네찌버러러 오과 우바.

23. But he continued, "You are from below; I am from above. You are of this world; I am not of this world.

24. N'echi chi chachwumaa nababura kwa mungashiba mwafira mwabibi byenyu. Kubinalyi, mw'ebi bibi byenyu mu munganafira akaba mutemerere mwa michima yenyu kwa nyono nyichwulao.

24. 너찌 찌 짜쭈마아 나바부라 과 무까씨바 롸피라 롸비비 벼뉴. 구비나레, 뭐비 비비 벼뉴 무 무까나피라 아가바 무더머러러 롸 미찌마 여뉴 과 뇨노 네쭈롸오.

24. I told you that you would die in your sins; if you do not believe that I am the one I claim to be, you will indeed die in your sins."

25. Chasinda bera kumubusa mbu: Woyo unde kasi? Yesu na imbu Nyono nyi n'oyu i n'oyu, ola nababura kutengera mira.

25. 짜시따 버라 구무부사 뿌: 오요 우떠 가시? 여수 나 이뿌 뇨노 네 노유 이 노유, 오롸 나바부라 구더떠라 미라.

25. "Who are you?" they asked. "Just what I have been claiming all along," Jesus replied.

26. Nyete myasi inene ya kubabura, kanji ya kubachinjibusa. Si ei myasi nenjire nababura inalyi era nomvaa era mw'ola wanyichwumaa. N'oyu wanyichwumaa, achwula wa kanangana.

26. 녀더 먀시 이너너 야 구바부라, 가찌 야 구바찌찌부사. 시 어이 먀시 너찌러 나바부라 이나레 어라 노빠아 어라 모롸 와네쭈마아. 노유 와네쭈마아, 아쭈롸 와 가나까나.

26. "I have much to say in judgment of you. But he who sent me is reliable, and what I have heard from him I tell the world."

27. Abu bandju chiro bakamenya kwa Yesu, era luulu s'eshe yi abaa abahambalyira.

27. 아부 바쭈 찌로 바가머냐 과 여수, 어라 루우루 서써 에 아바아 아바하빠레라.

27. They did not understand that he was telling them about his Father.

28. Bushi n'oku, Yesu era kubabura mbu: Mango munganyerusa kwa musaba

28. 부씨 노구, 여수 어라 구바부라 뿌: 마꼬 무까녀루사 과 무사바 네

28. So Jesus said, "When you have lifted up the Son of Man, then you will know

nyi mwana w'e mundju mu mango mungere mwamenyerera kanangana kwa kasi nyono nyi n'oyu kanji munganamenyerera kwa kutalyi kandju kasibya ka nenjire naira kwa kuhonda kwanyi nyeine. Si e myesi era nenjire nateta inalyi era tata anyikangilyisaa.

29. Ola wanyichwumaa atanyirekerere chiro na hicha, si anachwula alauma nanyi. Bushi e suku soshi, e kuhonda kwai ku nende nanaira.

30. Abere Yesu anachilyi ateta ei myasi, bandju banene kuna kumwemerera mwa michima yabo.

Yesu aenda e bwaka n'e bayuda

31. Chasinda, abu bayuda ba bemereraa, Yesu era kwire aburabo mbu: Ene myasi nenjire nabakangilyisa, mukende mwachwundai, elyi munalyi banafunzi banyi kanangana.

32. Mwa bacha, mungende mwamenya e myasi y'e kanangana. Nei myasi y'e kanangana i ingabakula mwa bucha.

33. Nabo mbu: chwubano

마나 워 무뚜 무 마꼬 무꺼러 먀머녀러라 가나꺄나 과 가시 뇨노 내 노유 가찌 무꺄나머녀러라 과 구다레 가꾸 가시뱌 가 너찌러 나이라 과 구호따 과네 녀이너. 시 어 며시 어라 너찌러 나더다 이나레 어라 다다 아네가삐쩨사아.

29. 오롸 와니쮸마아 아다니러거러러 찌로 나 히짜, 시 아나쮸롸 아롸우마 나니. 부씨 어 수구 소씨, 어 구호따 과이 구 너꺼 나나이라.

30. 아버러 여수 아나찌레 아더다 어이 먀시, 바꾸 바너너 구나 구뭐머러라 롸 미찌마 야보.

여수 아어따 어 봐가 너 바유다

31. 짜시따, 아부 바유다 바 버머러라아, 여수 어라 귀러 아부라보 뿌: 어너 먀시 너찌러 나바가삐쩨사, 무거꺼 먀쮸따이, 어레 무나레 바나푸씨 바네 가나꺄나.

32. 롸 바짜, 무꺼더 롸머냐 어 먀시 여 가나꺄나. 너이 먀시 여 가나꺄나 이 이꺄바구롸 롸 부짜.

33. 나보 뿌: 쮸바노 쮸쮸롸

---

that I am the one I claim to be and that I do nothing on my own but speak just what the Father has taught me.

29. The one who sent me is with me; he has not left me alone, for I always do what pleases him."

30. Even as he spoke, many put their faith in him.

31. To the Jews who had believed him, Jesus said, "If you hold to my teaching, you are really my disciples.

32. Then you will know the truth, and the truth will set you free."

33. They answered him, "We

chwuchwula bomwa lubuto lwa Aburahamu, kanji chwutafuraa kuba chwuungu chwa mundju usibya. Rero kute wenjire wateta mbu chwungatenga mwa bucha?

34. Nai mbu: Kubinalyi, nababura kwa chira mundju ola wende waira e bibi, i unachwula kaungu k'ebi bibi.

35. Mumenyaa kwa e kaungu katabera mwa nyumba ya enawabo e suku soshi. Si e mwana w'omwa nyumba yeke ende Aberamo e suku soshi.

36. Bushi n'oku, akaba nyi mwana nyingabakula mwa bucha, elyi mwanatengiremo kanangana.

37. Nyineshi kubuya kwa muchwula bomwa lubuto lwa Aburahamu. Si chiro bacha, mwahonda munyite bushi mwananyire e myasi era nenjire nakangilyisa.

38. Nyono bya nalolaako mango nabaa nyilyi na tata, bi nenjire nababura. Nenyu kunoku bya mwomvaa era mw'eho wenyu, bi nenyu mwenjire mwanaira.

39. Abu bayuda bera kuteta mbu: tata i Aburahamu. Yesu na imbu: Akaba mungabere benyi Aburahamu, mungenjire

---

보똬 루부도 똬 아부라하무, 가찌 쭈다푸라아 구바 쭈우꾸 똬 무뚜 우시뱌. 러로 구더 워찌러 와더다 뿌 쭈까더까 똬 부짜?

34. 나이 뿌: 구비나례, 나바부라 과 찌라 무뚜 오라 워떠 와이라 어 비비, 이 우나쭈라 가우꾸 거비 비비.

35. 무머냐아 과 어 가우꾸 가다버라 똬 뉴빠 야 어나와보 어 수구 소씨. 시 어 모나 오똬 뉴빠 여거 어너 아버라모 어 수구 소씨.

36. 부씨 노구, 아가바 니 모나 니까바구똬 똬 부짜, 어레 모나더띠러모 가나까나.

37. 니너씨 구부야 과 무쭈똬 보똬 루부도 똬 아부라하무. 시 찌로 바짜, 똬호따 무니더 부씨 모나니러 어 먀시 어라 너찌러 나가띠레사.

38. 뇨노 뱌 나로똬아고 마꼬 나바아 니레 나 다다, 비 너찌러 나바부라. 너뉴 구노구 뱌 모빠아 어라 뭐호 워뉴, 비 너뉴 뭐찌러 모나이라.

39. 아부 바유다 버라 구더다 뿌: 다다 이 아부라하무. 여수 나 이뿌: 아가바 무까버러 버니 아부라하무, 무꺼찌러

---

are Abraham's descendants and have never been slaves of anyone. How can you say that we shall be set free?"

34. Jesus replied, "I tell you the truth, everyone who sins is a slave to sin.

35. Now a slave has no permanent place in the family, but a son belongs to it forever.

36. So if the Son sets you free, you will be free indeed.

37. I know you are Abraham's descendants. Yet you are ready to kill me, because you have no room for my word.

38. I am telling you what I have seen in the Father's presence, and you do what you have heard from your father."

39. "Abraham is our father," they answered. "If you were Abraham's children," said Jesus, "then you would do

mwaira bya nai endee aira.

40. Si lwarero mwahonda kunyita, n'oku nababilyire mira e myasi y'e kanangana era nomvaa era mwa Ongo. Si Aburahamu yeke atendee aira bacha!

41. Mwabo, bya mwende mwa ira, binalyi by'eho wenyu nai ende anaira. Nabo mbu: chwubano, chwutachwula bana bomwa mbuwa. Tata muuma ichwunachwusa oshao. N'oyu tata i Ongo!

42. Yesu nai mbu: Akaba Ongo angabere eho wenyu, munganyisimire; bushi era mwai yi natengaa kwa kuika anola. Kanji ndabahire kwa buashi bwanyi nyeine, si iwanyichwumire.

43. Na cha chenjire chachwuma mutemerera kubuya e myasi era nenjire nababura, analyi bushi mutahonda kuimenyerera oshao.

44. Mwabo, eho wenyu i wamusimu. Rero nenyu munahonjire kunde mwaira ng'okwa achwula asimire. Kutengera mira, oyu eho wenyu anachwula mwiichi. Kanji ataira myasi ya

마이라 뱌 나이 어떠어 아이라.

40. 시 꽈러로 먀호따 구니다, 노구 나바비꼐러 미라 어 먀시 여 가나꽈나 어라 노빠아 어라 먀 오꼬. 시 아부라하무 여거 어더떠어 아이라 바짜!

41. 먀보, 뱌 뭐떠 먀 이라, 비나꼐 벼호 워뉴 나이 어떠 아나이라. 나보 뿌: 쭈바노, 쭈다쭈꽈 바나 보뫄 뿌와. 다다 무우마 이쭈나쭈사 오싸오. 노유 다다 이 오꼬!

42. 여수 나이 뿌: 아가바 오꼬 아꽈버러 어호 워뉴, 무꽈네시미러, 부씨 어라 먀이 에 나더꽈아 과 구이가 아노꽈. 가찌 따바히러 과 부아씨 봐니 녀이너, 시 이와네쭈미러.

43. 나 짜 쩌띠러 짜쭈마 무더머러라 구부야 어 먀시 어라 너띠러 나바부라, 아나꼐 부씨 무다호따 구이머녀러라 오싸오.

44. 먀보, 어호 워뉴 이 와무시무. 러로 너뉴 무나호띠러 구떠 먀이라 꼬과 아쭈꽈 아시미러. 구더꽈라 미라, 오유 어호 워뉴 아나쭈꽈 뮈이찌. 가찌 아다이라 먀시 야 가나꽈나,

the things Abraham did.

40. As it is, you are determined to kill me, a man who has told you the truth that I heard from God. Abraham did not do such things.

41. You are doing the things your own father does." "We are not illegitimate children," they protested. "The only Father we have is God himself."

42. Jesus said to them, "If God were your Father, you would love me, for I came from God and now am here. I have not come on my own; but he sent me.

43. Why is my language not clear to you? Because you are unable to hear what I say.

44. You belong to your father, the devil, and you want to carry out your father's desire. He was a murderer from the beginning, not holding to the truth, for there is no

kanangana, bushi kutalyi mwasi usibya wa kanangana ola uchwula mwa muchima wai. Na mango ende aba afula e bisha, e mitetere yai inachwula imuhuhire, bushi achwula mufusi wa bisha, kanji anaba eshe w'e bafusi b'e bisha boshi.

45. Si nyono oku nende nateta e myasi y'e kanangana, mutanganyemerera mwa michima yenyu!

46. Nde mu mwabo ola ungalosa e bibi bya nenjire naira? na akaba myasi ya kanangana i nenjire nateta chi chachwuma mutanyemerera?

47. Ola ulyi mundju wa Ongo, ende omvilyisa n'e myasi ya Ongo. Rero mwabo mutanyumvilyisa, bushi mutachwula bandju bai.

48. Abu bayuda bera kubura Yesu mbu: Kasi mango chwatetaa mbu ulyi musamariya, n'okwa wasimbirwe na bihwasi, chwabaa chwunasinganyire!

49. Yesu na imbu: Nyono ndasimbirwe na bihwasi, si nenjire nachwunda tata! si chiro bacha, kunyikena ku mwenjire mwananyikena.

50. Ndenjire nahonda e ngulu

부씨 구다뗴 먀시 우시뱌 와 가나빠나 오라 우쭈롸 먀 무찌마 와이. 나 마꼬 어더 아바 아푸롸 어 비싸, 어 미더더러 야이 이나쭈롸 이무후히러, 부씨 아쭈롸 무푸시 와 비싸, 가띠 아나바 어써 워 바푸시 버 비싸 보씨.

45. 시 뇨노 오구 너떠 나더다 어 먀시 여 가나빠나, 무다빠녀머러라 먀 미찌마 여뉴!

46. 떠 무 먀보 오롸 우빠로사 어 비비 뱌 너찌러 나이라? 나 아가바 먀시 야 가나빠나 이 너찌러 나더다 찌 짜쭈마 무다녀머러라?

47. 오롸 우레 무뿌 와 오꼬, 어떠 오삐레사 너 먀시 야 오꼬. 러로 먀보 무다뉴삐례사, 부씨 무다쭈롸 바뚜 바이.

48. 아부 바우다 버라 구부라 여수 뿌: 가시 마꼬 쫘더다아 뿌 우레 무사마리야, 노과 와시삐뤄 나 비화시, 쫘바아 쭈나시빠네러!

49. 여수 나 이뿌: 뇨노 따시삐뤄 나 비화시, 시 너찌러 나쭈따 다다! 시 찌로 바짜, 구네거나 구 뭐찌러 먀나네거나.

50. 떠찌러 나호따 어 꾸루

truth in him. When he lies, he speaks his native language, for he is a liar and the father of lies.

45. Yet because I tell the truth, you do not believe me!

46. Can any of you prove me guilty of sin? If I am telling the truth, why don't you believe me?

47. He who belongs to God hears what God says. The reason you do not hear is that you do not belong to God."

48. The Jews answered him, "Aren't we right in saying that you are a Samaritan and demon-possessed?"

49. "I am not possessed by a demon," said Jesus, "but I honor my Father and you dishonor me.

50. I am not seeking glory

yanyi nyeine, si kulyi ola wenjire wanyihonderai. N'oyu, iwete e buashi bw'e kuchinjibusa.

51. Kubinalyi, nababura kwa akaba e mundju angaendekera kunde achwunda e chinwa chanyi, atakafe chiro na hicha.

52. Abu bayuda kukwera kumubura mbu: Rero, chwelyire chwanachilorera kanangana kwa usimbirwe na bihwasi! si Aburahamu afire mira, n'e barebi, nabo si bafire mira. Si weke, wenjire wateta mbu ola ungende wachwunda e myasi yao, yeke atakafe chiro na hicha!

53. Woyo elyi u wera mukulu-kulu kurenza oyu hokulu wechwu Aburahamu? Si afire mira! Anabe n'e barebi nabo, si bafire mira! Rero woyo, wenjire wachitola nga nde?

54. Yesu na imbu: Akaba nyingachitonga nyeine, oku kuchitonga kwanyi, kutete mufa. Si tata iwenjire wanyitonga, na i nenyu mwenjire mwa teta mbu i Ongo wenyu.

55. Mwabo mutamwishi, si nyeke nyi nyimwishi! Rero,

야네 녀이너, 시 구례 오롸 워찌러 와네호뗘라이. 노유, 이워더 어 부아씨 뷔 구찌찌부사.

51. 구비나레, 나바부라 과 아가바 어 무뚜 아빠어떠거라 구떠 아쭈따 어 찌놔 짜녜, 아다가퍼 찌로 나 히짜.

52. 아부 바유다 구궈라 구무부라 뿌: 레로, 쮜례러 쫘나찌뢰러라 가나빠나 과 우시삐뤄 나 비화시! 시 아부라하무 아피러 미라, 너 바러비, 나보 시 바피러 미라. 시 워거, 워찌러 와더다 뿌 오롸 우어떠 와쭈따 어 먀시 야오, 여거 아다가퍼 찌로 나 히짜!

53. 오요 어례 우 워라 무구룩-구룩 구러싸 오유 호구룩 워쭈 아부라하무? 시 아피러 미라! 아나버 너 바러비 나보, 시 바피러 미라! 러로 오요, 워찌러 와찌도롸 빠 떠?

54. 여수 나 이뿌: 아가바 네빠찌도롸 녀이너, 오구 구찌도롸 과네, 구더더 무파. 시 다다 이워찌러 와네도롸, 나 이 너뉴 뭐찌러 롸 더다 뿌 이 오꼬 워뉴.

55. 뫄보 무다뮈씨, 시 녀거 네 네뮈씨! 러로, 아가바

for myself; but there is one who seeks it, and he is the judge.

51. I tell you the truth, if anyone keeps my word, he will never see death."

52. At this the Jews exclaimed, "Now we know that you are demon-possessed! Abraham died and so did the prophets, yet you say that if anyone keeps your word, he will never taste death.

53. Are you greater than our father Abraham? He died, and so did the prophets. Who do you think you are?"

54. Jesus replied, "If I glorify myself, my glory means nothing. My Father, whom you claim as your God, is the one who glorifies me.

55. Though you do not know him, I know him. If I

akaba nyingatechire mbu ndamwishi, nanyi nyingabere mufusi wa bisha kuuma nenyu. Si nyono nyimwishi, kanji nende nachwunda n'e myasi yai.

네ᄢᅡ더찌러 뿌 따뮈씨, 나네 네ᄢᅡ버러 무푸시 와 비싸 구우마 너뉴. 시 뇨노 네뮈씨, 가ᄽᅵ 너떠 나쭈따 너 먀시 야이.

said I did not, I would be a liar like you, but I do know him and keep his word.

56. Oyu eho wenyu Aburahamu, endee alangalyira na lumoo lunene alole kwa lusuku lw'e kubaha kwanyi. Na mango alulolaako, era kumowa busese.

56. 오유 어호 워뉴 아부라하무, 어떠어 아ᄙᅡᄢᅡᄙᅦ라 나 ᄙᅮ모오 ᄙᅮ너너 아ᄙᅩᄙᅥ 과 ᄙᅮ수구 ᄙᅯ 구바하 과네. 나 마ᅌᅩ 아ᄙᅮᄙᅩᄙᅡ아고, 어라 구모와 부서서.

56. Your father Abraham rejoiced at the thought of seeing my day; he saw it and was glad."

57. Chasinda, ba bayuda bera kwire bamubusa mbu: Era! Mangochi walolaa ku Aburahamu, n'oku utasa kuata chiro na myaka matano?

57. 짜시따, 바 바유다 버라 귀러 바무부사 뿌: 어라! 마ᅌᅩ찌 와ᄙᅩᄙᅡ아 구 아부라하무, 노구 우다사 구아다 찌로 나 먀가 마다노?

57. "You are not yet fifty years old," the Jews said to him, "and you have seen Abraham!"

58. Yesu nai mbu: Kubinalyi, nababura kwa mango Aburahamu abaa atasa kubuchibwa, nyono nyinachwulao.

58. 여수 나이 뿌: 구비나ᄙᅦ, 나바부라 과 마ᅌᅩ 아부라하무 아바아 아다사 구부찌봐, 뇨노 네나쭈ᄙᅡ오.

58. "I tell you the truth," Jesus answered, "before Abraham was born, I am!"

59. Bushi n'oku, bera kutolanga e makoi bamuhutangemo, si Yesu era kuchibisha na atenga mwa chibua ch'e luhu lwa Ongo.

59. 부씨 노구, 버라 구도ᄙᅡᄢᅡ 어 마고이 바무후다ᄢᅥ모, 시 여수 어라 구찌비싸 나 아더ᄢᅡ 모ᅡ 찌부아 쩌 ᄙᅮ후 ᄙᅪ 오ᅌᅩ.

59. At this, they picked up stones to stone him, but Jesus hid himself, slipping away from the temple grounds.

Yoana Chikono 9

요아나 찌고노 9

John Chapter 9[NIV]

Yesu alamya e muuta

여수 아ᄙᅡ먜 어 무우다

1. Mango Yesu abaa arenga, era kulola ku mundju muuma ola wabuchwaa alyi muuta.

1. 마ᅌᅩ 여수 아바아 아러ᄢᅡ, 어라 구ᄙᅩᄙᅡ 구 무ᅜᅮ 무우마 오ᄙᅡ 와부쫘아 아ᄙᅦ 무우다.

1. As he went along, he saw a man blind from birth.

2. E banafunzi bai bera kumu busa mbu: Mukangilyisi! Ndei wairaa e bibi bya byachwumaa ono mundju abuchwa alyi muuta? Elyi yeine, nesi abasere bai?

3. Yesu nai mbu: Ono mundju abuchwaa alyi muuta, ata bushi na bibi byai, nesi bya basere bai. Si abuchwaa bacha, chasiya e buashi bwa Ongo bulorekaneko mwa kalamo kai.

4. Chwemire kunde chwakola e mulyimo w'ola wanyichwumaa mango buchilyi busene, buchi e buchwufu bwahonda kwera. Na mango bungaba bwelyire, kutalyi mundju usibya ola ungachiala kukola.

5. Mango nyichilyi muno butala, nyono nyi narechire mw'e bulangare.

6. Abere Yesu era atetaa ei myasi, era kuchira-chira alashi. Amu mate, era kumahowa mwa butaka na abona bihoo bieke. Chasinda, era kwakabi kwa meho m'oyu muuta,

7. Na amubura mbu; Uyaa kwa chitomu cha silowamu, wowe era buso silowamu kukuteta mbu: Ola

2. 어 바나푼씨 바이 버라 구무 부사 뿌: 무가끼레시! 떠이 와이라아 어 비비 뱌 뱌쭈마아 오노 무뚜 아부좌 아레 무우다? 어레 여이너, 너시 아바서러 바이?

3. 여수 나이 뿌: 오노 무뚜 아부좌아 아레 무우다, 아다 부씨 나 비비 뱌이, 너시 뱌 바서러 바이. 시 아부좌아 바짜, 짜시야 어 부아씨 봐 오꼬 부로러가너고 뫄 가랴모 가이.

4. 쭤미러 구떠 좌고롸 어 무레모 올라 와네쭈마아 마꼬 부찌레 부서너, 부찌 어 부쭈푸 봐호따 궈라. 나 마꼬 부까바 뷔레러, 구다레 무뚜 우시뱌 올라 우까찌아롸 구고롸.

5. 마꼬 네찌레 무노 부다롸, 뇨노 네 나러찌러 뭐 부롸까러.

6. 아버러 여수 어라 아더다아 어이 먀시, 어라 구찌라-찌라 아꽈씨. 아무 마더, 어라 구마호와 뫄 부다가 나 아보나 비호오 비어거. 짜시따, 어라 과가비 과 머호 모유 무우다,

7. 나 아무부라 뿌; 우야아 과 찌도무 짜 시로와무, 오워 어라 부소 시로와무 구구더다 뿌: 오롸 와쭈미뤄. 오유

2. His disciples asked him, "Rabbi, who sinned, this man or his parents, that he was born blind?"

3. "Neither this man nor his parents sinned," said Jesus, "but this happened so that the work of God might be displayed in his life.

4. As long as it is day, we must do the work of him who sent me. Night is coming, when no one can work.

5. While I am in the world, I am the light of the world."

6. Having said this, he spit on the ground, made some mud with the saliva, and put it on the man's eyes.

7. "Go," he told him, "wash in the Pool of Siloam" (this word means Sent). So the man went and washed, and

wachwumirwe. Oyu muuta, era kunaya kwowa, na afuluka era alola. / 무우다, 어라 구나야 고와, 나 아푸루가 어라 아로롸. / came home seeing.

8. E balungu bai alauma, n'aba bendee balola kwa emeresa, bera kutangilyisa bateta mbu: Ewashe! Kasi ata ono mundju iwabaa wenjire waba wekese, emeresa? / 8. 어 바루꾸 바이 아롸우마, 나바 버떠어 바로롸 과 어머러사, 버라 구다삐레사 바더다 뿌: 어와써! 가시 아다 오노 무뚜 이와바아 워찌러 와바 워거서, 어머러사? / 8. His neighbors and those who had formerly seen him begging asked, "Isn't this the same man who used to sit and beg?"

9. Bauma mbu: Nechi! inoyu! N'e banji mbu: Nanga! Ata I yoyu! Si kumuhuha ku anamuhuhire. Si oyu mundju, yeine era kuteta mbu: Nyono ono. / 9. 바우마 뿌: 너찌! 이노유! 너 바찌 뿌: 나까! 아다 이 요유! 시 구무후하 구 아나무후히러. 시 오유 무뚜, 여이너 어라 구더다 뿌: 뇨노 오노. / 9. Some claimed that he was. Others said, "No, he only looks like him." But he himself insisted, "I am the man."

10. Bushi n'oku, bera kumubusa mbu: Era! kute e meho mao masibukalaa kasi? / 10. 부씨 노구, 버라 구무부사 뿌: 어라! 구더 어 머호 마오 마시부가롸아 가시? / 10. "How then were your eyes opened?" they demanded.

11. Nai mbu: Ola mulume mbu I Yesu iwahowaa bihoo bieke, na anyakabi kwa meho. Chasinda era kunyibura mbu nyiyaa kwa chitomu cha silowamu nyowe era buso. Nera kunayako, na nowa. Abere nera nowaa, unao-unao nera kutangilyisa na lola. / 11. 나이 뿌: 오롸 무루머 뿌 이 여수 이와호와아 비호오 비어거, 나 아냐가비 과 머호. 짜시따 어라 구내부라 뿌 네야아 과 찌도무 짜 시로와무 뇨워 어라 부소. 너라 구나야고, 나 노와. 아버러 너라 노와아, 우나오-우나오 너라 구다삐레사 나 로롸. / 11. He replied, "The man they call Jesus made some mud and put it on my eyes. He told me to go to Siloam and wash. So I went and washed, and then I could see."

12. Bera kuhuba kumubusa mbu: Oyu mulume, ngai u alyi? Nai mbu: Ndangamenya. / 12. 버라 구후바 구무부사 뿌: 오유 무루머, 까이 우 아레? 나이 뿌: 따까머냐. / 12. "Where is this man?" they asked him. "I don't know," he said.

E bafarisayo babusilyisa e muuta ola walamisibwaa / 어 바파리사요 바부시페뻽 어 무우다 오롸 와롸물습봅씹

13. Chasinda, abu bandju bera kwire beka oyu mundju wabaa muuta era mw'e bafarisayo.

14. N'e lusuku Yesu ahowaa e bihoo n'e kusibula e meho m'oyu mundju, lwabaa lusuku lwa sabato.

1.5 Bushi n'oku, e bafarisayo nabo bera kumubusa mbu: Era! Kute waikiraa walola? Nai mbu: Anyakaa chwa bihoo kwa meho. Chasinda, nera kuya kwowa era buso, rero nera nalola.

16. Bauma mw'abu bafarisayo bera kuteta mbu: Oyu mundju wairaa bacha, atatengaa era mwa Ongo, bushi atenjire achwunda e lusuku lw'e sabato. Si e banji beke bera kuteta mbu: E mukosi w'e mabi kute angabona e buashi bw'e kuira bisomerano bya bulyi ng'ebi? Bushi n'oku, ba bafarisayo, kuna kuberekanamo.

17. Chasinda, abu bafarisayo bera kubusa kanji oyu wabaa muuta mbu: woyo u oyu mundju asibula e meho. Rero nau, kute watechire era lulu sai? Nai mbu: Oyola alyi murebi!

18. Si abu bakulu-kulu b'e bayuda chiro bakemerera

---

13. 짜시따, 아부 바뚜 버라 귀러 버가 오유 무뚜 와바아 무우다 어라 뭐 바파리사요.

14. 너 루수구 여수 아호와아 어 비호오 너 구시부롸 어 머호 모유 무뚜, 롸바아 루수구 롸 사바도.

15. 부씨 노구, 어 바파리사요 나보 버라 구무부사 뿌: 어라! 구더 와이기라아 와로롸? 나이 뿌: 아냐가아 좌 비호오 과 머호. 짜시따, 너라 구야 교와 어라 부소, 러로 너라 나로롸.

16. 바우마 마부 바파리사요 버라 구더다 뿌: 오유 무뚜 와이라아 바짜, 아다더롸아 어라 마 오꼬, 부씨 아덴찌러 아쭈따 어 루수구 뤄 사바도. 시 어 바찌 버거 버라 구더다 뿌: 어 무고시 워 마비 구더 아꼬보나 어 부아씨 뷔 구이라 비소머라노 뱌 부쩨 뼈비? 부씨 노구, 바 바파리사요, 구나 구버러가나모.

17. 짜시따, 아부 바파리사요 버라 구부사 가찌 오유 와바아 무우다 뿌: 오요 우 오유 무뚜 아시부롸 어 머호. 러로 나우, 구더 와더찌러 어라 루루 사이? 나이 뿌: 오요롸 아레 무러비!

18. 시 아부 바구루-구루 버 바유다 찌로 바거머러라 교유

---

13. They brought to the Pharisees the man who had been blind.

14. Now the day on which Jesus had made the mud and opened the man's eyes was a Sabbath.

15. Therefore the Pharisees also asked him how he had received his sight. "He put mud on my eyes," the man replied, "and I washed, and now I see."

16. Some of the Pharisees said, "This man is not from God, for he does not keep the Sabbath." But others asked, "How can a sinner do such miraculous signs?" So they were divided.

17. Finally they turned again to the blind man, "What have you to say about him? It was your eyes he opened." The man replied, "He is a prophet."

18. The Jews still did not believe that he had been

kw'oyu mundju abaa achwula muuta, ola wera waola. Bera kwire bemerera mango bamaalaa e basere bai,

무뚜 아바아 아쭈롸 무우다, 오롸 워라 와오롸. 버라 귀러 버머러라 마꼬 바마아롸아 어 바서러 바이,

blind and had received his sight until they sent for the man's parents.

19. N'e kubabusa mbu: elyi onola analyi e mwana wenyu, ola mwenjire mwateta mbu abuchwaa alyi muuta? na akaba kunoku, rero kute ku eraa alyi?

19. 너 구바부사 뿌: 어레 오노롸 아나레 어 뫄나 워뉴, 오롸 뭐찌러 뫄더다 뿌 아부좌아 아레 무우다? 나 아가바 구노구, 러로 구더 구 어라아 아레?

19. "Is this your son?" they asked. "Is this the one you say was born blind? How is it that now he can see?"

20. Nabo mbu: chwuneshi kanangana kwa onola analyi mwana wechwu, kanji chwuneshi kwa abuchwaa alyi muuta.

20. 나보 뿌: 쭈너씨 가나꺄나 과 오노롸 아나레 뫄나 워쭈, 가찌 쭈너씨 과 아부좌아 아레 무우다.

20. "We know he is our son," the parents answered, "and we know he was born blind.

21. Si e kusibukala e meho kwai ku chwutangamenya kute kwabaa. Anabe n'ola wamusibulaamo, nai chwutanamwishi. Rero, mumubusaa yeine ababalyikisise e myasi yai. Si era mundju asene.

21. 시 어 구시부가롸 어 머호 과이 구 쭈다꺄머냐 구더 과바아. 아나버 노롸 와무시부롸아모, 나이 쭈다나뮈씨. 러로, 무무부사아 여이너 아바바레기시서 어 먀시 야이. 시 어라 무뚜 아서너.

21. But how he can see now, or who opened his eyes, we don't know. Ask him. He is of age; he will speak for himself."

22. Abu basere bai batetaa bacha, bushi babaa bobaa abu bakulu-kulu b'e bayuda. Bushi e bakulu-kulu b'e bayuda babaa bemeresanyise mira mbu e mundju ola ungemerera kwa Yesu i kirisito bangamubika era musike mwa bushenge bwabo.

22. 아부 바서러 바이 바더다아 바쨔, 부씨 바바아 보바아 아부 바구루-구루 버 바유다. 부씨 어 바구루-구루 버 바유다 바바아 버머러사네서 미라 뿌 어 무뚜 오롸 우꺼머러라 과 여수 이 기리시도 바꺄무비가 어라 무시거 뫄 부써꺼 봐보.

22. His parents said this because they were afraid of the Jews, for already the Jews had decided that anyone who acknowledged that Jesus was the Christ would be put out of the synagogue.

23. Echera chi chachwumaa e basere b'oyu mundju bateta mbu bamubusaa yeine, bushi

23. 어쩌라 찌 쨔쭈마아 어 바서러 보유 무뚜 바더다 뿌 바무부사아 여이너, 부씨

23. That was why his parents said, "He is of age; ask him."

era mundju asene.

24. Kanji abu bafarisayo bera kuhuba kwamaala oyu wabaa muuta e bwakabilyi, na bamubura mbu: Laisaa era muhondo sa Ongo! oyu mundju chwubano chwishi kwa alyi mukosi wa mabi!

25. Nai mbu: Akaba alyi mukosi wa mabi, nyono ndeshi. Si mwasi muuma ola nyishi i yono: Nyono nabaa muuta na silwarero nera nalola.

26. Bera kumubusa kanji mbu: Chiye chi akuilyira? na kute ku akusibulaa e meho?

27. Nai mbu: Nababilyire mira, si mutahonda kumva! Elyi mwahonda nyibabure kanji ei myasi inei? ngaba nenyu mwahonda mube banafunzi bai!

28. Unao-unao, abu bafarisayo bera kutangilyisa bamukamba-kamba, na bamubura mbu: Woyo umwanafunzi w'oyu mundju, si chwubano chwuchichwulyira banafunzi ba Musa!

29. Oyu Musa yeke, chwishi kwa Ongo endee ahambala nai. Si oyu mundju, chwuteshi chiro n'era aulukilyire.

어라 무뚜 아서너.

24. 가찌 아부 바파리사요 버라 구후바 과마아롸 오유 와바아 무우다 어 봐가비레, 나 바무부라 뿌: 롸이사아 어라 무호또 사 오꼬! 오유 무뚜 쭈바노 쮜씨 과 아레 무고시 와 마비!

25. 나이 뿌: 아가바 아레 무고시 와 마비, 뇨노 떠씨. 시 마시 무우마 오롸 니씨 이 요노: 뇨노 나바아 무우다 나 시롸러로 너라 나롤롸.

26. 버라 구무부사 가찌 뿌: 찌여 찌 아구이레라? 나 구더 구 아구시부롸아 어 머호?

27. 나이 뿌: 나바비레러 미라, 시 무다호따 구빠! 어레 먀호따 네바부러 가찌 어이 먀시 이너이? 까바 너뉴 롸호따 무버 바나푸씨 바이!

28. 우나오-우나오, 아부 바파리사요 버라 구다삐레사 바무가빠-가빠, 나 바무부라 뿌: 워요 우롸나푸씨 오유 무뚜, 시 쭈바노 쭈찌쭈레라 바나푸씨 바 무사!

29. 오유 무사 여거, 쮜씨 과 오꼬 어떠어 아하빠롸 나이. 시 오유 무뚜, 쭈더씨 찌로 너라 아우루기레러.

24. A second time they summoned the man who had been blind. "Give glory to God," they said. "We know this man is a sinner."

25. He replied, "Whether he is a sinner or not, I don't know. One thing I do know. I was blind but now I see!"

26. Then they asked him, "What did he do to you? How did he open your eyes?"

27. He answered, "I have told you already and you did not listen. Why do you want to hear it again? Do you want to become his disciples, too?"

28. Then they hurled insults at him and said, "You are this fellow's disciple! We are disciples of Moses!

29. We know that God spoke to Moses, but as for this fellow, we don't even know where he comes

30. Nai mbu: E myasi yenyu ilyi ya kushishasa! Muteshi era oyu mundju aulukilyira, n'oku anyisibure e meho mira!

31. chwishi kubuya kwa Ongo atomva e memo m'e bandju b'e mabi. Si ende omva chira mundju ola uchwula umuchwunjire, n'e kuira e kuhonda kwai.

32. Kanji chwutafuraa kumva chiro n'euma mbu kulyi ola wera usibwire e meho m'ola wabuchwaa alyi muuta.

33. Oyu mundju, akaba atatengaa era mwa Ongo, atangaalyire kuira chiro na kandju kasibya.

34. Nabo mbu: Elyi nao wahonda kuchwukangilyisa? Si mwa bibi mu wabuchwaa! Unao-unao, bera kwire bamukolokanya mwa bushenge bwabo.

E buuta b'omwa muchima

35. Oyu mundju wabaa muuta, Yesu era kumva e mwasi kwa bayuda bamukolokanyise mwa bushenge bwabo. Na mango Yesu abuananaa nai, era kumubusa mbu: Wemerere e mwana w'e mundju?

---

30. 나이 뿌: 어 먀시 여뉴 이례 야 구씨싸사! 무더씨 어라 오유 무뚜 아우루기례라, 노구 아네시부러 어 머호 미라!

31. 쮜씨 구부야 과 오꼬 아도빠 어 머모 머 바뚜 버 마비. 시 어어 오빠 찌라 무뚜 오롸 우쭈롸 우무쭈찌러, 너 구이라 어 구호따 과이.

32. 가찌 쭈다푸라아 구빠 찌로 너우마 뿌 구레 오롸 워라 우시뷔러 어 머호 모롸 와부쫘아 아레 무우다.

33. 오유 무뚜, 아가바 아다더빠아 어라 롸 오꼬, 아다빠아례러 구이라 찌로 나 가뚜 가시뱌.

34. 나보 뿌: 어례 나오 와호따 구쭈가삐례사? 시 롸 비비 무 와부쫘아! 우나오-우나오, 버라 귀러 바무고론가냐 롸 부써빠 보보.

어 부우다 보롸 무찌마

35. 오유 무뚜 와바아 무우다, 여수 어라 구빠 어 마시 과 바유다 바무고론가네서 롸 부써빠 보보. 나 마꼬 여수 아부아나나아 나이, 어라 구무부사 뿌: 워머러러 어 롸나 워 무뚜?

---

from."

30. The man answered, "Now that is remarkable! You don't know where he comes from, yet he opened my eyes.

31. We know that God does not listen to sinners. He listens to the godly man who does his will.

32. Nobody has ever heard of opening the eyes of a man born blind.

33. If this man were not from God, he could do nothing."

34. To this they replied, "You were steeped in sin at birth; how dare you lecture us!" And they threw him out.

35. Jesus heard that they had thrown him out, and when he found him, he said, "Do you believe in the Son of Man?"

36. Nai mbu: Ewalyiya oyu mwana w'e mundju i nde kasi? Unyiburaa, nanyi nyimwemerere mwa muchima wanyi!

37. Yesu na imbu: wamulolyireko mira, bushi ono wahambala nao, i yoyu.

38. Ola mundju, kukwera kuteta mbu: Enawechwu n'emerere. Chasinda, era kukoma e mafi era muhondo sa Yesu, na amwera.

39. Yesu era kuteta mbu: Naikire muno butala, nyirete mw'e buchinjibusi. Kuketeta mbu, e bauta balole, n'aba bachiremba mbu balola, bahube bauta.

40. Bafarisayo bauma ba babaa balyi aola, mango bomvaa kwei myasi ya Yesu bera kumubusa mbu: Era! wahonda kuteta mbu nechwu chwunalyi bauta?

41. Nai mbu: Mungabere bauta, mutangaachire bibi. Si bushi mwenjire mwachitonga mbu mwalola, chi chachwumire mwaendekera kuba mwa bibi.

36. 나이 뿌: 어와례야 오유 마나 워 무뚜 이 떠 가시? 우네부라아, 나니 네뭐머러러 마 무찌마 와네!

37. 여수 나 이뿌: 와무로로레러고 미라, 부씨 오노 와하빠라 나오, 이 요유.

38. 오꽈 무뚜, 구궈라 구더다 뿌: 어나워쭈 너머러러. 짜시따, 어라 구고마 어 마피 어라 무호또 사 여수, 나 아뭐라.

39. 여수 어라 구더다 뿌: 나이기러 무노 부다꽈, 네러더 뭐 부찌찌부시. 구거더다 뿌, 어 바우다 바로러, 나바 바찌러빠 뿌 바로꽈, 바후버 바우다.

40. 바파리사요 바우마 바 바바아 바례 아오꽈, 마꼬 보빠아 궈이 먀시 야 여수 버라 구무부사 뿌: 어라! 와호따 구더다 뿌 너쭈 쭈나례 바우다?

41. 나이 뿌: 무까버러 바우다, 무다아아찌러 비비. 시 부씨 뭐찌러 마찌도꽈 뿌 마로꽈, 찌 짜쭈미러 마어떠거라 구바 마 비비.

36. "Who is he, sir?" the man asked. "Tell me so that I may believe in him."

37. Jesus said, "You have now seen him; in fact, he is the one speaking with you."

38. Then the man said, "Lord, I believe," and he worshiped him.

39. Jesus said, "For judgment I have come into this world, so that the blind will see and those who see will become blind."

40. Some Pharisees who were with him heard him say this and asked, "What? Are we blind too?"

41. Jesus said, "If you were blind, you would not be guilty of sin; but now that you claim you can see, your guilt remains.

Yoana Chikono 10

E muanyi w'e mungere n'e mbulyi

1. Era nyuma s'ebi Yesu era kuteta mbu: Kubinalyi, nababura kwa akaba e mundju angareka kurengera kwa lwisi lw'e chikalyi, si aneruka kw'echi chikalyi, chasinda anatoweramo, mumenyaa kw'oyu mundju alyi mwisi kanji chilyi chihumusi.

2. Si ola warengere kwa lwisi yeke, imungere w'e mbulyi.

3. Rero oyola, i mulanzi ende aboorera e lwisi. Na mango e mungere ende amaala e mbulyi sai, unao-unao sanamumenyera kwa murenge wai. iwende wamaala chira mbulyi mw'e sina lyai, kanji iwende wanaulusasi era butala.

4. Mango ende aba era aulusaa esi mbulyi soshi era butala, ende ahondorerasi, nasi sanamukulyikira bushi sera sichwula sikomere e murenge wai.

5. Sitangakulyikira ola siteshi chiro na hicha. Si sende samuhaa, bushi siteshi e murenge wai.

요아나 찌고노 10

어 무아내 워 무꺼랸 너 뿌쀀

1. 어라 뉴마 서비 여수 어라 구더다 뿌: 구비나쀀, 나바부라 과 아가바 어 무뿌 아꺼러가 구러꺼라 과 뤼시 뤄 찌가쀀, 시 아너루가 궈찌 찌가쀀, 짜시따 아나도워라모, 무머냐아 교유 무뿌 아쀀 뮈시 가찌 찌쀀 찌후무시.

2. 시 오꽈 와러꺼러 과 뤼시 여거, 이무꺼러 워 뿌쀀.

3. 러로 오요꽈, 이 무꽈씨 어꺼 아보오러라 어 뤼시. 나 마꼬 어 무꺼러 어꺼 아마아꽈 어 뿌쀀 사이, 우나오-우나오 사나무머녀라 과 무러꺼 와이. 이워꺼 와마아꽈 찌라 뿌쀀 뭐 시나 꺄이, 가찌 이워꺼 와나우뤀사시 어라 부다꽈.

4. 마꼬 어꺼 아바 어라 아우뤀사아 어시 뿌쀀 소씨 어라 부다꽈, 어꺼 아호또러라시, 나시 사나무구쀀기라 부씨 서라 시쭈꽈 시고머러 어 무러꺼 와이.

5. 시다따구쀀기라 오꽈 시더씨 찌로 나 히짜. 시 서꺼 사무하아, 부씨 시더씨 어 무러꺼 와이.

John Chapter 10[NIV]

1. "I tell you the truth, the man who does not enter the sheep pen by the gate, but climbs in by some other way, is a thief and a robber.

2. The man who enters by the gate is the shepherd of his sheep.

3. The watchman opens the gate for him, and the sheep listen to his voice. He calls his own sheep by name and leads them out.

4. When he has brought out all his own, he goes on ahead of them, and his sheep follow him because they know his voice.

5. But they will never follow a stranger; in fact, they will run away from him because they do not recognize a

		stranger's voice."
6. Yesu aishiraa e bandju oyu muanyi, Si chiro bakamenya bya abaa ahonda kuteta.	6. 여수 아이씨라아 어 바ᅜᅮ 오유 무아네, 시 찌로 바가머냐 뱌 아바아 아호ᄕᅡ 구더다.	6. Jesus used this figure of speech, but they did not understand what he was telling them.
Yesu i mungere mubuya	*여수 이 무ᅁᅥ랸 무부야*	
7. Yesu era kwire ababura kanji mbu: Kubinalyi, nababura kwa nyono nyilyi nga lwisi lw'e chikali ch'e mbulyi.	7. 여수 어라 귀러 아바부라 가ᅜᅵ 뿌: 구비나ᄙᅦ, 나바부라 과 뇨노 네ᄙᅦ ᅁᅡ ᄙᅱ시 ᄙᅯ 찌가ᄙᅵ 쩌 뿌ᄙᅦ.	7. Therefore Jesus said again, "I tell you the truth, I am the gate for the sheep.
8. Si e banji boshi ba babahaa era muhondo sanyi, beke babaa besi, kanji bihumusi. Bushi n'oku, e mbulyi sitendee somva e myasi yabo.	8. 시 어 바ᅜᅵ 보씨 바 바바하아 어라 무호ᄕᅩ 사네, 버거 바바아 버시, 가ᅜᅵ 비후무시. 부씨 노구, 어 뿌ᄙᅦ 시더ᄕᅥ어 소ᄜᅡ 어 먀시 야보.	8. All who ever came before me were thieves and robbers, but the sheep did not listen to them.
9. Kanji nyono nyi lwisi. Ola wanyirengereko, kuika ananunulyibwe, oyola, yeke alyi nga mbulyi era ingende yauluka mwa chikalyi na yabona e bwaasi, kanji yanahuba kw'engilyiramo.	9. 가ᅜᅵ 뇨노 네 ᄙᅱ시. 오ᄙᅡ 와네러ᅁᅥ러고, 구이가 아나누누ᄙᅦ붜, 오요ᄙᅡ, 여거 아ᄙᅦ ᅁᅡ 뿌ᄙᅦ 어라 이ᅁᅥᄕᅥ 야우ᄙᅮ가 뫄 찌가ᄙᅦ 나 야보나 어 봐아시, 가ᅜᅵ 야나후바 궈ᅁᅵᄙᅦ라모.	9. I am the gate; whoever enters through me will be saved. He will come in and go out, and find pasture.
10. E mwisi ende aika bushi na kwiba, na kwita, na kukumbya. Si nyono, nyeke naikire chasiya e bandju babone e kalamo. N'aku kalamo, banakaate kanangana mwa ndanda sabo.	10. 어 뮈시 어ᄕᅥ 아이가 부씨 나 귀바, 나 귀다, 나 구구ᄜᅣ. 시 뇨노, 녀거 나이기러 짜시야 어 바ᅜᅮ 바보너 어 가ᄙᅡ모. 나구 가ᄙᅡ모, 바나가아더 가나ᅁᅡ나 뫄 ᄕᅡᄕᅡ 사보.	10. The thief comes only to steal and kill and destroy; I have come that they may have life, and have it to the full.
11. Kanji nyono nyi mungere mubuya. E mungere mubuya ende emerera kwana e kalamo kai bushi n'e mbulyi sai.	11. 가ᅜᅵ 뇨노 네 무ᅁᅥ러 무부야. 어 무ᅁᅥ러 무부야 어ᄕᅥ 어머러라 과나 어 가ᄙᅡ모 가이 부씨 너 뿌ᄙᅦ 사이.	11. "I am the good shepherd. The good shepherd lays down his life for the sheep.
12. Si ola wakorera e lwembo,	12. 시 오ᄙᅡ 와고러라 어	12. The hired hand is not

oyola atachwula mungere wa kanangana. Chiro n'e mbulyi sitachwula sai na mango ende alola kwa lushi bwabwa lwabahire, unao-unao anaamika e mbulyi, na achihaira. Chasinda, walushibwabwa anatabalyirasi, na ahandabanya e buso boshi.

13. Oyu mungere ende aira bacha, bushi olu lwembo lwai lu anachwula alaireko oshao, si atachwula alaire kwa mbulyi.

14. Nyono nyi mungere mubuya. Nyichwula nyishi e mbulyi sanyi, nasi sichwula sinyishi.

15. Ng'okwa tata nai achwula ananyishi n'okwa nyinachwula nyimwishi. Kanji esi mbulyi sanyi, nanyire e kalamo kanyi mira bushi nasi.

16. Nyete na sinji mbulyi sanyi, sa sitachwula mw'e chine chikalyi. Esera nasi, binyemire nyisirete, nasi sende somva e murenge wanyi. Chasinda, soshi sibe mubuso buuma, siate na mungere muuma.

17. Tata achwula anyisimire ngachi, bushi nemerere kwana e kalamo kanyi, chasiya nyihube kukabona.

뤄뙤, 오요퐈 아다쭈퐈 무뻐러 와 가나쌰나. 찌로 너 뿌레 시다쭈퐈 사이 나 마꼬 어뻐 아루퐈 과 루씨 봐봐 롸바히러, 우나오-우나오 아나아미가 어 뿌레, 나 아찌하이라. 짜시따, 와루씨봐봐 아나다바뻬라시, 나 아하따바냐 어 부소 보씨.

13. 오유 무뻐러 어뻐 아이라 바짜, 부씨 오루 뤄뙤 롸이 루 아나쭈퐈 아롸이러고 오싸오, 시 아다쭈퐈 아롸이러 과 뿌레.

14. 뇨노 네 무뻐러 무부야. 네쭈퐈 네씨 어 뿌레 사네, 나시 시쭈퐈 시네씨.

15. 꼬과 다다 나이 아쭈퐈 아나네씨 노과 네나쭈퐈 네뮈씨. 가찌 어시 뿌레 사네, 나네러 어 가퐈모 가네 미라 부씨 나시.

16. 녀더 나 시찌 뿌레 사네, 사 시다쭈퐈 뭐 찌너 찌가레. 어서라 나시, 비녀미러 네시러러, 나시 서뻐 소빠 어 무러뻐 와네. 짜시따, 소씨 시버 무부소 부우마, 시아더 나 무뻐러 무우마.

17. 다다 아쭈퐈 아네시미러 까찌, 부씨 너머러러 과나 어 가퐈모 가네, 짜시야 네후버 구가보나.

the shepherd who owns the sheep. So when he sees the wolf coming, he abandons the sheep and runs away. Then the wolf attacks the flock and scatters it.

13. The man runs away because he is a hired hand and cares nothing for the sheep.

14. "I am the good shepherd; I know my sheep and my sheep know me--

15. just as the Father knows me and I know the Father-- and I lay down my life for the sheep.

16. I have other sheep that are not of this sheep pen. I must bring them also. They too will listen to my voice, and there shall be one flock and one shepherd.

17. The reason my Father loves me is that I lay down my life--only to take it up again.

18. Kutalyi ola ungaala kunyinyaako. Si nyeine, nanyireko kwa kuhonda kwanyi. Nyete e buashi bw'e kuchana nyichibwe, nyete n'e kuhuba kubona e kalamo. Rero, echera chi tata anyiburaa mbu nyiiraa.

19. Ei myasi ya Yesu, yera kuchwuma e bayuta baberekanamo kanji.

20. Banene mubo bera kunde bateta mbu: Aaye! ono mundju asimbirwe na chihwasi! kubinalyi, asireire! Rero! chi chachwuma muchilyi mwa muteya e machi?

21. Si e banji beke mbu: Bisha byenyu! ei myasi itangatechwa n'ola usimbirwe n'e bihwasi. Kanji e bihwasi bitangaala kulamya e meho m'e muuta!

E bayuda banana Yesu

22. Mwa musi w'e yerusalemu, e lusuku lukulu lw'e kukengera e kwemera e luhu lwa Ongo lwera kuika. Kanji olu lusuku lwaikaa mwa suku s'e mbeo.

23. Mw'ebi bihangi, Yesu abaa arenga mwa luhu lwa Ongo, mwa chisusu cha bende belyika mbu: Chisusu cha solomono.

24. Unao-unao, e bayuda bera

---

18. 구다뤠 오롸 우꺄아꽈 구네냐고. 시 녀이너, 나니러고 과 구호따 과네. 녀더 어 부아씨 붜 구짜나 니찌붜, 녀더 너 구후바 구보나 어 가꽈모. 러로, 어쩌라 찌 다다 아네부라아 뿌 네이라아.

19. 어이 먀시 야 여수, 여라 구쭈마 어 바운다 바버러가나모 가찌.

20. 바너너 무보 버라 구떠 바더다 뿌: 아아여! 오노 무뚜 아시쁘뤄 나 찌화시! 구비나뤠, 아시러이러! 러로! 찌 짜쭈마 무찌뤠 롸 무더야 어 마찌?

21. 시 어 바찌 버거 뿌: 비싸 벼뉴! 어이 먀시 이다꽈더좌 노롸 우시쁘뤄 너 비화시. 가찌 어 비화시 비다꽈아꽈 구꽈먀 어 머호 머 무우다!

어 바유다 바나나 여수

22. 롸 무시 워 여루사꿔무, 어 루루수구 루꾸루뤄 뭐 구거꺼라 어 꿔머라 어 루후 꽈 오꾾 뭐라 구이가. 가찌 오루 루수구 꽈이가아 롸 수구 서 뻐오.

23. 뭐비 비하삐, 여수 아바아 아러꽈 롸 루후 꽈 오꾾, 롸 찌수수 짜 버떠 버뤠가 뿌: 찌수수 짜 소뤂모노.

24. 우나오-우나오, 어 바유다

---

18. No one takes it from me, but I lay it down of my own accord. I have authority to lay it down and authority to take it up again. This command I received from my Father."

19. At these words the Jews were again divided.

20. Many of them said, "He is demon-possessed and raving mad. Why listen to him?"

21. But others said, "These are not the sayings of a man possessed by a demon. Can a demon open the eyes of the blind?"

22. Then came the Feast of Dedication at Jerusalem. It was winter,

23. and Jesus was in the temple area walking in Solomon's Colonnade.

24. The Jews gathered

kumusungula na batangilyisa bamubusa mbu: Ukanaendekera kunde wachwusungulyisa e bwenge kuikira mangochi? Rero akaba woyo una kirisito, uchwuburaa changanama!

25. Yesu na imbu: Nababilyire mira, si mutenjire mwanyemerera! e bisomerano bya nenjire naira kwa buashi bwa tata, nabi byenjire byanalosa nyono nyilyi nde.

26. Si mwabo mutenjire mwanyemerera mwa michima yenyu, bushi mutachwula b'omwa mbulyi sanyi.

27. E mbulyi sanyi sende somva e murenge wanyi. Nyichwula nyisishi kubuya, nasi kunyikulyikira ku sende sananyikulyikira.

28. Nyono nyi nende neresasi e kalamo k'e suku n'e mango. Sitakaere chiro na hicha, kanji kutalyi chiro na mundju usibya ola ungaala kunyikulasi mwa mino.

29. Tata iwaiwanyeresaasi, i mukulu-kulu kurenza boshi. Rero kutalyi ola ungaala kumunyaa chiro na kandju.

30. Nyono na tata, chwunalyi muuma.

버라 구무수꾸롸 나 바다삐레사 바무부사 뿌: 우가나어떠거라 구더 와쭈수꾸레사 어 뷔머 구이기라 마ᄋ찌? 러로 아가바 오요 우나 기리시도, 우쭈부라아 짜까나마!

25. 여수 나 이뿌: 나바비레러 미라, 시 무더찌러 먀녀머러라! 어 비소머라노 뱌 너찌러 나이라 과 부아씨 봐 다다, 나비 벼찌러 뱌나로사 뇨노 네레 떠.

26. 시 먀보 무더찌러 먀녀머러라 먀 미찌마 여뉴, 부씨 무다쭈롸 보봐 뿌레 사니.

27. 어 뿌레 사니 서머 소빠 어 무러꺼 와네. 네쭈롸 네시씨 구부야, 나시 구네구레기라 구 서떠 사나네구레기라.

28. 뇨노 네 너떠 너러사시 어 가쫘모 거 수구 너 마ᄋ. 시다가어러 찌로 나 히짜, 가찌 구다레 찌로 나 무뚜 우시뱌 오라 우꺼아롸 구네구쫘시 먀 미노.

29. 다다 이와이와녀러사아시, 이 무구루-구루 구러쌰 보씨. 러로 구다레 오라 우꺼아롸 구무냐아 찌로 나 가꾸.

30. 뇨노 나 다다, 쭈나레 무우마.

around him, saying, "How long will you keep us in suspense? If you are the Christ, tell us plainly."

25. Jesus answered, "I did tell you, but you do not believe. The miracles I do in my Father's name speak for me,

26. but you do not believe because you are not my sheep.

27. My sheep listen to my voice; I know them, and they follow me.

28. I give them eternal life, and they shall never perish; no one can snatch them out of my hand.

29. My Father, who has given them to me, is greater than all; no one can snatch them out of my Father's hand.

30. I and the Father are one."

31. Bushi n'oku, e bayuda bera kuhuba kutolanga e makoi bamuumangemo.

32. Si Yesu era kwire ababura mbu: nabalosise myasi ibuya inene kwa buashi bwa tata. Rero mw'ei myasi, uye mui ola ungachwuma mwanyiumanga e makoi?

33. Nabo mbu: chwutakuumangamo mbu bushikulyi mabuya ma wailyire. Si chwakuumangamo bushi woyo wenjire wakamba Ongo. Kute uwishi kwa unalyi mundju wera ungachiira Ongo?

34. Yesu na imbu: si bichwula byanjikirwe mwa mwaso wenyu mbu Ongo atetaa kwa muchwula baongo!

35. Kanji chwunachwula chwishi kwa kutalyi chinwa chisibya cha chingaokolwa kwa maanjiko mabuya-buya. Rero, ba Ongo endee elyika mbu baongo, balyi ba echi chinwa chai chaikiraa.

36. Nyono e kuteta mbu nyilyi mwana wa Ongo, chi chinganachwuma mwateta mbu namukambira, n'oku anyilondore mira, n'e kunyichwuma muno butala?

---

31. 부씨 노구, 어 바유다 버라 구후바 구도롸꽈 어 마고이 바무우마꺼모.

32. 시 여수 어라 귀러 아바부라 뿌: 나바로시서 먀시 이부야 이너너 과 부아씨 봐 다다. 러로 뭐이 먀시, 우여 무이 오꽈 우꽈쭈마 마네우마꽈 어 마고이?

33. 나보 뿌: 쭈다구우마꽈모 뿌 부씨구레 마부야 마 와이레러. 시 좌구우마꽈모 부씨 오용 워찌러 와가꽈 오꼬. 구더 우위씨 과 우나레 무뚜 워라 우꽈찌이라 오꼬?

34. 여수 나 이뿌: 시 비쭈라 뱌찌기뤄 먀 먀소 워뉴 뿌 오꼬 아더다아 과 무쭈꽈 바오꼬!

35. 가찌 쭈나쭈라 쮜씨 과 구다레 찌나 찌시뱌 좌 찌꽈오고꽈 과 마아씨고 마부야-부야. 러로, 바 오꼬 어너어 어레가 뿌 바오꼬, 바레 바 어찌 찌나 짜이 짜이기라아.

36. 뇨노 어 구더다 뿌 네레 마나 와 오꼬, 찌 찌꽈나쭈마 먀더다 뿌 나무가뻬라, 노구 아네롣또러 미라, 너 구네쭈마 무노 부다꽈?

---

31. Again the Jews picked up stones to stone him,

32. but Jesus said to them, "I have shown you many great miracles from the Father. For which of these do you stone me?"

33. "We are not stoning you for any of these," replied the Jews, "but for blasphemy, because you, a mere man, claim to be God."

34. Jesus answered them, "Is it not written in your Law, 'I have said you are gods'?

35. If he called them 'gods,' to whom the word of God came--and the Scripture cannot be broken--

36. what about the one whom the Father set apart as his very own and sent into the world? Why then do you accuse me of blasphemy because I said, 'I

37. Rero akaba e milyimo era nakola itakulyikene n'e kuhonda kwa Tata, mutanyemererera mwa michima yenyu.

38. Si kuno nera naikola, mwiree mwemerera bushi nai, chiro angaba mbu nyono mutenjire mwanyemerera. Aola, mungera mwa menyerera kanangana kwa Tata alyi mwa ndanda sanyi, nanyi nanaba mwa ndanda sai.

39. Abu Bayuda bera kuhonda bamine Yesu kanji, si era kubafufumuka.

40. Chasinda, Yesu era kuya kanji kwa unji mushilyilya w'e Yorodani, ala Yowana endee abatisisa e bandju. Era kuberao.

41. Bandju banene bera kumuikira, bera kunde bateta mbu: Chiro angaba mbu Yowana atairaa chiro na chisomerano chisibya, si e myasi yoshi era endee ateta era luulu s'ono mundju, yanabaa ya kanangana.

42. Mw'echi chisiki, bandju banene bera kwire bemerera Yesu mwa michima yabo.

37. 러로 아가바 어 미꼐모 어라 나고꽈 이다구꼐거너 너 구호따 과 다다, 무다녀머러러라 롸 미찌마 여뉴.

38. 시 구노 너라 나이고꽈, 뭐러어 뭐머러라 부씨 나이, 찌로 아까바 뿌 뇨노 무더찌러 롸녀머러라. 아오꽈, 무꺼라 롸 머녀러라 가나까나 과 다다 아꼐 롸 따따 사네, 나네 나나바 롸 따따 사이.

39. 아부 바유다 버라 구호따 바미너 여수 가찌, 시 어라 구바푸푸무가.

40. 짜시따, 여수 어라 구야 가찌 과 우찌 무씨꼐랴 워 요로다니, 아라 요와나 어떠어 아바디시사 어 바뚜. 어라 구버라오.

41. 바뚜 바너너 버라 구무이기라, 버라 구떠 바더다 뿌: 찌로 아까바 뿌 요와나 아다이라아 찌로 나 찌소머라노 찌시뱌, 시 어 먀시 요씨 어라 어떠어 아더다 어라 루우루 소노 무뚜, 야나바아 야 가나까나.

42. 뭐찌 찌시기, 바뚜 바너너 버라 귀러 버머러라 여수 롸 미찌마 야보.

am God's Son'?

37. Do not believe me unless I do what my Father does.

38. But if I do it, even though you do not believe me, believe the miracles, that you may know and understand that the Father is in me, and I in the Father."

39. Again they tried to seize him, but he escaped their grasp.

40. Then Jesus went back across the Jordan to the place where John had been baptizing in the early days. Here he stayed

41. and many people came to him. They said, "Though John never performed a miraculous sign, all that John said about this man was true."

42. And in that place many believed in Jesus.

Yoana Chikono 11

E kufa kwa lasaro

1. Mwa musi w'e Betaniya mwabaa muchwula banyere babilyi. Muuma mubo iwabaa Mariya, n'e unji iwabaa Marta na mushishawabo iwabaa lasaro.

2. Oyu Mariya, iwakaa enawechwu e marashi kwa bihando, chasinda era kumahangula n'e mvilyi sai. Rero oyu mushishawabo, era kulaka.

3. Bushi n'oku, abu balyiwabo babilyi bera kwire bachwuma mundju muuma mbu ayaa kubura Yesu kwa mwira wai alakire.

4. Mango Yesu omvaa bacha, era kuteta mbu: Obu bulwala bwai, buta bwa kumwita, si bwamuikilyire chasiya Ongo aye ngulu, nanyi nyi Mwana wai nyiye ngulu kurengerabo.

5. Oyu lasaro n'abu balyiwabo babilyi, Yesu abaa achwula abasimire ngachi.

6. Si chiro bacha, mango omvaa kwa lasaro alakire, era kuhuba kumala sinji suku ebilyi era abaa alyi.

7. Chasinda, era kubura e banafunzi bai mbu: Tuyaa e

요아나 찌고노 11

어 구파 과 라쎌롄

1. 마 무시 워 버다니야 꽈바아 무쭈똬 바녀러 바비레. 무우마 무보 이와바아 마리야, 너 우찌 이와바아 마루다 나 무씨싸와보 이와바아 똬사로.

2. 오유 마리야, 이와가아 어나워쭈 어 마라씨 과 비하또, 짜시따 어라 구마하꾸똬 너 쁴레 사이. 러로 오유 무씨싸와보, 어라 구똬가.

3. 부씨 노구, 아부 바레와보 바비레 버라 귀러 바쭈마 무뚜 무우마 뿌 아야아 구부라 여수 과 뮈라 와이 아똬기러.

4. 마꼬 여수 오빠아 바짜, 어라 구더다 뿌: 오부 부똬똬 봐이, 부다 봐 구뮈다, 시 봐무이기레러 짜시야 오꼬 아여 꾸루, 나니 네 꽈나 와이 니여 꾸루 구러어라보.

5. 오유 똬사로 나부 바레와보 바비레, 여수 아바아 아쭈똬 아바시미러 꽈찌.

6. 시 찌로 바짜, 마꼬 오빠아 과 똬사로 아똬기러, 어라 구후바 구마똬 시찌 수구 어비레 어라 아바아 아레.

7. 짜시따, 어라 구부라 어 바나푸씨 바이 뿌: 두야아 어

John Chapter 11[NIV]

1. Now a man named Lazarus was sick. He was from Bethany, the village of Mary and her sister Martha.

2. This Mary, whose brother Lazarus now lay sick, was the same one who poured perfume on the Lord and wiped his feet with her hair.

3. So the sisters sent word to Jesus, "Lord, the one you love is sick."

4. When he heard this, Jesus said, "This sickness will not end in death. No, it is for God's glory so that God's Son may be glorified through it."

5. Jesus loved Martha and her sister and Lazarus.

6. Yet when he heard that Lazarus was sick, he stayed where he was two more days.

7. Then he said to his disciples, "Let us go back to

Yudeya kanji.

8. Nabo mbu: Mukagilyisi, si mwesine suku sine sine mw'e bayuda b'eyi babaa bahonda kukuumanga e makoi! Rero, kanji yi wahonda kuya?

9. Yesu era kubakula mbu: E mureerere achwusa saa ekumi n'ebilyi. Rero, akaba e mundju angaba aenda e mushi, atangasitala bushi asene kwa bulangare bo muno butala.

10. Si akaba angaba aende e buchwufu, ende asitala bushi ende aba atachilyi mwa bulangare.

11. Mango Yesu abaa era amalaa kuteta ei myasi, era kuhuba kubura e banafunzi bai mbu: Mwira wechwu lasaro aonjire, si naya kumususa.

12. Nabo mbu: Enawechwu, akaba kuonjira ku anaonjire, kasi angalama.

13. Batetaa bacha bushi beke bachichingaa mbu Yesu ateta mbu lasaro kuonjira ku aonjire, n'oku abaa ateta mbu Lasaro afire mira.

14. Yesu kukwera kubabura changanama mbu: Lasaro afire mira.

유데야 가찌.

8. 나보 뿌: 무가지례시, 시 뭐시너 수구 시너 시너 뭐 바유다 버에 바바아 바호따 구구우마까 어 마고이! 러로, 가찌 에 와호따 구야?

9. 여수 어라 구바구롸 뿌: 어 무러어러러 아쭈사 사아 어구미 너비례. 러로, 아가바 어 무뚜 아까바 아어따 어 무씨, 아다까시다롸 부씨 아서너 과 부롸까러 보 무노 부다롸.

10. 시 아가바 아까바 아어너 어 부쭈푸, 어너 아시다롸 부씨 어너 아바 아다찌례 롸 부롸까러.

11. 마끄 여수 아바아 어라 아마롸아 구더다 어이 먀시, 어라 구후바 구부라 어 바나푸씨 바이 뿌: 뮈라 워쭈 롸사로 아오찌러러, 시 나야 구무수사.

12. 나보 뿌: 어나워쭈, 아가바 구오찌라 구 아나오찌러러, 가시 아까롸마.

13. 바더다아 바짜 부씨 버거 바찌찌까아 뿌 여수 아더다 뿌 롸사로 구오찌라 구 아오찌러러, 노구 아바아 아더다 뿌 롸사로 아피러 미라.

14. 여수 구궈라 구바부라 짜까나마 뿌: 롸사로 아피러 미라.

Judea."

8. "But Rabbi," they said, "a short while ago the Jews tried to stone you, and yet you are going back there?"

9. Jesus answered, "Are there not twelve hours of daylight? A man who walks by day will not stumble, for he sees by this world's light.

10. It is when he walks by night that he stumbles, for he has no light."

11. After he had said this, he went on to tell them, "Our friend Lazarus has fallen asleep; but I am going there to wake him up."

12. His disciples replied, "Lord, if he sleeps, he will get better."

13. Jesus had been speaking of his death, but his disciples thought he meant natural sleep.

14. So then he told them plainly, "Lazarus is dead,

15. Rero, namoire bushi nenyu, bushi mango atowa e muchima, nabaa ndalyio. Byabere bacha, chasiya munyemerere mwa michima yenyu. Mwiree mwairaa chwuye era alyi!

16. Tomasi, ola basulaa e sina mbu i Maaha, era kwire abura banafunzi balyikabo mbu: Muiraa chwuende, netu chwuye kufira alauma na Enawechwu!

Yesu iwende wana e kalamo

17. Mango Yesu aikaa mwa musi w'e Betaniya, era kubuana Lasaro amala suku ene mwa shinda.

18. Kutengera e Betaniya kuika e Yerusalemu, byanabaa nga bilometere bihachwu oshao.

19. Bushi n'oku, bayuda banene bera kuika ala mwabo Marta na Mariya, baye kubasesa e michima, bushi n'e lufu l'oyu mushishawabo.

20. Mango Marta omvaa e mwasi kwa Yesu abahire, era kuya kumuhuukasa. Si Mariya, yeke era kushiba mwa nyumba.

21. Marta alolyire ku Yesu, era kwire amubura mbu: Enawechwu! Akaba ungabere

15. 러로, 나모이러 부씨 너뉴, 부씨 마꼬 아도와 어 무찌마, 나바아 따례오. 뱌버러 바짜, 짜시야 무녀머러러 와 미찌마 여뉴. 뮈러어 뫄이라아 쭈여 어라 아례!

16. 도마시, 오라 바수꽈아 어 시나 뿌 이 마아하, 어라 귀러 아부라 바나푸씨 바례가보 뿌: 무이라아 쭈어떠, 너두 쭈여 구피라 아꽈우마 나 어나워쭈!

여수 이워떠 와나 어 가꽈명

17. 마꼬 여수 아이가아 뫄 무시 워 버다니야, 어라 구부아나 꽈사로 아마꽈 수구 어너 뫄 씨따.

18. 구더꺼라 어 버다니야 구이가 어 여루사꺼무, 뱌나바아 까 비로머더러 비하쭈 오싸오.

19. 부씨 노구, 바유다 바너너 버라 구이가 아꽈 뫄보 마루다 나 마리야, 바여 구바서사 어 미찌마, 부씨 너 루푸 르오유 무씨싸와보.

20. 마꼬 마루다 오빠아 어 뫄시 과 여수 아바히러, 어라 구야 구무후우가사. 시 마리야, 여거 어라 구씨바 뫄 뉴빠.

21. 마루다 아로례러 구 여수, 어라 귀러 아무부라 뿌: 어나워쭈! 아가바 우까버러

15. and for your sake I am glad I was not there, so that you may believe. But let us go to him."

16. Then Thomas (called Didymus) said to the rest of the disciples, "Let us also go, that we may die with him."

17. On his arrival, Jesus found that Lazarus had already been in the tomb for four days.

18. Bethany was less than two miles from Jerusalem,

19. and many Jews had come to Martha and Mary to comfort them in the loss of their brother.

20. When Martha heard that Jesus was coming, she went out to meet him, but Mary stayed at home.

21. "Lord," Martha said to Jesus, "if you had been here, my brother would not have

anola, mushishawechwu atangafire!

22. Si chiro bacha, anabe mw'e chine chihangi, nyishi kwa choshi cha ungema Ongo, nganakweresachi.

23. Yesu na imbu: Mushishawenyu omwoka!

24. Marta na imbu: Nyishi kwa akomwoka mango e bafu boshi bakomwoka kwa lusuku lw'e businda.

25. Yesu era kwire amubura mbu: Nyono, nyi nende neresa e bandju e kalamo! ola wanyemerere mwa muchima wai kuika anabone e kalamo, chiro angaba mbu afire.

26. Kanji chira mundju woshi ola uchilyi muuma-uma ananyemerere mwa muchima wai, atakafe chiro na hicha. Ei myasi, wemererei?

27. Marta na imbu: Nechi Enawechwu! Nemerere kwa woyo u Kirisito, Kanji u Mwana wa Ongo, ola batetaa kwa akabaha mwa butala.

28. Abere Marta era amalaa kuteta ei myasi, era kuchiuma aya kwamaala mulumuna wai Mariya. Chasinda, era kumubura mwa byoo mbu: e Mukangilyisi era alyi kuno, akwamaere.

아노꽈, 무씨싸워쭈 아다까피러!

22. 시 찌로 바짜, 아나버 뭐 찌너 찌하끠, 니씨 과 쪼씨 짜 우꺼마 오꼬, 까나궈러사찌.

23. 여수 나 이뿌: 무씨싸워뉴 오모가!

24. 마루다 나 이뿌: 니씨 과 아고모가 마꼬 어 바푸 보씨 바고모가 과 루수구 뤄 부시따.

25. 여수 어라 귀러 아무부라 뿌: 뇨노, 네 너더 너러사 어 바뉴 어 가꽈모! 오라 와녀머러러 꽈 무찌마 와이 구이가 아나보너 어 가꽈모, 찌로 아까바 뿌 아피러.

26. 가찌 찌라 무뚜 오씨 오꽈 우찌레 무우마-우마 아나녀머러러 꽈 무찌마 와이, 아다가퍼 찌로 나 히짜. 어이 먀시, 워머러러이?

27. 마루다 나 이뿌: 너찌 어나워쭈! 너머러러 과 오요 우 기리시도, 가찌 우 꽈나 와 오꼬, 오꽈 바더다아 과 아가바하 꽈 부다꽈.

28. 아버러 마루다 어라 아마꽈아 구더다 어이 먀시, 어라 구찌우마 아야 과마아꽈 무루무나 와이 마리야. 짜시따, 어라 구무부라 꽈 보오 뿌: 어 무가끠레시 어라 아레 구노, 아과마어러.

died.

22. But I know that even now God will give you whatever you ask."

23. Jesus said to her, "Your brother will rise again."

24. Martha answered, "I know he will rise again in the resurrection at the last day."

25. Jesus said to her, "I am the resurrection and the life. He who believes in me will live, even though he dies;

26. and whoever lives and believes in me will never die. Do you believe this?"

27. "Yes, Lord," she told him, "I believe that you are the Christ, the Son of God, who was to come into the world."

28. And after she had said this, she went back and called her sister Mary aside. "The Teacher is here," she said, "and is asking for you."

29. Mariya omvire bacha, unao-unao kuna kubanzukala, aye era Yesu abaa alyi.

30. Mw'ebi bihangi, Yesu abaa atasa kw'engilyira mwa musi, si abaa achilyi ala Marta amubuanaa mango ayaa kumuhuukasa.

31. e Bayuda ba babaa balyi mwa nyumba alauma na Mariya kwa kumusesa e muchima, mango balolaa kwa abanzukala na achiuma era butala, bera kumukulyikira. Bairaa bacha, bushi bachichingaa mbu aya kulyilyira kwa shinda.

32. Mariya era kuika ala Yesu abaa alyi. Mwa kunamulolako, kuna kuya kuchihunda mwa bihando byai. Nai era kumubura mbu: Enawechwu! Akaba ungabere anola, mushishawechwu atangafire!

33. Mango Yesu alolaa kwa Mariya alauma n'abu Bayuda babaa bamwerekesise boshi balyira, e chifufu chera kumusimba. Era kusibuka busese.

34. Era kubusa mbu: Ngai u mwamutabiraa? Nabo mbu: Enawechwu! Bahaa ulole.

---

29. 마리야 오쀄러 바짜, 우나오-우나오 구나 구바누가꽈, 아여 어라 여수 아바아 아레.

30. 뭐비 비하삐, 여수 아바아 아다사 궈삐레라 뫄 무시, 시 아바아 아찌레 아꽈 마루다 아무부아나아 마꼬 아야아 구무후우가사.

31. 어 바유다 바 바바아 바레 뫄 뉴빠 아꽈우마 나 마리야 과 구무서사 어 무찌마, 마꼬 바로꽈아 과 아바누가꽈 나 아찌우마 어라 부다꽈, 버라 구무구레기라. 바이라아 바짜, 부씨 바찌찌까아 뿌 아야 구레레라 과 씨따.

32. 마리야 어라 구이가 아꽈 여수 아바아 아레. 뫄 구나무로꽈고, 구나 구야 구찌후따 뫄 비하도 뱌이. 나이 어라 구무부라 뿌: 어나워쭈! 아가바 우빠버러 아노꽈, 무씨싸워쭈 아다빠러!

33. 마꼬 여수 아로꽈아 과 마리야 아꽈우마 나부 바유다 바바아 바뭐러거시서 보씨 바레라, 어 찌푸푸 쩌라 구무시빠. 어라 구시부가 부서서.

34. 어라 구부사 뿌: 까이 우 뫄무다비라아? 나보 뿌: 어나워쭈! 바하아 우로쩌.

---

29. When Mary heard this, she got up quickly and went to him.

30. Now Jesus had not yet entered the village, but was still at the place where Martha had met him.

31. When the Jews who had been with Mary in the house, comforting her, noticed how quickly she got up and went out, they followed her, supposing she was going to the tomb to mourn there.

32. When Mary reached the place where Jesus was and saw him, she fell at his feet and said, "Lord, if you had been here, my brother would not have died."

33. When Jesus saw her weeping, and the Jews who had come along with her also weeping, he was deeply moved in spirit and troubled.

34. "Where have you laid him?" he asked. "Come and see, Lord," they replied.

35. Yesu muna malyira.

36. Bushi n'oku, abu bayuda bera kutangilyisa bateta mbu: Alyibwe! Musene kwa abaa amusimire ngachi!

37. Si bauma mubo, beke bera kutangilyisa bateta mbu: Ono mundju, si asibulaa e meho m'e muuta! Rero, chi chachwumaa atangika e lufu lwa lasaro!

Yesu omwola lasaro

38. Yesu e chifufu chera kumusimba kanji, era kusibuka busese na aya kwa shinda. Ei shinda, lwabaa lukunda, n'okwa chiso chalo kwabaa kuhukirwe e koi lyinene.

39. Yesu era kwire ateta mbu: Mukulaa elyi koi. Marta, mwalyi wabo Lasaro era kumwakula mbu: Enawechwu! Si suku ene sine amala mwa shinda, kubeya ku era abeya!
40. Yesu na imbu: Ndakubura kwa ukemerera mwa muchima wao, ungalola kwa buashi bwa Ongo?
41. Chasinda, bera kwire bakula ly'e koi. Yesu era kuchwumbikisa kwa nguba na ateta mbu: Tata, nakutonga bushi wanyumvire mira.
42. Nyineshi kanangana kwa

35. 여수 무나 마레라.

36. 부씨 노구, 아부 바유다 버라 구다삐레사 바더다 뿌: 아레붜! 무서너 과 아바아 아무시미러 까찌!

37. 시 바우마 무보, 버거 버라 구다삐레사 바더다 뿌: 오노 무뚜, 시 아시부롸아 어 머호 머 무우다! 러로, 찌 짜쭈마아 아다삐가 어 루푸 롸 롸사로!

여수 오모롸 롸뻴렌

38. 여수 어 찌푸푸 쩌라 구무시빠 가찌, 어라 구시부가 부서서 나 아야 과 씨따. 어이 씨따, 롸바아 루구따, 노과 찌소 짜로 과바아 구후기뤄 어 고이 레너너.

39. 여수 어라 귀러 아더다 뿌: 무구롸아 어레 고이. 마루다, 뫄레 와보 롸사로 어라 구뫄구롸 뿌: 어나워쭈! 시 수구 어너 시너 아마롸 뫄 씨따, 구버야 구 어라 아버야!
40. 여수 나 이뿌: 따구부라 과 우거머러라 뫄 무찌마 와오, 우까로롸 과 부아씨 뫄 오꼬?
41. 짜시따, 버라 귀러 바구롸 뤼어 고이. 여수 어라 구쭈삐기사 과 우바 나 아더다 뿌: 다다, 나구도꺄 부씨 와뉴삐러 미라.
42. 니너씨 가나꺄나 과 워떠

35. Jesus wept.

36. Then the Jews said, "See how he loved him!"

37. But some of them said, "Could not he who opened the eyes of the blind man have kept this man from dying?"

38. Jesus, once more deeply moved, came to the tomb. It was a cave with a stone laid across the entrance.

39. "Take away the stone," he said. "But, Lord," said Martha, the sister of the dead man, "by this time there is a bad odor, for he has been there four days."
40. Then Jesus said, "Did I not tell you that if you believed, you would see the glory of God?"
41. So they took away the stone. Then Jesus looked up and said, "Father, I thank you that you have heard me.
42. I knew that you always

wende wanyumva e suku soshi. Si natechire bacha bushi na bano bandju banyisungwire, chasiya bemerere mwa michima yabo kwa woyo u wananyichwumaa.

와뉴빠 어 수구 소씨. 시 나더찌러 바짜 부씨 나 바노 바뉴 바네수뀌러, 짜시야 버머러러 뫄 미찌마 야보 꽈 오요 우 와나네쭈마아.

hear me, but I said this for the benefit of the people standing here, that they may believe that you sent me."

43. Abere era amalaa kuteta ei myasi, era kuteta na murenge munene mbu: Lasaro! Tengaa omola!

43. 아버러 어라 아마롸아 구더다 어이 먀시, 어라 구더다 나 무러머 무너너 뿌: 롸사로! 더까아 오모라!

43. When he had said this, Jesus called in a loud voice, "Lazarus, come out!"

44. Unao-unao, walyi lasaro kuna kutenga mw'era shinda. E bihando n'e maboko mai, byabaa bichilyi biminyirwe mwa mirembe era bendee bamina mw'e bafu. N'e buso bwai, nabo bwabaa buchilyi buhukirwe n'e luchimba. Yesu kukwera kubura abu bandju mbu: Mumuboolaa esi njimba, mumureke aende.

44. 우나오-우나오, 와례 롸사로 구나 구더빠 뭐라 씨따. 어 비하또 너 마보고 마이, 뱌바아 비찌례 비미네뤄 뫄 미러뻐 어라 버떠어 바미나 뭐 바푸. 너 부소 바이, 나보 봐바아 부찌례 부후기뤄 너 루찌빠. 여수 구귀라 구부라 아부 바뉴 뿌: 무무보오롸아 어시 찌빠, 무무러거 아어떠.

44. The dead man came out, his hands and feet wrapped with strips of linen, and a cloth around his face. Jesus said to them, "Take off the grave clothes and let him go."

E lwango lw'e kwita Yesu

어 롸오 뤄 귀다 여수

45. Bayuda banene mw'aba babahaa ala mwa Mariya, mango balolaa kwa myasi era Yesu airaa, bera kwire bamwemerera mwa michima yabo.

45. 바유다 바너너 뫄바 바바하아 아롸 뫄 마리야, 마꼬 바롣롸아 꽈 먀시 어라 여수 아이라아, 버라 귀러 바뭐머러라 뫄 미찌마 야보.

45. Therefore many of the Jews who had come to visit Mary, and had seen what Jesus did, put their faith in him.

46. Si bauma mubo, beke bera kuya kubura e Bafarisayo bya Yesu airaa.

46. 시 바우마 무보, 버거 버라 구야 구부라 어 바파리사요 뱌 여수 아이라아.

46. But some of them went to the Pharisees and told them what Jesus had done.

47. Bushi n'oku, e bakulu-kulu b'e bakuhanyi, n'e Bafarisayo, bera kubuanyanya e

47. 부씨 노구, 어 바구루-구루 버 바구하네, 너 바파리사요, 버라 구부아냐냐

47. Then the chief priests and the Pharisees called a meeting of the Sanhedrin.

karubanda k'e bayuda. Bera kutangilyisa babusanya mbu: Bechwu! kute chwiree chwaira? Si ono mundju enjire aira bisomerano binene!

48. Rero, akaba chwungamureka aendekere kunde aira bacha, e bandju boshi bangamwemerera mwa michima yabo. Na mw'olu, e Baroma bangaika kuchwuhandjulyira luno luhu lwa Ongo, banalyinde basikya n'e lubaa lwechwu!

49. Mw'aku karubanda, mwabaa mulyi mundju muuma mbu i kayafa. Oyu kayafa, iwabaa mukulu-kulu w'e bakuhanyi mw'oyu mwaka. Era kubura balyikabo mbu: Mwabo, mutete cha mwishi!

50. Muteshi kwa e bandju boshi b'e lubaa lwechwu wa kusika, kungaba kukulu mundju muuma afe bushi nabo!

51. Oyu mwasi, kayafa atatetao kwa kuhonda kwai yeine. Si atetaao mu njira ya kureba, bushi iwabaa mukulu-kulu w'e bakuhanyi mw'oyu mwaka. N'obu burebi, bwabaa butechire kwa Yesu angafa bushi n'e lubaa lwe bayuda.

어 가루바따 거 바우다. 버라 구다삐레사 바부사냐 뿌: 버쭈! 구더 쮜러어 쫘이라? 시 오노 무뚜 어찌러 아이라 비소머라노 비너너!

48. 러로, 아가바 쭈까무러가 아어떠거러 구뜨 아이라 바짜, 어 바뚜 보씨 바까뭐머러라 마 미찌마 야보. 나 모룰, 어 바로마 바까이가 구쭈하뉴레라 루노 루후 똬 오끄, 바나레떠 바시갸 너 루바아 뭐쭈!

49. 뫄구 가루바따, 뫄바아 무레 무뚜 무우마 뿌 이 가야파. 오유 가야파, 이와바아 무구루-구루 워 바구하네 모유 뫄가. 어라 구부라 바레가보 뿌: 뫄보, 무더더 짜 뮈씨!

50. 무더씨 과 어 바뚜 보씨 버 루바아 뭐쭈 와 구시가, 구까바 구구루 무뚜 무우마 아퍼 부씨 나보!

51. 오유 뫄시, 가야파 아다더다오 과 구호따 과이 여이너. 시 아더다아오 무 찌라 야 구러바, 부씨 이와바아 무구루-구루 워 바구하네 모유 뫄가. 노부 부러비, 똬바아 부더찌러 과 여수 아까파 부씨 너 루바아 뭐 바우다.

"What are we accomplishing?" they asked. "Here is this man performing many miraculous signs.

48. If we let him go on like this, everyone will believe in him, and then the Romans will come and take away both our place and our nation."

49. Then one of them, named Caiaphas, who was high priest that year, spoke up, "You know nothing at all!

50. You do not realize that it is better for you that one man die for the people than that the whole nation perish."

51. He did not say this on his own, but as high priest that year he prophesied that Jesus would die for the Jewish nation,

52. Kanji atafe bushi n'olu lubaa lweine oshao, si bushi n'e banji bana ba Ongo ba bahandabanyire mwa binji bio, abuanyanyebo, babe mwa buuma.

53. Rero kutengera olu lusuku, abu bakulu-kulu b'e Bayuda, bera kwire baisa e lwango lw'e kwita Yesu.

54. Bushi n'oku, Yesu atendee achisungula changanama mwa bayuda. Era kutenga aola na aya mu musi muuma ola bende belyika mbu Efuraimu. Oyu musi, abaa achwula ofu n'e buyeye. Era kuberamo alauma n'e banafunzi bai.

55. E lusuku lukulu lw'e pasaka y'e bayuda lwabaa lwahonda kuika. Bushi n'oku, bandju banene bera kutangilyisa batenganga mwa misi yabo, berukiranga e Yerusalemu babe elyi bachikomise era muhondo olu lusuku lukulu luike.

56. Mango babaa bera balyi mwa luhu lwa Ongo, bera kutangilyisa bahonda Yesu. Bera kubusanya mbu: Kute musene? Elyi atanaike kw'oluno lusuku lukulu?

52. 가찌 아다퍼 부씨 노루 루바아 뤄이너 오싸오, 시 부씨 너 바찌 바나 바 오꼬 바 바하따바네러 롸 비찌 비오, 아부아냐녀보, 바버 롸 부우마.

53. 러로 구더뗘라 오루 루수구, 아부 바구루-구루 버 바유다, 버라 귀러 바이사 어 롸꼬 뤄 귀다 여수.

54. 부씨 노구, 여수 아더뗘어 아찌수꾸라 짜아나마 롸 바유다. 어라 구더꺄 아오롸 나 아야 무 무시 무우마 오롸 버떠 버쩨가 뿌 어푸라이무. 오유 무시, 아바아 아쭈롸 오푸 너 부여여. 어라 구버라모 아롸우마 너 바나푸씨 바이.

55. 어 루수구 루구루 뤄 파사가 여 바유다 롸바아 롸호따 구이가. 부씨 노구, 바뚜 바너너 버라 구다꺼레사 바더꺄꺄 롸 미시 야보, 버루기라꺄 어 여루사뻐무 바버 어쩨 바찌고미서 어라 무호또 오루 루수구 루구루 루이거.

56. 마꼬 바바아 버라 바쩨 롸 루후 롸 오꼬, 버라 구다꺼레사 바호따 여수. 버라 구부사냐 뿌: 구더 무서너? 어쩨 아다나이거 교루노 루수구 루구루?

52. and not only for that nation but also for the scattered children of God, to bring them together and make them one.

53. So from that day on they plotted to take his life.

54. Therefore Jesus no longer moved about publicly among the Jews. Instead he withdrew to a region near the desert, to a village called Ephraim, where he stayed with his disciples.

55. When it was almost time for the Jewish Passover, many went up from the country to Jerusalem for their ceremonial cleansing before the Passover.

56. They kept looking for Jesus, and as they stood in the temple area they asked one another, "What do you think? Isn't he coming to the Feast at all?"

57. E bakulu-kulu b'e bakuhanyi, n'e bafarisayo babaa babilyire e bandju mira kwa akaba kulyi ola ungamenya ala Yesu alyi, abahaa kubabura baye kumusimba.

57. 어 바구루-구루 버 바구하네, 너 바파리사요 바바아 바비례러 어 바쭈 미라 과 아가바 구례 오롸 우까머냐 아롸 여수 아례, 아바하아 구바부라 바여 구무시빠.

57. But the chief priests and Pharisees had given orders that if anyone found out where Jesus was, he should report it so that they might arrest him.

Yoana Chikono 12
Mariya akaba Yesu e marashi kwa bihando

요아나 찌고노 12
마리야 아가바 여수 어 마라씨 과 비하또

John Chapter 12[NIV]

1. Mango kwabaa kwashiba suku ndachwu e lusuku lukulu lw'e pasaka luike, Yesu era kuya mwa musi w'e Betaniya. Mw'oyu musi, mu lasaro abaa achwula, ola Yesu omwolaa.

1. 마오 과바아 과씨바 수구 따쭈 어 루수구 루구루 뭐 파사가 루이거, 여수 어라 구야 뫄 무시 워 버다니야. 모유 무시, 무 롸사로 아바아 아쭈롸, 오롸 여수 오모롸아.

1. Six days before the Passover, Jesus arrived at Bethany, where Lazarus lived, whom Jesus had raised from the dead.

2. Aikiremo, bera kumusheera e bilyo, na Marta iwabaaa weulyirabi e bandju. Lasaro nai, abaa alyi mwa ba babaa balya alauma na Yesu.

2. 아이기러모, 버라 구무써어라 어 비뵤, 나 마루다 이와바아아 워우례라비 어 바쭈. 롸사로 나이, 아바아 아례 뫄 바 바바아 바럇 아롸우마 나 여수.

2. Here a dinner was given in Jesus' honor. Martha served, while Lazarus was among those reclining at the table with him.

3. Chasinda, Mariya era kutola chimbi cha litere cha marashi ma chichiro chinene busese. Amu marashi, mabaa makunganyisibwe mwa bwaso bw'e muchi w'e narito oshao Era kumakaba Yesu kwa bihando, chasinda era kutangilyisa amahangula n'e mvilyi sai. E bumba bwamu

3. 짜시따, 마리야 어라 구도롸 찌뻬 짜 리더러 짜 마라씨 마 찌찌로 찌너너 부서서. 아무 마라씨, 마바아 마구까네시붜 뫄 봐소 붜 무찌 워 나리도 오싸오 어라 구마가바 여수 과 비하또, 짜시따 어라 구다끼례사 아마하우롸 너 쀄례 사이. 어 부빠 봐무 마라씨, 붜라

3. Then Mary took about a pint of pure nard, an expensive perfume; she poured it on Jesus' feet and wiped his feet with her hair. And the house was filled with the fragrance of the perfume.

marashi, bwera kwehula mwa nyumba yoshi.

4. Achwula isikarioti, muuma mwa banafunzi ba Yesu ola wabaa ungamurenganya, era kwire ateta mbu:

5. Chi chachwumaa mano marashi matausibwa? Si maana mahachwu ma dinari, mu mangafire chasiya maabirwe e bakene?

6. Ateta bacha, ata bushi abaa alaire kwa bakene, si bushi abaa achwula mwisi. Kanji oku iwendee walanga ehao, endee achitorera kwa buteya bwa bendee babikamo.

7. Si Yesu era kuteta mbu: Muchirekeraa ono mukasi! Ailyire bacha bushi n'e kukunganya e lusuku lw'e kutabwa kwanyi.

8. Abu bakene, bakanaba nenyu e suko soshi, si nyono ndakabe nenyu e suku soshi!

E lwango lw'e kwita lasaro nai

9. Luamba lunene lwa bayuda bera kumva e mwasi kwa Yesu alyi e Betaniya. Bushi n'oku, bera kuyayi. Batayaayi kulola ku Yesu yeine, si babaa bahonda balole ku lasaro nai ola Yesu omwolaa.

귀후롸 마 뉴빠 요씨.

4. 아쭈롸 이시가리오디, 무우마 롸 바나푸씨 바 여수 오롸 와바아 우까무러까냐, 어라 귀러 아더다 뿌:

5. 찌 짜쭈마아 마노 마라씨 마다우시봐? 시 마아나 마하쭈 마 디나리, 무 마까피러 짜시야 마아비뤄 어 바거너?

6. 아더다 바짜, 아다 부씨 아바아 아롸이러 과 바거너, 시 부씨 아바아 아쭈롸 뮈시. 가찌 오구 이워떠러 와롸까 어하오, 어떠어 아찌도러라 과 부더야 봐 버떠어 바비가모.

7. 시 여수 어라 구더다 뿌: 무찌러거라아 오노 무가시! 아이레러 바짜 부씨 너 구구까냐 어 루수구 뤄 구다봐 과네.

8. 아부 바거너, 바가나바 너뉴 어 수고 소씨, 시 뇨노 따가버 너뉴 어 수구 소씨!

어 롸꼬 뤄 귀다 롸쎕렌 나이

9. 루아빠 루너너 롸 바유다 버라 구빠 어 몫시 과 여수 아레 어 버다니야. 부씨 노구, 버라 구야에. 바다야아에 구로롸 구 여수 여이너, 시 바바아 바호따 바로뤄 구 롸사로 나이 오롸 여수

---

4. But one of his disciples, Judas Iscariot, who was later to betray him, objected,

5. "Why wasn't this perfume sold and the money given to the poor? It was worth a year's wages."

6. He did not say this because he cared about the poor but because he was a thief; as keeper of the money bag, he used to help himself to what was put into it.

7. "Leave her alone," Jesus replied. " It was intended that she should save this perfume for the day of my burial.

8. You will always have the poor among you, but you will not always have me."

9. Meanwhile a large crowd of Jews found out that Jesus was there and came, not only because of him but also to see Lazarus, whom he had raised from the dead.

오모꽈아.

10. Rero, e bakulu-kulu b'e bakuhanyi bera kwire baira e lwango lw'e kwita Lasaro nai,

10. 러로, 어 바구루-구루 버 바구하니 버라 귀러 바이라 어 꽈꼬 뤄 귀다 꽈사로 나이,

10. So the chief priests made plans to kill Lazarus as well,

11. bushi iwachwumaa bayuda banene bachikula kubo, na bemerera Yesu mwa michima yabo.

11. 부씨 이와쭈마아 바유다 바너너 바찌구꽈 구보, 나 버머러라 여수 꽈 미찌마 야보.

11. for on account of him many of the Jews were going over to Jesus and putting their faith in him.

Yesu engilyira mwa musi w'e Yerusalemu

여수 어삐레띱 꽈 무시 워 여루사꺼물

12. Abere mw'ei mishangya, e luamba lw'e bandju ba baikaa mwa musi w'e Yerusalemu kwa lusuku lukulu lw'e Pasaka, bera kumva e mwasi kwa Yesu nai alyi mwa njira aya e Yerusalemu.

12. 아버러 뭐이 미싸꺄, 어 루아빠 뤄 바꾸 바 바이가아 꽈 무시 워 여루사꺼무 과 루수구 루구루 뤄 파사가, 버라 구빠 어 꽈시 과 여수 나이 아례 꽈 씨라 아야 어 여루사꺼무.

12. The next day the great crowd that had come for the Feast heard that Jesus was on his way to Jerusalem.

13. Bushi n'oku, bera kutolanga e mangarara na batenga mwa musi baye kumuhuukasa. Bera kuenda bateta na murenge munene mbu: Hosana! Ono w'eshire kw'e sina lya enawechwu iwaahamyirwe! Kanji ina Mwami w'e Baisiraeli!

13. 부씨 노구, 버라 구도꽈꺼 어 마꺼라라 나 바더꺼 꽈 무시 바여 구무후우가사. 버라 구어따 바더다 나 무러꺼 무너너 뿌: 호사나! 오노 워씨러 궈 시나 꺄 어나워쭈 이와아하무에뤄! 가찌 이나 꽈미 워 바이시라어삐!

13. They took palm branches and went out to meet him, shouting, "Hosanna!" "Blessed is he who comes in the name of the Lord!" "Blessed is the King of Israel!"

14. Yesu era kubuana chana cha punda, na ekala kuchi, kukulyikana ng'okwa Maanjiko Mabuya-buya machwula matechire mbu:

14. 여수 어라 구부아나 짜나 짜 푸따, 나 어가꽈 구찌, 구구레가나 꼬과 마아찌고 마부야-부야 마쭈꽈 마더찌러 뿌:

14. Jesus found a young donkey and sat upon it, as it is written,

15. Mu besha mwa musi w'e Sayuni, mutobaaa! Mulolaa! e Mwami wenyu eshire, ekese kwa chana ch'e punda.

16. Mw'echi chihangi, e banfunzi ba Yesu babaa batasa kumenyereraa ei myasi yoshi. si mango Ongo erusaa Yesu mw'echwunda lyai, bera kwire bakengera kwa kasi ei myasi yabaa yaajikirwe era luulu sai mwa Maanjiko Mabuya-buya. Rero, kunoku ku banamukoreraa.

17. Cha chachwumaa bandju banene baya kuhuukasa Yesu bacha, bushi babaa bomvire mira kwa iwomwolaa Lasaro mwa kunamubura mbu atengaa mwa shinda.

18. Na ba bachiloreraa kw'echi chisomerano, bu babaa bafulyilyire e bandu kw'oyu mwasi mira.

19. Bushi n'oku, e Bafarisayo kukwera kuburana mbu: Ewashe! Mutasene kwa kutalyi cha mungachiira? Si musene kwa bandju boshi kumushemba kubamushemba!

Yesu ateta era luulu s'e kufa kwai

15. 무 버싸 먀 무시 워 사유니, 무도바아아! 무롤라아! 어 먀미 워뉴 어씨러, 어거서 과 짜나 쩌 푸따.

16. 뭐찌 찌하끼, 어 바누푸씨 바 여수 바바아 바다사 구머녀러라아 어이 먀시 요씨. 시 마꼬 오꼬 어루사아 여수 뭐쭈따 랴이, 버라 귀러 바거꺼라 과 가시 어이 먀시 야바아 야아지기뤄 어라 루우루 사이 먀 마아찌고 마부야-부야. 러로, 구노구 구 바나무고러라아.

17. 짜 짜쭈마아 바뚜 바너너 바야 구후우가사 여수 바짜, 부씨 바바아 보뼤러 미라 과 이오모꽈아 꽈사로 먀 구나무부라 뿌 아더꺼아 먀 씨따.

18. 나 바 바찌로러라아 궈찌 찌소머라노, 부 바바아 바푸레쪠러 어 바뚜 교유 먀시 미라.

19. 부씨 노구, 어 바파리사요 구궈라 구부라나 뿌: 어와써! 무다서너 과 구다레 짜 무꺼찌이라? 시 무서너 과 바뚜 보씨 구무써빠 구바무써빠!

여수 아더다 어라 뿌윰뿌 서 구파 과이

15. "Do not be afraid, O Daughter of Zion; see, your king is coming, seated on a donkey's colt."

16. At first his disciples did not understand all this. Only after Jesus was glorified did they realize that these things had been written about him and that they had done these things to him.

17. Now the crowd that was with him when he called Lazarus from the tomb and raised him from the dead continued to spread the word.

18. Many people, because they had heard that he had given this miraculous sign, went out to meet him.

19. So the Pharisees said to one another, "See, this is getting us nowhere. Look how the whole world has gone after him!"

20. Mw'abu bandju ba bayaa kwera Ongo e Yerusalemu kwa lusuku lukulu lw'e Pasaka, mwabaa mulyi bakiriki bauma.

20. 뫄부 바뉴 바 바야아 궈라 오꼬 어 여루사뤄무 과 루수구 루구루 뤠 파사가, 뫄바아 무뤠 바기리기 바우마.

20. Now there were some Greeks among those who went up to worship at the Feast.

21. Abu bakiriki, bera kuikira Filipo, mwesha mwa musi w'e Betesaita, mwa chio ch'e kalilaya. Bera kumubura mbu: e Walyiya! chwahonda chwulole ku Yesu.

21. 아부 바기리기, 버라 구이기라 피뤼포, 뭐싸 뫄 무시 워 버더사이다, 뫄 찌오 쩌 가뤼롸야. 버라 구무부라 뿌: 어 와뤠야! 좌호따 쭈롣뤄 구 여수.

21. They came to Philip, who was from Bethsaida in Galilee, with a request. "Sir," they said, "we would like to see Jesus."

22. Ei myasi, Filipo nai era kuya kuibura Andereya. Chasinda kwa banalyi babilyi, nabo bera kuya kuibura Yesu.

22. 어이 먀시, 피뤼포 나이 어라 구야 구이부라 아떠러야. 짜시따 과 바나뤠 바비뤠, 나보 버라 구야 구이부라 여수.

22. Philip went to tell Andrew; Andrew and Philip in turn told Jesus.

23. Yesu era kubaakula mbu: Rero e chihangi chaikire mira, cha nyono nyi Mwana w'e Mundju nyingerusibwa mw'e chwunda!

23. 여수 어라 구바아구롸 뿌: 러로 어 찌하삐 짜이기러 미라, 짜 뇨노 네 뫄나 워 무뚜 네떠루시봐 뭐 쭌따!

23. Jesus replied, "The hour has come for the Son of Man to be glorified.

24. Kubinalyi, nababura kwa e njimi y'e bulo, akaba itangatowera mwa lutaka na yafa, elyi inganaendekera kushiba njimi oshao. Si akaba ingafiramo, aola yera bifuma binene.

24. 구비나뤠, 나바부라 과 어 띠미 여 부로, 아가바 이다따도워라 뫄 루다가 나 야파, 어뤠 이따나어떠거라 구씨바 띠미 오싸오. 시 아가바 이따피라모, 아오롸 여라 비푸마 비너너.

24. I tell you the truth, unless a kernel of wheat falls to the ground and dies, it remains only a single seed. But if it dies, it produces many seeds.

25. Ola usimire e kalamo kai akaesako. Si ola ukakahomba mango achilyi muno butala, yeke akalangako kwa kubona e kalamo k'e suku n'e mango.

25. 오롸 우시미러 어 가롸모 가이 아가어사고. 시 오롸 우가가호빠 마꼬 아찌뤠 무노 부다롸, 여거 아가롸빠고 과 구보나 어 가롸모 거 수구 너 마꼬.

25. The man who loves his life will lose it, while the man who hates his life in this world will keep it for eternal life.

26. Akaba e mundju ahonda abe muanda wanyi, byemire anyikulyikire. N'e chisiki cha nyingabamo, mu nai anganaba. Na akaba e mundju anganyokorera, kuika Tata anamweresa e chwunda.

27. Rero, e bwenge bwanyisungulyire. Chi nyitetaa? Nyemaa tata anyinunule mwa myasi era yahonda kunyiikira mw'e chine chihangi? Si ei myasi, iyachwumaa nabaha!

28. Rero Tata, uiraa e sina lyao lyitongwe! Unao-unao, e murenge kuna kutenga kwa nguba, ola wabaa wateta mbu: Natongirelyi mira! Kanji nyinganalyitonga!

29. E bandju ba babaa balyi aola, mango bomvaa kw'oyu murenge, bauma bera kutangilyisa bateta mbu: Murasano oyola.

30. Si Yesu era kubabura mbu: Oyu murenge atomvikere bushi nanyi, si bushi nenyu.

31. Rero e chihangi cha Ongo ch'e kuchinjibusa e bandju bobuno butala chaikire mira. N'e mwami wabo nai, kumuuma ku Ongo angamuuma era mbuwa.

26. 아가바 어 무뚜 아호따 아버 무아따 와네, 벼미러 아네구례기러. 너 찌시기 짜 네따바모, 무 나이 아까나바. 나 아가바 어 무뚜 아까뇨고러라, 구이가 다다 아나뭐러사 어 쭈따.

27. 러로, 어 붸머 봐네수우례러. 찌 네더다아? 녀마아 다다 아네누누뿌러 마 먀시 어라 야호따 구네이기라 뭐 찌너 찌하뻬? 시 어이 먀시, 이야쭈마아 나바하!

28. 러로 다다, 우이라아 어 시나 랴오 례도워! 우나오-우나오, 어 무러뻐 구나 구더빠 과 우바, 오뽜 와바아 와더다 뿌: 나도삐러례 미라! 가찌 네까나례도뽜!

29. 어 바뚜 바 바바아 바례 아오뽜, 마꼬 보빠아 교유 무러뻐, 바우마 버라 구다삐례사 바더다 뿌: 무라사노 오요뽜.

30. 시 여수 어라 구바부라 뿌: 오유 무러뻐 아도삐거러 부씨 나네, 시 부씨 너뉴.

31. 러로 어 찌하뻬 짜 오꼬 쩌 구찌찌부사 어 바뚜 보부노 부다뽜 짜이기러 미라. 너 마미 와보 나이, 구무우마 구 오꼬 아까무우마 어라 뿌와.

26. Whoever serves me must follow me; and where I am, my servant also will be. My Father will honor the one who serves me.

27. "Now my heart is troubled, and what shall I say? 'Father, save me from this hour'? No, it was for this very reason I came to this hour.

28. Father, glorify your name!" Then a voice came from heaven, "I have glorified it, and will glorify it again."

29. The crowd that was there and heard it said it had thundered; others said an angel had spoken to him.

30. Jesus said, "This voice was for your benefit, not mine.

31. Now is the time for judgment on this world; now the prince of this world will be driven out.

32. Na mango nyingerusibwa natenga muno butala, mu mango nyingaira e bandju boshi babahe era mwanyi.

33. Cha chachwumaa Yesu atetaa bacha, kwabaa kubalosa kwa angafa.

34. Abu bandju, bera kumwakula mbu: e Mwaso achwula achwukangilyise mbu kirisito akanaendekera kubao e suku n'e mango! Rero, kute wera ungateta kanji mbu e Mwana w'e Mundju emire erusibwe atenga muno butala? N'oyu Mwana w'e Mundju, iwera nde?

35. Yesu nai mbu: Ola warechire e bulangare, achilyi mwa kachi-kachi kenyu ku bihangi bieke oshao. Rero, n'e bihangi bya muchilyi mwete obu bulangare, mundaa mwaenda mubo, e musimya angesha kubahukira. Bushi akaba e mundju aenda mwa musimya, atamenya era aya.

36. Oku ola warechire e bulangare anachilyi mwa kachi-kachi kenyu, mu mwemereraa mwa michima yenyu, kuikira mube bandju b'e bulangare. Mango Yesu abaa era amalaa kuteta ei myasi, era kubareka na aya

32. 나 마꼬 네꺼루시봐 나더꽈 무노 부다꽈, 무 마꼬 네까이라 어 바꾸 보씨 바바허 어라 마네.

33. 짜 짜쭈마아 여수 아더다아 바짜, 과바아 구바로사 과 아까파.

34. 아부 바꾸, 버라 구꽈구꽈 뿌: 어 꽈소 아쭈꽈 아쭈가꺼|레서 뿌 기리시도 아가나어떠거라 구바오 어 수구 너 마꼬! 러로, 구더 워라 우까더다 가찌 뿌 어 꽈나 워 무꾸 어미러 어루시봐 아더꽈 무노 부다꽈? 노유 꽈나 워 무꾸, 이워라 떠?

35. 여수 나이 뿌: 오라 와러찌러 어 부꽈까러, 아찌|레 꽈 가찌-가찌 거뉴 구 비하끼 비어거 오싸오. 러로, 너 비하끼 뱌 무찌|레 뭐더 오부 부꽈까러, 무따아 꽈어따 무보, 어 무시먀 아꺼싸 구바후기라. 부씨 아가바 어 무꾸 아어따 꽈 무시먀, 아다머냐 어라 아야.

36. 오구 오라 와러찌러 어 부꽈까러 아나찌|레 꽈 가찌-가찌 거뉴, 무 뭐머러라아 꽈 미찌마 여뉴, 구이기라 무버 바꾸 버 부꽈까러. 마꼬 여수 아바아 어라 아마꽈아 구더다 어이 먀시, 어라 구바러가 나 아야 구찌비싸 아부 바꾸.

32. But I, when I am lifted up from the earth, will draw all men to myself."

33. He said this to show the kind of death he was going to die.

34. The crowd spoke up, "We have heard from the Law that the Christ will remain forever, so how can you say, 'The Son of Man must be lifted up'? Who is this 'Son of Man'?"

35. Then Jesus told them, "You are going to have the light just a little while longer. Walk while you have the light, before darkness overtakes you. The man who walks in the dark does not know where he is going.

36. Put your trust in the light while you have it, so that you may become sons of light." When he had finished speaking, Jesus left and hid himself from them.

kuchibisha abu bandju.

Bayuda bauma banana kwemerera Yesu	*바유다 바우마 바나나 궈머러라 여수*	
37. Chiro angaba mbu Yesu airaa bisomerano binene era muhondo s'e bandju, chiro bakanamwemerera mwa michima yabo.	37. 찌로 아까바 뿌 여수 아이라아 비소머라노 비너너 어라 무호또 서 바뚜, 찌로 바가나뭐머러라 뫄 미찌마 야보.	37. Even after Jesus had done all these miraculous signs in their presence, they still would not believe in him.
38. Byabaa bacha, chasiya ene myasi iberere, era murebi Isaya atetaa mbu: Enawechwu! Nde ola wemereraa e myasi era chwatetaa? Si boshi banalolaa kwa buashi bwao?	38. 뱌바아 바짜, 짜시야 어너 먀시 이버러러, 어라 무러비 이사야 아더다아 뿌: 어나워쭈! 떠 오롸 워머러라아 어 먀시 어라 쫘더다아? 시 보씨 바나뢒롸아 과 부아씨 봐오?	38. This was to fulfill the word of Isaiah the prophet: "Lord, who has believed our message and to whom has the arm of the Lord been revealed?"
39. Echera chi chachwumaa abu bandju bataala kwemerera Yesu mwa michima yabo, kukulyikana n'ene myasi Isaya atetaa kanji mbu:	39. 어쩌라 찌 짜쭈마아 아부 바뚜 바다아롸 궈머러라 여수 뫄 미찌마 야보, 구구뤠가나 너너 먀시 이사야 아더다아 가찌 뿌:	39. For this reason they could not believe, because, as Isaiah says elsewhere:
40. Ongo abauchise, chasiya batendaa balola. Abakongobanyise n'e bwenge, chasiya batamenyereraa. Akaba bitangabere bacha, kulyi mango banganyialukilyire, nanyi nyingabalamise.	40. 오꼬 아바우찌서, 짜시야 바더따아 바뢒롸. 아바고꼬바네서 너 붜꺼, 짜시야 바다머녀러라아. 아가바 비다까버러 바짜, 구뤠 마꼬 바까네아루기뤠러, 나네 네까바롸미서.	40. "He has blinded their eyes and deadened their hearts, so they can neither see with their eyes, nor understand with their hearts, nor turn--and I would heal them."
41. Isaya atetaa ei myasi, bushi alolaa kwa bulangare bwa kirisito, na era ateta era lulu sai.	41. 이사야 아더다아 어이 먀시, 부씨 아뢒롸아 과 부롸까러 봐 기리시도, 나 어라 아더다 어라 루루 사이.	41. Isaiah said this because he saw Jesus' glory and spoke about him.

42. Si chiro bacha, banene mwa bakulu-kulu b'e Bayuda, bera kwemerera Yesu mwa michima yabo. Si bataendee balosa changanama kwa bamwemerere, bushi bendee bobaa e Bafarisayo bangesha kubakolokanya mwa mashenge mabo.

43. Bushi beke babaa bachwula basimire kunde batongibwa n'e bandju wa kutongibwa na Ongo.

Ba batachwunda e myasi ya Yesu bakachinjibusibwa

44. Chasinda, Yesu era kwire ateta na murenge munene mbu: Ola wanyemerere mwa muchima wai, ata nyemerere nyeine oshao, si emerere n'ola wanyichwumaa.

45. N'e mango anyilolyireko, elyi alolyire na kw'ola wanyichwumaa.

46. Nyono naikire muno butala nga mundju ola warechire e bulangare. Rero, ola wanyemerere atangachiba mwa musimya.

47. Si akaba e mundju angaba omvire e myasi yanyi, kanji anane e kuilanga mwa muchima wai, ata nyi nyingamuchinjibusa. Bushi ndaikire muno butala kwa

---

42. 시 찌로 바짜, 바너너 뫄 바구루-구루 버 바유다, 버라 궈머러라 여수 뫄 미찌마 야보. 시 바다어떠어 바로사 짜까나마 과 바뭐머러러, 부씨 버떠어 보바아 어 바파리사요 바꺼싸 구바고로가냐 뫄 마써꺼 마보.

43. 부씨 버거 바바아 바쭈꽈 바시미러 구너 바도꺼봐 너 바쭈 와 구도꺼봐 나 오꼬.

바 바다쭈따 어 먀시 야 여수 바가찌찌뵙습봄

44. 짜시따, 여수 어라 귀러 아더다 나 무러꺼 무너너 뿌: 오꽈 와녀머러러 뫄 무찌마 와이, 아다 녀머러러 녀이너 오싸오, 시 어머러러 노꽈 와네쭈마아.

45. 너 마꼬 아네로쩨러고, 어쩨 아로쩨러 나 교꽈 와네쭈마아.

46. 뇨노 나이기러 무노 부다꽈 꽈 무뚜 오꽈 와러찌러 어 부꽈꺼러. 러로, 오꽈 와녀머러러 아다꺼찌바 뫄 무시먀.

47. 시 아가바 어 무뚜 아꺼바 오뻬러 어 먀시 야네, 가찌 아나너 어 구이꽈꺼 뫄 무찌마 와이, 아다 네 네꺼무찌찌부사. 부씨 따이기러 무노 부다꽈 과

---

42. Yet at the same time many even among the leaders believed in him. But because of the Pharisees they would not confess their faith for fear they would be put out of the synagogue;

43. for they loved praise from men more than praise from God.

44. Then Jesus cried out, "When a man believes in me, he does not believe in me only, but in the one who sent me.

45. When he looks at me, he sees the one who sent me.

46. I have come into the world as a light, so that no one who believes in me should stay in darkness.

47. "As for the person who hears my words but does not keep them, I do not judge him. For I did not come to judge the world, but to save it.

kuchinjibusa e bandju, si naikiremo, chasiya nyibanunule.

구찌띠부사 어 바쭈, 시 나이기러모, 짜시야 내바누누뻐.

48. Si chiro bacha, akaba e mundju anganyinana, anane n'e myasi yanyi, ete ola ungamuchinjibusa. Bushi kwa lusuku lw'e businda, ei myasi nakangilyisaa e bandju iikanamuchinjibusa.

48. 시 찌로 바짜, 아가바 어 무뿌 아까네나나, 아나너 너 먀시 야네, 어더 오라 우까무찌띠부사. 부씨 과 루수구 뤄 부시따, 어이 먀시 나가까롄사아 어 바쭈 이이가나무찌띠부사.

48. There is a judge for the one who rejects me and does not accept my words; that very word which I spoke will condemn him at the last day.

49. Bushi ei myasi, ndatetaai kwa kuhonda kwanyi nyeine, si kwa kuhonda kwa Tata ola wanyichwumaa. Kanji iwanyiburaa bya nyemire kunde nakangilyisa.

49. 부씨 어이 먀시, 따더다아이 과 구호따 과내 녀이너, 시 과 구호따 과 다다 오라 와네쭈마아. 가찌 이와네부라아 뱌 녀미러 구떠 나가까롄사.

49. For I did not speak of my own accord, but the Father who sent me commanded me what to say and how to say it.

50. Kanji nyineshi kwa Mwaso wai iwende wareta e kalamo k'e suku n'e mango. Bushi n'oku, chira mwasi woshi ola nenjire nateta, nenjire natetao kukulyikana n'okwa tata ananyiburaa mbu nyitetaa.

50. 가찌 내너씨 과 뫄소 와이 이워떠 와러다 어 가쫘모 거 수구 너 마꼬. 부씨 노구, 찌라 먀시 옷씨 오라 너찌러 나더다, 너찌러 나더다오 구구롄가나 노과 다다 아나네부라아 뿌 네더다아.

50. I know that his command leads to eternal life. So whatever I say is just what the Father has told me to say."

Yoana Chikono 13
Yesu osa e banafunzi bai e bihando

요아나 찌고노 13
여수 오사 어 바나푼씨 바이 어 비하또

John Chapter 13[NIV]

1. Elusuku lukulu lw'e Pasaka, lwabaa lwahonda kuika. Yesu abaa amenyire mira kw'e bihangi byai by'e kutenga muno butala aya era mwa tata byaikire. Rero, bushi abaa achwula asimire e bandju bai bomuno butala, anaendekeraa abasima kuikira kwana businda.

2. Yesu n'e banafunzi bai babaa bera balya e bilyo by'e luolo-olo. Mw'echi chihangi, wamusimu abaa abikire mira e mianyisa ibi mwa muchima wa Yuda, mwenyi Simoni, isikariyota, mbu arenganyaa Yesu.

3. Yesu abaa aneshi kwa Ongo Tata amweresise mira e buashi kwa bindju byoshi. Kanji abaa aneshi kwa era mwa Ongo tata yatengaa, kanji yi anananahuba.

4. Yesu era kubachwuka ala abaa alyira, na akongola e luchimba lwa abaa achihukire. Era kutola e bwamve na achiminabo mwa binji.

5. Chasinda, era kubika e meshi mwa mbare, na atangilyisa osa e banfunzi bai e bihando. Obu bwamve abaa achiminyire mwa binji, bu

---

1. 어루수구 루구루 뤄 파사가, 똬바아 똬호따 구이가. 여수 아바아 아머네러 미라 궈 비하띠 뱌이 벼 구더따 무노 부다똬 아야 어라 똬 다다 뱌이기러. 러로, 부씨 아바아 아쭈똬 아시미러 어 바뚜 바이 보무노 부다똬, 아나어떠거라아 아바시마 구이기라 과나 부시따.

2. 여수 너 바나푸씨 바이 바바아 버라 바꺄 어 비뢴 벼 루오로-오로. 뭐찌 찌하띠, 와무시무 아바아 아비기러 미라 어 미아네사 이비 똬 무찌마 와 유다, 뭐네 시모니, 이시가리요다, 뿌 아러따냐아 여수.

3. 여수 아바아 아너씨 과 오꼬 다다 아뭐러시서 미라 어 부아씨 과 비뚜 뵤씨. 가찌 아바아 아너씨 과 어라 똬 오꼬 다다 야더따아, 가찌 에 아나따나후바.

4. 여수 어라 구바쭈가 아똬 아바아 아쎄라, 나 아고꼬똬 어 루찌빠 똬 아바아 아찌후기러. 어라 구도똬 어 봐뻐 나 아찌미나보 똬 비찌.

5. 짜시따, 어라 구비가 어 머씨 똬 빠러, 나 아다띠레사 오사 어 바누푸씨 바이 어 비하또. 오부 봐뻐 아바아 아찌미네러 똬 비찌, 부

---

1. It was just before the Passover Feast. Jesus knew that the time had come for him to leave this world and go to the Father. Having loved his own who were in the world, he now showed them the full extent of his love.

2. The evening meal was being served, and the devil had already prompted Judas Iscariot, son of Simon, to betray Jesus.

3. Jesus knew that the Father had put all things under his power, and that he had come from God and was returning to God;

4. so he got up from the meal, took off his outer clothing, and wrapped a towel around his waist.

5. After that, he poured water into a basin and began to wash his disciples' feet, drying them with the towel that was wrapped

abaa enjire abahangula mw'e meshi.

아바아 어찌러 아바하우꽈 뭐 머씨.

around him.

6. Abere aika ku Simoni Petero, petero yeke mbu: Enawechwu! Woyo u unganyosa kwa maulu?

6. 아버러 아이가 구 시모니 퍼더로, 퍼더로 여거 뿌: 어나워쭈! 오요 우 우까뇨사 과 마우루?

6. He came to Simon Peter, who said to him, "Lord, are you going to wash my feet?"

7. Yesu nai mbu: Bine naira, utangaala kubimenyerera mw'e bine bihangi, si ungabimenyerera era nyuma.

7. 여수 나이 뿌: 비너 나이라, 우다까아꽈 구비머녀러라 뭐 비너 비하삐, 시 우까비머녀러라 어라 뉴마.

7. Jesus replied, "You do not realize now what I am doing, but later you will understand."

8. Petero na imbu: Nanga walyiya! Woyo utanganyosa kwa maulu chiro na hicha! Yesu mbu: Rero akaba ndakwosise kwa maulu, kukuteta mbu ndete cha nyihangire nao.

8. 퍼더로 나 이뿌: 나까 와레야! 오요 우다까뇨사 과 마우루 찌로 나 히짜! 여수 뿌: 러로 아가바 따고시서 과 마우루, 구구더다 뿌 너더 짜 네하삐러 나오.

8. "No," said Peter, "you shall never wash my feet." Jesus answered, "Unless I wash you, you have no part with me."

9. Simoni petero kukwera ku mubura mbu: Enawechwu! Akaba kubilyi bacha, utachinyosaa kwa maulu meine, si wiree wanyosa n'okwa mino, unyose n'omwa echwe.

9. 시모니 퍼더로 구궈라 구 무부라 뿌: 어나워쭈! 아가바 구비레 바짜, 우다찌뇨사아 과 마우루 머이너, 시 위러어 와뇨사 노과 미노, 우뇨서 노와 어줘.

9. "Then, Lord," Simon Peter replied, "not just my feet but my hands and my head as well!"

10. Yesu na imbu: Ola wowire e mubilyi woshi mira, atangachihuba kwowa. Si kwa maulu kwemire kunowa oshao, bushi ende aba aatakachire mira. Rero, mwabo mwatakachire mira, chiro angaba mbu ata muboshi.

10. 여수 나 이뿌: 오꽈 오위러 어 무비레 오씨 미라, 아다까찌후바 고와. 시 과 마우루 궈미러 구노와 오싸오, 부씨 어떠 아바 아아다가찌러 미라. 러로, 꽈보 꽈다가찌러 미라, 찌로 아까바 뿌 아다 무보씨.

10. Jesus answered, "A person who has had a bath needs only to wash his feet; his whole body is clean. And you are clean, though not every one of you."

11. Cha chachwumaa Yesu ateta mbu ata boshi bu batakachire, bushi abaa amenyire mira ola ungamurenganya.

12. Mango Yesu abaa era amalaa kwosa abu banafunzi bai kwa maulu, era kuhuba kw'embala lwa luchimba lwai, na ahuba kw'ekala ala abaa alyira. Chasinda, era kubabusa mbu: Ebi nera nabailyiraa, mwabimenyerere?

13. Si mwabo mw'enjire mwanyelyika mbu: Mukangilyisi, kanji mbu: Enawenyu. Kw'echi munasinganyire, bushi kanangana nyilyi Mukangilyisi, kanji Enawenyu.

14. Rero, akaba nyono nyi Enawenyu kanji Mukangilyisi wenyu nabosise kwa maulu, nenyu ku munemire kunde mwosanya kwa maulu bacha.

15. Nabalosise mira kwa mungende mwaira, chasiya nenyu munde mwailyirana ng'okwa nabailyilyire.

16. Kubinalyi, nababura kwa e kaungu katachwula karenzise enawabo, n'ola wachwumwa nai atachwula arenzise ola wamuchwuma.

11. 짜 짜쭈마아 여수 아더다 뿌 아다 보씨 부 바다가찌러, 부씨 아바아 아머네러 미라 오라 우꺄무러꺄냐.

12. 마꼬 여수 아바아 어라 아마라아 교사 아부 바나푸씨 바이 과 마우루, 어라 구후바 궈빠꺄 꽈 루찌빠 꽈이, 나 아후바 궈가꺄 아꺄 아바아 아레라. 짜시따, 어라 구바부사 뿌: 어비 너라 나바이레라아, 꽈비머녀러러?

13. 시 꺄보 뭐찌러 꺄녀레가 뿌: 무가꺄레시, 가찌 뿌: 어나워뉴. 궈찌 무나시꺄네러, 부씨 가나꺄나 네레 무가꺄레시, 가찌 어나워뉴.

14. 러로, 아가바 뇨노 네 어나워뉴 가찌 무가꺄레시 워뉴 나보시서 과 마우루, 너뉴 구 무너미러 구떠 뫄사냐 과 마우루 바짜.

15. 나바론시서 미라 과 무꺼떠 뫄이라, 짜시야 너뉴 무떠 뫄이레라나 오과 나바이레레러.

16. 구비나레, 나바부라 과 어 가우꾸 가다쭈꺄 가러씨서 어나와보, 노꺄 와쭈꺄 나이 아다쭈꺄 아러씨서 오꺄 와무쭈꺄.

11. For he knew who was going to betray him, and that was why he said not every one was clean.

12. When he had finished washing their feet, he put on his clothes and returned to his place. "Do you understand what I have done for you?" he asked them.

13. "You call me 'Teacher' and 'Lord,' and rightly so, for that is what I am.

14. Now that I, your Lord and Teacher, have washed your feet, you also should wash one another's feet.

15. I have set you an example that you should do as I have done for you.

16. I tell you the truth, no servant is greater than his master, nor is a messenger greater than the one who sent him.

17. Rero ene myasi mwera muishi. Na akaba mungende mwaikulyikira, kuika munaahanyirwe.

Yesu atata kwa yuda angamurenganya

18. Yesu era kuendekera ateta mbu: Ene myasi yanyi, ndatetai bushi nenyu muboshi. Nyeine nyishi banachilondoreraa. Si byemire oyu mwasi aike. Bushi bichwula byanjikirwe mwa maanjiko Mabuya-buya mbu: Ola nahangiraa ebilyo byanyi ku mbare nguma nai, iwahubaa murenda wanyi.

19. Ei myasi Yoshi, nababilyirei lwarero, era muhondo iike, chasiya mango ingaika mumenyerere kwa nyono nyichwulao.

20. Kubinalyi, nababura kwa ola wahuukasise e mundju ola nachwumire, elyi nyono nyi anahuukasise. Nanyi kunoku, ola wanyihuukasise, elyi ahuukasise n'ola wanyichwumaa.

21. Mango Yesu amalaa kuteta ei myasi, e bwenge bwera kumusungulyira busese, na ababura changanama mbu: Kubinalyi, nababura kanangana kwa muuma mu

17. 러로 어너 먀시 뭐라 무이씨. 나 아가바 무머러 똬이구ퟀ기라, 구이가 무나아하니뤄.

여수 아다다 과 유다 아빠뮬랸빠넷

18. 여수 어라 구어떠거라 아더다 뿌: 어너 먀시 야네, 따더다이 부씨 너뉴 무보씨. 녀이너 네씨 바나찌론또러라아. 시 벼미러 오유 먀시 아이거. 부씨 비쭈똬 뱌찌기뤄 마 마아찌고 마부야-부야 뿌: 오똬 나하ꀀ라아 어비뤈 뱌네 구 빠러 꿈마 나이, 이와후바아 무러따 와네.

19. 어이 먀시 요씨, 나바비ퟀ러이 똬러로, 어라 무호또 이이거, 짜시야 마꼬 이ꀀ이가 무머녀러러 과 뇨노 네쭈똬오.

20. 구비나ퟀ, 나바부라 과 오똬 와후우가시서 어 무뿌 오똬 나쭈미러, 어레 뇨노 네 아나후우가시서. 나네 구노구, 오똬 와네후우가시서, 어레 아후우가시서 노똬 와네쭈마아.

21. 마꼬 여수 아마똬아 구더다 어이 먀시, 어 뷔머 뷔라 구무수꾸ퟀ라 부서서, 나 아바부라 짜빠나마 뿌: 구비나ퟀ, 나바부라 가나빠나 과 무우마 무 똬보

17. Now that you know these things, you will be blessed if you do them.

18. "I am not referring to all of you; I know those I have chosen. But this is to fulfill the scripture: 'He who shares my bread has lifted up his heel against me.'

19. "I am telling you now before it happens, so that when it does happen you will believe that I am He.

20. I tell you the truth, whoever accepts anyone I send accepts me; and whoever accepts me accepts the one who sent me."

21. After he had said this, Jesus was troubled in spirit and testified, "I tell you the truth, one of you is going to betray me."

mwabo anganyirenganya.

22. E banfunzi bai, na bera batabgilyisa basinderana, bushi batamenyaa nde I Yesu abaa ateta era lulu sai.

23. Muuma mubo, ola Yesu abaa achwula asimire busese, iwabaa wekese ala musike sai.

24. Simoni Petero, kukwera kumusimira, abuse Yesu mbu nde yateta era lulu sai.

25. Oyola nai kukwera kwerekera era Yesu abaa alyi. Na amubusa mbu: Enawechwu, nde iwateta era lulu sai kasi?

26. yesu nai mbu: Nyingatobesa chimbi cha mukati mwa mbare, n'ola nyigeresachi, iyoyu. Chasinda, Yesu kutola chimbi cha mukati, era kutobesachi mwa mbare, na angilyisachi Yuda, mwenyi simoni Isikariyota.

27. Mango Yuda abaa era angilyiraachi, unao-unao Wamusimu kuna kwengilyira mwa muchima wai. Yesu era kwire amubura mbu: Cha wahonda kuira, uiraachi fuba!

28. Oyu mwasi Yesu aburaa Yuda, kutabaa chiro na muuma mu balyikabo ba

아빠네러빠냐.

22. 어 바누푸씨 바이, 나 버라 바다부지쩨사 바시떠라나, 부씨 바다머냐아 떠 이 여수 아바아 아더다 어라 루루 사이.

23. 무우마 무보, 오라 여수 아바아 아쭈롸 아시미러 부서서, 이와바아 워거서 아롸 무시거 사이.

24. 시모니 퍼더로, 구궈라 구무시미라, 아부서 여수 뿌 떠 야더다 어라 루루 사이.

25. 오요롸 나이 구궈라 궈러거라 어라 여수 아바아 아롈. 나 아무부사 뿌: 어나워쭉, 떠 이와더다 어라 루루 사이 가시?

26. 여수 나이 뿌: 니빠도버사 찌뻬 짜 무가디 롸 빠러, 노롸 니거러사찌, 이요유. 짜시따, 여수 구도롸 찌뻬 짜 무가디, 어라 구도버사찌 롸 빠러, 나 아삐레사찌 유다, 뭐네 시모니 이시가리요다.

27. 마꼬 유다 아바아 어라 아삐레라아찌, 우나오-우나오 와무시무 구나 궈삐레라 롸 무찌마 와이. 여수 어라 귀러 아무부라 뿌: 짜 와호따 구이라, 우이라아찌 푸바!

28. 오유 뫄시 여수 아부라아 유다, 구다바아 찌로 나 무우마 무 바레가보 바

22. His disciples stared at one another, at a loss to know which of them he meant.

23. One of them, the disciple whom Jesus loved, was reclining next to him.

24. Simon Peter motioned to this disciple and said, "Ask him which one he means."

25. Leaning back against Jesus, he asked him, "Lord, who is it?"

26. Jesus answered, "It is the one to whom I will give this piece of bread when I have dipped it in the dish." Then, dipping the piece of bread, he gave it to Judas Iscariot, son of Simon.

27. As soon as Judas took the bread, Satan entered into him. "What you are about to do, do quickly," Jesus told him,

28. but no one at the meal understood why Jesus said this to him.

babaa balya ebi bilyo, ola wamenyereraa cha chachwumaa Yesu amuburao.

바바아 바퍄 어비 비료, 오퐈 와머녀러라아 짜 짜쭈마아 여수 아무부라오.

29. Bauma mubo bachichingaa mbu abunya Yesu amubilyire mbu ayaa kuula e bindju bya bangakoresa kw'olu lusuku lukulu lw'e Pasaka, nesi mbu ayaa kuasa e bakene, bushi iwendee walanga e hao.

29. 바우마 무보 바찌찌퐈아 뿌 아부냐 여수 아무비례러 뿌 아야아 구우퐈 어 비뿌 뱌 바빠고러사 교루 루수구 루구루 뤄 파사가, 너시 뿌 아야아 구아사 어 바거너, 부씨 이워떠어 와라빠 어 하오.

29. Since Judas had charge of the money, some thought Jesus was telling him to buy what was needed for the Feast, or to give something to the poor.

30. Mango Yuda abaa era atolaa cha chimbi ch'e mukati, unao-unao kuna kuuluka era butala. N'e buchwufu bwabaa bw'elyire mira.

30. 마꼬 유다 아바아 어라 아도퐈아 짜 찌삐 쩌 무가디, 우나오-우나오 구나 구우루가 어라 부다퐈. 너 부쭈푸 봐바아 뷔쮀러 미라.

Yesu ana e muomba muyayaya

여수 아나 어 무오빠 무야야야

31. Mango Yuda abaa aulukire mira, Yesu era kuteta mbu: Rero, nyi Mwana w'e Mundju neresibwe echwunda. Ongo nai, eresibwelyi mwa kunyirengerako.

31. 마꼬 유다 아바아 아우루기러 미라, 여수 어라 구더다 뿌: 러로, 네 뫄나 워 무뚜 너러시붜 어쭈따. 오꼬 나이, 어러시뷔쀄 뫄 구네러떠라고.

31. When he was gone, Jesus said, "Now is the Son of Man glorified and God is glorified in him.

32. Na akaba Ongo eresibwe echwunda kunyirengerako, echera chi chichwumire nanyi nyi Mwana, Ongo nai amberesalyi. Kanji atanemange kumberesalyi.

32. 나 아가바 오꼬 어러시붜 어쭈따 구네러떠라고, 어쩌라 찌 찌쭈미러 나니 네 뫄나, 오꼬 나이 아뻐러사쀄. 가지 아다너마떠 구뻐러사쀄.

32. If God is glorified in him, God will glorify the Son in himself, and will glorify him at once.

33. Rero bana banyi, nyichilyi alauma nenyu ku bihangi bieke oshao. Munganyihonda, si nababura lwarero kwa nanaburaa e Bayuda nabo:

33. 러로 바나 바네, 네찌쮀 아퐈루마 너뉴 구 비하삐 비어거 오싸오. 무빠네호따, 시 나바부라 퐈러로 과 나나부라아 어 바유다 나보:

33. "My children, I will be with you only a little longer. You will look for me, and just as I told the Jews, so I tell you now: Where I am

mutangaala kuika era naya.

무다꾸아꽈 구이가 어라
나야.

going, you cannot come.

34. Bushi n'oku, naberesise muomba muyayaya, nai yono: Mundaa mwasimana. Kwa nyichwula nyibasimire, ku nenyu mundaa mwanasimana.

34. 부씨 노구, 나버러시서 무오빠 무야야야, 나이 요노: 무따아 마시마나. 과 네쭈꽈 네바시미러, 구 너뉴 무따아 꽈나시마나.

34. "A new command I give you: Love one another. As I have loved you, so you must love one another.

35. Oku kusimana kw'enyu ku kungende kwachwuma e bandju boshi bamenyerera kanangana kwa munachwula banafunzi banyi.

35. 오구 구시마나 궈뉴 구 구꺼러 과쭈마 어 바뉴 보씨 바머녀러라 가나꾸나 과 무나쭈꽈 바나푸씨 바니.

35. By this all men will know that you are my disciples, if you love one another."

Yesu ateta mbu Petero angachakanai

여수 아더다 뿌 퍼더로 아꽈짓—낍일

36. Simoni petero kukwera kubusa Yesu mbu: Enawechwu, ngai iungaya kasi? Yesu nai mbu: Era nyingaya, utangafura kunyikulyikirayi, si era nyuma akananyikulyikira.

36. 시모니 퍼더로 구궈라 구부사 여수 뿌: 어나워쭈, 꽈이 이우꽈야 가시? 여수 나이 뿌: 어라 네꽈야, 우다꽈푸라 구네구레기라에, 시 어라 뉴마 아가나네구레기라.

36. Simon Peter asked him, "Lord, where are you going?" Jesus replied, "Where I am going, you cannot follow now, but you will follow later."

37. Petero era kumubusa kanji mbu: Enawechwu, chi chingachwuma ndakukulyikira mw'e chine chihangi? N'emerere kwana e kalamo kanyi bushi nao!

37. 퍼더로 어라 구무부사 가찌 뿌: 어나워쭈, 찌 찌꽈쭈마 따구구레기라 뭐 찌너 찌하삐? 너머러러 과나 어 가꽈모 가니 부씨 나오!

37. Peter asked, "Lord, why can't I follow you now? I will lay down my life for you."

38. Chasinjire, Yesu era kumwakula mbu: Wachikunganyise mira kwa ungana e kalamo kao bushi nanyi? Rero kubinalyi, nakubura kwa e luasi lungabika elyi woyo

38. 짜시찌러, 여수 어라 구꽈구꽈 뿌: 와찌구꽈네서 미라 과 우꽈나 어 가꽈모 가오 부씨 나니? 러로 구비나레, 나구부라 과 어 루꽈시 루꽈비가 어레 오요 와짜가나 뇨노 가하쭉!

38. Then Jesus answered, "Will you really lay down your life for me? I tell you the truth, before the rooster crows, you will disown me three times!

wachakana nyono kahachwu!

Yoana Chikono 14

Yesu I njira y'e kuya era mwa Tata

1. Yesu era kubura e banafunzi bai mbu: Mutendaa mwachilyibusa mwa michima yenyu. Mundaa mwemerera Ongo, nanyi mwanende mwanyemerera mwa michima yenyu.

2. Mwa nyumba ya tata, muchwula bisiki binene. akaba bitangabere bacha, ndangababilyire mbu naya kubakunganyisa e chisiki cha mukaberamo.

3. Na akaba nyingaya kubakunganyisa chi, nyikahuba kubaha nyibatole, chasiya e chisiki cha nyikabamo, nenyu mube muchi.

4. N'eyi nyingaya, mwishi enjira y'e kuyayi.

5. Mw'olu, tomasi era kubusa Yesu mbu: Enawechwu, si eyi ungaya, chwubeke chwuteshiyi! Rero, enjira y'e kuyayi, kute chwungere chwaimenya?

요아나 찌고노 14

여수 이 씨띱 여 구야 어라 와 다다

1. 여수 어라 구부라 어 바나푸씨 바이 뿌: 무더따아 마찌례부사 와 미찌마 여뉴. 무따아 뭐머러라 오꼬, 나니 와너떠 와녀머러라 와 미찌마 여뉴.

2. 와 뉴빠 야 다다, 무쭈라 비시기 비너너. 아가바 비다빠버러 바짜, 따빠바비례러 뿌 나야 구바구빠네사 어 찌시기 짜 무가버라모.

3. 나 아가바 네빠야 구바구빠네사 찌, 네가후바 구바하 네바도뚸, 짜시야 어 찌시기 짜 네가바모, 너뉴 무버 무찌.

4. 너에 네빠야, 뮈씨 어찌라 여 구야에.

5. 모루, 도마시 어라 구부사 여수 뿌: 어나워쭉, 시 어에 우빠야, 쭈버거 쭈더씨에! 러로, 어찌라 여 구야에, 구더 쭈어러 쫘이머냐?

John Chapter 14[NIV]

1. "Do not let your hearts be troubled. Trust in God; trust also in me.

2. In my Father's house are many rooms; if it were not so, I would have told you. I am going there to prepare a place for you.

3. And if I go and prepare a place for you, I will come back and take you to be with me that you also may be where I am.

4. You know the way to the place where I am going."

5. Thomas said to him, "Lord, we don't know where you are going, so how can we know the way?"

6. Yesu nai mbu: Nyono nyi njira, kanji nyi kanangana, kanji nyi kalamo! Kutalyi ola ungaalakuika era mwa tata, busira kunyirengerako.

6. 여수 나이 뿌: 뇨노 네 찌라, 가찌 네 가나ᅌ까나, 가찌 네 가ᄙᅡ모! 구다ᄙᅦ 오ᄙᅡ 우ᅌ까아ᄙᅡ구이가 어라 뫄 다다, 부시라 구네러ᅌ꺼라고.

6. Jesus answered, "I am the way and the truth and the life. No one comes to the Father except through me.

7. Akaba munganyimenyire na tata. Rero, kutengera lwarero mwamumenyire, mwanamulolireko!

7. 아가바 무ᅌ까네머네러 나 다다. 러로, 구더ᅌ꺼라 ᄙᅪ러로 뫄무머네러, 뫄나무ᄙᅩᄙᅵ러고!

7. If you really knew me, you would know my Father as well. From now on, you do know him and have seen him."

8. Firipo nai era kubura Yesu mbu: Enawechwu, uchwulosaa Tata, chasiya e michima yechwu ibambatale mwa bula.

8. 피리포 나이 어라 구부라 여수 뿌: 어나워쭈, 우쭈ᄙᅩ사아 다다, 짜시야 어 미찌마 여쭈 이바빠다ᄙᅥ 뫄 부ᄙᅡ.

8. Philip said, "Lord, show us the Father and that will be enough for us."

9. Yesu nai mbu: Era Firipo! Si suku sinene sine nyilyi alauma nenyu, utanafuraa kunyimenyerera kuikira lwarero? Ola wanyilolyireko, elyi alolyire na ku tata! Rero, kute uchilyi wateta kanji mbu nyibalosaa Tata?

9. 여수 나이 뿌: 어라 피리포! 시 수구 시너너 시너 네ᄙᅦ 아ᄙᅡ우마 너뉴, 우다나푸라아 구네머녀러라 구이기라 ᄙᅪ러로? 오ᄙᅡ 와네ᄙᅩᄙᅦ러고, 어ᄙᅦ 아ᄙᅩᄙᅦ러 나 구 다다! 러로, 구더 우찌ᄙᅦ 와더다 가찌 뿌 네바ᄙᅩ사아 다다?

9. Jesus answered: "Don't you know me, Philip, even after I have been among you such a long time? Anyone who has seen me has seen the Father. How can you say, 'Show us the Father'?

10. Woyo utemerere kwa nichwula mwa ndanda sa Tata, na Tata mwa ndanda sanyi? Bushi n'oku, e myasi era nenjire nababura, itatenganyire nanyi nyeine, si tata ola uchwula mwa ndanda sanyi, iwenjire wakola e milyimo yai.

10. 오요 우더머러러 과 니쭈ᄙᅡ 뫄 따따 사 다다, 나 다다 뫄 따따 사네? 부씨 노구, 어 먀시 어라 너찌러 나바부라, 이다더ᅌ까네러 나네 녀이너, 시 다다 오ᄙᅡ 우쭈ᄙᅡ 뫄 따따 사네, 이워찌러 와고ᄙᅡ 어 미ᄙᅦ모 야이.

10. Don't you believe that I am in the Father, and that the Father is in me? The words I say to you are not just my own. Rather, it is the Father, living in me, who is doing his work.

11. Ene myasi nababilyire kwa nyichwula mwa ndanda sa

11. 어너 먀시 나바비ᄙᅦ러 과 네쭈ᄙᅡ 뫄 따따 사 다다 나

11. Believe me when I say that I am in the Father and

Tata na Tata mwa ndanda sanyi, mwemereraai. Nesi mulumbaa mwanyemerere kukulyikana na bya nenjire naira.

12. Kubinalyi, nababura kwa ola unyemerere woshi, nai angende anaira bya nenjire naira. Kanji yeke, angende aira na binene kurenza bya nenjire naira, bushi nera naya era mwa Tata.

13. Kanji byoshi bya mungende mwema kw'e sina lyanyi, nyigende nanabiira, chasiya Tata ende aya ngulu kunyirengera nyi Mwana wai.

14. Kubinalyi, choshi cha mungende mwanyema kw'e sina lyanyi, nyigende nanairachi.

Yesu alaanya e ndjumwa sai e Muchima Mubuya-buya

15. Akaba muchwula munyisimire, mungende mwachwunda n'e miomba yanyi.

16. Nanyi, nyingema Tata aberese eunji ola ungende wabaasa, na kuendekera kuba alauma nenyu e suku soshi.

17. Oyola, i Muchima w'e kanangana. E bandju b'omwa butala, batangaala

다다 뫄 따따 사니, 뭐머러라아이. 너시 무루빠아 뫄녀머러러 구구레가나 나 뱌 너찌러 나이라.

12. 구비나레, 나바부라 과 오똬 우녀머러러 오씨, 나이 아꺼떠 아나이라 뱌 너찌러 나이라. 가찌 여거, 아꺼떠 아이라 나 비너너 구러싸 뱌 너찌러 나이라, 부씨 너라 나야 어라 뫄 다다.

13. 가찌 뵤씨 뱌 무꺼떠 뭐마 궈 시나 랸네, 네거떠 나나비이라, 짜시야 다다 어떠 아야 응루루 구네러꺼라 네 뫄나 와이.

14. 구비나레, 쪼씨 짜 무꺼떠 뫄녀마 궈 시나 랸네, 네거떠 나나이라찌.

여수 아똬씸냇 어 뚜뭄 사이 어 무찌마 무부야-부야

15. 아가바 무쭈똬 무네시미러, 무꺼떠 뫄쭈따 너 미오빠 야니.

16. 나니, 네꺼마 다다 아버러서 어우찌 오똬 우꺼떠 와바아사, 나 구어떠거라 구바 아똬우마 너뉴 어 수구 소씨.

17. 오요똬, 이 무찌마 워 가나꺄나. 어 바뚜 보뫄 부다똬, 바다꺄아똬

the Father is in me; or at least believe on the evidence of the miracles themselves.

12. I tell you the truth, anyone who has faith in me will do what I have been doing. He will do even greater things than these, because I am going to the Father.

13. And I will do whatever you ask in my name, so that the Son may bring glory to the Father.

14. You may ask me for anything in my name, and I will do it.

15. "If you love me, you will obey what I command.

16. And I will ask the Father, and he will give you another Counselor to be with you forever--

17. the Spirit of truth. The world cannot accept him, because it neither sees him

kumuhuukasa, bushi batachwula bamuseneko, kanji batachwula bamwishi. Si mwabo, mumwishi bushi achwula alauma nenyu, kanji akanalyinda anachwula mwa ndanda senyu.

구무후우가사, 부씨 바다쭈롸 바무서너고, 가찌 바다쭈롸 바뮈씨. 시 뫄보, 무뮈씨 부씨 아쭈롸 아롸우마 너뉴, 가찌 아가나뻬따 아나쭈롸 뫄 따따 서뉴.

nor knows him. But you know him, for he lives with you and will be in you.

18. Ndabareke nga fusi, si nyikabaha kanji ene mulyi.

18. 따바러거 까 푸시, 시 네가바하 가찌 어너 무레.

18. I will not leave you as orphans; I will come to you.

19. Era nyuma sa suku sieke, e bandju b'omuno butala batachinyiloleko, si mwabo mubeke mungende mwanyilolako. Rero, bushi nyilyi muuma-uma, nenyu munganaba bauma-uma.

19. 어라 뉴마 사 수구 시어거, 어 바쭈 보무노 부다롸 바다찌네로러고, 시 뫄보 무버거 무어러 뫄네로롸고. 러로, 부씨 네레 무우마-우마, 너뉴 무아나바 바우마-우마.

19. Before long, the world will not see me anymore, but you will see me. Because I live, you also will live.

20. Mw'esi suku, mu mungere mwamenyerera kanangana kwa nyichwula mwa ndanda sa Tata, nenyu mwa ndanda sanyi, nanyi mwa ndanda senyu.

20. 뭐시 수구, 무 무어러 뫄머녀러러 가나아나 과 네쭈롸 뫄 따따 사 다다, 너뉴 뫄 따따 사니, 나니 뫄 따따 서뉴.

20. On that day you will realize that I am in my Father, and you are in me, and I am in you.

21. Ola wemerere e miomba yanyi, na kunde achwundai, oyola iunyisimire. Ola unyisimire, i Tata nai angasima ngachi. Nanyi, nyinganamusima, kanji nyikende nachilosa kui.

21. 오롸 워머러러 어 미오빠 야네, 나 구떠 아쭈빠이, 오요롸 이우네시미러. 오롸 우네시미러, 이 다다 나이 아아시마 까찌. 나니, 네아나무시마, 가찌 네거떠 나찌로사 구이.

21. Whoever has my commands and obeys them, he is the one who loves me. He who loves me will be loved by my Father, and I too will love him and show myself to him."

22. Mw'olu, Yuda (si ata Yuta Isikariyota) era kubusa Yesu mbu: Enawechwu, chi chingachwuma ku chwubano ku anganachilosa oshao, si utachilose kwa banji bandju

22. 몰루, 유다 (시 아다 유다 이시가리요다) 어라 구부사 여수 뿌: 어나워쭉, 찌 찌까쭈마 구 쭈바노 구 아아나찌로사 오싸오, 시 우다찌로서 과 바찌 바쭈 보

22. Then Judas (not Judas Iscariot) said, "But, Lord, why do you intend to show yourself to us and not to the world?"

bo muno butala?

무노 부다ᄙᅡ?

23. Yesu nai mbu: Akaba e mundju anyisimire, kuika anachwunde e myasi yanyi. Oyu mundju, Tata angamusima, aola nyono na Tata chwungaya kubera alauma nai.

23. 여수 나이 뿌: 아가바 어 무ᅜᅮ 아네시미러, 구이가 아나쭈ᄕᅥ 어 먀시 야네. 오유 무ᅜᅮ, 다다 아ᅌᅡ무시마, 아오ᄙᅡ 뇨노 나 다다 쭈ᅌᅡ야 구버라 아ᄙᅡ우마 나이.

23. Jesus replied, "If anyone loves me, he will obey my teaching. My Father will love him, and we will come to him and make our home with him.

24. Si ola utanyisimire yeke, e myasi yanyi nai atanganaichwunda. N'ene myasi nababura, ita yanyi nyeine, si ilyi ya Tata ola wanyichwumaa.

24. 시 오ᄙᅡ 우다네시미러 여거, 어 먀시 야네 나이 아다ᅌᅡ나이쭈ᄕᅡ. 너너 먀시 나바부라, 이다 야네 녀이너, 시 이ᄙᅨ 야 다다 오ᄙᅡ 와네쭈마아.

24. He who does not love me will not obey my teaching. These words you hear are not my own; they belong to the Father who sent me.

25. Ei myasi Yoshi, nababilyirei, kuno nyichiri alauma nenyu.

25. 어이 먀시 요씨, 나바비ᄙᅨ러이, 구노 네찌리 아ᄙᅡ우마 너뉴.

25. "All this I have spoken while still with you.

26. Si kw'e sina lyanyi ku Tata angabachwumira e Muchima Mubuya-buya. N'oyu Muchima Mubuya-buya iungende wabaasa, na kunde abakangilyisa byoshi. Na chira mwasi woshi nababuraa, akende anabakengesao.

26. 시 궈 시나 ᄙᅣ네 구 다다 아ᅌᅡ바쭈미라 어 무찌마 무부야-부야. 노유 무찌마 무부야-부야 이우ᅌᅥᄕᅥ 와바아사, 나 구ᄕᅥ 아바가ᅌᅵᄙᅨ사 뵤씨. 나 찌라 뫄시 오씨 나바부라아, 아거ᄕᅥ 아나바거ᅌᅥ사오.

26. But the Counselor, the Holy Spirit, whom the Father will send in my name, will teach you all things and will remind you of everything I have said to you.

27. Nabarekere e boolo. N'obu boolo, nyinaberesisebo. Kanji butalyi ng'obwa bandju bo muno butala bende bana. Bushi n'oku, mutendaa mwachichilyibusa mwa michima yenyu, nesi mwachobaa.

27. 나바러거러 어 보오ᄙᅩ. 노부 보오ᄙᅩ, 네나버러시서보. 가ᅜᅵ 부다ᄙᅨ ᅌᅩ봐 바ᅜᅮ 보 무노 부다ᄙᅡ 버ᄕᅥ 바나. 부씨 노구, 무더ᄕᅡ아 뫄찌찌ᄙᅨ부사 뫄 미찌마 여뉴, 너시 뫄쪼바아.

27. Peace I leave with you; my peace I give you. I do not give to you as the world gives. Do not let your hearts be troubled and do not be afraid.

28. Si momvire kwa nababura kwa nyingaenda, n'okwa

28. 시 모삐러 과 나바부라 과 네ᅌᅡ어ᄕᅡ, 노과

28. "You heard me say, 'I am going away and I am

nyingafuluka kanji ene mulyi.
Rero akaba mwabaa
munyisimire, mungamoire
mwa kumva kwa nyingaya era
mwa tata, bushi imukulu-kulu
ku nyono.

29. Ei myasi Yoshi, nababilyirei
era muhondo ibe, chasiya
mango ingaberera,
munyemerere mwa michima
yenyu.

30. Ndachihambale nenyu inji
myasi inene, bushi e mwami
wobuno butala abahire. Si
chiro bacha, atete buashi
busibya ku nyono.

31. Si byemire e bandju
bomwa butala bemenye kwa
nyichwula nyisimire tata, na
bya anyichwumaa, bi nenjire
nanaira. Rero, mubachwukaa
tutenge anola.

네빠푸루가 가찌 어너 무쩨.
러로 아가바 마바아
무네시미러, 무빠모이러 마
구빠 과 네빠야 어라 마
다다, 부씨 이무구루루-구루 구
뇨노.

29. 어이 먀시 요씨,
나바비쩨러이 어라 무호또
이버, 짜시야 마꼬
이빠버러라, 무녀머러러 마
미찌마 여뉴.

30. 따찌하빠뻐 너뉴 이찌
먀시 이너너, 부씨 어 마미
오부노 부다라 아바히러. 시
찌로 바짜, 아더더 부아씨
부시뱌 구 뇨노.

31. 시 벼미러 어 바쭈 보와
부다랴 버머녀 과 네쭈롸
네시미러 다다, 나 뱌
아네쭈마아, 비 너찌러
나나이라. 러로, 무바쭈가아
두더뻐 아노롸.

---

coming back to you.' If you
loved me, you would be
glad that I am going to the
Father, for the Father is
greater than I.

29. I have told you now
before it happens, so that
when it does happen you
will believe.

30. I will not speak with you
much longer, for the prince
of this world is coming. He
has no hold on me,

31. but the world must learn
that I love the Father and
that I do exactly what my
Father has commanded me.
"Come now; let us leave.

Yoana Chikono 15
Yesu I muchi w'e musabibu
w'e kanangana

1. Nyono nyi muchi w'e
kanangana, na tata I muinzi.
2. Na akaba kulyi etabi lya
lyinyimelyreko, si lyiteka
bifuma, kuika anaishelyi. Si lya
lyende lyeka e bifuma, lyeke
ende alyihabulyira chasiya

요아나 찌고노 15
여수 이 무찌 워 무사비부 워
가나빠낍

1. 뇨노 네 무찌 워 가나빠나,
나 다다 이 무이씨.
2. 나 아가바 구레 어다비 랴
레네머뤼러고, 시 레더가
비푸마, 구이가 아나이써쩨.
시 랴 려너 려가 어 비푸마,
려거 어뻐 아쩨하부쩨라

Chapter John 15[NIV]

1. "I am the true vine, and
my Father is the gardener.
2. He cuts off every branch
in me that bears no fruit,
while every branch that
does bear fruit he prunes so
that it will be even more

Iyeke bifuma binene busese.

3. Rero nenyu, e myasi era nenjire nababura iyenjire yachwuma mwakomisibwa.

4. Muendekeraa kuba mwa ndanda sanyi, ng'okwa nanyi nyichwula mwa ndanda senyu. Bushi etabi ly'e musabibu, lyindangaala kweka bifuma lyeine, akaba lyitalyi kw'oyu muchi w'e musabibu. Rero nenyu mutangaala kweka chiro na chifuma chisibya akaba mutalyi mwa ndanda sanyi.

5. Nyono nyi muchi w'e musabibu, nenyu mu matabi. Ola waendekera kuba mwa ndanda sanyi, nanyi naba mwa ndanda sai, oyola iwende weka bifuma weka bifuma binene. Si busira nyono, mutangaala kuira kandju kasibya.

6. Na akaba e mundju atangaendekera kuba mwa ndanda sanyi, kuika anaumwe era butala. Aola, anaba ng'e tabi lya bakabulaa, na lyoma. N'e matabi ma momire, kumalunda-lunda ku bende bamalunda-lunda, na bamauma mwa mulyiro, chasinda manasirera.

짜시야 뗘거 비푸마 비너너 부서서.

3. 러로 너뉴, 어 먀시 어라 너찌러 나바부라 이여찌러 야쭈마 꽈고미시봐.

4. 무어떠거라아 구바 꽈 따따 사네, 꼬과 나네 네쭈롸 꽈 따따 서뉴. 부씨 어다비 뤼어 무사비부, 레따꽈아롸 궈가 비푸마 뗘이너, 아가바 레다레 교유 무찌 워 무사비부. 러로 너뉴 무다꽈아롸 궈가 찌로 나 찌푸마 찌시뱌 아가바 무다레 꽈 따따 사네.

5. 뇨노 네 무찌 워 무사비부, 너뉴 무 마다비. 오롸 와어떠거라 구바 꽈 따따 사네, 나네 나바 꽈 따따 사이, 오요롸 이워떠 워가 비푸마 워가 비푸마 비너너. 시 부시라 뇨노, 무다꽈아롸 구이라 가뚜 가시뱌.

6. 나 아가바 어 무뚜 아다꽈어떠거라 구바 꽈 따따 사네, 구이가 아나우뭐 어라 부다롸. 아오롸, 아나바 꺼 다비 롸 바가부롸아, 나 료마. 너 마다비 마 모미러, 구마룬따-룬따 구 버떠 바마룬따-룬따, 나 바마우마 꽈 무레로, 짜시따 마나시러라.

fruitful.

3. You are already clean because of the word I have spoken to you.

4. Remain in me, and I will remain in you. No branch can bear fruit by itself; it must remain in the vine. Neither can you bear fruit unless you remain in me.

5. "I am the vine; you are the branches. If a man remains in me and I in him, he will bear much fruit; apart from me you can do nothing.

6. If anyone does not remain in me, he is like a branch that is thrown away and withers; such branches are picked up, thrown into the fire and burned.

7. Si akaba munganaendekera mwaba mwa ndanda sanyi, n'e myasi yanyi yaendekera yaba mwa michima yenyu, aola mwera munganema tata choshi cha muhonjire, anaberesechi.

8. Akaba mungeka bifuma binene, Tata angaya ngulu busese. N'echi chi chingachwuma mwamenyeka kanangana kwa munalyi banafunzi banyi.

9. Kwa Tata achwula anyisimire, ku nanyi nyinachwula nyibasimire. Rero mwei nzii yanyi, mu munaendekera kuba.

10. Akaba mungachwunda e miomba yanyi, mukanaendekera kuba mwei nzii yanyi, ng'okwa nanyi nyichwula nyichwunjire e miomba ya Tata, n'e kuendekera kuba mwa nzii yai.

11. Ei myasi Yoshi, nababilyirei, chasiya e lumoo lwanyi luendekere kuba, kanji lunabe lunene busese.

12. Rero, e muomba ola naberesise I yono: Mundaa mwasimana, ng'okwa nanyi nyichwula nyibasimire.

7. 시 아가바 무빠나어떠거라 뫄바 뫄 따따 사네, 너 먀시 야네 야어떠거라 야바 뫄 미찌마 여뉴, 아오콰 뭐라 무빠너마 다다 쪼씨 짜 무호씨러, 아나버러서찌.

8. 아가바 무빠가 비푸마 비너너, 다다 아빠야 우루 부서서. 너찌 찌 찌빠쭈마 뫄머녀가 가나빠나 과 무나쩨 바나푸씨 바네.

9. 과 다다 아쭈콰 아네시미러, 구 나네 네나쭈콰 네바시미러. 러로 뭐이 씨이 야네, 무 무나어떠거라 구바.

10. 아가바 무빠쭈따 어 미오빠 야네, 무가나어떠거라 구바 뭐이 씨이 야네, 꼬과 나네 네쭈콰 네쭈씨러 어 미오빠 야 다다, 너 구어떠거라 구바 뫄 씨이 야이.

11. 어이 먀시 요씨, 나바비쩨러이, 짜시야 어 루모오 콰네 루어떠거러 구바, 가찌 루나버 루너너 부서서.

12. 러로, 어 무오빠 오라 나버러시서 이 요노: 무따아 뫄시마나, 꼬과 나네 네쭈콰 네바시미러.

7. If you remain in me and my words remain in you, ask whatever you wish, and it will be given you.

8. This is to my Father's glory, that you bear much fruit, showing yourselves to be my disciples.

9. "As the Father has loved me, so have I loved you. Now remain in my love.

10. If you obey my commands, you will remain in my love, just as I have obeyed my Father's commands and remain in his love.

11. I have told you this so that my joy may be in you and that your joy may be complete.

12. My command is this: Love each other as I have loved you.

13. Kutalyi mundju ola wete nzii inene kurenza ola wemerera kwana e kalamo kai bushi nabera bai.

14. Rero, mwabo mulyi bera banyi, akaba mungaira bya nababilyire.

15. Ndangachibelyika mbu mulyi baanda, bushi e muanda atamenya bya enawabo aira. Si mwabo, nera nabelyika bera banyi. Bushi byoshi bya Tata anyikangaa, nenyu nabalosisebi mira.

16. Mwabo ata mumwanyilondolaa, si nyono nyinabalondolaa, nera kubabura mbu muendaa, mweke n'e bifuma bya bitakawe. Bushi n'oku, choshi cha mungende mwema tata kw'e sina lyanyi, angende anaberesachi.

17. E muomba naberesise I yono: Mundaa mwasimana.

E bandju b'omwa butala bakahomba e banafunzi ba Yesu

18. Kanji Yesu era kuteta mbu: Akaba e bandju b'omwa butala babahombire, mumenyereraa kwa nyono nyi batangiraa kuhomba.

19. Akaba nenyu mungabere

---

13. 구다레 무뚜 오라 워더 씨이 이너너 구러싸 오라 워머라라 과나 어 가꾜모 가이 부씨 나버라 바이.

14. 러로, 마보 무레 버라 바네, 아가바 무까이라 뱌 나바비쪠러.

15. 따까찌버쪠가 뿌 무쪠 바아따, 부씨 어 무아따 아다머냐 뱌 어나와보 아이라. 시 먀보, 너라 나버쪠가 버라 바네. 부씨 뵤씨 뱌 다다 아네가까아, 너뉴 나바론시서비 미라.

16. 먀보 아다 무꽈네론또꽈아, 시 뇨노 네나바론또꽈아, 너라 구바부라 뿌 무어따아, 뭐거 너 비푸마 뱌 비다가워. 부씨 노구, 쪼씨 짜 무꺼너 뭐마 다다 궈 시나 꺄네, 아꺼너 아나버러사찌.

17. 어 무오빠 나버러시서 이 요노: 무따아 마시마나.

어 바뿌 보와 부다꽈 바가호빠 어 바나푸씨 바 여수

18. 가찌 여수 어라 구더다 뿌: 아가바 어 바뿌 보와 부다꽈 바바호쪠러, 무머녀러라아 과 뇨노 네 바다삐라아 구호빠.

19. 아가바 너뉴 무까버러

---

13. Greater love has no one than this, that he lay down his life for his friends.

14. You are my friends if you do what I command.

15. I no longer call you servants, because a servant does not know his master's business. Instead, I have called you friends, for everything that I learned from my Father I have made known to you.

16. You did not choose me, but I chose you and appointed you to go and bear fruit--fruit that will last. Then the Father will give you whatever you ask in my name.

17. This is my command: Love each other.

18. "If the world hates you, keep in mind that it hated me first.

19. If you belonged to the

bandju bo muno butala, beshamo bangabasimire nga banyakabo. Si mwabo, nabalondore mira n'e kubakula mwa kachi-kachi kabo. Rero echera chi chende chachwuma babahomba, bushi mutachichwula nabo.

20. Mundaa mwakengera cha chinwa nababuraa mbu: E muanda atarenzise enawabo. Rero, akaba banyilyibusaa kuika nenyu banabalyibuse. Kanji akaba bachwundaa e myasi era nendee nakangilyisa, kuika banachwunde n'e yenyu.

21. Bagende babalyibusa bacha bushi nanyi, kanji bushi bateshi ola wanyichwumaa.

22. Akaba nyeine ndaikaa kuhambala nabo, batangaachire chibi chisibya. Si rero, batachete cha chingachwuma mbu batete chibi.

23. Ola unyihombire, elyi ahombire na Tata.

24. Akaba ndangenjire naira bisomerano mwa kachi-kachi kabo, bya bitafuraa kuilyibwa na unji mundju, batangaachire chibi. Si rero, beine bachilorere kubi, si chiro bacha banachilyi

바뉴 보 무노 부다꾸라, 버싸모 바꾸바시미러 꾸 바냐가보. 시 마보, 나바로ㄸ러 미라 너 구바구꾸라 꾸 가찌-가찌 가보. 러로 어쩌라 찌 쩌떠 짜쭈마 바바호빠, 부씨 무다찌쭈라 나보.

20. 무따아 꽈거꺼라 짜 찌놔 나바부라아 뿌: 어 무아따 아다러씨서 어나와보. 러로, 아가바 바네쩨부사아 구이가 너뉴 바나바쩨부서. 가찌 아가바 바쭈따아 어 먀시 어라 너떠어 나가꾸쩨사, 구이가 바나쭈떠 너 여뉴.

21. 바거떠 바바쩨부사 바짜 부씨 나네, 가찌 부씨 바더씨 오꾸라 와네쭈마아.

22. 아가바 녀이너 따이가아 구하빠꾸라 나보, 바다꾸아아찌러 찌비 찌시뱌. 시 러로, 바다쩌더 짜 찌꾸쭈마 뿌 바더더 찌비.

23. 오꾸라 우네호삐러, 어쩨 아호삐러 나 다다.

24. 아가바 따꺼찌러 나이라 비소머라노 꽈 가찌-가찌 가보, 뱌 비다푸라아 구이쩨봐 나 우씨 무뚜, 바다꾸아아찌러 찌비. 시 러로, 버이너 바찌로러러 구비, 시

world, it would love you as its own. As it is, you do not belong to the world, but I have chosen you out of the world. That is why the world hates you.

20. Remember the words I spoke to you: 'No servant is greater than his master.' If they persecuted me, they will persecute you also. If they obeyed my teaching, they will obey yours also.

21. They will treat you this way because of my name, for they do not know the One who sent me.

22. If I had not come and spoken to them, they would not be guilty of sin. Now, however, they have no excuse for their sin.

23. He who hates me hates my Father as well.

24. If I had not done among them what no one else did, they would not be guilty of sin. But now they have seen these miracles, and yet they have hated both me and my

banyihombire, banahomba na Tata.

25. Si byabere bacha, chasiya cha chinwa chiberere, cha chichwula chanjikirwe mwa mwaso wabo

26. Chasinjire Yesu kukwera kubabura mbu: Nyingabachwumira e Muchima w'e kanangana, ola ukende wabaasa. Oyola angatengera era mwa tata. Na mango angaika, iukende wateta binene by'eshi era luulu sanyi.

27. Anabe nenyu, mungende mwahambala bya mwishi era luulu sanyi, bushi mu muchwula alauma nanyi kutengera endangilyiso.

Yoana Chikono 16

1. Ei myasi yoshi, nababilyirei mungesha kureka e bwemeresi bwenyu.
2. Bushi e bandju bangende babakolokanya mwa mashenge mabo. N'e suku singaika, sa e mundju ola wabechire, angende achichinga mbu Ongo iakorera.

찌로 바짜 바나찌꼐 바네호삐러, 바나호빠 나 다다.

25. 시 뱌버러 바짜, 짜시야 짜 찌놔 찌버러러, 짜 찌쭈롸 짜찌기뤄 뫄 뫄소 와보

26. 짜시찌러 여수 구궈라 구바부라 뿌: 네빠바쭈미라 어 무찌마 워 가나빠나, 오라 우거꺼 와바아사. 오요꽈 아빠더꺼라 어라 뫄 다다. 나 마꼬 아빠이가, 이우거꺼 와더다 비너너 벼씨 어라 루우루 사네.

27. 아나버 너뉴, 무꺼꺼 뫄하빠꽈 뱌 뮈씨 어라 루우루 사네, 부씨 무 무쭈꽈 아꽈우마 나네 구더꺼라 어따꼐쏘.

요아나 찌고노 16

1. 어이 먀시 요씨, 나바비꼐러이 무꺼싸 구러가 어 붜머러시 붜뉴.
2. 부씨 어 바뉴 바꺼꺼 바바고론가냐 뫄 마써꺼 마보. 너 수구 시빠이가, 사 어 무뉴 오꽈 와버찌러, 아꺼꺼 아찌찌빠 뿌 오꼬 이아고러라.

Father.

25. But this is to fulfill what is written in their Law: 'They hated me without reason.'

26. "When the Counselor comes, whom I will send to you from the Father, the Spirit of truth who goes out from the Father, he will testify about me.

27. And you also must testify, for you have been with me from the beginning.

John Chapter 16[NIV]

1. "All this I have told you so that you will not go astray.
2. They will put you out of the synagogue; in fact, a time is coming when anyone who kills you will think he is offering a service to God.

3. Bangende baira bacha, bushi batachwula banyishi, batachwula beshi na Tata.

4. Rero nababilyire ei myasi yoshi, chasiya mango e suku sa ikaika, mwanakengera kwa nabaa nababilyirei mira. Yesu era kuendekera ateta mbu: Ei myasi, ndababuraai bushi nabaa nyichilyi alauma nenyu.

Yesu ateta era luulu s'e mulyimo w'e Muchima Mubuya-buya

5. Rero nyingahuba era mw'ola wanyichwumaa. Si kutalyi chiro na muuma mu mwabo ola wanyibusise mbu ngai yi nyingaya!

6. Oku nababilyire ei myasi, mwaachire buyongwa bunene mwa michima yenyu.

7. Si chiro bacha, nababura kanangana kwa oku kuenda kwanyi imutoloke wenyu, bushi ndaenjire, ola ukende wabaasa atachibahe ene mulyi. Si nyikaenda, kuika nyinabachwumirei.

8. Na mango angaba aikire, angende alosa e bandju changanama kwa bauwirwe bushi n'e bibi byabo, na bushi n'e myasi era ichwungenene

3. 바꺼머 바이라 바짜, 부씨 바다쭈롸 바니씨, 바다쭈롸 버씨 나 다다.

4. 러로 나바비쩨러 어이 먀씨 요씨, 짜시야 마꼬 어수구 사 이가이가, 뫄나거꺼라 과 나바아 나바비쩨러이 미라. 여수 어라 구어떠거라 아더다 뿌: 어이 먀시, 따바부라아이 부씨 나바아 네찌쩨 아롸우마 너뉴.

여수 아더다 어라 뿌율뿌 서 무쩨명 워 무찌마 무부야-부야

5. 러로 네꺼후바 어라 뫄라 와네쭈마아. 시 구다쩨 찌로 나 무우마 무 뫄보 오롸 와네부시서 뿌 꺼이 에 네꺼야!

6. 오구 나바비쩨러 어이 먀시, 뫄아찌러 부요꽈 부너너 뫄 미찌마 여뉴.

7. 시 찌로 바짜, 나바부라 가나꺼나 과 오구 구어따 과네 이무도로거 워뉴, 부씨 따어찌러, 오롸 우거꺼 와바아사 아다찌바허 어너 무쩨. 시 네가어따, 구이가 네나바쭈미러이.

8. 나 마꼬 아꺼바 아이기러, 아꺼머 아론사 어 바쭈 짜꺼나마 과 바우위뤄 부씨 너 비비 뱌보, 나 부씨 너 먀시 어라 이쭈꺼너너 어라

3. They will do such things because they have not known the Father or me.

4. I have told you this, so that when the time comes you will remember that I warned you. I did not tell you this at first because I was with you.

5. "Now I am going to him who sent me, yet none of you asks me, 'Where are you going?'

6. Because I have said these things, you are filled with grief.

7. But I tell you the truth: It is for your good that I am going away. Unless I go away, the Counselor will not come to you; but if I go, I will send him to you.

8. When he comes, he will convict the world of guilt in regard to sin and righteousness and judgment:

era muhondo sa Ongo, na bushi n'e buchinjibusi bwa Ongo.

무호또 사 오꼬, 나 부씨 너 부찌끼부시 봐 오꼬.

9. Angende abalosa kwa bauwirwe bushi n'e bibi byabo, bushi batanyemerere mwa michima yabo.

9. 아꺼떠 아바로사 과 바우위뤄 부씨 너 비비 뱌보, 부씨 바다녀머러러 롸 미찌마 야보.

9. in regard to sin, because men do not believe in me;

10. Kanji angende abalosa kwa bauwirwe bushi n'ebya bichwungenene era muhondo sa Ongo, bushi naya era mwa Tata, era mutangachinyilorerako.

10. 가찌 아꺼떠 아바로사 과 바우위뤄 부씨 너뱌 비쭈꺼너너 어라 무호또 사 오꼬, 부씨 나야 어라 롸 다다, 어라 무다아찌네로러라고.

10. in regard to righteousness, because I am going to the Father, where you can see me no longer;

11. Kanji angende abalosa kwa bauwirwe bushi n'e buchinjibusi bwa Ongo, bushi e mwami w'obuno butala, achinjibusibwe mira.

11. 가찌 아꺼떠 아바로사 과 바우위뤄 부씨 너 부찌끼부시 봐 오꼬, 부씨 어 롸미 옾부노 부다롸, 아찌끼부시붜 미라.

11. and in regard to judgment, because the prince of this world now stands condemned.

12. Nyichilyi nyete myasi inene ya kubabura, si mutasa kuba ba kuimenyerera.

12. 녜찌레 녀더 먀시 이너너 야 구바부라, 시 무다사 구바 바 구이머녀러라.

12. "I have much more to say to you, more than you can now bear.

13. Si mango oyu Muchima w'e kanangana angaika, angende abalosa bya mwemire kuira mu chira mwasi w'e kanangana. Atakende ateta era luulu sai yeine, si e myasi era omvire, inai angende anateta. Kanji iungende wababura na bya bikaika.

13. 시 마꼬 오유 무찌마 워 가나아나 아까이가, 아꺼떠 아바로사 뱌 뭐미러 구이라 무 찌라 먀시 워 가나아나. 아다거떠 아더다 어라 루우루루 사이 여이너, 시 어 먀시 어라 오삐러, 이나이 아꺼떠 아나더다. 가찌 이우꺼떠 와바부라 나 뱌 비가이가.

13. But when he, the Spirit of truth, comes, he will guide you into all truth. He will not speak on his own; he will speak only what he hears, and he will tell you what is yet to come.

14. Na mango angende akula e myasi era mwanyi, n'e kubaburai, mw'olu angende

14. 나 마꼬 아꺼떠 아구꽈 어 먀시 어라 뫄니, 너 구바부라이, 뫀루 아꺼떠

14. He will bring glory to me by taking from what is mine and making it known

anyeresa echwunda.

아녀러사 어쭈따.

to you.

15. Bushi bya Tata achwusa byoshi, nanyi binachwula byanyi. N'echi chi chachwumaa nababura mbu e myasi era e Muchima Mubuya-buya angende ababura, era nyilyi yi angende aikula.

15. 부씨 뱌 다다 아쭈사 뵤씨, 나니 비나쭈퐈 뱌니. 너찌 찌 짜쭈마아 나바부라 뿌 어 먀시 어라 어 무찌마 무부야-부야 아꺼떠 아바부라, 어라 네레 에 아꺼떠 아이구퐈.

15. All that belongs to the Father is mine. That is why I said the Spirit will take from what is mine and make it known to you.

E businane bukabindjuka kuba lumoo

어 부시나너 부가비뿌— 구바 룸몊엪

16. Kanji Yesu era kuteta mbu: Era nyuma sa suku sieke, mutachinyiloleko, si kanji era nyuma sa suku sieke mungahuba kunyilolako.

16. 가찌 여수 어라 구더다 뿌: 어라 뉴마 사 수구 시어거, 무다찌네로러고, 시 가찌 어라 뉴마 사 수구 시어거 무까후바 구네로퐈고.

16. "In a little while you will see me no more, and then after a little while you will see me."

17. Bushi n'oku, banafunzi bai bauma bera kutangilyisa babusanya mbu: Enawechwu! Ekuteta mbu era nyuma sa suku sieke chwutachimuloleko, si kanji era nyuma sa suku sieke chwungahuba kumulolako bushi aya era mw'eshe kukwera kuteta kute oku?

17. 부씨 노구, 바나푸씨 바이 바우마 버라 구다찌레사 바부사냐 뿌: 어나워쭈! 어구더다 뿌 어라 뉴마 사 수구 시어거 쭈다찌무로러고, 시 가찌 어라 뉴마 사 수구 시어거 쭈까후바 구무로퐈고 부씨 아야 어라 뭐써 구궈라 구더다 구더 오구?

17. Some of his disciples said to one another, "What does he mean by saying, 'In a little while you will see me no more, and then after a little while you will see me,' and 'Because I am going to the Father'?"

18. N'e kuteta mbu: era nyuma sa suku sieke nako kukuteta kute? ebi byoshi atechire, si chwutabimenyerere!

18. 너 구더다 뿌: 어라 뉴마 사 수구 시어거 나고 구구더다 구더? 어비 뵤씨 아더찌러, 시 쭈다비머녀러러!

18. They kept asking, "What does he mean by 'a little while'? We don't understand what he is saying."

19. Yesu bushi abaa amenyire mira kwa bahonda kumubusa era luulu sei myasi, era kwire ababura mbu: Mwabusanya bushi n'ono mwasi nera kuteta mbu: Era nyuma sa suku sieke mutachinyiloleko, si kanji era nyuma sa suku sieke mungahuba kunyilolako?

20. Kubinalyi, nababura kwa mungalyira na kulyibuka busese, si e bandju bomuno butala beke, bangaba balyi mwa lumoo. Si chiro bacha, amu malyibuko menyu makabindjuka kuba lumoo.

21. Si mwishi kwa mango e mukasi ahonda kubuta, ende omva e mukero, bushi e bihangi byai by'e kubuta, ende omva e mukero, bushi e bihangi byai by'e kubuta byende byabaa byaikire mira. Na mango ende aba era abutaa, anebilyira oyu mukero, bushi n'e lumoo lw'e kubuta e mwana.

22. Rero nenyu kunoku, muchilyi mwalyibuka busese. Si nyingahuba kuika kubalolako. Aola, mungaba mwa lumoo. N'olu lumoo lwenyu, kutachibe chiro na mundju usibya ola ungahuba

19. 여수 부씨 아바아 아머네러 미라 과 바호따 구무부사 어라 루우루 서이 먀시, 어라 귀러 아바부라 뿌: 롸부사냐 부씨 노노 롸시 너라 구더다 뿌: 어라 뉴마 사 수구 시어거, 무다찌네로뻐고, 시 가찌 어라 뉴마 사 수구 시어거 무까후바 구네로롸고?

20. 구비나레, 나바부라 과 무까레라 나 구레부가 부서서, 시 어 바뉴 보무노 부다롸 버거, 바까바 바레 롸 루모오. 시 찌로 바쌰, 아무 마레부고 머뉴 마가비뉴가 구바 루모오.

21. 시 뮈씨 과 마꼬 어 무가시 아호따 구부다, 어떠 오빠 어 무거로, 부씨 어 비하꼐 뱌이 벼 구부다, 어떠 오빠 어 무거로, 부씨 어 비하꼐 뱌이 벼 구부다 벼떠 뱌바아 뱌이기러 미라. 나 마꼬 어떠 아바 어라 아부다아, 아너비레라 오유 무거로, 부씨 너 루모오 루워 구부다 어 롸나.

22. 러로 너뉴 구노구, 무찌레 롸레부가 부서서. 시 네까후바 구이가 구바로롸고. 아오롸, 무까바 롸 루모오. 노루 루모오 뤄뉴, 구다찌버 찌로 나 무뉴 우시뱌 오롸 우까후바 구바냐아로.

19. Jesus saw that they wanted to ask him about this, so he said to them, "Are you asking one another what I meant when I said, 'In a little while you will see me no more, and then after a little while you will see me'?

20. I tell you the truth, you will weep and mourn while the world rejoices. You will grieve, but your grief will turn to joy.

21. A woman giving birth to a child has pain because her time has come; but when her baby is born she forgets the anguish because of her joy that a child is born into the world.

22. So with you: Now is your time of grief, but I will see you again and you will rejoice, and no one will take away your joy.

kubanyaalo.

23. Mw'esi suku, mutakachinyibuse mwasi usibya. Kubinalyi, nababura kwa choshi cha mungende mwema Tata kw'e sina lyanyi, kuika angende anaberesachi.

24. Kuikira lwarero mutafuraa kwema kandju kasibya kw'e sina lyanyi. Rero, mundaa mwema elyi mwende mweresibwa, e lumoo lwenyu lube lunene.

Yesu aimire e myasi ibi y'e butala

25. Yesu era kuteta kanji mbu: Ei myasi yoshi, nababilyirei mwa mianyi. Si mwa suku sa s'eshire, ndachibaburei mwa mianyi. Si nyingere nende nababura changanama era luulu sa Tata.

26. Mw'esi suku, mu mubeine mungende mwema Tata kw'e sina lyanyi. Ndababilyire mbu nyono nyi nyigende nachibemera era mwai,

27. bushi Tata yeine achwula abasimire ngachi. Rero achwula abasimire bacha, bushi nenyu muchwula munyisimire busese na kwemerera mwa michima yenyu kwa era mwai yi

23. 뭐시 수구,
무다가찌네부서 먀시 우시뱌.
구비나뤠, 나바부라 과 쪼씨
짜 무꺼떠 뭐마 다다 궈 시나
쨔네, 구이가 아꺼떠
아나버러사찌.

24. 구이기라 꽈러로
무다푸라아 궈마 가꾸 가시뱌
궈 시나 쨔네. 러로, 무다아
뭐마 어뤠 뭐떠 뭐러시봐, 어
루우모오 뤈뉴 루버 루너너.

*여수 아이미러 어 먀시 이비
여 부다꽈*

25. 여수 어라 구더다 가찌
뿌: 어이 먀시 요씨,
나바비뤠러이 먀 미아네. 시
먀 수구 사 서씨러,
따찌바부러이 먀 미아네. 시
네꺼러 너떠 나바부라
짜꺄나마 어라 루우우루 사
다다.

26. 뭐시 수구, 무 무버이너
무꺼떠 뭐마 다다 궈 시나
쨔네. 따바비뤠러 뿌 뇨노 네
네거떠 나찌버머라 어라
꽈이,

27. 부씨 다다 여이너 아쭈꽈
아바시미러 꺼찌. 러로
아쭈꽈 아바시미러 바짜,
부씨 너뉴 무쭈꽈 무네시미러
부서서 나 궈머러라 먀
미찌마 여뉴 과 어라 꽈이 에
나나더꺼라아.

23. In that day you will no longer ask me anything. I tell you the truth, my Father will give you whatever you ask in my name.

24. Until now you have not asked for anything in my name. Ask and you will receive, and your joy will be complete.

25. "Though I have been speaking figuratively, a time is coming when I will no longer use this kind of language but will tell you plainly about my Father.

26. In that day you will ask in my name. I am not saying that I will ask the Father on your behalf.

27. No, the Father himself loves you because you have loved me and have believed that I came from God.

nanatengeraa.

28. Kubinalyi, era mwa tata yi nantengeraa, na naika muno butala. Rero buno butala, nyingabureka n'e kuhuba era mwai.

29. E banafunzi bai bera kwire bamubabura mbu: Aa bacha! Rero, watechire changanama busira kuteta mwa mianyi.

30. chwelyire chwamenya kwa uneshi byoshi, kanji utemire bakubusilyise myasi. Echera chi chachwumire chwemerera kanangana kwa era mwa Ongo yiwanatengeraa.

31. Yesu na imbu: Rero mwanyemerere mwa michima yenyu?

32. Mumenyaa! E suku singaika, sanaikire na mira sa bangabahandabanya. Na mu mango munganyamika nyeine na chira muuma mu mwabo anachiira mwa myasi yai. Si chiro bacha, ndashibe nyeine, bushi Tata alyi alauma nanyi.

33. Ei myasi yoshi, nababilyirei, chasiya mubone e boolo mwa kuendekera kuba mwa ndanda sanyi. Muno butala, mungalola

28. 구비나쩨, 어라 뫄 다다 에 나누더꺼라아, 나 나이가 무노 부다꽈. 러로 부노 부다꽈, 네꺼부러가 너 구후바 어라 뫄이.

29. 어 바나푸씨 바이 버라 귀러 바무바부라 뿌: 아아 바짜! 러로, 와더찌러 짜꺼나마 부시라 구더다 뫄 미아네.

30. 쭤쩨러러 쫘머냐 과 우너씨 뵤씨, 가찌 우더미러 바구부시쩨러 먀시. 어쩌라 찌 짜쭈미러 쭤머러라 가나꺼나 과 어라 뫄 오꼬 에와나더꺼라아.

31. 여수 나 이뿌: 러로 뫄녀머러러 뫄 미찌마 여뉴?

32. 무머냐아! 어 수구 시까이가, 사나이기러 나 미라 사 바꺼바하따바냐. 나 무 마꼬 무꺼냐미가 녀이너 나 찌라 무우마 무 뫄보 아나찌이라 뫄 먀시 야이. 시 찌로 바짜, 따씨버 녀이너, 부씨 다다 아쩨 아꽈우마 나네.

33. 어이 먀시 요씨, 나바비쩨러러이, 짜시야 무보너 어 보오뽀 뫄 구어더거라 구바 뫄 따따 사네. 무노

28. I came from the Father and entered the world; now I am leaving the world and going back to the Father."

29. Then Jesus' disciples said, "Now you are speaking clearly and without figures of speech.

30. Now we can see that you know all things and that you do not even need to have anyone ask you questions. This makes us believe that you came from God."

31. "You believe at last!" Jesus answered.

32. "But a time is coming, and has come, when you will be scattered, each to his own home. You will leave me all alone. Yet I am not alone, for my Father is with me.

33. "I have told you these things, so that in me you may have peace. In this world you will have trouble.

ku malyibuko manene. Si chiro bacha, mundaa mwasesa e michima, bushi e myasi ibi yoshi yo muno butala, naimirei.

부다꽈, 무까르꽈 구 마꿰부고 마녀너. 시 찌로 바짜, 무따아 먀서사 어 미찌마, 부씨 어 먀시 이비 요씨 요 무노 부다꽈, 나이미러이.

But take heart! I have overcome the world."

Yoana Chikono 17

Yesu achemera era mwa Ongo

1. Mango Yesu abaa era amalaa kuteta ei myasi, era kuchwumbikisa kwa nguba na ateta mbu: Tata, e chihangi chaikire mira. Rero, uraa wanyeresa e chwunda nyi Mwana wao, nanyi nyikwereselyi.

2. Bushi wanyeresise mira e buashi kwa bandju boshi, chasiya ba wanyeresise nanyi nyiberese e kalamo k'e suku n'e mango.

3. N'aku kalamo ku kakano: e bandju bakumenye kwa weine una Ongo w'e kanangana, bananyimenye nyono Yesu kirisito, nyi wachwumaa.

4. E mulyimo wanyichwumaa mbu nyiyaa kuira muno butala, naumalyire. Bushi n'oku, nakweresise e chwunda.

5. Rero Tata, ly'e chwunda nabaa nyichwusa era muhondo sao, mango e

요아나 찌고노 17

여수 아쩌머라 어라 꽈 오꼬

1. 마꼬 여수 아바아 어라 아마꽈아 구더다 어이 먀시, 어라 구쭈삐기사 과 꾸바 나 아더다 뿌: 다다, 어 찌하삐 짜이기러 미라. 러로, 우라아 와녀러사 어 쭈따 네 먀나 와오, 나네 네꿔러서꿰.

2. 부씨 와녀러시서 미라 어 부아씨 과 바뚜 보씨, 짜시야 바 와녀러시서 나네 네버러서 어 가꽈모 거 수구 너 마꼬.

3. 나구 가꽈모 구 가가노: 어 바뚜 바구머녀 과 워이너 우나 오꼬 워 가나꽈나, 바나네머녀 뇨노 여수 기리시도, 네 와쭈마아.

4. 어 무꿰모 와네쭈마아 뿌 네야아 구이라 무노 부다꽈, 나우마꿰러. 부씨 노구, 나꿔러시서 어 쭈따.

5. 러로 다다, 뛰어 쭈따 나바아 네쭈사 어라 무호또 사오, 마꼬 어 부다꽈 봐바아

John Chapter 17[NIV]

1. After Jesus said this, he looked toward heaven and prayed: "Father, the time has come. Glorify your Son, that your Son may glorify you.

2. For you granted him authority over all people that he might give eternal life to all those you have given him.

3. Now this is eternal life: that they may know you, the only true God, and Jesus Christ, whom you have sent.

4. I have brought you glory on earth by completing the work you gave me to do.

5. And now, Father, glorify me in your presence with the glory I had with you

butala bwabaa butasa kubumbwa, unyeresaalyi kanji.

부다사 구부빠, 우녀러사아쩨 가찌.

before the world began.

Yesu emera e banfunzi bai

여수 어머라 어 바누푸씨 바이

6. Yesu era kuteta mbu: Ongo tata, woyo, uwanyeresaa e bandju ba weine walondolaa mwa butala. Nanyi nera kunalyinda nabalosa woyo unde. Abu bandju babaa bao, si weine wera kunyeresabo. Nabo bera kunachwunda e chinwa chao.

6. 여수 어라 구더다 뿌: 오꼬 다다, 오요, 우와녀러사아 어 바뚜 바 워이너 와로또꽈아 뫄 부다꽈. 나니 너라 구나쩨따 나바로사 오요 우떠. 아부 바뚜 바바아 바오, 시 워이너 워라 구녀러사보. 나보 버라 구나쭈따 어 찌놔 짜오.

6. "I have revealed you to those whom you gave me out of the world. They were yours; you gave them to me and they have obeyed your word.

7. Rero, bera beshi kwa byoshi bya wambaa, era ulyi yi binatengire.

7. 러로, 버라 버씨 과 뵤씨 뱌 와빠아, 어라 우레 에 비나더삐러.

7. Now they know that everything you have given me comes from you.

8. Bushi e myasi era wanyichwumaa inanababilyire, nabo banayemerere mwa michima yabo. Bushi n'oku, belyire bamenya kanangana kwa era ulyi yi natengaa. Kanji banemerere kwa uwananyichwumaa.

8. 부씨 어 먀시 어라 와니쭈마아 이나나바비쩨러, 나보 바나여머러러 뫄 미찌마 야보. 부씨 노구, 버쩨러 바머냐 가나빠나 과 어라 우레 에 나더빠아. 가찌 바너머러러 과 우와나니쭈마아.

8. For I gave them the words you gave me and they accepted them. They knew with certainty that I came from you, and they believed that you sent me.

9. Abu wanyeresise, bu nenjire nemera, bushi beke bu bachwula bao. Si ndenjire nemera e bandju b'omwa butala.

9. 아부 와녀러시서, 부 너찌러 너머라, 부씨 버거 부 바쭈꽈 바오. 시 떠찌러 너머라 어 바뚜 보뫄 부다꽈.

9. I pray for them. I am not praying for the world, but for those you have given me, for they are yours.

10. E bandju ba nyichwusa boshi banachwula bao, na ba uchwusa boshi nabo banachwula banyi. Rero, kurengera abu bandju ku

10. 어 바뚜 바 니쭈사 보씨 바나쭈꽈 바오, 나 바 우쭈사 보씨 나보 바나쭈꽈 바니. 러로, 구러꺼라 아부 바뚜 구 너찌러 너러시봐 어 쭈따.

10. All I have is yours, and all you have is mine. And glory has come to me through them.

n'enjire neresibwa e chwunda.

11. Nyono, ndachibe muno butala bushi nyingahuba era ulyi. Si beke mubo mu banachilyi. Bushi n'oku, Ongo Tata u Mubuya-buya, nabo undaa wabalanga kwa buashi bw'e sina lyao wambaa. Echera chi chingachwuma nabo bende baba mwa buuma, ng'okwa nechwu chwu babilyi chwuchwula mwa buuma.

11. 뇨노, 따찌버 무노 부다롸 부씨 네까후바 어라 우레. 시 버거 무보 무 바나찌레. 부씨 노구, 오꼬 다다 우 무부야-부야, 나보 우따아 와바롸까 과 부아씨 뷔 시나 랴오 와빠아. 어쩌라 찌 찌까쭈마 나보 버떠 바바 뫄 부우마, 꼬과 너쭈 쭈 바비레 쭈쭈롸 뫄 부우마.

11. I will remain in the world no longer, but they are still in the world, and I am coming to you. Holy Father, protect them by the power of your name--the name you gave me--so that they may be one as we are one.

12. Mango nabaa nyilyi nabo, mwa buashi bw'elyi sina lyao wabaa mu nanabalangaa. Bushi n'oku. Kutalyi chiro na muuma mubo ola waelyire, kureka ola walawaa e kuera, chasiya bya by'anjikirwe mwa Maanjiko Mabuya-buya biberere.

12. 마꼬 나바아 네레 나보, 뫄 부아씨 뷔레 시나 랴오 와바아 무 나나바롸까아. 부씨 노구. 구다레 찌로 나 무우마 무보 오롸 와어레러, 구러가 오롸 와롸와아 어 구어라, 짜시야 뱌 뷔아찌기뤄 뫄 마아찌고 마부야-부야 비버러러.

12. While I was with them, I protected them and kept them safe by that name you gave me. None has been lost except the one doomed to destruction so that Scripture would be fulfilled.

13. Rero, nyono ono nera nahuba era ulyi. Si kuno nyichilyi muno butala, nyichilyi nateta ei myasi, chasiya e lumoo lwanyi lunene lwa nyete, nabo lube mwa michima yabo.

13. 러로, 뇨노 오노 너라 나후바 어라 우레. 시 구노 네찌레 무노 부다롸, 네찌레 나더다 어이 먀시, 짜시야 어 루모오 롸네 루너너 롸 녀더, 나보 루버 뫄 미찌마 야보.

13. "I am coming to you now, but I say these things while I am still in the world, so that they may have the full measure of my joy within them.

14. Nabakangilyise e myasi yao mira, n'e bandju b'omwa butala babahombire, bushi beke batachwula bobuno

14. 나바가끼레서 어 먀시 야오 미라, 너 바쭈 보뫄 부다롸 바바호삐러, 부씨 버거 바다쭈롸 보부노

14. I have given them your word and the world has hated them, for they are not of the world any more than

butala, ng'okwa nanyi ndanachwula wamwo.

부다꽈, 끄과 나네 따나쭈꽈 와모.

I am of the world.

15. Rero, ndakwemire mbu ubakulaa muno butala, si nakwema undaa wabalanga ku wamusimu.

15. 러로, 따꿔미러 뿌 우바구꽈아 무노 부다꽈, 시 나꿔마 우따아 와바꽈까 구 와무시무.

15. My prayer is not that you take them out of the world but that you protect them from the evil one.

16. Batachwula bobuno butala, ng'okwa nanyi ndanachwula wamo.

16. 바다쭈꽈 보부노 부다꽈, 끄과 나네 따나쭈꽈 와모.

16. They are not of the world, even as I am not of it.

17. Ubairaa kuba baanda bao kanangana. N'e chinwa chao chi chinachwula ch'e kanangana.

17. 우바이라아 구바 바아따 바오 가나까나. 너 찌놔 짜오 찌 찌나쭈꽈 쩌 가나까나.

17. Sanctify them by the truth; your word is truth.

18. Kwa wanyichwumaa muno butala, ku nanyi nanabachwumiremo.

18. 과 와네쭈마아 무노 부다꽈, 구 나네 나나바쭈미러모.

18. As you sent me into the world, I have sent them into the world.

19. Nachiilyire kuba muanda wao bushi nabo, chasiya nabo babe baanda bao kanangana.

19. 나찌이레러 구바 무아따 와오 부씨 나보, 짜시야 나보 바버 바아따 바오 가나까나.

19. For them I sanctify myself, that they too may be truly sanctified.

Yesu emera e bemeresi boshi

여수 어머라 어 버머러시 보씨

20. Yesu era kuendekera ema mbu: Ongo Tata, ata bano bandju beine bu nanemera oshao. Si nemera n'e banji ba bachilyi banganyemerera mwa michima yabo kurengera e myasi era banola bangende bateta era lulu sanyi.

20. 여수 어라 구어떠거라 어마 뿌: 오끄 다다, 아다 바노 바누 베이너 부 나너머라 오싸오. 시 너머라 너 바찌 바 바찌레 바까녀머러라 뫄 미찌마 야보 구러꺼라 어 먀시 어라 바노꽈 바꺼떠 바더다 어라 루루 사네.

20. "My prayer is not for them alone. I pray also for those who will believe in me through their message,

21. Bushi n'oku, Tata na kwema abu boshi bendee baba mwa buuma ng'okwa nyono nao chwuchwula mwa buuma. Kanji na kwema babe

21. 부씨 노구, 다다 나 꿔마 아부 보씨 버떠어 바바 뫄 부우마 끄과 뇨노 나오 쭈쭈꽈 뫄 부우마. 가찌 나 꿔마 바버

21. that all of them may be one, Father, just as you are in me and I am in you. May they also be in us so that the world may believe that

mwa buuma nechwu, chasiya e bandju b'omwa butala bemerere kwa woyo uwananyichwumaa.	짜시야 어 바ᅜᅮ 보뫄 부다ᄙᅡ 버머러러 과 오요 우와나네쭈마아.	you have sent me.
22. Echwunda lya wanyeresaa, nanyinaberesiselyi chasiya babe mwa buuma ng'okwa nechwu chwuchwula mubo.	22. 어쭈따 ᄙᅣ 와녀러사아, 나네나버러시서ᄙᅦ 짜시야 바버 뫄 부우마 ᅌᅩ과 너쭈 쭈쭈ᄙᅡ 무보.	22. I have given them the glory that you gave me, that they may be one as we are one:
23. Kukuteta mbu nyibe mwa buuma nabo, nao ube mwa buuma nanyi. Mw'olu, babe mw'obu buuma kanangana. N'echi chi chingachwuma e bandju b'omwa butala balyinda bamenya kanangana kwa uwanyichwumaa. Kanji bamenye n'okwa usimire abu bandju bao ng'okwa uchwula unyisimire.	23. 구구더다 ᄞᅮ 네버 뫄 부우마 나보, 나오 우버 뫄 부우마 나네. 뫄루, 바버 뫄부 부우마 가나ᅇᅡ나. 너찌 찌 찌ᅇᅡ쭈마 어 바ᅜᅮ 보뫄 부다ᄙᅡ 바ᄙᅦ따 바머냐 가나ᅇᅡ나 과 우와네쭈마아. 가ᄣᅵ 바머녀 노과 우시미러 아부 바ᅜᅮ 바오 ᅌᅩ과 우쭈ᄙᅡ 우네시미러.	23. I in them and you in me. May they be brought to complete unity to let the world know that you sent me and have loved them even as you have loved me.
24. Ongo Tata, abu bandju wanyeresise nahonda babe alauma nanyi mwa chisiki cha nyigabamo, chasiya balole kwa bulangare bwanyi. Obu bulangare, woyo uwambaabo, bushi wanyisimaa mango wabaa utasa kubumba e butala.	24. 오ᅌᅩ 다다, 아부 바ᅜᅮ 와녀러시서 나호따 바버 아ᄙᅡ우마 나네 뫄 찌시기 짜 네가바모, 짜시야 바로ᄙᅥ 과 부ᄙᅡᅇᅡ러 봐네. 오부 부ᄙᅡᅇᅡ러, 오요 우와빠아보, 부씨 와네시마아 마ᅌᅩ 와바아 우다사 구부빠 어 부다ᄙᅡ.	24. "Father, I want those you have given me to be with me where I am, and to see my glory, the glory you have given me because you loved me before the creation of the world.
25. Tata, woyo uwende waira e myasi era ichwungenene. E bandju b'omwa butala batachwula bakwishi, si nyeke nyikiwishi. Na bano wanyeresise, nabo banachwula beshi kwa uwananyichwumaa.	25. 다다, 오요 우워떠 와이라 어 먀시 어라 이쭈ᅇᅥ너너. 어 바ᅜᅮ 보뫄 부다ᄙᅡ 바다쭈ᄙᅡ 바귀씨, 시 녀거 네기위씨. 나 바노 와녀러시서, 나보 바나쭈ᄙᅡ 버씨 과 우와나네쭈마아.	25. "Righteous Father, though the world does not know you, I know you, and they know that you have sent me.

26. Nabalosise woyo unde. Kanji nyinganaendekera kubalosa woyo, chasiya ei nzii unyichwusako, nabo anaendekeraa kuba mwa ndanda sabo. Nanyi nyeine, nyinaendekere kuba mwa buuma nabo.

26. 나바롼시서 오요 우떠. 가찌 네따나어떠거라 구바롼사 오요, 짜시야 어이 씨이 우네쭈사고, 나보 아나어떠거라아 구바 롸 따따 사보. 나네 녀이너, 네나어떠거러 구바 롸 부우마 나보.

26. I have made you known to them, and will continue to make you known in order that the love you have for me may be in them and that I myself may be in them."

Yoana Chikono 18
Yesu asimbwa

1. Mango Yesu abaa amalaa kuteta ei myasi, era kutenga aola alauma n'e banafunzi bai. Bera kuhabuka e kabanda k'e kiteroni. Baikire kwa mushilyilya wako, bera kw'engilyira mw'ehwa lyiuma lya michi.

2. Ely'ehwa, yuda ola wamurenganyaa, abaa alyishi, bushi chira mango Yesu n'e banafunzi bai babaa bende babuanana aola.

3. Chasinda oyu yuda, era kuya mw'elyi ehwa alyi na chikembe cha basula alauma n'e balanzi ba babaa bachwumirwe n'e bakulu-kulu b'e bakuhanyi n'e bafarisayo. Abu bandju, babaa bakoresise e marata, n'e bimore, bete n'e

요아나 찌고노 18
여수 아시똬

1. 마꼬 여수 아바아 아마롸아 구더따 어이 먀시, 어라 구더따 아오롸 아롸우마 너 바나푼씨 바이. 버라 구하부가 어 가바따 거 기더로니. 바이기러 과 무씨쮈롸 와고, 버라 궈띠쮈라 뭐화 레우마 롸 미찌.

2. 어뤼어화, 유다 오롸 와무러먀냐아, 아바아 아쮀씨, 부씨 찌라 마꼬 여수 너 바나푼씨 바이 바바아 버떠 바부아나나 아오롸.

3. 짜시따 오유 유다, 어라 구야 뭐레 어화 아쮀 나 찌거뻐 짜 바수롸 아롸우마 너 바롸씨 바 바바아 바쭈미뤄 너 바구루-구루 버 바구하네 너 바파리사요. 아부 바쭈, 바바아 바고러시서 어 마라다, 너

John Chapter 18[NIV]

1. When he had finished praying, Jesus left with his disciples and crossed the Kidron Valley. On the other side there was an olive grove, and he and his disciples went into it.

2. Now Judas, who betrayed him, knew the place, because Jesus had often met there with his disciples.

3. So Judas came to the grove, guiding a detachment of soldiers and some officials from the chief priests and Pharisees. They were carrying torches, lanterns and weapons.

bindju by'e kulwa nabi.

4. Yesu bushi abaa amenyire mira e myasi Yoshi era ingamuikira, era kuchifunda ofu n'abu basula, na ababusa mbu: Nde imwahonda?

5. Nabo mbu Yesu w'e Nasareti. Yesu era kubabura mbu: Nyono ono. Yuda nai, iwamurenganya abaa emenze alauma n'abu basula.

6. Mango Yesu aburaa abu bandju mbu: Nyono ono, unao-unao bera kuenda chinyuma-nyuma, kuna kukumbaalanga.

7. Yesu era kubabusa kanji mbu: Nde imwahonda? Nabo kanji mbu: Yesu w'e Nasareti.

8. Yesu nai mbu: Nababilyire mira kwa nyono ono. Na akaba nyi mwahonda, murekaa bano nyilyi nabo bachiendere.

9. Byabaa bacha, chasiya e chinwa chiberere cha Yesu abaa atechire mira mbu: Mwa bawanyeresaa, ndaesise chiro na muuma mubo.

10. Simoni Petero abaa ete bombo. Era kubuhobola mwa lupota, kuna kuisha e kuchi kw'e kaungu k'e mukulu-kulu

비모러, 버더 너 비뿌 벼 구꽈 나비.

4. 여수 부씨 아바아 아머네러 미라 어 먀시 요씨 어라 이꾸무이기라, 어라 구찌푸따 오푸 나부 바수꽈, 나 아바부사 뿌: 떠 이뫄호따?

5. 나보 뿌 여수 워 나사러디. 여수 어라 구바부라 뿌: 뇨노 오노. 유다 나이, 이와무러꽈냐 아바아 어머써 아꽈우마 나부 바수꽈.

6. 마꼬 여수 아부라아 아부 바뚜 뿌: 뇨노 오노, 우나오-우나오 버라 구어따 찌뉴마-뉴마, 구나 구구빠아꽈꽈.

7. 여수 어라 구바부사 가찌 뿌: 떠 이뫄호따? 나보 가찌 뿌: 여수 워 나사러디.

8. 여수 나이 뿌: 나바비께러 미라 과 뇨노 오노. 나 아가바 네 뫄호따, 무러가아 바노 네께 나보 바쩌떠러.

9. 뱌바아 바짜, 짜시야 어 찌놔 찌버러러 짜 여수 아바아 아더찌러 미라 뿌: 뫄 바와녀러사아, 따어시서 찌로 나 무우마 무보.

10. 시모니 퍼더로 아바아 어더 보뽀. 어라 구부호보꽈 뫄 루포다, 구나 구이싸 어 구찌 궈 가우우 거 무구루-

4. Jesus, knowing all that was going to happen to him, went out and asked them, "Who is it you want?"

5. "Jesus of Nazareth," they replied. "I am he," Jesus said. (And Judas the traitor was standing there with them.)

6. When Jesus said, "I am he," they drew back and fell to the ground.

7. Again he asked them, "Who is it you want?" And they said, "Jesus of Nazareth."

8. "I told you that I am he," Jesus answered. "If you are looking for me, then let these men go."

9. This happened so that the words he had spoken would be fulfilled: "I have not lost one of those you gave me."

10. Then Simon Peter, who had a sword, drew it and struck the high priest's servant, cutting off his right

w'e bakuhanyi. Aku kaungu, e sina lyai iwabaa Maliko.

11. Si Yesu era kubura petero mbu: Hubyaa e bombo bwao mwa lupota! Uteshi kwa byemire nyirenge mwa malyibuko ma tata abaa anyikunganyisise mira?

Yesu aika era muhondo s'e mukulu-kulu Ana

12. Cha chikembe ch'e basula, n'e mukulu-kulu wabo, alauma n'aba balanzi b'e bakulu-kulu b'e Bayuda, kuna kusimba Yesu, na bamusalyinga.

13. Bera kumweka tanga era mw'e mukulu-kulu mbu i Anasi, sesala wa Kayafa. Oyu kayafa, iwabaa mukulu-kulu w'e bakuhanyi mw'oyu mwaka.

14. Kanji iweresaa e bakulu-kulu b'e bayuda eano kwa byemire kube mundju muuma ola ungafira e lubaa lwabo loshi.

Petero achakana Yesu

15. Simoni Petero alauma na unji mwanafunzi babaa bakulyikire Yesu katola nyuma. Oyu unji mwanafunzi, bushi abaa eshibwe n'e mukulu-kulu w'e bakuhanyi, era kwengilyira na Yesu mwa chikalyi ch'oyu mukulu-kulu.

구루 워 바구하네. 아구 가우꾸, 어 시나 랴이 이와바아 마삐고.

11. 시 여수 어라 구부라 퍼더로 뿌: 후뱌아 어 보쁘 봐오 롸 루포다! 우더씨 과 벼미러 니러러 롸 마레부고 롸 다다 아바아 아네구꽈네시서 미라?

여수 아이가 어라 무호또 서 무구루-구루 아나

12. 짜 찌거뻐 쩌 바수콰, 너 무구루-구루 와보, 아롸우마 나바 바롸씨 버 바구루-구루 버 바유다, 구나 구시뻐 여수, 나 바무사례꽈.

13. 버라 구뭐가 다꽈 어라 뭐 무구루-구루 뿌 이 아나시, 서사롸 와 가야파. 오유 가야파, 이와바아 무구루-구루 워 바구하네 모유 롸가.

14. 가찌 이워러사아 어 바구루-구루 버 바유다 어아노 과 벼미러 구버 무뚜 무우마 오롸 우꽈피라 어 루바아 콰보 로씨.

퍼더로 아짜가나 여수

15. 시모니 퍼더로 아롸우마 나 우찌 뫄나푸씨 바바아 바구레기러 여수 가도롸 뉴마. 오유 우찌 뫄나푸씨, 부씨 아바아 어씨붸 너 무구루-구루 워 바구하네, 어라 궈삐레라 나 여수 롸 찌가레 쪼유 무구루-구루.

ear. (The servant's name was Malchus.)

11. Jesus commanded Peter, "Put your sword away! Shall I not drink the cup the Father has given me?"

12. Then the detachment of soldiers with its commander and the Jewish officials arrested Jesus. They bound him

13. and brought him first to Annas, who was the father-in-law of Caiaphas, the high priest that year.

14. Caiaphas was the one who had advised the Jews that it would be good if one man died for the people.

15. Simon Peter and another disciple were following Jesus. Because this disciple was known to the high priest, he went with Jesus into the high priest's courtyard,

16. Si petero yeke era kwimanga era butala ofu n'e lwisi. Echera chera kuchwuma mulyikabo, ola wabaa wishibwe n'e mukulu-kulu w'e bakuhanyi auluka era mbuwa. Era kuhambala n'e mukasi ola wabaa walanga e lwisi lw'e chikalyi. Oyu mukasi, kukwera kw'engisa Petero.

17. Chasinda oyu mukasi era kubusa Petero mbu: Nau uta muuma mwa banafunzi b'ono mundju? Petero era kumwakula mbu: Nanga, nyono nda mwanfunzi w'oyu mundju.

18. Rero, bushi mw'esi suku e mbeo yabaa ya huunda busese, e chwuungu n'e balanzi babaa bakoresise mulyiro, bakalukala kuo banemenze. Petero nai abaa emenze alauma nabo, akalukala.

Yesu atongana era muhondo s'e mukulu-kulu w'e bakuhanyi

19. Era nyuma s'ebi, e mukulu-kulu w'e bakuhanyi, era kutangilyisa abusa Yesu era lulu s'e banafunzi bai. N'era lulu s'e myasi era abaa enjire akangilyisa e bandju.

16. 시 퍼더로 여거 어라 귀마꽈 어라 부다꽈 오푸 너 뤼시. 어쩌라 쩌라 구쭈마 무레가보, 오꽈 와바아 위씨붜 너 무구루-구루 워 바구하니 아우루가 어라 뿌와. 어라 구하빠꽈 너 무가시 오꽈 와바아 와꽈꽈 어 뤼시 뤄 찌가꼐. 오유 무가시, 구궈라 궈삐사 퍼더로.

17. 짜시따 오유 무가시 어라 구부사 퍼더로 뿌: 나우 우다 무우마 꽈 바나푸씨 보노 무뿌? 퍼더로 어라 구꽈구꽈 뿌: 나꽈, 뇨노 따 꽈누푸씨 오유 무뿌.

18. 러로, 부씨 뭐시 수구 어 뻐오 야바아 야 후우따 부서서, 어 쭈우웅 너 바꽈씨 바바아 바고러시서 무레로, 바가루가꽈 구오 바너머써. 퍼더로 나이 아바아 어머써 아꽈우마 나보, 아가루가꽈.

여수 아도꽈낍 어라 무호또 서 무구루-구루 워 바구하네

19. 어라 뉴마 서비, 어 무구루-구루 워 바구하네, 어라 구다삐꼐사 아부사 여수 어라 루루 서 바나푸씨 바이. 너라 루루 서 먀시 어라 아바아 어찌러 아가삐꼐사 어

16. but Peter had to wait outside at the door. The other disciple, who was known to the high priest, came back, spoke to the girl on duty there and brought Peter in.

17. "You are not one of his disciples, are you?" the girl at the door asked Peter. He replied, "I am not."

18. It was cold, and the servants and officials stood around a fire they had made to keep warm. Peter also was standing with them, warming himself.

19. Meanwhile, the high priest questioned Jesus about his disciples and his teaching.

바꾸.

20. Yesu era kumwakula mbu: Nabaa nenjire nakangilyisa e bandju boshi changanama mwa mashenge mabo, anabe n'omwa chibua ch'e luhu lwa Ongo. N'omu mu e Bayuda boshi bende babuanana. Kanji kutalyi chiro na mwasi usibya ola natetaa mwa bubisho-bisho.

20. 여수 어라 구꽈구꽈 뿌: 나바아 너찌러 나가삐레사 어 바꾸 보씨 짜까나마 마 마써꺼 마보, 아나버 노마 찌부아 쩌 루후 꽈 오끄. 노무 무 어 바유다 보씨 버꺼 바부아나나. 가찌 구다례 찌로 나 꽈시 우시뱌 오라 나더다아 마 부비쏘-비쏘.

20. "I have spoken openly to the world," Jesus replied. "I always taught in synagogues or at the temple, where all the Jews come together. I said nothing in secret.

21. Rero, chachwuma wanyibusa? E bandju ba babaa benjire b'omvilyisa e myasi era nabaa nenjire nababura bu ungabusise, bushi bu baishi kubuya.

21. 러로, 짜쭈마 와니부사? 어 바꾸 바 바바아 버지러 보삐례사 어 먀시 어라 나바아 너찌러 나바부라 부 우까부시서, 부씨 부 바이씨 구부야.

21. Why question me? Ask those who heard me. Surely they know what I said."

22. Muuma mwa balanzi ola wabaa wemenze ofu Yesu, omvire bacha, kuna kumumaasa, na ateta mbu: Ku wemire kwakula e mukulu-kulu w'e bakuhanyi bacha?

22. 무우마 꽈 바랸씨 오라 와바아 워머써 오푸 여수, 오삐러 바짜, 구나 구무마아사, 나 아더다 뿌: 구 워미러 과구꽈 어 무구루-구루 워 바구하니 바짜?

22. When Jesus said this, one of the officials nearby struck him in the face. "Is this the way you answer the high priest?" he demanded.

23. Yesu nai mbu: Akaba natechire bulio, ulosaabo. Si akaba natechire kubuya, chi chera chachwuma wanyimaasa?

23. 여수 나이 뿌: 아가바 나더찌러 부삐오, 우로사아보. 시 아가바 나더찌러 구부야, 찌 쩌라 짜쭈마 와네마아사?

23. "If I said something wrong," Jesus replied, "testify as to what is wrong. But if I spoke the truth, why did you strike me?"

24. Anasi kukwera kuchwuma Yesu anachilyi aminyirwe, era mwa kayafa, I mukulu-kulu w'e bakuhanyi.

24. 아나시 구귀라 구쭈마 여수 아나찌례 아미니뤄, 어라 꽈 가야파, 이 무구루-구루 워 바구하니.

24. Then Annas sent him, still bound, to Caiaphas the high priest.

Petero achakana Yesu kanji *퍼더로 아짜가나 여수 가찌*

25. Mw'ebi bihangi, Simoni Petero abaa anachilyi emenze aola akalukala kwa mulyiro. E bandju kukwera kumubusa kanji mbu: Elyi nao uta muuma mwa banafunzi b'ono mundju? Petero era kuchiakana kanji mbu: Nanga, nyono nda muuma nabo.

26. Aola abaa alyi kaungu kauma k'e mukulu-kulu w'e bakuhanyi. Aku kaungu, abaa munyakabo w'ola Petero aisha e kuchi. Nai era kubusa petero mbu: Era! Kasi ata unalolaako mango mwabaa mulyi na Yesu mw'ehwa ly'e michi?

27. Si petero era kuchakana kanji. Unao-unao. Elwaasi kuna kubika.

Yesu atongana era muhondo sa pilato

28. Abere lwera lumbulyi-mbulyi, e bakulu-kulu b'e bayuda bera kukula Yesu ala mwa kayafa, na bamweka mwa nyumba y'e Muroma Pilato, iwabaa mukulu-kulu w'e chio. Si beke chiro bakengilyiramo bushi batahondaa kuchaka e singa, echera chingachwumire balyikabo babanga mbu

25. 뭐비 비하끼, 시모니 퍼더로 아바아 아나찌쩨 어머서 아오롸 아가루루가롸 과 무쩨로. 어 바뚜 구궈라 구무부사 가찌 뿌: 어쩨 나오 우다 무우마 뫄 바나푸씨 보노 무뿌? 퍼더로 어라 구찌아가나 가찌 뿌: 나까, 뇨노 따 무우마 나보.

26. 아오롸 아바아 아쩨 가우꾸 가우마 거 무구루-구루 워 바구하네. 아구 가우꾸, 아바아 무냐가보 오롸 퍼더로 아이싸 어 구찌. 나이 어라 구부사 퍼더로 뿌: 어라! 가시 아다 우나로롸아고 마꼬 뫄바아 무쩨 나 여수 뭐화 뤼어 미찌?

27. 시 퍼더로 어라 구짜가나 가찌. 우나오-우나오. 어롸아시 구나 구비가.

여수 아도까낍 어라 무호또 사 피롸명

28. 아버러 뭐롸 루무쩨-뿌쩨, 어 바구루-구루 버 바유다 버라 구구롸 여수 아롸 뫄 가야파, 나 바뭐가 뫄 뉴빠 여 무로마 피롸도, 이와바아 무구루-구루 워 찌오. 시 버거 찌로 바거끼쩨라모 부씨 바다호따아 구짜가 어 시까, 어쩌라 찌까쭈미러 바쩨가보 바바까 뿌 바다롸아 과 비뾴 벼 파사가.

25. As Simon Peter stood warming himself, he was asked, "You are not one of his disciples, are you?" He denied it, saying, "I am not."

26. One of the high priest's servants, a relative of the man whose ear Peter had cut off, challenged him, "Didn't I see you with him in the olive grove?"

27. Again Peter denied it, and at that moment a rooster began to crow.

28. Then the Jews led Jesus from Caiaphas to the palace of the Roman governor. By now it was early morning, and to avoid ceremonial uncleanness the Jews did not enter the palace; they wanted to be able to eat the Passover.

batalyaa kwa bilyo by'e
Pasaka.

29. Bushi n'oku, Pilato kukwera kubabuana era mbua. Era kubabusa mbu: Myasi ichiye iyachwumire mwasitaka ono mundju?

30. Nabo mbu: Ono mundju atabaa mukosi wa mabi, chwutangamurechire ene ulyi.

31. Pilato era kubabura mbu: Mubeine mumwekaa muye kumuchinjibusa kukulyikana n'okwa e mwaso wenyu achwula atechire. Nabo mbu: chwubano, chwutete e loso lw'e kuteta mbu e mundju echibwaa.

32. Byabaa bacha, chasiya cha chinwa Yesu abaa atechire mira chiberere, kwa kulosa kwa angafa.

33. Chasinda, pilato era kuhuba mwa nyumba. Era kwamala Yesu na amubusa mbu: woyo umwami w'e Bayuda?

34. Yesu nai mbu: Oyu mwasi wanyibusise, elyi atengire mwa

---

29. 부씨 노구, 피롸도 구궈라 구바부아나 어라 뿌아. 어라 구바부사 뿌: 먀시 이찌여 이야쭈미러 먀시다가 오노 무뉴?

30. 나보 뿌: 오노 무뉴 아다바아 무고시 와 마비, 쭈다꺄무러찌러 어너 우웨.

31. 피롸도 어라 구바부라 뿌: 무버이너 무뭐가아 무여 구무찌찌부사 구구레가나 노과 어 먀소 워뉴 아쭈롸 아더찌러. 나보 뿌: 쭈바노, 쭈더더 어 로소 뤄 구더다 뿌 어 무뉴 어찌봐아.

32. 뱌바아 바짜, 짜시야 짜 찌놔 여수 아바아 아더찌러 미라 찌버러러, 과 구론사 과 아꺄파.

33. 짜시따, 피롸도 어라 구후바 먀 뉴빠. 어라 과마롸 여수 나 아무부사 뿌: 오요 우먀미 워 바유다?

34. 여수 나이 뿌: 오유 먀시 와네부시서, 어레 아더꼐러

---

29. So Pilate came out to them and asked, "What charges are you bringing against this man?"

30. "If he were not a criminal," they replied, "we would not have handed him over to you."

31. Pilate said, "Take him yourselves and judge him by your own law." "But we have no right to execute anyone," the Jews objected.

32. This happened so that the words Jesus had spoken indicating the kind of death he was going to die would be fulfilled.

33. Pilate then went back inside the palace, summoned Jesus and asked him, "Are you the king of the Jews?"

34. "Is that your own idea," Jesus asked, "or did others

mianyisa yao, nesi banji bandju bu bakuburaao era lulu sanyi?

35. Pilato nai mbu: Nyono ndachwula Muyuda! Si e bandju b'omwa lubaa lwao n'e bakulu-kulu b'e bakuhanyi, bu bakwanyire mwa mino sanyi! Chi wailyire kasi?

36. Yesu nai mbu: e Bwami bwanyi buta bwomuno butala. Bungabere bwomuno butala, e baanda banyi banganyilwilyire chasiya ndaanyibwaa mwamino sa bano Bayuda. Si e Bwami bwanyi, buta bwomuno butala.

37. Pilato kukwera kubusa Yesu kanji mbu: Kukuteta mbu ulyi mwami? Yesu nai mbu: Si weine watechire mira mbu nyilyi mwami! Nabuchwaa na kubaha muno butala, chasiya nyinde nateta bya nyishi era lulu s'e myasi y'e kanangana. Chira mundju woshi ola uchwula mwa myasi y'e kanagana, ende anyumvilyisa.

38. Pilato era kumubusa mbu: Ei myasi y'e kanangana i yera ichiye? Mango Pilato abaa era atetaa ei myasi, era kuhuba kuuluka era butala, na abura e Bayuda mbu: Nyono, ndasene ku chiro na chinwa chisibya

---

마 미아네사 야오, 너시 바찌 바뉴 부 바구부라아오 어라 루루 사니?

35. 피꽈도 나이 뿌: 뇨노 따쭈꽈 무유다! 시 어 바뉴 보마 루바아 롸오 너 바구루- 구루 버 바구하니, 부 바과네러 마 미노 사니! 찌 와이롈러 가시?

36. 여수 나이 뿌: 어 봐미 봐네 부다 보무노 부다꽈. 부빠버러 보무노 부다꽈, 어 바아따 바니 바빠네뤼렐러 짜시야 따아네봐아 마미노 사 바노 바유다. 시 어 봐미 봐네, 부다 보무노 부다꽈.

37. 피꽈도 구궈라 구부사 여수 가찌 뿌: 구구더다 뿌 우뤠 마미? 여수 나이 뿌: 시 워이너 와더찌러 미라 뿌 니뤠 마미! 나부쫘아 나 구바하 무노 부다꽈, 짜시야 네뉴 나더다 뱌 네씨 어라 루루 서 먀시 여 가나빠나. 찌라 무뉴 오씨 오라 우쭈꽈 마 먀시 여 가나가나, 어뉴 아뉴뻬렐러사.

38. 피꽈도 어라 구무부사 뿌: 어이 먀시 여 가나빠나 이 여라 이찌여? 마꼬 피꽈도 아바아 어라 아더다아 어이 먀시, 어라 구후바 구우루가 어라 부다꽈, 나 아부라 어 바유다 뿌: 뇨노, 따서너 구

---

talk to you about me?"

35. "Am I a Jew?" Pilate replied. "It was your people and your chief priests who handed you over to me. What is it you have done?"

36. Jesus said, "My kingdom is not of this world. If it were, my servants would fight to prevent my arrest by the Jews. But now my kingdom is from another place."

37. "You are a king, then!" said Pilate. Jesus answered, "You are right in saying I am a king. In fact, for this reason I was born, and for this I came into the world, to testify to the truth. Everyone on the side of truth listens to me."

38. "What is truth?" Pilate asked. With this he went out again to the Jews and said, "I find no basis for a charge against him.

cha chingachwuma nachinjibusa ono mundju.

찌로 나 찌놔 찌시뱌 짜 찌까쭈마 나찌찌부사 오노 무쭈.

Pilato ana e loso lw'e kwita Yesu

피꽈명 아나 어 로센 뭐 귀다 여수

39. Si kukulyikana n'e myanya yenyu, nende nababoorera mundju muuma wa buroko chira lusuku lukulu lw'e Pasaka. Rero, mwahonda nyibaboorere e mwami w'e Byuda?

39. 시 구구레가나 너 먀냐 여뉴, 너떠 나바보오러라 무쭈 무우마 와 부로고 찌라 루수구 루구루 뭐 파사가. 러로, 마호따 네바보오러러 어 먀미 워 뷰다?

39. But it is your custom for me to release to you one prisoner at the time of the Passover. Do you want me to release 'the king of the Jews'?"

40. Unao-unao, bera kutangilyisa balakanga na murenge munene mbu: Nanga, chwutahonda oyu mundju, si uchwubooreraa baraba! N'oku oyu Baraba, chabaa chihumusi.

40. 우나오-우나오, 버라 구다삐레사 바라가까 나 무러뻐 무너너 뿌: 나까, 쭈다호따 오유 무쭈, 시 우쭈보오러라아 바라바! 노구 오유 바라바, 짜바아 찌후무시.

40. They shouted back, "No, not him! Give us Barabbas!" Now Barabbas had taken part in a rebellion.

Yoana Chikono 19

요아나 찌고노 19

John Chapter 19[NIV]

1. Chasinda, Pilato era kwire abura e basula mbu basimbaa Yesu, bamuhute e chwuchi.

1. 짜시따, 피꽈도 어라 귀러 아부라 어 바수꽈 뿌 바시빠아 여수, 바무후더 어 쭈찌.

1. Then Pilate took Jesus and had him flogged.

2. Abu basula, bera kuluka e nzita mwa mihoi-hoi na bembasai Yesu kw'echwe. Bera kumwembasa n'e ropo lya mwola.

2. 아부 바수꽈, 버라 구루가 어 씨다 뫄 미호이-호이 나 버빠사이 여수 궈쭤. 버라 구뭐빠사 너 로포 꺄 몰꽈.

2. The soldiers twisted together a crown of thorns and put it on his head. They clothed him in a purple robe

3. Bera kunde bachifunda ofu nai, n'e kumubura mbu: Bwachere mwami w'e Bayuda! Kanji, bera kunde bamumaasanga.

4. Chasinda, pilato era kuhuba kuuluka era butala. Era kubura abu bayuda mbu: Munvaa! Nabareterai ano butala, mumenye kubuya kwa ndasene ku chiro na mwasi usibya ola ungachwuma nachinjibusa ono mundju.

5. Yesu era kwire auluka, anachilyi embere ei nzita y'e mihoi-hoi, n'e ly'e ropo ly'e mwola. Pilato era kubusa abu Bayuda mbu: Rero, ola mundju wenyu I yono!

6. Mango ba bakulu-kulu b'e bakuhanyi alauma n'e balanzi balolaa ku Yesu, kuna kutangilyisa balakanga mbu: Umumanyikaa kwa musalaba! Umumanyikaa kwa musalaba! Pilato kukwera kubabura mbu: Mubeine mumutolaa muye kumumanyika kwa musalaba, bushi nyono ndasene ku chiro na mwasi usibya ola ungachwuma namuchinjibusa.

7. Abu Bayuda nabo mbu: chwuchwusa mwaso wechwu. Rero kukulyikana n'oyu

---

3. 버라 구머 바찌푸따 오푸 나이, 너 구무부라 뿌: 봐쩌러 롸미 워 바유다! 가찌, 버라 구머 바무마아사짜.

4. 짜시따, 피롸도 어라 구후바 구우루가 어라 부다롸. 어라 구부라 아부 바유다 뿌: 무빠아! 나바러더라이 아노 부다롸, 무머녀 구부야 과 따서너 구 찌로 나 롸시 우시뱌 오롸 우짜쭈마 나찌띠부사 오노 무뚜.

5. 여수 어라 귀러 아우루가, 아나찌레 어뻐러 어이 씨다 여 미호이-호이, 너 뤼어 로포 뤼어 모롸. 피롸도 어라 구부사 아부 바유다 뿌: 러로, 오롸 무뚜 워뉴 이 요노!

6. 마앗 바 바구루-구루 버 바구하네 아롸우마 너 바롸씨 바르롸아 구 여수, 구나 구다띠레사 바롸가짜 뿌: 우무마네가아 과 무사롸바! 우무마네가아 과 무사롸바! 피롸도 구궈라 구바부라 뿌: 무버이너 무무도롸아 무여 구무마네가 과 무사롸바, 부씨 뇨노 따서너 구 찌로 나 롸시 우시뱌 오롸 우짜쭈마 나무찌띠부사.

7. 아부 바유다 나보 뿌: 쭈쭈사 롸소 워쭈. 러로 구구레가나 노유 롸소,

---

3. and went up to him again and again, saying, "Hail, king of the Jews!" And they struck him in the face.

4. Once more Pilate came out and said to the Jews, "Look, I am bringing him out to you to let you know that I find no basis for a charge against him."

5. When Jesus came out wearing the crown of thorns and the purple robe, Pilate said to them, "Here is the man!"

6. As soon as the chief priests and their officials saw him, they shouted, "Crucify! Crucify!" But Pilate answered, "You take him and crucify him. As for me, I find no basis for a charge against him."

7. The Jews insisted, "We have a law, and according to that law he must die,

mwaso, byemire ono mundju atenge mw'e muka, bushi enjire achitonga mbu I Mwana wa Ongo.

8. Pilato omvire oyu mwasi, era kuhuba kwobaa busese.

9. Era kwengira kanji mwa mwai, na abusa Yesu mbu: Ewashe, ulyi mwesha ngai? Si Yesu chiro akamwakula kandju.

10. Bushi n'oku, Pilato era kumubusa kanji mbu: Era! Utahonda kunyakula? Uteshi kwa nyete e buashe bw'e kukuboola, n'e bw'e kukumanyika kwa musalaba?

11. Yesu nai mbu: Bisha byao! Utangaata buashi busibya ku nyono akaba Ongo atakweresisebo. Bushi n'oku, e mundju ola wanyanyire ene ulyi, iwete bibi kukurenza.

12. Kutengera mw'echi chihangi, Pilato era kuhonda kute angabooresa Yesu. Si e Bayuda kanji bera kutangilyisa balakanga mbu: Ukanabooresa ono mundju, kukuteta kwa uta mwira wa mwami kaisari! Bushi chira mundju ola wachitonga kwa alyi mwami, elyi kaisari y'

벼미러 오노 무뚜 아더꺼 뭐 무가, 부씨 어찌러 아찌도꽈 뿌 이 뫄나 와 오끄.

8. 피꽈도 오삐러 오유 마시, 어라 구후바 곱바아 부서서.

9. 어라 궈끼라 가찌 뫄 마이, 나 아부사 여수 뿌: 어와써, 우뤠 뭐싸 까이? 시 여수 찌로 아가뫄구꽈 가뚜.

10. 부씨 노구, 피꽈도 어라 구무부사 가찌 뿌: 어라! 우다호따 구냐구꽈? 우더씨 과 녀더 어 부아써 붜 구구보오꽈, 너 붜 구구마네가 과 무사꽈바?

11. 여수 나이 뿌: 비싸 뱌오! 우다꽈아다 부아씨 부시뱌 구 뇨노 아가바 오끄 아다궈러시서보. 부씨 노구, 어 무뚜 오꽈 와냐니러 어너 우뤠, 이워더 비비 구구러싸.

12. 구더꺼라 뭐찌 찌하끼, 피꽈도 어라 구호따 구더 아꽈보오러사 여수. 시 어 바유다 가찌 버라 구다끼꽤사 바꽈가꽈 뿌: 우가나보오러사 오노 무뚜, 구구더다 과 우다 뮈라 와 뫄미 가이사리! 부씨 찌라 무뚜 오라 와찌도꽈 과 아뤠 뫄미, 어뤠 가이사리 위

---

because he claimed to be the Son of God."

8. When Pilate heard this, he was even more afraid,

9. and he went back inside the palace. "Where do you come from?" he asked Jesus, but Jesus gave him no answer.

10. "Do you refuse to speak to me?" Pilate said. "Don't you realize I have power either to free you or to crucify you?"

11. Jesus answered, "You would have no power over me if it were not given to you from above. Therefore the one who handed me over to you is guilty of a greater sin."

12. From then on, Pilate tried to set Jesus free, but the Jews kept shouting, "If you let this man go, you are no friend of Caesar. Anyone who claims to be a king opposes Caesar."

13. Pilato omvire bacha, era kuhuba kuulusa Yesu era butala. Era kwekala kwa ndebe yai y'e kuishira e manja, ala bende belyika mwa chi eburaniya mbu: Kabate kukuteta mbu: Sakafu ya Makoi.

14. Ei myasi yabaa e lusuku lw'e kuchikunganya kwa lusuku lukulu lw'e pasaka, nga mwa saa ndachwu s'e mushi. Pilato era kwire abura abu bayuda mbu: Rero e Mwami wenyu I yono.

15. Si bera kulakanga kanji mbu: Umukonolaa! umukonolaa! Umumanyikaa kwa musalaba! Pilato era kubabusa mbu: Ono mwami wenyu, mwahonda nyimumanyike kwa musalaba? Ebakulu-kulu b'e bakuhanyi nabo mbu: chwutachwusa unji mwami, kureka kaisari yeine!

16. Chasinjire, pilato era kwire aberesa Yesu, baye kumumanyika kwa musalaba. Chasinda, ba basula bera kunakusimba Yesu.

E basula bamanyika Yesu kwa musalaba

17. Na Yesu era kutenga mwa musi ete e musalaba wai yeine. Era kuika ala bende

13. 피라도 오뻬러 바짜, 어라 구후바 구우루사 여수 어라 부다따. 어라 궈가꽈 과 떠버 야이 여 구이씨라 어 마짜, 아꽈 버떠 버레가 뫄 찌 어부라니야 뿌: 가바더 구구더다 뿌: 사가푸 야 마고이.

14. 어이 먀시 야바아 어 루수구 뤄 구찌구꺄냐 과 루수구 루구루루 뤄 파사가, 꺄 뫄 사아 따쭈 서 무씨. 피꽈도 어라 귀러 아부라 아부 바유다 뿌: 러로 어 뫄미 워뉴 이 요노.

15. 시 버라 구꽈가꺄 가찌 뿌: 우무고노롸아! 우무고노롸아! 우무마네가아 과 무사꽈바! 피꽈도 어라 구바부사 뿌: 오노 뫄미 워뉴, 뫄호따 네무마네거 과 무사꽈바? 어바구루-구루 버 바구하네 나보 뿌: 쭈다쭈사 우찌 뫄미, 구러가 가이사리 여이너!

16. 짜시찌러, 피꽈도 어라 귀러 아버러사 여수, 바여 구무마네가 과 무사꽈바. 짜시따, 바 바수꽈 버라 구나구시빠 여수.

어 바수꽈 바마네— 여수 과 무사꽈밍

17. 나 여수 어라 구더꺄 뫄 무시 어더 어 무사꽈바 와이 여이너. 어라 구이가 아꽈

13. When Pilate heard this, he brought Jesus out and sat down on the judge's seat at a place known as the Stone Pavement (which in Aramaic is Gabbatha).

14. It was the day of Preparation of Passover Week, about the sixth hour. "Here is your king," Pilate said to the Jews.

15. But they shouted, "Take him away! Take him away! Crucify him!" "Shall I crucify your king?" Pilate asked. "We have no king but Caesar," the chief priests answered.

16. Finally Pilate handed him over to them to be crucified. So the soldiers took charge of Jesus.

17. Carrying his own cross, he went out to the place of the Skull (which in Aramaic

belyika mbu: kangasi kukuteta mbu: gologota mwa chieburaniya.

18. Abu basula baikire aola, bera kumanyika Yesu kwa musalaba. Bera kumanyika na banji balume babilyi kwa misalaba, muuma kwa lunda lw'e malyo n'e unji kwa lw'e marembe, na Yesu ala kachi-kachi kabo.

19. Pilato era kuteta mbu baanjikaa myasi kwa chihaki cha bangaya kubika kwa musalaba wa Yesu. Ei myasi yabaa yanjikirwe mbu: Yesu w'e Nasareti, Mwami w'e Bayuda.

20. Bayuda banene bera kunde basomai, bushi echi chisiki cha bamanyikiraamu Yesu, chichwula ofu n'e musi w'e Yerusalemu. Ei myasi yabaa yaanjikirwe mwa chieburaniya, n'omwa chilatini, n'omwa chikiriki.

21. Chasinda, e bakulu-kulu b'e bakuhanyi b'e Bayuda, bera kuya kubura Pilato mbu: Utangaanjikire mbu: Mwami w'e Bayuda, si wanjikaa mbu: Ono mundju, abaa enjire achitonga mbu I mwami w'e Bayuda.

22. Pilato nai mbu: Ebi

버떠 버쪠가 뿌: 가까시 구구더다 뿌: 고로고다 마 쩌부라니야.

18. 아부 바수똬 바이기러 아오똬, 버라 구마네가 여수 과 무사똬바. 버라 구마네가 나 바찌 바루머 바비쪠 과 미사똬바, 무우마 과 루따 뤄 마뢰 너 우찌 과 뤄 마러뻐, 나 여수 아똬 가찌-가찌 가보.

19. 피똬도 어라 구더다 뿌 바아찌가아 먀시 과 찌하기 짜 바까야 구비가 과 무사똬바 와 여수. 어이 먀시 야바아 야찌기뤄 뿌: 여수 워 나사러디, 먀미 워 바유다.

20. 바유다 바너너 버라 구떠 바소마이, 부씨 어찌 찌시기 짜 바마네기라아무 여수, 찌쭈따 오푸 너 무시 워 여루사뼈무. 어이 먀시 야바아 야아찌기뤄 마 쩌부라니야, 노마 찌똬디니, 노마 찌기리기.

21. 짜시따, 어 바구루루-구루뻐 버 바구하네 버 바유다, 버라 구야 구부라 피똬도 뿌: 우다까아찌기러 뿌: 먀미 워 바유다, 시 와찌가아 뿌: 오노 무뿌, 아바아 어찌러 아찌도똬 뿌 이 먀미 워 바유다.

22. 피똬도 나이 뿌: 어비

is called Golgotha).

18. Here they crucified him, and with him two others-- one on each side and Jesus in the middle.

19. Pilate had a notice prepared and fastened to the cross. It read:|sc JESUS OF NAZARETH, THE KING OF THE JEWS.

20. Many of the Jews read this sign, for the place where Jesus was crucified was near the city, and the sign was written in Aramaic, Latin and Greek.

21. The chief priests of the Jews protested to Pilate, "Do not write 'The King of the Jews,' but that this man claimed to be king of the Jews."

22. Pilate answered, "What I

naanjikisise, ku binashibaa bacha!

23. Mango e basula babaa bera bamanyikaa Yesu kwa musalaba, bera kutola e njimba sai, bera kuabasi mu myango ene, chasiya chira muuma mubo eke mwango muuma. Kanji bera kutola n'e ropo lyai. Elyi ropo, lyabaa lyitalyi ku mulando kutengera mw'e osi kuikira kwa maulu.

24. Bera kutangilyisa baburana mbu: Lyine ropo, chwutalyiberengangaa, si chwulyesheraa echoore, chwumenye nde ola ungekalyi. Byabaa bacha, chasiya e chinwa chiberere, cha Maanjiko Mabuya-buya machwula matechire mbu: Baabanaa e njimba sanyi. N'e luchimba lwanyi, bera kulweshera e chore. Ebyera by'e basula bairaa.

25. Nyina wa Yesu, na nyina mutoto, na Mariya muka keleopa, na Mariya w'omwa musi w'e Makatala babaa bemenze ofu n'e musalaba wai.

26. Mango Yesu alolaa kwa nyina emenze ofu n'e mwanafunzi ola abaa achwula asimire, era kubura nyina mbu:

나아찌기시서, 구 비나씨바아 바짜!

23. 마꼬 어 바수꽈 바바아 버라 바마네가아 여수 과 무사꽈바, 버라 구도꽈 어 찌빠 사이, 버라 구아바시 무 먀꼬 어너, 짜시야 찌라 무우마 무보 어거 먀꼬 무우마. 가찌 버라 구도꽈 너 로포 꺄이. 어레 로포, 꺄바아 레다레 구 무꽈또 구더꺼라 뭐 오시 구이기라 과 마우루.

24. 버라 구다삐레사 바부라나 뿌: 레너 로포, 쭈다레버러꺼까아아, 시 쭈껴써라아 어쪼오러, 쭈머녀 더 오꽈 우꺼가레. 뱌바아 바짜, 짜시야 어 찌나 찌버러러, 짜 마아찌고 마부야-부야 마쭈꽈 마더찌러 뿌: 바아바나아 어 찌빠 사니. 너 루찌빠 꽌니, 버라 구꿔써라 어 쪼러. 어벼라 벼 바수꽈 바이라아.

25. 네나 와 여수, 나 네나 무도도, 나 마리야 무가 거꺼오파, 나 마리야 옴마 무시 워 마가다꽈 바바아 버머써 오푸 너 무사꽈바 와이.

26. 마꼬 여수 아르꽈아 과 네나 어머써 오푸 너 먀나푸씨 오꽈 아바아 아쭈꽈 아시미러, 어라 구부라 네나

have written, I have written."

23. When the soldiers crucified Jesus, they took his clothes, dividing them into four shares, one for each of them, with the undergarment remaining. This garment was seamless, woven in one piece from top to bottom.

24. "Let's not tear it," they said to one another. "Let's decide by lot who will get it." This happened that the scripture might be fulfilled which said, "They divided my garments among them and cast lots for my clothing." So this is what the soldiers did

25. Near the cross of Jesus stood his mother, his mother's sister, Mary the wife of Clopas, and Mary Magdalene.

26. When Jesus saw his mother there, and the disciple whom he loved standing nearby, he said to

Mama, umenyaa kwa oyola I muala wao.

뿌: 마마, 우머냐아 과 오요롸 이 무아롸 와오.

his mother, "Dear woman, here is your son,"

27. Chasinda, era kubura n'oyu mwanafunzi mbu: Umenyaa kwa oyola I nyoko. Kutengera mw'echi chihangi, oyu mwanafunzi era kweka Mariya ala mwai.

27. 짜시따, 어라 구부라 노유 마나푸씨 뿌: 우머냐아 과 오요롸 이 뇨고. 구더뻐라 뭐찌 찌하삐, 오유 마나푸씨 어라 귀가 마리야 아롸 뫄이.

27. and to the disciple, "Here is your mother." From that time on, this disciple took her into his home.

E kufa kwa Yesu
어 구파 과 여수

28. Era nyuma s'ebi, Yesu era kumenya kwa e myasi Yoshi era yatechwaa mwa Maanjiko Mabuya-buya yaberere mira. Era kwire ateta mbu: Nafa chami.

28. 어라 뉴마 서비, 여수 어라 구머냐 과 어 먀시 요씨 어라 야더쫘아 뫄 마아찌고 마부야-부야 야버러러 미라. 어라 귀러 아더다 뿌: 나파 짜미.

28. Later, knowing that all was now completed, and so that the Scripture would be fulfilled, Jesus said, "I am thirsty."

29. Aola, abaa alyi chikai cha chabaa chehwire mu difai era ikalyire busese. Abu basula bera kutola e chiraka, na baminyirachi kwa katabi k'e isopo, na balobekachi mwei difai. Chasinda, bera kwerusisachi kwa bunu bwa Yesu.

29. 아오롸, 아바아 아레 찌가이 짜 짜바아 쩌휘러 무 디파이 어라 이가쩨러러 부서서. 아부 바수롸 버라 구도롸 어 찌라가, 나 바미네라찌 과 가다비 거 이소포, 나 바로버가찌 뭐이 디파이. 짜시따, 버라 귀루시사찌 과 부누 봐 여수.

29. A jar of wine vinegar was there, so they soaked a sponge in it, put the sponge on a stalk of the hyssop plant, and lifted it to Jesus' lips.

30. Mango Yesu abaa era anunusaa kwei difai, era kuteta mbu: Byoshi byaberere mira! Chasinjire, era kwinamilyisa echwe, na atowa e muchima.

30. 마오 여수 아바아 어라 아누누사아 귀이 디파이, 어라 구더다 뿌: 뵤씨 뱌버러러 미라! 짜시찌러, 어라 귀나미쎄사 어쭤, 나 아도와 어 무찌마.

30. When he had received the drink, Jesus said, "It is finished." With that, he bowed his head and gave up his spirit.

E musula abandanga e chirunda cha yesu mwa lukanga
어 무수롸 아바따꺄 어 찌루따 짜 여수 뫄 루—꺄

31. Olu lusuku, lwabaa lwa kuchikunganya kwa lusuku lw'e sabato. Rero kwa olu lusuku lu lwabaa lusuku lwabo lukulu, abu Bayuda batasimaa mbu e birunda byabu bamanyikibwaa bishibaa kwa misalaba. Bushi n'oku, bera kuya kwema Pilato mbu anaa e loso bafunangange e maulu m'abu bamanyikibwaa, chasiya bandasibwe fuba kwa misalaba.

32. Chasinda, e basula bera kuya kufunanganga e maulu m'aba balume babilyi ba bamanyikibwaa alauma na Yesu. Bera kutangilyira bafunanganga ma m'e mubere-bere, chasinda ma m'e wakabilyi.

33. Si mango baikaa ala Yesu abaa alyi, bera kulola kwa afire mira. Bushi n'oku, chiro bakachimufunanganga e maulu.

34. Si muuma mubo, era kubandanga Yesu e fumo mwa lukanga. Unao-unao, mw'olu lukanga mwera kushesheka mikira na meshi.

35. E mundju ola wachiloreraa kwei myasi, iwenjire wanyanyira e bubei bwai, bunalyi bwa kanangana. Oyu

31. 오루 루수구, 콰바아 콰 구찌구꽈냐 과 루수구 루워 사바도. 러로 과 오루 루수구 루 콰바아 루수구 콰보 루구루, 아부 바유다 바다시마아 뿌 어 비루따 뱌부 바마네기봐아 비씨바아 과 미사라바. 부씨 노구, 버라 구야 궈마 피라도 뿌 아나아 어 로소 바푸나까머 어 마우루 무아부 바마네기봐아, 짜시야 바따시붸 푸바 과 미사콰바.

32. 짜시따, 어 바수콰 버라 구야 구푸나까꽈 어 마우루 무아바 바루머 바비례 바 바마네기봐아 아꽈우마 나 여수. 버라 구다삐례라 바푸나까꽈 마 머 무버러- 버러, 짜시따 마 머 와가비례.

33. 시 마꼬 바이가아 아콰 여수 아바아 아례, 버라 구로콰 과 아피러 미라. 부씨 노구, 찌로 바가찌무푸나까꽈 어 마우루.

34. 시 무우마 무보, 어라 구바따꽈 여수 어 푸모 콰 루가꽈. 우나오-우나오, 모루 루가꽈 뭐라 구써써가 미기라 나 머씨.

35. 어 무뚜 오콰 와찌로러라라아 궈이 먀시, 이워찌러 와냐네라 어 부버이 봐이, 부나례 봐 가나꽈나.

31. Now it was the day of Preparation, and the next day was to be a special Sabbath. Because the Jews did not want the bodies left on the crosses during the Sabbath, they asked Pilate to have the legs broken and the bodies taken down.

32. The soldiers therefore came and broke the legs of the first man who had been crucified with Jesus, and then those of the other.

33. But when they came to Jesus and found that he was already dead, they did not break his legs.

34. Instead, one of the soldiers pierced Jesus' side with a spear, bringing a sudden flow of blood and water.

35. The man who saw it has given testimony, and his testimony is true. He knows that he tells the truth, and

mundju, aneshi kwa ebi enjire ateta binalyi bya kanagana, chasiya nenyu mwemerere.

오유 무ᅜᅮ, 아너씨 과 어비 어ᅜᅵ러 아더다 비나레 뱌 가나가나, 짜시야 너뉴 뭐머러러.

he testifies so that you also may believe.

36. Byabaa bacha, chasiya cha chinwa chiberere, cha Maanjiko Mabuya-buya machwula matechire mbu: Kutalyi chiro n'e kinya lyai lyikafunyika.

36. 뱌바아 바짜, 짜시야 짜 찌놔 찌버러러, 짜 마아ᅜᅵ고 마부야-부야 마쭈라 마더찌러 뿌: 구다레 찌로 너 기냐 랴이 레가푸네가.

36. These things happened so that the scripture would be fulfilled: "Not one of his bones will be broken,"

37. Kanji e Maanjiko Mabuya-buya machwula matechire mbu: Oyu babandangaa e fumo, bangamuchwumbikisa.

37. 가ᅜᅵ 어 마아ᅜᅵ고 마부야-부야 마쭈라 마더찌러 뿌: 오유 바바ᄕᅡᄓᅡ아 어 푸모, 바ᄓᅡ무쭈삐기사.

37. and, as another scripture says, "They will look on the one they have pierced."

Nikotemu na yosefu bataba Yesu

니고더무 나 요서푸 바다바 여수

38. Era nyuma s'ebi, mundju muuma w'omwa musi w'e Arimateya mbu i Yosefu, era kuya kwema Pilato mbu amuwaa e loso akule echirunda cha Yesu kwa musalaba. Oyu Yosefu, abaa mwanafunzi wa Yesu kwa bubisho-bisho, bushi endee obaa e bakulu-kulu b'e bayuda. Mango Pilato abaa amwemereraa, era kunaya kukula cha chirunda kwa musalaba.

38. 어라 뉴마 서비, 무ᅜᅮ 무우마 오뫄 무시 워 아리마더야 뿌 이 요서푸, 어라 구야 궈마 피라도 뿌 아무와아 어 로소 아구러 어찌루따 짜 여수 과 무사라바. 오유 요서푸, 아바아 뫄나푸씨 와 여수 과 부비쏘-비쏘, 부씨 어떠어 오바아 어 바구루-구루 버 바유다. 마ᄓᅩ 피라도 아바아 아뭐머러라아, 어라 구나야 구구라 짜 찌루따 과 무사라바.

38. Later, Joseph of Arimathea asked Pilate for the body of Jesus. Now Joseph was a disciple of Jesus, but secretly because he feared the Jews. With Pilate's permission, he came and took the body away.

39. Nikodemu, ola waikiraa Yesu lusuku luuma buchwufu, nai era kuika. Abaa ete chichwu cha marashi ma mabaa mahoonganyisibwe n'e

39. 니고더무, 오라 와이기라아 여수 루수구 루우마 부쭈푸, 나이 어라 구이가. 아바아 어더 찌쭈 짜 마라씨 마 마바아

39. He was accompanied by Nicodemus, the man who earlier had visited Jesus at night. Nicodemus brought a mixture of myrrh and aloes,

alowe. Echi chichwu chabaa chingaika ku biro mahachwu.

마호오까네시붜 너 아르워. 어찌 찌쭈 짜바아 찌까이가 구 비로 마하쭈.

about seventy-five pounds.

40. Abu babilyi, bera kutola e chirunda cha Yesu, na babunga-bungira kw'e mirembe alauma n'e marashi. Bushi e Bayuda ku bende baira bacha mwa kutaba e bafu.

40. 아부 바비례, 버라 구도롸 어 찌루따 짜 여수, 나 바부까-부끼라 궈 미러뻐 아롸우마 너 마라씨. 부씨 어 바유다 구 버떠 바이라 바짜 롸 구다바 어 바푸.

40. Taking Jesus' body, the two of them wrapped it, with the spices, in strips of linen. This was in accordance with Jewish burial customs.

41. Ala bamanyikiraa Yesu, abaa alyi ofu n'ehwa lyiuma. Mw'elyi ehwa, mwabaa mukunganyisibwe chinjifwa chiyayaya, cha babaa batafuraa kutaba mu chiro na mundju usibya.

41. 아롸 바마네기라아 여수, 아바아 아례 오푸 너화 례우마. 뭐례 어화, 마바아 무구까네시붜 찌찌퐈 찌야야야, 짜 바바아 바다푸라아 구다바 무 찌로 나 무쭈 우시뱌.

41. At the place where Jesus was crucified, there was a garden, and in the garden a new tomb, in which no one had ever been laid.

42. Rero, bushi e lusuku lw'e sabato lwabaa lwahonda kuika, kanji bushi echi chinjifwa chabaa chilyi ofu, bera kwire bataba mu Yesu.

42. 러로, 부씨 어 루수구 뤄 사바도 롸바아 롸혼따 구이가, 가찌 부씨 어찌 찌찌퐈 짜바아 찌례 오푸, 버라 귀러 바다바 무 여수.

42. Because it was the Jewish day of Preparation and since the tomb was nearby, they laid Jesus there.

Yoana Chikono 20
E komwoka kwa Yesu

1. Abere lw'einga lumbulyi-imbulyi, Mariya w'e Makatala era kuya kwa shinda ya yesu. Aikireko, era kulola kwa balangure ekoi lya babaa bahukire kwa chiso chei shinda.

요아나 찌고노 20
어 고모— 과 여수

1. 아버러 뤄이까 루뿔례-뿔례, 마리야 워 마가다롸 어라 구야 과 씨따 야 여수. 아이기러고, 어라 구로퐈 과 바롸우러 어고이 퍄 바바아 바후기러 과 찌소 쩌이 씨따.

John Chapter 20[NIV]

1. Early on the first day of the week, while it was still dark, Mary Magdalene went to the tomb and saw that the stone had been removed from the entrance.

2. Bushi n'oku, Mariya kuna kulyibita aya kuhonda simoni Petero, n'ola unji mwanafunzi Yesu abaa achwula asimire. Era kubabura mbu: Aaye! cha chirunda cha Enawechwu, bakulyirechi mwa chijifwa, chwuteshi n'era babikirechi!

3. Petero n'oyu unji mwanafunzi mulyikabo, bera kwire balyibichira kwa chinjifwa.

4. Mw'oku kulyibita kwa banalyi babilyi, oyu unji mwanafunzi yeke, era kurenza Petero e maulu, na aba mubere kuika kwa chinjifwa.

5. Aikireko, era kwinamirira, era kulungulyiramo, na alola kw'era mirembe yeine oshao iyanashibire alashi. Si chiro akengilyiramo.

6. Chasinda, simoni petero nai era kuika, unao-unao yeke kuna kw'engiliyiramo. Nai era kulola kwei mirembe ilyi alashi,

7. era kulola n'okwa luchimba lwa babaa bahukire kw'echwe lya Yesu, lubungilyirwe mwai-mwai.

---

2. 부씨 노구, 마리야 구나 구레비다 아야 구호따 시모니 퍼더로, 노롸 우찌 뫄나푸씨 여수 아바아 아쭈롸 아시미러. 어라 구바부라 뿌: 아아여! 짜 찌루따 짜 어나워쭈, 바구레러찌 롸 찌지퐈, 쭈더씨 너라 바비기러찌!

3. 퍼더로 노유 우찌 뫄나푸씨 무레가보, 버라 귀러 바레비찌라 과 찌찌퐈.

4. 모구 구레비다 과 바나레 바비레, 오유 우찌 뫄나푸씨 여거, 어라 구러싸 퍼더로 어 마우루, 나 아바 무버러 구이가 과 찌찌퐈.

5. 아이기러고, 어라 귀나미리라, 어라 구루우꿰라모, 나 아로롸 귀라 미러뻐 여이너 오싸오 이야나씨비러 아퐈씨. 시 찌로 아거끼레라모.

6. 짜시따, 시모니 퍼더로 나이 어라 구이가, 우나오-우나오 여거 구나 궈끼레라모. 나이 어라 구로롸 궈이 미러뻐 이레 아퐈씨,

7. 어라 구로롸 노과 루찌빠 롸 바바아 바후기러 궈쭤 퍄 여수, 루부끼레뤄 뫄이-뫄이.

---

2. So she came running to Simon Peter and the other disciple, the one Jesus loved, and said, "They have taken the Lord out of the tomb, and we don't know where they have put him!"

3. So Peter and the other disciple started for the tomb.

4. Both were running, but the other disciple outran Peter and reached the tomb first.

5. He bent over and looked in at the strips of linen lying there but did not go in.

6. Then Simon Peter, who was behind him, arrived and went into the tomb. He saw the strips of linen lying there,

7. as well as the burial cloth that had been around Jesus' head. The cloth was folded up by itself, separate from the linen.

8. Oyu unji mwanafunzi watangiraa kuika kwa chinjifwa, nai era kwire engelyiramo. Na mango yeine achiloreraa kw'ebi, era kwemerera mwa muchima wai.

9. Byabaa bacha, bushi e banafunzi babaa batanafuraa kumenyerera e myasi era Maanjiko Mabuya-buya machwula matechire kwa byemire Yesu omwoke.

10. Chasinjire, ba banafunzi babilyi bera kufuluka kwa wabo.

Yesu apamukira ku Mariya w'e Makatala

11. Mariya yeke, kwemanga ku abaa enemenze ofu n'e shinda, alyira. Abere anachilyi alyira, era kwinamilyira, nai achwumbikisemo.

12. Era kulola ku bamalaika babilyi balyimo bembesi njimba sa muoko-muoko. Babaa bekese ala chirunda cha Yesu chabaa chabikibwe. Muuma abaa alyi kwa lunda lw'echwe, n'e unji kwa lw'e maulu.

13. Abu bamalaika, bera kubusa Mariya mbu: E mama! chi walyilyira kasi? Nai mbu:

---

8. 오유 우찌 뫄나푸씨 와다삐라아 구이가 과 찌찌퐈, 나이 어라 귀러 어뻐레라모. 나 마꼬 여이너 아찌로러라아 궈비, 어라 궈머러라 뫄 무찌마 와이.

9. 뱌바아 바짜, 부씨 어 바나푸씨 바바아 바다나푸라아 구머녀러라 어 먀시 어라 마아찌고 마부야-부야 마쭈퐈 마더찌러 과 벼미러 여수 오모거.

10. 짜시찌러, 바 바나푸씨 바비뤠 버라 구푸룩가 과 와보.

여수 아파무기라 구 마리야 워 마가다퐈

11. 마리야 여거, 궈마꺄 구 아바아 어너머써 오푸 너 씨따, 아뤠라. 아버러 아나찌뤠 아뤠라, 어라 귀나미뤠라, 나이 아쭈삐기서모.

12. 어라 구룰퐈 구 바마퐈이가 바비뤠 바뤠모 버뻐시 찌빠 사 무오고- 무오고. 바바아 버거서 아퐈 찌루따 짜 여수 짜바아 짜비기붜. 무우마 아바아 아뤠 과 룬따 뤄쮀, 너 우찌 과 뤄 마우룩.

13. 아부 바마퐈이가, 버라 구부사 마리야 뿌: 어 마마! 찌 와뤠러라 가시? 나이 뿌:

---

8. Finally the other disciple, who had reached the tomb first, also went inside. He saw and believed.

9. (They still did not understand from Scripture that Jesus had to rise from the dead.)

10. Then the disciples went back to their homes,

11. but Mary stood outside the tomb crying. As she wept, she bent over to look into the tomb

12. and saw two angels in white, seated where Jesus' body had been, one at the head and the other at the foot.

13. They asked her, "Woman, why are you crying?" "They have taken my Lord away,"

Aaye! bakulyire e chirunda cha enawechwu omola, ndamenyire n'era babikirechi.

14. Mango Mariya abaa era atetaa ei myasi, era kubindjuka na alola kwa Yesu emenze aola. Si chiro akamenyerera kwa i yoyu.

15. Yesu era kumubusa mbu: mama! chi walyilyira? nde iwahonda kasi? Mariya era kuchichinga mbu oyu wamubusa bacha, i mulanzi w'elyi ehwa. Bushi n'oku, era kumwakula mbu: e Walyiya, akaba uwatolyire e chirunda chai, unyiburaa ngai u wabikirechi, nyiye kutolachi.

16. Yesu era kumubura mbu: Mariya! Unao-unao, Mariya kuna kubindjuka, na amubura mwa chieburaniya mbu: Raboni! Kukuteta mbu: Mukangilyisi.

17. Yesu era kumubura mbu: Utaereresaa wanyiumako, bushi ndasa kw'erukira era mwa Tata. Si uyaa kubura banyakechwu kwa nyingerukira tanga era mwa Tata, kanji ina Eho wenyu, I Ongo wanyi, kanji ina Ongo wenyu.

아아여! 바구쩨러 어 찌루따 짜 어나워쭈 오모롸, 따머니러 너라 바비기러찌.

14. 마꼬 마리야 아바아 어라 아더다아 어이 먀시, 어라 구비뿌가 나 아로롸 과 여수 어머써 아오롸. 시 찌로 아가머녀러라 과 이 요유.

15. 여수 어라 구무부사 뿌: 어 마마! 찌 와쩨쩨라? 떠 이와호따 가시? 마리야 어라 구찌찌꽈 뿌 오유 와무부사 바쨔, 이 무롸씨 워쩨 어화. 부씨 노구, 어라 구꽈구롸 뿌: 어 와쩨야, 아가바 우와도쩨러 어 찌루따 짜이, 우네부라아 꺄이 우 와비기러찌, 네여 구도롸찌.

16. 여수 어라 구무부라 뿌: 마리야! 우나오-우나오, 마리야 구나 구비뿌가, 나 아무부라 뫄 쩌부라니야 뿌: 라보니! 구구더다 뿌: 무가삐쩨시.

17. 여수 어라 구무부라 뿌: 우다어러러사아 와네우마고, 부씨 따사 꿔루기라 어라 뫄 다다. 시 우야아 구부라 바냐거쭈 과 네꺼루기라 다꺄 어라 뫄 다다, 가찌 이나 어호 워뉴, 이 오꼬 와니, 가찌 이나 오꼬 워뉴.

she said, "and I don't know where they have put him."

14. At this, she turned around and saw Jesus standing there, but she did not realize that it was Jesus.

15. "Woman," he said, "why are you crying? Who is it you are looking for?" Thinking he was the gardener, she said, "Sir, if you have carried him away, tell me where you have put him, and I will get him."

16. Jesus said to her, "Mary." She turned toward him and cried out in Aramaic, "Rabboni!" (which means Teacher).

17. Jesus said, "Do not hold on to me, for I have not yet returned to the Father. Go instead to my brothers and tell them, 'I am returning to my Father and your Father, to my God and your God.' "

18. Bushi n'oku, Mariya w'e Makatala era kunaya kubura e banafunzi mbu: Nyono nalolyire ku Enawechwu! N'e myasi era Yesu amuchwumaa, era kunababurai.

Yesu apamukira kwa banafunzi bai

19. Abere lwera luolo-olo lw'olu lusuku lw'einga, e banafunzi ba Yesu bera kubuanana mu nyumba nguma. Bera kuchinga e nyisi, bushi babaa bobaa e bakulu-kulu b'e Bayuda. Mw'olu, Yesu kuna kubapamukirako, na achikoma mwa kachi-kachi kabo. Era kubabura mbu: Mubaa n'e boolo!

20. Abere era atetaa bacha, era kutangilyisa abalosa e mino sai n'e lukanga lwai. Bushi n'oku, e banafunzi bera kumowa busese mwa kuhuba kulola ku Enawabo.

21. Yesu era kubabura kanji mbu: Mubaa n'e boolo! Rero, ng'okwa tata anyichwumaa, ku nanyi nanabachwuma.

22. Abere Yesu atetaa ei myasi, era kubabuira e muka, na ababura mbu: Mubonaa e Muchima Mubuya-buya.

---

18. 부씨 노구, 마리야 워 마가다라 어라 구나야 구부라 어 바나푸씨 뿌: 뇨노 나로레러 구 어나워쭈! 너 먀시 어라 여수 아무쭈마아, 어라 구나바부라이.

여수 아파무기라 과 바나푸씨 바이

19. 아버러 뤄라 루오로-오로 루오루 루수구 루워이까, 어 바나푸씨 바 여수 버라 구부아나나 무 뉴빠 응마. 버라 구찌까 어 니시, 부씨 바바아 보바아 어 바구루-구루 버 바유다. 모루, 여수 구나 구바파무기라고, 나 아찌고마 뫄 가찌-가찌 가보. 어라 구바부라 뿌: 무바아 너 보오로!

20. 아버러 어라 아더다아 바짜, 어라 구다삐레사 아바론사 어 미노 사이 너 루가까 롸이. 부씨 노구, 어 바나푸씨 버라 구모와 부서서 뫄 구후바 구로롸 구 어나와보.

21. 여수 어라 구바부라 가찌 뿌: 무바아 너 보오로! 러로, 끄과 다다 아네쭈마아, 구 나네 나나바쭈마.

22. 아버러 여수 아더다아 어이 먀시, 어라 구바부이라 어 무가, 나 아바부라 뿌: 무보나아 어 무찌마 무부야-부야.

---

18. Mary Magdalene went to the disciples with the news: "I have seen the Lord!" And she told them that he had said these things to her.

19. On the evening of that first day of the week, when the disciples were together, with the doors locked for fear of the Jews, Jesus came and stood among them and said, "Peace be with you!"

20. After he said this, he showed them his hands and side. The disciples were overjoyed when they saw the Lord.

21. Again Jesus said, "Peace be with you! As the Father has sent me, I am sending you."

22. And with that he breathed on them and said, "Receive the Holy Spirit.

23. E bandju boshi ba mungende mwababalyira e bibi byabo, bagende banababalyirwabi. Na ba mutagende mwababalyira e bibi byabo, batagende banababalyirwabi.

Yesu apamukira ku Tomasi

24. Mango Yesu apamukiraa kwa banafunzi bai, tomasi ola basulaa mbu i Maaha, kanji muuma mwa ndjumwa ekumi n'ebilyi sa Yesu, yeke abaa atalyi alauma na balyikabo.

25. Rero abu balyikabo, mango bamuburaa mbu: chwalolyire ku Enawechwu mira, era kubakula mbu: Ei myasi, nyono ndangayemerera chiro na hicha, akaba ndasa kuchilorera kwa nzuu s'e misumari mwa byaha byai, n'e kubika e mutoke wanyi ala bamukomaulyiraa e musumari, n'e kubika e mino yanyi mwa lukanga lwai.

26. Abere kwarenga einge lyiuma, e banafunzi ba Yesu babaa babuananyire kanji mwei nyumba. Rero, tomasi abaa alyi alauma nabo. Kanji babaa bachingire e nyisi. Si Yesu era kuhuba kubapamukirako, na achikoma

---

23. 어 바쭈 보씨 바 무머러 뫄바바쩨라 어 비비 뱌보, 바거러 바나바바쩨롸비. 나 바 무다거러 뫄바바쩨라 어 비비 뱌보, 바다거러 바나바바쩨롸비.

여수 아파무기라 구 도마시

24. 마꼬 여수 아파무기라아 과 바나푸씨 바이, 도마시 오롸 바수롸아 뿌 이 마아하, 가찌 무우마 뫄 쭈뫄 어구미 너비례 사 여수, 여거 아바아 아다례 아롸우마 나 바쩨가보.

25. 러로 아부 바례가보, 마꼬 바무부라아 뿌: 쫘로례러 구 어나워쭈 미라, 어라 구바구꽈 뿌: 어이 먀시, 뇨노 따꽈여머러라 찌로 나 히짜, 아가바 따사 구찌롣러라 과 누우 서 미수마리 뫄 뱌하 뱌이, 너 구비가 어 무도거 와네 아롸 바무고마우례라아 어 무수마리, 너 구비가 어 미노 야네 뫄 루가꽈 롸이.

26. 아버러 과러꽈 어이머 쩨우마, 어 바나푸씨 바 여수 바바아 바부아나네러 가찌 뭐이 뉴빠. 러로, 도마시 아바아 아례 아롸우마 나보. 가찌 바바아 바찌끼러 어 내시. 시 여수 어라 구후바 구바파무기라고, 나 아찌고마

---

23. If you forgive anyone his sins, they are forgiven; if you do not forgive them, they are not forgiven."

24. Now Thomas (called Didymus), one of the Twelve, was not with the disciples when Jesus came.

25. So the other disciples told him, "We have seen the Lord!" But he said to them, "Unless I see the nail marks in his hands and put my finger where the nails were, and put my hand into his side, I will not believe it."

26. A week later his disciples were in the house again, and Thomas was with them. Though the doors were locked, Jesus came and stood among them and said, "Peace be with you!"

mwa kachi-kachi kabo. Era
kubabura kanji mbu: Mubaa
n'e boolo!

27. Chasinda, era kubura
tomasi mbu: Bikaa e mutoke
wao, ulole n'omwa byaha
byanyi. Nanulaa n'e kuboko
kwaao, uchiumire mwa
lukanga lwanyi. Rero,
utachanganwaa, si wiree
wemerera mwa muchima wao!

28. Tomasi kukwera
kumwakula mbu: Woyo u
Enawechwu, kanji u Ongo
wanyi!

29. Chasinjire, Yesu era kwire
amubura mbu: Oku
wanyilolyireko kukwera
kwachwuma wanyemerera
mwa muchima wao? Rero,
baahanyirwe ba
banganyemerera busira
kunyilolako!

E myasi era chine chitabo
chahonda kuchwubura

30. Kulyi binji bisomerano
binene bya Yesu airaa mwa
meho m'e banafunzi bai. Si
byeke, bitaanjikirwe mw'e
chine chitabo.

31. Si ene myasi yanjikirwemo,
chasiya mwemerere kwa Yesu
ina kirisito, Mwana wa Ongo.
Na mukamwemerera mwa
michima yenyu, kuika

와 가찌-가찌 가보. 어라
구바부라 가찌 뿌: 무바아 너
보오롤!

27. 짜시따, 어라 구부라
도마시 뿌: 비가아 어 무도거
와오, 우롤러 노똬 뱌하 뱌녜.
나누똬아 너 구보고 과아오,
우찌우미러 똬 루가꽈 똬네.
러로, 우다짜까놔아, 시
위러어 워머러라 똬 무찌마
와오!

28. 도마시 구궈라 구똬구꽈
뿌: 오요 우 어나워쭈, 가찌
우 오꼬 와네!

29. 짜시찌러, 여수 어라 귀러
아무부라 뿌: 오구
와네롤레러고 구궈라 과쭈마
와녀머러라 똬 무찌마 와오?
러로, 바아하네뤄 바
바까녀머러라 부시라
구네롤꽈고!

어 먀시 어라 찌너 찌다보
짜호따 구쭈뷥띱

30. 구레 비찌 비소머라노
비너너 뱌 여수 아이라아 똬
머호 머 바나푸씨 바이. 시
벼거, 비다아찌기뤄 뭐 찌너
찌다보.

31. 시 어너 먀시 야찌기뤄모,
짜시야 뭐머러러 과 여수
이나 기리시도, 똬나 와 오꼬.
나 무가뭐머러라 똬 미찌마
여뉴, 구이가 무나보너 어

27. Then he said to Thomas,
"Put your finger here; see
my hands. Reach out your
hand and put it into my
side. Stop doubting and
believe."

28. Thomas said to him, "My
Lord and my God!"

29. Then Jesus told him,
"Because you have seen me,
you have believed; blessed
are those who have not
seen and yet have believed."

30. Jesus did many other
miraculous signs in the
presence of his disciples,
which are not recorded in
this book.

31. But these are written
that you may believe that
Jesus is the Christ, the Son
of God, and that by
believing you may have life

munabone e kalamo
kumurengerako.

가꽈모 구무러떠라고.

in his name.

Yoana Chikono 21
*Yesu apamukira kwa
banafunzi bai kwa nyanja*
1. Era nyuma s'ebi, Yesu era
kuhuba kupamukira kwa
banafunzi bai, kwa musike s'e
nyanja y'e Tiberiya. Rero,
bacha ku abapamukiraako:
2 .Simoni Petero abaa alyi
aola, alauma na tomasi ola
basulaa mbu Maaha, na
natanaeli, mwesha mwa musi
w'e kana, mwa chio ch'e
kalilaya, na baala ba sebetayo,
na banji banafunzi babilyi ba
Yesu.
3. Simoni petero era kubabura
balyikabo mbu: Nyono nera
nachiira kufuba efi. Nabo mbu:
Nechwu chwachiendera nao.
Bera kuna chiuma, na berukira
mu bwato buuma. Si mw'obu
buchwufu boshi, batabona
chiro n'e lyimboolo.
4. Abere luchilyi lumbulyi-
mbulyi, bera kulola ku Yesu
emenze kwa musike s'e
nyanja, si chiro bakamumenya.
5. Yesu era kubabusa mbu: E
bana banyi! Mutechire efi?

요아나 찌고노 21
*여수 아파무기라 과 바나푸씨
바이 과 냐짜*
1. 어라 뉴마 서비, 여수 어라
구후바 구파무기라 과
바나푸씨 바이, 과 무시거 서
냐짜 여 디버리야. 러로, 바짜
구 아바파무기라아고:
2. 시모니 퍼더로 아바아
아레 아오꽈, 아꽈우마 나
도마시 오꽈 바수꽈아 뿌
마아하, 나 나다나어리, 뭐싸
와 무시 워 가나, 와 찌오 쩌
가리꽈야, 나 바아꽈 바
서버다요, 나 바찌 바나푸씨
바비레 바 여수.
3. 시모니 퍼더로 어라
구바부라 바레가보 뿌: 뇨노
너라 나찌이라 구푸바 어피.
나보 뿌: 너쭈 쫘쩌떠라 나오.
버라 구나 찌우마, 나
버루기라 무 봐도 부우마. 시
모부 부쭈푸 보씨, 바다보나
찌로 너 레뗘오로르.
4. 아버러 루찌레 루뿌레-
뿌레, 버라 구르꽈 구 여수
어머써 과 무시거 서 냐짜,
시 찌로 바가무먀.
5. 여수 어라 구바부사 뿌: 어
바나 바니! 무더찌러 어피?

John Chapter 21[NIV]
1. Afterward Jesus appeared
again to his disciples, by the
Sea of Tiberias. It happened
this way:

2. Simon Peter, Thomas
(called Didymus), Nathanael
from Cana in Galilee, the
sons of Zebedee, and two
other disciples were
together.

3. "I'm going out to fish,"
Simon Peter told them, and
they said, "We'll go with
you." So they went out and
got into the boat, but that
night they caught nothing.

4. Early in the morning,
Jesus stood on the shore,
but the disciples did not
realize that it was Jesus.
5. He called out to them,
"Friends, haven't you any

Nabo mbu: Aaye! chiro n'e lyimboolo chwutanechirelyi!

6. Era kwire ababura mbu: Muumaa e kasira kenyu kwa lunda lw'e malyo lw'e bwato, elyi mweta efi. Bera kunakauma kw'olu lunda. Bera kwita efi sinene busese, bera kunaikira bafundjwa kukululyira e kasira mwa bwato.

7. Chasinda, e mwanafunzi ola Yesu abaa achwula asimire, era kubura petero mbu: Enawechwu onola! Simoni petero, omvire bacha, era kwembala e luchimba lwai, bushi abaa akongorelo mango abaa aloba, kuna kuchihunda kwa meshi.

8. Balyikabo, bera kumukulyikira n'e bwato, baenda bakulula e kasira ka kabaa k'ehwire mw'efi. Bushi babaa batachilyi n'okwa musike s'e nyanja, si babaa bera balyi ku metere singaika ku eyana oshao.

9. Abere baika kwa musike, bera kulola ku mukati, na makala ma makorera. Kw'amu makala, kwabaa kulyi efi.

10. Yesu era kubabura mbu: Munyireteraa kw'esi efi mwechire.

나보 뿌: 아아여! 찌로 너 레뭇오쯔 쭈다너찌러레!

6. 어라 귀러 아바부라 뿌: 무우마아 어 가시라 거뉴 과 루따 뤄 마료 뤄 봐도, 어레 뭐다 어피. 버라 구나가우마 교룪 루따. 버라 귀다 어피 시너너 부서서, 버라 구나이기라 바푼꽈 구구룪쩨라 어 가시라 롸 봐도.

7. 짜시따, 어 롸나푸씨 오롸 여수 아바아 아쭈롸 아시미러, 어라 구부라 퍼더로 뿌: 어나워쭈 오노롸! 시모니 퍼더로, 오쁘러 바짜, 어라 궈빠롸 어 룪찌빠 롸이, 부씨 아바아 아고꼬러로 마꼬 아바아 아룪바, 구나 구찌후따 과 머씨.

8. 바쩨가보, 버라 구무구쩨기라 너 봐도, 바어따 바구루롸 어 가시라 가 가바아 거휘러 뭐피. 부씨 바바아 바다찌레 노과 무시거 서 냐짜, 시 바바아 버라 바쩨 구 머더러 시빠이가 구 어야나 오싸오.

9. 아버러 바이가 과 무시거, 버라 구룪롸 구 무가디, 나 마가꽈 마 마고러라. 과무 마가꽈, 과바아 구레 어피.

10. 여수 어라 구바부라 뿌: 무네러더라아 궈시 어피 뭐찌러.

fish?" "No," they answered.

6. He said, "Throw your net on the right side of the boat and you will find some." When they did, they were unable to haul the net in because of the large number of fish.

7. Then the disciple whom Jesus loved said to Peter, "It is the Lord!" As soon as Simon Peter heard him say, "It is the Lord," he wrapped his outer garment around him (for he had taken it off) and jumped into the water.

8. The other disciples followed in the boat, towing the net full of fish, for they were not far from shore, about a hundred yards.

9. When they landed, they saw a fire of burning coals there with fish on it, and some bread.

10. Jesus said to them, "Bring some of the fish you have just caught."

11. Simoni petero era kwire erukira kanji mwa bwato, na akululyira e kasira kwa musike s'e nyanja. Aku kasira, kabaa k'ehwire efi sinene eyana na matano n'e hachwu. Si chiro angaba mbu sabaa silyi sinene bacha, aku kasira kabo chiro kakanabereka.

12. Yesu era kubabura mbu: Mubahaa mwekule. kutabaa chiro na muuma mubo, ola waereresaa amubusa mbu i nde, bushi babaa bamenyire mira kwa enawabo oyola.

13. Bushi n'oku, Yesu era kwire achifunda ofu nabo, era kutola e mukati na aberesao. chasinda, era kuberesa n'e s'efi.

14. Rero, oku kupamukira kwa Yesu apamukiraa kw'abu banafunzi bai, ku kwabaa kwa kahachwu kutengera mango omwokaa.

Yesu abura petero mbu amukoreraa

15. Mango babaa bera bakulaa, Yesu era kubusa simoni petero mbu: Simoni mwenyi Yowana! Elyi uchwula unyisimire kurenza ng'okwa bano banji nabo bachwula banyisimire? Nai mbu:

11. 시모니 퍼더로 어라 귀러 어루기라 가찌 뫄 봐도, 나 아구루쀄라 어 가시라 과 무시거 서 냐짜. 아구 가시라, 가바아 거휘러 어피 시너너 어야나 나 마다노 너 하쪽. 시 찌로 아까바 뿌 사바아 시례 시너너 바짜, 아구 가시라 가보 찌로 가가나버러가.

12. 여수 어라 구바부라 뿌: 무바하아 뭐구꿔. 구다바아 찌로 나 무우마 무보, 오롸 와어러러사아 아무부사 뿌 이 떠, 부씨 바바아 바머네러 미라 과 어나와보 오요롸.

13. 부씨 노구, 여수 어라 귀러 아찌푼따 오푸 나보, 어라 구도롸 어 무가디 나 아버러사오. 짜시따, 어라 구버러사 너 서피.

14. 러로, 오구 구파무기라 과 여수 아파무기라아 과부 바나푸씨 바이, 구 과바아 과 가하쪽 구더꺼라 마꼬 오모가아.

여수 아부라 퍼더로 뿌 아무고러라아

15. 마꼬 바바아 버라 바구꽈아, 여수 어라 구부사 시모니 퍼더로 뿌: 시모니 뭐네 요와나! 어레 우쭈롸 우니시미러 구러쌰 꼬과 바노 바찌 나보 바쭉꽈 바네시미러? 나이 뿌:

11. Simon Peter climbed aboard and dragged the net ashore. It was full of large fish, 153, but even with so many the net was not torn.

12. Jesus said to them, "Come and have breakfast." None of the disciples dared ask him, "Who are you?" They knew it was the Lord.

13. Jesus came, took the bread and gave it to them, and did the same with the fish.

14. This was now the third time Jesus appeared to his disciples after he was raised from the dead.

15. When they had finished eating, Jesus said to Simon Peter, "Simon son of John, do you truly love me more than these?" "Yes, Lord," he said, "you know that I love you." Jesus said, "Feed my

Enawechwu, si weine uneshi
kwa nyichwula nyikusimire.
Yesu era kumubura mbu:
Undaa weresa e byana by'e
mbulyi sanyi e bilyo.

16. Yesu era kumubusa e
bwakabilyi mbu: Simoni
mwenyi yowana! Elyi uchwula
unyisimire! Nai kanji mbu:
Nechi Enawechwu! si Weine
uneshi kwa nyichwula
nyikusimire. Yesu era
kumubura kanji mbu: Undaa
walanga e mbulyi sanyi.

17. chasinjire, Yesu era
kumubusa e bwakahachwu
mbu: Simoni mwenyi Yowana!
Elyi uchwula unyisimire! Petero
era kwire asibuka, bushi na
Yesu e kumubusa kahachwu
mbu elyi achwula amusimire.
Bushi n'oku, era kwire
amwakula mbu: Enawechwu, si
uchwula wishi byoshi! Rero,
uneshi kanangana kwa
nyichwula nyikusimire. Yesu
era kumubura kanji mbu:
Undaa weresa e mbulyi sanyi
e bilyo.

18. Kubinalyi, nakubura kwa
mango wabaa uchilyi
mutabana, wendee
wachembasa e mukaba wao
weine, kanji wendee waya era
unasimire. Si mango

어나워쭈, 시 워이너 우너씨
과 니쭈롸 네구시미러. 여수
어라 구무부라 뿌: 우따아
워러사 어 뱌나 벼 뿌레 사니
어 비료.

16. 여수 어라 구무부사 어
봐가비레 뿌: 시모니 뭐네
요와나! 어레 우쭈롸
우네시미러! 나이 가찌 뿌:
너찌 어나워쭈! 시 워이너
우너씨 과 네쭈롸
네구시미러. 여수 어라
구무부라 가찌 뿌: 우따아
와롸까 어 뿌레 사니.

17. 짜시찌러, 여수 어라
구무부사 어 봐가하쭈 뿌:
시모니 뭐네 요와나! 어레
우쭈롸 우네시미러! 퍼더로
어라 귀러 아시부가, 부씨 나
여수 어 구무부사 가하쭈 뿌
어레 아쭈롸 아무시미러.
부씨 노구, 어라 귀러
아똬구롸 뿌: 어나워쭈, 시
우쭈롸 위씨 뵤씨! 러로,
우너씨 가나꺄나 과 네쭈롸
네구시미러. 여수 어라
구무부라 가찌 뿌: 우따아
워러사 어 뿌레 사니 어
비료.

18. 구비나레, 나구부라 과
마꼬 와바아 우찌레
무다바나, 워떠어 와쩌빠사
어 무가바 와오 워이너, 가찌
워떠어 와야 어라
우나시미러. 시 마꼬

lambs."

16. Again Jesus said, "Simon
son of John, do you truly
love me?" He answered,
"Yes, Lord, you know that I
love you." Jesus said, "Take
care of my sheep."

17. The third time he said to
him, "Simon son of John, do
you love me?" Peter was
hurt because Jesus asked
him the third time, "Do you
love me?" He said, "Lord,
you know all things; you
know that I love you."

18. Jesus said, "Feed my
sheep. I tell you the truth,
when you were younger you
dressed yourself and went
where you wanted; but
when you are old you will

ukakunguwa, kunanula ku ukende wananula e maboko mao, unji mundju anakwebasa e mukaba, anakweka n'era utahonda.

19. Yesu ateta bacha, chasiya alose petero kwa akechibwa bushi n'e kweresa Ongo echwunda. Abere Yesu era amalaa kuteta ei myasi, era kubura petero mbu: Unyikulyikiraa!

Yesu n'e mwanafunzi ola achwula asimire

20. Petero era kubindjuka, na alola kwa mwanafunzi ola Yesu abaa achwula asimire abakulyikire. Oyu mwanafunzi iwabaa weyamire kwa chifuba cha Yesu mango babaa balya e bilyo by'e pasaka. Mwamu mango, mu abusaa Yesu mbu: Enawechwu, nde i ungakurenganya kasi?

21. Rero, mango Petero abaa era alolaa kw'oyu mulyikabo, era kubusa Yesu mbu: Enawechwu, n'ono nai, bate kasi?

22. Yesu na imbu: Akaba nahonda mbu ono mundju aendekeraa kuba muuma-uma, kuikira mango nyikabaha kanji, e byera bitakwerekere. Si woyo, kunyikulyikira ku

우가구꾸와, 구나누롸 구 우거머 와나누롸 어 마보고 마오, 우찌 무뚜 아나궈바사 어 무가바, 아나궈가 너라 우다호따.

19. 여수 아더다 바짜, 짜시야 아르서 퍼더로 과 아거찌봐 부씨 너 궈러사 오오 어쭈따. 아버러 여수 어라 아마롸아 구더다 어이 먀시, 어라 구부라 퍼더로 뿌: 우네구레기라아!

여수 너 먀나푸씨 오롸 아쭈롸 아시미러

20. 퍼더로 어라 구비뿌가, 나 아르롸 과 먀나푸씨 오롸 여수 아바아 아쭈롸 아시미러 아바구레기러. 오유 먀나푸씨, 이와바아 워야미러 과 찌푸바 짜 여수 마오 바바아 바랴 어 비료 벼 파사가. 먀무 마오, 무 아부사아 여수 뿌: 어나워쭈, 떠 이 우까구러꺄냐 가시?

21. 러로, 마오 퍼더로 아바아 어라 아르롸아 교유 무레가보, 어라 구부사 여수 뿌: 어나워쭈, 노노 나이, 바더 가시?

22. 여수 나 이뿌: 아가바 나호따 뿌 오노 무뚜 아어떠거라아 구바 무우마-우마, 구이기라 마오 니가바하 가찌, 어 벼라 비다궈러거러. 시 오요,

stretch out your hands, and someone else will dress you and lead you where you do not want to go."

19. Jesus said this to indicate the kind of death by which Peter would glorify God. Then he said to him, "Follow me!"

20. Peter turned and saw that the disciple whom Jesus loved was following them. (This was the one who had leaned back against Jesus at the supper and had said, "Lord, who is going to betray you?")

21. When Peter saw him, he asked, "Lord, what about him?"

22. Jesus answered, "If I want him to remain alive until I return, what is that to you? You must follow me."

unanyikulyikiraa!

구네구레기라 구
우나네구레기라아!

23. Mango Yesu aburaa Petero bacha, oyu mwasi era kunahandabana mwa bemeresi boshi kwa oyu mwanafunzi, yeke atakafe chiro na hicha. Si Yesu atamuburaa mbu oyu mwanafunzi atakafe, si amuburaa mbu: Akaba nahonda mbu ono mundju aendekera kuba muuma-uma, kuikira mango nyikabaha kanji, e byera bitakwerekere.

23. 마꼬 여수 아부라아 퍼더로 바짜, 오유 뫄시 어라 구나하따바나 뫄 버머러시 보씨 과 오유 뫄나푸씨, 여거 아다가퍼 찌로 나 히짜. 시 여수 아다무부라아 뿌 오유 뫄나푸씨 아다가퍼, 시 아무부라아 뿌: 아가바 나호따 뿌 오노 무뚜 아어떠거라 구바 무우마-우마, 구이기라 마꼬 네가바하가씨, 어 벼라 비다궈러거러.

23. Because of this, the rumor spread among the brothers that this disciple would not die. But Jesus did not say that he would not die; he only said, "If I want him to remain alive until I return, what is that to you?"

E myasi isinda

어 먀시 이시따

24. Oyu mwanafunzi, iwatetaa era luulu sei myasi, kanji iwanayanjikaa. Rero nechwu chwuneshi kwa inalyi ya kanangana.

24. 오유 뫄나푸씨, 이와더다아 어라 루우루 서이 먀시, 가씨 이와나야씨가아. 러로 너쭈 쭈너씨 과 이나례야 가나꽈나.

24. This is the disciple who testifies to these things and who wrote them down. We know that his testimony is true.

25. Kulyi inji myasi inene busese era Yesu airaa. Rero ei myasi, akaba yoshi bangayanjikire mwa bitabo, naanyisise kwa e butala boshi, bungabere bueke kwa kulangabi.

25. 구례 이찌 먀시 이너너 부서서 어라 여수 아이라아. 러로 어이 먀시, 아가바 요씨 바꺄야씨기러 뫄 비다보, 나아네시서 과 어 부다꽈 보씨, 부꺄버러 부어거 과 구꽈꺄비.

25. Jesus did many other things as well. If every one of them were written down, I suppose that even the whole world would not have room for the books that would be written.

E Mikolo ye Ndjumwa

어 미고로 여 뚜뫄

Acts

MIKOLO YE NDJUMWA

미고로 여 뚜뫄

Chikono 1

Yesu alaanya endjumwa sai e Muchima Mubuya-buya

여수 아파씹넷 어뉴몹 사이 어 무찌마 무부야-부야

1. Walyiya Teofile, mwa chitabu chanyi chiberi-beri, nakuandjikira eralulu s'e byoshi bya Yesu airaa na kukangilyisa kuetengera mango atangilyisa e mulyimo wai.

1. 와레야 더오피러, 똬 짜네 찌버리-버리, 나구아찌기라 어라룾룾 서 뵤씨 뱌 여수 아이라아 나 구가㎖레사 구어더떠라 마꼬 아다㎖레사 어 무레모 와이.

1. In my former book, Theophilus, I wrote about all that Jesus began to do and to teach

2. Kuikira olusiku lwa erusibwaa kwa nguba. N'era muhondo elyisibweko, abaa errsise endjuma sa alondolaa emiomba. Kuerengera e buashi bw'e Mchima Mubuya-buya.

2. 구이기라 오루시구 똬 어루시봐아 과 우바. 너라 무호또 어레시붜고, 아바아 어루시서 어뉴마 사 아로또똬라 어미오빠. 구어러떠라 어 부아씨 뷔 무찌마 무부야-부야.

2. until the day he was taken up to heaven, after giving instructions through the Holy Spirit to the apostles he had chosen.

3. Esi ndjumwa, abaa enjire achikangana era silyi ku njira sinene era nyuma s'e kufa kwai, kwa kusilosa kwa omwokire. Suku mane si airaa enjire apamukira kw'esi ndjuma na kunde asihambalyira kwa myasi era yekere eBwami bwa Ongo.

3. 어시 뉴똬, 아바아 어찌러 아찌가㎖나 어라 시레 구 찌라 시너너 어라 뉴마 서 구파 과이, 과 구시론사 과 오모기러. 수구 마너 시 아이라아 어찌러 아파무기라 궈시 뉴마 나 구더 아시하빠레라 과 먀시 어라 여거러 어봐미 봐 오꼬.

3. After his suffering, he showed himself to these men and gave many convincing proofs that he was alive. He appeared to them over a period of forty days and spoke about the kingdom of God.

4. Lusuku luuma mango abaa abwananyilyi nabo, era kubachichika mbu: Mutafura kute, nga mwono musi w'e Yerusalemu, mulyindjire cha chiraane Tata abawaa, cha mwendee mwuomva

4. 루수구 루우마 마꼬 아바아 아봐나네레 나보, 어라 구바찌찌가 뿌: 무다푸라 까 모노 무시 워 여루사꺼무, 무레찌러 짜 찌라아너 다다 아바와아, 짜 뭐떠어 무오빠 나바부라.

4. On one occasion, while he was eating with them, he gave them this command: "Do not leave Jerusalem, but wait for the gift my Father promised, which you have heard me speak about.

nababura.

5. Mwishi kwa Yowani mwa meshi mu endee abatisa ebandju. Si mu suku sieke, mubeke mungabatisibwa kwa mchima Mubuya-buya.

Yesu erusibwa kwa nguba

6. Mango Yesu abaa alyi mwa lubuanano n'e ndjumwa sai, sera kumubusa mbu: Enawetchu, utchubura akaba mwa kanokabilyi mu ungahuba kualulyira eBaisiraeli ebwami bwabo.

7. Era kubakula mbu: Ekumenyerera ebihangi nesi ebyanda, kutaberekere! Ongo angabawa e buashi.

8. Bushi n'oku, mungere mwaba babei banyi mwa musi w'e Yerusalemu, n'omwa chio choshi ch'e Yudeya, ne ch'e Samariya, kunaikira n'okwa bisinda-sinda by'e butala.

9. Abere era amalaa kuteta ebyera, nao banachilyi bamuchwumbikisa, Ongo era kumweresa mwa chanya mwanameho mabo, chiro bakachimulolako bushi n'e lumbumbu.

10. Mango babaa banachilyire bachwumbikilyisa mwa chanya

5. 뮈씨 과 요와니 뫄 머씨 무 어떠어 아바디사 어바뿌. 시 무 수구 시어거, 무버거 무까바디시봐 과 무찌마 무부야-부야.

여수 어루시봐 과 위밍

6. 마꼬 여수 아바아 아례 뫄 루부아나노 너 뚜봐 사이, 서라 구무부사 뿌: 어나워쭈, 우쭈부라 아가바 뫄 가노가비례 무 우까후바 구아루례라 어바이시라어삐 어봐미 봐보.

7. 어라 구바구봐 뿌: 어구머녀러라 어비하끼 너시 어뱌따, 구다버러거러! 오꼬 아까바와 어 부아씨.

8. 부씨 노구, 무꺼러 뫄바 바버이 바네 뫄 무시 워 여루사뻐무, 노봐 찌오 쪼씨 쩌 유더야, 너 쩌 사마리야, 구나이기라 노과 비시따-시따 벼 부다봐.

9. 아버러 어라 아마봐아 구더다 어벼라, 나오 바나찌례 바무쭘삐기사, 오꼬 어라 구뭐러사 뫄 짜냐 뫄나머호 마보, 찌로 바가찌무뽄봐고 부씨 너 룸뿌뿌.

10. 마꼬 바바아 바나찌례러 바쭘삐기례사 뫄 짜냐 무 여수

5. For John baptized with water, but in a few days you will be baptized with the Holy Spirit."

6. So when they met together, they asked him, "Lord, are you at this time going to restore the kingdom to Israel?"

7. He said to them: "It is not for you to know the times or dates the Father has set by his own authority.

8. But you will receive power when the Holy Spirit comes on you; and you will be my witnesses in Jerusalem, and in all Judea and Samaria, and to the ends of the earth."

9. After he said this, he was taken up before their very eyes, and a cloud hid him from their sight.

10. They were looking intently up into the sky as

mu Yesu abaa erukira, unao-unao, balume babilyi bera kupamukira era muhondo sabo. Abu balume, babaa bembese njimba sa Silangere.

11. Bera kubusa esi ndjuma mbu: Emu besha Kalilaya, chi chichwumire mwemanga bacha ne kutchumbikilyisa kwa nguba kw'oyu Yesu era kunerusibwa kwa nguba mwa meho menyu, ku akanahahuba kufuluka.

E ndjumwa salondola Matiya mw'echwe lya Yuda

12. Era nyuma s'ebi, endjumwa sera kwire satenga kwa ndjulungu y'e Mizeetuni. Ei ndjulungu ichwula ku chilometere chiuma n'e musi w'e Yerusalemu.

13. Mango baikaa mwa musi, bera kwerukira mwa chumba ch'okwa ngangamo mwa nyumba era Yowani, na Yakobo, na Andreya, na Filipo, na Simoni w'omwa chikembe ch'e Baselote, na Yuda mwenyi Yakobo.

14. Abu boshi babaa bachwula mwa buuma na kuata bushiru mwa kwema Ongo. Mwa kachi-kachi kabo

아바아 어루기라, 우나오-우나오, 바루머 바비레 버라 구파무기라 어라 무호또 사보. 아부 바루머, 바바아 띠빠 사 시라머러.

11. 버라 구부사 어시 뚜마 뿌: 어무 버싸 가릴라야, 찌 찌쭈미러 뭐마아 바짜 너 구쭈삐기레사 과 꾸바 교유 여수 어라 구너루시봐 과 꾸바 마 머호 머뉴, 구 아가나하후바 구푸루가.

어 뚜몹 사롤또롸 마디야 뭐줘 롸 유다

12. 어라 뉴마 서비, 어꾸롸 서라 귀러 사더빠 과 뚜루꾸 여 미저어두니. 어이 뚜루꾸 이쭈롸 구 찌롣머더러 찌우마 너 무시 워 여루사러무.

13. 마꼬 바이가아 롸 무시, 버라 귀루기라 롸 쭈빠 쪼과 빠빠모 롸 뉴빠 어라 요와니, 나 야고보, 나 안두러야, 나 피리포, 나 시모니 오롸 찌거뻐 쩌 바서롣더, 나 유다 뭐니 야고보.

14. 아부 보씨 바바아 바쭈롸 롸 부우마 나 구아다 부씨루 롸 귀마 오꼬. 롸 가찌-가찌 가보 롸바아 무쭈롸 나 바가시

he was going, when suddenly two men dressed in white stood beside them.

11. "Men of Galilee," they said, "why do you stand here looking into the sky? This same Jesus, who has been taken from you into heaven, will come back in the same way you have seen him go into heaven."

12. Then they returned to Jerusalem from the hill called the Mount of Olives, a Sabbath day's walk from the city.

13. When they arrived, they went upstairs to the room where they were staying. Those present were Peter, John, James and Andrew; Philip and Thomas, Bartholomew and Matthew; James son of Alphaeus and Simon the Zealot, and Judas son of James.

14. They all joined together constantly in prayer, along with the women and Mary the mother of Jesus, and

mwabaa muchwula na bakasi bauma, na Mariya nyina wa Yesu, na balumuna ba Yesu.

바우마, 나 마리야 니나 와 여수, 나 바루무나 바 여수.

with his brothers.

15. Mwesi suku, lusuku luuma bemeresi ba bangaika kueyana na makunyabilyi babaa balyi mu lubuanano. Petro era kwimanga mwa kachi-kachi kabo, na atangilyisa aburabo mbu:

15. 뭐시 수구, 루수구 루우마 버머러시 바 바까이가 구어야나 나 마구냐비쩨 바바아 바쩨 무 루부아나노. 퍼두로 어라 귀마까 똬 가찌-가찌 가보, 나 아다띠쩨사 아부라보 뿌:

15. In those days Peter stood up among the believers (a group numbering about a hundred and twenty)

16. E banyaketchu, kwabaa kunemire bya mchima mu buyabuya atetaa era luulu sa Yuda mwa maandjiko mabuya-buya, kurengera e bunu kwa tauni binabe! Oyu Yuda, iwahondoreraa engabo sa sayaa kusimba Yesu,

16. 어 바냐거쭈, 과바아 구너미러 뱌 무찌마 무 부야부야 아더다아 어라 루우루 사 유다 똬 마아찌고 마부야-부야, 구러꺼라 어 부누 과 다우니 비나버! 오유 유다, 이와호또러라아 어까보 사 사야아 구시빠 여수,

16. and said, "Brothers, the Scripture had to be fulfilled which the Holy Spirit spoke long ago through the mouth of David concerning Judas, who served as guide for those who arrested Jesus--

17. Kanji anabaa muuma womwa luamba lwechwu mwono mulyimo wa Ongo.

17. 가찌 아나바아 무우마 오똬 루아빠 뤄쭈 모노 무레모 와 오꼬.

17. he was one of our number and shared in this ministry."

18. Rero ebikulo bya abonaa mwa kukola amu mabi, erakuula mw'ehwa. Aba mw'elye ehwa mu anakumbalyiraa kufira-bwembe na achiberekera. Emyungo y'e bula bwai, yoshiyera kuhandabana.

18. 러로 어비구로 뱌 아보나아 똬 구고꾜 아무 마비, 어라구우꾜 뭐화. 아바 뭐쪄 어화 무 아나구빠쩨라아 구피라-뷔뼈 나 아찌버러거라. 어무유꼬 여 부꽈 봐이, 요씨여라 구하따바나.

18. (With the reward he got for his wickedness, Judas bought a field; there he fell headlong, his body burst open and all his intestines spilled out.

19. Besha Yerusalemu boshi bera kunomva kwoyu mwasi. Bushi n'oku, bera kwelyika elyi ehwa mw'e teta lyabo mbu? Hakelitama kukuteta mbu Ehwa ly'e mikira.

19. 버싸 여루사쩌무 보씨 버라 구노빠 고유 꽈시. 부씨 노구, 버라 귀쩨가 어쩨 어화 뭐 더다 쨔보 뿌? 하거꾀다마 구구더다 뿌 어화 쪄 미기라.

19. Everyone in Jerusalem heard about this, so they called that field in their language Akeldama, that is, Field of Blood.)

20. Petero erakunaendekera ateta mbu: bushi kubacha kubichwula byandjikirwi mwa chitabu cha saburi mbu: Enyumba yai bushi inashibaa muhaka, bushi kutanabaa na mundju ola ukasimbula mui. Kandji byandjikirwi mbu: N'e mulyimo aataa, kwemire undji mundju atoleo.

21. Rero, kwemire undji mundju muuma ola ungende wachwuasa kuhubanganyisa e bandju kwa Enawetchu Yesu omokire.

22. Oyu mundju, kwemire abe muuma mwa ba bendee bakulyikana netchu ebihangi byoshi, mango chwabaa chwulyi alauma na Enawetchu Yesu, kutengera mango abatisibwaa na Yowani, kuikira elusuku lwa atangaa mwa kachi-kachi ketchu erusibwa kwa nguba.

23. Ebemeresi bera kwira bana masina ma bandju babilyi: Yosefu ola bendee belyika mbu ibarisaba kandji ibasulaa esina lya Yusuto, n'ewa kabilyi iwabaa Matiya.

24. Chasinda, bera kwema Ongo mbu: Enawetchu, woyo uchwuula wishi cha chilyi mwa muchima wa chira mundju.

20. 퍼더로 어라구나어꺼거라 아더다 뿌: 부씨 구바짜 구비쭈롸 뱌찌기루위 롸 찌다부 짜 사부리 뿌: 어뉴빠 야이 부씨 이나씨바아 무하가, 부씨 구다나바아 나 무뚜 오라 우가시뿌롸 무이. 뱌찌기루위 뿌: 너 무레모 아아다아, 궈미러 우찌 무뚜 아도러오.

21. 러로, 궈미러 우찌 무뚜 무우마 오라 우꺼러 와쭈아사 구후바꺼네사 어 바뚜 과 어나워쭈 여수 오모기러.

22. 오유 무뚜, 궈미러 아버 무우마 롸 바 버꺼어 바구레가나 너쭈 어비하삐 뵤씨, 마꼬 쫘바아 쭈레 아롸우마 나 어나워쭈 여수, 구더꺼라 마꼬 아바디시봐아 나 요와니, 구이기라 어루수구 롸 아다꺼아 롸 가찌-가찌 거쭈 어루시봐 과 꾸바.

23. 어버머러시 버라 귀라 바나 마시나 마 바뚜 바비레: 요서푸 오라 버꺼어 버레가 뿌 이바리사바 가찌 이바수롸아 어시나 롸 유수도, 너와 가비레 이와바아 마디야.

24. 짜시따, 버라 궈마 오꼬 뿌: 어나워쭈, 오요 우쭈우롸 위씨 짜 찌레 롸 무찌마 와 찌라 무뚜.

20. "For," said Peter, "it is written in the book of Psalms,
" 'May his place be deserted; let there be no one to dwell in it,'
and,
" 'May another take his place of leadership.'

21. Therefore it is necessary to choose one of the men who have been with us the whole time the Lord Jesus went in and out among us,

22. beginning from John's baptism to the time when Jesus was taken up from us. For one of these must become a witness with us of his resurrection."

23. So they proposed two men: Joseph called Barsabbas (also known as Justus) and Matthias.

24. Then they prayed, "Lord, you know everyone's heart. Show us which of these two you have chosen

25. Rero, oku Yuda aire era abaa anganaire, uchwuloaa mwa bano balume babilyi nde iwalondwere kwa kukola emulyimo w'e kuba ndjumwa mwechwe ly'oyu Yuda. Chasindijire, bera kubeshera echoore.

26. Chachoore, kuna kusimba Matiya, era kubikwa mwa luamba lw'e ndjumwa ekumi na nguma.

25. 러로, 오구 유다 아이러 어라 아바아 아까나이러, 우쭈로아아 뫄 바노 바루머 바비례 떠 이와르뚜워러 과 구고콰 어무례모 워 구바 뚜뫄 뭐쭤 뛰오유 유다. 짜시띠지러, 버라 구버써라 어쪼오러.

26. 짜쪼오러, 구나 구시빠 마디야, 어라 구비과 뫄 루아빠 루워 뚜뫄 어구미 나 응마.

25. to take over this apostolic ministry, which Judas left to go where he belongs."

26. Then they cast lots, and the lot fell to Matthias; so he was added to the eleven apostles.

E Mikolo ye Ndjumwa Chikono 2

EMuchima Mubuya-buya andaalyira ebemeresi

1. Mango e lusuku lw'e Pendekosite lwaikaa, ebemeresi ba Yesu boshi babaa babuananyilyi mu chiuma.

2. Unao-unao, bera kumva mururumo munene atenga kwa nguba nga kuasi kasibu. Oyu mururumo, era kumvikana mwa nyumba yoshi era babaa balyimu.

3. Chasinda, bera kulola ku sabunya nyilyimi sa mulyiro saulukira. Esi nyilyimi, sera kuhandabanya na chira luuma lweya kuchikoma ku chira

어 미고론 여 뚜뫄 찌고노 2

어무찌마 무부야-부야 아따씸례띱 어버머러시

1. 마꼬 어 루수구 루워 퍼떠고시더 똰이가아, 어버머러시 바 여수 보씨 바바아 바부아나네례 무 찌우마.

2. 우나오-우나오, 버라 구빠 무루루모 무너너 아더까 과 꾸바 까 구아시 가시부. 오유 무루루모, 어라 구뻬가나 뫄 뉴빠 요씨 어라 바바아 바례무.

3. 짜시따, 버라 구르콰 구 사부냐 네례미 사 무례로 사우루끼라. 어시 네례미, 서라 구하따바냐 나 찌라 루우마 뤄야 구찌고마 구 찌라 무우마

Acts Chapter 2[NIV]

1. When the day of Pentecost came, they were all together in one place.

2. Suddenly a sound like the blowing of a violent wind came from heaven and filled the whole house where they were sitting.

3. They saw what seemed to be tongues of fire that separated and came to rest on each of them.

muuma mubo.

4. Boshi bera kubona emuchima mubuya buya, na bangangilyisa bateta mu mandji mateta, kukulyikana n'okwa emuchima mubuya-buya aneresabo ebuashi bw'ekuteta.

5. Rero, mwamusi w'e Yerusalemu mwabaa mulyi bayuda bauma ba babaa batchula batunjire Ongo, kandji batengeraa mwa bio byoshi by'e butala.

6. Mango bomwva kwoyu mururuma, eluamba loshi lw'ebandju lwera kuira lwachilunda alauma. Bera kusanwa busese, bushi chira muuma mubo abaa omvire kwa bemeresi bahambala mweteta lyai lyekubutchwa.

7. Bachwungwa na kushishala busese, na batangilyisa babusanya mbu: Ewashe! si besha Kalilaya bano boshi bahambala bacha!

8. Kute ku chira mundju mutchubano omvire bya bateta mweteta lyai ly'ekubutchwa

9. Mwa kachi-kachi kecthu mulyibesha mwa chio ch'e Pariti, ne ch'e Meti, n'e ch'e Elamu. Na bauma balyi besha

---

무보.

4. 보씨 버라 구보나 어무찌마 무부야 부야, 나 바빠삐레사 바더다 무 마찌 마더다, 구구레가나 노과 어무찌마 무부야-부야 아너러사보 어부아씨 붜구더다.

5. 러로, 똬무시 워 여루사뚜무 똬바아 무레 바유다 바우마 빠바바아 바쭈똬 바두찌러 오끄, 가찌 바더떠라아 똬 비오 뵤씨 벼 부다똬.

6. 마끄 보무우바 고유 무루루마, 어루아빠 로씨 루워바뚜 뭐라 구이라 똬찌루따 아똬우마. 버라 구사놔 부서서, 부씨 찌라 무우마 무보 아바아 오뻐러 버머러시 바하빠똬 뭐더다 똬이 려구부좌.

7. 바쭈똬 나 구씨싸똬 부서서, 나 바다삐레사 바부사냐 뿌: 어와써! 시 버싸 가띠똬야 바노 보씨 바하빠똬 바짜!

8. 구더 구 찌라 무뚜 무쭈바노 오뻐러 뱌 바더다 뭐더다 똬이 려구부좌

9. 똬 가찌-가찌 거쮸 무레버싸 똬 찌오 쩌 파리디, 너 쩌 머디, 너 쩌 어똬무. 나 바우마 바레 버싸 똬 찌오 쩌

---

4. All of them were filled with the Holy Spirit and began to speak in other tongues as the Spirit enabled them.

5. Now there were staying in Jerusalem God-fearing Jews from every nation under heaven.

6. When they heard this sound, a crowd came together in bewilderment, because each one heard them speaking in his own language.

7. Utterly amazed, they asked: "Are not all these men who are speaking Galileans?

8. Then how is it that each of us hears them in his own native language?

9. Parthians, Medes and Elamites; residents of Mesopotamia, Judea and Cappadocia, Pontus and

mwa chio ch'e Mesopotamiya, n'e ch'e Yudeya, n'e kapadokiya, n'e ch'e pondo, n'e ch'e Asiya,

10. Ne ch'e Furikiya, ne ch'e Pamufiriya, ne ch'e Misiri, na besha mwa bimbi by'e Kurene mwa chio ch'e Libiya. Na bandji batenga mwa musi w'e Roma,

11. N'e bandji kwa chisimba ch'e Kerete, ne bandji mwa chio ch'e Baarabu. Bauma balyi bayuda, n'e bandji balyi bandju ba sindji mbaa ba bemerere Ongo w'e bayuda. Si tchuboshi, tchunomvire kwa bateta emyasi y'e bisomerano bya Ongo mwa mateta metchu mekabutchwa!

12. Bushi n'oku kutungwa nekushishala busese, bera kutangilyisa bachitetembya mbu: Ewashi! kukwera kuteta kuti kuno?

13. Si ebandji beke, bera kutangilyisa basheka e bemerese mbu: Aaye, bano bandju mafu mubatamilyire!

Petero ahubanganya eMmwasi Mubuya-buya.

14. Chasinda, Petero kwira emanga mwa sindji ndjumwa ekumi na nguma, na auma e murenge mbu: Mu bayuda

머소포다미야, 너 쩌 유더야, 너 가파도기야, 너 쩌 포또, 너 쩌 아시야,

10. 너 쩌 푸리기야, 너 쩌 파무피리야, 너 쩌 미시리, 나 버싸 먀 비뼤 벼 구러너 먀 찌오 쩌 뤼비야. 나 바띠 바더꺄 먀 무시 워 로마,

11. 너 바띠 과 찌시빠 쩌 거러더, 너 바띠 먀 찌오 쩌 바아라부. 바우마 바레 바유다, 너 바띠 바레 바쭈 바 시띠 빠아 바 버머러러 오꼬 워 바유다. 시 쭈보씨, 쭈노뻬러 과 바더다 어먀시 여 비소머라노 뱌 오꼬 먀 마더다 머쭈 머가부쫘!

12. 부씨 노구 구두꽈 너구씨싸퐈 부서서, 버라 구다뼤레사 바찌더더빠 뿌: 어와씨! 구궈라 구더다 구디 구노?

13. 시 어바띠 버거, 버라 구다뼤레사 바써가 어 버머러서 뿌: 아아여, 바노 바쭈 마푸 무바다미뤠러!

퍼더로 아후바꺄낸 어무꽈시 무부야-부야.

14. 짜시따, 퍼더로 귀라 어마꺄 먀 시띠 쭈꽈 어구미 나 꾸마, 나 아우마 어 무러꺼 뿌: 무 바유다 무뤠 너쭈, 너뉴

10. Phrygia and Pamphylia, Egypt and the parts of Libya near Cyrene; visitors from Rome

11. (both Jews and converts to Judaism Cretans and Arabs--we hear them declaring the wonders of God in our own tongues!"

12. Amazed and perplexed, they asked one another, "What does this mean?"

13. Some, however, made fun of them and said, "They have had too much wine."

14. Then Peter stood up with the Eleven, raised his voice and addressed the crowd: "Fellow Jews and all

Asia,

mulyi netchu, nenyu muboshi mutchwula muno Yerusalemu, mumenyerera cha chilyi! Munyiteya e machi n'e kumvilyisa kubuya-buya cha nahonda kubabura:

15. Bano bandju batatamilyi mafu ngokwa mwanyisise, nanga! bushi sinera sichilyi saa ehatchwu sa mishangya-shangya.

16. Bine museneko, emurebi Yoweli abaa atechire era luulu sabi mira, mango atetaa mbu:

17. Bacha ku Ongo atechire: Mwa suku s'e businda, nyikandaasa eMuchima mubuya buya wanyi kwa bandju boshi, baala benyu na balyi banyu bakareba ebatabana benyu, nyikabalosa ku myasi iyayaya mu byabunya biroto, n'e bangumwa benyu nabo, nyikabalosai mwa biroto.

18. Kubinalyi, mwesi suku, Oyu muchima mubuya-buya wanyi, nyikandaasao kwa baanda n'e baandakasi banyi, nabo bakanareba.

19. Nyikalosa bisomerano mwa chanya kwa nguba, na bimenyeso mwa butala. E mikira ikashehekala, n'e

무보씨 무쭈콰 무노 여루사쩌무, 무머녀러라 짜 찌쩨! 무네더야 어 마찌 너 구뻬쩨사 구부여-부야 짜 나호따 구바부라:

15. 바노 바쭈 바다다미쩨 마푸 꼬과 마네시서, 나까! 부씨 시너라 시찌쩨 사아 어하쭈 사 미싸꺄-싸꺄.

16. 비너 무서너고, 어무러비 요워꾀 아바아 아더찌러 어라 루우루 사비 미라, 마꼬 아더다아 뿌:

17. 바짜 구 오꼬 아더찌러: 마 수구 서 부시따, 네가따아사 어무찌마 무부야 부야 와네 바쭈 보씨, 바아꽈 버뉴 나 바쩨 바뉴 바가러바 어바다바나 버뉴, 네가바쩌사 구 먀시 이야야야 무 뱌부냐 비로도, 너 바우꽈 버뉴 나보, 네가바쩌사이 마 비로도.

18. 구비나쩨, 뭐시 수구, 오유 무찌마 무부야-부야 와네, 네가따아사오 과 바아따 너 바아따가시 바네, 나보 바가나러바.

19. 네가쩌사 비소머라노 마 짜냐 과 우바, 나 비머녀소 마 부다라. 어 미기라 이가써허가꽈, 너 무쩨로

of you who live in Jerusalem, let me explain this to you; listen carefully to what I say.

15. These men are not drunk, as you suppose. It's only nine in the morning!

16. No, this is what was spoken by the prophet Joel:

17. " 'In the last days, God says, I will pour out my Spirit on all people. Your sons and daughters will prophesy, your young men will see visions, your old men will dream dreams.

18. Even on my servants, both men and women, I will pour out my Spirit in those days, and they will prophesy.

19. I will show wonders in the heaven above and signs on the earth below, blood and fire and billows of

mulyiro akabunga, n'e musi
akafumba munene.

20. Eramuhondo olulusuku
lukulu lwekulosa engulu ya
Enawetchwu luike, esuba
likahuba nga mikira.

21. Rero, chira mundju ola
ukamaala Enawetchu mbu
amununulaa, akanunulibwa?

22. Muba isiraeli, mumvilyisa
bine nahonda kubabura: si
mwishi kwa Yesu w'e Nasareti
airaa bisomerano na
bimanyiso binene mwa kachi-
kachi kenyu. Ebyera, bilosise
kanangana kwa Ongo
anamulondola.

23. Oyu Yesu, abikibwaa mwa
mino senyu kwa kuhonda kwa
Ongo yeine kutengera mira.
Aba mu mwanamwichisa mwa
kutchwuma ebandju babi mbu
bamumanyikaa kwa musalaba.

24. Si Ongo era kumwomola,
era kumununula mwa chisibu
cha wa lufu, bushi
bitangaalyikanyire mbu e lufu
luime.

25. Daudi nai abaa anatechire
mira era luulu soyu Yesu
mbu:Enawetchu, nendee
nalola kwa unatchula era

아가부빠, 너 무시 아가푸빠
무너너.

20. 어라무호또 오루루수구
루구루 뤄구로사 어우루 야
어나워쭈 루이거, 어수바
리가후바 빠 미기라.

21. 러로, 찌라 무뚜 오롸
우가마아롸 어나워쭈 뿌
아무누누롸아, 아가누누뤼봐?

22. 무바 이시라어리, 무뻬레사
비너 나호따 구바부라: 시
뮈씨 과 여수 워 나사러디
아이라아 비소머라노 나
비마네소 비너너 봐 가찌-가찌
거뉴. 어벼라, 비로시서
가나빠나 과 오꼬
아나무로또롸.

23. 오유 여수, 아비기봐아 봐
미노 서뉴 과 구호따 과 오꼬
여이너 구더뻐라 미라. 아바
무 뫄나뮈찌사 뫄 구쭈마
어바뚜 바비 뿌 바무마네가아
과 무사뢍봐.

24. 시 오꼬 어라 구모모롸,
어라 구무누누롸 뫄 찌시부 짜
와 루푸, 부씨
비다빠아레가네러 뿌 어 루푸
루이머.

25. 다우디 나이 아바아
아나더찌러 미라 어라 루우루
소유 여수 뿌:어나워쭈, 너떠어
나롸 과 우나쭈롸 어라

---

smoke.

20. The sun will be turned
to darkness and the moon
to blood before the coming
of the great and glorious
day of the Lord.

21. And everyone who calls
on the name of the Lord
will be saved.'

22. "Men of Israel, listen to
this: Jesus of Nazareth was
a man accredited by God to
you by miracles, wonders
and signs, which God did
among you through him, as
you yourselves know.

23. This man was handed
over to you by God's set
purpose and
foreknowledge; and you,
with the help of wicked
men, put him to death by
nailing him to the cross.

24. But God raised him
from the dead, freeing him
from the agony of death,
because it was impossible
for death to keep its hold
on him.

25. David said about him: "
'I saw the Lord always
before me. Because he is at
my right hand, I will not be

muhondo sanyi. Rero, bushi utchwula kwa lunda lwanyi lw'e malyo, ndangachikukumana.

26. Bushi noku, emuchima wanyi alyi mwa boolo n'e mitetere yanyi nai, yehwire n'elumoo. Anabe na mango nyikaba mwa shinda, e mubilyi wanyi mwa munyiro mu akaba anatchwula,

27. Bushi woyo, Enawetchwu, utakanyirekerere era kusimu, nesi wemerera mbu nyi mubuya-buya wao nyiboreraa mwa shinda.

28. Wanyilosise enjira sa singatchwuma nabona e kalamo k'e kunalyi, na mango nyikaba n'era nyilyi era muhondo sao, uukananyehusa n'e lumoo.

29. Rero banyaketchwu, mureka mureka nyibahambalyire kubuya-buya era lulu sa hokulu wetchwu Daudi. Oyu Daudi nai anafaa, era kutabwa, nakuikira lwarero, eshinda yai uinachitchwula.

30. Si bushi abaa atchwula murebi, abaa aneshi kwa Ongo amulaisisaa kwa akarekera mundju muuma womwa bula bwai e bwami.

무호또 사니. 러로, 부씨 우쭈롸 과 루따 롸네 루워마료, 따롸찌구구마나.

26. 부씨 노구, 어무찌마 와네 아쩨 롸 보오로 너 미더더러 야네 나이, 여휘러 너루우모오. 아나버 나 마꼬 네가바 롸 씨따, 어 무비쎄 와네 롸 무네로 무 아가바 아나쭈롸,

27. 부씨 오요, 어나워쭈, 우다가네러거러러 어라 구시무, 너시 워머러라 뿌 네 무부야-부야 와오 네보러라아 롸 씨따.

28. 와네로시서 어찌라 사 시롸쭈마 나보나 어 가롸모 거 구나쎄, 나 마꼬 네가바 너라 네쎄 어라 무호또 사오, 우우가나녀후사 너 루모오.

29. 러로 바냐거쭈, 무러가 무러가 네바하빠쎄러 구부야-부야 어라 루루 사 호구루 워쭈 다우디. 오유 다우디 나이 아나파아, 어라 구다봐, 나구이기라 롸러로, 어씨따 야이 우이나찌쭈롸.

30. 시 부씨 아바아 아쭈롸 무러비, 아바아 아너씨 과 오꼬 아무롸이시사아 과 아가러거라 무뿌 무우마 오롸 부롸 봐이 어 봐미.

shaken.

26. Therefore my heart is glad and my tongue rejoices; my body also will live in hope,

27. because you will not abandon me to the grave, nor will you let your Holy One see decay.

28. You have made known to me the paths of life; you will fill me with joy in your presence.'

29. "Brothers, I can tell you confidently that the patriarch David died and was buried, and his tomb is here to this day.

30. But he was a prophet and knew that God had promised him on oath that he would place one of his descendants on his throne.

31. Daudi, bushi nekumenyerera bya bikaba era muhondo, era kunahambala era luulu s'e kwomoka kwa Masiya mwa kuteta mbu: Ongo atamurekaa era kusimu, nemubilyi wai ataboreraa mwa shinda.

32. Rero oyu Yesu, tchwubanafunzi bai tchwuboshi tchwanachilorera n'e meho metchwu kwa Ongo amwomola.

33. Oyu Yesu, Ongo era kumweresa etchwunda mwa kumubika kwa malyo mayi, n'e kumweresa e muchima mubuya-buya ola amulaanyaa. Kandji oyu Yesu iutchwumire byaba ngokuno musene na ngokwa mwanomvire lwarero.

34. Bushi Daudi, ata iwerukiraa kwa nguba. Si bacha ku atetaa: Enawetchwu Ongo aburaa Enawetchwu mbu: wikala kwa lunda lwanyi lw'emalyo,

35. Kuikira nyikanalyinda nabika ebarenda bao mwa maulu mao bahube chisimachiro chao.

36. Rero, cha mu baisiraeli mwemire kumenyerera kubuya-buya chi chechine: Oyu Yesu mwamanyikaa kwa

31. 다우디, 부씨 너구머녀러라 뱌 비가바 어라 무호또, 어라 구나하빠꽈 어라 루우루 서 곰모가 과 마시야 뫄 구더다 뿌: 오꼬 아다무러가아 어라 구시무, 너무비례 와이 아다보러라아 뫄 씨따.

32. 러로 오유 여수, 쭈바나푸씨 바이 쭈보씨 좌나찌로러라 너 머호 머쭈 과 오꼬 아모모꽈.

33. 오유 여수, 오꼬 어라 구뭐러사 어쭈따 뫄 구무비가 과 마뢰 마에, 너 구뭐러사 어 무찌마 무부야-부야 오라 아무꽈아냐아. 가찌 오유 여수 이우쭈미러 뱌바 꼬구노 무서너 나 꼬과 뫄노삐러 꽈러로.

34. 부씨 다우디, 아다 이워루기라아 과 꾸바. 시 바짜 구 아더다아: 어나워쭈 오꼬 아부라아 어나워쭈 뿌: 위가꽈 과 루따 꽈네 루워마뢰,

35. 구이기라 네가나례따 나비가 어바러따 바오 뫄 마우루 마오 바후버 찌시마찌로 짜오.

36. 러로, 짜 무 바이시라어뢰 뭐미러 구머녀러라 구부야-부야 찌 쩌찌너: 오유 여수 뫄마네가아 과 무사꽈바, 오꼬

31. Seeing what was ahead, he spoke of the resurrection of the Christ, that he was not abandoned to the grave, nor did his body see decay.

32. God has raised this Jesus to life, and we are all witnesses of the fact.

33. Exalted to the right hand of God, he has received from the Father the promised Holy Spirit and has poured out what you now see and hear.

34. For David did not ascend to heaven, and yet he said, " 'The Lord said to my Lord: "Sit at my right hand

35. until I make your enemies a footstool for your feet." '

36. "Therefore let all Israel be assured of this: God has made this Jesus, whom you crucified, both Lord and

musalaba, Ongo amuilyire kuba Enawetchwu kandji Masiya.

37. Abere ebandju bera bomvaa ei myasi yoshi ya Petero, bera kulyibuka kusese mwa michima yabo. Bera kwire babusa Petero n'e sindji ndjumwa mbu: Ebanyaketchwu, kute tchwuiraa

38. Petero erakubala mbu: mibindjula e myanya yenyu, na chira mundju mu mwabo abatisibwa kw'e sina ly'a Yesu Kirisito, chasiya Ongo amubabalyire ebibi byai. Na bacha, Ongo angamuwa emuchima mubuya-buya nga lwembo.

39. Echi chiraane, Ongo aberesisechi n'e bana benyu, n'e bandji bandju boshi na butchwula burere nano, ba Enawetchwu Ongo achilyi akamaala?

40. Petero endee anababura na indji myasi ya kubana na ya kubasesa emichima, bacha ku endee ababura: muchitengeraa mwa bano bandju ba lwarero ba balyi mwa muero.

41. Olulusuku, ebandju babaa bangaika ku byumbi

아무이쪠러 구바 어나워쭈 가찌 마시야.

37. 아버러 어바뚜 버라 보빠아 어이 먀시 요씨 야 퍼더로, 버라 구쩨부가 구서서 먀 미찌마 야보. 버라 귀러 바부사 퍼더로 너 시찌 뚜먀 뿌: 어바냐거쭈, 구더 쭈이라아

38. 퍼더로 어라구바라 뿌: 미비뚜쫘 어 먀냐 여뉴, 나 찌라 무뚜 무 먀보 아바디시봐 귀 시나 랴 여수 기리시도, 짜시야 오꼬 아무바바쩨러 어비비 뱌이. 나 바짜, 오꼬 아까무와 어무찌마 무부야- 부야 까 뤄뽀.

39. 어찌 찌라아너, 오꼬 아버러시서찌 너 바나 버뉴, 너 바찌 바뚜 보씨 나 부쭈쫘 부러러 나노, 바 어나워쭈 오꼬 아찌쩨 아가마아쫘?

40. 퍼더로 어떠어 아나바부라 나 이찌 먀시 야 구바나 나 야 구바서사 어미찌마, 바짜 구 어떠어 아바부라: 무찌더꺼라아 먀 바노 바뚜 바 쫘러로 바 바쩨 먀 무어로.

41. 오루루수구, 어바뚜 바바아 바빠이가 구 뷰삐 비하쭈, 나

Christ."

37. When the people heard this, they were cut to the heart and said to Peter and the other apostles, "Brothers, what shall we do?"

38. Peter replied, "Repent and be baptized, every one of you, in the name of Jesus Christ for the forgiveness of your sins. And you will receive the gift of the Holy Spirit.

39. The promise is for you and your children and for all who are far off--for all whom the Lord our God will call."

40. With many other words he warned them; and he pleaded with them, "Save yourselves from this corrupt generation."

41. Those who accepted his message were baptized, and

bihatchwu, na bayamwa luamba lw'e bemeresi.

바야뫄 루아빠 루워 버머러시.

about three thousand were added to their number that day.

Ebemeresi baira byoshi mwa buuma

어버머러시 바이라 뵤씨 뫄 부우마

42. Ebemeresi bendee bachana busese mwa kunde bomvilyisa kwa ndjuma sabakangilyisa. Kandji baaa batchwula mwa buuma na kunde balyira ebilyo alauma. Na kwemera Ongo alauma.

42. 어버머러시 버떠어 바짜나 부서서 뫄 구떠 보삐레사 과 뚜마 사바가삐레사. 가찌 바아아 바쭈롸 뫄 부우마 나 구떠 바례라 어비뢒 아롸우마. 나 궈머라 오꼬 아롸우마.

42. They devoted themselves to the apostles' teaching and to the fellowship, to the breaking of bread and to prayer.

43. Kandji Ongo endee aira bisomerano binene kurengera endjumwa, bushi noku chira mundju era kunde asanwa busese mbu: Alyibwe!

43. 가찌 오꼬 어떠어 아이라 비소머라노 비너너 구러떠라 어뚜뫄, 부씨 노구 찌라 무뚜 어라 구떠 아사놔 부서서 뿌: 아례붜!

43. Everyone was filled with awe, and many wonders and miraculous signs were done by the apostles.

44. E bemeresi boshi bera kunasimika mwobu buuma kwabo, nomwa kuhangira ebindju byabo byoshi,

44. 어 버머러시 보씨 버라 구나시미가 뫄부 부우마 과보 노뫄 구하삐라 어비뚜 뱌보 뵤씨,

44. All the believers were together and had everything in common.

45. Kukuteta mbu: Emahwa, n'e bindju byabo, bera kunde banabiusa. Chasinda, bera kunde baana ebuteya byafaa kukulyikana n'e bulaye bwa chira mundju.

45. 구구더다 뿌: 어마화, 너 비뚜 뱌보, 버라 구떠 바나비우사. 짜시따, 버라 구떠 바아나 어부더야 뱌파아 구구레가나 너 부롸여 봐 찌라 무뚜.

45. Selling their possessions and goods, they gave to anyone as he had need.

46. Chira lusuku, bendee baendekera kubuanana mwa luhu lwa Ongo, kandji bendee babuanana mwa nyumba sabo kwa kuhangira e bilyo. Ne bibilyo byabo, bendee balyabi mwa lumoo n'e boolo.

46. 찌라 루수구, 버떠어 바어떠거라 구부아나나 뫄 루후 롸 오꼬, 가찌 버떠어 바부아나나 뫄 뉴빠 사보 과 구하삐라 어 비룐. 너 비비뢒 뱌보, 버떠어 바뢔비 뫄 루모오 너 보오뢒.

46. Every day they continued to meet together in the temple courts. They broke bread in their homes and ate together with glad and sincere hearts,

47. Bera kunde batonga Ongo na kusimisa ebandju boshi. Nachira lusuku, Enawetchwu era kunde abika ebandji bandju ba beende bemerera mwa chikembe ch'e bemeresi.

47. 버라 구떠 바도ᄜ 오ᄋᆞ 나구시미사 어바ᄔ 보씨. 나찌라 루수구, 어나워쭈 어라 구떠 아비가 어바찌 바ᄔ 바버어떠 버머러라 마 찌거뼈 쩌버머러시.

47. praising God and enjoying the favor of all the people. And the Lord added to their number daily those who were being saved.

E Mikolo ye Ndjumwa Chikono 3
어 미고론 여 ᄔ와 찌고노 3
Acts Chapter 3[NIV]

1. Petero na Yowani balamya echirema lusuku luuma, Petero na Yowani babaa baya mwa luhu lwa Ongo mwa saa mwenda se mushi, chin chabaa chihangi chekwema.

1. 퍼더로 나 요와니 바ᄬ마야어찌러마 루수구 루우마, 퍼더로 나 요와니 바바아 바야마 루후 롸 오ᄋᆞ 마 사아 서 무씨, 찌누 짜바아 찌하ᄜ 쩌꿔마.

1. One day Peter and John were going up to the temple at the time of prayer--at three in the afternoon.

2. Mwechi chihangi, bera kureta mulume muuma ola wabaa chirema kutengera ekubutwa kwai. Oyu mulume, chira lusuku bebdee bemureta na kumubika kwa chiso cholu luhu cha bendee berika mbu: chiso chikomire, chasiya eme ebandu ba bendee bengirira mwa luhu,

2. 뭬찌 찌하ᄜ, 버라 구러다 무루머 무우마 오롸 와바아 찌러마 구더ᄜ라 어구부돠 과이. 오유 무루머, 찌라 루수구 버부더어 버무러다 나 구무비가 과 찌소 쪼루 루후 짜 버떠어 버리가 ᄬ: 찌소 찌고미러, 짜시야 어머 어바ᄔ 바 버떠어 버ᄜ리라 마 루후,

2. Now a man crippled from birth was being carried to the temple gate called Beautiful, where he was put every day to beg from those going into the temple courts.

3. Alolire ku Petero na Yowana bera banengirira mwa luhu, kuna kutangirisa abema buses embu bamuwaa buteya.

3. 아론ᄜ러 구 퍼더로 나 요와나 버라 바너ᄜ리라 마 루후, 구나 구다ᄜ리사 아버마 부서수 어ᄬ 바무와아 부더야.

3. When he saw Peter and John about to enter, he asked them for money.

4. Petero na Yowani bera kumusonga busese, na Petero amubura mbu: utushinderaa

4. 퍼더로 나 요와니 버라 구무소ᄜ 부서서, 나 퍼더로 아무부라 ᄬ: 우두씨떠라아

4. Peter looked straight at him, as did John. Then Peter said, "Look at us!"

5. Oyu mulume, bushiabaaa aanyisa mbu bangamweresa

5. 오유 무루머, 부씨아바아아 아아네사 ᄬ 바ᄜ뭐러사 가ᄔ,

5. So the man gave them his attention, expecting to

kandu, era kunabasindera
busese.

6. Petero kukwera kumubura
mbu: Ebuteya, ndabwete. Si
cha nyete, chi nanakweresa:
kwa buashi bwesina Iya Yesu
Kirisitowe Nazareti, emangaa
uende?

7. Chasinda, Petero era
kumusimbira kwa min oye
malyo amwimanza. Unao-
unao, ebihando alauma n'e
bisi byola mulume kuna
kubona emisi.

8. Wamulume kuna
kubanzukala na atangirisa
achendera. Chshinda, era
kwingira mwa luhu alauma
nesi ndjumwa aenda auluka-
uluka ne kutonga Ongo.

9. Ebandju boshi bera
kunachilorera kwa achendera
nokwa atonga Ongo.

10. Mango abu bandju
bamenyereraa kwa echi
chirema chi chendee chekela
chemeresa kwecha chiso
che'luhu cha chitula chirikirwe
mbu chiso chikimire, bera
kwire basanwa na kutungwa
busese mwa kulola kwebya
byamuikiraa.

Petero ahubanganyisa
ebandju mwa luhu lwa Ongo

11. Mango abandju boshi

어라 구나바시떠라 부서서.

6. 퍼더로 구궈라 구무부라 뿌:
어부더야, 따붸더. 시 짜 녀더,
찌 나나궈러사: 과 부아씨
붜시나 랴 여수 기리시도워
나자러디, 어마빠아 우어떠?

7. 짜시따, 퍼더로 어라
구무시뻬라 과 미누 오여 마료
아뮈마싸. 우나오-우나오,
어비하또 아롸우마 너 비시
뵤롸 무루머 구나 구보나
어미시.

8. 와무루머 구나 구바누가롸
나 아다삐리사 아쩌러라.
찌씨따, 어라 귀삐라 뫄 루후
아롸우마 너시 뚜뫄 아어따
아우루가-우루가 너 구도빠
오꼬.

9. 어바누 보씨 버라
구나찌로러라 과 아쩌떠라
노과 아도빠 오꼬.

10. 마꼬 아부 바누
바머녀러라라아 과 어찌 찌러마
찌 쩌떠어 쩌거롸 쩌머러사
궈짜 찌소 쩌루후 짜 찌두롸
찌리기뤄 뿌 찌소 찌기미러,
버라 귀러 바사놔 나 구두꽈
부서서 뫄 구로롸 궈뱌
뱌무이기라아.

퍼더로 아후바빠내뻽 어바누
뫄 루흘 롸 오꼬

11. 마꼬 아바누 보씨

get something from them.

6. Then Peter said, "Silver or
gold I do not have, but
what I have I give you. In
the name of Jesus Christ of
Nazareth, walk."

7. Taking him by the right
hand, he helped him up,
and instantly the man's feet
and ankles became strong.

8. He jumped to his feet
and began to walk. Then he
went with them into the
temple courts, walking and
jumping, and praising God.

9. When all the people saw
him walking and praising
God,

10. they recognized him as
the same man who used to
sit begging at the temple
gate called Beautiful, and
they were filled with
wonder and amazement at
what had happened to him.

11. While the beggar held

balolaa kwa oyu mulume walamisibwa atachitengerera ku Petero na Yowani, bera kwire basanwa. Abu bandju, bera kulyibichira ala babaa balyi kwa banali bahatu mwa chisusu cha bendee berika mbu chisusu cha Solomono.

12. Petero alolire bacha, era kuuma emurenge ateta mbu: Emu banyaketu baisiraeli, chi chatuma mwasanwa bushi nebi chi chatchwuma mwatchwusonga bacha ata kwa buashi bw'etchwu tchwubeine nesi ebubuya bwetchwu era muhondo sa Ongo bu bwatchwumire tchwamulamya.

13. Ongo wa Abrahamu, na Isaka, na Yakobo, kukuteta mbu Ongo wa bahokulo betchwu, iwera kulosa ebuashi bw'e muanda wai Yesu. Oyu Yesu, mubeine mu mwamwanaa mbu echibwe, kandji mango pilato abaa ahonda kumuboola, mwera kunana.

14. Mwera kunana amubuya-buya ne wekunali, na mwateta, mbu bababooreraa emwichi webandju.

15. Oyu mwichisaa, iwende wana ekalamo. Si Ongo

바ퟣퟪ라아 과 오유 무루머 와ퟪ라미시봐 아다찌더ퟪ러라 구 퍼더로 나 요와니, 버라 귀러 바사놔. 아부 바뚜, 버라 구레비찌라 아퐈 바바아 바뤠 과 바나뤼 바하두 뫄 찌수수 짜 버ퟪ어 버리가 뿌 찌수수 짜 소ퟪ모노.

12. 퍼더로 아ퟣퟪ뤼러 바짜, 어라 구우마 어무러ퟪ어 아더다 뿌: 어무 바냐거두 바이시라어뤼, 찌 짜두마 뫄사놔 부씨 너비 찌 짜쭈마 뫄쭈소ퟪ 바짜 아다 과 부아씨 붜쭈 쭈버이너 너시 어부부야 붜쭈 어라 무호또 사 오ꙥ 부 봐쭈미러 쫘무퐈먀.

13. 오ꙥ 와 아부라하무, 나 이사가, 나 야고보, 구구더다 뿌 오ꙥ 와 바호구로 버쭈, 이워라 구로사 어부아씨 붜 무아따 와이 여수. 오유 여수, 무버이너 무 뫄뫄나아 뿌 어찌붜, 가찌 마ꙥ 피퐈도 아바아 아호따 구무보오퐈, 뭐라 구나나.

14. 뭐라 구나나 아무부야-부야 너 워구나뤼, 나 뫄더다, 뿌 바바보오러라아 어뮈찌 워바뚜.

15. 오유 뮈찌사아, 이워떠 와나 어가퐈모. 시 오ꙥ

on to Peter and John, all the people were astonished and came running to them in the place called Solomon's Colonnade.

12. When Peter saw this, he said to them: "Men of Israel, why does this surprise you? Why do you stare at us as if by our own power or godliness we had made this man walk?

13. The God of Abraham, Isaac and Jacob, the God of our fathers, has glorified his servant Jesus. You handed him over to be killed, and you disowned him before Pilate, though he had decided to let him go.

14. You disowned the Holy and Righteous One and asked that a murderer be released to you.

15. You killed the author of life, but God raised him

amwomwere mwa bafu na tchwubeine tchwanachiloreraa kwei myasi.

아모뭐러 와 바푸 나 쭈버이너 쫘나찌롼러라아 궈이 먀시.

from the dead. We are witnesses of this.

16. Si mwishi ono mulume museneko, kandji mwera kucholorera kwa abona emisi. Aibonyire, bushi ne bwemeresi bwai kwa buashi bwesina lya Yesu. Alamire ngokwa mwera kunachilorera mu beine, bushi ne kumlangalira eri sina.

16. 시 뮈씨 오노 무루머 무서너고, 가찌 뭐라 구쪼롤러라 과 아보나 어미시. 아이보녀러, 부씨 너 붜머러시 봐이 과 부아씨 붜시나 퍄 여수. 아롸미러 꼬과 뭐라 구나찌롼러라 무 버이너, 부씨 너 구무콰꽈뤼라 어리 시나.

16. By faith in the name of Jesus, this man whom you see and know was made strong. It is Jesus' name and the faith that comes through him that has given this complete healing to him, as you can all see.

17. Rero banyaketu, nyishi kwa mwabo alauma ne bakulu-kulu benyu, emabi ma mwairira Yesu, mwabuuta mu mwamairaa.

17. 러로 바냐거두, 네씨 과 뫄보 아롸우마 너 바구루-구루 버뉴, 어마비 마 뫄이리라 여수, 뫄부우다 무 뫄마이라아.

17. "Now, brothers, I know that you acted in ignorance, as did your leaders.

18. Si kutengera mira, Ongo abaa atechire kurengera kwa bunu bwebarebi boshi kwa masiya wai akalibuka.

18. 시 구더ㅺ러라 미라, 오꼬 아바아 아더찌러 구러ㅺ러라 과 부누 붜바라비 보씨 과 와이 아가뤼부가.

18. But this is how God fulfilled what he had foretold through all the prophets, saying that his Christ would suffer.

19. Bushi noko, mubindulaa emyanya yenyu, mualukire Ongo chasiya ababalire ebibi byenyu.

19. 부씨 노고, 무비뚜콰아 어먄냐 여뉴, 무아루기러 오꼬 짜시야 아바바뤼러 어비비 벼뉴.

19. Repent, then, and turn to God, so that your sins may be wiped out, that times of refreshing may come from the Lord,

20. Mukaira bacha, Enawetu angaberesa ebihangi byebolo, kandji angabatumira Masiya wai. Noyu Masiya i Yesu yeine.

20. 무가이라 바짜, 어나워두 아꽈버러사 어비하ㅺ 벼보롸, 가찌 아꽈바두미라 마시야 와이. 노유 마시야 이 여수 여이너.

20. and that he may send the Christ, who has been appointed for you--even Jesus.

21. Si mwesine suku, kwemire Yesu abere tanga kwa nguba, kuikira mango Ongo akaba akunganyise byoshi bya atetaa

21. 시 뭐시너 수구, 궈미러 여수 아버러 다꽈 과 ㅇ우바, 구이기라 마꼬 오꼬 아가바 아구꽈네서 뵤씨 뱌 아더다아

21. He must remain in heaven until the time comes for God to restore everything, as he promised

kutengera mira kurengera ebarebi bai babuya-buya.

22. Nokwa Musa atetaa mbu: Enawenyu Ongo akabatchwumira murebimuuma ola ukaba nga nyono. Oyu murebi, akaba muuma mu banyaketchwu. Bushi noku, kwemire munde mwomva byoshi bya akende ababura.

23. Chira mundju ola ukalaira kumva byoshi murebi akende ateta, Ongo akamukula mwa bandju bai ne kumwita.

24. Kutengera ku murebi Samweli ne bandji ba banamukulyikira, boshi banahambalaa era luulu s'emyasi era tchwera tuseneko lwarero.

25. Echilaano cha Ongo anaa kurengera e barebi chilyi chenyu. Necha airaa na bahokulu benyu nachi, chinachilyi elubuto lwao, chikahaanyira embaa soshi somwa butala.

26. Bushi noku, mwabo mu Ongo atchwumiraa tanga emuanda wai, abaahanyire kwa kukula chira muuma mu mwabo mwa mabi mai.

구더꺼라 미라 구러꺼라 어바러비 바이 바부야-부야.

22. 노과 무사 아더다아 뿌: 어나워뉴 오꼬 아가바쭈미라 무러비무우마 오롸 우가바 까 뇨노. 오유 무러비, 아가바 무우마 무 바냐거쭈. 부씨 노구, 궈미러 무떠 몸빠 뵤씨 뱌 아거떠 아바부라.

23. 찌라 무뚜 오롸 우가롸이라 구빠 뵤씨 무러비 아거떠 아더다, 오꼬 아가무구롸 롸 바뚜 바이 너 구뮈다.

24. 구더꺼라 구 무러비 사뭐리 너 바찌 바 바나무구레기라, 보씨 바나하빠롸아 어라 루우루 서먀시 어라 쭤라 두서너고 롸러로.

25. 어찌롸아노 짜 오꼬 아나아 구러꺼라 어 바러비 찌레 쩌뉴. 너짜 아이라아 나 바호구루 버뉴 나찌, 찌나찌레 어루부도 롸오, 찌가하아네라 어빠아 소씨 소롸 부다롸.

26. 부씨 노구, 롸보 무 오꼬 아쭈미라아 다까 어무아따 와이, 아바아하네러 과 구구롸 찌라 무우마 무 뫄보 롸 마비 마이.

long ago through his holy prophets.

22. For Moses said, 'The Lord your God will raise up for you a prophet like me from among your own people; you must listen to everything he tells you.

23. Anyone who does not listen to him will be completely cut off from among his people.'

24. "Indeed, all the prophets from Samuel on, as many as have spoken, have foretold these days.

25. And you are heirs of the prophets and of the covenant God made with your fathers. He said to Abraham, 'Through your offspring all peoples on earth will be blessed.'

26. When God raised up his servant, he sent him first to you to bless you by turning each of you from your wicked ways."

E Mikolo ye Ndjumwa Chikono 4

Petero na Yowani batongana era muhondo s'e karubanda

1. Abere Petero na Yowani banachilyii bahubanganyisa ebandju, unao-unao e bakuhanyi, na mukulu-kulu wabalanzi b'eluhu lwa Ongo alauma ne Basandukayo bera bapamukira ako.

2. Abu balume babaa basibukire busese bushi esi ndjumwa ebilyi sa Yesu sabaa sendji sakangilyisa kwa Yesu omwokire, nekulosa kwa kasi ebafu boshi nabo bakahomoka.

3. Bushi noku, bera kubasimba na babauma mwa buroko kuikira emishangya-shangya, bushi lwabaa lwera luoloolo.

4. Si banene mwa ba babaa bomvilyisa Petero na yowana bera kwemeresa Yesu. E muandjo w'e bemeresa era kuikira ku bandju bangaika ku byumbi bitano.

5. Abere mwei mishangya, ebakulukulu b'e bayuda, n'e bashamuka alauma n'e bakangilyisi b'e mwaso, boshi bera kubwanana mwa musi w'e Yerusalemu.

어 미고로 여 뚜똬 찌고노 4

퍼더로 나 요와니 바도똬낍 어라 무호또 서 가루바똬

1. 아버러 퍼더로 나 요와니 바나찌레이 바후바똬네사 어바뚜, 우나오-우나오 어 바구하네, 나 무구루-구루 와바똬씨 버루후 똬 오꼬 아똬우마 너 바사뚜가요 버라 바파무기라 아고.

2. 아부 바루머 바바아 바시부기러 부서서 부씨 어시 뚜똬 어비레 사 여수 사바아 서씨 사가똬레사 과 여수 오모기러, 너구론사 과 가시 어바푸 보씨 나보 바가호모가.

3. 부씨 노구, 버라 구바시빠 나 바바우마 똬 부로고 구이기라 어미싸땨-싸땨, 부씨 똬바아 뤄라 루오로오로.

4. 시 바너너 똬 바 바바아 보뻬레사 퍼더로 나 요와나 버라 궈머러사 여수. 어 무아쪼 워 버머러시 어라 구이기라 구 바뚜 바똬이가 구 뷰뻬 비다노.

5. 아버러 뭐이 미싸땨, 어바구루구루 버 바유다, 너 바싸무가 아똬우마 너 바가똬레시 버 마소, 보씨 버라 구봐나나 똬 무시 워 여루사뻐무.

Acts Chapter 4[NIV]

1. The priests and the captain of the temple guard and the Sadducees came up to Peter and John while they were speaking to the people.

2. They were greatly disturbed because the apostles were teaching the people and proclaiming in Jesus the resurrection of the dead.

3. They seized Peter and John, and because it was evening, they put them in jail until the next day.

4. But many who heard the message believed, and the number of men grew to about five thousand.

5. The next day the rulers, elders and teachers of the law met in Jerusalem.

---

6. Ba babaa balyi mwolu lubuanano bubabano: Anasi, iwabaa mukulu kulu wabakuhanyi, na Kayafa, na Yowani, na Alesanduro alauma na bandji bandju bomwa ngumo yoyu mukulu-kulu wabakohanyi.

7. Abere bera bemanzaa Petero na yowana era muhondo sabo, beraku babusa mbu: Oyu mundju, mwamulamisi kubuashi buchiye, nesi kwesina lyande?

8. Petero bushi abaa akoresibwe ne muchima mubuya-buya, erakubaakula mbu: Emubakulukulu b'e bayuda nenyu mubashamuka mumvaa:

9. Lwarero mwera mwatutonganya bushi ne mabuya matchwakorere ono mundju wabaa chirema.kandji mwatchwubusa mundjira ichiye tchwamulamise.

10. Rero muboshi, alauma ne baisiraeli boshi, chechine chi mwiraa mwamenyerera: Ono mundju wemenze era muhondo senyu anahaalukire, ebuashi bwesina lya Yesu Kirisitowe nasareti bu batumire alama. Noyu Yesu, analyi ola mwamanyikaa kwa

6. 바 바바아 바께 몰루 루부아나노 부바바노: 아나시, 이와바아 무구루 구루 와바구하니, 나 가야파, 나 요와니, 나 아뻐사뚜로 아라우마 나 바찌 바뚜 보와 꾸모 요유 무구루-구루 와바고하니.

7. 아버러 버라 버마싸아 퍼더로 나 요와나 어라 무호또 사보, 버라구 바부사 뿌: 오유 무뚜, 뫄무롸미시 구부아씨 부찌여, 너시 궈시나 랴더?

8. 퍼더로 부씨 아바아 아고러시붜 너 무찌마 무부야, 어라구바아구롸 뿌: 어무바구루구루 버 바유다 너뉴 무바싸무가 무빠아:

9. 롸러로 뭐라 뫄두도뜨냐 부씨 너 마부야 마쬬고러러 오노 무뚜 와바아 찌러마.가씨 롸쭈부사 무찌라 이찌여 쬬무롸미서.

10. 러로 무보씨, 아롸우마 너 바이시라어뤼 보씨, 쩌찌너 찌 뮈라아 뫄머녀러라: 오노 무뚜 워머써 어라 무호또 서뉴 아나하아루기러, 어부아씨 뷔시나 롸 여수 기리시도워 나사러디 부 바두미러 아롸마. 노유 여수, 아나레 오롸 뫄마네가아 과 무사롸바, 시

6. Annas the high priest was there, and so were Caiaphas, John, Alexander and the other men of the high priest's family.

7. They had Peter and John brought before them and began to question them: "By what power or what name did you do this?"

8. Then Peter, filled with the Holy Spirit, said to them: "Rulers and elders of the people!

9. If we are being called to account today for an act of kindness shown to a cripple and are asked how he was healed,

10. then know this, you and all the people of Israel: It is by the name of Jesus Christ of Nazareth, whom you crucified but whom God raised from the dead, that this man stands before you healed.

musalaba, si Ongo era kumwomola kutenga mwa bafu.

오꼬 어라 구모모롸 구더까 뫄 바푸.

11. Kandji oyu Yesu inoyu, yi emaandjiko mabuya-buya matechire era luulu sai mbu: Ekoi lya mwabo mu baimbi mwalangulaa, lilyahubire koi ly'emutoloke mwa kuimbirako.

11. 가찌 오유 여수 이노유, 에 어마아찌고 마부야-부야 마더찌러 어라 루우루 사이 뿌: 어고이 랴 뫄보 무 바이삐 뫄롸우롸아, 끼랴후비러 고이 껴무도롸거 뫄 구이삐라고.

11. He is " 'the stone you builders rejected, which has become the capstone.'

12. Bushi noku, ebununusi butangaboneka kurengera ku undji mundju. Bushi muno butala mutalyi lyindji sina lyisibya lya lingalamya ebandju kureka esina lya Yesu lyeine.

12. 부씨 노구, 어부누누시 부다까보너가 구러꺼라 구 우씨 무뚜. 부씨 무노 부다롸 무다레 레찌 시나 레시뱌 랴 끼까롸먀 어바쭈 구러가 어시나 랴 여수 껴이너.

12. Salvation is found in no one else, for there is no other name under heaven given to men by which we must be saved."

13. Ebashamuka boshi bomvire bacha, bera kusanwa busese bushi ne kulola kwa Petero na yowana bachitetera busira buba, noku bachichingaa mbu esi ndjumwa, banalyi bandju mwa bandji, kandji batasomire. Bera kwira bamenyerera kwa kasi babaa batchwula na Yesu.

13. 어바싸무가 보씨 보삐러 바짜, 버라 구사놔 부서서 부씨 너 구로롸 과 퍼더로 나 요와나 바찌더더라 부시라 부바, 노구 바찌찌까아 뿌 어시 쭈뫄, 바나레 바쭈 뫄 바찌, 가찌 바다소미러. 버라 귀라 바머녀러라 과 가시 바바아 바쭈롸 나 여수.

13. When they saw the courage of Peter and John and realized that they were unschooled, ordinary men, they were astonished and they took note that these men had been with Jesus.

14. Si kandji mwa kulola kwola mundju walamisibwa emenzi alauma na Petero na yowana, bera kwire banainacha cha bangachihuba kuteta.

14. 시 가찌 뫄 구로롸 고롸 무뿌 와롸미시뫄 어머씨 아롸우마 나 퍼더로 나 요와나, 버라 귀러 바나이나짜 짜 바까찌후바 구더다.

14. But since they could see the man who had been healed standing there with them, there was nothing they could say.

15. Abu bakulu-kulu kukwera kubabura mbu?bauluka tanga mwa lubuanano, nabo bera

15. 아부 바구루-구루 구귀라 구바부라 뿌?바우루가 다까 뫄라 루부아나노, 나보 버라 귀씨바

15. So they ordered them to withdraw from the Sanhedrin and then

kwishiba baya nama:

바야 나마:

conferred together.

16. Bera kutangilyisa babusanya mbu: kute tchwuira bano bandju bushi besha Yerusalemu boshibaneshi kanangana kwa kubaira e chisomerano cha chabaa. Netchwu tchwutangaereresa tchwalaira mbu chitabaa.

16. 버라 구다삐례사 바부사냐뭐: 구더 쭈이라 바노 바뚜 부씨 버싸 여루사뭐무 보씨바너씨 가나꾸나 과 구바이라 어 찌소머라노 짜 짜바아. 너쭈 쭈다꾸어러러사 좌롸이라 뿌 찌다바아.

16. "What are we going to do with these men?" they asked. "Everybody living in Jerusalem knows they have done an outstanding miracle, and we cannot deny it.

17. Si mwa kuhonda oyu mwasi atendekera ahandabana mwa bandju, tchwubananulaa e machi kwa batacheereresa bahambala era luulu sa Yesu.

17. 시 마 구호따 오유 뫄시 아더떠거라 아하따바나 뫄 바뚜, 쭈바나누롸아 어 마찌 과 바다쩌어러러사 바하빠롸 어라 루우루 사 여수.

17. But to stop this thing from spreading any further among the people, we must warn these men to speak no longer to anyone in this name."

18. Chasinda, bera kwamala Petero na yowana. Bera kubachichika mbu: bushi mutachereresa mwateta nesi mwakangilyisa ebandju era luulu soyu Yesu!

18. 짜시따, 버라 과마롸 퍼더로 나 요와나. 버라 구바찌찌가 뿌: 부씨 무다쩌러러사 뫄더다 너시 뫄가꾸례사 어바뚜 어라 루우루 소유 여수!

18. Then they called them in again and commanded them not to speak or teach at all in the name of Jesus.

19. Petero na yowana berakubala mbu: chiye chichikomire era muhondo sa Ongo: ekubatchwunda mwabo, nesi ekutchwunda Ongo cho! mubeine muteta!

19. 퍼더로 나 요와나 버라구바롸 뿌: 찌여 찌찌고미러 어라 무호또 사 오꼬: 어구바쭈따 뫄보, 너시 어구쭈따 오꼬 쪼! 무버이너 무더다!

19. But Peter and John replied, "Judge for yourselves whether it is right in God's sight to obey you rather than God.

20. Tchwubano, e kusilyira kwa mwasi tchwachumviraa nekuchilorerako, chitangalyikana chiro na hicha.

20. 쭈바노, 어 구시례라 과 뫄시 좌쭈뻬라아 너구찌뤈러라고, 찌다꾸례가나 찌로 나 히짜.

20. For we cannot help speaking about what we have seen and heard."

21. Ebakulu-kulu bomvire bacha berakuhuba kukalyiya

21. 어바구루-구루 보뻬러 바짜 버라구후바 구가례야

21. After further threats they let them go. They

Petero na Yowani busese. Bushi baina cha bangemangirako chasiya babachinjibuse, kandji bushi ebandju boshi babaa batonga Ongo kulola kwechi chisomerano bera kubalyikula.

22. Oyu mulume walamisibwaa kwa chisomerano, abaa era wa myaka inene ku mane.

E bemeresi bema Ongo mwa malyibuko

23. Mango Petero na Yowani babaa bera baboolwa, bera kua era balikabo babaa bali. Bera kubabalikisa emyasi yoshi era abakulukulu be bakuhanyi alauma ne bashamuka baburaabo.

24. Ebemeresi bomvire kwei myasi, boshi bera kuuma emirenge bema Ongo na muchima muuma mbu: enawetchwu, woyu uwabumbaa enguba, n'e butala, n'e nyanja, na byoshi bya bitchwula mubi.

25. Kanji enawetchwu, uweresa hokulu wetu Tauti emchima mubuya-buya wao mango atetaa mbu: chi chenjire chatchwuma ebandju be sinji mbaa bareta elwayo

퍼더로 나 요와니 부서서. 부씨 바이나 짜 바꺼마끼라고 짜시야 바바찌찌부서, 가찌 부씨 어바꾸 보씨 바바아 바도꺼 오꼬 구로뽜 귀찌 찌소머라노 버라 구바쀄구뫄.

22. 오유 무루머 와뫄미시봐아 과 찌소머라노, 아바아 어라 와 먀가 이너너 구 마너.

어 버머러시 버마 오꼬 뫄 마레뷥젤

23. 마꼬 퍼더로 나 요와니 바바아 버라 바보오뽜, 버라 구아 어라 바쀠가보 바바아 바쀠. 버라 구바바쀠기사 어먀시 요씨 어라 아바구룩구룩 버 바구하니 아뫄우마 너 바싸무가 바부라아보.

24. 어버머러시 보쁘러 귀이 먀시, 보씨 버라 구우마 어미러꺼 버마 오꼬 나 무찌마 무우마 뿌: 어나워쭈, 오유 우와부빠아 어꾸바, 너 부다뫄, 너 냐짜, 나 뵤씨 뱌 비쭈뫄 무비.

25. 가찌 어나워쭈, 우워러사 호구룩 워두 다우디 어무찌마 무부야-부야 와오 마꼬 아더다아 뿌: 찌 쩌찌러 짜쭈마 어바꾸 버 시찌 빠아 바러다 어뫄요 나 찌 찌꺼쭈마

could not decide how to punish them, because all the people were praising God for what had happened.

22. For the man who was miraculously healed was over forty years old.

23. On their release, Peter and John went back to their own people and reported all that the chief priests and elders had said to them.

24. When they heard this, they raised their voices together in prayer to God. "Sovereign Lord," they said, "you made the heaven and the earth and the sea, and everything in them.

25. You spoke by the Holy Spirit through the mouth of your servant, our father David: " 'Why do the nations rage and the peoples plot in vain?

na chi chingatchwuma
ebandju baya lwango mwa
myasi era bataale,

어바꾸 바야 똬꼬 똬 먀시
어라 바다아쩌,

26. Ebami be sinji mbaa
bachibikaa alauma, ebakulu-
kulu nabo, bera kuya lwango
kwa kulaira enawetchwu, ne
kulaira ola yeine alondola?

26. 어바미 버 시찌 빠아
바찌비가아 아똬우마,
어바구루-구루 나보, 버라
구야 똬꼬 과 구똬이라
어나워쭈, 너 구똬이라 오똬
여이너 아롣또똬?

26. The kings of the earth
take their stand and the
rulers gather together
against the Lord and
against his Anointed One.'

27. Kubinalyi, Herodi na
Pondiyo pilato ne baisiraeli
alauma n'e bandju nesindji
mbaa ba uananaa mwono
musi bushi na kuya lwango
lwa kulaira Yesu, imuanda wao
mubuya- buya ola walondolaa
kuba Kirisito.

27. 구비나쩨, 허로디 나
포띠요 피똬도 너
바이시라어찌 아똬우마 너
바꾸 너시찌 빠아 바
우아나나아 모노 무시 부시 나
구야 똬꼬 똬 구똬이라 여수,
이무아따 와오 무부야- 부야
오똬 와롣또똬아 구바
기리시도.

27. Indeed Herod and
Pontius Pilate met together
with the Gentiles and the
people of Israel in this city
to conspire against your
holy servant Jesus, whom
you anointed.

28. Mwolu, ebandu baira bya
weine wabaa wakunganyise
mira bibe mwa buashi bwao.

28. 모루, 어바꾸 바이라 뱌
워이너 와바아 와구꺄네서
미라 비버 똬 부아씨 봐오.

28. They did what your
power and will had decided
beforehand should happen.

29. Rero enawetu, abu bandu,
weine u'ulolaa kwa batulibusa.
Si tubano tu baanda bao,
utweresa emisi ye
kuhubanganya emwasi wao
busira buba,

29. 러로 어나워두, 아부 바꾸,
워이너 우우롣똬아 과
바두찌부사. 시 두바노 두
바아따 바오, 우뚸러사 어미시
여 구후바꺄냐 어똬시 와오
부시라 부바,

29. Now, Lord, consider
their threats and enable
your servants to speak your
word with great boldness.

30. Ulose ne buashi bwao
chasiya tchwinde tchwalamya
ebalwala ne kunde tchwaira
bindji bisomerano kwa buashi
bwesina lye muanda wao

30. 우롣서 너 부아씨 봐오
짜시야 쮜떠 똬똬먀 어바똬똬
너 구떠 똬이라 비찌
비소머라노 과 부아씨 뷔시나
쩌 무아따 와오 무부야-부야

30. Stretch out your hand to
heal and perform
miraculous signs and
wonders through the name
of your holy servant Jesus."

mubuya-buya Yesu. 여수.

31. Abere ebemeresi bamala kwema, echisiki cha babaa balyimo kuna kulyingitana. Boshi bera kubona ebuashi bw'e muchima mubuya-buya, na batangilyisa bahubanganya echinwa cha Ongo busira buba.

31. 아버러 어버머러시 바마꽈 궈마, 어찌시기 짜 바바아 바레모 구나 구레삐다나. 보씨 버라 구보나 어부아씨 붜 무찌마 무부야-부야, 나 바다삐레사 바후바까냐 어찌놔 짜 오끄 부시라 부바.

31. After they prayed, the place where they were meeting was shaken. And they were all filled with the Holy Spirit and spoke the word of God boldly.

Ebemeresi bahangira ebindju byabo

어버머러시 바하삐띱 어비뚜 뱌보

32. Ebemeresi boshi babaa beti muchima muuma na mianyisa iuma. Kutalyi chiro na muuma mubo ola wende wateta mbu byete binalyi byai yeine. Si ebi bindju byoshi, byanabaa byabo.

32. 어버머러시 보씨 바바아 버디 무찌마 무우마 나 미아니사 이우마. 구다레 찌로 나 무우마 무보 오꽈 워떠 와더다 뿌 벼더 비나레 뱌이 여이너. 시 어비 비뚜 뵤씨, 뱌나바아 뱌보.

32. All the believers were one in heart and mind. No one claimed that any of his possessions was his own, but they shared everything they had.

33. E ndjumwa sa Yesu nasi, emyasi yekuchilorera kwa enawetchwu Yesu omwokaa kutenga mwa bafu isabaa senjire sanahambalyira ebandju na buashi bunene. Ongo nai, era kunde anabahanyira boshi busese.

33. 어 뚜꽈 사 여수 나시, 어먀시 여구찌로러라 과 어나워쭈 여수 오모가아 구더꽈 마 바푸 이사바아 서찌러 사나하빠레라 어바뚜 나 부아씨 부너너. 오끄 나이, 어라 구떠 아나바하니라 보씨 부서서.

33. With great power the apostles continued to testify to the resurrection of the Lord Jesus, and much grace was upon them all.

34. Mwa bemerese mutabaa chiro na muuma ola wende wachifisa kandju, bushi ba babaa bete emahwa nesi e manyumba, bende banausa, nekureta ebuteya bwa mendee mafa 35 era muhondo s'e ndjumwa. Obu buteya, endjumwa nasi sera kunde sabuabira ebandju kukulyikana

35. Rero, mwa bemeresi mwabaa mutchwula mundju muuma womwa chirongo ch'e balawi mbuyi

36. Yosefu mwesha kwa chisimba ch'e chipuro, ola endjumwa sa sulaa esina lya Baranaba, kuteta mbu ola wende wasesa ebandju emichima,

37. Oyu Yosefu era kuusa ehwa lyai, ne buteya bwa lyafaa era kuretabo era muhondo s'e ndjumwa.

34. 꽈 버머러서 무다바아 찌로 나 무우마 오라 워떠 와찌피사 가뉴, 부씨 바 바바아 버더 어마화 너시 어 마뉴빠, 버더 바나우사, 너구러다 어부더야 봐 머떠어 마파 35 어라 무호또 서 뉴꽈. 오부 부더야, 어뉴꽈 나시 서라 구떠 사부아비라 어바뉴 구구꿰가나

35. 러로, 꽈 버머러시 꽈바아 무쭈꽈 무뉴 무우마 오꽈 찌로끄 쩌 바꽈위 뿌에

36. 요서푸 뭐싸 과 찌시빠 쩌 찌푸로, 오꽈 어뉴꽈 사 수라아 어시나 랴 바라나바, 구더다 뿌 오꽈 워떠 와서사 어바뉴 어미찌마,

37. 오유 요서푸 어라 구우사 어화 랴이, 너 부더야 봐 랴파아 어라 구러다보 어라 무호또 서 뉴꽈.

34. There were no needy persons among them. For from time to time those who owned lands or houses sold them, brought the money from the sales

35. and put it at the apostles' feet, and it was distributed to anyone as he had need.

36. Joseph, a Levite from Cyprus, whom the apostles called Barnabas (which means Son of Encouragement),

37. sold a field he owned and brought the money and put it at the apostles' feet.

E Mikolo ye Ndjumwa Chikono 5

어 미고론 여 뉴꽈 찌고노 5

Acts Chapter 5[NIV]

Emyasi ya Ananiya na Safira

어먀시 야 아나니야 나 사피라

1. Mwesi suku, mwa bemeresi mwabaa muli mulume muuma mbu i Ananiya. Abere oyu Ananiya era ayaa lwango na mukai mbu i Safira, nai era kuusa ehwa lyai,

1. 뭐시 수구, 꽈 버머러시 꽈바아 무뤼 무루머 무우마 뿌 이 아나니야. 아버러 오유 아나니야 어라 아야아 롸끄 나 무가이 뿌 이 사피라, 나이 어라 구우사 어화 랴이,

1. Now a man named Ananias, together with his wife Sapphira, also sold a piece of property.

2. Yeke era kubisha mwango muuma kwa buteya bwa lyafaa. Eunji mwango washibaa, era kwakao era muhondo se ndjumwa. Ei myasi, mukai nai abaa anaishi.

3. Petero erakwire abusa Ananiya mbu Era Ananiya! kute wemerere emusimu achionyera mwa mchima wao, kuikira ne chihangi weengeera emchima mubuya-buya, wera wabisha mwango kwa buteya bwa wausaa ehwa?

4. Mango wabaa utasaa kuusa eri ehwa, silyabaa linali lyao! na mango waliusaa, si ebuteya bwa lyafaa nabo bwanabaa bunali bwao! kute ku weraa wasima kuira mwasi ola ulingoyu Rero, umenyerera kwa ebi bisha, ataera muhondo se bandu iwafubire, si era muhondo sa Ongo!

5. Ananiya mwa kunomva kwei myasi, era kukumbalaa, kunakufa. Ebandu boshi ba bomva kwo yu myasi, bera kusimbibwa na buba bunene.

6. Ebatabana bera kuika na babungira echirunda chai mwa ngwaya. Chasinda, bera kumweka era butala, na baya kumutaba.

2. 여거 어라 구비싸 뫄꼬 무우마 과 부더야 봐 럐파아. 어우찌 뫄꼬 와씨바아, 어라 과가오 어라 무호또 서 뚜뫄. 어이 먀시, 무가이 나이 아바아 아나이씨.

3. 퍼더로 어라귀러 아부사 아나니야 뿌 어라 아나니야! 구더 워머러러 어무시무 아찌오녀라 뫄 무찌마 와오, 구이기라 너 찌하삐 워어꺼어라 어무찌마 무부야- 부야, 워라 와비싸 뫄꼬 과 부더야 봐 와우사아 어화?

4. 뫄꼬 와바아 우다사아 구우사 어리 어화, 시럐바아 삐나뤼 랴오! 나 뫄꼬 와뤼우사아, 시 어부더야 봐 럐파아 나보 봐나바아 부나뤼 봐오! 구더 구 워라아 와시마 구이라 마시 오꽈 우뤼꼬유 러로, 우머녀러라 과 어비 비싸, 아다어라 무호또 서 바뚜 이와푸비러, 시 어라 무호또 사 오꼬!

5. 아나니야 뫄 구노빠 궈이 먀시, 어라 구구빠랴아, 구나구파. 어바뚜 보씨 바 보빠 교 유 먀시, 버라 구시뻬봐 나 부바 부너너.

6. 어바다바나 버라 구이가 나 바부삐라 어찌루따 짜이 뫄 꽈야. 짜시따, 버라 구뭐가 어라 부다꽈, 나 바야 구무다바.

2. With his wife's full knowledge he kept back part of the money for himself, but brought the rest and put it at the apostles' feet.

3. Then Peter said, "Ananias, how is it that Satan has so filled your heart that you have lied to the Holy Spirit and have kept for yourself some of the money you received for the land?

4. Didn't it belong to you before it was sold? And after it was sold, wasn't the money at your disposal? What made you think of doing such a thing? You have not lied to men but to God."

5. When Ananias heard this, he fell down and died. And great fear seized all who heard what had happened.

6. Then the young men came forward, wrapped up his body, and carried him out and buried him.

7. Abere kwa renga saa singaika kwe'haut, safira nai era kwengirira busira kumenya emyasi era yabere.

8. Nai, Petero era kumubusa mbu unyiburaa kanangana, ebuteya bwafaa ehwa lyenyu buna boshi buno safira na imbu Eee! kutwanaliusaa bacha

9. Mbu: Petero kukwera kumubura mbu kute ku mwanaikiriraa mwalaana ne balo kwa kuereka emchima wa enawetu ulolaa, ebatabana ba betenga kutaba ebalo, bubano bali kwa chiso. Rero nao, bu banakweka.

10. Safira mwakunomva bacha, kuna kuchihunda mwa maulu ma Petero Nduuu! nai unao-unao kuna kufa. Ba batabana mwa kwengirira mwei nyumba, bera kubuana saf ira afire mira. Bera kumweka era butala, na baya kumutuba ala musike se'ba.

11. Bushi noku, ebemeresi boshi alauma ne bandji bandu boshi ba bomva kwoyu mwasi, bera kusimbibwa na buba benene.

Endjumwa sa Yesu saira e bisomerane

7. 아버러 과 러빠 사아 시빠이가 궈하우두, 사피라 나이 어라 궈삐리라 부시라 구머냐 어먀시 어라 야버러.

8. 나이, 퍼더로 어라 구무부사 뿌 우네부라아 가나빠나, 어부더야 봐파아 어화 려뉴 부나 보씨 부노 사피라 나 이뿌 어어어! 구돠나삐우사아 바짜

9. 뿌: 퍼더로 구궈라 구무부라 뿌 구더 구 먀나이기리라아 먀빠아나 너 바롣 과 구어러가 어무찌마 와 어나워두 우롣빠아, 어바다바나 바 버더빠 구다바 어바롣, 부바노 바삐 과 찌소. 러로 나오, 부 바나궈가.

10. 사피라 먀구노빠 바짜, 구나 구찌후따 마 마우룬 마 퍼더로 뚜우우! 나이 우나오- 우나오 구나 구파. 바 바다바나 먀 궈삐리라 뭐이 뉴빠, 버라 구부아나 사푸 이라 아피러 미라. 버라 구뭐가 어라 부다뺘, 나 바야 구무두바 아뺘 무시거 서바.

11. 부씨 노구, 어버머러시 보씨 아뺘우마 너 바찌 바뚜 보씨 바 보빠 교유 먀시, 버라 구시뻬봐 나 부바 버너너.

어뿌몹 사 여수 사이라 어 비소머라너

7. About three hours later his wife came in, not knowing what had happened.

8. Peter asked her, "Tell me, is this the price you and Ananias got for the land?" "Yes," she said, "that is the price."

9. Peter said to her, "How could you agree to test the Spirit of the Lord? Look! The feet of the men who buried your husband are at the door, and they will carry you out also."

10. At that moment she fell down at his feet and died. Then the young men came in and, finding her dead, carried her out and buried her beside her husband.

11. Great fear seized the whole church and all who heard about these events.

12. Endumwa sa Yesu sendee saira bisomerano na bimenyeso binene mwa bandu. Kanji mwa buuma, babaa bakomere kunde babuanana mwa chisusu che'lulu cha cherikirwe mbu chisusu cha solomono.

13. Si ola utabaa mwemeresi atendee aereresa akomerana nabo, chiro angaba mbu ebandu babaa benjire babatonga.

14. Si chiro bacha, bandu banene busese, abalume ne bakasi ba babaa banjire bemerera enawetu, emuanjo wabo era kuendekera aluwa busese.

15. Bushi noku, ebandu bera kunde baretanga ebalwala mwa nama ne kubaonjisanga kwa njingo nasi kwa mikeka chasiy amango Petero angende aba arenga, echimbusa cahi chinde chaika ku bauma mubo.

16. Bandu banene bendee batengera kwa misi era yabaa isungwire emusi we Yerusalemu, bera kunde bareteranga endumwa ebalwala, ne'ba basimbirwe nebihwasi. Boshi bera kunde banalama.

12. 어뚜뫄 사 여수 서뻐어 사이라 비소머라노 나 비머녀소 비너너 뫄 바뚜. 가찌 뫄 부우마, 바바아 바고머러 구뻐 바부아나나 뫄 찌수수 쩌루루 짜 쩌리기뤄 뿌 찌수수 짜 소로모노.

13. 시 오퐈 우다바아 뭐머러시 아더뻐어 아어러러사 아고머라나 나보, 찌로 아꺄바 뿌 어바뚜 바바아 버찌러 바바도꽈.

14. 시 찌로 바짜, 바뚜 바너너 부서서, 아바루머 너 바가시 바 바바아 바찌러 버머러라 어나워두, 어무아쪼 와보 어라 구어뻐거라 아루와 부서서.

15. 부씨 노구, 어바뚜 버라 구뻐 바러다꽈 어바꽈라 뫄 나마 너 구바오찌사꽈 과 찌꼬 나시 과 미거가 짜시위 아마꼬 퍼더로 아써뻐 아바 아러꽈, 어찌뿌사 시아히 찌뻐 짜이가 구 바우마 무보.

16. 바뚜 바너너 버뻐어 바더꺼라 과 미시 어라 야바아 이수뀌러 어무시 워 여루사퍼무, 버라 구뻐 바러더라꽈 어뚜뫄 어바꽈퐈, 너바 바시뼤뤄 너비화시. 보씨 버라 구뻐 바나퐈마.

12. The apostles performed many miraculous signs and wonders among the people. And all the believers used to meet together in Solomon's Colonnade.

13. No one else dared join them, even though they were highly regarded by the people.

14. Nevertheless, more and more men and women believed in the Lord and were added to their number.

15. As a result, people brought the sick into the streets and laid them on beds and mats so that at least Peter's shadow might fall on some of them as he passed by.

16. Crowds gathered also from the towns around Jerusalem, bringing their sick and those tormented by evil spirits, and all of them were healed.

Endjumwa sa Yesu salisibwa 어뿌몹 사 여수 사픠습뷥

17. Bushi noku, emukulu-kulu wa bakuhanyi* alauma ne bandu bai bomwa chikembe che basandukayo*, bera kufira endumwa mufula munene.

18. Bera kusimba esi ndumwa na baumasi mwa buroko.

19. Si abere bwera butufu, malaika wa enawetu era kuboola enyisi sobu buroko, era kusikulamo ne kuburasi mbu:

20. Muyaa mwa luhu lwa Ongo, mwanabalira ebandu emyasi yoshi era yerekere kanpo kalao kayayaya.

21. Esi ndumwa sera ku naira kwa sanaburwaa. Abere lumbuli-mbuli, sera kulamukira mwa luhu lwa Ongo, na tangairisa sakangirisa ebandu. Abere emukul-kulu wa bakuhanyi* alauma na balikabo bera baikaa, berakuamala ekarubanda ke bayuta*. Chasinda, bera kutumisa endumwa sa sabaabsiri mwa buroko.

22. Si ebalanzi ba batumwaa, baikire mwa buroko, chiro bakachibuanamo esi mundumwa. Bera kufuluka na

---

17. 부씨 노구, 어무구룹-구룹 와 바구하니* 아라우마 너 바뚜 바이 보뫄 찌거뻐 쩌 바사뚜가요*, 버라 구피라 어뚜뫄 무푸롸 무너너.

18. 버라 구시빠 어시 뚜뫄 나 바우마시 뫄 부로고.

19. 시 아버러 뷔롸 부두푸, 마롸이가 와 어나워두 어라 구보오롸 어니시 소부 부로고, 어라 구시구롸모 너 구부라시 뿌:

20. 무야아 뫄 루후 롸 오꼬, 뫄나바픠라 어바뚜 어먀시 요씨 어라 여러거러 가누포 가롸오 가야야야.

21. 어시 뚜뫄 서라 구 나이라 과 사나부롸아. 아버러 루뿌픠-뿌픠, 서라 구롸무기라 뫄 루후 롸 오꼬, 나 다꺄이리사 사가꺠리사 어바뚜. 아버러 어무구룹-구룹 와 바구하니* 아롸우마 나 바픠가보 버라 바이가아, 버라구아마롸 어가루바따 거 바유다*. 짜시따, 버라 구두미사 어뚜뫄 사 사바아부시리 뫄 부로고.

22. 시 어바롸씨 바 바두뫄아, 바이기러 뫄 부로고, 찌로 바가찌부아나모 어시 무뚜뫄. 버라 구푸룹가 나 바바픠기사

---

17. Then the high priest and all his associates, who were members of the party of the Sadducees, were filled with jealousy.

18. They arrested the apostles and put them in the public jail.

19. But during the night an angel of the Lord opened the doors of the jail and brought them out.

20. "Go, stand in the temple courts," he said, "and tell the people the full message of this new life."

21. At daybreak they entered the temple courts, as they had been told, and began to teach the people. When the high priest and his associates arrived, they called together the Sanhedrin--the full assembly of the elders of Israel--and sent to the jail for the apostles.

22. But on arriving at the jail, the officers did not find them there. So they went back and reported,

---

23. Twabwananyire eburoko bunachingirwe kubuya-buya, ebalanzi nabo babaa banemenzi kwa nyisi. Si mwa kuchungula, chiro tukabuananamo esi ndumwa.

24. Abere emukulu-kulu webalanzi beluhu lwa Ongo alauma ne bakulu-kulu be bakohanyi bomva bacha, ebwenge bwera kubasungulira. Bera kutangirisa bachibusa era kupamukira na ababura mbu ba balume mwauma mwa buroko, si mwa luhu lwa Ongo mu bali bakangirisa ebandu.

25. Unao-unao, oyu mukulu-kulu we balanzi be luhulwa Ongo alauma ne bandu bai, bera kuya kubinga esi ndumwa. Bera kubeka buke-buke bushi babaa bobaa ebandu bangesha kubahutanga emakoi.

26. Abere bera babaisa mwa karubanda ke bayuta*, bera kubemanza era muhondo se bandu. Emukulu-kulu we bakuhanyi* era kutangirisa

23. 돠봐나니러 어부로고 부나찌삐뤄 구부야-부야, 어바꽈씨 나보 바바아 바너머씨 과 네시. 시 뫄 구쭈우꽈, 찌로 두가부아나나모 어시 뚜뫄.

24. 아버러 어무구루-구루 워바꽈씨 버루후 꽈 오꼬 아꽈우마 너 바구루-구루 버 바고하네 보빠 바짜, 어붸어 붸라 구바수우삐라. 버라 구다삐리사 바찌부사 어라 구파무기라 나 아바부라 뿌 바 바루머 뫄우마 뫄 부로고, 시 뫄 루후 꽈 오꼬 무 바삐 바가삐리사 어바뚜.

25. 우나오-우나오, 오유 무구루-구루 워 바꽈씨 버 루후꽈 오꼬 아꽈우마 너 바뚜 바이, 버라 구야 구비빠 어시 뚜뫄. 버라 구버가 부거-부거 부씨 바바아 보바아 어바뚜 바삐싸 구바후다빠 어마고이.

26. 아버러 버라 바바이사 뫄 가루바따 거 바유다*, 버라 구버마싸 어라 무호또 서 바뚜. 어무구루-구루 워 바구하네* 어라 구다삐리사

23. "We found the jail securely locked, with the guards standing at the doors; but when we opened them, we found no one inside."

24. On hearing this report, the captain of the temple guard and the chief priests were puzzled, wondering what would come of this.

25. Then someone came and said, "Look! The men you put in jail are standing in the temple courts teaching the people."

26. At that, the captain went with his officers and brought the apostles. They did not use force, because they feared that the people

abaton ganya mwa kuteta mbu:

아바도누 가냐 먀 구더다 뿌: would stone them.

27. Si muneshi kwa twabangaa kwa mutachiereresaa mwakangirisa ebandu era luulu soyu mundu.

27. 시 무너씨 과 돠바까아 과 무다쩌러러사아 마가끼리사 어바누 어라 루우루 소유 무뚜.

27. Having brought the apostles, they made them appear before the Sanhedrin to be questioned by the high priest.

28. Rero, mwiree mwalola, emyasi mwenjire mwakangirisa, yene yehula mwono musi woshi we yerusalemeu. Kanji mwahonda elufu lwai lube kwetwe lyenu!

28. 러로, 뭐러어 먀로꽈, 어먀시 뭐찌러 먀가끼리사, 여너 여후꽈 모노 무시 올씨 워 여루사뗘머우. 가찌 먀호따 어루푸 꽈이 루버 궈뙈 뗘누!

28. "We gave you strict orders not to teach in this name," he said. "Yet you have filled Jerusalem with your teaching and are determined to make us guilty of this man's blood."

29. Petero alauma nesinji bdumwa bera kumwakula mbu: tubano, wakutunda ebandu, byemire tutunde Ongo!

29. 퍼더로 아꽈우마 너시찌 부두꽈 버라 구꽈구꽈 뿌: 두바노, 와구뚜따 어바누, 뼈미러 두두떠 오꼬!

29. Peter and the other apostles replied: "We must obey God rather than men!

30. Mumenyerera kwa oyu Yesu mwetaa mwa kumumanyika kwa musalaba, Ongo wa bahokulu amwomwere.

30. 무머녀러라 과 오유 여수 뭐다아 먀 구무마네가 과 무사꽈바, 오꼬 와 바호구루 아모뭐러.

30. The God of our fathers raised Jesus from the dead--whom you had killed by hanging him on a tree.

31. Kanji amuwere etunda ne kumubika lwa malyo mai, na kumuira mwami munene na mulamya, chasiya ebaisiraeli babone enjira yekubindula emyanya yabo, eri Ongo ababalire ebibi byabo.

31. 가찌 아무워러 어두따 너 구무비가 꽈 마뾰 마이, 나 구무이라 먀미 무너너 나 무꽈먀, 짜시야 어바이시라어뤼 바보너 어찌라 여구비뿌꽈 어먀냐 야보, 어리 오꼬 아바바뤼러 어비비 뱌보.

31. God exalted him to his own right hand as Prince and Savior that he might give repentance and forgiveness of sins to Israel.

32. Nei myasi, tubeine alauma ne muchima mubuya buya ola Ongo ersise ba batula

32. 너이 먀시, 두버이너 아꽈우마 너 무찌마 무부야 부야 오꽈 오꼬 어시서 바

32. We are witnesses of these things, and so is the Holy Spirit, whom God has

bamutunjire, twanachilorera kui.

33. Mango ba babaa bali mwa karubanda* bomva kwei myasi, ebute bwera kubasimba busese. Bera kwire bahonda kwita esi ndumwa.

34. Si mwolu lubuanano, mwabaa muli mufarisayo* muuma mbu ikamaliyeri. Oyu kamalire abaa mukangirisi we mwaso kanji ebandu boshi babaa batula bamutunjire. Era kwemanga na ateta mbu baulusaa esi ndumwa tanga.

35. Chasinda, era kubura abu balikabo mbu emu balume, mulolaa kui kubuya-buya!

36. Si mwishi kwa kutasa kurenga suku, mwomvire kwa myasi ya mulume muuma mbu i Teuta. Oyu Teuta, abaa enjire achitonga kwa yeine inandwali. Bandu bangaika kumaana mane bu babaa benjire bamushemba. Si ebandu bera kumwita.rero, ba chirembaa kunde bamushemba boshi, bera kuhandabana na lwarero emyasi yabo etanachomvikani.

바두똬 바무두띠러, 돠나찌똔러라 구이.

33. 마꼬 바 바바아 바삐 똬 가루바따* 보빠 궈이 먀시, 어부더 붜라 구바시빠 부서서. 버라 귀러 바호따 귀다 어시 뚜똬.

34. 시 모루 루부아나노, 똬바아 무뮈 무파리사요* 무우마 뿌 이가마삐여리. 오유 가마삐러 아바아 무가삐리시 워 똬소 가찌 어바뚜 보씨 바바아 바두똬 바무두띠러. 어라 궈마똬 나 아더다 뿌 바우루사아 어시 뚜똬 다똬.

35. 짜시따, 어라 구부라 아부 바삐가보 뿌 어무 바루머, 무똔똬아 구이 구부야-부야!

36. 시 뮈씨 과 구다사 구러똬 수구, 모뼤러 과 먀시 야 무루머 무우마 뿌 이 더우다. 오유 더우다, 아바아 어찌러 아찌도똬 과 여이너 이나똬삐. 바뚜 바똬이가 구마아나 마너 부 바바아 버찌러 바무써빠. 시 어바뚜 버라 구뮈다.러로, 바 찌러빠아 구떠 바무써빠 보씨, 버라 구하따바나 나 똬러로 어먀시 야보 어다나쪼뼤가니.

---

given to those who obey him."

33. When they heard this, they were furious and wanted to put them to death.

34. But a Pharisee named Gamaliel, a teacher of the law, who was honored by all the people, stood up in the Sanhedrin and ordered that the men be put outside for a little while.

35. Then he addressed them: "Men of Israel, consider carefully what you intend to do to these men.

36. Some time ago Theudas appeared, claiming to be somebody, and about four hundred men rallied to him. He was killed, all his followers were dispersed, and it all came to nothing.

37. Era nyuma sa Teuta, mwa suku se'fisi, kwera kuulukira mukalilaya muuma mbu iYuta. Era kutuma bandu banene bamushemba. Si nai ebandu bera kumwita. Ba bendee bachiremba kunde bamushemba boshi, nabo bera kunahandabana.

38. Rero banyaketu, mwiree mwova eano lya nabawa: mutachibikaa mwa myasi ya bano bandu! mubareka baende! bushi bya benjire baira akaba biri bya bandu juika nabi binafe buha.

39. Si akaba bitanganyire na Ongo, mumenyaa kwa mutangala kuba nga. Rero, mutaereresa mwalwa na Ongo! boshi bera kunemeresa ei myasi ya kamaliyeri.

40. Chsinda, bera kwemala kanji endumwa, na bateta mbu bahutaasi. Bera kuhuba kubangaa mbu batachiereresa kanji bahambala era luulu soyu Yesu, chasinjire, bera kubalikula.

41. Endumwa sera kutenga mwaku karubanda* saenda samowa, bushi Ongo emerera bakenyibwe mwa kulibukwa bushi na Yesu.

37. 어라 뉴마 사 더우다, 똬 수구 서피시, 궈라 구우룹기라 무가꿰롸야 무우마 뿌 이유다. 어라 구두마 바뚜 바너너 바무써빠. 시 나이 어바뚜 버라 구뮈다. 바 버떠어 바찌러빠 구떠 바무써빠 보씨, 나보 버라 구나하따바나.

38. 러로 바냐거두, 뮈러어 뫃바 어아노 쨔 나바와: 무다찌비가아 똬 먀시 야 바노 바뚜! 무바러가 바어떠! 부씨 뱌 버찌러 바이라 아가바 비리 뱌 바뚜 주이가 나비 비나퍼 부하.

39. 시 아가바 비다꺼네러 나 오꼬, 무머냐아 과 무다꺼롸 구바 꺼. 러로, 무다어러러사 꽈롸 나 오꼬! 보씨 버라 구너머러사 어이 먀시 야 가마꿰여리.

40. 찌시따, 버라 궈마롸 가찌 어뚜똬, 나 바더다 뿌 바후다아시. 버라 구후바 구바꺼아 뿌 바다쩌러러사 가찌 바하빠롸 어라 루우루 소유 여수, 짜시찌러, 버라 구바꿰구롸.

41. 어뚜똬 서라 구더꺼 똬구 가루바따* 사어따 사모와, 부씨 오꼬 어머러라 바거니붜 똬 구꿰부과 부씨 나 여수.

37. After him, Judas the Galilean appeared in the days of the census and led a band of people in revolt. He too was killed, and all his followers were scattered.

38. Therefore, in the present case I advise you: Leave these men alone! Let them go! For if their purpose or activity is of human origin, it will fail.

39. But if it is from God, you will not be able to stop these men; you will only find yourselves fighting against God."

40. His speech persuaded them. They called the apostles in and had them flogged. Then they ordered them not to speak in the name of Jesus, and let them go.

41. The apostles left the Sanhedrin, rejoicing because they had been counted worthy of suffering disgrace for the Name.

42. Chira lusuku, sera kunde sakangirisa ne kuhubanganyisa ebandu ewmasi mubuya-buya, mwa luhu lwa Ongo*, nomwa manyumba kwa Yesu i'masiya*.

42. 찌라 루수구, 서라 구떠 사가띠리사 너 구후바까네사 어바뿌 어우마시 무부야-부야, 꽈 루후 롸 오끄*, 노꽈 마뉴빠 과 여수 이마시야*.

42. Day after day, in the temple courts and from house to house, they never stopped teaching and proclaiming the good news that Jesus is the Christ.

E Mikolo ye Ndjumwa Chikono 6
Ebemeresi balondola bandju balyinda kwa kuasa endjumwa

어 미고론 여 뚜꽈 찌고노 6
어버머러시 바론또롸 바뚜 바레따 과 구아사 어뚜뫂

Acts Chapter 6[NIV]

1. Mwesi suku, emunanjo we bemeresi era kuendekera aluwa. Mwa kachi-kachi kabo, mwabaa muli bahumbakasi banene. Chira lusuku mango bendee baaba ebiyo, ebayuta ba bendee bateta echikiriki bera kuyongwa bushi ebahumbakasi ba bendee betat echieburaniya, bendee beresibwa mwango munene kurenza ebahumbakasi babo.

1. 뭐시 수구, 어무나쪼 워 버머러시 어라 구어러거라 아루와. 꽈 가찌-가찌 가보, 꽈바아 무뤼 바후빠가시 바너너. 찌라 루수구 마꼬 버떠어 바아바 어비요, 어바유다 바 버떠어 바더다 어찌기리기 버라 구요꽈 부씨 어바후빠가시 바 버떠어 버다두 어쩌부라니야, 버떠어 버러시봐 마꼬 무너너 구러싸 어바후빠가시 바보.

1. In those days when the number of disciples was increasing, the Grecian Jews among them complained against the Hebraic Jews because their widows were being overlooked in the daily distribution of food.

2. Bushi noko, esi ndumwa ekumi nebiri kukwera kubwanyanya ebemeresi boshi, na sabura bo mbu emulimo wa kweshibira twaabira ebandu ebiryo, atangatumwa tubano twarekera ekuhubanganya echinwa cha Ongo.

2. 부씨 노고, 어시 뚜꽈 어구미 너비리 구궈라 구봐냐냐 어버머러시 보씨, 나 사부라 보 뿌 어무뤼모 와 궈씨비라 돠아비라 어바뿌 어비료, 아다꺼두꽈 두바노 돠러거라 어구후바까냐 어찌놔 짜 오끄.

2. So the Twelve gathered all the disciples together and said, "It would not be right for us to neglect the ministry of the word of God in order to wait on tables.

3. Rero banyaketu, mulondola balume balinda mwa kachi-kachi keny. Abu balume babaa ba bete ngulu ibuya, kanji ba bakoresibwa ne mchima mubuya-buya, kanji ba bete bwenge abola, bu tungeresa oyu mulimo,

4. Netu tungere twachana mwa memo nomwa mulimo we kuhubanganyisa ebandu echinwa cha Ongo.

5. Ebandu boshi bera kumoera iyu mwasi. Bera kulondola tanga Sitefano. Oyu sitefano abaa atusa bwemeresi bunene, na kanji abaa akoresibwa ne mchima mubuya-buya. Bera kulondola na Filopo, na Porokoro, na Nikanora, na Timoni, na Parimena, na Nikolao. Oyu Nikolao, abaa atula mwesha mwa musi we Andiyokiya, si era kwemerera Ongo we bayuta.

6. Chasinda, abu balinda, ebemeresi bera kubemanza era muhondo se ndumwa, nasi sera kubemera mwa kubabika kwemino.

7. Bushi noku, bandu bera kumva echinwa cha Ongo. Ebemeresi nabo, bera kunaendekera baluwa busese

3. 러로 바냐거두, 무론또롸 바루머 바뢰따 뫄 가찌-가찌 거네. 아부 바루머 바바아 바 버더 위루 이부야, 가찌 바 바고러시봐 너 무찌마 무부야- 부야, 가찌 바 버더 붱머 아보롸, 부 두뻐러사 오유 무뢰모,

4. 너두 두뻐러 돠짜나 뫄 머모 노롸 무뢰모 워 구후바빠네사 어바뚜 어찌놔 짜 오꼬.

5. 어바뚜 보씨 버라 구모어라 이유 마시. 버라 구론또롸 다빠 시더파노. 오유 시더파노 아바아 아두사 붱머러시 부너너, 나 가찌 아바아 아고러시봐 너 무찌마 무부야- 부야. 버라 구론또롸 나 피론포, 나 포로고로, 나 니가노라, 나 디모니, 나 파리머나, 나 니고롸오. 오유 니고롸오, 아바아 아두롸 뭐싸 뫄 무시 워 아띠요기야, 시 어라 궈머러라 오꼬 워 바유다.

6. 짜시따, 아부 바뢰따, 어버머러시 버라 구버마싸 어라 무호또 서 뚜뫄, 나시 서라 구버머라 뫄 구바비가 궈미노.

7. 부씨 노구, 바뚜 버라 구빠 어찌놔 짜 오꼬. 어버머러시 나보, 버라 구나어떠거라 바루와 부서서 뫄 무시 워

3. Brothers, choose seven men from among you who are known to be full of the Spirit and wisdom. We will turn this responsibility over to them

4. and will give our attention to prayer and the ministry of the word."

5. This proposal pleased the whole group. They chose Stephen, a man full of faith and of the Holy Spirit; also Philip, Procorus, Nicanor, Timon, Parmenas, and Nicolas from Antioch, a convert to Judaism.

6. They presented these men to the apostles, who prayed and laid their hands on them.

7. So the word of God spread. The number of disciples in Jerusalem increased rapidly, and a

mwa musi we Yerusalemu. Na
luamba lunene lwa bakuhanyi
nalo, lwera kunemerera Yesu.

여루사쩌무. 나 루아빠 루너너
꽈 바구하니 나로, 뭐라
구너머러라 여수.

large number of priests
became obedient to the
faith.

E bakulu-kulu b'e Bayuda baminyisa Sitefano

어 바구루-구루 버 바유다 바미네뻬 시더파노

8. Sitefano abaa aahanyirwe
busese na Ongo, kanji abaa
ete na buashi bunene. Bushi
noko, era kunde aira
bisomerano na bimenyeso
binene mwa bandu.

8. 시더파노 아바아
아아하니뤄 부서서 나 오꼬,
가찌 아바아 어더 나 부아씨
부너너. 부씨 노고, 어라 구떠
아이라 비소머라노 나
비머녀소 비너너 꽈 바뚜.

8. Now Stephen, a man full
of God's grace and power,
did great wonders and
miraculous signs among the
people.

9. Si bandu bauma bera
kususa bwaka nai. Bauma
mubo babaa bayuta ba
bendee babuanana mu
bushenge buuma bwa
bwerikirwe mbu bushenge
bwe'ba batengire mwa bucha.
Mwa'bu bandu, mwabaa muli
ba batengere mwa musi we
Kurene, ne we Alesanduriya,
nomwa chio che Kirikiya, ne
banji mwa che Asiyz.

9. 시 바뚜 바우마 버라
구수사 봐가 나이. 바우마
무보 바바아 바유다 바 버떠어
바부아나나 무 부써어 부우마
봐 뭐리기뤄 뿌 부써어 뷔바
바더삐러 꽈 부짜. 꽈부 바뚜,
꽈바아 무삐 바 바더떠러 꽈
무시 워 구러너, 너 워
아쩌사뚜리야, 노꽈 찌오 쩌
기리기야, 너 바찌 꽈 쩌
아시위z.

9. Opposition arose,
however, from members of
the Synagogue of the
Freedmen (as it was called)-
-Jews of Cyrene and
Alexandria as well as the
provinces of Cilicia and
Asia. These men began to
argue with Stephen,

10. Si bushi endee ateta na
bwenge bunene, kanji bushi
emuchima mubuya-buya
iwendee wamweresa ebinwa,
batendee baala kumuima.

10. 시 부씨 어떠어 아더다 나
뷔써 부너너, 가찌 부씨
어무찌마 무부야-부야
이워떠어 와뭐러사 어비뇨,
바더떠어 바아꽈 구무이마.

10. but they could not
stand up against his
wisdom or the Spirit by
whom he spoke.

11. Bushi noku, bera kushirisa
bandu bauma, mbu batetaa
kwa bachumviraa kwa
Sitefano ateta myasi ya
kukamba Ongo na Musa.

11. 부씨 노구, 버라 구씨리사
바뚜 바우마, 뿌 바더다아 과
바쭈뻬라아 과 시더파노
아더다 먀시 야 구가빠 오꼬
나 무사.

11. Then they secretly
persuaded some men to
say, "We have heard
Stephen speak words of
blasphemy against Moses
and against God."

12. Chasinda, abu bayuta bera kushirisa ebandu, ne bashamuka, alauma ne bakangirisi be mwaso*mbu basimba Sitefano. Bera kunamutetula na ba mweka era muhondo se karubanda ke bayuta*.

12. 짜시따, 아부 바유다 버라 구씨리사 어바뚜, 너 바싸무가, 아라우마 너 바가끼리시 버 묘소*뿌 바시빠 시더파노. 버라 구나무더두라 나 바 뭐가 어라 무호또 서 가루바빠 거 바유다*.

12. So they stirred up the people and the elders and the teachers of the law. They seized Stephen and brought him before the Sanhedrin.

13. Bera kureta babei ba bisha. Abu ba bei bera kuteta mbu ono mundu atenjire areka kuteta bulio era luulu soluno luhu buya-buya lwa Ongo, nera luulu se mwaso wa Musa.

13. 버라 구러다 바버이 바 비싸. 아부 바 버이 버라 구더다 뿌 오노 무두 아더띠러 아러가 구더다 부뤼오 어라 루우루 소루노 루후 부야-부야 롸 오끄, 너라 루우루 서 묘소 와 무사.

13. They produced false witnesses, who testified, "This fellow never stops speaking against this holy place and against the law.

14. Kanji tubeine twanachimviraa kwa ateta mbu oyu mwesha Nasareti mbu i Yesu angahandula olu luhu, nekubindula emyanya era Musa aterukeraa.

14. 가찌 두버이너 돠나찌삐라아 과 아더다 뿌 오유 뭐싸 나사러디 뿌 이 여수 아까하뚜롸 오루 루후, 너구비뚜롸 어먀냐 어라 무사 아더루거라아.

14. For we have heard him say that this Jesus of Nazareth will destroy this place and change the customs Moses handed down to us."

15. Ebandu boshi ba babaa bali mwaku karubanda*, kutuubirisa ku babaa bera banatumbikirisa Sitefano. Bera kulola kwa ebuso bwai bwanabere pe-pe-pe nga bwa malaika*.

15. 어바뚜 보씨 바 바바아 바뀌 묘구 가루바빠*, 구두우비리사 구 바바아 버라 바나두삐기리사 시더파노. 버라 구론롸 과 어부소 봐이 봐나버러 퍼-퍼-퍼 까 봐 마똬이가*.

15. All who were sitting in the Sanhedrin looked intently at Stephen, and they saw that his face was like the face of an angel.

E Mikolo ye Ndjumwa Chikono 7
Sitefano achitetera era muhondo s'e karubanda k'e Bayuda

어 미고론 여 뚜롸 찌고노 7
시더파노 아찌더더라 어라 무호또 서 가루바빠 거 바유다

Acts Chapter 7[NIV]

1. Mango Sitefano abaa anachire era muhondo se bashamuka be bayuta, emukulu-kulu we bakuhanyi era kumubusa mbu unyiburaa, emyasi ebandu bakushitakirire inali ya kanangana?

2. Sitefano erakuakula mbu Ebanyeketu kanji mu batata, munyumvirisaa. Mango hokulu wetu Abrahamu abaa chiri mwa chio ceh Mesopotamiya, era muhondo abungire mwa che Harani, Ongo we'ngulu era kumipamukira'ko.

3. Era kubura Abrahamu mbu Utengaa mwechini chio chenyu, ureke banyakenyu, ubungire mwachio cha nyeine nyingakulosa.

4. Chasinda, Abrahamu era kutenga mwa chio che Babeli na abungira mwa che Harani. Era nyuma se'kufa kweshe, Ongo era kuhuba kumubura mbu atengaa eharani abungire mwechine chio mulimo lwarero.

5. Aola, Ongo abaa atasa kweresa Abrahamu chiro na kachibandja ne si kehwa ke koro liuma mbu imwandu mwechine chio. Si amulaanya kwa akanamuchi chibe chai,

1. 마꼬 시더파노 아바아 아나찌러 어라 무호또 서 바싸무가 버 바유다, 어무구루-구루 워 바구하니 어라 구무부사 뿌 우니부라아, 어먀시 어바누 바구씨다기리러 이나뤼 야 가나꺄나?

2. 시더파노 어라구아구꽈 뿌 어바녀거두 가찌 무 바다다, 무뉴삐리사아. 마꼬 호구루 워두 아부라하무 아바아 찌리 뫄 찌오 시어후 머소포다미야, 어라 무호또 아부꺼러 뫄 쩌 하라니, 오꼬 워꾸루 어라 구미파무기라고.

3. 어라 구부라 아부라하무 뿌 우더꺄아 뭐찌니 찌오 쩌뉴, 우러거 바냐거뉴, 우부꺼러 뫄찌오 짜 녀이너 네꺄구뽀사.

4. 짜시따, 아부라하무 어라 구더꺄 뫄 찌오 쩌 바버뤼 나 아부꺼라 뫄 쩌 하라니. 어라 뉴마 서구파 궈써, 오꼬 어라 구후바 구무부라 뿌 아더꺄아 어하라니 아부꺼러 뭐찌너 찌오 무뤼모 꽈러로.

5. 아오꽈, 오꼬 아바아 아다사 궈러사 아부라하무 찌로 나 가찌바짜 너 시 거화 거 고로 뤼우마 뿌 이뫄뚜 뭐찌너 찌오. 시 아무꽈아냐 과 아가나무찌 찌버 짜이, 찌버

1. Then the high priest asked him, "Are these charges true?"

2. To this he replied: "Brothers and fathers, listen to me! The God of glory appeared to our father Abraham while he was still in Mesopotamia, before he lived in Haran.

3. 'Leave your country and your people,' God said, 'and go to the land I will show you.'

4. "So he left the land of the Chaldeans and settled in Haran. After the death of his father, God sent him to this land where you are now living.

5. He gave him no inheritance here, not even a foot of ground. But God promised him that he and his descendants after him would possess the land,

chibe na chelubaa lwai mango akaba atachirio, n'oku mwamu mango Abrahamu abaa atasa kuata chiro na mwana asibya.

나 쩌루바아 롸이 마꼬 아가바 아다찌리오, 노구 뫄무 마꼬 아부라하무 아바아 아다사 구아다 찌로 나 뫄나 아시뱌.

even though at that time Abraham had no child.

6. Kanji Ongo era kumubura mbu Elubuto lwao lukabungira mu chinji chio. Ne chhi chio, besha chi bakabikalo mwa bucha na kulibusalo ku myaka maana mane.

6. 가찌 오꼬 어라 구무부라 뿌 어루부도 롸오 루가부ⅷ라 무 찌씨 찌오. 너 찌히 찌오, 버싸 찌 바가비가론 뫄 부짜 나 구릐부사론 구 먀가 마아나 마너.

6. God spoke to him in this way: 'Your descendants will be strangers in a country not their own, and they will be enslaved and mistreated four hundred years.

7. Si nyono Ongo nyikachicndjibusa besha echi chio, ba bakabika olu lubuto lwao mwobu bucha. Chasinda, bakatenga mwechi chio babahe kunde banyera mwechine chisiki.

7. 시 뇨노 오꼬 네가찌시찌부사 버싸 어찌 찌오, 바 바가비가 오루 루부도 롸오 모부 부짜. 짜시따, 바가더ⅷ 뭐찌 찌오 바바허 구떠 바녀라 뭐찌너 찌시기.

7. But I will punish the nation they serve as slaves,' God said, 'and afterward they will come out of that country and worship me in this place.'

8. Bushi noku, Ongo era kuira chilaano* na Abrahamu. Echimanyiso chechi chilaano*kwabaa kumona. Mwolu, Abrahamu era kubuta Isaka. Abere Isaka alumisa suku munane, eshe era kumumonya. Isaka nai era kumonya muala wai Yakobo, na Yakobo era kumonya baala bai ekumi na babiri, na bu bahubaa bahokulu betu.

8. 부씨 노구, 오꼬 어라 구이라 찌롸아노* 나 아부라하무. 어찌마네소 쩌찌 찌롸아노*과바아 구모나. 모루, 아부라하무 어라 구부다 이사가. 아버러 이사가 아루미사 수구 무나너, 어써 어라 구무모냐. 이사가 나이 어라 구모냐 무아롸 와이 야고보, 나 야고보 어라 구모냐 바아롸 바이 어구미 나 바비리, 나 부 바후뫄아 바호구루 버두.

8. Then he gave Abraham the covenant of circumcision. And Abraham became the father of Isaac and circumcised him eight days after his birth. Later Isaac became the father of Jacob, and Jacob became the father of the twelve patriarchs.

9. Abu bahokulu betu bera kufira mulumuna wabo Yosefu mufula, bera kunalinda bamukusa, na ekibwa kuba kaungu mwa chio che Misri. Si Ongo abaa anali alauma nai.

10. Era kumuasa mwa malibuko mai moshi. Kanji se kumweresa ngahanyi sekuba mundu wa bwenge, kanji se kumuira asimibwe na mwami Farao wechio che Misri. Oyu farao era kuira yosefu mwimangisi wechio chai chosi alauma ne chikali chai choshi.

11. Mwesi suku, ebulio bwera kuika mwa chio chosi che Misri nomwa che Kanana. Obu bulio, bwera kureta malibuko manene, nebahokulu betu bera kunalinda baina ekalyo ka balya.

12. Yakobo omvaa kwe misri yeke iri biryo, era kutumayi bahokulu betu ebubere-bere, baye kuula kwa biryo.

13. Abere bahubayi ebwakabiri, yosefu era kuchikangana era muhondo sabu banyakabu. Namumango farao eraa amenyerera banyakabo yosefu.

9. 아부 바호구루 버두 버라 구피라 무루무나 와보 요서푸 무푸꽈, 버라 구나삐따 바무구사, 나 어기봐 구바 시가우꾸 봐 찌오 쩌 미주리. 시 오꼬 아바아 아나삐 아꽈우마 나이.

10. 어라 구무아사 봐 마삐부고 마이 모씨. 가찌 서 구뭐러사 빠하네 서구바 무뚜 와 붸뻐, 가찌 서 구무이라 아시미붸 나 뫄미 파라오 워찌오 쩌 미주리. 오유 파라오 어라 구이라 요서푸 뮈마삐시 워찌오 짜이 쪼시 아꽈우마 너 찌가삐 짜이 쪼씨.

11. 뭐시 수구, 어부삐오 붜라 구이가 봐 찌오 쪼시 쩌 미주리 노봐 쩌 가나나. 오부 부삐오, 붜라 구러다 마삐부고 마너너, 너바호구루 버두 버라 구나삐따 바이나 어가뢴 가 바꺄.

12. 야고보 오빠아 궈 미주리 여거 이리 비료, 어라 구두마에 바호구루 버두 어부버러-버러, 바여 구우꽈 과 비료.

13. 아버러 바후바에 어봐가비리, 요서푸 어라 구찌가빠나 어라 무호또 사부 바냐가부. 나무마꼬 파라오 어라아 아머녀러라 바냐가보 요서푸.

9. "Because the patriarchs were jealous of Joseph, they sold him as a slave into Egypt. But God was with him

10. and rescued him from all his troubles. He gave Joseph wisdom and enabled him to gain the goodwill of Pharaoh king of Egypt; so he made him ruler over Egypt and all his palace.

11. "Then a famine struck all Egypt and Canaan, bringing great suffering, and our fathers could not find food.

12. When Jacob heard that there was grain in Egypt, he sent our fathers on their first visit.

13. On their second visit, Joseph told his brothers who he was, and Pharaoh learned about Joseph's family.

14. Chasinda, yosefu era kutumisa eshe Yakobo mbu abahaa eyera alauma nrngumu yai yoshi. Ei ngumo yabaa ya bandu malinda na batano.

15. Yakobo era kunandaalira eMirsi. Era kufirayi, nebanji bahokulu betu nabo bera kunafirayi.

16. Ebirunda byabo, bera kubifulusa mwa chio che Sekemu. Bera kutababi mwa chinjifwa cha Abrahamu aula ku benyi Hemora.

17. Mangoelusuku lwa cha chiraane Ongo eresaa Abrahamu lwabaa luli ofukuika, bahokulu betu bera kuendekera baluwa mwa chio che misri.

18. Mwechi chio, mwera kwema unji mwami ola ulautamenyaa yosefu.

19. Oyu mwami , era kunde aburabo mbu bendee berekerera etubonjo-bonjo twabo mwa mbuwa chasiya tuchifire.

14. 짜시따, 요서푸 어라 구두미사 어써 야고보 뿌 아바하아 어여라 아롸우마 누루윙무 야이 요씨. 어이 윙모 야바아 야 바뚜 마쀠따 나 바다노.

15. 야고보 어라 구나따아쀠라 어미시. 어라 구피라에, 너바씨 바호구루 버두 나보 버라 구나피라에.

16. 어비루따 뱌보, 버라 구비푸루사 마 찌오 쩌 서거무. 버라 구다바비 마 찌씨퐈 짜 아부라하무 아우퐈 구 버니 허모라.

17. 마꼬어루수구 롸 짜 찌라아너 오꼬 어러사아 아부라하무 롸바아 루쀠 오푸구이가, 바호구루 버두 버라 구어떠거라 바루와 마 찌오 쩌 미주리.

18. 뭐찌 찌오, 뭐라 궈마 우씨 먀미 오롸 우롸우다머냐아 요서푸.

19. 오유 먀미 , 어라 구떠 아부라보 뿌 버떠어 버러거러라 어두보노-보노 따보 마 뿌와 짜시야 두찌피러.

14. After this, Joseph sent for his father Jacob and his whole family, seventy-five in all.

15. Then Jacob went down to Egypt, where he and our fathers died.

16. Their bodies were brought back to Shechem and placed in the tomb that Abraham had bought from the sons of Hamor at Shechem for a certain sum of money.

17. "As the time drew near for God to fulfill his promise to Abraham, the number of our people in Egypt greatly increased.

18. Then another king, who knew nothing about Joseph, became ruler of Egypt.

19. He dealt treacherously with our people and oppressed our forefathers by forcing them to throw out their newborn babies so that they would die.

20. Mwesi suku, mu Musa abutwaa. Oyu musa, abaa mwana ola ukomire busese mwa meho ma Ongo. Myesi ehatu oshao yanaremberwa mwa mwabo.

21. Mwoku kumureka era mbua, mwali wa farao era kumubuula. Era kumurembera nga muala wai ola achibuchiraa.

22. Mwolu, musa era kukangirisibwa emyasi yoshi yebwenge bwa besha misri. Era kunaba ndwali mwa mietere nemwa mikorere yai.

23. Mango abaa alinga kulumisa myaka mane, era kuata emyanyisa yekuya kutangula banyakabu, ebaisiraeli.

24. Abere aika era bali, era kubuana munyakabo muuma anyisibwa na mwesha misri muuma. Unao-unao, mwa kufuna oyu munyakabo, kuna kwita ola mwesha misri wabaa wamulibusa.

25. Yeke abaa aanyisa mbu banyakabo bangamenyerera kwai Ongo atumire kwa kubanunula mwa bucha bwe misri, si chiro bakamenyechi.

20. 뭐시 수구, 무 무사 아부돠아. 오유 무사, 아바아 마나 오롸 우고미러 부서서 마머호 마 오꼬. 며시 어하두 오싸오 야나러뻐롸 마 뫄보.

21. 모구 구무러가 어라 뿌아, 뫄리 와 파라오 어라 구무부우롸. 어라 구무러뻐라 꺄 무아롸 와이 오롸 아찌부찌라아.

22. 모루, 무사 어라 구가삐리시뫄 어먀시 요씨 여뭐어 봐 버싸 미주리. 어라 구나바 똬리 마 미어더러 너뫄 미고러러 야이.

23. 마꼬 아바아 아삐꺄 구루미사 먀가 마녀, 어라 구아다 어먀네사 여구야 구다꿔라 바냐가부, 어바이시라어삐.

24. 아버러 아이가 어라 바리, 어라 구부아나 무냐가보 무우마 아네시봐 나 뭐싸 미주리 무우마. 우나오-우나오, 뫄 구푸나 오유 무냐가보, 구나 귀다 오롸 뭐싸 미주리 와바아 와무삐부사.

25. 여거 아바아 아아네사 뿌 바냐가보 바빠머녀러라 과이 오꼬 아두미러 과 구바누누롸 뫄 부짜 붜 미주리, 시 찌로 바가머녀찌.

20. "At that time Moses was born, and he was no ordinary child. For three months he was cared for in his father's house.

21. When he was placed outside, Pharaoh's daughter took him and brought him up as her own son.

22. Moses was educated in all the wisdom of the Egyptians and was powerful in speech and action.

23. "When Moses was forty years old, he decided to visit his fellow Israelites.

24. He saw one of them being mistreated by an Egyptian, so he went to his defense and avenged him by killing the Egyptian.

25. Moses thought that his own people would realize that God was using him to rescue them, but they did not.

26. Abere mwei mishangya, musa era kubuana baisiraeli babiri bu bera balwa. Era kuereka kubafunga na ababurabo mbu: emanzi bera banyi! si muli bauma, chimwera mwalwira?

27. Si ola wabaa wakunza mulikabo era kufumira musa nekumubura mbu: nde iwakuirire kuba mukulu-kulu na mususu wetu?

28. Wahonda unyite ngokwa wetaa ola mwesha misri mweolo?

29. Musa mwa kunomva bacha kuna kuhaa, na abungire mwa chio che mitiyani. Eyera, era kubuchirayi bana babiri ba busana.

30. Abere kwarenga myaka manne, malaika*erakupamukira ku musa mwa buyeye*, ofu ne'nfulungu ye Sinai. Oyu malaika* apamukiraa ku musa mu cahsi chehaka lya lyabaa lyakorera.

31. Musa alorire kwebi, era kusanwa busese. Si mango abaa era achifunda ofu nelu haka alole kubuya-buya, era kumva enawetu ateta mbu:

26. 아버러 뭐이 미싸蟀, 무사 어라 구부아나 바이시라어릐 바비리 부 버라 바롸. 어라 구어러가 구바푸싸 나 아바부라보 뿌: 어마씨 버라 바네! 시 무릐 바우마, 찌뭐라 뫄뤼라?

27. 시 오롸 와바아 와구싸 무릐가보 어라 구푸미라 무사 너구무부라 뿌: 떠 이와구이리러 구바 무구루-구루 나 무수수 워두?

28. 와호따 우네더 으과 워다아 오롸 뭐싸 미주리 뭐오롣?

29. 무사 뫄 구노빠 바짜 구나 구하아, 나 아부뻬러 뫄 찌오 쩌 미디야니. 어여라, 어라 구부찌라에 바나 바비리 바 부사나.

30. 아버러 과러빠 먀가 마누너, 마똬이가*어라구구파무기라 구 무사 뫄 부여여*, 오푸 너푸루우 여 시나이. 오유 마똬이가* 아파무기라아 구 무사 무 시아후시 쩌하가 뺘 뺘바아 뺘고러라.

31. 무사 아롣리러 궈비, 어라 구사놔 부서서. 시 마꼬 아바아 어라 아찌푸따 오푸 너루 하가 아롣러 구부야-부야, 어라 구빠 어나워두 아더다 뿌:

26. The next day Moses came upon two Israelites who were fighting. He tried to reconcile them by saying, 'Men, you are brothers; why do you want to hurt each other?'

27. "But the man who was mistreating the other pushed Moses aside and said, 'Who made you ruler and judge over us?

28. Do you want to kill me as you killed the Egyptian yesterday?'

29. When Moses heard this, he fled to Midian, where he settled as a foreigner and had two sons.

30. "After forty years had passed, an angel appeared to Moses in the flames of a burning bush in the desert near Mount Sinai.

31. When he saw this, he was amazed at the sight. As he went over to look more closely, he heard the Lord's voice:

32. Nyono nyi Ongo ola bahokulu bao bendee bera, nyi Ongo wa Abrahamu, kanji wa Isaka, kanji wa Yakobo. Musa omvire bacha, era kukukumana bushi nabuba, chiro akanachiereresa ahuba kuumayi emeho.

33. Chasinda, enawetu kukwera kumubura mbu: ukongolaa ebi birato btao, bushi echi chisiki wemangilirrmo, chiri chisiki chibuya-buya.

34. Nachilolerere kanangana kwa bandu banyi baenda mwa bine mwa chio che misri. Kanji nanomvire kwa balira. Echera chi chatumire nabaha nyibanunule. Rero, ureewaira nyikutume emisri.

35. Sitefano era kuendekera ateta mbu: oyu musa, ibaisiraeli bananaa mango bamubusaa mbu nde iwamuirire kuba mukulu-kulu na mususu wabo. Si abaa oyu musai Ongo anatumaa kuba mukulu-kulu, kanji kuba mutabasi kurengera emalaika* wa Ongo ola wamupamukiraako mwehaka.

---

32. 뇨노 네 오꼬 오꽈 바호구루 바오 버떠어 버라, 네 오꼬 와 아부라하무, 가찌 와 이사가, 가찌 와 야고보. 무사 오삐러 바짜, 어라 구구구마나 부씨 나부바, 찌로 아가나쩌러러사 아후바 구우마에 어머호.

33. 짜시따, 어나워두 구궈라 구무부라 뿌: 우고꼬꽈아 어비 비라도 부다오, 부씨 어찌 찌시기 워마삐삐루모, 찌리 찌시기 찌부야-부야.

34. 나찌롣러러러 가나꽈나 과 바뚜 바네 바어따 뫄 비너 뫄 찌오 쩌 미주리. 가찌 나노삐러 과 바뤼라. 어쩌라 찌 짜두미러 나바하 네바누누뻐. 러로, 우러어와이라 네구두머 어미주리.

35. 시더파노 어라 구어떠거라 아더다 뿌: 오유 무사, 이바이시라어삐 바나나아 마꼬 바무부사아 뿌 떠 이와무이리러 구바 무구루- 구루 나 무수수 와보. 시 아바아 오유 무사이 오꼬 아나두마아 구바 무구루루-구루, 가찌 구바 무다바시 구러꺼라 어마꽈이가* 와 오꼬 오꽈 와무파무기라아고 뭐하가.

---

32. 'I am the God of your fathers, the God of Abraham, Isaac and Jacob.' Moses trembled with fear and did not dare to look.

33. "Then the Lord said to him, 'Take off your sandals; the place where you are standing is holy ground.

34. I have indeed seen the oppression of my people in Egypt. I have heard their groaning and have come down to set them free. Now come, I will send you back to Egypt.'

35. "This is the same Moses whom they had rejected with the words, 'Who made you ruler and judge?' He was sent to be their ruler and deliverer by God himself, through the angel who appeared to him in the bush.

36. Aba inawanakulaa abu baisiraeli emisri mwa kuira ebisomerano mwechi chio, nokwa nyanja ye mwola, nomwabuyeye* kumyaka manee.

37. Oyu musa inoyu, iwanaburaa abu baisiraeli mbu: Ongo akabalonderera murebi ola ukashoka mwa lubaa lwenyu, ngokwa anyilondolaa.

38. Na mu chira lubuanano lwa bahokulu betu mwa buyeye, oyu musa inoyu iwendee waba ulinabo manho malaika endee auweresa emyasi yekalamo kwa ndulungu ye Sinai, nai era kunde atubalikisai.

39. Si abo bahokulu betu batahondaa kunde batunda musa, bera kumunana, nakuata myanyisi ya kuchihubira emisri,

40. Bera kuikira Haruni nekumubura mbu: utukunganyisaa ebaongo be bihuhanyi ba tungende twahondosa, bshi oyu musa tukula mwa chio che misri, tutamenyire kwa abere.

41. Mwolu, bera kwira bachikunganyisa beine chihuhanyi cha chana cha

36. 아바 이나와나구쫘아 아부 바이시라어쮜 어미주리 뫄 구이라 어비소머라노 뭐찌 찌오, 노과 냐쨔 여 뫄롸, 노뫄부여여* 구먀가 마너어.

37. 오유 무사 이노유, 이와나부라아 아부 바이시라어쮜 뿌: 오끄 아가바로너러라 무러비 오롸 우가쏘가 뫄 루바아 뤄뉴, 끄과 아네로또쫘아.

38. 나 무 찌라 루부아나노 롸 바호구루 버두 뫄 부여여, 오유 무사 이노유 이워떠어 와바 우뤼나보 마누호 마롸이가 어떠어 아우워러사 어먀시 여가롸모 과 뚜루우 여 시나이, 나이 어라 구떠 아두바쮜기사이.

39. 시 아보 바호구루 버두 바다호따아 구떠 바두따 무사, 버라 구무나나, 나구아다 먀네시 야 구찌후비라 어미주리,

40. 버라 구이기라 하루니 너구무부라 뿌: 우두구까네사아 어바오끄 버 비후하네 바 두떠러 돠호또사, 부씨 오유 무사 두구롸 뫄 찌오 쩌 미주리, 두다머네러 과 아버러.

41. 몰루, 버라 귀라 바찌구까네사 버이너 찌후하네 짜 짜나 짜 까푸 구바 오끄

36. He led them out of Egypt and did wonders and miraculous signs in Egypt, at the Red Sea and for forty years in the desert.

37. "This is that Moses who told the Israelites, 'God will send you a prophet like me from your own people.'

38. He was in the assembly in the desert, with the angel who spoke to him on Mount Sinai, and with our fathers; and he received living words to pass on to us.

39. "But our fathers refused to obey him. Instead, they rejected him and in their hearts turned back to Egypt.

40. They told Aaron, 'Make us gods who will go before us. As for this fellow Moses who led us out of Egypt-- we don't know what has happened to him!'

41. That was the time they made an idol in the form of a calf. They brought

ngafu kuba ongo wabo, echi chihuhanyi, bera kutulira emitulo*.

42. Ongo era kuberekerera. Erakunareka bende bera esuba, nemwesi alauma nengununu kukulikana nokwa byanjikwa mwa chitabo che barebi mbu: Emu baisirarli! mwa myaka manne mwairaa mwabuyeye*, mutangateta mbu nyonu nyi mwatulira enyama sa mochaa, nesi mbu mwanyitulira inji mitulo*.

43. Ehema lya ongo wenyu moleki limwendee mwatambana, alauma nechihubanyi che ngununu cha ongo wenyu refani. Ebi bihuhanyi, mwasimaa luchikunganyisa'bi, chasiya munde mwakomerabi emafi. Bushi noku, nyikabeka mwa bbuerere kutaluka emusi we Babeli.

44. Mango bahokulu betu babaa bali mwa buyeye* ehema lya bendee beka, lyabaa lya bubeyi era muhondo sabo, kanji lyabaa linakwisibwe kukulikana nokwa ola wahambalaa na musa amuburaa mbu analiiraa.

45. Eri hema lineli, e bahokulu

와보, 어찌 찌후하니, 버라 구두쮜라 어미두룐*.

42. 오꼬 어라 구버러거러라. 어라구나러가 버떠 버라 어수바, 너뭐시 아꽈우마 너꾸누누 구구쮜가나 노과 뱌찌과 마 찌다보 쩌 바러비 뿌: 어무 바이시라루쮜! 마 먀가 마누너 마이라아 마부여여*, 무다꽈더다 뿌 뇨누 네 먀두쮜라 어냐마 사 모짜아, 너시 뿌 마네두쮜라 이찌 미두룐*.

43. 어허마 랴 오꼬 워뉴 모꺼기 쮜뭐떠어 마다빠나, 아꽈우마 너찌후바니 쩌 꾸누누 짜 오꼬 워뉴 러파니. 어비 비후하니, 먀시마아 루쮜구꽈네사비, 짜시야 무떠 먀고머라비 어마피. 부씨 노구 네가버가 마 부부어러러 구다룽가 어무시 워 바버쮜.

44. 마꼬 바호구룽 버두 바바아 바쮜 마 부여여* 어허마 랴 버떠어 버가, 랴바아 랴 부버에 어라 무호또 사보, 가찌 랴바아 쮜나귀시붜 구구쮜가나 노과 오꽈 와하빠꽈아 나 무사 아무부라아 뿌 아나쮜이라아.

45. 어리 허마 쮜너쮜, 어

sacrifices to it and held a celebration in honor of what their hands had made.

42. But God turned away and gave them over to the worship of the heavenly bodies. This agrees with what is written in the book of the prophets: " 'Did you bring me sacrifices and offerings forty years in the desert, O house of Israel?

43. You have lifted up the shrine of Molech and the star of your god Rephan, the idols you made to worship. Therefore I will send you into exile' beyond Babylon.

44. "Our forefathers had the tabernacle of the Testimony with them in the desert. It had been made as God directed Moses, according to the pattern he had seen.

45. Having received the

ba Yoshuwa abaa emangirire, bera kulirekerwa. Nabo bera kwekali kukira mango banyaa ebio byesinji mbaa sa Ongo abakolokanyisaa. Lyabaa linatula mwa chio kuikira esuku sa Tauti emaa.

46. Oyu Tauti, Ongo era kumuahanyira. Nai era kwema Ongo wa Yakobo eloso lwekumuimbira enyumba.

47. Si muala wai Salomono iweraa waimbira Ongo ei nyumba.

48. Si kanji enyumba sa saimbwaa nebandu, Ongo wokwa nguba atangaba musi. Ebyera bitenganyire nokwa maanjiko me murebi matechire mbu:

49. Engubachi chitula chisiki chanyi che bwami, nebutala bu butula ndebe yanyi yekutamusisa kwemaulu. Rero, nyumba ichie imwera munganyiimbira nesi chisiki chichiye cha kutamukira cha munganyiimbira?

50. Si mutabukire kwa nyono nyi nabumbaa ebi bysohi!

51. Sitefano era kuendera ateta mbu: mwabo munatula bandu ba matwi masibu!mwanyire ebwemeresi,

바호구루 바 요쓰와 아바아 어마끼리러, 버라 구뀌러거롸. 나보 버라 궈가뀌 구기라 마꼬with them 바냐아 어비오 벼시찌 빠아 사 오꼬 아바고론가네사아. 럐바아 뤼나두롸 마 찌오 구이기라 어수구 사 다우디 어마아.

46. 오유 다우디, 오꼬 어라 구무아하네라. 나이 어라 궈마 오꼬 와 야고보 어론소 뤄구무이뼤라 어뉴빠.

47. 시 무아롸 와이 사론모노 이워라아 와이뼤라 오꼬 어이 뉴빠.

48. 시 가찌 어뉴빠 사 사이꽈아 너바뚜, 오꼬 옹과 우바 아다꺄바 무시. 어벼라 비더꺄네러 노과 마아찌고 머 무러비 마더찌러 뿌:

49. 어우바찌 찌두롸 찌시기 짜네 쩌 봐미, 너부다롸 부 부두롸 떠버 야네 여구다무시사 궈마우루. 러로, 뉴빠 이쩌 이뭐라 무꽈네이뼤라 너시 찌시기 찌찌여 짜 구다무기라 짜 무꽈네이뼤라?

50. 시 무다부기러 과 뇨노 네 나부빠아 어비 뷔소히!

51. 시더파노 어라 구어떠라 아더다 뿌: 꽈보 무나두롸 바뚜 바 마뒤 마시부!꽈네러 어붜머러시, 너 마뒤 마뉴

tabernacle, our fathers under Joshua brought it with them when they took the land from the nations God drove out before them. It remained in the land until the time of David,

46. who enjoyed God's favor and asked that he might provide a dwelling place for the God of Jacob.

47. But it was Solomon who built the house for him.

48. "However, the Most High does not live in houses made by men. As the prophet says:

49. " 'Heaven is my throne, and the earth is my footstool. What kind of house will you build for me? says the Lord. Or where will my resting place be?

50. Has not my hand made all these things?'

51. "You stiff-necked people, with uncircumcised hearts and ears! You are just like your fathers: You always

ne matwi manyu manaima ekumva emurenge wa Ongo. Bya muchima mubuya-buya ende ababura, kubilwisa ku wmenjire mwana biliwisa chira lusuku. Kwa bahokulu benyu nenyu kumunali.

마나이마 어구빠 어무러뻐 와 오꼬. 뱌 무찌마 무부야-부야 어떠 아바부라, 구비쀠사 구 우머띠러 뫄나 비뛰위사 찌라 루수구. 과 바호구루 버뉴 너뉴 구무나뛰.

resist the Holy Spirit!

52. Mwa barebi, nde ola bahokulu benyu batalibusaa bera kunalinda bata neba bendee bateta era luulu sekuika kwe maundu we kanangana. Noyu mundu imwabo mwarenganyaa ne kunamwita!

52. 똬 바러비, 떠 오똬 바호구루 버뉴 바다쀠부사아 버라 구나뛰따 바다 너바 버떠어 바더다 어라 루우루 서구이가 궈 마우뚜 워 가나뫄나. 노유 무뚜 이뫄보 뫄러빠냐아 너 구나뛰다!

52. Was there ever a prophet your fathers did not persecute? They even killed those who predicted the coming of the Righteous One. And now you have betrayed and murdered him--

53. Kanji mwabo, mu Ongo anatumira emwaso wai kurengera ebamalaika*, si mutatundaa'o.

53. 가찌 뫄보, 무 오꼬 아나두미라 어뫄소 와이 구러뻐라 어바마똬이가*, 시 무다두따아오.

53. you who have received the law that was put into effect through angels but have not obeyed it."

Ekufa kwa Sitefano

어구빠 과 시더파노

54. Mnago ebashamuka ba babaa bali mwa karubanda ke bayuta*bomvaa kwei myasi yoshi, ebute bwera kubasimba busese. Na bushi noku bute, bera kutangirisa bamukuuchira emeno.

54. 무나고 어바싸무가 바 바바아 바쀠 뫄 가루바따 거 바유다*보빠아 궈이 먀시 요씨, 어부더 뭐라 구바시빠 부서서. 나 부씨 노구 부더, 버라 구다삐리사 바무구우찌라 어머노.

54. When they heard this, they were furious and gnashed their teeth at him.

55. Si Sitefano yeke, abaa akoresibwa ne muchima mubuya-buya. Era kutumbukisa kwa nguba, na aola kwa bulangalre bwa Ongo.

55. 시 시더파노 여거, 아바아 아고러시봐 너 무찌마 무부야-부야. 어라 구두뿌기사 과 우바, 나 아오똬 과 부똬빠루러 봐 오꼬.

55. But Stephen, full of the Holy Spirit, looked up to heaven and saw the glory of God, and Jesus standing at the right hand of God.

56. Kanji era kuteta mbu:

56. 가찌 어라 구더다 뿌:

56. "Look," he said, "I see

' nyisene kwa nguba ibookere,' nokwa mwana we mundu emenze kwa malyo ma Ongo!

57. Abu bashamuka bomlvire bacha, unao-unao na basiba ematwi mabo. Bera kutangirisa bairanga elwayo busese, boshi kuna kuumbikira Sitefano.

58. Chasinda, bera kumukululira bure ne'musi, mwa kuhonda bamwite. Bera kukongolanga enjimba sabo na babikisasi mutabana muuma mbu i'Saulo.

59. Mango babaa bera banaumanga Sitefano emakoi, erakwema mbu Enawetu Yesu, wangiriraa emuchima wanyi!

60. Chasinda, era kukoma emafi, na auma emurenge mbu Enawetu, utabaanjira bine bibi! era nyuma se'kuteta bacha, kunakutowa emuchima. Olu lufu lwa Sitefano, Saulo nai abaa ali mwa lwango lwao.

내서너 과 꾸바 이보오거러, 노과 모나나 워 무뚜 어머써 과 마뮫 마 오꼬!

57. 아부 바싸무가 보무루루비러 바짜, 우나오-우나오 나 바시바 어마뒤 마보. 버라 구다띠리사 바이라까 어꽈요 부서서, 보씨 구나 구우삐기라 시더파노.

58. 짜시따, 버라 구무구루꾀라 부러 너무시, 똬 구호따 바뮈더. 버라 구고꼬꽈따 어찌빠 사보 나 바비기사시 무다바나 무우마 뿌 이사우로.

59. 마꼬 바바아 버라 바나우마까 시더파노 어마고이, 어라궈마 뿌 어나워두 여수, 와띠리라아 어무찌마 와네!

60. 짜시따, 어라 구고마 어마피, 나 아우마 어무러써 뿌 어나워두, 우다바아찌라 비너 비비! 어라 뉴마 서구더다 바짜, 구나구도와 어무찌마. 오루 루푸 꽈 시더파노, 사우로 나이 아바아 아뤼 똬 롸오 롸오.

heaven open and the Son of Man standing at the right hand of God."

57. At this they covered their ears and, yelling at the top of their voices, they all rushed at him,

58. dragged him out of the city and began to stone him. Meanwhile, the witnesses laid their clothes at the feet of a young man named Saul.

59. While they were stoning him, Stephen prayed, "Lord Jesus, receive my spirit."

60. Then he fell on his knees and cried out, "Lord, do not hold this sin against them." When he had said this, he fell asleep.

E Mikolo ye Ndjumwa Chikono 8

Saulo alyibusa ebemeresi

1. Mwolu lusuku lunolu, mu ebemeresi boshi ba babaa bali

어 미고로 여 뚜똬 찌고노 8

사우로 아페뷥뻽 어버머러시

1. 몰루 루수구 루노루, 무 어버머러시 보씨 바 바바아

Acts Chapter 8[NIV]

1. And Saul was there, giving approval to his

mwa musi we Yerusalemu batangirisa balibusibwa busese. Bushi noku, bera kuhandabana mwa ndambi sechio che Yuteya ne che Samariya. Endumwa seine si sanashibaa eYerusalemu.

2. Abere Sitefano era echibwaa, ebandu babaa batula batunjire Ongo, bera kumutaba na kumuirira mishibo inene.

3. Mwolu, Saulo yeke kusikya ku anaendekeraa asikya ebemeresi. Era kunde engirira mwa manyumba ahonderamo ebalume ne bakasi. Abu boshi, era kunde abaumanga mwa buroko.

Filipo ahubanganya emwasi mubuya-buya mwa musi w'e Samariya

4. Ba bemersi ba bahandabanaa bera kunde barenga muchira chisiki bahunganyisa ebandu emwasi mubuya-buya.

5. Muuma mubo mbu i Firipo, era kwandaliira mwa musi munene we samariya. Era kunde ahubanganyisa besha'mo era luulu sa Masiya*.

바삐 먀 무시 워 여루사쩌무 바다삐리리사 바삐부시봐 부서서. 부씨 노구, 버라 구하따바나 먀 따삐 서찌오 쩌 유더야 너 쩌 사마리야. 어뚜뫄 서이너 시 사나씨바아 어여루사쩌무.

2. 아버러 시더파노 어라 어찌봐아, 어바뚜 바바아 바두꽈 바두찌러 오꼬, 버라 구무다바 나 구무이리라 미씨보 이너너.

3. 모루, 사우로 여거 구시갸 구 아나어떠거라아 아시갸 어버머러시. 어라 구떠 어삐리라 먀 마뉴빠 아호떠라모 어바루머 너 바가시. 아부 보씨, 어라 구떠 아바우마꽈 먀 부로고.

피리펠 아후바꽈냇 어뫄시 무부야-부야 먀 무시 워 사마리야

4. 바 버머시 바 바하따바나아 버라 구떠 바러꽈 무찌라 찌시기 바후꽈네사 어바뚜 어뫄시 무부야-부야.

5. 무우마 무보 뿌 이 피리포, 어라 과따삐리라 먀 무시 무너너 워 사마리야. 어라 구떠 아후바꽈네사 버싸모 어라 루우루 사 마시야*.

death. On that day a great persecution broke out against the church at Jerusalem, and all except the apostles were scattered throughout Judea and Samaria.

2. Godly men buried Stephen and mourned deeply for him.

3. But Saul began to destroy the church. Going from house to house, he dragged off men and women and put them in prison.

4. Those who had been scattered preached the word wherever they went.

5. Philip went down to a city in Samaria and proclaimed the Christthere.

6. Bya endee ateta, ebandu boshi bera kunde babyumvirisa kubuya-buya, bushi nekulola kwa bisomerano bya abaa enijire aira.

7. Era kunde ambula ebihwasi ku bandu banene mubo. Ebi bihwasi, byera kunde byabatengako byaenda byalakanga busese. Kanji abaa enjire alamya na birema biene.

8. Bushi noku, besha mwoyu musi bera kunde baoa busese.

9. Rero mwoyu musi we samariya, mwabaa mutula mulume muuma mbu i Simoni. Oyu Simoni abaa erisa wmoyu musi, kanji abaa atula muhonga. Mwa kulaula kwai, era kwire ende achitonga era muhondo sa beshamo mbu yeine inamulume.

10. Ebandu boshi, emukulu ne mutoto, bera kunde bamuteya ematwi. Bera Kunde berika mbu: buashi bunene

11. Bendee nobu buhonga bwai ku suku sinene.

12. Si mango Firipo eraa

6. 뱌 어떠어 아더다, 어바뉴 보씨 버라 구너 바뷰삐리사 구부야-부야, 부씨 너구로롸 과 비소머라노 뱌 아바아 어니지러 아이라.

7. 어라 구너 아뿌롸 어비화시 구 바뉴 바너너 무보. 어비 비화시, 벼라 구너 뱌바더꺄고 뱌어따 뱌퐈가꺄 부서서. 가씨 아바아 어찌러 아퐈먀 나 비러마 비어너.

8. 부씨 노구, 버싸 모유 무시 버라 구너 바오아 부서서.

9. 러로 모유 무시 워 사마리야, 퐈바아 무두롸 무루머 무우마 뿌 이 시모니. 오유 시모니 아바아 어리사 우모유 무시, 가씨 아바아 아두롸 무호꺄. 롸 구퐈우퐈 과이, 어라 귀러 어너 아찌도꺄 어라 무호또 사 버싸모 뿌 여이너 이나무루머.

10. 어바뉴 보씨, 어무구루 너 무도도, 버라 구너 바무더야 어마뒤. 버라 구너 버리가 뿌: 부아씨 부너너

11. 버떠어 노부 부호꺄 봐이 구 수구 시너너.

12. 시 마꼬 피리포 어라아

6. When the crowds heard Philip and saw the miraculous signs he did, they all paid close attention to what he said.

7. With shrieks, evil spirits came out of many, and many paralytics and cripples were healed.

8. So there was great joy in that city.

9. Now for some time a man named Simon had practiced sorcery in the city and amazed all the people of Samaria. He boasted that he was someone great,

10. and all the people, both high and low, gave him their attention and exclaimed, "This man is the divine power known as the Great Power."

11. They followed him because he had amazed them for a long time with his magic.

12. But when they believed

ahubanganyisabo emwasi
mbuya-buya era luulu se
Bwami bwa Ongo*nera luulu
sa Yesu Kirisito, bera
kwemerera?.bushi noku,
ebalume ne bakasi bera
kubatisibwa.

13. Oyu Simoni nai era
kwemerera Yesu, na
abatisibwa. Chasinda, era
kutangirisa kuba luuma-luuma
na Firipo. Na mango endee
alola kwa bisomerano ne
bimenyeso bya abaa enjire
aira, era kunde asanwa
busese.

14. Mango endumwa sa Yesu
sa sabaa siri mwa musi we
Yerusalemu somvaa emwasi
kwa besha samariya nabo
bemerere echinwa cha Ongo,
sera kwire sabatumira Petero
na Yowani.

15. Abere baika esamariya,
bera kwemera ebemeresi
babone emuchima mubuya-
buya,

16. Bushi oyu mchima
mubuya-buya, abaa atasa
kwandalira chiro na muuma
mubo. Mwesi na lya enawetu
Yesu oshao mu abu besha
samariya babaa
banabatisibwe.

17. Chasinda, Petero na

아후바까네사보 어뫄시 뿌야-
부야 어라 루우루 서 봐미 봐
오꼬*너라 루우루 사 여수
기리시도, 버라 궈머러라?.부씨
노구, 어바루머 너 바가시
버라 구바디시봐.

13. 오유 시모니 나이 어라
궈머러라 여수, 나 아바디시봐.
짜시따, 어라 구다삐리사 구바
루우마-루우마 나 피리포. 나
마꼬 어떠어 아르퐈 과
비소머라노 너 비머녀소 뱌
아바아 어찌러 아이라, 어라
구떠 아사놔 부서서.

14. 마꼬 어뚜봐 사 여수 사
사바아 시리 뫄 무시 워
여루사러무 소빠아 어뫄시 과
버싸 사마리야 나보 버머러러
어찌놔 짜 오꼬, 서라 귀러
사바두미라 퍼더로 나 요와니.

15. 아버러 바이가 어사마리야,
버라 궈머라 어버머러시
바보너 어무찌마 무부야-부야,

16. 부씨 오유 무찌마 무부야-
부야, 아바아 아다사 과따삐라
찌로 나 무우마 무보. 뭐시 나
퍄 어나워두 여수 오싸오 무
아부 버싸 사마리야 바바아
바나바디시붜.

17. 짜시따, 퍼더로 나 요와니

Philip as he preached the
good news of the kingdom
of God and the name of
Jesus Christ, they were
baptized, both men and
women.

13. Simon himself believed
and was baptized. And he
followed Philip everywhere,
astonished by the great
signs and miracles he saw.

14. When the apostles in
Jerusalem heard that
Samaria had accepted the
word of God, they sent
Peter and John to them.

15. When they arrived, they
prayed for them that they
might receive the Holy
Spirit,

16. because the Holy Spirit
had not yet come upon any
of them; they had simply
been baptized into the
name of the Lord Jesus.

17. Then Peter and John

Yowani kukwera kubabika kwemino, nabo bera kubona emuchima mubuya-buya.

18. Ola Simoni mango alolaa kwa mchima mubuya-buya enjire abdaalira ebemresi ba endumwa sabikire kwe mino, era kuhonda erese Petero na Yowani ebuteya

19. Mwolu, era kubabuya mbu Ebetu, nanyi muumba kwobu buashi, cahsiya mundu ola nanyi nyingende nabika kwemino abone kwoyu mchima mubuya-buya.

20. Si Petero era kumwakula mbu ufe shambyo alauma ne buteya bwao! weke waanyisa mbu mwa buteya mu emundu angaula elwembo lwa Ongo

21. Umenyerera kwa uteti mwango nesi cha chikwerekere mwene myasi, bushi emuchima wao atatungene era muhondo sa Ongo.

22. Rero, ubindulaa emyanya yao ibi, wemerere enawetu, kuli emango anganakubabalira kwei myanyisa yao.

23. Nanyi nyeine nanachilorere kwa mwa muchima wao mwihwire mufula munebe, nokwa bibi

---

구궈라 구바비가 궈미노, 나보 버라 구보나 어무찌마 무부야-부야.

18. 오꽈 시모니 마꼬 아르꽈아 과 무찌마 무부야-부야 어찌러 아부다아뤼라 어버러시 바 어두와 사비기러 궈 미노, 어라 구호따 어러서 퍼더로 나 요와니 어부더야

19. 모루, 어라 구바부야 뿌 어버두, 나니 무우빠 곤부 부아씨, 시아후시야 무뚜 오꽈 나니 네어러 나비가 궈미노 아보너 곤유 무찌마 무부야-부야.

20. 시 퍼더로 어라 구꽈구꽈 뿌 우퍼 싸뾰 아꽈우마 너 부더야 봐오! 워거 와아네사 뿌 봐 부더야 무 어무뚜 아꽈우꽈 어뤄뾰 롸 오꼬

21. 우머녀러라 과 우더디 마꼬 너시 짜 찌궈러거러 먀시, 부씨 어무찌마 와오 아다두어너 어라 무호또 사 오꼬.

22. 러로, 우비뚜꽈아 어먀냐 야오 이비, 워머러러 어나워두, 구뤼 어마꼬 아꽈나구바바뤼라 궈이 먀네사 야오.

23. 나니 녀이너 나나찌뢰러러 과 봐 무찌마 와오 뮈휘러 무푸꽈 무너버, 노과 비비 비찌리 비구우이너러.

---

placed their hands on them, and they received the Holy Spirit.

18. When Simon saw that the Spirit was given at the laying on of the apostles' hands, he offered them money

19. and said, "Give me also this ability so that everyone on whom I lay my hands may receive the Holy Spirit."

20. Peter answered: "May your money perish with you, because you thought you could buy the gift of God with money!

21. You have no part or share in this ministry, because your heart is not right before God.

22. Repent of this wickedness and pray to the Lord. Perhaps he will forgive you for having such a thought in your heart.

23. For I see that you are full of bitterness and captive to sin."

bichiri bikuuinyire.

24. Simoni nai kukwera kubura Petero na Yowani mbu: munyemeraa era mwa enawetu nyingesha kusimbibwa na mwasi mwebi byoshi mwera kueta.

24. 시모니 나이 구궈라 구부라 퍼더로 나 요와니 뿌: 무녀머라아 어라 똬 어나워두 네꺼싸 구시삐봐 나 똬시 뭐비 뵤씨 뭐라 구어다.

24. Then Simon answered, "Pray to the Lord for me so that nothing you have said may happen to me."

25. Abere Petero na Yowani bamala kuhambalira enandu bya beine bachilorerako era luulu sa Yesu na kubahubanganyisan echinwa che enawetu, bera kuhuba eyerusalemu baenda bahubanganya emwasi mubuya-buya mu misi inene ye basamariya.

25. 아버러 퍼더로 나 요와니 바마똬 구하빠뤼라 어나뚜 뱌 버이너 바찌뽀러라고 어라 루우루 사 여수 나 구바후바까네사 어찌놔 쩌 어나워두, 버라 구후바 어여루사뤄무 바어따 바후바까냐 어똬시 무부야-부야 무 미시 이너너 여 바사마리야.

25. When they had testified and proclaimed the word of the Lord, Peter and John returned to Jerusalem, preaching the gospel in many Samaritan villages.

Filipo abatisa mukulu-kulu muuma w'e Etiyopiya

피뤼펠 아바디사 무구루-구루 무우마 워 어디요피야

26. Lusuku luuma, malaika* muuma wa enawetu era kubura Firipo mbu uchiteyanyaa uye kwa lunda lwera masina. Mwakuikeyi, wanatola enjira era itengire eyerusalemu yandaalira mwa musi we Kasa. (Ei njira, ebandu batachitula bakomere kurenga mui.)

26. 루수구 루우마, 마꽈이가* 무우마 와 어나워두 어라 구부라 피리포 뿌 우찌더야냐아 우여 과 루따 뤄라 마시나. 똬구이거에, 와나도똬 어찌라 어라 이더삐러 어여루사뤄무 야따아뤼라 똬 무시 워 가사. (어이 찌라, 어바뚜 바다찌두똬 바고머러 구러까 무이.)

26. Now an angel of the Lord said to Philip, "Go south to the road--the desert road--that goes down from Jerusalem to Gaza."

27. Unao-unao, Firipo kuna kuchiuma. Aikire mweinjire, era kubuanana na mukulu-kulu, iwabaa utula mwa chio

27. 우나오-우나오, 피리포 구나 구찌우마. 아이기러 뭐이찌러, 어라 구부아나나 나 무구루-구루, 이와바아 우두똬

27. So he started out, and on his way he met an Ethiopianeunuch, an important official in charge

che Etiyopia.

똬 찌오 쩌 어디요피아.

of all the treasury of Candace, queen of the Ethiopians. This man had gone to Jerusalem to worship,

28. Oyu mukulu-kulu, iwabaa utula wemangirire ebikulo bya Kandaki, mwamikasi wechi chio. Ongo eyrusalemu. Abaa ekere mwa mutukali wai aenda asoma echitabu cha murebi*Isaya aanjikaa.

28. 오유 무구루루-구루루, 이와바아 우두똬 워마삐리러 어비구로로 뱌 가따기, 똬미가시 워찌 찌오. 오끄 어위루사뤄무. 아바아 어거러 똬 무두가뤼 와이 아어따 아소마 어찌다부 짜 무러비*이사야 아아찌가아.

28. and on his way home was sitting in his chariot reading the book of Isaiah the prophet.

29. Emchima mubuya-buya kukwera kubura Firipo mbu uchifunda alamukari yolka ali.

29. 어무찌마 무부야-부야 구궈라 구부라 피리포 뿌 우찌푸따 아랴무가리 요루가 아뤼.

29. The Spirit told Philip, "Go to that chariot and stay near it."

30. Firipo era kunalibichira'o. Aikireo era kumva kwoyu mukulu-kulu asoma echitabu cha murebi *Isaya. Era kumubusa mbu Ewalyiya, ei myasi wasoma, uomvirei kubuya kwa itechire?

30. 피리포 어라 구나뤼비찌라오. 아이기러오 어라 구빠 고유 무구루루-구루루 아소마 어찌다부 짜 무러비 *이사야. 어라 구무부사 뿌 어와뤠야, 어이 먀시 와소마, 우오뻐러이 구부야 과 이더찌러?

30. Then Philip ran up to the chariot and heard the man reading Isaiah the prophet. "Do you understand what you are reading?" Philip asked.

31. Nai mbu chasinda, era kwire abura Firipo mbu erukaa mwa mutukari wai ekale alauma nai.

31. 나이 뿌 짜시따, 어라 귀러 아부라 피리포 뿌 어루가아 무두가리 와이 어가뿌 아똬우마 나이.

31. "How can I," he said, "unless someone explains it to me?" So he invited Philip to come up and sit with him.

32. Emilango ye maanjiko mabuya-buya ma abaa asoma, bacha ku yabaa utechire: Ekibwaa nga mbuli era baya kukera, kanji abaa nga chana cha mbuli cha chitama era

32. 어미똬끄 여 마아찌고 마부야-부야 마 아바아 아소마, 바짜 구 야바아 우더찌러: 어기봐아 꺄 뿌뤼 어라 바야 구거라, 가찌 아바아 꺄 짜나 짜 뿌뤼 짜

32. The eunuch was reading this passage of Scripture: "He was led like a sheep to the slaughter, and as a lamb before the shearer is silent, so he did not open his

768 E Mikolo ye Ndjumwa / 어 미고로로 여 누똬 / Acts

muhondo solka
waioshangachi eboya. Mwebi
byoshi, atanaboola ebubu
bwai.

33. Emereraa kukenyibwa, na
kwimibwa emwaso wai. Nde
iukateta era luulu se lubuto
lwai bushi bamwitaa kuno
butala.

34. Oyu mukulu-kulu kukwera
kubusa Firipo mbu Ewaliya,
nakwema unyibure:ono
murebi*Isaya atetaa ene myasi
era luulu sa nde ateta era
luulu sai yeine nesi era luulu
sa unjimundu?

35. Firipo mwa kumwakula,
aba ei myasi oyu mukulu-kulu
abaa asoma yanatangiriraa'ko
mwa kumubalikisisa emwasi
mubuya-buya era luulu sa
Yesu.

36. Abere banachire
baenzikanya, bera kuika mu
chisiki chiuma ala abaa ali
meshi. Oyu mukulu-kulu era
kwire abura Firipo mbu si
meshi mano mali anola! chi
chingatuma ndabatisibwa?

찌다마 어라 무호또 소루가
와이오싸까찌 어보야. 뭐비
뵤씨, 아다나보오롸 어부부
봐이.

33. 어머러라아 구거네봐, 나
귀미봐 어먀소 와이. 떠
이우가더다 어라 루우루 서
루부도 롸이 부씨 바뮈다아
구노 부다롸.

34. 오유 무구루루-구루 구궈라
구부사 피리포 뿌 어와쀠야,
나궈마 우네부러:오노
무러비*이사야 아더다아 어너
먀시 어라 루우루 사 떠
아더다 어라 루우루 사이
여이너 너시 어라 루우루 사
우찌무뚜?

35. 피리포 롸 구뫄구롸, 아바
어이 먀시 오유 무구루루-구루
아바아 아소마
야나다쀠리라아고 롸
구무바쀠기시사 어뫄시
무부야-부야 어라 루우루 사
여수.

36. 아버러 바나찌러
바어씨가냐, 버라 구이가 무
찌시기 찌우마 아롸 아바아
아쀠 머씨. 오유 무구루루-구루
어라 귀러 아부라 피리포 뿌
시 머씨 마노 마쀠 아노롸! 찌
찌까두마 따바디시봐?

mouth.

33. In his humiliation he
was deprived of justice.
Who can speak of his
descendants? For his life
was taken from the earth."

34. The eunuch asked Philip,
"Tell me, please, who is the
prophet talking about,
himself or someone else?"

35. Then Philip began with
that very passage of
Scripture and told him the
good news about Jesus.

36. As they traveled along
the road, they came to
some water and the eunuch
said, "Look, here is water.
Why shouldn't I be
baptized?"

37. Firipo na imbu akaba wemerere Yesu ne muchima wao woshi, unganabatisibwa. Bai mbu Nechi nemerere kwa Yesu kireisito anali mwana wa Ongo.)

38. Chasinda, ola mukulu-kulu era kuteta mbu bemaanza emutukali. Sinda, unao-unao, buana Firipo bera kwandalira mwa meshi. Firipo kunakumubatisa.

39. Abere bera batenga mwa meshi, emuchima wa enawetu kuna, kuna kuirimya Firipo. Oyu mukulu-kulu chiro akachimulolako, si era kunaendekera ne lubalamo lwai na lumoo lunene.

40. Firipo era kuchichingira era ali mwa musi we Asoto. Chasindjire, era kusungula mwa misi yoshi aenda ahubanganyisa ebandu emwasi mubuya-buya, kuikira mango aikaa mwa musi we kaisariya.

37. 피리포 나 이뿌 아가바 워머러러 여수 너 무찌마 와오 오씨, 우꽈나바디시봐. 바이 뿌 너찌 너머러러 과 여수 기러이시도 아나삐 뫄나 와 오꼬.)

38. 짜시따, 오롸 무구루-구루 어라 구더다 뿌 버마아싸 어무두가삐. 시따, 우나오-우나오, 부아나 피리포 버라 과따삐라 뫄 머씨. 피리포 구나구무바디사.

39. 아버러 버라 바더꽈 뫄 머씨, 어무찌마 와 어나워두 구나, 구나 구이리먀 피리포. 오유 무구루-구루 찌로 아가찌무롤롸고, 시 어라 구나어떠거라 너 루바꽈모 꽈이 나 루모오 루너너.

40. 피리포 어라 구찌찌삐라 어라 아삐 뫄 무시 워 아소도. 짜시띠러, 어라 구수꾸롸 뫄 미시 요씨 아어따 아후바꽈네사 어바누 어뫄시 무부야-부야, 구이기라 마꼬 아이가아 뫄 무시 워 가이사리야.

37. None

38. And he gave orders to stop the chariot. Then both Philip and the eunuch went down into the water and Philip baptized him.

39. When they came up out of the water, the Spirit of the Lord suddenly took Philip away, and the eunuch did not see him again, but went on his way rejoicing.

40. Philip, however, appeared at Azotus and traveled about, preaching the gospel in all the towns until he reached Caesarea.

E Mikolo ye Ndjumwa Chikono 9

Saulo emerera Yesu

1. Mwesi suku, Saulo abaa anachire ete emuchima mubi we kulibusa ne kwita ebanafunzi* ba Enawetu.

어 미고로 여 뚜꽈 찌고노 9

사우로 어머러라 여수

1. 뭐시 수구, 사우로 아바아 아나찌러 어더 어무찌마 무비 워 구삐부사 너 귀다 어바나푸씨* 바 어나워두.

Acts Chapter 9[NIV]

1. Meanwhile, Saul was still breathing out murderous threats against the Lord's disciples. He went to the

Lusuku luuma era kuendera ebakulu-kulu webakuhonyi*,

루수구 루우마 어라 구어떠라 어바구루-구루 워바구호네*,

high priest

2. Era kumwema emaruba me kuchikangana era muhondo se bakulu-kulu be mashenge me bayuta momwa musi we Tamasiki. Amu maruba, mabaa makumuwa loso lwa kumina ebemeresi, ebalume ne bakasi, abeke eyerusalemu.

2. 어라 구뭐마 어마루바 머 구찌가꺄나 어라 무호또 서 바구루-구루 버 마써꺼 머 바유다 모뫄 무시 워 다마시기. 아무 마루바, 마바아 마구무와 로소 롸 구미나 어버머러시, 어바루꺼 너 바가시, 아버거 어여루사꺼무.

2. and asked him for letters to the synagogues in Damascus, so that if he found any there who belonged to the Way, whether men or women, he might take them as prisoners to Jerusalem.

3. Abere era ali mwanjira ofu ne Tamasiki, unao-unao changasi chinene cha chatengera kwa n guba kuna kumusungula.

3. 아버러 어라 아찌 뫄지라 오푸 너 다마시기, 우나오-우나오 짜꺄시 찌너너 짜 짜더꺼라 과 누 구바 구나 구무수우꽈라.

3. As he neared Damascus on his journey, suddenly a light from heaven flashed around him.

4. Saulo kuna kuchihunda kwa chitaka. Era kumva emurenge amubura mbu Saulo! Saulo! chi chatuma wanyiribusa

4. 사우로 구나 구찌후따 과 찌다가. 어라 구빠 어무러꺼 아무부라 뿌 사우로! 사우로! 찌 짜두마 와네리부사

4. He fell to the ground and heard a voice say to him, "Saul, Saul, why do you persecute me?"

5. Saulo nai ubu woyo unde waliya noyu murenge mbu nyono Yesu nyiwalibusa.

5. 사우로 나이 우부 오요 우떠 와찌야 노유 무러꺼 뿌 뇨노 여수 네와찌부사.

5. "Who are you, Lord?" Saul asked. "I am Jesus, whom you are persecuting," he replied.

6. Wimangaa uye mwa musi, nomu mu bangakubwirira bya wemire kuira.

6. 위마꺄아 우여 뫄 무시, 노무 무 바꺄구뷔리라 뱌 워미러 구이라.

6. "Now get up and go into the city, and you will be told what you must do."

7. Ebandu ba babaa bali na Saulo, bera kwemanga batungwa busese. Batungwa bushi emurenge ibabaa banomvire oshao, si babaa batasene ku mundu asibya.

7. 어바뚜 바 바바아 바찌 나 사우로, 버라 궈마꺄 바두꽈 부서서. 바두꽈 부씨 어무러꺼 이바바아 바노삐러 오싸오, 시 바바아 바다서너 구 무뚜 아시뱌.

7. The men traveling with Saul stood there speechless; they heard the sound but did not see anyone.

8. Saulo era kubatuka. Si chiro angaba mbu abaa asibwire emeho, abaa atachisene ku kandu. Balikabo bera kwire bamuachirira kwa kuboko na bamutandaisa kuikira mwa musi we Tamasiki.

8. 사우뢒 어라 구바두가. 시 찌로 아까바 뿌 아바아 아시뷔러 어머호, 아바아 아다찌서너 구 가뚜. 바릐가보 버라 귀러 바무아찌리라 과 구보고 나 바무다따이사 구이기라 뫄 무시 워 다마시기.

8. Saul got up from the ground, but when he opened his eyes he could see nothing. So they led him by the hand into Damascus.

9. Era kumala suku ehatu ataola, atalya, atamwa na kandu kasibya.

9. 어라 구마롸 수구 어하두 아다오롸, 아다랴, 아다뫄 나 가뚜 가시뱌.

9. For three days he was blind, and did not eat or drink anything.

10. Mwoyu musi we Tamasiki mwabaa mutula mwemeresi muuma mbu i Ananiya. Oyu Ananiya, enawetu era kumwamaala mu byabunya biroto mbu Ananiya! nai mbu Karame Enawetu.

10. 뫄유 무시 워 다마시기 뫄바아 무두롸 뭐머러시 무우마 뿌 이 아나니야. 오유 아나니야, 어나워두 어라 구뫄마아롸 무 뱌부냐 비로도 뿌 아나니야! 나이 뿌 가라머 어나워두.

10. In Damascus there was a disciple named Ananias. The Lord called to him in a vision, "Ananias!" "Yes, Lord," he answered.

11. Enawetu era kumubura mbu Uyaa mwa mwengere ola utula wirekirwe mbu Mwengere Ushimire. Chasinda, ungengiraa mwa mwa Yuta, omola mu busisa mulume muuma mbu i Saulo, mwesha musi we Tariso. Oyu mulume, mwa memo mu ali mwebine bihangi.

11. 어나워두 어라 구무부라 뿌 우야아 뫄 뭐꺼러 오롸 우두롸 위러기뤄 뿌 뭐꺼러 우씨미러. 짜시따, 우꺼끼라아 뫄 뫄 유다, 오모롸 무 부시사 무루머 무우마 뿌 이 사우뢒, 뭐싸 무시 워 다리소. 오유 무루머, 뫄 머모 무 아릐 뭐비너 비하끼.

11. The Lord told him, "Go to the house of Judas on Straight Street and ask for a man from Tarsus named Saul, for he is praying.

12. Oyu Saulo nai alolire mwa nyumba amubike kwe mino, amwemere chasiya ahube kulola. Noyu mulume esina lyai i Ananiya.

12. 오유 사우뢒 나이 아뢒릐러 뫄 뉴빠 아무비거 궈 미노, 아뭐머러 짜시야 아후버 구뢒롸. 노유 무루머 어시나 랴이 이 아나니야.

12. In a vision he has seen a man named Ananias come and place his hands on him to restore his sight."

13. Ananiya era kumwakula mbu Enawetu! oyu mundu nomvire kwa ngulu yai ibi. Nebisibu byoshi bya alosise kwa bemeresi bao mwa musi we Yerusalemu, bandu banene banyibalikisise kubi.

14. Kanji aikire na mwono musi, ete ebuashi bekumina ebandu-bakulu kulu bebakuhanyi bu bamuwerebo.

15. Si enawetu na imbu unaendaa, bushi oyu Saulo nyeine nyi namulondwere mwa mulimo we kukangirisa ebandu era luulu sanyi era muhondo se bandu be sinji mbaa nera muhondo se bami babo nokwa baisiraeli.

16. Kanji nyeine nyi nyingamulosa kute angalibuka busese bushi nanyi.

17. Bushi noku, Ananiya era kunaneda. Aikire mwa Saulo abaa ali, era kumubika kwe'mino na amubura mbu: Enyaketu Saulo! enawetu Yesu ola wakupamukiraako mwanjira mango wabaa wabaha enera, iwanyitumire ene uli, bushi ahonda uhube kulola, ubone ne mchima mubuya-buya.

13. 아나니야 어라 구꽈구꽈 뿌 어나워두! 오유 무뚜 노삐러 과 꿀루 야이 이비. 너비시부 뵤씨 뱌 아뢰시서 과 버머러시 바오 꽈 무시 워 여루사뤄무, 바뚜 바너너 바네바삐기시서 구비.

14. 가찌 아이기러 나 몰노 무시, 어더 어부아씨 버구미나 어바뚜-바구루 구루 버바구하네 부 바무워러보.

15. 시 어나워두 나 이뿌 우나어따아, 부씨 오유 사우뢰 녀이너 네 나무뢴뚜워러 꽈 무삐모 워 구가삐리사 어바뚜 어라 뤼우루 사네 어라 무호또 서 바뚜 버 시찌 빠아 너라 무호또 서 바미 바보 노과 바이시라어삐.

16. 가찌 녀이너 네 네빠무뢰사 구더 아꽈삐부가 부서서 부씨 나네.

17. 부씨 노구, 아나니야 어라 구나너다. 아이기러 꽈 사우뢰 아바아 아삐, 어라 구무비가 궈미노 나 아무부라 뿌: 어냐거두 사우뢰! 어나워두 여수 오꽈 와구파무기라아고 꽈찌라 마꼬 와바아 와바하 어너라, 이와네두미러 어너 우삐, 부씨 아호따 우후버 구뢰꽈, 우보너 너 무찌마 무부야-부야.

13. "Lord," Ananias answered, "I have heard many reports about this man and all the harm he has done to your saints in Jerusalem.

14. And he has come here with authority from the chief priests to arrest all who call on your name."

15. But the Lord said to Ananias, "Go! This man is my chosen instrument to carry my name before the Gentiles and their kings and before the people of Israel.

16. I will show him how much he must suffer for my name."

17. Then Ananias went to the house and entered it. Placing his hands on Saul, he said, "Brother Saul, the Lord--Jesus, who appeared to you on the road as you were coming here--has sent me so that you may see again and be filled with the Holy Spirit."

18. Unao-unao, mwa meho ma Saulo mwera kutowanga byabunya byamba, kuna kutangirisa alola kanji. Chasinda era kwemuka na abatisibwa.

19. Chasinjire, era kulya na ahuba kuata misi. Saulo amalaa suku burebe alauma ne bemeresi ba babaa bali mwa musi we Tamasiki.

Saulo ahubanganya emwasi mubuya-buya mwa musi w'e Tamasiki

20. Busira kulinjira, era kutangirisa akangirisa ebandu mwa mashenge me bayuta mbu Yesu anali mwana wa Ongo.

21. Ebandu boshi babendee bomvirisa bya ateta, bera kunde basanwa busese ne kuburana mbu Ewashe! si ono mulume iwabaa wenjire walosa ebandu kwa kasibu ba batula batun jire Yesu mwa musi we Yerusalemu! kanji nechi chi chanamurechire nokono, chasiya abamine nekubeka era muhondo se bakulu-kulu be bakuhanyi!

18. 우나오-우나오, 뫄 머호 마 사우로 뭐라 구도와빠 뱌부냐 뱌빠, 구나 구다삐리사 아로뫄 가찌. 짜시따 어라 궈무가 나 아바디시봐.

19. 짜시찌러, 어라 구꺄 나 아후바 구아다 미시. 사우로 아마뫄아 수구 부러버 아뫄우마 너 버머러시 바 바바아 바삐 뫄 무시 워 다마시기.

사우로 아후바바삣냇 어뫄시 무부야-부야 뫄 무시 워 다마시기

20. 부시라 구삐찌라, 어라 구다삐리사 아가삐리사 어바뚜 뫄 마써삐어 머 바유다 뿌 여수 아나삐 뫄나 와 오꼬.

21. 어바뚜 보씨 바버떠어 보삐리사 뱌 아더다, 버라 구떠 바사놔 부서서 너 구부라나 뿌 어와써! 시 오노 무루머 이와바아 워찌러 와로사 어바뚜 과 가시부 바 바두뫄 바두누 지러 여수 뫄 무시 워 여루사뿌무! 가찌 너찌 찌 짜나무러찌러 노고노, 짜시야 아바미너 너구버가 어라 무호또 서 바구루-구루 버 바구하내!

18. Immediately, something like scales fell from Saul's eyes, and he could see again. He got up and was baptized,

19. and after taking some food, he regained his strength. Saul spent several days with the disciples in Damascus.

20. At once he began to preach in the synagogues that Jesus is the Son of God.

21. All those who heard him were astonished and asked, "Isn't he the man who raised havoc in Jerusalem among those who call on this name? And hasn't he come here to take them as prisoners to the chief priests?"

22. Si chero bacha, Saulo era kunaendekera aata buashi bunene mwa kutangangirisa ebandu echinwa cha Ongo. Ebayuta ba babaa batula eTamasiki bera kunde baina cha bangamwakula mango endee abalosa kanangana kwa Yesu ina masiya*.

23. Abere kwa renga suku burebe, aba yuta be Tamasiki bera kuya lwango bamulanyirire.

24. Boshi noku, eshi ne nutufu bendee bamulingira kwa biso bye misi chasiya bamwite.

25. Lusuku luuma butufu, ebanafunzi* ba Saulo, bera kumubika mwachitonga na bamwandasisa era nyuma se lusito lwemusi.

Saulo ahuba e Yerusalemu

26. Mango Saulo alikaa eYerusalemu, era kunde aereka kuchibika kwa banji bemeresi, si boshi bera kunde bamwobaa bushi batendee bemerera kanangana kwa kasi nai anera mwemeresi.

22. 시 쩌로 바짜, 사우로 어라 구나어떠거라 아아다 부아씨 부너너 뫄 구다빠끼리사 어바뚜 어찌놔 짜 오꼬. 어바유다 바 바바아 바두꽈 어다마시기 버라 구떠 바이나 짜 바빠뫄구꽈 마꼬 어떠어 아바로사 가나빠나 과 여수 이나 마시야*.

23. 아버러 과 러빠 수구 부러버, 아바 유다 버 다마시기 버라 구야 롸꼬 바무꽈네리러.

24. 보씨 노구, 어씨 너 누두푸 버떠어 바무링끼라 과 비소 벼 미시 짜시야 바뮈더.

25. 루수구 루우마 부두푸, 어바나푸씨* 바 사우로, 버라 구무비가 뫄찌도빠 나 바뫄따시사 어라 뉴마 서 루시도 뤄무시.

사우로 아후바 어 여루사뻐물

26. 마꼬 사우로 아삐가아 어여루사뻐무, 어라 구떠 아어러가 구찌비가 과 바찌 버머러시, 시 보씨 버라 구떠 바모봐아 부씨 바더떠어 버머러라 가나빠나 과 가시 나이 아너라 뭐머러시.

22. Yet Saul grew more and more powerful and baffled the Jews living in Damascus by proving that Jesus is the Christ.

23. After many days had gone by, the Jews conspired to kill him,

24. but Saul learned of their plan. Day and night they kept close watch on the city gates in order to kill him.

25. But his followers took him by night and lowered him in a basket through an opening in the wall.

26. When he came to Jerusalem, he tried to join the disciples, but they were all afraid of him, not believing that he really was a disciple.

27. Banarnaba era kwire amutole na amweka era muhondo sendumwa* era kubalikisisa kute kwa oyu Saulo abuanana na enawetu mango abaa ali mwa lubalamo lwe kuya e Tamasiki, na kute kwa Yesu yeine ahambalaa nai. Kanji era kubabalikisa kute kwa ahubanganyisaa besha Tamasiki era luulu sa Yesu busira buba.

28. Kutengera mwesi suku, Saulo erz kwire anaba alauma nabo nekunde asungula nabo mwa musi we Yerusalemu aenda ahubanganyisa ebandu era luulu sa enawetu Yesu busira buba.

29. Kanji abaa enjire aenda ebwaka ne bayuta ba bendee bateta echikiriki. Si beke babaa benjire banahonda kute bangamwita.

30. Mango bemeresi balikabo bomvaa kwoyu mwasi, bera kuMuhaisa ekaisariya, era kutengerayi bamutuma eTariso.

27. 바나루나바 어라 귀러 아무도러 나 아뭐가 어라 무호또 서뚜똬* 어라 구바삐기시사 구더 과 오유 사우로 아부아나나 나 어나워두 마꼬 아바아 아삐 똬 루바똬모 뭬 구야 어 다마시기, 나 구더 과 여수 여이너 아하빠똬아 나이. 가찌 어라 구바바삐기사 구더 과 아후바까네사아 버싸 다마시기 어라 루우루 사 여수 부시라 부바.

28. 구더꺼라 뭐시 수구, 사우로 어루주 귀러 아나바 아꼬우마 나보 너구떠 아수꾸똬 나보 똬 무시 워 여루사꺼무 아어따 아후바까네사 어바뚜 어라 루우루 사 어나워두 여수 부시라 부바.

29. 가찌 아바아 어찌러 아어따 어봐가 너 바유다 바 버떠어 바더다 어찌기리기. 시 버거 바바아 버찌러 바나호따 구더 바까뮈다.

30. 마꼬 버머러시 바삐가보 보빠아 굥유 똬시, 버라 구무하이사 어가이사리야, 어라 구더꺼라에 바무두마 어다리소.

27. But Barnabas took him and brought him to the apostles. He told them how Saul on his journey had seen the Lord and that the Lord had spoken to him, and how in Damascus he had preached fearlessly in the name of Jesus.

28. So Saul stayed with them and moved about freely in Jerusalem, speaking boldly in the name of the Lord.

29. He talked and debated with the Grecian Jews, but they tried to kill him.

30. When the brothers learned of this, they took him down to Caesarea and sent him off to Tarsus.

31. Mwesi suku, ebemeresi ba babaa bali mwa chio choshi che yuteya, ne che Kalilaya neche samariya babaa bali mwa bolo, echera chera kutuma babona emisi. Bera kulwa bushi ne kutunda enawetu, kanji bushi emchima mubuya-buya endee abasesa emichima.

Petero alamya Aineya

32. Mango Petero abaa enjire atambira ebemeresi boshi ba mwebi bio, lusuku luuma era kuya kuatangula ba babaa bali mwa musi we Luta.

33. Aikiremo, era kubuana'mo mulume muume muuma mbu i Aineya. Oyu aineya, abaa alamala myaka muane kwanjingo, bushi abaa aremere.

34. Petero era kumubura mbu Aineya, Yesu Kirisitoakulamisi! rero, batukaa uchihashulire enjiko yao weine. Unao-unao, aineya kuna kubatuka.

35. Besha mwa musi we luta alauma na besha mwa bulambo bwe Saroni boshi bera kulola kwa aineya alamisibwe. Bushi noku, bera kwemerera enawetu.

31. 뭐시 수구, 어버머러시 바 바바아 바뛰 똬 찌오 쪼씨 쩌 유더야, 너 쩌 가뀌롸야 너쩌 사마리야 바바아 바뛰 똬 보로, 어쩌라 쩌라 구두마 바보나 어미시. 버라 구꽈 부씨 너 구두따 어나워두, 가찌 부씨 어무찌마 무부야-부야 어떠어 아바서사 어미찌마.

퍼더로 아꽈맸 아이너야

32. 마꼬 퍼더로 아바아 어찌러 아다뻬라 어버머러시 보씨 바 뭐비 비오, 루수구 루우마 어라 구야 구아다꾸꽈 바 바바아 바뛰 똬 무시 워 루다.

33. 아이기러모, 어라 구부아나모 무루머 무우머 무우마 뿌 이 아이너야. 오유 아이너야, 아바아 아꽈마꽈 먀가 무아너 과찌꼬, 부씨 아바아 아러머러.

34. 퍼더로 어라 구무부라 뿌 아이너야, 여수 기리시도아구꽈미시! 러로, 바두가아 우찌하쑤뤼러 어찌고 야오 워이너. 우나오-우나오, 아이너야 구나 구바두가.

35. 버씨 똬 무시 워 루다 아꽈우마 나 버씨 똬 부꽈뽀 뭐 사로니 보씨 버라 구로꽈 과 아이너야 아꽈미시붜. 부씨 노구, 버라 궈머러라 어나워두.

31. Then the church throughout Judea, Galilee and Samaria enjoyed a time of peace. It was strengthened; and encouraged by the Holy Spirit, it grew in numbers, living in the fear of the Lord.

32. As Peter traveled about the country, he went to visit the saints in Lydda.

33. There he found a man named Aeneas, a paralytic who had been bedridden for eight years.

34. "Aeneas," Peter said to him, "Jesus Christ heals you. Get up and take care of your mat." Immediately Aeneas got up.

35. All those who lived in Lydda and Sharon saw him and turned to the Lord.

Petero omola Tabita

36. Mwa musi we Yope namo, mwabaa mutula mwemeresi muumua wa mukasi mbu i Tabika. Mwa chikiriki mbu iTorika kukuteta mbu Mburuko. Oyu mukasi abaa atusa myanya ibuya kanji endee aasa ne bakene.

37. Lusuku luuma era kulaka, chasinjire era kufa. Mango bemeresi balikabo babaa bera bamalaa kwosa echirunda chai, bera kubikachi mwa chumba chokwa ngangabo.

38. Rero, bushiemusi we Luta abaa atula ofu ne we Yope, ne bemeresi babaa bomvire emwasi mira kwa eLuta yi Petero ali. Bera kwire bamutuma ku balume babiri baye kumubura mbu utubabaliraa ubahe fuba ene mwetu!

39. Petero omvire bacha, kuna kuchiuma alauma nabo. Abere aika, bera kumwerusisa mwecha chumba. Ebahumbakasi boshi bera kuchifunda ala aba ali baenda balira. Bera kumulosa ne njimba qa Tabita endee alanjiraabo mango abaa achiri alauma nabo.

퍼더로 오모롸 다비다

36. 롸 무시 워 요퍼 나모, 롸바아 무두롸 뭐머러시 무우무아 와 무가시 뿌 이 다비가. 롸 찌기리기 뿌 이도리가 구구더다 뿌 뿌루고. 오유 무가시 아바아 아두사 먀냐 이부야 가찌 어떠어 아아사 너 바거너.

37. 루수구 루우마 어라 구롸가, 짜시찌러 어라 구파. 마꼬 버머러시 바삐가보 바바아 버라 바마롸아 교사 어찌루따 짜이, 버라 구비가찌 롸 쭈빠 쪼과 꽈꽈보.

38. 러로, 부씨어무시 워 루다 아바아 아두롸 오푸 너 워 요퍼, 너 버머러시 바바아 보삐러 어꽈시 미라 과 어루다 에 퍼더로 아뤼. 버라 귀러 바무두마 구 바루머 바비리 바여 구무부라 뿌 우두바바뤼라아 우바허 푸바 어너 뭐두!

39. 퍼더로 오삐러 바짜, 구나 구찌우마 아라우마 나보. 아버러 아이가, 버라 구뭐루시사 뭐짜 쭈빠. 어바후빠가시 보씨 버라 구찌푸따 아롸 아바 아뤼 바어따 바뤼라. 버라 구무로사 너 띠빠 구아 다비다 어떠어 아롸찌라아보 마꼬 아바아 아찌리 아롸우마 나보.

36. In Joppa there was a disciple named Tabitha (which, when translated, is Dorcas), who was always doing good and helping the poor.

37. About that time she became sick and died, and her body was washed and placed in an upstairs room.

38. Lydda was near Joppa; so when the disciples heard that Peter was in Lydda, they sent two men to him and urged him, "Please come at once!"

39. Peter went with them, and when he arrived he was taken upstairs to the room. All the widows stood around him, crying and showing him the robes and other clothing that Dorcas had made while she was still with them.

40. Petero kukwera kubura ebandu boshi mbu baulukaa era mbuwa. Era kukoma emafi na ema Ongo. Chasinda, era kwerekera era cha chirunda chabaa chiri na ateta mbu Tabita emukaa! unao-unao, Tabita kuna kubbola emeho.

41. Alolire ku Petero, era kwekala. Petero era kumuachirira kwa kuboko amwemuse.chasinda, era kwamaala ba bahumba-kasi alauma ne banji bemeresi, na abalosa Tabita era ali muuma-uma

42. Besha mwa musi we yope boshi, bera kunomva koyu mwasi, na banene mubo bera kwemerera enawetu.

43 Petero era kwekala mwoyu musi suku sinene mwa mwamulume muuma mbu i Simoni. Oyu Simoni abaa murenga wa kukunganya enyuu.

40. 퍼더로 구궈라 구부라 어바누 보씨 뿌 바우루가아 어라 뿌와. 어라 구고마 어마피 나 어마 오오. 짜시따, 어라 궈러거라 어라 짜 찌루따 짜바아 찌리 나 아더다 뿌 다비다 어무가아! 우나오-우나오, 다비다 구나 구부보꽈 어머호.

41. 아로끠러 구 퍼더로, 어라 궈가꽈. 퍼더로 어라 구무아찌리라 과 구보고 아뭐무서.짜시따, 어라 과마아꽈 바 바후빠-가시 아꽈우마 너 바찌 버머러시, 나 아바로사 다비다 어라 아끠 무우마-우마

42. 버싸 마 무시 워 요퍼 보씨, 버라 구노빠 고유 마시, 나 바너너 무보 버라 궈머러라 어나워두.

43 퍼더로 어라 궈가꽈 모유 무시 수구 시너너 마 마무루머 무우마 뿌 이 시모니. 오유 시모니 아바아 무러꽈 와 구구꺄냐 어뉴우.

40. Peter sent them all out of the room; then he got down on his knees and prayed. Turning toward the dead woman, he said, "Tabitha, get up." She opened her eyes, and seeing Peter she sat up.

41. He took her by the hand and helped her to her feet. Then he called the believers and the widows and presented her to them alive.

42. This became known all over Joppa, and many people believed in the Lord.

43. Peter stayed in Joppa for some time with a tanner named Simon.

E Mikolo ye Ndjumwa Chikono 10

Malaika ahambala ne mukulu-kulu w'e basula

어 미고로 여 뚜와 찌고노 10

마꽈일— 아하빠꽈 너 무구루-구루 워 바수꽈

10 Acts Chapter 10[NIV]

1. Mwa musi we kaisariya mwabaa mutula mulume muume mbu i Korneliyo. Oyu Korneliyo abaa mukulu-kulu kwa chikembe chiuma cha basula be Baroma cha chendee cherikwa mbu chikembe cha Bataliana.

2. Oyu mulume, abaa atula mundu wa kanangana kanji abaa atula atunjire Ongo alauma ne ngumo yai yoshi. Nomwa lubaa lwe bayuta, endee aasa mu bakene banene, kanji endee ema Ongo esuku soshi.

3. Lusuku luuma, ngomwa saa mwenda se mushi, era kuya mu byabunya biroto. Mwebi biroto, era kulola kubuya-buya ku malaika* muuma mwa Ongo engirira mwa mwai, nekumubura mbu Korneliyo!

4. Korneliyo, era kutumbikisa oyu malaika*na buba bunene, na amwakula mbu kute waliya! malaika nayi mbu Ememo mao wende waira, ne mabuya wende wairira ebakene, Ongo amowerere'mo. Bushi noku, akukengere.

---

1. 쫘 무시 워 가이사리야 쫘바아 무두쫘 무루머 무우머 뿌 이 고루너쫘요. 오유 고루너쫘요 아바아 무구루-구루 과 찌거뻐 찌우마 쫘 바수쫘 버 바로마 쫘 쩌너어 쩌리과 뿌 찌거뻐 쫘 바다쫘아나.

2. 오유 무루머, 아바아 아두쫘 무뚜 와 가나쫘나 가찌 아바아 아두쫘 아두씨러 오꼬 아쫘우마 너 꾸모 야이 요씨. 노마 루바아 뤄 바유다, 어떠어 아아사 무 바거너 바너너, 가찌 어떠어 어마 오꼬 어수구 소씨.

3. 루수구 루우마, 꼬마 사아 뭐따 서 무씨, 어라 구야 무 뱌부냐 비로도. 뭐비 비로도, 어라 구룬쫘 구부야-부야 구 마쫘이가* 무우마 쫘 오꼬 어끼리라 쫘 쫘이, 너구무부라 뿌 고루너쫘요!

4. 고루너쫘요, 어라 구두뻬기사 오유 마쫘이가*나 부바 부너너, 나 아마구쫘 뿌 구더 와쫘야! 마쫘이가 나에 뿌 어머모 마오 워떠 와이라, 너 마부야 워떠 와이리라 어바거너, 오꼬 아모워러러모. 부씨 노구, 아구거떠러.

---

1. At Caesarea there was a man named Cornelius, a centurion in what was known as the Italian Regiment.

2. He and all his family were devout and God-fearing; he gave generously to those in need and prayed to God regularly.

3. One day at about three in the afternoon he had a vision. He distinctly saw an angel of God, who came to him and said, "Cornelius!"

4. Cornelius stared at him in fear. "What is it, Lord?" he asked. The angel answered, "Your prayers and gifts to the poor have come up as a memorial offering before God.

5. Rero, kuno na murenge, wiree matuma ebandu mwa musi we Yope bakubingirire mulumemuuma mbu i Simoni Petero.

5. 러로, 구노 나 무러꺼, 위러어 마두마 어바뚜 꽈 무시 워 요퍼 바구비꺼리러 무루머무우마 뿌 이 시모니 퍼더로.

5. Now send men to Joppa to bring back a man named Simon who is called Peter.

6. Oyu Petero, atula mwa mwa mulume muuma mbu i'Simoni, murenga ola wende wakanganya enyuu. Ne nyumba yai, kwa musike wenjira kunitula.

6. 오유 퍼더로, 아두꽈 꽈 꽈 무루머 무우마 뿌 이시모니, 무러꺄 오라 워꺼 와가꺄냐 어뉴우. 너 뉴빠 야이, 과 무시거 워찌라 구니두꽈.

6. He is staying with Simon the tanner, whose house is by the sea."

7. Abere oyu malaika*era aenda, Korneliyo era kwamaala babir mwa baanda bai na musula muuma. Oyu musula, abaa muuma mwa ba bendee bamulanga, kanji abaa atula atunjire Ongo.

7. 아버러 오유 마꽈이가*어라 아어따, 고루너꿰요 어라 과마아꽈 바비루 꽈 바아따 바이 나 무수꽈 무우마. 오유 무수꽈, 아바아 무우마 꽈 바 버꺼어 바무꽈까, 가찌 아바아 아두꽈 아두찌러 오꼬.

7. When the angel who spoke to him had gone, Cornelius called two of his servants and a devout soldier who was one of his attendants.

8. Era kubalikisa abu bandu bai byoshi bya byamuikiraa. Chasinda, era kutuma eYope.

8. 어라 구바꿰기사 아부 바뚜 바이 뵤씨 뱌 뱌무이기라아. 짜시따, 어라 구두마 어요퍼.

8. He told them everything that had happened and sent them to Joppa.

Petero ahambala na Ongo mu byabunya biroto

퍼더로 아하빠꽈 나 오꼬 무 뱌부냐 비로도

9. Abere mwei mishangya, ngomwa saa ndatu se mushi, ebandu ba kornelito atumaa baa bahonda kuika ofu ne musi we Yopa. Mwechi chihangi, chinechi, Petero era kwerukira mwa chumba chokwa ngangamo eme Ongo.

9. 아버러 뭐이 미싸꺄, 꼬꽈 사아 따두 서 무씨, 어바뚜 바 고루너꿰도 아두마아 바아 바호따 구이가 오푸 너 무시 워 요파. 뭐찌 찌하꿰, 찌너찌, 퍼더로 어라 궈루기라 꽈 쭈빠 쪼과 까까모 어머 오꼬.

9. About noon the following day as they were on their journey and approaching the city, Peter went up on the roof to pray.

10. Si ebusinya bwera kumusimba, era kwire ahonda alye. Mango babaa bera

10. 시 어부시냐 붜라 구무시빠, 어라 궈러 아호따 아껴. 마꼬 바바아 버라

10. He became hungry and wanted something to eat, and while the meal was

bamutekera ebiyo, era kuya mu byabunya birito.

바무더거라 어비요, 어라 구야 무 뱌부냐 비리도.

being prepared, he fell into a trance.

11. Mwebi biroto, era kulola enguba ibbokere, na yabunya ngwaya inene yatenga mwa chanya, na yandaalira kwa chitaka. Ei ngwaya, yabaa isimbirirwe kwa mapembe mai mane.

11. 뭐비 비로도, 어라 구로롸 어꾸바 이부보거라, 나 야부냐 꽈야 이너너 야더꽈 롸 짜냐, 나 야따아뤼라 과 찌다가. 어이 꽈야, 야바아 이시삐리뤄 과 마퍼뼈 마이 마너.

11. He saw heaven opened and something like a large sheet being let down to earth by its four corners.

12. Kanji mui, mwabaa muli chira buko bwenyama se birenge bine, ne sa sende saendera kwa bula, alauma ne milango.

12. 가찌 무이, 롸바아 무뤼 찌라 부고 붜냐마 서 비러어 비너, 너 사 서떠 사어떠라 과 부롸, 아롸우마 너 미롸꼬.

12. It contained all kinds of four-footed animals, as well as reptiles of the earth and birds of the air.

13. Chasinda, era kumva emurenge amubura mbu Petero, emukaa, ukere, unaliye esi nyama!

13. 짜시따, 어라 구빠 어무러어 아무부라 뿌 퍼더로, 어무가아, 우거러, 우나뤼여 어시 냐마!

13. Then a voice told him, "Get up, Peter. Kill and eat."

14. Si Petero era kwakula mbu cha-cha! nanga enawetu! nyono ndafuraa kulya chiro na kandu ka mwaso wetu atula atolire nga katakomisibwe. *

14. 시 퍼더로 어라 과구롸 뿌 짜-짜! 나꽈 어나워두! 뇨노 따푸라아 구롁 찌로 나 가뚜 가 롸소 워두 아두롸 아도뤼러 꽈 가다고미시붜. *

14. "Surely not, Lord!" Peter replied. "I have never eaten anything impure or unclean."

15. Si oyu murenge era kuhuba kumubura mbu Bya Ongo airire kuba bibuya, utabyerikaa mbu bitakomisibwe*.

15. 시 오유 무러어 어라 구후바 구무부라 뿌 뱌 오꼬 아이리러 구바 비부야, 우다벼리가아 뿌 비다고미시붜*.

15. The voice spoke to him a second time, "Do not call anything impure that God has made clean."

16. Abere wa murenge abura Petero oyu mwasi muuma kahatu, unao-unao, era ngwaya kuna kuhuba kwerusibwa kwa nguba.

16. 아버러 와 무러어 아부라 퍼더로 오유 롸시 무우마 가하두, 우나오-우나오, 어라 꽈야 구나 구후바 궈루시봐 과 꾸바.

16. This happened three times, and immediately the sheet was taken back to heaven.

17. Mango Petero abaa anachire achibusa kute ebi biroto bitechire, mu mango ba balume Korneliyo abaa atumire nabo babaa bera bali kwa chiso. Abu balume, ebandu baibaa babalosise mira ala mwa Simoni.

18. Bera kubarangirira kwa chiso mbu awashe, mu Simoni ola bende berika mbu Petero atula muno

19. Mango Petero abaa anachiri achibusa era luula se bi birito, emuchima mubuya-buya era kumubura mbu umvaa! kwa lwisi kuli balume bahatu bakuhonda.

20. Rero, kuno na murenge, emangaa, wendaale unaenda nabo busira buba, bushi nyinabatumire.

21. Petero era kunandaala, na abura abu bandu mbu nyono onola mwahonda. Chi mwaendere kasi

22. Nabo mbu mukulu-kulu muuma we basula mbu i Korneliyo iwatutumire en uli.oyu Korneliyo, atula mundu wa kanangana kanji atula atunjire Ongo, ne lubaa loshi lwe bayuta lwende lwamutonga ngachi. Rero, malaika* wa Ongo amuikiraa,

17. 마꼬 퍼더로 아바아 아나찌러 아찌부사 구더 어비 비로도 비더찌러, 무 마꼬 바 바루머 고루너꾜 아바아 아두미러 나보 바바아 버라 바꺼 과 찌소. 아부 바루머, 어바뚜 바이바아 바바론시서 미라 아꽈 먀 시모니.

18. 버라 구바라끄리라 과 찌소 뿌 아와써, 무 시모니 오꽈 버떠 버리가 뿌 퍼더로 아두꽈 무노

19. 마꼬 퍼더로 아바아 아나찌리 아찌부사 어라 루우꽈 서 비 비리도, 어무찌마 무부야-부야 어라 구무부라 뿌 우빠아! 과 뤼시 구꾀 바루머 바하두 바구호따.

20. 러로, 구노 나 무러꺼, 어마까아, 워따아뤄 우나어빠 나보 부시라 부바, 부씨 네나바두미러.

21. 퍼더로 어라 구나따아꽈, 나 아부라 아부 바뚜 뿌 뇨노 오노꽈 먀호따. 찌 먀어떠러 가시

22. 나보 뿌 무구루-구루 무우마 워 바수꽈 뿌 이 고루너꾀요 이와두두미러 어누 우꾀.오유 고루너꾀요, 아두꽈 무뚜 와 가나까나 가찌 아두꽈 아두찌러 오꼬, 너 루바아 론씨 뤠 바유다 뤄떠 꽈무도까 까찌. 러로, 마꽈이가* 와 오꼬 아무이기라아, 어라 구무부라

17. While Peter was wondering about the meaning of the vision, the men sent by Cornelius found out where Simon's house was and stopped at the gate.

18. They called out, asking if Simon who was known as Peter was staying there.

19. While Peter was still thinking about the vision, the Spirit said to him, "Simon, three men are looking for you.

20. So get up and go downstairs. Do not hesitate to go with them, for I have sent them."

21. Peter went down and said to the men, "I'm the one you're looking for. Why have you come?"

22. The men replied, "We have come from Cornelius the centurion. He is a righteous and God-fearing man, who is respected by all the Jewish people. A holy angel told him to have you come to his house so that he could hear what

era kumubura mbu
akwamaala

뿌 아과마아롸

you have to say."

23. Petero era kubahuukasa
na bengirira mwa nyumba, era
kubalosa ala bangaonjira,
abere mwei mishangya, Petero
era kutangirisa elubalamo
alauma nabo. Bemeresi
bauma bomva bomwa musi
we yopa nabo, bera
kumwerekesayi.

23. 퍼더로 어라 구바후우가사
나 버끼리라 롸 뉴빠, 어라
구바로사 아롸 바꺄오찌라,
아버러 뭐이 미싸꺄, 퍼더로
어라 구다끼리사 어루바롸모
아롸우마 나보. 버머러시
바우마 보빠 보와 무시 워
요파 나보, 버라 구뭐러거사에.

23. Then Peter invited the
men into the house to be
his guests. The next day
Peter started out with them,
and some of the brothers
from Joppa went along.

Petero ahubanganyisa
ebandu besinje mbaa.

퍼더로 아후바꺼니쎕 어바뚜
버시쩌 빠씹.

24. Abere mweli lishisho,
Petero era kuka mwa musi we
kaisariya. Korneliyo abaa
abalanga alauma na
banyakabo na bera bai bokwa
muchima ba abaa alalikiri.

24. 아버러 뭐끼 끼씨쏘,
퍼더로 어라 구가 롸 무시 워
가이사리야. 고루너끼요
아바아 아바롸꺄 아롸우마 나
바냐가보 나 버라 바이 보과
무찌마 바 아바아 아롸끼기리.

24. The following day he
arrived in Caesarea.
Cornelius was expecting
them and had called
together his relatives and
close friends.

25. Mango Petero abaa
ahonda kwengirira mwa mwa
Korneliyo, Korneliyo era kuya
kumuhukasa.

25. 마꼬 퍼더로 아바아
아호따 궈끼리라 롸 롸
고루너끼요, 고루너끼요 어라
구야 구무후가사.

25. As Peter entered the
house, Cornelius met him
and fell at his feet in
reverence.

26. Si Petero era kumwimanza
ne kumubura mbu Emukaa,
bushi nanyi nyanali mundu
kuuma nao.

26. 시 퍼더로 어라 구뭐마싸
너 구무부라 뿌 어무가아,
부씨 나니 냐나끼 무뚜 구우마
나오.

26. But Peter made him get
up. "Stand up," he said, "I
am only a man myself."

27. Chasinda, Petero era
kwengirira mwa nyumba
aenda ahambala na Korneliyo.
Aikiremo, era kubuana bandu
banene babuaniriremo.

27. 짜시따, 퍼더로 어라
궈끼리라 롸 뉴빠 아어따
아하빠라 나 고루너끼요.
아이기러모, 어라 구부아나
바뚜 바너너 바부아니리러모.

27. Talking with him, Peter
went inside and found a
large gathering of people.

28. Era kubabura mbu bera banyi, mwishi kwa kukulikana ne mwaso wetu tu bayuta, tutumire kukomererana nesi kutambira mundu murebe wa lunji lubaa. Si Ongo yeine iwanyilosise kwa kutumire nyinde natola mundu muremba ngo utakomisibwe* nesi kumutobolola.

29. Echera chi chatumire nabaha busira kusinda-sinda kuno wanyamaere. Rero, cha chatumire mwanyamaala chi chamwiraa mwanyibura.

30. Korneliyo era kumwakula mbu suku ehatu sine sarenga nyire mwa memo muno mwanyi, mwa bihangi biri nge bine byesaa mwenda. Unao-unao, mundu muuma ola wabaa wembese njimba sa salangala busese, kuna kunyipamukirako, na emanga era muhondo sanyi.

31. Era kunyibura mbu Ememo mao wende waira, ne mabuya ma wende wairira ebakene, Ongo amowereremo. Bushi noku, akukengere.

32. Rero, wiree watuma ebandu mwa musi we Yopa, bakubingire mundu muuma mbu Isimoni, murenga ola wende wakunganya enyuu.

28. 어라 구바부라 뿌 버라 바네, 뮈씨 과 구구릐가나 너 꽈소 워두 두 바유다, 두두미러 구고머러라나 너시 구다뻬라 무뚜 무러버 와 룬찌 룬바아. 시 오꼬 여이너 이와네뽀시서 과 구두미러 네너 나도롸 무뚜 무러빠 꼬 우다고미시붜* 너시 구무도보뽀롸.

29. 어쩌라 찌 짜두미러 나바하 부시라 구시따-시따 구노 와냐마어러. 러로, 짜 짜두미러 마냐마아롸 찌 짜뮈라아 마네부라.

30. 고루너릐요 어라 구꽈구롸 뿌 수구 어하두 시너 사러꽈 네러 꽈 머모 무노 꽈네, 꽈 비하끼 비리 어 비너 벼사아 뮈따. 우나오-우나오, 무뚜 무우마 오롸 와바아 워뻐서 끼빠 사 사롸꺼롸 부서서, 구나 구네파무기라고, 나 어마꺼 어라 무호또 사네.

31. 어라 구네부라 뿌 어머모 마오 워떠 와이라, 너 마부야 마 워떠 와이리라 어바거너, 오꼬 아모워러러모. 부씨 노구, 아구거러러.

32. 러로, 위러어 와두마 어바뚜 꽈 무시 워 요파, 바구비뻬러 무뚜 무우마 뿌 이시모니, 무러꺼 오라 워떠 와구꺼냐 어뉴우. 너뉴빠 야이,

28. He said to them: "You are well aware that it is against our law for a Jew to associate with a Gentile or visit him. But God has shown me that I should not call any man impure or unclean.

29. So when I was sent for, I came without raising any objection. May I ask why you sent for me?"

30. Cornelius answered: "Four days ago I was in my house praying at this hour, at three in the afternoon. Suddenly a man in shining clothes stood before me

31. and said, 'Cornelius, God has heard your prayer and remembered your gifts to the poor.

32. Send to Joppa for Simon who is called Peter. He is a guest in the home of Simon the tanner, who lives by the sea.'

Nenyumba yai, kwa musike we nyanja kunitula.

33. Unao-unao, nera kutuma ebandu bakubinge. Nao wanakolire kuno waikire. Rero tuboshi bano tuli era muhondo sa Ongo kwa kumvirisa emyasi yoshi enawetu atumire utubure.

34. Petero era kwira auma mwa bunu mbu kubinali, nerire na menyerera kanangana kwa Ongo atatusa katobololo.

35. Si muchira lubaa, emundu woshi ola wende watunda Ongo nekuira bya bikomire mwa meho mai, oyola iwende wamusismisa.

36. Atumiraa ebaisiraeli emwasi kwa chira ola ukemerera Yesu kirisisto akabona ebolo. Noyu Yesu, ienawetu tu bandu boshi.

37. Era nyuma sa Yowani kuhubanganyisa ebandu era luulu se bubatiso, si muneshi emyasi era yarengaa mwa chio choshi che yuteya, era yatangiriraa ekaliliya.

38. Si kanji mutunabukire kwa Yesu we nasareti , Ongo amulondalaa mwa kumwehusa ne muchima mubuya-buya

과 무시거 워 냐짜 구니두롸.

33. 우나오-우나오, 너라 구두마 어바뚜 바구비어. 나오 와나고리러 구노 와이기러. 러로 두보씨 바노 두뛰 어라 무호또 사 옹오 과 구뻬리사 어먀시 요씨 어나워두 아두미러 우두부러.

34. 퍼더로 어라 귀라 아우마 롸 부누 뿌 구비나뛰, 너리러 나 머녀러라 가나ㅉ나 과 옹오 아다두사 가도보로로로.

35. 시 무찌라 루바아, 어무뚜 오씨 오라 워ㅁ 와두따 옹오 너구이라 뱌 비고미러 롸 머호 마이, 오요롸 이워ㅁ 와무시수미샤.

36. 아두미라아 어바이시라어뛰 어롸시 과 찌라 오롸 우거머러라 여수 기리시시도 아가보나 어보로. 노유 여수, 이어나워두 두 바뚜 보씨.

37. 어라 뉴마 사 요와니 구후바ㅁ네사 어바뚜 어라 루우루 서 부바디소, 시 무너씨 어먀시 어라 야러ㅁ아 롸 찌오 쪼씨 쩌 유더야, 어라 야다ㅁ리라아 어가뛰뛰야.

38. 시 가찌 무두나부기러 과 여수 워 나사러디 , 옹오 아무로ㄸ롸라아 롸 구뭐후사 너 무찌마 무부야-부야 아롸우마

33. So I sent for you immediately, and it was good of you to come. Now we are all here in the presence of God to listen to everything the Lord has commanded you to tell us."

34. Then Peter began to speak: "I now realize how true it is that God does not show favoritism

35. but accepts men from every nation who fear him and do what is right.

36. You know the message God sent to the people of Israel, telling the good news of peace through Jesus Christ, who is Lord of all.

37. You know what has happened throughout Judea, beginning in Galilee after the baptism that John preached--

38. how God anointed Jesus of Nazareth with the Holy Spirit and power, and how he went around doing good

alauma ne buashi. Abaa enjire
airira ebandu mabuya na
kunde alamya boshi ba babaa
bali mwa bucha bwe musimu.
Ebi byoshi, abaa enjire abiira
bushi Ongo

39. Kanji emyasi yoshi era
Yesu airaa mwa chio che
bayuta nomwa musi we
Yerusalemu, tubano
twanachiloreraa kui. Oyu Yesu,
iebandu baetaa mwa
kumumanyika kwa musalaba.

40. Ongo era kumwomola
elusuku lwa kahatu, na
amulosa era muhondo se
bandu.

41. Ata ebandu boshi bu
bamulolaa'ko, si tubano
oshao, tu Ongo alondolaa
tuchilorere kwei myasi. Kanji
tubano tu twabaa twenjire
twalya ne kumwa alauma nai
era se komwoka kwai.

42. Chasinda, era kututma
mbu tuenda kuhubanganyisa
ebandu, ne kuburabo kwa oyu
Yesu i Ongo alondolaa kwa
kuchinjibusa rbandu boshi:
babasene anabe ne ba bafiri
mira.

43. Era luulu soyu Yesu, ye
barebi boshi bateta mbu chira
mundu ola ukamwemerera
Ongo akamubabalira ebibi

너 부아씨. 아바아 어찌러
아이리라 어반두 마부야 나
구떠 아쫘먀 보씨 바 바바아
바삐 뫄 부짜 붸 무시무. 어비
뵤씨, 아바아 어찌러 아비이라
부씨 오꼬

39. 가찌 어먀시 요씨 어라
여수 아이라아 뫄 찌오 쩌
바유다 노뫄 무시 워
여루사뻐무, 두바노
똬나찌뢰러라아 구이. 오유
여수, 이어반두 바어다아 뫄
구무마네가 과 무사쫘바,

40. 오꼬 어라 구모모쫘
어루수구 쫘 가하두, 나
아무뢴사 어라 무호또 서
바뚜.

41. 아다 어반두 보씨 부
바무뢴쫘아고, 시 두바노
오싸오, 두 오꼬 아뢴또쫘아
두찌뢴러러 궈이 먀시. 가찌
두바노 두 똬바아 뛩찌러 똬쫘
너 구뫄 아쫘우마 나이 어라
서 고뫄 과이.

42. 짜시따, 어라 구두두마 뿌
두어따 구후바까네사 어반두,
너 구부라보 과 오유 여수 이
오꼬 아뢴또쫘아 과
구찌찌부사 루반두 보씨:
바바서너 아나버 너 바 바피리
미라.

43. 어라 뢴우뢴 소유 여수, 여
바러비 보씨 바더다 뿌 찌라
무뚜 오라 우가뭐머러라 오꼬
아가무바바삐라 어비비 부씨

and healing all who were
under the power of the
devil, because God was with
him.

39. "We are witnesses of
everything he did in the
country of the Jews and in
Jerusalem. They killed him
by hanging him on a tree,

40. but God raised him
from the dead on the third
day and caused him to be
seen.

41. He was not seen by all
the people, but by
witnesses whom God had
already chosen--by us who
ate and drank with him
after he rose from the dead.

42. He commanded us to
preach to the people and to
testify that he is the one
whom God appointed as
judge of the living and the
dead.

43. All the prophets testify
about him that everyone
who believes in him
receives forgiveness of sins

bushi ne buashi bwesina layi. *Ebandju besinji mbaa babona emuchima mubuya-buya.*

너 부아씨 붜시나 롸에. *어바뉴 버시씨 빠씸 바보나 어무찌마 무부야-부야.*

through his name."

44. Abere Petero anachiri ahambala, ebandu boshi ba babaa bomvirisa echinwa cha Ongo, bera kubona emchima mubuya-buya.

44. 아버러 퍼더로 아나찌리 아하빠롸, 어바뚜 보씨 바 바바아 보뻐리사 어찌놔 짜 오꼬, 버라 구보나 어무찌마 무부야-부야.

44. While Peter was still speaking these words, the Holy Spirit came on all who heard the message.

45. Ba bemeresi boshi be bayuta babaa berekesise Petero, bera kusanwa busese mwa kulola kwa Ongo eresise ebandu besinji mbaa nabo emchima mubuya-buya.

45. 바 버머러시 보씨 버 바유다 바바아 버러거시서 퍼더로, 버라 구사놔 부서서 뫄 구뢰롸 과 오꼬 어러시서 어바뉴 버시씨 빠아 나보 어무찌마 무부야-부야.

45. The circumcised believers who had come with Peter were astonished that the gift of the Holy Spirit had been poured out even on the Gentiles.

46. Basanwa bacha, bushi ne kumva kwa abu bandu bera bateta mu manji mateta mayayaya ne kutonga Ongo. Petero alolire bacha, era kwire ateta mbu:

46. 바사놔 바짜, 부씨 너 구빠 과 아부 바뉴 버라 바더다 무 마씨 마더다 마야야야 너 구도뫄 오꼬. 퍼더로 아롤뤼러 바짜, 어라 귀러 아더다 뿌:

46. For they heard them speaking in tongues and praising God. Then Peter said,

47. E banyaketu, bano bandu babonyire emchima mubuya-buya kuuma netu, kuchiri cha chingatuma batabatisibwa mwa meshi?

47. 어 바냐거두, 바노 바뉴 바보내러 어무찌마 무부야-부야 구우마 너두, 구찌리 짜 찌빠두마 바다바디시봐 뫄 머씨?

47. "Can anyone keep these people from being baptized with water? They have received the Holy Spirit just as we have."

48. Bushi noku, era kuteta mbu babatisibwa kwsina lya Yesu Kirisito. Nabo bera bamwema mbu ekalaa nabo sinji suku kurebe.

48. 부씨 노구, 어라 구더다 뿌 바바디시봐 구시나 뢌 여수 기리시도. 나보 버라 바뭐마 뿌 어가롸아 나보 시씨 수구 구러버.

48. So he ordered that they be baptized in the name of Jesus Christ. Then they asked Peter to stay with them for a few days.

E Mikolo ye Ndjumwa Chikono 11

Petero afulyira ebemeresi b'e Yerusalemu kwa myasi y'e mulyimo wai.

퍼더로 아푸페띱 어버머러시 버 여루사퍼물 과 먀시 여 무페명 와이.

1. Endumwa ne banji bemersi ba babaa batula eYuteya bomvaa emwasi kwa ebandu besinji mbaa nabo bemerere echinwa cha Ongo.

1. 어뚜꽈 너 바찌 버머시 바 바바아 바두꽈 어유더야 보빠아 어꽈시 과 어바뚜 버시찌 빠아 나보 버머러러 어찌냐 짜 오꼬.

1. The apostles and the brothers throughout Judea heard that the Gentiles also had received the word of God.

2. Rero, mango Petero afulikaa eYerusalemu, ebemeresi be bayuta bera kumuhubanganya mbu:

2. 러로, 마꼬 퍼더로 아푸퀴가아 어여루사퍼무, 어버머러시 버 바유다 버라 구무후바꺄냐 뿌:

2. So when Peter went up to Jerusalem, the circumcised believers criticized him

3. Era! chi chatumaa wengirira mwa nyumba ye bandu besinji mbaa, kanji wanalya nabo?

3. 어라! 찌 짜두마아 워삐리라 먀 뉴빠 여 바뚜 버시찌 빠아, 가찌 와나퍄 나보?

3. and said, "You went into the house of uncircumcised men and ate with them."

4. Petero ku kwera kutangirisa abatondosesa chiuma kwa chiuma emyasi yoshi kwa yanatangirisaa, era kuburabo mbu:

4. 퍼더로 구 궈라 구다삐리사 아바도또서사 찌우마 과 찌우마 어먀시 요씨 과 야나다삐리사아, 어라 구부라보 뿌:

4. Peter began and explained everything to them precisely as it had happened:

5. Nyono, nabaa nyire biroto. Mwebi biroto, nera kulola kuyabunya ngwaya inene yatenga mwa chanya, yandaalira kwa chitaka ala nabaa nyinali. Ei ngwaya, yabaa isimbirirwe kwa mapembe mai mane.

5. 뇨노, 나바아 녀러 비로도. 뭐비 비로도, 너라 구뢰꽈 구야부냐 꽈야 이너너 야더삐 꽈 짜냐, 야따아퀴라 과 찌다가 아롸 나바아 녀나퀴. 어이 꽈야, 야바아 이시뻬리뤄 과 마퍼뻐 마이 마너.

5. "I was in the city of Joppa praying, and in a trance I saw a vision. I saw something like a large sheet being let down from heaven by its four corners, and it came down to where I was.

6. Abere naihunda kwe meho, nera kulola muli chira buko kwa bifuana bya bitusa birengebine alauma ne nyuma somwerunga, ne sa sende

6. 아버러 나이후따 궈 머호, 너라 구뢰꽈 무퓌 찌라 부고 과 비푸아나 뱌 비두사 비러뻐비너 아롸우마 너 뉴마 소뭐루꽈, 너 사 서떠

6. I looked into it and saw four-footed animals of the earth, wild beasts, reptiles, and birds of the air.

saendera kwa bula, alauma ne milonge.

7. Chasinda, nera kumva murenge muuma anyibura mbu Petero, emuka, ukere, unalye esi nyama!

8. Si nera kwakula mbu nanga enawetu! nyono ndafuraa kulya chiro na kandu na mwaso wetu atula atolire nga katakomisibwe*.

9. Si oyu murenge wabaa watengera kwa nguba, era kuhuba kunyibura mbu bya Ongo airire kuba bibuya, utabyerikaa mbu bitakomisibwe*

10. Abere oyu murenge anyikirira kahatu, byoshi kuna kuhuba kwa nguba.

11. Unao-unao, balume bahatu bera kuika mwa nyumba era nabaa nyirimo. Abu balumle, batumwaa era nyiri kutengera ekaisariya?.

12. Emchima mubuya-buya nai, era kunyibura mbu nyienda alauma nabo busira kusinda- sinda. Na bano banyeketu nda museneko, bu banyerekesaa na twengirira mwa mwa mulume muuma mbu i Korneliyo.

13. Oyu Korneliyo, era kutubalikisa kute kwa malaika*

사어떠라 과 부롸, 아롸우마 너 미롱떠.

7. 짜시따, 너라 구빠 무러떠 무우마 아네부라 뿌 퍼더로, 어무가, 우거러, 우나뎌 어시 냐마!

8. 시 너라 과구롸 뿌 나꺄 어나워두! 뇨노 따푸라아 구럊 찌로 나 가뚜 나 뫄소 워두 아두롸 아도뢰러 꺄 가다고미시붜*.

9. 시 오유 무러떠 와바아 와더떠라 과 우바, 어라 구후바 구네부라 뿌 뱌 오꼬 아이리러 구바 비부야, 우다뼈리가아 뿌 비다고미시붜*

10. 아버러 오유 무러떠 아네기리라 가하두, 뵤씨 구나 구후바 과 우바.

11. 우나오-우나오, 바루머 바하두 버라 구이가 뫄 뉴빠 어라 나바아 네리모. 아부 바루무뤄, 바두뫄아 어라 네리 구더떠라 어가이사리야?.

12. 어무찌마 무부야-부야 나이, 어라 구네부라 뿌 네어따 아롸우마 나보 부시라 구시따- 시따. 나 바노 바녀거두 따 무서너고, 부 바녀러거사아 나 뚸삐리라 뫄 뫄 무루머 무우마 뿌 이 고루너쀠요.

13. 오유 고루너쀠요, 어라 구두바뢰기사 구더 과

7. Then I heard a voice telling me, 'Get up, Peter. Kill and eat.'

8. "I replied, 'Surely not, Lord! Nothing impure or unclean has ever entered my mouth.'

9. "The voice spoke from heaven a second time, 'Do not call anything impure that God has made clean.'

10. This happened three times, and then it was all pulled up to heaven again.

11. "Right then three men who had been sent to me from Caesarea stopped at the house where I was staying.

12. The Spirit told me to have no hesitation about going with them. These six brothers also went with me, and we entered the man's house.

13. He told us how he had seen an angel appear in his

aluukira mwa mwai ne kumubura mbu eraa atumaa ebandu be yupa, bamungire Simoni Petero,

14. Bushi oyu simoni, iungamubura emyasi era ingamuretera ekalomo kesuku ne mango alauma nengumi yai.

15. Abere nera nanatangirisa nahambala, abu bandu bera kubona emchima mubuya-buya ngokwa netu twanabonaa'o lyebere.

16. Mwechi chihangi, nera kuktengera echinwa cha enawetu Yesu atetaa mbu Yowani abatisaa ebandu mwa meshi, si mwabo mungabatisibwa kwa mchima mubuya-buya.

17. Mango twemereraa enawetu Yesu Kirisito, Ongo era kutweresa emchima mubuya-buya.rero, akaba nabo angaberesao nyono nyi nera nde wekulwisa Ongo?

18. Abu bemersi, abere bomva bacha, boshi chiro bakachihubanganya kanji. Bera kwire batangirisa batonga Ongo mbu kasi ebandu besinji mbaa nabo, Ongo ababoorere enjira ye kibindula emyanya yabo

---

마롸이가* 아루우기라 뫄 뫄이 너 구무부라 뿌 어라아 아두마아 어바뚜 버 유파, 바무삐러 시모니 퍼더로,

14. 부씨 오유 시모니, 이우꺄무부라 어먀시 어라 이꺄무러더라 어가론모 거수구 너 마꼬 아롸우마 너우미 야이.

15. 아버러 너라 나나다삐리사 나하빠롸, 아부 바뚜 버라 구보나 어무찌마 무부야-부야 꼬과 너두 돠나보나아오 쪄버러.

16. 뭐찌 찌하삐, 너라 구구더삐러라 어찌놔 짜 어나워두 여수 아더다아 뿌 요와니 아바디사아 어바뚜 뫄 머씨, 시 뫄보 무꺄바디시봐 과 무찌마 무부야-부야.

17. 마꼬 뚸머러라아 어나워두 여수 기리시도, 오꼬 어라 구뚸러사 어무찌마 무부야-부야.러로, 아가바 나보 아꺄버러사오 뇨노 네 너라 떠워구쀠사 오꼬?

18. 아부 버머시, 아버러 보빠 빠짜, 보씨 찌로 바가찌후바꺄냐 가찌. 버라 귀러 바다삐리사 바도꺄 오꼬 뿌 가시 어바뚜 버시찌 빠아 나보, 오꼬 아바보오러러 어찌라 여 기비뿌롸 어먀냐 야보 바보너 어가꽈모!

---

house and say, 'Send to Joppa for Simon who is called Peter.

14. He will bring you a message through which you and all your household will be saved.'

15. "As I began to speak, the Holy Spirit came on them as he had come on us at the beginning.

16. Then I remembered what the Lord had said: 'John baptized withwater, but you will be baptized with the Holy Spirit.'

17. So if God gave them the same gift as he gave us, who believed in the Lord Jesus Christ, who was I to think that I could oppose God?"

18. When they heard this, they had no further objections and praised God, saying, "So then, God has granted even the Gentiles repentance unto life."

babone ekalamo!

Emwasi mubuya-buya wa Yesu aika mwa musi w'e Antiyokiya.

어꽈시 무부야-부야 와 여수 아이가 꽈 무시 워 아띠욉굿엣.

19. Era nyuma se kufa kwa Sitefano, ebemersi barengaa mu malibuko manene. Bauma bera kuhandabana kuikira mwa chio che Foinikiya, ne banji kwa chisimba che Chepuro, nebanji bera kunaikira nomva musi we Andiyokiya. Mwebi bisiki byoshi, bera kunde banahubanganya echinwa cha Ongo kwa bayuta beien oshao.

19. 어라 뉴마 서 구파 과 시더파노, 어버머시 바러꽈아 무 마뤼부고 마너너. 바우마 버라 구하따바나 구이기라 꽈 찌오 쩌 포이니기야, 너 바찌 과 찌시빠 쩌 쩌푸로, 너바찌 버라 구나이기라 노빠 무시 워 아띠요기야. 뭐비 비시기 뵤씨, 버라 구떠 바나후방바꽈냐 어찌놔 짜 오꼬 과 바유다 버이어누 오싸오.

19. Now those who had been scattered by the persecution in connection with Stephen traveled as far as Phoenicia, Cyprus and Antioch, telling the message only to Jews.

20. Si mwabu bemeresi mwabaa muli besha chipuro, na besha mwa chio che kurene. Abere baika e Andiyokiya, bera kunde bahubanganyisa ebakiriki nabo emwasi mubya-buya wa enawetu

20. 시 꽈부 버머러시 꽈바아 무뤼 버싸 찌푸로, 나 버싸 꽈 찌오 쩌 구러너. 아버러 바이가 어 아띠요기야, 버라 구떠 바후바꽈네사 어바기리기 나보 어꽈시 무뱌-부야 와 어나워두

20. Some of them, however, men from Cyprus and Cyrene, went to Antioch and began to speak to Greeks also, telling them the good news about the Lord Jesus.

21. Ebemeresi babaa bete ebuashio bwa Ongo, echera chera kutuma bandu banene bemerera emwasi wa enawetu, na bamualukira.

21. 어버머러시 바바아 버더 어부아씨오 봐 오꼬, 어쩌라 쩌라 구두마 바뚜 바너너 버머러라 어꽈시 와 어나워두, 나 바무아루기라.

21. The Lord's hand was with them, and a great number of people believed and turned to the Lord.

22. Abere ebemeresi be Yerusalemu bomva kwoyu mwasi, bera kutuma Barnaba eAndiyokiya.

22. 아버러 어버머러시 버 여루사쩌무 보빠 교유 꽈시, 버라 구두마 바루나바 어아띠요기야.

22. News of this reached the ears of the church at Jerusalem, and they sent Barnabas to Antioch.

23. Oyu Barnaba abaa atula

23. 오유 바루나바 아바아

23. When he arrived and

mundu mubuya kanji abaa
akoresibwa ne mchima
mubuya-buya, abaa atusa na
bwemeresi bunene.

24. Rero, mango abaa era
aikaayi, era kucholorera
kanangana kwa Ongo aanyire
abu bandu. Era kumowa
busese na kubabura mbu
emichima yabo yabo boshi
ianendekeraa kusera mwa
kuchinyiira enawetu.

25. Chasinda, Barnaba era
kutenga e Andiyokiya, era
kuya kuhondera Saulo mwa
musi we Tariso.

26. Mango amulolaako, era
kumureta eAndiyokiya. Bera
kumalyi mwaka wa mutenga
nenjire babuanana ne
bemeresi, na kunde
bakangirisa bandu banene era
luulu sa Yesu. Mwoyu musi,
mu bemeresi batangiriraa
berikwa mbu baKirisito.

27. Mwesi suku si nesi-sinesi,
berebi bauma nabo bera
kutengera eyerusalemu
bandaalira e andiyokiya.

28. Muuma mubo mbu
iAkabo, era kwimanga ne
kutetangirisa areba nemisi ye
mchima mubuya-buya.Era

아두꽈 무뚜 무부야 가찌
아바아 아고러시봐 너 무찌마
무부야-부야, 아바아 아두사
나 붜머러시 부너너.

24. 러로, 마꼬 아바아 어라
아이가아에, 어라 구쪼뢰러라
가나빠나 과 오꼬 아아니러
아부 바뚜. 어라 구모와
부서서 나 구바부라 뿌
어미찌마 야보 야보 보씨
이아너떠거라아 구서라 먀
구찌네이라 어나워두.

25. 짜시따, 바루나바 어라
구더빠 어 아띠요기야, 어라
구야 구호떠라 사우뢰 먀 무시
워 다리소.

26. 마꼬 아무뢰꽈아고, 어라
구무러다 어아띠요기야. 버라
구마뤠 꽈가 와 무더빠 너찌러
바부아나나 너 버머러시, 나
구떠 바가빠리사 바뚜 바너너
어라 루우뢰 사 여수. 모유
무시, 무 버머러시
바다빠리라아 버리과 뿌
바기리시도.

27. 뭐시 수구 시 너시-시너시,
버러비 바우마 나보 버라
구더빠라 어여루사뭐무
바따아삐라 어 아띠요기야.

28. 무우마 무보 뿌 이아가보,
어라 귀마빠 너 구더다삐리사
아러바 너미시 여 무찌마
무부야-부야.어라 구더다 뿌

saw the evidence of the
grace of God, he was glad
and encouraged them all to
remain true to the Lord
with all their hearts.

24. He was a good man, full
of the Holy Spirit and faith,
and a great number of
people were brought to the
Lord.

25. Then Barnabas went to
Tarsus to look for Saul,

26. and when he found him,
he brought him to Antioch.
So for a whole year
Barnabas and Saul met with
the church and taught great
numbers of people. The
disciples were called
Christians first at Antioch.

27. During this time some
prophets came down from
Jerusalem to Antioch.

28. One of them, named
Agabus, stood up and
through the Spirit predicted
that a severe famine would

kuteta mbu mwa butala boshi mungaika bulio bunene. Obu bulio, bwera kunaika mango mwami kaulatiyo abaa emire mwa musi we Roma.

29. Bushi noku, ebemresi bera kwire bemeresanya kuira muholore kukulikana nokwa chira mundu angaala, babone kute bangaasa bemersi balikabo ba bonaa,

30. Bera kwesao Barnaba na Saulo, nabo bera kwekera ebamangirisi be bemersi be Yerusalemu.

와 부다쫘 보씨 무꽈이가 뿌쮜오 부너너. 오부 뿌쮜오, 뿨라 구나이가 마꼬 꽈미 가우쫘디요 아바아 어미러 꽈 무시 워 로마.

29. 부씨 노구, 어버러시 버라 귀러 버머러사냐 구이라 무호로러 구구쮜가나 노과 쮜라 무뚜 아꽈아쫘, 바보너 구더 바꽈아사 버머시 바쮜가보 바 보나아,

30. 버라 귀사오 바루나바 나 사우로, 나보 버라 귀거라 어바마쮜리시 버 버머시 버 여루사뿌무.

spread over the entire Roman world. (This happened during the reign of Claudius.)

29. The disciples, each according to his ability, decided to provide help for the brothers living in Judea.

30. This they did, sending their gift to the elders by Barnabas and Saul.

E Mikolo ye Ndjumwa Chikono 12

Yakobo echibwa na Petero aumwa mwa buroko

1. Mwesi suku, mwami Heroti era kutangirisa kunde alibusa bauma mwa bemeresi.

2. Era kwichisa Yakobo munyakabo Yowani mwa bomba.

3. Mango Heroti alolaa kwa echera chasimise ebayuta, era kuteta kwa basimbaa na Petero. Ebyera byabaa mwa suku sikulu sa serikirwe mbu suku se mikati era itali mu

어 미고론 여 뿌꽈 쮜고노 12

야고보 어쮜봐 나 퍼더로 아우꽈 와 부로고

1. 뭐시 수구, 꽈미 허로디 어라 구다쮜리사 구너 아쮜부사 바우마 와 버머러시.

2. 어라 귀쮜사 야고보 무냐가보 요와니 와 보빠.

3. 마꼬 허로디 아로쫘아 과 어쩌라 쨔시미서 어바유다, 어라 구더다 과 바시빠아 나 퍼더로. 어벼라 뱌바아 와 수구 시구루 사 서리기뤄 뿌 수구 서 미가디 어라 이다쮜

Acts Chapter 12[NIV]

1. It was about this time that King Herod arrested some who belonged to the church, intending to persecute them.

2. He had James, the brother of John, put to death with the sword.

3. When he saw that this pleased the Jews, he proceeded to seize Peter also. This happened during the Feast of Unleavened Bread.

chachu*

무 짜쭈*

4. Abere era asimba Petero, era kumuuma mwa buroko. Era kubura bikembe beine bya basula bane-bane mbu bamulangaa. Abu basula, bendee bakola bauma era nyuma se se banji. Airaa bacha, bushi abaa ahonda amutonganye era muhondo se bandu mango epasaka* ingaba yarengire.

4. 아버러 어라 아시빠 퍼더로, 어라 구무우마 뫄 부로고. 어라 구부라 비거뻐 버이너 뱌 바수꽈 바너-바너 뿌 바무꽈아아. 아부 바수꽈, 버떠어 바고꽈 바우마 어라 뉴마 서 서 바찌. 아이라아 바짜, 부씨 아바아 아호따 아무도꺄녀 어라 무호또 서 바뚜 마꼬 어파사가* 이까바 야러끼러.

4. After arresting him, he put him in prison, handing him over to be guarded by four squads of four soldiers each. Herod intended to bring him out for public trial after the Passover.

5. Petero era kunekala alangibwa mubu buroko, si ebemersi bera kunaendekera bamwemera era mwa Ongo na bushiru bunene.

5. 퍼더로 어라 구너가꽈 아롸끼봐 무부 부로고, 시 어버머시 버라 구나어떠거라 바뭐머라 어라 뫄 오꼬 나 부씨루 부너너.

5. So Peter was kept in prison, but the church was earnestly praying to God for him.

Malaika wa Enawechwu akula Petero mwa buroko

마꽈일— 와 어나워쭈 아구꽈 퍼더로 뫄 부로고

6. Ebutufu bwera muhondo se lusuku lwa Heroti abaa alalira kutonganya mu Petero, Petero abaa aonjire ala kachi-kachi ka basula babiri. Abaa aminyirirwe na mareure mabiri, nokwa chiso che buroko kwabaa kuli balanzi.

6. 어부두푸 붜라 무호또 서 루수구 꽈 허로디 아바아 아꽈삐라 구도꺄냐 무 퍼더로, 퍼더로 아바아 아오꼬러 아롸 가찌-가찌 가 바수꽈 바비리. 아바아 아미니리뤄 나 마러우러 마비리, 노과 찌소 쩌 부로고 과바아 구뤼 바롸씨.

6. The night before Herod was to bring him to trial, Peter was sleeping between two soldiers, bound with two chains, and sentries stood guard at the entrance.

7. Unao-unao, malaika*muuma wa Enawetu era kupamukira, nechasi kuna kulomekera mwa chumba cha

7. 우나오-우나오, 마꽈이가*무우마 와 어나워두 어라 구파무기라, 너짜시 구나 구뤂머거라 뫄 쭘빠 짜 바바아

7. Suddenly an angel of the Lord appeared and a light shone in the cell. He struck Peter on the side and woke

babaa balimo. Oyu malaika*,

8. Era kuhaanya-hanya Petero amususe, era kumubura mbu: batukaa fuba! ma mareure mabaa mamunyirire emaboko, kuna kuchitowangira.

9. Petero era kunauluka mwa burokoakulikira oyu malaika*si atamenyaa kwa bya malaika*abaa aira byabaa biri bya kanangana. Era kuchichinga mbu ali mu byabunya biroto.

10. Abere bera bahukaa echikembe chibere-bere che balanzi, ne chakabiri, bera kuika kwa lwisi lwechuma lwa lwabaa lwerekere mwa musi. Olu lwisi, kuna kuchiboola lweine mwa meho mabo, na bauluka. Bera kuenzikanya mu mwengere muuma, unao-unao ola malaika* era kumureka.

11. Abere Petero era ebwenge, era kuteta mbu: nerire namenyerera kanangana kwa enawetu iwatumaa malaika* wai anyinunula kutenga mwa mino sa Heroti ne mwa mabi moshi ma bayuta babaa

---

바뤼모. 오유 마콰이가*,

8. 어라 구하아냐-하냐 퍼더로 아무수서, 어라 구무부라 뿌: 바두가아 푸바! 마 마러우러 마바아 마무네리러 어마보고, 구나 구찌도와끼라.

9. 퍼더로 어라 구나우루가 콰 부로고아구릐기라 오유 마콰이가*시 아다머냐아 과 뱌 마콰이가*아바아 아이라 뱌바아 비리 뱌 가나꽈나. 어라 구찌찌까 뿌 아릐 무 뱌부냐 비로도.

10. 아버러 버라 바후가아 어찌거뻐 찌버러-버러 쩌 바콰씨, 너 짜가비리, 버라 구이가 과 뤼시 뤄쭈마 콰 콰바아 뤄러거러 콰 무시. 오루 뤼시, 구나 구찌보오콰 뤄이너 콰 머호 마보, 나 바우루가. 버라 구어씨가냐 무 뭐꺼러 무우마, 우나오-우나오 오콰 마콰이가* 어라 구무러가.

11. 아버러 퍼더로 어라 어붜꺼, 어라 구더다 뿌: 너리러 나머녀러라 가나꽈나 과 어나워두 이와두마아 마콰이가* 와이 아네누누콰 구더까 콰 미노 사 허로디 너 콰 마비 모씨 마 바우다 바바아 바호따 바네리러.

---

him up. "Quick, get up!" he said, and the chains fell off Peter's wrists.

8. Then the angel said to him, "Put on your clothes and sandals." And Peter did so. "Wrap your cloak around you and follow me," the angel told him.

9. Peter followed him out of the prison, but he had no idea that what the angel was doing was really happening; he thought he was seeing a vision.

10. They passed the first and second guards and came to the iron gate leading to the city. It opened for them by itself, and they went through it. When they had walked the length of one street, suddenly the angel left him.

11. Then Peter came to himself and said, "Now I know without a doubt that the Lord sent his angel and rescued me from Herod's clutches and from everything the Jewish people were anticipating."

bahonda banyirire.

12. Mango era amenyerera kubuya-buya byabyabere, era kuya ala mwa mariya nyina wa Yowani, ola wasulwaa esina lya Mariko. Mwei nyumba, mwabaa mubwanaanyire bandu banene bababaa bema Ongo,

13. Petero era kukongota kwa lwisi lwera butala. Muandakasi muuma mbu iRota era kuya komvirisa kwa lwisi.

14. Era kumenyerera emurenge wa Petero, si bushi ne lumoo chiro akachingula lwa lwisi. Era kulibichira mwa n yumba aya kubura ebandu kwa Petero iuliko.

15. Nabo bera kumwakula mbu Emwa! wasirire! si Rota na imbu: nechi betu! emurengewa Petero inomvire, bera kutangirisa bateta mbu: umh! oyola ali malaika* wa Petero

16. Petero kukwera kubasimira mwa mino mbu basiraa. Era kutangirisa abalikisabo kute ku enawetu amukula mwa buroko.

12. 마꼬 어라 아머녀러라 구부야-부야 뱌뱌버러, 어라 구야 아꽈 뫄 마리야 녜나 와 요와니, 오꽈 와수꽈아 어시나 랴 마리고. 뭐이 뉴빠, 뫄바아 무봐나아녜러 바뚜 바녀너 바바바아 버마 오꼬,

13. 퍼더로 어라 구고꼬다 과 뤼시 뤄라 부다꽈. 무아따가시 무우마 뿌 이로다 어라 구야 고뻬리사 과 뤼시.

14. 어라 구머녀러라 어무러꺼 와 퍼더로, 시 부씨 너 루모오 찌로 아가찌꾸꽈 꽈 뤼시. 어라 구뤼비찌라 뫄 누 유빠 아야 구부라 어바뚜 과 퍼더로 이우뤼고.

15. 나보 버라 구뫄구꽈 뿌 어뫄! 와시리러! 시 로다 나 이뿌: 너찌 버두! 어무러꺼와 퍼더로 이노뻬러, 버라 구다삐리사 바더다 뿌: 우무후!오요꽈 아뤼 마꽈이가* 와 퍼더로

16. 퍼더로 구귀라 구바시미라 뫄 미노 뿌 바시라아. 어라 구다삐리사 아바뤼기사보 구더 구 어나워두 아무구꽈 뫄 부로고.

12. When this had dawned on him, he went to the house of Mary the mother of John, also called Mark, where many people had gathered and were praying.

13. Peter knocked at the outer entrance, and a servant girl named Rhoda came to answer the door.

14. When she recognized Peter's voice, she was so overjoyed she ran back without opening it and exclaimed, "Peter is at the door!"

15. "You're out of your mind," they told her. When she kept insisting that it was so, they said, "It must be his angel."

16. But Peter kept on knocking, and when they opened the door and saw him, they were astonished.

17. Era kubabura kanji mbu: mubaliraa Yakobo nebanji bemeresi kwene myasi. Chasinjire, era kuuluka, era kuya mu chinji chisiki.

18. Abere mwei mishangya, ba basula ebwenge bwera kubasungulira busese. Bera kutangirisa babusanya mbu Ewashe! chi oyu Petero afire betu?

19. Heroti era kuteta mbu bamuhondaa, si chiro bakamulaako. Era kutonganya ebalanzi bababaa bamulanga, era kuteta mbu bechibwaa. Chasinda, heroti era kutenga eyuteya andalira mwa mus iwa kaisariya. Era kubera moyu musi suku burebi.

Ekufa kwa mwami Herode Akiripa

20. Mwesi suku, heroti abaa asibukirire besha mwa musi we Tiro ne we Sitone. Si besha ei misi, bera kulaana kuya kumulolako. Bera komvikana tanga na balasito iwabaa wemangirire ebakosi bomwa nyumba ya mwami. Bera kwema baate ebolo na mwami, bushi ebiyo bya

---

17. 어라 구바부라 가찌 뿌: 무바삐라아 야고보 너바찌 버머러시 궈너 먀시. 짜시띠러, 어라 구우루가, 어라 구야 무 찌찌 찌시기.

18. 아버러 뭐이 미싸꺄, 바 바수꽈 어붸꺼 붜라 구바수꾸삐라 부서서. 버라 구다삐리사 바부사냐 뿌 어와써! 찌 오유 퍼더로 아피러 버두?

19. 허로디 어라 구더다 뿌 바무호따야, 시 찌로 바가무라아고. 어라 구도꺄냐 어바꽈씨 바바바아 바무꽈꽈, 어라 구더다 뿌 버찌봐아. 짜시따, 허로디 어라 구더꽈 어유더야 아따삐라 꽈 무수 이와 가이사리야. 어라 구버라 모유 무시 수구 부러비.

어구파 과 꽈미 허로더 아기리파

20. 뭐시 수구, 허로디 아바아 아시부기리러 버싸 꽈 무시 워 디로 너 워 시도너. 시 버싸 어이 미시, 버라 구꽈아나 구야 구무론라고. 버라 고삐가나 다꽈 나 바꽈시도 이와바아 워마삐리러 어바고시 보꽈 뉴빠 야 꽈미. 버라 궈마 바아더 어보론 나 꽈미, 부씨 어비요 뱌 버띠어 바꺄, 꽈

---

17. Peter motioned with his hand for them to be quiet and described how the Lord had brought him out of prison. "Tell James and the brothers about this," he said, and then he left for another place.

18. In the morning, there was no small commotion among the soldiers as to what had become of Peter.

19. After Herod had a thorough search made for him and did not find him, he cross-examined the guards and ordered that they be executed. Then Herod went from Judea to Caesarea and stayed there a while.

20. He had been quarreling with the people of Tyre and Sidon; they now joined together and sought an audience with him. Having secured the support of Blastus, a trusted personal servant of the king, they asked for peace, because they depended on the king'

bendee balya, mwa chio chai 찌오 짜이 무 벼떠어 뱌더꺄.
mu byendee byatenga.

21. Abere elusuku lwa balaana lwaika, heroti era kwimbala enjimba sai se bwami. Era kwekala kwa ndbe yai ye bwami, casinda era kubura abandu myasi inene

21. 아버러 어루수구 꽈 바쫘아나 쫘이가, 허로디 어라 귀빠쫘 어찌빠 사이 서 봐미. 어라 궈가쫘 과 뚜버 야이 여 봐미, 시아시따 어라 구부라 아바뚜 먀시 이너너

21. On the appointed day Herod, wearing his royal robes, sat on his throne and delivered a public address to the people.

22. Abu bandu bera kutangirisa bauma emirenge mbu nechi! atachiri murenge wa mundumu wa enawetu kuna kuhuta heroti bulwala, bushi atokaa etunda lya Ongo kuba lyai.

22. 아부 바뚜 버라 구다삐리사 바우마 어미러꺼 뿌 너찌! 아다찌리 무러꺼 와 무뚜마 와 어나워두 구나 구후다 허로디 부쫘쫘, 부씨 아도가아 어두따 랴 오꼬 구바 쨔이.

22. They shouted, "This is the voice of a god, not of a man."

23. Bushi noku, enzoka somwa bula sera kumuluma, era kufa.

23. 부씨 노구, 어쏘가 소꽈 부쫘 서라 구무루마, 어라 구파.

23. Immediately, because Herod did not give praise to God, an angel of the Lord struck him down, and he was eaten by worms and died.

24. Si chiro bacha, echinwa cha Ongo chanaendekeraa kuya era muhondo na kuhandabana mu bisiki binene.

24. 시 찌로 바짜, 어찌놔 짜 오꼬 짜나어떠거라아 구야 어라 무호또 나 구하따바나 무 비시기 비너너.

24. But the word of God continued to increase and spread.

25. Mango Barnaba na Saulo babaa bera bamalaa emulimo wabo eyerusalemu, bera kutengayi alauma na Yowani ola wasula esina lya Mariko.

25. 마꼬 바루나바 나 사우론 바바아 버라 바마쫘아 어무쮜모 와보 어여루사뻐무, 버라 구더빠에 아쫘우마 나 요와니 오쫘 와수쫘 어시나 쨔 마리고.

25. When Barnabas and Saul had finished their mission, they returned from Jerusalem, taking with them John, also called Mark.

E Mikolo ye Ndjumwa Chikono 13

어 미고로 여 뚜똬 찌고노 13 Acts Chapter 13[NIV]

EMchima mubuya-buya alondola Barnaba na Saulo

어무찌마 무부야-부야
아로또똬 바루나바 나 사우로

1. Mwa bemersi ba babaa batula mwa musi we Andiyokiya, mwabaa muli barebi na bakangirisi:barnaba, na Simoni ola qasulwaa esina lya Nikeri, na lukiyo mwesha mwa musi we Kurene, na Saulo, na Mananeni ola wakuliraa aluama na mwami Heroti.

1. 똬 버머시 바 바바아 바두똬 똬 무시 워 아띠요기야, 똬바아 무뛰 바러비 나 바가끼리시:바루나바, 나 시모니 오똬 구아수똬아 어시나 랴 니거리, 나 루기요 뭐싸 똬 무시 워 구러너, 나 사우로, 나 마나너니 오똬 와구뤠라아 아루아마 나 똬미 허로디.

1. In the church at Antioch there were prophets and teachers: Barnabas, Simeon called Niger, Lucius of Cyrene, Manaen (who had been brought up with Herod the tetrarch) and Saul.

2. Lusuku luuma baba bali mwa lubuanano lw kutonga Enawetu, bali nomwa memo ma mende mairwa busira kulya. Ecmchima mubuya-buya era kueteta mbu munyibikiraa Barnaba na Saulo ala musiki bushi ne mulimo ola nabalonderere.

2. 루수구 루우마 바바 바뛰 똬 루부아나노 루우 구도똬 어나워두, 바뛰 노똬 머모 마 머떠 마이똬 부시라 구꺄. 어시무찌마 무부야-부야 어라 구어더다 뿌 무네비기라아 바루나바 나 사우로 아똬 무시기 부씨 너 무뤼모 오똬 나바로떠러러.

2. While they were worshiping the Lord and fasting, the Holy Spirit said, "Set apart for me Barnabas and Saul for the work to which I have called them."

3. Mango babaa banachiri mwa mumemo, bera kubabika kwe mino kwa kubemera, chasinda, bera kubareka baende.

3. 마꼬 바바아 바나찌리 똬 무머모, 버라 구바비가 꿔 미노 과 구버머라, 짜시따, 버라 구바러가 바어떠.

3. So after they had fasted and prayed, they placed their hands on them and sent them off.

Saulo na Barnaba bahubanganya e chinwa cha Ongo

사우로 나 바루나바 바후바똬넷 어 찌놔 짜 오꼬

4. Mango emchima mubuya-buya abaa era atumaa Barnaba na Saulo mwa mulimo, bera kwandalira mwa musi we sereukiya. Mwoyu musi, mu beraa batorera ebwato na bahubukira kwa chisimba che chipuro.

5. Abere baika mwa musi we salami, bera kunde bahubanganyisa ebandu echinwa cha Ongo mwa mashenge me bayuta. Yowani nai abaa alinabo kwa kunde abaasa.

6. Era nyuma se kusungula echi chisimba choshi, bera kuika mwa musi we Pafo. Bera kubuanamo muhonga muuma wa muyuta mbun i Bara-Yesu. Oyu Bara-Yesu abaa enjire achiira murebi*.

7. Oyu muhonga atula womwa chikali che mukulu-kulu wechi chisimba mbu i serikiyo paulusi. Oyu serikiyo, abaa mundu wa bwenge. Era kuteta mbu bamwa malira Barnaba na Saulo bushi abaa ahonda omve kwa chinwa cha Ongo.

8. Si oyu muhonga erema(ku esina lyai litechire bacha mwa chikiriki) era kunana emyasi yabo. Era kuhponda

---

4. 마꼬 어무찌마 무부야-부야 아바아 어라 아두마아 바루나바 나 사우로 꽈 무뢰모, 버라 과따뢰라 꽈 무시 워 서러우기야. 모유 무시, 무 버라아 바도러라 어봐도 나 바후부기라 과 찌시빠 쩌 찌푸로.

5. 아버러 바이가 꽈 무시 워 사꽈미, 버라 구너 바후바까니사 어바누 어찌놔 짜 오꼬 꽈 마써꺼 머 바유다. 요와니 나이 아바아 아뤼나보 과 구너 아바아사.

6. 어라 뉴마 서 구수우꽈 어찌 찌시빠 쪼씨, 버라 구이가 꽈 무시 워 파포. 버라 구부아나모 무호꽈 무우마 와 무유다 뿌누 이 바라-여수. 오유 바라-여수 아바아 어찌러 아찌이라 무러비*.

7. 오유 무호꽈 아두꽈 올꽈 찌가뤼 쩌 무구루-구루 워찌 찌시빠 뿌 이 서리기요 파우루씨. 오유 서리기요, 아바아 무뚜 와 붸꺼. 어라 구더다 뿌 바꽈 마뤼라 바루나바 나 사우로 부씨 아바아 아호따 오뻐 과 찌놔 짜 오꼬.

8. 시 오유 무호꽈 어러마(구 어시나 꺄이 뤼더찌러 바짜 꽈 찌기리기) 어라 구나나 어먀시 야보. 어라 구후포따

---

4. The two of them, sent on their way by the Holy Spirit, went down to Seleucia and sailed from there to Cyprus.

5. When they arrived at Salamis, they proclaimed the word of God in the Jewish synagogues. John was with them as their helper.

6. They traveled through the whole island until they came to Paphos. There they met a Jewish sorcerer and false prophet named Bar-Jesus,

7. who was an attendant of the proconsul, Sergius Paulus. The proconsul, an intelligent man, sent for Barnabas and Saul because he wanted to hear the word of God.

8. But Elymas the sorcerer (for that is what his name means) opposed them and tried to turn the proconsul

kukongobanya oyu mukulu-kulu angesha kwemerera Yesu. 구고ᄭᅡ바냐 오유 무구루-구루 아ᄭᅥ싸 궈머러라 여수. from the faith.

9. Rero, Saulo iwerikwaa mbu Paulo, bushi abaa akoresibwa ne mchima mubuya-buya, era kumutumbukisa.

9. 러로, 사우로 이워리과아 뿌파우로, 부씨 아바아 아고러시봐 너 무찌마 무부야-부야, 어라 구무두뿌기사.

9. Then Saul, who was also called Paul, filled with the Holy Spirit, looked straight at Elymas and said,

10. Era kumubura mbu: Eumuala wa wamusimu! mwa mchima wao mwehwire butebanyi ne burenzi bwa burengerese. Woyo utumva byoshi bya biri bye kanangana. Kanji utakanareke kunde waorombya e mwasi we kuli wa enawetu?

10. 어라 구무부라 뿌: 어우무아꽈 와 와무시무! 꽈 무찌마 와오 뭐휘러 부더바네 너 부러씨 봐 부러ᄭᅥ러서. 오요 우두빠 뵤씨 뱌 비리 뼈 가나ᄭᅡ나. 가찌 우다가나러거 구떠 와오로빠 어 뫄시 워 구찌 와 어나워두?

10. "You are a child of the devil and an enemy of everything that is right! You are full of all kinds of deceit and trickery. Will you never stop perverting the right ways of the Lord?

11. Rero, enawetu angakulosa kwa kasibu ungaba chiumi-umi, ku suku burebe utalole kwe suba. Unao- unao, emusimya kuna kuya mwa meho mai, kuikira kwa bihangi era kunaba chiumi-umi. Era kutangirisa amamata-mamata ahonda ola ungamutandaisa.

11. 러로, 어나워두 아ᄭᅡ구로사 과 가시부 우ᄭᅡ바 찌우미-우미, 구 수구 부러버 우다로러 궈 수바. 우나오-우나오, 어무시먀 구나 구야 와 머호 마이, 구이기라 과 비하ᄭᅵ 어라 구나바 찌우미-우미. 어라 구다띠리사 아마마다-마마다 아호따 오꽈 우ᄭᅡ무다따이샤.

11. Now the hand of the Lord is against you. You are going to be blind, and for a time you will be unable to see the light of the sun." Immediately mist and darkness came over him, and he groped about, seeking someone to lead him by the hand.

12. Mango oyu mukulu-kulu alolaa kwebya byabere, era kusanwa busese bushi nemyasi ya Enawetu. Bushi noku era kwemerera Yesu.

12. 마ᄭᅩ 오유 무구루-구루 아로꽈아 궈뱌 뱌버러, 어라 구사놔 부서서 부씨 너먀시 야 어나워두. 부씨 노구 어라 궈머러라 여수.

12. When the proconsul saw what had happened, he believed, for he was amazed at the teaching about the Lord.

Paulo na Barnaba mwa musi w'e Antiyokiya 파우로 나 바루나바 뫄 무시 워 아ᄯᅵ욉굿엣

13. Era n yuma qebi, Paulo na balikabo bera kutola ebwato batenga mwa musi we Pafo na bahubukira mwa we Perika mwa chio che Pamufiriya. Baikire mwoyu musi, Yowani ola wasulwaa esina lya Marko era kulikanuka nabo, era kuhuba eyerusalemu.

13. 어라 누 유마 구어비, 파우로 나 바ㄹ리가보 버라 구도ㄹ라 어봐도 바더ㅇ까 뫄 무시 워 파포 나 바후부기라 뫄 워 퍼리가 뫄 찌오 쩌 파무피리야. 바이기러 뫄유 무시, 요와니 오ㄹ라 와수ㄹ롸아 어시나 ㄹ랴 마루고 어라 구ㄹ리가누가 나보, 어라 구후바 어여루사ㄹ러무.

13. From Paphos, Paul and his companions sailed to Perga in Pamphylia, where John left them to return to Jerusalem.

14. Si Paulo na Barnaba beke, bera kutenga eperika, bera kuendekera ne lubalamo lwabo na baika e Andiyokiya mwa chio che pisitiya. Elusuku lwe sabato*, bera kwengirira mwa bushenge bwe bayuta*, bera kwekalamo.

14. 시 파우로 나 바루나바 버거, 버라 구더ㅇ까 어퍼리가, 버라 구어ㄸ거라 너 루바ㄹ라모 ㄹ롸보 나 바이가 어 아ㄸ이요기야 뫄 찌오 쩌 피시디야. 어루수구 뤄 사바도*, 버라 궈ㅇ기리라 뫄 부써ㅇ거 붜 바유다*, 버라 궈가ㄹ라모.

14. From Perga they went on to Pisidian Antioch. On the Sabbath they entered the synagogue and sat down.

15. Abere bamala kusoma mwa bitabu bwe mwaso wa musa ne bya barebi, ebakulu-kulu be bushenge be bayuta* bera kubatumira mundu muuma aye kubabura mbu: ebanayaketu, akaba mwete mwasi ola mungabalira ebandu mwa kubasesa emchima, mwiree mwateta.

15. 아버러 바마ㄹ라 구소마 뫄 비다부 붜 뫄소 와 무사 너 뱌 바러비, 어바구루-구루 버 부써ㅇ거 버 바유다* 버라 구바두미라 무뚜 무우마 아여 구바부라 뿌: 어바나야거두, 아가바 뭐더 뫄시 오ㄹ라 무ㅇ까바ㄹ리라 어바뚜 뫄 구바서사 어무찌마, 뮈러어 뫄더다.

15. After the reading from the Law and the Prophets, the synagogue rulers sent word to them, saying, "Brothers, if you have a message of encouragement for the people, please speak."

16. Paulo kukwera kubatuka era kubika emino mwa chanya kwa kubura ebandu mbu basiraa. Era kuteta mbu: emubenyi isiraeli, nyonu mu banji mu mutula mutunjire Ongo munyumvirisaa!

16. 파우로 구궈라 구바두가 어라 구비가 어미노 뫄 짜냐 과 구부라 어바뚜 뿌 바시라아. 어라 구더다 뿌: 어무버니 이시라어ㄹ리, 뇨누 무 바ㅉ지 무 무두ㄹ라 무두ㅉ지러 오ㅇ고 무뉴ㅃ미리사아!

16. Standing up, Paul motioned with his hand and said: "Men of Israel and you Gentiles who worship God, listen to me!

17. Ongo woluno lubaa lwe baisiraeli, iwalondolaa bahokulu betu. Era kubaira kuba lubaa lunene mango babaa bali baenyi mwa chio che Misri. Chasinda, era kubakula mwechi chio kwa buashi bai bunene.

18. Kanji era kuna balanga myaka ingaika ku mane mwa buyeye*.

19. Nera nyuma se kusikya mbaa sirinda somwa chio che kanana, era kweresabo echi chio kuba chabo esuku ne mango.

20. Ebi byoshi byamala myaka ingaika maana mane na matano. Chasinda, era kuberesa ebasusu kuikira esuku sa murebi* semweri.

21. Chasinda, bera kutangirisabema emwami.Ongo era kuberesa Saulo muala wa Kisi, womwa chirongo cha Benyamina. Oyu Saulo, era kwema myaka mane.

22. Era nyuma se kukula Saulo kwa bwami, Ongo era kwemika Tauti. Oyu Tauti iOngo atetaa era luulu sa imbu: nachilonderere Tauti mwenye Yese bushi ali mundu ola unyisimisise, kanji iukaira

17. 오꼬 올루노 루루바아 뤄 바이시라어삐, 이와르또쫘아 바호구루 버두. 어라 구바이라 구바 루루바아 루너너 마오 바바아 바삐 바어네 똬 찌오 쩌 미주리. 짜시따, 어라 구바구꽈 뭐찌 찌오 과 부아씨 바이 부너너.

18. 가찌 어라 구나 바꽈 먀가 이까이가 구 마너 똬 부여여*.

19. 너라 뉴마 서 구시갸 빠아 시리따 소똬 찌오 쩌 가나나, 어라 궈러사보 어찌 찌오 구바 짜보 어수구 너 마꼬.

20. 어비 뵤씨 뱌마쫘 먀가 이까이가 마아나 마너 나 마다노. 짜시따, 어라 구버러사 어바수수 구이기라 어수구 사 무러비* 서뭐리.

21. 짜시따, 버라 구다삐리사버마 어똬미.오꼬 어라 구버러사 사우로 무아꽈 와 기시, 오똬 찌로꼬 짜 버냐미나. 오유 사우로, 어라 궈마 먀가 마너.

22. 어라 뉴마 서 구구꽈 사우로 과 봐미, 오꼬 어라 궈미가 다우디. 오유 다우디 이오꼬 아더다아 어라 루우루 사 이뿌: 나찌로떠러러 다우디 뭐녀 여서 부씨 아삐 무뚜 오꽈 우네시미시서, 가찌

17. The God of the people of Israel chose our fathers; he made the people prosper during their stay in Egypt, with mighty power he led them out of that country,

18. he endured their conduct for about forty years in the desert,

19. he overthrew seven nations in Canaan and gave their land to his people as their inheritance.

20. All this took about 450 years. "After this, God gave them judges until the time of Samuel the prophet.

21. Then the people asked for a king, and he gave them Saul son of Kish, of the tribe of Benjamin, who ruled forty years.

22. After removing Saul, he made David their king. He testified concerning him: 'I have found David son of Jesse a man after my own heart; he will do everything I want him to do.'

ekuhonda kwa nyi koshi.

이우가이라 어구호따 과 네 고씨.

23. Nolu lubuto lwa Tauti, lu Ongo alondolaa mbu Yesu ashokaamo, na kumuira mununusi web a isiraeli, kukulikana ne chirane chai.

23. 노루 루부도 롸 다우디, 루 오꼬 아로또롸아 뿌 여수 아쏘가아모, 나 구무이라 무누누시 워부 아 이시라어삐, 구구삐가나 너 찌라너 짜이.

23. "From this man's descendants God has brought to Israel the Savior Jesus, as he promised.

24. Eramundo Yesu aike, Yowani abaa ahubanganyisise ebaisiraeli boshi kwa babindulaa emyanya yabo, babatisibwe.

24. 어라무또 여수 아이거, 요와니 아바아 아후바빠네시서 어바이시라어삐 보씨 과 바비뚜롸아 어먀냐 야보, 바바디시붸.

24. Before the coming of Jesus, John preached repentance and baptism to all the people of Israel.

25. Mango Yowani abaa ahonda okumala omulimo wai, era kunde abusa abandu mbu: mwenjire mwanyisqa mbu nyire nde mutachichinga mbu nyono muwende mwalinjira. Si si mumenyerra kwa eranyuma sanyi, kungaba mundu ola inanyi ndete kwanyiri kwa kungatuma nabona ebuashi bwe kuboola emirisi ye birato byai.

25. 마꼬 요와니 아바아 아호따 오구마롸 오무삐모 와이, 어라 구떠 아부사 아바뚜 뿌: 뭐찌러 모네수구아 뿌 니러 떠 무다찌찌빠 뿌 뇨노 무워떠 롸삐찌라. 시 시 무머녀라 과 어라뉴마 사니, 구빠바 무뚜 오롸 이나니 떠더 과네리 과 구빠두마 나보나 어부아씨 붸 구보오롸 어미리시 여 비라도 뱌이.

25. As John was completing his work, he said: 'Who do you think I am? I am not that one. No, but he is coming after me, whose sandals I am not worthy to untie.'

26. Banyeketu, mumwashoka ku Abrahamu, nenyu mu bandu besinji mbaa mu mutula mutunjire Ongo, mumenyereraa kwa tubano tu Ongo atumiraa ono mwasi webununusi.

26. 바녀거두, 무롸쏘가 구 아부라하무, 너뉴 무 바뚜 버시찌 빠아 무 무두롸 무두찌러 오꼬, 무머녀러라아 과 두바노 두 오꼬 아두미라아 오노 마시 워부누누시.

26. "Brothers, children of Abraham, and you God-fearing Gentiles, it is to us that this message of salvation has been sent.

27. Si besha eyrusalemu alauma ne bakulu-kulu babo, batamenyerera kwa Yesu ali mununusi. Kanji batendee

27. 시 버싸 어위루사러무 아롸우마 너 바구루-구루 바보, 바다머녀러라 과 여수 아삐 무누누시. 가찌 바더떠어

27. The people of Jerusalem and their rulers did not recognize Jesus, yet in condemning him they

bemerera ne maanjiko me barebi ma mendee masobibwa chira lusuku lwe sabato*.

28. Bushi noku, mwa kumuchichibusa mbu echibwa mu beree baira kwa mu maanjiko matula matechire.

29. Abere byoshi bya byanjikwaa era luulu sai byera byabaa, ebandu bera kwandaasa echirunda chai kwa musalaba na batabachi mwa chinjifwa.

30. Si Ongo era kumwomola.

31. Na ku suku sinene, Yesu abaa enjire achilosa kwa bandu ba baenda nai kutenga akalilaya berukira eyerusalemu. Nabo, bu bera benjire bahambalira ebanji baisiraeli emyasi bachilorerako era luulu sai.

32. Netu, oyu mwasi lubuya-buya ola Ongoi alaanya bahokulu betu itwabahubanganyisa.

33. Rero, mwa kwomola Yesu, Ongo erire alosa echi chilaano* ku tubano tu bana babo, kukulikana nokwa maanjiko matula matechire mwa chitabu cha saburi

버머러라 너 마아찌고 머 바러비 마 머떠어 마소비봐 찌라 룬수구 뤄 사바도*.

28. 부씨 노구, 뫄 구무찌찌부사 뿌 어찌봐 무 버러어 바이라 과 무 마아찌고 마두콰 마더찌러.

29. 아버러 뵤씨 뱌 뱌찌과아 어라 룬우루 사이 벼라 뱌바아, 어바뚜 버라 과따아사 어찌루따 짜이 과 무사콰바 나 바다바찌 뫄 찌찌퐈.

30. 시 오꼬 어라 구모모콰.

31. 나 구 수구 시너너, 여수 아바아 어찌러 아찌로사 과 바뚜 바 바어따 나이 구더꽈 아가릐콰야 버루기라 어여루사뤄무. 나보, 부 버라 버찌러 바하빠릐라 어바찌 바이시라어릐 어먀시 바찌론러라고 어라 룬우루 사이.

32. 너두, 오유 뫄시 룬부야-부야 오콰 오꼬이 아콰아냐 바호구룬 버두 이돠바후바꽈네사.

33. 러로, 뫄 고모콰 여수, 오꼬 어리러 아로사 어찌 찌콰아노* 구 두바노 두 바나 바보, 구구릐가나 노과 마아찌고 마두콰 마더찌러 뫄 찌다부 짜 사부리 찌삐 짜

fulfilled the words of the prophets that are read every Sabbath.

28. Though they found no proper ground for a death sentence, they asked Pilate to have him executed.

29. When they had carried out all that was written about him, they took him down from the tree and laid him in a tomb.

30. But God raised him from the dead,

31. and for many days he was seen by those who had traveled with him from Galilee to Jerusalem. They are now his witnesses to our people.

32. "We tell you the good news: What God promised our fathers

33. he has fulfilled for us, their children, by raising up Jesus. As it is written in the second Psalm: " 'You are my Son; today I have become your Father.'

chimbi cha kabiri mbu: woyu
wera muala wanyi, Nanyi
kutengera lwarero nyi nera
eho.

가비리 뿌: 오유 워라 무아뽜
와네, 나네 구더떠라 뽜러로
네 너라 어호.

34. Kanji bacha ku Ongo
atetaa bushi nekwomoka kwai
angesha kubolka mbu:
nyikakweresa engahanyi
sibuya-buya, kanji sa se
kanangana, sa nalaanya Tauti.

34. 가찌 바짜 구 오꼬
아더다아 부씨 너꼬모가 과이
아꺼싸 구보루가 뿌:
네가궈러사 어꺼하네 시부야-
부야, 가찌 사 서 가나꺼나, 사
나뽜아냐 다우디.

34. The fact that God raised
him from the dead, never to
decay, is stated in these
words: " 'I will give you the
holy and sure blessings
promised to David.'

35. Si Tauti, era nyuma se
kukola kukulikana nokuhonda
kwa Ongo mwa kalamo kai,
era kufa.

35. 시 다우디, 어라 뉴마 서
구고뽜 구구뤼가나 노구호따
과 오꼬 뫄 가뽜모 가이, 어라
구파.

35. So it is stated elsewhere:
" 'You will not let your Holy
One see decay.'

36. Chasinda, era kutabwa
alauma na bahokulu bai, era
kubola.

36. 짜시따, 어라 구다봐
아뽜우마 나 바호구루 바이,
어라 구보뽜.

36. "For when David had
served God's purpose in his
own generation, he fell
asleep; he was buried with
his fathers and his body
decayed.

37. Si Ongo omwolaa yake,
atabolaa.

37. 시 오꼬 오몰뽜아 야거,
아다보뽜아.

37. But the one whom God
raised from the dead did
not see decay.

38. Bushi noku banyaketu,
mumenyereraa kwa bushi
nonoyu Yesu ku emwasi we
bubabalire bwe bibu byenyu,
enjire ahubanganyisibwa. Obu
bubabalire mutabonaabo
kurengera emwaso wa musa.

38. 부씨 노구 바냐거두,
무머녀러라아 과 부씨 노노유
여수 구 어꽈시 워 부바바뤼러
뭐 비부 벼뉴, 어찌러
아후바꺼네시봐. 오부
부바바뤼러 무다보나아보
구러꺼라 어꽈소 와 무사.

38. "Therefore, my brothers,
I want you to know that
through Jesus the
forgiveness of sins is
proclaimed to you.

39. Kanji kurengera oyu Yesu,
ku chira mundu woshi ola wa
mwemerere ende abalirwa.

39. 가찌 구러꺼라 오유 여수,
구 찌라 무뚜 오씨 오뽜 와
뭐머러러 어떠 아바뤼롸.

39. Through him everyone
who believes is justified
from everything you could

not be justified from by the law of Moses.

40. Rero, muchilkangaa kubuya mungesha kusibibwa nene myasi ebarebi batetaa mbu:

40. 러로, 무찌루가ᄴ아 구부야 무ᅄ싸 구시비봐 너너 먀시 어바러비 바더다아 뿌:

40. Take care that what the prophets have said does not happen to you:

41. Mumvaa mu mwende mwakena ebanji, musanwa busese, munate nge nomwa meho manyi! bushi mwesine suku mulimo nyingaira mwasi, ola mutangemerera kwa kasi angaba, chiro mbu kungabere ola wabalikisa era luulu sao.

41. 무빠아 무 뭐ᄄ머 먀거나 어바ᄿ, 무사놔 부서서, 무나더ᄊ 노뫄 머호 마니! 부씨 뭐시너 수구 무ᄙ모 네ᅄ이라 먀시, 오ᄍ라 무다ᄴ머러라 과 가시 아아빠, 찌로 뿌 구ᅄ버러 오ᄍ라 와바ᄙ기사 어라 루우루 사오.

41. " 'Look, you scoffers, wonder and perish, for I am going to do something in your days that you would never believe, even if someone told you.'"

42. Mango Paulo na Barnaba babaa bera baulukaa mwa bushebge bwe bayuta*, ebandu bera kubema mbu bahubaa kuika kuhambala kwei myasi elusuku lwe sabato* kwa linji einga.

42. 마ᅉ 파우ᄙ 나 바루나바 바바아 버라 바우루가아 뫄 부써부거 붜 바유다*, 어바ᄄ 버라 구버먀 뿌 바후바아 구이가 구하빠ᄍ라 궈이 먀시 어루수구 뭐 사바도* 과 ᄙᄊ 어이ᄴ.

42. As Paul and Barnabas were leaving the synagogue, the people invited them to speak further about these things on the next Sabbath.

43. Abere ebandu bera bahandabana, ebayuta banene alauma nebnji bandu ba sinji mbaa ba bemerera etini lye bayuta, bera kukulikira Paulo na Barnaba. Esi ndumwa ebiri sabaa senjire sasesabo emchima kwa baendekera kusimika mwa kuchinyira obonjo bwa Ongo.

43. 아버러 어바ᄄ 버라 바하ᄄ따바나, 어바유다 바너너 아ᄍ라우마 너부ᄍ 바ᄄ 바 시ᄍ 빠아 바 버머러라 어디니 ᄙ 바유다, 버라 구구ᄙ기라 파우ᄙ 나 바루나바. 어시 ᄄ뫄 어비리 사바아 서ᄍ러 사서사보 어무ᄍ마 과 바어ᄄ거라 구시미가 뫄 구찌네라 오보ᄊ 봐 오ᅉ.

43. When the congregation was dismissed, many of the Jews and devout converts to Judaism followed Paul and Barnabas, who talked with them and urged them to continue in the grace of God.

44. Mango elunji lusuku lwe Sabato lwaikaa, bandu banene busese bomwa musi, bera

44. 마ᅉ 어루ᄍ 루수구 뭐 사바도 ᄍ아이가아, 바ᄄ 바너너 부서서 보뫄 무시, 버라

44. On the next Sabbath almost the whole city gathered to hear the word

kuhuba kubuanana kwa kumvirisa echinwa cha enawetu.

구후바 구부아나나 과 구뻬리사 어찌놔 짜 어나워두.

of the Lord.

45. Si mango ebayuta balolaa kwolu luamba lwabandu, bera kufa mufula munene. Bera kunana emyasi era Paulo abaa ateta, nekunamukamba.

45. 시 마꼬 어바유다 바로롸아 고루 루아빠 롸바누, 버라 구파 무푸롸 무너너. 버라 구나나 어먀시 어라 파우로 아바아 아더다, 너구나무가빠.

45. When the Jews saw the crowds, they were filled with jealousy and talked abusively against what Paul was saying.

46. Paulo na Barnaba kukwera kubabura busira bubaa mbu: mwabo mumungabere babere tanga kuhanganyisibwa echinwa cha Ongo. Si bushi mwana nyirechi, kanji musene nga ekalamo kesuku ne mango katabetere mufa, rero tubano, tungere twachiira atubwirire:

46. 파우로 나 바루나바 구궈라 구바부라 부시라 부바아 뿌: 롸보 무무까버러 바버러 다꺄 구하꺄니시봐 어찌놔 짜 오꼬. 시 부씨 뫄나 네러찌, 가찌 무서너 까 어가꺄모 거수구 너 마꼬 가다버더러 무파, 러로 두바노, 두꺼러 돠찌이라 아두붜리러:

46. Then Paul and Barnabas answered them boldly: "We had to speak the word of God to you first. Since you reject it and do not consider yourselves worthy of eternal life, we now turn to the Gentiles.

47. Nakuirire kuba bulangare bwembaa soshi, chasiya wekere ebandu boshi bomwa butala ebununusi.

47. 나구이리러 구바 부롸꺄러 붸빠아 소씨, 짜시야 워거러 어바누 보씨 보뫄 부다롸 어부누누시.

47. For this is what the Lord has commanded us: " 'I have made you a light for the Gentiles, that you may bring salvation to the ends of the earth.'"

48. Mango ebandu besinji mbaa bomvaa kwei myasi, bera kumowa busese na kutangirisa kutonga echinwa cha enawetu. Ebandu ba Ongo alondala kutengera mira kwakubona ekalamo ke suku ne mango, nabo bera kwemerera Yesu.

48. 마꼬 어바누 버시찌 빠아 보빠아 궈이 먀시, 버라 구모와 부서서 나 구다꺼리사 구도꺄 어찌놔 짜 어나워두. 어바누 바 오꼬 아로따롸 구더꺼라 미라 과구보나 어가꺄모 거 수구 너 마꼬, 나보 버라 궈머러라 여수.

48. When the Gentiles heard this, they were glad and honored the word of the Lord; and all who were appointed for eternal life believed.

49. Ebandu boshi ba mwechi chio, bera kumva echinwa cha enawetu.

50. Si ebayuta bera kushirisa ebashamuka be musi alauma na bakasi bauma ba babaa bete etunda, ka nji ba bendee bema Ongo. Bera kulisa Paulo na Barnaba busese, bera kunalinda babakolokanya mwa chio chabo.

51. Esi ndumwa sera kubakunguchira emukungu kutenga kwa bihando byabo, sera kuchiira elkonyiyo.

52. Ebemeresi be Andiyokiya beke, bera kushiba na lumoo lunene kanji babaa bakoresibwa ne mchima mubuya-buya.

49. 어바누 보씨 바 뭐찌 찌오,49. The word of the Lord 버라 구빠 어찌놔 짜 어나워두.

50. 시 어바유다 버라 구씨리사 어바싸무가 버 무시 아꽈우마 나 바가시 바우마 바 바바아 버더 어두따, 가 찌 바 버떠어 버마 오꼬. 버라 구꾀사 파우뢰 나 바루나바 부서서, 버라 구나꾀따 바바고뢰가냐 뫄 찌오 짜보.

51. 어시 뚜뫄 서라 구바구꾸찌라 어무구꾸 구더꽈 과 비하또 뱌보, 서라 구찌이라 어루고니요.

52. 어버머러시 버 아띠요기야 버거, 버라 구씨바 나 룸모 룬너너 가찌 바바아 바고러시봐 너 무찌마 무부야- 부야.

49. The word of the Lord spread through the whole region.

50. But the Jews incited the God-fearing women of high standing and the leading men of the city. They stirred up persecution against Paul and Barnabas, and expelled them from their region.

51. So they shook the dust from their feet in protest against them and went to Iconium.

52. And the disciples were filled with joy and with the Holy Spirit.

E Mikolo ye Ndjumwa Chikono 14

Paulo na Baranaba bahubanganya echinwa cha Ongo mwa musi w'e Ikoniyo

1. Mango Paulo na Baranaba baika mwa musi we Ikoniyo, namo byera kunaba ngokwa byanabaa e Andiyokiya. Mwoyu musi namo, bera kwengirira mwa bushenge bwe bayuta*. Bera kukangirisa ebandu echinwa cha Ongo

어 미고뢰 여 뚜뫄 찌고노 14

파우뢰 나 바라나바 바후바꽈낻 어찌놔 짜 오꼬 뫄 무시 워 이고니요

1. 마꼬 파우뢰 나 바라나바 바이가 뫄 무시 워 이고니요, 나모 벼라 구나바 꼬과 뱌나바아 어 아띠요기야. 모유 무시 나모, 버라 궈꾀리라 뫄 부써꺼 붜 바우다*. 버라 구가꾀리사 어바누 어찌놔 짜 오꼬 구이기라 과 비하꾀

Acts Chapter 14[NIV]

1. At Iconium Paul and Barnabas went as usual into the Jewish synagogue. There they spoke so effectively that a great number of Jews and Gentiles believed.

kuikira kwa bihangi bauyta na bakiriki banene bahubabemeresi.

바우위다 나 바기리기 바너너 바후바버머러시.

2. Si e bayuta ba bananaa kwemerera Yesu, bera kushiriisa ebandu besinji mbaa kuata muchima mubi kwa bemeresi.

2. 시 어 바유다 바 바나나아 궈머러라 여수, 버라 구씨리이사 어바뚜 버시찌 빠아 구아다 무찌마 무비 과 버머러시.

2. But the Jews who refused to believe stirred up the Gentiles and poisoned their minds against the brothers.

3. Si chiro bacha, Paulo na Baranaba bera kunekala suku sinene mwoyu musi. Babaa benjire bahubanganyisa ebandu echinwa cha Ongo busira buba, bushi enawetu abaa enjire eresabo ebuashi kwe kuira ebisomerano ne bimenyeso. Ebyera byera kunde byalosa kwa emyasi ye bonjo bai era bendee bahubanganya inali ya kanangana.

3. 시 찌로 바짜, 파우뢴 나 바라나바 버라 구너가짜 수구 시너너 모유 무시. 바바아 버찌러 바후바빠니사 어바뚜 어찌놔 짜 오꼬 부시라 부바, 부씨 어나워두 아바아 어찌러 어러사보 어부아씨 궈 구이라 어비소머라노 너 비머녀소. 어뼈라 뼈라 구떠 뱌뢴사 과 어먀시 여 보쪼 바이 어라 버떠어 바후바빠냐 이나삐 야 가나까나.

3. So Paul and Barnabas spent considerable time there, speaking boldly for the Lord, who confirmed the message of his grace by enabling them to do miraculous signs and wonders.

4. Besha ikoniyo bera kuberekanamo mbiriri ebiri: bauma bera kuba kwa lunda lwe bayuta, ne banji kwa lunda lwe ndumwa.

4. 버싸 이고니요 버라 구버러가나모 삐리리 어비리: 바우마 버라 구바 과 뤄뜨라 뤄 바유다, 너 바찌 과 뤄뜨라 뤄 뚜꽈.

4. The people of the city were divided; some sided with the Jews, others with the apostles.

5. Chasinda, ebayuta ne bandu besinji mbaa, alauma ne bakulu-kulu babo, bera kuya lwango lwa kuhonda kulibusa Paulo na Baranaba bera kumenya oyu mwasi.

5. 짜시따, 어바유다 너 바뚜 버시찌 빠아, 아꽈우마 너 바구뤀-구뤀 바보, 버라 구야 꽈꼬 꽈 구호따 구삐부사 파우뢴 나 바라나바 버라 구머냐 오유 꽈시.

5. There was a plot afoot among the Gentiles and Jews, together with their leaders, to mistreat them and stone them.

6. Bushi noku, bera kuhaira mwa chio che likaoniya, mwa musi we lisitara newe teribe, nomwa ndambi-ndambi sayi.

7. Mwei misi namo, bera kunde bahubanganyisa ebandu emwasi mubya-buya.
Paulo alamya echirema mwa musi w'e Lisitara.

8. Mwa musi we lisitara mwabaa mutula mulume muuma wa chirema. Kutengera ekubutwa kwai, abaa aatafura kubatuka bushi emaulu mai mabaa maremare.

9. Lusuku luuma, oyu mulume abaa omvirisa emyasi era Paulo abaa ateta. Paulo era kumutumbikirisa busese, era kumenyerera kwa oyu mundu ete bwemeresi bwa bungamulamya.

10. Paulo kukwera kumubura na murenge munene mbu: batuka, unemange chima-chima! unao-unao kuna kubanzukala na atangirisa achendera.

11. Mango ebandu balola kwa myasi era Paulo airire, bera kuuma emurenge mweteta lyabo lye Chilikaoniya mbu: Ebaongo bachihubise bandu na buberire batwandalira!

6. 부씨 노구, 버라 구하이라 뫄 찌오 쩌 릐가오니야, 뫄 무시 워 릐시다라 너워 더리버, 노뫄 따뻬-따뻬 사에.

7. 뭐이 미시 나모, 버라 구떠 바후바뫄네사 어바뚜 어뫄시 무뱌-부야.
파우롣 아퐈맫 어찌러마 뫄 무시 워 릐습닏띱.

8. 뫄 무시 워 릐시다라 뫄바아 무두롸 무루머 무우마 와 찌러마. 구더뻐라 어구부돠 과이, 아바아 아아다푸라 구바두가 부씨 어마우루 마이 마바아 마러마러.

9. 루수구 루우마, 오유 무루머 아바아 오뻬리사 어먀시 어라 파우롣 아바아 아더다. 파우롣 어라 구무두뻬기리사 부서서, 어라 구머녀러라 과 오유 무뚜 어더 뭐머러시 봐 부뻐무퐈먀.

10. 파우롣 구궈라 구무부라 나 무러뻐 무너너 뿌: 바두가, 우너마뻐 찌마-찌마! 우나오- 우나오 구나 구바누가퐈 나 아다뻬리사 아쩌떠라.

11. 마꼬 어바뚜 바롣롸 과 먀시 어라 파우롣 아이리리, 버라 구우마 어무러뻐 뭐더다 퍍보 뼈 찌릐가오니야 뿌: 어바오꼬 바찌후비서 바뚜 나 부버리러 바돠따릐라!

6. But they found out about it and fled to the Lycaonian cities of Lystra and Derbe and to the surrounding country,

7. where they continued to preach the good news.

8. In Lystra there sat a man crippled in his feet, who was lame from birth and had never walked.

9. He listened to Paul as he was speaking. Paul looked directly at him, saw that he had faith to be healed

10. and called out, "Stand up on your feet!" At that, the man jumped up and began to walk.

11. When the crowd saw what Paul had done, they shouted in the Lycaonian language, "The gods have come down to us in human form!"

12. Abu bandu bera kunde berika Baranaba esina lya Seu imukulu-kulu we baongo esina lya Herimesi iwabaa mutechi wai.

13. Eluhu lwa Seu lwabaa lutula mwa chifuna che Musi.rero kuhanyi wolu luhu alauma nebandu era kuhonda berese Paulo na Baranaba emitulo*. Bushi noku, era kureta mbanzi sa sitonyisibwe na bikanda bya bwaso kwa chiso cho luhu.

14. Si mango Paulo na Baranaba bomva kwoyu mwasi bera kuberenganga enjimba sabo kwa kulosa ebusinane bwabo. Bera bera kulibichira mwa luamba lwe bandu baenda balakanga mbu:

15. Ebanyaketu! chichatuma mwaira bacha si netu tunali bandu kuuma nenyu! kanji emwasi mubuya-buya ola twenjire twabahambalira, kuli kuburana kwa murekaa kunde mwera ebihuhanyi, mualukire Ongo we kalamo bushi iwabumbaa enguba nebutala, ne nyanja alauma na byoshi byabitula mubi.

16. Mwa suku sa srenga, Ongo arekereraa embaa soshi

---

12. 아부 바뚜 버라 구떠 버리가 바라나바 어시나 랴 서우 이무구루-구루 워 바오꼬 어시나 랴 허리머시 이와바아 무더찌 와이.

13. 어루후 롸 서우 롸바아 루두롸 마 찌푸나 쩌 무시.러로 구하네 오루 루후 아롸우마 너바뚜 어라 구호따 버러서 파우로 나 바라나바 어미두롼*. 부씨 노구, 어라 구러다 빠씨 사 시도네시붜 나 비가따 뱌 봐소 과 찌소 쪼 루후.

14. 시 마꼬 파우로 나 바라나바 보빠 굮유 마시 버라 구버러꺄까 어찌빠 사보 과 구롼사 어부시나너 봐보. 버라 버라 구뀌비찌라 마 루아빠 뤄 바뚜 바어따 바롸가까 뿌:

15. 어바냐거두! 찌짜두마 뫄이라 바짜 시 너두 두나뤼 바뚜 구우마 너뉴! 가찌 어뫄시 무부야-부야 오롸 뛰찌러 돠바하빠뤼라, 구뀌 구부라나 과 무러가아 구떠 뭐라 어비후하네, 무아루기러 오꼬 워 가롸모 부씨 이와부빠아 어우바 너부다롸, 너 냐짜 아롸우마 나 뵤씨 뱌비두롸 무비.

16. 뫄 수구 사 수러따, 오꼬 아러거러라아 어빠아 소씨

---

12. Barnabas they called Zeus, and Paul they called Hermes because he was the chief speaker.

13. The priest of Zeus, whose temple was just outside the city, brought bulls and wreaths to the city gates because he and the crowd wanted to offer sacrifices to them.

14. But when the apostles Barnabas and Paul heard of this, they tore their clothes and rushed out into the crowd, shouting:

15. "Men, why are you doing this? We too are only men, human like you. We are bringing you good news, telling you to turn from these worthless things to the living God, who made heaven and earth and sea and everything in them.

16. In the past, he let all nations go their own way.

kunde sakulikira enjira sabo beine.

구떠 사구뤼기라 어찌라 사보 버이너.

---

17. Si chiro bacha, atanarekaa kunde achilosa era mulimwa kubakorera emabuya. Kanji iwende waberesa emvula kutengera kwa nguba, na kubesesa emyaka kwa bianyiro bikomire, na kuberesa ekalyo, na kunde atuma mwaba mwa lumoo busese.

17. 시 찌로 바짜, 아다나러가아 구떠 아찌로사 어라 무뤼뫄 구바고러라 어마부야. 가찌 이워떠 와버러사 어뿌롸 구더뚸라 과 우바, 나 구버서사 어먀가 과 비아네로 비고미러, 나 구버러사 어가뢴, 나 구떠 아두마 뫄바 뫄 루모오 부서서.

17. Yet he has not left himself without testimony: He has shown kindness by giving you rain from heaven and crops in their seasons; he provides you with plenty of food and fills your hearts with joy."

---

18. Chiro mbu pauo na Baranaba batetaa ei myasi yoshi, bainaa kwa bangaangika abu bandu mbu bateresabo emitulo*.

18. 찌로 뿌 파우오 나 바라나바 바더다아 어이 먀시 요씨, 바이나아 과 바까아끼가 아부 바뚜 뿌 바더러사보 어미두뢴*.

18. Even with these words, they had difficulty keeping the crowd from sacrificing to them.

---

19. Chasinda, bayuta bauma bera kupamukira mwa musi we Andiyokiya ne we Ikoniya. Bera kushiirisa ebandu, baye kwa lunda lwabo. Bera kuumanga Paulo emakoi na bamukulurira era mbuwa se musi bushi bachichingaa mbu afire.

19. 짜시따, 바유다 바우마 버라 구파무기라 뫄 무시 워 아띠요기야 너 워 이고니야. 버라 구씨이리사 어바뚜, 바여 과 루따 롸보. 버라 구우마까 파우뢴 어마고이 나 바무구루리라 어라 뿌와 서 무시 부씨 바찌찌까아 뿌 아피러.

19. Then some Jews came from Antioch and Iconium and won the crowd over. They stoned Paul and dragged him outside the city, thinking he was dead.

---

20. Si mango ebemeresi bamusungulaa, era kubatuka, na ahuba kwangirira mwa musi. Chasinjire, mweli lishisho, era kuya na Baranaba mwa musi we Teribe.

20. 시 마꼬 어버머러시 바무수우롸아, 어라 구바두가, 나 아후바 과끼리라 뫄 무시. 짜시띠러, 뭐뤼 뤼씨쏘, 어라 구야 나 바라나바 더리버.

20. But after the disciples had gathered around him, he got up and went back into the city. The next day he and Barnabas left for Derbe.

Paulo na Baranaba bahunde mwa musi w'e Antiyokiya

파우뢴 나 바라나바 바후떠 뫄 무시 워 아띠윕굿앳

21. Mango Paulo na Baranaba babaa bera bahambaliraa ebandu echinwa cha Ongo mwa musi we Teribe na kubona bemeresi banene mubo, bera kuhuba mwa musi we Lisitara ne we Ikoniyo, ne we Andiyokiya.

22. Esi ndumwa sabaa senjire sasesa ebemeresi emchima nekunde sakangirisabo mbu bendaa bahangalira Yesu busese. Bacha ku sende seburabo: akaba twahonda kwengira mwa bwami bwao Ongo*, bitwemire kurenga mu malibuko manene.

23. Na mu chira chisiki cha chabaa chiri mu bemeresi, bera kubahondorera ebangumwa bekubemangira. Era nyuma se memo ma mende mairibwa busira kulya, bera kubemera era mwa enawtu ibaa bemerere, abalange.

24. Era kunyuma sebi, Paulo na Baranaba bera kurengera mwa chio che Pisitiya bahabukira mwa che Pamufiriya.

25. Abere bera bahubanganyisa ebandu echinwa cha Ongo mwa musi

21. 마꼬 파우로 나 바라나바 바바아 버라 바하빠릐라아 어바뚜 어찌냐 짜 오꼬 뫄 무시 워 더리버 나 구보나 버머러시 바너너 무보, 버라 구후바 뫄 무시 워 릐시다라 너 워 이고니요, 너 워 아띄요기야.

22. 어시 뚜뫄 사바아 서찌러 사서사 어버머러시 어무찌마 너구더 사가끼리사보 뿌 버따아 바하꺄릐라 여수 부서서. 바짜 구 서떠 서부라보: 아가바 돠호따 궈끼라 뫄 봐미 봐오 오꼬*, 비뚸미러 구러꺄 무 마릐부고 마너너.

23. 나 무 찌라 찌시기 짜 짜바아 찌리 무 버머러시, 버라 구바호또러라 어바꾸뫄 버구버마끼라. 어라 뉴마 서 머모 마 머너 마이리봐 부시라 구꺄, 버라 구버머라 어라 뫄 어나우두 이바아 버머러러, 아바꺄어.

24. 어라 구뉴마 서비, 파우로 나 바라나바 버라 구러꺄라 뫄 찌오 쩌 피시디야 바하부기라 뫄 쩌 파무피리야.

25. 아버러 버라 바후바바끼네사 어바뚜 어찌냐 짜 오꼬 뫄 무시 워 퍼리가, 버라 귀러

21. They preached the good news in that city and won a large number of disciples. Then they returned to Lystra, Iconium and Antioch,

22. strengthening the disciples and encouraging them to remain true to the faith. "We must go through many hardships to enter the kingdom of God," they said.

23. Paul and Barnabas appointed elders for them in each church and, with prayer and fasting, committed them to the Lord, in whom they had put their trust.

24. After going through Pisidia, they came into Pamphylia,

25. and when they had preached the word in Perga, they went down to Attalia.

we Perika, bera kwire bandaliramwa we Ataliya.

바따쯰라뫄 워 아다쯰야.

26. Kanji bera kutola ebwato batenga mwoyu musi, na bahabukira mwa Andiyokiya. Mwoyu musi mu bemerwaa engahanyi era mwa Ongo bushi ne mulimo ola babaa bera bakolaa.

26. 가찌 버라 구도롸 어봐도 바더꺄 모유 무시, 나 바하부기라 뫄 아띠요기야. 모유 무시 무 버머롸아 어꺄하네 어라 뫄 오꼬 부씨 너 무쮜모 오롸 바바아 버라 바고롸아.

26. From Attalia they sailed back to Antioch, where they had been committed to the grace of God for the work they had now completed.

27. Mango baikaa eAndiyokiya, bera kubuanyanya ebemeresi, bera kubalikisisabo byoshi bya Ongo airaa kubarengerako. Kanji bera kunalosa kute ku abooereraa ebandu ba batula bayuta enjira ye kwemerera Yesu.

27. 마꼬 바이가아 어아띠요기야, 버라 구부아냐냐 어버머러시, 버라 구바쮜기시사보 뵤씨 뱌 오꼬 아이라아 구바러꺄라고. 가찌 버라 구나롸사 구더 구 아보오어러라아 어바뚜 바 바두롸 바유다 어찌라 여 궈머러라 여수.

27. On arriving there, they gathered the church together and reported all that God had done through them and how he had opened the door of faith to the Gentiles.

28. Paulo na Baranaba bera kwekala suku sinene alauma ne bemeresi.

28. 파우로 나 바라나바 버라 궈가롸 수구 시너너 아롸우마 너 버머러시.

28. And they stayed there a long time with the disciples.

E Mikolo ye Ndjumwa Chikono 15
Elubuanano lw'e ndjumwa mwa musi w'e Yerusalemu

어 미고롣 여 뚜롸 찌고노 15
어루뷉씹낄녕 루웁 뚜몹 뫄 무시 워 여루사퍼물

Acts Chapter 15[NIV]

1. Mwesi suku, bandu bauma batengeraa mwa chio che Yuteya bera kwandaalira mwa musi we andiyokiya. Abu bandu bera kutangirisa kunde bakangirisa ebemeresi mbu

1. 뭐시 수구, 바뚜 바우마 바더꺄라아 뫄 찌오 쩌 유더야 버라 과따아쮜라 뫄 무시 워 아띠요기야. 아부 바뚜 버라 구다꺼리사 구떠 바가꺼리사 어버머러시 뿌 아가바

1. Some men came down from Judea to Antioch and were teaching the brothers: "Unless you are circumcised, according to the custom taught by Moses, you

akaba mutarengire mwa mwiya we kumona kukulikana nokwa mwaso wa Musa atula atechire, mutangabona ebununusi.

2. Oyu mwasi, Paulo na Baranaba bera kunanao. Bera kunde baenzabo bwaka bunene kusibu era luulu soyu mwasi. Bushi noku, ebemeresi bera kwemeresanya kutuma bauma

3. Alauma na Paulo na Baranaba baye eyerusalemu kuhambalirayi kwoyu mwasi alauma nesinji ndumwa*, ne bangumwa beluhu lwa Ongo.

4. Abere ebemeresi be andiyokiya bera batumaa'bo, bera kurengera mwa chio che Foinikiya neche Samariya, baenda babalikisa beshayi kwa bandu besinji mbaanabo bahubire bemeresi. Oyu mwasi era kunde asimisa ebemeresi oshi.

5. Mango Paulo na balikabo baikaa eyerusalemu, ebemeresi, ne ndumwa*, alauma ne bangumwa beluhu lwa Ongo, bera kubahukasa.

무다러삐러 롸 뮈야 워 구모나 구구쮜가나 노과 롸소 와 무사 아두꽈 아더찌러, 무다까보나 어부누누시.

2. 오유 롸시, 파우롣 나 바라나바 버라 구나나오. 버라 구떠 바어싸보 봐가 부너너 구시부 어라 루우루 소유 롸시. 부씨 노구, 어버머러시 버라 궈머러사냐 구두마 바우마

3. 아꽈우마 나 파우롣 나 바라나바 바여 어여루사꺼무 구하빠쮜라에 고유 롸시 아꽈우마 너시찌 뚜똬*, 너 바꾸마 버루후 꽈 오꼬.

4. 아버러 어버머러시 버 아띠요기야 버라 바두마아보, 버라 구러꺼라 롸 찌오 쩌 포이니기야 너쩌 사마리야, 바어따 바바쮜기사 버싸에 과 바뚜 버시찌 빠아나보 바후비러 버머러시. 오유 롸시 어라 구떠 아시미사 어버머러시 오씨.

5. 마꼬 파우롣 나 바쮜가보 바이가아 어여루사꺼무, 어버머러시, 너 뚜똬*, 아꽈우마 너 바우똬 버루후 꽈 오꼬, 버라 구바후가사.

cannot be saved."

2. This brought Paul and Barnabas into sharp dispute and debate with them. So Paul and Barnabas were appointed, along with some other believers, to go up to Jerusalem to see the apostles and elders about this question.

3. The church sent them on their way, and as they traveled through Phoenicia and Samaria, they told how the Gentiles had been converted. This news made all the brothers very glad.

4. When they came to Jerusalem, they were welcomed by the church and the apostles and elders, to whom they reported everything God had done through them.

5. Then some of the believers who belonged to the party of the Pharisees stood up and said, "The Gentiles must be

Chasinda, nabo bera kubabalikisa byoshi bya Ongo airaa kubarengerako

짜시따, 나보 버라 구바바릐기사 뵤씨 뱌 오꼬 아이라아 구바러꺼라고

circumcised and required to obey the law of Moses."

6. Si bandu bauma bomwa chikembe che Bafarisayo*ba bahubaa bemeresi, bera kwimanga na bateta mbu: byemire ebemeresi besinji mbaa nabo barenge mwa mwiya we kumona, na kubabura kwa bendaa batunda emwaso wa Musa.

6. 시 바뚜 바우마 보똬 찌거뻐 쩌 바파리사요*바 바후바아 버머러시, 버라 귀마꺄 나 바더다 뿌: 벼미러 어버머러시 버시찌 빠아 나보 바러어 똬 뮈야 워 구모나, 나 구바부라 과 버따아 바두따 어똬소 와 무사.

6. The apostles and elders met to consider this question.

7. Bushi noku, endumwa alauma ne bangumwa be luhu lwa Ongo, bera kwire babuanana chaisiya bahambale era luulu soyu mwasi,

7. 부씨 노구, 어뚜똬 아라우마 너 바우똬 버 루후 똬 오꼬, 버라 귀러 바부아나나 짜이시야 바하빠러 어라 루우루 소유 똬시,

7. After much discussion, Peter got up and addressed them: "Brothers, you know that some time ago God made a choice among you that the Gentiles might hear from my lips the message of the gospel and believe.

8. Petero alolire kwa bwaka bwanaendekere bwaluwa, era kuira emanga noku babura mbu: banyeketu! si mwishi kwa kutengera mira, Ongo anyilondwere mwa kachi-kachi kenyu, nyinde nyinde nahubanyanyisa ebandu besinji mbaa emwasi mubuya buya chasiya bomvi kuo, nabo babe bemeresi.

8. 퍼더로 아롤릐러 과 봐가 봐나어떠거러 봐루와, 어라 구이라 어마꺄 노구 바부라 뿌: 바녀거두! 시 뮈씨 과 구더꺼라 미라, 오꼬 아녜론뚜워러 똬 가찌-가찌 거뉴, 네떠 네떠 나후바냐네사 어바뚜 버시찌 빠아 어똬시 무부야 부야 짜시야 보삐 구오, 나보 바버 버머러시.

8. God, who knows the heart, showed that he accepted them by giving the Holy Spirit to them, just as he did to us.

9. Noyu Ongo yeine itula wishi emichima yebandu, iwalosise ekanangana kwa emerere ebandu besinji mbaa nabo, mwaku beresa emuchima mubya-buya ngokwa netu anatuwao.

10. Utali kalondo kasibya ka airire ala kachi-kachi ketu nabo, bushi kurengera ei njira yekuemerera Yesu, ku nabo akomise emichima yabo.

11. Rero, chi chera chingatuma mwaereka Ongo mwa kwesa abu bemeresi emusio ola bahokulu betu, netu tubeine twafundwa kweka?

12. Anabe netu tuneshi kwa twanunulibwe bushi nebonjo bwa Enawetu Yesu! nabo kunoku!

13. Ebandu boshi ba babaa bali mwolu lubuanano bera kwire basira. Bera kuteya Baranaba na Paulo ematwi, bomvirisa kwa myasi yebimenyeso ne bisomerano bya Ongo airaa kurengera'bo mwa kachi-kachi kebandu

9. 노유 오꼬 여이너 이두꽈 위씨 어미찌마 여바뚜, 이와론시서 어가나꽈나 과 어머러러 어바뚜 버시찌 빠아 나보, 꽈구 버러사 어무찌마 무뱌-부야 으과 너두 아나두와오.

10. 우다찌 가론또 가시뱌 가 아이리러 아꽈 가찌-가찌 거두 나보, 부씨 구러꺼러라 어이 찌라 여구어머러라 여수, 구 나보 아고미서 어미찌마 야보.

11. 러로, 찌 쩌라 찌꺼두마 꽈어러가 오꼬 꽈 궈사 아부 버머러시 어무시오 오꽈 바호구룬 버두, 너두 두버이너 돠푸꽈 궈가?

12. 아나버 너두 두너씨 과 돠누누찌붜 부씨 너보쪼 봐 어나워두 여수! 나보 구노구!

13. 어바뚜 보씨 바 바바아 바찌 몰루 룬부아나노 버라 귀러 바시라. 버라 구더야 바라나바 나 파우론 어마뒤, 보뻬리사 과 먀시 여비머녀소 너 비소머라노 뱌 오꼬 아이라아 구러꺼라보 꽈 가찌- 가찌 거바뚜 버시찌 빠아.

9. He made no distinction between us and them, for he purified their hearts by faith.

10. Now then, why do you try to test God by putting on the necks of the disciples a yoke that neither we nor our fathers have been able to bear?

11. No! We believe it is through the grace of our Lord Jesus that we are saved, just as they are."

12. The whole assembly became silent as they listened to Barnabas and Paul telling about the miraculous signs and wonders God had done among the Gentiles through them.

13. When they finished, James spoke up: "Brothers, listen to me.

besinji mbaa.

14. Abere bera bamala kuteta Yakobo nai era kuuma mwa bunu mbu: banyaketu, munyumvirisaa!

14. 아버러 버라 바마롸 구더다, 야고보 나이 어라 구우마 롸 부누 뿌: 바냐거두, 무뉴삐리사아!

14. Simon has described to us how God at first showed his concern by taking from the Gentiles a people for himself.

15. Simoni era atuburaa kwa kutengera mwa ndangiriso, Ongo yeine alondwere ebandu besnji mbaa, chasiya bauma mubo babe lubaa lwai.

15. 시모니 어라 아두부라아 과 구더꺼라 롸 따삐리소, 오꼬 여이너 아론뚜워러 어바뚜 버수씨 빠아, 짜시야 바우마 무보 바버 루바아 롸이.

15. The words of the prophets are in agreement with this, as it is written:

16. Echera chikulikene nemyasi era barebi*batetaa, bushi bacha ku emandjiko mabuya-buya matula matechire:

16. 어쩌라 찌구픠거너 너먀시 어라 바러비*바더다아, 부씨 바짜 구 어마씨고 마부야-부야 마두롸 마더찌러:

16. " 'After this I will return and rebuild David's fallen tent. Its ruins I will rebuild, and I will restore it,

17. Mwa suku sa sechire, nyono nyi Ongo, nyikahuba kubaha, kwa kwimanza kanji ebwami bwa Tauti, nyikahuba kumwemanza, ngokwa bende baimba, enyumba era yaibaa yasuukire.

17. 롸 수구 사 서찌러, 뇨노 네 오꼬, 네가후바 구바하, 과 귀마싸 가씨 어봐미 봐 다우디, 네가후바 구뭐마싸, 꼬과 버뻐 바이빠, 어뉴빠 어라 야이바아 야수우기러.

17. that the remnant of men may seek the Lord, and all the Gentiles who bear my name, says the Lord, who does these things'

18. Echera chi chikatuma ebandji bandu boshi banyialukira, chasiya ebandu bembaa soshi ba namaere, bandu banyi. Ku natechire bacha nyi nyamusinda.

18. 어쩌라 찌 찌가두마 어바씨 바뚜 보씨 바네아루기라, 짜시야 어바뚜 버빠아 소씨 바 나마어러, 바뚜 바네. 구 나더찌러 바짜 네 냐무시따.

18. that have been known for ages.

19. Kanji nyinalosaa ei myasi kutengera mira.

19. 가씨 네나롣사아 어이 먀시 구더꺼라 미라.

19. "It is my judgment, therefore, that we should not make it difficult for the Gentiles who are turning to God.

20. Yakobo era kunaendekera ateta mbu: bushi noku, nyono nyisene kwa ebandu besinji mbaa benjire be merera Ongo, tutemire kunde twalibusabo.

21. Si cha tuiraa, tubanjikiraa emaruba me kubabura kwa batendaa balya ebiyo bya byatulwa ebasimu, nesi kubanda ekiri, nesi kulya nyama era yachitumbiraa, nesi kulya mwambaa.

22. Bushi kutengera mira, emwaso wa Musa kusomwa kuende anasomibwa mwa mashenge me bayuta na kunde abalibwa chira lusuku lwa sabato*na chira musi.

E lwango kwa ba batachwula Bayuda

23. Chasinda, endumwa* nabangumwa beluhu lwa Ongo alauma ne bemeresi boshi bera kwire bemeresanya kwa kukomire balondele bandu bauma mwa kacho-kachi kabo ba bangeresa Paulo na Baranaba eAndiyokiya. Bera kulondola

20. 야고보 어라 구나어떠거라 아더다 뿌: 부씨 노구, 뇨노 니서너 과 어바뚜 버시찌 빠아 버찌러 버 머러라 오끄, 두더미러 구떠 돠쀠부사보.

21. 시 짜 두이라아, 두바찌기라아 어마루바 머 구바부라 과 바더따아 바쨔 어비요 뱌 뱌두똬 어바시무, 너시 구바따 어기리, 너시 구쨔 냐마 어라 야찌두쀄라아, 너시 구쨔 뫄빠아.

22. 부씨 구더꺼라 미라, 어뫄소 와 무사 구소똬 구어떠 아나소미봐 뫄 마써꺼 머 바유다 나 구떠 아바쀠봐 찌라 루수구 똬 사바도*나 찌라 무시.

어 똬끄 과 바 바다쭈똬 바유다

23. 짜시따, 어뚜뫄* 나바꾸뫄 버루후 똬 오끄 아꽈우마 너 버머러시 보씨 버라 귀러 버머러사냐 과 구고미러 바롣떠러 바뚜 바우마 뫄 가쪼-가찌 가보 바 바꺼러사 파우론 나 바라나바 어아찌요기야. 버라 구론또똬

20. Instead we should write to them, telling them to abstain from food polluted by idols, from sexual immorality, from the meat of strangled animals and from blood.

21. For Moses has been preached in every city from the earliest times and is read in the synagogues on every Sabbath."

22. Then the apostles and elders, with the whole church, decided to choose some of their own men and send them to Antioch with Paul and Barnabas. They chose Judas (called Barsabbas) and Silas, two men who were leaders among the brothers.

23. With them they sent the following letter: The apostles and elders, your brothers, To the Gentile believers in Antioch, Syria and Cilicia: Greetings.

Yuta ola sasulwaa esina lya Barisaba alauma na Sila. Mwa kachi-kachi ke bemeresi, abu bandu babiri babaa bete etunda

24. Bera kwesabo amu maruba, na bacha ku mabaa manjikirwe: Tubano tu ndumwa*, ne bangumwa beluhu lwa Ongo, alauma nebanji bemeresi, twabalamusise mu banyaketu bemeresi, mumutula bayuta, mumutula mwa musi we andiyokiya, nomwa chio che suriya, neche kirikiya.

25. Twomvaa emwasi kwa kuli bandu bauma ba batengaa ene mwetu baya kubabura myasi ya kubalibusa na kubasungulisa ebwenge. Abu bandu ata tutwabatumaa eyera.

26. Bushi noku, tuboshi twemeresanyise kulondola bandu babiri mwa kachi-kachi ketu, tutumebo eyi muli alauma na banyaketu basiirwa, Baranaba na Paulo,

27. Bu bemeresi kwana ekalamo kabo kwa kukorera enawetu Yesu Kirisito.

바리사바 아꽈우마 나 시꽈.
마 가찌-가찌 거 버머러시,
아부 바뚜 바비리 바바아 버더
어두따

24. 버라 궈사보 아무 마루바, 나 바짜 구 마바아 마찌기꿔: 두바노 두 뚜뫄*, 너 바구뫄 버루후 꽈 오꼬, 아꽈우마 너바찌 버머러시, 돠바꽈무시서 무 바냐거두 버머러시, 무무두꽈 바유다, 무무두꽈 뫄 무시 워 아띠요기야, 노뫄 찌오 쩌 수리야, 너쩌 기리기야.

25. 돔빠아 어뫄시 과 구리 바뚜 바우마 바 바더꽈아 어너 뭐두 바야 구바부라 먀시 야 구바뢰부사 나 구바수꾀뢰사 어붸꿔. 아부 바뚜 아다 두돠바두마아 어여라.

26. 부씨 노구, 두보씨 뚸머러사니서 구뢰또꽈 바뚜 바비리 뫄 가찌-가찌 거두, 두두머보 어에 무뢰 아꽈우마 나 바냐거두 바시이롸, 바라나바 나 파우로,

27. 부 버머러시 과나 어가꽈모 가보 과 구고러라 어나워두 여수 기리시도.

24. We have heard that some went out from us without our authorization and disturbed you, troubling your minds by what they said.

25. So we all agreed to choose some men and send them to you with our dear friends Barnabas and Paul--

26. men who have risked their lives for the name of our Lord Jesus Christ.

27. Therefore we are sending Judas and Silas to confirm by word of mouth what we are writing.

28. Rero ebandu twabatumire, bali Yuta na Sila. Abola bu bangababalikisa bunu kwa bunji binetwanjikire.

29. Kanji kukulikana neano lye mchima mubuya-buya, ne lyetu tubeine, twalolaa kwa kutakomire tubese enji misio, kureka bine byete mufa:

30. Mutenda mwalya ebiryo byabanadu batula ebasilu, nesi kulya mwamba, nesi kulya nyama sasachichumbiraa, nesi kubanda ekiri. Mukachilanga ekwebi mungaba eri mwairire kubuya. Muhanyirwaa!

31. Abere bera balaana, abu batumwaa bera kuchiuma bandaalira eandiyokiya. Baikireyi, nabo bera kubuanyanya ebemeresi nekubangirisa ma maruba.

32. Abere abu bemeresi bera bamasomaa, bera kumoa bushi emyasi era yabaa yanjikirwemo yabaa ya kubasesa emichima.

33. Yuta na Sila bushi babaa batula barebi*, bera kubura abu bemeresi balikabo, inji myasi inene ya kubasesa

28. 러로 어바뚜 돠바두미러, 바뤼 유다 나 시롸. 아보롸 부 바까바바뤼기사 부누 과 부찌 비너돠찌기러.

29. 가찌 구구쀠가나 너아노 려 무찌마 무부야-부야, 너 려두 두버이너, 돠뢰롸아 과 구다고미러 두버서 어찌 미시오, 구러가 비너 벼더 무파:

30. 무더따 뫄쨔 어비료 뱌바나두 바두롸 어바시루, 너시 구쨔 뫄빠, 너시 구쨔 냐마 사사쭈뻬라아, 너시 구바따 어기리. 무가찌롸까 어궈비 무까바 어리 뫄이리러 구부야. 무하니뢰아!

31. 아버러 버라 바롸아나, 아부 바두뫄아 버라 구찌우마 바따아쀠라 어아띠요기야. 바이기러에, 나보 버라 구부아냐냐 어버머러시 너구바쀠리사 마 마루바.

32. 아버러 아부 버머러시 버라 바마소마아, 버라 구모아 부씨 어먀시 어라 야바아 야찌기뤄모 야바아 야 구바서사 어미찌마.

33. 유다 나 시롸 부씨 바바아 바두롸 바러비*, 버라 구부라 아부 버머러시 바쀠가보, 이띠 먀시 이너너 야 구바서사

28. It seemed good to the Holy Spirit and to us not to burden you with anything beyond the following requirements:

29. You are to abstain from food sacrificed to idols, from blood, from the meat of strangled animals and from sexual immorality. You will do well to avoid these things. Farewell.

30. The men were sent off and went down to Antioch, where they gathered the church together and delivered the letter.

31. The people read it and were glad for its encouraging message.

32. Judas and Silas, who themselves were prophets, said much to encourage and strengthen the brothers.

33. After spending some time there, they were sent off by the brothers with the blessing of peace to return

emichima. / 어미찌마. / to those who had sent them.

34. Abere bamala suku burebi eyi eandiyokiya, ebemeresi bera kbalaa na kubabura mbu bafuluka nebolo era babatumaabo bali.

34. 아버러 바마퐈 수구 부러비 어에 어아띠요기야, 어버머러시 버라 구바퐈아 나 구바부라 뿌 바푸루가 너보로 어라 바바두마아보 바리.

34. None

35. (sis Sila yeke era kulola kwa kukomire ashibe eyera)

35. (시수 시롸 여거 어라 구로퐈 과 구고미러 아씨버 어여라)

35. But Paul and Barnabas remained in Antioch, where they and many others taught and preached the word of the Lord.

36. Paulo na Baranaba nabo bera kushiba eandiyokiya. Abu babiri alauma na banji bandu banene, bera kunde bakangirisa na kuhubanganya echinwa cha Enawetu.

36. 파우로 나 바라나바 나보 버라 구씨바 어아띠요기야. 아부 바비리 아퐈우마 나 바찌 바뚜 바너너, 버라 구떠 바가끼리사 나 구후바꽈냐 어찌놔 쨔 어나워두.

36. Some time later Paul said to Barnabas, "Let us go back and visit the brothers in all the towns where we preached the word of the Lord and see how they are doing."

Paulo na Baranaba balyikana mwa mulyimo

파우로 나 바라나바 바뻬—낍 와 무뤠명

37. Era nyuma sa suku burebi, Paulo era kubura Baranaba mbu: tuhubaa kanji mu chira musi ola twahubanganyaa mwa chinwa cha Enawetu, tutangule ebemeresi, tulole kunde baendekera.

37. 어라 뉴마 사 수구 부러비 파우로 어라 구부라 바라나바 뿌: 두후바아 가찌 무 찌라 무시 오퐈 돠후바꽈냐아 와 찌놔 쨔 어나워두, 두다꾸퍼 어버머러시, 두로꺼 구떠 바어떠거라.

37. Barnabas wanted to take John, also called Mark, with them,

38. Mwolu lubalamo, Baranaba era kuhonda mbu Yowani ola wasulwaa esina lya marko nai aende nabo.

38. 모루 루바퐈모, 바라나바 어라 구호따 뿌 요와니 오퐈 와수꽈아 어시나 쨔 마루고 나이 아어떠 나보.

38. but Paul did not think it wise to take him, because he had deserted them in Pamphylia and had not continued with them in the work.

39. Si Paulo yeke era kunana busese kwa batachiendaa noyu mundu, bushi mango babaa bali mwa chio che pamufiriya, achikulaa kubo, chiro akachikola kwa mulimo ola baenderaa.

40. Echera, chera kubaretera lubangano lunene busese, bera kunalinda balikana. Baranaba era kuenda na mariko, bera kutola ebwato, na bahabukira kwa chisimba che chipuro

41. Paulo nai kwire alondola Sila. Abere ebemeresi bera babemerera engahanyi era mwa enawetu, nabo bera kuchiuma. Bera kusungula mwa chio che suriya neche kirikiya baende besesa ebemeresi emichima.

39. 시 파우론 여거 어라 구나나 부서서 과 바다쩌따아 노유 무뚜, 부씨 마꼬 바바아 바뀌 마 찌오 쩌 파무피리야, 아찌구꽈아 구보, 찌로 아가찌고꽈 과 무뛰모 오꽈 바어떠라라아.

40. 어쩌라, 쩌라 구바러더라 루바까노 루너너 부서서, 버라 구나뤼따 바뤼가나. 바라나바 어라 구어따 나 마리고, 버라 구도꽈 어봐도, 나 바하부기라 과 찌시빠 쩌 찌푸로

41. 파우론 나이 귀러 아론또꽈 시꽈. 아버러 어버머러시 버라 바버머러라 어까하네 어라 마 어나워두, 나보 버라 구찌우마. 버라 구수꾸꽈 마 찌오 쩌 수리야 너쩌 기리기야 바어떠 버서사 어버머러시 어미찌마.

39. They had such a sharp disagreement that they parted company. Barnabas took Mark and sailed for Cyprus,

40. but Paul chose Silas and left, commended by the brothers to the grace of the Lord.

41. He went through Syria and Cilicia, strengthening the churches.

E Mikolo ye Ndjumwa Chikono 16

Timoteo aenda na Paulo na Sila mwa mulyimo

1. Paulo era kuka mwa musi we Teribe nomwa we Lisitara. Mwoyu musi we lisistara era kubuanana mumweresi muuma mbu i Timoteo. Oyu Timoteo abaa muala wa

어 미고론 여 뚜꽈 찌고노 16 Acts Chapter 16[NIV]

디모더오 아어따 나 파우론 나 시꽈 마 무레명

1. 파우론 어라 구가 마 무시 워 더리버 노꽈 워 뤼시다라. 모유 무시 워 뤼시수다라 어라 구부아나나 무뭐러시 무우마 뿌 이 디모더오. 오유 디모더오 아바아 무아꽈 와

1. He came to Derbe and then to Lystra, where a disciple named Timothy lived, whose mother was a Jewess and a believer, but whose father was a Greek.

muyutakasi muuma ola wahubaa mwemeresi, neshe abaa mukiriki.

2. Ebemeresi be Lisistara ne be Ikoniyo, bendee bateta kwa Timoteo atusa myanya ibuya.

3. Bushi noku, Paulo era kwire ahonda Timoteo ende amwerekesa mwa nyibalamo sai. Paulo era kumurenza tanga mwa mwiya wekumona, bushi ebayuta boshi ba babaa batula mwebi bitambi, babaa baneshi kweshe wa Timoteo atula mukiriki.

4. Mwa misi era bendee basungulamo, babaa benjire baenda babalikisisa ebemeresi kwa myasi era endumwa alauma nebangumwa beluhu lwa Ongo lwe Yerusalemu bafunjikaa. Kanji ei myasi, bera kubabura kwa benaa baikulikira kubuya.

5. Bushi noku, ebemersi bera kunaendekera basimika mwa bwemresi bwabo, na kuendekera baluwa chira lusuku.

Besha makedoniya balalyika Paulo

6. Paulo na balikabu bera kurenga mwa chio che Furikiya nomwa che Kalatiya,

---

무유다가시 무우마 오롸 와후바아 뭐머러시, 너써 아바아 무기리기.

2. 어버머러시 버 릐시수다라 너 버 이고니요, 버떠어 바더다 과 디모더오 아두사 먀냐 이부야.

3. 부씨 노구, 파우롣 어라 귀러 아호따 디모더오 어떠 아뭐러거사 롸 네바롸모 사이. 파우롣 어라 구무러싸 다따 롸 뮈야 워구모나, 부씨 어바유다 보씨 바 바바아 바두롸 뭐비 비다뻬, 바바아 바너씨 궈써 와 디모더오 아두롸 무기리기.

4. 롸 미시 어라 버떠어 바수우롸모, 바바아 버찌러 바어따 바바릐기시사 어버머러시 과 먀시 어라 어뚜롸 아롸우마 너바우롸 버룾후 롸 오으 뭐 여루사뭐무 바푸찌가아. 가찌 어이 먀시, 버라 구바부라 과 버나아 바이구릐기라 구부야.

5. 부씨 노구, 어버머시 버라 구나어떠거라 바시미가 롸 뭐러시 봐보, 나 구어떠거라 바룾와 찌라 룾수구.

버싸 마거도니야 바롸릐—
파우롣

6. 파우롣 나 바릐가부 버라 구러따 롸 찌오 쩌 푸리기야 노롸 쩌 가롸디야, 부씨

---

2. The brothers at Lystra and Iconium spoke well of him.

3. Paul wanted to take him along on the journey, so he circumcised him because of the Jews who lived in that area, for they all knew that his father was a Greek.

4. As they traveled from town to town, they delivered the decisions reached by the apostles and elders in Jerusalem for the people to obey.

5. So the churches were strengthened in the faith and grew daily in numbers.

6. Paul and his companions traveled throughout the region of Phrygia and

---

bushi emchima buya-buya angaabo mbu batahubanganyisa echinwa cha Ongo mwa chio che Asiya.

7. Mango baika ofu nechio che Misiya, bera kuata mianyisa ya kuya mwa musi we Bitiniya, si emuchima wa Yesu, era kwangabo kanji.

8. Bushi noku, bera kwire barenga mwa chio che Misiya na bandalira mwa musi we Torowa.

9. Abere bwera butufu, Paulo era kuya mu byabunya biroto. Era kulola ku mwesha maketoniya muuma emenze era muhondo sai amwema na bonjo bunene mbu: Urengeraa mwa chio che Maketoniya, utuase!

10. Era nyuma sebiroto, unao-unao twera kukunganya elubalamo lwekuya emaketoniya, bushi twabaa twemerere kanangana kwa Ongo iwatwamaere kuya kuhubanganyisa besha y emwasi mubuya-buya.

11. Era nyuma sebi, twera kutenga eTorowa mwa bwato, unao-unao na twahabukira kwa chisimba che Samotirake. Abere mwei mishnangya,

어무찌마 부야-부야 아꼬아아보 뿌 바다후바까네사 어찌놔 짜 오꼬 똬 찌오 쩌 아시야.

7. 마꼬 바이가 오푸 너찌오 쩌 미시야, 버라 구아다 미아네사 야 구야 똬 무시 워 비디니야, 시 어무찌마 와 여수, 어라 과꼬아보 가찌.

8. 부씨 노구, 버라 귀러 바러꼬 똬 찌오 쩌 미시야 나 바따쮜라 똬 무시 워 도로와.

9. 아버러 붜라 부두푸, 파우로ᄙ 어라 구야 무 뱌부냐 비로도. 어라 구로꽈 구 뭐싸 마거도니야 무우마 어머써 어라 무호또 사이 아뭐마 나 보쪼 부너너 뿌: 우러꼬라아 똬 찌오 쩌 마거도니야, 우두아서!

10. 어라 뉴마 서비로도, 우나오-우나오 뚀라 구구꼬냐 어루바꽈모 뤄구야 어마거도니야, 부씨 돠바아 뚀머러러 가나꼬나 과 오꼬 이와돠마어러 구야 구후바꼬네사 버싸 위 어똬시 무부야-부야.

11. 어라 뉴마 서비, 뚀라 구더꼬 어도로와 똬 봐도, 우나오-우나오 나 돠하부기라 과 찌시빠 쩌 사모디라거. 아버러 뭐이 미수후나꺄, 뚀라

Galatia, having been kept by the Holy Spirit from preaching the word in the province of Asia.

7. When they came to the border of Mysia, they tried to enter Bithynia, but the Spirit of Jesus would not allow them to.

8. So they passed by Mysia and went down to Troas.

9. During the night Paul had a vision of a man of Macedonia standing and begging him, "Come over to Macedonia and help us."

10. After Paul had seen the vision, we got ready at once to leave for Macedonia, concluding that God had called us to preach the gospel to them.

11. From Troas we put out to sea and sailed straight for Samothrace, and the next day on to Neapolis.

twera kuka mwa musi we Neyapoli.

구가 와 무시 워 너야포ᄙ리.

12. Twera kutenga eNeyapoli, na twaya mwa musi we Fripi iwabaa musi munene we chio che Maketoniya.oyu musi abaa ali mwa bucha bwe Baroma. Twera kumalamo suku burebi.

12. 뚸라 구더ᄬ 어너야포ᄙ리, 나 돠야 롸 무시 워 푸리피 이와바아 무시 무너너 워 찌오쩌 마거도니야.오유 무시 아바아 아ᄙ리 롸 부짜 붜 바로마. 뚸라 구마롸모 수구 부러비.

12. From there we traveled to Philippi, a Roman colony and the leading city of that district of Macedonia. And we stayed there several days.

13. Mango elusuku lwe Sabato* lwaikaa, twakutenga mwoyu musi, na twaya ofu ne lwishi, bushi twanyisaa kwa mwechi chisiki chisiki mwe bandu bendee bemera Ongo. Twakubuana bakasi bauma babuananyiremo, twera kwekala na twatangirisa twababura era luulu sa Yesu.

13. 마꼬 어루수구 뤄 사바도* ᄙ롸이가아, 돠구더ᄬ 모유 무시, 나 돠야 오푸 너 ᄅ뤼씨, 부씨 돠녜사아 과 뭐찌 찌시기 찌시기 뭐 바뚜 버떠어 버머라 오꼬. 돠구부아나 바가시 바우마 바부아나니러모, 뚸라 궈가라 나 돠다ᄬ리리사 돠바부라 어라 ᄅ우우ᄅ 사 여수.

13. On the Sabbath we went outside the city gate to the river, where we expected to find a place of prayer. We sat down and began to speak to the women who had gathered there.

14. Mwabu bakasi, mwabaa mili muuma mbu i Lutiya, mwesha mwa mus imbu iwe Tuwatera. Oyu Lutiya, abaa atula muchimbusi wa njimba sa bulimbi sa mwola, kanji abaa atula atunjire Ongo. Na mango Paulo abaa ahambala, enawetu era kuboola emchima wa Lutiya kukira echihangi emerera emyasi ya Paulo.

14. 롸부 바가시, 롸바아 미ᄙ리 무우마 뿌 이 ᄙ루디야, 뭐싸 롸 무수 이뿌 이워 두와더라. 오유 ᄙ루디야, 아바아 아두롸 무찌뿌시 와 ᄯ지빠 사 부ᄙ리ᄬ 사 모롸, 가찌 아바아 아두롸 아두ᄯ지러 오꼬. 나 마꼬 파우ᄅ로 아바아 아하빠라, 어나워두 어라 구보오롸 어무찌마 와 ᄙ루디야 구기라 어찌하ᄬ 어머러라 어먀시 야 파우ᄅ로.

14. One of those listening was a woman named Lydia, a dealer in purple cloth from the city of Thyatira, who was a worshiper of God. The Lord opened her heart to respond to Paul's message.

15. Chasinda, era kubatisibwa alauma na besha mwa mwai boshi.era kutwema mbu:mubahaa mwalolire kwa

15. 짜시따, 어라 구바디시봐 아롸우마 나 버싸 롸 뫄이 보씨.어라 구뚸마 뿌:무바하아 뫄ᄅ로ᄙ리러 과 너머러러

15. When she and the members of her household were baptized, she invited us to her home. "If you

nemerere enawetu kanangana, mubaha mubere mwa mwanyi. Era kunatwanjikirira twemerere.

Ebakulu-kulu b'e Baroma bauma Paulo na Sila mwa buroko

16. Lusuku luuma, twabaa twaya mwa chisiki che kwemeramo, twera kubuanana na muandakasi muuma wa munyere.oyu muandakasi, abaa atusa chihwasi cha chendee chamuasa kulaula. Oku kulaula kwai, kwera kutuma be nawabo kunde babona bikulo binene?.

17. Era kunde akulikira Paulo alauma netu aenda alanga mbu: bano bandu, bali bakosi ba Ongo wokkwa nguba. Benjire ba bahambalira era luulu senjira era mungabona mwe bununusi.

18. Era kunamala suku sinene enjire aira bacha. Chasinjire, Paulo ebute bwera kumusimba. Rero, lusuku luuma era kibindula na abura echi chihwasi mbu: natechire kwesina lya Yesu Kirisito, utengaa kwoyu munyere. Unao-unao, cha chihwasi kuna kumutengako.

19. Rero be nawabo ola

어나워두 가나빠나, 무바하 무버러 뫄 뫄네. 어라 구나돠찌기리라 뛰머러러.

어바구루-구루 버 바로마 바우마 파우뿐 나 시꽈 뫄 부로고

16. 루수구 루우마, 돠바아 돠야 뫄 찌시기 쩌 궈머라모, 뛰라 구부아나나 나 무아따가시 무우마 와 무녀러.오유 무아따가시, 아바아 아두사 찌화시 짜 쩌떠어 짜무아사 구꽈우꽈. 오구 구꽈우꽈 과이, 궈라 구두마 버 나와보 구떠 바보나 비구뽄 비너너?.

17. 어라 구떠 아구뤼기라 파우뿐 아꽈우마 너두 아어따 아꽈빠 뿌: 바노 바두, 바뤼 바고시 바 오꼬 옹구과 꾸바. 버찌러 바 바하빠뤼라 어라 루우뿐 서찌라 어라 무빠보나 뭐 부누누시.

18. 어라 구나마꽈 수구 시너너 어찌러 아이라 바짜. 짜시찌러, 파우뿐 어부더 뭐라 구무시빠. 러로, 루수구 루우마 어라 기비뚜꽈 나 아부라 어찌 찌화시 뿌: 나더찌러 궈시나 꽈 여수 기리시도, 우더빠아 고유 무녀러. 우나오-우나오, 짜 찌화시 구나 구무더빠고.

19. 러로 버 나와보 오꽈

consider me a believer in the Lord," she said, "come and stay at my house." And she persuaded us.

16. Once when we were going to the place of prayer, we were met by a slave girl who had a spirit by which she predicted the future. She earned a great deal of money for her owners by fortune-telling.

17. This girl followed Paul and the rest of us, shouting, "These men are servants of the Most High God, who are telling you the way to be saved."

18. She kept this up for many days. Finally Paul became so troubled that he turned around and said to the spirit, "In the name of Jesus Christ I command you to come out of her!" At that moment the spirit left her.

19. When the owners of the

munyere, balolire kwa emunyiiro wabo we kubona emutoloke kurengera oyu munyere awere, bera kwire basimba Paulo na Sila. Bera kubakulira era muhondo se baishi be manja ala bandu bendee babuanana.

20. Mango ba baisa era muhondo sabu baishi bemanja be baroma, bera kutangirisa bateta mbu: bano bandu bali bayuta, kanji barechire na lwayo lunene mwono musi wetu.

21. Ne myanya yebenjire bakangirisa ebandu, iri era tu baroma tutula tunanyisibwe kwemerera nesi kukulikira.

22. Eluamba lwe bandu momvire bacha, kuna kutabalira Paulo na Sila. Ebaishi be manja bera kubura ebasula mbu: mubakongola enjimba, mubahute etchi.

23. Abere bera babahutaa busese, bera kwire babauma mwa buroko. Bera kubura emulanzi wobu buroko mbu abalanga kubuya.

24. Kukulikana noyu mwasi, oyu mulanzi era kuumabo mwa chumba chomwa busese.era kubaminyira emaulu mwa biito.

무녀러, 바로삐러 과 어무네이로 와보 워 구보나 어무도로거 구러써라 오유 무녀러 아워러, 버라 귀러 바시빠 파우로 나 시쫘. 버라 구바구삐라 어라 무호또 서 바이씨 버 마짜 아쫘 바뚜 버떠어 바부아나나.

20. 마꼬 바 바이사 어라 무호또 사부 바이씨 버마짜 버 바로마, 버라 구다삐리사 바더다 뿌: 바노 바뚜 바삐 바유다, 가찌 바러찌러 나 쫘요 루너너 모노 무시 워두.

21. 너 먀냐 여버찌러 바가삐리사 어바뚜, 이리 어라 두 바로마 두두쫘 두나네시붜 궈머러라 너시 구구삐기라.

22. 어루아빠 뤄 바뚜 모삐러 바짜, 구나 구다바삐라 파우로 나 시쫘. 어바이씨 버 마짜 버라 구부라 어바수쫘 뿌: 무바고꼬쫘 어찌빠, 무바후더 어찌.

23. 아버러 버라 바바후다아 부서서, 버라 귀러 바바우마 뫄 부로고. 버라 구부라 어무쫘씨 오부 부로고 뿌 아바쫘꽈 구부야.

24. 구구삐가나 노유 뫄시, 오유 무쫘씨 어라 구우마보 뫄 쭈빠 쪼뫄 부서서.어라 구바미네라 어마우루 뫄 비이도.

---

slave girl realized that their hope of making money was gone, they seized Paul and Silas and dragged them into the marketplace to face the authorities.

20. They brought them before the magistrates and said, "These men are Jews, and are throwing our city into an uproar

21. by advocating customs unlawful for us Romans to accept or practice."

22. The crowd joined in the attack against Paul and Silas, and the magistrates ordered them to be stripped and beaten.

23. After they had been severely flogged, they were thrown into prison, and the jailer was commanded to guard them carefully.

24. Upon receiving such orders, he put them in the inner cell and fastened their feet in the stocks.

25. Mango kabaa kahonda kuba kachi-kachi ka butufu, Paulo na Sila babaa banachiri bema nekwima enyimbo sekutonga Ongo. Ebanji bandu bemulisi nabo, babaa babomvirisa,

26. Unao-unao, kwera kurenga musisi munene, era kulingitanya eburoko. Enyisi soshi sera kunachichungulanga, ne mareure ma mabaa maminyire ebandu bemulisi boshi, namo kuna kuchibookaliranga.

27. Emulanzi we buroko era kusuka. Alolire kwa nyisi se buroko sibookere, era kuhohola ebombo bwai achite, bushi achichingaa mbu ebandu bemulisi bongolokire.

28. Si Paulo era kuuma emurenge mbu: cha-cha! utachitaa, bushi tuboshi mutunali muno.

29. Oyu mulanzi, kwera kwema ekamore, era kulibichira mwecha chumba fuba, era kuchihunda mwa maulu ma Paulo na Sila, akukumana ne buba.

30. Chasinda, era kubeka era butala, na abusabo mbu: ebenawetu, chi nemire kuira chasiya nyobone ebununusi

25. 마꼬 가바아 가호따 구바 가찌-가찌 가 부두푸, 파우로 나 시롸 바바아 바나찌리 버마 너귀마 어네뾰 서구도와 오꼬. 어바씨 바뚜 버무퓌시 나보, 바바아 바보뻬리사,

26. 우나오-우나오, 궈라 구러꽈 무시시 무너너, 어라 구퓌미다냐 어부로고. 어네시 소씨 서라 구나쭈뀌콰꽈, 너 마러우러 마 마바아 마미네러 어바뚜 버무퓌시 보씨, 나모 구나 구찌보오가퓌리꽈.

27. 어무콰씨 워 부로고 어라 구수가. 아로퓌러 과 네시 서 부로고 시보오거러, 어라 구호호콰 어보뾰 봐이 아찌더, 부씨 아찌찌꽈아 뿌 어바뚜 버무퓌시 보꼬로기러.

28. 시 파우로 어라 구우마 어무러러꺼 뿌: 짜-짜! 우다찌다아, 부씨 두보씨 무두나퓌 무노.

29. 오유 무콰씨, 궈라 궈마 어가모러, 어라 구퓌비찌라 뭐짜 쭈빠 푸바, 어라 구찌후따 콰 마우루 마 파우로 나 시콰, 아구구마나 너 부바.

30. 짜시따, 어라 구버가 어라 부다콰, 나 아부사보 뿌: 어버나워두, 찌 너미러 구이라 짜시야 뇨보너 어부누누시

25. About midnight Paul and Silas were praying and singing hymns to God, and the other prisoners were listening to them.

26. Suddenly there was such a violent earthquake that the foundations of the prison were shaken. At once all the prison doors flew open, and everybody's chains came loose.

27. The jailer woke up, and when he saw the prison doors open, he drew his sword and was about to kill himself because he thought the prisoners had escaped.

28. But Paul shouted, "Don't harm yourself! We are all here!"

29. The jailer called for lights, rushed in and fell trembling before Paul and Silas.

30. He then brought them out and asked, "Sirs, what must I do to be saved?"

31. Nabo mbu: wemerera enawetu Yesu, ubone ebununusi alauma na besha mwa mwao.

32. Bera kumbubalira echinwa cha Enawetu, alauma na besha mwa mwai boshi.

33. Unao-unao, mwobu butufu, oyu mulanzi era kutola Paulo na Sila, era kubalonga ebyuulu, chasinda bera kumubatisa alauma nabesha mwa mwai boshi.

34. Chasinjire, era kubabura mbu berukiraa ala mawai, era kubasheera ebiryo. Yeinealauma na besha mwa mwai boshi bera kumowa busese bushi bemerere Ongo.

35. Mango bwabaa bwera bwachaa, ebaishi be manja be baroma bera kutumira oyu mulanzi endumwa mbu: uboolaa babandu.

36. Oyu lulanzi nai era kuya kubura Paulo mbu: ebaishi be manja banyitumirire emwasi kwa nybaboola. Rero, mwiree mwauluka, muchendere nebolo.

37. Si Paulo era kubura ba baretaa oyu mwasi mbu: abu baishi be manja batuhuchisaa

---

31. 나보 뿌: 워머러라 어나워두 여수, 우보너 어부누누시 아롸우마 나 버싸 마 마오.

32. 버라 구뿌바뤼라 어찌놔 짜 어나워두, 아롸우마 나 버싸 마 마이 보씨.

33. 우나오-우나오, 모부 부두푸, 오유 무롸씨 어라 구도롸 파우뢰 나 시롸, 어라 구바로ㅁ놔 어뷰우룾, 짜시따 버라 구무바디사 아롸우마 나버싸 마 마이 보씨.

34. 짜시찌러, 어라 구바부라 뿌 버루기라아 아롸 마와이, 어라 구바써어라 어비료. 여이너아롸우마 나 버싸 마 마이 보씨 버라 구모와 부서서 부씨 버머러러 오꼬.

35. 마꼬 봐바아 붜라 봐짜아, 어바이씨 버 마쨔 버 바로마 버라 구두미라 오유 무롸씨 어뚜놔 뿌: 우보오롸아 바바뚜.

36. 오유 루롸씨 나이 어라 구야 구부라 파우뢰 뿌: 어바이씨 버 마쨔 바네두미리러 어와시 과 네바보오롸. 러로, 뮈러어 마우룾가, 무쩌머러 너보뢰.

37. 시 파우뢰 어라 구부라 바 바러다아 오유 마시 뿌: 아부 바이씨 버 마쨔 바두후찌사아

---

31. They replied, "Believe in the Lord Jesus, and you will be saved--you and your household."

32. Then they spoke the word of the Lord to him and to all the others in his house.

33. At that hour of the night the jailer took them and washed their wounds; then immediately he and all his family were baptized.

34. The jailer brought them into his house and set a meal before them; he was filled with joy because he had come to believe in God--he and his whole family.

35. When it was daylight, the magistrates sent their officers to the jailer with the order: "Release those men."

36. The jailer told Paul, "The magistrates have ordered that you and Silas be released. Now you can leave. Go in peace."

37. But Paul said to the officers: "They beat us publicly without a trial, even

짜똬나마 부시라 구두도똬냐
다똬, 노구 너두 두나쀠
바로마! 버라 구나쀠따
바두우마 나 모부노 부로고.
러로, 구더 버라 바호따
구두보오똬 똬 부비쏘-비쏘
찌다똬쀠가나!
38. 아부 바뚜 바 바두똬 버라
구야 구바쀠라 어바이씨
버마짜 궈이 먀시. 아부
바이씨 버 마짜 보쀄러 과
가시 파우로 나 시똬 나보
바쀠 바로마, 버라 고바아
부서서.

39. 버라 궈러바야 구버마
어부바바쀠러 나 구바구똬 똬
부로고. 짜시따 버라 구부라
파우로 나 시똬 뿌 바더따
모유 무시.
40. 마꼬 파우로 나 시똬
바바아 버라 바더따아 똬
부로고, 버라 구야 아똬 똬
루디야. 버라 구다꾸똬
어버머러시 나 구바서사
어미찌마. 짜시쎠러 버라 궈러
바더따 모유 무시.

changanama busira
kututonganya tanga, noku
netu tnali baroma! bera
kunalinda batuuma na
mwobuno buroko. Rero, kute
bera bahonda kutuboola mwa
bubisho-bisho chitangalikana!
38. Abu bandu ba batumwa
bera kuya kubalira ebaishi
bemanja kwei myasi. Abu
baishi be manja bomvire kwa
kasi Paulo na Sila nabo bali
baroma, bera kwobaa busese.

39. Bera kwirebaya kubema
ebubabalire na kubakula mwa
buroko. Chasinda bera kubura
Paulo na Sila mbu batenga
mwoyu musi.
40. Mango Paulo na Sila
babaa bera batengaa mwa
buroko, bera kuya ala mwa
Lutiya. Bera kutangula
ebemeresi na kubasesa
emichima. Chasinjire bera
kwire batenga mwoyu musi.

though we are Roman
citizens, and threw us into
prison. And now do they
want to get rid of us
quietly? No! Let them come
themselves and escort us
out."
38. The officers reported
this to the magistrates, and
when they heard that Paul
and Silas were Roman
citizens, they were alarmed.

39. They came to appease
them and escorted them
from the prison, requesting
them to leave the city.

40. After Paul and Silas
came out of the prison,
they went to Lydia's house,
where they met with the
brothers and encouraged
them. Then they left.

E Mikolo ye Ndjumwa Chikono 17

어 미고로 여 뚜똬 찌고노 17 Acts Chapter 17[NIV]

Paulo na Sila mwa musi w'e Tesalonika

파우로 나 시똬 똬 무시 워 더사쪈늬—

1. Paulo na Sila bera kuendekera lwa lubuanano

1. 파우로 나 시똬 버라 구어떠거라 똬 루부아나노

1. When they had passed through Amphipolis and

lwabo, bera kurenga mwa musi we Amvipoli ne wa Apoloniya, bera kuka mwa we Tesalonika. Mwoyu musi mwabaa mutula bushenhe bwa bayuta.

꽈보, 버라 구러먀 먀 무시 워 아뻬포리 너 와 아포로니야, 버라 구가 먀 워 더사로니가. 모유 무시 마바아 무두꽈 부써누허 봐 바유다.

Apollonia, they came to Thessalonica, where there was a Jewish synagogue.

2. Rero, Paulo era kukulikanya suku ehatu sa sabato*enjire engirire mwa bushenge bwe bayuta*, bushi abaa akomere kwengiriremo. Mwobu ushenge baa nejire ahambala nebandu er aluulu se maanjiko mabuya-buya.

2. 러로, 파우로 어라 구구꿰가냐 수구 어하두 사 사바도*어찌러 어찌리러 먀 부써어 붜 바유다*, 부씨 아바아 아고머러 궈찌리리로모. 모부 우써어 바아 너지러 아하빠꽈 너바뚜 어루 아루우루 서 마아찌고 마부야- 부야.

2. As his custom was, Paul went into the synagogue, and on three Sabbath days he reasoned with them from the Scriptures,

3. Abaa enjire abakangirisa ne kubalosa kwa byabaa byemire Masiya* alibuke, anomwoke. Kanji era kunde ababura mbu: oyu Yesu nejire nabahambalire era luulu sahi, ina Masiya*.

3. 아바아 어찌러 아바가찌리사 너 구바로사 과 뱌바아 벼미러 마시야* 아찌부거, 아노모거. 가찌 어라 구떠 아바부라 뿌: 오유 여수 너지러 나바하빠찌러 어라 루우루 사히, 이나 마시야*.

3. explaining and proving that the Christ had to suffer and rise from the dead. "This Jesus I am proclaiming to you is the Christ," he said.

4. Bayuta bauma bera kwire bemerera na baya kwa lunda lwa Paulo na Sila. Nalunji luamba lwa bakiriki ba babaa batunjire Ongo, alauma na bakasi banene ba babaa bete tunda, nabo bera kunemerera.

4. 바유다 바우마 버라 귀러 버머러라 나 바야 과 루따 꽈 파우로 나 시꽈. 나루찌 루아빠 꽈 바기리기 바 바바아 바두찌러 오엇, 아꽈우마 나 바가시 바너너 바 바바아 버더 두따, 나보 버라 구너머러라.

4. Some of the Jews were persuaded and joined Paul and Silas, as did a large number of God-fearing Greeks and not a few prominent women.

5. Si bayuta bauma bera kufa mufula. Bera kubuanyanya bihusi biuma myomwa nama. Ber kuchibika alauma, nabatangirisa bareta lwayu mwa musi woshi. Mwolu, bera

5. 시 바유다 바우마 버라 구파 무푸꽈. 버라 구부아냐냐 비후시 비우마 무요봐 나마. 버루 구찌비가 아꽈우마, 나바다찌리사 바러다 꽈유 먀 무시 오씨. 모루, 버라 구야

5. But the Jews were jealous; so they rounded up some bad characters from the marketplace, formed a mob and started a riot in the city. They rushed to

kuya kutabalira enyumba ya Yasoni bahondere mu Paulo na Sila, chasiya babeke era munhondo se bandu.

6. Si chiro bakababuanamo. Bera kwire beka Yasoni alauma na banji bemeresi era muhondo se bakulu-kulu be musi. Bera kutangirisa balakanga mbu: banu banjo barechire lwayo mwa butala boshi, rero, bababano baika nokuko.

7. Nono Yasoni, iwabahukasa mwa mwai. Kanji kutali chiro namuuma mubo alamwenjire watunda omwaso wa mwami we baroma, bushi beke benjire bateta mbu kuli unji mwami mbi i Yesu.

8. Ei myasi yera kusibusa eluamba lwebandu alauma nebakululu be musi.

9. Yasoni na baliakabo bera kwana chikinja cha buteya buene era mxabu bakulu-kulu, era muhondo se kubalikula.

Paulo na Sila lwa musi w'e Beroya

10. Abere bwera butufu, ebemeresi bera kwerekesa Paulo na Sila mwa musi we Beroya. Baikiremo, bera kwengira mwa bushenge bwe

---

구다바삐리라 어뉴빠 야 야소니 바호러러 무 파우뤈 나 시꽈, 짜시야 바버거 어라 무누호또 서 바뚜.

6. 시 찌로 바가바부아나모. 버라 귀러 버가 야소니 아꽈우마 나 바찌 버머러시 어라 무호또 서 바구루-구루 버 무시. 버라 구다삐리사 바꽈가꽈 뿌: 바누 바쪼 바러찌러 꽈요 뫄 부다꽈 보씨, 러로, 바바바노 바이가 노구고.

7. 노노 야소니, 이와바후가사 뫄 마이. 가찌 구다삐 찌로 나무우마 무보 아꽈뭐삐러 와두따 오뫄소 와 뫄미 워 바로마, 부씨 버거 버찌러 바더다 뿌 구리 우씨 뫄미 삐 이 여수.

8. 어이 먀시 여라 구시부사 어루아빠 뤄바뚜 아꽈우마 너바구루루루 버 무시.

9. 야소니 나 바삐아가보 버라 과나 찌기짜 짜 부더야 부어너 어라 무x아부 바구루-구루, 어라 무호또 서 구바삐구꽈.

파우뤈 나 시꽈 꽈 무시 워 버로야

10. 아버러 뭐라 부두푸, 어버머러시 버라 귀러거사 파우뤈 나 시꽈 꽈 무시 워 버로야. 바이기러모, 버라 귀삐라 꽈 부써삐 뭐 바유다*.

Jason's house in search of Paul and Silas in order to bring them out to the crowd.

6. But when they did not find them, they dragged Jason and some other brothers before the city officials, shouting: "These men who have caused trouble all over the world have now come here,

7. and Jason has welcomed them into his house. They are all defying Caesar's decrees, saying that there is another king, one called Jesus."

8. When they heard this, the crowd and the city officials were thrown into turmoil.

9. Then they made Jason and the others post bond and let them go.

10. As soon as it was night, the brothers sent Paul and Silas away to Berea. On arriving there, they went to the Jewish synagogue.

bayuta*.

11. Besha beroya babaa bandu ba muchima mubuya-buya kurenza besha tesalonika, bushi beke bangirirraa echinwa cha Ongo na mchima muuuma. Chire lusuku benji basoma emaanjiko mabuyaubua mwakuhonda ba mereri akaba bya Paulo abaa enjire abura bo binali bya kanangana.

11. 버싸 버로야 바바아 바뚜 바 무찌마 무부야-부야 구러싸 버싸 더사쁘니가, 부씨 버거 바삐리라아 어찌놔 짜 오꼬 나 무찌마 무우우마. 찌러 쁘수구 버찌 바소마 어마아찌고 마부야우부아 똬구호따 바 머러리 아가바 뱌 파우쁘 아바아 어찌러 아부라 보 비나뤼 뱌 가나싸나.

11. Now the Bereans were of more noble character than the Thessalonians, for they received the message with great eagerness and examined the Scriptures every day to see if what Paul said was true.

12. Bayuta banene mubo, bera berakuhuba bemeresi, alauma na bandu banene besinji mbaa. Mwabu bandu, mwabamuli bakasi ba babaa bete tunda na balume.

12. 바유다 바너너 무보, 버라 버라구후바 버머러시, 아꽈우마 나 바뚜 바너너 버시찌 빠아. 똬부 바뚜, 똬바무뤼 바가시 바 바바아 버더 두따 나 바루머.

12. Many of the Jews believed, as did also a number of prominent Greek women and many Greek men.

13. Si ebayuta bomwa musi we tesalonika mango bomvaa kwa Paulo enjire ahubanganya echinwa cha Ongo e beroya namo, bera kuhuba kubakulikiramo. Bera kutangirisa bashiirisa ebandu, nekunalinda bareta lwayu lunene.

13. 시 어바유다 보똬 무시 워 더사쁘니가 마꼬 보빠아 과 파우쁘 어찌러 아후바아냐 어찌놔 짜 오꼬 어 버로야 나모, 버라 구후바 구바구뤼기라모. 버라 구다삐리사 바씨이리사 어바뚜, 너구나뤼따 바러다 꽈유 쁘너너.

13. When the Jews in Thessalonica learned that Paul was preaching the word of God at Berea, they went there too, agitating the crowds and stirring them up.

14. Bushi noku, ebemeresi bera kuira berekesa Paulo kuikira kwa chihabukiro. Si Sila na Timoteo beke, bera kweshiba eberoya.

14. 부씨 노구, 어버머러시 버라 구이라 버러거사 파우쁘 구이기라 과 찌하부기로. 시 시꽈 나 디모더오 버거, 버라 궈씨바 어버로야.

14. The brothers immediately sent Paul to the coast, but Silas and Timothy stayed at Berea.

15. Ebandu ba berekesa Paulo bera kunalinda bamuisa mwa musi we Atene. Mwa kuhuba

15. 어바뚜 바 버러거사 파우쁘 버라 구나뤼따 바무이사 똬 무시 워 아더너.

15. The men who escorted Paul brought him to Athens and then left with

eberoya, Paulo era kubalaira mbu baburaa Timoteo na Sila kwa bamubuanaa fuba.

마 구후바 어버로야, 파우로 어라 구바쫘이라 뿌 바부라아 디모더오 나 시쫘 과 바무부아나아 푸바.

instructions for Silas and Timothy to join him as soon as possible.

Paulo ahambala na besha Atene

파우로 아하빠쫘 나 버싸 아더너

16. Mango Paulo abaa anachiri alinjira Timoteo na Sila mwa musi we Atene, era kunde alola kwa wmoyu musi mwehwire bihuhanyi bya baongo, echere chera kumuluma busese kwa mchima.

16. 마꼬 파우로 아바아 아나찌리 아쮜찌라 디모더오 나 시쫘 마 무시 워 아더너, 어라 구떠 아로쫘 과 우모유 무시 뭐휘러 비후하네 뱌 바오꼬, 어쩌러 쩌라 구무루마 부서서 과 무찌마.

16. While Paul was waiting for them in Athens, he was greatly distressed to see that the city was full of idols.

17. Era kwire ende ahambala ne bayuta mwa bushenge bwabo alauma ne benji bandu besinji mbaa ba babaa batunjire Ongo. Kanji chire lusuku, era kunde ahambala nebandu ba bendee abuana mwa chisiki che kubuanano.

17. 어라 귀러 어떠 아하빠쫘 너 바유다 마 부써떠 봐보 아쫘우마 너 버찌 바뚜 버시찌 빠아 바 바바아 바두찌러 오꼬. 가찌 찌러 루수구, 어라 구떠 아하빠쫘 너바뚜 바 버떠어 아부아나 마 찌시기 쩌 구부아나노.

17. So he reasoned in the synagogue with the Jews and the God-fearing Greeks, as well as in the marketplace day by day with those who happened to be there.

18. Bakangirisa bauma bomwa chikembe che Baepukuriyo na banji bomwa che basitoiko nabo bera kutangirisa baenda ebwaka na Paulo. Bauma mubo, babaa benjire babusanya mbu: chiye chi ono katetera enjire ahonda kuteta ne banji mbu: Ali ngola wenjire wahubanganya era luulu sa baongo bauma ba chienyi. Bende babusa bacha bushi Paulo abaa

18. 바가쯰리사 바우마 보쫘 찌거뻐 쩌 바어푸구리요 나 바찌 보쫘 쩌 바시도이고 나보 버라 구다쯰리사 바어따 어봐가 나 파우로. 바우마 무보, 바바아 버찌러 바부사냐 뿌: 찌여 찌 오노 가더더라 어찌러 아호따 구더다 너 바찌 뿌: 아뤼 꼬쫘 워찌러 와후바까냐 어라 루우루 사 바오꼬 바우마 바 쩌네. 버떠 바부사 바짜 부씨 파우로 아바아 아후바까네사 어봐시

18. A group of Epicurean and Stoic philosophers began to dispute with him. Some of them asked, "What is this babbler trying to say?" Others remarked, "He seems to be advocating foreign gods." They said this because Paul was preaching the good news about J

ahubanganyisa emwasi mubuya-buya wa Yesu, nera luulu se komoka kwai.

무부야-부야 와 여수, 너라 루우루 서 고모가 과이.

19. Bushi noku bera kuya nai era muhondo se karubanda ka kerikibwe mbu Areyopako. Ebakulu-kulu baku karubanda bera kumubusa mbu:

19. 부씨 노구 버라 구야 나이 어라 무호또 서 가루바따 가 거리기붸 뿌 아러요파고. 어바구루-구루 바구 가루바따 버라 구무부사 뿌:

19. Then they took him and brought him to a meeting of the Areopagus, where they said to him, "May we know what this new teaching is that you are presenting?

20. Ei myasi iyayaya wenjire wenjire wahubanganyisa ebandu, tungasimire utukange kute ku itechire.

20. 어이 먀시 이야야야 워찌러 워찌러 와후바까네사 어바뚜, 두가시미러 우두가꺼 구더 구 이더찌러.

20. You are bringing some strange ideas to our ears, and we want to know what they mean."

21. Byabaa bacha bushi besha atene boshi alauma ne baenyi ba babaa batulamo, bende banarenza ebihangi byabo byoshi mwa kunde bomvirisa nesi kuteteresa era luulu se myasi iyayaya.

21. 뱌바아 바짜 부씨 버싸 아더너 보씨 아좌우마 너 바어네 바 바바아 바두좌모, 버떠 바나러싸 어비하끼 뱌보 보씨 먀 구떠 보뻬리사 너씨 구더더러사 어라 루우루 서 먀시 이야야야.

21. (All the Athenians and the foreigners who lived there spent their time doing nothing but talking about and listening to the latest ideas.)

22. Paulo era kwire emanga mwa kachi-kachi ke bakulu-kulu be karubanda ke yeropako, era kuteta mbu: Emu besha atene! nyisene kwa mubeke, mu chire kandu mutula muhondosise emyasi yetini busese!

22. 파우로 어라 귀러 어마까 먀 가찌-가찌 거 바구루-구루 버 가루바따 거 여로파고, 어라 구더다 뿌: 어무 버싸 아더너! 네서너 과 무버거, 무 찌러 가뚜 무두좌 무호또시서 어먀시 여디니 부서서!

22. Paul then stood up in the meeting of the Areopagus and said: "Men of Athens! I see that in every way you are very religious.

23. Natechire bacha, bushi mango nejire nasungula mwonu musi wenyu, nachilorera kwa bihuhanyi bya mwendee mwera. Ne kulola na kukahaha kauma kemitulo*

23. 나더찌러 바짜, 부씨 마꼬 너지러 나수꿔좌 모누 무시 워뉴, 나찌로러라 과 비후하네 뱌 무버떠어 뭐라. 너 구로좌 나 구가하하 가우마 거미두로* 바바아 버찌기러고 뿌: 가

23. For as I walked around and looked carefully at your objects of worship, I even found an altar with this inscription: TO AN UNKNOWN GOD. Now

ka babaa benjikireko mbu: ka ongo ola uteshibwe. Rero, oyu Ongo mwende mwera busira kumumenya, inoyu inenjire nabahubanganyisa.

오꼬 오롸 우더씨붜. 러로, 오유 오꼬 뭐떠 뭐라 부시라 구무머냐, 이노유 이너찌러 나바후바까네사.

what you worship as something unknown I am going to proclaim to you.

24. Ongo iwabumba ebutala nabyoshi bya bitulamo, kanji ina Ena enguba ne butala. Bushi noku, atekala mwa nyulu sa saimbwaa nebandu.

24. 오꼬 이와부빠 어부다롸 나뵤씨 뱌 비두롸모, 가찌 이나 어나 어꾸바 너 부다롸. 부씨 노구, 아더가롸 뫄 뉴루 사 사이뽜아 너바뚜.

24. "The God who made the world and everything in it is the Lord of heaven and earth and does not live in temples built by hands.

25. Kanji atatula alaire ku kuasibwa na mundu, bushi iwende weresa ebandu boshi omuka wekalamo, alauma ne bindu byoshi.

25. 가찌 아다두롸 아롸이러 구 구아시봐 나 무뚜, 부씨 이워떠 워러사 어바뚜 보씨 오무가 워가롸모, 아롸우마 너 비뚜 뵤씨.

25. And he is not served by human hands, as if he needed anything, because he himself gives all men life and breath and everything else.

26. Kanji ebandu bembaa soshi ba abumbaa, ku mundu muuma kubana shokaa chasiya behule mwa butala boshi. Era kubairira ne byanda, nenyi bibi sebio byabo.

26. 가찌 어바뚜 버빠아 소씨 바 아부빠아, 구 무뚜 무우마 구바나 쏘가아 짜시야 버후러 뫄 부다롸 보씨. 어라 구바이리라 너 뱌따, 너네 비비 서비오 뱌보.

26. From one man he made every nation of men, that they should inhabit the whole earth; and he determined the times set for them and the exact places where they should live.

27. Ongo airaa ebyera, bushi abaa ahonda ebandu bamulonde, banalinde bamubona chiro angaba mbu bamuhonda mwa kutala-tala. Si chiro bacha, Ongo atatula burerere na chira muuma mu tubano!

27. 오꼬 아이라아 어벼라, 부씨 아바아 아호따 어바뚜 바무로떠, 바나리떠 바무보나 찌로 아까바 뿌 바무호따 뫄 구다롸-다롸. 시 찌로 바짜, 오꼬 아다두롸 부러러러 나 찌라 무우마 무 두바노!

27. God did this so that men would seek him and perhaps reach out for him and find him, though he is not far from each one of us.

28. Bushi ebuashi bwai bu butumire twabao, twahaala, mumwabo ba bende banjika

28. 부씨 어부아씨 봐이 부 부두미러 돠바오, 돠하아롸, 무뫄보 바 버떠 바찌가 어먀시

28. 'For in him we live and move and have our being.' As some of your own poets

emyasi banjika mbu: netu, tunatula bana bai,

29. Rero, oku tuli bana ba Ongo, bitemire tunde twaanyisa mbu Ongo atula ahuhire nga bihuhanyi bya bandu bakwisaa kwa burenga mwa horo, nesi mwa miringa, nesi mwa makoi.

30. Bya bandu bendee baira mango babaa bali mwa buuta, Ongo asimaa kutabianja. Si rero, kubura ku era enjire abura ebandu boshi ba bali mu chira chisiki babindule emyanya yabo.

31. Bushi alondwere lusuku luuma lwa akachinjibusa mwabandu boshi busirakulondola mundu. Nobu buchinjibusi, bukemangirwa na mundu muuma ola Ongo yeine alondwere mira. Kanji Ongo alosise ebandu boshi echera mwa kwomola oyu mundu mwa bafu.

32. Abu bakulu-kulu, mango bomva kwa Paulo ahambala era luulu se kwomoka kwa bafu, bauma mubo, bera kutangirisa bamushekera. Si ebanji beke kumubura mbu: tungahuba kuka kumvirisa kwei myasi lunji lusuku.

33. Chasinjire, Paulo era

바찌가 뿌: 너두, 두나두롸 바나 바이,

29. 러로, 오구 두뤼 바나 바 오꼬, 비더미러 두떠 똬아니사 뿌 오꼬 아두롸 아후히러 까 비후하네 뱌 바뚜 바귀사아 과 부러롸 와 호로, 너시 와 미리까, 너시 와 마고이.

30. 뱌 바뚜 버떠어 바이라 마꼬 바바아 바뤼 와 부우다, 오꼬 아시마아 구다비아짜. 시 러로, 구부라 구 어라 어찌러 아부라 어바뚜 보씨 바 바뤼 무 찌라 찌시기 바비뚜뭐 어먀냐 야보.

31. 부씨 아룬뚜워러 루수구 루루마 롸 아가찌띠부사 롸바뚜 보씨 부시라구룬또롸 무뚜. 노부 부찌띠부시, 부거망이롸 나 무뚜 무우마 오롸 오꼬 여이너 아룬뚜워러 미라. 가찌 오꼬 아룬시서 어바뚜 보씨 어쩌라 와 고모롸 오유 무뚜 와 바푸.

32. 아부 바구루-구루, 마꼬 보빠 과 파우론 아하빠롸 어라 루우루 서 고모가 과 바푸, 바우마 무보, 버라 구다미리사 바무쎄거라. 시 어바찌 버거 구무부라 뿌: 두까후바 구가 구뻬리리사 궈이 먀시 룬찌 루수구.

33. 짜시찌러, 파우론 어라

have said, 'We are his offspring.'

29. "Therefore since we are God's offspring, we should not think that the divine being is like gold or silver or stone--an image made by man's design and skill.

30. In the past God overlooked such ignorance, but now he commands all people everywhere to repent.

31. For he has set a day when he will judge the world with justice by the man he has appointed. He has given proof of this to all men by raising him from the dead."

32. When they heard about the resurrection of the dead, some of them sneered, but others said, "We want to hear you again on this subject."

33. At that, Paul left the

kurekana nabo.	구러가나 나보.	Council.

34. Si chiro bacha, bandu bauma bera kuhuba bemeresi na baya kwa lunda lwa Paulo. Mwanu bandu,mwabaa muli Tiyonisiyo, muuma mwa ba babaa bali mwa karubanda ke Areyonisyo, na mukasi muuma mbu i Tamari, alauma na banji bandu.

34. 시 찌로 바짜, 바뚜 바우마 버라 구후바 버머러시 나 바야 과 루따 롸 파우로. 와누 바뚜,뫄바아 무릐 디요니시요, 무우마 뫄 바 바바아 바릐 뫄 가루바따 거 아러요니쇼, 나 무가시 무우마 뿌 이 다마리, 아롸우마 나 바찌 바뚜.

34. A few men became followers of Paul and believed. Among them was Dionysius, a member of the Areopagus, also a woman named Damaris, and a number of others.

E Mikolo ye Ndjumwa Chikono 18

어 미고로 여 뚜뫄 찌고노 18

Acts Chapter 18[NIV]

Paulo mwa musi w'e Korinto 파우로 뫄 무시 워 고리또

1. Era nyma sebi, Paulo era kutenga mw amusi we Atene, era kuya mwa we Korindo.

1. 어라 네마 서비, 파우로 어라 구더꽈 무우 아무시 워 아더너, 어라 구야 뫄 워 고리또.

1. After this, Paul left Athens and went to Corinth.

2. Aikiremo, era kubuana mu muyuta muuma mbu i Akila, mwesha mwa chio che Pondo. Oyu akila na mkai Purisila babaa batsa kweresa kwerisa batengire mwa chio Italiya, bushi mwami kalautiyo abaa aulusise ebayuta boshi mwa musi we Roma. Pailo era kuya kubatangula,

2. 아이기러모, 어라 구부아나 무 무유다 무우마 뿌 이 아기롸, 뭐싸 뫄 찌오 쩌 포또. 오유 아기롸 나 무가이 푸리시꽈 바바아 바두사 궈러사 궈리사 바더꿰러 뫄 찌오 이다릐야, 부씨 뫄미 가라우디요 아바아 아우루시서 어바유다 보씨 뫄 무시 워 로마. 파이로 어라 구야 구바다꿀롸,

2. There he met a Jew named Aquila, a native of Pontus, who had recently come from Italy with his wife Priscilla, because Claudius had ordered all the Jews to leave Rome. Paul went to see them,

3. Era kwire anekla nabo bushi emulimo wai newabo anabaa muuma. Noyu mulimo wabo abaa wa kukunganya

3. 어라 궈러 아너구꽈 나보 부씨 어무릐모 와이 너와보 아나바아 무우마. 노유 무릐모 와보 와보 아바아 와 구구꽈냐

3. and because he was a tentmaker as they were, he stayed and worked with them.

mahema.	마허마.	
4. Na chira lusuku lwa sabato*, Paulo abaa enjire engirira mwa bushenge bwe bayuta*. Era kunde aenda ebwaka ne bayuta alauma ne bakiriki era luulu se chinwa cha Ongo, chasiya babe bemeresi.	4. 나 찌라 루수구 롸 사바도*, 파우로 아바아 어지러 어끼리라 뫄 부써어 붜 바유다*. 어라 구떠 아어따 어봐가 너 바유다 아롸우마 너 바기리기 어라 루우루 서 찌놔 짜 오오, 짜시야 바버 버머러시.	4. Every Sabbath he reasoned in the synagogue, trying to persuade Jews and Greeks.
5. Mango Sila na Timoteo babaa bera baikaa batengera emaketoniya, Paulo era kwire anabika ebihangi byai byoshi mwa kunde ahubanganya echinwa cha Ongo. Era kunde abura ebayuta kwa Yesu ina Masiya*.	5. 마오 시롸 나 디모더오 바바아 버라 바이가아 바더어라 어마거도니야, 파우로 어라 귀러 아나비가 어비하끼 뱌이 뵤씨 뫄 구떠 아후바까냐 어찌놔 짜 오오. 어라 구떠 아부라 어바유다 과 여수 이나 마시야*.	5. When Silas and Timothy came from Macedonia, Paul devoted himself exclusively to preaching, testifying to the Jews that Jesus was the Christ.
6. Si ebayuta bera kunana emyasi ya Paulo nekumukamba. Era kwire abakunguchira enjimba ne kubabura mbu: akaba mwera mungaera, emikira yenyu iri kwetwe lwenyu. Nyono ndachete mwinda wa mundu. Na kutengera lwarero, nyingere nachira kukangirisa ebandu besinji mbaa.	6. 시 어바유다 버라 구나나 어먀시 야 파우로 너구무가빠. 어라 귀러 아바구우찌라 어지빠 너 구바부라 뿌: 아가바 뭐라 무까어라, 어미기라 여뉴 이리 궈뛔 뤄뉴. 뇨노 따쩌더 뮈따 와 무뚜. 나 구더어라 롸러로, 네어러 나찌라 구가끼리사 어바뚜 버시지 빠아.	6. But when the Jews opposed Paul and became abusive, he shook out his clothes in protest and said to them, "Your blood be on your own heads! I am clear of my responsibility. From now on I will go to the Gentiles."
7. Paulo era kutenga mwechi chisiki, era kuya mu nyumba nguma era yabaa iri ofu ne bushenge bwe bayuta*. Ei nyumba ya baa ya mulume muuma mbu i Tito Yusuto, oyu yusuto, abaa atula	7. 파우로 어라 구더까 뭐찌 찌시기, 어라 구야 무 뉴빠 우마 어라 야바아 이리 오푸 너 부써어 붜 바유다*. 어이 뉴빠 야 바아 야 무루머 무우마 뿌 이 디도 유수도, 오유 유수도, 아바아 아두롸	7. Then Paul left the synagogue and went next door to the house of Titius Justus, a worshiper of God.

atunjire Ongo.

8. Emukulu-kulu wobu bushenge mbu i Kirisipo era kwemerera enawetu alauma ,a besha mwa mawi boshi. Na besha korindo banene ba bendee bomvirisa emyasi ya Paulo, nabo bera kunde bemerera na kubatisibwa.

9. Lusuku luuma butufu, enawetu era kubura Paulo mubyabunya biroto mbu: utendaa woba nesi wasira! kuhubanganya ku unaendekera wa hubanganya,

10. Bushi nyiri alauma nao, kanji kutali mundu ola ungaerereresa kukuira bukumala mwaka muuma na myesi ndatu,

11. Woyu musi enjire akangirisa ebandu echinwa cha Ongo.

Paulo atongana era muhondo sa Kaliyo

12. Mangokaliyo abaa ali mukulu-kulu wechio che Akaya, ebayuta bera kuchibika alauma mwa lwango lwe kusimba Paulo na bamukululira era muhondo se banji be manja.

13. Bera kutangirisa bateta mbu: Ono mundu enjire ashiirisa ebandu mbu bendaa

---

아두찌러 오꼬.

8. 어무구루-구루 오부 부써꺼 뿌 이 기리시포 어라 궈머러라 어나워두 아꽈우마 ,아 버싸 마 마위 보씨. 나 버싸 고리또 바너너 바 버떠어 보삐리사 어먀시 야 파우론, 나보 버라 구떠 버머러라 나 구바디시봐.

9. 루수구 루우마 부두푸, 어나워두 어라 구부라 파우론 무뱌부냐 비로도 뿌: 우더따아 오바 너시 와시라! 구후바꽈냐 구 우나어떠거라 와 후바꽈냐,

10. 부씨 내리 아꽈우마 나오, 가찌 구다뜨리 무뚜 오꽈 우꽈어러러사 구구이라 부구마꽈 마가 무우마 나 며시 따두,

11. 오유 무시 어찌러 아가뜨리리사 어바뚜 어찌놔 짜 오꼬.

파우론 아도뜨낍 어라 무호또 사 가뜨위

12. 마꼬가뜨리요 아바아 아뜨리 무구루-구루 워찌오 쩌 아가야, 어바유다 버라 구찌비가 아꽈우마 마 꽈꼬 뭐 구시빠 파우론 나 바무구루뜨리라 어라 무호또 서 바찌 버 마짜.

13. 버라 구다뜨리리사 바더다 뿌: 오노 무뚜 어찌러 아씨이리사 어바뚜 뿌 버따아

---

8. Crispus, the synagogue ruler, and his entire household believed in the Lord; and many of the Corinthians who heard him believed and were baptized.

9. One night the Lord spoke to Paul in a vision: "Do not be afraid; keep on speaking, do not be silent.

10. For I am with you, and no one is going to attack and harm you, because I have many people in this city."

11. So Paul stayed for a year and a half, teaching them the word of God.

12. While Gallio was proconsul of Achaia, the Jews made a united attack on Paul and brought him into court.

13. "This man," they charged, "is persuading the people to worship God in

---

bera Ongo kunji-kunji kwa kutakulikene ne mwaso wetu.

14. Abere Paulo era alinga kuteta, kaliyo era kubura abu bayuta mbu: emu bayuta, akaba mwasitakaa ono mundu mbu akolire chibi chirebi nesi mbu airire mwasi mubi ola usitoire, aola nyingabomvirise.

15. Si bushi ebwaka bwenyu benerekere emiomba*, ne masina, ne mwaso wenyuebyera biberekere mubeine. Elubanji luli ngolu, nyono ndangaishalo.

16. Chasinda, era kuteta mbu bakolokanyaa abu bandu, batenge era muhondo se baishi be manja.

17. Mwolu, ebandu bera kuumbikira emukulu-kulu we bushenge bwe bayuta mbu i Sositene. Kuna kutangirisa bamupunjira mwa meho me baishi be manja. Si ebi byoshi, kaliyo chiro akanachiira kubi.

Paulo ahuba e Antiyokiya

18. Paulo era kumala sinji suku sinene mwoyu musi we korindo. Chasinda, era kulaa bemeresi balikabo, era kutola ebwato ahabukira mwa chio che Suriya atondokene na Purisila na Akila. Rero bushi

버라 오꼬 구띠-구띠 과 구다구뀌거너 너 뫄소 워두.

14. 아버러 파우로 어라 아쀠까 구더다, 가뀌요 어라 구부라 아부 바유다 뿌: 어무 바유다, 아가바 뫄시다가아 오노 무뚜 뿌 아고뀌러 찌비 찌러비 너시 뿌 아이리러 뫄시 무비 오롸 우시도이러, 아오롸 네꺄보쀄리서.

15. 시 부씨 어봐가 뷰뉴 버너러거러 어미오빠*, 너 마시나, 너 뫄소 워뉴어뼈라 비버러거러 무버이너. 어루바찌 루뀌 꼬루, 뇨노 따꺄이싸로.

16. 짜시따, 어라 구더다 뿌 바고로가냐아 아부 바뚜, 바더꺼 어라 무호또 서 바이씨 버 마짜.

17. 모루, 어바뚜 버라 구우쀄기라 어무구루-구루 워 부써꺼 뷰 바유다 뿌 이 소시더너. 구나 구다쀠리사 바무푸찌라 뫄 머호 머 바이씨 버 마짜. 시 어비 뵤씨, 가뀌요 찌로 아가나찌이라 구비.

파우로 아후바 어 아띠웝굿앳

18. 파우로 어라 구마퐈 시찌 수구 시너너 뫄유 무시 워 고리또. 짜시따, 어라 구퐈아 버머러시 바뀌가보, 어라 구도퐈 어봐도 아하부기라 뫄 찌오 쩌 수리야 아도또거너 나 푸리시퐈 나 아기롸. 러로

ways contrary to the law."

14. Just as Paul was about to speak, Gallio said to the Jews, "If you Jews were making a complaint about some misdemeanor or serious crime, it would be reasonable for me to listen to you.

15. But since it involves questions about words and names and your own law-- settle the matter yourselves. I will not be a judge of such things."

16. So he had them ejected from the court.

17. Then they all turned on Sosthenes the synagogue ruler and beat him in front of the court. But Gallio showed no concern whatever.

18. Paul stayed on in Corinth for some time. Then he left the brothers and sailed for Syria, accompanied by Priscilla and Aquila. Before he sailed, he had his hair cut

abaa alaisise mira kwa akakorera Ongo, era kukumulwaemviri era muhondo se kutenga kwa chihabukiro che kengureya.

19. Mango baikaa mwa musi we Efeso, Paulo era kurekana na Akila na Purisila. Yeke era kuya mwa bushenge bwe bayuta* na atangirisa ahambala nabo.

20. Bera kumwema mbu ekalaa nabo suku sinene, si era kunana.

21. Mango abaa eralaabo, era kubabura mbu: Ongo akasima nyingahuba kuika ene mwenyu. Chasinda era kutenga Efeso mwa bwato.

22. Abere era aikaa mwa musi we kaisariya, era kwerukira tanga eyerusalemu akese ebemeresi. Chasinda, era kwandaalira eAndiyokiya.

23. Abere amaala suku burebe mwoyu musi, era kuhuba kuchiuma aenda asungula mwa chio che kalatiya musi ku unji, kuikira mwa chio che Furikiya aenda asesa ebemeresi emuchima.

Apolo aika mwa musi w'e Efeso n'e Korinto

부씨 아바아 아꽈이시서 미라 과 아가고러라 오꼬, 어라 구구무꽈어삐리 어라 무호또 서 구더꽈 과 찌하부기로 쩌 거꾸러야.

19. 마꼬 바이가아 꽈 무시 워 어퍼소, 파우로 어라 구러가나 나 아기꽈 나 푸리시꽈. 여거 어라 구야 꽈 부써꺼 붸 바유다* 나 아다꾀리사 아하빠꽈 나보.

20. 버라 구뭐마 뿌 어가꽈아 나보 수구 시너너, 시 어라 구나나.

21. 마꼬 아바아 어라꽈아보, 어라 구바부라 뿌: 오꼬 아가시마 네꽈후바 구이가 어너 뭐뉴. 짜시따 어라 구더꽈 어퍼소 꽈 봐도.

22. 아버러 어라 아이가아 꽈 무시 워 가이사리야, 어라 궈루기라 다꽈 어여루사꺼무 아거서 어버머러시. 짜시따, 어라 과따아꾀라 어아띠요기야.

23. 아버러 아마아꽈 수구 부러버 모유 무시, 어라 구후바 구찌우마 아어따 아수꾸꽈 꽈 찌오 쩌 가꽈디야 무시 구 우찌, 구이기라 꽈 찌오 쩌 푸리기야 아어따 아서사 어버머러시 어무찌마.

아포로 아이가 꽈 무시 워 어퍼소 너 고리또

off at Cenchrea because of a vow he had taken.

19. They arrived at Ephesus, where Paul left Priscilla and Aquila. He himself went into the synagogue and reasoned with the Jews.

20. When they asked him to spend more time with them, he declined.

21. But as he left, he promised, "I will come back if it is God's will." Then he set sail from Ephesus.

22. When he landed at Caesarea, he went up and greeted the church and then went down to Antioch.

23. After spending some time in Antioch, Paul set out from there and traveled from place to place throughout the region of Galatia and Phrygia, strengthening all the disciples.

24. Mwa musi we Efeso mwaikaa muyuta muuma mbu i Apolo. Oyu Apolo abaa mwesha mwa musi we Alekisanduriya. Abaa ndechi ya mulume kanji abaa atula eshi emaanjiko mabuya-buya busese.

25. Ne njira ye kukulikira Enawetu, nai abaa akangirisibwei mira. Nai abaa enjire ahubanganyisa ebandu na kubakangirisa na bushuri bunene ekanangana kemyasi era yekere Yesu. Si ebubatiso bwa Yowani oshao bu abaa aneshi.

26. Era kuya mwa bushenge bwe bayuta*, na atangirisa ahubanganyisa ebandu echinwa cha Ongo busira buba. Abere Purisila na Akila bamvirisaa, bera kuya nai ala mwabo, chasiya bamukangirise enjira ye kukulikira Ongo.

27. Chasinda, Apolo era kuhonda aye mwa chio che Akaya. Ebemeresi bera kumuwa emisi yekusera mwoyu mwasi. Bera kwire banjikira ebemresi ba mwechi chio emaruba mbu bahuukasaa kubuya. Aikireyi, era kuachira mufamunene

24. 꽈 무시 워 어퍼소 꽈이가아 무유다 무우마 뿌 이 아포로. 오유 아포로 아바아 뭐싸 꽈 무시 워 아러기사누리야. 아바아 떠찌 야 무루머 가찌 아바아 아두롸 어씨 어마아찌고 마부야-부야 부서서.

25. 너 찌라 여 구구찌기라 어나워두, 나이 아바아 아가찌리시붜이 미라. 나이 아바아 어찌러 아후바싸네사 어바뿌 나 구바가찌리사 나 부쑤리 부너너 어가나싸나 거먀시 어라 여거러 여수. 시 어부바디소 봐 요오니 오싸오 부 아바아 아너씨.

26. 어라 구야 꽈 부써어 붜 바유다*, 나 아다찌리사 아후바싸네사 어바뿌 어찌놔 짜 오꼬 부시라 부바. 아버러 푸리시롸 나 아기롸 바삐리사아, 버라 구야 나이 아롸 꽈보, 짜시야 바무가찌리서 어찌라 여 구구찌기라 오꼬.

27. 짜시따, 아포로 어라 구호따 아여 꽈 찌오 쩌 아가야. 어버머러시 버라 구무와 어미시 여구서라 모유 꽈시. 버라 귀러 바찌기라 어버러시 바 뭐찌 찌오 어마루바 뿌 바후우가사아 구부야. 아이기러에, 어라 구아찌라 무파무너너 어바뿌

24. Meanwhile a Jew named Apollos, a native of Alexandria, came to Ephesus. He was a learned man, with a thorough knowledge of the Scriptures.

25. He had been instructed in the way of the Lord, and he spoke with great fervor and taught about Jesus accurately, though he knew only the baptism of John.

26. He began to speak boldly in the synagogue. When Priscilla and Aquila heard him, they invited him to their home and explained to him the way of God more adequately.

27. When Apollos wanted to go to Achaia, the brothers encouraged him and wrote to the disciples there to welcome him. On arriving, he was a great help to those who by grace had believed.

ebandu ba bahubaa beremeresi kwa buashi bwe bonjo bwa Ongo,

바 바후바아 버러머러시 과 부아씨 붜 보쪼 봐 오꼬,

28. Bushi yeke endee omya ebayuta emate changanama, mwa kubalosa kurengera emanjiko mabuya-buya kwa Yesu ina Masiya*.

28. 부씨 여거 어떠어 오먀 어바유다 어마더 짜꺄나마, 구바로사 구러꺼라 어마찌고 마부야-부야 과 여수 이나 마시야*.

28. For he vigorously refuted the Jews in public debate, proving from the Scriptures that Jesus was the Christ.

E Mikolo ye Ndjumwa Chikono 19

어 미고론 여 뚜봐 찌고노 19

Acts Chapter 19[NIV]

Paulo ahubanganya echinwa cha Ongo mwa musi w'e Efeso

파우론 아후바꺄낸 어찌놔 짜 오꼬 봐 무시 워 어퍼소

1. Mango Apolo abaa achiri ekorindo, Paulo nai abaa asungulanmwa miruko yebio bye Asiya. Chasinda, era kwandalira mwa musi we Efeso. Era kubuanamo bemresi bauma.

1. 마꼬 아포론 아바아 아찌리 어고리또, 파우론 나이 아바아 아수꾸롸누봐 미루고 여비오 벼 아시야. 짜시따, 어라 과따뢰라 봐 무시 워 어퍼소. 어라 구부아나모 버러시 바우마.

1. While Apollos was at Corinth, Paul took the road through the interior and arrived at Ephesus. There he found some disciples

2. Era kubabusa mbu:mango mwemereraa Yesu, mwabonaa emchima mubuya-buya nabo mbu: nanga, nekunomva kwa kutula mchima mubuya-buya, tutanafuraa kumvako.

2. 어라 구바부사 뿌:마꼬 뭐머러라아 여수, 봐보나아 어무찌마 무부야-부야 나보 뿌: 나까, 너구노빠 과 구두롸 무찌마 무부야-부야, 두다나푸라아 구빠고.

2. and asked them, "Did you receive the Holy Spirit when you believed?" They answered, "No, we have not even heard that there is a Holy Spirit."

3. Era kuhuba kubabusa mbu: ewashe! bubatiso buchiye bu mweraa mwabona mbeke nabo mbu: ebubatiso bwa Yowani akangirisaa.

3. 어라 구후바 구바부사 뿌: 어와써! 부바디소 부찌여 부 뭐라아 봐보나 뻐거 나보 뿌: 어부바디소 봐 요와니 아가뼈리사아.

3. So Paul asked, "Then what baptism did you receive?" "John's baptism," they replied.

4. Paulo kikwera kubabura mbu: Yowani abaa enjire abatisa ebandu ba bendee babinduka kutenga mwa bibi byabo. Kanji abaa enjire aburabo kwa bemereraa ola ungabaha era nyuma sai, noyu i Yesu.

5. Abere bera bomva kwei myasi, bera kubatisibwa kwesina lya enawetu Yesu.

6. Mango Paulo abaa anachiri ababikire kwemino,

7. Unao-unao emchima mubuya-buya nokuna baandalira.

8. Bera kuira myesi ehatu enjire engirira mwa bushenge bwe bayuta*. Era kunde ababura emyasi ye bwami bwa Ongo* na bushuri bunene, bushi abaa ahonda bayemerere.

9. Si bauma mubo, bera kuata mchima musibu, na banana kwemerera. Bera kutangirisa bakamba ei myasi era muhondo se bandu. Bushi noku, Paulo era kubareka, na aya ne bemeresi mu chumba chiuma, cha mulume muumabmbu i Tirano endee

4. 파우뽀 기궈라 구바부라 뿌: 요와니 아바아 어찌러 아바디사 어바뚸 바 버떠어 바비뚜가 구더꺄 롸 비비 뱌보. 가찌 아바아 어찌러 아부라보 과 버머러라아 오꽈 우꺄바하 어라 뉴마 사이, 노유 이 여수.

5. 아버러 버라 보빠 궈이 먀시, 버라 구바디시봐 궈시나 랴 어나워두 여수.

6. 마꼬 파우뽀 아바아 아나찌리 아바비기러 궈미노,

7. 우나오-우나오 어무찌마 무부야-부야 노구나 바아따꾀라.

8. 버라 구이라 며시 어하두 어찌러 어꾀리라 롸 부써어 봐유다*. 어라 구떠 아바부라 어먀시 여 봐미 봐 오꼬* 나 부쑤리 부너너, 부씨 아바아 아호따 바여머러러.

9. 시 바우마 무보, 버라 구아다 무찌마 무시부, 나 바나나 궈머러라. 버라 구다꾀리사 바가빠 어이 먀시 어라 무호또 서 바뚜. 부씨 노구, 파우뽀 어라 구바러가, 나 아야 너 버머러시 무 쭈빠 찌우마, 짜 무루머 무우마부뿌 이 디라노 어떠어

4. Paul said, "John's baptism was a baptism of repentance. He told the people to believe in the one coming after him, that is, in Jesus."

5. On hearing this, they were baptized into the name of the Lord Jesus.

6. When Paul placed his hands on them, the Holy Spirit came on them, and they spoke in tongues and prophesied.

7. There were about twelve men in all.

8. Paul entered the synagogue and spoke boldly there for three months, arguing persuasively about the kingdom of God.

9. But some of them became obstinate; they refused to believe and publicly maligned the Way. So Paul left them. He took the disciples with him and had discussions daily in the lecture hall of Tyrannus.

akangirisisa mwebandu.
Mwechi chumba, mu Paulo
abaa enjire akangirisisa
ebemeresi echinwa cha Ongo
chira lusuku.

10. Paulo era kunaendekera
aira basha ku myaka ebiri,
kuikira kwa chihangi ebayuta
ne bakiriki boshi ba babaa
batula mwa chio che Asiya
bomva echinwa cha enawetu.

*Baala ba Sikewa bahuchwa
n'echihwasi*

11. Ongo abaa enjire aira
bisomerano bya bitafura
kulorekano kurengera Paulo.

12. Ebandu bera kunde
batolanga ebitambara
nenjimba sa saumaa kwa
mubiri wa Paulo, bera kunde
babiretenga ebalwala na
balama. Ebihwasi nabi,
byakunde byanabatengako.

13. Kwabaa kuli bayuta bauma
ba babaa benjire barenga-
renga baenda bambula
ebihwasi kwa bandu. Nabo
mwa kwambula ebihwasi, bera
kunde barengera mwesina lya
enawetu Yesu mbu: kwesina
lya Yesu ola Paulo enjire
ahubanganya, nababwirire
mutengaa kwono mundu!

14. Mwa ba bendee baira ei

아가끼리시사 뭐바뚜. 뭐찌
쭈빠, 무 파우로 아바아
어찌러 아가끼리시사
어버머러시 어찌냐 짜 오꼬
찌라 루수구.

10. 파우로 어라 구나어떠거라
아이라 바싸 구 먀가 어비리,
구이기라 과 찌하끼 어바우다
너 바기리기 보씨 바 바바아
바두롸 뫄 찌오 쩌 아시야
보빠 어찌냐 짜 어나워두.

*바아롸 바 시거와 바후쫘
너찌화시*

11. 오꼬 아바아 어찌러
아이라 비소머라노 뱌
비다푸라 구로러가노 구러꺼라
파우로.

12. 어바뚜 버라 구떠
바도롸꽈 어비다빠라 너찌빠
사 사우마아 과 무비리 와
파우로, 버라 구떠 바비러더꽈
어바쫘롸 나 바쫘마. 어비화시
나비, 뱌구떠 뱌나바더꽈고.

13. 과바아 구찌 바유다
바우마 바 바바아 버찌러
바러꽈-러꽈 바어따 바뿌롸
어비화시 과 바뚜. 나보 뫄
과뿌롸 어비화시, 버라 구떠
바러꺼라 뭐시나 쨔 어나워두
여수 뿌: 귀시나 쨔 여수 오롸
파우로 어찌러 아후바꺼냐,
나바뷔리러 무더꽈아 굠노
무뚜!

14. 뫄 바 버떠어 바이라 어이

10. This went on for two
years, so that all the Jews
and Greeks who lived in the
province of Asia heard the
word of the Lord.

11. God did extraordinary
miracles through Paul,

12. so that even
handkerchiefs and aprons
that had touched him were
taken to the sick, and their
illnesses were cured and the
evil spirits left them.

13. Some Jews who went
around driving out evil
spirits tried to invoke the
name of the Lord Jesus over
those who were demon-
possessed. They would say,
"In the name of Jesus,
whom Paul preaches, I
command you to come
out."

14. Seven sons of Sceva, a

myasi, mwabaa muli baala ba sikewa balinda. Oyu sikewa, abaa muuma mwa bakulu-kulu be babakuhanyi be bayuta.

15. Lusuku luuma, echihwasi chabaa chiri ku mundu muuma. Na Paulo nai nyimwishi. Si mwabo, mu mwera bande

16. Mwolu, ola wabaa usimbirwe nechihwasi kuna kubaumbikira, era kubarenza nemisi boshi, kunakutangirisa abapunda-punda. Bera kunalinda baula mwa nyumba yoyu mulwala benda bahaa,bera bali butambara, bachikangire nebiulu.

17. Besha Efeso boshi, ebayuta ne bakiriki bera kunomva kwoyu mwasi. Ebula bwera kwire bwasimba boshi. Esina lya enawetu Yesu lyera kuya ngulu.

18. Rero, banene mwa bahubaa bemeresi, babaa benjire baika kuchiya changanama kwa mabi mabo era muhondo se bandu.

19. Banene mubo, ba bendee baula, nabo bera kunde bareta ebitabo bya bendee bakoresa mwa kulaula ne

마시, 롸바아 무뤼 바아롸 바 시거와 바뛰따. 오유 시거와, 아바아 무우마 롸 바구루루-구루 버 바바구하네 버 바유다.

15. 루수구 루우마, 어찌화시 짜바아 찌리 구 무뚜 무우마. 나 파우롣 바이 네뮈씨. 시 뫄보, 무 뭐라 바너

16. 모루, 오롸 와바아 우시삐뤄 너찌화시 구나 구바우삐기라, 어라 구바러싸 너미시 보씨, 구나구다삐리사 아바푸따-푸따. 버라 구나뛰따 바우롸 롸 뉴빠 요유 무롸롸 버따 바하아,버라 바뛰 부다빠라, 바찌가삐러 너비우룹.

17. 버싸 어퍼소 보씨, 어바유다 너 바기리기 버라 구노빠 교유 롸시. 어부롸 뭐라 귀러 봐시빠 보씨. 어시나 롸 어나워두 여수 뗘라 구야 읏룹.

18. 러로, 바너너 롸 바후바아 버머러시, 바바아 버찌러 바이가 구찌야 짜빠나마 과 마비 마보 어라 무호또 서 바뚜.

19. 바너너 무보, 바 버떠어 바우롸, 나보 버라 구떠 바러다 어비다보 뱌 버떠어 바고러사 롸 구롸우롸 너 구떠

Jewish chief priest, were doing this.

15. (One day) the evil spirit answered them, "Jesus I know, and I know about Paul, but who are you?"

16. Then the man who had the evil spirit jumped on them and overpowered them all. He gave them such a beating that they ran out of the house naked and bleeding.

17. When this became known to the Jews and Greeks living in Ephesus, they were all seized with fear, and the name of the Lord Jesus was held in high honor.

18. Many of those who believed now came and openly confessed their evil deeds.

19. A number who had practiced sorcery brought their scrolls together and burned them publicly. When

kunde babyochera era muhondo se bandu boshi. Mwa kulaula echichiro che bi bitabo, bera kulola kwa byabaa bingafa byumbi matano bya buteya.

바뵤쩌라 어라 무호또 서 바누 보씨. 똬 구꽈우꽈 어찌찌로 쩌 비 비다보, 버라 구뢴꽈 과 뱌바아 비빠파 뷰뻬 마다노 뱌 부텨야.

they calculated the value of the scrolls, the total came to fifty thousand drachmas.

20. Mwolu, echinwa cha enawetu chera kunandekera chahandabana mwa bisiki byoshi kwa buashi bwai, chaata na misi inene.

20. 모루, 어찌놔 짜 어나워두 쩌라 구나떠거라 짜하따바나 똬 비시기 뵤씨 과 부아씨 봐이, 짜아다 나 미시 이너너.

20. In this way the word of the Lord spread widely and grew in power.

Elwayo lwabo mwa musi w'e Efeso

어콰읩 콰별 똬 무시 워 어퍼소

21. Era nyuma sebi, Paulo era kulola kwa kukomire arengere mwa chio che maketoniya, ne che Akaya, chasinda erukireeyerusalemu. Kanji era kuteta mbu: era nyuma sekuika eyerusalemu, binganyema nyike nomwa musi we Roma namo.

21. 어라 뉴마 서비, 파우뢴 어라 구뢴꽈 과 구고미러 아러뻐러 똬 찌오 쩌 마거도니야, 너 쩌 아가야, 짜시따 어루기러어여루사뻐무. 가찌 어라 구더다 뿌: 어라 뉴마 서구이가 어여루사뻐무, 비빠녀마 네거 노똬 무시 워 로마 나모.

21. After all this had happened, Paul decided to go to Jerusalem, passing through Macedonia and Achaia. "After I have been there," he said, "I must visit Rome also."

22. Era kwire atola bandu babiri mwaba bendee bemwerekesa, Timoteo na Erasito mbu bamuhondoreraa emaketoniya. Si yeke era kwishiba tanga mwa chio che Asiya ku suku burebi.

22. 어라 귀러 아도꽈 바누 바비리 똬바 버떠어 버뭐러거사, 디모더오 나 어라시도 뿌 바무호또러라아 어마거도니야. 시 여거 어라 귀씨바 다빠 똬 찌오 쩌 아시야 구 수구 부러비.

22. He sent two of his helpers, Timothy and Erastus, to Macedonia, while he stayed in the province of Asia a little longer.

23. Rero mwesi suku, mwa musi we Efeso mwera kuba lyayo lunene bushi nemyasi ye kukulikira enawetu.

23. 러로 뭐시 수구, 똬 무시 워 어퍼소 뭐라 구바 랴요 루너너 부씨 너먀시 여 구구끠기라 어나워두.

23. About that time there arose a great disturbance about the Way.

24. Mwoyu musi mwabaa mutula murenga muuma mbu

24. 모유 무시 똬바아 무두꽈 무러빠 무우마 뿌 이

24. A silversmith named Demetrius, who made silver

i Temetiriyo. Oyu temetiriyo, abaa atusa mulimo wa kwesa bihuhanyi bieke-eke mwa biroto bya bihuhiri eluhu lwa ongo muuma mbu mutoloke munene.

25. Temetiriyo era kunde aretera kubuanyanya abu barenga alauma nebanji bandu ba bendee bakola emulimo ola uli ngoyu. Era kubabura mbu: ebetu! si mwishi kwono mlimo itula utubikire!

26. Rero, mbeine mwacholorere na kumchumvira kwa ono Paulo ashirise na kweka bandu banene muno musi we Efeso na mu bisiki binene byomuno chio choshi che Asiya. Enjire ateta mbu ebaongo ba bandu bende bakwisa, batatula ba ongo ba kanangana.

27. Rero, nyisene kwa ono mulimo wetubkufa kwa anjire afa. Ne luhu lwa ongo wetu munene Aritemi, nalo lutachilorekanako nga kandu, ne tunda layi, nali lingaera noku iongo ola ebandu boshi bomuno Aqiya nebmowa butala boshi bende bera.

28. Abu beranga bomvire bya

더머디리요. 오유 더머디리요, 아바아 아두사 무뢰모 와 귀사 비후하네 비어거-어거 뫄 비로도 뱌 비후히리 어루후 똬 오꼬 무우마 뿌 무도로거 무너너.

25. 더머디리요 어라 구떠 아러더라 구부아냐냐 아부 바러꺄 아퐈우마 너바찌 바뚜 바 버떠어 바고똬 어무뢰모 오똬 우뢰 꼬유. 어라 구바부라 뿌: 어버두! 시 뮈씨 굪노 무뢰모 이두똬 우두비기러!

26. 러로, 뻐이너 뫄쪼뢰러러 나 구무쭈뻬라 과 오노 파우뢰 아씨리서 나 귀가 바뚜 바너너 무노 무시 워 어퍼소, 나 무 비시기 비너너 뵤무노 찌오 쪼씨 쩌 아시야. 어찌러 아더다 뿌 어바오꼬 바 바뚜 버떠 바귀사, 바다두똬 바 오꼬 바 가나꺄나.

27. 러로, 네서너 과 오노 무뢰모 워두부구퐈 과 아씨러 아퐈. 너 루후 똬 오꼬 워두 무너너 아리더미, 나뢴 루다찌뢰러가나고 꺄 가뚜, 너 두따 똬에, 나뢰 뤼꺄어라 노구 이오꼬 오똬 어바뚜 보씨 보무노 아구이야 너부모와 부다똬 보씨 버너 버라.

28. 아부 버라꺄 보뻬러 뱌

---

shrines of Artemis, brought in no little business for the craftsmen.

25. He called them together, along with the workmen in related trades, and said: "Men, you know we receive a good income from this business.

26. And you see and hear how this fellow Paul has convinced and led astray large numbers of people here in Ephesus and in practically the whole province of Asia. He says that man-made gods are no gods at all.

27. There is danger not only that our trade will lose its good name, but also that the temple of the great goddess Artemis will be discredited, and the goddess herself, who is worshiped throughout the province of Asia and the world, will be robbed of her

28. When they heard this,

Temetiriyo abaa ateta, bera kusibuka busese na batangirisa balakanga mbu: Aritemi we Efeso aye ngulu!

더머디리요 아바아 아더다, 버라 구시부가 부서서 나 바다삐리사 바쫘가빠 뿌: 아리더미 워 어퍼소 아여 꾸룩!

they were furious and began shouting: "Great is Artemis of the Ephesians!"

29. Olu lwayu, lwera kunaendekera lwaluwa mwa musi woshi. Ebandu bera kusimba besha maketoniya babiri, kayo na arisitariko, bu bendee berekesa Paulo mwa mulimo. Kuna kubeka mwa nyumba inene era ebandu bendee babuananamo.

29. 오루 쫘유, 쭤라 구나어떠거라 쫘루와 마 무시 오씨. 어바누 버라 구시빠 버싸 마거도니야 바비리, 가요 나 아리시다리고, 부 버떠어 버러거사 파우뢰 마 무찌모. 구나 구버가 마 뉴빠 이너너 어라 어바누 버떠어 바부아나나모.

29. Soon the whole city was in an uproar. The people seized Gaius and Aristarchus, Paul's traveling companions from Macedonia, and rushed as one man into the theater.

30. Paulo abaa ahonda kuchikangana era muhondo sabu bandu, si ebemeresi bera kumwanga.

30. 파우뢰 아바아 아호따 구찌가꺄나 어라 무호또 사부 바누, 시 어버머러시 버라 구뫄꺄.

30. Paul wanted to appear before the crowd, but the disciples would not let him.

31. Bakulu-kulu bauma bomva chio che Asiya ba babaa batula bera bai, nabo bera kumutumira emwasi kwa ataereresa aya mwei nyumba.

31. 바구루-구루 바우마 보빠 찌오 쩌 아시야 바 바바아 바두쫘 버라 바이, 나보 버라 구무두미라 어뫄시 과 아다어러러사 아야 뭐이 뉴빠.

31. Even some of the officials of the province, friends of Paul, sent him a message begging him not to venture into the theater.

32. Mwolu lubuanano mwabaa muli lwayo lunene, bushi bandu bauma babaa balakanga kwabo, ne banji kwabo. Na banene mubo, babaa bataneshi cha chatumire babuanana.

32. 모루 루부아나노 뫄바아 무찌 쫘요 루너너, 부씨 바누 바우마 바바아 바쫘가꺄 과보. 너 바찌 과보. 나 바너너 무보, 바바아 바다너씨 짜 짜두미러 바부아나나.

32. The assembly was in confusion: Some were shouting one thing, some another. Most of the people did not even know why they were there.

33. Bauma mwa bayuta bera kubura mulume muuma mbu i Alesanduro mbu arengaa era muhondo se bandu aburebo bya biri. Nai kukwera kubika

33. 바우마 마 바유다 버라 구부라 무루머 무우마 뿌 이 아뤄사누로 뿌 아러꺄아 어라 무호또 서 바누 아부러보 뱌 비리. 나이 구꿔라 구비가

33. The Jews pushed Alexander to the front, and some of the crowd shouted instructions to him. He motioned for silence in

emino mwa chanya chasiya ebandu basire, bushi abaa ahonda achitetere yeine era muhondo sabo.

34. Si mango bamenyerera kwa kasi ali muyuta, boshi kuna kulakangirisa chakuuma kanji mbu: Aritemi web a Efeso aye ngulu! bera kumala saa singaika kwebiri benjire banateta bacha.

35. Chasinjire, ekaranyi we musi era kubanda kwabu bandu mbu: Emu besha Efeso, kuchiri ola uteshi kwa ono musi wetu iwende walanga eluhu lwa ongo munene aritemi ne chihuhanyi chai cha chatowaa kutengera kwa nguba?

36. Si kutali mundu ola unganana echera! bushi noku, mwiree mwasira, mutanalibichiraa kuira mwasi asibya busira kuanyisa.

37. Natechire bacha, bushi bano bandu mwarechire anola, batebire kandu mwa luhu, nesi kukamba ongo wetu aritemi.

38. Rero, akaba temetiriyo alauma na barenga balikabo bete lubanja. Eyera yi bemire kweka elubanja lwabo!

어미노 똬 짜냐 짜시야 어바뚜 바시러, 부씨 아바아 아호따 아찌더더러 여이너 어라 무호또 사보.

34. 시 마꼬 바머녀러라 과 가시 아픠 무유다, 보씨 구나 구꽈가끼리사 짜구우마 가끼 뿌: 아리더미 워부 아 어퍼소 아여 꾸루! 버라 구마꽈 사아 시꽈이가 궈비리 버찌러 바나더다 바짜.

35. 짜시찌러, 어가라네 워 무시 어라 구바따 과부 바뚜 뿌: 어무 버싸 어퍼소, 구찌리 오꽈 우더씨 과 오노 무시 워두 이워더 와꽈꽈 어루후 꽈 오꼬 무너너 아리더미 너 찌후하네 짜이 짜 짜도와아 구더꺼라 과 꾸바?

36. 시 구다픠 무뚜 오꽈 우꽈나나 어쩌라! 부씨 노구, 뮈러어 꽈시라, 무다나픠비찌라아 구이라 꽈시 아시뱌 부시라 구아네사.

37. 나더찌러 바짜, 부씨 바노 바뚜 꽈러찌러 아노꽈, 바더비러 가뚜 꽈 루후, 너시 구가빠 오꼬 워두 아리더미.

38. 러로, 아가바 더머디리요 아꽈우마 나 바러꽈 바픠가보 버더 루바짜. 어여라 에 버미러 궈가 어루바짜 꽈보!

order to make a defense before the people.

34. But when they realized he was a Jew, they all shouted in unison for about two hours: "Great is Artemis of the Ephesians!"

35. The city clerk quieted the crowd and said: "Men of Ephesus, doesn't all the world know that the city of Ephesus is the guardian of the temple of the great Artemis and of her image, which fell from heaven?

36. Therefore, since these facts are undeniable, you ought to be quiet and not do anything rash.

37. You have brought these men here, though they have neither robbed temples nor blasphemed our goddess.

38. If, then, Demetrius and his fellow craftsmen have a grievance against anybody, the courts are open and there are proconsuls. They

39. Kanji, akaba muchete chinji cha kuteta, mwa lubuanano lwa lutula lwishibe ne mwaso wetu muchingahambalibwako.

39. 가찌, 아가바 무쩌더 찌찌 짜 구더다, 똬 루부아나노 똬 루두똬 뤼씨버 너 똬소 워두 무찌ᄭ하빠뤼봐고.

39. If there is anything further you want to bring up, it must be settled in a legal assembly.

40. Mulolaa! emyasi era yabere lwarero, ingatuma twasitakibwa kwa tubano tu twarechire elwayo. Kanji kutali chiro na mwasi asibya ola tungalosa kwa iwatumire luno lubuaanano lwaba.

40. 무로똬아! 어먀시 어라 야버러 똬러로, 이ᄭ두마 똬시다기봐 과 두바노 두 똬러찌러 어똬요. 가찌 구다뤼 찌로 나 똬시 아시뱌 오똬 두ᄭ로사 과 이와두미러 루노 루부아아나노 똬바.

40. As it is, we are in danger of being charged with rioting because of today's events. In that case we would not be able to account for this commotion, since there is no reason for it."

41. Abere era amala kuteta bacha, era kwire abura ebandu mbu bafulikaa kwa musi.

41. 아버러 어라 아마똬 구더다 바짜, 어라 귀러 아부라 어바누 뿌 바푸뤼가아 과 무시.

41. After he had said this, he dismissed the assembly.

E Mikolo ye Ndjumwa Chikono 20

Paulo abalamira kanji mwa chio ch'e Makedoniya n'e Bukiriki

1. Mango elwayo lwabaa lwera lwawaa mwa musi we Efeso, Paulo era kubuanyanya ebemeresi, na abasesa emchima. Chasinda, era kubalaa, na aya mwa chio che maketoniya.

어 미고뢴 여 뚜똬 찌고노 20

파우뢴 아바똬믈띱 가찌 똬 찌오 쩌 마거도니야 너 부기리기

1. 마꾀 어똬요 똬바아 뤄라 똬와아 똬 무시 워 어퍼소, 파우뢴 어라 구부아냐냐 어버머러시, 나 아바서사 어무찌마. 짜시따, 어라 구바똬아, 나 아야 똬 찌오 쩌 마거도니야.

Acts Chapter 20[NIV]

1. When the uproar had ended, Paul sent for the disciples and, after encouraging them, said good-by and set out for Macedonia.

2. Era kurenga mwechi chio aenda abura ebemeresi myasi inene ya kubasesa emchima. Chasinda, era kuya mwa chio che bukiriki,

3. Na amalayi myesi ehatu. Mango abaa era ahonda kutola ebwato ahabukire mwa chio che suriya, ebayuta bera kumuira lwango. Bushi noku, byera kumwesha ahubekurengera emaketoniya.

4. Babano ku bamwerekesaa: Sopateri muala wa piro, mwesha beriya, na arisitano, na sekundo besha tesalonika, na kayo mwesha teribe, na timoteo, na tikiko, na torofimo, besha mwa chio che Asiya.

5. Abu bandu boshi, bera kutuhonderera mwa musi we torowa, batulinjiremo.

6. Mango elusuku lukulu lwemikati era itali muchachu*lwabaa lwera lwarengaa, tubano twera kutola ebwato twatenga mwa musi we firipi. Abere twamala suku etano mwolu lubanamo, twera kubuana abu baliketu mwa musi we torowa. Mwoyu musi namo, twera kumalamu inji einga lya mutenga.

Paulo omwola Eutiko

2. 어라 구러빠 뭐찌 찌오 아어따 아부라 어버머러시 먀시 이너너 야 구바서사 어무찌마. 짜시따, 어라 구야 꽈 찌오 쩌 부기리기,

3. 나 아마뽜에 며시 어하두. 마꼬 아바아 어라 아호따 구도꽈 어봐도 아하부기러 마 찌오 쩌 수리야, 어바유다 버라 구무이라 꽈꼬. 부씨 노구, 벼라 구뭐싸 아후버구러꺼라 어마거도니야.

4. 바바노 구 바뭐러거사아: 소파더리 무아꽈 와 피로, 뭐싸 버리야, 나 아리시다노, 나 서구또 버싸 더사뢰니가, 나 가요 뭐싸 더리버, 나 디모더오, 나 디기고, 나 도로피모, 버싸 꽈 찌오 쩌 아시야.

5. 아부 바뚜 보씨, 버라 구두호떠러라 꽈 무시 워 도로와, 바두뤼찌러모.

6. 마꼬 어루수구 루구루 뭠미가디 어라 이다뤼 무짜쭈*꽈바아 뭠라 꽈러꽈아, 두바노 뚸라 구도꽈 어봐도 돠더따 꽈 무시 워 피리피. 아버러 돠마꽈 수구 어다노 몰루 루바나모, 뚸라 구부아나 아부 바뤼거두 꽈 무시 워 도로와. 모유 무시 나모, 뚸라 구마꽈무 이찌 어이빠 꺄 무더따.

파우뢰 오모꽈 어우디고

2. He traveled through that area, speaking many words of encouragement to the people, and finally arrived in Greece,

3. where he stayed three months. Because the Jews made a plot against him just as he was about to sail for Syria, he decided to go back through Macedonia.

4. He was accompanied by Sopater son of Pyrrhus from Berea, Aristarchus and Secundus from Thessalonica, Gaius from Derbe, Timothy also, and Tychicus and Trophimus from the province of Asia.

5. These men went on ahead and waited for us at Troas.

6. But we sailed from Philippi after the Feast of Unleavened Bread, and five days later joined the others at Troas, where we stayed seven days.

7. Mango elweinga lwaikaa, twera kubuanana kwa kuhangira emukati. Rero, bushi byabaa byemire Paulo alamukire mwei mishangya, era kutangirisa ahubanganyisa ebandu echinwa cha Ongo kuikira kachi-kachi ka butufu.

8. Echumba cha twabaa tubwananyiremo, chabaa cha kahatu kwa ngangamo senyumba. Mwechi chumba mwabaa mwakorera tumore tunene.

9. Kwetirisha lyechi chumba, kwabaa kwekese mutabana muuma mbu iEutiko. Oyu eutiko, era kutangirisa asindana bushi Paulo amala bihangi biene akangirisa ebandu. Na mango ondoberaa mwa tulo, kuna kutowera amashi atengera kwechi chimbi cha kahatu chei nyumba. Ebandu bera kulibichira kumubatula, si bera kubuana afire mira.

10. Paulo era kwandala, era kwinamirira ku eutiko, era kumurembera. Chasinda, era kubura ebandu mbu: mutalira, bushi achiri aumula!

11. Era nyuma sebi, Paulo era kuhuba kwerukira mwechi chumba, era kuisha kanji mwa

7. 마꼬 어뤄이까 롸이가아, 뛰라 구부아나나 과 구하꼐라 어무가디. 러로, 부씨 뱌바아 벼미러 파우뢰 아롸무기러 뭐이 미싸꺄, 어라 구다꼐리사 아후바까니사 어바뚜 어찌놔 짜 오꼬 구이기라 가찌-가찌 가 부두푸.

8. 어쭈빠 짜 돠바아 두봐나니러모, 짜바아 짜 가하두 과 까까모 서뉴빠. 뭐찌 쭈빠 봐바아 마고러라 두모러 두너너.

9. 궈디리싸 려찌 쭈빠, 과바아 궈거서 무다바나 무우마 뿌 이어우디고. 오유 어우디고, 어라 구다꼐리사 아시따나 부씨 파우뢰 아마롸 비하꼐 비어너 아가꼐리사 어바뚜. 나 마꼬 오또버라아 봐 두로, 구나 구도워라 아마씨 아더꼐라 궈찌 찌뼤 짜 가하두 쩌이 뉴빠. 어바뚜 버라 구꾀비찌라 구무바두롸, 시 버라 구부아나 아피러 미라.

10. 파우뢰 어라 과따롸, 어라 궈나미리라 구 어우디고, 어라 구무러뼤라. 짜시따, 어라 구부라 어바뚜 뿌: 무다꾀라, 부씨 아찌리 아우무롸!

11. 어라 뉴마 서비, 파우뢰 어라 구후바 궈루기라 뭐찌 쭈빠, 어라 구이싸 가찌 봐

7. On the first day of the week we came together to break bread. Paul spoke to the people and, because he intended to leave the next day, kept on talking until midnight.

8. There were many lamps in the upstairs room where we were meeting.

9. Seated in a window was a young man named Eutychus, who was sinking into a deep sleep as Paul talked on and on. When he was sound asleep, he fell to the ground from the third story and was picked up dead.

10. Paul went down, threw himself on the young man and put his arms around him. "Don't be alarmed," he said. "He's alive!"

11. Then he went upstairs again and broke bread and ate. After talking until

mukati, na alyao. Kanji era kunaendekera akangirisa ebandu buhangi binene kuikira lumbuli-mbuli, chasinjire era kuuluka mwei nyumba na achiuma.

무가디, 나 아랴오. 가찌 어라 구나어떠거라 아가끼리사 어바뚜 부하끼 비너너 구이기라 루루뿌찌-뿌찌, 짜시찌러 어라 구우루가 뭐이 뉴빠 나 아찌우마.

daylight, he left.

12. Ebemeresi bera kwerekesa oyu eutiko kwa wabo era ali muuma-uma. Bera kusesibwa emuchima busese.

12. 어버머러시 버라 궈러거사 오유 어우디고 과 와보 어라 아찌 무우마-우마. 버라 구서시봐 어무찌마 부서서.

12. The people took the young man home alive and were greatly comforted.

Paulo abalamira mwa musi w'e Mileto

파우로 아바빠믈띱 똬 무시 워 미뻐몡

13. Paulo abaa ahonda kuya mwa musi we Asosi mwa maulu. Bushi noku, twera kwemeresanya kwa omola mutungabuanana nai. Twera kumureka na twamuhonderera mwa bwato.

13. 파우로 아바아 아호따 구야 똬 무시 워 아소시 똬 마우루. 부씨 노구, 뛰라 궈머러사냐 과 오모똬 무두까부아나나 나이. 뛰라 구무러가 나 똬무호떠러라 봐도.

13. We went on ahead to the ship and sailed for Assos, where we were going to take Paul aboard. He had made this arrangement because he was going there on foot.

14. Mango atubuanaa e Asosi, twera kumutola mwobu bwato, na twahabukira tunabo mwa musi we mitileni.

14. 마꼬 아두부아나아 어 아소시, 뛰라 구무도똬 모부 봐도, 나 똬하부기라 두나보 똬 무시 워 미디뻐니.

14. When he met us at Assos, we took him aboard and went on to Mitylene.

15. Abere elusuku lwa kabiri, twera kutenga kanji emitileni mwa bwato, na twahabukira ofu ne chisimba che Kiyo. Abere elusuku lwa kahatu, twera kuhabukira kwa chisimba che samoni. Chasinda, elusuku lwekane, twera kuhabukira mwa musi we mileto.

15. 아버러 어루수구 똬 가비리, 뛰라 구더까 가찌 어미디뻐니 똬 봐도, 나 똬하부기라 오푸 너 찌시빠 쩌 기요. 아버러 어루수구 똬 가하두, 뛰라 구하부기라 과 찌시빠 쩌 사모니. 짜시따, 어루수구 뛔가너, 뛰라 구하부기라 똬 무시 워 미뻐도.

15. The next day we set sail from there and arrived off Kios. The day after that we crossed over to Samos, and on the following day arrived at Miletus.

16. Paulo abaa ahonda mbu tunaulukanaa eEfeso mwa

16. 파우로 아바아 아호따 뿌 두나우루가나아 어어퍼소 똬

16. Paul had decided to sail past Ephesus to avoid

bwato busira kwimanga, bushi abaa atasumire ebihangi birengere mwa chio che Asiya. Kanji abaa alibichira eyerusalemu chasiya elusuku lukulu lwe pentekosite* lumubuaneyi, akaba bingaalikana.	봐도 부시라 귀마까, 부씨 아바아 아다수미러 어비하끼 비러꺼러 뫄 찌오 쪄 아시야. 가찌 아바아 아리비찌라 어여루사러무 짜시야 어루수구 루구루 뤄 퍼누더고시더* 루무부아너에, 아가바 비까아리가나.	spending time in the province of Asia, for he was in a hurry to reach Jerusalem, if possible, by the day of Pentecost.
Paulo ahambala n'e bangumwa b'e luhu lwa Ongo lw'e Efeso	***파우로 아하빠라 너 바우뭄 버 루훌 뢔 오오 루읍 어퍼소***	
17. Abere Paulo anachire emileto, era kutumisa ebangumwa belhu lwa Ongo lwe Efeso.	17. 아버러 파우로 아나찌러 어미러도, 어라 구두미사 어바우뫄 버루후 롸 오오 뤄 어퍼소.	17. From Miletus, Paul sent to Ephesus for the elders of the church.
18. Mango baikaa era abaa ali, era kubabura mbu: Kutengera elusuku lubere lwa naikaa mwechine chio che Asiya, mubeine muneshi kute emyanya yanyi yabaa iri.	18. 마오 바이가아 어라 아바아 아리, 어라 구바부라 뿌: 구더꺼라 어루수구 루버러 롸 나이가아 뭐찌너 찌오 쪄 아시야, 무버이너 무너씨 구더 어먀냐 야니 야바아 이리.	18. When they arrived, he said to them: "You know how I lived the whole time I was with you, from the first day I came into the province of Asia.
19. Mango nabaa nalibuka nendaane nesise bayuta, kukorera ku nabaa nenjire nanakorera enawetu mwa burembu boshi nomwa malira.	19. 마오 나바아 나리부가 너따아너 너시서 바유다, 구고러라 구 나바아 너찌러 나나고러라 어나워두 뫄 부러뿌 보씨 노뫄 마리라.	19. I served the Lord with great humility and with tears, although I was severely tested by the plots of the Jews.
20. Kanji muneshi kwa akaba kwabaa kuli mwasi ola wabaa ubetere mufa, ndababishaao chiro na hicha. Si nabaa nenjire nabahubanganyisa na kubakangirisa byoshi era muhondo se bandu, nomwa nyumba senyu.	20. 가찌 무너씨 과 아가바 과바아 구리 뫄시 오라 와바아 우버더러 무파, 따바비싸아오 찌로 나 히짜. 시 나바아 너찌러 나바후바까네사 나 구바가끼리사 뵤씨 어라 무호또 서 바뚜, 노뫄 뉴빠 서뉴.	20. You know that I have not hesitated to preach anything that would be helpful to you but have taught you publicly and from house to house.
21. Nabaa nenjire nabura	21. 나바아 너찌러 나부라	21. I have declared to both

ebayuta nebandu besinji mbaa changanama kwa babindukaa kutenga mwa bibi byabo baulukire Ongo, bemerere enawetu Yesu.

22. Rero nyono, ecmuchila lubuya-buya enjire anyibura kwa binyemire kuya eyerusalemu. Eyera, ndeshi emyasi era inganyikirayi,

23. Si cha nyishi kubuya-buya cheke, emuchima mubuya-buya anyilosise mira kwa chira musi ola nyingarengamo, ekuminwa ne kurenga mwa malibuko bibyanyiringamo, ekuminwa ne kurenga mwa malibuko bibyanyirinjira.

24. Si chiro bacha, ekalamo kanyi ndakaseneko nga kandu. Cha nahonda, kuli kumala emulimo wanyi ola enawetu Yesu anyeresise. Noyu mulimo, anali ola we kuhubanaganyisa ebandu emwasi mubuya-buya we bonjo bwa Ongo.

25. Kanji nabaa nejire nasungula mwa kachi-kachi kenyu naenda nabahubanganyisa era luulu se bwami bwa Ongo*. Si rero kutengera lwerero, nyono nyishi kwa kuatchiri chiro na muuma mu mwabo ola

어바유다 너바뚜 버시찌 빠아 짜아나마 과 바비뚜가아 구더아 마 비비 뱌보 바우루기러 오꼬, 버머러러 어나워두 여수.

22. 러로 뇨노, 어시무찌롸 루부야-부야 어찌러 아네부라 과 비녀미러 구야 어여루사뻐무. 어여라, 떠씨 어먀시 어라 이아네기라에,

23. 시 짜 네씨 구부야-부야 쩌거, 어무찌마 무부야-부야 아네론시서 미라 과 찌라 무시 오롸 네아러아모, 어구미놔 너 구러아 마 마뀌부고 비뱌네리아모, 어구미놔 너 구러아 마 마뀌부고 비뱌네리찌라.

24. 시 찌로 바짜, 어가롸모 가네 따가서너고 아 가뚜. 짜 나호따, 구뀌 구마롸 어무뀌모 와네 오롸 어나워두 여수 아녀러시서. 노유 무뀌모, 아나뀌 오라 워 구후바나가네사 어바뚜 어먀시 무부야-부야 워 보쪼 봐 오꼬.

25. 가찌 나바아 너지러 나수꿍롸 마 가찌-가찌 거뉴 나어따 나바후바꾸네사 어라 루우루 서 봐미 봐 오꼬*. 시 러로 구더어라 뤄러로, 뇨노 네씨 과 구아찌리 찌로 나 무우마 무 뫄보 오라 우가찌네뤈롸고.

Jews and Greeks that they must turn to God in repentance and have faith in our Lord Jesus.

22. "And now, compelled by the Spirit, I am going to Jerusalem, not knowing what will happen to me there.

23. I only know that in every city the Holy Spirit warns me that prison and hardships are facing me.

24. However, I consider my life worth nothing to me, if only I may finish the race and complete the task the Lord Jesus has given me-- the task of testifying to the gospel of God's grace.

25. "Now I know that none of you among whom I have gone about preaching the kingdom will ever see me again.

ukachinyilolako.

26. Bushi noku, cehchine chi nababura lwarero: mukere mwaera, emikira yenyu iri kwetwe lwenyu,

27. Bushi emyasi yoshi ye kuhonda kwa Ongo, nababwirirrei mira busira kubabisha kandu.

28. Rero, mundaa chilanga kubuya mubeine, mwanalanga neluamba loshi lwe bemeresi lwa emchima mbuya-buya aberesise mbu mubalangaa. Bushi abu bemeresi, Yesu iwanaa emikira yai kwa kubanunula.

29. Nyishi kwa era nyuma se kuenda kwanyi, ebandu ba bakaliire nga nyishibwabwa bangengirira mwa kachi-kachi kenyu, batanabafire bonjo.

30. Nomwa kachi-kachi kenyu mubeine, namo munachire munganaboneka banji, chasiya bakukulire ebemeresi kwa lunda lwabo.

31. Bushi noku, muchilanga kubuya! kanji mwanende mwakengera kwa kumyaka ehatu, emushi ne butufu, mwa malira ndarekaa kunde neresa chira muuma mu mwabo emano!

26. 부씨 노구, 시어후찌너 찌 나바부라 꽈러로: 무거러 먀어라, 어미기라 여뉴 이리 궈뚸 뤄뉴,

27. 부씨 어먀시 요씨 여 구호따 과 오꼬, 나바뷔리루러이 미라 부시라 구바비싸 가뚜.

28. 러로, 무따아 찌꽈따 구부야 무버이너, 마나꽈따 너루아빠 로씨 뤄 버머러시 꽈 어무찌마 뿌야-부야 아버러시서 뿌 무바꽈따아. 부씨 아부 버머러시, 여수 이와나아 어미기라 야이 과 구바누누꽈.

29. 네씨 과 어라 뉴마 서 구어따 과네, 어바뚜 바 바가뤼이러 따 네씨봐봐 바뤄삐리라 뫄 가찌-가찌 거뉴, 바다나바피러 보쪼.

30. 노뫄 가찌-가찌 거뉴 무버이너, 나모 무나찌러 무따나보너가 바찌, 짜시야 바구구뤼러 어버머러시 과 루따 꽈보.

31. 부씨 노구, 무찌꽈따 구부야! 가찌 먀너떠 뫄거뻐라 과 구먀가 어하두, 어무씨 너 부두푸, 뫄 마삐라 따러가아 구떠 너러사 찌라 무우마 무 뫄보 어마노!

26. Therefore, I declare to you today that I am innocent of the blood of all men.

27. For I have not hesitated to proclaim to you the whole will of God.

28. Keep watch over yourselves and all the flock of which the Holy Spirit has made you overseers. Be shepherds of the church of God, which he bought with his own blood.

29. I know that after I leave, savage wolves will come in among you and will not spare the flock.

30. Even from your own number men will arise and distort the truth in order to draw away disciples after them.

31. So be on your guard! Remember that for three years I never stopped warning each of you night and day with tears.

32. Rero, nababikire mwa maboko ma Ongo. Echinwa chai che bonjo nachi, chindaa chabalanga, bushi echi chinwa chichete ebuashi bwekubaasa kukula mwa bwemeresi, nekuberesa emwandu ola abikire ebandu bai boshi ba anunwire.

33. Kubinali!nyono ndahumiraa, buteya bwabene, nesi horo yabene, nesi njimba sabene.

34. Kanji mubeine muneshi kwa mwesine mino sanyi munendee nakola bushi nebilao byanyi ne bya baliketu ba nabaa nyiri nabo.

35. Mwa myasi yoshi, nabaa nenjire nabalosa kwa bitwemire twinde twashika endubano mwa kukola, chasiya tubone bya tuungasamo babatachirire. Mundaa mwakengera kwa enawetu Yesu yeine atetaa mbu: ola wana iuhanyirwe kurenza ola weresibwa.

36. Abere Paulo era amalaa kuteta ei myasi, era kukoma emafi alauma nabo boshi, era kwema Ongo.

37. Ebandu boshi bera kutangirisa bachiumanga mwa maboko mai, ne

---

32. 러로, 나바비기러 뫄 마보고 마 오꼬. 어찌냐 짜이 쩌 보쪼 나찌, 찌따아 짜바롸아, 부씨 어찌 찌냐 찌쩌더 어부아씨 붜구바아사 구구롸 뫄 붜머러시, 너구버러사 어뫄뚜 오롸 아비기러 어바뚜 바이 보씨 바 아누니위러.

33. 구비나릐!뇨노 따후미라아, 부더야 봐버너, 너시 호로 야버너, 너시 찌빠 사버너.

34. 가찌 무버이너 무너씨 과 뭐시너 미노 사니 무너떠어 나고롸 부씨 너비롸오 뱌네 너 뱌 바릐거두 바 나바아 니리 나보.

35. 뫄 먀시 요씨, 나바아 너찌러 나바로사 과 비뚸미러 뒤떠 돠씨가 어뚜바노 뫄 구고롸, 짜시야 두보너 뱌 두우꽈사모 바바다찌리러. 무따아 뫄거꺼라 과 어나워두 여수 여이너 아더다아 뿌: 오롸 와나 이우하니붜 구러쌰 오롸 워러시봐.

36. 아버러 파우로 어라 아마롸아 구더다 어이 먀시, 어라 구고마 어마피 아롸우마 나보 보씨, 어라 궈마 오꼬.

37. 어바뚜 보씨 버라 구다꾀리사 바찌우마꽈 뫄 마보고 마이, 너 구무오버라꽈

---

32. "Now I commit you to God and to the word of his grace, which can build you up and give you an inheritance among all those who are sanctified.

33. I have not coveted anyone's silver or gold or clothing.

34. You yourselves know that these hands of mine have supplied my own needs and the needs of my companions.

35. In everything I did, I showed you that by this kind of hard work we must help the weak, remembering the words the Lord Jesus himself said: 'It is more blessed to give than to receive.' "

36. When he had said this, he knelt down with all of them and prayed.

37. They all wept as they embraced him and kissed him.

kumuoberanga balira na busese.

바삐라 나 부서서.

---

38. Baliraa bacha, bushi aburaabo kwa batakachimuloleko. Chasinjire, bera kumwerekesa kuikira ala bwato bwe kumweka bwabaa buli.

38. 바삐라아 바짜, 부씨 아부라아보 과 바다가찌무로러고. 짜시띠러, 버라 구뭐러거사 구이기라 아꽈 봐도 뭐 구뭐가 봐바아 부삐.

38. What grieved them most was his statement that they would never see his face again. Then they accompanied him to the ship.

E Mikolo ye Ndjumwa Chikono 21

어 미고로 여 쭈똬 찌고노 21

Acts Chapter 21[NIV]

Paulo erukira eYerusalemu

파우똔 어루기라 어여루사삐물

1. Era nyuma sekukulikana nebangumwa beluhu lwa Ongo lwe Efeso,twera kutola ebwato na twahabukira kwa chisimba che Kosi. Mwei imshangya, twera kuhabukira kwa che Roto. Mwa kutenga kwechi chisimba che Roto, twera kuika mwa musi we Patara.

1. 어라 뉴마 서구구삐가나 너바우똬 버루후 똬 오꼬 뤄 어퍼소,뚸라 구도꽈 어봐도 나 돠하부기라 과 찌시빠 쩌 고시. 뭐이 이무싸꺄, 뚸라 구하부기라 과 쩌 로도. 똬 구더똬 궈찌 찌시빠 쩌 로도, 뚸라 구이가 똬 무시 워 파다라.

1. After we had torn ourselves away from them, we put out to sea and sailed straight to Cos. The next day we went to Rhodes and from there to Patara.

2. Mwoyu musi, twera kubuananmo bwato bwa bwabaa mwa chio che Foinikiya. Twera kuingira mubo na twachiuma.

2. 모유 무시, 뚸라 구부아나누모 봐도 똬 봐바아 똬 찌오 쩌 포이니기야. 뚸라 구이삐라 무보 나 돠찌우마.

2. We found a ship crossing over to Phoenicia, went on board and set sail.

3. Abere twera twalangusa kwa chisimba che Chipuro, twera kurekachi kwa lunda lwe marembe na twerekera mwa chio che Suriya. Twera kwemanga kwa chihabukiro che musi we Tiro, bushi mwoyu musi mwe bwato bwabaa bwemire kukanulira emisio era bwabaa bwete.

3. 아버러 뚸라 돠꽈우사 과 찌시빠 쩌 찌푸로, 뚸라 구러가찌 과 룬따 뤄 마러뻐 나 뚸러거라 뫄 찌오 쩌 수리야. 뚸라 궈마꽈 과 찌하부기로 쩌 무시 워 디로, 부씨 묘유 무시 뭐 봐도 봐바아 붜미러 구가누꿰라 어미시오 어라 봐바아 붜더.

3. After sighting Cyprus and passing to the south of it, we sailed on to Syria. We landed at Tyre, where our ship was to unload its cargo.

4. Twera kubuanana ne bemeresi boyu musi, twera kumala einga liuma nabo. Abu bemeresi, bushi babaa ba koresibwa no muchima mubuya-buya, berakubura Paulo mbu ataya eyerusalemu.

4. 뚸라 구부아나나 너 버머러시 보유 무시, 뚸라 구마꽈 어이꽈 뤼우마 나보. 아부 버머러시, 부씨 바바아 바 고러시봐 노 무찌마 무부야-부야, 버라구부라 파우로 뿌 아다야 어여루사꺼무.

4. Finding the disciples there, we stayed with them seven days. Through the Spirit they urged Paul not to go on to Jerusalem.

5. Si era nyuma sekumala eri einga liuma, twera kutanga e Tiro twendekera nolubalamo lwetu. Abu bemeresi boshi, alauma nebakasi, ne bana bera kutwerekesa kutengera mwa musi kuikira kwa chihabukiro. Twaikire kwechi chihabukiro, twera kukoma emafi na twema Ongo.

5. 시 어라 뉴마 서구마꽈 어리 어이꽈 뤼우마, 뚸라 구다꽈 어 디로 뚸뜨거라 노루바꽈모 뤄두. 아부 버머러시 보씨, 아꽈우마 너바가시, 너 바나 버라 구뚸러거사 구더꺼라 뫄 무시 구이기라 과 찌하부기로. 돠이기러 궈찌 찌하부기로, 뚸라 구고마 어마피 나 뚸마 오꼬.

5. But when our time was up, we left and continued on our way. All the disciples and their wives and children accompanied us out of the city, and there on the beach we knelt to pray.

6. Era kunyuma sekulaana, twera kwengira mwa bwato. Abu bemeresi nabo, berakuhuba mwa musi.

6. 어라 구뉴마 서구꽈아나, 뚸라 궈꿰라 뫄 봐도. 아부 버머러시 나보, 버라구후바 뫄 무시.

6. After saying good-by to each other, we went aboard the ship, and they returned home.

7. Kutengera e Tiro, twera kwendekera nolubuanano lwetu lokwa meshi mwa musi we Tolemai. Twaikire mwoyu musi, twera kulamusa banyetu bemeresi, twera kumala lusuku luuma alauma nabo.

8. Abere mwei mishangya, twere kwengirira mwa nyumba ya muhubanganyi Firipo, na twaberamo. Oyu Firipo abaa muuma mwa bandu balinda babalondolwa kwakwendi baasa endumwa*.

9. Abaa eti banyere bai banne ba babaa batasa kuhweribwa, kanji bendee bareba.

10. Abere twamala suku sitaseeke mwoyu musi we Kaisariya, mwera kuika murebi*muuma mbu i Akabo. Oyu akabo, abaa atengera mwa chio che yuteya.

11. Aikire alatwabaa tuli, erakutola emukaba wa Paulo, kuna kuchimina emaboko ne maulu muo. Era kuta ta mbu: mumvaa, omuchima mubuya-buya atechire mbu: Ena onu mukaba, kuebayuta be Yerusalemu bangamumina bacha ne kumwana mwa maboko me bandu besinji mbaa.

---

7. 구더꺼라 어 디로, 뚸라 궈꺼거라 노루부아나노 뤄두 로과 머씨 뫄 무시 워 도꺼마이. 돠이기러 모유 무시, 뚸라 구꽈무사 바녀두 버머러시, 뚸라 구마꽈 루수구 루우마 아꽈우마 나보.

8. 아버러 뭐이 미싸꺄, 뚸러 궈꺼리라 뫄 뉴빠 야 무후바꺼네 피리포, 나 돠바라모. 오유 피리포 아바아 무우마 뫄 바뚜 바꿰따 바바로또꽈 과궈띠 바아사 어뚜뫄*.

9. 아바아 어디 바녀러 바이 바누너 바 바바아 바다사 구훠리봐, 가찌 버떠어 바라바.

10. 아버러 돠마꽈 수구 시다서어거 모유 무시 워 가이사리야, 뭐라 구이가 무러비*무우마 뿌 이 아가보. 오유 아가보, 아바아 아더꺼라 뫄 찌오 쩌 유더야.

11. 아이기러 아꽈돠바아 두꿰, 어라구도꽈 어무가바 와 파우로, 구나 구찌미나 어마보고 너 마우루 무오. 어라 구다 다 뿌: 무빠아, 오무찌마 무부야-부야 아더찌러 뿌: 어나 오누 무가바, 구어바유다 버 여루사꺼무 바까무미나 바짜 너 구뫄나 뫄 마보고 머 바뚜 버시찌 빠아.

---

7. We continued our voyage from Tyre and landed at Ptolemais, where we greeted the brothers and stayed with them for a day.

8. Leaving the next day, we reached Caesarea and stayed at the house of Philip the evangelist, one of the Seven.

9. He had four unmarried daughters who prophesied.

10. After we had been there a number of days, a prophet named Agabus came down from Judea.

11. Coming over to us, he took Paul's belt, tied his own hands and feet with it and said, "The Holy Spirit says, 'In this way the Jews of Jerusalem will bind the owner of this belt and will hand him over to the Gentiles.' "

12. Twomvire bacha, tubano alauma ne banji bemeresi be kaisariyo, twera kwema Paulo buses embu ataya eyerusalemu.

13. Si yeke era kutwakula mbu: chichatuma mwalira nokuhonda kunyobairisa nyono, nachikunganyise mira kwakuenda kminwa eyerusalemu kwesina lya Enawetu Yesu. Na akaba kufa ,nanemereri kufa bushi nai.

14. Mangu twalolaa kwa atufunjire , twera kwire twateta mbu: ekuhonda kwa enawetu kukunabaa, na twasira.

15. Era nyuma sa suku burebi, twera kohola, na twerukira eyerusalemu.

16. Bemeresi bauma bomwa musi we kaisariya, bera kutwerekesa na batuisa kwe humbi ala mwa mulume muuma mbu i Munasoni. Oyu munasoni abaa mwesha kwa chisimba che chipuro, kanji abaa muuma mwa bemeresi babere-bere.

Paulo atambira Yakobo

17. Mangu twaika eyerusalemu, banyaketu bemeresi bera kutuhukasa na

---

12. 또뻬러 바짜, 두바노 아꽈우마 너 바찌 버머러시 버가이사리요, 뭐라 궈마 파우롣 부서수 어뿌 아다야 어여루사쩌무.

13. 시 여거 어라 구돠구꽈 뿌:찌짜두마 뫄뛰라 노구호따 구뇨바이리사 뇨노, 나찌구까니서 미라 과구어따 구미놔 어여루사쩌무 궈시나 꺄 어나워두 여수. 나 아가바 구파 ,나너머러리 구파 부씨 나이.

14. 마우 돠로뫄아 과 아두푸찌러 , 뭐라 귀러 돠더다 뿌: 어구호따 과 어나워두 구구나바아, 나 돠시라.

15. 어라 뉴마 사 수구 부러비, 뭐라 고호꽈, 나 뭐루기라 어여루사쩌무.

16. 버머러시 바우마 보뫄 무시 워 가이사리야, 버라 구뭐러거사 나 바두이사 궈 후뻬 아꽈 뫄 무루머 무우마 뿌 이 무나소니. 오유 무나소니 아바아 뭐싸 과 찌시빠 쩌 찌푸로, 가찌 아바아 무우마 뫄 버머러시 바버러-버러.

파우롣 아다뻬띱 야고보

17. 마우 돠이가 어여루사쩌무, 바냐거두 버머러시 버라 구두후가사 나 룻모오 루너너.

---

12. When we heard this, we and the people there pleaded with Paul not to go up to Jerusalem.

13. Then Paul answered, "Why are you weeping and breaking my heart? I am ready not only to be bound, but also to die in Jerusalem for the name of the Lord Jesus."

14. When he would not be dissuaded, we gave up and said, "The Lord's will be done."

15. After this, we got ready and went up to Jerusalem.

16. Some of the disciples from Caesarea accompanied us and brought us to the home of Mnason, where we were to stay. He was a man from Cyprus and one of the early disciples.

17. When we arrived at Jerusalem, the brothers received us warmly.

lumoo lunene.

18. Abere mwei mishangya, Paulo alauma netu twera kutambira Yakobo. Ebangumwa be luhu lwa Ongo boshi, nabu babaa babwananyire'o.

18. 아버러 뭐이 미싸쨔, 파우로 아롸우마 너두 뚸라 구다삐라 야고보. 어바꾸뫄 버 루후 롸 오꼬 보씨, 나부 바바아 바봐나니러오.

18. The next day Paul and the rest of us went to see James, and all the elders were present.

19. Paulo era kubalamusa nakubabalikisa chiuma kwa chiuma, byoshi bya Ongo abaa enjire aira mwa kachi-lachi ke bandu besinji mbaa, kurengera emulimo wai.

19. 파우로 어라 구바롸무사 나구바바뢰기사 찌우마 과 찌우마, 보씨 뱌 오꼬 아바아 어삐러 아이라 뫄 가찌-롸찌 거 바뚜 버시띠 빠아, 구러꺼라 어무뢰모 와이.

19. Paul greeted them and reported in detail what God had done among the Gentiles through his ministry.

20. Abu bangumwa bomvire bacha, bera ktonga Ongo, bera kwire babura Paulo mbu: Emunyaketu! ulola kwabayuta bangana babahubire bemeresi, kanji boshi banatula batunjire omwaso*wa Musa busese.

20. 아부 바꾸뫄 보삐러 바짜, 버라 구도까 오꼬, 버라 귀러 바부라 파우로 뿌: 어무냐거두! 우로롸 과바유다 바까나 바바후비러 버머러시, 가찌 보씨 바나두롸 바두띠러 오뫄소*와 무사 부서서.

20. When they heard this, they praised God. Then they said to Paul: "You see, brother, how many thousands of Jews have believed, and all of them are zealous for the law.

21. Rero, bomvire omwasi mira kwa oyu wenjire wakangirisa ebayuta boshi babatula mwa kachi-kachi kesinji mbaa kwa batendee batunda oyu mawaso*wa Musa. Kanji mbu wenjire wababura kwa batenda bachimonya ebana babo, nekubaanga kwa batenda bachikulikira emyanya yetu ye bayuta.

21. 러로, 보삐러 오뫄시 미라 과 오유 워찌러 와가삐리사 어바유다 보씨 바바두롸 뫄 가찌-가찌 거시띠 빠아 과 바더떠어 바두따 오유 마와소*와 무사. 가찌 뿌 워찌러 와바부라 과 바더따 바찌모냐 어바나 바보, 너구바아까 과 바더따 바찌구뢰기라 어먀냐 여두 여 바유다.

21. They have been informed that you teach all the Jews who live among the Gentiles to turn away from Moses, telling them not to circumcise their children or live according to our customs.

22. Kute twiree twaira abu bayuta banganomva omwasi kwa waikire kuno mira.

23. Bushi noku, chine twahonda kukubura chiunairaa: twende balume bane anola, ba balaisise era muhondu sa Ongo

24. Ubatolaa, wanaya nabo mwamwiya wekuchikomya*. Nabyoshi bya bangemibwa woyu ungabaongerabi chasiya bakumulwe. Echera chingalosa ebandu boshi kwa emyasi yabomva era luulu sao, iri ya bisha tenene. Kanji banganamenyerera ekanangana kwa kasi nao, unachire utunjire emwaso*wa Musa.

25. Kwa bya byerekere ebandu besinji mbaa ba bahubire bemeresi, twabanjikirire mira era luulu se lwango lwa twaishaa mbu batendaa bachira biryo bya byatulwaa ebasimu, nesi kulya mwamba, nesi kulya nyama era yachitumbiraa, nesi kubanda ekiri.

22. 구더 뒤러어 돠이라 아부 바유다 바빠노빠 오먀시 과 와이기러 구노 미라.

23. 부씨 노구, 찌너 돠호따 구구부라 찌우나이라아: 뛰떠 바루머 바너 아노쫘, 바 바퐈이시서 어라 무호뚜 사 오쯧

24. 우바도쫘아, 와나야 나보 뫄뮈야 워구찌고먀*. 나뵤씨 뱌 바뻐미봐 오유 우빠바오뻐라비 짜시야 바구무뤄. 어쩌라 찌빠쯘사 어바뚜 보씨 과 어먀시 야보빠 어라 루우루 사오, 이리 야 비싸 더너너. 가찌 바빠나머녀러라 어가나뫄나 과 가시 나오, 우나찌러 우두찌러 어뫄소*와 무사.

25. 과 뱌 벼러거러 어바뚜 버시찌 빠아 바 바후비러 버머러시, 돠바찌기리러 미라 어라 루우루 서 쫜오 쫜 돠이싸아 뿌 바더따아 바찌라 비료 뱌 뱌두쫜아 어바시무, 너시 구쨔 뫄빠, 너시 구쨔 냐마 어라 야찌두쁘라아, 너시 구바따 어기리.

22. What shall we do? They will certainly hear that you have come,

23. so do what we tell you. There are four men with us who have made a vow.

24. Take these men, join in their purification rites and pay their expenses, so that they can have their heads shaved. Then everybody will know there is no truth in these reports about you, but that you yourself are living in obedience to the law.

25. As for the Gentile believers, we have written to them our decision that they should abstain from food sacrificed to idols, from blood, from the meat of strangled animals and from sexual immorality."

26. Abere mwei mishangya, Paulo era kutola balume bane na aya nabo mwa mwiya wekuchikomya*. Chasinda era kuya mwa luhu lwa Ongo* abure ebandu mangochi oyu mwiya wabo angawa, ne mitulo*era inganyibwa bushi na chira muuma mubo.

E Bayuda basimba Paulo

27. Sa suku sirinda s'e kuchikomya mango sabaa sera sahonda kuwa, bayuta bauma ba babaa batengera mwa chio che Asiya, bera kulola ku Paulo mwa luhu lwa Ongo. Bera kushiirisa eluamba loshi lw'ebandju, na bamusimba.

28. Bera kubanda ebandu mbu: emu balume boshi be isiraeli, mubahaa mutuase! ola mulume ono, ola wenjire warenga mu chira chisiki aenda akangirisa ebandju boshi kwa bendaa batukena, na kubabura kwa batenda batunda emwaso wa musa, ne kukena luno luhu lubuya-buya lwa Ongo. Erire anabalasao mwa kwengisa mwebandu besinji mbaa.

26. 아버러 뭐이 미싸야, 파우로 어라 구도롸 바루머 바너 나 아야 나보 롸 뮈야 워구찌고먀*. 짜시따 어라 구야 롸 루후 롸 오꼬* 아부러 어바뚜 마꼬찌 오유 뮈야 와보 아꽈와, 너 미두로*어라 이꽈네봐 부씨 나 찌라 무우마 무보.

어 바유다 바시빠 파우로

27. 사 수구 시리따 서 구찌고먀 마꼬 사바아 서라 사호따 구와, 바유다 바우마 바 바바아 바더꺼라 롸 찌오 쩌 아시야, 버라 구로롸 구 파우로 롸 루후 롹 오꼬. 버라 구씨이리사 어루아빠 로씨 루워바뚜, 나 바무시빠.

28. 버라 구바따 어바뚜 뿌: 어무 바루머 보씨 버 이시라어삐, 무바하아 무두아서! 오롸 무루머 오노, 오롸 워찌러 와러꺼 무 찌라 찌시기 아어따 아가삐리사 어바뚜 보씨 과 버따아 바두거나, 나 구바부라 과 바더따 바두따 어롸소 와 무사, 너 구거나 루노 루후 루부야-부야 롹 오꼬. 어리러 아나바짜사오 롸 궈삐사 뭐바뚜 버시찌 빠아.

26. The next day Paul took the men and purified himself along with them. Then he went to the temple to give notice of the date when the days of purification would end and the offering would be made for each of them.

27. When the seven days were nearly over, some Jews from the province of Asia saw Paul at the temple. They stirred up the whole crowd and seized him,

28. shouting, "Men of Israel, help us! This is the man who teaches all men everywhere against our people and our law and this place. And besides, he has brought Greeks into the temple area and defiled this holy place."

29. Batetaa bacha, bushi balola kwa Paulo ali mwa musi na mwesha Efeso muuma mbu i Torofino. Bera kuchichinga mbu amwengisise mira mwa luhu lwa Ongo.

30. Elwayo lwera kwehula mwa musi we Yerusalemu. Ebandu bera kulibichiranga ala Paulo abaa ali, bera kumusimba bana mukulikira era butala. Unao-unao kunakuchikanga enyisi se luhu lwa Ongo.

31. Mango babaa bera bahonda kumwita, emukulu-kulu munene we basula be Baroma era kumva emwasi kwa olwayo lwehwire mwa musi woshi we yerusalamu.

32. Unao-unao, era kutola basula bai bauma alauma nebakulu-kulu babo, era kulyibichira nabo ala abu bandju babaa babuananyire. Elwamba lw'ebandju lwamulolyireko alauma nebasula bai, bera kwire bareka kupunda Paulo.

33. Oyu mukulu-kulu munene, kukwera kuchifunda ala Paulo abaa alyi. Era kumusimba ne kuteta kwa bamuminaa na mareure mabilyi. Chasinda, era kubusa ebandju: oyu mundju

29. 바더다아 바짜, 부씨 바르꽈 과 파우로 아뀌 꽈 무시 나 뭐싸 어퍼소 무우마 뿌 이 도로피노. 버라 꾸찌찌야 뿌 아뭐삐시서 미라 꽈 루후 꽈 오꼬.

30. 어꽈요 뭐라 궈후꽈 꽈 무시 워 여루사꺼무. 어바뚜 버라 구삐비찌라야 아꽈 파우로 아바아 아뤼, 버라 구무시빠 바나 무구뤼기라 어라 부다꽈. 우나오-우나오 구나구찌가야 어니씨 서 루후 꽈 오꼬.

31. 마꼬 바바아 버라 바호따 구뮈다, 어무구루-구루 무너너 워 바수꽈 버 바로마 어라 구빠 어마시 과 오꽈요 뭐휘러 꽈 무시 오씨 워 여루사꽈무.

32. 우나오-우나오, 어라 구도꽈 바수꽈 바이 바우마 아꽈우마 너바구루-구루 바보, 어라 구뤠비찌라 나보 아꽈 아부 바뚜 바바아 바부아나니러. 어꽈빠 루워바뚜 꽈무로뤠러고 아꽈우마 너바수꽈 바이, 버라 귀러 바러가 구푸따 파우로.

33. 오유 무구루-구루 무너너, 구궈라 구찌푸따 아꽈 파우로 아바아 아뤠. 어라 구무시빠 너 구더다 과 바무미나아 나 마러우러 마비뤠. 짜시따, 어라 구부사 어바뚜: 오유 무뚜

29. (They had previously seen Trophimus the Ephesian in the city with Paul and assumed that Paul had brought him into the temple area.)

30. The whole city was aroused, and the people came running from all directions. Seizing Paul, they dragged him from the temple, and immediately the gates were shut.

31. While they were trying to kill him, news reached the commander of the Roman troops that the whole city of Jerusalem was in an uproar.

32. He at once took some officers and soldiers and ran down to the crowd. When the rioters saw the commander and his soldiers, they stopped beating Paul.

33. The commander came up and arrested him and ordered him to be bound with two chains. Then he asked who he was and what he had done.

inde na chiye chi ailyire	이떠 나 찌여 찌 아이례러	
34. Si mwa kumwakula, abu bandju babaa balanga chira bauma kwabo-kwabo. Echera chatchwuma oyu mukulu-kulu w'e basula atachimerera kanangana cha chabere. Era kwira ateta mbu bekaa Paulo mwa chikali cha basula.	34. 시 뫄 구뫄구롸, 아부 바뉴 바바아 바롸ᅇ가 찌라 바우마 과보-과보. 어쩌라 짜쭈마 오유 무구루-구루 워 바수롸 아다찌머러라 가나ᅇ가나 짜 짜버러. 어라 귀라 아더다 뿌 버가아 파우로 뫄 찌가리 짜 바수롸.	34. Some in the crowd shouted one thing and some another, and since the commander could not get at the truth because of the uproar, he ordered that Paul be taken into the barracks.
35. Mango Paulo abaa era anahonda kwengirira mwechi chikali, ebasula bera kulola kwa byemire bamubatle, bushi ebandu babaa bakaliire busese.	35. 마ᅌ고 파우로 아바아 어라 아나호따 궈ᅇ이리라 뭬찌 찌가리, 어바수롸 버라 구로롸 과 벼미러 바무바두러, 부씨 어바뉴 바바아 바가리이러 부서서.	35. When Paul reached the steps, the violence of the mob was so great he had to be carried by the soldiers.
36. Boshi babaa bakulikire Paulo baenda bahonda ebandu mbu: mumukula mwemuka!	36. 보씨 바바아 바구리기러 파우로 바어따 바호따 어바뉴 뿌: 무무구롸 뭐무가!	36. The crowd that followed kept shouting, "Away with him!"
Paulo atongana era muhondo se bayuda	***파우로 아도ᅇ가깁 어라 무호또 서 바유다***	
37. Mango ebasula babaa bera bahonda kwengisa Paulo mwa chikali chabo, era kubusa emukulu-kulu wabo mbu: ewalyiya! unganyemerera nikubure chinwa chiuma na imbu: wishi chikiriki	37. 마ᅌ고 어바수롸 바바아 버라 바호따 궈ᅇ이사 파우로 뫄 찌가리 짜보, 어라 구부사 어무구루-구루 와보 뿌: 어와례야! 우ᅇ가녀머러라 니구부러 찌놔 찌우마 나 이뿌: 위씨 찌기리기	37. As the soldiers were about to take Paul into the barracks, he asked the commander, "May I say something to you?" "Do you speak Greek?" he replied.
38. Elyi ata woyu uola mwesha misiri wasinda kureta elwayo mwono musi, wera kweka nabyumbi bine bya bihumusi mwa buyeye?	38. 어례 아다 오유 우오롸 뭬싸 미시리 와시따 구러다 어롸요 뫄노 무시, 워라 궈가 나뷰삐 비너 뱌 비후무시 뫄 부여여?	38. "Aren't you the Egyptian who started a revolt and led four thousand terrorists out into the desert some time ago?"

39. Paulo na imbu: nyono, nyilyi muyuda, nyibutwa mwa musi we Tariso. Oyu musi, aire ngulu busese mwa chio che kirikiya. Rero waliya, nakwema unyemerera nihambale nabano bandju.

39. 파우로 나 이뿌: 뇨노, 네레 무유다, 네부돠 돠 무시 워 다리소. 오유 무시, 아이러 꿀루 부서서 돠 찌오 쩌 기리기야. 러로 와쀠야, 나꿔마 우녀머러라 니하빠쀠 나바노 바뚜.

39. Paul answered, "I am a Jew, from Tarsus in Cilicia, a citizen of no ordinary city. Please let me speak to the people."

40. Oyu mukulu-kulu era kwemerera mbu atetaa. Paulo era kwemangira kwa chiso, era kwemusa emino mwa chanya abura ebandju mbu barekaa elwayo. Abere boshi bera basiraa, Paulo kukwera kubabura mweteta lyabo boshi lye chi eburaniya mbu:

40. 오유 무구룰-구룰 어라 궈머러라 뿌 아더다아. 파우로 어라 궈마쀠라 과 찌소, 어라 궈무사 어미노 돠 짜냐 아부라 어바뚜 뿌 바러가아 어퇄요. 아버러 보씨 버라 바시라아, 파우로 구궈라 구바부라 뭐더다 랴보 보씨 려 찌 어부라니야 뿌:

40. Having received the commander's permission, Paul stood on the steps and motioned to the crowd. When they were all silent, he said to them in Aramaic:

E Mikolo ye Ndjumwa Chikono 22

어 미고로 여 뚜돠 찌고노 22

Acts Chapter 22[NIV]

1. Emu batata na banyaketchwu, mumvilyisaa bya nahonda kuteta era luulu sanyi nyeine era muhondo senyu!

1. 어무 바다다 나 바냐거쭈, 무쀠쩨사아 뱌 나호따 구더다 어라 룰우룰 사녜 녀이너 어라 무호또 서뉴!

1. "Brothers and fathers, listen now to my defense."

2. Abu bandju, mango bomvaa kwa mwa chieburania mu Paulo ateta, bera kwira banasira. Chasinda, era kubabura mbu:

2. 아부 바뚜, 마꼬 보빠아 과 돠 쩌부라니아 무 파우로 아더다, 버라 궈라 바나시라. 짜시따, 어라 구바부라 뿌:

2. When they heard him speak to them in Aramaic, they became very quiet. Then Paul said:

3. Nyono, nyire muyuta, nyibutwa mwa musi we Tariso, mwa chio che kirikiya. Si muno Yerusalemu munakuliraa. Kanji nabaa

3. 뇨노, 네러 무유다, 네부돠 돠 무시 워 다리소, 돠 찌오 쩌 기리기야. 시 무노 여루사쩌무 무나구쀠라아. 가찌 나바아

3. "I am a Jew, born in Tarsus of Cilicia, but brought up in this city. Under Gamaliel I was thoroughly trained in the

mwananfunzi wa kamaliyeri. Oyu kamaliyeri iwanyikangirisaa kubuya-buya kwa mwaso wa bahokulu betchwu atula atechire. Kanji nabaa nyitusa bushiru bunene mwa myasi ya Ongo ngokwa nenyu mubwete lwarero.

가마삐여리. 오유 가마삐여리 이와네가삐리사아 구부야-부야 과 먀소 와 바호구루 버쭈 아두꽈 아더찌러. 가찌 나바아 네두사 부씨루 부너너 먀 먀시 야 오꼬 꼬과 너뉴 무붜더 꽈러로.

law of our fathers and was just as zealous for God as any of you are today.

4. Kanji nabaa nenjire nalibusa busese ebandju babakulyikire enjira ya enawetchwu. Nera kunde namina ebalume ne bakasi nekubauma mwa buroko. Nabauma mubo, bera kunde banechibwa.

4. 가찌 나바아 너찌러 나삐부사 부서서 어바뿌 바바구꿰기러 어찌라 야 어나워쭉. 너라 구떠 나미나 어바루머 너 바가시 너구바우마 먀 부로고. 나바우마 무보, 버라 구떠 바너찌봐.

4. I persecuted the followers of this Way to their death, arresting both men and women and throwing them into prison,

5. Bine nateta, emukulu-kulu we bakuhanyi alauma nechikembe chosi che bashamuka be karubandake bayuda nabo, banagababura kwa binali bya kanangana. Abola bu babaa benjire banyeresa ne maruba me kwekera banyaketu bayuta bomwa musi we Tamasiki. . Nabaa benjire nayamo chasiya nyimine ebemeresi ne kubareta ene Yerusalemu bachinjibusibwe.

5. 비너 나더다, 어무구루-구루 워 바구하네 아꽈우마 너찌거뻐 쪼시 쩌 바싸무가 버 가루바따거 바유다 나보, 바나가바부라 과 비나삐 뱌 가나꺼나. 아보꽈 부 바바아 버찌러 바녀러사 너 마루바 머 궈거라 바냐거두 바유다 보봐 무시 워 다마시기. . 나바아 버찌러 나야모 짜시야 네미너 어버머러시 너 구바러다 어너 여루사꺼무 바찌띠부시붜.

5. as also the high priest and all the Council can testify. I even obtained letters from them to their brothers in Damascus, and went there to bring these people as prisoners to Jerusalem to be punished.

Paulo abalyikisa kute ahubaa mwemeresi

파우똔 아바꿰굿뻽 구더 아후바아 뭐머러시

6. Lusuku luuma, mango sabaa sahonda kuba saa ndatu sa mushi, abere nera

6. 루수구 루우마, 마꼬 사바아 사호따 구바 사아 따두 사 무씨, 아버러 너라 네나삐

6. "About noon as I came near Damascus, suddenly a bright light from heaven

nyinali ofu ne musi we tamasiki, unao-unao chilungere chinene chera kutenga kwa nguba na chalomekera ala nabaa nyilyi.

7. Nere kukumbala, unao-unao nera kumva murenge muua anyibura mbu: Saulo! Saulo! chi chatchwuma wanyiribusa?

8. Nanyi mbu! woyu u'nde waliya oyu murenge na imbu: nyono, nyi Yesu we nasareti nyiwalibusa.

9. Baliketu banaba nabalama nabo, bera kulola kwechi chilungere, si oyu murenge chiro bakomva kuo.

10. Nera kuira nambusa kanji mbu: enawetu, chi nemire kuira kasi na imbu:Emangaa uye mwa musi we tamasiki, omola mu bangakubwirira byoshi bya wemire kuira.

11. Mweshi chihangi nabaa ndachisene bushi nechi chulungere chabaa chanyisibire emeho. Abu baliketu, bera kwire banyiachilirira kwa kuboko, baenda banyitandaisa kuikira mwa musi we Tamasiki.

12. Wmoyu musi, mwabaa mulume muuma mbu iAnaniya. Oyu Ananiya, abaa

오푸 너 무시 워 다마시기, 우나오-우나오 찌루 어러 찌너너 쩌라 구더 과 우바 나 짜로 머거라 아 나바아 네레.

7. 너러 구구빠라, 우나오-우나오 너라 구빠 무러 어 무우아 아네부라 뿌: 사우로! 사우로! 찌 짜쭈마 와네리부사?

8. 나네 뿌! 오유 우너 와 야 오유 무러 어 나 이뿌: 뇨노, 네 여수 워 나사러디 네와 부사.

9. 바 거두 바나바 나바 라마 나보, 버라 구로 과 궈찌 찌루 어러, 시 오유 무러 어 찌로 바고빠 구오.

10. 너라 구이라 나뿌사 가찌 뿌: 어나워두, 찌 너미러 구이라 가시 나 이뿌:어마 아 우여 봐 무시 워 다마시기, 오모 무 바 구뷔리라 뵤씨 뱌 워미러 구이라.

11. 뭐씨 찌하 나바아 따찌서너 부씨 너찌 쭈루 어러 짜바아 짜네시비러 어머호. 아부 바 거두, 버라 귀러 바네아찌 리리라 과 구보고, 바어따 바네다 아이사 구이기라 봐 무시 워 다마시기.

12. 우모유 무시, 봐바아 무루머 무우마 뿌 이아나니야. 오유 아나니야, 아바아 아두사

flashed around me.

7. I fell to the ground and heard a voice say to me, 'Saul! Saul! Why do you persecute me?'

8. " 'Who are you, Lord?' I asked. " 'I am Jesus of Nazareth, whom you are persecuting,' he replied.

9. My companions saw the light, but they did not understand the voice of him who was speaking to me.

10. "'What shall I do, Lord?' I asked. "'Get up,' the Lord said, 'and go into Damascus. There you will be told all that you have been assigned to do.'

11. My companions led me by the hand into Damascus, because the brilliance of the light had blinded me.

12. "A man named Ananias came to see me. He was a devout observer of the law

atusa bushiru bunene bwekutunda emwaso wa musa. Kanji abaa atusa ngulu ibuya mwa kachi-kachi ke bayuta boshi ba mxoyu musi.

13. Ananiya era kuika alanaba nyire, nanyibura mbu: munyaketu Saulo, uhuba kulola! unao-unao, emeho manyi kuna kusibukala, na mamulolako,

14. Era kuhuba kunyibura mbu: Ongo wa bahokulu betu akulondwere umenyerera ekuhonda kwai, kanji uchilorere na kxola wende waira bya bitungene, echumvire nokwa murenge wai yeine.

15. Bushi emyasi wachiloreraako na kuchumvirako weine, ungende waibalikisisa ebandu boshi.

16. Rero, chi echiri walinjire wiree wemanga, weme enawetu akubabalire ebibi byao, chasinda ubatisibwe.

17. Era nyuma sebi, nera kuhuba eyerusalemu. Abere nyiriuwa luhu lwa Ongo* nema, nera kuya mu byabunya biroto.

부씨루 부너너 뭐구두따 어뫄소 와 무샤. 가찌 아바아 아두사 으루 이부야 뫄 가찌-가찌 거 바유다 보씨 바 무소유 무시.

13. 아나니야 어라 구이가 아쫘나바 네러, 나네부라 뿌: 무냐거두 사우로, 우후바 구로쫘! 우나오-우나오, 어머호 마네 구나 구시부가쫘, 나 마무르로쫘고,

14. 어라 구후바 구네부라 뿌: 오꼬 와 바호구루 버두 아구로뚜워러 우머녀러라 어구호따 과이, 가찌 우찌로러러 나 구소쫘 워너 와이라 뱌 비두어너, 어쭈삐러 노과 무러머 와이 여이너.

15. 부씨 어먀시 와찌로러라아고 나 구쭈삐라고 워이너, 우어따 와이바쀠기시사 어바뚜 보씨.

16. 러로, 찌 어찌리 와쀠씨러 위러어 워마따, 워머 어나워두 아구바바쀠러 어비비 뱌오, 짜시따 우바디시붜.

17. 어라 뉴마 서비, 너라 구후바 어여루사쩌무. 아버러 내리우와 루후 쫘 오꼬* 너마, 너라 구야 무 뱌부냐 비로도.

and highly respected by all the Jews living there.

13. He stood beside me and said, 'Brother Saul, receive your sight!' And at that very moment I was able to see him.

14. "Then he said: 'The God of our fathers has chosen you to know his will and to see the Righteous One and to hear words from his mouth.

15. You will be his witness to all men of what you have seen and heard.

16. And now what are you waiting for? Get up, be baptized and wash your sins away, calling on his name.'

17. "When I returned to Jerusalem and was praying at the temple, I fell into a trance

18. Mwebi biroto, nera kulola ku enawetu anyibura mbu: utengaa mwono musi we Yerusalemu fuba, bushi emyasi era uende wahubanganya beshamo, batayemerere.

19. Nera kwakula mbu: enawetu, si bano bandu boshi baneshi kubuya-buya kwa nyinabaa nenjire nasungula mwa mashenge me bayuta, naenda napunda ebemeresi bao ne kubauma mwa buroko!

20. Na mango betaa sitefano iwabaa wenjire wahubanganyisa ebandu era luulu sao, nanyi nyeine nabaa nyinalio. Nera kunaba mwa lwango mwekumwita. Na ba mwitaa, nyinabaaa nabalangira enjimba.

21. Si enawetu era kunyibura mbu: endaa, bushi nyingakutuma burerere, era mwebandu besinji mbaa.

18. 뭐비 비로도, 너라 구로꽈 구 어나워두 아니부라 뿌: 우더꽈아 모노 무시 워 여루사꺼무 푸바, 부씨 어먀시 어라 우어떠 와후바꽈냐 버싸모, 바다여머러러.

19. 너라 과구꽈 뿌: 어나워두, 시 바노 바뚜 보씨 바너씨 구부야-부야 과 네나바아 너찌러 나수우꽈 마 마써어 머 바유다, 나어따 나푸따 어버머러시 바오 너 구바우마 꽈 부로고!

20. 나 마꼬 버다아 시더파노 이와바아 워찌러 와후바꽈네사 어바뚜 어라 루우루 사오, 나니 녀이너 나바아 네나뤼오. 너라 구나바 마 롸꼬 뭐구뭐다. 나 바 뭐다아, 네나바아아 나바롸꼐라 어찌빠.

21. 시 어나워두 어라 구네부라 뿌: 어따아, 부씨 네꽈구두마 부러러러, 어라 뭐바뚜 버시찌 빠아.

18. and saw the Lord speaking. 'Quick!' he said to me. 'Leave Jerusalem immediately, because they will not accept your testimony about me.'

19. " 'Lord,' I replied, 'these men know that I went from one synagogue to another to imprison and beat those who believe in you.

20. And when the blood of your martyr Stephen was shed, I stood there giving my approval and guarding the clothes of those who were killing him.'

21. "Then the Lord said to me, 'Go; I will send you far away to the Gentiles.' "

Paulo abura ebandju kwa nai atchwula Muroma 파우론 아부라 어바뚜 과 나이 아쭈꽈 무로마

22. Ebandju bera kunomvirisa Paulo kubuya-buya. Si mango atetaa echi chinwa chisinda, bera kutangirisa bateta na murenge munene mbu: oyu mundu bamwitaa, bushi

22. 어바뚜 버라 구노뻬리사 파우론 구부야-부야. 시 마꼬 아더다아 어찌 찌냐 찌시따, 버라 구다뻬리사 바더다 나 무러어 무너너 뿌: 오유 무뚜 바뮈다아, 부씨 비더미러 뿌

22. The crowd listened to Paul until he said this. Then they raised their voices and shouted, "Rid the earth of him! He's not fit to live!"

bitemire mbu abaa muno butala!

23. Bera kubanda mwa twabwabwe busese, nengumanga enjimba sabu mwa chanya, baulusanga nemukungu.

24. Ola mukulu-kulu we basula era kwire abura ebasula bai mbu mbengisa Paulo mwa chikali chabo, era kubabura mbu bamuhuta etuchi, chasiya ababura chi chatuma ebandu bamukuwa-kuwa bacha.

25. Si mango abu basula babaa bera bamuminaa chasiya bamuhute etuchi, era kubura muuma mwa bakulu-kulu babo ola wabaa uli aola mbu: munyibura akaba mwete loso lwe kuhuta eMuroma busira kumenya akaba akolire lubanja!

26. Mango oyu mukulu-kulu omvaa era kuya kubura enawabo mbu: ewaliya, wabaa wauwirwe! ola mundu kasi nai ali muroma!

27. Enawabo omvire bacha, kukwera kuya kubusa Paulo mbu: unyibura ekanangana akaba unali muroma! na imbu: nechi, nyire muroma!

아바아 무노 부다롸!

23. 버라 구바따 롸 돠봐붸 부서서, 너우마꺄 어찌빠 사부 롸 짜냐, 바우루사꺄 너무구웃.

24. 오롸 무구루-구루 워 바수꽈 어라 귀러 아부라 어바수꽈 바이 뿌 뻐찌사 파우롣 롸 찌가뢰 짜보, 어라 구바부라 뿌 바무후다 어두찌, 짜시야 아바부라 찌 짜두마 어바뚜 바무구와-구와 바짜.

25. 시 마꼬 아부 바수꽈 바바아 버라 바무미나아 짜시야 바무후더 어두찌, 어라 구부라 무우마 롸 바구루-구루 바보 오롸 와바아 우뢰 아오꽈 뿌: 무네부라 아가바 뭐더 로소 뤄 구후다 어무로마 부시라 구머냐 아가바 아고뢰러 루바짜!

26. 마꼬 오유 무구루-구루 오빠아 어라 구야 구부라 어나와보 뿌: 어와뢰야, 와바아 와우위뤄! 오롸 무뚜 가시 나이 아뢰 무로마!

27. 어나와보 오뻬러 바짜, 구궈라 구야 구부사 파우롣 뿌: 우네부라 어가나꺄나 아가바 우나뢰 무로마! 나 이뿌: 너찌, 니러 무로마!

---

23. As they were shouting and throwing off their cloaks and flinging dust into the air,

24. the commander ordered Paul to be taken into the barracks. He directed that he be flogged and questioned in order to find out why the people were shouting at him like this.

25. As they stretched him out to flog him, Paul said to the centurion standing there, "Is it legal for you to flog a Roman citizen who hasn't even been found guilty?"

26. When the centurion heard this, he went to the commander and reported it. "What are you going to do?" he asked. "This man is a Roman citizen."

27. The commander went to Paul and asked, "Tell me, are you a Roman citizen?" "Yes, I am," he answered.

28. Chasinda, oyu mukulu-kulu era kubura Paulo mbu: nyono, mwa kuba muroma, naesaa buteya bunene. Si Paulo yeke, era kumbura mbu: nyono nyiri muroma wa kubutwa.

28. 짜시따, 오유 무구루루-구루 어라 구부라 파우르 뿌: 뇨노, 와 구바 무로마, 나어사아 부더야 부너너. 시 파우르 여거, 어라 구뿌라 뿌: 뇨노 네리 무로마 와 구부돠.

28. Then the commander said, "I had to pay a big price for my citizenship." "But I was born a citizen," Paul replied.

29. Unao-unao, ebasula ba babaa bahonda kuhuta Paulo etuchi, bera kwire bamureka. Wamukulu-kulu nai, mango amenyerera kwa kasi muroma yaminyire, era kwobaa.

29. 우나오-우나오, 어바수롸 바 바바아 바호따 구후다 파우르 어두찌, 버라 귀러 바무러가. 와무구루-구루 나이, 마꼬 아머녀러라 과 가시 무로마 야미네러, 어라 곤바아.

29. Those who were about to question him withdrew immediately. The commander himself was alarmed when he realized that he had put Paul, a Roman citizen, in chains.

Paulo atongana era muhondo se karubanda k'e bayuda

파우르 아도따낍 어라 무호또 서 가루바따 거 바유다

30. Abere mwei mishangya, emukulu-kulu we basula era kuhonda amenyerere kanangana echi chatumire ebayuta basitaka Paulo. Bushi noku, era kumuboola. Chasinda, era kuteta mbu ebakulu-kulu be bakuhanyi* alauma nekarubanda ke bayuta* koshi, babuananaa. . Chasinjire, era kureta Paulo nekumwemanza era muhondo sabo.

30. 아버러 뭐이 미싸꺄, 어무구루-구루 워 바수롸 어라 구호따 아머녀러러 가나꺄나 어찌 짜두미러 어바유다 바시다가 파우르. 부씨 노구, 어라 구무보오롸. 짜시따, 어라 구더다 뿌 어바구루-구루 버 바구하네* 아롸우마 너가루바따 거 바유다* 고씨, 바부아나나아. . 짜시찌러, 어라 구러다 파우르 너구뭐마싸 어라 무호또 사보.

30. The next day, since the commander wanted to find out exactly why Paul was being accused by the Jews, he released him and ordered the chief priests and all the Sanhedrin to assemble. Then he brought Paul and had him stand before them.

E Mikolo ye Ndjumwa Chikono 23

어 미고론 여 뚜롸 찌고노 23

Acts Chapter 23[NIV]

1. Mwechi chahangi, Paulo era

1. 뭐찌 짜하삐, 파우르 어라

1. Paul looked straight at

kutumbikisa abu bashamuka ba baa bali mwa karubanda ke bayuta*, era kubabura mbu: ebanyaketu, nyono ndasene ku chiro na chibi chisibya mwa muchima wanyi. Bushi kuikira lwarero, nyishi kwa nyimenze kubuya era muhondo sa Ongo.

2. Emukulu-kulu we bakohanyi mbu i Ananiya omvire bacha, era kubura ba babaa bali ofu na Paulo mbu bamumasaa kwa bunu.

3. Paulo era kwire abura oyu Ananiya mbu: nao, Ongo angakumasa! si woyo unekere aola kwakunyitonganya kukulikana nokwa mwaso* atula atechire. Rero, kute ku wera ungaisha mwoyu mwaso* mwa kuteta mbu manyimasaa?

4. Ebandu babaa bali ofu na Paulo, bera kumubusa mbu: era! utafanya honyi sekukamba emukulu-kulu we bakohanyi ba Ongo?

5. Nai mbu: Ebanyaketu, ndamenya kwa oyola imukulu-kulu we bakohanyi*, bushi emnjiko mabuya-buya matula matechire mbu: mutenda mwatakira emukulu-kulu ola ubemangirire!

구두뻬기사 아부 바싸무가 바바아 바뛰 뫄 가루바따 거 바유다*, 어라 구바부라 뿌: 어바냐거두, 뇨노 따서너 구 찌로 나 찌비 찌시뱌 뫄 무찌마 와네. 부씨 구이기라 똬러로, 네씨 과 네머써 구부야 어라 무호또 사 오꼬.

2. 어무구루루-구루 워 바고하네 뿌 이 아나니야 오뻬러 바짜, 어라 구부라 바 바바아 바뛰 오푸 나 파우로 뿌 바무마사아 과 부누.

3. 파우로 어라 귀러 아부라 오유 아나니야 뿌: 나오, 오꼬 아꽈구마사! 시 오요 우너거러 아오똬 과구네도꽈냐 구구뀌가나 노과 뫄소* 아두똬 아더찌러. 러로, 구더 구 워라 우꽈이싸 모유 뫄소* 뫄 구더다 뿌 마네마사아?

4. 어바누 바바아 바뛰 오푸 나 파우로, 버라 구무부사 뿌: 어라! 우다파냐 호네 서구가빠 어무구루루-구루 워 바고하네 바 오꼬?

5. 나이 뿌: 어바냐거두, 따머냐 과 오요똬 이무구루루-구루 워 바고하네*, 부씨 어무찌고 마부야-부야 마두똬 마더찌러 뿌: 무더따 뫄다기라 어무구루루-구루 오똬 우버마삐리러!

the Sanhedrin and said, "My brothers, I have fulfilled my duty to God in all good conscience to this day."

2. At this the high priest Ananias ordered those standing near Paul to strike him on the mouth.

3. Then Paul said to him, "God will strike you, you whitewashed wall! You sit there to judge me according to the law, yet you yourself violate the law by commanding that I be struck!"

4. Those who were standing near Paul said, "You dare to insult God's high priest?"

5. Paul replied, "Brothers, I did not realize that he was the high priest; for it is written: 'Do not speak evil about the ruler of your people.'"

6. Paulo abaa echi kwa bandu bauma mwaba babaa bali mwako karubanda ke bayuta*, babaa bomwa chikembe che basandukayo*, ne banji bomwa che bafarisayo* boshi noku, era kuuma emurenge mwa karubanda mbu: E banyaketu, nanyi nyire mufarisayo*, kanji mwala we ba

7. Mango Paulo abaa era kuteta ebyera, unao-unao ebarifarisayo* ne basandukayo*bera kuata bwaka bunene mwa kachi-kachi kabo, ne bandu ba babaa bali mwa lubuanano na baberakanamo.

8. Byabaa bacha, bushi ebasandukayo, batula bemereri kwe bafu bakomwoka, nesi kwa kutula bamalika* nesi bihwasi. Si ebarisayo* beke batula bemerere ebi byoshi.

9. Bushi noku, ebwaka bwera kunaba bunene, mwolu, mwolu bakangirisa bauma be mwaso*, bomwa chikembe che ba farisayo*bera kwimanga, nabatangirisa bateta na bukali bunene mbu: tubano tuta sene nakuchiro chibi chisiya kwono mundu.

6. 파우로 아바아 어찌 과바뚜 바우마 먀바 바바아 바뀌마고 가루바따 거 바유다*, 바바아 보뫄 찌거뻐 쩌 바사뚜가요*, 너 바찌 보뫄 쩌 바파리사요* 보씨 노구, 어라 구우마 어무러꺼 뫄 가루바따 뿌: 어 바냐거두, 나니 너려 무파리사요*, 가찌 뫄롸 워 바

7. 마꼬 파우로 아바아 어라 구더다 어벼라, 우나오-우나오 어바리파리사요* 너 바사뚜가요*버라 구아다 봐가 부너너 뫄 가찌-가찌 가보, 너 바뚜 바 바바아 바뀌 뫄 루부아나노 나 바버라가나모.

8. 뱌바아 바짜, 부씨 어바사뚜가요, 바두롸 버머러리 궈 바푸 바고모가, 너시 과 구두롸 바마뀌가* 너시 비화시. 시 어바리사요* 버거 바두롸 버머러러 어비 뵤씨.

9. 부씨 노구, 어봐가 붜라 구나바 부너너, 모루, 모루 바가뀌리사 바우마 버 뫄소*, 보뫄 찌거뻐 쩌 바 파리사요*버라 귀마까, 나바다뀌리사 바더다 나 부가뀌 부너너 뿌: 두바노 두다 서너 나구찌로 찌비 찌시야 고노 무두. 구뀌마꼬

6. Then Paul, knowing that some of them were Sadducees and the others Pharisees, called out in the Sanhedrin, "My brothers, I am a Pharisee, the son of a Pharisee. I stand on trial because of my hope in the resurrection of the dead."

7. When he said this, a dispute broke out between the Pharisees and the Sadducees, and the assembly was divided.

8. (The Sadducees say that there is no resurrection, and that there are neither angels nor spirits, but the Pharisees acknowledge them all.)

9. There was a great uproar, and some of the teachers of the law who were Pharisees stood up and argued vigorously. "We find nothing wrong with this man," they said. "What if a spirit or an angel has spoken to him?"

Kulimango chihwasi, nesi malaika* iwamuulikako.

10. Obu bwaka, mango bwabaa bwera bwarengeresa busese, emukulu-kulu we basula era kwobaa, bushi achichingaa mbu rero bangakonola Paulo. Era kwire abura ebasula bai mbu bataliraa mwa kachi-kachi ke bandu, banyahula Paulo mwa mino sabo, bamuhubye mwa chikali chabo.

11. Abere mwobu butufu, enawetu era kupamukira Paulo, na maubura mbu: esesaa emuchima! kwa wahambaliraa ebandu era luulu sanyi mwono musi we Yerusalemu, kubinakwemire kuira nomwa we Roma.

E Bayuda baya lwango lw'ekuita Paulo.

12. Abere mwei mishangya, bayuta bauma bera kuya lwango, bera kunalaisa kwa batalye batanamwe batasa kwita Paulo.

13. Ebandu ba baa mwolu lwango, babaa banene kumane.

14. Bere kuendera ebakulu-kulu be bakohanyi* nebashamuka be bayuta, bera kubabura mbu: tubano,

---

찌화시, 너시 마똬이가* 이와무우뤼가고.

10. 오부 봐가, 마꼬 봐바아 뭐라 봐러뻐러사 부서서, 어무구루-구루 워 바수똬 어라 곺바아, 부씨 아찌찌뻐아 뿌러로 바빠고노똬 파우뢰. 어라 귀러 아부라 어바수똬 바이 뿌 바다뤼라아 똬 가찌-가찌 거 바뚜, 바냐후똬 파우뢰 똬 미노 사보, 바무후벼 똬 찌가뤼 짜보.

11. 아버러 모부 부두푸, 어나워두 어라 구파무기라 파우뢰, 나 마우부라 뿌: 어서사아 어무찌마! 과 와하빠뤼라아 어바뚜 어라 루우루 사니 모노 무시 워 여루사뻐무, 구비나궈미러 구이라 노똬 워 로마.

어 바유다 바야 똬꼬 뤂끌읠닛 파우뢴.

12. 아버러 뭐이 미싸뺘, 바유다 바우마 버라 구야 똰꼬, 버라 구나똬이사 과 바다뼈 바다나뭐 바다사 귀다 파우뢴.

13. 어바뚜 바 바아 모루 똰꼬, 바바아 바너너 구마너.

14. 버러 구어뻐라 어바구루-구루 버 바고하네* 너바싸무가 버 바유다, 버라 구바부라 뿌: 두바노, 돠똬아시서 과

---

10. The dispute became so violent that the commander was afraid Paul would be torn to pieces by them. He ordered the troops to go down and take him away from them by force and bring him into the barracks.

11. The following night the Lord stood near Paul and said, "Take courage! As you have testified about me in Jerusalem, so you must also testify in Rome."

12. The next morning the Jews formed a conspiracy and bound themselves with an oath not to eat or drink until they had killed Paul.

13. More than forty men were involved in this plot.

14. They went to the chief priests and elders and said, "We have taken a solemn oath not to eat anything

twalaasise kwa tutangalya kandu kasibya akaba tutasa kwita Paulo!

15. Rero, nenyu alauma ne karubanda ke bayuta*, wmira mwaya kwema omukulu-kulu we basula aberesi oyu Paulo. Mungachira nga babahonda kmerera ekanangana emyasi era yatuma bamusitaka. Netu tungamulingirira mwanjira, tumwite era muhondo aike anola.

16. Si mwiwa muuma wa Paulo era kumva ekamesi-mesi kwolu lwango. Era kwire alibichira era chikali che basula chabaa chiri, era kwingiriramo, na balira Paulo kwoyu mwasi.

17. Chasinda, Paulo era kwire amaala muuma mwa bakulu-kulu be basula, era kumubura mbu: wekaa ono mutabana era mwenawenyu, bushi ete mwasi ola ahonda kumubura.

18. Oyu mukulu-kulu era kunatola wamutabna na aya nai era mwa enawabo. Era kubura oyu enawabo mbu: ewaliya, Paulo, ola mundu we buroko, anyamaalaa na anyibura mbu nyikureteraa ono mutabana bushi ete

두다까꺄 가뚜 가시뱌 아가바 두다사 귀다 파우로!

15. 러로, 너뉴 아롸우마 너 가루바따 거 바유다*, 우미라 마야 궈마 오무구루-구루 워 바수꽈 아버러시 오유 파우로. 무까찌라 까 바바호따 구머러라 어가나까나 어먀시 어라 야두마 바무시다가. 너두 두까무뤼끼리라 뫄찌라, 두뮈더 어라 무호또 아이거 아노롸.

16. 시 뮈와 무우마 와 파우로 어라 구빠 어가머시-머시 굘루 꽈꼬. 어라 귀러 아뤼비찌라 어라 찌가뤼 쩌 바수꽈 짜바아 찌리, 어라 귀끼리라모, 나 바뤼라 파우로 굘유 뫄시.

17. 짜시따, 파우로 어라 귀러 아마아꽈 무우마 뫄 바구루-구루 버 바수꽈, 어라 구무부라 뿌: 워가아 오노 무다바나 어라 뭐나워뉴, 부씨 어더 뫄시 오롸 아호따 구무부라.

18. 오유 무구루-구루 어라 구나도꽈 와무다부나 나 아야 나이 어라 뫄 어나와보. 어라 구부라 오유 어나와보 뿌: 어와뤼야, 파우로, 오롸 무뚜 워 부로고, 아냐마아롸아 나 아네부라 뿌 네구러더라아 오노 무다바나 부씨 어더 뫄시

15. Now then, you and the Sanhedrin petition the commander to bring him before you on the pretext of wanting more accurate information about his case. We are ready to kill him before he gets here."

16. But when the son of Paul's sister heard of this plot, he went into the barracks and told Paul.

17. Then Paul called one of the centurions and said, "Take this young man to the commander; he has something to tell him."

18. So he took him to the commander. The centurion said, "Paul, the prisoner, sent for me and asked me to bring this young man to you because he has something to tell you."

mwasi ola ahonda kukubura.

19. Ola enawabo era kusimbira ola mutabna kwa mino, era kuchifunda nai ala musike. Chasinda era kumubusa mbu: emusa! chiwahonda kunyibura?

20. Oyu mutabana na imbu: ebayuta bire lwango lwakuya kukukwema mbu ubaretera Paulo misnhangya mwa karubanda kabo. Bangachira nga bahonda kumenrera kanangana emyasi yai.

21. Si bya bangakubura, utabyemereraa, bushi ebandu bairire lwango kwa bangamulingira mwa njira. Nabu bandu bali banene ku mane. Kanji balaisese kwa batalye banatamwe batasa kwita Paulo. Rero, bachikunganyise mira, necha chingatenga mwa bunu bwao chi bera banalinjira.

22. Oyu mukulu-kulu era kumubura mbu: oyu mwasi wera kunyibura, utaererasa wabura unji mundu kwa wanyifulirire kuo mira.

Ebasula beeka Paulo era mwa Feliki

23. Chasinda, oyu mukulu-kulu munene we basula, era kwamala bakulu-kulu babiri

---

오꽈 아호따 구구부라.

19. 오꽈 어나와보 어라 구시뻬라 오꽈 무다부나 과 미노, 어라 구찌푸따 나이 아꽈 무시거. 짜시따 어라 구무부사 뿌: 어무사! 찌와호따 구네부라?

20. 오유 무다바나 나 이뿌: 어바유다 비러 꽈오 꽈구야 구구궈마 뿌 우바러더라 파우론 미수누하꺄 꽈 가루바따 가보. 바꽈찌라 꽈 바호따 구머누러라 가나꽈나 어먀시 야이.

21. 시 뱌 바꽈구부라, 우다벼머러라아, 부씨 어바뚜 바이리러 꽈오 과 바꽈무뀌끼라 꽈 띠라. 나부 바뚜 바뀌 바너너 구 마너. 가찌 바꽈이서서 과 바다뼈 바나다뭐 바다사 귀다 파우론. 러로, 바찌구꽈네서 미라, 너짜 찌꽈더꽈 꽈 부누 봐오 찌 버라 바나뀌찌라.

22. 오유 무구룬-구룬 어라 구무부라 뿌: 오유 먀시 워라 구네부라, 우다어러라사 와부라 우찌 무뚜 과 와네푸뀌리러 구오 미라.

어바수꽈 버어가 파우론 어라 꽈 퍼뀌굿

23. 짜시따, 오유 무구룬-구룬 무너너 워 바수꽈, 어라 과마꽈 바구룬-구룬 바비리 꽈

---

19. The commander took the young man by the hand, drew him aside and asked, "What is it you want to tell me?"

20. He said: "The Jews have agreed to ask you to bring Paul before the Sanhedrin tomorrow on the pretext of wanting more accurate information about him.

21. Don't give in to them, because more than forty of them are waiting in ambush for him. They have taken an oath not to eat or drink until they have killed him. They are ready now, waiting for your consent to their request."

22. The commander dismissed the young man and cautioned him, "Don't tell anyone that you have reported this to me."

23. Then he called two of his centurions and ordered them, "Get ready a

mwa basula bai. Era kubabura mbu: mutolaa basula maana mabiri ba bangaenda mwa maulu, mwanatola nabanji balinda ba bende balwa bali nokwa farasi, mwanatola na maana mabiri ma ba beshi kulwa mwa mafumo. Abu boshi, bangatenga kuno mwa saa ehatu se butufu, baye mwa musi we kaisariya.

24. Paulo nai, mukunganyaa efarasi se kumweka, aike butondo burerema era muhondo sa Feliki, imukulu-kulu we chio.

25. Oyu mukulu-kulu munene we basula era kanjika emaruba mbu:

26. Ewaliya Feliki, nyono nyi kalautiyo lusiya, nakulamusise!

27. Nahonda nyikubure kwoyu mundu, ebayuta bamusimbaa, bera kuhonda bamwite. Si mango nomvaa kwa ali muroma, nera kuya kumutabla alauma ne basula banyi.

28. Nera kwire namweka era muhondo se karubanda kabo, bushi nabaa nahonda nyimerere cha chatuma bamusitaka.

29. Naikiremo, nera kulola

바수꽈 바이. 어라 구바부라 뿌: 무도롸아 바수꽈 마아나 마비리 바 바까어따 꽈 마우루, 꽈나도롸 나바씨 바뤼따 바 버떠 바꽐 바뤼 노과 파라시, 꽈나도롸 나 마아나 마비리 마 바 버씨 구꽐 꽈 마푸모. 아부 보씨, 바까더따 구노 꽈 사아 어하두 서 부두푸, 바여 꽈 무시 워 가이사리야.

24. 파우롣 나이, 무구까냐아 어파라시 서 구뭐가, 아이거 부도또 부러러마 어라 무호또 사 퍼뤼기, 이무구루-구루 워 찌오.

25. 오유 무구루-구루 무너너 워 바수꽈 어라 가찌가 어마루바 뿌:

26. 어와뤼야 퍼뤼기, 뇨노 니 가꽈우디요 루시야, 나구꽈무시서!

27. 나호따 네구부러 고유 무뚜, 어바유다 바무시빠아, 버라 구호따 바뮈더. 시 마꼬 노빠아 과 아뤼 무로마, 너라 구야 구무다부롸 아롸우마 너 바수꽈 바니.

28. 너라 귀러 나뭐가 어라 무호또 서 가루바따 가보, 부씨 나바아 나호따 네머러러 짜 짜두마 바무시다가.

29. 나이기러모, 너라 구롣꽈

---

detachment of two hundred soldiers, seventy horsemen and two hundred spearmen to go to Caesarea at nine tonight.

24. Provide mounts for Paul so that he may be taken safely to Governor Felix."

25. He wrote a letter as follows:

26. Claudius Lysias, To His Excellency, Governor Felix: Greetings.

27. This man was seized by the Jews and they were about to kill him, but I came with my troops and rescued him, for I had learned that he is a Roman citizen.

28. I wanted to know why they were accusing him, so I brought him to their Sanhedrin.

29. I found that the

kwa kasi bamisitakaa bushi na bwaka bwa bwerekere emwaso wetini lyabo. Si kwabaa kutali chiro na chibi chisibya cha abaa airire, cha chingatuma bamumina nesi bamwita.

30. Na mango nomvaa emwasi kwa ebayuta bamulanyirire, nera kulola kwa kukomire nyikutumirei fuba. Chasinda, nera kubura ba bamusitakire kwa eyi uli, yi bayaa kumusitakira.

31. Ba basula bera kunaira ngokwa enawabo anababuraa, mwobu butufu bunobu, bera kutola, na baika nai mwa musi we andipatiri.

32. Mwei mishangya, ebasula ba baendaa mwa maulu mubo, bera kufuluka mwa chikali chabo. Bera kureka babaa bali kwa farasi bandekere nolubalamo alauma na Paulo.

33. Abere baika mwa musi we kaisariya, bera kwabgirisa mukulu-kulu we chio feliki ma maruba, bera kureta na Paulo era muhondo sai.

34. Abere emukulu-kulu era asoma amu maruba, era kubusa Paulo mbu: uli

---

과 가시 바미시다가아 부씨 나봐가 봐 붜러거러 어뫄소 워디니 랴보. 시 과바아 구다뛰 찌로 나 찌비 찌시뱌 짜 아바아 아이리러, 짜 찌빠두마 바무미나 너시 바뭐다.

30. 나 마꼬 노빠아 어마시 과 어바유다 바무꽈네리러, 너라 구로꽈 과 구고미러 네구두미러이 푸바. 짜시따, 너라 구부라 바 바무시다기러 과 어에 우뛰, 에 바야아 구무시다기라.

31. 바 바수꽈 버라 구나이라 꼬과 어나와보 아나바부라아, 몸부 부두푸 부노부, 버라 구도꽈, 나 바이가 나이 꽈 무시 워 아띠파디리.

32. 뭐이 미싸꺄, 어바수꽈 바 바어따아 꽈 마우루 무보, 버라 구푸루가 꽈 찌가뛰 짜보. 버라 구러가 바바아 바뛰 과 파라시 바떠거러 노루바꽈모 아꽈우마 나 파우로.

33. 아버러 바이가 꽈 무시 워 가이사리야, 버라 과부지리사 무구루-구루 워 찌오 퍼뛰기 마 마루바, 버라 구러다 나 파우로 어라 무호또 사이.

34. 아버러 어무구루-구루 어라 아소마 아무 마루바, 어라 구부사 파우로 뿌: 우뛰

---

accusation had to do with questions about their law, but there was no charge against him that deserved death or imprisonment.

30. When I was informed of a plot to be carried out against the man, I sent him to you at once. I also ordered his accusers to present to you their case against him.

31. So the soldiers, carrying out their orders, took Paul with them during the night and brought him as far as Antipatris.

32. The next day they let the cavalry go on with him, while they returned to the barracks.

33. When the cavalry arrived in Caesarea, they delivered the letter to the governor and handed Paul over to him.

34. The governor read the letter and asked what province he was from.

mwesha ngaye na imbu: nyiri mwesha kirikiya. Emukulu-kulu mango omvire bacha, era kwire amubura mbu:

35. Nyingakumvirisa mango ba bakusitakaa bangaika. Chaisnjire, era kubura ebasula bai mbu balanga Paulo mwa chikali cha mwami Herodi.

뭐싸 빠여 나 이뿌: 네리 뭐싸 기리기야. 어무구루-구루 마꼬 오뻬러 바짜, 어라 귀러 아무부라 뿌:

35. 네꾸구뻬리사 마꼬 바 바구시다가아 바빠이가. 짜이수찌러, 어라 구부라 어바수꽈 바이 뿌 바라빠 파우로 마 찌가뀌 짜 마미 허로디.

Learning that he was from Cilicia,

35. he said, "I will hear your case when your accusers get here." Then he ordered that Paul be kept under guard in Herod's palace.

E Mikolo ye Ndjumwa Chikono 24

어 미고로 여 뉴뫄 찌고노 24 Acts Chapter 24[NIV]

E Bayuda bashitaka Paulo era mwa Feliki

어 바유다 바씨다가 파우로 어라 뫄 퍼뤼긋

1. Era nyuma sa suku etano, emukulu-kulu we kuhanyi* Ananiya, era kwandaalira mwa musi we kaisariya alauma na bashamuka bauma be bayuta, ne mundu muuma wa kubatetera mbu i Teritulo. Bera kuika era muhondo sa Feliki, imukulu-kulu we chio, basitake Paulo.

2. Mango feliki abaa era amaala Paulo, teritulo era kutangirisa asitaka Paulo mbu: ewaliya, uutumire twabbona ebolo mwesine suku soshi. Kanji bushi nekwemangira ebandu kwao kubuya, ku kwatumire bindu binene byabinduka kuba kubuya kwa

1. 어라 뉴마 사 수구 어다노, 어무구루-구루 워 구하니* 아나니야, 어라 과따아뤼라 뫄 무시 워 가이사리야 아꽈우마 나 바싸무가 바우마 버 바유다, 너 무뚜 무우마 와 구바더더라 뿌 이 더리두뢰. 버라 구이가 어라 무호또 사 퍼뤼기, 이무구루-구루 워 찌오, 바시다거 파우로.

2. 마꼬 퍼뤼기 아바아 어라 아마아꽈 파우로, 더리두뢰 어라 구다삐리사 아시다가 파우로 뿌: 어와뀌야, 우우두미러 돠부보나 어보뢰 뭐시너 수구 소씨. 가찌 부씨 너꿔마삐라 어바뚜 과오 구부야, 구 과두미러 비뚜 비너너 뱌비뚜가 구바 구부야

1. Five days later the high priest Ananias went down to Caesarea with some of the elders and a lawyer named Tertullus, and they brought their charges against Paul before the governor.

2. When Paul was called in, Tertullus presented his case before Felix: "We have enjoyed a long period of peace under you, and your foresight has brought about reforms in this nation.

mutoloke wechine chio

과 무도로거 워찌너 찌오

3. Kwebi byoshi waliya feliki, esuku soshi ne muschira chisiki, kukutonga ku twende twakutonga.

3. 궈비 뵤씨 와리야 퍼리기, 어수구 소씨 너 무찌라 찌시기, 구구도까 구 뛔떠 돠구도까.

3. Everywhere and in every way, most excellent Felix, we acknowledge this with profound gratitude.

4. Rero, ndahonda kukutamya, si nera nakwema umvirise na mchima muuma ene myasi yeeke twahonda kuteta.

4. 러로, 따호따 구구다먀, 시 너라 나궈마 우삐리서 나 무찌마 무우마 어너 먀시 여어거 돠호따 구더다.

4. But in order not to weary you further, I would request that you be kind enough to hear us briefly.

5. Ono mundu, twalolire mire kwa ali ngabo ya mulume, bushi enjire akonga elwayo mwa kachi-kachi ke bayuta boshi bomwa butala. Kanji iutula mukulu-kulu we chikembe che banasareti.

5. 오노 무뚜, 돠로리러 미러 과 아리 까보 야 무루머, 부씨 어찌러 아고까 어롸요 뫄 가찌-가찌 거 바유다 보씨 보뫄 부다롸. 가찌 이우두롸 무구루-구루 워 찌거뻐 쩌 바나사러디.

5. "We have found this man to be a troublemaker, stirring up riots among the Jews all over the world. He is a ringleader of the Nazarene sect

6. Abaa ahonda na kubalasa eluhu lwa Ongo* twera kwire twamusimba. Twera kuhonda tumutonganye kukulikana nokwa mwaso*wetu atula atechire.

6. 아바아 아호따 나 구바롸사 어루후 롸 오꼬* 뛔라 궈러 돠무시빠. 뛔라 구호따 두무도까녀 구구리가나 노과 뫄소*워두 아두롸 아더찌러.

6. and even tried to desecrate the temple; so we seized him.

7. Si emukulu-kulu we basula, lusiya era kuika na atunyahulai.

7. 시 어무구루-구루 워 바수롸, 루습앳 어라 구이가 나 아두냐후롸일.

8. Era kuteta mbu ba basitakire Paulo, ene uli yibayaa. Rero nao, mango weine ungaba amutonganyise, mu mango ungamenyera kanangana cha chatuma twamusitaka.

8. 어라 구더다 뿌 바 바시다기러 파우로, 어너 우리 예바야아. 러로 나오, 마꼬 워이너 우까바 아무도까네서, 무 마꼬 우까머녀라 가나까나 짜 짜두마 돠무시다가.

8. By examining him yourself you will be able to learn the truth about all these charges we are bringing against him."

9. Ei myasi ta teritulo, ebayuta nabo bera kunateta mbu inali ya kanangana.

9. 어이 먀시 다 더리두로, 어바유다 나보 버라 구나더다 뿌 이나리 야 가나까나.

9. The Jews joined in the accusation, asserting that these things were true.

Paulo achitetera era
muhondo s'e mukulu-kulu
Feliki

파우론 아찌더더라 어라
무호또 서 무구룩-구룩 퍼픠굿

10. Chasinda, feliki era kusimira Paulo mbu nai eraa ateta. Nai kukwera kuuma mwa bunu mbu: nyishi kwa wamala myaka inene waisha manja mwechine chio. Bushi noku waliya, nyete lumoo lunene lwa kutongana era muhondo sao.

10. 짜시따, 퍼픠기 어라 구시미라 파우론 뿌 나이 어라아 아더다. 나이 구궈라 구우마 뫄 부누 뿌: 네씨 과 와마꺄 먀가 이너너 와이싸 마짜 뭐찌너 찌오. 부씨 노구 와픠야, 녀더 루모오 루너너 꺄 구도꺄나 어라 무호또 사오.

10. When the governor motioned for him to speak, Paul replied: "I know that for a number of years you have been a judge over this nation; so I gladly make my defense.

11. Weine unganabusa, banakubure kwa kutasa kurenga suku sinene kwekumi ne biri naikaa mwa musi we Yerusalemu, kuya kwera Ongo.

11. 워이너 우꺄나부사, 바나구부러 과 구다사 구러꺄 수구 시너너 궈구미 너 비리 나이가아 뫄 무시 워 여루사퍼무, 구야 궈라 오꼬.

11. You can easily verify that no more than twelve days ago I went up to Jerusalem to worship.

12. Na mwa bano bandu, mutali chiro na muuma ola wanyibuanaa naenda bwaka na mundu, nesi mbu nashiriisa bandu mbu baretaa lwayo: abe mwa luhu lwa Ongo*, nesi mwa mashenge me bayuta, nesi muchisiki chirebi mwoyu musi.

12. 나 뫄 바노 바뚜, 무다픠 찌로 나 무우마 오꽈 와네부아나아 나어따 봐가 나 무뚜, 너시 뿌 나씨리이사 바두 뿌 바러다아 꺄요: 아버 뫄 루후 꽈 오꼬*, 너시 마 마써꺼 머 바유다, 너시 무찌시기 찌러비 모유 무시.

12. My accusers did not find me arguing with anyone at the temple, or stirring up a crowd in the synagogues or anywhere else in the city.

13. Kanji waliya, bano bandu batangaala kukulosa kwa emyasi era banyisitakireko iri ya kanangana.

13. 가찌 와픠야, 바노 바뚜 바다꺄아꽈 구구론사 과 어먀시 어라 바네시다기러고 이리 야 가나꺄나.

13. And they cannot prove to you the charges they are now making against me.

14. Si cha nemerere era muhondo sao waliya, chichechine: nyono nyenjire nakorera Ongo wabahokulu betu, kukulikana nenjire era

14. 시 짜 너머러러 어라 무호또 사오 와픠야, 찌쩌찌너: 뇨노 녀찌러 나고러라 오꼬 와바호구룩 버두, 구구픠가나 너찌러 어라 버거 버찌러

14. However, I admit that I worship the God of our fathers as a follower of the Way, which they call a sect. I believe everything that

beke benjire bateta mbu iri ya bisha. Kanji byoshi bya bitula byerekre emwaso we bayuta, na bya bitula byanjikirwe mwa bitabo bye barebi*, nabi nyinatula nyibyemerere.

바다다 뿌 이리 야 비싸. 가찌 보씨 뱌 비두꽈 벼러구러 어꽈소 워 바유다, 나 뱌 비두꽈 뱌찌기뤄 꽈 비다보 벼 바러비*, 나비 네나두꽈 네벼머러러.

agrees with the Law and that is written in the Prophets,

15. Kanji, kwa bano balume bete emunyiiro kwa Ongo akomwola ebabi ne babuya, nanyi nanyi ku nyineteo.

15. 가찌, 과 바노 바루머 버더 어무네이로 과 오꼬 아고몰꽈 어바비 너 바부야, 나니 나니 구 네너더오.

15. and I have the same hope in God as these men, that there will be a resurrection of both the righteous and the wicked.

16. Bushi noku, chira lusuku nende nachisesa nyilorekaneko mubuya era muhondo sa Ongo nera muhondo se bandu.

16. 부씨 노구, 찌라 루수구 너떠 나찌서사 네뢰러가너고 무부야 어라 무호또 사 오꼬 너라 무호또 서 바뚜.

16. So I strive always to keep my conscience clear before God and man.

17. Rero waliya, era nyuma sa kumala myaka inene ndali mwa musi we Yerusalemu, nahubaamo nyiase banyaketu na mwango wa buteya, na kweresa Ongo emitulo*,

17. 러로 와뤼야, 어라 뉴마 사 구마라 먀가 이너너 따뤼 꽈 무시 워 여루사뗘무, 나후바아모 네아서 바냐거두 나 꽈꼬 와 부더야, 나 꿔러사 오꼬 어미두뢰*,

17. "After an absence of several years, I came to Jerusalem to bring my people gifts for the poor and to present offerings.

18. Ebyera binabaa naira mango banyibuanana mwa luhu lwa Ongo *. Kanji nabaa narengire mira nomwa mwiya wekuchikomya*. Na mwolu luhu, nabaa ndalimo na luambaa lwa bandu, kutali na lwayo lusibya lwa naretaamo.

18. 어벼라 비나바아 나이라 마꼬 바네부아나나 꽈 루후 꽈 오꼬 *. 가찌 나바아 나러뼈러 미라 노꽈 뮈야 워구찌고먀*. 나 모루 루후, 나바아 따뤼모 나 루아빠아 꽈 바뚜, 구다뤼 나 꽈요 루시뱌 꽈 나러다아모.

18. I was ceremonially clean when they found me in the temple courts doing this. There was no crowd with me, nor was I involved in any disturbance.

19. Si mwabaa munali bayuta bauma ba batengera mwa chio che asiya oshao. Abola beke bubanagira kunyisitaka ene muhondo sa akaba

19. 시 꽈바아 무나뤼 바유다 바우마 바 바더떠라 꽈 찌오 쩌 아시야 오싸오. 아보꽈 버거 부바나지라 구네시다가 어너 무호또 사 아가바 바녀더

19. But there are some Jews from the province of Asia, who ought to be here before you and bring charges if they have

banyete ku mwasi.

20. Rero, bano bandu bali anola nabo, beraa bateta akaba banyumvaa kumwasi mubi mango nabaa natongana era muhondo se karubanda kabo.

21. Nagaba cha banyumvaako bulio, chiri mango nalakangaa na murenge munene era muhondo sabo mbu: lwarero natongana era muhondo senyu bushi nyete emunyiiro kwa ebafu bakomwaka!

22. Feliki, bushi abaa omvire mira emyasi era yekere enjira ya Yesu, era kwimanza elubanja tanga. Era kuteta mbu: nyingabaishira luno lubnaja mango emukulu-kulu webasula, lusiya angaba aikire kuno!

23. Chasinda, era kubura emukulu-kulu we basula kwa alangaa Paulo mwa buroko, si enda amurekera bihangi bieke bya kuira bya ahonjire. Kanji atendaa angaika bera bai mango bangende baika kumuasa.

Feliki na mukai Turusila bomvilyisa Paulo

24. Era nyuma sa suku sieke, feliki na mukai turusila muyuta-kasi, bera kuika. Era

---

구 마시.

20. 러로, 바노 바두 바리 아노롸 나보, 버라아 바더다 아가바 바뉴빠아 구마시 무비 마꼬 나바아 나도꺄나 어라 무호또 서 가루바따 가보.

21. 나가바 짜 바뉴빠아고 부뢰오, 찌리 마꼬 나롸가꺄아 나 무러꺼 무너너 어라 무호또 사보 뿌: 롼러로 나도꺄나 어라 무호또 서뉴 부씨 녀더 어무네이로 과 어바푸 바고꽈가!

22. 퍼뢰기, 부씨 아바아 오삐러 미라 어먀시 어라 여거라 어씨라 야 여수, 어라 귀마싸 어룹바짜 다꺄. 어라 구더다 뿌: 네꺄바이씨라 루노 루부나자 마꼬 어무구룹-구룹 워바수롸, 루시야 아꺄바 아이기러 구노!

23. 짜시따, 어라 구부라 어무구룹-구룹 워 바수롸 과 아롸꺄아 파우로 마 부로고, 시 어따 아무러거라 비하꾀 비어거 뱌 구이라 뱌 아호찌러. 가씨 아더따아 아꺄이가 버라 바이 마꼬 바꺼러 바이가 구무아사.

퍼뢰굿 나 무가이 두루시롸 보삐례뻽 파우로

24. 어라 뉴마 사 수구 시어거, 퍼뢰기 나 무가이 두루시롸 무유다-가시, 버라 구이가.

---

anything against me.

20. Or these who are here should state what crime they found in me when I stood before the Sanhedrin--

21. unless it was this one thing I shouted as I stood in their presence: 'It is concerning the resurrection of the dead that I am on trial before you today.' "

22. Then Felix, who was well acquainted with the Way, adjourned the proceedings. "When Lysias the commander comes," he said, "I will decide your case."

23. He ordered the centurion to keep Paul under guard but to give him some freedom and permit his friends to take care of his needs.

24. Several days later Felix came with his wife Drusilla, who was a Jewess. He sent

---

kuteta mbu bamwamalira Paulo. Bera kumvirisa emyasi era Paulo abaa ateta era luulu se kwemerera Yesu Kirisito.

어라 구더다 뿌 바먀마뤼라 파우뤂. 버라 구뻬리리사 어먀시 어라 파우뤂 아바아 아더다 어라 룾우룾 서 궈머러라 여수 기리시도.

for Paul and listened to him as he spoke about faith in Christ Jesus.

25. Era kunaendekera abahambalira era luulu se buchinjibusi bwa Ongo bwa bukaika. Feliki omvire bacha, era kwobaa, era kwire abura Paulo mbu: uendaa tanga, nyingahuba kukwamala mango nyingabona ebinji bihnagi.

25. 어라 구나어떠거라 아바하빠뤼라 어라 룾우룾 서 부찌찌부시 봐 오꼬 봐 부가이가. 퍼뤼기 오뻬러 바짜, 어라 곤바아, 어라 귀러 아부라 파우뤂 뿌: 우어따아 다꺄, 네꺄후바 구과마꽈 마꼬 네꺄보나 어비찌 비후나지.

25. As Paul discoursed on righteousness, self-control and the judgment to come, Felix was afraid and said, "That's enough for now! You may leave. When I find it convenient, I will send for you."

26. Si feliki era kunde amaala Paulo bihangi biuma-biuma chasiya ahambale nai, bushi abaa aanyisa mbu Paulo angamweresa buteya.

26. 시 퍼뤼기 어라 구떠 아마아꽈 파우뤂 비하뀌 비우마-비우마 짜시야 아하빠러 나이, 부씨 아바아 아아네사 뿌 파우뤂 아꺄뭐러사 부더야.

26. At the same time he was hoping that Paul would offer him a bribe, so he sent for him frequently and talked with him.

27. Abere kwarenga myaka ebiri, porikiyo fesito era kwima mwetwe lya feliti. Si bushi feliki abaa ahonda kusimisa ebayuta, era kureka Paulo mwa buroko.

27. 아버러 과러꺄 먀가 어비리, 포리기요 퍼시도 어라 귀마 뭐뚜 랴 퍼뤼디. 시 부씨 퍼뤼기 아바아 아호따 구시미사 어바유다, 어라 구러가 파우뤂 뫄 부로고.

27. When two years had passed, Felix was succeeded by Porcius Festus, but because Felix wanted to grant a favor to the Jews, he left Paul in prison.

E Mikolo ye Ndjumwa Chikono 25

어 미고룾 여 뚜꽈 찌고노 25

Acts Chapter 25[NIV]

Paulo atongana era muhondo s'e mukulu-kulu Fesito

파우뤂 아도꺄낍 어라 무호또 서 무구룾-구룾 퍼시도

1. Mango fesito abaa amala suku ehatu aikire mwechi

1. 마꼬 퍼시도 아바아 아마꽈 수구 어하두 아이기러 뭐찌

1. Three days after arriving in the province, Festus went

chio, era kutenga mwa musi we kaisariya, erukira eyerusalemu.

찌오, 어라 구더꺄 뫄 무시 워 가이사리야, 어루기라 어여루사쩌무.

up from Caesarea to Jerusalem,

2. Aikireyi, ebakulu-kulu be bakohanyi* alauma ne bashamuka be bayuta bera kuya kusitaka Paulo era muhondo sai

2. 아이기러에, 어바구루-구루 버 바고하네* 아꽈우마 너 바싸무가 버 바유다 버라 구야 구시다가 파우로 어라 무호또 사이

2. where the chief priests and Jewish leaders appeared before him and presented the charges against Paul.

3. Bera kumwema mbu abasaa abahibise Paulo eyerusalemu, bushi babaa baire lwango kanji lwa kumwichira mwa njira.

3. 버라 구뭐마 뿌 아바사아 아바히비서 파우로 어여루사쩌무, 부씨 바바아 바이러 롼오 가찌 롸 구뭐찌라 뫄 찌라.

3. They urgently requested Festus, as a favor to them, to have Paul transferred to Jerusalem, for they were preparing an ambush to kill him along the way.

4. Fesito era kubakula mbu: Paulo aminyirirwe mwa buroko ekaisariya, nayi nyeine ndemanga kuhubayi.

4. 퍼시도 어라 구바구롸 뿌: 파우로 아미네리뤄 뫄 부로고 어가이사리야, 나에 녀이너 떠마꺄 구후바에.

4. Festus answered, "Paul is being held at Caesarea, and I myself am going there soon.

5. Mwiree mwaira twandaalireri na bakulu-kulu benyu bauma. Neyi yi bamusitakiraa, tumenye akaba kuli chibi cha airire.

5. 뭐러어 뫄이라 돠따아뙤러리 나 바구루-구루 버뉴 바우마. 너에 에 바무시다기라아, 두머녀 아가바 구뙤 찌비 짜 아이리러.

5. Let some of your leaders come with me and press charges against the man there, if he has done anything wrong."

6. Abere fesito amala suku singaika ku munane nesi ekumi alauma nabo, era kwire ahuba ekaisariya. Mwei mishangya, era kwiya kwikala kwa tiribinali, na ateta mbu bamureteraa Paulo.

6. 아버러 퍼시도 아마꽈 수구 시꺄이가 구 무나너 너시 어구미 아꽈우마 나보, 어라 귀러 아후바 어가이사리야. 뭐이 미싸꺄, 어라 귀야 귀가꽈 과 디리비나찌, 나 아더다 뿌 바무러더라아 파우로.

6. After spending eight or ten days with them, he went down to Caesarea, and the next day he convened the court and ordered that Paul be brought before him.

7. Mango Paulo aika aola, ba bayuta ba batengeraa eyerusalemu bera

7. 마꼬 파우로 아이가 아오꽈, 바 바유다 바 바더꺼라아 어여루사쩌무 버라

7. When Paul appeared, the Jews who had come down from Jerusalem stood

kumusungula. Bera kutangirisa bamusitaka na kumusindaira myasi inene era isitoire, kanji era beine babaa batangaanala kulosa kwairi ya kanangana.

8. Si Paulo era kuchitetera mbu: nyono, kutali chibi chisibya chanyifuraa kuira era luulu se mwaso we bayuta, nesi era luulu se luhu lwa Ongo*, nesi era luulu se kaisari*, mwami we baroma.

9. Fesito nai abaa ahonda kusimisa ebayuta. Bushi noku, era kubusa Paulo mbu: wahonda we rukire eyerusalemu uye kutonganyakirayi luno lubanja era muhondo sanyi?

10. Si Paulo era kumwakula mbu: mwabine bihangi nyire kwa tiribinali ya mwami we baroma. Rero, unao-unao ubinemire nyitonganyire. Si weine uneshi kwa kutali chibi chisibya cha nairire bano bayuta.

11. Nakaba nakolire mwasi ola ungatuma nechibwa, nanemrersi kufa. Si akaba kutali si akaba kutali mwasi wa kanangana ola bano bayuta banyisitakireko, umenyaa kwa kutali mundu

구무수우꽈. 버라 구다띠리사 바무시다가 나 구무시따이라 먀시 이너너 어라 이시도이러, 가찌 어라 버이너 바바아 바다꽈아나꽈 구론사 과이리 야 가나꽈나.

8. 시 파우로 어라 구찌더더라 뿌: 뇨노, 구다띄 찌비 찌시뱌 짜네푸라아 구이라 어라 루우루 서 뫄소 워 바유다, 너시 어라 루우루 서 루후 꽈 오끄*, 너시 어라 루우루 서 가이사리*, 뫄미 워 바로마.

9. 퍼시도 나이 아바아 아혼따 구시미사 어바유다. 부씨 노구, 어라 구부사 파우로 뿌: 와호따 워 루기러 어여루사꺼무 우여 구도꽈냐기라에 루노 루바짜 어라 무호또 사니?

10. 시 파우로 어라 구꽈구꽈 뿌: 뫄비너 비하띄 네러 과 디리비나띄 야 뫄미 워 바로마. 러로, 우나오-우나오 우비너미러 네도꽈네러. 시 워이너 우너씨 과 구다띄 찌비 찌시뱌 짜 나이리러 바노 바유다.

11. 나가바 나고띄러 뫄시 오꽈 우꽈두마 너찌봐, 나너러시 구파. 시 아가바 구다띄 시 아가바 구다띄 뫄시 와 가나꽈나 오꽈 바노 바유다 바네시다기러고, 우머냐아 과 구다띄 무뚜 오꽈 우꽈네비가

around him, bringing many serious charges against him, which they could not prove.

8. Then Paul made his defense: "I have done nothing wrong against the law of the Jews or against the temple or against Caesar."

9. Festus, wishing to do the Jews a favor, said to Paul, "Are you willing to go up to Jerusalem and stand trial before me there on these charges?"

10. Paul answered: "I am now standing before Caesar's court, where I ought to be tried. I have not done any wrong to the Jews, as you yourself know very well.

11. If, however, I am guilty of doing anything deserving death, I do not refuse to die. But if the charges brought against me by these Jews are not true, no one has the right to hand

ola unganyibika mwa mino sabo. Nyono, era mwa mwami we baroma yinahonda nyitonganyire!

와 미노 사보. 뇨노, 어라 와 마미 워 바로마 에나호따 네도까네러!

me over to them. I appeal to Caesar!"

12. Fesito era kwire aya nama ne bashamuka bai. Chasinda, era kwakula Paulo mbu: oku wemire kuya kutonganyira era mwa mwami we baroma, era yi ungere wanaya.

12. 퍼시도 어라 귀러 아야 나마 너 바싸무가 바이. 짜시따, 어라 과구꽈 파우로 뿌: 오구 워미러 구야 구도까네라 어라 와 마미 워 바로마, 어라 에 우꺼러 와나야.

12. After Festus had conferred with his council, he declared: "You have appealed to Caesar. To Caesar you will go!"

Paulo arechibwa era muhondo sa Agiripa na Bereniki

파우로 아러찌봐 어라 무호또 사 아지리파 나 버러니기

13. Abere kwa renga suku burebe, mwami akiripa alauma na mwami mwaliwabo mbu i bereniki bera kuika mwa musi we kaisariya baya kulamusa fesito.

13. 아버러 과 러꽈 수구 부러버, 마미 아기리파 아라우마 나 마미 마뤼와보 뿌 이 버러니기 버라 구이가 와 무시 워 가이사리야 바야 구꽈무사 퍼시도.

13. A few days later King Agrippa and Bernice arrived at Caesarea to pay their respects to Festus.

14. Bera kamalayi suku sinene. Na mwesi suku, fesito era kubalikisisa oyu mwa mwami kwa myasi ya Paulo. Era kumubura mbu: kunola kuli mulume muuma ola feliki arekaa mwa buroko.

14. 버라 가마꽈에 수구 시너너. 나 뭐시 수구, 퍼시도 어라 구바뤼기시사 오유 와 마미 과 먀시 야 파우로. 어라 구무부라 뿌: 구노꽈 구뤼 무루머 무우마 오꽈 퍼뤼기 아러가아 와 부로고.

14. Since they were spending many days there, Festus discussed Paul's case with the king. He said: "There is a man here whom Felix left as a prisoner.

15. Rero mango naikaa eyesrusalemu, ebakulu-kulu be bakohaanyi* alauma ne bashamuka be bayuta bera kubyibalikisisa kwa myasi era yatumaa bamusitaka. Bera kunyema mbu nyimuchinjibusaa.

15. 러로 마꼬 나이가아 어여수루사꺼무, 어바구루-구루 버 바고하아네* 아꽈우마 너 바싸무가 버 바유다 버라 구베바뤼기시사 과 먀시 어라 야두마아 바무시다가. 버라 구녀마 뿌 니무찌찌부사아.

15. When I went to Jerusalem, the chief priests and elders of the Jews brought charges against him and asked that he be condemned.

16. Nanyi nera kubakula mbu ebaroma batatusa mwanya wa kuchinjibusa emundu akabaa atasaa kuchitetera era muhondo se bandu ba bamusitakire.

17. Nera kwire nabaha nabo kuno. Mwei mishangya busira kwerisa, nera kwekala kwa tiribinali, nanateta mbu baretaa Paulo.

18. Abrere era aikaa, babamusitakaa mango babaa bera batetaa, nera kulola kwa kutali mwasi mubi ola bamusitakireko ngokwa nabaa nanyisa.

19. Bwaka bu babaa benjire banamuenza era luulu setini* lyabo oshao, nera luulu sa mundu muuma ola mafire mira mbu i Yesu. Noyu Yesu, i Paulo enjire abura ebandu kwa ali muuma-uma kanji.

20. Elubanja lwa luli ngulu, nainaa kwa nyingaishalo. Nera kwire nabusa Paulo akaba olu lubanja ungemerera kuya kutonganyiralo eyerusalemu.

21. Si era kuteta mbu era muhondo sa mwami wa

16. 나네 너라 구바구꽈 뿌 어바로마 바다두사 먀냐 와 구찌찌부사 어무뚜 아가바아 아다사아 구찌더더라 어라 무호또 서 바뚜 바 바무시다기러.

17. 너라 귀러 나바하 나보 구노. 뭐이 미싸꺄 부시라 귀리사, 너라 귀가꽈 과 디리비나삐, 나나더다 뿌 바러다아 파우뢰.

18. 아부러러 어라 아이가아, 바바무시다가아 마꼬 바바아 버라 바더다아, 너라 구뢰꽈 과 구다삐 먀시 무비 오꽈 바무시다기러고 꼬과 나바아 나네사.

19. 봐가 부 바바아 버찌러 바나무어싸 어라 루우루 서디니* 랴보 오싸오, 너라 루우루 사 무뚜 무우마 오꽈 마피러 미라 뿌 이 여수. 노유 여수, 이 파우뢰 어찌러 아부라 어바뚜 과 아삐 무우마-우마 가찌.

20. 어루바짜 롸 루삐 우루, 나이나아 과 네꽈이싸뢰. 너라 귀러 나부사 파우뢰 아가바 오루 루바짜 우꺼머러라 구야 구도꽈네라뢰 어여루사꺼무.

21. 시 어라 구더다 뿌 어라 무호또 사 먀미 와 바로마 에

16. "I told them that it is not the Roman custom to hand over any man before he has faced his accusers and has had an opportunity to defend himself against their charges.

17. When they came here with me, I did not delay the case, but convened the court the next day and ordered the man to be brought in.

18. When his accusers got up to speak, they did not charge him with any of the crimes I had expected.

19. Instead, they had some points of dispute with him about their own religion and about a dead man named Jesus who Paul claimed was alive.

20. I was at a loss how to investigate such matters; so I asked if he would be willing to go to Jerusalem and stand trial there on these charges.

21. When Paul made his appeal to be held over for

baroma yi ahonda atonganyire. Nanyi nera kwire nateta mbu bamulanga tanga mwa buroko, kuikira mango nyingamutuma era mwa mwami.

22. Akiripa kukwera kubura fesito mbu: oyu mundu, nanyi nyingasimire nyichumvire kwa ateta. Fesito na imbu: unganamovirisa mishangya.

Paulo atongana era muhondo sa Agiripa

23. Abere mwei mishangya, akiripa na bereniki bera kuika mwa lumoo lunene, bakulikene ne bakulu-kulu be basula, alauma ne bashamuka be musi, na bengirira mwa nyumba era bendee bahuukasisa mwa bakulu-kulu. Mwoyu, fesito era kuteta mbu bareta Paulo.

24. Chasinda, fesito era kuhuba kuteta mbu: mwami akiripa, nenyu muboshi mwabwananyire netu anola, mulola kwonu mundu! ebayuta boshi bamusitakaa era muhondo sanyi eyerusalemu. Kanji bera kunamusitaka nokuno kaisariya babanda mwa twabwabwe mbu bitemire ekale mwemuka.

아호따 아도따네러. 나니 너라 귀러 나더다 뿌 바무롸까 다마 와 부로고, 구이기라 마꼬 네따무두마 어라 와 먀미.

22. 아기리파 구궈라 구부라 퍼시도 뿌: 오유 무뚜, 나니 네따시미러 네쭈뻬러 과 아더다. 퍼시도 나 이뿌: 우따나모비리사 미싸뺘.

파우롣 아도따낍 어라 무호또 사 아지리파

23. 아버러 뭐이 미싸뺘, 아기리파 나 버러니기 버라 구이가 와 루모오 루너너, 바구뤼거너 너 바구룹-구루 버 바수롸, 아롸우마 너 바싸무가 버 무시, 나 버삐리라 와 뉴빠 어라 버떠어 바후우가시사 와 바구룹-구루. 모유, 퍼시도 어라 구더다 뿌 바러다 파우롣.

24. 짜시따, 퍼시도 어라 구후바 구더다 뿌: 먀미 아기리파, 너뉴 무보씨 뫄바나니러 너두 아노롸, 무롣롸 고누 무뚜! 어바유다 보씨 바무시다가아 어라 무호또 사니 어여루사뻐무. 가찌 버라 구나무시다가 노구노 가이사리야 바바따 와 돠봐붜 뿌 비더미러 어가뻐 뭐무가.

---

the Emperor's decision, I ordered him held until I could send him to Caesar."

22. Then Agrippa said to Festus, "I would like to hear this man myself." He replied, "Tomorrow you will hear him."

23. The next day Agrippa and Bernice came with great pomp and entered the audience room with the high ranking officers and the leading men of the city. At the command of Festus, Paul was brought in.

24. Festus said: "King Agrippa, and all who are present with us, you see this man! The whole Jewish community has petitioned me about him in Jerusalem and here in Caesarea, shouting that he ought not to live any longer.

25. Si nyeine nera kulola kwa kutali chiro na chiibi chisibya cha airire cha chingatuma echibwa. Si nai abaa anyemire mira mbu elubanja lwai, era mwa mwami we baroma yiluyaa. Nera kunalola kwa kukomire nyimutumirei.

26. Kanji nanyi nyeine, ndete mwasi wa kanangana era luulu sai, ola nyinganjikiraa mwami we baroma. Echara chi chatumire namureta ene muhondo senyu muboshi, nera muhondo sao mwami akiripa. Rero, nyingire nabona cha nyinganjika mango nao unagaba wamutonganyise,

27. Bushi nyisene kwa ekutuma emundu we buroko eRoma busira kumenyerera kubuya-buya emyasi era bamusitakirire, kutete mufa asibya.

25. 시 녀이너 너라 구로롸 과 구다뤼 찌로 나 찌이비 찌시뱌 짜 아이리러 짜 찌꺄두마 어찌봐. 시 나이 아바아 아녀미러 미라 뿌 어루바짜 롸이, 어라 마 마미 워 바로마 에루야아. 너라 구나로롸 과 구고미러 네무두미러이.

26. 가찌 나니 녀이너, 떠더 마시 와 가나꺄나 어라 루우루 사이, 오롸 네꺄찌기라아 마미 워 바로마. 어짜라 찌 짜두미러 나무러다 어너 무호또 서뉴 무보씨, 너라 무호또 사오 마미 아기리파. 러로, 네꺄러 나보나 짜 네꺄찌가 마꼬 나오 우나가바 와무도꺄네서,

27. 부씨 네서너 과 어구두마 어무뚜 워 부로고 어로마 부시라 구머녀러라 구부야-부야 어먀시 어라 바무시다기리러, 구더더 무파 아시뱌.

25. I found he had done nothing deserving of death, but because he made his appeal to the Emperor I decided to send him to Rome.

26. But I have nothing definite to write to His Majesty about him. Therefore I have brought him before all of you, and especially before you, King Agrippa, so that as a result of this investigation I may have something to write.

27. For I think it is unreasonable to send on a prisoner without specifying the charges against him."

E Mikolo ye Ndjumwa Chikono 26

1. Chasinda, akiripa era kubura Paulo mbu: nao nakweresise eloso le kuchitetera weine. Paulo kukwera kwemusa emino, na

어 미고로 여 뚜롸 찌고노 26

1. 짜시따, 아기리파 어라 구부라 파우로 뿌: 나오 나궈러시서 어로소 뤄 구찌더더라 워이너. 파우로 구궈라 궈무사 어미노, 나

Acts Chapter 26[NIV]

1. Then Agrippa said to Paul, "You have permission to speak for yourself." So Paul motioned with his hand and began his

atangirisa ateta mbu:

아다Ⓦ리리사 아더다 뿌:

defense:

2. Mwami Akiripa, lwarero namoire busese kwimanga era muhondo sao nyichitetere era luulu semyasi yoshi era bayuta benjire banyisitakako.

2. 꽈미 아기리파, 꽈러로 나모이러 부서서 귀마Ⓦ 어라 무호또 사오 네찌더더러 어라 루우루 서먀시 요씨 어라 바유다 버찌러 바네시다가고.

2. "King Agrippa, I consider myself fortunate to stand before you today as I make my defense against all the accusations of the Jews,

3.namoa bacha bushi weine utula wishi kubuya emyanya yoshi ye bayuta. Kanji uneshi emyasi era bende baenzanya kwe bwaka. Bushi noku waliya, nakwema unyomvirise busira kunyifira bute.

3.나모아 바짜 부씨 워이너 우두꽈 위씨 구부야 어먀냐 요씨 여 바유다. 가찌 우너씨 어먀시 어라 버더 바어싸냐 궈바가. 부씨 노구 와뤼야, 나궈마 우뇨Ⓦ리리서 부시라 구네피라 부더.

3. and especially so because you are well acquainted with all the Jewish customs and controversies. Therefore, I beg you to listen to me patiently.

4. Ebayuta boshi banatula beshi kute emyanya yanyi yabaa itula kutengera elyanetoto lyanyi. Kanji baneshi kute nendee nachitola ene mwetu, nomwa musi we Yerusalemu.

4. 어바유다 보씨 바나두꽈 버씨 구더 어먀냐 야니 야바아 이두꽈 구더Ⓦ라 어꺄너도도 꺄네. 가찌 바너씨 구더 너Ⓦ어 나찌도꽈 어너 뭐두, 노꽈 무시 워 여루사Ⓦ무.

4. "The Jews all know the way I have lived ever since I was a child, from the beginning of my life in my own country, and also in Jerusalem.

5. Kutengera mira abu bandu batula banyishi kubuya. Na akaba basimire, beine banganalosa kanangana kwa nabaa nyiytula muuma mwa chikembe che bafarisayo*. Nabu bafarisayo bu batula basimikire busese mwa myasi era yekere emyanya yetini* lyetu.

5. 구더Ⓦ라 미라 아부 바뚜 바두꽈 바네씨 구부야. 나 아가바 바시미러, 버이너 바Ⓦ나Ⓦ사 가나Ⓦ나 과 나바아 네위두꽈 무우마 꽈 찌거Ⓦ 쩌 바파리사요*. 나부 바파리사요 부 바두꽈 바시미기러 부서서 꽈 먀시 어라 여거러 어먀냐 여디니* 쪄두.

5. They have known me for a long time and can testify, if they are willing, that according to the strictest sect of our religion, I lived as a Pharisee.

6. Lwarero nera natongana, bushi nyitula nyilangalire

6. 꽈러로 너라 나도Ⓦ나, 부씨 네두꽈 네꽈Ⓦ뤼러 어찌라너

6. And now it is because of my hope in what God has

echirane cha Ongo alanyaa bahokulu betu.

7. Nechi chirane, embaa setu ekumi ne biri nasi, sinatula Silangalire kwa Ongo akanabalosachi. Nechi chi chende chatuma banamukorera emushi ne butufu. Rero waliya, oyu mulangaliro inoyu ituma bano bayuta banyisitaka lwarero.

8. Nenyu, chi chingatuma mwanana kwemerera kwa Ongo ende emwola ebafu

9. Nanyi era muhondo sebine, nabaa nyinasene kwa binyemire kunde naira byoshi bya nyingaala kwa kulwisanya esina lya Yesu we nasareti.

10. Nebi bi nanaira ne Yerusalemu. Ebakulu-kulu be bakuhanyi bera kumba nebuashi bwekunde naumanga bemeresi banene mwa buroko. Na mango bendee bateta mbu bechibwaa, nanyi nendee nanaba lwango luuma nabo.

11. Nabaa nenjire naya kbapunkira mwa mashenge me bayuta chasiya banane Yesu. Nabaa nyibete ku mungo munene busese, nera kunaika kwa chihangi naya kubaiya nomwa misi yebinje

---

짜 오꼬 아꽈냐아 바호구루 버두.

7. 너찌 찌라너, 어빠아 서두 어구미 너 비리 나시, 시나두꽈 시꽈꽈리러 과 오꼬 아가나바룬사찌. 너찌 찌 쩌너 짜두마 바나무고러라 어무씨 너 부두푸. 러로 와꾀야, 오유 무꽈꽈리로 이노유 이두마 바노 바유다 바네시다가 꽈러로.

8. 너뉴, 찌 찌꽈두마 모나나 궈머러라 과 오꼬 어떠 어모꽈 어바푸

9. 나네 어라 무호또 서비너, 나바아 네나서너 과 비녀미러 구떠 나이라 뵤씨 뱌 네꽈아꽈 과 구쀠사냐 어시나 꺄 여수 워 나사러디.

10. 너비 비 나나이라 너 여루사꺼무. 어바구루-구루 버 바구하네 버라 구빠 너부아씨 뭐구떠 나우마꽈 버머러시 바너너 뫄 부로고. 나 마꼬 버떠어 바더다 뿌 버찌뫄아, 나네 너떠어 나나바 꽈꼬 루우마 나보.

11. 나바아 너찌러 나야 구바푸누기라 뫄 마써꺼 머 바유다 짜시야 바나너 여수. 나바아 네버더 구 무꼬 무너너 부서서, 너라 구나이가 과 찌하꾀 나야 구바이야 노뫄 미시 여비꺼 비오.

---

promised our fathers that I am on trial today.

7. This is the promise our twelve tribes are hoping to see fulfilled as they earnestly serve God day and night. O king, it is because of this hope that the Jews are accusing me.

8. Why should any of you consider it incredible that God raises the dead?

9. "I too was convinced that I ought to do all that was possible to oppose the name of Jesus of Nazareth.

10. And that is just what I did in Jerusalem. On the authority of the chief priests I put many of the saints in prison, and when they were put to death, I cast my vote against them.

11. Many a time I went from one synagogue to another to have them punished, and I tried to force them to blaspheme. In my obsession against them, I even went to foreign cities

bio.

12. Lusuku luuma, ebakulu-kulu be bakuhanyi*bera kumba eloso lwekuya mwa musi we Tamasiki.

13. Rero mwami:abere nyinachiri mwa njira esuba limenze, kuna kulola ku chilungere chatenga kwa nguba. Echi chilungere, chabaa chalangala kurenza esuba, na chatulomokera enyinda soshi alauma nebandu ba nabaa nyire nabo mwa luenda.

14. Unao-unao, tuboshi kunakukumbaalanga. Chasinda, nera kumva murenge muumma anyibura mwa chieburaniya mbu: Saulo, Saulo! chi chatuma wanyiburisa woyu uli nga ngaafu era yachihuta kwa ngonyi ye nawabo. Umenyaa kwa chiribusa buha.

15. Nanyi nera kwire nabusa mbu:woyo unde enawetu na imbu: nyono nyi Yesu nyi walibusa.

16. Wiree wabatuka wimange. Nakupamukirireko bushi nahonda nyikuire kuba muanda wanyi. Ungende wabalikisisa ebandu kwa

---

12. 루수구 루우마, 어바구루-구루 버 바구하네*버라 구빠 어론소 뤄구야 롸 무시 워 다마시기.

13. 러로 롸미:아버러 네나찌리 롸 띠라 어수바 릐머써, 구나 구론롸 구 찌루머러 짜더롸 우바. 어찌 찌루머러, 짜바아 짜롸롸롸 구러싸 어수바, 나 짜두로모거라 어네따 소씨 아롸우마 너바뚜 바 나바아 네러 나보 롸 루어따.

14. 우나오-우나오, 두보씨 구나구구빠아롸롸. 짜시따, 너라 구빠 무러머 무우무마 아네부라 롸 쩌부라니야 뿌: 사우로, 사우로! 찌 짜두마 와네부리사 오유 우릐 롸 롸아푸 어라 야찌후다 과 꼬네 여 나와보. 우머냐아 과 찌리부사 부하.

15. 나네 너라 귀러 나부사 뿌:오요 우떠 어나워두 나 이뿌: 뇨노 네 여수 네 와릐부사.

16. 위러어 와바두가 위마써. 나구파무기리러고 부씨 나호따 네구이러 구바 무아따 와네. 우떠러 와바릐기시사 어바뚜 과 와네로리러고,

---

to persecute them.

12. "On one of these journeys I was going to Damascus with the authority and commission of the chief priests.

13. About noon, O king, as I was on the road, I saw a light from heaven, brighter than the sun, blazing around me and my companions.

14. We all fell to the ground, and I heard a voice saying to me in Aramaic, 'Saul, Saul, why do you persecute me? It is hard for you to kick against the goads.'

15. "Then I asked, 'Who are you, Lord?' " 'I am Jesus, whom you are persecuting,' the Lord replied.

16. 'Now get up and stand on your feet. I have appeared to you to appoint you as a servant and as a witness of what you have

---

wanyilorireko, nakubabalikisa ebinji bya nyingahuba kukulosa.

17. Nyingende nakutabala mwamaboko ma banyekenyu bayuta, nmwa bendu besinji mbaa. Abu bandu, bu nakutma era bali.

18. Chasiya ubaboole emeho, betenge mwa musimya, baye mwabulangare. Batenge mwa mino sa wamusimu, baalukire Ongo. Mwei jira, mubangababalirwa ebibi byabo, nakubona echiki alauma nebanji babuya-buya banyi, ba Ongo alondwere kwa njira yekunyemerera.

19. Bushi noku mwami Akiripa, ei myasi nomvaa mwa byabunya biroto yatengera kwa nguba, nera kunaira kwa yabaa yanyema.

20. Nera kwire nanatangirisa kuhubanganyisa besha Tamasiki mbu babinduka bendenge mwa bibi byabo baalukire Ongo, nemyanya yabo indaa yalosa kanangana kwa banindukire. Chasinda, neya kuya kuhubanganyisa besha Yerusalemu ei myasi enei-enei, nabesha mwachio

21. Rero bushi nei myasi, ebayuta bera kunyisimbira

17. 네뻐더 나구다바뻐 먀마보고 마 바녀거뉴 바유다, 누뫄 버뿌 버시띠 빠아. 아부 바뚜, 부 나구두마 어라 바뛰.

18. 짜시야 우바보오뤄 어머호, 버더뻐 먀 무시먀, 바여 먀부뽜뻐러. 바더뻐 먀 미노 사 와무시무, 바아룪기러 오으. 뭐이 지라, 무바뻐바바뛰러 어비비 먀보, 나구보나 어찌기 아뽜우마 너바띠 바부야-부야 바네, 바 오으 아뢴뚜워러 과 띠라 여구녀머러라.

19. 부씨 노구 먀미 아기리빠, 어이 먀시 노빠아 먀 먀부냐 비로도 야더뻐라 과 꾸바, 너라 구나이라 과 야바아 야녀마.

20. 너라 귀러 나나다뛰리사 구후바뻐네사 버싸 다마시기 뿌 바비뿌가 버뻐뻐 먀 비비 먀보 바아룪기러 오으, 너먀냐 야보 이따아 야뢴사 가나뻐나 과 바니뿌기러. 짜시따, 너야 구야 구후바뻐네사 버싸 여루사뻐무 어이 먀시 어너이-어너이, 나버싸 먀찌오

21. 러로 부씨 너이 먀시, 어바유다 버라 구네시뻐라 먀

seen of me and what I will show you.

17. I will rescue you from your own people and from the Gentiles. I am sending you to them

18. to open their eyes and turn them from darkness to light, and from the power of Satan to God, so that they may receive forgiveness of sins and a place among those who are sanctified by faith in me.'

19. "So then, King Agrippa, I was not disobedient to the vision from heaven.

20. First to those in Damascus, then to those in Jerusalem and in all Judea, and to the Gentiles also, I preached that they should repent and turn to God and prove their repentance by their deeds.

21. That is why the Jews seized me in the temple

mwa luhu lwa Ongo, nokubura banyita.

22. Sikuikira kwoluno lusuku lwa lwarero, Ongo kunyilanga kwa nachiri annyilanga. Bushi noku, nyinachiri naendekera kuhubanganyisa ebandu boshi, ebakulu-kulu ne batoto, emyasi era nachiloreako. Kutali inji mwasi isbbya era nenjire nahubanganyisa ebandu,

23. Abu boshi batetaa kwa byemire masiya* alibuke, abe na mubere kwomoka mwa bafu, chasiya ahubanganye ebwami bwe bulangare era mwa banyakabo bayuta, nera mwebandu besinji mbaa.

Paulo ahonda Agiripa emerere Yesu

24. Mango Paulo abaa nachiri achitetera, fesito era kumubura na murenge munene mbu: woyu Paulo wasireire! ekusoma kwa wasomire busese, kukwakurorobanyise ebwenge!

25. Si Paulo era kumwakula mbu: waliya fesito, nyono ndasimire. Emyasi era nateta iri ya kanangana, kanji iri ya mundu ola utungenene.

루후 롸 오꼬, 노구부라 바네다.

22. 시구이기라 골루노 루수구 롸 롸러로, 오꼬 구네롸아 과 나찌리 아누네롸아. 부씨 노구, 네나찌리 나어떠거라 구후바아네사 어바누 보씨, 어바구루-구루 너 바도도, 어먀시 어라 나찌로러라고. 구다뤼 이찌 마시 이수부뱌 어라 너찌러 나후바아네사 어바누,

23. 아부 보씨 바더다아 과 벼미러 마시야* 아뤼부거, 아버 나 무버러 고모가 롸 바푸, 짜시야 아후바아녀 어바미 붜 부롸아러 어라 롸 바냐가보 바유다, 너라 뭐바누 버시찌 빠아.

파우로 아호따 아지리파 어머러러 여수

24. 마꼬 파우로 아바아 나찌리 아찌더더라, 퍼시도 어라 구무부라 나 무러어 무너너 뿌: 오유 파우로 와시러이러! 어구소마 과 와소미러 부서서, 구과구로로바네서 어붜어!

25. 시 파우로 어라 구롸구롸 뿌: 와뤼야 퍼시도, 뇨노 따시미러. 어먀시 어라 나더다 이리 야 가나아나, 가찌 이리 야 무뚜 오롸 우두어너너.

courts and tried to kill me.

22. But I have had God's help to this very day, and so I stand here and testify to small and great alike. I am saying nothing beyond what the prophets and Moses said would happen--

23. that the Christ would suffer and, as the first to rise from the dead, would proclaim light to his own people and to the Gentiles."

24. At this point Festus interrupted Paul's defense. "You are out of your mind, Paul!" he shouted. "Your great learning is driving you insane."

25. "I am not insane, most excellent Festus," Paul replied. "What I am saying is true and reasonable.

26. Ei myasi, mwami akiripa nai anaishi kubuya-kubuya. Kanji nyishi kanangana kwa kutali cha abukire, bushi ei myasi itaribwaa mwa bubisho-bisho. Bushi noku, ndete buba busibya bwa kueta era muhondo sai.

26. 어이 먀시, 뫄미 아기리파 나이 아나이씨 구부야-구부야. 가지 네씨 가나ㅉ가나 과 구다끼짜 아부기러, 부씨 어이 먀시 이다리봐아 뫄 부비쏘-비쏘. 부씨 노구, 떠더 부바 부시뱌 봐 구어다 어라 무호또 사이.

26. The king is familiar with these things, and I can speak freely to him. I am convinced that none of this has escaped his notice, because it was not done in a corner.

27. Mwami akiripa, emyasi era barebi* batetaa, si utula uyemerere! nyineshi kanangana kwa unatula uyemerere.

27. 뫄미 아기리파, 어먀시 어라 바러비* 바더다아, 시 우두롸 우여머러러! 네너씨 가나ㅉ가나 과 우나두롸 우여머러러.

27. King Agrippa, do you believe the prophets? I know you do."

28. Akiripa era kwire abusa Paulo mbu waanyisa mbu unganyihubya muKirisito mwebine bihangi bieke

28. 아기리파 어라 귀러 아부사 파우로 뿌 와아네사 뿌 우ㅉ가네후뱌 무기리시도 뭐비너 비하ㅉ이 비어거

28. Then Agrippa said to Paul, "Do you think that in such a short time you can persuade me to be a Christian?"

29. Paulo na imbu:chiro bingaba bihangi byeke nesi binene, nema Ongo bushi nao, na bushi na bano banji bandu boshi babanyumvirisa lwa rero mube ngokwa nyiri. Si ndahonda munde mwaminwa ngokuno nyiminyirwe ne mareure.

29. 파우로 나 이뿌:찌로 비ㅉ가바 비하ㅉ이 벼거 너시 비너너, 너마 오ㄲ오 부씨 나오, 나 부씨 나 바노 바ㅉ이 바뚜 보씨 바바뉴삐리사 롸 러로 무버 ㄲ오과 네리. 시 따호따 무떠 뫄미놔 ㄲ오구노 네미네뤄 너 마러우러.

29. Paul replied, "Short time or long--I pray God that not only you but all who are listening to me today may become what I am, except for these chains."

30. Chasinda, mwami era kwire emanga, fesito, na bereniki ne banji bandu ba babaa bekese alauma nabo.

30. 짜시따, 뫄미 어라 귀러 어마ㅉ가, 퍼시도, 나 버러니기 너 바ㅉ이 바뚜 바 바바아 버거서 아롸우마 나보.

30. The king rose, and with him the governor and Bernice and those sitting with them.

31. Abere bera baulukaa, bera kutangirisa bateta mwa kachi-kachi kabo mbu: oyu mundu,

31. 아버러 버라 바우루가아, 버라 구다ㅉ이리사 바더다 뫄 가찌-가찌 가보 뿌: 오유 무뚜,

31. They left the room, and while talking with one another, they said, "This

kutali mwasi ola akolire ola ungatuma echibwa nesi aminwa.

32. Chasinjiren akiripa era kwire abura fesito mbu: oyu mundu, akaba atachemereraa yeine mbu ahonda kuya kutonganyira era muhondo sa mwami we baroma, abaa angaboolibwe.

구다릐 마시 오랴 아고릐러 오랴 우꽈두마 어찌봐 너시 아미놔.

32. 짜시띠러누 아기리파 어라 귀러 아부라 퍼시도 뿌: 오유 무뚜, 아가바 아다쩌머러라아 여이너 뿌 아호따 구야 구도꽈네라 어라 무호또 사 꽈미 워 바로마, 아바아 아꽈보오릐붜.

man is not doing anything that deserves death or imprisonment."

32. Agrippa said to Festus, "This man could have been set free if he had not appealed to Caesar."

E Mikolo ye Ndjumwa Chikono 27

Paulo aya kutonganyira eRoma

1. Chasinda, fesito era kuisha elwango kwa twekibwaa mwa chio che Italiya. Bera kubika Paulo na banji bandu bauma be buroko mwa mino sa mukulu-kulu muuma we basula mbu i Yuliyo. Oyu yuliyo, abaa womwa chikembe che basula cha bendee berika mbu chikembe chebasula ba mwami Okisito.

2. Twera kwerukira mu bwato buuma bwa bwabaa bwatengera mwa musi we Atiramiti. Obu bwato, bwabwaa bungemanga-emanga kwa bihabukiro bye chio che Asiya. Twera kuenda alauma na mwesha kaetoniya

어 미고론 여 뚜꽈 찌고노 27

파우론 아야 구도꽈네띱 어로마

1. 짜시따, 퍼시도 어라 구이싸 어꽈오꼬 과 뛰기봐아 봐 찌오 쩌 이다릐야. 버라 구비가 파우론 나 바찌 바뚜 바우마 버 부로고 봐 미노 사 무구루- 구루 무우마 워 바수꽈 뿌 이 유릐요. 오유 유릐요, 아바아 옴꽈 찌거뻐 쩌 바수꽈 짜 버뻐어 버리가 뿌 찌거뻐 쩌바수꽈 바 꽈미 오기시도.

2. 뚸라 궈루기라 무 봐도 부우마 봐 봐바아 봐더꺼라 무시 워 아디라미디. 오부 봐도, 봐봐아 부꺼마꽈-어마꽈 과 비하부기로 벼 찌오 쩌 아시야. 뚸라 구어따 아꽈우마 나 뭐싸 가어도니야

Acts Chapter 27[NIV]

1. When it was decided that we would sail for Italy, Paul and some other prisoners were handed over to a centurion named Julius, who belonged to the Imperial Regiment.

2. We boarded a ship from Adramyttium about to sail for ports along the coast of the province of Asia, and we put out to sea. Aristarchus, a Macedonian from Thessalonica, was with us.

muuma mbu i Arisitariko, womwa musi we tasalonike.

워 다사로니거.

3. Mwei ishangya, twera kuhabukira mwa musi we Sitona. Yuliyo, bushi endee akorera Paulo mabuya, era kulureka aye kulola ku bera bai chasiya bamweresi bya abaa alaireko.

3. 뭐이 이싸야, 뛰라 구하부기라 와 무시 워 시도나. 유리요, 부씨 어떠어 아고러라 파우로 마부야, 어라 구루러가 아여 구론롸 구 버라 바이 짜시야 바뭐러시 뱌 아바아 아롸이러고.

3. The next day we landed at Sidon; and Julius, in kindness to Paul, allowed him to go to his friends so they might provide for his needs.

4. Mwakutenga esitona, twera kurenga kwa musiki musiki we chisimba che chipuro, bushi noku ambuka emulaba ola wabaa watengera era muhondo setu.

4. 롸구더롸 어시도나, 뛰라 구러롸 과 무시기 무시기 워 찌시빠 쩌 찌푸로, 부씨 노구 아뿌가 어무롸바 오롸 와바아 와더뻐라 어라 무호또 서두.

4. From there we put out to sea again and passed to the lee of Cyprus because the winds were against us.

5. Twera kuhabuka enyanja twaenda twarenga kwa musike we chio che kirikiya neche pamufiriya. Chasinda, na twaika mwa musi we mira, mwa chio che Likiya.

5. 뛰라 구하부가 어냐짜 돠어따 돠러롸 과 무시거 워 찌오 쩌 기리기야 너쩌 파무피리야. 짜시따, 나 돠이가 롸 무시 워 미라, 롸 찌오 쩌 리기야.

5. When we had sailed across the open sea off the coast of Cilicia and Pamphylia, we landed at Myra in Lycia.

6. Oyu mukulu-kulu we basula, era kubuana bwato buuma wmoyu musi. Obu bwato, bwabaa bomwa musi we alesanduriya bwa bwabaa bwaya mwa chio che Italiya. Era kutwerusa mubo.

6. 오유 무구루-구루 워 바수롸, 어라 구부아나 봐도 부우마 우모유 무시. 오부 봐도, 봐바아 보롸 무시 워 아뻐사누리야 봐 봐바아 봐야 롸 찌오 쩌 이다뻐야. 어라 구뚸루사 무보.

6. There the centurion found an Alexandrian ship sailing for Italy and put us on board.

7. Twera kumala suku sinene kwa meshi, bushi twabaa twaenda mbala-mbala. Nera nyuma sa malibuko manene, twera kuika ofu ne musi we kinito. Mwa kutengamo, twera kwire twarengera kwa lunda

7. 뛰라 구마롸 수구 시너너 과 머씨, 부씨 돠바아 돠어따 빠롸-빠롸. 너라 뉴마 사 마뻐부고 마너너, 뛰라 구이가 오푸 너 무시 워 기니도. 롸 구더롸모, 뛰라 귀러 돠러뻐라 과 루따 뤄라 마시나 서

7. We made slow headway for many days and had difficulty arriving off Cnidus. When the wind did not allow us to hold our course, we sailed to the lee of Crete, opposite Salmone.

lwera masina se chisimba che kerete twerekera esalimuni, bushi echusi chatwangikaa kuendekera ne lubalamo kwolu lunda.

8. Twera kunaendekera ne lubalamo na malibuko manene, twaenda twarengera kwa musike-musike we nyanja. Chasinda, twera kuika mu chisiki chiuma cha chitula cherikirwe mbu Bihabukiro bibuya ofu ne musi we Laseya.

9. Abere twamala suku sinene mwolu lubalamo, twera kunalinda twaika mwa suku sa situla sikaramire mwa kubalama kwameshi. Kanji bushi olusuku lukulu lwememo ma mende mairwa busira kulya lwabaa lwarengire mira, Paulo era kwire abura balikabo mbu:

10. Abalume, nyisene kwa luno lubalamo lwetu lungaba lwa bisibu biene, bya bingatuma buno bwato alauma nene misio byakumba. Anabe netu, kuli mango tunganasika.

11. Eri eano lya Paulo, oyu mukulu-kulu era kulinana, era kukulikira emyanyisa yola wende waenza ebwato neya enabo.

찌시빠 쩌 거러더 뛰러거라 어사쮜무니, 부씨 어쭈시 짜돠삐가아 구어떠거라 너 루바꽈모 굘루 룬따.

8. 뛰라 구나어떠거라 너 루바꽈모 나 마쮜부고 마너너, 돠어따 돠러뤄라 과 무시거-무시거 워 냐짜. 짜시따, 뛰라 구이가 무 찌시기 찌우마 짜 찌두꽈 쩌리기뤄 뿌 비하부기로 비부야 오푸 너 무시 워 꽈서야.

9. 아버러 돠마꽈 수구 시너너 몰루 루바꽈모, 뛰라 구나쮜따 돠이가 똬 수구 사 시두꽈 시가라미러 똬 구바꽈마 과머씨. 가찌 부씨 오루수구 루구루 뤄메모 마 머떠 마이롸 부시라 구꺄 꽈바아 꽈러삐러 미라, 파우뢰 어라 귀러 아부라 바쮜가보 뿌:

10. 아바루머, 네서너 과 루노 루바꽈모 뤄두 루빠바 꽈 비시부 비어너, 뱌 비빠두마 부노 봐도 아꽈우마 너너 미시오 뱌구빠. 아나버 너두, 구쮜 마꼬 두빠나시가.

11. 어리 어아노 꺄 파우뢰, 오유 무구루루-구루 어라 구쮜나나, 어라 구구쮜기라 어먀네사 요꺄 워떠 와어싸 어봐도 너야 어나보.

8. We moved along the coast with difficulty and came to a place called Fair Havens, near the town of Lasea.

9. Much time had been lost, and sailing had already become dangerous because by now it was after the Fast. So Paul warned them,

10. "Men, I can see that our voyage is going to be disastrous and bring great loss to ship and cargo, and to our own lives also."

11. But the centurion, instead of listening to what Paul said, followed the advice of the pilot and of the owner of the ship.

12. Kanji echi chihabukiro chabaa chitakomire ebandu kubako mwa suku embeo. Bushi noku, banene mu tubano bera kwemeresanya kwa kutengaa kwolu lunda, tuike eFoinike akaba bingalikana, turenzeseyi esi suku. EFoinike chiri chihabukiro cha chitula cherekere kwa lunda esuba lyende lyachirowa.

Emulaba achihuta kwa nyanja

13. Chasinda, kwera kuulikira kausi kaeke ka kabaa katengera kwa lunda lwera masina. Besha ebwato bera kuchichinga mbu banganaendekera ne lubalamo ngokwa babaa basimire. Bushi noku, bera kwire berusa echuma cha chende chemanza ebwato. Twera kutenga aola, na twarenga kwa musike-musike wenyanja ofu ne chisimba che kerete.

14. Si abere kwa renga bihangi bieke, mwa miruko yechi chisimba mwera kuulikira chuusi chisibu, cha chabaa cha tenegra kwa lunda lwera luulu nokwa lunda esubalyende lyaulikira.

12. 가씨 어찌 찌하부기로 짜바아 찌다고미러 어바뚜 구바고 뫄 수구 어뻐오. 부씨 노구, 바너너 무 두바노 버라 궈머러사냐 과 구더꽈아 곤루 루따, 두이거 어포이니거 아가바 비꽈뛰가나, 두러써서에 어시 수구. 어포이니거 찌리 찌하부기로 짜 찌두롸 쩌러거러 과 루따 어수바 뗘떠 쟈찌로와.

어무롸밍 아찌후다 과 냐싸

13. 짜시따, 궈라 구우뛰기라 가우시 가어거 가 가바아 가더꺼라 과 루따 뭐라 마시나. 버싸 어봐도 버라 구찌찌꽈 뿌 바꽈나어떠거라 너 루바롸모 꼬과 바바아 바시미러. 부씨 노구, 버라 궈러 버루사 어쭈마 짜 쩌떠 쩌마싸 어봐도. 뗘라 구더꽈 아오롸, 나 돠러꽈 과 무시거-무시거 워냐싸 오푸 너 찌시빠 쩌 거러더.

14. 시 아버러 과 러꽈 비하찌 비어거, 뫄 미루고 여찌 찌시빠 뭐라 구우뛰기라 쭈우시 찌시부, 짜 짜바아 짜 더너구라 과 루따 뭐라 루우루 노과 루따 어수바뗘떠 쟈우뛰기라.

12. Since the harbor was unsuitable to winter in, the majority decided that we should sail on, hoping to reach Phoenix and winter there. This was a harbor in Crete, facing both southwest and northwest.

13. When a gentle south wind began to blow, they thought they had obtained what they wanted; so they weighed anchor and sailed along the shore of Crete.

14. Before very long, a wind of hurricane force, called the "northeaster," swept down from the island.

15. Echi chiusi chera kuruwa-ruwa obu bwato, bwera kunaina kute kwa bungalwisachi. Cha chusi, twera kwire twareka chitweke era chinahonjire kwa nyanja.

15. 어찌 찌우시 쩌라 구루와-루와 오부 봐도, 붜라 구나이나 구더 과 부까뤼사찌. 짜 쭈시, 뛰라 귀러 돠러가 찌뛰거 어라 찌나호ᄶ이러 과 냐ᄶ아.

15. The ship was caught by the storm and could not head into the wind; so we gave way to it and were driven along.

16. Twera kurenga kwa lunda lwera bfuli bwa kachisimba kaeke ka bende berika mbu Kauta. Aku kechisimba, kera kutulanga hicha kwechi chusi. Si twera kulibuka busese mwa kulanga eke bwato kaeke ka bwato bwa twabaa tulimo bwabaa bwakulula.

16. 뛰라 구러까 과 루따 뤄라 부푸리 봐 가찌시빠 가어거 가버떠 버리가 뿌 가우다. 아구 거찌시빠, 거라 구두라까 히짜 궈찌 쭈시. 시 뛰라 구리부가 부서서 뫄 구라까 어거 봐도 가어거 가 봐도 봐 돠바아 두리모 봐바아 봐구루라.

16. As we passed to the lee of a small island called Cauda, we were hardly able to make the lifeboat secure.

17. Abere bera bakerusisa mwa bwato, bera kubusungusa kwemirisi bungesha kubereka. Kanji bushi babaa bobaa kusinda kwa nundo ye chishee chokwa lunda lwechio che Libiya, bera kwendaasa echiito cha chende chemanza ebwato, bera kwire bamureka bwekibwe nechusi.

17. 아버러 버라 바거루시사 뫄 봐도, 버라 구부수우사 궈미리시 부어싸 구버러가. 가ᄶ이 부씨 바바아 보바아 구시따 과 누또 여 찌써어 쪼과 루따 뤄찌오 쩌 리비야, 버라 궈따아사 어찌이도 짜 쩌떠 쩌마ᄶ아 어봐도, 버라 귀러 바무러가 붜기붜 너쭈시.

17. When the men had hoisted it aboard, they passed ropes under the ship itself to hold it together. Fearing that they would run aground on the sandbars of Syrtis, they lowered the sea anchor and let the ship be driven along.

18. Emulaba era kunaendekera aruwa-ruwa ebwato busese. Mwei mishangya, bera kwire batangirisa baumanga emisio mwa nyanja.

18. 어무라바 어라 구나어떠거라 아루와-루와 어봐도 부서서. 뭐이 미싸갸, 버라 귀러 바다기리사 바우마까 어미시오 뫄 냐ᄶ아.

18. We took such a violent battering from the storm that the next day they began to throw the cargo overboard.

19. Abere mweli lishisho, nebinde bya bendee bakoresa mwa bwato, beine bera kunalinda bakabulangabi mwa nyanja.

19. 아버러 뭐리 리씨쏘, 너비떠 뱌 버떠어 바고러사 뫄 봐도, 버이너 버라 구나리따 바가부라까비 뫄 냐ᄶ아.

19. On the third day, they threw the ship's tackle overboard with their own hands.

20. Kwera kurenga suku sinene tutachilila kwesuba nesi kwa ngununu. Emulaba nao, era kunaendekera akarama busese. Netu twera kwire twanaesa emunyyiro we kulama.

21. Ebandu babaa bamala suku sinene busira kulya. Paulo era kwire emanga era muhondo sabo, na aburabo mbu: ebera banyi! Iyeano lyanyi, akaba mwemererali mango nababuraa mbu tutafura kutenga ekerete, tutangalolire kwe bine bisibu byoshi na kuesa ebi bindu.

22. Rero nera nabema musesaa emuchima, bushi kutali chiro na muuma mu mwabo ola ungafa, si ebwato bweine bu bunganakumba. Natechire bacha bushi nyiri muanda wa Ongo, kanji inende nera.

23. Na Iwarero mwa butufu, malaika*wai muuma anyipamikiraa,

24. Naanyibura mbu: epaulo! utobaa, bushi kwemire utonganyire era muhondo sa mwami we baroma. Kanji omerera kwa woyu na bano bandu boshi uli nabo, Ongo

20. 귀라 구러꺄 수구 시너너 두다찌끼꽈 귀수바 너시 과 우누누. 어무꽈바 나오, 어라 구나어꺼거라 아가라마 부서서. 너두 뚸라 귀러 돠나어사 어무네에로 워 구꽈마.

21. 어바뚜 바바아 바마꽈 수구 시너너 부시라 구꺌. 파우뾠 어라 귀러 어마꽈 어라 무호또 사보, 나 아부라보 뿌: 어버라 바네! 껴아노 꺄네, 아가바 뭐머러라끼 마꼬 나바부라아 뿌 두다푸라 구더꽈 어거러더, 두다꽈뾠끼러 궈 비너 비시부 보씨 나 구어사 어비 비뚜.

22. 러로 너라 나버마 무서사아 어무찌마, 부씨 구다끼 찌로 나 무우마 무 꽈보 오꽈 우꽈파, 시 어봐도 뷔이너 부 부꽈나구빠. 나더찌러 바짜 부씨 네리 무아따 와 오꼬, 가찌 이너너 너라.

23. 나 꽈러로 뫄 부두푸, 마꽈이가*와이 무우마 아네파미기라아,

24. 나아네부라 뿌: 어파우뾠! 우도바아, 부씨 궈미러 우도꽈네러 어라 무호또 사 꽈미 워 바로마. 가찌 오머러라 과 오유 나 바노 바뚜 보씨 우끼 나보, 오꼬 뫄

20. When neither sun nor stars appeared for many days and the storm continued raging, we finally gave up all hope of being saved.

21. After the men had gone a long time without food, Paul stood up before them and said: "Men, you should have taken my advice not to sail from Crete; then you would have spared yourselves this damage and loss.

22. But now I urge you to keep up your courage, because not one of you will be lost; only the ship will be destroyed.

23. Last night an angel of the God whose I am and whom I serve stood beside me

24. and said, 'Do not be afraid, Paul. You must stand trial before Caesar; and God has graciously given you the lives of all who sail with you.'

mwa bubuya bwai, angabasa mwolu lubalamo lwenyu.

25. Bushi noku, musesa emichima bushi bya Ongo anyiburaa, nyete emunyiiro kwa anganabiirira

26. Si chiro bacha, ebwato buchiri bunganaturowa ku chisimba chiuma.

27. Mwolu, twera kumama mainga mabiri emulaba aenda atweka yeyi-neyi kwa nyanja ya Atiriya. Abere kara kachi-kachi kabutufu bwe lusuku lwe kumi nene, ebakosi bomwa bwato bera kuchichinga mbu twahonda kuika kwa musiki we nyanja.

28. Bera kwire baabdasa echipimo era mubi cha chende chalosa ala meshi maikira, bera kulola kwa mwakuikira kwa chishee, sichiri metere mane. Abere bachifunda bure hicha, bera kuhuba kwandasa echipimo, na balola kwa mwa kuikira kwa chishee, sera metere mahatu.

29. Bera kobaa mbu ebwato bungasinda kwa makoi, kanji mwa kulinjira ebutufu buche, bera kwire baandasa byuma bine byera nyuma se bwato bya byende bya bwemanza.

부부야 봐이, 아빠바사 모루 루바꽈모 뤄뉴.

25. 부씨 노구, 무서사 어미찌마 부씨 뱌 오꼬 아네부라아, 녀더 어무네이로 과 아빠나비이리라

26. 시 찌로 바짜, 어봐도 부찌리 부빠나두로와 구 찌시빠 찌우마.

27. 모루, 뛰라 구마마 마이빠 마비리 어무꽈바 아어따 아뛰가 여에-너에 과 냐짜 야 아디리야. 아버러 가라 가찌-가찌 가부두푸 붜 루수구 뤄 구미 너너, 어바고시 보봐 봐도 버라 구찌찌빠 뿌 다호따 구이가 과 무시기 워 냐짜.

28. 버라 귀러 바아부다사 어찌피모 어라 무비 짜 쩌너 짜룬사 아꽈 머씨 마이기라, 버라 구룬꽈 과 꽈구이기라 과 찌써어, 시찌리 머더러 마너. 아버러 바찌푸따 부러 히짜, 버라 구후바 과따사 어찌피모, 나 바룬꽈 과 꽈 구이기라 과 찌써어, 서라 머더러 마하두.

29. 버라 고바아 뿌 어봐도 부빠시따 과 마고이, 가찌 꽈 구꿰찌라 어부두푸 부쩌, 버라 귀러 바아따사 뷰마 비너 벼라 뉴마 서 봐도 뱌 벼너 뱌 붜마싸. 버라 궈마 부쩌 푸바.

25. So keep up your courage, men, for I have faith in God that it will happen just as he told me.

26. Nevertheless, we must run aground on some island."

27. On the fourteenth night we were still being driven across the Adriatic Sea, when about midnight the sailors sensed they were approaching land.

28. They took soundings and found that the water was a hundred and twenty feet deep. A short time later they took soundings again and found it was ninety feet deep.

29. Fearing that we would be dashed against the rocks, they dropped four anchors from the stern and prayed for daylight.

Bera kwema buche fuba.

30. Mwolu, bera kuhonda bongoloke. Bera kwire bandasisa eke bwato kaeke kwa meshi mwa kuchengeeresa mbu baya kwandasa ebyuma byera muhondo mwa meshi byabyende byaemanza ebwato.

31. Paulo kukwera kubura emukulu-kulu we basula alauma ne basula bai mbu: bano balume bakatenga mwobuno bwato, mumenyaa kwanenyu mwasikire!

32. Ebasula bomvire bacha, kukwera kuishanga emirisi era yabaa iminirwe kwaku ke bwato kaeke na bakareka katowere mwa nyanja.

33. Abere ebutufu bwahonda kucha, Paulo era kubura ebandu mbu atangiraa kulya. Era kuteta mbu: mainga mabiri mano malumirire lwarero muli mwa malibuko, kanji mutalya na kalyo kasibya.

34. Rero nabema mulye kwa biryo, bushi bibingabaasa mungesha kufa. Si munyereraa kwa kutali muuma mu mwabo abaa angaesa chiro na lufiri kwetwe

30. 모루, 버라 구호따 보오로거. 버라 귀러 바따시사 어거 봐도 가어거 과 머씨 뫄 구쩌뻐어러사 뿌 바야 과따사 어뷰마 벼라 무호또 뫄 머씨 뱌벼너 뱌어마싸 어봐도.

31. 파우로 구궈라 구부라 어무구루루-구루 워 바수롸 아롸우마 너 바수롸 바이 뿌: 바노 바루머 바가더뽜 모부노 봐도, 무머냐아 과너뉴 롸시기러!

32. 어바수롸 보뻐러 바쨔, 구궈라 구이싸뽜 어미리시 어라 야바아 이미니뤄 과구 거 봐도 가어거 나 바가러가 가도워러 뫄 냐쨔.

33. 아버러 어부두푸 봐호따 구쨔, 파우로 어라 구부라 어바뉴 뿌 아다삐라아 구꺍. 어라 구더다 뿌: 마이뽜 마비리 마노 마루미리러 롸러로 무뾔 뫄 마뾔부고, 가씨 무다꺍 나 가룶 가시뱌.

34. 러로 나버마 무뗘 과 비료, 부씨 비비뻐바아사 무뻐싸 구파. 시 무녀러라아 과 구다삐 무우마 무 뫄보 아바아 아뻐어사 찌로 나 룾피리 궈뙤꺍이.

30. In an attempt to escape from the ship, the sailors let the lifeboat down into the sea, pretending they were going to lower some anchors from the bow.

31. Then Paul said to the centurion and the soldiers, "Unless these men stay with the ship, you cannot be saved."

32. So the soldiers cut the ropes that held the lifeboat and let it fall away.

33. Just before dawn Paul urged them all to eat. "For the last fourteen days," he said, "you have been in constant suspense and have gone without food--you haven't eaten anything.

34. Now I urge you to take some food. You need it to survive. Not one of you will lose a single hair from his head."

lyai.

35. Mango Paulo abaa era atetaa ei myasi, era kutola emukati, era kutonga Ongo era muhondo sabo. Chasinda, era kuisha muo, na atangirisa alya.

36. Bushi noku ebandu boshi bera kuhuba kusera emichima, nabo bera kutangirisa balya.

37. Mwobu bwato, twabaa tuli bandu maana mabiri na malinda na matano.

38. Abere chira mundu era alyaa, aneuchiri, bera kutangirisa baumanga emisio yebulo mwa nyanja, mwakuhonda ebwato bwanguwe.

Ebwato bwabereka

39. Mango ebutufu bwabaa bwera bwachaa, besha ebwato chiro bakamenyerera echio cha babaa balimo. Si bera kulola ku chisiki chiuma ala nyanja yabaa ichiumire kwa chio, kanji abaa ali na chihabukiro. Bera kuhonda kuruwa ebwato buye kusinda aola akaba bingalikana.

40. Bera kwire baboola emirisi yabya biito, na babitosangisa mwa nyanja. Bera kuboola nemirisi era yabaa eminyirwe kwa mbao sekuenza ebwato.

---

35. 마꼬 파우로 아바아 어라 아더다아 어이 먀시, 어라 구도롸 어무가디, 어라 구도꽈 오꼬 어라 무호또 사보. 짜시따, 어라 구이싸 무오, 나 아다꾀리사 아꺄.

36. 부씨 노구 어바뚜 보씨 버라 구후바 구서라 어미찌마, 나보 버라 구다꾀리사 바꺄.

37. 모부 봐도, 돠바아 두뤼 바뚜 마아나 마비리 나 마뤼따 나 마다노.

38. 아버러 찌라 무뚜 어라 아꺄아, 아너우찌리, 버라 구다꾀리사 바우마꽈 어미시오 여부로 봐 냐짜, 마구호따 어봐도 봐꾸워.

어봐도 봐버러가

39. 마꼬 어부두푸 봐바아 뷔라 봐짜아, 버싸 어봐도 찌로 바가머녀러라 어찌오 짜 바바아 바뤼모. 시 버라 구로롸 구 찌시기 찌우마 아롸 냐짜 야바아 이찌우미러 과 찌오, 가찌 아바아 아뤼 나 찌하부기로. 버라 구호따 구루와 어봐도 부여 구시따 아오롸 아가바 비꺄리가나.

40. 버라 귀러 바보오롸 어미리시 야뱌 비이도, 나 바비도사꾀사 봐 냐짜. 버라 구보오롸 너미리시 어라 야바아 어미네뤄 과 빠오

---

35. After he said this, he took some bread and gave thanks to God in front of them all. Then he broke it and began to eat.

36. They were all encouraged and ate some food themselves.

37. Altogether there were 276 of us on board.

38. When they had eaten as much as they wanted, they lightened the ship by throwing the grain into the sea.

39. When daylight came, they did not recognize the land, but they saw a bay with a sandy beach, where they decided to run the ship aground if they could.

40. Cutting loose the anchors, they left them in the sea and at the same time untied the ropes that held the rudders. Then they

Chasinda, bera kulina engwaya era muhondo se bwato mwa kuhonda echusi chibweke kwechi chihabukiro.

41. Si mwolu, echilbi chera muhondo che bwato chera kuchiukulira ku nundo ya chishee mwa kachi-kachi kemeshi, na chasinda aola. Si echimbi chera nyuma cheke, chera kuberekanga bushi nemulaba.

42. Ebasula bera kwire baata mianyisa ya kwita ebandju be buroko, kungesha kuba ola wahaa mwa kukaraba.

43. Si emukulu-kulu we basula yeke abaa ahonda alamye Paulo. Era kwanga abu basula mbu bataira bacha. Bushi noku, era kuteta mbu ba beshe kukaraba, bubabaa baberebere kuchiuma tanga kwa meshi bahabukire kwa mushirirya.

44. Nabangashiba batolaa embao, nesi kwa byande-ande bye bwato bahabuke nabi. Ku tuboshi twahabukiraa kwa mushirirya bacha nebolo.

서구어싸 어봐도. 짜시따, 버라 구리나 어꽈야 어라 무호또 서 봐도 콰 구호따 어쭈시 찌붜거 궈찌 찌하부기로.

41. 시 모루, 어찌루비 쩌라 무호또 쩌 봐도 쩌라 구찌우구리라 구 누또 야 찌써어 콰 가찌-가찌 거머씨, 나 짜시따 아오콰. 시 어찌삐 쩌라 뉴마 쩌거, 쩌라 구버러가꺄 부씨 너무콰바.

42. 어바수콰 버라 귀러 바아다 미아네사 야 귀다 어바뚜 버 부로고, 구써싸 구바 오콰 와하아 콰 구가라바.

43. 시 어무구루-구루 워 바수콰 여거 아바아 아호따 아콰며 파우로. 어라 과꺄 아부 바수콰 뿌 바다이라 바짜. 부씨 노구, 어라 구더다 뿌 바 버써 구가라바, 부바바아 바버러버러 구찌우마 다꺄 과 머씨 바하부기러 과 무씨리랴.

44. 나바꺄씨바 바도콰아 어빠오, 너시 과 뱌떠-아떠 벼 봐도 바하부거 나비. 구 두보씨 돠하부기라아 과 무씨리랴 바짜 너보로.

41. But the ship struck a sandbar and ran aground. The bow stuck fast and would not move, and the stern was broken to pieces by the pounding of the surf.

42. The soldiers planned to kill the prisoners to prevent any of them from swimming away and escaping.

43. But the centurion wanted to spare Paul's life and kept them from carrying out their plan. He ordered those who could swim to jump overboard first and get to land.

44. The rest were to get there on planks or on pieces of the ship. In this way everyone reached land in safety.

E Mikolo ye Ndjumwa Chikono 28

어 미고로 여 뚜콰 찌고노 28 Acts Chapter 28[NIV]

E njoka yomakilyira Paulo kwa mino

어 쪼— 요마기쪠띱 파우론 과 미노

1. Abere tchwera tchwafufumukaa elufu, tchwera tchwera kumenyerera kwa kasi echisimba cha tchwabaa tchwulyiko, bende belyika achi mbu Melita.

1. 아버러 쮜라 쫘푸푸무가아 어루푸, 쮜라 쮜라 구머녀러라 과 가시 어찌시빠 짜 쫘바아 쫉쪠고, 버떠 버쪠가 아찌 뿌 머쁘다.

1. Once safely on shore, we found out that the island was called Malta.

2. Besha kwechi chisimba batchwukoreraa mabuya manene. Bera kutchwukoresesa mulyiro na batchwubura mbu tchwubahaa tchwukalukale bushi emvula yabaa yera yatowa, nembeo nai yabaa yahuunda.

2. 버싸 궈찌 찌시빠 바쫉고러라아 마부야 마너너. 버라 구쫉고러서사 무쪠로 나 바쫉부라 뿌 쫘바하아 쫉가루가러 부씨 어뿌롸 야바아 여라 야도와, 너뻐오 나이 야바아 야후우따.

2. The islanders showed us unusual kindness. They built a fire and welcomed us all because it was raining and cold.

3. Paulo era kutola-tola mihalyi yeeke. Abere era abikaaikwa chiko, unao- unao- mwera kupamikira njoka bushi nechuka. Ei njoka kwomakilyira kwa mino yai.

3. 파우론 어라 구도롸-도롸 미하쪠 여어거. 아버러 어라 아비가아이과 찌고, 우나오- 우나오, 뭐라 구파미기라 쪼가 부씨 너쭈가. 어이 쪼가 고마기쪠라 과 미노 야이.

3. Paul gathered a pile of brushwood and, as he put it on the fire, a viper, driven out by the heat, fastened itself on his hand.

4. Besha melita balolyire kwei njoka yomakilyire kwa mino ya Paulo, bera kutangilyisa baburana mbu: kubinalyi, ono mulume analyi mwichi wa bandju. Bushi, chiro angaba mbu afufumikire elufu kwa nyanja, ebuchinjibusi bwa Ongo bwa bwe kunalyi, butanamwerere kubao.

4. 버싸 머쁘다 바롤쪠러 궈이 쪼가 요마기쪠러 과 미노 야 파우론, 버라 구다쀄쪠사 바부라나 뿌: 구비나례, 오노 무루머 아나례 뮈찌 와 바뚜. 부씨, 찌로 아까바 뿌 아푸푸미기러 어루푸 과 냐쨔, 어부찌찌부시 봐 오꼬 봐 붜 구나쪠, 부다나뭐러러 구바오.

4. When the islanders saw the snake hanging from his hand, they said to each other, "This man must be a murderer; for though he escaped from the sea, Justice has not allowed him to live."

5. Si Paulo era kukunguchira era njoka mwa mulyiro busira

5. 시 파우론 어라 구구꾸찌라 어라 쪼가 뫄 무쪠로 부시라

5. But Paul shook the snake off into the fire and

kufa kandju.

구파 가누.

suffered no ill effects.

6. Ebandju bera kulyinjira balole akaba Paulo angaimba e mubilyi, nesi angaba angakumbaala unao-unao anafe. Si abere bamala bihangi binene balyinjirira, bera kulola kwa kutalyi cha afire. Bera kwire babindjula e myanyisa yabo nekutangilyisa bateta mbu Paulo alyi muuma mwa baongo.

6. 어바누 버라 구레찌라 바르뤄 아가바 파우로 아까이빠 어 무비뤠, 너시 아까바 아까구빠아롸 우나오-우나오 아나퍼. 시 아버러 바마롸 비하끼 비너너 바뤠찌리라, 버라 구르롸 과 구다뤠 짜 아피러. 버라 귀러 바비누롸 어 먀네사 야보 너구다끼뤠사 바더다 뿌 파우로 아뤠 무우마 롸 바오꼬.

6. The people expected him to swell up or suddenly fall dead, but after waiting a long time and seeing nothing unusual happen to him, they changed their minds and said he was a god.

7. Ofu nala tchwabaa tchwulyi, abaa alyi mahwa me mukulu-kulu w'e chi chisimba mbu i Pupuliyo. Oyu pupuliyo, era kutchwuhukasa kubuya mwa mwai, tchwera kumalamu suku ehatchwu.

7. 오푸 나롸 쫘바아 쭈뤠, 아바아 아뤠 마화 머 무구루-구루 워 찌 찌시빠 뿌 이 푸푸뤼요. 오유 푸푸뤼요, 어라 구쭈후가사 구부야 롸 마이, 쭤라 구마롸무 수구 어하쭉.

7. There was an estate nearby that belonged to Publius, the chief official of the island. He welcomed us to his home and for three days entertained us hospitably.

8. Mwechi chihangi, eshe wa pupuliyo abaa aonjire kwa njingo, bushi eshushira yabaa yamusimbire, kanji abaa anya na mikira. Paulo era kuya kumutangula, era kumwemera amubikire kwe mino, na amulamya.

8. 뭐찌 찌하끼, 어써 와 푸푸뤼요 아바아 아오찌러 과 찌꼬, 부씨 어쑤씨라 야바아 야무시뻐러, 가찌 아바아 아냐 나 미기라. 파우로 어라 구야 구무다꿀롸, 어라 구뭐머라 아무비기러 궈 미노, 나 아무롸먀.

8. His father was sick in bed, suffering from fever and dysentery. Paul went in to see him and, after prayer, placed his hands on him and healed him.

9. Bushi noku, ebanji balwala boshi bababaa balyi kwechi chisimba, bera kunde baikiranga Paulo, nabo bera kunde banalama.

9. 부씨 노구, 어바찌 바롸롸 보씨 바바바아 바뤠 궈찌 찌시빠, 버라 구너 바이기라꺼 파우로, 나보 버라 구너 바나롸마.

9. When this had happened, the rest of the sick on the island came and were cured.

10. Ebandju bera kunde batchwutchwunda busese. Na

10. 어바누 버라 구너 바쭈쭈따 부서서. 나 마꼬

10. They honored us in many ways and when we

mango tchwabaa tchwera tchwahonda kuenda mwa bwato, bera kutchweresa byoshi bya tchwabaa tchwulaireko mwa lubalamo lwetchwu.

Paulo aika eRoma

11. Abere twamala myesi ehatu kwa chisimba che malita, twera kubalama mu bwato buuma bwa bwemangaa tanga kwechi chisimba, kwakulinjira esuku se mbeo sirenge. Obu bwato, bwabaa bomwa musi we alenduriya. Babaa baChikonoireko bihuhanyi bya maaha na baongo bauma.

12. Abere twaika mwa musi we sirakuse, twera kumalamu suku ehatu.

13. Mwa kutenga mwoyu musi, twera kurenga kwa musike-musike wenyanja, na twaika mwa musi we Rekiyo. Abere mwei mishangya, ekausi kakabaa katengera kwa lunda lwera bufuli kera kutangirisa karenga. Twera kwire twaira luendo lwa suku ebiri kwakuika mwa musi we puteyoli.

14. Twaikire mwoyo musi, twera kubwana mubanyaketu bemeresi bauma. Abu

좌바아 쭤라 좌호따 구어빠 뫄 봐도, 버라 구쭤러사 뵤씨 뱌 좌바아 쭈롸이러고 뫄 루바롸모 뤄쭈.

파우롣 아이가 어로마

11. 아버러 돠마롸 며시 어하두 과 찌시빠 쩌 마뤼다, 뚸라 구바롸마 무 봐도 부우마 봐 붜마꺄아 다꺄 궈찌 찌시빠, 과구뀌띠라 어수구 서 뻐오 시러꺼. 오부 봐도, 봐바아 보뫄 무시 워 아쩌뿌리야. 바바아 바찌고노이러고 비후하니 뱌 마아하 나 바오꼬 바우마.

12. 아버러 돠이가 뫄 무시 워 시라구서, 뚸라 구마롸무 수구 어하두.

13. 뫄 구더꺄 모유 무시, 뚸라 구러꺄 과 무시거-무시거 워냐쨔, 나 돠이가 뫄 무시 워 러기요. 아버러 뭐이 미쌰꺅, 어가우시 가가바아 가더꺄라 과 루따 뤄라 부푸뀌 거라 구다뀌리사 가러꺄. 뚸라 귀러 돠이라 루어또 콰 수구 어비리 과구이가 뫄 무시 워 푸더요뀌.

14. 돠이기러 모요 무시, 뚸라 구봐나 무바냐거두 버머러시 바우마. 아부 버머러시, 버라

were ready to sail, they furnished us with the supplies we needed.

11. After three months we put out to sea in a ship that had wintered in the island. It was an Alexandrian ship with the figurehead of the twin gods Castor and Pollux.

12. We put in at Syracuse and stayed there three days.

13. From there we set sail and arrived at Rhegium. The next day the south wind came up, and on the following day we reached Puteoli.

14. There we found some brothers who invited us to spend a week with them.

bemeresi, bera kutwema mbu tuma einga liuma nabo tanga. Chasinda, wmoku kutaira-taira, twera kunalinda twaika mwa musi we Roma.

15. Banyaketu bemeresi be Roma, mango bomvaa emwasi kwa twabahire, bauma bera kua kutulinjira mwesoko lye Apiyo, ne banji ala Tiretaberine. Paulo abahunjire kwemeho, era kutonga Ongo, chasinda era kuhuba kubona emisi.

16. Abere twaika eRoma, ebakulu-kulu bera kwemerera mbu Paulo aberaa mu yai nyumba, na musula muuma wa kumulanga abgesha kwongoloka.

Paulo ahubanganya echinwa cha Ongo eRoma

17. Abere kwarenga suku ehatchwu, Paulo era kwamaala e bashamuka be bayuda ba babaa batchwula eRoma. Mango babaa bera babuanana, era kutangilyisa ababura mbu: ebanyaketchwu, nyono naminwaa eyerusalemu, nera kwanyibwa mwa mino s'e baroma, noku ndailyiraa elubaa lwetchwu chiro na chibi chisibya, nesi kuuwa mwa myanya ya

구뚸마 뿌 두마 어이ⱄ 뾔우마 나보 다ⱄ. 짜시따, 우모구 구다이라-다이라, 뙤라 구나뾔따 다이가 뫄 무시 워 로마.

15. 바냐거두 버머러시 버 로마, 마꼬 보빠아 어마시 과 돠바히러, 바우마 버라 구아 구두뾔씨라 뭐소고 뗘 아피요, 너 바찌 아롸 디러다버리너. 파우뽀 아바후찌러 궈머호, 어라 구도ⱄ 오ꛝ, 짜시따 어라 구후바 구보나 어미시.

16. 아버러 돠이가 어로마, 어바구루-구루 버라 궈머러라 뿌 파우뽀 아버라아 무 야이 뉴빠, 나 무수퐈 무우마 와 구무롸ⱄ 아부거싸 괻ꛝ뽀가.

파우뽀 아후바ⱄ냿 어찌놔 짜 오ꛝ 어로마

17. 아버러 과러ⱄ 수구 어하쭈, 파우뽀 어라 과마아롸 어 바싸무가 버 바유다 바 바바아 바쭈롸 어로마. 마꼬 바바아 버라 바부아나나, 어라 구다ⱄ뻬싸 아바부라 뿌: 어바냐거쭉, 뇨노 나미놔아 어여루사뻐무, 너라 과녜봐 뫄 미노 서 바로마, 노구 따이뻬라라 어루바아 뭭쭉 찌로 나 찌비 찌시뱌, 너시 구우와 뫄 먀냐 야 바호구룩 버쭉.

And so we came to Rome.

15. The brothers there had heard that we were coming, and they traveled as far as the Forum of Appius and the Three Taverns to meet us. At the sight of these men Paul thanked God and was encouraged.

16. When we got to Rome, Paul was allowed to live by himself, with a soldier to guard him.

17. Three days later he called together the leaders of the Jews. When they had assembled, Paul said to them: "My brothers, although I have done nothing against our people or against the customs of our ancestors, I was arrested in Jerusalem and handed over

bahokulu betchwu.

18. Abu baroma, era nyuma sekunyitonganya, bera kuhonda kunyiboola, bushi batanyitolaa ku mwasi mubi ola ungatchwumire n'echibwa.

19. Si mango e bayuda bananaa mbu ndaboolwa, byera kwire byanyema nyiye kutonganyira eni roma, era muhondo sa mwami. Na mwebi boshi ndete chiro namyanyisa yakusitaka elubaa lwetchwu.

20. Echera chi chatchwumire nabamala nyihambale nenyu. Mumenyerera kwa nyiminyirwe mano mareure bushi ne munyiiro ola baisairaeli batchwusa.

21. Abu bashamuka bera kumwakula mbu: tchwubano, kutalyi maruba masibya matchwabonaa ma matengera eyerusalemu ma mahambere era luulu sao. Kanji kutalyi chiro namunyaketchwu muyuda ola waikaa enera kua kutchwubalyira mwasi, nesi kuteta bulyio era luulu sao.

22. Si tchwungasimire tchwuchumvire emyanyisa yao, bushi tchwishi kwa mwa bisiki byoshi ebandju benjire banana lyine tini lyao

18. 아부 바로마, 어라 뉴마 서구니도와냐, 버라 구호따 구네보오롸, 부씨 바다니도롸아 구 마시 무비 오롸 우꺄쭈미러 너찌봐.

19. 시 마꼬 어 바유다 바나나아 뿌 따보오롹, 벼라 귀러 뱌녀마 네여 구도꺄네라 어니 로마, 어라 무호또 사 꽈미. 나 뭐비 보씨 떠더 찌로 나먀네사 야구시다가 어루바아 뭐쭈.

20. 어쩌라 찌 짜쭈미러 나바마롸 네하빠뤄 너뉴. 무머녀러라 과 네미네뤄 마노 마러우러 부씨 너 무네이로 오롸 바이사이라어뤼 바쭈사.

21. 아부 바싸무가 버라 구꽈구롸 뿌: 쭈바노, 구다레 마루바 마시뱌 마쫘보나아 마 마더꺼라 어여루사꺼무 마 마하뻐러 어라 루우루루 사오. 가씨 구다레 찌로 나무냐거쭈 무유다 오롸 와이가아 어너라 구아 구쭈바뻬라 마시, 너시 구더다 부레오 어라 루우루루 사오.

22. 시 쭈꺄시미러 쭈쭈뻐러 어먀네사 야오, 부씨 쭤씨 과 꽈 비시기 뵤씨 어바쭈 버찌러 바나나 레너 디니 롺오 우구레기러.

18. They examined me and wanted to release me, because I was not guilty of any crime deserving death.

19. But when the Jews objected, I was compelled to appeal to Caesar--not that I had any charge to bring against my own people.

20. For this reason I have asked to see you and talk with you. It is because of the hope of Israel that I am bound with this chain."

21. They replied, "We have not received any letters from Judea concerning you, and none of the brothers who have come from there has reported or said anything bad about you.

22. But we want to hear what your views are, for we know that people everywhere are talking against this sect."

ukulyikire.

23. Chasinda, bera kulana elusuku kwa bangahuba kubuanana na Paulo mwei nyumba era abaa alyimo. Abere olu lusuku Iwaika, bandju banene bera kuika ala Paulo abaa abikire ehumbi. Era kumala mureerere wamutenga abahubanganyisa era luulu s'e Bwami bwa Ongo, nakubakangilyisa e myasi era barebi, busi abaa ahonda bemereri Yesu.

24. Ei myasi Paulo atetaa, bauma mubo bera kuyemerera, si ebanji beke bera kuchinanyirai.

25. Abere abu bayuda bera bahondabana busira kumvikana, Paulo era kuhuba kubabura ono unji mwasi:emuchima mubuya-buya abaa anasinganyire mango endee abura bahokulu benyu kurengera murebi Isaya mbu:

26. Uyaa era abu bandju balyi ababura kwa: kumva ku mukendi mwanomva, si mutakendi mwamenyerera. Kutchwumbikisa, kumukendi mwa tchwumbikisa, si mutakendi mwalola.

23. 짜시따, 버라 구꽈나 어루수구 과 바빠후바 구부아나나 나 파우뢰 뭐이 뉴빠 어라 아바아 아뤠모. 아버러 오루 루수구 롸이가, 바쭈 바너너 버라 구이가 아꽈 파우뢰 아바아 아비기러 어후삐. 어라 구마꽈 무러어러러 와무더빠 아바후바빠네사 어라 루우루 서 봐미 봐 오으, 나구바가삐뤠사 어 먀시 어라 바러비, 부시 아바아 아호따 버머러리 여수.

24. 어이 먀시 파우뢰 아더다아, 바우마 무보 버라 구여머러라, 시 어바씨 버거 버라 구찌나네라이.

25. 아버러 아부 바유다 버라 바호따바나 부시라 구뻬가나, 파우뢰 어라 구후바 구바부라 오노 우씨 먀시:어무찌마 무부야-부야 아바아 아나시빠네러 마꼬 어너어 아부라 바호구루 버뉴 구러빠라 무러비 이사야 뿌:

26. 우야아 어라 아부 바쭈 바뤠 아바부라 과: 구빠 구 무거띠 먀노빠, 시 무다거띠 먀머녀러라. 구쭈뻬기사, 구무거띠 먀 쭈뻬기사, 시 무다거띠 먀뢰꽈.

23. They arranged to meet Paul on a certain day, and came in even larger numbers to the place where he was staying. From morning till evening he explained and declared to them the kingdom of God and tried to convince them about Jesus from the Law of Moses

24. Some were convinced by what he said, but others would not believe.

25. They disagreed among themselves and began to leave after Paul had made this final statement: "The Holy Spirit spoke the truth to your forefathers when he said through Isaiah the prophet:

26. " 'Go to this people and say, "You will be ever hearing but never understanding; you will be ever seeing but never perceiving." '

27. Bushi bano bandju bailyire e michima yabo kuba isibu, belyire basiba e machi mabo, banasiba n'emeho mabo, akaba bataira bacha, emeho mabo mangenjire malola, n'e machi mabo mangenjire momva, n'e michima yabo ingenjire yabokola, banalyinde banyialukira, nanyi nyibalamye.

28. Kanji Paulo era kubabura mbu: rero, mwiree mwamenyerera kwa Ongo atchwumire ono mwasi w'e bununusi kwa bandju besinji mbaa. Abu bandju beke, banganamvao!

29. Abere Paulo era mala kuteta ei myasi, abu bayuda bera kuhandabana baenda baenzanya bwaka bunene.

30. Paulo era kumala myaka ebilyi mwera nyumba abaa atchwulamo yeine. Era kunde ahuukasisa mw'ebandju boshi ba bendee baika kumutangula.

31. Era kunde abahubanganyisa era luulu s'e Bwami bwa Ongo, nera luulu sa enawetchwu Yesu Kirisitobusira buba na busira changaiko.

27. 부씨 바노 바쭈 바이쩨러 어 미찌마 야보 구바 이시부, 버쩨러 바시바 어 마찌 마보, 바나시바 너머호 마보, 아가바 바다이라 바짜, 어머호 마보 마어찌러 마르롸, 너 마찌 마보 마어찌러 모빠, 너 미찌마 야보 이어찌러 야보고롸, 바나쩨떠 바네아루기라, 나니 네바롸며.

28. 가찌 파우르로 어라 구바부라 뿌: 러로, 뮈러어 뫄머녀러라 과 오꼬 아쭈미러 오노 뫄시 워 부누누시 과 바쭈 버시찌 빠아. 아부 바쭈 버거, 바빠나빠오!

29. 아버러 파우르로 어라 마롸 구더다 어이 먀시, 아부 바유다 버라 구하따바나 바어따 바어싸냐 봐가 부너너.

30. 파우르로 어라 구마롸 먀가 어비쩨 뭐라 뉴빠 아바아 아쭈롸모 여이너. 어라 구떠 아후우가시사 뭐바쭈 보씨 바 버떠어 바이가 구무다우롸.

31. 어라 구떠 아바후바바니너사 어라 루우루 서 봐미 봐 오꼬, 너라 루우루 사 어나워쭈 여수 기리시도부시라 부바 나 부시라 짜빠이고.

27. For this people's heart has become calloused; they hardly hear with their ears, and they have closed their eyes. Otherwise they might see with their eyes, hear with their ears, understand with their hearts and turn, and I would heal them.'

28. "Therefore I want you to know that God's salvation has been sent to the Gentiles, and they will listen!"

29. None

30. For two whole years Paul stayed there in his own rented house and welcomed all who came to see him.

31. Boldly and without hindrance he preached the kingdom of God and taught about the Lord Jesus Christ.

Ba Roma

바 로마

Rome

EMARUBA MA PAULO KWA BAROMA

어마루바 마 파우로 과 바로마

Ba Roma Chikono 1

Paulo alamusa e bemeresi b'e Roma

1 Nyono paulo, nyilyi muanda wa Yesu kirisito. Ongo anyamaere kuba ndjumwa, kanji anyilondwere chasiya nyinde nahubanganyisa ebandju emwasi mubuya-buya.

2 oyunmwasi mubuya-buya, Ongo abaa alaanyoseo mira kurengera e barebi bai mwa maanjiko mabuya-buya.

3 oyu mwasi ahambere era luulu s'e mwana wai ; enawetchwu Yesu kirisito. Yesu kirisito abutchwaa kwa njira y'e mubilyi, mwa chirongo cha mwami Daudi.

4 si kwa njira y'e muchima mubuya-buya, Ongo amuilyire kuba mwana wai na buashi bunene. Airaa bacha, mango amwomolaa mwa bafu.

5 kurengera Yesu kirisito, Ongo anyeresise engahanyi s'e kuba ndjumwa, chasiya nyinde nalosa ebandju boshi enjira y'e kumwemerera n'e yekunde baira kwa atechire. Mwa bacha, esina lyai lingende lyaya ngulu.

6 nenyu mulyi mwabu

바 로마 찌고노 1

파우쁜 아롸물쀈 어 버머러시 버 로마

1 뇨노 파우쁜, 네레 무아따 와 여수 기리시도. 오꼬 아냐마어러 구바 뚜먀, 가찌 아니롼뚜워러 짜시야 네너 나후바까네사 어바쭈 어먀시 무부야-부야.

2 오유누먀시 무부야-부야, 오꼬 아바아 아롸아뇨서오 미라 구러꺼라 어 바러비 바이 먀 마아찌고 마부야-부야.

3 오유 먀시 아하꺼러 어라 쁜우쁜 서 먀나 와이 ; 어나워쭈 여수 기리시도. 여수 기리시도 아부좌아 과 찌라 여 무비쩨, 먀 찌로꼬 짜 먀미 다우디.

4 시 과 찌라 여 무찌마 무부야-부야, 오꼬 아무이쩨러 구바 먀나 와이 나 부아씨 부너너. 아이라아 바쨔, 마꼬 아모모롸아 먀 바푸.

5 구러꺼라 여수 기리시도, 오꼬 아녀러시서 어꺄하네 서 구바 뚜먀, 짜시야 네너 나롼사 어바쭈 보씨 어찌라 여 구뭐머러라 너 여구떠 바이라 과 아더찌러. 먀 바쨔, 어시나 쨔이 찌꺼너 쨔야 우쁜.

6 너뉴 무쩨 먀부 바쭈 ; 바

Rome Chapter 1[NIV]

1. Paul, a servant of Christ Jesus, called to be an apostle and set apart for the gospel of God--

2. the gospel he promised beforehand through his prophets in the Holy Scriptures

3. regarding his Son, who as to his human nature was a descendant of David,

4. and who through the Spirit of holiness was declared with power to be the Son of God by his resurrection from the dead: Jesus Christ our Lord.

5. Through him and for his name's sake, we received grace and apostleship to call people from among all the Gentiles to the obedience that comes from faith.

6. And you also are among

bandju ; ba Yesu kirisito amaere.

여수 기리시도 아마어러.

those who are called to belong to Jesus Christ.

7 nabaanjikira muboshi mu mutchwula mwa musi w'e Roma, mu Ongo atchwula asimire, kanji abamaere chasiya mube bandju bai babuya-buya. Ongo Tata na enawetchwu Yesu kirisito, bendaa babaahanyira na kuberesa eboolo.

7 나바아찌기라 무보씨 무 무쭈똬 똬 무시 워 로마, 무 오꼬 아쭈똬 아시미러, 가찌 아바마어러 짜시야 무버 바뚜 바이 바부야-부야. 오꼬 다다 나 어나워쭈 여수 기리시도, 버따아 바바아하니러라 나 구버러사 어보오론.

7. To all in Rome who are loved by God and called to be saints: Grace and peace to you from God our Father and from the Lord Jesus Christ.

Paulo ahonda kuya kutangula ebemeresi b'e Roma

파우론 아호따 구야 구다위똬 어버머러시 버 로마

8 era muhondo sa byoshi, nateta mbu akoko era mwa Ongo wanyi kurengera Yesu kirisito bushi nenyu muboshi. Natechire bacha, bushi emyasi y'e bwemeresi bwenyu yaire ngulu mwa butala boshi.

8 어라 무호또 사 뵤씨, 나더다 뿌 아고고 어라 똬 오꼬 와네 구러떠라 여수 기리시도 부씨 너뉴 무보씨. 나더찌러 바짜, 부씨 어먀시 여 붜머러시 붜뉴 야이러 꾸루 똬 부다똬 보씨.

8. First, I thank my God through Jesus Christ for all of you, because your faith is being reported all over the world.

9 mango nende naba nahubanganya emwasi mubuya-buya w'e mwana wa Ongo, nende naba namukorera nomuchima wanyi woshi. Na Ongo yeine aneshi kwa nateta myasi ya kanangana. Esuku soshi, kubakengera ku nende nabakengera

9 마꼬 너더 나바 나후바아냐 어똬시 무부야-부야 워 똬나 와 오꼬, 너더 나바 나무고러라 노무찌마 와네 워씨. 나 오꼬 여이너 아너씨 과 나더다 먀시 야 가나아나. 어수구 소씨, 구바거떠라 구 너떠 나바거떠라

9. God, whom I serve with my whole heart in preaching the gospel of his Son, is my witness how constantly I remember you

10 mwa memo manyi. Kanji nenjire namwema akasima, anyiboorera enjira yekuya

10 똬 머모 마네. 가찌 너찌러 나뭐마 아가시마, 아네보오러라 어찌라 여구야

10. in my prayers at all times; and I pray that now at last by God's will the way

kubatangula.

구바다우꽈.

may be opened for me to come to you.

11 kubinalyi, nahonda busese nyibaloleko, nyibabalyikise kwa myasi era yatenga era mw'e mchima mubuya-buya, chasiya musuke.

11 구비나쩨, 나호따 부서서 네바로꺼고, 네바바쩨기서 과 먀시 어라 야더꽈 어라 뭐 무찌마 무부야-부야, 짜시야 무수거.

11. I long to see you so that I may impart to you some spiritual gift to make you strong--

12 kulyi kuteta kwa nahonda kusesanye emichima kurengera ebwemeresi bwetchwu.

12 구쩨 구더다 과 나호따 구서사녀 어미찌마 구러꺼라 어뭐머러시 붜쭈.

12. that is, that you and I may be mutually encouraged by each other's faith.

13 banyaketchwu, nahonda mumenyere kwa chira mango, nenjire nalalyira kuya kubangula. Nahonda nyilole akaba emulyimo wanyi nakola mwa kachi-kachi kenyu era ete bifuma ngokwa ete bi mwa kachi-kachi ka ba batchwula bayuda. Si kuikira lwarero, nyichete byangiko.

13 바냐거쭈, 나호따 무머녀러 과 찌라 마꼬, 너찌러 나꽈쩨라 구야 구바우꽈. 나호따 네로꺼 아가바 어무쩨모 와네 나고꽈 꽈 가찌-가찌 거뉴 어라 어더 비푸마 꼬과 어더 비 꽈 가찌-가찌 가 바 바쭈꽈 바유다. 시 구이기라 꽈러로, 네쩌더 뱌꼬.

13. I do not want you to be unaware, brothers, that I planned many times to come to you (but have been prevented from doing so until now) in order that I might have a harvest among you, just as I have had among the other Gentiles.

14 binyemire nyinde naya kukorera ebandju boshi: ebasamba na ba bata basamba, ba basomire na ba batasomire.

14 비녀미러 네떠 나야 구고러라 어반쭈 보씨: 어바사빠 나 바 바다 바사빠, 바 바소미러 나 바 바다소미러.

14. I am obligated both to Greeks and non-Greeks, both to the wise and the foolish.

15 echera chi chitchwumire nahonda busese nyiye kubahubanyisa nenyu emwasi mubuya-buya, mu mutchwula eRoma.

15 어쩌라 찌 찌쭈미러 나호따 부서서 네여 구바후바네사 너뉴 어꽈시 무부야-부야, 무 무쭈꽈 어로마.

15. That is why I am so eager to preach the gospel also to you who are at Rome.

Ebuashi bw'e mwasi mubuya-buya

어부아씨 붜 꽈시 무부야-부야

16 nyono ndenjire nafa honyi sa kuhubanganya emwasi mubuya-buya. Bushi oyu mwasi, bubuashi Ongo ende akorera kwa kununula chira mundju woshi ola wemerere: e bayuda tanga, chasinda ba batchwula bayuda.

17 kubinalyi, emwasi mubuya-buya ewende walosa kute Ongo ende aira ebandju kuba ba batchwungenene era muhondo sai. Oku kutchwunganana kwende kwalyikana kurengera ebwemeresi bweine oshao. Ebyera bikulyikene nokwa bitchwula bianjikirwe mwa maanjiko mabuya-buya mbu: Ola utchwungenene era muhondo sanyi, emibere yai ingende yamangira kwa bwemeresi.

Ongo ende achinjibusa ebakosi b'e bibi

18 kutengera kwa nguba, Ongo ende alosa kwa asibukirire ebandju boshi ba bende baira ebibi, n'emyasi era itatchwungenene. Bushi ei myasi yabo yende yangika ebandju bangamenya emyasi ye kanangana.

---

16 뇨노 떠찌러 나파 호네 사 구후바빠냐 어뫄시 무부야-부야. 부씨 오유 뫄시, 부부아씨 오꼬 어떠 아고러라 과 구누누롸 찌라 무뚜 옹씨 오롸 워머러러: 어 바유다 다빠, 짜시따 바 바쭈롸 바유다.

17 구비나레, 어뫄시 무부야-부야 어워떠 와로사 구더 오꼬 어떠 아이라 어바뚜 구바 바 바쭈떠너너 어라 무호또 사이. 오구 구쭈빠나나 궈떠 과레가나 구러떠라 어붜머러시 붜이너 오싸오. 어벼라 비구쩨거너 노과 비쭈롸 비아찌기뤄 뫄 마아찌고 마부야-부야 뿌: 오롸 우쭈떠너너 어라 무호또 사니, 어미버러 야이 이떠너 야마삐라 과 붜머러시.

오꼬 어떠 아찌삐뷉뻽 어바고시 버 비비

18 구더떠라 과 응바, 오꼬 어떠 아로사 과 아시부기리러 어바뚜 보씨 바 버떠 바이라 어비비, 너먀시 어라 이다쭈떠너너. 부씨 어이 먀시 야보 여떠 야삐가 어바뚜 바빠머냐 어먀시 여 가나빠나.

---

16. I am not ashamed of the gospel, because it is the power of God for the salvation of everyone who believes: first for the Jew, then for the Gentile.

17. For in the gospel a righteousness from God is revealed, a righteousness that is by faith from first to last, just as it is written: "The righteous will live by faith."

18. The wrath of God is being revealed from heaven against all the godlessness and wickedness of men who suppress the truth by their wickedness,

19 kubinalyi, emyasi era bandju bangamenya era luulu sa Ongo, itchwula ichilosise kubuya-buya era muhondo sabu, bushi Ongo yeine abalosise yi changanama.

20 kutengera ala Ongo abumbiraa ebutala, emyanya yai era italorekanako, kukuteta mbu: ebuashi bwai bwesuku n'e mango, n'ekuba Ongo kwai, byende byalorekana ko kurengera bya abumbaa. Bushi noku, abu bandju batete njira ya kuchokolola kwa bya bairaa.

21 chiro angaba mbu batchwula beshi Ongo, si batamutonga nesi kumubura mbu akoko ngokwa binemire. Si emianyisa yabo yelyire yaba kwa myasi ye buha-buha, n'e michima yabo ye buuta yelyire yanachibera mwa musimya.

22 bende bachiremba mbu balyi bandju ba beshi myasi, si bahubire basire.

23 kanji kwakunde bera Ongo iutchwulao esuku ne mango, bera kunde bera ebihuhanyi bya bikunganyisibwe kwe hulu ly'emundju w'ekufa, nesi lyemilonge, nesi lye nyama se

19 구비나례, 어먀시 어라 바쭈 바빠머냐 어라 루우루 사 오꼬, 이쭈라 이찌로시서 구부야-부야 어라 무호또 사부 부씨 오꼬 여이너 아바로시서 에 짜빠나마.

20 구더뻐라 아라 오꼬 아부삐라아 어부다라, 어먀냐 야이 어라 이다로러가나고, 구구더다 뿌: 어부아씨 봐이 뭐수구 너 마꼬, 너구바 오꼬 과이, 벼뻐 뱌로러가나 고 구러뻐라 뱌 아부빠아. 부씨 노구, 아부 바쭈 바더더 찌라 야 구쪼고로뽜 과 뱌 바이라아.

21 찌로 아빠바 뿌 바쭈뽜 버씨 오꼬, 시 바다무도빠 너시 구무부라 뿌 아고고 꼬고 비너미러. 시 어미아네사 야보 여례러 야바 과 먀시 여 부하- 부하, 너 미찌마 야보 여 부우다 여례러 야나찌버라 마 무시먀.

22 버떠 바찌러빠 뿌 바례 바쭈 바 버씨 먀시, 시 바후비러 바시러.

23 가찌 과구떠 버라 오꼬 이우쭈뽜오 어수구 너 마꼬, 버라 구떠 버라 어비후하네 뱌 비구빠네시뭐 궈 후루 뛰어무뿌 워구파, 너시 려미로뻐, 너시 려 냐마 서 비러뻐 비너, 너시 려냐마 사

19. since what may be known about God is plain to them, because God has made it plain to them.

20. For since the creation of the world God's invisible qualities--his eternal power and divine nature--have been clearly seen, being understood from what has been made, so that men are without excuse.

21. For although they knew God, they neither glorified him as God nor gave thanks to him, but their thinking became futile and their foolish hearts were darkened.

22. Although they claimed to be wise, they became fools

23. and exchanged the glory of the immortal God for images made to look like mortal man and birds and animals and reptiles.

birenge bine, nesi lyenyama sa sende saendekera kwa bula.

24 bushi noku, Ongo abarekeraa bachake esinga beine mwakunde bakulyikira ebuhuma-huma bw'e michima yabo, kuikira echihangi beine kwa beine baira myasi ya honyi.

25 emyasi y'e kanangana era itechire era luulu sa Ongo, bende baibindjula kuba ya bisha. Ebindju bya byabumbwaa bi bende bera wa kwera chibumbi yeine, iwemire kutongibwa esuku n'e mango. Bibe bacha!

26 bushi noku Ongo abarekeraa bende bakulyikira ebuhuma-huma bwabo bwekubeta ehonyi. Bakasi babo bendee bareka kuonjira n'e balume babo, na baya kubanda ekilyi beine kwa beine. Ekuira bacha, kutakulyikene nokwa byemire kuba.

27 ne balume nabo kunoku. Banende bareka kuonjira na bakasi babo, na kunde baaata mianyisa isibu yakuhonda kubanda ekilyi beine kwa beine. Nei, iri myasi ya honyi. Mwakuira bacha, banere

---

서떠 사어떠거라 과 부퐈.

24 부씨 노구, 오꼬 아바러거라아 바짜거 어시빠 버이너 뫄구떠 바구꿰기라 어부후마-후마 붜 미찌마 야보, 구이기라 어찌하삐 버이너 과 버이너 바이라 먀시 야 호네.

25 어먀시 여 가나빠나 어라 이더찌러 어라 뤂우뤂 사 오꼬, 버떠 바이비뿌퐈 구바 야 비싸. 어비뿌 뱌 뱌부빠아 비 버떠 버라 와 궈라 찌부삐 여이너, 이워미러 구도삐봐 어수구 너 마꼬. 비버 바짜!

26 부씨 노구 오꼬 아바러거라아 버떠 바구꿰기라 어부후마-후마 봐보 어호네. 바가시 바보 버떠어 바러가 구오찌라 너 바루머 바보, 나 바야 구바따 어기꿰 버이너 과 버이너. 어구이라 바짜, 구다구꿰거너 노과 벼미러 구바.

27 너 바루머 나보 구노구. 바너떠 바러가 구오찌라 나 바가시 바보, 나 구떠 바아아다 미아네사 이시부 야구호따 구바따 어기꿰 버이너 과 버이너. 너이, 이리 먀시 야 호네. 뫄구이라 바짜,

---

24. Therefore God gave them over in the sinful desires of their hearts to sexual impurity for the degrading of their bodies with one another.

25. They exchanged the truth of God for a lie, and worshiped and served created things rather than the Creator--who is forever praised. Amen.

26. Because of this, God gave them over to shameful lusts. Even their women exchanged natural relations for unnatural ones.

27. In the same way the men also abandoned natural relations with women and were inflamed with lust for one another. Men committed indecent acts with other men, and

bende bachinjibusibwa kukulikana nei myanya yabo ibi, era yabakula mwa njira era itungenene.

28 abu bandu babaa batahonda kumenya Ongo. Era kwire arekabo bakulyikire ebwenge bwabo bwebuha-buha, chasiya bende baira bya batemire kuira.

29 mwa michima yabo mutchwula mwehwire chira myasi yoshi era itchwungenene, ne mabi, n'ebuhuma-huma n'e bubi. Kanji mutchwula mwehwire emufula, nebwichi, nembangano, ne bwengeere, ne burenzi. Batchwula bandju ba bende basinga ebanji e myasi era batailyire.

30 bende bamaana ebanji bulyi, batchwula barenda ba Ongo, batchwula bandju ba kukunza ebanji, batchwula bandju berume kanji ba kuchilola. Bende bakoresa enjira soshi mwa kuira emabi, batatchwunda ne basere babo,

31 batatchwusa bwenge, bataira cha chabalaanya emundju, batatchwusa chamba, batatchwusa na

---

바너러 버뻐 바찌띠부시봐 구구뤠가나 너이 먀냐 야보 이비, 어라 야바구꽈 먀 띠라 어라 이두뻐너너.

28 아부 바두 바바아 바다호따 구머냐 오끄. 어라 귀러 아러가보 바구레기러 어붜뻐 봐보 붜부하-부하, 짜시야 버뻐 바이라 뱌 바더미러 구이라.

29 먀 미찌마 야보 무쭈꽈 뭐휘러 찌라 먀시 요씨 어라 이쭈뻐너너, 너 마비, 너부후마-후마 너 부비. 가찌 무쭈꽈 뭐휘러 어무푸꽈, 너뷔찌, 너빠뻐노, 너 붱뻐어러, 너 부러씨. 바쭈꽈 바뚜 바 버뻐 바시빠 어바찌 어 먀시 어라 바다이뻬러.

30 버뻐 바마아나 어바찌 부레, 바쭈꽈 바러따 바 오끄, 바쭈꽈 바뚜 바 구구싸 어바찌, 바쭈꽈 바뚜 버루머 가찌 바 구찌로꽈. 버뻐 바고러사 어띠라 소씨 먀 구이라 어마비, 바다쭈따 너 바서러 바보,

31 바다쭈사 붱뻐, 바다이라 짜 짜바뽜아냐 어무뚜, 바다쭈사 짜빠, 바다쭈사 나 보쪼.

---

received in themselves the due penalty for their perversion.

28.. Furthermore, since they did not think it worthwhile to retain the knowledge of God, he gave them over to a depraved mind, to do what ought not to be done.

29. They have become filled with every kind of wickedness, evil, greed and depravity. They are full of envy, murder, strife, deceit and malice. They are gossips,

30. slanderers, God-haters, insolent, arrogant and boastful; they invent ways of doing evil; they disobey their parents;

31. they are senseless, faithless, heartless, ruthless.

bonjo.

32 noku baneshi ebuchinjibusi bwa Ongo kwa bandju ba bende baira ei myasi bemire kufa. Si chiro bacha, banachire baendekera kuira ei myasi, na kunde bemeresa ba benjire bairai.

32 노구 바너씨 어부찌찌부시 봐 오꼬 과 바뚜 바 버너 바이라 어이 먀시 버미러 구파. 시 찌로 바짜, 바나찌러 바어떠거라 구이라 어이 먀시, 나 구떠 버머러사 바 버찌러 바이라이.

32. Although they know God's righteous decree that those who do such things deserve death, they not only continue to do these very things but also approve of those who practice them.

Ba Roma Chikono 2
Ongo akachinjibusa ebandju

1 Rero woyu u wenjire wachinjibusa ebanji, utete kwa ungachokolola chiro mbu unde. Mango achinjibusa ebanji, eri eine uwachinjibusa. Bushi emyasi era wachinjibusako, inao wenjire wanaira.

바 로마 찌고노 2
오꼬 아가찌찌뷥뻡 어바뚜

1 러로 오유 우 워찌러 와찌찌부사 어바찌, 우더더 과 우까쪼고로롸 찌로 뿌 우너. 마꼬 아찌찌부사 어바찌, 어리 어이너 우와찌찌부사. 부씨 어먀시 어라 와찌찌부사고, 이나오 워찌러 와나이라.

1. You, therefore, have no excuse, you who pass judgment on someone else, for at whatever point you judge the other, you are condemning yourself, because you who pass judgment do the same things.

2 ba bende baira emyasi era iri ngei, tuneshi kwa Ongo enjire achinjibusabo kukulikana ne kanangana.

2 바 버너 바이라 어먀시 어라 이리 꺼이, 두너씨 과 오꼬 어찌러 아찌찌부사보 구구꾀가나 너 가나꺼나.

2. Now we know that God's judgment against those who do such things is based on truth.

3 woyu wenjire wachinibusa ba bende baira ei myasi, noku nao wenjire wanairai. Waanyisa mbu ungafufumuka ebuchinjibusi bwa Ongo?

3 오유 워찌러 와찌니부사 바 버너 바이라 어이 먀시, 노구 나오 워찌러 와나이라이. 와아니에사 뿌 우까푸푸무가 어부찌찌부시 봐 오꼬?

3. So when you, a mere man, pass judgment on them and yet do the same things, do you think you will escape God's judgment?

4 oku Ongo atula mubuya busese, atusa na muchima wa kulinjirira, atanalibichira kuchinjibusa ebandu, ebyera

4 오구 오꼬 아두롸 무부야 부서서, 아두사 나 무찌마 와 구꾀찌리라, 아다나꾀비찌라 구찌찌부사 어바뚜, 어벼라 비

4. Or do you show contempt for the riches of his kindness, tolerance and patience, not realizing that

bi byrera byatuma wamukena? uteshi kwa abu bu buya bwai bu bungatuma wabinduka kutenga mwa bibi byao?

5 si woyu wete matwi masibu na muchima ola utahonda kubinduka atenge mwa bibi. Bushi noku, weine wachikulilira buchinjibusi benene, elusuku lwa Ongo akalosa ebute bwai kwa bandu, ne kuchinjibusabo busira kalondo.

6 olu lusuku, Ongo akemba chira mundu kukulikana nabya ende aira.

7 ba bende baira emabuya busira kutama, mwa kuhonda Ongo aberesi engulu, netunda ne kalamo ka katete nzinjiro, akeresabo ekalamo ke suku ne mango.

8 si ba batatunda Ongo beke na kunde banana kukulikira emyasi ye kanangana, na kunde bakoresibwa na mabi, Ongo akalosabo kwa kasibu ke bute bwai.

9 chira mundu ola wende waira emabi, Ongo akamulosa kumalibuko na malio: ebayuta tanga, chasinda ba batatula bayuta.

10 si chira mundu woshi ola

뷔러라 뱌두마 와무거나? 우더씨 과 아부 부 부야 봐이 부 부빠두마 와비뚜가 구더빠 꽈 비비 뱌오?

5 시 오유 워더 마뒤 마시부 나 무찌마 오롸 우다호따 구비뿌가 아더뼈 꽈 비비. 부씨 노구, 워이너 와찌구릴릴라 부찌찌부시 버너너, 어루수구 꽈 오꼬 아가론사 어부더 봐이 과 바뚜, 너 구찌찌부사보 부시라 가로또.

6 오루 루수구, 오꼬 아거빠 찌라 무뚜 구구릐가나 나뱌 어떠 아이라.

7 바 버떠 바이라 어마부야 부시라 구다마, 꽈 구호따 오꼬 아버러시 어우루, 너두따 너 가롸모 가 가더더 씨찌로, 아거러사보 어가롸모 거 수구 너 마꼬.

8 시 바 바다두따 오꼬 버거 나 구떠 바나나 구구릐기라 어먀시 여 가나빠나, 나 구떠 바고러시봐 나 마비, 오꼬 아가론사보 과 가시부 거 부더 봐이.

9 찌라 무뚜 오롸 워떠 와이라 어마비, 오꼬 아가무론사 구마릐부고 나 마릐오: 어바유다 다따, 짜시따 바 바다두롸 바유다.

10 시 찌라 무뚜 오씨 오롸

God's kindness leads you toward repentance?

5. But because of your stubbornness and your unrepentant heart, you are storing up wrath against yourself for the day of God's wrath, when his righteous judgment will be revealed.

6. God "will give to each person according to what he has done."

7. To those who by persistence in doing good seek glory, honor and immortality, he will give eternal life.

8. But for those who are self-seeking and who reject the truth and follow evil, there will be wrath and anger.

9. There will be trouble and distress for every human being who does evil: first for the Jew, then for the Gentile;

10. but glory, honor and

wende waira emabuya, Ongo akamweresa engulu, netunda nebolo: ebayuta tanga, chasinda babatatula bayuta.

11 bushi atatusa kalondo.

12 boshi babende baira ebibi busira kumenyerera emwaso* wa musa, bakaya mwa muero busirz kuchinjibusibwa noyu mwaso* wa musa, beke bakachinjibusibwa kukulikana noyu mwaso*

13 bushi ata ba bende bomvirisa kwa mwaso* wa musa atula etchire oshao, bu Ongo ende atola nga bandu ba batungene era muhondo sai, si ba bende baira kwa oyu mwaso*atechire.

14 ba batatula bayuta batatusa emwaso*wa musa. Si chiro bacha, bauma mubo mubo bende baira kwa oyu mwaso* atula atechire busira kumenya. Mwakuira bacha, bende balosa kwa beine baneshi bya bemire kuira noku batete oyu mwaso*.

15 mwa bacha, bende balosa kwe miomba* ye mwaso* yanjikirwe mwa michima yabo. Kanji bende yabasitaka nesi yende ya batetera.

워더 와이라 어마부야, 오꼬 아가뭐러사 어꾸루, 너두따 너보론: 어바유다 다따, 짜시따 바바다두롸 바유다.

11 부씨 아다두사 가론또.

12 보씨 바버더 바이라 어비비 부시라 구머녀러라 어뫄소* 와 무사, 바가야 뫄 무어로 부시루주 구찌찌부시봐 노유 뫄소* 와 무사, 버거 바가찌찌부시봐 구구끠가나 노유 뫄소*

13 부씨 아다 바 버더 보뻬리사 과 뫄소* 와 무사 아두롸 어찌러 오싸오, 부 오꼬 어떠 아도롸 까 바뚜 바 바두꺼너 어라 무호또 사이, 시 바 버머 바이라 과 오유 뫄소*아더찌러.

14 바 바다두롸 바유다 바다두사 어뫄소*와 무사. 시 찌로 바짜, 바우마 무보 무보 버더 바이라 과 오유 뫄소* 아두롸 아더찌러 부시라 구머냐. 뫄구이라 바짜, 버더 바론사 과 버이너 바너씨 뱌 버미러 구이라 노구 바더더 오유 뫄소*.

15 뫄 바짜, 버더 바론사 궈 미오빠* 여 뫄소* 야찌기뭐 뫄 미찌마 야보. 가찌 버더 야바시다가 너시 여더 야 바더더라.

peace for everyone who does good: first for the Jew, then for the Gentile.

11. For God does not show favoritism.

12. All who sin apart from the law will also perish apart from the law, and all who sin under the law will be judged by the law.

13. For it is not those who hear the law who are righteous in God's sight, but it is those who obey the law who will be declared righteous.

14. (Indeed, when Gentiles, who do not have the law, do by nature things required by the law, they are a law for themselves, even though they do not have the law,

15. since they show that the requirements of the law are written on their hearts, their consciences also bearing witness, and their thoughts now accusing, now even

defending them.)

16 ebyera bikalorekanako kubuya elusuku lwe buchinjibusi. Kukulikana nokwa emwasi mubuya-buya ola nenjire nahubanganya atechire, olu lusuku Ongo akachinjibusa emyasi era ibishirwe mwa michima ye bandu. Akaira bacha, kurengera Yesu kirsito.

E Bayuda n'e Mwaso

17 woyu wende wacherika mbu uli muyuta, kanji mbu utula ulangalire emwaso*na kunde wachitonga mbu uli luuma-luuma na Ongo.

18 kanji wende wachitonga mbu utula wishi ekuhonda kwai, ne mwaso akukangirise kute ungaala kumenyerera bya byete mufa.

19 wende wachitola kuba mundu ola wende watandaisa ebiumi-umi, na kuba bulanganre kwa bandu ba bali mwa musimya.

20 kanji mbu utula mukangirisi we bandu ba bateshi kandu, kanji mukangirisi web ana, bushi kurengera emwaso* wishi

16 어벼라 비가뢰러가나고 구부야 어루수구 뤄 부찌찌부시. 구구뤠가나 노과 어뫄시 무부야-부야 오롸 너찌러 나후바까냐 아더찌러, 오루 루수구 오꼬 아가찌찌부사 어먀시 어라 이비씨뤄 뫄 미찌마 여 바뚜. 아가이라 바짜, 구러뻐라 여수 기시도.

어 바유다 너 뫄소

17 오유 워떠 와쩌리가 뿌 우뤠 무유다, 가찌 뿌 우두롸 우롸까뤠러 어뫄소*나 구더 와찌도까 뿌 우뤠 루우마-루우마 나 오꼬.

18 가찌 워떠 와찌도까 뿌 우두롸 위씨 어구호따 과이, 너 뫄소 아구가삐리서 구더 우까아롸 구머녀러라 뱌 벼더 무파.

19 워떠 와찌도롸 구바 무뚜 오롸 워떠 와다따이사 어비우미-우미, 나 구바 부롸까누러 과 바뚜 바 바뤼 뫄 무시먀.

20 가찌 뿌 우두롸 무가삐리시 워 바뚜 바 바더씨 가뚜, 가찌 무가삐리시 워부 아나, 부씨 구러뻐라 어뫄소* 위씨 어먀시 여붜뻐 너 여가나까냐.

16. This will take place on the day when God will judge men's secrets through Jesus Christ, as my gospel declares.

17. Now you, if you call yourself a Jew; if you rely on the law and brag about your relationship to God;

18. if you know his will and approve of what is superior because you are instructed by the law;

19. if you are convinced that you are a guide for the blind, a light for those who are in the dark,

20. an instructor of the foolish, a teacher of infants, because you have in the law the embodiment of knowledge and truth--

932 Ba Roma / 바 로마 / Rome

kubuya emyasi yebwenge ne
yekanangana.

21 rero woyu wende
wakangirisa ebanji, chi
chingatuma utachikangirisa
weine? woyu wende
wahubanganya mbu bitemire
kwiba, chi chera chende
chatuma weba?

21 러로 오유 워떠 와가삐리사
어바찌, 찌 찌까두마
우다찌가삐리사 워이너? 오유
워떠 와후바까냐 뿌 비더미러
귀바, 찌 쩌라 쩌떠 짜두마
워바?

21. you, then, who teach
others, do you not teach
yourself? You who preach
against stealing, do you
steal?

22 woyu uwende wanga
ebanji mbu batenda babanda
ekiri, chi chera chende
chatuma wabandali? woyu
uutula uaire ibihuhanyi bye
ba ongo, chi chera chende
chatuma weba ebindu mwa
tuhumiro twabo?

22 오유 우워떠 와까 어바찌
뿌 바더따 바바따 어기리, 찌
쩌라 쩌떠 짜두마 와바따삐?
오유 우우두라 우아이러
이비후하니 벼 바 오꼬, 찌
쩌라 쩌떠 짜두마 워바 어비뚜
뫄 두후미로 돠보?

22. You who say that people
should not commit adultery,
do you commit adultery?
You who abhor idols, do
you rob temples?

23 wende wachotonga mbu
utula wishi emwaso*, si
wende wa kena Ongo mwa
kutaira kwoyu mwaso* atula
tachire!

23 워떠 와쪼도까 뿌 우두라
위씨 어뫄소*, 시 워떠 와 거나
오꼬 뫄 구다이라 교유 뫄소*
아두라 다찌러!

23. You who brag about the
law, do you dishonor God
by breaking the law?

24 kubinali, bitula byanjikirwe
mwa maanjiko mabuya-buya
mbu: mwabo mu mwende
mwatuma ba batatula bayuta
bakamba Ongo.

24 구비나삐, 비두라 뱌찌기뤄
뫄 마아찌고 마부야-부야 뿌:
뫄보 무 뭐떠 뫄두마 바
바다두라 바유다 바가빠 오꼬.

24. As it is written: "God's
name is blasphemed among
the Gentiles because of
you."

25 kubinali, ekumonyisibwa
kwete mufa akaba ungaira
ngokwa mwaso* atula
atechire. Si akaba utenjire
waira ngokwa mwaso atula
atechire, ola unali ngola

25 구비나삐, 어구모니시봐
궈더 무파 아가바 우까이라
꼬과 뫄소* 아두라 아더찌러.
시 아가바 우더찌러 와이라
꼬과 뫄소 아두라 아더찌러,
오롸 우나삐 꼬롸

25. Circumcision has value if
you observe the law, but if
you break the law, you have
become as though you had
not been circumcised.

utamonyisibwe.	우다모네시붜.	

26 akaba ola utamonyisibwe angaira ngokwa emiomba* yemwaso* itula itechire, muteshi kwa Ongo angamutola ngola umonyisibwe?

26 아가바 오롸 우다모네시붜 아빠이라 꼬과 어미오빠* 여마소* 이두롸 이더찌러, 무더씨 과 오꼬 아빠무도롸 꼬롸 우모네시붜?

26. If those who are not circumcised keep the law's requirements, will they not be regarded as though they were circumcised?

27 ola utamonyisibwe kwa mubiri, si enjire aira ngokwa mwaso*atula atechire, akachinjibubusa chiro waira ngokwa mwaaso* atula atechire. Akakuchinjibusa chiro mbu umonyisibwe, wete ne mwaso*ola wanjikirwe.

27 오롸 우다모네시붜 과 무비리, 시 어찌러 아이라 꼬과 마소*아두롸 아더찌러, 아가찌찌부부사 찌로 와이라 꼬과 마아소* 아두롸 아더찌러. 아가구찌찌부사 찌로 뿌 우모네시붜, 워더 너 마소*오롸 와찌기뤄.

27. The one who is not circumcised physically and yet obeys the law will condemn you who, even though you have the written code and circumcision, are a lawbreaker.

28 bushi okulorekanako nga muyuta kwa njira yemubiri oshao, atakuba muyuta kanangana. Ne kumonyisibwa kwa mubiri oshao, ata ku kumonyisibwa kwe kanangana.

28 부씨 오구로러가나고 빠 무유다 과 찌라 여무비리 오싸오, 아다구바 무유다 가나빠나. 너 구모네시봐 과 무비리 오싸오, 아다 구 구모네시봐 궈 가나빠나.

28.. A man is not a Jew if he is only one outwardly, nor is circumcision merely outward and physical.

29 si emuyuta we kanangana, ali ola uli muyuta mwa mchima, kanji ola umonyisibwe kwa kwekanangana. Oku kumonyisiwa ku kutenganyire ne mchima mubuya-buya mwa mchima we mundu, si ata kurengera emwaso* ola wanjikirwe. Rero emundu ola uli ngoyu, ata ebandu bu bende bamutonga, si Ongo

29 시 어무유다 워 가나빠나, 아찌 오롸 우찌 무유다 마 무찌마, 가찌 오롸 우모네시붜 과 궈가나빠나. 오구 구모네시와 구 구더빠네러 너 무찌마 무부야-부야 마 무찌마 워 무뚜, 시 아다 구러뻐라 어마소* 오롸 와찌기뤄. 러로 어무뚜 오롸 우찌 꼬유, 아다 어바뚜 부 버뻐 바무도빠, 시 오꼬 이워뻐 와무도빠.

29. No, a man is a Jew if he is one inwardly; and circumcision is circumcision of the heart, by the Spirit, not by the written code. Such a man's praise is not from men, but from God.

iw ende wamutonga.

<table>
<tr><td>

Ba Roma Chikono 3
Ongo anatchwula
wakuchinyirwa

1 Rero, ekuba muyuta ne
kumonyisibwa kwete
mutoloke muchiye?

2 nechi, ebyera byeta
mutoloke munene kwa njira
soshi: kwa bayuta tanga,
bushi bu Ongo aresaa
echinwa chai chasiya
bemerechi.

3 chi twiree twateta kasi?
akaba bandu bauma
mwabayuta babaa bata
bakuchinyiirwaa?

4 nanga chrio na hicha! chiro
mbu ebandu boshi batula
bafusi ba bisha, si Ongo yeke,
kanangana kuende anateta,
ngokwa bitula byan jikirwe
mwa maanjiko mabuya-buya
mbu: Ongo Tata! ebandu
bendaa bamenya kwa bya
wende wateta binatula
bitungene. Kanji mango
wasitakibwa, u'uendaa
wanasingana!

</td><td>

바 로마 찌고노 3
오꼬 아나쭈라 와구찌네롭

1 러로, 어구바 무유다 너
구모네시봐 궈더 무도쯔거
무찌여?

2 너찌, 어벼라 벼다 무도쯔거
무너너 과 찌라 소씨: 과
바유다 다꺄, 부씨 부 오꼬
아러사아 어찌놔 짜이 짜시야
버머러찌.

3 찌 뒤러어 돠더다 가시?
아가바 바뚜 바우마 뫄바유다
바바아 바다 바구찌네이롸아?

4 나꺄 찌리오 나 히짜! 찌로
뿌 어바뚜 보씨 바두꽈 바푸시
바 비싸, 시 오꼬 여거,
가나꺄나 구어떠 아나더다,
꼬과 비두꽈 뱌누 지기뤄 뫄
마아찌고 마부야-부야 뿌: 오꼬
다다! 어바뚜 버따아 바머냐
과 뱌 워떠 와더다 비나두꽈
비두뻐너. 가찌 마꼬
와시다기봐, 우우어따아
와나시뻐나!

</td><td>

Rome Chapter 3[NIV]

1. What advantage, then, is
there in being a Jew, or
what value is there in
circumcision?

2. Much in every way! First
of all, they have been
entrusted with the very
words of God.

3. What if some did not
have faith? Will their lack of
faith nullify God's
faithfulness?

4. Not at all! Let God be
true, and every man a liar.
As it is written: "So that you
may be proved right when
you speak and prevail when
you judge."

</td></tr>
</table>

5 akaba kurengera emabi ma twende twaira, Ongo ende alorekanako kuba ola wende waira bya bitungenene mango atukemera? anola, nateta nga mundu.

5 아가바 구러꺼라 어마비 마 뛰꺼 돠이라, 오꼬 어너 아로러가나고 구바 오롸 워꺼 와이라 뱌 비두꺼너너 마꼬 아두거머라? 아노롸, 나더다 꺼 무뚜.

5. But if our unrighteousness brings out God's righteousness more clearly, what shall we say? That God is unjust in bringing his wrath on us? (I am using a human argument.)

6 nanga chiro na hicha!bushi akaba Ongo angenjire aira bya bitatungenene, kute angenjire achinjibusa ebandu be butala?

6 나꺼 찌로 나 히짜!부씨 아가바 오꼬 아꺼찌러 아이라 뱌 비다두꺼너너, 구더 아꺼찌러 아찌찌부사 어바누 버 부다롸?

6. Certainly not! If that were so, how could God judge the world?

7 si akaba kurengera ebisha byanyi, ekanangana ka Ongo kenjire kalorekanako kubuya nekulosa etunda lyai, rero chi chera chingatuma nachinjibusibwa nga mundu wa bibi?

7 시 아가바 구러꺼라 어비싸 뱌네, 어가나꺼나 가 오꼬 거찌러 가로러가나고 구부야 너구로사 어두따 랴이, 러로 찌 쩌라 찌꺼두마 나찌찌부시봐 꺼 무뚜 와 비비?

7. Someone might argue, "If my falsehood enhances God's truthfulness and so increases his glory, why am I still condemned as a sinner?"

8 akaba ku biri bacha, twiree twateta mbu: tundaa twaira emabi chasiya amu mabi mabute emabuya? bushi kulu bandu bauma ba benjire banyisinga mbu ku nenjire nateta bacha. Abola bu bangachinjibusibwa, bushi kuhubanganairwa bacha!
Kutalyi mundju ola utchwungenene era muhondo sa Ongo

8 아가바 구 비리 바짜, 뒤러어 돠더다 뿌: 두따아 돠이라 어마비 짜시야 아무 마비 마부더 어마부야? 부씨 구루 바뚜 바우마 바 버찌러 바네시꺼 뿌 구 너찌러 나더다 바짜. 아보롸 부 바꺼찌찌부시봐, 부씨 구후바꺼나이롸 바짜!
구다뗴 무뚜 오롸 우쭈꺼냘냘 어라 무호또 사 오꼬

8. Why not say--as we are being slanderously reported as saying and as some claim that we say--"Let us do evil that good may result"? Their condemnation is deserved.

9 rero chi tutetaa? ta bayuta, chiye turenzise ebanji bandu? tutabarenzise chiro na kandu kasibya! bushi nabalosise mire kwe bayuta na ba batula bayuta, boshi banali mwa bucha bwebibi.

10 kunali ngokwa bitula byanjikirwe mwa maanjiko mabuya-buya mbu: kutali chiro na mundu ola utula utungenene era muhondo sa Ongo, chiro na mundu asibya.

11 kutali chiro na mundu ola wete bwenge bwe kumva, kanji kutalu chiro na muuma ola wende wahonda Ongo.

12 boshi berekire enjira ibuya, boshi baierere alauma. Kutali chiro na muuma ola wende waira emabuya, chiro na mundu asibya.

13 Emimiro yabo inachitulira nga shinda era ibookere. Enyirimi sabo sinatula sa kwengeera ebandu oshao. Kwa bieta byabo, sumu ikaliire nga ya njoka, iinatulako.

14 mwa bunu bwabo, bitaki na binwa bya kulumya ebanji emihima, bi binatula byehwiremo.

9 러로 찌 두더다아? 다 바유다, 찌여 두러씨서 어바찌 바뚜? 두다바러씨서 찌로 나 가뚜 가시뱌! 부씨 나바로시서 미러 궈 바유다 나 바 바두롸 바유다, 보씨 바나뢰 먀 부짜 붜비비.

10 구나뢰 으과 비두롸 뱌찌기뤄 먀 마아찌고 마부야-부야 뭇: 구다뢰 찌로 나 무뚜 오롸 우두롸 우두꺼너너 어라 무호또 사 오끄, 찌로 나 무뚜 아시뱌.

11 구다뢰 찌로 나 무뚜 오롸 워더 붜꺼 붜 구빠, 가찌 구다루 찌로 나 무우마 오롸 워떠 와호따 오끄.

12 보씨 버러기러 어찌라 이부야, 보씨 바이어러러 아롸우마. 구다뢰 찌로 나 무우마 오롸 워떠 와이라 어마부야, 찌로 나 무뚜 아시뱌.

13 어미미로 야보 이나찌두뢰라 꺄 씨따 어라 이보오거러. 어네리미 사보 시나두롸 사 궈꺼어라 어바누 오싸오. 과 비어다 뱌보, 수무 이가뢰이러 꺄 야 쪼가, 이이나두롸고.

14 먀 부누 봐보, 비다기 나 비뇨 뱌 구루먀 어바찌 어미히마, 비 비나두롸 벼휘러모.

9. What shall we conclude then? Are we any better? Not at all! We have already made the charge that Jews and Gentiles alike are all under sin.

10. As it is written: "There is no one righteous, not even one;

11. there is no one who understands, no one who seeks God.

12. All have turned away, they have together become worthless; there is no one who does good, not even one."

13. "Their throats are open graves; their tongues practice deceit." "The poison of vipers is on their lips."

14. "Their mouths are full of cursing and bitterness."

15 Emaulu mabo, manatula ma kulibichira kushesha emikira.

16 chira ala banarengire oshi, kukumbya ku bende banakumbya na kurekao buanya.

17 batachitulira beshi njira ya kureta bolo.

18 kanji batobaa Ongo chiro na hicha.

19 noku kwisha kwa bya mwaso* atula atechire binatula byerekere ba bemire kuira ngokwa atula atechire .aola, ktachiri ola ukaboola ebunu mbu achokolola. Mwa bacha, ebutala boshi bukalorekanako kwa bwemire kuchinjibusibwa era muhondo sa Ongo.

20 bushi kutali ola ungatolibwa nga mundu utungenene era muhondo sa Ongo bushi aira ngokwa mwaso*atula atechire. Si emwaso* anatula wa kuasa emundu kumenyerera kwa akolire bibi.

Ekutchwunganana era muhondo sa Ongo

21 Rero Ongo erire alosa ebandu enjira era ingatuma batunganana era muhondo sai, busira kurengera kwa

---

15 어마우루 마보, 마나두꽈 마 구뀌비찌라 구쎠싸 어미기라.

16 찌라 아꽈 바나러삐러 오씨, 구구빠 구 버뉘 바나구빠 나 구러가오 부아냐.

17 바다찌두뛰라 버씨 띠라 야 구러다 보뤄.

18 가찌 바도바아 오끄 찌로 나 히짜.

19 노구 귀싸 과 뱌 뫄소* 아두꽈 아더찌러 비나두꽈 벼러거러 바 버미러 구이라 끄과 아두꽈 아더찌러 .아오꽈, 구다찌리 오라 우가보오꽈 어부누 뿌 아쪼고뤄꽈. 뫄 바짜, 어부다꽈 보씨 부가뤄러가나고 과 뷔미러 구찌삐부시봐 어라 무호또 사 오끄.

20 부씨 구다뛰 오꽈 우꽈도뛰봐 까 무뚜 우두뼈너너 어라 무호또 사 오끄 부씨 아이라 끄과 뫄소*아두꽈 아더찌러. 시 어뫄소* 아나두꽈 와 구아사 어무뚜 구머녀러라 과 아고뛰러 비비.

어구쭈까낍낍 어라 무호또 사 오끄

21 러로 오끄 어리러 아뤄사 어바뉘 어찌라 어라 이까두마 바두꽈나나 어라 무호또 사이, 부시라 구러꺼라 과 뫄소*.

---

15. "Their feet are swift to shed blood;

16. ruin and misery mark their ways,

17. and the way of peace they do not know."

18. "There is no fear of God before their eyes."

19. Now we know that whatever the law says, it says to those who are under the law, so that every mouth may be silenced and the whole world held accountable to God.

20. Therefore no one will be declared righteous in his sight by observing the law; rather, through the law we become conscious of sin.

21. But now a righteousness from God, apart from law, has been made known, to which the Law and the

mwaso*. Ebi byoshi binatula bilosibwe mwa mwaso*nomwa maanjiko me barebi*.

어비 보씨 비나두롸 비로시붜 롸 마소*노롸 마아찌고 머 바러비*.

Prophets testify.

22 ebandu ba Ongo ende atolanga bu batungenene era muhondo sai, bali ba batusa ebwemeresi mwa ndanda sa Yesu kirisito. Ende aira bacha busira kalondo, kwa bandu boshi ba bamwemerere.

22 어바뉴 바 오꼬 어떠 아도롸꽈 부 바두꺼너너 어라 무호또 사이, 바삐 바 바두사 어붜머러시 롸 따따 사 여수 기리시도. 어떠 아이라 바짜 부시라 가론또, 과 바뉴 보씨 바 바뭐머러러.

22. This righteousness from God comes through faith in Jesus Christ to all who believe. There is no difference,

23 bushi ebandu boshi bairire ebibi, beribe baina ebulangare bwa Ongo.

23 부씨 어바뉴 보씨 바이리러 어비비, 버리버 바이나 어부롸꺼러 봐 오꼬.

23. for all have sinned and fall short of the glory of God,

24 si Ongo mwa bubuya bwai, ende airabo kuba ba batungenene era muhondo sai kwa buha, kurengera Yesu kirisito iwende wanunulabo mwa bibi.

24 시 오꼬 롸 부부야 봐이, 어떠 아이라보 구바 바 바두꺼너너 어라 무호또 사이 과 부하, 구러꺼라 여수 기리시도 이워떠 와누누롸보 롸 비비.

24. and are justified freely by his grace through the redemption that came by Christ Jesus.

25 oyu kirisito iOngo anaa kuba mitulo*, chasiya kurengera emikra yai, ba bamwemerere bende bababalirwa ebibi anaira bya bitungenene. Kwa mira, endee abangola utasene kwa bibi bya bandu bendee baira, bushi abaa atusa mchima wakulinjirira.

25 오유 기리시도 이오꼬 아나아 구바 미두로*, 짜시야 구러꺼라 어미구라 야이, 바 바뭐머러러 버떠 바바바삐롸 어비비 아나이라 뱌 비두꺼너너. 과 미라, 어떠어 아바꼬꽈 우다서너 과 비비 뱌 바뉴 버떠어 바이라, 부씨 아바아 아두사 무찌마 와구삐씨리라.

25. God presented him as a sacrifice of atonement, through faith in his blood. He did this to demonstrate his justice, because in his forbearance he had left the sins committed beforehand unpunished--

26 si mwesine suku, erire alosa kwa yeke ende aira bya bitungenene, chasiya alorekaneko kwa anatula airabo kuba ba batungenene

26 시 뭐시너 수구, 어리러 아로사 과 여거 어떠 아이라 뱌 비두꺼너너, 짜시야 아로러가너고 과 아나두꽈 아이라보 구바 바 바두꺼너너

26. he did it to demonstrate his justice at the present time, so as to be just and the one who justifies those who have faith in Jesus.

era muhondo sai. 어라 무호또 사이.

27 Ewashe! kunachiri cha chingatuma mundu achitonga? nanga chiro na hicha! bushi na chiye? bushi emwasi ola wete mufa kuta kuira ngokwa mwaso* atula atechire, si ekwemerera Yesu oshao.

27 어와써! 구나찌리 짜 찌까두마 무뚜 아찌도까? 나까 찌로 나 히짜! 부씨 나 찌여? 부씨 어뫄시 오롸 워더 무파 구다 구이라 꼬과 뫄소* 아두롸 아더찌러, 시 어궈머러라 여수 오싸오.

27. Where, then, is boasting? It is excluded. On what principle? On that of observing the law? No, but on that of faith.

28 bushi twanyisa kwa mundu ende atalibwa ngola utungenene era muhondo sa Ongo kurengera ebwemeresi, si ata kurengera ekuira ngokwa mwaso atula atechire kweine.

28 부씨 돠네사 과 무뚜 어떠 아다뤼봐 꼬라 우두꺼너너 어라 무호또 사 오꼬 구러꺼라 어붜머러시, 시 아다 구러꺼라 어구이라 꼬과 뫄소 아두롸 아더찌러 궈이너.

28.. For we maintain that a man is justified by faith apart from observing the law.

29 Ongo anatula Ongo we bayuta beine? atatula Ongo we banji bandu nabo? nechi, anatula Ongo we banji bandu nabo.

29 오꼬 아나두롸 오꼬 워 바유다 버이너? 아다두롸 오꼬 워 바찌 바뚜 나보? 너찌, 아나두롸 오꼬 워 바찌 바뚜 나보.

29. Is God the God of Jews only? Is he not the God of Gentiles too? Yes, of Gentiles too,

30 bushi Ongo anatula muuma oshao. Na iukaira ebandu ba bamwemerere kuba ba batungenene era muhondo sai, abe muyuta nesi ola uta muyuta.

30 부씨 오꼬 아나두롸 무우마 오싸오. 나 이우가이라 어바뚜 바 바뭐머러러 구바 바 바두꺼너너 어라 무호또 사이, 아버 무유다 너시 오롸 우다 무유다.

30. since there is only one God, who will justify the circumcised by faith and the uncircumcised through that same faith.

31 rero, mwanyiisa mbu bushi twete ebwemeresi twiree twatola emwaso* nga kandu ka katete mufa? nanga chiro

31 로로, 뫄네이사 뿌 부씨 뛰더 어붜머러시 뒤러어 돠도롸 어뫄소* 까 가뚜 가 가더더 무파? 나까 찌로 나

31. Do we, then, nullify the law by this faith? Not at all! Rather, we uphold the law.

na hicha! mwa kuata
ebwemeresi mu twenjire
tweresa emwaso emufa wai
woshi

히짜! 뫄 구아다 어뭐머러시
무 뛰찌러 뛰러사 어뫄소
어무파 와이 올씨

Ba Roma Chikono 4
*Ebwemeresi bwa
Aburahamu*

바 로마 찌고노 4
어뭐머러시 봐 아부라하무

Rome Chapter 4[NIV]

1 Rero, chi tutetaa era luulu
sa hokulu wetu Aburahamu?
chiye chi abonaa nga
mundu?

1 러로, 찌 두더다아 어라
루우루 사 호구루 워두
아부라하무? 찌여 찌 아보나아
꽈 무뚜?

1. What then shall we say
that Abraham, our
forefather, discovered in this
matter?

2 akaba Aburahamu
atolibwaa ngola utungenene
bushi na bya endee aira,
angaachire cha
angachitongera. Si kanangana
atetecha angachitongera era
muhondo sa Ongo.

2 아가바 아부라하무
아도뤼봐아 꼬꽈 우두꺼너너
부씨 나 뱌 어떠어 아이라,
아꽈아찌러 짜 아꽈찌도꺼라.
시 가나꽈나 아더더짜
아꽈찌도꺼라 어라 무호또 사
오꼬.

2. If, in fact, Abraham was
justified by works, he had
something to boast about--
but not before God.

3 bushi emaanjiko mabuya-
buya matula amtechire mbu:
Aburahamu abaa atula
emrere Ongo. Bushi noku,
Ongo era kumutola ngola
utungenene era muhondo
sai.

3 부씨 어마아찌고 마부야-
부야 마두꽈 아무더찌러 뿌:
아부라하무 아바아 아두꽈
어러러 오꼬. 부씨 노구, 오꼬
어라 구무도꽈 꼬꽈
우두꺼너너 어라 무호또 사이.

3. What does the Scripture
say? "Abraham believed
God, and it was credited to
him as righteousness."

4 Emukosi ende alipibwa kwa
mulimo wai. Oku kulipibwa
kutaanjibwa nga muhobore,
sikali kandu ka emire
kweresibwa.

4 어무고시 어떠 아뤼피봐 과
무뤼모 와이. 오구 구뤼피봐
구다아찌봐 꽈 무호보러,
시가뤼 가뚜 가 어미러
궈러시봐.

4. Now when a man works,
his wages are not credited
to him as a gift, but as an
obligation.

5 si akaba emmundu atetecha ende aira, si emerere kwa Ongo ende aira emundu webibi kuba ola utungenene, aola ebwemeresi boyu mundu bwende bwatuma Ongo amutola ngola utungenene.

6 kunoku ku mwami Tauti nai atechire mwa maanjiko mabuya-buya, era luulu se ngahanyi se mundu ola Ongo ende atola ngola utungenene, busira kulaa kwa bya ende aira. Bacha ku Tauti atechire:

7 Baahanyirwe ebandu ba Ongo ababalire emabi mabo, ne bibi byabo byakulibwe.

8 Aahanyirwe emundu ola enawetu atamwanjira ebibi byai.

9 Esi ngahanyi sitatula kwa bandu ba bamonyisibwe beine oshao, si situla nokwa bandu ba batamonyisibwe. Bushi twatechire mira kwa Ongo atolaa Aburahamu ngola utungenene kurengera ebwemeresi bwai.

10 mangochi kasi mu Ongo atolaa Aburahamu bacha? mango abaa amonyisibwe mira, nesi mango abaa atasa kumonyisibwa? ata mango

5 시 아가바 어무무뚜 아더더짜 어떠 아이라, 시 어머러러 과 오꼬 어떠 아이라 어무뚜 워비비 구바 오롸 우두떠너너, 아오롸 어뭐머러시 보유 무뚜 뭐떠 봐두마 오꼬 아무도롸 꼬롸 우두떠너너.

6 구노구 구 뫄미 다우디 나이 아더찌러 뫄 마아찌고 마부야-부야, 어라 루우루 서 까하네 서 무뚜 오롸 오꼬 어떠 아도롸 꼬롸 우두떠너너, 부시라 구롸아 과 뱌 어떠 아이라. 바짜 구 다우디 아더찌러:

7 바아하네뤄 어바뚜 바 오꼬 아바바뤼러 어마비 마보, 너 비비 뱌보 뱌구찌뷔.

8 아아하네뤄 어무뚜 오롸 어나워두 아다뫄찌라 어비비 뱌이.

9 어시 까하네 시다두롸 과 바뚜 바 바모네시뷔 버이너 오쌰오, 시 시두롸 노과 바뚜 바 바다모네시뷔. 부씨 돠더찌러 미라 과 오꼬 아도롸아 아부라하무 꼬롸 우두떠너너 구러러라 어뭐머러시 봐이.

10 마꼬찌 가시 무 오꼬 아도롸아 아부라하무 바짜? 마꼬 아바아 아모네시뷔 미라, 너시 마꼬 아바아 아다사 구모네시봐? 아다 마꼬 아바아

5. However, to the man who does not work but trusts God who justifies the wicked, his faith is credited as righteousness.

6. David says the same thing when he speaks of the blessedness of the man to whom God credits righteousness apart from works:

7. "Blessed are they whose transgressions are forgiven, whose sins are covered.

8. Blessed is the man whose sin the Lord will never count against him."

9. Is this blessedness only for the circumcised, or also for the uncircumcised? We have been saying that Abraham's faith was credited to him as righteousness.

10. Under what circumstances was it credited? Was it after he was circumcised, or before? It was not after, but before!

abaa amonyisibwe mira, si
mango abaa tasa
kumonyisibwa.

11 era nyuma sebi,
aburahamu era kwire
amonyisibwa. Oku
kumonyisibwa kwai ku kabaa
kalorero kekulosa kanangana
kwa Ongo amutola nga
mundu ola utungenene
kurengera ebwemeresi bwai.
Mwa bacha, aburahamu era
kwire abaa eshe webandu
boshi ba bemerere, chiro
mbu batamonyisibwe, chasiya
nabo Ongo abatole nga ba
batungenene.
12 kanji aburahamu ali eshe
webandu ba bamonyisibwe,
bakulikire enjire ye bwemeresi
bwai. Ei njira itata aburahamu
nai abaa atula akulikre
mango abaa atasa
kumonyisibwa.

*Echiraane cha Ongo chilyi
kwa bemeresi boshi*
13 Ongo alaanyaa
aburahamu ne lubuto lwai
kwa akaberesa ebutala kuba
mwandu wabo. Echi chirane,
Ongo atairaachi kwa bushi
Aburahamu endee aira
ngokwa mwaso*atula

아모네시붜 미라, 시 마꼬
아바아 다사 구모네시봐.

11 어라 뉴마 서비,
아부라하무 어라 귀러
아모네시봐. 오구 구모네시봐
과이 구 가바아 가뤄러로
거구뤄사 가나꽈나 과 오꼬
아무도롸 꽈 무뚜 오롸
우두꺼너너 구러꺼라
어붜머러시 봐이. 꽈 바짜,
아부라하무 어라 귀러 아바아
어써 워바뚜 보씨 바
버머러러, 찌로 뿌
바다모네시붜, 짜시야 나보
오꼬 아바도꺼 꽈 바
바두꺼너너.
12 가찌 아부라하무 아뤼 어써
워바뚜 바 바모네시붜,
바구뤼기러 어찌러 여
붜머러시 봐이. 어이 띠라
이다다 아부라하무 나이
아바아 아두롸 아구뤼구러
마꼬 아바아 아다사
구모네시봐.

*어찌라아너 짜 오꼬 찌쩨 과
버머러시 보씨*
13 오꼬 아롸아냐아
아부라하무 너 루부도 롸이 과
아가버러사 어부다롸 구바
꽈뚜 와보. 어찌 찌라너, 오꼬
아다이라아찌 과 부씨
아부라하무 어떠어 아이라
꼬과 꽈소*아두롸 아더찌러.

11. And he received the sign
of circumcision, a seal of the
righteousness that he had
by faith while he was still
uncircumcised. So then, he
is the father of all who
believe but have not been
circumcised, in order that
righteousness might be
credited to them.

12. And he is also the father
of the circumcised who not
only are circumcised but
who also walk in the
footsteps of the faith that
our father Abraham had
before he was circumcised.

13. It was not through law
that Abraham and his
offspring received the
promise that he would be
heir of the world, but
through the righteousness
that comes by faith.

atechire. Nanga! si airaachi, bushi abaa atolire aburahamu ngola utungenene kurengera ebwemeresi bwai.

나까! 시 아이라아찌, 부씨 아바아 아도찌러 아부라하무 꼬라 우두꺼너너 구러꺼라 어붜머러시 봐이.

14 bushi akaba ebandu ba bende baira ngokwa mwaso*atula atechire bu bakabona bya Ongo alaanyaa, aola ebwemeresi butachete mufa asibya, nechiraane cha Ongo nachi, chinali cha busha.

14 부씨 아가바 어바누 바 버너 바이라 꼬과 먀소*아두퐈 아더찌러 부 바가보나 뱌 오꼬 아퐈아냐아, 아오퐈 어붜머러시 부다쩌더 무파 아시뱌, 너찌라아너 짜 오꼬 나찌, 찌나퀴 짜 부싸.

14. For if those who live by law are heirs, faith has no value and the promise is worthless,

15 bushi ekutaira kwa mwaso* atula atechire, kwende kwatuma Ongo afira ebandu bute. Na akaba emwaso* atali, nakutaira ngokwa atula atechire nako kutanali.

15 부씨 어구다이라 과 먀소* 아두퐈 아더찌러, 궈너 과두마 오꼬 아피라 어바누 부더. 나 아가바 어먀소* 아다퀴, 나구다이라 꼬과 아두퐈 아더찌러 나고 구다나퀴.

15. because law brings wrath. And where there is no law there is no transgression.

16 bushi noku, echiraane chitenganyire nobwemeresi, chasiya ebandu babonechi nga lwembo lwa Ongo, chiatena mufa kanangana kwa luboto loshi lwa aburahamu. Echi chiraane chitali kwa ba bende baira ngokwa mwaso*atula atechire oshao, si chiri nokwa bandu babatusa ebwemeresi nga aburahamu, itata wetu tuboshi.

16 부씨 노구, 어찌라아너 찌더꼬네러 노붜머러시, 짜시야 어바누 바보너찌 꺼 뭐꾜 퐈 오꼬, 찌아더나 무파 가나까나 과 루보도 로씨 퐈 아부라하무. 어찌 찌라아너 찌다퀴 과 바 버너 바이라 꼬과 먀소*아두퐈 아더찌러 오싸오, 시 찌리 노과 바누 바바두사 어붜머러시 꺼 아부라하무, 이다다 워두 두보씨.

16. Therefore, the promise comes by faith, so that it may be by grace and may be guaranteed to all Abraham's offspring--not only to those who are of the law but also to those who are of the faith of Abraham. He is the father of us all.

17 ebyera bikulikene nokwa bitula byabjikirwe mwa maanjiko mabuya-buya mbu: nakuirire eshi we mbaa sinene. Aburahamu ali tata era muhondo sa Ongo, iabaa atusa emerere. Woyu Ongo iwabaa wende womola ebafu, kanji iwende wa teta mbu ebindu bya byabaa bitatula bibaa.

18 aburahamu aataa enwemeresi na kulanagalira emyasi era itangalika kulangalirwa. Bushi noku, era kwire abaa eshe wa mbaa sinene, kukulikana nene myasi Ongo amuburaa mbu:Elubuto lwao lukaba lunene busese.

19 aburahamu abaa era ete myaka era ingaika kweyana. Abaa eshi kwa mubiri wai era ali ngola walinga kufa. Kanji abaa eshi kwa mukai Sara atula ngumba.

20 Si chero bacha, era kunaendekera se chiraane cha Ongo amweresaa, nesi ataesaa emunyiiro. Si ebwemeresi bwai bwameresaa emisi, era kutonga Ongo.

17 어벼라 비구꾀거너 노과 비두꽈 뱌부지기뤄 똬 마야찌고 마부야-부야 뿌: 나구이리러 어씨 워 빠아 시너너. 아부라하무 아꾀 다다 어라 무호또 사 오꼬, 이아바아 아두사 어머러러. 올유 오꼬 이와바아 워떠 온모꽈 어바푸, 가찌 이워떠 와 더다 뿌 어비뚜 뱌 뱌바아 비다두꽈 비바아.

18 아부라하무 아아다아 어누워머러시 나 구꽈나가꾀라 어먀시 어라 이다꽈꾀라 구꽈꽈꾀롸. 부씨 노구, 어라 귀러 아바아 어써 와 빠아 시너너, 구구꾀가나 너너 먀시 오꼬 아무부라아 뿌:어룹부도 꽈오 루가바 루너너 부서서.

19 아부라하무 아바아 어라 어더 먀가 어라 이꽈이가 궈야나. 아바아 어씨 과 무비리 와이 어라 아꾀 끄꽈 와꾀꽈 구파. 가찌 아바아 어씨 과 무가이 사라 아두꽈 우빠.

20 시 쩌로 바짜, 어라 구나어떠거라 서 찌라아너 짜 오꼬 아뭐러사아, 너시 아다어사아 어무네이로. 시 어붜머러시 봐이 봐머러사아 어미시, 어라 구도꽈 오꼬.

17. As it is written: "I have made you a father of many nations." He is our father in the sight of God, in whom he believed--the God who gives life to the dead and calls things that are not as though they were.

18. Against all hope, Abraham in hope believed and so became the father of many nations, just as it had been said to him, "So shall your offspring be."

19. Without weakening in his faith, he faced the fact that his body was as good as dead--since he was about a hundred years old-- and that Sarah's womb was also dead.

20. Yet he did not waver through unbelief regarding the promise of God, but was strengthened in his faith and gave glory to God,

21 abaa aneshi kanangana kwa Ongo ete ebuashi kwe kuira bya alaanyaa.

22 bushi noku, Ongo era kumutola ngola utungenene.

23 si oyu mwesi utechire mbu: Ongo era kumutola ngola utungenene. Ataajikibwaa bushi na aburahamu yeine oshao,

24 si kanji aanjikibwaa bushi netu, tu Ongo akatola nga bandu ba batunganene, tu tutula twemerere kwa iwomwolaa enawetu Yesu mwa bafu.

25 Ongo amwanaa chasiya afe bushi ne bibi byetu. Si era kumwomola , chasiya atuire kuba bandu ba batunganene era muhondo sai.

21 아바아 아너씨 가나꺄나 과 오꼬 어더 어부아씨 궈 구이라 뱌 아롸아냐아.

22 부씨 노구, 오꼬 어라 구무도롸 꼬롸 우두꺼너너.

23 시 오유 뭐시 우더찌러 뿌: 오꼬 어라 구무도롸 꼬롸 우두꺼너너. 아다아지기봐아 부씨 나 아부라하무 여이너 오싸오,

24 시 가찌 아아찌기봐아 부씨 너두, 두 오꼬 아가도롸 꺄 바뚜 바 바두꺼너너, 두 두두롸 뛰머러러 과 이오모롸아 어나워두 여수 꽈 바푸.

25 오꼬 아뫄나아 짜시야 아퍼 부씨 너 비비 벼두. 시 어라 구모모롸 , 짜시야 아두이러 구바 바뚜 바 바두꺄너너 어라 무호또 사이.

21. being fully persuaded that God had power to do what he had promised.

22. This is why "it was credited to him as righteousness."

23. The words "it was credited to him" were written not for him alone,

24. but also for us, to whom God will credit righteousness--for us who believe in him who raised Jesus our Lord from the dead.

25. He was delivered over to death for our sins and was raised to life for our justification.

Ba Roma Chikono 5
Yesu kirsito atuhubise mwa buuma na Ongo

1 Kubinali, Ongo atuirire kuba bandu ba batungenene era muhondo sai kurengera ebwemeresi. Rero twera tuli mwa bolo nai kurengera enawetu Yesu kirisito.

바 로마 찌고노 5
여수 기시도 아두후비서 꽈 부우꺄 나 오꼬

1 구비나삐, 오꼬 아두이리러 구바 바뚜 바 바두꺼너너 어라 무호또 사이 구러꺼라 어붜머러시. 러로 뛰라 두삐 꽈 보론 나이 구러꺼라 어나워두 여수 기리시도.

Rome Chapter 5[NIV]

1. Therefore, since we have been justified through faith, wehave peace with God through our Lord Jesus Christ,

2 na kurengera Obu bwemeresi, Yesu atweresise ebusahi bwe kuchifunda ofu ne bonjo bwa Ongo. Na mwobu bonjo, mutunachiri lwarero. Bushi noku, twenjire twamowa, bushi twete emunyiiro kwa tukabona kwa bulangare bwa Ongo.

2 나 구러ᅇᅥ라 오부 붜머러시, 여수 아뚸러시서 어부사히 붜 구찌푸ᄕᅡ 오푸 너 보ᄶᅩ 봐 오ᅁᅩ. 나 모부 보ᄶᅩ, 무두나찌리 ᄙᅪ러로. 부씨 노구, 뚸ᄡᅵ러 돠모와, 부씨 뚸더 어무네이로 과 두가보나 과 부ᄙᅡᅇᅡ러 봐 오ᅁᅩ.

2. through whom we have gained access by faith into this grace in which we now stand. And we rejoice in the hope of the glory of God.

3 alauma nebi byoshi, kanji twenjire twamowa mwa malibuko ma twarengamo. Bushi twishi kwa amu malibuko mumende matuma twaata ebushibirisi.

3 아ᄙᅡ우마 너비 뵤씨, 가ᄡᅵ 뚸ᄡᅵ러 돠모와 뫄 마ᄙᅵ부고 마 돠러ᅇᅡ모. 부씨 뒤씨 과 아무 마ᄙᅵ부고 무머ᄕᅥ 마두마 돠아다 어부씨비리시.

3. Not only so, but we also rejoice in our sufferings, because we know that suffering produces perseverance;

4 nobu bushibirishi bu bwende bwatuma twaba bandu ba kuchinyiirwa kanangana. Noku kuchinyiirwa kukwende kwatuma twata emunyiiro.

4 노부 부씨비리씨 부 붜ᄕᅥ 봐두마 돠바 바뚜 바 구찌네이롸 가나ᅇᅡ나. 노구 구찌네이롸 구궈ᄕᅥ 과두마 돠다 어무네이로.

4. perseverance, character; and character, hope.

5 noyu munyiiro atatufuna emchima, bushi Ongo abikire enzii yai mira mwa michima yetu kurengera emchima mubuya-buya ola atweresise.

5 노유 무네이로 아다두푸나 어무찌마, 부씨 오ᅁᅩ 아비기러 어ᄡᅵ이 야이 미라 뫄 미찌마 여두 구러ᅇᅥ라 어무찌마 무부야-부야 오ᄙᅡ 아뚸러시서.

5. And hope does not disappoint us, because God has poured out his love into our hearts by the Holy Spirit, whom he has given us.

6 Bushi kwa bihangi bya Ongo abaa akunganyise mira, na mango twabaa tuchiri tutete chiro na misi eisibya, kirirsito era kufira ebandu be mabi.

6 부씨 과 비하ᅇᅵ 뱌 오ᅁᅩ 아바아 아구ᅇᅡ네서 미라, 나 마ᅁᅩ 돠바아 두찌리 두더더 찌로 나 미시 어이시뱌, 기리시도 어라 구피라 어바뚜 버 마비.

6. You see, at just the right time, when we were still powerless, Christ died for the ungodly.

7 bitula bisibuire kwa mundu kwemerera kufira eunji, chiro angaba mbu oyu unji atungenene. Ngaba mundu angachana kufira eunji ola wende waira emubuya.

8 si Ongo yeke alosise changanama kwa ba bbibi,kirisito era kufa bushi netu.

9 rero kurengera emikra yai, Ongo atuirire kuba bandu ba batungenene. Echera chalosa kanangana kwa Yesu akatununula mango twabaa tuli barenda ba Ongo, era kutuhubya mwa buuma nai kurengera ekufa kwe mwana wai.

10 Rero bushi twera tuli mwa buuma nai, akatununula kurengera ekalamo koyu mwana wai

11 kanji ata ebyera oshao, si twenjire twamoera Ongo kurengera enawetu Yesu kirisito, iwerire watuhubya mwa buuma na Ongo.

Adamu na Yesu Kilyisito

7 비두롸 비시부이러 과 무뚜 궈머러라 구피라 어우찌, 찌로 아까바 뿌 오유 우찌 아두꺼너너. 까바 무뚜 아까짜나 구피라 어우찌 오롸 워떠 와이라 어무부야.

8 시 오꼬 여거 아로시서 짜까나마 과 바 부비비,기리시도 어라 구파 부씨 너두.

9 러로 구러꺼라 어미구라 야이, 오꼬 아두이리러 구바 바뚜 바 바두꺼너너. 어쩌라 짜로사 가나까나 과 여수 아가두누누롸 마꼬 돠바아 두뛰 바러따 바 오꼬, 어라 구두후뱌 마 부우마 나이 구러꺼라 어구파 궈 꽈나 와이.

10 러로 부씨 뛰라 두뛰 마 부우마 나이, 아가두누누롸 구러꺼라 어가꽈모 고유 꽈나 와이

11 가찌 아다 어벼라 오싸오, 시 뛰찌러 돠모어라 오꼬 구러꺼라 어나워두 여수 기리시도, 이워리러 와두후뱌 마 부우마 나 오꼬.

아다무 나 여수 기뤠습명

7. Very rarely will anyone die for a righteous man, though for a good man someone might possibly dare to die.

8. But God demonstrates his own love for us in this: While we were still sinners, Christ died for us.

9. Since we have now been justified by his blood, how much more shall we be saved from God's wrath through him!

10. For if, when we were God's enemies, we were reconciled to him through the death of his Son, how much more, having been reconciled, shall we be saved through his life!

11. Not only is this so, but we also rejoice in God through our Lord Jesus Christ, through whom we have now received reconciliation.

12 Rero, bushi namundu muuma, ebibi byengiriraa mwabutala. Ne bi bibi byera kureta olofu. Mwa bacha, elufu lwaikire kwa bandu boshi, bushi boshi bairire bibi.

13 ebi bibi byabaa byera binatula mwa butala mango Ongo abaa atasa kwersa Musa emwaso*, si bushi emwaso* abaa atasa kuba, Ongo abaa ataholabi.

14 si kutengera ku Adamu kuikira ku Musa, elufu lwendee lwanaikira ebandu boshi. Lwendee lwanaikira ne bandu babatairire bibi, ngokwa Atamu airaa bya Ongo amwanga mbu atairaa. Oyu atamu anabaa ehhuhi lyola wanabaa wemire kubaha.

15 si elwembo lwe buha lwa Ongo ende ana, lutali kuuma nechi chibi cha atamu chiro na hicha. Bandu banene bafa bushi nechi choyu mundu muuma. Si obon jo bwa Ongo bweke bunatula bunene busese. Nolu lwembo lwe buha lweresa bandu bandu benene kurengera mundu muuma, Yesu kirisito, lulwete mufa munene.

12 러로, 부씨 나무뚜 무우마, 어비비 벼ᄢ리리아아 뫄부다ᄙᅡ. 너 비 비비 벼라 구러다 오로루. 마 바짜, 어루푸 ᄙᅪ이기러 과 바뚜 보씨, 부씨 보씨 바이리러 비비.

13 어비 비비 뱌바아 벼라 비나두ᄙᅪ 마 부다ᄙᅡ 마ᄭᅩ 오ᄭᅩ 아바아 아다사 궈루사 무사 어뫄소*, 시 부씨 어뫄소* 아바아 아다사 구바, 오ᄭᅩ 아바아 아다호ᄙᅡ비.

14 시 구더ᄭᅥ라 구 아다무 구이기라 구 무사, 어루푸 뤄떠어 ᄙᅪ나이기라 어바뚜 보씨. 뤄떠어 ᄙᅪ나이기라 너 바뚜 바바다이리러 비비, ᄭᅩ과 아다무 아이라아 뱌 오ᄭᅩ 아뫄ᄭᅡ 뿌 아다이라아. 오유 아다무 아나바아 어후후히 료ᄙᅡ 와나바아 워미러 구바하.

15 시 어뤔모 뤄 부하 ᄙᅪ 오ᄭᅩ 어떠 아나, 루다ᄙᅵ 구우마 너찌 찌비 짜 아다무 찌로 나 히짜. 바뚜 바너너 바파 부씨 너찌 쪼유 무뚜 무우마. 시 오보누 조 봐 오ᄭᅩ 붜거 부나두ᄙᅪ 부너너 부서서. 노루 뤔모 뤄 부하 뤄러사 바뚜 바뚜 버너너 구러ᄭᅥ라 무뚜 무우마, 여수 기리시도, 루뤌더 무파 무너너.

12. Therefore, just as sin entered the world through one man, and death through sin, and in this way death came to all men, because all sinned--

13. for before the law was given, sin was in the world. But sin is not taken into account when there is no law.

14. Nevertheless, death reigned from the time of Adam to the time of Moses, even over those who did not sin by breaking a command, as did Adam, who was a pattern of the one to come.

15. But the gift is not like the trespass. For if the many died by the trespass of the one man, how much more did God's grace and the gift that came by the grace of the one man, Jesus Christ, overflow to the many!

16 kanji olwembo lwa Ongo mutali kuuma nemyasi era yarechibwaa nechibi choyu mundu muuma. Bushi echibi chai chichatuma ebandu baishirwa elubanja mbu bachinjibusibwaa. Si elwembo lwebuha lwa Ongo ende ana lu lwerire lwatuma ebandu batunagnana era mundo sai, chiro chiro angaba mbu emabi mabo mali manene.

17 kubinali, elufu lwataa ebuashi kwa bandu kurengera mundu muuma, bushi nemabi moyu mundu muuma. Si kanji kurengera mundu muuma, Yesu kirisito, ebandu bende babona bindu binene kutenga era mwa Ongo. Ende afirabo bonjo bunene, na kubatola nga babatungenene. Kanji kurengera oyu mundu muuma, yesu kirisito, bakaata ekalamo na kwima.

18 rero ngokwa chibi cha mundu muuma, atamu chatumaa ebandu boshi bachinjibusibwaa, kunoku ku emulimo ola ebandu boshi utungenene wa mundu muuma, Yesu kirisito, atumire ebandu boshi batangaaena era muhondo sa Ongo na

16 가찌 오뤄뗀 롸 오꼬 무다뤼 구우마 너먀시 어라 야러찌봐아 너찌비 쪼유 무뚜 무우마. 부씨 어찌비 짜이 찌짜두마 어바뚜 바이씨롸 어루바짜 뿌 바찌띠부시봐아. 시 어뤄뗀 뤄부하 롸 오꼬 어떠 아나 루 뤄리러 롸두마 어바뚜 바두나구나나 어라 무또 사이, 찌로 찌로 아꺼바 뿌 어마비 마보 마뛰 마너너.

17 구비나뤼, 어루푸 롸다아 어부아씨 과 바뚜 구러꺼라 무뚜 무우마, 부씨 너마비 모유 무뚜 무우마. 시 가찌 구러꺼라 무뚜 무우마, 여수 기리시도, 어바뚜 버떠 바보나 비뚜 비너너 구더꺼 어라 롸 오꼬. 어떠 아피라보 보쪼 부너너, 나 구바도롸 꺼 바바두꺼너너. 가찌 구러꺼라 오유 무뚜 무우마, 여수 기리시도, 바가아다 어가롸모 나 귀마.

18 러로 꼬과 찌비 짜 무뚜 무우마, 아다무 짜두마아 어바뚜 보씨 바찌띠부시봐아, 구노구 구 어무뛰모 오롸 어바뚜 보씨 우두꺼너너 와 무뚜 무우마, 여수 기리시도, 아두미러 어바뚜 보씨 바다꺼아어나 어라 무호또 사 오꼬 나 구보나 어가롸모.

16. Again, the gift of God is not like the result of the one man's sin: The judgment followed one sin and brought condemnation, but the gift followed many trespasses and brought justification.

17. For if, by the trespass of the one man, death reigned through that one man, how much more will those who receive God's abundant provision of grace and of the gift of righteousness reign in life through the one man, Jesus Christ.

18. Consequently, just as the result of one trespass was condemnation for all men, so also the result of one act of righteousness was justification that brings life for all men.

kubona ekalamo.

19 na kukulikana nokwa mundu muuma, atamu, iwananaakuira kwa Ongo atechiri, bandu banene berire baba bandu ba bibi. Kunoku, kukulikana na mundu muuma, Yesu kiristo, iwairaa kwa Ongo atechire, bandu banene bakere baanjibwa nga ba batungenene era muhondo sa Ongo.

20 emwaso* aikaa, era kutuma emabi maluwa. Si ala bibi byabaa byaendekera byaluwa, ebonjo bwa Ongo nabo bwera kunaendekera bwaluwa busese.

21 rero, kukulikana nokwa bibi byabaa byete ebuashi bwekwita, kunoku ku ebonjo bwa Ongo butusa ebuashi bwe kuira ebandu kuba ba batunganene, na kutweresa ekalamo kesuku nemango kuregera enawetu Yesu kirirsito.

19 나 구구끠가나 노과 무뚜 무우마, 아다무, 이와나나아구이라 과 오꼬 아더찌리, 바뚜 바너너 버리러 바바 바뚜 바 비비. 구노구, 구구끠가나 나 무뚜 무우마, 여수 기리시도, 이와이라아 과 오꼬 아더찌러, 바뚜 바너너 바거러 바아찌봐 까 바 바두꺼너너 어라 무호또 사 오꼬.

20 어뫄소* 아이가아, 어라 구두마 어마비 마루와. 시 아꽈 비비 뱌바아 뱌어꺼거라 뱌루와, 어보쪼 봐 오꼬 나보 뭐라 구나어꺼거라 봐루와 부서서.

21 러로, 구구끠가나 노과 비비 뱌바아 뼈더 어부아씨 뭐귀다, 구노구 구 어보쪼 봐 오꼬 부두사 어부아씨 뭐 구이라 어바뚜 구바 바 바두꺼너너, 나 구뛰러사 어가꽈모 거수구 너마꼬 구러거라 어나워두 여수 기리시도.

19. For just as through the disobedience of the one man the many were made sinners, so also through the obedience of the one man the many will be made righteous.

20. The law was added so that the trespass might increase. But where sin increased, grace increased all the more,

21. so that, just as sin reigned in death, so also grace might reign through righteousness to bring eternal life through Jesus Christ our Lord.

Ba Roma Chikono 6
Ekufa ne kuba muuma-uma alauma na kirisito

바 로마 찌고노 6
어구파 너 구바 무우마-우마 아꽈윰맆 나 기리시도

Rome Chapter 6[NIV]

1 Rero, chi tuteta? tuendekeraa kuba mwa bibi chasiya ebonjo bwa Ongo buendekera bwaluwa?

2 nanga chiro na hicha! mwa myasi era yekere ebibi, tubano tuli nga babafiri mira. Rero kute tungahuba kanji kuba mwa bibi?

3 si mwishi kanangana kwa tuboshi twabatisibwaa, chasibuya tube mwa buuma na Yesu kirisito. Namwoku kubatisibwa, twera kwire twabaa mwa buuma nai kurengera olufu lwai.

4 rero mwa kubatisibwa, twabaa ngaba bafire na kutabwa alauma nai, chasiya ngokwa kirisito* omwolibwa mwa bafu kwa buashi bwengulu ya Tata, netu kunoku tuate kalamo kayayaya.

5 akaba twabaa mwa buuma nai kurengera ekufa ngokwa nai afaa, kunoku ku kutukaba mwa buuma nai kurengera ekwomolibwa ngokwa nai omwolibwaa.

6 twishi kwemibere yetu yokwa mira yamanyikibwaa kwa mmusalaba alauma na kirisito*. Mwa bacha, ei mibere ye bibi yahandulibwe,

---

1 러로, 찌 두더다?
두어떠거라아 구바 뫄 비비
짜시야 어보쪼 봐 오꼬
부어떠거라 봐루와?

2 나꼬 찌로 나 히짜! 뫄 먀시
어라 여거러 어비비, 두바노
두뤼 꽈 바바피리 미라. 러로
구더 두꽈후바 가찌 구바 뫄
비비?

3 시 뮈씨 가나꽈나 과 두보씨
돠바디시봐아, 짜시부야 두버
뫄 부우마 나 여수 기리시도.
나모구 구바디시봐, 뛰라 귀러
돠바아 뫄 부우마 나이
구러꺼라 오루푸 꽈이.

4 러로 뫄 구바디시봐, 돠바아
꽈바 바피러 나 구다봐
아꽈우마 나이, 짜시야 꼬과
기리시도* 오모뤼봐 뫄 바푸
과 부아씨 뭐우루 야 다다,
너두 구노구 두아더 가꽈모
가야야야.

5 아가바 돠바아 뫄 부우마
나이 구러꺼라 어구파 꼬과
나이 아파아, 구노구 구
구두가바 뫄 부우마 나이
구러꺼라 어고모뤼봐 꼬과
나이 오모뤼봐아.

6 뒤씨 궈미버러 여두 요과
미라 야마네기봐아 과
무무사꽈바 아꽈우마 나
기리시도*. 뫄 바짜, 어이
미버러 여 비비 야하누뤼붜,

---

1. What shall we say, then? Shall we go on sinning so that grace may increase?

2. By no means! We died to sin; how can we live in it any longer?

3. Or don't you know that all of us who were baptized into Christ Jesus were baptized into his death?

4. We were therefore buried with him through baptism into death in order that, just as Christ was raised from the dead through the glory of the Father, we too may live a new life.

5. If we have been united with him like this in his death, we will certainly also be united with him in his resurrection.

6. For we know that our old self was crucified with him so that the body of sin might be done away with, that we should no longer be

chasiya tutachibaa tuungu* twebibi.

7 bushi emundu akafa, ende abona ebuhuru bwekutenga mwa bibi.

8 rero, akaba twafire alauma na kirisito*, twete ebwemeresi kwa netu tukaata ekalamo alauma nai.

9 twishi kwa kirisito*, omokire mira, atakanachife, ne lufu lutachete buashi era luulu sai.

10 mwa kufa, afaa euma oshao kwa kuhandula ebusahi bwebibi. Rero era ali muuma-uma, bushi na Ongo.

11 nenyu kunoku: mwa mmyasi era yekere ebibi, mundaa mwachitola nga ba bafire, kanji nga ba bali bauma-uma bushi na Ongo, kure,gera ebuuma bwenyu na Yesu kirisito.

12 rero, mutachemerera ebibi kunde byaata buashi kwa mubiri wenyu wekufa, mwa kunde mwalukira ebuhuma-uma bwai bubi.

13 mutenda mwana ebitera byelubiri wenyu kwa kuira ebibi, mwa kubikoresa nga bindu bya kuira mabi. Si mundaa mwachana mubeine

짜시야 두다찌바아 두우꾸* 뚸비비.

7 부씨 어무뚜 아가파, 어더 아보나 어부후루 붜구더까 뫄 비비.

8 러로, 아가바 돠피러 아꽈우마 나 기리시도*, 뚸더 어붜머러시 과 너두 두가아다 어가꽈모 아꽈우마 나이.

9 뒤씨 과 기리시도*, 오모기러 미라, 아다가나찌퍼, 너 루푸 루다쩌더 부아씨 어라 루우루 사이.

10 뫄 구파, 아파아 어우마 오싸오 과 구하두꽈 어부사히 뷔비비. 러로 어라 아꾀 무우마-우마, 부씨 나 오꼬.

11 너뉴 구노구: 뫄 무먀시 어라 여거러 어비비, 무따아 꽈찌도꽈 까 바 바피러, 가찌 까 바 바꾀 바우마-우마 부씨 나 오꼬, 구러,거라 어부우마 뷔뉴 나 여수 기리시도.

12 러로, 무다쩌머러라 어비비 구더 뱌아다 부아씨 과 무비리 워뉴 워구파, 뫄 구더 꽈루기라 어부후마-우마 봐이 부비.

13 무더따 뫄나 어비더라 뼈루비리 워뉴 과 구이라 어비비, 뫄 구비고러사 까 비뚜 뱌 구이라 마비. 시 무따아 꽈짜나 무버이너 과

slaves to sin--

7. because anyone who has died has been freed from sin.

8. Now if we died with Christ, we believe that we will also live with him.

9. For we know that since Christ was raised from the dead, he cannot die again; death no longer has mastery over him.

10. The death he died, he died to sin once for all; but the life he lives, he lives to God.

11. In the same way, count yourselves dead to sin but alive to God in Christ Jesus.

12. Therefore do not let sin reign in your mortal body so that you obey its evil desires.

13. Do not offer the parts of your body to sin, as instruments of wickedness, but rather offer yourselves to God, as those who have

kwa kukorera Ongo nga bandu ba bomolibwe, mwa kunde mwakoresa ebitera bye mubiri wenyu nga bindu bya kuira myasi era itungenene.

14 ebibi bitaendaa byachiaata buashi era luulu enyu, bushi mutachiri era bufuli se mwaso*, si mwera muli era bufuli se bonjo bwa Ongo.

Ekuira emyasi era itchwungenene

15 Chiye chi tutetaa kasi? tuendekeraa kunde twaira ebibi bushi tutachiri era bufuli se mwaso*, si era bufuli se bonjo bwa Ongo? nanga chiro na hicha!

16 mwshi kanangana kwa mango mwende mwachana kwa kukorera mundu murebe nga tuung, twai, mwende mwaira ngokwa atechire. Aola mwande mwanaba kanangana tuungu* twai. Rero akaba mungaba tuungu* twebibi, ebusinda lunali lufu. Si akaba mungendi mwaira ngokwa Ongo atechire, ebusinda kunali kwata mubere era itunganene.

구고러라 오꼬 꺄 바뚜 바 보모뤼붜, 꽈 구떠 꽈고러사 어비더라 벼 무비리 워뉴 꺄 비뚜 뱌 구이라 먀시 어라 이두꺼너너.

14 어비비 비다어따아 뱌찌아아다 부아씨 어라 루우루루 어뉴, 부씨 무다찌리 어라 부푸뤼 서 꽈소*, 시 뭐라 무뤼 어라 부푸뤼 서 보쪼 봐 오꼬.

어구이라 어먀시 어라 이쭈꺼날날

15 찌여 찌 두더다아 가시? 두어떠거라아 구떠 돠이라 어비비 부씨 두다찌리 어라 부푸뤼 서 꽈소*, 시 어라 부푸뤼 서 보쪼 봐 오꼬? 나꽈 찌로 나 히짜!

16 무씨 가나꽈나 과 마꼬 뭐떠 꽈짜나 과 구고러라 무뚜 무러버 꺄 두우꾸, 돠이, 뭐떠 꽈이라 꼬과 아더찌러. 아오꽈 돠이. 러로 아가바 무꽈바 두우꾸* 뚸비비, 어부시따 루뤼 루푸. 시 아가바 무꺼띠 꽈이라 꼬과 오꼬 아더찌러, 어부시따 구나뤼 과다 무버러 어라 이두꺼너너.

been brought from death to life; and offer the parts of your body to him as instruments of righteousness.

14. For sin shall not be your master, because you are not under law, but under grace.

15. What then? Shall we sin because we are not under law but under grace? By no means!

16. Don't you know that when you offer yourselves to someone to obey him as slaves, you are slaves to the one whom you obey-- whether you are slaves to sin, which leads to death, or to obedience, which leads to righteousness?

17 Kweine Ongo atongwe bushi mwabaa mwa bucha bwe byaa mwera kuna tehwunda mwa michima yenyu bwenge bwa mwabaa munabikirwemo era masina sabo.

18 Abere mwa bolyibwa ne kubikibwa bure ne byaa mwera kuba mwa bucha bwe kanangana (mabuya).

19 nahambala nenyu nga mundu bushi nyishi ekuina emisi kwenyu. Kwa mira mwendee mwachana busese nga tuungu*mwakwende mwakorera ebitera byenyu kwakuira emyasi era yende yabaka esinga, nakuira emabi. Ebi byoshi, bibyendee byatuma mwaata mibere era itasimise Ongo. Kunoku ku mwiraa mwende mwachana kuba tuungu* mwa kunde mwaira emyasi era itungenene, chasiya emibere yenyu inde yasimisa Ongo.

20 mango twabaa muchiri tuungu* twebibi, ekuira emyasi era itungenene kwabaa kutaberekere.

21 rero, mutoloke muchiye mwendee mwabona mwa kuira emyasi era yera yabeta honyi lwarero? bushi

---

17 궈이너 오꼬 아도워 부씨 먀바아 와 부짜 붜 뱌아 뭐라 구나 더후웊따 와 미찌마 여뉴 붜꺼 봐 먀바아 무나비기뤄모 어라 마시나 사보.

18 아버러 와 보꼐봐 너 구비기봐 부러 너 뱌아 뭐라 구바 와 부짜 붜 가나꺄나 (마부야).

19 나하빠랴 너뉴 꺄 무뚜 부씨 네씨 어구이나 어미시 궈뉴. 과 미라 뭐떠어 먀짜나 부서서 꺄 두우꾸*먀궈떠 마고러라 어비더라 벼뉴 과구이라 어먀시 어라 여떠 야바가 어시꺄, 나구이라 어마비. 어비 뵤씨, 비벼떠어 뱌두마 먀아다 미버러 어라 이다시미서 오꼬. 구노구 구 뮈라아 뭐떠 먀짜나 구바 두우꾸* 와 구떠 먀이라 어먀시 어라 이두꺼너너, 짜시야 어미버러 여뉴 이떠 야시미사 오꼬.

20 마꼬 돠바아 무찌리 두우꾸* 뚸비비, 어구이라 어먀시 어라 이두꺼너너 과바아 구다버러거러.

21 러로, 무도뤈거 무찌여 뭐떠어 먀보나 와 구이라 어먀시 어라 여라 야버다 호네 꽈러로? 부씨 어부시따 붜이

---

17. But thanks be to God that, though you used to be slaves to sin, you wholeheartedly obeyed the form of teaching to which you were entrusted.

18. You have been set free from sin and have become slaves to righteousness.

19. I put this in human terms because you are weak in your natural selves. Just as you used to offer the parts of your body in slavery to impurity and to ever-increasing wickedness, so now offer them in slavery to righteousness leading to holiness.

20. When you were slaves to sin, you were free from the control of righteousness.

21. What benefit did you reap at that time from the things you are now ashamed of? Those things

ebusinda bwei myasi luli
elufu!

먀시 루ᄙᅵ 어루푸!

result in death!

22 si rero mwerire mwatenga
mwa bucha bwebibi, mwera
muli tuungu* twa Ongo.
Mwera mwete emutoloke
wekuata mibere era isimise
Ongo. Nokwa businda,
mukabona ekalamo kesuku
nemango.

22 시 러로 뭐리러 뫄더ᅁᅡ 뫄
부짜 붜비비, 뭐라 무ᄙᅵ
두우ᅁᅮ* 돠 오ᅁᅩ. 뭐라 뭐더
어무도ᄙᅩ거 워구아다 미버러
어라 이시미서 오ᅁᅩ. 노과
부시따, 무가보나 어가ᄙᅡ모
거수구 너마ᅁᅩ.

22. But now that you have
been set free from sin and
have become slaves to God,
the benefit you reap leads
to holiness, and the result is
eternal life.

23 bushi emukosi we bibi
ende alipibwa elufu. Si
emuholore ola Ongo ende
ana yeke, kali ekalamo
kesuku ne mango kurengera
ebuuma bwetu na enawetu
Yesu kirisito.

23 부씨 어무고시 워 비비
어떠 아ᄙᅵ피봐 어루푸. 시
어무호ᄙᅩ러 오ᄙᅡ 오ᅁᅩ 어떠
아나 여거, 가ᄙᅵ 어가ᄙᅡ모
거수구 너 마ᅁᅩ 구러ᅁᅥ라
어부우마 붜두 나 어나워두
여수 기리시도.

23. For the wages of sin is
death, but the gift of God is
eternal life in Christ Jesus
our Lord.

Ba Roma Chikono 7

*Ebemeresi batengire mwa
bucha bw'e mwaso wa
Musa*

바 로마 찌고노 7

*어버머러시 바더ᅁᅵ랸 뫄 부짜
붜 뫄소 와 무사*

Rome Chapter 7[NIV]

1 Banyaketu, oku mutula
mwishi emwaso*, ene myasi
nahonda kubabura, muishi
kubuya-buya. Emwaso* atusa
ebuashi kwa mundu mango
mundu achirio.

1 바냐거두, 오구 무두ᄙᅡ 뮈씨
어뫄소*, 어너 먀시 나호따
구바부라, 무이씨 구부야-부야.
어뫄소* 아두사 어부아씨 과
무뚜 마ᅁᅩ 무뚜 아찌리오.

1. Do you not know,
brothers--for I am speaking
to men who know the law--
that the law has authority
over a man only as long as
he lives?

2 binali kuuma ne mukasi ola
uhwesibwe: oyu mukasi,
emwaso ende aba
amuminyirire kweba mango
oyu eba achirio. Si akaba oyu

2 비나ᄙᅵ 구우마 너 무가시
오ᄙᅡ 우훠시붜: 오유 무가시,
어뫄소 어떠 아바
아무미녜리러 궈바 마ᅁᅩ 오유
어바 아찌리오. 시 아가바

2. For example, by law a
married woman is bound to
her husband as long as he
is alive, but if her husband
dies, she is released from

eba angafa, wamukasi anatenga era bufuli soyu mwaso wabaa umunyirire kweba.

3 rero akaba oyu mukasi angatolibwa na unji mulume mango eba achirio, anerikibwa musingisi. Si akaba eba angafa, oyu mukasi anatenga era bufuli soyu mwaso. Na akaba era angatolibwa na unji mulume angacherikibwa musingisi.

4 nenyu banyeketu, kubinali bacha ku mwabo. Kukulikana ne myasi era yekere emwaso* wa Musa, mwera muli nga bafiri mira, bushi mwabere mwa buuma ne mubuiri wa kirisito iwafaa. Mwerire mwatolibwa na unji mundu. Noyu mundu iwomokaa mwa bafu, chasiya tunde twaira bya bisimise Ongo.

5 bushi manho twabaa tuchiri twende twaira ekuhonda kwemubiri, emwaso*wamusa ende asusa mwa ndanda setu emianyisa yekuira ebibi. Nei mianyisa ibi, era yende yakola mwa ndanda setu iyatureteraa elufu.

6 si rero twatengire mwa bucha bwoyu mwaso*, bushi kukulikana bemyasi era yabaa

오유 어바 아ᄴ파, 와무가시 아나더ᄽ 어라 부푸리 소유 ᄁ소 와바아 우무네리러 궈바.

3 러로 아가바 오유 무가시 아ᄴ도리봐 나 우찌 무루머 마ᄁ 어바 아찌리오, 아너리기봐 무시ᄞ시. 시 아가바 어바 아ᄴ파, 오유 무가시 아나더ᄽ 어라 부푸리 소유 ᄁ소. 나 아가바 어라 아ᄴ도리봐 나 우찌 무루머 아ᄴ쩌리기봐 무시ᄞ시.

4 너뉴 바녀거두, 구비나리 바짜 구 ᄁ보. 구구ᄈ가나 너 ᄝ시 어라 여거러 어ᄁ소* 와 무사, ᄆ라 무ᄈ ᄽ 바피리 미라, 부씨 ᄁ버러 와 부우마 너 무부이리 와 기리시도 이와파아. ᄆ리러 ᄁ도리봐 나 우찌 무뚜. 노유 무뚜 이오모가아 와 바푸, 짜시야 두ᄄ 돠이라 뱌 비시미서 오ᄁ.

5 부씨 마누호 돠바아 두찌리 ᄆᄄ 돠이라 어구호ᄽ 궈무비리, 어ᄁ소*와무사 어ᄃ 아수사 와 ᄄᄄ 서두 어미아네사 여구이라 어비비. 너이 미아네사 이비, 어라 여ᄃ 야고롸 와 ᄄᄄ 서두 이야두러더라아 어루푸.

6 시 러로 돠더ᄞ러 와 부짜 보유 ᄁ소*, 부씨 구구ᄈ가나 버ᄝ시 어라 야바아

the law of marriage.

3. So then, if she marries another man while her husband is still alive, she is called an adulteress. But if her husband dies, she is released from that law and is not an adulteress, even though she marries another man.

4. So, my brothers, you also died to the law through the body of Christ, that you might belong to another, to him who was raised from the dead, in order that we might bear fruit to God.

5. For when we were controlled by the sinful nature, the sinful passions aroused by the law were at work in our bodies, so that we bore fruit for death.

6. But now, by dying to what once bound us, we have been released from the

ituminyire, twera tuli nga ba bafire. Mwa bacha, twera tungakorera Ongo mwa kukulikira enjira iyayaya, era yakoresibwa ne muchima mubuya-buya, si atachiri mwa kukulikira enjira yokwa mira era yakoresibwa nemyasi era yanjikirwe mwa mwaso*.

EMwaso wa Musa ne bibi

7 Chi twairaavtwatetavkasi? emwaso* wa Musa biri bibi? nanga chiro na hicha! si ndangamenyire ebibi chiri chiye, akaba emwaso* atangabere. Kanji ndangamenyire ebuhuma-huma chiri chiye akaba emwaso* atangatechire mbu: Utendaa wahumira ebyabene.

8 ebibi byabonaa enjira kurengera emuomba*, kwa kususa chira buhuma-huma mwa mchima wanyi. Bushi akaba emwaso* atangabere, ebibibingabere bifire.

9 kwa mira, mango nabaa ndasa kumenya emwaso*, nabaa nyiri muuma-uma. Si mango emuomba* aikaa, ebibi byera kulorekanako,

10 nanyi nera kunafa. Aola, emuomba* ola wabaa unganyiretere ekalamo, era kwire anyiretere elufu.

이두미네러, 뛰라 두뀌 까 바 바피러. 먀 바짜, 뛰라 두꽈고러라 오꼬 먀 구구뀌기라 어찌라 이야야야, 어라 야고러시봐 너 무찌마 무부야-부야, 시 아다찌리 꽈 구구뀌기라 어찌라 요꽈 미라 어라 야고러시봐 너먀시 어라 야찌기뤄 먀 먀소*.

어꽈소 와 무사 너 비비

7 찌 돠이라아부돠더더다부가시? 어꽈소* 와 무사 비리 비비? 나꽈 찌로 나 히짜! 시 따까머니러 어비비 찌리 찌여, 아가바 어꽈소* 아다까버러. 가찌 따까머니러 어부후마-후마 찌리 찌여 아가바 어꽈소* 아다꽈더찌러 뿌: 우더따아 와후미라 어뱌버너.

8 어비비 뱌보나아 어찌라 구러꿔라 어무오빠*, 과 구수사 찌라 부후마-후마 꽈 무찌마 와니. 부씨 아가바 어꽈소* 아다까버러, 어비비비까버러 비피러.

9 과 미라, 마꼬 나바아 따사 구머냐 어꽈소*, 나바아 니리 무우마-우마. 시 마꼬 어무오빠* 아이가아, 어비비 뼈라 구뢰러가나고,

10 나니 너라 구나파. 아오꽈, 어무오빠* 오꽈 와바아 우까네러더러 어가꽈모, 어라 귀러 아니러더러 어루푸.

law so that we serve in the new way of the Spirit, and not in the old way of the written code.

7. What shall we say, then? Is the law sin? Certainly not! Indeed I would not have known what sin was except through the law. For I would not have known what coveting really was if the law had not said, "Do not covet."

8. But sin, seizing the opportunity afforded by the commandment, produced in me every kind of covetous desire. For apart from law, sin is dead.

9. Once I was alive apart from law; but when the commandment came, sin sprang to life and I died.

10. I found that the very commandment that was intended to bring life actually brought death.

11 bushi kurengera oyu muomba* inoyu, ebibi byabonaa enira yekunyengeera, nekunyita.

12 kubinali, emwaso* atula mubuya-buya. Ne muomba* nao anatula mubuya-buya, kanji atula atungenene, kanji atula mubuya.

13 rero, echibindu chibuya chi cherire chanyiretera elufu? nanga chiro na hicha! ebibi bi byanyiretere elufu. Mwabacha, byerire byanalorekako kwa binali bibi kanangana, mwa kurengera kwa chindu chibuya kwa kunyiretera elufu. Rero, kurengera emuomba*, ebibi byachilosise kwa binali bibi busese.

Emabi mende malwisa emabuya mwa muchima w'e mundju

14 Twishi kwe mwaso* iri myasi ya mchima, si nyono nyinali mundu wa mubiri, bushi nausibwe mira chasiya nyibe kaungu* kebibii.

15 kubinali, bya nende naira ndabishi. Bushi bya nende nahonda kuira, ata bi nende naira. Si bya nyitula nyiayire,

11 부씨 구러꺼라 오유 무오빠* 이노유, 어비비 뱌보나아 어니라 여구녀꺼어라, 너구네다.

12 구비나삐, 어꽈소* 아두꽈 무부야-부야. 너 무오빠* 나오 아나두꽈 무부야-부야, 가찌 아두꽈 아두꺼너너, 가찌 아두꽈 무부야.

13 러로, 어찌비뚜 찌부야 찌 쩌리러 쨔네러더라 어루푸? 나꽈 찌로 나 히짜! 어비비 비 뱌네러더라 어루푸. 마바짜, 벼리러 뱌나로러가고 과 비나삐 비비 가나꽈나, 마 구러꺼라 과 찌뚜 찌부야 과 구네러더라 어루푸. 러로, 구러꺼라 어무오빠*, 어비비 뱌찌로시서 과 비나삐 비비 부서서.

어마비 머너 마뤼쁩 어마부야 와 무찌마 워 무뚜

14 뒤씨 궈 꽈소* 이리 먀시 야 무찌마, 시 뇨노 니나삐 무뚜 와 무비리, 부씨 나우시붜 미라 쨔시야 네버 가우우* 거비비이.

15 구비나삐, 뱌 너떠 나이라 따비씨. 부씨 뱌 너떠 나호따 구이라, 아다 비 너떠 나이라. 시 뱌 니두꽈 네아에러, 비떠

11. For sin, seizing the opportunity afforded by the commandment, deceived me, and through the commandment put me to death.

12. So then, the law is holy, and the commandment is holy, righteous and good.

13. Did that which is good, then, become death to me? By no means! But in order that sin might be recognized as sin, it produced death in me through what was good, so that through the commandment sin might become utterly sinful.

14. We know that the law is spiritual; but I am unspiritual, sold as a slave to sin.

15. I do not understand what I do. For what I want to do I do not do, but what I hate I do.

binde naira.

나이라.

16 na akaba bya nyitula nyiayire bi nende naira, echera chilosise kwa nemere kwa mwaso* atula mubuya.

16 나 아가바 뱌 네두롸 네아에러 비 너머 나이라, 어쩌라 찌로시서 과 너머러 과 뫄소* 아두롸 무부야.

16. And if I do what I do not want to do, I agree that the law is good.

17 rero, atechire nyono nyi nende naira ebyera, si ebibi bya bitula mwa ndanda sanyi nyinachiberere mundu wa mubiri oshao.

17 러로, 아더찌러 뇨노 네 너머 나이라 어벼라, 시 어비비 뱌 비두롸 뫄 따따 사니 네나찌버러러 무뚜 와 무비리 오쌰오.

17. As it is, it is no longer I myself who do it, but it is sin living in me.

18 Kubinali bacha, bushi nyitusa emchima wekuhonda kuira emabuya, si ndaala kuiramo.

18 구비나릐 바쨔, 부씨 네두사 어무찌마 워구호롸 구이라 어마부야, 시 따아롸 구이라모.

18. I know that nothing good lives in me, that is, in my sinful nature. For I have the desire to do what is good, but I cannot carry it out.

19 bushi emabuya ma nende nahonda kuira, atamunende naira. Si emabi ma ndahonda kuira , munende naira.

19 부씨 어마부야 마 너머 나호롸 구이라, 아다무너머 나이라. 시 어마비 마 따호롸 구이라 , 무너머 나이라.

19. For what I do is not the good I want to do; no, the evil I do not want to do-- this I keep on doing.

20 rero, akaba nende naira bya bitula mwa ndanda sanyi bi byende byairabi.

20 러로, 아가바 너머 나이라 뱌 비두롸 뫄 따따 사니 비 벼머 뱌이라비.

20. Now if I do what I do not want to do, it is no longer I who do it, but it is sin living in me that does it.

21 chechine chi nerire namenyerera kanangana: mango nahonda kuira emabuya, unao-unao nanachichingira nairire emabi.

21 쩌찌너 찌 너리러 나머녀러라 가나껑나: 마꼬 나호롸 구이라 어마부야, 우나오-우나오 나나찌찌끠라 나이리러 어마비.

21. So I find this law at work: When I want to do good, evil is right there with me.

22 si nyisene kwa mwa mubiri wanyi mutula unji mwaso ola wende walwisa

22 시 네서너 과 뫄 무비리 와니 무두롸 우찌 뫄소 오라 워뗘 와뤠사 어뫄소* 오롸

22. For in my inner being I delight in God's law;

emwaso* ola nyitula nyisimire.

네두퐈 네시미러.

23 Noyu mwaso anyirire kuba mundu wa mulisi we mwaso we bibi ola wende wakola mwa ndanda sanyi.

23 노유 먀소 아네리러 구바 무뚜 와 무삐시 워 먀소 워 비비 오퐈 워떠 와고퐈 먀 따따 사네.

23. but I see another law at work in the members of my body, waging war against the law of my mind and making me a prisoner of the law of sin at work within my members.

24 nyono nyiri mwanya! nde iukanyinunula kutenga mwono mubiri we kunyeka mwa lufu?

24 뇨노 네리 먀냐! 떠 이우가네누누퐈 구더따 모노 무비리 워 구녀가 먀 루푸?

24. What a wretched man I am! Who will rescue me from this body of death?

25 Ongo atognwe kurengera enawetu Yesu kirisito! rero, kurengeresa ebwenge bwanyi, byiri kaungu* ke mwaso*wa Ongo. Si kanji bushi nyinali mundu wa mubiri, nyiri kaungu*ke mwaso webibi.

25 오꼬 아도구누워 구러떠라 어나워두 여수 기리시도! 러로, 구러떠러사 어붸떠 봐네, 베리 가우꾸* 거 먀소*와 오꼬. 시 가찌 부씨 네나삐 무뚜 와 무비리, 네리 가우꾸*거 먀소 워비비.

25. Thanks be to God-- through Jesus Christ our Lord! So then, I myself in my mind am a slave to God's law, but in the sinful nature a slave to the law of sin.

Ba Roma Chikono 8
Ekukoresibwa n'e mchima Mubuya-buya

바 로마 찌고노 8
어구고러시봐 너 무찌마 무부야-부야

Rome Chapter 8[NIV]

1 Bushi noku, rero kutachiri buchinjibusi busibya kwa bandu ba bali mwa buuma na Yesu kirisito.

1 부씨 노구, 러로 구다찌리 부찌띠부시 부시뱌 과 바뚜 바 바삐 먀 부우마 나 여수 기리시도.

1. Therefore, there is now no condemnation for those who are in Christ Jesus,

2 bushi emwaso we muchima Mubuya-buya iwende wana ekalamo kwa bandu ba bali mwa buuma na Yesu kirirsito.

2 부씨 어먀소 워 무찌마 무부야-부야 이워떠 와나 어가퐈모 과 바뚜 바 바삐 먀 부우마 나 여수 기리시도.

2. because through Christ Jesus the law of the Spirit of life set me free from the law of sin and death.

Oyu mwaso, akukulikre mwa bucha bwe mwaso webibi nelufu.

오유 마소, 아구구꾀구러 뫄 부짜 붜 마소 워비비 너루푸.

3 emwaso* wa Musa ataala kuira echera bushi nekuima emisi kwemundu. Si Ongo yeke airaachi: atuma emwana wai ahube mundu nga tubano tu bandu bebibi, chasiya atununule mwabibi. Mwei njira mu Ongo achinjibusaa ebibi bya byende byakola mwa bandu.

3 어마소* 와 무사 아다아꽈 구이라 어쩌라 부씨 너구이마 어미시 궈무뚜. 시 오꼬 여거 아이라아찌: 아두마 어뫄나 와이 아후버 무뚜 까 두바노 두 바뚜 버비비, 짜시야 아두누누꿔 뫄비비. 뭐이 끼라 무 오꼬 아찌끼부사아 어비비 뱌 벼너 뱌고꽈 뫄 바뚜.

3. For what the law was powerless to do in that it was weakened by the sinful nature, God did by sending his own Son in the likeness of sinful man to be a sin offering. And so he condemned sin in sinful man,

4 mwa bacha, chira mwasi woshi ola oyu mwaso* abaa ahonda, era kwire aberera mwa ndanda setu. Kanji tutachikoresibwa nemyasi yemubiri, si twera twende twakoresibwa ne Muchima Mubuya-buya.

4 뫄 바짜, 찌라 뫄시 오씨 오꽈 오유 마소* 아바아 아호따, 어라 귀러 아버러라 뫄 따따 서두. 가찌 두다찌고러시봐 너먀시 여무비리, 시 뚸라 뚸너 똬고러시봐 너 무찌마 무부야-부야.

4. in order that the righteous requirements of the law might be fully met in us, who do not live according to the sinful nature but according to the Spirit.

5 bushi ba bende bakoresibwa ne myasi ye mubiri, emyanyisa yabu inachitula kwa myasi ye mubiri. Si ba bende bakoresibwa ne mchima mubuya-buya, beke emyanyisa yabo itula kwa myasi ye mchima mubuya-buya.

5 부씨 바 버너 바고러시봐 너 먀시 여 무비리, 어먀네사 야부 이나찌두꽈 과 먀시 여 무비리. 시 바 버너 바고러시봐 너 무찌마 무부야-부야, 버거 어먀네사 야보 이두꽈 과 먀시 여 무찌마 무부야-부야.

5. Those who live according to the sinful nature have their minds set on what that nature desires; but those who live in accordance with the Spirit have their minds set on what the Spirit desires.

6 ekubika emyanyisa kwa myasi yemubiri, kwende kwareta elufu. Si ekubika emyanyisa kwa myasi ye mchima mubuya-buya, kweke kwende kwareta ekalamo ne bolo.

7 bushi ba bende babika emyanyisa kwa myanyisa ye mubiri, batula barenda ba Ongo. Bataira kwa mwaso* wa Ongo atula atechire, batanganaala kuirako chiro na hicha.

8 ebandu ba bende bakulikira emyasi ye mubiri, batangaala kusimisa Ongo.

9 si mwabo, mutachikulikira emyasi ye mubiri, si mwera mwende mwakulikira emyasi ye mchima wa Ongo, akaba oyu mchima wai ali mwa ndanda senyu. Na akaba mundu atete emchima wa kirisito* mwa ndanda sai, oyola ata mundu wa kirisito*

10 si akaba kirisito* ali mwa ndanda senyu chiro angaba mbu emubiri wenyu akafa bushi ne bibi, si emchima mubuya-buya akaberesa ekalamo, bushi Ongo abairire kuba bandu ba batungenene.

6 어구비가 어먀네사 과 먀시 여무비리, 궈떠 과러다 어루푸. 시 어구비가 어먀네사 과 먀시 여 무찌마 무부야-부야, 궈거 과러다 어가꽈모 너 보론.

7 부씨 바 버떠 바비가 어먀네사 과 먀네사 여 무비리, 바두꽈 바러따 바 오꼬. 바다이라 과 마소* 와 오꼬 아두꽈 아더찌러, 바다꺼나아꽈 구이라고 찌로 나 히짜.

8 어바뚜 바 버떠 바구꿰기라 어먀시 여 무비리, 바다꺼아꽈 구시미사 오꼬.

9 시 먀보, 무다찌구꿰기라 어먀시 여 무비리, 시 뭐라 뭐떠 뫄구꿰기라 어먀시 여 무찌마 와 오꼬, 아가바 오유 무찌마 와이 아꿰 먀 따따 서뉴. 나 아가바 무뚜 아더더 어무찌마 와 기리시도* 뫄 따따 사이, 오요꽈 아다 무뚜 와 기리시도*

10 시 아가바 기리시도* 아꿰 먀 따따 서뉴 찌로 아꺼바 뿌 어무비리 워뉴 아가파 부씨 너 비비, 시 어무찌마 무부야-부야 아가버러사 어가꽈모, 부씨 오꼬 아바이리러 구바 바뚜 바 바두꺼너너.

6. The mind of sinful man is death, but the mind controlled by the Spirit is life and peace;

7. the sinful mind is hostile to God. It does not submit to God's law, nor can it do so.

8. Those controlled by the sinful nature cannot please God.

9. You, however, are controlled not by the sinful nature but by the Spirit, if the Spirit of God lives in you. And if anyone does not have the Spirit of Christ, he does not belong to Christ.

10. But if Christ is in you, your body is dead because of sin, yet your spirit is alive because of righteousness.

11 kanji akaba emchima wa Ongo iwomolaa Yesu mwa bafu ali mwandanda senyu, kukuteta mbu oyu womolaa kirisito* akeresa emubiri wenyu wekufa ekalamo. Akaira bacha, kurengera echima wai ola utula mwa ndanda senyu.

12 rero banyaketu, tuli mu mwinda. Si tutali mu mwinda we mubiri, kuikira echihangi ekalamo ketu kende kakoresibwa ne kuhonda kwe mubiri.

13 bushi akaba mwa kalamo kenyu, mungendi mwa koresibwa nemyasi yemubiri, mungafa. Si akaba mungeta emyanya ye mubiri kurengera ebuashi bwe mchima mubuya-buya, mungaba bauma-bauma.

14 boshi be bende bakoresibwa nemchima wa Ongo, bu bana ba Ongo.

15 bushi muteresibwaa wa kubaira tuunga*, nesi wa kubobairisa, si al iwa kubaira bana ba Ongo. Na kurenegera oyu mchima ku twende twamaala Ongo mbu " Aba, Tata! "

11 가찌 아가바 어무찌마 와 오꼬 이오모롸아 여수 롸 바푸 아뤼 롸따따 서뉴, 구구더다 뿌 오유 온모롸아 기리시도* 아거러사 어무비리 워뉴 워구파 어가롸모. 아가이라 바짜, 구러써라 어찌마 와이 오롸 우두롸 롸 따따 서뉴.

12 러로 바냐거두, 두뤼 무 뮈따. 시 두다뤼 무 뮈따 워 무비리, 구이기라 어찌하삐 어가롸모 거두 거떠 가고러시봐 너 구호따 궈 무비리.

13 부씨 아가바 롸 가롸모 거뉴, 무써띠 롸 고러시봐 너먀시 여무비리, 무빠파. 시 아가바 무써다 어먀냐 여 무비리 구러써라 어부아씨 붜 무찌마 무부야-부야, 무빠바 바우마-바우마.

14 보씨 버 버떠 바고러시봐 너무찌마 와 오꼬, 부 바나 바 오꼬.

15 부씨 무더러시봐아 와 구바이라 두우빠*, 너시 와 구보바이리사, 시 아루 이와 구바이라 바나 바 오꼬. 나 구러너거라 오유 무찌마 구 뛰떠 돠마아롸 오꼬 뿌 " 아바, 다다! "

11. And if the Spirit of him who raised Jesus from the dead is living in you, he who raised Christ from the dead will also give life to your mortal bodies through his Spirit, who lives in you.

12. Therefore, brothers, we have an obligation--but it is not to the sinful nature, to live according to it.

13. For if you live according to the sinful nature, you will die; but if by the Spirit you put to death the misdeeds of the body, you will live,

14. because those who are led by the Spirit of God are sons of God.

15. For you did not receive a spirit that makes you a slave again to fear, but you received the Spirit of sonship. And by him we cry, "Abba, Father."

16 kanji oyu mchima mubuya-buya yeine ende ateta kananga a mwa mchima yetu kwa tubano tunali bana ba Ongo.

17 rero, akaba tunali bana bai, kukuteta mbu tukabona mwango kwa mwandu ola alaanyaa ebandu bai. Kanji oyu mwandu, tkahangirao na kirirsito.bushi akaba tungalibusibwa alauma nai, kunoku ku tukaneresibwa netunda alauma nai.

Ebandju ba Ongo alondola kutengera mira

18 nyoono nyisene kwe malibuko ma twarengamo mwesine suku, mali maeke kurenza etunda lya Ongo akatulosa.

19 ebutala boshi kulinjira ku bwanalinjirira busese echihangi cha Ongo akalosa changanama ba bali bana bai kanangana.

20 bushi buno butala bwabikirwe era bufuli se buashi bwa butete mufa. Ata kwa kuhonda kwe butala bweine, si bushi na Ongo iwabikaabo era bufuli sobu buashi. Si chiro bacha, ono munyiiro anachirio:

16 가찌 오유 무찌마 무부야-부야 여이너 어더 아더다 가나꺄 아 뫄 무찌마 여두 과 두바노 두나뤼 바나 바 오꼬.

17 러로, 아가바 두나뤼 바나 바이, 구구더다 뿌 두가보나 뫄꼬 과 뫄뿌 오라 아롸아냐아 어바뿌 바이. 가찌 오유 뫄뿌, 두가하꾜라오 나 기리시도.부씨 아가바 두꺄뤼부시봐 아롸우마 나이, 구노구 구 두가너러시봐 너두따 아롸우마 나이.

어바뿌 바 오꼬 아롣또롸 구더꺼띱 미라

18 뇨오노 네서너 궈 마뤼부고 마 돠러꺄모 뭐시너 수구, 마뤼 마어거 구러싸 어두따 랴 오꼬 아가두로사.

19 어부다라 보씨 구뤼찌라 구 봐나뤼찌리라 부서서 어찌하꼐 짜 오꼬 아가로사 짜꺄나마 바 바뤼 바나 바이 가나꺄나.

20 부씨 부노 부다롸 봐비기뤄 어라 부푸뤼 서 부아씨 봐 부더더 무파. 아다 과 구호따 궈 부다롸 붸이너, 시 부씨 나 오꼬 이와비가아보 어라 부푸뤼 소부 부아씨. 시 찌로 바짜, 오노 무네이로 아나찌리오:

16. The Spirit himself testifies with our spirit that we are God's children.

17. Now if we are children, then we are heirs--heirs of God and co-heirs with Christ, if indeed we share in his sufferings in order that we may also share in his glory.

18. I consider that our present sufferings are not worth comparing with the glory that will be revealed in us.

19. The creation waits in eager expectation for the sons of God to be revealed.

20. For the creation was subjected to frustration, not by its own choice, but by the will of the one who subjected it, in hope

21 lusuku luuma, buno butala nabo bukaboolibwa. Bukatenga mwa bucha bwe buashi bwa bwende bwakumbyabo, na bwengira mwa buhuru nomwetunda lyebana ba Ongo.

22 twishi kwa kukira lwarero, ebutala boshi kulakanga ku bwanalakanga na kulibuka ne mukero.

23 kanji ata ebutala weine oshao bu bwalakanga bacha, si netu tu twera twete emchima mbuya-buya nga mwango mubere-bere kwa bindu bya Ongo akatweresa. Twenjire twachilakangira mwa michima yetu, mwa kulinjira Ongo atuire kuba bana bai, na kutununula loshi.

24 bushi emyanyiiro itunete oshao kwa twanunulibwe. Mango mundu asene kwa kandu ka abaa achinyiire, oyola atachire munyiiro. Ndeiungaendekera achinyiira ekandu ka aseneko?

25 si akaba tungachinyiira ekandu ka tutaseneko, twende twalinjirako na bushibirisi bunene.

21 루수구 루우마, 부노 부다꽈 나보 부가보오리봐. 부가더꽈 봐 부짜 붜 부아씨 봐 붜떠 봐구뺘보, 나 붜끼라 뫄 부후루 노뭐두따 껴바나 바 오꼬.

22 뒤씨 과 구기라 꽈러로, 어부다꽈 보씨 구꽈가꽈 구 봐나꽈가꽈 나 구끠부가 너 무거로.

23 가찌 아다 어부다꽈 워이너 오싸오 부 봐라가꽈 바짜, 시 너두 두 뛰라 뛰더 어무찌마 뿌야-부야 꽈 뫙꼬 무버러-버러 과 비뚜 뱌 오꼬 아가뛰러사. 뛰끠러 돠찌꽈가끼라 뫄 미찌마 여두, 뫄 구끠찌라 오꼬 아두이러 구바 바나 바이, 나 구두누누꽈 로씨.

24 부씨 어먀네이로 이두너더 오싸오 과 돠누누끠붜. 마꼬 무뚜 아서너 과 가뚜 가 아바아 아찌네이러, 오요꽈 아다찌러 무네이로. 떠이우꽈어떠거라 아찌네이라 어가뚜 가 아서너고?

25 시 아가바 두꽈찌네이라 어가뚜 가 두다서너고, 뛰떠 돠끠찌라고 나 부씨비리시 부너너.

21. that the creation itself will be liberated from its bondage to decay and brought into the glorious freedom of the children of God.

22. We know that the whole creation has been groaning as in the pains of childbirth right up to the present time.

23. Not only so, but we ourselves, who have the firstfruits of the Spirit, groan inwardly as we wait eagerly for our adoption as sons, the redemption of our bodies.

24. For in this hope we were saved. But hope that is seen is no hope at all. Who hopes for what he already has?

25. But if we hope for what we do not yet have, we wait for it patiently.

26 kanji kunoku, ku emchima mubuya-buya ende atuasa ngokwa byemire. Si emchima mubuya-buya yeine ende atwemera busese era mwa Ongo, nga mundu ola waneka kwa kutangamanyisibwa.

27 na Ongo iwende walola kwa myasi era iri mwa mchima yetu, atula eshi emyanyisa ye muchima uubuya-buya.oyu mchima mubuya-buya ende emera ebandu ba Ongo, kukulikana ne kuhonda kwa Ongo.

28 twishi kwa mwa myasi yoshi, Ongo ende akola kwa mufa webandu ba batula bamusimire. Abola, bu amaere kukulikana ne bya aanyisa kuira.

29 bushi abu bandu, Ongo alondolaabo kutengera mira. Kanji atolaa elwango kutengera mira kwa akairabo kuba bandu ba bahuhene ne mwana wai. Airaa bacha, chasiya oyu mwana wai abe fula ya banyakabo banene.

30 abu bandu ba Ongo atolaa elwango era luulu sabo kutenegera mira, abamaalaa. Nabu amaalaa, era kubaira kuba ba

26 가찌 구노구, 구 어무찌마 무부야-뿌야 어떠 아두아사 꼬과 벼미러. 시 어무찌마 무부야-뿌야 여이너 어떠 아뛰머라 부서서 어라 먀 오꼬, 까 무뚜 오퐈 와너가 과 구다까마니시봐.

27 나 오꼬 이워떠 와롸 과 먀시 어라 이리 먀 무찌마 여두, 아두퐈 어씨 어마네사 여 무찌마 우우부야-뿌야.오유 무찌마 무부야-뿌야 어떠 어머라 어바뚜 바 오꼬, 구구삐가나 너 구호따 과 오꼬.

28 뒤씨 과 먀 먀시 요씨, 오꼬 어떠 아고퐈 과 무파 워바뚜 바 바두퐈 바무시미러. 아보퐈, 부 아마어러 구구삐가나 너 뱌 아아네사 구이라.

29 부씨 아부 바뚜, 오꼬 아롸또퐈아보 구더떠라 미라. 가찌 아도퐈아 어퐈꼬 구더떠라 미라 과 아가이라보 구바 바뚜 바 바후허너 너 먀나 와이. 아이라아 바짜, 짜시야 오유 먀나 와이 아버 푸퐈 야 바냐가보 바너녀.

30 아부 바뚜 바 오꼬 아도퐈아 어퐈꼬 어라 류우루 사보 구더너거라 미라, 아바마아퐈아. 나부 아마아퐈아, 어라 구바이라

26. In the same way, the Spirit helps us in our weakness. We do not know what we ought to pray for, but the Spirit himself intercedes for us with groans that words cannot express.

27. And he who searches our hearts knows the mind of the Spirit, because the Spirit intercedes for the saints in accordance with God's will.

28. And we know that in all things God works for the good of those who love him, who have been called according to his purpose.

29. For those God foreknew he also predestined to be conformed to the likeness of his Son, that he might be the firstborn among many brothers.

30. And those he predestined, he also called; those he called, he also justified; those he justified, he also glorified.

batungenene era muhondo sai. Nabu airaa kuba batungenene, era kweresabo etunda lyai.

구바 바 바두꺼너너 어라 무호또 사이. 나부 아이라아 구바 바두꺼너너, 어라 궈러사보 어두따 랴이.

Enzii ya Ongo

어씨일 야 오꼬

31 rero chi twairaa twahuba kuteta? akaba Ongo ali kwa lunda lwetu, nde iungaala kutulwisa?

31 러로 찌 돠이라아 돠후바 구더다? 아가바 오꼬 아쀠 과 루따 뤄두, 떠 이우꽈아꽈 구두쮜사?

31. What, then, shall we say in response to this? If God is for us, who can be against us?

32 bushi Ongo atasichiraa kwa mwana wai wechihwa, si amwanaa bushi netu tuboshi. Rero ngokwa atweresaa oyu mwana wai, ku akatweresa ne bindu byoshi.

32 부씨 오꼬 아다시찌라아 과 뫄나 와이 워찌화, 시 아뫄나아 부씨 너두 두보씨. 러로 꼬과 아뚸러사아 오유 뫄나 와이, 구 아가뚸러사 너 비뚜 뵤씨.

32. He who did not spare his own Son, but gave him up for us all--how will he not also, along with him, graciously give us all things?

33 ebandu ba Ongo alondwere, nde iungasitakabo? bushi Ongo yeine iwende wairabo kuba ba batungenene era muhondo sai.

33 어바뚜 바 오꼬 아뢰뚜워러, 떠 이우꽈시다가보? 부씨 오꼬 여이너 이워떠 와이라보 구바 바 바두꺼너너 어라 무호또 사이.

33. Who will bring any charge against those whom God has chosen? It is God who justifies.

34 nde iungachinjibusabo? kutali! bushi Yesu kirisito afaa, era kunomwomoka, na lwarero ali kwa malyo ma Ongo, atwemera.

34 떠 이우꽈찌찌부사보? 구다뤼! 부씨 여수 기리시도 아파아, 어라 구노모모가, 나 꽈러로 아쀠 과 마뢒 마 오꼬, 아뚸머라.

34. Who is he that condemns? Christ Jesus, who died--more than that, who was raised to life--is at the right hand of God and is also interceding for us.

35 chiye chi chingatulikanya era kirisito* atutusako? eri ebuanya? nasi ebusinane? nesi ekulibusibwa? nesi ebulio? nesi ekuina enjimba? nesi ekasibu? nesi elufu?

35 찌여 찌 찌꽈두뤼가냐 어라 기리시도* 아두두사고? 어리 어부아냐? 나시 어부시나너? 너시 어구쀠부시봐? 너시 어부뤼오? 너시 어구이나 어찌빠? 너시 어가시부? 너시 어뤂푸?

35. Who shall separate us from the love of Christ? Shall trouble or hardship or persecution or famine or nakedness or danger or sword?

36 biri ngokwa bitula banjikirwe mwa maanjiko mabuya-buya mbu: "chira lusuku, benjire bahonda kutwita bushi nao. Benjire batutola nga mbuli sa saya kukeribwa."

37 si mwei myasi yoshi, twenjire twaima loshi kurengera oyu watusimaa.

38 kubinali, nyishi kanangana kwa kutali kandu kasibya ka kangatulikanya nenzii era Ongo atutusako: abe elufu, nesi ekalamo, nesi ebamalaika*, nesi ba bemire, nesi emyasi yesine suku, nesi emyasi era ikaika, nesi ba byete ebuashi,

39 nesi bya byete buashi mwa chanya, nesi bya byete ebuashi era bufuli se butala, nesi chira kandu koshi ka kabumbwaa, katangaala kutulikanya nenzii ya Ongo, era atulosaa kurengera enawetu Yesu kirisito.

---

36 비리 오과 비두롸 바찌기뤄와 마아찌고 마부야-부야 뿌: "찌라 룻수구, 버찌러 바호따 구뒤다 부씨 나오. 버찌러 바두도롸 따 뿌쬐 사 사야 구거리봐."

37 시 뭐이 먀시 요씨, 뛰찌러 돠이마 롣씨 구러뻐라 오유 와두시마아.

38 구비나쬐, 네씨 가나따나과 구다쬐 가뉴 가시뱌 가 가따두쬐가냐 너씨이 어라 오꼬 아두두사고: 아버 어루푸, 너시 어가랴모, 너시 어바마쫘이가*, 너시 바 버미러, 너시 어먀시 여시너 수구, 너시 어먀시 어라 이가이가, 너시 바 벼더 어부아씨,

39 너시 뱌 벼더 부아씨 뫄 쨔냐, 너시 뱌 벼더 어부아씨 어라 부푸쬐 서 부다롸, 너시 찌라 가뉴 고씨 가 가부꽈아, 가다따아쫘 구두쬐가냐 너씨이야 오꼬, 어라 아두롣사야 구러뻐라 어나워두 여수 기리시도.

---

36. As it is written: "For your sake we face death all day long; we are considered as sheep to be slaughtered."

37. No, in all these things we are more than conquerors through him who loved us.

38. For I am convinced that neither death nor life, neither angels nor demons, neither the present nor the future, nor any powers,

39. neither height nor depth, nor anything else in all creation, will be able to separate us from the love of God that is in Christ Jesus our Lord.

Ba Roma Chikono 9
Ebana ba Ongo kanangana

바 로마 찌고노 9
어바나 바 오꼬 가나따낍

Rome Chapter 9[NIV]

1 Ene myasi nahonda kuteta mwesina lya Yesu kirisito iri ya kanangana, ndafula bisha. Kurengera emchima mubuya-buya, emyanisa era yatenga mwa mchima wanyi yenjire yanyilosa kwa ndafula bisha.
2 netu businane bunene na malibuko manene mwa mchima.
3 kungabere kukulunyichifire shambyo, kanji nyirekane na kirisito*, kwa utoloke wa banyaketu ba tubutwa nabo mulubaa luuma.
4 abu banyaketu, bali be lubaa lwe baisiraeli. Ongo airaabo kuba bana bai, era kubalosa ne bulangare bwai. Kanji era kuira ebilaano nabo, na kweresabo emwaso*. Era kulosabo enjira era bangende bamweramo, na kweresabo ebirani byai.
5 abu banyaketu bali bomwa lubuto lwa bahokulu betu ba baire ngulu. Na mwolu lubuto mu kirisito* abutwaa kwa njira ye mubiri. Oyu kirisito*, iOngo utula era luulu sa byoshi, kanji iwende watongibwa esuku ne mango. Bibe bacha!

1 어너 먀시 나호따 구더다 뭐시나 먀 여수 기리시도 이리 야 가나따나, 따푸롸 비싸. 구러꺼라 어무찌마 무부야-부야, 어먀니사 어라 야더꽈 와 무찌마 와네 여찌러 야네론사 과 따푸롸 비싸.
2 너두 부시나너 부너너 나 마뛰부고 마너너 와 무찌마.
3 구꽈버러 구구루네찌피러 싸뾰, 가찌 네러가너 나 기리시도*, 과 우도론거 와 바냐거두 바 두부똬 나보 무루바아 루우마.
4 아부 바냐거두, 바뛰 버 루바아 뤄 바이시라어삐. 오꼬 아이라아보 구바 바나 바이, 어라 구바론사 너 부롸꺼러 바이. 가찌 어라 구이라 어비롸아노 나보, 나 궈러사보 어꽈소*. 어라 구론사보 어찌라 어라 바꺼러 바뭐라모, 나 궈러사보 어비라니 뱌이.
5 아부 바냐거두 바뛰 보꽈 루부도 롸 바호구루 버두 바 바이러 꾸루. 나 몰루 루부도 무 기리시도* 아부똬아 과 찌라 여 무비리. 오유 기리시도*, 이오꼬 우두롸 어라 루우루 사 뵤씨, 가찌 이워떠 와도삐봐 어수구 너 마꼬. 비버 바짜!

1. I speak the truth in Christ--I am not lying, my conscience confirms it in the Holy Spirit--

2. I have great sorrow and unceasing anguish in my heart.

3. For I could wish that I myself were cursed and cut off from Christ for the sake of my brothers, those of my own race,

4. the people of Israel. Theirs is the adoption as sons; theirs the divine glory, the covenants, the receiving of the law, the temple worship and the promises.

5. Theirs are the patriarchs, and from them is traced the human ancestry of Christ, who is God over all, forever praised! Amen.

6 ndatechire mbu echiraane cha Ongo chafire buha. Bushi ata ebandu boshi bomwa lubuto lwa Isiraeli, buna ba isiraeli kanangana.

7 kanji ata eaandu boshi bomwa lubuto lwa aburahamu buna bana ba aburahamu kanangana. Bushi Ongo aburaa aburahamu mbu: elubuto lwa nakulanyaa, ukabonalo kurengera Isaka.

8 kukuteta mbu ata ba babutwaa kwa njira yemubiri bu bende batolibwa nga bu bana ba Ongo. Si ba bende batolibwa nga bu bana bai kanangana, bali ba babutwaa kukulikana nechiraane chai.

9 chechine chi chiraane Ongo ersaa aburahamu: nyishi kwa nyingahuba kuika kuno wao mwa chinyiro cha chiri ngechini, eri Sara era ete mwana wa busana.

10 kanji ata echera cheine, tulolaa nokwa myasi ya Rebeka nai.

11 Abutaa maaha. Amu maaha, mango mabaa matasa kubutwa, matasa kuira chiro na chibuya nesi chibi chisibya,

6 따더찌러 뿌 어찌라아너 짜 오꼬 짜피러 부하. 부씨 아다 어바뚜 보씨 보봐 루부도 꽈 이시라어삐, 부나 바 이시라어삐 가나꽈나.

7 가찌 아다 어아아뚜 보씨 보봐 루부도 꽈 아부라하무 부나 바나 바 아부라하무 가나꽈나. 부씨 오꼬 아부라아 아부라하무 뿌: 어루부도 꽈 나구꽈냐아, 우가보나로 구러꺼라 이사가.

8 구구더다 뿌 아다 바 바부돠아 과 찌라 여무비리 부 버떠 바도삐봐 꽈 부 바나 바 오꼬. 시 바 버떠 바도삐봐 꽈 부 바나 바이 가나꽈나, 바삐 바 바부돠아 구구삐가나 너찌라아너 짜이.

9 쩌찌너 찌 찌라아너 오꼬 어루사아 아부라하무: 네씨 과 네꽈후바 구이가 구노 와오 꽈 찌네로 짜 찌리 꺼찌니, 어리 사라 어라 어더 뫄나 와 부사나.

10 가찌 아다 어쩌라 쩌이너, 두로꽈라 노과 먀시 야 러버가 나이.

11 아부다아 마아하. 아무 마아하, 마꼬 마바아 마다사 구부돠, 마다사 구이라 찌로 나 찌부야 너시 찌비 찌시뱌,

6. It is not as though God's word had failed. For not all who are descended from Israel are Israel.

7. Nor because they are his descendants are they all Abraham's children. On the contrary, "It is through Isaac that your offspring will be reckoned."

8. In other words, it is not the natural children who are God's children, but it is the children of the promise who are regarded as Abraham's offspring.

9. For this was how the promise was stated: "At the appointed time I will return, and Sarah will have a son."

10. Not only that, but Rebekah's children had one and the same father, our father Isaac.

11. Yet, before the twins were born or had done anything good or bad--in order that God's purpose in election might stand:

12 Ongo era kubura Rebeka mbu: chikuru akaba mukosi wa chitoto. Atetaa bacha chasiya alose kwa yeke ende alondola ebandu ngokwa anasimire. Atalondolabo kukulikana nebya bende baira, si kukulikana nokwa yeine anamaalaabo.

13 bushi bitula byanjikirwe mwa maanjiko mabuya- buya mbu: nasima Yakobo imweresi, na nahomba Esau ifula.

14 rero chi tutetaa? Ongo atula wa kalondo? nanga, chiro na hicha!

15 bushi bacha ku aburaa Musa: ola nyisimire kufira ebonjo, inyinganafirabo. Nola nyisimire kuachira echahamba, inyinhanaachirachi.

16 mwa bacha, ebubuya bwa Ongo, butatenganyire nekuhonda kwebandu nesi nekuchisesa kwabo, si butenganyire nabonjo bwai.

17 bushi mwa maanjiko mabuya-buya, bacha ku Ongo aburaa mwami Farao: nakwemikaa chasiya linde lyahubanyisibwa mwa butala boshi.

12 오꼬 어라 구부라 러버가 뿌: 찌구루 아가바 무고시 와 찌도도. 아더다아 바짜 짜시야 아로서 과 여거 어머 아로또롸 어바뚜 꼬과 아나시미러. 아다로또롸보 구구릐가나 너뱌 버떠 바이라, 시 구구릐가나 노과 여이너 아나마아롸아보.

13 부씨 비두롸 뱌찌기륔 마 마아찌고 마부야- 부야 뿌: 나시마 야고보 이뭐러시, 나 나호빠 어사우 이푸롸.

14 러로 찌 두더다아? 오꼬 아두롸 와 가로또? 나꺄, 찌로 나 히짜!

15 부씨 바짜 구 아부라아 무사: 오롸 네시미러 구피라 어보뽀, 이네꺄나피라보. 노롸 네시미러 구아찌라 어짜하빠, 이네누하나아찌라찌.

16 롸 바짜, 어부부야 봐 오꼬 부다더꺄네러 너구호따 궈바뚜 너시 너구찌서사 과보, 시 부더꺄네러 나보쪼 봐이.

17 부씨 롸 마아찌고 마부야- 부야, 바짜 구 오꼬 아부라아 롸미 파라오: 나궈미가아 짜시야 릐떠 롹후바네시봐 롸 부다롸 보씨.

12. not by works but by him who calls--she was told, "The older will serve the younger."

13. Just as it is written: "Jacob I loved, but Esau I hated."

14. What then shall we say? Is God unjust? Not at all!

15. For he says to Moses, "I will have mercy on whom I have mercy, and I will have compassion on whom I have compassion."

16. It does not, therefore, depend on man's desire or effort, but on God's mercy.

17. For the Scripture says to Pharaoh: "I raised you up for this very purpose, that I might display my power in you and that my name might be proclaimed in all the earth."

18 rero, echera chalosa kwa akaba Ongo asimire kufira emundu ebonjo, ende anamufirabo. Na akaba asimire mbu mundu aataa matwi masibu, ende anaatamo.

Ongo ende alondola ebandju kwa asimire

19 kuli mango unganyibusa mbu: akaba ku biri bacha, chichera chende chatuma Ongo akaliira ebandu? bushi kutali ola ungaala kulwisa ekuhonda kwai.

20 rero u'mundu, uli nde kwa kunana bya Ongo atechire? echindu cha chabumbwaa mwe bumba chitangaala kubusa ola wabumbaachi mbu: chichatuma wanyibumba bacha?

21 emubumbi, kwa asimire ku ende anaira ebumba. Mu chitosa chiuma cha bumba, angabumba mu chindu cha chete etunda na chinji cha kukoresibwa chira chihangi.

22 rero, Ongo abaa ahonda kulosa abute bwai na kukangana ebandu ebuashi bwai. Si era kuata mchima wa kulinjirira ebandu ba abaa emire kufira ebute na kulosabo kwa kasibu.

---

18 러로, 어쩌라 짜로사 과 아가바 오꼬 아시미러 구피라 어무뚜 어보쪼, 어떠 아나무피라보. 나 아가바 아시미러 뿌 무뚜 아아다아 마뒤 마시부, 어떠 아나아다모.

오꼬 어떠 아론또롸 어바쭈 과 아시미러

19 구뤼 마꼬 우빠네부사 뿌: 아가바 구 비리 바짜, 찌쩌라 쩌떠 짜두마 오꼬 아가뤼이라 어바쭈? 부씨 구다뤼 오롸 우빠아롸 구뤼사 어구호따 과이.

20 러로 우무뚜, 우뤼 떠 과 구나나 뱌 오꼬 아더찌러? 어찌뚜 짜 짜부빠아 뭐 부빠 찌다아아롸 구부사 오롸 와부빠아찌 뿌: 찌짜두마 와네부빠 바짜?

21 어무부뻬, 과 아시미러 구 어떠 아나이라 어부빠. 무 찌도사 찌우마 짜 부빠, 아빠부빠 무 찌뚜 짜 쩌더 어두따 나 찌찌 짜 구고러시봐 찌라 찌하뻬.

22 러로, 오꼬 아바아 아호따 구로사 아부더 봐이 나 구가빠나 어바쭈 어부아씨 봐이. 시 어라 구아다 무찌마 와 구뤼찌리라 어바쭈 바 아바아 어미러 구피라 어부더 나 구로사보 과 가시부.

---

18. Therefore God has mercy on whom he wants to have mercy, and he hardens whom he wants to harden.

19. One of you will say to me: "Then why does God still blame us? For who resists his will?"

20. But who are you, O man, to talk back to God? "Shall what is formed say to him who formed it, 'Why did you make me like this?' "

21. Does not the potter have the right to make out of the same lump of clay some pottery for noble purposes and some for common use?

22. What if God, choosing to show his wrath and make his power known, bore with great patience the objects of his wrath--prepared for destruction?

23 kanji abaa ahonda alose ebandu ba afiraa ebonjo, kwa ngulu yai inatula inene. Abu bandu, bu abaa akunganyise mira chasiya nabo babone kwei ngulu yai.

23 가찌 아바아 아호따 아론서 어바누 바 아피라아 어보쪼, 과 응우루 야이 이나두꽈 이너너. 아부 바누, 부 아바아 아구까네서 미라 짜시야 나보 바보너 궈이 응우루 야이.

23. What if he did this to make the riches of his glory known to the objects of his mercy, whom he prepared in advance for glory--

24 nabu bandu, bali tubano. Atatulondolaa mwa bayuta beine oshao, si nomwa banji bandu.

24 나부 바누, 바리 두바노. 아다두론또라아 뫄 바유다 버이너 오싸오, 시 노뫄 바찌 바누.

24. even us, whom he also called, not only from the Jews but also from the Gentiles?

25 ei myasi ikulikene nokwa Ongo atechire mwa chitabo cha murebi Oseya mbu: " Elibaa lwa lutabaa lwanyi, nyikalwerika mbu: lubaa lwanyi. Ne lubaa lwa nabaa ndatula nyisimire, nyikere nerikalo mbu: lubaa lwanyi lusiirwa.

25 어이 먀시 이구꾀거너 노과 오꼬 아더찌러 뫄 찌다보 짜 무러비 오서야 뿌: " 어리바아 롸 루다바아 롸니, 네가꿔리가 뿌: 루바아 롸니. 너 루바아 롸 나바아 따두꽈 네시미러, 네거러 너리가로 뿌: 루바아 롸니 루시이롸.

25. As he says in Hosea: "I will call them 'my people' who are not my people; and I will call her 'my loved one' who is not my loved one,"

26. na la berikibwaa mbu: mutatula bandu banyi! aola bakere berikibwa mbu: bana ba Ongo ola uli muuma-uma.

26. 나 롸 버리기뵈아 뿌: 무다두꽈 바누 바니! 아오꽈 바거러 버리기뵈 뿌: 바나 바 오꼬 오꽈 우뀌 무우마-우마.

26. and, "It will happen that in the very place where it was said to them, 'You are not my people,' they will be called 'sons of the living God.' "

27 murebi* Isaya nai bacha ku atetaa na murenge munene era luulu selubaa lwe ba isiraeli: " chiro angaba mbu ebaisiraeli bangaba banene nga mishee yomwa nyanja, si baeke mubo oshao bu bakanunulibwa.

27 무러비* 이사야 나이 바짜 구 아더다아 나 무러꺼 무너너 어라 루우루루 서루바아 뤄 바 이시라어뤼: " 찌로 아까바 뿌 어바이시라어뤼 바까바 바너너 까 미써어 요뫄 냐짜, 시 바어거 무보 오싸오 부 바가누누뤼봐.

27. Isaiah cries out concerning Israel: "Though the number of the Israelites be like the sand by the sea, only the remnant will be saved.

28. bushi cha enawetu atetaa era luulu se bandu be butala,

28. 부씨 짜 어나워두 아더다아 어라 루우루 서 바누

28.. For the Lord will carry out his sentence on earth

atemanga kuirachi.

29 ebyeya bikulikene nokwa murebi*Isaya ahubaa kuteta mbu: akaba enawetu Ongo iwabumbaa byoshi atangaturekere bana bauma, bingatuberere ngoknwa byaberaa besha mwa musi we Sotomo ne we Komora.

Ekutchwunganana kurengera ebwemeresi

30 rero chi tuteta kasi? ebandju besinji mbaa babaa batahonda kutunganana era muhondo sa Ongo. Si rero kurengera ebwemeresi, berire batunganana era muhondo sai.

31 si ebaisiraeli beke, babaa bahonda kutunganana era muhondo sa Ongo mwakunde baira ngokwa mwaso*atula atechire, si bitaalikanaa.

32 chi chatumaa bitalikaana kasi? bitaalikana bushi babaa batenjire bahonda kutunganana era muhondo sa Ongo kurengera ebwemeresi, si bahondaa kutunganana kurengera emyanya yabo oshao. Mwa bacha, bera kwire basitala kwe "ekoi lya lyende lyakumbaasa ebandu",

버 부다꽈, 아더마애 구이라찌.

29 어벼야 비구뤼거너 노과 무러비*이사야 아후바아 구더다 뿌: 아가바 어나워두 오꼬 이와부빠아 뵤씨 아다빠두러거러 바나 바우마, 비빠두버러러 꼬구놔 뱌버라아 버싸 뫄 무시 워 소도모 너 워 고모라.

어구쭈빠낍낍 구러뻐띱 어붜머러시

30 러로 찌 두더다 가시? 어바쭈 버시씨 빠아 바바아 바다호따 구두빠나나 어라 무호또 사 오꼬. 시 러로 구러뻐라 어붜머러시, 버리러 바두빠나나 어라 무호또 사이.

31 시 어바이시라어뤼 버거, 바바아 바호따 구두빠나나 어라 무호또 사 오꼬 먀구떠 바이라 꼬과 뫄소*아두꽈 아더찌러, 시 비다아뤼가나아.

32 찌 짜두마아 비다뤼가아나 가시? 비다아뤼가나 부씨 바바아 바더찌러 바호따 구두빠나나 어라 무호또 사 오꼬 구러뻐라 어붜머러시, 시 바호따아 구두빠나나 구러뻐라 어먀냐 야보 오싸오. 뫄 바짜, 버라 귀러 바시다꽈 귀 "어고이 꺄 려떠 꺄구빠아사 어바뚜",

with speed and finality."

29. It is just as Isaiah said previously: "Unless the Lord Almighty had left us descendants, we would have become like Sodom, we would have been like Gomorrah."

30. What then shall we say? That the Gentiles, who did not pursue righteousness, have obtained it, a righteousness that is by faith;

31. but Israel, who pursued a law of righteousness, has not attained it.

32. Why not? Because they pursued it not by faith but as if it were by works. They stumbled over the "stumbling stone."

33 ngokwa bitula byanjikirwe mwa maanjiko mabuya-buya mbu: mulolaa, mwa musi we sayuni, mu nabikire ekoi lye kusitasa ebandu. Neri koi, liri lya kukumbaasa. Si ola ukachiachirisa kuli, yeke atakafunyike emchima

33 끄과 비두롸 뱌찌기뤄 마 마아찌고 마부야-부야 뿌: 무뢰롸아, 마 무시 워 사유니, 무 나비기러 어고이 펴 구시다사 어바뚜. 너리 고이, 리리 랴 구구빠아사. 시 오롸 우가찌아찌리사 구리, 여거 아다가푸네거 어무찌마

33. As it is written: "See, I lay in Zion a stone that causes men to stumble and a rock that makes them fall, and the one who trusts in him will never be put to shame."

Ba Roma Chikono 10

1 Banyaketu, cha nenjire nahonda kwa mchima wanyi woshi na kwema Ongo bushi ne bayuta chi chechine:nabo banunulibwe.

2 nyeine nachilorere kananganana kwa bete bushiru bunene mwa myasi ya Ongo. Si obu bushiru, bateshi kute bangakoresabo.

3 batamenyerera kute Ongo ende aira ebandu kuba ba batungenene era muhondo sai. Bera kwire bachilondorera yabo njira era ingatuma batunganana era muhondo sa Ongo. Mwa bacha, bera kunana kukulikira enjira era Ongo ende aira mwebandu kuba ba batungenene.

4 bushi kirisito aisise emwaso wa Musa kwa nzinjiro yao, chasiya chira mundu ola

바 로마 찌고노 10

1 바냐거두, 짜 너찌러 나호따 과 무찌마 와니 오씨 나 궈마 오끄 부씨 너 바유다 찌 쩌찌너:나보 바누누뤼붜.

2 녀이너 나찌뢰러러 가나빠나나 과 버더 부씨루 부너너 마 먀시 야 오끄. 시 오부 부씨루, 바더씨 구더 바빠고러사보.

3 바다머녀러라 구더 오끄 어떠 아이라 어바뚜 구바 바 바두어너너 어라 무호또 사이. 버라 귀러 바찌뢰또러라 야보 찌라 어라 이빠두마 바두빠나나 어라 무호또 사 오끄. 마 바짜, 버라 구나나 구구뤼기라 어찌라 어라 오끄 어떠 아이라 뭐바뚜 구바 바 바두어너너.

4 부씨 기리시도 아이시서 어마소 와 무사 과 씨찌로 야오, 짜시야 찌라 무뚜 오롸

Rome Chapter 10[NIV]

1. Brothers, my heart's desire and prayer to God for the Israelites is that they may be saved.

2. For I can testify about them that they are zealous for God, but their zeal is not based on knowledge.

3. Since they did not know the righteousness that comes from God and sought to establish their own, they did not submit to God's righteousness.

4. Christ is the end of the law so that there may be righteousness for everyone

wemerere ende atolibwa
ngola utungenene era
muhondo sa Ongo.
Chira mundju ola wemerere
enawetchwu Yesu
anganunulyibwa

5 enera imyasi Musa aanjikaa
era luulu sekuhonda kuba
mundu ola utungenene era
muhondo sa Ongo kurengera
emwaso*. Ola wende waira
kwa miomba* ye mwaso*
itula itechire, angabona
ekalamo kurengera oyu
mwaso*.

6 si bacha kwemaanjiko
matula matechire era luulu se
kutunganana era muhondo
sa Ongo kurengera
ebwemeresi: utendaa
wachibusa mwa mchimawao
mbu: nde iungeruka kwa
nguba? kukuteta mbu
kwandaasa kirisito* atengeko.

7 nesi utendaa wachibusa
mbu:nde iungandaala era
kusimu? kukuteta mbu
kwerusa kirisito*atenge mwa
bafu.

8 ei myasi, kuitechire? itechite
mbu: echinwa cha Ongo chiri
chinwa, ali emwasi ola
twenjire twahubanganyisa
ebandu era luulu
sebwemeresi.

워머러러 어떠 아도삐봐 으롸
우두머너너 어라 무호또 사
오꼬.
찌라 무뿌 오롸 워머러러
어나워쭈 여수 아빠늅늅레봡

5 어너라 이먀시 무사
아아찌가아 어라 루우루
서구호따 구바 무뿌 오롸
우두머너너 어라 무호또 사
오꼬 구러머라 어먀소*. 오롸
워떠 와이라 과 미오빠* 여
먀소* 이두롸 이더찌러,
아빠보나 어가롸모 구러머라
오유 먀소*.

6 시 바짜 궈마아찌고 마두롸
마더찌러 어라 루우루 서
구두빠나나 어라 무호또 사
오꼬 구러머라 어뭐머러시:
우더따아 와찌부사 먀
무찌마와오 뿌: 떠 이우머루가
과 꾸바? 구구더다 뿌
과따아사 기리시도* 아더머고.

7 너시 우더따아 와찌부사
뿌:떠 이우빠따아롸 어라
구시무? 구구더다 뿌 궈루사
기리시도*아더머 먀 바푸.

8 어이 먀시, 구이더찌러?
이더찌더 뿌: 어찌놔 짜 오꼬
찌리 찌놔, 아삐 어먀시 오롸
뭐찌러 돠후바빠니세사 어바뚜
어라 루우루 서뭐머러시.

who believes.

5. Moses describes in this
way the righteousness that
is by the law: "The man who
does these things will live
by them."

6. But the righteousness
that is by faith says: "Do not
say in your heart, 'Who will
ascend into heaven?'" (that
is, to bring Christ down)

7. "or 'Who will descend
into the deep?'" (that is, to
bring Christ up from the
dead).

8. But what does it say?
"The word is near you; it is
in your mouth and in your
heart," that is, the word of
faith we are proclaiming:

9 akaba ungateta mwa bunu bwao weine mbu Yesu ienawetu, nakuemerera mwa mchima wao kwa Ongo omwomolaa mwa bafu, unganunulibwa.

10 ola wemerersi kwa mchima wai woshi, Ongo ende amuira kuba ola utungenene era muhondo sai. Na mango emundu ende ateta mwa bunu bwai yeine kwa emrere, Ongo ende amununula.

11 bushi eamanjiko mabuya-buya matula matechire mbu: chira mundu ola mwemerere atakafunyike muchima.

12 mwa bacha, kutachiri bayuta, kutachiri na ba batatula bayuta, bushi enawetu tuboshi anali muuma. Kanji ende aahayira busese boshi ba bende bamwema.

13 ebyera bikulikene nokwa maanjiko mabuya-buya matula matechire mbu: chira mundu ola ungende wema enawetu, anganunulibwa.

14 rero, kute bangema enawetu ola batemareraa? nakute bangamwemerere, noku batafuraa kumva kwa myasi yai, na kute

---

9 아가바 우꺼더다 뫄 부누 봐오 워이너 뿌 여수 이어나워두, 나구어머러라 뫄 무찌마 와오 과 오꼬 오모모롸아 뫄 바푸, 우꺼누누삐봐.

10 오롸 워머러시 과 무찌마 와이 오씨, 오꼬 어떠 아무이라 구바 오롸 우두꺼너너 어라 무호또 사이. 나 마꼬 어문두 어떠 아더다 뫄 부누 봐이 여이너 과 어러러, 오꼬 어떠 아무누누롸.

11 부씨 어아마찌고 마부야-부야 마두롸 마더찌러 뿌: 찌라 무뚜 오롸 뭐머러러 아다가푸네거 무찌마.

12 뫄 바짜, 구다찌리 바우다, 구다찌리 나 바 바다두롸 바유다, 부씨 어나워두 두보씨 아나삐 무우마. 가찌 어떠 아아하에라 부서서 보씨 바 버떠 바뭐마.

13 어뵈라 비구삐거너 노과 마아찌고 마부야-부야 마두롸 마더찌러 뿌: 찌라 무뚜 오롸 우꺼떠 워마 어나워두, 아꺼누누삐봐.

14 러로, 구더 바꺼마 어나워두 오롸 바더마러라아? 나구더 바꺼뭐머러러, 노구 바다푸라아 구빠 과 먀시 야이, 나 구더 바오삐러 과

---

9. That if you confess with your mouth, "Jesus is Lord," and believe in your heart that God raised him from the dead, you will be saved.

10. For it is with your heart that you believe and are justified, and it is with your mouth that you confess and are saved.

11. As the Scripture says, "Anyone who trusts in him will never be put to shame."

12. For there is no difference between Jew and Gentile--the same Lord is Lord of all and richly blesses all who call on him,

13. for, "Everyone who calls on the name of the Lord will be saved."

14. How, then, can they call on the one they have not believed in? And how can they believe in the one of whom they have not heard?

bangomvire kwa myasi yai, kutali nola wabahubanganyisai?

먀시 야이, 구다뾔 노롸 와바후바까네사이?

And how can they hear without someone preaching to them?

15 na kute bangahubanganya akaba batatumirwe? ei myasi ikulikene nokwa bitula byanjikirwe mwa maanjiko mabuya-buya mbu: Ekuika kwe bandu ba bareta emyasi ibuya-buya, lutula lumoo lunene!

15 나 구더 바까후바까냐 아가바 바다두미뤄? 어이 먀시 이구뾔거너 노과 비두롸 뱌찌기뤄 롸 마아찌고 마부야-부야 뿌: 어구이가 궈 바뚜 바 바러다 어먀시 이부야-부야, 루두롸 루모오 루너너!

15. And how can they preach unless they are sent? As it is written, "How beautiful are the feet of those who bring good news!"

16 si chiro bacha, ata ebandu boshi bu bemereraa oyu mwasi mubuya-buya. Ebyera bikulikene nokwa murebi Isaya atetaa mbu: enawetu, nde iwemereraa emyasi era twahubanganyaa?

16 시 찌로 바짜, 아다 어바뚜 보씨 부 버머러라아 오유 먀시 무부야-부야. 어벼라 비구뾔거너 노과 무러비 이사야 아더다아 뿌: 어나워두, 떠 이워머러라아 어먀시 어라 돠후바까냐아?

16. But not all the Israelites accepted the good news. For Isaiah says, "Lord, who has believed our message?"

17 mwa bacha, ebwemeresi bwende bwetengana nekumva emwasi. Noyu mwasi, chiri echinwa cha Kirisito*.

17 롸 바짜, 어붜머러시 붜떠 붜더까나 너구빠 어먀시. 노유 먀시, 찌리 어찌놔 짜 기리시도*.

17. Consequently, faith comes from hearing the message, and the message is heard through the word of Christ.

18 rero nabusa: ebayuta batomvaa kwoyu mwasi? nechi, bomvaa kuo! bushi emanajiko mabuya-buya matula matechire mbu: emirenge yebandu ba bende bahubanganya, yomvikere mwa butala boshi. Emyasi yabo, yaikire kwa nyinda soshi se butala.

18 러로 나부사: 어바유다 바도빠아 궈유 먀시? 너찌, 보빠아 구오! 부씨 어마나지고 마부야-부야 마두롸 마더찌러 뿌: 어미러꺼 여바뚜 바 버떠 바후바까냐, 요삐거러 롸 부다롸 보씨. 어먀시 야보, 야이기러 과 네따 소씨 서 부다롸.

18. But I ask: Did they not hear? Of course they did: "Their voice has gone out into all the earth, their words to the ends of the world."

19 kanji nabusa: ebaisiraeli batamenyereraa? bushi Ongo abaa atechire mira kurengera Musa mbu: nyingabaira munde mwafira emufula ebandu ba beta lubaa kanangana. Nyi gabaira munde mwafira ebute ebandu ba batete bwenge.

20 kanji Ongo abaa atechire mira kurengera murebi *Isaya mbu: Eabndu ba babaa batanyihonda, bu berire banyibona, nachilosise kwa bandu ba babaa banyibusa mwasi.

21 si bacha ku Ongo atechire era luulu se baisisraeli: emushi woshi, nabaa nenjire na nateya emino sanyi kwa bandu ba bataira kwa natechire, kanji bande baenzanya ebwaka.

19 가찌 나부사: 어바이시라어쀠 바다머녀러러아? 부씨 오꼬 아바아 아더찌러 미라 구러꺼라 무사 뿌: 네꺼바이라 무떠 콰피라 어무푸콰 어바누 바 버다 루부바아 가나꺼나. 네 가바이라 무떠 콰피라 어부더 어바누 바 바더더 붸꺼.

20 가찌 오꼬 아바아 아더찌러 미라 구러꺼라 무러비 *이사야 뿌: 어아부누 바 바바아 바다네호따, 부 버리러 바네보나, 나찌론시서 과 바누 바 바바아 바네부사 콰시.

21 시 바짜 구 오꼬 아더찌러 어라 루우루 서 바이시수라어쀠: 어무씨 오씨, 나바아 너찌러 나 나더야 어미노 사네 과 바누 바 바다이라 과 나더찌러, 가찌 바떠 바어싸냐 어봐가.

19. Again I ask: Did Israel not understand? First, Moses says, "I will make you envious by those who are not a nation; I will make you angry by a nation that has no understanding."

20. And Isaiah boldly says, "I was found by those who did not seek me; I revealed myself to those who did not ask for me."

21. But concerning Israel he says, "All day long I have held out my hands to a disobedient and obstinate people."

Ba Roma Chikono 11
Ongo atarekerere elubaa lw'e Isiraeli

1 Rero nabusa: Ongo akabulire elubaa lwai? nanga, chiro na hicha! bushi anabe nanyi, nyiri muisiraeli womwa lubuto lwa aburahamu, mwa

바 로마 찌고노 11
오꼬 아다러거러러 어뤀밍쒭 뤄 이시라어쀠

1 러로 나부사: 오꼬 아가부쀠러 어뤀바아 롸이? 나꺼, 찌로 나 히짜! 부씨 아나버 나네, 네리 무이시라어쀠 옹콰 루부도 롸

Rome Chapter 11[NIV]

1. I ask then: Did God reject his people? By no means! I am an Israelite myself, a descendant of Abraham, from the tribe of Benjamin.

chirongo cha Benyamine.

2 Ongo atakabulira elubaa lwai, lwa achilondoreraa kutengera mira. Mutechi kute emaanjiko mabuya-buya matuma matechire mango murebi* Eliya abaa achanya era muhondo sa Ongo bushi ne lubaa lwe baisiraeli? atetaa mbu: Aaye enawetu, bechire ebarebi

3 *bao, banahandula ne kahaha kao kemitulo*. Nyine oshao nyinanashibire, si nanyi bahonda kunyita.

4 kute ku Ongo amwakulaa kasi? amwakulaa mbu: " nachibikirire bandu byumbi birinda ba bananyire kufukama era muhondo sa ongo ola bende berika mbu bali. "

5 anabe mwesine suku, ku binali bacha. Kweshiba banji bandu baeke ba Ongo alondwere kurengera ebonjo bwai.

6 alondolaabo kurengera ebonjo bwai, si ata kurengera bya bende baira. Akaba bingabere bacha, obu bonjo butangachibere bonjo kanangana.

아부라하무, 꽈 찌로끄 짜 버냐미너.

2 오끄 아다가부삐라 어루바아 꽈이, 꽈 아찌로또러라아 구더꺼라 미라. 무더찌 구더 어마아찌고 마부야-부야 마두마 마더찌러 마오 무러비* 어삐야 아바아 아짜냐 어라 무호또 사 오끄 부씨 너 루바아 뤄 바이시라어삐? 아더다아 뿌: 아아여 어나워두, 버찌러 어바러비

3 *바오, 바나하뚜꽈 너 가하하 가오 거미두뜬*. 니너 오싸오 니나나씨비러, 시 나니 바호따 구니다.

4 구더 구 오끄 아꽈구꽈아 가시? 아꽈구꽈아 뿌: " 나찌비기리러 바뚜 뷰삐 비리따 바 바나니러 구푸가마 어라 무호또 사 오끄 오꽈 버떠 버리가 뿌 바삐. "

5 아나버 뭐시너 수구, 구 비나삐 바짜. 궈씨바 바찌 바뚜 바어거 바 오끄 아뤈뚜워러 구러꺼라 어보쬬 봐이.

6 아뤈또꽈아보 구러꺼라 어보쬬 봐이, 시 아다 구러꺼라 뱌 버떠 바이라. 아가바 비꽈버러 바짜, 오부 보쬬 부다까찌버러 보쬬 가나꽈나.

2. God did not reject his people, whom he foreknew. Don't you know what the Scripture says in the passage about Elijah--how he appealed to God against Israel:

3. "Lord, they have killed your prophets and torn down your altars; I am the only one left, and they are trying to kill me"?

4. And what was God's answer to him? "I have reserved for myself seven thousand who have not bowed the knee to Baal."

5. So too, at the present time there is a remnant chosen by grace.

6. And if by grace, then it is no longer by works; if it were, grace would no longer be grace.

7 chi twiraa twateta kasi? elubaa lweisisraeli lutabonaa cha lwabaa lwahonda. Si ba Ongo alondola oshao, bubababonaachi. Ebanji ba bashibaa beke, bera kuira emchima yabo kuba isibu.
8 ebyera bikulikene nokwa maanjiko mabuya-buya matula matechire mbu: " Ongo aberesise michima isibu, na meho ma matalola, na matwi ma matomva. Na kubanachiri bacha, kuira lwarero.
9 mwami Tauti naiatechire mbu: ebiryo byabo byesuku sikulu, bindaa byabaalukira kuba muteo wa kubasimba, binda byabaalukira kuba buya bwa bangende batoweramo, na bachinjibusibwa.
10 emeho mabo mendaa manaya mwe musimya, chasiya batalolaa, ne miongo yabo inekalaa ichionyire esuku soshi.
11 rero nabusa: ebayuta basitalaa chasiya bakumbaale loshi? nanga, chiro na hicha! emabi mabo mu maboorere enjira kwa ba batatula bayuta nabo, banunulibwe, chasiya abu bayuta bende bafirabo emufulu.

7 찌 뒤라아 돠더다 가시? 어루바아 뤠이시수라어뢰 루다보나아 짜 롸바아 롸호따. 시 바 오꼬 아룬또롸 오싸오, 부바바보나아찌. 어바찌 바 바씨바아 버거, 버라 구이라 어무찌마 야보 구바 이시부.
8 어벼라 비구뤼거너 노과 마아찌고 마부야-부야 마두롸 마더찌러 뿌: " 오꼬 아버러시서 미찌마 이시부, 나 머호 마 마다로롸, 나 마뒤 마 마도빠. 나 구바나찌리 바짜, 구이라 롸러로.
9 뫄미 다우디 나이아더찌러 뿌: 어비료 뱌보 벼수구 시구룩, 비따아 뱌바아루기라 구바 무더오 와 구바시빠, 비따 뱌바아루기라 구바 부야 봐 바꺼러 바도워라모, 나 바찌찌부시봐.
10 어머호 마보 머따아 마나야 뭐 무시먀, 짜시야 바다로롸아, 너 미오꼬 야보 이너가롸아 이찌오네러 어수구 소씨.
11 러로 나부사: 어바유다 바시다롸아 짜시야 바구빠아뤄 론씨? 나꺄, 찌로 나 히짜! 어마비 마보 무 마보오러러 어찌라 과 바 바다두롸 바유다 나보, 바누누뤼붜, 짜시야 아부 바유다 버떠 바피라보 어무푸룩.

7. What then? What Israel sought so earnestly it did not obtain, but the elect did. The others were hardened,

8. as it is written: "God gave them a spirit of stupor, eyes so that they could not see and ears so that they could not hear, to this very day."

9. And David says: "May their table become a snare and a trap, a stumbling block and a retribution for them.

10. May their eyes be darkened so they cannot see, and their backs be bent forever."

11. Again I ask: Did they stumble so as to fall beyond recovery? Not at all! Rather, because of their transgression, salvation has come to the Gentiles to make Israel envious.

12 mwa bacha, emabi me bayuta marechire ngahanyi sinene muno butala. Nekuimwa kwabo, kwareterere ba batatula bayuta ngahanyi sinene. Rero, sikaba ngahanyi sinene mango e bayuda boshi bakanunulibwa.	12 뫄 바짜, 어마비 머 바유다 마러찌러 ᅇᅡ하네 시너너 무노 부다ᄙᅡ. 너구이뫄 과보, 과러더러러 바 바다두ᄙᅡ 바유다 ᅇᅡ하네 시너너. 러로, 시가바 ᅇᅡ하네 시너너 마ᅌᅩ 어바유다 보씨 바가누누ᄙᅵ봐.	12. But if their transgression means riches for the world, and their loss means riches for the Gentiles, how much greater riches will their fullness bring!
Kute ku ba batatchwula bayuda bende banunulyibwa	***구더 구 바 바다쭈ᄙᅡ 바유다 버떠 바누누ᄙᅨ봅***	
13 nera nateta nenyu mu mutatula bayuta: nyono, nyiri ndumwa* ya kirisito* kwa ba batatula bayuta. Kanji nende namoera oyu mulimo wanyi.	13 너라 나더다 너뉴 무 무다두ᄙᅡ 바유다: 뇨노, 네리 뚜뫄* 야 기리시도* 과 바 바다두ᄙᅡ 바유다. 가씨 너떠 나모어라 오유 무ᄙᅵ모 와네.	13. I am talking to you Gentiles. Inasmuch as I am the apostle to the Gentiles, I make much of my ministry
14 mwa bacha, nanyiisa kwa banyaketu bayuta bangende babafira mufula, chasiya nyinunule bauma mubo.	14 뫄 바짜, 나네이사 과 바냐거두 바유다 바ᅇᅥ떠 바바피라 무푸ᄙᅡ, 짜시야 네누누ᄙᅥ 바우마 무보.	14. in the hope that I may somehow arouse my own people to envy and save some of them.
15 kubinali, mango Ongo asiikaabo, era kwire abika ebuuma ala kachi-kachi kai nebandu bomwa butala. Rero kute bikere byabaa mango ebayuta bakahuba kwemererwa era muhondo sa Ongo? kukaba nga kwomoka kwa bafu!	15 구비나ᄙᅵ, 마ᅌᅩ 오ᅌᅩ 아시이가아보, 어라 귀러 아비가 어부우마 아ᄙᅡ 가찌-가찌 가이 너바뚜 보뫄 부다ᄙᅡ. 러로 구더 비거러 뱌바아 마ᅌᅩ 어바유다 바가후바 궈머러롸 어라 무호또 사 오ᅌᅩ? 구가바 ᅇᅡ 고모가 과 바푸!	15. For if their rejection is the reconciliation of the world, what will their acceptance be but life from the dead?
16 akaba endumwa atulire Ongo echimbi chibere-bere che muakati, kukuteta mbu emukati woshi anera wa Ongo. Na akaba emundu	16 아가바 어뚜뫄 아두ᄙᅵ러 오ᅌᅩ 어찌삐 찌버러-버러 쩌 무아가디, 구구더다 뿌 어무가디 온씨 아너라 와 오ᅌᅩ. 나 아가바 어무뚜	16. If the part of the dough offered as firstfruits is holy, then the whole batch is holy; if the root is holy, so are the branches.

atulire Ongo echisina che muchi, kukuteta mbu nendabi nasi sanera sa Ongo.

아두뭬러 오꼬 어찌시나 쩌 무찌, 구구더다 뿌 너따비 나시 사너라 사 오꼬.

17 elubaa lwe baisiraeli luli nga muchi wa museituni ola waingwaa, ola baishire ku ndabi siuma. Nenyu mu mutatula bayuta, muli nga ndabi sa unji muchi womwerungu. Ne ndabi soyu muchi womwerungu, sera kwomakirisibwa ala esinji saishibwaa kwa muchi we museituni. Rero, emasisi ma mende matenga mwa misi-misi yoyu museituni, mu menjire maberesa nenyu emisi.

17 어루바아 뤠 바이시라어뤼 루뤼 까 무찌 와 무서이두니 오라 와이꽈아, 오롸 바이씨러 구 따비 시우마. 너뉴 무 무다두롸 바유다, 무뤼 까 따비 사 우찌 무찌 오뭐루꽈. 너 따비 소유 무찌 오뭐루꽈, 서라 곧마기리시봐 아롸 어시찌 사이씨봐아 과 무찌 워 무서이두니. 러로, 어마시시 마 머떠 마더까 와 미시-미시 요유 무서이두니, 무 머찌러 마버러사 너뉴 어미시.

17. If some of the branches have been broken off, and you, though a wild olive shoot, have been grafted in among the others and now share in the nourishing sap from the olive root,

18 bushi noku, esi ndabi sa saishibwaa, mutenda mwakenasi. Mwabo mutete cha mungachitongera, bushiata mu muachirise echisina che muchi, si echi chisina chi chibaachirise.

18 부씨 노구, 어시 따비 사 사이씨봐아, 무더따 먀거나시. 뫄보 무더더 쨔 무까찌도꺼라, 부씨아다 무 무아찌리서 어찌시나 쩌 무찌, 시 어찌 찌시나 쩌 찌바아찌리서.

18. do not boast over those branches. If you do, consider this: You do not support the root, but the root supports you.

19 kuli mango ungateta mbu: Esi ndabi saishibwaa, chasiya nyono nyomakirisibwa ala satengaa.

19 구뤼 마꼬 우까더다 뿌: 어시 따비 사이씨봐아, 쨔시야 뇨노 뇨마기리시봐 아롸 사더꽈아.

19. You will say then, "Branches were broken off so that I could be grafted in."

20 kubinali bacha. Baishaasi bushi sabaa sitete bwemeresi, si woyo uli mwechi chisiki bushi ne bwemeresi bwao. Rero, utendaa wachitonga, si

20 구비나뤼 바짜. 바이싸아시 부씨 사바아 시더더 뷔머러시, 시 오요 우뤼 뭬찌 찌시기 부씨 너 뷔머러시 봐오. 러로, 우더따아 와찌도까, 시

20. Granted. But they were broken off because of unbelief, and you stand by faith. Do not be arrogant, but be afraid.

undaa wachilanga-langa.

21 bushi akaba Ongo atasichiraa kwa bayuta, bu bali nga matabi me muchi ola waingwaa, ne nyu atanabasichireko.

22 rero, mundaa mwaanyisa era luulu sebubuya bwa Ongo ne bukali bwai. Atula mukali kwa bandu ba bengirire mwa bibi, si atula mubuya ku woyo, akaba ungendekera kwekala mwobu bubuya bwai. Bitabere bacha, nao ungaishibwa.

23 si akaba ebayuta bangahuba kwemerera, Ongo angahuba kwomakirisabo ala babaa bali byebere. Bushi ete ebuashi bwe kuira echera.

24 woyo uutatula muyuta, ulinga lutabi lwa muchi wa museituni womwerungu. Chasinda, olu luabi lwera kwomakirisibwa kwa muchi wemuseituni ola waingwaa. Echera, chisibuire. Si ebayuta beke, bali ngandabi Ongo oyu muchi ola waingwaa. Rero, bibofuire busese era mwa Ongo, kwa kuhuba kwomakirisa esi ndabi kwa muchi ola sameraako.

E Baisiraeli bachilyi

와찌꽈아-꽈꽈.

21 부씨 아가바 오꼬 아다시찌라아 과 바유다, 부 바삐 아 마다비 머 무찌 오꽈 와이꽈아, 너 뉴 아다나바시찌러고.

22 러로, 무따아 꽈아니사 어라 루우루 서부부야 봐 오꼬 너 부가삐 봐이. 아두꽈 무가삐 과 바뚜 바 버삐리러 꽈 비비, 시 아두꽈 무부야 구 오요, 아가바 우꺼떠거라 귀가꽈 몸부 부부야 봐이. 비다버러 바짜, 나오 우꽈이씨봐.

23 시 아가바 어바유다 바꽈후바 귀머러라, 오꼬 아꽈후바 곰마기리사보 아꽈 바바아 바삐 벼버러. 부씨 어더 어부아씨 붜 구이라 어쩌라.

24 오요 우우다두꽈 무유다, 우삐꽈 루다비 꽈 무찌 와 무서이두니 옴뭐루꼬. 짜시따, 오루 루아비 뭐라 곰마기리시봐 과 무찌 웜무서이두니 오꽈 와이꽈아. 어쩌라, 찌시부이러. 시 어바유다 버거, 바삐 꽈따비 오꼬 오유 무찌 오꽈 와이꽈아. 러로, 비보푸이러 부서서 어라 봐 오꼬, 과 구후바 곰마기리사 어시 따비 과 무찌 오꽈 사머라아고.

어 바이시라어삐 바찌쩨

---

21. For if God did not spare the natural branches, he will not spare you either.

22. Consider therefore the kindness and sternness of God: sternness to those who fell, but kindness to you, provided that you continue in his kindness. Otherwise, you also will be cut off.

23. And if they do not persist in unbelief, they will be grafted in, for God is able to graft them in again.

24. After all, if you were cut out of an olive tree that is wild by nature, and contrary to nature were grafted into a cultivated olive tree, how much more readily will these, the natural branches, be grafted into their own olive tree!

25 banyaketu ndahonda mbu mwikalaa busira kumenya ono mwasi Ongo abaa abishire, mungesha kwende mwachitola ingabandu ba bete bwenge bunene. Noyu mwai iyoni: baisiraeli bauma bakanaendekera kunde baira icmichima yabo kuba isibu, kuikira mango emuanjo webandu esinji mbaa ba Ongo alondwere bengirire mwa bwami bwai.

26 chasinda, elubaa loshi lwebaisiraeli lukanunulibwa kukulikana nokwa maanjiko mabuya-buya matechire mbu: emununusi akatengera esayuni, akakula emchima musibu mwa lubuto lwa Yakobo.

27 echera chi chilaano* nyikaira nabo, mango nyikakula ebibi byabo.

28 ebayuta bahubire barenda ba Ongo bushi nekunana emwasi mubuya-buya. Noku kunanao kwabo, iwabere mutoloke wenyu mu mutatula bayuta. Si chiro bacha, Ongo anasimirebo, kukulikana nokula alondolabo kurengera bahokulu babo.

25 바냐거두 따호따 뿌 뮈가롸아 부시라 구머냐 오노 똬시 오꼬 아바아 아비씨러, 무꺼싸 궈떠 똬찌도롸 이꺄바뚜 바 버더 붱꺼 부너너. 노유 똬이 이요니: 바이시라어꾀 바우마 바가나어떠거라 구떠 바이라 이시미찌마 야보 구바 이시부, 구이기라 마꼬 어무아쪼 워바뚜 어시끼 빠아 바 오꼬 아룬뚜워러 버꾀리러 똬 봐미 봐이.

26 짜시따, 어루바아 론씨 뤄바이시라어꾀 루가누누꾀봐 구구꾀가나 노과 마아찌고 마부야-부야 마더찌러 뿌: 어무누누시 아가더꺼라 어사유니, 아가구롸 어무찌마 무시부 똬 루부도 롸 야고보.

27 어쩌라 찌 찌롸아노* 네가이라 나보, 마꼬 네가구롸 어비비 뱌보.

28 어바우다 바후비러 바러따 바 오꼬 부씨 너구나나 어똬시 무부야-부야. 노구 구나나오 과보, 이와버러 무도론거 워뉴 무 무다두롸 바유다. 시 찌로 바짜, 오꼬 아나시미러보, 구구꾀가나 노구롸 아룬또롸보 구러꺼라 바호구룩 바보.

25. I do not want you to be ignorant of this mystery, brothers, so that you may not be conceited: Israel has experienced a hardening in part until the full number of the Gentiles has come in.

26. And so all Israel will be saved, as it is written: "The deliverer will come from Zion; he will turn godlessness away from Jacob.

27. And this is my covenant with them when I take away their sins."

28.. As far as the gospel is concerned, they are enemies on your account; but as far as election is concerned, they are loved on account of the patriarchs,

29 bushi Ongo atanyaa bya abaa anyire mira, atbindula nemyanyisa yai kwa bandu ba amaere mira.

30 kwa mira, mwendee mwanana kuira bya Ongo atechire. Si erire abalosa ebonjo bwai kukulikana nokwa bayuta nabo. Bananaa kuira kwa Ongo atechire,

31 chasiya mu mutatula bayuta, Ongo abalose ebonjo bwai. Rero, obu bonjo bwai, bu anganalosa nabo.

32 Ongo airire ebandu boshi kuba nga bandu ba buroko bushi ne kunana kunde baira bya atechire. Airire bacha, chasiya alose ebonjo bwai kwa bandu boshi.

Myasi ya kutonga Ongo

33 ebuare bwa Ongo, nekumenya emyasi kwai, nebwenge bwai, bitangamaanyisibwa! kutali ola ungaala kumenya kute ku ende aisha emyasi, nesi kumenya enjira sai.

34 ebyera bikulikene nokwa maanjiko mabuya-buya matula matechire mbu: nde iwamenyaa emyanyisa ya enawetu? nde iwamweresa

---

29 부씨 오꼬 아다냐아 뱌 아바아 아니러 미라, 아두비뿌롸 너먀네사 야이 과 바뚜 바 아마어러 미라.

30 과 미라, 뭐떠어 모나나 구이라 뱌 오꼬 아더찌러. 시 어리러 아바론사 어보쪼 봐이 구구뀌가나 노과 바유다 나보. 바나나아 구이라 과 오꼬 아더찌러,

31 짜시야 무 무다두롸 바유다, 오꼬 아바론서 어보쪼 봐이. 러로, 오부 보쪼 봐이, 부 아까나론사 나보.

32 오꼬 아이리러 어바뚜 보씨 구바 까 바뚜 바 부로고 부씨 너 구나나 구떠 바이라 뱌 아더찌러. 아이리러 바짜, 짜시야 아론서 어보쪼 봐이 과 바뚜 보씨.

먀시 야 구도꺄 오꼬

33 어부아러 봐 오꼬, 너구머냐 어먀시 과이, 너붜어 봐이, 비다꺄마아네시봐! 구다뀌 오롸 우꺄아롸 구머냐 구떠 구 어꺼 아이싸 어먀시, 너시 구머냐 어찌라 사이.

34 어벼라 비구뀌거너 노과 마아찌고 마부야-부야 마두롸 마더찌러 뿌: 떠 이와머냐아 어먀네사 야 어나워두? 떠 이와뭐러사 어아노?

---

29. for God's gifts and his call are irrevocable.

30. Just as you who were at one time disobedient to God have now received mercy as a result of their disobedience,

31. so they too have now become disobedient in order that they too may now receive mercy as a result of God's mercy to you.

32. For God has bound all men over to disobedience so that he may have mercy on them all.

33. Oh, the depth of the riches of the wisdom and knowledge of God! How unsearchable his judgments, and his paths beyond tracing out!

34. "Who has known the mind of the Lord? Or who has been his counselor?"

eano?

35 nde iwaalaa kweresa Ongo kandu tangu, chasiya Ongo amufulusiseko?

36 bushi ebindu byoshi era mwai yibyende byatenga, byoshi bitulao kwa buashi bwai, kanji bushi nai, Ongo endaa atongibwa esuku nemango. Bibe bacha!

35 떠 이와아꽈아 궈러사 오끄 가뚜 다우, 짜시야 오끄 아무푸루시서고?

36 부씨 어비뚜 뵤씨 어라 롸이 에벼떠 뱌더꽈, 뵤씨 비두꽈오 과 부아씨 봐이, 가찌 부씨 나이, 오끄 어따아 아도삐봐 어수구 너마끄. 비버 바짜!

35. "Who has ever given to God, that God should repay him?"

36. For from him and through him and to him are all things. To him be the glory forever! Amen.

Ba Roma Chikono 12
Ekuchana kwa kukorera Ongo

1 Rero banyaketu, bushi nobonjo bwa Ongo atulosise, nabema mundaa mwana emibiri yenyu kuba mitulo* era iri iuma-uma, ibuya-buya, kanji era imusimisise. Eyera injira ye kanangana yekumwera.

2 mutandaa mwakulikira emyanya yebandu besine suku. Si mureka Ongo ababindule mwakuhuba kuira ebwenge bwenyu kuba buyayaya. Mwa bacha, mungaala kunde mwamenyerera bya Ongo ahonda: byabiri bibuya, bya bimusimisise, nebya bilumirire.

바 로마 찌고노 12
어구짜나 과 구고려라 오끄

1 러로 바냐거두, 부씨 노보쪼 봐 오끄 아두똔시서, 나버마 무따아 롸나 어미비리 여뉴 구바 미두똔* 어라 이리 이우마-우마, 이부야-부야, 가찌 어라 이무시미시서. 어여라 이찌라 여 가나꽈나 여구뭐라.

2 무다따아 롹구뀌기라 어먀냐 여바뚜 버시너 수구. 시 무러가 오끄 아바비뚜뗘 롹구후바 구이라 어붜뗘 붜뉴 구바 부야야야. 롸 바짜, 무꽈아꽈 구너 롸머녀러라 뱌 오끄 아호따: 뱌비리 비부야, 뱌 비무시미시서, 너뱌 비루미리러.

Rome Chapter 12[NIV]

1. Therefore, I urge you, brothers, in view of God's mercy, to offer your bodies as living sacrifices, holy and pleasing to God--this is your spiritual act of worship.

2. Do not conform any longer to the pattern of this world, but be transformed by the renewing of your mind. Then you will be able to test and approve what God's will is--his good, pleasing and perfect will.

3 bushi nengahanya sa Ongo anyeresise, bacha ku nababura muboshi: kutabaa mundu ola undaa wachitola nga iwete mufa kurenza kwa ali. Si mundaa mwachitola ngokwa munali, chira mundu kukulikana ne chipimo che bwemeresi bwa Ongo amweresise.

4 emubiri atula muuma, si atusa bitera binene. Na chira chitera, chitusa wai mulimo.

5 netu kutunali bacha. Chiro mbu tuli banene, si tunali mubiri muuma kurengera ebuuma bwetu na kirisito*. Tuboshi tuli mwa buuma nga bitera bya mubiri muuma.

6 rero, mwa bubuya bwai, atweresise nyembo sa sirengan yire. Rero, ola weresibwe elwembo lwekureba, endaa areba kukulikana nebwemeresi bwai.

7 ola weresibwe elwembo lwekuba mukosi, endaa akola. Ola weresibwe elwembo lwekuknagirisa, endaa akangirisa.

---

3 부씨 너꺄하냐 사 오꼬 아녀러시서, 바짜 구 나바부라 무보씨: 구다바아 무뚜 오롸 우따아 와찌도롸 꺄 이워더 무파 구러쌰 과 아뢰. 시 무따아 뫄찌도롸 꼬과 무나뢰, 찌라 무뚜 구구뢰가나 너 찌피모 쩌 뷔머러시 봐 오꼬 아뭐러시서.

4 어무비리 아두롸 무우마, 시 아두사 비더라 비너너. 나 찌라 찌더라, 찌두사 와이 무뢰모.

5 너두 구두나뢰 바짜. 찌로 뿌 두뢰 바너너, 시 두나뢰 무비리 무우마 구러꺼라 어부우마 붜두 나 기리시도*. 두보씨 두뢰 뫄 부우마 꺄 비더라 뱌 무비리 무우마.

6 러로, 뫄 부부야 봐이, 아뭐러시서 녀뽀 사 시러꺄누 에러. 러로, 오롸 워러시붜 어뭐뽀 붜구러바, 어따아 아러바 구구뢰가나 너붜머러시 봐이.

7 오롸 워러시붜 어뭐뽀 붜구바 무고시, 어따아 아고롸. 오롸 워러시붜 어뭐뽀 붜구구나지리사, 어따아 아가삐리사.

---

3. For by the grace given me I say to every one of you: Do not think of yourself more highly than you ought, but rather think of yourself with sober judgment, in accordance with the measure of faith God has given you.

4. Just as each of us has one body with many members, and these members do not all have the same function,

5. so in Christ we who are many form one body, and each member belongs to all the others.

6. We have different gifts, according to the grace given us. If a man's gift is prophesying, let him use it in proportion to his faith.

7. If it is serving, let him serve; if it is teaching, let him teach;

8 ola weresibibwe elwembo lwekusesa ebanji emchima , endaa abasesao. Ola weresibibwe elwembo lwekwana, endaa ana na mchima muuma. Ola wemangirire ebanji, endaa emangirabo na bushiru. Nola weresibibwe lwembo lwe kuasa ba balaire, endaa aasabo na lumoo.

9 enzii yenyu indaa yanaba ya kanangana. Mundaa mwanyaa emabi, si mundaa mwasimika mwa mabuya.

10 mutendaa mwafulussisa emundu emabi kwa manji. Mundaa mwaira bya bandu boshi basene mundaa mwasimana busese nga bauma, na kunde mwaata bushiru mwa kweresanya etunda.

11 mutabaa ngalisi, si mundaa mwakorera enawetu na bushiru kanji namuchima muuma.

12 mundaa mwamowa bushi nemunyiiro ola mutusa. Mundaa mwaata ebushibirisi mwa malibuko, na kunde mwema busira kutama.

13 mundaa mwaasa ebandu ba Ongo mwa malae mabo, na kunde mwahukaasa

8 오라 워러시비붜 어뤄뽀 뤄구서사 어바찌 어무찌마 , 어따아 아바서사오. 오롸 워러시비붜 어뤄뽀 뤄과나, 어따아 아나 나 무찌마 무우마. 오롸 워마삐리러 어바찌, 어따아 어마삐라보 나 부씨루. 노롸 워러시비붜 뤄뽀 뤄 구아사 바 바롸이러, 어따아 아아사보 나 루모오.

9 어씨이 여뉴 이따아 야나바 야 가나따나. 무따아 모나야 어마비, 시 무따아 모시미가 뫄 마부야.

10 무더따아 뫄푸루씨사 어무뚜 어마비 과 마찌. 무따아 모이라 뱌 바뚜 보씨 바서너 무따아 모시마나 부서서 뫄 바우마, 나 구떠 뫄아다 부씨루 뫄 궈러사냐 어두따.

11 무다바아 따찌시, 시 무따아 모고러라 어나워두 나 부씨루 가찌 나무찌마 무우마.

12 무따아 뫄모와 부씨 너무네이로 오롸 무두사. 무따아 모아다 어부씨비리시 뫄 마찌부고, 나 구떠 뭐마 부시라 구다마.

13 무따아 모아사 어바뚜 바 오꼬 뫄 마롸어 마보, 나 구떠 뫄후가아사 바어네.

8. if it is encouraging, let him encourage; if it is contributing to the needs of others, let him give generously; if it is leadership, let him govern diligently; if it is showing mercy, let him do it cheerfully.

9. Love must be sincere. Hate what is evil; cling to what is good.

10. Be devoted to one another in brotherly love. Honor one another above yourselves.

11. Never be lacking in zeal, but keep your spiritual fervor, serving the Lord.

12. Be joyful in hope, patient in affliction, faithful in prayer.

13. Share with God's people who are in need. Practice hospitality.

baenyi.

14 mundaa mwahanyira ba bende babalibusa. Mundaa mwanyirabo, si mutendaa mwabatakira.

14 무따아 뫄하네라 바 버뻐 바바쀠부사. 무따아 뫄네라보, 시 무더따아 뫄바다기라.

14. Bless those who persecute you; bless and do not curse.

15 mundaa mwamowa na ba bamowa. Mundaa mwalira na babalira.

15 무따아 뫄모와 나 바 바모와. 무따아 뫄쀠라 나 바바쀠라.

15. Rejoice with those who rejoice; mourn with those who mourn.

16 mundaa mwomvikana mwa kachi-kachi kenyu. Mutendaa mwaata mianyisa ya kucherusa, si mundaa mwakomerana ne barembu.

16 무따아 뫔삐가나 뫄 가찌-가찌 거뉴. 무더따아 뫄아다 미아네사 야 구쩌루사, 시 무따아 뫄고머라나 너 바러뿌.

16. Live in harmony with one another. Do not be proud, but be willing to associate with people of low position. Do not be conceited.

17 Mutendaa mwachitola nga ba bete bwenge bunene. kwa bikomire.

17 무더따아 뫄찌도롸 까 바 버더 붜꺼 부너너. 과 비고미러.

17. Do not repay anyone evil for evil. Be careful to do what is right in the eyes of everybody.

18 akaba bingalikana, kukulikana nebuashi bwenyu, mundaa mwabaa mwa bolo nebandu boshi.

18 아가바 비까쀠가나, 구구쀠가나 너부아씨 붜뉴, 무따아 뫄바아 뫄 보로 너바뚜 보씨.

18. If it is possible, as far as it depends on you, live at peace with everyone.

19 banyaketu basiirwa, mutenda mwachifuna. Si mundaa mwendaa mwarekera Ongo echihangi chekubafuna kukulikana ne bute bwai. Bushi byanjikirwe mwa maanjiko mabuya-buya mbu: nyono, nyi nyikafuna ebandu na kwemba chira mundu kukulikana na bya airaa.

19 바냐거두 바시이롸, 무더따 뫄찌푸나. 시 무따아 뭐따아 뫄러거라 오꼬 어찌하삐 쩌구바푸나 구구쀠가나 너 부더 봐이. 부씨 뱌찌기뤄 뫄 마아찌고 마부야-부야 뿌: 뇨노, 네 네가푸나 어바뚜 나 귀빠 찌라 무뚜 구구쀠가나 나 뱌 아이라아.

19. Do not take revenge, my friends, but leave room for God's wrath, for it is written: "It is mine to avenge; I will repay,"says the Lord.

20 si kanji byanjikirwe mbu: akaba emurenda wao afa

20 시 가찌 뱌찌기뤄 뿌: 아가바 어무러따 와오 아파

20. On the contrary: "If your enemy is hungry, feed him;

businya, umweresa ebiryo. Na kaba afa chami, umweresaa ebyekumwa. Ekuira bacha, kuli ngokwa bangamubika engala-ngala sa sakorera buseses kwe twe.

21 utendaa wemerera kuimwa ne mabi, si undaa waimamo mwa kuira emabuya

부시냐, 우뭐러사 어비료. 나 가바 아파 짜미, 우뭐러사아 어벼구뫄. 어구이라 바짜, 구삐 꼬과 바까무비가 어까롸-까롸 사 사고러라 부서서수 궈 뒈.

21 우더따아 워머러라 구이뫄 너 마비, 시 우따아 와이마모 뫄 구이라 어마부야

if he is thirsty, give him something to drink. In doing this, you will heap burning coals on his head."

21. Do not be overcome by evil, but overcome evil with good.

Ba Roma Chikono 13
Ekuira kwa bakulu-kulu batechire

1 Chirabmundu emire kunde aira kwa bakulu-kulu ba bemire batechire. Bushi Ongo yeine iwende waira emundu kuba mukulu-kulu. Nebakulu-kulu ba bemire, Ongo iwemikaabo.

2 bushi noku, ola walwisa ebakulu-kulu, eri alwisa emuomba* wa Ongo. Ne bandu ba banana kuira kwa bakulu-kulu batechire, bamenya kwa bachikululira ebuchinjibusi beine.

3 mango mundu aira emabuya, atangobaa ebakulu-kulu. Si emundu akobaa ebakulu-kulu, mango aira emabi. Utahonda kunde

바 로마 찌고노 13
어구이라 과 바구루-구루 바더찌러

1 찌라부무뚜 어미러 구너 아이라 과 바구루-구루 바 버미러 바더찌러. 부씨 오꼬 여이너 이워떠 와이라 어무뚜 구바 무구루루-구루. 너바구루루-구루 바 버미러, 오꼬 이워미가아보.

2 부씨 노구, 오롸 와뤼사 어바구루루-구루, 어리 아뤼사 어무오빠* 와 오꼬. 너 바뚜 바 바나나 구이라 과 바구루루-구루 바더찌러, 바머냐 과 바찌구루뤼라 어부찌찌부시 버이너.

3 마꼬 무뚜 아이라 어마부야, 아다꼬바아 어바구루루-구루. 시 어무뚜 아고바아 어바구루루-구루, 마꼬 아이라 어마비. 우다호따 구너 오바아

Rome Chapter 13[NIV]

1. Everyone must submit himself to the governing authorities, for there is no authority except that which God has established. The authorities that exist have been established by God.

2. Consequently, he who rebels against the authority is rebelling against what God has instituted, and those who do so will bring judgment on themselves.

3. For rulers hold no terror for those who do right, but for those who do wrong. Do you want to be free from fear of the one in authority?

wobaa ebakulu-kulu? rero, undaa waira emabuya, chasiya bende bakutonga.

어바구루-구루? 러로, 우따아 와이라 어마부야, 짜시야 버너 바구도따.

Then do what is right and he will commend you.

4 ebakulu-kulu batula bakose ba Ongo kwakuasa ebandu bende baira emabuya. Si akaba ungaira emabi, kuika unobae bushi bete ebuashi bwekukuchinjibusa. Bende bakorera Ongo kwa kulosa ebute bwai kwabakosi be mabi.

4 어바구루-구루 바두따 바고서 바 오끄 과구아사 어바뚜 버너 바이라 어마부야. 시 아가바 우까이라 어마비, 구이가 우노바어 부씨 버더 어부아씨 붜구구찌띠부사. 버너 바고러라 오끄 과 구룻사 어부더 봐이 과바고시 버 마비.

4. For he is God's servant to do you good. But if you do wrong, be afraid, for he does not bear the sword for nothing. He is God's servant, an agent of wrath to bring punishment on the wrongdoer.

5 bushi noku, byemire munde mwaira kwa bakulu-kulu batechire. Atabushi nekwobaa ebute bwa Ongo oshao, si kanji bushi mwa michia yetu bitwemire kunde twaira bacha.

5 부씨 노구, 벼미러 무너 똬이라 과 바구루-구루 바더찌러. 아다부씨 너굘바아 어부더 봐 오끄 오싸오, 시 가찌 부씨 똬 미찌아 여두 비뭐미러 구너 돠이라 바짜.

5. Therefore, it is necessary to submit to the authorities, not only because of possible punishment but also because of conscience.

6 kanji echera chi chende chatuma mwafuta embarata. Bushi abu bdende bakola oyu mulimo, Ongo ibende bakorera.

6 가찌 어쩌라 찌 쩌너 짜두따 똬푸다 어빠라다. 부씨 아부 부더너 바고똬 오유 무뢰모, 오끄 이버너 바고러라.

6. This is also why you pay taxes, for the authorities are God's servants, who give their full time to governing.

7 mundaa mweresa chira mundu bya emire kweresibwa: emufichisi we mbarata, embarata ; emufichisi we mukoro, emukoro ; ola wemire kweresibwa etunda, etunda ; ola wemire kutongibwa, atongibwaa.

7 무따아 뭐러사 찌라 무두 뱌 어미러 궈러시봐: 어무피찌시 워 빠라다, 어빠라다 ; 어무피찌시 워 무고로, 어무고로 ; 오똬 워미러 궈러시봐 어두따, 어두따 ; 오똬 워미러 구도띠봐, 아도띠봐아.

7. Give everyone what you owe him: If you owe taxes, pay taxes; if revenue, then revenue; if respect, then respect; if honor, then honor.

Ekusimana

어구시마나

8 mutendaa mwaata mwinda wa chiro na mundu asibya. Si mwinda muuma imwemire kuata oshao, kuli ekusimana. Bushi ola usimire mulikabo, eri aira kwa mwaso* woshi atula atechire.

9 bushi ene miomba *itula itechire mbu: utendaa wabanda ekiri, utenda weta, utendaa weba, utendaa wahumira ebyabene. Ei miomba alauma neinji yoshi, ifinjikirwe mwono muomba* muuma ola techire mbu: undaa wasima mulikenyu ngokwa utula uchisimire weine.

10 emundu ola usimire mulikabo, atangamukorera mabi. Bushi noku, ola wete nzii eri aira kwa Mwaso *woshi atula atechire.

Ekuchikunganya kwa kufuluka kwa kirisito

11 Mwishi esuku sa twera tulimo. Ebihangi byenyu byekutenga mwa tulo byaikire. Bushi elusuku lwa Ongo angatununula lwera luli ofu, kurenza ngokwa byabaa biri mango twemerera.

12 ebutufu bwahonda kucha, nemushi ali ofu. Rero,

8 무더따아 롸아다 뮈따 와 찌로 나 무뚜 아시뱌. 시 뮈따 무우마 이뭐미러 구아다 오싸오, 구뢰 어구시마나. 부씨 오롸 우시미러 무뢰가보, 어리 아이라 과 롸소* 옷씨 아두롸 아더찌러.

9 부씨 어너 미오빠 *이두롸 이더찌러 뿌: 우더따아 와바따 어기리, 우더따 워다, 우더따아 워바, 우더따아 와후미라 어뱌버너. 아이 미오빠 아롸우마 너이찌 요씨, 이피찌기뤄 모노 무오빠* 무우마 오롸 더찌러 뿌: 우따아 와시마 무뢰거뉴 꼬과 우두롸 우찌시미러 워이너.

10 어무뚜 오롸 우시미러 무뢰가보, 아다빠무고러라 마비. 부씨 노구, 오롸 워더 씨이 어리 아이라 과 롸소 *옷씨 아두롸 아더찌러.

어구찌구빠냇 과 구푸루— 과 기리시도

11 뮈씨 어수구 사 뚸라 두뢰모. 어비하삐 벼뉴 벼구더빠 롸 두로 뱌이기러. 부씨 어룩수구 롸 오꼬 아빠두누누롸 뤄라 루뢰 오푸, 구러싸 꼬과 뱌바아 비리 마꼬 뚸머러라.

12 어부두푸 봐호따 구짜, 너무씨 아뢰 오푸. 러로,

8. Let no debt remain outstanding, except the continuing debt to love one another, for he who loves his fellowman has fulfilled the law.

9. The commandments, "Do not commit adultery," "Do not murder," "Do not steal," "Do not covet," and whatever other commandment there may be, are summed up in this one rule: "Love your neighbor as yourself."

10. Love does no harm to its neighbor. Therefore love is the fulfillment of the law.

11. And do this, understanding the present time. The hour has come for you to wake up from your slumber, because our salvation is nearer now than when we first believed.

12. The night is nearly over; the day is almost here. So

tkabuliraa bure emyasi era yende yairwa mwa musimya, twanatola ebikaya byekulwa nabi mwa bulangare.

13 tundaa twaata myanya ibuya era yemire kuiribwa mwa bihangi byemushi. Tundaa twachilanga nekulya kwa kurengerese ne butamisi, ne buhungu ne lusingi, ne mbangano ne mufula.

14 mubaa nga enawetu Yesu kirisito, mutendaa mwachemerera kukululwa nemyanyisa yenyu ibi, kukira echihangi yabeka mwa bibi.

두가부뛰라아 부러 어먀시 어라 여떠 야이롸 마 무시먀, 돠나도롸 어비가야 벼구꽌 나비 마 부롸따러.

13 두따아 돠아다 먀냐 이부야 어라 여미러 구이리봐 마 비하삐 벼무씨. 두따아 돠찌꽈아 너구꺄 과 구러떠러서 너 부다미시, 너 부후익 너 루시삐, 너 빠아노 너 무푸꽈.

14 무바아 따 어나워두 여수 기리시도, 무더따아 먀쩌머러라 구구루꽌 너먀네사 여뉴 이비, 구기라 어찌하삐 야버가 마 비비.

let us put aside the deeds of darkness and put on the armor of light.

13. Let us behave decently, as in the daytime, not in orgies and drunkenness, not in sexual immorality and debauchery, not in dissension and jealousy.

14. Rather, clothe yourselves with the Lord Jesus Christ, and do not think about how to gratify the desires of the sinful nature.

Ba Roma Chikono 14
Utendaa wachinjibusa munyakenyu

1 Munda mwangirira ola utasimikiri mwa bwemeresi, busira kuemanza bwaka era luulu semyannyisa yai.

2 kuli omundu ola ebwemeresi bwai bumubwirire kwa anganalya chira kalyo. Si eunji yeke, kukulikana ne bwemeresi bwai bwa butasimikire, ende alya enyanyi oshao.

3 ola wende walya chira kalyo, atmire kunde achinjibusa ola wende walya

바 로마 찌고노 14
우더따씹 와찌씨뵙뻼 무냐거뉴

1 무따 마삐리라 오롸 우다시미기리 마 붸머러시, 부시라 구어마싸 봐가 어라 루우루 서먀누네사 야이.

2 구뛰 오무뚜 오롸 어붸머러시 봐이 부무뷔리러 과 아까나꺄 찌라 가꾜. 시 어우씨 여거, 구구뛰가나 너 붸머러시 봐이 봐 부다시미기러, 어떠 아꺄 어냐네 오싸오.

3 오롸 워더 와꺄 찌라 가꾜, 아두미러 구더 아찌씨부사 오롸 워더 와꺄 찌로 가꾜,

Rome Chapter 14[NIV]

1. Accept him whose faith is weak, without passing judgment on disputable matters.

2. One man's faith allows him to eat everything, but another man, whose faith is weak, eats only vegetables.

3. The man who eats everything must not look down on him who does not,

chiro kalyo, bushi Ongo amwangirire.

부씨 오꼬 아뫄삐리러.

and the man who does not eat everything must not condemn the man who does, for God has accepted him.

4 woyu uli nde, uwachinjibusa emukosi wenji mundu? akaba oyu mukosi angasimika bushi enawetu ete ebuashi bwekumuasa.

4 오유 우릐 떠, 우와찌씨부사 어무고시 원찌 무뚜? 아가바 오유 무고시 아꺄시미가 부씨 어나워두 어더 어부아씨 뷔구무아사.

4. Who are you to judge someone else's servant? To his own master he stands or falls. And he will stand, for the Lord is able to make him stand.

5 kuli emundu ola wende watola suku siuma nga ste mufa kurenza esinji. Si eu nji yeke, ende atola esuku nga sinali kuuma. Rero, chira mundu endaa anemangira kwebya muchima wai amuburire.

5 구릐 어무뚜 오롸 워떠 와도롸 수구 시우마 꺄 수더 무파 구러롸 어시씨. 시 어우 씨 여거, 어더 아도롸 어수구 꺄 시나릐 구우마. 러로, 찌라 무뚜 어따아 아너마삐라 귀뱌 무찌마 와이 아무부리러.

5. One man considers one day more sacred than another; another man considers every day alike. Each one should be fully convinced in his own mind.

6 ola utula utolire lusuku lurebe nga luwete mufa kurenza esinji , ende aira ebyera kwa kutonga enawetu. Nola wende walya chira kalyo, nai ende aira bacha kwa kutonga enawetu. Endee aira bacha kwa kuteta mbu akoko era mwa Ongo bushi nesi biryo. Nola utalya kalyo, nai ende aira bacha kwa kutonga enawetu, na kuteta mbu akoko era mwa Ongo.

6 오롸 우두롸 우도픠러 루수구 루러버 꺄 루웨더 무파 구러롸 어시씨 , 어더 아이라 어뷰라 과 구도꺄 어나워두. 노롸 워떠 와롸 찌라 가료, 나이 어더 아이라 바짜 과 구도꺄 어나워두. 어떠어 아이라 바짜 과 구더다 뿌 아고고 어라 뫄 오꼬 부씨 너시 비료. 노롸 우다롸 가료, 나이 어더 아이라 바짜 과 구도꺄 어나워두, 나 구더다 뿌 아고고 어라 뫄 오꼬.

6. He who regards one day as special, does so to the Lord. He who eats meat, eats to the Lord, for he gives thanks to God; and he who abstains, does so to the Lord and gives thanks to God.

7 kubinali, kutali chiro na mundu asibya mu tubano ola uli muuma-uma kwa mufa

7 구비나릐, 구다릐 찌로 나 무뚜 아시뱌 무 두바노 오롸 우릐 무우마-우마 과 무파

7. For none of us lives to himself alone and none of us dies to himself alone.

wai yeine. Nesi kutali ola wende wafa kwa mufa wai yeine.

8 bushi akaba tuli bauma-uma, tuli bauma-uma kwa mufa wa enawetu. Na akaba tungafa, twende twafa kwa mufa wa enawetu. Rero, akaba tuli bauma-uma, nesi akaba tungafa, tubano tunali bandu ba enwaetu.

9 bushi kirisito*afaa nekwomoka, chasiya abe enawetu tuboshi tu tuli bauma-uma na ba bafire.

10 si woyo, chi chatuma wachinjibusa munyakenyu? nao, chi chatuma wakena munyakenyu? bushi toboshi tukatongana era muhondo se tiribinali ya Ongo.

11 bushi byanjikirwe mwa maanjiko mabuya-buya mbu: enawetu alaisise mbu: kukulikana nokwa nyinatula muuma-uma, chira mundu woshi akakoma emafi era muhondo sanyi. Na chira mundu woshi akateta mbu nyiri Ongo.

12 chira mundu akachitetera yeine era muhondo sa Ongo era luulu se bya airaa.

와이 여이너. 너시 구다뤼 오롸 워뚜 와파 과 무파 와이 여이너.

8 부씨 아가바 두뤼 바우마-우마, 두뤼 바우마-우마 과 무파 와 어나워두. 나 아가바 두까파, 뛰뚜 돠파 과 무파 와 어나워두. 러로, 아가바 두뤼 바우마-우마, 너시 아가바 두까파, 두바노 두나뤼 바뚜 바 어놔어두.

9 부씨 기리시도*아파아 너고모가, 짜시야 아버 어나워두 두보씨 두 두뤼 바우마-우마 나 바 바피러.

10 시 오요, 찌 짜두마 와찌띠부사 무냐거뉴? 나오, 찌 짜두마 와거나 무냐거뉴? 부씨 도보씨 두가도까나 어라 무호또 서 디리비나뤼 야 오꼬.

11 부씨 뱌찌기뤄 마 마아찌고 마부야-부야 뿌: 어나워두 아롸이시서 뿌: 구구뤼가나 노과 내나두롸 무우마-우마, 찌라 무뚜 오씨 아가고마 어마피 어라 무호또 사네. 나 찌라 무뚜 오씨 아가더더라 뿌 네리 오꼬.

12 찌라 무뚜 아가찌더더라 여이너 어라 무호또 사 오꼬 어라 루우루 서 뱌 아이라아.

8. If we live, we live to the Lord; and if we die, we die to the Lord. So, whether we live or die, we belong to the Lord.

9. For this very reason, Christ died and returned to life so that he might be the Lord of both the dead and the living.

10. You, then, why do you judge your brother? Or why do you look down on your brother? For we will all stand before God's judgment seat.

11. It is written: " 'As surely as I live,' says the Lord, 'every knee will bow before me; every tongue will confess to God.' "

12. So then, each of us will give an account of himself to God.

Utendaa watchwuma mulyikenyu aya mwa bibi

우더따씹 와쭈립 무레개닐 아야 뫄 비비

13 rero, tureka kunde twachinjibusanya. Kanji mutendaa mwaira mwasi asibya ola ungatuma munyakenyu asitala na aya mwa bibi.

13 러로, 두러가 구머 돠찌찌부사냐. 가찌 무더따아 뫄이라 뫄시 아시뱌 오라 우빠두마 무냐거뉴 아시다빠 나 아야 뫄 비비.

13. Therefore let us stop passing judgment on one another. Instead, make up your mind not to put any stumbling block or obstacle in your brother's way.

14 kukulikana nokwa nyitula mwa buuma na enawetu Yesu, nyishi kanangana kwa kutali kandu ka katula baiirre. Si ekandu kende kabiya kukulikana nola ukatolire nga kali kabi.

14 구구삐가나 노과 네두빠 뫄 부우마 나 어나워두 여수, 니씨 가나빠나 과 구다삐 가뚜 가 가두빠 바이이루러. 시 어가뚜 거거 가비야 구구삐가나 노빠 우가도삐러 빠 가삐 가비.

14. As one who is in the Lord Jesus, I am fully convinced that no food is unclean in itself. But if anyone regards something as unclean, then for him it is unclean.

15 akaba ungasibusa munyakenyu bushi nebiryo bya walya, kukuteta mbu atakoresibwa nenzii. Bushi ne biryo byao, bitemire mbu uesaa emundu ola kirisito* afiraa.

15 아가바 우빠시부사 무냐거뉴 부씨 너비료 뱌 와퍄, 구구더다 뿌 아다고러시봐 너씨이. 부씨 너 비료 뱌오, 비더미러 뿌 우어사아 어무뚜 오빠 기리시도* 아피라아.

15. If your brother is distressed because of what you eat, you are no longer acting in love. Do not by your eating destroy your brother for whom Christ died.

16 rero, ekandu kamuseneko kwa kakomire, mumenyaa ebandu bangesha kunde bamaanako bulio.

16 러로, 어가뚜 가무서너고 과 가고미러, 무머냐아 어바뚜 바빠싸 구머 바마아나고 부삐오.

16. Do not allow what you consider good to be spoken of as evil.

17 bushi ebwami bwa Ongo* butatula bwerekere ebyekulya nesi ebye kumwa. Si butula bwerekere emyasi era itungenene, ne bolo, ne lumoo. Ebi byoshi byatenga era mwe mchima mubuya-buya.

17 부씨 어봐미 봐 오꼬* 부다두빠 붜러거러 어벼구퍄 너시 어벼 구뫄. 시 부두빠 붜러거러 어먀시 어라 이두뻐너너, 너 보룯, 너 룯모오. 어비 뵤씨 뱌더빠 어라 뭐 무찌마 무부야-부야.

17. For the kingdom of God is not a matter of eating and drinking, but of righteousness, peace and joy in the Holy Spirit,

18 ola wende wakorera

18 오빠 워더 와고러라

18. because anyone who

kirisito* mwei njira ende asimisa Ongo, kanji aata ngulu ibuya mwa bandu.

19 bushi noku, tundaa twahonda emyasi era ingatuma twabamwa bolo, kanji era ingutuasa kukula alauma mwa bwemresi.

20 utendaa weta emulimo wa Ongo bushi nemyasi era yekere ebiryo. Kubinali, ebiryo byoshi binganalibwa. Si kutakomire ekulya ebiryo bya bingatuma eunji aya mwa mabi.

21 cha chikomire kuli kunana kulya enyama , na kumwa etifai, nakuchulanga kuchira kandu koshi kakangatuma munyakenyu aya mwabibi.

22 bya utula wemrere era luulu sei myasi, undaa walangabi mwa mchima wao weine era muhondo sa Ongo. Aahanyirwe, ola utachiya mwa mchima buhi bya aira.

23 si ola wahungwa-hungwa era luulu sebiryo bya alya, Ongo ende amuchinjibusa, bushi bya aira bitakulikene ne bwemeresi. Na chira mwasi ola wairbwa, atanakulikene ne bwemeresi, chiri chibi.

기리시도* 뭐이 띠라 어떠 아시미사 오꼬, 가찌 아아다 꾸루 이부야 먀 바뉴.

19 부씨 노구, 두따아 됴호따 어먀시 어라 이빠두마 됴바먀 보론, 가찌 어라 이꾸두아사 구구꽈 아꽈우마 먀 붜러시.

20 우더따아 워다 어무찌모 와 오꼬 부씨 너먀시 어라 여거러 어비료. 구비나뤼, 어비료 뵤씨 비빠나뤼봐. 시 구다고미러 어구꺄 어비료 뱌 비빠두마 어우찌 아야 먀 마비.

21 짜 찌고미러 구뤼 구나나 구꺄 어냐마 , 나 구봐 어디파이, 나구쭈꽈빠 구찌라 가뉴 고씨 가가빠두마 무냐거뉴 아야 먀비비.

22 뱌 우두꽈 워러러 어라 루우루 서이 먀시, 우따아 와꽈빠비 먀 무찌마 와오 워이너 어라 무호또 사 오꼬. 아아하니뤄, 오꽈 우다찌야 먀 무찌마 부히 뱌 아이라.

23 시 오꽈 와후꽈-후꽈 어라 루우루 서비료 뱌 아꺄, 오꼬 어떠 아무찌찌부사, 부씨 뱌 아이라 비다구뤼거너 너 붜머러시. 나 찌라 마시 오꽈 와이루봐, 아다나구뤼거너 너 붜머러시, 찌리 찌비.

---

serves Christ in this way is pleasing to God and approved by men.

19. Let us therefore make every effort to do what leads to peace and to mutual edification.

20. Do not destroy the work of God for the sake of food. All food is clean, but it is wrong for a man to eat anything that causes someone else to stumble.

21. It is better not to eat meat or drink wine or to do anything else that will cause your brother to fall.

22. So whatever you believe about these things keep between yourself and God. Blessed is the man who does not condemn himself by what he approves.

23. But the man who has doubts is condemned if he eats, because his eating is not from faith; and everything that does not come from faith is sin.

Ba Roma Chikono 15

Ekusimisa balyiketchwu

1 Tubano tu tusimikire mwa bwemeresi, tutemire kunde twaira bya bitusimise tubeine, si twemire kunde twaasa ba batasimikire mwa bwemweresi.

2 chira mundu mwa kachi-kachi ketu emire kunde asimisa mulikabo chasiya aendekere akula mwa bwmeresi.

3 bushi anabe na kirisito* atendee aira bya bimusimisise yeine. Si kukulikana nokwa bitula byanjikirwe mwa maanjiko mabuya-buya mbu: engambo sa bangakukambire, nyono nyi berire bakambasi.

4 emyasi yoshi era yaanjikwaa kwa mira mwa maanjiko mabuya-buya, yaanjikwaa kwa mira mwa maanjiko tuate ebushibirishi na kutusesa emuchima, chasiya tuate elunyiiro.

5 Ongo iwende watuma ebandu baata ebushibirisi na kusesabo emuchima, endaa aberesa emuchima we kunde mwomvikana mwa kachi-kachi kenyu, ngokwa Yesu

바 로마 찌고노 15

어구시미사 바례개쭈

1 두바노 두 두시미기러 롸 붜머러시, 두더미러 구너 돠이라 뱌 비두시미서 두버이너, 시 뚸미러 구너 돠아사 바 바다시미기러 롸 붜뭐러시.

2 찌라 무뚜 롸 가찌-가찌 거두 어미러 구너 아시미사 무뤼가보 짜시야 아어떠거러 아구꽈 롸 부우머러시.

3 부씨 아나버 나 기리시도* 아더떠어 아이라 뱌 비무시시서 여이너. 시 구구뤼가나 노과 비두꽈 뱌찌기뤄 롸 마아찌고 마부야- 부야 뿌: 어까뽀 사 바까구가뻐러, 뇨노 네 버리러 바가빠시.

4 어먀시 요씨 어라 야아찌과아 과 미라 롸 마아찌고 마부야-부야, 야아찌과아 과 미라 롸 마아찌고 두아더 어부씨비리씨 나 구두서사 어무찌마, 짜시야 두아더 어루네이로.

5 오꼬 이워떠 와두마 어바뚜 바아다 어부씨비리시 나 구서사보 어무찌마, 어따아 아버러사 어무찌마 워 구너 몸뻬가나 롸 가찌-가찌 거뉴, 꼬과 여수 기리시도 어떠어

Rome Chapter 15[NIV]

1. We who are strong ought to bear with the failings of the weak and not to please ourselves.

2. Each of us should please his neighbor for his good, to build him up.

3. For even Christ did not please himself but, as it is written: "The insults of those who insult you have fallen on me."

4. For everything that was written in the past was written to teach us, so that through endurance and the encouragement of the Scriptures we might have hope.

5. May the God who gives endurance and encouragement give you a spirit of unity among yourselves as you follow Christ Jesus,

kirisito endee aira.

아이라.

6 mwa bacha, muboshi alauma na muchima muuma, kanji na murenge muuma mungende mwatonga Ongo, eshe wa enawetu Yesu kirisito.

6 와 바짜, 무보씨 아꺄우마 나 무찌마 무우마, 가찌 나 무러꺼 무우마 무꺼떠 먀도꽈 오꼬, 어써 와 어나워두 여수 기리시도.

6. so that with one heart and mouth you may glorify the God and Father of our Lord Jesus Christ.

Mwasi mubuya-buya kwa mbaa soshi

먀시 무부야-부야 과 빠씹 소씨

7 bushi noku, mundaa mwahuukasanya ngokwa kirisito*nai abahukasaa, chasiya Ongo aye ngulu.

7 부씨 노구, 무따아 먀후우가사냐 꼬과 기리시도*나이 아바후가사아, 짜시야 오꼬 아여 꾸루.

7. Accept one another, then, just as Christ accepted you, in order to bring praise to God.

8 nababura kwa kirisito* achirire kuba mukosi we bayuta, chasiya ebiraane bya Ongo eresaa bahokulu betu biberere. Airire bacha, chasiya alose kanangana kwa Ongo ende anaira bya alanyaa.

8 나바부라 과 기리시도* 아찌리러 구바 무고시 워 바유다, 짜시야 어비라아너 뱌 오꼬 어러사아 바호구루 버두 비버러러. 아이리러 바짜, 짜시야 아로쎄 가나꽈나 과 오꼬 어떠 아나이라 뱌 아꺄냐아.

8. For I tell you that Christ has become a servant of the Jewson behalf of God's truth, to confirm the promises made to the patriarchs

9 kanji aikaa, chasiya ba batatula bayuta bende batonga Ongo bushi ne bubuya bwai, kukulikana nokwa bitula byanjikirwe mwa maanjiko mabuya-buya mbu: echera chi chingende Chatuma nakutonga mwa bandu besinji mbaa. Nyingende nemba enyimbo sekutonga esina lyao.

9 가찌 아이가아, 짜시야 바 바다두꽈 바유다 버떠 바도꽈 오꼬 부씨 너 부부야 봐이, 구구끠가나 노과 비두꽈 뱌찌기뤄 먀 마아찌고 마부야- 부야 뿌: 어쩌라 찌 찌꺼떠 짜두마 나구도꽈 먀 바뚜 버시찌 빠아. 니꺼떠 너빠 어네뽀 서구도꽈 어시나 랴오.

9. so that the Gentiles may glorify God for his mercy, as it is written: "Therefore I will praise you among the Gentiles; I will sing hymns to your name."

10 kanji byanjikirwe mbu: mubandu besinnji mbaa, mundaa mwamowaa alauma ne lubaa lwa Ongo!

11 kanji byanjikirwe mbu: mu bandu besinji mbaa luboshi, mundaa mwatonga enawetu. Mu bandu boshi, mundaa mwamutonga!

12 murebi*Isaya nai atechire mbu: mwalubuto lwa Yese, mungatengera mundu muuma, ola ungemangira ebandu besinji mbaa. Nabu bandu, bangamulangalira.

13 Ongo iutula shokororo yeminyiiro, endaa abika elimoo nebolo bwa bunalumirere mwa michima yenyu kurengera ebwemeresi bwenyu. Endaa aira bacha, chasiya emunyiiro wenyu aendekere aluwa kurengera ebuashi bwe mchima mubuya-buya.

Emulyimo wa Paulo mwa bandju ba batatchwula bayuda

14 Banyaketu, nyeine nyineshi kanangana kwa muli bandu babuya busese, kanji mutula mwishi byoshi bya byemire kumenyeka, kanji mungaala kunde mweresanya emano.

15 si chiro bacha,

---

10 가찌 뱌찌기뤄 뿌: 무바뚜 버시누찌 빠아, 무따아 뫄모와아 아꽈우마 너 루바아 꽈 오끄!

11 가찌 뱌찌기뤄 뿌: 무 바뚜 버시찌 빠아 루보씨, 무따아 뫄도𝄴 어나워두. 무 바뚜 보씨, 무따아 뫄무도𝄴!

12 무러비*이사야 나이 아더찌러 뿌: 뫄루부도 꽈 여서, 무𝄴더러라 무뚜 무우마, 오꽈 우꺼마𝄴라 어바뚜 버시찌 빠아. 나부 바뚜, 바𝄴무꽈𝄴찌라.

13 오끄 이우두꽈 쏘고로로 여미네이로, 어따아 아비가 어찌모오 너보르 봐 부나루미러러 뫄 미찌마 여뉴 구러꺼라 어뭐머러시 뭐뉴. 어따아 아이라 바짜, 짜시야 어무네이로 워뉴 아어꺼거러 아루와 구러꺼라 어부아씨 뭐 무찌마 무부야-부야.

어무뤠명 와 파우르 뫄 바뚜 바 바다쭈꽈 바유다

14 바냐거두, 녀이너 니너씨 가나𝄴나 과 무뤼 바뚜 바부야 부서서, 가찌 무두꽈 뮈씨 보씨 뱌 벼미러 구머녀가, 가찌 무𝄴아꽈 구떠 뭐러사냐 어마노.

15 시 찌로 바짜,

---

10. Again, it says, "Rejoice, O Gentiles, with his people."

11. And again, "Praise the Lord, all you Gentiles, and sing praises to him, all you peoples."

12. And again, Isaiah says, "The Root of Jesse will spring up, one who will arise to rule over the nations; the Gentiles will hope in him."

13. May the God of hope fill you with all joy and peace as you trust in him, so that you may overflow with hope by the power of the Holy Spirit.

14. I myself am convinced, my brothers, that you yourselves are full of goodness, complete in knowledge and competent to instruct one another.

15. I have written you quite

nabaanjikiraa busira kubabisha kandu era luulu sa myasi yuma-yuma, chasiya nyihube kubakengesai. Nairaa bacha, kukulikana no bonjo bwa Ongo,

나바아씨기라아 부시라 구바비싸 가뚜 어라 루우루 사 먀시 유마-유마, 짜시야 네후버 구바거어사이. 나이라아 바짜, 구구뤼가나 노 보쪼 봐 오꼬,

boldly on some points, as if to remind you of them again, because of the grace God gave me

16 iwanyirire kuba mukosi wa Yesu kirisito kwa ba batatula bayuta. Anyilondwere, chasiya nyinde nahubanganyasabo emwasi Mubuya-buya. Mwa bacha, abu bandu bangere baba mitulo* era isimisise Ongo, kanji era ikomisibwe* na mchima mubuya-buya.

16 이와네리러 구바 무고시 와 여수 기리시도 과 바 바다두롸 바유다. 아네뤄뚜워러, 짜시야 네떠 나후바빠냐사보 어뫄시 무부야-부야. 똬 바짜, 아부 바뚜 바어러 바바 미두뤈* 어라 이시미시서 오꼬, 가찌 어라 이고미시붜* 나 무찌마 무부야-부야.

16. to be a minister of Christ Jesus to the Gentiles with the priestly duty of proclaiming the gospel of God, so that the Gentiles might become an offering acceptable to God, sanctified by the Holy Spirit.

17 rero , kurengera ebuuma bwanyi na kirisito*, nyingachitonga bushi nono mulimo na korera Ongo.

17 러로 , 구러뻐라 어부우마 봐네 나 기리시도*, 네빠찌도롸 부씨 노노 무뤼모 나 고러라 오꼬.

17. Therefore I glory in Christ Jesus in my service to God.

18 Bushi ndangaereresa kuteta era luulu sa unji mwasi, kureka emwasi ola kirisito*aira mwakunyirengerako, chasiya ebandu ba batatula bayuta bende batunda Ongo. Airaa bacha, kurengera byanabaa nenjire nateta na byanabaa nenjire naira.

18 부씨 따빠어러러사 구더다 어라 루우루 사 우찌 뫄시, 구러가 어뫄시 오롸 기리시도*아이라 똬구네러뻐라고, 짜시야 어바뚜 바 바다두롸 바유다 버뻐 바두따 오꼬. 아이라아 바짜, 구러뻐라 뱌나바아 너찌러 나더다 나 뱌나바아 너찌러 나이라.

18. I will not venture to speak of anything except what Christ has accomplished through me in leading the Gentiles to obey God by what I have said and done--

19 kurengera ebushi bwe bimenyeso ne bishishalo, nakurengera ebushi bwe mchima mubuya-buya. Mwei njira munahubanganyisaa ebandu emwasi mubuya-buya

19 구러뻐라 어부씨 붜 비메녀소 너 비씨싸뢴, 나구러뻐라 어부씨 붜 무찌마 무부야-부야. 뭐이 찌라 무나후바빠네사아 어바뚜 어뫄시 무부야-부야 와

19. by the power of signs and miracles, through the power of the Spirit. So from Jerusalem all the way around to Illyricum, I have fully proclaimed the gospel

wa kirisito*mwa bisiki byoshi, 기리시도*똬 비시기 뵤씨, of Christ.
kutengera eyerusalemu 구더뻐라 어여루사뻐무
kuikira mwa chio che Iliriko. 구이기라 똬 찌오 쩌
이뻐리고.

20 mwasi muuma inabaa 20 똬시 무우마 이나바아 20. It has always been my
nyiseriremo, abaa 네서리러모, 아바아 ambition to preach the
wakuhubanganya emwasi 와구후바빠냐 어똬시 무부야- gospel where Christ was not
mubuya-buya, mwa bisiki bya 부야, 똬 비시기 뱌 known, so that I would not
kirisito*abaa atasa 기리시도*아바아 아다사 be building on someone
kwomvikalamo oshao. Nairaa 꼬삐가꽈모 오싸오. 나이라아 else's foundation.
bacha, bushi nabaa ndahonda 바짜, 부씨 나바아 따호따
kukola mwa bisiki bya banji 구고라 똬 비시기 뱌 바찌
babaa bakoliremo mira. 바바아 바고뻐러모 미라.

21 mwa bacha, nairaa kwa 21 똬 바짜, 나이라아 과 21. Rather, as it is written:
maanjiko mabuya-buya 마아찌고 마부야-부야 마두꽈 "Those who were not told
matula matechire mbu: 마더찌러 뿌: 어바뚜 바 about him will see, and
Ebandu ba babaa batasa 바바아 바다사 구부롸 어먀시 those who have not heard
kuburwa emyasi yai, 야이, 바빠무뤄라고. 나 나 바 will understand."
bangamulolako. Na na ba 바바아 바다푸라아 구빠 과
babaa batafuraa kumva kwa 먀시 야이, 바꼬빠 구이.
myasi yai, bangomva kui.

Paulo ahonda kubalamira **파우뤈 아호따 구바꽈믈띱 똬**
mwa musi w'e Roma **무시 워 로마**

22 echera chi chabaa chenjire 22 어쩌라 찌 짜바아 쩌찌러 22. This is why I have often
chanyangika chaira mango, 짜냐삐가 짜이라 마꼬, 나이가 been hindered from coming
ndaika ei mwenyu. 어이 뭐뉴. to you.

23 kanji kwarenga myaka 23 가찌 과러빠 먀가 이너너, 23. But now that there is no
inene, nyete mbuha yekuya 녀더 뿌하 여구야 구바다우꽈, more place for me to work
kubatangula, si rero namalire 시 러로 나마뻐러 어무뾔모 in these regions, and since I
emulimo wanyi mwebi bio, 와니 뭐비 비오, have been longing for many
years to see you,

24 bushi noku, nyingere naika 24 부씨 노구, 네뻐러 나이가 24. I plan to do so when I
eyi mwenyu mango nyingaya 어에 뭐뉴 마꼬 네꽈야 똬 go to Spain. I hope to visit
mwa chio che Sipaniya. Nyete 찌오 쩌 시파니야. 녀더 you while passing through
emunyiiro kwa mwa kurenga 어무네이로 과 똬 구러빠 어이 and to have you assist me

ei mwenyu, nyingabalolako. Nera nyuma se kumowa alauma nenyu kubihangi bieke, nyingasimire munyiase mwolu lubalamo.

25 si mwebine bihangi, naya tanga eyerusalemu kwa kuasa ebandu ba Ongo.

26 bushi ebemeresi bomwa chio che maketoniya ne che akaya balolaa kwa kukomire baire muholore kwa kuasa ebakene ba bali mwa kachi-kachi ke bemeresi bomwa musi we yerusalemu.

27 bairaa bacha kwa kuhonda kwabo beine, si kanji babaa bete mwinda mwa kuasabo. Ebandu ba batatula bayuta babonyire kwa ngahanyi semyasi yebwemeresi bwe bayuta. Rero, abu batula bayuta nabo, bemire kunde baasa ebayuta kurengera ebuare bwa bete.

28 mango nyingaba namalire oyu mulimo, nakuisa bo kwebindu bya byahololwaa, nyingere narengera eyi mwenyu mwa kuya mwa chio che sipaniya.

29 nyishi kwa mango nyingaika eyi mwenyu, nyingabaretera ngahanyi sinene sa satenga era mwa

뭐뉴, 네ㅆ바로ㄹ꽈고. 너라 뉴마 서 구모와 아꽈우마 너뉴 구비하ㅣ 비어거, 네ㅆ시미러 무네아서 모루 루바꽈모.

25 시 뭐비너 비하ㅣ, 나야 다ㅆ아 어여루사꺼무 과 구아사 어바뚜 바 오ㄲ.

26 부씨 어버머러시 보봐 찌오 쩌 마거도니야 너 쩌 아가야 바로ㄹ꽈아 과 구고미러 바이러 무호로러 과 구아사 어바거너 바 바ㄹ리 봐 가찌-가찌 거 버머러시 보봐 무시 워 여루사꺼무.

27 바이라아 바짜 과 구호따 과보 버이너, 시 가찌 바바아 버더 뮈따 봐 구아사보. 어바뚜 바 바다두꽈 바유다 바보니러 과 ㅆ하니 서먀시 여붸머러시 붸 바유다. 러로, 아부 바두꽈 바유다 나보, 버미러 구ㄸ 바아사 어바유다 구러ㅆ라 어부아러 봐 버더.

28 마ㄲ 네ㅆ바 나마ㄹ러 오유 무ㄹ모, 나구이사 보 궈비뚜 뱌 뱌호로ㄹ꽈아, 네ㅆ러 나러ㅆ라 어에 뭐뉴 봐 구야 봐 찌오 쩌 시파니야.

29 네씨 과 마ㄲ 네ㅆ이가 어에 뭐뉴, 네ㅆ바러더라 ㅆ하니 시너너 사 사더ㅆ 어라 봐 기리시도*

on my journey there, after I have enjoyed your company for a while.

25. Now, however, I am on my way to Jerusalem in the service of the saints there.

26. For Macedonia and Achaia were pleased to make a contribution for the poor among the saints in Jerusalem.

27. They were pleased to do it, and indeed they owe it to them. For if the Gentiles have shared in the Jews' spiritual blessings, they owe it to the Jews to share with them their material blessings.

28.. So after I have completed this task and have made sure that they have received this fruit, I will go to Spain and visit you on the way.

29. I know that when I come to you, I will come in the full measure of the blessing of Christ.

kirirsito*

30 banyaketu, nabema busese kurengera enawetu Yesu kirisito, nakurengera enzii ye mchima mubuya-buya, kwa mundaa mwalwisa alauma nanyi mwa kunyemerera era mwa Ongo.

31 mundaa mwa nyemerera, chasiya mango nyingaika mwa chio che yuteya, nyinunulibwe mwa mino se bandu ba batemerere kirisito*. Kanji munyemereraa, chasiya ebandu ba Ongo be yerusalemu banhirire kubuya emuholore ola nakerabo.

32 mwa bacha, Ongo akasima, nyingaika eyi mwenyu na lumoo, ku tamukira kubuya mwa kachi-kachi kenyu.

33 Ongo iwende weresa ebandu eboli, endaa aba alauma nenyu muboshi. Bibe bacha!

---

30 바냐거두, 나버마 부서서 구러꺼라 어나워두 여수 기리시도, 나구러꺼라 어씨이 여 무찌마 무부야-부야, 과 무따아 똬뤄사 아롸우마 나니 똬 구녀머러라 어라 똬 오끄.

31 무따아 똬 녀머러라, 짜시야 마꼬 네꺼이가 똬 찌오 쩌 유더야, 네누누뤼뷔 똬 미노 서 바뚜 바 바더머러러 기리시도*. 가찌 무녀머러라아, 짜시야 어바뚜 바 오끄 버 여루사꺼무 바누히리러 구부야 어무호뢰러 오롸 나거라보.

32 똬 바짜, 오끄 아가시마, 네꺼이가 어에 뭐뉴 나 루모오, 구 다무기라 구부야 똬 가찌-가찌 거뉴.

33 오끄 이워떠 워러사 어바뚜 어보뤼, 어따아 아바 아롸우마 너뉴 무보씨. 비버 바짜!

---

30. I urge you, brothers, by our Lord Jesus Christ and by the love of the Spirit, to join me in my struggle by praying to God for me.

31. Pray that I may be rescued from the unbelievers in Judea and that my service in Jerusalem may be acceptable to the saints there,

32. so that by God's will I may come to you with joy and together with you be refreshed.

33. The God of peace be with you all. Amen.

Ba Roma Chikono 16
Paulo akesa ebemeresi b'e Roma

1 Nabatchwumilire mwalyiwetchwu Foibe. Alyi mukosi mubuya mwa

---

바 로마 찌고노 16
파우뢴 아거사 어버머러시 버 로마

1 나바쭈미뤼러 똬뤠워쭈 포이버. 아뤠 무고시 무부야 똬 버머러시 보똬

Rome Chapter 16[NIV]

1. I commend to you our sister Phoebe, a servant of the church in Cenchrea.

bemeresi bomwa musi w'e Kengureya.

무시 워 거꾸러야.

2 Mumuhukasaa kubuya kwesina lya Enawetchwu, ngokwa ebandju ba Ongo bemire kuira. Mango angende aba alaire ku kandju karebe, mundaa mwamweresako. Bushi nai aasise bandju banene, anabe nanyi ananyiasise.

2 무무후가사아 구부야 궈시나 퍄 어나워쭈, 꼬과 어바뚜 바 오꼬 버미러 구이라. 마꼬 아꺼러 아바 아퐈이러 구 가뚜 가러버, 무따아 뫄뭐러사고. 부씨 나이 아아시서 바뚜 바너너, 아나버 나니 아나네아시서.

2. I ask you to receive her in the Lord in a way worthy of the saints and to give her any help she may need from you, for she has been a great help to many people, including me.

3 Munyikesesaa Purisila na Akila, bu nenjire nakola nabo emulimo wa Yesu kirisito.

3 무네거서사아 푸리시퐈 나 아기퐈, 부 너찌러 나고퐈 나보 어무퓌모 와 여수 기리시도.

3. Greet Priscilla and Aquila, my fellow workers in Christ Jesus.

4 abu babiri baburaa bafa bushi nanyi. Natechire mbu akoko era bali. Ata na nyeine nyinachitechire bacha, si anabe ne bemeresi boshi ba batatula bayuta.

4 아부 바비리 바부라아 바파 부씨 나니. 나더찌러 뿌 아고고 어라 바퓌. 아다 나 녀이너 네나찌더찌러 바짜, 시 아나버 너 버머러시 보씨 바 바다두퐈 바유다.

4. They risked their lives for me. Not only I but all the churches of the Gentiles are grateful to them.

5 munyikesesaa ne bemeresi ba benjire babuanana mwa mwa Akila na Purisila. Mwananyikesesaa na munyaketchwu musiirwa Epeneto. Oyu Epeneto, iwabaa mubere-bere kwemerera kirisito mwa chio ch'e Asiya.

5 무네거서사아 너 버머러시 바 버찌러 바부아나나 뫄 뫄 아기퐈 나 푸리시퐈. 뫄나네거서사아 나 무냐거쭈 무시이롸 어퍼너도. 오유 어퍼너도, 이와바아 무버러-버러 궈머러라 기리시도 뫄 찌오 쩌 아시야.

5. Greet also the church that meets at their house. Greet my dear friend Epenetus, who was the first convert to Christ in the province of Asia.

6 munyikesesaa na Mariya. Oyu Mariya, abaa enjire

6 무네거서사아 나 마리야. 오유 마리야,

6. Greet Mary, who worked very hard for you.

ashika endjubano kwa kubakorera. / 아바아 어찌러 아씨가 어쿠바노 과 구바고러라.

7 munyikesesaa na Andoroniko na Yuniya bomwa lubaa lwetchwu, bu tchwabaa tchwuminyirwe nabo mwa buroko. Abu babilyi, bete ngulu ibuya mwa kachi-kachi kendjumwa. Kanji bu babaa baberebere kwemerera kirisito era muhondo sanyi.

7 무네거서사아 나 아또로니고 나 유니야 보과 루바아 뤄쭈, 부 좌바아 쭈미니뤄 나보 과 부로고. 아부 바비례, 버더 꾸루 이부야 과 가찌-가찌 거쭈꽈. 가찌 부 바바아 바버러버러 궈머러라 기리시도 어라 무호또 사니.

7. Greet Andronicus and Junias, my relatives who have been in prison with me. They are outstanding among the apostles, and they were in Christ before I was.

8 munyikesesaa na Ambuliyato, munyaketchwu musirwa kurengera ebuuma bwetchwu na kirisito.

8 무네거서사아 나 아뿌례야도, 무냐거쭈 무시롸 구러뻐라 어부우마 뷔쭈 나 기리시도.

8. Greet Ampliatus, whom I love in the Lord.

9 munyikesesaa na Urubano, itchwenjire tchwakola nai emulyimo wa kirisito. Mwananyikesesaa na munyaketchwu musiirwa Sitaki.

9 무네거서사아 나 우루바노, 이쭤찌러 좌고롸 나이 어무례모 와 기리시도. 뫄나네거서사아 나 무냐거쭉 무시이롸 시다기.

9. Greet Urbanus, our fellow worker in Christ, and my dear friend Stachys.

10 Munyikesesa na Apele. Oyu apele alosise ekanangana kwa emerere kirisito mwananyikesesa na basha mwa Aristobulo.

10 무네거서사 나 아퍼뤄. 오유 아퍼뤄 아뢰시서 어가나꺄나 과 어머러러 기리시도 뫄나네거서사 나 바싸 뫄 아리시도부뢰.

10. Greet Apelles, tested and approved in Christ. Greet those who belong to the household of Aristobulus.

11 munyikesesa ne Herotiyo mwomwa lubaa lwetu. Mwananyikesesa ne bemeresi be enawetchwu ba batchwula mwa mwa narikiso.

11 무네거서사 너 허로디요 모꽈 루바아 뤄두. 뫄나네거서사 너 버머러시 버 어나워쭉 바 바쭈롸 뫄 뫄 나리기소.

11. Greet Herodion, my relative. Greet those in the household of Narcissus who are in the Lord.

12 munyikeksesa na tirifena na tirifosa. Abu bakasi babiri benjire bashika endjubano mwa kukorera enawetchwu. Mwana nyikesesa na mwalyi wetchwu musiirwa peresi. Oyu peresi nai endee ashika endjubano mwa kukorera enawetchwu.

13 munyikesesa na rufo, iwende wakorera enawetchwu na bushiru bunene. mwana nyikesesa na nyina. Bushi nanyi, nyinatchwula nyimutolyire nga mama.

14 munyikesesa na asinikirisito, na fulengo, na herene, na paturoba, na herema na banyaketchwu ba batchwula nabo.

15 munyikesesa filongo na yuliya, na nereo, na mwalyi wabo, na olimba n'e bemeresi boshi ba balyi nabo.

16 mundaa mwakesanya mwa kuoberana nga bauma, kurengera ebuuma bwenyu na kirisito. Ebandju boshi bomwa nyulu sa kirisito, babakesise.

Eano Iyisinda

12 무네거구서사 나 디리퍼나 나 디리포사. 아부 바가시 바비리 버찌러 바씨가 어꾸바노 와 구고러라 어나워쭈. 뫄나 네거서사 나 뫄레워쭈 무시이롸 퍼러시. 오유 퍼러시 나이 어어어 아씨가 어꾸바노 와 구고러라 어나워쭈.

13 무네거서사 나 루포, 이워떠 와고러라 어나워쭈 나 부씨루 부너너. 뫄나 네거서사 나 네나. 부씨 나네, 네나쭈롸 네무도뤠러 꽈 마마.

14 무네거서사 나 아시니기리시도, 나 푸꿔오, 나 허러너, 나 파두로바, 나 허러마 나 바냐거쭈 바 바쭈롸 나보.

15 무네거서사 피로오 나 유뤼야, 나 너러오, 나 뫄레 와보, 나 오뤼빠 너 버머러시 보씨 바 바뤠 나보.

16 무따아 뫄거사냐 뫄 구오버라나 꽈 바우마, 구러꺼라 어부우마 붜뉴 나 기리시도. 어바꾸 보씨 보와 뉴룹 사 기리시도, 바바거시서.

어아노 뤠습따

12. Greet Tryphena and Tryphosa, those women who work hard in the Lord. Greet my dear friend Persis, another woman who has worked very hard in the Lord.

13. Greet Rufus, chosen in the Lord, and his mother, who has been a mother to me, too.

14. Greet Asyncritus, Phlegon, Hermes, Patrobas, Hermas and the brothers with them.

15. Greet Philologus, Julia, Nereus and his sister, and Olympas and all the saints with them.

16. Greet one another with a holy kiss. All the churches of Christ send greetings.

17 banayaketchwu nabema busese, mundaa mwachilanga kwabandju ba benjire balyikanya ebemeresi. Abu bandju benjire bateta bulyio era luulu s'e myasi era mwakangilyisibwaa. Nechi chenjire chaesa ebemeresi. Rero, murekana nabo.

17 바나야거쭈 나버마 부서서, 무따아 뫄찌롸ㅁㅏ 과바뚜 바 버찌러 바페가냐 어버머러시. 아부 바뚜 버찌러 바더다 부페오 어라 루우루 서 먀시 어라 뫄가ㅁㅣ페시봐아. 너찌 쩌찌러 짜어사 어버머러시. 러로, 무러가나 나보.

17. I urge you, brothers, to watch out for those who cause divisions and put obstacles in your way that are contrary to the teaching you have learned. Keep away from them.

18 bushi ebandju ba balyi ngabo batakorera enawetchwu kirisito, si bende bakorera emola mabo beine. Kanji kurengera emyasi yabo era ilokerera kanji ya kuchisimisa, bende bengeera ebandju ba batakalangire.

18 부씨 어바뚜 바 바페 ㅁㅏ보 바다고러라 어나워쭈 기리시도, 시 버떠 바고러라 어모롸 마보 버이너. 가찌 구러ㅁㅓ라 어먀시 야보 어라 이로거러라 가찌 야 구찌시미사, 버떠 버ㅁㅓ어라 어바뚜 바 바다가롸ㅁㅣ러.

18. For such people are not serving our Lord Christ, but their own appetites. By smooth talk and flattery they deceive the minds of naive people.

19 ebandju boshi baneshi kwa mwende mwaira ngokwa enawetchwu atechire. Echera chi chenjire chatchwuma namowa bushi nenyu. Si nahonda mubaa benge kwa kunde mwaira emabuya, na kunde mwachilanga kwa mabi.

19 어바뚜 보씨 바너씨 과 뭐떠 마이라 ㅇ꼬과 어나워쭈 아더찌러. 어쩌라 찌 쩌찌러 짜쭈마 나모와 부씨 너뉴. 시 나호따 무바아 버떠 과 구떠 마이라 어마부야, 나 구떠 뫄찌롸ㅁㅏ 과 마비.

19. Everyone has heard about your obedience, so I am full of joy over you; but I want you to be wise about what is good, and innocent about what is evil.

20 Ongo iwende weresa ebandju eboolo, atemange kufungorera wa musimu era chibanda s'e maulu menyu. Enawetchwu Yesu kirisito

20 오꼬 이워떠 워러사 어바뚜 어보오른, 아더마떠 구푸으러라 와 무시무 어라 찌바따 서 마우루 머뉴. 어나워쭈

20. The God of peace will soon crush Satan under your feet. The grace of our Lord Jesus be with you.

endaa abaahanyira

21 Timoteo, inenjire nakola nai, abakesise. Lukiyo na Yasona na Sosipateri, bomwa lubaa lwetchwu, nabo babakesise.

22 nanyi Teritiyo, nyi naanjikaa mano maruba, nabakesise kwesina lya Enawetchwu.

23 kayo iwanyihuukasaa kanji anachilyi ahuukasa ebemeresi boshi ba bende babuanana ala mwai, abakesise. Erasito, iwende walanga ehao y'emusi, na munyaketchwu kwarito, nabo babakesise.

24 enawetchwu Yesu kirisito endaa abaahanyira muboshi. Bibe bacha!

E myasi era yabaa ibishirwe yelyire yabihukala

25 Ongo atongwe, iwete ebuashi bwa bungatchwuma mwasimika mwa bwemeresi, kukulyikana nokwa mwasi mubuya-buya atechire, ola nenjire nahubanganya era

21 디모더오, 이너찌러 나고꽈 나이, 아바거시서. 루기요 나 야소나 나 소시파더리, 보와 루바아 뤄쭉, 나보 바바거시서.

22 나내 더리디요, 네 나아찌가아 마노 마루바, 나바거시서 궈시나 꺄 어나워쭉.

23 가요 이와네후우가사아 가찌 아나찌께 아후우가사 어버머러시 보씨 바 버너 바부아나나 아꽈 마이, 아바거시서. 어라시도, 이워떠 와꽈빠 어하오 여무시, 나 무냐거쭉 과리도, 나보 바바거시서.

24 어나워쭉 여수 기리시도 어따아 아바아하네라 무보씨. 비버 바짜!

어 먀시 어라 야바아 이비씨뤄 여쩨럇 야비후가꽈

25 오꼬 아도워, 이워더 어부아씨 봐 부꽈쭈마 먀시미가 마 붜머러시, 구구께가나 노과 먀시 무부야-부야 아더찌러, 오꽈 너찌러 나후바꽈냐

21. Timothy, my fellow worker, sends his greetings to you, as do Lucius, Jason and Sosipater, my relatives.

22. I, Tertius, who wrote down this letter, greet you in the Lord.

23. Gaius, whose hospitality I and the whole church here enjoy, sends you his greetings. Erastus, who is the city's director of public works, and our brother Quartus send you their greetings.

24. None

25. Now to him who is able to establish you by my gospel and the proclamation of Jesus Christ, according to the revelation of the mystery hidden for long ages past,

luulu sa Yesu kirisito. Oyu
mwasi mubuya-buya iwenjire
wabihula emyasi era Ongo
abaa atula abishire kutengera
mira.

어라 루우루 사 여수
기리시도. 오유 먀시
무부야-부야 이워찌러
와비후롸 어먀시 어라
오꼬 아바아 아두롸
아비씨러 구더꺼라 미라.

26 si rero ei myasi yerire
yabihulibwa kurengera
emaanjiko me barebi,
kukulikana ne loso lwa Ongo
iutulao esuku n'e mango.Ei
myasi yabihulibwe kwa bandu
bembaa soshi, chasiya
bamwemerere na kunde baira
ngokwa atechire.

26 시 러로 어이 먀시
여리러 야비후뤼봐
구러꺼라 어마아씨고 머
바러비, 구구뤼가나 너
로소 롸 오꼬 이우두롸오
어수구 너 마꼬.어이 먀시
야비후뤼붜 과 바뚜
버빠아 소씨, 짜시야
바뭐머러러 나 구떠
바이라 꼬과 아더찌러.

26. but now revealed and made
known through the prophetic
writings by the command of the
eternal God, so that all nations
might believe and obey him--

27 Ongo yeine iutusa
ebwenge, endaa atongibwa
esuku ne mango kurengera
Yesu kirisito! bibe bacha!

27 오꼬 여이너 이우두사
어붜꺼, 어따아 아도삐봐
어수구 너 마꼬 구러꺼라
여수 기리시도! 비버
바짜!

27. to the only wise God be
glory forever through Jesus
Christ! Amen.

1 E Bakorinto

1 어 바고리또

1 Corinthians

E BAKORINDO BA BEREBERE

(1 CORINTHIANS)

어 바고리또 바 버러버러

(1 고리띠아뚜)

1. Paolo ola waamalzaa kuba ndjumwa ya Yesu Kiristito kwa bwaashi bwa Nyakabumbi na munyakabu Sositene

2. Kwa luhu lwa Ongo lwa lwaba lulyi era Korindo bala baahanyirwaa mu Yesu Kirisito, babaamalwaa kuba babuyabuya, alauma ne bandju bala babikire e sina lya Yesu Kirisito era muhondo kuba ena wabu na Enawetchu.

3. O mwisha abaa lauma nenyu ne boolo. Ola utengire era mwa Ongo tata nera mwa ena wetchu Kirisito.

4. Natongire Kabumbi e bihangi byoshi bushi nenyu, kukulyikana no mwisha wa Kabumbi ola mweeresibwaa kurengera Yesu Kirisito.

5. Kwa bushi mu tchira mwasi mwaalyiri kumurengera, mwa myaasi yoshi alauma no bwenge boshi

6. nga bubei bwa Kirisito bula bukootchire era mwenyu

7. Mutakeerwa no bwaashi, emangu mwalyindjira okumenya o burebi bwa ena

---

1. 파오로 오롸 와아마루자아 구바 ﾞﾞ 뚸 야 여수 기리시도 과 봐아씨 봐 냐가부뻬 나 무냐가부 소시더너

2. 과 루후 똬 오끄 똬 똬바 루쀄 어라 고리또 바똬 바아하네롸아 무 여수 기리시도, 바바아마똬아 구바 바부야부야, 아똬우마 너 바뚜 바똬 바비기러 어 시나 뺘 여수 기리시도 어라 무호또 구바 어나 와부 나 어나워쭈.

3. 오 뮈싸 아바아 똬우마 너뉴 너 보오롣. 오롸 우더삐러 어라 똬 오끄 다다 너라 똬 어나 워쭈 기리시도.

4. 나도삐러 가부뻬 어 비하삐 뵤씨 부씨 너뉴, 구구쀄가나 노 뮈싸 와 가부뻬 오롸 뭐어러시봐아 구러쩌라 여수 기리시도.

5. 과 부씨 무 찌라 마시 똬아쩨리 구무러쩌라, 똬 먀아시 요씨 아똬우마 노 뷔삐 보씨

6. 삐 부버이 봐 기리시도 부똬 부고오찌러 어라 뭐뉴

7. 무다거어롸 노 봐아씨, 어마우 똬쩨찌라 오구머냐 오 부러비 봐 어나 워쭈 여수

---

1. Paul, called to be an apostle of Christ Jesus by the will of God, and our brother Sosthenes,

2. To the church of God in Corinth, to those sanctified in Christ Jesus and called to be holy, together with all those everywhere who call on the name of our Lord Jesus Christ--their Lord and ours:

3. Grace and peace to you from God our Father and the Lord Jesus Christ.

4. I always thank God for you because of his grace given you in Christ Jesus.

5. For in him you have been enriched in every way--in all your speaking and in all your knowledge--

6. because our testimony about Christ was confirmed in you.

7. Therefore you do not lack any spiritual gift as you eagerly wait for our Lord

wetchu Yesu Kirisito.

8. Ola angabawa e misi kuikira e businda mungesha kwaaibwa o lusiku lula Enawetchu Yesu Kirisito.

9. Ongo alyi mwemeresi ola mwaamaerwe nayi lyi mwaata o bwira na mwaala wayi Yesu Kirisito Enawetchu

10. Kwa bushi noku banyaketchu, nabeemire kurengera e sina lya enawetchu Yesu Kirisito mwaata e teta lyiuma kutanabaa na katootanyi ala kakatchi kenyu, si mushibiraa mu mwaanyisa muuma na lwango luuma.

11. Kwa bushi, banayaketchu, nabulyirwe e myasi yenyu kutengera e bandju bala balamire mwa luhu lwa Kulde nambu mulyi burenda era mwenyu.

12. Kwetchi, o mufa wanyi ahondjire tchira muuma mu mwaabu atetaa nambu: nyono nyilyi wa Paolo, nanyi nyilyi wa Apolo, nanyi nyilyi wa Kefa, nanyi nyilyi wa Kirisito.

13. Tchwabusise elyi Kirisito aabirwe'mo? Elyi Paolo abikibwaa kwa tchimanyi bushi nenyu? Nesi mwabatisibwaa kwe sina lya Paolo?

기리시도.

8. 오라 아까바와 어 미시 구이기라 어 부시따 무워싸 과아이봐 오 루시구 루롸 어나워쭈 여수 기리시도.

9. 오꼬 아레 뭐머러시 오롸 롸아마어뤄 나에 레 롸아다 오 뷔라 나 롸아롸 와에 여수 기리시도 어나워쭈

10. 과 부씨 노구 바냐거쭈, 나버어미러 구러워라 어 시나 롸 어나워쭈 여수 기리시도 롸아다 어 더다 레우마 구다나바아 나 가도오다네 아롸 가가찌 거뉴, 시 무씨비라아 무 롸아네사 무우마 나 롸꼬 루우마.

11. 과 부씨, 바나야거쭈, 나부레뤄 어 먀시 여뉴 구더워라 어 바뚜 바롸 바롸미러 롸 루후 롸 구루더 나뿌 무레 부러따 어라 뭐뉴.

12. 귀찌, 오 무파 와네 아호찌러 찌라 무우마 무 롸아부 아더다아 나뿌: 뇨노 네레 와 파오로, 나니 네레 와 아포로, 나니 네레 와 거파, 나니 네레 와 기리시도.

13. 쫘부시서 어레 기리시도 아아비뤄모? 어레 파오로 아비기봐아 과 찌마네 부씨 너뉴? 너시 롸바디시봐아 귀 시나 롸 파오로?

Jesus Christ to be revealed.

8. He will keep you strong to the end, so that you will be blameless on the day of our Lord Jesus Christ.

9. God, who has called you into fellowship with his Son Jesus Christ our Lord, is faithful.

10. I appeal to you, brothers, in the name of our Lord Jesus Christ, that all of you agree with one another so that there may be no divisions among you and that you may be perfectly united in mind and thought.

11. My brothers, some from Chloe's household have informed me that there are quarrels among you.

12. What I mean is this: One of you says, "I follow Paul"; another, "I follow Apollos"; another, "I follow Cephas"; still another, "I follow Christ."

13. Is Christ divided? Was Paul crucified for you? Were you baptized into the name of Paul?

14. Natongire, kwa bushi ndabatisaa mundju era mwenyu seri Kirisipo na Gayo oshao.

14. 나도삐러, 과 부씨 따바디사아 무뚜 어라 뮤뉴 서리 기리시포 나 가요 오싸오.

14. I am thankful that I did not baptize any of you except Crispus and Gaius,

15. Kutabaaa ola wateta nambu abatisibwaa kwe sina lyanyi.

15. 구다바아아 오롸 와더다 나뿌 아바디시봐아 궈 시나 랴니.

15. so no one can say that you were baptized into my name.

16. Kandji, nabatisaa e bandju bo mwa luhu lwa Sitefano, banene kwa bano, ndeshi elyi kulyi undji ola nabatisaa.

16. 가찌, 나바디사아 어 바뿌 보 뫄 루후 롸 시더파노, 바너너 과 바노, 떠씨 어레 구뤠 우씨 오롸 나바디사아.

16. (Yes, I also baptized the household of Stephanas; beyond that, I don't remember if I baptized anyone else.)

17. Kwa bushi Kirisito atanyitchumaa kubatisa selyi bushi no kuiirisa o mwaasi mubuyabuya, kandji kuta kwa burembi bwe binwa. E tchimanyi tcha Yesu tchitarengao buha.

17. 과 부씨 기리시도 아다네쭈마아 구바디사 서뤠 부씨 노 구이이리사 오 뫄아시 무부야부야, 가찌 구다 과 부러삐 붜 비놔. 어 찌마네 짜 여수 찌다러뫄오 부하.

17. For Christ did not send me to baptize, but to preach the gospel--not with words of human wisdom, lest the cross of Christ be emptied of its power.

18. Bushi e tchinwa tche tchimanyi bulyi buuta kwa bala berire si tchuthcwanunulyibwe ilyi misi ya kabumbi kwa bushi

18. 부씨 어 찌놔 쩌 찌마네 부뤠 부우다 과 바롸 버리러 시 쭈쭈와누누뤠붜 이뤠 미시야 가부삐 과 부씨

18. For the message of the cross is foolishness to those who are perishing, but to us who are being saved it is the power of God.

19. byaandjikirwe nambu Ongo angakumbya bala batchitolyire na benge, nesi e beete e bwenge e myanyisa inene.

19. 뱌아찌기뤄 나뿌 오꼬 아까구뺘 바롸 바찌도레러 나 버뭐, 너시 어 버어더 어 뭐뭐 어 먀네사 이너너.

19. For it is written: "I will destroy the wisdom of the wise; the intelligence of the intelligent I will frustrate."

20. ngayi yi angaboneka ola weete e bwenge? ngai ula alyi o mwaandjiki, ngai wa alyi o mweenzi wa baaka ba mwesini siku kasi elyi Ongo ataalulaa e bwenge bwo mwa butala,

20. 까에 에 아까보너가 오롸 워어더 어 뭐뭐? 까이 우롸 아뤠 오 뫄아찌기, 까이 와 아뤠 오 뭐어씨 와 바아가 바뭐씨니 시구 가시 어뤠 오꼬 아다아루롸아 어 뭐뭐 보 뫄

20. Where is the wise man? Where is the scholar? Where is the philosopher of this age? Has not God made foolish the wisdom of the world?

kuba buuta?

21. Kwa bushi mwa bwenge, e bandju be butala bakaba batamuteerere kwa bwenge bwai, Ongo ahondaa kununula e beemeresi bai kurengera e kanengereso ke tchinwa bairisibwaa.

22. Kwa bushi e Bayahuti bahonda kulosa e bisomerani ne Bayunani bahonda e bwenge

23. Bushi tchubanu tchwahubanganya o mwaasi wa Kirisito ola wamanyikibwaa, si kwa Bayahuti alyi mwaasi wa businani, nera mwa Bayunani kalyi kanengereso.

24. Seri kwa bala baamaerwe, Wayahuti ne Bayunani, Kirisito yi miisi ya Kabumbi ne bwenge bwai.

25. Kwa bushi, e buuta bwa Kabumbi bwete e bwenge kurengera e bana be mikira no butambukare bwa Ongo bukootchire kurenga e bana be mikira.

26. Bushi banyaketchu, mulolaa kula mwaamalwaa kuteta ata boshi bete bwenge nesi e miisi, nesi e tchisiki bu baamalyibwaa.

부다꽈, 구바 부우다?

21. 과 부씨 먀 붸꺼, 어 바꾸 버 부다꽈 바가바 바다무더어러러 과 붸꺼 봐이, 오꼬 아호따아 구누누꽈 어 버어머러시 바이 구러꺼라 어 가너꺼러소 거 찌냐 바이리시봐아.

22. 과 부씨 어 바야후디 바호따 구론사 어 비소머라니 너 바유나니 바호따 어 붸꺼

23. 부씨 쭈바누 좌후바따냐 오 마아시 와 기리시도 오꽈 와마네기봐아, 시 과 바야후디 아례 마아시 와 부시나니, 너라 먀 바유나니 가쪠 가너꺼러소.

24. 서리 과 바꽈 바아마어뤄, 와야후디 너 바유나니, 기리시도 에 미이시 야 가부쎄 너 붸꺼 봐이.

25. 과 부씨, 어 부우다 봐 가부쎄 붸더 어 붸꺼 구러꺼라 어 바나 버 미기라 노 부다뿌가러 봐 오꼬 부고오찌러 구러따 어 바나 버 미기라.

26. 부씨 바냐거쭈, 무론꽈아 구꽈 먀아마꽈아 구더다 아다 보씨 버더 붸꺼 너시 어 미이시, 너시 어 찌시기 부 바아마례봐아.

---

21. For since in the wisdom of God the world through its wisdom did not know him, God was pleased through the foolishness of what was preached to save those who believe.

22. Jews demand miraculous signs and Greeks look for wisdom,

23. but we preach Christ crucified: a stumbling block to Jews and foolishness to Gentiles,

24. but to those whom God has called, both Jews and Greeks, Christ the power of God and the wisdom of God.

25. For the foolishness of God is wiser than man's wisdom, and the weakness of God is stronger than man's strength.

26. Brothers, think of what you were when you were called. Not many of you were wise by human standards; not many were

27. Seri Ongo alondolaa e
bindju byo buhabuha byo
butala, kwa kukosa e bandju
be myaanyisa e honyi, kandji
Ongo era kulondola e bindju
bitambukare byo butala lyi
akose ehonyi bira byeete
emiisi.

28. Kandji Ongo era kulondola
e bindju byo bukene munu
butala nebira bakenyire noku e
bindju bira bitalyi kwa
kubiinganya nebira bilyi.

29. Tchira ola wete o mubiri
atatchitongaa era muhondo sa
kabuubi

30. Si kumurengera, mwabo
mwaeresibwe o mwisha
wokuba na Yesu Kirisito ola
wairwa bwenge bwetchu
kutenga era mwa kabumbi
kwa buuma uma, kwa
bwemeresi no bununusi.

31. Kwa bushi, ngo kula
byaandjikirwe, ola
ungatchitonga, atatchitongera
mu Ongo.

---

27. 서리 오꼬 아로오또롸아 어
비뚜 뵤 부하부하 뵤 부다롸,
과 구고사 어 바뚜 버
먀아니사 어 호니, 가찌 오꼬
어라 구로오또롸 어 비뚜
비다뿌가라 뵤 부다롸 레
아고서 어호네 비라 벼어더
어미이시.

28. 가찌 오꼬 어라 구로오또롸
어 비뚜 뵤 부거너 무누
부다롸 너비라 바거니러 노구
어 비뚜 비라 비다레 과
구비이꽈냐 너비라 비레.

29. 찌라 오롸 워더 오
무비리 아다찌도꽈아 어라
무호또 사 가부우비

30. 시 구무러꺼라, 먀보
먀어러시붜 오 뮈싸 오구바
나 여수 기리시도 오롸
와이라 붜머 붜쭈 구더꽈
어라 먀 가부뻬 과 부우마
우마, 과 붜머러시 노
부누누시.

31. 과 부씨, 꼬 구롸
뱌아찌기뤄, 오롸 우꽈찌도꽈,
아다찌도꺼라 무 오꼬.

---

27. But God chose the
foolish things of the world
to shame the wise; God
chose the weak things of the
world to shame the strong.

28. He chose the lowly
things of this world and the
despised things--and the
things that are not--to
nullify the things that are,

29. so that no one may
boast before him.

30. It is because of him that
you are in Christ Jesus, who
has become for us wisdom
from God--that is, our
righteousness, holiness and
redemption.

31. Therefore, as it is written:
"Let him who boasts boast
in the Lord."

---

1 E Bakorinto Chikono 2

1. Banyaketchu e mangu
naikaa era mwenyu, naeshaa

---

1 어 바고리또 찌고노 2

1. 바냐거쭈 어 마꾸
나이가아 어라 뮈뉴,

**1 Corinthians Chapter 2
[NIV]**

1. When I came to you,
brothers, I did not come

---

kubaiirisa bibishirwe na Kabumbi kurengera e myaasi inene nesi ye bwenge

2. Bushi nairiraa kuba nga ola uteshi tchiro no mwasi ula ubaerekere si ola werekere okumanyikwa kwa Yesu Kirisito.

3. Nnanyi nabaa era mwenyu mwa bufundjwa no mwa buba, ne ngukumanyi inene

4. Ne mwaasi wanyi ne mikangilyiso yanyi itabaa myaasi ye bwenge yeku shiirisa e bandju selyi mwa mikangilyiso ye mutchima ne miisi.

5. Ne bweemeresi bwenyu butabaa, wa bwenge bwe bandju selyi mwa miisi ya Ongo

6. Selyi thwatetchire e bwenge mwa kakatchi ke bemeresi, selyi buta bwengi bu buno butala, nesi amaangilyire buno butala kubindjuka buha.

7. Selyi tchwateta kwe bwengi bwa Ongo bwa bubisho, nobu bwenge bwabaa bwabishirwe bula Ongo atchindjibusaa kutengera mira mwa bwaashi bwetchu.

나어싸아 구바이이리사 비비씨뤄 나 가부삐 구러뮈라 어 먀아시 이너너 너시 여 붜뮈

2. 부씨 나이리라아 구바 뮈 오롸 우더씨 찌로 노 뫄시 우롸 우바어러거러 시 오롸 워러거러 오구마네과 과 여수 기리시도.

3. 나네 나바아 어라 뮈뉴 뫄 부푸좌 노 뫄 부바, 너 우구마네 이너너

4. 너 뫄아시 와네 너 미가삐레소 야네 이다바아 먀아시 여 붜뮈 여구 씨이리사 어 바뉴 서뤠 뫄 미가삐레소 여 무찌마 너 미이시.

5. 너 붜어머러시 붜뉴 부다바아, 와 붜뮈 붜 바쭈 서뤠 뫄 미이시 야 오꼬

6. 서뤠 좌더찌러 어 붜뮈 뫄 가가찌 거 버머러시, 서뤠 부다 붜삐 부 부노 부다롸, 너시 아마아삐레러 부노 부다롸 구비뿌가 부하.

7. 서뤠 좌더다 귀 붜삐 봐 오꼬 봐 부비쏘, 노부 붜뮈 봐바아 봐비씨뤄 부롸 오꼬 아찌씨부사아 구더뮈라 미라 뫄 봐아씨 붜쭈.

with eloquence or superior wisdom as I proclaimed to you the testimony about God.

2. For I resolved to know nothing while I was with you except Jesus Christ and him crucified.

3. I came to you in weakness and fear, and with much trembling.

4. My message and my preaching were not with wise and persuasive words, but with a demonstration of the Spirit's power,

5. so that your faith might not rest on men's wisdom, but on God's power.

6. We do, however, speak a message of wisdom among the mature, but not the wisdom of this age or of the rulers of this age, who are coming to nothing.

7. No, we speak of God's secret wisdom, a wisdom that has been hidden and that God destined for our glory before time began.

8. Ne beemangisi bobuno butala bata neeshi, kwa bushi akaba banga menyire batangamutchindjibuse omwana we bwaashi

9. Selyi ngokula emaandjiko matetchire, bira e meho matalolaa'ko ne makutchu matoonvaa'ko, nesi bitalyi mwa mutchima wo mwana we mikira, bi Ongo akunganyisaa e bamusimiri.

10. Selyi Ongo atchuboorere kwa mutchima, bushi Ongo ende amaamaa byoshi, anabi nebira yeine abishiri kwa mutchima wai

11. bushi kutalyi o mwana we mikira ola e byerekere o undji mwana we mikira akaba ata o mutchima ola ulyi mwa ndanda sai?

12. Tchubanu tchutawebwaa o mutchima wo bunu butala si o mutchima utengire era mwa kabumbi lyi tchwateerera e myaasi ya Ongo kukulyikana no bwaashi bwai

13. Tchwendjiri thwanabihambala, ata kwa nyiiriso se bwenge bwe bandju si e so mutchima mubuyabuya ola wakoresa e mitetere yo

8. 너 버어마끼시 보부노 부다꽈 바다 너어씨, 과 부씨 아가바 바꾜 머니러 바다꾜무찌찌부서 오모나 워 봐아씨

9. 서레 꼬구꽈 어마아씨고 마더찌러, 비라 어 머호 마다롸아고 너 마구쭈 마도오빠아고, 너시 비다레 뫄 무찌마 오 모나 워 미기라, 비 오꼬 아구꺄네사아 어 바무시미리.

10. 서레 오꼬 아쭈보오러러 과 무찌마, 부씨 오꼬 어너 아마아마아 뵤씨, 아나비 너비라 여이너 아비씨리 과 무찌마 와이

11. 부씨 구다레 오 모나 워 미기라 오꽈 어 벼려거러 오 우찌 모나 워 미기라 아가바 아다 오 무찌마 오꽈 우레 뫄 따따 사이?

12. 쭈바누 쭈다워봐아 오 무찌마 올 부누 부다꽈 시 오 무찌마 우더끼러 어라 뫄 가부삐 레 좌더어러라 어 먀아시 야 오꼬 구구레가나 노 봐아씨 봐이

13. 쮀찌리 좌나비하빠꽈, 아다 과 네이리소 서 붸꺼 붸 바꾸 시 어 소 무찌마 무부야부야 오꽈 와고러사 어 미더더러 요 무찌마 과 비꾸

8. None of the rulers of this age understood it, for if they had, they would not have crucified the Lord of glory.

9. However, as it is written: "No eye has seen, no ear has heard, no mind has conceived what God has prepared for those who love him"--

10. but God has revealed it to us by his Spirit. The Spirit searches all things, even the deep things of God.

11. For who among men knows the thoughts of a man except the man's spirit within him? In the same way no one knows the thoughts of God except the Spirit of God.

12. We have not received the spirit of the world but the Spirit who is from God, that we may understand what God has freely given us.

13. This is what we speak, not in words taught us by human wisdom but in words taught by the Spirit, expressing spiritual truths in

mutchima kwa bindju byerekere o mutchima.

14. Si omwana we mikira ateemerera e bindju bitanganyire ne myaasi ya Ongo bushi yendi yamubera nga myaasi ya siri, alaungaiteerera kwa bushi yende yamenyeka kwa bala beete e myaanyisa ya Ongo ku banga biteerara.

15. O mundju ulyi mu Ongo yeke endi a maamirisa tchira mwaasi ne yeine atanga tchimenya yeene.

16. indi yi ushi e myaanyisa ya Walyia, ne ku ikangirisa? si tchubanu thweete emyaanyisa ya Kirisito.

벼러거러 오 무찌마.

14. 시 오꽈나 워 미기라 아더어머러라 어 비뿌 비다빠니러 너 먀아시 야 오꼬 부씨 여띠 야무버라 빠 먀아시 야 시리, 아꽈우빠이더어러라 과 부씨 여너 야머녀가 과 바꽈 버어더 어 먀아네사 야 오꼬 구 바빠 비더어라라.

15. 오 무뿌 우쩨 무 오꼬 여거 어띠 아 마아미리사 찌라 꽈아시 너 여이너 아다빠 찌머냐 여어너.

16. 이띠 에 우씨 어 먀아네사 야 와쩨아, 너 구 이가빠리사? 시 쭈바누 쭤어더 어먀아네사 야 기리시도.

spiritual words.

14. The man without the Spirit does not accept the things that come from the Spirit of God, for they are foolishness to him, and he cannot understand them, because they are spiritually discerned.

15. The spiritual man makes judgments about all things, but he himself is not subject to any man's judgment:

16. "For who has known the mind of the Lord that he may instruct him?" But we have the mind of Christ.

1 E Bakorinto Chikono 3

1. Kwa myaanyisa yanyi, banyaketchu na balyibetchu, ndatetaa nenyu nga bandju babaongoswa ne mutchima mubuyabuya si nga bandju babaongoswa nebendju beinibeini, nga bana mwa bwemeresi bwa Kirisito.

2. Kwa bushi noku, nabawaa e mata siate bilyo, bikootchire,

1 어 바고리또 찌고노 3

1. 과 먀아네사 야니, 바냐거쭈 나 바쩨버쭈, 따더다아 너뉴 빠 바쭈 바바오꼬솨 너 무찌마 무부야부야 시 빠 바쭈 바바오꼬솨 너버쭈 버이니버이니, 빠 바나 마 뭐머러시 봐 기리시도.

2. 과 부씨 노구, 나바와아 어 마다 시아더 비뵤,

1 Corinthians Chapter 3 [NIV]

1. Brothers, I could not address you as spiritual but as worldly--mere infants in Christ.

2. I gave you milk, not solid food, for you were not yet

bushi mutangaalyire kubi eshibira

3. bushi mulyi nga bandju balabaanyirwe ku beine. Mangu mutasimana mubeini kubeini, mweete e mbangano ne kuabana, si mwaongoswa ne bandju.

4. Mangu muuma atetaa: "nyoono natchiomakirisise era mwa Paolo"nenyu: "nyono mwa Apolo". Mutalyi mwa tchirongosi tche bandju?

5. Indi i Apolo na indi yi Paolo? Balyi baanda ba Ongo babakangirisaaa endjira ye kuemerera Kirisito, kukulyikana ne lwembo lwa Enawetchu aeresise muuma mu tchubano.

6. Nyono naingaa, Apolo erakunde ahuira e meshi, si Ongo iwamesaa

7. Ata ola waingaa nola wahuiraa huiree e meshi beteti mufa, si Ongo iwete mufa bushi iwende wamesa

8. Ola waingaa, nola wahuiraa huiree e meshi, boshi kuuma kubanalyi, na tchira muuma mubu, Ongo akamweresa e lweembo kukulyikana ne mulyimo wai.

9. Tchubano, tchulyi baanda babendjire bakola na Ongo.

비고오찌러, 부씨 무다꽈아쪠러 구비 어씨비라

3. 부씨 무레 까 바쭈 바꽈바아니뤄 구 버이너. 마위 무다시마나 무버이니 구버이니, 뭐어더 어 빠까노 너 구아바나, 시 뫄오꼬솨 너 바쭈.

4. 마위 무우마 아더다아: "뇨오노 나찌오마기리시서 어라 뫄 파오로"너뉴: "뇨노 뫄 아포로". 무다쪠 뫄 찌로꼬시 쩌 바쭈?

5. 이띠 이 아포로 나 이띠 에 파오로? 바레 바아따 바 오꼬 바바가끼리사아아 어찌라 여 구어머러라 기리시도, 구구쪠가나 너 뤄뽀 롸 어나워쭈 아어러시서 무우마 무 쭈바노.

6. 뇨노 나이까아, 아포로 어라구떠 아후이라 어 머씨, 시 오꼬 이와머사아

7. 아다 오롸 와이까아 노롸 와후이라아 후이러러 어 머씨 버더디 무파, 시 오꼬 이워더 무파 부씨 이워더 와머사

8. 오롸 와이까아, 노롸 와후이라아 후이러러 어 머씨, 보씨 구우마 구바나쪠, 나 찌라 무우마 무부, 오꼬 아가뭐러사 어 뤄어뽀 구구쪠가나 너 무레모 와이.

9. 쭈바노, 쭈쪠 바아따 바버찌러 바고롸 나 오꼬.

ready for it. Indeed, you are still not ready.

3. You are still worldly. For since there is jealousy and quarreling among you, are you not worldly? Are you not acting like mere men?

4. For when one says, "I follow Paul," and another, "I follow Apollos," are you not mere men?

5. What, after all, is Apollos? And what is Paul? Only servants, through whom you came to believe--as the Lord has assigned to each his task.

6. I planted the seed, Apollos watered it, but God made it grow.

7. So neither he who plants nor he who waters is anything, but only God, who makes things grow.

8. The man who plants and the man who waters have one purpose, and each will be rewarded according to his own labor.

9. For we are God's fellow workers; you are God's field,

Nenyu mulyi ehwa layi, kandji mwanaba tchiibo tcha Ongo.

11. Kukulyikana ne ngahanyi sa Ongo anyeresise nga murengi ola ushi kuimba, nemanzise emusingi, no kwoyu musingi, undji mundju emire kunde amenyerera kubuya kuti angendi au imbira'ko.

10. Kutalyi undji mundju ola ungaimanza e undji musingi. Noyu musingi alyi Yesu Kirisito.

12. Kwoyu musingi emundju ne horo, ne buteya, ne makai netchicthiro tchinene, nemitchi, ne bukere nesi ne maungu.

13. Si tchiru batcha, e mulyimo wa tchira mundju akanalorekana'ko tchanganama kwa lusuku lwe businda, bushi kwolu lusuku, e mulyimo watchira mundju akarenzibwa mwa mulyimo. Noyu mulyimo i ukareka ne kulosa we mulyimo wa tchira mundju.

14. Akaba e mulyimo ola e mundju aimbaa kwoyu musingi atasirire, oyola iukabona elweembo

15. Si ola emulyimo wai asireraa, yeke atakabone

너뉴 무레 어화 꽈에, 가찌 뫄나바 찌이보 짜 오꼬.

11. 구구레가나 너 꽈하네 사 오꼬 아녀러시서 꽈 무러이 오꽈 우씨 구이빠, 너마씨서 어무시삐, 노 굥유 무시삐, 우씨 무쭈 어미러 구떠 아머녀러라 구부야 구디 아뻐삐 아우 이삐라고.

10. 구다레 우씨 무쭈 오꽈 우꽈이마싸 어 우씨 무시삐. 노유 무시삐 아레 여수 기리시도.

12. 굥유 무시삐 어무쭈 너 호로, 너 부더야, 너 마가이 너찌찌로 찌너너, 너미찌, 너 부거러 너시 너 마우꾸.

13. 시 찌루 바짜, 어 무레모 와 찌라 무쭈 아가나뢰러가나고 짜꽈나마 과 루수구 뤠 부시따, 부씨 굥루 루수구, 어 무레모 와찌라 무쭈 아가러씨봐 뫄 무레모. 노유 무레모 이 우가러가 너 구뢰사 워 무레모 와 찌라 무쭈.

14. 아가바 어 무레모 오꽈 어 무쭈 아이빠아 굥유 무시삐 아다시리러, 오요꽈 이우가보나 어뭐어뽄

15. 시 오꽈 어무레모 와이 아시러라아, 여거 아다가보너

God's building.

10. By the grace God has given me, I laid a foundation as an expert builder, and someone else is building on it. But each one should be careful how he builds.

11. For no one can lay any foundation other than the one already laid, which is Jesus Christ.

12. If any man builds on this foundation using gold, silver, costly stones, wood, hay or straw,

13. his work will be shown for what it is, because the Day will bring it to light. It will be revealed with fire, and the fire will test the quality of each man's work.

14. If what he has built survives, he will receive his reward.

15. If it is burned up, he will suffer loss; he himself will be

lwembo. Si tchiru batcha yeine akanunulyibwa, si akaba ngola wafufumukirwe mwa mulyimo.

뭐뚄. 시 찌루 바짜 여이너 아가누누레봐, 시 아가바 꼬롸 와푸푸무기뤄 마 무레모.

saved, but only as one escaping through the flames.

16. Muteshi kwa mwabu mulyi nyumba ya Kabumbi ne mutchima wai atchula mwa ndanda senyu?

16. 무더씨 과 뫄부 무레 뉴빠 야 가부삐 너 무찌마 와이 아쭈롸 마 따따 서뉴?

16. Don't you know that you yourselves are God's temple and that God's Spirit lives in you?

17. Ola ukahonda e luhu lwa kabumbi, kabumbi naye akamuhonda, kwa bushi e luhu lwa kabumbi lulyi lubuyabuya, naku munalyi batcha.

17. 오롸 우가호따 어 루후 롸 가부삐, 가부삐 나여 아가무호따, 과 부씨 어 루후 롸 가부삐 루레 루부야부야, 나구 무나레 바짜.

17. If anyone destroys God's temple, God will destroy him; for God's temple is sacred, and you are that temple.

18. Emundju atendaa atchiteba yeine! Akaba mundju mwa katchikatchi kenyu angende aanyisa alyi mwengi mwa myaasi ye butala, emire kunde atchitola nga mbuta, tchasiya abe mundju wa bwenge kanangana.

18. 어무뚄 아더따아 아찌더바 여이너! 아가바 무뚄 뫄 가찌가찌 거뉴 아꺼너 아아니사 아레 뭥이 뫄 먀아시 여 부다롸, 어미러 구떠 아찌도롸 까 뿌다, 짜시야 아버 무뚄 와 붜꺼 가나꺼나.

18. Do not deceive yourselves. If any one of you thinks he is wise by the standards of this age, he should become a "fool" so that he may become wise.

19. Kwa bushi e bwenge bomuno butala, bulyi buuta era muhondo sa Kabumbi. Bushi bitchula biandjikirwe mwa maandjika mabuyabuya: "Kabumbi enda simbira ebandju be bwenge kwa bukalange bwabu beine".

19. 과 부씨 어 붜꺼 보무노 부다롸, 부레 부우다 어라 무호또 사 가부삐. 부씨 비쭈롸 비아찌기뤄 마 마아찌가 마부야부야: "가부삐 어따 시삐라 어바뚄 버 붜꺼 과 부가롸꺼 봐부 버이너".

19. For the wisdom of this world is foolishness in God's sight. As it is written: "He catches the wise in their craftiness";

20. kandji bitchula biandjikirwe mbu: "Enawetchu atchula eshi emyaanyisa ye bandju be bwenge: eneeshi kwa inatchula ya buha itete mufa".

20. 가찌 비쭈롸 비아찌기뤄 뿌: "어나워쭈 아쭈롸 어씨 어먀아니사 여 바뚄 버 붜꺼: 어너어씨 과 이나쭈롸 야 부하 이더더 무파".

20. and again, "The Lord knows that the thoughts of the wise are futile."

21. Bushi noku, kutabaa ola undaa watchitongera ebandju bushi byoshi binalyi byenyu.

22. Aabe Paolo, nesi Apolo, nesi Petero, nesi ebutala, nesi ekalamo, nesi elufu, nesi emyaasi ye sine siku, nesi emyaasi era ikaika. Ebi byoshi binalyi byenyu.

23. Nenyu munalyi bandju ba Kirisito na Kirisito analyi wa Kabumbi.

21. 부씨 노구, 구다바아 오롸 우따아 와찌도꿔라 어바쭈 부씨 뵤씨 비나뤠 벼뉴.

22. 아아버 파오롣, 너시 아포롣, 너시 퍼더로, 너시 어부다롸, 너시 어가롸모, 너시 어루푸, 너시 어먀아시 여 시너 시구, 너시 어먀아시 어라 이가이가. 어비 뵤씨 비나뤠 벼뉴.

23. 너뉴 무나뤠 바쭈 바 기리시도 나 기리시도 아나뤠 와 가부삐.

21. So then, no more boasting about men! All things are yours,

22. whether Paul or Apollos or Cephas or the world or life or death or the present or the future--all are yours,

23. and you are of Christ, and Christ is of God.

1 E Bakorinto Chikono 4

1 어 바고리또 찌고노 4

1 Corinthians Chapter 4 [NIV]

1. Rero, mundqq mwatchutola nga bakosi ba Kirisito kandji bala bemangisi ba beresibwe e mulyimo wekunde bakangirisa e bandju a myaasi ya Kabumbi era yabaa ibishirwe.

2. Emwaasi ola abandju bendi bahonda kwa mwimangisi, kutchula kuba mundju mubuya.

3. Kwa yanyi myaanyisa, kutalyi mwaasi asibya akaba mungacthindjibusa nesi kutchindjibusibwa ne Tiribinalyi ye bandju. Nanyi nyeine kutalyi mwaasi nendjire natchisita'ko.

1. 러로, 무뚜구구 뫄쭈도롸 까 바고시 바 기리시도 가찌 바롸 버마꺼시 바 버러시붜 어 무뤠모 워구떠 바가꺼리사 어 바뉴 아 먀아시 야 가부삐 어라 야바아 이비씨뤄.

2. 어뫄아시 오롸 아바뉴 버띠 바호따 과 뮈마꺼시, 구쭈롸 구바 무뚜 무부야.

3. 과 야네 먀아네사, 구다뤠 뫄아시 아시뱌 아가바 무까찌띠부사 너시 구찌띠부시봐 너 디리비나뤠 여 바뉴. 나네 녀이너 구다뤠 뫄아시 너띠러 나찌시다고.

1. So then, men ought to regard us as servants of Christ and as those entrusted with the secret things of God.

2. Now it is required that those who have been given a trust must prove faithful.

3. I care very little if I am judged by you or by any human court; indeed, I do not even judge myself.

4. Mwa muchima wanyi, mutalyi chiro kasibya ka nenjire na chishitako. Si chiro bacha ndatechire mbu nyi chungenene, enawetchu yuka nyi chinjibusa.

5. Bushi noku, mutendaa mwalyibicbhira kunyibusa e banju ne bihangi by aka bumbi bitasa kuika, mundaa mwalyinjira e lu siku enawetchu akabaha bushi akabika emyasi Yoshi changanama, era ilyi mwa michima yabo. Kanji aka bihula na myaanyisa era ilyi mwa michima yabo. Chasinda, kabumbi akatonga chira munju ola weemirwe kutongibwa kukulikana ne bya akolaa.

6. Banyakechu, ei myaasi nababurirei, mwa kuchi ishira kwe wanyi mwanyi nyeine chuna Apolo chusiya munde mwachulorera'ko, ne kunde mwamenyerera nonu unji mwanyi utechire mbu"mutendaa mwaya bure na maanjiko, chasiya kutabaa munju mwa kachi kachi kenyu ola ungendi wa chitonga mbu olyi munju wa rebe, ne kunde akena unji.

7. Inde iwa kuirire kuba

4. 꽈 무찌마 와네, 무다쥐 찌로 가시뱌 가 너찌러 나 찌씨다고. 시 찌로 바짜 따더찌러 뿌 네 쭈어너너, 어나워쭈 유가 네 찌찌부사.

5. 부씨 노구, 무더따아 꽈쥐비시부히라 구네부사 어 바뚜 너 비하삐 뷔 아가 부삐 비다사 구이가, 무따아 꽈쥐찌라 어 쭈 시구 어나워쭈 아가바하 부씨 아가비가 어먀시 요씨 짜아나마, 어라 이쥐 꽈 미찌마 야보. 가찌 아가 비후쮜 나 먀아네사 어라 이쥐 꽈 미찌마 야보. 짜시따, 가부삐 아가도꽈 찌라 무뿌 오쮜 워어미뤄 구도삐봐 구구쮜가나 너 뱌 아고쮜아.

6. 바냐거쭈, 어이 먀아시 나바부리러이, 꽈 구찌 이씨라 궈 와네 꽈네 녀이너 쭈나 아포로 쭈시야 무떠 꽈쭈쮜러라고, 너 구떠 꽈머녀러라 노누 우씨 꽈네 우더찌러 뿌"무더따아 꽈야 부러 나 마아찌고, 짜시야 구다바아 무뿌 꽈 가찌 가찌 거뉴 오쮜 우떠씨 와 찌도꽈 뿌 오쮜 무뿌 와 러버, 너 구떠 아거나 우씨.

7. 이떠 이와 구이리러 구바

4. My conscience is clear, but that does not make me innocent. It is the Lord who judges me.

5. Therefore judge nothing before the appointed time; wait till the Lord comes. He will bring to light what is hidden in darkness and will expose the motives of men's hearts. At that time each will receive his praise from God.

6. Now, brothers, I have applied these things to myself and Apollos for your benefit, so that you may learn from us the meaning of the saying, "Do not go beyond what is written." Then you will not take pride in one man over against another.

7. For who makes you

mukulu kulu kurenze E banji? Byoshi bya wete, si kabumbi iwa kweeresaa'bi? Na akaba kabumbi iwa kweresa bi, chichera chinga chuma wachitonga ng'o la uteresibwaa bi?

8. Rero mwabonyire mira bya mwa baa mulaire 'ko! Mwera mulyi bami, chiro angaba mbu chubano chuta bami, nyingasimire muube bami: nyingasimire muube bani kanangana, chasiya nechu chuime alamu nenyu.

9. Bushi nyiseni kwa chubano chu njumwa, kabumbi achuirire kuba baunda. Bendi bachutola nga ba bumire kuichibwa era muhondo se banju. E banju bomwa butala, ne bamalaika benjire basanwa mwa ku chulola'ko.

10. Chubano chulyi mbuta bushi na kristo, si mwabo mulyi bengi kurengera ebuuma bwenyu na kristo. Chubano chuteete misi si mwabo mu mueete misi. Tchunjire chwa kenyibwa, si mwabo mwenjire mweresibwe 'e chunda.

11. Anabi kuikira mwechine chihangi, chwalyibuka

무구루 구루 구러써 어 바씨? 뵤씨 뱌 워더, 시 가부뻬 이와 궈어러사아비? 나 아가바 가부뻬 이와 궈러사 비, 찌쩌라 찌꺄 쭈마 와찌도꺄 꼬 롸 우더러시봐아 비?

8. 러로 먀보네러 미라 뱌 먀 바아 무퐈이러 고! 뭐라 무레 바미, 찌로 아꺄바 뿌 쭈바노 쭈다 바미, 네꺄시미러 무우버 바미: 네꺄시미러 무우버 바니 가나꺄나, 짜시야 너쭈 쭈이머 아퐈무 너뉴.

9. 부씨 네서니 과 쭈바노 쭈 뚜꽈, 가부뻬 아쭈이리러 구바 바우따. 버띠 바쭈도꺄 꺄 바 부미러 구이찌봐 어라 무호또 서 바쭈. 어 바쭈 보꽈 부다롸, 너 바마퐈이가 버찌러 바사냐 꽈 구 쭈로롸고.

10. 쭈바노 쭈레 뿌다 부씨 나 기리시도, 시 먀보 무레 버띠 구러어라 어부우마 뭐뉴 나 기리시도. 쭈바노 쭈더어더 미시 시 먀보 무 무어어더 미시. 쭈찌러 쫘 거네봐, 시 먀보 뭐찌러 뭐러시봐 어 쭈따.

11. 아나비 구이기라 뭐찌너 찌하삐, 쫘레부가 너부시냐,

different from anyone else? What do you have that you did not receive? And if you did receive it, why do you boast as though you did not?

8. Already you have all you want! Already you have become rich! You have become kings--and that without us! How I wish that you really had become kings so that we might be kings with you!

9. For it seems to me that God has put us apostles on display at the end of the procession, like men condemned to die in the arena. We have been made a spectacle to the whole universe, to angels as well as to men.

10. We are fools for Christ, but you are so wise in Christ! We are weak, but you are strong! You are honored, we are dishonored!

11. To this very hour we go hungry and thirsty, we are in

nebusinya, ne chaami ne kuina cha chireembala, kanji chwalyibusibwa, ne kulowalowa tchuteti ala chungabera.

너 짜아미 너 구이나 짜 찌러어빠롸, 가끼 좌쀄부시봐, 너 구롸와롸와 쭈더디 아롸 쭈빠버라.

rags, we are brutally treated, we are homeless.

12. Chuenjire chiuaeshika e njubano kwa kubona ekalyo. Mangu tchuwa kambibwa, chubano chuenjire chaahanyira ne mangu chwalyi bubwa, chwenjire chasese'emuchima.

12. 쭈어씨러 찌우아어씨가 어 쀼바노 과 구보나 어가룐. 마우 쭈와 가삐봐, 쭈바노 쭈어씨러 짜아하네라 너 마우 좌쀄 부봐, 쥐씨러 짜서서어무찌마.

12. We work hard with our own hands. When we are cursed, we bless; when we are persecuted, we endure it;

13. Mungu bachusinge'emyaasi, chubano chwenjiri chwaakula ne burembo. Kuikira lwarero chura churi chenjiri chwabibwa nga chafu chamwa butala, kanji chira munju achuseneko nge' singa.

13. 무우 바쭈시어어먀아시, 쭈바노 쥐씨리 좌아구롸 너 부러뽀. 구이기라 뢀러로 쭈라 쭈리 쩌씨리 좌비봐 까 짜푸 짜와 부다롸, 가끼 씨라 무뚜 아쭈서너고 어 시꺄.

13. when we are slandered, we answer kindly. Up to this moment we have become the scum of the earth, the refuse of the world.

14. Ndabaandjikiriri eni myaasi kwa ku betchise'ehonyi, si kwa kuberesa eyano nga bana banyi

14. 따바아찌기리리 어니 먀아시 과 구 버찌서어호네, 시 과 구버러사 어야노 꺄 바나 바네

14. I am not writing this to shame you, but to warn you, as my dear children.

15. ba bendjire babakangirisa emyaasi ya Kirisito, si ehu wenyu analyi muuma oshao. Bushi mangu nabahubanganyisaa emwaasi mubuya-buya, mu mango nababutaa kurengera Yesu Kirisito.

15. 바 버찌러 바바가끼리사 어먀아시 야 기리시도, 시 어후 워뉴 아나쀄 무우마 오싸오. 부씨 마우 나바후바까네사아 어꽈아시 무부야-부야, 무 마꼬 나바부다아 구러꺼라 여수 기리시도.

15. Even though you have ten thousand guardians in Christ, you do not have many fathers, for in Christ Jesus I became your father through the gospel.

16. Rero, nabeema busese kwa mundaa mwaba beyi

16. 러로, 나버어마 부서서 과 무따아 꽈바 버에

16. Therefore I urge you to imitate me.

17. Etchera tchi tchatchuma nabatchumira Timoteo. Oyu

17. 어쩌라 찌 짜쭈마 나바쭈미라 디모더오. 오유

17. For this reason I am sending to you Timothy, my

Timoteo alyi mwana wanyi mussirwa, kandji atchula atchungenene mwa myaasi ya Enawetchu. Angenda abakengesa endjira era nendee nakulyikira mwa kalamo kanyi kurengera ebuuma bwanyi na Yesu Kirisito. Nesi ndjira, sinesndjire nakangirisa ebandju mwa nyuhu sa Kabumbi soshi.

디모더오 아쩨 먀나 와네 무씨롸, 가찌 아쭈롸 아쭈꺼너너 먀 먀아시 야 어나워쭈. 아꺼따 아바거꺼사 어찌라 어라 너떠어 나구쩨기라 먀 가롸모 가네 구러꺼라 어부우마 봐네 나 여수 기리시도. 너시 띠라, 시너띠러 나가끼리사 어바꾸 먀 뉴후 사 가부삐 소씨.

son whom I love, who is faithful in the Lord. He will remind you of my way of life in Christ Jesus, which agrees with what I teach everywhere in every church.

18. Bandju bauma mu mwabu bendjiri batchitonga mwa kutchitchonga mbu ndatchihube kuika eyi mwenyu kubatangula.

18. 바꾸 바우마 무 먀부 버찌리 바찌도꺼 먀 구찌쪼꺼 뿌 따찌후버 구이가 어에 뭐뉴 구바다꾸롸.

18. Some of you have become arrogant, as if I were not coming to you.

19. Si Enawetchu akasima, ndeemange kuika eyi mwenyu. Aola nyingamenyerera emyaasi yabu bendjire batchitonga, ne kutchilorera kwa butchula bwabo!

19. 시 어나워쭈 아가시마, 떠어마꺼 구이가 어에 뭐뉴. 아오롸 네꺼머녀러라 어먀아시 야부 버찌러 바찌도꺼, 너 구찌롣러라 과 부쭈롸 봐보!

19. But I will come to you very soon, if the Lord is willing, and then I will find out not only how these arrogant people are talking, but what power they have.

20. Bushi ebwami bwa Kabumbi butatchula bwemangirire kwa bunu, si butchula bwemangirire kwa bwaashi bwai.

20. 부씨 어봐미 봐 가부삐 부다쭈롸 붜마끼리러 과 부누, 시 부쭈롸 붜마끼리러 과 봐아씨 봐이.

20. For the kingdom of God is not a matter of talk but of power.

21. Tchi mwahonda kasi? Mwahonda nyiike eni mwenyu nyeete ne katchi? Nesi mwahonda nyiike ne mutchima wa nzii inee kandji wa burembo?

21. 찌 먀호따 가시? 먀호따 네이거 어니 뭐뉴 녀어더 너 가찌? 너시 먀호따 네이거 너 무찌마 와 씨이 이너어 가찌 와 부러뽀?

21. What do you prefer? Shall I come to you with a whip, or in love and with a gentle spirit?

1 E Bakorinto Chikono 5

1. Rero, emwaasi ahandabanyire mira mwa bandju boshi kwa mwa katchi-katchi kenu mulyi bandju ba bendjire baira elusingi. Ne lusingi lwa lulyi ngolu, anabi ne bandju babateshi Ongo batangaira'lo. Bushi kulyi muuma mu mwabu ola watolyire muke'eshi.

2. Kandji mutchiri bandju ba kutchitonga busese? Mwaabu, kultira kumwabaa mwemire kulyira, ne kukolokanya oyu mundju mwa katchi-katchi kenyu.

3. Tchiro angaba mbu nyilyi bure nenyu kwa ndjira ye mubiri, se mucthima wanyi analyi alauma nenyu. Rero oyu mundju wairire batcha, nyono namutchindjibusise mira, ngokwa nyingamutchindjibusise akaba nyingabere eyera.

4. Mangu mungabwaanana kwe sina lya Enawetchu Yesu, nanyi nyingaba nyilyi alauma nenyu kwa ndjira ye mutchima. Ne buashi bwa Enawetchu Yesu nabo bungaba bunalyi aola.

1 어 바고리또 찌고노 5

1. 러로, 어뫄아시 아하따바네러 미라 뫄 바뚜 보씨 과 뫄 가찌-가찌 거누 무꼐 바뚜 바 버찌러 바이라 어루시삐. 너 루시삐 롸 루레 꼬루, 아나비 너 바뚜 바바더씨 오꼬 바다꽈이라룐. 부씨 구레 무우마 무 뫄부 오롸 와도레러 무거어씨.

2. 가찌 무찌리 바뚜 바 구찌도꽈 부서서? 뫄아부, 구루디라 구뫄바아 뭐미러 구레라, 너 구고룐가냐 오유 무뿌 뫄 가찌-가찌 거뉴.

3. 찌로 아꽈바 뿌 네레 부러 너뉴 과 찌라 여 무비리, 서 무찌마 와네 아나레 아롸우마 너뉴. 러로 오유 무뿌 와이리러 바짜, 뇨노 나무찌찌부시서 미라, 꼬과 네꽈무찌찌부시서 아가바 네꽈버러 어여라.

4. 마꾸 무꽈봐아나나 궈 시나 랴 어나워쭈 여수, 나니 네꽈바 네레 아롸우마 너뉴 과 찌라 여 무찌마. 너 부아씨 봐 어나워쭈 여수 나보 부꽈바 부나레 아오롸.

1 Corinthians Chapter 5 [NIV]

1. It is actually reported that there is sexual immorality among you, and of a kind that does not occur even among pagans: A man has his father's wife.

2. And you are proud! Shouldn't you rather have been filled with grief and have put out of your fellowship the man who did this?

3. Even though I am not physically present, I am with you in spirit. And I have already passed judgment on the one who did this, just as if I were present.

4. When you are assembled in the name of our Lord Jesus and I am with you in spirit, and the power of our Lord Jesus is present,

5. Rero mangu mungabwaanana, oyu mundju mumubikaa mwa mino sa musimu. Muiraa batcha, tchasiya amubiri ahandjulibwe, si emutchima wai anunulyibwe emusuku lwa Enawetchu Yesu akabaha.

6. Ekutchitonga kwenyu kutakomiri: muteshi kwa ekwaamba kwe hye kandju hitcha kwende kwaambya e tchungu tchoshi?

7. Bushi noku, ehi hye komba hyokwa mira, mukulaa'hi mwa katchi-katchi kenyu, tchasiya muube bandju babakomisibwe. Mukaira batcha, mungaba tchitchu tchiyayaya. Reru ku mwera mukomisibwe batcha bushi Kirisito aanyirwe mira kuba mutchulo era ikeribwe bushi netchu, nga mwana we mbulyi ola wendi warekibwa kwa lusuku lukulu lwe Pasaka.

8. Bushi noku mwakulya elyinye lye Pasaka, tchutendaa tchwakoresa emikate era ibikirwe mwe tchatchu, kuteta mbu tchundaa tchwalya elyi lyinye na mutchima ola ukomisibwe nomwa kanangana.

---

5. 러로 마꿔 무빠봐아나나, 오유 무뚜 무무비가아 뫄 미노 사 무시무. 무이라아 바짜, 짜시야 아무비리 아하뚜삐붜, 시 어무찌마 와이 아누누뤠붜 어무수구 똴 어나워쭈 여수 아가바하.

6. 어구찌도꽈 궈뉴 구다고미리: 무더씨 과 어과아빠 궈 혀 가뚜 히짜 궈떠 과아빠 어 쭈워 쪼씨?

7. 부씨 노구, 어히 혀 고빠 효과 미라, 무구똬아히 뫄 가찌-가찌 거뉴, 짜시야 무우버 바뚜 바바고미시붜. 무가이라 바짜, 무빠바 쭈 찌야야. 러루 구 뭐라 무고미시붜 바짜 부씨 기리시도 아아내뤄 미라 구바 무쭈론 어라 이거리붜 부씨 너쭈, 꽈 뫄나 워 뿌뤠 오라 워띠 와러기봐 과 루수구 루구루 뭐 파사가.

8. 부씨 노구 뫄구꺄 어뤠녀 뗘 파사가, 쭈더따아 똬고러사 어미가더 어라 이비기뤄 뭐 짜쭈, 구더다 뿌 쭈따아 똬꺄 어뤠 뤠녀 나 무찌마 오라 우고미시붜 노똬 가나꽈나.

---

5. hand this man over to Satan, so that the sinful nature may be destroyed and his spirit saved on the day of the Lord.

6. Your boasting is not good. Don't you know that a little yeast works through the whole batch of dough?

7. Get rid of the old yeast that you may be a new batch without yeast--as you really are. For Christ, our Passover lamb, has been sacrificed.

8. Therefore let us keep the Festival, not with the old yeast, the yeast of malice and wickedness, but with bread without yeast, the bread of sincerity and truth.

9. Mwa maruba nabatchumiraa, nabaandjikiraa kwa mutendaa mwakomerana ne bakiri-kiri.

9. 꽈 마루바 나바쭈미라아, 나바아씨기라아 꽈 무더따아 꽈고머라나 너 바기리-기리.

9. I have written you in my letter not to associate with sexually immoral people--

10. Ekubabura batcha, kuta kutete kanangana mbu mutendaa mwakomerana nebandju boshi bomunu butala: bakiri-kiri (basingisi), baisya-siya, ne bihumisi, ne bala bende beera ebasimu. Bsuhi abu bandju boshi akutchikula kubo, bingabeemire mbu mutengaa muno butala.

10. 어구바부라 바짜, 구다 구더더 가나따나 뿌 무더따아 꽈고머라나 너바쭈 보씨 보무누 부다롸: 바기리-기리 (바시끼시), 너 바이샤-시야, 너 비후미시, 너 바롸 버떠 버어라 어바시무. 부수히 아부 바쭈 보씨 아구찌구꽈 구보, 비까버어미러 뿌 무더따아 무노 부다롸.

10. not at all meaning the people of this world who are immoral, or the greedy and swindlers, or idolaters. In that case you would have to leave this world.

11. Si nabaandjikirire kwa mutendaa mwakomerana na tchira mundju woshi ola watchitonga mbu alyi munyaketchu mwemeresi, noku alyi musingisi, nesi musiya-siya, nesi mundju wa kweera ebasimu, nesi mundju ola wende wakamba abandji, nesi mutamisi, nesi tchihumisi. E mundju ola ulyi ngo'yu, nekulya mutendaa mwanalya nai.

11. 시 나바아씨기리러 꽈 무더따아 꽈고머라나 나 찌라 무뚜 올씨 오롸 와찌도까 뿌 아뤠 무냐거쭈 뭐머러시, 노구 아뤠 무시끼시, 너시 무시야-시야, 너시 무뚜 와 꿔어라 어바시무, 너시 무뚜 오롸 워떠 와가빠 아바찌, 너시 무다미시, 너시 찌후미시. 어 무뚜 오롸 우뤠 꼬유, 너구꺄 무더따아 꽈나꺄 나이.

11. But now I am writing you that you must not associate with anyone who calls himself a brother but is sexually immoral or greedy, an idolater or a slanderer, a drunkard or a swindler. With such a man do not even eat.

12. Ebandji ba bata bemeresi, ekutchindjibusa'bo kutanyeerekere, si Kabumbi yeine iukatchindjibusa'bo. Si mwabo mweemire kunde mwatchindjibusa ebandju bomwa tchikembe tchenyu

12. 어바씨 바 바다 버머러시, 어구찌씨부사보 구다녀어러거러, 시 가부삐 여이너 이우가찌씨부사보. 시 꽈보 뭐어미러 구떠 꽈찌씨부사 어바쭈 보꽈 찌거뻐 쩌뉴 쩌 버어머러시.

12. What business is it of mine to judge those outside the church? Are you not to judge those inside?

tche beemeresi.

13. E mandjik mabuya-buya matchula matetchire mbu: "emundju mubi, mumukolokanyaa mwa katchi-katchi kenyu".	13. 어 마찌구 마부야-부야 마쭈롸 마더찌러 뿌: "어무뿌 무비, 무무고론가냐아 뫄 가찌-가찌 거뉴".	13. God will judge those outside. "Expel the wicked man from among you."

1 E Bakorinto Chikono 6 | 1 어 바고리또 찌고노 6 | 1 Corinthians Chapter 6 [NIV]

1. Mangu mundju mu mwabo eete lubangano ne munya mwemeresi, anga ereresa kumushitajka era muhondo se baishi be mandja ba bateshi Kabumbi? eemire kumushitaka era muhondo sa bemeresi balyikabu.	1. 마우 무뿌 무 뫄보 어어더 루바꺄노 너 무냐 뭐머러시, 아아 어러러사 구무씨다가 어라 무호또 서 바이씨 버 뫄짜 바 바더씨 가부뻬? 어어미러 구무씨다가 어라 무호또 사 버머러시 바레가부.	1. If any of you has a dispute with another, dare he take it before the ungodly for judgment instead of before the saints?
2. Muteshi kwe bandju ba Kabumbi bu bakatchindjibusa ebandju be butala? Na akaba mwabu mumukatchindjibusa ebandju be butala, mutangaala kundemwaamala emyaalyi ye buha-buha era ilyi mwa katchi-katchi kenyu?	2. 무더씨 궈 바뚜 바 가부뻬 부 바가찌찌부사 어바뚜 버 부다롸? 나 아가바 뫄부 무무가찌찌부사 어바뚜 버 부다롸, 무다아아롸 구떠뫄아마롸 어먀아레 여 부하-부하 어라 이레 뫄 가찌-가찌 거뉴?	2. Do you not know that the saints will judge the world? And if you are to judge the world, are you not competent to judge trivial cases?
3. Muteshi kwa tchubanu tchu tchukatchindjibusa ne bamalaika? Mwa batcha tchungaala kunde tchwamala emyaasi era yerekere kano kalamo ketchu.	3. 무더씨 과 쭈바누 쭈 쭈가찌찌부사 너 바마롸이가? 뫄 바짜 쭈꺄아롸 구떠 쫘마롸 어먀아시 어라 여러거러 가노 가롸모 거쭈.	3. Do you not know that we will judge angels? How much more the things of this life!
4. Rero mangu mweete mbangano sa siri ngesi	4. 러로 마우 뭐어더 빠꺄노 사 시리 꺼시 찌꺄쭈마 뭐띠	4. Therefore, if you have disputes about such matters,

tchingatchuma mwendi mweeka si era muhondo se basihi be mandja ba bakenyibwe mwa katchi-katchi ke bemeresi!

5. Natetchire batcha, kwa kubetchise ehonyi. Mwa katchi-katchi kenyu mutanalyi tchiro ne mundju asibya ola weete bwenge, ola ungendi wamalyira banyakabu bemeresi embangano?

6. Si mwabo, emwemeresi kunaya kushitaka mwemeresi mulyikabu era muhondo se basihi be mandja ba bateemere Kirisito!

7. Kubinalyi! Oku kushitakana kwenyu, kwalosise mira kwa mwaimirwe kanangana: Kungakomire munde mwasesa emitchima mangu babakorera emabi. Kandji kungakomire munde mwemerera kunyaibwa bya mweete!

8. Si mwabo, mu mwendjire mwakorera ebandji emabi, ne kubanyaa ebikulo byabo. Nabu mwendjire mwakorera batcha, banalyi banyakenyu bemeresi.

9. Muteshi kwe ebakosi be mabi batakabone kwa mwaandju we bwami bwa Kabumbi? Mutendaaa mwatchiteba, bushi abasingisi,

---

뭐어가 시 어라 무호또 서 바시히 버 마짜 바 바거네뭐 와 가찌-가찌 거 버머러시!

5. 나더찌러 바짜, 과 구버찌서 어호네. 롸 가찌-가찌 거뉴 무다나레 찌로 너 무쭈 아시뱌 오롸 워어더 뭐어, 오롸 우어띠 와마레라 바냐가부 버머러시 어빠아노?

6. 시 롸보, 어뭐머러시 구나야 구씨다가 뭐머러시 무쩨가부 어라 무호또 서 바시히 버 마짜 바 바더어머러 기리시도!

7. 구비나레! 오구 구씨다가나 궈뉴, 과로시서 미라 과 롸이미뤄 가나아나: 구까고미러 무머 롸서사 어미찌마 마꾸 바바고러라 어마비. 가찌 구까고미러 무머 뭐머러라 구냐이봐 뱌 뭐어더!

8. 시 롸보, 무 뭐찌러 롸고러라 어바찌 어마비, 너 구바냐야 어비구로 뱌보. 나부 뭐찌러 롸고러라 바짜, 바나쩨 바냐거뉴 버머러시.

9. 무더씨 궈 어바고시 버 마비 바다가보너 과 롸아꾸 워 봐미 봐 가부뻬? 무더따아아 롸찌더바, 부씨 아바시띠시, 나바 버떠

---

appoint as judges even men of little account in the church!

5. I say this to shame you. Is it possible that there is nobody among you wise enough to judge a dispute between believers?

6. But instead, one brother goes to law against another--and this in front of unbelievers!

7. The very fact that you have lawsuits among you means you have been completely defeated already. Why not rather be wronged? Why not rather be cheated?

8. Instead, you yourselves cheat and do wrong, and you do this to your brothers.

9. Do you not know that the wicked will not inherit the kingdom of God? Do not be deceived: Neither the sexually immoral nor

naba bende beera ebasimu, ne bihungu, nesi emulume ola wende waira elusingi na mulume mulyikabo, ne mukasi ola wende waira elusingi na mukasi mulyikabo.

버어라 어바시무, 너 비후우, 너시 어무루머 오롸 워떠 와이라 어루시삐 나 무루머 무쩨가보, 너 무가시 오롸 워떠 와이라 어루시삐 나 무가시 무쩨가보.

idolaters nor adulterers nor male prostitutes nor homosexual offenders

10. Ne besi, ne basiya-siya, ne batamisi naba bende bakamba ebandji, ne bihumisi, abu boshi batakabone kwa mwandju we bwami bwa Kabumbi.

10. 너 버시, 너 바시야-시야, 너 바다미시 나바 버떠 바가빠 어바찌, 너 비후미시, 아부 보씨 바다가보너 과 마뚜 워 봐미 봐 가부뻬.

10. nor thieves nor the greedy nor drunkards nor slanderers nor swindlers will inherit the kingdom of God.

11. Ne bauma mu mwabo nabo, ku kabaa banatchu batcha. Si Kabumbi

11. 너 바우마 무 먀보 나보, 구 가바아 바나쭈 바짜. 시 가부뻬

11. And that is what some of you were. But you were washed, you were sanctified, you were justified in the name of the Lord Jesus Christ and by the Spirit of our God.

12. Bandju bauma mu mwabo bendji bateta mbu: "nyeete loso lwa kuira tchira kandju". Kubinalyi! Si ata tchira kandju ku kabeetere mufa! Kandji tchiro mbu yeete loso lwa kuira tchira kandju, ndangemerera kuba era nyuma sa tchira mundju.

12. 바뚜 바우마 무 먀보 버찌 바다다 뿌: "녀어더 로소 롸 구이라 찌라 가뚜". 구비나쪠! 시 아다 찌라 가뚜 구 가버어더러 무파! 가찌 찌로 뿌 여어더 로소 롸 구이라 찌라 가뚜, 따꺼머러라 구바 어라 뉴마 사 찌라 무뚜.

12. "Everything is permissible for me"--but not everything is beneficial. "Everything is permissible for me"--but I will not be mastered by anything.

13. Kandji mwende mwateta mbu: "ebilyo byabumbwaa bushi nebula, nebula nabumbwaa bushi nebilyo" Kubinalyi! Mumenyaa kwa ebilyo nebula Kabumbi akahandjula'bi. Si emubiri

13. 가찌 뭐떠 뫄더다 뿌: "어비룐 뱌부꽈아 부씨 너부롸, 너부롸 나부꽈아 부씨 너비룐" 구비나쪠! 무머냐아 과 어비룐 너부롸 가부뻬 아가하뚜꽈비. 시 어무비리 아다부꽈아 부씨 너

13. "Food for the stomach and the stomach for food"-- but God will destroy them both. The body is not meant for sexual immorality, but for the Lord, and the Lord for the body.

atabumbwaa bushi ne kuira elusingi, si abumbwaa bushi Enawetchu, kandji anatchula wai.

14. Kabumbi iwoomalaa Enawetchu Yesu, netchu akanatchoomola kurengera ebuashi bwai.

15. Muteshi kwemubiri yenyu bilyi bitera bye mubiri wa Kirisito? Rero, etchitera tchemubiri wa Kirisito tchi nyiiraa kuba tchitera tche tchihungu kasi? Bisha byenyu.

16. Muteshi kwe mundju ola waira elusingi ne tchihungukasi, ende aba mundju muma natchi? Bushi bitchula byaandjikirwe mwa Maandjiko mabuya-buya mbu: "Abu babiri banera mubilyi muuma".

17. Si ola ulyi mwa buuma na Enawetchu, ende aba mundju muuma nai kwa ndjira ye mutchima.

18. Mundaa mwahaa elusingi! Bsuhi emandji mabi moshi ma mundju ende aira, matauma kwa mubiri wai. Si ola waira ebuhungu, ende aba airire mabi era luulu se mubiri wai yeine.

19. Muteshi kwe mubiri, lu luhu lwe Mutchima mubuya-

구이라 어루시띠, 시 아부빠아 부씨 어나워쭈, 가찌 아나쭈롸 와이.

14. 가부삐 이오오마롸아 어나워쭈 여수, 너쭈 아가나쪼오모롸 구러떠라 어부아씨 봐이.

15. 무더씨 궈무비리 여뉴 비레 비더라 벼 무비리 와 기리시도? 러로, 어찌더라 쩌무비리 와 기리시도 찌 네이라아 구바 찌더라 쩌 찌후꾸 가시? 비싸 벼뉴.

16. 무더씨 궈 무뿌 오롸 와이라 어루시띠 너 찌후꾸가시, 어떠 아바 무뿌 무마 나찌? 부씨 비쭈롸 뱌아찌기뤄 롸 마아찌고 마부야-부야 뿌: "아부 바비리 바너라 무비레 무우마".

17. 시 오롸 우레 롸 부우마 나 어나워쭈, 어떠 아바 무뿌 무우마 나이 과 띠라 여 무찌마.

18. 무따아 롸하아 어루시띠! 부수히 어마찌 마비 모씨 마 무뿌 어떠 아이라, 마다우마 과 무비리 와이. 시 오롸 와이라 어부후꾸, 어떠 아바 아이리러 마비 어라 루우루 서 무비리 와이 여이너.

19. 무더씨 궈 무비리, 루 루후 뤄 무찌마 무부야-부야?

14. By his power God raised the Lord from the dead, and he will raise us also.

15. Do you not know that your bodies are members of Christ himself? Shall I then take the members of Christ and unite them with a prostitute? Never!

16. Do you not know that he who unites himself with a prostitute is one with her in body? For it is said, "The two will become one flesh."

17. But he who unites himself with the Lord is one with him in spirit.

18. Flee from sexual immorality. All other sins a man commits are outside his body, but he who sins sexually sins against his own body.

19. Do you not know that your body is a temple of the

buya? Rero, emubiri wenyu atatchiri wenyu mubeine.

20. Ongo abaulyire mira ku tchitchiro tchinene busese. Rero, mundaa mwakoresa emubiri wenyu kwe tchunda lya kabumbi.

러로, 어무비리 워뉴 아다찌리 워뉴 무버이너.

20. 오꼬 아바우례러 미라 구 찌찌로 찌너너 부서서. 러로, 무따아 마고러사 어무비리 워뉴 궈 쭈따 랴 가부삐.

Holy Spirit, who is in you, whom you have received from God? You are not your own;

20. you were bought at a price. Therefore honor God with your body.

1 E Bakorinto Chikono 7

1 어 바고리또 찌고노 7

1 Corinthians Chapter 7 [NIV]

1. Rero kukulyikana ne myaasi mwanyaandjikiraa, batchaku nababura: kukomire emulume atahwera,

2. Si bushi nekutchilanga kwa lusingi, kweemire tchira mulume aate mukai na tchira mukasi tcheemira aate eba wai.

3. Emulume eemire kunde airira mukai bira aemire kumuilyira nga eba wai. Nemukasi nai, eemire kunde airira eba wai bya eemire kumuilyira nga mukai.

4. Emukasi ateete ebuashi kwa mubiri wai, bushi alyi mubiri weba wai. Ne mulume nai ateete buashi kwa mubiri wai, bushi alyi mubiri wa mukai.

1. 러로 구구께가나 너 먀아시 먄냐아찌기라아, 바짜구 나바부라: 구고미러 어무루머 아다훠라,

2. 시 부씨 너구찌롸아 과 루시삐, 궈어미러 찌라 무루머 아아더 무가이 나 찌라 무가시 쩌어미라 아아더 어바 와이.

3. 어무루머 어어미러 구떠 아이리라 무가이 비라 아어미러 구무이쩨라 꽈 어바 와이. 너무가시 나이, 어어미러 구떠 아이리라 어바 와이 뱌 어어미러 구무이쩨라 꽈 무가이.

4. 어무가시 아더어더 어부아씨 과 무비리 와이, 부씨 아쩨 무비리 워바 와이. 너 무루머 나이 아더어더 부아씨 과 무비리 와이, 부씨 알리 무비리 와 무가이.

1. Now for the matters you wrote about: It is good for a man not to marry.

2. But since there is so much immorality, each man should have his own wife, and each woman her own husband.

3. The husband should fulfill his marital duty to his wife, and likewise the wife to her husband.

4. The wife's body does not belong to her alone but also to her husband. In the same way, the husband's body does not belong to him

아ᄙᅨ 무비리 와 무가이.

alone but also to his wife.

5. Bushi noku, mutendaa mweemana. Mungeemana bihangi byeeke oshao bya mwemeresanyise'ko bushi nekubone bihangi bye kuema. Nera nyuma se kuema, mwanahuba kubwaanana? Bitabere batcha, mutabone emisi ye kutchilanga, aola wamusimu anabone endjire ye kubaereka.

5. 부씨 노구, 무더따아
뭐어마나. 무ᅇᅥ어마나 비하ᅇᅵ
벼어거 오싸오 뱌
뭐머러사네서고 부씨
너구보너 비하ᅇᅵ 벼 구어마.
너라 뉴마 서 구어마,
뫄나후바 구봐아나나?
비다버러 바짜, 무다보너
어미시 여 구찌ᄙᅡᅇᅡ, 아오ᄙᅡ
와무시무 아나보너 어ᄡᅵ러 여
구바어러가.

5. Do not deprive each other except by mutual consent and for a time, so that you may devote yourselves to prayer. Then come together again so that Satan will not tempt you because of your lack of self-control.

6. Ei myaasi nababulyire, ata kusesibwa si kujkomire akaba mungaira batcha.

6. 어이 먀아시 나바부ᄙᅨ러,
아다 구서시봐 시 구고미러
아가바 무ᅇᅡ이라 바짜.

6. I say this as a concession, not as a command.

7. Kubinalyi, nyingasimire abandju boshi baabe bashimba nga nyonu. Si tchira mundju eete alwai lweembo lwa Kabumbi amweresise. Mundju muuma angaata luno lweembo, ne undji anaata lolula.

7. 구비나ᄙᅨ, 네ᅇᅡ시미러
아바ᅜᅮ 보씨 바아버 바씨빠
ᅇᅡ 뇨누. 시 찌라 무ᅜᅮ
어어더 아ᄙᅪ이 ᄙᅯ어뽄 ᄙᅪ
가부뻬 아뭐러시서. 무ᅜᅮ
무우마 아ᅇᅡ아다 ᄙᅮ노
ᄙᅯ어뽄, 너 우ᄡᅵ 아나아다
ᄙᅩᄙᅮᄙᅡ.

7. I wish that all men were as I am. But each man has his own gift from God; one has this gift, another has that.

8. Rero, abashimba nebahumbakasi, naburaa'bo kwa kungakomire baendekere kweekala nga nyono.

8. 러로, 아바씨빠
너바후빠가시, 나부라아보 과
구ᅇᅡ고미러 바어ᄠᅥ거러
궈어가ᄙᅡ ᅇᅡ 뇨노.

8. Now to the unmarried and the widows I say: It is good for them to stay unmarried, as I am.

9. Si akaba batangaala kunde babika emibiri yabo, kukomire bahwere ne kuhweribwa. Bushi ekuhwera nekuhweribwa ku kukulu kwa kunde balyibuka busese ne myaanyisa ye kuira elusingi.

9. 시 아가바 바다ᅇᅡ아ᄙᅡ
구ᄠᅥ 바비가 어미비리 야보,
구고미러 바훠러 너
구훠리봐. 부씨 어구훠라
너구훠리봐 구 구구ᄙᅮ 과
구ᄠᅥ 바ᄙᅨ부가 부서서 너
먀아네사 여 구이라
어ᄙᅮ시ᅇᅵ.

9. But if they cannot control themselves, they should marry, for it is better to marry than to burn with passion.

10. Kwa bala bera bahwelyire, nesi kuhweribwa, naberesa onu .... Ata nyonu nyinaberesa'o si Enawetchu yeine: emukasi eteemire kurekana neba wai.

11. Si akaba emukasi angarekana neba, atatchihweribwaa, nesi koonvikana nai. Emulume nai biteemire kukolokanya mukai.

12. Ebandji bandju, eni myaasi naburaa'bu ilyi yanyi nyeine, si itatengilyi era mwa Enawetchu akaba emulume ola ulyi mwemeresi eete mukasi ola uta mwemeresi, noyu mukasi aneemerere kweekala nai, oyu mulume atarekanaa nai.

13. Ne mukasi ola ulyi mwemeresi, ani akaba eete mulume ola uta mwemeresi, noyu mulume aneemerere kweekala nai, oyu mukasi atarekanaa nai.

14. Bushi emulume ola uta mwemeresi, ende aba mwa buuma na Kabumbi kurengera ebuuma bwai na mukai. Ne mukasi ola uta mwemeresi nai, ende aba mwa buuma na

10. 과 바꽈 버라 바훠쪠러, 너시 구훠리봐, 나버러사 오누 .... 아다 뇨누 네나버러사오 시 어나워쭈 여이너: 어무가시 어더어미러 구러가나 너바 와이.

11. 시 아가바 어무가시 아꽈러가나 너바, 아다찌훠리봐아, 너시 고오뻬가나 나이. 어무루머 나이 비더어미러 구고로가냐 무가이.

12. 어바찌 바뿌, 어니 먀아시 나부라아부 이쪠 야네 녀이너, 시 이다더삐쪠 어라 꽈 어나워쭈: 아가바 어무루머 오꽈 우쪠 뭐머러시 어어더 무가시 오꽈 우다 뭐머러시, 노유 무가시 아너어머러러 궈어가꽈 나이, 오유 무루머 아다러가나아 나이.

13. 너 무가시 오꽈 우쪠 뭐머러시, 아니 아가바 어어더 무루머 오꽈 우다 뭐머러시, 노유 무루머 아너어머러러 궈어가꽈 나이, 오유 무가시 아다러가나아 나이.

14. 부씨 어무루머 오꽈 우다 뭐머러시, 어떠 아바 꽈 부우마 나 가부뻬 구러꺼라 어부우마 봐이 나 무가이. 너 무가시 오꽈 우다 뭐머러시 나이, 어떠 아바 꽈 부우마

10. To the married I give this command (not I, but the Lord): A wife must not separate from her husband.

11. But if she does, she must remain unmarried or else be reconciled to her husband. And a husband must not divorce his wife.

12. To the rest I say this (I, not the Lord): If any brother has a wife who is not a believer and she is willing to live with him, he must not divorce her.

13. And if a woman has a husband who is not a believer and he is willing to live with her, she must not divorce him.

14. For the unbelieving husband has been sanctified through his wife, and the unbelieving wife has been sanctified through her believing husband.

Kabumbi kurengera ebuuma bwai neba wai. Akaba bitangabere batcha, ebana babo bangatolyibwe nga bandju ba balyi bure na Kabumbi. Si kanangana abu bana banalyi bandju ba Kabumbi.

나 가부삐 구러써라 어부우마 봐이 너바 와이. 아가바 비다까버러 빠짜, 어바나 바보 바까도레붜 까 바쭈 바 바레 부러 나 가부삐. 시 가나까나 아부 바나 바나레 바쭈 바 가부삐.

Otherwise your children would be unclean, but as it is, they are holy.

15. Si akaba emulume nesi emukasi ola uta mwemeresi angahonda kurekana nemwemeresi ola bahweranyire nai, anarekanaa nai. Mwa myaasi ilyi nge'i, emulume nesi emukasi ola ulyi mwemeresi ea alyi mwa buhuru, bushi Kabumbi abaamaere tchasiya mweekale mwa boolo.

15. 시 아가바 어무루머 너시 어무가시 오라 우다 뭐머러시 아까호따 구러가나 너뭐머러시 오라 바훠라니러 나이, 아나러가나아 나이. 똬 먀아시 이레 써이, 어무루머 너시 어무가시 오라 우레 뭐머러시 어아 아레 똬 부후루, 부씨 가부삐 아바아마어러 짜시야 뭐어가뻐 똬 보오르.

15. But if the unbeliever leaves, let him do so. A believing man or woman is not bound in such circumstances; God has called us to live in peace.

16. Woyu u mukasi mwemeresi, tchi tchingalosa akaba ungaala kununula eba'o? Nau u mulume mwemeresi, tchi tchingalosa kwa ungaala kununula mukasi'au?

16. 오유 우 무가시 뭐머러시, 찌 찌까르사 아가바 우까아롸 구누누롸 어바오? 나우 우 무루머 뭐머러시, 찌 찌까르사 과 우까아롸 구누누롸 무가시아우?

16. How do you know, wife, whether you will save your husband? Or, how do you know, husband, whether you will save your wife?

17. Mangu Kabumbi abaamalaa, mwabaa mulyi mwa mwango ola Enwawetchu aberesaa. Rero, kureka ebi bera natetaa, tchira mundju tcheemire kuendekera kuba moyu mwango. Oyola alyi ndjira ye butondeki nakangirisa mwa nyuhu sa

17. 마꾸 가부삐 아바아마뫄아, 똬바아 무레 똬 마꼬 오라 어놔워쭈 아버러사아. 러로, 구러가 어비 버라 나더다아, 찌라 무뿌 쩌어미러 구어떠거라 구바 모유 뫄꼬. 오요롸 아레 찌라 여 부도떠기 나가끼리사 똬 뉴후 사 가부삐 소씨.

17. Nevertheless, each one should retain the place in life that the Lord assigned to him and to which God has called him. This is the rule I lay down in all the churches.

Kabumbi soshi.

18. Akaba mundju abaa amonyisibwe mira Kabumbi amwaamalaa, anashibaa batcha. Na akaba mundju abaa atasa kumonyisibwa mango Kabumbi amwaamalaa, athondaa kumonyisibwa.

19. Ekumonyisibwa, nesi ekutakumonyisibwa, kutete mufa asibya. Si tcha tcheete mufa, kulyi kuira tcha Kabumbi atetchire.

20. Tchira mundju eemire kuishiba ngokwa abaa analyi mango Kabumbi amuamalaa

21. Akaba wabaa ulyi kapundjwa Kabumbi amwaamalaa, etchera tchitakulyibusaa. Si akaba ungabona emuisha we kutenga mwa butcha, uteesaa'u.

22. Bushi emundju ola wabaa ulyi kapundjwa mangu Enawetchu amwaalaa, era alyi mwa buhuru mwa ndanda sa Enawetchu. Nola wabaa ulyi mwa buhuru mangu Enawetchu amwaamalaa, era alyi kapundjwa ka Kirisito.

23. Kabumbi abaulyire ku tchitchiro tchinene busese. Bushi noku mutatcheemereraa kuba tchupundjwa tchwa

18. 아가바 무뚜 아바아 아모네시봐 미라 가부삐 아마아마롸아, 아나씨바아 바짜. 나 아가바 무뚜 아바아 아다사 구모네시봐 마꼬 가부삐 아마아마롸아, 아쏘따아 구모네시봐.

19. 어구모네시봐, 너시 어구다구모네시봐, 구더더 무파 아시뱌. 시 짜 쩌어더 무파, 구레 구이라 짜 가부삐 아더찌러.

20. 찌라 무뚜 어어미러 구이씨바 꼬과 아바아 아나레 마꼬 가부삐 아무아마롸아

21. 아가바 와바아 우레 가푸롸 가부삐 아마아마롸아, 어쩌라 찌다구레부사아. 시 아가바 우빠보나 어무이싸 워 구더빠 봐 부짜, 우더어사아우.

22. 부씨 어무뚜 오롸 와바아 우레 가푸롸 마뀌 어나워쭈 아마아롸아, 어라 아레 뫄 부후루 뫄 따따 사 어나워쭈. 노롸 와바아 우레 뫄 부후루 마뀌 어나워쭈 아마아마롸아, 어라 아레 가푸롸 가 기리시도.

23. 가부삐 아바우레러 구 찌찌로 찌너너 부서서. 부씨 노구 무다쩌어머러라아 구바 쭈푸롸 좌 바뚜.

18. Was a man already circumcised when he was called? He should not become uncircumcised. Was a man uncircumcised when he was called? He should not be circumcised.

19. Circumcision is nothing and uncircumcision is nothing. Keeping God's commands is what counts.

20. Each one should remain in the situation which he was in when God called him.

21. Were you a slave when you were called? Don't let it trouble you--although if you can gain your freedom, do so.

22. For he who was a slave when he was called by the Lord is the Lord's freedman; similarly, he who was a free man when he was called is Christ's slave.

23. You were bought at a price; do not become slaves of men.

bandju.

24. Rero banyaketchu, tchira mundju anaendekeraa kuba mwa buuma bwai na Kabumbi ne kushiba ngokwa abaa analyi mangu Kabumbi amwaamalaa.

25. Rero, bushi nemyaasi era yeerekere ba batasa kuhwera nesi kuhweribwa, ndeete byakubasesa (;;;;;;;;) byakutenga era mwa Enawetchu ola nyingeeresa'bo. Si eyanyi myaanyisa ineeresa'bo, bushi nanyi nyiri mundju ola wemire kweemererwa kukulyikana ne bondjo bwa Enawetchu.

26. Rero, bushi ne malyibuko me sini suku, nyisene kwa kukomire tchira mundju ashibe ngokwa analyi

27. Akaba weete mukasi, utahondaa kurekana nai, na akaba utasa kuhwera, utahondaa mukasi.

28. Si akaba ungahwera, utairiri tchibi. Na akaba emunyerenai angahweribwa, atairiri tchibi. Si ebandju ba bahwerantire bangalola ku malyibuko manene mwa kalamo kabu. Rero amu malyibuko, nahonda nyibaambuse namu.

24. 러로 바냐거쭈, 찌라 무뚜 아나어떠거라아 구바 봐 부우마 봐이 나 가부삐, 너 구씨바 꼬과 아바아 아나레 마우 가부삐 아뫄아마꽈아.

25. 러로, 부씨 너먀아시 어라 여어러거러 바 바다사 구훠라 너시 구훠리봐, 떠어더 뱌구바서사 (;;;;;;;;) 뱌구더꽈 어라 봐 어나워쭈 오라 네뻐어러라사보. 시 어야네 먀아네사 이너어러사보, 부씨 나네 네리 무뚜 오라 워미러 궈어머러롸 구구레가나 너 보쪼 봐 어나워쭈.

26. 러로, 부씨 너 마레부고 머 시니 수구, 네서너 과 구고미러 찌라 무뚜 아씨버 꼬과 아나레

27. 아가바 워어더 무가시, 우다호따아 구러가나 나이, 나 아가바 우다사 구훠라, 우다호따아 무가시.

28. 시 아가바 우꽈훠라, 우다이리리 찌비. 나 아가바 어무녀러나이 아꽈훠리봐, 아다이리리 찌비. 시 어바뿌 바 바훠라띠러 바꽈르꽈 구 마레부고 마너너 뫄 가꽈모 가부. 러로 아무 마레부고, 나호따 네바아뿌서 나무.

24. Brothers, each man, as responsible to God, should remain in the situation God called him to.

25. Now about virgins: I have no command from the Lord, but I give a judgment as one who by the Lord's mercy is trustworthy.

26. Because of the present crisis, I think that it is good for you to remain as you are.

27. Are you married? Do not seek a divorce. Are you unmarried? Do not look for a wife.

28. But if you do marry, you have not sinned; and if a virgin marries, she has not sinned. But those who marry will face many troubles in this life, and I want to spare you this.

29. Banyeketchu, tchitchini tchinahonda kubabura: ebihangi bya byashiba bilyi byeeke. Rero, kutengera lwarero, ebanju ba beete ebakasi bakoreraa Kabumbi nga balabateete'bo,

30. na bala balyira baa nga batalyira, bala balyi mwa lumoo babaa nga batalyi mu lumo, na bala baula ebindju, babaa nga beteete kandju.

31. Nabala bakoresa bakoresa ebikulo byomuno butala, babaa nga batakoresa'bi. Bushi buno butala bwahonda kuwa.

32. Nyingasimire mutendaa muanyisa bye kubalyibusa. Emundju ola utahwerire , ende atchianya mwa myaasi ya Enawetchu, ende ahonda amusimise.

33. Si ola uhwerire, yeke ende alyibukira emyaasi ye'butala, bushi ahonda asimise mukai.

34. Aola, ende aba ngola watchiabire'mu kabiri. Ne mukasi ola utahweribwe nesi emunyere, ende atchianya loshi mwa myaasi ya Enawetchu, tchasiya aabe mukasi mubuya-buya kwa

---

29. 바녀거쭈, 찌찌니 찌나호따 구바부라: 어비하삐 뱌 뱌씨바 비례 벼어거. 러로, 구더뼈라 롸러로, 어바쭈 바 버어더 어바가시 바고러라아 가부뻬 까 바롸바더어더보,

30. 나 바롸 바례라 바아 까 바다례라, 바롸 바례 뫄 루모오 바바아 까 바다례 무 루모, 나 바롸 바우롸 어비쭈, 바바아 까 버더어더 가누.

31. 나바롸 바고러사 바고러사 어비구롣 뵤무노 부다롸, 바바아 까 바다고러사비. 부씨 부노 부다롸 뵤호따 구와.

32. 네까시미러 무더따아 무아네사 벼 구바례부사. 어무누 오라 우다훠리러 , 어떠 아찌아냐 뫄 먀아시 야 어나워쭈, 어떠 아호따 아무시미서.

33. 시 오라 우훠리러, 여거 어떠 아례부기라 어먀아시 여부다롸, 부씨 아호따 아시미서 무가이.

34. 아오롸, 어떠 아바 꼬롸 와찌아비러무 가비리. 너 무가시 오롸 우다훠리붜 너시 어무녀러, 어떠 아찌아냐 롣씨 뫄 먀아시 야 어나워쭈, 짜시야 아아버 무가시 무부야-부야 과 찌라

---

29. What I mean, brothers, is that the time is short. From now on those who have wives should live as if they had none;

30. those who mourn, as if they did not; those who are happy, as if they were not; those who buy something, as if it were not theirs to keep;

31. those who use the things of the world, as if not engrossed in them. For this world in its present form is passing away.

32. I would like you to be free from concern. An unmarried man is concerned about the Lord's affairs--how he can please the Lord.

33. But a married man is concerned about the affairs of this world--how he can please his wife--

34. and his interests are divided. An unmarried woman or virgin is concerned about the Lord's affairs: Her aim is to be devoted to the Lord in both body and spirit. But a

ndjira yemubiri ne ye mutchima. Si emukasi ola uhweribwe yeke ende atchianya mwa myaasi yomuno butala, bushi ende ahonda asimise eba wai.

35. Nababurire ei myaasi, kwa mutoloke wenyu, si ndahonda kubabikira emyereko. Nahonda munde mwaata endjira era itchungenene, kandji yomuno butala, bushi ende ahonda asimise eba wai.

36. Akaba emutabana angaba akukumanyira emurakasi busese, kandji asene kwa ahonda kumuirira mwaasi ola utakomire, noku ahonda amuhwere, banahweranaa. Wamutabana akahwera murakasi wai, angaba atakolyire tchibi.

37. Si akaba emutabana mwa mutchima wai yeine angateta busira kumutchitchika mbu atatchihonda kuhwera murakasi, kandji anemerere kutchishibira mushimba, aola angaba airire kubuya.

38. Rero, emutabana ola wahwerira murakasi eri airire kubuya. Si emutabana ola wanana kuhwera murakasi, eri

여무비리 너 여 무찌마. 시 어무가시 오꽈 우훠리붸 여거 어너 아찌아냐 똬 먀아시 요무노 부다꽈, 부씨 어너 아호따 아시미서 어바 와이.

35. 나바부리러 어이 먀아시, 과 무도로꺼 워뉴, 시 따호따 구바비기라 어머러고. 나호따 무떠 똬아다 어찌라 어라 이쭈떠너너, 가찌 요무노 부다꽈, 부씨 어너 아호따 아시미서 어바 와이.

36. 아가바 어무다바나 아빠바 아구구마네라 어무라가시 부서서, 가찌 아서너 과 아호따 구무이리라 똬아시 오꽈 우다고미러, 노구 아호따 아무훠러, 바나훠라나아. 와무다바나 아가훠라 무라가시 와이, 아빠바 아다고께러 찌비.

37. 시 아가바 어무다바나 똬 무찌마 와이 여이너 아빠더다 부시라 구무찌찌가 뿌 아다찌호따 구훠라 무라가시, 가찌 아너머러러 구찌씨비라 무씨빠, 아오꽈 아빠바 아이리러 구부야.

38. 러로, 어무다바나 오꽈 와훠리라 무라가시 어리 아이리러 구부야. 시 어무다바나 오꽈 와나나

married woman is concerned about the affairs of this world--how she can please her husband.

35. I am saying this for your own good, not to restrict you, but that you may live in a right way in undivided devotion to the Lord.

36. If anyone thinks he is acting improperly toward the virgin he is engaged to, and if she is getting along in years and he feels he ought to marry, he should do as he wants. He is not sinning. They should get married.

37. But the man who has settled the matter in his own mind, who is under no compulsion but has control over his own will, and who has made up his mind not to marry the virgin--this man also does the right thing.

38. So then, he who marries the virgin does right, but he who does not marry her does even better.

airire kubuya busese.

39. Emukasi ola wahwerirwe ende aba aminyirwe kwe'ba mangu oyu eba abaa atchiri alama. Si akaba angafa, oyu mukasi angatchilondorera yeine ola ungamuhwera ne mulume ne mulume ola asimire. Si oyu mulume wamuhwera, tcheemire aba mwerersi.

40. Si kwa myaanyisa yanyi, akaba oyu muhumba-kasi angeekala ngokwa analyi, angaahanyirwa busese. Nanyi, naanyisa kwa nakoresibwa ne Mutchima wa Kabumbi.

구훠라 무라가시, 어리
아이리러 구부야 부서서.

39. 어무가시 오라 와훠리뤄
어뻐 아바 아미네뤄 궈바
마우 오유 어바 아바아
아찌리 아롸마. 시 아가바
아까파, 오유 무가시
아까찌로또러라 여이너 오롸
우까무훠라 너 무루머 너
무루머 오롸 아시미러. 시
오유 무루머 와무훠라,
쩌어미러 아바 뭐러시.

40. 시 과 먀아네사 야니,
아가바 오유 무후빠-가시
아뻐어가롸 쪼과 아나레,
아까아하네롸 부서서. 나니,
나아네사 과 나고러시봐 너
무찌마 와 가부삐.

---

39. A woman is bound to her husband as long as he lives. But if her husband dies, she is free to marry anyone she wishes, but he must belong to the Lord.

40. In my judgment, she is happier if she stays as she is--and I think that I too have the Spirit of God.

---

1 E Bakorinto Chikono 8

1. Rero kukulyikana nebya byeerekere anyama sa bandju batchuilaa ebasimu, tchwishi kwa mwende mwateta mbu: "Tchuboshi tchutchula tchwishi myaasi". Si ekumenya emyaasi kwende kwatchuma emundju aata erume. Si enzii yeke, yende yatchuma ebandju bakula mwa bwemeresi.

---

1 어 바고리또 찌고노 8

1. 러로 구구께가나 너뱌
벼어러거러 아냐마 사 바뚜
바쭈이롸아 어바시무, 쮜씨
과 뭐더 머더다 뿌: "쭈보씨
쭈쭈롸 쮜씨 먀아시". 시
어구머냐 어먀아시 궈떠
과쭈마 어무뿌 아아다
어루머. 시 어씨이 여거, 여떠
야쭈마 어바뿌 바구롸 뫄
뷔머러시.

---

1 Corinthians Chapter 8 [NIV]

1. Now about food sacrificed to idols: We know that we all possess knowledge. Knowledge puffs up, but love builds up.

2. Akaba mundju angatchitchinga mbu eshi kandju karebe, eri atasa kumenya'ku nokwa byeemire kumenyerera.

3. Si mundju ola usimire Ongo oyola eeshibwe na Ongo!!

4. Rero, kukulyikana ne mwaasi werekere ekulya enyama se bandju batchulaa ebasimu, tchwishi kwe basimu kata kandju muno butala kandji tchwishi kanangana kwa kunatchula Ongo muuma pwere.

5. Kanangana, mwatchana, kwa nguba nokuno butala kulyi bindju binene bye bandju batchula batolyire nga baongo. Kandji kulyi baongo banene, kwanaba na baenawetchu banene.

6. Si tchiro batcha, tchubano tchunatchusa Ongo muuma oshao. Oyola i Tata wabumbaa byoshi. Kandji tchulyi bauma-uma bushi nai. Kutchula na Enawetchu muuma oshao i Yesu Kirisito. Nokumurengera'ko, Ongo abumbaa ebindju byoshi, ne buashi bwai bubutchumire thwaba bauma-uma.

7. Oyu mwaasi, ata ebemeresi

---

2. 아가바 무뚜 아까찌찌까뿌 어씨 가꾸 가러버, 어리 아다사 구머냐구 노과 벼어미러 구머녀러라.

3. 시 무뚜 오꽈 우시미러 오꼬 오요꽈 어어씨붜 나 오꼬!!

4. 러로, 구구쭈레가나 너 꽈아시 워러거러 어구꺄 어냐마 서 바뚜 바쭈꽈아 어바시무, 쮜씨 궈 바시무 가다 가꾸 무노 부다꽈 가찌 쮜씨 가나까나 과 구나쭈꽈 오꼬 무우마 풔러.

5. 가나까나, 꽈짜나, 과 우바 노구노 부다꽈 구레 비뚜 비너너 벼 바뚜 바쭈꽈 바도쩨러 까 바오꼬. 가찌 구레 바오꼬 바너너, 과나바 나 바어나워쭈 바너너.

6. 시 찌로 바짜, 쭈바노 쭈나쭈사 오꼬 무우마 오싸오. 오요꽈 이 다다 와부빠아 뵤씨. 가찌 쮜레 바우마-우마 부씨 나이. 구쭈꽈 나 어나워쭈 무우마 오싸오 이 여수 기리시도. 노구무러꺼러라고, 오꼬 아부빠아 어비뚜 뵤씨, 너 부아씨 봐이 부부쭈미러 쫘바 바우마-우마.

7. 오유 꽈아시, 아다

---

2. The man who thinks he knows something does not yet know as he ought to know.

3. But the man who loves God is known by God.

4. So then, about eating food sacrificed to idols: We know that an idol is nothing at all in the world and that there is no God but one.

5. For even if there are so-called gods, whether in heaven or on earth (as indeed there are many "gods" and many "lords"),

6. yet for us there is but one God, the Father, from whom all things came and for whom we live; and there is but one Lord, Jesus Christ, through whom all things came and through whom we live.

7. But not everyone knows

boshi babuishi. Bushi kulyi bauma mubo ba babaa bakomire kunde beeya ebasimu. Kuikira lwarero, abu bandju mwa kulya esi nyama, bendjire baanyisa kanangana mbu oyu musimu mbu oyu musimu. Mwa kuba bera balya'si, banatangirisa batchiaya mwa mitchima yabu.

8. Si kanangana, ebilyo bitangatchuma tchwaba ofu na Ongo. Akaba tchunganana kulya'bi, kutalyi tchatchungaba tchwaesise. Na akaba tchungalya'bi kutalyi tcha tchungaba tchwaingukire.

9. Si mumenyaa ebuhuru bwenyu bungesha kutchuma ba batasimikire mwa bwemeresi baya mwa mabi.

10. Bushi akaba emundju ola utasimikire mwa bwemeresi angalola kwa u mundju wishi myaasi walyira enyama kwa kahumiro, utasene kwa etchera tchingatchuma nai lya enyama se bandju batchulaaa ebasimu?

11. Rero bushi noku kumenya emyaasi kwao, kukwanatchuma oyu munyakenyu mwemeresi ola

어버머러시 보씨 바부이씨. 부씨 구레 바우마 무보 바 바바아 바고미러 구너 버어야 어바시무. 구이기라 롸러로, 아부 바뉴 먀 구꺄 어시 냐마, 버찌러 바아니싸 가나빠나 뿌 오유 무시무 뿌 오유 무시무. 먀 구바 버라 바꺄시, 바나다삐리사 바찌아야 먀 미찌마 야부.

8. 시 가나빠나, 어비료 비다빠쭈마 쫘바 오푸 나 오꼬. 아가바 쭈빠나나 구꺄비, 구다레 짜쭈빠바 쫘어시서. 나 아가바 쭈빠꺄비 구다레 짜 쭈빠바 쫘이꾸기러.

9. 시 무머냐아 어부후루 뷰뉴 부빠싸 구쭈마 바 바다시미기러 먀 뷰머러시 바야 먀 마비.

10. 부씨 아가바 어무뉴 오꺄 우다시미기러 먀 뷰머러시 아빠로꽈 과 우 무뉴 위씨 먀아시 와레라 어냐마 과 가후미로, 우다서너 과 어쩌라 찌빠쭈마 나이 꺄 어냐마 서 바뉴 바쭈꽈아아 어바시무?

11. 러로 부씨 노구 구머냐 어먀아시 과오, 구과나쭈마 오유 무냐거뉴 뭐머러시 오꺄 우다시미기러 아야 먀

this. Some people are still so accustomed to idols that when they eat such food they think of it as having been sacrificed to an idol, and since their conscience is weak, it is defiled.

8. But food does not bring us near to God; we are no worse if we do not eat, and no better if we do.

9. Be careful, however, that the exercise of your freedom does not become a stumbling block to the weak.

10. For if anyone with a weak conscience sees you who have this knowledge eating in an idol's temple, won't he be emboldened to eat what has been sacrificed to idols?

11. So this weak brother, for whom Christ died, is destroyed by your knowledge.

utasimikire aya mwa mulyiro, noku Kirisito amufiraa.

무쎄로, 노구 기리시도 아무피라아.

12. Mango mwende mwairira abu banyaketchu bemeresi emabi, ne kutchuma mwalyibukira mwa mitchima, mumenyaa kwa Yesu Kirisito yeine imwende mwaba mwailyira emabi

12. 마꼬 뭐떠 마이리라 아부 바냐거쭈 버머러시 어마비, 너 구쭈마 솨쎄부기라 솨 미찌마, 무머냐아 과 여수 기리시도 여이너 이뭐떠 솨바 솨이쎄라 어마비

12. When you sin against your brothers in this way and wound their weak conscience, you sin against Christ.

13. Bushi noku, akaba biryo birebe bingatchuma munyaketchu mwemeresi aya mwa mabi, ndakatchiryе tchiro ne hitcha, nyingesha kutchuma oyu munyaketchu aya mwa mabi.

13. 부씨 노구, 아가바 비료 비러버 비까쭈마 무냐거쭈 뭐머러시 아야 솨 마비, 따가찌루여 찌로 너 히짜, 네떠싸 구쭈마 오유 무냐거쭈 아야 솨 마비.

13. Therefore, if what I eat causes my brother to fall into sin, I will never eat meat again, so that I will not cause him to fall.

1 E Bakorinto Chikono 9

1 어 바고리또 찌고노 9

1 Corinthians Chapter 9 [NIV]

1. Nyono nyilyi mwa buhuru, kandji nyiri ndjumwa. Nyeine natchiloreraa ku Enawetchu Yesu Kirisito. Ne mulyimo wa Enawetchu ola nakolaa mwa katchi-katchi kenyu, iwatchumire mwamwerera.

1. 뇨노 네쎄 솨 부후루, 가찌 네리 뚜솨. 녀이너 나찌또러라아 구 어나워쭈 여수 기리시도. 너 무쎄모 와 어나워쭈 오솨 나고솨아 솨 가찌-가찌 거뉴, 이와쭈미러 솨뭐러라.

1. Am I not free? Am I not an apostle? Have I not seen Jesus our Lord? Are you not the result of my work in the Lord?

2. Tchiru angaba mbu abandji bandju kwa nyiri ndjumwa, si mwabo muneshi kwa nyiri ndjumwa kubinalyi! Ekuba kwenyu mwa buuma na Enawetchu ku kuosise

2. 찌루 아까바 뿌 아바찌 바뚜 과 네리 뚜솨, 시 솨보 무너씨 과 네리 뚜솨 구비나쎄! 어구바 궈뉴 솨 부우마 나 어나워쭈 구 구오시서 가나까나 과 네쎄

2. Even though I may not be an apostle to others, surely I am to you! For you are the seal of my apostleship in the Lord.

kanangana kwa nyilyi ndjumwa.

3. Mango ebandju bende banyishitaka, nende nabaakula mbu:

4. Netchu, kasi tchuteete eloso lwe kunde tchweeresibwa ebiryo, ne bye kumwa byoshi ne mulyimo ola tchwakola?

5. Nesi tchuteete eloso lwa kunde tchwabalama ne mukasi mwememresi, ngokwa esindji ndjumwa sende saira, ne banyakabo Enawetchu, anabe na Petero?

6. Nesi nyono na Baranabo oshao, tchutchunemire kunde tchwatchikorera tchasiya tchubone bya tchulaire'ko.

7. Kutalyi ola wende wakoresa ebikulo byai yeine mwa mulyimo we tchisula. Kutalyi nola wende wainga ehwa lyai lye misabibu mbu atalyaa nokwa bifuma byalyi. Kutalyi na Mulanzi ola utamwa kwa mata mebifuana bira alanga.

8. Mutatchitchingaa mbu natetchire ei myaasi kukulyikana nokwa bitchula mwa katchi-katchi ke bandju, si e mwaso wa Musa nao ku anatchula atetchire batcha.

9. Bushi mwoyu mwaso,

누꽈.

3. 마꼬 어바누 버너 바네씨다가, 너떠 나바아구꽈 뿌:

4. 너쭈, 가시 쭈더어더 어로소 뤠 구더 쭤어러시봐 어비료, 너 벼 구꽈 뵤씨 너 무레모 오라 쫘고꽈?

5. 너시 쭈더어더 어로소 꽈 구더 쫘바라마 너 무가시 뭐머러시, 꼬과 어시찌 누꽈 서떠 사이라, 너 바냐가보 어나워쭈, 아나버 나 퍼더로?

6. 너시 뇨노 나 바라나보 오싸오, 쭈쭈너미러 구더 쫘찌고러라 짜시야 쭈보너 뱌 쭈꽈이러고.

7. 구다레 오라 워떠 와고러사 어비구로 뱌이 여이너 마 무레모 워 찌수꽈. 구다레 노꽈 워떠 와이꽈 어화 꺄이 려 미사비부 뿌 아다꺄아 노과 비푸마 뱌레. 구다레 나 무꽈씨 오라 우다꽈 과 마다 머비푸아나 비라 아꽈꽈.

8. 무다찌찌꽈아 뿌 나더찌러 어이 먀아시 구구레가나 노과 비쭈꽈 마 가찌-가찌 거 바누, 시 어 뫄소 와 무사 나오 구 아나쭈꽈 아더찌러 바짜.

9. 부씨 모유 뫄소, 비쭈꽈

3. This is my defense to those who sit in judgment on me.

4. Don't we have the right to food and drink?

5. Don't we have the right to take a believing wife along with us, as do the other apostles and the Lord's brothers and Cephas?

6. Or is it only I and Barnabas who must work for a living?

7. Who serves as a soldier at his own expense? Who plants a vineyard and does not eat of its grapes? Who tends a flock and does not drink of the milk?

8. Do I say this merely from a human point of view? Doesn't the Law say the same thing?

9. For it is written in the Law

bitchula byaandjikirwe mbu: "mango ambanzi yakola kwa kushebula, utaiminaa ebunu mbu italyaaa kwa bulo". Mwishi Ongo ei myaasi bushi nekulaa kwa ngafu?

10. Atetaa batcha bushi netchu. Kubinalyi, oyu mwasi aandjikibwaa bushi netchu. Byemire emundju ola wainga ehwa, nola waumba boshi bakole beete ne munyiiro we kubona ewabo mwango kwa mwaka.

11. Tchubani tchwaingaa atchinwa tcha Ongo mwa ndanda senyu. Rero etchibi ngai utchiri akaba netchu tchungende tchwabona kwa bindju bya mweete?

12. Akaba ebandji bu bete eloso lwekubona kwe bya mweete, si tchuba o tchu tchweete'lu kurenza'bu! Si tchiro batcha, tchutatetaa mbu mutchweeresaa bya mweete kwe loso. Si tchwendjire tchwaata ebushibirisi mwa myaasi yoshi, tchasiya emwaasu mubuya-buya wa Yesu Kirisito atabonaa tchaangiko.

13. Mwishi kwa ba bende bakola mwa luhu lwa Ongo, mwolu luhu mu bende

뱌아찌기뤄 뿌: "마꼬 아빠씨 야고꽈 과 구써부꽈, 우다이미나아 어부누 뿌 이다랴아아 과 부로". 뮈씨 오꼬 어이 먀아시 부씨 너구꽈아 과 까푸?

10. 아더다아 바짜 부씨 너쭈 구비나쩨, 오유 마시 아아찌기봐아 부씨 너쭈. 벼미러 어무뚜 오랴 와이꽈 어화, 노꽈 와우빠 보씨 바고꿔 버어더 너 무네이로 워 구보나 어와보 먀꼬 과 꽈가.

11. 쭈바니 쫘이꽈아 아찌놔 짜 오꼬 꽈 따따 서뉴. 러로 어찌비 꽈이 우찌리 아가바 너쭈 쭈꺼떠 쫘보나 과 비뿌 뱌 뭐어더?

12. 아가바 어바찌 부 버더 어로쏘 뤄구보나 궈 뱌 뭐어더, 시 쭈바 오 쭈 쭤어더루 구러싸부! 시 찌로 바짜, 쭈다더다아 뿌 무쭤어러사아 뱌 뭐어더 궈 로쏘. 시 쭤찌러 쫘아다 어부씨비리시 꽈 먀아시 요씨, 짜시야 어꽈아수 무부야-부야 와 여수 기리시도 아다보나아 짜아꼬.

13. 뮈씨 과 바 버떠 바고꽈 꽈 루후 꽈 오꼬, 모루 루후 무 버떠 바나쩨라. 나 버떠

of Moses: "Do not muzzle an ox while it is treading out the grain." Is it about oxen that God is concerned?

10. Surely he says this for us, doesn't he? Yes, this was written for us, because when the plowman plows and the thresher threshes, they ought to do so in the hope of sharing in the harvest.

11. If we have sown spiritual seed among you, is it too much if we reap a material harvest from you?

12. If others have this right of support from you, shouldn't we have it all the more? But we did not use this right. On the contrary, we put up with anything rather than hinder the gospel of Christ.

13. Don't you know that those who work in the temple get their food from

banalyira. Na bende bakola mwa kwaana emitchulo kwa kahaha, kwaku kahaha kunabo bende banabonera ewabu mwango kwa mitchulo era yende yetchulwa'ko.

14. Kunoku ku Enawetchu atetaa mbu ba bende bahubanganya emwasi mubuya-buya beemire kunde babona bya balaire'ko mwa kalamo kabo kurengera oyu mwasi mubuya-buya.

15. Si nyono, mwebi byoshibya nyeete kwe loso, ndeemire mu cthiro na tchiuma: nesi ndabaandjikirire batcha kwa kuhonda munyeerese'bi. Bushi nyono, ekufa ku kukulu, wakunyianga mbu natchitonga bushi nebi.

16. Si tchiro batcha, ndeemire kunde natchitonga bushi nendjire nahubanganya ne mwasi mubuya-buya. Oyola, alyi musio ola neesibwe. Rero bulyi buanya ku nyono, akaba ndangahubanganya e mwasi mubuya-buya!

17. Bingabee mbu nyeine nyinatchilondoreraa oyu mulyimo, nyingendjire neeresibwa elwembo. Si bushi alyi mulyimo ola neresibwe, binemire nyinde nakola'o.

바고꽈 와 과아나 어미쭈롣 과 가하하, 과구 가하하 구나보 버머 바나보너라 어와부 뫄끄 과 미쭈롣 어라 여머 여쭈꽈고.

14. 구노구 구 어나워쭈 아더다아 뿌 바 버머 바후바꺄냐 어뫄시 무부야-부야 버어미러 구머 바보나 뱌 바꽈이러고 뫄 가꽈모 가보 구러꺼라 오유 뫄시 무부야-부야.

15. 시 뇨노, 뭐비 뵤씨뱌 녀어더 귀 롣소, 떠어미러 무 찌로 나 찌우마: 너시 따바아찌기리러 바짜 과 구호따 무녀어러서비. 부씨 뇨노, 어구파 구 구구루, 와구네아꺼 뿌 나찌도꺼 부씨 너비.

16. 시 찌로 바짜, 떠어미러 구머 나찌도꺼 부씨 너찌러 나후바꺄냐 너 뫄시 무부야-부야. 오요꽈, 아꼐 무시오 오꽈 너어시붜. 러로 부꼐 부아냐 구 뇨노, 아가바 따꺼후바꺄냐 어 뫄시 무부야-부야!

17. 비꺼버어 뿌 녀이너 네나찌롣또러라아 오유 무꼐모, 네꺼찌러 너어러시봐 어뤄뽇. 시 부씨 아꼐 무꼐모 오꽈 너러시붜, 비너미러 네떠 나고꽈오.

the temple, and those who serve at the altar share in what is offered on the altar?

14. In the same way, the Lord has commanded that those who preach the gospel should receive their living from the gospel.

15. But I have not used any of these rights. And I am not writing this in the hope that you will do such things for me. I would rather die than have anyone deprive me of this boast.

16. Yet when I preach the gospel, I cannot boast, for I am compelled to preach. Woe to me if I do not preach the gospel!

17. If I preach voluntarily, I have a reward; if not voluntarily, I am simply discharging the trust committed to me.

18. Rero, elwembo lwanyi tchiri tchiye? Elwembo lwanyi, kulyi kunde nahubanganyisa ebandju eMwasi mubuya-buya kwa buha, busira kweema'bo bya neemire kubona mwa kubahubanganyisa'o.

18. 러로, 어뤄뙤 똬네 찌리 찌여? 어뤄뙤 똬네, 구레 구떠 나후바빠니사 어바뿌 어마시 무부야-부야 과 부하, 부시라 귀어마보 뱌 너어미러 구보나 똬 구바후바빠네사오.

18. What then is my reward? Just this: that in preaching the gospel I may offer it free of charge, and so not make use of my rights in preaching it.

19. Nyono, nyiri mwa buhuru, ndalyi kaungu ka mundju asibya. Si natcjiirire kaungu ke bandju boshi, tchasiya nyibone bandju banene.

19. 뇨노, 네리 똬 부후루, 따레 가우꾸 가 무뚜 아시뱌. 시 나찌이리러 가우꾸 거 바뚜 보씨, 짜시야 네보너 바뚜 바너너.

19. Though I am free and belong to no man, I make myself a slave to everyone, to win as many as possible.

20. Mango nende naba nyiri mwa Bayuta, nende natchitola nga muyuta tchasiya nabo nyibone'bo. Na mango nyiri mwa ba bende ba tchunda e mwaso wa Musa, nanyi nanatchunda'o tchiro angaba mbu ndalyi era bufulyi so'yu mwaso. Nende naira batcha tchasiya nabo nyibone'bo.

20. 마꼬 너더 나바 네리 똬 바유다, 너더 나찌도똬 빠 무유다 짜시야 나보 네보너보. 나 마꼬 네리 똬 바 버떠 바 쭈따 어 마소 와 무사, 나네 나나쭈따오 찌로 아빠바 뿌 따레 어라 부푸레 소유 마소. 너더 나이라 바짜 짜시야 나보 네보너보.

20. To the Jews I became like a Jew, to win the Jews. To those under the law I became like one under the law (though I myself am not under the law), so as to win those under the law.

21. Na mango nende naba nyiri mwa ba bateshi e Mwaso wa Musa, nende natchitola nga nanyi ndauishi, tchasiya nyobone'bo. Ekuira batcha kutakuteta mbu ndatchundjire e Mwaso wa Ongo, bushi nyitchula nyicthundjire e Mwaso wa Kirisito.

21. 나 마꼬 너더 나바 네리 똬 바 바더씨 어 마소 와 무사, 너더 나찌도똬 빠 나네 따우이씨, 짜시야 뇨보너보. 어구이라 바짜 구다구더다 뿌 따쭈띠러 어 마소 와 오꼬, 부씨 네쭈똬 네쭈띠러 어 마소 와 기리시도.

21. To those not having the law I became like one not having the law (though I am not free from God's law but am under Christ's law), so as to win those not having the law.

22. Na mango nende naba nyiri mwa ba batasimikire mwa bwemeresi, nende natchitola nga nanyi ndasimikire mubo,

22. 나 마꼬 너더 나바 네리 똬 바 바다시미기러 똬 뭐머러시, 너더 나찌도똬 빠 나네 따시미기러 무보,

22. To the weak I became weak, to win the weak. I have become all things to all men so that by all possible

tchasiya nabo nyibone'bo.
Mwa bandju boshi, nende
natchisesa kuba muuma nabo,
tchasiya mwa ndjira soshi,
nyinunule bauma mubo.

23. Ebi bysohi nende nabiira
ne Mwasi Mubuya-buya,
tchasiya nanyi nyibone
mwango kwa ngahanyi sa
atchusa.

24. Si mwishi kwa mango
ebandju bende baira ekaimano
ke malyibita, boshi bende
banalyibita, si muuma oshao
iwende weeresibwa elwembo!
Rero mundaa mwalyibita,
tchasiya mubone elwembo.

25. Ebandju boshi ba bende
baira ekaimano mu mahata
marebe, bende batchilanga ku
bindju binene. Bende baira
batcha tchasiya babone enzita
era itemanga kukumba. Si
tchubano tchwende tchwaira
batcha, tchasiya tchubone
enzita era itakakumbe tchiro
ne hitcha.

26. Bushi noku, nendjire
nalyibita, bushi nahonda
nyiimane. Nyono, ndalyi ngola
wahuta emangumi mwa
mbusi.

27. Si nyeine nalyibusa emubiri

짜시야 나보 네보너보. 먀
바꾸 보씨, 너떠 나찌서사
구바 무우마 나보, 짜시야 먀
띠라 소씨, 네누누뭐 바우마
무보.

23. 어비 뷔소히 너떠
나비이라 너 마시 무부야-
부야, 짜시야 나네 네보너
먀꼬 과 꺄하네 사 아쭈사.

24. 시 뮈씨 과 마꼬 어바꾸
버떠 바이라 어가이마노 거
마레비다, 보씨 버떠
바나레비다, 시 무우마
오싸오 이워떠 워어러시봐
어뭐뽀! 러로 무따아
먀레비다, 짜시야 무보너
어뭐뽀.

25. 어바꾸 보씨 바 버떠
바이라 어가이마노 무 마하다
마러버, 버떠 바찌롸꺄 구
비꾸 비너너. 버떠 바이라
바짜 짜시야 바보너 어씨다
어라 이더마꺄 구구빠. 시
쭈바노 쭤떠 좌이라 바짜,
짜시야 쭈보너 어씨다 어라
이다가구뻐 찌로 너 히짜.

26. 부씨 노구, 너찌러
나레비다, 부씨 나호따
네이마너. 뇨노, 따레 꼬롸
와후다 어마꾸미 먀 뿌시.

27. 시 녀이너 나레부사

means I might save some.

23. I do all this for the sake
of the gospel, that I may
share in its blessings.

24. Do you not know that in
a race all the runners run,
but only one gets the prize?
Run in such a way as to get
the prize.

25. Everyone who competes
in the games goes into strict
training. They do it to get a
crown that will not last; but
we do it to get a crown that
will last forever.

26. Therefore I do not run
like a man running aimlessly;
I do not fight like a man
beating the air.

27. No, I beat my body and

wanyi na kukoresa'o busese. Nendjire naira batcha, nyingesha kunanyibwa noku nyinabaa nendjira nahubanganyisa ebandji bandju e Mwasi mubuya-buya.

어무비리 와네 나 구고러사오 부서서. 너찌러 나이라 바짜, 네써 구나니봐 노구 네나바아 너찌라 나후바마니사 어바찌 바뉴 어 봐시 무부야-부야.

make it my slave so that after I have preached to others, I myself will not be disqualified for the prize.

1 E Bakorinto Chikono 10

1 어 바고리또 찌고노 10

1 Corinthians Chapter 10 [NIV]

1. Bnayaketchu, nahonda mukengere emyasi era yaikiraa bahokulu betchu. Boshi babaa balangibwa ne lumbumbu, kandji boshi banahabukaa enyandja ye Mwola.

1. 부나야거쭈, 나호따 무거꺼러 어먀시 어라 야이기라아 바호구루 버쭈. 보씨 바바아 바꺄ㅔ봐 너 루뿌뿌, 가찌 보씨 바나하부가아 어냐짜 여 모롸.

1. For I do not want you to be ignorant of the fact, brothers, that our forefathers were all under the cloud and that they all passed through the sea.

2. Boshi banabatisibwaa mwolu lumbumbu na mwei nyandja, tchasiya baabe mwa buuma na Musa.

2. 보씨 바나바디시봐아 모루 루뿌뿌 나 뭐이 냐짜, 짜시야 바아버 와 부우마 나 무사.

2. They were all baptized into Moses in the cloud and in the sea.

3. Boshi bendee banalya bilyo biuma bye mutchima.

3. 보씨 버떠어 바나쨔 비뾴 비우마 벼 무찌마.

3. They all ate the same spiritual food

4. Kandji boshi bendee banamwa meshi mauma ne mutchima. Bushi amu meshi mendee matenga mwekoi lya lyabaa lyiberekesise mwa lubalamo. Neri koi, abaa Kirisito yeine.

4. 가찌 보씨 버떠어 바나마 머씨 마우마 너 무찌마. 부씨 아무 머씨 머떠어 마더꽈 뭐고이 꺄 꺄바아 쩨버러거시서 와 루바꽈모. 너리 고이, 아바아 기리시도 여이너.

4. and drank the same spiritual drink; for they drank from the spiritual rock that accompanied them, and that rock was Christ.

5. Si banene mubo batendee basimisa Ongo. Bushi noku, bera kufira mwa buyeye.

5. 시 바너너 무보 바더떠어 바시미사 오꼬. 부씨 노구, 버라 구피라 와 부여여.

5. Nevertheless, God was not pleased with most of them; their bodies were

scattered over the desert.

6. Ei myasi yaikiraa'bo kwa kutchukangirisa tchasiya tchutendaa tchwaata mianyisa ya kuira mabi ngokwa nabo bendee baata'i.

7. Mutendaa mwera ebasimu ngokwa bauma mubo bendee baira. Bushi bitchula byaandjikirwe mwa maandjiko mabuya-buya mbu: "ebandju bera kweekala baalye banamwe, tchasinda bera kubatchuka na batangirisa batchimores

8. Tchutendaa tchwaira elusingi ngokwa bauma mubo bendee baira'lo, na ku lusuku luuma oshao, mwa katchi-katchi kabo mwera kufa bandju biumbi namakunyabiri na bahatchu.

9. Tchutendaa tchwaereka Kirisito ngokwa bauma mubo bende baira, endjoka sera kuita'bo.

10. Mutendaa watchaanya ngokwa bauma mubo bende baira, emalaika ola wende weta era kusikya'bo.

6. 어이 먀시 야이기라아보 과 구쭈가끼리사 짜시야 쭈더따아 쫘아다 미아네사 야 구이라 마비 꼬과 나보 버떠어 바아다이.

7. 무더따아 뭐라 어바시무 꼬과 바우마 무보 버떠어 바이라. 부씨 비쭈좌 뱌아씨기뤄 좌 마아씨고 마부야-부야 뿌: "어바뚜 버라 궈어가좌 바아쪄 바나뭐, 짜시따 버라 구바쭈가 나 바다끼리사 바찌모러수

8. 쭈더따아 쫘이라 어루시끼 꼬과 바우마 무보 버떠어 바이라뢷, 나 구 루수구 루우마 오싸오, 좌 가찌-가찌 가보 뭐라 구파 바뚜 비우뻬 나마구냐비리 나 바하쭈.

9. 쭈더따아 쫘어러가 기리시도 꼬과 바우마 무보 버떠 바이라, 어쏘가 서라 구이다보.

10. 무더따아 와짜아냐 꼬과 바우마 무보 버떠 바이라, 어마좌이가 오라 워떠 워다 어라 구시갸보.

6. Now these things occurred as examples to keep us from setting our hearts on evil things as they did.

7. Do not be idolaters, as some of them were; as it is written: "The people sat down to eat and drink and got up to indulge in pagan revelry."

8. We should not commit sexual immorality, as some of them did--and in one day twenty-three thousand of them died.

9. We should not test the Lord, as some of them did--and were killed by snakes.

10. And do not grumble, as some of them did--and were killed by the destroying angel.

11. Ei myasi yoshi yaikiraa bahokulu betchu tchasiya inde yatchukangirisa. Kandji yaandjikibwa mwa Maandjiko mabuya-buya tchasiya inde yatchweresa emaano, bushi tchwera tchulyi mwa suku se businda.

12. Bushi noku, ola waanyisa mbu emeenze kubuya, amenyaa angeesha kukumbaala!

13. Emiereko era yendjire yabaikira, iyende yanaikira nebandji bandju. Si bushi Ongo ende aira bira alanyaa, atangabarekerera mukeribwe kurenza emisi yenyu. Na mango emuereko ende abaikira, Ongo anaberesa emisi ye kusesa emitchima, ne ndjira yekutenga muo.

14. Bushi noku bera banyi basiirwa, mundaa mwatchilanga kwa kunde mwera ebasimu.

15. Nahambala nenyunga bandju ba bete bwenge. Rero, mubeine mutetaa kwa muanyisise era luulu sei myasi natetchire.

11. 어이 먀시 요씨 야이기라아 바호구루 버쭈 짜시야 이떠 야쭈가끼리사. 가찌 야아찌기봐 봐 마아찌고 마부야-부야 짜시야 이떠 야쭤러사 어마아노, 부씨 쭤라 쭈레 봐 수구 서 부시따.

12. 부씨 노구, 오꽈 와아네사 뿌 어머어써 구부야, 아머냐아 아꺼어싸 구구빠아꽈!

13. 어미어러고 어라 여찌러 야바이기라, 이여떠 야나이기라 너바찌 바쭈. 시 부씨 오꼬 어떠 아이라 비라 아꽈냐아, 아다꽈바러거러라 무거리붜 구러싸 어미시 여뉴. 나 마꼬 어무어러고 어떠 아바이기라, 오꼬 아나버러사 어미시 여 구서사 어미찌마, 너 찌라 여구더꽈 무오.

14. 부씨 노구 버라 바네 바시이롸, 무따아 뫄찌꽈꽈 과 구떠 뭐라 어바시무.

15. 나하빠꽈 너뉴꽈 바쭈 바 버더 붜어. 러로, 무버이너 무더다아 과 무아네시서 어라 루우루 서이 먀시 나더찌러.

11. These things happened to them as examples and were written down as warnings for us, on whom the fulfillment of the ages has come.

12. So, if you think you are standing firm, be careful that you don't fall!

13. No temptation has seized you except what is common to man. And God is faithful; he will not let you be tempted beyond what you can bear. But when you are tempted, he will also provide a way out so that you can stand up under it.

14. Therefore, my dear friends, flee from idolatry.

15. I speak to sensible people; judge for yourselves what I say.

16. Tchwende tchwatonga Ongo bushi ne ngumbu ye ngahanyi. Muteshi kwa mango tchwama ei ngumbu, tchwende tchwaba mwa buuma nemikira ya Kirisito? Na mango tchwaishanga mwa mukati ne kulya'o, tchwende tchwaba mwa buuma ne mubiri wa Kirisito?

17. Emukati anatchula muuma oshao. Netchu tchiro mbu tchulyi banene, si tchunalyi mundju muuma bushi oyu mukati itchwende tchwanahangira.

18. Muloreraa kwa Ba Isiraeli: ebandju ba bende balya enyama sa satchulwaa kwa kahaha ke mitchulo, bende baba mwa bauma na Ongo

19. Tchi nahonda kuteta kasi? Enyama se bandju bende batchula ebihwa sinatchusa mufa? Nesi ebi bihwasi nabi, binete mufa?

20. Naanga! Si nahonda kubabura kwa mango ebandju ba bateshi Ongo bende baana emitchulo yabo, bende baitchula ebasimu, si ata Ongo ibende baitchula. Rero, nahonda mbu mundaa mwaba mwa buuma ne basimu.

16. 쮜떠 좌도ᄴ 오ᄋ 부씨 너 ᄋ뿌 여 ᄴ하니. 무더씨 과 마ᄋ 좌마 어이 ᄋ뿌, 쮜떠 좌바 ᄆ 부우마 너미기라 야 기리시도? 나 마ᄋ 좌이싸ᄴ ᄆ 무가디 너 구랴오, 쮜떠 좌바 ᄆ 부우마 너 무비리 와 기리시도?

17. 어무가디 아나쮜좌 무우마 오싸오. 너쮜 찌로 뿌 쮜레 바너너, 시 쮜나레 무뚜 무우마 부씨 오유 무가디 이쮜떠 좌나하ᄴ라.

18. 무로러라아 과 바 이시라어뀌: 어바ᄂ 바 버너 바랴 어냐마 사 사쮜뫄아 과 가하하 거 미쮜로, 버떠 바바 ᄆ 바우마 나 오ᄋ

19. 찌 나호따 구더다 가시? 어냐마 서 바ᄂ 버너 바쮜좌 어비화 시나쮜사 무파? 너시 어비 비화시 나비, 비너더 무파?

20. 나아ᄴ! 시 나호따 구바부라 과 마ᄋ 어바ᄂ 바 바더씨 오ᄋ 버떠 바아나 어미쮜로 야보, 버떠 바이쮜좌 어바시무, 시 아다 오ᄋ 이버떠 바이쮜좌. 러로, 나호따 뿌 무따아 ᄆ바 ᄆ 부우마 너 바시무.

16. Is not the cup of thanksgiving for which we give thanks a participation in the blood of Christ? And is not the bread that we break a participation in the body of Christ?

17. Because there is one loaf, we, who are many, are one body, for we all partake of the one loaf.

18. Consider the people of Israel: Do not those who eat the sacrifices participate in the altar?

19. Do I mean then that a sacrifice offered to an idol is anything, or that an idol is anything?

20. No, but the sacrifices of pagans are offered to demons, not to God, and I do not want you to be participants with demons.

21. Mutangaala kunde mwamwa kwa ngumbu ya Enawetchu, na mwamwa noku ngumbu ye basimu. Kandji mutangaala kunde mwalya kwa bilyo bya Enawetchu, mwalya nokwa biryo bye musimu.

22. Nesi tchwahonda kukunza Enawetchu tchasiya afe mufula? Mwaanyisa mbu tchutchweete emisi kumurenza.

23. Bandju bauma mu mwabo bende bateta mbu: "nyeete loso lwa kuira tchira kandju". Kubinalyi! Si ata tchira kandju kukabeetere mufa! Kandji tchiro mbu nyeete loso lwa kuira tchira kandju, si ata tchira kandju ku kabeetere mufa kwa kukusa ebwemeresi bwe bandju.

24. Emundju atendaa ahonda emutoloke wai yeine, si endaa ahonda newebandji

25. Mulyi mwa buhuru bwekulya enyama soshi sa sausibwa mwesoko busira kubusabusa myasi era ingabalyibusisa mwa mitchima.

26. Bushi ebutala na byoshi bitchula'mo biri bya Enawetchu

21. 무다까아롸 구떠 뫄뫄 과 꾸뿌 야 어나워쭈, 나 뫄뫄 노구 꾸뿌 여 바시무. 가찌 무다까아롸 구떠 뫄럊 과 비룭 뱌 어나워쭈, 뫄럊 노과 비료 뼈 무시무.

22. 너시 쫘호따 구구싸 어나워쭈 짜시야 아퍼 무푸롸? 뫄아네사 뿌 쭤어더 어미시 구무러싸.

23. 바꾸 바우마 무 뫄보 버떠 바더다 뿌: "녀어더 로소 롸 구이라 찌라 가꾸". 구비나롃! 시 아다 찌라 가꾸 구가버어더러 무파! 가찌 찌로 뿌 녀어더 로소 롸 구이라 찌라 가꾸, 시 아다 찌라 가꾸 구 가버어더러 무파 과 구구사 어붜머러시 붜 바꾸.

24. 어무뿌 아더따아 아호따 어무도로거 와이 여이너, 시 어따아 아호따 너워바찌

25. 무롃 뫄 부후루 붜구럊 어냐마 소씨 사 사우시봐 뭐소고 부시라 구부사부사 먀시 어라 이까바뤠부시사 뫄 미찌마.

26. 부씨 어부다롸 나 뵤씨 비쭈롸모 비리 뱌 어나워쭈

21. You cannot drink the cup of the Lord and the cup of demons too; you cannot have a part in both the Lord's table and the table of demons.

22. Are we trying to arouse the Lord's jealousy? Are we stronger than he?

23. "Everything is permissible"--but not everything is beneficial. "Everything is permissible"--but not everything is constructive.

24. Nobody should seek his own good, but the good of others.

25. Eat anything sold in the meat market without raising questions of conscience,

26. for, "The earth is the Lord's, and everything in it."

27. Akaba emundju ola uteshi Ongo anagabalalyika mbu muyaa kulya kwa biryo, namweemerera kwenda, munalyaa byoshi bya angabasheera busira kubusabusa myasi era ingatchuma mwalyibukira mwa mitchima

27. 아가바 어무뚜 오꽈 우더씨 오꼬 아나가바꽈쩨가 뿌 무야아 구꺄 과 비료, 나뭐어머러라 궈따, 무나꺄아 뵤씨 뱌 아까바써어라 부시라 구부사부사 먀시 어라 이까쭈마 꽈쩨부기라 꽈 미찌마

27. If some unbeliever invites you to a meal and you want to go, eat whatever is put before you without raising questions of conscience.

28. Si akaba mundju murebe angababura mbu: "bine biryo byatchulwaa ebasimu", mutalyaa'bi mungesha kulyibusa emutchima woyu wabakengesaa.

28. 시 아가바 무뚜 무러버 아까바부라 뿌: "비너 비료 뱌쭈꽈아 어바시무", 무다꺄아비 무꺼싸 구레부사 어무찌마 오유 와바거꺼사아.

28. But if anyone says to you, "This has been offered in sacrifice," then do not eat it, both for the sake of the man who told you and for conscience' sake--

29. Ndatetchire mu mwabo mungalyibukira mwa mitchima, si oyu wabakengesaa rero, tchitchingatchuma ekulyibukira mwa mutchima kwe undji mundju kwanyaangika tcha nyeete kwe buhuru?

29. 따더찌러 무 꽈보 무까레부기라 꽈 미찌마, 시 오유 와바거꺼사아 러로, 찌찌까쭈마 어구레부기라 꽈 무찌마 궈 우씨 무뚜 과냐아끼가 짜 녀어더 궈 부후루?

29. the other man's conscience, I mean, not yours. For why should my freedom be judged by another's conscience?

30. Akaba natongire Ongo mira bushi ne biryo bya nalyaa, tchitchingatchuma ebandji bandju banyiamana bulyio bushi nabi?

30. 아가바 나도꺼러 오꼬 미라 부씨 너 비료 뱌 나꺄아, 찌찌까쭈마 어바찌 바꾸 바네아마나 부쩨오 부씨 나비?

30. If I take part in the meal with thankfulness, why am I denounced because of something I thank God for?

31. Mwa batcha, akaba mungalya nesi mwamwa, nesi mwaira tchira mwasi woshi, mundaa mwaira byoshi kwe tchunda lya Ongo.

31. 꽈 바짜, 아가바 무까꺄 너시 꽈꽈, 너시 꽈이라 찌라 꽈시 옷씨, 무따아 꽈이라 뵤씨 궈 쭈따 꺄 오꼬.

31. So whether you eat or drink or whatever you do, do it all for the glory of God.

32. Mutendaa mwaira tchatchingatchuma e mundju aya mwa mabi: abe muyuta, abe mukiri-kiri, nesi e bandju bomwa luhu lwa Ongo.

32. 무더따아 먀이라 짜찌빠쭈마 어 무뚜 아야 먀 마비: 아버 무유다, 아버 무기리-기리, 너시 어 바뚜 보와 루후 롸 오꼬.

32. Do not cause anyone to stumble, whether Jews, Greeks or the church of God--

33. Mundaa mwatchitola nga nyono, nende natchisesa kusimisa e bandju boshi mwa myasi yoshi. Ndahonda emutoloke wanyi nyeine, si nende nahonda e mutoloke we bandju boshi tchasiya nabu banunulyibwe.

33. 무따아 먀찌도롸 빠 뇨노, 너떠 나찌서사 구시미사 어 바뚜 보씨 먀 먀시 요씨. 따호따 어무도로꺼 와네 녀이너, 시 너떠 나호따 어 무도로꺼 워 바뚜 보씨 짜시야 나부 바누누레붜.

33. even as I try to please everybody in every way. For I am not seeking my own good but the good of many, so that they may be saved.

1 E Bakorinto Chikono 11

1 어 바고리또 찌고노 11

1 Corinthians Chapter 11 [NIV]

1. Mundaa mwamenya ngokwa nanyi nyende neeya Kirisito

1. 무따아 먀머냐 꼬과 나네 녀떠 너어야 기리시도

1. Follow my example, as I follow the example of Christ.

2. Nabatonga bushi mwendjire mwanyikengera mwa myasi yoshi kandji bushi mutchiri mukulyikire emyasi era nabakangirisa

2. 나바도꽈 부씨 뭐찌러 먀네거꺼러라 먀 먀시 요씨 가찌 부씨 무찌리 무구레기러 어먀시 어라 나바가삐리사

2. I praise you for remembering me in everything and for holding to the teachings, just as I passed them on to you.

3. Si tchiro batcha tchitchine tchi nahonda mumenyerere: Kirisito lyi tchwe lya tchira mulume, ne mulume lyi tchwe lya mukai, na Ongo lyi tchwe lya Kirisito

3. 시 찌로 바짜 찌찌너 찌 나호따 무머녀러러: 기리시도 레 쮀 랴 찌라 무루머, 너 무루머 레 쮀 랴 무가이, 나 오꼬 레 쮀 랴 기리시도

3. Now I want you to realize that the head of every man is Christ, and the head of the woman is man, and the head of Christ is God.

4. Bushi noku, tchira mulume woshi ola wahukira etchwe lyai mango eema Ongo, nesi mango era aaba ereba, eri

4. 부씨 노구, 찌라 무루머 오씨 오롸 와후기라 어쮀 랴이 마꼬 어어마 오꼬, 너시 마꼬 어라 아아바 어러바,

4. Every man who prays or prophesies with his head covered dishonors his head.

Kirisito lyi tchwe lyai yeetchisa ehonyi

어리 기리시도 레 쭤 쨔이 여어찌사 어호네

5. Si tchira mukasi ola utahukire etchwe lyai mango eema Ongo, nesi mango era areba, eri eba lyi tchwe lyai yeetchisa ehonyi, aola enda aba ngola ukumulyibwe emviri.

5. 시 찌라 무가시 오라 우다후기러 어쭤 쨔이 마꼬 어어마 오꼬, 너시 마꼬 어라 아러바, 어리 어바 레 쭤 쨔이 여어찌사 어호네, 아오라 어따 아바 꼬쫘 우구무레붜 어삐리.

5. And every woman who prays or prophesies with her head uncovered dishonors her head--it is just as though her head were shaved.

6. Akaba emukasi atangahukira etchwe lyai, eemire akumulyibwe! Si bushi silyi honyi kwa mukasi ekuishibwa kwa mviri, nesi kukumulyibwa, rero eemire kunde ahukira etchwe.

6. 아가바 어무가시 아다까후기라 어쭤 쨔이, 어어미러 아구무레붜! 시 부씨 시레 호네 과 무가시 어구이씨봐 과 삐리, 너시 구구무레봐, 러로 어어미러 구떠 아후기라 어쭤.

6. If a woman does not cover her head, she should have her hair cut off; and if it is a disgrace for a woman to have her hair cut or shaved off, she should cover her head.

7. Emulume ateemire kunde ahukira etchwe, bushi alyi huhi kandji anaba etchunda lya Ongo. Si emukasi alyi etchunda lye mulume.

7. 어무루머 아더어미러 구떠 아후기라 어쭤, 부씨 아레 후히 가찌 아나바 어쭈따 쨔 오꼬. 시 어무가시 아레 어쭈따 려 무루머.

7. A man ought not to cover his head, since he is the image and glory of God; but the woman is the glory of man.

8. Bushi emulume atabumbwaa kutengera kwa mukasi, si emukasi iwabumbwaa kutengera kwa mulume

8. 부씨 어무루머 아다부꽈아 구더꺼라 과 무가시, 시 어무가시 이와부꽈아 구더꺼라 과 무루머

8. For man did not come from woman, but woman from man;

9. Kandji emulume atabumbwa bushi ne mukasi, si emukasi abumbwaa bushi ne mulume.

9. 가찌 어무루머 아다부꽈 부씨 너 무가시, 시 어무가시 아부꽈아 부씨 너 무루머.

9. neither was man created for woman, but woman for man.

10. Etchera tchitchitchumire emukasi eemire kuata kalorero ke buashi kwetchwe busihi ne ndonyi (bamalaika)

10. 어쩌라 찌쭈미러 어무가시 어어미러 구아다 가로러로 거 부아씨 궈쭤 부시히 너 또네 (바마쫘이가)

10. For this reason, and because of the angels, the woman ought to have a sign of authority on her head.

11. Si mwa buuma bwetchu na Enawetchu, kutangaba mukasi busira mulume, kutangaba ne mulume busira mukasi.

12. Bushi ngokwa emukasi abumbwaa kutengera kwa mulume, kunoku kwe mulume nai ende abutchwaa ne mukasi. Byoshi era mwa Ongo i bitengire.

13. Mubeine mutetaa kute musene, akaba kunakomire emukasi kunde eema Ongo atanahukire etchwe!

14. Kubinalyi! Kukulyikana nokwa Ongo abumbaa ebandju, kunalosise kwa siri honyi kwa mulume ekuata emviri sirerere

15. Si emukasi yeke, ekuata emviri sirerere lyi tchunda lyai bushi eeresibwaa'si, tchasiya sinde sahukira etchwe lyai.

16. Si akaba mundju ahonda kuira bwaka era luulu soyu mwasi, amenyereraa kwa tchubano nenyuhu sa Ongo, tchutatchusa undji mwasi.

17. Kukulyikana ne maano ma nahonda kubeeresa, ndabatonga, bushi mango mwendjire mwabwaanana, enyibwaanano senyu wakunde sa baasa, sendjire sabalyibusa.

11. 시 꽈 부우마 붜쭈 나 어나워쭈, 구다빠바 무가시 부시라 무루머, 구다빠바 너 무루머 부시라 무가시.

12. 부씨 꼬과 어무가시 아부빠아 구더뻐라 과 무루머, 구노구 궈 무루머 나이 어더 아부좌아 너 무가시. 뵤씨 어라 꽈 오꼬 이 비더삐러.

13. 무버이너 무더다아 구더 무서너, 아가바 구나고미러 어무가시 구더 어어마 오꼬 아다나후기러 어쮀!

14. 구비나뤠! 구구뤠가나 노과 오꼬 아부빠아 어바뉴, 구나로시서 과 시리 호네 과 무루머 어구아다 어뻬리 시러러러

15. 시 어무가시 여거, 어구아다 어뻬리 시러러러 레 쭈따 랴이 부씨 어어러시봐아시, 짜시야 시너 사후기라 어쮀 랴이.

16. 시 아가바 무뉴 아호따 구이라 봐가 어라 루우루 소유 꽈시, 아머녀러라아 과 쭈바노 너뉴후 사 오꼬, 쭈다쭈사 우씨 꽈시.

17. 구구뤠가나 너 마아노 마 나호따 구버어러사, 따바도꽈, 부씨 마꼬 뭐찌러 꽈봐아나나, 어네봐아나노 서뉴 와구더 사 바아사, 서찌러 사바뤠부사.

11. In the Lord, however, woman is not independent of man, nor is man independent of woman.

12. For as woman came from man, so also man is born of woman. But everything comes from God.

13. Judge for yourselves: Is it proper for a woman to pray to God with her head uncovered?

14. Does not the very nature of things teach you that if a man has long hair, it is a disgrace to him,

15. but that if a woman has long hair, it is her glory? For long hair is given to her as a covering.

16. If anyone wants to be contentious about this, we have no other practice--nor do the churches of God.

17. In the following directives I have no praise for you, for your meetings do more harm than good.

18. Ne tchiberebere tchi tchitchini: noonvire emwasi kwa mango mwendjire mwabwaanana, mwendjire mwaberekana'mo. Ku lunda luula, nanyi naemerere kwa eyi myasi inalyi ya kanangana.

19. Ekuberekana'mo kweemire kunabe wa katchi-katchi kenyu, tchasiya ebandju ba bangatchinyiirwa mu mwabo.

20. Mango mwendjire mwabwaanana, bita biryo byakukengera Enawetchu bi mwendjire mwalya

21. Bushi mango mwalya, tchira muuma endjire alyibitchira kulya ebiro byai, noku bauma mu mwabo bafe ne businya, ne bandji batamirira.

22. Mwabo, mutatchusa nyumba sakulyira'mo, nesi kumwera'mo? Nesi kukena ku mwahonda mukene eluhu lwa Ongo? Balyikenyu bateete kalyo, bu mwendjire mwahonda muitchise? Tchi nyibaburaa kandji? Mwahonda nyibatonge? Ebyera, bitangatchuma nabatonga tchiro na hitcha.

18. 너 찌버러버러 찌 찌찌니: 노오삐러 어뫄시 꽈 마꼬 뭐찌러 뫄봐아나나, 뭐찌러 뫄버러가나모. 구 룬따 루우꽈, 나네 나어머러러 꽈 어에 먀시 이나쩨 야 가나까나.

19. 어구버러가나모 궈어미러 구나버 와 가찌-가찌 거뉴, 짜시야 어바뿌 바 바까찌네이라 무 뫄보.

20. 마꼬 뭐찌러 뫄봐아나나, 비다 비료 뱌구거꺼라 어나워쭈 비 뭐찌러 뫄퍄

21. 부씨 마꼬 뫄퍄, 찌라 무우마 어찌러 아쩨비찌라 구퍄 어비로 뱌이, 노구 바우마 무 뫄보 바퍼 너 부시냐, 너 바찌 바다미리라.

22. 뫄보, 무다쭈사 뉴빠 사구쩨라모, 너시 구뭐라모? 너시 구거나 구 뫄호따 무거너 어루후 꽈 오꼬? 바쩨거뉴 바더어더 가료, 부 뭐찌러 뫄호따 무이찌서? 찌 네바부라아 가찌? 뫄호따 네바도꺼? 어벼라, 비다까쭈마 나바도까 찌로 나 히짜.

18. In the first place, I hear that when you come together as a church, there are divisions among you, and to some extent I believe it.

19. No doubt there have to be differences among you to show which of you have God's approval.

20. When you come together, it is not the Lord's Supper you eat,

21. for as you eat, each of you goes ahead without waiting for anybody else. One remains hungry, another gets drunk.

22. Don't you have homes to eat and drink in? Or do you despise the church of God and humiliate those who have nothing? What shall I say to you? Shall I praise you for this? Certainly not!

23. Kwa bushi nanyi emyasi era Enawetchu anyikangirisaa inanyi nanabakangirisaa: Ebutchufu bwa Enawetchu Yesu aanyibwaa mu atolaa emukati.

24. Nera nyuma sekutonga Ongo era kuisha muo era kuteta mbu: "Onola i mubiri wanyi, ola waanyirwe bushi nenyu mundaa mwaira batcha kwakunyikengera"

25. Kunoku, era nyuma sekulya, era kutola nengumbu, era kuteta mbu: "eni ngumbu tchiri tchilaano tchiyayaya kurengera e mikira yanyi tchira mango ma mungende mwamwa, mundaa mwaira batcha kwakunyikengera".

26. Bushi tchira mango mwakuba mwalya onu mukati nekumwa eni ngumbu, mungende mwaba mwabalyira ebanju emwasi we kufa kwa Enawetchu kuikira mango akafuluka.

27. Bushi noku, tchira mundju ola walya kwa mukati wa Enawetchu, nesi amwa kwa ngumbu yai kwa kutatchungenene eri airire tchibi era luulu se mubiri, ne mikira ya Enawetchu.

---

23. 과 부씨 나니 어먀시 어라 어나워쭈 아니가끼리사아 이나니 나나바가끼리사아: 어부쭈푸 봐 어나워쭈 여수 아아니봐아 무 아도롸아 어무가디.

24. 너라 뉴마 서구도롸 오꼬 어라 구이싸 무오 어라 구더다 뿌: "오노롸 이 무비리 와니, 오롸 와아니눼 부씨 너뉴 무따아 마이라 바짜 과구네거어라"

25. 구노구, 어라 뉴마 서구례, 어라 구도롸 너꾸뿌, 어라 구더다 뿌: "어니 꾸뿌 찌리 찌롸아노 찌야야야 구러꺼라 어 미기라 야네 찌라 마꼬 마 무꺼러 롸롸, 무따아 마이라 바짜 과구네거어라".

26. 부씨 찌라 마꼬 롸구바 롸롍 오누 무가디 너구롸 어니 꾸뿌, 무꺼러 롸바 롸바쿀라 어반쭈 어롸시 워 구파 과 어나워쭈 구이기라 마꼬 아가푸룩가.

27. 부씨 노구, 찌라 무뚜 오롸 와롂 과 무가디 와 어나워쭈, 너시 아롸 과 꾸뿌 야이 과 구다쭈꺼너너 어리 아이리러 찌비 어라 루우룩 서 무비리, 너 미기라 야 어나워쭈.

---

23. For I received from the Lord what I also passed on to you: The Lord Jesus, on the night he was betrayed, took bread,

24. and when he had given thanks, he broke it and said, "This is my body, which is for you; do this in remembrance of me."

25. In the same way, after supper he took the cup, saying, "This cup is the new covenant in my blood; do this, whenever you drink it, in remembrance of me."

26. For whenever you eat this bread and drink this cup, you proclaim the Lord's death until he comes.

27. Therefore, whoever eats the bread or drinks the cup of the Lord in an unworthy manner will be guilty of sinning against the body and blood of the Lord.

28. Rero, tchira mundju endaa aanyisa tanga era luulu se myanya yai. Tchasinda aneere alya konu mukati nakumwa kweni ngumbu.

29. Bushi emundju oyu mukati nakumwa kwei ngumbu, busira kumenya kwa oyola alyi mubiri wa Enawetchu, eri yeine atchikulyira ebutchindjibusi.

30. Etchera tchi tchitchumire banene mumwabo balyi balwala, kandji batambukalyisa, na benene bafire.

31. Si akaba tchubeinetchungendjire tchwaanyisa tanga era luulu se myanya yetchu, Ongo atangatchutchindjibusise.

32. Si Enawetchu endaa atchutchindjibusa kwa kutchukemera, tchungesha kutchindjibusibwa alauma ne bandju bomuno butala.

33. Bushi noku banyaketchu, mango mungende mwabwaanana kwa kulya e biryo bya kukengera Enawetchu, mundaa mwalyindjirana.

28. 러로, 찌라 무뚜 어따아 아아니사 다따 어라 루우루루 서 먀냐 야이. 짜시따 아너어러 아럊 고누 무가디 나구똬 궈니 응뿍.

29. 부씨 어무뚜 오유 무가디 나구똬 궈이 응뿍, 부시라 구머냐 과 오요똘 아뤠 무비리 와 어나워쭈, 어리 여이너 아찌구뤠라 어부찌띠부시.

30. 어쩌라 찌 쭈미러 바너너 무똬보 바뤠 바똹똪, 가찌 바다뿌가뤠사, 나 버너너 바피러.

31. 시 아가바 쭈버이너쭈어띠러 좌아네사 다따 어라 루우루루 서 먀냐 여쭈, 오꼬 아다따쭈찌띠부시서.

32. 시 어나워쭈 어따아 아쭈찌띠부사 과 구쭈거머라, 쭈어싸 구찌띠부시똬 아랒우마 너 바뚜 보무노 부다똹.

33. 부씨 노구 바냐거쭈, 마꼬 무어떠 똬보아나나 과 구럊 어 비료 뱌 구거떠라 어나워쭈, 무따아 똬뤠띠라나.

28. A man ought to examine himself before he eats of the bread and drinks of the cup.

29. For anyone who eats and drinks without recognizing the body of the Lord eats and drinks judgment on himself.

30. That is why many among you are weak and sick, and a number of you have fallen asleep.

31. But if we judged ourselves, we would not come under judgment.

32. When we are judged by the Lord, we are being disciplined so that we will not be condemned with the world.

33. So then, my brothers, when you come together to eat, wait for each other.

34. Akaba mundju afa businya, endaa alyira mwa mwai. Mwabatcha, Ongo atabatchindjibuse mango mungende mwabwaanana. Eindji myasi era ishibire, nyingabaakula kui, mango nyingaika ei mwenyu.

34. 아가바 무뚜 아파 부시냐, 어따아 아레라 뫄 뫄이. 뫄바짜, 오꼬 아다바찌찌부서 뫄꼬 무꺼머 뫄봐아나나. 어이찌 먀시 어라 이씨비러, 네꺄바아구꽈 구이, 뫄꼬 네꺄이가 어이 뭐뉴.

34. If anyone is hungry, he should eat at home, so that when you meet together it may not result in judgment. And when I come I will give further directions.

1 E Bakorinto Chikono 12

1 어 바고리또 찌고노 12

1 Corinthians Chapter 12 [NIV]

1. Rero tchutahambalaa era luulu se myasi ere yeerekere enyembo se Mutchima Mubuya-buya. Banyeketchu, nahonda mumenyerere kubuya emyasi yesi nyembo.

1. 러로 쭈다하빠랴아 어라 루우루 서 먀시 어러 여어러거러 어녀뽀 서 무찌마 무부야-부야. 바녀거쭈, 나호따 무머녀러러 구부야 어먀시 여시 녀뽀.

1. Now about spiritual gifts, brothers, I do not want you to be ignorant.

2. Mwishi kwa mango mwabaa mutasaa kumenya Ongo, mwendee mwakululyibwa na kutebwa na myasi ye kwera ebihuhanyi bya bitateta.

2. 뮈씨 과 마꼬 뫄바아 무다사아 구머냐 오꼬, 뭐떠어 뫄구루레봐 나 구더봐 나 먀시 여 궈라 어비후하니 뱌 비다더다.

2. You know that when you were pagans, somehow or other you were influenced and led astray to mute idols.

3. Bushi noku, nababura kanangana kwa kutalyi mundju ola wakoresibwa ne Mutchima wa Ongo, ola ungateta mbu: "Yesu afe shambyo! "Kandji kutalyi mundju ola ungateta mbu: "Yesu i Enawetchu", akaba atakoresibwa ne Mutchima Mubuya-buya.

3. 부씨 노구, 나바부라 가나꺄나 과 구다레 무뚜 오라 와고러시봐 너 무찌마 와 오꼬, 오라 우꺄더다 뿌: "여수 아퍼 싸뽀! "가찌 구다레 무뚜 오라 우꺄더다 뿌: "여수 이 어나워쭈", 아가바 아다고러시봐 너 무찌마 무부야-부야.

3. Therefore I tell you that no one who is speaking by the Spirit of God says, "Jesus be cursed," and no one can say, "Jesus is Lord," except by the Holy Spirit.

4. Enyembo sitchula sirenzenye, si e Mutchima Mubuya-buya ola wende

4. 어녀뽀 시쭈꽈 시러떠녀, 시 어 무찌마 무부야-부야 오꽈 워떠 와아나시,

4. There are different kinds of gifts, but the same Spirit.

waana'si, anatchula muuma. 아나쭈롸 무우마.

5. Emikorere irenzenye, si
Enawetchu anatchula muuma.

5. 어미고러러 이러써녀, 시
어나워쭈 아나쭈롸 무우마.

5. There are different kinds
of service, but the same
Lord.

6. Ne mirimo nai irenzenye, si
Ongo anatchula muuma,
iwende waira byoshi mwa
bandju boshi.

6. 너 미리모 나이 이러써녀,
시 오꼬 아나쭈롸 무우마,
이워떠 와이라 뵤씨 뫄 바뚜
보씨.

6. There are different kinds
of working, but the same
God works all of them in all
men.

7. Emutchima Mubuya-buya
ende eeresa tchira mundju
lweembo lurebe, kwa
mutoloke we bandju boshi.

7. 어무찌마 무부야-부야
어떠 어어러사 찌라 무뚜
뤄어뽀 루러버, 과 무도로거
워 바뚜 보씨.

7. Now to each one the
manifestation of the Spirit is
given for the common good.

8. EMutchima Mubuya-buya
ende eerea mundju muuma
elwembo lwe kuata ebuashi
bwe kuteta myasi ya bwenge.
Oyu Mutchima inoyu, aneeresa
ne undji mundju elweembo
lwe kuata ebuashi
bwekumenyerera emyasi.

8. 어무찌마 무부야-부야
어떠 어어러아 무뚜 무우마
어뤄뽀 뤄 구아다 어부아씨
뷔 구더다 먀시 야 뷔어.
오유 무찌마 이노유,
아너어러사 너 우찌 무뚜
어뤄어뽀 뤄 구아다 어부아씨
뷔구머녀러라 어먀시.

8. To one there is given
through the Spirit the
message of wisdom, to
another the message of
knowledge by means of the
same Spirit,

9. Oyu Mutchima Mubuya-
buya inoyu ende eeresa eundji
mundju elweembo lwe kiuata
ebwemeresi, ne undji elwe
kulamya ebalwala.

9. 오유 무찌마 무부야-부야
이노유 어떠 어어러사 어우찌
무뚜 어뤄어뽀 뤄 기우아다
어뷔머러시, 너 우찌 어뤄
구롸먀 어바롸롸.

9. to another faith by the
same Spirit, to another gifts
of healing by that one Spirit,

10. Ne undji anamweresa
elweembo lwe kuira
ebisomerane, ne undji
elwekureba, ne undji
elwekumenyerera e myasi era
itengire nera itatengire era
mwe Mutchima Mubuya-buya,
ne undji elwe kuteta mu
mateta ma mateshibwe, ne

10. 너 우찌 아나뭐러사
어뤄어뽀 뤄 구이라
어비소머라너, 너 우찌
어뤄구러바, 너 우찌
어뤄구머녀러라 어 먀시 어라
이더삐러 너라 이다더삐러
어라 뭐 무찌마 무부야-부야,
너 우찌 어뤄 구더다 무
마더다 마 마더씨뷔, 너 우찌

10. to another miraculous
powers, to another
prophecy, to another
distinguishing between
spirits, to another speaking
in different kinds of tongues,
and to still another the
interpretation of tongues.

undji elwe kuanunula amu mateta.

11. Eyi myasi yoshi, oyu Mutchima Mubuya-buya, yeine iwende wanaira'i mwa kweeresa tchira mundju elwai lweembo ngokwa anasimire.

12. Emubiri atchula muuma si atchusa bitera binene. Tchiro anagaba mbu ebitera bye mubiri biri binene, si binaychula bya mubiri muuma. Rero, Kirisito nai ku anatchula batcha.

13. Bushi, aabe e Bayuta, nesi ba batchula Bayutan nesi etchuungu, nesi e bandju ba balyi mwa buhuru, tchuboshi tchwanabatisibwaa mzoyu Mutchima Mubuya-buya muuma, tchasiya tchube mundju muuma. Kandji tchuboshi, kwa shokororo yoyu Mutchima Mubuya-buya muuma ku tchwanamweraa.

14. Emubiri atatchusa tchitera tchiuma oshai, si atchusa bitera binene.

15. Akaba wakuulu angateta mbu: "nyono bushi nda mino, nda tchitera tche mubiri", ekuteta batcha, kutangatchuma ataba tchitera tche mubiri.

어뭐 구아누누똬 아무 마더다.

11. 어에 먀시 요씨, 오유 무찌마 무부야-부야, 여이너 이워떠 와나이라이 똬 궈어러사 찌라 무뚜 어똻이 뤄어뽀 끄과 아나시미러.

12. 어무비리 아쭈똬 무우마 시 아쭈사 비더라 비너너. 찌로 아나가바 뿌 어비더라 벼 무비리 비리 비너너, 시 비나이쭈똬 뱌 무비리 무우마. 러로, 기리시도 나이 구 아나쭈똬 바짜.

13. 부찌, 아아버 어 바유다, 너시 바 바쭈똬 바유다누 너시 어쭈우뿌, 너시 어 바뉴 바 바례 똬 부후루, 쭈보씨 똬나바디시봐아 쏘유 무찌마 무부야-부야 무우마, 짜시야 쭈버 무뚜 무우마. 가찌 쭈보씨, 과 쏘고로로 요유 무찌마 무부야-부야 무우마 구 똬나뭐라아.

14. 어무비리 아다쭈사 찌더라 찌우마 오싸이, 시 아쭈사 비더라 비너너.

15. 아가바 와구우루루 아꽈더다 뿌: "뇨노 부씨 따 미노, 따 찌더라 쩌 무비리", 어구더다 바짜, 구다꽈쭈마 아다바 찌더라 쩌 무비리.

11. All these are the work of one and the same Spirit, and he gives them to each one, just as he determines.

12. The body is a unit, though it is made up of many parts; and though all its parts are many, they form one body. So it is with Christ.

13. For we were all baptized by one Spirit into one body--whether Jews or Greeks, slave or free--and we were all given the one Spirit to drink.

14. Now the body is not made up of one part but of many.

15. If the foot should say, "Because I am not a hand, I do not belong to the body," it would not for that reason cease to be part of the body.

16. Na akaba wakuulu angateta mbu: "nyono bushi nda lyiho, nda tchitera tche mubiri", ekuteta batcha kutangatchuma ataba tchitera tche mubiri.

17. Akaba emubiri woshi angabere lyiho, kute emundju angendjire omva? Na kaba emundju woshi angabere kutchu, kute emundju angendjire aunyirisa?

18. Si rero Ongo atondekaa tchira tchitera tche mubiri ngokwa abaa ahondjire.

19. Akaba ebitera byoshi bingebere tchitera tchiuma, emubiri atangabere

20. Rero ebitera biri binene, si emubiri anatchula muuma.

21. Walyiho atangabura wamino mbu: "Ndakumaire'ko!"Nesi etchwe lyitangabura emaulu mbu: "Ndakulaire'ko!".

22. Si tchiro batcha, ebitera bye mubiri bya bitchula biseneke'ko nga bitete misi, binatchusa mufa.

23. Kandji ebitera bya tchwende tchwatola nga bitete etchunda, bi tchwende

---

16. 나 아까더다 뿌: "뇨노 부씨 따 레호, 따 찌더라 쩌 무비리", 어구더다 바짜 구다까쭈마 아다바 찌더라 쩌 무비리.

17. 아가바 어무비리 올씨 아까버러 레호, 구더 어무뿌 아꺼씨러 오빠? 나 가바 어무뿌 올씨 아까버러 구쭈, 구더 어무뿌 아꺼씨러 아우네리사?

18. 시 러로 오꼬 아도더가아 찌라 찌더라 쩌 무비리 꼬과 아바아 아호씨러.

19. 아가바 어비더라 뵤씨 비꺼버러 찌더라 찌우마, 어무비리 아다까버러

20. 러로 어비더라 비리 비너너, 시 어무비리 아나쭈롸 무우마.

21. 와레호 아다까부라 와미노 뿌: "따구마이러고!"너시 어쮀 레다까부라 어마우루 뿌: "따구롸이러고!".

22. 시 찌로 바짜, 어비더라 벼 무비리 뱌 비쭈롸 비서너거고 까 비더더 미시, 비나쭈사 무파.

23. 가찌 어비더라 뱌 쮀더 좌도롸 까 비더더 어쭈따, 비 쮀더 쮀어러사 어쭈따

---

16. And if the ear should say, "Because I am not an eye, I do not belong to the body," it would not for that reason cease to be part of the body.

17. If the whole body were an eye, where would the sense of hearing be? If the whole body were an ear, where would the sense of smell be?

18. But in fact God has arranged the parts in the body, every one of them, just as he wanted them to be.

19. If they were all one part, where would the body be?

20. As it is, there are many parts, but one body.

21. The eye cannot say to the hand, "I don't need you!" And the head cannot say to the feet, "I don't need you!"

22. On the contrary, those parts of the body that seem to be weaker are indispensable,

23. and the parts that we think are less honorable we treat with special honor. And

tchweeresa etchunda busese.
Ne bitera bya tchwende
tchwabisha, bi tchwende
tchwalanga kubuya.

24. Noku ebitera bya
tchutabisha, byeke bitchula
bilaire ku kulangibwa kubuya.
Bushi mango Ongo
oomotanyaa emubiri, ebitera
bya byabaa bitete tchunda, era
kweeresa'bi etchunda lyinene.

25. Airaa batcha tchasiya
ebitera bye mubiri
bitaberekanaa'mo, si tchira
tchitera tchinde tchalaa ku
tchirikabo.

26. Akaba tchitera tchiuma
tchingalyibuka, ebindji bitera
byoshi, nabi byanalyibuka
alauma natchi. Na akaba
tchitera tchiuma
tchingeeresibwa etchunda,
ebindji bitera byanamowa
alauma natchi.

27. Mwabo mulyi mubiri wa
Kirisito. Na tchira muuma mu
mwabo alyi tchitera tchoyu
mubiri.

28. Mwa luhu lwa Ongo,
etchiberebere, Ongo abikaa
endjumwa, etcha kabiri era
kubika ebarebi, etcha kahatchu
era kubika ebakangirisi.
Tchasinda era kubika ebandju

부서서. 너 비더라 뱌 쭤떠
좌비싸, 비 쭤떠 좌롸아
구부야.

24. 노구 어비더라 뱌
쭈다비싸, 벼거 비쭈롸
비롸이러 구 구롸에봐
구부야. 부씨 마꼬 오꼬
오오모다냐아 어무비리,
어비더라 뱌 뱌바아 비더더
쭈따, 어라 궈어러사비
어쭈따 레너너.

25. 아이라아 바짜 짜시야
어비더라 벼 무비리
비다버러가나아모, 시 찌라
찌더라 찌떠 짜롸아 구
찌리가보.

26. 아가바 찌더라 찌우마
찌꺄레부가, 어비찌 비더라
뵤씨, 나비 뱌나레부가
아롸우마 나찌. 나 아가바
찌더라 찌우마 찌어어러시봐
어쭈따, 어비찌 비더라
뱌나모와 아롸우마 나찌.

27. 꽈보 무레 무비리 와
기리시도. 나 찌라 무우마 무
꽈보 아레 찌더라 쪼유
무비리.

28. 꽈 루후 롸 오꼬,
어찌버러버러, 오꼬 아비가아
어누꽈, 어짜 가비리 어라
구비가 어바러비, 어짜
가하쭈 어라 구비가
어바가에리시. 짜시따 어라

the parts that are
unpresentable are treated
with special modesty,

24. while our presentable
parts need no special
treatment. But God has
combined the members of
the body and has given
greater honor to the parts
that lacked it,

25. so that there should be
no division in the body, but
that its parts should have
equal concern for each
other.

26. If one part suffers, every
part suffers with it; if one
part is honored, every part
rejoices with it.

27. Now you are the body of
Christ, and each one of you
is a part of it.

28. And in the church God
has appointed first of all
apostles, second prophets,
third teachers, then workers
of miracles, also those
having gifts of healing,

ba bende baira ebisomerane. Kwa businda era kubika ba batchusa elweembo lwe kulamya ebalwala, nesi elwekuasa ebandji, nesi elwekweemangira ebandji, nesi elwekuteta mu mateta ma mateshibwe.

29. Boshi sita ndjumwa, boshi bata barebi, bosi bata bakangirisi, boshi bataira bisomerane.

30. Boshi batete elweembo lwa kulamya ebalwala, nesi elwe kueta mwa mateta ma mateshibwe, nesi elwe kuanunula amu mateta.

31. Mundaa mwahonda busese enyeembo sa sete mufa munene. Si rero nyingabalosa endjira era ikomire busese era irenzise esindji soshi.

구비가 어바쑤 바 버떠 바이라 어비소머라너. 과 부시따 어라 구비가 바 바쭈사 어뤄어뽀 뤄 구꽈마 어바꽈꽈, 너시 어뤄구아사 어바씨, 너시 어뤄궈어마끼라 어바씨, 너시 어뤄구더다 무 마더다 마 마더씨붜.

29. 보씨 시다 뚜꽈, 보씨 바다 바러비, 보시 바다 바가끼리시, 보씨 바다이라 비소머라너.

30. 보씨 바더더 어뤄어뽀 꽈 구꽈먀 어바꽈꽈, 너시 어뤄 구어다 먀 마더다 마 마더씨붜, 너시 어뤄 구아누누꽈 아무 마더다.

31. 무따아 먀호따 부서서 어녀어뽀 사 서더 무파 무너너. 시 러로 네까바로사 어씨라 어라 이고미러 부서서 어라 이러씨서 어시끼 소씨.

those able to help others, those with gifts of administration, and those speaking in different kinds of tongues.

29. Are all apostles? Are all prophets? Are all teachers? Do all work miracles?

30. Do all have gifts of healing? Do all speak in tongues? Do all interpret?

31. But eagerly desire the greater gifts. And now I will show you the most excellent way.

1 E Bakorinto Chikono 13

1 어 바고리또 찌고노 13

1 Corinthians Chapter 13 [NIV]

1. tchiro nyingaata ebuashi bwe kuteta mwa mateta me bandju ne be malaika, akaba ndete nzii, eri bya nateta bainalyi bya buha nga lwayo lwa ngoma, nesi ngo lwa mbeere.

1. 찌로 네까아다 어부아씨 붜 구더다 먀 마더다 머 바뚜 너 버 마꽈이가, 아가바 떠더 씨이, 어리 뱌 나더다 바이나레 뱌 부하 꺄 꽈요 꽈 꼬마, 너시 꼬 꽈 뻐어러.

1. If I speak in the tongues of men and of angels, but have not love, I am only a resounding gong or a clanging cymbal.

2. kandji tchiro nyingaata elweembo lwe kureba, nyiate ne buashi bwekumenyerera tchira mwasi woshi ola ubishirwe, nyiate nebwenge boshi, nyiate na bwemeresi bunene bwe kubatchula endjulungu no kweeka'si mu tchindji tchisiki, si akaba ndete nzii, eri nyinalyi buha?

3. Kandji tchiro nyingaabira ebakene ebikulo byanyi byoshi, naikira nokwa tchihangi naana emubiri wanyi tchasiya nyitchitongen si akaba ndete nzii, ebyera bitanyetere mufa.

4. Enzii itchusa bushibirisi, yende yairana emabuya. Enzii itafa mufula, itatchilola, itatchusa ne rume.

5. Enzii itaina kuata etchunda, itahonda emutoloke wai yeine, itasibuka fuba, itabika na mungo.

6. Enzii itamoera mabi, si yende yamoera ekanangana.

7. Enzii itahola byoshi, yende yemerera byoshin yende yatchinyiira byoshi, na kuata bushibirisi mwa byoshi.

2. 가찌 찌로 네까아다 어뤄어뼈 뭐 구러바, 네아더 너 부아씨 뷔구머녀러라 찌라 마씨 옹씨 오롸 우비씨뤄, 네아더 너뷔꺼 보씨, 네아더 나 뷔머러시 부너너 뷔 구바쭈롸 어뚜루꾸 노 궈어가시 무 찌찌 찌시기, 시 아가바 떠더 씨이, 어리 네나레 부하?

3. 가찌 찌로 네까아비라 어바거너 어비구로 뱌니 뵤씨, 나이기라 노과 찌하끼 나아나 어무비리 와니 짜시야 네찌도꺼누 시 아가바 떠더 씨이, 어벼라 비다녀더러 무파.

4. 어씨이 이쭈사 부씨비리시 여떠 야이라나 어마부야. 어씨이 이다파 무푸롸, 이다찌로롸, 이다쭈사 너 루머.

5. 어씨이 이다이나 구아다 어쭈따, 이다호따 어무도로거 와이 여이너, 이다시부가 푸바, 이다비가 나 무꼬.

6. 어씨이 이다모어라 마비, 시 여떠 야모어라 어가나까나.

7. 어씨이 이다호롸 뵤씨, 여떠 여머러라 뵤씨 여떠 야찌네이라 뵤씨, 나 구아다 부씨비리시 뫄 뵤씨.

2. If I have the gift of prophecy and can fathom all mysteries and all knowledge, and if I have a faith that can move mountains, but have not love, I am nothing.

3. If I give all I possess to the poor and surrender my body to the flames, but have not love, I gain nothing.

4. Love is patient, love is kind. It does not envy, it does not boast, it is not proud.

5. It is not rude, it is not self-seeking, it is not easily angered, it keeps no record of wrongs.

6. Love does not delight in evil but rejoices with the truth.

7. It always protects, always trusts, always hopes, always perseveres.

8. Enzii iri esuku ne mango. Si ekureba kukawa ne lweembo lwe kuteta mu mateta ma mateshibwe nalo, lukawa, ne bwenge nabo, bukanawa.

8. 어씨이 이리 어수구 너 마꼬. 시 어구러바 구가와 너 뤄어뽀 뤄 구더다 무 마더다 마 마더씨붜 나롤, 루가와, 너 붜꺼 나보, 부가나와.

8. Love never fails. But where there are prophecies, they will cease; where there are tongues, they will be stilled; where there is knowledge, it will pass away.

9. Bushi bya tchwishi bitalumirire, nebya tchwende tchwareba bitalumirire.

9. 부씨 뱌 쮜씨 비다뤼미리러, 너뱌 쮜꺼 쫘러바 비다뤼미리러.

9. For we know in part and we prophesy in part,

10. Si mango bya bilumirire bikaika mu mango bya bitalumirire bikawa.

10. 시 마꼬 뱌 비루미리러 비가이가 무 마꼬 뱌 비다뤼미리러 비가와.

10. but when perfection comes, the imperfect disappears.

11. Mango nabaa nyitchiri mwama, nedee nateta nga mwana, nendee naanyisa nga mwana, ne bwenge bwanyi bwanabaa bunalyo nga bwa mwanwa. Si mango nabaa nera mundju nyisene nera kura nareka ei myasi ye lyanetoto.

11. 마꼬 나바아 네찌리 뫄마, 너더어 나더다 꺼 뫄나, 너뻐어 나아네사 꺼 뫄나, 너 붜꺼 봐네 봐나바아 부나뢒 꺼 봐 뫄놔. 시 마꼬 나바아 너라 무뚜 네서너 너라 구라 나러가 어이 먀시 여 랴너도도.

11. When I was a child, I talked like a child, I thought like a child, I reasoned like a child. When I became a man, I put childish ways behind me.

12. Bushi mwesine suku, tchutchiri tchwaola bimbunye mbunye nga mundju ola watchisonga mwa tchiyo tcha tchitalosa kubuya. Si mwa suku sa seshire, tchungalola meho kwa mandji. Mwesine suku, bya nyishi bitalumirir, si mwa suku sa seshire nyingamenyerera kwa kulumirire, ngokwa Ongo atchula anyiishi.

12. 부씨 뭐시너 수구, 쮜찌리 쫘오롸 비뿌녀 뿌녀 꺼 무뚜 오롸 와찌소꺼 뫄 찌요 짜 찌다롒사 구부야. 시 뫄 수구 사 서씨러, 쮜꺼롞롸 머호 과 마찌. 뭐시너 수구, 뱌 네씨 비다뤼미리루, 시 뫄 수구 사 서씨러 네꺼머녀러라 과 구뤼미리러, 꼬과 오꼬 아쮜롸 아네이씨.

12. Now we see but a poor reflection as in a mirror; then we shall see face to face. Now I know in part; then I shall know fully, even as I am fully known.

13. Rero, ene myasi ehatchu iri

13. 러로, 어너 먀시 어하쮜

13. And now these three

kandji ikanaendekera inatchula: ebwemeresi, emunyiiro, ne nzii. Si mwebi bihatchu, emwasi ola urenzise irikabo busese, iri enzii.

이리 가찌 이가나어떠거라 이나쭈좌: 어붸머러시, 어무네이로, 너 씨이. 시 뭐비 비하쭈, 어롸시 오롸 우러씨서 이리가보 부서서, 이리 어씨이.

remain: faith, hope and love. But the greatest of these is love.

1 E Bakorinto Chikono 14

1. Muhondaa tanga kunde mwasimana. Kandji mundaa mwasima busese kubona enyeembo se Mutchima Mubuya-buya, si tanga elweembo lwe kureba.

2. Emundju ola wateta mu mateta ma mateshibwe, ende aba atateta ne bandju, si ende aba ateta na Ongo, bushi kutalyi ola wende wabawomvire bira ateta. Kurengera ebuashi bwe Mutchima Mubuya-buya, oyu mundju ende aba ateta myasi era ibishirwe.

3. Si ola wareba, ende aba abura ebandju myasi ya kubakusa mwa bwemeresi kandji ya kubasesa emitchima na kuberesa emisi.

4. Emundju ola wateta mu mateta ma mateshibwe, ende aba akusa ebwemeresi bwai yeine. Si ola wareba, ende aba

1 어 바고리또 찌고노 14

1. 무호따아 다까 구너 롸시마나. 가찌 무따아 롸시마 부서서 구보나 어녀어뽀 서 무찌마 무부야-부야, 시 다까 어뤠어뽀 뤄 구러바.

2. 어무뚜 오롸 와더다 무 마더다 마 마더씨붸, 어떠 아바 아다더다 너 바뚜, 시 어떠 아바 아더다 나 오꼬, 부씨 구다뤠 오롸 워떠 와바오쀄러 비라 아더다. 구러꺼라 어부아씨 붸 무찌마 무부야-부야, 오유 무뚜 어떠 아바 아더다 먀시 어라 이비씨뤄.

3. 시 오롸 와러바, 어떠 아바 아부라 어바뚜 먀시 야 구바구사 뫄 붸머러시 가찌 야 구바서사 어미찌마 나 구버러사 어미시.

4. 어무뚜 오롸 와더다 무 마더다 마 마더씨붸, 어떠 아바 아구사 어붸머러시 봐이 여이너. 시 오롸 와러바, 어떠

1 Corinthians Chapter 14 [NIV]

1. Follow the way of love and eagerly desire spiritual gifts, especially the gift of prophecy.

2. For anyone who speaks in a tongue does not speak to men but to God. Indeed, no one understands him; he utters mysteries with his spirit.

3. But everyone who prophesies speaks to men for their strengthening, encouragement and comfort.

4. He who speaks in a tongue edifies himself, but he who prophesies edifies the church.

akusa abandju bomwa luhu lwa Ongo mwa bwemeresi.

5. Nyingasimire muboshi munde mwateta mu mateta ma mateshibwe si nyingasimire busese munde mwareba, bushi ola wareba iwete mufa kwola wateta mu mateta ma mateshibwe. Si oyu mateta mu mateta ma mateshibwe nai aneete mufa akaba kulyi undji mundju ola waanulula bya ateta, tchasiya bikuse ebandju bomwa luhu lwa Ongo mwa bwemeresi.

6. Rero banyaketchu, mufa mutchiye nyingabaatchira, akaba nyingaika eyi mwenyu, na natangirisa nateta nenyu mu mateta ma mateshibwe? Ndangabaatchira mufa asibya akaba ngangafulyira myasi era yabaa ibishirwe era Ongo anyilosaa, nesi myasi ya bwenge, nesi ya burebi nesi yakubakangirisa.

7. Kubinalyi batcha nokwa bindju bye musiki, ngakuno emurumbu, nesi enzenze. Ebi bindju, akaba bitangana mirenge era irenzenye, kute emundju angamenyerera elwimbo lwa lwaombibwa ne murumbu nesi ne nzenze.

아바 아구사 아바뉴 보똬 루후 똬 오꼬 똬 뭐머러시.

5. 네빠시미러 무보씨 무떠 똬더다 무 마더다 마 마더씨붸 시 네빠시미러 부서서 무떠 똬러바, 부씨 오똬 와러바 이워더 무파 꼴똬 와더다 무 마더다 마 마더씨붸. 시 오유 마더다 무 마더다 마 마더씨붸 나이 아너어더 무파 아가바 구레 우찌 무뚜 오똬 와아누루똬 뱌 아더다, 짜시야 비구서 어바뉴 보똬 루후 똬 오꼬 똬 뭐머러시.

6. 러로 바냐거쭈, 무파 무찌여 네빠바아찌라, 아가바 네빠이가 어에 뮤뉴, 나 나다삐리사 나더다 너뉴 무 마더다 마 마더씨붸? 따빠바아찌라 무파 아시뱌 아가바 빠빠푸레라 먀시 어라 야바아 이비씨뤄 어라 오꼬 아네로사아, 너시 먀시 야 붸삐, 너시 야 부러비 너시 야구바가삐리사.

7. 구비나레 바짜 노과 비뿌 벼 무시기, 빠구노 어무루뿌, 너시 어써써. 어비 비뿌, 아가바 비다빠나 미러뼈 어라 이러써녀, 구더 어무뿌 아빠머녀러라 어뤼뽀 똬 똬오삐봐 너 무루뿌 너시 너 써써.

5. I would like every one of you to speak in tongues, but I would rather have you prophesy. He who prophesies is greater than one who speaks in tongues, unless he interprets, so that the church may be edified.

6. Now, brothers, if I come to you and speak in tongues, what good will I be to you, unless I bring you some revelation or knowledge or prophecy or word of instruction?

7. Even in the case of lifeless things that make sounds, such as the flute or harp, how will anyone know what tune is being played unless there is a distinction in the notes?

8. Ne kaperere nako, akaba katabandjibwe'mo kwa kuundjukere, nde iungatchikunganya kuya kwa bita?

9. Rero nenyu kubinalyi batcha. Akaba mungateta mu mateta ma mateshibwe, kute ebandju bangamenyerera bya mwateta, noku bitaundjukere? Mwa kuira batcha, mungaba naga ba bateta ne mbusi.

10. Mwa butala mulyi mateta manene busese ma marenzenye, si kutalyi tchiro na liuma lya lyitete kwa lyitetchire.

11. Akaba ndeshi teta lyirebe, nanaba nga muenyi era muhondo sola wateta'lyi, nai anaba nga muenyi era muhondo sanyi.

12. Rero, nenyu oku mutchula musimire kubona enyembo se Mutchima Mubuya-buya, mundaa mwatchisesa kuhonda busese sa singaasa ebandju bomwa luhu lwa Ongo kukula mwa bwemeresi.

13. Bushi noku, ola wateta mwa mateta ma mateshibwe, emaa Ongo amweerese ne lweembo lwe kunde aanulula'o.

14. Bushi akaba nema Ongo

8. 너 가퍼러러 나고, 아가바 가다바씨붜모 과 구우뚜거러, 떠 이우까찌구까냐 구야 과 비다?

9. 러로 너뉴 구비나레 바짜. 아가바 무까더다 무 마더다 마 마더씨붜, 구더 어바뉴 바까머녀러라 뱌 뫄더다, 노구 비다우뚜거러? 뫄 구이라 바짜, 무까바 나가 바 바더다 너 뿌시.

10. 뫄 부다꽈 무레 마더다 마너너 부서서 마 마러써녀, 시 구다레 찌로 나 찌우마 꺄 레더더 과 레더찌러.

11. 아가바 떠씨 더다 레러버, 나나바 까 무어네 어라 무호또 소꽈 와더다레, 나이 아나바 까 무어네 어라 무호또 사니.

12. 러로, 너뉴 오구 무쭈꽈 무시미러 구보나 어녀뽀 서 무찌마 무부야-부야, 무따아 꽈찌서사 구호따 부서서 사 시까아사 어바뉴 보뫄 루후 꽈 오꼬 구구꽈 뫄 붜머러시.

13. 부씨 노구, 오꽈 와더다 뫄 마더다 마 마더씨붜, 어마아 오꼬 아뭐어러서 너 뭐어뽀 뭐 구더 아아누루꽈오.

14. 부씨 아가바 너마 오꼬

8. Again, if the trumpet does not sound a clear call, who will get ready for battle?

9. So it is with you. Unless you speak intelligible words with your tongue, how will anyone know what you are saying? You will just be speaking into the air.

10. Undoubtedly there are all sorts of languages in the world, yet none of them is without meaning.

11. If then I do not grasp the meaning of what someone is saying, I am a foreigner to the speaker, and he is a foreigner to me.

12. So it is with you. Since you are eager to have spiritual gifts, try to excel in gifts that build up the church.

13. For this reason anyone who speaks in a tongue should pray that he may interpret what he says.

14. For if I pray in a tongue,

mu mateta ma mateshibwe, e
Mutchima wanyi iwende waba
weema, si ebwenge bwanyi
bwande bwa butakola.

15. Rero, tchii nyiraa?
Nyingende nema Ongo mwa
mutchima wanyi,
nanamweema nokwa
kungomvikala. Nyingende
namwembira mwa mutchima
wanyi nanamwembira nokwa
kungomvikana.

16. Akaba watonga Ongo mwa
mutchima wao oshaao,
emundju ola ulyi mwa
lubwaanano atangamenya bya
waira. Rero kute angaala
kwaakula mbu: "bibe
batcha"noku atomvire bya
wateta?

17. Tchiro angaba mbu amu
meemo mao mekutonga
Ongo makomire busese
matangakusa ebwemeresi bwe
undji mundju

18. Natonga Ongo bushi
nateta mu mateta ma
mateshibwe kubarenza
muboshi.

19. Si mango nyiri mwa
lubwaanano mwa luhu lwa
Ongo nyitchula nyisimire
kuteta binwa bitano bya
bandju bangoomva, tchasiya
nyibakangirise, wakuteta

무 마더다 마 마더씨붜, 어
무찌마 와네 이워떠 와바
워어마, 시 어붜어 봐네 봐떠
봐바 부다고꽈.

15. 러로, 찌이 네라아?
네꺼떠 너마 오꼬 꽈 무찌마
와네, 나나뭐어마 노과
구꼬삐가꽈. 네꺼떠 나뭐삐라
꽈 무찌마 와네 나나뭐삐라
노과 구꼬삐가나.

16. 아가바 와도꽈 오꼬 꽈
무찌마 와오 오싸아오,
어무뚜 오라 우뤠 꽈
루봐아나노 아다꽈머냐 뱌
와이라. 러로 구더 아꽈아꽈
과아구꽈 뿌: "비버 바짜"노구
아도삐러 뱌 와더다?

17. 찌로 아꽈바 뿌 아무
머어모 마오 머구도꽈 오꼬
마고미러 부서서 마다꽈구사
어붜머러시 붸 우찌 무뚜

18. 나도꽈 오꼬 부씨 나더다
무 마더다 마 마더씨붜
구바러싸 무보씨.

19. 시 마꼬 네리 꽈
루봐아나노 꽈 루후 꽈 오꼬
네쭈꽈 네시미러 구더다 비놔
비다노 뱌 바뚜 바오오빠,
짜시야 네바가꽈리서,
와구더다 뷰삐 아구미 뱌

my spirit prays, but my mind
is unfruitful.

15. So what shall I do? I will
pray with my spirit, but I will
also pray with my mind; I
will sing with my spirit, but I
will also sing with my mind.

16. If you are praising God
with your spirit, how can
one who finds himself
among those who do not
understand say "Amen" to
your thanksgiving, since he
does not know what you are
saying?

17. You may be giving
thanks well enough, but the
other man is not edified.

18. I thank God that I speak
in tongues more than all of
you.

19. But in the church I would
rather speak five intelligible
words to instruct others than
ten thousand words in a
tongue.

byumbi akumi bya binwa mu mateta ma mateshibwe.

비놔 무 마더다 마 마더씨붜.

---

20. Banyaketchu mutendaa mwaanyisa nga bana batoto. Mwa myasi ibi, mundaa mwatchitola nga bana batoto, si emianyisa yenyu indaa yaba nga bandju ba bera basene

21. Bitchula byaandjikirwe mwa mwaso mbu: "Enawetchu atetchire batcha: nyingende nateta noluno lubaa kurengera ebandju ba batengera burerere, ba bateta mateta ma tchienyi, si tchiro batcha, batakende banyumvira.

22. Bushi noku, ekuteta mwa mateta ma mateshibwe, kalyi kalorero kwa batata bemeresi, si kata kalorero kwa bemeresi. Ne kureba kalyi kalorero kwa bemeresi, si kata kalorero kwaba bata bemeresi.

23. Muumwaa, ebemeresi boshi bangaba balyi mwa lubwaanano na boshi batangirisa bateta mu mateta ma mateshibwe. Tchasiya mwolu lubwaanano, mwaneengirira bandju ba bateshi bya mwaira, nesi ba bata bemeresi. Mutasene kwabu bandju bangatchitchinga mbu

---

20. 바냐거쭈 무더따아 꽈아니사 까 바나 바도도. 꽈 먀시 이비, 무따아 꽈찌도롸 까 바나 바도도, 시 어미아네사 여뉴 이따아 야바 까 바뉴 바 버라 바서너

21. 비쭈롸 뱌아찌기뤄 꽈 마소 뿌: "어나워쭈 아더찌러 바짜: 네꺼떠 나더다 노루노 루바아 구러꺼라 어바뉴 바 바더꺼라 부러러러, 바 바더다 마더다 마 쩌네, 시 찌로 바짜, 바다거떠 바뉴쁘라.

22. 부씨 노구, 어구더다 꽈 마더다 마 마더씨붜, 가쩨 가론러로 과 바다 버머러시, 시 가다 가론러로 과 버머러시. 너 구러바 가쩨 가론러로 과 버머러시, 시 가다 가론러로 과바 바다 버머러시.

23. 무우꽈아, 어버머러시 보씨 바까바 바쩨 꽈 루봐아나노 나 보씨 바다꺼리사 바더다 무 마더다 마 마더씨붜. 짜시야 모루 루봐아나노, 꽈너어꺼리라 바뉴 바 바더씨 뱌 꽈이라, 너시 바 바다 버머러시. 무다서너 과부 바뉴 바까찌찌꺼 뿌 꽈시러이러?

---

20. Brothers, stop thinking like children. In regard to evil be infants, but in your thinking be adults.

21. In the Law it is written: "Through men of strange tongues and through the lips of foreigners I will speak to this people, but even then they will not listen to me," says the Lord.

22. Tongues, then, are a sign, not for believers but for unbelievers; prophecy, however, is for believers, not for unbelievers.

23. So if the whole church comes together and everyone speaks in tongues, and some who do not understand or some unbelievers come in, will they not say that you are out of your mind?

mwasireire?

24. Si boshi bangareba.
Emundju ola uta mwemeresi
nesi ola uteshi bya mwaira
aneengiriraa mwa lubwaanano.
Rero byoshi bya angomva bi
bingatchuma amenyerera
kanangana kwa alyi mukosi wa
mabi. Aola, angatchuumva
ngola watchindjibusiwe na
boshi

25. Mwolu, emyasi era abaa
abishire mwa mutchima wai
yanabihukala. Mwa batcha,
angafukama era muhondo sa
Ongo na kumwera, mwa
kuteta mbu: "Kubinalyi! Ongo
analyi mwa katchi-katchi
kenyu!

26. Enawetchu, tchi nyitetaa
kasi? Mango mulyi mwa
lubwaanano , mundju muuma
mu mwabo angeemba lwimbo
ne undji angakangirisa
etchinwa tcha Ongo, ne undji
angateta myasi era Ongo
amubihulyiraa, era yabaa
ibishirwe, ne undji angateta
mu mateta ma mateshibwe, ne
undji angaanulula amu mateta.
Nebi byoshi, byeemire kunde
byairibwa kwa kuhonda
kukusa ebemeresi mwa
bwemeresi bwabo.

27. Akaba kulyi bandju ba

24. 시 보씨 바빠러바. 어무뚜
오라 우다 뭐머러시 너시
오라 우더씨 뱌 마이라
아너어삐리라아 뫄
루봐아나노. 러로 뵤씨 뱌
아꼬빠 비 비빠쭈마
아머녀러라 가나빠나 과 아레
무고시 와 마비. 아오롸,
아빠쭈우빠 꼬롸
와찌뼈부시워 나 보씨

25. 모루, 어먀시 어라 아바아
아비씨러 뫄 무찌마 와이
야나비후가꺄. 뫄 바짜,
아빠푸가마 어라 무호또 사
오꼬 나 구뭐라, 뫄 구더다
뿌: "구비나레! 오꼬 아나레
뫄 가찌-가찌 거뉴!

26. 어나워쭈, 찌 니더다아
가시? 마꼬 무레 뫄
루봐아나노 , 무뚜 무우마 무
뫄보 아뻐어어빠 뤼뽀, 너 우찌
아빠가삐리사 어찌놔 짜
오꼬, 너 우찌 아빠더다 먀시
어라 오꼬 아무비후레라아,
어라 야바아 이비씨뤄, 너
우찌 아빠더다 무 마더다 마
마더씨붜, 너 우찌
아빠아누루롸 아무 마더다.
너비 뵤씨, 벼어미러 구너
뱌이리봐 과 구호따 구구사
어버머러시 뫄 붜머러시
봐보.

27. 아가바 구레 바뚜 바

24. But if an unbeliever or
someone who does not
understandcomes in while
everybody is prophesying,
he will be convinced by all
that he is a sinner and will
be judged by all,

25. and the secrets of his
heart will be laid bare. So he
will fall down and worship
God, exclaiming, "God is
really among you!"

26. What then shall we say,
brothers? When you come
together, everyone has a
hymn, or a word of
instruction, a revelation, a
tongue or an interpretation.
All of these must be done
for the strengthening of the
church.

27. If anyone speaks in a

bateta mu mateta ma mateshibwe, biteemire babe banene ku babiri nesi bahatchu. Nomwa kuteta, bemire kuteta muuma-muuma. Kandji byeemire kube mundju ola ungende waanulula bya bateta.

28. Akaba kutalyi mundju wa kuanulula, rero ba bateta mwa mateta ma mateshibwe basiraa mwa lubwaanano. Aola, tchira muuma ateteraa mwa mutchima wai yeine buna Ongo.

29. Kwa bya byeerekere ekureba, biteemire kube bandju banene ku baibiri nesi bahatchu ba bateta. Ne bandji banalola kubuyabuya akaba bya bateta binalyi bya kanangana.

30. Si akaba kulyi mundju ola wateta, tchasinda undji mundju ola ulyi mwa lubwaanano, Ongo anamubihulyira myasi, oyu wabaa wateta, asiraa.

31. Muboshi munganareba muuma-muuma tchasiya ebandju boshi bakangiribwe, ne kusesibwa emitchima.

32. Elweembo lwe kureba lweemire kunde lwaba era tchibanda se buashi bwola

---

바더다 무 마더다 마 마더씨붸, 비더어미러 바버 바너너 구 바비리 너시 바하쭈. 노봐 구더다, 버미러 구더다 무우마-무우마. 가찌 벼어미러 구버 무뚜 오롸 우꺼너 와아누룰롸 뱌 바더다.

28. 아가바 구다례 무뚜 와 구아누룰롸, 러로 바 바더다 롸 마더다 마 마더씨붸 바시라아 롸 룹봐아나노. 아오롸, 찌라 무우마 아더더라아 롸 무찌마 와이 여이너 부나 오꼬.

29. 과 뱌 벼어러거러 어구러바, 비더어미러 구버 바뚜 바너너 구 바이비리 너시 바하쭈 바 바더다. 너 바찌 바나룰롸 구부야부야 아가바 뱌 바더다 비나례 뱌 가나꺄나.

30. 시 아가바 구례 무뚜 오롸 와더다, 짜시따 우찌 무뚜 오롸 우레 롸 룹봐아나노, 오꼬 아나무비후쩨라 먀시, 오유 와바아 와더다, 아시라아.

31. 무보씨 무꺄나러바 무우마-무우마 짜시야 어바뚜 보씨 바가꺄리리붸, 너 구서시봐 어미찌마.

32. 어뤄어뽀 뤄 구러바 뤄어미러 구더 꽈바 어라 찌바따 서 부아씨 볼롸

---

tongue, two--or at the most three--should speak, one at a time, and someone must interpret.

28. If there is no interpreter, the speaker should keep quiet in the church and speak to himself and God.

29. Two or three prophets should speak, and the others should weigh carefully what is said.

30. And if a revelation comes to someone who is sitting down, the first speaker should stop.

31. For you can all prophesy in turn so that everyone may be instructed and encouraged.

32. The spirits of prophets are subject to the control of prophets.

weresibwe'lo

워러시붸로

33. Bushi Ongo atatchula Ongo wa kafango, si atchula wa boolo. Ngokwa byendjire byanairibwa mwa nyuhu sa Ongo soshi.

33. 부씨 오꼬 아다쭈롸 오꼬 와 가파꼬, 시 아쭈롸 와 보오로. 꼬과 벼찌러 뱌나이리봐 뫄 뉴후 사 오꼬 소씨.

33. For God is not a God of disorder but of peace. As in all the congregations of the saints,

34. Ebakasi beemire kunde basira mwa nyibwaanano. Bateresibwe loso lwa kuteta, si beemire kunde batchirembeka ngokwa mwaso atchula atetchire.

34. 어바가시 버어미러 구떠 바시라 뫄 네봐아나노. 바더러시붸 로소 롸 구더다, 시 버어미러 구떠 바찌러뻐가 꼬과 뫄소 아쭈롸 아더찌러.

34. women should remain silent in the churches. They are not allowed to speak, but must be in submission, as the Law says.

35. Akaba bahonda bamenye mwasi murebe, babusao beba babo mwa mahosi mabo. Bushi siri honyi kwa mukasi ekuteta mwa luhu lwa Ongo

35. 아가바 바호따 바머녀 뫄시 무러버, 바부사오 버바 바보 뫄 마호시 마보. 부씨 시리 호네 과 무가시 어구더다 뫄 루후 롸 오꼬

35. If they want to inquire about something, they should ask their own husbands at home; for it is disgraceful for a woman to speak in the church.

36. Mwaanyisa mbu eyi mwenyu yetchinwa tcha Ongo tchatengeraa? Nesi mbu mubeine oshao mu tchanaikirire?

36. 뫄아네사 뿌 어에 뭐뉴 여찌놔 짜 오꼬 짜더뻐라아? 너시 뿌 무버이너 오싸오 무 짜나이기리러?

36. Did the word of God originate with you? Or are you the only people it has reached?

37. Akaba emundju aanyisa kwa murebi, nesi mbu ete lweembo lwe mutchima Mubuya-buya, eemire kumenyerera kwa ene myesi nabaandjikirire, alyi muomba wa Enawetchu.

37. 아가바 어무뿌 아아네사 과 무러비, 너시 뿌 어더 뤄어뽀 뤄 무찌마 무부야-부야, 어어미러 구머녀러라 과 어너 며시 나바아찌기리러, 아쀄 무오빠 와 어나워쭈.

37. If anybody thinks he is a prophet or spiritually gifted, let him acknowledge that what I am writing to you is the Lord's command.

38. Akaba oyu mundju ateshi ei myasi, eri nai Ongo atamwishi

38. 아가바 오유 무뿌 아더씨 어이 먀시, 어리 나이 오꼬 아다뮈씨

38. If he ignores this, he himself will be ignored.

39. Bushi noku banyaketchu,

39. 부씨 노구 바냐거쭈,

39. Therefore, my brothers,

mundaa mwahonda busese elweembe lwe kureba si tchiro batcha, mutendaa mwaangika ebandju kunde bateta mwa mateta ma mateshibwe.

40. Si emyasi yoshi, indaa yairibwa mwa ndjira era itchungenene, kandji era ilongomanyire.

무따아 먀호따 부서서 어뤄어뻐 뤄 구러바 시 찌로 바짜, 무더따아 먀아께가 어바꾸 구떠 바더다 먀 마더다 마 마더씨붜.

40. 시 어먀시 요씨, 이따아 야이리봐 먀 띠라 어라 이쭈어너너, 가찌 어라 이로꼬마네러.

be eager to prophesy, and do not forbid speaking in tongues.

40. But everything should be done in a fitting and orderly way.

1 E Bakorinto Chikono 15

1 어 바고리또 찌고노 15

1 Corinthians Chapter 15 [NIV]

1. Banyaketchun nahonda nyibakengese era luulu se mwasi Mubuya-buya, ola nabakangirisaa. Mwera kwemerera'o, kandji munasimikire muo.

2. Kurengera oyu mwasi ku mwendjire mwanunulyiba emango mwalyibukirao ngokwa nanabakangirisaa. Si akaba bitakyi batcha, eri ebwemeresi bwenyu bunalyi bwa buha.

3. Era muhondo sabyoshi, nabakangirisa emyasi era nanyi nakangirisibwaa: Kirisito afaa bushi ne bibi byetchu, kukulyikana nokwa maandjiko Mabuya-buya mabaa matetchire mira.

4. Era kutabwa na koomoka kwa lusuku lwa kahatchu era

1. 바냐거쭈 나호따 네바거어서 어라 루우루 서 먀시 무부야-부야, 오라 나바가께리리사아. 뭐라 궈머러라오, 가찌 무나시미기러 무오.

2. 구러어라 오유 먀시 구 뭐찌러 먀누누쪠바 어마꼬 뫄쪠부기라오 꼬과 나나바가께리리사아. 시 아가바 비다게 바짜, 어리 어붜머러시 붜뉴 부나쪠 봐 부하.

3. 어라 무호또 사뵤씨, 나바가께리리사 어먀시 어라 나니 나가께리리시봐아: 기리시도 아파아 부씨 너 비비 벼쭈, 구구쪠가나 노과 마아찌고 마부야-부야 마바아 마더찌러 미라.

4. 어라 구다봐 나 고오모가 과 루수구 뢈 가하쭈 어라

1. Now, brothers, I want to remind you of the gospel I preached to you, which you received and on which you have taken your stand.

2. By this gospel you are saved, if you hold firmly to the word I preached to you. Otherwise, you have believed in vain.

3. For what I received I passed on to you as of first importance: that Christ died for our sins according to the Scriptures,

4. that he was buried, that he was raised on the third

nyuma se kufa kwai,
kukulyikana nokwa Maaandjiko
Mabuya-buya bamaa
matetchire mira.

5. Era kupamukira ku Petero,
tchasinda era kupamukira kwa
ndjumwa ekumi nebiri.

6. Era nyuma sebi, era
kupamukira ku bemeresi
banene ku maana matano ku
tchihangi tchiuma. Na banene
mubo banatchiri'o, si ebandji
bafire mira.

7. Era nyuma sebi, era
kupamukira ku Yakobo,
tchasinda kwa ndjumwa soshi

8. Tchasindjire, era nyuma
sabu boshi, era
kunyipamukira'ko nanyi, nyi
nyiri nga mwana ola
wabutchirwa atasa kulumisa
ne myesi.

9. Bushi nyono nyi mueke
mwa ndjumwa. Tchiro
ndanemira kwerikibwa mbu
ndjumwa, bushi nyinabaa
nendjire nalyibusa eluhu lwa
Ongo.

10. Si kwa bondjo bwa Ongo,
ku kutchumire naba ngokwa
nyiri. Obu bondjo butabaa
bwa buha, bushi nakolaa
busese kurenza esindji
ndjumwa soshi. Kanangana ata

뉴마 서 구파 과이,
구구레가나 노과 마아아찌고
마부야-부야 바마아 마더찌러
미라.

5. 어라 구파무기라 구
퍼더로, 짜시따 어라
구파무기라 과 뿌똬 어구미
너비리.

6. 어라 뉴마 서비, 어라
구파무기라 구 버머러시
바너너 구 마아나 마다노 구
찌하삐 찌우마. 나 바너너
무보 바나찌리오, 시 어바찌
바피러 미라.

7. 어라 뉴마 서비, 어라
구파무기라 구 야고보,
짜시따 과 뿌똬 소씨

8. 짜시띠러, 어라 뉴마 사부
보씨, 어라 구네파무기라고
나니, 네 니리 똬 모나 오똬
와부찌라 아다사 구루미사 너
며시.

9. 부씨 뇨노 네 무어거 똬
뿌똬. 찌로 따너미라
궈리기똬 뿌 뿌똬, 부씨
네나바아 너찌러 나레부사
어루후 똬 오꼬.

10. 시 과 보쪼 똬 오꼬, 구
구쭈미러 나바 꼬과 니리.
오부 보쪼 부다바아 똬 부하,
부씨 나고똬아 부서서 구러싸
어시찌 뿌똬 소씨. 가나똬나
아다 네나고똬, 시 어보쪼 똬

day according to the
Scriptures,

5. and that he appeared to
Peter, and then to the
Twelve.

6. After that, he appeared to
more than five hundred of
the brothers at the same
time, most of whom are still
living, though some have
fallen asleep.

7. Then he appeared to
James, then to all the
apostles,

8. and last of all he
appeared to me also, as to
one abnormally born.

9. For I am the least of the
apostles and do not even
deserve to be called an
apostle, because I
persecuted the church of
God.

10. But by the grace of God
I am what I am, and his
grace to me was not without
effect. No, I worked harder
than all of them--yet not I,
but the grace of God that

nyinakola, si ebondjo bwa Ongo bu bwendjire bwakola mwa ndanda sanyi.

11. Rero, abe nyono, abe abu bandju, oyu mwasi Mubuya-buya muuma, itchwendjire tchwanahubanganyisa ebandju, na imwaneemerere.

12. Tchwendjire tchwakangirisa ebandju mbu Kirisito omwokaa mwa bafu. Rero, kute bauma mu mwabo bendjire bateta mbu ebafu batakoomwoke?

13. Akaba kanangana ebafu batakoomwoke, kukuteta mbu Kirisito nai atoomwokaa

14. Na akaba Kirisito atoomwokaa, kukuteta mbu ne myasi era tchwendjire tchwahubanganyisa ebandju iri ya buha, ne bwemeresi bwenyu nabo, bunalyi bwa buha!

15. KAndji akaba kanangana ebafu batakoomwoke, kuteta mbu Ongo atoomwolaa Kirisito. Aola tchuseneke'ko nga babei ba beekera Ongo bisha, bushi tchwendjire tchwateta mbu oomwolaa Kirisito.

16. Bushi akaba ebafu batakoomwoke, kukuteta mbu Kirisito nai atoomwokaa.

오꼬 부 붸찌러 봐고롸 봐 따따 사니.

11. 러로, 아버 뇨노, 아버 아부 바뉴, 오유 마시 무부야-부야 무우마, 이쮀찌러 쫘나후바빠네사 어바뉴, 나 이뫄너어머러러.

12. 쮀찌러 쫘가끼리사 어바뉴 뿌 기리시도 오모가아 봐 바푸. 러로, 구더 바우마 무 뫄보 버찌러 바더다 뿌 어바푸 바다고오모거?

13. 아가바 가나빠나 어바푸 바다고오모거, 구구더다 뿌 기리시도 나이 아도오모가아

14. 나 아가바 기리시도 아도오모가아, 구구더다 뿌 너 먀시 어라 쮀찌러 쫘후바빠네사 어바뉴 이리 야 부하, 너 붸머러시 붸뉴 나보, 부나쩨 봐 부하!

15. 가찌 아가바 가나빠나 어바푸 바다고오모거, 구더다 뿌 오꼬 아도오모롸아 기리시도. 아오롸 쭈서너거고 빠 바버이 바 버어거라 오꼬 비싸, 부씨 쮀찌러 쫘더다 뿌 오오모롸아 기리시도.

16. 부씨 아가바 어바푸 바다고오모거, 구구더다 뿌 기리시도 나이 아도오모가아.

was with me.

11. Whether, then, it was I or they, this is what we preach, and this is what you believed.

12. But if it is preached that Christ has been raised from the dead, how can some of you say that there is no resurrection of the dead?

13. If there is no resurrection of the dead, then not even Christ has been raised.

14. And if Christ has not been raised, our preaching is useless and so is your faith.

15. More than that, we are then found to be false witnesses about God, for we have testified about God that he raised Christ from the dead. But he did not raise him if in fact the dead are not raised.

16. For if the dead are not raised, then Christ has not been raised either.

17. Kandji akaba Kirisito atoomwokaa, kukuteta mbu ebwemeresi bwenyu bulyi bwa buha, munatchiri nomwa bibi byenyu.

18. Kandji kukuteta mbu ebandju ba bafire bemeerere Kirisito, kuera ku baerire.

19. Akaba tchutchinyiirire Kirisito bushi na kano kalamo ka tchweete lwarero oshao, eri tchulyi baanya kurenza ebandju boshi.

20. Si kanangana Kirisito omwokaa mwa bafu, etchera tchi tchalosa kanangana kwe bandji bafu nabo bakanoomwoka.

21. Bushi ngokwa walufu aretchibwaa na mundju muuma, kunoku ku ekoomwoka kwe bafu nako, kwaretchibwaa na mudju muuma.

22. Rero, ngokwa ebandju boshi bende bafa bushi ne buuma bwabo na Atamu, kunoku ku ebandju boshi bakanahuba kuba bauma-uma bushi ne buuma bwabo na Kirisito.

23. Si tchira mundju ete tchai tchihangi tche koomwoka, na Kirisito imuberebere. Tchasinda

---

17. 가찌 아가바 기리시도 아도오모가아, 구구더다 뿌 어뭐머러시 뭐뉴 부레 봐 부하, 무나찌리 노롸 비비 벼뉴.

18. 가찌 구구더다 뿌 어바뉴 바 바피러 버머어러러 기리시도, 구어라 구 바어리러.

19. 아가바 쭈찌네이리러 기리시도 부씨 나 가노 가롸모 가 줘어더 롸러로 오싸오, 어리 쭈레 바아냐 구러싸 어바뉴 보씨.

20. 시 가나꽈나 기리시도 오모가아 롸 바푸, 어쩌라 찌 짜롸사 가나꽈나 궈 바찌 바푸 나보 바가노오모가.

21. 부씨 꼬과 와루푸 아러찌봐아 나 무뚜 무우마, 구노구 구 어고오모가 궈 바푸 나고, 과러찌봐아 나 무주 무우마.

22. 러로, 꼬과 어바뉴 보씨 버머 바파 부씨 너 부우마 봐보 나 아다무, 구노구 구 어바뉴 보씨 바가나후바 구바 바우마-우마 부씨 너 부우마 봐보 나 기리시도.

23. 시 찌라 무뚜 어더 짜이 찌하께 쩌 고오모가, 나 기리시도 이무버러버러.

---

17. And if Christ has not been raised, your faith is futile; you are still in your sins.

18. Then those also who have fallen asleep in Christ are lost.

19. If only for this life we have hope in Christ, we are to be pitied more than all men.

20. But Christ has indeed been raised from the dead, the firstfruits of those who have fallen asleep.

21. For since death came through a man, the resurrection of the dead comes also through a man.

22. For as in Adam all die, so in Christ all will be made alive.

23. But each in his own turn: Christ, the firstfruits; then, when he comes, those who

ebandju bai nabo bakoomwoka mango akabaha.

24. Nera nyuma sebi, enzindjiro ikaika. Mwa mu mango Kirisito akahandjula byoshi bya biimire, na byoshi bye byeete ebuashi, na byoshi bye byeete emisi. Tchasinda, akaalulyira Ongo Tata ebwami.

25. Bushi byeemire Kirisito aendekere kwiima kuikira mango Ongo akaba abikire ebarenda bai boshi kuba tchisimatchiro tchai.

26. Ne murenga musinda ola ukahandjulibwa, alyi walufu.

27. Bushi bitchula byaandjikirwe mwa maandjika Mabuya-buya mbu: "Ongo airire byoshi tchisimatchiro tchai". Si byoshi byairibwe kuba tchisimatchiro tchai kureka Ongo yeine oshao, bushi iwabikire byoshi era tchibanda se buashi bwa Kirisito.

28. Na mango akaba abikire byoshi era tchibanda se buashi bwe Mwana wai, mu mango oyu Mwana nai akeri atchibika era tchibanda se buashi bwa Ongo, iwabikaa byoshi era tchibanda se buashi bwai. Mwa batcha, Ongo anere eema loshi era luulu sa byoshi.

짜시따 어바뿌 바이 나보 바고오모가 마꼬 아가바하.

24. 너라 뉴마 서비, 어씨찌로 이가이가. 롸 무 마꼬 기리시도 아가하뿌롸 뵤씨 뱌 비이미러, 나 뵤씨 벼 벼어더 어부아씨, 나 뵤씨 벼 벼어더 어미시. 짜시따, 아가아루쩨라 오꼬 다다 어봐미.

25. 부씨 벼어미러 기리시도 아어더거러 귀이마 구이기라 마꼬 오꼬 아가바 아비기러 어바러따 바이 보씨 구바 찌시마찌로 짜이.

26. 너 무러까 무시따 오롸 우가하뿌뤼봐, 아레 와루푸.

27. 롸 마아씨가 마부야-부야 뿌 "오꼬 아이리러 뵤씨 찌시마찌로 짜이". 시 뵤씨 뱌이리붜 구바 찌시마찌로 짜이 구러가 오꼬 여이너 오싸오, 부씨 이와비기러 뵤씨 어라 찌바따 서 부아씨 봐 기리시도.

28. 나 마꼬 아가바 아비기러 뵤씨 어라 찌바따 서 부아씨 붜 모나 와이, 무 마꼬 오유 모나 나이 아거리 아찌비가 어라 찌바따 서 부아씨 봐 오꼬, 이와비가아 뵤씨 어라 찌바따 서 부아씨 봐이. 롸 바짜, 오꼬 아너러 어어마 로씨 어라 루우루 사 뵤씨.

belong to him.

24. Then the end will come, when he hands over the kingdom to God the Father after he has destroyed all dominion, authority and power.

25. For he must reign until he has put all his enemies under his feet.

26. The last enemy to be destroyed is death.

27. For he "has put everything under his feet." Now when it says that "everything" has been put under him, it is clear that this does not include God himself, who put everything under Christ.

28. When he has done this, then the Son himself will be made subject to him who put everything under him, so that God may be all in all.

29. Rero akaba ebafu batakoomwoke, kute bikaba kwabu bendjire babatisibwa bushi nabo? Kandji akaba kanangana ebafu batakoomwoke, tchi tchingatchuma ebandju bendjire babatsisibwa bushi nabo?

30. Anabe netchu tchubeine, tchi tchingatchuma tchira tchihangi tchwaendekera kubika ekalamo ketchu mwa kasibu?

31. Banyaketchu, tchira lusuku nendjire nabura nafa. Nababura batcha bushi nendjire natchitongera mwabo mwa buuma bwetchu na Enawetchu Yesu Kirisito.

32. Anabe nomwa musi we Efeso, nalwaa ne nyama ngalyi. Rero, akaba nyingalwire nasi bushi ne kuhonda ebindju byomuno butala oshaao, mutoloke mutchiye nyingabonyire? Akaba ebafu batakoomwoke, rero: "Tchulyaa mishanga tchungafa"

33. Mutendaa mweengerwa!"Ebera babi bende batchuma ebandju babuya baira emabi".

34. Mutchihubaa'ko ngokwa bineemire, murekaa kunde

---

29. 러로 아가바 어바푸 바다고오모거, 구더 비가바 과부 버찌러 바바디시봐 부씨 나보? 가찌 아가바 가나아나 어바푸 바다고오모거, 찌 찌까쭈마 어바쭈 버찌러 바바찌시봐 부씨 나보?

30. 아나버 너쭈 쭈버이너, 찌 찌까쭈마 찌라 찌하삐 쫘어떠거라 구비가 어가꽈모 거쭈 꽈 가시부?

31. 바냐거쭈, 찌라 루수구 너찌러 나부라 나파. 나바부라 바짜 부씨 너찌러 나찌도꺼라 꽈보 꽈 부우마 붜쭈 나 어나워쭈 여수 기리시도.

32. 아나버 노꽈 무시 워 어퍼소, 나꽈아 너 냐마 까레. 러로, 아가바 네까뤼러 나시 부씨 너 구호따 어비뉴 뵤무노 부다꽈 오싸아오, 무도로꺼 무찌여 네까보니러? 아가바 어바푸 바다고오모거, 러로: "쭈꺄아 미싸까 쭈까파"

33. 무더따아 뭐어꺼라!"어버라 바비 버떠 바쭈마 어바푸 바부야 바이라 어마비".

34. 무찌후바아고 꼬과 비너어미러, 무러가아 구떠

---

29. Now if there is no resurrection, what will those do who are baptized for the dead? If the dead are not raised at all, why are people baptized for them?

30. And as for us, why do we endanger ourselves every hour?

31. I die every day--I mean that, brothers--just as surely as I glory over you in Christ Jesus our Lord.

32. If I fought wild beasts in Ephesus for merely human reasons, what have I gained? If the dead are not raised, "Let us eat and drink, for tomorrow we die."

33. Do not be misled: "Bad company corrupts good character."

34. Come back to your senses as you ought, and

mwaira emabi, bushi bauma mu mwabo bateshi Ongo. Ekubabura batcha, siri honyi senyu.

35. Si kulyi mango mundju angabusa mbu: "kute ebafu bakoomwoka? Na Mubiri mutchiye ibakoomwokana?"

36. Eu mbuta! Mango wende wainga embuto, ei mbuta itangamera itasakufa tanga.

37. Kandji tcha wende wainga, atatchula emwaka ola ungamera, si wainga endjimi. Ei ndjimi ingaba ya bulo nesi ndjimi ya indji mbuto.

38. Tchasinda, Ongo ende aeresai ehuhi ngokwa yeine aisimire. Ende eeresa tchira ndjimi elyai huhi.

39. Emibiri ya byoshi bya byabumbwaa itchula irenzenye. Ebandju batchusa wabo mubiri, ne nyama sanaata wabo, ne milonge yanaata wabo, nefi sanaata wabo.

40. Kutchula mibiri yokwa nguba ne mibiri yomuno butala. Emibiri yokwa nguba itchusa bwabo bulangare, nemibiri yomuno butala, nai yanaata bwabo bulangare.

마이라 어마비, 부씨 바우마 무 먀보 바더씨 오꼬. 어구바부라 바짜, 시리 호니 서뉴.

35. 시 구레 마꼬 무뚜 아까부사 뿌: "구더 어바푸 바고오모가? 나 무비리 무찌여 이바고오모가나?"

36. 어우 뿌다! 마꼬 워떠 와이까 어뿌도, 어이 뿌다 이다까머라 이다사구파 다까.

37. 가찌 짜 워떠 와이까, 아다쭈라 어마가 오라 우까머라, 시 와이까 어찌미. 어이 찌미 이까바 야 부로 너시 찌미 야 이찌 뿌도.

38. 짜시따, 오꼬 어떠 아어러사이 어후히 꼬과 여이너 아이시미러. 어떠 어어러사 찌라 찌미 어랴이 후히.

39. 어미비리 야 뵤씨 뱌 뱌부빠아 이쭈라 이러써녀. 어바뉴 바쭈사 와보 무비리, 너 냐마 사나아다 와보, 너 미로꺼 야나아다 와보, 너피 사나아다 와보.

40. 구쭈짜 미비리 요과 우바 너 미비리 요무노 부다짜. 어미비리 요과 우바 이쭈사 뵤보 부라까러, 너미비리 요무노 부다짜, 나이 야나아다 뵤보 부라까러.

stop sinning; for there are some who are ignorant of God--I say this to your shame.

35. But someone may ask, "How are the dead raised? With what kind of body will they come?"

36. How foolish! What you sow does not come to life unless it dies.

37. When you sow, you do not plant the body that will be, but just a seed, perhaps of wheat or of something else.

38. But God gives it a body as he has determined, and to each kind of seed he gives its own body.

39. All flesh is not the same: Men have one kind of flesh, animals have another, birds another and fish another.

40. There are also heavenly bodies and there are earthly bodies; but the splendor of the heavenly bodies is one kind, and the splendor of the earthly bodies is another.

41. Esuba lyitchusa bwai bulangare, ne mwesi anaata bwai, ne ngunuru nasi sanaata bwabo. Na tchira ngunuru inatchusa ebwai bulangare.

42. Rero, ekoomwoka ku kukanaba batcha. Mango emubiri atchabwa, ende aba alyi wakubola, si mango ende aomwolibwa, ende aba atatchiri wakubola.

43. Ende achabwa mwa kukenyibwa, si ende oomwoka mwe tchunda. Kandji ende atchabwa mwa kukenyibwa, ende oomwolyibwa ete misi

44. Ende atchabwa alyi mubiri wa mundju, si ende oomwolyibwa, era mubiri ola weeresibwe ekalamo kurengera eMutchima Mubuya-buya. Kulyi emubiri we mundju, kwanaba ne mubiri ola weeresibwe ekalamo kurengera eMutchima Mubuya-buya.

45. Bushi bitchula byaandjikirwe mwa Maandjiko Mabuya-buya mbu: "Emundju muberebere, Atamu abaa mundju ola weete kalamo"Si"Atamu musinda sinda", i Mutchima, ola wende weeresa abandju ekalamo.

41. 어수바 레쭈사 봐이 부롸까러, 너 뭐시 아나아다 봐이, 너 우누누 나시 사나아다 봐보. 나 찌라 우누누 이나쭈사 어봐이 부롸까러.

42. 러로, 어고오모가 구 구가나바 바짜. 마꼬 어무비리 아짜봐, 어너 아바 아레 와구보롸, 시 마꼬 어너 아오모릐봐, 어너 아바 아다찌리 와구보롸.

43. 어너 아짜봐 마 구거네봐, 시 어너 오오모가 뭐 쭈따. 가찌 어너 아짜봐 마 구거네봐, 어너 오오모레봐 어더 미시

44. 어너 아짜봐 아레 무비리 와 무뚜, 시 어너 오오모레봐, 어라 무비리 오롸 워어러시붸 어가꽈모 구러꺼라 어무찌마 무부야-부야. 구레 어무비리 워 무뚜, 과나바 너 무비리 오롸 워어러시붸 어가꽈모 구러꺼라 어무찌마 무부야-부야.

45. 부씨 비쭈롸 뱌아찌기뤄 마 마아찌고 마부야-부야 뿌: "어무뚜 무버러버러, 아다무 아바아 무뚜 오롸 워어더 가꽈모"시"아다무 무시따 시따", 이 무찌마, 오롸 워어러사 아바뉴 어가꽈모.

41. The sun has one kind of splendor, the moon another and the stars another; and star differs from star in splendor.

42. So will it be with the resurrection of the dead. The body that is sown is perishable, it is raised imperishable;

43. it is sown in dishonor, it is raised in glory; it is sown in weakness, it is raised in power;

44. it is sown a natural body, it is raised a spiritual body. If there is a natural body, there is also a spiritual body.

45. So it is written: "The first man Adam became a living being"; the last Adam, a life-giving spirit.

46. Emubiri ola weeresibwe ekalamo kurengera eMutchima Mubuya-buya, ata iwatangiraa-kubao, si mubiri we mundju iwatangiraa. Tchasinda, emubiri ola weeresibwe ekalamo kurengera eMutchima Mubuya-buya, nao era kwire aba'o.

46. 어무비리 오꽈 워어러시붜 어가꽈모 구러꺼라 어무찌마 무부야-부야, 아다 이와다삐라아 구바오, 시 무비리 워 무뚜 이와다삐라아. 짜시따, 어무비리 오꽈 워어러시붜 어가꽈모 구러꺼라 어무찌마 무부야-부야, 나오 어라 귀러 아바오.

46. The spiritual did not come first, but the natural, and after that the spiritual.

47. Emundju muberebere abumbwaa mwa butaka, kandji abalyi we butala. Si emundju wa kabiri, yeke atengaa kwa nguba.

47. 어무뚜 무버러버러 아부꽈아 뫄 부다가, 가찌 아바레 워 부다꽈. 시 어무뚜 와 가비리, 여거 아더꽈아 과 꾸바.

47. The first man was of the dust of the earth, the second man from heaven.

48. Ebandju be butala, batchula bauhire ola wabumbwaa mwabutaka, nebandju bokwa nguba batchula bauhire ola watengaa kwa nguba

48. 어바뚜 버 부다라, 바쭈꽈 바우히러 오꽈 와부꽈아 꽈부다가, 너바뚜 보과 꾸바 바쭈꽈 바우히러 오꽈 와더꽈아 과 꾸바

48. As was the earthly man, so are those who are of the earth; and as is the man from heaven, so also are those who are of heaven.

49. Rero ngokwa tchutchula tchuuhire oyu mundju wabumbwaa mwa butaka, kunoku ku tchukanauha ola watengaa kwa nguba.

49. 러로 끄과 쭈쭈꽈 쭈우히러 오유 무뚜 와부꽈아 뫄 부다가, 구노구 구 쭈가나우하 오꽈 와더꽈아 과 꾸바.

49. And just as we have borne the likeness of the earthly man, so shall we bear the likeness of the man from heaven.

50. Banyaketchu, batcha kunatetchire: tchoshi tcha tchabumbwaa mwa mubiri ne mikira, tchitangangerira mwa bwami bwa Ongo. Na tchoshi tcha tchiri tche kubola tchitangaata ekalamo ke suku ne mango.

50. 바냐거쭈, 바짜 구나더찌러: 쪼씨 짜 짜부꽈아 뫄 무비리 너 미기라, 찌다꽈꺼리라 뫄 봐미 봐 오끄. 나 쪼씨 짜 찌리 쩌 구보꽈 찌다꽈아다 어가꽈모 거 수구 너 마끄.

50. I declare to you, brothers, that flesh and blood cannot inherit the kingdom of God, nor does the perishable inherit the imperishable.

51. Rero, nera bababibihulyira

51. 러로, 너라 바바비후레라

51. Listen, I tell you a

onu mwasi wabaa ubishibwe: tchuboshi tchutakafe, si tchuboshi tchukabundjulyibwa.

52. Ebyera bikaba mu bihangi byeeke, ngokwa mundju ende asiba ne kusibula elyiho mango ekaperere kasinda sinda kakabandjibwa'mo. Bushi mango kakabandjibwa'mo ebafu bakoomwoka, kandji batakatchibe ba kubola, netchu tchukabindjulibwa (kualusibwa) emibiri.

53. Bushi byeemire onu mubiri we kubola abindjulibwe kuba mubiri ola uta wekubola. Ne mubiri wekufa, byeemire abindjulibwe kuba mubiri ola uta wekufa.

54. Na mango onu mubiri we kubola akabindjulyibwa kuba ola uta wekubola, nemubiri wekufa mango akabindjulyibwa kuba ola uta wekufa, mu mango etchinwa tchikaberera tcha tchitchula tchiandjikirwe mwa Maandjiko Mabuya-buya: "Walufu asikire, aimirwe loshi?".

55."Era walufu, ekuimana kwao, ngai yi kulyi? Era walufu, ebuashi bwau bwe kuita ngai yi bulyi?"

56. Walufu ende abona

오누 똬시 와바아 우비씨붜: 쭈보씨 쭈다가퍼, 시 쭈보씨 쭈가부뉴쮀봐.

52. 어벼라 비가바 무 비하삐 벼어거, 꼬과 무뚜 어떠 아시바 너 구시부퐈 어쩨호 마꼬 어가퍼러러 가시따 시따 가가바찌봐모. 부씨 마꼬 가가바찌봐모 어바푸 바고오모가, 가찌 바다가찌버 바 구보퐈, 너쭈 쭈가비뉴쮀봐 (구아루시봐) 어미비리.

53. 부씨 벼어미러 오누 무비리 워 구보퐈 아비뉴쮀붜 구바 무비리 오퐈 우다 워구보퐈. 너 무비리 워구파, 벼어미러 아비뉴쮀붜 구바 무비리 오퐈 우다 워구파.

54. 나 마꼬 오누 무비리 워 구보퐈 아가비뉴쮀봐 구바 오퐈 우다 워구보퐈, 너무비리 워구파 마꼬 아가비뉴쮀봐 구바 오퐈 우다 워구파, 무 마꼬 어찌놔 찌가버러라 짜 쭈퐈 찌아찌기뤄 똬 마아시고 마부야-부야: "와루푸 아시기러, 아이미뤄 로씨?".

55."어라 와루푸, 어구이마나 과오, 까이 에 구쩨? 어라 와루푸, 어부아씨 봐우 붜 구이다 까이 에 부쩨?"

56. 와루푸 어떠 아보나

mystery: We will not all sleep, but we will all be changed--

52. in a flash, in the twinkling of an eye, at the last trumpet. For the trumpet will sound, the dead will be raised imperishable, and we will be changed.

53. For the perishable must clothe itself with the imperishable, and the mortal with immortality.

54. When the perishable has been clothed with the imperishable, and the mortal with immortality, then the saying that is written will come true: "Death has been swallowed up in victory."

55. "Where, O death, is your victory? Where, O death, is your sting?"

56. The sting of death is sin,

ebuashi kurengera ebibi. Nebibi byende byabona ebuashi kurengera e Mwaso.	어부아씨 구러꺼라 어비비. 너비비 벼떠 뱌보나 어부아씨 구러꺼라 어 뫄소.	and the power of sin is the law.
57. Si Ongo atongwe, bushi iwende watchuma tchwaimana kurengera Enawetchu Yesu Kirisito.	57. 시 오꼬 아도눠, 부씨 이워떠 와쭈마 쫘이마나 구러꺼라 어나워쭈 여수 기리시도.	57. But thanks be to God! He gives us the victory through our Lord Jesus Christ.
58. Bushi noku banyaketchu basiirwa, musimikaa busese busira kulyiya-lyiya. Muendekeraa era muhondo mwa kukorera Enawetchu esuku soshi, bushi mwishi kwe malyibuko ma mwalola'ko bushi nai, matakafe buha.	58. 부씨 노구 바냐거쭈 바시이롸, 무시미가아 부서서 부시라 구레야-레야. 무어떠거라아 어라 무호또 뫄 구고러라 어나워쭈 어수구 소씨, 부씨 뮈씨 궈 마레부고 마 뫄롸고 부씨 나이, 마다가퍼 부하.	58. Therefore, my dear brothers, stand firm. Let nothing move you. Always give yourselves fully to the work of the Lord, because you know that your labor in the Lord is not in vain.

1 E Bakorinto Chikono 16	**1 어 바고리또 찌고노 16**	**1 Corinthians Chapter 16 [NIV]**
1. Rero, bushi ne muholore we kuasa e bandju ba Ongo bomwa musi we Yerusalemu, nenyu munairaa ngokwa naburaa ebemeresi bomwa tchio tche Kataliya.	1. 러로, 부씨 너 무호롸러 워 구아사 어 바쭈 바 오꼬 보뫄 무시 워 여루사꺼무, 너뉴 무나이라아 꼬과 나부라아 어버머러시 보뫄 찌오 쩌 가다리야.	1. Now about the collection for God's people: Do what I told the Galatian churches to do.
2. Tchira lweinga, tchira muuma mu mwabo emire kunde abika mwango kwa bikulo byai, kukulyikana nokwa abonaa. Mwa batcha mango nyingaika, kutatchibe myasi ya kuholosa.	2. 찌라 뤄이꺄, 찌라 무우마 무 뫄보 어미러 구떠 아비가 뫄꼬 과 비구로 뱌이, 구구레가나 노과 아보나아. 뫄 바짜 마꼬 네꺄이가, 구다찌버 먀시 야 구호롸사.	2. On the first day of every week, each one of you should set aside a sum of money in keeping with his income, saving it up, so that when I come no collections will have to be made.
3. Mango nyingaika, nyingeesa ebandju ba mungaba mwalondore emaruba kwa	3. 마꼬 네꺄이가, 네꺼어사 어바쭈 바 무까바 뫄롸또러 어마루바 과 궈어거	3. Then, when I arrive, I will give letters of introduction to the men you approve and

kweeke emuholore wenyu e Yerusalemu.

4. Akaba kukomire nanyi nyiiye'yi, bangabalama alauma nanyi

5. Nyingaika eyi mwenyu mango nyingaba natengire eMaketoniya, bushi eyi Maketoniya yi nahonda nyirengere.

6. Kulyi mango nyingamala suku burebe alauma nenyu, nesi nyinganarenzesa esuku soshi se mbeo eyi mwenyu, tchasiya munyiase nyiendekere ne lubalama lwanyi.

7. Ndahonda nyibalole'ko mwa kunaulukana oshaao. Bushi nyeete munyiiro kwa nyingamala suku burebe alauma nenyu, akaba Enawetchu ahondjire.

8. Si nyitchiri muno musi we Efeso, kuikira lwa lusuku lukulu lwe Pendekosite.

9. Bushi mwonu misi, Ongo anyiboorere endjira ye kukola mulyimo munene, tchiro angaba mbu ebarenda balyi banene.

10. Timoteo akaika eyi mwenyu, Mutchisesaa kumuhuukasa kubuya, bushi nai endjire anakola emulyimo

어무호로러 워뉴 어 여루사러무.

4. 아가바 구고미러 나내 네이여에, 바까바짜마 아짜우마 나내

5. 네까이가 어에 뭐뉴 마꼬 네까바 나더끼러 어마거도니야, 부씨 어에 마거도니야 에 나호따 네러꺼러.

6. 구레 마꼬 네까마짜 수구 부러버 아짜우마 너뉴, 너시 네까나러써사 어수구 소씨 서 뼤오 어에 뭐뉴, 짜시야 무네아서 네어떠거러 너 루바짜마 꽈내.

7. 따호따 네바로꺼러고 꽈 구나우루가나 오싸아오. 부씨 녀어더 무네이로 과 네까마짜 수구 부러버 아짜우마 너뉴, 아가바 어나워쭈 아호찌러.

8. 시 네찌리 무노 무시 워 어퍼소, 구이기라 꽈 루수구 루구루 뤄 퍼더고시더.

9. 부씨 모누 미시, 오꼬 아네보오러러 어찌라 여 구고꽈 무쩨모 무너너, 찌로 아까바 뿌 어바러따 바쩨 바너너.

10. 디모더오 아가이가 어에 뭐뉴, 무찌서사아 구무후우가사 구부야, 부씨 나이 어찌러 아나고꽈

send them with your gift to Jerusalem.

4. If it seems advisable for me to go also, they will accompany me.

5. After I go through Macedonia, I will come to you--for I will be going through Macedonia.

6. Perhaps I will stay with you awhile, or even spend the winter, so that you can help me on my journey, wherever I go.

7. I do not want to see you now and make only a passing visit; I hope to spend some time with you, if the Lord permits.

8. But I will stay on at Ephesus until Pentecost,

9. because a great door for effective work has opened to me, and there are many who oppose me.

10. If Timothy comes, see to it that he has nothing to fear while he is with you, for he is carrying on the work

wa Enawetchu kuuma nanyi.

어무뤠모 와 어나워쭈 구우마 나니.

of the Lord, just as I am.

11. Kutabaa tchiro na mundju asibya ola umukenaa! Si kumuasa kumumuasaa aendekere ne lubalamo lwai mwa boolo tchasiya afuluke eni nyiri. Bushi nyonu, alauma na banyaketchu bemeresi tchwamulyindjira.

11. 구다바아 찌로 나 무쭈 아시뱌 오롸 우무거나아! 시 구무아사 구무무아사아 아어떠거러 너 루바라모 롸이 뫄 보오롣 짜시야 아푸루거 어니 니리. 부씨 뇨누, 아롸우마 나 바냐거쭈 버머러시 쫘무뤠찌라.

11. No one, then, should refuse to accept him. Send him on his way in peace so that he may return to me. I am expecting him along with the brothers.

12. Rero bushi ne myasi era yerekere munyaketchu Apolo, namwemaa buses embu ayaa eyi mwenyu alauma ne bandji banyaketchu bemeresi. Si atahonda kuya eyera mwakanu kabiri. Atchiri ahonda mango angabona abihangi.

12. 러로 부씨 너 먀시 어라 여러거러 무냐거쭈 아포롣, 나뭐마아 부서수 어뿌 아야아 어에 뭐뉴 아롸우마 너 바찌 바냐거쭈 버머러시. 시 아다호따 구야 어여라 뫄가누 가비리. 아찌리 아호따 마꼬 아꽈보나 아비하끼.

12. Now about our brother Apollos: I strongly urged him to go to you with the brothers. He was quite unwilling to go now, but he will go when he has the opportunity.

13. Mundaa mwatchilanga langa ne kusimika busese mwa bwemeresi. Kandji mundaa mwatchisimba nga balume na kuata emisi.

13. 무따아 뫄찌롸꺄 롸꺄 너 구시미가 부서서 뫄 뭐머러시. 가찌 무따아 뫄찌시빠 꺄 바루머 나 구아다 어미시.

13. Be on your guard; stand firm in the faith; be men of courage; be strong.

14. Mundaa mwaira byoshi mwa nzii.

14. 무따아 뫄이라 뵤씨 뫄 씨이.

14. Do everything in love.

15. Si mwishi kwa mwa tchio tchoshi tche Akaya, Sitafanasi alauma na besha mwa mwai bu babaaa beberebere kweemerera Kirisito. Kandji bende batchiana kwa kukorera ebandju ba Ongo. Bushi noku banyaketchu, nabeema busese,

15. 시 뮈씨 과 뫄 찌오 쪼씨 쩌 아가야, 시다파나시 아롸우마 나 버싸 뫄 뫄이 부 바바아아 버버러버러 궈어머러라 기리시도. 가찌 버떠 바찌아나 과 구고러라 어바쭈 바 오꼬. 부씨 노구 바냐거쭈, 나버어마 부서서,

15. You know that the household of Stephanas were the first converts in Achaia, and they have devoted themselves to the service of the saints. I urge you, brothers,

16. mundaa mwatchunda ebandju ba balyi nga'bu. Mundaa mwatchunda ne bandji boshi ba bendjire bakola busese alauma nabo.

17. Namoire busese bushi nekuika kwa Sitefanasi na Foritunato, na Akaiko. Abu bandju baire mwetchwe lyenyu kwa kunyiasa.

18. Bushi banyisesise emutchima ngokwa nenyu banabasesaa'o. Rero, ebandju ba balyi ngabano, mundaa mwemenyerera emufa wabo.

19. Ebemeresi bomwa tchio tche Asiya babalamusise. Akila na Purisila, alauma ne bemeresi ba bendjire babwaanana mwa mabu, nabu babalamusise kwe sina lya Enawetchu.

20. Banyaketchu bemeresi boshi ba balyi anola, nabu babalamusise. Mulamusanyaa mwa kuoberana nga bauma.

21. Eni myasi yekubalamusa, nyono Paolo nyi nabaandjikirire'i ne mino yanyi nyeine.

22. Akaba mundju murebe atatchula asimire Enawetchu, afe (ataata boolo). Maranatha Enawetchu ubahaa.

23. Enawetchu Yesu endaa

16. 무따아 먀쭈따 어바뉴 바 바쩨 따부. 무따아 먀쭈따 너 바찌 보씨 바 버찌러 바고꽈 부서서 아꽈우마 나보.

17. 나모이러 부서서 부씨 너구이가 과 시더파나시 나 포리두나도, 나 아가이고. 아부 바뉴 바이러 뭐쭤 쪄뉴 과 구네아사.

18. 부씨 바네서시서 어무찌마 꼬과 너뉴 바나바서사아오. 러로, 어바뉴 바 바쩨 따바노, 무따아 뭐머녀러라 어무파 와보.

19. 어버머러시 보꽈 찌오 쩌 아시야 바바꽈무시서. 아기꽈 나 푸리시꽈, 아꽈우마 너 버머러시 바 버찌러 바봐아나나 먀 마부, 나부 바바꽈무시서 궈 시나 꺄 어나워쭈.

20. 바냐거쭈 버머러시 보씨 바 바쩨 아노꽈, 나부 바바꽈무시서. 무꽈무사냐아 먀 구오버라나 따 바우마.

21. 어니 먀시 여구바꽈무사, 뇨노 파오뢴 네 나바아찌기리러이 너 미노 야네 녀이너.

22. 아가바 무뚜 무러버 아다쭈꽈 아시미러 어나워쭈, 아퍼 (아다아다 보오뢴). 마라나따 어나워쭈 우바하아.

23. 어나워쭈 여수 어따아

16. to submit to such as these and to everyone who joins in the work, and labors at it.

17. I was glad when Stephanas, Fortunatus and Achaicus arrived, because they have supplied what was lacking from you.

18. For they refreshed my spirit and yours also. Such men deserve recognition.

19. The churches in the province of Asia send you greetings. Aquila and Priscilla greet you warmly in the Lord, and so does the church that meets at their house.

20. All the brothers here send you greetings. Greet one another with a holy kiss.

21. I, Paul, write this greeting in my own hand.

22. If anyone does not love the Lord--a curse be on him. Come, O Lord!

23. The grace of the Lord

abaahanyira

24. Nyibasimire muboshi kurengera ebuuma bwetchu na Yesu Kiristo.

아바아하네라

24. 네바시미러 무보씨 구러꺼라 어부우마 붸쭈 나 여수 기리시도.

Jesus be with you.

24. My love to all of you in Christ Jesus. Amen.

2 E Bakorinto

2 어 바고리또

2 Corinthians

E BAKORINDO BA KABIRI
(2 CORINTHIANS)

어 바고리또 바 가비리
(2 고리띠아쭈)

2 E Bakorinto Chikono 1

1. Paulo ndjumwa wa Yesu kirisitonkwa kuhonda kwa Ongo, na Timoteo munyeketchu kwa luhu lwa Ongo lwalulyi mwa Korindo, alauma ne babuyabuya boshi babalyi mwa tchiuo tchoshi tche Akaya.

2. O mwisha abaa alauma nenyu ne buolo kutenga era mwa Kabumbi Tata mwetchu na Enawetchu Yesu Kirisito.

3. Kabumbi atongwe, Enawabo Enawetchu Yesu Kirisito, Tata we bubabalyire, Ongo we lumoo loshi.

4. Uutchuwere e lumo mwa malyibuko metchu moshi lyi netchu tchuase babalyi mwa malyibuko ma tchira mbinda ekubona e lumoo, koluno lumoo tchweereswaa na Ongo.

5. kwa boshi kula e malyibuko ma Yesu Kirisito marengeresisi era mwetchu kune lumoo lwetchu lungalorekana'ko kurengera endjira ya Kirisito.

6. Si akaba tchubano tchulyi

2 어 바고리또 찌고노 1

1. 파우론 ㄴ쭈똬 와 여수 기리시도똬 구호따 과 오꼬, 나 디모더오 무녀거쭈 과 루후 똬 오꼬 똬루꿰 똬 고리또, 아똬우마 너 바부야부야 보씨 바바꿰 똬 찌우오 쪼씨 쩌 아가야.

2. 오 뮈싸 아바아 아똬우마 너뉴 너 부오론 구더따 어라 똬 가부뻬 다다 뭐쭈 나 어나워쭈 여수 기리시도.

3. 가부뻬 아도워, 어나와보 어나워쭈 여수 기리시도, 다다 워 부바바꿰러, 오꼬 워 루모오 론씨.

4. 우우쭈워러 어 루모 똬 마꿰부고 머쭈 모씨 꿰 너쭈 쭈아서 바바꿰 똬 마꿰부고 마 찌라 뻬따 어구보나 어 루모오, 고루노 루모오 쭤어러솨아 나 오꼬.

5. 과 보씨 구똬 어 마꿰부고 마 여수 기리시도 마러따러시시 어라 뭐쭈 루모오 뭐쭈 루따로러가나고 구러따라 어찌라 야 기리시도.

6. 시 아가바 쭈바노 쭈꿰 똬

2 Corinthians Chapter 1 [NIV]

1. Paul, an apostle of Christ Jesus by the will of God, and Timothy our brother, To the church of God in Corinth, together with all the saints throughout Achaia:

2. Grace and peace to you from God our Father and the Lord Jesus Christ.

3. Praise be to the God and Father of our Lord Jesus Christ, the Father of compassion and the God of all comfort,

4. who comforts us in all our troubles, so that we can comfort those in any trouble with the comfort we ourselves have received from God.

5. For just as the sufferings of Christ flow over into our lives, so also through Christ our comfort overflows.

6. If we are distressed, it is

mwa malyibuko, iri kwa bushi ne lumoo lwenyu elwaira emikolo yayi ne bushibirisi bwe malyibuko amola moola tchwalolaa'ko.

7. Ebulangalyire bwetchu kwa bushi nenyu bweemangire busira kushiula alauma ne kumenya kwa Ongo kula ebaanda bamu malyibuko noku mwanabere baanda be lumoo

8. Kwa bushi munyetchu, tchutahonda mutamenyaa emwaasi we malyibuko malatchwalolaa'ko mwa Azia. Kwa bushi thwalyibukire busese kurengera emisi yetchu, kuikira kwa bihangi bwe kuisha emitchinyiiro ye kulama.

9. Naam, tchubeeru thwabaa tchweete ebutchindjibusi bwelufu mwamitchima yetchu yoshi lyi tchuta tchilangalyiraa mwa mitchima yetchu, si tchulangalyiraa Ongo, muomosi we birunda.

10. Emununusi wetchu kutenga mwebi birunda, kandji anganatchununula kandji tchulangalyire kwa atchiri akanatchununula.

마레부고, 이리 과 부씨 너 루모오 뤄뉴 어꽈이라 어미고로 야에 너 부씨비리시 뷔 마레부고 아모꽈 모오꽈 쫘로꽈아고.

7. 어부꽈ퟁ레러 뷔쭈 과 부씨 너뉴 뷔어마삐러 부시라 구씨우꽈 아꽈우마 너 구머냐 과 오끄 구꽈 어바아따 바무 마레부고 노구 모나버러 바아따 버 루모오

8. 과 부씨 무녀쭈, 쭈다호따 무다머냐아 어꽈아시 워 마레부고 마꽈쫘로꽈아고 꽈 아지아. 과 부씨 쫘레부기러 부서서 구러ퟁ라 어미시 여쭈, 구이기라 과 비하삐 뷔 구이싸 어미찌네이로 여 구꽈마.

9. 나아무, 쭈버어루 쫘바아 쭤어더 어부찌찌부시 뷔루푸 마미찌마 여쭈 요씨 레 쭈다 찌꽈ퟁ레라아 꽈 미찌마 여쭈, 시 쭈꽈ퟁ레라아 오끄, 무오모시 워 비루따.

10. 어무누누시 워쭈 구더ퟁ 뮈비 비루따, 가찌 아ퟁ나쭈누누꽈 가찌 쭈꽈ퟁ레러 과 아찌리 아가나쭈누누꽈.

for your comfort and salvation; if we are comforted, it is for your comfort, which produces in you patient endurance of the same sufferings we suffer.

7. And our hope for you is firm, because we know that just as you share in our sufferings, so also you share in our comfort.

8. We do not want you to be uninformed, brothers, about the hardships we suffered in the province of Asia. We were under great pressure, far beyond our ability to endure, so that we despaired even of life.

9. Indeed, in our hearts we felt the sentence of death. But this happened that we might not rely on ourselves but on God, who raises the dead.

10. He has delivered us from such a deadly peril, and he will deliver us. On him we have set our hope that he will continue to deliver us,

11. Nenyu mwendjire mwatchwaasa kwa lweemo, mwa batcha, angende aakula elwemo lwa lwairwaa ne bandju banene bushi netchu, ne kutchwiirira emabuya. Aola, bandju banene bangatonga Ongo bushi netchu.

12. Tchubano emyasi tchwendjire tchwatchitongera, ne mitchima yetchu yalosa kwa inalyi ya kananagana yeene: Tchwabaa tchwendjire tchwatchitola mwa bandju, tanga mwa katchikatchi kenyu ne mutchima we burembi, kandji kwa butchungenene bwokutenga era mwa Ongo. Enyera byabaa bitatenganyire na bwenge bwa mundju, si byabaa bitenganyire ne bondjo bwa Ongo.

13. Mwa maruba metchu, tchwendjire tchwabaandjikira emyaasi era mwa soma ne kuunva oshaao. Nyeete mutchinyiiro kwa munganomva ene myaasi kubuyabuya.

14. Bushi mwonvire'i bimbi-imbi, ne myaasi iyene: Elusuku lwa Enawetchu akafuluka, mukatchitonga bushi netchu, netchu tchwanatchitonga bushi nenyu.

11. 너뉴 뭐찌러 마좌아사 과 뭐어모, 뫄 바짜, 아어떠 아아구꽈 어뭐모 뫄 꽈이롸아 너 바뚜 바너너 부씨 너쭈, 너 구쮜이리라 어마부야. 아오꽈, 바뚜 바너너 바아도꽈 오꼬 부씨 너쭈.

12. 쭈바노 어먀시 쮜찌러 좌찌도어라, 너 미찌마 여쭈 야로사 과 이나께 야 가나나가나 여어너: 좌바아 쮜찌러 좌찌도꽈 뫄 바뚜, 다꽈 뫄 가찌가찌 거뉴 너 무찌마 워 부러삐, 가찌 과 부쭈어너너 보구더꽈 어라 뫄 오꼬. 어녀라 뱌바아 비다더꽈네러 나 뭐어 뫄 무뚜, 시 뱌바아 비더꽈네러 너 보쪼 뫄 오꼬.

13. 뫄 마루바 머쭈, 쮜찌러 좌바아찌기라 어먀아시 어라 뫄 소마 너 구우빠 오싸아오. 녀어더 무찌네이로 과 무꽈노빠 어너 먀아시 구부야부야.

14. 부씨 몬삐러이 비삐-이삐, 너 먀아시 이여너: 어루수구 꽈 어나워쭈 아가푸루가, 무가찌도꽈 부씨 너쭈, 너쭈 좌나찌도꽈 부씨 너뉴.

11. as you help us by your prayers. Then many will give thanks on our behalf for the gracious favor granted us in answer to the prayers of many.

12. Now this is our boast: Our conscience testifies that we have conducted ourselves in the world, and especially in our relations with you, in the holiness and sincerity that are from God. We have done so not according to worldly wisdom but according to God's grace.

13. For we do not write you anything you cannot read or understand. And I hope that,

14. as you have understood us in part, you will come to understand fully that you can boast of us just as we will boast of you in the day of the Lord Jesus.

15. Nabaa nyishi eyi myaasi kubuya-buya. Bushi noku, nabaa nahonda nyike tanga eyi mwenyu, tchasiya mwaahanyirwe ebwakabiri.

16. No'mwakutenga eyi wenyu nyingaire e Maketoniya, tchasinda mwakutenga E Maketoniya, nyingahubire kurenga eyi mwenyu tchasiya munyiase kwa byanyilaire'ko mwa lubalamo lwe'kuya e Yuteya.

17. Rero mango natolaa eyi myaanyisa, nabaa ndaserire mui? Nesi, mango natolaa e lwangolurebe, nende nakoresa bwenge bwa bandju, kuikira nemerera nesi na nanaa e myaasi kutchihangi tchiuma?

18. Na Ongo aneeshi kanangana kwa emyaasi era tchwababuraa itabaa ya kwemerera nesi kunana ku tchihangi tchiuma.

19. Bushi Yesu Kirisito, e Mwana wa Ongo ola nyono, na Sirifano, na Timoteo tchwabahubanganyisaa ataikaa kwa kunde emeerera na kunana ku tchihangi tchiuma. Si anatchula wa kweemerera.

20. Bushi kurengera Yesu, ku

---

15. 나바아 네씨 어에 먀아시 구부야-부야. 부씨 노구, 나바아 나호따 네거 다까 어에 뭐뉴, 짜시야 롸아하니뤄 어봐가비리.

16. 노꽈구더까 어에 워뉴 네까이러 어 마거도니야, 짜시따 롸구더까 어 마거도니야, 네까후비러 구러까 어에 뭐뉴 짜시야 무네아서 과 뱌네롸이러고 롸 루바롸모 뤄구야 어 유더야.

17. 러로 마꼬 나도롸아 어에 먀아네사, 나바아 따서리러 무이? 너시, 마꼬 나도롸아 어 롸꼬루러버, 너떠 나고러사 뭐떠 봐 바뚜, 구이기라 너머러라 너시 나 나나아 어 먀아시 구찌하께 찌우마?

18. 나 오꼬 아너어씨 가나까나 과 어먀아시 어라 쫘바부라아 이다바아 야 궈머러라 너시 구나나 구 찌하께 찌우마.

19. 부씨 여수 기리시도, 어 롸나 와 오꼬 오롸 뇨노, 나 시리파노, 나 디모더오 쫘바후바까네사아 아다이가아 과 구떠 어머어러라 나 구나나 구 찌하께 찌우마. 시 아나쭈롸 와 궈어머러라.

20. 부씨 구러꺼라 여수, 구

---

15. Because I was confident of this, I planned to visit you first so that you might benefit twice.

16. I planned to visit you on my way to Macedonia and to come back to you from Macedonia, and then to have you send me on my way to Judea.

17. When I planned this, did I do it lightly? Or do I make my plans in a worldly manner so that in the same breath I say, "Yes, yes" and "No, no"?

18. But as surely as God is faithful, our message to you is not "Yes" and "No."

19. For the Son of God, Jesus Christ, who was preached among you by me and Silas and Timothy, was not "Yes" and "No," but in him it has always been "Yes."

20. For no matter how many

Ongo ende aira byoshi bya atchulaanyaa. Rero, kurengera Yesu Kirisito, kutchwende tchwateta mbu: "bibe batcha", kwa kweeresa Ongo etchunda.

21. Tchubano alauma nenyu, Ongo yeine wende watchweeresa emisi ye'kusimika mwabuuma bwetchu na Kirisito. Kandji Ongo iwatchulondolaa.

22. Na kutchubika kwe kalorero kakola kwe tchulyi bandju bayi. Abikire ne mutchima mubuya-buya mwa ndanda setchu, abe tchikindja tche bindju bya atchula atchubikirire.

23. nyono nalaisise era muhondo sa Ongo, akaba nafula bisha anyiitaa. Natolaa kwa kukomire eyi Korindon bushi ne'kubafira e bondjo.

24. Tchutahonda kubatchitchika emyaasi era mweemire kweemerera, bushi musimikire kwa bwemeresi. Si tchwahonda kukola alauma nenyu tchasiya munde mwamowa.

2 E Bakorinto Chikono 2

1. Nyono natolaa kwa

오꼬 어떠 아이라 뵤씨 뱌 아쭈꽈아나야아. 러로, 구러떠라 여수 기리시도, 구쭤떠 쫘더다 뿌: "비버 바짜", 과 궈어러사 오꼬 어쭈따.

21. 쭈바노 아꽈우마 너뉴, 오꼬 여이너 워떠 와쭤어러사 어미시 여구시미가 뫄부우마 뷔쭈 나 기리시도. 가찌 오꼬 이와쭈론도꽈아.

22. 나 구쭈비가 궈 가로러로 가고꽈 궈 쭈레 바뉴 바에. 아비기러 너 무찌마 무부야- 부야 뫄 따따 서쭈, 아버 찌기꽈 쩌 비뉴 뱌 아쭈꽈 아쭈비기리러.

23. 뇨노 나꽈이시서 어라 무호또 사 오꼬, 아가바 나푸꽈 비싸 아녜이다아. 나도꽈아 과 구고미러 어에 고리또누 부씨 너구바피라 어 보쏘.

24. 쭈다호따 구바찌찌가 어먀아시 어라 뭐어미러 궈어머러라, 부씨 무시미기러 과 뷔머러시. 시 쫘호따 구고꽈 아꽈우마 너뉴 짜시야 무떠 뫄모와.

2 어 바고리또 찌고노 2

1. 뇨노 나도꽈아 과

---

promises God has made, they are "Yes" in Christ. And so through him the "Amen" is spoken by us to the glory of God.

21. Now it is God who makes both us and you stand firm in Christ. He anointed us,

22. set his seal of ownership on us, and put his Spirit in our hearts as a deposit, guaranteeing what is to come.

23. I call God as my witness that it was in order to spare you that I did not return to Corinth.

24. Not that we lord it over your faith, but we work with you for your joy, because it is by faith you stand firm.

2 Corinthians Chapter 2 [NIV]

1. So I made up my mind

kutakomire nyihube kurengera eyi mwenyu, nyingesha kubasibusa.

2. Bushi nyikabasibusa, inde iungatchuma nahuba kubona elumoo akaba ata mwabo mu nasibusaa?

3. Rero, etchera tchi tchatchumaa nabaandjikira bushi nabaa ndahonda mbu mwa kuika eyi mwenyu munyisibuse, noku mu mwabaa mungatchuma naata elumoo, bushi nyineshi kanangana kwa mango nyiri mwa lumoo, nenyu eri munalyi mwa lumoo.

4. Kubinalyi! Mango nabaandjikiraa, nabaa nyeete businane bunene, ne mutchima wanyi abaa afunyikire busese, kandji kulyira kunabaa nalyira. Mwe'bi, nabaa ndahonda nyibasibuse, si nabaa nahonda mumenyi kwa nyibasimire busese.

5. Akaba mundju murebe angatengera ky mwai wa kusibusa eri ata nyeine nyi asibusise, si muboshi mu asibusise. No mwa kutarengeresa, eri asibusise bauma mu mwabo.

6. Oyu mundju, eemire

구다고미러 네후버 구러꺼라 어에 뭐뉴, 네꺼싸 구바시부사.

2. 부씨 네가바시부사, 이떠 이우까쭈마 나후바 구보나 어루모오 아가바 아다 뫄보 무 나시부사아?

3. 러로, 어쩌라 찌 짜쭈마아 나바아찌기라 부씨 나바아 따호따 뿌 뫄 구이가 어에 뭐뉴 무네시부서, 노구 무 뫄바아 무까쭈마 나아다 어루모오, 부씨 네너씨 가나까나 과 마꼬 네리 뫄 루모오, 너뉴 어리 무나레 뫄 루모오.

4. 구비나레! 마꼬 나바아찌기라아, 나바아 녀어더 부시나너 부너너, 너 무찌마 와네 아바아 아푸네기러 부서서, 가찌 구레라 구나바아 나레라. 뭐비, 나바아 따호따 네바시부서, 시 나바아 나호따 무머네 과 네바시미러 부서서.

5. 아가바 무뚜 무러버 아까더꺼라 게 뫄이 와 구시부사 어리 아다 녀이너 네 아시부시서, 시 무보씨 무 아시부시서. 노 뫄 구다러꺼러사, 어리 아시부시서 바우마 무 뫄보.

6. 오유 무뚜, 어어미러

that I would not make another painful visit to you.

2. For if I grieve you, who is left to make me glad but you whom I have grieved?

3. I wrote as I did so that when I came I should not be distressed by those who ought to make me rejoice. I had confidence in all of you, that you would all share my joy.

4. For I wrote you out of great distress and anguish of heart and with many tears, not to grieve you but to let you know the depth of my love for you.

5. If anyone has caused grief, he has not so much grieved me as he has grieved all of you, to some extent--not to put it too severely.

6. The punishment inflicted

kukemerwa na bandju banene mwa tchikembe tchenyu.

7. Si kungakomire kumubabalyira nakumusesa e mutchima, angesha kuesa emucthinyiiro bushi ne businane bunene.

8. Bushi noku, nabeemire busese mundaa mwalosa oyu mundju kwa mu musimire

9. Bushi tcha tchatchumaa nabaandjikira, kwabaa kuhonda nyimenye kanangana akaba muneete e mutchima we kunde mwanyitchunda mwa myaasi yoshi.

10. Mango mwababalyira mundju murebe, nanyi eri nanamubabalyire, na akaba ndababalyire kutchiri na mwaasi ola neemire kubabalyira, nanababalyira era muhondo sa Kirisito bushi neyu.

11. Mwa batcha, wa musimu atabone endjira yekutchuteba, bushi tchutchula tchwishi emyaanyisa yai.

12. Mango naikaa mwa musi we Torowa kwa kuhubanganyisa ebandju emwaasi mubuya-buya wa Kirisito, nalolaa kwa Enawetchu anyiboorere endjira inene ye kukola oyu mulyimo, mwo'yu

---

구거머롸 나 바뚜 바너너 뫄 찌거뻐 쩌뉴.

7. 시 구꽈고미러 구무바바례라 나구무서사 어 무찌마, 아꺼싸 구어사 어무찌네이로 부씨 너 부시나너 부너너.

8. 부씨 노구, 나버어미러 부서서 무따아 뫄로사 오유 무뚜 과 무 무시미러

9. 부씨 짜 짜쭈마아 나바아찌기라, 과바아 구호따 네머녀 가나꽈나 아가바 무너어더 어 무찌마 워 구꺼 꽈네쭈따 뫄 먀아시 요씨.

10. 마꼬 뫄바바례라 무뚜 무러버, 나네 어리 나나무바바례러, 나 아가바 따바바례러 구찌리 나 뫄아시 오꽈 너어미러 구바바례라, 나나바바례라 어라 무호또 사 기리시도 부씨 너유.

11. 뫄 바짜, 와 무시무 아다보너 어찌라 여구쭈더바, 부씨 쭈쭈롸 쮜씨 어먀아네사 야이.

12. 마꼬 나이가아 뫄 무시 워 도로와 과 구후바까네사 어바뚜 어뫄아시 무부야-부야 와 기리시도, 나르롸아 과 어나워쭈 아네보오러러 어찌라 이너너 여 구고꽈 오유 무레모, 모유 무시.

---

on him by the majority is sufficient for him.

7. Now instead, you ought to forgive and comfort him, so that he will not be overwhelmed by excessive sorrow.

8. I urge you, therefore, to reaffirm your love for him.

9. The reason I wrote you was to see if you would stand the test and be obedient in everything.

10. If you forgive anyone, I also forgive him. And what I have forgiven--if there was anything to forgive--I have forgiven in the sight of Christ for your sake,

11. in order that Satan might not outwit us. For we are not unaware of his schemes.

12. Now when I went to Troas to preach the gospel of Christ and found that the Lord had opened a door for me,

musi.

13. Si nabaa ndete lumoo mwa mutchima, bushi ndabuanaa munyaketchu Tito. Bushi noku, nera kulaa besha'mo, na naya mwa tchiuo tche Maketoniya.

14. Ongo atongwe, bushi iwende watchweresa e buashi bwe kuimana sohi kurengera e buuma bwetchu na Kirisito? Kandji mwa kutchurengera'ko, endjire atchuma Kirisito amenyeka mwa bisiki byoshi nga marashi ma mauka mwa bisiski byoshi.

15. Bushi tchubano tchulyi marashi ma mauka ma Kirisito atchulaa Ongo. Na'mu marashi mene maukira ebandju ba Ongo anumwire na babalyi mwa muero.

16. kwa bandju ba balyi mwa muero, e bumba bwamu marashi bulyi bwalufu, kwa kureta elufu. Si kwa ba banunulyibwe, bulyi bumba bwakalamo kwa kureta e kalamo. Rero, nde mundju ola wete ebuashi bwe'kuira'emulyimo ulyingo'yu?

17. Bushi tchubano tchutalyi nga bandji bandju banene ba bendjire baira ebutchimbusi

13. 시 나바아 떠더 루모오 와 무찌마, 부씨 따부아나아 무냐거쭈 디도. 부씨 노구, 너라 구롸아 버싸모, 나 나야 와 찌우오 쩌 마거도니야.

14. 오꼬 아도뭐, 부씨 이워떠 와쭤러사 어 부아씨 붜 구이마나 소히 구러꺼라 어 부우마 붜쭈 나 기리시도? 가찌 와 구쭈러꺼라고, 어찌러 아쭈마 기리시도 아머녀가 와 비시기 뵤씨 까 마라씨 마 마우가 와 비시기 뵤씨.

15. 부씨 쭈바노 쭈뻬 마라씨 마 마우가 마 기리시도 아쭈롸아 오꼬. 나무 마라씨 머너 마우기라 어바뉴 바 오꼬 아누뮈러 나 바바뻬 롸 무어로.

16. 과 바뉴 바 바뻬 롸 무어로, 어 부빠 봐무 마라씨 부뻬 봐루푸, 과 구러다 어루푸. 시 과 바 바누누뻬붜, 부뻬 부빠 봐가롸모 과 구러다 어 가롸모. 러로, 떠 무뉴 오롸 워더 어부아씨 붜구이라어무뻬모 우뻬꼬유?

17. 부씨 쭈바노 쭈다뻬 까 바찌 바뉴 바너너 바 버찌러 바이라 어부찌뿌시 롸 찌놔

13. I still had no peace of mind, because I did not find my brother Titus there. So I said good-by to them and went on to Macedonia.

14. But thanks be to God, who always leads us in triumphal procession in Christ and through us spreads everywhere the fragrance of the knowledge of him.

15. For we are to God the aroma of Christ among those who are being saved and those who are perishing.

16. To the one we are the smell of death; to the other, the fragrance of life. And who is equal to such a task?

17. Unlike so many, we do not peddle the word of God for profit. On the contrary,

mwa tchinwa tcha Ongo! Si bushi Ongo iwatchitchumaa, tchwendjire tchwateta ekanangana ka katenga era mwa Ongo, era muhondo sai, mwa buuma bwetchu na Kirisito.

짜 오꼬! 시 부씨 오꼬 이와쭈마아, 쭤찌러 쫘더다 어가나와나 가 가더와 어라 마 오꼬, 어라 무호또 사이, 마 부우마 붜쭈 나 기리시도.

in Christ we speak before God with sincerity, like men sent from God.

2 E Bakorinto Chikono 3

2 어 바고리또 찌고노 3

2 Corinthians Chapter 3 [NIV]

1. Eri bithcweemire kandji kunde tchwatchikangana era mulyi? nesi tchunde tchwabaretera maruba ma malosa kwa tchunalyi baanda kangana ngo'kwa ebandji bendjire baira? Nesi byemire tchunde thwabeema'mo?

1. 어리 비쭈워어미러 가찌 구떠 좌찌가마나 어라 무례? 너시 쭈너 쫘바러더라 마루바 마 마로사 과 쭈나례 바아따 가따나 끄고 어바씨 버찌러 바이라? 너시 벼미러 쭈떠 쫘버어마모?

1. Are we beginning to commend ourselves again? Or do we need, like some people, letters of recommendation to you or from you?

2. Mwaabo mu mulyi nga maruba metchu, ma maandjikirwe mwa mitchima yetchu. Amu matuba, e bandju boshi bangasoma'mu banamenya bya biri'mo.

2. 뫄아보 무 무례 따 마루바 머쭈, 마 마아찌기뤄 뫄 미찌마 여쭈. 아무 마두바, 어 바꾸 보씨 바따소마무 바나머냐 뱌 비리모.

2. You yourselves are our letter, written on our hearts, known and read by everybody.

3. Kanangana, mwabo mu mulyi nga maruba ma Kirisito aandjikaa na kumatchuma kurengera emulyimo wetchu. Amu maruba mataandjikwaa mwa bwino, si maandjikwaa kurengera e Mutchima wa Ongo ola utchula muma-uma. Amu maruba, mataandjikwaa kwa makoi ma malyi nga nyipao, si maandjikwaa mwa

3. 가나따나, 뫄보 무 무례 따 마루바 마 기리시도 아아찌가아 나 구마쭈마 구러어라 어무례모 워쭈. 아무 마루바 마다아찌과아 뫄 뷔노, 시 마아찌과아 구러어라 어 무찌마 와 오꼬 오퐈 우쭈퐈 무마-우마. 아무 마루바, 마다아찌과아 과 마고이 마 마례 따 니파오, 시 마아찌과아 뫄 미찌마 여

3. You show that you are a letter from Christ, the result of our ministry, written not with ink but with the Spirit of the living God, not on tablets of stone but on tablets of human hearts.

mitchima ye bandju.

바쭈.

4. Tchwatetchire batcha bushi ne mitchinyiiro era thweete era muhondo sa Ongo, kurengera Kirisito.

4. 쫘더찌러 바짜 부씨 너 미찌네이로 어라 쭤어더 어라 무호또 사 오꼬, 구러뻐라 기리시도.

4. Such confidence as this is ours through Christ before God.

5. Tchungateta mbu e mulyimo ola tchwakola'o kwa buashi bwetchu tchubeine, si Ongo iwendjire watchweeresa e buashi bwe kukola'o.

5. 쭈빠더다 뿌 어 무레모 오라 쫘고꽈오 과 부아씨 붜쭈 쭈버이너, 시 오꼬 이워찌러 와쭤어러사 어 부아씨 붜 구고꽈오.

5. Not that we are competent in ourselves to claim anything for ourselves, but our competence comes from God.

6. Ongo iwatchweresaa e buashi bwekuba baanda be tchilaano tchiyayaya. Netchi tchilaano, tchitatenganyire ne mwaso ola waandjikwaa, si tchitenganyire ne mutchima mubuya buya. Bushi e mwasi ola waandjikwaa ende areta elufu, si e mutchima mubuya-buya yeki ende areta e kalamo.

6. 오꼬 이와쭤러사아 어 부아씨 붜구바 바아따 버 찌라아노 찌야야야. 너찌 찌꽈아노, 찌다더따네러 너 마소 오꽈 와아씨과아, 시 찌더따네러 너 무찌마 무부야 부야. 부씨 어 마시 오꽈 와아씨과아 어떠 아러다 어루푸, 시 어 무찌마 무부야-부야 여기 어떠 아러다 어 가꽈모.

6. He has made us competent as ministers of a new covenant--not of the letter but of the Spirit; for the letter kills, but the Spirit gives life.

7. Oyu mwaso, aandjikikwaa kwa makoyi ma malyi nga nyipao ne bulangare bwa Ongo bwalangalaa mwesi suku. Ebuso bwa Musa nabo bwera kulangala kuikira etchihangi e ba Isiraeli bataalaa kumutchumbikisa era buso bushi no'bu bulangare tchiro angaba mbu bwabaa bwa bihangi byeeki. Akaba a mulyimo we mwaso ola wende wareta elufu, abaa eete bulangare bwa bulyi ngo'bu.

7. 오유 마소, 아아씨기과아 과 마고에 마 마레 따 네파오 너 부꽈라러 봐 오꼬 봐꽈따꽈아 뭐시 수구. 어부소 봐 무사 나보 붜라 구꽈따라 구이기라 어찌하띠 어 바 이시라어뤼 바다아꽈아 구무쭈뻬기사 어라 부소 부씨 노부 부꽈따러 찌로 아따바 뿌 봐바아 봐 비하띠 벼어기. 아가바 아 무레모 워 마소 오꽈 워떠 와러다 어루푸, 아바아 어어더 부꽈따러 봐 부레 꼬부.

7. Now if the ministry that brought death, which was engraved in letters on stone, came with glory, so that the Israelites could not look steadily at the face of Moses because of its glory, fading though it was,

8. Rero kute abulangalare bwe'mulyimo we'mutchima mubuya-buya, bukaba bungana?

9. Emulyimo we mwaso ola wende watchindjibusa e bandju aba eete bulangare. Rero emulyimo we mutchima mubuya-buya, ola wende watchuma a bandju batchunganane era muhondo sa Ongo, iungaata bulangare bunene busese.

10. Bushi ebulangare bwa bwalomekaa kwamira butangalyinganyisibwa ne bulangare bwa lwarero, bushi bweke burengerese

11. Akaba emyasi ye kurenga yabaa yeete bulangare, rero emyaasi ye kwerisa iyete bulangare bunene

12. Rero bushi tchweete oyu mutchinyiiro, tchwendjire tchwateta na bushiru bunene.

13. Tchubano tchutendjire tchwaira nga Musa iwendee wahukira ebuso bwai netchitambara kwa kwaangika eba Isiraeli batalolaa kwa businda bwe bulangare bwe bihangi byeke.

14. Abu ba Isiraeli bairaa e mitchima yabo kuba isibu kwa kuumva, bushi kuikira lwarero,

---

8. 러로 구더 아부꽈까꽈러 붜무레모 워무찌마 무부야-부야, 부가바 부까나?

9. 어무레모 워 마소 오꽈 워떠 와찌찌부사 어 바뉴 아바 어어더 부꽈꺼러. 러로 어무레모 워 무찌마 무부야-부야, 오꽈 워떠 와쭈마 아 바뉴 바쭈까나너 어라 무호또 사 오꼬, 이우꽈아다 부꽈꺼러 부너너 부서서.

10. 부씨 어부꽈꺼러 봐 봐로머가아 과미라 부다까레꺼네시봐 너 부꽈꺼러 봐 꽈러로, 부씨 붜거 부러꺼러서

11. 아가바 어먀시 여 구러까 야바아 여어더 부꽈꺼러, 러로 어먀아시 여 궈리사 이여더 부꽈꺼러 부너너

12. 러로 부씨 쮀어더 오유 무찌네이로, 쮀찌러 쫘더다 나 부씨루 부너너.

13. 쭈바노 쭈더찌러 쫘이라 까 무사 이워떠어 와후기라 어부소 봐이 너찌다빠라 과 과아끼가 어바 이시라어뤼 바다로꽈아 과 부시따 붜 부꽈꺼러 붜 비하끼 벼거.

14. 아부 바 이시라어뤼 바이라아 어 미찌마 야보 구바 이시부 과 구우빠, 부씨

---

8. will not the ministry of the Spirit be even more glorious?

9. If the ministry that condemns men is glorious, how much more glorious is the ministry that brings righteousness!

10. For what was glorious has no glory now in comparison with the surpassing glory.

11. And if what was fading away came with glory, how much greater is the glory of that which lasts!

12. Therefore, since we have such a hope, we are very bold.

13. We are not like Moses, who would put a veil over his face to keep the Israelites from gazing at it while the radiance was fading away.

14. But their minds were made dull, for to this day the same veil remains when

---

mango basoma ebitabu bye tchilaano tchokwa mira, e bwenge bwabo bwende bwaba bunatchiri buhukirwe mwa buso bwe mundju emango alyi mwa buuma na Kirisito.

15. Anabe kuikira lwarero, mango bende basoma ebitabu bya Musa, etchitambara tchende tchaba tchihukire e bwenge bwabo.

16. Si ngokwa bitchula biandjikirwe mwa maandjiko mabuya-buya: "mango mundju ende aalukira Enawetchu, etchitambara tchanahukulyibwa".

17. Anola, Enawetchu, i mucthima mubuya-buya. Nola mutchima wa Enawetchu alyi, eri alyi buhuru.

18. Rero tchuboshi tchu ebuso bwetchu butahukirwe, tchwende tchwalosa ebulangare bwa Enawetchu nga tchiyo. Mwa batcha, tchwende tchwa bindjulyibwa tchasiya tchuuhe Enawetchu. Aola, bwanaya mu bindju bwa bulyi bunene busese. Ebyera bi Enawetchu i Mutchima mubuya-buya ende aira.

구이기라 똭러로, 마꼬 바소마 어비다부 벼 찌롸아노 쪼과 미라, 어 붜꺼 봐보 붜떠 봐바 부나찌리 부후기뤄 똴 부소 붜 무뚜 어마꼬 아레 똴 부우마 나 기리시도.

15. 아나버 구이기라 똭러로, 마꼬 버떠 바소마 어비다부 뱌 무사, 어찌다빠라 쩌떠 짜바 찌후기러 어 붜꺼 봐보.

16. 시 꼬과 비쭈롸 비아찌기뤄 똴 마아찌고 마부야-부야: "마꼬 무뚜 어떠 아아루기라 어나워쭈, 어찌다빠라 짜나후구꿰봐".

17. 아노롸, 어나워쭈, 이 무찌마 무부야-부야. 노롸 무찌마 와 어나워쭈 아레, 어리 아레 부후루.

18. 러로 쭈보씨 쭈 어부소 붜쭈 부다후기뤄, 쮜떠 쫘로사 어부롸롸러 봐 어나워쭈 꽈 찌요. 똴 봐짜, 쮜떠 쫘 비뚜꿰봐 짜시야 쭈우허 어나워쭈. 아오롸, 봐나야 무 비뚜 봐 부꿰 부너너 부서서. 어벼라 비 어나워쭈 이 무찌마 무부야-부야 어떠 아이라.

the old covenant is read. It has not been removed, because only in Christ is it taken away.

15. Even to this day when Moses is read, a veil covers their hearts.

16. But whenever anyone turns to the Lord, the veil is taken away.

17. Now the Lord is the Spirit, and where the Spirit of the Lord is, there is freedom.

18. And we, who with unveiled faces all reflect the Lord's glory, are being transformed into his likeness with ever-increasing glory, which comes from the Lord, who is the Spirit.

2 E Bakorinto Chikono 4	2 어 바고리또 찌고노 4	2 Corinthians Chapter 4 [NIV]
1. Ongo atchweresise onu mulyimo mwa bubuya bwai. Bushi no'ku, tchutangafunyika emitchima.	1. 오ᅌᅩ 아쮜러시서 오누 무례모 뫄 부부야 봐이. 부씨 노구, 쭈다ᄢᅡ푸네가 어미찌마.	1. Therefore, since through God's mercy we have this ministry, we do not lose heart.
2. Tchwa nanyire kunde tchwaira myaasi ya bubisho-bisho, kandji era ingeeta honyi. Tchutaira myaasi ya butebanyi, kandji tchutabindjula ne'tchinwa tcha Ongo ngo'kwa tchitetchire. Si tchwendjire tchwakangirisa e bandju kubuya-buya ekanangana, tchasiya tchira mundju amenyerere mwa mutchima wai era muhondo sa Ongo, kwa tchunalyi bandju ba kutchinyiirwa.	2. 쫘 나네러 구ᄠᅥ 쫘이라 먀아시 야 부비쏘-비쏘, 가ᄡᅵ 어라 이ᄢᅥ어다 호네. 쭈다이라 먀아시 야 부더바네, 가ᄡᅵ 쭈다비ᄂᆢ쥴라 너찌놔 쨔 오ᅌᅩ ᅌᅩ과 찌더찌러. 시 쮜ᄡᅵ러 쫘가끼리사 어 바ᄂᆢ 구부야-부야 어가나까나, 쨔시야 찌라 무ᄂᆢ 아머녀러러 뫄 무찌마 와이 어라 무호또 사오ᅌᅩ, 과 쭈나례 바ᄂᆢ 바구찌네이롸.	2. Rather, we have renounced secret and shameful ways; we do not use deception, nor do we distort the word of God. On the contrary, by setting forth the truth plainly we commend ourselves to every man's conscience in the sight of God.
3. Rero akaba e mwaasi mubuya-buya ola mwendjire tchwakangirisa abishirwe, abishirwe kwa bandju ba balyi mwa ndjira ye muero.	3. 러로 아가바 어 뫄아시 무부야-부야 오ᄙᅡ 뭐ᄡᅵ러 쫘가끼리사 아비씨뤄, 아비씨뤄 과 바ᄂᆢ 바 바례 뫄 ᄡᅵ라 여 무어로.	3. And even if our gospel is veiled, it is veiled to those who are perishing.
4. Abu bandju batete bwemeresi bushi wamusimu, i Ongo wobuno butala, ahukire e bwenge bwabo ende abangika bangesha kulola kwa tchilungere tche mwaasi mubuya-buya we bulangare bwa Kirisito. Noyu Kirisito yi utchusa e huhi lya Ongo.	4. 아부 바ᄂᆢ 바더더 붜머러시 부씨 와무시무, 이 오ᅌᅩ 오부노 부다ᄙᅡ, 아후기러 어 붜ᄢᅥ 봐보 어떠 아바끼가 바ᄢᅥ싸 구ᄛᅮᄙᅡ 과 찌루ᄢᅥ러 쪄 뫄아시 무부야-부야 워 부ᄙᅡ까러 봐 기리시도. 노유 기리시도 에 우쭈사 어 후히 ᄙᅣ 오ᅌᅩ.	4. The god of this age has blinded the minds of unbelievers, so that they cannot see the light of the gospel of the glory of Christ, who is the image of God.
5. Kubiri batcha, tchutendjire	5. 구비리 바짜, 쭈더ᄡᅵ러	5. For we do not preach

tchwakangirisa e myaasi yetchu tchubeine. Si tchwendjire tchwakangirisa kwa Yesu Kirisito i Enawetchu, netchu tchunalyi baanda benyu bushi nayi.

6. Ongo atetaa mbu: "Ebulangare bulomekaa mwa musimya" Ongo ino'yu iwalomekaa mwa mitchima yetchu nakutcweresa e buashi bwe kumenyerera ebulangare bai bwa bwende bwalangala kwa buso bwa Kirisito.

7. Si tchubano tchu tchweete obu bware bwe mutchima mwa ndanda setchu, tchubwete ngabware bulyi mwa bindju bya bikunganyisibwe mwe bumba. Biri batcha, tchasiya e bandju bamenye kubuya-buya kwa tchu bwasi bwa butangalyingalanyisibwa, bwatenga era mwa Ongo, si butatenganyire netchu.

8. E bandju batchutabulyira mundjira sinene, si tchiro batcha, tchutendjire tchwaimwa. Kandji bendjire batchulyibusa busese, si tchiro batcha, tchutendjire thwaesa e mitchinyiiro.

9. Bendjire batchulyibusa, si tchiro batcha, batendjire

좌가끼리사 어 먀아시 여쭈 쭈버이너. 시 쭤찌러 좌가끼리사 과 여수 기리시도 이 어나워쭈, 너쭈 쭈나레 바아따 버뉴 부씨 나에.

6. 오꼬 아더다아 뿌: "어부롸까러 부롣머가아 마 무시먀" 오꼬 이노유 이와롣머가아 마 미찌마 여쭈 나구쭤러사 어 부아씨 붸 구머녀러라 어부롸까러 바이 봐 붸떠 봐롸까롸 과 부소 봐 기리시도.

7. 시 쭈바노 쭈 쭤어더 오부 봐러 붸 무찌마 마 따따 서쭈, 쭈붸더 까바러 부레 마 비뉴 뱌 비구까네시붸 뭐 부빠. 비리 바짜, 짜시야 어 바뉴 바머녀 구부야-부야 과 쭈 봐시 봐 부다까레까롸네시봐, 봐더까 어라 마 오꼬, 시 부다더까니러 너쭈.

8. 어 바뉴 바쭈다부레라 무찌라 시너너, 시 찌로 바짜, 쭈더찌러 좌이봐. 가찌 버찌러 바쭈레부사 부서서, 시 찌로 바짜, 쭈더찌러 좌어사 어 미찌네이로.

9. 버찌러 바쭈레부사, 시 찌로 바짜, 바더찌러 바쮜다.

---

ourselves, but Jesus Christ as Lord, and ourselves as your servants for Jesus' sake.

6. For God, who said, "Let light shine out of darkness," made his light shine in our hearts to give us the light of the knowledge of the glory of God in the face of Christ.

7. But we have this treasure in jars of clay to show that this all-surpassing power is from God and not from us.

8. We are hard pressed on every side, but not crushed; perplexed, but not in despair;

9. persecuted, but not abandoned; struck down,

but not destroyed.

batchwita.

10. Tchira lusuku tchwendjire tchweeka e malyibuko me'lufu lwa Yesu mwa mibiri yetchu mu tchira tchisiki, tchasiya ekalamo kai nako kende kalorekana'ko mwa mibiri yetchu.

10. 찌라 루수구 쮀찌러 쮀어가 어 마레부고 머루푸 콰 여수 콰 미비리 여쭈 무 찌라 찌시기, 짜시야 어가콰모 가이 나고 거머 가로러가나고 콰 미비리 여쭈.

10. We always carry around in our body the death of Jesus, so that the life of Jesus may also be revealed in our body.

11. Bushi, tchiro angaba mbu tchulyi bauma-uma, si tchira lusuku tchwendjire tchwalola kwa lufu era muhondo setchu bushi na Yesu. Byendjire byaba batcha, tchasiya ekalamo kai nako kalorekane'ko mwa mubiri wetchu we'kufa.

11. 부씨, 찌로 아까바 뿌 쮀레 바우마-우마, 시 찌라 루수구 쮀찌러 좌로라 과 루푸 어라 무호또 서쭈 부씨 나 여수. 벼찌러 뱌바 바짜, 짜시야 어가콰모 가이 나고 가로러가너고 콰 무비리 워쭈 워구파.

11. For we who are alive are always being given over to death for Jesus' sake, so that his life may be revealed in our mortal body.

12. Mwa batcha, elufu lutchuyli era muongo, na bushi noku, mwebo mwendjire mwabona ekalamo.

12. 콰 바짜, 어루푸 루쭈이릴 어라 무오꼬, 나 부씨 노구, 뭐보 뭐찌러 콰보나 어가콰모.

12. So then, death is at work in us, but life is at work in you.

13. E maandjiko mabuya-buya matetchire mbu: "neemerere, noku kweemerera kukwatchuma nateta". Rero netchu bushi tchweete obu bwemeresi, ku kwendjire kwatchuma tchwateta.

13. 어 마아찌고 마부야-부야 마더찌러 뿌: "너어머러러, 노구 궈어머러라 구과쭈마 나더다". 러로 너쭈 부씨 쮀어더 오부 붜머러시, 구 궈찌러 과쭈마 좌더다.

13. It is written: "I believed; therefore I have spoken." With that same spirit of faith we also believe and therefore speak,

14. Tchwishi kwa Ongo iwoomwolaa Enawetchu Yesu, netchu akanatchuomwola alauma na Yesu. Kandji tchubano nenyu, akatchubika era muhondo sa Yesu.

14. 쮀씨 과 오꼬 이오오몰라아 어나워쭈 여수, 너쭈 아가나쭈오몰라 아라우마 나 여수. 가찌 쭈바노 너뉴, 아가쭈비가 어라 무호또 사 여수.

14. because we know that the one who raised the Lord Jesus from the dead will also raise us with Jesus and present us with you in his presence.

15. Ebi byoshi byendjire byatchuikira bushi nenyu,

15. 어비 뵤씨 벼찌러 뱌쭈이기라 부씨 너뉴,

15. All this is for your benefit, so that the grace

tchasiya ebubuya bwa Ongo buendekere kuluwa ku bandju banene esuku soshi. Mwa batcha, bandju banene banende bateta mbu akoko era mwa Ongo kwa kulosa ebulangare bwai.

짜시야 어부부야 봐 오꼬 부어떠거러 구루와 구 바뚜 바너너 어수구 소씨. 봐 바짜, 바뚜 바너너 바너떠 바더다 뿌 아고고 어라 봐 오꼬 과 구루사 어부꽈까러 봐이.

that is reaching more and more people may cause thanksgiving to overflow to the glory of God.

16. Bushi noku, tchutendjire tchwafunyika e mutchima tchiro angaba mbu e mibiri yetchu yaenda yakunguwa, si e mitchima yetchu yendjire yairibwa kuba iya-yaya tchira lusuku.

16. 부씨 노구, 쭈더찌러 쫘푸네가 어 무찌마 찌로 아까바 뿌 어 미비리 여쭈 야어따 야구꾸와, 시 어 미찌마 여쭈 여찌러 야이리봐 구바 이야-야야 찌라 루수구.

16. Therefore we do not lose heart. Though outwardly we are wasting away, yet inwardly we are being renewed day by day.

17. E malyibuko ma tchwarenga'mo lwarero, maanguire mwa kumalyingamanya ne busito bwa butangalyingamanyisibwa bwe bulangare bwe suku ne mango, bwa matchukunganyisa.

17. 어 마레부고 마 쫘러까모 꽈러로, 마아꾸이러 봐 구마레까마냐 너 부시도 봐 부다꽈레까마네시봐 봐 부꽈러러 봐 수구 너 마꼬, 봐 마쭈구꽈네사.

17. For our light and momentary troubles are achieving for us an eternal glory that far outweighs them all.

18. Tchubano tchutabika e mianyisa yetchu kwa bindju byabiseneke'ko, si kwa bindju bya bitaseneke'ko. Bushi e bindju bya biseneke'ko, binaltchula bya bbihangi byeeke. Si ebindju bya biseneke'ko byeke, bitchula bye suku ne mango.

18. 쭈바노 쭈다비가 어 미아네사 여쭈 과 비뚜 뱌비서너거고, 시 과 비뚜 뱌 비다서너거고. 부씨 어 비뚜 뱌 비서너거고, 비나루쭈꽈 뱌 부비하삐 벼어거. 시 어비뚜 뱌 비서너거고 벼거, 비쭈꽈 벼 수구 너 마꼬.

18. So we fix our eyes not on what is seen, but on what is unseen. For what is seen is temporary, but what is unseen is eternal.

2 E Bakorinto Chikono 5	2 어 바고리또 찌고노 5	2 Corinthians Chapter 5 [NIV]
1. Kwa bushi tchushi kwa kasi enyumba ye butala ne hema lyetchu lyikahandjibwa tchweete e kaimbo kakutenga era mwa Ongo, e kaimbi kakatairirwe kwa minu ye suku ne mango ya ilyi mwa mbingu.	1. 과 부씨 쭈씨 과 가시 어뉴ᄜᅡ 여 부다ᄙᅡ 너 허마 ᄙᅧ쭈 ᄙᅦ가하ᄕᅵ봐 쭤어더 어 가이ᄜᅩ 가구더ᅌᅡ 어라 뫄 오ᅌᅩ, 어 가이ᄜᅵ 가가다이리뤄 과 미누 여 수구 너 마ᅌᅩ 야 이ᄙᅦ 뫄 ᄜᅵᅌᅮ.	1. Now we know that if the earthly tent we live in is destroyed, we have a building from God, an eternal house in heaven, not built by human hands.
2. Kwa bushi kanangana, mwene tchwalyibuka, ne kutchinyiira kusiu kweembwaswa e tchisiki tchetchu tchekutenga mwa mbingu.	2. 과 부씨 가나ᅌᅡ나, 뭐너 짜ᄙᅦ부가, 너 구찌네이라 구시우 궈어ᄜᅪ솨 어 찌시기 쩌쭈 쩌구더ᅌᅡ 뫄 ᄜᅵᅌᅮ.	2. Meanwhile we groan, longing to be clothed with our heavenly dwelling,
3. E mangu tchungaba tchweembasiswe tchutatchilorekane'ku ngabala balyi buteeembala.	3. 어 마ᅌᅮ 쭈ᅌᅡ바 쭤어ᄜᅡ시숴 쭈다찌ᄙᅩ러가너구ᅌᅡ바ᄙᅡ 바ᄙᅦ 부더어어ᄜᅡᄙᅡ.	3. because when we are clothed, we will not be found naked.
4. Kwa bushi kanangana tchubano tchutchulyi mwelyine hema tchwalyibuka kwa kuabiranwa, si ata kwa bushi tchwahonda e ndjimba sine kukongolyibwa, si elyi tchwahonda kuembwaswa kwa bushi ebilyi bye lufu bimilyibwee ne'ebye kalamo.	4. 과 부씨 가나ᅌᅡ나 쭈바노 쭈쭈ᄙᅦ 뭐ᄙᅦ너 허마 짜ᄙᅦ부가 과 구아비라놔, 시 아다 과 부씨 짜호ᄕᅡ 어 ᄕᅵᄜᅡ 시너 구고ᅌᅩᄙᅦ봐, 시 어ᄙᅦ 짜호ᄕᅡ 구어ᄜᅪ솨 과 부씨 어비ᄙᅦ 벼 ᄙᅮ푸 비미ᄙᅦ붜어 너어벼 가ᄙᅡ모.	4. For while we are in this tent, we groan and are burdened, because we do not wish to be unclothed but to be clothed with our heavenly dwelling, so that what is mortal may be swallowed up by life.
5. Kwa bushi ola watchukungaanyaa tcbubano kwa bushi noonu mwaasi wa Ongo ola atchuwa tchubano (arabuni) yo mutchima.	5. 과 부씨 오ᄙᅡ 와쭈구ᅌᅡ아냐아 쭈부바노 과 부씨 노오누 뫄아시 와 오ᅌᅩ 오ᄙᅡ 아쭈와 쭈바노 (아라부니) 요 무찌마.	5. Now it is God who has made us for this very purpose and has given us the Spirit as a deposit, guaranteeing what is to come.

6. Kwa bushi tchweete e molo esiku nemango, tchukamenyerera kwa kasi tchukaaba mwa mubiri, tchungaaba burerere na tata.

7. Kwa bushibwa tchwaenda kwa byeemeresi si ata kwa kulola

8. Si eryi tchweete e molo netchu tchusimire busibu kutenga mwa mubiri, ne kweeshiba alauma na Enawetchu

9. Kwa bushibwa ne'ebi, tchweereka kumusimisa, bushibwa nga tchulyi anola, nesi tchukaba tchutalyi anola.

10. Kwa bushi bitchwemire tchubano ekulorekanaku ala muhondo se tchifumbi tche bicthindjibusi tcha Kirisito, na tchira mundju abone e mwaasi yra akolaa mwa mubiri, kwa ngokwa akolaa, nga mabuya nesi mabi.

11. Bushi tchukamenya ebuba bwe Enawetchu tchwanakula e bandju, lakini tchubano tchu eshikeni tchanganama era muhondo sa Ongo: tchunatchilangalyire tchweeshikeni mwa myaanyisa yenyu batcha batcha.

12. Tchutatchitonga era muhondo senyu kandji, lakini

6. 과 부씨 쭤어더 어 모로 어시구 너마꼬, 쭈가머녀러라 과 가시 쭈가아바 똬 무비리, 쭈꽈아바 부러러러 나 다다.

7. 과 부씨봐 쫘어따 과 벼어머러시 시 아다 과 구로꽈

8. 시 어에 쭤어더 어 모로 너쭈 쭈시미러 부시부 구더똬 똬 무비리, 너 궈어씨바 아꽈우마 나 어나워쭈

9. 과 부씨봐 너어비, 쭤어러가 구무시미사, 부씨봐 꽈 쭈쩨 아노꽈, 너시 쭈가바 쭈다쩨 아노꽈.

10. 과 부씨 비쭤미러 쭈바노 어구로러가나구 아꽈 무호또 서 찌푸삐 쩌 비찌띠부시 쨔 기리시도, 나 찌라 무뚜 아보너 어 뫄아시 이라 아고꽈아 똬 무비리, 과 꼬과 아고꽈아, 똬 마부야 너시 마비.

11. 부씨 쭈가머냐 어부바 붜 어나워쭈 쫘나구꽈 어 바두, 꽈기니 쭈바노 쭈 어씨거니 쨔꽈나마 어라 무호또 사 오꼬: 쭈나찌꽈꽈쩨러 쭤어씨거니 똬 먀아니사 여뉴 바쨔 바쨔.

12. 쭈다찌도꽈 어라 무호또 서뉴 가찌, 꽈기니

6. Therefore we are always confident and know that as long as we are at home in the body we are away from the Lord.

7. We live by faith, not by sight.

8. We are confident, I say, and would prefer to be away from the body and at home with the Lord.

9. So we make it our goal to please him, whether we are at home in the body or away from it.

10. For we must all appear before the judgment seat of Christ, that each one may receive what is due him for the things done while in the body, whether good or bad.

11. Since, then, we know what it is to fear the Lord, we try to persuade men. What we are is plain to God, and I hope it is also plain to your conscience.

12. We are not trying to commend ourselves to you

thwabeeresise mwaabu kwa bushi ne kutchitonga kwenyu kwabushibwa netchu, mubone kwaata emwaasi yeku akula abu batchitonga kwa myaasi yera butala, si ata kwa myaasi ye mutchima.	쫘버어러시서 뫄아부 과 부씨 너 구찌도ᅌ가 궈뉴 과부씨봐 너쭈, 무보너 과아다 어뫄아시 여구 아구ᄙᅡ 아부 바찌도ᅌ가 과 먀아시 여라 부다ᄙᅡ, 시 아다 과 먀아시 여 무찌마.	again, but are giving you an opportunity to take pride in us, so that you can answer those who take pride in what is seen rather than in what is in the heart.
13. Kwa bushi nga tchungaba tchwaulukirwe ne bwenge bwetchu, bushibwa na Ongom wala nga tchungaata e bwenge bwetchu boshi alyi kwabushi nenyu.	13. 과 부씨 ᅌ가 쭈ᅌ가바 쫘우루기뤄 너 붜ᅌ거 붜쭈, 부씨봐 나 오ᅌ고무 와ᄙᅡ ᅌ가 쭈ᅌ가아다 어 붜ᅌ거 붜쭈 보씨 아ᄙᅦ 과부씨 너뉴.	13. If we are out of our mind, it is for the sake of God; if we are in our right mind, it is for you.
14. Kwa bushi emasimani ma Kirisito, watchuandjirisise tchubano: kwa bushibwa tchutchindjibusibwe batcha, kwakasi, nga muuma afaa kwa bushi na boshi, sasa boshi berakufa ;	14. 과 부씨 어마시마니 마 기리시도, 와쭈아ᅜᅵ리시서 쭈바노: 과 부씨봐 쭈찌ᅜᅵ부시붜 바짜, 과가시, ᅌ가 무우마 아파아 과 부씨 나 보씨, 사사 보씨 버라구파 ;	14. For Christ's love compels us, because we are convinced that one died for all, and therefore all died.
15. Kandji afiraa boshi ne abalamire bata tchilamaa kandji kwe beene beene, lakini kwa bushi nayi yeeni afaa neku omolyibwa kwabushi nabu.	15. 가ᅜᅵ 아피라아 보씨 너 아바ᄙᅡ미러 바다 찌ᄙᅡ마아 가ᅜᅵ 궈 버어너 버어너, ᄙᅡ기니 과 부씨 나에 여어니 아파아 너구 오모ᄙᅦ봐 과부씨 나부.	15. And he died for all, that those who live should no longer live for themselves but for him who died for them and was raised again.
16. Batcha, kutengera mwebini bihangi, tchubano tchuteshi mundju kwa murengeri womubiri tchirombu tchungaba tchwishi Kirisito kwa halyi yo mubiri, si elyi sasa tchutatchimwishi kandji batcha.	16. 바짜, 구더ᅌ거라 뭐비니 비하ᅌ기, 쭈바노 쭈더씨 무ᅜᅮ 과 무러ᅌ거리 오무비리 찌로ᄪᅮ 쭈ᅌ가바 쮜씨 기리시도 과 하ᄙᅦ 요 무비리, 시 어ᄙᅦ 사사 쭈다찌뮈씨 가ᅜᅵ 바짜.	16. So from now on we regard no one from a worldly point of view. Though we once regarded Christ in this way, we do so no longer.
17. Batcha nga emundju	17. 바짜 ᅌ가 어무ᅜᅮ 아ᅌ가바	17. Therefore, if anyone is in

angaba alyi mu Kirisito yewi alyi tchireemu (kiumbe) tchiyayaya ; emyaasi ya miramira ya rengire, lolaa, e myaasi yoshi ye bere iya yaya.

18. Ne myaasi yoshi neindji yatenga era mwa Ongo, iwahubire kucthubika mwa buuma nayi kurengera Kirisito. Kwandji Ongo iwatchweresise e mulyimo we kuhuba kubika e bandji bandju mwa buuma nayi.

19. Kubinalyi Ongo yeine iwahubaa kubika ebandju boshi mwa buuma nayi kurengera Yesu Kirisito, busira kuandja emabi mabo. Rero, atchweeresise e mulyimo wekunde tchwahubanganya emwaasi we kuhuba kubika e bandju mwa buuma nayi.

20. Rero tchubano tchwendjire tchwateta mwesina lya Kirisito. Ongo yeine iwabamaalaa kutchurengera'ko. Bushi noku, tchwebema kwe sina lya Kirisito. Mwemereraa kunde mwahuba kuba mwa buuma na Ongo.

21. Kirisito atairaa tchiro na tchibi tchisibya ; si Ongo amuesaa emusio webibi byetchu, tchasiya mwa

---

아레 무 기리시도 여위 아레 찌러어무 (기우뻐) 찌야야야 ; 어먀아시 야 미라미라 야 러삐러, 로롸아, 어 먀아시 요씨 여 버러 이야 야야.

18. 너 먀아시 요씨 너이찌 야더빠 어라 뫄 오꼬, 이와후비러 구쮸비가 뫄 부우마 나에 구러뻐라 기리시도. 과찌 오꼬 이와쭤러시서 어 무쪠모 워 구후바 구비가 어 바찌 바꾸 뫄 부우마 나에.

19. 구비나레 오꼬 여이너 이와후바아 구비가 어바꾸 보씨 뫄 부우마 나에 구러뻐라 여수 기리시도, 부시라 구아짜 어마비 마보. 러로, 아쭤러러시서 어 무쪠모 워구떠 쫘후바빠냐 어먀아시 워 구후바 구비가 어 바꾸 뫄 부우마 나에.

20. 러로 쭈바노 쭤찌러 쫘더다 뭐시나 퍄 기리시도. 오꼬 여이너 이와바마아롸아 구쭈러뻐라고. 부씨 노구, 쭤버마 궈 시나 퍄 기리시도. 뭐머러라아 구떠 뫄후바 구바 뫄 부우마 나 오꼬.

21. 기리시도 아다이라아 찌로 나 찌비 찌시뱌 ; 시 오꼬 아무어사아 어무시오 워비비 벼쭈, 짜시야 뫄

Christ, he is a new creation; the old has gone, the new has come!

18. All this is from God, who reconciled us to himself through Christ and gave us the ministry of reconciliation:

19. that God was reconciling the world to himself in Christ, not counting men's sins against them. And he has committed to us the message of reconciliation.

20. We are therefore Christ's ambassadors, as though God were making his appeal through us. We implore you on Christ's behalf: Be reconciled to God.

21. God made him who had no sin to be sin for us, so that in him we might become the righteousness

kumurengera'ko tchuube bandju ba batchungenene era muhondo sa Ongo.

구무러어라고 쭈우버 바뚜 바of God.
바쭈어너너 어라 무호또 사
오꼬.

2 E Bakorinto Chikono 6

2 어 바고리또 찌고노 6

2 Corinthians Chapter 6 [NIV]

1. Rero bushi thcwakola alauma na Ongo, tchwabema mutaesaa abondjo bwayi buha-buha.

1. 러로 부씨 쭈와고꽈 아꽈우마 나 오꼬, 쫘버마 무다어사아 아보쪼 봐에 부하-부하.

1. As God's fellow workers we urge you not to receive God's grace in vain.

2. Bushi Ongo yeene atetaa na Ongo mwa maandjiko mabuya-buya mbu: "kwa bihangi bya byabaa bikomire, naakulaa ememo mao, ne lusuku lwe bununusi mango lwaikaa nera kukutabala". Rero, binera bi bihangi bikomire, kandji lu lusuku lwe bununusi.

2. 부씨 오꼬 여어너 아더다아 나 오꼬 뫄 마아찌고 마부야-부야 뿌: "과 비하꾀 뱌 뱌바아 비고미러, 나아구꽈아 어머모 마오, 너 루수구 뤄 부누누시 마꼬 꽈이가아 너라 구구다바꽈". 러로, 비너라 비 비하꾀 비고미러, 가찌 루 루수구 뤄 부누누시.

2. For he says, "In the time of my favor I heard you, and in the day of salvation I helped you." I tell you, now is the time of God's favor, now is the day of salvation.

3. Tchubano, tchutahonda kusibusa tchiro na mundju asibya, e bandjubangesha kunde bakena emulyimo wetchu.

3. 쭈바노, 쭈다호따 구시부사 찌로 나 무뚜 아시뱌, 어 바뚜바어싸 구너 바거나 어무레모 워쭈.

3. We put no stumbling block in anyone's path, so that our ministry will not be discredited.

4. Si mwa byoshi, tchwendjire tchwalosa ebandju kwa tchulyi tchwalosa ebandju kwa tchulyi bakosi ba Ongo mwa kuata bushibiri si bunene, kurengera ebuanya nemalyibuko ne kunde tchwo bairisibwa.

4. 시 뫄 뵤씨, 쮀찌러 쫘르어사 어바뚜 과 쭈레 쫘르어사 어바뚜 과 쭈레 바고시 바 오꼬 뫄 구아다 부씨비리 시 부너너, 구러어라 어부아냐 너마레부고 너 구너 쪼 바이리시봐.

4. Rather, as servants of God we commend ourselves in every way: in great endurance; in troubles, hardships and distresses;

5. Ne kunde tchwapundwa, nekunde batchuuma mwa

5. 너 구너 쫘푸똬, 너구너 바쭈우마 뫄 부로고, 너 구너

5. in beatings, imprisonments and riots; in

buroko, ne kunde tchwatabalyirwa, ne bitamu-tamu, ne kutasibya lukoyi, ne kunde tchwatchiima ebiryo.

6. Tchwendjire tchwalosa kwa tchulyi bakosi ba Ongo kurengera ekukomya e mitchima yetchu, na kurengera e bwenge bwetchu, ne kusesa emutchima nomwa kuira emabuya, na kurengera e mutchima mubuya-buya, na kurengera e nzii yetchu ye kanangana.

7. Na kurengera e kukangirisa e mwaasi we kanangana na kurengera ebuashi bwa Ongo, tchwendjire tchwakoresa ekutanganana era muhondo sa Ongo nga kandju tche kulwisanya natchi kandji tchakutchilanga natchi.

8. Tchwendjire tchwalosa kwa tchulyi bakosi ba Ongo mango tchweresibwa etchunda na mango tchwakenyibwa, mango batchwamaana kubuya na mango batchwamaana bulyio, mango batchutola nga bafusi ba bisha tchiro angaba mbu tchwendjire tchwateta e kanangana.

9. Bendjire batchutola nga bandju ba bateshibwe, noku tchwishibwe kubuya-buya.

좌다바페롸, 너 비다무-다무, 너 구다시뱌 루고에, 너 구떠 좌찌이마 어비료.

6. 쭤찌러 좌로사 과 쭈페 바고시 바 오꼬 구러꺼라 어구고먀 어 미찌마 여쭈, 나 구러꺼라 어 붜꺼 붜쭈, 너 구서사 어무찌마 노와 구이라 어마부야, 나 구러꺼라 어 무찌마 무부야-부야, 나 구러꺼라 어 씨이 여쭈 여 가나꺼나.

7. 나 구러꺼라 어 구가꺼리사 어 뫄아시 워 가나꺼나 나 구러꺼라 어부아씨 봐 오꼬, 쭤찌러 좌고러사 어구다꺼나나 어라 무호또 사 오꼬 꺼 가뿌 쩌 구뤼사냐 나찌 가찌 짜구찌롸꺼 나찌.

8. 쭤찌러 좌로사 과 쭈페 바고시 바 오꼬 마꼬 쭤러시봐 어쭈따 나 마꼬 좌거네봐, 마꼬 바좌마아나 구부야 나 마꼬 바좌마아나 부페오, 마꼬 바쭈도롸 꺼 바푸시 바 비싸 찌로 아꺼바 뿌 쭤찌러 좌더다 어 가나꺼나.

9. 버찌러 바쭈도롸 꺼 바뚜 바 바더씨붜, 노구 쮜씨붜 구부야-부야. 버찌러

hard work, sleepless nights and hunger;

6. in purity, understanding, patience and kindness; in the Holy Spirit and in sincere love;

7. in truthful speech and in the power of God; with weapons of righteousness in the right hand and in the left;

8. through glory and dishonor, bad report and good report; genuine, yet regarded as impostors;

9. known, yet regarded as unknown; dying, and yet we live on; beaten, and yet not

Bendjire batchutola nga ba bahonda kufa, noku tchutchiri bauma-uma. Bendjire batchupunda busese, si batatchwiita.

10. Bendjire batchusibusa, si tchunalyi mwa lumoo esuku soshi. Tchwalorekana'ko nga bakene, si tchwendjire tchwatchuma bandju banene baba baare. Tchwendjire tchwalorekana'ko nga tchutete kandju, noku tchweete byoshi.

11. Rero mubesha Korindo, tchwahambere nenyu busira kubabisha kandju, kandji e mucthima wetchu anatchiri abookere busese era muhondo senyu ;

12. Tchubano, tchubete ku tchaamba tchinene, si etchi tchaamba ; mwananyiretchi mwa mitchima yenyu.

13. Nahambala nenyu nga bana banyi: nenyu mutchubooreraa e micthima yenyu busese.

14. Mutendaa mwaba mwa buuma ne bandju ba bata bemeresi. Bushi buuma butchiye bwa bungaba ala katchi-katchi ke myaasi era icthungenene ne myaasi ibi? Kandji buuma bucthiye bwa bungaba ala katchi-katchi ke

바쭈도롸 까 바 바호따 구파, 노구 쭈찌리 바우마-우마. 버찌러 바쭈푸따 부서서, 시 바다쮜이다.

10. 버찌러 바쭈시부사, 시 쭈나레 뫄 루모오 어수구 소씨. 좌로러가나고 까 바거너, 시 쮀찌러 좌쭈마 바쭈 바너너 바바 바아러. 쮀찌러 좌로러가나고 까 쭈더더 가뚜, 노구 쮀어더 뵤씨.

11. 러로 무버싸 고리또, 좌하뻐러 너뉴 부시라 구바비싸 가뚜, 가찌 어 무찌마 워쭈 아나찌리 아보오거러 부서서 어라 무호또 서뉴 ;

12. 쭈바노, 쭈버더 구 짜아빠 찌너너, 시 어찌 짜아빠 ; 뫄나내러찌 뫄 미찌마 여뉴.

13. 나하빠롸 너뉴 까 바나 바네: 너뉴 무쭈보오러라아 어 미찌마 여뉴 부서서.

14. 무더따아 뫄바 뫄 부우마 너 바쭈 바 바다 버머러시. 부씨 부우마 부찌여 봐 부빠바 아똬 가찌-가찌 거 먀아시 어라 이쮸뻐너너 너 먀아시 이비? 가찌 부우마 부찌여 봐 부빠바 아똬 가찌- 가찌 거 부똬뻐러 너 무시먀?

killed;

10. sorrowful, yet always rejoicing; poor, yet making many rich; having nothing, and yet possessing everything.

11. We have spoken freely to you, Corinthians, and opened wide our hearts to you.

12. We are not withholding our affection from you, but you are withholding yours from us.

13. As a fair exchange--I speak as to my children-- open wide your hearts also.

14. Do not be yoked together with unbelievers. For what do righteousness and wickedness have in common? Or what fellowship can light have with darkness?

bulangare ne musimya?

15. Boomvitane bucthiye bwa bungaba ala katci-katchi ka Kirisito na Berilai? Nesi buuma butchiye bwa bungaba ala katchi-katchi ke mwemeresi nola uta mwemeresi?

16. Buuma butchiye bwa bulyi ala katchi-katchi ke luhu lwa Ongo ne bihuhanyi? Bushi tchubano tchulyi luhu lwa Ongo ola ulyi muuma-uma, ngokwa atetaa mbu: "Nyingaba mwa katchi-katchi kabo, na kunde natamba alauma nabo. Nyingaba Ongo wabo, nabo banaba lubaa lwanyi".

17. Bushi noku, Enawetchu atetchire mbu: "Mutengaa mwa katchi-katchi kabo, merekanaa nabo. Mutendaa mwauma ku kandju ka kaseneke'ko nga katakomisibwe, nanyi nyingabahuukasa".

18. Enawetchu we buashi boshi atecthire kandji mbu: "Nyingaaba eho wenyu, nenyu mwanaba baala banyi na balyi banyi".

15. 보오삐다너 부찌여 봐 부꾸바 아롸 가찌-가찌 가 기리시도 나 버리꽈이? 너시 부우마 부찌여 봐 부꾸바 아롸 가찌-가찌 거 뭐머러시 노롸 우다 뭐머러시?

16. 부우마 부찌여 봐 부레 아롸 가찌-가찌 거 루후 꽈 오꼬 너 비후하니? 부씨 쭈바노 쭈레 루후 꽈 오꼬 오롸 우레 무우마-우마, 꼬과 아더다아 뿌: "네꾸바 봐 가찌-가찌 가보, 나 구꺼 나다빠 아롸우마 나보. 네꾸바 오꼬 와보, 나보 바나바 루바아 꽈니".

17. 부씨 노구, 어나워쭈 아더찌러 뿌: "무더따아 봐 가찌-가찌 가보, 머러가나아 나보. 무더따아 봐우마 구 가뚜 가 가서너거고 까 가다고미시붸, 나니 네꾸바후우가사".

18. 어나워쭈 워 부아씨 보씨 아더찌러 가찌 뿌: "네꾸아바 어호 워뉴, 너뉴 봐나바 바아롸 바니 나 바레 바니".

15. What harmony is there between Christ and Belial? What does a believer have in common with an unbeliever?

16. What agreement is there between the temple of God and idols? For we are the temple of the living God. As God has said: "I will live with them and walk among them, and I will be their God, and they will be my people."

17. "Therefore come out from them and be separate, says the Lord. Touch no unclean thing, and I will receive you."

18. "I will be a Father to you, and you will be my sons and daughters, says the Lord Almighty."

2 E Bakorinto Chikono 7

1. Banyaketchu basiirwa, ebi birane biri byetchu ; bushi noku tchundaa tchwatchikomya kwa myaasi yoshi era yende ya tchwaaka esinga kwa mubiri nokwa mutchima. Kandji tchundaatchwatchisesa kuba babuya-buya kanangana mwa kunde tchwatchunda Ongo.

2. MUtchubooreraa emitchima yenyu! kutalyi mundju ola tchwairiraa tchibi, kutalyi nola tchwaesaa mwa bwemeresi, kutalyi nola tchwengeeraa tchasiya tchumubone kwe mutoloke mwa bukalange.

3. Ndatetchire batcha kwa kuhonda nyibatchindjibuse. Bushi nabaa nababurire mira kwa mulyi kwa mitchima yetchu, abe mwa kufa nesi mwa kulama.

4. Nyitchula nyitchinyiire mwabo busese na kunde natchitonga bushi nenyu, mwa mano malyibuko metchu moshi, nendjire nasesibwa emutchima na kuata luoo lunene.

5. Bushi anabe mango tchwaikaa e Maketoniya, tchutabonaa tchiro na

2 어 바고리또 찌고노 7

1. 바냐거쭈 바시이라, 어비 비라너 비리 벼쭈 ; 부씨 노구 쭈따아 쫘찌고먀 과 먀아시 요씨 어라 여너 야 쫘아가 어시빠 과 무비리 노과 무찌마. 가찌 쭈따아쫘찌서사 구바 바부야-부야 가나빠나 먀 구너 쫘쭈따 오꼬.

2. 무쭈보오러라아 어미찌마 여뉴! 구다뤠 무뚜 오롸 쫘이리라아 찌비, 구다뤠 노라 쫘어사아 먀 붸머러시, 구다뤠 노라 쭤뻐어라아 짜시야 쭈무보너 궈 무도로거 먀 부가롸뻐.

3. 따더찌러 바짜 과 구호따 네바찌찌부서. 부씨 나바아 나바부리러 미라 과 무뤠 과 미찌마 여쭈, 아버 먀 구파 너시 먀 구롸마.

4. 네쭈롸 네찌네이러 먀보 부서서 나 구너 나찌도빠 부씨 너뉴, 먀 마노 마뤠부고 머쭈 모씨, 너찌러 나서시봐 어무찌마 나 구아다 루오오 루너너.

5. 부씨 아나버 마꼬 쫘이가아 어 마거도니야, 쭈다보나아 찌로 나 찌하삐

2 Corinthians Chapter 7 [NIV]

1. Since we have these promises, dear friends, let us purify ourselves from everything that contaminates body and spirit, perfecting holiness out of reverence for God.

2. Make room for us in your hearts. We have wronged no one, we have corrupted no one, we have exploited no one.

3. I do not say this to condemn you; I have said before that you have such a place in our hearts that we would live or die with you.

4. I have great confidence in you; I take great pride in you. I am greatly encouraged; in all our troubles my joy knows no bounds.

5. For when we came into Macedonia, this body of ours had no rest, but we

tchihangi tchakutamuka, tchwarengaa mumalyibuko ma tchira ndjira: ebandju babaa bendjire batchubanganya nomwa mitchima yetchu, mwabaa mulyi buba.

6. Si Ongo iwende weresa e bandju ba bafunyikiri emitchima emisi, atchusesaa e mitchima kurengera ekuika kwa Tito.

7. Ata ekuika kwa Tito kweine ku kwatchusesaa e mutchima, si kandji kukulyikana nokwa nenyu mwamusesaa emutchima. Tito atchubalyikisise kwa mwete mbuha inene ye kuhuba kunyilola'ko. Kandji atchubalyirire nokwa malyira mwa mweete nokwa mwenjire mwatchana bushi nanyi. Bushi noku bahubiri kumowa busese.

8. Rero, akaba ematuba nabatchumiraa mabasibusaa, ndatchanya ku kandju. Nanatchanyaa mango namenyereraa kwa amu maruba mabasibusaa tchiro angaba mbu mabasibusaa ku bihangi bieke.

9. Rero nyiri mwa lumoo atabu nabasibusaa ; si bushi ebusinane bwenyu, bwatchumire mwabindjula e

짜구다무가, 쫘러꺄아 무마레부고 마 찌라 띠라: 어바쭈 바바아 버찌러 바쭈바꺄냐 노봐 미찌마 여쭈, 마바아 무레 부바.

6. 시 오꼬 이워떠 워러사 어 바쭈 바 바푸네기리 어미찌마 어미시, 아쭈서사아 어 미찌마 구러꺼라 어구이가 과 디도.

7. 아다 어구이가 과 디도 궈이너 구 과쭈서사아 어 무찌마, 시 가찌 구구레가나 노과 너뉴 먀무서사아 어무찌마. 디도 아쭈바레기시서 과 뭐더 뿌하 이너너 여 구후바 구네롤롸고. 가찌 아쭈바레리러 노과 마레라 먀 뭐어더 노과 뭐찌러 먀짜나 부씨 나니. 부씨 노구 바후비리 구모와 부서서.

8. 러로, 아가바 어마두바 나바쭈미라아 마바시부사아, 따짜냐 구 가뉴. 나나짜냐아 마꼬 나머녀러라아 과 아무 마루바 마바시부사아 찌로 아꺄바 뿌 마바시부사아 구 비하꼐 비어거.

9. 러로 네리 먀 루모오 아다부 나바시부사아 ; 시 부씨 어부시나너 붜뉴, 봐쭈미러 마비뉴꽈 어 미찌마

were harassed at every turn--conflicts on the outside, fears within.

6. But God, who comforts the downcast, comforted us by the coming of Titus,

7. and not only by his coming but also by the comfort you had given him. He told us about your longing for me, your deep sorrow, your ardent concern for me, so that my joy was greater than ever.

8. Even if I caused you sorrow by my letter, I do not regret it. Though I did regret it--I see that my letter hurt you, but only for a little while--

9. yet now I am happy, not because you were made sorry, but because your sorrow led you to

mitchima yenyu. Bushi obu businane bwebaa butenganyire nekuhonda kwa Ongo. Aola kutalyi tchiro na tchibi tchisibya tcha tchwabakorera.	여뉴. 부씨 오부 부시나너 붜바아 부더까네러 너구호따 과 오꼬. 아오롸 구다례 찌로 나 찌비 찌시뱌 짜 쫘바고러라.	repentance. For you became sorrowful as God intended and so were not harmed in any way by us.
10. Kubinalyi, ebusinane bwa butenganyire ne kuhonda kwa Ongo, bwende bwatchuma emundju abindjula emucthima wayi na kununulyibwa busira kutchanya bushi nobu businane. Si e businane bwa butenganyire ne myaasi ye butala, bweke bwende bwareta elufu!	10. 구비나례, 어부시나너 봐 부더까네러 너 구호따 과 오꼬, 붜떠 봐쭈마 어무쭈 아비쭈롸 어무찌마 와에 나 구누누례봐 부시라 구짜냐 부씨 노부 부시나너. 시 어 부시나너 봐 부더까네러 너 먀아시 여 부다롸, 붜거 붜떠 봐러다 어루푸!	10. Godly sorrow brings repentance that leads to salvation and leaves no regret, but worldly sorrow brings death.
11. Kubinalyi, obu businane bwenyu butenganyire nekuhonda kwa Ongo. Rero mulolaa kwa myaasi ibuya era babaretere: bwatchumire mwaata bushiru bunene, na kunde mwa tchitetera, na kunde mwalosa kwa muyongirwe, na kunde mwabaa mutete tchiro na tchibi tchisibya mweyi myaasi.	11. 구비나례, 오부 부시나너 붜뉴 부더까네러 너구호따 과 오꼬. 러로 무로롸아 과 먀아시 이부야 어라 바바러더러: 봐쭈미러 뫄아다 부씨루 부너너, 나 구떠 뫄 찌더더라, 나 구떠 뫄로사 과 무요이뤄, 나 구떠 뫄바아 무더더 찌로 나 찌비 찌시뱌 뭐에 먀아시.	11. See what this godly sorrow has produced in you: what earnestness, what eagerness to clear yourselves, what indignation, what alarm, what longing, what concern, what readiness to see justice done. At every point you have proved yourselves to be innocent in this matter.
12. Rero ndabaandjikiraa bushi ne mundju ola wairaa emabi, nesi bushi nola bairiraa'mo ; si nabaandjikiraa, tchasiya mumenyerere kubua-buya era muhondo sa Ongo, ebushiru bwa mutchwete'ko.	12. 러로 따바아찌기라아 부씨 너 무쭈 오롸 와이라아 어마비, 너시 부씨 노롸 바이리라아모 ; 시 나바아찌기라아, 짜시야 무머녀러러 구부아-부야 어라 무호또 사 오꼬, 어부씨루 봐 무쭤더고.	12. So even though I wrote to you, it was not on account of the one who did the wrong or of the injured party, but rather that before God you could see for yourselves how devoted to us you are.
13. Etchera tchatchumire	13. 어쩌라 짜쭈미러	13. By all this we are

tchwasesibwa emutchima. Tchutasesibwaa e mutchima oshaao, si kandji elumoo lwetchu lwatengeresaa, bushi ne lumoo lwa Tito abaa ete kukulyikana nokwa muboshi mwamubambatasaa emutchima.

14. Natchitonga hitcha era muhondo sayi bushi nenyu, mutanyiitaa honyi. Rero kukulyikana nokwa tchwabaa tchwendjire tchwabura ekanangana mwa byoshi, kunoku ku ekutchitonga kwanyi era muhondo sa Tio bushi nenyu kwalorekanyire'ko kwa kunalyi kwa kanangana.

15. Enzii era Tito abete'ko yendjire yaendekera yaluwa, mango akengera kwa muboshi mwabaa mwendjire mwaira bya ababurire nokwa mwamuhuukasaa mwabuba ne mwetchunda lyinene.

16. Nyimoire busese bushi nyibalangalyire mwa myaasi yoshi!

좌서시봐 어무찌마. 쭈다서시봐아 어 무찌마 오싸아오, 시 가찌 어루모오 뤄쭈 콰더꺼러사아, 부씨 너 루모오 콰 디도 아바아 어더 구구레가나 노과 무보씨 콰무바빠다사아 어무찌마.

14. 나찌도꽈 히짜 어라 무호또 사에 부씨 너뉴, 무다네이다아 호네. 러로 구구레가나 노과 좌바아 쭤찌러 좌부라 어가나꽈나 마 보씨, 구노구 구 어구찌도꽈 과네 어라 무호또 사 디오 부씨 너뉴 과뤄러가네러고 과 구나레 과 가나꽈나.

15. 어씨이 어라 디도 아버더고 여찌러 야어꺼거라 야루와, 마꼬 아거꺼라 과 무보씨 콰바아 뭐찌러 콰이라 뱌 아바부리러 노과 콰무후우가사아 콰부바 너 뭐쭈따 레너너.

16. 네모이러 부서서 부씨 네바콰꽈레러 콰 먀아시 요씨!

---

encouraged. In addition to our own encouragement, we were especially delighted to see how happy Titus was, because his spirit has been refreshed by all of you.

14. I had boasted to him about you, and you have not embarrassed me. But just as everything we said to you was true, so our boasting about you to Titus has proved to be true as well.

15. And his affection for you is all the greater when he remembers that you were all obedient, receiving him with fear and trembling.

16. I am glad I can have complete confidence in you.

---

2 E Bakorinto Chikono 8

1. Banyaketchu, tchwahonda mumenye kute Ongo alosise

---

2 어 바고리또 찌고노 8

1. 바냐거쭈, 좌호따 무머녀 구더 오꼬 아로시서 어부부야

---

2 Corinthians Chapter 8 [NIV]

1. And now, brothers, we want you to know about the

ebubuya bwayi kwa bikembe byebemeresi bomwa tchiuo tche Maketoniya.

봐에 과 비거뻐 벼버머러시 보봐 찌우오 쩌 마거도니야.

grace that God has given the Macedonian churches.

2. Abu bandju baerekibwaa busese kurengera emalyibuko ma berengaa'mo. Si banaendekeraa kuata lumoo lunene, kuikira etchi tchihangi baata e mucthima we kwana kurenza ebuashi bwabo, tchiro angaba mbu babaa balyi bakene.

2. 아부 바뚜 바어러기봐아 부서서 구러뻐라 어마레부고 마 버러꺼아모. 시 바나어떠거라아 구아다 루모오 루너너, 구이기라 어찌 찌하끼 바아다 어 무찌마 워 과나 구러싸 어부아씨 봐보, 찌로 아꺼바 뿌 바바아 바레 바거너.

2. Out of the most severe trial, their overflowing joy and their extreme poverty welled up in rich generosity.

3. Natetaa bya nyishi era luulu sabo, kwa banaa kukulyikana nokwa babaa bangaala. Bera kuikira etchihangi banakurenza nokwa babaa bangaala busira kutchitchikibwa.

3. 나더다아 뱌 네씨 어라 루우루 사보, 과 바나아 구구께가나 노과 바바아 바꺼아꽈. 버라 구이기라 어찌하끼 바나구러싸 노과 바바아 바꺼아꽈 부시라 구찌찌기봐.

3. For I testify that they gave as much as they were able, and even beyond their ability. Entirely on their own,

4. Batchwemaa busese mbu nabo bahonda bmererwe kuhangira kwa mulyimo we kuasa ebandju ba Ongo.

4. 바쭤마아 부서서 뿌 나보 바호따 부머러뤄 구하끼라 과 무레모 워 구아사 어바뚜 바 오꼬.

4. they urgently pleaded with us for the privilege of sharing in this service to the saints.

5. Banaa kurenza ngokwa tchwabaa tchulangalyire. Batchanaa tangaa era mwa Enawetchu, tchasinda bera kutchana beine netchu kurengera ekuhonda kwa Ongo.

5. 바나아 구러싸 꼬과 쫘바아 쭈꽈꺼께러. 바짜나아 다꺼아 어라 뫄 어나워쭈, 짜시따 버라 구짜나 베이너 너쭈 구러뻐라 어구호따 과 오꼬.

5. And they did not do as we expected, but they gave themselves first to the Lord and then to us in keeping with God's will.

6. Etchera tchitchatchumaa tchwema Tito mbu ayaa eyi mwenyu, tchasiya amalyirise oyu mulyimo mubuya wekunde mwana kwa kuasa

6. 어쩌라 찌짜쭈마아 쭤마 디도 뿌 아야아 어에 뮤뉴, 짜시야 아마레리서 오유 무레모 무부야 워구너 뫄나 과 구아사 어바뚜 바 오꼬,

6. So we urged Titus, since he had earlier made a beginning, to bring also to completion this act of grace on your part.

ebandju ba Ongo, ngokwa anatangirisaa'o.

꼬과 아나다삐리사아오.

7. Mwabo mulyi baare mwa myaasi yoshi: mwete bwemeresi, mulyi ndetchi, mwishi myaasi, mwete ebushiru mu tchira mwaasi, kandji mutchwete kwe nzii. Rero, tchwabema mubaa baare nomwa kuata e mutchima we kunde mwana.

7. 먀보 무쩨 바아러 먀 먀아시 요씨: 뭐더 붜머러시, 무쩨 떠찌, 뮈씨 먀아시, 뭐더 어부씨루 무 찌라 먀아시, 가찌 무쭤더 궈 씨이. 러로, 쫘버마 무바아 바아러 노콰 구아다 어 무찌마 워 구너 먀나.

7. But just as you excel in everything--in faith, in speech, in knowledge, in complete earnestness and in your love for us--see that you also excel in this grace of giving.

8. Ndatetchire batcha kwa kuberesa muomba ; si nabaa nahonda kubalosa ebushiru bwe bandji bemeresi. Mwa kuira batcha, naberesise endjira yekulosa kwa enzii yenyu inalyi ya kanangana.

8. 따더찌러 바짜 과 구버러사 무오빠 ; 시 나바아 나호따 구바로사 어부씨루 붜 바찌 버머러시. 먀 구이라 바짜, 나버러시서 어찌라 여구로사 과 어씨이 여뉴 이나쩨 야 가나빠나.

8. I am not commanding you, but I want to test the sincerity of your love by comparing it with the earnestness of others.

9. Bushi mwishi ebubuya bwa Enawetchu Yesu Kirisito, tchiro angaba mbu abaa muare, si yeine atchiira mukene bushi nenyu, tchasiya mube baare kurengera obu bukene bwayi.

9. 부씨 뮈씨 어부부야 봐 어나워쭈 여수 기리시도, 찌로 아빠바 뿌 아바아 무아러, 시 여이너 아찌이라 무거너 부씨 너뉴, 짜시야 무버 바아러 구러써라 오부 부거너 봐에.

9. For you know the grace of our Lord Jesus Christ, that though he was rich, yet for your sakes he became poor, so that you through his poverty might become rich.

10. Mwa batcha, naberesa emianyisa yanyi mweyi myaasi kukomire muendekere kuata ebushibirisi, bushi mu mwabaa babere-bere kuana, kandji mu mwatangirisaa oyu mulyimo kutengera mwa mwaka ola warengaa.

10. 먀 바짜, 나버러사 어미아네사 야니 뭐에 먀아시: 구고미러 무어떠거러 구아다 어부씨비리시, 부씨 무 먀바아 바버러-버러 구아나, 가찌 무 먀다삐리사아 오유 무쩨모 구더써라 먀 먀가 오빠 와러빠아.

10. And here is my advice about what is best for you in this matter: Last year you were the first not only to give but also to have the desire to do so.

11. Rero, oyu mulyimo,

11. 러로, 오유 무쩨모,

11. Now finish the work, so

muisaa'o kwa businda. Kwa mwabaa munete emutchima we kukola'u, ku munaisaa'o kwa businda batcha, kukulyikana ne buashi bwa mweete.

12. Bushi akaba emundju ete emutchima we kwana, Ongo ende emerera etchindju tcha aanyire kukulyikana na tcha oyu mundju eete, si ata kukulyikana na tcha ateete.

13. Emyaanyisa yanyi, ita ya kuhonda kubalyibusa kwa kuasa ebandji bandju, si nahonda ebandju boshi bende batolyibwa kuuma.

14. Mwesine suku, mweete abu bwaare bunene. Rero abu bwaare bwenyu, bundaa bwaasa ebandji ba balyi mwa malayi. Mwa batcha, nabi mango bangaba babonyire bindju binene busese, bangebe babaasa mango mukaba mwa bulae. Mweyi ndjira ebandju boshi bangende batolyibwa kuuma.

15. Kukulyikana nokwa maandjika maubuya-buya matchula matetchire mbu: "ola watla-tolaa binene, atabonaa binene kurenza nola watola-tolaa bieke atabonaa bieke busese".

무이사아오 과 부시따. 과 꽈바아 무너더 어무찌마 워 구고꽈우, 구 무나이사아오 과 부시따 바짜, 구구꿰가나 너 부아씨 봐 뭐어더.

12. 부씨 아가바 어무뚜 어더 어무찌마 워 과나, 오꼬 어더 어머러라 어찌뉴 짜 아아니러 구구꿰가나 나 짜 오유 무뚜 어어더, 시 아다 구구꿰가나 나 짜 아더어더.

13. 어먀아네사 야니, 이다 야 구호따 구바꿰부사 과 구아사 어바찌 바뿌, 시 나호따 어바뉴 보씨 버떠 바도꿰봐 구우마.

14. 뭐시너 수구, 뭐어더 봐아러 부너너. 러로 아부 봐아러 뭐뉴, 부따아 봐아사 어바찌 바 바꿰 봐 마꽈에. 꽈 바짜, 나비 마꼬 바꽈바 바보네러 비뚜 비너너 부서서, 바꺼버 바바아사 마꼬 무가바 봐 부꽈어. 뭐에 띠라 어바뉴 보씨 바꺼떠 바도꿰봐 구우마.

15. 구구꿰가나 노과 마아찌가 마우부야-부야 마쭈꽈 마더찌러 뿌: "오꽈 와두꽈-도꽈아 비너너, 아다보나아 비너너 구러싸 노꽈 와도꽈-도꽈아 비어거 아다보나아 비어거 부서서".

that your eager willingness to do it may be matched by your completion of it, according to your means.

12. For if the willingness is there, the gift is acceptable according to what one has, not according to what he does not have.

13. Our desire is not that others might be relieved while you are hard pressed, but that there might be equality.

14. At the present time your plenty will supply what they need, so that in turn their plenty will supply what you need. Then there will be equality,

15. as it is written: "He who gathered much did not have too much, and he who gathered little did not have too little."

16. Akoko era mwa Ongo iweresaa Tito bushiru bunene kwa kubaasa ngokwa nanyi nyinete'bo!

17. Tito emerere kuya eyi mwenyu kukulyikana nokwa tchwamwemaa. Kandji kwa bushitu bwayi bunene, atchikunganyise mira kwa kuya eyi mwenyu kukulyikana ne kuhonda kwayi yeine.

18. Tchwamutchumire na undji munyaketchu muuma mwa bemeresi boshi, bushi ne mulyimo wayi we kunde ahubanganyisa ebandju e mwaasi mubuya-buya.

19. kandji oyu munyaketchu, alondolyibwa ne bemeresi kwa kunde atchwerekesa mwa nyibalamo se kuaba emiholore era yaanyibwaa na mutchima mubuya-buya. Tchwendjire tchwakola oyu mulyimo kwe tchunda lya Enwawetchu, na kulasa e mutchima wetchu mubuya we kuasa ebandji bandju.

20. Kandji tchutahonda mbu ebandju bendaa batchwamaana bulyio, kukulyikana nokwa tchwendjire tchwaaba bine bikuli bingana bitcha.

21. bushi tchwahonda kuira

16. 아고고 어라 뫄 오꼬 이워러사아 디도 부씨루 부너너 과 구바아사 꼬과 나니 니너더보!

17. 디도 어머러러 구야 어에 뭐뉴 구구레가나 노과 좌뭐마아. 가찌 과 부씨두 봐에 부너너, 아찌구꺄네서 미라 과 구야 어에 뭐뉴 구구레가나 너 구호따 과에 여이너.

18. 좌무쭈미러 나 우찌 무냐거쭈 무우마 뫄 버머러시 보씨, 부씨 너 무레모 와에 워 구떠 아후바꺄네사 어바뉴 어 뫄아시 무부야-부야.

19. 가찌 오유 무냐거쭈, 아르또레봐 너 버머러시 과 구떠 아쒀러거사 뫄 네바꽈모 서 구아바 어미호르러 어라 야아네봐아 나 무찌마 무부야-부야. 쮜찌러 좌고롸 오유 무레모 궈 쭈따 랴 어놔워쭈, 나 구꽈사 어 무찌마 워쭈 무부야 워 구아사 어바찌 바뉴.

20. 가찌 쭈다호따 뿌 어바뉴 버따아 바쫘마아나 부레오, 구구레가나 노과 쮜찌러 좌아바 비너 비구뤼 비꺄나 비짜.

21. 부씨 좌호따 구이라

16. I thank God, who put into the heart of Titus the same concern I have for you.

17. For Titus not only welcomed our appeal, but he is coming to you with much enthusiasm and on his own initiative.

18. And we are sending along with him the brother who is praised by all the churches for his service to the gospel.

19. What is more, he was chosen by the churches to accompany us as we carry the offering, which we administer in order to honor the Lord himself and to show our eagerness to help.

20. We want to avoid any criticism of the way we administer this liberal gift.

21. For we are taking pains

emabuya, ata era muhondo sa Enawetchu yeine oshao, si nera muhondo se bandju.

22. Tcwatchumire na undji munyaketchu mwemeresi muuma alauma nabo. Oyu munyaketchu, mu ndjira sinene, tchwede tchwalola kwa atchusa bushiru bunene. Rero obu bushirubwayi bweire bwanarengeresa bushi abalangalyiri busese.

23. Rero kwabya byeerekere Tito, alyi mundju ola wende wanyekerekesa mwa mulyimo. Ende akola mwa katchi-katchi kenyu mwetchwe lyanyi. Nabu bandji banyaketchu ba bamwerekesise, batchumirwe ne bikembe bye bemeresi. Bende bakola kwe tchunda kya kirisito.

24. Bushi noku mulosaa era muhondo se bikembe bye bemeresi kwa mubasimire kanangana, na kulosa'bo kwa tchwabaa tchusinganyire ekunde tchwatchitonga bushi nenyu.

어마부야, 아다 어라 무호또 사 어나워쭈 여이너 오싸오, 시 너라 무호또 서 바쭈.

22. 좌쭈미러 나 우찌 무냐거쭈 뭐머러시 무우마 아롸우마 나보. 오유 무냐거쭈, 무 찌라 시너너, 쭤더 좌로롸 과 아쭈사 부씨루 부너너. 러로 오부 부씨루봐에 뷔이러 봐나러어러사 부씨 아바롸까레리 부서서.

23. 러로 과뱌 벼어러거러 디도, 아레 무뚜 오라 워너 와녀거러거사 뫄 무레모. 어떠 아고롸 뫄 가찌-가찌 거뉴 뭐쭤 랴니. 나부 바찌 바냐거쭈 바 바뭐러거시서, 바쭈미뤄 너 비거뻐 벼 버머러시. 버떠 바고롸 궈 쭈따 갸 기리시도.

24. 부씨 노구 무로사아 어라 무호또 서 비거뻐 벼 버머러시 과 무바시미러 가나까나, 나 구로사보 과 좌바아 쭈시까너러 어구떠 좌찌도까 부씨 너뉴.

to do what is right, not only in the eyes of the Lord but also in the eyes of men.

22. In addition, we are sending with them our brother who has often proved to us in many ways that he is zealous, and now even more so because of his great confidence in you.

23. As for Titus, he is my partner and fellow worker among you; as for our brothers, they are representatives of the churches and an honor to Christ.

24. Therefore show these men the proof of your love and the reason for our pride in you, so that the churches can see it.

2 E Bakorinto Chikono 9

2 어 바고리또 찌고노 9

2 Corinthians Chapter 9 [NIV]

1. Nyisene kwa kutabetere

1. 내서너 과 구다버더러

1. There is no need for me

mufa asibya, ekubaandjikira era luulu se lweembo lwekuya kuasa ebandju ba Ongo

2. Bushi nyishi kwa mweete mutchima mubuya wakuasa'bo. Nendjire natchitonga bushi nenyu era muhondo sa besha Maketoniya mbu: "ebemeresi bomwa tchio tche Akaya batchikunganyise mira kwa kwana kutengera mwa mwaka ola warengaa". Mwa batcha, kurengera obu bushiru bwenyu, mwatchumire banene mubo nabo baata emutchima we kunde baana.

3. Si tchiro batcha, nabatchumirire bano banyaketchu, tchasiya ekutchitonga kwetchu bushi nenyu kutalorekanaa'ko nga kandju buha. Bushi noku nahonda mwiikale mwatchikunganyise kukulyikana nokwa natetaa.

4. Bushi akaba nyingabaha eyi mwenyu alauma na besha Maketoniya, tchasinda tchanaba buana mutatchikunganyise, aola tchungafa honyi busese kukulyikana nokwa tchwabaa tchubalangalyire. Anabe nenyu

무파 아시뱌, 어구바아찌기라 어라 루우루 서 뤄어뽀 뤄구야 구아사 어바뉴 바 오오.

2. 부씨 네씨 과 뭐어더 무찌마 무부야 와구아사보. 너띠러 나찌도꺄 부씨 너뉴 어라 무호또 사 버싸 마거도니야 뿌: "어버머러시 보꽈 찌오 쩌 아가야 바찌구꺄네서 미라 과 과나 구더꺼라 꽈 꽈가 오꽈 와러꺄아". 꽈 바짜, 구러꺼라 오부 부씨루 뷰뉴, 꽈쭈미러 바너너 무보 나보 바아다 어무찌마 워 구떠 바아나.

3. 시 찌로 바짜, 나바쭈미리러 바노 바냐거쭈, 짜시야 어구찌도꺄 궈쭈 부씨 너뉴 구다로러가나아고 꺄 가뉴 부하. 부씨 노구 나호꺄 뮈이가꺼 꽈찌구꺄네서 구구레가나 노과 나더다아.

4. 부씨 아가바 네꺄바하 어에 뭐뉴 아꺄우마 나 버싸 마거도니야, 짜시따 짜나바 부아나 무다찌구꺄네서, 아오꽈 쭈꺄파 호네 부서서 구구레가나 노과 좌바아 쭈바꺄꺄레러. 아나버 너뉴 무버이너 무꺄나파시.

to write to you about this service to the saints.

2. For I know your eagerness to help, and I have been boasting about it to the Macedonians, telling them that since last year you in Achaia were ready to give; and your enthusiasm has stirred most of them to action.

3. But I am sending the brothers in order that our boasting about you in this matter should not prove hollow, but that you may be ready, as I said you would be.

4. For if any Macedonians come with me and find you unprepared, we--not to say anything about you--would be ashamed of having been so confident.

mubeine munganafa'si.

5. Etxhera tchi tchatchumaa naanyisa kwa byemire nyibure banu banyaketchu banyihondorere eyi mwenyu tanga, tchasiya baaye kukunganya e lweembo lwa mwalaanyaa. Aola lungaba lwakunganyisibwe mira, netchi tchi tchingalosa kwa mwaanaa'lo na mutchima muuma, si mutaanaa'lo na mitchima ebiri.

6. Mundaa mwakengera ene myaasi: Emundju ola wainga bieke, angashebula bieke ; nola wainga binene, angashebula binene.

7. Tchira mundju emire kunde aana kukulyikana nokwa abaa aanyisise mira mwa mutchima wayi, busira businane kandji busira kutchitchikibwa. Bushi Ongo atchula asimire emundju ola waana na lumoo.

8. Ongo eete ebuashi bwe kubaahanyira mwa nyira soshi, tchasiya munde mwabona byoshi bya mulaire'ko esuku soshi. Kandji mungaendekera kuata binene busese kwakunde mwakola tchira mulyimo woshi mubuya.

9. Etchera tchikulyikene nokwa

5. 어두x허라 찌 짜쭈마아 나아네사 과 벼미러 내부러 바누 바냐거쭈 바네호또러러 어에 뭐뉴 다빠, 짜시야 바아여 구구빠냐 어 뤄어뽀 롸 롸라아냐아. 아오롸 루빠바 롹구빠네시붜 미라, 너찌 찌 찌빠로사 과 롸아나아로 나 무찌마 무우마, 시 무다아나아로 나 미찌마 어비리.

6. 무따아 롸거꺼라 어너 먀아시: 어무뚜 오롸 와이빠 비어거, 아빠써부롸 비어거 ; 노롸 와이빠 비너너, 아빠써부롸 비너너.

7. 찌라 무뚜 어미러 구떠 아아나 구구레가나 노과 아바아 아아네시서 미라 롸 무찌마 와에, 부시라 부시나너 가찌 부시라 구찌찌기봐. 부씨 오꼬 아쭈롸 아시미러 어무뚜 오롸 와아나 나 루모오.

8. 오꼬 어어더 어부아씨 붜 구바아하네라 롸 네라 소씨, 짜시야 무너 롸보나 뵤씨 뱌 무롸이러고 어수구 소씨. 가찌 무빠어떠거라 구아다 비너너 부서서 과구떠 롸고롸 찌라 무레모 올씨 무부야.

9. 어쩌라 찌구레거너 노과

5. So I thought it necessary to urge the brothers to visit you in advance and finish the arrangements for the generous gift you had promised. Then it will be ready as a generous gift, not as one grudgingly given.

6. Remember this: Whoever sows sparingly will also reap sparingly, and whoever sows generously will also reap generously.

7. Each man should give what he has decided in his heart to give, not reluctantly or under compulsion, for God loves a cheerful giver.

8. And God is able to make all grace abound to you, so that in all things at all times, having all that you need, you will abound in every good work.

9. As it is written: "He has

bitchula biandjikirwe mwa maandjiko mabuya-buya mbu: "Eresaa ebakene bindju binene aira bya bitchungenene esuku ne mango"

10. Ongo iwende weresa emuinzi embuto, kndji iwende weresa abandju akalyo. Rero nenyu, anganaberesa embuto, na kunde aalula'yi na kumesa'yi, tchasiya ekuira kwenyu bya bitchungenene, kunde kweka bifuma binene.

11. Mwa batcha Ongo angabaira kuba baare mwa bindju byoshi, tchasiya esuku soshi munde mwalosa emutchima we kuana. Aola, bandju banene bangende bateta mbu akoko kalyi tchiumbi era mwa Ongo bushi ne lweembo lwa tchwendjire tchwabaesa'ko, lwa lwatenga era mwenyu.

12. Bushi onu mulyimo we kuholola etete mufa oshao kwa kweresa ebandju ba Ongo bya balaire'ko, si kandji mweyi ndjira, banene mwabu bandju bangende bateta mbu akoko kalyi tchiumbi era mwa Ongo.

13. Bushi ne mufa woyu mulyimo, banju banene bangende batonga Ongo mwa

비쭈꽈 비아찌기뤄 똬 마아찌고 마부야-부야 뿌: "어러사아 어바거너 비쭈 비너너 아이라 뱌 비쭈꺼너너 어수구 너 마꼬"

10. 오꼬 이워떠 워러사 어무이씨 어뿌도, 구찌 이워떠 워러사 아바쭈 아가꾜. 러로 너뉴, 아까나버러사 어뿌도, 나 구떠 아아루꽈에 나 구머사에, 짜시야 어구이라 귀뉴 뱌 비쭈꺼너너, 구떠 귀가 비푸마 비너너.

11. 똬 바짜 오꼬 아까바이라 구바 바아러 똬 비뿌 뵤씨, 짜시야 어수구 소씨 무떠 꽈로사 어무찌마 워 구아나. 아오꽈, 비뿌 바너너 바꺼떠 바다다 뿌 아고고 가레 찌우뻬 어라 똬 오꼬 부씨 너 뤄어뽀 꽈 쭤찌러 꽈바어사고, 꽈 꽈더까 어라 뭐뉴.

12. 부씨 오누 무레모 워 구호로꽈 어더더 무파 오싸오 과 귀러사 어바쭈 바 오꼬 뱌 바꽈이러고, 시 가찌 뭐에 찌라, 바너너 꽈부 바쭈 바꺼떠 바다다 뿌 아고고 가레 찌우뻬 어라 똬 오꼬.

13. 부씨 너 무파 오유 무레모, 바쭈 바너너 바꺼떠 바도까 오꼬 똬 구로꽈 과

scattered abroad his gifts to the poor; his righteousness endures forever."

10. Now he who supplies seed to the sower and bread for food will also supply and increase your store of seed and will enlarge the harvest of your righteousness.

11. You will be made rich in every way so that you can be generous on every occasion, and through us your generosity will result in thanksgiving to God.

12. This service that you perform is not only supplying the needs of God's people but is also overflowing in many expressions of thanks to God.

13. Because of the service by which you have proved yourselves, men will praise

kulola kwa mwendjire mwayira kwa mwaasi mubuya-buya wa Kirisito atetchire. Kandji bangende bamutonga mwakulola kwa mutchima we kuana ola mwete mwa kunde mweeresaa'bo kwa bikulo byenyu, mweresa ne bandji bandju boshi.

뭐찌러 뫄에라 과 뫄아시 무부야-부야 와 기리시도 아더찌러. 가찌 바꺼머 바무도꺼 뫄구로꽈 과 무찌마 워 구아나 오꽈 뭐더 뫄 구너 뭐어러사아보 과 비구로 벼뉴, 뭐러사 너 바찌 바누 보씨.

God for the obedience that accompanies your confession of the gospel of Christ, and for your generosity in sharing with them and with everyone else.

14. Kandji bangende ba bemera na nzii inene bushi ne bubuya bunene busese bwa Ongo abetee'ko.

14. 가찌 바꺼머 바 버머라 나 씨이 이너너 부씨 너 부부야 부너너 부서서 봐 오꼬 아버더어고.

14. And in their prayers for you their hearts will go out to you, because of the surpassing grace God has given you.

15. Akoko era mwa Ongo bushi ne lweembo lwayi lwa lutangalyingamanyisibwa!

15. 아고고 어라 뫄 오꼬 부씨 너 뤄어뽀 뢔에 꽈 루다꺼레꺼마네시봐!

15. Thanks be to God for his indescribable gift!

2 E Bakorinto Chikono 10

2 어 바고리또 찌고노 10

2 Corinthians Chapter 10 [NIV]

1. Nyono Paulo nyeine nabema kurengera eburembu ne bubuya bwa Kirisito. E bandju bendjire bateta mbu mango nyiri mwa katchi-katchi kenyu nende naba murembu si mango nyiri nenyu, nanalosa kwa nyete misi.

1. 뇨노 파우로 녀이너 나버마 구러꺼라 어부러뿌 너 부부야 봐 기리시도. 어 바누 버찌러 바더다 뿌 마꼬 내리 뫄 가찌-가찌 거뉴 너꺼 나바 무러뿌 시 마꼬 내리 너뉴, 나나로사 과 녀더 미시.

1. By the meekness and gentleness of Christ, I appeal to you--I, Paul, who am "timid" when face to face with you, but "bold" when away!

2. Nabeema busese kwa mango nyingaika eyi mwenyu, mutairaa mwaasi ola unatchuma nalosa kwa nyeete misi. Bushi nysisi kanangana kwe eyi misi, nyingalosayi

2. 나버어마 부서서 과 마꼬 내꺼이가 어에 뭐뉴, 무다이라아 뫄아시 오꽈 우나쭈마 나로사 과 녀어더 미시. 부씨 내시시 가나꺼나 궈 어에 미시, 네꺼로사에

2. I beg you that when I come I may not have to be as bold as I expect to be toward some people who think that we live by the standards of this world.

kwabu bandjire baanyisa mbu emyanya yetchu iri ya mubiri.

3. Bushi tchiro mbu tchulyi mwa mubiri, si tchutendjire tchwalwa ebita kwa ndjira ye mubiri

4. Ebindju bya tchwendjire tchwakoresa mwa kulwa, bita bindju bya mubiri. Si ebuashi bwebi binsju butengire era mwa Ongo kwa kuhandjula ebikalyi bisibu bye barenda. Tchwendjire tchwahandjula ne myaanyisa yabo era itaye kanangana.

5. Na kuhandjula emianyisa yoshi yerume era yende yaangika ebandju kutamenya Ongo. Tchwendjire tchwasimba emianyisa yoshi ye bandju tchasiya inde yatchunda Kirisito.

6. Mango mungalosa kwa mutchundjire ene myaasi kanangana, mu mango tchungakemera tchira mundju ola utndjire watchunda'i.

7. Mwabo, mwendjire mwatola ebindju ngokwa binaseneke'ko. Tchira mundju woshi ola wendjire watchiandja kwa alyi mundju wa Kirisito, yeine ahubaa kumenyerera onu mwaasi: akaba alyi mundju wa Kirisito, netchu tchunalyi

과부 바찌러 바아네사 뿌 어먀냐 여쭈 이리 야 무비리.

3. 부씨 찌로 뿌 쭈레 먀 무비리, 시 쭈더찌러 좌똬 어비다 과 찌라 여 무비리

4. 어비뚜 뱌 쮀찌러 좌고러사 먀 구똬, 비다 비뚜 뱌 무비리. 시 어부아씨 붸비 비뚜 부더찌러 어라 먀 오꼬 과 구하뚜똬 어비가레 비시부 벼 바러따. 쮀찌러 좌하뚜똬 너 먀아네사 야보 어라 이다여 가나똬나.

5. 나 구하뚜똬 어미아네사 요씨 여루머 어라 여떠 야아끼가 어바뚜 구다머냐 오꼬. 쮀찌러 좌시빠 어미아네사 요씨 여 바뚜 짜시야 이떠 야쭈따 기리시도.

6. 마꼬 무똬로사 과 무쭈찌러 어너 먀아시 가나똬나, 무 마꼬 쭈똬거머라 찌라 무뚜 오똬 우두찌러 와쭈따이.

7. 와보, 뭐찌러 마도똬 어비뚜 꼬과 비나서너거고. 찌라 무뚜 온씨 오똬 워찌러 와찌아짜 과 아레 무뚜 와 기리시도, 여이너 아후바아 구머녀러라 오누 먀아시: 아가바 아레 무뚜 와 기리시도, 너쭈 쭈나레 바뚜

3. For though we live in the world, we do not wage war as the world does.

4. The weapons we fight with are not the weapons of the world. On the contrary, they have divine power to demolish strongholds.

5. We demolish arguments and every pretension that sets itself up against the knowledge of God, and we take captive every thought to make it obedient to Christ.

6. And we will be ready to punish every act of disobedience, once your obedience is complete.

7. You are looking only on the surface of things. If anyone is confident that he belongs to Christ, he should consider again that we belong to Christ just as much as he.

bandju ba Kirisito.

8. Bushi ndafaa honyi sisibya akaba na tchitongaa bushi ne buashi bwa Enawetchu atchweresise. Bushi obu buashi bulyi bwa kuimba e bwemeresi bwenyu, si buta bwa kubahandjula.

9. Ndahonda kulorekana'ko ngo'la wahonda kubobairisa kurengera emaruba manyi.

10. Bushi ebandju bendjire bateta mbu: "Emaruba ma Paulo matchula makaalyiire kandji masitoire. Si mango ende aba alyi mwa katchi-katchi ketchu, ende aba nga mutambukalyisa, ne mitetere yai yende yaba yakukenyibwa".

11. Emundju ola wendjire wateta batcha, tchetchine tchi emire kumenyerera: myaasi era tchwendjire tchwaandjika mwa maruba metchu manago tchulyi bure nenyu, inei itchunganaira mango tchungaba alauma nenyu.

12. Kanangana, tchubano tchutangaereresa kunde tchwatchitola nesi tchwatchiringamanya ne bandju ba bende batchitonga beine. Abola siri mbuta. Bendjire batchipima kukulyikana ne tchipimo

바 기리시도.

8. 부씨 따파아 호니 시시뱌 아가바 나 찌도₩아 부씨 너 부아씨 봐 어나워쭈 아쭤러시서. 부씨 오부 부아씨 부레 봐 구이빠 어 붜머러시 붜뉴, 시 부다 봐 구바하쭈롸.

9. 따호따 구롸러가나고 꼬롸 와호따 구보바이리사 구러뻐라 어마루바 마네.

10. 부씨 어바쭈 버찌러 바더다 뿌: "어마루바 마 파우로 마쭈롸 마가아레이러 가찌 마시도이러. 시 마꼬 어떠 아바 아레 봐 가찌-가찌 거쭈, 어떠 아바 까 무다뿌가레사, 너 미더더러 야이 여떠 야바 야구거네봐".

11. 어무뿌 오롸 워찌러 와더다 바짜, 쩌찌너 찌 어미러 구머녀러라: 먀아시 어라 쭤찌러 쫘아찌가 봐 마루바 머쭈 마나고 쭈레 부러 너뉴, 이너이 이쭈₩아나이라 마꼬 쭈₩바 아롸우마 너뉴.

12. 가나₩아나, 쭈바노 쭈다₩어러러사 구떠 쫘찌도롸 너시 쫘찌리₩아마냐 너 바뉴 바 버떠 바찌도₩ 비이너. 아보롸 시리 뿌다. 버찌러 바찌피마 구구레가나 너 찌피모 짜보 비이너 나 구찌리₩아마냐 비이너 과

8. For even if I boast somewhat freely about the authority the Lord gave us for building you up rather than pulling you down, I will not be ashamed of it.

9. I do not want to seem to be trying to frighten you with my letters.

10. For some say, "His letters are weighty and forceful, but in person he is unimpressive and his speaking amounts to nothing."

11. Such people should realize that what we are in our letters when we are absent, we will be in our actions when we are present.

12. We do not dare to classify or compare ourselves with some who commend themselves. When they measure themselves by themselves and compare themselves with themselves, they are not wise.

tchabo beine na kutchiringamanya beine kwa beine.

13. Si tchubano tchutangatchitonga kurenza etchipimo. Tchwahonda tchunde tchwakoresa etchipimo tche mulyimo ola Ongo atcweresaa. Noyu mulyimo iwatchuisaa eyi mwenyu.

14. Tchutahabukaa enyibibi ngokwa bingabere akaba tchungaikire eyi mwenyu. Bushi tchwaikaa kubahubanganyisa emwaasi mubuya-buya wa Kirisito.

15. Rero, tchutatchitonga kurenza e tchipimo bushi ne mulyimo we bandji bandju. Si tchweete emunyiiro kwa mango ebwemeresi bwenyu bungaendekera bwaluwa, tchungakola mulyimo munene mwa katchi-katchi kenyu, kukulyikana nenyibibi sa Ongo atchubikirire.

16. Tchasinda, tchungaya kuhubanganya e mwaasi mubuya-buya, mwa bindji biuo bya biri bure ne tchiuo tchenyu. Tchutahonda kukola mwabisiki bya bandji babaa bakolyire'mo nakutchitongera emulyimo ola babaa bakolyire

---

버이너.

13. 시 쭈바노 쭈다ᄊ찌도ᄊ 구러싸 어찌피모. 쫘호ᄄ 쭈ᄄ 쫘고러사 어찌피모 쩌 무례모 오라 오ᄁ 아쭤러사아. 노유 무례모 이와쭈이사아 어에 뭐뉴.

14. 쭈다하부가아 어네비비 ᄁ과 비ᄄ버러 아가바 쭈ᄊ이기러 어에 뭐뉴. 부씨 쫘이가아 구바후바ᄊ나네사 어ᄆ아아시 무부야-부야 와 기리시도.

15. 러로, 쭈다찌도ᄊ 구러싸 어 찌피모 부씨 너 무례모 워 바ᄊ 바뉴. 시 쭤어더 어무네이로 과 마ᄁ 어ᄇ머러시 뷔뉴 부ᄊ어ᄄ거라 봐루와, 쭈ᄊ고ᄊ 무례모 무너너 ᄆ 가찌-가찌 거뉴, 구구ᄊ게가나 너네비비 사 오ᄁ 아쭈비기리러.

16. 짜시ᄄ, 쭈ᄊ야 구후바ᄊ나ᄒ 어 ᄆ아아시 무부야-부야, ᄆ 비ᄊ 비우오 뱌 비리 부러 너 찌우오 쩌뉴. 쭈다호ᄄ 구고ᄊ ᄆ아비시기 뱌 바ᄊ 바바아 바고ᄊ러모 나구찌도ᄊ라 어무례모 오ᄊ 바바아

---

13. We, however, will not boast beyond proper limits, but will confine our boasting to the field God has assigned to us, a field that reaches even to you.

14. We are not going too far in our boasting, as would be the case if we had not come to you, for we did get as far as you with the gospel of Christ.

15. Neither do we go beyond our limits by boasting of work done by others. Our hope is that, as your faith continues to grow, our area of activity among you will greatly expand,

16. so that we can preach the gospel in the regions beyond you. For we do not want to boast about work already done in another man's territory.

mira.

17. Bushi e maandjiko mabuya-buya matchula matetchire nambu: "akaba emundju ahonda kutchitonga, endaa atchitonga bushi na Enawetchu".

18. Bushi ata emundju ola wende watchitonga yeine iwende waba wemererwe era muhondo sa Ongo, si ola watongibwa na Enawetchu.

바고레러 미라.

17. 부씨 어 마아찌고 마부야-부야 마쭈라 마더찌러 나뿌: "아가바 어무뚜 아호따 구찌도따, 어따아 아찌도따 부씨 나 어나워쭈".

18. 부씨 아다 어무뚜 오꽈 워떠 와찌도따 여이너 이워떠 와바 워머러뤄 어라 무호또 사 오꼬, 시 오꽈 와도삐봐 나 어나워쭈.

17. But, "Let him who boasts boast in the Lord."

18. For it is not the one who commends himself who is approved, but the one whom the Lord commends.

2 E Bakorinto Chikono 11

1. Ebetchu! Nabema busese munyemerere nyihambale nenyu nga musire ; munyemerereaa betchu!

2. nendjire nabafira lui lunene, nulu lui, era mwa Ongo yi lutengire. Bushi mwabo, mulyi nga munyere ola utafuraa kumenya balume, ola ukomisibwe, ola nalaanyise kuabira mulume muuma oshao. Noyu mulume i Kirisito.

3. Si mukengeraa kute wandjoka atebaa Efa kurengera ebukalabge bwai. Rero nobaa nenyu mungesha kutebwa, kuikira etchihangi mwaesa ekutchindjirwa ne

2 어 바고리또 찌고노 11

1. 어버쭈! 나버마 부서서 무녀머러러 네하빠러 너뉴 따 무시러 ; 무녀머러러아아 버쭈!

2. 너찌러 나바피라 루이 루너너, 누루 루이, 어라 뫄 오꼬 에 루더삐러. 부씨 뫄보, 무녀려 오꽈 우다푸라아 구머냐 바루머, 오꽈 우고미시붜, 오꽈 나꽈아네서 구아비라 무루머 무우마 오싸오. 노유 무루머 이 기리시도.

3. 시 무거머라아 구더 와또가 아더바아 어파 구러떠라 어부가꽈부거 봐이. 러로 노바아 너뉴 무꺼싸 구더봐, 구이기라 어찌하삐 뫄어사 어구찌찌롸 너

2 Corinthians Chapter 11 [NIV]

1. I hope you will put up with a little of my foolishness; but you are already doing that.

2. I am jealous for you with a godly jealousy. I promised you to one husband, to Christ, so that I might present you as a pure virgin to him.

3. But I am afraid that just as Eve was deceived by the serpent's cunning, your minds may somehow be led astray from your sincere and pure devotion to Christ.

kukomisibwa kwa mutchusa
mwa buuma bwenyu na
Kirisito.

4. Ebyera bitenganyire nokwa
mwendjire mwemerera mbu
undji mundju aikaa
kubahubanganyisa era luulu sa
undji-undji yesu, kureka ola
tchwabahubanganyisaa. Kandji
mwendjire mwaba bangula
mwangiriraa, na kwangirira
undji-undji mwaasi mubuya-
buya ola utalyi ngola
mwaangiriraa kutenga era
tchulyi.

5. Naanyisa kwa abu
mwendjire mwatola ngabu
bakulu-kulu busese mwa
ndjumwa, batanyirenzise mu
tchiro na mwasi asibya.

6. Kubinalyi, tchiro angaba
mbu ndatchula nysihsi kuteta
si kwa bya byerekere emyaasi
ye bwenge, nyibishi kubuya.
Ebyera tchwanabalosaa'bi
kubuya-buya tchira mango
nomwa myaasi yoshi.

7. Nyono nabahubanganyisaa
emwaasi mubuya-buya wa
Ongo busira kubema kandju.
Natchandaasa batcha, nairaa
tchibi?

8. Mango nabaa nakola mwa
katchi-katchi kenyu, nabaa
nendjire nayipibwa ne bindji

구고미시봐 과 무쭈사 뫄
부우마 뭐뉴 나 기리시도.

4. 어벼라 비더꺼네러 노과
뭐찌러 뭐머러라 뿌 우찌
무뚜 아이가아
구바후바꺼네사 어라 루우루
사 우찌-우찌 여수, 구러가
오꽈 좌바후바꺼네사아. 가찌
뭐찌러 뫄바 바위꽈
뫄찌리라아, 나 과찌리라
우찌-우찌 뫄아시 무부야-
부야 오꽈 우다레 꼬꽈
뫄아찌리라아 구더꺼 어라
쭈레.

5. 나아네사 과 아부 뭐찌러
뫄도꽈 꺼부 바구루-구루
부서서 뫄 뚜뫄,
바다네러씨서 무 찌로 나
뫄시 아시뱌.

6. 구비나레, 찌로 아꺼바 뿌
따쭈꽈 네시후시 구더다 시
과 뱌 벼러거러 어먀아시 여
뭐꺼, 네비씨 구부야. 어벼라
좌나바로사아비 구부야-부야
찌라 마꼬 노뫄 먀아시 요씨.

7. 뇨노 나바후바꺼네사아
어먀아시 무부야-부야 와
오꼬 부시라 구버마 가뚜.
나짜따아사 바짜, 나이라아
찌비?

8. 마꼬 나바아 나고꽈 뫄
가찌-가찌 거뉴, 나바아
너찌러 나에피봐 너 비찌

4. For if someone comes to
you and preaches a Jesus
other than the Jesus we
preached, or if you receive a
different spirit from the one
you received, or a different
gospel from the one you
accepted, you put up with it
easily enough.

5. But I do not think I am in
the least inferior to those
"super-apostles."

6. I may not be a trained
speaker, but I do have
knowledge. We have made
this perfectly clear to you in
every way.

7. Was it a sin for me to
lower myself in order to
elevate you by preaching
the gospel of God to you
free of charge?

8. I robbed other churches
by receiving support from
them so as to serve you.

bikembe bye bemeresi. Mwa kuira batcha, nabaa ngola wanyaa ebikulo byabu bemeresi na kukoresa'bi bushi nenyu.

9. Mango nabaa nyiri mwa katchi-katchi kenyu, ndasitoweraa tchiro na mundju asibya mwa malae manyi. Bushi banyaketchu ba batengaa e maketoniya, banyireteraa byoshi bya nabaa nyilaire'ko. Mwa myaasi yoshi, natchilangaa busese nyingesha kubasitoera. Kandji nyingaendekera kunde natchilanga.

10. Kukulyikana ne kanangana ka Kirisito ka kalyi mwa ndanda sanyi, nalaisa kwa kutalyi tchiro na mundju asibya ola unganyianga mbu ndatchitongaa bushi noyu mwaasi mwa tchiuo tchoshi tche Akaya.

11. Tchi tchatchumire nateta batcha? Eri bushi ndabasimire? Ongo yeine aneshi.

12. Bya naira lwarero, bi nyinganaendekera kuira, tchasiya nyaangike e bandju boshi ba bendjire bahonda kutchitonga kwa nabo bakola kuuma netchu.

비거뻐 벼 버머러시. 뫄 구이라 바짜, 나바아 끄롸 와냐아 어비구롣 뱌부 버머러시 나 구고러사비 부씨 너뉴.

9. 마끄 나바아 네리 뫄 가찌-가찌 거뉴, 따시도워라아 찌로 나 무뚜 아시뱌 뫄 마퐈어 마니. 부씨 바냐거쭈 바 바더뫄아 어 마거도니야, 바네러더라아 뵤씨 뱌 나바아 네퐈이러고. 뫄 먀아시 요씨, 나찌퐈뫄아 부써서 네뻐싸 구바시도어라. 가찌 네뻐어떠거라 구뗘 나찌퐈뺘.

10. 구구례가나 너 가나뫄나 가 기리시도 가 가례 뫄 따따 사네, 나퐈이사 과 구다례 찌로 나 무뚜 아시뱌 오롸 우뫄네아뺘 뿌 따찌도뫄아 부씨 노유 뫄아시 뫄 찌우오 쪼씨 쩌 아가야.

11. 찌 짜쭈미러 나더다 바짜? 어리 부씨 따바시미러? 오끄 여이너 아너씨.

12. 뱌 나이라 퐈러로, 비 네뫄나어떠거라 구이라, 짜시야 냐아끼거 어 바뚜 보씨 바 버찌러 바호따 구찌도뫄 과 나보 바고롸 구우마 너쭈.

---

9. And when I was with you and needed something, I was not a burden to anyone, for the brothers who came from Macedonia supplied what I needed. I have kept myself from being a burden to you in any way, and will continue to do so.

10. As surely as the truth of Christ is in me, nobody in the regions of Achaia will stop this boasting of mine.

11. Why? Because I do not love you? God knows I do!

12. And I will keep on doing what I am doing in order to cut the ground from under those who want an opportunity to be considered equal with us in the things they boast about.

13. Abu bandju sita ndjumwa kanangana, kandji balyi bakosi ba bateteta e kanangana. Bendjire bwatchiira nga siri ndjumwa sa Kirisito.

14. Oyu mwaasi ata wakushishasa bushi anabe wamusimu yeine nai ende atchiira kuba ndonyi wa bulangare.

15. Rero ata mwaasi wakushishasa akaba ebakosi be myaasi era itchungenene. Kwa businda, bakembibwa kukulyikana ne bya bende baira.

16. Nateta kanji: kutabaa mundju ola watchitchinga mbu nyiri musire! Akaba bitalyi batcha, munyemereraa nga musire tchasiya nanyi nyitchitonge hitcha.

17. Bine nateta kwa kutchitonga, bitatenganyire ne kuhonda kwa Enawetchu, si natetaa'bi nga musire.

18. Rero bushi bandju banene bendjire batchitonga kwa ndjira ye mubiri, nanyi nyingatchitonga

19. Mwabo mu mwishi myaasi, mwendjire mwa mowera kweemerera ebasire!

20. Bushi mwendjire mweemerera emundju ola

---

13. 아부 바뚜 시다 뚜꽈 가나꽈나, 가찌 바레 바고시 바 바더더다 어 가나꽈나. 버찌러 봐찌이라 꽈 시리 뚜꽈 사 기리시도.

14. 오유 꽈아시 아다 와구씨싸사 부씨 아나버 와무시무 여이너 나이 어너 아찌이라 구바 또네 와 부꽈꽈러.

15. 러로 아다 꽈아시 와구씨싸사 아가바 어바고시 버 먀아시 어라 이쭈꺼너너. 과 부시따, 바거삐봐 구구레가나 너 뱌 버뎌 바이라.

16. 나더다 가찌: 구다바아 무뚜 오꽈 와찌찌꽈 뿌 네리 무시러! 아가바 비다레 바짜, 무녀머러라아 꽈 무시러 짜시야 나네 네찌도꺼 히짜.

17. 비너 나더다 과 구찌도꽈, 비다더꽈네러 너 구호따 과 어나워쭈, 시 나더다아비 꽈 무시러.

18. 러로 부씨 바뚜 바너너 버찌러 바찌도꽈 과 띠라 여 무비리, 나네 네꽈찌도꽈

19. 꽈보 무 뮈씨 먀아시, 뭐찌러 꽈 모워라 궈어머러라 어바시러!

20. 부씨 뭐찌러 뭐어머러라 어무뚜 오꽈 와바도꽈 꽈

---

13. For such men are false apostles, deceitful workmen, masquerading as apostles of Christ.

14. And no wonder, for Satan himself masquerades as an angel of light.

15. It is not surprising, then, if his servants masquerade as servants of righteousness. Their end will be what their actions deserve.

16. I repeat: Let no one take me for a fool. But if you do, then receive me just as you would a fool, so that I may do a little boasting.

17. In this self-confident boasting I am not talking as the Lord would, but as a fool.

18. Since many are boasting in the way the world does, I too will boast.

19. You gladly put up with fools since you are so wise!

20. In fact, you even put up with anyone who enslaves

wabatola nga tchuungu, ola wabatola mwe mutoloke mwa bukalange, ola wabanyaa ebikulo byenyu, ola wabakengula, ola wabamaasa era muso.

21. Naataa honyi sakuteta ene myaasi: tchubano tchutete misi ya kuira batcha. Si akaba mundju murene angaereresa kutchitonga bushi na kandju karebe, nanyi nyinganaereresa.

22. Abu bandju balyi Baeburaniya? Nanyi nyinalyi Mueburaniya. Balyi ba Isiraeli? Nanyi nyinalyi mu Isiraeli! Balyi bomwa lubuto lwa Aburahamu? Nanyi nyinalyi womwa lubuto lwai!

23. Balyi baanda ba Kirisito? Nyono nyiri muanda wai kubarenza. Aola, nanatetchire kandji nga mbuta. Nakolaa mirimo inene kurenzabo, naminwaa mbiso sinene kurenzabo, napundjwaa biso sinene busese kurenzabo, na bihangi binene elufu lwabaa lunyiri era muongo.

24. Ku mbiso etano, eBayuta banyi hutaa biboko mahatu na mwenda.

쭈우우, 오라 와바도롸 뭐 무도로거 롸 부가롸뼈, 오롸 와바냐아 어비구롣 벼뉴, 오롸 와바거우롸, 오롸 와바마아사 어라 무소.

21. 나아다아 호네 사구더다 어너 먀아시: 쭈바노 쭈더더 미시 야 구이라 바짜. 시 아가바 무뚜 무러너 아꺄어러러사 구찌도꺄 부씨 나 가꾸 가러버, 나네 네꺄나어러러사.

22. 아부 바꾸 바롙 바어부라니야? 나네 네나롙 무어부라니야. 바롙 바 이시라어뤼? 나네 네나롙 무 이시라어뤼! 바롙 보뫄 루부도 롹 아부라하무? 나네 네나롙 옴뫄 루부도 롸이!

23. 바롙 바아따 바 기리시도? 뇨노 네리 무아따 와이 구바러싸. 아오롸, 나나더찌러 가찌 꺄 뿌다. 나고꾀아 미리모 이너너 구러싸보, 나미놔아 뻬소 시너너 구러싸보, 나푸꾀아 비소 시너너 부서서 구러싸보, 나 비하뼈 비너너 어루푸 롹바아 루네리 어라 무오꼬.

24. 구 뻬소 어다노, 어바유다 바네 후다아 비보고 마하두 나 뭐따.

you or exploits you or takes advantage of you or pushes himself forward or slaps you in the face.

21. To my shame I admit that we were too weak for that! What anyone else dares to boast about--I am speaking as a fool--I also dare to boast about.

22. Are they Hebrews? So am I. Are they Israelites? So am I. Are they Abraham's descendants? So am I.

23. Are they servants of Christ? (I am out of my mind to talk like this.) I am more. I have worked much harder, been in prison more frequently, been flogged more severely, and been exposed to death again and again.

24. Five times I received from the Jews the forty lashes minus one.

25. Napundjwaa kahathu mwa thuchi, nahuthwaa emakoi euma, nasikaa kahathu mwa nyanja, nairaa buthufu buuma na lusuku lwa mutenga mwa nyanja.

25. 나푸좌아 가하쭈 뫄 쭈찌, 나후좌아 어마고이 어우마, 나시가아 가하쭈 뫄 냐짜, 나이라아 부후푸 부우마 나 루수구 꽈 무더까 뫄 냐짜.

25. Three times I was beaten with rods, once I was stoned, three times I was shipwrecked, I spent a night and a day in the open sea,

26. Nairaa nyibalamo mbiso sinene. Mwesi nyibalamo, nrengaa mwa bisibu byemwihuso wenyishi sinenene, mwa bisibu byekutabalyirwa nebihumusi, mwa bisibu byekutabalyirwa na banyakethu Bayuta, mwa bisibu byekutabalirwa neba batathula Bayuta. Narengaa mwa bisibu mwa misi, nomwa buyeye, nokwa nyanja inene, nomwa kachi-kachi kebandju ba benjire bacherika mbu balyi banyakethu noku bata banyakethu.

26. 나이라아 네바꽈모 삐소 시너너. 뭐시 네바꽈모, 누러꺄아 뫄 비시부 벼뮈후소 워네씨 시너너너, 뫄 비시부 벼구다바꼐롸 너비후무시, 뫄 비시부 벼구다바꼐롸 나 바냐거쭈 바유다, 뫄 비시부 벼구다바뢰라 너바 바다쭈꽈 바유다. 나러꺄아 뫄 비시부 뫄 미시, 노뫄 부여여, 노과 냐짜 이너너, 노뫄 가찌-가찌 거바쭈 바 버찌러 바쩌리가 뿌 바꼐 바냐거쭈 노구 바다 바냐거쭈.

26. I have been constantly on the move. I have been in danger from rivers, in danger from bandits, in danger from my own countrymen, in danger from Gentiles; in danger in the city, in danger in the country, in danger at sea; and in danger from false brothers.

27. Natamaa nemirimo isito. Bihangi binene nanaa ethulo, bihangi binene nafa neebusinya alauma nechaami, bihangi binene nachiimaa ebiryo. Nalyibukaa nembeo na kuina enjimba.

27. 나다마아 너미리모 이시도. 비하끼 비너너 나나아 어쭈롣, 비하끼 비너너 나파 너어부시냐 아꽈우마 너짜아미, 비하끼 비너너 나찌이마아 어비료. 나꼐부가아 너뻐오 나 구이나 어찌빠.

27. I have labored and toiled and have often gone without sleep; I have known hunger and thirst and have often gone without food; I have been cold and naked.

28. Kanji busira kutondosa einji myasi yoshi era iri ngei, chira lusuku emuchima wanyi enjire aanyisa busese era luulu sebikembe byoshi

28. 가찌 부시라 구도또사 어이찌 먀시 요씨 어라 이리 꺼이, 찌라 루수구 어무찌마 와네 어찌러 아아네사 부서서 어라 루우루 서비거뻐 뵤씨

28. Besides everything else, I face daily the pressure of my concern for all the churches.

byebemeresi.

29. Mango mundju murebe aina emisi, nanyi ndachumva nainyirei? Mango mundju murebe aya mwa mabi, echera chitanyocha kwa muchima?

30. Akaba byeemire nyichitonge, nyingende nachitonga bushi nekuina emisi kwanyi.

31. Ongo, Eshe wa Enawethu Yesu, iwende watongibwa esuku nemango aneshi kwa ndafula bisha.

32. Mango nabaanyiri mwa musi we Tamasiki, emukulu-kulu ola mwami Aretaa baaemikiremo era kubika ebalanzi mwoyu musi chasiya banyisimbe.

33. Si ebandju bera kunyibika mwa chitonga, bera kunyirenzesa mwa tirisha na banyandaasisa kwa lusimbo lwemusi. Rero, kunafufumukaa bacha kutenga mwa mino yoyu mukulu-kulu.

2 E Bakorinto Chikono 12

1. Mwa batcha, nyingaendekera kunde na tchitonga mbu ekutchitonga

---

벼버머러시.

29. 마꼬 무뚜 무러버 아이나 어미시, 나네 따쭈빠 나이네러이? 마꼬 무뚜 무러버 아야 먀 마비, 어쩌라 찌다뇨짜 과 무찌마?

30. 아가바 벼어미러 네찌도꺼, 네어떠 나찌도꽈 부씨 너구이나 어미시 과네.

31. 오꼬, 어써 와 어나워쭈 여수, 이워떠 와도삐봐 어수구 너마꼬 아너씨 과 따푸롸 비싸.

32. 마꼬 나바아네리 먀 무시 워 다마시기, 어무구루-구루 오롸 마미 아러다아 바아어미기러모 어라 구비가 어바롸씨 모유 무시 짜시야 바네시뻐.

33. 시 어바누 버라 구네비가 먀 찌도꽈, 버라 구네러써사 먀 디리싸 나 바냐따아시사 과 루시뽀 뤄무시. 러로, 구나푸푸무가아 바짜 구더꽈 먀 미노 요유 무구루-구루.

2 어 바고리또 찌고노 12

1. 먀 바짜, 네꺼어떠거라 구떠 나 찌도꽈 뿌 어구찌도꽈 구더더 무파.

---

29. Who is weak, and I do not feel weak? Who is led into sin, and I do not inwardly burn?

30. If I must boast, I will boast of the things that show my weakness.

31. The God and Father of the Lord Jesus, who is to be praised forever, knows that I am not lying.

32. In Damascus the governor under King Aretas had the city of the Damascenes guarded in order to arrest me.

33. But I was lowered in a basket from a window in the wall and slipped through his hands.

2 Corinthians Chapter 12 [NIV]

1. I must go on boasting. Although there is nothing to be gained, I will go on to

kutete mufa. Rero nera nahonda kuteta era luulu se bya byende byalorekana'ko nga byabunya biroto ne myaasi era Enawetchu anyibihulyiraa.

2. Nyishi mundju muuma ola wabaa ulyi mwa buuma na Kirisito. Rero kwarenga myaka ekuni ne'ene oyu mundju erusibwe kuikira kwa nguba ya kahatchu. Ndeshi akaba oyu mundju erusibwaa alyi mwa mubiri nesi abaa atalyi mwa mubiri. Ongo yeine oshao yi uneshi.

3. Kandji nyishi kwa oyu mundju erusibwa, si ndeshi akaba erusibwaa alyi mwa mubiri nesi atalyi mwa mubiri. Ongo yeine oshao yi uneshi.

4. Oyu mundju erusibwaa kuikira mwa paratiso. Era kuumva ku myaasi ya kushishaa era emundju atete loso lwa kubalyikisa.

5. Emundju ola ulyi ngoyu, inyingatchingera. Si nyono ndatchitonge bushi nanyi nyeine, kureka ekuina emisi kwanyi.

6. Akaba nyingasimire kunde na tchitonga, ndangabere musire, bushi nyingendjire nanateta ekanangana. Si

러로 너라 나호따 구더다 어라 룻우룻 서 뱌 벼너 뱌롣러가나고 까 뱌부냐 비로도 너 먀아시 어라 어나워쭈 아네비후레라아.

2. 네씨 무뚜 무우마 오롸 와바아 우레 뫄 부우마 나 기리시도. 러로 과러까 먀가 어구니 너어너 오유 무뚜 어루시붜 구이기라 과 꾸바 야 가하쭈. 떠씨 아가바 오유 무뚜 어루시봐아 아레 뫄 무비리 너시 아바아 아다레 뫄 무비리. 오꼬 여이너 오싸오 에 우너씨.

3. 가찌 네씨 과 오유 무뚜 어루시봐, 시 떠씨 아가바 어루시봐아 아레 뫄 무비리 너시 아다레 뫄 무비리. 오꼬 여이너 오싸오 에 우너씨.

4. 오유 무뚜 어루시봐아 구이기라 뫄 파라디소. 어라 구우빠 구 먀아시 야 구씨싸아 어라 어무뚜 아더더 로소 똬 구바레기사.

5. 어무뚜 오롸 우레 꼬유, 이네까찌꺼라. 시 뇨노 따찌도꺼 부씨 나내 녀이너, 구러가 어구이나 어미시 과내.

6. 아가바 네까시미러 구떠 나 찌도까, 따까버러 무시러, 부씨 네꺼찌러 나나더다 어가나까나. 시 떠찌러

visions and revelations from the Lord.

2. I know a man in Christ who fourteen years ago was caught up to the third heaven. Whether it was in the body or out of the body I do not know--God knows.

3. And I know that this man--whether in the body or apart from the body I do not know, but God knows--

4. was caught up to paradise. He heard inexpressible things, things that man is not permitted to tell.

5. I will boast about a man like that, but I will not boast about myself, except about my weaknesses.

6. Even if I should choose to boast, I would not be a fool, because I would be speaking the truth. But I

ndendjire nasima kutchitonga, e bandju bangesha kunde banyerusa busese kurenza bya basene nendjire naira nesi bya bendjire bomva nateta.

7. Si kwakuhonda ndarengeresa mwa kunde na tchitonga bushi ne myaasi ye kushishaa era Ongo anyibihulyiraa, nabibkibwaa kandju mwa mubiri ka kendjire kanyibabasa nga muhoi-hoi. Aku kandju kalyi nga ndjumwa ya wamusimu kwa kunyihuta na kunyaangika nyingesha kurengeresa mwa kunde na tchitonga.

8. Neema Emawetchu kahatchu, tchasiya akule amu malyibuko mwanda sanyi.

9. Si era kuakula mbu: "e bondjo bwanyi bulumirire era ulyi. Bushi ebuashi bwanyi bwende bwalorekana'ko mango emundju ainyire misi". Rero, nyingende natchitongera ekuina emisi kwanyi, tchasiya ebuashi bwa Kirisito bube mwa ndanda sanyi.

10. Bushi noku, nendjire nomowera ekuina emisi, ne kukambibwa, nekulyibukira mwa mutchima, ne kulyibusibwa, ne kwobairisibwa bushi na Kirisito. Bushi mango

---

나시마 구찌도꺄, 어 바꾸 바꺼싸 구떠 바녀루사 부서서 구러싸 뱌 바서너 너띠러 나이라 너시 뱌 버띠러 보빠 나더다.

7. 시 과구호따 따러꺼러사 뫄 구떠 나 찌도꺄 부씨 너 먀아시 여 구씨싸아 어라 오꼬 아네비후꿰라아, 나비부기봐아 가꾸 뫄 무비리 가 거띠러 가네바바사 꺄 무호이-호이. 아구 가꾸 가뼤 꺄 꾸뫄 야 와무시무 과 구네후다 나 구냐아끼가 네꺼싸 구러꺼러사 뫄 구떠 나 찌도꺄.

8. 너어마 어마워쭈 가하쭈, 짜시야 아구꿔 아무 마뼤부고 뫄따 사네.

9. 시 어라 구아구꽈 뿌: "어 보쪼 봐네 부루미리러 어라 우꿰. 부씨 어부아씨 봐네 붸떠 봐로러가나고 마꼬 어무꾸 아이네러 미시". 러로, 네꺼떠 나찌도꺼라 어구이나 어미시 과네, 짜시야 어부아씨 봐 기리시도 부버 뫄 따따 사네.

10. 부씨 노구, 너띠러 노모워라 어구이나 어미시, 너 구가뼤봐, 너구꿰부기라 뫄 무찌마, 너 구꿰부시봐, 너 곱바이리시봐 부씨 나 기리시도. 부씨 마꼬

---

refrain, so no one will think more of me than is warranted by what I do or say.

7. To keep me from becoming conceited because of these surpassingly great revelations, there was given me a thorn in my flesh, a messenger of Satan, to torment me.

8. Three times I pleaded with the Lord to take it away from me.

9. But he said to me, "My grace is sufficient for you, for my power is made perfect in weakness." Therefore I will boast all the more gladly about my weaknesses, so that Christ's power may rest on me.

10. That is why, for Christ's sake, I delight in weaknesses, in insults, in hardships, in persecutions, in difficulties. For when I am weak, then I am strong.

nainyire emisi, mumango nende naba munyake.

11. Rero, nerire nanaba nga musire! Si mumwatchumire naba batcha. Mwabo mu mwabaa mwemire kunde mwalosa kwanyiri nde. Bushi tchiro angaba mbu nyiri mundju wabuha-buha, si esi ndjumwa senyu sa mwendjire mwatola nga buhakulu-kulu busese sitanyirenzise kandju kasibya.

12. Emyaasi era yalosa kwa nyinalyi ndjumwa kanangana, yairibwaa mwa katchi-katchi kenyu na bushibirisi bunene? Neyi myaasi iyene: Ekuira ebisomerane, ne bishishalo, ne bimenyeso.

13. Tchimwakeerwaa natchi kurenza ebinji bikembe bye bemeresi, kureka nyono ekutabasitowera? Rero, munyiobabalyiraa kwoyu mwaasi utatchungenen!

14. Natchikunganyisa mira kwa kuika eyi mwenyu ebwakahatchu, ndanabasitowere. Bushi ata ebikulo byenyu bi nahonda, si mwabo mu nahonda. Bushi ata ebana bu bemire kunde babikira ebaere babi ebwaare, si ebasere bu bemire kunde

나이네러 어미시, 무마꼬 너떠 나바 무냐거.

11. 러로, 너리러 나나바 까 무시러! 시 무뫄쭈미러 나바 바짜. 뫄보 무 뫄바아 뭐미러 구떠 뫄르사 과네리 떠. 부씨 찌로 아까바 뿌 네리 무뚜 와부하-부하, 시 어시 뚜뫄 서뉴 사 뭐띠러 뫄도롸 까 부하구루-구루 부서서 시다네러씨서 가뚜 가시뱌.

12. 어먀아시 어라 야르사 과 네나레 뚜뫄 가나까나, 야이리봐아 뫄 가찌-가찌 거뉴 나 부씨비리시 부너너? 너에 먀아시 이여너: 어구이라 어비소머라너, 너 비씨싸르, 너 비머녀소.

13. 찌뫄거어롸아 나찌 구러싸 어비찌 비거뻐 벼 버머러시, 구러가 뇨노 어구다바시도워라? 러로, 무네오바바레라아 교유 뫄아시 우다쭈꺼너!

14. 나찌구까네사 미라 과 구이가 어에 뭐뉴 어봐가하쭈, 따나바시도워러. 부씨 아다 어비구르 벼뉴 비 나호따, 시 뫄보 무 나호따. 부씨 아다 어바나 부 버미러 구떠 바비기라 어봐어러 바비 어봐아러, 시 어바서러 부 버미러 구떠 바비기라보

11. I have made a fool of myself, but you drove me to it. I ought to have been commended by you, for I am not in the least inferior to the "super-apostles," even though I am nothing.

12. The things that mark an apostle--signs, wonders and miracles--were done among you with great perseverance.

13. How were you inferior to the other churches, except that I was never a burden to you? Forgive me this wrong!

14. Now I am ready to visit you for the third time, and I will not be a burden to you, because what I want is not your possessions but you. After all, children should not have to save up for their parents, but parents for their children.

babikira'bo ebana babo.

어바나 바보.

15. Si nyono nyingamowa kukoresa ebikulo byanyi na kwaana ekalamo kanyi nyeine bushi nenyu. Rero akaba nyibasimire busese batcha, munganyiataa'ku nzii yeeke?

15. 시 뇨노 녜까모와 구고러사 어비구로 뱌네 나 과아나 어가짜모 가네 녀이너 부씨 너뉴. 러로 아가바 네바시미러 부서서 바짜, 무까네아다아구 씨이 여어거?

15. So I will very gladly spend for you everything I have and expend myself as well. If I love you more, will you love me less?

16. Muneshi kubuya-buya kwa nyono ndabasitoweraa. Si bandju bauma bendjire bamenya mbu nyiri mukalange, kandji nasimbire'bo kurengera ebakalange.

16. 무너씨 구부야-부야 과 뇨노 따바시도워라아. 시 바쭈 바우마 버찌러 바머냐 뿌 녜리 무가짜머, 가찌 나시삐러보 구러꺼라 어바가짜머.

16. Be that as it may, I have not been a burden to you. Yet, crafty fellow that I am, I caught you by trickery!

17. Munyiburaa: nababanaaku mutoloke mwa bukalange kurengera muuuma mwa bandju ba nabatchumiraa?

17. 무네부라아: 나바바나아구 무도로거 마 부가짜머 구러꺼라 무우우마 마 바쭈 바 나바쭈미라아?

17. Did I exploit you through any of the men I sent you?

18. Neema Tito buses embu ayaa eyi mwenyu, nera kumutchuma na undji munyaketchu muuma. Munyiburaa, kulyi mutoloke ola Tito ababonaa'ko mwa bukalange? Nyono alauma nai, tchwaba tchutaneete mianyisa yiuma na myanya yiuma?

18. 너어마 디도 부서수 어뿌 아야아 어에 뮤뉴, 너라 구무쭈마 나 우씨 무냐거쭈 무우마. 무네부라아, 구레 무도로거 오라 디도 아바보나아고 마 부가짜머? 뇨노 아짜우마 나이, 쫘바 쭈다너어더 미아네사 에우마 나 먀냐 에우마?

18. I urged Titus to go to you and I sent our brother with him. Titus did not exploit you, did he? Did we not act in the same spirit and follow the same course?

19. Kutengera mira, mwaabo mwende mwaantisa mbu tchubano tchwendjire tchwahonda kutchitetera era muhondo senyu. Tchwendjire tchwateta era muhondo sa Ongo kukulyikana ne buuma

19. 구더꺼라 미라, 뫄아보 뭐떠 뫄아띠사 뿌 쭈바노 쮜찌러 쫘호따 구찌더더라 어라 무호또 서뉴. 쮜찌러 쫘더다 어라 무호또 사 오꼬 구구레가나 너 부우마 붜쭈 나 기리시도. 가찌 바냐거쭈

19. Have you been thinking all along that we have been defending ourselves to you? We have been speaking in the sight of God as those in Christ; and everything we do, dear friends, is for your

bwetchu na Kirisito. Kandji banyaketchu bassirwa, tchwendjire tchwaira eyi myaasi yoshi tchasiya mukule mwa bwemeresi.

20. Bushi nobaa kwamango nyingaika eyi mwenyu, ndababuane mulyi ngokwa nahonda, nenyu mutanyibuane nyiri ngokwa mwahonda. Nabaa nyingesha kubabuana mulyi mwa mbangano, mwafirana mufula, musibukirirane, mweteneku mutchima mubi wakaimano, mwakambana, mwamaanana bulyio, mwatchilola, mulyi nomwa kafango.

21. Kandji nobaa kwa mango nyingahuba kuika eyi mwenyu, Ongo wanyi anganyiitchisa honyi era muhondo senyu. Aola, nyingalyira bushi na bandju banene mwaba bairaa ebibi kwa mira, batanabindjukaa batenge mwa myaasi ye kutcha esinga, nomwa buhungu, nomwa lusingi.

바씨롸, 쭤찌러 좌이라 어에 먀아시 요씨 짜시야 무구꿔 롸 뭐머러시.

20. 부씨 노바아 과마꼬 네까이가 어에 뭐뉴, 따바부아너 무레 꼬과 나호따, 너뉴 무다네부아너 네리 꼬과 먀호따. 나바아 네꺼싸 구바부아나 무레 롸 빠까노, 롸피라나 무푸롸, 무시부기리라너, 뭐더너구 무찌마 무비 와가이마노, 롸가빠나, 롸마아나나 부레오, 롸찌로롸, 무레 노롸 가파꼬.

21. 가찌 노바아 과 마꼬 네까후바 구이가 어에 뭐뉴, 오꼬 와네 아까네이찌사 호네 어라 무호또 서뉴. 아오롸, 네까레라 부씨 나 바뚜 바너너 롸바 바이라아 어비비 과 미라, 바다나비뚜가아 바더꺼 롸 먀아시 여 구짜 어시까, 노롸 부후우, 노롸 루시끼.

strengthening.

20. For I am afraid that when I come I may not find you as I want you to be, and you may not find me as you want me to be. I fear that there may be quarreling, jealousy, outbursts of anger, factions, slander, gossip, arrogance and disorder.

21. I am afraid that when I come again my God will humble me before you, and I will be grieved over many who have sinned earlier and have not repented of the impurity, sexual sin and debauchery in which they have indulged.

2 E Bakorinto Chikono 13

2 어 바고리또 찌고노 13

2 Corinthians Chapter 13 [NIV]

1. Lunola lu lubalamo lwanyi lwa kahatchu nakunganya lwe

1. 루노롸 루 루바롸모 꽈네 꽈 가하쭈 나구꺄냐 뤄 구야

1. This will be my third visit to you. "Every matter must

kuya eyi mwenyu. Ngokwa maandjiko mabuya-buya matchula matetchire mbu: "tchira mwasi ende emererwa kwa alyi wa kanangana kwa bubei bwa bandju babilyi nesi bihatchu".

2. Nakengesa ebandju ba bairaa emabi lyebere alauma ne bandji boshi emwaasi ola nabaa na babwirire mira mwa lubalamo lwanyi lwa kabiri. Rero kuno nitchire bure nenyu, nahubaa kubaburao era muhondo nyiike, kwa mango nyingaika eyi mwenyu, ndafire tchiro na mundju asibya bondjo.

3. Nyingaira batcha, bushi mwendjire mwahonda mulole kanangana eri Kirisito iwendjire kunyirengeraa'ko. Kwalunda lwenyu, Kirisito atatchula mutambukalyisa, si ende alosa ebuashi bwai mwa katchi-katchi kenyu.

4. Kubinalyi! Mango Kirisito amanyikibwaa kwa tchimanyi, abaa alimwa butambukare bwe mubiri. Si rero, era muuma-uma kurengera ebuashi bwa Ongo. Netchu, tchulyi mwa butambukare bwe mubiri kurengera ebuuma bwetchu nai. Si tchukaba bauma-uma

어에 뭐뉴. 꼬과 마아찌고 마부야-부야 마쭈롸 마더찌러 뿌: "찌라 마시 어너 어머러롸 과 아레 와 가나와나 과 부버이 봐 바쭈 바비레 너시 비하쭈".

2. 나거워사 어바쭈 바 바이라아 어마비 쪄버러 아롸우마 너 바찌 보씨 어꽈아시 오롸 나바아 나 바뷔리러 미라 봐 루바쫘모 똬네 똬 가바리. 러로 구노 니찌러 부러 너뉴, 나후바아 구바부라오 어라 무호또 네이거, 과 마꼬 네아이가 어에 뭐뉴, 따피러 찌로 나 무뿌 아시뱌 보쪼.

3. 네와이라 바쨔, 부씨 뭐찌러 뫄호따 무롸쪄 가나와나 어리 기리시도 이워찌러 구네러워라아고. 과루따 뭐뉴, 기리시도 아다쭈롸 무다뿌가레사, 시 어너 아롹사 어부아씨 봐이 봐 가찌-가찌 거뉴.

4. 구비나레! 마꼬 기리시도 아마네기봐아 과 찌마네, 아바아 아뢰롸 부다뿌가러 붜 무비리. 시 러로, 어라 무우마-우마 구러워라 어부아씨 봐 오꼬. 너쭈, 쭈레 봐 부다뿌가러 붜 무비리 구러워라 어부우마 붜쭈 나이. 시 쭈가바 바우마-우마

be established by the testimony of two or three witnesses."

2. I already gave you a warning when I was with you the second time. I now repeat it while absent: On my return I will not spare those who sinned earlier or any of the others,

3. since you are demanding proof that Christ is speaking through me. He is not weak in dealing with you, but is powerful among you.

4. For to be sure, he was crucified in weakness, yet he lives by God's power. Likewise, we are weak in him, yet by God's power we will live with him to serve you.

alauma nai kwa buashi bwa Ongo kwa mufa wenyu.	아롸우마 나이 과 부아씨 봐 오ᅌ고 과 무파 워뉴.	
5. Mutchibusaa mwa micthima yenyu mubeine, mumenye akaba musimikire mwa bwemeresi. Mubeine mucthilolaa'ko kubuya-buya mwa mitchima yenyu. Si mwishi kwa Yesu Kirisito atchula mwa ndanda senyu! Akaba bitalyi batcha, kuteta mbu mwaimirwe.	5. 무찌부사아 뫄 미찌마 여뉴 무버이너, 무머녀 아가바 무시미기러 뫄 붜머러시. 무버이너 무찌로롸아고 구부야-부야 뫄 미찌마 여뉴. 시 뮈씨 과 여수 기리시도 아쭈롸 뫄 따따 서뉴! 아가바 비다례 바짜, 구더다 뿌 뫄이미뤄.	5. Examine yourselves to see whether you are in the faith; test yourselves. Do you not realize that Christ Jesus is in you--unless, of course, you fail the test?
6. Si nyete emunyiiro kwa mungamenyerera kwa tchubano tchutaimirwe.	6. 시 녀더 어무네이로 과 무ᅌ가머녀러라 과 쭈바노 쭈다이미뤄.	6. And I trust that you will discover that we have not failed the test.
7. Tchwabeemera era mwa Ongo, tchasiya kutabaa tchiro na mwassi mubi ola mungaira. Tchutahonda kubalosa kwa tchwutchwaimire mwa kukola emabuya. Si tchwahonda munde mwaira emabuya tchiro angaba mbu tchwendjire tchwalorekana'ko nga tchwaimirwe.	7. 쫘버어머라 어라 뫄 오ᅌ고, 짜시야 구다바아 찌로 나 뫄씨 무비 오롸 무ᅌ가이라. 쭈다호따 구바로사 과 쭈쫘이미러 뫄 구고롸 어마부야. 시 쫘호따 무떠 뫄이라 어마부야 찌로 아ᅌ가바 뿌 쭤찌러 쫘로러가나고 ᅌ가 쫘이미뤄.	7. Now we pray to God that you will not do anything wrong. Not that people will see that we have stood the test but that you will do what is right even though we may seem to have failed.
8. Bushi kutalyi tchiro na mwaasi asibya olatchungaira kwa kwaangika ekanangana. Si tchunganaira, kunalyi kukola kwa mufa we kanangana.	8. 부씨 구다례 찌로 나 뫄아시 아시뱌 오롸쭈ᅌ가이라 과 과아ᅌ기가 어가나ᅌ가나. 시 쭈ᅌ가나이라, 구나례 구고롸 과 무파 워 가나ᅌ가나.	8. For we cannot do anything against the truth, but only for the truth.
9. Tchwendjire tchwa mowa mwakuba tchubano tchwainyire emisi, si mwaabo mweete misi. Bushi noku, tchwendjire tchwabemera	9. 쭤찌러 쫘 모와 뫄구바 쭈바노 쫘이네러 어미시, 시 뫄아보 뭐어더 미시. 부씨 노구, 쭤찌러 쫘버머라 무버 바쭈 바 바루미리러	9. We are glad whenever we are weak but you are strong; and our prayer is for your perfection.

mube bandju ba balumirire kanangana.

10. Etchera tchitatchumire nabaandjikira eni myaasi kuno nyicthiri bure nenyu, tchasiya mango nyingaika eyi mwenyu, ndabaa mukalyi kukulyikana ne buashi bwa Enawetchu anyeresise. Bushi obu buashi, bulyi kwa kuimba, si buta bwa kuhandjula.

11. Rero banyaketchu mwakumala, mundaa mwaba mwa lumoo. Mutchisesaa kunde mwaba bandju ba balumiriri. Mundaaa mwasesanya e mitchima, nakuata mianyisa yiuma. Mubaa mwaboolo, na Ongo wenzii kandji we boolo angaba alauma nenyu.

12. Mundaa mwakesanya mwa kwoberana nga bauma. Ebandju ba Ongo boshi babakesise.

13. E bondjo bwa Enawetchu Yesu Kirisito, ne nzii ya Ongo ne buuma bwe mutchima mubuya-buya, bindaaa byaba alauma nenyu muboshi.

가나빠나.

10. 어쩌라 찌다쭈미러 나바아씨기라 어니 먀아시 구노 네찌리 부러 너뉴, 짜시야 마오 네빠이가 어에 뮤뉴, 따바아 무가쩨 구구쩨가나 너 부아씨 봐 어나워쭈 아녀러시서. 부씨 오부 부아씨, 부쩨 과 구이빠, 시 부다 봐 구하누쫘.

11. 러로 바냐거쭈 먀구마쫘, 무따아 먀바 먀 루모오. 무찌서사아 구떠 먀바 바누 바 바루미리리. 무따아아 먀서사냐 어 미찌마, 나구아다 미아네사 에우마. 무바아 먀보오론, 나 오오 워씨이 가찌 워 보오론 아빠바 아쫘우마 너뉴.

12. 무따아 먀거사냐 먀 곱버라나 빠 바우마. 어바누 바 오오 보씨 바바거시서.

13. 어 보쪼 봐 어나워쭈 여수 기리시도, 너 씨이 야 오오 너 부우마 붜 무찌마 무부야-부야, 비따아아 뱌바 아쫘우마 너뉴 무보씨.

10. This is why I write these things when I am absent, that when I come I may not have to be harsh in my use of authority--the authority the Lord gave me for building you up, not for tearing you down.

11. Finally, brothers, good-by. Aim for perfection, listen to my appeal, be of one mind, live in peace. And the God of love and peace will be with you. Greet one another with a holy kiss.

12. All the saints send their greetings.

13. May the grace of the Lord Jesus Christ, and the love of God, and the fellowship of the Holy Spirit be with you all.

E Bakalatiya

어 바가짜디야

Galatians

E MARUBA ME NDJUMWA POOLO
ERA MWE BAKALATIA

어 마루바 머 뚜와 포오로
어라 뭐 바가짜디아

E Bakalatiya Chikono 1

1. Poolo ndjumwa atalyi wa bandju nesi era mwa mundju si era mwa Yesu Kirisito na Kabumbi tata ola wamuomolaa kutenga mwa birunda.

2. Na banyaketchu boshi babaa balyi nanyi. Era nyuhu sa Ongo era Bakalatiya.

3. E mwisha abaa era mwenyu nebolo bwekutenga era mwa Kabumbi tata nera mwa Enawetchu Yesu Kirisito.

4. Ola watchana kwabushi mobunu nebibi byetchu kwa kutchununula mobunu butala.

5. Ebuashi bwesiku ne mangu. Bibe batcha!

6. Natchihalyimire busese kwa kulola kwa mwamurekire fubafuba batcha oyu waba barangira kwa muisha wa Kirisito. Mwera kualuka mwa myasi ibuya-buya ya kundjikundji.

7. Itaindji myasi: seri kulyi bandju bala babatebaa mwabo: bala bahonda kualula emyasi ibuya-buya ya Kirisito.

어 바가꽈디야 찌고노 1

1. 포오로 뚜뫄 아다뤠 와 바뚜 너시 어라 뫄 무뚜 시 어라 뫄 여수 기리시도 나 가부뻬 다다 오꽈 와무오모꽈아 구더까 뫄 비루따.

2. 나 바냐거쭈 보씨 바바아 바레 나네. 어라 뉴후 사 오꼬 어라 바가꽈디야.

3. 어 뮈싸 아바아 어라 뭐뉴 너보로 뭐구더까 어라 뫄 가부뻬 다다 너라 뫄 어나워쭈 여수 기리시도.

4. 오꽈 와짜나 과부씨 모부누 너비비 벼쭈 과 구쭈누누꽈 모부누 부다꽈.

5. 어부아씨 뭐시구 너 마꾸. 비버 바짜!

6. 나찌하뤠미러 부서서 과 구뢰꽈 과 뫄무러기러 푸바푸바 바짜 오유 와바 바라끼라 과 무이싸 와 기리시도. 뭐라 구아루가 뫄 먀시 이부야-부야 야 구찌구찌.

7. 이다이찌 먀시: 서리 구뤠 바뚜 바꽈 바바더바아 뫄보: 바꽈 바호따 구아루꽈 어먀시 이부야-부야 야 기리시도.

Galatians Chapter 1[NIV]

1. Paul, an apostle--sent not from men nor by man, but by Jesus Christ and God the Father, who raised him from the dead--

2. and all the brothers with me, To the churches in Galatia:

3. Grace and peace to you from God our Father and the Lord Jesus Christ,

4. who gave himself for our sins to rescue us from the present evil age, according to the will of our God and Father,

5. to whom be glory for ever and ever. Amen.

6. I am astonished that you are so quickly deserting the one who called you by the grace of Christ and are turning to a different gospel--

7. which is really no gospel at all. Evidently some people are throwing you into confusion and are trying to pervert the

8. Seri tchubano nesi endonyi sera nguba tchukaba irisa emyasi ibuya-buya ya itahuhene nera tchwabairisa mwabo bwanya era mwai.

9. Ngokula tchwatangirisa kuteta: kandji natetchire ebwa kabiri : Emundju woshi ola ungabairisa mwabo emyasi ibuyabuya era itahuhene nera moomva, alyi mwanya.

10. Kwabushi noku, eri ekuhonda kwe bandju kunyisimaa, nesi ekuhonda kwa Ongo? Nesi nahonda kusimisa ebandju? Kwa bushi nyikasimisa ebandju ndangaba mwaanda wa Kirisito.

11. Nabakengesa banyaketchu emyasi ibuya buya era nabaiirisa ita ya bandju.

12. Kwabushi, ndaibona, ndanaiirisibwa ii myasi nebandju, seri kurengera emiboolo ya Yesu Kirisito

13. Kwa bushi moonvire emyasi ya mikorere yanyi lyamiramira mwa lunda lwa Bayuta, ngokula nalyibusaa busese elwandaa lwa Ongo, nekuluhanda.

---

8. 서리 쭈바노 너시 어또네 서라 우바 쭈가바 이리사 어먀시 이부야-부야 야 이다후허너 너라 쫘바이리사 먀보 봐냐 어라 먀이.

9. 오구꽈 쫘다삐리사 구더다: 가찌 나더찌러 어봐 가비리 : 어무뚜 오씨 오꽈 우까바이리사 먀보 어먀시 이부야부야 어라 이다후허너 너라 모오빠, 아뤠 먀냐.

10. 과부씨 노구, 어리 어구호따 궈 바뚜 구네시마아, 너시 어구호따 과 오꼬? 너시 나호따 구시미사 어바뚜? 과 부씨 네가시미사 어바뚜 따까바 먀아따 와 기리시도.

11. 나바거써사 바냐거쭈 어먀시 이부야 부야 어라 나바이이리사 이다 야 바뚜.

12. 과부씨, 따이보나, 따나이이리씨봐 이이 먀시 너바뚜, 서리 구러꺼라 어미보오롣 야 여수 기리시도

13. 과 부씨 모오삐러 어먀시 야 미고러러 야네 럄미라미라 먀 루따 꽈 바우다, 오구꽈 나뤠부사아 부서서 어꽈따아 꽈 오꼬, 너구루하따.

---

gospel of Christ.

8. But even if we or an angel from heaven should preach a gospel other than the one we preached to you, let him be eternally condemned!

9. As we have already said, so now I say again: If anybody is preaching to you a gospel other than what you accepted, let him be eternally condemned!

10. Am I now trying to win the approval of men, or of God? Or am I trying to please men? If I were still trying to please men, I would not be a servant of Christ.

11. I want you to know, brothers, that the gospel I preached is not something that man made up.

12. I did not receive it from any man, nor was I taught it; rather, I received it by revelation from Jesus Christ.

13. For you have heard of my previous way of life in Judaism, how intensely I persecuted the church of God and tried to destroy it.

14. Nanyi nahondorera mwa lwaanda lye Bayuta kuluha ebandji, babaa mwa bihangi byanyi, mwa lwaanda lwanyi, nera kuba wa mufula busese kusima enyaano sa bahukulyisa.

15. Seri Ongo ola wanyirekanya mwabula bwa mama, era kunyamaala kwa mwisha mwa kunyilorera evondjo bwai

16. Asima kubola emwana wai kunyirengera'mu, eri nabona kuiirisa emyasi yayi mwa bapakani, mwetchi tchihangi ndaira tchilaano nebandju ba mubiri nesi bandju ba mikira.

17. Ndanerukira kuya mwa yerusalemu era mwabu balababaanda era muhondo sanyi , seri natchiendera mwa tcheu tche baarabu , nerakufulukanji era Damasiki

18. Eranyuma semiaka ehatchu nerakueruka kuya era yerusalemu kulolanaku tchu na KEFA , nera kwekala Era mwai siku ekumi netano.

19. Seri ndalolaa kubanji baantchu kure ka YAKOBO munyakabo Enawetchu.

14. 나니 나호또러라 뫄 꽈아따 쪄 바유다 구루하 어바찌, 바바아 뫄 비하삐 뱌네, 뫄 꽈아따 꽌네, 너라 구바 와 무푸라 부서서 구시마 어냐아노 사 바후구쩨사.

15. 서리 오꼬 오라 와네러가냐 뫄부꽈 봐 마마, 어라 구냐마아꽈 과 뮈싸 뫄 구네뤄러라 어보쪼 봐이

16. 아시마 구보꽈 어뫄나 와이 구네러꺼라무, 어리 나보나 구이이리사 어먀시 야에 뫄 바파가니, 뭐찌 찌하삐 따이라 찌꽈아노 너바쭈 바 무비리 너시 바쭈 바 미기라.

17. 따너루기라 구야 뫄 여루사꺼무 어라 뫄부 바꽈바바아따 어라 무호또 사네 , 서리 나쩌떠라 뫄 쩌우 쩌 바아라부 , 너라구푸루가찌 어라 다마시기 .

18. 어라뉴마 서미아가 어하쭈 너라구어루가 구야 어라 여루사꺼무 구룐꽈나구 쭈 나 거파 , 너라 궈가꽈 어라 뫄이 시구 어구미 너다노.

19. 서리 따롣꽈 구바찌 바아쭈 구러 가 야고보 무냐가보 어나워쭈.

14. I was advancing in Judaism beyond many Jews of my own age and was extremely zealous for the traditions of my fathers.

15. But when God, who set me apart from birth and called me by his grace, was pleased

16. to reveal his Son in me so that I might preach him among the Gentiles, I did not consult any man,

17. nor did I go up to Jerusalem to see those who were apostles before I was, but I went immediately into Arabia and later returned to Damascus.

18. Then after three years, I went up to Jerusalem to get acquainted with Peter and stayed with him fifteen days.

19. I saw none of the other apostles--only James, the Lord's brother.

20. Nemyasi nabaanjikira mwabo , mulolaa, Eramuhondo sa kabumbi (ongo)ndatetaabisha.

21. Kanji n'erakuenda era musiki se SURIA ne KILIKIA.

22. Seri Ebusu bwanyi butamenyekana nenyiiriso se bayuta sasiri mwandanda sa kirisitu.

23. Seri banonva nambu alawatchulibusaalyamira -mira Reruera airirisa , Ebwemeresi bwa ahonda lyamiramira.

24. Bera kutongo Ongo kwa bushi nanyi .

20. 너먀시 나바아찌기라 먀보 , 무롸로아, 어라무호또사 가부삐 (오꼬)따더다아비싸.

21. 가찌 너라구어따 어라 무시기 서 수리아 너 기끼기아.

22. 서리 어부수 봐니 부다머녀가나 너네이리소 서 바유다 사시리 먀따따 사 기리시도.

23. 서리 바노빠 나뿌 아롸와쭈끼부사아랴미라 - 미라 러루어라 아이리리사 , 어뭐머러시 봐 아호따 랴미라미라.

24. 버라 구도꼬 오꼬 과 부씨 나니 .

20. I assure you before God that what I am writing you is no lie.

21. Later I went to Syria and Cilicia.

22. I was personally unknown to the churches of Judea that are in Christ.

23. They only heard the report: "The man who formerly persecuted us is now preaching the faith he once tried to destroy."

24. And they praised God because of me.

E Bakalatiya Chikono 2

1. Emangu kwabaa kwarenga byanda ekumi na bine, nerakuya kandji era Yerusalemu alauma na Barinaba, Nerakuenda na Tchito alauma nanyi :

2. Nanyi nera kuenda mwa byabowerwe nera kubahubanganyisa emyasi ibuyabuya nahubanganyisa bala bata bemeresi. Seri mwa bushobisho kwabala bete etchunda, bitabaa ubunga nalyibitchi buha, mulyi

어 바가꺄디야 찌고노 2

1. 어마우 과바아 과러꺄 꺄따 어구미 나 비너, 너라구야 가찌 어라 여루사꺼무 아꺄우마 나 바리나바, 너라구어따 나 찌도 아꺄우마 나니 :

2. 나니 너라 구어따 먀 꺄보워뤄 너라 구바후바꺄네사 어먀시 이부야부야 나후바꺄네사 바꺄 바다 버머러시. 서리 먀 부쏘비쏘 과바꺄 버더 어쭈따, 비다바아 우부꺄 나꼐비찌 부하, 무꼐

Galatians Chapter 2[NIV]

1. Fourteen years later I went up again to Jerusalem, this time with Barnabas. I took Titus along also.

2. I went in response to a revelation and set before them the gospel that I preach among the Gentiles. But I did this privately to those who seemed to be leaders, for fear that I was running or had run my race

nabiritchirire buha.

3. Seri Tchito iwaba alauma nanyi, iwaba ulyi mugiriki. Atatchitchikwa kumonyisibwa.

4. Kwabushi na banyaketchu beki bebisha bala bengisibwa mwa bubishobisho, banu bengisibwa mwa bubisho bishop, basisimbe ebolo bwetchu tchwete mwandanda sa Yesu Kirisito, batchubike mwa butcha.

5. Si tchiro ne tchihangi tchiuma tchula tchibikaa era masina sabu; tchasiya ekanangana ke mwasi mubuyabuya kabaa alauma nenyu.

6. Emangu bahamitongo balorekanaa'ku ngabandju bakulukulu, ebakulukulu bwabu katanakandju era mwanyi. Kabumbi ataandja bulangare bwa mundju. Natetchire banu ba bahamitongo batanyibulyire kandju.

7. Si era nyuma seni myasi bera kulola kwa nabikirwe kwa myasi ibuya yabalabamonyisibwa. Ngokula Petero abikibwa kwa myasi ibuya yabala bamonyisibwa.

나비리찌리러 부하.

3. 서리 찌도 이와바 아롸우마 나니, 이와바 우레 무지리기. 아다찌찌과 구모네시봐.

4. 과부씨 나 바냐거쭈 버기 버비싸 바롸 버삐시봐 마 부비쏘비쏘, 바누 버삐시봐 마 부비쏘 비쏘부, 바시시뻐 어보롣 뷔쭈 줴더 마따따 사 여수 기리시도, 바쭈비거 마 부짜.

5. 시 찌로 너 찌하삐 찌우마 쭈롸 찌비가아 어라 마시나 사부; 짜시야 어가나빠나 거 마시 무부야부야 가바아 아롸우마 너뉴.

6. 어마우 바하미도꼬 바로러가나아구 빠바뉴 바구루루구루, 어바구루루구루 봐부 가다나가쭈 어라 마니. 가부뻬 아다아짜 부롸빠러 봐 무뉴. 나더찌러 바누 바 바하미도꼬 바다니부뻬러 가쭈.

7. 시 어라 뉴마 서니 먀시 버라 구롣롸 과 나비기뤄 과 먀시 이부야 야바롸바모네시봐. 꼬구롸 퍼더로 아비기봐 과 먀시 이부야 야바롸 바모네시봐.

in vain.

3. Yet not even Titus, who was with me, was compelled to be circumcised, even though he was a Greek.

4. This matter arose because some false brothers had infiltrated our ranks to spy on the freedom we have in Christ Jesus and to make us slaves.

5. We did not give in to them for a moment, so that the truth of the gospel might remain with you.

6. As for those who seemed to be important--whatever they were makes no difference to me; God does not judge by external appearance--those men added nothing to my message.

7. On the contrary, they saw that I had been entrusted with the task of preaching the gospel to the Gentiles, just as Peter had been to the Jews.

8. Kwabushi ola waira Petero kuba mwaanda wabala bamonyisibwa, inoyo-inoyo iwanyiira kuenda era mwe bala batemerere.

9. NA kandji mangu baba bera bamenyerera ebondjo bambaa, Yakobo na Kefa alauma na Yooni, bera kumenyeka mbungaa bi bikondo, bera kunyeresa nyono na Barinaba eminu ye malyo era yo buumauma: nambu tchubano tchutchuya era mwa bala bata bemeresi, nabu banaya era mwa babatamonyisibwe (ebasira).

10. Seri mwasi muuma batchuemire nambu tchukengera ebakeni, nonumwasi inahonda kuira busese.

11. Nemangu Petero aika mwa Andiokia nera kuabiranwa nai meho kwa meho kwa bushi abaa alyi mundju wa munyororo.

12. Kwa bushi era muhondo sekubaha kwe bandju banene, balabatengaa era mwa Yakobu balyira alauma na bala bata bemeresi, seri emangu aika, arakuhuba era nyuma, era kutchilangula, era kubobaa balabamonyire.

8. 과부씨 오롸 와이라 퍼더로 구바 마아따 와바롸 바모네시봐, 이노요-이노요 이와네이라 구어따 어라 뭐 바롸 바더머러러.

9. 나 가씨 마우 바바 버라 바머녀러라 어보쪼 바빠아, 야고보 나 거파 아롸우마 나 요오니, 버라 구머녀가 뿌까아 비 비고또, 버라 구녀러사 뇨노 나 바리나바 어미누 여 마룔 어라 요 부우마우마: 나뿌 쭈바노 쭈쭈야 어라 마 바롸 바다 버머러시, 나부 바나야 어라 마 바바다모네시붜 (어바시라).

10. 서리 마시 무우마 바쭈어미러 나뿌 쭈거꺼라 어바거니, 노누마시 이나호따 구이라 부서서.

11. 너마우 퍼더로 아이가 마 아띠오기아 너라 구아비라놔 나이 머호 과 머호 과 부씨 아바아 아례 무뿌 와 무뇨로로.

12. 과 부씨 어라 무호또 서구바하 궈 바뿌 바너너, 바롸바더까아 어라 마 야고부 바례라 아롸우마 나 바롸 바다 버머러시, 서리 어마우 아이가, 아라구후바 어라 뉴마, 어라 구찌롸우꽈, 어라 구보바아 바롸바모네러.

8. For God, who was at work in the ministry of Peter as an apostle to the Jews, was also at work in my ministry as an apostle to the Gentiles.

9. James, Peter and John, those reputed to be pillars, gave me and Barnabas the right hand of fellowship when they recognized the grace given to me. They agreed that we should go to the Gentiles, and they to the Jews.

10. All they asked was that we should continue to remember the poor, the very thing I was eager to do.

11. When Peter came to Antioch, I opposed him to his face, because he was clearly in the wrong.

12. Before certain men came from James, he used to eat with the Gentiles. But when they arrived, he began to draw back and separate himself from the Gentiles because he was afraid of those who belonged to the

13. Na Bayuta bala beshi batchaalula alauma nayi, tchiru Barinaba ekibwa nekutchaalula mbunga alyi wabu.

14. Nemangu nyono nalolaa kwendjira sabu sitaenda kubuyabuya ne kanangana ke myasi ibuyabuya, nera kubura Petero era muhondo sebandju boshi: akaba woyo ulyi Muyuta, wakulyikira emyanya ya bala bata bemeresi, si ita myanya ye Bayuta, kwabushi netchii ungesesa bala bata bemeresi kukulyira emyanya ye Bayuta.

15. Tchubano tchulyi Bayuta bekabutchwa, si tchutabakosi ba mabi, mwasindji mwaa.

16. Tchukamenya kwe mundju ata mubuya kurengera etchwasi tchwe mwaso, seri ekurengera ebwemeresi bwa Yesu Kirisito netchu tchubanu tchu tchwemerere Yesu Kirisito elyi tchwatchundjibwa mwa bwemeresi bwa Kirisito si ata mwa tchwasi tchwe bwemeresi. Kwabushi kutalyi mundju ola baandjire etchwasi mwa bwemeresi.

13. 나 바유다 바꽈 버씨 바짜아루꽈 아꽈우마 나에, 찌루 바리나바 어기봐 너구짜아루꽈 뿌까 아례 와부.

14. 너마우 뇨노 나로꽈아 궈찌라 사부 시다어따 구부야부야 너 가나까나 거 먀시 이부야부야, 너라 구부라 퍼더로 어라 무호또 서바뉴 보씨: 아가바 오요 우레 무유다, 와구례기라 어먀냐 야 바꽈 바다 버머러시, 시 이다 먀냐 여 바유다, 과부씨 너찌이 우꺼서사 바꽈 바다 버머러시 구구례라 어먀냐 여 바유다.

15. 쭈바노 쭈례 바유다 버가부꽈, 시 쭈다바고시 바 마비, 마시찌 마아.

16. 쭈가머냐 궈 무뿌 아다 무부야 구러꺼라 어좌시 쭤 마소, 서리 어구러꺼라 어뿨머러시 봐 여수 기리시도: 너쭈 쭈바누 쭈 쭤머러러 여수 기리시도 어례 좌쭈찌봐 마 뿨머러시 봐 기리시도 시 아다 마 좌시 쭤 뿨머러시. 과부씨 구다례 무뿌 오꽈 바아찌러 어좌시 마 뿨머러시.

13. The other Jews joined him in his hypocrisy, so that by their hypocrisy even Barnabas was led astray.

14. When I saw that they were not acting in line with the truth of the gospel, I said to Peter in front of them all, "You are a Jew, yet you live like a Gentile and not like a Jew. How is it, then, that you force Gentiles to follow Jewish customs?

15. "We who are Jews by birth and not 'Gentile sinners'

16. know that a man is not justified by observing the law, but by faith in Jesus Christ. So we, too, have put our faith in Christ Jesus that we may be justified by faith in Christ and not by observing the law, because by observing the law no one will be justified.

17. Seri tchubeene tchwabaa tchwahonda kuanyibwa kuba babatchungenene mwandanda sa Kirisitu, tchwera kulorekana'ko nga bandju ba bayaa, na Kirisito abere mukosi wa byaa? Nanga tchiro nehitcha.

17. 서리 쭈버어너 짜바아 짜호따 구아네봐 구바 바바쭈ㅶ어너너 뫄따따 사 기리시도, 쭤라 구롤러가나고 ㅶ가 바뿌 바 바야아, 나 기리시도 아버러 무고시 와 뱌아? 나ㅶ가 찌로 너히짜.

17. "If, while we seek to be justified in Christ, it becomes evident that we ourselves are sinners, does that mean that Christ promotes sin? Absolutely not!

18. Kwabushi nyikahubirira emyasi nahandaa, natchilosise nyeine mukosi wa wabi.

18. 과부씨 네가후비리라 어먀시 나하따아, 나찌롤시서 녀이너 무고시 와 와비.

18. If I rebuild what I destroyed, I prove that I am a lawbreaker.

19. Kwabushi nebutchungenene, nyono nafaa mwa butchungenene, eri nabona ekalamu era mwa Kabumbi.

19. 과부씨 너부쭈ㅶ어너너, 뇨노 나파아 뫄 부쭈ㅶ어너너, 어리 나보나 어가롸무 어라 뫄 가부삐.

19. For through the law I died to the law so that I might live for God.

20. Nalyibusibwa alauma na Kirisito, seri Kalamu: Seri atanyono si Kirisito i kalamu mwandanda sanyi. Ne kalamui nyete kulwarero mwa mubiri bulyi bolo bwe bwemeresi bwa mwenyi Kabumbi ola asima era kutchana ekalamu kai busbhi nanyi.

20. 나례부시봐 아롸우마 나 기리시도, 서리 가롸무: 서리 아다뇨노 시 기리시도 이 가롸무 뫄따따 사네. 너 가롸무이 녀더 구뢀러로 뫄 무비리 부례 보롤 붜 붜머러시 봐 뭐네 가부삐 오롸 아시마 어라 구짜나 어가롸무 가이 부수부히 나네.

20. I have been crucified with Christ and I no longer live, but Christ lives in me. The life I live in the body, I live by faith in the Son of God, who loved me and gave himself for me.

21. Ndainganyise emwisha wa Ongo kwabushi ebutchungenen bwababaa mwa mwaso kasi Kirisito afaa buha.

21. 따이ㅶ가네서 어뮈싸 와 오꼬 과부씨 어부쭈ㅶ어너 봐바아 뫄 뫄소 가시 기리시도 아파아 부하.

21. I do not set aside the grace of God, for if righteousness could be gained through the law, Christ died for nothing!"

E Bakalatiya Chikono 3

어 바가롸디야 찌고노 3

Galatians Chapter 3[NIV]

1. Emu bakalatiya mutete

1. 어무 바가롸디야 무더더

1. You foolish Galatians! Who

bwenge, nde iwabaloire mwabu, mutemerera ekanangana, mumwabaa na Yesu Kirisitu, ola walyibusibwa era muhondo semeho menyu?

2. Nahonda kumenya tchini tchinwa tchiuma era mwenyu. Mwabone emutchima kurengera emikolo ye lwaso, mulyi kwa kumvwa mwa bwemeresi.

3. Mwabo mu mbuta sira siri batcha? Mwaanaza mwa mutchima, mwahonda mamalaa mwa mubiri?

4. Mwalyibuswa na myasi inene batcha buha? Akaba buha kanangana?

5. Kwa bushi noku, ola waberesa emutchima nekuira emikolo yemisi mu mwabo, ailyire batcha mwa mikorere ye lwaso, mulyi ekunva mwa bwemeresi?

6. Ngoku Aburaamu aba alyi mwa bwemeresi bwa Kabumbi, erakuandjirwa elwaso.

7. Mumenyerera kwa bala bemerereaa, banola balyi ban aba Aburaamu.

8. Ne muandjiko alorekana'ko kutengera mira kwa Kabumbi akaandja elwaso; bala bata

---

뭐어, 떠 이와바뢰이러 먀부, 무더머러라 어가나까나, 무먀바아 나 여수 기리시도, 오꽈 와쩨부시봐 어라 무호또 서머호 머뉴?

2. 나호따 구머냐 찌니 찌놔 찌우마 어라 뭐뉴. 먀보너 어무찌마 구러꺼라 어미고론 여 꽈소, 무뤠 과 구꽈 먀 뭐머러시.

3. 먀보 무 뿌다 시라 시리 바짜? 먀아나자 먀 무찌마, 먀호따 마마꽈아 먀 무비리?

4. 먀뤠부쏴 나 먀시 이너너 바짜 부하? 아가바 부하 가나까나?

5. 과 부씨 노구, 오롸 와버러사 어무찌마 너구이라 어미고론 여미시 무 먀보, 아이뤠러 바짜 먀 미고러러 여 꽈소, 무뤠 어구빠 먀 뭐머러시?

6. 오구 아부라아무 아바 아뤠 먀 뭐머러시 봐 가부뻬, 어라구아씨러 어꽈소.

7. 무머녀러라 과 바꽈 버머러러아아, 바노꽈 바뤠 바누 아바 아부라아무.

8. 너 무아찌고 아뢰러가나고 구더꺼라 미라 과 가부뻬 아가아꽈 어꽈소; 바꽈 바다

---

has bewitched you? Before your very eyes Jesus Christ was clearly portrayed as crucified.

2. I would like to learn just one thing from you: Did you receive the Spirit by observing the law, or by believing what you heard?

3. Are you so foolish? After beginning with the Spirit, are you now trying to attain your goal by human effort?

4. Have you suffered so much for nothing--if it really was for nothing?

5. Does God give you his Spirit and work miracles among you because you observe the law, or because you believe what you heard?

6. Consider Abraham: "He believed God, and it was credited to him as righteousness."

7. Understand, then, that those who believe are children of Abraham.

8. The Scripture foresaw that God would justify the Gentiles by faith, and

bemeresi erav kubura
Aburaamu mwasi mubuya era
muhondo, tchatetaa:
kwabushi nao ebapakani
bangaahanyisibwa.

버머러시 어라부 구부라
아부라아무 마시 무부야 어라
무호또, 짜더다아: 과부씨
나오 어바파가니
바까아하네시봐.

announced the gospel in
advance to Abraham: "All
nations will be blessed
through you."

9. Bushi noku ebemeresi baka
ahanyisibwa alauma na
Aburaamu i mwemeresi.

9. 부씨 노구 어버머러시
바가 아하네시봐 아롸우마 나
아부라아무 이 뭐머러시.

9. So those who have faith
are blessed along with
Abraham, the man of faith.

10. Kwa bushi abu boshi bete
emikolo yelwaso balyi era
bufulyi se bwanya. Kwa kuba
kwaandjikirwe: bwanya bwa
tchira mundju ola utasimikire
mu byoshi bya andjikwa mwa
tchitabu tche lwaso afire
shambyo.

10. 과 부씨 아부 보씨 버더
어미고로 여똬소 바례 어라
부푸레 서 봐냐. 과 구바
과아찌기뤄: 봐냐 봐 찌라
무쭈 오롸 우다시미기러 무
보씨 뱌 아찌과 똬 찌다부 쩌
똬소 아피러 싸뾰.

10. All who rely on observing
the law are under a curse, for
it is written: "Cursed is
everyone who does not
continue to do everything
written in the Book of the
Law."

11. Tchilosise kwa kutalyi
mundju ola wandjirwa elwaso
era muhondo semeho ma
Kabumbi. Kwabushi bala
beshe lwaso bakalama mwa
bwemeresi.

11. 찌로시서 과 구다례 무쭈
오롸 와찌롸 어똬소 어라
무호또 서머호 마 가부삐.
과부씨 바롸 버써 똬소
바가똬마 똬 뭐머러시.

11. Clearly no one is justified
before God by the law,
because, "The righteous will
live by faith."

12. Nelwaso atamwa
bwemeresi seri emundju
alawakola bini binwa
angalama mwei myasi.

12. 너똬소 아다똬 뭐머러시
서리 어무쭈 아롸와고롸 비니
비놔 아까롸마 뭐이 먀시.

12. The law is not based on
faith; on the contrary, "The
man who does these things
will live by them."

13. Kirisito atchununulaa mwa
bwanya bwe lwaso akaba
airwa mwanya bushi netchu,
ngoku kwaandjikirwe: Bwanya
era mwatchira mundju olawa
wamanyikibwa kwa mutchi.

13. 기리시도 아쭈누누롸아
똬 봐냐 붜 똬소 아가바
아이롸 마냐 부씨 너쭈, 오구
과아찌기뤄: 봐냐 어라
똬찌라 무쭈 오롸와
와마네기봐 과 무찌.

13. Christ redeemed us from
the curse of the law by
becoming a curse for us, for
it is written: "Cursed is
everyone who is hung on a
tree."

14. Esi ngahanyi sa
Aburaamu siikiiraa ebapakani
eramwa Yesu Kirisito,

14. 어시 까하네 사
아부라아무 시이기이라아
어바파가니 어라똬 여수

14. He redeemed us in order
that the blessing given to
Abraham might come to the

kanbonakurengera ebwemeresi tchukabona tchilaano tcho mutchima mwa bwemeresi.

15. Banyaketchu nateta ngokula ebandju balyi, tchiro etchilaano tche bandju tchingemereswe, emundju atangaalula tchi tchilaano nesi ekulumisisa kwe tchindji.s

16. Si era mwa Aburaamu tchilaano tchatetchwa, nokwa lubaa. Nambu enyibaa sinene, ngokwa angaba muma, elubaa lyao lyi Kirisitu.

17. Natetchire eni myasi, efulao era yetetchwa era muhondo sa Kabumbi mwandanda sa Yesu Kirisito, elwaso lwalwabaa mwa byanda. Maana mane na mahatchu, era businda itangaala kuyalusa, tchiro nekualula etchilaano.

18. Kwabushi efulao ikaba kwa loso itatchiri mwa tchilaano, seri Aburaamu eresibwa etchilaano tcha Kabumbi.

19. Elwaso tchitchii kandji? Lwairibwa kwabushi nebyaa

기리시도, 가누보나구러어라 어뭐머러시 쭈가보나 찌롸아노 쪼 무찌마 롸 뭐머러시.

15. 바냐거쭈 나더다 꼬구롸 어바쭈 바레, 찌로 어찌롸아노 쩌 바쭈 찌어머러쉬, 어무쭈 아다꽈아루롸 찌 찌롸아노 너시 어구루미시사 궈 찌씨.수

16. 시 어라 롸 아부라아무 찌롸아노 짜더좌, 노과 루바아. 나뿌 어니바아 시너너, 꼬과 아꽈바 무마, 어루바아 랴오 레 기리시도.

17. 나더찌러 어니 먀시, 어푸롸오 어라 여더좌 어라 무호또 사 가부삐 롸따따 사 여수 기리시도, 어꽈소 롸꽈바아 롸 뱌따. 마아나 마너 나 마하쭈, 어라 부시따 이다꽈아롸 구야루사, 찌로 너구아루롸 어찌롸아노.

18. 과부씨 어푸롸오 이가바 과 로소 이다찌리 롸 찌롸아노, 서리 아부라아무 어러시봐 어찌롸아노 짜 가부삐.

19. 어꽈소 찌찌이 가씨? 롸이리봐 과부씨 너뱌아

Gentiles through Christ Jesus, so that by faith we might receive the promise of the Spirit.

15. Brothers, let me take an example from everyday life. Just as no one can set aside or add to a human covenant that has been duly established, so it is in this case.

16. The promises were spoken to Abraham and to his seed. The Scripture does not say "and to seeds," meaning many people, but "and to your seed," meaning one person, who is Christ.

17. What I mean is this: The law, introduced 430 years later, does not set aside the covenant previously established by God and thus do away with the promise.

18. For if the inheritance depends on the law, then it no longer depends on a promise; but God in his grace gave it to Abraham through a promise.

19. What, then, was the purpose of the law? It was

kuikira emangu emubutchwa
wekulangalyirwa akaika, ola
weresibwa etchilaano;
tchatchatetchwa ne ndonyi
mwa maboko me baanyi.

20. Ola wamwaana ata
mwaanyi wa museri Kabumbi
analyi muuma.

21. Nesi elwaso lutasimbeni
netchilaano tcha Kabumbi?
Nanga tchiru nehitcha,
kwabushi akaba elwaso
lungaanyirwe kwakureta
ekalamu, kanangana
kangaanyirwe kwakureta
ekalamu, ekanangana
kangabere kwa lwaso.

22. Seri emaandjiko maminaa
boshi era bufulyi bwe mabi
kwabushi ebemeresi
beeresibwa efulao kwa
bwemeresi bwa Yesu Kirisitu.

23. Seri era muhondo se
kubaha kwe bwemeresi,
tchwabikikibwa era bufulyi bwe
lwaso, tchwahwekwa kwa
bwemeresi bwa
bukaboolyibwa era businda.

24. Mwa batcha elwaso
lwabaa ngaa mwirisi
wakutchwiisa era mwa Kirisito
tchwereesibwa elwaso mwa

구이기라 어마우 어무부좌
워구꽈싸쩨롸 아가이가, 오롸
워러시봐 어찌꽈아노;
짜짜더좌 너 또네 마 마보고
머 바아네.

20. 오롸 와마아나 아다
마아네 와 무서리 가부쀄
아나쩨 무우마.

21. 너시 어꽈소 루다시뻐니
너찌꽈아노 짜 가부쀄? 나꽈
찌루 너히짜, 과부씨 아가바
어꽈소 루꽈아네뤄 과구러다
어가꽈무, 가나꽈나
가꽈아네뤄 과구러다
어가꽈무, 어가나꽈나
가꽈버러 과 꽈소.

22. 서리 어마아찌고
마미나아 보씨 어라 부푸쩨
붜 마비 과부씨 어버머러시
버어러시봐 어푸꽈오 과
붜머러시 봐 여수 기리시도.

23. 서리 어라 무호또 서
구바하 궈 붜머러시,
좌비기봐 어라 부푸쩨 붜
꽈소, 좌훠과 과 붜머러시 봐
부가보오쩨봐 어라 부시따.

24. 마 바짜 어꽈소 꽈바아
꽈아 뮈리시 와구쮜이사 어라
마 기리시도 쭤러어시봐
어꽈소 마 붜머러시.

added because of
transgressions until the Seed
to whom the promise
referred had come. The law
was put into effect through
angels by a mediator.

20. A mediator, however,
does not represent just one
party; but God is one.

21. Is the law, therefore,
opposed to the promises of
God? Absolutely not! For if a
law had been given that
could impart life, then
righteousness would certainly
have come by the law.

22. But the Scripture declares
that the whole world is a
prisoner of sin, so that what
was promised, being given
through faith in Jesus Christ,
might be given to those who
believe.

23. Before this faith came, we
were held prisoners by the
law, locked up until faith
should be revealed.

24. So the law was put in
charge to lead us to Christ
that we might be justified by
faith.

bwemeresi.

25. Seri rero Ebwemeresi bwerisa bwabahire, tchutatchiri kandji era bufulyi se muirisi.

26. Kwabushi muboshi mulyi ban aba Kabumbi, mwa bwemeresi mwandanda sa Yesu Kirisitu.

27. Kwabushi muboshi mwa batisibwa neku engirisibwa mwandanda sa Kirisito, mwamwembere Kirisito.

28. Bushi noku kutatchilyi muyuta nesi Mukirikiri nesi kaungu, nesi muhuru kutalyi mulume nesi mukasi, kwabushi muboshi mwera mundju muuma mwandanda sa Yesu Kirisito.

29. Na akaba mwabo mulyi ba Kirisito, kasi mweramulyi lubuto lwa Aburaamu, ne mwandju alaanywa.

25. 서리 러로 어붸머러시 붜리사 봐바히러, 쭈다찌리 가찌 어라 부푸레 서 무이리시.

26. 과부씨 무보씨 무레 바누 아바 가부삐, 뫄 붜머러시 뫄따따 사 여수 기리시도.

27. 과부씨 무보씨 뫄 바디시봐 너구 어삐리시봐 뫄따따 사 기리시도, 뫄뭐뻐러 기리시도.

28. 부씨 노구 구다찌레 무유다 너시 무기리기리 너시 가우꾸, 너시 무후루 구다레 무루머 너시 무가시, 과부씨 무보씨 뭐라 무뿌 무우마 뫄따따 사 여수 기리시도.

29. 나 아가바 뫄보 무레 바 기리시도, 가시 뭐라무레 루부도 꽈 아부라아무, 너 뫄뿌 아꽈아네와.

25. Now that faith has come, we are no longer under the supervision of the law.

26. You are all sons of God through faith in Christ Jesus,

27. for all of you who were baptized into Christ have clothed yourselves with Christ.

28. There is neither Jew nor Greek, slave nor free, male nor female, for you are all one in Christ Jesus.

29. If you belong to Christ, then you are Abraham's seed, and heirs according to the promise.

E Bakalatiya Chikono 4

1. Seri natetchire emwana ola ukalya emwatchu weshi, emangu abaatchiri mwana mutoto alorekana'ko nga kaungu tchiru mbu yena byoshi.

2. Seri enda aba alyi bufulyi

어 바가꽈디야 찌고노 4

1. 서리 나더찌러 어뫄나 오꽈 우가꺄 어뫄쭈 워씨, 어마꾸 아바아찌리 뫄나 무도도 아로러가나고 까 가우꾸 찌루 뿌 여나 뵤씨.

2. 서리 어따 아바 아레

Galatians Chapter 4[NIV]

1. What I am saying is that as long as the heir is a child, he is no different from a slave, although he owns the whole estate.

2. He is subject to guardians

sebemangire bai nebete ebwenge tchiru nambu ebihangi byabaa byatetchwire na Tata.

부푸레 서버마삐러 바이 너버더 어붸뭐 찌루 나뿌 어비하삐 뱌바아 뱌더쮜러 나 다다.

and trustees until the time set by his father.

3. Anabe netchu mangu tchwabaa tchutchiri bana, tchwahwekwa era busfulyi bwe lwaso lwe butala.

3. 아나버 너쭈 마우 좌바아 쭈찌리 바나, 좌훠과 어라 부수푸레 붜 똽소 뤄 부다똬.

3. So also, when we were children, we were in slavery under the basic principles of the world.

4. Seri mangu ebihangi bayika Ongo erakutchuma emwaala ola wabutchwa nemukasi, ola wabutchwa era bufulyi se lwaso.

4. 서리 마우 어비하삐 바에가 오꼬 어라구쭈마 어뫄아똬 오라 와부좌 너무가시, 오똬 와부좌 어라 부푸레 서 똽소.

4. But when the time had fully come, God sent his Son, born of a woman, born under law,

5. Tchasiya anunule ba babaa balyi era bufulyi sebuashi. Eri tchwabone emwaso tchasiya tchube bana ba Ongo.

5. 짜시야 아누누뤄 바 바바아 바레 어라 부푸레 서부아씨. 어리 좌보너 어뫄소 짜시야 쭈버 바나 바 오꼬.

5. to redeem those under law, that we might receive the full rights of sons.

6. Seri kwabushi mwabu mulyi baanda bala Ongo atchuma emutchima mubuyabuya we mwaala mwandanda se mitchima yetchu yalyilyira nambu: "Aba", Tata.

6. 서리 과부씨 뫄부 무레 바아따 바똬 오꼬 아쭈마 어무찌마 무부야부야 워 뫄아똬 뫄따따 서 미찌마 여쭈 야레레라 나뿌: "아바", 다다.

6. Because you are sons, God sent the Spirit of his Son into our hearts, the Spirit who calls out, "Abba, Father."

7. Batcha, woyo utatchiri Kaungu. Seri wera mwana: nesi ulyi mwana wai akakweresa kwa mwandju wa Kabumbi era mwa Kirisito.

7. 바짜, 오요 우다찌리 가우꾸. 서리 워라 뫄나: 너시 우레 뫄나 와이 아가꿔러사 과 뫄꾸 와 가부뻬 어라 뫄 기리시도.

7. So you are no longer a slave, but a son; and since you are a son, God has made you also an heir.

8. Seri emango etchihangi tcha muteshi Kabumbi ola mwakorera mwabaa mwakorera ebasimu bala batatchula Ongo

8. 서리 어뫄꼬 어찌하삐 짜 무더씨 가부뻬 오똬 뫄고러라 뫄바아 뫄고러라 어바시무 바똬 바다쭈똬 오꼬 워가나삐나.

8. Formerly, when you did not know God, you were slaves to those who by nature are not gods.

wekanangana.

9. Seri rero akaba mwamenyerere Ongo nesi mwamenyekire na Ongo, kwa bushi netchii mwahubirire kandji mwa myasi yebuoshi nebukene mwahonda kubikorera kandji?

9. 서리 러로 아가바 뫄머녀러러 오꼬 너시 뫄머녀기러 나 오꼬, 과 부씨 너찌이 뫄후비리러 가ᄡᅵ 뫄 먀시 여부오씨 너부거너 뫄호따 구비고러라 가ᄡᅵ?

9. But now that you know God--or rather are known by God--how is it that you are turning back to those weak and miserable principles? Do you wish to be enslaved by them all over again?

10. Mwatolyire esiku nemyesi nebihangi nemwaka.

10. 뫄도례러 어시구 너며시 너비하ᅇᅵ 너뫄가.

10. You are observing special days and months and seasons and years!

11. Nabobaire mwabu, itaba nga naesise ebihangi byanyi kwabuha.

11. 나보바이러 뫄부, 이다바 ᅇᅡ 나어시서 어비하ᅇᅵ 뱌니 과부하.

11. I fear for you, that somehow I have wasted my efforts on you.

12. Nabeemire banyaketchu, mubaa nga nyono, kwabushi nyiri nga mwabo, mutanyikorere tchiro netchaa tchiuma.

12. 나버어미러 바냐거쭈, 무바아 ᅇᅡ 뇨노, 과부씨 네리 ᅇᅡ 뫄보, 무다네고러러 찌로 너짜아 찌우마.

12. I plead with you, brothers, become like me, for I became like you. You have done me no wrong.

13. Seri mwishi kwa mwa booshi bwe mubiri nabairisa tanga emyasi ibuyabuya.

13. 서리 뮈씨 과 뫄 보오씨 붜 무비리 나바이리사 다ᅇᅡ 어먀시 이부야부야.

13. As you know, it was because of an illness that I first preached the gospel to you.

14. Nemweereko owaba ulyi mwa mubiri wanyi, mutakenaa'u nesi mutanaa, seri mukanyihuukasa nga ndonyi ya Ongo, kandji nga Yesu Kirisito.

14. 너뭐어러고 오와바 우례 뫄 무비리 와네, 무다거나아우 너시 무다나아, 서리 무가네후우가사 ᅇᅡ 또네야 오꼬, 가ᄡᅵ ᅇᅡ 여수 기리시도.

14. Even though my illness was a trial to you, you did not treat me with contempt or scorn. Instead, you welcomed me as if I were an angel of God, as if I were Christ Jesus himself.

15. Kandji ngai we lumoo lwenyu lulyi? Kwabushi nabatongire

15. 가ᄡᅵ ᅇᅡ이 워 루모오 뤄뉴 루례? 과부씨 나바도ᅇᅵ러 ᅇᅡ비ᅇᅡ아례거너,

15. What has happened to all your joy? I can testify that, if you could have done so, you

ngabingaalyikene, mungakulyire emeho menyu, munyerese'omo.

무까구꿰러 어머호 머뉴, 무녀러서오모.

would have torn out your eyes and given them to me.

16. nahubire murenda wenyu kwabushi nababulyire ekanangana.

16. 나후비러 무러따 워뉴 과부씨 나바부꿰러 어가나까나.

16. Have I now become your enemy by telling you the truth?

17. Ebushiro bwabete era mulyi, buta bwalukoo, seri bahonda kubakula mutchubano, erinmwaate ebushiro era mwabo.

17. 어부씨로 봐버더 어라 무꿰, 부다 봐루꼬오, 서리 바호따 구바구꽈 무쭈바노, 어리누꽈어더 어부씨로 어라 꽈보.

17. Those people are zealous to win you over, but for no good. What they want is to alienate you from us, so that you may be zealous for them.

18. Seri tchulyi tchakanangana kuate ebushiro kwa mabuya ebihangi byoshi saate mangu ma nyinalyi nenyu.

18. 서리 쭈꿰 짜가나까나 구아더 어부씨로 과 마부야 어비하끼 뵤씨 사아더 마꾸 마 니나꿰 너뉴.

18. It is fine to be zealous, provided the purpose is good, and to be so always and not just when I am with you.

19. Bana banyi basiirwa, munyetere etchamba kuikira emangu Kirisito angamenyekana mwa ndanda senyu.

19. 바나 바네 바시이롸, 무녀더러 어짜빠 구이기라 어마꾸 기리시도 아까머녀가나 꽈 따따 서뉴.

19. My dear children, for whom I am again in the pains of childbirth until Christ is formed in you,

20. Netchi, nahonda kuba alauma nenyu, rero nekualula emurenge wanyi kwabushi ndabalangalyire mwa mihambare yenyu.

20. 너찌, 나호따 구바 아꽈우마 너뉴, 러로 너구아루꽈 어무러꺼 와니 과부씨 따바꽈까꿰러 꽈 미하빠러 여뉴.

20. how I wish I could be with you now and change my tone, because I am perplexed about you!

21. Munyiburaa mwabo mumwahonda kuba era bufulyi se mwaso, mutonvire kwa lwaso?

21. 무네부라아 꽈보 무꽈호따 구바 어라 부푸꿰 서 꽈소, 무도뼤러 과 꽈소?

21. Tell me, you who want to be under the law, are you not aware of what the law says?

22. Kwabushi kwaandjikirwe; Aburaamu abaa ete bana babilyi, muma we mukasi we kaungu, neundji we mukasi

22. 과부씨 과아찌기뤄; 아부라아무 아바아 어더 바나 바비꿰, 무마 워 무가시 워 가우꾸, 너우찌 워 무가시

22. For it is written that Abraham had two sons, one by the slave woman and the other by the free woman.

wai muberebere ola
wetchiranga tchai.

와이 무버러버러 오꽈
워찌라까 짜이.

23. Seri oyu we kaungu
abutchibwa kwa mubiri: noyo
we bolo abutchibwa kwa
mwandju.

23. 서리 오유 워 가우꾸
아부찌봐 과 무비리: 노요 워
보로 아부찌봐 과 꽈쭈.

23. His son by the
slave woman was born in the
ordinary way; but his son by
the free woman was born as
the result of a promise.

24. Eni mwasi ilyi mwasi ela
ilosise kwabanu bakasi balyi
myandju ebiri; muuma
kutenga kwa ndjulundu ye
Sinai lilya butchibwa mwa
butcha, esina lyai i Akari.

24. 어니 꽈시 이레 꽈시
어꽈 이로시서 과바누 바가시
바레 먀쭈 어비리; 무우마
구더까 과 쭈루쭈 여 시나이
리랴 부찌봐 꽈 부짜, 어시나
랴이 이 아가리.

24. These things may be
taken figuratively, for the
women represent
two covenants.
One covenant is from Mount
Sinai and bears children who
are to be slaves: This is
Hagar.

25. Kwabushi Akari ilyi
ndjulungu ye Sinai era ilyi
mwa Arabiya, ihuhanyire ne
Yerusalemu ya kulwarero, nayi
inalyi mwa butcha nebana
bai.

25. 과부씨 아가리 이레
쭈루꾸 여 시나이 어라 이레
꽈 아라비야, 이후하니러 너
여루사러무 야 구꽈러로,
나에 이나레 꽈 부짜 너바나
바이.

25. Now Hagar stands for
Mount Sinai in Arabia and
corresponds to the present
city of Jerusalem, because
she is in slavery with her
children.

26. Seri e Yerusalemu year
lulu ilyi mwa bolo, eyera
mama wetchu tchuboshi.

26. 서리 어 여루사러무 여라
루루 이레 꽈 보로, 어여라
마마 워쭈 쭈보씨.

26. But the Jerusalem that is
above is free, and she is our
mother.

27. Kwabushi byaandjikirwe
nambu: umoha ulyi, ngumba,
uutabuta, uukulaa emurenge
ulyire, woyo utete malyibuko.
Kwabushi ebana bola
warekibwa bubanene kuluha
bala bola wete emulume.

27. 과부씨 뱌아찌기뤄 나뿌:
우모하 우레, 꾸빠,
우우다부다, 우우구꽈아
어무러꺼 우레러, 오요
우더더 마레부고. 과부씨
어바나 보꽈 와러기봐
부바너너 구루하 바꽈 보꽈
워더 어무루머.

27. For it is written: "Be glad,
O barren woman, who bears
no children; break forth and
cry aloud, you who have no
labor pains; because more
are the children of the
desolate woman than of her
who has a husband."

28. Tchubano, banyaketchu, akaba Isaka bana bamwandju.

28. 쭈바노, 바냐거쭈, 아가바 이사가 바나 바마뉴.

28. Now you, brothers, like Isaac, are children of promise.

29. Seri mwebi bihangi ola wabutchibwa kwa mubiri, alyibusa ola wabutchibwa kwa mutchima, kunoko kunoko na mangaseni.

29. 서리 뭐비 비하삐 오라 와부찌봐 과 무비리, 아께부사 오롸 와부찌봐 과 무찌마, 구노고 구노고 나 마빠서니.

29. At that time the son born in the ordinary way persecuted the son born by the power of the Spirit. It is the same now.

30. Emaandjiko kute matetchire? Kolokanya ekaungu ne mwana wi kwabushi omwana we kaungu ataboni kwa mwatcdju alauma nemwana we bolo.

30. 어마아찌고 구더 마더찌러? 고로가냐 어가우우 너 뫄나 위 과부씨 오뫄나 워 가우우 아다보니 과 뫄두시주 아롸우마 너뫄나 워 보로.

30. But what does the Scripture say? "Get rid of the slave woman and her son, for the slave woman's son will never share in the inheritance with the free woman's son."

31. kasi banyaketchu, tchubano tchutalyi ban aba kahungu, seri tchulyi bana bola wete ebolo.

31. 가시 바냐거쭈, 쭈바노 쭈다레 바누 아바 가후우, 서리 쭈뻬 바나 보롸 워더 어보로.

31. Therefore, brothers, we are not children of the slave woman, but of the free woman.

E Bakalatiya Chikono 5

어 바가꽈디야 찌고노 5

Galatians Chapter 5[NIV]

1. Kirisito atchuira babuya lwa bolo. Kasi mwemangaa mutatchihubaa mwa butcha bwe musimu.

1. 기리시도 아쭈이라 바부야 롸 보로. 가시 뭐마빠아 무다찌후바아 뫄 부짜 붜 무시무.

1. It is for freedom that Christ has set us free. Stand firm, then, and do not let yourselves be burdened again by a yoke of slavery.

2. Munyisonga, nyono Paulo nababulyire mwabo, nambu; mukamonyisibwa, Kirisito atabaatchire mufa.

2. 무네소빠, 뇨노 파우로 나바부레러 뫄보, 나뿌; 무가모네시봐, 기리시도 아다바아찌러 무파.

2. Mark my words! I, Paul, tell you that if you let yourselves be circumcised, Christ will be of no value to you at all.

3. Nanemeresise kandjio, kwa tchira mundju ola wamonyisibwe, tchimwemire kuira elwaso loshi.

3. 나너머러시서 가찌오, 과 찌라 무뚜 오롸 와모네시붜, 찌뭐미러 구이라 어꽈소 로씨.

3. Again I declare to every man who lets himself be circumcised that he is obligated to obey the whole law.

4. Mwarekanyire na Kirisito, mumuhonda kuandjirwa emwaso mwa lwaso: Mwakumbeere nekutenga mwa mwiisha.

5. Kwabushi tchubano mwabwemeresi bwa tchwalyindjira ne mutchima we mulangalyiro we lwaso.

6. Kwabushi mwandanda sa Kirisito Yesu ekumonyisibwa nekutakumonyisibwa kata kandju: Seri abwemeresi bubwakole ekasi mwa busimene.

7. Mwabaa mwalyibita fubafuba kubuya kasi inde ola wabangaa nambu mutemerera ekanangana?

8. Kunokushiirisibwa kutabahire na Ongo ola wababarangiraa.

9. Ebyaambisa byeeke byende byaambya etchitchu tchoshi.

10. Nete emulangalyiro era mulyi mwandanda sa Tata, nambu mutabone indji myanyisa, seri ola wabakunza angabone emalyibuko mayi moshi.

11. Nanyi banyaketchu, nyika iirisa emwasi yakumonyisibwa, kwabushi netchii nalyibusibwa kuikira

4. 먀러가네러 나 기리시도, 무무호따 구아찌러 어먀소 뫄 똸소: 먀구뻐어러 너구더까 뫄 뮈이싸.

5. 과부씨 쭈바노 먀붜머러시 봐 쫘레찌라 너 무찌마 워 무뫄까레로 워 똸소.

6. 과부씨 먀따따 사 기리시도 여수 어구모네시봐 너구다구모네시봐 가다 가뚜: 서리 아붜머러시 부봐고꿔 어가시 뫄 부시머너.

7. 먀바아 먀레비다 푸바푸바 구부야 가시 이너 오뫄 와바까아 나뿌 무더머러라 어가나까나?

8. 구노구씨이리시봐 구다바히러 나 오꼬 오뫄 와바바라꿰라아.

9. 어뱌아삐사 벼어거 벼너 뱌아뺘 어쭈 쪼씨.

10. 너더 어무뫄까레로 어라 무레 먀따따 사 다다, 나뿌 무다보너 이찌 먀네사, 서리 오뫄 와바구싸 아까보너 어마레부고 마에 모씨.

11. 나네 바냐거쭈, 네가 이이리사 어먀시 야구모네시봐, 과부씨 너찌이 나레부시봐 구이기라

4. You who are trying to be justified by law have been alienated from Christ; you have fallen away from grace.

5. But by faith we eagerly await through the Spirit the righteousness for which we hope.

6. For in Christ Jesus neither circumcision nor uncircumcision has any value. The only thing that counts is faith expressing itself through love.

7. You were running a good race. Who cut in on you and kept you from obeying the truth?

8. That kind of persuasion does not come from the one who calls you.

9. "A little yeast works through the whole batch of dough."

10. I am confident in the Lord that you will take no other view. The one who is throwing you into confusion will pay the penalty, whoever he may be.

11. Brothers, if I am still preaching circumcision, why am I still being persecuted? In that case the offense of

kulwarero? Batcha emalyibuko me etchimanyi mawere?

12. Nyingahondjire banu bandju babalyibusa, bangatchilore ekalamu kabu beine.

13. Kwabushi mwabu banyaketchu, mwaamalwa mubone ebolo. Seri ebolo bwenyu butabaa ndjira yo kukulyikira emubiri, seri mukorerana kwa masimano.

14. Kwabushi elwaso loshi lwairibwa mwa mwasi muuma, oyu mwasi uyono: usimaa munyakenyu ngokula utchisimire weine.

15. Seri mukalumana nekulyana, mulolaa mutalyibusanya mubeine.

16. Kasi nahambere batcha: mundaa kwa mutchima mubuyabuya; seri mutasimisisaa ekuhonola kwe mubiri.

17. Kwabushi o mubiri ahonda aimana ne mutchima, ne mutchima aimana ne mubiri. Kwabushi bini byombi byalwisanya, mutangaala kuira ebibuya bira mwahonda kuira.

구똬러로? 바짜 어마쪠부고 머 어찌마니 마워러?

12. 네까호씨러 바누 바뚜 바바쪠부사, 바까찌로러 어가똬무 가부 버이너.

13. 과부씨 먀부 바냐거쭈, 먀아마똬 무보너 어보로. 서리 어보로 뷔뉴 부다바아 씨라 요 구구쪠기라 어무비리, 서리 무고러라나 과 마시마노.

14. 과부씨 어똬소 로씨 똬이리봐 먀 마시 무우마, 오유 마시 우요노: 우시마아 무냐거뉴 꼬구똬 우찌시미러 워이너.

15. 서리 무가루마나 너구쨔나, 무로똬아 무다쪠부사냐 무버이너.

16. 가시 나하뻐러 바짜: 무따아 과 무찌마 무부야부야; 서리 무다시미시사아 어구호노똬 궈 무비리.

17. 과부씨 오 무비리 아호따 아이마나 너 무찌마, 너 무찌마 아이마나 너 무비리. 과부씨 비니 뵤뻬 뱌뤼사냐, 무다까아똬 구이라 어비부야 비라 먀호따 구이라.

the cross has been abolished.

12. As for those agitators, I wish they would go the whole way and emasculate themselves!

13. You, my brothers, were called to be free. But do not use your freedom to indulge the sinful nature; rather, serve one another in love.

14. The entire law is summed up in a single command: "Love your neighbor as yourself."

15. If you keep on biting and devouring each other, watch out or you will be destroyed by each other.

16. So I say, live by the Spirit, and you will not gratify the desires of the sinful nature.

17. For the sinful nature desires what is contrary to the Spirit, and the Spirit what is contrary to the sinful nature. They are in conflict with each other, so that you do not do what you want.

18. Serimukakoresibwa nemutchima mubuyabuya, mutalyi era masina se lwaso.

19. Kasi etchwasi tchwe mubiri, tchuseneke'oko, utchutchuno : ekukunda: ebwafu nekiri

20. Ekukomera ebihuhanyi emafi, ebulosi, eburenda, ekubangana, emufula, ekusinana, ne mutchima we kaimano, ekuhombana nekutonvana.

21. Nekutcaanyira, nebwitchi mwe mundju nebutamisi, ne kusiya ebilyo, nebindji byabihuhene nebinwa bilyi ngebini. Kukulyikana neni myasi: nababulyire lwabo era muhondo. Ngokula nababura mwabo lyamiramira. Abu bandju bakolaaa emyanya ilyi ngei, batakeeresibwe kwa mwandju we bwami bwa Kabumbi.

22. Seri elwembo lula lutenganyire ne mwasi yomutchima mubuyabuya uyene : Emasimano, ne lumoo, ne bolo, nebusibirisi, nebubuya, netchamba: ne bwemeresi.

23. Ebwemeresi nokutchilanga kwa bibi

18. 서리무가고러시봐 너무찌마 무부야부야, 무다레 어라 마시나 서 봚소.

19. 가시 어좌시 쮜 무비리, 쮸서너거오고, 우쭈쭈노 : 어구구따: 어봐푸 너기리

20. 어구고머라 어비후하네 어마피, 어부로시, 어부러따, 어구바빠나, 어무푸봐, 어구시나나, 너 무찌마 워 가이마노, 어구호빠나 너구도빠나.

21. 너구두시아아네라, 너뷔찌 뭐 무뚜 너부다미시, 너 구시야 어비뢴, 너비찌 뱌비후허너 너비봐 비레 뻐비니. 구구레가나 너니 먀시: 나바부레러 봠보 어라 무호또. 끄구봐 나바부라 봐보 럄미라미라. 아부 바뚜 바고봐아아 어먀냐 이레 뻐이, 바다거어러시붜 과 봐뚜 워 봐미 봐 가부뻬.

22. 서리 어뤄뽀 루봐 루더빠네러 너 봐시 요무찌마 무부야부야 우여너 : 어마시마노, 너 루모오, 너 보뢴, 너부시비리시, 너부부야, 너짜빠: 너 붜머러시.

23. 어붜머러시 노구찌봐빠 과 비비 구다레 어봚소 봐

18. But if you are led by the Spirit, you are not under law.

19. The acts of the sinful nature are obvious: sexual immorality, impurity and debauchery;

20. idolatry and witchcraft; hatred, discord, jealousy, fits of rage, selfish ambition, dissensions, factions

21. and envy; drunkenness, orgies, and the like. I warn you, as I did before, that those who live like this will not inherit the kingdom of God.

22. But the fruit of the Spirit is love, joy, peace, patience, kindness, goodness, faithfulness,

23. gentleness and self-control. Against such things

kutalyi elwaso lwa lulyi era luulu seni myasi.

ᄙᅮᄙᅦ 어라 ᄙᅮ우ᄙᅮ 서니 먀시.

there is no law.

24. Nabala balyi bandju ba Kirisito balyibusa emubiri alauma nemyaanyisa ibi alauma ne buhumahuma bubi bwa bubehure mwa mitchima.

24. 나바ᄙᅡ 바ᄙᅦ 바쭈 바 기리시도 바ᄙᅦ부사 어무비리 아ᄙᅡ우마 너먀아네사 이비 아ᄙᅡ우마 너 부후마후마 부비 봐 부버후러 뫄 미찌마.

24. Those who belong to Christ Jesus have crucified the sinful nature with its passions and desires.

25. Akaba tchweekere kwa mutchima, tchunaenda nokwa mutchima.

25. 아가바 쭤어거러 과 무찌마, 쭈나어따 노과 무찌마.

25. Since we live by the Spirit, let us keep in step with the Spirit.

26. Tchutatchitongaa: Tchunatchilyi tchwahondana kwe butokotoko, tchwahonderanako nekiri.

26. 쭈다찌도ᅇᅡ아: 쭈나찌ᄙᅦ 쫘호따나 궈 부도고도고, 쫘호떠라나고 너기리.

26. Let us not become conceited, provoking and envying each other.

E Bakalatiya Chikono 6

어 바가ᄙᅡ디야 찌고노 6

Galatians Chapter 6[NIV]

1. Banyaketchu, akaba emundju angabonekana mu tchira tchaa tchoshi, mwabumubantchu Be mutchima mu mubuyabuya, mufulusa onu mutchilangaa nau weine emutchima wau angesha kuengilira mwa muereko.

1. 바냐거쭈, 아가바 어무쭈 아ᅇᅡ보너가나 무 찌라 짜아 쪼씨, 뫄부무바쭈 버 무찌마 무 무부야부야, 무푸ᄙᅮ사 오누 무찌ᄙᅡᅇᅡ아 나우 워이너 어무찌마 와우 아ᅇᅥ싸 구어ᅇᅵᄙᅵ라 뫄 무어러고.

1. Brothers, if someone is caught in a sin, you who are spiritual should restore him gently. But watch yourself, or you also may be tempted.

2. Muasanya kwa misuu yenyu, mwabacha mungalumisa elwaso lwa kirisitu.

2. 무아사냐 과 미수우 여뉴, 뫄바짜 무ᅇᅡᄙᅮ미사 어ᄙᅪ소 ᄙᅪ 기리시도.

2. Carry each other's burdens, and in this way you will fulfill the law of Christ.

3. Kwabushi o mundju ahonda nambu alyi kandju, nayi ata kandju kutchiteba kwana tchiteba yeine.

3. 과부씨 오 무쭈 아호따 나뿌 아ᄙᅦ 가쭈, 나에 아다 가쭈 구찌더바 과나 찌더바 여이너.

3. If anyone thinks he is something when he is nothing, he deceives himself.

4. Seri tchira mundju aetreka ekasi kayi yeine, tchasinda angaata tchira anga tchitongera yeine seri atabaa kwa bondjo bwa bandju boshi.

5. Kwabushi tchira mundju akabatchula emusiu wayi yeine.

6. Seri ola waiirisibwa mwa tchinwa, nai airisa ebandji boshoi emyasi yoshi ibuyabuya.

7. Mutatebwa : Kabumbi Ongo atakenyerwa meno : Tchamundju aingaa tchaakanashebula.

8. Kwabushi alawainga kwa mubiri wai yeine, nokwa mubiri wai kwa akanashebula emabi mai yezine. Seri ola waingaa kwa mutchima wai nokwa mutchima wai yeine kwa akanashebula ekalamu ke suku ne mangu.

9. Nomwa kuira emabuya, tchutatamaa kwabushi mwabihangi byai, tchungashebula emangu etchihangi tchai tchingaika.

10. Nesi tchukalola kwa mundju: tchuire emabuya era mwe ebandju boshi, seri busese bala bomwanyumba ye bwemeresi.

4. 서리 찌라 무뚜 아어두러가 어가시 가에 여이너, 짜시따 아까아다 찌라 아까 찌도꺼라 여이너 서리 아다바아 과 보쪼 봐 바뚜 보씨.

5. 과부씨 찌라 무뚜 아가바쭈롸 어무시우 와에 여이너.

6. 서리 오롸 와이이리시봐 뫄 찌놔, 나이 아이리사 어바찌 보쏘이 어먀시 요씨 이부야부야.

7. 무다더봐 : 가부삐 오꼬 아다거녀롸 머노 : 짜무뚜 아이까아 짜아가나써부롸.

8. 과부씨 아롸와이까 과 무비리 와이 여이너, 노과 무비리 와이 과 아가나써부롸 어마비 마이 여지너. 서리 오롸 와이까아 과 무찌마 와이 노과 무찌마 와이 여이너 과 아가나써부롸 어가롸무 거 수구 너 마꾸.

9. 노뫄 구이라 어마부야, 쭈다다마아 과부씨 뫄비하끼 뱌이, 쭈까써부롸 어마꾸 어찌하끼 짜이 찌꽈이가.

10. 너시 쭈가롣롸 과 무뚜: 쭈이러 어마부야 어라 뭐 어바뚜 보씨, 서리 부서서 바롸 보꽈뉴빠 여 붜머러시.

4. Each one should test his own actions. Then he can take pride in himself, without comparing himself to somebody else,

5. for each one should carry his own load.

6. Anyone who receives instruction in the word must share all good things with his instructor.

7. Do not be deceived: God cannot be mocked. A man reaps what he sows.

8. The one who sows to please his sinful nature, from that naturewill reap destruction; the one who sows to please the Spirit, from the Spirit will reap eternal life.

9. Let us not become weary in doing good, for at the proper time we will reap a harvest if we do not give up.

10. Therefore, as we have opportunity, let us do good to all people, especially to those who belong to the family of believers.

11. Mulolaa mwa maandjiko manenene nabaandjikirire mwabo mwa mino yanyi nyeine :

12. Boshi bala balorekanyire'ko kuba babuyabjuya kwa mubiri, babasesise mwabu kumonyisibwa, batalyibusibwa kwa bushi netchimanyi tcha Kirisito.

13. Naabu bamonyisibwa batemerere elwaso : seri bahonda mwabu mumonyisibwa: eri babona kwa batchitonga kwa mibilyi yenyu.

14. Seri nyono ndatchitonga tchiru nehitcha kwabushi na kandju seri etchimanyi tche Enawetchu Yesu Kirisito ku murengeraa'ko bunu butala bwalyibusibwa era mwanyi, nanyi kwa butala.

15. Kwabushi mwandanda sa Kirisito Yesu, ekumonyisibwa katalyi kandju nesi ekutamonyisibwa katalyi na kandju seri ekuba mundju ola ubumbirwe buyaya.

16. Na boshi balabakulyikire tchini tchilaano Ongo abalorera ebondjo nekubalorera nen mwiisha, nera mwa Isiraeli wa Ongo.

---

11. 무룬꽈아 꽈 마아찌고 마너너너 나바아찌기리러 꽈보 꽈 미노 야네 녀이너 :

12. 보씨 바꽈 바룐러가네러고 구바 바부야부주야 과 무비리, 바바서시서 꽈부 구모네시봐, 바다쩨부시봐 과 부씨 너찌마네 짜 기리시도.

13. 나아부 바모네시봐 바더머러러 어꽑소 : 서리 바호따 꽈부 무모네시봐: 어리 바보나 과 바찌도꽈 과 미비쩨 여뉴.

14. 서리 뇨노 따찌도꽈 찌루 너히짜 과부씨 나 가뚜 서리 어찌마네 쩌 어나워쭈 여수 기리시도 구 무러꺼라아고 부누 부다꽈 봐쩨부시봐 어라 꽈네, 나네 과 부다꽈.

15. 과부씨 꽈따따 사 기리시도 여수, 어구모네시봐 가다쩨 가뚜 너시 어구다모네시봐 가다쩨 나 가뚜 서리 어구바 무뚜 오꽈 우부삐뤄 부야야.

16. 나 보씨 바꽈바구쩨기러 찌니 찌꽈아노 오꼬 아바룐러라 어보쪼 너구바룐러라 너 뮈이싸, 너라 꽈 이시라어뢰 와 오꼬.

---

11. See what large letters I use as I write to you with my own hand!

12. Those who want to make a good impression outwardly are trying to compel you to be circumcised. The only reason they do this is to avoid being persecuted for the cross of Christ.

13. Not even those who are circumcised obey the law, yet they want you to be circumcised that they may boast about your flesh.

14. May I never boast except in the cross of our Lord Jesus Christ, through which the world has been crucified to me, and I to the world.

15. Neither circumcision nor uncircumcision means anything; what counts is a new creation.

16. Peace and mercy to all who follow this rule, even to the Israel of God.

17. Kutengera kulwarero emundju ata nyilyibusaa kwabushi, nehuhilyira lya mubiri wanyi lyihuhira Enawetchu Yesu.

18. Banyaketchu, ebolo bwe Enawecthu Yesu Kirisito bubaa alauma ne mitchima yenyu. Bibe batcha!

17. 구더써라 구롸러로 어무뿌 아다 네쩨부사아 과부씨, 너후히쩨라 랴 무비리 와네 쩨후히라 어나워쭈 여수.

18. 바냐거쭈, 어보로 뭐 어나워쮸 여수 기리시도 부바아 아롸우마 너 미찌마 여뉴. 비버 바짜!

17. Finally, let no one cause me trouble, for I bear on my body the marks of Jesus.

18. The grace of our Lord Jesus Christ be with your spirit, brothers. Amen.

E Baefeso

어 바어퍼소

Ephesians

BAEFESO
(EPHESIANS)

바어퍼소
(어퍼시아뚜)

E Baefeso Chikono 1

1. Nyono Paulo, nyilyi ndjumwa ya Yesu Kirisito kwa kuhonda kwa Ongo. Nabaandjikira mu bandju ba Ongo bomwa musi we Efeso. Mulyi bandju babuya-buya mwa buuma bwenyu na Yesu Kirisito.

2. Ongo Tata na Enawetchu Yesu Kirisito, bendaa babaahanyira na kuberesa ebolo!
Engahanyi sa tchwende tchwabona kurengera Kirisito

3. Tchundaa tchwatonga Ongo, Eshe wa Enawethu Yesu Kirisito! Bushi iwatchweresise engahanyi soshi se muchima kutenga kwa nguba kurengera ebuuma bwetchu na Kirisito.

4. Era muhondo sekubumbwa kwe butala, Ongo abaa atchulondwere mira, tchube bandju bai kurengera ebuuma bwetchu na Kirisito. Airaa bacha, chasiya tchube bandju babuya-buya kandji ba batete tchibi tchisibya era muhondo sai. Rero bushi Ongo atchula atchusimire,

5. atchulondolaa kutengera

어 바어퍼소 찌고노 1

1. 뇨노 파우로, 네레 뿌뫄 야 여수 기리시도 과 구호따 과 오꼬. 나바아찌기라 무 바뚜 바 오꼬 보뫄 무시 워 어퍼소. 무레 바뚜 바부야-부야 뫄 부우마 붜뉴 나 여수 기리시도.

2. 오꼬 다다 나 어나워쭈 여수 기리시도, 버따아 바바아하네라 나 구버러사 어보로!
어꼬하네 사 쮜떠 좌보나 구러써라 기리시도

3. 쭈따아 좌도뫄 오꼬, 어써 와 어나워쭈 여수 기리시도! 부씨 이와쮜러시서 어꼬하네 소씨 서 무찌마 구더뫄 과 우바 구러써라 어부우마 붜쭈 나 기리시도.

4. 어라 무호또 서구부뫄 궈 부다뫄, 오꼬 아바아 아쭈로뿌워러 미라, 쭈버 바뚜 바이 구러써라 어부우마 붜쭈 나 기리시도. 아이라아 바짜, 짜시야 쭈버 바뚜 바부야-부야 가찌 바 바더더 찌비 찌시뱌 어라 무호또 사이. 러로 부씨 오꼬 아쭈뫄 아쭈시미러,

5. 아쭈로또뫄아 구더써라

Ephesians Chapter 1[NIV]

1. Paul, an apostle of Christ Jesus by the will of God, To the saints in Ephesus, the faithful in Christ Jesus:

2. Grace and peace to you from God our Father and the Lord Jesus Christ.

3. Praise be to the God and Father of our Lord Jesus Christ, who has blessed us in the heavenly realms with every spiritual blessing in Christ.

4. For he chose us in him before the creation of the world to be holy and blameless in his sight. In love

5. he predestined us to be

mira tchube bana bai kurengera emulyimo wa Yesu Kirisito. Asimaa kuira bacha mwa bubuya bwai.

6. Bushi noku, tchundaa tchwatonga Ongo kwa bondjo bwai bunene bwa atchufiraa kurengera eMwana wai musiirwa.

7. Bushi Kirisito atchufiraa, tchwanunulyibwe na kubabalyirwa emabi metchu. Aola, Ongo alosise ebwingi bwebondjo bwai,

8. mwa kutchweresa ebuashi bwekumenyerera emyasi, anatchweresa na bwenge bwa bulumirire.

9. Ongo atchulosise emyasi yai era yabaa ibishirwe yekuhonda kwai, era abaa ahonda kuira kutenga mira kurengera Kirisito.

10. Abaa ahonda kuira ei myasi kwa bihangi bya abaa alondwere, kukuteta mbu byoshi bya bitchula kwa nguba no'muno butala angabikabi mwa mino sa Kirisito, emangirebi.

11. Ongo ende aira chira kandju kukulyikana nekuhonda kwai. Atchulondolaa kutengera mira tchube bandju bai kurengera

---

미라 쭈버 바나 바이 구러ᄧ라 어무ᄲ모 와 여수 기리시도. 아시마아 구이라 바짜 마 부부야 바이.

6. 부씨 노구, 쭈따아 쫘도ᄭ아 오ᄭ 과 보ᄍ 바이 부너너 봐 아쭈피라아 구러ᄧ라 어뫄나 와이 무시이롸.

7. 부씨 기리시도 아쭈피라아, 쫘누누레봐 나 구바바ᄤ롸 어마비 머쭈. 아오똬, 오ᄭ 아로ᄉ시서 어뷔ᄭ 봐보ᄍ 봐이,

8. 똬 구쭤러사 어부아씨 봐구머녀러라 어먀시, 아나쭤러사 나 봐ᄭ 봐 부루미리러.

9. 오ᄭ 아쭈로ᄉ시서 어먀시 야이 어라 야바아 이비씨뤄 여구호따 과이, 어라 아바아 아호따 구이라 구더ᄭ 미라 구러ᄧ라 기리시도.

10. 아바아 아호따 구이라 어이 먀시 과 비하ᄭ 뱌 아바아 아로뚜워러, 구구더다 뿌 보씨 뱌 비쭈똬 과 우바 노무노 부다똬 아ᄭ아비가비 똬 미노 사 기리시도, 어마ᄭ이러비.

11. 오ᄭ 어너 아이라 찌라 가ᄶ 구구ᄤ가나 너구호따 과이. 아쭈로ᄠ똬아 구더ᄧ라 미라 쭈버 바ᄶ 바이 구러ᄧ라 어부우마 봐쭈 나

---

adopted as his sons through Jesus Christ, in accordance with his pleasure and will--

6. to the praise of his glorious grace, which he has freely given us in the One he loves.

7. In him we have redemption through his blood, the forgiveness of sins, in accordance with the riches of God's grace

8. that he lavished on us with all wisdom and understanding.

9. And he made known to us the mystery of his will according to his good pleasure, which he purposed in Christ,

10. to be put into effect when the times will have reached their fulfillment--to bring all things in heaven and on earth together under one head, even Christ.

11. In him we were also chosen, having been predestined according to the plan of him who works out everything in conformity with

ebuuma bwetchu na Kirisito.

12. Rero tchu tchwabaa babere-bere kuchinyiira Kirisito, tchundaa tchwatonga Ongo bushi nengulu yai!

13. Nenyu, mango momvaa emwasi wekanangana, kukuteta mbu eMwasi Mubuya-buya ola wabareteraa ebununusi, mwera kwemerera Kirisito. Chasinda, Ongo era kubabika kwekalorero kai ka kalosa kwa munalyi bandju bai. Naku kalorero, alyi eMuchima Mubuya-buya ola alaanyaa.

14. Oyu Muchima Mubuya-buya, alyi chikinja chebindju bya tchukabona era mwa Ongo. Echera chalosa kanangana kwa tchukabonbi mango Ongo akanunula ebandju bai loshi. Bushi noku, tchundaa tchwamutonga bushi nengulu yai!

15. Rero, kutengera mango nomvaa emwasi kwa mwemerere Enawetchu Yesu, nokwa musimire ebandju ba Ongo boshi,

16. echera chi chendjire chatchuma natonga Ongo bushi nenyu busira kutama. Nendjire nabakengera mwa memo manyi.

기리시도.

12. 러로 쭈 쫘바아 바버러-버러 구찌네이라 기리시도, 쭈따아 쫘도꽈 오꼬 부씨 너꾸루 야이!

13. 너뉴, 마꼬 모빠아 어꽈시 워가나꽈나, 구구더다 뿌 어꽈시 무부야-부야 오라 와바러더라아 어부누누시, 뭐라 궈머러라 기리시도. 짜시따, 오꼬 어라 구바비가 궈가뢰러로 가이 가 가뢰사 과 무나례 바쭈 바이. 나구 가뢰러로, 아레 어무찌마 무부야-부야 오라 아라아냐아.

14. 오유 무찌마 무부야-부야, 아레 찌기짜 쩌비뿌 뱌 쭈가보나 어라 꽈 오꼬. 어쩌라 짜뢰사 가나꽈나 과 쭈가보누비 마꼬 오꼬 아가누누꽈 어바뿌 바이 뢰씨. 부씨 노구, 쭈따아 쫘무도꽈 부씨 너꾸루 야이!

15. 러로, 구더꺼라 마꼬 노빠아 어꽈시 과 뭐머러러 어나워쭈 여수, 노과 무시미러 어바뿌 바 오꼬 보씨,

16. 어쩌라 찌 쩌찌러 짜쭈마 나도꽈 오꼬 부씨 너뉴 부시라 구다마. 너찌러 나바거꺼라 꽈 머모 마네.

the purpose of his will,

12. in order that we, who were the first to hope in Christ, might be for the praise of his glory.

13. And you also were included in Christ when you heard the word of truth, the gospel of your salvation. Having believed, you were marked in him with a seal, the promised Holy Spirit,

14. who is a deposit guaranteeing our inheritance until the redemption of those who are God's possession--to the praise of his glory.

15. For this reason, ever since I heard about your faith in the Lord Jesus and your love for all the saints,

16. I have not stopped giving thanks for you, remembering you in my prayers.

17. Nendjire nema Ongo wa Enawetu Yesu Kirisito, Tata webulangare, aberese emuchima wekumenyerera emyasi, na kunde achilosa era mulyi chasiya mumumenye kanangana.

18. Kandji nendjire namwema abalomekere mwa michima yenyu, munde mwalola kwa bulangare bwai. Mwa bacha, mungamenyerera emunyiiro ola aberesaa mango abamaalaa. Kandji mungamenyerera engulu yebuare bwemwandju bwa abikirire ebandju bai.

19. Kandji mungamenyerera kwa emisi yebuashi bwai itchula inene ku tchubano tchu tchumwemerere. Ei misi yebuashi bwai inei

20. iOngo akoresaa mango omwolaa Kirisito nekumwekasa kwa lunda lwai lwemalyo kwa nguba.

21. Mwa bacha, Kirisito i'ulyi era luulu sebakulu-kulu boshi, ba bete buashi boshi, na ba bete misi, nebami boshi, nera luulu sa chira esina mwobuno butala bwa lwarero nomwa butala bwa bukabaha.

17. 너찌러 너마 오꼬 와 어나워두 여수 기리시도, 다다 워부콰꽈러, 아버러서 어무찌마 워구머녀러라 어먀시, 나 구떠 아찌론사 어라 무뤠 짜시야 무무머녀 가나꽈나.

18. 가찌 너찌러 나뭐마 아바론머거러 똬 미찌마 여뉴, 무떠 똬론콰 과 부콰꽈러 바이. 똬 바짜, 무꽈머녀러라 어무네이로 오콰 아버러사아 마꼬 아바마아꽈라아. 가찌 무꽈머녀러라 어꾸루 여부아러 뷔똬뉴 봐 아비기리러 어바뉴 바이.

19. 가찌 무꽈머녀러라 과 어미시 여부아씨 봐이 이쭈콰 이너너 구 쭈바노 쭈 쭈뭐머러러. 어이 미시 여부아씨 봐이 이너이

20. 이오꼬 아고러사아 마꼬 오모콰라 기리시도 너구뭐가사 과 루따 콰이 뤄마료 과 꾸바.

21. 똬 바짜, 기리시도 이우뤠 어라 루우루루 서바구루-구루 보씨, 바 버더 부아씨 보씨, 나 바 버더 미시, 너바미 보씨, 너라 루우루루 사 찌라 어시나 모부노 부다꽈 봐 콰러로 노와 부다꽈 봐 부가바하.

17. I keep asking that the God of our Lord Jesus Christ, the glorious Father, may give you the Spirit of wisdom and revelation, so that you may know him better.

18. I pray also that the eyes of your heart may be enlightened in order that you may know the hope to which he has called you, the riches of his glorious inheritance in the saints,

19. and his incomparably great power for us who believe. That power is like the working of his mighty strength,

20. which he exerted in Christ when he raised him from the dead and seated him at his right hand in the heavenly realms,

21. far above all rule and authority, power and dominion, and every title that can be given, not only in the present age but also in the one to come.

22. Ongo abikire ebindju byoshi kuba chisimachiro cha Kirisito. Kandji amubikire era luulu sa byoshi na kumuira etchwe lyebemeresi.
23. Abu bemeresi imubiri wa Kirisito. Kirisito atchula mwa ndanda sabo, na iwende walumisabo tenene, kanji iwende walumisa chira chindju.

22. 오꼬 아비기러 어비뉴 뵤씨 구바 찌시마찌로 짜 기리시도. 가찌 아무비기러 어라 루우루 사 뵤씨 나 구무이라 어쮜 려버머러시.
23. 아부 버머러시 이무비리 와 기리시도. 기리시도 아쭈롸 마 따따 사보, 나 이워떠 와루미사보 더너너, 가찌 이워떠 와루미사 찌라 찌뉴.

22. And God placed all things under his feet and appointed him to be head over everything for the church,
23. which is his body, the fullness of him who fills everything in every way.

E Baefeso Chikono 2

1. Kwa mira, mwabaa muli bafu mwa myasi ye'muchima bushi ne'bibi byenyu binene.
2. Mwabaa mulyi mwa mabi mwa kunde mwakulyikira emyanya ibi yomuno butala. Mwendee mwathunda emukulu-kulu webihwasi bya bitchusa ebuashi mwa chanya. Rero oyu mukulu-kulu, iwimire kwa bandju ba batatchunda Ongo.
3. Kwa mira, netchu tchuboshi ku tchwabaa tchunalyi ngabu bandju. Tchwendee tchwakulyikira ebuhuma-huma bwetchu bwemubiri, tchwendee tchwaira ekuhonda kwemibiri yetchu nekuhonda kwemianyisa yetchu ibi. Rero

어 바어퍼소 찌고노 2

1. 과 미라, 마바아 무뤼 바푸 마 먀시 여무찌마 부씨 너비비 벼뉴 비너너.
2. 마바아 무뤠 마 마비 마 구떠 마구뤠기라 어먄냐 이비 요무노 부다롸. 뭐떠어 롸쭈따 어무구룩-구룩 워비화시 뱌 비쭈사 어부아씨 마 짜냐. 러로 오유 무구룩-구룩, 이위미러 과 바뉴 바 바다쭈따 오꼬.
3. 과 미라, 너쭈 쭈보씨 구 롸바아 쭈나뤠 따부 바뉴. 쭤떠어 롸구뤠기라 어부후마-후마 뷔쭈 뷔무비리, 쭤떠어 롸이라 어구호따 궈미비리 여쭈 너구호따 궈미아네사 여쭈 이비. 러로 부씨 너이 먄냐 여쭈 여무비리, 롸바아

Ephesians Chapter 2[NIV]

1. As for you, you were dead in your transgressions and sins,
2. in which you used to live when you followed the ways of this world and of the ruler of the kingdom of the air, the spirit who is now at work in those who are disobedient.
3. All of us also lived among them at one time, gratifying the cravings of our sinful nature and following its desires and thoughts. Like the rest, we were by nature objects of wrath.

bushi nei myanya yetchu yemubiri, tchwabaa tchwemire kuchinjibusibwa kuuma nebandji.

쮜미러 구찌씨부시봐 구우마 너바찌.

4. Si Ongo atchula wa bondjo bunene, kandji atchula atchusimire na nzii inene.

4. 시 오꼬 아쭈롸 와 보쪼 부너너, 가찌 아쭈롸 아쭈시미러 나 씨이 이너너.

4. But because of his great love for us, God, who is rich in mercy,

5. Bushi noku, era kutchwomola alauma na Kirisito, tchutchwabaa tchwafire mwa myasi yemuchima bushi nemabi metchu. Kwa bonjo bwa Ongo ku mwanunulyibwe.

5. 부씨 노구, 어라 구쪼모롸 아롸우마 나 기리시도, 쭈좌바아 좌피러 와 먀시 여무찌마 부씨 너마비 머쭈. 과 보쪼 봐 오꼬 구 뫄누누레붜.

5. made us alive with Christ even when we were dead in transgressions--it is by grace you have been saved.

6. Kurengera ebuuma bwetchu na Yesu Kirisito, Ongo atchwomwere alauma nai, tchwime alauma nai kwa nguba.

6. 구러뻐라 어부우마 붜쭈 나 여수 기리시도, 오꼬 아쪼뭐러 아롸우마 나이, 쮜머 아롸우마 나이 과 꾸바.

6. And God raised us up with Christ and seated us with him in the heavenly realms in Christ Jesus,

7. Mwakutchulosa ebubuya bwai kurengera Yesu Kirisito, abaa ahonda alose enyibuto sa sikaika kwa bwingi bwebuare bwebonjdo bwai bwa butangamaanyibwa.

7. 뫄구쭈롯사 어부부야 봐이 구러뻐라 여수 기리시도, 아바아 아호따 아롯서 어네부도 사 시가이가 과 뷔삐 붜부아러 붜보뚜도 봐이 봐 부다까마아니봐.

7. in order that in the coming ages he might show the incomparable riches of his grace, expressed in his kindness to us in Christ Jesus.

8. Bushi mwanunulyibwe kwa bondjo bwa Ongo, kurengera ebwemeresi. Echera chitatenganyire nenyu, si lulyi lwembo lwa Ongo.

8. 부씨 뫄누누레붜 과 보쪼 봐 오꼬, 구러뻐라 어붜머러시. 어쩌라 찌다더까네러 너뉴, 시 루레 뤄뚜 꽈 오꼬.

8. For it is by grace you have been saved, through faith-- and this not from yourselves, it is the gift of God--

9. Ata bushi nebya mwende mwaira, kungesha kuba mundju ola wachitonga.

9. 아다 부씨 너뱌 뭐떠 뫄이라, 구뻐싸 구바 무뚜 오롸 와찌도까.

9. not by works, so that no one can boast.

10. Bushi tchubano tchwabumbwaa na Ongo. Na

10. 부씨 쭈바노 좌부꽈아 나 오꼬. 나 구러뻐라 어부우마

10. For we are God's workmanship, created in

kurengera ebuuma bwetchu na Yesu Kirisito, atchubumbire chasiya tchunde tchwakola emabuya mwa kalamo ketchu. Amu mabuya, Ongo akunganyaamo kutengera mira chasiya tchunde tchwairamo.

뭐쭈 나 여수 기리시도, 아쭈부삐러 짜시야 쭈너 짜고라 어마부야 마 가라모 거쭈. 아무 마부야, 오꼬 아구까냐아모 구더꺼라 미라 짜시야 쭈너 짜이라모.

Christ Jesus to do good works, which God prepared in advance for us to do.

11. Mwabo mu mutatula Bayuta, mukengeraa kute mwabaa mulyi kwa mira. eBayuta bende bamona, noku kumona kwende kwairibwa kwa mubiri oshao. Nechi chi chende chatuma mango ba babamaana, bende baberika mbu: "mutamonyire".

11. 뫄보 무 무다두롸 바유다, 무거꺼라아 구더 뫄바아 무례 과 미라. 어바유다 버러 바모나, 노구 구모나 꿔러 과이리봐 과 무비리 오싸오. 너찌 찌 쩌너 짜두마 마꼬 바 바바마아나, 버러 바버리가 뿌: "무다모네러".

11. Therefore, remember that formerly you who are Gentiles by birth and called "uncircumcised" by those who call themselves "the circumcision" (that done in the body by the hands of men)--

12. Mwesi suku, mwabaa muli bure na Kirisito, mwabaa mutanalyi nomwa bandju ba Ongo alondolaa, mwabaa baenyi mwa kachi-kachi kabo. Kandji mwabaa mutete na mwango kwa bilaano bya Ongo alaanyaa eBaisiraeli. Mwabaa mulyi mwa butala busira munyiiro, kanji busira Ongo.

12. 뭐시 수구, 뫄바아 무리 부러 나 기리시도, 뫄바아 무다나례 노봐 바뉴 바 오꼬 아로또롸아, 뫄바아 바어네 뫄 가찌-가찌 가보. 가찌 뫄바아 무더더 나 뫄꼬 과 비롸아노 뱌 오꼬 아롸아냐아 어바이시라어례. 뫄바아 무례 뫄 부다롸 부시라 무네이로, 가찌 부시라 오꼬.

12. remember that at that time you were separate from Christ, excluded from citizenship in Israel and foreigners to the covenants of the promise, without hope and without God in the world.

13. Si rero kurengera ebuuma bwenyu na Yesu Kirisito, mu bandu mwabaa mulyi bure, mwera muli ofu bushi nemikira ya Kirisito.

13. 시 러로 구러꺼라 어부우마 뭐뉴 나 여수 기리시도, 무 바뉴 뫄바아 무례 부러, 뭐라 무례 오푸 부씨 너미기라 야 기리시도.

13. But now in Christ Jesus you who once were far away have been brought near through the blood of Christ.

14. Kirisito yeine iwaturetere ebolo, mwa kuira eBayuta na

14. 기리시도 여이너 이와두러더러 어보로, 뫄

14. For he himself is our peace, who has made the

ba batatula Bayuta kuba lubaa luuma. Mwa kwana emubiri wai, ahandjwire eburenda bwa bwabaa bulyi nga lusito lwa lwabaa lulyikanyisebo.

구이라 어바유다 나 바 바다두롸 바유다 구바 루바아 루우마. 롸 과나 어무비리 와이, 아하뉴위러 어부러따 봐 봐바아 부레 따 루시도 롸 롸바아 루레가네서보.

two one and has destroyed the barrier, the dividing wall of hostility,

15. Ahandjwire emufa weMwaso weBayuta nemiomba yao, nemyasi era itechirwemo. Airire bacha, chasiya eBayuta na ba batathula Bayuta, babe bandu ba lubaa luuma luyayaya. Mwei njira mu Kirisito arechire ebolo.

15. 아하뉴위러 어무파 워마소 워바유다 너미오빠 야오, 너먀시 어라 이더찌뤄모. 아이리러 바짜, 짜시야 어바유다 나 바 바다쭈롸 바유다, 바버 바뚜 바 루바아 루우마 루야야야. 뭐이 띠라 무 기리시도 아러찌러 어보롯.

15. by abolishing in his flesh the law with its commandments and regulations. His purpose was to create in himself one new man out of the two, thus making peace,

16. Ekufa kwa Kirisito kwa musalaba, ku kwerire kwathuma abu boshi baba mundju muuma na kubabika mwa buuma na Ongo. Kurengera oyu musalaba, ahandjwire eburenda.

16. 어구파 과 기리시도 과 무사롸바, 구 궈리러 과쭈마 아부 보씨 바바 무뚜 무우마 나 구바비가 롸 부우마 나 오읏. 구러뼈라 오유 무사롸바, 아하뉴위러 어부러따.

16. and in this one body to reconcile both of them to God through the cross, by which he put to death their hostility.

17. Rero, Kirisito aikaa kuhubanganya eMwasi Mubuya-buya webolo, kwa ba babaa balyi bure na Ongo, na kwa ba babaa balyi ofu nai.

17. 러로, 기리시도 아이가아 구후바빠냐 어먀시 무부야-부야 워보롯, 과 바 바바아 바레 부러 나 오읏, 나 과 바 바바아 바레 오푸 나이.

17. He came and preached peace to you who were far away and peace to those who were near.

18. Bushi kurengera Kirisito, thuboshi thwera thungaika era muhondo sa Ongo Tata, kwa njira ye'Muchima Mubuya-buya muuma.

18. 부씨 구러뼈라 기리시도, 쭈보씨 쭤라 쭈빠이가 어라 무호또 사 오읏 다다, 과 띠라 여무찌마 무부야-부야 무우마.

18. For through him we both have access to the Father by one Spirit.

19. Bushi noku, mu mutatula Bayuta, mutachiri baenyi nesi babunga. Si mwera muli

19. 부씨 노구, 무 무다두롸 바유다, 무다찌리 바이네 너시 바부빠. 시 뭐라 무삐

19. Consequently, you are no longer foreigners and aliens, but fellow citizens with God's

besha chio alauma nebandju ba Ongo, kanji mwera mulyi bandju bomwa ngumo yai.

20. Mwera mulyi nga nyumba era iimbirwe kwa musingi ola ndjumwa nebarebi bemanzaa. Yesu Kirisito yeine lyi koi lyinene lyokwa pembe.

21. Mwa kuba mwa buuma nai mu enyumba yoshi isimikire kubuya, na kuendekera yehula chasiya lube luhu lubuya-buya lwa Enawethu.

22. Kanji kurengera ebuuma bwenyu na Kirisito, nenyu mwera muli mwa buuma nebanji bandJu boshi, chasiya mube nyumba era Ongo alyimo, kurengera eMuchima wai.

버싸 찌오 아꽈우마 너바쭈 바 오꼬, 가찌 뭐라 무레 바쭈 보와 꾸모 야이.

20. 뭐라 무레 까 뉴빠 어라 이이삐뤄 과 무시끼 오꽈 쭈꽈 너바러비 버마싸아. 여수 기리시도 여이너 레 고이 레너너 뢌과 퍼뻐.

21. 와 구바 와 부우마 나이 무 어뉴빠 요씨 이시미기러 구부야, 나 구어떠거라 여후꽈 짜시야 루버 루후 루부야-부야 꽈 어나워쭈.

22. 가찌 구러꺼라 어부우마 붜뉴 나 기리시도, 너뉴 뭐라 무꾀 와 부우마 너바씨 바쭈 보씨, 짜시야 무버 뉴빠 어라 오꼬 아뻬모, 구러꺼라 어무찌마 와이.

people and members of God's household,

20. built on the foundation of the apostles and prophets, with Christ Jesus himself as the chief cornerstone.

21. In him the whole building is joined together and rises to become a holy temple in the Lord.

22. And in him you too are being built together to become a dwelling in which God lives by his Spirit.

E Baefeso Chikono 3

1. Bushi noku, nyono Paulo nenjire nema Ongo. Nyiri mundu wa buroko wemulimo wa Yesu Kirisito bushi nenyu mu mutatula Bayuta.

2. Mwomvire emwasi kanangana kwa Ongo anyiahanyire mwa kunyeresa emulyimo wekunde nabakorera.

어 바어퍼소 찌고노 3

1. 부씨 노구, 뇨노 파우뢰 너찌러 너마 오꼬. 내리 무뚜 와 부로고 워무꾀모 와 여수 기리시도 부씨 너뉴 무 무다두꽈 바유다.

2. 모뻬러 어마시 가나까나 과 오꼬 아네아하네러 와 구녀러사 어무뻬모 워구떠 나바고러라.

Ephesians Chapter 3[NIV]

1. For this reason I, Paul, the prisoner of Christ Jesus for the sake of you Gentiles--

2. Surely you have heard about the administration of God's grace that was given to me for you,

3. Bushi Ongo anyilosaa emyasi era yabaa ibishirwe, ngokwa nabaa nabaanjikirei mira mu binwa bieke.

4. Mwa kusomai, mungamenyerera kwa kasi nyishi emyasi ya Kirisito era yabaa ibishirwe.

5. Kwa mira, ei myasi yabaa ibishirwe, Ongo atalosaai ebandju ngokwa erire alosai endjumwa nebarebi bai babuya-buya kurengera eMuchima wai.

6. Ei myasi yabaa ibishirwe iyene: kurengera eMwasi Mubuya-buya, ba batathula Bayuta neBayuta, boshi bahangire kwa mwandju ola Ongo abikirire ebandju bai. Abu bandju bera balyi bitera bya mubiri muuma. Nabo banganabona kwa chiraane cha Ongo alanyaa ebandju kurengera Yesu Kirisito.

7. Ongo mwa bubuya bwai, anyeresise elwembo lwekuba mukosi weMwasi Mubuya-buya. Airire bacha, kukulyikana nemulimo webuashi bwai.

8. Nyono nyi mueke mwa bandju boshi ba Ongo. Si Ongo anyeresise elwembo

3. 부씨 오꼬 아네로싸아 어먀시 어라 야바아 이비씨뤄, 꼬과 나바아 나바아찌기러이 미라 무 비놔 비어거.

4. 마 구소마이, 무까머녀러라 과 가시 네씨 어먀시 야 기리시도 어라 야바아 이비씨뤄.

5. 과 미라, 어이 먀시 야바아 이비씨뤄, 오꼬 아다로싸아이 어바뚜 꼬과 어리러 아로싸이 어뚜먀 너바러비 바이 바부야-부야 구러꺼라 어무찌마 와이.

6. 어이 먀시 야바아 이비씨뤄 이여너: 구러꺼라 어마시 무부야-부야, 바 바다쭈롸 바유다 너바유다, 보씨 바하꺼러 과 먀뚜 오롸 오꼬 아비기리러 어바뚜 바이. 아부 바뚜 버라 바께 비더라 뱌 무비리 무우마. 나보 바까나보나 과 찌라아너 짜 오꼬 아퐈냐아 어바뚜 구러꺼라 여수 기리시도.

7. 오꼬 먀 부부야 봐이, 아녀러시서 어뤄뽀 뤄구바 무고시 워먀시 무부야-부야. 아이리러 바짜, 구구께가나 너무뛰모 워부아씨 봐이.

8. 뇨노 네 무어거 먀 바뚜 보씨 바 오꼬. 시 오꼬 아녀러시서 어뤄뽀 뤄구머

3. that is, the mystery made known to me by revelation, as I have already written briefly.

4. In reading this, then, you will be able to understand my insight into the mystery of Christ,

5. which was not made known to men in other generations as it has now been revealed by the Spirit to God's holy apostles and prophets.

6. This mystery is that through the gospel the Gentiles are heirs together with Israel, members together of one body, and sharers together in the promise in Christ Jesus.

7. I became a servant of this gospel by the gift of God's grace given me through the working of his power.

8. Although I am less than the least of all God's people, this grace was given me: to

lwekunde nahubanganyisa ba batathula Bayuta eMwasi Mubuya-buya webuare bwa Kirisito bwa butakawe.

9. Nemire kunde nalosa ebandju boshi kubuya-buya kute Ongo iwabumbaa byoshi ende aira emyasi era abaa akunganyise, era abaa abishire kutengera mira.

10. Rero kurengera ebemeresi, ba bathula bemire nebakulu-kulu ba bete buashi mwa chanya, bende bamenyerera ebwenge bwa Ongo. Obu bwenge, Ongo ende alosabo mu njira sinene.

11. Ongo airire bacha, kukulyikana nokwa abaa ahonjire kutengera mira, kurengera Enawetu Yesu Kirisito.

12. Rero, bushi tulyi mwa buuma na Yesu Kirisito kanji thumwemerere, thwera thwete ebuuru bwekuika era muhondo sa Ongo na munyiiro munene.

13. Bushi noku, nabema mutendaa mwafunyika emuchima bushi nemalyibuko ma narengamo bushi nenyu. Amu malyibuko menjire maberesa ethunda.

나후바까네사 바 바다쭈꽈 바유다 어먀시 무부야-부야 워부아러 봐 기리시도 봐 부다가워.

9. 너미러 구떠 나롤사 어바뉴 보씨 구부야-부야 구더 오꼬 이와부빠아 뵤씨 어떠 아이라 어먀시 어라 아바아 아구까네서, 어라 아바아 아비씨러 구더꺼라 미라.

10. 러로 구러꺼라 어버머러시, 바 바쭈꽈 버미러 너바구룹-구루 바 버더 부아씨 꽈 짜냐, 버떠 바머녀러라 어뿨꺼 봐 오꼬. 오부 뷔꺼, 오꼬 어너 아롤사보 무 찌라 시너너.

11. 오꼬 아이리러 바짜, 구구레가나 노과 아바아 아호찌러 구더꺼라 미라, 구러꺼라 어나워두 여수 기리시도.

12. 러로, 부씨 두쪠 꽈 부우마 나 여수 기리시도 가찌 쭈뭐머러러, 쮜라 쮜더 어부우루 뷔구이가 어라 무호또 사 오꼬 나 무네이로 무너너.

13. 부씨 노구, 나버마 무더따아 꽈푸네가 어무찌마 부씨 너마쪠부고 마 나러까모 부씨 너뉴. 아무 마쪠부고 머찌러 마버러사 어쭈따.

preach to the Gentiles the unsearchable riches of Christ,

9. and to make plain to everyone the administration of this mystery, which for ages past was kept hidden in God, who created all things.

10. His intent was that now, through the church, the manifold wisdom of God should be made known to the rulers and authorities in the heavenly realms,

11. according to his eternal purpose which he accomplished in Christ Jesus our Lord.

12. In him and through faith in him we may approach God with freedom and confidence.

13. I ask you, therefore, not to be discouraged because of my sufferings for you, which are your glory.

14. Echera chi chenjire chathuma nakoma emafi era muhondo sa Tata,
15. ishokororo ya chira ngumo era ilyi kwa nguba nera iri muno butala.
16. Nenjire namwema kukulyikana nebwingi bwetunda lyai, abasese emichima kurengera eMuchima wai.
17. Kanji Kirisito endaa ekala mwa michima yenyu bushi mumwemerere. Musimikaa na kusera mwa nzii.

18. Mwa bacha, mungaala kumenyerera alauma nebandju boshi ba Ongo, kwa nzii ya Kirisito ilyi ingana, nokwa ilyi ireya, nokwa itowamire mwa chanya nokwa ilyi ireya mwa kwandaala.
19. Kanji mungamenyerera ei nzii yai era ithalukire ebwenge boshi, chasiya mube bandju ba balumirire tenene ngokwa Ongo anathula.
20. Ongo iwende wakola mwa ndanda sethu ete ebuashi bwekuira bindju binene busese kurenza bya twamwema nesi bya twaanyisa.
21. Endaa atongibwa mwa

14. 어쩌라 찌 쩌찌러 짜쭈마 나고마 어마피 어라 무호또 사 다다,
15. 이쏘고로로 야 찌라 꾸모 어라 이쩨 과 꾸바 너라 이리 무노 부다ﬁ.
16. 너찌러 나뭐마 구구쩨가나 너뷔찌 뭐두따 ﬁ이, 아바서서 어미찌마 구러찌러라 어무찌마 와이.
17. 가찌 기리시도 어따아 어가ﬁ 마 미찌마 여뉴 부씨 무뭐머러러. 무시미가아 나 구서라 마 씨이.

18. 마 바짜, 무찌아아ﬁ 구머녀러라 아ﬁ아우마 너바쭈 보씨 바 오꼬, 과 씨이 야 기리시도 이쩨 이ﬁ나, 노과 이쩨 이러야, 노과 이도와미러 마 짜냐 노과 이쩨 이러야 마 과따아ﬁ.
19. 가찌 무찌머녀러라 어이 씨이 야이 어라 이따루기러 어뭐찌 보씨, 짜시야 무버 바쭈 바 바루미리러 더너너 꼬과 오꼬 아나쭈ﬁ.
20. 오꼬 이워너 와고ﬁ 마 따따 서쭈 어더 어부아씨 뭐구이라 비쭈 비너너 부서서 구러싸 뱌 돠뭐마 너시 뱌 돠아네사.
21. 어따아 아도찌봐 마

14. For this reason I kneel before the Father,
15. from whom his whole family in heaven and on earth derives its name.
16. I pray that out of his glorious riches he may strengthen you with power through his Spirit in your inner being,
17. so that Christ may dwell in your hearts through faith. And I pray that you, being rooted and established in love,
18. may have power, together with all the saints, to grasp how wide and long and high and deep is the love of Christ,
19. and to know this love that surpasses knowledge-- that you may be filled to the measure of all the fullness of God.
20. Now to him who is able to do immeasurably more than all we ask or imagine, according to his power that is at work within us,
21. to him be glory in the

kachi-kachi kebemeresi kurengera Yesu Kirisito, mwa nyibuto soshi esuku nemango. Bibe bacha!

가찌-가찌 거버머러시 구러꺼라 여수 기리시도, 뫄 네부도 소씨 어수구 너마꼬. 비버 바짜!

church and in Christ Jesus throughout all generations, for ever and ever! Amen.

E Baefeso Chikono 4

1. Nyiminyirwe bushi nende nakorera Enawethu. Rero nabema busese munde mwaata mibere era ithungenene kukulyikana nokwa Ongo abamaalaa.
2. Mundaa mwachirembeka na kuba balomvu na kunde mwaata ebushibirisi. Kanji mundaa mwasesa emuchima wekuba alauma mwa nzii.
3. Muchisesaa kuba mwa buuma ngokwa eMuchima Mubuya-buya athula atubikire mwa buuma. Kanji mundaa mwalanga ebolo bwa bubabikire mwobu buuma.
4. Kutula mubiri muuma, kwanaba na Muchima Mubuya-buya muuma. Nemunyiiro ola Ongo abamaaliraa, nao anathula muuma.
5. Enawethu anathula muuma, nebwemeresi bunathula buuma nebubatiso nabo bunathula buuma.
6. Ongo anathula muuma,

어 바어퍼소 찌고노 4

1. 네미네뤄 부씨 너떠 나고러라 어나워쭈. 러로 나버마 부서서 무떠 뫄아다 미버러 어라 이쭈꺼너너 구구레가나 노과 오꼬 아바마아롸아.
2. 무따아 뫄찌러뻐가 나 구바 바롿뿌 나 구떠 뫄아다 어부씨비리시. 가찌 무따아 뫄서사 어무찌마 워구바 아롸우마 뫄 씨이.
3. 무찌서사아 구바 뫄 부우마 꼬과 어무찌마 무부야-부야 아쭈롸 아두비기러 뫄 부우마. 가찌 무따아 뫄롸꺄 어보롿 봐 부바비기러 모부 부우마.
4. 구두롸 무비리 무우마, 과나바 나 무찌마 무부야-부야 무우마. 너무네이로 오롸 오꼬 아바마아뢰라아, 나오 아나쭈롸 무우마.
5. 어나워쭈 아나쭈롸 무우마, 너붜머러시 부나쭈롸 부우마 너부바디소 나보 부나쭈롸 부우마.
6. 오꼬 아나쭈롸 무우마,

Ephesians Chapter 4[NIV]

1. As a prisoner for the Lord, then, I urge you to live a life worthy of the calling you have received.

2. Be completely humble and gentle; be patient, bearing with one another in love.

3. Make every effort to keep the unity of the Spirit through the bond of peace.

4. There is one body and one Spirit--just as you were called to one hope when you were called--

5. one Lord, one faith, one baptism;

6. one God and Father of all,

iShe webandju boshi. Iuthula wemire kwa bandju boshi, na iwende wakola kurengera ebandju boshi, kanji iunathula mwa ndanda sa boshi.

7. Si chira mundju mwa kachi-kachi kethu eresibwe elwai Iwembo kukulikana nemwango ola Kirisito amuabiraa.

8. Nechi chikulyikene nokwa Maanjiko Mabuya-buya mathula matechire mbu:

Mango erukaa mwa chanya, ekaa ebarenda bai ba asimbaa, era kweresa ebandju enyembo.

9. Ekweruka mwa chanya, kukuteta kute Kulyi kuteta mbu andaalyiraa muno butala, era kunalyinda aika nera bufulyi busese.

10. Oyu wandaalyiraa muno butala, inoyu kanji iwanerukaa mwa chanya busese kwa nguba, chasiya alumirire mwa butala boshi.

11. Yeine iweresise ebandju enyembo. Airire bauma kuba ndujmwa, nebanji kuba barebi, nebanji kuba bandju ba kunde bahubanganya eMwasi Mubuya-buya, nebanji kuba balanzi na bakangirisi.

이써 워바뚜 보씨. 이우쭈롸 워미러 과 바뚜 보씨, 나 이워떠 와고롸 구러뻐라 어바뚜 보씨, 가띠 이우나쭈롸 뫄 따따 사 보씨.

7. 시 찌라 무뚜 뫄 가찌-가찌 거쭈 어러시붜 어롸이 뤄뽀 구구뤠가나 너뫄오 오롸 기리시도 아무아비라아.

8. 너찌 찌구뤠거너 노과 마아찌고 마부야-부야 마쭈롸 마더찌러 뿌:

마오 어루가아 뫄 짜냐, 어가아 어바러따 바이 바 아시빠아, 어라 궈러사 어바뚜 어녀뽀.

9. 어궈루가 뫄 짜냐, 구구더다 구더 구뤠 구더다 뿌 아따아뤠라아 무노 부다롸, 어라 구나뤠따 아이가 너라 부푸뤠 부서서.

10. 오유 와따아뤠라아 무노 부다롸, 이노유 가띠 이와너루가아 뫄 짜냐 부서서 과 꾸바, 짜시야 아루미리라 뫄 부다롸 보씨.

11. 여이너 이워러시서 어바뚜 어녀뽀. 아이리러 바우마 구바 뚜j뫄, 너바찌 구바 바러비, 너바찌 구바 바뚜 바 구떠 바후바까냐 어뫄시 무부야-부야, 너바찌 구바 바롸씨 나 바가삐리시.

who is over all and through all and in all.

7. But to each one of us grace has been given as Christ apportioned it.

8. This is why it says: "When he ascended on high, he led captives in his train and gave gifts to men."

9. (What does "he ascended" mean except that he also descended to the lower, earthly regions?

10. He who descended is the very one who ascended higher than all the heavens, in order to fill the whole universe.)

11. It was he who gave some to be apostles, some to be prophets, some to be evangelists, and some to be pastors and teachers,

12. Airire bacha, kwa kukunganya ebandju ba Ongo, bakole emulyimo wai, chasiya emubiri wa Kirisito aimbibwe.

12. 아이리러 바짜, 과
구구ㆁ가냐 어바쑤 바 오ᅌᅩ,
바고롸 어무레모 와이,
짜시야 어무비리 와 기리시도
아이삐붜.

12. to prepare God's people for works of service, so that the body of Christ may be built up

13. Mwa bacha, thuboshi thungaikirira kuba mwa buuma bwebwemeresi bwethu, na kumenya eMwana wa Ongo kanangana. Aola, tungaba bandju ba bakula kuikirira thwaba ngokwa Kirisito yeine athula.

13. 뫄 바짜, 쭈보씨
쭈ㆁ가이기리라 구바 뫄 부우마
붜붜머러시 붜쭈, 나 구머냐
어뫄나 와 오ᅌᅩ 가나ㆁ가나.
아오롸, 두ㆁ가바 바쑤 바
바구롸 구이기리라 쫘바 ᅌᅩ과
기리시도 여이너 아쭈롸.

13. until we all reach unity in the faith and in the knowledge of the Son of God and become mature, attaining to the whole measure of the fullness of Christ.

14. Rero thutachibe nga bana batoto ba bekibwa na chira kausi. Kanji thutachengeerwe nemyasi yebisha era bandju benjire bakangirisa mwa bukalange bwabo.

14. 러로 쭈다찌버 ㆁ가 바나
바도도 바 버기봐 나 찌라
가우시. 가ᄡᅵ 쭈다쩌ㆁ거어뤄
너먀시 여비싸 어라 바쑤
버ᄡᅵ러 바가ㆁ기리사 뫄
부가롸ㆁ거 봐보.

14. Then we will no longer be infants, tossed back and forth by the waves, and blown here and there by every wind of teaching and by the cunning and craftiness of men in their deceitful scheming.

15. Si akaba thungende thwateta ekanangana mwa nzii, thungakula mwa myasi yoshi. Tungaikirira nokwa chihangi thwaba nga Kirisito, iuthula ethwe.

15. 시 아가바 쭈ㆁ거떠 쫘더다
어가나ㆁ가나 뫄 ᄶᅵ이,
쭈ㆁ가구롸 뫄 먀시 요씨.
두ㆁ가이기리라 노과 찌하ㆁ기
쫘바 ㆁ가 기리시도, 이우쭈롸
어쮜.

15. Instead, speaking the truth in love, we will in all things grow up into him who is the Head, that is, Christ.

16. Kanji iwende wathuma ebitera byoshi byemubiri woshi byasimbana kubuya. Emubiri woshi anasimbana kubuya kurengera emvunyiro soshi. Rero, mango chira chitera chende chakola kwa binemire, emubiri woshi ende

16. 가ᄡᅵ 이워떠 와쭈마
어비더라 뵤씨 벼무비리 오씨
뱌시빠나 구부야. 어무비리
오씨 아나시빠나 구부야
구러ㆁ거라 어뿌네로 소씨.
러로, 마ᅌᅩ 찌라 찌더라 쩌떠
짜고롸 과 비너미러,
어무비리 오씨 어떠 어후가

16. From him the whole body, joined and held together by every supporting ligament, grows and builds itself up in love, as each part does its work.

ehuka na kukula mwa nzii.

17. Rero cha nabema busese kwesina Iya Enawethu chi chechine: mutachiataa mibere era ilyi nga yebandju ba bateshi Ongo, ba bende bakulyikira emianyisa yabo yebuha-buha.

18. Ebwenge bwabo, buthula mwa musimya. Abu bandju, batete mwango kwa kalamo ka Ongo ende ana, bushi silyi mbuta kanji balyi ba michima isibu.

19. Kanji batachifa honyi sisibya. Bende baira ebuhungu na kunde baira chira mwasi mubi busira lubibi.

20. Si mwabo, ata kumwakangirisibwaa era luulu sa Kirisito bacha.

21. Kubinalyi, mwomvire emyasi era ihambere era luulu sai. Kanji bushi muli bemeresi, mwakangirisibwe emyasi yekanangana era iyi mwa ndanda sa Yesu Kirisito.

22. Bushi noku, mwemire kureka emyanya yenyu yokwa mira. Kanji murekanaa nemibere yenyu yokwa mira yebuhuma-huma

---

나 구구꽈 먀 씨이.

17. 러로 짜 나버마 부서서 궈시나 랴 어나워쭈 찌 쩌찌너: 무다찌아다아 미버러 어라 이쩨 꺄 여바뉴 바 바더씨 오꼬, 바 버너 바구쩨기라 어미아네사 야보 여부하-부하.

18. 어붸어 봐보, 부후꽈 먀 무시먀. 아부 바뉴, 바더더 꽈꼬 과 가꽈모 가 오꼬 어너 아나, 부씨 시쩨 뿌다 가찌 바쩨 바 미찌마 이시부.

19. 가찌 바다찌파 호네 시시뱌. 버너 바이라 어부후우 나 구너 바이라 찌라 먀시 무비 부시라 루비비.

20. 시 뫄보, 아다 구꽈가찌리시봐아 어라 루우루 사 기리시도 바짜.

21. 구비나쩨, 뫃뻬러 어먀시 어라 이하뻐러 어라 루우루 사이. 가찌 부씨 무꿰 버머러시, 뫄가찌리시붜 어먀시 여가나꺄나 어라 이에 꽈 따따 사 여수 기리시도.

22. 부씨 노구, 뭐미러 구러가 어먀냐 여뉴 요과 미라. 가찌 무러가나아 너미버러 여뉴 요과 미라 여부후마-후마 여붜꺼어러 어라 여꺼어

---

17. So I tell you this, and insist on it in the Lord, that you must no longer live as the Gentiles do, in the futility of their thinking.

18. They are darkened in their understanding and separated from the life of God because of the ignorance that is in them due to the hardening of their hearts.

19. Having lost all sensitivity, they have given themselves over to sensuality so as to indulge in every kind of impurity, with a continual lust for more.

20. You, however, did not come to know Christ that way.

21. Surely you heard of him and were taught in him in accordance with the truth that is in Jesus.

22. You were taught, with regard to your former way of life, to put off your old self, which is being corrupted by its deceitful desires;

yebwengeere era yendee
yabeka mwa muero.

23. Muiribwaa bayayaya mwa michima nomwa mianyisa yenyu.

24. Kanji muhubaa bandju bayayaya, ba babumbirwe kwehuhi lya Ongo, mwa kunde mwaata mibere era ithungenene, kanji ibuya-buya era itenganyire nekanangana.

25. Bushi noku, murekaa kunde mwafula ebisha. Chira mundu endaa abura mulyikabo ekanangana, bushi thulyi bitera bya mubiri muuma.

26. Emango musibukire, mumenyaa mwengira mwa bibi. Ekusibuka kwenyu kwemire kuwe era muhondo esuba lyichirowe.

27. Mutabooreraa Wamusimu enjira.

28. Rero, ola wabaa wenjire weba, arekaa ebwisi. Achisesaa kunde achikorera mwa njira sa sithungenene, chasiya abone cha angaasamu ba balyi mwa bulae.

29. Mwa bunu bwenyu mutendaa mwatenga myasi ibi. Si mundaa mwateta myasi ibuya, era ingaasa ebanji mwa

야버가 뫄 무어로.

23. 무이리봐아 바야야야 뫄 미찌마 노뫄 미아네사 여뉴.

24. 가찌 무후바아 바뚜 바야야야, 바 바부삐뤄 궈후히 랴 오꼬, 뫄 구떠 뫄아다 미버러 어라 이쭈꺼너너, 가찌 이부야-부야 어라 이더꽈네러 너가나꽈나.

25. 부씨 노구, 무러가아 구떠 뫄푸롸 어비싸. 찌라 무뚜 어따아 아부라 무레가보 어가나꽈나, 부씨 쭈레 비더라 뱌 무비리 무우마.

26. 어마꼬 무시부기러, 무머냐아 뭐꾀라 뫄 비비. 어구시부가 궈뉴 궈미러 구워 어라 무호또 어수바 레찌로워.

27. 무다보오러라아 와무시무 어찌라.

28. 러로, 오롸 와바아 워찌러 워바, 아러가아 어뷔시. 아찌서사아 구떠 아찌고러라 뫄 띠라 사 시쭈꺼너너, 짜시야 아보너 짜 아꽈아사무 바 바꿰 뫄 부롸어.

29. 뫄 부누 붸뉴 무더따아 뫄더꽈 먀시 이비. 시 무따아 뫄더다 먀시 이부야, 어라 이꽈아사 어바찌 뫄 마롸어

23. to be made new in the attitude of your minds;

24. and to put on the new self, created to be like God in true righteousness and holiness.

25. Therefore each of you must put off falsehood and speak truthfully to his neighbor, for we are all members of one body.

26. "In your anger do not sin": Do not let the sun go down while you are still angry,

27. and do not give the devil a foothold.

28. He who has been stealing must steal no longer, but must work, doing something useful with his own hands, that he may have something to share with those in need.

29. Do not let any unwholesome talk come out of your mouths, but only what is helpful for building

malae mabo, kanji era ingareta ngahanyi kwa ba bakwomvirisa.

30. Mutendaa mwasibusa eMuchima Mubuya-buya wa Ongo. Oyu Muchima Mubuya-buya, ku kalorero Ongo ababikireko kwa kulosa kwa munalyi bandju bai kuikira elusuku lwa akabanunula.

31. Ene myasi yoshi mukabuliraai bure: ekubikirana emungo, ebute, nebusibuke, nebwaka nengambo. Ebi byoshi alauma nebukalyi, murekanaa nabi.

32. Mundaa mwairirana emabuya na kuatana kwechamba. Mundaa mwababalyirana ngokwa Ongo nai anabababalyiraa kurengera Kirisito.

E Baefeso Chikono 5

1. Rero bushi muli bana basiirwa ba Ongo, mundaa mwamweya.

2. Mundaa mwasimana mwa kalamo kenyu ngokwa Kirisito nai anathusimaa. Anaa ekalamo kai bushi nethu nga mithulo kanji nga mithulo era yende yasiresibwa kwa

---

마보, 가찌 어라 이까러다 까하네 과 바 바고삐리사.

30. 무더따아 마시부사 어무찌마 무부야-부야 와 오꼬. 오유 무찌마 무부야-부야, 구 가로러로 오꼬 아바비기러고 과 구로사 과 무나께 바뚜 바이 구이기라 어루수구 똬 아가바누누똬.

31. 어너 먀시 요씨 무가부삐러아아이 부러: 어구비기라나 어무꼬, 어부더, 너부시부거, 너봐가 너까뾪. 어비 뵤씨 아똬우마 너부가께, 무러가나아 나비.

32. 무따아 먀이리라나 어마부야 나 구아다나 궈짜빠. 무따아 먀바바께라나 꼬과 오꼬 나이 아나바바바께라아 구러꺼라 기리시도.

어 바어퍼소 찌고노 5

1. 러로 부씨 무뤼 바나 바시이롸 바 오꼬, 무따아 먀뭐야.

2. 무따아 먀시마나 똬 가롸모 거뉴 꼬과 기리시도 나이 아나쭈시마아. 아나아 어가똬모 가이 부씨 너쭈 까 미쭈로 가찌 까 미쭈로 어라 여러 야시러시봐 과 가하하,

---

others up according to their needs, that it may benefit those who listen.

30. And do not grieve the Holy Spirit of God, with whom you were sealed for the day of redemption.

31. Get rid of all bitterness, rage and anger, brawling and slander, along with every form of malice.

32. Be kind and compassionate to one another, forgiving each other, just as in Christ God forgave you.

Ephesians Chapter 5[NIV]

1. Be imitators of God, therefore, as dearly loved children

2. and live a life of love, just as Christ loved us and gave himself up for us as a fragrant offering and sacrifice to God.

kahaha, era yauka kubuya kanji isimise Ongo.

3. Rero kukulikana nokwa ebandju ba Ongo bemire kuba, emyasi yelusingi na chira mwasi wa buhungu, nebuhuma-huma, bitendaa byomvikala mwa kachi-kachi kenyu.

4. Kanji mwa kachi-kachi kenyu, mutendaa mwomvikala myasi ya ngambo, nesi ya buha-buha, nesi ya honyi, bushi ebyera bitakomire. Si cha chikomire, kuli ekutonga Ongo.

5. Mumenyereraa kanangana kwa chira musingisi, nechihungu, nemuhuma-huma webikulo batakengirire mwa bwami bwa Kirisito na Ongo. Bushi ebuhuma-huma inalyi njira ya kwera ebihuhanyi.

6. Kutabaa mundu ola wabengeera na myasi ya buha-buha. Bushi emyasi era ilyi ngei iyende yathuma Ongo asibukira ebandju ba batathula bamuthundjire.

7. Rero ebandju ba balyi ngabu, mutakomeranaa nabo.

8. Kwa mira, mwabaa mutuhla mwa musimya. Si mwera mulyi mwa bulangare bushi

어라 야우가 구부야 가찌 이시미서 오꼬.

3. 러로 구구끼가나 노과 어바뚜 바 오꼬 버미러 구바, 어먀시 여루시끼 나 찌라 먀시 와 부후꾸, 너부후마-후마, 비더따아 뵤삐가꽈 마 가찌-가찌 거뉴.

4. 가찌 먀 가찌-가찌 거뉴, 무더따아 뫂삐가꽈 먀시 야 꺄뽀, 너시 야 부하-부하, 너시 야 호네, 부씨 어벼라 비다고미러. 시 짜 찌고미러, 구끼 어구도꽈 오꼬.

5. 무머녀러라아 가나꺄나 과 찌라 무시끼시, 너찌후꾸, 너무후마-후마 워비구로 바다거끼리러 마 바미 봐 기리시도 나 오꼬. 부씨 어부후마-후마 이나레 찌라 야 꿔라 어비후하네.

6. 구다바아 무뚜 오꽈 와버꺼어라 나 먀시 야 부하-부하. 부씨 어먀시 어라 이레 꺼이 이여떠 야쭈마 오꼬 아시부기라 어바뚜 바 바다쭈꽈 바무쭈찌러.

7. 러로 어바뚜 바 바레 꺄부 무다고머라나아 나보.

8. 과 미라, 먀바아 무두후꽈 먀 무시먀. 시 뭐라 무레 마 부꽈꺄러 부씨 무레 마

3. But among you there must not be even a hint of sexual immorality, or of any kind of impurity, or of greed, because these are improper for God's holy people.

4. Nor should there be obscenity, foolish talk or coarse joking, which are out of place, but rather thanksgiving.

5. For of this you can be sure: No immoral, impure or greedy person--such a man is an idolater--has any inheritance in the kingdom of Christ and of God.

6. Let no one deceive you with empty words, for because of such things God's wrath comes on those who are disobedient.

7. Therefore do not be partners with them.

8. For you were once darkness, but now you are light in the Lord. Live as

mulyi mwa buuma na
Enawethu Bushi noku,
mundaa mwachitola nga bana
ba bulangare.

9. Ebulangare bu bwende
bwabuta emabuya, nemyasi
era ithungenene
neyekanangana.

10. Muchisesaa kunde
mwamenyerera emyasi era
isimise Enawethu.

11 Mutendaa mwengirira
mwa myasi yemusimya era
itete mufa, si mundaa
mwalosai changanama.

12. Bushi bya abu bandju
bende baira mwa bubisho-
bisho, byende byeta honyi
mwa kubihambalako.

13. Si mango ei myasi yende
yalosibwa changanama,
yanalorekanako mwa
bulangare.

14. Bushi byoshi bya byende
byalorekanako mwa
bulangare, byende byahuba
bulangare. Echera chi chende
chathuma bateta mbu: Sukaa,
uulyi mwa thulo! Omwokaa
utenge mwa bafu, na Kirisito
angakulomekera.

15. Rero muchilangaa kwa
myanya yenyu. Mutendaa
mwachitola nga mbuta, si
mundaa mwachitola nga

부우마 나 어나워쭈 부씨
노구, 무따아 뫄찌도롸 빠
바나 바 부롸빠러.

9. 어부롸빠러 부 뷔떠
봐부다 어마부야, 너먀시
어라 이쭈빠너너
너여가나빠나.

10. 무찌서사아 구떠
뫄머녀러라 어먀시 어라
이시미서 어나워쭈.

11 무더따아 뭐삐리라 뫄
먀시 여무시먀 어라 이더더
무파, 시 무따아 뫄로싸이
짜빠나마.

12. 부씨 뱌 아부 바뚜 버떠
바이라 뫄 부비쏘-비쏘, 벼떠
벼다 호네 뫄 구비하빠롸고.

13. 시 마꼬 어이 먀시 여떠
야로시봐 짜빠나마,
야나로러가나고 뫄 부롸빠러.

14. 부씨 뵤씨 뱌 벼떠
뱌로러가나고 뫄 부롸빠러,
벼떠 뱌후바 부롸빠러.
어쩌라 찌 쩌떠 짜쭈마
바더다 뿌: 수가아, 우우레 뫄
쭈로! 오모가아 우더떠 뫄
바푸, 나 기리시도
아빠구로머거라.

15. 러로 무찌롸빠아 과 먀냐
여뉴. 무더따아 뫄찌도롸 빠
뿌다, 시 무따아 뫄찌도롸 빠
바뚜 바 버씨 먀시.

children of light

9. (for the fruit of the light consists in all goodness, righteousness and truth)

10. and find out what pleases the Lord.

11. Have nothing to do with the fruitless deeds of darkness, but rather expose them.

12. For it is shameful even to mention what the disobedient do in secret.

13. But everything exposed by the light becomes visible,

14. for it is light that makes everything visible. This is why it is said: "Wake up, O sleeper, rise from the dead, and Christ will shine on you."

15. Be very careful, then, how you live--not as unwise but as wise,

bandju ba beshi myasi.

16. Mundaa mwakoresa kubuya ebihangi bya mwabonyire, bushi sine suku thulyimo silyi sibi.

16. 무따아 먀고러사 구부야 어비하삐 뱌 먀보네러, 부씨 시너 수구 쭈레모 시레 시비.

16. making the most of every opportunity, because the days are evil.

17. Bushi noku, mutabaa mbuta, si muchisesaa kumenya bya Enawethu ahonda munde mwaira.

17. 부씨 노구, 무다바아 뿌다, 시 무찌서사아 구머냐 뱌 어나워쭈 아호따 무머 먀이라.

17. Therefore do not be foolish, but understand what the Lord's will is.

18. Mutendaa mwatamira etifai, bushi ebutamisi bwende bwathuma ebandju baira bya bitalongomanyire. Si mundaa mwakoresibwa neMuchima Mubuya-buya.

18. 무더따아 먀다미라 어디파이, 부씨 어부다미시 붜머 봐쭈마 어바뉴 바이라 뱌 비다롱오마네러. 시 무따아 먀고러시봐 너무찌마 무부야-부야.

18. Do not get drunk on wine, which leads to debauchery. Instead, be filled with the Spirit.

19. Mundaa mwasesanya emichima mwa kwemba enyimbo se'kutonga Enawethu na sinji nyimbo sekumwera sa sitenganyire neMuchima Mubuya-buya. Mundaa mwamwembira na kumutonga kwa muchima wenyu woshi.

19. 무따아 먀서사냐 어미찌마 먀 궈빠 어네뽀 서구도따 어나워쭈 나 시찌 네뽀 서구뭐라 사 시더따네러 너무찌마 무부야-부야. 무따아 봐뭐뻬라 나 구무도따 과 무찌마 워뉴 오씨.

19. Speak to one another with psalms, hymns and spiritual songs. Sing and make music in your heart to the Lord,

20. Esuku soshi, mundaa mwateta mbu akoko era mwa Ongo Tata mu chira mwasi, kwesina lya Enawetu Yesu Kirisito.

20. 어수구 소씨, 무따아 먀더다 뿌 아고고 어라 봐 오쪼 다다 무 찌라 마시, 궈시나 랴 어나워두 여수 기리시도.

20. always giving thanks to God the Father for everything, in the name of our Lord Jesus Christ.

21. Mundaa mweresanya ethunda, bushi nethunda lya muthusa ku Kirisito.

21. 무따아 뭐러사냐 어쭌다, 부씨 너쭌따 랴 무쭈사 구 기리시도.

21. Submit to one another out of reverence for Christ.

22. Mu bakasi, mundaa mwathunda beba benyu,

22. 무 바가시, 무따아 먀쭈따 버바 버뉴, 쪼과 무쭈롸

22. Wives, submit to your husbands as to the Lord.

ngokwa muthula muthunjire Enawethu.

무쭈찌러 어나워쭈.

23. Bushi emulume lithwe lyemukasi ngokwa Kirisito lyithwe lyebemeresi. Kanji yeine iMununusi wabu bemeresi, bu balyi mubiri wai.

23. 부씨 어무루머 뤼줘 려무가시 꼬과 기리시도 뤠줘 려버머러시. 가찌 여이너 이무누누시 와부 버머러시, 부 바뤠 무비리 와이.

23. For the husband is the head of the wife as Christ is the head of the church, his body, of which he is the Savior.

24. Rero, ngokwa bemeresi bende bathunda Kirisito, kunoku ku ebakasi nabo bemire kunde bathunda beba babo mu chira mwasi.

24. 러로, 꼬과 버머러시 버떠 바쭈따 기리시도, 구노구 구 어바가시 나보 버미러 구떠 바쭈따 버바 바보 무 찌라 먀시.

24. Now as the church submits to Christ, so also wives should submit to their husbands in everything.

25. Nenyu mu balume, mundaa mwasima bakasi benyu ngokwa Kirisito nai asimaa ebemeresi, kuikira echihangi ana ekalamo kai bushi nabo.

25. 너뉴 무 바루머, 무따아 먀시마 바가시 버뉴 꼬과 기리시도 나이 아시마아 어버머러시, 구이기라 어찌하삐 아나 어가롸모 가이 부씨 나보.

25. Husbands, love your wives, just as Christ loved the church and gave himself up for her

26. Airaa bacha, chasiya airebo kuba babuya-buya na kubakomya kurengera emeshia na kurengera eChinwa

26. 아이라아 바짜, 짜시야 아이러보 구바 바부야-부야 나 구바고먀 구러꺼라 어머씨아 나 구러꺼라 어찌놔

26. to make her holy, cleansing her by the washing with water through the word,

27. Abaa ahonda acherese yeine ebemeresi ba bee bulangare kanji babuya-buya, ba batete nesinga, nesi mifunyenye, nesi burema busibya.

27. 아바아 아호따 아쩌러서 여이너 어버머러시 바 버어 부롸꺼러 가찌 바부야-부야, 바 바더더 너시빠, 너시 미푸녀녀, 너시 부러마 부시뱌.

27. and to present her to himself as a radiant church, without stain or wrinkle or any other blemish, but holy and blameless.

28. Kunoku kwebalume nabo bemire kunde basima bakasi babo ngokwa beine bathula basimire emibiri yabo. Bushi ola usimire mukai, eri achisimire yeine.

28. 구노구 궈바루머 나보 버미러 구떠 바시마 바가시 바보 꼬과 버이너 바쭈롸 바시미러 어미비리 야보. 부씨 오롸 우시미러 무가이, 어리 아찌시미러 여이너.

28. In this same way, husbands ought to love their wives as their own bodies. He who loves his wife loves himself.

29. Bushi kutalyi ola uthula uhombire emubiri wai! Si ende alyisao, na kulangao kubuya, ngokwa Kirisito nai ende airira ebemeresi,

30. bushi thulyi bitera byemubiri wai.

31. eMaanjiko Mabuya-buya mathula matechire mbu: "Echera chi chende chatuma emulume areka eshe na nyina, anaba mwa buuma na mukai. Abu babiri banere baba mundju muuma."

32. Ono mwasi abishire bindju binene, si nyono nateta era luulu sa Kirisito nebemeresi.

33. Si chiro bacha, kwa bya biberekere nenyu, chira mulume emire kunde asima mukai, ngokwa athula achisimire yeine. Na chira mukasi emire kunde athunda eba.

29. 부씨 구다례 오라 우쭈롸 우호뻬러 어무비리 와이! 시 어떠 아레사오, 나 구롸꽈오 구부야, 꼬과 기리시도 나이 어떠 아이리라 어버머러시,

30. 부씨 쭈례 비더라 벼무비리 와이.

31. 어마아찌고 마부야-부야 마쭈롸 마더찌러 뿌: "어쩌라 찌 쩌떠 짜두마 어무루머 아러가 어써 나 니나, 아나바 롸 부우마 나 무가이. 아부 바비리 바너러 바바 무뿌 무우마."

32. 오노 롸시 아비씨러 비뿌 비너너, 시 뇨노 나더다 어라 루우루 사 기리시도 너버머러시.

33. 시 찌로 바짜, 과 뱌 비버러거러 너뉴, 찌라 무루머 어미러 구더 아시마 무가이, 꼬과 아쭈롸 아찌시미러 여이너. 나 찌라 무가시 어미러 구떠 아쭈따 어바.

29. After all, no one ever hated his own body, but he feeds and cares for it, just as Christ does the church--

30. for we are members of his body.

31. "For this reason a man will leave his father and mother and be united to his wife, and the two will become one flesh."

32. This is a profound mystery--but I am talking about Christ and the church.

33. However, each one of you also must love his wife as he loves himself, and the wife must respect her husband.

E Baefeso Chikono 6

1. Mu bana, mundaa mwatunda ebasere benyu kurengera ebuuma bwenyu na Enawethu, bushi echera chithungenene.

2. "Undaa wathunda eho na nyoko." Oyola imuomba

어 바어퍼소 찌고노 6

1. 무 바나, 무따아 뫄두따 어바서러 버뉴 구러떠라 어부우마 붜뉴 나 어나워쭈, 부씨 어쩌라 찌쭈떠너너.

2. "우따아 와쭈따 어호 나 뇨고." 오요롸 이무오빠

Ephesians Chapter 6[NIV]

1. Children, obey your parents in the Lord, for this is right.

2. "Honor your father and mother"--which is the first

mubere ola utalyikirwe kwechiraane

무버러 오롸 우다레기뤄 궈찌라아너

commandment with a promise--

3. "chasiya uahanyirwe na kuba kwa butala suku sinene."

3. "짜시야 우아하네뤄 나 구바 과 부다롸 수구 시너너."

3. "that it may go well with you and that you may enjoy long life on the earth."

4. Nenyu mu batata, mutendaa mwakunza ebana benyu. Si muremberaa'bo mwa kunde mwakemera'bo na kunde mweresa'bo emano ma matenga era mwa Enawetu.

4. 너뉴 무 바다다, 무더따아 롸구싸 어바나 버뉴. 시 무러뻐라아보 롸 구떠 롸거머라보 나 구떠 뭐러사보 어마노 마 마더따 어라 롸 어나워두.

4. Fathers, do not exasperate your children; instead, bring them up in the training and instruction of the Lord.

Mano kwa tuungu na be'nawabo

마노 과 두우꾸 나 버나와보

5 Nenyu mu tuungu*, mundaa mwaira bya be'nawenyu bo'muno butala bababwirire. Mundaa mwobaa'bo na kunde mwatunda'bo na muchima mubuya, ngo'kwa mutula mutunjire Kirisito*.

5 너뉴 무 두우꾸*, 무따아 롸이라 뱌 버나워뉴 보무노 부다롸 바바뷔리러. 무따아 모바아보 나 구떠 롸두따보 나 무찌마 무부야, 꼬과 무두롸 무두띠러 기리시도*.

5. Slaves, obey your earthly masters with respect and fear, and with sincerity of heart, just as you would obey Christ.

6 Mutendaa mwakola mango babasene'ko oshao kwa kuhonda mubasimise. Si mundaa mwachitola nga tuungu* twa Kirisito*, mwa kunde mwaira kwa muchima wenyu woshi bya Ongo asimire.

6 무더따아 롸고롸 마꼬 바바서너고 오싸오 과 구호롸 무바시미서. 시 무따아 롸찌도롸 따 두우꾸* 돠 기리시도*, 롸 구떠 롸이라 과 무찌마 워뉴 오씨 뱌 오꼬 아시미러.

6. Obey them not only to win their favor when their eye is on you, but like slaves of Christ, doing the will of God from your heart.

7 Mundaa mwakorera bena wenyu na muchima mubuya, nga bandu ba bakorera Enawetu yeine, si batakorera bandu.

7 무따아 롸고러라 버나 워뉴 나 무찌마 무부야, 따 바두 바 바고러라 어나워두 여이너, 시 바다고러라 바두.

7. Serve wholeheartedly, as if you were serving the Lord, not men,

8 Mumenyaa kwa Enawetu akemba chira mundu kukulikana ne'mabuya ma akolaa, kabe kaungu* nesi mundu ola uli mwa buhuru.

9 Nenyu mu benawabo etuungu*, ku mundaa mwanairira etuungu* twenyu bacha. Mutendaa mwakanyira'to. Mumenyaa kwa mwabo ala'uma no'tu tuungu*, munete Enawenyu muuma kwa nguba, ataira na kalondo kasibya.c

Ebita bye'mwemeresi

10 Kwa kumala, mundaa mwasimika mwa buuma bwenyu na Enawetu, kurengera emisi ye'buashi bwai bunene.

11 Mundaa mwembala ebindu byoshi bya Ongo ende aberesa kwa kulwa ebita, chasiya muchimange'ko mwa kulwisa emyasi ye'bukalange bwa Wamusimu*.

12 Bushi, tutalwisa bandu bo'muno butala, si twenjire twalwa ne'bihwasi bya bitula mwa chanya, ne'bakulu-kulu, na ba bete buashi na ba bemire muno butala bwe'musimya.

13 Bushi no'ku, mutolaa

---

8 무머냐아 과 어나워두 아거빠 찌라 무뚜 구구삐가나 너마부야 마 아고롸아, 가버 가우우* 너시 무뚜 오롸 우삐 롸 부후루.

9 너뉴 무 버나와보 어두우우*, 구 무따아 롸나이리라 어두우우* 뛰뉴 바짜. 무더따아 롸가네라도. 무머냐아 과 롸보 아롸우마 노두 두우우*, 무너더 어나워뉴 무우마 과 우바, 아다이라 나 가로또 가시뱌.시

어비다 벼뭐머러시

10 과 구마롸, 무따아 롸시미가 와 부우마 뷔뉴 나 어나워두, 구러뻐라 어미시 여부아씨 봐이 부너너.

11 무따아 뭐빠롸 어비뚜 뵤씨 뱌 오꼬 어머 아버러사 과 구롹 어비다, 짜시야 무찌마뻐고 롸 구뤼사 어먀시 여부가롸뻐 봐 와무시무*.

12 부씨, 두다뤼사 바뚜 보무노 부다롸, 시 뛰찌러 돫롸 너비화시 뱌 비두롸 롸 짜냐, 너바구루-구루, 나 바 버더 부아씨 나 바 버미러 무노 부다롸 뷔무시먀.

13 부씨 노구, 무도롸아

---

8. because you know that the Lord will reward everyone for whatever good he does, whether he is slave or free.

9. And masters, treat your slaves in the same way. Do not threaten them, since you know that he who is both their Master and yours is in heaven, and there is no favoritism with him.

10. Finally, be strong in the Lord and in his mighty power.

11. Put on the full armor of God so that you can take your stand against the devil's schemes.

12. For our struggle is not against flesh and blood, but against the rulers, against the authorities, against the powers of this dark world and against the spiritual forces of evil in the heavenly realms.

13. Therefore put on the full

ebindu byoshi bya Ongo ende aberesa kwa kulwa ebita. Mwa bacha, mungachimanga'ko mango elusuku lubi lungabaikira. Na mango mungaba mwalwire kuikira kwa businda, mungasimika kubuya-buya.

14. Rero, muchikunganyaa. Mundaa mwatola emyasi ye'kanangana, ibe nga mukaba ola mungende mwembala mwa mbinji. Mundaa mwatola bya bitungenene, bibe nga mbenzi ya kubalanga ebifuba.

15. Mundaa mwatola ebushiru bwekuhubanganya eMwasi Mubuya-buya webolo, bube nga bi birato byenyu byekwembala.

16. Mwa bihangi byoshi, mundaa mwatola ebwemeresi bube nga mbezi yekwaangika emyeera ya Wamusimu era yeete mulyiro.

17. Mundaa mwatola ebununusi bube nga isapo yechuma kwa kubalanga, mwanatola neChinwa cha Ongo chibe nga bu bombo bwa Muchima Mubuya-buya aberesise.

18. Mundaa mwema Ongo chira mango mwa

어비뚜 뵤씨 뺘 오꼬 어너 아버러사 과 구롸 어비다. 뫄 바짜, 무꽈찌마꺄고 마꼬 어루수구 루비 루꽈바이기라. 나 마꼬 무꽈바 뫄뤼러 구이기라 과 부시따, 무꽈시미가 구부야-부야.

14. 러로, 무찌구꽈냐아. 무따아 뫄도롸 어먀시 여가나꽈나, 이버 꽈 무가바 오롸 무꺼너 뭐빠롸 뫄 삐씨. 무따아 뫄도롸 뱌 비두꺼너너, 비버 꽈 뻐씨 야 구바롸꽈 어비푸바.

15. 무따아 뫄도롸 어부씨루 뷔구후바꽈냐 어먀시 무부야- 부야 워보로, 부버 꽈 비 비라도 뱌뉴 벼궈빠롸.

16. 뫄 비하꼐 뵤씨, 무따아 뫄도롸 어뷔머러시 부버 꽈 뻐지 여과아꼐가 어머어라 야 와무시무 어라 여어더 무레로.

17. 무따아 뫄도롸 어부누누시 부버 꽈 이사포 여쭈마 과 구바롸꽈, 뫄나도롸 너찌놔 짜 오꼬 찌버 꽈 부 보뽀 봐 무찌마 무부야-부야 아버러시서.

18. 무따아 뭐마 오꼬 찌라 마꼬 뫄 구고러시봐 너무찌마

---

armor of God, so that when the day of evil comes, you may be able to stand your ground, and after you have done everything, to stand.

14. Stand firm then, with the belt of truth buckled around your waist, with the breastplate of righteousness in place,

15. and with your feet fitted with the readiness that comes from the gospel of peace.

16. In addition to all this, take up the shield of faith, with which you can extinguish all the flaming arrows of the evil one.

17. Take the helmet of salvation and the sword of the Spirit, which is the word of God.

18. And pray in the Spirit on all occasions with all kinds of

kukoresibwa neMuchima Mubuya-buya. Mundaa mwamwema na kumusengera. Muchilanga-langaa busese na kuendekera mwemera ebandju ba Ongo boshi.

19. Nanyi mundaa mwanyemera Ongo anyerese emyasi yekuteta. Mwa bacha, nyingaala kunde nabalyikisisa ebandju na bushiru bunene emyasi ibishirwe ye'Mwasi Mubuya-buya.

20. Nyono, nyithumirwe kwa kunde nahubanganya eMwasi Mubuya-buya, chiro angaba mbu lwarero nyilyi mwa buroko. Rero, munyemeraa chasiya nyinde nateta busira buba ngokwa binanyemire kuteta.

21. Nahonda nenyu mumenye emyasi yanyi nebya naira. Munyakethu musiirwa Tikiko, muanda mubuya wa Enawethu, iungabafulyira ei emyasi yoshi.

22. Echera chi chathuma nabathumirai, chasiya abafulyire kwa myasi yethu na kubasesa emichima.

23. Ongo Tata na Enawethu Yesu Kirisito bendaa beresa banyakethu ebemeresi boshi

무부야-부야. 무따아 롸뭐마 나 구무서떠라. 무찌롸까-롸까아 부서서 나 구어떠거라 뭐머라 어바뉴 바 오꼬 보씨.

19. 나네 무따아 롸녀머라 오꼬 아녀러서 어먀시 여구더다. 롸 바짜, 네까아롸 구떠 나바풰기시사 어바뉴 나 부씨루 부너너 어먀시 이비씨뤄 여롸시 무부야-부야.

20. 뇨노, 네쭈미뤄 과 구떠 나후바까냐 어롸시 무부야-부야, 찌로 아까바 뿌 롸러로 네퀘 롸 부로고. 러로, 무녀머라아 짜시야 네떠 나더다 부시라 부바 오꼬과 비나녀미러 구더다.

21. 나호따 너뉴 무머녀 어먀시 야네 너뱌 나이라. 무냐거쭈 무시이롸 디기고, 무아따 무부야 와 어나워쭈, 이우까바푸퀘라 어이 어먀시 요씨.

22. 어쩌라 찌 짜쭈마 나바쭈미라이, 짜시야 아바푸퀘러 과 먀시 여쭈 나 구바서사 어미찌마.

23. 오꼬 다다 나 어나워쭈 여수 기리시도 버따아 버러사 바냐거쭈 어버머러시 보씨

prayers and requests. With this in mind, be alert and always keep on praying for all the saints.

19. Pray also for me, that whenever I open my mouth, words may be given me so that I will fearlessly make known the mystery of the gospel,

20. for which I am an ambassador in chains. Pray that I may declare it fearlessly, as I should.

21. Tychicus, the dear brother and faithful servant in the Lord, will tell you everything, so that you also may know how I am and what I am doing.

22. I am sending him to you for this very purpose, that you may know how we are, and that he may encourage you.

23. Peace to the brothers, and love with faith from God the Father and the Lord

ebolo nenzii nebwemeresi.　어보롣 너씨이 너뭐머러시.　Jesus Christ.

24. Ongo endaa aahanyira ebandju boshi ba bathula basimire Enawethu Yesu Kirisito na nzii era itakawe chiro ne hicha.

24. 오끄 어따아 아아하네라 어바뚜 보씨 바 바쭈꽈 바시미러 어나워쭈 여수 기리시도 나 씨이 어라 이다가워 찌로 너 히짜.

24. Grace to all who love our Lord Jesus Christ with an undying love.

E Bafilipi

어 바피뤠피

Philipians

BAFIRIPI
(PHILLIPIANS)

바피리피
(피루뤠피아뚜)

E Bafilipi Chikono 1

1. Nyono Paulo na Timoteo, thulyi baanda ba Yesu Kirisito. Nabaanjikira kurengera ebuuma bwenyu na Yesu Kirisito, mu bandju ba Ongo boshi bomwa musi weFiripi, nebangumwa beluhu lwa Ongo, alauma na ba bende baasabo.

2. Ongo Tata, na Enawetchu Yesu Kirisito bendaa babaahanyira na kuberesa ebolo!

3. Chira chihangi mango nende nabakengera, nende nateta mbu akoko era mwa Ongo wanyi.

4. Kanji chira chihangi mango nabeemera muboshi, nende nema na lumoo,

5. bushi mwenjire mwanyiasa mwa kuhubanganya eMwasi Mubuya-buya kutengera elusuku lubere-bere mwomvaa kuo, kunaikira lwarero.

6. Nyishi kwa Ongo iwatangirisaa oyu mulyimo mubuya mwa kachi-kachi kenyu, anganaisao kwa businda kuikira elusuku

어 바피피피 찌고노 1

1. 뇨노 파우로 나 디모더오, 쭈레 바아따 바 여수 기리시도. 나바아찌기라 구러뻐라 어부우마 뷰뉴 나 여수 기리시도, 무 바뚜 바 오꼬 보씨 보와 무시 워피리피, 너바우뫄 버루후 롸 오꼬, 아롸우마 나 바 버떠 바아사보.

2. 오꼬 다다, 나 어나워쭈 여수 기리시도 버따아 바바아하네라 나 구버러사 어보로!

3. 찌라 찌하삐 마꼬 너떠 나바거뻐라, 너떠 나더다 뿌 아고고 어라 뫄 오꼬 와네.

4. 가찌 찌라 찌하삐 마꼬 나버어머라 무보씨, 너떠 너마 나 루모오,

5. 부씨 뭐찌러 뫄네아사 뫄 구후바따냐 어뫄시 무부야-부야 구더뻐라 어루수구 루버러-버러 모빠아 구오, 구나이기라 롸러로.

6. 네씨 과 오꼬 이와다삐리사아 오유 무레모 무부야 뫄 가찌-가찌 거뉴, 아빠나이사오 과 부시따 구이기라 어루수구

Philippians Chapter 1[NIV]

1. Paul and Timothy, servants of Christ Jesus, To all the saints in Christ Jesus at Philippi, together with the overseers and deacons:

2. Grace and peace to you from God our Father and the Lord Jesus Christ.

3. I thank my God every time I remember you.

4. In all my prayers for all of you, I always pray with joy

5. because of your partnership in the gospel from the first day until now,

6. being confident of this, that he who began a good work in you will carry it on to completion until the day of Christ Jesus.

Iwekufuluka kwa Yesu Kirisito. 붜구푸루가 과 여수 기리시도.

7. Ku binanyeemire nyinde nachumva bacha era luulu senyu muboshi, bushi munyithula kwa muchima, kanji bushi muboshi mwenjire mwabona kwa ngahanyi sa Ongo anyeresise. Abe kuno nyiri mwa buroko, abe mango nenjire nalosa tenene kwa Mwasi Mubuya-buya, analyi wakanangana.

7. 구 비나녀어미러 네너 나쭈빠 바짜 어라 루우루 서뉴 무보씨, 부씨 무네쭈롸 과 무찌마, 가찌 부씨 무보씨 붜찌러 뫄보나 과 꺄하네 사 오꼬 아녀러시서. 아버 구노 네리 뫄 부로고, 아버 마꼬 너찌러 나롸사 더너너 과 뫄시 무부야-부야, 아나쩨 와가나꺄나.

7. It is right for me to feel this way about all of you, since I have you in my heart; for whether I am in chains or defending and confirming the gospel, all of you share in God's grace with me.

8. Kubinalyi! Na Ongo aneeshi kwa nyithula nyibasimire muboshi na nzii era yatengera era mwa Yesu Kirisito.

8. 구비나쩨! 나 오꼬 아너어씨 과 네쭈롸 네바시미러 무보씨 나 씨이 어라 야더꺼라 어라 뫄 여수 기리시도.

8. God can testify how I long for all of you with the affection of Christ Jesus.

9. Cha nenjire nabeemera era mwa Ongo chi chechine: muendekeraa kunde mwasimana busese, na kunde mwamenyerera na kuumva ebindju kubuya-buya,

9. 짜 너찌러 나버어머라 어라 뫄 오꼬 찌 쩌찌너: 무어머거라아 구떠 뫄시마나 부서서, 나 구떠 뫄머녀러라 나 구우빠 어비뿌 구부야-부야,

9. And this is my prayer: that your love may abound more and more in knowledge and depth of insight,

10. chasiya muate ebuashi bwekunde mwamenyerera cha chiri chibuya busese. Mwa bacha, mungaba bandju ba bakomisibwe, kanji ba batete chiro na mwasi mubi ola bangabasitako kuikira elusuku lwa Kirisito akafuluka.

10. 짜시야 무아더 어부아씨 붜구떠 뫄머녀러라 짜 찌리 찌부야 부서서. 뫄 바짜, 무꺄바 바뚜 바 바고미시붜, 가찌 바 바더더 찌로 나 뫄시 무비 오롸 바꺄바시다고 구이기라 어루수구 롸 기리시도 아가푸루가.

10. so that you may be able to discern what is best and may be pure and blameless until the day of Christ,

11. Na Yesu Kirisito endaa aberesa ebuashi bwekunde mwaata myanya era ithungenene. Na mango

11. 나 여수 기리시도 어따아 아버러사 어부아씨 붜구떠 뫄아다 먀냐 어라 이쭈꺼너너. 나 마꼬 어바뿌 바꺼머

11. filled with the fruit of righteousness that comes through Jesus Christ--to the glory and praise of God.

ebandju bangende balola kwei myanya, bangende balosa engulu ya Ongo na kumutonga.

바로롸 궈이 먀냐, 바어떠 바로사 어우루 야 오끄 나 구무도롸.

eMwasi Mubuya-buya aendekera

어롸시 무부야-부야 아어떠거라

12. Banyakethu, nahonda mumenyerere kubuya kwemyasi era yanyiikirire yathumire eMwasi Mubuya-buya aendekera era muhondo.

12. 바냐거쭈, 나호따 무머녀러러 구부야 궈먀시 어라 야네이기리러 야쭈미러 어롸시 무부야-부야 아어떠거라 어라 무호또.

12. Now I want you to know, brothers, that what has happened to me has really served to advance the gospel.

13. Kukulyikana nebi, ebalanzi boshi bomwa chikalyi cha mwami, alauma nebanji bandju boshi, baneeshi kanangana kwa nyiminyirwe bushi nakorera Kirisito.

13. 구구뤠가나 너비, 어바롸씨 보씨 보롸 찌가뤠 쨔 롸미, 아롸우마 너바씨 바뉴 보씨, 바너어씨 가나롸나 과 네미니뤄 부씨 나고러라 기리시도.

13. As a result, it has become clear throughout the whole palace guard and to everyone else that I am in chains for Christ.

14. Kanji bushi noku kuminwa kwanyi, banene mwa bemeresi berire balangalyira Enawetchu busese. Baachire bushiru bunene bwekunde bahubanganyisa ebandju eChinwa cha Ongo busira buba.

14. 가찌 부씨 노구 구미놔 과네, 바너너 롸 버머러시 버리러 바롸롸뤠라 어나워쭈 부서서. 바아찌러 부씨루 부너너 붜구떠 바후바롸네사 어바뉴 어찌놔 쨔 오끄 부시라 부바.

14. Because of my chains, most of the brothers in the Lord have been encouraged to speak the word of God more courageously and fearlessly.

15. Kanangana, kulyi bauma mubo ba benjire bahubanganya emyasi ya Kirisito na muchima wa mufula na wa kaimano. Si ebanji beke, benjire bahubanganya na muchima mubuya.

15. 가나롸나, 구뤠 바우마 무보 바 버찌러 바후바롸냐 어먀시 야 기리시도 나 무찌마 와 무푸롸 나 와 가이마노. 시 어바찌 버거, 버찌러 바후바롸냐 나 무찌마 무부야.

15. It is true that some preach Christ out of envy and rivalry, but others out of goodwill.

16. Abola benjire bakangirisa

16. 아보롸 버찌러

16. The latter do so in love,

mwa nzii, bushi beshi kwa emulyimo wanyi enera, kulyi kulosa kwa eMwasi Mubuya-buya analyi wa kanagana.

17. Si abu banji benjire bakangirisa emyasi ya Kirisito na muchima wa kaimano, na mianyisa era itakomire. Benjire baira bacha, chasiya emalyibuko manyi marengerese mwono mulyisi nyirimo.

18. Kutalyi bwaka! Emianyisa yabo ibe ibi, ibe ibuya, echemutoloke kulyi kulola kwa emyasi era yerekere Kirisito yabalyibwa. Na bushi nechi, nyimoire kanji nyinganaendekera namowa,

19. bushi nyineshi kwa kurengera ememo menyu na kurengera ebuashi bweMuchima wa Yesu Kirisitoa nyingaboolyibwa.

20. Kukulyikana nokwa nalyinjirira busese nemunyiiro ola nyete, kutalyi mwasi asibya ola unganyita honyi. Si lwarero anabe nesuku soshi, nyilangalyire kubuya-buya kwa Kirisito angatongibwa mwa kalamo kanyi, abe mwa kulama kwanyi abe mwa kufa

바가끼리사 똬 씨이, 부씨 버씨 과 어무쀄모 와네 어너라, 구쀄 구론사 과 어똬시 무부야-부야 아나쀄 와 가나가나.

17. 시 아부 바찌 버찌러 바가끼리사 어똬시 야 기리시도 나 무찌마 와 가이마노, 나 미아네사 어라 이다고미러. 버찌러 바이라 바짜, 짜시야 어마쀄부고 마네 마러꺼러서 모노 무쀄시 네리모.

18. 구다쀄 봐가! 어미아네사 야보 이버 이비, 이버 이부야, 어쩌무도론거 구쀄 구론꽈 과 어똬시 어라 여러거러 기리시도 야바쀄봐. 나 부씨 너찌, 네모이러 가찌 네까나어떠거라 나모와,

19. 부씨 네너씨 과 구러꺼라 어머모 머뉴 나 구러꺼라 어부아씨 붜무찌마 와 여수 기리시도아 네까보오쀄봐.

20. 구구쀄가나 노과 나쀄찌리라 부서서 너무네이로 오꽈 녀더, 구다쀄 똬시 아시뱌 오꽈 우까네다 호네. 시 꽐러로 아나버 너수구 소씨, 네꽈까쀄러 구부야-부야 과 기리시도 아까도끼봐 똬 가꽈모 가네, 아버 똬 구꽈마 과네 아버 똬

knowing that I am put here for the defense of the gospel.

17. The former preach Christ out of selfish ambition, not sincerely, supposing that they can stir up trouble for me while I am in chains.

18. But what does it matter? The important thing is that in every way, whether from false motives or true, Christ is preached. And because of this I rejoice. Yes, and I will continue to rejoice,

19. for I know that through your prayers and the help given by the Spirit of Jesus Christ, what has happened to me will turn out for my deliverance.

20. I eagerly expect and hope that I will in no way be ashamed, but will have sufficient courage so that now as always Christ will be exalted in my body, whether by life or by death.

kwanyi.

구파 과네.

21. Rero ku nyono, Kirisito ku kalamo kanyi. Nekufa kunyiberere mutoloke.

21. 러로 구 뇨노, 기리시도 구 가롸모 가네. 너구파 구네버러러 무도로거.

21. For to me, to live is Christ and to die is gain.

22. Si akaba ekubao kwanyi muno butala kuchiri kwete mutoloke bushi nemulyimo wanyi, aola ndachimenyire chiye cha nyilondolaa.

22. 시 아가바 어구바오 과네 무노 부다롸 구찌리 궈더 무도로거 부씨 너무레모 와네. 아오롸 따찌머네러 찌여 짜 네로또롸아.

22. If I am to go on living in the body, this will mean fruitful labor for me. Yet what shall I choose? I do not know!

23. Ene myasi ebiri yenjire yanyisungulyisa ebwenge: nyingasimire nyichifire nyiye kwekala alauma na Kirisito, echera chi chikulu.

23. 어너 먀시 어비리 여찌러 야네수꾸레사 어붱어: 네까시미러 네찌피러 네여 궈가롸 아롸우마 나 기리시도, 어쩌라 찌 찌구루.

23. I am torn between the two: I desire to depart and be with Christ, which is better by far;

24. Si bushi nenyu, kwemire nyiendekere kuba muno butala.

24. 시 부씨 너뉴, 궈미러 네어떠거러 구바 무노 부다롸.

24. but it is more necessary for you that I remain in the body.

25. Rero nyishi kwa kubinganaba bacha, nyineshi kanangana kwa nyichiri nyingaendekera kubao. Nyingaba alauma nenyu muboshi, nyinde nabaasa chasiya muendekere kulangalyira Ongo, na kuata lumoo bushi mumweemerere.

25. 러로 네씨 과 구비까나바 바짜, 네너씨 가나까나 과 네찌리 네아어떠거라 구바오. 네까바 아롸우마 너뉴 무보씨, 네떠 나바아사 짜시야 무어떠거러 구롸까레라 오꼬, 나 구아다 루모오 부씨 무뭐어머러러.

25. Convinced of this, I know that I will remain, and I will continue with all of you for your progress and joy in the faith,

26. Aola, mango nyingahuba kuika eyi mwenyu, mungamowa busese bushi nanyi, kurengera ebuuma bwenyu na Yesu Kirisito.

26. 아오롸, 마꼬 네까후바 구이가 어에 뭐뉴, 무까모와 부서서 부씨 나네, 구러꺼라 어부우마 붜뉴 나 여수 기리시도.

26. so that through my being with you again your joy in Christ Jesus will overflow on account of me.

27. Rero cha nabeema chi chechine: mundaa mwaata myanya era ikulyikene

27. 러로 짜 나버어마 찌 쩌찌너: 무따아 뫄아다 먀냐 어라 이구레거너 너꽈시

27. Whatever happens, conduct yourselves in a manner worthy of the gospel

neMwasi Mubuya-buya wa Kirisito. Abe nyiike, abe ndaikire, nahonda nyinomve kwa munasimikire na muchima muuma, kanji mwalwisa alauma bushi nebwemeresi bwa butenganyire neMwasi Mubuya-buya.

28. Mutendaa mwobaa ebarenda benyu chiro na hicha. Echera chi chingalosabo kwa beke baerire, si mwabo, kununulyibwa ku mwanunulyibwe. Nebi byoshi era mwa Ongo yibitengire.

29. Bushi Ongo atabeeresise engahanyi sekweemerera Kirisito oshao, si kanji mungende mwalola nokwa malyibuko bushi nai.

30. Rero, ebita bya mwalolaa nenjire nalwa, nenyu bi mwera mwalwako. Na ngokwa mwenjire mwanomva, anabe na lwarero, kulwisa ku nyinachiri nalwisa.

무부야-부야 와 기리시도. 아버 네이거, 아버 따이기러, 나호따 네노뻐 과 무나시미기러 나 무찌마 무우마, 가찌 먀뤄사 아롸우마 부씨 너붜머러시 봐 부더따네러 너마시 무부야-부야.

28. 무더따아 모바아 어바러따 버뉴 찌로 나 히짜. 어쩌라 찌 찌따뢰사보 과 버거 바어리러, 시 먀보, 구누누뤠봐 구 마누누뤠붜. 너비 뵤씨 어라 마 오꼬 에비더띠러.

29. 부씨 오꼬 아다버어러시서 어따하네 서궈어머러라 기리시도 오싸오, 시 가찌 무뻐러 먀뢰롸 노과 마뤠부고 부씨 나이.

30. 러로, 어비다 뱌 먀뢰롸아 너찌러 나똬, 너뉴 비 뭐라 먀똬고. 나 오꽈 뭐찌러 마노빠, 아나버 나 똬러로, 구뤼사 구 네나찌리 나뤼사.

of Christ. Then, whether I come and see you or only hear about you in my absence, I will know that you stand firm in one spirit, contending as one man for the faith of the gospel

28. without being frightened in any way by those who oppose you. This is a sign to them that they will be destroyed, but that you will be saved--and that by God.

29. For it has been granted to you on behalf of Christ not only to believe on him, but also to suffer for him,

30. since you are going through the same struggle you saw I had, and now hear that I still have.

E Bafilipi Chikono 2

1. Ebuuma bwenyu na Kirisito bwenjire bwaberesa emisi, nenzii yai yenjire yabasesa

어 바피삐피 찌고노 2

1. 어부우마 붜뉴 나 기리시도 붜찌러 봐버러사 어미시, 너씨이 야이 여찌러

Philippians Chapter 2[NIV]

1. If you have any encouragement from being united with Christ, if any

emichima! Kanji mulyi mwa buuma neMuchima Mubya-buya, mwete na muchima wa kunde mwasimana na kufirana bonjo!

2. Rero mundaa mwomvikana, na kusimana, na kuata muchima muuma na mianyisa iuma. Mwa kuira bacha, mungende mwathuma namowa busese.

3. Mutendaa mwaira chiro na mwasi asibya na muchima wa kaimano, nesi wa kuchilola kwa kutete mufa. Si mundaa mwaba barembu, na chira mundju endaa aanja mulyikabo ngaiumurenzise.

4. Chira muuma mu mwabo, atendaa ahonda emutoloke wai yeine oshao, si endaa ahonda newebanji.

5. Mwa kachi-kachi kenyu, mundaa mwachitola ngokwa Yesu Kirisito abaa achitolyire.

6. Kutengera mira anathula kuuma na Ongo, si chiro bacha, oku kuba kwai kuuma na Ongo, atalolaa nga kali kandu ka kuchiminyirirako.

7. Si ebi byoshi, yeine eemereraa kurekabi, era kuchiira muanda, era kuchiira kuba mundju. Era kunalorekanako ete ehuhe

---

야바서사 어미찌마! 가찌 무레 와 부우마 너무찌마 무뱌-부야, 뭐더 나 무찌마 와 구떠 먀시마나 나 구피라나 보쏘!

2. 러로 무따아 몸삐가나, 나 구시마나, 나 구아다 무찌마 무우마 나 미아네사 이우마. 먀 구이라 바짜, 무뻐머 먀쭈마 나모와 부서서.

3. 무더따아 먀이라 찌로 나 먀시 아시뱌 나 무찌마 와 가이마노, 너시 와 구찌로롸 과 구더더 무파. 시 무따아 먀바 바러뿌, 나 찌라 무뚜 어따아 아아짜 무레가보 꺄이우무러씨서.

4. 찌라 무우마 무 먀보, 아더따아 아호따 어무도르거 와이 여이너 오싸오, 시 어따아 아호따 너워바찌.

5. 먀 가찌-가찌 거뉴, 무따아 먀찌도롸 꼬과 여수 기리시도 아바아 아찌도쮀러.

6. 구더뻐라 미라 아나쭈롸 구우마 나 오꼬, 시 찌로 바짜, 오구 구바 과이 구우마 나 오꼬, 아다르롸아 꺄 가삐 가뚜 가 구찌미네리라고.

7. 시 어비 뵤씨, 여이너 어어머러라아 구러가비, 어라 구찌이라 무아따, 어라 구찌이라 구바 무뚜. 어라 구나로러가나고 어더 어후허

---

comfort from his love, if any fellowship with the Spirit, if any tenderness and compassion,

2. then make my joy complete by being like-minded, having the same love, being one in spirit and purpose.

3. Do nothing out of selfish ambition or vain conceit, but in humility consider others better than yourselves.

4. Each of you should look not only to your own interests, but also to the interests of others.

5. Your attitude should be the same as that of Christ Jesus:

6. Who, being in very nature God, did not consider equality with God something to be grasped,

7. but made himself nothing, taking the very nature of a servant, being made in human likeness.

lyemundju,

8. na kuchandaasa busese.
Era kuthunda kuikira kwa lufu,
lufu lokwa musalaba.

8. 나 구짜따아사 부서서.
어라 구쭈따 구이기라 과
루푸, 루푸 로과 무사빠바.

8. And being found in
appearance as a man, he
humbled himself and
became obedient to death--
even death on a cross!

9. Echera chi chathumaa
Ongo amubika era luulu
busese, na kumweresa esina
lya lirenzise emanji masina
moshi,

9. 어쩌라 찌 짜쭈마아 오꼬
아무비가 어라 루우루 부서서,
나 구뭐러사 어시나 랴
삐러씨서 어마찌 마시나 모씨,

9. Therefore God exalted him
to the highest place and
gave him the name that is
above every name,

10. chasiya kwa kuthunda eri
sina lya Yesu, byoshi bya
byabumbwaa,bya bithula kwa
nguba,na bya bithula muno
butala, na bya bitula ekusimu,
binde byafukama era
muhondo sai.

10. 짜시야 과 구쭈따 어리
시나 랴 여수, 뵤씨 뱌
뱌부빠아,뱌 비쭈라 과
우바,나 뱌 비쭈라 무노
부다랴, 나 뱌 비두빠
어구시무, 비떠 뱌푸가마 어라
무호또 사이.

10. that at the name of Jesus
every knee should bow, in
heaven and on earth and
under the earth,

11. Na chira mundju atete
changanama,kwa Yesu Kirisito
iEnawetchu, chasiya Ongo
Tata atongibwe.

11. 나 찌라 무뚜 아더더
짜빠나마,과 여수 기리시도
이어나워쭈, 짜시야 오꼬 다다
아도삐붜.

11. and every tongue confess
that Jesus Christ is Lord, to
the glory of God the Father.

12. Rero, banyakethu basiirwa,
kwa mwabaa mwenjire
mwanathunda mango nabaa
nyiri alauma nenyu, mwiree
mwanaendekera busese
kunde mwaira bacha kuno
ndachiri alauma nenyu.
Mundaa mwaata mibere era
yalosa kwa mwanunulyibwe.
Mundaa mwaira bacha, mwa
burembu na mwa kuthunda
Ongo busese.

12. 러로, 바냐거쭈 바시이롸,
과 뫄바아 뭬찌러 뫄나쭈따
마꼬 나바아 네리 아롸루마
너뉴, 뭬러어 뫄나어떠거라
부서서 구떠 뫄이라 바짜
구노 따찌리 아롸우마 너뉴.
무따아 뫄아다 미버러 어라
야론사 과 뫄누누쀄붜. 무따아
뫄이라 바짜, 뫄 부러뿌 나 뫄
구쭈따 오꼬 부서서.

12. Therefore, my dear
friends, as you have always
obeyed--not only in my
presence, but now much
more in my absence--
continue to work out your
salvation with fear and
trembling,

13. Bushi Ongo iwenjire

13. 부씨 오꼬 이워찌러

13. for it is God who works

wakola mwa ndanda senyu, na kuberesa emuchima wekuhonda nekuira bya bimusimise.

14. Byoshi bya mwaira, mundaa mwairabi busira kuchaanya, na busira bwaka.

15. Mwa bacha, mungaba bandju ba batete chiro na mwasi mubi asibya ola bangabasitakako, kanji mungaba bandju ba bakomisibwe. Aola, mungaba bana ba Ongo ba batete bubi busibya mwa kachi-kachi kebandju babi kanji bakosi ba mabi busese bomuno butala bwa lwarero. Mungende mwalomeka mwa kachi-kachi kabo ngokwa ngunumu sende salomeka kwa nguba,

16. mwa kuhubanganyisabo emwasi wekalamo. Mwa kuira bacha, nanyi nyikabona cha nachitongera elusuku lwa Kirisito akafuluka. Echera chi chikalosa kanangana kwa emulyimo wanyi netamo lyanyi mwa kachi-kachi kenyu bitafire buha.

17. Ekweemerera Ongo kwenyu, kuliy nga mithulo. Rero, kulyi mango nyingeechibwa. Bikaba bacha, emikira yanyi ingatalyikibwa

14. 뵤씨 뱌 먀이라, 무따아 먀이라비 부시라 구짜아냐, 부시라 봐가.

15. 뫄 빠짜, 무따바 바뚜 바 바더더 찌로 나 뫄시 무비 아시뱌 오롸 바따바시다가고, 가찌 무따바 바뚜 바 바고미시붜. 아오롸, 무따바 바나 바 오꼬 바 바더더 부비 부시뱌 뫄 가찌-가찌 거바뚜 바비 가찌 바고시 바 마비 부서서 보무노 부다롸 봐 꽈러로. 무따떠 뫄로머가 뫄 가찌-가찌 가보 꼬과 꾸누누 서떠 사로머가 과 꾸바,

16. 뫄 구후바꽈네사보 어뫄시 워가꽈모. 뫄 구이라 바짜, 나니 네가보나 짜 나찌도꾸라 어루수구 꽈 기리시도 아가푸루가. 어쩌라 찌 찌가로사 가나따나 과 어무레모 와니 너다모 랴네 뫄 가찌-가찌 거뉴 비다피러 부하.

17. 어꿔어머러라 오꼬 귀뉴, 구뤼위 따 미쭈로. 러로, 구레 마꼬 네어어찌봐. 비가바 바짜, 어미기라 야네 이따다레기봐 귀이 미쭈로

in you to will and to act according to his good purpose.

14. Do everything without complaining or arguing,

15. so that you may become blameless and pure, children of God without fault in a crooked and depraved generation, in which you shine like stars in the universe

16. as you hold out the word of life--in order that I may boast on the day of Christ that I did not run or labor for nothing.

17. But even if I am being poured out like a drink offering on the sacrifice and service coming from your faith, I am glad and rejoice

kwei mithulo yenyu. Aola, nyingamowa busese, na kumowa alauma nenyu.

18. Nenyu mundaa mwamowa alauma nanyi.

19. Nyilangalyire kwa era nyuma sa suku sieke, Enawetchu Yesu akasima nyingabathumira Timoteo, chasiya emyasi era anganyibalyira era luulu senyu, inyisese emuchima.

20. Bushi yeine oshao iuneete emianyisa era iri ngeyanyi, kanji iunalaire busese kwa myasi era ibeerekere.

21. Ebanji boshi, mutoloke wabo beine ibenjire banahonda, si batalaire kwa myasi ya Yesu Kirisito.

22. Si mubeine muneeshi kwa Timoteo alosaa kwa analyi mukosi wa kanangana. Akolaa alauma nanyi emulyimo wekuhubanganya eMwasi Mubuya-buya, ngokwa mwana ende anakola neshe.

23. Rero, nyilangalyire kwa nyingamuthuma eyi mulyi mango nyingaba namenyire kubuya kute emyasi yanyi yabere.

24. Anabe nanyi nyeine, nyinalangalyire Enawetchu

여뉴. 아오롸, 네꺄모와 부서서, 나 구모와 아롸우마 너뉴.

18. 너뉴 무따아 뫄모와 아롸우마 나니.

19. 네롸꺄레러 과 어라 뉴마 사 수구 시어거, 어나워쭈 여수 아가시마 네꺄바쭈미라 디모더오, 쨔시야 어먀시 어라 아꺄네바레라 어라 루우루 서뉴, 이네서서 어무찌마.

20. 부씨 여이너 오싸오 이우너어더 어미아네사 어라 이리 꺄야네, 가찌 이우나롸이러 부서서 과 먀시 어라 이버어러거라.

21. 어바찌 보씨, 무도루거 와보 베이너 이버찌러 바나호따, 시 바다롸이러 과 먀시 야 여수 기리시도.

22. 시 무버이너 무너어씨 과 디모더오 아로사아 과 아나레 무고시 와 가나꺄나. 아고롸아 아롸우마 나니 어무풰모 워구후바꺄냐 어뫄시 무부야- 부야, 꼬과 뫄나 어너 아나고롸 너써.

23. 러로, 네롸꺄레러 과 네꺄무쭈마 어에 무풰 마꾜 네꺄바 나머네러 구부야 구더 어먀시 야네 야버러.

24. 아나버 나니 녀이너, 네나롸꺄레러 어나워쭈 과

with all of you.

18. So you too should be glad and rejoice with me.

19. I hope in the Lord Jesus to send Timothy to you soon, that I also may be cheered when I receive news about you.

20. I have no one else like him, who takes a genuine interest in your welfare.

21. For everyone looks out for his own interests, not those of Jesus Christ.

22. But you know that Timothy has proved himself, because as a son with his father he has served with me in the work of the gospel.

23. I hope, therefore, to send him as soon as I see how things go with me.

24. And I am confident in the Lord that I myself will come

kwa era nyuma sa suku sieke, nyingaika eyi.

어라 뉴마 사 수구 시어거, 네까이가 어에.

soon.

25. Si nalolaa kwa kukomire nyibathumire munyakethu Epafurotito, mulyikethu mwa mulyimo kanji ithwende thwalwisa alauma nai mwa kuhubanganya eMwasi Mubuya-buya. Mwamuthumaa enera chasiya anyiretere elweembo kukulyikana nebulae bwa nabaa nyete.

25. 시 나로라아 과 구고미러 네바쭈미러 무냐거쭈 어파푸로디도, 무레거쭈 와 무레모 가찌 이쭤떠 쫘뛰사 아라우마 나이 롸 구후바까냐 어롸시 무부야-부야. 롸무쭈마아 어너라 짜시야 아니러더러 어뤠어뽀 구구레가나 너부롸어 봐 나바아 녀더.

25. But I think it is necessary to send back to you Epaphroditus, my brother, fellow worker and fellow soldier, who is also your messenger, whom you sent to take care of my needs.

26. Nahonda kubathumirai bushi bacha ku era anabafula muboshi. Kanji alyibuka mwa muchima bushi mwomvaa emwasi kwa alyi mulwala.

26. 나호따 구바쭈미라이 부씨 바짜 구 어라 아나바푸롸 무보씨. 가찌 아레부가 롸 무찌마 부씨 뫃빠아 어롸시 과 아레 무롸롸.

26. For he longs for all of you and is distressed because you heard he was ill.

27. Kubinalyi, abaa alyi mulwala wa mareka-reka, si Ongo amufiraa bonjo. Ata na yeine oshao, si nanyi ananyifirabo, emalyibuko manyi mangesha kuya kwemanji.

27. 구비나레, 아바아 아레 무롸롸 와 마러가-러가, 시 오꼬 아무피라아 보쪼. 아다 나 여이너 오싸오, 시 나니 아나네피라보, 어마레부고 마네 마꺼싸 구야 꿔마찌.

27. Indeed he was ill, and almost died. But God had mercy on him, and not on him only but also on me, to spare me sorrow upon sorrow.

28. Echera chi chathuma nahonda kumuthuma fuba eyi mulyi, chasiya mango mungahuba kumulolako mumowe, nanyi emuchima wanyi abambatale.

28. 어쩌라 찌 짜쭈마 나호따 구무쭈마 푸바 어에 무레, 짜시야 마꼬 무꺼후바 구무로롸고 무모워, 나네 어무찌마 와네 아바빠다러.

28. Therefore I am all the more eager to send him, so that when you see him again you may be glad and I may have less anxiety.

29. Rero, mumwangiriraa na lumoo lunene kurengera

29. 러로, 무롸끼리라아 나 루모오 루너너 구러꺼라

29. Welcome him in the Lord with great joy, and honor

ebuuma bwenyu na
Enawetchu. Ebandju ba balyi
ngoyu, mweemire kunde
mweeresabo ethunda,
30. bushi abaa ahonda kufa
bushi nemulyimo wa Kirisito.
Abaa angafa bacha mwa
kunyiretera elweembo lwa
mubeine mwabaa
mutangaalyire kuisa ene nyiri.

어부우마 뷔뉴 나 어나워쭈.
어바뉴 바 바쩨 꼬유,
뭐어미러 구떠 뭐어러사보
어쭈따,
30. 부씨 아바아 아호따 구파
부씨 너무쩨모 와 기리시도.
아바아 아까파 바짜 마
구네러더라 어뭐어쁘 롸
무버이너 마바아
무다까아쩨러 구이사 어너
네리.

men like him,

30. because he almost died
for the work of Christ, risking
his life to make up for the
help you could not give me.

E Bafilipi Chikono 3

1. Rero banyakethu, kwa
kumalyirisa, mundaa
mwamowa bushi nebuuma
bwenyu na Enawetchu. Ene
myasi nabaa nabaanjikirirei
mira, si chiro bacha ekuhuba
kubaanjikirai kutanyita bute
busibya, bushi iri ya
kubalanga.
2. Mundaa mwachilanga kwa
bakosi babi, esi ngunda sa
senjire seemangira kwa myasi
yemwiya wekuchiisha kwa
mubiri oshao.
3. Tubano thu thumonyire
emwiya wekanangana, bushi
thu thwende thweera Ongo
mwa kukoresibwa neMuchima
wai. Kanji thwende
thwachitongera Yesu Kirisito,
si thutathula thuchinyiire

어 바피삐피 찌고노 3

1. 러로 바냐거쭈, 과
구마쩨리사, 무따아 마모와
부씨 너부우마 뷔뉴 나
어나워쭈. 어너 먀시 나바아
나바아찌기리러이 미라, 시
찌로 바짜 어구후바
구바아찌기라이 구다네다
부더 부시뱌, 부씨 이리 야
구바롸까.
2. 무따아 마찌롸까 과
바고시 바비, 어시 꾸따 사
서찌러 서어마삐라 과 먀시
여뮈야 워구찌이싸 과 무비리
오싸오.
3. 두바노 쭈 쭈모네러
어뮈야 워가나까나, 부씨 쭈
쭤떠 쭤어라 오꼬 마
구고러시봐 너무찌마 와이.
가찌 쭤떠 좌찌도러라 여수
기리시도, 시 쭈다쭈롸
쭈찌네이러 어먀시 여무비리.

Philippians Chapter 3[NIV]

1. Finally, my brothers,
rejoice in the Lord! It is no
trouble for me to write the
same things to you again,
and it is a safeguard for you.

2. Watch out for those dogs,
those men who do evil,
those mutilators of the flesh.

3. For it is we who are the
circumcision, we who
worship by the Spirit of God,
who glory in Christ Jesus,
and who put no confidence
in the flesh--

emyasi yemubiri.

4. Ei myasi yemubiri, anabe nanyi nyinganachinyiirai. Akaba kulyi ola wenjire wachichinga mbu iwete eloso lwekuchinyiira emyasi yemubiri, amenyaa kwa nyono nyi nyingachinyiirai busese kumurenza.

5. Bushi nyono nyiri womwa lubaa lweBaisiraeli, nyiri Mueburaniya bwereko, womwa lubuto lwa Benyamina. Na mango nabaa nalumisa suku munane nyibuchirwe, nera kumonyisibwa. Nemyasi era ithula yeerekere eMwaso weBayuta, nyono nabaa nyithunjirei busese, bushi nabaa nyithula Mufarisayo.

6. Nabaa nyiri mutaata-taata mwa kulosa ebemeresi kwa kasibu. Akaba kuanja ba bendee bakulyikira kwa Mwaso atechire, kutalyi chiro na mwasi asibya ola banyisitakaako mbu naishire muo.

7. Si emyasi yoshi era yabaa inyeetere mufa, nera nende naitola nga buha bushi nekukulyikira Kirisito.

8. Kubinalyi! Ebi byoshi

4. 어이 먀시 여무비리, 아나버 나니 네꺼나찌네이라이. 아가바 구레 오롸 워씨러 와찌찌꺼 뿌 이워더 어로소 뤄구찌네이라 어먀시 여무비리, 아머냐아 과 뇨노 네 네꺼찌네이라이 부서서 구무러싸.

5. 부씨 뇨노 네리 옴와 루바아 뤄바이시라어리, 네리 무어부라니야 붜러고, 옴와 루부도 롸 버냐미나. 나 마꼬 나바아 나루미사 수구 무나너 네부찌뤄, 너라 구모네시봐. 너먀시 어라 이쭈롸 여어러거러 어롸소 워바유다, 뇨노 나바아 네쭈씨러이 부서서, 부씨 나바아 네쭈롸 무파리사요.

6. 나바아 네리 무다아다- 다아다 뫄 구로사 어버머러시 과 가시부. 아가바 구아짜 바 버떠어 바구레기라 과 뫄소 아더찌러, 구다레 찌로 나 뫄시 아시뱌 오롸 바네시다가아고 뿌 나이씨러 무오.

7. 시 어먀시 요씨 어라 야바아 이녀어더러 무파, 너라 너러 나이도롸 꺄 부하 부씨 너구구레기라 기리시도.

8. 구비나레! 어비 뵤씨

4. though I myself have reasons for such confidence. If anyone else thinks he has reasons to put confidence in the flesh, I have more:

5. circumcised on the eighth day, of the people of Israel, of the tribe of Benjamin, a Hebrew of Hebrews; in regard to the law, a Pharisee;

6. as for zeal, persecuting the church; as for legalistic righteousness, faultless.

7. But whatever was to my profit I now consider loss for the sake of Christ.

8. What is more, I consider

nenjire nabitola nga buha, bushi nemutoloke munene wekumenyerera Enawetchu Yesu Kirisito. Kanji bushi nai, naesise byoshi, na kunde nabitola nga masi, chasiya nyikulyikire Kirisito,

9. na kuba mwa buuma nai tenene. Ndathungenene era muhondo sa Ongo bushi nekuthunda eMwaso, si nyithungenene bushi nemerere Kirisito. Bushi ekuba mundju ola uthungenene, kwende kwatenga era mwa Ongo. Nemundju ola wemerere Kirisito, iOngo ende aanja nga mundju ola Uthungenene era muhondo sai.

10. Echindu chananahonda, kulyi kumenya Kirisito na kumenya ebuashi bwekwomoka kwai. Kanji nahonda nyiribuke ngokwa nai analyibukaa, nyinafe ngokwa nai anafaa.

11. Aola, nyilangalyire kwa nanyi nyikanomwoka.

12. Ebi byoshi, ndatechire mbu nabibonyire mira, nesi mbu nera nyiri mundju ola ulumirire. Si mwa malyibita mu nyinachiri chasiya

너찌러 나비도롸 ꄲ 부하, 부씨 너무도뜨거 무너너 워구머녀러라 어나워쭈 여수 기리시도. 가찌 부씨 나이, 나어시서 뵤씨, 나 구떠 나비도롸 ꄲ 마시, 짜시야 네구쩨기러 기리시도,

9. 나 구바 뫄 부우마 나이 더너너. 따쭈머너너 어라 무호또 사 오꼬 부씨 너구쭈따 어뫄소, 시 네쭈머너너 부씨 너머러러 기리시도. 부씨 어구바 무뚜 오롸 우쭈머너너, 궈떠 과더ꄲ 어라 뫄 오꼬. 너무뚜 오롸 워머러러 기리시도, 이오꼬 어떠 아아짜 ꄲ 무뚜 오롸 우쭈머너너 어라 무호또 사이.

10. 어찌뚜 짜나나호따, 구레 구머냐 기리시도 나 구머냐 어부아씨 붜굥모가 과이. 가찌 나호따 네리부거 꼬과 나이 아나레부가아, 네나퍼 꼬과 나이 아나파아.

11. 아오롸, 네롸ꄲ쩨러 과 나니 네가노뫃가.

12. 어비 뵤씨, 따더찌러 뿌 나비보네러 미라, 너시 뿌 너라 네리 무뚜 오롸 우루미리러. 시 뫄 마쩨비다 무 네나찌리 짜시야 네이마너,

everything a loss compared to the surpassing greatness of knowing Christ Jesus my Lord, for whose sake I have lost all things. I consider them rubbish, that I may gain Christ

9. and be found in him, not having a righteousness of my own that comes from the law, but that which is through faith in Christ--the righteousness that comes from God and is by faith.

10. I want to know Christ and the power of his resurrection and the fellowship of sharing in his sufferings, becoming like him in his death,

11. and so, somehow, to attain to the resurrection from the dead.

12. Not that I have already obtained all this, or have already been made perfect, but I press on to take hold of that for which Christ Jesus

nyiimane, nyibone elweembo, bushi Yesu Kirisito anyitolyire mira nyibe mundju wai.

13. Nanga banyakethu, olu lweembo ndatechire mbu nalubonyire mira. Si chindju chiuma chi nenjire naira, na chi chechine: nenjire nebirira bya byarengire mira, nanende nalyibichira bya biri era muhondo.

14. Bushi noku, nyinachiri nasesa eluendo kuikira kwa businda, chasiya nyibone elweembo lwa Ongo athwamaltiraa kwa nguba kurengera Yesu Kirisito.

15. Rero, thuboshi thu thwera bandju thukulyire mwa bwemeresi, ei mianyisa iuma ithundaa thwanaata. Na akaba bauma mu mwabo bachete inji mianyisa, Ongo angabalosai kubuya-buya.

16. Si chiro bacha, ano thwaikira, thunaendekeraa mu njira nguma.

17. E banyaketu, mundaa mwanyeya. Thubano thwalosaa emyanya era byeemire kukulyikira. Rero, mundaa mwalorera kwaba benjire bakulyikira ei myanya.

18. Ono mwasi, nababwirireo

내보너 어뭐어뽀, 부씨 여수 기리시도 아네도뤠러 미라 네버 무뿌 와이.

13. 나아 바냐거쭈, 오루 뭐어뽀 따더찌러 뿌 나루보네러 미라. 시 찌뿌 찌우마 찌 너지러 나이라, 나 찌 쩌찌너: 너찌러 너비리라 뱌 뱌러꼐러 미라, 나너떠 나뤠비찌라 뱌 비리 어라 무호또.

14. 부씨 노구, 네나찌리 나서사 어루어또 구이기라 과 부시따, 짜시야 네보너 어뭐어뽀 콰 오꼬 아쫘마루디라아 과 우바 구러꺼라 여수 기리시도.

15. 러로, 쭈보씨 쭈 쭤라 바뿌 쭈구꿰러 와 붜머러시, 어이 미아네사 이우마 이쭈따아 쫘나아다. 나 아가바 바우마 무 뫄보 바쩌러 이찌 미아네사, 오꼬 아까바로사이 구부야-부야.

16. 시 찌로 바짜, 아노 쫘이기라, 쭈나어떠거라아 무 찌라 우마.

17. 어 바냐거두, 무따아 뫄녀야. 쭈바노 쫘로사아 어먀냐 어라 벼어미러 구구꿰기라. 러로, 무따아 뫄로러라 과바 버찌러 바구꿰기라 어이 먀냐.

18. 오노 뫄시, 나바뷔리러오

took hold of me.

13. Brothers, I do not consider myself yet to have taken hold of it. But one thing I do: Forgetting what is behind and straining toward what is ahead,

14. I press on toward the goal to win the prize for which God has called me heavenward in Christ Jesus.

15. All of us who are mature should take such a view of things. And if on some point you think differently, that too God will make clear to you.

16. Only let us live up to what we have already attained.

17. Join with others in following my example, brothers, and take note of those who live according to the pattern we gave you.

18. For, as I have often told

mira. Na lwarero nalyira mwa kuhuba kubaburao. Kulyi bandju banene ba benjire balosa kurengera emyanya yabo kwekufa kwa Kirisito kwa musalaba, kutabetere mufa asibya.

19. Ebusinda bwabo kunalyi kuya mwa muero, bushi ongo wabo, kulyi ekwiucha emwola mabo. Emyasi era ingabeechisa honyi, ibenjire bachitongera. Nemianyisa yabo, kwa bindju byomuno butala ku inachithulyira oshao.

20. Si thubano, thuchiberere bandju bokwa nguba. Kwei nguba, kuthwalinjira eMununusi wethu, Enawetchu Yesu Kirisito atengere.

21. Na mango akabaha, akabindjula ene mibiri yethu yebutambukare kanji ya kufa, na kuirai ibe ngemubiri wai webulangare. Akaira ebyera, kurengera ebuashi bwende eemangira mwebindju byoshi.

미라. 나 꽈러로 나쩨라 먀 구후바 구바부라오. 구쩨 바뉴 바너너 바 버띠러 바른사 구러뻐라 어먀냐 야보 귀구파 과 기리시도 과 무사꽈바, 구다버더러 무파 아시뱌.

19. 어부시따 봐보 구나쩨 구야 먀 무어로, 부씨 오꼬 와보, 구쩨 어귀우짜 어모꽈 마보. 어먀시 어라 이빠버어찌사 호네, 이버띠러 바찌도뻐라. 너미아네사 야보, 과 비뉴 뵤무노 부다꽈 구 이나찌쭈쩨라 오싸오.

20. 시 쭈바노, 쭈찌버러러 바뉴 보과 우바. 귀이 우바, 구꽈띠씨라 어무누누시 워쭈, 어나워쭈 여수 기리시도 아더뻐러.

21. 나 마꼬 아가바하, 아가비뉴꽈 어너 미비리 여쭈 여부다뿌가러 가찌 야 구파, 나 구이라이 이버 뻐무비리 와이 워부꽈뻐러. 아가이라 어뼈라, 구러뻐라 어부아씨 뭐떠 어어마삐라 뭐비뉴 뵤씨.

you before and now say again even with tears, many live as enemies of the cross of Christ.

19. Their destiny is destruction, their god is their stomach, and their glory is in their shame. Their mind is on earthly things.

20. But our citizenship is in heaven. And we eagerly await a Savior from there, the Lord Jesus Christ,

21. who, by the power that enables him to bring everything under his control, will transform our lowly bodies so that they will be like his glorious body.

E Bafilipi Chikono 4

1. Bushi noku banyakethu basiirwa, nyete mbuha inene yekuhuba kubalolako. Mwabo mu mwende mwathuma

어 바피끠피 찌고노 4

1. 부씨 노구 바냐거쭈 바시이롸, 녀더 뿌하 이너너 여구후바 구바른라고. 먀보 무 뭐떠 먀쭈마 나모와, 가찌 무

Philippians Chapter 4[NIV]

1. Therefore, my brothers, you whom I love and long for, my joy and crown, that is how you should stand firm in

namowa, kanji mu mulyi nzita 무쩨 씨다 야네 여구이마나. the Lord, dear friends!
yanyi yekuimana. Rero 러로 바냐거쭈 바시이롸,
banyakethu basiirwa, mundaa 무따아 뫄시미가 롸 부우마
mwasimika mwa buuma 뷰뉴 나 어나워쭈.
bwenyu na Enawetchu.

2. Woyo Ewotiya nao Sindike, 2. 오요 어우디야 나오 2. I plead with Euodia and I
nabeema busese mundaa 시띠거, 나버어마 부서서 plead with Syntyche to agree
mwomvirisanya bushi mulyi 무따아 뫔삐리사냐 부씨 무쩨 with each other in the Lord.
mwa buuma na Enawetchu. 롸 부우마 나 어나워쭈.

3. Nao mukosi mulyikethu 3. 나오 무고시 무쩨거쭈 3. Yes, and I ask you, loyal
mubuya, nakweema busese 무부야, 나궈어마 부서서 과 yokefellow, help these
kwa uasaa abu bakasi babiri, 우아사아 아부 바가시 바비리,women who have contended
bushi balyibukaa busese 부씨 바쩨부가아 부서서 at my side in the cause of
alauma nanyi mwa 아롸우마 나네 롸 구후바아냐 the gospel, along with
kuhubanganya eMwasi 어뫄시 무부야-부야. 구쩨 나 Clement and the rest of my
Mubuya-buya. Kulyi na 거러마 나 바찌 바고시 fellow workers, whose names
Kelema na banji bakosi 바쩨거쭈 바 어마시나 마보 are in the book of life.
balyikethu ba emasina mabo 마아찌기뤄 롸 찌다보
maanjikirwe mwa chitabo 쩌가롸모.
chekalamo.

4. Mundaa mwamowa esuku 4. 무따아 뫄모와 어수구 4. Rejoice in the Lord always.
soshi kurengera ebuuma 소씨 구러뻐라 어부우마 뷰뉴 I will say it again: Rejoice!
bwenyu na Enawetchu. Kanji 나 어나워쭈. 가찌 나더쩌러
natechire kwa mundaa 과 무따아 뫄모와.
mwamowa.

5. Eburembu bwenyu bundaa 5. 어부러뿌 뷰뉴 부따아 5. Let your gentleness be
bwamenyeka nebandju boshi. 봐머녀가 너바뉴 보씨. evident to all. The Lord is
Enawetchu alyi ofu kufuluka. 어나워쭈 아쩨 오푸 구푸루가.near.

6. Mutendaa mwachiribusa 6. 무더따아 뫄찌리부사 부씨 6. Do not be anxious about
bushi na mwasi asibya. Si 나 뫄시 아시뱌. 시 어마뢔어 anything, but in everything,
emalae menyu moshi, 머뉴 모씨, 무따아 뭐머라모 by prayer and petition, with
mundaa mwemeramo era 어라 롸 오꼬, 나 구떠 thanksgiving, present your
mwa Ongo, na kunde 뫄무도꺼 무 찌라 뫄시. requests to God.
mwamutonga mu chira
mwasi.

7. Mwa bacha, Ongo angaberesa ebolo bwa bandju batangaala kumenyerera. Obu bolo bundaa bwaba mwa michima nomwa mianyisa yenyu kurengera ebuuma bwenyu na Yesu Kirisito.

8. Rero banyakethu kwa businda, emyasi yoshi era mundaa mwaanyisako ibaa: emyasi yekanangana, nera ingareta ethunda, nera ithungenene, nera ikomisibwe, nera ingasimisa, nera ingatongibwa, neye kulosa ebubuya.

9. Byoshi bya nabakangirisaa, na bya mwabonaa era nyiri, na bya mwomvaa nateta, na bya mwalolaa naira, nenyu bi mundaa mwanaira. Na Ongo iwende wana ebolo angaba alauma nenyu.

10. Natongaa Enawetchu na kumowa busese bushi nekulola kwa mwahubaa kukengera kunyiasa. Nyishi kwa mwabaa mutanyebirire, si enjira yekulosa echera, imwabaa mwainyire.

11. Ndatechire bacha mbu bushi nyiri mwa malae. Nyono nera nyithula nyikomere kumowa mwa myasi yoshi era yanyiikirire.

---

7. 꽈 바짜, 오꼬 아까버러사 어보로 봐 바쭈 바다까아꽈 구머녀러라. 오부 보로 부따아 봐바 꽈 미찌마 노꽈 미아네사 여뉴 구러꺼라 어부우마 뷔뉴 나 여수 기리시도.

8. 러로 바냐거쭈 과 부시따, 어먀시 요씨 어라 무따아 꽈아네사고 이바아: 어먀시 여가나꽈나, 너라 이까러다 어쭈따, 너라 이쭈꺼너너, 너라 이고미시붸, 너라 이까시미사, 너라 이까도꒐봐, 너여 구로사 어부부야.

9. 뵤씨 뱌 나바가꒐리사아, 나 뱌 꽈보나아 어라 네리, 나 뱌 모빠아 나더다, 나 뱌 꽈로꽈아 나이라, 너뉴 비 무따아 꽈나이라. 나 오꼬 이워떠 와나 어보로 아까바 아꽈우마 너뉴.

10. 나도까아 어나워쭈 나 구모와 부서서 부씨 너구로꽈 과 꽈후바아 구거꺼라 구네아사. 네씨 과 꽈바아 무다녀비리러, 시 어찌라 여구로사 어쩌라, 이꽈바아 꽈이네러.

11. 따더찌러 바짜 뿌 부씨 네리 꽈 마꽈어. 뇨노 너라 네쭈꽈 네고머러 구모와 꽈 먀시 요씨 어라 야네이기리러.

---

7. And the peace of God, which transcends all understanding, will guard your hearts and your minds in Christ Jesus.

8. Finally, brothers, whatever is true, whatever is noble, whatever is right, whatever is pure, whatever is lovely, whatever is admirable--if anything is excellent or praiseworthy--think about such things.

9. Whatever you have learned or received or heard from me, or seen in me--put it into practice. And the God of peace will be with you.

10. I rejoice greatly in the Lord that at last you have renewed your concern for me. Indeed, you have been concerned, but you had no opportunity to show it.

11. I am not saying this because I am in need, for I have learned to be content whatever the circumstances.

12. Nyithula nyishi kutle nyingachisimba mwa bukene na kute nyingachisimba mwa buare. Nachikangirise mira ekunde namowa mu chira chisiki na mu chira mwasi. Abe mwa mwaako abe mwa bulyio.

13. Nende naala ebi byoshi, kurengera Kirisito iwende wanyeresa emisi.

14. Si chiro bacha, mwairaa kubuya ekunyiasa mwa malyibuko manyi.

15. Mubesha Firipi, mubeine muneeshi kubuya-buya kwa nabaa nyiri mango natangirisaa kunde nahubanganyisa ebandju eMwasi Mubuya-buya. Mango natengaa mwa chio chenyu cheMaketoniya, kutalyi banji bemeresi ba thwabaa thulyi luuma-luuma nabo mwa myasi yekwana ebindju nekubyangirira, si mubeine oshao.

16. Bushi mango nabaa nyiri mwa musi weTesalonika, mwabaa mwenjire mwanyithumira ebindju kwa kunyiasa mwa malae manyi, kanji lyita neuma.

12. 네쭈롸 네씨 구두뻐 네빠찌시빠 롸 부거너 나 구더 네빠찌시빠 롸 부아러. 나찌가삐리서 미라 어구떠 나모와 무 찌라 찌시기 나 무 찌라 롸시. 아버 롸 롸아고 아버 롸 부뤠오.

13. 너떠 나아롸 어비 뵤씨, 구러뻐라 기리시도 이워떠 와녀러사 어미시.

14. 시 찌로 바짜, 롸이라아 구부야 어구네아사 롸 마뤠부고 마네.

15. 무버싸 피리피, 무버이너 무너어씨 구부야-부야 과 나바아 네리 마꼬 나다삐리사아 구떠 나후바삐네사 어바쭈 어롸시 무부야-부야. 마꼬 나더롸아 롸 찌오 쩌뉴 쩌마거도니야, 구다뤠 바찌 버머러시 바 좌바아 쭈뤠 루우마-루우마 나보 롸 먀시 여과나 어비쭈 너구뱌삐리라, 시 무버이너 오싸오.

16. 부씨 마꼬 나바아 네리 롸 무시 워더사롼니가, 롸바아 뭐찌러 롸네쭈미라 어비쭈 과 구네아사 롸 마롸어 마네, 가찌 뤠다 너우마.

12. I know what it is to be in need, and I know what it is to have plenty. I have learned the secret of being content in any and every situation, whether well fed or hungry, whether living in plenty or in want.

13. I can do everything through him who gives me strength.

14. Yet it was good of you to share in my troubles.

15. Moreover, as you Philippians know, in the early days of your acquaintance with the gospel, when I set out from Macedonia, not one church shared with me in the matter of giving and receiving, except you only;

16. for even when I was in Thessalonica, you sent me aid again and again when I was in need.

17. Ndatechire bacha mbu bushi nahonda munde mwaanyisa. Si nahonda Ongo ende abaahanyira kwa nyeembo senyu.

18. Ebindju byoshi, bya mwanyithumiraa kurengera Epafurotito, nabonyirebi. Byanyiasise kumala emalae manyi moshi, nebinji byanashibireko. Ebi bindju biri nga mithulo ya marashi ma mauka kubuya, kanji biri nga mithulo ya kusiresibwa era Ongo emerere inamusimise.

19. Rero nenyu, Ongo wanyi angende abamalyira emalae menyu moshi, kukulyikana nengulu yebuare bwai bunene kurengera Yesu Kirisito.

20. Ongo Tata endaa atongibwa esuku nemango! Bibe bacha!

21. Munyilamusisaa ebandju ba Ongo boshi, kwesina lya Yesu Kirisito. Banyakethu ba tulyi nabo anola, nabo babalamusise.

22. Ebandju ba Ongo boshi babalamusise. Na ba bende bakola mwa chikalyi cha mwami, nabo babalamusise busese.

23. Enawetchu Yesu Kirisito

---

17. 따더찌러 바짜 뿌 부씨 나호따 무떠 롸아네사. 시 나호따 오꼬 어떠 아바아하네라 과 녀어뿐 서뉴.

18. 어비뉴 뵤씨, 뱌 롸네쭈미라아 구러뻐라 어파푸로디도, 나보네러비. 뱌네아시서 구마롸 어마뫄어 마니 모씨, 너비찌 뱌나씨비러고. 어비 비뉴 비리 뫄 미쭈론 야 마라씨 마 마우가 구부야, 가찌 비리 뫄 미쭈론 야 구시러시봐 어라 오꼬 어머러러 이나무시미서.

19. 러로 너뉴, 오꼬 와네 아뻐떠 아바마뼤라 어마뫄어 머뉴 모씨, 구구뼤가나 너우뿌 여부아러 봐이 부너너 구러뻐라 여수 기리시도.

20. 오꼬 다다 어따아 아도삐봐 어수구 너마꼬! 비버 바짜!

21. 무네뫄무시사아 어바뉴 바 오꼬 보씨, 궈시나 뺘 여수 기리시도. 바냐거쭈 바 두뤠 나보 아노롸, 나보 바바뫄무시서.

22. 어바뉴 바 오꼬 보씨 바바뫄무시서. 나 바 버떠 바고롸 뫄 찌가뼤 짜 롸미, 나보 바바뫄무시서 부서서.

23. 어나워쭈 여수 기리시도

---

17. Not that I am looking for a gift, but I am looking for what may be credited to your account.

18. I have received full payment and even more; I am amply supplied, now that I have received from Epaphroditus the gifts you sent. They are a fragrant offering, an acceptable sacrifice, pleasing to God.

19. And my God will meet all your needs according to his glorious riches in Christ Jesus.

20. To our God and Father be glory for ever and ever. Amen.

21. Greet all the saints in Christ Jesus. The brothers who are with me send greetings.

22. All the saints send you greetings, especially those who belong to Caesar's household.

23. The grace of the Lord

endaa abaahanyira.   어따아 아바아하니라.   Jesus Christ be with your
                                                          spirit. Amen.

E Bakolosai

어 바고로로사이

Colossians

BAKOLOSAYI
(COLOSIANS)

바고로로사에
(고로시아쭈)

E Bakolosai Chikono 1

1. Nyono Paulo, nyri ndjumwa ya Yesu Kirisito kwa kuhonda kwa Ongo. Nyono na munyaketchu Timoteo,

2 tchu tchwabaandjikira mu bandju ba Ongo bomwa musi weKolosayi. Mwabo, mulyi banyaketchu ba bmenze kubuya mwa bwemeresi mwa ndanda sa Kirisito. Ongo Tata ndaa baahanyira, na kuberesa eboolo!

3. Chira chihangi mango tchwabemera, tchwendjire tchwateta mbu akoko era mwa Ongo, Eshi wa Enawethu Yesu Kirisito.

4. Tchwendjire tchwaira bacha, bushi tchwomvire emwasi kwa mwemerere Yesu Kirisito, nokwa musimire ebandju ba Ongo boshi.

5. Ebyera bitenganyire nemunyiiro webya Ongo atchula ababikirire kwa nguba. Oyu munyiiro, imoomvaa bateta era luulu sao, mango babahubanganyisaa eMwasi Mubuya-buya wekanangana.

6. Oyu Mwasi Mubuya-buya ahandabanyire mwa butala

어 바고로사이 찌고노 1

1. 뇨노 파우로, 네리 뚜꽈 야 여수 기리시도 과 구호따 과 오꼬. 뇨노 나 무냐거쭈 디모더오,

2 쭈 쫘바아찌기라 무 바뚜 바 오꼬 보꽈 무시 워고로사에. 꽈보, 무쀄 바냐거쭈 바 부머써 구부야 꽈 붸머러시 꽈 따따 사 기리시도. 오꼬 다다 따아 바아하네라, 나 구버러사 어보오롣!

3. 찌라 찌하삐 마꼬 쫘버머라, 쮀찌러 쫘더다 뿌 아고고 어라 꽈 오꼬, 어씨 와 어나워쭈 여수 기리시도.

4. 쮀찌러 쫘이라 바짜, 부씨 쪼삐러 어꽈시 과 뭐머러러 여수 기리시도, 노과 무시미러 어바뚜 바 오꼬 보씨.

5. 어벼라 비더따네러 너무네이로 워바 오꼬 아쭈꽈 아바비기리러 과 꾸바. 오유 무네이로, 이모오빠아 바더다 어라 루우루 사오, 마꼬 바바후바따네사아 어꽈시 무부야-부야 워가나꽈나.

6. 오유 꽈시 무부야-부야 아하따바네러 꽈 부다꽈 보씨.

Colossians Chapter 1[NIV]

1. Paul, an apostle of Christ Jesus by the will of God, and Timothy our brother,

2. To the holy and faithful brothers in Christ at Colosse: Grace and peace to you from God our Father.

3. We always thank God, the Father of our Lord Jesus Christ, when we pray for you,

4. because we have heard of your faith in Christ Jesus and of the love you have for all the saints--

5. the faith and love that spring from the hope that is stored up for you in heaven and that you have already heard about in the word of truth, the gospel

6. that has come to you. All over the world this gospel is

boshi. Kanji enjire athuma ebandju baata myanya ibuya, ngokwa enjire anaira mwa kachi-kachi kenyu, kutengera mango mwomvaa na kumenyerera emyasi yekanangana yebonjo bwa Ongo.

7. Ei myasi, Epafura mukosi mulyikethu musiirwa iwabakangirisaai. Oyu Epafura alyi mukosi mubuya wa Yesu Kirisito, na iwenjire wakola emulyimo ola thungakolyire mwa kachi-kachi kenyu.

8. Kanji iwathuburaa kwa eMuchima-Mubuya enjire aberesa ebuashi bwekunde mwasimana.

9. Bushi noku, kutengera mango thwomvaa kwei myasi, thwenjire thwabeemera era mwa Ongo busira kutama. Thwenjire thwamwema, chasiya eMuchima Mubuya-buya abeerese ebwenge boshi bwekunde mwamenyerera kubuya-buya ekuhonda kwa Ongo.

10. Mwa bacha, mungaata mibere era yeresa Enawethu ethunda, yamusimisa nomwa byoshi. Kanji mungende mwaira chira mwasi mubuya,

---

가찌 어찌러 아쭈마 어바꾸 바아다 먀냐 이부야, 꼬과 어찌러 아나이라 먀 가찌-가찌 거뉴, 구더꺼라 마꼬 몸빠아 나 구머녀러라 어먀시 여가나꺼나 여보쪼 봐 오꼬.

7. 어이 먀시, 어파푸라 무고시 무레거쭈 무시이롸 이와바가꺼리사아이. 오유 어파푸라 아레 무고시 무부야 와 여수 기리시도, 나 이워찌러 와고롸 어무레모 오롸 쭈꺼고레러 먀 가찌-가찌 거뉴.

8. 가찌 이와쭈부라아 과 어무찌마-무부야 어찌러 아버러사 어부아씨 뭐구떠 마시마나.

9. 부씨 노구, 구더꺼라 마꼬 찌오빠아 궈이 먀시, 쭤찌러 쫘버어머라 어라 먀 오꼬 부시라 구다마. 쭤찌러 쫘뭐마 짜시야 어무찌마 무부야-부야 아버어러서 어뭐꺼 보씨 뭐구떠 먀머녀러라 구부야-부야 어구호꺼 과 오꼬.

10. 먀 바짜, 무꺼아다 미버러 어라 여러사 어나워쭈 어쭈따, 야무시미사 노와 뵤씨. 가찌 무꺼떠 먀이라 찌라 마시 무부야, 나 구어떠거라 좌구롸

---

bearing fruit and growing, just as it has been doing among you since the day you heard it and understood God's grace in all its truth.

7. You learned it from Epaphras, our dear fellow servant, who is a faithful minister of Christ on our behalf,

8. and who also told us of your love in the Spirit.

9. For this reason, since the day we heard about you, we have not stopped praying for you and asking God to fill you with the knowledge of his will through all spiritual wisdom and understanding.

10. And we pray this in order that you may live a life worthy of the Lord and may please him in every way: bearing fruit in every

na kuendekera mwakula mwa kumenya Ongo.

11. Ongo endaa aberesa misi inene kurengera ebuashi bwethunda lyai, chasiya munde mwasesa emichima na kuata bushibirisi mu chira mwasi woshi.

12. Mundaa mwateta mbu akoko era mwa Ongo Tata na lumoo lunene, bushi iwabairire kuba bandju ba bemire kubona mwango kwa mwandju ola abikirire ebandju bai, mwa bwami bwebulangare.

13. Bushi athununwire thutenge mwa buashi bwemusimya, na kuthweka mwa bwami bweMwana wai musiirwa.

14. Rero kurengera oyu Mwana wai, thwanunulyibwe na kubabalyirwa ebibi byethu.

15. Kirisito iuthusa ehuhe lya Ongo, ola utalorekanako. Kanji ifula era ithula era luulu sa byoshi bya byabumbwaa.

16. Bushi kurengera Kirisito, Ongo abumbaa ebindju byoshi, bya bithula kwa nguba, na bya bithula muno butala, bya bisenekeko na bya bitasenekeko, nesi basimu ba

와 구머냐 오꼬.

11. 오꼬 어따아 아버러사 미시 이너너 구러꺼라 어부아씨 붜쭈따 랴이, 짜시야 무떠 먀서사 어미찌마 나 구아다 부씨비리시 무 찌라 먀시 올씨.

12. 무따아 먀더다 뿌 아고고 어라 먀 오꼬 다다 나 루모오 루너너, 부씨 이와바이리러 구바 바뉴 바 버미러 구보나 먀꼬 과 먀뉴 오롸 아비기리러 어바뉴 바이, 먀 봐미 붜부롸꺼러.

13. 부씨 아쭈누니위러 쭈더꺼 먀 부아씨 붜무시먀, 나 구줘가 먀 봐미 붜먀나 와이 무시이롸.

14. 러로 구러꺼라 오유 먀나 와이, 쫘누누레붜 나 구바바레롸 어비비 벼쭈.

15. 기리시도 이우쭈사 어후허 랴 오꼬, 오롸 우다롸러가나고. 가찌 이푸롸 어라 이쭈롸 어라 루우루 사 뵤씨 뱌 뱌부꽈아.

16. 부씨 구러꺼라 기리시도, 오꼬 아부빠아 어비뉴 뵤씨, 뱌 비쭈롸 과 뉴바, 나 뱌 비쭈롸 무노 부다롸, 뱌 비서너거고 나 뱌 비다서너거고, 너시 바시무 바

good work, growing in the knowledge of God,

11. being strengthened with all power according to his glorious might so that you may have great endurance and patience, and joyfully

12. giving thanks to the Father, who has qualified you to share in the inheritance of the saints in the kingdom of light.

13. For he has rescued us from the dominion of darkness and brought us into the kingdom of the Son he loves,

14. in whom we have redemption, the forgiveness of sins.

15. He is the image of the invisible God, the firstborn over all creation.

16. For by him all things were created: things in heaven and on earth, visible and invisible, whether thrones or powers or rulers or authorities; all things

bete buashi na ba bemire. Byoshi byabumbwaa nai, kanji bushi nai.

17 Kanji mango ebi byoshi byabaa bitasa kubumbwa, Kirisito anathula. Nebuashi bwai bu buthumire ebi byoshi byabao.

18. Eluhu lwa Ongo lu luthula mubiri wa Kirisito. Nai yeine lithwe. Kanji Kirisito indangiriso, na imubere-bere kwoomoka mwa bafu, chasiya abe mubere-bere mwa byoshi.

19. Bushi Ongo asimaa mbu eMwana wai anabaa kuuma nai mwa byoshi.

20. Kanji kurengera oyu Mwana wai, Ongo asimaa ahube kuba mwa buuma na byoshi bya byabumbwaa. Mwa bacha, arechire eboolo mwa butala nokwa nguba, kurengera emikira yeMwana wai era yasheshekalaa kwa musalaba.

21. Kwamira, nenyu mwabaa mulyi bure na Ongo, na kuba barenda bai, bushi nemianyisa yenyu ibi nemyanya yenyu ibi.

22. Si Ongo erire ahuba kuba mwa buuma nenyu, kurengera eMwana wai ola wafaa kwa njira yemubiri. Airaa bacha,

버더 부아씨 나 바 버미러. 뵤씨 뱌부꽈아 나이, 가찌 부씨 나이.

17 가찌 마꼬 어비 뵤씨 뱌바아 비다사 구부꽈, 기리시도 아나쭈꽈. 너부아씨 봐이 부 부후미러 어비 뵤씨 뱌바오.

18. 어루후 똬 오꼬 루 루쭈꽈 무비리 와 기리시도. 나이 여이너 띄줘. 가찌 기리시도 이따띠리소, 나 이무버러-버러 굠오모가 똬 바푸, 짜시야 아버 무버러-버러 똬 뵤씨.

19. 부씨 오꼬 아시마아 뿌 어꽈나 와이 아나바아 구우마 나이 똬 뵤씨.

20. 가찌 구러꺼라 오유 꽈나 와이, 오꼬 아시마아 아후버 구바 똬 부우마 나 뵤씨 뱌 뱌부꽈아. 똬 바짜, 아러찌러 어보오롣 똬 부다꽈 노과 꿔바, 구러꺼라 어미기라 여꽈나 와이 어라 야써써가꽈아 과 무사꽈바.

21. 과미라, 너뉴 꽈바아 무레 부러 나 오꼬, 나 구바 바러따 바이, 부씨 너미아니싸 여뉴 이비 너먀냐 여뉴 이비.

22. 시 오꼬 어리러 아후바 구바 똬 부우마 너뉴, 구러꺼라 어꽈나 와이 오꽈 와파아 과 띠라 여무비리.

were created by him and for him.

17. He is before all things, and in him all things hold together.

18. And he is the head of the body, the church; he is the beginning and the firstborn from among the dead, so that in everything he might have the supremacy.

19. For God was pleased to have all his fullness dwell in him,

20. and through him to reconcile to himself all things, whether things on earth or things in heaven, by making peace through his blood, shed on the cross.

21. Once you were alienated from God and were enemies in your minds because of your evil behavior.

22. But n ow he has reconciled you by Christ's physical body through death to present

chasiya muike era muhondo sai mulyi babuya-buya, kanji mube busira chibi chisibya, na busira mwasi mubi asibya ola bangabasitako.

아이라아 바짜, 짜시야 무이거 어라 무호또 사이 무레 바부야-부야, 가찌 무버 부시라 찌비 찌시뱌, 나 부시라 먀시 무비 아시뱌 오롸 바빠바시다고.

you holy in his sight, without blemish and free from accusation--

23. Si mwemire kunde mwasimika na kuata misi mwa bwemeresi bwenyu. Mutendaa mwatenga mwa munyiiro ola eMwasi Mubuya-buya ende aana. Oyu Mwasi Mubuya-buya imwomvaako, na iwahubanganyisibwaa kwa bandju boshi bomwa butala. Rero nanyi Paulo, nera mukosi wa kunde nahubanganyao.

23. 시 뭐미러 구너 먀시미가 나 구아다 미시 먀 뷔머러시 뷔뉴. 무더따아 먀더빠 먀 무네이로 오롸 어먀시 무부야-부야 어떠 아아나. 오유 먀시 무부야-부야 이뫃빠아고, 나 이와후바빠니시봐아 과 바쭈 보씨 보먀 부다롸. 러로 나니 파우롣, 너라 무고시 와 구너 나후바빠냐오.

23. if you continue in your faith, established and firm, not moved from the hope held out in the gospel. This is the gospel that you heard and that has been proclaimed to every creature under heaven, and of which I, Paul, have become a servant.

24. Rero namowa kwa nalyibuka bushi nenyu. Nalyibuka kwa mubiri, chasiya nyiendekere kuhangira kwa malyibuko ma Kirisito alolaako bushi neluhu lwa Ongo. Nolu luhu, imubiri wai.

24. 러로 나모와 과 나레부가 부씨 너뉴. 나레부가 과 무비리, 짜시야 니어떠거러 구하빠라 과 마레부고 마 기리시도 아롣빠아고 부씨 너루후 롸 오꼬. 노루 루후, 이무비리 와이.

24. Now I rejoice in what was suffered for you, and I fill up in my flesh what is still lacking in regard to Christ's afflictions, for the sake of his body, which is the church.

25. Nyono banyiirire kuba mukosi weluhu lwa Ongo, kwa kukola emulyimo ola Ongo anyeresaa bushi nenyu. Noyu mulyimo, alyi wekunde nahubanganyisa ebandju eChinwa chai choshi.

25. 뇨노 바네이리러 구바 무고시 워루후 롸 오꼬, 과 구고롸 어무레모 오롸 오꼬 아녀러사아 부씨 너뉴. 노유 무레모, 아레 워구떠 나후바빠니사 어바쭈 어찌놔 짜이 쪼씨.

25. I have become its servant by the commission God gave me to present to you the word of God in its fullness--

26. Echi Chinwa, imyasi era abaa athula abishire ebandju kutengera mira. Si rero, erire

26. 어찌 찌놔, 이먀시 어라 아바아 아쭈롸 아비씨러 어바쭈 구더빠라 미라. 시

26. the mystery that has been kept hidden for ages and generations, but is now

abihulyirai ebandju bai.

27. Bushi Ongo abaa ahonda ebandju bai bamenyerere kwa ei myasi ithusa buare bunene, na bulangare kwa bandju ba batathula bamwishi. Nei myasi bacha ku itechire: Kirisito atula mwa ndanda senyu, mwete nemunyiiro kwa mukabona mwango kwethunda lya Ongo.

28. Oyu Kirisito ithwenjire thwahubanganyisa ebandju boshi era luulu sai. Thwenjire thweresa chira mundju eano na kumukangirisa nebwenge boshi, chasiya thuase ebandju boshi kukula mwa buuma bwabo na Kirisito.

29. Echera chichenjire chathuma nashika endubano na kulwisanya kurengera emisi era Kirisito anyeresise. Nei misi iyenjire yakola nebuashi mwa ndanda sanyi.

러로, 어리러 아비후뤠라이 어바쭈 바이.

27. 부씨 오꼬 아바아 아호따 어바쭈 바이 바머녀러러 과 어이 먀시 이쭈사 부아러 부너너, 나 부퐈마러 과 바쭈 바 바다쭈퐈 바뮈씨. 너이 먀시 바짜 구 이더찌러: 기리시도 아두퐈 마 따따 서뉴, 뭐더 너무네이로 과 무가보나 먀꼬 궈쭈따 퍄 오꼬.

28. 오유 기리시도 이쮀찌러 좌후바마네사 어바쭈 보씨 어라 루우루 사이. 쮀찌러 쮀러사 찌라 무뿌 어아노 나 구무가끼리사 너붸어 보씨, 짜시야 쭈아서 어바쭈 보씨 구구퐈 마 부우마 봐보 나 기리시도.

29. 어쩌라 찌쩌찌러 짜쭈마 나씨가 어뚜바노 나 구뤼사냐 구러어라 어미시 어라 기리시도 아녀러시서. 너이 미시 이여찌러 야고퐈 너부아씨 퐈 따따 사니.

disclosed to the saints.

27. To them God has chosen to make known among the Gentiles the glorious riches of this mystery, which is Christ in you, the hope of glory.

28. We proclaim him, admonishing and teaching everyone with all wisdom, so that we may present everyone perfect in Christ.

29. To this end I labor, struggling with all his energy, which so powerfully works in me.

E Bakolosai Chikono 2

1. Nahonda mumenyereraa kubuya kwa nenjire nalwisanya busese bushi nenyu, na bushi nebemeresi bomwa musi we Laotikiya, na bushi nebanji boshi ba

어 바고뽀사이 찌고노 2

1. 나호따 무머녀러러라아 구부야 과 너찌러 나뤼사냐 부서서 부씨 너뉴, 나 부씨 너버머러시 보뫄 무시 워 퐈오디기야, 나 부씨 너바찌 보씨 바 바다푸라아

Colossians Chapter 2[NIV]

1. I want you to know how much I am struggling for you and for those at Laodicea, and for all who have not met me personally.

batafuraa kunyilolako.	구네로ᄙᅡ고.	
2. Nenjire naira bacha, chasiya basesibwe emichima na kunde basimana mwa buuma, na kuata ebwenge boshi. Mwa kuira bacha, bangamenyerera kanangana emyasi yoshi era Ongo abaa athula abishire. Nei myasi, alyi Kirisito yeine.	2. 너띠러 나이라 바짜, 짜시야 바서시ᄇᆎ 어미찌마 나 구떠 바시마나 뫄 부우마, 나 구아다 어ᄇᆎᅌᅥ 보씨. 뫄 구이라 바짜, 바ᅌᅡ머녀러라 가나ᅌᅡ나 어먀시 요씨 어라 오ᅌᅩ 아바아 아쭈ᄙᅡ 아비씨러. 너이 먀시, 아ᄙᅦ 기리시도 여이너.	2. My purpose is that they may be encouraged in heart and united in love, so that they may have the full riches of complete understanding, in order that they may know the mystery of God, namely, Christ,
3. Bushi mwa ndanda sai mu muthula mubishirwe emwandju woshi wekumenyerera emyasi newekuata ebwenge.	3. 부씨 뫄 따따 사이 무 무쭈ᄙᅡ 무비씨ᄅᆎ 어뫈쭈 오씨 워구머녀러라 어먀시 너워구아다 어ᄇᆎᅌᅥ.	3. in whom are hidden all the treasures of wisdom and knowledge.
4. Nababulyire bacha, chasiya kutabaa chiro na mundju asibya ola wabengeera na myasi yai ya bukalange.	4. 나바부ᄙᅦ러 바짜, 짜시야 구다바아 찌로 나 무쭈 아시뱌 오ᄙᅡ 와버ᅌᅥ어라 나 먀시 야이 야 부가ᄙᅡᅌᅥ.	4. I tell you this so that no one may deceive you by fine-sounding arguments.
5. Bushi chiro angaba nyiri bure nenyu kwa njira yemubiri, si kwa njira yemuchima nyinalyi alauma nenyu. Kanji nenjire namowa busese mwakulola kwa muchiri mwaira myasi era ilongomanyire, nebwemeresi bwenyu bunachiri busimikire mwa ndanda sa Kirisito.	5. 부씨 찌로 아ᅌᅡ바 네리 부러 너뉴 과 띠라 여무비리, 시 과 띠라 여무찌마 네나ᄙᅦ 아ᄙᅡ우마 너뉴. 가띠 너띠러 나모와 부서서 뫄구로ᄙᅡ 과 무찌리 뫄이라 먀시 어라 이로ᅌᅩ마네러, 너ᄇᆎ머러시 ᄇᆎ뉴 부나찌리 부시미기러 뫄 따따 사 기리시도.	5. For though I am absent from you in body, I am present with you in spirit and delight to see how orderly you are and how firm your faith in Christ is.
6. Rero, ngokwa mweemerere kwa Yesu Kirisito iEnawenyu, ku munaendekeraa kuba mwa buuma nai.	6. 러로, ᅌᅩ과 ᄆᆎ어머러러 과 여수 기리시도 이어나워뉴, 구 무나어떠거라아 구바 뫄 부우마 나이.	6. So then, just as you received Christ Jesus as Lord, continue to live in him,
7. Musimikaa mwa ndanda sai ngokwa emisi-misi yende	7. 무시미가아 뫄 따따 사이 ᅌᅩ과 어미시-미시 여떠 야쭈마	7. rooted and built up in him, strengthened in the

yathuma emuchi asimika mwa chitaka. Kanji imwendaa mwaimbira kwekalamo kenyu ngokwa bende baimbira endaana kwa musingi. Mundaa mwasimika busese mwa bwemeresi bwenyu, kukulyikana nokwa banabakangirisaa, na kunde mwaendekera kuteta mbu akoko era mwa Ongo.

8. Mumenyaa, kungesha kuba mundju ola wabatasa mwa myasi yai yebwenge, kanji ya bwengeere. Ei myasi yebuha-buha, ithula itenganyire nemyanya yebandju yekabuthwa, nokwa basimu ba bemire muno butala. Si itathula itenganyire na Kirisito.

9. Bushi ebuashi boshi bwa Ongo athusa, bu bunathula nomwa mubiri wa Kirisito.

10. Rero nenyu mwabonyire byoshi kurengera ebuuma bwenyu na Kirisito. Oyu Kirisito iuthula era luulu sa byoshi bya bimire nebya byete buashi.

11. Kanji kurengera ebuuma bwenyu na Kirisito, mwamonyisibwe. Oku kumonyisibwa kwenyu, kutairwaa na bandju, si Kirisito yeine iwabamonyise,

어무찌 아시미가 똬 찌다가. 가찌 이뭐따아 똬이뼤라 궈가꽈모 거뉴 꼬과 버떠 바이뼤라 어따아나 과 무시삐. 무따아 똬시미가 부서서 똬 뭐머러시 뭐뉴, 구구레가나 노과 바나바가삐리사아, 나 구떠 똬어떠거라 구더다 뿌 아고고 어라 똬 오꼬.

8. 무머냐아, 구떠싸 구바 무뚜 오라 와바다사 똬 먀시 야이 여뭐떠, 가찌 야 뭐떠어러. 어이 먀시 여부하-부하, 이쭈라 이더따네러 너먀냐 여바뚜 여가부화, 노과 바시무 바 버미러 무노 부다라. 시 이다쭈라 이더따네러 나 기리시도.

9. 부씨 어부아씨 보씨 봐 오꼬 아쭈사, 부 부나쭈라 노똬 무비리 와 기리시도.

10. 러로 너뉴 똬보네러 뵤씨 구러떠라 어부우마 뭐뉴 나 기리시도. 오유 기리시도 이우쭈라 어라 루우루 사 뵤씨 뱌 비미러 너뱌 벼더 부아씨.

11. 가찌 구러떠라 어부우마 뭐뉴 나 기리시도, 똬모네시뭐. 오구 구모네시봐 궈뉴, 구다이롸아 나 바뚜, 시 기리시도 여이너 이와바모네서, 똬 구바아구꽈

faith as you were taught, and overflowing with thankfulness.

8. See to it that no one takes you captive through hollow and deceptive philosophy, which depends on human tradition and the basic principles of this world rather than on Christ.

9. For in Christ all the fullness of the Deity lives in bodily form,

10. and you have been given fullness in Christ, who is the head over every power and authority.

11. In him you were also circumcised, in the putting off of the sinful nature, not with a circumcision done by the hands of men but with the circumcision done by

mwa kubaakula mwa myasi yemubiri era yendee yabeka mwa mabi.

꽈 먀시 여무비리 어라 여떠어 야버가 꽈 마비.

Christ,

12. Kurengera ekubatisibwa, mwatabwaa alauma na Kirisito. Kanji mwomolyibwe alauma nai, bushi mwemerere ebuashi bwa Ongo, iwamwoomolaa.

12. 구러꺼라 어구바디시봐, 꽈다봐아 아꽈우마 나 기리시도. 가찌 모모례붸 아꽈우마 나이, 부씨 뭐머러러 어부아씨 봐 오꼬, 이와모오모꽈라.

12. having been buried with him in baptism and raised with him through your faith in the power of God, who raised him from the dead.

13. Kwa mira, mwabaa musenekeko nga bandju ba bafire mira, bushi nemabi menyu, kanji bushi mwabaa mutamonyisibwe. Si Ongo erire abaira kuba bauma-uma alauma na Kirisito, na kubabalyira emabi methu moshi.

13. 과 미라, 꽈바아 무서너거고 까 바뚜 바 바피러 미라, 부씨 너마비 머뉴, 가찌 부씨 꽈바아 무다모네시붸. 시 오꼬 어리러 아바이라 구바 바우마-우마 아꽈우마 나 기리시도, 나 구바바례라 어마비 머쭈 모씨.

13. When you were dead in your sins and in the uncircumcision of your sinful nature, God made you alive with Christ. He forgave us all our sins,

14. Nethuratasi thweminda yethu era yendee yathusitaka era muhondo sai, aberengangireto mwa kukomerarato kwa musalaba.

14. 너쭈라다시 쮀미따 여쭈 어라 여떠어 야쭈시다가 어라 무호또 사이, 아버러꽈꺼러도 꽈 구고머라라도 과 무사꽈바.

14. having canceled the written code, with its regulations, that was against us and that stood opposed to us; he took it away, nailing it to the cross.

15. Mwa kuira bacha, Ongo anyaire ebuashi bwebasimu ba babaa bemire. Abeechise honyi mwa kubatambaisa changanama nga bandju ba mulyisi. Echera chalosa kwa aimirebo kurengera emusalaba weMwana wai.

15. 꽈 구이라 바짜, 오꼬 아냐이러 어부아씨 붸바시무 바 바바아 버미러. 아버어찌서 호네 꽈 구바다빠이사 짜꽈나마 까 바뚜 바 무례시. 어쩌라 짜로사 과 아이미러보 구러꺼라 어무사꽈바 워꽈나 와이.

15. And having disarmed the powers and authorities, he made a public spectacle of them, triumphing over them by the cross.

16. Bushi noku, mutendaa mweemerera mbu kubaa chiro na mundju asibya ola

16. 부씨 노구, 무더따아 뭐어머러라 뿌 구바아 찌로 나 무뚜 아시뱌 오꽈

16. Therefore do not let anyone judge you by what you eat or drink, or with

wabachinjibusa bushi nebya mwalya, nesi bya mwamwa, nesi bushi mutenjire mwathunda esuku sikulu seBayuta, ngakuno elusuku lukulu lwekubaluka kwemwesi, nesi elusuku lweSabato.

17. Bushi ebi byoshi, chinalyi chimbusa chemyasi era ikaika. Si ekanangana kemyasi, alyi Kirisito.

18. Kanji mutendaa mweemerera kuchinjibusibwa na chiro na mundju asibya, ola wachilosa mbu alyi murembu, enjire eera ne ndonyi. Bushi emundju ola ulyi ngoyu, ende abika emianyisa yai yoshi mwebya enjire alolako mwa biroto. Ende achitongera emianyisa yai yebuha-buha yemubiri.

19. Oyu mundu atemerera kuba mwa buuma na Kirisito, lyithwe lyemubiri. Bushi kurengera Kirisito, emubiri woshi ende alyisibwa kubuya na kwoomatanyisibwa alauma kurengera emvunyiro nemisi-misi. Aola, anakula kukulyikana nokwa Ongo asimire.

20. Mwabo mwafire alauma na Kirisito, kanji mwanunulyibwe kutenga mwa

와바찌띠부사 부씨 너뱌 먀퍄, 너시 뱌 먀먀, 너시 부씨 무더띠러 먀쭈따 어수구 시구루 서바유다, 퍄구노 어루수구 루구루루 뭐구바루가 귀뭐시, 너시 어루수구 뭐사바도.

17. 부씨 어비 뵤씨, 찌나레 찌뿌사 쩌먀시 어라 이가이가. 시 어가나퍼나 거먀시, 아레 기리시도.

18. 가띠 무더따아 뭐어머러라 구찌띠부시뫄 나 찌로 나 무뿌 아시뱌, 오롸 와찌로사 뿌 아레 무러뿌, 어띠러 어어라 너 또네. 부씨 어무뿌 오롸 우레 꼬유, 어떠 아비가 어미아네사 야이 요씨 뭐뱌 어띠러 아롸롸고 뫄 비로도. 어떠 아찌도떠라 어미아네사 야이 여부하-부하 여무비리.

19. 오유 무뿌 아더머러라 구바 뫄 부우마 나 기리시도, 레쭤 려무비리. 부씨 구러떠라 기리시도, 어무비리 옹씨 어떠 아레시뫄 구부야 나 꼬오마다네시뫄 아롸우마 구러떠라 어뿌네로 너미시-미시. 아오롸, 아나구롸 구구레가나 노과 오꼬 아시미러.

20. 뫄보 뫄피러 아롸우마 나 기리시도, 가띠 뫄누누레뷔 구더퍼 뫄 부아씨 뷔바시무

regard to a religious festival, a New Moon celebration or a Sabbath day.

17. These are a shadow of the things that were to come; the reality, however, is found in Christ.

18. Do not let anyone who delights in false humility and the worship of angels disqualify you for the prize. Such a person goes into great detail about what he has seen, and his unspiritual mind puffs him up with idle notions.

19. He has lost connection with the Head, from whom the whole body, supported and held together by its ligaments and sinews, grows as God causes it to grow.

20. Since you died with Christ to the basic principles of this world, why, as

buashi bwebasimu ba bathula bemire muno butala. Rero, chichera chingathuma mwaata mibere era iri nga yebandju bomuno butala, mwa kweemerera bende babaminyirira emiomba era itechire mbu:

21. "Utendaa walya chine! Utendaa watoma kwechi! Utendaa wauma kwechira!"

22. Ei miomba yoshi yerekere ebindju bya byende byakumba mwa kuba byera byakoresibwaa. Ei myasi benjire bakangirisa, inalyi miomba era yairwaa nebandju.

23. Ei miomba yende yalorekanako nga iri myasi ya bwenge, bushi yende yathuma ebandju bachiremba kweera Ongo, mwa kuchiira barembu na kulyibusa emibiri yabo. Si ebi byoshi bitathusa mufa kwa kwaangikabo kutakulyikira emianyisa yabo ibi yemubiri.

바 바쭈롸 버미러 무노 부다롸. 러로, 찌 쩌라 찌꺄쭈마 뫄아다 미버러 어라 이리 꺄 여바쭈 보무노 부다롸, 뫄 궈어머러라 버떠 바바미니리라 어미오빠 어라 이더찌러 뿌:

21. "우더따아 와롸 찌너! 우더따아 와도마 궈찌! 우더따아 와우마 궈찌라!"

22. 어이 미오빠 요씨 여러거러 어비쭈 뱌 벼떠 뱌구빠 뫄 구바 벼라 뱌고러시봐아. 어이 먀시 버찌러 바가꺼리사, 이나례 미오빠 어라 야이롸아 너바쭈.

23. 어이 미오빠 여너 야로러가나고 꺄 이리 먀시 야 붸어, 부씨 여너 야쭈마 어바쭈 바찌러빠 궈어라 오꽃, 뫄 구찌이라 바러뿌 나 구례부사 어미비리 야보. 시 어비 뵤씨 비다쭈사 무파 과 과아꺼가보 구다구례기라 어미아네사 야보 이비 여무비리.

though you still belonged to it, do you submit to its rules:

21. "Do not handle! Do not taste! Do not touch!"?

22. These are all destined to perish with use, because they are based on human commands and teachings.

23. Such regulations indeed have an appearance of wisdom, with their self-imposed worship, their false humility and their harsh treatment of the body, but they lack any value in restraining sensual indulgence.

E Bakolosai Chikono 3

1. Rero bushi mwomolyibwe alauma na Kirisito, mundaa mwahonda ebindju bya biri

어 바고로사이 찌고노 3

1. 러로 부씨 모모례붸 아롸우마 나 기리시도, 무따아 뫄호따 어비쭈 뱌 비리 과

Colossians Chapter 3[NIV]

1. Since, then, you have been raised with Christ, set your hearts on things above,

kwa nguba. Okola ku Kirisito ekese kwa lunda lwemalyo ma Ongo.

우바. 오고꽈 구 기리시도 어거서 과 루따 뤄마뢴 마 오꼬.

where Christ is seated at the right hand of God.

2. Ebi bindju byokwa nguba, bi mundaa mwaanyisako busese, si mutendaa mwaanyisa kwa bindju byomuno butala.

2. 어비 비쭈 뵤과 우바, 비 무따아 뫄아네사고 부서서, 시 무더따아 뫄아네사 과 비쭈 뵤무노 부다꽈.

2. Set your minds on things above, not on earthly things.

3. Bushi mwafire mira, nekalamo kenyu kabishirwe alauma na Kirisito mwa ndanda sa Ongo.

3. 부씨 뫄피러 미라, 너가꽈모 거뉴 가비씨뤄 아꽈우마 나 기리시도 뫄 따따 사 오꼬.

3. For you died, and your life is now hidden with Christ in God.

4. Kirisito ku kalamo kenyu. Mango akalorekanako, nenyu mukanalorekanako alauma nai, mwa bulangare bwai.

4. 기리시도 구 가꽈모 거뉴. 마꼬 아가뢰러가나고, 너뉴 무가나뢰러가나고 아꽈우마 나이, 뫄 부꽈꽈러 봐이.

4. When Christ, who is your life, appears, then you also will appear with him in glory.

5. Bushi noku, emyasi ibi yomuno butala, era ithula mwa ndanda senyu, murekanaa nai loshi. Nei myasi iyeene: elusingi, nemyasi yemahunga, nemianyisa yelusingi, nebuhuma-huma. Kanji murekaa kunde mwahumira ebikulo, bushi oku kuhumira ebikulo kwende kwathuma ebandju babitola nga iongo wabo.

5. 부씨 노구, 어먀시 이비 요무노 부다꽈, 어라 이쭈꽈 뫄 따따 서뉴, 무러가나아 나이 뢴씨. 너이 먀시 이여어너: 어루시삐, 너먀시 여마후꽈, 너미아네사 여루시삐, 너부후마-후마. 가찌 무러가아 구너 뫄후미라 어비구뢴, 부씨 오구 구후미라 어비구뢴 궈너 과쭈마 어바누 바비도꽈 꽈 이오꼬 와보.

5. Put to death, therefore, whatever belongs to your earthly nature: sexual immorality, impurity, lust, evil desires and greed, which is idolatry.

6. Ebyera bi bikathluma Ongo achinjibusa ba bende banana kumuthunda.

6. 어벼라 비 비가찌루마 오꼬 아찌찌부사 바 버너 바나나 구무쭈따.

6. Because of these, the wrath of God is coming.

7. Nenyu ku mwabaa munathula bacha kwa mira, mango mwabaa muchiri

7. 너뉴 구 뫄바아 무나쭈꽈 바짜 과 미라, 마꼬 뫄바아 무찌리 뫄무 마비.

7. You used to walk in these ways, in the life you once lived.

mwamu mabi.

8. Si rero, murekaa ene myasi ibi yoshi: ebusinane, nekufa ebute, nebukalyi, nekusinga emundju cha atairaa. Na mwa bunu bwenyu, mutendaa mwatenga myasi ya ngambo.

8. 시 러로, 무러가아 어너 먀시 이비 요씨: 어부시나너, 너구파 어부더, 너부가레, 너구시빠 어무뿌 짜 아다이라아. 나 뫄 부누 뷔뉴, 무더따아 뫄더빠 먀시 야 까뽀.

8. But now you must rid yourselves of all such things as these: anger, rage, malice, slander, and filthy language from your lips.

9. Mutendaa mweengeerana, bushi mutachiri ngokwa mwabaa muthula kwa mira, mwarekire nemyanya yenyu ibi era mwabaa muthusa.

9. 무더따아 뭐어꺼어라나, 부씨 무다찌리 끄과 뫄바아 무쭈꽈 과 미라, 뫄러기러 너먀냐 여뉴 이비 어라 뫄바아 무쭈사.

9. Do not lie to each other, since you have taken off your old self with its practices

10. Mwera bandju bayayaya. Na Ongo iwenjire wabaira kuba bayayaya chira lusuku, chasiya muhuuhane nai na kunde mwamumenyerera kanangana.

10. 뭐라 바뚜 바야야야. 나 오끄 이워찌러 와바이라 구바 바야야야 찌라 루수구, 짜시야 무후우하너 나이 나 구떠 뫄무머녀러라 가나빠나.

10. and have put on the new self, which is being renewed in knowledge in the image of its Creator.

11. Bushi noku, kutachiri Bayuta nesi Bakiriki, nesi banduj ba bamonyisibwe na ba batamonyisibwe, nesi babunga, nesi ba bata basamba, nesi thuungu na ba batathula thuungu. Si Kirisito iuthula era luulu sa byoshi, kanji iunathula mwa michima yebandju bai boshi.

11. 부씨 노구, 구다찌리 바우다 너시 바기리기, 너시 바뚜j 바 바모네시붜 나 바 바다모네시붜, 너시 바부빠, 너시 바 바다 바사빠, 너시 쭈우끄 나 바 바다쭈꽈 쭈우끄. 시 기리시도 이우쭈꽈 어라 루우루 사 뵤씨, 가찌 이우나쭈꽈 뫄 미찌마 여바뚜 바이 뵤씨.

11. Here there is no Greek or Jew, circumcised or uncircumcised, barbarian, Scythian, slave or free, but Christ is all, and is in all.

12. Ongo abalondore mira chasiya mube bandju bai basiirwa. Bushi noku, mundaa mwafirana bonjo, na kunde mwairirana emabuya. Kanji

12. 오끄 아바롣또러 미라 짜시야 무버 바뚜 바이 바시이롸. 부씨 노구, 무따아 뫄피라나 보쯔, 나 구떠 뫄이리라나 어마부야. 가찌

12. Therefore, as God's chosen people, holy and dearly loved, clothe yourselves with compassion, kindness, humility,

mundaa mwachirembeka na kuba balomvu na kunde mwasesa emichima.

무따아 뫄찌러뻐가 나 구바 바르로뿌 나 구떠 뫄서사 어미찌마.

gentleness and patience.

13. Mutendaa mwakulyikirana ku chira mwasi, si mundaa mwaata emuchima wekuba nebandju. Akaba mundju ete mwasi na mulyikabo, mundaa mwababalyirana ngokwa Enawethu nai anabababalyiraa.

13. 무더따아 뫄구레기라나 구 찌라 뫄시, 시 무따아 뫄아다 어무찌마 워구바 너바쭈. 아가바 무뿌 어더 뫄시 나 무레가보, 무따아 뫄바바레라나 끄과 어나워쭈 나이 아나바바바레라아.

13. Bear with each other and forgive whatever grievances you may have against one another. Forgive as the Lord forgave you.

14. Si emwasi munene mwebi byoshi kunalyi ekunde mwasimana. Bushi ekusimana ku kwende kwathuma ebandju baba mwa buuma bwekanangana.

14. 시 어뫄시 무너너 뭐비 뵤씨 구나레 어구떠 뫄시마나. 부씨 어구시마나 구 궈떠 과쭈마 어바쭈 바바 뫄 부우마 뭐가나뫄나.

14. And over all these virtues put on love, which binds them all together in perfect unity.

15. Eboolo bwa Kirisito bundaa bwakoresa emichima yenyu. Bushi obu boolo, bu bwathumaa Ongo abamaala, chasiya mube mubiri muuma. Mundaa mwateta mbu akoko era mwai.

15. 어보오르로 뫄 기리시도 부따아 뫄고러사 어미찌마 여뉴. 부씨 오부 보오르로, 부 뫄쭈마아 오끄 아바마아꽈, 짜시야 무버 무비리 무우마. 무따아 뫄더다 뿌 아고고 어라 뫄이.

15. Let the peace of Christ rule in your hearts, since as members of one body you were called to peace. And be thankful.

16. Emyasi ya Kirisito nebuare bwai, bindaa byaba mwa michima yenyu. Mundaa mwakangirisanya na kweeresanya emano mwa bwenge boshi. Mundaa mwateta mbu akoko era mwa Ongo mwa kumwimbira kwa michima yenyu yoshi. Mundaa

16. 어먀시 야 기리시도 너부아러 봐이, 비따아 뱌바 뫄 미찌마 여뉴. 무따아 뫄가삐리사냐 나 궈어러사냐 어마노 뫄 뭐써 보씨. 무따아 뫄더다 뿌 아고고 어라 뫄 오끄 뫄 구미뻬라 과 미찌마 여뉴 요씨. 무따아 뫄뮈뻬라 어네뽀 서사부리,

16. Let the word of Christ dwell in you richly as you teach and admonish one another with all wisdom, and as you sing psalms, hymns and spiritual songs with gratitude in your hearts to God.

mwamwimbira enyimbo sesaburi, nesekumutonga, nesa satenga era mweMuchima Mubuya-buya.	너서구무도꺄, 너사 사더꺄 어라 뭐무찌마 무부야-부야.	
17. Byoshi bya mungende mwaira mwa mitetere nesi mwa mikorere, mundaa mwairabi kwesina lya Enawethu Yesu. Na kumurengerako, mundaa mwateta mbu akoko era mwa Ongo Tata.	17. 뵤씨 뱌 무꺼떠 뫄이라 뫄 미더더러 너시 뫄 미고러러, 무따아 뫄이라비 궈시나 랴 어나워쭈 여수. 나 구무러꺼라고, 무따아 뫄더다 뿌 아고고 어라 뫄 오꼬 다다.	17. And whatever you do, whether in word or deed, do it all in the name of the Lord Jesus, giving thanks to God the Father through him.
18. Mu bakasi, mundaa mwathunda beba benyu ngokwa binemire era muhondo sa Enawethu.	18. 무 바가시, 무따아 뫄쭈따 버바 버뉴 꼬과 비너미러 어라 무호또 사 어나워쭈.	18. Wives, submit to your husbands, as is fitting in the Lord.
19. Nenyu mu balume, mundaa mwasima bakasi benyu. Kanji mutendaa mwabatola nga thuungu.	19. 너뉴 무 바루머, 무따아 뫄시마 바가시 버뉴. 가찌 무더따아 뫄바도롸 꺄 쭈우꾸.	19. Husbands, love your wives and do not be harsh with them.
20. Nenyu mu bana, mundaa mwathunda ebasere benyu mwa myasi yoshi. Bushi echera chende chasimisa Enawethu.	20. 너뉴 무 바나, 무따아 뫄쭈따 어바서러 버뉴 뫄 먀시 요씨. 부씨 어쩌라 쩌떠 짜시미사 어나워쭈.	20. Children, obey your parents in everything, for this pleases the Lord.
21. Nenyu mu batata, mutendaa mwasibusa ebana benyu, bangesha kunde bafunyika emichima.	21. 너뉴 무 바다다, 무더따아 뫄시부사 어바나 버뉴, 바꺼싸 구떠 바푸네가 어미찌마.	21. Fathers, do not embitter your children, or they will become discouraged.
22. Nenyu mu thuungu, mundaa mwathunda benawenyu bomuno butala mwa myasi yoshi. Mutendaa mwaira bacha mango	22. 너뉴 무 쭈우꾸, 무따아 뫄쭈따 버나워뉴 보무노 부다롸 뫄 먀시 요씨. 무더따아 뫄이라 바짜 마꼬 바바서너고 오싸아오, 과	22. Slaves, obey your earthly masters in everything; and do it, not only when their eye is on you and to win their favor, but with sincerity

babaseneko oshaao, kwa kuhonda mubasimise. Si mundaa mwathundabo na muchima mubuya, bushi mwende mwathunda Enawethu.

구호따 무바시미서. 시 무따아 마쭈따보 나 무찌마 무부야, 부씨 뭐떠 마쭈따 어나워쭈.

of heart and reverence for the Lord.

23. Na chira mulyimo woshi ola mungende mwakola, mundaa mwakolao na muchima muuma, nga bandju ba bakorera Enawethu, si batakorera mundju.

23. 나 찌라 무례모 오씨 오롸 무뻐떠 마고롸, 무따아 마고롸오 나 무찌마 무우마, 아 바뚜 바 바고러라 어나워쭈, 시 바다고러라 무뚜.

23. Whatever you do, work at it with all your heart, as working for the Lord, not for men,

24. Bushi mwishi kwa Enawethu Kirisito imwakorera, na iukaberesa elweembo lwa athula abikirire ebandju bai.

24. 부씨 뮈씨 과 어나워쭈 기리시도 이마고러라, 나 이우가버러사 어뤠어뽀 롸 아쭈롸 아비기리러 어바뚜 바이.

24. since you know that you will receive an inheritance from the Lord as a reward. It is the Lord Christ you are serving.

25. Si emundju ola wende wakola emabi, akaneembibwa kukulyikana nemabi mai. Bushi Ongo atathusa kalondo.

25. 시 어무뚜 오롸 워떠 와고롸 어마비, 아가너어삐봐 구구례가나 너마비 마이. 부씨 오꼬 아다쭈사 가론또.

25. Anyone who does wrong will be repaid for his wrong, and there is no favoritism.

E Bakolosai Chikono 4

1. Nenyu mu benawabo etHuungu, mundaa mwasimbato kubuya kwa njira era ithungenene kanji ya kanangana. Bushi nenyu mwishi kwa mwete Enawenyu kwa nguba.

어 바고론사이 찌고노 4

1. 너뉴 무 버나와보 어쭈우꾸, 무따아 마시빠도 구부야 과 띠라 어라 이쭈뻐너너 가찌 야 가나꽈나. 부씨 너뉴 뮈씨 과 뭐더 어나워뉴 과 꾸바.

Colossians Chapter 4[NIV]

1. Masters, provide your slaves with what is right and fair, because you know that you also have a Master in heaven.

2. Mundaa mwema Ongo busira kutama na kubika emianyisa yenyu yoshi mwamu memo. Mundaa

2. 무따아 뭐마 오꼬 부시라 구다마 나 구비가 어미아네사 여뉴 요씨 마무 머모. 무따아 마더다 뿌 아고고 어라 마이.

2. Devote yourselves to prayer, being watchful and thankful.

mwateta mbu akoko era
mwai.

3. Nethu, mundaa mwathwemera, chasiya Ongo athuboorere enjira yekunde thwahubanganyisa ebandju eChinwa chai, na kubabalyikisisa emyasi ya Kirisito era ibishirwe. Ei myasi iithumire naba muno buroko.

4. Mundaa mwanyemera chasiya nyinde nakangirisa kubuya-buya ei myasi yai, ngokwa binanyemire.

5. Mundaa mwachitola na bwenge mwa kachi-kachi kebandju ba batathula bemeresi, mwa kukoresa kubuya ebihangi bya mwabonyire.

6. Emitetere yenyu, esuku soshi indaa yaba ya kuahanyira, kanji era ilokerere. Mwa bacha, mungende mwamenyerera kute mungaakula chira mundju.

7. Emyasi yanyi yoshi, munyakethu musiirwa Tikiko, iungababalyikisisai. Oyu Tikiko alyi mukosi mulyikethu mubuya mwa mulyimo wa Enawethu.

3. 너쭈, 무따아 뫄쭤머라, 짜시야 오꼬 아쭈보오러러 어찌라 여구떠 쫘후바까네사 어바쭈 어찌놔 짜이, 나 구바바뤠기시사 어먀시 야 기리시도 어라 이비씨뤄. 어이 먀시 이이쭈미러 나바 무노 부로고.

4. 무따아 뫄녀머라 짜시야 네떠 나가끼리사 구부야-부야 어이 먀시 야이, 꼬과 비나녀미러.

5. 무따아 뫄찌도롸 나 붸어 뫄 가찌-가찌 거바쭈 바 바다쭈롸 버머러시, 뫄 구고러사 구부야 어비하끼 뱌 뫄보네러.

6. 어미더더러 여뉴, 어수구 소씨 이따아 야바 야 구아하네라, 가찌 어라 이로거러러. 뫄 바쨔, 무어러 뫄머녀러라 구더 무까아구롸 찌라 무뿌.

7. 어먀시 야네 요씨, 무냐거쭈 무시이롸 디기고, 이우까바바뤠기시사이. 오유 디기고 아뤠 무고시 무뤠거쭈 무부야 뫄 무뤠모 와 어나워쭈.

3. And pray for us, too, that God may open a door for our message, so that we may proclaim the mystery of Christ, for which I am in chains.

4. Pray that I may proclaim it clearly, as I should.

5. Be wise in the way you act toward outsiders; make the most of every opportunity.

6. Let your conversation be always full of grace, seasoned with salt, so that you may know how to answer everyone.

7. Tychicus will tell you all the news about me. He is a dear brother, a faithful minister and fellow servant in the Lord.

8. Nabathumiraai chasiya ababalyikisise kwa myasi yethu, abasese nemichima.

9. Angabaha na munyakethu musiirwa Onesimo. Oyu Onesimo, alyi mwesha eyi mwenyu, kanji mundju wa kuchinyiirawa. Abu babiri, bu bangababalyikisisa emyasi yoshi era yarenga enera.

10. Mulyikethu Arisitariko ola thuminyirwe nai, abalamusise. Mariko, musala wa Baranaba, nai abalamusise. Akaika eyi mwenyu, mumuhuukasaa kubuya ngokwa nanababuraa.

11. Yesu ola bende berika kanji mbu Yusuto, nai abalamusise. Mwa Bayuta ba beemerere Kirisito, abu bandju bahathu oshaao bu banakola nanyi mwa mulyimo ola werekere ebwamwi bwa Ongo. Banyisesise emuchima busese.

12. Epafura, mwesha eyi mwenyu, nai abalamusise. Nai anathula mukosi wa Yesu Kirisito. Kanji athusa bushiru bunene bwekubemera era mwa Ongo, chasiya musimike na kukula mwa bwemeresi, na

8. 나바쭈미라아이 짜시야 아바바페기시서 과 먀시 여쭈, 아바서서 너미찌마.

9. 아까바하 나 무냐거쭈 무시이롸 오너시모. 오유 오너시모, 아페 뭐싸 어에 뭐뉴, 가찌 무뚜 와 구찌네이라와. 아부 바비리, 부 바까바바페기시사 어먀시 요씨 어라 야러까 어너라.

10. 무페거쭈 아리시다리고 오롸 쭈미네뤄 나이, 아바짜무시서. 마리고, 무사꽈 와 바라나바, 나이 아바라무시서. 아가이가 어에 뭐뉴, 무무후우가사아 구부야 꼬과 나나바부라아.

11. 여수 오롸 버떠 버리가 가찌 뿌 유수도, 나이 아바짜무시서. 롸 바유다 바 버어머러러 기리시도, 아부 바뚜 바하쭈 오싸아오 부 바나고꽈 나네 롸 무페모 오롸 워러거러 어봐뮈 봐 오꼬. 바네서시서 어무찌마 부서서.

12. 어파푸라, 뭐싸 어에 뭐뉴, 나이 아바짜무시서. 나이 아나쭈꽈 무고시 와 여수 기리시도. 가찌 아쭈사 부씨루 부너너 뭐구버머라 어라 롸 오꼬, 짜시야 무시미거 나 구구꽈 롸 뭐머러시, 나

8. I am sending him to you for the express purpose that you may know about our circumstances and that he may encourage your hearts.

9. He is coming with Onesimus, our faithful and dear brother, who is one of you. They will tell you everything that is happening here.

10. My fellow prisoner Aristarchus sends you his greetings, as does Mark, the cousin of Barnabas. (You have received instructions about him; if he comes to you, welcome him.)

11. Jesus, who is called Justus, also sends greetings. These are the only Jews among my fellow workers for the kingdom of God, and they have proved a comfort to me.

12. Epaphras, who is one of you and a servant of Christ Jesus, sends greetings. He is always wrestling in prayer for you, that you may stand firm in all the will of God, mature and fully assured.

kweemerera loshi kunde mwaira chira mwasi woshi ola Ongo asimire.

13. Oyu Epafura, enjire akola busese bushi nenyu, na bushi na banyakethu bemeresi bomwa musi we Laotikiya, nebomwa musi we Hiyerapoli. Natechire bacha bushi nachilorere kwei myasi.

14. Munyakethu musiirwa, munganga Luka, na Tema, nabo babalamusise.

15. Mulamusaa banyakethu bomwa musi we Laotikiya. Mwanalamusa na Nimufa, alauma nebemeresi ba benjire babuanana mwa mwai.

16. Mango mungaba mwasomire mano maruba mira, mwanaira emisi yenyu yoshi maye kusomibwa mwa kachi-kachi kebemeresi bomwa musi we Laotikiya. Nemaruba ma nathumiraabo, nenyu babathumiraamo mumasome.

17. Muburaa Arikipo mbu akolaa kubuya emulyimo ola Enawethu amweresise, kuikira amalyiriseo.

18. Ene myasi yekubalamusa, nyono Paulo nyi nabaanjikirirei mwa mino yanyi nyeine. Mutebiriraa kwa

---

궈어머러라 른씨 구떠 먀이라 찌라 먀시 온씨 오롸 오꼬 아시미러.

13. 오유 어파푸라, 어찌러 아고롸 부서서 부씨 너뉴, 나 부씨 나 바냐거쭈 버머러시 보먀 무시 워 롸오디기야, 너보먀 무시 워 히여라포릐. 나더찌러 바짜 부씨 나찌론러러 궈이 먀시.

14. 무냐거쭈 무시이롸, 무까까 루가, 나 더마, 나보 바바롸무시서.

15. 무롸무사아 바냐거쭈 보먀 무시 워 롸오디기야. 먀나롸무사 나 니무파, 아롸우마 너버머러시 바 버찌러 바부아나나 먀 마이.

16. 마꼬 무까바 먀소미러 마노 마루바 미라, 먀나이라 어미시 여뉴 요씨 마여 구소미봐 먀 가찌-가찌 거버머러시 보먀 무시 워 롸오디기야. 너마루바 마 나쭈미라아보, 너뉴 바바쭈미라아모 무마소머.

17. 무부라아 아리기포 뿌 아고롸아 구부야 어무뤠모 오롸 어나워쭈 아뭐러시서, 구이기라 아마뤠리서오.

18. 어너 먀시 여구바롸무사, 뇨노 파우론 네 나바아찌기리러이 먀 미노 야니 녀이너. 무더비리라아 과

---

13. I vouch for him that he is working hard for you and for those at Laodicea and Hierapolis.

14. Our dear friend Luke, the doctor, and Demas send greetings.

15. Give my greetings to the brothers at Laodicea, and to Nympha and the church in her house.

16. After this letter has been read to you, see that it is also read in the church of the Laodiceans and that you in turn read the letter from Laodicea.

17. Tell Archippus: "See to it that you complete the work you have received in the Lord."

18. I, Paul, write this greeting in my own hand. Remember my chains. Grace be with you.

nyichiri mwa buroko. Ongo
endaa abaahanyira!

네찌리 마 부로고. 오꼬
어따아 아바아하네라!

1 E Batesalonika

1 어 바더사룐니가

1 Thessalonians

BATESALONIKA BA BEREBERE

(1 TESALONIANS)

바더사룐니가 바 버러버러

(1 더사룐니아뚜)

1 E Batesalonika Chikono 1

1. Nyono Paulo alauma na Sirifano na Timoteo, tchutchwa baandjikiraa manu maruba, mu beemeri ba mwa musi we Tesalonika. Mwabo mulyi bandju ba Kabumbi Tata, kandji mwanaba bandju ba ewawetchu Yesu Kirisito. Kabumbi Tata endaa abaahanyira ne kubeeresa eboolo.

2. Tchwendjire tchwateta mbu akoko era mwa Kabumbi esuku soshi bushi nenyu muboshi, nekunde tchwabakengera mwa meemo metchu.

3. Tchwendjire tchwabakengera busira kutama bushi ebwemeresi bwenyu kukola ku bwanakola, ne nzii yenyu yendjire yatchuma mwalyibuka busese nemirimo, kandji bushi musimikire mwa munyiiro ola mucthusa mwa ndanda sa Enawetchu.

4. Banyaketchu, tchwishi kwa Kabumbi atchula abasimire, kandji abalondoree mira mube bandju bai.

5. Bushi mangu tchwabahubanganyisaa emwaasi mubuya-buya,

1 어 바더사뤄니가 찌고노 1

1. 뇨노 파우뤄 아퐈우마 나 시리파노 나 디모더오, 쭈쫘 바아씨기라아 마누 마루바, 무 버어머리 바 뫄 무시 워 더사뤄니가. 뫄보 무뤠 바뉴 바 가부쀄 다다, 가찌 뫄나바 바뉴 바 여와워쭈 여수 기리시도. 가부쀄 다다 어따아 아바아하네라 너 구버어러사 어보오뤄.

2. 쭤찌러 쫘더다 뿌 아고고 어라 뫄 가부쀄 어수구 소씨 부씨 너뉴 무보씨, 너구떠 쫘바거어라 뫄 머어모 머쭈.

3. 쭤찌러 쫘바거어라 부시라 구다마 부씨 어뷔머러시 뷔뉴 구고꽈 구 봐나고꽈, 너 씨이 여뉴 여찌러 야쭈마 뫄뤠부가 부서서 너미리모, 가찌 부씨 무시미기러 뫄 무네이로 오꽈 무쭊사 뫄 따따 사 어나워쭈.

4. 바냐거쭈, 쮜씨 과 가부쀄 아쭈꽈 아바시미러, 가찌 아바뤄또러어 미라 무버 바뉴 바이.

5. 부씨 마꾸 쫘바후바꽈네사아 어뫄아시 무부야-부야,

1 Thessalonians Chapter 1 [NIV]

1. Paul, Silas and Timothy, To the church of the Thessalonians in God the Father and the Lord Jesus Christ: Grace and peace to you.

2. We always thank God for all of you, mentioning you in our prayers.

3. We continually remember before our God and Father your work produced by faith, your labor prompted by love, and your endurance inspired by hope in our Lord Jesus Christ.

4. For we know, brothers loved by God, that he has chosen you,

5. because our gospel came to you not simply with words, but also with power,

tchubahubanganyisaa'wo kwa bieta oshao si tchwabahubanganyisaa'wo ne buashi nekuasibwa nemutchima mubuya-buya kandji tchwabaa tchuneshi kubuya kwa analyi mwaasi wa kanangana. Nenyu muneshi kubuya kute tchwabaa tchwendjire tchwatchitola mwa katchi-katchi kenyu, tchasiya tchubaatchire mufa.

쭈바후바빠네사아오 과 비어다 오싸오 시 좌바후바빠네사아오 너 부아씨 너구아시봐 너무찌마 무부야-부야 가찌 좌바아 쭈너씨 구부야 과 아나쩨 봐아시 와 가나빠나. 너뉴 무너씨 구부야 구더 좌바아 쭤찌러 좌찌도롸 마 가찌- 가찌 거뉴, 짜시야 쭈바아찌러 무파.

with the Holy Spirit and with deep conviction. You know how we lived among you for your sake.

6. Nenyu mwerire mweeya emyanya yetchu, ne kweeya emyanya ya Enawetchu. Kandji tchiro angaba mbu mwangiriraa etchinwa tcha Kabumbi mu malyibuko manene, si mwana angiriraa'cthi ne lumoo, lwe mutchima mubuya-buya enda aana.

6. 너뉴 뭐리러 뭐어야 어먀냐 여쭈, 너 귀어야 어먀냐 야 어나워쭈. 가찌 찌로 아빠바 뿌 뫄이리라아 어찌놔 짜 가부삐 무 마쩨부고 마너너, 시 뫄나 아삐리라아찌 너 루모오, 뤠 무찌마 무부야-부야 어따 아아나.

6. You became imitators of us and of the Lord; in spite of severe suffering, you welcomed the message with the joy given by the Holy Spirit.

7. Mwa kuira batcha, mwerire mwalosa emyanya ibuya kwa bemeresi boshi bomwa tchiio tche Maketoniya ne tcha Akaya.

7. 뫄 구이라 바짜, 뭐리러 뫄로사 어먀냐 이부야 과 버머러시 보씨 보뫄 찌이오 쩌 마거도니야 너 짜 아가야.

7. And so you became a model to all the believers in Macedonia and Achaia.

8. Bushi eyi mwenyu yi etchinwa tcha Enawetchu tchatengeraa, na tchahandabana mwebi biio bibiri. Kandji ata na mwebi biio bibiri byeine, si na mwa bindji bisiki byoshi, e bandju baneshi

8. 부씨 어에 뭐뉴 에 어찌놔 짜 어나워쭈 짜더빠라아, 나 짜하따바나 뭐비 비이오 비비리. 가찌 아다 나 뭐비 비이오 비비리 벼이너, 시 나 뫄 비찌 비시기 보씨, 어 바뉴 바너씨 과 무쭈롸

8. The Lord's message rang out from you not only in Macedonia and Achaia--your faith in God has become known everywhere. Therefore we do not need to say anything about it,

kwa mutchula mwemerere Kabumbi. Rero, tchutatete tcha tchatchungahuba kuteta era luulu sobu bwemeresi bwenyu.

9. Bushi abu bandju beine bendjire babalyikisa kwa mwatchuhuukasaa mango tchwaikaa eyi mwenyu, nokwa mwarekire kunde mweera ebasimu, mwemerera kabumbi, ne kunde mwamukorera bushi iutchula muuma-uma, kandji iwe kanangana.

10. Kandji kulyindjira ku mwera mwalyindjira emwana wai Yesu atenga kwa nguba. Oyola i Ongo oomolaa mwa bafu na iwende watchununula kwa bucthindjibusi bwa Kabumbi bwa bweeshire.

뭐머러러 가부삐. 러로, 쭈다더더 짜 짜쭈까후바 구더다 어라 루우루 소부 뭐머러시 뷔뉴.

9. 부씨 아부 바쭈 버이너 버찌러 바바레기사 과 마쭈후우가사아 마꼬 짜이가아 어에 뭐뉴, 노과 마러기러 구떠 뭐어라 어바시무, 뭐머러라 가부삐, 너 구떠 마무고러라 부씨 이우쭈짜 무우마-우마, 가찌 이워 가나까나.

10. 가찌 구레찌라 구 뭐라 마레찌라 어마나 와이 여수 아더까 과 꾸바. 오요짜 이 오꼬 오오모라아 마 바푸 나 이워떠 와쭈누누짜 과 부찌찌부시 봐 가부삐 봐 뭐어씨러.

9. for they themselves report what kind of reception you gave us. They tell how you turned to God from idols to serve the living and true God,

10. and to wait for his Son from heaven, whom he raised from the dead--Jesus, who rescues us from the coming wrath.

1 E Batesalonika Chikono 2

1 어 바더사로니가 찌고노 2

1 Thessalonians Chapter 2 [HIV]

1. E banyeketchu! Si mubeine muneeshi kwa ekubalamira kwetchu eyi mwenyu kwabaa kwete mutoloke.

1. 어 바녀거쭈! 시 무버이너 무너어씨 과 어구바짜미라 궈쭈 어에 뭐뉴 과바아 궈더 무도로거.

1. You know, brothers, that our visit to you was not a failure.

2. Bushi mwishi kwa era muhondo tchuike eyi mwenyu, besha mwa musi we Firiei batchulosaa kwa kasibu ne kutchukamba-kamba. Si tchiro angaba mbu e bandju batchulwisaa busese, Kabumbi

2. 부씨 뮈씨 과 어라 무호또 쭈이거 어에 뭐뉴, 버싸 마 무시 워 피리어이 바쭈로사아 과 가시부 너 구쭈가빠-가빠. 시 찌로 아까바 뿌 어 바쭈 바쭈뤼사아 부서서, 가부삐

2. We had previously suffered and been insulted in Philippi, as you know, but with the help of our God we dared to tell you his gospel in spite of strong opposition.

era kucthweeresa ebushiru bwe kubahubanganyisa emwaasi mubuya-buya.

3. Emyaasi era tchwendjire tchwahubanganyisa ebandju, ita ya bisha. Kandji italyi lu mianyisa ibi nesi butebanyi.

4. Si kabumbi yeine iwatchweeresaa oyu mwaasi mubuya-buya, bushi alolaa kwa tchutchungenene era muhondo sai. O mwa kuhubanganya'wo tchutendjire tchwahonda kusimisa bandju, si Kabumbi bushi iwishi bya biri mwa mitchima yetchu.

5. Mubeine muneshi kubuyabuya kwa kutalyi lusuku lwa tchwatetaa myaasi ya butebanyi era muhondo se bandju nesi ya kuhonda mutoloke we bikulo. Kabumbi alyi mubei wetchu.

6. Kandji tchwaba tchutahonda ebandju batchutonge, abe mwabo, nesi bandji bandji

7. Mango tchwabaa tchulyi mwa katchi-katchi kenyu, kutchimanga'ku ku tchungendjire tchwatchiimanga'ku era muhondo seny, tchubone bya

어라 구쭤어러사 어부씨루 뭐 구바후바꺄네사 어먀아시 무부야-부야.

3. 어먀아시 어라 쭤찌러 쫘후바꺄네사 어바쭈, 이다 야 비싸. 가찌 이다레 루 미아네사 이비 너시 부더바네.

4. 시 가부쀄 여이너 이와쭤어러사아 오유 먀아시 무부야-부야, 부씨 아르꽈아 과 쭈쭈꺄너너 어라 무호또 사이. 오 먀 구후바꺄냐옷 쭈더찌러 쫘호따 구시미사 바쭈, 시 가부쀄 부씨 이위씨 뱌 비리 꽈 미찌마 여쭈.

5. 무버이너 무너씨 구부야부야 과 구다레 루수구 꽈 쫘더다아 먀아시 야 부더바네 어라 무호또 서 바쭈 너시 야 구호따 무도르거 워 비구르. 가부쀄 아레 무버이 워쭈.

6. 가찌 쫘바 쭈다호따 어바쭈 바쭈도꺼, 아버 먀보, 너시 바찌 바쭈

7. 마꼬 쫘바아 쭈레 먀 가찌-가찌 거뉴, 구찌마꺄구 구 쭈꺼찌러 쫘찌이마꺄구 어라 무호또 서네, 쭈보너 뱌 쭈꽈이러구, 부씨 쭈레 누꽈 사 기리시도. 시

3. For the appeal we make does not spring from error or impure motives, nor are we trying to trick you.

4. On the contrary, we speak as men approved by God to be entrusted with the gospel. We are not trying to please men but God, who tests our hearts.

5. You know we never used flattery, nor did we put on a mask to cover up greed-- God is our witness.

6. We were not looking for praise from men, not from you or anyone else. As apostles of Christ we could have been a burden to you,

7. but we were gentle among you, like a mother caring for her little children.

tchulaire'ku, bushi tchulyi ndjumwa sa Kirisito. Si tchwabalosaaa eburembi ngoka emukasi ende alosa ebondjo kwa bana bai.

8. Tchubasimire busese batcha ata mwakubangirisa emwaasi mubuya-buya wa Kabumbi weine oshao, si kandji tchwabaa tchwemerere kwana ne kalamo kute bushi nenyu. Kubinalyi, tchwera tchubasimire ngatchi.

9. Banyaketchu, si mutchikengere kwa mango tchwabaa tchwendjire tchwabakangirisa emwaasi mubuya-buya wa Kabumbi, ndjubano itchwabaa tchwendjire tchweeshika ne mirimo emushi ne butchufu. Tchwairaa batcha, bushi thwabaa tchutahonda kusitowera mundju asibya mwa malae metchu.

10. Mango tchwabaa tchulyi mwa katchi-katchi kenyu mu bemeresi, tchwbaa tchwendjire tchwabalosa myanya ibuya, kandji era itchungenene, kandji era bandju batanga tchushitaka'ku tchiro na mwaasi mubi asibya, mubeine mwana tchiloreraa kui, na kabumbi nai anailolaa'ku.

좌바로사아아 어부러삐 끄가 어무가시 어떠 아로사 어보쪼 과 바나 바이.

8. 쭈바시미러 부서서 바짜 아다 꽈구바삐리사 어뫄아시 무부야-부야 와 가부삐 워이너 오쌰오, 시 가끼 좌바아 쭤머러러 과나 너 가꽈모 구더 부씨 너뉴. 구비나레, 쭤라 쭈바시미러 까찌.

9. 바냐거쭈, 시 무찌거어러 과 마끄 좌바아 쭤찌러 좌바가삐리사 어뫄아시 무부야-부야 와 가부삐, 쑤바노 이좌바아 쭤찌러 쭤어씨가 너 미리모 어무씨 너 부쭈푸. 좌이라아 바짜, 부씨 좌바아 쭈다호따 구시도워라 무뚜 아시뱌 뫄 마꽈어 머쭈.

10. 마끄 좌바아 쭤레 뫄 가찌-가찌 거뉴 무 버머러시, 좌바아 쭤찌러 좌바로사 먀냐 이부야, 가찌 어라 이쭈떠너너, 가찌 어라 바뿌 바다따 쭈씨다가구 찌로 나 뫄아시 무비 아시뱌, 무버이너 뫄나 찌로러라아 구이, 나 가부삐 나이 아나이로꽈아구.

8. We loved you so much that we were delighted to share with you not only the gospel of God but our lives as well, because you had become so dear to us.

9. Surely you remember, brothers, our toil and hardship; we worked night and day in order not to be a burden to anyone while we preached the gospel of God to you.

10. You are witnesses, and so is God, of how holy, righteous and blameless we were among you who believed.

11. Kandji muneshi kubuya-kubuya kwa tchwabaa tchwendjire tchwatola tchira muuma mu mwabo ngokwa eshi web ana enda anatola ebana bai.

12. Tchwabaa tchwendjire tchwabasesa emutchima, ne kuberesa emaano. Kandji tchwabaa tchwendjire tchwabeema buses embu mundaa mwaata mibere era isimisi Kabumbi. Bushi oyu Kambumbi iwendjire wabaamaala ; tchasiya mwengirire mwa bwami bwai, na kuikala mwa bulangare bwai.

13. Etchindji tcha tchandjire tchatchuma tchwateta mbu akoko era mwa Kabumbi esuku soshi, tchi tchitchine : mango tchwabareteraa e cthinwa tchai, mutangiriraa tchi nga tchiri tcha bandju, si mwangiriraa'tchi kwa tchunalyi tcha Kabumbi kanangana. Ne'tchi tchinwa, tchi tchendjire tchakola mwa mitchima yenyu, mu beemeresi.

14. Rero banyaketchu, mwalyibusibwaa na besha eyi mwenyu, ngokwa ebemeresi bo mwa nyuhu sa Kabumbi somwa chiio tche Yuteya, nabo

11. 가찌 무너씨 구부야-구부야 과 쫘바아 쭤찌러 쫘도롸 찌라 무우마 무 뫄보 꼬과 어씨 워부 아나 어따 아나도롸 어바나 바이.

12. 쫘바아 쭤찌러 쫘바서사 어무찌마, 너 구버러사 어마아노. 가찌 쫘바아 쭤찌러 쫘버어마 부서수 어뿌 무따아 뫄아다 미버러 어라 이시미시 가부쁴. 부씨 오유 가뿌쁴 이워찌러 와바아마아롸 ; 짜시야 뭐ㅉ리리러 뫄 봐미 봐이, 나 구이가롸 뫄 부롸ㅉ러 봐이.

13. 어찌찌 짜 짜찌러 짜쭈마 쫘더다 뿌 아고고 어라 뫄 가부쁴 어수구 소씨, 찌 찌찌너 : 마꼬 쫘바러더라아 어 찌뇨 짜이, 무다ㅉ리라아 찌 ㄸ 찌리 짜 바뚜, 시 마ㅉ리리아아찌 과 쭈나레 짜 가부쁴 가나바나. 너찌 찌뇨, 찌 쩌찌러 짜고롸 뫄 미찌마 여뉴, 무 버어머러시.

14. 러로 바냐거쭈, 마레부시봐아 나 버싸 어에 뭐뉴, 꼬과 어버머러시 보 뫄 뉴후 사 가부쁴 소뫄 찌이오 쩌 유더야, 나보

11. For you know that we dealt with each of you as a father deals with his own children,

12. encouraging, comforting and urging you to live lives worthy of God, who calls you into his kingdom and glory.

13. And we also thank God continually because, when you received the word of God, which you heard from us, you accepted it not as the word of men, but as it actually is, the word of God, which is at work in you who believe.

14. For you, brothers, became imitators of God's churches in Judea, which are in Christ Jesus: You suffered from your own countrymen

babalyibusibwaa na banyakabo
Bayuta.

바바쩨부시봐아 나 바냐가보
바유다.

the same things those churches suffered from the Jews,

15. Abu Bayuta bu baneetaa Enawetchu Yesu ne kunde beeta ebarebi anabe netchu, banatchulosaa kwa kasibu mwa kuira, bendjire basibusa Kabumbi, ne kuba barenda be bandju boshi.

15. 아부 바유다 부 바너어다아 어나워쭈 여수 너 구떠 버어다 어바러비 아나버 너쭈, 바나쭈로사아 과 가시부 뫄 구이라, 버찌러 바시부사 가부삐, 너 구바 바러따 버 바쭈 보씨.

15. who killed the Lord Jesus and the prophets and also drove us out. They displease God and are hostile to all men

16. Bendjire batchwaanganyika mbu tchutahubanganyisaa ebandju ba bateshi Kabumbi emyassi era ingatchuma nabu banunulyibwa aola, bendjire batchuma ebibi bye bende baira esuku soshi byerengeresa. Si ebusinane bwa Kabumbi kwetchwe lyabo ku bwera bulyi.

16. 버찌러 바쫘아안네가 뿌 쭈다후바까네사아 어바쭈 바 바더씨 가부삐 어먀씨 어라 이까쭈마 나부 바누누쩨봐 아오롸, 버찌러 바쭈마 어비비 벼 버더 바이라 어수구 소씨 벼러어러사. 시 어부시나너 봐 가부삐 궈쭤 쨔보 구 붜라 부쎼.

16. in their effort to keep us from speaking to the Gentiles so that they may be saved. In this way they always heap up their sins to the limit. The wrath of God has come upon them at last.

17. Banyeketchu, tchwerekanaa nenyu kwa mubiri ku suku sieke, si kwa mucthima tchwabaa tchunalyi alauma. Bushi noku, tchwairaa emisi yetchu, tchasiya tchuhube kubalola'ku.

17. 바녀거쭈, 쭤러가나아 너뉴 과 무비리 구 수구 시어거, 시 과 무찌마 쫘바아 쭈나쩨 아롸우마. 부씨 노구, 쫘이라아 어미시 여쭈, 짜시야 쭈후버 구바를롸구.

17. But, brothers, when we were torn away from you for a short time (in person, not in thought), out of our intense longing we made every effort to see you.

18. Tchwabaa tchwahonda tchuhube kuika eyi mwenyu. Na nyono Paulo tanga ; nakunganyaa elubalamo mbiso sinene, si wamusimu era kunde atchwaaangika.

18. 쫘바아 쫘호따 쭈후버 구이가 어에 뮤뉴. 나 뇨노 파우롣 다까 ; 나구까냐아 어뤂바꽈모 쎼소 시너너, 시 와무시무 어라 구떠 아쫘아아끼가.

18. For we wanted to come to you--certainly I, Paul, did, again and again--but Satan stopped us.

19. Kanangana, mwabo mu mutchumire tchwaata

19. 가나까나, 뫄보 무 무쭈미러 쫘아다 어무네이로,

19. For what is our hope, our joy, or the crown in

emunyiiro, ne lumoo. Kandji mwabo mu mulyi nga nzita era tchuka tchitongera era muhondo sa Enawetchu Yesu mango akafuluka.	너 룰모오. 가ᄣᅵ 와보 무 무ᄙᅦ ᄢᅡ ᄣᅵ다 어라 쭈가 찌도ᄢᅥ라 어라 무호ᄯᅩ 사 어나워쭈 여수 마ᅇᅩ 아가푸룰가.	which we will glory in the presence of our Lord Jesus when he comes? Is it not you?
20. Kubinalyi! Mwabo mwendjire mwatchuma tchwatchitonga ne kuata elumoo.	20. 구비나ᄙᅦ! 와보 뭐ᄣᅵ러 와쭈마 쫘찌도ᄢᅡ 너 구아다 어룰모오.	20. Indeed, you are our glory and joy.

1 E Batesalonika Chikono 3	**1 어 바더사뢀니가 찌고노 3**	**1 Thessalonians Chapter 3 [HIV]**
1. Kuire tchwashiba mwa misi we Atene	1. 구이러 쫘씨바 와 미시 워아더너	1. So when we could stand it no longer, we thought it best to be left by ourselves in Athens.
2. Oyu Timoteo alyi mukosi mulyiketchu ola tchwendjire tchwakola nai emulyimo wa Kabumbi, mwa kuhubanganyisa ebandju emwaasi mubuya-buya wa Yesu Kirisito, tchwabatchumirire'i, aabse kusimika ne kubasesa emitchima mwa bwemeresi bwenyu.	2. 오유 디모더오 아ᄙᅦ 무고시 무ᄙᅦ거쭈 오ᄙᅡ 쭤ᄣᅵ러 쫘고ᄙᅡ 나이 어무ᄙᅦ모 와 가부ᄤᅦ, 와 구후바ᄢᅡ네사 어바ᄶᅮ 어와아시 무부야-부야 와 여수 기리시도, 쫘바쭈미리러이, 아아부서 구시미가 너 구바서사 어미찌마 와 붜머러시 붜뉴.	2. We sent Timothy, who is our brother and God's fellow workerin spreading the gospel of Christ, to strengthen and encourage you in your faith,
3. Tchasiya tchutabaa tchiro ne mundju asibya mwa katchi-katchi kenyu, ola ungalyiya lyiya mwa bwemeresi bushi na mano malyibuko tchwarengere'mu. Si mubeine	3. 짜시야 쭈다바아 찌로 너 무ᄶᅮ 아시뱌 와 가찌-가찌 거뉴, 오ᄙᅡ 우ᄢᅡᄙᅦ야 ᄙᅦ야 와 붜머러시 부씨 나 마노 마ᄙᅦ부고 쫘러ᄢᅥ러무. 시 무버이너 무너씨 과 아무	3. so that no one would be unsettled by these trials. You know quite well that we were destined for them.

muneshi kwa amu malyibuko, manalyi mwa kwa kuhonda kwa kabumbi.

마레부고, 마나레 뫄 과 구호따 과 가부뻬.

4. Mango tchwabaa tchutchiri eyi mwenyu, tchwabaa tchwendjire tchwababura kwa byeemire tchunde tchwalyibuka busese. Rero, ku byanabere ngokwa munasene.

4. 마꼬 쫘바아 쭈찌리 어에 뮈뉴, 쫘바아 쭤찌러 쫘바부라 과 벼어미러 쭈떠 쫘레부가 부서서. 러로, 구 뱌나버러 꼬과 무나서너.

4. In fact, when we were with you, we kept telling you that we would be persecuted. And it turned out that way, as you well know.

5. Bushi noku, mango nalolaa kwa ndangatchiala kulyindjirira, nera kuire nabatchumira Timoteo, tchasiya nyimenyerere emyaasi ye bwemeresi bwenyu. Bushi nabaa nobaa mbu abunya wa musimu aerekire ebwemeresi bwenyu, kuikira etchihangi si emulyimo tchwakolaa mwa katchi-katchi kenyu afire buha.

5. 부씨 노구, 마꼬 나로쫘아 과 따빠찌아쫘 구레찌리라, 너라 구이러 나바쭈미라 디모더오, 짜시야 녜머녀러러 어먀아시 여 뷔머러시 뷔뉴. 부씨 나바아 노바아 뿌 아부냐 와 무시무 아어러기러 어뷔머러시 뷔뉴, 구이기라 어찌하삐 시 어무레모 쫘고쫘아 뫄 가찌- 가찌 거뉴 아피러 부하.

5. For this reason, when I could stand it no longer, I sent Timothy to find out about your faith. I was afraid that in some way the tempter might have tempted you and our efforts might have been useless.

6. Si rero, Timoteo era aikaa kutenga eyi mwenyu, ne mwaasi ola atchuretere luulu se bwemeresi bwenyu, ne nzii yenyu alyi mwaasi mubuya. Kandji atchubwirire mbu munatchiri mwendjire mwatchufula busese esuku soshi, ngokwa netchu tchwete embuha ye kuhuba kubalola'ku.

6. 시 러로, 디모더오 어라 아이가아 구더빠 어에 뮈뉴, 너 뫄아시 오쫘 아쭈러더러 뤂우뤂 서 뷔머러시 뷔뉴, 너 씨이 여뉴 아레 뫄아시 무부야. 가찌 아쭈뷔리러 뿌 무나찌리 뮈찌러 뫄쭈푸쫘 부서서 어수구 소씨, 꼬과 너쭈 쭤더 어뿌하 여 구후바 구바로쫘구.

6. But Timothy has just now come to us from you and has brought good news about your faith and love. He has told us that you always have pleasant memories of us and that you long to see us, just as we also long to see you.

7. Bushi noku banyaketchu, tchiro angaba mbu tchwarenga mu bisibu binene ne malyibuko, emitchima yetchu

7. 부씨 노구 바냐거쭈, 찌로 아빠바 뿌 쫘러빠 무 비시부 비너너 너 마레부고, 어미찌마 여쭈 야서시뷔 뫄

7. Therefore, brothers, in all our distress and persecution we were encouraged about you because of your faith.

yasesibwe mwa kumva emyaasi 구빠 어먀아시 여 뭐머러시
ye bwemeresi bwenyu. 뭐뉴.

8. Rero bushi mucthiri
musimikire mwa buua bwenyu
na Enwawetchu, tchwatchumire
emitchima ya fumbamire.

8. 러로 부씨 무찌리
무시미기러 롸 부우아 뭐뉴
나 어놔워쭈, 좌쭈미러
어미찌마 야 푸빠미러.

8. For now we really live,
since you are standing firm
in the Lord.

9. Tchwainyire tcha tchungateta
kwa kubura Kabumi mbu
akoko, bushi ne luno lumoo
loshi lwa tchweete era
muhondo sai bushi nenyu.

9. 좌이네러 짜 쭈아더다 과
구부라 가부미 뿌 아고고,
부씨 너 루노 루모오 로씨
롸 쭤더러 어라 무호또 사이
부씨 너뉴.

9. How can we thank God
enough for you in return for
all the joy we have in the
presence of our God
because of you?

10. Kuema ku tchwendire
tchwaneema Kabumbi mbu
busese emushi ne butchufu,
atchuboreera endjira ye
kuhuba kulolana'ku nenyu,
tchubaase ku cthiravkandju ka
mutchiri muinyire mwa
bwemeresi bwenyu.

10. 구어마 구 쭤띠러
좌너어마 가부삐 뿌 부서서
어무씨 너 부쭈푸,
아쭈보러어라 어찌라 여
구후바 구롸나구 너뉴,
쭈바아서 구 찌라부가뉴 가
무찌리 무이네러 롸
뭐머러시 뭐뉴.

10. Night and day we pray
most earnestly that we may
see you again and supply
what is lacking in your faith.

11. Kabumbi tata yeine, ne
Enawetchu Yesu,
batchubooreraa endjira ye
kuika eyi mwenyu.

11. 가부삐 다다 여이너, 너
어나워쭈 여수,
바쭈보오러라아 어찌라 여
구이가 어에 뮈뉴.

11. Now may our God and
Father himself and our Lord
Jesus clear the way for us to
come to you.

12. Enawetchu aendekeraa
kunde akusa e nzii era
mwetene'ku, nera mweete kwa
bandji bandju boshi. Ei nzii
indaa yanaba ngera
tchubatchusa'ku.

12. 어나워쭈 아어떠거라아
구떠 아구사 어 씨이 어라
뮈더너구, 너라 뮈어더 과
바찌 바뉴 보씨. 어이 씨이
이따아 야나바 꺼라
쭈바쭈사구.

12. May the Lord make your
love increase and overflow
for each other and for
everyone else, just as ours
does for you.

13. Mwa batcha, endaa
abasesa emitchima ne mango
Enawetchu Yeshu akaika alyi ne
bandju bai boshi, mukaba
baubuyabuya era muhondo sa

13. 롸 바짜, 어따아
아바서사 어미찌마 너 마꾜
어나워쭈 여쑤 아가이가
아레 너 바뉴 바이 보씨,
무가바 바우부야부야 어라

13. May he strengthen your
hearts so that you will be
blameless and holy in the
presence of our God and
Father when our Lord Jesus

Kabumbi, kutakabe tchiro ne mwaasu mubi ola bakabashitaka'ku.

무호또 사 가부삐, 구다가버 찌로 너 꽈아수 무비 오꽈 바가바씨다가구.

comes with all his holy ones.

1 E Batesalonika Chikono 4

1 어 바더사뿐니가 찌고노 4

1 Thessalonians Chapter 4 [HIV]

1. Banyeketchu, kwa kumala, tchwabeema tchwabeema mwa sina lya Enawetchu Yesu, kwa beemire kunde mwaata myanya era isimise Kabumbi mwa kalamo kenyu, ngokwa tchwanabangirisaa. Kubinalyi! Etchera tchi mwendjire mwanaira. Rero, tchwabatchitchi kwa munarengeresa kunde mwaira batcha.

1. 바녀거쭈, 과 구마꽈, 꽈버어마 꽈버어마 꽈 시나 꺄 어나워쭈 여수, 과 버어미러 구너 꽈아다 먀냐 어라 이시미서 가부삐 꽈 가꽈모 거뉴, 꼬과 꽈나바끼리사아. 구비나꿰! 어쩌라 찌 뭐띠러 꽈나이라. 러로, 꽈바찌찌 과 무나러꺼러사 구너 꽈이라 바짜.

1. Finally, brothers, we instructed you how to live in order to please God, as in fact you are living. Now we ask you and urge you in the Lord Jesus to do this more and more.

2. Bushi mwishi emiomba era tchwarekaa tchwabatchitchikire kwe sina lya Enawetchu Yesu.

2. 부씨 뮈씨 어미오빠 어라 꽈러가아 꽈바찌찌기러 궈 시나 꺄 어나워쭈 여수.

2. For you know what instructions we gave you by the authority of the Lord Jesus.

3. Kabumbi ahonda mube bandju bai boshi. Rero, mundaa mwatchilanga kwa lusingi.

3. 가부삐 아호따 무버 바쭈 바이 보씨. 러로, 무따아 꽈찌꽈까 과 루시끼.

3. It is God's will that you should be sanctified: that you should avoid sexual immorality;

4. Tchira mulumeeemire kunde eekala na mukai kwa ndjira ibuya-buya, kandji era ingareta etchunda.

4. 찌라 무루머어어미러 구너 어어가꽈 나 무가이 과 띠라 이부야-부야, 가찌 어라 이까러다 어쭈따.

4. that each of you should learn to control his own body in a way that is holy and honorable,

5. Busira kutchirekerera kunde eekibwa na mianyi si ibi ye lusingi ngokwa ebandju ba bateshi Kabumbi bende baira.

5. 부시라 구찌러거러라 구너 어어기봐 나 미아니 시 이비 여 루시끼 꼬과 어바쭈 바 바더씨 가부삐 버너 바이라.

5. not in passionate lust like the heathen, who do not know God;

6. Rero kukulyikana nei myaasi kutabaa tchiro ne mundju asibya ola undaa wirira munyakabo mabi ; nesi kumweengeere. Bushi tchwabaa tchwaba burire mira na kubatchitchika kwa boshi ba bendjire baira batcha, Enawetchu akabatchindjibusa.

7. Bushi Kabumbi atchwamaalaa tchunde tchwaira emabi, si atatchwamaalaa tchube bandju bai boshi

8. Bushi noku, emundju ola wananaa ene miomba, amenyaa kwa atananyire miomba ya mundju, si ananyire emiomba ya Kabumbi ; ola wende wa beeresa emutchima mubuya.

9. Mutatchilaire ku myaasi ya kuteta mbu bahubaa kubandjikira era luulu se kunde mwasima banyakenyu beemeresi, bushi Kabumbi yeine abakangirisise mira ekunde mwasina.

10. Kubinalyi, ku mwendjire mwasimaa banyaketchu bemeresi boshi bomwa tchioo tchoshi tche Maketoniya batcha. Rero, tchwabeema munarengeresaa busese kunde masimana.

6. 러로 구구쀄가나 너이 먀아시 구다바아 찌로 너 무뿌 아시뱌 오롸 우따아 위리라 무냐가보 마비 ; 너시 구뭐어뻐어러. 부씨 쫘바아 쫘바 부리러 미라 나 구바찌찌가 과 보씨 바 버찌러 바이라 바짜, 어나워쭈 아가바찌찌부사.

7. 부씨 가부쀄 아쫘마아롸아 쭈떠 쫘이라 어마비, 시 아다쫘마아롸아 쭈버 바뚜 바이 보씨

8. 부씨 노구, 어무뿌 오롸 와나나아 어너 미오빠, 아머냐아 과 아다나니러 미오빠 야 무뚜, 시 아나니러 어미오빠 야 가부쀄 ; 오롸 워떠 와 버어러사 어무찌마 무부야.

9. 무다찌롸이러 구 먀아시 야 구더다 뿌 바후바아 구바찌기라 어라 룻우뤀 서 구떠 롸시마 바냐거뉴 버어머러시, 부씨 가부쀄 여이너 아바가삐리시서 미라 어구떠 롸시나.

10. 구비나쀄, 구 뭐찌러 롸시마아 바냐거쭈 버머러시 보씨 보똬 찌오오 쪼씨 쩌 마거도니야 바짜. 러로, 쫘버어마 무나러뻐러사아 부서서 구떠 마시마나.

6. and that in this matter no one should wrong his brother or take advantage of him. The Lord will punish men for all such sins, as we have already told you and warned you.

7. For God did not call us to be impure, but to live a holy life.

8. Therefore, he who rejects this instruction does not reject man but God, who gives you his Holy Spirit.

9. Now about brotherly love we do not need to write to you, for you yourselves have been taught by God to love each other.

10. And in fact, you do love all the brothers throughout Macedonia. Yet we urge you, brothers, to do so more and more.

11. Mundaa mwahonda kuba mwa boolo, kandji mutendaa mwengira mu myaasi era itabeerekere si mundaa mwalya bya mubeine mwakoreraa, ngokwa tchwana batchitchikaa.

12. Mwa kuira batcha, ebandju ba batemerere Yesu bangende ba beeresa etchunda. Kandji, mutasitowera tchio ne mundju asibya.

13. Banyaketchu, tchwahonda mumenyerere ekanangana era luulu se bandju ba bafire mira, mungeesha kunde mwaba mwa businane nga bandji bandju ba batatchusa munyiiro.

14. Bushi tchutchula tchweemerere kwa Yesu afaa, era kunoomoka. Kunoku, kutchutchula thweemerere kwa Kabumbi akana omola ebandju ba bafaa bemerere Yesu, tchasiya baabe alauma nai.

15. Kubinalyi! Kukulyikana ne myaasi ya Enawetchu, tchetchine tchi tchwababura : tchubano tchu tchukaba tchutchiri bauma-uma mango, akafuluka, tchutakangire ba bafire mira.

16. Mwamu mango,

11. 무따아 뫄호따 구바 뫄 보오로, 가찌 무더따아 뭐끼라 무 먀아시 어라 이다버어러거러 시 무따아 뫄꺄 뱌 무버이너 뫄고러라아, 오과 쫘나 바찌찌가아.

12. 뫄 구이라 바짜, 어바뉴 바 바더머러러 여수 바꺼너 바 버어러사 어쭈따. 가찌, 무다시도워라 찌오 너 무뉴 아시뱌.

13. 바냐거쭈, 쫘호따 무머녀러러 어가나꺄나 어라 루우루 서 바뉴 바 바피러 미라, 무어어싸 구너 뫄바 뫄 부시나너 꺄 바찌 바뉴 바 바다쭈사 무네이로.

14. 부찌 쭈쭈롸 쮜어머러러 과 여수 아파아, 어라 구노오모가. 구노구, 구쭈쭈롸 쮜어머러러 과 가부뻬 아가나 오모롸 어바뉴 바 바파아 버머러러 여수, 짜시야 바아버 아롸우마 나이.

15. 구비나뤠! 구구뤠가나 너 먀아시 야 어나워쭈, 쩌찌너 찌 쫘바부라 : 쭈바노 쭈 쭈가바 쭈찌리 바우마-우마 마오, 아가푸루가, 쭈다가끼러 바 바피러 미라.

16. 뫄무 마오, 구고오뻬가나

11. Make it your ambition to lead a quiet life, to mind your own business and to work with your hands, just as we told you,

12. so that your daily life may win the respect of outsiders and so that you will not be dependent on anybody.

13. Brothers, we do not want you to be ignorant about those who fall asleep, or to grieve like the rest of men, who have no hope.

14. We believe that Jesus died and rose again and so we believe that God will bring with Jesus those who have fallen asleep in him.

15. According to the Lord's own word, we tell you that we who are still alive, who are left till the coming of the Lord, will certainly not precede those who have fallen asleep.

16. For the Lord himself will

kukoomvikana murenge ola waana emuomba, ne murenge we mukulukulu we bamalaika, ne murenge we kaperere ka Kabumbi. Mwolu, Enawetchu yeine akaandaala kutenga kwa nguba. Rero, ebandju ba bafaa bemerere Kirisito ba koomoka tanga.

17. Tchasinda, netchu tchu tchukaba tchutchiri bauma-uma, unaounao tchukerusibwa alauma nabo mwa lumbumbu, tchubuanane na Enawetchu mwa tchanya. Kutchukanaendekera kuba alauma na Enawetchu batcha esuku ne mango.

18. Rero kurengera ene myaasi mundaa mwasesanya e mitchima.

come down from heaven, with a loud command, with the voice of the archangel and with the trumpet call of God, and the dead in Christ will rise first.

17. After that, we who are still alive and are left will be caught up together with them in the clouds to meet the Lord in the air. And so we will be with the Lord forever.

18. Therefore encourage each other with these words.

무러꺼 오롸 와아나 어무오빠, 너 무러꺼 워 무구룯구루 워 바마똬이가, 너 무러꺼 워 가퍼러러 가 가부삐. 모루, 어나워쭈 여이너 아가아따아롸 구더꽈 과 우바. 러로, 어바누 바 바파아 버머러러 기리시도 바 고오모가 다꽈.

17. 짜시따, 너쭈 쭈 쭈가바 쭈찌리 바우마-우마, 우나오우나오 쭈거루시봐 아롸우마 나보 봐 룸뿌뿌, 쭈부아나너 나 어나워쭈 꽈 짜냐. 구쭈가나어떠거라 구바 아롸우마 나 어나워쭈 바짜 어수구 너 마꾜.

18. 러로 구러꺼라 어너 먀아시 무따아 마서사냐 어 미찌마.

---

1 E Batesalonika Chikono 5

1 어 바더사롼니가 찌고노 5

1 Thessalonians Chapter 5 [HIV]

1. Rero banyaketchu, mutatchilaire ku myaasi ya kuteta mbu bahubaa kubaandjikira era luulu se lusuku nesi etchihangi tcha Enawetchu akafuluka.

2. Bushi mubeine mwishi kwa elusuku lwe kufuluka kwai, lukaika ngokwa mwisi endaika

1. 러로 바냐거쭈, 무다찌똬이러 구 먀아시 야 구더다 뿌 바후바아 구바아찌기라 어라 루우루 서 루수구 너시 어찌하꾀 짜 어나워쭈 아가푸루가.

2. 부씨 무버이너 뮈씨 과 어루수구 뤠 구푸룯가 과이, 루가이가 꼬과 뮈시

1. Now, brothers, about times and dates we do not need to write to you,

2. for you know very well that the day of the Lord will come like a thief in the

ebutchufu.

3. Mango ebandju bakaba bendjire bateta mbu " tchilyi mwa boolo, kandji tchutambatere ", mu mango ekasibu kakabaikira tchimbate, ngokwa emukure ende alumwa ne mukero. Kandji batakanafufumuke tchiro ne hitcha.

4. Si mwabo banyaketchu, mutalyi mwa musimya. Rero olu lusuku, lutabaikire tchimbate nga mwisi.

5. Bushi muboshi mulyi bandju ba balyi mwa bulangare, kandji ba balyi mwa mushi. Tchubano tchuta bandju ba balyi mwa butchufu, nesi ba balyi mwa musimya.

6. Bushi noku, tchutaondjiraa nga ebandji bandju si tchundaa tchwatchilanga kwa mabi.

8. Bushi ba balyi tchulo, bende baondjira ebutchufune batamisi nabo bende batamirira ebutchufu.

7. Si tchubano, oku tchunalyi bandju ba balyi mwa mushi, tchundaa tchwatchilanga kwa mabi. Tchundaa tchwaata nga mbenzi ye kutchianga. Kandji tchundaa tchwaata ne

어빠이가 어부쭈푸.

3. 마꼬 어바뉴 바가바 버찌러 바더다 뿌 " 찌레 롸 보오롣, 가찌 쭈다빠더러 ", 무 마꼬 어가시부 가가바이기라 찌빠더, 끄과 어무구러 어떠 아룹롸 너 무거로. 가찌 바다가나푸푸무거 찌로 너 히짜.

4. 시 뫄보 바냐거쭈, 무다레 롸 무시먀. 러로 오룻 룯수구, 룯다바이기러 찌빠더 롸 뮈시.

5. 부씨 무보씨 무레 바뉴 바 바레 롸 부롸꺄러, 가찌 바 바레 롸 무씨. 쭈바노 쭈다 바뉴 바 바레 롸 부쭈푸, 너시 바 바레 롸 무시먀.

6. 부씨 노구, 쭈다오씨라아 롸 어바찌 바뉴 시 쭈따아 좌찌롸꺄 과 마비.

8. 부씨 바 바레 쭈롣, 버떠 바오씨라 어부쭈푸너 바다미시 나보 버떠 바다미리라 어부쭈푸.

7. 시 쭈바노, 오구 쭈나레 바뉴 바 바레 롸 무씨, 쭈따아 좌찌롸꺄 과 마비. 쭈따아 좌아다 롸 뻐씨 여 구찌아꺄. 가찌 쭈따아 좌아다 너 무네이로 과

night.

3. While people are saying, "Peace and safety," destruction will come on them suddenly, as labor pains on a pregnant woman, and they will not escape.

4. But you, brothers, are not in darkness so that this day should surprise you like a thief.

5. You are all sons of the light and sons of the day. We do not belong to the night or to the darkness.

6. So then, let us not be like others, who are asleep, but let us be alert and self-controlled.

7. For those who sleep, sleep at night, and those who get drunk, get drunk at night.

8. But since we belong to the day, let us be self-controlled, putting on faith and love as a breastplate, and the hope of salvation as a helmet.

munyiiro kwa tchukanunulyibwa, aabe nga sapo ye tchuma yeku tchilanga kwa ngabo.

9. Bushi Kabumbi atatchulondolaa mbu atchutchindjibuse mwa businane bwai, si atchulondolaa tchasiya tchununulyibwe kurengera Enawetchu Yesu Kirisito.

10. Bushi Yesu Kirisito afaa kwabushi netchu lyi tchulame alauma nayi, tchwaesa nesi kuondjira.

11. Bushi noku, mundaa mwasesanya emitchima ne kunde mwasasanya kusimika mwa bweemeresi, ngokwa mwera mwendjire mwanaira.

12. Banyaketchu, tchwabeema busese kwa mundaa mwatchunda ebemangisi ba bendjire balyibuka busese ne mulyimo mwa katchi-katchi kenyu. Abola bu Enawetchu abeerisise kwa kunde baberesa emaano.

13. Mundaa mwa tchunda bo busese ne kusima bo boshi ne mulyimo ola baokla. Mubaa ne boolo mwa katchi-katchi kenyu.

14. Banyaketchu, tchwabeema busese kwa mundaa

쭈가누누레봐, 아아버 까 사포 여 쭈마 여구 찌롸까 과 까보.

9. 부씨 가부뻬 아다쭈롣또롸아 뿌 아쭈찌띠부서 마 부시나너 봐이, 시 아쭈롣또롸아 짜시야 쭈누누레붜 구러꺼라 어나워쭈 여수 기리시도.

10. 부씨 여수 기리시도 아파아 과부씨 너쭈 레 쭈롸머 아라우마 나에, 좌어사 너시 구오씨라.

11. 부씨 노구, 무따아 마서사냐 어미찌마 너 구떠 마사사냐 구시미가 마 붜어머러시, 꼬과 뭐라 뭐찌러 뫄나이라.

12. 바냐거쭈, 좌버어마 부서서 과 무따아 마쭈따 어버까l시 바 버찌러 바레부가 부서서 너 무레모 마 가찌-가찌 거뉴. 아보롸 부 어나워쭈 아버어러시서 과 구떠 바버러사 어마아노.

13. 무따아 마 쭈따 보 부서서 너 구시마 보 보씨 너 무레모 오롸 바오구롸. 무바아 너 보오롣 마 가찌-가찌 거뉴.

14. 바냐거쭈, 좌버어마 부서서 과 무따아

9. For God did not appoint us to suffer wrath but to receive salvation through our Lord Jesus Christ.

10. He died for us so that, whether we are awake or asleep, we may live together with him.

11. Therefore encourage one another and build each other up, just as in fact you are doing.

12. Now we ask you, brothers, to respect those who work hard among you, who are over you in the Lord and who admonish you.

13. Hold them in the highest regard in love because of their work. Live in peace with each other.

14. And we urge you, brothers, warn those who

mwakalyiira engalyisi. Naba batatchiserira emitchima, munda mwa basesa'i. ba batatchete misi nabo mundaa mwaasa'bu, mundaa mwaata emutchima we kuba ne bandju boshi.

15. Mumenyaa! Akaba tchiro ne mundju asibya mwa katchi-katchi kenyu ola ungende wa tchifuna kwa mabi bamukorere. Si esuku soshi mundaa mwahonda kuirira mo ebandju boshi.

16. Mundaa mwamowa esuku soshi

17. Mundaa mweema Kabumbi busira kutama

18. Namu tchira mwaasi, mwateta mbu akoko era mwa Kabumbi. Bushi ebyera bi ahonda munde mwaira, mu mulyi mwa buuma na Yesu Kirisito.

19. Mutendaa mwaangika emulyimo we mutchima mubuya-buya.

20. Kandji mutendaa mwakena emyaasi ye burebi

21. Si mundaa mwalola kwa myaasi yoshi kubuya, mwanasimba wera iri ibuya

22. Mundaa mwatchilanga ku tchira mwaasi mubi

23. Kbumbi we boolo yeine

마가꼐이라 어빠꼐시. 나바 바다찌서리라 어미찌마, 무따 마 바서사이. 바 바다쩌더 미시 나보 무따아 마아사부, 무따아 마아다 어무찌마 워 구바 너 바뉴 보씨.

15. 무머냐아! 아가바 찌로 너 무뿌 아시뱌 마 가찌-가찌 거뉴 오라 우꺼더 와 찌푸나 과 마비 바무고러러. 시 어수구 소씨 무따아 마호따 구이리라 모 어바뉴 보씨.

16. 무따아 마모와 어수구 소씨

17. 무따아 뭐어마 가부뻬 부시라 구다마

18. 나무 찌라 마아시, 마더다 뿌 아고고 어라 마 가부뻬. 부씨 어벼라 비 아호따 무더 마이라, 무 무뤠 마 부우마 나 여수 기리시도.

19. 무더따아 마아끼가 어무뤠모 워 무찌마 무부야-부야.

20. 가찌 무더따아 마거나 어먀아시 여 부러비

21. 시 무따아 마료라 과 먀아시 요씨 구부야, 마나시빠 워라 이리 이부야

22. 무따아 마찌롸꺼 구 찌라 마아시 무비

23. 구부뻬 워 보오뤈 여이너

---

are idle, encourage the timid, help the weak, be patient with everyone.

15. Make sure that nobody pays back wrong for wrong, but always try to be kind to each other and to everyone else.

16. Be joyful always;

17. pray continually;

18. give thanks in all circumstances, for this is God's will for you in Christ Jesus.

19. Do not put out the Spirit's fire;

20. do not treat prophecies with contempt.

21. Test everything. Hold on to the good.

22. Avoid every kind of evil.

23. May God himself, the

abaira kuba bandju bai boshi. Endaa alaga ekalamo kenyu koshi, imitcha yenyu, ne myaanyisa yenyu, ne mibiri yenyu. Aola mwanera mwaba busira mwaasi mubi asibya ola batangabashitaka'ku mwango Enawetchu Yesu Kirisito akafuluka.

24. Oyu wabamaala iukaira ebyera bushi yeke ende anaira bya alaanyaa.

25. Si banyaketchu! Netchu mundaa mwatchweemera era mwa Kabumbi

26. Mukesaa ebemeresi boshi mwa kwoobera'bu nga bauma

27. Nabatchitchika kwe sina lya Enawetchu, mano maruba, mumasomeraa ebemeresi boshi.

28. Enawetchu Yesu Kirisito endaa abaahanyira.

아바이라 구바 바쭈 바이 보씨. 어따아 아꽈가 어가꽈모 거뉴 고씨, 이미짜 여뉴, 너 먀아네사 여뉴, 너 미비리 여뉴. 아오꽈 먀너라 먀바 부시라 먀아시 무비 아시뱌 오꽈 바다까바씨다가구 먀꼬 어나워쭈 여수 기리시도 아가푸루가.

24. 오유 와바마아꽈 이우가이라 어벼라 부씨 여거 어떠 아나이라 뱌 아꽈아냐아.

25. 시 바냐거쭈! 너쭈 무따아 먀쭤어머라 어라 먀 가부삐

26. 무거사아 어버머러시 보씨 먀 고오버라부 까 바우마

27. 나바찌찌가 궈 시나 랴 어나워쭈, 마노 마루바, 무마소머라아 어버머러시 보씨.

28. 어나워쭈 여수 기리시도 어따아 아바아하네라.

God of peace, sanctify you through and through. May your whole spirit, soul and body be kept blameless at the coming of our Lord Jesus Christ.

24. The one who calls you is faithful and he will do it.

25. Brothers, pray for us.

26. Greet all the brothers with a holy kiss.

27. I charge you before the Lord to have this letter read to all the brothers.

28. The grace of our Lord Jesus Christ be with you.

2 E Batesalonika

2 어 바더사롣니가

2 Thessalonians

E BATESALONIKA BAKABIRI

(2 THESSALONIANS)

어 바더사롣니가 바가비리

(2 더싸롣니아뚜)

2 E Batesalonika Chikono 1

1. Nyono Paulo, alauma na Sirifano na Timoteo tchutchwabaandjikira mu bemeresi bomwa musi we Tesalonika. Mwabo mutchula bandju ba Kabumbi tata, kandji mwanaba bandju ba Enawetchu Yesu Kirisito:

2. Kabumbi Tata na Enawetchu Yesu Kirisito bendaa ba baahanyira, na kubeeresa eboolo!

3. Banyeketchu, tchweemire kunde tchwateta mbu akoko era mwa Kabumbi esuku soshi bushi nenyu. Tchweemire kunde tchwaira batcha bushi ebweemeresi bwenyu kukula ku bwaendekere bwakula. Ne nzii era mwetene'ku nai kuyanaendekera yaluwa busese.

4. Bushi noku, tchwendjire tchwatchitongera mwaabo era muhondo se bandji bemeresi bomwa nyuhu sa kabumbi. Bushi tchiro angaba mwalyibusibwa ne kulosibwa kwa kasibu, munatchiri mweete bushibirisi, ne kusimika mwa bweemeresi.

2 어 바더사로니가 찌고노 1

1. 뇨노 파우로, 아꽈우마 나 시리파노 나 디모더오 쭈좌바아씨기라 무 버머러시 보와 무시 워 더사로니가. 마보 무쭈좌 바뉴 바 가부삐 다다, 가찌 먀나바 바뉴 바 어나워쭈 여수 기리시도:

2. 가부삐 다다 나 어나워쭈 여수 기리시도 버따아 바 바아하네라, 나 구버어러사 어보오로!

3. 바녀거쭈, 쮜어미러 구떠 좌더다 뿌 아고고 어라 먀 가부삐 어수구 소씨 부씨 너뉴. 쮜어미러 구떠 좌이라 바짜 부씨 어붜어머러시 붜뉴 구구좌 구 봐어떠거러 봐구좌. 너 씨이 어라 뭐더너구 나이 구야나어떠거라 야루와 부서서.

4. 부씨 노구, 쮜찌러 좌찌도꺼라 먀아보 어라 무호또 서 바찌 버머러시 보와 뉴후 사 가부삐. 부씨 찌로 아꺼바 먀레부시봐 너 구로시봐 과 가시부, 무나찌리 뭐어더 부씨비리시, 너 구시미가 먀 붜어머러시.

2 Thessalonians Chapter 1 [HIV]

1. Paul, Silas and Timothy, To the church of the Thessalonians in God our Father and the Lord Jesus Christ:

2. Grace and peace to you from God the Father and the Lord Jesus Christ.

3. We ought always to thank God for you, brothers, and rightly so, because your faith is growing more and more, and the love every one of you has for each other is increasing.

4. Therefore, among God's churches we boast about your perseverance and faith in all the persecutions and trials you are enduring.

5. Amu malyibuko malosise kwa Kabumbi enda atchindjibusa ebandju kwa kutchungenene, bushi mu munabaira kuba bandju ba beemire kuingirira mwa bwami bwai, bwa bwatchuma malyibuba batcha.

6. Kubinalyi! Oku Kabumbi ende aira bya bitchungenene, akalyibusa ba bendjire babulyisa.

7. Na mumwalyibuka, akabatamusisa alauma netchu. Ebyera bikaba, mango Enawetchu Yesu akaika kutenga kwa nguba, alauma ne ba Malaika bai ba beete abuashi.

8. Akaika alyi mwa tchasi tche mulyiro, kuya kutchindjibusa ebandju ba batahonda kumenya Kabumbi, ne kunde batchundaa emwaasi mubuya-buya wa Enawetchu Yesu.

9. Abunbadju, ebutchundjibusi bwa bakabona bububunu: baaba mwa muero esuku ne mango, bure na Enawetchu, kandji bure ne tchunde lye buashi bwai.

10. Ei myaasi ikaba elusuku lwa Enawetchu akaika. Nolu lusuku, ebandju bai boshi

---

5. 아무 마뤠부고 마뢴시서 과 가부뻬 어따 아찌띠지부사 어바뚜 과 구쭈에너너, 부씨 무 무나바이라 구바 바뚜 바 버어미러 구이삐리라 롸봐미 봐이, 봐 봐쭈마 마뤠부바 바짜.

6. 구비나뤠! 오구 가부뻬 어떠 아이라 뱌 비쭈에너너, 아가뤠부사 바 버찌러 바부뤠사.

7. 나 무롸뤠부가, 아가바다무시사 아롸우마 너쭈. 어벼라 비가바, 마꼬 어나워쭈 여수 아가이가 구더꽈 과 꾸바, 아롸우마 너 바 마롸이가 바이 바 버어더 아부아씨.

8. 아가이가 아뤠 롸 짜시 쩌 무뤠로, 구야 구찌띠부사 어바뚜 바 바다호따 구머냐 가부뻬, 너 구떠 바쭈따아 어롸아시 무부야-부야 와 어나워쭈 여수.

9. 아부빠쭈, 어부쭈띠부시 봐 바가보나 부부부누: 바아바 봐 무어로 어수구 너 마꼬, 부러 나 어나워쭈, 가찌 부러 너 쭈떠 려 부아씨 봐이.

10. 어이 먀아시 이가바 어루수구 꽈 어나워쭈 아가이가. 노루 루수구,

---

5. All this is evidence that God's judgment is right, and as a result you will be counted worthy of the kingdom of God, for which you are suffering.

6. God is just: He will pay back trouble to those who trouble you

7. and give relief to you who are troubled, and to us as well. This will happen when the Lord Jesus is revealed from heaven in blazing fire with his powerful angels.

8. He will punish those who do not know God and do not obey the gospel of our Lord Jesus.

9. They will be punished with everlasting destruction and shut out from the presence of the Lord and from the majesty of his power

10. on the day he comes to be glorified in his holy people and to be marveled

bakamutonga, neba bamwerere boshi bakasanwa busese bushi nai. Rero, nenyu mukanaba alaum nabu, bushi mwemerere emyassi era tchwabahubanganyisaa era luulu sai.

어바꾸 바이 보씨 바가무도까, 너바 바뭐러러 보씨 바가사놔 부서서 부씨 나이. 러로, 너뉴 무가나바 아라우무 나부, 부씨 뭐머러러 어먀씨 어라 쫘바후바까니사아 어라 루우루 사이.

at among all those who have believed. This includes you, because you believed our testimony to you.

11. Bushi noku, kwema ku tchwendjire tchwana beemera ebihangi byoshi, tchasiya Kabumbi wetchu abeerese emisi ye kuata mibere era ikulyikene ne myaasi era yatchumaaa abaamaala. Kandji tchwendjire tchwamweema tchasiya kurengera e buashi bwai abaase kunde mwakola emabuya moshi ma mwanahonda kuira, bushi mutchula mu mweemerere.

11. 부씨 노구, 궈마 구 쭤찌러 쫘나 버어머라 어비하끼 뵤씨, 짜시야 가부삐 워쭈 아버어러서 어미시 여 구아다 미버러 어라 이구례거너 너 먀아시 어라 야쭈마아아 아바아마아라. 가찌 쭤찌러 쫘뭐어마 짜시야 구러꺼라 어 부아씨 봐이 아바아서 구떠 뫄고라 어마부야 모씨 마 뫄나호따 구이라, 부씨 무쭈라 무 뭐어머러러.

11. With this in mind, we constantly pray for you, that our God may count you worthy of his calling, and that by his power he may fulfill every good purpose of yours and every act prompted by your faith.

12. Mwa batcha, mungende mwatonga esina lya Enawetchu Yesu, nai anende abatonga ebi byoshi byalosa ebubuya bwa Kabumbi wetchu, na Enawetchu Yesu Kirisito.

12. 뫄 바짜, 무꺼떠 뫄도까 어시나 랴 어나워쭈 여수, 나이 아너떠 아바도까 어비 뵤씨 뱌로사 어부부야 봐 가부삐 워쭈, 나 어나워쭈 여수 기리시도.

12. We pray this so that the name of our Lord Jesus may be glorified in you, and you in him, according to the grace of our God and the Lord Jesus Christ.

2 E Batesalonika Chikono 2

2 어 바더사로니가 찌고노 2

2 Thessalonians Chapter 2 [HIV]

1. Banyaketchu, Enawetchu Yesu Kiristito akafuluka na tchukabwaanana nai. Rero

1. 바냐거쭈, 어나워쭈 여수 기리시도 아가푸루가 나 쭈가봐아나나 나이. 러로

1. Concerning the coming of our Lord Jesus Christ and our being gathered to him,

bushi nei myaasi, tchetchine tchi tchabeema.

2. Akaba mungomva mbu elusuku lwa kufuluka kwa Enawetchu lwaikire mira, ebwenge butabasungulyiraa fuba, nesi kufa fuba. Kulyi mango ei myasi, bangababura mbu yatenga era mwa Kabumbi, nesi myaasi era bendjire bakangirisa, nesi maruba ma bisha mbu tchu tchwaandjikaa.

3. Muteemerereaa kwaba mundju ola wabateba mu tchiro na ndjira isibya. Bushi era muhondo olu lusuku luike, bandju banene bakanana kunde batchunda Kabumbi ; nolu mukosi we mabi nai akalorekana'ku. Oyola, iwalawaa kuya mwa muero.

4. Oyu mukosi we mabi alwisa byoshi bya bandju bnde batonga na byoshi bye bende beera na kunde atchitonga mbu iulyi era luulu sebi byoshi. Akanalyinda aya kweekala mwa luhu lwa Kabumbi, ne kunde atchihuta ala kabalyi mbu ina Kabumbi yeine.

5. Mutatchikengee kwa mango nabaa nyiri alauma nenyu, nabaa nendjire nababura era

부씨 너이 먀아시, 쩌찌너 찌 짜버어마.

2. 아가바 무꼬빠 뿌 어루수구 똬 구푸루가 과 어나워쭈 똬이기러 미라, 어붜꺼 부다바수우꼐라아 푸바, 너시 구파 푸바. 구레 마꼬 어이 먀시, 바까바부라 뿌 야더꺄 어라 롸 가부뼤, 너시 먀아시 어라 버찌러 바가꺼리사, 너시 마루바 마 비싸 뿌 쭈 똬아찌가아.

3. 무더어머러라아 과바 무뚜 오롸 와바더바 무 찌로 나 찌라 이시뱌. 부씨 어라 무호또 오루 루수구 루이거, 바뚜 바너너 바가나나 구더 바쭈따 가부뼤 ; 노루 무고시 워 마비 나이 아가롸러가나구. 오요롸, 이와롸와아 구야 롸 무어로.

4. 오유 무고시 워 마비 아뤄사 뵤씨 뱌 바뚜 버너 바도꺄 나 뵤씨 뼈 버떠 버어라 나 구더 아찌도꺄 뿌 이우레 어라 루우루 서비 뵤씨. 아가나뼤따 아야 궈어가꽈 롸 루후 똬 가부뼤, 너 구떠 아찌후다 아롸 가바뤠 뿌 이나 가부뼤 여이너.

5. 무다찌거꺼어 과 마꼬 나바아 너리 아꽈우마 너뉴, 나바아 너찌러 나바부라

we ask you, brothers,

2. not to become easily unsettled or alarmed by some prophecy, report or letter supposed to have come from us, saying that the day of the Lord has already come.

3. Don't let anyone deceive you in any way, for (that day will not come) until the rebellion occurs and the man of lawlessness is revealed, the man doomed to destruction.

4. He will oppose and will exalt himself over everything that is called God or is worshiped, so that he sets himself up in God's temple, proclaiming himself to be God.

5. Don't you remember that when I was with you I used to tell you these things?

luulu sei myaasi? 어라 루우루 서이 먀아시?

6. Oyu mukosi we mabi, mwishi tcha tchitchiri tchimwaangikire atalorekana'ku era muhodo se tchihangi tcha alondorerwe.

6. 오유 무고시 워 마비, 뮈씨 짜 찌찌리 찌꽈아ⴰ기러 아다뢰러가나구 어라 무호도 서 찌하ⴰ 짜 아뢰또러뤄.

6. And now you know what is holding him back, so that he may be revealed at the proper time.

7. Si tchiro batcha, ebuashi bwai kukola kubwere bwanakola emilyimo mwa bubisho-bisho. Ne mango oyu umwaangikire akaba atatchiri'u, mu mango akere ende akola emulyimo wai tchanganama.

7. 시 찌로 바짜, 어부아씨 봐이 구고꽈 구붜러 봐나고꽈 어미례모 꽈 부비쏘-비쏘. 너 마꾜 오유 우꽈아ⴰ기러 아가바 아다찌리우, 무 마꾜 아거러 어떠 아고꽈 어무례모 와이 짜꽈나마.

7. For the secret power of lawlessness is already at work; but the one who now holds it back will continue to do so till he is taken out of the way.

8. Tchasinda, akere alorekana'ku kubuya-buya. Si mango Enawetchu Yesu akaika, akamuita mwa kunamubuwa kwe muka, ne kumumalyirisa kurengera ebuashi bwa akaika'mu.

8. 짜시따, 아거러 아뢰러가나구 구부야-부야. 시 마꾜 어나워쭈 여수 아가이가, 아가무이다 꽈 구나무부와 궈 무가, 너 구무마례리사 구러꺼라 어부아씨 봐 아가이가무.

8. And then the lawless one will be revealed, whom the Lord Jesus will overthrow with the breath of his mouth and destroy by the splendor of his coming.

9. Mango oyu mukosi we mabi akaika, mwa buashi bwawa musimu mu anende aira ebisomerane ne bishishalo tchasiya atebe ebandju.

9. 마꾜 오유 무고시 워 마비 아가이가, 꽈 부아씨 봐와 무시무 무 아너떠 아이라 어비소머라너 너 비씨싸뢰 짜시야 아더버 어바쭈.

9. The coming of the lawless one will be in accordance with the work of Satan displayed in all kinds of counterfeit miracles, signs and wonders,

10. Akende akoresa tchira bubi boshi, tchasiya atebe ebandju ba balyi mwa muero. Abu bandju bakaya mwa muero, bushi bateemereraa ne kusima emyaasi ye kanangana ingabanunwire.

10. 아거떠 아고러사 찌라 부비 보씨, 짜시야 아더버 어바쭈 바 바례 꽈 무어로. 아부 바쭈 바가야 꽈 무어로, 부씨 바더어머러라아 너 구시마 어먀아시 여 가나꽈나 이까바누니위러.

10. and in every sort of evil that deceives those who are perishing. They perish because they refused to love the truth and so be saved.

11. Etchera tchi tchatchumire

11. 어쩌라 찌 짜쭈미러

11. For this reason God

atchumira'bu ebuashi bwe kuteba, tchaisya bende beemerera emyaasi ye bisha.

12. Rero, boshi ba bateemereraa emyaasi ye kanangana, si kumowa ku bendee bamoera kuira emabi, kuika banatchindjibusibwe.

13. Banyeketchu bassirwa ba Enawetchu, tchweemire kunde tchwateta mbu akoko era mwa Kabumbi esuku soshi bushi nenyu. Bushi kutengera endangiriso, Kabumbi abalondolaa tchasiya abanunule. Rero, mwanunulyibwe bushi emutchima mubuya-buya ende abakomya, kandji bushi mutchula muemerere emyaasi ye kanangana.

14. Ebyera bi byatchumaa abaamaala kurengera emwaasi mubuya-buya ola tchwabahubanganyisaa, tchasiya nenyu muhangire kwe tchunda lya Enawetchu yesu Kirisito.

15. Rero banyaketchu, mundaa mwasimika ne kulanga busese emyaasi era tchwabakangirisaa bunu kwa bundji, nesi era

아쭈미라부 어부아씨 붜 구더바, 짜이샤 버떠 버어머러라 어먀아시 여 비싸.

12. 러로, 보씨 바 바더어머러라아 어먀아시 여 가나까나, 시 구모와 구 버떠어 바모어라 구이라 어마비, 구이가 바나찌띠부시붜.

13. 바녀거쭈 바씨롸 바 어나워쭈, 쭤어미러 구떠 좌더다 뿌 아고고 어라 뫄 가부삐 어수구 소씨 부씨 너뉴. 부씨 구더꺼라 어따끼리소, 가부삐 아바로또롸아 짜시야 아바누누꺼. 러로, 뫄누누레붸 부씨 어무찌마 무부야-부야 어떠 아바고먀, 가찌 부씨 무쭈롸 무어머러러 어먀아시 여 가나까나.

14. 어벼라 비 뱌쭈마아 아바아마아롸 구러꺼라 어뫄아시 무부야-부야 오롸 좌바후바까네사아, 짜시야 너뉴 무하끼러 궈 쭈따 꺄 어나워쭈 여수 기리시도.

15. 러로 바냐거쭈, 무따아 마시미가 너 구롸까 부서서 어먀아시 어라 좌바가끼리사아 부누 과

sends them a powerful delusion so that they will believe the lie

12. and so that all will be condemned who have not believed the truth but have delighted in wickedness.

13. But we ought always to thank God for you, brothers loved by the Lord, because from the beginning God chose you to be saved through the sanctifying work of the Spirit and through belief in the truth.

14. He called you to this through our gospel, that you might share in the glory of our Lord Jesus Christ.

15. So then, brothers, stand firm and hold to the teachings we passed on to you, whether by word of

tchwabaandjikiraa.

16. Kabumbi Tata atchusimaa, ne kurengera ebondjo bwai atchusesise emitchima esuku ne manbu. Kandji atchweeresise ne munyiiro mubuya. Rero, yeine alauma na Enawetchu Yesu Kirisito.

17. Bendaa babasesa emitchima na kubeeresa emisi ye kunde mwaira emabuya esuku soshi mwa mikorere nomwa mitetere.

부찌, 너시 어라
쫘바아찌기라아.

16. 가부삐 다다 아쭈시마아, 너 구러꺼라 어보쬬 봐이 아쭈서시서 어미찌마 어수구 너 마뿌. 가찌 아쭤어러시서 너 무네이로 무부야. 러로, 여이너 아롸우마 나 어나워쭈 여수 기리시도.

17. 버따아 바바서사 어미찌마 나 구버어러사 어미시 여 구떠 마이라 어마부야 어수구 소씨 마 미고러러 노와 미더더러.

mouth or by letter.

16. May our Lord Jesus Christ himself and God our Father, who loved us and by his grace gave us eternal encouragement and good hope,

17. encourage your hearts and strengthen you in every good deed and word.

2 E Batesalonika Chikono 3

2 어 바더사로니가 찌고노 3

2 Thessalonians Chapter 3 [HIV]

1. Rero banyeketchu, mwa kumala, tchwabasengerere mundaa mwatchweemera, tchasiya etchinwa tcha Enawetchu tchihandabane fuba mwa bandju, na kunde batchunda'tchi ngokwa nenyu mwendjire mwatchunda'tchi.

1. 러로 바녀거쭈, 와 구마라, 쫘바서꺼러러 무따아 마쭤어머라, 짜시야 어찌놔 짜 어나워쭈 찌하따바너 푸바 와 바뉴, 나 구떠 바쭈따찌 꼬과 너뉴 뭐찌러 마쭈따찌.

1. Finally, brothers, pray for us that the message of the Lord may spread rapidly and be honored, just as it was with you.

2. Kandji mundaa mweema Kabumbi atchununule mwa mino se bandju babi kandji bakosi ba mabi busese. Bushi ata ebandju bu batchusa ebweemeresi.

2. 가찌 무따아 뭐어마 가부삐 아쭈누누꺼 와 미노 서 바뉴 바비 가찌 바고시 바 마비 부서서. 부씨 아다 어바뉴 부 바쭈사 어붜어머러시.

2. And pray that we may be delivered from wicked and evil men, for not everyone has faith.

3. Si tchiro batcha, Enawetchu ende anaira bya alaanyaa. Angende aberesa emisi, ne

3. 시 찌로 바짜, 어나워쭈 어떠 아나이라 뱌 아롸아냐아. 아꺼떠 아버러사

3. But the Lord is faithful, and he will strengthen and protect you from the evil

kunde abalanga ku wamusimu.

4. Kandji kurengera ebuuma bwetchu na Enawetchu, tchuneeshi kwa bya tchwabathitchikaa bi mwendjire mwaira, nebi munganaendekera kunde mwaira

5. Enawetchuendaa akoresa emitchima yenyu, munde mwasima Kabumbi ne kuata ebushibirisi nga Kirisito.

6. Banyaketchu, tchitchine tchi tchwabatchitchika kwe sina lya Enawetchu Yesu Kirisito: muyendaa mwakomerana na tchira munyaketchu mwemeresi woshi ola ulyi nglyisi, kandji atatchunda ne myaasi era tchwabakangirisaa.

7. Mubeine mwishi kute ku mweemire kunde mwatchweya. Bushi mango tchwabaa tchulyi mwa katchi-katchi kenyu, tchutabaa ngalyisi tchiro ne hitcha.

8. Tchubano, tchatalyaa kalyo ka mundju asibya kwa buha. Si emushi ne butchufu, kukola ku tchwabaa tchwendjire tchwakola busese ne kutama busese, tchasiya tchutasitowera tchiro ne mundju mwa katchi-katchi

어미시, 너 구떠 아바꽈꽈 구 와무시무.

4. 가찌 구러꺼라 어부우마 붜쭈 나 어나워쭈, 쭈너어씨 꽈 뱌 쫘바찌찌가아 비 뭐찌러 뫄이라, 너비 무꺄나어떠거라 구떠 뫄이라

5. 어나워쭈어따아 아고러사 어미찌마 여뉴, 무떠 뫄시마 가부삐 너 구아다 어부씨비리시 꽈 기리시도.

6. 바냐거쭈, 찌찌너 찌 쫘바찌찌가 궈 시나 랴 어나워쭈 여수 기리시도: 무여따아 뫄고머라나 나 찌라 무냐거쭈 뭐머러시 오씨 오롸 우레 무레씨, 가찌 아다쭈따 너 먀아시 어라 쫘바가꺼리리사아.

7. 무버이너 뮈씨 구더 구 뭐어미러 구떠 뫄줘야. 부씨 마꼬 쫘바아 쭈레 뫄 가찌-가찌 거뉴, 쭈다바아 꺼레시 찌로 너 히짜.

8. 쭈바노, 짜다뺘아 가뢴 가 무뚜 아시뱌 과 부하. 시 어무씨 너 부쭈푸, 구고롸 구 쫘바아 줘찌러 쫘고롸 부서서 너 구다마 부서서, 짜시야 쭈다시도워라 찌로 너 무뚜 뫄 가찌-가찌 거뉴.

one.

4. We have confidence in the Lord that you are doing and will continue to do the things we command.

5. May the Lord direct your hearts into God's love and Christ's perseverance.

6. In the name of the Lord Jesus Christ, we command you, brothers, to keep away from every brother who is idle and does not live according to the teaching you received from us.

7. For you yourselves know how you ought to follow our example. We were not idle when we were with you,

8. nor did we eat anyone's food without paying for it. On the contrary, we worked night and day, laboring and toiling so that we would not be a burden to any of you.

kenyu.

9. Ekuira batcha, kuta kuteta mbu tchwabaa tchutangaasibwa nenyu. Si tchwabaa tchwahonda kubalosa kwa mweemire kunde mwaira, tchasiya munde mwatchweya.

10. Kubinalyi, mango tchwabaa tchulyi eyi mwenyu, tchwabaa tchwendjire tchwabatchitchika mbu: "emundju ola utahonda kukola atanalyaa!".

11. Tchwatcthire batcha, bushi tchoomvire emwaasi mira kwa bandju bauma mwa katchi-katchi kenyui siri ngalyisi, na wa kunde bakola, bandjire baya mwa myaasi era itabeerekere.

12. Abu bandju, tchwabatchitchika ne kubeeresa eyano kwe sina lya Enawetchu Yesu Kirisito mbu bendaa bakola mwa boolo, tchasiya bende balya bya neine bakoreraa.

13. Si mwabo banyaketchu, mutendaa mwatama mwa kuira emabuya.

14. Rero, akaba mundju murebe anaganana kutchunda ene myaasi tchwabaaandjikirire mwa mano maruba

9. 어구이라 바짜, 구다 구더다 뿌 좌바아 쭈다빠아시봐 너뉴. 시 좌바아 좌호따 구바로사 과 뭐어미러 구떠 뫄이라, 짜시야 무떠 뫄쭤야.

10. 구비나레, 마오 좌바아 쭈레 어에 뭐뉴, 좌바아 쭤찌러 좌바찌찌가 뿌: "어무뿌 오롸 우다호따 구고롸 아다나뺘아!".

11. 좌찌러 바짜, 부씨 쪼오삐러 어뫄아시 미라 과 바뚜 바우마 뫄 가찌-가찌 거뉴이 시리 빠레시, 나 와 구떠 바고롸, 바찌러 바야 뫄 먀아시 어라 이다버어러거러.

12. 아부 바뚜, 좌바찌찌가 너 구버어러사 어야노 궈 시나 롸 어나워쭈 여수 기리시도 뿌 버따아 바고롸 뫄 보오롣, 짜시야 버떠 바뺘 뱌 너이너 바고러라아.

13. 시 뫄보 바냐거쭈, 무더따아 뫄다마 뫄 구이라 어마부야.

14. 러로, 아가바 무뿌 무러버 아나가나나 구쭈따 어너 먀아시 좌바아찌기리러 뫄 마노 마루바

9. We did this, not because we do not have the right to such help, but in order to make ourselves a model for you to follow.

10. For even when we were with you, we gave you this rule:"If a man will not work, he shall not eat."

11. We hear that some among you are idle. They are not busy; they are busybodies.

12. Such people we command and urge in the Lord Jesus Christ to settle down and earn the bread they eat.

13. And as for you, brothers, never tire of doing what is right.

14. If anyone does not obey our instruction in this letter, take special note of him. Do not associate with him, in

mumumenyereraa kubuya. Kandji mutanakomeranaa nai, tchasiya aafe honyi.

무무머녀러라아 구부야. 가찌 무다나고머라나아 나이, 짜시야 아아퍼 호니.

order that he may feel ashamed.

15. Si tchiro batcha, mutamutolaa nga murenda, si mundaa mwamukalyiira nga munyakenyu

15. 시 찌로 바짜, 무다무도롸아 빠 무러따, 시 무따아 뫄무가쩨이라 빠 무냐거뉴

15. Yet do not regard him as an enemy, but warn him as a brother.

16. Enawetchu iwende waana eboolo, yeine andaa abeeresa obu boolo esuku soshi, ne muctchira mwaasi woshi! Kandji endaa anaba alauma nenyu muboshi!

16. 어나워쭈 이워떠 와아나 어보오로, 여이너 아따아 아버어러사 오부 보오로 어수구 소씨, 너 무찌라 뫄아시 옷씨! 가찌 어따아 아나바 아롸우마 너뉴 무보씨!

16. Now may the Lord of peace himself give you peace at all times and in every way. The Lord be with all of you.

17. Ene myaasi ye kubalamusa, nyono Paulo nyeine nyi nabaandjikirire'i ne mino yanyi. Ne maruba manyi moshi, ku nende nansinye'mu batcha, na kunende nanaandjika batcha.

17. 어너 먀아시 여 구바롸무사, 뇨노 파우로 녀이너 네 나바아찌기리러이 너 미노 야네. 너 마루바 마네 모씨, 구 너떠 나씨녀무 바짜, 나 구너떠 나나아찌가 바짜.

17. I, Paul, write this greeting in my own hand, which is the distinguishing mark in all my letters. This is how I write.

18. Enawetchu Yesu Kirisito endaa abaahanyira muboshi!

18. 어나워쭈 여수 기리시도 어따아 아바아하네라 무보씨!

18. The grace of our Lord Jesus Christ be with you all.

1 Timoteo

1 디모더오

1 Timothy

TIMOTEO WA KWANZA
(1 TIMOTHY)

디모더오 와 콰싸
(1 디모씨)

1 Timoteo Chikono 1

1. Poolo, ndjumwa ya Yesu Kirisito kwa kutchitchika kwa kabumbi, Mununusi wetchu na Kirisito Yesu Mulangalyiro wetchu.

2. Era mwa Timoteo, mwana wanyi we kanangana mwa bwemeresi : Ebubuya no bondjo ne boolo kutenga era mwa Kabumboi tata na Kirisito Yesu Enawetchu

3. Ngukula nakuana kwawekala mwa musi wera Efeso, emangu naya era Maketoniya unange ebandji bandju bata irisa sindji nyiiriso sira sita tchungenene.

4. Ngokula batakulyikira enyaano nei myasi ya bahokulyisa era itete kuokeresa, era yendi yareta ebwaka ; seri italyi ngokula ekuhonda kwa kabumbi era ilyi mwa bwemeresi, tchasiya uira ekulyingo'ku.

5. Seri ekutchitchika ebandju kulyikuhonda emasimano mala matamekutenga mwa mutchima mubuyabuya ne

1 디모더오 찌고노 1

1. 포오로, 뿌와 야 여수 기리시도 과 구찌찌가 과 가부쀄, 무누누시 워쭈 나 기리시도 여수 무롸빠레로 워쭈.

2. 어라 롸 디모더오, 롸나 와내 워 가나빠나 롸 붜머러시 : 어부부야 노 보쪼 너 보오로 구더빠 어라 롸 가부쁂이 다다 나 기리시도 여수 어나워쭈

3. 우구롸 나구아나 과워가롸 롸 무시 워라 어퍼소, 어마우 나야 어라 마거도니야 우나뻐 어바찌 바뿌 바다 이리사 시찌 네이리소 시라 시다 쭈뻐너너.

4. 오구롸 바다구레기라 어냐아노 너이 먀시 야 바호구레사 어라 이더더 구오거러사, 어라 여뼈 야러다 어봐가 ; 서리 이다레 오구롸 어구호빠 과 가부쀄 어라 이레 롸 붜머러시, 짜시야 우이라 어구레오구.

5. 서리 어구찌찌가 어바뿌 구레구호빠 어마시마노 마롸 마다머구더빠 롸 무찌마 무부야부야 너 미아내사

1 Timothy Chapter 1[NIV]

1. Paul, an apostle of Christ Jesus by the command of God our Savior and of Christ Jesus our hope,

2. To Timothy my true son in the faith: Grace, mercy and peace from God the Father and Christ Jesus our Lord.

3. As I urged you when I went into Macedonia, stay there in Ephesus so that you may command certain men not to teach false doctrines any longer

4. nor to devote themselves to myths and endless genealogies. These promote controversies rather than God's work--which is by faith.

5. The goal of this command is love, which comes from a pure heart and a good conscience and a sincere faith.

mianyisa ibuyabuya, nebwemeresi bula butete butebanyi busibya.

6. Ebandji bakaina kweni myasi, baneshibira mwa myasi ye buha-buha.

7. Emangu bahonda nambu babaa bakangirisi be lwaso lwa Kabumbi seri emyasi era bendjire bateta, nera bendjire basimika'mu bataiiishi.

8. Seri tchwishi e lwaso lula lukomire akaba emundju elukoresa mwa ndjira sira sikomire (sithchungenene)

9. Seri tchumenyereraa kwe lwaso lutabikwa bushi nebandju bala batchungenene. Seri lwabikwa kwa bandju bala batatchirembeka kandji batanakulyikira elwaso. Nokwabala batoobaa Kabumbi nebandju bala be byaa, kandji atchula erekere era mwe bandju bala batatchunda ebinndju bibuyabuya nabala betaa beshi nesi banyina nebandji betchi boshi.

10. Nebasingisi, ne balume bala bende basingira nebalume balyikabo, nesi ebakasi balyikabo ne bendi beeba ebandju nebafusi

이부야부야, 너뭐머러시 부꽈 부더더 부더바네 부시뱌.

6. 어바찌 바가이나 궈니 먀시, 바너씨비라 뫄 먀시 여 부하-부하.

7. 어마꾸 바호따 나뿌 바바아 바가끼리시 버 롸소 꽈 가부뻬 서리 어먀시 어라 버찌러 바더다, 너라 버찌러 바시미가무 바다이이이씨.

8. 서리 쮜씨 어 롸소 루꽈 루고미러 아가바 어무뚜 어루고러사 뫄 찌라 시라 시고미러 (시쭈뻐너너)

9. 서리 쭈머녀러라아 궈 롸소 루다비과 부씨 너바뚜 바꽈 바쭈뻐너너. 서리 롸비과 과 바뚜 바꽈 바다찌러뻐가 가찌 바다나구꿰기라 어롸소. 노과바꽈 바도오바아 가부뻬 너바뚜 바꽈 버 뱌아, 가찌 아쭈꽈 어러거러 어라 뭐 바뚜 바꽈 바다쭈따 어비뚜 비부야부야 나바꽈 버다아 버씨 너시 바네나 너바찌 버찌 보씨.

10. 너바시삐시, 너 바루머 바꽈 버더 바시삐라 너바루머 바꿰가보, 너시 어바가시 바꿰가보 너 버찌 버어바 어바뚜 너바푸시

6. Some have wandered away from these and turned to meaningless talk.

7. They want to be teachers of the law, but they do not know what they are talking about or what they so confidently affirm.

8. We know that the law is good if one uses it properly.

9. We also know that law is made not for the righteous but for lawbreakers and rebels, the ungodly and sinful, the unholy and irreligious; for those who kill their fathers or mothers, for murderers,

10. for adulterers and perverts, for slave traders and liars and perjurers--and for whatever else is contrary to the sound doctrine

bebisha, nabala bende balaisa emyasi era ye bisha, ne bandji boshi bala bendi baira nebira bitakulyikene ne myasi ye kanangana.

11. Ngokula ei myasi ye kanangana itchula mwa mwasi ola Kabumbi anyeeresaa. Noyu mwasi alyi mubuyabuya ola wende walosa ebulangare bwa Ongo kwa mundju ola uwahanyisibwe.

12. Nanyi nendjire natonga Yesu Kirisito Enawetchu, ola wanyeresa emisi era yatchuma nakola emulyimo wanyi, nendjire namutonga batcha bushi nayitolyire nga mundju ola alangalyire, kandji anyibikire mwa mulyimo wai.

13. Nyono kwa miramira nabaa mutetchi wabulyio na mulyibusi we bandji, namwicthi, si tchiro na batcha Ongo era kunyilorera ebondjo, bushi nabaa ndasa kumwemerera mwa mutchima wanyi, nei myasi yoshi naiira mwa buuta ; nokutamumenyerera.

14. Nengahanyi senawetchu sinanendekera busese

버비싸, 나바꽈 버떠 바꽈이사 어먀시 어라 여 비싸, 너 바찌 보씨 바꽈 버띠 바이라 너비라 비다구꿰거너 너 먀시 여 가나꽈나.

11. 꼬구꽈 어이 먀시 여 가나꽈나 이쭈꽈 마 마시 오꽈 가부삐 아녀어러사아. 노유 마시 아레 무부야부야 오꽈 워떠 와로사 어부꽈꽈러 봐 오꼬 과 무뚜 오꽈 우와하니시붜.

12. 나니 너띠러 나도꽈 여수 기리시도 어나워쭈, 오꽈 와녀러사 어미시 어라 야쭈마 나고꽈 어무레모 와니, 너띠러 나무도꽈 바짜 부씨 나에도꿰러 꽈 무뚜 오꽈 아꽈꽈꿰러, 가찌 아녜비기러 마 무레모 와이.

13. 뇨노 과 미라미라 나바아 무더찌 와부꿰오 나 무꿰부시 워 바찌, 나뮈찌, 시 찌로 나 바짜 오꼬 어라 구니로러라 어보쪼, 부씨 나바아 따사 구뭐머러라 마 무찌마 와니, 너이 먀시 요씨 나이이라 마 부우다 ; 노구다무머녀러라.

14. 너꽈하니 서나워쭈 시나너떠거라 부서서

---

11. that conforms to the glorious gospel of the blessed God, which he entrusted to me.

12. I thank Christ Jesus our Lord, who has given me strength, that he considered me faithful, appointing me to his service.

13. Even though I was once a blasphemer and a persecutor and a violent man, I was shown mercy because I acted in ignorance and unbelief.

14. The grace of our Lord was poured out on me abundantly,

alauma nebwemeresi, nemasimano mala malyi mwa ndanda sa Yesu Kirisito.

15. Onu mwasi alyi wa kanangana, ne bandju bemire kwemerera oyu mwasi mwa mitchima yabo. Noyu mwasi, uyono : Yesu Kirisito abaha munu butala, tchasiya anunule ebandju bala be mabi, arero nyono nyi mundju mukosi we mabi busese kurenga ebandji boshi.

16. Seri anyilorera ebondjo, bushi mwakunyirengera 'ko muberebere Yesu Kirisito alosaa eburembe bwai kwamu mabuya nebamwemerere, mwa mitchima yabu, babonyire ekalamu kesiku ne mangu.

17. Arero era mwa Ongo mwami we siku nemangu, ola utaala kulola kwa byaa, ola utalolyibwa'ku, Ongo ola wete ebwenge yeine lyibaa etchungan nekumutonga esiku nemangu. Bibe batcha.

18. Nakutchitchikire mwana wanyi Timoteo, kukulyikana neburebi, kukulyikana nemyasi yoburebi. Era era yahambalwa era luulu sau. Ei

---

아롸우마 너붜머러시, 너마시마노 마롸 마레 와 따따 사 여수 기리시도.

15. 오누 마시 아레 와 가나꽈나, 너 바뚜 버미러 궈머러라 오유 마시 마 미찌마 야보. 노유 마시, 우요노 : 여수 기리시도 아바하 무누 부다꽈, 짜시야 아누누러 어바뚜 바롸 버 마비, 아러로 뇨노 니 무뚜 무고시 워 마비 부서서 구러꽈 어바찌 보씨.

16. 서리 아네뢰러라 어보쪼, 부씨 꽈구니러꺼라 고 무버러버러 여수 기리시도 아로사아 어부러뻐 봐이 과무 마부야 너바뭐머러러, 꽈 미찌마 야부, 바보네러 어가롸무 거시구 너 마웃.

17. 아러로 어라 꽈 오꼬 마미 워 시구 너마웃, 오롸 우다아롸 구로롸 과 뱌아, 오롸 우다뢰레봐구, 오꼬 오롸 워더 어붜머 여이너 레바아 어쭈꺼누 너구무도꽈 어시구 너마웃. 비버 바짜.

18. 나구찌찌기러 뫄나 와네 디모더오, 구구레가나 너부러비, 구구레가나 너먀시 요부러비. 어라 어라 야하빠롸 어라 루우루 사우.

---

along with the faith and love that are in Christ Jesus.

15. Here is a trustworthy saying that deserves full acceptance: Christ Jesus came into the world to save sinners-- of whom I am the worst.

16. But for that very reason I was shown mercy so that in me, the worst of sinners, Christ Jesus might display his unlimited patience as an example for those who would believe on him and receive eternal life.

17. Now to the King eternal, immortal, invisible, the only God, be honor and glory for ever and ever. Amen.

18. Timothy, my son, I give you this instruction in keeping with the prophecies once made about you, so that by following them you may fight the good

myasi, wendaa waikulyikira, bushi ingakweeresa emisi yekunde walwisa emabi nobushiro.

19. Wendaa wasimika mwa bwemeresi bwao nekuata emianyisa ibuyabuya mwa mutchima wau. Kubinalyi ! Ei mianyisa ibuyabuya bandju bauma batatchitchula bailaire'ku. Boshi noku ebwemeresi bwabo bwelyire bwaokeresa (bwawa).

20. Mwaabu mu bandju mulyi Himeneo na Alesanduro. Abu bandju babiri nababikire mira mwa minu semusima; tchasiya babanunule ematchi bushi batathiereresa bakamba Ongo.

어이 먀시, 워따아 와이구뤠기라, 부씨 이까궈어러사 어미시 여구떠 와뤼사 어마비 노부씨로.

19. 워따아 와시미가 먀 붜머러시 봐오 너구아다 어미아네사 이부야부야 먀 무찌마 와우. 구비나뤠 ! 어이 미아네사 이부야부야 바뉴 바우마 바다쭈롸 바이롸이러구. 보씨 노구 어붜머러시 봐보 붜뤠러 봐오거러사 (봐와).

20. 먀아부 무 바뉴 무뤠 히머너오 나 아뤄사뉴로. 아부 바뉴 바비리 나바비기러 미라 먀 미누 서무시마; 짜시야 바바누누뤄 어마찌 부씨 바다쩌러러사 바가빠 오꼬.

fight,

19. holding on to faith and a good conscience. Some have rejected these and so have shipwrecked their faith.

20. Among them are Hymenaeus and Alexander, whom I have handed over to Satan to be taught not to blaspheme.

1 Timoteo Chikono 2

1. Rero, era muhondo sa byoshi, eano lyaneresise ebemeresi lyilyilyine : mwenda kweemera ebandju boshi era mwa Kabumbi. Mwendaa mwa mweema nokumubura kwenda abaasa nekunde mwa mwemwa nobondjo. Kandji nekumutonga kwa mabuya mai.

1 디모더오 찌고노 2

1. 러로, 어라 무호또 사 뵤씨, 어아노 랴너러시서 어버머러시 레뤠레뤠너 : 뭐따 궈어머라 어바뉴 보씨 어라 먀 가부뻬. 뭐따아 먀 뭐어마 노구무부라 궈따 아바아사 너구떠 먀 뭐먀 노보쪼. 가찌 너구무도빠 과 마부야 마이.

1 Timothy Chapter 2[NIV]

1. I urge, then, first of all, that requests, prayers, intercession and thanksgiving be made for everyone--

2. Mundaa mwemera abami nebandji bakulukulu boshi bala bemikirwe, tchasiya ememo metchu mabe mwa bolo nomwa buhaluke mwa kunde tchwaira bira bisimise Ongo nekuata emyanya era ingatchuma tchweresibwa etchunda.

2. 무따아 뭐머라 아바미 너바찌 바구루구루 보씨 바꽈 버미기뤄, 짜시야 어머모 머쭈 마버 뫄 보론 노뫄 부하루거 뫄 구떠 좌이라 비라 비시미서 오꼬 너구아다 어먀냐 어라 이까쭈마 쭤러시봐 어쭌따.

2. for kings and all those in authority, that we may live peaceful and quiet lives in all godliness and holiness.

3. Ekwemerera ebandju kutchula kukomire ngatchi kandji kwende kwasimisa Kabumbi i mununusi wetchu.

3. 어궈머러라 어바쭈 구쭈꽈 구고미러 까찌 가찌 궈떠 과시미사 가부삐 이 무누누시 워쭈.

3. This is good, and pleases God our Savior,

4. Bushi yeke ahonda ebandju boshi abanunule baikire kwa tchihangi bamenyerere emiyanyisa ye kanangana.

4. 부씨 여거 아호따 어바쭈 보씨 아바누누뤄 바이기러 과 찌하삐 바머녀러러 어미야네사 여 가나까나.

4. who wants all men to be saved and to come to a knowledge of the truth.

5. Bushi kunatchula Ongo muuma oshao. Kwanaba na mundju muuma oshao ola wende wabika ebandju mwa buuma bwa Ongo noyu mundju i Yesu Kirisito.

5. 부씨 구나쭈꽈 오꼬 무우마 오싸오. 과나바 나 무쭈 무우마 오싸오 오라 워떠 와비가 어바쭈 뫄 부우마 봐 오꼬 노유 무쭈 이 여수 기리시도.

5. For there is one God and one mediator between God and men, the man Christ Jesus,

6. Yeke iwaane ekalamu kai yeine, tchasiya anunule ebandju boshi mwa kuira batcha Yesu analosa kwa Kabumbi ahonda, anunule ebandju boshi. Aira batcha mwa bihangi nya Ongo abaa alondolyibwe mira.

6. 여거 이와아너 어가꽈무 가이 여이너, 짜시야 아누누뤄 어바쭈 보씨 뫄 구이라 바짜 여수 아나롯사 과 가부삐 아호따, 아누누뤄 어바쭈 보씨. 아이라 바짜 뫄 비하삐 냐 오꼬 아바아 아루또례붜 미라.

6. who gave himself as a ransom for all men--the testimony given in its proper time.

7. Kwa bushi nei myasi iyatchumire Ongo nayiira ndjumwa yai. Era

7. 과 부씨 너이 먀시 이야쭈미러 오꼬 나에이라 뚜뫄 야이. 어라 구네쭈마

7. And for this purpose I was appointed a herald and an apostle--I am telling the truth,

kunyitchuma nambu nenda nahubanganyisa ebandju bala batamumenyerere nokubakangirisa emyasi ye kanangana ye bwemeresi. Eni myasi nateta ilyi ya kanangana seri ita yabisha. Emyanya ye balume nebakasi mwa lubwaanano.	나뿌 너따 나후바까네사 어바꾸 바꽈 바다무머녀러러 노구바가끼리사 어먀시 여 가나꽈나 여 붜머러시. 어니 먀시 나더다 이레 야 가나꽈나 서리 이다 야비싸. 어먀냐 여 바루머 너바가시 와 루봐아나노.	I am not lying--and a teacher of the true faith to the Gentiles.
8. Rero, nahonda ebalume beine, Kabumbi mutchira tchisiki bomosise nemino mwa tchanya mwa kuba sine mino sikomisibwe. Bendaa baira batcha busira kufa bute, nesi kuira bwaka.	8. 러로, 나호따 어바루머 버이너, 가부삐 무찌라 찌시기 보모시서 너미노 와 짜냐 와 구바 시너 미노 시고미시붜. 버따아 바이라 바짜 부시라 구파 부더, 너시 구이라 봐가.	8. I want men everywhere to lift up holy hands in prayer, without anger or disputing.
9. Nebakasi nabu, nahonda bendaa baata emiimbalyire era itchungenene kandji era itarengeresa kandji era itangabeeta honyi, nekutchibika kwe bulyimbi kwabu kutendaa kwaba kwa kusukibwa envilyi kwakurengerea nesi kwa kweembala ebindju bira bihunganyisibwe mwa Hooro, nesi mwa mikofu nesi mwa ndjimba sira setchitchiro tchinene.	9. 너바가시 나부, 나호따 버따아 바아다 어미이빠레러 어라 이쭈꺼너너 가찌 어라 이다러꺼러사 가찌 어라 이다까버어다 호니, 너구찌비가 궈 부레삐 과부 구더따아 과바 과 구수기봐 어삐레 과구러꺼러러아 너시 과 궈어빠꽈 어비꾸 비라 비후까네시붜 와 호오로, 너시 와 미고푸 너시 와 찌빠 시라 서찌찌로 찌너너.	9. I also want women to dress modestly, with decency and propriety, not with braided hair or gold or pearls or expensive clothes,
10. Seri ekutchibika kwe bulyimbi kwabo, kwendaa kwaba mwa kuira emabuya ngokula bineemire kwa bakasi bala bende	10. 서리 어구찌비가 궈 부레삐 과보, 궈따아 과바 와 구이라 어마부야 꼬구꽈 비너어미러 과 바가시 바꽈 버너 바찌도까 나뿌 바쭈꽈	10. but with good deeds, appropriate for women who profess to worship God.

batchitonga nambu batchula 바쭈찌러 오꼬.
batchundjire Ongo.

11. Emukasi atchiirisa mwa busirire mwa kutchunda mwa ndjira soshi.	11. 어무가시 아찌이리사 똬 부시리러 똬 구쭈따 똬 씨라 소씨.	11. A woman should learn in quietness and full submission.
12. Na kandji nderesise emukasi lwaso nambu endaa akangirisa nesi nambu endaa emangira ebalume, si tcheemire kunde areka elwayo.	12. 나 가찌 떠러시서 어무가시 똬소 나뿌 어따아 아가삐리사 너시 나뿌 어따아 어마삐라 어바루머, 시 쩌어미러 구떠 아러가 어똬요.	12. I do not permit a woman to teach or to have authority over a man; she must be silent.
13. Bushi Atamu iwabaa muberebere kubumbibwa tchasinda Efa.	13. 부씨 아다무 이와바아 무버러버러 구부삐봐 짜시따 어파.	13. For Adam was formed first, then Eve.
14. Kandji ata Atamu iwatebwaa si emukasi tchiro akatchunda Kabumbi.	14. 가찌 아다 아다무 이와더봐아 시 어무가시 찌로 아가쭈따 가부삐.	14. And Adam was not the one deceived; it was the woman who was deceived and became a sinner.
15. Si tchiru nabatcha, emukasi akanunulyibwa kurengera elubuto lwai, akaba angeendekera kusimika mwa bwemeresi bwai nakunde asima ebandji, na kuata emikorere era itchungenene kandji era isimise Ongo.	15. 시 찌루 나바짜, 어무가시 아가누누쪠봐 구러꺼라 어루뿌도 똬이, 아가바 아꺼어떠거라 구시미가 똬 붜머러시 봐이 나구떠 아시마 어바찌, 나 구아다 어미고러러 어라 이쭈꺼너너 가찌 어라 이시미서 오꼬.	15. But women will be saved through childbearing--if they continue in faith, love and holiness with propriety.

1 Timoteo Chikono 3	1 디모더오 찌고노 3	1 Timothy Chapter 3[NIV]
1. Onu mwasi alyi wa kanangana : Akaba emundju ahonda ekaasi komwa luhu lwa Ongo, eri ahonda	1. 오누 똬시 아쪠 와 가나따나 : 아가바 어무뚜 아호따 어가아시 고똬 루후 똬 오꼬, 어리 아호따	1. Here is a trustworthy saying: If anyone sets his heart on being an overseer, he desires a noble task.

emulyimo oma ukomire.

2. Bushi noku emungumwa we luhu lwa Kabumbi emire abaa mundju ola utomvikana'ku na mwasi mubi. Kandji tcheemire abaa mulume ola wete mukasi muuma pwere ; kandji abaa mundju ola wende watchilanga mwa mabi, na kandji endaa atchilanga kwa mabi nekunde aata miyanyisa ibuya. Nekuba mundju ola wende weresibwa etchunda, ola wende waangirira ebaenyi kubuya na kandji abaa mundju ola wishi kukangirisa.

3. Atabaa mundju mutamisi nemafu kandji atabaa mundju ola wende walwa nebandji, nesi ola wende wabanganya ebandji, si abaa murembi, kandji atabaa mundju ola utchula usimire ebuteya.

4. Nakandji abaa mundju ola wemangirire engumu yai kubuya. Nebana bai batemire kuba batengu, si bemire kunde bamutchunda mwa byoshi.

5. Bushi akaba mundju angafundjwa kwemangira engumu yai rero kute

어무레모 오마 우고미러.

2. 부씨 노구 어무꾸와 워 루후 롸 가부삐 어미러 아바아 무뚜 오롸 우도삐가나구 나 뫄시 무비. 가찌 쩌어미러 아바아 무루머 오롸 워더 무가시 무우마 풔러 ; 가찌 아바아 무뚜 오롸 워떠 와찌롸빠 뫄 마비, 나 가찌 어따아 아찌롸빠 과 마비 너구떠 아아다 미야네사 이부야. 너구바 무뚜 오롸 워떠 워러시봐 어쭈따, 오롸 워떠 와아삐리라 어바어네 구부야 나 가찌 아바아 무뚜 오롸 위씨 구가삐리사.

3. 아다바아 무뚜 무다미시 너마푸 가찌 아다바아 무뚜 오롸 워떠 와롸 너바찌, 너시 오롸 워떠 와바빠냐 어바찌, 시 아바아 무러삐, 가찌 아다바아 무뚜 오롸 우쭈롸 우시미러 어부더야.

4. 나가찌 아바아 무뚜 오롸 워마삐리러 어꾸무 야이 구부야. 너바나 바이 바더미러 구바 바더우, 시 버미러 구떠 바무쭈따 뫄 보씨.

5. 부씨 아가바 무뚜 아빠푸롸 궈마삐라 어꾸무 야이 러로 구더 아빠아롸

2. Now the overseer must be above reproach, the husband of but one wife, temperate, self-controlled, respectable, hospitable, able to teach,

3. not given to drunkenness, not violent but gentle, not quarrelsome, not a lover of money.

4. He must manage his own family well and see that his children obey him with proper respect.

5. (If anyone does not know how to manage his own family, how can he take care of

angaala kulanga eluhu lwa Ongo ?

구롸까 어루후 똬 오꼬 ?

God's church?)

6. Kandji atemire kuba mwemeresi muyayaya, angeshakunde atchilola, tchasinda anatchindjibuswa ngokula wamusimu nai atchindjibuswaa.

6. 가찌 아더미러 구바 뭐머러시 무야야야, 아꺼싸구떠 아찌뤈롸, 짜시따 아나찌찌부솨 꼬구롸 와무시무 나이 아찌찌부솨아.

6. He must not be a recent convert, or he may become conceited and fall under the same judgment as the devil.

7. Kandji abaa mundju ola utchusa ngulu ibuya mwa bandju ba bata bemeresi, angesha kukenyibwa tchasinda anatowera mwa mwiita we musimu.

7. 가찌 아바아 무뚜 오롸 우쭈사 꿍루 이부야 똬 바뚜 바 바다 버머러시, 아꺼싸 구거네봐 짜시따 아나도워라 똬 뮈이다 워 무시무.

7. He must also have a good reputation with outsiders, so that he will not fall into disgrace and into the devil's trap.

8. Batcha ebakasi ba Kabumbi tchibeemire baata emyanya eraingatchuma beresibwa etchunda. Bateemire kuba batebanyi, nesi batamisi, nesi bandju bakuhonda ebikulo mwa ndjira sibi.

8. 바짜 어바가시 바 가부삐 찌버어미러 바아다 어먄냐 어라이꺼쭈마 버러시봐 어쭈따. 바더어미러 구바 바더바네, 너시 바다미시, 너시 바뚜 바구호따 어비구뤈 똬 찌라 시비.

8. Deacons, likewise, are to be men worthy of respect, sincere, not indulging in much wine, and not pursuing dishonest gain.

9. Bakasimika mwa mwasi we kanangana mwa mianyisa ibuyabuya.

9. 바가시미가 똬 마시 워 가나꺼나 똬 미아네사 이부야부야.

9. They must keep hold of the deep truths of the faith with a clear conscience.

10. Nabanu bakasi tcheemira kubaereka emyanya yabu tanga: tchasinda eribakola omulyimo wa Ongo. Balorekanyire oku batete busira bitaki.

10. 나바누 바가시 쩌어미라 구바어러가 어먄냐 야부 다꺄: 짜시따 어리바고롸 오무뤠모 와 오꼬. 바뤈러가네러 오구 바더더 부시라 비다기.

10. They must first be tested; and then if there is nothing against them, let them serve as deacons.

11. Batcha nebakasi babaa bandju bakutchitchunda; batabaa beki babisha, batabaaa bandju bakuamana

11. 바짜 너바가시 바바아 바뚜 바구쭈따; 바다바아 버기 바비싸, 바다바아아 바뚜 바구아마나 어비찌

11. In the same way, their wives are to be women worthy of respect, not malicious talkers but temperate and

ebindji bulyio, seri babaa bakutchulanga kwa mabi moshi.

부레오, 서리 바바아 바구쭈롸아 과 마비 모씨.

trustworthy in everything.

12. Tchira mukosi woshi abaa mulume ola wete mukasi muuma pwere, balange ebana babu kubuya nebihyaala byabu byoshi?

12. 찌라 무고시 오씨 아바아 무루머 오라 워더 무가시 무우마 풔러, 바라워 어바나 바부 구부야 너비햐아롸 뱌부 뵤씨?

12. A deacon must be the husband of but one wife and must manage his children and his household well.

13. Kwabushi balabakola emulyimo wa Kabumbi kubuya, bende batcheresa etchunda lyibuya nemisi bushi mwa bwemeresi bula bulyi mwa ndanda sa Kirisito.

13. 과부씨 바롸바고롸 어무레모 와 가부삐 구부야, 버떠 바쩌러사 어쭈따 레부야 너미시 부씨 롸 붜머러시 부라 부레 롸 따따 사 기리시도.

13. Those who have served well gain an excellent standing and great assurance in their faith in Christ Jesus.

14. Nni myasi nakuandjikira nyilangalyire kuika era mwoo fubafuba

14. 누니 먀시 나구아찌기라 네롸워레러 구이가 어라 모오 푸바푸바

14. Although I hope to come to you soon, I am writing you these instructions so that,

15. Seri nyikerisa, umenyerera busese tchitatchi kwemire kuira mwa luhu lwa Kabumbi ola uhalukire, engulyiro, nenzimikiro ye kanangana.

15. 서리 네거리사, 우머녀러라 부서서 찌다찌 궈미러 구이라 롸 루후 롸 가부삐 오롸 우하루끼러, 어우레로, 너씨미기로 여 가나워나.

15. if I am delayed, you will know how people ought to conduct themselves in God's household, which is the church of the living God, the pillar and foundation of the truth.

16. Kubinalyi! Rero, mwunvaa emyasi era thuboshi thuthula thwemerere. Emwasi munene ola Ongo athubihulyire, athula wa kushishasa busese! Noyu mwasi iyono: Kirisito ahubaa mundju. Oyu Kirisito, eMuchima Mubuyabuya era kunalosa kwa athula athungenene. Kandji era kunalorekanako ne ndonyi.

16. 구비나레! 러로, 무빠아 어먀시 어라 쭈보씨 쭈쭈롸 쭤머러러. 어먀시 무너너 오롸 오꼬 아쭈비후레러, 아쭈롸 와 구씨싸사 부서서! 노유 먀시 이요노: 기리시도 아후바아 무뚜. 오유 기리시도, 어무찌마 무부야부야 어라 구나로사 과 아쭈롸 아쭈워너너. 가찌 어라 구나로러가나고 너

16. Beyond all question, the mystery of godliness is great: He appeared in a body, was vindicated by the Spirit, was seen by angels, was preached among the nations, was believed on in the world, was taken up in glory.

Era kuhubanganyisibwa mwa bandju ba bateshi Ongo. Era kweemererwa na bandju banene mwa butala. Chasinda era kwerusibwa kwa nguba mwa bulangare.

또니. 어라 구후바꺄네시봐 봐 바뚜 바 바더씨 오꼬. 어라 궈어머러롸 나 바뚜 바너너 봐 부다뢔. 짜시따 어라 궈루시봐 과 꾸바 봐 부롸꺄러.

1 Timoteo Chikono 4

1. Reru emutchima mubuyabuya atetchire tchanganama nambu mwa siku sebusinda bandju banene bakareka ebwemeresi seri bakomvirisa emyasi ye mitchima ye kuengeerana nekunfirisa enyiiriso sira sitenganyire nebihwasi.

2. Bangende bahambala emyasi yobutebanyi ; ei myanya yabu yotchirwe netchuma tchira tcha taata.

3. Bendjire babure ebandju nambu batahwera nesi kuhweribwa. Nekunde baanga ebandju nambu batendaa balya nebilyo byomubyuma bira Ongo abumba. Tchasiya ebemeresi bubeshi emyasi ye kanangana bendaa babilya mwa kumutonga.

4. Kwa bushi byoshi bira Kabumbi abumbaa bitchula

1 디모더오 찌고노 4

1. 러루 어무찌마 무부야부야 아더찌러 짜꺄나마 나뿌 봐 시구 서부시따 바뚜 바너너 바가러가 어붜머러시 서리 바고뻬리사 어먀시 여 미찌마 여 구어꺼어라나 너구뻬리사 어네이리소 시라 시더꺄네러 너비화시.

2. 바꺼떠 바하빠뢔 어먀시 요부더바네 ; 어이 먀냐 야부 요찌뤄 너쭈마 찌라 짜 다아다.

3. 버찌러 바부러 어바뚜 나뿌 바다훠라 너시 구훠리봐. 너구떠 바아꺄 어바뚜 나뿌 바더따아 바뢔 너비꾠 뵤무뷰마 비라 오꼬 아부빠. 짜시야 어버머러시 부버씨 어먀시 여 가나꺄나 버따아 바비꺄 봐 구무도꺄.

4. 과 부씨 뵤씨 비라 가부뻬 아부빠아 비쭈롸

1 Timothy Chapter 4[NIV]

1. The Spirit clearly says that in later times some will abandon the faith and follow deceiving spirits and things taught by demons.

2. Such teachings come through hypocritical liars, whose consciences have been seared as with a hot iron.

3. They forbid people to marry and order them to abstain from certain foods, which God created to be received with thanksgiving by those who believe and who know the truth.

4. For everything God created is good, and nothing is to be

bikomire. Seri kutalyi tchira ebandju bendaa banana. Seri ebibyoshi tcheemire kunde bamutonga era muhondo sokubyaangirira.

5. Kwa bushi tchira tchindju tcheemererwe era muhondo sa Ongo mwa memo.

6. Eri ungakengesa munyakenyu ei myasi, ungaba mwaanda mubuya wa Yesu Kirisito. Bushi weine, ei myasi ya Kabumbi era tchwemerere iyakukusa, alauma nemyasi ya ye kanangana erawende wakangirisibwa, ei myasi wendjire wakulyikira kubuya.

7. Seri utemerera emyasi ye nyiano se buhabuha sira sitalyi mwa bwemeresi nesi sira se bakosi bala be Baekulu. Nau wenda watchikomeresa mwa myasi era isimisi Ongo.

8. Kwabushi okukola busese nemisi yomubiri, kweete mufa mueke siri ekuira bira bisimise Kabumbi bitchusa mufa bwa bindju byoshi, kwa bushi etchera tchende tchatchweresa etchiraane tchekubona ekalamu mwesine siku nekalamu kesiku nemangu.

비고미러. 서리 구다뤠 찌라 어바뚜 버따아 바나나. 서리 어비뵤씨 쩌어미러 구너 바무도빠 어라 무호또 소구뱌아끼리라.

5. 과 부씨 찌라 찌뚜 쩌어머러뤄 어라 무호또 사 오꼬 먀 머모.

6. 어리 우빠거어사 무냐거뉴 어이 먀시, 우빠바 뫄아따 무부야 와 여수 기리시도. 부씨 워이너, 어이 먀시 야 가부뻬 어라 쭤머러러 이야구구사, 아빠우마 너먀시 야 여 가나빠나 어라워머 와가끼리시봐, 어이 먀시 워찌러 와구쀄기라 구부야.

7. 서리 우더머러라 어먀시 여 네아노 서 부하부하 시라 시다뤠 뫄 붜머러시 너시 시라 서 바고시 바빠 버 바어구룩. 나우 워빠 와찌고머러사 뫄 먀시 어라 이시미시 오꼬.

8. 과부씨 오구고꽈 부서서 너미시 요무비리, 궈어더 무파 무어거 시리 어구이라 비라 비시미서 가부뻬 비쮸사 무파 봐 비뚜 뵤씨, 과 부씨 어쩌라 쩌떠 짜쭤러사 어찌라아너 쩌구보나 어가꽈무 뭐시너 시구 너가꽈무 거시구 너마뀌.

rejected if it is received with thanksgiving,

5. because it is consecrated by the word of God and prayer.

6. If you point these things out to the brothers, you will be a good minister of Christ Jesus, brought up in the truths of the faith and of the good teaching that you have followed.

7. Have nothing to do with godless myths and old wives' tales; rather, train yourself to be godly.

8. For physical training is of some value, but godliness has value for all things, holding promise for both the present life and the life to come.

9. Onu mwasi alyi wa kanangana tchineemire kwemererwa nebandju boshi.

10. Kwa bushi noku tchwakola busese nekulwisa bushi thculangalyire Kabumbi, ola utchula muuma-uma, kandji imununusi we bandju boshi, si alyi tanga mununusi wabala ba mwemerere.

11. Eni myasi iwemire kunde watchitchika nekuikangirisa ebandju.

12. Kutabaa mundju ola wakene etabana lyau, seri uate emyanya ibuya-buya era muhondo se ebemeresi, mwa myasi yobwemeresi nokurengera emikorere yau (emyanya), ne nzii yau kurengera ebwemeresi bwau nebulangare bwau.

13. Natchiru nyinganabaha utchisesa busese ekunde wairisa ebandju emaandjiko mabuya-buya nekunde wabasesa emutchima nekubakangirisa.

14. Utareka ekukoresa elwembo lula lulyi mwa mutchima wau lula weresibwa mwa burebi emangu ebangumwa beluhu

---

9. 오누 먀시 아레 와 가나까나 찌너어미러 궈머러롸 너바쭈 보씨.

10. 과 부씨 노구 쫘고롸 부서서 너구뛰사 부씨 쭈우롸까레러 가부삐, 오롸 우쭈롸 무우마-우마, 가찌 이무누누시 워 바쭈 보씨, 시 아레 다까 무누누시 와바롸 바 뭐머러러.

11. 어니 먀시 이워미러 구더 와찌찌가 너구이가끼리사 어바쭈.

12. 구다바아 무뚜 오롸 와거너 어다바나 랴우, 서리 우아더 어먀냐 이부야-부야 어라 무호또 서 어버머러시, 먀 먀시 요붜머러시 노구러꺼라 어미고러러 야우 (어먀냐), 너 씨이 야우 구러꺼라 어붜머러시 봐우 너부롸까러 봐우.

13. 나찌루 네까나바하 우찌서사 부서서 어구떠 와이리사 어바쭈 어마아찌고 마부야-부야 너구떠 와바서사 어무찌마 너구바가끼리사.

14. 우다러가 어구고러사 어뤄뽀 루롸 루레 먀 무찌마 와우 루롸 워러시봐 먀 부러비 어마우 어바우먀 버루후 똬 가부삐 바구가 궈

---

9. This is a trustworthy saying that deserves full acceptance

10. (and for this we labor and strive), that we have put our hope in the living God, who is the Savior of all men, and especially of those who believe.

11. Command and teach these things.

12. Don't let anyone look down on you because you are young, but set an example for the believers in speech, in life, in love, in faith and in purity.

13. Until I come, devote yourself to the public reading of Scripture, to preaching and to teaching.

14. Do not neglect your gift, which was given you through a prophetic message when the body of elders laid their hands on you.

lwa Kabumbi bakuka kwe mino.

15. Waanyisa kwei myasi Yoshi, kandji utchanaa loshi kweni myasi, tchasiya ebandju boshi balola tchanganama kwa weendekera mwaku kasi ke bwemeresi bwau.

16. Utchilangaa weine nobubuirisi bwau usesa mwei myasi. Kwabushi mwa kuira batcha, ungatchinunula weine alauma nabala bendjire bakumvirisa.

미노.

15. 와아네사 궈이 먀시 요씨, 가찌 우짜나아 론씨 궈니 먀시, 짜시야 어바뉴 보씨 바로라 짜까나마 과 워어떠거라 마구 가시 거 뭐머러시 봐우.

16. 우찌롸까아 워이너 노부부이리시 봐우 우서사 뭐이 먀시. 과부씨 뫄 구이라 바짜, 우까찌누누롸 워이너 아롸우마 나바롸 버찌러 바구삐리사.

15. Be diligent in these matters; give yourself wholly to them, so that everyone may see your progress.

16. Watch your life and doctrine closely. Persevere in them, because if you do, you will save both yourself and your hearers.

1 Timoteo Chikono 5

1. Utendaa wakaliire emungumwa, seri wendaaa wamuaana ngokuno tata, nebatabana wana batola nga banyaketchu.

2. Nebakasi bala be baekulu ubatola nga balyi ba mama, ne banyere ubatola ngokula ungatola balyi benyu busira kubaata'ku mianyisa ibiire.

3. Utchundaa ebahumbakasi bala be kanangana

4. Seri akaba emuhumbakasi eete ebana nesi ebehukulu,

1 디모더오 찌고노 5

1. 우더따아 와가찔이러 어무꾸뫄, 서리 워따아아 와무아아나 꼬구노 다다, 너바다바나 와나 바도롸 까 바냐거쭈.

2. 너바가시 바롸 버 바어구룹 우바도롸 까 바쪠 바 마마, 너 바녀러 우바도롸 꼬구롸 우까도롸 바쪠 버뉴 부시라 구바아다구 미아네사 이비이러.

3. 우쭈따아 어봐후빠가시 바롸 버 가나까나

4. 서리 아가바 어무후빠가시 어어더 어바나

1 Timothy Chapter 5[NIV]

1. Do not rebuke an older man harshly, but exhort him as if he were your father. Treat younger men as brothers,

2. older women as mothers, and younger women as sisters, with absolute purity.

3. Give proper recognition to those widows who are really in need.

4. But if a widow has children or grandchildren, these should

abola bemire kunde batchikangirisa kulosa etchunda mwa tchihaala tchabu beine ne kufulusisa ebasere babu boshi : kwabushi onu mwasi akomire, bakaira batcha onu mwasi angeemererwa na Tata Kabumbi.

5. Seri ola ulyin muhumbakasi ola we kanangana nekurekibwa yeine yeke ende aba aalangalyire Kabumbi yeine. Kandji kusalyira kwende anasalyira emushi ne butchufu Kabumbi amuaasa mwa byaha byai.

6. Seri ola wende watchisimisa mwa miasi yomuno butala oshao, yeke ende aba afire mira mwa miasi yoshi ye mitchima, tchiro angaba nambu angaba muuma-uma we mubiri wai.

7. Bushi noku tcheemire utchitchika ebahumbakasi eniu miasi tchasiya kutabaa tchiru nomwasi mubi ola ungatchuma baba takira.

8. Seri akaba emundju ataalyire kulanga bala balyi bai nesi ebandju bomwa tchahaala tchai yeine, onola

너시 어버후구루, 아보꽈 버미러 구떠 바찌가꼐리사 구루사 어쭈따 마 찌하아꽈 짜부 버이너 너 구푸루시사 어바서러 바부 보씨 : 과부씨 오누 꽈시 아고미러, 바가이라 바짜 오누 꽈시 아꼐어머러롸 나 다다 가부삐.

5. 서리 오꽈 우레누 무후빠가시 오꽈 워 가나꽈나 너구러기봐 여이너 여거 어떠 아바 아아꽈꽈레러 가부삐 여이너. 가찌 구사꼐라 궈떠 아나사꼐라 어무씨 너 부쭈푸 가부삐 아무아아사 꽈 뱌하 뱌이.

6. 서리 오꽈 워떠 와찌시미사 꽈 미아시 요무노 부다꽈 오싸오, 여거 어떠 아바 아피러 미라 꽈 미아시 요씨 여 미찌마, 찌로 아꽈바 나뿌 아꽈바 무우마-우마 워 무비리 와이.

7. 부씨 노구 쩌어미러 우찌찌가 어바후빠가시 어니우 미아시 짜시야 구다바아 찌루 노꽈시 무비 오꽈 우꽈쭈마 바바 다기라.

8. 서리 아가바 어무뚜 아다아꼐러 구꽈아 바꽈 바레 바이 너시 어바뚜 보꽈 짜하아꽈 짜이 여이너,

learn first of all to put their religion into practice by caring for their own family and so repaying their parents and grandparents, for this is pleasing to God.

5. The widow who is really in need and left all alone puts her hope in God and continues night and day to pray and to ask God for help.

6. But the widow who lives for pleasure is dead even while she lives.

7. Give the people these instructions, too, so that no one may be open to blame.

8. If anyone does not provide for his relatives, and especially for his immediate family, he has denied the faith and is

ananyire ebwemeresi, nonu mundju alyi mundju mubi kuluha emundju ola utalyi mwa bwemeresi.

오노꽈 아나네러 어뭐머러시, 노누 무뚜 아쩨 무뚜 무비 구루하 어무뚜 오꽈 우다쩨 꽈 뭐머러시.

worse than an unbeliever.

9. Emuhumbakasi ata andjikwa mwa bahumbakasi balyikabo akaba atasa kulumisa ebiro tchiratchu, na kandji abaa mukasi ola wabaa uhwelyirwe na mulume muuma (atabaa mukasi ola uhweltirwe kwa lwalyi).

9. 어무후빠가시 아다 아찌과 꽈 바후빠가시 바쩨가보 아가바 아다사 구루미사 어비로 찌라쭈, 나 가찌 아바아 무가시 오꽈 와바아 우훠쩨뤄 나 무루머 무우마 (아다바아 무가시 오꽈 우훠루디뤄 과 꽈쩨).

9. No widow may be put on the list of widows unless she is over sixty, has been faithful to her husband,

10. Na kandji abaa mundju ola wemererwe ne bandju kwabushi nemabuya mai, kandji arembera nebana bai, kandji ende aangilyira ebaenyi, akaba ende osa emaulu me bakosi ba Ongo, kandji alyi mundju ola wende waasa bala balyoi mwa bulai, na kandji akaba atchusa ebushiro bunene mukunde aira tchira mabuya moshi.

10. 나 가찌 아바아 무뚜 오꽈 워머러뤄 너 바뚜 과부씨 너마부야 마이, 가찌 아러뻐라 너바나 바이, 가찌 어떠 아아끼쩨라 어바어네, 아가바 어떠 오사 어마우루 머 바고시 바 오꽁, 가찌 아쩨 무뚜 오꽈 워떠 와아사 바꽈 바룐이 꽈 부꽈이, 나 가찌 아가바 아쭈사 어부씨로 부너너 무구떠 아이라 찌라 마부야 모씨.

10. and is well known for her good deeds, such as bringing up children, showing hospitality, washing the feet of the saints, helping those in trouble and devoting herself to all kinds of good deeds.

11. Seri ebahumbakasi bala batchiri banyere beke utababika mwa mwaandjo we bahumbakasi, bala beemirwe kuasibwa kwabushi kulyi emangu emubiri wabu angabatchuma kuata mianyisa ye kureka Kirisito nekuhonda kuhwerana.

11. 서리 어바후빠가시 바꽈 바찌리 바녀러 버거 우다바비가 꽈 꽈아쪼 워 바후빠가시, 바꽈 버어미뤄 구아시봐 과부씨 구쩨 어마꾸 어무비리 와부 아꺄바쭈마 구아다 미아네사 여 구러가 기리시도 너구호따 구훠라나.

11. As for younger widows, do not put them on such a list. For when their sensual desires overcome their dedication to Christ, they want to marry.

12. Mwa kuira batcha nabu

12. 꽈 구이라 바짜 나부

12. Thus they bring judgment

bangatchindjibusibwa
kwabushi nokureka
etchilaano tchabu na Kirisito.

13. Nokwa bushi noku,
ebuoshi bwabu berabendjire
bauna-una mwa bihaala
(nyumba) byebene seri ata
nebooshi bweine oshau, seri
bendi bekala mamaana
maanebandji bandju nekunde
batchiingisa mwa miasi era
itaberekere nokuteta bira
bitatchungenene.

14. Bushi noku nyingasimire
ebahumbakasi bala batchiri
banyere bahweranaa
banabutaa nebana,
balangaa'bu ne kuemangirira
emahosimabu kubuya
tchasiya ebarenda batabona
tchihangi tcha kutchuteta
bulyiyo (kutchuamana).

15. Kwa bushi kulyi
bahumbakasi bauma-uma
bala baerire mira bushi
nokukulyikira emusimu.

16. Akaba emulume nesi
emukasi ola ulyi mwa
bwemeresi ete ebahumbakasi
mwa tchihaala tchai, abaasa
neluhu lwa kabumbi
lutalyibuka mwa kuasa banu
balyi bahumbakasi bala balyi
be kanangana.

17. Ebangumwa bala

바까찌띠부시봐 과부씨
노구러가 어찌퐈아노 짜부
나 기리시도.

13. 노과 부씨 노구,
어부오씨 봐부 버라버띠러
바우나-우나 퐈 비하아퐈
(뉴빠) 벼버너 서리 아다
너보오씨 뭐이너 오싸우,
서리 버띠 버가퐈 마마아나
마아너바찌 바뚜 너구떠
바찌이띠사 퐈 미아시 어라
이다버러거러 노구더다 비라
비다쭈어너너.

14. 부씨 노구 네까시미러
어바후빠가시 바퐈 바찌리
바녀러 바훠라나아
바나부다아 너바나,
바퐈까아부 너 구어마띠리라
어마호시마부 구부야 짜시야
어바러따 바다보나 찌하띠
짜 구쭈더다 부레요
(구쭈아마나).

15. 과 부씨 구레
바후빠가시 바우마-우마
바퐈 바어리러 미라 부씨
노구구레기라 어무시무.

16. 아가바 어무루머 너시
어무가시 오퐈 우레 퐈
뭐머러시 어더 어바후빠가시
퐈 찌하아퐈 짜이, 아바아사
너루후 롸 가부뻬
루다레부가 퐈 구아사 바누
바레 바후빠가시 바퐈 바레
버 가나까나.

17. 어바꾸롸 바퐈

on themselves, because they
have broken their first pledge.

13. Besides, they get into the
habit of being idle and going
about from house to house.
And not only do they become
idlers, but also gossips and
busybodies, saying things they
ought not to.

14. So I counsel younger
widows to marry, to have
children, to manage their
homes and to give
the enemy no opportunity for
slander.

15. Some have in fact already
turned away to follow Satan.

16. If any woman who is a
believer has widows in her
family, she should help them
and not let the church be
burdened with them, so that
the church can help those
widows who are really in need.

17. The elders who direct the

bemangirire eluhu lwa
Kabumbi kubjuya ; tcheemire
kunde batchundjibwa kabiri,
nekueresibwa elwembo lula
lunabalumirire, seri tcheemire
tanga kutangirira kwa bala
batchaanyire busesemwa
tchinwa nomwa nyiiriso.

18. Kwa bushi, emaandjiko
matetchire bathca : utamina
ebunu bwe mbanzi emangu
yesimatanga ebulu nakandji
emungere nesi emukosi
tcheemire kunde eresibwa
elwembo lwai.

19. Utasimba mutchira mwasi
ola bahobekire emungumwa
seri mwa bunu bwa bebei
babiri nesi bahatchu.

20. Nabu bakosi be mabi,
ubakalyiira era muhondo se
bandju boshi tchasiya ebandji
bendaa bobaa kuira e byaa.

21. NAkutchitchikire era
muhondo sa Kabumbi nera
muhondo sa Kirisito nera
muhondo seba Malaika bai
bala balondolwa ; wendaa
wakulyikira (weemisa) eni
myasi busira kabolo na
busira kuira kalondo mwa
bandju boshi.

22. Utalyibitchira kweeresa

버마삐리러 어루후 똬
가부삐 구부주야 ; 쩌어미러
구떠 바쭈찌봐 가비리,
너구어러시봐 어뤄뽀 루똬
루나바루미리러, 서리
쩌어미러 다따 구다삐리라
과 바똬 바짜아니러
부서서똬 찌나 노똬
네이리소.

18. 과 부씨, 어마아찌고
마더찌러 바쭈아 : 우다미나
어부누 붜 빠씨 어마꾸
여시마다따 어부루 나가찌
어무뻐러 너시 어무고시
쩌어미러 구떠 어러시봐
어뤄뽀 똬이.

19. 우다시빠 무찌라 마시
오똬 바호버기러 어무꾸똬
서리 똬 부누 봐 버버이
바비리 너시 바하쭈.

20. 나부 바고시 버 마비,
우바가례이라 어라 무호또
서 바쭈 보씨 짜시야 어바씨
버따아 보바아 구이라 어
뱌아.

21. 나구찌찌기러 어라
무호또 사 가부삐 너라
무호또 사 기리시도 너라
무호또 서바 마똬이가 바이
바똬 바로또똬 ; 워따아
와구례기라 (워어미사) 어니
먀시 부시라 가보뜨 나
부시라 구이라 가로또 똬
바쭈 보씨.

22. 우다례비찌라 궈어러사

affairs of the church well are
worthy of double honor,
especially those whose work is
preaching and teaching.

18. For the Scripture says, "Do
not muzzle the ox while it is
treading out the grain," and
"The worker deserves his
wages."

19. Do not entertain an
accusation against an elder
unless it is brought by two or
three witnesses.

20. Those who sin are to be
rebuked publicly, so that the
others may take warning.

21. I charge you, in the sight of
God and Christ Jesus and the
elect angels, to keep these
instructions without partiality,
and to do nothing out of
favoritism.

22. Do not be hasty in the

emunsju emulyimo mwa luhu Iwa Kabumbi nesi wamubika kwe mino fubafuba. Utanaata buuma nebandji bandju, be bakosi be mabi, utchilanga weine kubuyabuya kwa mabi.	어무뿌 어무쪠모 좌 루후 좌 가부뻬 너시 와무비가 궈 미노 푸바푸바. 우다나아다 부우마 너바찌 바쭈, 버 바고시 버 마비, 우찌좌꽈 워이너 구부야부야 꽈 마비.	laying on of hands, and do not share in the sins of others. Keep yourself pure.
23. Kutengera kulwarero, utendaa wamwa emeshi meine oshao, seri wendaa wamwa ne tifai yeke kwabushi ne malumwa mala wende wonvwa mwa bula bwaon nakandji wende walakirisa tchira mangu.	23. 구더꺼라 구꽈러로, 우더따아 와꽈 어머씨 머이너 오싸오, 서리 워따아 와꽈 너 디파이 여거 과부씨 너 마루꽈 마꽈 워더 오누봐 꽈 부꽈 봐오누 나가찌 워더 와꽈기기사 찌라 마꾸.	23. Stop drinking only water, and use a little wine because of your stomach and your frequent illnesses.
24. Ebyaa bya bandju bauma-bauma byende byalorekana'ku tchanganama era muhondo se kutchindjibusibwa. Si ebandji bandju ebibi byabu byende byalorekana'ko era nyuma.	24. 어뱌아 뱌 바쭈 바우마- 바우마 벼더 뱌뢰러가나구 짜꽈나마 어라 무호또 서 구찌찌부시봐. 시 어바찌 바쭈 어비비 뱌부 벼더 뱌뢰러가나고 어라 뉴마.	24. The sins of some men are obvious, reaching the place of judgment ahead of them; the sins of others trail behind them.
25. Kunoku kunoko kwe mabuya namu manatchula mende malorekana'ko unau-unau tchanganama. Seri kunalyi emabi mala matalorekana'ko unau-unau tchanganama, matangekala matchibishire.	25. 구노구 구노고 궈 마부야 나무 마나쭈꽈 머더 마뢰러가나고 우나우-우나우 짜꽈나마. 서리 구나쪠 어마비 마꽈 마다뢰러가나고 우나우-우나우 짜꽈나마, 마다꺼가꽈 마찌비씨러.	25. In the same way, good deeds are obvious, and even those that are not cannot be hidden.

1 Timoteo Chikono 6	**1 디모더오 찌고노 6**	**1 Timothy Chapter 6[NIV]**
1. Ebandju boshi bala balyi tchuungu beemire klunde	1. 어바쭈 보씨 바꽈 바쪠 쭈우꾸 버어미러 구루꺼	1. All who are under the yoke of slavery should consider their

batola bee'nawabo nga bandju bala beemire kueresibwa etchunda mwa byoshi tchasiya esina lya Kabumbi nemyasi era tchwendjire tchwakangirisa ingesha kukambibwa.

바도ᄙᅡ 버어나와보 ㅇ까 바뇨 바ᄙᅡ 버어미러 구어러시봐 어쭈따 뫄 뵤씨 짜시야 어시나 ᄙᅣ 가부뻬 너먀시 어라 쭤ᄡᅵ러 쫘가ㅇ끼리사 이ㅇ꺼싸 구가뻬봐.

masters worthy of full respect, so that God's name and our teaching may not be slandered.

2. Kandji etchuungu tchula beenawabo balyi bemeresi tchuteemire kunde tchwabakena nambu bushi balyi banyakabu mwa bwemeresi. Si tchibeemire kunde bakorera beenawabo bkubuya busese, bushin bala bendjire bainguka kurengera emulyimo wabu mubuya balyi banyakabo basiirwa. Ei myasi iwemire kunde wakangirisa ne kuhubanganyisa ebandju.

2. 가ᄡᅵ 어쭈우ㅇ꾸 쭈ᄙᅡ 버어나와보 바ᄙᅦ 버머러시 쭈더어미러 구떠 쫘바거나 나뿌 부씨 바ᄙᅦ 바냐가부 뫄 뷖머러시. 시 찌버어미러 구떠 바고러라 버어나와보 부구부야 부서서, 부씨 바ᄙᅡ 버ᄡᅵ러 바이ㅇ꾸가 구러ㅇ꺼라 어무ᄙᅦ모 와부 무부야 바ᄙᅦ 바냐가보 바시이롸. 어이 먀시 이워미러 구떠 와가ㅇ끼리사 너 구후바ㅇ까네사 어바뇨.

2. Those who have believing masters are not to show less respect for them because they are brothers. Instead, they are to serve them even better, because those who benefit from their service are believers, and dear to them. These are the things you are to teach and urge on them.

3. Akaba emundju angaiirisa indji myasi, kandji atemerere emyasi ye kanangana era ye'Enawetchu Yesu Kirisito, nesi era ikulyikene nebwemeresi.

3. 아가바 어무뇨 아ㅇ까이이리사 이ᄡᅵ 먀시, 가ᄡᅵ 아더머러러 어먀시 여 가나ㅇ까나 어라 여어나워쭈 여수 기리시도, 너시 어라 이구ᄙᅦ거너 너뷖머러시.

3. If anyone teaches false doctrines and does not agree to the sound instruction of our Lord Jesus Christ and to godly teaching,

4. Oyola endjire atcheeka, ateshi netchinwa tchisibya nakandji alyi mundju olawete ebulwala bula bwekuira ebwaka era luulu wemyasi ye buha-buha. Nebi bibyende byareta emufula nembangano, ne ngambo, ne

4. 오요ᄙᅡ 어ᄡᅵ러 아쩌어가, 아더씨 너찌놔 찌시뱌 나가ᄡᅵ 아ᄙᅦ 무뇨 오ᄙᅡ워더 어부ᄙᅪᄙᅡ 부ᄙᅡ 뷖구이라 어봐가 어라 루우루 워먀시 여 부하-부하. 너비 비벼떠 뱌러다 어무푸ᄙᅡ 너빠ㅇ까노, 너 ㅇ까뽀, 너 먀네사

4. he is conceited and understands nothing. He has an unhealthy interest in controversies and quarrels about words that result in envy, strife, malicious talk, evil suspicions

myanyisa ibiire. 이비이러.

5. Nekuira ebwaka kwe bandju bala ebwenge bwabo bulyi ngobula burorobanyire kuikira nomwa tchihangi be bilyira nemyasi ye kanangana ne kunde batchitchinga nambu ekwemerera Kabumbi ilyi ndjira yakuba muare, urekana ne bandju balyi ngabu.

5. 너구이라 어봐가 궈 바쭈 바롸 어붸꿔 봐보 부쩨 꼬부롸 부로로바녜러 구이기라 노똬 찌하꼐 버 비쩨라 너먀시 여 가나똬나 너 구떠 바찌찌꽈 나뿌 어궈머러라 가부삐 이쩨 씨라 야구바 무아러, 우러가나 너 바쭈 바쩨 꽈부.

5. and constant friction between men of corrupt mind, who have been robbed of the truth and who think that godliness is a means to financial gain.

6. Seri ebwemeresi alauma nelumoo alyi muinguki munene

6. 서리 어붸머러시 아꽈우마 너루모오 아쩨 무이꾸기 무너너

6. But godliness with contentment is great gain.

7. Kwa bushi tchutabaha na kandju munu butala na kandji tchutakanaende na kandju

7. 과 부씨 쭈다바하 나 가쭈 무누 부다꽈 나 가찌 쭈다가나어떠 나 가쭈

7. For we brought nothing into the world, and we can take nothing out of it.

8. Seri akaba tchungabona ekalyo nesi endjimb. Kwe bini bindju tchusimaa busese.

8. 서리 아가바 쭈꽈보나 어가꾜 너시 어찌꿰. 궈 비니 비쭈 쭈시마아 부서서.

8. But if we have food and clothing, we will be content with that.

9. Seri abandju bala bahonda kuata ebikulo binene bende beeengirira mwa miereko nokusimbwa mwa miita era ibiire yatchira buhuma-huma boshi bye buuta, kandji bula bubi. Nobu buhuma-huma bubwende bwabeka muero nokubeta boshi.

9. 서리 아바누 바롸 바호따 구아다 어비구론 비너너 버떠 버어어꿰리라 똬 미어러고 노구시꽈 똬 미이다 어라 이비이러 야찌라 부후마-후마 보씨 벼 부우다, 가찌 부롸 부비. 노부 부후마-후마 부붸떠 봐버가 무어로 노구버다 보씨.

9. People who want to get rich fall into temptation and a trap and into many foolish and harmful desires that plunge men into ruin and destruction.

10. Kwabushi eshokororo nguma yaye mabi moshi kulyi kusima ebuteya;

10. 과부씨 어쏘고로로 꿔마 야여 마비 모씨 구쩨 구시마 어부더야; 너바찌 바가시마

10. For the love of money is a root of all kinds of evil. Some people, eager for money, have

nebandji bakasima ebuteya banatchikula mwa bwemeresi, nekutchootcha beine kwabushi nobute bunene.

11. Seri woyo uulyi mwaanda wa Kabumbi wendaa waha ei myasi ibi, ukulyikire emyasi ye kanangana, usimika mwa ndanda sa Kabumbi ubaaa mwemeresi, uataa emasimano kwa bandji, uataa ebushibiris, ubaa murembi era muhondo sebandji kandji ubaa namurembi.

12. Ulwisa kubuya kwa kulanga ebwemeresin bwau tchasiya ubone ekalamukesiku nemangu, naku kalamu ku Kabumbi akuamalyira ubone emangu walosa ebwemeresi bwau era muhondo se babei banene.

13. Nakutchitchika era muhondo sa Kabumbi, ola weeresa ebindju byoshi ekalamu: near muhondo sa Kirisito Yesu I mubei ola watetaa tchanganama era muhondo sa Posio Pirato.

어부더야 바나찌구꽈 먀 뭐머러시, 너구쪼오짜 버이너 과부씨 노부더 부너너.

11. 서리 오요 우우레 먀아따 와 가부삐 워따아 와하 어이 먀시 이비, 우구레기러 어먀시 여 가나꽈나, 우시미가 먀 따따 사 가부삐 우바아아 뭐머러시, 우아다아 어마시마노 과 바찌, 우아다아 어부씨비리수, 우바아 무러삐 어라 무호또 서바찌 가찌 우바아 나무러삐.

12. 우뤼사 구부야 과 구꽈꽈 어뭐머러시누 봐우 짜시야 우보너 어가꽈무거시구 너마꾸, 나구 가꽈무 구 가부삐 아구아마레라 우보너 어마꾸 와로사 어뭐머러시 봐우 어라 무호또 서 바버이 바너너.

13. 나구찌찌가 어라 무호또 사 가부삐, 오꽈 워어러사 어비뿌 뵤씨 어가꽈무: 너라 무호또 사 기리시도 여수 이 무버이 오꽈 와더다아 짜꽈나마 어라 무호또 사 포시오 피라도.

wandered from the faith and pierced themselves with many griefs.

11. But you, man of God, flee from all this, and pursue righteousness, godliness, faith, love, endurance and gentleness.

12. Fight the good fight of the faith. Take hold of the eternal life to which you were called when you made your good confession in the presence of many witnesses.

13. In the sight of God, who gives life to everything, and of Christ Jesus, who while testifying before Pontius Pilate made the good confession, I charge you

14. Unalanga eni Amri ikomire busese busira tchitaki tchisibya kuikira elusiku lula Enawetchu Yesu Kirisito akabaha.

15. Kwa bushi kuikira mwesi siku sai, sini siku sikalosibwa nai yeine, ola wahanyisibwe ka misi Yoshi yai yeine, emwami webami nai Enawetchu ola wabe'Enawetcchu.

16. Ina yeine oshao iutakafe kandji atchula m:wa bulangare bula butalyi mundju ola ungala kubuikilyira, kutalyi nesi mundju ola wamulolyire'ko nesi nambu angaala kumulola'ko yeine yene etchundan nebwaashi bwe siku nemangu bibe batcha.

17. Utchitchika bala balyi bare munu butala batendaa batchilola nesi batchinyiira ebwaare bwabu, bula bungaera mwa tchihangi tchiuma seri tchutchinyiira Kabumbi yeine kwabushi iwendjire watchweeresa ebindju byoshi tchubimoera.

14. 우나빠빠 어니 아무리 이고미러 부서서 부시라 찌다기 찌시뱌 구이기라 어루시구 루빠 어나워쭈 여수 기리시도 아가바하.

15. 과 부씨 구이기라 뭐시 시구 사이, 시니 시구 시가로시봐 나이 여이너, 오빠 와하네시뷔 가 미시 요씨 야이 여이너, 어마미 워바미 나이 어나워쭈 오빠 와버어나워쭈.

16. 이나 여이너 오싸오 이우다가퍼 가찌 아쭈빠 뫄 부빠빠러 부빠 부다뤠 무뚜 오빠 우빠빠 구부이기쩨라, 구다뤠 너시 무뚜 오빠 와무뢰쩨러고 너시 나뿌 아빠아빠라 구무뢰빠고 여이너 여너 어쭈따누 너봐아씨 뷔 시구 너마뀌 비버 바짜.

17. 우찌찌가 바빠 바뤠 바러 무누 부다빠 바더따아 바찌뢰빠 너시 바찌네이라 어봐아러 봐부, 부빠 부빠어라 뫄 찌하삐 찌우마 서리 쭈찌네이라 가부삐 여이너 과부씨 이워찌러 와쭤어러사 어비뿌 뵤씨 쭈비모어라.

14. to keep this command without spot or blame until the appearing of our Lord Jesus Christ,

15. which God will bring about in his own time--God, the blessed and only Ruler, the King of kings and Lord of lords,

16. who alone is immortal and who lives in unapproachable light, whom no one has seen or can see. To him be honor and might forever. Amen.

17. Command those who are rich in this present world not to be arrogant nor to put their hope in wealth, which is so uncertain, but to put their hope in God, who richly provides us with everything for our enjoyment.

18. Abu bare bendaa baira emabuya kandji baneshibira kuba baareb mwa korero ibuya, kandji banaba bare mwabu mabuya mabu, baase ebandji na mutchima muuma ne kuata enzii nebandji bandju.

19. Mwa kuira batcha bangaba batchibikilyire emwandju we nzimiko mubuya ola utakawe mwa siku sira seeshire tchasiya babone ekalamu kala ke kanangana.

20. Timoteo ulangaa byoshi bira Ongo akueresa nga mwandju, kandji wendaa wanatchilanga kubuya kwa bandju bala bendjire baira ebwaka era lulu semyasi yobuha-buha era itakulyikene nebwemeresi bwetchu kwabushi ei myasi bendjire bbahambala nambu ilyi ya bwenge seri kanangana inalyi myasi ya bisha.

21. Kwabushi ebandji bemeresi bauma bala baikulyikira; molu barekire ebwemeresi bwabu. Emwiisha abaa alauma nau.

18. 아부 바러 버따아 바이라 어마부야 가찌 바너씨비라 구바 바아러부 와 고러로 이부야, 가찌 바나바 바러 뫄부 마부야 마부, 바아서 어바찌 나 무찌마 무우마 너 구아다 어씨이 너바찌 바뚜.

19. 뫄 구이라 바짜 바까바 바찌비기께러 어뫄뚜 워 씨미고 무부야 오롸 우다가워 뫄 시구 시라 서어씨러 짜시야 바보너 어가롸무 가롸 거 가나까나.

20. 디모더오 우롸까아 뵤씨 비라 오꼬 아구어러사 까 뫄뚜, 가찌 워따아 와나찌롸바 구부야 과 바뚜 바롸 버찌러 바이라 어봐가 어라 루루 서먀시 요부하- 부하 어라 이다구쩨거너 너붜머러시 붜쭈 과부씨 어이 먀시 버찌러 부바하빠롸 나뿌 이쩨 야 붜꺼 서리 가나까나 이나쩨 먀시 야 비싸.

21. 과부씨 어바찌 버머러시 바우마 바롸 바이구쩨기라; 모루 바러기러 어붜머러시 봐부. 어뮈이싸 아바아 아롸우마 나우.

18. Command them to do good, to be rich in good deeds, and to be generous and willing to share.

19. In this way they will lay up treasure for themselves as a firm foundation for the coming age, so that they may take hold of the life that is truly life.

20. Timothy, guard what has been entrusted to your care. Turn away from godless chatter and the opposing ideas of what is falsely called knowledge,

21. which some have professed and in so doing have wandered from the faith. Grace be with you.

2 Timoteo

2 디모더오

2 Timothy

TIMOTEO WA KABIRI

(2 TIMOTHY)

디모더오 와 가비리
(2 디모씨)

2 Timoteo Chikono 1

1. Poolo ndjumwa ya Yesu Kirisito kwa kuhonda Kabumbi kwa kulangalyira ekalamu ke siku nemangu kala kalyi mwa ndanda sa Kirisito Yesu.

2. Eram wau Timoteo mwana wanyi we nzii busese : emwiisha nobondjo nebolo kutenga era mwa Kabumbi itata nera mwa Kirisito Yesu.

3. Kandji natongire Kabumbi ola nendee nakorera kutengera kubahokulu mwa mianyisa ibuya-buya, nyikakengera esiku soshi sememo manyi ebutchufu nemushi.

4. Nyikakengera emalyira mau, nyete etchami tchinene tchekukulola'ko, tchasiya nyimowe busese.

5. Kandji nyikakengera ebwemeresi bwau bula bwe kanangana, bwa bwabaa bulyi mwandanda sa nyokulu wau Loisi nomwa ndanda so Nyoko Euniki babaa balyi bemeresi busese, rero, nyineshi kwa kanangana nau

2 디모더오 찌고노 1

1. 포오로 뚜봐 야 여수 기리시도 과 구호따 가부뻬 과 구꽈꽈레라 어가꽈무 거 시구 너마꾸 가꽈 가레 봐 따따 사 기리시도 여수.

2. 어라무 와우 디모더오 봐나 와네 워 씨이 부서서 : 어뮈이싸 노보쪼 너보로 구더꽈 어라 봐 가부뻬 이다다 너라 봐 기리시도 여수.

3. 가찌 나도삐러 가부뻬 오꽈 너떠어 나고러라 구더꺼라 구바호구루 봐 미아네사 이부야-부야, 네가거꺼라 어시구 소씨 서머모 마네 어부쭈푸 너무씨.

4. 네가거꺼라 어마쩨라 마우, 녀더 어짜미 찌너너 쩌구구로꽈고, 짜시야 네모워 부서서.

5. 가찌 네가거꺼라 어뭐머러시 봐우 부꽈 붜 가나봐나, 봐 봐바아 부쩨 봐따따 사 뇨구루 와우 로이시 노봐 따따 소 뇨고 어우니기 바바아 바쩨 버머러시 부서서, 러로, 네너씨 과 가나봐나 나우

2 Timothy Chapter 1[NIV]

1. Paul, an apostle of Christ Jesus by the will of God, according to the promise of life that is in Christ Jesus,

2. To Timothy, my dear son: Grace, mercy and peace from God the Father and Christ Jesus our Lord.

3. I thank God, whom I serve, as my forefathers did, with a clear conscience, as night and day I constantly remember you in my prayers.

4. Recalling your tears, I long to see you, so that I may be filled with joy.

5. I have been reminded of your sincere faith, which first lived in your grandmother Lois and in your mother Eunice and, I am persuaded, now lives in you also.

kuuma mwemerere batcha.

구우마 뭐머러러 바짜.

6. Kwa bushi noku, nakukengesa, ususa elwemba lwa Kabumbi lula lulyi mwandanda sau emangu nakwemerferaa mwakuka kwe minu sanyi.

6. 과 부씨 노구, 나구거어사,우수사 어뤄빠 똬 가부삐 루똬 루똀 뫄따따 사우 어마우 나궈머루퍼라아 똬구가 궈 미누 사니.

6. For this reason I remind you to fan into flame the gift of God, which is in you through the laying on of my hands.

7. Kwa bushi Kabumbi atatchweresa mutchima wabuba : seri atchueresa emutchima ola wete emisi nola wete enzii nola wete ebuashi bwe kunde tchwasimana nekutchilanga kwa mabi.

7. 과 부씨 가부삐 아다쭤러사 무찌마 와부바 : 서리 아쭈어러사 어무찌마 오똬 워더 어미시 노똬 워더 어씨이 노똬 워더 어부아씨 붜 구떠 쫘시마나 너구찌똬따 과 마비.

7. For God did not give us a spirit of timidity, but a spirit of power, of love and of self-discipline.

8. Kandji utataa honyi mwa kutonga Enawetchu kunyirengera'ku nyinyiri mwa mwa munyororo wai, seri ulyibuka alauma nanyi ; ei myasi ibuya-buya era itengire mwa misi ya Kabumbi.

8. 가찌 우다다아 호네 똬 구도따 어나워쭈 구네러떠라구 네네리 똬 똬 무뇨로로 와이, 서리 우뤠부가 아똬우마 나네 ; 어이 먀시 이부야-부야 어라 이더삐러 똬 미시 야 가부삐.

8. So do not be ashamed to testify about our Lord, or ashamed of me his prisoner. But join with me in suffering for the gospel, by the power of God,

9. Bushi Ongo yeine iwatchununulaa iwanatchuamalaa kwa murenge mubuya-buya, seri atabaa kwa mikorere yetchu, seri kukulyikana nekuhonda kwai yeine nokwa muisha wetchu ola tchweeresibwa mwandanda sa Kirisito Yesu era muhondo se miaka ya miramira

9. 부씨 오꼬 여이너 이와쭈누누똬아 이와나쭈아마똬아 과 무러떠 무부야-부야, 서리 아다바아 과 미고러러 여쭈, 서리 구구뤠가나 너구호따 과이 여이너 노과 무이싸 워쭈 오똬 쭤어러시봐 뫄따따 사 기리시도 여수 어라 무호또 서 미아가 야 미라미라

9. who has saved us and called us to a holy life--not because of anything we have done but because of his own purpose and grace. This grace was given us in Christ Jesus before the beginning of time,

10. Onu muisha aboolyibwe

10. 오누 무이싸 아보오뤠붜

10. but it has now been

nekulorekana'ko nemununusi 너구ᄙ러가나고 너무누누시 revealed through the
wetchu Yesu Kirisito 워쭈 여수 기리시도 과부씨 appearing of our Savior, Christ
kwabushi Yesu aimire wa 여수 아이미러 와 루푸. 나 Jesus, who has destroyed
lufu. Na kurengera emwasiu 구러꺼라 어꽈시우 무부야- death and has brought life and
mubuya-buya kandji analosa 부야 가찌 아나로사 궈바쭈 immortality to light through
kwebandju bakabona 바가보나 어가꽈무 거시구 the gospel.
ekalamu kesiku nemangu. 너마우.

11. Oyu mwasi mubuya-buya 11. 오유 꽈시 무부야-부야 11. And of this gospel I was
inoyu iwatchumaa Kabumbi 이노유 이와쭈마아 가부뻬 appointed a herald and an
anyibika kuba muirisi, 아네비가 구바 무이리시, apostle and a teacher.
nakuba ndjumwa nekuenda 나구바 쭈꽈 너구어따
nahubanganya oyu mwasi 나후바꽈나 오유 꽈시 과
kwa bandju bala batalyi mwa 바쭈 바꽈 바다뤠 꽈
bwemeresi. 붜머러시.

12. Nokwa bushi nai 12. 노과 부씨 나이 12. That is why I
iwatchuma narenga mwa 이와쭈마 나러꽈 꽈 마누 am suffering as I am. Yet I am
manu malyibuko moshi. 마뤠부고 모씨. not ashamed, because I know
Kunokokunoko, si tchiro 구노고구노고, 시 찌로 나뿌 whom I have believed, and am
nambu batcha, nyono 바짜, 뇨노 떠찌러 나파 호네 convinced that he is able to
ndendjire nafa honyi 과부씨 오유 네쭈꽈 guard what I have entrusted to
kwabushi oyu nyitchula 너머러러 꽈 무찌마 와네 him for that day.
nemerere mwa mutchima 네뮈씨 구부야. 가찌 네너씨
wanyi nyimwishi kubuya. 가나꽈나 과 쪼씨 찌라
Kandji nyineshi kanangana 아녀러사 어더 어부아씨
kwa tchoshi tchira anyeresa 붜구꽈까찌 구이기라 구륻
ete ebuashi bwekulanga'tchi 루시구 루꽈 아가바하.
kuikira kulo lusiku lula
akabaha.

13. Usimikaa busese mwei 13. 우시미가아 부서서 뭐이 13. What you heard from me,
myasi yoshi ei nendjire 먀시 요씨 어이 너찌러 keep as the pattern of sound
nakukangirisa, unaitchundaa, 나구가삐리사, 우나이쭈따아, teaching, with faith and love in
kwabushi ilyi myasi ya 과부씨 이뤠 먀시 야 Christ Jesus.
kanangana. Kandji wendaa 가나꽈나. 가찌 워따아
wasimika mwa bwemeresi 와시미가 꽈 붜머러시 봐우,
bwau, nomwa nzii era 노꽈 씨이 어라 쭈쭈사

tchutchusa kurengera
ebuuma bwetchu na Kirisito
Yesu.

구러꺼라 어부우마 붜쭈 나
기리시도 여수.

14. Kwabushi noku ulangaa
emyasi ibuya yoshi era
weresibwe na Kabumbi
uilanga kubuya kurenga
ebwaasshi bwe mutchima
mubuya-buya. Kwabusbhi
atchula mwa ndanda setchu.

14. 과부씨 노구 우롸꺼아
어먀시 이부야 요씨 어라
워러시붜 나 가부삐
우이롸꺼 구부야 구러꺼
어봐아씨 붜 무찌마 무부야-
부야. 과부수부히 아쭈롸 마
따따 서쭈.

14. Guard the good deposit
that was entrusted to you--
guard it with the help of the
Holy Spirit who lives in us.

15. Seri uneshi eni myasi kwa
balyiketchu boshi bala
bomwa tchio tche Asiya
banyirekerere, namubu mulyi
Fingeloi na Herimongene.

15. 서리 우너씨 어니 먀시
과 바레거쭈 보씨 바롸 보롸
찌오 쩌 아시야
바네러거러러, 나무부 무레
피꺼로이 나 허리모꺼너.

15. You know that everyone in
the province of Asia has
deserted me, including
Phygelus and Hermogenes.

16. Enawetchu abalorera
ebondjo nekubahanyira bala
balyi mwa tchihaal atcha
Onesiforo, kwabushi oyu
Onesiforo abaa endjire
abaha kunyisese emutchima
mwa malyibuku manyi,
kandji atabaa ende anyifira
honyi kwabushi nyihwekirwe
neni minyororo.

16. 어나워쭈 아바로러라
어보쪼 너구바하네라 바롸
바레 마 찌하아루 아짜
오너시포로, 과부씨 오유
오너시포로 아바아 어찌러
아바하 구네서서 어무찌마
마 마레부구 마네, 가찌
아다바아 어떠 아네피라
호네 과부씨 내훠기뤄 너니
미뇨로로.

16. May the Lord show mercy
to the household of
Onesiphorus, because he often
refreshed me and was
not ashamed of my chains.

17. Nemangu aika mwa musi
we Roma, erakunaira emisi
yai yoshi anyihondaa era
kuna nyibona

17. 너마우 아이가 롸 무시
워 로마, 어라구나이라
어미시 야이 요씨
아네호따아 어라 구나
네보나

17. On the contrary, when he
was in Rome, he searched hard
for me until he found me.

18. Enawetchu amuloreraa
ebondjo era mwa Tata mwesi
siku sobusinda.

18. 어나워쭈 아무로러라아
어보쪼 어라 롸 다다 뭐시
시구 소부시따.

18. May the Lord grant that he
will find mercy from the Lord
on that day! You know very
well in how many ways he
helped me in Ephesus.

2 Timoteo Chikono 2

1. Woyo mwananyi, usilika mwa ngahanyi sasitchula mu Kirisito Yesu.

2. Nei myasi era onvaako era mwanyi era muhondo se babei banene, nao wabaa wendjire wanayunva'ko. Rero nao uikangirisa ebandju bala utchilangalyire bala bangaala nabo kuikangirisa ebandji bandju.

3. Nau wenda wasesa emutchima mwakulyibukira alauma ne bandji nda musula mubuya wakirisito Yesu.

4. Bushi kutatchula musula ola wende waya mwa mulyimo nambu kandji angende atchibika muindji myasi yomunu butala seri ahonda asimise enawabo olawamweeresa ekasi.

5. Akaba emundju ola ulyi mwa kaimano, nayi akaba angahonda aimane mwandjiora era itatchungenene atangaembasibwa enziita era yokulosa kute kwaimanyire.

6. Emuinzi ola wende watchilyibusa mwa kukola tcheemire abaa muberebere kulya. Emwangu muberebere

2 디모더오 찌고노 2

1. 오요 먀나네, 우시쀠가 먀 빠하네 사시쭈롸 무 기리시도 여수.

2. 너이 먀시 어라 오빠아고 어라 마네 어라 무호또 서 바버이 바너너, 나오 와바아 워찌러 와나유봐'고. 러로 나오 우이가쀠리사 어바쭈 바롸 우찌롸빠레러 바롸 바빠아롸 나보 구이가쀠리사 어바찌 바뿌.

3. 나우 워따 와서사 어무찌마 마구궤부기라 아롸우마 너 바찌 따 무수롸 무부야 와기리시도 여수.

4. 부씨 구다쭈롸 무수롸 오롸 워떠 와야 먀 무레모 나뿌 가찌 아꺼떠 아찌비가 무이찌 먀시 요무누 부다롸 서리 아호따 아시미서 어나와보 오롸와뭐어러사 어가시.

5. 아가바 어무뿌 오롸 우레 먀 가이마노, 나에 아가바 아빠호따 아이마너 먀찌오라 어라 이다쭈꺼너너 아다빠어빠시봐 어씨이다 어라 요구로싸 구더 과이마네러.

6. 어무이씨 오롸 워떠 와찌레부사 먀 구고롸 쩌어미러 아바아 무버러버러 구롸. 어롸우 무버러버러

2 Timothy Chapter 2[NIV]

1. You then, my son, be strong in the grace that is in Christ Jesus.

2. And the things you have heard me say in the presence of many witnesses entrust to reliable men who will also be qualified to teach others.

3. Endure hardship with us like a good soldier of Christ Jesus.

4. No one serving as a soldier gets involved in civilian affairs--he wants to please his commanding officer.

5. Similarly, if anyone competes as an athlete, he does not receive the victor's crown unless he competes according to the rules.

6. The hardworking farmer should be the first to receive a share of the crops.

kwei myaka yai.

7. Uanyisa busese eyi myasi nendjire nateta kwa bushi Enawetchu yeine akweresise ebuashi bula bwekumenyerera byoshi.

8. Ukengera Yesu Kirisito ola woomoka mwa bafu ola wabutchibwa mwa lubutu lwa mwai Tauti; oyola I mwasi mubuya-buya nendjire naenda nahubanganyisa ebandju.

9. Nanyi kandji inoyo iwanatchuma nalyibuka batcha. Nahwekibwa neni minyororo mbungaa tchihumusi. Sitchiru batcha, emwasi wa Kabumbi yeke ataminyirwe.

10. Kwabushi noku nendjire nasesa emutchima mwa myasi Yoshi. Tchasiya ebandju bala balondolyiobwa na Kabumbi banunulyibwe kurengera Kirisito Yesu. Tchasinda bakabona netchunda lyesiku nemangu.

11. Onu mwasi alyi mwasi wa kanangana: kwabushi akaba tchungafa alauma nayi eri tchukanabona ekalamu alauma nayi.

12. Nakandji tchukasesa emutchima, eritchukanema

귀이 먀가 야이.

7. 우아니사 부서서 어에 먀시 너끼러 나더다 과 부씨 어나워쭈 여이너 아꿔러시서 어부아씨 부롸 뭐구머녀러라 뵤씨.

8. 우거꺼라 여수 기리시도 오롸 오오모가 롸 바푸 오롸 와부찌봐 롸 루부두 롹 마이 다우디; 오요롸 이 먀시 무부야-부야 너끼러 나어따 나후바까네사 어바뉴.

9. 나네 가끼 이노요 이와나쭈마 나레부가 바짜. 나훠기봐 너니 미뇨로로 뿌꺼아 찌후무시. 시찌루 바짜, 어롸시 와 가부삐 여거 아다미네뤄.

10. 과부씨 노구 너끼러 나서사 어무찌마 롸 먀시 요씨. 짜시야 어바뉴 바롸 바룬또레오봐 나 가부삐 바누누레뷔 구러꺼라 기리시도 여수. 짜시따 바가보나 너쭈따 려시구 너마우.

11. 오누 먀시 아례 먀시 와 가나꺼나: 과부씨 아가바 쭈꺼파 아롸우마 나에 어리 쭈가나보나 어가롸무 아롸우마 나에.

12. 나가끼 쭈가서사 어무찌마, 어리쭈가너마

---

7. Reflect on what I am saying, for the Lord will give you insight into all this.

8. Remember Jesus Christ, raised from the dead, descended from David. This is my gospel,

9. for which I am suffering even to the point of being chained like a criminal. But God's word is not chained.

10. Therefore I endure everything for the sake of the elect, that they too may obtain the salvation that is in Christ Jesus, with eternal glory.

11. Here is a trustworthy saying: If we died with him, we will also live with him;

12. if we endure, we will also reign with him. If we disown

alauma nayi. Seri akaba tchungamunana seri nayi akanatchunana.

13. Kandji akaba tchubano tchutamwemerere ula ulyi mwemeresi, kwabushi yeke atangatchinana yeine.

14. Ubakengesa eni myasi Yoshi nokubatchitchika era muhondo s'Enawetchu, batendaa baenda ebwaka mwa myasi era itete mufa asibya, seri ebwaka bulyi batcha butete mufa asibya.

15. Usera mwakunde watchilosanya era muhondo sa Ongo ngokula emundju olawaire eburebi, ngokula ekaungu kala katafa honyi mwa kuiirisa kubuya-buya emwasi wa Ongo we kanangana.

16. Seri utchilangaa kwa myasi era itete mufa, kandji itanalyi ya luhu lwa Ongo, kwabushi nakaneshibira bakulyikira busese endjira era italyi ya Ongo.

17. Na kandji ei myasi yabu ingatondera mbungaa tchuulu. Namwabanu bandju bala bendjire baira batcha mulyi Himeneo na Fileto

18. Abu babiri barekire mira emyasi ye kanangana, mwa

아롸우마 나에. 서리 아가바 쭈까무나나 서리 나에 아가나쭈나나.

13. 가찌 아가바 쭈바노 쭈다뭐머러러 우롸 우레 뭐머러시, 과부씨 여거 아다까찌나나 여이너.

14. 우바거꺼사 어니 먀시 요씨 노구바찌찌가 어라 무호또 서나워쭈, 바더따아 바어따 어봐가 뫄 먀시 어라 이더더 무파 아시뱌, 서리 어봐가 부레 바짜 부더더 무파 아시뱌.

15. 우서라 뫄구꺼 와찌롸사냐 어라 무호또 사 오꼬 꼬구롸 어무뚜 오롸와이러 어부러비, 꼬구롸 어가우꾸 가라 가다파 호네 뫄 구이이리사 구부야-부야 어뫄시 와 오꼬 워 가나까나.

16. 서리 우찌롸까아 과 먀시 어라 이더더 무파, 가찌 이다나레 야 루후 롸 오꼬, 과부씨 나가너씨비라 바구레기라 부서서 어찌라 어라 이다레 야 오꼬.

17. 나 가찌 어이 먀시 야부 이까도떠러 뿌까아 쭈우룩. 나뫄바누 바뉴 바롸 버찌러 바이라 바짜 무레 히머너오 나 피뗘도

18. 아부 바비리 바러기러 미라 어먀시 여 가나까나, 뫄

him, he will also disown us;

13. if we are faithless, he will remain faithful, for he cannot disown himself.

14. Keep reminding them of these things. Warn them before God against quarreling about words; it is of no value, and only ruins those who listen.

15. Do your best to present yourself to God as one approved, a workman who does not need to be ashamed and who correctly handles the word of truth.

16. Avoid godless chatter, because those who indulge in it will become more and more ungodly.

17. Their teaching will spread like gangrene. Among them are Hymenaeus and Philetus,

18. who have wandered away from the truth. They say that

kunde bateta mbu ekwomoka kwe bafu kwabere mira. Rero, bathumire bandju bauma bareka ebwemeresi bwabo.

19. Si tchiro batcha emyasi ya Kabumbi iaknaendekera kusiminga nga nzimiko era isibuire era baandjikire'ko nambu: "Enawetchu atchula, aneshi bala balyi bai" nakandji byaandjikirwe nambu: "tchira mundju woshi ola wende watchitonga nambu alyi mundju wa Enawetchu, tchimweemire kunde atchilanga kwa mabi".

20. Seri mwanyumbainene, mutchula bindju bya tchira mulala. Na mwebi bindju byuma-byuuma bitchula bikunganyisibwe mwa Horo, nebinsji mwa Milinga, arero ebyera bibyende byakoresibwa netchunda mu ndjira sinene, mwanaba na bindji bindju bira bikunganyisibwe mwa mitchi, nomwe ebumbwa seri ebyeke byende byakoresibwa tchita tchihangi busira etchunda.

21. Kunoko, akaba emundju angende atchikomya mwakuba atchilanga kwa

구떠 바더다 뿌 어고모가 궈 바푸 과버러 미라. 러로, 바쭈미러 바누 바우마 바러가 어붜머러시 봐보.

19. 시 찌로 바짜 어먀시 야 가부삐 이아구나어떠거라 구시미꺄 꺄 씨미고 어라 이시부이러 어라 바아찌기러고 나뿌: "어나워쭈 아쭈롸, 아너씨 바롸 바레 바이" 나가찌 뱌아찌기뤄 나뿌: "찌라 무뚜 옴씨 오롸 워러 와찌도꽈 나뿌 아레 무뚜 와 어나워쭈, 찌뭐어미러 구떠 아찌롸꺄 과 마비".

20. 서리 먀뉴빠이너너, 무쭈롸 비뚜 뱌 찌라 무롸롸. 나 뭐비 비뚜 뷰마-뷰우마 비쭈롸 비구꺄네시붜 뫄 호로, 너비지 뫄 미뤼꺄, 아러로 어뼈라 비뼈너 뱌고러시봐 너쭈따 무 찌라 시너너, 뫄나바 나 비찌 비뚜 비라 비구꺄네시붜 뫄 미찌, 노뭐 어부빠 서리 어뼈거 뼈러 뱌고러시봐 찌다 찌하삐 부시라 어쭈따.

21. 구노고, 아가바 어무뚜 아머러 아찌고먀 뫄구바 아찌롸꺄 과 뱌아 어리

the resurrection has already taken place, and they destroy the faith of some.

19. Nevertheless, God's solid foundation stands firm, sealed with this inscription: "The Lord knows those who are his," and, "Everyone who confesses the name of the Lord must turn away from wickedness."

20. In a large house there are articles not only of gold and silver, but also of wood and clay; some are for noble purposes and some for ignoble.

21. If a man cleanses himself from the latter, he will be an instrument for noble purposes,

byaa eri angaba mbungaa tchindju tchira tchende tchakoresibwa netchunda. Kandji alyi mundju ola walondorwe mira n'Enawetchu na kandji anganamwaatchira mufa mwakunde aira tchiran mulyimo woshi ola ulyi mubuya-buya.

22. Seri wendaa wahaa emyanya ibi yo kusingira yetabana, kandji wendaa wasimika mwa myasi erfa itchungenene era muhondo sa Ongo nomwa bwemeresi, nomwa nzii, nomwa bolo alauma nebandji bandju boshi, nabala bende bema Enawetchu nomutchima mubuya-buya.

23. NAkandji wenda watchilanga, utendaa waenda ebwaka bula bwende bwatchuma embuta sareka ebwemeresi bwabu bushi weke wishi kwe ebyera bibyende byareta embangano mwa bandju.

24. Tchitaneemire emwaanda w'Enawetchu etemire kunde alwa, si emire kuba murembi era muhondo se bandju boshi, nakandji abaa mundju ola wishi kuiirisa, na kunde

아빠바 뿌까아 찌뚜 찌라 쩌머 짜고러시봐 너쭈따. 가찌 아레 무뚜 오라 와로또뤄 미라 너나워쭈 나 가찌 아까나뫄아찌라 무파 뫄구떠 아이라 찌라누 무레모 온씨 오꽈 우레 무부야-부야.

22. 서리 워따아 와하아 어먀냐 이비 요 구시꼐라 여다바나, 가찌 워따아 와시미가 뫄 먀시 어루파 이쭈꺼너너 어라 무호또 사 오꼬 노뫄 붜머러시, 노뫄 씨이, 노뫄 보로 아꺄우마 너바찌 바꾸 보씨, 나바꽈 버떠 버마 어나워쭈 노무찌마 무부야-부야.

23. 나가찌 워따 와찌꽈까, 우더따아 와어따 어봐가 부꽈 붜떠 봐쭈마 어뿌다 사러가 어붜머러시 봐부 부씨 워거 위씨 궈 어뼈라 비뼈떠 뱌러다 어빠까노 뫄 바꾸.

24. 찌다너어미러 어뫄아따 워나워쭈 어더미러 구떠 아꽈, 시 어미러 구바 무러뻬 어라 무호또 서 바꾸 보씨, 나가찌 아바아 무뚜 오꽈 위씨 구이이리사, 나 구떠

made holy, useful to the Master and prepared to do any good work.

22. Flee the evil desires of youth, and pursue righteousness, faith, love and peace, along with those who call on the Lord out of a pure heart.

23. Don't have anything to do with foolish and stupid arguments, because you know they produce quarrels.

24. And the Lord's servant must not quarrel; instead, he must be kind to everyone, able to teach, not resentful.

asesa emutchima mwakuba bamubanganya.

25. Ne mangu ebandju mbu bamulwise tcheemire kunde aberesa eano namutchima weburembi kwabushi kulye emangui Ongo angabaasa na baaluka loshi kutenga mwa bibi byabu baikira bamenyerera nemyasi ye kanangana.

26. Nemangu bende baba bafulusise emyaanyisa, bana fufumuka mwa mifa yemusimu. Bushi abu bandju baminyirwe nawa musimu mira, kandji erendjire anabakoresa ngokula anasimire.

아서사 어무찌마 꽈구바 바무바까냐.

25. 너 마꾸 어바뉴 뿌 바무뤼서 쩌어미러 구더 아버러사 어아노 나무찌마 워부러삐 과부씨 구껴 어마꾸이 오꼬 아꺄바아사 나 바아루가 로씨 구더꺄 꽈 비비 뱌부 바이기라 바머녀러라 너먀시 여 가나꺄나.

26. 너마꾸 버떠 바바 바푸뤼시서 어먀아네사, 바나 푸푸무가 꽈 미파 여무시무. 부씨 아부 바뉴 바미네뤄 나와 무시무 미라, 가찌 어러씨러 아나바고러사 꼬구꽈 아나시미러.

25. Those who oppose him he must gently instruct, in the hope that God will grant them repentance leading them to a knowledge of the truth,

26. and that they will come to their senses and escape from the trap of the devil, who has taken them captive to do his will.

2 Timoteo Chikono 3

1. Reru, umenyereraa kwa mwasiku sebusinda, sikaba siku samalyibuko busese.

2. Kwa bushi ebandju bakaba bakutchisima beine kandji bakaba bala basimire e bikulo (ebuteya) busese, bakaba bandju bala batchisimire beine nokunde basima ebuteya ngatchi. Bakende batchitonga nekuate erume, nekunde

2 디모더오 찌고노 3

1. 러루, 우머녀러라아 과 꽈시구 서부시마, 시가바 시구 사마례부고 부서서.

2. 과 부씨 어바뉴 바가바 바구찌시마 버이너 가찌 바가바 바꽈 바시미러 어 비구룬 (어부더야) 부서서, 바가바 바뉴 바꽈 바찌시미러 버이너 노구더 바시마 어부더야 꺄찌. 바거떠 바찌도꺄 너구아더 어루머, 너구떠 바가빠 오꼬,

2 Timothy Chapter 3[NIV]

1. But mark this: There will be terrible times in the last days.

2. People will be lovers of themselves, lovers of money, boastful, proud, abusive, disobedient to their parents, ungrateful, unholy,

bakamba Ongo, bala batatchundjire ebasere babu, bakaba bandju bala batakende basima kandji bakende balaa kwa myasi ya Kabumbi.

바롸 바다쭈띠러 어바서러 바부, 바가바 바뚜 바롸 바다거떠 바시마 가찌 바거떠 바롸아 과 먀시 야 가부삐.

3. Batakende basimana, kandji batakende bafirana bondjo, bakende bafulire ebandji ebisha, kandji bakende batchilanga kwa mabi, bakende kalyiira busese, batakende basima kuira emabuya.

3. 바다거떠 바시마나, 가찌 바다거떠 바피라나 보쪼, 바거떠 바푸쀠러 어바찌 어비싸, 가찌 바거떠 바찌롸애 과 마비, 바거떠 가레이라 부서서, 바다거떠 바시마 구이라 어마부야.

3. without love, unforgiving, slanderous, without self-control, brutal, not lovers of the good,

4. Balyi bandju bakunde barenganye ebandji, balyi bandju bala bete emakutchu masibu, nekunde batchilola, bende batchilola, nekunde batchimoera mwa myasi yomubiri kuluha Ongo.

4. 바레 바뚜 바구떠 바러애녀 어바찌, 바레 바뚜 바롸 버더 어마구쭈 마시부, 너구떠 바찌롣롸, 버떠 바찌롣롸, 너구떠 바찌모어라 와 먀시 요무비리 구루하 오꼬.

4. treacherous, rash, conceited, lovers of pleasure rather than lovers of God--

5. Bende balorekana'ko ndjingaa bandju bala bobaa Ongo, seri bakenyire ebuashi bwai. Rero abu bandju balyi batcha utaesa ukakomerana'nabo.

5. 버떠 바롣러가나고 띠애아 바뚜 바롸 보바아 오꼬, 서리 바거네러 어부아씨 봐이. 러로 아부 바뚜 바레 바짜 우다어사 우가고머라나나보.

5. having a form of godliness but denying its power. Have nothing to do with them.

6. Kwa bushi bauma mwabu bandju bendjire batchibisha-bisha mwa nyumba sabene, nokunde bashiirisa ebakasi bala batete bwenge. Arero abu bakasi belyire banarengeresa nebibi, bendjire bakoresibwa ne

6. 과 부씨 바우마 먀부 바뚜 버찌러 바찌비싸-비싸 와 뉴빠 사버너, 노구떠 바씨이리사 어바가시 바롸 바더더 뷔떠. 아러로 아부 바가시 버레러 바나러애러사 너비비, 버찌러 바고러시봐 너 부후마-후마 부비 무

6. They are the kind who worm their way into homes and gain control over weak-willed women, who are loaded down with sins and are swayed by all kinds of evil desires,

buhuma-huma bubi mu ndjira sinene.

띠라 시너너.

7. Kandji beerisa bendi bakangirisibwa, seri batatchusa ebuashi bwe kuikira bamenyerera emyasi ye Kanangana.

7. 가띠 버어리사 버띠 바가끼리시봐, 서리 바다쭈사 어부아씨 뭐 구이기라 바머녀러라 어먀시 여 가나꺄나.

7. always learning but never able to acknowledge the truth.

8. Kumlyingokula Yane buna Yambure banana emyasi ya Musa. Kunoku kunoku banu bandju babilyi ebwenge bwabu bwalorekanyire'ko mira, nebwemeresi bwabu bwananyirwe loshi.

8. 구무레꼬구꽈 야너 부나 야뿌러 바나나 어먀시 야 무사. 구노구 구노구 바누 바뉴 바비레 어뷔꺼 봐부 봐뢰러가네러고 미라, 너뷔머러시 봐부 봐나니뤄 로씨.

8. Just as Jannes and Jambres opposed Moses, so also these men oppose the truth--men of depraved minds, who, as far as the faith is concerned, are rejected.

9. Na tchiro batcha batanga endekera mwamu mabi mabu: kwabushi ebuuta bwabu, butchilyi bukalorekana'ko ne bandju boshi, ngokula balola lyamira-mira kwa byaa bya Yene buna Yambure.

9. 나 찌로 바짜 바다꺄 어떠거라 먀무 마비 마부: 과부씨 어부우다 봐부, 부찌레 부가뢰러가나고 너 바뉴 보씨, 꼬구꽈 바뢰꽈 꺄미라-미라 과 뱌아 뱌 여너 부나 야뿌러.

9. But they will not get very far because, as in the case of those men, their folly will be clear to everyone.

10. Seri woyo uwendjire wakulyikira kubuya-buya emyasi yanyi, uuneshi nemyanya yanyi, uneshi nebyanende nahonda, uneshi namwasi nera lulu se bwemeresi bwanyi, kandji nera lulu se kusesa emutchima kwanyi, nera lulu-ulu se nzii yanyi, nera lulu se bushibirisi bwanyi.

10. 서리 오요 우워찌러 와구레기라 구부야-부야 어먀시 야녜, 우우너씨 너먀냐 야녜, 우너씨 너뱌너떠 나호따, 우너씨 나뫄시 너라 루루 서 뷔머러시 봐녜, 가띠 너라 루루 서 구서사 어무찌마 과녜, 너라 루루-우루 서 씨이 야녜, 너라 루루 서 부씨비리시 봐녜.

10. You, however, know all about my teaching, my way of life, my purpose, faith, patience, love, endurance,

11. Kandji uneshi kute nendjire nalyibusibwa,

11. 가띠 우너씨 구더 너찌러 나레부시봐, 노구뢰꽈

11. persecutions, sufferings--what kinds of things happened

nokulola kwa bisibu, kandji uneshi natchira mwasi oshi ola banyikorera mwa musi we Andiyokiya nomwa musi we Ikoniyo, nomwa musi we Lisitara noku naataa ebushibirisi mwamu malyibuko moshi, si tchiro batcha, mwebini byoshi, Enawetchu era kuna nyinunula mu byoshi.

12. Kubinalyi nebandji bandju boshi bala bahonda kutchunda Ongo, kurengera Kiristito Yesu, bamenyerera kwa nabu bangende balosibwa kwa bisibu.

13. Seri ebandju babi nebatebanyi banaendekera kuba babi busese, bende batebana sinabo bakende banatebwa.

14. Woyo, usera busese mwa myasi era wendaa wairisibwa, ne kubwuunva kwa kanangana nokumenyerera ola wakuirisa eyi myasi.

15. Na kutengera elyanetoto lyau unathcula uneshi emaandjiko mabuya-buya kubuiuya, namu maandjiko mu mangaala kukuira mwenge kuikira emangu unganunulyibwa kurengera

과 비시부, 가찌 우너씨 나찌라 먀시 오씨 오롸 바네고러라 뫄 무시 워 아띠요기야 노뫄 무시 워 이고니요, 노뫄 무시 워 뢰시다라 노구 나아다아 어부씨비리시 뫄무 마뤠부고 모씨, 시 찌로 바짜, 뭐비니 뵤씨, 어나워쭈 어라 구나 네누누롸 무 뵤씨.

12. 구비나뤠 너바찌 바뚜 보씨 바롸 바호따 구쭈따 오끄, 구러뻐라 기리시도 여수, 바머녀러라 과 나부 바뻐떠 바뢰시봐 과 비시부.

13. 서리 어바뚜 바비 너바더바네 바나어떠거라 구바 바비 부서서, 버뻐 바더바나 시나보 바거떠 바나더봐.

14. 오요, 우서라 부서서 뫄 먀시 어라 워따아 와이리시봐, 너 구부웅우빠 과 가나빠나 노구머녀러라 오롸 와구이리사 어에 먀시.

15. 나 구더뻐라 어뺘너도도 뺘우 우나쭈우롸 우너씨 어마아찌고 마부야-부야 구부이우야, 나무 마아찌고 무 마빠아롸 구구이라 뭐뻐 구이기라 어마꾸 우빠누누뤠봐 구러뻐라

to me in Antioch, Iconium and Lystra, the persecutions I endured. Yet the Lord rescued me from all of them.

12. In fact, everyone who wants to live a godly life in Christ Jesus will be persecuted,

13. while evil men and impostors will go from bad to worse, deceiving and being deceived.

14. But as for you, continue in what you have learned and have become convinced of, because you know those from whom you learned it,

15. and how from infancy you have known the holy Scriptures, which are able to make you wise for salvation through faith in Christ Jesus.

ebwemeresi bwa bwa Kirisito Yesu.

16. E maandjiko mabuya-buya moshi maandjikwa mwa kukoresibwa nebwaashi bwa Ongo. Kandji mete na mufa munene ngatchi mwa kukangilyisa ebandju nekubeeresa emaano,

17. bushi nemabi mabo, nomwa kubakemera nokubalosa tchoira mwasi woshi ola ucthungenene era muhondoi sa Ongo.

2 Timoteo Chikono 4

1. Nakutchitchikire era muhondo sa Ongo nera mw'Enawetchu Yesu Kirisito yeine iukanatchindjibusa ebandju bala basen,e, nabala bafire mira nekulorekana'ko kwai, nokwa bwami bwai.

2. Bushi noku waata ebushiro ne bihangi bya kuiirisa etchinwa tcha Ongo, unaata nebihangi bye kubakangilyisa etchinwa mwa tchihangi tchikomire, nesi mwa tchihangi tchira tchitakomire. Wendaa wabakalyiira kwa mabi mabo, wendaa wabakolobola bushi

---

어뭐머러시 봐 봐 기리시도 여수.

16. 어 마아찌고 마부야-부야 모씨 마아찌과 봐 구고레시봐 너봐아씨 봐 오꼬. 가찌 머더 나 무파 무너너 까찌 봐 구가삐레사 어바쭈 너구버어러사 어마아노,

17. 부씨 너마비 마보, 노봐 구바거머라 노구바로사 쪼이라 봐시 옷씨 오롸 우쮸뻐너너 어라 무호또이 사 오꼬.

2 디모더오 찌고노 4

1. 나구찌찌기러 어라 무호또 사 오꼬 너라 뭐나워쭈 여수 기리시도 여이너 이우가나찌찌부사 어바쭈 바롸 바서누,어, 나바롸 바피러 미라 너구로러가나고 과이, 노과 봐미 봐이.

2. 부씨 노구 와아다 어부씨로 너 비하삐 뱌 구이이리사 어찌놔 짜 오꼬, 우나아다 너비하삐 벼 구바가삐레사 어찌놔 봐 찌하삐 찌고미러, 너시 봐 찌하삐 찌라 찌다고미러. 워따아 와바가쩨이라 과 마비 마보, 워따아 와바고론보롸 부씨 나무

---

16. All Scripture is God-breathed and is useful for teaching, rebuking, correcting and training in righteousness,

17. so that the man of God may be thoroughly equipped for every good work.

2 Timothy Chapter 4[NIV]

1. In the presence of God and of Christ Jesus, who will judge the living and the dead, and in view of his appearing and his kingdom, I give you this charge:

2. Preach the Word; be prepared in season and out of season; correct, rebuke and encourage--with great patience and careful instruction.

namu mabi mabo, unabasesaa emitchima mwa kubairisa mwa bushibirisi boshi.

3. Kwa bushi mwa bihangi bira byeshire ebandju batangendi bemera kundi boonvirisa emyasi ye kanangana, kwabushi nobuhuma-huma bwabo bubi, bangende batchihondera bairisi banene, tchasiya bende bakangirisa'bo emyasi era beine basimire kuiteya ematchi.

4. Banganana kuonvirisa emyasi ye kanangana, seri bangende balangalyira enyaano se bishabisha.

5. Seri woyu, ucthilangalanga mwa myasi yoshi, wendaa wasesa emutchima mwa malyibuko moshi, unaendekera aira ekasi kau kala kebuirisi bwe mwasi mubuya-buya. Nekunde waira byoshi bira bitchungenene mwa mulyimo wau.

6. Kwabushi nyoono nyiri mwa kwanyibwa nga mutchulo kwabushi ebihangi byanyi byekutenga munu butala byaikire mira.

마비 마보, 우나바서사아 어미찌마 똬 구바이리사 똬 부씨비리시 보씨.

3. 과 부씨 똬 비하꾀 비라 벼씨러 어바뉴 바다꺼띠 버머라 구띠 보오뻬리사 어먀시 여 가나꺄나, 과부씨 노부후마-후마 봐보 부비, 바꺼떠 바찌호떠라 바이리시 바너너, 짜시야 버떠 바가꾀리사보 어먀시 어라 버이너 바시미러 구이더야 어마찌.

4. 바꺄나나 구오뻬리사 어먀시 여 가나꺄나, 서리 바꺼떠 바꽈꺼쪠라 어냐아노 서 비싸비싸.

5. 서리 오유, 우찌꽈꺼꽈꺼 똬 먀시 요씨, 워따아 와서사 어무찌마 똬 마쪠부고 모씨, 우나어떠거라 아이라 어가시 가우 가꽈 거부이리시 붜 먀시 무부야-부야. 너구떠 와이라 뵤씨 비라 비쭈꺼너너 똬 무쪠모 와우.

6. 과부씨 뇨오노 내리 똬 과내봐 꺼 무쭈롣 과부씨 어비하꾀 뱌네 벼구더꺄 무누 부다꽈 뱌이기러 미라.

3. For the time will come when men will not put up with sound doctrine. Instead, to suit their own desires, they will gather around them a great number of teachers to say what their itching ears want to hear.

4. They will turn their ears away from the truth and turn aside to myths.

5. But you, keep your head in all situations, endure hardship, do the work of an evangelist, discharge all the duties of your ministry.

6. For I am already being poured out like a drink offering, and the time has come for my departure.

7. Nalwire ebita bibuya, namalyire elwendo lwanyi kandji nyinatchiri nalanga ebwemeresi bwanyi.

7. 나뤼러 어비다 비부야, 나마뢔러 어뤄또 롸네 가찌 네나찌리 나롸까 어뭐머러시 봐네.

7. I have fought the good fight, I have finished the race, I have kept the faith.

8. Era businda sebine byoshi, nyibikilyirwe elwembo lwekuimana, lwula boshi bala batchungenene era muhondo s'Enawetchu bakabona, kandji akananyeresa'lo kulu lusuku lula akabaha, kwabushi akanyibusa ebandju mwa ndjira era icthungenene, ata nyono nyeine oshao nyinyikalubona seri nebandji boshi bala batchusa etchami tchira tchekulyindjira ekubaha kwai.

8. 어라 부시따 서비너 뵤씨, 네비기뢔뤄 어뤄뽀 뤄구이마나, 룰롸 보씨 바롸 바쭈꺼너너 어라 무호또 서나워쭈 바가보나, 가찌 아가나녀러사롸 구뤄 룩수구 룩롸 아가바하, 과부씨 아가네부사 어바뉴 롸 띠라 어라 이쮸꺼너너, 아다 뇨노 녀이너 오싸오 네네가룩보나 서리 너바찌 보씨 바롸 바쭈사 어짜미 찌라 쩌구뢔찌라 어구바하 과이.

8. Now there is in store for me the crown of righteousness, which the Lord, the righteous Judge, will award to me on that day--and not only to me, but also to all who have longed for his appearing.

9. Reru, uire misi yau yoshi unyibahire fuba-fuba.

9. 러루, 우이러 미시 야우 요씨 우네바히러 푸바-푸바.

9. Do your best to come to me quickly,

10. Bushi Tema anyirekire mira, bushi nokusima emyasi yobutala, nekutchiira mwa musi we Tesalonika Kereseke nai aire mwa tchio tche Kalatia mira, na Tito aire mwa tchio tche Talimatia.

10. 부씨 더마 아네러기러 미라, 부씨 노구시마 어먀시 요부다롸, 너구찌이라 롸 무시 워 더사롸니가 거러서거 나이 아이러 롸 찌오 쩌 가롸디아 미라, 나 디도 아이러 롸 찌오 쩌 다뤼마디아.

10. for Demas, because he loved this world, has deserted me and has gone to Thessalonica. Crescens has gone to Galatia, and Titus to Dalmatia.

11. Luka yeine oshao, itchwanashibire nai anola emangu ungabaha mubahaa na Mariko, kwabushi anyetere mufa munene mwa mulyimo wanyi.

11. 루가 여이너 오싸오, 이쫘나씨비러 나이 아노롸 어마꾸 우까바하 무바하아 나 마리고, 과부씨 아녀더러 무파 무너너 롸 무뢰모 와네.

11. Only Luke is with me. Get Mark and bring him with you, because he is helpful to me in my ministry.

12. Seri Tikiko namutchumire mwa musi we Efeso.

13. Emangu mala ungabaha, unyiretera lyira kotchi narekaa mwa musi we Torowa mula mwa Karido, unanyiretera nebira bitabu si kandji bira bikunganyisibwe mwa nyuu.

14. Alesanduru ola mwesi we byuma anyilosa kwa kasibu? Reru bushi nook Enawetchu angamulosa kwa bisibu nai.

15. Nau utchilanga busese kubu bwaneshi, kwabushi abaa mukalyi busese mwakuhonda aangike emyasi yetchu.

16. Bushi emangu natangilyisaa kunde natchitetera era muhondo se beshi be mandja kutabonekaa na mundju asibya ola waika kunyiasa si boshi bera kunanyireka bushi noku Ongo ababalyira.

17. Si tchiro batcha, Enawetchu yeke abaa analyi alauma nanyi erakunyeresa nemisi. Bushi noku nendjire nahubanganya emwasi mubuya-buya mwa bandju bala bateshi Kabumbi. Kuikira boshi nabo

---

12. 서리 디기고 나무쭈미러 와 무시 워 어퍼소.

13. 어마웆 마꽈 우꺄바하, 우네러더라 쪠라 고찌 나러가아 와 무시 워 도로와 무꽈 와 가리도, 우나네러더라 너비라 비다부 시 가찌 비라 비구꺄네시뭐 와 뉴우.

14. 아꿔사뚜루 오꽈 뭐시 워 뷰마 아네쯔사 과 가시부? 러루 부씨 노오구 어나워쭈 아꺄무쯘사 과 비시부 나이.

15. 나우 우찌꽈꺄 부서서 구부 봐너씨, 과부씨 아바아 무가쪠 부서서 꽈구호꺄 아아끼거 어먀시 여쭈.

16. 부씨 어마웆 나다끼쪠사아 구떠 나찌더더라 어라 무호또 서 버씨 버 마꽈 구다보너가아 나 무뿌 아시뱌 오라 와이가 구네아사 시 보씨 버라 구나네러가 부씨 노구 오꼳 아바바쪠라.

17. 시 찌로 바짜, 어나워쭈 여거 아바아 아나쪠 아꽈우마 나내 어라구녀러사 너미시. 부씨 노구 너찌러 나후바꺄냐 어먀시 무부야- 부야 와 바뚜 바꽈 바더씨 가부뻬. 구이기라 보씨 나보 바나쪠꺄 보빠아오. 가찌

---

12. I sent Tychicus to Ephesus.

13. When you come, bring the cloak that I left with Carpus at Troas, and my scrolls, especially the parchments.

14. Alexander the metalworker did me a great deal of harm. The Lord will repay him for what he has done.

15. You too should be on your guard against him, because he strongly opposed our message.

16. At my first defense, no one came to my support, but everyone deserted me. May it not be held against them.

17. But the Lord stood at my side and gave me strength, so that through me the message might be fully proclaimed and all the Gentiles might hear it. And I was delivered from the lion's mouth.

banalyinda bonvaa'o. kandji anyinunulaa nomwa bunu se ngoromolyi.

18. Enawetchu anganyinunula mwa kasi koshi kala ke mabi, nekuna nyilanga tchasiya nyinaika mwa bwami bwai bula bwe bolo, bushi ne kunde atongibwa esiku nemangu; Bibe batcha!

19. Unyikesesaa Purisila na Akila ne ngumu sira silyi mwa mwa Onesiforo.

20. Erasito ashibire mwamusi we Korindo na Torofimo nai na murekaa alakira mwa musi we Mileto

21. Uira emisi yau Yoshi uike enera era muhondo setchihangi, kuno esiku sembeo sitakuika. Eubulo na Punde na Kalautia alauma nebandji banyaketchu bemeresi boshi nabo banakukesise.

22. Enawetchu Yesu Kirisito abaa alauma nemutchima wao, nebubuya bwai bubaa alauma nenyu.

아네누누똬아 노똬 부누 서 쯔로모례.

18. 어나워쭈 아까네누누똬 똬 가시 고씨 가똬 거 마비, 너구나 네똬까 짜시야 네나이가 똬 봐미 봐이 부똬 뭐 보로, 부씨 너 구떠 아도삐봐 어시구 너마꾸; 비버 바짜!

19. 우네거서사아 푸리시똬 나 아기똬 너 꾸무 시라 시례 똬 똬 오너시포로.

20. 어라시도 아씨비러 똬무시 워 고리또 나 도로피모 나이 나 무러가아 아똬기라 똬 무시 워 미뗘도

21. 우이라 어미시 야우 요씨 우이거 어너라 어라 무호또 서찌하삐, 구노 어시구 서뻐오 시다구이가. 어우부로 나 푸떠 나 가똬우디아 아똬우마 너바찌 바냐거쭈 버머러시 보씨 나보 바나구거시서.

22. 어나워쭈 여수 기리시도 아바아 아똬우마 너무찌마 와오, 너부부야 봐이 부바아 아똬우마 너뉴.

18. The Lord will rescue me from every evil attack and will bring me safely to his heavenly kingdom. To him be glory for ever and ever. Amen.

19. Greet Priscilla and Aquila and the household of Onesiphorus.

20. Erastus stayed in Corinth, and I left Trophimus sick in Miletus.

21. Do your best to get here before winter. Eubulus greets you, and so do Pudens, Linus, Claudia and all the brothers.

22. The Lord be with your spirit. Grace be with you.

Tito

디도

Titus

TITO
(TITUS)

디도
(디두)

Tito Chikono 1

1. Poolo muaanda wa Ongo kandji nyiri ndjumwa ya Yesu Kirisito, mwa bwemeresi bwa balaa balondolyibwa na Ongo tchasiya bamwemerere, banamenyerere nemyasi ye kanangana, nei myasi ingende ya baasa kuata nzimiko era isimise.

2. Nomwa kuata emalangalyisa mekubona ekalamu kesiku nemangu. Naku kalamu Ongo ola utafula bisha iwatchulaanya'ko emangu abaa atasa kubumba ebutala.

3. Seri era kuboola etchinwa tchai mwa bihangi byai kurengera enyiiriso sira anyiburaa nambu nendaa nahubanganyisa ebandju kukulyikana nebutondokeke bwa Ongo yi Enawetchu.

4. Era uwau Tito, mwananyi ola we kanangana, mwa bwemeresi bula butchubikire alauma, emuisha nobondjo, noboolo bokutenga era mwa Ongo i Tata wetchu, nera mwa Kirisito Yesu y'Enawetchu.

디도 찌고노 1

1. 포오ᄙᅩ 무아아ᄯᅡ 와 오ᅌ고 가ᄡᅵ 네리 ᅜᅮ뫄 야 여수 기리시도, 뫄 붸머러시 봐 바ᄙᅡ아 바ᄙᅩᄯᅩᄙᅦ봐 나 오ᅌ고 짜시야 바뭐머러러, 바나머녀러러 너먀시 여 가나ᅁᅡ나, 너이 먀시 이ᅁᅥᄯᅥ 야 바아사 구아다 씨미고 어라 이시미서.

2. 노뫄 구아다 어마ᄙᅡᅁᅡᄙᅦ사 머구보나 어가ᄙᅡ무 거시구 너마ᅌ구. 나구 가ᄙᅡ무 오ᅌ고 오ᄙᅡ 우다푸ᄙᅡ 비싸 이와쭈ᄙᅡ아냐고 어마ᅌ구 아바야 아다사 구부빠 어부다ᄙᅡ.

3. 서리 어라 구보오ᄙᅡ 어찌놔 짜이 뫄 비하ᅁᅵ 뱌이 구러ᅁᅥ라 어네이리소 시라 아네부라아 나뿌 너ᄯᅡ아 나후바ᅁᅡ네사 어바ᅜᅮ 구구ᄙᅦ가나 너부도ᄯᅩ거거 봐 오ᅌ고 에 어나워쭈.

4. 어라 우와우 디도, 뫄나니 오ᄙᅡ 워 가나ᅁᅡ나, 뫄 붸머러시 부ᄙᅡ 부쭈비기러 아ᄙᅡ우마, 어무이싸 노보ᅜᅩ, 노보오ᄙᅩ 보구더ᅁᅡ 어라 뫄 오ᅌ고 이 다다 워쭈, 너라 뫄 기리시도 여수 여나워쭈.

Titus Chapter 1[NIV]

1. Paul, a servant of God and an apostle of Jesus Christ for the faith of God's elect and the knowledge of the truth that leads to godliness--

2. a faith and knowledge resting on the hope of eternal life, which God, who does not lie, promised before the beginning of time,

3. and at his appointed season he brought his word to light through the preaching entrusted to me by the command of God our Savior,

4. To Titus, my true son in our common faith: Grace and peace from God the Father and Christ Jesus our Savior.

5. Kwabushi noku nakurekaa kwa tchisimba tche Kereto, tchasiya ukunganyaa ei myasi era yashiba nekubika ebangumwa bala bangemangira eluhu lwa Ongo, kukulyikana ngokula nekutchitchika.

6. Akaba kwabonekire emundju ola utonvikana'ko tchira na mwasi mubi kandji anabaa mulume ola unetee mukasi muuma, nebana bai babaa bemeresi, kandji bataata ngulu ibi : nesi ya butamisi nesi kuba batengu.

7. Bushi batcha tchemire emungumwa ola wemangilyire emulyimo wa Ongo, tchitamwemire mbubendaa onvikana'ko mwasi mubi : kandji ataemire kuba mundju we rume, nesi wakusinana fuba-fuba nesi mutamisi, nesi kalaha, nesi mundju wakuhonda bikulo mwandjira sira sitakomire.

8. Seri abaa mundju ola wekuangilyira ebaenyi, abaa mundju ola usimire emabuya, abaa mundju ola wete ebwenge, ola wete alwaso, abaa mundju mwemeresi mubuya-buya, nekunde

5. 과부씨 노구 나구러가아 과 찌시빠 쩌 거러도, 짜시야 우구빠냐아 어이 먀시 어라 야씨바 너구비가 어바우꽈 바꽈 바꺼마끼라 어루후 꽈 오쯔, 구구레가나 쯔구꽈 너구찌찌가.

6. 아가바 과보너기러 어무뿌 오꽈 우도삐가나고 찌라 나 꽈시 무비 가찌 아나바아 무루머 오꽈 우너더어 무가시 무우마, 너바나 바이 바바아 버머러시, 가찌 바다아다 우루 이비 : 너시 야 부다미시 너시 구바 바더우.

7. 부씨 바짜 쩌미러 어무우꽈 오꽈 워마끼레러 어무레모 와 오쯔, 찌다뭐미러 뿌버따아 오삐가나고 꽈시 무비 : 가찌 아다어미러 구바 무뿌 워 루머, 너시 와구시나나 푸바- 푸바 너시 무다미시, 너시 가꽈하, 너시 무뿌 와구호따 비구롣 꽈찌라 시라 시다고미러.

8. 서리 아바아 무뿌 오꽈 워구아끼레라 어바어네, 아바아 무뿌 오꽈 우시미러 어마부야, 아바아 무뿌 오꽈 워더 어붜꺼, 오꽈 워더 아꽐소, 아바아 무뿌 뭐머러시 무부야-부야,

5. The reason I left you in Crete was that you might straighten out what was left unfinished and appoint elders in every town, as I directed you.

6. An elder must be blameless, the husband of but one wife, a man whose children believe and are not open to the charge of being wild and disobedient.

7. Since an overseer is entrusted with God's work, he must be blameless--not overbearing, not quick-tempered, not given to drunkenness, not violent, not pursuing dishonest gain.

8. Rather he must be hospitable, one who loves what is good, who is self-controlled, upright, holy and disciplined.

atchilanga kwa mabi.

9. Kandji tcheemire kuba mundju ola usimikire mwa mwasi we kanangana nekuima bala bendjire bamuenza ebuaka kwa bauwirwe

10. Kwabushi kunalyi bandju banene bala batana tchundjire tchiro na mundju asibya, nekunde bateba ebandju kurengera emyasi yabo era yebuha-buha, seri banene mubo balyi Ebayuta bala bemerera Yesu Kirisito.

11. Kwabushi noko, tcheemire kubamina ebunu bwabu abu bendjire bakangirisa emyasi era itatchungenene, bera bendjire batchuma ebandju boshi mu ngumu suma-suma bera bareka ebwemeresi bwabo, bera bendjire baira batcha tchasiya babonaa ebuteya mwa ndjira sira sitakomire.

12. Mundju muuma murebi wera mwabo era kuteta mbu : " Besha kerete banatchula bafusi babisha besiku soshi. Kandji banatchula ngalyi, banaba baoshi-oshi, kandji banaba bandarenza kalyo ".

13. Bubu bubei bunalyi bwa

너구떠 아찌롸애 과 마비.

9. 가찌 쩌어미러 구바 무뚜 오라 우시미기러 와 먀시 워 가나까나 너구이마 바롸 버찌러 바무어싸 어부아가 과 바우위뤄

10. 과부씨 구나레 바뚜 바너너 바롸 바다나 쭈찌러 찌로 나 무뚜 아시뱌, 너구떠 바더바 어바뚜 구러떠라 어먀시 야보 어라 여부하-부하, 서리 바너너 무보 바레 어바우다 바롸 버머러라 여수 기리시도.

11. 과부씨 노고, 쩌어미러 구바미나 어부누 봐부 아부 버찌러 바가끼리사 어먀시 어라 이다쭈떠너너, 버라 버찌러 바쭈마 어바뚜 보씨 무 꾸무 수마-수마 버라 바러가 어붜머러시 봐보, 버라 버찌러 바이라 바짜 짜시야 바보나아 어부더야 와 찌라 시라 시다고미러.

12. 무뚜 무우마 무러비 워라 먀보 어라 구더다 뿌 : " 버싸 거러더 바나쭈롸 바푸시 바비싸 버시구 소씨. 가찌 바나쭈롸 까레, 바나바 바오씨-오씨, 가찌 바나바 바따러싸 갸료 ".

13. 부부 부버이 부나레 봐

9. He must hold firmly to the trustworthy message as it has been taught, so that he can encourage others by sound doctrine and refute those who oppose it.

10. For there are many rebellious people, mere talkers and deceivers, especially those of the circumcision group.

11. They must be silenced, because they are ruining whole households by teaching things they ought not to teach--and that for the sake of dishonest gain.

12. Even one of their own prophets has said, "Cretans are always liars, evil brutes, lazy gluttons."

13. This testimony is true.

kanangana, kwabushi noko ubakalyira busese-busese tchasiya basimike kubuya mwa bwemeresi bwe kanangana.

14. Batenda banakulyikira emyasi yenganu se Bayuta nesi kukulyikira emyasi ye bandju bala bendjire banana ne kureta emyasi ye kanangana.

15. Ebindju byoshi byabumbwa ba Ongo, binakomisibwe kwa bandju, batchikomise; seri bibiire kwa bandju bala babiire, batalyi na bemeresi. Kwabushi ebwenge bwabu ne buashi bwabu bwekumenyerera etchibuya netchibi bilyi mwe singa.

16. Abu bandju bende batchitonga nambu beshi Ongo, seri emyaanyisa yabu yende yaba ibalosise kanangana kwa bata muishi. Kandji balyi bandju bala bende bakola bira bitakolwa, batatchunda na mundju asibya, bataala nakuira tchiro namwasi mubuya asibya.

가나까나, 과부씨 노고 우바가쩨라 부서서-부서서 짜시야 바시미거 구부야 뫄 붜머러시 붜 가나까나.

14. 바더따 바나구쩨기라 어먀시 여까누 서 바유다 너시 구구쩨기라 어먀시 여 바쭈 바꽈 버찌러 바나나 너 구러다 어먀시 여 가나까나.

15. 어비쭈 뵤씨 뱌부까 바 오꼬, 비나고미시붜 과 바쭈, 바찌고미서; 서리 비비이러 과 바쭈 바꽈 바비이러, 바다쩨 나 버머러시. 과부씨 어붸어 봐부 너 부아씨 봐부 붜구머녀러라 어찌부야 너찌비 비쩨 뭐 시까.

16. 아부 바쭈 버떠 바찌도까 나뿌 버씨 오꼬, 서리 어먀아네사 야부 여떠 야바 이바론시서 가나까나 과 바다 무이씨. 가찌 바쩨 바쭈 바꽈 버떠 바고꽈 비라 비다고꽈, 바다쭈따 나 무쭈 아시뱌, 바다아꽈 나구이라 찌로 나뫄시 무부야 아시뱌.

Therefore, rebuke them sharply, so that they will be sound in the faith

14. and will pay no attention to Jewish myths or to the commands of those who reject the truth.

15. To the pure, all things are pure, but to those who are corrupted and do not believe, nothing is pure. In fact, both their minds and consciences are corrupted.

16. They claim to know God, but by their actions they deny him. They are detestable, disobedient and unfit for doing anything good.

Tito Chikono 2

1. Seri woyo : wendaa

디도 찌고노 2

1. 서리 오요 : 워따아

Titus Chapter 2 [NIV]

1. You must teach what is in

wakangilyisa ebemeresi emyasi era ikulyikene ne bwiirisi bwe kanangana.	와가ᅌᅵᄙᅦ사 어버머러시 어먀시 어라 이구ᄙᅦ거너 너 뷔이리시 붜 가나ᅌᅡ나.	accord with sound doctrine.
2. Ebalume bala bera bangumwa, wendaa wabakangirisa mbu batchilangaa kwa mabi kandji benda bataa emyanya era ingatchuma beeresibwa etchunda, kandji benda baata emianyisa ibuy; nakandji ubakangirisa mbu benda basimika mwa bwemeresi nomwa nzii nomwa bushibirisi.	2. 어바루머 바ᄙᅡ 버라 바ᅌᅮ뫄, 워따아 와바가ᅌᅵ리사 뿌 바찌ᄙᅡᅌᅡ아 과 마비 가ᄶᅵ 버따 바다아 어먀냐 어라 이ᅌᅡ쭈마 버어러시봐 어쭈따, 가ᄶᅵ 버따 바아다 어미아네사 이부에; 나가ᄶᅵ 우바가ᅌᅵ리사 뿌 버따 바시미가 뫄 붜머러시 노뫄 ᄶᅵ이 노뫄 부씨비리시.	2. Teach the older men to be temperate, worthy of respect, self-controlled, and sound in faith, in love and in endurance.
3. Ne bakasi bala be baekulu nabo wenda wabakangirisa mbu benda batchitola mbunga bandju babuya-buya, batemire kunde baamana ebandji bulyiu, nesi kuba batamisi, si beemire kunde baana emaano mala makomire.	3. 너 바가시 바ᄙᅡ 버 바어구루 나보 워따 와바가ᅌᅵ리사 뿌 버따 바찌도ᄙᅡ 뿌ᅌᅡ 바ᅜᅮ 바부야-부야, 바더미러 구떠 바아마나 어바ᄶᅵ 부ᄙᅦ우, 너시 구바 바다미시, 시 버어미러 구떠 바아나 어마아노 마ᄙᅡ 마고미러.	3. Likewise, teach the older women to be reverent in the way they live, not to be slanderers or addicted to much wine, but to teach what is good.
4. Tchasiya bendaa bakangirisa ebakasi bala batchiri banyere mbu bendaa basima beba babu nekusima ebana babo.	4. 짜시야 버따아 바가ᅌᅵ리사 어바가시 바ᄙᅡ 바찌리 바녀러 뿌 버따아 바시마 버바 바부 너구시마 어바나 바보.	4. Then they can train the younger women to love their husbands and children,
5. Na kandji benda baanabo mbu bendaa baata emyanyisa ibuya-buya nekunde batchilanga kwa buhungu kandji beemire kunde bakola emilyimo kubuya mwa	5. 나 가ᄶᅵ 버따 바아나보 뿌 버따아 바아다 어먀네사 이부야-부야 너구떠 바찌ᄙᅡᅌᅡ 과 부후ᅌᅮ 가ᄶᅵ 버어미러 구떠 바고ᄙᅡ 어미ᄙᅦ모 구부야 뫄 마호시	5. to be self-controlled and pure, to be busy at home, to be kind, and to be subject to their husbands, so that no one will malign the word of God.

mahosi mabo, nekunde
bakorera ebandji bandju
emabuya nakutchunda beba
babu; tcheemire bendaa baira
batcha bushi ebandju
bangesha kukamba etchinwa
tcha Ongo.

마보, 너구떠 바고러라
어바찌 바뚜 어마부야
나구쭈따 버바 바부;
쩌어미러 버따아 바이라
바짜 부씨 어바뚜 바꺼싸
구가빠 어찌뇨 짜 오꼬.

6. Nebatabana nabo undaa
wabaana mbu bendaa
babookala ebwenge mwa
bindju byoshi.

6. 너바다바나 나보 우따아
와바아나 뿌 버따아
바보오가꺄 어붜어 먀 비뚜
뵤씨.

6. Similarly, encourage the
young men to be self-
controlled.

7. Mwa binwa byoshi, woyo
nau wendaa waira emabuya
tchasiya ebandji bandju
bakulorere'ko, nomwa kuirisa
kwau wendaa walosa
ekanangana utendaa wakuba
mwaalyo.

7. 먀 비뇨 뵤씨, 오요 나우
워따아 와이라 어마부야
짜시야 어바찌 바뚜
바구로러러고, 노먀 구이리사
과우 워따아 와로사
어가나까나 우더따아 와구바
먀아료.

7. In everything set them an
example by doing what is
good. In your teaching show
integrity, seriousness

8. Wendaa wa balyikisa
nemyasi era ingareta kalamo
era ebandju
batangakuenza'ku na bwaka
busibya : tchasiya oyu
mweenzi we bwaka afe
ehonyi. Kwabushi atatchibone
na mwasi mubi ola angateta
era luulu setchu.

8. 워따아 와 바뤠기사
너먀시 어라 이꺄러다
가꺄모 어라 어바뚜
바다꺄구어싸구 나 봐가
부시뱌 : 짜시야 오유 뭐어씨
워 봐가 아퍼 어호네. 과부씨
아다찌보너 나 먀시 무비
오꽈 아꺄더다 어라 루우루
서쭈.

8. and soundness of speech
that cannot be condemned,
so that those who oppose
you may be ashamed because
they have nothing bad to say
about us.

9. Wendaa waana etchuungu
mbu bendaa batchunda
beenawabo nekubasimisa mu
tchira mwasi kandji batabaa
na bandju bakuira bwaka
nababu enawabo.

9. 워따아 와아나 어쭈우꾸
뿌 버따아 바쭈따
버어나와보 너구바시미사 무
찌라 먀시 가찌 바다바아 나
바뚜 바구이라 봐가 나바부
어나와보.

9. Teach slaves to be subject
to their masters in everything,
to try to please them, not to
talk back to them,

10. Kandji batabaa besi seri
balyi bandju bakulosa kwa

10. 가찌 바다바아 버시 서리
바뤠 바뚜 바구로사 과 바뤠

10. and not to steal from
them, but to show that they

balyi bandju bakutchinyiirwa mu byoshi, bakaira batcha, byoshi bira bangende baira bingaba byeresise, emyasi yoshi ye mununusi wetchu Ongo etchunda lyira tchwendjire tchwabakangirisa.

11. Kubinalyi, kwa bushi ebondjo bwa Ongo bwa anganunula mwe bandju boshi, bwalorekene'ko.

12. Kurengera obu bondjo, bitchuemire kunde tchwanana ekunde tchwaira bira bitamusimisise nekunana ekukulyikira emyasi ye buhuma-huma bomuno butala. Seri emangu tchutchiri munu butala bwakulwarero tchuata mianyisa ibuya nekuira bira bisimise Ongo.

13. Mwakuira batcha; tchasiya tchulyindjiraa elusuku lubuya lula tchutchula tchulangalyire, olu lusuku lwe Emununusi wetchu Yesu Kirisito i Ongo wetchu munene akabaha mwa bulangare bwai.

14. Oyu Yesu atchaana yeine bushi netchu. Atchaana batcha tchasiya atchununule mwa mabi nmetchu moshi nekutchuira bandju bai bala bakomisibwe; kandji bala bete ebushiro bwekuira

바쭈 바구찌네이라 무 뵤씨, 바가이라 바짜, 뵤씨 비라 바꺼러 바이라 비까바 벼러시서, 어먀시 요씨 여 무누누시 워쭈 오꼬 어쭈따 레라 쭤찌러 쫘바가꺼리사.

11. 구비나레, 과 부씨 어보쪼 봐 오꼬 봐 아꺼누누롸 뭐 바쭈 보씨, 봐로러거너고.

12. 구러꺼라 오부 보쪼, 비쭈어미러 구뻐 쫘나나 어구뻐 쫘이라 비라 비다무시미시서 너구나나 어구구레기라 어먀시 여 부후마-후마 보무노 부다롸. 서리 어마꾸 쭈찌리 무누 부다롸 봐구꽈러로 쭈아다 미아네사 이부야 너구이라 비라 비시미서 오꼬.

13. 먀구이라 바짜; 짜시야 쭈레찌라아 어루수구 루부야 루꽈 쭈쭈꽈 쭈꽈꺼레러, 오루 루수구 뭐 어무누누시 워쭈 여수 기리시도 이 오꼬 워쭈 무너너 아가바하 먀 부롸꺼러 바이.

14. 오유 여수 아짜아나 여이너 부씨 너쭈. 아짜아나 바짜 짜시야 아쭈누누뻐 먀 마비 누머쭈 모씨 너구쭈이라 바쭈 바이 바꽈 바고미시붜; 가찌 바꽈 버더 어부씨로 붜구이라 어마부야.

can be fully trusted, so that in every way they will make the teaching about God our Savior attractive.

11. For the grace of God that brings salvation has appeared to all men.

12. It teaches us to say "No" to ungodliness and worldly passions, and to live self-controlled, upright and godly lives in this present age,

13. while we wait for the blessed hope--the glorious appearing of our great God and Savior, Jesus Christ,

14. who gave himself for us to redeem us from all wickedness and to purify for himself a people that are his very own, eager to do what is good.

emabuya.

15. Rero mwana wanyi mwana wanyi, ei myasi iweemire kunde wakangirisa ebandju ne kubasesa emitchima nekubakalyira; wendaa waira ebi byoshi nebuashi bwao boshi; wendaa wemerera nambu kubaa tchiro na mundju asibya ola ukukenaa.	15. 러로 먀나 와네 먀나 와네, 어이 먀시 이워어미러 구떠 와가삐리사 어바뚜 너 구바서사 어미찌마 너구바가쪠라; 워따아 와이라 어비 뵤씨 너부아씨 봐오 보씨; 워따아 워머러라 나뿌 구바아 찌로 나 무뚜 아시뱌 오롸 우구거나아.	15. These, then, are the things you should teach. Encourage and rebuke with all authority. Do not let anyone despise you.

Tito Chikono 3 / 디도 찌고노 3 / Titus Chapter 3[NIV]

1. Wendaa wakengesa ebandju mbu bendaa ba tchirembeka era muhondo se bami, nera muhondo sebakulu-kulu ? Tcheemire kuba tchunda ne kutchirembeka mwa kuira tchira mwasi mubuya.	1. 워따아 와거써사 어바뚜 뿌 버따아 바 찌러뻐가 어라 무호또 서 바미, 너라 무호또 서바구루-구루 ? 쩌어미러 구바 쭌다 너 구찌러뻐가 마 구이라 찌라 먀시 무부야.	1. Remind the people to be subject to rulers and authorities, to be obedient, to be ready to do whatever is good,
2. Kandji ubaburaa nambu bataendaa bakamba mundju nesi kunde babangana. Si tchibeemire babaa mwa boolo, banaendekera kuba barembu era muhondo se bandju boshi.	2. 가찌 우바부라아 나뿌 바다어따아 바가빠 무뚜 너시 구떠 바바빠나. 시 찌버어미러 바바야 마 보오롣, 바나어떠거라 구바 바러뿌 어라 무호또 서 바뚜 보씨.	2. to slander no one, to be peaceable and considerate, and to show true humility toward all men.
3. Kwabushi kwamira netchu tchwanabaa tchutete bwenge busibya, tchutendaa tchwatchunda Ongo, tchwatebibwaa mwa kunde	3. 과부씨 과미라 너쭈 쫜나바아 쭈더더 뷔꺼 부시뱌, 쭈더따아 쫜쭈따 오꼳, 쫜더비봐아 마 구떠 쫜고러라 어미비리 여쭈	3. At one time we too were foolish, disobedient, deceived and enslaved by all kinds of passions and pleasures. We lived in malice and envy,

tchwakorera emibiri yetchu oshao, nekutchiira tchuungu tchwa kutchisimisa mu tchira buhuma-huma bubi. Kandji tchwabaa tchwera tchunatchitchulyira bandju babi na kunde tchwafira ebandji emufula. Ebandju bendee batchuhomba netchu tchwanahombana.

오싸오, 너구찌이라 쭈우꾸 좌 구찌시미사 무 찌라 부후마-후마 부비. 가찌 좌바아 쮜라 쭈나쭈레라 바뚜 바비 나 구떠 좌피라 어바찌 어무푸롸. 어바뚜 버떠어 바쭈호빠 너쭈 좌나호빠나.

being hated and hating one another.

4. Seri emango Ongo i mununusi wetchu alosaa ebubuya bwai nenzii yai kwa bandju.

4. 서리 어마꼬 오꼬 이 무누누시 워쭈 아로사아 어부부야 봐이 너씨이 야이 과 바쭈.

4. But when the kindness and love of God our Savior appeared,

5. Mwakutchununula ataraa batcha kwabushi tchwendee tchwaira bira bitchungenene era muhondo sai, nanga : si kwabushi atchufiraa ebondjo era kutchununula mwa bondjo bwai yeine, mwakoosibwa buyayaya, nekubutchibwa bwa kabiri kurengera emutchima mubuya-buya.

5. 콰구쭈누누롸 아다이라아 바짜 과부씨 쮜떠어 좌이라 비라 비쭈꺼너너 어라 무호또 사이, 나꺄 : 시 과부씨 아쭈피라아 어보쏘 어라 구쭈누누롸 와 보쏘 봐이 여이너, 마고오시봐 부야야야, 너구부찌봐 봐 가비리 구러꺼라 어무찌마 무부야-부야.

5. he saved us, not because of righteous things we had done, but because of his mercy. He saved us through the washing of rebirth and renewal by the Holy Spirit,

6. Oyu mutchima Mubuya-buya Ongo atchuboshi kurengera emwana wayi Yesu Kirisito i mununusi wetchu.

6. 오유 무찌마 무부야-부야 오꼬 아쭈보씨 구러꺼라 어마나 와에 여수 기리시도 이 무누누시 워쭈.

6. whom he poured out on us generously through Jesus Christ our Savior,

7. Aira batcha, tchuata emwisha wekubona ekalamu kesiku nemangi. Ebi byoshi bya alyikana bushi kurengera ebondjo bwai, era kunatchuira kuba bandju bala

7. 아이라 바짜, 쭈아다 어뮈싸 워구보나 어가꽈무 거시구 너마삐. 어비 뵤씨 뱌 아레가나 부씨 구러꺼라 어보쏘 봐이, 어라 구나쭈이라 구바 바쭈 봐롸

7. so that, having been justified by his grace, we might become heirs having the hope of eternal life.

batchungenene era muhondo sai.

8. Onu mwasi alyi mwasi wokunalyi nanyi nahonda unasese mwei myasi, tchasiya bala bemerere Ongo, batcheresa ebushiro bwe kumukorera ekasi kabuya-buya. Eni myasi iikomire, kandji inete na mufa kwa bandju boshi.

9. Seri utendaa wengira mu tchira bwaka bwa buuta, na bwaka era luulu se myasi ye masimana era luulu se mwaso kwabushi ebyera binatchula byabuha-buha, bitete na mufa asibya.

10. Emundju ola wendjire watchuma ebemeresi baberekana'mo; umubandaa'ko euma, nesi kabiri. Akaba atakuumvire; umubika, urekanaa nai.

11. Na ukamenya emundju ulyi ngoyu, umenyaa kwakuera ku aelyire, kandji mabi ma era endire aendekera kuira. No mwakuira batcha yeine atchi tchindjibuse.

12. Emangu nyikatchuma Artema era mwao, nesi Tikiko, ucthisesa busese uike era nyilyi, tchiru nyingaba era

바쭈ㅆ어너너 어라 무호또 사이.

8. 오누 먀시 아레 먀시 옹구나레 나니 나호따 우나서서 뭐이 먀시, 짜시야 바롸 버머러러 오꼬, 바쩌러사 어부씨로 붜 구무고러라 어가시 가부야-부야. 어니 먀시 이이고미러, 가찌 이너더 나 무파 과 바쭈 보씨.

9. 서리 우더따아 워께라 무 찌라 봐가 봐 부우다, 나 봐가 어라 ㄹㅜ우ㄹㅜ 서 먀시 여 마시마나 어라 ㄹㅜ우ㄹㅜ 서 꽈소 과부씨 어벼라 비나쭈롸 뱌부하-부하, 비더더 나 무파 아시뱌.

10. 어무뿌 오롸 워찌러 와쭈마 어버머러시 바버러가나모; 우무바빠아고 어우마, 너시 가비리. 아가바 아다구우쀄러; 우무비가, 우러가나아 나이.

11. 나 우가머냐 어무뿌 우레 꼬유, 우머냐아 과구어라 구 아어레러, 가찌 마비 마 어라 어띠러 아어떠거라 구이라. 노 꽈구이라 바짜 여이너 아찌 찌찌부서.

12. 어마웃 네가쭈마 라더마 어라 꽈오, 너시 디기고, 우찌서사 부서서 우이거 어라 네레, 찌루 네빠바 어라

8. This is a trustworthy saying. And I want you to stress these things, so that those who have trusted in God may be careful to devote themselves to doing what is good. These things are excellent and profitable for everyone.

9. But avoid foolish controversies and genealogies and arguments and quarrels about the law, because these are unprofitable and useless.

10. Warn a divisive person once, and then warn him a second time. After that, have nothing to do with him.

11. You may be sure that such a man is warped and sinful; he is self-condemned.

12. As soon as I send Artemas or Tychicus to you, do your best to come to me at Nicopolis, because I have

Nikopolil. Kwabushi eyera inyihondjire kuekala mwa siku sembeo.

니고포릐이. 과부씨 어여라 이네호끠러 구어가꽈 뫄 시구 서뻐오.

decided to winter there.

13. Uira emisi yau yoshi, uasa Apolo alauma nola musus Senas, tchasiya bataina kandju kasibya mwa lubwaanano lwabo.

13. 우이라 어미시 야우 요씨, 우아사 아포로 아꽈우마 노꽈 무수 서나, 짜시야 바다이나 가뚜 가시뱌 뫄 루봐아나노 꽈보.

13. Do everything you can to help Zenas the lawyer and Apollos on their way and see that they have everything they need.

14. Banyaketchu nabo, tcheemire batchikangilyisa nekutchaana mwa kuira emabuya, mwabatcha bangende baasa ebandji bandju bala balyi mwa bulayi. Mwakuira batcha, akalamu kabo kangaata mufa.

14. 바냐거쭈 나보, 쩌어미러 바찌가끠례사 너구짜아나 뫄 구이라 어마부야, 뫄바짜 바꺼떠 바아사 어바끠 바뚜 바꽈 바례 뫄 부꽈에. 뫄구이라 바짜, 아가꽈무 가보 가까아다 무파.

14. Our people must learn to devote themselves to doing what is good, in order that they may provide for daily necessities and not live unproductive lives.

15. Ebandju boshi bala nyilyi nabo anola bakukesise. Nau unyikesesaa banyaketchu bemeresi. Emuisha wa Ongo abaa alauma nenyu muboshi.

15. 어바뚜 보씨 바꽈 네례 나보 아노꽈 바구거시서. 나우 우네거서사아 바냐거쭈 버머러시. 어무이싸 와 오꼬 아바아 아꽈우마 너뉴 무보씨.

15. Everyone with me sends you greetings. Greet those who love us in the faith. Grace be with you all.

Filemoni

피려모니

Philemon

FILEMONO
(PHILEMON)

피려모노
(피려모누)

Filemoni Chikono 1

1. Nyono Poolo, nyilyi munyororo mwa Yesu Kirisito, nyono na munyaketchu TIMOTEO, tchutchwa kuandjikira musirwa Filemono, mukosi mulyiketchu.

2. Nera mwa Apiya ii mwalyi wetchu na ARIKIPO i musula wekutchuasa kwa bita, nowa luhu lwa Ongo lula lulyi lwau.

3. Emuisha, neboolo bira bitengire era mwa Ongo i Tata wetchu, weera mwe'Enawetchu Yesu Kirisito.

4. Natongire Ongo wanyi, esiku soshi, nendjire nakukengera mwa memo manyi.

5. Kwabushi nonvire emyasi yau ye nzii neye bwemeresi bula utchusa era mwe'Enawetchu Yesu nokwa bemeresi boshi.

6. Nendjire nema Ongo, obu buuma tchwete kurengera ebwemeresi bwau buira emulyimo wai mwa kumenyerera emabuya moshi mala tchwete mwa buuma bwetchu na Kirisito Yesu.

7. Kwabushi tchwete lumoo

피러모니 찌고노 1

1. 뇨노 포오로, 네레 무뇨로로 먀 여수 기리시도, 뇨노 나 무냐거쭈 디모더오, 쭈좌 구아씨기라 무시롸 피러모노, 무고시 무레거쭈.

2. 너라 먀 아피야 이이 먀레 워쭈 나 아리기포 이 무수롸 워구쭈아사 과 비다, 노와 루후 롸 오끄 루롸 루레 롸우.

3. 어무이싸, 너보오로 비라 비더끼러 어라 먀 오끄 이 다다 워쭈, 워어라 뭐어나워쭈 여수 기리시도.

4. 나도끼러 오끄 와네, 어시구 소씨, 너찌러 나구거어라 먀 머모 마네.

5. 과부씨 노삐러 어먀시 야우 여 씨이 너여 뭐머러시 부롸 우쭈사 어라 뭐어나워쭈 여수 노과 버머러시 보씨.

6. 너찌러 너마 오끄, 오부 부우마 쭤더 구러꺼라 어뭐머러시 봐우 부이라 어무레모 와이 먀 구머녀러라 어마부야 모씨 마롸 쭤더 먀 부우마 뭐쭈 나 기리시도 여수.

7. 과부씨 쭤더 루모오 루너너

Philemon Chapter 1[NIV]

1. Paul, a prisoner of Christ Jesus, and Timothy our brother, To Philemon our dear friend and fellow worker,

2. to Apphia our sister, to Archippus our fellow soldier and to the church that meets in your home:

3. Grace to you and peace from God our Father and the Lord Jesus Christ.

4. I always thank my God as I remember you in my prayers,

5. because I hear about your faith in the Lord Jesus and your love for all the saints.

6. I pray that you may be active in sharing your faith, so that you will have a full understanding of every good thing we have in Christ.

7. Your love has given me

lunene nemisi inene bushi nenzii yau. Na kandji emitchima ye bemeresi ba Ongo yamoire busese nokuumula busese.

8. Kwa bushi noku, natchiro nyingaata emisi era mwandanda sa Kirisito, nakutchitchikire koyu mwasi we kanangana.

9. Si tchsiro batcha, kusengera kunahonda nyikusengere kurengera enzii era tchwetene'ko. Nyono Poolo, nera mungumwa, kandji nyilyi bwa buroko kwabushi nyilyi mukosi wa Yesu Kirisito.

10. Nakusengera, bushi nonu mwana wanyi ola nabuta mangu nabaa nyilyi munyororo wanyi, esina lyai ii ONESIMO.

11. Mwesi siku sira sarenga abaa atakwetere tchiro na mufa asibya. Si mwesine siku era mundju ola utchwetera mufa tchubabilyi.

12. Arero nakualulyira ii, nau unamuangilyira kwabushi alyi ngokula nyingana kweeresa emutchima wanyi.

13. Nanyi nabaa nahonda angashibire alauma nanyi, tchasiya anyikorere ngokula

너미시 이너너 부씨 너씨이 야우. 나 가찌 어미찌마 여 버머러시 바 오꼬 야모이러 부서서 노구우무꽈 부서서.

8. 과 부씨 노구, 나찌로 네꽈아다 어미시 어라 꽈따따 사 기리시도, 나구찌찌기러 고유 꽈시 워 가나꽈나.

9. 시 찌시로 바짜, 구서꺼라 구나호따 네구서꺼러 구러꺼라 어씨이 어라 쮀더너고. 뇨노 포오루, 너라 무꿔꽈, 가찌 네레 봐 부로고 과부씨 네레 무고시 와 여수 기리시도.

10. 나구서꺼라, 부씨 노누 꽈나 와네 오꽈 나부다 마꾸 나바아 네레 무뇨로로 와네, 어시나 랴이 이이 오너시모.

11. 뭐시 시구 시라 사러꽈 아바아 아다궈더러 찌로 나 무파 아시뱌. 시 뭐시너 시구 어라 무뚜 오꽈 우쮀더라 무파 쭈바비뻬.

12. 아러로 나구아루뻬라 이이, 나우 우나무아꾀레라 과부씨 아레 꼬구꽈 네꽈나 궈어러사 어무찌마 와네.

13. 나네 나바아 나호따 아꽈씨비러 아꽈우마 나네, 짜시야 아네고러러 꼬구꽈

great joy and encouragement, because you, brother, have refreshed the hearts of the saints.

8. Therefore, although in Christ I could be bold and order you to do what you ought to do,

9. yet I appeal to you on the basis of love. I then, as Paul--an old man and now also a prisoner of Christ Jesus--

10. I appeal to you for my son Onesimus, who became my son while I was in chains.

11. Formerly he was useless to you, but now he has become useful both to you and to me.

12. I am sending him--who is my very heart--back to you.

13. I would have liked to keep him with me so that he could take your place in

wabaa wendjire wanyikorera kwe byawoyo ungendjire wanyaasa'ko. Angendjire anyaasa batcha, bushi nyitchilyi mwa buroko bushi nokuhubanganya emwasi mubuya-buya.

와바아 워찌러 와네고러라 궈 뱌오요 우꺼찌러 와냐아사고. 아꺼찌러 아냐아사 바짜, 부씨 네찌레 먀 부로고 부씨 노구후바꺄냐 어먀시 무부야-부야.

helping me while I am in chains for the gospel.

14. Si ndahondaa kuira tchiro na mwasi asibya, ola utemerere kwabushi ndahonda kukuandjira nambu unyiiriraa emabuya. Seri umaira kwakuhonda kwau weine.

14. 시 따호따아 구이라 찌로 나 먀시 아시뱌, 오라 우더머러러 과부씨 따호따 구구아찌라 나뿌 우네이리라아 어마부야. 서리 우마이라 과구호따 과우 워이너.

14. But I did not want to do anything without your consent, so that any favor you do will be spontaneous and not forced.

15. Abunya onu ONESIMO alyikanyisibwaa nau tanga ku biro byeeke, tchasiya urawanekala nai loshi.

15. 아부냐 오누 오너시모 아레가네시봐아 나우 다꺼 구 비로 벼어거, 짜시야 우라와너가꺄 나이 로씨.

15. Perhaps the reason he was separated from you for a little while was that you might have him back for good--

16. Reru, atatchilyi nga kaungu, oshau, si era mundju ola wete mufa kurenga ekaungu ; bushi era munyaketchu musiirwa. Nyono nyimusimire ngatchi nau ungana musima busese, ungamusima tanga nga mundju, kandji nga munyaketchu mwemeresi.

16. 러루, 아다찌레 꺼 가우꾸, 오싸우, 시 어라 무뚜 오라 워더 무파 구러꺼 어가우꾸 ; 부씨 어라 무냐거쭈 무시이롸. 뇨노 네무시미러 꺼찌 나우 우꺄나 무시마 부서서, 우꺼무시마 다꺼 꺼 무뚜, 가찌 꺼 무냐거쭈 뭐머러시.

16. no longer as a slave, but better than a slave, as a dear brother. He is very dear to me but even dearer to you, both as a man and as a brother in the Lord.

17. Rero akaba utchula unyitolyire nga mwira wao, umuhuukasaa ngokwa unganyihuukasise nyeine.

17. 러로 아가바 우쭈꽈 우네도레러 꺼 뮈라 와오, 우무후우가사아 꼬과 우꺼나네후우가시서 녀이너.

17. So if you consider me a partner, welcome him as you would welcome me.

18. Na akaba kulyi mwasi mubi akukoreraa, nesi akaba

18. 나 아가바 구레 먀시 무비 아구고러라아, 너시

18. If he has done you any wrong or owes you anything,

alyi mu mwinda wau nyono nyi uufusaa.

19. Nyono Poolo, nyeine nyinaandjikire ene myasi mwa mino yanyi nyeine kwa nyono nyingakufuwa. Si tchiro batcha, nakukengesa kwa nau ulyi mu mwinda wanyi, noyo mwinda kalyi ekalamu kau.

20. Reru, munyaketchu, unyiiriraa bira nakuemire busi na Enawetchu, tchasiya unyisese emutchima kurengera ebuuma bwetchu na Kirisito.

21. Kuno nakuandjikira manu maruba, nyineshi kwa ebi nakuemire bi unganaira, ungaira na binene kurenza ebyera.

22. Kandji nahonda unyikunganyisa ala nyingende na ondjira nyete emulangaro kwa kurengera ememo menyu, Ongo angahuba kunyifulusa ei mwenyu.

23. Epafura itchwa hwekanai muno buroko bushi tchulyi bakosi ba Yesu Kirisitu akusesise.

24. Bakosi balyiketchu : Marko na Aritisitariko na Tema na Luka nabo bakulamusise (bakusesise).

25. Enawetchu Yesu Kirisito

아가바 아레 무 뮈따 와우 뇨노 니 우우푸사아.

19. 뇨노 포오로, 녀이너 네나아찌기러 어너 먀시 롸 미노 야네 녀이너 과 뇨노 네따구푸와. 시 찌로 바짜, 나구거어사 과 나우 우레 무 뮈따 와네, 노요 뮈따 가레 어가퐈무 가우.

20. 러루, 무냐거쭈, 우네이리라아 비라 나구어미러 부시 나 어나워쭈, 짜시야 우네서서 어무찌마 구러어라 어부우마 붸쭈 나 기리시도.

21. 구노 나구아찌기라 마누 마루바, 네너씨 과 어비 나구어미러 비 우따나이라, 우따이라 나 비너너 구러싸 어벼라.

22. 가찌 나호따 우네구따네사 아롸 네어떠 나 오찌라 녀더 어무퐈따로 과 구러어라 어머모 머뉴, 오꼬 아따후바 구네푸루싸 어이 뮈뉴.

23. 어파푸라 이쫘 훠가나이 무노 부로고 부씨 쭈레 바고시 바 여수 기리시도 아구서시서.

24. 바고시 바레거쭈 : 마루고 나 아리디시다리고 나 더마 나 루가 나보 바구퐈무시서 (바구서시서).

25. 어나워쭈 여수 기리시도

charge it to me.

19. I, Paul, am writing this with my own hand. I will pay it back--not to mention that you owe me your very self.

20. I do wish, brother, that I may have some benefit from you in the Lord; refresh my heart in Christ.

21. Confident of your obedience, I write to you, knowing that you will do even more than I ask.

22. And one thing more: Prepare a guest room for me, because I hope to be restored to you in answer to your prayers.

23. Epaphras, my fellow prisoner in Christ Jesus, sends you greetings.

24. And so do Mark, Aristarchus, Demas and Luke, my fellow workers.

25. The grace of the Lord

endaa abaahanyisa.　　　　어따아 아바아하네사.　　　　Jesus Christ be with
　　　　　　　　　　　　　　　　　　　　　　　　　your spirit.

E Baebrania

어 바어부라니아

Hebrews

BAEBURANIYA

(HEBREWS)

바어부라니야

(허부루수)

E Baebrania Chikono 1

1. Kwa mira, Ongo endee ahambala na bahokulu bethu mbiso sinene, mu njira sinene kurengera ebarebi.

2. Si mwesine suku sebusinda, elyire ahambala nethu kurengera eMwana wai. Kurengera oyu Mwana, ku Ongo abumbaa ebutala boshi, kanji amulondwere chasiya abe ena ebindju byoshi.

3. Oyu Mwana, ebulangare bwengulu ya Ongo, bwende bwalorekanako mwa ndanda sai, kanji iuthusa ehuhi lya Ongo kanangana. Nebuashi bwechinwa chai, bu buachirise ebutala boshi. Akomise ebandju mwa kubakula mwa bibi, nera nyuma sebi alyire aya kweekala kwa nguba, kwa lunda lwemalyo ma Ongo webuashi boshi.

4. Oyu Mwana ailyiibwe kuba mukulukulu busese kurenza endonyi, kukulyikana nesina lya Ongo amweresaa, lya lyirenzise emasina mabo.

5. Bushi kutalyi chiro na muuma mwa ndonyi ola Ongo afuraa kubura mbuWoyo, uMwana wanyi, lwarero nabere Eho.Kanji kutalyi ndonyi ola

어 바어부라니아 찌고노 1

1. 과 미라, 오꼬 어떠어 아하빠롸 나 바호구루 버쭈 뼤소 시너너, 무 찌라 시너너 구러꺼라 어바러비.

2. 시 뭐시너 수구 서부시따, 어레러 아하빠롸 너쭈 구러꺼라 어마나 와이. 구러꺼라 오유 마나, 구 오꼬 아부빠아 어부다롸 보씨, 가찌 아무로뚜워러 짜시야 아버 어나 어비뚜 보씨.

3. 오유 마나, 어부롸꺼러 뭐꾸루 야 오꼬, 뭐떠 봐로러가나고 마 따따 사이, 가찌 이우쭈사 어후히 롸 오꼬 가나꺼나. 너부아씨 뭐찌놔 짜이, 부 부아찌리서 어부다롸 보씨. 아고미서 어바뚜 마 구바구롸 마 비비, 너라 뉴마 서비 아레러 아야 궈어가롸 과 꿔바, 과 루따 뭐마뢒 마 오꼬 워부아씨 보씨.

4. 오유 마나 아이레이뭐 구바 무구루꾸구루 부서서 구러싸 어또니, 구구레가나 너시나 롸 오꼬 아뭐러사아, 롸 레러씨서 어마시나 마보.

5. 부씨 구다레 찌로 나 무우마 마 또니 오라 오꼬 아푸라아 구부라 뿌오요, 우마나 와니, 롸러로 나버러 어호.가찌 구다레 또니 오라

Hebrews Chapter 1[NIV]

1. In the past God spoke to our forefathers through the prophets at many times and in various ways,

2. but in these last days he has spoken to us by his Son, whom he appointed heir of all things, and through whom he made the universe.

3. The Son is the radiance of God's glory and the exact representation of his being, sustaining all things by his powerful word. After he had provided purification for sins, he sat down at the right hand of the Majesty in heaven.

4. So he became as much superior to the angels as the name he has inherited is superior to theirs.

5. For to which of the angels did God ever say, "You are my Son; today I have become your Father"? Or again, "I will be his

Ongo afuraa kubura mbu
Nyono nyingaba eshe, nai
angaba Mwana wanyi.

6. Si mango Ongo athumaa
eFula yai muno butala, atetaa
mbu Endonyi ba Ongo boshi,
beemire kunde bamwera

7. Kwa bya byerekere endonyi,
Ongo atetaa mbu Ongo ende
aira endonyisai kuba nga
mbusi. Ende aira abu baanda
bai kuba nga byasi bya
mulyiro.

8. Si kwa bya byerekere
eMwana wai, Ongo atetaa
mbu Woyo Ongo, endebe yao
yebwwami ikanaendekera
inathulao esuku nemango.
Uthala wimire mwa bwami
bwao, kukulyikana nemyasi era
ithungenene.

9. Uthula usimire bya
bithungenene, si uthula uaire
emabi. Echera chi chathumaa
Ongo, Ongo wao akulondola,
mwa kukwaakaba emafuta
melumoo, na kukweeresa
ethunda, mwa kukubika era
luulu busese kurenza
balyikenyu.

10. Kanji Ongo atetaa mbu
Mwa ndangilyiso, woyo
Enawethu u wabumbaa
ebutala. Emino sao si

오꼬 아푸라아 구부라 뿌
뇨노 네까바 어써, 나이
아까바 뫄나 와니.

6. 시 마꼬 오꼬 아쭈마아
어푸꽈 야이 무노 부다꽈,
아더다아 뿌 어또네 바 오꼬
보씨, 버어미러 구떠 바뭐라

7. 꽈 뱌 벼러거러 어또네,
오꼬 아더다아 뿌 오꼬 어떠
아이라 어또네사이 구바 까
뿌시. 어떠 아이라 아부
바아따 바이 구바 까 뱌시 뱌
무꿰로.

8. 시 꽈 뱌 벼러거러 어뫄나
와이, 오꼬 아더다아 뿌 우요
오꼬, 어떠버 야오 여부와미
이가나어떠거라 이나쭈꽈오
어수구 너마꼬. 우따꽈 위미러
꽈 봐미 봐오, 구구꿰가나
너먀시 어라 이쭈꺼너너.

9. 우쭈꽈 우시미러 뱌
비쭈꺼너너, 시 우쭈꽈
우아이러 어마비. 어쩌라 찌
짜쭈마아 오꼬, 오꼬 와오
아구로또꽈, 꽈 구과아가바
어마푸다 머루모오, 나
구궈어러사 어쭈따, 꽈
구구비가 어라 루우루 부서서
구러싸 바꿰거뉴.

10. 가찌 오꼬 아더다아 뿌 꽈
따끼레소, 우요 어나워쭈 우
와부빠아 어부다꽈. 어미노
사오 시 사부빠아 어우바.

Father, and he will be my
Son"?

6. And again, when God
brings his firstborn into the
world, he says, "Let all God's
angels worship him."

7. In speaking of the angels
he says, "He makes his
angels winds, his servants
flames of fire."

8. But about the Son he
says, "Your throne, O God,
will last for ever and ever,
and righteousness will be
the scepter of your
kingdom.

9. You have loved
righteousness and hated
wickedness; therefore God,
your God, has set you
above your companions by
anointing you with the oil
of joy."

10. He also says, "In the
beginning, O Lord, you laid
the foundations of the
earth, and the heavens are

sabumbaa enguba.

11. Ebi byoshi bikailyima, si woyo ukekala unathlao. Kubinalyi, enguba nebutala bikakunguwa nga luchimba.

12. Ukabungabungaabi ngokwa bende babunga ekochi, kanji bikainganyisibwa nga njimba. Si woyo, unathula unoyu. Nekalamo kao katakawe chiro na hicha.

13. Ongo atafuraa kubura chiro na muuma mwa ndonyi mbu Ekalaa kwa lunda lwanyi lwemalyo, kuikira mango nyingaba nalyire ebarenda bao kuba chisimachiro chao.

14. Endonyi balyi bande kasi? Boshi, inathula michima era yende yakorera Ongo. Ende athumabo baye kuasa ebandju ba beemire kubona ebununusi. Thutendaa thwakena ebununusi bwethu

11. 어비 뵤씨 비가이레마, 시오요 우거가꺄 우나찌꺄오. 구비나레, 어우바 너부다꺄 비가구우와 꺄 루찌빠.

12. 우가부꺄부꺄아비 으과 버떠 바부꺄 어고찌, 가찌 비가이꺄네시봐 꺄 띠빠. 시오요, 우나쭈꺄 우노유. 너가꺄모 가오 가다가워 찌로 나 히짜.

13. 오꼬 아다푸라아 구부라 찌로 나 무우마 꺄 또니 뿌 어가꺄아 과 루따 꽈니 뭐마료, 구이기라 마꼬 네꺄바 나레러 어바러따 바오 구바 찌시마찌로 짜오.

14. 어또니 바레 바떠 가시? 보씨, 이나쭈꺄 미찌마 어라 여떠 야고러라 오꼬. 어떠 아쭈마보 바여 구아사 어바뚜 바 버어미러 구보나 어부누누시. 쭈더따아 쫘거나 어부누누시 뭐쭈

the work of your hands.

11. They will perish, but you remain; they will all wear out like a garment.

12. You will roll them up like a robe; like a garment they will be changed. But you remain the same, and your years will never end."

13. To which of the angels did God ever say, "Sit at my right hand until I make your enemies a footstool for your feet"?

14. Are not all angels ministering spirits sent to serve those who will inherit salvation?

E Baebrania Chikono 2 — 어 바어부라니아 찌고노 2 — Hebrews Chapter 2[NIV]

1. Bushi noku, thweemire kunde thwasimika busese mwa mwasi ola thoomvaa, thungesha kwaabuka enjira.

2. Emwasi weMwaso ola Endonyi babalaaa, anachilosaa kwa analyi wa kanangana. Na chira mundju ola utendee

1. 부씨 노구, 쮀어미러 구더 꽈시미가 부서서 꺄 마시 오꺄 쏘오빠아, 쮸어싸 과아부가 어찌라.

2. 어꺄시 워꺄소 오꺄 어또네 바바꺄아아, 아나찌로사아 과 아나레 와 가나꺄나. 나 찌라 무뚜 오꺄 우더떠어 와이라

1. We must pay more careful attention, therefore, to what we have heard, so that we do not drift away.

2. For if the message spoken by angels was binding, and every violation and disobedience received

waira ngokwa atechire, endee achinjibusibwa ngokwa binamwemire.

꼬과 아더찌러, 어뻐어 아찌찌부시봐 꼬과 비나뭐미러.

its just punishment,

3. Rero thubano, kute thukafufumuka ebuchinjibusi akaba thungende thwakena ebununusi bungana ngobu? Emyasi yobu bununusi, Enawethu yeine iwatangilyiisaa kubalyirai ebandju. Chasinda, ba bendee boomvilyisa kwei myasi, nabo bera kunathubura kwa inalyi ya kanangana.

3. 러로 쭈바노, 구더 쭈가푸푸무가 어부찌찌부시 아가바 쭈뻐떠 좌거나 어부누누시 부뻐나 꼬부? 어먀시 요부 부누누시, 어나워쭈 여이너 이와다삐레이사아 구바쩨라이 어바쭈. 짜시따, 바 버떠어 보오삐쩨사 궈이 먀시, 나보 버라 구나쭈부라 과 이나쩨 야 가나뻐나.

3. how shall we escape if we ignore such a great salvation? This salvation, which was first announced by the Lord, was confirmed to us by those who heard him.

4. Na Ongo nai era kunde analosa kwebubei bwabu bandju bunalyi bwa kanangana, kurengera ebimenyeso, nebishishalo nebisomerano bya njira sinene. Kanji aabilyire ebandju enyembo seMuchima Mubuyabuya, ngokwa abaa anahonda.

4. 나 오꼬 나이 어라 구떠 아나르사 궈부버이 봐부 바뚜 부나쩨 봐 가나뻐나, 구러뻐라 어비머녀소, 너비씨싸르 너비소머라노 뱌 찌라 시너너. 가찌 아아비쩨러 어바쭈 어녀뽀 서무찌마 무부야부야, 꼬과 아바아 아나호따.

4. God also testified to it by signs, wonders and various miracles, and gifts of the Holy Spirit distributed according to his will.

5. Anola, thwahambala era luulu sebutala bwa bukaika. Obu butala, Ongo ateeresise Endonyi ebuashi bwekwiimangirabo.

5. 아노꽈, 좌하빠꽈 어라 루우루 서부다꽈 봐 부가이가. 오부 부다꽈, 오꼬 아더어러시서 어또네 어부아씨 붜귀이마삐라보.

5. It is not to angels that he has subjected the world to come, about which we are speaking.

6. .Mwa Maanjiko Mabuyabuya, mundju muuma atetaa mbu Ongo Tata, emundju alyi nde, chasiya unde wamukengera?

6. .봐 마아찌고 마부야부야, 무뚜 무우마 아더다아 뿌 오꼬 다다, 어무뚜 아쩨 너, 짜시야 우떠 와무거뻐라?

6. But there is a place where someone has testified: "What is man that you are mindful of him, the son of man that you care for him?

7. Wamubikaa era chibanda sendonyi ku bihangi bieke. Chasinda, wera kumweresa engulu na thunda lyinene.

8. Wamweresise ebuashi era luulu sebindju byoshi. Mango byatechibwa kwa Ongo eeresaa emundju ebuashi era luulu sebindju byoshi, kutalyi chiro na kandju kasibya ka arekaa. Si chiro bacha, ebindju byoshi ngokwa bilyi lwarero, thutasene nga emundju eete ebuashi era luulu sabi byoshi.

9. Si cha thuseneko, chi chechine: Yesu abikibwaa era chibanda se ndonyi ku bihangi bieke, chasiya kurengera ebonjo bwa Ongo, alyibusibwe na kweechibwa bushi nebandu boshi. Rero kurengera olu lufu lwai, eresibwe engulu nethunda.

10. Ongo iwabumbaa ebindju byoshi, kanji byoshi binalyi byai. Ailyire Yesu kuba ola unalumilyire kurengera emalyibuko, chasiya arete bana banene mwa bulangare bwa Ongo. Bushi Yesu iwende waisa ebandju kwa bununusi.

11. Yesu iwende wakomya ebandju batenge mwa bibi byabo. Yesu nebandju ba ende akomya, boshi banlyi bana ba

7. 와무비가아 어라 찌바따 서또네 구 비하삐 비어거. 짜시따, 워라 구뭐러사 어꾸룹 나 쭈따 쀄너너.

8. 와뭐러시서 어부아씨 어라 루우룹 서비뉴 뵤씨. 마꼬 뱌더찌봐 과 오꼬 어어러사아 어무뉴 어부아씨 어라 루우룹 서비뉴 뵤씨, 구다쀄 찌로 나 가뉴 가시뱌 가 아러가아. 시 찌로 바짜, 어비뉴 뵤씨 꼬과 비쀄 롸러로, 쭈다서너 까 어무뉴 어어더 어부아씨 어라 루우룹 사비 뵤씨.

9. 시 짜 쭈서너고, 찌 쩌찌너: 여수 아비기봐아 어라 찌바따 서 또네 구 비하삐 비어거, 짜시야 구러꺼라 어보쪼 봐 오꼬, 아쀄부시붜 나 궈어찌봐 부씨 너바뉴 뵤씨. 러로 구러꺼라 오루 루푸 롸이, 어러시붜 어우룹 너쭈따.

10. 오꼬 이와부빠아 어비뉴 뵤씨, 가찌 뵤씨 비나쀄 뱌이. 아이쀄러 여수 구바 오롸 우나루미쀄러 구러꺼라 어마쀄부고, 짜시야 아러더 바나 바너너 뫄 부롸까러 봐 오꼬. 부씨 여수 이워떠 와이사 어바뉴 과 부누누시.

11. 여수 이워떠 와고먀 어바뉴 바더꺼 뫄 비비 뱌보. 여수 너바뉴 바 어떠 아고먀, 뵤씨 바누쀄 바나 바 다다

7. You made him a little lower than the angels; you crowned him with glory and honor

8. and put everything under his feet?In putting everything under him, God left nothing that is not subject to him. Yet at present we do not see everything subject to him.

9. But we see Jesus, who was made a little lower than the angels, now crowned with glory and honor because he suffered death, so that by the grace of God he might taste death for everyone.

10. In bringing many sons to glory, it was fitting that God, for whom and through whom everything exists, should make the author of their salvation perfect through suffering.

11. Both the one who makes men holy and those who are made holy are of the same family. So Jesus is

Tata muuma. Bushi noku, Yesu atafa honyi sa kuberika mbu balyi banyakabo.

무우마. 부씨 노구, 여수 아다파 호네 사 구버리가 뿌 바레 바냐가보.

not ashamed to call them brothers.

12. Bushi atechire mbu E Ongo, nyingende nabalyikisa esina lyao era mwa banyakethu. Nyingende nakutonga mwa lubuanano lwebandju bao.

12. 부씨 아더찌러 뿌 어 오꼬, 네꺼머 나바레기사 어시나 럐오 어라 뫄 바냐거쭈. 네꺼머 나구도꺄 뫄 루부아나노 뤄바쭈 바오.

12. He says, "I will declare your name to my brothers; in the presence of the congregation I will sing your praises."

13. Kanji atechire mbu Nyingende nachinyiira Ongo. Kanji anateta mbu Unyilyiano, alauma nebandju ba Ongo anyeresise kuba nga bana banyi.

13. 가찌 아더찌러 뿌 네꺼머 나찌네이라 오꼬. 가찌 아나더다 뿌 우네례아노, 아롸우마 너바쭈 바 오꼬 아녀러시서 구바 꺄 바나 바네.

13. And again, "I will put my trust in him." And again he says, "Here am I, and the children God has given me."

14. Rero, bushi abu bana balyi bandju ba bete emubilyi nemikira, chi chathumaa Yesu nai, abaha kwa njira yemubilyi nemikira kuuma nabo. Airaa bacha, chasiya kurengera ekufa kwai, asise Wamusimu, iwabaa wete ebuashi bwekwiita ebandju.

14. 러로, 부씨 아부 바나 바레 바쭈 바 버더 어무비레 너미기라, 찌 짜쭈마아 여수 나이, 아바하 과 띠라 여무비레 너미기라 구우마 나보. 아이라아 바짜, 짜시야 구러꺼라 어구파 과이, 아시서 와무시무, 이와바아 워더 어부아씨 뷔귀이다 어바쭈.

14. Since the children have flesh and blood, he too shared in their humanity so that by his death he might destroy him who holds the power of death--that is, the devil--

15. Abolaa nebandju ba babaa balyi nga thuungu mwa kalamo kabo koshi, bushi nekwobaa elufu.

15. 아보롸아 너바쭈 바 바바아 바레 꺄 쭈우꾸 뫄 가롸모 가보 고씨, 부씨 너곱바아 어루푸.

15. and free those who all their lives were held in slavery by their fear of death.

16. Kubinalyi, Yesu atabahaa kuasa endonyi, si abahaa kuasa elubuto lwa Aburahamu.

16. 구비나레, 여수 아다바하아 구아사 어또네, 시 아바하아 구아사 어루부도 롸 아부라하무.

16. For surely it is not angels he helps, but Abraham's descendants.

17. Bushi noku, byabaa binamwemire ahuhe

17. 부씨 노구, 뱌바아 비나뭐미러 아후허 바냐가보

17. For this reason he had to be made like his brothers

banyakabo mwa myasi yoshi.
Mwa bacha, elyire aba
Mukulukulu webakuhanyi ola
wete chamba, kanji ola
ungachinyiirwa mwa mulyimo
wa Ongo, chasiya ebibi
byebandju bibabalyirwe.
18. Kanji bushi yeine
aerekibwaa na kulyibusibwa,
angaala kunde aasa ba benjire
baerekibwa.

마 먀시 요씨. 마 바짜,
어레러 아바 무구루구루
워바구하네 오롸 워더 짜빠,
가찌 오롸 우까찌네이롸 마
무레모 와 오끄, 짜시야
어비비 벼바뉴 비바바레뤄.

18. 가찌 부씨 여이너
아어러기봐아 나 구레부시봐,
아까아롸 구더 아아사 바
버찌러 바어러기봐.

in every way, in order that
he might become a merciful
and faithful high priest in
service to God, and that he
might make atonement
forthe sins of the people.

18. Because he himself
suffered when he was
tempted, he is able to help
those who are being
tempted.

E Baebrania Chikono 3
1. Banyakethu, Ongo
abamaere kanji abairire kuba
bandju bai kuuma nethu.
Bushi noku, mundaa
mwaanyisa busese era luulu sa
Yesu, iwathumwaa na Ongo,
kanji iMukulukulu
webakuhanyi webwemeresi
bwa thwende
thwahubanganyisa ebandju.
2. Abaa alyi wakuchinyiirwa
era muhondo sa Ongo
iwamubikaa mwa mulyimo,
ngokwa Musa abaa alyi
wakuchinyiirwa mwa nyumba
ya Ongo yoshi.
3. Si chiro bacha, Yesu
iweemire kuya ngulu busese
kurenza Musa. Bushi emundju
ola waimba enyumba iwende

어 바어부라니아 찌고노 3
1. 바냐거쭈, 오끄 아바마어러
가찌 아바이리러 구바 바뉴
바이 구우마 너쭈. 부씨 노구,
무따아 뫄아니사 부서서 어라
루우루 사 여수, 이와쭈뫄아
나 오끄, 가찌 이무구루구루
워바구하네 워붜머러시 봐
쮀떠 좌후바까네사 어바뉴.

2. 아바아 아레 와구찌네이롸
어라 무호또 사 오끄
이와무비가아 마 무레모, 끄과
무사 아바아 아레
와구찌네이롸 마 뉴빠 야
오끄 요씨.

3. 시 찌로 바짜, 여수
이워어미러 구야 꾸루 부서서
구러싸 무사. 부씨 어무뉴
오롸 와이빠 어뉴빠 이워떠

Hebrews Chapter 3[NIV]
1. Therefore, holy brothers,
who share in the heavenly
calling, fix your thoughts on
Jesus, the apostle and high
priest whom we confess.

2. He was faithful to the
one who appointed him,
just as Moses was faithful in
all God's house.

3. Jesus has been found
worthy of greater honor
than Moses, just as the
builder of a house has

weresibwa ethunda busese kurenza enyumba era aimba.
4. Kubinalyi, chira nyumba inathusa ola waimbaai, si Ongo iwaimbaa byoshi.
5. Musa abaa mukosi ola weemire kuchinyiirwa mwa nyumba ya Ongo yoshi, chasiya aane ebubeyi era luulu semyasi era Ongo abaa akateta era nyuma.
6. Si Kirisito iweemire kuchinyiirwa nga Mwana ola wemangilyire enyumba ya Ongo. Rero thubano, thu thulyi ei nyumba, akaba thungaendekera kusesa emuchima na kumoera emunyiiro ola thuthusa.
7. Rero, kukulyikana nokwa eMuchima Mubuyabuya ateta mbu Lwarero akaba mungomva emurenge wa Ongo,
8. mutairaa emichima yenyu kuba isibu, ngokwa bahokulu benyu bairaa mango bananaa kuira bya Ongo atechire, kwolwa lusuku mango bamuerekaa mwa buyeye.
9. Kanji Ongo atechire mbu: Chiro angaba mbu bahokulu benyu bachiloreraa kwa byoshi bya nairaa ku myaka mane mwa buyeye, si banyierekaa

워러시봐 어쭈따 부서서 구러싸 어뉴빠 어라 아이빠.
4. 구비나뤠, 찌라 뉴빠 이나쭈사 오롸 와이빠아이, 시 오꼬 이와이빠아 뵤씨.
5. 무사 아바아 무고시 오롸 워어미러 구찌네이롸 먀 뉴빠 야 오꼬 요씨, 짜시야 아아너 어부버에 어라 루우루 서먀시 어라 오꼬 아바아 아가더다 어라 뉴마.
6. 시 기리시도 이워어미러 구찌네이롸 ㅺ 먀나 오롸 워마ㅺ뤠러 어뉴빠 야 오꼬. 러로 쭈바노, 쭈 쭈뤠 어이 뉴빠, 아가바 쭈ㅺ어너거라 구서사 어무찌마 나 구모어라 어무네이로 오롸 쭈쭈사.
7. 러로, 구구뤠가나 노과 어무찌마 무부야부야 아더다 뿌 롸러로 아가바 무꼬빠 어무러ㅺ 와 오꼬,
8. 무다이라아 어미찌마 여뉴 구바 이시부, 꼬과 바호구루 버뉴 바이라아 마꼬 바나나아 구이라 뱌 오꼬 아더찌러, 고롸 루수구 마꼬 바무어러가아 먀 부여여.
9. 가찌 오꼬 아더찌러 뿌: 찌로 아ㅺ바 뿌 바호구루 버뉴 바찌뢰러라아 과 뵤씨 뱌 나이라아 구 먀가 마너 뫄 부여여, 시 바네어러가아

greater honor than the house itself.
4. For every house is built by someone, but God is the builder of everything.
5. Moses was faithful as a servant in all God's house, testifying to what would be said in the future.
6. But Christ is faithful as a son over God's house. And we are his house, if we hold on to our courage and the hope of which we boast.
7. So, as the Holy Spirit says: "Today, if you hear his voice,
8. do not harden your hearts as you did in the rebellion, during the time of testing in the desert,
9. where your fathers tested and tried me and for forty years saw what I did.

chasiya balole cha nyingaira.

10. Bushi noku, abu bandju besi suku, nera kwire nasibukirabo, nera kuteta mbu: Bano bandju, emichima yabo yende yeengeerwa esuku soshi, batamenyerera na bya nahonda bende baira.

11. Rero mwobu busibuke bwanyi, nera kulaisa mbu: Batakengilyire chiro na hicha mwa chisiki chekutamukira cha nabakunganyisise.

12. Rero, banyakethu mumenyaa Mwakachikachi kenyu mutabaa chiro na mundju ola undaa waata muchima mubi wekuteemerera, kuikira echihangi aya bure na Ongo iuthula Muumauma.

13. Si mundaa mwasesanya emichima chira lusuku, mango chine chinwa lwarero cha chitechirwe, chichilyi chithweerekere. Mwa bacha, ebibi bitangende byachibengeera, nomwa kachikachi kenyu mutachibe mundju ola waata mathwi masibu.

14. Bushi thubano thwakola na Kirisito, akaba thungalanga emunyiiro ola thwabonaa mwa ndangiriso yebwemeresi

짜시야 바롤러 짜 네ᄴᅡ이라.

10. 부씨 노구, 아부 바뉴 버시 수구, 너라 귀러 나시부기라보, 너라 구더다 뿌: 바노 바뉴, 어미찌마 야보 여떠 여어러어롸 어수구 소씨, 바다머녀러라 나 뱌 나호따 버떠 바이라.

11. 러로 모부 부시부거 봐네, 너라 구퐈이사 뿌: 바다거끼ᄙᅦ러 찌로 나 히짜 봐 찌시기 쩌구다무기라 짜 나바구싸네시서.

12. 러로, 바냐거쭈 무머냐아 뫄가찌가찌 거뉴 무다바아 찌로 나 무뚜 오라 우따아 와아다 무찌마 무비 워구더어머러라, 구이기라 어찌하ᄢᅵ 아야 부러 나 오ᅇᅩ 이우쭈퐈 무우마우마.

13. 시 무따아 뫄서사냐 어미찌마 찌라 ᄙᅮ수구, 마ᅌᅩ 찌너 찌놔 ᄣᅡ러로 짜 찌더찌뤄, 찌찌ᄙᅦ 찌쭤어러거러. 뫄 바짜, 어비비 비다ᄴᅥ러 뱌찌버ᄴᅥ어라, 노뫄 가찌가찌 거뉴 무다찌버 무뚜 오퐈 와아다 마쮜 마시부.

14. 부씨 쭈바노 쫘고퐈 나 기리시도, 아가바 쭈싸퐈싸 어무네이로 오퐈 쫘보나아 뫄 따ᄢᅵ리소 여붜머러시 붜쭈,

10. That is why I was angry with that generation, and I said, 'Their hearts are always going astray, and they have not known my ways.'

11. So I declared on oath in my anger, 'They shall never enter my rest.' "

12. See to it, brothers, that none of you has a sinful, unbelieving heart that turns away from the living God.

13. But encourage one another daily, as long as it is called Today, so that none of you may be hardened by sin's deceitfulness.

14. We have come to share in Christ if we hold firmly till the end the confidence we had at first.

bwethu, kuikira kwa businda.　구이기라 과 부시따.

15. eMaanjiko Mabuya-buya mathula matechire mbu lwarero, akaba mungomva emurenge wa Ongo, mutairaa emichima yenyu kuba isibu, ngokwa bahokulu benyu bairaa, mango bananaa kuira bya Ongo atechire.

15. 어마아찌고 마부야-부야 마쭈꽈 마더찌러 뿌 롸러로, 아가바 무끄빠 어무러꺼 와 오끄, 무다이라아 어미찌마 여뉴 구바 이시부, 끄과 바호구루 버뉴 바이라아, 마끄 바나나아 구이라 뱌 오끄 아더찌러.

15. As has just been said: "Today, if you hear his voice, do not harden your hearts as you did in the rebellion."

16. Bandu bachiye bu bendee boomva kwa murenge wa Ongo, na banana kuira bya atechire? Si banalyi ba bandju boshi ba Musa abaa emangilyire abakula mwa chio cheMisiri

16. 바뚜 바찌여 부 버더어 보오빠 과 무러꺼 와 오끄, 나 바나나 구이라 뱌 아더찌러? 시 바나쩨 바 바뚜 보씨 바 무사 아바아 어마끼레러 아바구꽈 먀 찌오 쩌미시리

16. Who were they who heard and rebelled? Were they not all those Moses led out of Egypt?

17. Kanji bandju bachiye bu basibusaa Ongo ku miaka mane? Si banalyi ba bandju ba bairaa ebibi, na bafira mwa buyeye!

17. 가찌 바뚜 바찌여 부 바시부사아 오끄 구 미아가 마너? 시 바나쩨 바 바뚜 바 바이라아 어비비, 나 바피라 먀 부여여!

17. And with whom was he angry for forty years? Was it not with those who sinned, whose bodies fell in the desert?

18. Kanji bandju bachiye bu Ongo alaisisaa mbu batakeengilyire mwa chisiki chekutamukiramo cha abakunganyisise? Si banalyi ba bandju ba bananaa kuira bya atechire!

18. 가찌 바뚜 바찌여 부 오끄 아꽈이시사아 뿌 바다거어끼레러 먀 찌시기 쩌구다무기라모 짜 아바구꽈네시서? 시 바나쩨 바 바뚜 바 바나나아 구이라 뱌 아더찌러!

18. And to whom did God swear that they would never enter his rest if not to those who disobeyed?

19. Kubinalyi, thusene kwa abu bandju bataalaa kweengilyira mwechi chisiki chekutamukira,

19. 구비나쩨, 쭈서너 과 아부 바뚜 바다아꽈아 귀어끼레라 뭐찌 찌시기 쩌구다무기라,

19. So we see that they were not able to enter, because of their unbelief.

bushi nekutemerera kwabo.　부씨 너구더머러라 과보.

E Baebrania Chikono 4

1. Ongo athulanyaa kwa thukeengilyira mwa chisiki chai chekutamukira. Bushi noku, thundaa thwachilanga, chasiya kutabaa chiro na muuma mu mwabo ola ukaina kweengiriramo.

2. Bushi anabe nethu, thwahubanganyisibwe eMwasi Mubuyabuya, ngokwa abu bahokulu bethu ba babaa balyi mwa buyeye, nabo banahubanganyisibwaao. Si beke oyu Mwasi boomvaa, atabaanjiraa chiro na mufa asibya, bushi ba boomvaao batangilyiraao na bwemeresi.

3. Si thubano, thu thweemerere thu thukeengilyira mwechi chisiki chekutamukira, cha Ongo atetaa era luulu sachi mbu: Bushi noku, nera kulaisa mwa busibuke bwanyi mbu: Batakeengilyire chiro na hicha mwa chisiki chekutamukira cha nabakunganyisise Ongo atetaa bacha, chiro angaba mbu abaa amalyire mira emulyimo wai kutengera mango abumbaa ebutala.

어 바어부라니아 찌고노 4

1. 오꼬 아쭈꽈냐아 과 쭈거어삐레라 꽈 찌시기 짜이 쩌구다무기라. 부씨 노구, 쭈따아 좌찌롸꽈, 짜시야 구다바아 찌로 나 무우마 무 꽈보 오롸 우가이나 궈어삐리라모.

2. 부씨 아나버 너쭈, 좌후바꽈네시붜 어마시 무부야부야, 꼬과 아부 바호구루 버쭈 바 바바아 바레 꽈 부여여, 나보 바나후바꽈네시봐아오. 시 버거 오유 마시 보오빠아, 아다바아찌라아 찌로 나 무파 아시뱌, 부씨 바 보오빠아오 바다삐레라아오 나 붸머러시.

3. 시 쭈바노, 쭈 쭤어머러러 쭈 쭈거어삐레라 뭐찌 찌시기 쩌구다무기라, 짜 오꼬 아더다아 어라 루우루 사찌 뿌: 부씨 노구, 너라 구롸이사 꽈 부시부거 봐네 뿌: 바다거어삐레러 찌로 나 히짜 꽈 찌시기 쩌구다무기라 짜 나바구꽈네시서 오꼬 아더다아 바짜, 찌로 아꽈바 뿌 아바아 아마레러 미라 어무레모 와이 구더뻐라 마꼬 아부빠아 어부다롸.

Hebrews Chapter 4[NIV]

1. Therefore, since the promise of entering his rest still stands, let us be careful that none of you be found to have fallen short of it.

2. For we also have had the gospel preached to us, just as they did; but the message they heard was of no value to them, because those who heard did not combine it with faith.

3. Now we who have believed enter that rest, just as God has said, "So I declared on oath in my anger, 'They shall never enter my rest.' " And yet his work has been finished since the creation of the world.

4. Bushi mwa Maanjiko Mabuyabuya mulyi ala bahambere era luulu selusuku lwa kalyinda mbu Emulyimo wai woshi ola Ongo akolaa, abaa amalyiriseo mira elusuku lwa kalyinda. Olu lusuku, era kutamuka.

5. Kanji mwamu Maanjiko, Ongo atechire mbu Batakeengilyire chiro na hicha mwa chisiki chanyi chekutamukira.

6. Ebandju ba babaa baberebere kuhubanganyisibwa eMwasi Mubuyabuya, bateengilyiraa mwechi chisiki chekutamukira, bushi bananaa kuira bya Ongo ateta. Si chiro bacha, ebanji bandju bachilyi bangeengilyiramo.

7. Bushi noku, Ongo elyire ahuba kubika lunji lusuku lwa lweelyikibwe mbu: lwarero. Atetaa era luulu solu lusuku, era nyuma sa myaka inene kurengera Daudi, kukulyikana na mano Maanjiko ma matechirweko mira mbu: Lwarero, akaba mungomva emurenge wa Ongo, mutairaa emichima yenyu kuba isibu.

8. Bushi akaba Yoshuwa

---

4. 부씨 뫄 마아찌고 마부야부야 무뤠 아꽈 바하뻐러 어라 루우루 서루수구 꽈 가뤠따 뿌 어무뤠모 와이 오씨 오꽈 오꼬 아고꽈아, 아바아 아마뤠리서오 미라 어루수구 꽈 가뤠따. 오루 루수구, 어라 구다무가.

5. 가찌 뫄무 마아찌고, 오꼬 아더찌러 뿌 바다거어꼐리뤠러 찌로 나 히짜 뫄 찌시기 짜니 쩌구다무기라.

6. 어바뚜 바 바바아 바버러버러 구후바꺄네시봐 어뫄시 무부야부야, 바더어꼐뤠라아 뭐찌 찌시기 쩌구다무기라, 부씨 바나나아 구이라 뱌 오꼬 아더다. 시 찌로 바짜, 어바찌 바뚜 바찌뤠 바여어꼐뤠라모.

7. 부씨 노구, 오꼬 어뤠러 아후바 구비가 루찌 루수구 꽈 뭐어뤠기붜 뿌: 꽈러로. 아더다아 어라 루우루 소루 루수구, 어라 뉴마 사 먀가 이너너 구러꺼라 다우디, 구구뤠가나 나 마노 마아찌고 마 마더찌뤄고 미라 뿌: 꽈러로, 아가바 무꼬빠 어무러꺼 와 오꼬, 무다이라아 어미찌마 여뉴 구바 이시부.

8. 부씨 아가바 요쑤와

---

4. For somewhere he has spoken about the seventh day in these words: "And on the seventh day God rested from all his work."

5. And again in the passage above he says, "They shall never enter my rest."

6. It still remains that some will enter that rest, and those who formerly had the gospel preached to them did not go in, because of their disobedience.

7. Therefore God again set a certain day, calling it Today, when a long time later he spoke through David, as was said before: "Today, if you hear his voice, do not harden your hearts."

8. For if Joshua had given

(continued) angaisise ebandju mwa chisiki chekutamukira kanangana, era nyuma sebi Ongo atangachitechire era luulu sa lunji lusuku lwa kutamuka.

9. Echera chilosise kwebandju ba Ongo bachilyi babikilyirwe ekutamuka, kwa kuhuhanyisibwe nekutamuka kweluusuku lwa kalyinda.

10. Bushi emundju ola wengilyire mwa chisiki chekutamukira cha Ongo, ende atamuka bushi amalyire emilyimo yai, ngokwa Ongo nai atamukaa mango amalaa emiyimo yai.

11. Bushi noku, thuiraa emisi yethu yoshi thwiingilyire mwechi chisiki chekutamukiramo, chasiya kutabaa chiro na muuuma muthubano ola wakumbaala, bushi nekunana kuira kwa Ongo atechire, ngokwa bahokulu bethu bairaa.

12. Kubinalyi, eChinwa cha Ongo, chithula chiumauma, chithusa na misi. Kanji chithula chikalyiire busese kurenza eboombo bwa moyi mabilyi. Chende cheenya busese, chanalyinda chalyikanya ekalamo nemuchima, na kulyikanya emvunyiro

---

아빠이시서 어바뚜 마 찌시기 찌구다무기라 가나빠나, 어라 뉴마 서비 오꼬 아다빠찌더찌러 어라 루우루 사 루찌 루수구 롸 구다무가.

9. 어쩌라 찌로시서 궈바뚜 바 오꼬 바찌레 바비기레뤄 어구다무가, 과 구후하니시붜 너구다무가 궈루우수구 롸 가레따.

10. 부씨 어무뚜 오롸 워삐레러 마 찌시기 찌구다무기라 짜 오꼬, 어떠 아다무가 부씨 아마레러 어미레모 야이, 꼬과 오꼬 나이 아다무가아 마꼬 아마롸아 어미에모 야이.

11. 부씨 노구, 쭈이라아 어미시 여쭈 요씨 쮜이삐레러 뭐찌 찌시기 찌구다무기라모, 짜시야 구다바아 찌로 나 무우우마 무쭈바노 오롸 와구빠아롸, 부씨 너구나나 구이라 과 오꼬 아더찌러, 꼬과 바호구루 버쭈 바이라아.

12. 구비나레, 어찌놔 짜 오꼬, 찌쭈롸 찌우마우마, 찌쭈사 나 미시. 가찌 찌쭈롸 찌가레이러 부서서 구러싸 어보오뽀 봐 모에 마비레. 쩌더 쩌어냐 부서서, 짜나레따 짜레가냐 어가롸모 너무쪼마, 나 구레가냐 어뿌네로 너무꼬푸. 쩌더 짜비후롸 뵤씨 뱌 무뚜

---

them rest, God would not have spoken later about another day.

9. There remains, then, a Sabbath-rest for the people of God;

10. for anyone who enters God's rest also rests from his own work, just as God did from his.

11. Let us, therefore, make every effort to enter that rest, so that no one will fall by following their example of disobedience.

12. For the word of God is living and active. Sharper than any double-edged sword, it penetrates even to dividing soul and spirit, joints and marrow; it judges the thoughts and attitudes of the heart.

nemungofu. Chende chabihula byoshi bya mundju ahonda kuira na kubihula emianyisa era ilyi mwa muchima wai.

13. Kutalyi chiro na kandju kasibya ka kabishirwe era muhondo sa Ongo. Byoshi bya abumbaa, byende byanalorekanako changanama era muhondo sai. Kanji era muhondo sai, yi thukatetera era luulu semyasi yoshi era thwairaa.

14. Rero thwete eMukulukulu webakuhanyi ola waire kwa nguba, na iYesu, Mwana wa Ongo. Bushi noku, thusimikaa busese mwa bwemeresi bwethu.

15. eMukulukulu webakuhanyi ola thwete, ende athufira bonjo mwa kuina emisi kwethu. Bushi nai anaerekibwaa mwa njira soshi kuuma nethu, si yeke atairaa bibi.

16. Bushi noku, thundaa thwachifunda ofu nendebe ya Ongo busira buba. Aola, uthungabonera ebubabalyire nebubuya bwai, chasiya athuase mwa bihangi bya bikomire.

아호따 구이라 나 구비후꽈 어미아네사 어라 이쪠 꽈 무찌마 와이.

13. 구다쪠 찌로 나 가꾸 가시뱌 가 가비씨뤄 어라 무호또 사 오꼬. 뵤씨 뱌 아부빠아, 벼떠 뱌나로러가나고 짜까나마 어라 무호또 사이. 가찌 어라 무호또 사이, 에 쭈가더더라 어라 루우루 서먀시 요씨 어라 짜이라아.

14. 러로 쭤더 어무구루구루 워바구하네 오꽈 와이러 과 꾸바, 나 이여수, 뫄나 와 오꼬. 부씨 노구, 쭈시미가아 부서서 뫄 붜머러시 붜쭈.

15. 어무구루구루 워바구하네 오꽈 쭤더, 어떠 아쭈피라 보쏘 뫄 구이나 어미시 궈쭈. 부씨 나이 아나어러기봐아 뫄 띠라 소씨 구우마 너쭈, 시 여거 아다이라아 비비.

16. 부씨 노구, 쭈따아 짜찌푸따 오푸 너떠버 야 오꼬 부시라 부바. 아오꽈, 우쭈까보너라 어부바바뤠러 너부부야 와이, 짜시야 아쭈아서 뫄 비하끼 뱌 비고미러.

13. Nothing in all creation is hidden from God's sight. Everything is uncovered and laid bare before the eyes of him to whom we must give account.

14. Therefore, since we have a great high priest who has gone through the heavens, Jesus the Son of God, let us hold firmly to the faith we profess.

15. For we do not have a high priest who is unable to sympathize with our weaknesses, but we have one who has been tempted in every way, just as we are--yet was without sin.

16. Let us then approach the throne of grace with confidence, so that we may receive mercy and find grace to help us in our time of need.

E Baebrania Chikono 5

1. Chira Mukulukulu webakuhanyi ende alondolyibwa mwa bandju, na kubikibwa mwa mulyimo, akorere Ongo kwa mufa wabu bandju. Iwende wathula Ongo ebindju bya bandju bamureteraa bushi nebibi byabo.

2. Oyu Mukulukulu webakuhanyi angaala kunde afira ebandju bonjo, ba benjire baera busira kumenya, bushi nai ende anaina emisi kuuma nabo.

3. Kanji bushi nai ende anaina emisi, eemire kunde ana emithulo ata bushi nebibi byebanji bandju oshao, si kanji bushi nebibi byai yeine.

4. Kutalyi mundju ola wende wacheresa yeine ethunda lyekuba Mukulukulu webakuhanyi. Si eemire kwamalyibwa na Ongo, ngokwa Haruni nai aamaalyibwaa.

5. Rero kunoku, Kirisito nai atacheresaa ethunda yeine lyekuba Mukulukulu webakuhanyi. Si Ongo yeine iwamweresaalyi mwa

어 바어부라니아 찌고노 5

1. 찌라 무구루구루 워바구하니 어머 아르또레봐 봐 바쭈, 나 구비기봐 봐 무레모, 아고러러 오꼬 과 무파 와부 바쭈. 이워머 와쭈롸 오꼬 어비뚜 뱌 바쭈 바무러더라아 부씨 너비비 뱌보.

2. 오유 무구루구루 워바구하니 아까아롸 구머 아피라 어바뚜 보쪼, 바 버찌러 바어라 부시라 구머냐, 부씨 나이 어머 아나이나 어미시 구우마 나보.

3. 가찌 부씨 나이 어머 아나이나 어미시, 어어미러 구머 아나 어미쭈르 아다 부씨 너비비 뎌바찌 바쭈 오싸오, 시 가찌 부씨 너비비 뱌이 여이너.

4. 구다레 무뚜 오롸 워머 와쩌러사 여이너 어쭈따 뎌구바 무구루구루 워바구하니. 시 어어미러 과마레봐 나 오꼬, 꼬과 하루니 나이 아아마아레봐아.

5. 러로 구노구, 기리시도 나이 아다쩌러사아 어쭈따 여이너 뎌구바 무구루구루 워바구하니. 시 오꼬 여이너 이와뭐러사아레 봐 구무부라

Hebrews Chapter 5[NIV]

1. Every high priest is selected from among men and is appointed to represent them in matters related to God, to offer gifts and sacrifices for sins.

2. He is able to deal gently with those who are ignorant and are going astray, since he himself is subject to weakness.

3. This is why he has to offer sacrifices for his own sins, as well as for the sins of the people.

4. No one takes this honor upon himself; he must be called by God, just as Aaron was.

5. So Christ also did not take upon himself the glory of becoming a high priest. But God said to him, "You are my Son; today I have

kumubura mbu Woyo uMwana wanyi, lwarero nabere Eho.	뿌 오요 우뫄나 와네, 롸러로 나버러 어호.	become your Father."

6. Kanji mwa Maanjiko Mabuyabuya, mulyii na anji ala atechire mbu Woyo, ukanaendekera uthula kuhanyi esuku nemango, nga Melyikiseteki

6. 가찌 뫄 마아찌고 마부야부야, 무례이 나 아찌 아롸 아더찌러 뿌 오요, 우가나어떠거라 우쭈롸 구하네 어수구 너마꼬, 까 머레기서더기

6. And he says in another place, "You are a priest forever, in the order of Melchizedek."

7. Mango Yesu abaa achilyi muno butala, emaa Ongo na kumusengera na murenge munene mwa kutosangya emalyira. Aira bacha, bushi Ongo yeine iwabaa ungaala kumununula mwa lufu. Ongo era kumva ememo mai, bushi Yesu endee amuthunda.

7. 마꼬 여수 아바아 아찌레 무노 부다롸, 어마아 오꼬 나 구무서뻐라 나 무러뻐 무너너 뫄 구도사꺄 어마레라. 아이라 바짜, 부씨 오꼬 여이너 이와바아 우꺄아롸 구무누누롸 뫄 루푸. 오꼬 어라 구뺘 어머모 마이, 부씨 여수 어떠어 아무쭈따.

7. During the days of Jesus' life on earth, he offered up prayers and petitions with loud cries and tears to the one who could save him from death, and he was heard because of his reverent submission.

8. Chiro angaba mbu Yesu abaa alyi Mwana wa Ongo, si achikangilyiisaa ekuira kwa Ongo atechire kurengera emalyibuko ma alolaako.

8. 찌로 아꺄바 뿌 여수 아바아 아레 뫄나 와 오꼬, 시 아찌가꺠레이사아 어구이라 과 오꼬 아더찌러 구러뻐라 어마레부고 마 아뢰롸아고.

8. Although he was a son, he learned obedience from what he suffered

9. Ongo amuiraa kuba ola ulumirire. Rero, ba bende baira kwa Kirisito atechire, bende babona ebununusi bwesuku nemango mwa kumurengerako.

9. 오꼬 아무이라아 구바 오롸 우루미리러. 러로, 바 버더 바이라 과 기리시도 아더찌러, 버더 바보나 어부누누시 붜수구 너마꼬 뫄 구무러뻐라고.

9. and, once made perfect, he became the source of eternal salvation for all who obey him

10. Mwa bacha, Ongo amuilyire Mukulukulu webakuhanyi, nga Merikiseteki.

10. 뫄 바짜, 오꼬 아무이례러 무구루꾸구루 워바구하네, 까 머리기서더기.

10. and was designated by God to be high priest in the order of Melchizedek.

Tutendaa thwaba nga bana batoto mwa myasi ya Ongo	두더따아 쫘바 까 바나 바도도 뫄 먀시 야 오꼬

11. Thucheete binene bya kuhambala era luulu sei myasi si ekubabalyikisisabi kusibuire, bushi mutaika moomva.

12. Rero mwesine suku soshi, mwabo mwabaa mwera mweemire kuba bakangilyisi, si munachilyi mweemire kukangilyisibwa emyasi iberebere yechinwa cha Ongo. Mwabere nga ba beemire kwonga emabere, si batangaala kutafuna bilyo bya bisibuire!

13. Chira mundju ola wende wamoera ekwonga emabere atangaala kumenyerera emyasi era ithungenene, bushi alyi mwana mutoto.

14. Si ebilyo bya bisibuire bilyi byebandju ba bera basene. Bushi emyasi era barengiremo mwa kalamo kabo yende yaberesa ebuashi bwekumenya echibi nechibuya.

E Baebrania Chikono 6
1. Bushi noku, thuendekeraa era muhondo, mwa kunde thwachikangirisa emyasi era bandju ba bera basene bangachikangirisa. Thuteshibiraa oshao kwa

---

11. 쯔쩌어더 비너너 뱌 구하빠꽈 어라 루우루 서이 먀시, 시 어구바바례기시사비 구시부이러, 부씨 무다이가 모오빠.

12. 러로 뭐시너 수구 소씨, 먀보 먀바아 뭐라 뭐어미러 구바 바가꾀레시, 시 무나찌레 뭐어미러 구가꾀레시봐 어먀시 이버러버러 여찌놔 짜 오꾰. 먀버러 꽈 바 버어미러 굦꽈 어마버러, 시 바다꽈아꽈 구다푸나 비뾰 뱌 비시부이러!

13. 찌라 무뿌 오롸 워떠 와모어라 어굦꽈 어마버러 아다꽈아꽈 구머녀러라 어먀시 어라 이쭈떠너너, 부씨 아례 뫄나 무도도.

14. 시 어비뾰 뱌 비시부이러 비례 벼바뉴 바 버라 바서너. 부씨 어먀시 어라 바러꾀러모 뫄 가꽈모 가보 여떠 야버러사 어부아씨 뭐구머냐 어찌비 너찌부야.

어 바어부라니아 찌고노 6
1. 부씨 노구, 쭈어떠거라아 어라 무호또, 뫄 구너 쫘찌가꾀리사 어먀시 어라 바뉴 바 버라 바서너 바꽈찌가꾀리사. 쭈더씨비라아 오싸오 과 먀시 이버러 버러

---

11. We have much to say about this, but it is hard to explain because you are slow to learn.

12. In fact, though by this time you ought to be teachers, you need someone to teach you the elementary truths of God's word all over again. You need milk, not solid food!

13. Anyone who lives on milk, being still an infant, is not acquainted with the teaching about righteousness.

14. But solid food is for the mature, who by constant use have trained themselves to distinguish good from evil.

Hebrews Chapter 6[NIV]
1. Therefore let us leave the elementary teachings about Christ and go on to maturity, not laying again the foundation of repentance from acts that

myasi ibere-bere era thwachikangirisaa era luulu sa Kirisito, nga kuno ekubindjula emichima yenyu itenge mwa myanya ibi era yende yareta elufu, nesi emyasi era itechire era luulu sekweemerera Ongo,

2. nesi era luulu semyasi era yerekere enjira soshi sekubatisa ebandju,a nesi era luulu sekwemera ebandju mwa kubabika kwemino, nesi era luulu sekwoomoka kwebafu, nesi era luulu sebuchinjibusi bwesuku nemango.

3. Rero Ongo akasima thungere thwende thwakangirisa emyasi yebandju ba bera basene.

4. Kulyi bandju ba balomekerwe mira nebulangare bwa Ongo, na kutoma kwa lweembo lwa lwatenga kwa nguba, na kubona ebuashi bweMuchima Mubuya-buya.

5. Kanji abu bandju batomire nokwa buloke bwechinwa cha Ongo nebuashi bwebutala bwa bukaika.

6. Si chiro bacha, barekire ebwemeresi. Abu bandju, ekufulusabo kutangachalyikana kuikira echihangi bahuba kubindjuka

어라 좌찌가ᄞ리사아 어라 루우루 사 기리시도, ᄯᅡ 구노 어구비ᄲᅪ 어미찌마 여뉴 이더머 뫄 먀냐 이비 어라 여ᄯᅥ 야러다 어루푸, 너시 어먀시 어라 이더찌러 어라 루우루 서궈어머러라 오ᄭᅩ,

2. 너시 어라 루우루 서먀시 어라 여러거러 어찌라 소씨 서구바디사 어바쮸,아 너시 어라 루우루 서궈머라 어바쮸 뫄 구바비가 궈미노, 너시 어라 루우루 서고오모가 궈바푸, 너시 어라 루우루 서부찌찌부시 붜수구 너마ᄭᅩ.

3. 러로 오ᄭᅩ 아가시마 쭈머러 쭤ᄯᅥ 좌가ᄞ리사 어먀시 여바쮸 바 버라 바서너.

4. 구레 바쮸 바 바롬머거뤄 미라 너부ᄙᅡ아러 봐 오ᄭᅩ, 나 구도마 과 뤄어마 봐 ᄯᅪ더마 과 우바, 나 구보나 어부아씨 붜무찌마 무부야-부야.

5. 가찌 아부 바쮸 바도미러 노과 부록거 붜찌놔 짜 오ᄭᅩ 너부아씨 붜부다ᄭᅡ 봐 부가이가.

6. 시 찌로 바짜, 바러기러 어붜머러시. 아부 바쮸, 어구푸루사보 구다마짜레가나 구이기라 어찌하의 바후바 구비ᄠᅮ가 바더마 뫄 먀냐

lead to death, and of faith in God,

2. instruction about baptisms, the laying on of hands, the resurrection of the dead, and eternal judgment.

3. And God permitting, we will do so.

4. It is impossible for those who have once been enlightened, who have tasted the heavenly gift, who have shared in the Holy Spirit,

5. who have tasted the goodness of the word of God and the powers of the coming age,

6. if they fall away, to be brought back to repentance, becauseto their loss they are crucifying the Son of God all over again and

batenga mwa myanya yabo ibi. Bushi beine bende baba bamanyikire eMwana wa Ongo ebwakabiri na kuthuma ebandju bamukena.

7. Echitaka cha chatowera kwemvula chira mango, na kukusisa ebainzi emyaka era ikomire, chende chaba chaahanyirwe na Ongo.

8. Si akaba echi chitaka chingamesa mihoi-hoi nechashingi, eri chitete mufa asibya. Aola, chende chaba chiri ofu kutakirwa na Ongo, nebusinda bwachi kulyi kwochibwa.

9. Banyakethu basiirwa, chiro angaba mbu thwatechire bacha, si tuneeshi kanangana kwa mukulyikire enjira era ikomire busese, yebununusi.

10. Ongo ende aira bya bithungenene. Atangeebirira emulyimo wenyu, nenzii era mwalosaa bushi nesina lyai, kukulyikana nokwa mwaasaa ebandju bai, nokwa munachiri mwaendekera kuasabo.

11. Si kanji thwahonda chira muuma mu mwabo aendekeraa kuata obu bushiru kuikira kwa businda, chasiya ei myasi muthula muchinyiire

야보 이비. 부씨 버이너 버머 바바 바마니기러 어마나 와 오꼬 어봐가비리 나 구쭈마 어바쭈 바무거나.

7. 어찌다가 짜 짜도워라 궈뿌꽈 찌라 마꼬, 나 구구시사 어바이씨 어먀가 어라 이고미러, 쩌떠 짜바 짜아하니뤄 나 오꼬.

8. 시 아가바 어찌 찌다가 찌꽈머사 미호이-호이 너짜씨삐, 어리 찌더더 무파 아시뱌. 아오꽈, 쩌떠 짜바 찌리 오푸 구다기롸 나 오꼬, 너부시따 봐찌 구뤠 굄찌봐.

9. 바냐거쭈 바시이롸, 찌로 아꽈바 뿌 좌더찌러 바짜, 시 두너어씨 가나꽈나 과 무구뤠기러 어찌라 어라 이고미러 부서서, 여부누누시.

10. 오꼬 어떠 아이라 뱌 비쭈뻐너너. 아다뻐어비리라 어무뤠모 워뉴, 너씨이 어라 퐈론사아 부씨 너시나 랴이, 구구뤠가나 노과 퐈어사아 어바쭈 바이, 노과 무나찌리 퐈어떠거라 구아사보.

11. 시 가찌 좌호따 찌라 무우마 무 퐈보 아어떠거라아 구아다 오부 부씨루 구이기라 과 부시따, 짜시야 어이 먀시 무쭈꽈 무찌네이러 이버러러

subjecting him to public disgrace.

7. Land that drinks in the rain often falling on it and that produces a crop useful to those for whom it is farmed receives the blessing of God.

8. But land that produces thorns and thistles is worthless and is in danger of being cursed. In the end it will be burned.

9. Even though we speak like this, dear friends, we are confident of better things in your case--things that accompany salvation.

10. God is not unjust; he will not forget your work and the love you have shown him as you have helped his people and continue to help them.

11. We want each of you to show this same diligence to the very end, in order to make your hope sure.

iberere kanangana.

12. Rero mutabaa ngalyisi, si mundaa mweeya ba beemerere, bete nebushibirisi. Abola bu bende babona bya Ongo alaanyaa.

13. Mango Ongo eeresaa Aburahamu echiraane, akulyikisaachi kwekulaisa. Rero, bushi kutalyi unji mundju ola ulyi mukulu-kulu kurenza Ongo, chasiya alaise era muhondo sai, Ongo era kuri alaisa kwesina lyai yeine.

14. Era kuteta mbu: "Kanangana, nyikakuahanyira busese, nelubuto lwao, nyikairalo kuba lunene busese."

15. Era nyuma sekulyinjirira na bushibirisi, Aburahamu era kwire abona bya Ongo amulaanyaa.

16. Bushi mango ebandju balaisa, bende balaisa kwesina lyemundju ola ulyi mukulu-kulu kurenzabo. Mwa bacha, oku kulaisa kwabo kwanalosa ekanangana kebya bateta, kwanamala nebwaka mwa kachi-kachi kabo.

17. Ongo abaa ahonda alose changanama ba bakabona bya alanyaa, kwa atangabindjula

---

가나까나.

12. 러로 무다바아 까레시, 시 무따아 뭐어야 바 버어머러러, 버더 너부씨비리시. 아보롸 부 버더 바보나 뱌 오꼬 아롸아나야.

13. 마꼬 오꼬 어어러사아 아부라하무 어찌라아너, 아구레기사아찌 궈구퐈이사. 러로, 부씨 구다레 우찌 무뚀 오롸 우레 무구루-구루 구러쌰 오꼬, 쨔시야 아퐈이서 어라 무호또 사이, 오꼬 어라 구리 아퐈이사 궈시나 랴이 여이너.

14. 어라 구더다 뿌: "가나까나, 네가구아하네라 부서서, 너루부도 퐈오, 네가이라로 구바 루너너 부서서."

15. 어라 뉴마 서구레찌리라 나 부씨비리시, 아부라하무 어라 궈러 아보나 뱌 오꼬 아무퐈아냐아.

16. 부씨 마꼬 어바뉴 바퐈이사, 버더 바퐈이사 궈시나 려무뚀 오롸 우레 무구루-구루 구러쌰보. 마 바쨔, 오구 구퐈이사 과보 과나로사 어가나까나 거뱌 바더다, 과나마롸 너봐가 마 가찌-가찌 가보.

17. 오꼬 아바아 아호따 아로서 쨔까나마 바 바가보나 뱌 아퐈냐아, 과 아다까비뉴퐈

---

12. We do not want you to become lazy, but to imitate those who through faith and patience inherit what has been promised.

13. When God made his promise to Abraham, since there was no one greater for him to swear by, he swore by himself,

14. saying, "I will surely bless you and give you many descendants."

15. And so after waiting patiently, Abraham received what was promised.

16. Men swear by someone greater than themselves, and the oath confirms what is said and puts an end to all argument.

17. Because God wanted to make the unchanging nature of his purpose very

emwasi ola afunjikaa chiro na hicha. Bushi noku, era kure akulyikisa echiraane chai kwekulaisa.

18. Kuthula myasi ebiri era itabindjuka: echiraane, nekulaisa. Na kwa bya byerekere ei myasi, chitangaalyikana mbu Ongo afule bisha. Rero, echera chi chende chathusesa emuchima busese. Bushi noku, thwarekire byoshi na kusimika mwa munyiiro ola Ongo athulaanyise.

19. Oyu munyiiro, alyi ngechuma cha chende chathuma emashuwa masimika kwa meshi mango memangire, bushi iwende wathuma ekalamo kethu kasimika na kusera. Kanji oyu munyiiro, aulukanyire mira mwa ngwaya era yahumba mwa luhu lwa Ongo kwa nguba, na eengirira mwa Chisiki Chibuya-buya busese.

20. Aola, uYesu engiriraa mubere-bere bushi nethu, chasiya ende athwaasa. Rero iwerire waba Mukulu-kulu wethu webakuhanyi esuku nemango nga Merikiseteki.

어롸시 오롸 아푸찌가아 찌로 나 히짜. 부씨 노구, 어라 구러 아구뻬기사 어찌라아너 짜이 꿔구꽈이사.

18. 구쭈꽈 먀시 어비리 어라 이다비부가: 어찌라아너, 너구꽈이사. 나 과 뱌 벼러거러 어이 먀시, 찌다꽈아쩨가나 뿌 오꼬 아푸퍼 비싸. 러로, 어찌라 찌 쩌떠 짜쭈서사 어무찌마 부서서. 부씨 노구, 쫘러기러 뵤씨 나 구시미가 롸 무네이로 오롸 오꼬 아쭈꽈아니서.

19. 오유 무네이로, 아뼤 꺼쭈마 짜 쩌떠 짜쭈마 어마쑤와 마시미가 과 머씨 마꼬 머마꼐러, 부씨 이워떠 와쭈마 어가꽈모 거쭈 가시미가 나 구서라. 가찌 오유 무네이로, 아우루가너러 미라 롸 꽈야 어라 야후빠 롸 루후 꽈 오꼬 과 꾸바, 나 어어꼐리라 롸 찌시기 찌부야-부야 부서서.

20. 아오롸, 우예수 어꼐리라아 무버러-버러 부씨 너쭈, 짜시야 어떠 아쫘사. 러로 이워리러 와바 무구루- 구루 워쭈 워바구하니 어수구 너마꼬 꽈 머리기서더기.

clear to the heirs of what was promised, he confirmed it with an oath.

18. God did this so that, by two unchangeable things in which it is impossible for God to lie, we who have fled to take hold of the hope offered to us may be greatly encouraged.

19. We have this hope as an anchor for the soul, firm and secure. It enters the inner sanctuary behind the curtain,

20. where Jesus, who went before us, has entered on our behalf. He has become a high priest forever, in the order of Melchizedek.

E Baebrania Chikono 7

1. Oyu Merikiseteki abaa mwami wemusi we Salemi, kanji abaa athula kuhanyi wa Ongo ola ulyi era luulu sa byoshi. Mango Aburahamu abaa atenga kwa bita bya aimaa mu bami bauma, Merikiseteki era kuya kumuhuukasa na amuahanyira.

2. Aburahamu era kumweresa echiuma chekumi cha byoshi bya abonaa mwa bita. Rero esina lya Merikiseteki, kukuteta tanga mbu: "Mwami ola wende waira bya bithungenene." Kanji alyi mwami weSalemi, kukuteta mbu: "Mwami wa boolo."

3. Kutalyi ola wishi eshe nesi nyina, nesi elubuto lwa ashokaamo. Nelusuku lwekubuchibwa nelwekufa kwai, nalo luteshibwe. Alyi kuhanyi esuku nemango nga kuno eMwana wa Ongo.

4. Musene kute oyu mundju abaa alyi mukulu-kulu busese! Anabe na Aburahamu, hokulu wethu munene anamweresaa echiuma chekumi chebindju bya bikomire busese, bya anyaa mwa bita.

어 바어부라니아 찌고노 7

1. 오유 머리기서더기 아바아 마미 워무시 워 사뻐미, 가찌 아바아 아쭈롸 구하네 와 오꼬 오롸 우뤠 어라 루우루루 사 뵤씨. 마꼬 아부라하무 아바아 아더빠 과 비다 뱌 아이마아 무 바미 바우마, 머리기서더기 어라 구야 구무후우가사 나 아무아하네라.

2. 아부라하무 어라 구뭐러사 어찌우마 쩌구미 짜 뵤씨 뱌 아보나아 롸 비다. 러로 어시나 럐 머리기서더기, 구구더다 다빠 뿌: "마미 오롸 워떠 와이라 뱌 비쭈뻐너너." 가찌 아뤠 마미 워사뻐미, 구구더다 뿌: "마미 와 보오뤀."

3. 구다뤠 오롸 위씨 어써 너시 니나, 너시 어룪부도 롸 아쏘가아모. 너룪수구 뤄구부찌봐 너뤄구파 과이, 나로 루더씨붜. 아뤠 구하네 어수구 너마꼬 빠 구노 어뫄나 와 오꼬.

4. 무서너 구더 오유 무뚜 아바아 아뤠 무구룪-구루 부서서! 아나버 나 아부라하무, 호구룪 워쭈 무너너 아나뭐러사아 어찌우마 쩌구미 쩌비뚜 뱌 비고미러 부서서, 뱌 아냐아

Hebrews Chapter 7[NIV]

1. This Melchizedek was king of Salem and priest of God Most High. He met Abraham returning from the defeat of the kings and blessed him,

2. and Abraham gave him a tenth of everything. First, his name means "king of righteousness"; then also, "king of Salem" means "king of peace."

3. Without father or mother, without genealogy, without beginning of days or end of life, like the Son of God he remains a priest forever.

4. Just think how great he was: Even the patriarch Abraham gave him a tenth of the plunder!

와 비다.

5. eMwaso athula aanyire eloso kwa bandju bomwa lubuto lwa Lawi, ba beeresibwe emulyimo webukuhanyi kunde baholosa echi chiuma chekumi mwa kachi-kachi ka banyakabo Baisiraeli. Bende baira bacha, chiro angaba mbu nabo balyi bomwa lubuto lwa Aburahamu.

5. 어뫄소 아쭈롸 아아니러 어르소 과 바뚜 보뫄 루부도 롸 롸위, 바 버어러시붜 어무레모 워부구하네 구떠 바호롸사 어찌 찌우마 쩌구미 뫄 가찌-가찌 가 바냐가보 바이시라어릐. 버러 바이라 바짜, 찌로 아꺄바 뿌 나보 바뤠 보뫄 루부도 롸 아부라하무.

5. Now the law requires the descendants of Levi who become priests to collect a tenth from the people--that is, their brothers--even though their brothers are descended from Abraham.

6. Oyu Merikiseteki atabaa womwa lubuto lwa Lawi, si Aburahamu amweeresaa echiuma chekumi. Chasinda, Merikiseteki era kuahanyira Abrahamu iOngo eeresise echiraane.

6. 오유 머리기서더기 아다바아 옴뫄 루부도 롸 롸위, 시 아부라하무 아뭐어러사아 어찌우마 쩌구미. 짜시따, 머리기서더기 어라 구아하네라 아부라하무 이오꼬 어어러시서 어찌라아너.

6. This man, however, did not trace his descent from Levi, yet he collected a tenth from Abraham and blessed him who had the promises.

7. Kubinalyi, ola waahanyira iulyi era luulu sola waahanyirwa.

7. 구비나뤠, 오롸 와아하네라 이우뤠 어라 루우루 소롸 와아하네롸.

7. And without doubt the lesser person is blessed by the greater.

8. Ebakuhanyi ba bende baholosa echiuma chekumi, nabo banalyi bandju ba bende bafa. Si Merikiseteki iweeresibwaa echiuma chekumi, yeke anachiri muuma-uma kukulyikana nokwa Maanjiko Mabuya-buya mathula matechire.

8. 어바구하네 바 버떠 바호롸사 어찌우마 쩌구미, 나보 바나뤠 바뚜 바 버떠 바파. 시 머리기서더기 이워어러시봐아 어찌우마 쩌구미, 여거 아나찌리 무우마-우마 구구뤠가나 노과 마아찌고 마부야-부야 마쭈롸 마더찌러.

8. In the one case, the tenth is collected by men who die; but in the other case, by him who is declared to be living.

9. Rero, thungateta mbu mango Aburahamu anaa echiuma chekumi chebikulo

9. 러로, 쭈꺄더다 뿌 마꼬 아부라하무 아나아 어찌우마 쩌구미 쩌비구롣 뱌이, 롸위

9. One might even say that Levi, who collects the tenth, paid the tenth through

byai, Lawi nai ananaachi kumurengerako.	나이 아나나아찌 구무러꺼라고.	Abraham,
10. Bushi chiro angaba mbu Lawi abaa atasa kubuthwa, si abaa era analyi mwa mikira ya hokulu wai Aburahamu, mango Merikiseteki ayaa kumuhuukasa.	10. 부씨 찌로 아까바 뿌 롸위 아바아 아다사 구부화, 시 아바아 어라 아나뤠 뫄 미기라 야 호구루 와이 아부라하무, 마오 머리기서더기 아야아 구무후우가사.	10. because when Melchizedek met Abraham, Levi was still in the body of his ancestor.
11. Mwa Mwaso weBaisiraeli, ebandju bomwa ngumo ya Lawi bu bendee balondolyibwa mwebakuhanyi. Bendee baba bakuhanyi nga kuno Haruni. Si obu bukuhanyi bwabo, bwabaa butalumirire. Bushi akaba bungabere bulumirire, ekubika eunji kuhanyi ola ulyi nga Merikiseteki, kutangachiachire mufa.	11. 뫄 뫄소 워바이시라어뤼, 어반쭈 보뫄 우모 야 롸위 부 번떠어 바로또뤠봐 뭐바구하니. 번떠어 바바 바구하니 까 구노 하루니. 시 오부 부구하니 봐보, 봐바아 부다루미리러. 부씨 아가바 부까버러 부루미리러, 어구비가 어우찌 구하니 오롸 우뤠 까 머리기서더기, 구다까찌아찌러 무파.	11. If perfection could have been attained through the Levitical priesthood (for on the basis of it the law was given to the people), why was there still need for another priest to come--one in the order of Melchizedek, not in the order of Aaron?
12. Mango ebukuhanyi bwende bwabindjulyibwa, eMwaso nao, ende eema abindjulyibwe.	12. 마오 어부구하니 뷔떠 봐비쭈뤠봐, 어뫄소 나오, 어떠 어어마 아비쭈뤠뷔.	12. For when there is a change of the priesthood, there must also be a change of the law.
13. Bushi Enawethu Yesu ola ei myasi yerekere, abaa mundju wa chinji chirongo. Kanji kutalyi chiro na mundju asibya womwa chirongo chai, ola wendee wakola emulyimo webukuhanyi kwa kahaha kemithulo.	13. 부씨 어나워쭈 여수 오롸 어이 먀시 여러거러, 아바아 무쭈 와 찌찌 찌로오. 가찌 구다뤠 찌로 나 무쭈 아시뱌 오뫄 찌로오 짜이, 오롸 워떠어 와고롸 어무뤠모 워부구하니 과 가하하 거미쭈로.	13. He of whom these things are said belonged to a different tribe, and no one from that tribe has ever served at the altar.
14. Kubinalyi, ebandju boshi baneeshi kanangana kwoyu	14. 구비나뤠, 어바쭈 보씨 바너어씨 가나까나 고유	14. For it is clear that our Lord descended from Judah,

Enawethu ashokaa mwa chirongo cha Yuta. Nera luulu sechi chirongo, Musa atatetaa chiro na mwasi asibya ola werekere ebukuhanyi.

15. Oyu mwasi alorekanyireko changanama bushi kwaulukirire unji kuhanyi ola uhuhanyisibwe na Merikiseteki.

16. Oyola yeke atairibwe kuba kuhanyi kukulyikana nemiomba yebandju bomwa chirongo cha Lawi. Si airibwe kuba kuhanyi kukulyikana nebuashi bwekalamo ka katakakumbe.

17. Bushi eMaanjiko Mabuya-buya mathula matechire mbu: "Woyo, ukanaendekera uthula kuhanyi esuku nemango, nga Merikiseteki."

18. Rero, emuomba wokwa mira abindjulyibwaa bushi abaa atete misi, kanji abaa atete mufa,

19. bushi kutalyi kandju ka kalumirire, keMwaso aretaa. Si thwerire thwabona unji munyiiro ola urenzise ola wokwa mira, na kurengera oyu munyiiro, thwera thungachifunda ofu na Ongo.

20. Kanji ei myasi yairwaa kukulyikana nekulaisa kwa

어나워쭈 아쏘가아 뫄 찌로으 짜 유다. 너라 루우루 서찌 찌로으, 무사 아다더다아 찌로 나 먀시 아시뱌 오꽈 워러거러 어부구하네.

15. 오유 먀시 아뢰러가네러고 짜꾸나마 부씨 과우루기리러 우찌 구하네 오꽈 우후하네시뷔 나 머리기서더기.

16. 오요꽈 여거 아다이리뷔 구바 구하네 구구꿰가나 너미오빠 여바쭈 보뫄 찌로으 짜 꽈위. 시 아이리뷔 구바 구하네 구구꿰가나 너부아씨 뷔가꽈모 가 가다가구뻐.

17. 부씨 어마아찌고 마부야- 부야 마쭈꽈 마더찌러 뿌: "오요, 우가나어떠거라 우쭈꽈 구하네 어수구 너마으, 꽈 머리기서더기."

18. 러로, 어무오빠 오과 미라 아비뉴꿰봐아 부씨 아바아 아더더 미시, 가찌 아바아 아더더 무꽈,

19. 부씨 구다뤠 가뉴 가 가루미리러, 거봐소 아러다아. 시 쮜리러 쫘보나 우찌 무네이로 오꽈 우러씨서 오꽈 오과 미라, 나 구러뻐라 오유 무네이로, 쮜라 쭈꽈찌푸따 오푸 나 오으.

20. 가찌 어이 먀시 야이롸아 구구꿰가나 너구꽈이사 과

and in regard to that tribe Moses said nothing about priests.

15. And what we have said is even more clear if another priest like Melchizedek appears,

16. one who has become a priest not on the basis of a regulation as to his ancestry but on the basis of the power of an indestructible life.

17. For it is declared: "You are a priest forever, in the order of Melchizedek."

18. The former regulation is set aside because it was weak and useless

19. (for the law made nothing perfect), and a better hope is introduced, by which we draw near to God.

20. And it was not without an oath! Others became

Ongo alaisaa. Si abu banji bakuhanyi bomwa chirongo cha Lawi, mango bendee babikibwa kwa bukuhanyi, kutalyi ola wendee walaisa.

21. Si Yesu airibwe kuba kuhanyi kurengera ekulaisa kwa Ongo alaisaa mango amuburaa mbu: "Enawethu alaisise, kanji atangabindjula na cha atechire mbu: Woyo, ukanaendekera uthula kuhanyi esuku nemango?"

22. Mwa bacha, Yesu erire aba chikinja chechilaano cha chikomire busese kurenza echilaano chokwa mira.

23. Kanji abu banji bakuhanyi babaa banene, bushi ekufa kwendee kwathuma bataendekera nemulyimo wabo.

24. Si Yesu yeke anathula muuma-uma esuku nemango, nebukuhanyi bwai butakawe chiro na hicha.

25. Echera chi chithumire angaala kununula boshi ba benjire bachifunda ofu na Ongo mwa kumurengerako. Bushi alyi muuma-uma esuku nemango, chasiya ende eemerabo era mwa Ongo.

오꼬 아롸이사아. 시 아부 바찌 바구하니 보먀 찌로꼬 짜 롸위, 마꼬 버떠어 바비기뫄 과 부구하니, 구다레 오롸 워떠어 와롸이사.

21. 시 여수 아이리붸 구바 구하니 구러뻐라 어구롸이사 과 오꼬 아롸이사아 마꼬 아무부라아 뿌: "어나워쭈 아롸이시서, 가찌 아다빠비뿌롸 나 짜 아더찌러 뿌: 오요, 우가나어떠거라 우쭈롸 구하니 어수구 너마꼬?"

22. 먀 바짜, 여수 어리러 아바 찌기짜 쩌찌롸아노 짜 찌고미러 부서서 구러싸 어찌롸아노 쪼과 미라.

23. 가찌 아부 바찌 바구하니 바바아 바너너, 부씨 어구파 궈떠어 과쭈마 바다어떠거라 너무레모 와보.

24. 시 여수 여거 아나쭈롸 무우마-우마 어수구 너마꼬, 너부구하니 봐이 부다가워 찌로 나 히짜.

25. 어쩌라 찌 찌쭈미러 아빠아롸 구누누롸 보씨 바 버찌러 바찌푸따 오푸 나 오꼬 먀 구무러뻐라고. 부씨 아레 무우마-우마 어수구 너마꼬, 짜시야 어더 어어머라보 어라 먀 오꼬.

priests without any oath,

21. but he became a priest with an oath when God said to him: "The Lord has sworn and will not change his mind: 'You are a priest forever.' "

22. Because of this oath, Jesus has become the guarantee of a better covenant.

23. Now there have been many of those priests, since death prevented them from continuing in office;

24. but because Jesus lives forever, he has a permanent priesthood.

25. Therefore he is able to save completely those who come to God through him, because he always lives to intercede for them.

26. Kubinalyi! Yesu iMukulu-kulu webakuhanyi ola uthweetere mufa. Yeke athula mubuya-buya, atete chiro na chibi chisibya, atathusa nesinga. Abikibwe bure nebandju bebibi, na kwerusibwa mwa chanya busese kwa nguba.

27. Yeke atalyi kuuma nebanji Bakulu-kulu bebakuhanyi. Atathula alaire ku kwana mithulo chira lusuku ngokwa abu banji bende baira bushi nebibi byabo beine nebye banji bandju. Si Yesu yeke achanaa kuba mithulo euma oshao, mango yeine eemereraa kufa.

28. eMwaso wa Musa ende abika ebandju ba batete misi kuba Bakulu-kulu bebakuhanyi. Si kukulyikana nekulaisa kwa Ongo alaisaa era nyuma sekubika oyu Mwaso, eMwana iuthula ulumirire esuku nemango, erire airibwa kuba Mukulu-kulu webakuhanyi.

26. 구비나레! 여수 이무구루-구루 워바구하네 오라 우쮀어더러 무파. 여거 아쭈롸 무부야-부야, 아더더 찌로 나 찌비 찌시뱌, 아다쭈사 너시꽈. 아비기붜 부러 너바쭈 버비비, 나 궈루시봐 뫄 쨔냐 부서서 과 우바.

27. 여거 아다레 구우마 너바찌 바구루-구루 버바구하네. 아다쭈롸 아롸이러 구 과나 미쭈로 찌라 루수구 꼬과 아부 바찌 버떠 바이라 부씨 너비비 뱌보 버이너 너뼈 바찌 바쭈. 시 여수 여거 아쨔나아 구바 미쭈로 어우마 오싸오, 마꼬 여이너 어어머러라아 구파.

28. 어뫄소 와 무사 어떠 아비가 어바쭈 바 바더더 미시 구바 바구루-구루 버바구하네. 시 구구레가나 너구롸이사 과 오꼬 아롸이사아 어라 뉴마 서구비가 오유 뫄소, 어뫄나 이우쭈롸 우루미리러 어수구 너마꼬, 어리러 아이리봐 구바 무구루-구루 워바구하네.

26. Such a high priest meets our need--one who is holy, blameless, pure, set apart from sinners, exalted above the heavens.

27. Unlike the other high priests, he does not need to offer sacrifices day after day, first for his own sins, and then for the sins of the people. He sacrificed for their sins once for all when he offered himself.

28. For the law appoints as high priests men who are weak; but the oath, which came after the law, appointed the Son, who has been made perfect forever.

E Baebrania Chikono 8

1. Emwasi munene busese mwa bya twhahonda kuteta, iyoono: thwete eMukulu-kulu

어 바어부라니아 찌고노 8

1. 어뫄시 무너너 부서서 뫄 뱌 똬호따 구더다, 이요오노: 쮀더 어무구루-구루

Hebrews Chapter 8[NIV]

1. The point of what we are saying is this: We do have such a high priest, who sat

webakuhanyi ola ulyi ngoyu
thwahambereko. Oyola,
iwekese kwa nguba kwa lunda
lwemalyo ma Ongo webuashi
boshi.

2. Akola mwa Chisiki Chibuya-
buya, kukuteta mbu mwa
hema lyekanangana. Eri hema,
lyitakomibwaa na mundju, si
Enawethu yeine iwakomaalyi.

3. Chira Mukulu-kulu
webakuhanyi ende abikwa
chasiya akole emulyimo
wekunde ana emithulo. Bushi
noku, oyu Mukulu-kulu wethu
webakuhanyi, nai abaa emire
aate kandju ka kwana.

4. Akaba Kirisito angabere
muno butala, atangabere
kuhanyi chiro na hicha. Bushi
kulyi bakuhanyi ba benjire
bana emithulo kukulyikana
nokwa Mwaso wa Musa athula
atechire.

5. Emulyimo ola abu
bakuhanyi benjire baira, chiri
chimbusa kanji kalorero ka
kalosa emyasi kanangana era
yakolyibwa kwa nguba. Ei
myasi, iri ngera Musa
alosibwaa. Bushi mango Musa
abaa alyi ofu kuimba ehema,
Ongo era kumuchichika mbu:
"Ulolaa kubuya, chasiya

워바구하네 오라 우뤠 꼬유
쫘하뻐러고. 오요라, 이워거서
과 우바 과 루따 뤄마룬 마
오꼬 워부아씨 보씨.

2. 아고꽈 뫄 찌시기 찌부야-
부야, 구구더다 뿌 뫄 허마
뗘가나빠나. 어리 허마,
뤠다고미봐아 나 무뚜, 시
어나워쭈 여이너
이와고마아뤠.

3. 찌라 무구루-구루
워바구하네 어떠 아비과
쫘시야 아고뤄 어무뤠모
워구떠 아나 어미쭈룬. 부씨
노구, 오유 무구루-구루 워쭈
워바구하네, 나이 아바아
어미러 아아더 가뚜 가 과나.

4. 아가바 기리시도 아빠버러
무노 부다꽈, 아다빠버러
구하네 찌로 나 히꽈. 부씨
구뤠 바구하네 바 버찌러
바나 어미쭈룬 구구뤠가나
노과 뫄소 와 무사 아쭈꽈
아더찌러.

5. 어무뤠모 오꽈 아부
바구하네 버찌러 바이라, 찌리
찌뿌사 가찌 가룬러로 가
가룬사 어먀시 가나빠나 어라
야고뤠봐 과 우바. 어이 먀시,
이리 뻐라 무사 아룬시봐아.
부씨 마꼬 무사 아바아 아뤠
오푸 구이빠 어허마, 오꼬
어라 구무찌찌가 뿌:
"우룬꽈아 구부야, 짜시야

down at the right hand of
the throne of the Majesty in
heaven,

2. and who serves in the
sanctuary, the true
tabernacle set up by the
Lord, not by man.

3. Every high priest is
appointed to offer both
gifts and sacrifices, and so it
was necessary for this one
also to have something to
offer.

4. If he were on earth, he
would not be a priest, for
there are already men who
offer the gifts prescribed by
the law.

5. They serve at a sanctuary
that is a copy and shadow
of what is in heaven. This is
why Moses was warned
when he was about to build
the tabernacle: "See to it
that you make everything
according to the pattern
shown you on the
mountain."

ukunganye chira kandju
kukulyikana nokwa
nanakulosaa kwa ndjulungu."

6. Si rero, Yesu eeresibwe
emulyimo ola urenzise busese
emulyimo wabu bakuhanyi,
bushi iwabikire ebandju mwa
buuma na Ongo kurengera
echilaano cha chikomire
busese kurenza cha chibere-
bere. Echi chilaano cheke,
chithula chemangirire kwa
biraane bya bikomire busese.

7. Akaba echi chilaano
chibere-bere chingabere
chilumirire,
chitangainganyisibwe necha
kabiri.

8. Si Ongo era kunde akalyiira
ebandju bai mwa kubabura
mbu: "Enawethu atechire mbu:
Mwa suku sa seshire, nyingaira
chilaano chiyayaya nelubaa
lweBaisiraeli, alauma nelubaa
lwa Yuta.

9. Echi chilaano cheke, chitabe
ngecha nairaa na bahokulu
babo, mango nabaa
nyibaachirire kwa mino,
nabakula mwa chio cheMisiri.
Si batendee baira kwa echi
chilaano chabaa chitechire.
Bushi noku, nera kwire
narekererabo."

우구ᄊ녀 찌라 가뉴
구구ᄙ레가나 노과
나나구ᄙ로사아 과 뉴ᄙ루ᄋ."

6. 시 러로, 여수 어어러시붜
어무ᄙ레모 오롸 우러씨서
부서서 어무ᄙ레모 와부
바구하네, 부씨 이와비기러
어바뉴 과 부우마 나 오ᄋ오
구러ᄊ라 어찌롸아노 짜
찌고미러 부서서 구러ᄊ 짜
찌버러-버러. 어찌 찌롸아노
쩌거, 찌쭈롸 쩌마ᄋ이리러 과
비라아너 뱌 비고미러 부서서.

7. 아가바 어찌 찌롸아노
찌버러-버러 찌ᄊ버러
찌루ᄋ미리러, 찌다ᄊ아이ᄊ네시붜
너짜 가비리.

8. 시 오ᄋ오 어라 구ᄕ어
아가ᄙ레이라 어바뉴 바이 ᄆ롸
구바부라 뮤: "어나워쭈
아더찌러 뮤: 롸 수구 사
서씨러, 네ᄊ아이라 찌롸아노
찌야야야 너루바아
ᄙ뮈바이시라어ᄙ리, 아롸우마
너루바아 ᄅ롸 유다.

9. 어찌 찌롸아노 쩌거,
찌다버 ᄊ쩌짜 나이라아 나
바호구루ᄙ 바보, 마ᄋ오 나바아
네바아찌리러 과 미노,
나바구ᄅ롸 과 찌오 쩌미시리.
시 바더ᄕ어 바이라 과 어찌
찌롸아노 짜바아 찌더찌러.
부씨 노구, 너라 귀러
나러거러라보."

6. But the ministry Jesus has
received is as superior to
theirs as the covenant of
which he is mediator is
superior to the old one, and
it is founded on better
promises.

7. For if there had been
nothing wrong with that
first covenant, no place
would have been sought for
another.

8. But God found fault with
the people and said: "The
time is coming, declares the
Lord, when I will make a
new covenant with the
house of Israel and with the
house of Judah.

9. It will not be like the
covenant I made with their
forefathers when I took
them by the hand to lead
them out of Egypt, because
they did not remain faithful
to my covenant, and I
turned away from them,
declares the Lord.

10. Kanji Enawethu atechire mbu: "Echilaano cha nyingaira nelubaa lweBaisiraeli era nyuma sesi suku chi chechine: Nyingabika eMwaso wanyi mwa mianyisa yabo,na kuanjikao mwa michima yabo. Nyingaba Ongo wabo, nabo banaba bandju banyi.

11. Kutachibe mundju ola wakangirisa mulyikabo, nesi ola wabura munyakabo mbu: ?Kwemire umenye Enawethu!? Bushi ebandju boshi banganyimenya, kutengera kwa mutoto, kuikira kwa mukulu.

12. Bushi nyingababalyira emabi mabo, kanji ndachikengere nebibi byabo."

13. Mango Ongo ateta era luulu sechi chilaano chiyayaya, kulyi kuteta mbu abindjwire echilaano chibere-bere, kuba chokwa mira. Na chira kandju koshi ka kalyi kokwa mira, katachete na mutoloke, kende kaikirira kwa chihangi kawekerera.

10. 가찌 어나워쭈 아더찌러 뿌: "어찌롸아노 짜 네까이라 너루바아 뤄바이시라어삐 어라 뉴마 서시 수구 찌 쩌찌너: 네까비가 어뫄소 와네 뫄 미아네사 야보,나 구아찌가오 뫄 미찌마 야보. 네까바 오꼬 와보, 나보 바나바 바뉴 바네.

11. 구다찌버 무뚜 오롸 와가끼리사 무뤠가보, 너시 오롸 와부라 무냐가보 뿌: ?궈미러 우머녀 어나워쭈!? 부씨 어바뉴 보씨 바까네머냐, 구더꺼라 과 무도도, 구이기라 과 무구룩.

12. 부씨 네까바바바삐라 어마비 마보, 가찌 따찌거꺼러 너비비 뱌보."

13. 마꼬 오꼬 아더다 어라 루우룩 서찌 찌롸아노 찌야야야, 구뤠 구더다 뿌 아비뉴위러 어찌롸아노 찌버러-버러, 구바 쪼과 미라. 나 찌라 가뉴 고씨 가 가뤠 고과 미라, 가다쩌더 나 무도롱거, 거꺼 가이기리라 과 찌하끼 가워거러라.

10. This is the covenant I will make with the house of Israel after that time, declares the Lord. I will put my laws in their minds and write them on their hearts. I will be their God, and they will be my people.

11. No longer will a man teach his neighbor, or a man his brother, saying, 'Know the Lord,' because they will all know me, from the least of them to the greatest.

12. For I will forgive their wickedness and will remember their sins no more."

13. By calling this covenant "new," he has made the first one obsolete; and what is obsolete and aging will soon disappear.

1. Mwa chilaano chibere-bere, bahambere era luulu semiomba yekweera Ongo, nera luulu sechisiki chekweereramo, cha chaimbwaa nebandju.

2. Bushi noku, bera kukoma ehema. Mweri hema, mwabaa mulyi echumba chibere-bere cha bendee berika mbu Chisiki Chibuya-buya. Na mwechi chumba, mu mwabaa muthula ekakondo kekubika kwetara, nemesa mekubika kwemikati era bathulaa Ongo.

3. Chasinda, kwabaa kulyi ngwaya era yabaa ilyikanyise echi chumba chibere-bere, nechumba cha kabiri cha bendee berika mbu Chisiki Chibuya-buya Busese.

4. Mwechi chumba mu mwabaa muthula ekahaha kemithulo ka kabaa kakunganyisibwe mwa horo. Kwaku kahaha ku bendee basiresesa emarashi. Kanji mwabaa muthula nesanduku yechilaano, era yabaa yakabirwe kwehoro kwa nyinda soshi. Na mwei sanduku, mwabaa mulyi ngumbu era yabaa ikunganyisibwe mwa horo. Nomwa ndanda sei ngumbu,

1. 롸 찌롸아노 찌버러-버러, 바하뻐러 어라 루우루 서미오빠 여궈어라 오꼬, 너라 루우루 서찌시기 쩌궈어러라모, 짜 짜이빡아 너바쭈.

2. 부씨 노구, 버라 구고마 어허마. 뭐리 허마, 롸바아 무레 어쭈빠 찌버러-버러 짜 버떠어 버리가 뿌 찌시기 찌부야-부야. 나 뭐찌 쭈빠, 무 롸바아 무쭈롸 어가고또 거구비가 궈다라, 너머사 머구비가 궈미가디 어라 바쭈롸아 오꼬.

3. 짜시따, 과바아 구레 꽈야 어라 야바아 이레가네서 어찌 쭈빠 찌버러-버러, 너쭈빠 짜 가비리 짜 버떠어 버리가 뿌 찌시기 찌부야-부야 부서서.

4. 뭐찌 쭈빠 무 롸바아 무쭈롸 어가하하 거미쭈또 가 가바아 가구빡네시붜 롸 호로. 과구 가하하 구 버떠어 바시러서사 어마라씨. 가찌 롸바아 무쭈롸 너사뚜구 여찌롸아노, 어라 야바아 야가비뤄 궈호로 과 네따 소씨. 나 뭐이 사뚜구, 롸바아 무레 우뿌 어라 야바아 이구빡네시붜 롸 호로. 노롸 따따 서이 우뿌, 롸바아 무레 마나. 가찌 뭐이 사뚜구 롸바아 무레 어가찌 가

1. Now the first covenant had regulations for worship and also an earthly sanctuary.

2. A tabernacle was set up. In its first room were the lampstand, the table and the consecrated bread; this was called the Holy Place.

3. Behind the second curtain was a room called the Most Holy Place,

4. which had the golden altar of incense and the gold-covered ark of the covenant. This ark contained the gold jar of manna, Aaron's staff that had budded, and the stone tablets of the covenant.

mwabaa mulyi mana. Kanji mwei sanduku mwabaa mulyi ekachi ka Haruni, ka kahowaa kwebwaso. Mwabaa mulyi na makoi mabiri ma mabaa maanjikirwe kwemyasi yechilaano.	하루니, 가 가호와아 궈봐소. 뫄바아 무례 나 마고이 마비리 마 마바아 마아찌기뤄 궈먀시 여찌롸아노.	
5. Nera luulu sei sanduku, yabaa iri bihuhanyi bibiri bya makerubi, ba bendee balosa kanangana kwa uOngo analyi aola. Ebibaba byabo, byabaa bihukire echisiki cha bendee batulyira mu Ongo emikira bushi nekubabalyira ebibi byebandju. Si rero chitasa kuba chihangi cha kubalyikisa ei myasi yoshi muuma kwa muuma.	5. 너라 룰우룰 서이 사뚜구, 야바아 이리 비후하니 비비리 뱌 마거루비, 바 버떠어 바로사 가나까나 과 우오오 아나례 아오롸. 어비바바 뱌보, 뱌바아 비후기러 어찌시기 짜 버떠어 바두례라 무 오오 어미기라 부씨 너구바바례라 어비비 벼바쭈. 시 러로 찌다사 구바 찌하끼 짜 구바례기사 어이 먀시 요씨 무우마 과 무우마.	5. Above the ark were the cherubim of the Glory, overshadowing the atonement cover. But we cannot discuss these things in detail now.
6. Mango ebi bindju byoshi byendee byaba byatondekibwe kubuya, mu mango ebakuhanyi bendee beengirira chira lusuku mwechi chumba chibere-bere, kwa kukola emulyimo wabo.	6. 마오 어비 비쭈 뵤씨 벼떠어 뱌바 뱌도떠기뷰 구부야, 무 마오 어바구하니 버떠어 버어끼리라 찌라 룰수구 뭐찌 쭈빠 찌버러-버러, 과 구고롸 어무례모 와보.	6. When everything had been arranged like this, the priests entered regularly into the outer room to carry on their ministry.
7. Si eMukulu-kulu webakuhanyi yeine oshao iwendee wengira mwa chumba cha kabiri. Endee eengiramo euma kwa mwaka oshao, ete emikira yenyama yekuthula bushi nebibi byai yeine, na bushi nebibi byebanji bandju, bya bakolaa busira kumenya.	7. 시 어무구룰-구룰 워바구하니 여이너 오싸오 이워떠어 워끼라 뫄 쭈빠 짜 가비리. 어떠어 어어끼라모 어우마 과 뫄가 오싸오, 어더 어미기라 여냐마 여구쭈롸 부씨 너비비 뱌이 여이너, 나 부씨 너비비 벼바찌 바쭈, 뱌 바고롸아 부시라 구머냐.	7. But only the high priest entered the inner room, and that only once a year, and never without blood, which he offered for himself and for the sins the people had committed in ignorance.

8. Mwebi byoshi, eMuchima Mubuya-buya abaa ahonda alose kwenjira yekweengirira mwa Chisiki Chibuya-buya busese yabaa itasa kuboolyibwa mwesi suku soshi sa hema lyibere-bere lyabaa lyichiri limangire.

9. Ei myasi, chiri chimbusa chemyasi era iri lwarero. Yalosa kwemithulo era bandju bende bathula Ongo, itangaala kukomya emuchima wemundju ola wanai.

10. Ebi byoshi, inalyi miomba era itechire era luulu semubiri, kwa myasi era yerekere ebiryo, nebyekumwa, alauma nemyanya yekuchikomya mu njira sinene. Ei miomba yaataa mufa kuikira kwa chihangi cha Ongo abindjulaa ebindju byoshi kuba biyayaya.

11. Si Kirisito aikire kuba Mukulu-kulu webakuhanyi kwa kuthweresa ebindju bibuya bya biri lwarero. Ehema lyaulukanyiremo, lyeke liri lyinene busese kanji lya lyilumirire. Eri hema, litairwaa na bandju, kukuteta mbu lyita lyomuno butala.

12. Kirisito eengirire eri neuma mwa Chisiki Chibuya-buya Busese. Atathulaa mikira ya

8. 뭐비 뵤씨, 어무찌마 무부야-부야 아바아 아호따 아로서 궈씨라 여궈어삐리라 와 찌시기 찌부야-부야 부서서 야바아 이다사 구보오쩨봐 뭐시 수구 소씨 사 허마 쩨버러-버러 쨔바아 쩨찌리 삐마삐러.

9. 어이 먀시, 찌리 찌뿌사 쩌먀시 어라 이리 쫘러로. 야로사 궈미쭈론 어라 바쭈 버러 바쭈쫘 오꼬, 이다따아쫘 구고먀 어무찌마 워무뿌 오롸 와나이.

10. 어비 뵤씨, 이나레 미오빠 어라 이더찌러 어라 루우루 서무비리, 과 먀시 어라 여러거러 어비료, 너벼구뫄, 아쫘우마 너먀냐 여구찌고먀 무 찌라 시너너. 어이 미오빠 야아다아 무파 구이기라 과 찌하삐 쨔 오꼬 아비뿌쫘아 어비뿌 뵤씨 구바 비야야야.

11. 시 기리시도 아이기러 구바 무구루-구루 워바구하니 과 구쭤러사 어비뿌 비부야 뱌 비리 쫘러로. 어허마 쨔우루가네러모, 쪄거 삐리 쩨너너 부서서 가찌 쨔 쩨루미리러. 어리 허마, 삐다이롸아 나 바쭈, 구구더다 뿌 쩨다 룐무노 부다쫘.

12. 기리시도 어어삐리러 어리 너우마 와 찌시기 찌부야-부야 부서서. 아다쭈쫘아

8. The Holy Spirit was showing by this that the way into the Most Holy Place had not yet been disclosed as long as the first tabernacle was still standing.

9. This is an illustration for the present time, indicating that the gifts and sacrifices being offered were not able to clear the conscience of the worshiper.

10. They are only a matter of food and drink and various ceremonial washings--external regulations applying until the time of the new order.

11. When Christ came as high priest of the good things that are already here, he went through the greater and more perfect tabernacle that is not man-made, that is to say, not a part of this creation.

12. He did not enter by means of the blood of goats and calves; but he

chikolya, nesi ya chana cha ngaafu, si emikira yai yeine. Airaa bacha, chasiya athununule esuku nemango.

미기라 야 찌고ᄙᅣ, 너시 야 짜나 짜 ᅁᅡ아푸, 시 어미기라 야이 여이너. 아이라아 바짜, 짜시야 아쭈누누ᄙᅥ 어수구 너마ᅌᅩ.

entered the Most Holy Place once for all by his own blood, having obtained eternal redemption.

13. Ebandju ba bendee babalaka, bendee bamamairisibwa kwemikira yechikolya, neyembanzi, alauma nelufufu lwengaafu sa sasiresibwaa, kwa kukomya emibiri yabo.

13. 어바ᅜᅮ 바 버ᄕᅥ어 바바ᄙᅡ가, 버ᄕᅥ어 바마마이리시봐 궈미기라 여찌고ᄙᅣ, 너여빠ᅜᅵ, 아ᄙᅡ우마 너루푸푸 뤄ᅁᅡ아푸 사 사시러시봐아, 과 구고먀 어미비리 야보.

13. The blood of goats and bulls and the ashes of a heifer sprinkled on those who are ceremonially unclean sanctify them so that they are outwardly clean.

14. Akaba kubiri bacha, mutasene kwemikira ya Kirisito iyete buashi bunene bwekukomya ebandju kurenza emikira yenyama? Bushi Kirisito achanaa yeine era mwa Ongo kurengera ebuashi bweMuchima Mubuya-buya iuthulao esuku nemango. Era kuba mithulo era itete chibi chisibya. Nemikira yai yende yakomya emichima yethu, itenge mwa myanya era itakomire era yende yareta elufu, chasiya thunde thwakorera Ongo iuthula muuma-uma.

14. 아가바 구비리 바짜, 무다서너 궈미기라 야 기리시도 이여더 부아씨 부너너 붜구고먀 어바ᅜᅮ 구러ᄴ 어미기라 여냐마? 부씨 기리시도 아짜나아 여이너 어라 뫄 오ᅌᅩ 구러ᅁᅥ라 어부아씨 붜무찌마 무부야-부야 이우쭈ᄙᅡ오 어수구 너마ᅌᅩ. 어라 구바 미쭈ᄙᅩ 어라 이더더 찌비 찌시뱌. 너미기라 야이 여ᄕᅥ 야고먀 어미찌마 여쭈, 이더ᅁᅥ 뫄 먀냐 어라 이다고미러 어라 여ᄕᅥ 야러다 어루푸, 짜시야 쭈ᄕᅥ 쫘고러라 오ᅌᅩ 이우쭈ᄙᅡ 무우마-우마.

14. How much more, then, will the blood of Christ, who through the eternal Spirit offered himself unblemished to God, cleanse our consciences from acts that lead to death, so that we may serve the living God!

15. Bushi noku, Kirisito iwabikire ebandju mwa buuma na Ongo, kurengera echilaano chiyayaya. Kanji kurengera ekufa kwai, anunwire ebandju kutenga mwa bibi bya bairaa

15. 부씨 노구, 기리시도 이와비기러 어바ᅜᅮ 뫄 부우마 나 오ᅌᅩ, 구러ᅁᅥ라 어찌ᄙᅡ아노 찌야야야. 가ᅜᅵ 구러ᅁᅥ라 어구파 과이, 아누니워러 어바ᅜᅮ 구더ᅁᅡ 뫄 비비 뱌

15. For this reason Christ is the mediator of a new covenant, that those who are called may receive the promised eternal inheritance--now that he

mango babaa bachiri mwa chilaano chibere-bere. Airire bacha, chasiya ebandju ba Ongo amaere babone emwandju wesuku nemango ola abalanyaa.

16. Mwa myasi era yerekere efulao yekulya emwandju, byemire kulosa kanangana kwa ola warekaai afire mira.

17. Efulao yekulya emwandju, yende yakola mango emundju ola wairai ende aba afire mira, si itangakola mango achirio.

18. Kunoku, kwechilaano chibere-bere cha Ongo airaa nebandju, chitakolaa busira kushesha mikira.

19. Musa abalyiraa tanga eBaisiraeli boshi kwa miomba yoshi yeMwaso ithula itechire. Chasinda, era kure atola ematabi memuchi weisopo ma maminyirirwe ku boya bwa mwola bwa mbulyi. Era kulobekamo mwa mikira yebyana byengaafu neyebikolya, era ihoonganyisibwe mwemeshi. Era kumamairisai kwa chitabo cheMwaso nokwa lubaa loshi lweBaisiraeli.

20. Era kuteta mbu: "Enera imikira era yalosa kanangana

바이라아 마꼬 바바아 바찌리 묘 찌라아노 찌버러-버러. 아이리러 바짜, 짜시야 어바누 바 오꼬 아마어러 바보너 어뫄누 워수구 너마꼬 오롸 아바롸냐아.

16. 뫄 먀시 어라 여러거러 어푸롸오 여구럐 어뫄누, 벼미러 구로사 가나롸나 과 오롸 와러가아이 아피러 미라.

17. 어푸롸오 여구럐 어뫄누, 여떠 야고롸 마꼬 어무누 오롸 와이라이 어떠 아바 아피러 미라, 시 이다롸고롸 마꼬 아찌리오.

18. 구노구, 궈찌롸아노 찌버러-버러 짜 오꼬 아이라아 너바누, 찌다고롸아 부시라 구써싸 미기라.

19. 무사 아바레라아 다롸 어바이시라어리 보씨 과 미오빠 요씨 여뫄소 이쭈롸 이더찌러. 짜시따, 어라 구러 아도롸 어마다비 머무찌 워이소포 마 마미네리뤄 구 보야 봐 모롸 봐 뿌레. 어라 구로버가모 뫄 미기라 여뱌나 벼꺄아푸 너여비고롸, 어라 이호오꺄네시붜 뭐머씨. 어라 구마마이리사이 과 찌다보 쩌뫄소 노과 루바아 로씨 뤄바이시라어리.

20. 어라 구더다 뿌: "어너라 이미기라 어라 야로사

has died as a ransom to set them free from the sins committed under the first covenant.

16. In the case of a will, it is necessary to prove the death of the one who made it,

17. because a will is in force only when somebody has died; it never takes effect while the one who made it is living.

18. This is why even the first covenant was not put into effect without blood.

19. When Moses had proclaimed every commandment of the law to all the people, he took the blood of calves, together with water, scarlet wool and branches of hyssop, and sprinkled the scroll and all the people.

20. He said, "This is the blood of the covenant,

echilaano cha Ongo airire nenyu."

21. Kanji Musa era kumamairisa ei mikira kwa hema, nokwa bindju byoshi bya bendee bakoresa mwa kwera Ongo.

22. Rero, kukulyikana noyu Mwaso, ebindju byoshi byende byakomisibwa kurengera emikira. Nebibi bitangababalyirwa busira kusheshekala kwa mikira.

23. Mwa bacha, ebi bindju byomuno butala binalyi nga chimbusa chemyasi era yairibwa kwa nguba. Ebi bindju, byabaa byemire kunde byakomisibwa kurengera emikira yenyama. Si emyasi yekanangana yokwa nguba yemire kukomisibwa kurengera emithulo era ikomire busese kurenza era ibere-bere.

24. Bushi Kirisito ateengiriraa mwa Chisiki Chibuya-buya cha chairwaa nebandju, cha chiri nga chimbusa cheChisiki Chibuya-buya chekanangana. Si yeine eengiriraa kwa nguba, mwa chisiki chemenzemo lwarero era muhondo sa Ongo, chasiya ende athutetera.

가나ⵡ나 어찌롸아노 짜 오ㄲ 아이리러 너뉴."

21. 가찌 무사 어라 구마마이리사 어이 미기라 과 허마, 노과 비뿌 뵤씨 뱌 버더어 바고러사 롸 궈라 오ㄲ.

22. 러로, 구구뤠가나 노유 롸소, 어비뿌 뵤씨 벼더 뱌고미시봐 구러ⵡ라 어미기라. 너비비 비다ⵡ바바뤠롸 부시라 구써써가꽈 과 미기라.

23. 롸 바짜, 어비 비뿌 뵤무노 부다퐈 비나뤠 ⵡ 찌뿌사 쩌먀시 어라 야이리봐 과 우바. 어비 비뿌, 뱌바아 벼미러 구더 뱌고미시봐 구러ⵡ라 어미기라 여냐ⵡ. 시 어먀시 여가나ⵡ나 요과 우바 여미러 구고미시봐 구러ⵡ라 어미쭈로 어라 이고미러 부서서 구러ㅆ 어라 이버러- 버러.

24. 부씨 기리시도 아더어ⵡ리리라아 롸 찌시기 찌부야-부야 짜 짜이롸아 너바뿌, 짜 찌리 ⵡ 찌뿌사 쩌찌시기 찌부야-부야 쩌가나ⵡ나. 시 여이너 어어ⵡ리리라아 과 우바, 롸 찌시기 쩌머써모 퐈러로 어라 무호또 사 오ㄲ, 짜시야 어머 아쭈더더라.

---

which God has commanded you to keep."

21. In the same way, he sprinkled with the blood both the tabernacle and everything used in its ceremonies.

22. In fact, the law requires that nearly everything be cleansed with blood, and without the shedding of blood there is no forgiveness.

23. It was necessary, then, for the copies of the heavenly things to be purified with these sacrifices, but the heavenly things themselves with better sacrifices than these.

24. For Christ did not enter a man-made sanctuary that was only a copy of the true one; he entered heaven itself, now to appear for us in God's presence.

25. eMukulu-kulu webakuhanyi weBayuta ende eengira mwa Chisiki Chibuya-buya Busese chira mwaka, ete emikira yenyama. Si Kirisito ateengiriraa mbiso sinene kwa nguba chasiya ende achaana kuba mithulo chira mango.

26. Akaba bingabere bacha, bingamwemire alyibusibwe mbiso sinene kutengera ekubumbwa kwebutala. Si rero, mwesine suku sebusinda, erire aulukira eri neuma, chasiya akule ebibi byebandju kurengera ekuchana kwai yeine kuba mithulo.

27. Chira mundju abikirirwe kufa euma oshao, nera nyuma sekufa anachinjibusibwa na Ongo.

28. Rero kunoku, ku Kirisito nai achaanaa euma oshao, chasiya akule bibi bya bandju banene. Akahuba kubaha ebwakabiri, ata kwa kukula ebibi, si kwa kununula ebandju ba bamulyinjira.

25. 어무구루-구루 워바구하네 워바유다 어떠 어어삐라 뫄 찌시기 찌부야-부야 부서서 찌라 뫄가, 어더 어미기라 여냐마. 시 기리시도 아더어삐리라아 삐소 시너너 과 응바 짜시야 어떠 아짜아나 구바 미쭈로 찌라 마오.

26. 아가바 비까버러 바짜, 비까뭐미러 아레부시붜 삐소 시너너 구더뻐라 어구부꽈 궈부다꽈. 시 러로, 뭐시너 수구 서부시따, 어리러 아우루기라 어리 너우마, 짜시야 아구뻐 어비비 벼바쭈 구러뻐라 어구짜나 과이 여이너 구바 미쭈로.

27. 찌라 무뿌 아비기리뤄 구파 어우마 오싸오, 너라 뉴마 서구파 아나찌띠부시봐 나 오오.

28. 러로 구노구, 구 기리시도 나이 아짜아나아 어우마 오싸오, 짜시야 아구뻐 비비 뱌 바쭈 바너너. 아가후바 구바하 어봐가비리, 아다 과 구구꽈 어비비, 시 과 구누누꽈 어바쭈 바 바무레찌라.

25. Nor did he enter heaven to offer himself again and again, the way the high priest enters the Most Holy Place every year with blood that is not his own.

26. Then Christ would have had to suffer many times since the creation of the world. But now he has appeared once for all at the end of the ages to do away with sin by the sacrifice of himself.

27. Just as man is destined to die once, and after that to face judgment,

28. so Christ was sacrificed once to take away the sins of many people; and he will appear a second time, not to bear sin, but to bring salvation to those who are waiting for him.

E Baebrania Chikono 10   **어 바어부라니아 찌고노 10**   **Hebrews Chapter 10[NIV]**

1. eMwaso wa Musa chinalyi chimbusa chemabuya me ndonyi, si ata kukalorero kanangana ka kalosa amu mabuya. Bushi noku, eMwaso atangaala chiro na hicha kuira ebandju kuba ba banalumirire, ba bahonda kuchifunda ofu na Ongo, kurengera emithulo era yende yaanyibwa chira mwaka.

1. 어뫄소 와 무사 찌나례 찌뿌사 쪄마부야 머 또네, 시 아다 구가료러로 가나꺄나 가 가료사 아무 마부야. 부씨 노구, 어뫄소 아다꺄아롸 찌로 나 히짜 구이라 어바쭈 구바 바 바나루미리러, 바 바호따 구찌푸따 오푸 나 오꼬, 구러꺼라 어미쭈로 어라 여떠 야아네봐 찌라 뫄가.

1. The law is only a shadow of the good things that are coming--not the realities themselves. For this reason it can never, by the same sacrifices repeated endlessly year after year, make perfect those who draw near to worship.

2. Akaba ba benjire beera Ongo mwei njira, bangakomisibwe ebibi byabo eri neuma oshao, batangenjire bachiribukira mwa michima bushi nebibi byabo. Aola, ei mithulo bangarekire kunde banai.

2. 아가바 바 버찌러 버어라 오꼬 뭐이 찌라, 바꺄고미시붜 어비비 뱌보 어리 너우마 오싸오, 바다꺼찌러 바찌리부기라 뫄 미찌마 부씨 너비비 뱌보. 아오롸, 어이 미쭈로 바꺄러기러 구떠 바나이.

2. If it could, would they not have stopped being offered? For the worshipers would have been cleansed once for all, and would no longer have felt guilty for their sins.

3. Si oku kwana ei mithulo chira mwaka, kwende kwakengesa ebandju ebibi byabo.

3. 시 오구 과나 어이 미쭈로 찌라 뫄가, 궈떠 과거꺼사 어바쭈 어비비 뱌보.

3. But those sacrifices are an annual reminder of sins,

4. Bushi emikira yebanzi neyebikolya, itangaala kukula ebibi.

4. 부씨 어미기라 여바찌 너여비고랴, 이다꺄아롸 구구롸 어비비.

4. because it is impossible for the blood of bulls and goats to take away sins.

5. Bushi noku, mango Kirisito abaa alyi mu kubaha muno butala, aburaa Ongo mbu: "Woyo, utasima mbu ebandju bakuthulaa mithulo. Si wanyimbasaa emubiri.

5. 부씨 노구, 마꼬 기리시도 아바아 아례 무 구바하 무노 부다롸, 아부라아 오꼬 뿌: "오요, 우다시마 뿌 어바쭈 바구쭈롸아 미쭈로. 시 와네빠사아 어무비리.

5. Therefore, when Christ came into the world, he said: "Sacrifice and offering you did not desire, but a body you prepared for me;

6 .Utamoeraa mithulo ya nyama sa sisiresibwe, nesi mithulo ya kubabalyira ebibi.

6 .우다모어라아 미쭈로 야 냐마 사 시시러시붜, 너시 미쭈로 야 구바바례라 어비비.

6. with burnt offerings and sin offerings you were not pleased.

7. Nera kure nateta mbu: Unyiri ano, Ongo Tata nabahire kuira ekuhonda kwao, kukulyikana nokwa byanjikirwe era luulu sanyi mwa chibungo chechitabo.?

7. 너라 구러 나더다 뿌: 우네리 아노, 오꼬 다다 나바히러 구이라 어구호따 과오, 구구쀄가나 노과 뱌찌기뤄 어라 루우루 사네 뫄 찌부꼬 쩌찌다보.?

7. Then I said, 'Here I am--it is written about me in the scroll-- I have come to do your will, O God.' "

8. Kirisito atetaa tanga mbu: "Utasima nesi utamoeraa mbu ebandju bakuthulaa mithulo, nesi mithulo ya nyama sa sisiresibwe, nesi mithulo ya kubabalyira ebibi." Atetaa bacha, chiro angaba mbu ei mithulo yoshi yendee yaanyibwa kukulyikana nokwa Mwaso athula atechire.

8. 기리시도 아더다아 다까 뿌: "우다시마 너시 우다모어라아 뿌 어바뉴 바구쭈롸아 미쭈론, 너시 미쭈론 야 냐마 사 시시러시붸, 너시 미쭈론 야 구바바롄라 어비비." 아더다아 바짜, 찌로 아까바 뿌 어이 미쭈론 요씨 여떠어 야아네봐 구구쀄가나 노과 뫄소 아쭈롸 아더찌러.

8. First he said, "Sacrifices and offerings, burnt offerings and sin offerings you did not desire, nor were you pleased with them" (although the law required them to be made).

9. Chasinda, era kure ateta mbu: "Unyiri ano, nabahire kuira ekuhonda kwao." Mwa bacha, ahandjure ei emithulo ibere-bere na kuinganya nekuchaana kwai yeine.

9. 짜시따, 어라 구러 아더다 뿌: "우네리 아노, 나바히러 구이라 어구호따 과오." 뫄 바짜, 아하뉴러 어이 어미쭈론 이버러-버러 나 구이까냐 너구짜아나 과이 여이너.

9. Then he said, "Here I am, I have come to do your will." He sets aside the first to establish the second.

10. Yesu Kirisito airaa ekuhonda kwa Ongo, era kuchaana yeine kuba mithulo euma oshao. Mwa bacha, ebibi byethu byakulyibwe, chasiya thube bandju ba bakomisibwe.

10. 여수 기리시도 아이라아 어구호따 과 오꼬, 어라 구짜아나 여이너 구바 미쭈론 어우마 오싸오. 뫄 바짜, 어비비 벼쭈 뱌구쀄붸, 짜시야 쭈버 바뉴 바 바고미시붸.

10. And by that will, we have been made holy through the sacrifice of the body of Jesus Christ once for all.

11. Chira kuhanyi ende eemanga chira lusuku kwa kukola emulyimo wekwera Ongo. Chira mango, ende aana ei mithulo inei-inei, si ei

11. 찌라 구하네 어떠 어어마까 찌라 루수구 과 구고롸 어무롐모 워꿔라 오꼬. 찌라 마꼬, 어떠 아아나 어이 미쭈론 이너이-이너이, 시

11. Day after day every priest stands and performs his religious duties; again and again he offers the same sacrifices, which can

mithulo itangaala kukula ebibi chiro na hicha.

12. Si Kirisito yeke, athulaa mithulo yiuma oshao bushi nebibi. Chasinda, era kwire aya kwikala esuku nemango kwa lunda lwemalyo ma Ongo.

13. Rero aola, alyinjirira kuikira Ongo aire ebarenda bai kuba chisimachiro chai.

14. Kurengera ei mithulo yiuma era athulaa, airire ebandju ba bakomisibwe kuba ba balumirire esuku nemango.

15. eMuchima Mubuya-buya, nai enjire anateta mbu ei myasi inalyi ya kanangana. Atetaa tanga mbu:

16. "Enawethu atechire mbu: Chechine chi chilaano nyingaira nabo mwa suku sa seshire: Nyingabika eMwaso wanyi mwa emichima yabo, na kwanjikao mwa mianyisa yabo."

17. Kanji atechire mbu: "Ndakanachikengere ebibi byabo, nesi emabi mabo chiro na hicha."

18. Rero, mango ebibi byende byaba byababalyirwe, kutachiba myasi ya kwana

어이 미쭈론 이다꺄아롸 구구롸 어비비 찌로 나 히짜.

12. 시 기리시도 여거, 아쭈롸아 미쭈론 에우마 오싸오 부씨 너비비. 짜시따, 어라 귀러 아야 귀가롸 어수구 너마꼬 과 룬따 뤠마룐 마 오꼬.

13. 러로 아오롸, 아뤠찌리라 구이기라 오꼬 아이러 어바러따 바이 구바 찌시마찌로 짜이.

14. 구러꺼라 어이 미쭈론 에우마 어라 아쭈롸아, 아이리러 어바뉴 바 바고미시붜 구바 바 바루미리러 어수구 너마꼬.

15. 어무찌마 무부야-부야, 나이 어찌러 아나더다 뿌 어이 먀시 이나뤠 야 가나꺄나. 아더다아 다꺄 뿌:

16. "어나워쭈 아더찌러 뿌: 쩌찌너 찌 찌롸아노 네꺄이라 나보 먀 수구 사 서씨러: 네꺄비가 어뫄소 와네 먀 어미찌마 야보, 나 과찌가오 먀 미아네사 야보."

17. 가찌 아더찌러 뿌: "따가나찌거꺼러 어비비 뱌보, 너시 어마비 마보 찌로 나 히짜."

18. 러로, 마꼬 어비비 벼떠 뱌바 뱌바바뤠뤄, 구다찌바 먀시 야 과나 미쭈론 과

never take away sins.

12. But when this priest had offered for all time one sacrifice for sins, he sat down at the right hand of God.

13. Since that time he waits for his enemies to be made his footstool,

14. because by one sacrifice he has made perfect forever those who are being made holy.

15. The Holy Spirit also testifies to us about this. First he says:

16. "This is the covenant I will make with them after that time, says the Lord. I will put my laws in their hearts, and I will write them on their minds."

17. Then he adds: "Their sins and lawless acts I will remember no more."

18. And where these have been forgiven, there is no longer any sacrifice for sin.

mithulo kwa kukulabi. 구구쫘비.

19. Banyakethu, thwera thwete ebuhuru bwekweengirira mwa Chisiki Chibuya-buya busese kurengera emikira ya Yesu.

19. 바냐거쭈, 쭤라 쭤더 어부후루 붜궈어삐리라 먀 찌시기 찌부야-부야 부서서 구러어라 어미기라 야 여수.

19. Therefore, brothers, since we have confidence to enter the Most Holy Place by the blood of Jesus,

20. Athuboorere njira iyayaya ya kalamo era iulukanyire mwa ngwaya era yabaa yahumba mwa luhu lwa Ongo, kukuteta mbu emubiri wai yeine.

20. 아쭈보오러러 씨라 이야야야 야 가쫘모 어라 이우루가녀러 먀 꽈야 어라 야바아 야후빠 먀 루후 쫘 오꼬, 구구더다 뿌 어무비리 와이 여이너.

20. by a new and living way opened for us through the curtain, that is, his body,

21. Kanji thwera thwete eMukulu-kulu webakuhanyi ola wimangirire enyumba ya Ongo.

21. 가찌 쭤라 쭤더 어무구루-구루 워바구하니 오라 위마삐리러 어뉴빠 야 오꼬.

21. and since we have a great priest over the house of God,

22. Emichima yethu yakomisibwe kutenga mu chira mianyisa ibi era yende yathulyibusisa mwa ndanda. Nemibiri yethu yalongibwe mwa meshi ma matathwangire. Bushi noku, thundaa thwachifunda ofu na Ongo na muchima muuma, na kuata bwemeresi bwa bulumirire.

22. 어미찌마 여쭈 야고미시붜 구더빠 무 찌라 미아네사 이비 어라 여너 야쭈레부시사 먀 따따. 너미비리 여쭈 야론삐붜 먀 머씨 마 마다쫘삐러. 부씨 노구, 쭈따아 쫘찌푸따 오푸 나 오꼬 나 무찌마 무우마, 나 구아다 붜머러시 봐 부루미리러.

22. let us draw near to God with a sincere heart in full assurance of faith, having our hearts sprinkled to cleanse us from a guilty conscience and having our bodies washed with pure water.

23. Tundaa thwasimika busese mwa munyiiro ola thwende thwateta era luulu sao era muhondo sebandju busira kutama, bushi Ongo ende anaira bya alanyaa.

23. 두따아 쫘시미가 부서서 먀 무네이로 오라 쭤더 쫘더다 어라 루우루 사오 어라 무호또 서바쭈 부시라 구다마, 부씨 오꼬 어너 아나이라 뱌 아쫘냐아.

23. Let us hold unswervingly to the hope we profess, for he who promised is faithful.

24. Kanji thundaa thwaanyisa kute ku thungeresanya emisi, mwa kunde thwasima ebandju

24. 가찌 쭈따아 쫘아네사 구더 구 쭈떠러사냐 어미시, 먀 구떠 쫘시마 어바쭈 노와

24. And let us consider how we may spur one another on toward love and good

nomwa kuira emabuya.

25. Thutarekaa kunde thwaika kwa nyibuanano sebemeresi, ngokwa bandju bauma bathula bakomere. Si thundaa thwasesanya emichima busese, bushi ngokwa munasene, elusuku lwekufuluka kwa Enawethu lulyi ofu.

26. Thwakangirisibwe mira ekumenyerera emyasi yekanangana. Rero, akaba thungaendekera kunde thwairirira ebibi, aola kutachiri mithulo era ingachiala kukula ebi bibi.

27. Mwa bacha, kwanashiba kulyinjirira na buba bunene ebuchinjibusi bwa Ongo, nemarunga memulyiro ma makwocha ebarenda bai.

28. Mango emundju endee anana kuira kwa Mwaso wa Musa atechire, endee eechibwa busira bonjo akaba bandju babiri nesi bahathu bangateta mbu bachiloreraa kwa aishaa muo.

29. Rero, emundju ola wende wakena eMwana wa Ongo, mutasene kwa akachinjibusibwa busese? Oyu mundju, atathunda emikira yechilaano era yamukomyaa kutenga mwa bibi. Kanji ende

구이라 어마부야.

25. 쭈다러가아 구떠 쫘이가 과 내부아나노 서버머러시, 꼬과 바쮸 바우마 바쭈쫘 바고머러. 시 쭈따아 쫘서사냐 어미찌마 부서서, 부씨 꼬과 무나서너, 어루수구 뭐구푸루가 과 어나워쭈 루레 오푸.

26. 쫘가삐리시붜 미라 어구머녀러라 어먀시 여가나꺄나. 러로, 아가바 쭈까어떠거라 구떠 쫘이리리라 어비비, 아오쫘 구다찌리 미쭈뢴 어라 이까찌아쫘 구구꽈 어비 비비.

27. 와 바짜, 과나씨바 구레찌리라 나 부바 부너너 어부찌찌부시 봐 오꼬, 너마루까 머무레로 마 마꼬짜 어바러따 바이.

28. 마꼬 어무뚜 어떠어 아나나 구이라 과 묘소 와 무사 아더찌러, 어떠어 어어찌봐 부시라 보쪼 아가바 바뉴 바비리 너시 바하쭈 바까더다 뿌 바찌뢴러라아 과 아이싸아 무오.

29. 러로, 어무뚜 오쫘 워떠 와거나 어뫄나 와 오꼬, 무다서너 과 아가찌찌부시봐 부서서? 오유 무뚜, 아다쭈따 어미기라 여찌쫘아노 어라 야무고먀아 구더까 뫄 비비. 가찌 어떠 아가빠 어무찌마

deeds.

25. Let us not give up meeting together, as some are in the habit of doing, but let us encourage one another--and all the more as you see the Day approaching.

26. If we deliberately keep on sinning after we have received the knowledge of the truth, no sacrifice for sins is left,

27. but only a fearful expectation of judgment and of raging fire that will consume the enemies of God.

28. Anyone who rejected the law of Moses died without mercy on the testimony of two or three witnesses.

29. How much more severely do you think a man deserves to be punished who has trampled the Son of God under foot, who has treated as an unholy thing the blood of the covenant

akamba eMuchima Mubuya-buya ola wende wathukangirisa ebubuya bwa Ongo.

30. Kubinalyi, thwishi ola watetaa mbu: "Ekuchifuna kulyi kwanyi. Nyono nyi nyikeemba chira muuma kukulyikana na bya emire kweembibwa." Kanji atetaa mbu: "Enawethu akachinjibusa elubaa lwai."

31. Chiri chisibu busese ekutowera mwa mino sa Ongo, iuthula muuma-uma!

32. Mukengeraa emyasi era yabaikiraa kwa mira mango ebulangare bwa Ongo bwabalomekeraa. Mwesi suku, mwarengaa mu malyibuko manene busese, si mwera kunasimika.

33. Bihangi biuma mwakambibwaa na kulyibusibwa changanama. Na binji bihangi mwera kuba kwa lunda lwa ba balyibusibwa.

34. Mwalyibukaa alauma nebandju bemulyisi mwa malyibuko mabo. Mwanyaibwaa ebindju byenyu, mwera kweemerera kuesabi na lumoo. Bushi mwaba mwishi kwa mwete buare bunene

무부야-부야 오라 워떠 와쭈가삐리사 어부부야 봐 오꼬.

30. 구비나레, 쮜씨 오롸 와더다아 뿌: "어구찌푸나 구레 과내. 뇨노 네 네거어빠 찌라 무우마 구구레가나 나 뱌 어미러 궈어삐봐." 가찌 아더다아 뿌: "어나워쭈 아가찌씨부사 어루바아 롸이."

31. 찌리 찌시부 부서서 어구도워라 마 미노 사 오꼬, 이우쭈롸 무우마-우마!

32. 무거떠라아 어먀시 어라 야바이기라아 과 미라 마꼬 어부롸따러 봐 오꼬 봐바로머거라라. 뭐시 수구, 롸러따아 무 마레부고 마너너 부서서, 시 뭐라 구나시미가.

33. 비하삐 비우마 롸가삐봐아 나 구레부시봐 짜따나마. 나 비찌 비하삐 뭐라 구바 과 루따 롸 바 바레부시봐.

34. 롸레부가아 아롸우마 너바쭈 버무레시 마 마레부고 마보. 마냐이봐아 어비쭈 벼뉴, 뭐라 궈어머러라 구어사비 나 루모오. 부씨 롸바아 뮈씨 과 뭐더 부아러 부너너 구러싸 어벼라, 가찌

that sanctified him, and who has insulted the Spirit of grace?

30. For we know him who said, "It is mine to avenge; I will repay," and again, "The Lord will judge his people."

31. It is a dreadful thing to fall into the hands of the living God.

32. Remember those earlier days after you had received the light, when you stood your ground in a great contest in the face of suffering.

33. Sometimes you were publicly exposed to insult and persecution; at other times you stood side by side with those who were so treated.

34. You sympathized with those in prison and joyfully accepted the confiscation of your property, because you knew that you yourselves had better and lasting possessions.

kurenza ebyera, kanji bwa
butakawe.

35. Rero, mutaesaa emunyiiro
wenyu, bushi iukathuma
mwabona lweembo lunene.

36. Mwemire kuata bushibirisi,
chasiya munde mwaira
ekuhonda kwa Ongo, mubone
bya alanyaa.

37. Bushi eMaanjiko Mabuya-
buya mathula matechire mbu:
"Mu bihangi bieke, bieke
busese, oyu wemire kubaha,
angabaha, nekubaha kwai
kuteerise!"
38. Ongo atechire mbu:
"Emundju ola uthungenene
era muhondo sanyi, emibere
yai ingende yeemangira kwa
bwemeresi. Si akaba angahuba
era nyuma, ndangasimisibwa
nai."
39. Tubano thuta bandju ba
kuhuba era nyuma, na kuya
mwa muero. Si thulyi bandju
ba bete bwemeresi, kanji ba
balyi mwa njira
yekununulyibwa.

봐 부다가워.

35. 러로, 무다어사아
어무네이로 워뉴, 부씨
이우가쭈마 뫄보나 뤄어뽀
루너너.

36. 뭐미러 구아다
부씨비리시, 짜시야 무떠
뫄이라 어구호따 과 오꼬,
무보너 뱌 아꽈냐아.

37. 부씨 어마아찌고 마부야-
부야 마쭈꽈 마더찌러 뿌: "무
비하삐 비어거, 비어거
부서서, 오유 워미러 구바하,
아꽈바하, 너구바하 과이
구더어리서!"
38. 오꼬 아더찌러 뿌: "어무뚜
오꽈 우쭈어너너 어라 무호또
사니, 어미버러 야이 이어떠
여어마삐라 과 뷔머러시. 시
아가바 아꽈후바 어라 뉴마,
따꽈시미시봐 나이."

39. 두바노 쭈다 바뚜 바
구후바 어라 뉴마, 나 구야 뫄
무어로. 시 쭈꼐 바뚜 바 버더
뷔머러시, 가찌 바 바꼐 뫄
찌라 여구누누꼐봐.

35. So do not throw away
your confidence; it will be
richly rewarded.

36. You need to persevere
so that when you have
done the will of God, you
will receive what he has
promised.

37. For in just a very little
while, "He who is coming
will come and will not delay.

38. But my righteous one
will live by faith. And if he
shrinks back, I will not be
pleased with him."

39. But we are not of those
who shrink back and are
destroyed, but of those who
believe and are saved.

E Baebrania Chikono 11   **어 바어부라니아 찌고노 11**   **Hebrews Chapter 11[NIV]**

1. Ekuata ebwemeresi mu Ongo, kulyi kuata ekanangana kebindju bya mundju alangalyire. Kanji kulyi kweemerera kanangana kwa bya bitasenekeko bithulao.

2. Obu bwemeresi, bu bwendee bwathuma bahokulu basimisa Ongo.

3. Ebwemeresi bu bwende bwathuma thwamenyerera kanangana kwa Ongo abumbaa byoshi kurengera echinwa chai. Mwa bacha, ebindju bya bisenekeko byairwaa kutengera kwa bya bitasenekeko.

4. Ebwemeresi bwa Aberi bu bwathumaa eeresa Ongo emithulo era ikomire busese, kurenza era ya Kaini. Obu bwemeresi bwai, bu bwathumaa Ongo amutola nga mundju ola uthungenene, bushi Ongo amoeraa emithulo yai. Kanji obu bwemeresi bwa Aberi bu bwathuma emyasi yai ichiri yomvikala, chiro mbu afire mira.

5. Ebwemeresi bwa Enoki bu bwathumaa erusibwa kwa nguba busira kufa. Kutalyi chiro na mundju asibya ola wachihubaa kumulolako, bushi

1. 어구아다 어뭐머러시 무 오쯔, 구레 구아다 어가나빠나 거비쭈 뱌 무뚜 아롸빠레러. 가찌 구레 궈어머러라 가나빠나 과 뱌 비다서너거고 비쭈롸오.

2. 오부 뭐머러시, 부 뭐떠어 봐쭈마 바호구루 바시미사 오쯔.

3. 어뭐머러시 부 뭐떠 봐쭈마 쫘머녀러라 가나빠나 과 오쯔 아부빠아 뵤씨 구러뻐러 어찌냐 짜이. 마 바쨔, 어비쭈 뱌 비서너거고 뱌이롸아 구더뻐라 과 뱌 비다서너거고.

4. 어뭐머러시 봐 아버리 부 봐쭈마아 어어러사 오쯔 어미쭈론 어라 이고미러 부서서, 구러싸 어라 야 가이니. 오부 뭐머러시 봐이, 부 봐쭈마아 오쯔 아무도롸 빠 무뚜 오라 우쭈뻐너너, 부씨 오쯔 아모어라아 어미쭈론 야이. 가찌 오부 뭐머러시 봐 아버리 부 봐쭈마 어먀시 야이 이찌리 요뻬가롸, 찌로 뿌 아피러 미라.

5. 어뭐머러시 봐 어노기 부 봐쭈마아 어루시봐 과 우바 부시라 구파. 구다레 찌로 나 무뚜 아시뱌 오라 와찌후바아 구무론라고, 부씨 오쯔 아바아

1. Now faith is being sure of what we hope for and certain of what we do not see.

2. This is what the ancients were commended for.

3. By faith we understand that the universe was formed at God's command, so that what is seen was not made out of what was visible.

4. By faith Abel offered God a better sacrifice than Cain did. By faith he was commended as a righteous man, when God spoke well of his offerings. And by faith he still speaks, even though he is dead.

5. By faith Enoch was taken from this life, so that he did not experience death; he could not be found, because God had taken him

Ongo abaa amwerusise mira kwa nguba. eMaanjiko Mabuya-buya mathula matechire mbu era muhondo Enoki erusibwe kwa nguba, endee asimisa Ongo.

6. Kutalyi mundju ola ungaala kunde asimisa Ongo akaba atete ebwemeresi. Bushi ola wahonda kuchifunda ofu na Ongo, emire kweemerera kwa Ongo alyio, na kweemerera kwa Ongo ende eeresa ba bamuhonda elweembo.

7. Ebwemeresi bwa Nowa bu bwathumaa athunda emyasi era Ongo amuburaa era luulu sebya byabaa byemire kuika, bya byabaa bitasa kulorekanako. Era kwaanga emashuwa kwa kununula engumo yai. Mwa bacha, mu achinjibusaa ebandju bomwa butala. Kanji obu bwemeresi bwai, bu bwathumaa Ongo amutola nga mundju ola uthungenene.

8. Ebwemeresi bwa Aburahamu bu bwathumaa aira bya Ongo amuburaa, mango amwamaalaa. Era kuya mwa chio cha Ongo abaa emire kumweresa kuba mwandju. Era kunaenda busira kumenya era aya.

아뭐루시서 미라 과 우빠.
어마아찌고 마부야-부야
마쭈콰 마더찌러 뿌 어라
무호또 어노기 어루시붜 과
우빠, 어떠어 아시미사 오꼬.

6. 구다레 무뚜 오라 우빠아콰
구떠 아시미사 오꼬 아가바
아더더 어뷔머러시. 부씨 오콰
와호따 구찌푸따 오푸 나
오꼬, 어미러 귀어머러라 과
오꼬 아레오, 나 귀어머러라
과 오꼬 어떠 어어러사 바
바무호따 어뤄어뽀.

7. 어뷔머러시 봐 노와 부
봐쭈마아 아쭈따 어먀시 어라
오꼬 아무부라아 어라 루우루
서뱌 뱌바아 벼미러 구이가,
뱌 뱌바아 비다사
구로러가나고. 어라 과아빠
어마수와 과 구누누콰 어꾸모
야이. 봐 바짜, 무
아찌찌부사아 어바뚜 보봐
부다콰. 가찌 오부 붜머러시
봐이, 부 봐쭈마아 오꼬
아무도콰 빠 무뚜 오콰
우쭈뻐너너.

8. 어뷔머러시 봐 아부라하무
부 봐쭈마아 아이라 뱌 오꼬
아무부라아, 마꼬
아뫄마아콰아. 어라 구야 봐
찌오 짜 오꼬 아바아 어미러
구뭐러사 구바 뫄뚜. 어라
구나어따 부시라 구머냐 어라
아야.

away. For before he was taken, he was commended as one who pleased God.

6. And without faith it is impossible to please God, because anyone who comes to him must believe that he exists and that he rewards those who earnestly seek him.

7. By faith Noah, when warned about things not yet seen, in holy fear built an ark to save his family. By his faith he condemned the world and became heir of the righteousness that comes by faith.

8. By faith Abraham, when called to go to a place he would later receive as his inheritance, obeyed and went, even though he did not know where he was going.

9. Ebwemeresi bwai bu bwathumaa ekala nga mubunga mwa chio cha Ongo amulanyaa. Era kubera mwa hema, ngokwa Isaka, na Yakobo banaberaamo. Abola nabo, Ongo aneeresaabo echi chiraane.

10. Aburahamu abaa alyinjira kwikala mwa musi ola wimbirwe kwa musingi ukoochire busese. Oyu musi, Ongo yeine iwaataa emianyisa kute angaimbwa kanji iwanaimbaao.

11. Ebwemeresi bwa Sara, muka Aburahamu bu bwathumaa Ongo amweresa ebuashi bwekubuta emwana, chiro angaba mbu abaa era mweekulu busese kanji abaa athula ngumba. Abaa aneeshi kanangana kwa Ongo ende aira bya alaanyaa.

12. Rero, kurengera Aburahamu iwabaa wahonda kufa, kwera kubuchibwa mbaa sinene busese nga ngununu sokwa nguba, kanji nga mishee yokwa musike senyanja, era itangaanjibwa.

13. Abu bandju boshi, bafaa bete ebwemeresi mwa ndanda sa Ongo. Batabonaa ebindju bya Ongo alanyaabo. Si

9. 어붜머러시 봐이 부 봐쭈마아 어가퐈 ㄲ 무부ㄲ 롸 찌오 짜 오꼬 아무퐈냐아. 어라 구버라 롸 허마, 꼬과 이사가, 나 야고보 바나버라아모. 아보퐈 나보, 오꼬 아너어러사아보 어찌 찌라아너.

10. 아부라하무 아바아 아뤠찌라 귀가퐈 롸 무시 오롸 위뻬뤄 과 무시ㄲ 우고오찌러 부서서. 오유 무시, 오꼬 여이너 이와아다아 어미아네사 구더 아까이뺘 가찌 이와나이빠아오.

11. 어붜머러시 봐 사라, 무가 아부라하무 부 봐쭈마아 오꼬 아뭐러사 어부아씨 붜구부다 어롸나, 찌로 아까바 뿌 아바아 어라 뭐어구루 부서서 가찌 아바아 아쭈롸 꾸빠. 아바아 아너어씨 가나까나 과 오꼬 어떠 아이라 뱌 아퐈아냐아.

12. 러로, 구러꺼라 아부라하무 이와바아 와호ㄸ 구파, 궈라 구부찌봐 빠아 시너너 부서서 ㄲ 꾸누누 소과 꾸바, 가찌 ㄲ 미써어 요과 무시거 서냐짜, 어라 이다까아찌봐.

13. 아부 바뉴 보씨, 바파아 버더 어붜머러시 롸 따따 사 오꼬. 바다보나아 어비꾸 뱌 오꼬 아퐈냐아보. 시

9. By faith he made his home in the promised land like a stranger in a foreign country; he lived in tents, as did Isaac and Jacob, who were heirs with him of the same promise.

10. For he was looking forward to the city with foundations, whose architect and builder is God.

11. By faith Abraham, even though he was past age-- and Sarah herself was barren--was enabled to become a father because he considered him faithful who had made the promise.

12. And so from this one man, and he as good as dead, came descendants as numerous as the stars in the sky and as countless as the sand on the seashore.

13. All these people were still living by faith when they died. They did not receive the things promised;

babiloreraako marerere, na kumoerabi. Batetaa changanama mbu balyi baenyi kanji barenganjira muno butala.

14. Abu bandju mwa kuteta bacha, balosa kanangana kwa bahonda echabo chio.

15. Akaba bangenjire bafula echio cha batengaamo, kutalyi cha chingabangikire ekufulukamo.

16. Si kanangana echio cha chikomire busese kurenza echera, chi babaa bahonda, kukuteta mbu echio chokwa nguba. Bushi noku, Ongo atafa honyi sa kwerikibwa mbu alyi Ongo wabo. Kanji akunganyisisebo mira emusi.

17. Ebwemeresi bwa Aburahamu bu bwathumaa aana emuala Isaka kuba mithulo ya kusiresibwa, mango Ongo aerekaa ebwemeresi bwai.

18. Ongo abaa amulaanyise mira mbu: "Kurengera Isaka ku ukabona enyibuto sa nakulaanyaa. "Si chiro bacha, Aburahamu abaa aneemerere kwaana oyu mwana wai wechihwa.

바비� 로러라아고 마러러러, 나 구모어라비. 바더다아 짜까나마 뿌 바레 바어네 가찌 바러까찌라 무노 부다꽈.

14. 아부 바쭈 똬 구더다 짜, 바룬사 가나까나 꽈 바호따 어짜보 찌오.

15. 아가바 바꺼찌러 바푸꽈 어찌오 짜 바더까아모, 구다레 짜 찌까바꺼기러 어구푸루가모.

16. 시 가나까나 어찌오 짜 찌고미러 부서서 구러싸 어쩌라, 찌 바바아 바호따, 구구더다 뿌 어찌오 쪼꽈 우바. 부씨 노구, 오끄 아다파 호네 사 궈리기봐 뿌 아레 오끄 와보. 가찌 아구까네시서보 미라 어무시.

17. 어붜머러시 봐 아부라하무 부 봐쭈마아 아아나 어무아꽈 이사가 구바 미쭈룬 야 구시러시봐, 마끄 오끄 아어러가아 어붜머러시 봐이.

18. 오끄 아바아 아무꽈아네서 미라 뿌: "구러꺼라 이사가 구 우가보나 어네부도 사 나구꽈아냐아. "시 찌로 바짜, 아부라하무 아바아 아너어머러러 과아나 오유 꽈나 와이 워찌화.

they only saw them and welcomed them from a distance. And they admitted that they were aliens and strangers on earth.

14. People who say such things show that they are looking for a country of their own.

15. If they had been thinking of the country they had left, they would have had opportunity to return.

16. Instead, they were longing for a better country--a heavenly one. Therefore God is not ashamed to be called their God, for he has prepared a city for them.

17. By faith Abraham, when God tested him, offered Isaac as a sacrifice. He who had received the promises was about to sacrifice his one and only son,

18. even though God had said to him, "It is through Isaac that your offspring will be reckoned."

19. Aburahamu abaa aneeshi kanangana kwa Ongo ete ebuashi bwekoomwola Isaka mwa bafu. Bushi noku, Ongo era kumufulusisa oyu mwana wai, era kunaba ngola womwokire mwa bafu.

20. Ebwemeresi bwa Isaka bu bwathumaa aahanyira Yakobo na Esau kukulyikana nemyasi era ikabaikira.

21. Ebwemeresi bwa Yakobo bu bwathumaa mango abaa ahonda kutowa emuchima, aahanyira ebana babiri ba Yosefu. Era kweeyamira kwa chikoma chai, na era Ongo.

22. Ebwemeresi bwa Yosefu bu bwathumaa mango abaa ahonda kutowa emuchima, ateta era luulu sechihangi cha Baisiraeli bakatenga mwa chio cheMisiri. Era kueresabo emiomba era luulu semakinya mai.l

23. Ebwemeresi bwebasere ba Musa bu bwathumaa bamala myesi ehathu bamubishire era nyuma sekubuchibwa kwai. Bairaa bacha, bushi balolaa kwa alyi mwana ola wete huhe lya lyikomire busese, kanji batoobaa emuomba wa mwami weMisiri.

19. 아부라하무 아바아 아너어씨 가나꺄나 과 오꼬 어더 어부아씨 붜고오모롸 이사가 마 바푸. 부씨 노구, 오꼬 어라 구무푸루시사 오유 먀나 와이, 어라 구나바 꼬롸 오모기러 마 바푸.

20. 어붜머러시 봐 이사가 부 봐쭈마아 아아하니라 야고보 나 어사우 구구롖가나 너먀시 어라 이가바이기라.

21. 어붜머러시 봐 야고보 부 봐쭈마아 마꼬 아바아 아호따 구도와 어무찌마, 아아하니라 어바나 바비리 바 요서푸. 어라 궈어야미라 과 찌고마 짜이, 나 어라 오꼬.

22. 어붜머러시 봐 요서푸 부 봐쭈마아 마꼬 아바아 아호따 구도와 어무찌마, 아더다 어라 루우루 서찌하삐 짜 바이시라어삐 바가더따 마 찌오 쩌미시리. 어라 구어러사보 어미오빠 어라 루우루 서마기냐 마이.루

23. 어붜머러시 붜바서러 바 무사 부 봐쭈마아 바마롸 며시 아하쭈 바무비씨러 어라 뉴마 서구부찌봐 과이. 바이라아 바짜, 부씨 바롣롸아 과 아뗴 먀나 오롸 워더 후허 롸 롖고미러 부서서, 가찌 바도오바아 어무오빠 와 먀미 워미시리.

19. Abraham reasoned that God could raise the dead, and figuratively speaking, he did receive Isaac back from death.

20. By faith Isaac blessed Jacob and Esau in regard to their future.

21. By faith Jacob, when he was dying, blessed each of Joseph's sons, and worshiped as he leaned on the top of his staff.

22. By faith Joseph, when his end was near, spoke about the exodus of the Israelites from Egypt and gave instructions about his bones.

23. By faith Moses' parents hid him for three months after he was born, because they saw he was no ordinary child, and they were not afraid of the king's edict.

24. Ebwemeresi bwa Musa bu bwathumaa mango abaa era mundju asene, ananaa kunde erikibwa mbu alyi muala wa mwalyi wa mwami weMisiri.

25. Era kulondola ekulyibukira alauma nebandju ba Ongo, wakuchimoeresa mwa bibi ku bihangi bieke.

26. Alolaa kwekukenyibwa ngokwa Masiya akenyibwaa, ku kwete mufa munene busese kurenza ebuare bweMisiri. Airaa bacha, bushi abaa abikire emuchima kwa lweembo lwa Ongo akamweresa.

27. Ebwemeresi bwa Musa bu bwathumaa atenga mwa chio cheMisiri busira kwoobaa ebukalyi bwa mwami. Asimikaa busese nga mundju ola usene ku Ongo noku Ongo atalorekanako.

28. Ebwemeresi bwai bu bwathumaa aba mubere kutangirisa elusuku lukulu lwePasaka. Kanji era kubura eBaisiraeli mbu bamamairisaa emikira yembulyi kwa nyisi senyumba sabo, chasiya mango endonyi ola wende wasikya ebandju angarenga, atetaa efula seBaisiraeli.

24. 어뷔머러시 봐 무사 부 봐쭈마아 마꼬 아바아 어라 무뚜 아서너, 아나나아 구너 어리기봐 뿌 아레 무아꽈 와 꽈레 와 꽈미 워미시리.

25. 어라 구론또꽈 어구레부기라 아꽈우마 너바꾸 바 오꼬, 와구찌모어러사 꽈 비비 구 비하삐 비어거.

26. 아론꽈아 궈구거네봐 꼬과 마시야 아거네봐아, 구 궈더 무파 무너너 부서서 구러싸 어부아러 붜미시리. 아이라아 바짜, 부씨 아바아 아비기러 어무찌마 과 뤄어뽀 꽈 오꼬 아가뭐러사.

27. 어뷔머러시 봐 무사 부 봐쭈마아 아더꽈 꽈 찌오 쩌미시리 부시라 교오바아 어부가레 봐 꽈미. 아시미가아 부서서 꽈 무뚜 오라 우서너 구 오꼬 노구 오꼬 아다로러가나고.

28. 어뷔머러시 봐이 부 봐쭈마아 아바 무버러 구다삐리사 어루수구 루구루 뤄파사가. 가씨 어라 구부라 어바이시라어삐 뿌 바마마이리사아 어미기라 여뿌레 과 네시 서뉴빠 사보, 짜시야 마꼬 어또네 오꽈 워떠 와시갸 어바꾸 아꽈러꽈, 아더다아 어푸꽈

24. By faith Moses, when he had grown up, refused to be known as the son of Pharaoh's daughter.

25. He chose to be mistreated along with the people of God rather than to enjoy the pleasures of sin for a short time.

26. He regarded disgrace for the sake of Christ as of greater value than the treasures of Egypt, because he was looking ahead to his reward.

27. By faith he left Egypt, not fearing the king's anger; he persevered because he saw him who is invisible.

28. By faith he kept the Passover and the sprinkling of blood, so that the destroyer of the firstborn would not touch the firstborn of Israel.

서바이시라어휘.

29. Ebwemeresi bweBaisiraeli bu bwathumaa bahabuka enyanja yeMwola nga bandju ba barenga kwa chitaka ala akalyire. Si mango besha Misiri baerekaa kurengao, beke bera kusika.

29. 어붜머러시 붜바이시라어휘 부 봐쭈마아 바하부가 어냐아 여모롸 빠 바꾸 바 바러빠 과 찌다가 아롸 아가렐러. 시 마꼬 버싸 미시리 바어러가아 구러봐오, 버거 버라 구시가.

29. By faith the people passed through the Red Sea as on dry land; but when the Egyptians tried to do so, they were drowned.

30. Ebwemeresi bu bwathumaa elusimbo lwa lwabaa lusungwire emusi weYeriko lwakundjuka, mango eBaisiraeli babaa bera basungulaalo ku suku sirinda.

30. 어붜머러시 부 봐쭈마아 어루시뽀 롸 롸바아 루수뒤러 어무시 워여리고 롸구뚜가, 마꼬 어바이시라어휘 바바아 버라 바수뚜롸아로 구 수구 시리따.

30. By faith the walls of Jericho fell, after the people had marched around them for seven days.

31. Ebwemeresi bwa Rahaba, cha chihungukasi, bu bwathumaa atasikira alauma nebandju ba bananaa kuira kwa Ongo atechire. Bushi yeke ahuukasaa eBaisiraeli mwa boolo, ba bathumwaa kubusirisa emyasi yechio.

31. 어붜머러시 봐 라하바, 짜 찌후꾸가시, 부 봐쭈마아 아다시기라 아롸우마 너바꾸 바 바나나아 구이라 과 오꼬 아더찌러. 부씨 여거 아후우가사아 어바이시라어휘 롸 보오롣, 바 봐쭈마아 구부시리사 어먀시 여찌오.

31. By faith the prostitute Rahab, because she welcomed the spies, was not killed with those who were disobedient.

32. Rero chi nyihubaa kuteta? Ebihangi byanyikeere byekuteta era luulu sa Kiteoni, na Barakaq, na Samusoni, na Yefuta, na mwami Tauti, na Samweri, nebarebi.

32. 러로 찌 네후바아 구더다? 어비하삐 뱌네거러러 벼구더다 어라 루우우루 사 기더오니, 나 바라가구, 나 사무소니, 나 여푸다, 나 뫄미 다우디, 나 사뭐리, 너바러비.

32. And what more shall I say? I do not have time to tell about Gideon, Barak, Samson, Jephthah, David, Samuel and the prophets,

33. Ebwemeresi bwabu bandju bu bwathumaa baima ebio byebanji bami, na kunde baira bya bithungenene, na kubona bya Ongo alanyaa. Baminaa emonu mengoromolyi,

33. 어붜머러시 봐부 바꾸 부 봐쭈마아 바이마 어비오 벼바찌 바미, 나 구떠 바이라 뱌 비쭈뻐너너, 나 구보나 뱌 오꼬 아롸냐아. 바미나아 어모누 머꼬로모쩨,

33. who through faith conquered kingdoms, administered justice, and gained what was promised; who shut the mouths of lions,

34. na kusimya emarunga memulyiro, na kufufumuka kwiichibwa mwa boombo. Babaa bainyire emisi, si bera kuba banyake. Bera kuba ndjwalyi mwa bita kuikira echihangi bakolokanya ebasula bebinji bio.

35. Ebwemeresi bu bwathumaa bakasi bauma bahuba kulola kwa bafu babo boomwolyibwa na kuhuba kubafulusisabo bera balyi bauma-uma. Ebanji bendee balyibusibwa busese kuikira kwa chihangi beechibwa, si bera kunde banana kuboolyibwa. Babaa bahonda bomwolyibwe mwa bafu, babone kanji kalamo ka kakomire busese.

36. Nebanji bendee bashekerwa na kupundjwa busese nethuchi. Nebanji bera kunde baminwa neminyororo na kuumwa mwa buroko.

37. Nebanji bera kunde beechibwa mwa kuhuthwanga emakoi. Nebanji bera kunde baishibwamo kabiri mwa sii. Nebanji bera kunde beechibwa mwa boombo. Bendee balua-lua bembese enyuu sembulyi, nesi enyuu

34. 나 구시먀 어마루꽈 머무레로, 나 구푸푸무가 귀이찌봐 봐 보오뽄. 바바아 바이니러 어미시, 시 버라 구바 바냐거. 버라 구바 꽈레 봐 비다 구이기라 어찌하꿰 바고론가냐 어바수꽈 버비찌 비오.

35. 어붜머러시 부 봐쭈마아 바가시 바우마 바후바 구론꽈 과 바푸 바보 보오몯레봐 나 구후바 구바푸루시사보 버라 바레 바우마-우마. 어바찌 버떠어 바레부시봐 부서서 구이기라 과 찌하꿰 버어찌봐, 시 버라 구떠 바나나 구보오레봐. 바바아 바호따 보몯레붜 봐 바푸, 바보너 가찌 가꽈모 가 가고미러 부서서.

36. 너바찌 버떠어 바써거롸 나 구푸꽈 부서서 너쭈찌. 너바찌 버라 구떠 바미뇨 너미뇨로로 나 구우봐 봐 부로고.

37. 너바찌 버라 구떠 버어찌봐 봐 구후꽈꽈 어마고이. 너바찌 버라 구떠 바이써봐모 가비리 봐 시이. 너바찌 버라 구떠 버어찌봐 봐 보오뽄. 버떠어 바루아-루아 버써서 어뉴우 서뿐레, 너시 어뉴우 서뻐너. 버떠어

34. quenched the fury of the flames, and escaped the edge of the sword; whose weakness was turned to strength; and who became powerful in battle and routed foreign armies.

35. Women received back their dead, raised to life again. Others were tortured and refused to be released, so that they might gain a better resurrection.

36. Some faced jeers and flogging, while still others were chained and put in prison.

37. They were stoned; they were sawed in two; they were put to death by the sword. They went about in sheepskins and goatskins, destitute, persecuted and mistreated--

sembene. Bendee baba mwa bukene, na kulyibusibwa, na kunde bakorerwa emabi.

38. Ebandju babuya ba balyi ngabu, babaa batemire kuba mwobuno butala! Bendee balua-lua mwa buyeye nomwa miruko, na kwikala mwa nyikunda nomwa fumbi mwa chitaka.

39. Abu bandju boshi bemererwaa era muhondo sa Ongo, bushi nebwemeresi bwabo. Si chiro bacha, batabonaa bya Ongo alaanyaabo.

40. Bushi Ongo abaa athukunganyisise mira bindju bya bikomire busese. Echera chi chathumaa bataba bandju ba balumirire busira thubano.

E Baebrania Chikono 12

1. Rero, thusungwirwe na luamba lunene lwabu bendee balosa ebwemeresi bwabo. Bushi noku, nethu thurekanaa loshi nebindju byoshi bya bingathuma thutaendekera era muhondo, thwanarekana nebibi bya byenjire byathwangika fuba. Aola, thwanere thwalyibita na bushiru bunene mwa kaimano ka thweresibwe.

바바 마 부거너, 나 구레부시봐, 나 구떠 바고러롸 어마비.

38. 어바누 바부야 바 바뤠 까부, 바바아 바더미러 구바 모부노 부다꽈! 버떠어 바루아-루아 마 부여여 노롸 미루고, 나 귀가꽈 마 네구따 노롸 푸쀼 마 찌다가.

39. 아부 바누 보씨 버머러롸아 어라 무호또 사 오끄, 부씨 너붜머러시 봐보. 시 찌로 바짜, 바다보나아 뱌 오끄 아꽈아냐아보.

40. 부씨 오끄 아바아 아쭈구까네시서 미라 비누 뱌 비고미러 부서서. 어쩌라 찌 짜쭈마아 바다바 바누 바 바루미리러 부시라 쭈바노.

어 바어부라니아 찌고노 12

1. 러로, 쭈수위뤄 나 루아빠 루너너 꽈부 버떠어 바로사 어붜머러시 봐보. 부씨 노구, 너쭈 쭈러가나아 로씨 너비누 보씨 뱌 비까쭈마 쭈다어떠거라 어라 무호또, 쫘나러가나 너비비 뱌 벼찌러 뱌쫘께가 푸바. 아오꽈, 쫘너러 쫘쀄비다 나 부씨루 부너너 마 가이마노 가 쭤러시붜.

38. the world was not worthy of them. They wandered in deserts and mountains, and in caves and holes in the ground.

39. These were all commended for their faith, yet none of them received what had been promised.

40. God had planned something better for us so that only together with us would they be made perfect.

Hebrews Chapter 12[NIV]

1. Therefore, since we are surrounded by such a great cloud of witnesses, let us throw off everything that hinders and the sin that so easily entangles, and let us run with perseverance the race marked out for us.

2. Thundaa thwasindera Yesu, ishokororo yebwemeresi bwethu, kanji iwende waira obu bwemeresi bwethu kuba bwa bunalumirire. Yeine eemereraa kufa kwa musalaba, busira kulaa kwa honyi sa sitenganyire nelufu lwa lulyi ngolu. Airaa bacha, bushi abaa eshi kwa abikirirwe lumoo. Na lwarero ekese kwa lunda lwemalyo mendebe ya Ongo.

2. 쭈따아 쫘시떠라 여수, 이쏘고로로 여붜머러시 붜쭈 가찌 이워떠 와이라 오부 붜머러시 붜쭈 구바 봐 부나루미리라. 여이너 어어머러라아 구파 과 무사꽈바, 부시라 구꽈아 과 호네 사 시더꽈내러 너루푸 꽈 루쩨 오룰. 아이라아 바짜, 부씨 아바아 어씨 과 아비기리뤄 루모오. 나 꽈러로 어거서 과 루따 뤄마뀰 머떠버 야 오꼬.

2. Let us fix our eyes on Jesus, the author and perfecter of our faith, who for the joy set before him endured the cross, scorning its shame, and sat down at the right hand of the throne of God.

3. Mundaa mwakengera kute Yesu asesaa emuchima, mango ebandju bebibi bamuhombaa. Bushi noku, mutendaa mwatama nesi mwafunyika emichima.

3. 무따아 꽈거꺼라 구더 여수 아서사아 어무찌마, 마꼬 어바뚜 버비비 바무호빠아. 부씨 노구, 무더따아 꽈다마 너시 꽈푸네가 어미찌마.

3. Consider him who endured such opposition from sinful men, so that you will not grow weary and lose heart.

4 Bushi ebita bya mwalwa kwa kuima ebibi, mutasa kulwabi kuikira kwa lufu.

4 부씨 어비다 뱌 꽈롸 과 구이마 어비비, 무다사 구꽈비 구이기라 과 루푸.

4. In your struggle against sin, you have not yet resisted to the point of shedding your blood.

5. Mwebirire lyine eano Ongo aberesaa nga bana bai? "Mwana wanyi, mango Enawethu akukemera, utendaa wakena oku kukemera kwai. Nesi utendaa wafunyika emuchima, mango akukalyiira.

5. 뭐비리러 례너 어아노 오꼬 아버러사아 꽈 바나 바이? "꽈나 와네, 마꼬 어나워쭈 아구거머라, 우더따아 와거나 오구 구거머라 과이. 너시 우더따아 와푸네가 어무찌마, 마꼬 아구가쩨이라.

5. And you have forgotten that word of encouragement that addresses you as sons: "My son, do not make light of the Lord's discipline, and do not lose heart when he rebukes you,

6. Bushi Enawethu ende akemera emundju ola asimire, kanji ende ahuta chira mundju woshi ola eshi kwa alyi mwana

6. 부씨 어나워쭈 어너 아거머라 어무뚜 오라 아시미러, 가찌 어너 아후다 찌라 무뚜 오씨 오롸 어씨 과

6. because the Lord disciplines those he loves, and he punishes everyone he accepts as a son."

wai."

7. Mundaa mwasesa emuchima mwa malyibuko mango mwakalyirwa, bushi Ongo ende abatola nga bana bai. Nde mwana ola utakalyirwa neshe?

8. Akaba Ongo atangabakalyira, ngokwa ende akalyira ebana bai boshi, kukuteta mbu muta bana bai kanangana, si mulyi bana bomwa mbuwa.

9. Thukengeraa, ebatata bomuno butala, mango bendee bathukalyira, thwendee twathundabo. Rero, Ongo Tata wokwa nguba ithwemire kunde thwathunda busese, chasiya thuate ekalamo.

10. Abu batata, bendee bathukalyira ku suku sieke kukulyikana nokwa bahonjire. Si Ongo Tata, yeke ende athukalyira kwa mufa wethu, chasiya thube babuya-buya kuuma nai.

11. Echihangi ebandju bakalyirwa, chitathula cha lumoo, si chithula cha businane. Si kwa businda, ba bakangirisibwaa mwoku kukalyirwa, bende baba bandju ba bathungenene, na

아레 마나 와이."

7. 무따아 마서사 어무찌마 마 마레부고 마꼬 마가레라, 부씨 오꼬 어더 아바도롸 빠 바나 바이. 더 마나 오롸 우다가레라 너써?

8. 아가바 오꼬 아다빠바가레라, 꼬과 어더 아가레라 어바나 바이 보씨, 구구더다 뿌 무다 바나 바이 가나빠나, 시 무레 바나 보와 뿌와.

9. 쭈거꺼라아, 어바다다 보무노 부다롸, 마꼬 버더어 바쭈가레라, 쭤더어 돠쭈따보. 러로, 오꼬 다다 오과 꾸바 이쭤미러 구더 쫘쭈따 부서서, 짜시야 쭈아더 어가롸모.

10. 아부 바다다, 버더어 바쭈가레라 구 수구 시어거 구구레가나 노과 바호찌러. 시 오꼬 다다, 여거 어더 아쭈가레라 과 무파 워쭈, 짜시야 쭈버 바부야-부야 구우마 나이.

11. 어찌하삐 어바누 바가레롸, 찌다쭈롸 짜 루모오, 시 찌쭈롸 짜 부시나너. 시 과 부시따, 바 바가삐리시봐아 모구 구가레롸, 버더 바바 바누 바 바쭈꺼너너, 나 뭐이 띠라

7. Endure hardship as discipline; God is treating you as sons. For what son is not disciplined by his father?

8. If you are not disciplined (and everyone undergoes discipline), then you are illegitimate children and not true sons.

9. Moreover, we have all had human fathers who disciplined us and we respected them for it. How much more should we submit to the Father of our spirits and live!

10. Our fathers disciplined us for a little while as they thought best; but God disciplines us for our good, that we may share in his holiness.

11. No discipline seems pleasant at the time, but painful. Later on, however, it produces a harvest of righteousness and peace for those who have been trained by it.

mwei njira banaata eboolo mwa kalamo kabo.

12. Bushi noku, muhubaa kusesa emino senyu sa sitamire, mwanasesa nemafi menyu ma matamire.

13. Muchikunganyisaa enjira sa silambukere, chasiya emundju ola uremere emaulu atachilabukaa, si alamisibwe.

14. Muchisesaa kunde mwaba mwa boolo nebandju boshi, na kuba babuya-buya mwa kalamo kenyu. Bushi busira kuba mwobu bubuya-buya, kutalyi ola ukalola ku Enawethu.

15. Mumenyaa! Kutabaa chiro na mundju ola warekana nebubuya bwa Ongo! Nesi kutabaa mundju ola ulyi nga mwaka, ola wende weka ebifuma bya byalula, na kureta ekafango mwa kachi-kachi kenyu, na kwaukisa ebanji.

16. Kanji mumenyaa! Kutabaa chiro na muuma mu mwabo ola undaa waira elusingi. Kanji mutendaa mwakena ebindju bibuya-buya, nga Esau iwausaa engahanyi sai sekuba fula, bushi na kalyo kaeke oshao.

바나아다 어보오**르** 마 가**짜**모 가보.

12. 부씨 노구, 무후바아 구서사 어미노 서뉴 사 시다미러, 뫄나서사 너마피 머뉴 마 마다미러.

13. 무찌구**까**네사아 어**찌**라 사 시라**뿌**거러, **짜**시야 어무**쭈** 오**짜** 우러머러 어마우**루** 아다**찌짜**부가아, 시 아**짜**미시**붜**.

14. 무**찌**서사아 구**떠** 뫄바 뫄 보오**르** 너바**쭈** 보씨, 나 구바 바부야-부야 뫄 가**짜**모 거뉴. 부씨 부시라 구바 모부 부부야-부야, 구다**레** 오**짜** 우가**르짜** 구 어나워**쭈**.

15. 무머냐아! 구다바아 **찌**로 나 무**쭈** 오**짜** 와러가나 너부부야 봐 오**꼬**! 너시 구다바아 무**쭈** 오**짜** 우레 **짜** 뫄가, 오**짜** 워**떠** 워가 어비푸마 뱌 뱌루**짜**, 나 구러다 어가파**꼬** 뫄 가**찌**- 가**찌** 거뉴, 나 과우기사 어바**찌**.

16. 가**찌** 무머냐아! 구다바아 **찌**로 나 무우마 무 뫄보 오**짜** 우**따**아 와이라 어루시**삐**. 가**찌** 무더**따**아 뫄거나 어비**쭈** 비부야-부야, **짜** 어사우 이와우사아 어**까**하네 사이 서구바 푸**짜**, 부씨 나 가**룐** 가어거 오**싸**오.

12. Therefore, strengthen your feeble arms and weak knees.

13. "Make level paths for your feet," so that the lame may not be disabled, but rather healed.

14. Make every effort to live in peace with all men and to be holy; without holiness no one will see the Lord.

15. See to it that no one misses the grace of God and that no bitter root grows up to cause trouble and defile many.

16. See that no one is sexually immoral, or is godless like Esau, who for a single meal sold his inheritance rights as the oldest son.

17. Si muneshi kwa era nyuma sebi, mango abaa era ahonda eshe amuahanyire, eshe era kunana. Abaa atachete njira ya kubindjula emwasi ola airaa, chiro angaba mbu ahondaa esi ngahanyi mwa kulyira.

18. Mango mwabo mwaikiriraa ofu na Ongo, mutaikaa ofu na ndjulungu era ingaumibwako ngokwa eBaisiraeli baikiriraa ofu nendjulungu yeSinai. Kwei ndjulungu kweke, kwabaa kwakorera marunga ma mulyiro, kwabaa kulyi musimya tendere, kanji kwabaa kwarenga kausi kasibu.

19. Boomvaa ku murenge wa kaperere na murenge ola waruruma busese. Mango eBaisiraeli boomvaa kwoyu murenge wa Ongo, bera kumwema busese mbu atachihubaa kubabura chinwa.

20. Batetaa bacha, bushi bataalaa kuthunda ono muomba beeresibwaa mbu: "Chira mundju woshi ola ungauma kwene ndjulungu, echibwaa mwa kumuumanga emakoi, na chiro mbu chingaba chifuana."

17. 시 무너씨 과 어라 뉴마 서비, 마꼬 아바아 어라 아호따 어써 아무아하니러, 어써 어라 구나나. 아바아 아다쩌더 띠라 야 구비뿌롸 어롸시 오롸 아이라아, 찌로 아까바 뿌 아호따아 어시 까하네 롸 구레라.

18. 마꼬 뫄보 뫄이기리라아 오푸 나 오꼬, 무다이가아 오푸 나 뚜루꾸 어라 이까우미봐고 꼬과 어바이시라어릐 봐이기리라아 오푸 너뚜루꾸 여시나이. 궈이 뚜루꾸 궈거, 과바아 과고러라 마루까 마 무레로, 과바아 구레 무시먀 더떠러, 가찌 과바아 과러까 가우시 가시부.

19. 보오빠아 구 무러꺼 와 가퍼러러 나 무러꺼 오롸 와루루마 부서서. 마꼬 어바이시라어릐 보오빠아 고유 무러꺼 와 오꼬, 버라 구뭐마 부서서 뿌 아다찌후바아 구바부라 찌놔.

20. 바더다아 바짜, 부씨 바다아롸아 구쭈따 오노 무오빠 버어러시봐아 뿌: "찌라 무뚜 오씨 오롸 우까우마 궈너 뚜루꾸, 어찌봐아 뫄 구무우마까 어마고이, 나 찌로 뿌 찌까바 찌푸아나."

17. Afterward, as you know, when he wanted to inherit this blessing, he was rejected. He could bring about no change of mind, though he sought the blessing with tears.

18. You have not come to a mountain that can be touched and that is burning with fire; to darkness, gloom and storm;

19. to a trumpet blast or to such a voice speaking words that those who heard it begged that no further word be spoken to them,

20. because they could not bear what was commanded: "If even an animal touches the mountain, it must be stoned."

21. Ei myasi balolaako, yabaa ya kwoobairisa busese, kuikira echihangi Musa ateta mbu: Nakukumana nebuba!

22. Si mwabo, mwaikirire ofu nendjulungu ye Sayuni, kanji ofu nemusi wa Ongo iulyi muuma-uma. Oyola alyi emusi weYerusalemu yokwa nguba, kwa ebyumbi nebyumbi byendonyi babuananyire mwa lyinye.

23. Mwaikirire mwa lubuanano lwelumoo lwefula sa Ongo, sa masina mabo maanjikirwe kwa nguba. Kanji mwaikirire ofu na Ongo, iuthula muisha manja webandju boshi. Kanji mwaikirire ofu nemichima yebandju ba bafire mira, ba babaa bathungenene, kanji ba Ongo airire kuba bandju ba balumirire.

24. Mwaikirire ofu na Yesu iwende wabika ebandju mwa buuma na Ongo, kurengera echilaano chiyayaya. Kanji mwaikirire ofu nemikira yai era yasheshekalaa, era yateta kubuya kurenza emikira ya Aberi.

25. Rero, mumenyaa! Mutendaa mwanana kuumvirisa Ongo iwateta

---

21. 어이 먀시 바로롸아고, 야바아 야 교오바이리사 부서서, 구이기라 어찌하삐 무사 아더다 뿌: 나구구마나 너부바!

22. 시 먀보, 마이기리러 오푸 너뚜루꾸 여 사유니, 가찌 오푸 너무시 와 오꼬 이우레 무우마-우마. 오요롸 아레 어무시 워여루사뻐무 요과 우바, 과 어뷰삐 너뷰삐 벼또네 바부아나니러 롸 레녀.

23. 마이기리러 롸 루부아나노 뤄루푸롸 사 오꼬, 사 마시나 마보 마아찌기뤄 과 우바. 가찌 마이기리러 오푸 나 오꼬, 이우쭈롸 무이싸 마짜 워바뚜 보씨. 가찌 마이기리러 오푸 너미찌마 여바뚜 바 바피러 미라, 바 바바아 바쭈써너너, 가찌 바 오꼬 아이리러 구바 바뚜 바 바루미리러.

24. 마이기리러 오푸 나 여수 이워떠 와비가 어바뚜 마 부우마 나 오꼬, 구러써라 어찌롸아노 찌야야야. 가찌 마이기리러 오푸 너미기라 야이 어라 야써써가롸아, 어라 야더다 구부야 구러싸 어미기라 야 아버리.

25. 러로, 무머냐아! 먀나나 구우뻬리사 오꼬 이와더다 너뉴. 부씨

---

21. The sight was so terrifying that Moses said, "I am trembling with fear."

22. But you have come to Mount Zion, to the heavenly Jerusalem, the city of the living God. You have come to thousands upon thousands of angels in joyful assembly,

23. to the church of the firstborn, whose names are written in heaven. You have come to God, the judge of all men, to the spirits of righteous men made perfect,

24. to Jesus the mediator of a new covenant, and to the sprinkled blood that speaks a better word than the blood of Abel.

25. See to it that you do not refuse him who speaks. If they did not escape when

nenyu. Bushi eBaisiraeli ba bendee banana kumuumvirisa, iwendee weresabo emano muno butala, batafufumukaa emalyibuko. Thubano, Ongo iwenjire wathweresa emano kutenga kwa nguba. Mutasene kwa echera chalosa changanama kwa nethu akaba thungende thwanana kumumvirisa, thutakafufumuke amu malyibuko?

26. Kwa mira, emurenge wa Ongo endee alyingitanya ebutala. Si lwarero, athulaanyise mbu: "Nyingahuba kulyingitanya ebutala lyinji euma, ata ebutala bweine si nenguba nai!"

27. Chine chinwa "lyinji euma" chilosise kwa ebindju bya byabumbwaa bingalyingitanyisibwa, na byairima. Mwa bacha, ebindju bya bitangalyingitanyisibwa bi bikaendekera kubao esuku nemango.

28. Rero thundaa thwateta mbu akoko era mwa Ongo, bushi iwathweresise ebwami bwa butangalyingitanyisibwa. Oku kuteta mbu akoko, thundaa thwalosako mwa kumukorera mwa njira era

어바이시라어뤼 바 버떠어 바나나 구무우뻬리사, 이워떠어 워러사보 어마노 무노 부다꽈, 바다푸푸무가아 어마뤠부고. 쭈바노, 오꼬 이워찌러 와쭤러사 어마노 구더꽈 과 꾸바. 무다서너 과 어쩌라 짜뤈사 짜까나마 과 너쭈 아가바 쭈꺼떠 쫘나나 구무뻬리사, 쭈다가푸푸무거 아무 마뤠부고?

26. 과 미라, 어무러꺼 와 오꼬 어떠어 아뤠미다냐 어부다꽈. 시 꽐러로, 아쭈꽈아니서 뿌: "네까후바 구뤠미다냐 어부다꽈 레찌 어우마, 아다 어부다꽈 붸이너 시 너우바 나이!"

27. 찌너 찌놔 "레찌 어우마" 찌뤈시서 과 어비부 뱌 뱌부꽈아 비까뤠미다네시봐, 나 뱌이리마. 똬 바짜, 어비부 뱌 비다까뤠미다네시봐 비 비가어떠거라 구바오 어수구 너마꼬.

28. 러로 쭈따아 쫘더다 뿌 아고고 어라 똬 오꼬, 부씨 이와쭤러시서 어바미 봐 부다까뤠미다네시봐. 오구 구더다 뿌 아고고, 쭈따아 쫘뤈사고 똬 구무고러라 똬 찌라 어라 이무시미서,

they refused him who warned them on earth, how much less will we, if we turn away from him who warns us from heaven?

26. At that time his voice shook the earth, but now he has promised, "Once more I will shake not only the earth but also the heavens."

27. The words "once more" indicate the removing of what can be shaken--that is, created things--so that what cannot be shaken may remain.

28. Therefore, since we are receiving a kingdom that cannot be shaken, let us be thankful, and so worship God acceptably with reverence and awe,

imusimise, alauma
nekumuthunda nekumwoobaa.
29. Bushi Ongo wethu athula
nga mulyiro ola wende
wasiresa!

아롸우마 너구무쭈따
너구모오바아.
29. 부씨 오꼬 워쭈 아쭈롸 ㅁ29. for our "God is a
무례로 오롸 워떠 와시러사! consuming fire."

E Baebrania Chikono 13

1. Muendekeraa kunde
mwasimana nga bauma.

2. Mutebiriraa kunde
mwahuukasa ebaenyi kubuya.
Bushi mwa kuira bacha,
bandju bauma bahuukasaa
endonyi busira kumenya.

3. Mundaa mwakengera
ebandju ba baminyirwe, mwa
kunde mwachitola nga ba
baminyirwe alauma nabo.
Mundaa mwakengera na ba
balyibusibwa, mwa kunde
mwachitola nga ba
balyibusibwa kuuma nabo.

4. Ebuya bwemire kunde
bwathunjibwa nebandju boshi.
Emulume na mukai batemire
kunde baya mwa mbuwa.
Bushi Ongo akachinjibusa ba
bende baya mwa mbuwa noku
bera bahweranyire,
anachinjibusa nebashimba ba
benjire baira elusingi.

5. Mutendaa mwachirekerera
kuba mwa bucha bwekusima

어 바어부라니아 찌고노 13

1. 무어떠거라아 구떠
롸시마나 ㅁ 바우마.

2. 무더비리라아 구떠
롸후우가사 어바어네 구부야.
부씨 롸 구이라 바짜, 바뚜
바우마 바후우가사아 어또네
부시라 구머냐.

3. 무따아 마거떠라 어바뚜 바
바미네뤄, 롸 구떠 롸찌도롸
ㅁ 바 바미네뤄 아롸우마
나보. 무따아 마거떠라 나 바
바례부시봐, 롸 구떠 롸찌도롸
ㅁ 바 바례부시봐 구우마
나보.

4. 어부야 뭐미러 구떠
봐쭈찌봐 너바뚜 보씨.
어무루머 나 무가이 바더미러
구떠 바야 롸 뿌와. 부씨 오꼬
아가찌찌부사 바 버떠 바야
롸 뿌와 노구 버라
바훠라니러, 아나찌찌부사
너바씨빠 바 버찌러 바이라
어루시ㅁ.

5. 무더따아 롸찌러거러라
구바 롸 부짜 붜구시마

Hebrews Chapter 13[NIV]

1. Keep on loving each
other as brothers.

2. Do not forget to
entertain strangers, for by
so doing some people have
entertained angels without
knowing it.

3. Remember those in
prison as if you were their
fellow prisoners, and those
who are mistreated as if you
yourselves were suffering.

4. Marriage should be
honored by all, and the
marriage bed kept pure, for
God will judge the adulterer
and all the sexually
immoral.

5. Keep your lives free from
the love of money and be

ebuteya busese. Si mundaa mwamoera bya mwete. Bushi Ongo yeine atetaa mbu: "Ndakakulyikulyire chiro na hicha, nesi ndakakurekerere chiro na hicha."

6. Bushi noku, thungaala kunde thwateta na bushiru bunene mbu: "Enawethu iwende wanyitabala! Ndangobaa kandju! Chiye chemundju anganyiira?"

7. Mundaa mwakengera ebemangisi benyu, ba babahubanganyisaa eChinwa cha Ongo. Mundaa mwalola kubuya kute bendee bachitola mwa kalamo kabo nokwa bendee bafa. Mundaa mweeya ebwemeresi bwabo.

8. Yesu Kirisito anathula inoyu inoyu: mweolo, na lwarero, nesuku nemango.

9. Mutendaa mweengeerwa na chira myasi yoshi ya cheenyi era benjire ba bakangirisa. Emichima yethu yemire kunde yasimika kurengera ebonjo bwa Ongo, si ata kwa kuthunda emiomba era yerekere ebiryo. Ei miomba, itafuraa kuata chiro na mufa asibya kwa ba benjire bathundai.

10. Thubano, thwete ekethu

어부더야 부서서. 시 무따아 마모어라 뱌 뭐더. 부씨 오꼬 여이너 아더다아 뿌: "따가구레구레러 찌로 나 히짜, 너시 따가구러거러러 찌로 나 히짜."

6. 부씨 노구, 쭈따아파 구떠 좠다다 나 부씨루 부너너 뿌: "어나워쭈 이워떠 와네다바퐈! 따꼬바아 가쭈! 찌여 쩌무뿌 아퐈네이라?"

7. 무따아 퐈거어라 어버마삐시 버뉴, 바 바바후바퐈네사아 어찌놔 짜 오꼬. 무따아 퐈로퐈 구부야 구더 버떠어 바찌도퐈 퐈 가퐈모 가보 노과 버떠어 바파. 무따아 뭐어야 어뭐머러시 봐보.

8. 여수 기리시도 아나쭈퐈 이노유 이노유: 뭐오로, 나 퐈러로, 너수구 너마꼬.

9. 무더따아 뭐어떠어러롸 나 찌라 먀시 요씨 야 쩌어네 어라 버찌러 바 바가삐리사. 어미찌마 여쭈 여미러 구떠 야시미가 구러떠라 어보쪼 봐 오꼬, 시 아다 과 구쭈따 어미오빠 어라 여러거러 어비료. 어이 미오빠, 이다푸라아 구아다 찌로 나 무파 아시뱌 과 바 버찌러 바쭈따이.

10. 쭈바노, 쭤더 어거쭈

content with what you have, because God has said, "Never will I leave you; never will I forsake you."

6. So we say with confidence, "The Lord is my helper; I will not be afraid. What can man do to me?"

7. Remember your leaders, who spoke the word of God to you. Consider the outcome of their way of life and imitate their faith.

8. Jesus Christ is the same yesterday and today and forever.

9. Do not be carried away by all kinds of strange teachings. It is good for our hearts to be strengthened by grace, not by ceremonial foods, which are of no value to those who eat them.

10. We have an altar from

kahaha kemithulo.
Nebakuhanyi beBayuta, ba
bende bakola mwa Chisiki
Chibuya-buya batete eloso
lwekulya mwango kwa bindju
bya byenjire byathulwa kwako
kahaha.

11. EMukulu-kulu weBakuhanyi
ende eka emikira yenyama
mwa Chisiki Chibuya-buya
busese chasiya aanei kuba
mithulo bushi nekubabalyira
ebibi. Si enyama yoshi yende
yaya kusiresibwa bure nemusi.

12. Echera chi chathumaa Yesu
nai afira bure nemusi, chasiya
akomye ebandju bai kurengera
emikira yai yeine.

13. Rero, nethu thuyaa era alyi,
bure nemusi, thwemereraa
kukenyibwa ngokwa nai
anakenyibwaa.

14. Bushi muno butala, thutete
musi ola ukaendekera kubao
esuku nemango. Si emusi ola
ukabaha ithwahonda.

15. Rero kurengera Yesu,
thundaa thweeresa Ongo
emithulo yekumutonga esuku
soshi, kukuteta mbu thundaa
thwabura ebandju kwa
thubano thuthula thwemerere
esina lyai.

가하하 거미쭈로. 너바구하네
버바유다, 바 버떠 바고꽈 와
찌시기 찌부야-부야 바더더
어로소 뭐구려 마꼬 과 비뉴
뱌 벼찌러 뱌쭈꽈 과고
가하하.

11. 어무구루루-구루 워바구하네
어떠 어가 어미기라 여냐마
와 찌시기 찌부야-부야
부서서 짜시야 아아너이 구바
미쭈로 부씨 너구바바례라
어비비. 시 어냐마 요씨 여떠
야야 구시러시봐 부러 너무시.

12. 어쩌라 찌 짜쭈마아 여수
나이 아피라 부러 너무시,
짜시야 아고며 어바뉴 바이
구러꺼라 어미기라 야이
여이너.

13. 러로, 너쭈 쭈야아 어라
아례, 부러 너무시,
쭤머러라아 구거네봐 꼬과
나이 아나거네봐아.

14. 부씨 무노 부다꽈, 쭈더더
무시 오꽈 우가어떠거라
구바오 어수구 너마꼬. 시
어무시 오꽈 우가바하
이쫘호따.

15. 러로 구러꺼라 여수,
쭈따아 쭤어러사 오꼬
어미쭈로 여구무도뼈 어수구
소씨, 구구더다 뿌 쭈따아
쫘부라 어바뉴 과 쭈바노
쭈쭈꽈 쭤머러러 어시나 랴이.

which those who minister at
the tabernacle have no right
to eat.

11. The high priest carries
the blood of animals into
the Most Holy Place as a sin
offering, but the bodies are
burned outside the camp.

12. And so Jesus also
suffered outside the city
gate to make the people
holy through his own blood.

13. Let us, then, go to him
outside the camp, bearing
the disgrace he bore.

14. For here we do not have
an enduring city, but we are
looking for the city that is
to come.

15. Through Jesus,
therefore, let us continually
offer to God a sacrifice of
praise--the fruit of lips that
confess his name.

16. Kanji mutendaa mwebirira kukorerana emabuya na kunde mwaasanya. Bushi emithulo era iri ngei, yende yasimisa Ongo.

17. Mundaa mwathunda ebemangisi benyu, na kunde mwaira bya bababurire. Abola bu bende balanga emichima yenyu, bushi Ongo akabusabo era luulu semulyimo ola bakolaa. Akaba mungende mwathundabo, bangakola emulyimo wabo na lumoo lunene. Si akaba mutangende mwathundabo, bangakolao na businane. Nekukolao bacha, kutabaachire chiro na mufa asibya.

18. Mundaa mwathwemera. Thwishi kanangana kwa mwa michima yethu mutalyi chiro na chibi chisibya cha thwenjire thwachisitakako, bushi thwahonda thunde thwata myanya ibuya mwa myasi yoshi.

19. Nabema busese mwemaa Ongo, nyihube kuika eyi mwenyu fuba.

20. Ongo iwende wathweresa eboolo. Oomwolaa Enawethu Yesu mwa bafu. Oyu Yesu iMulanzi Munene wembulyi. Nemikira yai, iyairire echilaano

16. 가찌 무더따아 뭐비리라 구고러라나 어마부야 나 구너 먀아사냐. 부씨 어미쭈론 어라 이리 써이, 여뻐 야시미사 오꼬.

17. 무따아 뫄쭈따 어버마께시 버뉴, 나 구머 마이라 뱌 바바부리러. 아보쫘 부 버너 바쫘꺄 어미찌마 여뉴, 부씨 오꼬 아가부사보 어라 루우루 서무쩨모 오쫘 바고쫘아. 아가바 무꺼머 뫄쭈따보, 바까고쫘 어무쩨모 와보 나 루모오 루너너. 시 아가바 무다꺼머 뫄쭈따보, 바까고쫘오 나 부시나너. 너구고쫘오 바짜, 구다바아찌러 찌로 나 무파 아시뱌.

18. 무따아 뫄쭤머라. 쮜씨 가나꺼나 과 뫄 미찌마 여쭈 무다쩨 찌로 나 찌비 찌시뱌 짜 쮜찌러 쫘찌시다가고, 부씨 쫘호따 쭈너 쫘다 먀냐 이부야 뫄 먀시 요씨.

19. 나버마 부서서 뭐마아 오꼬, 네후버 구이가 어에 뭐뉴 푸바.

20. 오꼬 이워더 와쭤러사 어보오론. 오오몰쫘아 어나워쭈 여수 뫄 바푸. 오유 여수 이무쫘씨 무너너 워뿌쩨. 너미기라 야이, 이야이리러

16. And do not forget to do good and to share with others, for with such sacrifices God is pleased.

17. Obey your leaders and submit to their authority. They keep watch over you as men who must give an account. Obey them so that their work will be a joy, not a burden, for that would be of no advantage to you.

18. Pray for us. We are sure that we have a clear conscience and desire to live honorably in every way.

19. I particularly urge you to pray so that I may be restored to you soon.

20. May the God of peace, who through the blood of the eternal covenant brought back from the dead our Lord Jesus, that great

chesuku nemango ala kachi-kachi kebandju na Ongo.

21. Ongo endaa aberesa ebuashi bwekuira chira mwasi mubuya, chasiya munde mwaira ekuhonda kwai. Kanji endaa aira bya bimusimise mwa ndanda sethu kurengera Yesu Kirisito. Yesu endaa atongibwa esuku nemango. Bibe bacha!

22. Banyakethu, nabema busese, muumvaa kubuya ene myasi nabaanjikiririre kwa kubasesa emuchima. Bushi nabaanjikirirei kwa kuneeshangira.

23. Nahonda nyibakengese kwa munyakethu Timoteo abooIyibwe mira. Akaika fuba, nyingabaha thunai kuya kubatangula.

24. Munyikesesaa ebemangisi benyu boshi, alauma nebandju ba Ongo boshi. Banyakethu bomwa chio che Italyiya, babakesise.

25. Ongo endaa abaahanyira muboshi!

어찌퐈아노 쩌수구 너마꼬 아퐈 가찌-가찌 거바뿌 나 오꼬.

21. 오꼬 어따아 아버러사 어부아씨 붜구이라 찌라 먀시 무부야, 짜시야 무떠 먀이라 어구호따 과이. 가찌 어따아 아이라 뱌 비무시미서 뫄 따따 서쭈 구러꺼라 여수 기리시도. 여수 어따아 아도띠봐 어수구 너마꼬. 비버 바짜!

22. 바냐거쭈, 나버마 부서서, 무우빠아 구부야 어너 먀시 나바아찌기리러 과 구바서사 어무찌마. 부씨 나바아찌기리러이 과 구너어싸띠라.

23. 나호따 네바거꺼서 과 무냐거쭈 디모더오 아보오뤠붜 미라. 아가이가 푸바, 네까바하 쭈나이 구야 구바다꿔롸.

24. 무네거서사아 어버마띠시 버뉴 보씨, 아퐈우마 너바뚜 바 오꼬 보씨. 바냐거쭈 보봐 찌오 쩌 이다뤠야, 바바거시서.

25. 오꼬 어따아 아바아하네라 무보씨!

Shepherd of the sheep,

21. equip you with everything good for doing his will, and may he work in us what is pleasing to him, through Jesus Christ, to whom be glory for ever and ever. Amen.

22. Brothers, I urge you to bear with my word of exhortation, for I have written you only a short letter.

23. I want you to know that our brother Timothy has been released. If he arrives soon, I will come with him to see you.

24. Greet all your leaders and all God's people. Those from Italy send you their greetings.

25. Grace be with you all.

Yakobo

야고보

James

YAKOBO
(JAMES)

야고보
(자이쓰)

Yakobo Chikono 1

1. Nyono Yakobo, muanda wa Ongo. Kandji wa Enawetchu Yesu Kirisito, nabalamusise mu bandju ba Ongo muhandabanyire mwa butala boshi.

2. Banyaketchu, mango mwarenga mwa miereko ya tchira ndjira mundaa mwatchumva nga mulyi mwa lumoo.

3. Bushi mwishi, kwa ekuerekibwa kwe bwemeresi bwenyu, ku kwende kwatchuma mwaata ebushibilyisi.

4. Si obu bushibilyisi kwemire bukole emulyimo wai kuikira kwa businda, tchasiya mube bandju ba batete tchibi tchisibya, kandji babanalumilyire mwa byoshi, batainyire ne kandju kasibya.

5. Rero akaba muuma mu mwabo ainyire ebwenge, emaabu era mwa Ongo. Na Ongo angamwemeresa'bu, bushi iwende weresa ebandju boshi ne mutchima muuma kandji busira kalondo.

6. Si oyu mundju emire

야고보 찌고노 1

1. 뇨노 야고보, 무아따 와 오꼬. 가찌 와 어나워쭈 여수 기리시도, 나바라무시서 무 바뚜 바 오꼬 무하따바네러 뫄 부다꽈 보씨.

2. 바냐거쭈, 마꼬 뫄러꽈 뫄 미어러고 야 찌라 띠라 무따아 뫄쭈빠 마 무뤠 뫄 루모오.

3. 부씨 뮈씨, 과 어구어러기봐 귀 붜머러시 붜뉴, 구 궈떠 과쭈마 뫄아다 어부씨비뤠시.

4. 시 오부 부씨비뤠시 귀미러 부고뤄 어무뤠모 와이 구이기라 과 부시따, 짜시야 무버 바뚜 바 바더더 찌비 찌시뱌, 가찌 바바나룬미뤠러 뫄 뵤씨, 바다이네러 너 가뉴 가시뱌.

5. 러로 아가바 무우마 무 뫄보 아이네러 어붸어, 어마아부 어라 뫄 오꼬. 나 오꼬 아꽈뭐머러사부, 부씨 이워떠 워러사 어바뚜 보씨 너 무찌마 무우마 가찌 부시라 가릇또.

6. 시 오유 무뚜 어미러

James Chapter 1[NIV]

1. James, a servant of God and of the Lord Jesus Christ, To the twelve tribes scattered among the nations: Greetings.

2. Consider it pure joy, my brothers, whenever you face trials of many kinds,

3. because you know that the testing of your faith develops perseverance.

4. Perseverance must finish its work so that you may be mature and complete, not lacking anything.

5. If any of you lacks wisdom, he should ask God, who gives generously to all without finding fault, and it will be given to him.

6. But when he asks, he must

kwema ne bwemeresi busira kuhungwa-hungwa? Busbhi emundju ola wahungwa-hungwa ahuhanyisibwa ne mulaba kwa myanya inene ola wekibwa ne tchusi ne kuuma emeshi yeyi ne yi.

7. Emundju ola ulyi ngoyu atatchitchingaa mbu angabona kandju era mwa Enawetchu.

8. Bushi alyi mundju ola wete mitchima abilyi kandji wakubindjuka bindjuka mwa myasi era aira.

9. Munyaketchu mwemeresi ola ulyi mukene endaa amowa bushi Ongo amwerusise.

10. Ne munyaketchu mwemeresi ola ulyi muare, endaa amowa bushi Ongo amwaandasise. Bushi emuare kurenga ku arenga nga bwaso bwan bitchi.

11. Esuba lyende lyaulukira, etchuka tchalyi tchanomya nemyaka. Ebwaso bweyi myaka bwanatchitowangira, ne bulyimbi bwobu bwaso boshi bwanakumba. Rero, ne muare nai ku akanalyima batcha mwa mirimo yai.

12. Aahanyirwe emundju ola waata ebushibilyisi mwa

궈마 너 뭐머러시 부시라 구후꽈-후꽈? 부수부히 어무뚜 오롸 와후꽈-후꽈 아후하네시봐 너 무롸바 과 먀냐 이너너 오롸 워기봐 너 쭈시 너 구우마 어머씨 여에 너 에.

7. 어무뚜 오롸 우레 꼬유 아다찌찌꽈아 뿌 아꽈보나 가뚜 어라 뫄 어나워쭈.

8. 부씨 아레 무뚜 오롸 워더 미찌마 아비레 가찌 와구비뚜가 비뚜가 뫄 먀시 어라 아이라.

9. 무냐거쭈 뭐머러시 오롸 우레 무거너 어따아 아모와 부씨 오꼬 아뭐루시서.

10. 너 무냐거쭈 뭐머러시 오롸 우레 무아러, 어따아 아모와 부씨 오꼬 아뫄아따시서. 부씨 어무아러 구러꽈 구 아러꽈 꽈 봐소 봐누 비찌.

11. 어수바 려떠 랴우루기라, 어쭈가 짜레 짜노먀 너먀가. 어봐소 뭐에 먀가 봐나찌도와끼라, 너 부레삐 보부 봐소 보씨 봐나구빠. 러로, 너 무아러 나이 구 아가나레마 바짜 뫄 미리모 야이.

12. 아아하네뤄 어무뚜 오롸 와아다 어부씨비레시 뫄

believe and not doubt, because he who doubts is like a wave of the sea, blown and tossed by the wind.

7. That man should not think he will receive anything from the Lord;

8. he is a double-minded man, unstable in all he does.

9. The brother in humble circumstances ought to take pride in his high position.

10. But the one who is rich should take pride in his low position, because he will pass away like a wild flower.

11. For the sun rises with scorching heat and withers the plant; its blossom falls and its beauty is destroyed. In the same way, the rich man will fade away even while he goes about his business.

12. Blessed is the man who perseveres under trial, because

miereko, bushi era nyuma se kuimai akabona enzita era Ongo alaanyaa ba batchula bamusimire.

13. Akaba mundju murebe angaerekibwa, atateta mbu: Ongo iwanyierekire. Bushi Ongo atangaerekibwa ne mabi, nesi atangaereka mundju asibya;

14. Si tchira mundju ende aerekibwa mango akululwa ne kweengerwa, ne mianyisa yai ibi ye buhumahuma.

15. Tchasinda, obu buhumahuma mango bungakula bwanabuta ebibi, ebi bibi nabi mango bingakula byanabuta elufu.

16. Banyaketchu basiirwa, mutendaa mwengerwa!

17. Bushi tchira lwembo lubuya na tchira lwembo lwa lulumilyire, lwende lwatenga kwa nguba era mwa Ongo Tata iwabumbaa ebimore byoshi bya bitchula ku. Era mwa Ongo itatchula buaku aluka nesi bya biri nga tchimbusa.

18. Kukulyikana ne kuhonda kwai, atchweresise ekalamo kurengera etchinwa tchai tche kanangana, tchasiya tchube

미어러고, 부씨 어라 뉴마 서 구이마이 아가보나 어씨다 어라 오꼬 아라아냐아 바 바쭈롸 바무시미러.

13. 아가바 무뚜 무러버 아빠어러기봐, 아다더다 뿌: 오꼬 이와네어러기러. 부씨 오꼬 아다빠어러기봐 너 마비, 너시 아다빠어러가 무뚜 아시뱌;

14. 시 찌라 무뚜 어어 아어러기봐 마꼬 아구루롸 너 궈어뻐라, 너 미아니사 야이 이비 여 부후마후마.

15. 짜시따, 오부 부후마후마 마꼬 봐나부다 어비비, 어비 비비 나비 마꼬 비빠구롸 뱌나부다 어루푸.

16. 바냐거쭈 바시이롸, 무더따아 뭐뻐롸!

17. 부씨 찌라 뭐뽀 루부야 나 찌라 뭐뽀 롸 루루미쩨러, 뭐뻐 롹더빠 과 꾸바 어라 롸 오꼬 다다 이와부빠아 어비모러 뵤씨 뱌 비쭈롸 구. 어라 롸 오꼬 이다쭈롸 부아구 아루가 너시 뱌 비리 빠 찌뿌사.

18. 구구쩨가나 너 구호따 과이, 아쭤러시서 어가롸모 구러뻐라 어찌놔 짜이 쩌 가나빠나, 짜시야 쭈버

when he has stood the test, he will receive the crown of life that God has promised to those who love him.

13. When tempted, no one should say, "God is tempting me." For God cannot be tempted by evil, nor does he tempt anyone;

14. but each one is tempted when, by his own evil desire, he is dragged away and enticed.

15. Then, after desire has conceived, it gives birth to sin; and sin, when it is full-grown, gives birth to death.

16. Don't be deceived, my dear brothers.

17. Every good and perfect gift is from above, coming down from the Father of the heavenly lights, who does not change like shifting shadows.

18. He chose to give us birth through the word of truth, that we might be a kind of firstfruits of all he created.

kaumbe ka byoshi bya abumbaa.

	가우뻐 가 뵤씨 뱌 아부빠아.	

19. Banyaketchu basiirwa mundaa mwamenyerera ono mwasi: tchira mundju emire kubwa mwangu wa kumvwa si atabaa mwangu mwa kuteta nesi kusinana.

19. 바냐거쭈 바시이롸 무따아 마머녀러라 오노 마시: 찌라 무뿌 어미러 구봐 마우 와 구빠 시 아다바아 마우 마 구더다 너시 구시나나.

19. My dear brothers, take note of this: Everyone should be quick to listen, slow to speak and slow to become angry,

20. Bushi emundju kusinana ataala kuira bya bitchungenene era muhondo sa Ongo.

20. 부씨 어무뿌 구시나나 아다아빠 구이라 뱌 비쭈머너너 어라 무호또 사 오꼬.

20. for man's anger does not bring about the righteous life that God desires.

21. Bushi noku, mukabulyiraa emyasi Yoshi era yenfde yabaaka esinga na tchira myasi Yoshi ya bubi bwa burengererese. Mwaangilyiraa etchinwa tcha Ongo mwa burembu tcha tchabikirwe mwa mitchima yenyu, bushoi tchi tchete ebuashi bwe kununula.

21. 부씨 노구, 무가부뤠라아 어먀시 요씨 어라 여누푸더 야바아가 어시빠 나 찌라 먀시 요씨 야 부비 봐 부러꺼러러서. 뫄아삐뤠라아 어찌냐 짜 오꼬 마 부러뿌 짜 짜비기뤄 마 미찌마 여뉴, 부쏘이 찌 쩌더 어부아씨 붜 구누누롸.

21. Therefore, get rid of all moral filth and the evil that is so prevalent and humbly accept the word planted in you, which can save you.

22. Mutendaa mwa tchiteba mubeine mwa kunde mwanomvilyisa oshao etchinwa tcha Ongo. Si mundaa mwaira ngokwa tchitetchire.

22. 무더따아 뫄 찌더바 무버이너 뫄 구떠 뫄노삐뤠사 오싸오 어찌냐 짜 오꼬. 시 무따아 뫄이라 꼬과 찌더찌러.

22. Do not merely listen to the word, and so deceive yourselves. Do what it says.

23. Bushi emundju ola wende womvilyisa etchinwa tcha Ongo oshao busira kuira ngokwa tchitetchire, ahuhanyisibwe nola wasonga ebuso bwai mwa tchiyo.

23. 부씨 어무뿌 오롸 워떠 올삐뤠사 어찌냐 짜 오꼬 오싸오 부시라 구이라 꼬과 찌더찌러, 아후하네시붜 노롸 와소빠 어부소 봐이 뫄 찌요.

23. Anyone who listens to the word but does not do what it says is like a man who looks at his face in a mirror

24. Era nyuma seku

24. 어라 뉴마 서구 찌소빠,

24. and, after looking at

tchisonga, anatchendera unao unao anebilyira kute ku ahuhire.

25. Si emundju ola wende watchikangilyisa kubuyabuya emwaso ola ulumilyire, kandji ola wende wabika ebandji mwa buhuru, ne kuendekera kusimika muo, si kuta kumvuilyisa oshao tchasinda anebilyira'u, si ende aira ngokwa atetchire, oyu mundju aahanyirwe na Ongo mwa myasi yai Yoshi.

26. Akaba emundju angatchitola mbu alyi mundju wa tini, noku ataala kulanga elulyimi lwai, elyi kutchiteba kwana tchiteba yeine. Nelyi tini lyai lyitete mufa asibya.

27. Etini lya lyikomire lyitete ne tchibi tchisibya era muhondo sa Ongo lyi lyelyine: kulyi kuasa efusi, ne bahumbakasi, mwa malyibuko mabo ne kutchilanga kwa myasi era angabaaka esinga.

아나쩌뻐라 우나오 우나오 아너비뻬라 구더 구 아후히러.

25. 시 어무뚜 오퐈 워뻐 와찌가삐뻬사 구부야부야 어퐈소 오퐈 우루미뻬러, 가찌 오퐈 워뻐 와비가 어바찌 퐈 부후루, 너 구어뻐거라 구시미가 무오, 시 구다 구뿌이뻬사 오싸오 짜시따 아너비뻬라우, 시 어뻐 아이라 꼬과 아더찌러, 오유 무뚜 아아하네뤄 나 오꼬 퐈 먀시 야이 요씨.

26. 아가바 어무뚜 아꺄찌도퐈 뿌 아뻬 무뚜 와 디니, 노구 아다아퐈 구꽈삐 어루뻬미 퐈이, 어뻬 구찌더바 과나 찌더바 여이너. 너뻬 디니 퍄이 뻬더더 무파 아시뱌.

27. 어디니 퍄 뻬고미러 뻬더더 너 찌비 찌시뱌 어라 무호또 사 오꼬 뻬 퍄뻬너: 구뻬 구아사 어푸시, 너 바후꺄가시, 퐈 마뻬부고 마보 너 구찌퐈꺄 과 먀시 어라 아꺄바아가 어시꺄.

himself, goes away and immediately forgets what he looks like.

25. But the man who looks intently into the perfect law that gives freedom, and continues to do this, not forgetting what he has heard, but doing it--he will be blessed in what he does.

26. If anyone considers himself religious and yet does not keep a tight rein on his tongue, he deceives himself and his religion is worthless.

27. Religion that God our Father accepts as pure and faultless is this:
to look after orphans and widows in their distress and to keep oneself from being polluted by the world.

Yakobo Chikono 2
1. Banyaketchu, kukulyikana nokwa mutchula mwemerere Enawetchu Yesu Kirisito, we

야고보 찌고노 2
1. 바냐거쭈, 구구뻬가나 노과 무쭈퐈 뭐머러러 어나워쭈 여수 기리시도, 워

James Chapter 2[NIV]
1. My brothers, as believers in our glorious Lord Jesus Christ, don't show favoritism.

bulangare, mutendaa mwaira kalondo mwa bandju kwa kusimilyira.

2. Mulolaa: akaba mundju murebe angengelyira mwa lubwaanano lwenyu, embese malinga we horo, ne ndjimba sa langala. Tchasinda, kwanengilyira ne mukenen ola wembese biramba.

3. Rero oyu wembese endjimba salangala, mwanamweresa etchunda mwa kumubura mbu: Ekalaa anola mwa tchisiki tchikomire! Si emukene yeke, mwanamubura mbu: Woyo, emangaa, nesi ekalaa alashi mwa maulu mendji.

4. Mwa kuira batcha, mutasene kwa kalondo ku mwaira mwa katchi-katchi kenyu? Kandji mwa kuira batcha, mutasene kwa mwakoresibwa ne mianyisa ibi?

5. Banyeketchu basiirwa mumva: Ongo atalondolaa, ebakene muno butala, tchasiya babe baare mwa bwemeresi, babone ne mwandjo we bwami bwa alaanyaa ebandju ba batchula bamusimire.

6. Si emukene, mwabo

부짜쌔러, 무더따아 먀이라
가르오또 마 바뿌 과
구시미쩨라.

2. 무로쨔아: 아가바 무뿌
무러버 아쌔쌔쩨라 먀
루봐아나노 뤼뉴, 어쎄서
마찌쌔 워 호로, 너 띠빠 사
쨔쌔쨔. 쨔시따, 과너쌔쩨라
너 무거너 오꽈 워쎄서
비라빠.

3. 러로 오유 워쎄서 어찌빠
사쨔쌔쨔, 먀나뭐러사
어쭈따 먀 구무부라 뿌:
어가쨔아 아노꽈 먀 찌시기
찌고미러! 시 어무거너 여거,
먀나무부라 뿌: 오요,
어마쌔아, 너시 어가쨔아
아꽈씨 먀 마우루 머찌.

4. 먀 구이라 바짜, 무다서너
과 가르오또 구 먀이라 먀
가찌-가찌 거뉴? 가찌 먀
구이라 바짜, 무다서너 과
먀고러시봐 너 미아니싸
이비?

5. 바녀거쭈 바시이롸 무빠:
오꼬 아다르오또쨔아,
어바거너 무노 부다꽈,
쨔시야 바버 바아러 먀
뷔머러시, 바보너 너 먀쪼
워 바미 봐 아쨔아냐아
어바뿌 바 바쭈꽈
바무시미러.

6. 시 어무거너, 먀보

2. Suppose a man comes into your meeting wearing a gold ring and fine clothes, and a poor man in shabby clothes also comes in.

3. If you show special attention to the man wearing fine clothes and say, "Here's a good seat for you," but say to the poor man, "You stand there" or "Sit on the floor by my feet,"

4. have you not discriminated among yourselves and become judges with evil thoughts?

5. Listen, my dear brothers: Has not God chosen those who are poor in the eyes of the world to be rich in faith and to inherit the kingdom he promised those who love him?

6. But you have insulted

mwendjire mwamukena! Abu baare, ata bu bendjire babaenza mwe bine ne kunde ba basitaka kwa lutchiko (timirari).

7. Kandji ata bu bendjire bakamba esina lyibuya lya mweresibwe?

8. Mwendjire mwaira kubuya akaba mungaira kwa ono mwaso we bwami atchula atetchire mwa mwaandjiko mabuyabuya mbu: usimaa mulyikenyu kwa ucthula utchisimire mweine.

9. Si akaba mungende maira ekalondo elyi mwailyire tchibi. Aola, mumenyaa kwa mwatchindjibusibwe ne mwaso bushi mutatchundjire'u.

10. Bushi akaba emundju endjire aira kwa miomba yoshi, mwaso atetchite, tchasinda anaisha mu muuma oshao, elyi aishire mwa myasi yoshi.

11. Bushi ola watetaa mbu: utendaa wabanda ekilyi iwanatetaa kandji mbu: utendaa weta. Rero, tchiro mbu utabanyire ekilyi, si wetchire, umenyaa kwa waishire mwa mwaso.

12. Mwa batcha, mango

뫄무거나! 아부 바아러, 아다 부 버찌러 바바어싸 뭐 비너 구떠 바 바시다가 과 루찌고 (디미라리).

7. 가씨 아다 부 버찌러 바가빠 어시나 레부야 랴 뭐러시붜?

8. 뭐찌러 뫄이라 구부야 아가바 무짜이라 과 오노 뫄소 워 바미 아쭈쫘 아더찌러 뫄 뫄아찌고 마부야부야 뿌: 우시마아 무쩨거뉴 과 우쮸쫘 우찌시미러 뭐이너.

9. 시 아가바 무떠러 마이라 어가론또 어쩨 뫄이쩨러 찌비. 아오쫘, 무머냐아 과 뫄찌찌부시붜 너 뫄소 부씨 무다쭈찌러우.

10. 부씨 아가바 어무뉴 어찌러 아이라 과 미오빠 요씨, 뫄소 아더찌더, 짜시따 아나이싸 무 무우마 오싸오, 어쩨 아이씨러 뫄 먀시 요씨.

11. 부씨 오쫘 와더다아 뿌: 우더따아 와바따 어기쩨 이와나더다아 가씨 뿌: 우더따아 워다. 러로, 찌로 뿌 우다바네러 어기쩨, 시 워찌러, 우머냐아 과 와이씨러 뫄 뫄소.

12. 뫄 바짜, 마꼬 뫄더다

the poor. Is it not the rich who are exploiting you? Are they not the ones who are dragging you into court?

7. Are they not the ones who are slandering the noble name of him to whom you belong?

8. If you really keep the royal law found in Scripture, "Love your neighbor as yourself," you are doing right.

9. But if you show favoritism, you sin and are convicted by the law as lawbreakers.

10. For whoever keeps the whole law and yet stumbles at just one point is guilty of breaking all of it.

11. For he who said, "Do not commit adultery," also said, "Do not murder." If you do not commit adultery but do commit murder, you have become a lawbreaker.

12. Speak and act as those

mwateta nesi mwaira mwasi murebe, mundaa mwakengera kwa Ongo akabatchindjibusa kukulyikana ne mwaso ola wende watchweresa ebolo.

13. Bushi ebandju ba batatchusa bondjo mango batchindjibusa ebandji, Ongo nai atakabafire'bu. Si ola wende wafira ebandji ebondjo atobaa ebutchindjibusi.

14. Banyaketchu, mutoloke mutchiye ola mundju angabona mango ateta mbu ete bwemeresi, noku atendjire alosa'bu kurengera bya aira? Obu bwemeresi bungamununula?

15. Muumvaa, akaba munyakenyu nesi mwalyiwenyu mwa bwemeresi ainyire tchembala nesi tcha abalya.

16. Tchasinda, muuma mu mwabo anamubura mbu: wendaa ne bolo, uye kukalukala kwa mulyiro, uneute! Oyu mwasi ete mufa mutchiye emango utamuasise netcha alaire'ko?

17. Rero ebwemeresi nabu kunoku. Ebwemeresi bwa butendjire bwalorekana'ku

너시 마이라 꽈시 무러버, 무따아 꽈거꺼라 과 오꼬 아가바찌띠부사 구구레가나 너 꽈소 오꽈 워떠 와쮜러사 어보롣.

13. 부씨 어바뚜 바 바다쭈사 보쪼 마꼬 바찌띠부사 어바씨, 오꼬 나이 아다가바피러부. 시 오꽈 워떠 와피라 어바씨 어보쪼 아도바아 어부찌띠부시.

14. 바냐거쭈, 무도로거 무찌여 오꽈 무뚜 아빠보나 마꼬 아더다 뿌 어더 뷔머러시, 노구 아더띠러 아로사부 구러빠라 뱌 아이라? 오부 뷔머러시 부빠무누누꽈?

15. 무우빠아, 아가바 무냐거뉴 너시 꽈레워뉴 꽈 뷔머러시 아이니러 쩌빠뺘 너시 짜 아바뺘.

16. 짜시따, 무우마 무 꽈보 아나무부라 뿌: 워따아 너 보롣, 우여 구가루가뺘 과 무레로, 우너우더! 오유 꽈시 어더 무빠 무찌여 어마꼬 우다무아시서 너짜 아빠이러고?

17. 러로 어뷔머러시 나부 구노구. 어뷔머러시 봐 부더띠러 봐로러가나구

who are going to be judged by the law that gives freedom,

13. because judgment without mercy will be shown to anyone who has not been merciful. Mercy triumphs over judgment!

14. What good is it, my brothers, if a man claims to have faith but has no deeds? Can such faith save him?

15. Suppose a brother or sister is without clothes and daily food.

16. If one of you says to him, "Go, I wish you well; keep warm and well fed," but does nothing about his physical needs, what good is it?

17. In the same way, faith by itself, if it is not accompanied by action, is dead.

kurengera emyanya, eri bufire?	구러ᄢᅥ라 어먀냐, 어리 부피러?	
18. Emundju angateta mbu: woyo wete bwemeresi, nanyinyete myanya ibuya. Unyilosaa ebwemeresi bwanyi kurengera emyanya ibuya.	18. 어무ᅜᅮ 아ᄢᅡ더다 뿌: 오요 워더 붜머러시, 나네녀더 먀냐 이부야. 우네ᄙᅩ사아 어붜머러시 봐네 구러ᄢᅥ라 어먀냐 이부야.	18. But someone will say, "You have faith; I have deeds." Show me your faith without deeds, and I will show you my faith by what I do.
19. Woyo wemerere kwa kutchula Ongo muuma oshao. Kubinalyi! Anabe ne bihwasi nabi binemerere oyu mwasi, kandji byende byanakukumana ne buba!	19. 오요 워머러러 과 구쭈ᄙᅡ 오ᅌᅩ 무우마 오싸오. 구비나ᄙᅦ! 아나버 너 비화시 나비 비너머러러 오유 뫄시, 가ᄧᅵ 벼ᄠᅥ 뱌나구구마나 너 부바!	19. You believe that there is one God. Good! Even the demons believe that--and shudder.
20. Woyo ulyi mbuta! Wahonda bakulose kwa ebwemeresi bwa butete myanya ibuya butete mufa?	20. 오요 우ᄙᅦ 뿌다! 와호ᄠᅡ 바구ᄙᅩ서 과 어붜머러시 봐 부더더 먀냐 이부야 부더더 무파?	20. You foolish man, do you want evidence that faith without deeds is useless?
21. Tata wetchu Aburahamu alorekanaa'ku ka walyi mundju ola utchungenene era muhondo sa Ongo kurengera emyanya yai ibuya, bushi atchulaa emwana wai Isaka nga mitchulo yakusiresa kwa kahaha.	21. 다다 워쭈 아부라하무 아ᄙᅩ러가나아구 가 와ᄙᅦ 무ᅜᅮ 오ᄙᅡ 우쭈ᄢᅥ너너 어라 무호ᄯᅩ 사 오ᅌᅩ 구러ᄢᅥ라 어먀냐 야이 이부야, 부씨 아쭈ᄙᅡ아 어뫄나 와이 이사가 ᄢᅡ 미쭈ᄙᅩ 야구시러사 과 가하하.	21. Was not our ancestor Abraham considered righteous for what he did when he offered his son Isaac on the altar?
22. Rero, utasene kwe bwemeresi bwa Aburahamu bwalorekanaa'ku kurengera emyanya yai ibuya, na mwei ndjira bwera kuba bwa bunalumilyire kanangana.	22. 러로, 우다서너 궈 붜머러시 봐 아부라하무 봐ᄙᅩ러가나아구 구러ᄢᅥ라 어먀냐 야이 이부야, 나 뭐이 ᄧᅵ라 붜라 구바 봐 부나ᄙᅮ미ᄙᅦ러 가나ᄢᅡ나.	22. You see that his faith and his actions were working together, and his faith was made complete by what he did.
23. Batcha kwe myasi itchula yandjikirwde mwa maandjiko mabuyabjuya yabereraa:	23. 바짜 궈 먀시 이쭈ᄙᅡ 야ᄧᅵ기루더 뫄 마아ᄧᅵ고 마부야부주야 야버러라아:	23. And the scripture was fulfilled that says, "Abraham believed God, and it was

Aburahamu emereraa Ongo, na Ongo era kumuandja kwa alyi mundju ola utchungenene era muhondo sai. Kandji era kumwelyika mbu alyi mwira wai.

24. Sin musene kwa kasi emundju ende alorekana'ku kwa atchungenene era muhondo sa Ongo kurengera bya aira, si ata kurengera ebwemeresi oshao.

25. Na Rahabu nai, tcha tchihungakasi kubyanabaa batcha. Ongo amutolaaa nga mundju ola utchungenene era muhondo sai mango ahuukasaa endjumwa sa Baisiraeli, tchasinda era kwongolosa'bu kurengera indji ndjira.

26. Kubinalyi! Emubilyi busira mutchima elyi afire. Kunoku ebwemeresi bwa butalorekana'ku kurengera emyanya nabo elyi bufire.

아부라하무 어머러라아 오꼬, 나 오꼬 어라 구무아짜 과 아쪠 무뚜 오꽈 우쭈꺼너너 어라 무호또 사이. 가찌 어라 구뭐쪠가 뿌 아쪠 뭐라 와이.

24. 시누 무서너 과 가시 어무뚜 어떠 아뢰러가나구 과 아쭈꺼너너 어라 무호또 사 오꼬 구러꺼라 뱌 아이라, 시 아다 구러꺼라 어붜머러시 오싸오.

25. 나 라하부 나이, 짜 찌후꺼가시 구뱌나바아 바짜. 오꼬 아무도롸아아 꺼 무뚜 오꽈 우쭈꺼너너 어라 무호또 사이 마꼬 아후우가사아 어뚜뫄 사 바이시라어쮜, 짜시따 어라 곤꼬롸사부 구러꺼라 이찌 찌라.

26. 구비나쪠! 어무비쪠 부시라 무찌마 어쪠 아피러. 구노구 어붜머러시 봐 부다뢰러가나구 구러꺼라 어먀냐 나보 어쪠 부피러.

credited to him as righteousness," and he was called God's friend.

24. You see that a person is justified by what he does and not by faith alone.

25. In the same way, was not even Rahab the prostitute considered righteous for what she did when she gave lodging to the spies and sent them off in a different direction?

26. As the body without the spirit is dead, so faith without deeds is dead.

Yakobo Chikono 3

1. Banyaketchu mwa katchikatchi kenyu, mutabaa bandju banene ba bahonda kuba bakangilyisi bushi mwishi kwa tchu bakangilyisi tchukatchindjibusibwa busese

야고보 찌고노 3

1. 바냐거쭈 뫄 가찌가찌 거뉴, 무다바아 바뚜 바너너 바 바호따 구바 바가꼐쪠시 부씨 뮈씨 과 쭈 바가꼐쪠시 쭈가찌찌부시봐 부서서 구러싸 어바찌.

James Chapter 3[NIV]

1. Not many of you should presume to be teachers, my brothers, because you know that we who teach will be judged more strictly.

kurenza ebandji.

2. Tchuboshi tchwende tchwaira mabi mu ndjira sinene. Emundju ola utauwa mwa mitetere yai, oyola alyi mundju ola ulumilyire kanangana, ete ne buashi bwe kulanga emubilyi wai woshi.

3. Tchwende tchwabika tchuma tchieke mwa bunu bwe farasi tchasiya sitchutchunde. Mwa kuira batcha tchwanaala kweka si era tchunasimire.

4. Mulolaa: ne bwato nabo, tchiro angaba mbu malyi manene busese, kandji mekibwa ne tchusi tchikalyire, si mende maenzibwa naka tchimbi kaeke ketchihaki na kwerekera era ola wende waenza mu asimire.

5. Kunoku, elulyimi nalo tchiri tchitera tchieke tche mubilyi si lungatchitonga ku myasi inene. Mutolaa engunyikunyi ye mulyiro yende yotcha eluira lunene.

6. Rero elulyimi lulyinga mulyiro. Thilyi tchitera tchieke tche mubilyi tcha tchehwire mu tchira bubi kandji tchende tchaaka emubilyi woshi esinga. Elulyimi lwende

2. 쭈보씨 쭤떠 좌이라 마비 무 찌라 시너너. 어무뿌 오랴 우다우와 먀 미더더러 야이, 오요롸 아뤠 무뿌 오랴 우루미뤠러 가나꽈나, 어더 너 부아씨 붜 구롸와 어무비뤠 와이 오씨.

3. 쭤떠 좌비가 쭈마 쩌거 먀 부누 붜 파라시 짜시야 시쭈쭈떠. 먀 구이라 바짜 좌나아롸 궈가 시 어라 쭈나시미러.

4. 무로롸아: 너 봐도 나보, 찌로 아꽈바 뿌 마뤠 마너너 부서서, 가찌 머기봐 너 쭈시 찌가뤠러, 시 머너 마어씨봐 나가 찌뻬 가어거 거찌하기 나 궈러거라 어라 오롸 워떠 와어싸 무 아시미러.

5. 구노구, 어루뤠미 나롣 찌리 찌더라 쩌거 쩌 무비뤠 시 루꽈찌도꽈 구 먀시 이너너. 무도롸아 어꾸네구네 여 무뤠로 여떠 요짜 어루이라 루너너.

6. 러로 어루뤠미 루뤠꽈 무뤠로. 찌뤠 찌더라 쩌거 쩌 무비뤠 짜 쩌휘러 무 찌라 부비 가찌 쩌떠 짜아가 어무비뤠 오씨 어시꽈. 어루뤠미 뤄떠 꽈시러러사

2. We all stumble in many ways. If anyone is never at fault in what he says, he is a perfect man, able to keep his whole body in check.

3. When we put bits into the mouths of horses to make them obey us, we can turn the whole animal.

4. Or take ships as an example. Although they are so large and are driven by strong winds, they are steered by a very small rudder wherever the pilot wants to go.

5. Likewise the tongue is a small part of the body, but it makes great boasts. Consider what a great forest is set on fire by a small spark.

6. The tongue also is a fire, a world of evil among the parts of the body. It corrupts the whole person, sets the whole course of his life on fire, and is itself set on fire by hell.

lwasiresa ekalamo ketchu, nalo lweine lwanasirera kurengera emulyiro ola watenga era kusimu.

어가롸모 거쭈, 나로 뤄이너 롸나시러라 구러꺼라 어무뤠로 오롸 와더까 어라 구시무.

7. Ebandju bende baala kulanga tchira buku bwa nyama so mwerungu, ne milonge ne sa sende saendera kwa bula, nefi. Ebyera, ebandju bera banalangalyire'bi.

7. 어바뉴 버떠 바아롸 구롸까 찌라 부구 봐 냐마 소 뭐루우, 너 미로꺼 너 사 서떠 사어떠라 과 부롸, 너피. 어벼라, 어바뉴 버라 바나롸까뤠러비.

7. All kinds of animals, birds, reptiles and creatures of the sea are being tamed and have been tamed by man,

8. Si elulyimi lweke, kutalyi mundju asibya ola ungaala kuklanga 'lu, bushi kalyi kandju kabi ka katatchibombeka. Kandji lutchula lwehuremu busunga bwa kuita.

8. 시 어루뤠미 뤄거, 구다뤠 무뉴 아시뱌 오롸 우까아롸 구구롸까 루, 부씨 가뤠 가뉴 가비 가 가다찌보뻐가. 가찌 루쭈롸 뤄후러무 부수까 봐 구이다.

8. but no man can tame the tongue. It is a restless evil, full of deadly poison.

9. Kurengera elulyimi tchwende tchwatonga Enawetchu ONgo; kandji i Tata. Kandji kurengera olu lulyimi lunolu, tchwende tchwatakira abandju ba Ongo abumbaa kwe huhe lyai.

9. 구러꺼라 어루뤠미 쮜떠 쫘도까 어나워쭈 오꼬; 가찌 이 다다. 가찌 구러꺼라 오루 루뤠미 루노루, 쮜떠 쫘다기라 아바뉴 바 오꼬 아부빠아 궈 후허 랴이.

9. With the tongue we praise our Lord and Father, and with it we curse men, who have been made in God's likeness.

10. mwa bunu buuma mwende mwatenga myasin ya ngahanyi, mwanatenga ne ye bitaki. Rero banyaketchu bitemire kunde byaba batcha.

10. 뫄 부누 부우마 뭐떠 뫄더까 먀시누 야 까하니, 뫄나더까 너 여 비다기. 러로 바냐거쭈 비더미러 구떠 뱌바 바짜.

10. Out of the same mouth come praise and cursing. My brothers, this should not be.

11. Shokororo nguma itangakula meshi ma malokire ne ma malula.

11. 쏘고로로 우마 이다까구롸 머씨 마 마로기러 너 마 마루롸.

11. Can both fresh water and salt water flow from the same spring?

12. Banyaketchu, emutchi we Tini angeka bifuma byo

12. 바냐거쭈, 어무찌 워 디니 아꺼가 비푸마 뵤

12. My brothers, can a fig tree bear olives, or a grapevine

Miseituni? Nesi emutchi we Musabibu angeka ebifuma bye Tini? Kunoku ku eshokororo era yende yaana emeshi me munyumunyu itangaala kuana emeshi ma malokire.	미서이두니? 너시 어무찌 워 무사비부 아꺼가 어비푸마 벼 디니? 구노구 구 어쏘고로로 어라 여떠 야아나 어머씨 머 무뉴무뉴 이다까아롸 구아나 어머씨 마 마롣기러.	bear figs? Neither can a salt spring produce fresh water.
13. Nde mwa katchikatchi kenyu ola ulyi mundju wa bwenge? Endaa alosa bu kurengera emyanya ibuya ne bya aira mwa burembu nomwa bwenge.	13. 떠 뫄 가찌가찌 거뉴 오롸 우뤠 무뀻 와 붜꺼? 어따아 아롣사 부 구러꺼라 어먀냐 이부야 너 뱌 아이라 뫄 부러뿌 노뫄 붜꺼.	13. Who is wise and understanding among you? Let him show it by his good life, by deeds done in the humility that comes from wisdom.
14. Si akaba mwa mitchima yenyu mungaba mwehure mufula, mwanaba na mutchima wakaimano, aola murekaa kunde mwa tchitonga mbu mulyi benge. Bushi ekuira batcha kulyi kubindjula ekanangana kuba bisha.	14. 시 아가바 뫄 미찌마 여뉴 무까바 뭐후러 무푸롸, 뫄나바 나 무찌마 와가이마노, 아오롸 무러가아 구떠 뫄 찌도까 뿌 무뤠 버꺼. 부씨 어구이라 바짜 구뤠 구비뀻롸 어가나까나 구바 비싸.	14. But if you harbor bitter envy and selfish ambition in your hearts, do not boast about it or deny the truth.
15. Ebwenge bwa bulyi ngobu butatengire kwa nguba, si bunalyi bwomuno butala kandji bwa bandju, bwanaba na bwa musimu.	15. 어붜꺼 봐 부뤠 옸부 부다더끼러 과 응구바, 시 부나뤠 봐무노 부다롸 가지 봐 바뀻, 봐나바 나 봐 무시무.	15. Such "wisdom" does not come down from heaven but is earthly, unspiritual, of the devil.
16. Bushi ala mufula ne mutchima wa kaimano bilyi, we kafango na tchira bubi boshi nabi byende byanaba.	16. 부씨 아롸 무푸롸 너 무찌마 와 가이마노 비뤠, 워 가파옸 나 찌라 부비 보씨 나비 벼떠 뱌나바.	16. For where you have envy and selfish ambition, there you find disorder and every evil practice.
17. Si ebwenge bwa butengire kwa nguba butchuila tanga:	17. 시 어붜꺼 봐 부더끼러 과 응구바 부쭈이롸 다까: 부고미시붜, 가지 부쭈롸 봐	17. But the wisdom that comes from heaven is first of all pure; then peace-loving,

bukomisibwe, kandji butchula bwa kureta bolo ne kuira emundju kuba murembu kandji butchula bwa kwaana ebandju ba batchusa obu bwenge bende bafirana ebondjo busese ne kukorerana emabuya. Batatchusa kalondo batatchusa na butebanyi.

구러다 보로 너 구이라 어무뿌 구바 무러뿌 가찌 부쭈롸 봐 과아나 어바뚜 바 바쭈사 오부 붜뻐 버뻐 바피라나 어보쪼 부서서 너 구고러라나 어마부야. 바다쭈사 가롣또 바다쭈사 나 부더바네.

considerate, submissive, full of mercy and good fruit, impartial and sincere.

18. Ba bende babika ebandju mwa buuma, bende bainga eboolo. Nabola bende bareta ebuolo.

18. 바 버뻐 바비가 어바뚜 뫄 부우마, 버뻐 바이까 어보오롣. 나보롸 버뻐 바러다 어부오롣.

18. Peacemakers who sow in peace raise a harvest of righteousness.

Yakobo Chikono 4

1. Emalwa ne mbangano bya bilyi mwa katchi-katchi ken yu, nagi yi bitengire? Bitengere mwa myasi ye kutchifindja-findja, ere yendjire yalwisanya mwa mitchima yenyu.

야고보 찌고노 4

1. 어마뫄 너 빠까노 뱌 비레 뫄 가찌-가찌 거누 유, 나지 에 비더끼러? 비더뻐러 뫄 먀시 여 구찌피짜-피짜, 어러 여찌러 야뤼사냐 뫄 미찌마 여뉴.

James Chapter 4[NIV]

1. What causes fights and quarrels among you? Don't they come from your desires that battle within you?

2. Ekutchanyirane mwita mwita ne kufa mufula mutete na kandju tcha mwahonda bushi noku mwendjire mwalwa ne kubangana, mutendjire mwabona tcha mwahonda bushi mutendjire mwema ea mwa Ongo.

2. 어구짜네라너 뮈다 뮈다 너 구파 무푸롸 무더더 나 가뚜 짜 뫄호따 부씨 노구 뭐찌러 뫄뫄 너 구바까나, 무더찌러 뫄보나 짜 뫄호따 부씨 무더찌러 뭐마 어아 뫄 오꼬.

2. You want something but don't get it. You kill and covet, but you cannot have what you want. You quarrel and fight. You do not have, because you do not ask God.

3. Mango mwema?utendjire mwabona kandju bushi mwendjire mwema bulyio mwa kuhonda kumisa ebuhumahuma bwenyu.

4. Emu babanzi bekiri, mteshi kwa ekuba mwira webutala kulyi kucthiira murenda waOngo? Bushi emundju ola ulyi mwira we butala amenyaa lkwa atchiilyire murenda wa Ongo.

5. Mutatchitchingaa mbu: Ongo ende afa mufula busese bushi ne mutchima mubuyabuya ola abikire mwa ndanda senyu.

6. Si Ongo atchuilyirire mabuya manene bushi emaandjiko mabuyabuya matchula matetchire mbu: Ongo ende alwisa ebandju be rume, si ebarembu ende abailyira emabuya.

7. Bushi noku, mundaa mwatchirembeka era muhondo sa Ongo ne kunde mwalwisa emisimu, mwa batcha angende ahaira bure nenyu.

8. Mundaa mwatchifunda ofu na Ongo, ani angatchifunda ofu nennyu mu bandju be mitchima ebilyi, mundaa mwakomya emitchima yenyu.

3. 마꼬 뭐마?우더찌러 뫄보나 가뚜 부씨 뭐찌러 뭐마 부레오 뫄 구호따 구미사 어부후마후마 뷔뉴.

4. 어무 바바씨 버기리, 떠씨과 어구바 뮈라 워부다롸 구레 구찌이라 무러따 와오꼬? 부씨 어무뚜 오롸 우레 뮈라 워 부다롸 아머냐아 루과 아찌이레러 무러따 와 오꼬.

5. 무다찌찌까아아 뿌: 오꼬 어떠 아파 무푸롸 부서서 부씨 너 무찌마 무부야부야 오롸 아비기러 뫄 따따 서뉴.

6. 시 오꼬 아쭈이레리러 마부야 마너너 부씨 어마아찌고 마부야부야 마쭈롸 마더찌러 뿌: 오꼬 어떠 아뤼사 어바뚜 버 루머, 시 어바러뿌 어떠 아바이레라 어마부야.

7. 부씨 노구, 무따아 뫄찌러뻐가 어라 무호또 사 오꼬 너 구떠 뫄뤼사 어미시무, 뫄 바짜 아어떠 아하이라 부러 너뉴.

8. 무따아 뫄찌푼따 오푸 나 오꼬, 아니 아까찌푼따 오푸 너뉴 무 바뚜 버 미찌마 어비레, 무따아 마고먀 어미찌마 여뉴.

3. When you ask, you do not receive, because you ask with wrong motives, that you may spend what you get on your pleasures.

4. You adulterous people, don't you know that friendship with the world is hatred toward God? Anyone who chooses to be a friend of the world becomes an enemy of God.

5. Or do you think Scripture says without reason that the spirit he caused to live in us envies intensely?

6. But he gives us more grace. That is why Scripture says: "God opposes the proud but gives grace to the humble."

7. Submit yourselves, then, to God. Resist the devil, and he will flee from you.

8. Come near to God and he will come near to you. Wash your hands, you sinners, and purify your hearts, you double-minded.

9. Mubaa mwa businane, mulyiraa ne kutchanya! Emasheka menyu mabindjukaa kuba malyira! Ne lumoo lwenyu lubindjukaa kuba businane!

10. Mundaa mwatchandaasa era muhondo sa Enawetchu, ani anagabeerusa

11. Banyaketchu, mutendaa mwaamanana bulyio. Bushi ola wateta bulyio era lulu sa munyakabo nesi amutchindjibusa elyi atetchire bulyio era lulu se mwaso kwa kuira ngokwa atetchire.

12. Ongo yeine oshao, iwabikaa emwaso kandji yeine oshao iunete ebuashi bwe kutchindjibusa. Kandji yeine iunete ebuashi bwe kununula ne kuita. Rero, woyo ulyi nde kwa ku tchindjibusa mulyikenyu?

13. Rero, munyumvilyisaa mu mwendjire mwateta mbu: lwarero nesi mishangya tchungaya mu musi murebe, tchungamala mu tchanda tcha mutenga tchu tchimbule ne kubone mutoloke.

14. Si muteshi kute ekalamo kenyu kangaba mishangya! Bushi mulyi nga musi ola

9. 무바아 똬 부시나너, 무레라아 너 구짜냐! 어마써가 머뉴 마비쭈가아 구바 마레라! 너 루모오 뤄뉴 루비쭈가아 구바 부시나너!

10. 무따아 똬짜따아사 어라 무호또 사 어나워쭈, 아니 아나가버어루사

11. 바냐거쭈, 무더따아 똬아마나나 부레오. 부씨 오똬 와더다 부레오 어라 루루 사 무냐가보 너시 아무찌찌부사 어레 아더찌러 부레오 어라 루루 서 먀소 과 구이라 꼬과 아더찌러.

12. 오꼬 여이너 오싸오, 이와비가아 어먀소 가찌 여이너 오싸오 이우너더 어부아씨 붜 구찌찌부사. 가찌 여이너 이우너더 어부아씨 붜 구누누똬 너 구이다. 러로, 오요 우레 떠 과 구 찌찌부사 무레거뉴?

13. 러로, 무뉴삐레사아 무 뭐찌러 먀더다 뿌: 똬러로 너시 미싸꺄 쭈따야 무 무시 무러버, 쭈까마똬 무 짜따 짜 무더따 쭈 찌뿌러 너 구보너 무도뤄거.

14. 시 무더씨 구더 어가꽈모 거뉴 가까바 미싸꺄! 부씨 무레 따 무시

9. Grieve, mourn and wail. Change your laughter to mourning and your joy to gloom.

10. Humble yourselves before the Lord, and he will lift you up.

11. Brothers, do not slander one another. Anyone who speaks against his brother or judges him speaks against the law and judges it. When you judge the law, you are not keeping it, but sitting in judgment on it.

12. There is only one Lawgiver and Judge, the one who is able to save and destroy. But you--who are you to judge your neighbor?

13. Now listen, you who say, "Today or tomorrow we will go to this or that city, spend a year there, carry on business and make money."

14. Why, you do not even know what will happen tomorrow. What is

useneke ku ku bihangi bieke anaokerera.

오라 우서너거 구 구 비하Ⓜ 비어거 아나오거러라.

your life? You are a mist that appears for a little while and then vanishes.

15. Mwamo mungendjire mwateta mbu: Enawetchu akasima tchungaba'u nekuira tchetchine nesi tchinera.

15. 먀모 무ⓦ찌러 먀더다 뿌: 어나워쭈 아가시마 쭈ⓜ바우 너구이라 쩌찌너 너시 찌너라.

15. Instead, you ought to say, "If it is the Lord's will, we will live and do this or that."

16. Si rero mwendjire mwatchihuta ala kabalyi ne kutchitonga, ekutchitonga kwa kulyi ngoku ku kutakomire.

16. 시 러로 뭐찌러 먀찌후다 아ⓦ 가바레 너 구찌도ⓦ, 어구찌도ⓦ 과 구레 Ⓜ구 구 구다고미러.

16. As it is, you boast and brag. All such boasting is evil.

17. Rero akaba emundju eshi kuira emabuya, si ataira'mu, aola amenyaa kwa ailyire byaa.

17. 러로 아가바 어무뉴 어씨 구이라 어마부야, 시 아다이라무, 아오ⓦ 아머냐아 과 아이ⓦ러 뱌아.

17. Anyone, then, who knows the good he ought to do and doesn't do it, sins.

Yakobo Chikono 5

1. Rero mwabu mu baare mumvilyisaa! Mulyiraa ne kutchana bushi ne buanya bwa bungabaikira.

야고보 찌고노 5

1. 러로 먀부 무 바아러 무ⓟ레사아! 무레라아 너 구짜나 부씨 너 부아냐 봐 부ⓜ바이기라.

James Chapter 5[NIV]

1. Now listen, you rich people, weep and wail because of the misery that is coming upon you.

2. Ebuare bwenyu bwabolyire ne ndjimba senyu salyirwe ne kaembe.

2. 어부아러 붜뉴 봐보레러 너 찌ⓜ바 서뉴 사레뤄 너 가어ⓟ.

2. Your wealth has rotted, and moths have eaten your clothes.

3. Ehoro ne buteya bwenyu byahukirwe ne luhwarenge, nolu luhwarenbe bu bukanaba bubei bwi myasi. Kandji bu bukanasingonola emibilyi yenyu ngokwa mulyiro ende anasingonosa. Mwatchibikilyire emwandju

3. 어호로 너 부더야 붜뉴 뱌후기뤄 너 루화러ⓦ, 노루 루화러누버 부 부가나바 부버이 뷔 먀시. 가찌 부 부가나시Ⓜ노ⓦ 어미비레 여뉴 Ⓜ과 무레로 어ⓤ 아나시Ⓜ노사. 먀찌비기레러 어먀뉴 뭐 시너 수구 서

3. Your gold and silver are corroded. Their corrosion will testify against you and eat your flesh like fire. You have hoarded wealth in the last days.

mwe sine suku se businda
bwe butala.

4. Mulolaa, mwananyire
kufuwa ebakosi ba
babakoreraa mwa mahwa
menyu. Rero kulyira ku
balyira, emilakango yabu
bakosi yanaikire mwa matchi
ma Enawetchu Ongo
iwabumbaa byoshi.

5. Mwabaa mulyi mwa muako
ne kunde mwatchimoeresa
mwa kalamo kenyu kwa
butala, mwabaa mwendjire
mwatchifesa nga nyama sa
salyindjira elusuku lwe
kukelyibwa.

6. Mwa tchindjibusaa ne kuita
ebandju ba batchungenene
nesi ata naira katalyi nenyu.

7. Rero banyaketchu mundaa
mwaata ebushibilyisi kuikira
mangi Enawetchu akafuluka.
Mulolaa kute kwa muinzi
enda alyindjira ashebule
emyaka era yete mutoloke
munene mwehwa lyai. Ende
alyindjilyira kuikira mango
emvula siberebere ne si
sindasinda sitowe.

8. Nenyu mundaa mwaata
bushibilyisi ne kusesa
emutchima bushi Enawetchu
alyi ofu kufuluka.

부시따 뭐 부다롸.

4. 무뤄롸아, 먀나니러
구푸와 어바고시 바
바바고러라아 롸 마화 머뉴.
러로 구례라 구 바례라,
어미롸가꼬 야부 바고시
야나이기러 롸 마찌 마
어나워쭈 오꼬 이와부빠아
뵤씨.

5. 뫄바아 무레 롸 무아고
너 구떠 뫄찌모어러사 뫄
가롸모 거뉴 과 부다롸,
뫄바아 뭐띠러 뫄찌퍼사 빠
냐마 사 사례띠라 어루수구
뤄 구거례봐.

6. 뫄 찌띠부사아 너 구이다
어바쭈 바 바쭈꺼너너 너시
아다 나이라 가다례 너뉴.

7. 러로 바냐거쭈 무따아
뫄아다 어부씨비례시
구이기라 마삐 어나워쭈
아가푸루가. 무뤄롸아 구더
과 무이씨 어따 아례띠라
아써부뤄 어먀가 어라 여더
무도뤄거 무너너 뭐화 롸이.
어떠 아례띠례라 구이기라
마꼬 어뿌롸 시버러버러 너
시 시따시따 시도워.

8. 너뉴 무따아 뫄아다
부씨비례시 너 구서사
어무찌마 부씨 어나워쭈
아레 오푸 구푸루가.

4. Look! The wages you failed
to pay the workmen who
mowed your fields are crying
out against you. The cries of
the harvesters have reached
the ears of the Lord Almighty.

5. You have lived on earth in
luxury and self-indulgence.
You have fattened yourselves
in the day of slaughter.

6. You have condemned and
murdered innocent men, who
were not opposing you.

7. Be patient, then, brothers,
until the Lord's coming. See
how the farmer waits for the
land to yield its valuable crop
and how patient he is for the
autumn and spring rains.

8. You too, be patient and
stand firm, because the Lord's
coming is near.

9. Banyaketchu, mutendaa mwasibukirana, Ongo angesha kuba tchindjibuso. Mulolaa emusihi we mandja kwa tchiso ku era alyi!

9. 바냐거쭈, 무더따아 마시부기라나, 오꼬 아꺼싸 구바 찌찌부소. 무로롸아 어무시히 워 마짜 과 찌소 구 어라 아뤠!

9. Don't grumble against each other, brothers, or you will be judged. The Judge is standing at the door!

10. Banyeketchu, mundaa mwakengera ebarebi ba bendee bareba kwe sina lya Enawetchu. Mulolaa kwa bendee baata ebushibilyisi mwa malyibuko, nenyu mundaaa mweye'bu.

10. 바녀거쭈, 무따아 퐈거꺼라 어바러비 바 버떠어 바라바 궈 시나 퍄 어나워쭈. 무로롸아 과 버떠어 바아다 어부씨비뤠시 퐈 마뤠부고, 너뉴 무따아아 뭐여부.

10. Brothers, as an example of patience in the face of suffering, take the prophets who spoke in the name of the Lord.

11. Tchwende tchwateta mbu abu bandju baahanyirwe bushi babaa bete bushibilyisi. Mwomvire kute Yobu abaa atchusa ebushibilyisi kandji mushi nokwa Enawetchu amuilyiraa kwa businda. Kubinalyi, Enawetchu atchula wa bondjo bunene kandji atchula mubuya.

11. 쮀떠 좌더다 뿌 아부 바뉴 바아하니뤄 부씨 바바아 버더 부씨비뤠시. 모뻬러 구더 요부 아바아 아쭈사 어부씨비뤠시 가찌 무씨 노과 어나워쭈 아무이뤠라아 과 부시따. 구비나뤠, 어나워쭈 아쭈롸 와 보쪼 부너너 가찌 아쭈롸 무부야.

11. As you know, we consider blessed those who have persevered. You have heard of Job's perseverance and have seen what the Lord finally brought about. The Lord is full of compassion and mercy.

12. Rero era muhondo sa byoshi banyeketchu, mutendaa mwalaisa, nesi kwe sina lya kandji kandju koshi. Ekwemerera kunabaa kwemerera, ne kunana kunabaa kunana, Ongo angesha kubatchindjibusa.

12. 러로 어라 무호또 사 뵤씨 바녀거쭈, 무더따아 퐈라이사, 너시 궈 시나 퍄 가찌 가뉴 고씨. 어궈머러라 구나바아 궈머러라, 너 구나나 구나바아 구나나, 오꼬 아꺼싸 구바찌찌부사.

12. Above all, my brothers, do not swear--not by heaven or by earth or by anything else. Let your "Yes" be yes, and your "No," no, or you will be condemned.

13. Mwa katchikatchi kenyu mulyi mundju ola walyibuka? Emaa Ongo. Kulyi ola ulyi mwa lumoo? Embaa nyimbo sa kutonga Ongo.

13. 퐈 가찌가찌 거뉴 무뤠 무뉴 오롸 와뤠부가? 어마아 오꼬. 구뤠 오롸 우뤠 퐈 루모오? 어빠아 니뽀 사 구도꽈 오꼬.

13. Is any one of you in trouble? He should pray. Is anyone happy? Let him sing songs of praise.

14. Mwa katchikatchi kenyu mulyi mulwala? Amaalaa ebangumwa be luhu lwa Ongo, bamwemere ne kumwakaba emafuta kwe sina lya Enawetchu Yesu Kirisito.

15. Bakema ne bwemeresi oyu mulwala angalama bushi Enawetchu angahuba kumwenamula. Na akaba akolyire byaa, angababalyirwa.

16. Rero mundaa mwatchiaya kwa byaa byenyu, tchira mundju era muhondo sa mulyikabo, ne kunde mwemerana tchasiya mulamisibwe. Ememo me mundju ola utchungenene era muhondo sa Ongo, matchusa buashi bunene.

17. Eliya abaa mundju kuuma netchu. Era kwema Ongo nebushiru mbu emvula itatowaa, emvula tchiro ikatoa kwa tchitaka ku byanda bihatchu na biranga ndatchu.

18. Tchasinda, era kuhuba kwema, enguba year kutosa emvula ne tchitaka tchera kwesa emyaka.

19. Banyaketchu, akaba muuma mu mwabo aire bure ne myasi ye kanangana, tchasinda undji mundju

14. 먀 가찌가찌 거뉴 무레 무똬퐈? 아마아퐈아 어바우똬 버 루후 똬 오꼬, 바뭐머러 너 구똬가바 어마푸다 궈 시나 퍄 어나워쭈 여수 기리시도.

15. 바거마 너 붜머러시 오유 무똬퐈 아똬퐈마 부씨 어나워쭈 아똬후바 구뭐나무똬. 나 아가바 아고레러 뱌아, 아똬바바레롸.

16. 러로 무따아 똬찌아야 과 뱌아 벼뉴, 찌라 무뚜 어라 무호또 사 무레가보, 너 구떠 뭐머라나 짜시야 무똬미시붜. 어머모 머 무뚜 오라 우쭈써너너 어라 무호또 사 오꼬, 마쭈사 부아씨 부너너.

17. 어퓌야 아바아 무뚜 구우마 너쭈. 어라 궈마 오꼬 너부씨루 뿌 어뿌퐈 이다도와아, 어뿌퐈 찌로 이가도아 과 찌다가 구 뱌따 비하쭈 나 비라퐈 따쭈.

18. 짜시따, 어라 구후바 궈마, 어우바 여라 구도사 어뿌퐈 너 찌다가 쩌라 궈사 어먀가.

19. 바냐거쭈, 아가바 무우마 무 먀보 아이러 부러 너 먀시 여 가나똬나, 짜시따 우찌 무뚜 아나후바

14. Is any one of you sick? He should call the elders of the church to pray over him and anoint him with oil in the name of the Lord.

15. And the prayer offered in faith will make the sick person well; the Lord will raise him up. If he has sinned, he will be forgiven.

16. Therefore confess your sins to each other and pray for each other so that you may be healed. The prayer of a righteous man is powerful and effective.

17. Elijah was a man just like us. He prayed earnestly that it would not rain, and it did not rain on the land for three and a half years.

18. Again he prayed, and the heavens gave rain, and the earth produced its crops.

19. My brothers, if one of you should wander from the truth and someone should bring him back,

anahuba kumufulusa.

20. Mumenyaa kwa ola wafulusise emukasi we byaa kutenga mwa ndjira yai ibi, angaba anunwire ekalamo koyu mundju mwa lufu na Ongo angamubabalyira ku mabi manene.

구무푸루사.

20. 무머냐아 과 오라 와푸루시서 어무가시 워 뱌아 구더까 뫄 띠라 야이 이비, 아까바 아누니위러 어가쫘모 고유 무뚜 뫄 루푸 나 오꼬 아까무바바례라 구 마비 마너너.

20. remember this: Whoever turns a sinner from the error of his way will save him from death and cover over a multitude of sins.

1 Petero

1 퍼더로

1 Peter

PETERO MUBEREBERE

(1 PETER)

퍼더로 무버러버러
(1 퍼더로)

1 Petero Chikono 1

1. Nyono Petero, ndjumwa ya Yesu Kirisito nyina andjika manu maruba. Nabaandjikira mwabo mu Ongo alondore, mu muhundo banyire mwa tchio tche Pondo ne tche Kalatiya netche Kapatokiya ne tche Asiya nomwa tche Bitiniya.

2. Ongo Tata abalondolaa kukulyikana nokwa abaa afundjikire emwasi mira. Abairire kuba bandju bai kurengera emutchima mubuya-buya tchasiya munde mwatchunda Yesu Kirisito, nakukomisibwa kurengera emikira yai.

3. Tchundaa tchwatonga Ongo, eshe wa Enawetchu Yesu Kirisito kurengera ebondjo bwai bunene atchweresise kalamo kayayaya mwa komola Yesu Kirisito. Mwa batcha tchwabonyire emunyiiro ola utakawe.

4. Kandji mwa batcha tchwalyindjirira engahanyi sa Ongo abikirire ebandju bai ; esi ngahanyi Ongo ababikirire'si kwa nguba, okola sitakabole nesi kuya

1 퍼더로 찌고노 1

1. 뇨노 퍼더로, 쑤롸 야 여수 기리시도 네나 아찌가 마누 마루바. 나바아찌기라 롸보 무 오꼬 아롣또러, 무 무후또 바네러 롸 찌오 쩌 포또 너 쩌 가롸디야 너쩌 가파도기야 너 쩌 아시야 노롸 쩌 비디니야.

2. 오꼬 다다 아바롣또롸아 구구쩨가나 노과 아바아 아푸찌기러 어롸시 미라. 아바이리러 구바 바쑤 바이 구러꺼라 어무찌마 무부야- 부야 짜시야 무떠 롸쭈따 여수 기리시도, 나구고미시봐 구러꺼라 어미기라 야이.

3. 쭈따아 쫘도꺼 오꼬, 어써 와 어나워쭈 여수 기리시도 구러꺼라 어보쪼 봐이 부너너 아쮀러시서 가롸모 가야야야 롸 고모롸 여수 기리시도. 롸 바짜 쫘보네러 어무네이로 오롸 우다가워.

4. 가찌 롸 바짜 쫘쩨찌리라 어꺼하네 사 오꼬 아비기리러 어바쑤 바이 ; 어시 꺼하네 오꼬 아바비기리러시 과 꾸바, 오고롸 시다가보러 너시

1 Peter Chapter 1[NIV]

1. To the elders among you, I appeal as a fellow elder, a witness of Christ's sufferings and one who also will share in the glory to be revealed:

2. Be shepherds of God's flock that is under your care, serving as overseers--not because you must, but because you are willing, as God wants you to be; not greedy for money, but eager to serve;

3. not lording it over those entrusted to you, but being examples to the flock.

4. And when the Chief Shepherd appears, you will receive the crown of glory that will never fade away.

kwe singa nesi ku kunguwa.

5. Kurengera ebwemeresi bwenyu Ongo endjire abalanga kwa buashi bwai tchasiya abanunule, obu bununusi bukalorekana'ku mwa suku se businda.

6. Rero, mundaa mwamowa busese tchiro angaba mbu bitchiri bibemire kulyibuka ku bihangi bieke bushi ne miereko ya tchira ndjira era mwarenga'mo.

7. Amu malyibuko malyi ma makuereka ebwemeresi bwenyu. Ehoro kalyi kandju ka kende kakumba, si tchiro batcha yende ya erekibwa mwa kuirenza mwa mulyiro. Rero ebwemeresi bwenyu bu bweete mufa munene kurenza ehoro. Si nabo buneemire kuerekibwa, tchasiya bulorekane'ku kwa bunalyi bwa kanangana. Etchera tchi tchingatchuma mwatongibwa nekuya ngulu ne kweeresibwa etchunda mango Yesu Kirisito akahuba kubaha.

8. Mwabo mutafuraa kulola ku Yesu, si mumusimire. Kandji mutamusene'ku si

구야 궈 시싸 너시 구 구우와.

5. 구러ᄶᅥ라 어붸머러시 붜뉴 오꼬 어찌러 아바짜와 과 부아씨 봐이 짜시야 아바누누ᄲᅥ, 오부 부누누시 부가ᄙᅩ러가나구 봐 수구 서 부시ᄯᅡ.

6. 러로, 무ᄯᅡ아 봐모와 부서서 찌로 아까바 뿌 비찌리 비버미러 구ᄶᅦ부가 구 비하끼 비어거 부씨 너 미어러고 야 찌라 띠라 어라 뫄러까모.

7. 아무 마ᄶᅦ부고 마ᄶᅦ 마 마구어러가 어붸머러시 붜뉴. 어호로 가ᄶᅦ 가ᄶᅮ 가 거ᄯᅥ 가구빠, 시 찌로 바짜 여ᄯᅥ 야 어러기봐 뫄 구이러싸 뫄 무ᄶᅦ로. 러로 어붸머러시 붜뉴 부 붜어더 무파 무너너 구러싸 어호로. 시 나보 부너어미러 구어러기봐, 짜시야 부ᄙᅩ러가너구 과 부나ᄶᅦ 봐 가나까나. 어쩌라 찌 찌까쭈마 뫄도끼봐 너구야 어꾸루 너 궈어러시봐 어쭈ᄯᅡ 마꼬 여수 기리시도 아가후바 구바하.

8. 뫄보 무다푸라아 구ᄙᅩ짜 구 여수, 시 무무시미러. 가찌 무다무서너구 시

5. Young men, in the same way be submissive to those who are older. All of you, clothe yourselves with humility toward one another, because, "God opposes the proud but gives grace to the humble."

6. Humble yourselves, therefore, under God's mighty hand, that he may lift you up in due time.

7. Cast all your anxiety on him because he cares for you.

8. Be self-controlled and alert. Your enemy the devil prowls around like a

mumweemerere. Etchera tchi tcheendjire tchatchuma mwaba mu lumoo lunene busese lwa lutangamaanyibwa.

9. Mwete olu lumoo, bushi mwaikirire kwa lweembo lwe bwemeresi bwenyu, nolu lwembo kulyi ekununulyibwa kwenyu.

10. Ebarebi batchisesaa kuhonda bamenyerere ekanangana emyasi era yeerekere obununusi. Bera kunareba era luulu se lwembo lwa Ongo angaberesise.

11. Emutchima wa Kirisito ola abu barebi babaa beete abaa atetchire mira era luulu se malyibuko ma Kirisito akabona ne tchunda lya akabona era nyuma samu malyibuko. Abu barebi batchaanaa busese bamenyerere mangotchi namu ndjira itchiye mu ei myasi ikaba.

12. Ongo alosaa abu barebi kwa emwasi ola babaa bendjire babala abaa aterekere'bu, si mwabo mu abaa erekere. Rero oyu mwasi mwomnire'u

무뭐어머러러. 어쩌라 찌 쩌어찌러 짜쭈마 마바 무 루루모오 루너너 부서서 꽈 루다까마아니봐.

9. 뭐더 오루 루모오, 부씨 마이기리러 과 뭐어뽀 뭐 뷰머러시 뷰뉴, 노루 뭐뽀 구쩨 어구누누쩨봐 궈뉴.

10. 어바러비 바찌서사아 구호따 바머녀러러 어가나까나 어먀시 어라 여어러거러 오부누누시. 버라 구나러바 어라 루우루 서 뭐뽀 꽈 오꼬 아까버러시서.

11. 어무찌마 와 기리시도 오꽈 아부 바러비 바바아 버어더 아바아 아더찌러 미라 어라 루우루 서 마쩨부고 마 기리시도 아가보나 너 쭈따 꺄 아가보나 어라 뉴마 사무 마쩨부고. 아부 바러비 바짜아나아 부서서 바머녀러러 마꼬찌 나무 찌라 이찌여 무 어이 먀시 이가바.

12. 오꼬 아론사아 아부 바러비 과 어뫄시 오꽈 바바아 버찌러 바바꽈 아바아 아더러거러부, 시 뫄보 무 아바아 어러거러. 러로 오유 먀시 모무니러우

roaring lion looking for someone to devour.

9. Resist him, standing firm in the faith, because you know that your brothers throughout the world are undergoing the same kind of sufferings.

10. And the God of all grace, who called you to his eternal glory in Christ, after you have suffered a little while, will himself restore you and make you strong, firm and steadfast.

11. To him be the power for ever and ever. Amen.

12. With the help of Silas, whom I regard as a faithful brother, I have written to you briefly, encouraging you and testifying that this is the true grace of God. Stand fast in

kurengera ba bendjire
bahubanganya etchinwa tcha
Ongo kwa buashi bwe
Mutchima Mubuya-buya ola
watchumwaa kutenga kwa
nguba. Oyu mwasi endonyi
nabo bendjire bahonda
bamenyerere'u.

구러써라 바 버찌러
바후바까냐 어찌놔 짜 오끄
과 부아씨 붜 무찌마
무부야-부야 오롸 와쭈뫄아
구더까 과 우바. 오유 뫄시
어또네 나보 버찌러 바호따
바머녀러러우.

it.

13. Bushi noku
mutchikunganyaa kwakukola
emulyimo. Mutchilanga-
langaa nekubika emunyiiro
wenyu woshi kwa lwembo
lwa mukabona mango Yesu
Kirisito akahuba kubaha.

13. 부씨 노구 무찌구까냐아
과구고롸 어무레모.
무찌롸까-롸까아 너구비가
어무네이로 워뉴 오씨 과
뤄뫋 롸 무가보나 마쯔
여수 기리시도 아가후바
구바하.

13. She who is in Babylon,
chosen together with you,
sends you her greetings, and
so does my son Mark.

14. Mundaa mwatchunda
Ongo, mutatchihubiriraa
emianyisa yenyu ibi era
mwabaa mutchusa kwa mira,
mango mwabaa mutchiri
mwa buuta.

14. 무따아 뫄쭈따 오끄,
무다찌후비리라아
어미아네사 여뉴 이비 어라
뫄바아 무쭈사 과 미라,
마쯔 뫄바아 무찌리 뫄
부우다.

14. Greet one another with a
kiss of love. Peace to all of you
who are in Christ.

15. Si kwa Ongo ola
wabaamaala atchula
mubuya-buya, nenyu
kumunabaa babuyabuya
mwa myanya yenyu yoshi.

15. 시 과 오끄 오롸
와바아마아롸 아쭈롸
무부야-부야, 너뉴
구무나바아 바부야부야 뫄
먀냐 여뉴 요씨.

15. But just as he who called
you is holy, so be holy in all
you do;

16. Bushi emaandjiko
mabuyabuya matchula
matetchire mbu : mubaa
babuya buya bushi nyeine
nyilyi mubuya buya.

16. 부씨 어마아찌고
마부야부야 마쭈롸
마더찌러 뿌 : 무바아
바부야 부야 부씨 녀이너
네레 무부야 부야.

16. for it is written: "Be holy,
because I am holy."

17. Mwa meemo menyu
mwende mwelyika mbu : Tata
ola wende watchindjibusa
ebandju busira kalondo

17. 뫄 머어모 머뉴 뭐떠
뭐레가 뿌 : 다다 오롸 워떠
와찌찌부사 어바뉴 부시라
가롣또 구구레가나 너 먀냐

17. Since you call on a Father
who judges each man's work
impartially, live your lives as
strangers here in reverent fear.

kukulyikana ne myanya yenyu indaa yalosa kwa mumutchundjire.

여뉴 이따아 야로사 과 무무쭈찌러.

18. Mwishi kwe myanya era bakulukulu benyu babarekeraa itchula ya buha buha, kandji mwishi kwa Ongo atabanunwire kurengera ebindju bya bende byakumba ngakuno ehoro nesi emiringa.

18. 뮈씨 귀 먀냐 어라 바구루구루 버뉴 바바러거라아 이쭈꽈 야 부하 부하, 가찌 뮈씨 과 오꼬 아다바누니위러 구러꺼라 어비뿌 뱌 버버 뱌구빠 까구노 어호로 너시 어미리꽈.

18. For you know that it was not with perishable things such as silver or gold that you were redeemed from the empty way of life handed down to you from your forefathers,

19. Si abanunwire kurengera emikira ye tchitchiro tchinene ya Kirisito, iulyi nga mwana we mbulyi ola utete burema nesi tchibi tchisibya.

19. 시 아바누니위러 구러꺼라 어미기라 여 찌찌로 찌너너 야 기리시도, 이우레 까 먀나 워 뿌레 오꽈 우더더 부러마 너시 찌비 찌시뱌.

19. but with the precious blood of Christ, a lamb without blemish or defect.

20. Oyu Kirisito Ongo amulondolaa era muhondo se kubumbwa kwe butala ne kubalosa'i tchasiya mumumenye kwa mutoloke wenyu mwe sine suku se businda.

20. 오유 기리시도 오꼬 아무로또꽈라아 어라 무호또 서 구부빠 귀 부다꽈 너 구바로사이 짜시야 무무머녀 과 무도로거 워뉴 뭐 시너 수구 서 부시따.

20. He was chosen before the creation of the world, but was revealed in these last times for your sake.

21. Kurengera Kirisito, ku mwemerere Ongo iwamwomolaa ne kumweresa etchunda. Etchera tchi tchitchumire mwemerera Ongo ne kumulangalyira.

21. 구러꺼라 기리시도, 구 뭐머러러 오꼬 이와모모꽈라아 너 구뭐러사 어쭈따. 어쩌라 찌 쭈미러 뭐머러라 오꼬 너 구무꽈까레라.

21. Through him you believe in God, who raised him from the dead and glorified him, and so your faith and hope are in God.

22. Mwabo mwakomisibwe mira kurengera ekutchunda emyasi ye kanangana tchasiya munde mwasima

22. 꽈보 꽈고미시붜 미라 구러꺼라 어구쭈따 어먀시 여 가나꽈나 짜시야 무떠 꽈시마 바냐거쭈 버머러시

22. Now that you have purified yourselves by obeying the truth so that you have sincere love for your brothers, love one

banyaketchu bemeresi busira
butebanyi. Mundaa
mwasimana busese ne
mutchima wenyu yoshi.

23. Mwabutchirwe buyayaya
kurengera etchinwa tcha
Ongo. Etchi tchinwa tchitalyi
nga mbuto era yende
yakumba. Si tchiri tchiuma-
uma tchitangana kumba
kandji tchikanaendekera kuba
esuku ne mango.

24. Bushi emaandjiko
mabuyabuya matchula
matetchire mbu : ebandju
boshi balyi nga bicthi ne
tchunda lyabo boshi lyilyi
nga bwaso, ebitchi byomire,
ebitchi byende byoma, ne
bwaso bwana tchitowangira.

25. Si etchinwa tcha
Enawetchu tcheke
tchinatchula'o esuku ne
mango. Netchi tchinwa analyi
mwasi mubuyabuya ola
mwahubanganyisibwa.

부시라 부더바네. 무따아
마시마나 부서서 너 무찌마
워뉴 요씨.

23. 롸부찌뤄 부야야야
구러꺼라 어찌냐 짜 오꼬.
어찌 찌냐 찌다레 꺼 뿌도
어라 여떠 야구빠. 시 찌리
찌우마-우마 찌다꺼나 구빠
가찌 찌가나어떠거라 구바
어수구 너 마꼬.

24. 부씨 어마아찌고
마부야부야 마쭈꽈
마더찌러 뿌 : 어바뉴 보씨
바레 꺼 비찌 너 쭈따 랴보
보씨 레레 꺼 봐소, 어비찌
뵤미러, 어비찌 벼떠 뵤마,
너 봐소 봐나 찌도와꺼라.

25. 시 어찌냐 짜 어나워쭈
쩌거 찌나쭈꽈오 어수구 너
마꼬. 너찌 찌냐 아나레
마시 무부야부야 오꽈
롸후바꺼네시봐.

another deeply, from the heart.

23. For you have been born
again, not of perishable seed,
but of imperishable, through
the living and enduring word of
God.

24. For, "All men are like grass,
and all their glory is like the
flowers of the field; the grass
withers and the flowers fall,

25. but the word of the Lord
stands forever." And this is the
word that was preached to you.

1 Petero Chikono 2

1. Rero murekaa kunde
mwaira tchira tchibi.
Mutendaa mwafula bisha,
mutabaa batebanyi,
mutendaa mwafa mufula,
mutendaa mwamaana

1 퍼더로 찌고노 2

1. 러로 무러가아 구떠
롸이라 찌라 찌비. 무더따아
롸푸꽈 비싸, 무다바아
바더바네, 무더따아 롸파
무푸꽈, 무더따아 롸마아나
어바찌 부레요.

1 Peter Chapter 2[NIV]

1. Therefore, rid yourselves of
all malice and all deceit,
hypocrisy, envy, and slander of
every kind.

ebandji bulyiyo.

2. Ngokwa etchubondjobondjo tchwabutchwa batchilyindja emango me etchinwa tcha Ongo. Etchi tchinwa, tchiri nga mbere ma matahoonganyisibwe. Rero mwa kwoongamo, mungakula ne kununulyibwa.

2. 꼬과 어쭈보뇨보뇨 쫘부좌 바찌레쨔 어마꼬 머 어찌놔 짜 오오. 어찌 찌놔, 찌리 까 뻐러 마 마다호오꺄네시붜. 러로 뫄 고오꺄모, 무꺄구꽈 너 구누누레봐.

2. Like newborn babies, crave pure spiritual milk, so that by it you may grow up in your salvation,

3. Bushi emaandjiko mabuyabuya matchula matetchire mbu mubeine mwatchilorere mira kwa Enawetchu atchula mubuya.

3. 부씨 어마아찌고 마부야부야 마쭈꽈 마더찌러 뿌 무버이너 꽈찌로러러 미라 과 어나워쭈 아쭈꽈 무부야.

3. now that you have tasted that the Lord is good.

4. Mundaa mwaba ofu na Enawetchu bushi lyi koi lye kalamo, elyi koi, ebandju bakabulyira'lyi si Ongo alyi londolaa lyiri na lya tchiro tchinene busese era muhondo sai.

4. 무따아 꽈바 오푸 나 어나워쭈 부씨 레 고이 뗘 가꽈모, 어레 고이, 어바뿌 바가부뗴라레 시 오꼬 아레 로또꽈아 레리 나 꺄 찌로 찌너너 부서서 어라 무호또 사이.

4. As you come to him, the living Stone--rejected by men but chosen by God and precious to him--

5. rero nenyu mubaa nga makoi ma meete ekalamo, tchasiya mukoresibwe kwa kuimba enyumba ye mutchima mubuyabuya. Kandji mungaba bajungu babuyabuya ba bangende bakola emulyimo we kueresa Ongo emitchulo kukulyikana ne mutchima mubuyabuya wai. Ei mitchulo, Ongo angende ayemerera kurengera Yesu Kirisito.

5. 러로 너뉴 무바아 꺄 마고이 마 머어더 어가꽈모, 짜시야 무고러시붜 과 구이빠 어뉴빠 여 무찌마 무부야부야. 가찌 무꺄바 바주우 바부야부야 바 바꺼떠 바고꽈 어무레모 워 구어러사 오꼬 어미쭈로 구구떼가나 너 무찌마 무부야부야 와이. 어이 미쭈로, 오꼬 아꺼떠 아여머러라 구러꺼라 여수 기리시도.

5. you also, like living stones, are being built into a spiritual house to be a holy priesthood, offering spiritual sacrifices acceptable to God through Jesus Christ.

6. Bushi yaandjikirwe mwa maandjiko mabuyabuya mbu : Mulolaa nashingire ekoi lyinene lyokwa musike lyemikirwe lye tchunda. Nola uka mwemeravatakafe honyi cthiro na hitcha.

7. Rero etchunda lyinera lyilyi lyenyu mu mwemerere si kwabala batalremerere ekoyi lyabalaira ebatengu, lyabere lyinene kwa musiki.

8. Kandji byaandjikirwe mbu: Elyi koi lyiri lya kusitabu kwe kuulu kandji lyilyi lundandalyi lwa kukumbaasa bushi lya sitasa kwa tchinwa, bata emerea'tchi nabo babikwa bushi babone'tchi. Abu bandju bendjire basitala bushi bende banana kwemerera etchinwa tcha Ongo, etchera tchi banalawaa kutengera mira.

9. Si mwabo mulyi bandju ba Ongo alondore, kandji mulyi bakuhanyi ba mwami, kandji mulyi lubaa lubuyabuya. Abailyire kuba lubaa lwai tchasiya munde mwabalyira ebandju emyasi ye bisomerane era ende aira. Oyola iwabamaaalaa mutenge mwa musimya na

6. 부씨 야아찌기뤄 똬 마아찌고 마부야부야 뿌 : 무로콰아 나씨삐러 어고이 레너너 료과 무시거 려미기뤄 려 쭈따. 노라 우가 뭐머라바다가퍼 호니 찌로 나 히짜.

7. 러로 어쭈따 레너라 레레 려뉴 무 뭐머러러 시 과바콰 바다뤄러머러러 어고에 퍄바콰이라 어바더우, 퍄버러 레너너 과 무시기.

8. 가찌 바아찌기뤄 뿌: 어레 고이 레리 퍄 구시다부 궈 구우루 가찌 레레 루따따레 콰 구구빠아사 부씨 퍄 시다사 과 찌나, 바다 어머러아찌 나보 바비과 부씨 바보너찌. 아부 바쭈 버찌러 바시다퐈 부씨 버떠 바나나 궈머러라 어찌나 짜 오꼬, 어쩌라 찌 바나퐈와아 구더떠라 미라.

9. 시 똬보 무레 바쭈 바 오꼬 아로또러, 가찌 무레 바구하니 바 똬미, 가찌 무레 루바아 루부야부야. 아바이레러 구바 루바아 콰이 짜시야 무떠 똬바레라 어바쭈 어먀시 여 비소머라너 어라 어떠 아이라. 오요퐈 이와바마아아퐈아 무더떠

6. For in Scripture it says: "See, I lay a stone in Zion, a chosen and precious cornerstone, and the one who trusts in him will never be put to shame."

7. Now to you who believe, this stone is precious. But to those who do not believe, "The stone the builders rejected has become the capstone,"

8. and, "A stone that causes men to stumble and a rock that makes them fall." They stumble because they disobey the message--which is also what they were destined for.

9. But you are a chosen people, a royal priesthood, a holy nation, a people belonging to God, that you may declare the praises of him who called you out of darkness into his wonderful light.

kubeengisa mwa bulangare
bwai bwebisomerane.

10. Kwa mira, mwabaa
mutatchula bandju ba Ongo,
si lwarero mwera bandju bai.
Kandji kwa mira Ongo abaa
atabafira bondjo si lwarero
endjire abafira'bu.

11. Bera banyi Basiirwa mulyi
baenyi kandji bandju ba
babungirire muno butala.
Bushi noku nabeema busese
mutendaa mwakulyoikira
emyasi ye buumauma ye
mubiri era yendjire yabalwisa.

12. Mundaa mwaata myanya
ibuya mwa katchikatchi ke
bandju be sinyi mbaa.
Mundaa mwanaira batcha
tchasiya mango bangende
babasinga mbu mwailyire
mabi, banende batchilorera
kwei myanya yenyu ibuya.
Mwa batcha mango Ongo
akaiba, banamutonga.

13. Bushi ne'Enawetchu
mundaa mwatchundaa
ebakulukulu ba bemire
mutchundaa, mwami bushi
iwete ebuashi kwa bandju
boshi.

14. Mwanatchunda ne
bakulukulu ba bemikirwe ne

마 무시먀 나 구버어찌사
마 부꽈찌러 봐이
뭐비소머라너.

10. 과 미라, 마바아
무다쭈꽈 바뉴 바 오꼬, 시
꽈러로 뭐라 바뉴 바이.
가찌 과 미라 오꼬 아바아
아다바피라 보쪼 시 꽈러로
어찌러 아바피라부.

11. 버라 바네 바시이롸
무꿰 바어네 가찌 바뉴 바
바부찌리러 무노 부다꽈.
부씨 노구 나버어마 부서서
무더따아 마구뾔이기라
어먀시 여 부우마우마 여
무비리 어라 여찌러
야바뤼사.

12. 무따아 마아다 먀냐
이부야 마 가찌가찌 거
바뉴 버 시니 빠아. 무따아
마나이라 바짜 짜시야 마꼬
바찌떠 바바시아 뿌
마이쮀러 마비, 바너떠
바찌뾴러라 궈이 먀냐 여뉴
이부야. 마 바짜 마꼬 오꼬
아가이바, 바나무도꽈.

13. 부씨 너어나워쭈 무따아
마쭈따아 어바구룩구룩 바
버미러 무쭈따아, 마미 부씨
이워더 어부아씨 과 바뉴
보씨.

14. 마나쭈따 너 바구룩구룩
바 버미기뤄 너 마미 과 구

10. Once you were not a
people, but now you are the
people of God; once you had
not received mercy, but now
you have received mercy.

11. Dear friends, I urge you, as
aliens and strangers in the
world, to abstain from sinful
desires, which war against your
soul.

12. Live such good lives among
the pagans that, though they
accuse you of doing wrong,
they may see your good deeds
and glorify God on the day he
visits us.

13. Submit yourselves for the
Lord's sake to every authority
instituted among men: whether
to the king, as the supreme
authority,

14. or to governors, who are
sent by him to punish those

mwami kwa ku tchindjibusa ebakosi be mabi ne kutonga ba bende bakola emabuya.

15. Bushi Ongo ahonda munde mlwaira emabuya kwa kubanda kwa myasi ye buuta ye bandju ba bateshi kandju.

16. Mundaa mwa tchilanga bandju ba balyi mwa buolo. Seri batalyi mobo buolo kwaku sita emabi (singa) ndjumwa sa Ongo. Si mundaa mwatchitola nga bakosi ba Ongo.

17. Mutendaa mwakena mundju mundaa mwasima banyakenyu bemeresi nekunde mwobaa Ongo na kutchunda mwami.

18. Mu baanda, mundaa mwatchunda bee'Enawenyu busese. Elyi tchunda lyitabaa kwabatchusa emyanya ibuya kandji barembu oshao, si lyibaa nokwa batchula bakalyiire.

19. Muahanyirwe akaba mungasesa emutchima mango mwalyibusibwa bushi ne kutchunda Ongo, noku mutailyire tchiro na tchibi tchisibya.

20. Etchunda lyitchiye lyi mungabona akaba

찌찌부사 어바고시 버 마비 너 구도꽈 바 버떠 바고꽈 어마부야.

15. 부씨 오꼬 아호따 무떠 무꽈이라 어마부야 과 구바따 과 먀시 여 부우다 여 바쭈 바 바더씨 가뉴.

16. 무따아 마 찌롸꽈 바뉴 바 바레 마 부오뢰. 서리 바다레 모보 부오뢰 과구 시다 어마비 (시꽈) 뉴꽈 사 오꼬. 시 무따아 꽈찌도롸 꽈 바고시 바 오꼬.

17. 무더따아 뫄거나 무뉴 무따아 마시마 바냐거뉴 버머러시 너구떠 몰바아 오꼬 나 구쭈따 뫄미.

18. 무 바아따, 무따아 꽈쭈따 버어어나워뉴 부서서. 어레 쭈따 레다바아 과바쭈사 어먀냐 이부야 가씨 바러뿌 오싸오, 시 레바아 노과 바쭈롸 바가레이러.

19. 무아하니뤄 아가바 무꽈서사 어무찌마 마꼬 꽈레부시봐 부씨 너 구쭈따 오꼬, 노구 무다이레러 찌로 나 찌비 찌시뱌.

20. 어쭈따 레찌여 레 무꽈보나 아가바 무꽈서서

---

who do wrong and to commend those who do right.

15. For it is God's will that by doing good you should silence the ignorant talk of foolish men.

16. Live as free men, but do not use your freedom as a cover-up for evil; live as servants of God.

17. Show proper respect to everyone: Love the brotherhood of believers, fear God, honor the king.

18. Slaves, submit yourselves to your masters with all respect, not only to those who are good and considerate, but also to those who are harsh.

19. For it is commendable if a man bears up under the pain of unjust suffering because he is conscious of God.

20. But how is it to your credit if you receive a beating for

mungasese emitchima
mango mwapundjwa bushi
mwakolyire mabi? Si akaba
mungasesa emitchima
mango mwalyibusibwa bushi
mwailyire emabuya, oyu
mwasi ende asimisa Ongo.

21. Rero etchera tchi
tchatchuma Ongo abamaala,
bushi Kirisito nai
analyibusibwaa bushi nenyu.
Alyibukaa batcha tchasiya
tchumulorere'ku tchukulyikire
endjira yai.

22. Atairaa tchiro ne tchibi
tchisibya, kutalyi na mwasi
wa bisha, ola watengaa mwa
bunu bwai.

23. Mango bamukambaa
atarokaa, si atchibikaa mwa
amino sa Ongo iwende
watchindjibusa ebandju mwa
kanangana.

24. Kirisito yeine ekaa ebibi
byetchu mwa mubiri wai,
mango etchibwaa kwa
tchimanyi. Airaa batcha
tchasiya tchurekana ne bibi
byoshi tchuate emibere era
icthungenene era muhondo
sa Ongo. Rero kurengera
ekubabasibwa kwai
mwalamisibwe.

어미찌마 마꼬 꽈푸돠 부씨
마고레러 마비? 시 아가바
무까서사 어미찌마 마꼬
꽈레부시봐 부씨 마이레러
어마부야, 오유 마시 어떠
아시미사 오꼬.

21. 러로 어쩌라 찌 짜쭈마
오꼬 아바마아롸, 부씨
기리시도 나이
아나레부시봐아 부씨 너뉴.
아레부가아 바짜 짜시야
쭈무로러러구 쭈구레기러
어찌라 야이.

22. 아다이라아 찌로 너
찌비 찌시뱌, 구다레 나
마시 와 비싸, 오롸
와더꺼아 마 부누 봐이.

23. 마꼬 바무가빠아
아다로가아, 시 아찌비가아
마 아미노 사 오꼬 이워떠
와찌찌부사 어바뚜 마
가나꺼나.

24. 기리시도 여이너 어가아
어비비 벼쭈 마 무비리
와이, 마꼬 어찌봐아 과
찌마네. 아이라아 바짜
짜시야 쭈러가나 너 비비
뵤씨 쭈아더 어미버러 어라
이쮸꺼너너 어라 무호또 사
오꼬. 러로 구러꺼라
어구바바시봐 과이
꽈라미시붜.

doing wrong and endure it?
But if you suffer for doing
good and you endure it, this is
commendable before God.

21. To this you were called,
because Christ suffered for you,
leaving you an example, that
you should follow in his steps.

22. "He committed no sin, and
no deceit was found in his
mouth."

23. When they hurled their
insults at him, he did not
retaliate; when he suffered, he
made no threats. Instead, he
entrusted himself to him
who judges justly.

24. He himself bore our sins in
his body on the tree, so that
we might die to sins and live
for righteousness; by his
wounds you have been healed.

25. Bushi mwabaa mulyi nga mbulyi sa saelyire, si mwelyire mwafulukira era mwe mungere wenyu ola wende walanga ekalamo kenyu.

25. 부씨 먀바아 무레 퐈 뿌레 사 사어레러, 시 뭐레러 먀푸루기라 어라 뭐 무꺼러 워뉴 오롸 워꺼 와롸꺄 어가롸모 거뉴.

25. For you were like sheep going astray, but now you have returned to the Shepherd and Overseer of your souls.

1 Petero Chikono 3

1. Nenyu mu bakasi mundaa mwatchunda beba benyu, mukaira batcha, bauma mubo tchiro angaba mbu batemerere etchinwa tcha Ongo, si mwa kulola kwa myanya yenyu ibuya, banemerera'tchui mutanababwilrire tchiro na mwasi.

2. Bangende bemerera'tchi mwa kutchilorera kwa myanya yenyu ibuya kandji era yete etchunda.

3. Ekutchibika kwe bulyimbi kwenyu kutendaa kwaba kwe bya biseneke'ku kwa mubilyi ngakuno ekusukibwa emviri kwa kurengereseen ekwemala bitanga bya bikunganyisibwe mwa horo nesi kwembala nyimba sa tchitchiro tchinene.

4. Si emulyimbi bwenyu bwemire kuba bomwa mucthima, mutchima wa

1 퍼더로 찌고노 3

1. 너뉴 무 바가시 무따아 먀쭈따 버바 버뉴, 무가이라 바짜, 바우마 무보 찌로 아꺄바 뿌 바더머러러 어찌냐 짜 오꼬, 시 먀 구뢰롸 과 먀냐 여뉴 이부야, 바너머러라쭈이 무다나바뷔루리러 찌로 나 먀시.

2. 바꺼러 버머러라찌 먀 구찌뢰러라 과 먀냐 여뉴 이부야 가찌 어라 여더 어쭈따.

3. 어구찌비가 궈 부레삐 궈뉴 구더따아 과바 궈 뱌 비서너거구 과 무비레 꺄구노 어구수기봐 어뻬리 과 구러꺼러서어누 어궈마롸 비다꺄 뱌 비구꺄네시뷔 먀 호로 너시 궈빠롸 네빠 사 찌찌로 찌너너.

4. 시 어무레삐 뷔뉴 뷔미러 구바 보봐 무찌마, 무찌마 와 보오뢴 나와 부러뿌.

1 Peter Chapter 3[NIV]

1. Wives, in the same way be submissive to your husbands so that, if any of them do not believe the word, they may be won over without words by the behavior of their wives,

2. when they see the purity and reverence of your lives.

3. Your beauty should not come from outward adornment, such as braided hair and the wearing of gold jewelry and fine clothes.

4. Instead, it should be that of your inner self, the unfading beauty of a gentle and

boolo nawa burembu. Obola bu bulyimbi bwa bwete mufa munene era muhondo sa Ongo kandji butaka kumbe.

5. Rero ebakasi bo mwa mira ba babaa bemerere Ongo ne kumulangalyira, ku bendee balosa ebulyimbi bwabo batcha mwa kutchunda beba babo.

6. Mwa kuira batcha, ngokwa Sara endee atchunda Aburahamu mwa kumwerika mbu enawabo. Nenyu mwera mulyi balyi boyu Sarah akaba mungende mwaira emabuya busira kwobaisibwa na kandju.

7. Nenyu mu balume, mundaa mwekala na bakasi benyu eri muneshi kwa batete misi kuuma nenyu. Mundaa mweresa'bu etchunda bushi nabu Ongo akeeresa'bu elwembo lwe kalamo ke siku ne mango alauma nenyu. Mundaa mwaira batcha tchasiya ememo menyu matabonaa byangiko era muhondo sa Ongo.

8. Kwa kumala, muboshi mundaa mwonvikana ne kuata myanyisa iuma, mundaa mwafirane bondjo,

오보퐈 부 부례뻬 봐 붜더 무파 무너너 어라 무호또 사 오꼬 가찌 부다가 구뻐.

5. 러로 어바가시 보 퐈 미라 바 바바아 버머러러 오꼬 너 구무퐈까례라, 구 버너어 바로사 어부례뻬 봐보 바짜 퐈 구쭈따 버바 바보.

6. 퐈 구이라 바짜, 꼬과 사라 어떠어 아쭈따 아부라하무 퐈 구뭐리가 뿌 어나와보. 너뉴 뭐라 무쩨 바쩨 보유 사라후 아가바 무꺼러 퐈이라 어마부야 부시라 고바이시봐 나 가꾸.

7. 너뉴 무 바루머, 무따아 뭐가퐈 나 바가시 버뉴 어리 무너씨 과 바더더 미시 구우마 너뉴. 무따아 뭐러사부 어쭈따 부씨 나부 오꼬 아거어러사부 어뭐뽀 뭐 가퐈모 거 시구 너 마꼬 아퐈우마 너뉴. 무따아 퐈이라 바짜 짜시야 어머모 머뉴 마다보나아 뱌꼬 어라 무호또 사 오꼬.

8. 과 구마퐈, 무보씨 무따아 모쀄가나 너 구아다 먀네사 이우마, 무따아 퐈피라너 보쪼, 무따아

quiet spirit, which is of great worth in God's sight.

5. For this is the way the holy women of the past who put their hope in God used to make themselves beautiful. They were submissive to their own husbands,

6. like Sarah, who obeyed Abraham and called him her master. You are her daughters if you do what is right and do not give way to fear.

7. Husbands, in the same way be considerate as you live with your wives, and treat them with respect as the weaker partner and as heirs with you of the gracious gift of life, so that nothing will hinder your prayers.

8. Finally, all of you, live in harmony with one another; be sympathetic, love as brothers, be compassionate and humble.

mundaa mwasimana nga bauma mwa bwemeresi ne kuba bandju ba bete tchamba kwa bandji barembu.

9. Mutendaa mwafulusa mabi kwa mandji nesi ngambo kwa sindji. Si mundaaa mwemerana engahanyi. Bushi etchera tchi tchatchumaa Ongo abamalaa, tchasiya mubone engahanyi.

10. Bushi emaandjiko mabuya buya matchula matetchire mbu ola wahonda kuloola ku suku sibuya, ne kuata lumoo mwa kalamo kai, emire kunde alanga ebunu bwai, butendaa bwateta myasi ibi nesi kufula bisha.

11. Endaa ahaa emabi ne kunde aira emabuya. Endaa aata bushibilyisi kuhonda ebolo

12. Bushi emeho ma Enawetchu matchula malyi kwa bandju ba bende baira bya bitchungenene. Ne matchi mai mende mwonvilyisa ememo mabo. Si ba bende baira emabi, Enawetchu atomva mbu barengaa mwa meho mai.

마시마나 빠 바우마 뫄 뭐머러시 너 구바 바뉴 바 버더 짜빠 과 바찌 바러뿌.

9. 무더따아 뫄푸루사 마비 과 마찌 너시 빠뾰 과 시찌 시 무따아아 뭐머라나 어빠하니. 부씨 어쩌라 찌 짜쭈마아 오꼬 아바마꽈아, 짜시야 무보너 어빠하니.

10. 부씨 어마아찌고 마부야 부야 마쭈꽈 마더찌러 뿌 오꽈 와호따 구료오꽈 구 수구 시부야, 너 구아다 루모오 뫄 가꽈모 가이, 어미러 구떠 아꽈빠 어부누 봐이, 부더따아 봐더다 먀시 이비 너시 구푸꽈 비싸.

11. 어따아 아하아 어마비 너 구떠 아이라 어마부야. 어따아아 아아다 부씨비꼐시 구호따 어보료

12. 부씨 어머호 마 어나워쭈 마쭈꽈 마꼐 과 바뉴 바 버더 바이라 뱌 비쭈뻐너너. 너 마찌 마이 머떠 모삐꼐사 어머모 마보. 시 바 버떠 바이라 어마비, 어나워쭈 아도빠 뿌 바러빠아 뫄 머호 마이.

9. Do not repay evil with evil or insult with insult, but with blessing, because to this you were called so that you may inherit a blessing.

10. For, "Whoever would love life and see good days must keep his tongue from evil and his lips from deceitful speech.

11. He must turn from evil and do good; he must seek peace and pursue it.

12. For the eyes of the Lord are on the righteous and his ears are attentive to their prayer, but the face of the Lord is against those who do evil."

13. Nde ola ungabaumaku bulyiu akaba mwete mutchima wa bushiru we kunde mwaira emabuya?

14. Tchiro mungalyibuka bushi ne kuira bya bitchungenene, muahanyirwe. Mutendaa mwobaa ebandji bandju ne bwenge butendaa bwabasungulyira.

15. Si mundaa mwatchunda Kirisito mwa mitchima yenyu nga Enawenyu mundaa mutchiteyanyise kutchitetera era muhondo sa tchira mundju ola wababusa tchi tchitchumire mwaata emunyiro.

16. I mundaa mwaakula ne burembu ne tchunda. Kandji mutendaa mwaata tchibi mwa mutchima tcha munga tchisitaka'ku. Mwa batcha, ba bendjire ba basinga emyasi neku kamba bushi ne myanya yenyu ibuya kurengera ebuuma bwenyu na Kirisito, bangafa honyi.

17. Kubinalyi, ekulyibuka bushi ne kuira emabuya akaba ku kuhonda kwa Ongo, ku kukulu kwa kulyibuka bushi ne kuira emabi.

13. 너 오롸 우꾜바우마구 부뤠우 아가바 뭐더 무찌마 와 부씨루 워 구너 먀이라 어마부야?

14. 찌로 무꾜뤠부가 부씨 너 구이라 뱌 비쭈꺼너너, 무아하니뤄. 무더따아 모바아 어바찌 바뚜 너 뷔꺼 부더따아 봐바수우뤠라.

15. 시 무따아 먀쭈따 기리시도 롸 미찌마 여뉴 꾜 어나워뉴 무따아 무찌더야네서 구찌더더라 어라 무호또 사 찌라 무뚜 오롸 와바부사 찌 쭈미러 먀아다 어무네로.

16. 이 무따아 마아구롸 너 부러뿌 너 쭈따. 가찌 무더따아 마아다 찌비 롸 무찌마 짜 무꾜 찌시다가구. 롸 바짜, 바 버찌러 바 바시꾜 어먀시 너구 가빠 부씨 너 먀냐 여뉴 이부야 구러꺼라 어부우마 뷔뉴 나 기리시도, 바꾜파 호네.

17. 구비나뤠, 어구뤠부가 부씨 너 구이라 어마부야 아가바 구 구호따 과 오꼬, 구 구구루 과 구뤠부가 부씨 너 구이라 어마비.

13. Who is going to harm you if you are eager to do good?

14. But even if you should suffer for what is right, you are blessed. "Do not fear what they fear; do not be frightened."

15. But in your hearts set apart Christ as Lord. Always be prepared to give an answer to everyone who asks you to give the reason for the hope that you have. But do this with gentleness and respect,

16. keeping a clear conscience, so that those who speak maliciously against your good behavior in Christ may be ashamed of their slander.

17. It is better, if it is God's will, to suffer for doing good than for doing evil.

18. Bushi Kirisito afaa euma oshao bushi nebibi byetchu, abaa atete tchibi tchisibya, si era kufira ebandju be mabi, tchasiya abarete era mwa Ongo. Etchibwaa kwa mubilyi. Si emutchima mubuyabuya era kumuhubya kuba muuma uma.

19. Kurengera ebuashi bwoyu mutchima era kuya hubanganya etchinwa tcha Ongo kwa mitchima era buroko

20. Ei mitchima, iyananaa kutchunda Ongo. Kutengera mira, mango abaa alyindjilyira mwa siku sa Nowa abaa aanga emashuwa manene. Bandju munane oshao bu banengilyiraa mwamu mashuwa manene ne kununulyibwa kwa meshi.

21. Rero amu meshi mahuhanyisibwa ne bubatiso bwa bwanunula nenyu lwarero, obu bubatiso buta bwa kukula esinga kwa mubilyi, si ilyi ndjira ya kwema Ongo aberese mianyisa ibuya mwa mitchima yenyu. Kandji bu bwendjire banunula kurengera ekwomoka kwa

18. 부씨 기리시도 아파아 어우마 오쌰오 부씨 너비비 벼쭈, 아바아 아더더 찌비 찌시뱌, 시 어라 구피라 어바쭈 버 마비, 짜시야 아바러더 어라 와 오꼬. 어찌봐아 과 무비쩨. 시 어무찌마 무부야부야 어라 구무후뱌 구바 무우마 우마.

19. 구러뻐라 어부아씨 보유 무찌마 어라 구야 후바뻐냐 어찌냐 짜 오꼬 과 미찌마 어라 부로고

20. 어이 미찌마, 이야나나아 구쭈따 오꼬. 구더뻐라 미라, 마꼬 아바아 아쩨찌쩨라 와 시구 사 노와 아바아 아아뻐 어마쑤와 마너너. 바쭈 무나너 오쌰오 부 바너삐쩨라아 뫄무 마쑤와 마너너 너 구누누쩨봐 과 머씨.

21. 러로 아무 머씨 마후하니시봐 너 부바디소 봐 봐누누뻐 너뉴 쫘러로, 오부 부바디소 부다 봐 구구뽜 어시뻐 과 무비쩨, 시 이쩨 찌라 야 궈마 오꼬 아버러서 미아네사 이부야 봐 미찌마 여뉴. 가찌 부 봒찌러 바누누뽜 구러뻐라 어고모가 과 여수 기리시도.

18. For Christ died for sins once for all, the righteous for the unrighteous, to bring you to God. He was put to death in the body but made alive by the Spirit,

19. through whom also he went and preached to the spirits in prison

20. who disobeyed long ago when God waited patiently in the days of Noah while the ark was being built. In it only a few people, eight in all, were saved through water,

21. and this water symbolizes baptism that now saves you also--not the removal of dirt from the body but the pledge of a good conscience toward God. It saves you by the resurrection of Jesus Christ,

Yesu Kirisito.

22. Oyu Yesu Kirisito aire, kwa ngumba ekese kwa lunda lwe malyo ma Ongo. Okwola, emire era luulu se ndonyi, nera luulu se bakulukulu, nera luulu sa ba bete buashi.

22. 오유 여수 기리시도 아이러, 과 웅빠 어거서 과 루따 뤄 마료 마 오꼬. 오고롸, 어미러 어라 루우루 서 또니, 너라 루우루 서 바구루구루, 너라 루우루 사 바 버더 부아씨.

22. who has gone into heaven and is at God's right hand--with angels, authorities and powers in submission to him.

1 Petero Chikono 4

1. Tchiwshi kwa Kirisito alyibuka mango abaa ?t? emubilyi we mundju bushi noku nenyu mutchiatchirisaa ne mianyisa era ilyinga yai. Bushi emundju ola wasesa emutchima mwa kulyibuka kwa ndjira ye mubilyi, byemire areke kunde aira ebibi.

2. Mwa batcha, esuku sa mutchiri muno butala mutendaa mwakulyikira emyasi ye buuma uma ye mubilyi si mundaa mwakulyikira ekuhonda kwa Ongo.

3. Kubinalyi mwaesaa bihangi binenemwa kunde mwaira bya bisimise ebandju ba batemerere Ongo. Mwabaa mukomerekunde mwaira elusingi ne kuata ebuuma

1 퍼더로 찌고노 4

1. 찌씨 과 기리시도 아례부가 마꼬 아바아 ?두? 어무비례 워 무뚜 부씨 노구 너뉴 무찌아찌리사아 너 미아니사 어라 이례까 야이. 부씨 어무뚜 오롸 와서사 어무찌마 롸 구례부가 과 띠라 여 무비례, 벼미러 아러거 구더 아이라 어비비.

2. 롸 바짜, 어수구 사 무찌리 무노 부다롸 무더따아 롸구례기라 어먀시 여 부우마 우마 여 무비례 시 무따아 롸구례기라 어구호따 과 오꼬.

3. 구비나례 롸어사아 비하끼 비너너롸 구더 롸이라 뱌 비시미서 어바뉴 바 바더머러러 오꼬. 롸바아 무고머러구더 롸이라 어루시끼 너 구아다

1 Peter Chapter 4[NIV]

1. Therefore, since Christ suffered in his body, arm yourselves also with the same attitude, because he who has suffered in his body is done with sin.

2. As a result, he does not live the rest of his earthly life for evil human desires, but rather for the will of God.

3. For you have spent enough time in the past doing what pagans choose to do--living in debauchery, lust, drunkenness, orgies, carousing and detestable idolatry.

uma ne kunde mwatamira, mwendee mwama ne kumwa kwa kurengeresan ne kunde mwakola bya bitakolwa mwa kwera ebasimu.

4. Rero abu bandju bendjire basanwa mwakulola kwa mutatchiri luuma luuma nabo mwa mibere yabo ye honyi era irengerers. Etchera tchi tchendjire tchatchuma ba bakamba.

5. Si batatongana bushi ne myanya yabo era muhondo sa Ongo, iwatchukunganyise mira kwa kutchindjibusa ba bafire neba babtchilyi bauma uma.

6. Etchera tchi tchatchumaa Kirisito aya kuhubanganya emwasi Mubuya buya kwa bafu. Mbu bafu batchindjibusibwaa kuuma ne bandji bandju, ku kulyikana ne bya bendee baira mwa butala. Si rero kurengera emutchima mabuyabuya, bera bete kalamo ka kakulyikene ne kuhonda kwa Ongo.

7. Ebusinda bwe bindju byoshi bulyi ofu. Bushi noku, mwaataa mianyisa ibuya ne kutchilanga kwa mabi, tchasiya munde mwaala

어부우마 우마 너 구떠 꽈다미라, 뭐떠어 꽈마 너 구꽈 과 구러꺼러사 너 구떠 꽈고꽈 뱌 비다고꽈 꽈 궈라 어바시무.

4. 러로 아부 바뚜 버띠러 바사놔 꽈구뽀꽈 과 무다찌리 루우마 루우마 나보 꽈 미버러 야보 여 호네 어라 이러꺼러수. 어쩌라 찌 쩌띠러 짜쭈마 바 바가빠.

5. 시 바다도꺼나 부씨 너 먀냐 야보 어라 무호또 사 오꾿, 이와쭈구꺼네서 미라 과 구찌띠부사 바 바피러 너바 바부찌레 바우마 우마.

6. 어쩌라 찌 짜쭈마아 기리시도 아야 구후바꺼냐 어꽈시 무부야 부야 과 바푸. 뿌 바푸 바찌띠부시봐아 구우마 너 바찌 바뚜, 구 구레가나 너 뱌 버떠어 바이라 꽈 부다꽈. 시 러로 구러꺼라 어무찌마 마부야부야, 버라 버더 가꽈모 가 가구레거너 너 구호따 과 오꾿.

7. 어부시따 붜 비뚜 뵤씨 부레 오푸. 부씨 노구, 꽈아다아 미아네사 이부야 너 구찌꽈까 과 마비, 짜시야 무떠 꽈아꽈 궈마

4. They think it strange that you do not plunge with them into the same flood of dissipation, and they heap abuse on you.

5. But they will have to give account to him who is ready to judge the living and the dead.

6. For this is the reason the gospel was preached even to those who are now dead, so that they might be judged according to men in regard to the body, but live according to God in regard to the spirit.

7. The end of all things is near. Therefore be clear minded and self-controlled so that you can pray.

kwema Ongo.　　　　　　오꼬.

8. Era muhondo sa byoshi mundaa mwasimana busira kutama bushi emasimano kwende kwa tchuma ebandju ba babalyirana ku bibi binene.

8. 어라 무호또 사 뵤씨 무따아 먀시마나 부시라 구다마 부씨 어마시마노 궈떠 과 쭈마 어바쭈 바 바바쩨라나 구 비비 비너너.

8. Above all, love each other deeply, because love covers over a multitude of sins.

9. Mundaa mwamoerana mubeine kwa mubeine busira kutokolana

9. 무따아 먀모어라나 무버이너 과 무버이너 부시라 구도고퐈나

9. Offer hospitality to one another without grumbling.

10. Tchira muuma mu mwabo, endaa akoresa elwembo lwa Ongo amweresesa kwa mufa we bandji. Mwa batcha mungaba bemangisi babuya ba beshi kulanga tchira lwembo lwa Ongo aberesise.

10. 찌라 무우마 무 먀보, 어따아 아고러사 어뭬뽀 콰 오꼬 아뭐러서사 과 무파 워 바찌. 콰 바짜 무꽈바 버마₩시 바부야 바 버씨 구꽈꽈 찌라 뤄뽀 콰 오꼬 아버러시서.

10. Each one should use whatever gift he has received to serve others, faithfully administering God's grace in its various forms.

11. Emundju ola wabahubanganya endaa ahubanganya emyasi ya Ongo ngokwa inalyi. Nola waasa ebandji endaa aasabu kukulyikana nemisi era Ongo amweresise. Bendaa baira batcha, tchasiya Ongo ende atongibwa mwa byoshi kurengera Yesu Kirisito iene ensulu ne buashi ekuku ne mango!

11. 어무쭈 오퐈 와바후바꽈냐 어따아 아후바꽈냐 어먀시 야 오꼬 꼬과 이나쩨. 노라 와아사 어바찌 어따아 아아사부 구구쩨가나 너미시 어라 오꼬 아뭐러시서. 버따아 바이라 바짜, 짜시야 오꼬 어떠 아도꾀봐 콰 뵤씨 구러꺼라 여수 기리시도 이어너 어누수룩 너 부아씨 어구구 너 마꼬!

11. If anyone speaks, he should do it as one speaking the very words of God. If anyone serves, he should do it with the strength God provides, so that in all things God may be praised through Jesus Christ. To him be the glory and the power for ever and ev

12. Bera banyi basiirwa! Mutendaa mwasanwa bushi ne miereko isibu era mwarenga'mu, ei miereko mutaitolaa nga ilyi myasi ya tchienyi.

13. Si mundaa mwamowa bushi nenyu mwahangira kwa malyibuko ma Kirisito, tchasiya mango akafuluka mwa bulangare bwai mumowe busese.

14. Akaba bangabakamba bushi mukulyikire Kirisito muahanyirwe bushi mwete emutchima we bulangare wa Ongo.

15. Mwa katchikatchi kenyu, mutabaa mundju ola walyibuka bushi alyi mwitchi, nesi mwisi, nesi mukosi wa mabi, nesi mundju wakutchibika mwa myasi era itawerekere.

16. Si akaba emundju angalyibuka bushi alyi mukirisito, atafaa honyi, si endaa atonga Ongo bushi ne kwerikibwa elyi sina.

17. Kubinalyi, etchihangi tche butchundjibusi tchaikire. Nobu butchindjibusi, bungatangilyira kwa bandju ba Ongo ku bukatangilyira

12. 버라 바네 바시이롸! 무더따아 뫄사놔 부씨 너 미어러고 이시부 어라 뫄러까무, 어이 미어러고 무다이도롸아 까 이레 먀시 야 쩌네.

13. 시 무따아 뫄모와 부씨 너뉴 뫄하끼라 과 마레부고 마 기리시도, 짜시야 마꼬 아가푸루가 뫄 부롸까러 봐이 무모워 부서서.

14. 아가바 바까바가빠 부씨 무구께기러 기리시도 무아하니뤄 부씨 뭐더 어무찌마 워 부롸까러 와 오꼬.

15. 뫄 가찌가찌 거뉴, 무다바아 무뚜 오롸 와레부가 부씨 아레 뮈찌, 너시 뮈시, 너시 무고시 와 마비, 너시 무뚜 와구찌비가 뫄 먀시 어라 이다워러거러.

16. 시 아가바 어무뚜 아까레부가 부씨 아레 무기리시도, 아다파아 호네, 시 어따아 아도까 오꼬 부씨 너 궈리기봐 어레 시나.

17. 구비나레, 어찌하끼 쩌 부쭈찌부시 짜이기러. 노부 부찌찌부시, 부까다끼레라 과 바뚜 바 오꼬 구 부가다끼레라 다까, 러로 과

12. Dear friends, do not be surprised at the painful trial you are suffering, as though something strange were happening to you.

13. But rejoice that you participate in the sufferings of Christ, so that you may be overjoyed when his glory is revealed.

14. If you are insulted because of the name of Christ, you are blessed, for the Spirit of glory and of God rests on you.

15. If you suffer, it should not be as a murderer or thief or any other kind of criminal, or even as a meddler.

16. However, if you suffer as a Christian, do not be ashamed, but praise God that you bear that name.

17. For it is time for judgment to begin with the family of God; and if it begins with us, what will the outcome be for those who do not obey the

tanga, rero kwa businda kute bikere byaba kwaba bende banana kwemerera emwasi mubuyabuya wa Ongo?

18. Kandji bilyi ngokwa maandjiko mabuyabuya matchula matetchire mbu akaba ekununulyibwa kwe bandju ba batchungenene era muhondo sa Ongo kusibuire. Rero kute bikaba kwa bandjun babi kandji bakosi ba mabi?

19. Ebandju ba balyibuka bushi bendjire baira ekuhonda kwa Ongo, banaendekeraa kunde baira emabu. Batchibika mwamino sa Ongo iwababumbwaa, kandji ende anaira bya alaanyaa.

부시따 구더 비거러 뱌바 과바 버떠 바나나 궈머러라 어꽈시 무부야부야 와 오꼬?

18. 가찌 비례 꼬과 마아찌고 마부야부야 마쭈꽈 마더찌러 뿌 아가바 어구누누례봐 궈 바뚜 바 바쭈꺼너너 어라 무호또 사 오꼬 구시부이러. 러로 구더 비가바 과 바뚜누 바비 가찌 바고시 바 마비?

19. 어바뚜 바 바례부가 부씨 버찌러 바이라 어구호따 과 오꼬, 바나어떠거라아 구더 바이라 어마부. 바찌비가 마미노 사 오꼬 이와바부꽈아, 가찌 어떠 아나이라 뱌 아꽈아냐아.

gospel of God?

18. And, "If it is hard for the righteous to be saved, what will become of the ungodly and the sinner?"

19. So then, those who suffer according to God's will should commit themselves to their faithful Creator and continue to do good.

1 Petero Chikono 5

1. Nera neresa ebangumwa be luhu lwa Ongo ba balyi mwa katchikatchi kenyu emano. Nanyi nyiri mungumwa mulyikenyu, nyirina mubei we malyibuko ma Kirisito. Kandji nyikabona mwango alauma nenyu kwe tchunda lya Kirisito, lya Ongo akalosa ebandju.

1 퍼더로 찌고노 5

1. 너라 너러사 어바우꽈 버 루후 꽈 오꼬 바 바례 꽈 가찌가찌 거뉴 어마노. 나니 네리 무우꽈 무례거뉴, 네리나 무버이 워 마례부고 마 기리시도. 가찌 네가보나 꽈오 아꽈우마 너뉴 궈 쭈따 꺄 기리시도, 꺄 오꼬 아가로사 어바뚜.

1 Peter Chapter 5[NIV]

1. To the elders among you, I appeal as a fellow elder, a witness of Christ's sufferings and one who also will share in the glory to be revealed:

2. Rero nabema busese kwa mundaa mwalanga kubuya etchi tchikembe tch Ongo aberesise, ngokwa munyere ende alanga ebuso bwai. Kutabaa kwa kwandjilyirwa, si kutengaa mwa mitchima yenyu ku kukulyikana ne kuhonda kwa Ongo. Mutendaa mwakola ne mutchima mubuya.

3. Etchi tchikembe Ongo aberesise, mutendaa mwemangira tchi kwa misi si mundaa mwaata myanya ibuya era bangende beya.

4. Ne mango emungere mukulukulu akaika mukabona enzita ye bulangare era itaka kumbe.

5. Nenyu mu batabana, mundaa mwatchunda ebangumwa. Muboshi mundaa mwalosanya eburembu mwa katchikatchi kenyu bushi emaandjiko mabuyabuya matchuma matetchire mbu: Ongo ende alwisa ebandju be rume. Si ebarembi ende abailyira emabuya.

6. Bushi noku mundaa mwatchirembeka era muhondo sa Ongo wa buashi tchasiya ende

---

2. 러로 나버마 부서서 과 무따아 롸롸까 구부야 어찌 찌거뻐 찌 오꼬 아버러시서, 꼬과 무녀러 어너 아롸까 어부소 봐이. 구다바아 과 과찌쩨롸, 시 구더따아 롸 미찌마 여뉴 구 구구쩨가나 너 구호따 과 오꼬. 무더따아 롸고롸 너 무찌마 무부야.

3. 어찌 찌거뻐 오꼬 아버러시서, 무더따아 뭐마삐라 찌 과 미시 시 무따아 롸아다 먀냐 이부야 어라 바뻐너 버야.

4. 너 마꼬 어무뻐러 무구루구루 아가이가 무가보나 어씨다 여 부롸까러 어라 이다가 구뻐.

5. 너뉴 무 바다바나, 무따아 롸쭈따 어바우롸. 무보씨 무따아 롸르사냐 어부러뿌 롸 가찌가찌 거뉴 부씨 어마아찌고 마부야부야 마쭈마 마더찌러 뿌: 오꼬 어너 아뤼사 어바쭈 버 루머. 시 어바러뼤 어너 아바이쩨라 어마부야.

6. 부씨 노구 무따아 롸찌러뻐가 어라 무호또 사 오꼬 와 부아씨 짜시야 어너 아버나무롸 과 비하삐

---

2. Be shepherds of God's flock that is under your care, serving as overseers--not because you must, but because you are willing, as God wants you to be; not greedy for money, but eager to serve;

3. not lording it over those entrusted to you, but being examples to the flock.

4. And when the Chief Shepherd appears, you will receive the crown of glory that will never fade away.

5. Young men, in the same way be submissive to those who are older. All of you, clothe yourselves with humility toward one another, because, "God opposes the proud but gives grace to the humble."

6. Humble yourselves, therefore, under God's mighty hand, that he may lift you up in due time.

abenamula kwa bihangi bya alondwere.

7. Mundaa mwamuretera emiango yenyu Yoshi bushi iwende wabalanga.

8. Muataa bwenge nekunde mwatchilangalanga bushi emurenda wenyu wamusimu endjire asunsungula nga ngoromolyi era yaruruma yahonda ola inga hahanyula.

9. Mundaa mwa mulwisa mwa kusimika mwa bwemeresi mumenyerera kwa mwa butala boshi banyakenyu bemeresi nabo kubanalyibuka batcha.

10. Mutchilyi mungalyibuka ku suku sieke, si Ongo iutchusa ebondjo boshi, abamaere tchasiya mube luumaluuma nai mwa bulangare bwai bwe suku ne mango kurengera ebuuma bwenyu naye Yesu Kirisito. Yeine angahuba kubaira kuba bandju ba balumilyire ne kubakusa mwa bwemeresi, ne kubasesa emitchima ne kuberesa emisi ye kusimika busese.

11. Yeine iwete ebuashi esuku ne mango. Bibe batcha !

12. Nabaandjikilyire mano

바 아로뚜워러.

7. 무따아 뫄무러더라 어미아꼬 여뉴 요씨 부씨 이워떠 와바꽈따.

8. 무아다아 뷔머 너구떠 뫄찌꽈따꽈따 부씨 어무러따 워뉴 와무시무 어찌러 아수누우꽈 따 꼬로모레 어라 야루루마 야호따 오꽈 이까 하하뉴꽈.

9. 무따아 뫄 무뤼사 뫄 구시미가 뫄 뷔머러시 무머녀러라 과 뫄 부다꽈 보씨 바냐거뉴 버머러시 나보 구바나쩨부가 바짜.

10. 무찌쩨 무꽈쩨부가 구 수구 시어거, 시 오꼬 이우쭈사 어보쪼 보씨, 아바마어러 짜시야 무버 루우마뤄우마 나이 뫄 부꽈꽈러 봐이 뷔 수구 너 마꼬 구러꺼라 어부우마 뷔뉴 나여 여수 기리시도. 여이너 아꽈후바 구바이라 구바 바쭈 바 바루미쩨러 너 구바구사 뫄 뷔머러시, 너 구바서사 어미찌마 너 구버러사 어미시 여 구시미가 부서서.

11. 여이너 이워더 어부아씨 어수구 너 마꼬. 비버 바짜 !

12. 나바아찌기쩨러 마노

7. Cast all your anxiety on him because he cares for you.

8. Be self-controlled and alert. Your enemy the devil prowls around like a roaring lion looking for someone to devour.

9. Resist him, standing firm in the faith, because you know that your brothers throughout the world are undergoing the same kind of sufferings.

10. And the God of all grace, who called you to his eternal glory in Christ, after you have suffered a little while, will himself restore you and make you strong, firm and steadfast.

11. To him be the power for ever and ever. Amen.

12. With the help of Silas,

<table>
<tr><td>maruba maeke mwa
kuasibwa nasila, inyitchula
nyitolyire nga munyaketchu
mubuya. Nahonda nyibasese
emitchima ne kubabura kwa
emyasi era yerekere ebondjo
bwa Ongo inalyi ya
kanangana. Rero mutarekaa
kunde mwaikulyikira.</td><td>마루바 마어거 뫄 구아시봐
나시롸, 이네쭈롸 네도례러
먀 무냐거쭈 무부야. 나호따
네바서서 어미찌마 너
구바부라 과 어먀시 어라
여러거러 어보졷 봐 오옹
이나례 야 가나먀나. 러로
무다러가아 구떠
뫄이구례기라.</td><td>whom I regard as a
faithful brother, I have written
to you briefly, encouraging you
and testifying that this is the
true grace of God. Stand fast in
it.</td></tr>
<tr><td>13. Ebemeresi bo mwa musi
we Babeli ba Ongo alondore
kuuma nenyu, ba balamusise.
Na Mariko mwana wanyi nai
abalamusise.</td><td>13. 어버머러시 보 뫄 무시
웨 바버리 바 오옹
아론도러 구우마 너뉴, 바
바롸무시서. 나 마리고 뫄나
와네 나이 아바롸무시서.</td><td>13. She who is in Babylon,
chosen together with you,
sends you her greetings, and
so does my son Mark.</td></tr>
<tr><td>14. Mundaa mwalamusanya
ne lumoo lunene nga bauma
mu bandju ba Kirisito
muboshi, mubaa ne bolo.</td><td>14. 무따아 뫄롸무사냐 너
루모오 루너너 먀 바우마
무 바쭈 바 기리시도
무보씨, 무바아 너 보로.</td><td>14. Greet one another with a
kiss of love. Peace to all of you
who are in Christ.</td></tr>
</table>

2 Petero

2 퍼더로

2 Peter

PETERO WAKABIRI

(2 PETER)

퍼더로 와가비리
(2 퍼더로)

2 Petero Chikono 1

1. Nyono Simoni Petero, muanda kandji ndjumwa wa Yesu Kirisito, nabandjikira mu mwete ebwemeresi mwa ndanda sai nga tchubano. Obu bwemeresi bulyi bwa tchitchiro tchinene busese. Yesu iwairaa ebyera bushi netchu, bushi ende aira bya bitchungenene oyu Yesu i Ongo kandji I mununusi wetchu mu Yesu Kirisito.

2. Ongo endaa abaahanyira busese ne kuberesa ebolo busese kukulyikana nokwa mwaendekere mwamumenya ne kumenya Enawetchu Yesu.

3. Ongo atchweresise byoshi bya tchutchula tchulaire'ku mwa kalamo ketchu kwa buashi bwai tchasiya tchuate mibui era imusimise. Airaa batcha kwa kutchubika mwa buuma nai tchunde tchwamenyerera oyu watchwamaere tchasiya tchubone mwango kwe tchunda ne bubuya bwai.

4. Ku kulyikana nebi, Ongo atchweresise bindju bya byete mufa munene bya atchulanyaa. Ailyire batcha

2 퍼더로 찌고노 1

1. 뇨노 시모니 퍼더로, 무아따 가찌 뚜꽈 와 여수 기리시도, 나바찌기라 무 뭐더 어뷔머러시 꽈 따따 사이 꺄 쭈바노. 오부 뷔머러시 부레 봐 찌찌로 찌너너 부서서. 여수 이와이라아 어벼라 부씨 너쭈, 부씨 어떠 아이라 뱌 비쭈꺼너너 오유 여수 이 오꼬 가찌 이 무누누시 워쭈 무 여수 기리시도.

2. 오꼬 어따아 아바아하네라 부서서 너 구버러사 어보롣 부서서 구구쩨가나 노과 꽈어떠거러 꽈무머냐 너 구머냐 어나워쭈 여수.

3. 오꼬 아쭤러시서 뵤씨 뱌 쭈쭈꽈 쭈꽈이러구 꽈 가꽈모 거쭈 과 부아씨 봐이 짜시야 쭈아더 미부이 어라 이무시미서. 아이라아 바짜 과 구쭈비가 꽈 부우마 나이 쭈떠 쫘머녀러라 오유 와쫘마어러 짜시야 쭈보너 꽈꼬 궈 쭈따 너 부부야 봐이.

4. 구 구쩨가나 너비, 오꼬 아쭤러시서 비부 뱌 벼더 무파 무너너 뱌 아쭈꽈냐아. 아이쩨러 바짜 짜시야

2 Peter Chapter 1[NIV]

1. Simon Peter, a servant and apostle of Jesus Christ, To those who through the righteousness of our God and Savior Jesus Christ have received a faith as precious as ours:

2. Grace and peace be yours in abundance through the knowledge of God and of Jesus our Lord.

3. His divine power has given us everything we need for life and godliness through our knowledge of him who called us by his own glory and goodness.

4. Through these he has given us his very great and precious promises, so that through them you may participate in the

tchasiya kurengera ebi biraane mufufumuke ekasibu ka katenganyire ne buumauma bubi bomuno butala mube ngokwa atchula.

5. Bushi noku mundaa mwatchisesa busese mwa kunde mwatalyika emabuya kwa bwemeresi bwenyu na kwamu mabuya mwatalyika kwe bwenge.

6. Nokwo bu bwenge mwanatalyika kwe kutchilanga kwa mabi noku kutchilanga kwa mabi mwanatalyika kwe bushibilyisi nokwo bu bushibilyisi mwanatalyika kwe bushiru bwe kunde mwaira bya bisimise Ongo.

7. Na kwobu bushiru mwanatalyika kwe buuma ne nzii

8. Bushi akaba mungaata ei myanya Yoshi nekuira kwa itetchire ingabaasa kuikala ne kuendekera mwamenyerera Enawetchu Yesu Kirisito.

9. Si ola utete ei myanya ibuya alyi nga mundju ola utalola, kukuteta mbu atalola burerere. Ende ebilyira kwa akomisibwe ebibi byai

구러꺼라 어비 비라아너 무푸푸무거 어가시부 가 가더따니러 너 부우마우마 부비 보무노 부다꽈 무버 끄과 아쭈꽈.

5. 부씨 노구 무따아 꽈찌서사 부서서 과 구떠 꽈다뻬가 어마부야 과 붜머러시 붜뉴 나 과무 마부야 꽈다뻬가 궈 붜꺼.

6. 노고 부 붜꺼 꽈나다뻬가 궈 구찌꽈까 과 마비 노구 구찌꽈까 과 마비 꽈나다뻬가 궈 부씨비뻬시 노고 부 부씨비뻬시 꽈나다뻬가 궈 부씨루 붜 구떠 꽈이라 뱌 비시미서 오끄.

7. 나 고부 부씨루 꽈나다뻬가 궈 부우마 너 씨이

8. 부씨 아가바 무까아다 어이 먀냐 요씨 너구이라 과 이더찌러 이까바아사 구이가꽈 너 구어떠거라 꽈머녀러라 어나워쭈 여수 기리시도.

9. 시 오꽈 우더더 어이 먀냐 이부야 아쩨 까 무뚜 오꽈 우다론꽈, 구구더다 뿌 아다론꽈 부러러러. 어떠 어비뻬라 과 아고미시붜

divine nature and escape the corruption in the world caused by evil desires.

5. For this very reason, make every effort to add to your faith goodness; and to goodness, knowledge;

6. and to knowledge, self-control; and to self-control, perseverance; and to perseverance, godliness;

7. and to godliness, brotherly kindness; and to brotherly kindness, love.

8. For if you possess these qualities in increasing measure, they will keep you from being ineffective and unproductive in your knowledge of our Lord Jesus Christ.

9. But if anyone does not have them, he is nearsighted and blind, and has forgotten that he has been cleansed from his past sins.

byokwa mira.

10. Rero, bunyaketchu, Ongo abalondore kandji abamaere. Bushi noku mundaa mwatchisesa ebyera bilorekane'ku kubuya. Bushi mukaira batcha, mutengilyire mu tchiro na tchibi tchisibya.

11. Mwei ndjira mu mungabona eloso lwe kwengilyira kanangana mwa bwami bwe suku ne mango bwa Enawetchu Yesu Kirisito, e mununusi wetchu.

12. Bushi noku nyingaendekera kuṇde na bakengesa eni myasi tchira lusuku tchiro angaba mbu mwera muishi ne kusimika kubuya mwa myasi ye kanangana era mwangilyiraa.

13. NYisene kwa kukomire nyinde na bakengesa ei myasi kuno nyicthiri muuma uma tchasiya muhube kuanyisa era lulu sai.

14. Bushi nyishi kwa ebihangi byanyi bye kufa bilyi ofu ngokwa Enawetchu Yesu Kirisito anyilosaa.

15. Nyingatchisesa busese kuberesa endjira ye kunde mwakengera ene myasi esuku soshi era nyuma se kufa kwanyi.

어비비 뱌이 뵤과 미라.

10. 러로, 부냐거쭈, 오꼬 아바롣또러 가찌 아바마어러. 부씨 노구 무따아 마찌서사 어뼈라 비로러가너구 구부야. 부씨 무가이라 바짜, 무더꼐레러 무 찌로 나 찌비 찌시뱌.

11. 뭐이 씨라 무 무까보나 어로소 뤄 귀꼐레라 가나까나 뫄 뱌미 뷔 수구 너 마꼬 봐 어나워쭈 여수 기리시도, 어 무누누시 워쭈.

12. 부씨 노구 네꺄어떠거라 구떠 나 바거어사 어니 먀시 찌라 루수구 찌로 아까바 뿌 뭐라 무이씨 너 구시미가 구부야 뫄 먀시 여 가나까나 어라 뫄꼐레라아.

13. 네서너 과 구고미러 네떠 나 바거어사 어이 먀시 구노 네찌리 무우마 우마 짜시야 무후버 구아네사 어라 룰루 사이.

14. 부씨 네씨 과 어비하꾀 뱌네 벼 구파 비레 오푸 꼬과 어나워쭈 여수 기리시도 아네로사아.

15. 네까찌서사 부서서 구버러사 어찌라 여 구떠 뫄거어라 어너 먀시 어수구 소씨 어라 뉴마 서 구파 과네.

10. Therefore, my brothers, be all the more eager to make your calling and election sure. For if you do these things, you will never fall,

11. and you will receive a rich welcome into the eternal kingdom of our Lord and Savior Jesus Christ.

12. So I will always remind you of these things, even though you know them and are firmly established in the truth you now have.

13. I think it is right to refresh your memory as long as I live in the tent of this body,

14. because I know that I will soon put it aside, as our Lord Jesus Christ has made clear to me.

15. And I will make every effort to see that after my departure you will always be able to remember these things.

16. Mango tchwabakangilyisaa era lulu se buashi bwa Enawetchu . yesu Kirisito nera luulu se kufuluka kwai tchutakoresaa nyaano sa bisha sa bundju bende batchifulyira ne bwenge bwabo. Si tchubeine tchwanatchiloreraa kwa buashi bwai.	16. 마꼬 짜바가끼레사아 어라 루루 서 부아씨 봐 어나워쭈 . 여수 기리시도 너라 루우루 서 구푸루가 과이 쭈다고러사아 냐아노 사 비싸 사 부쭈 버떠 바찌푸레라 너 붜꺼 봐보. 시 쭈버이너 짜나찌로러라아 과 부아씨 봐이.	16. We did not follow cleverly invented stories when we told you about the power and coming of our Lord Jesus Christ, but we were eyewitnesses of his majesty.
17. Kubinalyi Ongo Tata amweresaa etchunda ne buashi, mango emurenge wa Ongo we buashi atetaa mbu: onola I mwana wanyi musiirwa iutchula unyisimise nanyi.	17. 구비나레 오꼬 다다 아뭐러사아 어쭈따 너 부아씨, 마꼬 어무러꺼 와 오꼬 워 부아씨 아더다아 뿌: 오노라 이 뫄나 와니 무시이롸 이우쭈라 우네시미서 나니.	17. For he received honor and glory from God the Father when the voice came to him from the Majestic Glory, saying, "This is my Son, whom I love; with him I am well pleased."
18. Tchubeine tchwanatchomvira kwoyu murenge wabaa watenga kwa nguba mango tchwabaa tchulyi na Yesu kwa ndjulungu ibuya-buya.	18. 쭈버이너 짜나쪼삐라 꾸유 무러꺼 와바아 와더까 과 우바 마꼬 짜바아 쭈레 나 여수 과 누루우 이부야-부야.	18. We ourselves heard this voice that came from heaven when we were with him on the sacred mountain.
19. Kandfji tchutchula tchwemerere kanangana emyasi era barebi batetaa. Rero nenyu akaba mungende mwatchunda'i mungaba eri mwailyire kubuya. Bushi ei myasi ilyi nge tara lya lyalomeka mwa musimya kuikira ebutchufu butche ne ngununu ye lumbulyimbulyi ilomeke mwa mitchima yenyu.	19. 가뚜푸지 쭈쭈라 쭤머러러 가나까나 어먀시 어라 바러비 바더다아. 러로 너뉴 아가바 무꺼떠 뫄쭈따이 무까바 어리 뫄이레러 구부야. 부씨 어이 먀시 이레 꺼 다라 랴 랴로머가 뫄 무시먀 구이기라 어부쭈푸 부쩌 너 우누누 여 루뿌레뿌레 이로머거 뫄 미찌마 여뉴.	19. And we have the word of the prophets made more certain, and you will do well to pay attention to it, as to a light shining in a dark place, until the day dawns and the morning star rises in your hearts.

20. Era muhondo sa byoshi, tchetchine tchi mwemire kumenya: kutalyi mundju ola ungaala yeine kuanunula kubuya eburebi bwa bulyi mwa maandjiko mabuyabuya.

21. Buhi kutalyi tchiro ne burebi busibya bwa bwanyibwaa kwa kuhonda kwa mundju si kurengera ebuashi bwe mutchima mubuyabuya ku ebandju bendee bateta emyasi era yatenga era mwa Ongo.

20. 어라 무호또 사 뵤씨, 쩌찌너 찌 뭐미러 구머냐: 구다례 무뚜 오롸 우롸아롸 여이너 구아누누롸 구부야 어부러비 봐 부례 롸 마아찌고 마부야부야.

21. 부히 구다례 찌로 너 부러비 부시뱌 봐 봐니봐아 과 구호따 과 무뚜 시 구러러라 어부아씨 붜 무찌마 무부야부야 구 어바뚜 버떠어 바더다 어먀시 어라 야더빠 어라 롸 오꼬.

20. Above all, you must understand that no prophecy of Scripture came about by the prophet's own interpretation.

21. For prophecy never had its origin in the will of man, but men spoke from God as they were carried along by the Holy Spirit.

2 Petero Chikono 2

1. Kwa mira mwa lubaa lwe Baisiraeli, mwaulukiraa barebi ba bisha. Rero kunoku ku ebakangilyisi be bisha nabo banganaulukira mwa katchikatchi kenyu. Bangende babakangilyisa nokwa tchihangi banana Enawetchu ola wabanunulaa ! Mwa kuira batcha bangatchikululyira kasibu ka kangatchuma basika fuba.

2. Bandju banene bangende bakulyikira'bu mwa myanyan yabo ibi. Kandji bushi nabu

2 퍼더로 찌고노 2

1. 과 미라 롸 루바아 뤄 바이시라어뤼, 롸우루기라아 바러비 바 비싸. 러로 구노구 구 어바가삐례시 버 비싸 나보 바롸나우루뤼라 롸 가찌가찌 거뉴. 바떠떠 바바가삐례사 노과 찌하삐 바나나 어나워쭈 오롸 와바누누롸아 ! 롸 구이라 바짜 바롸찌구루례라 가시부 가 가까쭈마 바시가 푸바.

2. 바뚜 바너너 바떠떠 바구레기라부 롸 먀냐누 야보 이비. 가찌 부씨 나부

2 Peter Chapter 2[NIV]

1. But there were also false prophets among the people, just as there will be false teachers among you. They will secretly introduce destructive heresies, even denying the sovereign Lord who bought them--bringing swift destruction on themselves.

2. Many will follow their shameful ways and will bring the way of truth into disrepute.

emyasi ye kanangana ya Enawetchu ingende yakambibwa.

3. Nabushi nebahumahuma bubi bwe bikolo abu bakangilyisi be bisha bangende babakula kwa bya mwete mwa kulokeresa ebieta. Si kutengera mira Ongo akunganyisise bu ebutchindjibusi ne kusika kwabo nkutatchiri burerere.

4. Anabe ne ndonyi ba bairaa emabi, Ongo atafiraa bu bondjo si abakabulaa era kusimu. Eyera balangibwa baminyirwe mwa musimya munene kwa kulyindjira elusuku lwe butchindjibusi.

5. Ongo atarekaa ne bandju bo kwa mira busira kutchindjibusa bu. Si mango asikyaa ebandju babi mwa mwihuso we meshi era kulanga Nowa alauma ne bandji bandju balyinda, iwendee wahubanganyisa ebandju emyasi era icthungenene ya Ongo.

6. Kandji Ongo atchindjibusaa emisi ye Sotoma ne Komora, mwa kuisiresa. Airaa batcha tchasiya alose emyasi era

어먀시 여 가나까나 야 어나워쭈 이꺼떠 야가뻬봐.

3. 나부씨 너바후마후마 부비 붸 비고로 아부 바가끼꼐시 버 비싸 바꺼떠 바바구꽈 과 뱌 뭐더 봐 구로거러사 어비어다. 시 구더꺼라 미라 오꼬 아구까네시서 부 어부찌끼부시 너 구시가 과보 꾸다찌리 부러러러.

4. 아나버 너 또네 바 바이라아 어마비, 오꼬 아다피라아 부 보쪼 시 아바가부꽈아 어라 구시무. 어여라 바꽈끼봐 바미니뤄 봐 무시먀 무너너 과 구꼐끼라 어루수구 뭐 부찌끼부시.

5. 오꼬 아다러가아 너 바쭈 보 과 미라 부시라 구찌끼부사 부. 시 마꼬 아시갸아 어바쭈 바비 봐 뮈후소 워 머씨 어라 구꽈까 노와 아꽈우마 너 바찌 바쭈 바꼐따, 이워떠어 와후바까네사 어바쭈 어먀시 어라 이쮸꺼너너 야 오꼬.

6. 가찌 오꼬 아찌끼부사아 어미시 여 소도마 너 고모라, 봐 구이시러사. 아이라아 바짜 짜시야 아로서 어먀시 어라

3. In their greed these teachers will exploit you with stories they have made up. Their condemnation has long been hanging over them, and their destruction has not been sleeping.

4. For if God did not spare angels when they sinned, but sent them to hell, putting them into gloomy dungeons to be held for judgment;

5. if he did not spare the ancient world when he brought the flood on its ungodly people, but protected Noah, a preacher of righteousness, and seven others;

6. if he condemned the cities of Sodom and Gomorrah by burning them to ashes, and made them an example of what is going to happen to the

ikaikira ebakosi be mabi.	이가이기라 어바고시 버 마비.	ungodly;
7. Si anunulaa Loti bushi endee aira bya bitchungenene era muhondo sai. Yeke ebwenge bwendee bwa musungulyira mwa kulola kwa myanya ibi yabu bakosi be mabi.	7. 시 아누누롸아 로디 부씨 어떠어 아이라 뱌 비쭈머너너 어라 무호또 사이. 여거 어붸머 붜떠어 봐 무수꾸레라 봐 구로롸 과 먀냐 이비 야부 바고시 버 마비.	7. and if he rescued Lot, a righteous man, who was distressed by the filthy lives of lawless men
8. Rero, Loti iwendee waira bya bitchungenene bushi abaa atchula alauma nabu bandju be mabi tchiralusuku endee atchilorera ne kutchimvira kwa myasi ibi era bendee baira. Ei myasi year kunde yamulyibusa busese kwa mutchima.	8. 러로, 로디 이워떠어 와이라 뱌 비쭈머너너 부씨 아바아 아쭈롸 아롸우마 나부 바쭈 버 마비 찌라루수구 어떠어 아찌로러라 너 구찌삐라 과 먀시 이비 어라 버떠어 바이라. 어이 먀시 여라 구떠 야무레부사 부서서 과 무찌마.	8. (for that righteous man, living among them day after day, was tormented in his righteous soul by the lawless deeds he saw and heard)--
9. Etchera tchilosise kwa Enawetchu atchula eshi endjira ye kununula ebandju mwa miereko, ba batchungenene era muhondo sai. Kandji atchula eshi kulanga ebandju babi tchasiya abalose kwa kasibu kwa lusuku lwe butchindjibusi.	9. 어쩌라 찌로시서 과 어나워쭈 아쭈롸 어씨 어찌라 여 구누누롸 어바쭈 과 미어러고, 바 바쭈머너너 어라 무호또 사이. 가찌 아쭈롸 어씨 구롸꽈 어바쭈 바비 짜시야 아바로서 과 가시부 과 루수구 뤄 부찌찌부시.	9. if this is so, then the Lord knows how to rescue godly men from trials and to hold the unrighteous for the day of judgment, while continuing their punishment.
10. Si abu bendjire bakulyikira emyanya yabo ibi ye kutchanyira kurenza bakena ebukulukulu bwa Ongo bu akatchindjibusa busese kurenza ebandji	10. 시 아부 버찌러 바구레기라 어먀냐 야보 이비 여 구짜네라 구러롸 바거나 어부구루꾸루 봐 오꼬 부 아가찌찌부사 부서서 구러롸 어바찌 바쭈.	10. This is especially true of those who follow the corrupt desire of the sinful nature and despise authority. Bold and arrogant, these men are not afraid to slander celestial

bandju. Abu bakangilyisi be bisha, batchusa erume ne kunde batcherusa busese. Kandji batatchunda ne besha kwa nguba ba batchusa ebulangare si bende bakamba'bu.	아부 바가ᅌ기ᄙᅦ시 버 비싸, 바쭈사 어루머 너 구ᄕᅥ 바쩌루사 부서서. 가ᅜᅵ 바다쭈ᄕᅡ 너 버싸 과 ᅌ구바 바 바쭈사 어부ᄙᅪᅌ가러 시 버ᄕᅥ 바가빠부.	beings;
11. Si tchiro batcha endonyi ba barenzise bu emisi ne buashi batabasitaka bulyio mwa ku kamba era muhondo sa Enawetchu.	11. 시 찌로 바짜 어ᄕᅩ니 바 바러ᅛᅵ서 부 어미시 너 부아씨 바다바시다가 부ᄙᅦ오 뫄 구 가빠 어라 무호ᄕᅩ 사 어나워쭈.	11. yet even angels, although they are stronger and more powerful, do not bring slanderous accusations against such beings in the presence of the Lord.
12. Si abu bakangilyisi be bisha batchula nga nyama so mwe rungu sa sende sa butchibwa tchasiya sisimbibwe kwa miteo sinetchibwe. Bende bakamba emyasi era bateshi. Rero basene tchibwange si nyama esuba.	12. 시 아부 바가ᅌ기ᄙᅦ시 버 비싸 바쭈ᄙᅪ ᅌ가 냐마 소 뭐 루ᅌ구 사 서ᄕᅥ 사 부찌봐 짜시야 시시삐뷔 과 미더오 시너찌뷔. 버ᄕᅥ 바가빠 어먀시 어라 바더씨. 러로 바서너 찌봐ᅌ거 시 냐마 어수바.	12. But these men blaspheme in matters they do not understand. They are like brute beasts, creatures of instinct, born only to be caught and destroyed, and like beasts they too will perish.
13. Akola ku kasibu bakalola'ku bushi ne mabi bendee bakola. Bende bamoera kuira ekuhonda kwe mubiri wabu tchanganama esuba lyimenzi. Kandji emango mwalya elinye alauma nabu bende bamoera ekubengeera. Etchera tchende tcheta honyi ne kurenza mahunga.	13. 아고ᄙᅪ 구 가시부 바가ᄙᅩᄙᅪ구 부씨 너 마비 버ᄕᅥ어 바고ᄙᅪ. 버ᄕᅥ 바모어라 구이라 어구호ᄕᅡ 궈 무비리 와부 짜ᅌ가나마 어수바 ᄙᅦ머ᅛᅵ. 가ᅜᅵ 어마ᅌ고 뫄ᄙᅣ 어ᄙᅵ녀 아ᄙᅪ우마 나부 버ᄕᅥ 바모어라 어구버ᅌ거어라. 어쩌라 쩌ᄕᅥ 쩌다 호네 너 구러싸 마후ᅌ가.	13. They will be paid back with harm for the harm they have done. Their idea of pleasure is to carouse in broad daylight. They are blots and blemishes, reveling in their pleasures while they feast with you.
14. Emeho mabo kwa buhungu ku	14. 어머호 마보 과 부후ᅌ구 구 마나쭈ᄙᅦ라. 바다나다마	14. With eyes full of adultery, they never stop sinning; they

manatchitchulyira. Batanatama kunde baira ebibi bateya ebandju ba batasimikire mwa bwemeresi. Barengerese mwa kutchaanyira bwe kubona ebikulo. Kubinalyi, Ongo atakire bu mira.	구ᄕᅥ 바이라 어비비 바더야 어바ᅜᅮ 바 바다시미기러 뫄 붸머러시. 바러ᅌᅥ러서 뫄 구짜아네라 붸 구보나 어비구ᄙᅩ. 구비나ᄙᅦ, 오ᅌ고 아다기러 부 미라.	seduce the unstable; they are experts in greed--an accursed brood!
15. Barekire endjira ye kanangana na baera mwa ku kulyikira endjira era balama mwenyi Beori akulyikiraa. Oyu Balama, asimaa kubona ebikulo mwa ndjira era itatchungenene.	15. 바러기러 어ᅜᅵ라 여 가나ᅌᅡ나 나 바어라 뫄 구 구ᄙᅦ기라 어ᅜᅵ라 어라 바ᄙᅡ마 뭬네 버오리 아구ᄙᅦ기라아. 오유 바ᄙᅡ마, 아시마아 구보나 어비구ᄙᅩ 뫄 ᅜᅵ라 어라 이다쭈ᅌᅥ너너.	15. They have left the straight way and wandered off to follow the way of Balaam son of Beor, who loved the wages of wickedness.
16. Si era kukalyiirwa bushi ne bubi bwai. E ndokomi ye tchikasi era itateta yera kuteta nga mundju, na yangika emwasi mubi we buuta ola murebi Balama abaa ahonda kuira.	16. 시 어라 구가ᄙᅦ이롸 부씨 너 부비 봐이. 어 ᄕᅩ고미 여 찌가시 어라 이다더다 여라 구더다 ᅌᅡ 무ᅜᅮ, 나 야ᅌᅵ가 어뫄시 무비 웨 부우다 오ᄙᅡ 무러비 바ᄙᅡ마 아바아 아호ᄕᅡ 구이라.	16. But he was rebuked for his wrongdoing by a donkey--a beast without speech--who spoke with a man's voice and restrained the prophet's madness.
17. Abu bakangilyisi balyi nga shokororo sa somire kandji balyi nga lumbumbu lwa lwekibwa ne tchusi tcha tchikalyiire. Ongo abakunganyisise etchisiki tcha tchiri mwa musimya tenene.	17. 아부 바가ᅌᅵᄙᅦ시 바ᄙᅦ ᅌᅡ 쏘고로로 사 소미러 가ᅜᅵ 바ᄙᅦ ᅌᅡ 루뿌뿌 ᄙᅪ ᄙᅰ기봐 너 쭈시 짜 찌가ᄙᅦ이러. 오ᅌ고 아바구ᅌᅡ네시서 어찌시기 짜 찌리 뫄 무시먀 더너너.	17. These men are springs without water and mists driven by a storm. Blackest darkness is reserved for them.
18. Bende batchitonga tchanganama mwakuteta myasi ye buhabuha. Kandji bende baereka kuteya	18. 버ᄕᅥ 바찌도ᅌᅡ 짜ᅌᅡ나마 뫄구더다 먀시 여 부하부하. 가ᅜᅵ 버ᄕᅥ 바어러가 구더야 어바ᅜᅮ 바 버라 바더ᅌᅡ아	18. For they mouth empty, boastful words and, by appealing to the lustful desires of sinful human nature, they

ebandju ba bera batengaa mwa tchikembe tcha bandju ba bateshi emyasi yabo ye buhumahuma bwe lusingi.

19. Mwebi bende balaanya ebandju mbu bangaba mwa bolo noku beine batchilyi mwa butcha bwe myasi ye muero ! Bushi tchira mundju anatchula kaungu ke mwanya ola wende wamukoresa.

20. Ebandju banunulyibwe kutenga mwa buhumahuma bubi bo muno butala bushi ne kumenya Enawetchu Yesu Kirisito kandji imununusi. Si akaba bangemerera kuhuba kukorisibwa nobuhumahuma, aola ebusinda bwabo bwanera bwaba bubi busese kurenza kwa babaa lyamira.

21. Abu bandju, kungabere kukulu akaba batangamenyire endjira ya myasi era itchungenene, wa kuimenya tchasinda banareka emuomba mubuyabuya ola beresibwaa.

22. Rero ebi byabaikilyire, bilosise kanangana emuanyi ola utchula utetchire mbu : Engunda yahubire kulya bya yahalaa, kandji mbu :

마 찌거뻐 짜 바뉴 바 바더씨 어먀시 야보 여 부후마후마 붜 루시끼.

19. 뭐비 버떠 바롸아냐 어바뉴 뿌 바까바 마 보로 노구 버이너 바찌쩨 마 부짜 붜 먀시 여 무어로 ! 부씨 찌라 무뉴 아나쭈롸 가우꾸 거 먀냐 오롸 워떠 와무고러사.

20. 어바뉴 바누누레붜 구더까 마 부후마후마 부비 보 무노 부다롸 부씨 너 구머냐 어나워쭈 여수 기리시도 가찌 이무누누시. 시 아가바 바꺼머러라 구후바 구고리시봐 노부후마후마, 아오롸 어부시따 봐보 봐너라 봐바 부비 부서서 구러싸 과 바바아 쨔미라.

21. 아부 바뉴, 구까버러 구구루 아가바 바다까머니러 어찌라 야 먀시 어라 이쭈꺼너너, 와 구이머냐 짜시따 바나러가 어무오빠 무부야부야 오롸 버러시봐아.

22. 러로 어비 뱌바이기쩨러, 비로시서 가나까나 어무아네 오롸 우쭈롸 우더찌러 뿌 : 어꾸따 야후비러 구꺄 뱌

entice people who are just escaping from those who live in error.

19. They promise them freedom, while they themselves are slaves of depravity--for a man is a slave to whatever has mastered him.

20. If they have escaped the corruption of the world by knowing our Lord and Savior Jesus Christ and are again entangled in it and overcome, they are worse off at the end than they were at the beginning.

21. It would have been better for them not to have known the way of righteousness, than to have known it and then to turn their backs on the sacred command that was passed on to them.

22. Of them the proverbs are true: "A dog returns to its vomit,"and, "A sow that is washed goes back to her wallowing in the mud."

Engulube era bosaa yahubire 야하퐈아, 가찌 뿌 :
kutchifufusa mwa bihoo. 어위루버 어라 보사아
야후비러 구찌푸푸사 뫄
비호오.

---

2 Petero Chikono 3

1. Bera banyi basiirwa !
Manola mu maruba makabiri
nabandjikira. Mwa mu
maruba mabiri, nahonda
kuba kengesa munde
mwaanyisa kubuya kwe bya
nabaandjikilyire.

2. Nahonda munde
mwakengera bya barebi
babuyabuya batetaa kwa
mira. Kandji mundaa
mwakengera nola muomba
wa Enawetchu kandji i
mununusi wetchu ola
endjumwa sa bakangilyisaa.

3. Era muhondo sa byoshi,
mumenyereraa kwa mwa
suku se businda, kukaulukira
bandju ba bakende
batchitola kukulyikana ne
myasu yabo ibi ye
buhumahuma. Abu bandju
bakende babashekera.

4. mwa kuteta mbu :
Abalaanyaa kwa akafuluka !
Rero ngai alyi ? Bushi
kutengera ala ba hokulu

---

2 퍼더로 찌고노 3

1. 버라 바네 바시이롸 !
마노퐈 무 마루바 마가비리
나바찌기라. 뫄 무 마루바
마비리, 나호따 구바 거써사
무떠 뫄아네사 구부야 궈
뱌 나바아찌기레러.

2. 나호따 무떠 뫄거써라 뱌
바러비 바부야부야
바더다아 과 미라. 가찌
무따아 뫄거써라 노퐈
무오빠 와 어나워쭈 가찌
이 무누누시 워쭈 오퐈
어뿌뫄 사 바가찌레사아.

3. 어라 무호또 사 뵤씨,
무머녀러라아 과 뫄 수구
서 부시따, 구가우루기라
바뿌 바 바거떠 바찌도퐈
구구레가나 너 먀수 야보
이비 여 부후마후마. 아부
바뿌 바거떠 바바써거라.

4. 뫄 구더다 뿌 :
아바퐈아나냐아 과
아가푸루가 ! 러로 아이
아레 ? 부씨 구더써라 아퐈

---

2 Peter Chapter 3[NIV]

1. Dear friends, this is now my
second letter to you. I have
written both of them as
reminders to stimulate you to
wholesome thinking.

2. I want you to recall the
words spoken in the past by
the holy prophets and the
command given by our Lord
and Savior through your
apostles.

3. First of all, you must
understand that in the last days
scoffers will come, scoffing and
following their own evil desires.

4. They will say, "Where is this
'coming' he promised? Ever
since our fathers died,
everything goes on as it has

betchu bafiraa kuikira
lwarero, emyasi yoshi
inatchilyi ngokwa yabaa
inatchula kutengera
ekukumbwa kwe butala !

5. Mwa kuteta batcha,
banatchebilyisa kwa
kutengera mira, Ongo
abumbaa enguba ne butala
kurengera etchinwa oshao.
Ebutala bwa kulyibwaa mwe
meshi kandji bwabumbwaa
kurengera emeshi.

6. Kandji kurengera amu
meshi, kwe butala bokwa
mira bwasikaa ne mwihuso.

7. Si kandji kurengera etchi
tchinwa tchinetchi, enguba
ne butala bya lwarero,
bibikilyirwe kusiresibwa mwa
mulyiro. Byalyindjirisibwa
kuikira elusuku lwa Ongo
akatchindjibusa ne kusikya
ebakosi be mabi.

8. Rero bera bandji basiirwa,
kulyi mwaisi muuma ola
mutemire kunde mwebilyira.
Oyu mwasi, kulyi kuteta kwa
era mwa Enawetchu, lusuku
luuma lulyi nga byanda
tchumbi, ne byanda tchumbi
ilyi nga lusuku luuma.

9. Enawetchu atelyisa kuira
bya alaanyaa ngokwa bandju

바 호구루 버쭈 바피라아
구이기라 똬러로, 어먀시
요씨 이나찌레 꼬과 야바아
이나쭈똬 구더뼈라
어구구똬 궈 부다똬 !

5. 똬 구더다 바짜,
바나쩌비레사 과 구더뼈라
미라, 오꼬 아부빠아 어우바
너 부다똬 구러뼈라 어찌놔
오싸오. 어부다똬 봐
구레봐아 뭐 머씨 가찌
봐부똬아 구러뼈라 어머씨.

6. 가찌 구러뼈라 아무
머씨, 궈 부다똬 보과 미라
봐시가아 너 뮈후소.

7. 시 가찌 구러뼈라 어찌
찌놔 찌너찌, 어우바 너
부다똬 봐 똬러로,
비비기레뤄 구시러시봐 똬
무레로. 뱌레찌리시봐
구이기라 어루수구 똬 오꼬
아가찌찌부사 너 구시갸
어바고시 버 마비.

8. 러로 버라 바찌
바시이롸, 구레 뫄이시
무우마 오롸 무더미러 구뎌
뭐비뗴라. 오유 뫄시, 구레
구더다 과 어라 똬
어나워쭈, 루수구 루우마
루뗴 똬 뱌따 쭈뻬, 너 뱌따
쭈뻬 이레 똬 루수구
루우마.

9. 어나워쭈 아더뗴사
구이라 뱌 아똬아냐아 꼬과

since the beginning
of creation."

5. But they deliberately forget
that long ago by God's word
the heavens existed and
the earth was formed out
of water and by water.

6. By these waters also the
world of that time was deluged
and destroyed.

7. By the same word the
present heavens and earth are
reserved for fire, being kept for
the day of judgment and
destruction of ungodly men.

8. But do not forget this one
thing, dear friends: With the
Lord a day is like a thousand
years, and a thousand years are
like a day.

9. The Lord is not slow in
keeping his promise, as some

bauma baanyisa. Atchilyi alyindjilyira bushi nenyu bushi atahonda mbu kubaa tchiro ne mundju asibya ola uera. Si ahonda ebandju boshi babindjuke kutenga mwa bibi byabo.

10. Si elusuku lwe kufuluka kwa Enawetchu lukaika ngokwa mwisi enda aika. Olu lusuku, enguba ikairima mu lusindo lunene busese. Nabyoshi byabumbwaa bya bitchula kwa nguba bikashenga ne mulyiro. Ebutala na byoshi bya bitchula'mo bikatchindjibusibwa.

11. Rero bushi ebindju bikakumba batcha, mwabo mwemire kuata mikorere ibuyabuya era isimise Ongo.

12. Mundaa mwaira batcha mu mwalyindjilyira olu lusuku lwa Ongo luike fuba. Mwolu lusuku enguba ikashenga nebidnju byoshi byababumbwaa, bya bitchula kwa nguba, nabi bikanashenga ne mulyiro.

13. Si kutengera mira, Ongo abaa atchulaanyise kwa kukaba nguba iyaya ne

바쭈 바우마 바아네사. 아찌레 아레찌레라 부씨 너뉴 부씨 아다호따 뿌 구바아 찌로 너 무뉴 아시뱌 오롸 우어라. 시 아호따 어바쭈 보씨 바비쭈거 구더따 롸 비비 뱌보.

10. 시 어루수구 뤄 구푸룩가 과 어나워쭈 룩가이가 꼬과 뮈시 어따 아이가. 오루 룩수구, 어꾸바 이가이리마 무 룩시또 룩너너 부서서. 나뇨씨 뱌부빠아 뱌 비쭈롸 과 꾸바 비가써따 너 무레로. 어부다롸 나 뇨씨 뱌 비쭈롸모 비가찌찌부시봐.

11. 러로 부씨 어비쭈 비가구빠 바쨔, 뫄보 구아다 미고러러 이부야부야 어라 이시미서 오꼬.

12. 무따아 뫄이라 바쨔 무 뫄레찌레라 오루 룩수구 롸 오꼬 룩이거 푸바. 모루 룩수구 어꾸바 이가써따 너비쭈 뇨씨 뱌바부빠아, 뱌 비쭈롸 과 꾸바, 나비 비가나써따 너 무레로.

13. 시 구더따라 미라, 오꼬 아바아 아쭈롸아네서 과 구가바 꾸바 이야야 너

understand slowness. He is patient with you, not wanting anyone to perish, but everyone to come to repentance.

10. But the day of the Lord will come like a thief. The heavens will disappear with a roar; the elements will be destroyed by fire, and the earth and everything in it will be laid bare.

11. Since everything will be destroyed in this way, what kind of people ought you to be? You ought to live holy and godly lives

12. as you look forward to the day of God and speed its coming. That day will bring about the destruction of the heavens by fire, and the elements will melt in the heat.

13. But in keeping with his promise we are looking forward to a new heaven and a

butala buyaya bya bikaba mwe myasi yoshi era itchungenene. Rero ebyera bitchwalyindjira.

부다꽈 부야야 뱌 비가바 뭐 먀시 요씨 어라 이쭈꺼너너. 러로 어벼라 비쫘쩨찌라.

new earth, the home of righteousness.

14. Bushi noku ku bera banyi basiirwa, mango mutchilyi mwalyindjira ei myasi mutchisesaa kuba bandju babuyabuya, ba batete tchiro ne tchibi tchisibya era muhondo sa Ongo, balyi nomwa bolo nai.

14. 부씨 노구 구 버라 바네 바시이롸, 마꼬 무찌쩨 똬쩨찌라 어이 먀시 무찌서사아 구바 바쭈 바부야부야, 바 바더더 찌로 너 찌비 찌시뱌 어라 무호또 사 오꼬, 바쩨 노롸 보로 나이.

14. So then, dear friends, since you are looking forward to this, make every effort to be found spotless, blameless and at peace with him.

15. Kandji mumenyereraa kwa oku kulyindjirira kwa Enawetchu, bilyi bihangi bibuya bya aberesise tchasiya mununulyibwe. Ebyera bikulyikene ne myasi era munyaketchu mussirwa Paulo abaandjikiraa, mwa kukoresibwa ne bwenge bwa Ongo amweresise.

15. 가찌 무머녀러라아 과 오구 구쩨찌리라 과 어나워쭈, 비쩨 비하꾀 비부야 뱌 아버러시서 짜시야 무누누쩨붜. 어벼라 비구쩨거너 너 먀시 어라 무냐거쭈 무씨롸 파우로 아바아찌기라아, 뫄 구고러시봐 너 붜꺼 봐 오꼬 아뭐러시서.

15. Bear in mind that our Lord's patience means salvation, just as our dear brother Paul also wrote you with the wisdom that God gave him.

16. Ei myasi i Paulo aandjikaa mwa maruba mai moshi ma atchula atetchire mu era luulu sebi. Mwamu maruba, mutchula myasi inene era ikootchira kuumva. Rero embuta neba batakangilyisibwe bende babindjula ei myasi kwa itetchire ngokwa bende banaibindjula ebindji bimbi bye maandjiko mabuyabuya. Mwa kuira batcha, bendjire

16. 어이 먀시 이 파우로 아아찌가아 뫄 마루바 마이 모씨 마 아쭈꽈 아더찌러 무 어라 루우루 서비. 뫄무 마루바, 무쭈꽈 먀시 이너너 어라 이고오찌라 구우빠. 러로 어뿌다 너바 바다가꾀쩨시붜 버떠 바비뿌꽈 어이 먀시 과 이더찌러 꼬과 버떠 바나이비뿌꽈 어비찌 비뻬 뱌 마아찌고 마부야부야. 뫄 구이라 바짜, 버찌러

16. He writes the same way in all his letters, speaking in them of these matters. His letters contain some things that are hard to understand, which ignorant and unstable people distort, as they do the other Scriptures, to their own destruction.

batchiuma mwa muero beine.

17. Rero bera banyi basiirwa, mwelyire mwamenyerera ei myasi. Bushi noku, mundaa mwatchilanga mungesha kwengeerwa bushi ne kuuwa kwe bakosi be mabi. Muakira batcha, mungasimika busese mwa bwemeresi bwenyu.

18. Muendekeraa kusimika mwa myasi ya Enawetchu Yesu Kirisito, kandji imununusi wetchu tchasiya mumenyerere busese nai enda abaahanyira busese. Endaa atongibwa kutengera lwarero kuikira esuku ne mango. Bibe batcha!

바찌우마 뫄 무어로 버이너.

17. 러로 버라 바네 바시이롸, 뭐례러 뫄머녀러라 어이 먀시. 부씨 노구, 무따아 뫄찌롸롸 무꺼싸 궈꺼어롸 부씨 너 구우와 궈 바고시 버 마비. 무아기라 바쨔, 무뫄시미가 부서서 뫄 뭐머러시 뭐뉴.

18. 무어떠거라아 구시미가 뫄 먀시 야 어나워쭈 여수 기리시도, 가찌 이무누누시 워쭈 짜시야 무머녀러러 부서서 나이 어따 아바아하네라 부서서. 어따아 아도꺼봐 구더꺼라 꽈러로 구이기라 어수구 너 마꼬. 비버 바쨔!

17. Therefore, dear friends, since you already know this, be on your guard so that you may not be carried away by the error of lawless men and fall from your secure position.

18. But grow in the grace and knowledge of our Lord and Savior Jesus Christ. To him be glory both now and forever! Amen.

1 Yoana

1 요아나

1 John

YOWANI MUBEREBERE

(1 JOHN)

요와니 무버러버러

(1 조후누)

1 Yoana Chikono 1

1. Thwabaanjikira era luulu sa Wachinwa chekalamo. Oyu Wachinwa abaa anathula kutengera mwa ndangilyiso yebindu byoshi. Thubeine thwachuumviraa kwa bya abaa enjire ateta, thwera kunachimuloreraako nemeho methu, na kumuthumbikisa kubuya-buya, thwera kunamuumako nemino sethu.

2. Oyu Wakalamo abaa anathula alauma na Ongo Tata. Rero, Ongo athulosise i mira. Bushi noku, thwenjire thwateta bya thwishi era luulu sai, kwa mwa ndanda sai mu munathula ekalamo kesuku nemango.

3. Oyu thwachiloreraako na kuchumvira bya atetaa, nenyu ithwenjire thwabahubanganyisa era luulu sai, chasiya mube mwa buuma nethu. Kanji thuboshi thube mwa buuma na Tata, neMwana wai Yesu Kirisito.

4. Thwabaanjikirire ene myasi, chasiya thumowe loshi.

5. Emwasi ola thomvaa Yesu Kirisito ateta, inenyu thwenjire thwanabakangirisa. Noyu mwasi iyono: Ongo

1 요아나 찌고노 1

1. 쫘바아찌기라 어라 루우루 사 와찌냐 쩌가꺄모. 오유 와찌냐 아바아 아나쭈꽈 구더꺼라 뫄 따삐레쏘 여비뿌 뽀씨. 쭈버이너 쫘쭈우뻬라아 과 뱌 아바아 어찌러 아더다, 쮀라 구나찌무뢰러라고 너머호 머쭈, 나 구무쭈뻬기사 구부야-부야, 쮀라 구나무우마고 너미노 서쭈.

2. 오유 와가꺄모 아바아 아나쭈꽈 아꺄우마 나 오꼬 다다. 러로, 오꼬 아쭈로시서 이 미라. 부씨 노구, 쮀찌러 쫘더다 뱌 쮀씨 어라 루우루 사이, 과 뫄 따따 사이 무 무나쭈꽈 어가꺄모 거수구 너마꼬.

3. 오유 쫘찌뢰러라아고 나 구쭈뻬라 뱌 아더다아, 너뉴 이쮀찌러 쫘바후바뱌니새사 어라 루우루 사이, 짜시야 무버 뫄 부우마 너쭈. 가찌 쭈보씨 쭈버 뫄 부우마 나 다다, 너뫄나 와이 여수 기리시도.

4. 쫘바아찌기리러 어너 먀시, 짜시야 쭈모워 로씨.

5. 어뫄시 오라 쏘빠아 여수 기리시도 아더다, 이너뉴 쮀찌러 쫘나바가삐리사. 노유 뫄시 이요노: 오꼬

1 John Chapter 1[NIV]

1. That which was from the beginning, which we have heard, which we have seen with our eyes, which we have looked at and our hands have touched--this we proclaim concerning the Word of life.

2. The life appeared; we have seen it and testify to it, and we proclaim to you the eternal life, which was with the Father and has appeared to us.

3. We proclaim to you what we have seen and heard, so that you also may have fellowship with us. And our fellowship is with the Father and with his Son, Jesus Christ.

4. We write this to make our joy complete.

5. This is the message we have heard from him and declare to you: God is light; in him there is no darkness

ibulangare, nomwa ndanda sai mutathula musimya chiro na hicha.

6. Akaba thungachiremba kuteta mbu thulyi mwa buuma na Ongo, noku bya thwaira bilyi bya musimya, elyi thwafula bisha. Aola, emyanya yethu yalosa kwa thutaira myasi ya kanangana.

7. Si akaba thulyi mwa bulangare, ngokwa Ongo yeine athula bulangare, aola thwanaba mwa buuma thubeine kwa thubeine, nemikira yeMwana wai Yesu, yanende yakomya ebibi byethu byoshi.

8. Akaba thungachiremba kuteta mbu thutete bibi, elyi thwachengeera thubeine, nemyasi yekanangana, italyi mwa ndanda sethu.

9. Si akaba thungachiaya kwa bibi byethu, thuneshi kanangana kwa Ongo angathubabalyira, bushi yeke ende aira bya alanyaa, kanji ende aira bya bithungenene. Na chira mabi moshi ma malyi mwa ndanda sethu, anamakomya.

10. Akaba thungateta mbu thutakola mabi, elyi thwarire Ongo kuba mufusi wa bisha,

---

이부꽈마레러, 노마 따따 사이 무다쭈꽈 무시먀 찌로 나 히짜.

6. 아가바 쭈꽈찌러빠 구더다 뿌 쭈레 마 부우마 나 오꼬, 노구 뱌 쫘이라 비레 뱌 무시먀, 어레 쫘푸꽈 비싸. 아오꽈, 어먀냐 여쭈 야로사 과 쭈다이라 먀시 야 가나꽈나.

7. 시 아가바 쭈레 마 부꽈마레러, 꼬과 오꼬 여이너 아쭈꽈 부꽈마레러, 아오꽈 쫘나바 마 부우마 쭈버이너 과 쭈버이너, 너미기라 여마나 와이 여수, 야너머 야고먀 어비비 벼쭈 뵤씨.

8. 아가바 쭈꽈찌러빠 구더다 뿌 쭈더더 비비, 어레 쫘쩌꺼어라 쭈버이너, 너먀시 여가나꽈나, 이다레 마 따따 서쭈.

9. 시 아가바 쭈꽈찌아야 과 비비 벼쭈, 쭈너씨 가나꽈나 과 오꼬 아꽈쭈바바레라, 부씨 여거 어떠 아이라 뱌 아꽈냐야, 가찌 어떠 아이라 뱌 비쭈꺼너너. 나 찌라 마비 모씨 마 마레 마 따따 서쭈, 아나마고먀.

10. 아가바 쭈꽈더다 뿌 쭈다고꽈 마비, 어레 쫘리러 오꼬 구바 무푸시 와 비싸,

---

at all.

6. If we claim to have fellowship with him yet walk in the darkness, we lie and do not live by the truth.

7. But if we walk in the light, as he is in the light, we have fellowship with one another, and the blood of Jesus, his Son, purifies us from all sin.

8. If we claim to be without sin, we deceive ourselves and the truth is not in us.

9. If we confess our sins, he is faithful and just and will forgive us our sins and purify us from all unrighteousness.

10. If we claim we have not sinned, we make him out to be a liar and his word has no

nechinwa chai elyi chitalyi mwa ndanda sethu.

너찌놔 짜이 어레 찌다례 봐 따따 서쭈.

place in our lives.

1 Yoana Chikono 2

1. Mu bana banyi, nabaanjikira ene myasi, mungesha kunde mwaira mabi. Si akaba kungaba mundju ola wairiremo, thuthusa ola wende wathutetera era muhondo sa Tata. Noyu, iYesu Kirisito, iuthula uthungenene era muhondo sai.

2. Oyu Yesu iwachanaa yeine nga mithulo kwa kubabalyira ebibi byethu. Ata ebibi byethu byeine oshao byende ababalyira, si anabe nebyebanji bandju boshi bo mwa butala.

3. Thwende thwamenyerera kanangana kwa thwishi Ongo, mango thwthunda emiombayai.

4. Si akaba mundju angateta mbu nyithula nyishi Ongo, noku atenjire athunda emiombayai, elyi alyi mufusi wa bisha, nemyasi yekanangana italyi mwa ndanda sai.

1 요아나 찌고노 2

1. 무 바나 바네, 나바아찌기라 어너 먀시, 무꺼싸 구떠 뫄이라 마비. 시 아가바 구꾸바 무뚜 오롸 와이리러모, 쭈쭈사 오롸 워떠 와쭈더더라 어라 무호또 사 다다. 노유, 이여수 기리시도, 이우쭈롸 우쭈꺼너너 어라 무호또 사이.

2. 오유 여수 이와짜나아 여이너 꺄 미쭈로 과 구바바례라 어비비 벼쭈. 아다 어비비 벼쭈 벼이너 오싸오 벼떠 아바바례라, 시 아나버 너벼바찌 바뚜 보씨 보 봐 부다롸.

3. 쮜떠 좌머녀러라 가나꺄나 과 쮜씨 오꼬, 먀꼬 찌우쭈따 어미오빠야이.

4. 시 아가바 무뚜 아꺄더다 뿌 네쭈롸 네씨 오꼬, 노구 아더찌러 아쭈따 어미오빠야이, 어레 아레 무푸시 와 비싸, 너먀시 여가나꺄나 이다레 봐 따따 사이.

1 John Chapter 2[NIV]

1. My dear children, I write this to you so that you will not sin. But if anybody does sin, we have one who speaks to the Father in our defense--Jesus Christ, the Righteous One.

2. He is the atoning sacrifice for our sins, and not only for ours but also for the sins of the whole world.

3. We know that we have come to know him if we obey his commands.

4. The man who says, "I know him," but does not do what he commands is a liar, and the truth is not in him.

5. Si emundju ola wende waira kwa Ongo atechire, enzii yai ku Ongo yende yaba yalumisibwe kanangana. Nechi chi chende chathulosa kwa thulyi mwa buuma na Ongo.

6. Akaba mundju angateta mbu athula mwa buuma na Ongo, emire kunde achitola ngokwa Yesu nai abaa athula achitolyre.

7. Bera banyi basiirwa, emuomba ola nabaanjikira anola, ata muomba muyayaya, si alyi wokwa mira ola muthula muneshi kutengera mango mwemereraa Enawethu. Kanji oyu muomba wokwa mira chilyi echinwa cha Ongo cha momvaa kutengera mira.

8. Si chiro bacha, emuomba ola nabaanjikira anola, analyi muyayaya. Echera chisenekeko kurengera emyanya era Yesu abaa athusa. Nemyanya yenyu nai yalosa kanangana kwa oyu muomba analyi muyayaya. Bushi emusimya arengire mira, nebandju bera basene kwa bulangare bwekanangana.

9. Emundju ola wateta mbu alyi mwa bulangare, noku

5. 시 어무뚜 오롸 워떠 와이라 과 오꼬 아더찌러, 어씨이 야이 구 오꼬 여너 야바 야루미시붜 가나마나. 너찌 찌 쩌떠 짜쭈론사 과 쭈레 뫄 부우마 나 오꼬.

6. 아가바 무뚜 아까더다 뿌 아쭈롸 뫄 부우마 나 오꼬, 어미러 구떠 아찌도롸 꼬과 여수 나이 아바아 아쭈롸 아찌도뤼러.

7. 버라 바네 바시이롸, 어무오빠 오롸 나바아찌기라 아노롸, 아다 무오빠 무야야야, 시 아레 옹과 미라 오롸 무쭈롸 무너씨 구더꺼라 마꼬 뭐머러라아 어나워쭈. 가찌 오유 무오빠 옹과 미라 찌레 어찌뇨 짜 오꼬 짜 모빠아 구더꺼라 미라.

8. 시 찌로 바짜, 어무오빠 오롸 나바아찌기라 아노롸, 아나레 무야야야. 어쩌라 찌서너거고 구러꺼라 어먀냐 어라 여수 아바아 아쭈사. 너먀냐 여뉴 나이 야론사 가나마나 과 오유 무오빠 아나레 무야야야. 부씨 어무시먀 아러끼러 미라, 너바쭈 버라 바서너 과 부롸꺼라 붜가나마나.

9. 어무뚜 오롸 와더다 뿌 아레 뫄 부롸꺼라, 노구

5. But if anyone obeys his word, God's love is truly made complete in him. This is how we know we are in him:

6. Whoever claims to live in him must walk as Jesus did.

7. Dear friends, I am not writing you a new command but an old one, which you have had since the beginning. This old command is the message you have heard.

8. Yet I am writing you a new command; its truth is seen in him and you, because the darkness is passing and the true light is already shining.

9. Anyone who claims to be in the light but hates his

ahombire munyakabo, elyii mwa musimya mu anachilyi kuikira lwarero.

10. Emundju ola usimire munyakabo elyi alyi mwa bulangare. Nomwa ndanda sai mutalyi chiro na kandju kasibya ka kangathuma akumbaala.

11. Si ola uhombire munyakabo, elyi mwa musimya mu alyi, atangaala kumenya nera aya bushi emusimya amusibise emeho.

12. Nabaanjikira mu bana banyi, bushi ebibi byenyu byababalyirwe kurengera esina lya Yesu Kirisito.

13. Nabaanjikira mu batata, bushi muthula mwishi ola uthulao kutengera mwa ndangiriso yebindju byoshi. Nabaanjikira mu batabana, bushi mwaimire ola Mukosi wemabi.

14. Nabaanjikira mu bana banyi, bushi muthula mwishi Tata. Nabaanjikira mu batata, bushi muthula mwishi ola uthulao kutengera mwa ndangiriso yebindju byoshi.

아호삐러 무냐가보, 어레이 먀 무시먀 무 아나찌레 구이기라 롸러로.

10. 어무뚜 오롸 우시미러 무냐가보 어레 아레 먀 부롸까러. 노롸 따따 사이 무다레 찌로 나 가꾸 가시뱌 가 가꾸마 아구빠아롸.

11. 시 오롸 우호삐러 무냐가보, 어레 먀 무시먀 무 아레, 아다까아롸 구머냐 너라 아야 부씨 어무시먀 아무시비서 어머호.

12. 나바아찌기라 무 바나 바네, 부씨 어비비 벼뉴 뱌바바레뤄 구러꺼라 어시나 랴 여수 기리시도.

13. 나바아찌기라 무 바다다, 부씨 무쭈롸 뮈씨 오롸 우쭈롸오 구더꺼라 먀 따꺼리소 여비뿌 뵤씨. 나바아찌기라 무 바다바나, 부씨 롸이미러 오롸 무고시 워마비.

14. 나바아찌기라 무 바나 바네, 부씨 무쭈롸 뮈씨 다다. 나바아찌기라 무 바다다, 부씨 무쭈롸 뮈씨 오롸 우쭈롸오 구더꺼라 먀 따꺼리소 여비뿌 뵤씨.

brother is still in the darkness.

10. Whoever loves his brother lives in the light, and there is nothing in him to make him stumble.

11. But whoever hates his brother is in the darkness and walks around in the darkness; he does not know where he is going, because the darkness has blinded him.

12. I write to you, dear children, because your sins have been forgiven on account of his name.

13. I write to you, fathers, because you have known him who is from the beginning. I write to you, young men, because you have overcome the evil one. I write to you, dear children, because you have known the Father.

14. I write to you, fathers, because you have known him who is from the beginning. I write to you, young men, because you are strong, and the word of God

Nabaanjikira mu batabana, bushi muthusa misi, nechinwa cha Ongo, chithula mwa michima yenyu, mwaimire nola Mukosi wemabi. Biteemire kusima ebindju bibi byomuno butala.

나바아찌기라 무 바다바나, 부씨 무쭈사 미시, 너찌놔 짜 오꼬, 찌쭈콰 마 미찌마 여뉴, 콰이미러 노라 무고시 워마비. 비더어미러 구시마 어비뉴 비비 뵤무노 부다콰.

lives in you, and you have overcome the evil one.

15. Mutendaa mwasima buno butala, nesi chira kandju kabi ka kathulamo. Akaba mundju angasima ebutala, atangaala kusima Tata.

15. 무더따아 콰시마 부노 부다콰, 너시 찌라 가뉴 가비 가 가쭈콰모. 아가바 무뉴 아꽈시마 어부다콰, 아다꾸아꽈 구시마 다다.

15. Do not love the world or anything in the world. If anyone loves the world, the love of the Father is not in him.

16. Emyasi yebutala iyeene: ekuira emyasi ibi era mubilyi ahonda, nekuhumira bya mundju aseneko, neekuchilola bushi nebuare. Ebi byoshi, bitatengire era mwa Tata, si bitengire muno butala.

16. 어먀시 여부다콰 이여어너: 어구이라 어먀시 이비 어라 무비쩨 아호따, 너구후미라 뱌 무뉴 아서너고, 너어구찌쫀콰 부씨 너부아러. 어비 뵤씨, 비다더삐러 어라 콰 다다, 시 비더삐러 무노 부다콰.

16. For everything in the world--the cravings of sinful man, the lust of his eyes and the boasting of what he has and does--comes not from the Father but from the world.

17. Ebutala nemyasi era bandju bende bahumiramo, byoshi kurenga ku byarenga. Si emundju ola waira ekuhonda kwa Ongo, yeke ete ekalamo kesuku nemango.

17. 어부다콰 너먀시 어라 바뉴 버떠 바후미라모, 뵤씨 구러꾸 구 뱌러꾸. 시 어무뉴 오콰 와이라 어구호따 과 오꼬, 여거 어더 어가꽈모 거수구 너마꼬.

17. The world and its desires pass away, but the man who does the will of God lives forever.

18. Bana banyi, sinera sera suku sa businda sobuno butala. Mwomvaa kanangana kwa Murenda wa Kirisito akabaha. Rero, barenda banene ba Kirisito balorekanyireko mira. Bushi noku, thwamenyerere kanangana kwa sinera sera

18. 바나 바네, 시너라 서라 수구 사 부시따 소부노 부다콰. 몸빠아 가나꾸나 과 무러따 와 기리시도 아가바하. 러로, 바러따 바너너 바 기리시도 바쪼러가네러고 미라. 부씨 노구, 쫘머녀러러 가나꾸나 과 시너라 서라 시나쩨 수구

18. Dear children, this is the last hour; and as you have heard that the antichrist is coming, even now many antichrists have come. This is how we know it is the last hour.

sinalyi suku sa businda sobuno butala.

사 부시따 소부노 부다라.

19. Abu bandju, bachikulaa mwa kachi-kachi kethu, si batabaa bauma nethu. Bushi akaba bangabere bauma nethu, batangachikulyire ku thubano. Echera, chilosise kanangana kwa boshi batanabaa bauma nethu.

19. 아부 바뚜, 바찌구롸아 마 가찌-가찌 거쭈, 시 바다바아 바우마 너쭈. 부씨 아가바 바까버러 바우마 너쭈, 바다까찌구레러 구 쭈바노. 어쩌라, 찌로시서 가나까나 과 보씨 바다나바아 바우마 너쭈.

19. They went out from us, but they did not really belong to us. For if they had belonged to us, they would have remained with us; but their going showed that none of them belonged to us.

20. Si mwabo, mwabonyire eMuchima Mubuya-buya ola Kirisito aberesise. Nechi chithumire mwamenyerera emyasi yekanangana.

20. 시 먀보, 먀보네러 어무찌마 무부야-부야 오롸 기리시도 아버러시서. 너찌 찌쭈미러 먀머녀러라 어먀시 여가나까나.

20. But you have an anointing from the Holy One, and all of you know the truth.

21. Ndabanjikirire mbu bushi muteshi emyasi yekanangana. Si nabanjikirire bushi muishi. Kanji mwishi kwa mwei myasi yekanangana, mutangatenga chiro na mwasi wabisha.

21. 따바찌기리러 뿌 부씨 무더씨 어먀시 여가나까나. 시 나바찌기리러 부씨 무이씨. 가찌 뮈씨 과 뭐이 먀시 여가나까나, 무다까더까 찌로 나 먀시 와비싸.

21. I do not write to you because you do not know the truth, but because you do know it and because no lie comes from the truth.

22. Nde imufusi webisha kasi? Alyi ola wanana mbu Yesu ata iKirisito. Emundu ola ulyi ngoyu, iMurenda wa Kirisito, bushi ananyire Tata, ananana neMwana wai.

22. 떠 이무푸시 워비싸 가시? 아레 오롸 와나나 뿌 여수 아다 이기리시도. 어무뚜 오롸 우레 꼬유, 이무러따 와 기리시도, 부씨 아나네러 다다, 아나나나 너먀나 와이.

22. Who is the liar? It is the man who denies that Jesus is the Christ. Such a man is the antichrist--he denies the Father and the Son.

23. Bushi ola wanana eMwana, elyi ananyire na Tata. Si ola wemerere eMwana, elyi emerere na Tata.

23. 부씨 오롸 와나나 어먀나, 아레 아나네러 나 다다. 시 오롸 워머러러 어먀나, 아레 어머러러 나 다다.

23. No one who denies the Son has the Father; whoever acknowledges the Son has the Father also.

24. Bushi noku, emyasi era mwomvaa kutengera mango mwemereraa Enawethu,

24. 부씨 노구, 어먀시 어라 모빠아 구더러라 마꼬 뭐머러라아 어나워쭈, 무따아

24. See that what you have heard from the beginning remains in you. If it does,

mundaa mwalangai kubuya 꽈꽈꽈이 구부야 꽈 미찌마 you also will remain in the
mwa michima yenyu. Bushi ei 여뉴. 부씨 어이 먀시 몸빠아 Son and in the Father.
myasi mwomvaa kutengera 구더뻐라 마꼬 뭐머러라아,
mango mwemereraa, akaba 아가바 무빠이꽈꽈 꽈 미찌마
mungailanga mwa michima 여뉴, 무빠바 꽈 부우마
yenyu, mungaba mwa buuma 너꽈나, 꽈나바 노꽈 부우마
neMwana, mwanaba nomwa 나 다다.
buuma na Tata.

25. Nechiraane cha Kirisito 25. 너찌라아너 짜 기리시도 25. And this is what he
atweresise kalyi ekalamo 아뚸러시서 가례 어가꽈모 promised us--even eternal
kesuku nemango. 거수구 너마꼬. life.

26. Nasimaa busese 26. 나시마아 부서서 26. I am writing these things
kubanjikira ei myasi, bushi 구바찌기라 어이 먀시, 부씨 to you about those who are
kulyi bandju bauma ba benjire 구례 바뚜 바우마 바 버찌러 trying to lead you astray.
bahonda kubengeera. 바호따 구버뻐어라.

27. Si mwabo, Kirisito 27. 시 꽈보, 기리시도 27. As for you, the anointing
aberesise eMuchima Mubuya- 아버러시서 어무찌마 무부야- you received from him
buya mira. Noyu Muchima 부야 미라. 노유 무찌마 remains in you, and you do
Mubuya-buya anathula mwa 무부야-부야 아나쭈꽈 꽈 not need anyone to teach
ndanda senyu. Bushi noku, 따따 서뉴. 부씨 노구, you. But as his anointing
mutalaire ku mundju 무다꽈이러 구 무뚜 teaches you about all things
wakubakangirisa, bushi oyu 와구바가삐리사, 부씨 오유 and as that anointing is real,
Muchima Mubuya-buya, 무찌마 무부야-부야, 이워뻐 not counterfeit--just as it has
iwende wabakangirisa byoshi. 와바가삐리사 뵤씨. 나 찌라 taught you, remain in him.
Na chira mwasi woshi ola 꽈시 올씨 오꽈 어뻐
ende abakangirisa, anathula 아바가삐리사, 아나쭈꽈 와
wa kanangana, si atawa bisha. 가나빠나, 시 아다와 비싸.
Rero, mundaa mwaba mwa 러로, 무따아 꽈바 꽈 부우마
buuma na Kirisito ngokwa 나 기리시도 꼬과 어무찌마
eMuchima Mubuya-buya 무부야-부야
anabakangirisaa. 아나바가삐리사아.

28. Rero bana banyi, 28. 러로 바나 바네, 28. And now, dear children,
muendekeraa kuba mwa 무어떠거라아 구바 꽈 부우마 continue in him, so that
buuma na Kirisito. Mango 나 기리시도. 마꼬 when he appears we may be
akalorekanako, thukabona 아가꾠러가나고, 쭈가보나 confident and unashamed

emunyiiro kanangana,
thutakafe na honyi era
muhondo sai kwolu lusuku.

어무네이로 가나까나,
쭈다가퍼 나 호네 어라
무호또 사이 곤루 루수구.

before him at his coming.

29. Mwera mwishi kwa Kirisito
athula athungenene era
muhondo sa Ongo. Rero
mumenyereraa kwa chira
mundju woshi ola wende
waira bya bithungenene era
muhondo sa Ongo, imwana
wai.

29. 뭐라 뮈씨 과 기리시도
아쭈꽈 아쭈꺼너너 어라
무호또 사 오꼬. 러로
무머녀러라아 과 찌라 무뚜
오씨 오꽈 워떠 와이라 뱌
비쭈꺼너너 어라 무호또 사
오꼬, 이꽈나 와이.

29. If you know that he is
righteous, you know that
everyone who does what is
right has been born of him.

1 Yoana Chikono 3
1. Mulolaa kwa Tata
athusimaa busese kuikira
echihangi thwelyikibwa bana
ba Ongo. Kubinalyi Thubano
thunalyi bana bai. Nechi chi
chithumire ebandju bomwa
butala batathumenya, bushi
bateshi na Tata.
2. Rero bera banyi basiirwa,
thwera thlyi bana ba Ongo. Si
kwa thukaba, thutasa
kumenyako. Si thuneshi kwa
mango Kirisito akalorekanako,
thukahuha kuuma nai, bushi
thukamulolako ngokwa
anathula.
3. Rero chira mundju ola wete
oyu munyiiro mwa ndanda sa
Kirisito, ende achikomya

1 요아나 찌고노 3
1. 무로꽈아 과 다다
아쭈시마아 부서서 구이기라
어찌하끼 쭤뤠기봐 바나 바
오꼬. 구비나뤠 쭈바노
쭈나뤠 바나 바이. 너찌 찌
찌쭈미러 어바뚜 보봐 부다꽈
바다쭈머냐, 부씨 바더씨 나
다다.
2. 러로 버라 바네 바시이롸,
쭤라 찌뤠 바나 바 오꼬. 시
과 쭈가바, 쭈다사 구머냐고.
시 쭈너씨 과 마꼬 기리시도
아가뤼러가나고, 쭈가후하
구우마 나이, 부씨
쭈가무로꽈고 꼬과 아나쭈꽈.
3. 러로 찌라 무뚜 오꽈 워더
오유 무네이로 봐 따따 사
기리시도, 어떠 아찌고먀

1 John Chapter 3[NIV]
1. How great is the love the
Father has lavished on us,
that we should be called
children of God! And that is
what we are! The reason the
world does not know us is
that it did not know him.
2. Dear friends, now we are
children of God, and what
we will be has not yet been
made known. But we know
that when he appears,we
shall be like him, for we shall
see him as he is.
3. Everyone who has this
hope in him purifies himself,
just as he is pure.

ngokwa Kirisito yeine athula akomisibwe

꼬과 기리시도 여이너 아쭈롸 아고미시붜

4. Chira mundju ola wende waira ebibi, elyi kulwisa ku alwisa Ongo. Bushi ekuira ebibi, kuthula kulwisa Ongo.

4. 찌라 무뚜 오롸 워떠 와이라 어비비, 어레 구뤼사 구 아뤼사 오꼬. 부씨 어구이라 어비비, 구쭈롸 구뤼사 오꼬.

4. Everyone who sins breaks the law; in fact, sin is lawlessness.

5. Mwishi kwa Kirisito abahaa, chasiya aye kukula ebibi byethu. Nomwa ndanda sai, mutathula chiro na bibi bisibya.

5. 뮈씨 과 기리시도 아바하아, 짜시야 아여 구구롸 어비비 벼쭈. 노롸 따따 사이, 무다쭈롸 찌로 나 비비 비시뱌.

5. But you know that he appeared so that he might take away our sins. And in him is no sin.

6. Mwa bacha, chira mundju woshi ola ulyi mwa buuma nai atachiira mabi. Si chira mundju ola wende waira emabi, atafuraa kumulolako atanamwishi.

6. 롸 바짜, 찌라 무뚜 오씨 오롸 우레 롸 부우마 나이 아다찌이라 마비. 시 찌라 무뚜 오롸 워떠 와이라 어마비, 아다푸라아 구무롤롸고 아다나뮈씨.

6. No one who lives in him keeps on sinning. No one who continues to sin has either seen him or known him.

7. Bana banyi, mumenyaa kungesha kuba mundju ola wabengeera Emundju ola wende waira bya bithungenene, iunathula uthungenene ngokwa Kirisito nai anathula athungenene.

7. 바나 바네, 무머냐아 구꺼싸 구바 무뚜 오롸 와버꺼어라 어무뚜 오롸 워떠 와이라 뱌 비쭈어너너, 이우나쭈롸 우쭈꺼너너 꼬과 기리시도 나이 아나쭈롸 아쭈꺼너너.

7. Dear children, do not let anyone lead you astray. He who does what is right is righteous, just as he is righteous.

8. Emundju ola wende waira ebibi, alyi mundju wa Wamusimu, bushi Wamusimu ende aira ebibi kutengera mwa ndangiriso yebindju byoshi. Si eMwana wa Ongo aikaa kuhandjula emilyimo ya Wamusimu.

8. 어무뚜 오롸 워떠 와이라 어비비, 아레 무뚜 와 와무시무, 부씨 와무시무 어떠 아이라 어비비 구더꺼라 롸 따꺼리소 여비뚜 뵤씨. 시 어롸나 와 오꼬 아이가아 구하뚜롸 어미레모 야 와무시무.

8. He who does what is sinful is of the devil, because the devil has been sinning from the beginning. The reason the Son of God appeared was to destroy the devil's work.

9. Chira mundju ola wera ulyi mwana wa Ongo atachiira

9. 찌라 무뚜 오롸 워라 우레 롸나 와 오꼬 아다찌이라

9. No one who is born of God will continue to sin,

bibi, bushi echinwa cha Ongo chithula mwa muchima wai. Kanji bushi alyi mwana wa Ongo, atangachiendekera kunde aira ebibi.

10. Cha chende chalosa ebana ba Ongo neba Wamusimu chi chechine: emundju ola utaira bya bithungenene nesi ola utathula usimire munyakabo, oyola atamwana wa Ongo.

11. Emwasi ola mwomvaa kutengera mango mwemereraa Enawethu iyono thundaa thwasimana.

12. Thutendaa thwaba nga Kaini iwabaa mundju wola Mukosi wemabi, era kwita munyakabo. Chi chathumaa amwita? Amwitaa bushi emyanya yai yabaa ibi, si eya munyakabo yeke yabaa ithungenene.

13. Rero banyakethu, mutendaa mwasanwa akaba ebandju bomwa butala bangabahomba.

14. Thubano thwishi kwa thwatengire mwa lufu thwaya mwa kalamo bushi thuthula thusimire banyakethu. Emundju ola utathula usimire banyakabo elyi atasa kutenga

비비, 부씨 어찌냐 짜 오꼬 찌쭈롸 롸 무찌마 와이. 가찌 부씨 아레 롸나 와 오꼬, 아다까쩌떠거라 구떠 아이라 어비비.

10. 짜 쩌떠 짜로사 어바나 바 오꼬 너바 와무시무 찌 쩌찌너: 어무뚜 오롸 우다이라 뱌 비쭈떠너너 너시 오롸 우다쭈롸 우시미러 무냐가보, 오요롸 아다롸나 와 오꼬.

11. 어롸시 오롸 모롸아 구더떠라 마꼬 뭐머러라아 어나워쭈 이요노 쫘시마나.

12. 쭈더따아 쫘바 까 가이니 이와바아 무뚜 오롸 무고시 워마비, 어라 귀다 무냐가보. 찌 짜쭈마아 아뭐다? 아뭐다아 부씨 어먀냐 야이 야바아 이비, 시 어야 무냐가보 여거 야바아 이쭈떠너너.

13. 러로 바냐거쭈, 무더따아 롸사놔 아가바 어바뚜 보롸 부다롸 바까바호빠.

14. 쭈바노 쮜씨 과 쫘더삐러 롸 루푸 쫘야 롸 가롸모 부씨 쭈쭈롸 쭈시미러 바냐거쭈. 어무뚜 오롸 우다쭈롸 우시미러 바냐가보 어레 아다사 구더까 롸 루푸.

because God's seed remains in him; he cannot go on sinning, because he has been born of God.

10. This is how we know who the children of God are and who the children of the devil are: Anyone who does not do what is right is not a child of God; nor is anyone who does not love his brother.

11. This is the message you heard from the beginning: We should love one another.

12. Do not be like Cain, who belonged to the evil one and murdered his brother. And why did he murder him? Because his own actions were evil and his brother's were righteous.

13. Do not be surprised, my brothers, if the world hates you.

14. We know that we have passed from death to life, because we love our brothers. Anyone who does not love remains in death.

mwa lufu.

15. Chira mundju woshi ola uhombire munyakabo, alyi mwichi. Si mwishi kwa kutalyi chiro na mwichi ola wete ekalamo kesuku nemango.

16. Thubano, thwera thwishi enzii chilyi chiye kurengera ene myasi Yesu Kirisito anaa ekalamo kai bushi nethu. Rero nethu thwemire kunde thwemerera kwana ekalamo kethu bushi na banyakethu.

17. Akaba mundju angaba alyi muare, asene nokwa munyakabo alyi mwa bulae, atanahonda kumufira bonjo, oyu mundju anganachiremba kuteta mbu athula asimire Ongo?

18. Mu bana banyi, ekusimana kwethu, kutendaa kwaba kwa bieta oshao, si kundaa kwaba kwa kanangana, kanji kundaa kwalorekanako kurengera emyanya.

19. Kurengera ebyera, ku thungamenyerera kwa thulyi bandju ba kanangana, nemichima yethu ingabambatala era muhondo sa Ongo.

20. Bushi chiro angaba mbu bya bilyi mwa michima yethu byende byathushitaka,

15. 찌라 무뚜 오씨 오롸 우호삐러 무냐가보, 아레 뮈찌. 시 뮈씨 과 구다레 찌로 나 뮈찌 오롸 워더 어가롸모 거수구 너마꼬.

16. 쭈바노, 쮀라 쮜씨 어씨이 찌레 찌여 구러꺼라 어너 먀시 여수 기리시도 아나아 어가롸모 가이 부씨 너쭈. 러로 너쭈 쮀미러 구더 쮀머러라 과나 어가롸모 거쭈 부씨 나 바냐거쭈.

17. 아가바 무뚜 아빠바 아레 무아러, 아서너 노과 무냐가보 아레 롸 부롸어, 아다나호따 구무피라 보쪼, 오유 무뚜 아빠나찌러빠 구더다 뿌 아쭈롸 아시미러 오꼬?

18. 무 바나 바네, 어구시마나 궈쭈, 구더따아 과바 과 비어다 오싸오, 시 구따아 과바 과 가나빠나, 가찌 구따아 과롤러가나고 구러꺼라 어먀냐.

19. 구러꺼라 어벼라, 구 쭈빠머녀러라 과 쭈레 바뉴 바 가나빠나, 너미찌마 여쭈 이빠바빠다롸 어라 무호또 사 오꼬.

20. 부씨 찌로 아빠바 뿌 뱌 비레 롸 미찌마 여쭈 벼너 뱌쭈씨다가, 쭈너씨 과 오꼬

15. Anyone who hates his brother is a murderer, and you know that no murderer has eternal life in him.

16. This is how we know what love is: Jesus Christ laid down his life for us. And we ought to lay down our lives for our brothers.

17. If anyone has material possessions and sees his brother in need but has no pity on him, how can the love of God be in him?

18. Dear children, let us not love with words or tongue but with actions and in truth.

19. This then is how we know that we belong to the truth, and how we set our hearts at rest in his presence

20. whenever our hearts condemn us. For God is greater than our hearts, and

thuneshi kwa Ongo athala era luulu sebi byoshi, aneshi na byoshi.

21. Bera banyi basiirwa Akaba bya bilyi mwa michima yethu bitathushitaka, aola, thwete munyiiro era muhondo sa Ongo.

22. Thwende thwabona chira kandju koshi ka thwamwema, bushi thwende thwathunda emiomba yai na kuira bya bimusimise.

23. Nemuomba wai iyono thundaa thwemerera esina lyeMwana wai Yesu Kirisito na kunde thwasimana ngokwa Kirisito anathuburaa.

24. Emundju ola uthunjire emiomba ya Ongo, elyi alyi mwa buuma na Ongo, na Ongo anaba mwa buuma nai. Thwende thwamenyerera kwa thulyi mwa buuma na Ongo kurengera eMuchima Mubuya-buya ola athweresaa.

아따롸 어라 루우루 서비 뵤씨, 아너씨 나 뵤씨.

21. 버라 바네 바시이롸 아가바 뱌 비레 롸 미찌마 여쭈 비다쭈씨다가, 아오롸, 쭤더 무네이로 어라 무호또 사 오꼬.

22. 쭤더 좌보나 찌라 가뉴 고씨 가 좌뭐마, 부씨 쭤더 좌쭈따 어미오빠 야이 나 구이라 뱌 비무시미서.

23. 너무오빠 와이 이요노 쭈따아 쭤머러라 어시나 려롸나 와이 여수 기리시도 나 구떠 좌시마나 꼬과 기리시도 아나쭈부라아.

24. 어무뉴 오롸 우쭈찌러 어미오빠 야 오꼬, 어레 아레 롸 부우마 나 오꼬, 나 오꼬 아나바 롸 부우마 나이. 쭤더 좌머녀러라 과 쭈레 롸 부우마 나 오꼬 구러꺼라 어무찌마 무부야-부야 오롸 아쭤러사아.

he knows everything.

21. Dear friends, if our hearts do not condemn us, we have confidence before God

22. and receive from him anything we ask, because we obey his commands and do what pleases him.

23. And this is his command: to believe in the name of his Son, Jesus Christ, and to love one another as he commanded us.

24. Those who obey his commands live in him, and he in them. And this is how we know that he lives in us: We know it by the Spirit he gave us.

1 Yoana Chikono 4

1. Bera banyi basiirwa, mutendaa mwemerera chira mundju ola wateta mbu Nyeete eMuchima Mubuya-buya. Si mundaa mwalola

1 요아나 찌고노 4

1. 버라 바네 바시이롸, 무더따아 뭐머러라 찌라 무뉴 오롸 와더다 뿌 녀어더 어무찌마 무부야-부야. 시 무따아 뫄로롸 구부야-부야,

1 John Chapter 4[NIV]

1. Dear friends, do not believe every spirit, but test the spirits to see whether they are from God, because many false prophets have

kubuya-buya, mumenye akaba emuchima ola oyu mundju ete anatengire era mwa Ongo. Bushi barebi banene ba bisha bahandabanyire mwa butala.

2. Cha chingathuma mwamenyerera eMuchima wa Ongo chi chechine chira mundju ola wemerere kwa Yesu Kirisito ahubaa mundju kanangana, oyola iwete eMuchima wa Ongo.

3. Si chira mundju woshi ola utemerere Yesu, elyi atete Muchima wa Ongo, si ete emuchima weMurenda wa Kirisito. Mwomvaa mira kwa eMurenda wa Kirisito akabaha. Rero era alyi muno butala.

4. E bana banyi Mulyi bandju ba Ongo, mwaimire nebarebi bebisha. Bushi ola ulyi mwa ndanda senyu iwete ebuashi kurenza ola uthula mwa bandju bomwa butala.

5. Abu barebi bebisha, balyi bandju bebutala. Nemyasi era bende bateta inathula yebutala. Nebandju bomwa butala bu bende bomvirisabo.

6. Si thubano, thuchiberere bandju ba Ongo. Emundju ola wishi Ongo, iwende womva

무머녀 아가바 어무찌마 오롸 오유 무뚜 어더 아나더삐러 어라 와 오꼬. 부씨 바러비 바너녀 바 비싸 바하따바네러 와 부다롸.

2. 짜 찌빠쭈마 뫄머녀러라 어무찌마 와 오꼬 찌 쩌찌너 찌라 무뚜 오롸 워머러러 과 여수 기리시도 아후바아 무뚜 가나빠나, 오요롸 이워더 어무찌마 와 오꼬.

3. 시 찌라 무뚜 올씨 오롸 우더머러러 여수, 어레 아더더 무찌마 와 오꼬, 시 어더 어무찌마 워무러따 와 기리시도. 뫼빠아 미라 과 어무러따 와 기리시도 아가바하. 러로 어라 아레 무노 부다롸.

4. 어 바나 바니 무레 바뚜 바 오꼬, 뫄이미러 너바러비 버비싸. 부씨 오롸 우레 뫄 따따 서뉴 이워더 어부아씨 구런싸 오롸 우쭈롸 뫄 바뚜 보뫄 부다롸.

5. 아부 바러비 버비싸, 바레 바뚜 버부다롸. 너먀시 어라 버떠 바더다 이나쭈롸 여부다롸. 너바뚜 보뫄 부다롸 부 버떠 보뻬리사보.

6. 시 쭈바노, 쭈찌버러러 바뚜 바 오꼬. 어무뚜 오롸 위씨 오꼬, 이워떠 옴빠 뱌

gone out into the world.

2. This is how you can recognize the Spirit of God: Every spirit that acknowledges that Jesus Christ has come in the flesh is from God,

3. but every spirit that does not acknowledge Jesus is not from God. This is the spirit of the antichrist, which you have heard is coming and even now is already in the world.

4. You, dear children, are from God and have overcome them, because the one who is in you is greater than the one who is in the world.

5. They are from the world and therefore speak from the viewpoint of the world, and the world listens to them.

6. We are from God, and whoever knows God listens to us; but whoever is not

bya thwateta. Si ola utamundju wa Ongo, yeke atomva bya thwateta. Rero bacha kuthwende thwamenyerera eMuchima wekanangana, newebisha.

7. Bera banyi basiirwa, thundaa thwasimana. Bushi enzii yende yatenga era mwa Ongo. Chira mundju ola uthula usimire ebanji, imwana wa Ongo, kanji iuneshi Ongo.

8. Si emundju ola utathula usimire ebanji, atafuraa kumenya Ongo, bushi Ongo inzii.

9. Bacha ku Ongo alosaa enzii yai athumaa eMwana wai wechihwa muno butala, chasiya kurengera oyu Mwana thubone ekalamo kekanangana.

10. Nei nzii iyene Atathubano thuthwasimaa Ongo, si yeine iwathusimaa. Era kuthuma eMwana wai, achane nga mithulo kwa kubabalyira ebibi byethu.

11. Rero bera banyi basiirwa, oku Ongo athusimaa bacha, nethu thwemire kunde thwasimana.

12. Kutalyi mundju ola ufuraa kulola ku Ongo. Si akaba thungende thwasimana, Ongo

---

좌더다. 시 오라 우다무뉴 와 오꼬, 여거 아도빠 뱌 좌더다. 러로 바짜 구쭤머 좌머녀러라 어무찌마 워가나빠나, 너워비싸.

7. 버라 바네 바시이롸, 쭈따아 좌시마나. 부씨 어씨이 여너 야더빠 어라 롸 오꼬. 찌라 무뉴 오라 우쭈롸 우시미러 어바찌, 이마나 와 오꼬, 가찌 이우너씨 오꼬.

8. 시 어무뉴 오라 우다쭈롸 우시미러 어바찌, 아다푸라아 구머냐 오꼬, 부씨 오꼬 이씨이.

9. 바짜 구 오꼬 아르사아 어씨이 야이 아쭈마아 어뫄나 와이 워찌화 무노 부다롸, 짜시야 구러뭐라 오유 뫄나 쭈보너 어가뫄모 거가나빠나.

10. 너이 씨이 이여너 아다쭈바노 쭈좌시마아 오꼬, 시 여이너 이와쭈시마아. 어라 구쭈마 어뫄나 와이, 아짜너 빠 미쭈른 과 구바바뼤라 어비비 벼쭈.

11. 러로 버라 바네 바시이롸, 오구 오꼬 아쭈시마아 바짜, 너쭈 쭤미러 구떠 좌시마나.

12. 구다뤠 무뉴 오롸 우푸라아 구른롸 구 오꼬. 시 아가바 쭈뭐떠 좌시마나,

---

from God does not listen to us. This is how we recognize the Spirit of truth and the spirit of falsehood.

7. Dear friends, let us love one another, for love comes from God. Everyone who loves has been born of God and knows God.

8. Whoever does not love does not know God, because God is love.

9. This is how God showed his love among us: He sent his one and only Son into the world that we might live through him.

10. This is love: not that we loved God, but that he loved us and sent his Son as an atoning sacrifice for our sins.

11. Dear friends, since God so loved us, we also ought to love one another.

12. No one has ever seen God; but if we love one another, God lives in us and

anaba mwa buuma nethu, nenzii yai ku thubano yanende yalorekanako mwa kachi-kachi kethu ngokwa binemire.

오꼬 아나바 똬 부우마 너쭈, 너씨이 야이 구 쭈바노 야너떠 야로러가나고 똬 가찌-가찌 거쭈 꼬과 비너미러.

his love is made complete in us.

13. Cha chende chathuma thwamenyerera kwa thulyi mwa buuma na Ongo, nai alyi mwa buuma nethu chi chechine Athweresise eMuchima wai.

13. 짜 쩌떠 짜쭈마 쫘머녀러라 과 쭈레 똬 부우마 나 오꼬, 나이 아레 똬 부우마 너쭈 찌 쩌찌너 아쮜러러시서 어무찌마 와이.

13. We know that we live in him and he in us, because he has given us of his Spirit.

14. Thubeine, thwanachiloreraa, kanji thwenjire thwanateta kwa Tata athumaa eMwana wai, chasiya abe Mununusiwebutala.

14. 쭈버이너, 쫘나찌로러라아, 가찌 쮜찌러 쫘나더다 과 다다 아쭈마아 어똬나 와이, 짜시야 아버 무누누시워부다똬.

14. And we have seen and testify that the Father has sent his Son to be the Savior of the world.

15. Emundju ola wemerere kwa Yesu alyi Mwana wa Ongo, Ongo ende aba mwa buuma nai, nai anaba mwa buuma na Ongo.

15. 어무뚜 오똬 워머러러 과 여수 아레 똬나 와 오꼬, 오꼬 어떠 아바 똬 부우마 나이, 나이 아나바 똬 부우마 나 오꼬.

15. If anyone acknowledges that Jesus is the Son of God, God lives in him and he in God.

16. Thubano thwishi, kanji thunemerere kwa Ongo athula athusimire. Ongo inzii. Emundju ola wete nzii iwende waba mwa buuma na Ongo, na Ongo anaba mwa buuma nai.

16. 쭈바노 쮜씨, 가찌 쭈너머러러 과 오꼬 아쭈똬 아쭈시미러. 오꼬 이씨이. 어무뚜 오똬 워더 씨이 이워떠 와바 똬 부우마 나 오꼬, 나 오꼬 아나바 똬 부우마 나이.

16. And so we know and rely on the love God has for us. God is love. Whoever lives in love lives in God, and God in him.

17. Akaba enzii ingalorekanako loshi mwa ndanda sethu, thukaata emunyiiro mango Ongo akachinjibusa ebandju, bushi ekalamo kethu kanalyi ngekalamo ka Yesu Kirisito

17. 아가바 어씨이 이까로러가나고 로씨 똬 따따 서쭈, 쭈가아다 어무네이로 마꼬 오꼬 아가찌찌부사 어바뚜, 부씨 어가똬모 거쭈 가나레 꺼가똬모 가 여수 기리시도 아바아 어더 무노

17. In this way, love is made complete among us so that we will have confidence on the day of judgment, because in this world we are like him.

abaa ete muno butala.

18. Mwa nzii mutathula buba. Enzii yekanangana, yende yakolokanya ebuba. Emufi webuba alyi mundju ola utalumirire mwa nzii, bushi ende afa ebuba emango eshi kwa alyi wa kuchinjibusibwa.

19. Thubano thwende thwasimana, bushi Ongo iwabaa mubere kuthusima.

20. Akaba mundju angateta mbu athula asimire Ongo, noku ahombire munyakabo, elyi alyi mufusi wa bisha. Bushi emundju ola utasimire munyakabo, ola aseneko, atangaala kusima Ongo, ola ataseneko.

21. Rero emuomba ola Kirisito athweresise iyono: emundju ola usimire Ongo, emire kunde asima na munyakabo.

부다쫘.

18. 먀 씨이 무다쭈쫘 부바. 어씨이 여가나냐나, 여떠 야고롣가냐 어부바. 어무피 워부바 아쮀 무뚜 오롸 우다뤀미리러 먀 씨이, 부씨 어떠 아파 어부바 어마꼬 어씨 과 아쀒 와 구찌씨부시봐.

19. 쭈바노 쮀떠 좌시마나, 부씨 오꼬 이와바아 무버러 구쭈시마.

20. 아가바 무뚜 아꺠더다 뿌 아쭈롸 아시미러 오꼬, 노구 아호쀒러 무냐가보, 어쀒 아쀒 무푸시 와 비싸. 부씨 어무뚜 오롸 우다시미러 무냐가보, 오롸 아서너고, 아다꺠아꺠 구시마 오꼬, 오롸 아다서너고.

21. 러로 어무오빠 오롸 기리시도 아쮀러시서 이요노: 어무뚜 오롸 우시미러 오꼬, 어미러 구떠 아시마 나 무냐가보.

18. There is no fear in love. But perfect love drives out fear, because fear has to do with punishment. The one who fears is not made perfect in love.

19. We love because he first loved us.

20. If anyone says, "I love God," yet hates his brother, he is a liar. For anyone who does not love his brother, whom he has seen, cannot love God, whom he has not seen.

21. And he has given us this command: Whoever loves God must also love his brother.

1 Yoana Chikono 5

1. Chira mundju woshi ola wemerere kwa Yesu iKirisito, oyu mundju alyi mwana wa Ongo. Na chira mundju ola usimire eshe webana eri asimire nebana bai.

1 요아나 찌고노 5

1. 찌라 무뚜 올씨 오롸 워머러러 과 여수 이기리시도, 오유 무뚜 아쀒 먀나 와 오꼬. 나 찌라 무뚜 오롸 우시미러 어써 워바나 어리 아시미러 너바나 바이.

1 John Chapter 5[NIV]

1. Everyone who believes that Jesus is the Christ is born of God, and everyone who loves the father loves his child as well.

2. Thwende thwamenyerera kwa thuthula thusimire ebana ba Ongo mwa kunde thwasima Ongo yeine, nomwa kunde thwathunda emiomba yai.

3. Bushi ekusima Ongo, kuthula kuira kwa miomba yai itechire. Nei miomba yai, itathula isitoire.

4. Bushi chira mundju ola ulyi mwana wa Ongo, ende aima emyasi yebutala. Nei myasi, thwende thwaimai kurengera ebwemeresi bwethu.

5. Nde kasi iwende waima emyasi yebutala? Analyi emundju ola uthula wemerere kwa Yesu alyi Mwana wa Ongo.

6. Yesu Kirisito abahaa kwa njira yeemeshi neyemikira. Atabahaa kwa njira yemeshi meine oshao, si abahaa nokwa njira yemikira. Nemyasi era eMuchima Mubuya-buya ende ateta era luulu sebi, inalyi ya kanangana, bushi oyu Muchima anathula wa kanangana.

7. Kulyi babei bahathu ba balosa kwa Yesu iMwana wa Ongo

8. eMuchima Mubuya-buya,

---

2. 쮀떠 쫘머녀러라 과 쭈쭈롸 쭈시미러 어바나 바 오꼬 롸 구떠 쫘시마 오꼬 여이너, 노롸 구떠 쫘쭈따 어미오빠 야이.

3. 부씨 어구시마 오꼬, 구쭈롸 구이라 과 미오빠 야이 이더찌러. 너이 미오빠 야이, 이다쭈롸 이시도이러.

4. 부씨 찌라 무뚜 오라 우레 마나 와 오꼬, 어떠 아이마 어먀시 여부다롸. 너이 먀시, 쮀떠 쫘이마이 구러꺼라 어붸머러시 붸쭈.

5. 떠 가시 이워떠 와이마 어먀시 여부다롸? 아나레 어무뚜 오라 우쭈롸 워머러러 과 여수 아레 마나 와 오꼬.

6. 여수 기리시도 아바하아 과 찌라 여어머씨 너여미기라. 아다바하아 과 찌라 여머씨 머이너 오싸오, 시 아바하아 노고과 찌라 여미기라. 너먀시 어라 어무찌마 무부야-부야 어떠 아더다 어라 루우루 서비, 이나레 야 가나꺼나, 부씨 오유 무찌마 아나쭈롸 와 가나꺼나.

7. 구레 바버이 바하쭈 바 바로사 과 여수 이마나 와 오꼬

8. 어무찌마 무부야-부야,

---

2. This is how we know that we love the children of God: by loving God and carrying out his commands.

3. This is love for God: to obey his commands. And his commands are not burdensome,

4. for everyone born of God overcomes the world. This is the victory that has overcome the world, even our faith.

5. Who is it that overcomes the world? Only he who believes that Jesus is the Son of God.

6. This is the one who came by water and blood--Jesus Christ. He did not come by water only, but by water and blood. And it is the Spirit who testifies, because the Spirit is the truth.

7. For there are three that testify:

8. the Spirit, the water and

nemeshi, nemikira. Nabu babei kwa banalyi bahathu, ebubei bwabo bunathula buuma.

9. Mango mundju ende ana ebubei era luulu sa mwasi murebe, thwende thwemererabo. Rero, ebubei bwa Ongo burenzise ebwebandju. Anola Ongo yeine iwanaabo era luulu seMwana wai.

10. Emundju ola wemerere eMwana wa Ongo, athusa obu bubei mwa ndanda sai. Si emundju ola utemerere Ongo, ende aba ailyire Ongo kuba mufusi wa bisha. Bushi atemerere ebubei bwa Ongo anaa era luulu seMwana wai.

11. Nobu bubei, bu bobuno Ongo athweresise ekalamo kesuku nemango, naku kalamo, thwende thwakabona kurengera eMwana wai.

12. Emundju ola ulyi mwa buuma neMwana wa Ongo, iuthusa aku kalamo. Si ola utalyi mwa buuma neMwana wa Ongo, yeke atete ekalamo.

Ekalamo kesuku nemango

너머씨, 너미기라. 나부 바버이 과 바나레 바하쭈, 어부버이 봐보 부나쭈꽈 부우마.

9. 마꼬 무뚜 어너 아나 어부버이 어라 루우루루 사 꽈시 무러버, 쮀머 쮀머러라보. 러로, 어부버이 봐 오꼬 부러씨서 어붸바꾸. 아노꽈 오꼬 여이너 이와나아보 어라 루우루루 서꽈나 와이.

10. 어무뚜 오꽈 워머러러 어꽈나 와 오꼬, 아쭈사 오부 부버이 꽈 따따 사이. 시 어무뚜 오꽈 우더머러러 오꼬, 어떠 아바 아이쩨러 오꼬 구바 무푸시 와 비싸. 부씨 아더머러러 어부버이 봐 오꼬 아나아 어라 루우루루 서꽈나 와이.

11. 노부 부버이, 부 보부노 오꼬 아쮀러시서 어가꽈모 거수구 너마꼬, 나구 가꽈모, 쮀떠 쫘가보나 구러꺼라 어꽈나 와이.

12. 어무뚜 오꽈 우레 꽈 부우마 너꽈나 와 오꼬, 이우쭈사 아구 가꽈모. 시 오꽈 우다쩨 꽈 부우마 너꽈나 와 오꼬, 여거 아더더 어가꽈모.

어가꽈모 거수구 너마꼬

the blood; and the three are in agreement.

9. We accept man's testimony, but God's testimony is greater because it is the testimony of God, which he has given about his Son.

10. Anyone who believes in the Son of God has this testimony in his heart. Anyone who does not believe God has made him out to be a liar, because he has not believed the testimony God has given about his Son.

11. And this is the testimony: God has given us eternal life, and this life is in his Son.

12. He who has the Son has life; he who does not have the Son of God does not have life.

13. Nabanjikirire ene myasi, mu muthula mwemerere esina lye Mwana wa Ongo, chasiya mumenyerere kwa mwete ekalamo kesuku nemango.

14. Emunyiiro ola thwete era muhondo sa Ongo iyono: thwishi kwa choshi cha thwamwema kukulyikana nekuhonda kwai, ende anathumva.

15. Rero bushi thwishi kwa ende anathumva mango thwamwema, thuneshi kanangana kwa thwende thwabona choshi cha thwamweemire.

16. Akaba mundju angalola kwa munyakabo aira chibi cha chitangamuisa kwa lufu, emire kumwemera era mwa Ongo. Na Ongo angamweresa ekalamo. Ei myasi, inerekere ebandju ba bailyire emabi ma matangabaisa kwa lufu. Kuthula chibi cha chende chaisa emundju kwa lufu. Rero ndatechire mbu echi chibi chi emire kumwemerako.

17. Choshi cha chitathungenene era muhondo sa Ongo, chilyi chibi. Si chiro bacha, kuthula emabi ma matangaisa

13. 나바찌기리러 어너 먀시, 무 무쭈콰 뭐머러러 어시나 펴 먀나 와 오꼬, 짜시야 무머녀러러 과 뭐더 어가꽈모 거수구 너마꼬.

14. 어무네이로 오콰 쮀더 어라 무호또 사 오꼬 이요노: 쮀씨 과 쪼씨 짜 좌뭐마 구구레가나 너구호따 과이, 어떠 아나쭈빠.

15. 러로 부씨 쮀씨 과 어너 아나쭈빠 마꼬 좌뭐마, 쭈너씨 가나꽈나 과 쮀떠 좌보나 쪼씨 짜 좌뭐어미러.

16. 아가바 무뚜 아꽈른콰 과 무냐가보 아이라 찌비 짜 찌다꽈무이사 과 루푸, 어미러 구뭐머라 어라 콰 오꼬. 나 오꼬 아꽈머러사 어가꽈모. 어이 먀시, 이너러거러 어바뚜 바 바이뤠러 어마비 마 마다꽈바이사 과 루푸. 구쭈콰 찌비 짜 쩌떠 짜이사 어무뚜 과 루푸. 러로 따더찌러 뿌 어찌 찌비 찌 어미러 구뭐머라고.

17. 쪼씨 짜 찌다쭈어너너 어라 무호또 사 오꼬, 찌레 찌비. 시 찌로 바짜, 구쭈콰 어마비 마 마다꽈이사 어무뚜 과 루푸.

13. I write these things to you who believe in the name of the Son of God so that you may know that you have eternal life.

14. This is the confidence we have in approaching God: that if we ask anything according to his will, he hears us.

15. And if we know that he hears us--whatever we ask-- we know that we have what we asked of him.

16. If anyone sees his brother commit a sin that does not lead to death, he should pray and God will give him life. I refer to those whose sin does not lead to death. There is a sin that leads to death. I am not saying that he should pray about that.

17. All wrongdoing is sin, and there is sin that does not lead to death.

emundju kwa lufu.

18. Thwishi kwa chira mundju woshi ola ulyi mwana wa Ongo atachiendekera kuira mabi, bushi eMwana wa Ongo ende aba amulanga. Nola Mukosi wemabi atangachimuira kandju.

18. 쮜씨 과 찌라 무뚜 옴씨 오롸 우레 뫄나 와 오꼬 아다쩌떠거라 구이라 마비, 부씨 어뫄나 와 오꼬 어떠 아바 아무롸까. 노롸 무고시 워마비 아다까찌무이라 가뚜.

18. We know that anyone born of God does not continue to sin; the one who was born of God keeps him safe, and the evil one cannot harm him.

19. Thubano thwishi kwa thulyi bana ba Ongo. Si ebutala boshi bulyi mwa mino soyu Mukosi wemabi.

19. 쭈바노 쮜씨 과 쭈레 바나 바 오꼬. 시 어부다롸 보씨 부레 뫄 미노 소유 무고시 워마비.

19. We know that we are children of God, and that the whole world is under the control of the evil one.

20. Kanji thuneshi kwa eMwana wa Ongo aikire mira, athweresise nebwenge bwekunde thwamenyerera Ongo wekanangana. Rero, thwera thulyi mwa buuma nai kurengera eMwana wai Yesu Kirisito. Yesu Kirisito iOngo wekanangana, kanji ikalamo kesuku nemango.

20. 가찌 쭈너씨 과 어뫄나 와 오꼬 아이기러 미라, 아쮜러시서 너붜꺼 붜구떠 쫘머녀러라 오꼬 워가나뫄나. 러로, 쮜라 쭈레 뫄 부우마 나이 구러꺼라 어뫄나 와이 여수 기리시도. 여수 기리시도 이오꼬 워가나뫄나, 가찌 이가롸모 거수구 너마꼬.

20. We know also that the Son of God has come and has given us understanding, so that we may know him who is true. And we are in him who is true--even in his Son Jesus Christ. He is the true God and eternal life.

21. Rero bana banyi, mumenyaa Mutendaa mwakulyikira ebango.

21. 러로 바나 바네, 무머냐아 무더따아 뫄구레기라 어바꼬.

21. Dear children, keep yourselves from idols.

2 Yoana

2 요아나

2 John

YOWANI WA KABIRI

(2 JOHN)

요와니 와 가비리
(2 조후누)

2 Yoana Chikono 1

1. Nyono Mungumwa weluhu lwa Ongo, nyi nakuanjikira mano maruba woyo Mama alauma nebana bao, uwalondolyibwe na Ongo. Abu bana, nyithula nyibasimire kanangana.a Ata nyeine oshao nyi nyithula nyibasimire muboshi, si nebanji bandju boshi ba bathula beshi emyasi yekanangana, nabo banathula babasimire,

2. bushi ei myasi yekanangana ithula mwa michima yethu. Nei myasi ikanaendekera kuba mwa michima yethu esuku nemango.

3. Ongo Tata, neMwana wai Yesu Kirisito bendaa bathweresa engahanyi, na kuthufira bonjo na kutweresa ebolo chasiya tube mwa kanangana nomwa nzii.

4. Namowaa busese mango nomvaa emwasi kwa bana bao bauma bathula bakulyikire emyasi yekanangana, kukulyikana nokwa Tata anathuburaa.

2 요아나 찌고노 1

1. 뇨노 무우와 워루후 롸 오꼬, 네 나구아찌기라 마노 마루바 오요 마마 아롸우마 너바나 바오, 우와로꼬레뷔 나 오꼬. 아부 바나, 네쭈롸 네바시미러 가나꺄나.아 아다 녀이너 오싸오 네 네쭈롸 네바시미러 무보씨, 시 너바찌 바꾸 보씨 바 바쭈롸 버씨 어먀시 여가나꺄나, 나보 바나쭈롸 바바시미러,

2. 부씨 어이 먀시 여가나꺄나 이쭈롸 롸 미찌마 여쭈. 너이 먀시 이가나어떠거라 구바 롸 미찌마 여쭈 어수구 너마꼬.

3. 오꼬 다다, 너롸나 와이 여수 기리시도 버따아 바쭤러사 어꺄하네, 나 구쭈피라 보쯔 나 구뚀러사 어보로 짜시야 두버 롸 가나꺄나 노롸 씨이.

4. 나모와아 부서서 마꼬 노빠아 어롸시 과 바나 바오 바우마 바쭈롸 바구레기러 어먀시 여가나꺄나, 구구레가나 노과 다다 아나쭈부라아.

2 John Chapter 1[NIV]

1. The elder, To the chosen lady and her children, whom I love in the truth--and not I only, but also all who know the truth -

2. because of the truth, which lives in us and will be with us forever:

3. Grace, mercy and peace from God the Father and from Jesus Christ, the Father's Son, will be with us in truth and love.

4. It has given me great joy to find some of your children walking in the truth, just as the Father commanded us.

5. Rero Mama, nakwema busese kwa thndaa thwasimana. Echera atamuomba muyayaya inakwanjikilyire si analyi ola thwabonaa kutengera mango thwemereraa Enawethu.

6. Nenzii kulyi kuthunda bya miomba ya Ongo itechire. Onola imuomba mwomvaa kutengera endangilyiso mundaa mwaba mwa nzii Mutendaa mwahuukasa ebatebanyi

7. Batebanyi banene bahandabanyire mwa butala. Abu batebanyi bende banana kwemerera kwa Yesu Kirisito ahubaa mundju kanangana. Rero abu bandju bu bafusi bebisha kanji bu barenda ba Kirisito.

8. Bushi noku, mundaa mwachilanga-langa, chasiya etamo lyemulyimo wenyu lyitafaa buha, si mubone elwembo lwa lunalumilyire.

9. Chira mundu woshi ola utasimikire mwa mwasi ola Kirisito akangilyisaa, nekuya bure nao, oyola atalyi mwa buuma na Ongo. Si ola usimikire mwoyu mwasi yeke, iulyi mwa buuma na Tata anaba nomwa buuma

5. 러로 마마, 나궈마 부서서 과 찌따아 쫘시마나. 어쩌라 아다무오빠 무야야야 이나과씨기껠러 시 아나쩨 오롸 쫘보나아 구더꺼라 마꼬 쮀머러라아 어나워쭈.

6. 너씨이 구쩨 구쭈따 뱌 미오빠 야 오꼬 이더찌러. 오노롸 이무오빠 모빠아 구더꺼라 어따꺼쩨소 무따아 먀바 먀 씨이 무더따아 먀후우가사 어바더바네

7. 바더바네 바너너 바하따바네러 먀 부다롸. 아부 바더바네 버떠 바나나 궈머러라 과 여수 기리시도 아후바아 무뚜 가나꺼나. 러로 아부 바쭈 부 바푸시 버비싸 가찌 부 바러따 바 기리시도.

8. 부씨 노구, 무따아 먀찌롸꺼-롸꺼, 쨔시야 어다모 려무꼐모 워뉴 쩨다파아 부햐, 시 무보너 어뤄뙈 롸 루나루미쩨러.

9. 찌라 무뚜 오씨 오롸 우다시미기러 먀 먀시 오롸 기리시도 아가꺼쩨사아, 너구야 부러 나오, 오요롸 아다쩨 먀 부우마 나 오꼬. 시 오롸 우시미기러 모유 먀시 여거, 이우쩨 먀 부우마 나 다다 아나바 노먀 부우마

5. And now, dear lady, I am not writing you a new command but one we have had from the beginning. I ask that we love one another.

6. And this is love: that we walk in obedience to his commands. As you have heard from the beginning, his command is that you walk in love.

7. Many deceivers, who do not acknowledge Jesus Christ as coming in the flesh, have gone out into the world. Any such person is the deceiver and the antichrist.

8. Watch out that you do not lose what you have worked for, but that you may be rewarded fully.

9. Anyone who runs ahead and does not continue in the teaching of Christ does not have God; whoever continues in the teaching has both the Father and the Son.

neMwana.

10. Akaba mundu murebe angaika eyi mwenyu, akangilyiisa unji-unji mwasi ola utakulyikene nemwasi ola Kirisito akangilyisaa, mutamuhuukasaa mwa nyumba senyu. Nekumukesa, mutanamukesaa.

11. Bushi ola wakesise emundju ola ulyingoyu, elyi abere luuma-luuma nai mwa myanya yai ibi.

12. Nyichete myasi inene yakubabura, si ndahonda kubanjikirai mwa kukoresa ekaratasi nebwino. Nyete emunyiiro kwa nyingaika eyi mwenyu thuhambale bunu kwa bunji chasiya tumowe busese.

13. Ebana ba mama muuma ola nai alondolyibwe na Ongo, bakukesise.

너뫄나.

10. 아가바 무뚜 무러버 아빠이가 어에 뮈뉴, 아가삐뗴이사 우찌-우찌 뫄시 오꽈 우다구뗴거너 너뫄시 오꽈 기리시도 아가삐뗴사아, 무다무후우가사아 뫄 뉴빠 서뉴. 너구무거사, 무다나무거사아.

11. 부씨 오꽈 와거시서 어무뚜 오꽈 우뗴꼬유, 어뗴 아버러 루우뫄-루우뫄 나이 뫄 먀냐 야이 이비.

12. 네쩌더 먀시 이너너 야구바부라, 시 따호따 구바찌기라이 뫄 구고러사 어가라다시 너뷔노. 녀더 어무네이로 과 네빠이가 어에 뮈뉴 쭈하빠뗘 부누 과 부찌 짜시야 두모워 부서서.

13. 어바나 바 마마 무우마 오꽈 나이 아뢰또뗴뷔 나 오꼬, 바구거시서.

10. If anyone comes to you and does not bring this teaching, do not take him into your house or welcome him.

11. Anyone who welcomes him shares in his wicked work.

12. I have much to write to you, but I do not want to use paper and ink. Instead, I hope to visit you and talk with you face to face, so that our joy may be complete.

13. The children of your chosen sister send their greetings.

3 Yoana

3 요아나

3 John

YOWANI WA KAHATCHU

(3 JOHN)

요와니 와 가하쭈
(3 조후누)

3 Yoana Chikono 1

1. Nyono mungumwa weluhu lwa Ongo nyina kuanjikira munyakethu Kayo, musiirwa wanyi kanangana.

2. Mwira wanyi musiirwa, nahonda emyasi yoshi inde yanakubera kubuya. Emaala mao mendaa manahaaluka ngokwa emuchima wao nao, anathula ahaalukire.

3. Namowaa busese mango banyakethu bauma baikaa kunyibalyira emwasi, kwa uthula mundju mubuya mwa myasi yekanangana, nokwa uthula ukulyikire ekanangana.

4. Kutalyi mwasi ola wenjire wanyisimisa, nga ekuumva mbu ebana banyi bakulyikire emyasi yekanangana.

5. Mwira wanyi musiirwa, uthula mundju mubuya bushi nemulyimo wao wekuunde waasa banyakethu bemeresi, nebanji banyakethu bemeresi bomwa binji bisiki.

6. Abu banyakethu bachiteteraa beine era luulu senzii yao, era muhondo sebemeresi bomwa luhu lwethu. Rero nakweema busese ubaasaa ngokwa binemire era muhondo sa

3 요아나 찌고노 1

1. 뇨노 무우와 워루후 롸 오끄 네나 구아찌기라 무냐거쭈 가요, 무시이롸 와니 까나까나.

2. 뮈라 와네 무시이롸, 나호따 어먀시 요씨 이떠 야나구버라 구부야. 어마아꽈 마오 머따아 마나하아루가 끄과 어무찌마 와오 나오, 아나쭈롸 아하아루기러.

3. 나모와아 부서서 마끄 바냐거쭈 바우마 바이가아 구네바뻬라 어먀시, 과 우쭈롸 무뚜 무부야 뫄 먀시 여가나와나, 노과 우쭈롸 우구레기러 어가나와나.

4. 구다뻬 먀시 오롸 워찌러 와네시미사, 꽈 어구우빠 뿌 어바나 바네 바구뻬기러 어먀시 여가나와나.

5. 뮈라 와네 무시이롸, 우쭈롸 무뚜 무부야 부씨 너무뻬모 와오 워구우떠 와아사 바냐거쭈 버머러시, 너바씨 바냐거쭈 버머러시 보뫄 비찌 비시기.

6. 아부 바냐거쭈 바찌더더라아 버이너 어라 루우루 서씨이 야오, 어라 무호또 서버머러시 보뫄 뤄후 뤄쭈. 러로 나궈어마 부서서 우바아사아 끄과 비너미러 어라 무호또 사 오끄,

3 John Chapter 1[NIV]

1. The elder, To my dear friend Gaius, whom I love in the truth.

2. Dear friend, I pray that you may enjoy good health and that all may go well with you, even as your soul is getting along well.

3. It gave me great joy to have some brothers come and tell about your faithfulness to the truth and how you continue to walk in the truth.

4. I have no greater joy than to hear that my children are walking in the truth.

5. Dear friend, you are faithful in what you are doing for the brothers, even though they are strangers to you.

6. They have told the church about your love. You will do well to send them on their way in a manner worthy of God.

Ongo, baendekere nelubalamo lwabo.

7. Batangirisaa olu lubalamo lwabo, bushi nekuya kukola emulyimo wa Kirisito, busira kwemerera kandju kutenga mwa mino sebandju ba bateshi Ongo.

8. Rero ebandju ba balyi ngabo, thwemire kunde twaasabo, chasiya thube luuma-luuma nabo mwa mulyimo wekuhubanganya emwasi wekanangana.

9. Naanjikirire ebemeresi bomwa luhu lwenyu myasi yeeke. Si Tiyotirefe, iuthula usimire kweemangira ebanji, ateendjire alaa kwebya nateta.

10. Bushi noku, mango nyingaika eyera, nyingbalosa changanama emabi mai moshi maenjire akola. Enjire athusinga myasi ibi. Atenebi byeine oshao, si na mango banyakethu benjire babalamira eyera, enjire anana kubahuukasa. Na ba bahonda kuhuukasabo, enjire angikabo na kukolokanyabo mwa luhu lwa Ongo.

11. Mwira wanyi musiirwa Utendaa weeya emabi, si undaa weeya emabuya.

바어떠거러 너루바짜모 꽈보.

7. 바다끼리사아 오루 루바짜모 꽈보, 부씨 너구야 구고꽈 어무레모 와 기리시도, 부시라 궈머러라 가뉴 구더까 와 미노 서바뉴 바 바더씨 오꼬.

8. 러로 어바뉴 바 바레 까보, 쭤미러 구떠 돠아사보, 짜시야 쭈버 루우마-루우마 나보 와 무레모 워구후바까냐 어뫄시 워가나까나.

9. 나아찌기리러 어버머러시 보와 루후 뤠뉴 먀시 여거. 시 디요디러퍼, 이우쭈꽈 우시미러 궈어마끼라 어바찌, 아더어찌러 아꽈아 궈뱌 나더다.

10. 부씨 노구, 마꼬 네까이가 어여라, 네뉘바로사 짜까나마 어마비 마이 모씨 마어찌러 아고꽈. 어찌러 아쭈시까 먀시 이비. 아더너비 벼이너 오싸오, 시 나 마꼬 바냐거쭈 버찌러 바바꽈미라 어여라, 어찌러 아나나 구바후우가사. 나 바 바호따 구후우가사보, 어찌러 아끼가보 나 구고로가냐보 와 루후 꽈 오꼬.

11. 뮈라 와네 무시이롸 우더따아 워어야 어마비, 시 우따아 워어야 어마부야.

---

7. It was for the sake of the Name that they went out, receiving no help from the pagans.

8. We ought therefore to show hospitality to such men so that we may work together for the truth.

9. I wrote to the church, but Diotrephes, who loves to be first, will have nothing to do with us.

10. So if I come, I will call attention to what he is doing, gossiping maliciously about us. Not satisfied with that, he refuses to welcome the brothers. He also stops those who want to do so and puts them out of the church.

11. Dear friend, do not imitate what is evil but what is good. Anyone who does

Emundju ola wende wakola emabuya, alyi mwana wa Ongo. Si ola wende wakola emabi ateshi Ongo.

12. Temetiriyo yeke, ebandju boshi benjire banateta kubuya era luulu sai. Nemyanya yai inalosise kwa bya benjire bateta era luulu sai, binalyi bya kanangana. Anabe nethu, thwenjire thwanateta kubuya era luulu sai, nebi thwenjire thwateta, uneeshi kwa binalyi bya kanangana.

13. Nyichete myasi inene ya kukubura. Si ndahonda kukuanjikirai mwa kukoresa ekalamu kebwino.

14. Nyicheete emunyiiro kwa ndemange kuhuba kukulolako. Na mango nyingakulolako, thungahambala bunu kwa bunji.

15. Uba neboolo Bera bao ba nyilyi nabo enera bakulamusise. Nao uthulamusisaa bera bethu ba balyi eyera, chira mundju kwesina lyai.

어무뚜 오꽈 워떠 와고꽈 어마부야, 아레 마나 와 오꼬. 시 오꽈 워떠 와고꽈 어마비 아더씨 오꼬.

12. 더머디리요 여거, 어바뚜 보씨 버찌러 바나더다 구부야 어라 루우루 사이. 너먀냐 야이 이나로씨서 과 뱌 버찌러 바더다 어라 루우루 사이, 비나레 뱌 가나꽈나. 아나버 너쭈, 쮀찌러 쫘나더다 구부야 어라 루우루 사이, 너비 쮀찌러 쫘더다, 우너어씨 과 비나레 뱌 가나꽈나.

13. 네쩌더 먀시 이너너 야 구구부라. 시 따호따 구구안찌기라이 뫄 구고러사 어가꽈무 거뷔노.

14. 네쩌어더 어무네이로 과 떠마떠 구후바 구구론꽈고. 나 마꼬 네까구론꽈고, 쭈까하빠꽈 부누 과 부찌.

15. 우바 너보오론 버라 바오 바 네레 나보 어너라 바구꽈무시서. 나오 우쭈꽈무시사아 버라 버쭈 바 바레 어여라, 찌라 무뚜 궈시나 꺄이.

what is good is from God. Anyone who does what is evil has not seen God.

12. Demetrius is well spoken of by everyone--and even by the truth itself. We also speak well of him, and you know that our testimony is true.

13. I have much to write you, but I do not want to do so with pen and ink.

14. I hope to see you soon, and we will talk face to face.

15. Peace to you. The friends here send their greetings. Greet the friends there by name.

Yuda
유다
Jude

YUTA

(JUDE)

유다

(주더)

Yuda Chikono 1

1. Nyono Yuta, nyilyi muanda wa Yesu Kirisito, kanji nyilyi munyakabo Yakobo. Nabanjikira mwabo mu Ongo Tata alondwere mira, kanji athula abasimire, na Yesu Kirisito ende abalanga.

2. Ongo endaa abafira bonjo, na kuberesa eboolo nenzii. Endaa aberesa ebi byoshi busese.

Ebuchinjibusi bwebakangirisi bebisha

3. Banyakethu basiirwa, mango nabaa naira emisi yekubaanjikira era luulu semyasi yebununusi bwa thuthula thuhangire thuboshi, nera kulola kwa byeemire nyibaanjikire kwa kubasesa emichima chasiya mulange ebwemeresi bwenyu. Obu bwemeresi, Ongo eresaabo ebandju bai loshi.

4. Nabaanjikirire bacha, bushi kulyi bandju babi, ba bachifurerekire mwa kachi-kachi kenyu. Abu bandju benjire baorombya emyasi era ihambere era luulu sebonjo bwa Ongo, chasiya babone enjira yekunde baira elusingi. Mwa kuira bacha,

유다 찌고노 1

1. 노노 유다, 네레 무아따 와 여수 기리시도, 가찌 네레 무냐가보 야고보. 나바찌기라 롸보 무 오꼬 다다 아로뚜워러 미라, 가찌 아쭈롸 아바시미러, 나 여수 기리시도 어떠 아바롸까.

2. 오꼬 어따아 아바피라 보노, 나 구버러사 어보오로 너씨이. 어따아 아버러사 어비 뵤씨 부서서.

어부찌씨뷥습 붜바가끼룻습 버비싸

3. 바냐거쭈 바시이롸, 마꼬 나바아 나이라 어미시 여구바아찌기라 어라 루우루 서먀시 여부누누시 봐 쭈쭈롸 쭈하끼러 쭈보씨, 너라 구로롸 과 벼어미러 네바아찌기러 과 구바서사 어미찌마 짜시야 무롸꺼 어붜머러시 붜뉴. 오부 붜머러시, 오꼬 어러사아보 어바뚜 바이 로씨.

4. 나바아찌기리러 바짜, 부씨 구레 바뚜 바비, 바 바찌푸러러기러 롸 가찌-가찌 거뉴. 아부 바뚜 버찌러 바오로뺘 어먀시 어라 이하뻐러 어라 루우루 서보꼬 봐 오꼬, 짜시야 바보너 어찌라 여구떠 바이라 어루시끼. 롸 구이라 바짜,

Jude Chapter 1[NIV]

1. Jude, a servant of Jesus Christ and a brother of James, To those who have been called, who are loved by God the Father and kept by Jesus Christ:

2. Mercy, peace and love be yours in abundance.

3. Dear friends, although I was very eager to write to you about the salvation we share, I felt I had to write and urge you to contend for the faith that was once for all entrusted to the saints.

4. For certain men whose condemnation was written about long ago have secretly slipped in among you. They are godless men, who change the grace of our God into a license for immorality and deny Jesus Christ our only Sovereign and Lord.

benjire banana Yesu Kirisito, iuthula Mukulu-kulu wethu yeine kanji Enawethu. Kutengera mira, eMaanjiko Mabuya-buya mabaa matechire era luulu sebuchinjibusi bwa abu bandju bakabona.

5. Chiro angaba mbu mwera mwishi kubuya-buya ene myasi yoshi, nahonda nyibakengese kute kwa Enawethu anunulaa eBaisiraeli loshi, kutenga mwa chio che Misiri. Si babananaa kumwemerera, era kubasikya.

6. Anabe noomwa bamalaika, bauma mubo bananaa kulanga ethunda lya Ongo eresaabo, bera kutenga mwa bisiki byabo. Bushi noku, Ongo era kubamina mwa mareure nekuumabo mwa musimya, balyinjirire mwelusuku lukulu lwebuchinjibusi.

7. Mukengeraa na besha mwa musi weSotomo, neweKomora, na besha mwa misi era yabaa ibasungwire. Nabo babaa benjire banachitola ngabu bamalaika. Bera kunde baira myasi ya honyi mwakuira elusingi ebalume kwa balume.a Bushi

버찌러 바나나 여수 기리시도, 이우쭈꽈 무구루-구루 워쭈 여이너 가찌 어나워쭈. 구더꺼라 미라, 어마아찌고 마부야-부야 마바아 마더찌러 어라 루우루 서부찌찌부시 봐 아부 바쭈 바가보나.

5. 찌로 아꽈바 뿌 뭐라 뮈씨 구부야-부야 어너 먀시 요씨, 나호따 네바거꺼서 구더 과 어나워쭈 아누누꽈아 어바이시라어뤼 로씨, 구더꽈 봐 찌오 쩌 미시리. 시 바바나나아 구뭐머러라, 어라 구바시갸.

6. 아나버 노오와 바마꽈이가, 바우마 무보 바나나아 구꽈꽈 어쭈따 랴 오꼬 어러사아보, 버라 구더꽈 봐 비시기 뱌보.. 부씨 노구, 오꼬 어라 구바미나 봐 마러우러 너구우마보 봐 무시먀, 바레찌리러 뭐루루수구 루구루 뭐부찌찌부시.

7. 무거꺼라아 나 버싸 봐 무시 워소도모, 너워고모라, 나 버싸 봐 미시 어라 야바아 이바수쀠러. 나보 바바아 버찌러 바나찌도꽈 꽈부 바마꽈이가. 버라 구너 바이라 먀시 야 호네 꽈구이라 어루시삐 어바루머 과 바루머.아 부씨 노구, 버라

5. Though you already know all this, I want to remind you that the Lord delivered his people out of Egypt, but later destroyed those who did not believe.

6. And the angels who did not keep their positions of authority but abandoned their own home--these he has kept in darkness, bound with everlasting chains for judgment on the great Day.

7. In a similar way, Sodom and Gomorrah and the surrounding towns gave themselves up to sexual immorality and perversion. They serve as an example of those who suffer the punishment of eternal fire.

noku, bera balyibukira mwa mulyiro wesuku nemango. Rero, echera chindaa chakangirisa ebandju boshi.

8. Abu bandju babi, nabo ku benjire banachitola bacha. Ebiroto bya benjire balota, byenjire byathuma baaka esinga kwa mibilyi yabo. Benjire bakena ebuashi bwa Ongo, na kunde bakamba ebamalaika bebulangare.

9. Anabe na Mikaelyi, imukulu-kulu we ndonyi, mango abanganaa na Wamusimu bushi nechirunda cha Musa, ataereresaa amukamba mwa kumuchinjibusa. Si anamuburaa oshao mbu: "Enawethu yeine akukalyiiraa!"

10. Si abu bandju babi, benjire bakamba emyasi era bateshi. Anabe nemyasi era beshi, banaishi nga nyama somwerungu, sa sitathusa bwenge. Rero echera, chi chenjire chathuma basika.

11. Abu bandju balyi banya, bushi emyanya ya Kaini ibakulyikire. Kanji bushi nekuhonda ebikulo, bengirire mwa mabi ma Balama airaa.

바례부기라 먀 무례로 워수구 너마꼬. 러로, 어쩌라 찌따아 짜가끼리사 어바뉴 보씨.

8. 아부 바뉴 바비, 나보 구 버찌러 바나찌도롸 바짜. 어비로도 뱌 버찌러 바로다, 뱌찌러 뱌쭈마 바아가 어시꺄 과 미비례 야보. 버찌러 바거나 어부아씨 봐 오꼬, 나 구떠 바가빠 어바마롸이가 버부롸꺄러.

9. 아나버 나 미가어레, 이무구루-구루 워 또네, 마꼬 아바꺄나아 나 와무시무 부씨 너찌루따 짜 무사, 아다어러러사아 아무가빠 먀 구무찌찌부사. 시 아나무부라아 오싸오 뿌: "어나워쭈 여이너 아구가례이라아!"

10. 시 아부 바뉴 바비, 버찌러 바가빠 어먀시 어라 바더씨. 아나버 너먀시 어라 버씨, 바나이씨 꺄 냐마 소뭐루꾸, 사 시다쭈사 붜꺼. 러로 어쩌라, 찌 쩌찌러 짜쭈마 바시가.

11. 아부 바뉴 바레 바냐, 부씨 어먄냐 야 가이니 이바구례기러. 가찌 부씨 너구호따 어비구롣, 버끼리러 먀 마비 마 바롸마 아이라아.

8. In the very same way, these dreamers pollute their own bodies, reject authority and slander celestial beings.

9. But even the archangel Michael, when he was disputing with the devil about the body of Moses, did not dare to bring a slanderous accusation against him, but said, "The Lord rebuke you!"

10. Yet these men speak abusively against whatever they do not understand; and what things they do understand by instinct, like unreasoning animals--these are the very things that destroy them.

11. Woe to them! They have taken the way of Cain; they have rushed for profit into Balaam's error; they have been destroyed in Korah's

Rero basikire bushi nekutatunda Ongo, ngokwa Kora nai atamuthundaa.

12. Abu bandju bende bareta ekafango ala mwalyira ebiryo byenyu mwa buuma. Bende balya binene na kweuta busese busira honyi, batanalaa kwa banji bandju. Balyi nga lumbumbu lwa lwekibwa nechusi, si lutatosa mvula isibya. Kanji balyi nga michi era iteka bifuma, chiro angaba mbu echianyiro chekushebula chaikire. Balyi nga michi era yashungulyibwe mira na ya chifira.

13. Kanji balyi nga mulaba munene wokwa nyanja. Bende bafubula emyasi yabo yehonyi ngokwa nyanja yende yauma emifumba yemulaba kwa musike. Kanji balyi nga ngununu sa satalatala. Rero, Ongo abikilyirebo mira echisiki mwa musimya munene esuku nemango.

14. Enoki, hokulu wethu wa kalyinda kutengera ku Adamu, abaa arebire mira era luulu sabo mbu Muumvaa Enawethu akabaha na biumbi na biumbi byebamalaika bai babuya-buya,

러로 바시기러 부씨 너구다두따 오꼬, 꼬과 고라 나이 아다무쭈따아.

12. 아부 바뉴 버떠 바러다 어가파꼬 아롸 뫄레라 어비료 벼뉴 뫄 부우마. 버떠 바퍄 비너너 나 귀우다 부서서 부시라 호네, 바다나롸아 꽈 바찌 바뉴. 바레 꺄 루뿌뿌 롸 뤄기봐 너쭈시, 시 루다도사 뿌롸 이시뱌. 가찌 바레 꺄 미찌 어라 이더가 비푸마, 찌로 아꺄바 뿌 어찌아네로 쩌구써부롸 쨔이기러. 바레 꺄 미찌 어라 야쑤꾸레붜 미라 나 야 찌피라.

13. 가찌 바레 꺄 무롸바 무너너 오꽈 냐쨔. 버떠 바푸부롸 어먀시 야보 여호네 꼬과 냐쨔 여떠 야우마 어미푸빠 여무롸바 꽈 무시거. 가찌 바레 꺄 꾸누누 사 사다롸-다롸. 러로, 오꼬 아비기레러보 미라 어찌시기 뫄 무시먀 무너너 어수구 너마꼬.

14. 어노기, 호구루 워쭈 와 가레따 구더뗘라 구 아다무, 아바아 아러비러 미라 어라 루우루 사보 뿌 무우빠아 어나워쭈 아가바하 나 비우삐 나 비우삐 벼바마롸이가 바이 바부야-부야,

rebellion.

12. These men are blemishes at your love feasts, eating with you without the slightest qualm--shepherds who feed only themselves. They are clouds without rain, blown along by the wind; autumn trees, without fruit and uprooted--twice dead.

13. They are wild waves of the sea, foaming up their shame; wandering stars, for whom blackest darkness has been reserved forever.

14. Enoch, the seventh from Adam, prophesied about these men: "See, the Lord is coming with thousands upon thousands of his holy ones

15. chasiya aye kuchinjibusa ebandju boshi. Akachinjibusa ebakosi bemabi boshi kwa mabi ma bakolaa mwa kutathunda Ongo. Kanji akachinjibusabo bushi nemyasi yoshi ibi era ikalyiire, era bendee bateta era luulu sai.

16. Esuku soshi, abu bandju batathusa lumoo, kuchaanya ku bende banachaanya bushi batamoera kwa balyi. Bende bakulyikira emyasi yabo ibi yebuhuma-huma. Bende bateta myasi ya kuchitonga, na kulokeresa ebunu era muhondo sebandju chasiya babakule kwekandju.

17. Si mwabo banyakethu basiirwa, mutendaa mwa bilyira emyasi era ndumwa sa Enawethu Yesu Kirisito sababuraa mira.

18. Sababuraa mbu Mwa suku sebusinda, kukaulukira bandju ba bakende ba bashekera na kunde banana kuthunda Ongo, mwa kukulyikira emyasi yabo ibi yebuhuma-huma.

19. Abola, bu bende bathuma ebemeresi baberekanamo. Kanji bende bakoresibwa nemyasi yemubilyi, si

15. 짜시야 아여 구찌찌부사 어바뚜 보씨. 아가찌찌부사 어바고시 버마비 보씨 과 마비 마 바고롸아 뫄 구다쭈따 오꼬. 가찌 아가찌찌부사보 부씨 너먀시 요씨 이비 어라 이가레이러, 어라 버떠어 바더다 어라 루우루 사이.

16. 어수구 소씨, 아부 바뚜 바다쭈사 루모오, 구짜아냐 구 버떠 바나짜아냐 부씨 바다모어라 과 바례. 버떠 바구레기라 어먀시 야보 이비 여부후마-후마. 버떠 바더다 먀시 야 구찌도따, 나 구롲거러사 어부누 어라 무호또 서바뚜 짜시야 바바구러 궈가뚜.

17. 시 먀보 바냐거쭈 바시이롸, 무더따아 뫄 비례라 어먀시 어라 뚜뫄 사 어나워쭈 여수 기리시도 사바부라아 미라.

18. 사바부라아 뿌 뫄 수구 서부시따, 구가우룬기라 바뚜 바 바거떠 바 바써거라 나 구떠 바나나 구쭈따 오꼬, 뫄 구구레기라 어먀시 야보 이비 여부후마-후마.

19. 아보롸, 부 버떠 바쭈마 어버머러시 바버러가나모. 가찌 버떠 바고러시봐 너먀시 여무비례, 시 바다쭈사

15. to judge everyone, and to convict all the ungodly of all the ungodly acts they have done in the ungodly way, and of all the harsh words ungodly sinners have spoken against him."

16. These men are grumblers and faultfinders; they follow their own evil desires; they boast about themselves and flatter others for their own advantage.

17. But, dear friends, remember what the apostles of our Lord Jesus Christ foretold.

18. They said to you, "In the last times there will be scoffers who will follow their own ungodly desires."

19. These are the men who divide you, who follow mere natural instincts and do not have the Spirit.

batathusa eMuchima wa Ongo.

20. Si mwabo banyakethu basiirwa, musimikaa busese mwa bwemeresi bwenyu bubuya-buya. Mango mwema Ongo, mundaa mwareka eMuchima Mubuya-buya endee abaasa.

21. Emibere yenyu ibaa ya bandju ba beshi kwa Ongo abasimire. Bindaa byaba bacha, mwa kulyinjirira Enawethu Yesu Kirisito iungabeeresa ekalamo kesuku nemango, kurengera ebonjo bwai.

22. Mundaa mwaata muchima wa bonjo kwaba bachilyi bahungwa-hungwa,

23. Mu banunule batenge mwa mulyiro. Ebanji nabo, mundaa mwabafira bonjo, si muchilangaa kubo. Mutaereresaa mwauma nokwa njimba sabo sa bakabire kwesinga kurengera emyasi yabo ibi yebuhuma-huma.

24. Ongo atongwe bushi iwathununulaa kurengera Enawethu Yesu Kirisito Yeine endaa abalanga mungesha kwengilyira mwa mabi.

어무찌마 와 오꼬.

20. 시 뫄보 바냐거쭈 바시이롸, 무시미가아 부서서 뫄 붜머러시 붜뉴 부부야-부야. 마꼬 뭐마 오꼬, 무따아 뫄러가 어무찌마 무부야-부야 어떠어 아바아사.

21. 어미버러 여뉴 이바아 야 바뚜 바 버씨 과 오꼬 아바시미러. 비따아 뱌바 바짜, 뫄 구쩨찌리라 어나워쭈 여수 기리시도 이우꺄버러러사 어가꺄모 거수구 너마꼬, 구러꺼라 어보쪼 봐이.

22. 무따아 뫄아다 무찌마 와 보쪼 과바 바찌쩨 바후꽈-후꽈,

23. 무 바누누퍼 바더꺼 뫄 무쩨로. 어바찌 나보, 무따아 뫄바피라 보쪼, 시 무찌꽈꺄아 구보. 무다어러러사아 뫄우마 노과 띠꺄 사보 사 바가비러 궈시꺄 구러꺼라 어먀시 야보 이비 여부후마-후마.

24. 오꼬 아도워 부씨 이와쭈누누꽈아 구러꺼라 어나워쭈 여수 기리시도 여이너 어따아 아바꽈꺄 무꺼싸 궈꺼쩨라 뫄 마비.

---

20. But you, dear friends, build yourselves up in your most holy faith and pray in the Holy Spirit.

21. Keep yourselves in God's love as you wait for the mercy of our Lord Jesus Christ to bring you to eternal life.

22. Be merciful to those who doubt;

23. snatch others from the fire and save them; to others show mercy, mixed with fear- -hating even the clothing stained by corrupted flesh.

24. To him who is able to keep you from falling and to present you before his glorious presence without fault and with great joy--

25. Endaa abemanza na lumoo lunene era muhondo sai mwa bulangere busira chibi chisibya. Endaa atongibwa na kweresibwa ethunda, nemisi, kutengera mira, na lwarero, nesuku nemango. Bibe bacha.

25. 어따아 아버마싸 나 루모오 루너너 어라 무호또 사이 뫄 부퐈ᄊ러 부시라 찌비 찌시뱌. 어따아 아도ᄈ봐 나 궈러시뫄 어쭈따, 너미시, 구더ᄊ라 미라, 나 쫘러로, 너수구 너마ᄋ. 비버 바짜.

25. to the only God our Savior be glory, majesty, power and authority, through Jesus Christ our Lord, before all ages, now and forevermore! Amen.

Byaboolyibwa

뱌보오례봐

Revelation

BYABOERWE
(REVELATION)

뱌보어뤄
(러버꽈디오누)

Byaboolyibwa Chikono 1

1. Enera ilyi myasi era Yesu Kirisito abihulaa. Na Ongo yeine iwamweresaai, alose ebaanda bai bya bikaika. Ei myasi, Yesu iwathumaa endonyi wai alosei emuanda wai Yowani.

2. Yowani nai atetaa era luulu semyasi yoshi era achiloreraako. Nei myasi, chinalyi eChinwa cha Ongo. Kanji inalyi myasi era Yesu Kirisito alosaa kanangana.

3. Rero, ene myasi yandjikibwe mwechine chitabo inalyi ya burebi. Ola waisomera ebanji, na ba bomvirisai, na kuithunda, kuika boshi banaahanyirwe. Bushi ebihangi byekuba kwai, bilyi ofu. Yowani alamusa bemeresi ba nyuhu sirinda sa Ongo.

4. Nyono nyi Yowani, nyi nabandjikira mu bemeresi benyuhu sirinda sa Ongo sa sithula mwa chio che Asiya. Ongo ola wabaa uthula, kanji iunathula, kanji iunachiri ukabaha, endaa aberesa engahanyi nebolo. Ebyera,

뱌보오쮀봐 찌고노 1

1. 어너라 이쮀 먀시 어라 여수 기리시도 아비후퐈아. 나 오꼬 여이너 이와뭐러사아이, 아로서 어바아따 바이 뱌 비가이가. 어이 먀시, 여수 이와쭈마아 어또네 와이 아로서이 어무아따 와이 요와니.

2. 요와니 나이 아더다아 어라 루우루 서먀시 요씨 어라 아찌로러라아고. 너이 먀시, 찌나쮀 어찌뇨 짜 오꼬. 가찌 이나쮀 먀시 어라 여수 기리시도 아로사아 가나빠나.

3. 러로, 어너 먀시 야찌기붸 뭐찌너 찌다보 이나쮀 야 부러비. 오퐈 와이소머라 어바찌, 나 바 보뻬리사이, 나 구이쭈따, 구이가 보씨 바나아하니붜뤄. 부씨 어비하삐 벼구바 과이, 비쮀 오푸. 요와니 아퐈무사 버머러시 바 뉴후 시리따 사 오꼬.

4. 뇨노 내 요와니, 네 나바찌기라 무 버머러시 버뉴후 시리따 사 오꼬 사 시쭈퐈 뫄 찌오 쩌 아시야. 오꼬 오퐈 와바아 우쭈퐈, 가찌 이우나쭈퐈, 가찌 이우나찌리 우가바하, 어따아 아버러사 어빠하니 너보로,

Revelation Chapter 1[NIV]

1. The revelation of Jesus Christ, which God gave him to show his servants what must soon take place. He made it known by sending his angel to his servant John,

2. who testifies to everything he saw--that is, the word of God and the testimony of Jesus Christ.

3. Blessed is the one who reads the words of this prophecy, and blessed are those who hear it and take to heart what is written in it, because the time is near.

4. John, To the seven churches in the province of Asia: Grace and peace to you from him who is, and who was, and who is to come, and from the seven spirits before his throne,

kanji mundaa mwanabibona kutengera kwa michima erinda era ithula era muhondo sendebe yai yebwami.

어벼라, 가찌 무따아 먀나비보나 구더꺼라 과 미찌마 어리따 어라 이쭈꽈 어라 무호또 서떠버 야이 여봐미.

5. Kanji mundaa mwanabibona kutenga era mwa Yesu Kirisito, iwatetaa kanangana era luulu sebya achiloreraako era mwa Ongo. Kanji iwabaa mubere kwomoka, kanji iunathula mukulu-kulu webami boshi bomwa butala. Oyu Yesu Kirisito, athula athusimire ngachi. Atunuwire mira mwa bibi byethu, kurengera emikira yai.

5. 가찌 무따아 먀나비보나 구더꺼 어라 먀 여수 기리시도, 이와더다아 가나꺼나 어라 루우루 서뱌 아찌로러라아고 어라 먀 오꼬. 가찌 이와바아 무버러 고모가, 가찌 이우나쭈꽈 무구루-구루 워바미 보씨 보먀 부다꽈. 오유 여수 기리시도, 아쭈꽈 아쭈시미러 까찌. 아두누니위러 미라 먀 비비 뱌쭈, 구러꺼라 어미기라 야이.

5. and from Jesus Christ, who is the faithful witness, the firstborn from the dead, and the ruler of the kings of the earth. To him who loves us and has freed us from our sins by his blood,

6. Anathuira kuba bandju bomwa bwami bwa Ongo, kanji anathuira kuba mikosi thunde twakorera Eshe Ongo. Endaa aya ngulu na kuata ebuashi esuku nemango! Bibe bacha.

6. 아나쭈이라 구바 바뚜 보먀 봐미 봐 오꼬, 가찌 아나쭈이라 구바 미고시 쭈떠 돠고러라 어써 오꼬. 어따아 아야 꾸루 나 구아다 어부아씨 어수구 너마꼬! 비버 바짜.

6. and has made us to be a kingdom and priests to serve his God and Father--to him be glory and power for ever and ever! Amen.

7. Mulolaa! Yola wabaha mwa lumbumbu. Ebandju boshi bangamulolako, anabe na ba bamubandaa efumo, nabo banganamulolako. Nembaa soshi somwa butala singalyira busese bushi nai. Nechi! Bibe bacha!

7. 무로꽈아! 요꽈 와바하 먀 루뿌뿌. 어바뚜 보씨 바꺼무로꽈고, 아나버 나 바 바무바따아 어푸모, 나보 바꺼나무로꽈고. 너꺼아 소씨 소먀 부다꽈 시꺼례라 부서서 부씨 나이. 너찌! 비버 바짜!

7. Look, he is coming with the clouds, and every eye will see him, even those who pierced him; and all the peoples of the earth will mourn because of him. So shall it be! Amen.

8. Enawethu Ongo, webuashi boshi bacha ku atechire:

8. 어나워쭈 오꼬, 워부아씨 보씨 바짜 구 아더찌러: "뇨노

8. "I am the Alpha and the Omega," says the Lord God,

"Nyono nyi Alufa, kanji nyi Omeka! Nyono nabaa nyitula, kanji nyinathula, kanji nyi nyichiri nyikabaha!"

9. Nyono Yowani, nyiri munyakenyu bushi nebuuma bwethu mu Yesu, kanji bushi nebwami bwa Ongo. Narenga mwa malyibuko kuuma nenyu na kunde nata ebushibirisi. Rero, bushi nekunde nahubanganyisa ebandju eChinwa cha Ongo, na kunde nateta bya nyishi era luulu sa Yesu, chi chathumire banyipereka kwechine chisimba chePatimo.

10. Lusuku luuma lwa Enawethu, eMuchima Mubuya-buya anyandalyiraa. Unao-unao, na nomva era nyuma sanyi yatengera murenge munene ola walyira nga wa kaperere.

11. Oyu murenge, era kunyibura mbu: "Byoshi bya ungalolako, waanjikaabi mwa chitabo. Chasinda, wanathumirachi ebemeresi besine nyuhu sirinda sa Ongo. Nesi nyuhu sisesine: eluhu lwe Efeso, ne lwe Simirina, ne lwe Perikamu, ne lwe Tuwatera, ne lwe Sariti, ne lweFilatelifiya, ne lwe Laotikiya."

네 아루파, 가찌 네 오머가! 뇨노 나바아 네두롸, 가찌 네나쭈롸, 가찌 네 네찌리 네가바하!"

9. 뇨노 요와니, 네리 무냐거뉴 부씨 너부우마 붜쭈무 여수, 가찌 부씨 너봐미 봐 오꼬. 나라꽈 봐 마레부고 구우마 너뉴, 나 구떠 나다 어부씨비리시. 러로, 부씨 너구떠 나후바꽈네사 어바누 어찌놔 짜 오꼬, 나 구떠 나다다 뱌 네씨 어라 루우루 사 여수, 찌 짜쭈미러 바네퍼러가 궈찌너 찌시빠 쩌파디모.

10. 루수구 루우마 꽈 어나워쭈, 어무찌마 무부야-부야 아냐따레라아. 우나오-우나오, 나 노빠 어라 뉴마 사네 야더꺼라 무러꺼 무너너 오롸 와례라 꽈 와 가퍼러러.

11. 오유 무러꺼, 어라 구네부라 뿌: "뵤씨 뱌 우가로롸고, 와아찌가아비 꽈 찌다보. 짜시따, 와나쭈미라찌 어버머러시 버시너 뉴후 시리따 사 오꼬. 너시 뉴후 시서시너: 어루후 뤄 어퍼소, 너 뤄 시미리나, 너 뤄 퍼리가무, 너 뤄 두와더라, 너 뤄 사리디, 너 뤄피꽈더뤠피퍄, 너 뤄

"who is, and who was, and who is to come, the Almighty."

9. I, John, your brother and companion in the suffering and kingdom and patient endurance that are ours in Jesus, was on the island of Patmos because of the word of God and the testimony of Jesus.

10. On the Lord's Day I was in the Spirit, and I heard behind me a loud voice like a trumpet,

11. which said: "Write on a scroll what you see and send it to the seven churches: to Ephesus, Smyrna, Pergamum, Thyatira, Sardis, Philadelphia and Laodicea."

12. Unao-unao, kuna kubindjuka nyilole nde iwahambala nanyi. Abere nera nabindjukaa, nera kulola ku thukondo thulinda thwa matara thwa tukunganyisibwe mwa horo.

12. 우나오-우나오, 구나 구비뉴가 니로러 떠 이와하빠롸 나니. 아버러 너라 나비뉴가아, 너라 구로롸 구 쭈고또 쭈리따 좌 마다라 좌 두구네시붜 마 호로.

12. I turned around to see the voice that was speaking to me. And when I turned I saw seven golden lampstands,

13. Nomwa kachi-kachi kamo, nera kulola mwemangire mundju muuma ola wabaa ulyi nga "eMwana weMundju", embese ropo lya lyabaa lyiikirire kwana maulu. Kandji abaa eembere na mukaba wa horo mwa chifuba.

13. 노롸 가찌-가찌 가모, 너라 구로롸 뭐마러 무뚜 무우마 오라 와바아 우레 "어먀나 워무뚜", 어뻐서 로포 랴 랴바아 레이기리러 과나 마우루. 가찌 아바아 어어뻐러 나 무가바 와 호로 롸 찌푸바.

13. and among the lampstands was someone "like a son of man,"dressed in a robe reaching down to his feet and with a golden sash around his chest.

14. Ethwe lyai, lyabaa lyehwire emvi salangala nga pamba, kandji sa muoko-muoko nga luthwa. Nemeho mai mabaa mengengenya nga nyirimi sa mulyiro.

14. 어쮀 랴이, 랴바아 려휘러 어삐 사롸롸 파빠, 가찌 사 무오고-무오고 루좌. 너머호 마이 마바아 머머냐 니리미 사 무레로.

14. His head and hair were white like wool, as white as snow, and his eyes were like blazing fire.

15. Ne maulu mai mabaa malangala na kwengengenya busese nga miringa era bakomise mwa kuirenza mwa mulyiro. Nemurenge wai abaa auma nga chiira.

15. 너 마우루 마이 마바아 마롸롸 나 궈머냐 부서서 미리 어라 바고미서 롸 구이러싸 롸 무레로. 너무러 와이 아바아 아우마 찌이라.

15. His feet were like bronze glowing in a furnace, and his voice was like the sound of rushing waters.

16. Mwa mino yai ye malyo, abaa eete mu ngununu sirinda. Nomwa bunu bwai, mwera kutenga bombo bwa moyi mabiri. Ne buso bwai, bwabaa bwalangala busese ngesuba limenze.

16. 롸 미노 야이 여 마룐, 아바아 어어더 무 꾸누누 시리따. 노롸 부누 바이, 뭐라 구더 보뾘 봐 모에 마비리. 너 부소 바이, 봐바아 봐롸롸 부서서 수바 뤼머.

16. In his right hand he held seven stars, and out of his mouth came a sharp double-edged sword. His face was like the sun shining in all its brilliance.

17. Mango nanamulolaako, unao-unao kuna kukumbaala kafulyi-bwembe mwa maulu mai, na naba ngola wafire. Si era kunyibika kwemino yai yemalyo na anyibura mbu: "Utobaa! Nyono nyi Mubere, kanji nyi Musinda.

18. Kanji nyi nyithula muuma-uma. Chiro mbu nafaa, si rero nera nyiri muuma-uma wesuku nemango! Nera nyete nebuashi era luulu se lufu, nera luulu se Kusimu.

19. "Bushi noku, byoshi bya ungalolako, ubiandjikaa: bya biri lwarero, nebya bikaika.

20. Rero, sa ngunu sirinda mwera kulola nyete mwa mino yanyi yemalyo, alauma na thwa thukondo thulyinda twe matara thwa thukunganyisibwe mwa horo, kulyi kuteta mbu esi ngunu sirinda, balyi donyi besa nyuhu sirinda sa Ongo. Nothu thukondo thulyinda thwamo matara natho, balyi ebemeresi besi nyuhu sirinda."

17. 마꼬 나나무롤롸아고, 우나오-우나오 구나 구구빠아롸 가푸레-붸뻐 마 마우루 마이, 나 나바 꼬롸 와피러. 시 어라 구네비가 궈미노 야이 여마롼 나 아내부라 뿌: "우도바아! 뇨노 네 무버러, 가찌 네 무시따.

18. 가찌 네 네쭈롸 무우마-우마. 찌로 뿌 나파아, 시 러로 너라 네리 무우마-우마 워수구 너마꼬! 너라 녀더 너부아씨 어라 루우루 서 루푸, 너라 루우루 서 구시무.

19. "부씨 노구, 보씨 뱌 우빠롤롸고, 우비아찌가아: 뱌 비리 롸러로, 너뱌 비가이가.

20. 러로, 사 꾸누누 시리따 뭐라 구롤롸 녀더 마 미노 야네 여마롼, 아롸우마 나 좌 쭈고또 쭈레따 뛰 마다라 좌 쭈구꽈네시붸 마 호로, 구레 구더다 뿌 어시 꾸누누 시리따, 바레 도네 버사 뉴후 시리따 사 오꼬. 노쭈 쭈고또 쭈레따 좌모 마다라 나쏘, 바레 어버머러시 버시 뉴후 시리따."

17. When I saw him, I fell at his feet as though dead. Then he placed his right hand on me and said: "Do not be afraid. I am the First and the Last.

18. I am the Living One; I was dead, and behold I am alive for ever and ever! And I hold the keys of death and Hades.

19. "Write, therefore, what you have seen, what is now and what will take place later.

20. The mystery of the seven stars that you saw in my right hand and of the seven golden lampstands is this: The seven stars are the angels of the seven churches, and the seven lampstands are the seven churches.

Byaboolyibwa Chikono 2

1. "Uanjikiraa endonyi weluhu lwa Ongo lwa luthula mwa

뱌보오레봐 찌고노 2

1. "우아찌기라아 어또네 워루후 롸 오꼬 롸 루쭈롸 마

Revelation Chapter 2[NIV]

1. "To the angel of the church in Ephesus write:

musi we Efeso mbu: "Ene myasi, yatengera era mwola wete sangununu sirinda mwa mino yai yemalyo. Nathwa thukondo thulyinda thwa ma matara thwa thukunganyisibwe mwa horo, iwenjire wasungula mwa kachi-kachi katho.

2. "Emyanya yenyu nyiishi. Kanji nyineshi kwa mwenjire mwashika endjubano mui, nokwa mwenjire mwaata ebushibirisi. Kanji nyineshi kwa mutenjire mwemerera emyasi yebandju babi. Anabe na ba benjire bachitonga mbu siri ndjumwa sanyi, mwaerekaabo mwera kulola kwa balyi bafusi ba bisha.

3. Chiro angaba mbu mwalyibuka busese bushi nesina lyanyi, munachiri musimikire, mwanata nebushibirisi busira kutama.

4. "Si nyisene kwa mwa kachi-kachi kenyu, muchiri mwasi muuma ola utanyisimise. Noyu mwasi iyono: enzii yenyu era mwabaa muthusa lyebere mwairekire.

5. Mukengeraa kwa mwabaa muthula lyebere na kute mwahubire era nyuma busese. Rero, mubindjukaa kutenga

무시 워 어퍼소 뿌: "어너 먀시, 야더뻐라 어라 몰롸 워더 사우누누 시리따 롸 미노 야이 여마룐. 나좌 쭈고또 쭈뤠따 좌 마 마다라 좌 쭈구까네시붜 롸 호로, 이워띠러 와수우롸 롸 가찌-가찌 가쏘.

2. "어먀냐 여뉴 네이씨. 가찌 네너씨 과 뭐띠러 롸씨가 어뿌바노 무이, 노과 뭐띠러 롸아다 어부씨비리시. 가찌 네너씨 과 무더띠러 뭐머러라 어먀시 여반쭈 바비. 아나버 나 바 버찌러 바찌도까 뿌 시리 누롸 사네, 롸어러가아보 뭐라 구로롸 과 바뤠 바푸시 바 비싸.

3. 찌로 아까바 뿌 롸뤠부가 부서서 부씨 너시나 랸네, 무나찌리 무시미기러, 롸나다 너부씨비리시 부시라 구다마.

4. "시 네서너 과 롸 가찌-가찌 거뉴, 무찌리 롸시 무우마 오롸 우다네시미서. 노유 롸시 이요노: 어씨이 여뉴 어라 롸바아 무쭈사 뗘버러 롸이러기러.

5. 무거뻐라아 과 롸바아 무쭈롸 뗘버러 나 구더 롸후비러 어라 뉴마 부서서. 러로, 무비뿌가아 구더까 롸

These are the words of him who holds the seven stars in his right hand and walks among the seven golden lampstands:

2. I know your deeds, your hard work and your perseverance. I know that you cannot tolerate wicked men, that you have tested those who claim to be apostles but are not, and have found them false.

3. You have persevered and have endured hardships for my name, and have not grown weary.

4. Yet I hold this against you: You have forsaken your first love.

5. Remember the height from which you have fallen! Repent and do the things you did at first. If you do

mwa bibi byenyu, muhube kunde mwaira bya mwendee mwaira lyebere. Na akaba mutangachiaya kwebi bibi byenyu, nyingaika kukula ekakondo ketara ala kathula.

6. Si chiro bacha, mwa kachi-kachi kenyu muchiri undji mwasi ola unyisimise. Noyu mwasi iyono: muthula muaire busese emyanya ye Banikolayia ngokwa nanyi nyinathula nyinaairei.

7. "Ola wete mathi, oomvaa ene myasi eMuchima Mubuya-buya abura ebemeresi! Ola ukaimana, nyikamweresa eloso lwekulya kwa bifuma byemuchi wekwana ekalamo, ola uthula mwa Paratiso ya Ongo."

8. "Waanjikiraa endonyi we luhu lwa Ongo lwa luthula mwa musi we Simirina mbu: "Ene myasi, yatengera era mwola uthula Mubere, kanji Musinda. Oyola iwafaa, si era kwomoka.

9. "Nyishi emalyibuko menyu, nebukene bwenyu. Si chiro bacha, mulyi baare. Kanji nyineshi kwa mwende mwekerwa ebisha na ba bende bachitonga mbu bathula Bayuta. Abola,

비비 벼뉴, 무후버 구떠 마이라 뱌 뭐떠어 마이라 려버러. 나 아가바 무다까찌아야 궈비 비비 벼뉴, 네마이가 구구롸 어가고또 거다라 아롸 가쭈롸.

6. 시 찌로 바짜, 똬 가찌-가찌 거뉴 무찌리 우찌 마시 오라 우네시미서. 노유 마시 이요노: 무쭈롸 무아이러 부서서 어먀냐 여 바니고롸에아 꼬과 나네 네나쭈롸 네나아이러이.

7. "오롸 워더 마찌, 오오빠아 어너 먀시 어무찌마 무부야-부야 아부라 어버머러시! 오롸 우가이마나, 네가뭐러사 어로소 뭐구롸 과 비푸마 벼무찌 워과나 어가롸모, 오롸 우쭈롸 똬 파라디소 야 오꼬."

8. "와아찌기라아 어또네 워 루후 롸 오꼬 롸 루쭈롸 똬 무시 워 시미리나 뿌: "어너 먀시, 야더떠라 어라 뫄롸 우쭈롸 무버러, 가찌 무시따. 오요롸 이와파아, 시 어라 꼬모가.

9. "네씨 어마레부고 머뉴, 너부거너 붜뉴. 시 찌로 바짜, 무레 바아러. 가찌 네너씨 과 뭐떠 뭐거롸 어비싸 나 바 버떠 바찌도꽈 뿌 바쭈롸 바유다. 아보롸, 바다쭈롸 바유다, 시 바쭈롸 보뫄

not repent, I will come to you and remove your lampstand from its place.

6. But you have this in your favor: You hate the practices of the Nicolaitans, which I also hate.

7. He who has an ear, let him hear what the Spirit says to the churches. To him who overcomes, I will give the right to eat from the tree of life, which is in the paradise of God.

8. "To the angel of the church in Smyrna write: These are the words of him who is the First and the Last, who died and came to life again.

9. I know your afflictions and your poverty--yet you are rich! I know the slander of those who say they are Jews and are not, but are a synagogue of Satan.

batathula Bayuta, si bathula bomwa bushenge bwa Wamusimu!

10. "Mumenyaa kwa bauma mu mwabo, Wamusimu angende abaumanga mwa buroko, abaereke. Na mwobu buroko, bangalola kwa malyibuko ku suku ekumi. Si amu malyibuko, mutobaaamo. Na chiro mungechibwa bushi nanyi, munasimikaa mwa bwemeresi bwenyu, munaimane nanyi nyingabemba enzita. Ei nzita, kalyi ekalamo kesuku nemango.

11. "Ola wete mathi, omvaa ene myasi eMuchima Mubuya-buya abura ebemeresi! Ola ukaimana, atakachilole kwa malyibuko melufu lwakabiri."

12. "Uanjikiraa endonyi weluhu lwa Ongo lwa luthula mwa musi we Perikamu mbu: "Ene myasi, yatengera era mwola wete bwa bombo bukalyire busese bwa bwete moyi mabiri:

13. "Nyishi kubuya echisiki cha muthulamo. Echi chisiki, chi Wasimu akomire mwendebe yai yebwami. Si chiro bacha, munachiri munyikulikire

부써써 봐 와무시무!

10. "무머냐아 과 바우마 무 뫄보, 와무시무 아떠러 아바우마까 봐 부로고, 아바어러거. 나 모부 부로고, 바까루뢔 과 마레부고 구 수구 어구미. 시 아무 마레부고, 무도바아아모. 나 찌로 무써찌봐 부씨 나니, 무나시미가아 봐 붜머러시 붜뉴, 무나이마너 나니 네까버빠 어씨다. 어이 씨다, 가레 어가롸모 거수구 너마꼬.

11. "오롸 워더 마찌, 오빠아 어너 먀시 어무찌마 무부야-부야 아부라 어버머러시! 오롸 우가이마나, 아다가찌뢰뻐 과 마레부고 머루푸 뢔가비리."

12. "우아찌기라아 어또네 워루후 롸 오꼬 롸 루쭈롸 봐 무시 워 퍼리가무 뿌: "어너 먀시, 야더써라 어라 몰롸 워더 봐 보뽀 부가레러 부서서 봐 붜더 모에 마비리:

13. "네씨 구부야 어찌시기 짜 무쭈뢔모. 어찌 찌시기, 찌 와시무 아고미러 뭐떠버 야이 여봐미. 시 찌로 바짜, 무나찌리 무네구쀠기러

10. Do not be afraid of what you are about to suffer. I tell you, the devil will put some of you in prison to test you, and you will suffer persecution for ten days. Be faithful, even to the point of death, and I will give you the crown of life.

11. He who has an ear, let him hear what the Spirit says to the churches. He who overcomes will not be hurt at all by the second death.

12. "To the angel of the church in Pergamum write: These are the words of him who has the sharp, double-edged sword.

13. I know where you live-- where Satan has his throne. Yet you remain true to my name. You did not renounce your faith in me, even in the

kubuya. Anabe mango betaa Andipa, mubei wanyi mubuya, mutarekaa ebwemeresi bwenyu ku nyono.

14 "Si mwa kachi-kachi kenyu, muchiri myasi yiuma era itanyisimise. Bushi, kuli bandju bauma mu mwabo ba benjire bakulikira emyasi era Balama endee akangirisa. Oyu Balama, iwendee wakangirisa Balaki mbu atebaa eBaisiraeli bende bakola emabi. Amu mabi, kwabaa kulya ebiryo bya byatulwaa ebasimu, na kubanda ekiri.

15 Kanji kuli na banji bauma mu mwabo ba benjire bakulikira emyasi ibi era eBanikolayi benjire bakangirisa.

16 "Rero, mubindjukaa kutenga mwa bibi byenyu. Bitabere bacha, era nyuma sa bihangi bieke, nabaikira nyilwise abu bandju mwobuno bombo nyete mwa bunu.

17 "Ola wete mathi, omvaa ene myasi eMuchima Mubuya-buya abura ebemeresi! Ola ukaimana, nyikamweresa kwa biryo bya bibishirwe, bya bende berika mbu mana. Kanji

구부야. 아나버 마꼬 버다아 아띠파, 무버이 와네 무부야, 무다러가아 어붸머러시 붜뉴 구 뇨노.

14 "시 똬 가찌-가찌 거뉴, 무찌리 먀시 에우마 어라 이다네시미서. 부씨, 구쀠 바쭈 바우마 무 똬보 바 버찌러 바구쀠기라 어먀시 어라 바꽈마 어너어 아가삐리사. 오유 바꽈마, 이워너어 와가삐리사 바꽈기 뿌 아더바아 어바이시라어쀠 버너 바고꽈 어마비. 아무 마비, 과바아 구꺄 어비료 뱌 뱌두똬아 어바시무, 나 구바따 어기리.

15 가찌 구쀠 나 바찌 바우마 무 똬보 바 버찌러 바구쀠기라 어먀시 이비 어라 어바니고꽈에 버찌러 바가삐리사.

16 "러로, 무비뿌가아 구더따 똬 비비 벼뉴. 비다버러 바짜, 어라 뉴마 사 비하삐 비어거, 나바이기라 내쀠서 아부 바쭈 몹부노 보뽀 녀더 똬 부누.

17 "오꽈 워더 마찌, 오빠아 어너 먀시 어무찌마 무부야-부야 아부라 어버머러시! 오꽈 우가이마나, 내가뭐러사 과 비료 뱌 비비씨뤄, 뱌 버러 버리가 뿌 마나. 가찌 네까뭐러사 나 고이 꺄

days of Antipas, my faithful witness, who was put to death in your city--where Satan lives.

14. Nevertheless, I have a few things against you: You have people there who hold to the teaching of Balaam, who taught Balak to entice the Israelites to sin by eating food sacrificed to idols and by committing sexual immorality.

15. Likewise you also have those who hold to the teaching of the Nicolaitans.

16. Repent therefore! Otherwise, I will soon come to you and will fight against them with the sword of my mouth.

17. He who has an ear, let him hear what the Spirit says to the churches. To him who overcomes, I will give some of the hidden manna. I will also give him a white stone with a new name

nyingamweresa na koi lya
muoko-muoko. Na kweri koi,
kwanjikirwe sina liyayaya. Neri
sina, kutalyi chiro na mundju
asibya ola ungalyimenya,
kureka ola baneresaalyi."

무오고-무오고. 나 궈리 고이,
과씨기뤄 시나 뤠야야야. 너리
시나, 구다뤠 찌로 나 무뚀
아시뱌 오꽈 우꺄뤠머냐,
구러가 오꽈 바너러사아뤠."

written on it, known only to
him who receives it.

18. "Uanjikiraa endonyi
weluhu lwa Ongo lwa luthula
mwa musi we Tuwatera mbu:
"Ene myasi, era mweMwana
wa Ongo yiyatengera. Oyu
Mwana, emeho mai mende
mengengenya nga chasi cha
mulyiro. Nemaulu mai mende
malangala na kwengengenya
busese nga miringa era
bakomise mwa kuirenza mwa
mulyiro.

18. "우아씨기라아 어또네
워루후 꽈 오꼬 꽈 루쭈꽈 마
무시 워 두와더라 뿌: "어너
먀시, 어라 뭐마나 와 오꼬
에야더꺼라. 오유 뫄나,
어머호 마이 머떠 머꺼꺼냐
꺄 짜시 짜 무레로. 너마우루
마이 머떠 마꽈꺄꽈 나
궈꺼꺼냐 부서서 꺄 미리꺄
어라 바고미서 꽈 구이러싸
꽈 무레로.

18. "To the angel of the
church in Thyatira write:
These are the words of the
Son of God, whose eyes are
like blazing fire and whose
feet are like burnished
bronze.

19. "Nyishi emyanya yenyu,
nenzii yenyu, nebwemeresi
bwenyu, nemulyimo wenyu,
nebushibirisi bwenyu. Kanji
nyishi kwa bya mwera
mwenjire mwaira, biri binene
kurenza bya mwendee mwaira
lyebere.

19. "네씨 어먀냐 여뉴, 너씨이
여뉴, 너뷔머러시 붜뉴,
너무레모 워뉴, 너부씨비리시
붜뉴. 가씨 네씨 과 뱌 뭐라
뭐씨러 뫄이라, 비리 비너너
구러싸 뱌 뭐떠어 뫄이라
뗘버러.

19. I know your deeds, your
love and faith, your service
and perseverance, and that
you are now doing more
than you did at first.

20. "Si mwa kachi-kachi kenyu,
muchiri mwasi muuma ola
utanyisimise. Bushi mwenjire
mwemerera kuba nola mukasi
mbu iYesebeli, ola wende
wafula ebisha mbu alyi
murebi. Noku, mwa
kukangirisa kwai, enjire
ashiirisa ebaanda banyi mbu

20. "시 꽈 가찌-가찌 거뉴,
무찌리 마시 무우마 오라
우다네시미서. 부씨 뭐씨러
뭐머러라 구바 노꽈 무가시
뿌 이여서버뤠, 오꽈 워떠
와푸꽈 어비싸 뿌 아뤠
무러비. 노구, 꽈 구가꺄리사
과이, 어찌러 아씨이리사
어바아따 바네 뿌 버따아

20. Nevertheless, I have this
against you: You tolerate
that woman Jezebel, who
calls herself a prophetess. By
her teaching she misleads
my servants into sexual
immorality and the eating of
food sacrificed to idols.

bendaa babanda ekiri, na kunde balya ebiryo bya byathulwaa ebasimu.

21. Rero, namurekeraa ebihangi abindjuke kutenga mwolu lusingi lwai, si atanahonda kurekalo.

22. "Bushi noku, nyingamuhunda bulwala bwa bungamuonyera kwa njingo, na kumulosa kwa kasibu. Nabu bandju boshi ba enjire aira nabo olu lusingi, nabo kuika banalyibukire alauma nai, akaba batangabindjuka kutenga mwoyu mwanya wabo mubi.

23. Nyingeta nebana bai, chasiya ebemeresi boshi bamenyerere kwa nyi nyithula nyishi byoshi bya biri mwa michima yebandju, nomwa mianyisa yabo. Bushi chira muuma mu mwabo, nyikamwemba kukulyikana nebya endee aira.

24. "Si mu banji bemeresi bomwa musi we Tuwatera, mubeke mutakulyikiraa emyasi ibi yoyu Yesebeli. Kanji muteshi emyasi era bende berika mbu: ?myasi ibishirwe ya Wamusimu? Rero, chechine chi nababura: ndangachibesa unji musio,

바바따 어기리, 나 구떠 바퍄 어비료 뱌 뱌쭈꽈아 어바시무.

21. 러로, 나무러거라아 어비하삐 아비뉴거 구더따 몰루 루시삐 꽈이, 시 아다나호따 구러가롣.

22. "부씨 노구, 네삐무후따 부꽈꽈 봐 부삐무오녀라 과 찌꼬, 나 구무로사 과 가시부. 나부 바뉴 보씨 바 어찌러 아이라 나보 오루 루시삐, 나보 구이가 바나례부기러 아꽈우마 나이, 아가바 바다삐비뉴가 구더따 모유 먀냐 와보 무비.

23. 네뼈다 너바나 바이, 짜시야 어버머러시 보씨 바머녀러러 과 네 네쭈꽈 네씨 뵤씨 뱌 비리 뫄 미찌마 여바뉴, 노뫄 미아네사 야보. 부씨 찌라 무우마 무 뫄보, 네가뭐빠 구구례가나 너뱌 어떠어 아이라.

24. "시 무 바찌 버머러시 보뫄 무시 워 두와더라, 무버거 무다구례기라아 어먀시 이비 요유 여서버삐. 가찌 무더씨 어먀시 어라 버떠 버리가 뿌: ?먀시 이비씨뤄 야 와무시무? 러로, 쩌찌너 찌 나바부라: 따삐찌버사 우찌 무시오,

21. I have given her time to repent of her immorality, but she is unwilling.

22. So I will cast her on a bed of suffering, and I will make those who commit adultery with her suffer intensely, unless they repent of her ways.

23. I will strike her children dead. Then all the churches will know that I am he who searches hearts and minds, and I will repay each of you according to your deeds.

24. Now I say to the rest of you in Thyatira, to you who do not hold to her teaching and have not learned Satan's so-called deep secrets (I will not impose any other burden on you):

25. si munaendekeraa kusimika mwa myasi era mwachikangirisaa, kuikira mango nyikabaha.

26. "Ola ukaimana, na kuendekera aira ekuhonda kwanyi kuikira kwa businda, nyikamweresa ebuashi bwekwimangira ebandju bembaa soshi.

27 ?Akabemangira mwa kunde abaenza mwa mafi, na kubafungolanga, ngokwa bende bafungoola enyungu sa sikunganyisibwe mwebumba?

28. Rero ola ukaimana, nyikamuwa obu buashi ngokwa Tata ananyeresaabo. Kanji nyikamweresa nengununu era yende yakorera kuikira elumbulyi-mbulyi, bushi aimanyire.

29. "Ola wete matchi, omvaa ene myasi eMuchima Mubuya-buya abura ebemeresi!"

---

25. 시 무나어떠거라아 구시미가 똬 먀시 어라 똬찌가삐리사아, 구이기라 마꼬 네가바하.

26. "오똬 우가이마나, 나 구어떠거라 아이라 어구호따 과내 구이기라 과 부시따, 네가뭐러사 어부아씨 뭐귀마삐라 어바쭈 버빠아 소씨.

27 ?아가버마삐라 똬 구떠 아바어싸 똬 마피, 나 구바푸꼬똬까, 꼬과 버떠 바푸꼬오똬 어뉴우 사 시구까네시뭐 뭐부빠?

28. 러로 오똬 우가이마나, 네가무와 오부 부아씨 꼬과 다다 아나녀러사아보. 가찌 네가뭐러사 너꾸누누 어라 여떠 야고러라 구이기라 어루뿌뤠-뿌뤠, 부씨 아이마네러.

29. "오똬 워더 마찌, 오빠아 어너 먀시 어무찌마 무부야-부야 아부라 어버머러시!"

---

25. Only hold on to what you have until I come.

26. To him who overcomes and does my will to the end, I will give authority over the nations--

27. 'He will rule them with an iron scepter; he will dash them to pieces like pottery'-- just as I have received authority from my Father.

28. I will also give him the morning star.

29. He who has an ear, let him hear what the Spirit says to the churches.

Byaboolyibwa Chikono 3

1. "Uanjikiraa endonyi weluhu lwa Ongo lwa luthula mwa musi we Sariti mbu: "Ene myasi, yatengera era mwola uthula wete era michima erinda era yende yakorera

뱌보오뤠봐 찌고노 3

1. "우아찌기라아 어또네 워루후 똬 오꼬 똬 루쭈똬 똬 무시 워 사리디 뿌: "어너 먀시, 야더떠라 어라 몰똬 우쭈똬 워더 어라 미찌마 어리따 어라 여떠 야고러라

Revelation Chapter 3[NIV]

1. "To the angel of the church in Sardis write: These are the words of him who holds the seven spiritsof God and the seven stars. I know your deeds; you have

Ongo. Kanji iwete nesa ngunu sirinda. Emyasi yoshi mwenjire mwaira, nyiishi. Kanji chiro angaba mbu benjire babatonga mbu mulyi bauma-uma, si mwafire mira.

2. "Muchilanga-langaa! Musimike mwa bwemeresi bwenyu bwa mweshibana, oku bwalyinga kufa loshi. Bushi nyisene kwa bya mwenjire mwaira bitalumirire era muhondo sa Ongo wanyi.

3. Rero, era myasi mwomvaa ba bakangirisa na mwemererai mwa michima yenyu, eyera imundaa mwakengera na kunde mwaithunda. Nebibi byenyu, mundaa mwabindjuka kutenga mubi nekubireka loshi. Bushi akaba mutangachilanga-langa, nyingabaikira chimbate nga mwisi mwa bihangi bya muteshi.

4. "Si chiro bacha, mwa musi we Sariti, muchiri bandju baeke ba batakaa esinga kwa njimba sabo mwa kunde baira emabi. Abola bu beemire kunde batamba nanyi, bembese na njimba sa muoko-muoko.

5. "Rero, ola ukaimana, nai akembasibwa njimba sa

오꼬. 가찌 이워더 너사 우누누 시리따. 어먀시 요씨 뭐찌러 마이라, 네이씨. 가찌 찌로 아까바 뿌 버찌러 바바도꽈 뿌 무레 바우마-우마, 시 뫄피러 미라.

2. "무찌꽈-꽈까아! 무시미거 뫄 뷔머러시 뷔뉴 봐 뭐씨바나, 오구 봐레꽈 구파 로씨. 부씨 네서너 과 뱌 뭐찌러 뫄이라 비다루미리러 어라 무호또 사 오꼬 와니.

3. 러로, 어라 먀시 모빠아 바 바가꺼리사 나 뭐머러라이 뫄 미찌마 여뉴, 어여라 이무따아 뫄거꺼라 나 구떠 마이쭈따. 너비비 벼뉴, 무따아 뫄비뿌가 구더꽈 무비 너구비러가 로씨. 부씨 아가바 무다꽈찌꽈-꽈까, 네꽈바이기라 찌빠더 꽈 뮈시 뫄 비하꼐 뱌 무더씨.

4. "시 찌로 바짜, 뫄 무시 워 사리디, 무찌리 바뿌 바어거 바 바다가아 어시꽈 과 찌빠 사보 뫄 구떠 바이라 어마비. 아보꽈 부 버어미러 구떠 바다빠 나니, 버뻐서 나 찌빠 사 무오고-무오고.

5. "러로, 오라 우가이마나, 나이 아거빠시봐 찌빠 사

a reputation of being alive, but you are dead.

2. Wake up! Strengthen what remains and is about to die, for I have not found your deeds complete in the sight of my God.

3. Remember, therefore, what you have received and heard; obey it, and repent. But if you do not wake up, I will come like a thief, and you will not know at what time I will come to you.

4. Yet you have a few people in Sardis who have not soiled their clothes. They will walk with me, dressed in white, for they are worthy.

5. He who overcomes will, like them, be dressed in

muoko-muoko. Nesina Iyai, ndakasimyeri chiro na hicha mwa chitabo chekalamo. Si nyikateta mbu nyimwishi era muhondo sa Tata, nera muhondo sendonyi sai.

6. "Ola wete matchi, omvaa ene myasi eMuchima Mubuya-buya abura ebemeresi."

7. "Uanjikiraa endonyi weluhu lwa Ongo lwa luthula mwa musi we Filatelifiya mbu: "Ene myasi, yatengera era mwola uthula Mubuya-buya. Kanji iuthula wekanangana, kanji iuthusa nokwa lufunguro lwa mwami Tauti. Akaba angaboola elwisi, kutalyi unji mundju asibya ola ungachingalo. Na akaba angachingalo, kutalyi ola ungaboolalo.

8. "Emyasi yoshi mwenjire mwaira, nyiishi. Kanji nyishi kwa mutathusa misi inene. Si chiro bacha, munachiri mwakulyikira eChinwa chanyi, kanji mutenjire mwanana nesina lyanyi. Mulolaa! Nababoorere elwisi, kutalyi nola ungachiereresa achingalo.

9. "Mumvaa! Kulyi bandju ba bathula mwa bushenge bwa

무오고-무오고. 너시나 꺄이, 따가시며리 찌로 나 히짜 뫄 찌다보 쩌가롸모. 시 네가더다 뿌 네뮈씨 어라 무호또 사 다다, 너라 무호또 서또네 사이.

6. "오롸 워더 마찌, 오빠아 어너 먀시 어무찌마 무부야-부야 아부라 어버머러시."

7. "우아찌기라아 어또네 워루후 꽈 오꼬 꽈 루쭈롸 뫄 무시 워 피롸더뤼피야 뿌: "어너 먀시, 야더뻐라 어라 모롸 우쭈롸 무부야-부야. 가찌 이우쭈롸 워가나나나, 가찌 이우쭈사 노과 루푸꾸로 꽈 뫄미 다우디. 아가바 아꽈보오롸 어뤼시, 구다뤠 우찌 무뿌 아시뱌 오롸 우꽈찌꽈롣. 나 아가바 아꽈찌꽈롣, 구다뤠 오롸 우꽈보오롸롣.

8. "어먀시 요씨 뭐찌러 뫄이라, 네이씨. 가찌 네씨 과 무다쭈사 미시 이너너. 시 찌로 바짜, 무나찌리 뫄구뤠기라 어찌놔 짜네, 가찌 무더띠러 뫄나나 너시나 꺄네. 무롣꽈아! 나바보오러러 어뤼시, 구다뤠 노롸 우꽈쩌러러사 아찌꽈롣.

9. "무빠아! 구뤠 바뚜 바 바쭈롸 뫄 부써뻐 봐

white. I will never blot out his name from the book of life, but will acknowledge his name before my Father and his angels.

6. He who has an ear, let him hear what the Spirit says to the churches.

7. "To the angel of the church in Philadelphia write: These are the words of him who is holy and true, who holds the key of David. What he opens no one can shut, and what he shuts no one can open.

8. I know your deeds. See, I have placed before you an open door that no one can shut. I know that you have little strength, yet you have kept my word and have not denied my name.

9. I will make those who are of the synagogue of Satan,

Wamusimu, kanji bende bachitonga mbu bathula Bayuta, noku bata Bayuta. Rero abu bandju, bu nyingaberesa bakome emafi era muhondo senyu. Aola, bangamenyerera kanangana kwa mwabo, nyithula nyibasimire ngachi.

10. Rero, oku mubeke mwathundaa emyasi era nababuraa kwa mubaa mwa bushibirisi, nanyi nyinganabalanga kwa malyibuko memuereko ma mangaikira ebandju boshi bomwa butala.

11. "Nyiri mu kubaha! Bushi noku, muendekeraa kusimika mwa cha mwete, kungesha kuba mundju ola wabanyaa enzita yenyu yekwimana.

12. "Ola ukaimana, nyikamuira kuba ngulyiro yeluhu lwa Ongo wanyi. Kanji atakanachitengemo chiro na hicha. Kanji nyikamuanjika kwesina lya Ongo wanyi, nelyemusi weYerusalemu iyayaya, ola Ongo akathuma kutenga kwa nguba andaalyira mwa butala. Nesina lyanyi lyiyayaya nalyi, nyikanalyianjika kui.

13. "Ola wete matchi, omvaa

와무시무, 가찌 버떠 바찌도빠뿌 바쭈롸 바유다, 노구 바다 바유다. 러로 아부 바쭈, 부 네빠버러사 바고머 어마피 어라 무호또 서뉴. 아오롸, 바빠머녀러라 가나냐나 과 뫄보, 네쭈롸 네바시미러 빠찌.

10. 러로, 오구 무버거 뫄쭈따아 어먀시 어라 나바부라아 과 무바아 뫄 부씨비리시, 나니 네빠나바롸빠 과 마레부고 머무어러고 마 마빠이기라 어바뿌 보씨 보뫄 부다롸.

11. "네리 무 구바하! 부씨 노구, 무어떠거라아 구시미가 뫄 짜 뭐더, 구뻐싸 구바 무뿌 오롸 와바냐아 어씨다 여뉴 여귀마나.

12. "오롸 우가이마나, 네가무이라 구바 꿔레로 여루후 롸 오꼬 와네. 가찌 아다가나찌더뻐모 찌로 나 히짜. 가찌 네가무아찌가 궈시나 롸 오꼬 와네, 너려무시 워여루사꿔무 이야야야, 오롸 오꼬 아가쭈마구더빠 과 꾸바 아따아레라 뫄 부다롸. 너시나 롸네 레야야야 나레, 네가나레아찌가 구이.

13. "오롸 워더 마찌, 오빠아

who claim to be Jews though they are not, but are liars--I will make them come and fall down at your feet and acknowledge that I have loved you.

10. Since you have kept my command to endure patiently, I will also keep you from the hour of trial that is going to come upon the whole world to test those who live on the earth.

11. I am coming soon. Hold on to what you have, so that no one will take your crown.

12. Him who overcomes I will make a pillar in the temple of my God. Never again will he leave it. I will write on him the name of my God and the name of the city of my God, the new Jerusalem, which is coming down out of heaven from my God; and I will also write on him my new name.

13. He who has an ear, let

ene myasi eMuchima
Mubuya-buya abura
ebemeresi."

14. "Waanjikiraa endonyi
weluhu lwa Ongo lwa luthula
mwa musi weLaotikiya mbu:
"Ene myasi, yatengera era
mwola bende berika
mbu: ?Amina? Oyola, iwatetaa
kanangana era luulu sebya
achiloreraako era mwa Ongo.
Kanji iuthula ndangiriso
yebindju byoshi bya Ongo
abumbaa.

15. "Byoshi bya mwenjire
mwaira, nyibishi. Mwabo,
mutaaha, mutanataata. Rero
mwebi bibiri, kungakomire
muchihowe chiuma.

16. Si bushi mulyi nga meshi
ma chibembere, nyingabahala
mutenge mwa bunu bwanyi.

17. "Mwabo, mwenjire
mwachitonga mbu muthula
baare, mwera mwete na
bikulo binene, mutachilaire na
ku kandju kasibya. Kasi
muteshi kwa mulyi banya,
kanji balaisa, kanji bakene,
kanji bauta, kanji mulyi
butambara!

18. "Rero, eano lya naberesa
lilyeline: mubahaa ene nyiri
muule kwa horo era

어너 먀시 어무찌마 무부야-
부야 아부라 어버머러시."

14. "와아찌기라아 어또네
워루후 똬 오꼬 똬 루쭈똬 마
무시 워똬오디기야 뿌: "어너
먀시, 야더꺼라 어라 모똬
버떠 버리가 뿌: ?아미나?
오요똬, 이와더다아 가나꺼나
어라 루우루 서뱌
아찌로러라라고 어라 마 오꼬.
가찌 이우쭈똬 따꺼리소
여비뚜 뵤씨 뱌 오꼬
아부빠아.

15. "뵤씨 뱌 뭐찌러 먀이라,
네비씨. 뫄보, 무다아하,
무다나다아다. 러로 뭐비
비비리, 구빠고미러 무찌호워
찌우마.

16. 시 부씨 무쪠 꺼 머씨 마
찌버뻐러, 네꺼바하똬 무더꺼
뫄 부누 봐네.

17. "뫄보, 뭐찌러 뫄찌도꺼 뿌
무쭈똬 바아러, 뭐라 뭐더 나
비구론 비너너, 무다찌똬이러
나 구 가뚜 가시뱌. 가시
무더씨 과 무쪠 바냐, 가찌
바똬이사, 가찌 바거너, 가찌
바우다, 가찌 무쪠 부다빠라!

18. "러로, 어아노 똬 나버러사
뤼뤼너: 무바하아 어너 니리
무우뭐 과 호로 어라

him hear what the Spirit
says to the churches.

14. "To the angel of the
church in Laodicea write:
These are the words of the
Amen, the faithful and true
witness, the ruler of God's
creation.

15. I know your deeds, that
you are neither cold nor
hot. I wish you were either
one or the other!

16. So, because you are
lukewarm--neither hot nor
cold--I am about to spit you
out of my mouth.

17. You say, 'I am rich; I
have acquired wealth and
do not need a thing.' But
you do not realize that you
are wretched, pitiful, poor,
blind and naked.

18. I counsel you to buy
from me gold refined in the
fire, so you can become

yakomisibwe mwa mulyiro, mube baare. Muulaa, nenjimba semuoko-muoko, mwembalesi mungesha kunde mwafa honyi bushi nebutambara bwenyu era muhondo sebandju. Chasinda, muulaa nebufumu mububike mwa meho menyu, chasiya munde mwalola.

19. "Ebandju boshi ba nyithula nyisimire, bu neresa eano na kubakemera. Bushi noku, muchisesaa, mubindjuke kutenga mwa bibi byenyu!

20. Rero mumvaa! Kwa lwisi ku nyimenze, nakongota. Na akaba emundju angomva emurenge wanyi, anyiboorere nelwisi, nyingengirira mwa mwai. Chasinda, nyingahangira ebiryo alauma nai.

21. "Ola ukaimana, nyikamweresa eloso lwekwekala alauma nanyi kwa ndebe yanyi yebwami, ngokwa nanyi naimanaa na nekala alauma na Tata kwa ndebe yai yebwami.

22. "Ola wete matchi, omvaa ene myasi eMuchima Mubuya-buya abura ebemeresi."

야고미시붜 뫄 무롈로, 무버 바아러. 무우롸아, 너띠빠 서무오고-무오고, 뭐빠뤄시 무꺼싸 구더 뫄파 호네 부씨 너부다빠라 붜뉴 어라 무호또 서바뉴. 짜시따, 무우롸아 너부푸무 무부비거 뫄 머호 머뉴, 짜시야 무떠 뫄롤롸.

19. "어바뉴 보씨 바 네쭈롸 네시미러, 부 너러사 어아노 나 구바거머라. 부씨 노구, 무찌서사아, 무비뉴거 구더꺄 뫄 비비 벼뉴!

20. 러로 무빠아! 과 뤼시 구 네머써, 나고꼬다. 나 아가바 어무뉴 아꼬빠 어무러어 와네, 아네보오러러 너뤼시, 네꺼께리라 뫄 마이. 짜시따, 네꺄하께라 어비료 아롸우마 나이.

21. "오롸 우가이마나, 네가뭐러사 어로쏘 뤄궈가롸 아롸우마 나네 과 떠버 야네 여봐미, 꼬과 나네 나이마나아 나 너가롸 아롸우마 나 다다 과 떠버 야이 여봐미.

22. "오롸 워더 마찌, 오빠아 어너 먀시 어무찌마 무부야-부야 아부라 어버머러시."

---

rich; and white clothes to wear, so you can cover your shameful nakedness; and salve to put on your eyes, so you can see.

19. Those whom I love I rebuke and discipline. So be earnest, and repent.

20. Here I am! I stand at the door and knock. If anyone hears my voice and opens the door, I will come in and eat with him, and he with me.

21. To him who overcomes, I will give the right to sit with me on my throne, just as I overcame and sat down with my Father on his throne.

22. He who has an ear, let him hear what the Spirit says to the churches."

Byaboolyibwa Chikono 4

1. Era nyuma sebi, nera kuthumbikisa, na nalola kwa nguba kulyi lwisi luuma lwa lubookere. Nera kumva kwola murenge wabaa ulyi nga wa kaperere, anyibura kanji mbu: "Erukira kuno, nyikulose bya bingahuba kuika."

2. Unao-unao, eMuchima Mubuya-buya era kunyandaalyira, nera kulola kwa ndebe yebwami kwa nguba. Kwei ndebe, kwabaa kwekese mundju muuma.

3. Oyu mundju, abaa engengenya nga makoi ma chichiro chinene ma mauhire mwola, kanji mauhire nga chihoho chibishi-bishi. Kanji ei ndebe yabaa isungurwe na mungere ola wabaa walangala busese nga koi lya chichiro chinene.

4. Kanji ei ndebe yabaa isungurwe na sinji ndebe sa bwami makunyabiri nene. Kwesi ndebe nako, kwabaa kwekese bangumwa makunyabiri na bane. Abu bangumwa, babaa bembese njimba sa muoko-muoko, bembese na nzita sa

뱌보오쀄봐 찌고노 4

1. 어라 뉴마 서비, 너라 구쭈뻬기사, 나 나쁘롸 과 우바 구쀄 뤼시 루우마 롸 뤂보오거러. 너라 구빠 곤롸 무러어 와바아 우쀄 까 와 가퍼러러, 아내부라 가찌 뿌: "어루기라 구노, 네구쁘서 뱌 비꺄후바 구이가."

2. 우나오-우나오, 어무찌마 무부야-부야 어라 구냐따아쀄라, 너라 구쁘롸 과 떠버 여봐미 과 우바. 궈이 떠버, 과바아 궈거서 무뿌 무우마.

3. 오유 무뚜, 아바아 어어어냐 까 마고이 마 찌찌로 찌너너 마 마우히러 몰롸, 가찌 마우히러 까 찌호호 찌비씨-비씨. 가찌 어이 떠버 야바아 이수꾸뤄 나 무어러 오롸 와바아 와롸꺄롸 부서서 까 고이 롸 찌찌로 찌너너.

4. 가찌 어이 떠버 야바아 이수꾸뤄 나 시찌 떠버 사 봐미 마구냐비리 너너. 궈시 떠버 나고, 과바아 궈거서 바꾸봐 마구냐비리 나 바너. 아부 바꾸봐, 바바아 버뻐서 끼빠 사 무오고-무오고, 버뻐서 나 씨다 사 시구꺄네시붜 뫄 호로 과

Revelation Chapter 4[NIV]

1. After this I looked, and there before me was a door standing open in heaven. And the voice I had first heard speaking to me like a trumpet said, "Come up here, and I will show you what must take place after this."

2. At once I was in the Spirit, and there before me was a throne in heaven with someone sitting on it.

3. And the one who sat there had the appearance of jasper and carnelian. A rainbow, resembling an emerald, encircled the throne.

4. Surrounding the throne were twenty-four other thrones, and seated on them were twenty-four elders. They were dressed in white and had crowns of gold on their heads.

sikunganyisibwe mwa horo kwa metwe mabo.

머뚸 마보.

5. Mwei ndebe yebwami, mwabaa mwenjire mwatengera thulimya-limya, na mirasano, na mikungulo. Nera muhondo sai, yabaa iri bimore birinda bya byabaa byakorera busese. Ebi bimore, iithula michima erinda era yende yakorera Ongo.

5. 뭐이 떠버 여봐미, 마바아 뭐찌러 마더어라 쭈뤼먀-뤼먀, 나 미라사노, 나 미구우로. 너라 무호또 사이, 야바아 이리 비모러 비리따 뱌 뱌바아 뱌고러라 부서서. 어비 비모러, 이이쭈꽈 미찌마 어리따 어라 여뭐 야고러라 오꼬.

5. From the throne came flashes of lightning, rumblings and peals of thunder. Before the throne, seven lamps were blazing. These are the seven spirits of God.

6. Nera muhondo sei ndebe yebwami, nera kulola ku yabunya nyanja, era yabaa yarenga mwemeho nga chiraulyi. Kanji ei ndebe yebwami, oku yabaa iri mwa kachi-kachi, yabaa isungwirwe na bindju bine bya biri biuma-uma kanji bya kushishasa. Ebi bindju, byabaa byete meho chibere-bere era muhondo nera nyuma.

6. 너라 무호또 서이 떠버 여봐미, 너라 구뤄꽈 구 야부냐 냐짜, 어라 야바아 야러꽈 뭐머호 까 찌라우레. 가찌 어이 떠버 여봐미, 오구 야바아 이리 마 가찌-가찌, 야바아 이수뀌뤄 나 비쭈 비너 뱌 비리 비우마-우마 가찌 뱌 구씨싸사. 어비 비쭈, 뱌바아 벼더 머호 찌버러- 버러 어라 무호또 너라 뉴마.

6. Also before the throne there was what looked like a sea of glass, clear as crystal. In the center, around the throne, were four living creatures, and they were covered with eyes, in front and in back.

7. Echibere-bere mubi, chabaa chiuhire nga ngoromoli. Necha kabiri, chabaa chihuhire nga mbanzi. Necha kahathu, chabaa chete ebuso nga bwa mundju. Necha kane, chabaa chihuhire nga nzu era yauluka.

7. 어찌버러-버러 무비, 짜바아 찌우히러 까 꼬로모뤼. 너짜 가비리, 짜바아 찌후히러 까 빠씨. 너짜 가하쭈, 짜바아 쩌더 어부소 까 봐 무뚜. 너짜 가너, 짜바아 찌후히러 까 누 어라 야우루가.

7. The first living creature was like a lion, the second was like an ox, the third had a face like a man, the fourth was like a flying eagle.

8. Chira chiuma mwebi bindju bine bya biri biuma-uma, chabaa chete bibaba ndathu-ndathu. Nebi bibaba byabaa byehwire kwemeho kwa

8. 찌라 찌우마 뭐비 비쭈 비너 뱌 비리 비우마-우마, 짜바아 쩌더 비바바 따쭈- 따쭈. 너비 비바바 뱌바아 벼휘러 궈머호 과 무오꼬

8. Each of the four living creatures had six wings and was covered with eyes all around, even under his wings. Day and night they

muongo nomwandanda. Ebi bindju kuimba ku byabaa byenjire byanemba emushi nebuthufu mbu: "Enawethu Ongo webuashi boshi, athula Mubuya-buya, athula Mubuya-buya, athula Mubuya-buya! Iwabaa uthula, iunathula, kanji iunachiri ukabaha!"

9. Oyu wekese kwei ndebe yebwami, iunathulao esuku nemango. Nenyimbo sa ebi bindju bine bya biri biuma-uma byende byemba chira chihangi, sinathula sa kumweresa engulu, nethunda, nekumutonga. Rero chira chihangi cha ebi bindju byende byaira bacha,

10. abu bangumwa makunyabiri na bane nabo, bende bera mwa kufukama era muhondo soyu uthulao esuku nemango. Kanji bende baya kuumanga enzita sabo era muhondo sendebe yai, na kuteta mbu:

11. "Enawethu Ongo! Woyo uwemire kunde waya ngulu, weresibwa nethunda, nebuashi, bushi ebindju byoshi bya bithulao, uwasimaa mbu bibaao, wera kuna bibumba."

노마따따. 어비 비뉴 구이빠구 뱌바아 벼찌러 뱌너빠 어무씨 너부후푸 뿌: "어나워쭈 오꼬 워부아씨 보씨, 아쭈롸 무부야-부야, 아쭈롸 무부야-부야, 아쭈롸 무부야-부야! 이와바아 우쭈롸, 이우나쭈롸, 가찌 이우나찌리 우가바하!"

9. 오유 워거서 궈이 떠버 여봐미, 이우나쭈롸오 어수구 너마꼬. 너네뽀 사 어비 비뉴 비너 뱌 비리 비우마-우마 벼떠 벼빠 찌라 찌하끼, 시나쭈롸 사 구뭐러사 어꾸루, 너쭈따, 너구무도까. 러로 찌라 찌하끼 쨔 어비 비뉴 벼떠 뱌이라 바쨔,

10. 아부 바꾸롸 마구냐비리 나 바너 나보, 버떠 버라 롸 구푸가마 어라 무호또 소유 우쭈롸오 어수구 너마꼬. 가찌 버떠 뱌야 구우마까 어씨다 사보 어라 무호또 서떠버 야이, 나 구더다 뿌:

11. "어나워쭈 오꼬! 옷요 우워미러 구떠 와야 꾸루, 워러시봐 너쭈따, 너부아씨, 부씨 어비뉴 보씨 뱌 비쭈롸오, 우와시마아 뿌 비바아오, 워라 구나 비부빠."

never stop saying: "Holy, holy, holy is the Lord God Almighty, who was, and is, and is to come."

9. Whenever the living creatures give glory, honor and thanks to him who sits on the throne and who lives for ever and ever,

10. the twenty-four elders fall down before him who sits on the throne, and worship him who lives for ever and ever. They lay their crowns before the throne and say:

11. "You are worthy, our Lord and God, to receive glory and honor and power, for you created all things, and by your will they were created and have their being."

Byaboolyibwa Chikono 5

1. Chasinda, nera kulola oyu wabaa wekese kwa ndebe yebwami ete ku chibungo cha chitabo mwa mino yai yemalyo. Echi chitabo, chabaa chianjikirwe mwa ndanda nokwa muongo, kanji chabaa chomatanyisibwe kalyinda nekasuku nga thwashe chingesha kuboolyibwa na unji mundju.

2. Nera kulola ku ndonyi muuma ola wabaa wete misi. Oyu ndonyi, abaa abusa na murenge munene mbu: "Ewashe! Echi chibungo chechitabo, nde iwemire kulyikanya aku kasuku ka kaminyirechi kalyinda nga thwashe, aboolechi?"

3. Si kutabaa chiro na mundju asibya ola waala kuboolachi, mbu alole muchi, abe wokwa nguba, nesi womwa butala, nesi wekusimu.

4. Rero, bushi kutabaa chiro na mundju asibya ola wabaa wemire kuboola echi chibungo, na kulolamo, nera kwire nalyira busese.

뱌보오례봐 찌고노 5

1. 짜시따, 너라 구로콰 오유 와바아 워거서 과 떠버 여봐미 어더 구 찌부꼬 짜 찌다보 뫄 미노 야이 여마룐. 어찌 찌다보, 짜바아 찌아찌기뤄 뫄 따따 노과 무오꼬, 가찌 짜바아 쪼마다네시붜 가례따 너가수구 꺄 좌써 찌꺼싸 구보오례봐 나 우찌 무뚜.

2. 너라 구로콰 구 또네 무우마 오라 와바아 워더 미시. 오유 또네, 아바아 아부사 나 무러꺼 무너너 뿌: "어와써! 어찌 찌부꼬 쩌찌다보, 떠 이워미러 구례가냐 아구 가수구 가 가미네러찌 가례따 꺄 좌써, 아보오꿔찌?"

3. 시 구다바아 찌로 나 무뚜 아시뱌 오라 와아롸 구보오롸찌, 뿌 아론뤄 무찌, 아버 옹과 우바, 너시 옹뫄 부다롸, 너시 워구시무.

4. 러로, 부씨 구다바아 찌로 나 무뚜 아시뱌 오라 와바아 워미러 구보오롸 어찌 찌부꼬 나 구로콰모, 너라 귀러 나례라 부서서.

Revelation Chapter 5[NIV]

1. Then I saw in the right hand of him who sat on the throne a scroll with writing on both sides and sealed with seven seals.

2. And I saw a mighty angel proclaiming in a loud voice, "Who is worthy to break the seals and open the scroll?"

3. But no one in heaven or on earth or under the earth could open the scroll or even look inside it.

4. I wept and wept because no one was found who was worthy to open the scroll or look inside.

5. Si muuma mwabu bangumwa, era kunyibura mbu: "Utalyiraa! Ulolaa kwola bende berika mbu: ?Ngoromoli yomwa lubaa lwa Yuta?, kanji ola ushoka mwa chirongo cha mwami Tauti, aimire ebarenda bai mira. Oyola yeine, iunganaala kulyikanya aku kasuku ka kaminyirechi kalyinda nga thwashe, aboolechi."

6. Aola, mwa kachi-kachi kera ndebe yebwami, nera kulola mwemenze Mwana wa Mbulyi. Oyu Mwana weMbulyi abaa asungurwe na bya bindju bine bya biri biuma-uma kanji bya kushishasa, kanji abaa asungurwe na ba bangumwa. Abaa asenekeko ngola ukeribwe. Kanji abaa ete membe malyinda, na meho malyinda. Amu meho, iithula era michima erinda yekwera Ongo, era athumaa mwa butala boshi.

7. Oyu Mwana weMbulyi, era kuya kutola cha chibungo chechitabo. Mwa mino yemalyo yola wabaa wekese kwa ndebe yebwami mu chabaa chiri.

5. 시 무우마 뫄부 바우뫄, 어라 구내부라 뿌: "우다례라아! 우로뢔아 고롸 버떠 버리가 뿌: ?꼬로모푀 요뫄 루바아 롸 유다?, 가찌 오롸 우쏘가 뫄 찌로꼬 짜 뫄미 다우디, 아이미러 어바러따 바이 미라. 오요롸 여이너, 이우꺄나아롸 구례가냐 아구 가수구 가 가미네러찌 가례따 꺄 좌써, 아보오러찌."

6. 아오롸, 뫄 가찌-가찌 거라 떠버 여바미, 너라 구로롸 뭐머써 뫄나 와 뿌례. 오유 뫄나 워뿌례 아바아 아수우뤄 나 뱌 비뿌 비너 뱌 비리 비우마-우마 가찌 뱌 구씨싸사, 가찌 아바아 아수우뤄 나 바 바우뫄. 아바아 아서너거고 꼬롸 우거리붜. 가찌 아바아 어더 머뻐 마례따, 나 머호 마례따. 아무 머호, 이이쭈롸 어라 미찌마 어리따 여궈라 오꼬, 어라 아쭈마아 뫄 부다롸 보씨.

7. 오유 뫄나 워뿌례, 어라 구야 구도롸 짜 찌부꼬 쩌찌다보. 뫄 미노 여마료 요롸 와바아 워거서 과 떠버 여봐미 무 짜바아 찌리.

5. Then one of the elders said to me, "Do not weep! See, the Lion of the tribe of Judah, the Root of David, has triumphed. He is able to open the scroll and its seven seals."

6. Then I saw a Lamb, looking as if it had been slain, standing in the center of the throne, encircled by the four living creatures and the elders. He had seven horns and seven eyes, which are the seven spirits of God sent out into all the earth.

7. He came and took the scroll from the right hand of him who sat on the throne.

8. Abere era atolaachi, unao-unao bya bindju bine bya biri biuma-uma kanji bya kushishasa, alauma na ba bangumwa makunyabiri na bane, boshi kuna kufukama era muhondo sai. Chira muuma mubo abaa ete nzenze, na ngumbu sa sabaa sikunganyisibwe mwa horo, sehwire mu marashi. Amu marashi, mu mathula memo mebandju ba Ongo.

8. 아버러 어라 아도롸아찌, 우나오-우나오 뱌 비쭈 비너 뱌 비리 비우마-우마 가찌 뱌 구씨싸사, 아롸우마 나 바 바웅와 마구냐비리 나 바너, 보씨 구나 구푸가마 어라 무호또 사이. 찌라 무우마 무보 아바아 어더 써써, 나 웅뿌 사 사바아 시구꺄네시붜 와 호로, 서휘러 무 마라씨. 아무 마라씨, 무 마쭐롸 머모 머바쭈 바 오꼬.

8. And when he had taken it, the four living creatures and the twenty-four elders fell down before the Lamb. Each one had a harp and they were holding golden bowls full of incense, which are the prayers of the saints.

9. Abu boshi babaa bembira eMwana weMbulyi lwimbo luyayaya, lwa lutechire mbu: "Woyo, uunemire kutola echi chitabo, na kulyikanya aku kasuku ka kwomatanyisechi, bushi woyo uwakeribwaa. Na kurengera emikira yao, ku wanunuliraa Ongo ebandju, bembaa soshi, nemateta moshi, nenyibuto soshi, nebio byoshi.

9. 아부 보씨 바바아 버삐라 어와나 워뿌뤠 뤼뽀 루야야야, 롸 루더찌러 뿌: "오요, 우우너미러 구도롸 어찌 찌다보, 나 구뤠가냐 아구 가수구 가 꼬마다네서찌, 부씨 오요 우와거리봐아. 나 구러꺼라 어미기라 야오, 구 와누누뤼라아 오꼬 어바쭈, 버빠아 소씨, 너마더다 모씨, 너네부도 소씨, 너비오 뵤씨.

9. And they sang a new song: "You are worthy to take the scroll and to open its seals, because you were slain, and with your blood you purchased men for God from every tribe and language and people and nation.

10. Abu boshi, woyo uwabairire kuba bandju bomwa bwami bwa Ongo wethu, babe bakuhanyi ba kunde bamukorera, na bu bakanalyinda bema kwa bandju boshi bomwa butala."

10. 아부 보씨, 오요 우와바이리러 구바 바쭈 보와 봐미 봐 오꼬 워쭈, 바버 바구하네 바 구떠 바무고러라, 나 부 바가나뤠따 버마 과 바쭈 보씨 보와 부다롸."

10. You have made them to be a kingdom and priests to serve our God, and they will reign on the earth."

11. Chasinda, nera kuhuba kuthumbikisa, na nomva ku mirenge katayamuanjo ya

11. 짜시따, 너라 구후바 구쭈삐기사, 나 노빠 구 미러꺼 가다야무아뇨 야

11. Then I looked and heard the voice of many angels, numbering thousands upon

bandonyi ba babaa basungwire era ndebe yebwami, nebya bindju bine bya biri biuma-uma kanji bya kushishasa, alauma naba bangumwa.

12. Nabo babaa bemba na murenge munene mbu: "eMwana weMbulyi ola wakeribwaa, iwemire kweresibwa ebuashi, nebuare, nebwenge, nemisi, nethunda, nengulu, nekutongibwa!"

13. Nera kuhuba kumva kwa byoshi bya byabumbwaa, bya bithula kwa nguba, na bya bithula mwa butala, na bya bithula ekusimu, na bya bithula mwa nyanja, byemba mbu: "Oyu wekese kwa ndebe yebwami, noyu Mwana weMbulyi, bendaa batongibwa, na kweresibwa ethunda, nengulu, nebuashi, esuku nemango!"

14. Bya bindju bine bya biri biuma-uma kanji bya kushishasa, byomvire bacha, byera kwakula mbu: "Bibe bacha!" Ba bangumwa nabo bera kufukama na batangirisa bera Ongo.

바또니 바 바바아 바수뀌러 어라 떠버 여봐미, 너뱌 비뚜 비너 뱌 비리 비우마-우마 가찌 뱌 구씨싸사, 아꽈우마 나바 바꿔마.

12. 나보 바바아 버빠 나 무러꺼 무너너 뿌: "어마나 워뿌레 오꽈 와거리봐아, 이워미러 궈러시봐 어부아씨, 너부아러, 너붜꺼, 너미시, 너쭈따, 너꿔루, 너구도뎨봐!"

13. 너라 구후바 구빠 과 뵤씨 뱌 뱌부꽈아, 뱌 비쭈꽈 과 꿔바, 나 뱌 비쭈꽈 마 부다꽈, 나 뱌 비쭈꽈 어구시무, 나 뱌 비쭈꽈 마 냐짜, 벼빠 뿌: "오유 워거서 과 떠버 여봐미, 노유 마나 워뿌레, 버따아 바도뎨봐, 나 궈러시봐 어쭈따, 너꿔루, 너부아씨, 어수구 너마꼬!"

14. 뱌 비뿌 비너 뱌 비리 비우마-우마 가찌 뱌 구씨싸사, 뵤뻬러 바짜, 벼라 과구꽈 뿌: "비버 바짜!" 바 바꿔마 나보 버라 구푸가마 나 바다뎨리사 버라 오꼬.

thousands, and ten thousand times ten thousand. They encircled the throne and the living creatures and the elders.

12. In a loud voice they sang: "Worthy is the Lamb, who was slain, to receive power and wealth and wisdom and strength and honor and glory and praise!"

13. Then I heard every creature in heaven and on earth and under the earth and on the sea, and all that is in them, singing: "To him who sits on the throne and to the Lamb be praise and honor and glory and power, for ever and ever!"

14. The four living creatures said, "Amen," and the elders fell down and worshiped.

Byaboolyibwa Chikono 6

1. Chasinda, mwaka kasuku ka kabaa komomatanyise cha chitabo kalyinda nga thwashe, nera kulola kwa Mwana weMbulyi alyikanya ekashe kabere-bere. Kanji nera kumva kwa chiuma mwebya bindju bine bya biri biuma-uma kanji bya kushishasa, chateta na murenge munene ola wabaa ulyi nga mukungulo mbu: "Bahaa!"

2. Mwolu, nera kuthumbikisa, na nalola ku farasi nguma ya muoko-muoko! Nola wabaa ulyi kui, abaa ete butachi mwa mino, bera kumweresa na nzita. Era kuchiuma aya kuimana kanji, noku abaa aimanyire mira.

3. Mango oyu Mwana weMbulyi alyikanyaa ekashe ka kabiri, nera kumva cha chindju cha kabiri cha chiri chiuma-uma kanji cha kushishasa, nachi chateta mbu: "Bahaa!"

4. Unao-unao, kwera kuulukira farasi ya mwola! Nola wabaa ulyi kui, bera kumweresa bombo burerere. Bera kumuwa nebuashi bwekunde ahombanya ebandju mwa

뱌보오쪠봐 찌고노 6

1. 짜시따, 뫄가 가수구 가 가바아 고모마다니서 짜 찌다보 가례따 까 좌써, 너라 구르롸 과 뫄나 워뿌쪠 아쪠가냐 어가써 가버러-버러. 가찌 너라 구빠 과 찌우마 뭐뱌 비뚜 비너 뱌 비리 비우마-우마 가찌 뱌 구씨싸사, 짜더다 나 무러꺼 무너너 오롸 와바아 우쪠 까 무구꾸론 뿌: "바하아!"

2. 모루, 너라 구쭈삐기사, 나 나르롸 구 파라시 우마 야 무오고-무오고! 노롸 와바아 우쪠 구이, 아바아 어더 부다찌 뫄 미노, 버라 구뭐러사 나 씨다. 어라 구찌우마 아야 구이마나 가찌, 노구 아바아 아이마네러 미라.

3. 마꼬 오유 뫄나 워뿌쪠 아쪠가냐아 어가써 가 가비리, 너라 구빠 짜 찌뚜 짜 가비리 짜 찌리 찌우마-우마 가찌 짜 구씨싸사, 나찌 짜더다 뿌: "바하아!"

4. 우나오-우나오, 궈라 구우루기라 파라시 야 모롸! 노롸 와바아 우쪠 구이, 버라 구뭐러사 보뽀 부러러러. 버라 구무와 너부아씨 붜구떠 아호빠냐 어바뚜 뫄 부다롸,

Revelation Chapter 6[NIV]

1. I watched as the Lamb opened the first of the seven seals. Then I heard one of the four living creatures say in a voice like thunder, "Come!"

2. I looked, and there before me was a white horse! Its rider held a bow, and he was given a crown, and he rode out as a conqueror bent on conquest.

3. When the Lamb opened the second seal, I heard the second living creature say, "Come!"

4. Then another horse came out, a fiery red one. Its rider was given power to take peace from the earth and to make men slay each other. To him was given a large

butala, chasiya bende betana.

5. Mango eMwana weMbulyi alyikanyaa ekashe ka kahathu, nera kumva cha chindju cha kahathu cha chiri chiuma-uma kanji cha kushishasa, nachi chateta mbu: "Bahaa!" Abere nathumbikisa, kuna kulola ku farasi irafulu! Nola wabaa ulyi kui, abaa ete chipimo mwa mino.

6. Mwa kachi-kachi kebi bindju bine bya biri biuma-uma kanji bya kushishasa, nera kumva mwatengera wabunya murenge ola wabaa wateta mbu: "Echiro chiuma chebulo, chinafaa ebutea bwa bangemba emundju ku mubisi muuma. Nebiro bihathu byeshano yeshahiri nabi binafaa buteya bwa bangemba emukosi ku mubisi muuma. Si emafuta netifai, byeke utaereresaa wabiumaako!"

7. Mango eMwana weMbulyi alyikanyaa ekashe ka kane, unao-unao nera kumva kwa chindju cha kane cha chiri chiuma-uma kanji cha kushishasa, nachi chateta mbu: "Bahaa!"

짜시야 버떠 버다나.

5. 마꼬 어뫄나 워뿌레 아레가냐아 어가써 가 가하쭈 너라 구빠 짜 찌뉴 짜 가하쭈 짜 찌리 찌우마-우마 가찌 짜 구씨싸사, 나찌 짜더다 뿌: "바하아!" 아버러 나쭈삐기사, 구나 구론롸 구 파라시 이라푸루! 노롸 와바아 우레 구이, 아바아 어더 찌피모 뫄 미노.

6. 뫄 가찌-가찌 거비 비뉴 비너 뱌 비리 비우마-우마 가찌 뱌 구씨싸사, 너라 구빠 뫄더뼈라 와부냐 무러뼈 오롸 와바아 와더다 뿌: "어찌로 찌우마 쩌부르로, 찌나파아 어부더아 봐 바뼈빠 어무뉴 구 무비시 무우마. 너비로 비하쭈 벼싸노 여싸히리 나비 비나파아 부더야 봐 바뼈빠 어무고시 구 무비시 무우마. 시 어마푸다 너디파이, 벼거 우다어러러사아 와비우마아고!"

7. 마꼬 어뫄나 워뿌레 아레가냐아 어가써 가 가너, 우나오-우나오 너라 구빠 과 찌뉴 짜 가너 짜 찌리 찌우마-우마 가찌 짜 구씨싸사, 나찌 짜더다 뿌: "바하아!"

sword.

5. When the Lamb opened the third seal, I heard the third living creature say, "Come!" I looked, and there before me was a black horse! Its rider was holding a pair of scales in his hand.

6. Then I heard what sounded like a voice among the four living creatures, saying, "A quart of wheat for a day's wages, and three quarts of barley for a day's wages, and do not damage the oil and the wine!"

7. When the Lamb opened the fourth seal, I heard the voice of the fourth living creature say, "Come!"

8. Nera kuthumbikisa, unao-unao kuna kulola ku farasi ya lufufu-lufufu! Nola wabaa ulyi kui, esina lyai iwabaa Halufu, na ena kusimu amukulyikire. Abu babiri, bera kweresibwa ebuashi bwekwita chimbi chiuma chekane chebandju boshi ba balyi mwa butala, mwa bombo, nesi nebulyio, nesi mwa malwala ma makalyiire, nesi mwa nyama ngalyi somwerungu.

9. Mango eMwana weMbulyi alyikanyaa ekashe ka katano, unao-unao na nalola kwa michima yebandju ba bafire mira, iri mwa ndanda sekahaha kemithulo. Ei michima, iri yebandju ba bechibwaa bushi neChinwa cha Ongo na bushi nekuteta era luulu sachi.

10. Yabaa yalakanga na murenge munene mbu: "Enawethu, uthula Mubuya-buya, kanji uthula wa kanangana! Rero, ukaendekera walyinjira kuikira mangochi, uchinjibuse, unafune nemikira yethu kwa bandju bomwa butala ba bathwitaa?"

11. Chira muuma mubo, bera kumweresa eropo lya muoko-muoko. Bera kubabura mbu

---

8. 너라 구쭈삐기사, 우나오-우나오 구나 구로롸 구 파라시 야 루푸푸-루푸푸! 노롸 와바아 우레 구이, 어시나 랴이 이와바아 하루푸, 나 어나 구시무 아무구레기러. 아부 바비리, 버라 궈러시봐 어부아씨 붜귀다 찌삐 찌우마 쩌가너 쩌바뉴 보씨 바 바레 뫄 부다롸, 뫄 보뽀, 너시 너부레오, 너시 뫄 마롸롸 마 마가레이러, 너시 뫄 냐마 꺄레 소뭐루우.

9. 마오 어뫄나 워뿌레 아레가냐아 어가써 가 가다노, 우나오-우나오 나 나로롸 과 미찌마 여바뉴 바 바피러 미라, 이리 뫄 따따 서가하하 거미쭈로. 어이 미찌마, 이리 여바뉴 바 버찌봐아 부씨 너찌놔 짜 오꼬 나 부씨 너구더다 어라 루우루 사찌.

10. 야바아 야롸가꺄 나 무러머 무너너 뿌: "어나워쭈, 우쭈롸 무부야-부야, 가찌 우쭈롸 와 가나꺄나! 러로, 우가어더거라 와레찌라 구이기라 마오찌, 우찌찌부서, 우나푸너 너미기라 여쭈 과 바뉴 보뫄 부다롸 바 바쮜다아?"

11. 찌라 무우마 무보, 버라 구뭐러사 어로포 랴 무오고-무오고. 버라 구바부라 뿌

---

8. I looked, and there before me was a pale horse! Its rider was named Death, and Hades was following close behind him. They were given power over a fourth of the earth to kill by sword, famine and plague, and by the wild beasts of the earth.

9. When he opened the fifth seal, I saw under the altar the souls of those who had been slain because of the word of God and the testimony they had maintained.

10. They called out in a loud voice, "How long, Sovereign Lord, holy and true, until you judge the inhabitants of the earth and avenge our blood?"

11. Then each of them was given a white robe, and they were told to wait a little

balyinjiraa hicha tanga, kuikira emuanjo wa bakosi balyikabo na banyakabo ba bachiri bangechibwa ngokwa nabo bechibwaa, alumirire.

12. Chasinda, nera kulola kwoyu Mwana weMbulyi alyikanya ekashe ka ndathu. Unao-unao, mwa butala boshi na mwarenga musisi munene. Esuba lyera kubindjuka lirafulu nga musimya. Nemwesi nao, era kubindjuka mwola nga mikira.

13. Engununu, nasi sera kutowangiranga mwa butala, ngokwa bifuma bya bitasa kwera byende byatowanga kwa muchi wetini mango echusi chikalyiire chende chalyingitanyao.

14. Enguba yera kubungwa-bungwa, ngokwa bende babunga-bunga emukeka, kuna kuirima. Endjulungu soshi, nebisimba byoshi, nabi byera kuna kulyibwa mwa bisiki bithulamo.

15. Mwolu, ebami boshi bomwa butala, nebatambo, nebakulu-kulu bebasula, nebaare, na ba bete ebuashi, nebanji bandju boshi: ethuungu, neba batathula thuungu, boshi bera kuya

바쩨찌라아 히짜 다따, 구이기라 어무아쪼 와 바고시 바쩨가보, 나 바냐가보 바 바찌리 바꺼찌봐 쪼과 나보 버찌봐아, 아루미리러.

12. 짜시따, 너라 구쯘짜 고유 마나 워뿌쩨 아쩨가냐 어가쌔 가 따쭈. 우나오-우나오, 마 부다쫘 보씨 나 마러까 무시시 무너너. 어수바 쪄라 구비쭈가 쫴라푸루 까 무시먀. 너뭐시 나오, 어라 구비쭈가 몰쫘 까 미기라.

13. 어꾸누누, 나시 서라 구도와까라까 마 부다쫘, 쪼과 비푸마 뱌 비다사 궈라 벼버 뱌도와까 과 무찌 워디니 마꼬 어쭈시 찌가쩨이러 쩌떠 짜쩨까다냐오.

14. 어꾸바 여라 구부꽈-부꽈, 쪼과 버떠 바부까-부까 어무거가, 구나 구이리마. 어꾸루꾸 소씨, 너비시빠 뵤씨, 나비 벼라 구나 구쩨봐 쫘 비시기 비쭈쫘모.

15. 몰루, 어바미 보씨 보봐 부다쫘, 너바다뗘, 너바구루-구루 버바수쫘, 너바아러, 나 바 버더 어부아씨, 너바찌 바누 보씨: 어쭈우꾸, 너바 바다쭈쫘 쭈우꾸, 보씨 버라 구야 구찌비싸 마 너구따

longer, until the number of their fellow servants and brothers who were to be killed as they had been was completed.

12. I watched as he opened the sixth seal. There was a great earthquake. The sun turned black like sackcloth made of goat hair, the whole moon turned blood red,

13. and the stars in the sky fell to earth, as late figs drop from a fig tree when shaken by a strong wind.

14. The sky receded like a scroll, rolling up, and every mountain and island was removed from its place.

15. Then the kings of the earth, the princes, the generals, the rich, the mighty, and every slave and every free man hid in caves and among the rocks of the mountains.

kuchibisha mwa nyikunda nomwa birimbi mwa miruko.

노봐 비리삐 봐 미루고.

16. Boshi bera kutangirisa babura endjulungu, nebirimbi mbu: "Muthutowerangaa, muthubishe thungesha kulorekanako mwa meho mwoyu wekese kwa ndebe yebwami, thulame ebusinane bwoyu Mwana weMbulyi!

16. 보씨 버라 구다삐리사 바부라 어쀼루우, 너비리삐 뿌: "무쭈도워라봐아, 무쭈비써 쭈써싸 구로러가나고 봐 머호 모유 워거서 과 떠버 여봐미, 쭈롸머 어부시나너 보유 봐나 워뿌레!

16. They called to the mountains and the rocks, "Fall on us and hide us from the face of him who sits on the throne and from the wrath of the Lamb!

17. Bushi elusuku lunene lwekulosa ebusinane bwabo, lwaikire mira. Kutalyi nola ungaalana nalo."

17. 부씨 어루수구 루너너 뤄구로사 어부시나너 봐보, 롸이기러 미라. 구다레 노롸 우봐아롸나 나르."

17. For the great day of their wrath has come, and who can stand?"

Byaboolyibwa Chikono 7

1. Era nyuma sebi, nera kulola kuba ndonyi bane bemenze kwa nyinda ene sebutala. Babaa bangika echusi cha chatengera kwesi nyinda ene sebutala, chingesha kurenga kwa nyanja, nesi mwa butala, nokwa michi.

2. Nera kulola kwaindji ndonyi yatengera era suba lyende lyaulukira erukira kwa nguba. Abaa ete ekashe ka Ongo ola uthula muuma-uma. Oyu ndonyi, era kulakangira abu balyikabo bane na murenge munene. Abola, bu beresibwaa ebuashi

뱌보오레봐 찌고노 7

1. 어라 뉴마 서비, 너라 구로롸 구바 또니 바너 버머써 과 내따 어너 서부다롸. 바바아 바삐가 어쭈시 짜 짜더써라 궈시 내따 어너 서부다롸, 찌써싸 구러봐 과 냐녀, 너시 봐 부다롸, 노과 미찌.

2. 너라 구로롸 과이찌 또니 야더써라 어라 수바 려너 롸우루기라 어루기라 과 우바. 아바아 어더 어가써 가 오꼬 오롸 우쭈롸 무우마-우마. 오유 또니, 어라 구롸가삐라 아부 바레가보 바너 나 무러써 무너너. 아보롸, 부 버러시봐아 어부아씨

Revelation Chapter 7[NIV]

1. After this I saw four angels standing at the four corners of the earth, holding back the four winds of the earth to prevent any wind from blowing on the land or on the sea or on any tree.

2. Then I saw another angel coming up from the east, having the seal of the living God. He called out in a loud voice to the four angels who had been given power to harm the land and the sea:

bwekukumbya ebutala nenyanja.

3. Era kubabura mbu: "Chacha! Mutafuraa kukumbya ebutala, nenyanja, nemichi thutanasa na kuhuta ekashe kwa malanga mebaanda ba Ongo wethu."

4. Abu baanda ba babaa bahuchirwe kwekashe ka Ongo, nera kumva kwa emuanjo wabo aikire ku bandju byumbi eyana na mane na bane. Abu bandju, mwa mbaa soshi seBaisiraeli mu babaa batengera.

5. Mubo boshi, byumbi ekumi na bibiri babaa bomwa lubuto lwa Yuta, na binji byumbi ekumi na bibiri bomwa lubuto lwa Rubeni, na binji byumbi ekumi na bibiri bomwa lubuto lwa Kati,

6. na binji byumbi ekumi na bibiri bomwa lubuto lwa Aseri, na binji byumbi ekumi na bibiri bomwa lubuto lwa Nafutalyi, na binji byumbi ekumi na bibiri bomwa lubuto lwa Manasi,

7. na binji byumbi ekumi na bibiri bomwa lubuto lwa Simeoni, na binji byumbi ekumi na bibiri bomwa lubuto lwa Lawi, na binji byumbi

뷔구구뺘 어부다롸 너냐짜.

3. 어라 구바부라 뿌: "짜짜! 무다푸라아 구구뺘 어부다롸, 너냐짜, 너미찌 쭈다나사 나 구후다 어가써 과 마롸와 머바아따 바 오꼬 워쭈."

4. 아부 바아따 바 바바아 바후찌뤄 궈가써 가 오꼬, 너라 구뺘 과 어무아쪼 와보 아이기러 구 바뚜 뷰삐 어야나 나 마너 나 바너. 아부 바뚜, 마 빠아 소씨 서바이시라어릐 무 바바아 바더뻐라.

5. 무보 보씨, 뷰삐 어구미 나 비비리 바바아 보뫄 루부도 롸 유다, 나 비찌 뷰삐 어구미 나 비비리 보뫄 루부도 롸 루버니, 나 비찌 뷰삐 어구미 나 비비리 보뫄 루부도 롸 가디,

6. 나 비찌 뷰삐 어구미 나 비비리 보뫄 루부도 롸 아서리, 나 비찌 뷰삐 어구미 나 비비리 보뫄 루부도 롸 나푸다뤠, 나 비찌 뷰삐 어구미 나 비비리 보뫄 루부도 롸 마나시,

7. 나 비찌 뷰삐 어구미 나 비비리 보뫄 루부도 롸 시머오니, 나 비찌 뷰삐 어구미 나 비비리 보뫄 루부도 롸 롸위, 나 비찌 뷰삐

3. "Do not harm the land or the sea or the trees until we put a seal on the foreheads of the servants of our God."

4. Then I heard the number of those who were sealed: 144,000 from all the tribes of Israel.

5. From the tribe of Judah 12,000 were sealed, from the tribe of Reuben 12,000, from the tribe of Gad 12,000,

6. from the tribe of Asher 12,000, from the tribe of Naphtali 12,000, from the tribe of Manasseh 12,000,

7. from the tribe of Simeon 12,000, from the tribe of Levi 12,000, from the tribe of Issachar 12,000,

ekumi na bibiri bomwa lubuto lwa Isakari,

8. na binji byumbi ekumi na bibiri bomwa lubuto lwa Sabuloni, na binji byumbi ekumi na bibiri bomwa lubuto lwa Yosefu, na binji byumbi ekumi na bibiri bomwa lubuto lwa Benyamina. Bandju chibere-bere bemenze era muhondo sendebe ya Ongo

9. Era nyuma sebi, nera kuhuba kuthumbikisa na nalola ku bandju chibere-bere, kutalyi chiro na mundju asibya ola wabaa ungaala kubaanja. Babaa bemenze era muhondo sendebe yebwami, nera muhondo seMwana weMbulyi. Abu bandju, babaa batengera mwa bio byoshi, nomwa mbaa soshi, nomwa nyibuto soshi, nomwa mateta moshi. Babaa bembese maropo ma muoko-muoko, betange na mangarara mwa mino.

10. Bacha ku babaa bateta na murenge munene: "Ebununusi, era mwa Ongo wethu, yibwende bwatenga, ola uthula wekese kwa ndebe yebwami. Kanji bwende bwatenga nera mweMwana weMbulyi!"

어구미 나 비비리 보봐 루부도 롸 이사가리,

8. 나 비찌 뷰뻬 어구미 나 비비리 보봐 루부도 롸 사부로니, 나 비찌 뷰뻬 어구미 나 비비리 보봐 루부도 롸 요서푸, 나 비찌 뷰뻬 어구미 나 비비리 보봐 루부도 롸 버냐미나. 바쭈 찌버러-버러 버머써 어라 무호또 서너버 야 오꼬

9. 어라 뉴마 서비, 너라 구후바 구쭈뻬기사 나 나롤롸 구 바쭈 찌버러-버러, 구다뤠 찌로 나 무뚜 아시뱌 오롸 와바아 우까아롸 구바아짜. 바바아 버머써 어라 무호또 서너버 여봐미, 너라 무호또 서뫄나 워뿌뤠. 아부 바쭈, 바바아 바더꺼라 뫄 비오 뵤씨, 노뫄 빠아 소씨, 노뫄 내부도 소씨, 노뫄 마더다 모씨. 바바아 버뻐서 마로포 마 무오고-무오고, 버다꺼 나 마까라라 뫄 미노.

10. 바짜 구 바바아 바더다 나 무러꺼 무너너: "어부누누시, 어라 뫄 오꼬 워쭈, 에붸너 봐더꽈, 오롸 우쭈롸 워거서 과 떠버 여봐미. 가찌 뷔너 봐더꽈 너라 뭐뫄나 워뿌뤠!"

8. from the tribe of Zebulun 12,000, from the tribe of Joseph 12,000, from the tribe of Benjamin 12,000.

9. After this I looked and there before me was a great multitude that no one could count, from every nation, tribe, people and language, standing before the throne and in front of the Lamb. They were wearing white robes and were holding palm branches in their hands.

10. And they cried out in a loud voice: "Salvation belongs to our God, who sits on the throne, and to the Lamb."

11. Ebandonyi boshi nabo babaa basungwire ei ndebe yebwami, na ba bangumwa, nebya bindju bine bya biri biuma-uma kanji bya kushishasa. Abu bandonyi, bera kufukama kuikira kwana chitaka era muhondo sei ndebe yebwami, bera Ongo mbu:

11. 어바또네 보씨 나보 바바아 바수뮈러 어이 떠버 여봐미, 나 바 바우뫄, 너뱌 비쭈 비너 뱌 비리 비우마-우마 가찌 뱌 구씨싸사. 아부 바또네, 버라 구푸가마 구이기라 과나 찌다가 어라 무호또 서이 떠버 여봐미, 버라 오꼬 뿌:

11. All the angels were standing around the throne and around the elders and the four living creatures. They fell down on their faces before the throne and worshiped God,

12. "Bibe bacha! Ongo wethu, iena ebulangare, nengulu! Kanji iutusa nebwenge! Kanji iwekutongibwa! Kanji ina ena ethunda! Kanji ina ena emisi! Kanji ina ena ebuashi! Kuikira esuku nemango. Bibe bacha!"

12. "비버 바짜! 오꼬 워쭈, 이어나 어부롸꽈러, 너우루! 가찌 이우두사 너붜꿔! 가찌 이워구도꿰봐! 가찌 이나 어나 어쭈따! 가찌 이나 어나 어미시! 가찌 이나 어나 어부아씨! 구이기라 어수구 너마꼬. 비버 바짜!"

12. saying: "Amen! Praise and glory and wisdom and thanks and honor and power and strength be to our God for ever and ever. Amen!"

13. Chasinda mwabu bangumwa, muuma era kunyibusa mbu: "Ewashe! Bano bembese emaropo memuoko-muoko bacha, bu bera bande kasi? Na ngai yi batengera?"

13. 짜시따 뫄부 바우뫄, 무우마 어라 구네부사 뿌: "어와써! 바노 버뻐서 어마로포 머무오고-무오고 바짜, 부 버라 바떠 가시? 나 까이 에 바떠꿔라?"

13. Then one of the elders asked me, "These in white robes—who are they, and where did they come from?"

14. Nanyi mbu: "Ewalyiya, si woyo uungamenya!" Nai era kwire anyibura mbu: "Bano bandju, bu batenga mwa malyibuko masibu. Rero bafulirire emaropo mabo mwa mikira yeMwana weMbulyi. Na chi chathumire maba muoko-muoko bacha.

14. 나니 뿌: "어와꼐야, 시 오요 우우까머냐!" 나이 어라 귀러 아니부라 뿌: "바노 바뚜, 부 바더꽈 뫄 마꼐부고 마시부. 러로 바푸끼리러 어마로포 마보 뫄 미기라 여뫄나 워뿌꼐. 나 찌 짜쭈미러 마바 무오고-무오고 바짜.

14. I answered, "Sir, you know." And he said, "These are they who have come out of the great tribulation; they have washed their robes and made them white in the blood of the Lamb.

15. Kanji echera chi chithumire bemenga era muhondo sendebe yebwami bwa Ongo, na kuendekera bamukorera mwa Luhu lwai emushi nebuthufu. Noyu wekese kwa ndebe yebwami, iungalangabo mwa hema lyai.

16. Batakachife businya, nesi chami. Kanji echuka chesuba chitakachiboche chiro na hicha,

17. bushi oyu Mwana weMbulyi ola ulyi mwa kachi-kachi kendebe yebwami, iukende wabalanga, kanji iukende wabeka era shokororo semeshi ma mende mana ekalamo siri. Ongo nai akabahangula emalyira mabo moshi."

15. 가찌 어쩌라 찌 찌쭈미러 버머빠 어라 무호또 서떠버 여봐미 봐 오꼬, 나 구어떠거라 바무고러라 뫄 루후 롸이 어무씨 너부후푸. 노유 워거서 과 떠버 여봐미, 이우빠롸빠보 뫄 허마 롸이.

16. 바다가찌퍼 부시냐, 너시 짜미. 가찌 어쭈가 쩌수바 찌다가찌보쩌 찌로 나 히짜,

17. 부씨 오유 마나 워뿌레 오롸 우레 뫄 가찌-가찌 거떠버 여봐미, 이우거떠 와바롸빠, 가찌 이우거떠 와바가 어라 쏘고로로 서머씨 마 머떠 마나 어가롸모 시리. 오꼬 나이 아가바하꾸롸 어마레라 마보 모씨."

15. Therefore, "they are before the throne of God and serve him day and night in his temple; and he who sits on the throne will spread his tent over them.

16. Never again will they hunger; never again will they thirst. The sun will not beat upon them, nor any scorching heat.

17. For the Lamb at the center of the throne will be their shepherd; he will lead them to springs of living water. And God will wipe away every tear from their eyes."

Byaboolyibwa Chikono 8

1. Mango eMwana weMbulyi alyikanyaa ekashe ka kalyinda, kwa nguba na kwaba "pii" ku bihangi bingaika ku chimbi cha saa nguma.

2. Kanji nera kuhuba kulola kwa bandonyi balyinda ba bende bemanga era muhondo sa Ongo. Bera kweresibwa

뱌보오레봐 찌고노 8

1. 마꼬 어뫄나 워뿌레 아레가냐아 어가써 가 가레따, 과 우바 나 과바 "피이" 구 비하삐 비빠이가 구 찌뻬 짜 사아 우마.

2. 가찌 너라 구후바 구로롸 과 바또네 바레따 바 버떠 버마빠 어라 무호또 사 오꼬. 버라 궈러시봐 쭈퍼러러

Revelation Chapter 8[NIV]

1. When he opened the seventh seal, there was silence in heaven for about half an hour.

2. And I saw the seven angels who stand before God, and to them were given seven trumpets.

thuperere thulyinda.

3. Chasinda, undji ndonyi muuma era kubaha ete ngumbu era ikunganyisibwe mwa horo. Era kuya kwimanga era muhondo sendebe ya Ongo, ofu nekahaha kemithulo, ka kabaa kakunganyisibwe mwa horo. Bera kumweresa marashi manene, ocheremo kwako kahaha amathule Ongo, mabere alauma nememo mebandju boshi ba Ongo.

4. Emusi wamu marashi alauma nememo mebandju ba Ongo, kuna kutenga mwa mino soyu ndonyi, na byerukira era mwa Ongo.

5. Era nyuma sebi, kanji oyu ndonyi era kutola mulyiro kwako kahaha, era kwehusao mwei ngumbu. Chasinda, era kuumao mwa butala. Unao-unao, ethulimya-limya kuna kurenga, nemirasano, nemikungulo, alauma nemusisi.

6. Abu bandonyi balyinda ba babaa bete thwa thuperere thulyinda, bera kuchikunganya babande muto.

7. Mango endonyi mubere-bere abandaa mwa kai, unao-unao mwa butala mwera

---

쭈쩨따.

3. 짜시따, 우찌 또네 무우마 어라 구바하 어더 꾸뿌 어라 이구까네시붜 똬 호로. 어라 구야 귀마까 어라 무호또 서뻐버 야 오꼬, 오푸 너가하하 거미쭈롣, 가 가바아 가구까네시붜 똬 호로. 버라 구뭐러사 마라씨 마너너, 오쩌러모 과고 가하하 아마쭈뤄 오꼬, 마버러 아쩨우마 너머모 머바뉴 보씨 바 오꼬.

4. 어무시 와무 마라씨 아쩨우마 너머모 머바뉴 바 오꼬, 구나 구더까 똬 미노 소유 또네, 나 벼루기라 어라 똬 오꼬.

5. 어라 뉴마 서비, 가찌 오유 또네 어라 구도똬 무쩨로 과고 가하하, 어라 궈후사오 뭐이 꾸뿌. 짜시따, 어라 구우마오 똬 부다똬. 우나오-우나오, 어쭈쮜먀-쮜먀 구나 구러까, 너미라사노, 너미구꾸롣, 아쩨우마 너무시시.

6. 아부 바또네 바쩨따 바 바바아 버더 똬 쭈퍼러러 쭈쩨따, 버라 구찌구까냐 바바떠 무도.

7. 마꼬 어또네 무버러-버러 아바따아 똬 가이, 우나오-우나오 똬 부다똬 뭐라

---

3. Another angel, who had a golden censer, came and stood at the altar. He was given much incense to offer, with the prayers of all the saints, on the golden altar before the throne.

4. The smoke of the incense, together with the prayers of the saints, went up before God from the angel's hand.

5. Then the angel took the censer, filled it with fire from the altar, and hurled it on the earth; and there came peals of thunder, rumblings, flashes of lightning and an earthquake.

6. Then the seven angels who had the seven trumpets prepared to sound them.

7. The first angel sounded his trumpet, and there came hail and fire mixed with

kutowera mvula ya luthwa na mulyiro ola uhoonganyire nemikira. Mwolu, ola mulyiro kuna kusiresa chimbi chiuma chekahathu chebutala, na kukumbya emichi, nebichi bibishi.

8. Chasinda, endonyi wa kabiri nai, era kubanda mwa kai kaperere. Abere era abandaa muko, kwera kulorekanako chindju chiuma cha chiri nga ndjulungu inene, cha chabunga nga mulyiro. Cha chindju, kuna kuumwa mwa nyanja. Unao-unao, chimbi chiuma chekahathu chei nyanja kuna kubindjuka mikira.

9. Na mwechi chimbi chenyanja, ebindju byoshi kuna kusika. Nemashuwa moshi namo kuna kukumba.

10. Mango endonyi wa kahathu nai abandaa mwa kai kaperere, kwa nguba kwera kutowa ngununu inene, era yabaa yakorera nga chimore. Era ngununu, kuna kutowera ku chimbi chiuma chekahathu chenyishi, necheshokororo.

11. Nesina lyei ngununu, iyabaa "Kalulu". Mwolu, chimbi chiuma chekahathu chesi

구도워라 뿌꽈 야 루좌 나 무쩨로 오꽈 우호오까네러 너미기라. 모루, 오꽈 무쩨로 구나 구시러사 찌삐 찌우마 쩌가하쭈 쩌부다꽈, 나 구구뺘 어미찌, 너비찌 비비씨.

8. 짜시따, 어또네 와 가비리 나이, 어라 구바따 뫄 가이 가퍼러러. 아버러 어라 아바따아 무고, 궈라 구르러가나고 찌뿌 찌우마 짜 찌리 꺄 뚜루우 이너너, 짜 짜부꺄 꺄 무쩨로. 짜 찌뿌, 구나 구우뫄 뫄 냐자. 우나오-우나오, 찌삐 찌우마 쩌가하쭈 쩌이 냐짜 구나 구비뿌가 미기라.

9. 나 뭐찌 찌삐 쩌냐짜, 어비뿌 뵤씨 구나 구시가. 너마쑤와 모씨 나모 구나 구구뺘.

10. 마꼬 어또네 와 가하쭈 나이 아바따아 뫄 가이 가퍼러러, 과 꾸바 궈라 구도와 꾸누누 이너너, 어라 야바아 야고러라 꺄 찌모러. 어라 꾸누누, 구나 구도워라 구 찌삐 찌우마 쩌가하쭈 쩌네씨, 너쩌쏘고로로.

11. 너시나 쪄이 꾸누누, 이야바아 "가루루". 모루, 찌삐 찌우마 쩌가하쭈 쩌시 네씨,

blood, and it was hurled down upon the earth. A third of the earth was burned up, a third of the trees were burned up, and all the green grass was burned up.

8. The second angel sounded his trumpet, and something like a huge mountain, all ablaze, was thrown into the sea. A third of the sea turned into blood,

9. a third of the living creatures in the sea died, and a third of the ships were destroyed.

10. The third angel sounded his trumpet, and a great star, blazing like a torch, fell from the sky on a third of the rivers and on the springs of water--

11. the name of the star is Wormwood. A third of the waters turned bitter, and

nyishi, unao-unao kuna kutangirisa salula. Bandju banene ba bendee bamwa kwa meshi masi, bera kunde bafanga bushi mabaa mera malula.

12. Mango endonyi wa kane nai abandaa mwa kai kaperere, unao-unao chimbi chiuma chekahathu chesuba, kuna kuukulyirwa. Bushi noku, chimbi chiuma chekahathu chemushi, chera kunalyinda chaina ebulangare. Na chimbi chiuma chekahathu chemwesi, nechengununu, nabi byera kuna ukulyirwa. Rero, chimbi chiuma chekahathu chebuthufu, nachi chera kunalyinda chaina ebulangare.

13. Abere nyinachiri nathumbikisa, nera kumva nzu nguma yauluka mwa byanya bibiri. Ei nzu, yabaa yateta na murenge munene mbu: "Buanya! Buanya! Bungaba buanya kwa bandju boshi ba bathula mwa butala, mango abu banji bandonyi bahathu ba beshiba, nabo bangabanda mwa thwabo thuperere!"

우나오-우나오 구나 구다삐리사 사루쫘. 바뚜 바너녀 바 버떠어 바뫄 과 머씨 마시, 버라 구떠 바파꽈 부씨 마바아 머라 마루쫘.

12. 마꼬 어또네 와 가너 나이 아바따아 뫄 가이 가퍼러러, 우나오-우나오 찌뻬 찌우마 쩌가하쭈 쩌수바, 구나 구우구쿠레롸. 부씨 노구, 찌뻬 찌우마 쩌가하쭈 쩌무씨, 쩌라 구나쿠레따 짜이나 어부쫘꽈러. 나 찌뻬 찌우마 쩌가하쭈 쩌뭐시, 너쩌꾸누누, 나비 벼라 구나 우구쿠레롸. 러로, 찌뻬 찌우마 쩌가하쭈 쩌부후푸, 나찌 쩌라 구나쿠레따 짜이나 어부쫘꽈러.

13. 아버러 네나찌리 나쭈뻬기사, 너라 구빠 누 우마 야우루가 뫄 뱌냐 비비리. 어이 누, 야바아 야더다 나 무러꺼 무너너 뿌: "부아냐! 부아냐! 부꽈바 부아냐 과 바쭈 보씨 바 바쭈롸 뫄 부다쫘, 마꼬 아부 바찌 바또네 바하쭈 바 버씨바, 나보 바꽈바따 뫄 쫘보 쭈퍼러러!"

many people died from the waters that had become bitter.

12. The fourth angel sounded his trumpet, and a third of the sun was struck, a third of the moon, and a third of the stars, so that a third of them turned dark. A third of the day was without light, and also a third of the night.

13. As I watched, I heard an eagle that was flying in midair call out in a loud voice: "Woe! Woe! Woe to the inhabitants of the earth, because of the trumpet blasts about to be sounded by the other three angels!"

Byaboolyibwa Chikono 9

1. Mango endonyi wa katano

뱌보오쿠례봐 찌고노 9

1. 마꼬 어또네 와 가다노

Revelation Chapter 9[NIV]

1. The fifth angel sounded

nai abandaa mwa kai kaperere, unao-unao kuna kulola ku ngunuu nguma era yabaa yatengera kwa nguba yatowera mwa butala. Bera kweresai elufunguro lwekuboola efumbi irerere yekusimu.

2. Wangununu, mango aboolaa ei fumbi, unao-unao mwera kutenga musi munene, ola wabaa ulyi nga musi wa luira. Oyu musi, era kwangika esuba nenguba bitachilomekera ebutala.

3. Mwoyu musi, mwera kuulukira myuuku, na yahandabana mwa butala. Ei myuku, bera kweresai ebuashi bwekunde yakomotola nga nguthu.

4. Bera kuburai mbu itakumbyaa chiro na chichi chisibya, nesi muchi asibya, nesi mwaka asibya. Si inatabalyiraa ebandju ba batahuchirwe kwekashe ka Ongo era malanga.

5. Kanji iteresibwaa eloso lwekunde yeta abu bandju, si indaa yanabalyibusa busese ku myesi etano oshao. Nebandju ba bangende bakomotolyibwa nei myuuku, bangende bomva emalumwa

나이 아바따아 뫄 가이 가퍼러러, 우나오-우나오 구나 구로롸 구 꾸누누 꾸마 어라 야바아 야더꺼라 과 꾸바 야도워라 뫄 부다롸. 버라 궈러사이 어루푸꾸로 뤄구보오롸 어푸삐 이러러러 여구시무.

2. 와꾸누누, 마꼬 아보오롸아 어이 푸삐, 우나오-우나오 뭐라 구더꺼 무시 무너너, 오롸 와바아 우레 꺼 무시 와 루이라. 오유 무시, 어라 과끼가 어수바 너꾸바 비다찌로머거라 어부다롸.

3. 모유 무시, 뭐라 구우루기라 무유우구, 나 야하따바나 뫄 부다롸. 어이 무유구, 버라 궈러사이 어부아씨 뭐구떠 야고모도롸 꺼 꾸쭈.

4. 버라 구부라이 뿌 이다구빠아 찌로 나 찌찌 찌시뱌, 너시 무찌 아시뱌, 너시 뫄가 아시뱌. 시 이나다바레라아 어바꾸 바 바다후찌뤄 궈가써 가 오꼬 어라 마롸꺼.

5. 가찌 이더러시봐아 어로소 뤄구떠 여다 아부 바꾸, 시 이따아 야나바레부사 부서서 구 며시 어다노 오싸오. 너바꾸 바 바꺼더 바고모도레봐 너이 무유우구, 바꺼더 보빠 어마루봐 꼬과

his trumpet, and I saw a star that had fallen from the sky to the earth. The star was given the key to the shaft of the Abyss.

2. When he opened the Abyss, smoke rose from it like the smoke from a gigantic furnace. The sun and sky were darkened by the smoke from the Abyss.

3. And out of the smoke locusts came down upon the earth and were given power like that of scorpions of the earth.

4. They were told not to harm the grass of the earth or any plant or tree, but only those people who did not have the seal of God on their foreheads.

5. They were not given power to kill them, but only to torture them for five months. And the agony they suffered was like that of the sting of a scorpion when it strikes a man.

ngokwa nguthu yende
yanakomotola emundju.

6. Rero kwei myesi etano,
ebandju bangende bahonda
walufu, si batangende
bamulolako. Kanji bangende
bahonda bachifire, si walufu
angende abahaa.

7. Ei myuuku, yabaa ihuhire
nga farasi, sa sakunganyisibwe
mira siye kwa bita. Nokwa
mithwe yeyi myuuku, kwabaa
kulyi bindju bya biri nga nzita
sa sikunganyisibwe mwa horo.
Nebuso bwai, bwabaa bulyi
nga bwa bandju.

8. Nemviri sai, sabaa siri nga
sa bakasi. Nemeno mai,
mabaa malyi nga meno ma
ngoromolyi.

9. Nomwa bifuba byai, yabaa
yembese bindju bya biri nga
mbenzi sa sikunganyisibwe
mwa chuma. Mango yendee
yahaanya ebibaba byai,
kwendee komvikala sindo sa
siri nga sa farasi sinene sa
sakulula mithukalyi,
salyibichira kwa bita.

10. Ei myuuku, yabaa yete
misemba era iri nga ya
nguthu. Rero mwei misemba,
mu yabaa yenjire
yakomaulyira ebandju. Kanji

우쭈 여떠 야나고모도롸
어무뚜.

6. 러로 궈이 며시 어다노,
어바뚜 바꺼떠 바호따 와루푸,
시 바다꺼떠 바무롣롸고. 가찌
바꺼떠 바호따 바찌피러, 시
와루푸 아꺼떠 아바하아.

7. 어이 무유우구, 야바아
이후히러 까 파라시, 사
사구까네시붜 미라 시여 과
비다. 노과 미쭤 여에
무유우구, 과바아 구레 비뚜
뱌 비리 까 씨다 사
시구까네시붜 마 호로. 너부소
봐이, 봐바아 부레 까 봐
바뚜.

8. 너뻐리 사이, 사바아 시리
까 사 바가시. 너머노 마이,
마바아 마레 까 머노 마
으로모레.

9. 노콰 비푸바 뱌이, 야바아
여꺼서 비뚜 뱌 비리 까 뻐씨
사 시구까네시붜 마 쭈마.
마으 여떠어 야하아냐
어비바바 뱌이, 궈떠어
고뻬가롸 시또 사 시리 까 사
파라시 시너너 사 사구루롸
미쭈가레, 사레비찌라 과
비다.

10. 어이 무유우구, 야바아
여더 미서빠 어라 이리 까 야
우쭈. 러로 뭐이 미서빠, 무
야바아 여찌러 야고마우레라
어바뚜. 가찌 뭐이 미서빠,

6. During those days men
will seek death, but will not
find it; they will long to die,
but death will elude them.

7. The locusts looked like
horses prepared for battle.
On their heads they wore
something like crowns of
gold, and their faces
resembled human faces.

8. Their hair was like
women's hair, and their
teeth were like lions' teeth.

9. They had breastplates like
breastplates of iron, and the
sound of their wings was
like the thundering of many
horses and chariots rushing
into battle.

10. They had tails and stings
like scorpions, and in their
tails they had power to
torment people for five
months.

mwei misemba, mwebuashi bwekulyibusa ebandju kwei myesi etano bwendee bwatengera.

11. Nola ndonyi wabaa wemangirire era fumbi irerere yekusimu, iwabaa mwami wei myuuku. Nesina lyai mwa Chieburaniya i Abitani, nomwa Chikiriki i Apoliyoni, kukuteta mbu "Mukumbya."

12. Rero amu malyibuko mabere-bere, ku marengaa bacha. Kanji mumvaa! Era nyuma samo, kuchiri kungaika manji mabiri.

13. Chasinda, endonyi wa ndathu, nai era kubanda mwa kai kaperere. Nera kumva murenge muuma atengera kwa membe ma mabaa malyi kwa pembe ene sako kahaha kemithulo. Ako kahaha, kabaa kakunganyisibwe mwa horo, kalyi era muhondo sa Ongo.

14. Oyu murenge, era kubura oyu ndonyi wandathu, wabaa wete ekaperere mbu: "Abu bandonyi bane baminyirirwe kwa musike selwishi lunene lweFurati, uboolabo."

15. Unao-unao, ba bandonyi bane kuna kuboolyibwa, bushi babaa bakunganyisibwe mira

뭐부아씨 붜구뤠부사 어바쭈 궈이 며시 어다노 붜떠어 봐더꺼라.

11. 노롸 또네 와바아 워마삐리러 어라 푸삐 이러러러 여구시무, 이와바아 꺄미 워이 무유우구. 너시나 꺄이 마 쩌부라니야 이 아비다니, 노롸 찌기리기 이 아포쀠요니, 구구더다 뿌 "무구뺘."

12. 러로 아무 마뤠부고 마버러-버러, 구 마러꺄아 바짜. 가찌 무빠아! 어라 뉴마 사모, 구찌리 구꺄이가 마찌 마비리.

13. 짜시따, 어또네 와 따쭈, 나이 어라 구바따 마 가이 가퍼러러. 너라 구빠 무러꺼 무우마 아더꺼라 과 머뻬 마 마바아 마뤠 과 퍼뻬 어너 사고 가하하 거미쭈룬. 아고 가하하, 가바아 가구꺄네시붜 뫄 호로, 가뤠 어라 무호또 사 오꼬.

14. 오유 무러꺼, 어라 구부라 오유 또네 와따쭈, 와바아 워더 어가퍼러러 뿌: "아부 바또네 바너 바미니리뤄 과 무시거 서쀠씨 루너너 뤄푸라디, 우보오롸보."

15. 우나오-우나오, 바 바또네 바너 구나 구보오쀄봐, 부씨 바바아 바구꺄네시붜 미라 과

11. They had as king over them the angel of the Abyss, whose name in Hebrew is Abaddon, and in Greek, Apollyon.

12. The first woe is past; two other woes are yet to come.

13. The sixth angel sounded his trumpet, and I heard a voice coming from the horns of the golden altar that is before God.

14. It said to the sixth angel who had the trumpet, "Release the four angels who are bound at the great river Euphrates."

15. And the four angels who had been kept ready for this very hour and day and

kwa kwita chimbi chiuma chekahathu chebandju boshi, mwechi chihangi chinechi, na mwolu lusuku lunolu, na mwoyu mwesi inoyu, na mwoyu mwaka inoyu.

16. Nera kumva banyibura mbu emuanjo webasula ba bende balwa balyi kwa farasi, alyi miriyoni maana mabiri.

17. Rero mwebi byabunya biroto, mu naloreraa kwabu basula boshi, nesi farasi babaa balyiko. Abu basula, babaa bete mbenzi sa mwola sa siri nga byasi bya mulyiro, kanji sa kanyiki, kanji sa muhombo nga chibirichi. Emithwe yesi farasi yabaa iri nga ya ngoromolyi. Nomwa bunu bwasi, mwabaa mwatenganga mulyiro, na musi, na ngunye-kunye sa chibirichi.

18. Mano malyibuko mahathu: mulyiro, nemusi, nengunye-kunye sechibirichi, mera kunalyinda meta chimbi chiuma chekahathu chebandju boshi.

19. Byabaa bacha, bushi esi farasi, ebuashi bwasi, mwa bunu nomwa misemba mu bwabaa bulyi. Bushi ei misemba, nai yabaa iri nga njoka, yete na mithwe era

귀다 찌삐 찌우마 쩌가하쭈 쩌바뉴 보씨, 뭐찌 찌하삐 찌너찌, 나 모루 루수구 루노루, 나 모유 뭐시 이노유, 나 모유 뫄가 이노유.

16. 너라 구빠 바네부라 뿌 어무아쬬 워바수롸 바 버떠 바롸 바레과 파라시, 아레 미리요니 마아나 마비리.

17. 러로 뭐비 뱌부냐 비로도, 무 나롤러라아 과부 바수롸 보씨, 너시 파라시 바바아 바레고. 아부 바수롸, 바바아 버더 뻐씨 사 모롸 사 시리 롸 뱌시 뱌 무쩨로, 가찌 사 가네기, 가찌 사 무호뽀 롸 찌비리찌. 어미쭤 여시 파라시 야바아 이리 롸 야 꼬로모레. 노뫄 부누 봐시, 뫄바아 뫄더롸롸 무쩨로, 나 무시, 나 우녀-구녀 사 찌비리찌.

18. 마노 마레부고 마하쭈: 무쩨로, 너무시, 너우녀-구녀 서찌비리찌, 머라 구나레따 머다 찌삐 찌우마 쩌가하쭈 쩌바뉴 보씨.

19. 뱌바아 바짜, 부씨 어시 파라시, 어부아씨 봐시, 뫄 부누 노뫄 미서빠 무 봐바아 부레. 부씨 어이 미서빠, 나이 야바아 이리 롸 쪼가, 여더 나 미쭤 어라 야바아 여찌러

month and year were released to kill a third of mankind.

16. The number of the mounted troops was two hundred million. I heard their number.

17. The horses and riders I saw in my vision looked like this: Their breastplates were fiery red, dark blue, and yellow as sulfur. The heads of the horses resembled the heads of lions, and out of their mouths came fire, smoke and sulfur.

18. A third of mankind was killed by the three plagues of fire, smoke and sulfur that came out of their mouths.

19. The power of the horses was in their mouths and in their tails; for their tails were like snakes, having heads with which they inflict injury.

yabaa yenjire yakomotola mwebandju.

20. Ebandju ba bashibaa, chiro angaba mbu beke batafaa mwamu malyibuko, batarekaa kunde bera ebasimu, na kwera ebihuhanyi bya beine bachikunganyisaa mwa horo, nomwa bichere byebuteya, nomwa miringa, nomwa makoi, nomwa michi. Noku ebi bihuhanyi byabo, bitalola, bitanomva, bitanaenda.

21. Abu bandju, chiro batanarekaa ebibi byabo byebwichi, nesi byebulosi, nesi byelusingi, nesi byebwisi.

야고모도롸 뭐바뚜.

20. 어바뚜 바 바씨바아, 찌로 아까바 뿌 버거 바다파아 롸무 마례부고, 바다러가아 구떠 버라 어바시무, 나 궈라 어비후하니 뱌 버이너 바찌구까네사아 롸 호로, 노롸 비쩌러 벼부더야, 노롸 미리까, 노롸 마고이, 노롸 미찌. 노구 어비 비후하니 뱌보, 비다로롸, 비다노빠, 비다나어따.

21. 아부 바뚜, 찌로 바다나러가아 어비비 뱌보 벼뷔찌, 너시 벼부로시, 너시 벼루시끼, 너시 벼뷔시.

20. The rest of mankind that were not killed by these plagues still did not repent of the work of their hands; they did not stop worshiping demons, and idols of gold, silver, bronze, stone and wood--idols that cannot see or hear or walk.

21. Nor did they repent of their murders, their magic arts, their sexual immorality or their thefts.

Byaboolyibwa Chikono 10

1. Era nyuma sebi, nera kulola ku unji ndonyi ola wete buashi, atenga kwa nguba. Oyu ndonyi, elumbumbu lwabaa lumusungwire, nemungere abaa asungwire ethwe lyai. Nebuso bwai, bwabaa bwalangala ngesuba. Nemaulu mai mabaa malyi nga ngulyiro sa mulyiro.

2. Nomwa mino yai, mwabaa mulyi kachibungo ka chitabo kaeke ka kabaa kaboolyibwe. Era kubika ekuulu kwai

뱌보오풰봐 찌고노 10

1. 어라 뉴마 서비, 너라 구론롸 구 우씨 또네 오롸 워더 부아씨, 아더까 과 우바. 오유 또네, 어루뿌뿌 롸바아 루무수뉘러, 너무꺼러 아바아 아수뉘러 어쮀 랴이. 너부소 봐이, 봐바아 봐롸까롸 꺼수바. 너마우루 마이 마바아 마례 까 우풰로 사 무풰로.

2. 노롸 미노 야이, 롸바아 무풰 가찌부꼬 가 찌다보 가어거 가 가바아 가보오풰붜. 어라 구비가 어구우루 과이

Revelation Chapter 10[NIV]

1. Then I saw another mighty angel coming down from heaven. He was robed in a cloud, with a rainbow above his head; his face was like the sun, and his legs were like fiery pillars.

2. He was holding a little scroll, which lay open in his hand. He planted his right foot on the sea and his left

kwemalyo kwa nyanja, nekwemarembe, kwa chio.

궈마룬 과 냐짜, 너궈마러뻐, 과 찌오.

foot on the land,

3. Chasinda, era kulakanga na murenge munene ola ulyi nga mururomo wa ngoromolyi. Abere era alakangaa, nera kumva mikungulo ya mirasano erinda yateta.

3. 짜시따, 어라 구꽈가꽈 나 무러뻐 무너너 오꽈 우레 꽈 무루로모 와 꼬로모레. 아버러 어라 아꽈가꽈아, 너라 구빠 미구꾸룬 야 미라사노 어리따 야더다.

3. and he gave a loud shout like the roar of a lion. When he shouted, the voices of the seven thunders spoke.

4. Mango ei mikungulo yabaa yera yatetaa, nera kuhonda kwanjika bya yabaa yateta. Si unao-unao, kuna kumva unji murenge atenga kwa nguba, na anyibura mbu: "Emyasi era ei mikungulo erinda yera kuteta, utaanjikaai, si uibishaa mwa muchima."

4. 마꼬 어이 미구꾸룬 야바아 여라 야더다아, 너라 구호따 과씨가 뱌 야바아 야더다. 시 우나오-우나오, 구나 구빠 우씨 무러뻐 아더꽈 과 꾸바, 나 아네부라 뿌: "어먀시 어라 어이 미구꾸룬 어리따 여라 구더다, 우다아찌가아이, 시 우이비싸아 뫄 무찌마."

4. And when the seven thunders spoke, I was about to write; but I heard a voice from heaven say, "Seal up what the seven thunders have said and do not write it down."

5. Mwolu, ola ndonyi nalolaako emenze kwa nyanja nokwa chio, era kwemusa emino yai yemalyo mwa chanya,

5. 모루, 오꽈 또니 나로꽈아고 어머써 과 냐짜 노과 찌오, 어라 궈무사 어미노 야이 여마룬 뫄 짜냐,

5. Then the angel I had seen standing on the sea and on the land raised his right hand to heaven.

6. na alaisa kwesina lya Ongo. Oyu Ongo, iuthulao esuku nemango, kanji iwabumbaa enguba nebutala, nenyanja, na byoshi bya bithulamo. Oyu ndonyi, era kuteta mbu: "Kutachiri bihangi bya kulyinjira!

6. 나 아꽈이사 궈시나 꽈 오꼬. 오유 오꼬, 이우쭈꽈오 어수구 너마꼬, 가씨 이와부빠아 어꾸바 너부다꽈, 너냐짜, 나 뵤씨 뱌 비쭈꽈모. 오유 또니, 어라 구더다 뿌: "구다찌리 비하꿰 뱌 구레찌라!

6. And he swore by him who lives for ever and ever, who created the heavens and all that is in them, the earth and all that is in it, and the sea and all that is in it, and said, "There will be no more delay!

7. Bushi mango endonyi wa kalyinda nai angabanda mwa kai kaperere, unao-unao emyasi yoshi era Ongo abaa aanyisise kuira, kanji era yabaa

7. 부씨 마꼬 어또네 와 가레따 나이 아꽈바따 뫄 가이 가퍼러러, 우나오-우나오 어먀시 요씨 어라 오꼬 아바아 아아네시서 구이라,

7. But in the days when the seventh angel is about to sound his trumpet, the mystery of God will be accomplished, just as he

iteshibwe nebandju, ingere yaberera. Ebi byoshi bingaberera kukulyikana nokwa abaa abwirire ebarebi bai mira, ba bendee bamukorera."

가찌 어라 야바아 이더씨붜 너바쭈, 이꺼러 야버러라. 어비 뵤씨 비꺼버러라 구구쀄가나 노과 아바아 아붜리러 어바러비 바이 미라, 바 버떠어 바무고러라."

announced to his servants the prophets."

8. Chasinda, ola murenge nomvaa atengera kwa nguba, kanji era kunyibura mbu: "Uyaa kutola aku kechitabo kaeke ka kabungulyibwe, ka kalyi mwa mino soyu ndonyi wemenze kwa nyanja nokwa chio."

8. 짜시따, 오라 무러꺼 노빠아 아더꺼라 과 꾸바, 가찌 어라 구네부라 뿌: "우야아 구도롸 아구 거찌다보 가어거 가 가부우쀄붜, 가 가쀄 롸 미노 소유 또니 워머써 과 냐쨔 노과 찌오."

8. Then the voice that I had heard from heaven spoke to me once more: "Go, take the scroll that lies open in the hand of the angel who is standing on the sea and on the land."

9. Nomvire bacha, nera kunachifunda ala oyu ndonyi abaa alyi, na namwema ka kechitabo. Nai era kunyibura mbu: "Tolaako, unalyeko. Mango kangaba kachiri mwa bunu, kangaba kaloka nga buki, si mango kangaika mwa bula, kulula ku kangalula."

9. 노삐러 바짜, 너라 구나찌푸따 아롸 오유 또니 아바아 아쀄, 나 나뭐마 가 거찌다보. 나이 어라 구네부라 뿌: "도롸아고, 우나려고. 마꾜 가까바 가찌리 롸 부누, 가까바 가롣가 까 부기, 시 마꾜 가까이가 롸 부롸, 구루롸 구 가까루롸."

9. So I went to the angel and asked him to give me the little scroll. He said to me, "Take it and eat it. It will turn your stomach sour, but in your mouth it will be as sweet as honey."

10. Mwolu, nera kutola ka kechitabo mwa mino soyu ndonyi, kuna kulyako. Mango kabaa kanachiri mwa bunu, nera kunomva kwa kaloka nga buki. Si mango kabaa kera kanatoweraa mwa bula, nera kumva kwa kera kalula.

10. 모루, 너라 구도롸 가 거찌다보 롸 미노 소유 또니, 구나 구럊고. 마꾜 가바아 가나찌리 롸 부누, 너라 구노빠 과 가롣가 까 부기. 시 마꾜 가바아 거라 가나도워라아 롸 부롸, 너라 구빠 과 거라 가루롸.

10. I took the little scroll from the angel's hand and ate it. It tasted as sweet as honey in my mouth, but when I had eaten it, my stomach turned sour.

11. Chasinjire, bera kwire banyibura mbu: "Bichiri bikwemire uhube kureba era

11. 짜시지러, 버라 귀러 바네부라 뿌: "비찌리 비궈미러 우후버 구러바 어라

11. Then I was told, "You must prophesy again about many peoples, nations,

luulu sa mbaa sinene, na bio binene, na mateta manene, na bami banene."

루우루 사 빠아 시너너, 나 비오 비너너, 나 마더다 마너너, 나 바미 바너너."

languages and kings."

Byaboolyibwa Chikono 11

1. Era nyuma sebi, bera kunyeresa lusheke lwa kupima burerere bwa kandju karebe. Bera kunyibura mbu: "Bathukaa, uye kupima eluhu lwa Ongo, nekahaha kemithulo ka kathulamo, uanje nebandju ba bende bereramu Ongo.

2. Si echibua cholu luhu cheke, utapimaachi bushi beresisechi mira ebandju ba batathula beshi Ongo. Abu bandju, bangamala myesi mane nebiri bachinyeesesa mwa musi mubuya-buya.

3. Rero nanyi, nyingathuma bandju banyi babiri ba bangateta era luulu sanyi. Abu bandju babiri, bangaba bembese njimba sa chiriyo. Bangamala suku chumbi na maana mabiri na chiratu benjire bareba."

4. Abu bandju babiri, bu bathula era michi ebiri yemiseituni, era imenze era muhondo sa Ena ebutala boshi. Kanji bu ma matara

뱌보오레봐 찌고노 11

1. 어라 뉴마 서비, 버라 구녀러사 루써거 롸 구피마 부러러러 봐 가뚜 가러버. 버라 구네부라 뿌: "바쭈가아, 우여 구피마 어루후 롸 오꼬, 너가하하 거미쭈롣 가 가쭈롸모, 우아써 너바뉴 바 버떠 버러라무 오꼬.

2. 시 어찌부아 쪼루 루후 쩌거, 우다피마아찌 부씨 버러시서찌 미라 어바뉴 바 바다쭈롸 버씨 오꼬. 아부 바뉴, 바까마롸 며시 마너 너비리 바찌녀어서사 뫄 무시 무부야-부야.

3. 러로 나네, 네까쭈마 바뉴 바네 바비리 바 바까더다 어라 루우루 사니. 아부 바뉴 바비리, 바까바 버뻐서 끼빠 사 찌리요. 바까마롸 수구 쭈뻬 나 마아나 마비리 나 찌라두 버찌러 바러바."

4. 아부 바뉴 바비리, 부 바쭈롸 어라 미찌 어비리 여미서이두니, 어라 이머써 어라 무호또 사 어나 어부다롸 보씨. 가찌 부 마

Revelation Chapter 11[NIV]

1. I was given a reed like a measuring rod and was told, "Go and measure the temple of God and the altar, and count the worshipers there.

2. But exclude the outer court; do not measure it, because it has been given to the Gentiles. They will trample on the holy city for 42 months.

3. And I will give power to my two witnesses, and they will prophesy for 1,260 days, clothed in sackcloth."

4. These are the two olive trees and the two lampstands that stand before the Lord of the earth.

mabiri ma memenze era
muhondo sai.

5. Akaba barenda barebe
bangahonda kuira abu bandju
bulio, emulyiro angatenga
mwa bunu bwabo, na asiresa
abu barenda unao-unao. Rero
ku chira mundju woshi ola
ungahonda kubaira bulio,
angechibwa bacha.

6. Kanji abu bandju bete
ebuashi bwekwanga emvula
mango bangende baba
bareba. Bete nebuashi
bwekubindjula emeshi kuba
mikira, nebwekureta chira
malyibuko moshi mwa butala.
Ebi byoshi, bangende babiira
mango banasimire.

7. Mango bangaba bamalyire
kureba, enyama ngalyi era
yatenga mwera fumbi irerere
yekusimu, ingaya kubalwisa
nekulyinda yabaima. Chasinda,
ingetabo.

8. Ebirunda byabo,
bingashibanga mwa nama
semusi munene, ola bende
berika mwa uranya mbu
Sotomo, nesi kanji mbu Misiri.
Mwoyu musi, inoyu-inoyu, mu
bamanyikiraa Enawabo kwa
musalaba.

9. Ebi birunda, bingamala
suku ehatu na chimbi, bandju

마다라 마비리 마 머머써
어라 무호또 사이.

5. 아가바 바러따 바러버
바까호따 구이라 아부 바뚜
부뀨오, 어무레로 아까더까 꽈
부누 봐보, 나 아시러사 아부
바러따 우나오-우나오. 러로
구 찌라 무뚜 오씨 오꽈
우까호따 구바이라 부뀨오,
아꺼찌봐 바짜.

6. 가찌 아부 바뚜 버더
어부아씨 붜과꽈 어뿌꽈 마꼬
바꺼떠 바바 바러바. 버더
너부아씨 붜구비뿌과 어머씨
구바 미기라, 너붜구러다 찌라
마레부고 모씨 꽈 부다꽈.
어비 뵤씨, 바꺼떠 바비이라
마꼬 바나시미러.

7. 마꼬 바까바 바마레러
구러바, 어냐마 까레 어라
야더꽈 뭐라 푸삐 이러러러
여구시무, 이까야 구바뷔사
너구레따 야바이마. 짜시따,
이꺼다보.

8. 어비루따 뱌보, 비까씨바꽈
꽈 나마 서무시 무너너, 오꽈
버떠 버리가 꽈 우라냐 뿌
소도모, 너시 가찌 뿌 미시리.
묘유 무시, 이노유-이노유, 무
바마네기라아 어나와보 과
무사꽈바.

9. 어비 비루따, 비까마꽈
수구 어하두 나 찌뻬, 바뚜

5. If anyone tries to harm
them, fire comes from their
mouths and devours their
enemies. This is how anyone
who wants to harm them
must die.

6. These men have power to
shut up the sky so that it
will not rain during the time
they are prophesying; and
they have power to turn the
waters into blood and to
strike the earth with every
kind of plague as often as
they want.

7. Now when they have
finished their testimony, the
beast that comes up from
the Abyss will attack them,
and overpower and kill
them.

8. Their bodies will lie in the
street of the great city,
which is figuratively called
Sodom and Egypt, where
also their Lord was crucified.

9. For three and a half days
men from every people,

bauma bembaa soshi, nenyibuto soshi, nemateta moshi, nebomwa bio byoshi benjire babisonganga. Kanji batanemerere mbu bitabwaa.	바우마 버빠아 소씨, 너네부도 소씨, 너마더다 모씨, 너보와 비오 뵤씨 버ᄧᅵ러 바비소ᄢᅡᄢᅡ. 가ᄧᅵ 바다너머러러 뿌 비다봐아.	tribe, language and nation will gaze on their bodies and refuse them burial.
10. Rero mwa kusonga ebirunda byabu barebi babiri, abu bandju boshi bomwa butala bangende bamowa ngachi. Na bushi nolu lumoo lwabo, bangende balya lyinye na kunde bathumirana enyembo, bushi abu barebi babiri bu babaa benjire babalyibusa muno butala.	10. 러로 뫄 구소ᄢᅡ 어비루ᄠᅡ 뱌부 바러비 바비리, 아부 바ᅜᅮ 보씨 보뫄 부다ꥤᅡ 바ᄢᅥᄠᅥ 바모와 ᄢᅡ찌. 나 부씨 노루 루모오 ᄙᅪ보, 바ᄢᅥᄠᅥ 바ꥤᅣ ꥤᅦ녀 나 구ᄠᅥ 바쭈미라나 어녀뽀, 부씨 아부 바러비 바비리 부 바바아 버ᄧᅵ러 바바ꥤᅦ부사 무노 부다ꥤᅡ.	10. The inhabitants of the earth will gloat over them and will celebrate by sending each other gifts, because these two prophets had tormented those who live on the earth.
11. Si sa suku ehathu na chimbi, abere sawa, Ongo era kuhuba kubika emuka mwabu barebi babiri, na bahuba kuba bauma-uma, kuna kwemanga. Ebandju ba babalolaako, bera kwobaa busese.	11. 시 사 수구 어하쭈 나 찌삐, 아버러 사와, 오ᄋᆢ 어라 구후바 구비가 어무가 뫄부 바러비 바비리, 나 바후바 구바 바우마-우마, 구나 궈마ᄢᅡ. 어바ᅜᅮ 바 바바ᄙᅩꥤᅡ아고, 버라 ᄏᆢ바아 부서서.	11. But after the three and a half days a breath of life from God entered them, and they stood on their feet, and terror struck those who saw them.
12. Chasinda, abu barebi, kwa banalyi babiri, bera kumva murenge munene atenga kwa nguba, na aburabo mbu: "Mwerukiraa enera!" Unao-unao, ba barebi babiri kuna kwerukira kwa nguba mwa lumbumbu, na ba barenda babo banasene.	12. 짜시ᄠᅡ, 아부 바러비, 과 바나ꥤᅦ 바비리, 버라 구빠 무러ᄢᅥ 무너너 아더ᄢᅡ 과 ᅌᅮ바, 나 아부라보 뿌: "뭐루기라아 어너라!" 우나오-우나오, 바 바러비 바비리 구나 궈루기라 과 ᅌᅮ바 뫄 루뿌뿌, 나 바 바러ᄠᅡ 바보 바나서너.	12. Then they heard a loud voice from heaven saying to them, "Come up here." And they went up to heaven in a cloud, while their enemies looked on.
13. Mwechi chihangi chinechi, mwa butala mwera kurenga musisi munene. Mwolu,	13. 뭐찌 찌하ᄢᅵ 찌너찌, 뫄 부다ꥤᅡ 뭐라 구러ᄢᅡ 무시시 무너너. 뫄루, 찌삐 찌우마	13. At that very hour there was a severe earthquake and a tenth of the city

chimbi chiuma chekumi choyu musi kuna kukundjuka. Unao-unao, bandju byumbi birinda kuna kufa. Naba bafufumukaa, bera kwobaa busese, na batangirisa batonga Ongo wokwa nguba.

찌구미 쪼유 무시 구나 구구뚜가. 우나오-우나오, 바뚜뷰삐 비리따 구나 구파. 나바 바푸푸무가아, 버라 곤바아 부서서, 나 바다삐리사 바도빠 오꼬 옹과 꾸바.

collapsed. Seven thousand people were killed in the earthquake, and the survivors were terrified and gave glory to the God of heaven.

14. Rero, emalyibuko ma kabiri, namo ku marengaa bacha. Kanji mumvaa! Emalyibuko ma kahathu namo, malyi ofu kuika.

14. 러로, 어마레부고 마 가비리, 나모 구 마러빠아 바짜. 가씨 무빠아! 어마레부고 마 가하쭈 나모, 마레 오푸 구이가.

14. The second woe has passed; the third woe is coming soon.

15. Chasinda, endonyi wa kalyinda nai, era kubanda mwa kai kaperere. Unao-unao, kwa nguba kwera kumvikala mirenge inene era yabaa yateta mbu: "Rero ebwimi bwebutala, bwera bulyi mwa mino sa Enawethu Ongo, alauma na Masiya wai. Kanji, akanaendekera kwima esuku nemango."

15. 짜시따, 어또네 와 가레따 나이, 어라 구바따 뫄 가이 가퍼러러. 우나오-우나오, 과 꾸바 궈라 구뻬가꺄 미러뻐 이너너 어라 야바아 야더다 뿌: "러로 어뷔미 붜부다라, 붜라 부뻬 뫄 미노 사 어나워쭈 오꼬, 아롸우마 나 마시야 와이. 가씨, 아가나어떠거라 귀마 어수구 너마꼬."

15. The seventh angel sounded his trumpet, and there were loud voices in heaven, which said: "The kingdom of the world has become the kingdom of our Lord and of his Christ, and he will reign for ever and ever."

16. Ba bangumwa makunyabiri na bane, ba bekese kwa ndebe sabo sebwami era muhondo sa Ongo, bera kufumaka kuikira kwana chitaka na bamwera,

16. 바 바꾸뫄 마구냐비리 나 바너, 바 버거서 과 떠버 사보 서뵈미 어라 무호또 사 오꼬, 버라 구푸마가 구이기라 과나 찌다가 나 바뭐라,

16. And the twenty-four elders, who were seated on their thrones before God, fell on their faces and worshiped God,

17. mwa kuteta mbu: "Enawethu Ongo webuashi boshi, uwabaao, uunachirio. Twateta akoko era ulyi, bushi watolire ebuashi bwao bunene

17. 뫄 구더다 뿌: "어나워쭈 오꼬 워부아씨 보씨, 우와바아오, 우우나찌리오. 돠더다 아고고 어라 우레, 부씨 와도뾔러 어부아씨 봐오

17. saying: "We give thanks to you, Lord God Almighty, the One who is and who was, because you have taken your great power and

mira, nekutangirisa wema.

18. Ebandju ba batathula bakwishi, babaa basibukire. Si rero, ebusinane bwao bu bwerire bwaika.Sinera sera suku sa kuchinjibusa ebandju ba bafire mira. Boshi ba babaa benjire balosa ebandju bomwa butala kwa kasibu, rero nabo uungabalosa kuko. Si ebakosi bao bebarebi, beke kwemba ku ungembabo, alauma nebanji bandju bao ba walondwere, ba bende bathunda esina lyao, kutangirira kwa baunda, kuikira kwa bakulu-kulu."

19. Chasinjire, eluhu lwa Ongo lwa luthula kwa nguba, lwera kubookala. Mwolu luhu, esanduku yechilaano chai yera kulorekanako. Unao-unao, kwera kurenga thulimya-limya, na lwayo, na mikungulo, na misisi. Kwera kutowa na mvula inene ya luthwa.

부너너 미라, 너구다ᄜ리사 워마.

18. 어바뉴 바 바다쭈봐 바귀씨, 바바아 바시부기러. 시 러로, 어부시나너 봐오 부 뭐리러 봐이가.시너라 서라 수구 사 구찌찌부사 어바뷰 바 바피러 미라. 보씨 바 바바아 버찌러 바뤄사 어바뉴 보봐 부다봐 과 가시부, 러로 나보 우우ᄭ바뤄사 구고. 시 어바고시 바오 버바러비, 버거 궈빠 구 우ᄱ빠보, 아라우마 너바찌 바뉴 바오 바 와뤄뚜워러, 바 버너 바쭈ᄯ 어시나 랴오, 구다ᄜ리리라 과 바우ᄯ, 구이기라 과 바구루- 구루."

19. 짜시찌러, 어루후 롸 오오 롸 루쭈롸 과 우바, 뤄라 구보오가봐. 모루 루후, 어사뚜구 여찌롸아노 짜이 여라 구뤄러가나고. 우나오- 우나오, 궈라 구러ᄭ 쭈ᄳ먀- 리먀, 나 롸요, 나 미구우뤈, 나 미시시. 궈라 구도와 나 뿌롸 이너너 야 루쫘.

have begun to reign.

18. The nations were angry; and your wrath has come. The time has come for judging the dead, and for rewarding your servants the prophets and your saints and those who reverence your name, both small and great-- and for destroying those who destroy the earth."

19. Then God's temple in heaven was opened, and within his temple was seen the ark of his covenant. And there came flashes of lightning, rumblings, peals of thunder, an earthquake and a great hailstorm.

Byaboolyibwa Chikono 12
1. Era nyuma sebi, kwa nguba kwera kulorekanako chisomerano chiuma chinene. Nechi chisomerano chi chechine: mukasi muuma

뱌보오레봐 찌고노 12
1. 어라 뉴마 서비, 과 우바 궈라 구뤄러가나고 찌소머라노 찌우마 찌너너. 너찌 찌소머라노 찌 쩌찌너: 무가시 무우마

Revelation Chapter 12[NIV]
1. A great and wondrous sign appeared in heaven: a woman clothed with the sun, with the moon under her feet and a crown of

abaa embese esuba nga luchimba. Abaa alyibachire nemwesi. Nokwethwe lyai, abaa embese ku nzita era yabaa yete ngununu ekumi nebiri.

2. Kanji abaa ete bukure bwa bwabaa bwera bwamuluma. Rero bushi nemukero, era kunde achilakangira.

3. Kanji kwa nguba, kwera kulorekanako chinji chisomerano chiuma. Nechi chisomerano chi chechine: njoka anguma inene busese ya mwola yabaa yete mithwe erinda, na membe ekumi. Na ku chira ethwe, kwabaa kulyi ka nzita kaeke.

4. Emusemba wei njoka, era kuuruthula chimbi chiuma chekahathu chengununu sokwa nguba kuna kuumangasi mwa butala. Chasinda, yera kuya kwimanga era muhondo soyu mukasi wabaa wabuta, chasiya mango angabuta, unao-unao irye emwana.

5. Oyu mukasi, era kubuta mwana wa busana, ola ukemangira embaa soshi mwa kubaenzesa mwa mafi. Na mango abuthwaa, unao-unao kuna kwerusibwa ala Ongo

어수바 꾜 루찌빠. 아바아 아레바찌러 너뭐시. 노궈쭤 랴이, 아바아 어뻐서 구 씨다 어라 야바아 여더 우누누 어구미 너비리.

2. 가찌 아바아 어더 부구러 봐 봐바아 붜라 봐무루마. 러로 부씨 너무거로, 어라 구뻐 아찌롸가끼라.

3. 가찌 과 우바, 궈라 구뢰러가나고 찌씨 찌소머라노 찌우마. 너찌 찌소머라노 찌 쩌찌너: 쪼가 아우마 이너너 부서서 야 몰롸 야바아 여더 미쭤 어리따, 나 머뻐 어구미. 나 구 찌라 어쭤, 과바아 구레 가 씨다 가어거.

4. 어무서빠 워이 쪼가, 어라 구우루쭈롸 찌뻬 찌우마 쩌가하쭈 쩌우누누 소과 우바 구나 구우마까시 뫄 부다롸. 짜시따, 여라 구야 귀마꺄 어라 무호쪼 소유 무가시 와바아 와부다, 짜시야 마꼬 아꺄부다, 우나오-우나오 이루여 어뫄나.

5. 오유 무가시, 어라 구부다 뫄나 와 부사나, 오라 우거마끼라 어빠아 소씨 뫄 구바어써사 뫄 마피. 나 마꼬 아부화아, 우나오-우나오 구나 궈루시봐 아롸 오꼬 아바아

twelve stars on her head.

2. She was pregnant and cried out in pain as she was about to give birth.

3. Then another sign appeared in heaven: an enormous red dragon with seven heads and ten horns and seven crowns on his heads.

4. His tail swept a third of the stars out of the sky and flung them to the earth. The dragon stood in front of the woman who was about to give birth, so that he might devour her child the moment it was born.

5. She gave birth to a son, a male child, who will rule all the nations with an iron scepter. And her child was snatched up to God and to his throne.

abaa ekese kwa ndebe yai yebwami.

6. Ola mukasi nai, era kuhaira mwa buyeye. Era kuika mwa chisiki cha Ongo abaa amukunganyisise mira, chasiya ende amuasisamo kuikira ku suku chumbi na maana mabiri na chirathu.

7. Chasinda, kwa nguba kwera kuba ndambala isibu. Mikaeri nebandonyi bai, bera kutabalyira era njoka inene. Ei njoka, nai alauma nebandonyi bai, bera kunalwa nabo.

8. Si wanjoka era kuimwa. Bushi noku, bitachialyikanaa mbu aendekere kwekala kwa nguba nabu bandonyi bai.

9. Chasinda, era kwire aumwa mwa butala. Rero, oyola iuthula era njoka inene yokwa mira, era bende berika mbu "Wamusimu" nesi mbu "Shetani" ola wende wengeera ebandju boshi bomwa butala. Na mango abaa era aumwaa mwa butala alauma nabu bandonyi bai,

10. nera kumva murenge munene atengera kwa nguba mbu: "Rero, ebununusi bwa Ongo bwaikire! Ebwimi nebuashi bwai, nabi

어거서 과 떠버 야이 여봐미.

6. 오파 무가시 나이, 어라 구하이라 봐 부여여. 어라 구이가 봐 찌시기 짜 오오 아바아 아무구빠네시서 미라, 짜시야 어더 아무아시사모 구이기라 구 수구 쭈삐 나 마아나 마비리 나 찌라쭈.

7. 짜시따, 과 꾸바 궈라 구바 따빠롸 이시부. 미가어리 너바또네 바이, 버라 구다바뻬라 어라 쪼가 이너너. 어이 쪼가, 나이 아롸우마 너바또네 바이, 버라 구나롸 나보.

8. 시 완쪼가 어라 구이봐. 부씨 노구, 비다찌아뻬가나아 뿌 아어떠거러 궈가롸 과 꾸바 나부 바또네 바이.

9. 짜시따, 어라 귀러 아우봐 봐 부다롸. 러로, 오요파 이우쭈롸 어라 쪼가 이너너 요과 미라, 어라 버떠 버리가 뿌 "와무시무" 너시 뿌 "써다니" 오파 워떠 워뻐어라 어바쭈 보씨 보봐 부다롸. 나 마꼬 아바아 어라 아우봐아 봐 부다롸 아롸우마 나부 바또네 바이,

10. 너라 구빠 무러뻐 무너너 아더뻐라 과 꾸바 뿌: "러로, 어부누누시 봐 오꼬 봐이기러!어뷔미 너부아씨 봐이, 나비 뱌나이기러. 나 기리시도 와이

6. The woman fled into the desert to a place prepared for her by God, where she might be taken care of for 1,260 days.

7. And there was war in heaven. Michael and his angels fought against the dragon, and the dragon and his angels fought back.

8. But he was not strong enough, and they lost their place in heaven.

9. The great dragon was hurled down--that ancient serpent called the devil, or Satan, who leads the whole world astray. He was hurled to the earth, and his angels with him.

10. Then I heard a loud voice in heaven say: "Now have come the salvation and the power and the kingdom of our God, and the

byanaikire. Na Kirisito wai iwemire. Bushi ola wabaa wenjire wasitaka banyakethu emushi nebuthufu era muhondo sa Ongo, aumirwe mira ereshi.

이워미러. 부씨 오ᄙᅡ 와바아 워ᅜᅵ러 와시다가 바냐거쭈 어무씨 너부후푸 어라 무호또사 오ᅌᅩ, 아우미뤄 미라 어러씨.

authority of his Christ. For the accuser of our brothers, who accuses them before our God day and night, has been hurled down.

11. Abu banyaketu, bamuimire kurengera emikira yeMwana weMbulyi, na kurengera bya bendee bateta era luulu sai bya bachiloreraako. Kanji beke, batasimaa ekalamo kabo, si bemereraa kwichibwa.

11. 아부 바냐거두, 바무이미러 구러ᅌᅥ라 어미기라 여뫄나 워ᄜᅮᄙᅦ, 나 구러ᅌᅥ라 뱌 버ᄕᅥ어 바더다 어라 ᄙᅮ우ᄙᅮ 사이 뱌 바찌ᄙᅩ러라아고. 가ᅜᅵ 버거, 바다시마아 어가ᄙᅡ모 가보, 시 버머러라아 귀찌봐.

11. They overcame him by the blood of the Lamb and by the word of their testimony; they did not love their lives so much as to shrink from death.

12. Bushi noku, enguba ibaa mwa lumoo, alauma nenyu muboshi mu muthulako! Si buanya kwa ba bathula mwa butala, nomwa nyanja, bushi Wamusimu, eyi mulyi yiandalyire. Kanji asibukire busese, bushi aneshi kwesuku sa samweshibira, sikeire."

12. 부씨 노구, 어ᅌᅮ바 이바아 뫄 ᄙᅮ모오, 아ᄙᅡ우마 너뉴 무보씨 무 무쭈ᄙᅡ고! 시 부아냐 과 바 바쭈ᄙᅡ 뫄 부다ᄙᅡ, 노뫄 냐ᅜᅡ, 부씨 와무시무, 어에 무ᄙᅦ 에아ᄕᅡᄙᅦ러. 가ᅜᅵ 아시부기러 부서서, 부씨 아너씨 궈수구 사 사뭐씨비라, 시거이러."

12. Therefore rejoice, you heavens and you who dwell in them! But woe to the earth and the sea, because the devil has gone down to you! He is filled with fury, because he knows that his time is short."

13. Mango ei njoka inene yalolaa kwa yaumirwe mwa butala, yera kutangirisa yaiya ola mukasi wabutaa ola mwana webusana.

13. 마ᅌᅩ 어이 ᅜᅩ가 이너너 야ᄙᅩᄙᅡ아 과 야우미뤄 뫄 부다ᄙᅡ, 여라 구다ᅌᅵ리사 야이야 오ᄙᅡ 무가시 와부다아 오ᄙᅡ 뫄나 워부사나.

13. When the dragon saw that he had been hurled to the earth, he pursued the woman who had given birth to the male child.

14. Si wamukasi era kweresibwa bibaba bibiri bya biri nga byanzu inene, chasiya aulukire mwobwa buyeye. Bushi omola mweke, mu ei njoka inene yabaa itangaika.

14. 시 와무가시 어라 궈러시봐 비바바 비비리 뱌 비리 ᅌᅡ 뱌ᅜᅮ 이너너, 짜시야 아우ᄙᅮ기러 뫄봐 부여여. 부씨 오모ᄙᅡ 뭐거, 무 어이 ᅜᅩ가 이너너 야바아 이다ᅌᅡ이가.

14. The woman was given the two wings of a great eagle, so that she might fly to the place prepared for her in the desert, where she would be taken care of for a

Kanji mu Ongo abaa amukunganyisise mira kwa mu angamuasisa ku myaka ehathu na chimbi.

15. Chasinda, era njoka yera kufubula meshi manene busese matenga mwa bunu bwai. Amu meshi mabaa mahenda nga lwishi lunene era nyuma soyu mukasi, chasiya lumuhenze.

16. Unao-unao, echitaka mwa kubookala cheine, chera kumulamya. Lwa lwishi loshi, lwa lwabaa lwatengera mwa bunu bwera njoka, na chamiralo.

17. Wanjoka alolyire bacha, era kusibukira ola mukasi busese. Era kwire aya kulwisa ebandju ba bashibaa boshi bomwa lubuto lwoyu mukasi. Nabu bandju, bu bende bathunda emiomba ya Ongo, nekulanga kubuya-buya emyasi era Yesu Kirisito endee ateta.

18. Chasinjire, wanjoka era kwire aya kwimanga kwa chishee, kwa musike senyanja.

Byaboolyibwa Chikono 13

1. Chasinda, mwera nyanja, nera kulola mwaulukira nyama ngalyi. Ei nyama, yabaa yete

가찌 무 오꼬 아바아 아무구꽈네시서 미라 과 무 아까무아시사 구 먀가 어하쭈 나 찌뻬.

15. 짜시따, 어라 쪼가 여라 구푸부라 머씨 마너너 부서서 마더꽈 마 부누 봐이. 아무 머씨 마바아 마허따 까 뤼씨 루너너 어라 뉴마 소유 무가시, 짜시야 루무허써.

16. 우나오-우나오, 어찌다가 마 구보오가꽈 쩌이너, 쩌라 구무꽈먀. 꽈 뤼씨 로씨, 꽈 꽈바아 꽈더꺼라 마 부누 붜라 쪼가, 나 짜미라로.

17. 와쪼가 아뢰레러 바짜, 어라 구시부기라 오꽈 무가시 부서서. 어라 귀러 아야 구뤼사 어바쭈 바 바씨바아 보씨 보꽈 루부도 뢰유 무가시. 나부 바쭈, 부 버러 바쭈따 어미오빠 야 오꼬, 너구꽈까 구부야-부야 어먀시 어라 여수 기리시도 어떠어 아더다.

18. 짜시찌러, 와쪼가 어라 귀러 아야 귀마까 과 찌써어, 과 무시거 서냐짜.

뱌보오꿰봐 찌고노 13

1. 짜시따, 뭐라 냐짜, 너라 구로꽈 마우루기라 냐마 까레. 어이 냐마, 야바아 여더 미쮜

time, times and half a time, out of the serpent's reach.

15. Then from his mouth the serpent spewed water like a river, to overtake the woman and sweep her away with the torrent.

16. But the earth helped the woman by opening its mouth and swallowing the river that the dragon had spewed out of his mouth.

17. Then the dragon was enraged at the woman and went off to make war against the rest of her offspring--those who obey God's commandments and hold to the testimony of Jesus.

18. None

Revelation Chapter 13[NIV]

1. And the dragon stood on the shore of the sea. And I saw a beast coming out of

mithwe erinda na membe ekumi. Na ku chira embe, kwabaa kulyi kanzita kaeke, na ku chira ethwe kwabaa kuanjikirwe esina lya kukamba Ongo.

2. Ei nyama nalolaako, yabaa ihuhire nga kakiri. Si ebibumbu byai byabaa biri nga bya lushibwabwa. Nebunu bwai, bwabaa bulyi nga bwa ngoromoli. Era njoka inene, yera kumweresa ebwimi bwai, nendebe yai yebwami, chasiya eme na buashi bunene.

3. Mwa mithwe yei nyama ngalyi, lyiuma lyabaa lyiri nga lyikomangibwe chiulu cha chabaa chingeta, si chabaa chalamire mira. Bushi noku, ebandju boshi bomwa butala bera kusanwa na batangirisa kunde baikulyikira.

4. Rero, abu bandju boshi bera kutangirisa kunde bera ei njoka inene bushi yabaa yeresise ei nyama ebuashi bwai. Kanji bera kunde bera nei nyama mwa kuitonga mbu: "Ene nyama, nde ola ungalyingamanyisibwa nai? Nande ola ungaala kulwa nai?"

어리따 나 머뼈 어구미. 나 구 찌라 어뼈, 과바아 구레 가씨다 가어거, 나 구 찌라 어쭤 과바아 구아씨기뤄 어시나 랴 구가빠 오옹.

2. 어이 냐마 나로쫘아고, 야바아 이후히러 꽈 가기리. 시 어비부뿌 뱌이 뱌바아 비리 꽈 뱌 루씨봐봐. 너부누 봐이, 봐바아 부레 꽈 봐 꼬로모삐. 어라 쪼가 이너너, 여라 구뭐러사 어뷔미 봐이, 너더버 야이 여봐미, 짜시야 어머 나 부아씨 부너너.

3. 꽈 미쭤 여이 냐마 꽈레, 레우마 랴바아 레리 꽈 레고마삐붜 찌우뤀 짜 짜바아 찌꺼다, 시 짜바아 짜랴미러 미라. 부씨 노구, 어바쭈 보씨 보봐 부다퐈 버라 구사놔 나 바다삐리사 구떠 바이구레기라.

4. 러로, 아부 바쭈 보씨 버라 구다삐리사 구떠 버라 어이 쪼가 이너너 부씨 야바아 여러시서 어이 냐마 어부아씨 봐이. 가씨 버라 구떠 버라 너이 냐마 꽈 구이도꽈 뿌: "어너 냐마, 떠 오라 우꽈레꽈마네시봐 나이? 나떠 오라 우꽈아퐈 구퐈 나이?"

the sea. He had ten horns and seven heads, with ten crowns on his horns, and on each head a blasphemous name.

2. The beast I saw resembled a leopard, but had feet like those of a bear and a mouth like that of a lion. The dragon gave the beast his power and his throne and great authority.

3. One of the heads of the beast seemed to have had a fatal wound, but the fatal wound had been healed. The whole world was astonished and followed the beast.

4. Men worshiped the dragon because he had given authority to the beast, and they also worshiped the beast and asked, "Who is like the beast? Who can make war against him?"

5. Ei nyama ngalyi, bera kuyeresa eloso lwekunde yateta myasi ya chirume-rume kanji ya kukamba Ongo. Kanji bera kuyeresa nebuashi bwekwima ku myesi mane nebiri.

6. Bushi noku, yera kutangirisa kunde yakamba Ongo, yakamba nesina lyai. Kanji yera kutangirisa yakamba nechisiki cha athulamo, na kukamba boshi ba bathula nai kwa nguba.

7. Kanji ei nyama ngalyi, bera kweresai eloso lwekulwisa ebandju ba Ongo na kubaima. Kanji bera kweresai nebuashi bwekwimangira ebandju bembaa soshi, nebenyibuto soshi, nebemateta moshi, nebebio byoshi.

8. Ei nyama, ebandju boshi bomwa butala bakende berai, kureka ba masina mabo maanjikwaa kutengera ekubumbwa kwebutala, mwa chitabo chekalamo cheMwana weMbulyi ola wakeribwaa.

9. Ola wete matchi, omvaa!

10. Akaba emundju alawaa mbu akaminyibwa, eri kuminyibwa ku akanaminyibwa. Na akaba

5. 어이 냐마 까레, 버라 구여러사 어로소 뤄구떠 야더다 먀시 야 찌루머-루머 가찌 야 구가빠 오끄. 가찌 버라 구여러사 너부아씨 뭐귀마 구 며시 마너 너비리.

6. 부씨 노구, 여라 구다삐리사 구떠 야가빠 오끄, 야가빠 너시나 럐이. 가찌 여라 구다삐리사 야가빠 너찌시기 짜 아쭈롸모, 나 구가빠 보씨 바 바쭈롸 나이 과 우바.

7. 가찌 어이 냐마 까레, 버라 궈러사이 어로소 뭐구뤼사 어바뚜 바 오끄 나 구바이마. 가찌 버라 궈러사이 너부아씨 뭐귀마삐라 어바뚜 버빠아 소씨, 너버네부도 소씨, 너버마더다 모씨, 너버비오 뵤씨.

8. 어이 냐마, 어바뚜 보씨 보먀 부다롸 바거떠 버라이, 구러가 바 마시나 마보 마아씨과아 구더뻐라 어구부빠 궈부다롸, 먀 찌다보 쩌가롸모 쩌먀나 워뿌레 오롸 와거리봐아.

9. 오롸 워더 마찌, 오빠아!

10. 아가바 어무뚜 아롸와아 뿌 아가미네봐, 어리 구미네봐 구 아가나미네봐. 나 아가바 아롸와아 뿌 아거찌봐 먀

5. The beast was given a mouth to utter proud words and blasphemies and to exercise his authority for forty-two months.

6. He opened his mouth to blaspheme God, and to slander his name and his dwelling place and those who live in heaven.

7. He was given power to make war against the saints and to conquer them. And he was given authority over every tribe, people, language and nation.

8. All inhabitants of the earth will worship the beast--all whose names have not been written in the book of life belonging to the Lamb that was slain from the creation of the world.

9. He who has an ear, let him hear.

10. If anyone is to go into captivity, into captivity he will go. If anyone is to be killed with the sword, with

alawaa mbu akechibwa mwa bombo, eri mwa bombo mu akanechibwa. Bushi noku, ebandju ba Ongo bemire kunde baata ebushibirisi na kuendekera baata ebwemeresi.

11. Chasinda, nera kulola ku inji nyama yatenga mwa chitaka. Ei nyama, yeke yabaa yete membe mabiri ma malyi nga membe ma chana cha mbulyi. Si yabaa yenjire yateta nga njoka inene.

12. Kanji nai, yabaa yete ebuashi boshi bwera nyama ibere-bere, era yabaa yete cha chiulu chingeta si chera kulama. Obu buashi, yera kunde yabukoresa mwana meho moyu mulyikabo. Bushi noku, ei nyama ya kabiri yera kubura ebandju boshi bomwa butala mbu bendaa bera ei nyama ibere-bere.

13. Kanji yabaa yenjire yaira bisomerano binene. Yera kunalyinda yenjire yandaasa mulyiro kwa nguba yatosesao mwa butala era muhondo sebandju.

14. Rero bushi nekuata ebuashi bwekuira ebi bisomerano era muhondo sa mulyikabo, yera kwire yende

보뽀, 어리 먀 보뽀 무 아가너찌봐. 부씨 노구, 어바쭈 바 오꼬 버미러 구떠 바아다 어부씨비리시 나 구어떠거라 바아다 어뭐머러시.

11. 짜시따, 너라 구르롸 구 이찌 냐마 야더꾸 먀 찌다가. 어이 냐마, 여거 야바아 여더 머뻐 마비리 마 마레 꾸 머뻐 마 짜나 짜 뿌레. 시 야바아 여찌러 야더다 꾸 쪼가 이너너.

12. 가찌 나이, 야바아 여더 어부아씨 보씨 붜라 냐마 이버러-버러, 어라 야바아 여더 짜 찌우루 찌어다 시 쩌라 구롸마. 오부 부아씨, 여라 구떠 야부고러사 모나 머호 모유 무레가보. 부씨 노구, 어이 냐마 야 가비리 여라 구부라 어바쭈 보씨 보봐 부다롸 뿌 버바아 버라 어이 냐마 이버러-버러.

13. 가찌 야바아 여찌러 야이라 비소머라노 비너너. 여라 구나레따 여찌러 야따아사 무레로 과 우바 야도서사오 먀 부다롸 어라 무호또 서바쭈.

14. 러로 부씨 너구아다 어부아씨 붜구이라 어비 비소머라노 어라 무호또 사 무레가보, 여라 귀러 여떠

the sword he will be killed. This calls for patient endurance and faithfulness on the part of the saints.

11. Then I saw another beast, coming out of the earth. He had two horns like a lamb, but he spoke like a dragon.

12. He exercised all the authority of the first beast on his behalf, and made the earth and its inhabitants worship the first beast, whose fatal wound had been healed.

13. And he performed great and miraculous signs, even causing fire to come down from heaven to earth in full view of men.

14. Because of the signs he was given power to do on behalf of the first beast, he deceived the inhabitants of

yengeera ebandju bomwa
butala mbu bakunganyaa
echihuhanyi kwa kuthunda
mulyikabo ola
wakomangibwaa mwa bombo,
si era kulama.

15. Chasinda, ei nyama ya
kabiri bera kweresai ebuashi
bwekubuwa emuka wekalamo
mwechi chihuhanyi chenyama
ibere-bere, chibone ebuashi
bwekunde chateta na kwichisa
ebandju ba bangende banana
kwerachi.

16. Kanji yera kubura ebandju
boshi mbu babikibwaa
ekalorero kwa mino sabo
semalyo, nesi kwa malanga,
kutangirira kwa baunda,
kuikira kwa bakulu-kulu, kwa
baare kuikira kwa bakene, kwa
thuungu kuikira kwa ba
batathula thuungu.

17. Rero, kutabaa chiro na
mundju asibya ola weresibwaa
loso lwa kuula nesi kuusa
kandju, akaba atasa kubikibwa
kwekalorero. Kanji ako
kalorero, lilyabaa esina nesi
emuanjo ola ulyingene nesina
lyei nyama ibere-bere.

18. Aola, ebandju bemire
kuata bwenge. Bushi ola wete
bwenge, iungamenyerera

여꺼어라 어바뚜 보뫄 부다꽈
뿌 바구꺄냐아 어찌후하네 과
구쭈따 무레가보 오꽈
와고마삐봐아 뫄 보뽄, 시
어라 구꽈마.

15. 짜시따, 어이 냐마 야
가비리 버라 궈러사이
어부아씨 뷔구부와 어무가
워가꽈모 뭐찌 찌후하네
쩌냐마 이버러-버러, 찌보너
어부아씨 뷔구떠 짜더다 나
궈찌사 어바뚜 바 바꺼떠
바나나 궈라찌.

16. 가찌 여라 구부라 어바뚜
보씨 뿌 바비기봐아
어가로러로 과 미노 사보
서마뾰, 너시 과 마꽈까,
구다삐리라 과 바우따,
구이기라 과 바구루-구루, 과
바아러 구이기라 과 바거너,
과 쭈우꾸 구이기라 과 바
바다쭈꽈 쭈우꾸.

17. 러로, 구다바아 찌로 나
무누 아시뱌 오꽈 워러시봐아
로소 꽈 구우꽈 너시 구우사
가뚜, 아가바 아다사 구비기봐
궈가로러로. 가찌 아고
가로러로, 삐꺄봐아 어시나
너시 어무아쪼 오꽈 우레꺼너
너시나 꺄이 냐마 이버러-
버러.

18. 아오꽈, 어바뚜 버미러
구아다 뷔꺼. 부씨 오꽈 워더
뷔꺼, 이우꺄머녀러라

---

the earth. He ordered them
to set up an image in honor
of the beast who was
wounded by the sword and
yet lived.

15. He was given power to
give breath to the image of
the first beast, so that it
could speak and cause all
who refused to worship the
image to be killed.

16. He also forced everyone,
small and great, rich and
poor, free and slave, to
receive a mark on his right
hand or on his forehead,

17. so that no one could
buy or sell unless he had
the mark, which is the name
of the beast or the number
of his name.

18. This calls for wisdom. If
anyone has insight, let him
calculate the number of the

kanangana kute oyu muanjo wei nyama atechire. Kanji oyu muanjo wai, alyi muanjo wa mundju. Noyu muanjo alyi wa maana ndathu na chirathu na ndathu.

가나빠나 구더 오유 무아쪼 워이 냐마 아더찌러. 가찌 오유 무아쪼 와이, 아레 무아쪼 와 무뚜. 노유 무아쪼 아레 와 마아나 따쭈 나 찌라쭈 나 따쭈.

beast, for it is man's number. His number is 666.

Byaboolyibwa Chikono 14

1. Era nyuma sebi, nera kulola kwola Mwana weMbulyi achiri emenze kwa ndjulungu ye Sayuni, alyi alauma na ba bandju byumbi eyana na mane na bane. Nokwa malanga mabo, esina lyai nelyeShe mu mabaa maanjikirweko.

2. Nera kumva murenge atenga kwa nguba, ola wabaa wauma nga chiira. Kanji abaa akungula nga murasano. Kanji abaa enjire omvikala nga murenge wa nzenze sa bandju basiya.

3. Abu bandju boshi babaa bemenze era muhondo sendebe yebwami, nera muhondo sebya bindju bine bya biri biuma-uma kanji bya kushishasa, nera muhondo sa ba bangumwa bemba lwimbo luyayaya. Nolu lwimbo, kutalyi mundju asibya ola wabaa

뱌보오레봐 찌고노 14

1. 어라 뉴마 서비, 너라 구론똬 골똬 마나 워뿌레 아찌리 어머써 과 뚜루우우 여 사유니, 아레 아똬우마 나 바 바뚜 뷰삐 어야나 나 마너 나 바너. 노과 마똬빠 마보, 어시나 랴이 너려써 무 마바아 마아찌기뤄고.

2. 너라 구빠 무러써 아더빠 과 우바, 오똬 와바아 와우마 빠 찌이라. 가찌 아바아 아구우똬 빠 무라사노. 가찌 아바아 어찌러 오삐가똬 빠 무러써 와 써써 사 바뚜 바시야.

3. 아부 바뚜 보씨 바바아 버머써 어라 무호또 서더버 여봐미, 너라 무호또 서뱌 비뚜 비너 뱌 비리 비우마-우마 가찌 뱌 구씨싸사, 너라 무호또 사 바 바우똬 버빠 뤼뽀 루야야야. 노루 뤼뽀, 구다레 무뚜 아시뱌 오똬 와바아 우빠아똬

Revelation Chapter 14[NIV]

1. Then I looked, and there before me was the Lamb, standing on Mount Zion, and with him 144,000 who had his name and his Father's name written on their foreheads.

2. And I heard a sound from heaven like the roar of rushing waters and like a loud peal of thunder. The sound I heard was like that of harpists playing their harps.

3. And they sang a new song before the throne and before the four living creatures and the elders. No one could learn the song except the 144,000 who had been redeemed from the earth.

ungaala kuchikangirisalo, kureka abu bandju byumbi eyana na mane na bane oshao, ba banunulibwe na Ongo mwa butala.	구찌가ᅁᅵ리사ᄙᅩ, 구러가 아부 바ᅜᅮ 뷰ᄜᅵ 어야나 나 마너 나 바너 오싸오, 바 바누누ᄙᅵ붸 나 오ᅁᅩ 와 부다ᄙᅡ.	
4. Abola beke, batakolaa chiro na chibi chisibya mwa kuonjiraa nebakasi, bushi beke bachishibiraa ngokwa banabuthwaa. Na bu bende bakulyikira eMwana weMbulyi mu chira chisiki choshi cha ende anayamo. Rero abola, bu banunulyibwe mira mwa banji, nekuba babere kwanyibwa nga mithulo era mwa Ongo, nera mwoyu Mwana weMbulyi.	4. 아보ᄙᅡ 버거, 바다고ᄙᅡ아 찌로 나 찌비 찌시뱌 와 구오ᅜᅵ라아 너바가시, 부씨 버거 바찌씨비라아 ᅁᅩ과 바나부화아. 나 부 버ᄗᅥ 바구ᄙᅦ기라 어와나 워ᄜᅮᄙᅦ 무 찌라 찌시기 쪼씨 짜 어ᄗᅥ 아나야모. 러로 아보ᄙᅡ, 부 바누누ᄙᅦ붸 미라 와 바ᅜᅵ, 너구바 바버러 과네봐 ᅁᅡ 미쭈ᄙᅩ 어라 와 오ᅁᅩ, 너라 뫄유 와나 워ᄜᅮᄙᅦ.	4. These are those who did not defile themselves with women, for they kept themselves pure. They follow the Lamb wherever he goes. They were purchased from among men and offered as firstfruits to God and the Lamb.
5. Kanji abu bandju, mwa bunu bwabo mutafuraa kutenga chiro na mwasi wa bisha. Kanji batathusa chiro na chibi chisibya.	5. 가ᅜᅵ 아부 바ᅜᅮ, 와 부누 봐보 무다푸라아 구더ᅁᅡ 찌로 나 와시 와 비싸. 가ᅜᅵ 바다쭈사 찌로 나 찌비 찌시뱌.	5. No lie was found in their mouths; they are blameless.
6. Chasinda, nera kulola ku unji ndonyi auluka mwa byanya bibiri. Oyu ndonyi, abaa ete eMwasi Mubuya-buya wesuku nemango. Abaa aya kuhubanganyisao ebandju boshi bomwa butala: chira chio, na chira mbaa, na chira eteta, na chira lubuto.	6. 짜시ᄗᅡ, 너라 구ᄙᅩᄙᅡ 구 우ᅜᅵ ᄗᅩ네 아우ᄙᅮ가 와 뱌냐 비비리. 오유 ᄗᅩ네, 아바아 어더 어와시 무부야-부야 워수구 너마ᅁᅩ. 아바아 아야 구후바ᅁᅡ네사오 어바ᅜᅮ 보씨 보와 부다ᄙᅡ: 찌라 찌오, 나 찌라 ᄜᅡ아, 나 찌라 어더다, 나 찌라 ᄙᅮ부도.	6. Then I saw another angel flying in midair, and he had the eternal gospel to proclaim to those who live on the earth--to every nation, tribe, language and people.
7. Era kuteta na murenge munene mbu: "Mundaa mwathunda Ongo, na kunde	7. 어라 구더다 나 무러ᅁᅥ 무너너 ᄜᅮ: "무ᄗᅡ아 와쭈ᄗᅡ 오ᅁᅩ, 나 구ᄗᅥ 와무도ᅁᅡ! 부씨	7. He said in a loud voice, "Fear God and give him glory, because the hour of

mwamutonga! Bushi ebihangi
byai byekuchinjibusa ebandju,
byaikire mira. Mundaa
mwamwera bushi iwabumbaa
enguba nechitaka, nenyanja,
neshokororo semeshi."

8. Endonyi wa kabiri, era
kukulyikira oyu mubere-bere.
Nai era kuteta mbu: "Emusi
weBabiloni ola wabaa waire
ngulu, rero akundjukire.
Kubinalyi, akundjukire mira!
Iwabaa wenjire watamisa
ebandju boshi bomwa butala
nelusingi lwai. Olu lusingi, lulyi
nga mafu ma makalyiire
busese."

9. Endonyi wa kahathu nai era
kukulyikira abu balyikabo
babiri. Nai era kuteta na
murenge munene mbu: "Ola
wera ei nyama ngalyi, era
nechihuhanyi chai, nola
wabikibweko ka kalorero kai
ala malanga, nesi kwa mino
yai,

10. amenyaa kwa Ongo
akamulosa kwa businane
bwai. Obu businane, bukalyiire
busese nga mafu ma
mafukirwe mwa ngumbu mira
busira meshi. Oyu mundju,
mulyiro nengunye-kunye
sechibirichi bikende
byamulosa kwa kasibu, era

어비하삐 뱌이 벼구찌찌부사
어바뉴, 뱌이기러 미라.
무따아 뫄뭐라 부씨
이와부빠아 어우바 너찌다가,
너냐짜, 너쏘고로로 서머씨."

8. 어또네 와 가비리, 어라
구구쩨기라 오유 무버러-버러.
나이 어라 구더다 뿌: "어무시
워바비로니 오롸 와바아
와이러 우루, 러로
아구뉴기러. 구비나뤠,
아구뉴기러 미라! 이와바아
워찌러 와다미사 어바뉴 보씨
보롸 부다롸 너루시삐 롸이.
오루 루시삐, 루뤠 롸 마푸 마
마가쩨이러 부서서."

9. 어또네 와 가하쭈 나이
어라 구구쩨기라 아부
바뤠가보 바비리. 나이 어라
구더다 나 무러뭐 무너너 뿌:
"오롸 워라 어이 냐마 롸뤠,
어라 너찌후하니 짜이, 노롸
와비기붜고 가 가뢰루로 가이
아롸 마롸롸, 너시 과 미노
야이,

10. 아머냐아 과 오꼬
아가무로사 과 부시나너 봐이.
오부 부시나너, 부가쩨이러
부서서 롸 마푸 마 마푸기붜
롸 우뿌 미라 부시라 머씨.
오유 무뉴, 무뤠로 너우녀-
구녀 서찌비리찌 비거뭐
뱌무로사 과 가시부, 어라
무호또 서바또네 바부야-부야,

---

his judgment has come.
Worship him who made the
heavens, the earth, the sea
and the springs of water."

8. A second angel followed
and said, "Fallen! Fallen is
Babylon the Great, which
made all the nations drink
the maddening wine of her
adulteries."

9. A third angel followed
them and said in a loud
voice: "If anyone worships
the beast and his image and
receives his mark on the
forehead or on the hand,

10. he, too, will drink of the
wine of God's fury, which
has been poured full
strength into the cup of his
wrath. He will be tormented
with burning sulfur in the
presence of the holy angels
and of the Lamb.

muhondo sebandonyi babuya-buya, nera muhondo sola Mwana weMbulyi.	너라 무호또 소롸 뫄나 워뿌레.	
11. Mango abu bandju bakaba balorera kwa kasibu mwoyu mulyiro, emusi wao akanaendekera kunde afumba esuku nemango. Kanji, batakatamuke emushi nebuthufu chiro na hicha. Rero, kubikaba bacha kwa bandju ba bendee bera ei nyama ngalyi, bera nechihuhanyi chai, nekubikibwako ekalorero kesina lyai."	11. 마오 아부 바쭈 바가바 바로러라 과 가시부 모유 무레로, 어무시 와오 아가나어떠거라 구떠 아푸빠 어수구 너마오. 가찌, 바다가다무거 어무씨 너부후푸 찌로 나 히짜. 러로, 구비가바 바짜 과 바쭈 바 버떠어 버라 어이 냐마 아레, 버라 너찌후하니 짜이, 너구비기봐고 어가로러로 거시나 랴이."	11. And the smoke of their torment rises for ever and ever. There is no rest day or night for those who worship the beast and his image, or for anyone who receives the mark of his name."
12. Bushi noku, ba bende bathunda emiomba ya Ongo nekulanga ebwemeresi bwabo mu Yesu, bemire kunde bachisesa mwa bushibirisi.	12. 부씨 노구, 바 버떠 바쭈따 어미오빠 야 오오 너구라아 어붜머러시 봐보 무 여수, 버미러 구떠 바찌서사 뫄 부씨비리시.	12. This calls for patient endurance on the part of the saints who obey God's commandments and remain faithful to Jesus.
13. Kanji nera kumva unji murenge atenga kwa nguba, anyibura mbu: "Uanjikaa mbu: Kutengera chine chihangi, baahanyirwe ba bende bafa balyi mwa buuma na Enawethu!" eMuchima Mubuya-buya nai, era kuteta mbu: "Kubinalyi! Bakatamuka kwa malyibuko mabo, nemyanya yabo ikanabakulyikira."	13. 가찌 너라 구빠 우찌 무러어 아더아 과 우바, 아네부라 뿌: "우아찌가아 뿌: 구더어라 찌너 찌하이, 바아하네뤄 바 버떠 바파 바레 뫄 부우마 나 어나워쭈!" 어무찌마 무부야-부야 나이, 어라 구더다 뿌: "구비나레! 바가다무가 과 마레부고 마보, 너먀냐 야보 이가나바구레기라."	13. Then I heard a voice from heaven say, "Write: Blessed are the dead who die in the Lord from now on." "Yes," says the Spirit, "they will rest from their labor, for their deeds will follow them."
14. Chasinda, nera kuhuba kulola ku lumbumbu lwa	14. 짜시따, 너라 구후바 구로라 구 루뿌뿌 롸 무오고-	14. I looked, and there before me was a white

muoko-muoko. Kwolu lumbumbu, kwabaa kwekese ola uhuhire ngeMwana weMundju. Nokwethwe lyai, abaa embese nzita era bakunganyise mwa horo. Kanji mwa mino yai, abaa ete mu karoko ka kakalyiire.

15 Unji ndonyi era kutenga mwa luhu lwa Ongo lwa luthula kwa nguba. Oyu ndonyi, era kuuma emurenge abura oyu wabaa wekese kwolu lumbumbu mbu: "Chasaa ekaroko kao, utangirise washebula, bushi ebihangi byekushebula emyaka mwa butala byaikire mira."

16. Unao-unao, oyu wabaa wekese kwolu lumbumbu, kuna kurenza ka karoko kai mwa butala, na ashebula ei myaka.

17. Mwolu luhu lwa Ongo lunolu-lunolu, lwa luthula kwa nguba, mwera kutenga unji ndonyi. Nai abaa ete kanji karoko ka kakalyiire.

18. Chasinda, kwa kahaha kemithulo, nako kwera kuulukira unji ndonyi muuma. Oyu ndonyi, iwabaa uthula wemangirire emulyiro. Nai era

무오고. 곤루 루뿌뿌, 과바아 궈거서 오롸 우후히러 꺼마나 워무뿌. 노궈줘 랴이, 아바아 어뻐서 씨다 어라 바구까네서 롸 호로. 가찌 롸 미노 야이, 아바아 어더 무 가로고 가 가가쩨이러.

15 우찌 또네 어라 구더까 롸 루후 롸 오꼬 롸 루쭈롸 과 꾸바. 오유 또네, 어라 구우마 어무러꺼 아부라 오유 와바아 워거서 곤루 루뿌뿌 뿌: "짜사아 어가로고 가오, 우다끼리서 와써부롸, 부씨 어비하끼 벼구써부롸 어먀가 롸 부다롸 뱌이기러 미라."

16. 우나오-우나오, 오유 와바아 워거서 곤루 루뿌뿌, 구나 구러싸 가 가로고 가이 롸 부다롸, 나 아써부롸 어이 먀가.

17. 몰루 루후 롸 오꼬 루노루-루노루, 롸 루쭈롸 과 꾸바, 뭐라 구더까 우찌 또네. 나이 아바아 어더 가찌 가로고 가 가가쩨이러.

18. 짜시따, 과 가하하 거미쭈롣, 나고 궈라 구우루기라 우찌 또네 무우마. 오유 또네, 이와바아 우쭈롸 워마끼리러 어무쩨로. 나이

cloud, and seated on the cloud was one "like a son of man" with a crown of gold on his head and a sharp sickle in his hand.

15. Then another angel came out of the temple and called in a loud voice to him who was sitting on the cloud, "Take your sickle and reap, because the time to reap has come, for the harvest of the earth is ripe."

16. So he who was seated on the cloud swung his sickle over the earth, and the earth was harvested.

17. Another angel came out of the temple in heaven, and he too had a sharp sickle.

18. Still another angel, who had charge of the fire, came from the altar and called in a loud voice to him who had the sharp sickle, "Take

kuuma emurenge abura mulyikabo ola wabaa wete ka karoko kakalyiire mwa mino mbu: "Tolaa ekaroko kao, uye mwehwa lyemisabibu lya liri mwa butala. Uishaa ematabi ma malyi kwethufuma thwemisabibu, wanalunda-lundaamo. Bushi ethufuma thwa thulyiko thwerire mira."

어라 구우마 어무러ᄞᅥ 아부라 무ᄙᅨ가보 오ᄙᅪ 와바아 워더 가 가로고 가가ᄙᅨ이러 뫄 미노 쁘: "도ᄙᅪ아 어가로고 가오, 우여 뭐화 ᄙᅧ미사비부 ᄙᅣ ᄙᅵ리 뫄 부다ᄙᅪ. 우이싸아 어마다비 마 마ᄙᅨ 궈쭈푸마 쭤미사비부, 와나루ᄠᅡ-루ᄠᅡ아모. 부씨 어쭈푸마 쫘 쭈ᄙᅨ고 쭤리러 미라."

your sharp sickle and gather the clusters of grapes from the earth's vine, because its grapes are ripe."

19. Unao-unao, ola ndonyi kuna kurenza ekaroko kai mwehwa lyemisabibu era yabaa iri mwa butala, na ashebulai. Chasinda, thwa thufuma era kuumatho mu mufumbi munene. Oyu mufumbi ahuhanyisibwe nebusinane bwa Ongo.

19. 우나오-우나오, 오ᄙᅪ 또니 구나 구러ᄡᅡ 어가로고 가이 뭐화 ᄙᅧ미사비부 어라 야바아 이리 뫄 부다ᄙᅪ, 나 아써부ᄙᅪ이. 짜시ᄠᅡ, 쫘 쭈푸마 어라 구우마쏘 무 무푸삐 무너너. 오유 무푸삐 아후하네시붜 너부시나너 봐 오ᅁᅩ.

19. The angel swung his sickle on the earth, gathered its grapes and threw them into the great winepress of God's wrath.

20. Bera kuikanjira mwoyu mufumbi, bure nemusi. Mwera kuulukira mikira era yabaa yashenda kuikira ku bilometere bingaika ku mana mahathu. Nebunenene kuya mwa chanya bwei mikira, bwabaa bungaika ku metere nguma na chimbi.

20. 버라 구이가ᄡᅵ라 뫄유 무푸삐, 부러 너무시. 뭐라 구우ᄙᅮ기라 미기라 어라 야바아 야써ᄠᅡ 구이기라 구 비ᄙᅩ머더러 비ᄞᅡ이가 구 마나 마하쭈. 너부너너너 구야 뫄 짜냐 붜이 미기라, 봐바아 부ᄞᅡ이가 구 머더러 ᅁᅮ마 나 찌삐.

20. They were trampled in the winepress outside the city, and blood flowed out of the press, rising as high as the horses' bridles for a distance of 1,600 stadia.

Byaboolyibwa Chikono 15

1. Era nyuma sebi, nera kulola ku chinji chisomerano chinene kwa nguba kanji cha kushishasa busese. Nechi

뱌보오ᄙᅰ봐 찌고노 15

1. 어라 뉴마 서비, 너라 구ᄙᅩᄙᅪ 구 찌ᄡᅵ 찌소머라노 찌너너 과 ᅁᅮ바 가ᄡᅵ 짜 구씨싸사 부서서. 너찌

Revelation Chapter 15[NIV]

1. I saw in heaven another great and marvelous sign: seven angels with the seven last plagues--last, because

chisomerano chi chechine: kwabaa kulyi bandonyi balyinda ba babaa bete na malyibuko malyinda mwa mino. Rero, amu malyibuko mu masinda, bushi mu Ongo angakoresa kwa kumalyirisa ebusinane bwai.

2. Kanji nera kulola ku yabunya nyanja era yabaa yarenga mwemeho nga chirauli. Kanji ei nyanja yabaa ihoonganyisibwe mwemulyiro. Nera musike sai, nera kuhuba kulola kwa ba bandju ba baimaa era nyama ngalyi alauma nechihuhanyi chai, nemuanjo wesina lyai. Abu bandju babaa bete nzenze mwa mino sa Ongo eresaabo.

3. Babaa bemba elwimbo lwemuanda wai Musa, nelwimbo lwola Mwana weMbulyi. Olu lwimbo, bacha ku lwabaa lutechire: "Enawethu Ongo webuashi boshi! Byoshi bya wende waira, bithula binene, kanji bya kushishasa! Nenjira sao sinathula sa kanangana, kanji sinathula sithungenene! Woyo uuthula Mwami wembaa soshi!

찌소머라노 찌 쩌찌너: 과바아 구레 바또네 바레따 바 바바아 버더 나 마레부고 마레따 와 미노. 러로, 아무 마레부고 무 마시따, 부씨 무 오쪼 아빠고러사 과 구마페리사 어부시나너 봐이.

2. 가찌 너라 구로롸 구 야부냐 냐짜 어라 야바아 야러빠 뭐머호 빠 찌라우뤼. 가찌 어이 냐짜 야바아 이호오빠네시붜 뭐무풰로. 너라 무시거 사이, 너라 구후바 구로롸 과 바 바뚜 바 바이마아 어라 냐마 빠레 아롸우마 너찌후하니 짜이, 너무아쪼 워시나 랴이. 아부 바뚜 바바아 버더 써써 뫄 미노 사 오쪼 어러사아보.

3. 바바아 버빠 어뤼뽀 뤄무아따 와이 무사, 너뤼뽀 롤롸 모나 워뿌레. 오루 뤼뽀, 바짜 구 롸바아 루더찌러: "어나워쭈 오쪼 워부아씨 보씨! 뵤씨 뱌 워더 와이라, 비쭈롸 비너너, 가찌 뱌 구씨싸사! 너찌라 사오 시나쭈롸 사 가나빠나, 가찌 시나쭈롸 시쭈어너너! 오요 우우쭈롸 뫄미 워빠아 소씨!

with them God's wrath is completed.

2. And I saw what looked like a sea of glass mixed with fire and, standing beside the sea, those who had been victorious over the beast and his image and over the number of his name. They held harps given them by God

3. and sang the song of Moses the servant of God and the song of the Lamb: "Great and marvelous are your deeds, Lord God Almighty. Just and true are your ways, King of the ages.

4. Enawethu! Nde ola utangende wakwobaa? Nesi nde ola unganana kunde atonga esina lyao? Bushi weine oshao, uunathula Mubuya-buya. Kanji ebandju bembaa soshi bakende baika kukwera, bushi balolyire kwemirimo yao ithula ithungenene."

5. Chasinda, nera kulola kwa luhu lwa Ongo lwachungukala kwa nguba. Kanji olu luhu, lyilyinathula hema lyelubuanano.

6. Ba bandonyi balyinda, ba babaa bete na ma malyibuko malyinda mwa mino, bera kuuluka mulo. Enjimba sa babaa bembese sabaa sitakachire kanji sengengenya busese. Nemikaba era babaa bembere mwa bifuba byabo, yabaa ikunganyisibwe mwa horo.

7. Chiuma mwabya bindju bine bya biri biuma-uma kanji bya kushishasa, chera kwangirisa abu bandonyi balyinda ngumbu sirinda sa sabaa sikunganyisibwe mwa horo. Mwesi ngumbu, mwabaa mwehwire ebusinane bwa Ongo. Noyu Ongo inoyu-inoyu iuthulao esuku

4. 어나워쭈! 떠 오롸 우다꺼떠 와고바아? 너시 떠 오롸 우꺼나나 구떠 아도꺼 어시나 랴오? 부씨 워이너 오싸오, 우우나쭈롸 무부야-부야. 가찌 어바뚜 버빠아 소씨 바거떠 바이가 구궈롸, 부씨 바로쩨러 궈미리모 야오 이쭈롸 이쭈꺼너너."

5. 짜시따, 너라 구로롸 과 루후 롸 오꼬 롸쭈꾸가롸 과 우바. 가찌 오루 루후, 쩨쩨나쭈롸 허마 쩌루부아나노.

6. 바 바또네 바쩨따, 바 바바아 버더 나 마 마쩨부고 마쩨따 롸 미노, 버라 구우루가 무로. 어찌빠 사 바바아 버뻐서 사바아 시다가찌러 가찌 서꺼꺼냐 부서서. 너미가바 어라 바바아 버뻐러 롸 비푸바 뱌보, 야바아 이구꺼네시붜 롸 호로.

7. 찌우마 뫄뱌 비뚜 비너 뱌 비리 비우마-우마 가찌 뱌 구씨싸사, 쩌라 과꺼리사 아부 바또네 바쩨따 꾸뿌 시리따 사 사바아 시구꺼네시붜 롸 호로. 뭐시 꾸뿌, 뫄바아 뭐휘러 어부시나너 롸 오꼬. 노유 오꼬 이노유-이노유 이우쭈롸오 어수구 너마꼬.

4. Who will not fear you, O Lord, and bring glory to your name? For you alone are holy. All nations will come and worship before you, for your righteous acts have been revealed."

5. After this I looked and in heaven the temple, that is, the tabernacle of the Testimony, was opened.

6. Out of the temple came the seven angels with the seven plagues. They were dressed in clean, shining linen and wore golden sashes around their chests.

7. Then one of the four living creatures gave to the seven angels seven golden bowls filled with the wrath of God, who lives for ever and ever.

nemango.

8. Unao-unao, lwa luhu lwa Ongo, kuna kwehula mwemusi ola watengera mwa bulangare nomwa buashi bwai. Bushi noku, kutabaa chiro na mundju asibya ola waalaa kwengiriramo kuikira mango ma malyibuko malyinda, ma ba bandonyi balyinda baretaa, mabaa mawere.

8. 우나오-우나오, 롸 루후 롸 오꼬, 구나 궈후롸 뭐무시 오롸 와더꺼라 롸 부롸꺼러 노롸 부아씨 봐이. 부씨 노구, 구다바아 찌로 나 무쭈 아시뱌 오롸 와아롸아 궈꺼리리라모 구이기라 마꼬 마 마레부고 마레따, 마 바 바또네 바쩨따 바러다아, 마바아 마워러.

8. And the temple was filled with smoke from the glory of God and from his power, and no one could enter the temple until the seven plagues of the seven angels were completed.

Byaboolyibwa Chikono 16

1. Era nyuma sebi, nera kumva murenge atengera mwa luhu lwa Ongo. Oyu murenge, abaa abura abu bandonyi balyinda mbu: "Ebusinane bwa Ongo, bwa bulyi mwesi ngumbu sirinda, muyaa kushesherabo mwa butala!"

2. Endonyi mubere-bere era kuya kusheshera eyai ngumbu mwa butala. Ebandju boshi ba babaa babikibwe kwekalorero kera nyama ngalyi, na kunde bera echihuhanyi chai, unao-unao kuna kumeranga ku bisimba bisibu. Ebi bisimba, byabaa byenjire bya balosa kwa kasibu.

3. Endonyi wa kabiri, nai era kuya kusheshera eyai ngumbu

뱌보오쩨봐 찌고노 16

1. 어라 뉴마 서비, 너라 구빠 무러꺼 아더꺼라 롸 루후 롸 오꼬. 오유 무러꺼, 아바아 아부라 아부 바또네 바쩨따 뿌: "어부시나너 봐 오꼬, 롸 부쩨 뭐시 우뿌 시리따, 무야아 구써써라보 롸 부다롸!"

2. 어또네 무버러-버러 어라 구야 구써써라 어야이 우뿌 롸 부다롸. 어바뉴 보씨 바 바바아 바비기붜 궈가로러로 거라 냐마 꺼레, 나 구떠 버라 어찌후하네 짜이, 우나오- 우나오 구나 구머라꺼 구 비시빠 비시부. 어비 비시빠, 뱌바아 벼찌러 뱌 바로사 과 가시부.

3. 어또네 와 가비리, 나이 어라 구야 구써써라 어야이

Revelation Chapter 16[NIV]

1. Then I heard a loud voice from the temple saying to the seven angels, "Go, pour out the seven bowls of God's wrath on the earth."

2. The first angel went and poured out his bowl on the land, and ugly and painful sores broke out on the people who had the mark of the beast and worshiped his image.

3. The second angel poured out his bowl on the sea, and

mwa nyanja. Unao-unao, era nyanja kuna kuhuba nga mikira ya mundju ola wafire. Chasinda, na byoshi bya bithulamo kuna kusika.

4. Endonyi wa kahathu, nai era kuya kusheshera eyai ngumbu mwa nyishi, nomwa shokororo. Unao-unao, nabi kuna kubindjuka mikira.

5. Mwolu, nera kumva endonyi ola uthula wemangirire emeshi moshi ateta mbu: "Woyo uthula utungenene! Uwabaa, kanji uunachitula! Weke, kwa binemire ku wende wanachinjibusa ebandju.

6. Bushi, emikira yebarebi neyebanji bandju bao, bano bandju bu baisheshaa. Rero, kubamwesa ku wabamwesise emikira ngokwa byabaa binemire ubakorere."

7. Chasinda, nera kumva emurenge atengera kwa kahaha kemithulo ola wabaa wekirisa mbu: "Kubinalyi! Enawethu Ongo webuashi boshi, weke wende wachinjibusa ebandju kwa binemire. Nebuchinjibusi bwao, bunathula bwa kanangana!"

8. Endonyi wa kane, nai era

꾸뿌 먀 냐짜. 우나오-우나오, 어라 냐짜 구나 구후바 까 미기라 야 무뚜 오라 와피러. 짜시따, 나 뵤씨 뱌 비쭈롸모 구나 구시가.

4. 어또네 와 가하쭈, 나이 어라 구야 구써써라 어야이 꾸뿌 먀 네씨, 노롸 쏘고로로. 우나오-우나오, 나비 구나 구비뿌가 미기라.

5. 모루, 너라 구빠 어또네 오라 우쭈롸 워마삐리러 어머씨 모씨 아더다 뿌: "오요 우쭈롸 우두꺼너너! 우와바아, 가찌 우우나찌두롸! 워거, 과 비너미러 구 워떠 와나찌찌부사 어바뚜.

6. 부씨, 어미기라 여바러비 너여바찌 바뚜 바오, 바노 바뚜 부 바이써싸아. 러로, 구바뭐사 구 와바뭐시서 어미기라 꼬과 뱌바아 비너미러 우바고러러."

7. 짜시따, 너라 구빠 어무러꺼 아더꺼라 과 가하하 거미쭈로 오롸 와바아 워기리사 뿌: "구비나례! 어나워쭈 오꼬 워부아씨 뵤씨, 워거 워떠 와찌찌부사 어바뚜 과 비너미러. 너부찌찌부시 봐오, 부나쭈롸 봐 가나까나!"

8. 어또네 와 가너, 나이 어라

---

it turned into blood like that of a dead man, and every living thing in the sea died.

4. The third angel poured out his bowl on the rivers and springs of water, and they became blood.

5. Then I heard the angel in charge of the waters say: "You are just in these judgments, you who are and who were, the Holy One, because you have so judged;

6. for they have shed the blood of your saints and prophets, and you have given them blood to drink as they deserve."

7. And I heard the altar respond: "Yes, Lord God Almighty, true and just are your judgments."

8. The fourth angel poured

kuya kusheshera eyai ngumbu kwesuba. Unao-unao, lyesuba kuna kubona ebuashi bwekunde lyababa ebandju nechuka chalyi.

구야 구써써라 어야이 우뿌 궈수바. 우나오-우나오, 려수바 구나 구보나 어부아씨 뷔구떠 랴바바 어바쭈 너쭈가 짜례.

out his bowl on the sun, and the sun was given power to scorch people with fire.

9. Rero bushi echi chuka chabaa chikalyiire, chera kubaba ebandju busese. Si chiro bacha, batanabindjukaa kutenga mwa bibi byabo mbu batonge Ongo. Si bera kutangirisa bakamba-kamba esina lyai, bushi iwabaa wete ebuashi era luulu samu malyibuko.

9. 러로 부씨 어찌 쭈가 짜바아 찌가례이러, 쩌라 구바바 어바쭈 부서서. 시 찌로 바짜, 바다나비쭈가아 구더따 롸 비비 뱌보 뿌 바도떠 오꼬. 시 버라 구다띠리사 바가빠-가빠 어시나 랴이, 부씨 이와바아 워더 어부아씨 어라 루우루 사무 마례부고.

9. They were seared by the intense heat and they cursed the name of God, who had control over these plagues, but they refused to repent and glorify him.

10. Endonyi wa katano, nai era kuya kusheshera eyai ngumbu kwa ndebe yebwami yera nyama ngalyi. Unao-unao bwa bwami bwai, kuna kuba mu musimya munene busese. Ebandju bera kutangirisa bachikuutanga enyirimi bushi nemalumwa.

10. 어또네 와 가다노, 나이 어라 구야 구써써라 어야이 우뿌 과 떠버 여뫄미 여라 냐마 따례. 우나오-우나오 봐 뫄미 봐이, 구나 구바 무 무시먀 무너너 부서서. 어바쭈 버라 구다띠리사 바찌구우다따 어네리미 부씨 너마루롸.

10. The fifth angel poured out his bowl on the throne of the beast, and his kingdom was plunged into darkness. Men gnawed their tongues in agony

11. Rero bushi namo malumwa, alauma nebya bisimba, bera kunaendekera bakamba-kamba Ongo ola uthula kwa nguba. Si batanabindjukaa chiro na hicha kutenga mwa bibi byabo.

11. 러로 부씨 나모 마루롸, 아롸우마 너뱌 비시빠, 버라 구나어떠거라 바가빠-가빠 오꼬 오롸 우쭈롸 과 우바. 시 바다나비쭈가아 찌로 나 히짜 구더따 롸 비비 뱌보.

11. and cursed the God of heaven because of their pains and their sores, but they refused to repent of what they had done.

12. Endonyi wa ndathu, nai era kuya kusheshera eyai ngumbu mwa lwishi lunene

12. 어또네 와 따쭈, 나이 어라 구야 구써써라 어야이 우뿌 롸 뤼씨 루너너 뤄

12. The sixth angel poured out his bowl on the great river Euphrates, and its

iwe Furati. Lwa lwishi kuna kwoma, chasiya ihube njira era bami ba batengera era suba lyende lyaulukira, bangarengamo.

13. Chasinda, nera kulola ku bihwasi bihatu bya bihuhire nga myota. Ebi bihwasi, byabaa byatenga mwa bunu bwera njoka inene, nomwa bunu bwera nyama ngalyi, nomwa bunu bwola murebi webisha.

14. Rero, ebi bihwasi byebasimu, byabaa byenjire byaira bisomerano. Kanji byera kunde byaya era mwebami boshi bomwa butala, bibuanyanyebo, bachikunganye kwa kulwa endambala era ikaika kwolwa lusuku lunene lwa Ongo webuashi boshi.

15. Mumvaa! Enawethu atechire mbu: "Nyikabaha chimbate nga mwisi. Rero, aahanyirwe chira mundju woshi ola wachilanga-langa, alanga neluchimba lwai kubuya, angesha kuenda butambara, na kufa honyi era muhondo sebandju."

16. Bya bihwasi, byera kunabuanyanya ba bami mwa chisiki cha bende berika mwa

푸라디. 롸 뤼씨 구나 굠마, 짜시야 이후버 띠라 어라 바미 바 바더ㄸ라 어라 수바 려ㄸ러 랴우루기라, 바ㄸ러ㄸ모.

13. 짜시따, 너라 구롼라 구 비화시 비하두 뱌 비후히러 ㄸ 무요다. 어비 비화시, 뱌바아 뱌더ㄸ 마 부누 붜라 쪼가 이너너, 노롸 부누 붜라 냐마 ㄸ레, 노롸 부누 볼라 무러비 워비싸.

14. 러로, 어비 비화시 뱌바시무, 뱌바아 뱌찌러 뱌이라 비소머라노. 가찌 뱌라 구떠 뱌야 어라 뭐바미 보씨 보롸 부다롸, 비부아냐녀보, 바찌구ㄸ녀 과 구롸 어따빠롸 어라 이가이가 굠롸 루수구 루너너 롸 오꼬 워부아씨 보씨.

15. 무빠아! 어나워쭈 아더찌러 뿌: "네가바하 찌빠더 ㄸ 뮈시. 러로, 아아하니뤄 찌라 무뿌 옹씨 오롸 와찌롸ㄸ-롸ㄸ, 아롸ㄸ 너루찌빠 롸이 구부야, 아ㄸ싸 구어따 부다롸라, 나 구파 호네 어라 무호또 서바뚜."

16. 뱌 비화시, 뱌라 구나부아냐냐 바 바미 롸 찌시기 짜 버ㄸ 버리가 롸

water was dried up to prepare the way for the kings from the East.

13. Then I saw three evil spirits that looked like frogs; they came out of the mouth of the dragon, out of the mouth of the beast and out of the mouth of the false prophet.

14. They are spirits of demons performing miraculous signs, and they go out to the kings of the whole world, to gather them for the battle on the great day of God Almighty.

15. "Behold, I come like a thief! Blessed is he who stays awake and keeps his clothes with him, so that he may not go naked and be shamefully exposed."

16. Then they gathered the kings together to the place that in Hebrew is called

Chieburaniya mbu: "Harimaketoni."

17. Endonyi wa kalyinda, nai era kuya kuhuira eyai ngumbu mwa chanya. Chasinda, mwa ndebe yebwami bwa Ongo era ithula mwa luhu lwai, mwera kutenga murenge ola wateta mbu: "Rero byoshi, byaberere mira!"

18. Unao-unao, kwera kurenga thulimya-limya alauma nemikungulo, na mirasano. Mwa butala, mwera kurenga musisi munene busese. Rero, kutengera ala ebandju baberaa mwa butala kuikira lwarero, kutafuraa kurenga musisi ola wera ubulyingitanyise bacha.

19. Unao-unao, ola musi munene kuna kuberekamo bimbi bihathu, neinji misi yembaa soshi, yera kuhandjukalanga. Ola musi munene we Babiloni, Ongo era kukengerao, mwa kumwesao engumbu sa sehwire mwebusinane bwai. Nobu businane, bwabaa bukalyiire busese nga tifai era ikalyire!

20. Mwolu, ebisimba byoshi byera kuirima. Nendjulungu nasi, sitanachilorekanaako.

쩌부라니야 뿌: "하리마거도니."

17. 어또네 와 가롄따, 나이 어라 구야 구후이라 어야이 우뿌 롸 짜냐. 짜시따, 롸 떠버 여봐미 봐 오꼬 어라 이쭈롸 롸 루후 롸이, 뭐라 구더빠 무러어 오라 와더다 뿌: "러로 뵤씨, 뱌버러러 미라!"

18. 우나오-우나오, 궈라 구러빠 쭈뀌먀-뀌먀 아롸우마 너미구우뽀, 나 미라사노. 롸 부다롸, 뭐라 구러빠 무시시 무너너 부서서. 러로, 구더빠라 아롸 어바쭈 바버라아 롸 부다롸 구이기라 롸러로, 구다푸라아 구러빠 무시시 오롸 워라 우부롒이다니서 바짜.

19. 우나오-우나오, 오롸 무시 무너너 구나 구버러가모 비삐 비하쭈, 너이씨 미시 여빠아 소씨, 여라 구하쭈가롸빠. 오롸 무시 무너너 워 바비로니, 오꼬 어라 구거빠라오, 롸 구뭐사오 어우뿌 사 서휘러 뭐부시나너 봐이. 노부 부시나너, 봐바아 부가롒이러 부서서 빠 디파이 어라 이가롒러!

20. 몰루, 어비시빠 뵤씨 벼라 구이리마. 너쭈루우 나시, 시다나찌로러가나아고.

Armageddon.

17. The seventh angel poured out his bowl into the air, and out of the temple came a loud voice from the throne, saying, "It is done!"

18. Then there came flashes of lightning, rumblings, peals of thunder and a severe earthquake. No earthquake like it has ever occurred since man has been on earth, so tremendous was the quake.

19. The great city split into three parts, and the cities of the nations collapsed. God remembered Babylon the Great and gave her the cup filled with the wine of the fury of his wrath.

20. Every island fled away and the mountains could not be found.

21. Chasinjire, kwa nguba kwera kutowa mvula ya luthwa lunenene. Chira luthwa, lwabaa lwete biro bingaika ku mane. Mango olu luthwa lwabaa lwenjire lwatoweranga kwa bandju, bera kunde bakamba-kamba Ongo, bushi amu malyibuko mabaa makalyiire busese.

21. 짜시끼러, 과 우바 궈라 구도와 뿌꽈 야 루좌 루너너너. 찌라 루좌, 꽈바아 뭐더 비로 비까이가 구 마너. 마꼬 오루 루좌 꽈바아 뭐끼러 꽈도워라까 과 바뚜, 버라 구떠 바가빠-가빠 오꼬, 부씨 아무 마레부고 마바아 마가페이러 부서서.

21. From the sky huge hailstones of about a hundred pounds each fell upon men. And they cursed God on account of the plague of hail, because the plague was so terrible.

Byaboolyibwa Chikono 17

1. Chasinda, muuma mwaba bandonyi balyinda ba babaa bete sa ngumbu sirinda, era kuika kunyibura mbu: "Ubahaa nyikulose kwa Ongo angachinjibusa cha chihungukasi. Nechi chihungukasi, imusi munene ola wimbirwe kwa musike wa nyishi sinene.

2. Ebami boshi bomwa butala babanjire ekiri nachi. Nebandju bamo, nabo berire banatamirira mwoku kunde babanda ekiri nachi."

3. Unao-unao, eMuchima Mubuya-buya era kunyandaalyira, ola ndonyi kuna kunyeka mwa buyeye. Mwobu buyeye, nera kulola ku mukasi muuma ekese ku nyama nguma ngalyi ya

뱌보오페봐 찌고노 17

1. 짜시따, 무우마 꽈바 바도니 바레따 바 바바아 버더 사 우뿌 시리따, 어라 구이가 구네부라 뿌: "우바하아 네구로서 과 오꼬 아까찌찌부사 짜 찌후우가시. 너찌 찌후우가시, 이무시 무너너 오꽈 위뻬뤄 과 무시거 와 네씨 시너너.

2. 어바미 보씨 보봐 부다꽈 바바찌러 어기리 나찌. 너바뚜 바모, 나보 버리러 바나다미리라 모구 구떠 바바따 어기리 나찌."

3. 우나오-우나오, 어무찌마 무부야-부야 어라 구냐따아페라, 오꽈 또네 구나 구녀가 봐 부여여. 모부 부여여, 너라 구로꽈 구 무가시 무우마 어거서 구 냐마 우마 까레 야 모꽈. 어이

Revelation Chapter 17[NIV]

1. One of the seven angels who had the seven bowls came and said to me, "Come, I will show you the punishment of the great prostitute, who sits on many waters.

2. With her the kings of the earth committed adultery and the inhabitants of the earth were intoxicated with the wine of her adulteries."

3. Then the angel carried me away in the Spirit into a desert. There I saw a woman sitting on a scarlet beast that was covered with blasphemous names and had seven heads and ten

mwola. Ei nyama, yabaa yete mithwe erinda, na membe ekumi. Nokwa mubiri wai woshi, kwabaa kwanjikirwe masina ma kukamba Ongo.

4. Oyu mukasi, abaa embese ndjimba sa mikerembende, kanji sa mwola. Abaa achibikire kwebulyimbi, mwa kuimbala bindju bya byabaa bikunganyisibwe mwa horo, nomwa makoi ma makomire kanji ma chichiro chinene, na mikofu ya chichiro chinene. Nomwa mino yai, abaa ete ngumbu era yabaa ikunganyisibwe mwa horo. Mwei ngumbu, mwabaa mwehwire bindju byemianyisa yelusingi lwai, kanji mwabaa mwehwire na binji bya bitasimise Ongo.

5. Nala malanga mai, abaa aanjikirwe esina lya myasi yai ibishirwe. Eri sina, lyabaa lyitechire mbu: "Nyono nyi musi munene weBabiloni, nyi nyina webihungukasi byoshi, kanji nyi nyina wa ba bende baira emyasi era itasimise Ongo."

6. Nera kulola kwa oyu mukasi atamirire emikira yebandju ba Ongo, neyebandju ba bechibwaa bushi nekundee

냐마, 야바아 여더 미쭤 어리따, 나 머뻐 어구미. 노과 무비리 와이 오씨, 과바아 과찌기뤄 마시나 마 구가빠 오꼬.

4. 오유 무가시, 아바아 어뻐서 띠빠 사 미거러뻐떠, 가찌 사 몰롸. 아바아 아찌비기러 궈부레뻬, 롸 구이빠롸 비쭈 뱌 뱌바아 비구까네시붜 롸 호로, 노롸 마고이 마 마고미러 가찌 마 찌찌로 찌너너, 나 미고푸 야 찌찌로 찌너너. 노롸 미노 야이, 아바아 어더 우뿌 어라 야바아 이구까네시붜 롸 호로. 뭐이 우뿌, 롸바아 뭐휘러 비쭈 벼미아네사 여루시꺼 롸이, 가찌 롸바아 뭐휘러 나 비찌 뱌 비다시미서 오꼬.

5. 나롸 마롸까 마이, 아바아 아아찌기뤄 어시나 랴 먀시 야이 이비씨뤄. 어리 시나, 랴바아 레더찌러 뿌: "뇨노 네 무시 무너너 워바비로니, 네 네나 워비후꾸가시 뵤씨, 가찌 네 네나 와 바 버떠 바이라 어먀시 어라 이다시미서 오꼬."

6. 너라 구론롸 과 오유 무가시 아다미리러 어미기라 여바누 바 오꼬, 너여바누 바 버찌봐아 부씨 너구떠어

horns.

4. The woman was dressed in purple and scarlet, and was glittering with gold, precious stones and pearls. She held a golden cup in her hand, filled with abominable things and the filth of her adulteries.

5. This title was written on her forehead: MYSTERY BABYLON THE GREAT THE MOTHER OF PROSTITUTES AND OF THE ABOMINATIONS OF THE EARTH.

6. I saw that the woman was drunk with the blood of the saints, the blood of those who bore testimony to

bateta kwa bya bachiloreraako era luulu sa Yesu. Namulolyireko, nera kusanwa busese.

7. Chasinda, oyu ndonyi era kunyibusa mbu: "Era! Chi chathumire wasanwa kasi? Rero nakubura emyasi era ibishirwe yoyu mukasi, neyei nyama ngalyi ekeseko, era yete mithwe erinda, na membe ekumi.

8. "Ei nyama wera kulolako, yabaa ithula kwamira, si lwarero itachirio. Si chiro bacha, ingeruka yatenga mwera fumbi irerere yekusimu, chasinda yanaya kwichibwa. Ebandju boshi bomwa butala, ba emasina mabo matafuraa kwanjikibwa mwa chitabo chekalamo kutengera ekubumbwa kwebutala, mango bangailolako bangasanwa busese, bushi ei nyama yabaa ithula kwa mira si lwarero itachirio. Si ingahuba kulorekanako.

9. "Anola, byemire emundju amenyerere ene myasi, ate bwenge bunene. Bushi ei mithwe erinda, siri ndjulungu sirinda sa oyu mukasi ekeseko. Kanji ei mithwe

바더다 과 뱌 바찌로러라아고 어라 루우루 사 여수. 나무로께레고, 너라 구사놔 부서서.

7. 짜시따, 오유 또네 어라 구네부사 뿌: "어라! 찌 짜쭈미러 와사놔 가시? 러로 나구부라 어먀시 어라 이비씨뤄 요유 무가시, 너여이 냐마 까레 어거서고, 어라 여더 미쭤 어리따, 나 머뻐 어구미.

8. "아이 냐마 워라 구로똬고, 야바아 이쭈똬 과미라, 시 똬러로 이다찌리오. 시 찌로 바짜, 이꺼루가 야더따 뭐라 푸뻬 이러러러 여구시무, 짜시따 야나야 귀찌봐. 어바뚜 보씨 보봐 부다똬, 바 어마시나 마보 마다푸라아 과찌기봐 봐 찌다보 쩌가똬모 구더꺼라 어구부똬 귀부다똬, 마꼬 바까이로똬고 바까사놔 부서서, 부씨 어이 냐마 야바아 이쭈똬 과 미라 시 똬러로 이다찌리오. 시 이까후바 구로러가나고.

9. "아노똬, 벼미러 어무뿌 아머녀러러 어너 먀시, 아더 뷔머 부너너. 부씨 어이 미쭤 어리따, 시리 뚜루우 시리따 사 오유 무가시 어거서고. 가찌 어이 미쭤 어리따, 바레

Jesus. When I saw her, I was greatly astonished.

7. Then the angel said to me: "Why are you astonished? I will explain to you the mystery of the woman and of the beast she rides, which has the seven heads and ten horns.

8. The beast, which you saw, once was, now is not, and will come up out of the Abyss and go to his destruction. The inhabitants of the earth whose names have not been written in the book of life from the creation of the world will be astonished when they see the beast, because he once was, now is not, and yet will come.

9. "This calls for a mind with wisdom. The seven heads are seven hills on which the woman sits.

erinda, balyi bami balyinda.

10. Mwabu bami, batano mubo, emami mabo mahandjukere mira. Si muuma yeke, achiri emire. Na unji muuma, atasa kwika. Si mango angaika, angema ku suku sieke oshao.

11. "Ei nyama ngalyi era yabaa ithula kwa mira, si lwarero itachirio, imwami wa munane. Oyola, nai analyi muuma mwabu bami balyinda, si nai kwichibwa ku anganechibwa.

12. "Namu membe ekumi wera kulolako, balyi bami ekumi ba batasa kwima. Abola bu bangeresibwa ebuashi bwekwima ku saa nguma oshao, alauma nei nyama ngalyi.

13. Abu bami boshi, mwasi muuma ibanete. Kanji bangeresa ei nyama ngalyi emisi yabo, nebuashi bwabo.

14. "Chasinda, bangaya kulwisa eMwana weMbulyi. Si angaimabo, bushi I Enawethu webaenawethu, kanji iMwami webami. Na mango angaimabo, angaba alyi nebandju bai babuya, ba yeine achilondoreraa mira nekubamaala."

바미 바쮀따.

10. 뫄부 바미, 바다노 무보, 어마미 마보 마하누거러 미라. 시 무우마 여거, 아찌리 어미러. 나 우찌 무우마, 아다사 귀가. 시 마꼬 아빠이가, 아머마 구 수구 시어거 오싸오.

11. "어이 냐마 빠쮀 어라 야바아 이쭈롸 과 미라, 시 롸러로 이다찌리오, 이뫄미 와 무나너. 오요롸, 나이 아나쮀 무우마 뫄부 바미 바쮀따, 시 나이 귀찌봐 구 아빠너찌봐.

12. "나무 머뻐 어구미 워라 구론롸고, 바쮀 바미 어구미 바 바다사 귀마. 아보롸 부 바뻐러시봐 어부아씨 붜귀마 구 사아 꾸마 오싸오, 아롸우마 너이 냐마 빠쮀.

13. 아부 바미 보씨, 뫄시 무우마 이바너더. 가찌 바뻐러사 어이 냐마 빠쮀 어미시 야보, 너부아씨 봐보.

14. "짜시따, 바빠야 구뤼사 어마나 워뿌쮀. 시 아빠이마보, 부씨 이 어나워쭈 워바어나워쭈, 가찌 이뫄미 워바미. 나 마꼬 아빠이마보, 아빠바 아쮀 너바쭈 바이 바부야, 바 여이너 아찌론또러라아 미라 너구바마아롸."

10. They are also seven kings. Five have fallen, one is, the other has not yet come; but when he does come, he must remain for a little while.

11. The beast who once was, and now is not, is an eighth king. He belongs to the seven and is going to his destruction.

12. "The ten horns you saw are ten kings who have not yet received a kingdom, but who for one hour will receive authority as kings along with the beast.

13. They have one purpose and will give their power and authority to the beast.

14. They will make war against the Lamb, but the Lamb will overcome them because he is Lord of lords and King of kings--and with him will be his called, chosen and faithful followers."

15. Oyu ndonyi, era kunyibura kanji mbu: "Esi nyishi wera kulolako, ala echi chihungukasi chekese, balyi ebandju ba batengera mu mbaa sinene, na mu bikembe binene, na mu nyibuto sinene na mu mateta manene.

16. "Nei nyama ngalyi wera kulolako, namu membe ekumi, bingahomba echi chihungukasi. Bingamunyaa na byoshi bya athusa, na kulyinda bamureka butambara. Chasinda, bangamulya nekusiresa ebukombo-kombo bwai mwa mulyiro.

17. Bushi abu bami ekumi, Ongo iwababikaa mwemianyisa yekuata oyu mwasi muuma, kanji baire ekuhonda kwai, berese nei nyama ngalyi ebuashi bwemami mabo, kuikira emyasi ya Ongo inaberere.

18. "Noyu mukasi wera kulolako, imusi munene ola uthula wemangirire ebami boshi bomwa butala."

15. 오유 또네, 어라 구네부라 가찌 뿌: "어시 니씨 워라 구로콰고, 아콰 어찌 찌후꾸가시 쩌거서, 바레 어바뉴 바 바더꾸라 무 빠아 시너너, 나 무 비거뻐 비너너, 나 무 네부도 시너너 나 무 마더다 마너너.

16. "너이 냐마 까레 워라 구로콰고, 나무 머뻐 어구미, 비까호빠 어찌 찌후꾸가시. 비까무냐아 나 뵤씨 뱌 아쭈사, 나 구레따 바무러가 부다빠라. 짜시따, 바까무꺄 너구시러사 어부고뽀-고뽀 봐이 봐 무레로.

17. 부씨 아부 바미 어구미, 오꼬 이와바비가아 뭐미아네사 여구아다 오유 콰시 무우마, 가찌 바이러 어구호따 과이, 버러서 너이 냐마 까레 어부아씨 붜마미 마보, 구이기라 어먀시 야 오꼬 이나버러러.

18. "노유 무가시 워라 구로콰고, 이무시 무너너 오콰 우쭈콰 워마끼리러 어바미 보씨 보봐 부다콰."

15. Then the angel said to me, "The waters you saw, where the prostitute sits, are peoples, multitudes, nations and languages.

16. The beast and the ten horns you saw will hate the prostitute. They will bring her to ruin and leave her naked; they will eat her flesh and burn her with fire.

17. For God has put it into their hearts to accomplish his purpose by agreeing to give the beast their power to rule, until God's words are fulfilled.

18. The woman you saw is the great city that rules over the kings of the earth."

Byaboolyibwa Chikono 18

1. Era nyuma sebi, nera kulola ku unji ndonyi atenga kwa

뱌보오례봐 찌고노 18

1. 어라 뉴마 서비, 너라 구로콰 구 우찌 또네 아더꽈

Revelation Chapter 18[NIV]

1. After this I saw another angel coming down from

nguba. Oyu ndonyi abaa ete buashi bunene busese. Ebulangare bwai, bwera kulomekera ebutala boshi.

2. Era kuteta na murenge munene mbu: "Aaye! Emusi munene weBabiloni akundjukire! Kubinalyi, akundjukire mira! Rero, erire anahuba chisiki chebasimu boshi, nebihwasi, na chira mulonge na nyama yoshi era italyibwa.

3. Kubinalyi, oyu musi, ebami bomwa bio byoshi, bairire elusingi nao. Nolu lusingi, lwera kutamisa ebandju boshi nga tifai era ikalyiire. Nebachimbusi bebi bio byoshi, nabo banaingukire bushi nekunde bausisamo chira ngulo ya chichiro chinene."

4. Chasinda, nera kumva unji murenge atenga kwa nguba nekuteta mbu: "Mu bandju banyi, mutengaa mwoyu musi fuba, mungesha kuhangira kwa bibi byao, na kuhangira kwa malyibuko mao,

5. bushi ebibi bya byairwamo, kuluwa ku byanaenda byaluwa busese, kuikira kwa nguba. Na Ongo anachiri abikengere.

과 우바. 오유 또네 아바아 어더 부아씨 부너너 부서서. 어부꽈머러 봐이, 붜라 구로머거라 어부다라 보씨.

2. 어라 구더다 나 무러어 무너너 뿌: "아아여! 어무시 무너너 워바비로니 아구뿌기러! 구비나레, 아구뿌기러 미라! 러로, 어리러 아나후바 찌시기 쩌바시무 보씨, 너비화시, 나 찌라 무로어 나 냐마 요씨 어라 이다레봐.

3. 구비나레, 오유 무시, 어바미 보봐 비오 뵤씨, 바이리러 어루시에 나오. 노루 루시에, 뤄라 구다미사 어바누 보씨 꽈 디파이 어라 이가레이러. 너바찌뿌시 버비 비오 뵤씨, 나보 바나이우기러 부씨 너구떠 바우시사모 찌라 우로 야 찌찌로 찌너너."

4. 짜시따, 너라 구빠 우찌 무러어 아더꽈 과 우바 너구더다 뿌: "무 바누 바니, 무더꽈아 모유 무시 푸바, 무어싸 구하에라 과 비비 뱌오, 나 구하에라 과 마레부고 마오,

5. 부씨 어비비 뱌 뱌이롸모, 구루와 구 뱌나어따 뱌루와 부서서, 구이기라 과 우바. 나 오꼬 아나찌리 아비거어러.

heaven. He had great authority, and the earth was illuminated by his splendor.

2. With a mighty voice he shouted: "Fallen! Fallen is Babylon the Great! She has become a home for demons and a haunt for every evil spirit, a haunt for every unclean and detestable bird.

3. For all the nations have drunk the maddening wine of her adulteries. The kings of the earth committed adultery with her, and the merchants of the earth grew rich from her excessive luxuries."

4. Then I heard another voice from heaven say: "Come out of her, my people, so that you will not share in her sins, so that you will not receive any of her plagues;

5. for her sins are piled up to heaven, and God has remembered her crimes.

6. Rero, kwa akoreraa ei inji misi, ku nao munamukoreraa. Kanji, muchifunaa kabiri kwa mabi ma abakoreraa. Na mwera ngumbu ahonganyisaa mwetifai yai, nai munomu mu munamuhonganyisaa mweinji era ikalyiire kabiri kurenza era aberesaa.

7. Kanji ngokwa abaa enjire achitonga nekuba mwa muako, kunoku ku munalosaao kwa kasibu, nekubikao mwa malyira. Oyu musi enjire atetera kwa muchima mbu: ?Nyono, nyekese kwa ndebe yebwami nga mwamikasi! Ndanamuhumba-kasi, ndakanalole ku chiro na malyira masibya?

8. Bushi noku, oyu musi angatabalyirwa na mano malyibuko moshi ku lusuku luuma oshao: elufu, nemalyira, nebulio. Chasinda, angasirera mwa mulyiro, bushi Enawethu Ongo webuashi boshi iwachinjibusiseo mira."

9. Rero, ebami bomwa butala, ba bendee babanda ekiri noyu musi, na kuchimoeresa mu binene mwa buare bwao, bangalyirirao na kuata

6. 러로, 과 아고러라아 어이 이찌 미시, 구 나오 무나무고러라아. 가찌, 무찌푸나아 가비리 과 마비 마 아바고러라아. 나 뭐라 우뿌 아호ㅺ네사아 뭐디파이 야이, 나이 무노무 무 무나무호ㅺ네사아 뭐이찌 어라 이가쩨이러 가비리 구러싸 어라 아버러사아.

7. 가찌 ㅇ과 아바아 어찌러 아찌도ㅺ 너구바 뫄 무아고, 구노구 구 무나른사아오 과 가시부, 너구비가오 뫄 마쩨라. 오유 무시 어찌러 아더더라 과 무찌마 뿌: ?뇨노, 녀거서 과 떠버 여봐미 ㅺ 마미가시! 따나무후빠-가시, 따가나른뤄 구 찌로 나 마쩨라 마시뱌?

8. 부씨 노구, 오유 무시 아ㅺ다바쩨라 나 마노 마쩨부고 모씨 구 루수구 루우마 오싸오: 어루푸, 너마쩨라, 너부쩨오. 짜시따, 아ㅺ시러라 뫄 무쩨로, 부씨 어나워쭈 오ㅇ 워부아씨 보씨 이와찌찌부시서오 미라."

9. 러로, 어바미 보뫄 부다ㅉ, 바 버떠어 바바따 어기리 노유 무시, 나 구찌모어러사 무 비너너 뫄 부아러 봐오, 바ㅺ쩨리리라오 나 구아다

6. Give back to her as she has given; pay her back double for what she has done. Mix her a double portion from her own cup.

7. Give her as much torture and grief as the glory and luxury she gave herself. In her heart she boasts, 'I sit as queen; I am not a widow, and I will never mourn.'

8. Therefore in one day her plagues will overtake her: death, mourning and famine. She will be consumed by fire, for mighty is the Lord God who judges her.

9. "When the kings of the earth who committed adultery with her and shared her luxury see the smoke of her burning, they

businane bunene, mango bangalola kwa musi wemulyiro ola ungasiresao enjire afumba mwa chanya.

10. Bangemangira marerere bushi nekwobaa amu malyibuko, na bangatangirisa bateta mbu: "Aaye! Buanya, buanya kwa musi munene we Babiloni! Woyo wabaa ndjwalyi!Si mu saa nguma oshao, mu wanachinjibusibwe!"

11. Ebachimbusi bomwa butala, nabo bangalyirirao na businane bunene, bushi ebindju bya bendee bachimbula, kutachiri ola ungachibaulyirabi.

12. Na mwebi bindju, mulyi ehoro, nebuteya, nemakoi ma makomire mechichiro chinene, nemikofu. Mulyi na njimba sikomire sa saterera nesemikerebende, nesemwola. Mulyi na chira michi era yende yauka-uka kubuya. Mulyi na bindju bya bikunganyisibwe mwa membe menjofu. Na binji bya bikunganyisibwe mu michi ya chichiro chinene. Mulyi na chira kandju koshi ka kakunganyisibwe mwa miringa, nomwa chuma. Mulyi

부시나너 부너너, 마꼬 바까로꽈 과 무시 워무레로 오꽈 우까시리사오 어찌러 아푸빠 마 짜냐.

10. 바꺼마끼라 마러러러 부씨 너곤바아 아무 마레부고, 나 바까다끼리사 바더다 뿌: "아아여! 부아냐, 부아냐 과 무시 무너너 워 바비로니! 오요 와바아 꽈레!시 무 사아 우마 오싸오, 무 와나찌찌부시붜!"

11. 어바찌뿌시 보꽈 부다꽈, 나보 바까레리라오 나 부시나너 부너너, 부씨 어비뉴 뱌 버떠어 바찌뿌꽈, 구다찌리 오꽈 우까찌바우레라비.

12. 나 뭐비 비뉴, 무레 어호로, 너부더야, 너마고이 마 마고미러 머찌찌로 찌너너, 너미고푸. 무레 나 띠빠 시고미러 사 사더러라 너서미거러버떠, 너서뫃꽈. 무레 나 찌라 미찌 어라 여너 야우가-우가 구부야. 무레 나 비뉴 뱌 비구까네시붜 뫄 머뻐 머쏘푸. 나 비찌 뱌 비구까네시붜 무 미찌 야 찌찌로 찌너너. 무레 나 찌라 가뚜 고씨 가 가구까네시붜 뫄 미리까, 노뫄 쭈마. 무레 나 비찌 뱌 비구까네시붜 뫄 마고이 마 마고미러 부서서

will weep and mourn over her.

10. Terrified at her torment, they will stand far off and cry: " 'Woe! Woe, O great city, O Babylon, city of power! In one hour your doom has come!'

11. "The merchants of the earth will weep and mourn over her because no one buys their cargoes any more--

12. cargoes of gold, silver, precious stones and pearls; fine linen, purple, silk and scarlet cloth; every sort of citron wood, and articles of every kind made of ivory, costly wood, bronze, iron and marble;

na binji bya bikunganyisibwe
mwa makoi ma makomire
busese kanji mabengirwe.

13. Kanji mwebi bindju,
mwabaa mulyi kasuku, na
marashi, na tifai, na mafuta,
na shano ibuya, na bulo, na
ngaafu, na mbulyi, na farasi,
na mithukalyi era yende
yakululwa, na thuungu, anabe
nebandju beburoko.

14. Mwesi suku, abu
bachimbusi bakatangirisa
babura oyu musi mbu: "Rero,
byoshi bya wabaa wenjire
wacheka nabi, byakuwerere.
Kanji ebuare, nebindju
bikomire-komire, byechichiro
chinene bya byalangala
busese, nabi byanakuwerere.
Bitakanachilorekeko chiro na
hicha."

15. Ebachimbusi ba babonaa
ebuare mwa kuchimbulyira
mwoyu musi, bangemangira
marerere mwa kwobaa
emalyibuko mao. Bangalyirirao
na kuata businane bunene.

16. Bangende balakanga mbu:
"Aaye! Buanya, buanya kwa
musi munene! Weine, uwabaa
wenjire wembala njimba sa
sikunganyisibwe mwa usi
sikomire, na sinji njimba
semikerebende, na sinji sa

가찌 마버띠뤄.

13. 가찌 뭐비 비쑤, 꽈바아
무레 가수구, 나 마라씨, 나
디파이, 나 마푸다, 나 싸노
이부야, 나 부뢰, 나 까아푸,
나 뿌레, 나 파라시, 나
미쭈가뻬 어라 여머 야구루뽜,
나 쭈우웇, 아나버 너바쭈
버부로고.

14. 뭐시 수구, 아부 바찌뿌시
바가다띠리사 바부라 오유
무시 뿌: "러로, 뵤씨 뱌
와바아 워띠러 와쩌가 나비,
뱌구워러러. 가찌 어부아러,
너비쭈 비고미러-고미러,
뼈찌찌로 찌너너 뱌 뱌꽈까꽈
부서서, 나비 뱌나구워러러.
비다가나찌뢰러거고 찌로 나
히짜."

15. 어바찌뿌시 바 바보나아
어부아러 꽈 구찌뿌뻬라 모유
무시, 바꺼마띠라 마러러러 꽈
곧바아 어마뻬부고 마오.
바까뻬리리라오 나 구아다
부시나너 부너너.

16. 바꺼너 바롸가까 뿌:
"아아여! 부아냐, 부아냐 과
무시 무너너! 워이너,
우와바아 워띠러 워빠롸 띠빠
사 시구꺼네시붜 꽈 우시
시고미러, 나 시찌 띠빠
서미거러버떠, 나 시찌 사

13. cargoes of cinnamon
and spice, of incense, myrrh
and frankincense, of wine
and olive oil, of fine flour
and wheat; cattle and sheep;
horses and carriages; and
bodies and souls of men.

14. "They will say, 'The fruit
you longed for is gone from
you. All your riches and
splendor have vanished,
never to be recovered.'

15. The merchants who sold
these things and gained
their wealth from her will
stand far off, terrified at her
torment. They will weep and
mourn

16. and cry out: " 'Woe!
Woe, O great city, dressed
in fine linen, purple and
scarlet, and glittering with
gold, precious stones and
pearls!

mwola busese. Kanji wabaa wenjire wachibika kwebulyimbi mwa kuembala ebindju bya byalangala, bya bikunganyisibwe mwa horo, nomwa makoi makomire mechichiro chinene, na mikofu ya chichiro chinene busese.

17. Si ku saa nguma oshao, ku obu buare bwao boshi, bwakumbirire!" Boshi ba bende baenza emato, alauma nebanji bandju boshi ba bende babalama nabo, na boshi ba bende bakola mwa mato, na boshi ba bende baira ebuchimbusi kwa nyanja, nabo bera kwemangira marerere nao.

18. Na mango abu boshi balolaa kwa musi wemulyiro woyu musi, enjire afumba, bera kutangirisa bachanya mbu: "Ono musi munene, kuchiri unji ola wabaa ungalyingamanyisibwa nao?"

19. Abu boshi, bera kunde bachibikanga emukungu mwethwe kwa kulosa ebusinane bwabo, na kulyirirao mbu: "Aaye! Buanya, buanya kwa musi munene! Bushi ba babaa bete emato ma mendee machimbulyira kwa nyanja, boshi babaa

모롸 부서서. 가찌 와바아	
워찌러 와찌비가 궈부레삐 마	
구어빠롸 어비뉴 뱌 뱌롸까롸,	
뱌 비구까네시붜 마 호로,	
노롸 마고이 마고미러	
머찌찌로 찌너너, 나 미고푸	
야 찌찌로 찌너너 부서서.	

17. 시 구 사아 우마 오싸오, 구 오부 부아러 봐오 보씨, 봐구삐리러!" 보씨 바 버너 바어싸 어마도, 아롸우마 너바찌 바뉴 보씨 바 버너 바바롸마 나보, 나 보씨 바 버너 바고롸 마 마도, 나 보씨 바 버너 바이라 어부찌뿌시 과 냐짜, 나보 버라 궈마삐라 마러러러 나오.

18. 나 마꼰 아부 보씨 바로롸아 과 무시 워무레로 오유 무시, 어찌러 아푸빠, 버라 구다삐리사 바짜냐 뿌: "오노 무시 무너너, 구찌리 우찌 오롸 와바아 우까레까마네시봐 나오?"

19. 아부 보씨, 버라 구더 바찌비가까 어무구꾸 뭐쭤 과 구르사 어부시나너 봐보, 나 구레리라오 뿌: "아아여! 부아냐, 부아냐 과 무시 무너너! 부씨 바 바바아 버더 어마도 마 머떠어 마찌뿌레라 과 냐짜, 보씨 바바아 버찌러 바이우가 봐 부아러 봐오. 시

17. In one hour such great wealth has been brought to ruin!' "Every sea captain, and all who travel by ship, the sailors, and all who earn their living from the sea, will stand far off.

18. When they see the smoke of her burning, they will exclaim, 'Was there ever a city like this great city?'

19. They will throw dust on their heads, and with weeping and mourning cry out: " 'Woe! Woe, O great city, where all who had ships on the sea became rich through her wealth! In one hour she has been brought to ruin!

benjire bainguka mwa buare bwao. Si ku saa nguma oshao, woshi akumbire!"

구 사아 우마 오싸오, 오씨 아구삐러!"

20. Si woyo nguba umowaa, bushi oyu musi akundukire! Nenyu mu ndjumwa, alauma nebarebi, nebanji bandju ba Ongo boshi, nenyu munamowaa, bushi emabi ma oyu musi abaa enjire abakorera, Ongo achinjibusiseo bushi namo.

20. 시 오요 우바 우모와아, 부씨 오유 무시 아구뚜기러! 너뉴 무 쭈뫄, 아롸우마 너바러비, 너바찌 바쭈 바 오꼬 보씨, 너뉴 무나모와아, 부씨 어마비 마 오유 무시 아바아 어찌러 아바고러라, 오꼬 아찌찌부시서오 부씨 나모.

20. Rejoice over her, O heaven! Rejoice, saints and apostles and prophets! God has judged her for the way she treated you.' "

21. Chasinda, ndonyi muuma ola wete buashi era kwemusa koi lyalyabaa lyiri nga lusho lunene. Era kuumalyi mwa nyanja na ateta mbu: "Ku emusi munene weBabiloni anganaumwa ereshi bacha nemisi, atakanachilorekaneko chiro na hicha!

21. 짜시따, 또네 무우마 오롸 워더 부아씨 어라 궈무사 고이 랴랴바아 례리 으가 루쏘 루너너. 어라 구우마례 뫄 냐쨔 나 아더다 뿌: "구 어무시 무너너 워바비로니 아ㄲ나우와 어러씨 바짜 너미시, 아다가나찌로러가너고 찌로 나 히짜!

21. Then a mighty angel picked up a boulder the size of a large millstone and threw it into the sea, and said: "With such violence the great city of Babylon will be thrown down, never to be found again.

22. Mwa musi weBabiloni, mutakanachomvikane nyimbo sa ba bende babanda mwa mirumbu, nesi mwa thuperere, nesi sa ba bende basiya enzenze, nesi mirenge ya bandju ba bemba. Kanji mwoyu musi, mutakanachomvikane sindo sa muthuta. Kanji mutakanachilorekeneko chiro na murenga asibya.

22. 뫄 무시 워바비로니, 무다가나쪼삐가너 네뽀 사 바 버떠 바바따 뫄 미루뿌, 너시 뫄 쭈퍼러러, 너시 사 바 버떠 바시야 어써써, 너시 미러ㅇ여 야 바쭈 바 버빠. 가찌 모유 무시, 무다가나쪼삐가너 시또 사 무쭈다. 가찌 무다가나찌로러거너고 찌로 나 무러ㅇ가 아시뱌.

22. The music of harpists and musicians, flute players and trumpeters, will never be heard in you again. No workman of any trade will ever be found in you again. The sound of a millstone will never be heard in you again.

23. Kanji mwoyu musi, ebulangare bwetara

23. 가찌 모유 무시, 어부롸ㅇ가러 붜다라

23. The light of a lamp will never shine in you again.

butakanachilorekaneko chiro na hicha. Kanji mutakanachomvikane chiro na murenge wa muya-mukasi nesi wa muya-mulume. Rero bikaba bacha, bushi ebachimbusi bao, bu babaa baire ngulu mwa butala boshi. Nomwa bulosi bwao, mu endee atebera ebandju bembaa soshi."

24. Nemikira yebarebi ba Ongo neyebabuya-buya bai na ba bendee bechibwa mwa butala, mwoyu musi mu yendee yalorekanako.

부다가나찌로러가너고 찌로 나 히짜. 가찌 무다가나쪼삐가너 찌로 나 무러머 와 무야-무가시 너시 와 무야-무루머. 러로 비가바 바짜, 부씨 어바찌뿌시 바오, 부 바바아 바이러 으루 마 부다롸 보씨. 노와 부로시 봐오, 무 어떠어 아더버라 어바누 버빠아 소씨."

24. 너미기라 여바러비 바 오쯔 너여바부야-부야 바이 나 바 버떠어 버찌봐 마 부다롸, 모유 무시 무 여떠어 야로러가나고.

The voice of bridegroom and bride will never be heard in you again. Your merchants were the world's great men. By your magic spell all the nations were led astray.

24. In her was found the blood of prophets and of the saints, and of all who have been killed on the earth."

Byaboolyibwa Chikono 19

1. Era nyuma sebi, nera kumva murenge munene ola ulyi nga murenge wa chikembe cha bandju banene busese atenga kwa nguba mbu: "Ongo atongwe! Ebununusi, nethunda, nebuashi biri bya Ongo wethu!

2. Bushi yeke, ende achinjibusa ebandju kukulyikana nemyasi yekanangana kanji era ithungenene. Achinjibusise bwa bwaneshe bwecha chihungukasi, cha chabaa

뱌보오쩨봐 찌고노 19

1. 어라 뉴마 서비, 너라 구바 무러머 무너너 오롸 우쩨 마 무러머 와 찌거뻐 짜 바누 바너너 부서서 아더마 과 으바 뿌: "오쯔 아도워! 어부누누시, 너쭈따, 너부아씨 비리 뱌 오쯔 워쭈!

2. 부씨 여거, 어떠 아찌찌부사 어바누 구구쩨가나 너먀시 여가나마나 가찌 어라 이쭈머너너. 아찌찌부시서 봐 봐너써 붜짜 찌후으가시, 짜 짜바아 쩌찌러 짜 씨이리사

Revelation Chapter 19[NIV]

1. After this I heard what sounded like the roar of a great multitude in heaven shouting: "Hallelujah! Salvation and glory and power belong to our God,

2. for true and just are his judgments. He has condemned the great prostitute who corrupted the earth by her adulteries. He has avenged on her the blood of his servants."

chenjire cha shiirisa ebandju bomwa butala mwa myasi yai yelusingi. Kubinalyi! Ongo afunyire emikira yebaanda bai ba echi chihungukasi chasikyaa."

3. Abu bandju boshi, bera kuteta kanji mbu: "Ongo atongwe! Emusi wemulyiro ola waochaa oyu musi munene, akanaendekera afumba, kuikira kwana nguba esuku nemango."

4. Ba bangumwa makunyabiri na bane, alauma nebya bindju bine bya biri biuma-uma kanji bya kushishasa, bera kufukama era muhondo sa Ongo, ola wekese kwa ndebe yai yebwami. Bera kumwera na murenge munene mbu: "Ongo atongwe! Bibe bacha!"

5. Chasinda, mwei ndebe yebwami, mwera kutenga ola wabaa wateta mbu: "Mutongaa Ongo wethu, mu baanda bai, mu mwende mwamuthunda, kutengera kwa baunda, kuikira kwa bakulu-kulu!"

6. Chasinda, nera kumva ku unji murenge munene, ola ulyi nga murenge wa chikembe cha bandju banene busese. Kanji abaa auma nga chiira,

어바뉴 보뫄 부다롸 뫄 먀시 야이 여루시메. 구비나레! 오꼬 아푸네러 어미기라 여바아따 바이 바 어찌 찌후꾸가시 짜시갸아."

3. 아부 바뉴 보씨, 버라 구더다 가찌 뿌: "오꼬 아도붜! 어무시 워무레로 오롸 와오짜아 오유 무시 무너너, 아가나어떠거라 아푸빠, 구이기라 과나 꾸바 어수구 너마꼬."

4. 바 바꾸뫄 마구냐비리 나 바너, 아롸우마 너뱌 비뉴 비너 뱌 비리 비우마-우마 가찌 뱌 구씨싸사, 버라 구푸가마 어라 무호또 사 오꼬, 오롸 워거서 과 떠버 야이 여봐미. 버라 구붜라 나 무러뗘 무너너 뿌: "오꼬 아도붜! 비버 바짜!"

5. 짜시따, 뮈이 떠버 여봐미, 뭐라 구더따 오롸 와바아 와더다 뿌: "무도따아 오꼬 워쭈, 무 바아따 바이, 무 뭐떠 뫄무쭈따, 구더뗘라 과 바우따, 구이기라 과 바구루-구루!"

6. 짜시따, 너라 구빠 구 우찌 무러뗘 무너너, 오롸 우레 따 무러뗘 와 찌거뻐 짜 바뉴 바너너 부서서. 가찌 아바아 아우마 따 찌이라, 아구꾸롸

3. And again they shouted: "Hallelujah! The smoke from her goes up for ever and ever."

4. The twenty-four elders and the four living creatures fell down and worshiped God, who was seated on the throne. And they cried: "Amen, Hallelujah!"

5. Then a voice came from the throne, saying: "Praise our God, all you his servants, you who fear him, both small and great!"

6. Then I heard what sounded like a great multitude, like the roar of rushing waters and like loud peals of thunder, shouting:

akungula nga murasano. Abu bandju bera kuteta mbu: "Ongo atongwe! Bushi iEnawethu webuashi boshi, kanji iwatangirise kwima.

7. Thundaa thwahaaluka na kumowa, kanji thundaa thwamutonga, bushi ebuya bweMwana weMbulyi bwaikire mira. Nemuya, achikunganyise mira.

8. Oyu muya, eresibwe luchimba lwa lwakunganyisibwaa mu chiraka cha chaterera, chitakachire kanji chalangala busese." (Olu luchimba, luhuhanyisibwe nemyanya ibuya yebandju ba Ongo. Nei myanya iithungenene era muhondo sai.)

9. Chasinda, oyu ndonyi era kunyibura mbu: "Uanjikaa mbu: ?Baahanyirwe babalalyikibwe kwa buya bweMwana weMbulyi!?" Kanji era kunyibura mbu: "Ene myasi nakubwirire, iri ya kanangana, kanji yatengera era mwa Ongo."

10. Unao-unao, na naya kufukama era muhondo sai, nyimwere. Si era kunyibura mbu: "Chacha! Utairaa bacha, bushi nanyi nyinalyi muanda

와 무라사노. 아부 바쭈 버라 구더다 뿌: "오꼬 아도눠! 부씨 이어나워쭈 워부아씨 보씨, 가찌 이와다)리러서 귀마.

7. 쭈따아 쫘하아루가 나 구모와, 가찌 쭈따아 쫘무도따, 부씨 어부야 붜마나 워뿌레 봐이기러 미라. 너무야, 아찌구까네서 미라.

8. 오유 무야, 어러시붜 루찌빠 롸 롸구까네시봐아 무 찌라가 짜 짜더러라, 찌다가찌러 가찌 짜롸아라 부서서." (오루 루찌빠, 루후하네시붜 너먀냐 이부야 여바쭈 바 오꼬. 너이 먀냐 이이쭈어너너 어라 무호또 사이.)

9. 짜시따, 오유 또네 어라 구네부라 뿌: "우아찌가아 뿌: ?바아하네붜 바바롸레기붜 과 부야 붜마나 워뿌레!?" 가찌 어라 구네부라 뿌: "어너 먀시 나구뷔리러, 이리 야 가나따나, 가찌 야더어라 어라 와 오꼬."

10. 우나오-우나오, 나 나야 구푸가마 어라 무호또 사이, 네뭐러. 시 어라 구네부라 뿌: "짜짜! 우다이라아 바짜, 부씨 나네 네나레 무아따 구우마

"Hallelujah! For our Lord God Almighty reigns.

7. Let us rejoice and be glad and give him glory! For the wedding of the Lamb has come, and his bride has made herself ready.

8. Fine linen, bright and clean, was given her to wear." (Fine linen stands for the righteous acts of the saints.)

9. Then the angel said to me, "Write: 'Blessed are those who are invited to the wedding supper of the Lamb!' " And he added, "These are the true words of God."

10. At this I fell at his feet to worship him. But he said to me, "Do not do it! I am a fellow servant with you and with your brothers who hold

kuuma nao, kanji kuuma na banyakenyu ba bende bateta bya balolaako era luulu sa Yesu. Rero, Ongo yeine iundaa wera! Bushi ba bende bateta bya bachiloreraako era luulu sa Yesu, bunabo-bunabo bu banathula barebi." Ola ulyi kwa farasi yemuoko-muoko aimanyire.

11. Chasinda, nera kulola enguba ibookere. Mwolu, kwera kuulukira farasi ya muoko-muoko. Nola wabaa ulyi kui, iMubuya, kanji iKanangana. Bushi yeke ende achinjibusa ebandju na kulwa ebita kukulyikana nemyasi era ithungenene.

12. Emeho mai, mabaa mengengenya nga chasi cha mulyiro. Nokwethwe lyai, kwabaa kulyi nzita sa bami. Babaa bamuanjikireko sina lyiuma, lya kutalyi chiro na mundju asibya ola ulyishi. Si yeine iunathula ulyishi.

13. Kanji abaa embese luchimba lwa lulobekirwe mwa mikira. Nelyinji sina lyai: iChinwa cha Ongo.

14. Ebasula bokwa nguba, babaa benjire bamukulyikira bikembe-bikembe balyi kwa farasi sa muoko-muoko.

나오, 가찌 구우마 나 바냐거뉴 바 버떠 바더다 뱌 바로똬아고 어라 루우루 사 여수. 러로, 오꼬 여이너 이우따아 워라! 부씨 바 버떠 바더다 뱌 바찌로러라아고 어라 루우루 사 여수, 부나보-부나보 부 바나쭈똬 바러비." 오똬 우레 과 파라시 여무오고-무오고 아이마네러.

11. 짜시따, 너라 구로똬 어꾸바 이보오거러. 모룰, 궈라 구우루기라 파라시 야 무오고-무오고. 노똬 와바아 우레 구이, 이무부야, 가찌 이가나똬나. 부씨 여거 어너 아찌찌부사 어바뉴 나 구똬 어비다 구구레가나 너먀시 어라 이쭈떠너너.

12. 어머호 마이, 마바아 머떠떠냐 까 짜시 짜 무레로. 노궈줘 랴이, 과바아 구레 씨다 사 바미. 바바아 바무아씨기러고 시나 레우마, 랴 구다레 찌로 나 무뚜 아시뱌 오똬 우레씨. 시 여이너 이우나쭈똬 우레씨.

13. 가찌 아바아 어뻐서 루찌빠 똬 루로버기뤄 마 미기라. 너레찌 시나 랴이: 이찌놔 짜 오꼬.

14. 어바수똬 보과 우바, 바바아 버찌러 바무구레기라 비거뻐-비거뻐 바레 과 파라시 사 무오고-무오고.

to the testimony of Jesus. Worship God! For the testimony of Jesus is the spirit of prophecy."

11. I saw heaven standing open and there before me was a white horse, whose rider is called Faithful and True. With justice he judges and makes war.

12. His eyes are like blazing fire, and on his head are many crowns. He has a name written on him that no one knows but he himself.

13. He is dressed in a robe dipped in blood, and his name is the Word of God.

14. The armies of heaven were following him, riding on white horses and dressed in fine linen, white and

Babaa bembese njimba sa muoko-muoko busese, sitakachire kanji saterera.

바바아 버뻐서 띠빠 사 무오고-무오고 부서서, 시다가찌러 가찌 사더러라.

clean.

15. Mwa bunu bwai mwera kutenga bombo bukalyiire busese. Obu bombo, bwabaa bwa kuima ebandju bembaa soshi. "Abu bandju, angemangirabo mwa kubaenzesa mwa mafi." Nebusinane bwa Ongo webuashi boshi, angalosabo mwa kubakanjira mwa mufumbi ngokwa bende bakanda etifai mwa misabibu.

15. 똬 부누 똬이 뭐라 구더아 보뽀 부가레이러 부서서. 보뽀, 똬바아 똬 구이마 어바뉴 버빠아 소씨. "아부 바뉴, 아꺼마끼라보 똬 구바어써사 똬 마피." 너부시나너 똬 오꼬 워부아씨 보씨, 아까로사보 똬 구바가찌라 똬 무푸삐 꼬과 버떠 바가따 어디파이 똬 미사비부.

15. Out of his mouth comes a sharp sword with which to strike down the nations. "He will rule them with an iron scepter." He treads the winepress of the fury of the wrath of God Almighty.

16. Na kwolu luchimba lwai, nokwa chibero chai, kwabaa kuanjikirwe esina lya lyitechire mbu: Mwami webami, na Enawethu webaenawethu.

16. 나 고루 루찌빠 롸이, 노과 찌버로 짜이, 과바아 구아찌기뤄 어시나 랴 레더찌러 뿌: 똬미 워바미, 나 어나워쭈 워바어나워쭈.

16. On his robe and on his thigh he has this name written: KING OF KINGS AND LORD OF LORDS.

17. Chasinda, nera kulola ku ndonyi muuma emenze mwesuba. Oyu ndonyi, abaa alakanga na murenge munene. Era kubura emilonge yoshi era yabaa yauluka mwa byanya bibiri mbu: "Mubahaa enera mubwaanane kwa lyinye lyinene lya Ongo,

17. 짜시따, 너라 구로롸 구 또니 무우마 어머써 뭐수바. 오유 또니, 아바아 아롸가까 나 무러꺼 무너너. 어라 구부라 어미로꺼 요씨 어라 야바아 야우루가 똬 뱌냐 비비리 뿌: "무바하아 어너라 무봐아나너 과 레녀 레너너 랴 오꼬,

17. And I saw an angel standing in the sun, who cried in a loud voice to all the birds flying in midair, "Come, gather together for the great supper of God,

18. mulye ebirunda byebami, nebyebakulu-kulu bebasula, nebyendwalyi, nebyefarasi, nebyebandju ba babaa balyi kusi. Kanji, mungalya ebirunda byebandju boshi: ethuungu na

18. 무려 어비루따 뱌바미, 너뱌바구루-구루 버바수롸, 너뱌꽈레, 너뱌파라시, 너뱌바뉴 바 바바아 바레 구시. 가찌, 무까랴 어비루따 뱌바뉴 보씨: 어쭈우꾸 나 바

18. so that you may eat the flesh of kings, generals, and mighty men, of horses and their riders, and the flesh of all people, free and slave, small and great."

ba batathula thuungu,
ebaunda nebakulu-kulu."

19. Era nyuma sebi, nera
kulola kwa era nyama ngalyi
yabuananyire nebami bebinji
bio byoshi nebasula babo,
baye kulwisa oyu wabaa
wekese kwa farasi alauma
nebasula bai.

20. Si ei nyama ngalyi, alauma
nola murebi webisha, bera
kusimbibwa. Oyu murebi,
inoyu inoyu iwendee waira
ebisomerano kwa buashi bwei
nyama na kunde ateba
ebandju ba babikibwe
kwekalorero kei nyama
nekuera echihuhanyi chei
nyama. Rero, ei nyama ngalyi
noyu murebi webisha, bera
kuumwa bauma-uma mwa
marunga ma mabunga busese
alauma nengunye-kunye
sechibirichi.

21. Chasinda, ebanji basula
babo boshi ba bashibaa, nabo
bera kwechibwa mwa bombo
bwa bwabaa bwatenga mwa
bunu boyu wabaa wekese kwa
farasi. Chasinjire, emilonge
yoshi, yera kulya ebirunda
byabo, na yeuta busese.

바다쭈꽈 쭈우위, 어바우따
너바구루-구루."

19. 어라 뉴마 서비, 너라
구루꽈 과 어라 냐마 까레
야부아나니러 너바미 버비찌
비오 뵤씨 너바수꽈 바보,
바여 구뤼사 오유 와바아
워거서 과 파라시 아꽈우마
너바수꽈 바이.

20. 시 어이 냐마 까레,
아꽈우마 노꽈 무러비 워비싸,
버라 구시삐봐. 오유 무러비,
이노유 이노유 이워떠어
와이라 어비소머라노 과
부아씨 뷔이 냐마 나 구떠
아드바 어바쮸 바 바비기붜
궈가로러로 거이 냐마
너구어라 어찌후하니 쩌이
냐마. 러로, 어이 냐마 까레
노유 무러비 워비싸, 버라
구우꽈 바우마-우마 꽈
마루꽈 마 마부꽈 부서서
아꽈우마 너위녀-구녀
서찌비리찌.

21. 짜시따, 어바찌 바수꽈
바보 뵤씨 바 바씨바아, 나보
버라 궈찌봐 꽈 보뾰 봐
봐바아 봐더꽈 꽈 부누 보유
와바아 워거서 과 파라시.
짜시찌러, 어미로어 요씨,
여라 구꺄 어비루따 뱌보, 나
여우다 부서서.

19. Then I saw the beast
and the kings of the earth
and their armies gathered
together to make war
against the rider on the
horse and his army.

20. But the beast was
captured, and with him the
false prophet who had
performed the miraculous
signs on his behalf. With
these signs he had deluded
those who had received the
mark of the beast and
worshiped his image. The
two of them were thrown
alive into the fiery lake of
burning sulfur.

21. The rest of them were
killed with the sword that
came out of the mouth of
the rider on the horse, and
all the birds gorged
themselves on their flesh.

Byaboolyibwa Chikono 20	뱌보오레봐 찌고노 20	Revelation Chapter 20[NIV]
1. Era nyuma sebi, nera kulola ku ndonyi muuma andaala kwa nguba. Oyu ndonyi, abaa ete elufunguro mwa mino, lwekuboola era fumbi irerere yekusimu. Kanji abaa ete na bureure bunene busese.	1. 어라 뉴마 서비, 너라 구로롸 구 또네 무우마 아따아롸 과 우바. 오유 또네, 아바아 어더 어루푸우로 뫄 미노, 뤄구보오롸 어라 푸삐 이러러러 여구시무. 가찌 아바아 어더 나 부러우러 부너너 부서서.	1. And I saw an angel coming down out of heaven, having the key to the Abyss and holding in his hand a great chain.
2. Unao-unao, kuna kuumbikira era njoka inene yokwa mira, era bende berika mbu "Wamusimu", nesi mbu "Shetani." Oyu ndonyi, kuna kuisalyinga ku myaka chumbi.	2. 우나오-우나오, 구나 구우삐기라 어라 쪼가 이너너 요과 미라, 어라 버떠 버리가 뿌 "와무시무", 너시 뿌 "써다니." 오유 또네, 구나 구이사례까 구 먀가 쭈삐.	2. He seized the dragon, that ancient serpent, who is the devil, or Satan, and bound him for a thousand years.
3. Era kuiuma mwera fumbi irerere yekusimu, na ahukirai, chasinda era kumina kwechifundo nga kashe. Aola, itakachengeere ebandju, kuikira kwei myaka chumbi. Nera nyuma sei myaka chumbi, bikema iboolyibwe ku bihangi bieke oshao.	3. 어라 구이우마 뭐라 푸삐 이러러러 여구시무, 나 아후기라이, 짜시따 어라 구미나 궈찌푸또 까 가써. 아오롸, 이다가쩌꺼어러 어바쭈, 구이기라 궈이 먀가 쭈삐. 너라 뉴마 서이 먀가 쭈삐, 비거마 이보오레뷔 구 비하끼 비어거 오싸오.	3. He threw him into the Abyss, and locked and sealed it over him, to keep him from deceiving the nations anymore until the thousand years were ended. After that, he must be set free for a short time.
4. Chasinda, nera kulola ku ndebe sa bwami. Neba ba babaa bekese kusi, bera kweresibwa ebuashi bwekuchinjibusa. Kanji nera kulola nokwa michima yebandju ba bakeribwaa bushi neChinwa cha Ongo, nemyasi era bendee bateta era luulu sa Yesu. Abu bandju, beke	4. 짜시따, 너라 구로롸 구 떠버 사 봐미. 너바 바 바바아 버거서 구시, 버라 궈러시봐 어부아씨 뷔구찌찌부사. 가찌 너라 구로롸 노과 미찌마 여바쭈 바 바거리봐아 부씨 너찌놔 짜 오오, 너먀시 어라 버떠어 바더다 어라 루우루 사 여수. 아부 바쭈, 버거 바다바아 뫄바 버떠어 버라	4. I saw thrones on which were seated those who had been given authority to judge. And I saw the souls of those who had been beheaded because of their testimony for Jesus and because of the word of God. They had not worshiped the beast or his image and had

batabaa mwaba bendee bera era nyama ngalyi, nesi cha chihuhanyi chai. Kanji batabikibwaako ekalorero kai kwa malanga mabo, nesi kwa mino sabo. Bera kwomoka na bema alauma na Kirisito, kuikira kwei myaka chumbi.

5. Rero, oku kwomoka kwabo, kukuthula kwomoka kubere-bere. Si ebanji bafu, beke batomwokaa mwoku kwomoka kubere-bere mango ei myaka chumbi yabaa itasa kulumirira.

6. Rero, ba bomwokire mwoku kwomoka kubere-bere bu baahanyirwe! Kanji balyi babuya-buya. Abu bandju, elufu lwa kabiri lutakachate chiro na buashi busibya era luulu sabo. Bakaba bakuhanyi ba Ongo, na bakuhanyi ba Kirisito. Kanji bakema alauma nai, kwei myaka chumbi.

7. Mango ei myaka chumbi ikaba yalumirire mira, Wasimu akaboolyibwa atenge mwa buroko bwai.

8. Unao-unao akaya kwa nyinda ene sebutala, engeere ebandju bebio byoshi, abakurumanye kwa kulwa ebita. Bakaba banene busese

어라 냐마 까레, 너시 짜 찌후하네 짜이. 가찌 바다비기봐아고 어가뤄러로 가이 과 마꽈까 마보, 너시 과 미노 사보. 버라 꼬모가 나 버마 아꽈우마 나 기리시도, 구이기라 궈이 먀가 쭈삐.

5. 러로, 오구 꼬모가 과보, 구구쭈꽈 꼬모가 구버러-버러. 시 어바찌 바푸, 버거 바도모가아 모구 꼬모가 구버러-버러 마꼬 어이 먀가 쭈삐 야바아 이다사 구루미리라.

6. 러로, 바 보모기러 모구 꼬모가 구버러-버러 부 바아하네뤄! 가찌 바레 바부야-부야. 아부 바뉴, 어루푸 꽈 가비리 루다가짜더 찌로 나 부아씨 부시뱌 어라 루우루 사보. 바가바 바구하네 바 오꼬, 나 바구하네 바 기리시도. 가찌 바거마 아꽈우마 나이, 궈이 먀가 쭈삐.

7. 마꼬 어이 먀가 쭈삐 이가바 야루미리러 미라, 와시무 아가보오레봐 아더꺼 봐 부로고 봐이.

8. 우나오-우나오 아가야 과 니따 어너 서부다꽈, 어꺼어러 어바뉴 버비오 뵤씨, 아바구루마녀 과 구꽈 어비다. 바가바 바너너 부서서 까

not received his mark on their foreheads or their hands. They came to life and reigned with Christ a thousand years.

5. (The rest of the dead did not come to life until the thousand years were ended.) This is the first resurrection.

6. Blessed and holy are those who have part in the first resurrection. The second death has no power over them, but they will be priests of God and of Christ and will reign with him for a thousand years.

7. When the thousand years are over, Satan will be released from his prison

8. and will go out to deceive the nations in the four corners of the earth--Gog and Magog--to gather them for battle. In number they

nga mishee yomwa nyanja. 미써어 요뫄 냐짜. 너마시나 are like the sand on the

Nemasina mabo mu mamano 마보 무 마마노 "고기 나 seashore.

"Koki na Makoki." 마고기."

9. Ba bandju, bera kwehula 9. 바 바쮸, 버라 궈후쫘 뫄 9. They marched across the

mwa butala boshi, na baya 부다쫘 보씨, 나 바야 breadth of the earth and

kusungula ekambi kebandju 구수꿀라 어가삐 거바쮸 바 surrounded the camp of

ba Ongo, nemusi wai ola 오꼬, 너무시 와이 오라 God's people, the city he

athula asimire. Si kwa nguba, 아쭈쫘 아시미러. 시 과 우바, loves. But fire came down

kwera kutenga mulyiro, unao- 궈라 구더꽈 무쮀로, 우나오- from heaven and devoured

unao kuna kubasiresa. 우나오 구나 구바시러사. them.

10. Chasinda, Wasimu ola 10. 짜시따, 와시무 오쫘 10. And the devil, who

wendee wengeera abu bandju, 워떠어 워꺼어라 아부 바쮸, deceived them, was thrown

kuna kuumwa mwa marunga, 구나 구우뫄 뫄 마루꽈, 마 into the lake of burning

ma mabunga busese alauma 마부꽈 부서서 아라우마 sulfur, where the beast and

nengunye-kunye sechibirichi. 너우녀-구녀 서찌비리찌. the false prophet had been

Rero mwamu marunga, mu 러로 뫄무 마루꽈, 무 어라 냐마 thrown. They will be

era nyama ngalyi, nola murebi 꽈쩨, 노쫘 무러비 워비싸, tormented day and night for

webisha, nabo babaa balorera 나보 바바아 바로러라 과 ever and ever.

kwa kasibu. Abu boshi, 가시부. 아부 보씨,

bakanaendekera kunde 바가나어떠거라 구떠

balyibukiramo ebuthufu 바쩨부기라모 어부후푸

nemushi kuikira esuku 너무씨 구이기라 어수구

nemango. 너마꼬.

11. Chasinda, nera kulola ku 11. 짜시따, 너라 구뢰쫘 구 11. Then I saw a great white

ndebe inene ya bwami. Ei 떠버 이너너 야 봐미. 어이 throne and him who was

ndebe, yabaa ya muoko- 떠버, 야바아 야 무오고- seated on it. Earth and sky

muoko busese. Nera kulola na 무오고 부서서. 너라 구뢰쫘 fled from his presence, and

kwola wabaa wekeseko. 나 고쫘 와바아 워거서고. there was no place for

Ebutala nenguba, unao-unao 어부다쫘 너우바, 우나오- them.

kuna kuirima era muhondo 우나오 구나 구이리마 어라

sai, chiro bikanachilorekanako. 무호또 사이, 찌로

비가나찌뢰러가나고.

12. Kanji nera kulola nokwa 12. 가찌 너라 구뢰쫘 노과 12. And I saw the dead,

bandju ba bafire mira, 바쮸 바 바피러 미라, great and small, standing

ebaunda nebakulu-kulu, bemenze era muhondo seindebe yebwami. Mwolu, ebitabo byera kuboolyibwanga. Na chinji chitabo chiuma, nachi chera kuboolyibwa. Echera cheke, chi chithula chitabo chekalamo. Ba babaa bafire mira, bera kuchinjibusibwa ku kulyikana nemyanya yabo, ngokwa byabaa byanjkirwe mwebi bitabo.

13. Ba bafiraa mwa nyanja, yera kufulusabo. Walufu na ena kusimu, nabo bera kufulusa ebafu ba babaa balyi mwa mino sabo. Chira mundju, era kuchinjibusibwa ku kulyikana nemyanya yai.

14. Chasinjire, Walufu na ena kusimu, nabo bera kuumwa mwamu marunga. Namu marunga, lu lufu lwa kabiri.

15. Na chira mundju woshi ola esina lyai lyitalorekanaako mwa chitabo chekalamo, nai era kuumwa mwa mu murunga.

어바우따 너바구루-구루, 버머써 어라 무호또 서이머버 여봐미. 모루, 어비다보 벼라 구보오레봐아. 나 찌찌 찌다보 찌우마, 나찌 쩌라 구보오레봐. 어쩌라 쩌거, 찌 찌쭈라 찌다보 쩌가꽈모. 바 바바아 바피러 미라, 버라 구찌찌부시봐 구 구레가나 너먀냐 야보, 꼬과 뱌바아 뱌쭈기뤄 뭐비 비다보.

13. 바 바피라아 마 냐짜, 여라 구푸루사보. 와루푸 나 어나 구시무, 나보 버라 구푸루사 어바푸 바 바바아 바레 마 미노 사보. 찌라 무뚜, 어라 구찌찌부시봐 구 구레가나 너먀냐 야이.

14. 짜시찌러, 와루푸 나 어나 구시무, 나보 버라 구우뫄 뫄무 마루뺘. 나무 마루뺘, 루 루푸 똬 가비리.

15. 나 찌라 무뚜 오씨 오꽈 어시나 랴이 레다로러가나아고 뫄 찌다보 쩌가꽈모, 나이 어라 구우뫄 뫄 무 무루뺘.

before the throne, and books were opened. Another book was opened, which is the book of life. The dead were judged according to what they had done as recorded in the books.

13. The sea gave up the dead that were in it, and death and Hades gave up the dead that were in them, and each person was judged according to what he had done.

14. Then death and Hades were thrown into the lake of fire. The lake of fire is the second death.

15. If anyone's name was not found written in the book of life, he was thrown into the lake of fire.

Byaboolyibwa Chikono 21

1. Chasinda, nera kulola ku nguba iyayaya na butala buyayaya. Bushi enguba ibere-

뱌보오레봐 찌고노 21

1. 짜시따, 너라 구로꽈 구 꾸바 이야야야 나 부다꽈 부야야야. 부씨 어꾸바

1. Then I saw a new heaven and a new earth, for the first heaven and the first

bere nebutala bubere-bere, byabaa byarengire mira. Nenyanja, nai yabaa itanachirio.

2. Nera kulola kwa Yerusalemu iyayaya imusi mubuya-buya, andaala kutenga kwa nguba, era mwa Ongo. Oyu musi, abaa akunganyisibwe kubuya, ngokwa muya ende achibika kwebulyimbi, mwa kuhonda asimise eba wai.

3. Mwera ndebe yebwami, nera kumva mwatengera murenge munene ola wabaa wateta mbu: "Rero, enyumba ya Ongo, yera iri alauma nebandju. Kanji akanaendekera kuba mwa kachi-kachi kabo. Nabo, bakaba bandju bai, nai anaba Ongo wabo.

4. Akahangula emalyira mabo moshi. Kutakanachibe lufu, nesi malyira, nesi milakango, nesi malumwa. Bushi emyasi yokwa mira ikaba yarengire mira. "

5. Chasinda, oyu wabaa wekese kwa ndebe yebwami era kwire ateta mbu: " Mulolaa! Bya bithulao byoshi, nabiirire kuba biyayaya! " Kanji era kunyibura mbu: " Ene myasi, uianjikaa bushi iri

---

이버러-버러 너부다꽈 부버러-버러, 뱌바아 뱌러의러 미라. 너냐쨔, 나이 야바아 이다나찌리오.

2. 너라 구로꽈 과 여루사러무 이야야야 이무시 무부야-부야, 아따아꽈 구더꽈 과 우바, 어라 뫄 오꼬. 오유 무시, 아바아 아구꽈네시붜 구부야, 꼬과 무야 어떠 아찌비가 궈부레삐, 뫄 구호따 아시미서 어바 와이.

3. 뭐라 떠버 여봐미, 너라 구빠 뫄더어라 무러어 무너너 오꽈 와바아 와더다 뿌: "러로, 어뉴빠 야 오꼬, 여라 이리 아꽈우마 너바쀼. 가찌 아가나어떠거라 구바 뫄 가찌-가찌 가보. 나보, 바가바 바쀼 바이, 나이 아나바 오꼬 와보.

4. 아가하우꽈 어마레라 마보 모씨. 구다가나찌버 루푸, 너시 마레라, 너시 미꽈가꼬, 너시 마루뫄. 부씨 어먀시 요과 미라 이가바 야러의러 미라. "

5. 짜시따, 오유 와바아 워거서 과 떠버 여봐미 어라 귀러 아더다 뿌: " 무로꽈! 뱌 비쭈꽈오 뵤씨, 나비이리러 구바 비야야야! " 가찌 어라 구네부라 뿌: " 어너 먀시, 우이아찌가아 부씨 이리 야

---

earth had passed away, and there was no longer any sea.

2. I saw the Holy City, the new Jerusalem, coming down out of heaven from God, prepared as a bride beautifully dressed for her husband.

3. And I heard a loud voice from the throne saying, "Now the dwelling of God is with men, and he will live with them. They will be his people, and God himself will be with them and be their God.

4. He will wipe every tear from their eyes. There will be no more death or mourning or crying or pain, for the old order of things has passed away."

5. He who was seated on the throne said, "I am making everything new!" Then he said, "Write this down, for these words are trustworthy and true."

ya kanangana, kanji iri ya kwemererwa. "

가나ᅌᅡ나, 가ᄡᅵ 이리 야 궈머러롸. "

6. Era kuhuba kunyibura mbu: " Byoshi byairibwe mira! Nyono, nyi Alufa kanji nyi Omeka! Nyi mubere kanji nyi musinda! Akaba emundju afa chaami, nyono nyinyingamweresa emeshi mekumwa kwa buha, ma matenga mwa shokororo yemeshi ma mende maana ekalamo.

6. 어라 구후바 구네부라 뿌: " 뵤씨 뱌이리붜 미라! 뇨노, 네 아ᄛᅮ파 가ᄡᅵ 네 오머가! 네 무버러 가ᄡᅵ 네 무시ᄕᅡ! 아가바 어무ᅜᅮ 아파 짜아미, 뇨노 네네ᅌᅡ뭐러사 어머씨 머구뫄 과 부하, 마 마더ᅌᅡ 뫄 쏘고로로 여머씨 마 머ᄕᅥ 마아나 어가ᄙᅡ모.

6. He said to me: "It is done. I am the Alpha and the Omega, the Beginning and the End. To him who is thirsty I will give to drink without cost from the spring of the water of life.

7. Chira mundju ola ukaimana, nyikamweresa oyu mwandju woshi. Rero, nyono nyikaba Ongo wai, nai anaba mwana wanyi.

7. 찌라 무ᅜᅮ 오ᄙᅡ 우가이마나, 네가뭐러사 오유 뫄ᅜᅮ 오씨. 러로, 뇨노 네가바 오ᅌᅩ 와이, 나이 아나바 뫄나 와네.

7. He who overcomes will inherit all this, and I will be his God and he will be my son.

8. Si ebafi bebuba, na babatathusa bwemeresi, na ba bende bakola ebitakolwa, nebechi bebandju, nebasingisi, nebalosi, na ba bende bera ebihuhanyi, nebafusi bebisha, abu boshi echisiki chabo beke chikaba mwa marunga ma makorera busese alauma nengunye-kunye sechibirichi. Rero olola, lulukaba lufu lwa kabiri. "

8. 시 어바피 버부바, 나 바바다쭈사 붜머러시, 나 바 버ᄕᅥ 바고ᄙᅡ 어비다고ᄙᅪ, 너버찌 버바ᅜᅮ, 너바시ᅌᅵ시, 너바ᄛᅩ시, 나 바 버ᄕᅥ 버라 어비후하네, 너바푸시 버비싸, 아부 보씨 어찌시기 짜보 버거 찌가바 뫄 마루ᅌᅡ 마 마고러라 부서서 아ᄙᅡ우마 너ᅌᅮ녀-구녀 서찌비리찌. 러로 오ᄛᅩᄙᅡ, ᄛᅮᄛᅮ가바 ᄛᅮ푸 ᄛᅪ 가비리. "

8. But the cowardly, the unbelieving, the vile, the murderers, the sexually immoral, those who practice magic arts, the idolaters and all liars--their place will be in the fiery lake of burning sulfur. This is the second death."

9. Chasinda, muuma mwaba bandonyi balyinda, bababaa bete sa ngumbu sirinda sa sabaa sehuiremo mamalyibuko malyinda

9. 짜시ᄕᅡ, 무우마 뫄바 바ᄯᅩ네 바ᄙᅨᄕᅡ, 바바바아 버더 사 ᅌᅮ뿌 시리ᄕᅡ 사 사바아 서후이러모 마마ᄙᅨ부고 마ᄙᅨᄕᅡ 마시ᄕᅡ, 어라 구찌푸ᄕᅡ

9. One of the seven angels who had the seven bowls full of the seven last plagues came and said to me, "Come, I will show you the

masinda, era kuchifunda ofu nanyi. Era kunyibura mbu: "Bahaa nyikulose emuya, muka eMwana weMbulyi. "

10. Chasinda, eMuchima Mubuya-buya era kunyandaalyira. Mwolu, oyu ndonyi, kuna kunyeka kundjulungu nguma inene era itowamire busese. Era kunyilosa ola musi mubuya-buya weYerusalemu, ola wabaa wandaala kutenga kwa nguba, era mwa Ongo.

11. Oyu musi, abaa ete ebulangare bwa Ongo, bushi noku abaa alangala busese. Kanji abaa engengenya nga makoi ma chichiro chinene ma mahuhire muola, kanji mahuhire nga chihoho chibishi-bishi. Abaa arenga mwemeho nga chirauli.

12. Kanji oyu musi abaa asungwirwe na lusito lunene lwa lutowamire busese. Olu lusito, lwabaa lwete nyisi ekumi nebiri, sa sabaa salangibwa na bandonyi ekumi na babiri. Kanji kwesi nyisi, kwabaa kuanjikirwe emasina membaa ekumi nebiri se Baisieraeli.

오푸 나네. 어라 구네부라 뿌:
"바하아 네구로써 어무야,
무가 어마나 워뿌레. "

10. 짜시따, 어무찌마 무부야-부야 어라 구냐따아레라. 모루, 오유 또네, 구나 구녀가 구뚜루우 우마 이너너 어라 이도와미러 부서서. 어라 구네로사 오라 무시 무부야-부야 워여루사뤄무, 오라 와바아 와따아롸 구더까 과 우바, 어라 뫄 오꼬.

11. 오유 무시, 아바아 어더 어부롸따러 봐 오꼬, 부씨 노구 아바아 아롸까롸 부서서. 가찌 아바아 어어머냐 까 마고이 마 찌찌로 찌너너 마 마후히러 무오롸, 가찌 마후히러 까 찌호호 찌비씨-비씨. 아바아 아러꽈 뭐머호 까 찌라우뤼.

12. 가찌 오유 무시 아바아 아수뀌뤄 나 루시도 루너너 롸 루도와미러 부서서. 오루 루시도, 롸바아 뤄더 네시 어구미 너비리, 사 사바아 사롸끼봐 나 바또네 어구미 나 바비리. 가찌 궈시 네시, 과바아 구아찌기뤄 어마시나 머빠아 어구미 너비리 서 바이시어라어뤼.

bride, the wife of the Lamb."

10. And he carried me away in the Spirit to a mountain great and high, and showed me the Holy City, Jerusalem, coming down out of heaven from God.

11. It shone with the glory of God, and its brilliance was like that of a very precious jewel, like a jasper, clear as crystal.

12. It had a great, high wall with twelve gates, and with twelve angels at the gates. On the gates were written the names of the twelve tribes of Israel.

13 Mwesi nyisi, ehathu sabaa serekere era esuba lyende lyaulukira. Na sinji ehathu, era lyende lyachirowa. Na sinji ehathu, kwa lunda lwera luulu. Na sinji ehathu, kwa lunda lwera masina.

14. Olu lusito lunene, lwabaa luimbirirwe kumisingi ekumi nebiri. Na kwei misingi, ku babaa baanjikire emasina mendjumwa ekumi nebiri seMwana weMbulyi.

15. Oyu ndonyi, wabaa wateta nanyi, abaa ete kachi mwa mino kakabaa kakunganyisibwe mwa horo, aaye kupima oyu musi, alauma nenyisi sao, nelusito lwa lwabaa lusungwireo.

16. Oyu musi, abaa ete nyinda ene. Nesi nyinda soshi sabaa sinalyingene. Mango oyu ndonyi apimaao naka kachi, era kulola kweburere bwa chira lunda bwabaa bungaika ku bilometere byumbi bibiri na mana mabiri. Esi nyinda ene soshi kutengera era chibanda kuikira era luulu, sabaa sinalyingene.

17. Kanji oyu ndonyi era kupima ebunenene bwolu lusito nalo. Era kulola kwa lwete metere malyinda

13 뭐시 네시, 어하쭈 사바아 서러거러 어라 어수바 려너 랴우루루기라. 나 시찌 어하쭈, 어라 려너 랴찌로와. 나 시찌 어하쭈, 과 루따 뤄라 루우루. 나 시찌 어하쭈, 과 루따 뤄라 마시나.

14. 오루 루시도 루너너, 롸바아 루이삐리뤄 구미시삐 어구미 너비리. 나 궈이 미시삐, 구 바바아 바아찌기러 어마시나 머뿌뫄 어구미 너비리 서뫄나 워뿌뤠.

15. 오유 또네, 와바아 와더다 나네, 아바아 어더 가찌 뫄 미노 가가바아 가구따네시붸 뫄 호로, 아아여 구피마 오유 무시, 아롸우마 너네시 사오, 너루시도 롸 롸바아 루수뀌러오.

16. 오유 무시, 아바아 어더 네따 어너. 너시 네따 소씨 사바아 시나뤠머너. 마꼬 오유 또네 아피마아오 나가 가찌, 어라 구뢴롸 궈부러러 봐 찌라 루따 봐바아 부따이가 구 비로머더러 뷰삐 비비리 나 마나 마비리. 어시 네따 어너 소씨 구더뻐라 어라 찌바따 구이기라 어라 루우루, 사바아 시나뤠머너.

17. 가찌 오유 또네 어라 구피마 어부너너너 보루 루시도 나뢰. 어라 구뢴롸 과 뤄더 머더러 마뤠따 너비비리.

13. There were three gates on the east, three on the north, three on the south and three on the west.

14. The wall of the city had twelve foundations, and on them were the names of the twelve apostles of the Lamb.

15. The angel who talked with me had a measuring rod of gold to measure the city, its gates and its walls.

16. The city was laid out like a square, as long as it was wide. He measured the city with the rod and found it to be 12,000 stadiain length, and as wide and high as it is long.

17. He measured its wall and it was 144 cubits thick, by man's measurement, which the angel was using.

nebibiri. Echipimo cha oyu ndonyi akoresaa, chiebandju nabo bende bakoresa.

18. Elusito lwoyu musi, lwabaa luimbirwe na makoi ma Yasipi. Nemusi nao, abaa aimbirwe mwa horo yeine oshi ao, era yalangala busese nga chiraulyi.

19. Emusingi ola babaa baimbirireko olu lusito, abaa abikirwe kwebulyimbi na chira mulala wa makoi ma chichiro chinene. Emusingi muberebere, abaa abikirwe kwebulyimbi bwemakoi me Yasipi. Newakabiri, abaa abikirwe kwebulyimbi bwemakoi me Safilo. Newakahathu abaa abikirwe kwebulyimbi bwemakoi me Kaletonyi. Newakane, abaa abikirwe kwebulyimbi bwemakoi bwe Sumariti.

20. Newakatano, abaa abikirwe kwebulyimbi bwemakoi me Satoniki. Newandathu, abaa abikirwe kwebulyimbi bwemakoi me Akiki. Newakalyinda, abaa abikirwe kwebulyimbi bwemakoi me Kirisolite. Newamunane, abaa abikirwe kwebulyimbi bwemakoi me Belulo. Newamwenda, abaa

어찌피모 짜 오유 또네 아고러사아, 쩌바쭈 나보 버떠 바고러사.

18. 어루시도 롸유 무시, 롸바아 루이삐뤄 나 마고이 마 야시피. 너무시 나오, 아바아 아이삐뤄 롸 호로 여이너 오씨 아오, 어라 야롸따롸 부서서 롸 찌라우쮀.

19. 어무시삐 오롸 바바아 바이삐리러고 오루 루시도, 아바아 아비기뤄 궈부쮀삐 나 찌라 무라롸 와 마고이 마 찌찌로 찌너너. 어무시삐 무버러-버러, 아바아 아비기뤄 궈부쮀삐 뷔마고이 머 야시피. 너와가비리, 아바아 아비기뤄 궈부쮀삐 뷔마고이 머 사피론. 너와가하쭈 아바아 아비기뤄 궈부쮀삐 뷔마고이 머 가쩌도네. 너와가너, 아바아 아비기뤄 궈부쮀삐 뷔마고이 뷔 수마리디.

20. 너와가다노, 아바아 아비기뤄 궈부쮀삐 뷔마고이 머 사도니기. 너와따쭈, 아바아 아비기뤄 궈부쮀삐 뷔마고이 머 아기기. 너와가쮀따, 아바아 아비기뤄 궈부쮀삐 뷔마고이 머 기리소쮀더. 너와무나너, 아바아 아비기뤄 궈부쮀삐 뷔마고이 머 버루로. 너와뭐따, 아바아 아비기뤄

18. The wall was made of jasper, and the city of pure gold, as pure as glass.

19. The foundations of the city walls were decorated with every kind of precious stone. The first foundation was jasper, the second sapphire, the third chalcedony, the fourth emerald,

20. the fifth sardonyx, the sixth carnelian, the seventh chrysolite, the eighth beryl, the ninth topaz, the tenth chrysoprase, the eleventh jacinth, and the twelfth amethyst.

abikirwe kwebulyimbi bwemakoi me Topaso. Newekumi, abaa abikirwe kwebulyimbi bwemakoi me Kirisoparaso. Newekumi na muuma, abaa abikirwe kwebulyimbi bwemakoi me Haikindo. Newekumi nebiri, abaa abikirwe kwebulyimbi bwemakoi me Amasito.

귀부쩨삐 붜마고이 머 도파소. 너워구미, 아바아 아비기뤄 귀부쩨삐 붜마고이 머 기리소파라소. 너워구미 나 무우마, 아바아 아비기뤄 귀부쩨삐 붜마고이 머 하이기또. 너워구미 너비리, 아바아 아비기뤄 귀부쩨삐 붜마고이 머 아마시도.

21. Esi nyisi ekumi nebiri soyu musi, thwabaa thutare ekumi na thubiri thwa chichiro chinene busese. Chira lwisi, lwabaa lukunganyisibwe mukatare kauma kanenene. Nemyengere yoyu musi, yanabaa ya horo yeine oshi ao, kanji yabaa yarenga mwemeho busese nga chiraulyi.

21. 어시 네시 어구미 너비리 소유 무시, 쫘바아 쭈다러 어구미 나 쭈비리 쫘 찌찌로 찌너너 부서서. 찌라 뤼시, 쫘바아 루구까네시붜 무가다러 가우마 가너너너. 너며꺼러 요유 무시, 야나바아 야 호로 여이너 오씨 아오, 가찌 야바아 야러까 뭐머호 부서서 까 찌라우쩨.

21. The twelve gates were twelve pearls, each gate made of a single pearl. The great street of the city was of pure gold, like transparent glass.

22. Mwoyu musi, ndalolaamo kuluhu lwa Ongo, bushi Enawethu Ongo webuashi boshi, alauma neMwana weMbulyi beine bubanathula luhu lwamo.

22. 모유 무시, 따쫀쫘아모 구루후 쫘 오끄, 부씨 어나워쭈 오끄 워부아씨 보씨, 아쫘우마 너마나 워뿌쩨 버이너 부바나쭈쫘 루후 쫘모.

22. I did not see a temple in the city, because the Lord God Almighty and the Lamb are its temple.

23. Oyu musi, atathula alaire kubulangare bwesuba, nesi bwa mwesi. Bushi ebulangare bwa Ongo, bubwende bwalomekerao. Noyu Mwana weMbulyi, lyirithula etara lyamo.

23. 오유 무시, 아다쭈쫘 아쫘이러 구부쫘까러 붜수바, 너시 봐 뭐시. 부씨 어부쫘까러 봐 오끄, 부붜떠 봐쫀머거라오. 노유 마나 워뿌쩨, 쩨리쭈쫘 어다라 쨔모.

23. The city does not need the sun or the moon to shine on it, for the glory of God gives it light, and the Lamb is its lamp.

24. Na mwobu bulangare bwai, muebandju bembaa soshi bangende batamba. Nebami bomwa butala boshi, bangende baretamo ebuare bwabo.

25. Enyisi soyu musi, sitakachingibwe chiro na hicha, bushi mutakabe buthufu busibya.

26. Kanji mwoyu musi, ebandju bebio byoshi bangende bareta mwebuare bwabo, nebindju bya bikomire.

27. Kutalyi chiro na chindju chisisbya cha chibiire, cha chikalyibatamo, nesi ola wende wakola ebitakolwa nesi mufusi wa bisha. Si ba bakanengiriramo, banalyi ba emasina mabo maanjikwaa mwa chitabo chekalamo cheMwana weMbulyi.

24. 나 모부 부꽈아러 봐이, 무어바뉴 버빠아 소씨 바꺼너 바다빠. 너바미 보뫄 부다꽈 보씨, 바꺼너 바러다모 어부아러 봐보.

25. 어네시 소유 무시, 시다가찌삐붜 찌로 나 히짜, 부씨 무다가버 부후푸 부시뱌.

26. 가찌 모유 무시, 어바뉴 버비오 뵤씨 바꺼너 바러다 뭐부아러 봐보, 너비뿌 뱌 비고미러.

27. 구다레 찌로 나 찌뿌 찌시뱌 짜 찌비이러, 짜 찌가레바다모, 너시 오라 워꺼 와고꽈 어비다고꽈 너시 무푸시 와 비싸. 시 바 바가너끼리라모, 바나레 바 어마시나 마보 마아찌과아 뫄 찌다보 쩌가꽈모 쩌뫄나 워뿌레.

24. The nations will walk by its light, and the kings of the earth will bring their splendor into it.

25. On no day will its gates ever be shut, for there will be no night there.

26. The glory and honor of the nations will be brought into it.

27. Nothing impure will ever enter it, nor will anyone who does what is shameful or deceitful, but only those whose names are written in the Lamb's book of life.

Byaboolyibwa Chikono 22
1. Chasinda, oyu ndonyi era kunyilosa elwishi lwa luthusa emeshi mekalamo. Olu lwishi, lwabaa lwalangala busese nga chiyo. Kanji lwabaa lushokire mwa ndebe yebwami bwa Ongo, nomwa ye Mwana

뱌보오레봐 찌고노 22
1. 짜시따, 오유 또네 어라 구네로사 어뤼씨 꽈 루쭈사 어머씨 머가꽈모. 오루 뤼씨, 꽈바아 꽈라꺼라 부서서 까 찌요. 가찌 꽈바아 루쏘기러 뫄 떠버 여봐미 봐 오끄, 노뫄 여 뫄나 워뿌레.

Revelation Chapter 22[NIV]
1. Then the angel showed me the river of the water of life, as clear as crystal, flowing from the throne of God and of the Lamb

weMbulyi.

2. Kanji lwabaa lwahenda mwa kachi-kachi kemwengere munene busese woyu musi. Nokwa misike ebiri yalo, kwabaa kumerire emuchi wekalamo. Oyu muchi, endee eka ebifuma kalyi ekumi na kabiri kwa mwaka, kukuteta mbu endee eka bifuma ku chira mwesi. Nebihoho byao, buthula bufumu bwa kulamya ebandju bembaa soshi.

3. Mwoyu musi, mutakachibe chiro na kandju kasibya ka katakirwe. Si endebe yebwami bwa Ongo neyeMwana weMbulyi, bi bikanabamo. Nebaanda bai, kumwera ku bakende banamwera,

4. bamuseneko meho kwa manji. Nesina lyai, lyikanaanjikibwa kwa malanga mabo.

5. Mwoyu musi, mutakabe buthufu, nesi ebandju batakachilae ku bulangare bwetara, nesi bwesuba, bushi Enawethu Ongo yeine, iukaba wenjire wabalomekera. Na kwima ku bakanaendekera bema esuku nemango.

6. Chasinda, oyu ndonyi era kunyibura mbu: "Ene myasi, iri

2. 가찌 똬바아 똬허따 똬 가찌-가찌 거뭐뼈러 무너너 부서서 오유 무시. 노과 미시거 어비리 야롣, 과바아 구머리러 어무찌 워가똬모. 오유 무찌, 어머어 어가 어비푸마 가뤠 어구미 나 가비리 과 똬가, 구구더다 뿌 어머어 어가 비푸마 구 찌라 뭐시. 너비호호 뱌오, 부후똬 부푸무 봐 구똬먀 어바쭈 버빠아 소씨.

3. 모유 무시, 무다가찌버 찌로 나 가쭈 가시뱌 가 가다기뤄. 시 어떠버 여봐미 봐 오꼬 너여뫄나 워뿌뤠, 비 비가나바모. 너바아따 바이, 구뭐라 구 바거떠 바나뭐라,

4. 바무서너고 머호 과 마찌. 너시나 랴이, 뤠가나아찌기봐 과 마똬빠 마보.

5. 모유 무시, 무다가버 부후푸, 너시 어바쭈 바다가찌똬어 구 부똬빠러 뭐다라, 너시 붜수바, 부씨 어나워쭈 오꼬 여이너, 이우가바 워찌러 와바뢰머거라. 나 귀마 구 바가나어떠거라 버마 어수구 너마꼬.

6. 짜시따, 오유 또네 어라 구네부라 뿌: "어너 먀시, 이리

2. down the middle of the great street of the city. On each side of the river stood the tree of life, bearing twelve crops of fruit, yielding its fruit every month. And the leaves of the tree are for the healing of the nations.

3. No longer will there be any curse. The throne of God and of the Lamb will be in the city, and his servants will serve him.

4. They will see his face, and his name will be on their foreheads.

5. There will be no more night. They will not need the light of a lamp or the light of the sun, for the Lord God will give them light. And they will reign for ever and ever.

6. The angel said to me, "These words are

ya kanangana, kanji ya kwemererwa. Bushi Enawethu Ongo, ola weresaa ebarebi ebuashi bweMuchima Mubuya-buya, iwathumaa endonyi wai, aye kubura ebaanda bai chira mwasi ola byemire aike era nyuma sa suku sieke."

7. Yesu atechire mbu: "Mulolaa! Nyiri mu kufuluka! Baahanyirwe ba bende bathunda emyasi yeburebi era yaanjikirwe mwechine chitabo."

8. Ei myasi yoshi, nyono Yowani nyeine nyinachumviraa na kuchilorera kui. Na mango nabaa nera nachumviraa na kuchilorera kui, nera kufukama era muhondo soyu ndonyi nyimwere bushi iwanyilosaai.

9. Si era kunyibura mbu: "Chacha! Utairaa bacha, bushi nanyi nyinalyi muanda kuuma nao, kanji kuuma na banyakenyu barebi, nebanji bandju boshi ba bende bathunda ene myasi yanjikirwe mwechine chitabo. Ongo yeine iwemire kunde wera!"

야 가나까나, 가찌 야 궈머러롸. 부씨 어나워쭈 오끄, 오롸 워러사아 어바러비 어부아씨 붜무찌마 무부야-부야, 이와쭈마아 어도네 와이, 아여 구부라 어바아따 바이 찌라 마시 오롸 벼미러 아이거 어라 뉴마 사 수구 시어거."

7. 여수 아더찌러 뿌: "무로롸아! 네리 무 구푸루가! 바아하니뤄 바 버더 바쭈따 어먀시 여부러비 어라 야아찌기뤄 뭐찌너 찌다보."

8. 어이 먀시 요씨, 뇨노 요와니 녀이너 네나쭈뻬라아 나 구찌로러라 구이. 나 마꼬 나바아 너라 나쭈뻬라아 나 구찌로러라 구이, 너라 구푸가마 어라 무호또 소유 또니 네뭐러 부씨 이와네로사아이.

9. 시 어라 구네부라 뿌: "짜짜! 우다이라아 바짜, 부씨 나네 네나뗴 무아따 구우마 나오, 가찌 구우마 나 바냐거뉴 바러비, 너바찌 바뚜 보씨 바 버더 바쭈따 어너 먀시 야찌기뤄 뭐찌너 찌다보. 오끄 여이너 이워미러 구너 워라!"

trustworthy and true. The Lord, the God of the spirits of the prophets, sent his angel to show his servants the things that must soon take place."

7. "Behold, I am coming soon! Blessed is he who keeps the words of the prophecy in this book."

8. I, John, am the one who heard and saw these things. And when I had heard and seen them, I fell down to worship at the feet of the angel who had been showing them to me.

9. But he said to me, "Do not do it! I am a fellow servant with you and with your brothers the prophets and of all who keep the words of this book. Worship God!"

10. Chasinda, oyu ndonyi era kunyibura kanji mbu: "Ene myasi yeburebi era yanjikirwe mwechine chitabo, utaereresaa wabikai kwa muchima, bushi ebihangi bya ingabereramo, byera biri ofu.

11. "Emundju mubi anaendekeraa kunde akola emabi! Nola wende wakola ebitakolwa, nai anaendekeraa kunde akolabi! Si ola wende wakola ebithungenene era muhondo sa Ongo, yeke anaendekeraa kunde akolabi! Nola ulyi mubuya-buya, nai anaendekeraa kuba mubuya-buya"

12. Yesu atechire kanji mbu: "Mulolaa kubuya! Nyiri mu kufuluka! Na mango nyingafuluka, nyingabaha nelwembo, nyembe chira mundju kukulyikana na bya endee aira.

13. Nyono nyi Alufa kanji nyi Omeka! Nyi Mubere kanji nyi Musinda! Nyi Ndangiriso kanji nyi Businda!"

14. Baahanyirwe ba bende bafura enjimba sabo, bushi bakeresibwa eloso lwekulya kwa bifuma byola muchi

10. 짜시따, 오유 또네 어라 구네부라 가찌 뿌: "어너 먀시 여부러비 어라 야찌기뤄 뭐찌너 찌다보, 우다어러러사아 와비가이 과 무찌마, 부씨 어비하끼 뱌 이까버러라모, 벼라 비리 오푸.

11. "어무뚜 무비 아나어떠거라아 구떠 아고롸 어마비! 노롸 워떠 와고롸 어비다고롸, 나이 아나어떠거라아 구떠 아고롸비! 시 오롸 워떠 와고롸 어비쭈꺼너너 어라 무호또 사 오꼬, 여거 아나어떠거라아 구떠 아고롸비! 노롸 우뤠 무부야-부야, 나이 아나어떠거라아 구바 무부야-부야"

12. 여수 아더찌러 가찌 뿌: "무롿롸아 구부야! 네리 무 구푸루가! 나 마꼬 네까푸루가, 네까바하 너뤄뾰, 녀뻐 찌라 무뚜 구구뤠가나 나 뱌 어떠어 아이라.

13. 뇨노 네 아루파 가찌 네 오메가! 네 무버러 가찌 네 무시따! 네 따끼리소 가찌 네 부시따!"

14. 바아하니뤄 바 버떠 바푸라 어찌빠 사보, 부씨 바거러시봐 어론소 뤄구롸 과 비푸마 뵤롸 무찌 워가라모,

10. Then he told me, "Do not seal up the words of the prophecy of this book, because the time is near.

11. Let him who does wrong continue to do wrong; let him who is vile continue to be vile; let him who does right continue to do right; and let him who is holy continue to be holy."

12. "Behold, I am coming soon! My reward is with me, and I will give to everyone according to what he has done.

13. I am the Alpha and the Omega, the First and the Last, the Beginning and the End.

14. "Blessed are those who wash their robes, that they may have the right to the tree of life and may go

wekalamo, kanji bakeresibwa 가찌 바거러시봐 어로소 through the gates into the
eloso lwekurengera kwa nyisi 뭐구러꺼라 과 내시 버끼리라 city.
bengirira mwoyu musi. 모유 무시.

15. Si ba bende bakola 15. 시 바 버떠 바고롸 15. Outside are the dogs,
ebitakolwa bekea, nebalosi, 어비다고꽈 버거아, 너바로시, those who practice magic
nebasingisi, nebechi bebandju, 너바시끼시, 너버찌 버바뚜, arts, the sexually immoral,
na ba bende bera ebihuhanyi, 나 바 버떠 버라 어비후하니, the murderers, the idolaters
na ba bathula basimire ebisha 나 바 바쭈롸 바시미러 and everyone who loves
nekufulabi, abu boshi era 어비싸 너구푸롸비, 아부 보씨 and practices falsehood.
mbuwa yi bakanashiba. 어라 뿌와 에 바가나씨바.

16. Nyono Yesu nathumire 16. 뇨노 여수 나쭈미러 16. "I, Jesus, have sent my
endonyi wanyi mira, afulyire 어또네 와네 미라, 아푸레러 angel to give you this
ebemeresi boshi kwei myasi. 어버머러시 보씨 궈이 먀시. testimony for the churches. I
Nyono, nyishoka mwa lubuto 뇨노, 내쏘가 롸 루부도 꽈 am the Root and the
lwa mwami Tauti! Kanji nyono 롸미 다우디! 가찌 뇨노 네 Offspring of David, and the
nyi bende berika 버떠 버리가 뿌: ?끄누누 어라 bright Morning Star."
mbu: ?Ngunuu era yende 여떠 야고러라 부서서
yakorera busese kuikira 구이기라 어루뿌레-뿌레"
elumbulyi-mbulyi"

17. EMuchima Mubuya-buya, 17. 어무찌마 무부야-부야, 17. The Spirit and the bride
alauma nemuya bateta mbu: 아롸우마 너무야 바더다 뿌: say, "Come!" And let him
"Bahaa!" Nola womvire kwene "바하아!" 노롸 옴삐러 궈너 who hears say, "Come!"
myasi, nai emire atete mbu: 먀시, 나이 어미러 아더더 뿌: Whoever is thirsty, let him
"Bahaa!" Nola wafa echami, "바하아!" 노롸 와파 어짜미, come; and whoever wishes,
nai anabahaa. Abahaa 나이 아나바하아. 아바하아 let him take the free gift of
achifomere kwa meshi 아찌포머러 과 머씨 머가롸모 the water of life.
mekalamo mebuha kwa 머부하 과 아나시미러.
anasimire.

18. Nyono Yowani, natechire 18. 뇨노 요와니, 나더찌러 뿌 18. I warn everyone who
mbu chira mundju woshi, ola 찌라 무뚜 오씨, 오롸 워끼러 hears the words of the
wenjire womva kwene myasi 옴빠 궈너 먀시 여부러비 prophecy of this book: If
yeburebi era yanjikirwe 어라 야끼기뤄 뭐찌너 찌다보, anyone adds anything to
mwechine chitabo, akaba 아가바 아꽈다레가고 우찌 them, God will add to him
angatalyikako unji mwasi, 먀시, 아머냐아 과 오꼬 the plagues described in
amenyaa kwa Ongo 아가무다레기라 어마레부고 this book.

akamutalyikira emalyibuko ma 마 마찌기뤄모.
manjikirwemo.

19. Kanji ene myasi yobuno burebi era yanjikirwe mwechine chitabo, akaba mundju murebe angaokola ku chinwa, nai amenyaa kwa Ongo akaokola ewai mwango kwa bifuma byemuchi wekalamo, na kumunyaa echai chisiki mwoyu musi mubuya-buya, kukulyikana ngokwa byanjikirwe mwechine chitabo.	19. 가찌 어너 먀시 요부노 부러비 어라 야찌기뤄 뭐찌너 찌다보, 아가바 무뚜 무러버 아빠오고롸 구 찌놔, 나이 아머냐아 과 오꼬 아가오고롸 어와이 뫄꼬 과 비푸마 벼무찌 워가꽈모, 나 구무냐아 어짜이 찌시기 모유 무시 무부야-부야, 구구쩨가나 꼬과 뱌뚜기뤄 뭐찌너 찌다보.	19. And if anyone takes words away from this book of prophecy, God will take away from him his share in the tree of life and in the holy city, which are described in this book.
20. Yesu atechire mbu ene myasi yoshi iri ya kanangana. Kanji atechire mbu: "Kubinalyi! Nyiri mu kubaha!" Bibe bacha! Enawethu Yesu, bahaa!	20. 여수 아더찌러 뿌 어너 먀시 요씨 이리 야 가나빠나. 가찌 아더찌러 뿌: "구비나쩨! 네리 무 구바하!" 비버 바짜! 어나워쭈 여수, 바하아!	20. He who testifies to these things says, "Yes, I am coming soon." Amen. Come, Lord Jesus.
21. Engahanyi sa Enawethu Yesu, sindaa saba alauma nenyu muboshi!	21. 어빠하네 사 어나워쭈 여수, 시따아 사바 아꽈우마 너뉴 무보씨!	21. The grace of the Lord Jesus be with God's people. Amen.

아프리카 피그미족 신약성경

CHIRAANE CHIYAYAYA 찌라아너 찌야야야 New Testament

2025년 6월 26일 처음 펴냄

엮은이 | 작은손선교회
편집인 | 최관신

발행처 | 도서출판 동연
발행인 | 김영호
등 록 | 제1-1383(1992. 6. 12.)
주 소 | 서울시 마포구 월드컵로 163-3, 2층
전 화 | 02-335-2630 팩스 | 02-335-2640
이메일 | yh4321@gmail.com

작은손선교회 후원계좌: 농협 301-0168-2312-51(예금주 에이취에프엘)
연락처: 010-3164-7282 / 010-8401-7011

ISBN 978-89-6447-116-6   03230
정가 70,000원 (50.00 USD)